Who's Who
in
Canadian Sport

Edition 4

Bob Ferguson

Fitzhenry & Whiteside

Who's Who in Canadian Sport
Copyright © 2005 Bob Ferguson

Fitzhenry and Whiteside Limited
195 Allstate Parkway
Markham, Ontario L3R 4T8

In the United States:
121 Harvard Avenue, Suite 2
Allston, Massachusetts 02134
www.fitzhenry.ca godwit@fitzhenry.ca

Fitzhenry & Whiteside acknowledges with thanks the Canada Council for the Arts, the Government of Canada through its Book Publishing Industry Development Program, and the Ontario Arts Council for their support of our publishing program.

Library and Archives Canada Cataloguing in Publication

Ferguson, Bob, 1931-
Who's who in Canadian sport, volume 4 / Bob Ferguson. — 4th ed.
ISBN 1-55041-855-6
1. Athletes—Canada—Biography. 2. Sports—Canada—Biography. I. Title.
GV697.A1F47 2005   796'.092'271 C2005-904353-6

United States Cataloging-in-Publication Data

Ferguson, Bob, 1931-
Who's who in Canadian sport / Bob Ferguson. 4th ed.
Originally published: Toronto: Summerhill Press, 1985.
[656] p. : cm.
Includes index.
Summary: An alphabetical listing of almost 5,000 Canadian athletes, coaches and officials, including their biographies and career highlights.
ISBN 1-55041-855-6
1. Sports — Canada — Biography. 2. Athletes—Canada—Biography. I. Title.
796/.092/2 B dc22   GV697.A1F46 2005

Interior design by Denise Pittuck
Cover design by David Drummond
Cover Images: top and middle Getty Images Royalty Free;
bottom Comstock Royalty Free.

Printed and bound in Canada

1 3 5 7 9 10 8 6 4 2

*To Aaron, Alex, Taylor, Jordan and Darien, grandchildren of whom
I am extremely proud.*

*And, to Scott and Shane, sons of whom any father would be proud and
daughters-in-law Alison and Lindsey, for providing the adhesive that
holds it all together.*

*To my editorial team of Pam McFarlane, Graham and Ron Cox and Denise
Pittuck for their encouragement and a job well done.*

*And, of course, to the sports personalities whose exploits have made
this book so necessary.*

Contents

Introduction vii

Credits ix

Alphabetic Listing of Biographies 1

List of Abbreviations 491

Cross Reference Index by Sport 498

List of Candian Champions, Award Winners, and Medallists 525

Information Sheet for Future Candidates 579

Introduction

One would have to reside in a vacuum not to be even remotely aware of the athletic exploits of a Wayne Gretzky, Barbara Ann Scott, Gordie Howe, Nancy Greene, Ferguson Jenkins, Gaetan Boucher, Sandra Schmirler, Russ Jackson, Marilyn Bell, Tom Longboat or Paul Henderson. Like eternal flames their magnificent achievements shine perpetually in Canadian sport annals. And, well they should.

But, what of the multitude of athletes, native or otherwise, who have enjoyed their fleeting moments of glory only to fade into obscurity's twilight zone? Does the passage of time diminish their deeds or just the memories?

Edition Four of *Who's Who* is yet another step in an effort to recognize Canada's glorious sports heritage. The efforts and achievements of close to 5,000 athletes and sports figures, amateur and professional, living and dead, and representing virtually every sport, are included.

As is always the case in efforts of this nature there are omissions. In some instances the tracing of individuals deserving inclusion, or their relatives, struck a dead end. In other instances exclusion resulted from reluctance on the part of the contacted to reply to requests for information.

It is my hope that you, the reader, will assist in the ongoing search for names, addresses and additional information so that a future edition will include many more worthy persons who have had an impact on the Canadian sports scene. Any correspondence should be directed to *Who's Who in Canadian Sport*, 5 Catterick Cresc., Kanata, ON, K2K 3M5. You may also contact me by telephone at (613) 271-8690 or by e-mail at fergwho@rogers.com.

This work can never be definitive. It is, however, another major step along the path of preserving Canada's proud sports heritage.

— **Bob Ferguson**

Credits

Editors & Research
Terry Baker
Graham Cox
Ron Cox
Ray Lauzon
Pam MacFarlane

Computer guru
Rob Murray

Text Layout
Denise Pittuck

Contributors
Alexis Redmond, Canadian Football League
Allan Stewart, Canada's Sports Hall of Fame
Allison MacNeill, Ottawa hockey
Al Mann, Wallaceburg Sports Hall of Fame
Allison Neill, Canadian Equestrian Federation
Al Rae, Basketball, business advisor
Al Weiss, Canadian Press Toronto
Andre Brin, Hockey Canada
Andre Lachance, Baseball Canada
Andre Leclerc, Horseshoe Canada
Andrew Exner, CODA
Anita McCallum, London Free Press librarian
Ann Deavy, Shooting Federation of Canada
Anne MacRae, Mississauga Sports Hall of Fame
Anne Merklinger, Canadian Canoe Association
Arash Modani, Ottawa Renegades
Arleen Noga, Regina, Canadian women's baseball
Arnold Midgley, Canadian Ski Museum
Atila Ozkaplan, Canadian Olympic Association
Barb MacDonald, Skate Canada
Barb Wilson, Canadian Figure Skating Association
Barre Campbell, Ottawa Sun
Bernard Voyer, Biathlon Canada
Betty Bawden Bowen, Edmonton Grads
Bev Miller, Gymnastics Canada
Bill Charlick, Sarnia/Lambton Sports Hall of Fame
Bill Knight, Detroit Red Wings Alumni
Bill McNulty, Athletics, Vancouver, B.C.
Bill Plouffe, DCRA
Bill Rayner, St. Thomas, baseball historian
Bill Steinburg, RCGA
Bob Gage, London sport historian
Bob Stauffer, University of Alberta
Bonnie Shepherd, U of T
Brad Pascall, Hockey Canada
Brenda Gorman, Skate Canada
Brian McFalone, Guelph hockey historian
Bruce Huff, London journalist
Bruce Murray, Ontario Jockey Club
Bruce Walker, Ontario Jockey Club
Bruce Wylie, Brockville Sports Hall of Fame
Carla King, Canadian Ski Museum
Caroline Sharp, Volleyball Canada
Cecil Smith, Athletics Canada historian
Chantal Benoit, Wheelchair Basketball

Charlie Kitts, Almonte basketball
Cheri Morrison, Canadian Sportfishing Productions
Cheryl Henhawke, Six Nations of the Grand River
Cheryl Reilly, Canadian Curling Hall of Fame
Chris Dornan, CODA
Christine Brown, International Triathlon Union
Cindy Kistner, Saskatchewan Roughriders
Clara Shamanski, Langara College Foundation
Colin Kirk, Canadian Orienteering Federation
Danny Lamoureux, Curl Canada
David Bandla, University of Alberta
David Blaikie, ultramarathon historian
David Hart, Water Polo Canada
David Menary, Cambridge Reporter
David Silverman, WTF Taekwondo Association of Canada
Debbie Butt, B.C. Lions
Debbie Chevarie, Canada's Sports Hall of Fame
Deborah Williams, New Brunswick Sports Hall of Fame
Dennis 'Dee' Murphy, St. John's, Nfld.
Diana Ranken, OFSAA
Diane Imrie, Northwestern Ontario Sports Hall of Fame
Dick Pound – COA Montreal
Dina Bell-Laroche, Spirit of Sport Foundation
Dr. Sidney Soames, Figure Skating historian
Don Hilsendager, North Battleford Sports Hall o Fame
Donna Rochon, pistol shooting
Doug Lomberg, Cornwall Sports Hall of Fame
Earl McRae, Ottawa Sun
Earl Zukerman, McGill University
Ed Arnold, Peterborough Examiner
Ed Grenda, Kingston soccer, snowshoe authority
Eddi Chittaro, Windsor/Essex County Sports Hall of Fame
Elizabeth Dagg, Canadian Football Hall of Fame
Emery Leger, Skate Canada Hall of Fame archivist
Eric Holmes, Toronto Argonauts
Eugene Reimer, Abbotsford Paralympian
Fiona Morrow, Canadian Cycling Association
Fran Rider, Ontario Women's Hockey Association
Fred Rams, Ontario Aquatic Hall of Fame
Gillian Holter, Langara College Foundation
Glen McCurdy, Hockey Canada
Glynne Jenkins – Triathlon Canada
Greg Fulton, Canadian Football League
Greg Hamilton, Baseball Canada
Greg Lagace, Canadian Paralympics
Greg Mathieu, Canadian Amateur Wrestling Association
Guy Bertrand, Trail Daily Times
Howard Starkman, Toronto Blue Jays Baseball Club
Hugh Wilson, Athletics Canada
Ian Kennedy, Vancouver Rugby
Ian Moss, Badminton Canada
Ian Walker, Vancouver Sun sports
Jack Jordan, Football Canada
Jack Wylie, Oshawa Sports Hall of Fame
Jacqueline Affleck, Charlottetown Guardian
Jamie Cartmell, Edmonton Eskimos
Jan Coates, Racquetball Canada
Jane Livingston, Hockey Canada
Jane Rodney, Hockey Hall of Fame

Janice Smith, Canadian Football Hall of Fame
Jeff Domenic, Canadian Football League
Jeff Roy, Ottawa/North Bay
Jeff Timson, Labatt Brier
Jeffrey Reed, London Intercounty baseball
Jennifer Jones, University of Toronto
Jennifer Ward, Canadian Equestrian Federation
Jim Baba, Baseball Canada
Jim McAuley, Ottawa sports historian
Jim Shearon, Kanata baseball historian
Jocelyn Langlois, Shooting Federation of Canada
Joe Foley, Canadian Boxing Hall of Fame
John Bales, Coaching Association of Canada
John Bulmer, Collingwood Sports Hall of Fame
John Craig, Athletics Ontario
John Gosset, Canadian Basketball Hall of Fame
John Loaring Jr., Windsor-Essex Sports Hall of Fame
John Trager, Canadian 10-Pin Bowling Federation
Jon Braun, Soloway Jewish Community of Ottawa Hall of
    Fame
Josh Oubadia, Canadian Football League
Julie Jardine, Campbellton Sports Hall of Fame
June Takahashi, Judo Canada
Karen Hewson, Canadian Golf Hall of Fame
Karl Balisch, Gymnastics Canada
Kate Dwyer, Northwestern Ontario Sports Hall of Fame
Kathleen Millar, Federation of Canadian Archers
Kathy Ladouceur, Ringette Canada
Kathy Meagher, New Brunswick Sports Hall of Fame
Keith Tanton, Prince Edward Island Sports Hall of Fame
Kelly McKay, New Brunswick Sports Hall of Fame
Ken Doucette, Canadian Forces Sports Hall of Fame
Kevin Jepson, Canadian 5-Pin Bowlers' Association
Kevin Penny, Triathlon Canada
Kim Ali, Tennis Canada
Kim Conway, Manitoba Sports Hall of Fame
Laurie Alpern, Tennis Canada
Leane Swales, Canadian Cycling Association
Lefty Reid, Peterborough historian
Linda Petryna, Saskatchewan Sports Hall of Fame
Lisa Burke, Synchronized Swimming Canada
Lise Gosselin-Simard, Gymnastics Canada
Lisette Stapley, Softball Canada
Liz Shaughnessy, Linda Hiles, Equestrian Sport
Loretto Vella, Tennis Canada
Louise Frogett, Canadian Football Hall of Fame
Louis-Philippe Dorais, Montreal Alouettes
Lucie Leclerc-Rose, Canadian Olympic Association
Luc Robert, Canadian Paralympics
Lynn Clifford-Ward, Canadian Figure Skating Hall of
    Fame
Marguerite Grant, Gymnastics Canada
Marilyn Haley, Alberta Sports Hall of Fame
Martha Fournier, B.C. Sports Hall of Fame
Martin Cleary, Ottawa Citizen
Mary Fraser, Canadian Freestyle Ski Association
Matt Charbonneau, Swimming Canada
Matt Mizerski, Boxing Canada

Michelle Lalonde, Calgary Stampeders
Mike Lachapelle, Canadian Lacrosse Association
Mitch Geller, Diving Canada
Merv Bonney, Ottawa
Moira Lassen, Canadian Weightlifting Federation
Monique Giroux, Montreal Expos
Morgan Quarry, Soccer Canada
Nancy Irvin, Water Ski Canada
Natalie Monette, Canadian Canoe Association
Norma Foster, Canadian Karate
Pam Rene, Canadian Olympic Association
Pat Armstrong, B.C. Sports Hall of Fame
Pat Hall, Greater Victoria Sports Hall of Fame
Patti Hutchison, Nova Scotia Sports Hall of Fame
Paul Ramlow, U.S. Trotting Association
Paul Stone, Canadian Golf Hall of Fame
Paul Thomas, Basketball, Windsor, Ont.
Paula Lally, Hockey Canada
Penny Joyce, Athletics Canada
Peter Vaughn, Dominion of Canada Rifle Association
Phil Legault, Ottawa Senators
Phil Pritchard, Hockey Hall of Fame
Rachel Delaney, Canadian Curling Association
Reg McClellan, Wheelchair Basketball, technical advisor
Rene Leroux, Embrun broomball, hockey
Rick Brownlee, Manitoba Sports Hall of Fame
Robert Bolduc, Speed Skating Association
Robin Turnbull, Spirit of Sport Foundation
Robin Wilson, Scott Tournament of Hearts
Roch Pilon, Speed Skating Canada
Ron Gallinger, Softball Canada
Ron Jackson, Canada's Sports Hall of Fame
Ron Lebsack, Alberta Sports Hall of Fame
Ron Skronski, Smiths Falls Recreation Hall of Fame
Roy McGregor, National Post
Ruth Krall, Canadian Professional Rodeo Association
Sandra Boutilier, Pacific Newspaper Group Library
Sarah Storey, Canadian Bobsleigh & Luge Association
Sean O'Donnell, Canadian Cycling Association
Shauna Flath, Squash Canada
Sheila Carr, Canadian 5-pin Bowlers' Association
Sheila Kelly, Saskatchewan Sports Hall of Fame
Sheila Robertson, Canadian Association for the
    Advancement of Women and Sport and Physical
    Activity
Stephen Coutts, Nova Scotia Sport Hall of Fame
Steve Kehoe, Ottawa Senators
Steve Parker, Canadian Commonwealth Games
Steve Tuckwood, UBC
Sue Cadieux, Sport North
Sue Hylland, Canadian Olympic Association
Susan Flanagan, B.C. Blind Sports
Susan Fulford Hearn, Water Polo Canada
Susan Stern, UBC Public Affairs
Suzanne Judd, Volleyball Canada
Suzanne Nicholson, Field Hockey Canada
Sylvie Clark, Badminton Canada
Sylvie Doucette, Canadian Olympic Association

Terry Baker, London sports authority
Terry Wheatley-Magee, Field Hockey Canada
Tim Sample, Barrie Sports Hall of Fame
Tom Boreski, Canadian Olympic Association
Tom Casey, Ottawa Citizen
Tom Sweet, Nova Scotia sports historian
Tom Valcke, Canadian Baseball Hall of Fame
Tom West, Calgary Olympic Hall of Fame
Toni Scheier, Cross Country Canada
Traci House, Gymnastics Canada
Vaughan Baird, Canadian Aquatic Hall of Fame
Violet Le Blanc, Canadian Table Tennis Association
Wayne Kondro, Ottawa, basketball historian
Wayne Scanlan, Ottawa Citizen
Wendy Vallillee, Lanark Era

A

ABBOTT, Bill Jr. (sailing); b. 21 May 1954, Sarnia, Ont.; m. Joanne Gray; c. Bill, Cam, Chris, Katie; boat builder; with father Bill Sr., brother Larry soling gold '77 Governor's Cup, silver '77 President's Cup, '79 NA, '82 US nationals, '83 PAG; 4 CORK bronze; 4 ntl soling class titles; with wife Joanne, Brad Boston won '93 CORK silver; bronze '97 world championships; 2-time Olympian; res. Sarnia, Ont.

ABBOTT, Colin (softball); b. 1 Oct 1970, St. John's, Nfld.; m. Michelle Ghent; Memorial, BA, BCom; salesman; outfielder with big bat; mem. Lloydminster Liners, Rempel Bros, Green Bay All Car; 2 ntl jr. titles with Lloydminster; ntl championships '94 Rempel Bros team, '97 Victoria, '98 Halifax Jaguars; MVP '94 ISC Green Bay world title team; with Green Bay All-Car '95-97, Madison, Wisc. Farm Tavern '98-99; PAG gold team '99; ISC MVP, 1st team all-star '94; ASA all-American '94; 2 St. John's athlete-of-yr awards; Team Canada '04; res. Portugal Cove, Nfld.

ABBOTT, Jack (baseball); b. 16 Sep 1890, Dufferin, Man.; d. 12 Jul 1950, North Battleford, Sask.; m. Mary Leask; UofT BPharm.; pharmacist; mem. Retail Merchants Assn, Board of Trade, Rotary Club, Agricultural Society; long association with North Battleford Curling Club, North Battleford Beaver hockey, baseball clubs as player, organizer, exec. mem.; sr. hockey team won prov., Western Cdn titles and lost Allan Cup final to Sudbury '37; charter pres. baseball club '47; home field bore his name; following his death team he established won 5 titles; mem. North Battleford Sports Hall of Fame.

ABBOTT, Joanne (sailing); b. 25 Apr 1955, Sarnia, Ont.; m. Bill Jr.; c. Bill, Cam, Chris, Katie; chartered accountant; sailed with husband several years before taking break to raise children; formed own crew to compete in '85, '91 world championships; re-teamed with husband and Brad Boston to win '93 CORK silver; bronze '97 world championships; 1st woman to compete in soling class at Olympics '96; res. Sarnia, Ont.

ABBOTT, Marni (wheelchair basketball); b. 10 Nov 1965, Nelson, B.C.; m. Richard Peter; Coaches Assn. of BC; downhill ski accident '83 left her a paraplegic; still qualified for ntl swim team where she earned 4 gold, silver '86 PAG; began playing wheelchair basketball '88; mem. ntl team from '92; flag-bearer '96 Paralympics; helped Canada to 43-game undefeated streak; 3 Paralympic, world gold; 1 Paralympic bronze; mem. Western Grizzlies ntl NWWBA gold medal team '98; 4 silver, 3 bronze ntl competitions; certified Level 3 coach; head coach Team BC '03 Canada Games; Queen's Jubilee medal; BCWSA athlete of '92; BC athlete with disability award '96; BC Wheelchair Sports female athlete of millennium; BC Women in Sport leaders & legends award; res. Vancouver, B.C.

ABBRUZZI, Pat (football); b. 29 Aug 1932, Providence, R.I.; given name: Pasquale; m. Philomena Andreozzi; c. Diane, Debra, Michael, Mary, Julie, Jane; Rhode Island, BSc; teacher, restaurateur; HS all-state '48-49; all-prep Marianapolis '50; all-Yankee conf. '51-54; little all-America '52, '54; all-New England '52-54; 10 RI, NE records including 306yds single game, 99yd td run; 4yr. college rushing record 3389yds; all-pro Montreal '55-58; CFL records 20 tds single season '52, 182 carries, 1248yds, 17 tds '56; EFC scoring title '56; coached 7 Warren HS title teams; state team record 32 consecutive victories; pres. RI Football Coaches Assn. '72-73; R.I. athlete of '54; RI Italian athlete of '53-54; RI coach of '75; mem. U of RI. Hall of Fame; res. Warren, R.I.

ABDO, Reema (swimming); b. 19 May 1963, Aden, South Yemen; Arizona State, UofT; Ont. Provincial Police; backstroke specialist; broke onto ntl scene '81; 14 ntl championship medals, 7 gold, 4 silver, 3 bronze; Cdn record short-course 100m, 200m backstroke; represented Canada USSR-Germany-Canada tri-meet, Cwlth, FISU Games, '84 Olympics; Pan-Pacific championships; FISU games 4x100 medley relay bronze '83; gold France's Diana Invitational '84; Olympic 4x100 medley relay bronze; coached for several yrs at age-group, university levels; active triathlete, long distance runner; Olympic champion award '85; mem. Ont. Aquatic Hall of Fame; res. Caledon, Ont.

ABDOU, Justin (wrestling); b. 18 Jan 1971, Moose Jaw, Sask.; SFU BA; coach; competing at 85kg won 4 NAIA , '91 US university titles; SFU record: 204 wins; gold Romanian Open, NYAC open, Sunkist Invitational, Canada Cup, '94 CG, Polish GP, US GP, US Espoir, '87 world cadet; competed '00 Olympics; ret'd from ntl team '02; 2 ntl bantam, 2 cadet, 2 jr., 2 espoir, 9 sr. titles; 2 Canada Games gold; mem. Burnaby Mountain Wrestling Club; asst. coach SFU; coached ntl jr., World Cup teams '02; res. Vancouver, B.C.

ABEL, Sid (hockey); b. 22 Feb 1918, Melville, Sask.; d. 8 Feb 2000, Farmington, Mich; given name: Sidney Gerald; m. Gloria Moranday; c. Gerry, Linda; hockey broadcaster; Flin Flon Man. Sr. League; Detroit (NHL) '38-43, '45-52; team capt. at 24; centred Liniment Line of Don Grosso, Eddie Wares, Production Line of Gordie Howe, Ted Lindsay; Canadian Forces '43-45; playing-coach Chicago '52-54; NHL playing record: 612 scheduled games, 189g, 283a, 97 playoff games, 28g, 30a; mem. 3 Stanley Cup winners; Hart Trophy (MVP) '49; Detroit coach '57-58; GM '62-71; coach St. Louis '71, GM '72-73; GM Kansas City Scouts '73; NHL coaching record: 382w, 423l, 155t, 9 playoffs, no titles; Red Wings ret. jersey 8; *Hockey News* coach of '53; NHL all-star coach '63; mem. Sask Sports, Hockey halls of fame.

ABELSON, Jess (all-around); b. 14 Apr 1892, Cleveland, Ohio; d. 22 Nov 1975, Ottawa, Ont.; m. Mollie; c. Sylvia, Lawrence (d), Stanley, Alan, Bob; flying wing Ottawa Football Club 1910-20; mem. 1913-14 league title teams; mem. 1913 Britannia Cdn war canoe titlists; playing-mgr. Ottawa rugby league team; capt. Ottawa Senators YMCA sr. basketball city title teams '13-14, mem. Cdn champions '14; top-ranked handball player '13-14; track standout early in career; involved with YMCA program 60 yrs; owner, mgr., occasional player Strathconas semipro softball team; sponsored Ottawa Primrose hockey club; founder, pres. Tel Aviv Tennis Club '34; formed 39th Boy Scout Troop; mem. Ottawa Jewish, Ottawa Sports halls of fame.

ABENDSCHAN, Jack (football); b. 1942, New Mexico; given name: John Jacob; m. Virginia Lomax; c. Christina, Shelley, John; New Mexico, BA; personnel dir.; og/de/pk, 2nd team AP all-American; pro Sask. Roughriders '65-75; CFL record: 312 converts, 159 field goals, 74 singles, 863 points; sat out '74 campaign with knee injury; quit Riders '68 for AFL Denver trial, when cut rejoined Riders; 7 times WFC all-star, 5 times all-Canadian; 2 WFC, 1 CFL scoring title; res. Abilene, Tex.

ABRAMOWITZ, Moe (basketball); b. 5 Aug 1903, Montreal, Que.; d. 2 Jan 1991, Montreal, Que.; m. Lilian Lessor; c. Mark; company treas.; despite 5'4" stature veritable court wizard; player/coach/administrator '19-54; record 88 free throws in 101 attempts '22; numerous Montreal area scoring titles, YMHA title teams; coach from '35; 4 Que., 3 Eastern, 3 ntl titles; coached McGill '49-52, Montreal league title, Dodds Cup; with Bob Osborne co-coach '48 Olympic basketball team; former YMHA basketball chair.; charter mem. Que. Board of Referees; 1st athlete inducted into Montreal YM-YWHA Sports Hall of Fame.

ACKLES, Bob (football); b. 16 Sep 1938, Sarnia, Ont.; given name: Robert William; m. Kay; c. Steve, Scott; football exec.; UNLV; mem. jr. Blue Bombers; joined BC at '54 inception; water boy, equipment mgr., dir. player personnel, AGM, club historian, GM '75-86, pres./CEO '02-04; GM Dallas (NFL) '86-92; AGM Arizona '93-94; dir. of football operations, Philadelphia '95; dir. football operations, Miami '96-00; GM XFL Las Vegas Outlaws (XFL) '00; only man to hold exec. positions in CFL, NFL, XFL; Schenley award-of-excellence; mem. BC Lions Wall, Cdn Football Hall of Fame; res. Vancouver, B.C.

ACOOSE, Paul (t&f); b. 1883 Sakimay Reserve, Sask.; d. 30 Apr 1978, Sakimay Reserve, Sask.; m. Madeleine Osoup; c. 9; band councilor, farmer; began competing in late teens at Grenfell area sport days; 3-, 5-mile Sask. road race titles; Western Canada 5-mile track title; won Regina 10.5-mile race '08 beating best Sask. runners by 8 minutes; won '08 Manitoba 5-mile title; turned pro '09; beat England's Fred Appleby in 1st pro race setting world 15-mile record 1:22:22; 2nd Madison Square Garden 20-mile race vs. top international field '10; beat Tom Longboat in 12-mile race at Toronto to close pro career '10; mem. Sask, First Nations Sports halls of fame.

ACTON, Keith (hockey); b. 15 Apr 1958, Stouffville, Ont.; given name: Keith Edward; m. Susan; c. Brooke, Elisa, William, Robert; coach; centre Peterborough (OHA) '76-78, Nova Scotia (AHL) '78-80; claimed in '78 amateur draft by Montreal; played in NHL with Montreal '79-83, Minnesota '83-88, Edmonton '88-89, Philadelphia '89-93, Washington '93, NYI '93-94; NHL record: 15 seasons, 1023 scheduled games, 226g, 358a, 66 playoff games, 12g,

21a; mem. 1 Stanley Cup winner; AHL all-star '80; played in NHL all-star game '82; asst./assoc. coach Philadelphia '94-98; asst. coach NYR '98-00; asst. coach TML '00-03; res. Toronto, Ont.

ADAIR, Colin (squash); b. 4 Nov 1942, Montreal, Que.; given name: Colin John; m. Margot Jean Lafleur; c. Jacqueline, Gregor, Dylan; McGill, BA; investment banker; from '60 earned more than 100 major tournament titles in US, Canada; US singles '68, '71; twice ntl singles champion; 1st Canadian to win US doubles '74; 4 ntl doubles titles; McGill athlete of '64; Squash Canada distinguished service award; res. Montreal, Que.

ADAMS, Diane (curling); b. 7 Jan 1965, Baudette, Minn.; given name: Diane Janet Wolanicki; m. Jim Adams; provincial civil servant; skipped NWO jr title rink '83; played second for Heather Houston's Cdn. women's title rink '88-89, world champions '89; conducted jr. curling clinics in NWO '91; exec. mem Thunder Bay Major League '88-91; mem. Ont. team of '89; mem. NWO Sports, Cdn Curling halls of fame; res. Thunder Bay, Ont.

ADAMS, Dick (football); b. 13 Feb 1948, Athens, Ohio; given name: Richard Earl; div.; c. Timothy Eugene, Anthony William; m. Catherine Patterson; c. Rachel, Daniel Chelsey; Miami of Ohio, BSc; football coach; all-Southeastern Ohio '63-66, all-Southern Ohio baseball '66; with Miami all-Mid-American Conf. '69-70, best db, MVP twice; *UPI* all-American 2nd team '69-70, athlete of '70; Mid-Am. Conf. defensive player '70; 14 Miami school records; dh/p Ottawa '72-75; 4yrs EFC, all-Canadian; led EFC punt returners '72 with 92 for 608yds; mem. '73 Grey Cup winners; coached HS in Ohio '71, asst. coach Carleton, Mount Allison, UofOtt '76-82; Calgary '83, Ottawa '84-86, '95, Saskatchewan '87-92, Murray State '92, head coach Bethel College '93-94, asst. Winnipeg '96-99; res. Winnipeg, Man.

ADAMS, Harry (curling); b. 7 Dec 1932, D'Arcy, Sask.; d. 27 Jul 2000, Ottawa, Ont.; m. Shirley Goodwin; c. Ken, Connie, Debbie, Lisa; businessman; established reputation in mixed curling winning Salls Trophy, Canadian Branch Lady Gilmour competition, OVCA mixed '75; twice Ont. mixed champion; won Branch Governor-General's, OCA Silver Tankard (double rink); finalist OCA Intermediates; 4 times men's provincial finals; Red Anderson Memorial Trophy '73, *Curl 4 TV* series '78, City of Ottawa grand aggregate shield '78, Ottawa Masters '78, North Bay Jamaica 'spiel '78, Capital Challenge series '77.

ADAMS, Jack (hockey); b. 14 Jun 1895, Ft. William, Ont.; d. 1 May 1968, Detroit, Mich.; given name: John James; m. Helen; hockey exec.; Ft. William, Peterborough, Sarnia amateur; pro ctr Toronto Arenas '18; Vancouver 3 seasons; Pacific Coast League scoring title '20 with 24g, 18a in 24 games; Toronto St. Pats '22-26, Ottawa (NHL) '26-27 Stanley Cup winners; Detroit mgr. '27; 18yrs mgr. and/or coach, 12 league titles, 7 in succession, 7 Stanley Cups; coached 1st, 2nd NHL all-star teams once each; innovator of hockey farm system; Central Pro League pres. '62-68; mem. Hockey, Canada's, Mich., NWO Sports halls of fame.

ADAMS, Jeff (t&f); b. 15 Nov 1970, Brampton, Ont.; motivational speaker; wheelchair track athlete in distances from 100m to marathon; silver 800m, 4x400m '92 Paralympics; 800m gold, 400m silver, 4x400m relay bronze '96 Paralympics; competed '92 Olympics but withdrew with 300m remaining due to mechanical difficulties; 2 gold, 2 silver, 1 bronze '00 Paralympics; 2 ntl 10km. marathon titles; '94 CG 800, 1500m gold; IAAF 1500m gold '95; 3 Stoke-Mandeville Games gold, 5 Ian Hume Invitational gold '95, 4 Black Top Invitational gold '96; 5 Canberra Interclub meet gold, 3 silver '96; 1 gold, 3 silver '94 IPC Worlds; world 1500m silver '01; res. Don Mills, Ont.

ADAMS, Robert (t&f); b. 20 Dec 1924, Alsask, Sask,; m. Marjorie Pascoe; c. Janice, Murray; UofSask, BA, BEd; ret'd. HS phys-ed supervisor; decathlete '52 Olympics; capt. '54 BEG track team; Fred Rowell Trophy AAU of C outstanding field event athlete '54; ntl sr. native discus record 148'10" '49; sr. native decathlon record 6636 points '52; t&f team coach '58 Commonwealth, '64 Olympic, '68 Trinidad Games; 5yrs coach Royal Canadian Legion coaching clinic Guelph; head judge pole vaulting '76 Olympics; vertical jumps referee '78 , '94, '01 Commonwealth Games, '79 World Cup; Bob Adams Foundation to assist aspiring t&f athletes initiated by STFA '83; Centennial Medal; hon. mem. Commonwealth Games Assn. Of Canada; mem. Cdn Olympic, Sask., Saskatoon Sports halls of fame; res. Victoria, B.C.

ADAMSON, Gail (builder/synchronized swimming); b. 26 Jul 1936, Winnipeg, Man.; d. 4 Apr 1996, Winnipeg, Man.; m. John; c. 4 daughters, 2 sons; drawn into sport by daughters she became ultimate volunteer; v-p Synchro Man. '74, pres. '76-77; Level 1 coach; dir. Man, Sports Fed. 10yrs; ntl dir. from '76; v-p Synchro Canada '78, pres. '81-83, p-pres '83-85; personnel chair. Synchro Can. 12yrs; led Synchro Can. steering comm. Human Resources audit '89-90; mem. Man. Sports Hall of Fame.

ADELMAN, Louis (football); b. 13 Jan 1905, Devil's Lake, N.D.; d. 3 Jul 1987, Palmdale Calif.; m. Molly Rosenblat; c. David, Howard, Robert, Sheila; HS football to Tammany Tigers (forerunners Winnipeg Blue Bombers); ctr '24-38; 4 Grey Cup finals, 1 winner; capt. '35 team which brought Grey Cup West 1st time; mgr. Winnipeg club '39-45; inducted with '35 team into Manitoba Sports Hall of Fame.

ADKIN, Dennis (builder); b. 6 Jun 1919, Monitor, Alta.; m. Alison Ronalda Fortune; c. Dennis Monte, Laurie Elizabeth, David Roderick; ret'd. newspaper exec.; during 19yrs as reporter/editor *London Free Press* instrumental in establishing and developing London Ski Club; club pres. 9yrs, dir. 6yrs; moving to Saskatoon exec. editor *Star-Phoenix* '65-67, Federated Co-Ops Ltd. in-house publication editor '68-82; key role in development Blackstrap Hill for '71 Saskatoon Winter Games; established, edited *Sask. Ski Journal* '74-87; pres. Sask. Div. CSA 11yrs; life mem. London Ski Club, Sask. Ski Assn.; mem. Cdn. Skiing, Sask. Sports halls of fame; res. Victoria, B.C.

ADLHOCH, Hans (shooting); b. 10 Apr 1935, Heidelberg, Ger.; carpenter; '72, '77 ntl smallbore 3-position champion; '74 ntl smallbore prone title; silver, bronze '78 Benito Juarez International; silver smallbore air rifle team '79 PAG; mem. '76 Olympic team; Longueuil athlete of '75; SFC golden anniversary award; distinguished life mem. USNRA; res. Victoria, B.C.

AGER, Barry (basketball); b. 29 Jan 1938, London, Ont.; given name: Barry Laurence; m. Catherine Mutsch; c. David, Robert, Carolyn; UWO BA, McMaster U, BPhE, Ithaca College, MSc.; HS v.-principal; London Dist. HS all-star '56; mem. Western Colts jr. title team '57; UWO Mustangs '58; London Lounge Int. A '59, Tillsonburg Livingstons ntl sr. A champs, Olympic team '60; CIAU all-star McMaster '61; Ottawa Joe Feller's Sr. A team '62; Ottawa ACT basketballer of year; Ottawa Lapointes Sr. A team '63, Bert Marshall Trophy; coached Ridgemont Spartans to Ottawa HS, Valley titles '69; res. Nepean, Ont.

AH YOU, Junior (football); b. 30 Dec 1948, American Samoa; Arizona State; all-around athlete at Arizona State starring in football, basketball, volleyball, t&f; named outstanding lineman Fiesta Bowl, MVP '70 Peach Bowl; sought by NE Patriots but opted for CFL Montreal '72-81; de; 4 all-East, 2 all-Cdn de; 5 Grey Cup finals, 2 winners; top def. player '74 Grey Cup; 2 CFL tds; mem. Cdn Football, Ariz. State halls of fame; res. Laie, Hawaii.

AHEARN, Frank (hockey); b. 10 May 1886, Ottawa, Ont.; d. 17 Nov 1962, Ottawa, Ont.; jr., sr. hockey promoter; bought Ottawa Senators from Tommy Gorman '24 and assembled powerful team which included Jack Adams, George Boucher, Alex Connell, Hec Kilrea, Frank Nighbor, Syd Howe, Hooley Smith; won '27 Stanley Cup; depression years forced him to sell his arena, star players in series of deals considered spectacular at time; mem. Ottawa, Hockey halls of fame.

AIRD, Stu (lacrosse/football); b. 14 Apr 1957, Oakville, Ont.; given name: Samuel Stuart; m. Laura Ramsay; c. Emily, Samuel, Neil; UWO BA, UWindsor LL.B, lawyer; mem. UWO Vanier Cup CIAU finalists '77, '79, winner '77; began playing lacrosse age 5; mem. Mississauga Jr A '75-78, Vancouver Burrards '79-80, Owen Sound North Stars '81-90, Buffalo Bandits '93-94; ntl team from '83; mem. 3 Cdn teams at World championships; mem. '83 international championships; 2 Owen Sound North Stars, Mississauga jr A MVP awards; OLA sr., jr league all-star; mem. major indoor league champion Buffalo Bandits '93; 2nd team MILL all-star '94; MILL rookie of '93 and unsung hero '93-95; ret'd. from competitive ranks '95; res. Ancaster, Ont.

AITCHISON, Gordon (basketball); b. 1909, North Bay, Ont.; d. 6 Jan 1990, Windsor, Ont.; m. Melba Malott; c. Andy, Peggy; Detroit, Assumption College, BA, UofT; ret'd HS principal; ntl interscholastic pole vault record; mem. UofD, Windsor Alumni, Assumption, Windsor Fords teams; ntl sr. finalist '34, Eastern, Cdn sr. titles '35; mem. silver medal team '36 Olympics; played at UofT '38; player-coach Portage La Prairie while mem. RCAF WW2; coached football, basketball, t&f, CO Cornwall cadet corps '45; mem. Cdn Basketball Hall of Fame.

AITKEN, Don (curling); b. 16 May 1945, Tillsonburg, Ont.; given name: Donald John; m. Terry; c. Bruce; self-employed; mem. 8 Brier rinks; 2nd for Jim Ursel's '77 Que. ntl champions; mem. '75 *CBC* Classic, '77-79 Kronenbourg Trophy (Switzerland) winning rinks; mem. Cdn Curling Hall of Fame; res. Mount Royal, Que.

AKERVALL, Henry (all-around); b. 24 Aug 1937, Port Arthur, Ont.; d. 8 Feb 2000, Thunder Bay, Ont; m. Lorna

Mahan; c. Christopher, Kelli; Mich. Tech, BSc, N.Mich, MEd, N.Colo EdD; ret'd. educator; HS jr pole vault record holder; active hockey defenceman '50-72 Port Arthur Jr. A champs, Hamilton Jr. A; 3yrs mem. US ntl college all-star teams, Western Collegiate all-star, NCAA Div. 1 champs, all-American; playing coach Tampere, Finland; capt. '64 Cdn Olympic hockey team; mem. Port Arthur Sr. Bearcats, 3 city titles, 1 MVP award; all-star champion Marquette Iron Rangers; mem. Thunder Bay Twins; utility baseball player '52-64 with champion Port Arthur senior Giants, Red Sox; utility fastball player, '64-75 champion Port Arthur Dairyman, MVP '66, twice all-star 3rd baseman, sr. champ Club 17 team; with Tom Luck Jr. won '72 TB dist. Red Rock pro-am golf title; active curler, skier, bowler, squash player, paddler; HS football, hockey, t&f coach; co-ordinator NWO hockey clinics; 2yrs AD Lakehead U; coach GPAC champion Lakehead U hockey team; Lakehead U fastball, paddling, speed skating coach; Port Arthur minor hockey coach, CAHA level 5 instructor; x-country ski instructor; TB male athlete-of-yr '63; Celebration '88 fed. govt. medal; mem. North Shore Steelhead Assn., pres. '85-87; bd. mem. Big Thunder ski training centre; mem. Lakehead U Hall of Fame selection comm.; mem. NWO Sports Hall of Fame.

ALBERT, Herb (archery); b. 17 Jan 1905, Germany; d. (circa 1990), Clearbrook, B.C.; m. Marjorie Docherty; c. Edward, Sonja, Elizabeth, Sandra; ret'd. manufacturer, engraver; 1st official competition '14 winning distance event with homemade bow, arrows; considered Canada's finest long distance shooter in modern flight archery; from '50 held all Canadian flight records, including 613yds with 50lb light bow; high altitude shooting in California surpassed this mark with 702yds, but not recognized Cdn record; B.E. flight records; helped form Canadian Archery Assn. '51; p-pres. FCA, mem. Alta. Sports Hall of Fame.

ALBRECHT, Grant (luge); b. 29 Jan 1981, Red Deer, Alta.; carpenter; doubles specialist with Eric Pothier from '02, previous partner Mike Moffat; ntl team from '98; bronze '99, silver '00 jr. worlds; 6th '01 worlds, 11th '03; 12th '02 Olympics; started the '02/03 WC circuit with 2 4th place finishes, had four more top-10 results and ended the season with WC 9th ranking; 3 ntl titles; res. Calgary, Alta.

ALBRECHT, J.I. (football/soccer); b. 15 Feb 1931, St. James, N.Y.; m. Anna Maria Johnson; c. Roderick, Hunter, Dean; Georgia Military College, BA, MA, PhD; football exec.; asst. coach Tennessee '50-52; teams competed in '50, '52 Cotton Bowl, '51 Sugar Bowl; '51 US ntl title; coach Southern Cal, Maryland, Wyoming, South Carolina '53-58 with teams participating in Rose, Orange, Sun Bowls; AFL talent consultant '59; mem. Montreal staff '60-62; business mgr., AGM AFL Oakland '63; helped establish Quebec Rifles UFL '64; chief scout San Francisco ''65-67; scout Denver '68-70; rejoined Alouettes '70, GM '72-73; player personnel dir. New England '74; dir. personnel Toronto '75-77; GM Argos '00; GM Toronto Croatia soccer club '78; instrumental in Maritimes bid for CFL franchise '79; opinionated broadcaster, newspaper sports columnist; AD Cape Breton College '89-90; special advisor '93 Ottawa , '94 Shreveport Pirates; nicknamed "Bird Dog or Super Scout"; author *Just J.I.: A Sports Odyssey*; res. Halifax, N.S.

ALBRIGHT, Debbie (figure skating); b. 11 Jul 1958, Kamloops, B.C.; given name: Deborah Lee; m. David Islam; c. Mitchell, Rachel; UofT, BSc. MHSc.; exec. dir. Alzheimer Society of Greater Simcoe County; ntl. jr. ladies title '76; bronze Nebelhorn '76, Prague Skate '77, ntl srs. figures Otto Gold Memorial Trophy '79; Ont. Achievement Award, 3 Toronto Cricket, Skating and Curling Club McCordic Memorial awards; rep. Canada internationally through '80; athlete rep. CFSA board '80-86; COA athletes' advisory council '81-85; CFSA judge from '78, ISU judge from '95; res. Barrie, Ont.

ALDAG, Roger (football); b. 6 Oct 1953, Gull Lake, Sask.; given name: Roger Louis; m. Joanne; c. Sherri, Kris, Kelley; mgr. public awareness Trans Gas; began amateur career with Gull Lake Lions; 4 seasons all-star dt/ctr Regina Rams; Man.-Sask. Junior League outstanding lineman '76; twice Rams MVP; CFL Saskatchewan og '76-92; 271 games played through '92; 8 all-Western, 5 all-CFL; Schenley outstanding offensive lineman award '86, '88; West Div. Becket-DeMarco Memorial Trophy outstanding offensive lineman award '86, '88; mem. '89 Grey Cup winner; nicknamed "Dog"; jersey #44 ret'd by Sask; mem. Sask. Roughriders Plaza of Honour, Cdn Football Hall of Fame; res. Regina Beach, Sask.

ALDRIDGE, Dick (football); b. 19 Jan 1941, Toronto, Ont.; given name: Richard Frederick; m. Elisabeth van Haastrecht; c. Jodi Elisabeth, Richard Todd; Waterloo, BA, BPHe; ret'd HS teacher; mem. OFSAA basketball champions '59-61; MVP Lakeshore Bears jr. ORFU '62; twice Waterloo football MVP, once basketball, outstanding athlete '66; from '66 Dick Aldridge Trophy awarded annually to Waterloo football MVP; drafted BC, traded to Hamilton '64; star lb Argos '65-73; Hamilton '74; led Argos punt returns '65, 7 interceptions '70; career record 19 interceptions 127 scheduled games; head coach York U '76-77, Etobicoke Argonauts '78-79; head boys' physical and health education Banting Memorial HS Alliston, Ont.; mem. OUAA Football Hall of Fame; res. Alliston, Ont.

ALEXANDER, Jeremy (shooting): b. 31 Jan 1948, Liverpool, Eng.; c. Michael; boilermaker; became mem. Calgary Rifle & Pistol Club '58; Calgary jr. small-bore champ '59; Alberta jr. small-bore prone title '64; won Cotteslee Vase Bisley while attending school in England '63; BC TR title '90, '96; DCRA Champlain agg. '96; qualified 4 Cdn Bisley teams; res. Victoria, B.C.

ALEXANDER, Keith (golf); b. 23 Jul 1930, Vulcan, Alta.; given name: Robert Keith; m. Vanessa Ramsay; c. Robert Brent, Marc Christopher, Jonathan Phillip, Susan Jolie Maitland, Andrea Denise, Jennifer Carrie; Colorado, BA, Wharton School of Finance, securities management certificate; investment exec., politician; ntl amateur title '60; 6 Alta. amateur, 2 Alta. open, 2 International Oilmen's titles; mem. 26 Willingdon Cup teams, 4 titles; 4 times Willingdon Cup medalist; 8 Calgary amateur, 5 Calgary open, 2 Edmonton amateur, 1 Edmonton open, 6 Calgary tournament of champions, 2 Alta. Canada Dry Challenge Cup, 6 Lethbridge Chinook Classic, 3 Mayfair GC titles; only Albertan to win prov. titles 4 different decades; mem. 6 World amateur (Eisenhower), 5 Americas Cup, 3 Commonwealth Cup, 1 Humberto de Almeida Brazil Cup,

1 Bogota Colombia International, 1 Paris International, French Amateur teams; Big 7 conf. title '53, low amateur '61 Azalea Open, competed '61 Masters; Colorado College title '56; 2 Guadalajara International titles; twice all-American; officer AGA '68-82, pres. '77; MLA (PC) Edmonton Whitemud from '82; mem. Alta., RCGA halls of fame; res. Edmonton, Alta.

ALEXANDER, Kevin (lacrosse); b. 18 Nov 1955, Victoria, B.C.; real estate agent; began playing age 6; considered Wayne Gretzky of lacrosse; mem. Victoria Shamrocks '79-86, Victoria Royal Waxmen '80-86; ntl team '81-90; mem. 7 ntl field, 3 box title teams; '76 Minto Cup, '79, '83 Mann Cup champions; Minto Cup MVP '76; mem. MILL titlist Buffalo Bandits '92-93; selected to all-world team '86; midfielder of '86; in 300 scheduled games amassed 797g, 584a; set or tied 31 box lacrosse records including most game-winning goals (40), most hat tricks 1 season (24), most powerplay goals 1 season (30), fastest 3 goals by individual player (13 seconds); coach/player ntl men's field team; asst. coach jr ntl team; coach Syracuse Smash (NLL) '98; nicknamed "Spanky"; mem. Cdn Lacrosse, Greater Victoria Sports halls of fame; res. Victoria, B.C.

ALEXANDER, Lisa (synchro swim); b. 22 Sep 1968, Toronto, Ont.; UofT HBA; Olympic coach; mgr. Cara Operations; competitive age-level swimmer completing all Red Cross programs to age 12 before entering synchro swimming at age 8; gold solo, figures '92 Scottish Open; team silver, duet (Kathy Glen) bronze '91 worlds; gold solo, duet (Erin Woodley) '94 CG; solo, duet (Woodley), team silver '95 worlds; team capt., team silver '96 Olympics; Helen Vanderburg Cdn top overall swimmer award '91; Ont. female athlete of '96; res. Mississauga, Ont.

ALEXANDER, Ray (football); b. 8 Jan 1962, Miami, Fla.; m. Mariel; c. Cardan, Amber; Florida A&M; wr; drafted Tampa Bay USFL '84; signed Denver NFL '84; Calgary CFL '85-86; Dallas NFL '87-89; BC CFL '90-94, '96; Ottawa CFL '95; CFL record 114g, 556recept, 8842yds, 41tds; 4 all-Western, 1 all-Cdn; mem. '94 Grey Cup champions; res. Talahassee, Fla.

ALFREDSSON, Daniel (hockey); b. 11 Dec 1972, Gothenburg, Sweden; m. Birgitta (Bibbi) Backman; c. Hugo; right wing Molndal Sweden '91-92, Vastra Frolunda Swedish Elite League '92-95; mem. Swedish ntl team Nissan Cup winners, World championship silver medal team '95; also competed for Sweden '96 World Cup, World championships, '98, '02 Olympics; drafted 5th by Ottawa '94 NHL entry draft; Calder Memorial Trophy '96; NHL all-rookie team '96; 2 NHL all-star teams; named team capt. '01; Ottawa NHLPA player rep.; NHL record (through '04): 629 scheduled games, 219g, 350a, 69 playoff games, 27g, 21a; played in Sweden during '04 labor dispute; res. Partille, Sweden/Ottawa, Ont.

ALIE, Caroll-Ann (boardsailing); b. 6 Jul 1960, Gracefield, Que.; m. Steve Rosenberg; c. Jacob; UofOtt, BSc. (2), Mich., CalState MSc (2); personal trainer LPGA; mem. Que., ntl women's boardsailing team; dist. 13 windsurfer champion '82-84; 2nd overall Australian windsurfer championships '83; Florida dist. windsurfer overall champion '84; Eastern midwinter windsurfer FS champion '84; ntl boardsailing overall champion '84-91; Western hemisphere windsurfer triangle champion '84; PAG gold '95, silver '87, '99; US, Cdn women's titles '91; 3 world Mistral, windsurfer overall titles; Cdn Mistral title '93; mem. '92, '96 Olympic Games teams; Ottawa ACT athlete of '85; 2 CYA, 1 QSF female-athlete-of-yr awards; mem. Cdn. Olympic Sports Hall of Fame; res. Huntington Beach, Calif.

ALLAN, Maurice (weightlifting); b. 17 Apr 1927, Montreal, Que.; d. 11 Jan 1990, Montreal, Que.; m. Pierrette Laroche; c. Michel, Lucie, Jean; Laval, BA; program-marketing mgr. Air Canada; operated Gymnase Hercule; Que. shot put, hammer throw titles '50; weightlifting coach '50-68; pres. Canadian Weightlifting Fed. '60-70; category I international lifting referee; coach '64 Olympics, mgr. '66 CG team; tech. advisor Canada Winter Games '67, PAG '67, Canada Summer Games '69; CdM Mexico Little Olympics '67, asst. CdM '68 Olympics, CdM '72, '76 Olympics; v-p IWF '72-80, COA director from '60, sec.-treas. from '77; hon. life pres. CWA '70; pres. AAU of C '70-71, v-p. SFC '70-71; '67 Centennial medal, gold medal for 25 years in weightlifting, Foley award sport administrator of '67, Air Canada merit award '67; mem. Order of Canada, Canadian Olympic, Que. Sports halls of fame.

ALLAN, Robert (lacrosse); b. 19 Sep 1934, Orillia, Ont.; m. Patricia Nickels; c. 3 daughters; UofT, mem. 4 Mann Cup title teams; 3 MVP awards; 3 scoring titles while playing Peterborough Jr., Sr. A, Nanaimo Sr. A '53-68; record 89 goals single season '56; coached 6 Ont. title teams; coached ntl team to world field title '78; coached Phildelphia Wings (NL) '74-75, Peterborough '64-72; OLA/ICLL/NLA pro sr. record: 192 scheduled games, 406g, 308a, 101 playoff games, 133g, 124a; Maitland trophy '56; Denny Huddleston Memorial trophy '57; Bucko McDonald trophy '59; Mike Kelly Memorial medal '64; mem. Cdn, Ont. Lacrosse halls of fame; res. Orillia, Ont.

ALLAN, Wanda (archery); b. 24 Jan 1955, Victoria, B.C.; given name: Wanda Marie; m. Bud Sadegur; received bow for 11th birthday and became seriously involved in archery '66; ntl jr. girls' title '69-72; twice runnerup senior nationals; mem. '76, '84 Olympic, 4 all-Americas, 3 worlds teams; 5 BC titles; gold '75, bronze '78 Western Canada Games; bronze target '74 all-Americas Puerto Rico; res. Kamloops, B.C.

ALLBON, Ackie (baseball); b. 8 Nov 1905, Springhill, N.S.; d. 27 Apr 2001, Springhill, N.S.; given name: Alfred George; m. Lillian Matthews; ret'd. town clerk; made sr. baseball debut at 16, pitching 14-inning victory; p/cf Springhill Fencebusters 1922-34; participated in 3 longest games in NS baseball history, 15, 14, 13 innings; registered 21 strikeouts in losing cause '29; mem. 4 NS, 2 Maritime title teams; pres. Springhill Minor Baseball Association; baseball columnist *Springhill Citizen*; level 1 ntl coaching certificate; award of merit '80; mem. NS Sports Hall of Fame.

ALLEN, Damon (football); b. 29 Jul 1963, San Diego, Calif.; CalState (Fullerton); m. Desiree; c. Amanda, Alyssa, Ateya; football player; pro qb Edmonton '85-88, '93-94; Ottawa '89-91; Hamilton '92-94; Memphis (CFL) Mad Dogs '95; BC '96-'02; Toronto '03-05; CFL record:

(through '04): 303 games, 89td, 5cvt, 539pts; 1652 carries, 11,241yds, 89td; 8187 passes, 4563 completed, 64,240yds, 252int, 346td; 5 Grey Cup finals, 3 winners; offensive star of '87, MVP '93, '04 game awards; 1 Eastern, Western all-star; all-time CFL passing leader '00; surpassed 60,000 passing yds 1 Aug '03; pitching tryout with Pittsburgh organization '94; brother of NFL star rb Marcus Allen; res. Stone Mountain, Ga.

ALLEN, Keith (builder/hockey); b. 21 Aug 1923, Saskatoon, Sask.; given name: Courtney Keith; m. Joyce; c. Brad, Blake, Traci; hockey exec.; played for Cdn navy team; 13 pro seasons AHL Buffalo, Springfield, Syracuse; QHL Sherbrooke; WHL Edmonton, Brandon; parts of 2 with NHL Detroit; mem. '54 Detroit Stanley Cup winner; 10yrs coach/ GM/bookkeeper/publicist Seattle Totems (WHL); league title '59; *HN* minor league exec. of '60; joined Philadelphia '66 as coach; became GM '70 and drafted-traded Flyers into a powerhouse in the '70s and '80s, 1ˢᵗ expansion team to win a Stanley Cup '74; repeated '75; team reached 4 more finals; set pro sports record of staying unbeaten for 35 games '79-80 season; stepped down as GM '83 to become exec. v-p; *HN* NHL exec. of '80; Lester Patrick trophy '88; nicknamed: "Bingo"; mem. Flyers, AHL, Hockey halls of fame; res. Bryn Mawr, Pa.

ALLETSON, Kim (figure skating); b. 30 Jun 1958, Brockville, Ont.; given name: Patricia Kim; m. Philip Henderson; c. John Charles Philip; UNB, BA, Dalhousie, LLB; lawyer; moved through Minto Skating Club ranks to win Eastern Ontario titles at each level of competition '68-78 before turning pro teaching in Ottawa, Fredericton; ntl jr. champion '74; twice runnerup srs.; Skate Canada '76; mem. '76 Olympic, several worlds teams; attended International Olympic Academy Greece; res. London, Eng.

ALLEYNE, Jeff (boxing); b. 25 Jun 1938, St. Philip, Barbados; given name: Jeffrey O'Neale; m. Carmen Goodridge; c. Derek, Michael; Concordia; telecommunications technician; moved to Canada '55; Golden Gloves champion '56-60, ntl 156lb title '60; mem. '60 Olympic team; following 4-yr retirement lost split decision in final in bid for '64 team berth; career ring record 83 wins, 4 losses; 1 year sr. football; coached Michel Prevost, Roger Fortin to '76 Olympic team; Prevost won '75 Pan-Am silver, Fortin '78 Commonwealth gold; operator Lafleche Boxing Club; Optimist International service to youth award; res. Greenfield Park, Que.

ALLISON, Ian (basketball); b. 26 Jul 1909, Greenock, Scotland; d. 4 Aug 1990, London, Ont.; given name: Ian Alaistair; m. Jean Reid; c. Heather, Jane; Assumption College, UWO, OCE; ret'd Walkerville CI athletic dir.; mem. 5 WOSSA soccer champions, 4 WOSSA, Ont. title basketball teams, Eastern Canadian title '28; WOSSA 440 titlist; all-conf. hb Assumption, mem. Assumption Ont. basketball champions; ORFU football St. Michael's; mem. UofT basketball champions, Windsor Alumni, Ford V8s ntl title; mem. '36 Olympic silver medal team; coached Ont. basketball titlists, WOSSA track, volleyball champions, HS football; Windsor Coaches Assn. award for outstanding contribution to HS athletics; Alpha Kai Omega fraternity award for service in junior sport; National Basketball Assn. of Coaches award for contributions to Canadian basketball;

city of Windsor award for outstanding contribution to HS athletics; mem. Cdn Basketball; Windsor-Essex County Sports halls of fame.

ALOMAR, Robbie (baseball); b. 5 Feb. 1968, Ponce, Puerto Rico; given name: Roberto Velazquez; father Sandy, brother Sandy Jr. both major leaguers; 2b; launched pro career '85 Charleston (A); '86 Reno (A), Baseball America all-star; '87 Wichita (AA); '88 Las Vegas (AAA); joined San Diego Padres '88; youngest player on ML roster '89 opening day; traded to Toronto '91 becoming integral part of '92-93 World Series champions; through '03 mem. 12 all-star teams; 10 Gold Glove awards; Toronto BBWAA, Labatt's player-of-yr awards '91; ALCS MVP '92; all-star game MVP '98; signed as free agent by Baltimore '96-98, Cleveland '99-01, NY Mets '02-03, Chicago WS '03, '04, Arizona '04, Tampa Bay '05; spitting (on umpire) incident '96 led to suspension to start '97 season; MBL record (through '04): 2379 scheduled games, 9073ab, 1508r, 2724h, 504db, 80tr, 210hr, 474sb, 1134rbi, .300ba; res. Salinas, PR.

ALOU, Felipe (baseball): b. 12 May 1935, Haina, Dominican Republic; m. Lucie Gagnon; c. Moises, Jose, Valerie, Felipe Jr.; baseball manager; of; represented Dominican Republic '54 PAG in baseball, javelin; minor league stints '56-58 with Lake Charles, Cocoa, Minneapolis, Springfield, Phoenix; major leagues '58-74 with San Francisco, Milwaukee, Atlanta, Oakland, NY Yankees, Montreal; ML record: 2082 games, 7339ab, 985r, 2101h, 359db, 49tr, 206hr, 852rbi, 423bob, 705k, 107sb, .286ba; 3 all-star games, '62 World Series; made history '63 appearing in same outfield with younger brothers Jesus and Matty for Giants; 31ˢᵗ player in history to record at least 2000 hits, 200 homers; turned to managing '77 posting 884-751 minor league record with West Palm Beach, Memphis, Denver, Wichita, Indianapolis '77-91; coach Montreal '79-80, '84, '92; mgr. Montreal '92-01; San Francisco Giants '03-05; consultant Detroit '02; established Expos club managerial record with 1127 games, 600 victories '99; hon. citizen Laval; *AP* mgr of '94; res. Lake Worth, Fla.

ALSOP, Amy (goalball); b. 30 Jun 1978, Saskatoon, Sask.; given name: Amy Lynn; USask BComm.; full-time athlete; born with rare genetic condition which left her visually impaired; first athletic competition came as swimmer in '93 Canadian Games; swimming not her thing; switched to goalball, in which she quickly showed considerable talent; competed for Team Sask. ntl championships from '94, 5 gold, 2 silver, 1 bronze; 3 Ottawa Invitational gold; 1 NA gold; 5 ntl championships MVP awards; SBSA rookie of '94, 3 female-athlete-of-yr awards, 1 team-of-yr award; Investors Group bursary recipient; profiled in book *Making a Difference, Profiles in Abilities* mem. Team Canada from '97; Paralympic gold '00; 2 Helmacy Memorial gold, 1 silver; London International gold, silver; IBSA worlds, PAG silver; chair athlete advisory council Cdn Sport Centre Sask.; mem. Team Sport Speakers Bureau; '02 Sask. Winter Games mission staff; res. Saskatoon, Sask

ALTMANN, Fred (shooting); b. 13 Feb 1935, Stuttgart, W.Germany; given name: Fred Max; m. Helga Kloster; c. Cindy, Monique; painting contractor; skeet shooting specialist; silver '77-78 Canadian team trials; team gold, individual bronze '80 German grand prix; team gold '82

CG; mem. '78, '82 Commonwealth, '79 PAG, 5 world, 6 Benito Juarez championships teams; federal govt. excellence award '83; res. Toronto, Ont.

AMATT, John (mountaineering); b. 19 May 1945, Manchester, Eng.; given name: John Robert; m. Peggy Hagel; c. Jillian; UCal, BEd, U of Durham, Eng. Dip. Ed; pres. One Step Beyond World Wide; lecturer, teacher, management consultant; emigrated to Canada '68; Cdn citizen from '73; more than 30yrs experience climbing, mountain hiking Britain, Norway, France, Italy, Germany, Austria, Greenland, Peru, Mexico, Nepal, China, USA, Canada; mem./principal organizer successful Cdn Mount Everest expedition '82; leader 1st Cdn China mountaineering expedition '81; chair. Alexander Mackenzie Canada Sea-to-Sea bicentennial expeditions '89-93; qualified pro mountain guide, photo journalist; founder Banff Festival of Mountain Films; 2 Alta achievement awards, SFC Cdn sports award; mem. advisory board Banff Centre for Mountain Culture; mem. Alpine Club of Canada, Assn. Cdn Mountain Guides, Meeting Planners Intl, Intl Platform Assn.; Alta. Sports Hall of Fame special award; res. Canmore, Alta.

AMBROSE, John (baseball); b. 20 Jun 1929, Vineland, N.J.; given name: John Francis; m. Beatrice Neale; c. Neal, Philip, Cathy, Nancy, Edward; ret'd. plumbing contractor; p/if/of; pro Boston Braves organization '48-53; twice Quebec City (Provincial League) all-star; amassed variety of all-star, pitching, batting honors St.Thomas, London Sr. IC '54-66; mgr. St. Thomas team; mem. IC title teams '54-55, '58; IC MVP '58; mem. 2 all-Ont. St. Thomas basketball title teams; res. St. Thomas, Ont.

AMES, Stephen (golf); b. 28 Apr 1964, San Fernando, Trinidad & Tabago; m. Jodi; c. Justin, Ryan Michael; Boca Raton; following lead of grandmother who won 20 T&T titles pursued golf career from teens; won Barbados Hoerman Cup at 16 with course record 66; turned pro '87 competing on Hogan, Nike, European, US PGA tours; won Pensacola Open (Hogan) '91; multiple winner European tour '93-97; became Cdn citizen; mem. 2 Cdn World Cup teams; scored 1st PGA tour win at Cialis Western Open '04; competed '05 Masters; res. Calgary, Alta.

AMEY, Jessica (swimming): b. 15 Nov 1976, Montreal, Que.; butterfly specialist; 7 ntl titles; 6 ntl records; silver 4x100 medley relay '95 world short course championships; bronze 100m fly '95, 50m FS '93 Pan-Pacific; 2 bronze '94 CG; 2 silver, 1 bronze '96 World Cup III short course; res. Calgary, Alta.

AMUNDRUD, Gail (swimming); b. 6 Apr 1957, Toronto, Ont.; m. Jim Beattie; c. Lauren; Arizona State; software co. applications engineer; began competitive swimming Ottawa Kingfish '67 moving to Vancouver Dolphins '74; 1st ntl age-group (11-12) 100m backstroke title '70; 1st ntl record :54.0 in 100yd FS '73; 1st Canadian girl to swim 100m FS under one minute (:59.8) '73 world championships; two gold, silver, bronze '74 CG; two gold, two silver, bronze '74 Ont. finals; bronze '74, gold, bronze '77 AAU finals; 7 gold '76 ntls; 2 silver, bronze '76 Olympics; two bronze '79 PAG; AIWA 100m, 200m FS champion '78-79; 10 ntl FS records during career; mem. '75, '79 Pan-Am, '76 Olympic, '74, '78 CG; 4 yrs. all-American; coached 6yrs; competed as triathlete '88-

90; masters competitor; mem. Ottawa Sports, BC Swimming, Ariz. State halls of fame; res. Calgary, Alta.

AMYOT, Frank (canoeing); b. 14 Sep 1904, Thornhill, Ont.; d. 21 Nov 1962, Ottawa, Ont.; m. Mary Kelly; civil servant; one of six children of Dr. John Amyot, Canada's first deputy minister of health and pensions; mem. Rideau Aquatic, Britannia Boating Clubs; big man who required custom built racing shell; Canadian Canoe Assn. int. singles '23; 6 ntl sr. singles, 1 double-blade title; capt., mgr., coach Canadian canoe team '36 Olympics; only Canadian ever to win gold in 1000m Canadian singles setting Olympic record 5:32.1; instrumental in saving 3 lives, including footballer Dave Sprague, in Ottawa River boating mishap; helped organize Rideau Canoe Club; mem. Ottawa, Cdn Olympic, Ottawa CSRA, Canada's Sports halls of fame.

ANAKIN, Doug (bobsleigh); b. 6 Nov 1930, Chatham, Ont.; given name: Douglas Thomas; m. Mary Jane Mosker; c. Megan Grace, Bridget Susan; Queen's, BA, SUNY College, MA, OCE; teacher John Abbott Coll.; intercollegiate wrestling, skiing, mountaineering; selected by Vic Emery for number two spot on '64 Olympic bobsleigh gold medal team; pioneered Cdn luge program; mem. Cdn Winter Olympic, Cdn Olympic, Canada's Sports halls of fame; res. Windermere, B.C.

ANDERSEN, Dale (boxing); b. 21 May 1953, Yellowknife, N.W.T.; given name: Dale Irwin; div; derrickman; mem. Rocky Legion boxing club, coached by father Gunner; ntl amateur featherweight, 4 Alta., 1 BC Golden Gloves titles; mem. '71 Pan-Am, '72 Olympic, '74 CG teams; bronze '74 CG; silver '73 Tournament of Europeans East Berlin; 3 silver medals NA championships; boxer-of-yr, runnerup Canadian male athlete of '74; several provincial achievement awards; res. Rocky Mountain House, Alta.

ANDERSEN, Roxy (t&f/builder); b. 26 Jun 1912, Montreal, Que.; d. 6 Sep 2002, San Francisco, Calif.; given name: Roxanne Atkins; m. Einar Andersen; UofT; City College of San Francisco; track exec.; several Ont. hurdles, relay titles early '30s with Laurel Ladies AC, club she founded; ntl indoor 50yd hurdles, 80m FS, 440yd outdoor relay records; US indoor 50yd hurdles, US indoor 440 relay title team '34-36; mem. '36 Olympic, '34 BEG, women's world games teams; pres.-sec. Ont. Women's Amateur Athletic Fed., Ont. Ladies' Hockey League, Queen City Softball League; US citizen; commissioned by Pacific AAU to organize N. California women's t&f program; during 26-year period did same in Central California, Oregon, Colorado; pioneered ntl age-group program; chair. Olympic women's t&f committee '53-57; mgr. US women's t&f team '56 Olympics; 1st woman rep. AAU men's t&f comm.; former pres. Pacific AAU; chair. emeritus Athletic Congress; former chair. AAU women's t&f comm.; author, composer, raconteur; Norman Craig Memorial Trophy Award outstanding Ont. female athlete '34; Bay area distinguished woman award '65; '00 women of achievement award '74; President's meritorious service award '82; *World's Who's Who of Women, Who's Who in America*; mem. US t&f Hall of Fame.

ANDERSON, Andy (softball); b. 25 Oct 1933, Windsor, Ont.; d. 12 Nov 1994, Ottawa, Ont.; given name: Albert

Garnet; m. Joyce Hill; c. Andrew, Bonnie Jean, Patricia; ret'd. RCMP officer, City of Ottawa security dir.; began pitching at 16 with Amherstburg SKD Manufacturing; pitched for Loretto Bros. Wr. Sr. League, Ottawa Wajax, Westmount RCMP, Snowdon, Toronto Beaches Major Fastball Leagues, Oshawa Tony's, Vancouver Sr. League, Gatineau Ambassadors, RCMP National Defence League; league career record 407 wins, 216 losses; mem. 2 all-Cdn World tournament teams; rookie-of-yr finalist Snowdon League; frequent Most Valuable Pitcher honors Toronto, Ottawa, Montreal leagues; mem. 11 league, playoff champions; 2 Cdn title teams; 19 career no-hitters, 39 1-hitters, competed in 30 tournaments; pitched in 4 games vs. Eddie Feigner's King and His Court; with another pitcher combined for record 15-inning 35 strikeouts (he had 18); ret'd from game '78.

ANDERSON, Dave (all-around); b. 29 Oct 1932, Winnipeg, Man.; given name: David Frederick; m. Ann Cameron Spencer; c. Ian, Dorothy; UCLA, BSc., MSc., Northern Colorado, EdD; administrator, professor; varsity football, rugby, soccer UCLA; twice all-America soccer goaler; NCAA all-America goaler '54; mem. '53 Rose Bowl, '54 Hula Bowl teams; pro LA Rams '54-55; HS coach '54-63; football coach UCLA '57-59, Manitoba provincial team coach '61-63; mem. National Advisory Council '67-69; chair. Man. sport advisory council '70-73; chair./sect.-treas. Man. boxing, wrestling commission '71-73; former pres. University Athletic Directors Assn.; 16yrs dir. athletic camp; exec. mem. Man. Sports Fed. '74-75; CIAU dir. '73-76; res. Winnipeg, Man.

ANDERSON, Gabby (baseball); b. 29 Nov 1929, Detroit, Mich.; given name: Stanley Robert; m. Lorella Talbot; c. Jeffrey, Richard, Lisa; ret'd. inspector automobile quality control; pro ball Pony League, '50 rookie-of-yr batting .335 Peoria, Ill.; Class D Olean, NY '54-55, .355 in '54; quit pro ball, London Majors (Sr.IC) briefly '55; Great Lakes-Niagara League batting title '57 with .403, also MVP; with London rejoined IC '58; runnerup '58 batting race with .398, '59 with .420; won '60 batting crown with .391; IC MVP '59; twice led IC in doubles, once each home runs, runs batted in; 12-year IC average .339; mgr. London '63; v-p Eager Beaver Baseball League (Little League) '65-66, pres. '67-68; helped launch Tyke Div. (9-10 year olds) '68; coached minor, girls hockey from '73; res. London, Ont.

ANDERSON, Gary (swimming): b. 7 Apr 1969, Montreal, Que.; Southern Cal; near drowning age 4 led to swimming lessons; 8 ntl titles; broke John Naber's 13-yr school 200yd backstroke record '90 NCAA's; mem. ntl team '87-95; mem. '88, '92 Olympic, '91 World aquatic, '93 Pan-Pacific, world short course championship teams; gold 200m backstroke, 200m IM, silver 100m backstroke '90 CG; competed '94 CG, '95 PAG; does hospital volunteer work in L.A.; competed '03 US masters; res. Manhattan Beach, Calif.

ANDERSON, George (soccer); b. 23 Jun 1890, Fraserburgh, Aberdeenshire, Scotland; d. 30 May 1985, Winnipeg, Man.; compositor; organized, managed Caledonia junior, juvenile, midget teams; 10yrs mem. Man. Jr. Soccer Assn. exec., 4yrs. exec. Man. Sr. Soccer Assn.; involved in reactivation Dominion Football Assn. '46, exec. capacities '51-68; key role Canada's 1st World Cup entry '57; CFA delegate to FIFA '61, '66 World Congress; key role Canada's '68 Olympic soccer entry; organizer, mgr. Expo '67 soccer tournament; active in '67 Winnipeg Pan-Am tournament; sect.-treas. Rockwood unit 303 ANAF veterans minor soccer program; mem. Man., Canada's Sports halls of Fame.

ANDERSON, Glenn (hockey); b. 2 Oct 1960, Vancouver, B.C.; given name: Glenn Chris; div. Patricia O'Connor; c. Nicholas; Denver U; Seattle (WHL) '79-80; mem. Olympic team '80; 3rd Edmonton draft pick, 69th overall '79; pro NHL Edmonton '80-91, '96, Toronto '91-94, NYR '94, St. Louis '95-96; topped 50-goal plateau '83-84, '85-86 with 54 goals each time; NHL record: 1129 scheduled games, 498g, 601a, 225 playoff games, 93g, 121a; played briefly in Germany '94, '96, Finland '94, Switzerland '97; 4 NHL all-star games; mem. Team Canada '84, '95; mem. 6 Stanley Cup winners; mem. B.C. Hockey Hall of Fame; res. Vancouver, B.C.

ANDERSON, Jasey Jay (snowboarding); b. 13 Apr 1975, Montreal, Que.; John Abbott Coll.; giant slalom specialist; began snowboarding age 13; gold Sugarloaf GP '96, Snowmass GP '97; silver NA championships '97; bronze FIS World Cup '96, gold '01; 13 medals '01-02 WC tour; 4 world titles; 20 WC victories; 2 world championship gold '05; 2 ntl parallel GS titles; competed '98, '02 Olympics; John Semmelink award; res. Mont. Tremblant, Que.

ANDERSON, Jerry (golf); b. 22 Sep 1955, Montreal, Que.; m. Barbara; c. Chirysse; Texas; pro golfer; turned pro '78; qualified for USPGA tour '89; mem. 2 Dunhill Cup, 2 World Cup teams; won Cdn TPC, Windsor Charity Classic, '87 CPGA title, '84 European Masters, '82-83 Quebec Open, '79 Sask., Ont., Man. Opens; du Maurier Order of Merit '89; competed on US, Europe, Australia/NZ, Asia, South America, South Africa, Cdn PGA tours; res. Scarborough, Ont.

ANDERSON, Kate (t&f): b. 9 Jan 1968, Kingston, Jamaica; given name: Keturah; hurdler; ntl jr 100m, 200m titles '86; competed '87 worlds, '88 (as sprinter), '92, '96 Olympics, '90, '98 Commonwealth, '99 Pan-Am, '93 FISU Games, world championships as hurdler; gold '96 Georgia Tech Reebok Invitational, '94 Alabama relays; bronze '98 CGs; '99 indoor worlds; 3 ntl titles; res. Toronto, Ont./Tuscaloosa, Ala.

ANDERSON, Les (archery); b. 31 May 1940, Wells, B.C.; given name: Leslie Ernest; m. Lorraine Marie DeLong; senior electrical technical assistant; from '61 won 16 Sask., 3 Alta. titles, 20 invitational tournaments; runnerup field events '73 ntl championships; '73 Championship of Americas field event title; ntl indoor champion '76, outdoor '78; certificate of recognition for outstanding achievement in amateur sport from Western Christian College, Weyburn, Sask., '76; mem. Sask Sports Hall of Fame; res. Prince Albert, Sask.

ANDERSON, Nint (builder/curling): b. 2 Sep 1917, Fredericton, N.B.; d. 28 May 1988, Newcastle, N.B.,; given name: Millicent; m. William Anderson; served curling at club, provincial, ntl administrative levels; instrumental in formation NB mixed curling assn in '60s; 1st and only woman to chair NB men's Ganong Cup '74; NB Ladies' CA v-p, secty '63-73, pres. '74-76; 1st from NB to receive CLCA appreciation award; hon. mem. Chatham CC; mem. NB Sports Hall of Fame.

ANDERSON, Patrick (wheelchair basketball); b. 22 Aug 1979, Edmonton, Alta.; Illinois; began playing wheelchair basketball '90; following outstanding junior career moved to ntl team '98 where he became a consummate team player and leader by example; mem. Twin City Spinners; gold '97, '01 jr. worlds; world cup bronze '98; 1 CWBL gold, 2 silver; 3 ntl championship gold, 2 silver; Paralympic gold '00, '04; 6 tournament MVP awards; 5 all-star teams; res. Fergus, Ont.

ANDERSON, Randy (volleyball); b. 19 Feb 1957, Winnipeg, Man.; given name: Randall Barry; UMan, BPhE.; Man. sports consultant; 17 hockey seasons Winnipeg region; mem. 3 Man. jr. lacrosse champions, 3 ntl Jr. B champions; mem. '77 Canada Games lacrosse; mem. Man. HS volleyball champions '72, '76; ntl jr. titlists '74; mem. Canada Winter Games '75 silver medal team; ntl jr. team '75-76; mem. 4 Great Plains Conf. champions, '78, '80 CIAU champions; ntl men's team '80-81; mem. '80 Canada Games gold medal team; Bill Masterton Trophy for athletic-academic excellence in HS; 3 times Great Plains all-star, twice CIAU all-Canadian; 5 times major tournament all-star; res. Winnipeg, Man.

ANDERSON, Ricky (boxing); b. 28 Oct 1960, Halifax, N.S.; given name: Rick Kenneth; m. Effie Washington; c. Torres, Shay; St. Mary's BA; motivational speaker; ntl jr. light welterweight title '75, int. '76, sr. '80-81; silver '79 world jr. championship; gold Acropolis Greece tournament, 3 European tour competitions '80; bronze Finland Tammer tournament, NZ Games; ntl gold, 2 world silver; 8 NS titles; mem. '80 Olympic team; athletes rep. Olympic advisory comm.; as pro from '82 posted 19-2 record and held Cdn welter title '85-86; authored *Win in the Arena of Life*; NS athlete of '80; mem. Cdn Boxing, NS Sports halls of fame; res. Halifax, N.S.

ANDERSON, Steve (karate): b. 29 Mar 1955, Toledo, O; Southwestern Coll; San Diego State, BSc.; karate instructor; nickname "Nasty"; began training under world kickboxing champion Chicken Gabriel and earned black belt status '80; US champion '80-87; Cdn titles '88-90; WAKO world titles England '83-84, '85-86, Germany '87-89. Italy '90-92; charter mem. 1st pro karate team '87; NASKA fighter of '80s; *Kick Illustrated* fighter of '83; selected for 1st issue commemorative karate cards '91; California Karate League competitor of '80-81; NASKA lifetime achievement award '90; active fund-raiser for juvenile diabetes; set marathon fighting records; NASKA living legend award '95; record 6 US Capital Classics tournament titles; more than 60 major tournament victories; NA number 1 karate fighter since '80; mem. Fighter Magazine, Black Belt halls of fame; res. Orleans, Ont.

ANDERSON, Tamara (ringette); b. 12 Sep 1973, Calgary, Alta.; admin. asst.; goalie '91 Canada Winter Games gold medal team; playing for Team Alberta 7 ntl titles, as mem. Team Canada 3 world titles; 2 1st team, 1 2nd team ntl championship all-star; res. Calgary, Alta.

ANDERSON, Verne (skiing); b. 1937, Rossland, B.C.; d. 30 Sep 1983, Boulder, Colo; given name: Verne Ralph; m. Ardys Klinzing; c. Beverley, Sherri; business consultant; Western Cdn jr. downhill '53; ntl downhill '58-59; mem.

'60 Olympic team; top Cdn male competitor '61 European, NA circuits; hampered by injuries competing '62 FIS championships France; men's ntl team coach '62-64; coached Nancy Greene; women's ntl team coach '66-68; mem. Canadian Skiing Hall of Fame.

ANDREW, Trevor (snowboarding); b. 31 Aug 1979, Kentville, N.S.; began snowboarding age 11; halfpipe specialist; 2 ntl titles; 1 WC gold, silver, bronze; competed '98 Olympics; res. Falmouth, N.S.

ANDREWS, Porky (basketball); b. 18 Sep 1917, Victoria, B.C.; given name: George Lloyd; m. Marion Kennedy; c. Wayne Murray, Janet Louise, Scott Alexander; Oregon, BSc.; teacher; 3 Victoria HS track titles; ntl high hurdles record; mem. BC rugby, softball, lacrosse title teams; Royal Colwood Golf Club championship; 2 decades one of nation's top basketballers; mem. ntl title teams '35, '46; player-coach Victoria Dominoes; pro Vancouver Hornets, Alberni Athletics, team he started '49; 2yrs. capt. Oregon team, all-Coast Guard, all-American; coach Victoria Hudson Bay Sr. A women's team 2yrs., Victoria HS boys to 3 provincial titles, Victoria HS girls 1 provincial title; governor BC Boys HS Basketball Assn.; mem. BC, Greater Victoria Sports halls of fame; res. Victoria, B.C.

ANDREYCHUK, Dave (hockey); b. 29 Sep 1963, Hamilton, Ont.; m. Sue; c. Taylor, Caci; lw Oshawa Generals; mem. Team Canada jr. worlds '83; 1st choice Buffalo '82 draft; Buffalo '82-92, '01; Toronto '92-96; New Jersey '96-99, Boston '99, Colorado '00, Tampa Bay '01-04 (capt.); topped 50-goal plateau 54 '93, 53 '94; eclipsed TML record 49 goals for left winger set by Frank Mahovlich with 53 '94; achieved 500g plateau '97; NHL record: (through '04) 1597 scheduled games, 634g, 686a, 162 playoff games, 43g, 54a; 1 Stanley Cup winner; active with American Cancer Society; res. Buffalo, N.Y.

ANDRU, John (fencing); b. 20 Nov 1932, Toronto, Ont; div. Joan Davies; c. Reina; UofT; restaurateur; best overall competitive record by any native-born fencer in Canada; 9 ntl individual, 4 team titles, medalist 34 times, 8 Eastern Cdn, 14 Ont. titles; only husband-wife pair to win ntl individual foils titles same year '63; mem. 2 Olympic, 4 Pan-Am, 4 CG teams; 6 Commonwealth, 3 Pan-Am medals; mgr., capt. '68 Olympic, '70 Commonwealth, '71 PAG, world youth teams; CdM '72 world youth team; international dir., judge '72, '76 Olympics; 1st Canadian qualified Class A pres. of jury by Federation Internationale d'Escrime; AAU of C Central Ont. dir.; established CFA as ntl incorporated body following demise of AAU of C, pres. '67-73; CFA tech., exec. dir. '73-80; COA dir. '67-72, AAU of C '67-71; v-p Commonwealth Fencing Fed. '70-74; Centennial Medal '67; Norton Crowe medal '69; 3 Ont. achievement awards; 6 OFA Don Collinge awards; mem. Canadian Olympic Sports Hall of Fame; res. Toronto, Ont.

ANDRUSYSHYN, Zenon (football/t&f); b. 25 Feb 1947, Gunzburg, Germany; m. Sue Johnson; c. Zoe, Zuriel; UCLA; state dir. Fellowship of Christian Athletes; Cdn jr., men's javelin records; mem '66 CG team; track scholarship UCLA; switched to football, set UCLA punting, field goal records; *Sporting News* all-American '67, '69; noted as showboat wearing golden kicking boot; pro Toronto Argos

'71-77, '80-82, Kansas City Chiefs (NFL) '78, Hamilton '79, Edmonton '82, Tampa Bay (USFL) '83-85; shared EFC scoring title with Bernie Ruoff '80; 11-year CFL record 213 converts, 201 field goals, 139 singles, 955 points; 6 times CFL all-star; several Argos club kicking records; mem. Athletes in Action; nicknamed "Big Z"; res. Tampa, Fla.

ANTHONY, Matt (football/coaching); b. 12 Feb 1921, St. Catharines, Ont.; d. 13 Jul 2000, Ottawa, Ont.; given name: Matt Lloyd; m. Marilyn Feeney; c. Judith (d), Darryl, Pamela, Valerie; electrical contractor; versatile athlete; capt. Cdn jr. basketball title team; mem. UofOtt, Barrett's Lumber sr. basketball teams; played lacrosse St. Catharines Ont. minor title teams, Ont. sr. league Orillia Tigers, Ottawa St. Anthony, pro Quebec Montagnards; as rower stroke 1st Cdn HS coxless 4s to win NA title at Cdn Henley; mem. St. Catharines sr. baseball/softball teams; football with Hamilton Wildcats '40, Montreal '46, Ottawa '47-48, '51-53, Sask. '49-50; Big Four/Ted Reeves all-Cdn '50; mem. '51 Grey Cup champions; head coach UofOtt 15yrs; asst/head coach jr Ottawa Sooners; 4yrs Cdn Navy; recipient Burma Star; UofO football award bears his name.

ANTOFT, Kell (skiing/administration); b. 24 Jul 1923, Roskilde, Denmark; d. 8 Jan 2005, Bridgewater, N.S.; div. Kit Burns; m. Mary Lou Courtney; c. Asta, Susan, Nick, Tim; King's County Academy, Dalhousie BA, MA; adjunct prof. Henson Coll.; dir. Dalhousie U Institute of Public Affairs; emigrated to Canada '30; avid skier; co-founder Nancy Greene Ski League; founding pres. NS Ski Areas Assn., Ski Atlantic Srs. Club; served on board Cdn Ski Assn; life mem. Cdn Ski Instructors' Alliance; founded/sold 2 successful businesses; RCAF navigator; asst. ED ntl Cancer Institute; active Cdn Hostelling Assn.; pres. Katimivik program '86-89; co-founder Veterans Agains Nuclear Arms; WW2 Victory, Defence, Voluntary Services, Christian X (Denmark) medals; mem. Order of Canada, Order of NS, NS Sports Hall of Fame.

ANTON, Ron (curling); b. 7 Aug 1941, Medicine Hat, Alta.; given name: Ronald Michael; m. Sharon Dew; c. Michael, Douglas, Lorna, Margo; UofAlta, BA. educator; p/if Medicine Hat baseball teams '53-63, 2 no-hitters; HS football qb; HS football coach '65-75, 2 Edmonton city titles; competitive curler '58-76 winning variety of major events; at 19 youngest mem. Brier winner playing 3rd for Hec Gervais; mem. Brier winners '61, '74, runnerup '62; mem. '64-67 Northern Alta. champions; skipped Alta. mixed titlist, ntl runnerup '73; Curl Canada ntl course conductor; mem. Curl Canada certification comm.; all-star Brier 3rd '61, '74; 1st pres. Alta. Assn. of Competitive Curlers; tech. co-ordinator '92 Olympic curling team; mem. Canadian Curling Hall of Fame; res. Spruce Grove, Alta.

APPLEBY, Elizabeth (speed skating); b. 25 Nov 1958, Winnipeg, Man.; m. Gordon Levin; c. Eric; Health Science Centre RN; nurse; Cdn jr. champion '74; mem. ntl team '74-79; set variety of Man., ntl and one world record during 16-yr career; world jr champ '76; Cdn sr women's title '77-79; named to world sprint, all-round teams '74-75; mem. '76 Olympic team; mem. Wpg women's sr softball title team '73; mem. gold medal women's cycle team Western Cdn Games '79; mem. Cdn Speed Skating, Man. Sports halls of fame; res. Winnipeg, Man.

APPS, Syl Sr. (hockey/t&f); b. 18 Jan 1915, Paris, Ont.; d. 24 Dec. 1998, Kingston, Ont.; given name: Charles Joseph Sylvanus; m. Mary Josephine Marshall; c. Joanne, Robert, Carol, Sylvanus Jr., Janet; McMaster, BA; ret'd. brick manufacturer, ret'd politician; ntl pole vault, '34 BEG titles; mem. '36 Olympic team; capt. McMaster intercollegiate football title team; sr. hockey Hamilton Tigers; pro Toronto '36-48; led NHL in assists, 2nd overall scoring '36-37, '37-38; Calder Trophy rookie-of-year; Lionel Conacher trophy '37; centred line of Busher Jackson, Gordie Drillon, later Drillon, Bob Davidson; ret'd. as Leaf capt.; NHL record: 423 scheduled games, 201g, 231a, 69 playoff games, 25g, 29a; Lady Byng Trophy '41-42 with no penalty minutes; twice 1st, 3 times 2nd team all-star; mem. 3 Stanley Cup winners; Ont. Athletic Commissioner '46-48; PC MLA for Kingston and the Islands '63-80; Minister Correctional Services '71-74; jersey 10 ret'd by Leafs; Paris, Ont. rink, trophy honoring Ont. athlete-of-yr bear his name; mem. Order of Canada, Hockey, Copps Coliseum, Royal Canadian Legion, McMaster, Canadian Olympic, Canada's Sports halls of fame.

ApSIMON, John (fencing); b. 5 Aug 1935, England; div. Claire Manning, c. Joanne, Paul, Michele, m. Karen Bergenstein; c. Megan, Noah; Liverpool, BSc, PhD; v-p. research and external affairs Carleton; capt. Liverpool fencing team '57-59; UK ntl universities champion '58; Northwestern Section champion '58; emigrated to Canada and ranked class A fencer in foil, sabre, épée '60-72; 4 times McFarland 3-weapon trophy, Governor-General's épée titlist '69; mem. RA Les Spadassins 3 team gold, 2 silver, 2 bronze in épée, 2 gold, silver, 4 bronze in foil, 5 silver, 2 bronze in sabre; '71 Ont. foil title, Ont. Winter Games foil, team titles; from '60 coach Les Spadassins, Carleton; guided Carleton to intercollegiate titles '67-68; coached individual OUAA champions '67-69, '74; FIE class B dir. 3 weapons; Don Collinge Trophy OFA '71; pres. RA Les Spadassins, v-p CFA '68-73, pres. '73-76, v-p CFA elite '78; mgr. '72 Olympic, '74, '78-79 jr. world title, '75 Ont. Canada Winter Games, '79 PAG teams; judge '76 Olympics; competed world sr games Toronto; assists son Paul as UofOtt coach; life mem. Ottawa CSRA; res. Ottawa, Ont.

ARAKGI, Nick (football); b. 9 Aug 1955, Cairo, Egypt; m. Suzanne; c. Nicholas, Michelle; Bishop's; salesman Imperial Tobacco; te Montreal '79-85; outstanding blocker; club record 89 receptions for 1062yds, 6tds '82; record 269 receptions, 3590yds, 22tds; EFC all-star '82, '84; Montreal player of '82; Schenley outstanding Canadian award '84; res. Kirkland, Que.

ARBOUR, Al (hockey); b. 1 Nov 1932, Sudbury, Ont.; given name: Alger Joseph; m. Claire Sabourin; c. Joanne, Jay, Julie, Janice; Assumption College; ret'd. hockey exec; dfc Windsor jrs; NHL Detroit '53-58, Chicago '58-61, Toronto '61-66, St. Louis '67-71; NHL playing record: 626 scheduled games, 12g, 58a, 86 playoff games, 1g, 8a; mem. 3 Stanley Cup winners; coach/AGM St. Louis '70-73, scout Atlanta; coach NYI '73-86, '88-94; v-p, consultant to GM Islanders from '95; 4 consec. Stanley Cups; NHL coach-of-yr '78-79; NHL milestone 15 Apr '92 coaching 1438th game, passing Dick Irvin; NHL coaching record: ('79-94) 1606 games, 781-577-248; Hockey Hall of Fame selection comm; mem. Hockey Heritage

North, Hockey halls of fame; res. Cold Spring Harbor, N.Y./Sarasota, Fla.

ARCHIBALD, Joan (fencing); b. 3 Mar 1913, Montreal, Que.; given name: Helen Joan; m. John Riddell; c. John Jr., Joanna, Michael, Edward, Christie; Royal Academy of Music, London, Eng.; variety of provincial, ntl fencing titles prior to '32; mem. '32 Olympic team; turned to horse breeding and produced colt which won Governor-General's, Lt.-Governor's Cups Royal Winter Fair; senior horse show judge; res. Mt. Uniacke, N.S.

ARCHIBALD, Nancy (fencing); b. 7 Dec 1911, Montreal, Que.; d. Apr 1996, Vancouver, B.C.; m. Werner Joeck; c. Nancy, Susan, Ian, Neil; social worker; fenced several years MAAA, competing at provincial, ntl levels; Que. champion '34-35; runnerup ntl ladies' foil '37; mem. ntl fencing team '36 Olympics.

ARMITAGE, Roly (harness racing); b. 8 Feb 1925, South March, Ont.; given name: Roland Montgomery; m. Mary Spearman (d); c. Maxwell Anne, Anne Elizabeth, Blake, James, Don; m. Karen; UofT; veterinarian; pres. Canadian Standardbred Society '73-74; pres. CTA '75-81; pres./GM Rideau Carleton Raceway '81-90; horse show judge; veterinarian of '82 award; Pontiac County citizen of yr '62; unsuccessful in initial bid in provincial political arena '87; mem. Cdn Horse Racing, Ottawa Sports halls of fame; res. Dunrobin, Ont.

ARMSTRONG, Brian (t&f); b. 9 Sep 1948, Toronto, Ont.; given name: Brian Joseph; UofT, BA, LLB; lawyer; from '69-74 represented Canada in international x-country, marathon races; 2nd Canadian marathon, Olympic trials '72; Detroit Motor City, Western Hemisphere marathons '72; runnerup '73 Canadian, Fukuoka Japan marathons; ranked 3rd among world marathoners '73 by *Track & Field News*; mem '74 CG team; res. Toronto, Ont.

ARMSTRONG, Charles (coaching); b. 10 Oct 1906, Stratford, Ont.; d. 29 May 2001, Windsor, Ont.; Assumption College; RC priest; regarded as "Spirit of Assumption"; coach, athletic dir, 1935-72; an innovator he became 1st Canadian coach to use T-formation popularized by George Halas and Sid Luckman in US; mem. Windsor/Essex County Sports Hall of Fame.

ARMSTRONG, George (hockey); b. 6 Jul 1930, Skead, Ont.; given name: George Edward; m. Betty Shannon; c. Brian, Betty Ann, Fred, Lorne; ret'd hockey coach/scout; nicknamed "Chief"; jr., sr. Toronto Marlboros; Allan Cup winner; Maple Leafs centre '52-71; 13yrs team capt.; NHL record: 1187 scheduled games, 296g, 417a, 110 playoff games, 26g, 34a; 7 all-star games; mem. 4 Stanley Cup winners; coached Marlboros to 2 Memorial Cups; coach Toronto '88-89; scout TML; mem. Hockey Heritage North, Hockey halls of fame; res. Toronto, Ont.

ARMSTRONG, Jim (curling); b. 30 Jun 1950, Victoria, B.C.; given name: James Peter; m. Carleen; c. Gregory, Jayne, Jody; dentist; mem. BC men's title rinks '73-74, '83-84, '87, '92; skipped BC mixed title rink '73, BC jr. titlist '71, BC HS titlist '67; all-star 3rd '87 Brier; Ross Harstone award '83, '87; active curling official at numerous

ntl championships; mem. Canadian Curling Hall of Fame; res. Richmond, B.C.

ARMSTRONG, Ken (diving); b. 12 Oct 1953, Ingersoll, Ont.; given name: Kenneth Robert; m. Brenda Tifts; c. Jaymi; Texas; diving coach; ntl diving team '73-80; 20 ntl titles; mem. '73, '75 world championships, '78 Pan-Am, '74, '78 CG, '76 Olympic teams; mem. youth camp '72 Olympics, qualified for '80 boycotted Olympics; silver 10m board '78 CG; res.Woodland, Tex.

ARMSTRONG, Lesley (builder); b. 18 Jun 1929, Saint John, N.B.; given name: Lesley Jean Fraser; m. Nigel Armstrong; c. 2 daughters; home economist; competitive figure skater '47-54; childhood bout of polio hampered career; won city titles '49-53; began coaching '55; mem. NB FS exec. '78; dir. CanSkate pgm. '78; mem. National Core comm. '85; formed Sussex Skating Club '56; longest serving dir. NB section CFSA; NB FS volunteer of '86, CFSA award of excellence, Town of Sussex achievement, community service award '86; mem. NB Sports Hall of Fame; res. Sussex, N.B.

ARMSTRONG, Neil (hockey/officiating); b. 29 Dec 1932, Plympton Twp, Ont.; m. Margaret Scott; c. Douglas, Lezleigh; hockey scout; began officiating minor hockey at 15; in early '50s became OHA certified official; became part-time NHL official '57; officiated in NHL 21yrs in 1733 regular season, 208 Stanley Cup playoff (48 finals), 10 all-star games; known as "ironman" for not missing single assignment due to injury in 16 seasons; following retirement became Montreal Canadiens scout; mem. Hockey, Sarnia-Lambton Sports, Waterloo County halls of fame; res. Sarnia, Ont.

ARMSTRONG, Paul (coaching, basketball); b. 14 Aug 1955, Fredericton, N.B.; given name: Paul Maurice; m. Ann Anderson; c. Thomas, Katharine; Carleton, BA; mgr. communication, community relations Carleton U; 1 jr., 2 sr Ottawa title teams with Lisgar HS; Carleton varsity '73-77, '79-80; 3 OUAA all-star; at graduation 3rd all-time scorer (1602), 1st all-time assists (358); mem. '77 ntl men's B team; Carleton MVP '74-75; head coach Carleton women '81-83, men '83-99; OUAA east title '87-88; 2 OUAA east coach of yr; NCCP levels I & II basketball course conductor; high performance initative '88; res. Ottawa, Ont.

ARNOLD, Don (rowing); b. 14 Jul 1935, Kelowna, B.C.; given name: Donald John; m. Gwendolyn Mary Amor (d); c. Malcolm, Graham, Andrew; m. Linda; UBC, BPhE., San Francisco State, MSc; Indiana, PhD; exec-dir. Rowing BC; mem. UBC gold medal jr. varsity 8s, '55 Pacific Coast sprint champion; stroke UBC-VRC 4-oared coxless crew '56 unofficial world record 6:05.8 over 2000m course; stroked same crew to '56 Olympic gold; gold 8s, silver coxed 4s '58 CG; '58 Grand Challenge Cup Bedford, Eng. regatta; asst. coach UBC-VRC 8s silver medalists '59 PAG; mem. '60 Olympic silver medal 8s; Heather MacDonald Memorial Award, runnerup BC athlete of '58, Robert Gaul Memorial award UBC outstanding graduating student '62, Indiana outstanding graduating student '70, Indiana citation from US Olympic comm.; Ont. contribution to sport citation '74, BC Sports Fed. contribution to sport citation '76, CARA medal of honor for outstanding contribution to rowing 1880-1980;

mem. Canadian Olympic, Canada's Sports halls of fame; res. Richmond, B.C.

ARNOLD, Sherman (shooting); b. 12 Feb 1938, Waters, Ont.; given name: Sherman Stanley; m. Mary Ann Hlewka; c. Sharon, Tim, Sherman Jr.; sheet metal mechanic; handgun specialist; mem. ntl standard pistol team '75-85; Ont. pistol team '76-94; intl. black powder Cdn team '93-99; ntl centrefire team '78-87; 11 ntl, 8 Ont. centrefire titles; 9 ntl standard pistol titles; 1 ntl air pistol title; 2 NY state centrefire, 1 air pistol titles; 2 NRA air pistol , 4 centrefire, 2 standard pistol titles; 5 ntl, Ont. black powder pistol titles; 3 ntl muzzle loading assn. titles; accumulated more than 500 medals and awards; ntl record 592 old style targets centrefire outdoors 25m; ntl muzzle loading team record '96; team gold, individual bronze '97 Pacific zone championships; 6 ntl achievement, 4 Ont. championship awards; res. St. Catharines, Ont.

ARNOTT, Jan (curling); b. 17 Apr 1956, Winnipeg, Man.; given name: Janet Elizabeth Laliberte; m. Douglas Arnott; Red River Community College; accounting co-ordinator; began curling age 11; lead for sister Connie '84, Cdn, World, '92, '95 Cdn champions; participated 3 Man. mixed championships; through '95 mem. 12 major cashspiel winners; mem. 2 Winnipeg Super League titlists; exec. mem. Winnipeg Business Women's League, Women's Competitive Curling Assn.; mem. Cdn Curling, Man. Sports halls of fame; res. Winnipeg, Man.

ARNOTT, Jason (hockey); b. 11 Oct 1974, Collingwood, Ont.; center OJHL jr. C Stayner '89-90, jr. B Lindsay '90-91, jr. A Oshawa '91-93; CHL all-star game '93; 1st draft Edmonton '93; NHL Edmonton '93-98, New Jersey '98-02, Dallas '02-04; Team Canada '94 world championship gold; '94 NHL all-rookie team; named *Hockey News, Sporting News, Beckett Publication* rookie of year; played in '97 all-star game; scored overtime Stanley Cup winning goal game 6 '00; NHL record: (through '04) 743 scheduled games, 244g, 324a, 86 playoff games, 25g, 32a; res. Wasaga Beach, Ont.

ARSENAULT, Lise (gymnastics); b. 14 Dec 1954, Cartierville, Que.; given name: Lise Isabelle; m. David Goertz; c. Natalie, Lyne; York, BA, NY State, MEd.; teacher; 4 Que. sr. titles; 3 OWIAA, 2 CWIAU title teams; youngest mem. Cdn team '70 world championships; 2 bronze '71 PAG; mem. '72, '76 Olympics, '73 FISU; variety of gold, silver, bronze medals Ont. ntl championships; McMaster gym coach '76-78; coach Sparks gym club St. Catharines; HS female athlete-of-yr; Vaudreuil Sports Centre female athlete of '70; co-winner York female athlete '73-74; life mem. Cdn Gymnastics Fed.; mem. York Sports Hall of Fame; res. St. Catharines, Ont.

ARSENAULT, Paul (coaching); b. 8 Aug 1939, Halifax, N.S.; m. Cathi; c. Klay, Holly; UNB, BPhE, Oregon, MSc.; entrepeneur; ex-coach; football, hockey UNB; hockey coach Sir George Williams '63-72, Loyola '72-75, Concordia '75-90; 4th all-time NA college hockey coaches victory list; reached 500 victory plateau '84; 17 league titles; twice CIAU coach of year; 3 Que. hockey coach-of-yr awards; mem. Canadian student team coaching staff '77-78; res. Charlottetown, P.E.I.

ARUSOO, Toomas (swimming); b. 22 Jul 1948, Sweden; div. Angela Coughlan; c. Jessica, Lee, Kate; m. Diane; c. Toomas Jr.; Michigan, BSc.; swim coach, businessman; mem. ntl team '65-71; mem. '66, '70 CG, '67, '71 Pan-Am, '68 Olympic teams; silver 200m butterfly '67 Pan-Ams; gold 200m, silver 100m butterfly '70 CG; coach ntl team '75 Pan-Ams; Montreal Camo SC '77-78; St. John's, Nfld. Aquarama '78-80; Montreal POM '80-81; UofMtl Champions SC from '82; mem. Canadian Aquatic Hall of Fame; res. Birmingham, Mich.

ASH, Gord (administration/baseball); b. 20 Dec 1951, Toronto, Ont.; York BA; baseball exec.; following 4yrs service with CIBC joined Blue Jays organization as ticket office employee '78; became grounds crew operations supervisor '79; asst. dir. operations '80; administrator player personnel '84; attended Michigan human resource management seminar '88, Queen's industrial relations seminar '90; AGM '89; v-p baseball/GM '94; v-p/GM '97-01; radio baseball analyst '01-02; AGM Milwaukee Brewers '03; 1 of 4 Cdns to serve as ML GM; mem. Cdn Special Olympics advisory board; res. Toronto, Ont.

ASHCROFT, Christina (shooting); b. 28 Jun 1964, Kitchener, Ont.; given name: Christina Schulze; m. Michael Ashcroft; c. Alexandra; Ont. standard rifle 3-position title '82; mem. '81 Championship of Americas, '82, '86, '90, '94, '98 worlds, Benito Juarez, '83, '87, '91, '95, '99 Pan-Am, '84, '88, '92 Olympic, '94, '98 CG teams; 4 silver, 4 bronze PAG; 3 gold, 1 silver, 3 bronze CG; 1 ntl, 1 World Cup gold; 2 SFC female athlete-of-yr; Gil Boa Memorial award '90; 3 Sheila MacQuarrie Memorial awards; mem. Ottawa CSRA Sports Hall of Fame; res. Courtenay, B.C.

ASHCROFT, Michael (shooting); b. 7 Dec 1964, Leeds, Eng.; given name: Michael James; m. Christina Schulze; c. Alexandra; RMC, BEng.; CF major, aerospace engineer; began shooting as cadet in Hamilton; ntl prone rifle champion '84, '88, '89, '91; team gold '86 CG, '87 PAG, '85, '92 World Cups; team silver '90 CG; individual silver '85, bronze '89 World Cup; 8th '88 Olympics; SFC male athlete of '88, '89; Cdn Forces male athlete of '87; Cdn flagbearer '91 PAG; avid cycle road racer; mem. Ottawa CSRA, Cdn Forces Sports halls of fame; res. Courtenay, B.C.

ASHLEY, John (hockey/officiating); b. 5 Mar 1930, Galt, Ont.; m. June Millman; c. Kristine, Tom; ret'd. salesman; Jr. A Galt Red Wings, Toronto Marlboros, Guelph Biltmores '46-50; AHL Pittsburgh, Syracuse '50-53; Sr. OHA Stratford '55-58; NHL referee '59-72, 622 scheduled games, 58 playoff games; 5ys NHL scout, councilor for referees; mem. Cambridge, Waterloo County, Hockey halls of fame; res. Kitchener, Ont.

ASHTON, Elizabeth (equestrian); b. 16 Mar 1950, Darwen, Eng.; m. Carl Eriksen; UofT, hons. BPHE; Med, Central Mich, MA, Texas(Austin) PhD; pres. Camosun Coll.; mem. ntl jumping team '67-74; gold President's Cup (Washington), Rothman's International (Toronto), B&W Puissance, McKee International Stakes '72; leading international rider Washington, Royal Horse Show, Toronto '72; from '72 mem. Canadian 3-day team event; team gold, individual bronze Bromont mini-Olympics '75; team silver 3-day event '75 PAG; alternate mem. '72, '76 Olympic team; mem. '84 Olympic team; ntl 3-day event title '77; team gold 3-day event '78 world championships, '82 Leitchroff Farm trials; bronze Chesterland Horse Trials '79; Canadian horsewoman of '76; Dick Ellis Memorial Trophy '78; res. Victoria, B.C.

ASSELIN, Marie-Claude (skiing); b. 1 Apr 1962, Montreal, Que.; accomplished alpine skier with love of acrobatics; jr. women's Shell Cup FS titles '77-78 sweeping moguls, ballet, aerials, combined; sr. Shell Cup titles '79-80, '82; joined World Cup circuit '81, dominated competition; '81-82 WC grand prix titles, '81-83 WC aerials; won 9 WC events '82-83 season; ntl champion '77-79; NA aerial, combined titles '80; freestyle skier of '79, '81; Julien Trophy French Canadian athlete of '81; Elaine Tanner award '82; federal government achievement award '83; mem. Cdn Ski Hall of Fame; res. Baie James, Que.

ASTRA, Duke (darts); b. 6 Oct 1947, Germany; d. 6 May 1978, Ottawa, Ont.; given name: Vytautas; m. Florence; c. Stephanie, Jennifer; hardware store mgr.; pitched baseball Pembroke 7yrs; mem. HS jr. basketball title team; HS athlete-of-yr award; began playing darts as lunch-break recreation '72; helped organize, competed in Central Canada DL; with Bob Dupere won '76 ntl doubles title, 5th in worlds; won ntl singles, 4th in worlds '77; Ottawa ACT award '76-77.

ATCHISON, Ron (football); b. 30 Apr 1930, Central Butte, Sask.; given name: Ronald William; div. Monica Manwaring; c. Margaret, Gordon, Kathy; m. Brenda Joy Lloyd; c. Michael; ret'd. cabinet maker; rental property business; Saskatoon Jr. Hilltops '47-49; mg/dt Sask. '52-68; noted for toughness, durability; 2 Grey Cups, 1 winner; 5 times WFC all-star; club record most fumble recoveries; honored by fans with "night" '63; Hilltops training field, club house bear his name; Northern Sask. Lake, Regina St. bears his name; Saskatoon award of merit; 2 Stack Tibbits Roughriders MV Cdn awards; all-time Roughriders all-star; mem. Roughriders Plaza of Honor, Sask., Saskatoon Sports, Cdn Football halls of fame; res. Regina, Sask.

ATHANS, Gary (skiing); b. 12 Jun 1961, Kelowna, B.C.; given name: Gary Wayne; div. Leanne; c. Jesse, Kaylee; ski resort owner, operator; following family tradition excelled on skis both on slopes and water; ntl juve. alpine, waterski champion '75; Western Cdn juve. boys overall waterski titlist '76-77; mem. ntl alpine 8yrs, waterski teams; ntl boys, men's waterski jump records; ret'd from water skiing '80 to concentrate on alpine World, Europa Cup circuit specializing in slalom, giant slalom; 2nd overall ntl men's alpine championships '80; silver, bronze FIS GS '83; mem. '84 Olympic team; recurring leg circulatory problem led to retirement from competition '84; res. Kelowna, B.C.

ATHANS, George Jr. (water skiing); b. 6 Jul 1952, Kelowna, B.C.; div. Claire Suzanne Sicotte; c. Shawn Sacha; m. Sandrine Debanne; c. Cassandra, Sydney; Concordia (SGW campus), BA, McGill; TV producer/dir., pres. Athans Communications; sports commentator *CBC* 16yrs; mem.ntl waterski team '66-75; ntl sr. champion '65-75; Western Hemisphere titles '68, '70; world slalom record

'69-72; 4 world titles; 33 ntl titles among more than 100 championships; 1st foreign competitor to win US Masters; world journalist games slalom title '85; above average alpine skier; rejected '69 invitation to join ntl alpine team; with father George Sr., 1st father-son combination in Canadian Olympic Sports Hall of Fame; BC athlete of '71; with Bruce Robertson co-holder Norton Crowe award; Que. athlete of '73; 2 BC special merit awards; 2 ntl amateur athlete of yr awards; ntl sporting goods assn. athlete of yr award; hon. life mem. CWSA; author *Water Skiing* '75; Que. Athlete of decade award '78; mem. Order of Canada; mem. Cdn Olympic, BC, Que., Canada's Sports, Intl Water Ski Fed., Water Ski/Wakeboard Canada halls of fame; res. Ile des Soeurs, Que.

ATHANS, George Sr. (diving); b. 4 Jan 1921, Vancouver, B.C.; given name: George Demetrie; div. Irene Hartzell; c. George, Greg, Gary; Washington, BA, McGill, MD; ret'd. physician; 1st of 10 ntl titles, berth on Olympic team '36; Pacific Coast diving titles '40-44; BEG title '50; bronze '38 BEG; 7th '48 Olympics; diving coach '54 BEG, '60 Olympics; with son George Jr., mem. Canadian Olympic, BC Sports, Canadian Aquatic halls of fame; res. Kelowna, B.C.

ATHANS, Greg (skiing); b. 18 Jun 1955, Kelowna, B.C.; div. Lyn Cowan; c. Carly; m. Peggy Meyers; c. Zoe; UBC; advertising photographer; equally proficient on snow or water skis; only Canadian athlete to win gold both winter, summer Canada Games ('71 alpine slalom, '73 water ski tricks); 8 ntl water ski titles; mem. ntl water ski team '73, '75 world championships; world pro FS alpine champion '76, '80; world pro freestyle mogul, ballet champion '78; world mogul champion '80; author *Ski Free*; res. Vancouver, B.C.

ATKINSON, Bill (baseball); b. 4 Oct 1954, Chatham, Ont.; given name: William Cecil Glenn; m. Marlene Theresa Houle; c. William David; mechanic; a product of Chatham minor baseball program, he also excelled in football, basketball and t&f; signed initial pro baseball contract on his birthday '71; saw minor league service with Jamestown (A), West Palm Beach (A), Quebec (AA), Memphis (AAA), Denver (AAA) before joining Montreal '76-79; joined ChiSox organization '80-83 playing mostly in minors; mem. AAA Denver title teams '76, '83, Appleton A title team '83; ML record: 98 scheduled games, 11-4, 11sv, 99k, 62bob, 3.42era; winning pitcher, scored winning run in 1st Pearson Cup clash between Expos and Blue Jays; '78; coach/mgr. Chatham minor/sr. baseball program '84-98; res. Chatham, Ont.

ATKINSON, Lorne (cycling); b. 8 Jun 1921, Vancouver, B.C.; given name: Lorne Charles; m. Evelyn Mary Speer; c. Daniel Lorne, Janis Marie; ret'd. bicycle merchant; BC jr. title '39; 4 sr. titles; 4 Pacific Coast 25-mile titles; 4 BC 5-mile track titles; 3 Redmond Derby Pacific Northwest titles; 2 BC 25-mile road titles; ntl 25, 10-mile track titles '49; Que. mile title '45; mem. '48 Olympic, '50, '54 BEG teams; ret'd from competition '64; life mem. Vancouver Velo Vets Cycling Club; annual race bears his name; mem. BC Sports Hall of Fame; res. Vancouver, B.C.

ATKINSON, Ted (horse racing); b. 18 Sep 1911, Toronto, Ont.; ret'd jockey; raised in NY state; while working at Brooklyn chemical plant as teenager, 98lber encouraged to become jockey; mounted 1st horse taking lessons at Bronx riding academy; worked at Greentree Stables but considered too old (past 20) to be apprentice jockey; struck out on own riding at bush tracks in Midwest; attracted ntl attention in New England at 23; graduated to NY circuit rejoining Greentree as contract jockey; US riding titles '44 (287 wins), '46 (233); rode '53 horse of year Tom Fool; '49 Preakness, Belmont Stakes with Capot but missed Kentucky Derby; 1st jockey to win $1M in single yr '46; record: 3795 wins in 23,661 starts, $17,449,360 in purses; nicknamed "Slasher" by fans, "Professor" by peers; George Woolf memorial award; back injury forced '59 retirement; mem. US Jockeys, Cdn Horse Racing halls of fame; res. New York.

ATTFIELD, Roger (horse racing); b. 28 Nov 1939, Newbury, Eng.; div. Tracie; c. John; horse trainer; accomplished show jump and amateur steeplechase rider in Eng., before moving to Canada '70; trained horses for Charles Baker, David Willmot, Earle Mack, Allan Dragone, Frank Stronach; trained 3 of only 5 Cdn Triple Crown winners (With Approval, Izvestia, Peteski); 7 Queen's Plate winners; 6 Cdn horse-of-yr winners; 5 Cdn trainer-of-yr Sovereign awards; led Kinghaven Farms to 1st place among NA leading owners with earnings in excess of $5M '90; regarded as one of top trainers in NA; 1300+ winners, $75M+ in purses; mem. Cdn Horse Racing Hall of Fame; res. Nobleton, Ont.

AU, On-Kow (lawn bowling); b. 7 Jan 1942, Hong Kong; m. Chung-Pack Au; c. Ernest, Constance; Hong Kong U, BA; broadcaster, journalist; Hong Kong women's singles title '89; moved to BC winning BC Week singles title '92; 2 Indoor Foreman singles titles; V&D singles crown '95; 3 BC fours, 3 singles, 1 pairs silver; mem. ntl team '95-96; Cdn indoor singles bronze '96; bowler-of-week award '92; res. Vancouver, B.C.

AUBIN, Jack (swimming); b. 29 Jun 1907, Twickenham, Eng.; d. (circa 1995), Toronto, Ont.; given name: John Ernest; m. Merion Margaret King; c. Jane Anne; magazine editor; swimming standout in '20s, early '30s; gold 200yd breaststroke '30 BEG; 3 ntl titles; Central YMCA award of merit '27; BE Medal '45; International Council of Industrial Editors achievement awards '57, '63; mem. Cdn Aquatic Hall of Fame.

AUBIN, Marc (harness racing); b. 31 Jul 1933, Quebec City, Que.; ret'd. RCAF, private detective, steamship agent, night club singer; launched driving career at Connaught Park winning 1st race 1959; ranked among leading West Coast drivers during '70s; shifted to Chicago circuit during '80s; returned briefly to California before settling in Pompano Beach, Fla. '93; guided Magna Bird to season's record for 4yr-old trotters '86; through '95 2898 victories with purses exceeding $13M; res. Hollywood, Fla.

AUBUT, Marcel (builder); b. 1 May 1948, Quebec City, Que.; m. Francine Vallee; c. Melanie, Julie, Catherine; Laval LLB, LLM; lawyer QC; key role in bringing NHL to Quebec City with foundation of Nordiques of which he was chair./CEO/co-owner; prominent role in merger of WHL with NHL; lead promoter Rendez-Vous '87; in early '80s one of most influential NHL governors credited with bringing about some of league's proudest moments of last few decades;

pres./CEO Productions Trans-Amerique Ltee; creator/chair. Fondation Nordiques; sits on boards of several Cdn companies; instrumental in furthering country's business development; actively involved in community organizations and major national social causes such as Canadian Cancer Society, MS Society, Heart & Stroke Foundation, Quebec Special Olympics, Red Cross, Jean Lapointe Foundation; honored by Quebec National Assembly; twice *La Presse* person of week; *HN* manager of yr; among *McLean's* 12 people of year '87; Quebec Hoteliers' Assn person of '87 award; *Le Monde Juridique* business lawyer of '98 award; Officer Order of Canada; mem. Canada's Sports Hall of Fame; res. Sillery, Que.

AUCH, Susan (speed skating); b. 1 Mar 1966, Winnipeg, Man.; UCal; real estate broker; motivational speaker, TV commentator, coach; began skating age 10; switched to long- from short-track after '88 Olympics; 3 NA junior titles; 15 ntl titles; 2 Canada Games gold; 2g, 2s, 1b '85 FISU Games; short-track world 3000 relay record '86; CR 1000m '97; '88 Olympic bronze 3000 relay (demo) short-track; '94 Olympic silver 500m; Canada Cup 500m gold; 3g, 2s Italian World Cup; 3 Cdn sprint titles; Cdn 500m record; beat Bonnie Blair for 3 World Cup 500m gold '95; mem. Winnipeg Speed Skating Club; ret'd from competition '98 but returned to competition '99-02; '85 sports excellence award, '89 world champion award; CASSA female athlete of year '90, '91; long-track female athlete of '90-92, '94-95; Bobbie Rosenfeld trophy '95; Bruce Kidd award '99; Calgary female athlete of yr award; active in YM-YWCA youth programs; Canada Games sports council, CAAWS, COA committees; mem. Cdn Athletes Assn. Board '94-98; mem. Man. Order of Buffalo Hunt, Alta. Sports, Cdn Speed Skating halls of fame; res. Calgary, Alta.

AUDETTE, Julien (soaring); b. 6 Jun 1914, Radville, Sask.; d. 28 Oct 1986, Regina, Sask.; given name: Julien Joseph; m. Myrtle Dewsom; c. Ray, Joan, Robert, Douglas, Michelle; pioneered sport in Sask.; founding mem. Regina Gliding and Soaring Club, dir., pres., chief pilot; instrumental in organizing 3 ntl championships in Sask.; originated gliding scholarship program for air cadets; all 8 ntl soaring records, including 6 simultaneously; 7 ntl, 5 international awards; 1st Canadian awarded Federation Aeronautique Internationale Gold C pin with 3 diamonds; Canadian diamond badge; mem. Sask. Sports Hall of Fame.

AUDLEY, Gordon (speed skating); b. 20 Apr 1928, Winnipeg, Man.; given name: Gordon Vernon; m. Grace MacKenzie; c. Karey, Rocky; ret'd CPR machinist, auto insurance agent; first competition Man. Open age 10, won 110-, 220yd events in provincial record times; '40-44 competed both speed skating, hockey; '44 Man. jr. speed skating title; '45 Man., Detroit int. titles, 220yd record Sask.; '46 ntl, Man. int. Open, Closed titles; Man. sr. titles '50, '53-57; mem. '48, '52, '56 Olympic, '56 world championships teams; Canadian flag-bearer, bronze 500m '52 Olympics; ret'd from competition '57; officiated '60 Olympics; mem. Canadian Speed Skating, Man., Winnipeg Sports, Cdn Olympic halls of fame; res. Long Beach, Calif.

AURIE, Larry (hockey); b. 8 Feb 1905, Sudbury, Ont.; d. 12 Dec 1952, Detroit, Mich.; given name: Lawrence Harry; m. Ivy Annie Cluney; salesman; diminutive (5'6") rw with great scoring touch and skating skills; jr. hockey Sudbury, Galt, London; claimed by Detroit '27 draft; capt. Red Wings '32-33; led league scorers '37; mem. 2 Stanley Cup winners; played 1ˢᵗ NHL all-star game; NHL totals 489 scheduled games, 147g, 129a, 24 playoff goals, 6g, 9a; Red Wings owner Jim Norris was so impressed with Aurie he ret'd his jersey 6 although Detroit club does not officially honor this fact; ret'd from NHL '38 and was player/coach Pittsburgh (AHL) '38-44; nicknamed "Little Dempsey" or "Little Rag Man"; mem. Hockey Heritage North Hall of Fame.

AVERY, Earle (harness racing); b. 4 Feb 1894, Knowlesville, N.B.; d. 6 Nov 1977, Woodstock, N.B.; given name: Earle Bradford; m. Elizabeth Kinney; c. Robert, Blair; horseman, potato farmer; active driver, trainer '19-72; 1252 victories, purses totalling more than $3.5 million; American Pacing Classic (Meadow Skipper '64), American Trotting Classic (Porterhouse '63), Cane Pace (Meadow Skipper '63); best time 1:57 4/5 with Meadow Skipper; 21 2:00 or less miles; 7 world record driving performances; US Harness Writers' Clem McCarthy Good Guy award '63; mem. NB Sports, Canadian Horse Racing, US Harness Racing halls of fame.

AVERY, Frank (curling); b. 25 Feb 1902, Austin, Man.; d. 25 May 1997, Vancouver, B.C.; m. Freda (d); c. Brian; ret'd; Vancouver's Mr. Curling through work in pioneering, promoting game on coast; BC title '35, '43; 3ʳᵈ BC Brier entries '37, '39, '42; skipped BC Brier entry '46; mem. BC entry ntl men's seniors championships '66-67; instrumental in founding Pacific Coast Curling Assn., Vancouver Curling Club; mgr. Vancouver CC '58-66; hon. mem. Canadian Curling Reporters; life mem. Vancouver CC, Pacific Coast CA; mem. Governor-General's CC; mem. Canadian Curling, BC Sports halls of Fame.

AVERY, Jeff (football); b. 28 Mar 1953, Ottawa, Ont.; given name: Jeffrey Clarke; div. Jocelyn Brown; m. Sharon Fitzmaurice; UofOtt, BA, financial consultant; 4 UofOtt, seasons gained 1973yds on 110 receptions, 15tds; 3 times OUAA all-star, 2 all-Canadian; Frank Tindall award MVP '75 Central Bowl; 3 times UofOtt most valuable receiver, once leadership award winner; mem. '75 Yates (OUAA), Vanier (CIAU) Cup title teams; pro Ottawa '76-82; 2 Grey Cup finals, 1 winner; EFC all-star '77-78; wr/sb/reserve punter; CFL record: 169 reception for 2609 yds, 15tds, 102 league games; asst. coach UofOtt '83-84; Rough Riders radio color commentator '89-96; mem. UofO Football Hall of Fame; res. Kanata, Ont.

AWREY, Don (hockey); b. 18 Jul 1943, Kitchener, Ont.; given name: Donald William; m. Marie; bus-tour company owner; def; Niagara Falls Jrs; minor league stints with Minneapolis (CPHL), Hershey, Boston (AHL); NHL with Boston '63-73, St. Louis '73-74, Montreal '74-76, Pittsburgh '76-77, NYR '77-78, Colorado '78-79; Team Canada '72 Summit Series; NHL record: 16 seasons, 979 scheduled games, 31g, 158a, 1065pim, 71 playoff games, 0g, 18a, 150pim; mem. 2 Stanley Cup winners; plays with Boston alumni; nicknamed "Bugsy"; res. Hooksett, N.H.

B

BABBITT, Ethel (tennis); b. 13 Jul 1876, Fredericton, N.B.; d. 20 Aug 1969, Fredericton, N.B.; given name: Ethel Mary Hatt; m. Harold Babbitt; c. Isabel, John David; standout tennis player '08-27; 14 NB championships, 3 Maritime titles in ladies' singles, mixed doubles; ntl honors '10; mem. NB Sports Hall of Fame.

BABBITT, John (tennis); b. 2 Feb 1908, Fredericton, N.B.; d. (circa 1990), Ottawa, Ont.; given name: John David; m. Dorothy Elizabeth Rooney; c. David, Robert (d), Susan, Cynthia, James, Andrew (d); UNB, Oxford; ret'd NRC physicist; like mother Ethel and sister Isabel, prominent tennis star in Maritimes; NB singles titles '28-29; Maritime championship '29; Oxford on Rhodes Scholarship; 6yrs. mem. ice hockey team; mem. UNB rugger team, capt. '28; 2 McTier Trophy title teams.

BABITS, Laslo (t&f); b. 17 Apr 1958, Oliver, B.C.; Washington State; javelin specialist; father former European boxing champion, mother former European swimming champion; BC HS champion '76-77; gold '77 Canada Games, '79 BC championships, '81 Modesto Relays, '82 Pac10 Conf., Can-Ita-Jpn tri meet; '83 PAG gold; '82 CG silver; mem. '84 Olympic team; fed. govt. excellence award '84; res. Kalenden, B.C.

BABYCH, Dave (hockey); b. 23 May 1961, Edmonton, Alta.; given name: David Michael; div. Sherrey Buffie; m. Diana; c. Terence, Ty, Kolton, Jaret, Cal; def. Portland Jr. (WHL) '79-80; 1st pick Winnipeg '80 draft; NHL with Winnipeg '80-85, Hartford '85-91, Vancouver '91-97, Philadelphia '97-98, Los Angeles '99; WHL 1st team all-star; 2 NHL all-star games; NHL record: 1195 scheduled games, 142g, 581a, 114 playoff games, 21g. 41a; operates summer hockey school; awarded $1.37M in suit vs. Flyers; launched Babych & Friends Anglers Challenge charity auction; res. North Vancouver, B.C.

BABYCH, Wayne (hockey); b. 6 Jun 1958, Edmonton, Alta.; given name: Wayne Joseph; m. Shelley Buffie (sister to Sherrey which for a time made Dave his brother and brother-in-law); carpentry, furniture business owner; ex-golf course owner; jr. Spruce Grove, Edmonton, Portland Winter Hawks; twice WHL 1st team all-star rw; Team Canada '77-70; 1st pick St. Louis, 3rd overall '78 draft; topped 50-goal plateau with 54 '80-81 season; mem. St. Louis '78-84, Pittsburgh '84-85, Quebec '85, Hartford '86-87; NHL record: 519 scheduled games, 192g, 246a, 41 playoff games, 7g, 9a; Emery award '85; plays on NHL Oldtimers Challenge tour; res. Winnipeg, Man.

BACK, Len (football); b. 21 Jul 1900, Hamilton, Ont.; d. 16 Mar 1982, Florida; given name: Leonard Percival; m. Lillian (d.); c. Beverly; m. Grace; football exec.; Hamilton Tigers jrs. '18-19 before skull fracture ended playing days; team mgr. '20; mgr. Hamilton Tigers intermediates '21-26; mgr. Tiger sr. ORFU team '28-40; joined Brian Timmis as mgr. Hamilton Wildcats, won '43 Grey Cup; rejoined Tigers following WWll, on hand when Tigers and Wildcats combined; mgr. Ticats from '50; honored by Grey Cup comm. '61, City of Hamilton, Ticats FC; mem. Cdn Football, Copps Coliseum halls of fame.

BACKHOUSE-SHARPE, Claire (badminton); b. 13 May 1958, Vancouver, B.C.; m. Douglas Sharpe; c. Megan, Jaime, Kieran; UBC; with variety of partners ranked as one of Canada's top doubles competitors; ntl competitor from '76; 1 ntl single, 6 ladies' doubles, 3 mixed doubles titles; Mexican Open, Eastern, Western, Pan-Am championships, US Open ladies' doubles titles; 2 Pan-Am championships, 2 Pepsi-Cola, 8 US, 2 Cdn Open titles; '86 CG singles silver; with Johanne Falardeau '82 CG ladies' doubles gold; with Jane Youngberg '78 CG ladies' doubles silver, team silver; mem. '78 Uber Cup, 5 CG, '88 Olympics, 5 All-England, 5 world championships, 2 Scottish International, 2 Sweden Open, 3 Danish Open teams; participated '88 Olympics as demonstration sport; Badminton Canada athlete of '94; BC Leaders & Legends in Sport award; mem. BC Sports Hall of Fame; res. Victoria, B.C.

BACKSTROM, Ralph (hockey); b. 18 Sep 1937, Kirkland Lake, Ont.; given name: Ralph Gerald; m. Fran; c. Martin, Diana, Andrew; hockey executive; capt. Hull-Ottawa Jr. Canadiens Memorial Cup winner; ctr Canadiens '58-71; Calder Memorial Trophy NHL rookie of year; Los Angeles '71-72; Chicago '73; WHA Chicago Cougars '73-75, Denver Spurs '76, New England Whalers '77; most sportsmanlike player '74; most popular Cougar award '73-74; WHA all-star once; starred with Team Canada '74 in losing series vs USSR; NHL record: 1032 scheduled games, 278g, 361a, 116 playoff games, 27g, 32a; WHA record: 304 games, 100g, 153a; asst. coach Kings; head coach Denver U, Spencer Penrose coach-of-yr award; coach IHL Phoenix Roadrunners '90-92; comissioner Roller Hockey International from '93; co-owner/ GM Colorado Eagles (CHL); mem. Hockey Heritage North Hall of Fame; res. Windsor, Colo.

BAERG, Cameron (rowing); b. 17 Oct. 1972, Saskatoon, Sask.; given name: Cameron Walter; carpenter, construction; '94 Royal Cdn. Henley int. single champion; gold men's single '97 Canada Cup; 3rd men's fours, 4th men's single '97 US ntls; competed men's fours '98 worlds; 4th men's eights '99 PAG; competed men's pairs '02 worlds; joined men's fours winning gold '03 worlds, Lucerne World Cup, Royal Henley Regatta; gold '04 Munich World Cup, Duisburg Regatta, silver Lucerne World Cup, Athens Olympics; res. Victoria, B.C.

BAERT, Jean-Paul (t&f); b. 6 Oct 1942, Paris, France; mem. French jr. javelin team; moved to Canada '66; guest prof. UofQue; throws coach UofMtrl, Que. provincial coach; dir-gen. Que. T&f Federation; CTFA throws coach; master coach; authored *The Throws*; coach pre-Olympic US training camp, Americas team World Cup '77, '79; ntl team coach '74, '78 Commonwealth, '75, '79 Pan-Am, '76, '80 Olympic Games teams; *Radio-Canada* Olympic bobsleigh analyst; mem. organizing comm. IAAF world youth championships; res. Laval, Que.

BAGGULEY, Howard (ski jumping/x-country); b. 31 May 1909, Ottawa, Ont.; d. 11 Dec 1999, Prescott, Ont.; given name: Douglas Howard; m. Maysel Jean Bradley (d); c. Douglas, David (d); ret'd fed. govt.; jr., int., sr. jumping, x-country titles Ottawa, Montreal regions; Que. jumping champion; 2 Ont., 1 ntl jumping titles; Eastern record 227' jump; Eastern US Class B jumping champion; mem. '32 Olympic team; several US pro jumping events; perfect 450 5-pin string '46, Brunswick award; 426 in '62 RA Molson Award.

BAGLEY, June (golf); b. 25 Jun 1928, Winnipeg, Man.; given name: June Baker; m. Ralph Bagley; c. Keith, Dennis, Nancy; following lead of golf pro father Arthur at Canoe Club she became 1st Manitoban golfer to win 3 championship categories, junior '48, women's amateur '52, seniors '79 & '81; longevity as top-flight golfer saw her win titles and/or play on provincial teams 6 consec. decades '48-93; mem. 5 Man. Amateur teams, 9 sr. prov. teams, 4 ntl low net titles; won Winnipeg & district crown '65; with Nancy won 6 MLGA North American Life mother-daughter titles; pres. Ladies section Canoe Club; active as volunteer prov. jr. golf; trophy for most improved lady golfer Canoe Club bears her name; ranked by CLGA among top sr. women golfers of century; mem. Man. Sports Hall of Fame; res. Winnipeg, Man.

BAGNELL, Norm (softball); b. 11 May 1926, Toronto, Ont.; d. Jun 1987, Toronto, Ont.; given name: Norman James; m. Joan Fraser; c. Ken, Karen, Kim; employee General Motors; pitched 1st of 54 career no-hitters age 11 Essex playground; at 15 sr. Toronto's top team Prince of Wales; noted for ambidextrous pitching; mem. more than 25 title teams, 3 world tournament teams while playing on more than 20 clubs throughout Ont.; averaged 20 strikeouts per game while toiling for Oshawa Pedlars, twice Sr. B titlists; defeated Eddie Feigner's King and His Court; mem. Kincardine OASA Int. titlists '54 posting 510 strikeouts in 35 games and batting .333; Oshawa Tony's 2 Sr. B, 1 Sr. A title, world tournament MVP; '39-72 more than 1000 victories, 26 perfect games among 54 no-hitters, 41 one-hitters, 37 two-hitters, 32 strikeouts in single game, 39 consecutive scoreless innings, 510 strikeouts in 35 games, 17 consecutive wins, back-to-back no-hitters at age 45, lifetime batting average of .300; managed Filtro Perks, Canada's entry in women's world tournament '62; mem. Canadian Softball Hall of Fame.

BAILEY, Ace (hockey); b. 13 Jun 1948, Lloydminster, Sask.; d. 11 Sep 2001, New York, N.Y.; given name: Garnet Edward; m. Katherine; c. Todd; dir. pro scouting LA Kings; began jr. career at 15 Edmonton '65-67; CHL Oklahoma City '67-68, '71, Houston '79-80, Wichita '80-81; AHL Hershey '68-69; WHA Edmonton '78-79; NHL Boston '68-73, Detroit '73-74, St. Louis '74-75, Washington '75-78; NHL record 568 scheduled games, 107g, 171a, 15 playoff games, 2g, 4a; Memorial Cup; 2 Stanley Cups as player Boston, 5 as scout Edmonton; coached Houston, Wichita; 13ys scout Edmonton, 8yrs Los Angeles; killed by terrorists who crashed plane into World Trade Centre.

BAILEY, Ace (hockey); b. 3 Jul 1903, Bracebridge, Ont.; d. 7 Apr 1992, Toronto, Ont.; given name: Irvin Wallace; m. Gladys Rowan; c. Audrey, Joyce, Joanne; salesman; jr. Bracebridge, St. Mary's, Toronto; sr. Peterborough Petes '24-26; pro Maple Leafs 1926-34; Stanley Cup winner '32,

scoring title '28-29 for which he was dubbed Ace by sports writers; twice team MVP; career terminated in Boston Dec '33 when he sustained severe head injuries when checked by Eddie Shore; jersey No. 6 ret'd by Leafs, but reactivated at his request and given to Ron Ellis; NHL totals: 111g, 82a; mem. Hockey Hall of Fame.

BAILEY, Angela (t&f); b. 28 Feb 1962, Coventry, Eng.; UofT; sprint specialist; '78, '82, '86 CG 4x100 relay silver; 2 Colgate meet records; 2 ntl jr., sr. records; 3 Pacific Conf. Games golds; mem. '80, '84, '88 Olympic, '81 World Cup, '83 world championships, '99 PAG teams; 10 4x100 relay, 9 100m, 5 200m, 3 50m, 1 60m titles; mem. 4x100 women's silver relay team '84 Olympics; Elaine Tanner trophy '81; Olympic champions award '85; mem. Mississauga Sports Hall of Fame; res. Mississauga, Ont.

BAILEY, By (football); b. 12 Oct 1930, Omaha, Neb.; d. 18 Jan 1998, Winfield, B.C.; given name: Byron; m. Diana Churchill (d); c. Laurel, Lynn; m. Sandra Hyslop; Washington State, BEd; marketing mgr.; all-Pacific Coast honors WSU rb; pro Detroit '52 NFL championship team; Green Bay '53; charter mem. BC '54 scoring 1st td ever by a Lion and 1st Lions td ever in a winning cause; all-Cdn hb '57, MVP, WIFU all-star team; 1st Lion honored by 'night' '60; mem. BC Grey Cup champions '64; 29 CFL tds; exec. mem., trustee, BC Sports Hall of Fame, mem. BC Place Wall of Fame; BC Sports, Canadian Football halls of fame.

BAILEY, Dave (t&f); b. 17 Mar 1945, Toronto, Ont.; given name: David George; m. Barbara Gillespie; c. Karen Joanne, Brian David, Scott Andrew; UofT, BSc., MSc., PhD.; sr. investigator, drug research and development, Smith, Kline, French Canada Ltd.; 4:07.5 mile world record for 17-year-old '62; toured Europe with EYTC '63; 11 Jun '66 became 1st Canadian to crack 4-minute mile barrier with 3:59.1 at San Diego; Canadian mile record 3:57.7 Toronto Police Games '67; bronze '67 PAG; gold California relays; silver FISU Games; disappointing '68 Olympic 1500 performance brought retirement; '70 comeback produced 3rd California relays; while preparing for '72 Olympics broke ankle and ret'd from active competition; coached Saskatoon TC '76-78; res. North York, Ont.

BAILEY, Donovan (t&f); b. 16 Dec 1967, Manchester, Jamaica; marketing consultant; sprint specialist; emigrated to Canada '81; began competing '90; Ont. indoor 60m title, silver 100m Harry Jerome Classic '91; PAG 4x100m relay silver '91, '99; ntl indoor 60m title '92; silver 100m '94 Francophone Games; mem. '94 CG gold record 4x100m relay team; world 100m title '95 (9.97), mem. world 4x100 gold medal relay team '95-97; world indoor 50m record 5.56 '96; ntl 100m, 200m records; '96 Olympic gold 100m in world record 9.84, 4x100m relay gold; 2 Norton Crowe trophies; 2 Cdn men's team of yr awards; Ont. athlete of '96, Lionel Conacher, Lou Marsh trophies '96; handily defeated Olympic 200-, 400m record-holder Michael Johnson of US in $1.5M 150m match race '97; mem. Phoenix TC; ret'd from competition '01; mem. Canada's Sports, Canadian Olympic halls of fame ('96 Oly gold 4x100 relay team); res. Oakville, Ont.

BAILEY, Marguerite (basketball); b. 31 Oct 1906, Toronto, Ont.; d. 28 Oct 1992, Vancouver, B.C.; div. Horace Jacobs;

ret'd exec. secty.; mem. famed Edmonton Grads '26-27; mem. Canadian Basketball, Alta. Sports halls of fame.

BAILEY, Marjorie (t&f); b. 21 Nov 1947, Lockeport, N.S.; given name: Marjorie Evalena; m. James Brown; c. Anthony Bobby George; Manitoba Institute of Technology; public health nurse; sprint specialist; ntl team '64-76; mem. '66, '74 Commonwealth, '75 PAG teams; bronze 100m (11.42), 4x100m relay '76 Olympics; ntl record 200m 23.06 '76; mem. NS Sports Hall of Fame; res. Lockeport, N.S.

BAILLIE, Charlie (football); b. 14 Feb 1935, Montreal, Que.; given name: Charles Bishop; m. Alyce O'Connor; c. Sharon, Steven, Scott, Peter, Christine; Sir George Williams; mgr. manufacturing Northern Telecom; hockey Jr. Royals '53-54; mem. '53 ntl sr. champion Lakeshore Flyers football team; pro Montreal '54, '56-57, '60-61, '65, Quebec Rifles (UFL) '64, Montreal Beavers (Continental FL) '66; head coach Chomedey (Que. Sr. League) '62; coach TMR Jr. Lions '63; line coach McGill '67-69; offensive co-ordinator SGW '70-71; head football coach McGill '72-00; Montreal HS League football MVP '51; 4 OQIFC football coach-of-yr awards; res. Dollard des Ormeaux, Que.

BAIN, Dan (all-around); b. 14 Feb 1874, Belleville, Ont.; d. 15 Aug. 1962, Winnipeg, Man.; given name: Donald Henderson; wholesale merchant; excelled in hockey, cycling, gymnastics, figure skating, roller skating, golf, trap and skeet shooting; first athletic medal, Man. 3-mile roller skating title, at 13; last athletic medal figure skating at 56; mem. Winnipeg hockey team winning 9 of 11 matches vs. East 1893; capt. Winnipeg Victorias Stanley Cup champions 1896; ret'd from top-flight hockey '01 after team won 2nd Stanley Cup; ntl trapshooting title Toronto '03; enjoyed wildfowl shooting, owned shoreline of Grant's Lake, one of best goose lakes in Man. flyway, turned property over to Ducks Unlimited; at 70 gave skate waltzing exhibitions with partners half century his junior; mem. Canada's, Man. Sports, Hockey, Man. Hockey halls of fame.

BAIRD, Vaughan (builder); b. 6 Sep 1927, Winnipeg, Man.; UMan., BA, Dalhousie, LL.B, U Paris, diploma, UofWpg, doctorate; lawyer, QC; competed in boxing, diving, swimming but gained prominence for organizational skills; founding dir. Manitoba Sports Federation; founding/present chairman Cdn Aquatic Hall of Fame and Museum; founding pres. Cdn Amateur Diving Assn.; founding dir. Aquatic Fed. of Can.; mem. COA '69-72; v-p CG Assn.; dir. FINA, ASUA; mem. '67 PAG comm.; led crusade to get Pan-Am pool enclosed; life mem. MSF; Air Canada exec. of '71; Silver Jubilee medal '77; CM; authored *A Canadian History of the Art and Sport of Diving*; Schroeder IASMHOF award; mem. Order of Canada; Man. Sports Hall of Fame; res. Winnipeg, Man.

BAJIN, Boris (gymnastics); b. 20 Mar 1933, Yugoslavia; given name: Borislav; m. Natasa; c. Alexandar, Sanja; U of Belgrade, BSc., MPhE.; gymnastics coach, fitness dir. Ont. Tennis Assn., Thornhill Chamber Music Institute; international competitor prior to '60; Yugoslavian ntl coach '60-73; coached competitors in FISU, Balkan, Mediterannean Games, European, world championships, Olympic, CG; Canadian ntl women's coach '74; authored several books, numerous articles on gymnastics; extensive

teaching career Europe, Canada; lecturer '76 USGF Congress; head coach '77 ntl coaches' seminar for Australian GF, lecturer NZ ntl gymnastics clinics, also England, Puerto Rico, US; coach 4 Olympic, 5 European, 6 world championships, 2 FISU, 1 Commonwealth, 1 PAG teams; res. King City, Ont.

BAKER, Alison (t&f); b. 6 Aug 1964, Ballymena, N. Ireland; McMaster, PhD; environmental engineer; racewalk specialist; came to Canada '68; started competing at 17; Ont. 3km title; silver Pan-Am jr. '82; competed for Canada '82 America's Cup, '85, '89, '93 World Cup, '85 Canada Games, '87, '93 worlds, '85, '89 FISU; '89, '93 World indoor, '90, '94 CG; ntl 10km title '93; bronze Spanish, Czech 10km events '92; Cdn record 44:30.1 for 10km walk '92; res. Kingston/Guelph, Ont.

BAKER, Bill (football); b. 23 Apr 1945, Sheridan, Man.; m. Cathy; c. 3 daughters; Otterbein Coll; jr. Regina Rams '63; off/def tackle, lb at Otterbein; twice Ohio Conf. all-star, MVP '67; joined CFL Saskatchewan '68-73, '77-78, BC '75-76; missed '74 season with ankle injury; nicknamed "The Undertaker" for ferocious pass rush; 5 all-West, 4 all-Cdn de; 2 BC most-valuable-lineman, most-inspirational-player awards; Dr. Beattie Martin trophy '76, 2 Norm Fieldgate trophies, Schenley defensive player award '76; mem. 2 Grey Cup winners; CFL pres./CEO '89; mem. Roughriders Plaza of Honor, Cdn Football Hall of Fame; res. Kelowna, B.C.

BAKER, Brad (softball); b. 10 May 1965, Oshawa, Ont.; given name: Brad Daniel; m. Jan Simpson; records officer; lhp; started sr. softball at 19 with Penn Corp.; played 4yrs US leagues; played with various Cdn teams from '90; Toronto Gators '94-96, Madison, Wisc. Farm Tavern '97-98, Oshawa Gators '99; during winter months competed in Wellington, N.Z. from '90; 2 ntl, 1 world title; res. Wellington, N.Z./ Oshawa, Ont.

BAKER, Charles (equestrian); b. 10 Jun 1920, Toronto, Ont.; m. Susanne Elizabeth Gaby; c. Charles III, Susanne; Upper Canada College, UofT; advertising co. owner; operated Norcliffe stables; sr. exec. officer, board chairman Ontario Jockey Club '67-85; mem. ntl equestrian team '47-57; Chef d'equipe Olympic bronze entry, Pan-Am gold medal team, '60 Olympic team; owner individual gold winner Natan '59 PAG; res. King, Ont.

BAKER, Joann (swimming); b. 24 Nov 1960, Moose Jaw, Sask.; given name: Joann Elaine; m. Scott Anderson; c. Ryan, Sean, Troy; Arizona State; backstroke, IM specialist; launched career with Thunderbolts SC '72; silver 200m breaststroke, 4x100 medley relay '75 PAG; 7 ntl titles; '75 world trials 200m breaststroke, '76 Olympic trials 100m breaststroke; mem. '75, '79 Pan-Am, '76 Olympic Games, Canada-Russia, Canada-West Germany dual meet teams, winning 3 silver, 1 bronze; Man. sr. champion '77; 6 ntl sr., 2 Commonwealth records; competed 2 NCAA championships; ret'd from competition '80; 2 Thunder Bay athlete-of-yr awards; mem. NWO Sports, Ont. Aquatic halls of fame; res. Phoenix, Ariz.

BAKER, Mary (baseball/softball); b. 10 Jul 1919, Regina, Sask.; d. 17 Dec 2003, Regina, Sask.; ret'd sportscaster;

catcher for Blue Sox in P.K. Wrigley's All-American Girls Baseball League '43; proved feminity and top-notch baseball were a solid combination; became league's most publicized player earning nickname "Pretty Bonnie Baker"; 3 times all-star catcher; only full-time woman manager Kalamazoo Lassies '51; returning to Regina led Regina Legion team to provincial, Western Cdn, world women's softball titles; distinction of becoming 1st female sportscaster in Canada with *CKRM* '64-65; mem. Sask. Sports Hall of Fame; honored by Cooperstown, Cdn Baseball halls of fame.

BAKER, Norm (basketball); b. 17 Feb. 1923, Victoria, B.C.; d. 23 Apr 1989, Victoria, B.C.; m. Nancy; c. Norman Jr.; police chief; joined sr. ranks with five-time ntl champ Victoria Dominoes at 16; mem. 5 ntl sr. title teams; 38-point single game record; pro Chicago Stags newly-formed Basketball Association of America; with Vancouver Hornets dominated scoring 2yrs setting record 1862 points 70-game schedule; Portland '48 pro playoffs; 1st player written pact with Abe Saperstein of Harlem Globetrotters; toured Europe, North Africa with Stars of World '50; 1 pro season Boston; mem. New Westminster Adanacs Mann Cup lacrosse champs '47; Victoria Shamrocks through '54, coached Shamrocks '59-60 before retiring; *CP* poll Canadian basketballer of half century '50; Centennial medal '67; mem. Canada's, BC Sports, Cdn Basketball, Greater Victoria Sports halls of fame.

BAKER, Terry (football); b. 8 May 1962, Bridgewater, N.S.; m. Krista; c. Natasha, Ashley, Brianna; Mount Allison; owner Admiral Benbow Trading Co. gift shop Lunenburg, NS; drafted Montreal Concordes '84 CIAU draft; jockeyed around in CFL with Edmonton, Toronto, Montreal '85-86 before seeing first action Saskatchewan '87-89; Ottawa '90-95, Toronto '95, Montreal '96-02; CFL record: 278gp. 454 fg, 557 cvt, 205s, 2126pts, 2031punts, 87,528yds, 960kickoffs, 56,786 yds; 2 CFL scoring titles; 3 CFL punting avg. titles, 2 Eastern; 1 CFL all-star; mem. '89, '02 Grey Cup winner; res. Bridgewater, NS.

BAKONYI, Peter (fencing); b. 10 Jul 1933, Budapest, Hungary; d. 26 Aug 1997, Vancouver, B.C.; m. Vera Biaitz; c. Debbie, Ronnie, David; UBC law school; regional real estate manager; 16 BC titles in épée, foil, sabre; 7 ntl titles; bronze épée team '62 BEG; 6th individual épée '63 Pan-Am; silver team épée, 4th individual '66 BEG; 5th '67 Pan-Am; among top 20, highest by Canadian fencer, '68 Olympics; silver '61, '69 Maccabiah Games; bronze épée team, 4th individual '70 BEG; referee '71 Pan-Am, '72, '76 Olympic Games; ret'd from competition '73; active role with Maccabiah Games '65-89; team mgr. '75 PAG; ntl jr. development chair. '72-76, ntl jr. Olympic chair. '72-76; v-p CFA 3 terms.

BALA, Ray Sr. (bowling); b. 21 Feb 1931, Windsor, Ont.; m. Marjorie Budolowski; c. Ronald, Jo-Ann, Ray Jr.; U of Windsor, Ont., Cdn Police College; ret'd. staff inspector Windsor City Police; city school hj title '44; Border Cities tournament singles title '55; Ont., ntl 10-pin singles titles '55 (set record), '58; competed US Masters '55, '58, world tournament '58; 10th place highest ever by Canadian '57 ABC tournament; 2 Windsor city ntl champion medals; mem. Windsor/Essex/Kent County 10-pin, Windsor/Essex Sports halls of fame; res. Windsor, Ont.

BALD, Kathy (swimming); b. 19 Dec 1963, Etobicoke, Ont.; given name: Katherine Ann; m. Kevin Renard; CEO asst 3-D Medical Co.; ntl 12-year-old 100m FS record '76; mem. ntl team '81-84, '85-92; gold 100m breaststroke, silver 200m breaststroke '82 CG; 1 gold, 2 silver, 1 bronze '83 PAG; 1 Canada Games, 4 Canada Cup, 2 Swedish Games gold; 1 CG, 5 ntl sr. records; 5 1sts '83 Ont. championships; 5 ntl titles; competed '88 Olympics; 3 fed. govt. excellence awards; Ottawa ACT athlete of '83; masters competitor; mem. Nepean Wall of Fame; res. Mississauga, Ont.

BALDING, Al (golf); b. 29 Apr 1924, Toronto, Ont.; m. Moreen Lyttle; c. Allan, Erin; following overseas stint WWll turned pro '49 as summer starter Toronto Oakdale; asst. pro Burlington GC '50; asst. Islington GC '51-52; head pro Credit Valley '54-56; Ont. Assistants' title '50; won Que. Open '52, 4 Cdn match play titles, CPGA championships '55, '63, '70; 1st Canadian to win PGA tour event '55 Mayfair Open; USPGA tour regular '57; West Palm Beach, Miami Opens, Havana Invitational '57; Mexican Open '63; Alta. Open '73; twice low Cdn in Canadian Open; individual champion and with George Knudson won World Cup team title Rome '68; rotator cuff operations curtailed play '65, '70, '77; twice Ont. athlete of year; competes on PGA Srs. circuit; CPGA seniors title '00; mem. Etobicoke, RCGA, Canada's Sports halls of fame; res. Sebring, Fla./ Mississauga, Ont.

BALDWIN, Bill (shooting); b. 31 Oct 1943, Pincher Creek, Alta.; given name: Wilfred William; div.; c. Linda, Tanya, Billy; welding contractor; competitive shooter from '77; Alta. muzzle-loading pistol, rifle champion '77; KOCR-MRA club champion '78-80; 84 match titles through '86; 4 time Bisley qualifier; with Alain Marion won '86 CG pairs gold; won Governor-General's prize '84 DCRA matches; team silver '92 Palma matches; Sask. athlete for Jul '86 award; life mem. DCRA; mem. SPRA, NSR-MRA, SFC; certified shooting coach; res. Kanata, Ont.

BALDWIN, Frank (coaching/basketball); b. 23 Dec 1920, Halifax, N.S.; d. 30 Apr 1999, Halifax, N.S.; given name: Francis Vincent; development co-ordinator Basketball NS; began coaching '39; coached ntl juv titlists '50; launched St. Mary's U program; program dir. Cdn Martyrs Parish Centre '63; founding mem. Halifax juv basketball league; development co-ordinator Basketball NS from '71; coached NS Canada Games teams '71, '75; played softball 10yrs, involved in summer camp programs 15yrs; conductor numerous basketball clinics throughout NS.; National Assn. Basketball Coaches merit award '76. NS school Athletic Fed. award '80; mem. Canadian Basketball, Nova Scotia Sports halls of fame.

BALDWIN, Matt (curling); b. 3 May 1926, Blucher, Sask.; given name: Matthew Martyn; m. Betty Jean Hamilton; c. Susan, Sally, Leslie; UofAlta., BSc.; ret'd petroleum engineer; 8 Northern Alta., 5 Alta titles; 3 Brier titles; '54 Edmonton carspiel; Keen Ice Singles curling TV series 7 of 10 years; dir. Eskimos Football Club 5yrs, club pres.; mem. Governor-General's Curling Club, Alta., Edmonton, UofAlta., Canada's Sports, Canadian Curling halls of fame; res. Edmonton, Alta.

BALDWIN, Ralph (harness racing); b. 25 Feb 1916, Lloydminster, Sask.; d. 26 Sep 1982, Pompano Beach, Fla.; m. Jeanette; harness race driver, trainer; apprenticed with father, becoming second trainer, later for Harry Fitzpatrick, before opening public stables; began racing in '30s shifting to US tracks '46 after serving in US army; more than 1100 winners with purses totalling more than $5 million; major victories include 2 Hambletonians (Speedy Scott '63, Flirth '73), 5 Kentucky Futurities, 2 Westbury Futurities, 2 Realization Trots, Messenger Stakes; head trainer Castleton Farms, Lexington, Ky. '60-69; following year's absence returned to racing as head trainer, sometimes driver, Arden Homestead Stables, Goshen, N.Y.; mem. Cdn Horse Racing, USTA Living halls of fame.

BALES, John (canoeing/administration); b. 6 Jul 1950, Lachine, Que.; m. Penny Werthner; c. Neill, Elena; McMaster, BA, BPhE, MBA, European Institute Business Administration; pres. Coaching Assn. of Canada; ntl Juvenile boys' singles canoe champion '67; head coach Rideau Canoe Club from '70; Canadian club title '73; CCA ntl team coach '73 world, jr. European championships, '74-75, '77 worlds, '76 Olympics; instrumental in establishing Ntl Sports Centre in Ottawa, Ntl Coaching Institute in Calgary; chair. Cdn Sport Centre Calgary; res. Ottawa, Ont.

BALL, James (t&f); b. May 7 1903, Dauphin, Man.; d. 2 Jul 1988, Victoria, B.C.; m. Violet Laird Parker; c. Jacqueline Allan; UofM; pharmacist; Man., Western Canadian Intercollegiate titles; '27 ntl quarter-mile title, anchored winning mile relay team; '28 Olympic trials 400m in record 48.6 breaking 49.4 standard he had set in heat 1 hour earlier; silver with 48-second run '28 Olympics, team bronze mile relay; Glasgow quarter-mile, Dublin relay, set Irish 200m mark breaking standard set 20 years earlier by Hamilton's Bobby Kerr; mem. relay team which won '29 Madison Square Gardens Millrose Games medley relay; anchored Commonwealth relay team in victory over England; ntl 400yd record stood 37 years; relay bronze '32 Olympics; competed in 1st Maple Leaf Gardens indoor championships, 1st BEG Hamilton; 3 Cdn 300yd, 400m titles; outstanding performer Dublin, Ireland, meet (Tailteam Queen trophy), '33 Canadian amateur athlete-of-yr (Norton Crowe Trophy), Winnipeg Jockey Club sterling silver Grecian urn for contribution to sport; silver medal ntl snowshoe race; mem. Cdn Olympic, Canada's, Man. Sports halls of fame.

BALLANTINE, Bonny (bowling); b. 10 Feb 1939, Regina, Sask.; given name: Bonny Bonnell; m. William Ballantine; c. Drew, Grey, Dawne, Jaye, Brad; secretary; began as 5-pinner; mixed championship team '55; Western Canadian team championship '61; moved to 10-pin winning Regina mixed doubles; mem. women's championship teams '63, '65; city, provincial women's doubles titles '64, '65, '66; Regina, Sask., Canadian O'Keefe Open singles titles '66; certified AMF 10-pin bowling instructor, began working with youth leagues '67; Regina scratch singles, all-events, ladies' team '68, city, provincial, ntl open singles '69; competed world championship '69; city, provincial all-events, city, provincial open singles '71; Regina Lakeshore Lions sportswoman of '66; mem. Sask. Sports Hall of Fame; res. Regina Beach, Sask.

BALLARD, Harold (entrepreneur); b. 30 Jul 1905; Toronto, Ont.; d. 11 Apr 1990, Toronto, Ont.; given name: Harold Edwin; m. Dorothy Biggs (d); c. William, Harold Garner, Mary Elizabeth; Upper Canada College; pres. Maple Leaf Gardens; champion powerboat racer, speed skater; ntl speedboat record 63mph Rice Lake; Toronto 220-, 440-, 880yd speed skating titles; following footsteps of skate manufacturing father, became involved with all aspects of hockey at early age; managed Toronto Sea Fleas to Allan Cup, Toronto Nationals to Memorial Cup; principal exec/financial backer Marlboro organization in '30s; Marlies won record 7 Memorial Cups; sr. team '50 Allan Cup; part-owner Maple Leafs '62-63; principal owner '71; owner CFL's Tiger-Cats from '77; noted for charitable work; recipient OHA goldstick; newsworthy personality with many detractors; involved with initial Team Canada '72; spent 1yr of 3-yr sentence Millhaven Penitentiary for misappropriation of Leafs funds; mem. Cdn Football, Hockey halls of fame.

BALON, Dave (hockey); b. 2 Aug 1938, Wakaw, Sask.; given name: David Alexander; m. Gwen; c. Jodi, Jeff; tour boat owner; lw Prince Albert Mintos, Vancouver, Saskatoon (WHL), Trois-Rivieres, Kitchener-Waterloo (EPHL), Houston (CPHL); NHL '59-73 with Montreal, NYR, Minnesota, Vancouver; NHL record: 776 scheduled games, 192g, 222a, 78 playoff games, 14g, 21a; mem. 2 Stanley Cup winners; rated top 2-way player in NHL '70-71; Que. (WHA) '73-74; coached Humboldt Jrs '72-80; diagnosed as having multiple sclerosis '78; res. Prince Albert, Sask.

BANNON, Paul (t&f); b. 22 Mar 1956, Glasgow, Scotland; given name: Paul Patrick; Memphis State, BA; chartered accountant; Scottish schools 1500m champion '71; British jr. 3000m champion '72; 5 times NCAA All-American '73-77, Canadian 5000-, 10,000m champion '77; bronze '78 CG marathon; PB: 800m (2:01); 1500m (3:57); mile (4:11); 5000m (13:49); 10,000m (28:36); marathon (2h: l6:03); res. Mississauga, Ont.

BANOS, Jean-Marie (fencing); b. 10 Feb 1962, Lavelanet, France; m. Caitlin Bilodeau; c. Justin, Sebastien; UofMtl; educator; sabre specialist; mem. 1st non-European sabre team to place in top 8 world championships '82; 4 ntl individual, 3 team titles; 2 Governor-General's Cup, Eastern Canadian, London Heroes titles, 1 Heineken, Terre des Hommes title; mem. 2 world youth, 2 world championships, '81, '83 FISU, '83, '91 Pan-Am, '84, '88, '92 Olympic Games teams; best ever showing by Canadian fencing team 6th '91 World Championships; mem. Montreal team of year '90; res. MacMasterville, Que.

BANOS, Jean-Paul (fencing); b. 27 Jan 1961, Lavelanet, France; UofMtl; tech. dir. Que. Fencing Federation; sabre specialist; mem. ntl team from '78; 24 ntl titles; best sabre showing by Canadian individual, team 7th '84 Olympics; mem. '84, '88, '92 Olympic, '87, '91 PAG teams; individual, team gold '90 Commonwealth championships; 2 ntl individual, team titles; individual gold '87 Pan-Ams; capt. '91 sabre team which posted best Cdn result (6th) at Sr. Worlds; mem. Montreal team of '91; Sport Excellence Award '89; res. Montreal, Que.

BAPTIE, Norval (speed skating); b. 1879, Bethany, Ont.; d. 1966, Baltimore Md.; m. Gladys Lamb; showman; at 14

North Dakota speed champion, at 16 defeated Winnipeg's Jack McCulloch for world title; shattered all speed records as amateur and pro; remained in competition more than 25yrs winning close to 5000 races at distances from 220yds to 5 miles; turned to stunt and figure skating, setting record for barrel jumping, skating backwards, broad jumping, skating on stilts; after WW1 launched touring ice shows; directed first shows featuring Sonja Henie; ret'd from active skating '39, 1st pro coach Washington, D.C. Figure Skating Club; diabetes led to amputation of both legs by '58; continued to coach in Baltimore, Washington; with Miss Henie became 1st skaters named to US Ice Skating Hall of Fame; mem. Canada's Sports Hall of Fame.

BAPTISTE, Sheridon (bobsleigh): b. 6 Jan 1964, Georgetown, Guyana; m. Andrea; Queen's BA; personal trainer; standout football player drafted Ottawa Rough Riders '88 but elected to become competitive sprinter, long jumper and bobsleigher; mem. ntl bobsleigh team from '89; brakeman for Chris Lori 4-man team; competed '92, '94, '98 Winter Olympics; 1 silver, 4 World Cup race bronze; CIAU indoor male t&f athlete-of-yr award; res. Ottawa, Ont.

BARBER, Bill (hockey): b. 11 Jul 1952, Callander, Ont.; given name: William Charles; m. Jenny (d); c. Kerri, Brooks; hockey exec.; jr. Kitchener Rangers; Philadelphia's 1st choice, 7th overall '72 amateur draft; 1 1st team, 2 2nd team all-star lw; 50g single season '75-76 season; passed 400 NHL career goal plateau '83-84 season; mem. 2 Stanley Cup winners, 6 NHL all-star games; Team Canada '76, NHL all-stars '79 Challenge Cup; ret'd following '84-85 season; head coach Hershey '84-85, '95-96; asst Philadelphia '94-95, dir. pro scouting '88-96; head coach Philadelphia Phantoms (AHL) '96-'00; head coach Flyers '00-02; won Calder Cup '98; head coach Planet USA AHL all-stars; 13yr NHL record 420g, 463a in 903 scheduled games, 53g, 55a in 129 playoff games; player personnel dir. Tampa Bay '02; jersey No. 7 ret'd. by Flyers; mem. Flyers, Hockey Heritage North, Hockey halls of fame; res. Cherry Hill, N.J.

BARBER, Darren (rowing): b. 26 Dec 1968, Victoria, B.C.; UVic; grandson of Hockey Hall of Famer Syl Apps; mem. jr. ntl team '86, sr. ntl team from '87; fastest man in Canada on rowing ergometer (which measures strength & stamina) and ranked 2nd in world '92; 6:21 fastest Cdn time ever in pairs '94 worlds; mem. ntl schoolboy 8s gold '85, '92 Olympic gold 8s; 9 Cdn Henley, 5 international, 2 ntl, 1 FISU regatta gold; competed '89 FISU, '92, '96 Olympic Games, '89, '90, '91, '94 worlds; '91 BC Premier's athletic award, '92 CARA centennial medal; mem. Canada's Sports, Cdn Olympic halls of fame; res. Victoria, B.C.

BARBER, Jack (speed skating): b. 9 Jan 1895, Ottawa, Ont.; d. 4 Jul, 1993, Ottawa, Ont.; given name: Jack Alexander; m. Anna Twedley (d); c. Dorothy; ret'd. National Capital Commission; too small to pursue hockey career so following WWI launched competitive career at 31; won numerous city, provincial titles; pres., meet dir., fund raiser EOSSA '47-65; pres. OSSA; did much to foster sport among youngsters; Ottawa ACT sportsman of '82; mem. Ottawa Sports, Canadian Speed Skating halls of fame.

BARBER, Sara (swimming): b. 25 Jan 1941, Brantford, Ont.; m. Donald Jenkins; c. David, Robert, Margie;

McMaster, BA, BHE; teacher; mem. ntl swim teams '54-62 competing '54, '58, '62 BEG, '55, '59 Pan-Am, '56, '60 Olympic Games; '59 world record 100m backstroke; silver '59 PAG; silver, bronze in relays '58, '62 BEG; finalist backstroke, butterfly '56 Olympics; 8 ntl backstroke titles; ret'd from competition '62; Ross Gold trophy; mem. McMaster Sports, Ont. Aquatic halls of Fame, Brantford Area Sports Hall of Recognition; res. Orillia, Ont.

BARBER, Wendy (synchro swim): b. 20 Oct 1962, Mississauga, Ont.; UCal; mem. Calgary Aquabelles; mem. ntl title team '81; with Sue Clarke '83 Spanish, French Open duet titles; 2 Spanish, 1 Swiss, French Open, Pan-Pacific, Eastern div. team titles; '82 Spanish Open figures, '83 French Open solo titles; res. Mississauga, Ont.

BARCLAY, Ann (tennis): b. 31 Jan 1940, Vancouver, B.C.; UBC, BA, BEd.; teacher; won 1st title in US age 11; claimed BC -13, -15, -18, women's singles, doubles titles; at 15 ranked 5th nationally in singles, won ntl women's doubles; won ntl open/closed -13, -15 ntl titles in singles/doubles; won several Pacific Northwest -13, -15, -18 singles doubles titles; at 15 1st ranked BC women's singles; ranked 2nd nationally women's singles at 20; 3 ntl women's singles titles; competed at Forest Hills, Wimbledon, reaching doubles 1/4 finals; played 2yrs Florida-Caribbean circuit, 2yrs European circuit; won several Ont./Que. titles; injuries sustained in car accident curtailed play in later years; mem. Cdn Tennis Hall of Fame; res. N. Vancouver, B.C.

BARDSLEY, Jim (basketball/tennis): b. 19 Nov 1913, New York, N.Y.; d. Dec 1993, Vancouver, B.C.; given name: James Milton Albert; m. Jean Eckardt; c. James Anthony, Robert Eckardt; UBC, BApSc, BEd.; teacher; mem. 5 ntl title basketball teams '37-48; toured Japan with '39 team; coached sr. men's, HS teams '39-74; teaching tennis pro '46-59; numerous city, provincial, ntl titles; rep. Canada at Wimbledon '70-71, seniors doubles semifinals '70; mem. BC, UBC Sports halls of fame.

BARIL, Benoit (speed skating): b. 7 Oct 1960, Quebec City, Que.; international competitive debut '77 NA indoor championships; gold world short-track 1000m, all-around '81; Dick Ellis Memorial Trophy team of '81, CASSA skater of '81; mem. Cdn Speed Skating Hall of Fame; res. Windsor, Que.

BARILKO, Bill (hockey): b. 25 Mar 1927, Timmins, Ont.; d. 26 Aug 1951, near Cochrane, Ont.; given name: William; def. Timmins, Porcupine (NOHA) '44-45, Hollywood (PCHL) '45-47; NHL Toronto '46-51; 3 NHL all-star; 3 Stanley Cup winners; scored historic overtime goal vs. Montreal to give Toronto Stanley Cup '51; died in plane crash while on off-season fishing trip; NHL totals 252 scheduled games, 26g, 36a, 47 playoff games, 5g, 7a; nicknamed "Bashin' Bill"; mem. Hockey Heritage North Hall of Fame.

BARLOW, Wendy (tennis): b. 7 May 1960, North Bay, Ont.; m. Brad Pattenden; Brigham Young.; tennis pro; 5 ntl age-group singles, 4 doubles titles; gold '77 Canada Games; ntl women's doubles title '77, singles '80; 4th '79 PAG; '80 championship of the Americas title; mem. ntl team '74-80, Continental Cup '76-78, Soisbault Cup '78,

'80, Federation Cup '77-78, '80, Chiquita Cup teams '80; Cedar Springs Racquet Club pro Burlington '80-81; OTA clinic assessor '81; Moon Mountain School Phoenix athlete of '74; American Legion outstanding student award '74; Victoria athlete of '79, runnerup BC athlete of year; all-American BYU '79; res. Victoria, B.C.

BARNES, Bev (basketball); b. 9 Aug 1951, Ottawa, Ont.; given name: Beverly; UBC; BPhE; teacher; mem. ntl team '71-76; Moscow FISU Games, Bogota World Championships, Mexico City PAG, Montreal Olympics; mem. BC entry ntl sr. women's championships '80-81; Div. II soccer; res. Roberts Creek, B.C.

BARNES, Kirsten (rowing); b. 26 Mar 1968, London, Eng.; m. Terry Dillon; UVic BA, Bristol PhD; sport psychology consultant; aspiring figure skater who outgrew her male partners (6'2" on skates); began rowing in HS '83; mem. '85 Cdn HS 8s championship crew, ntl team from '87; '87 PAG pairs gold; competed '88, '92 Olympics; 3 US Ntls, 3 San Diego, 3 Cdn Henley, 2 Augusta, 1 Vienna, 1 Amsterdam titles; '91 world 8s and 4s gold; sport excellence award '89, CARA Centennial medal '91; 2 Dick Ellis Memorial awards; UVic female athlete of year '89-91; Greater Victoria female athlete of '90, university rowing's most valuable rower '87-90; also figure skating coach and judge; UVic distinguished alumni award; mem. British Olympic Assn. Psychology steering group; helped Oxford crew beat Cambridge in '00 race; mem. Cdn Olympic, Greater Victoria halls of fame; res. England.

BARNES, Rolph (t&f); b. 16 Jul 1904, Hamilton, Ont., d. 6 Oct 1982, Waterdown, Ont.; given name: William Rolph; m. Charlotte Innes (d.); c. Bill, Rennie, Peter, Bruce; m. Marnie Wilmot Holton; c. Gerry, Margot; Princeton; industrialist; mem. '24 Olympic team; Hamilton and District badminton singles, doubles, mixed doubles champion '32-34; Savanah Club, Barbardos Tennis Club title team '72.

BARR, Dave (golf); b. 1 Mar 1952, Kelowna, B.C.; given name: David Allen; m. LuAnn Busch; c. Brent Jason, Teryn Amber; Oral Roberts U.; pro golfer; all-star pitcher Little League, Babe Ruth baseball; def Jr. A Kelowna Buckaneers; runnerup Canadian amateur golf championship '72; '73 Oklahoma State Amateur, 5 college tournament titles, 2nd-team all-American '73; pro '74; 3 BC, Que., 2 Kamloops Opens; Canadian TPC; BCPGA, Alta., Man., Cariboo, Washington State Opens once each; BC Sun match champion '77; twice runnerup Canadian tournament of champions; CPGA open champion; mem. 4 Dunhill Cup teams; mem. Canadian amateur world team; mem. 9 Canadian world cup pro teams, with Dan Halldorson '85 winner; low individual '83; USPGA tour '78-98; won '81 Quad Cities, Victoria Opens, '87 Atlanta Classic; 2 holes-in-one; 4 Canadian Tour Order of Merit titles; '85 CPGA title; runnerup US Open; with Dawn Coe won '89-90 Canadian Airlines International mixed; qualified for PGA Srs tour '02; 1st Cdn to win on Champions (Sr.) tour taking '03 Royal Caribbean Classic; 2 Canadian tour stroke-average awards; 8 *SCORE* player of year awards; joined Champions tour '02; won Royal Caribbean Classic '02; 10 career aces; mem. Cdn Golf Hall of Fame; res. Coquitlam, B.C.

BARR, Doris (baseball); b. 26 Aug 1921, Starbuck, Man.; given name: Mary Doris; ret'd hospital accounting dept; lhp; played softball before joining AAGPBL South Bend '43-45, Racine '45-47, Springfield '48, Muskegon '49, Kalamazoo '50; best season 20-8 leading Racine to '46 title; mem. Man. Baseball Hall of Fame; honored by Cooperstown, Cdn Baseball halls of fame; res. Winnipeg, Man.

BARR, Irene (swimming); b. 3 Sep 1923, Hamilton, Ont.; m. Van Fleet; c. 2; born with acroydenia, which causes malfunction of muscular system; began swimming as therapy and soon joined Hamilton Aquatic Club; by age 14 was strong candidate for medal at '40 Olympics; but war intervened; set 6 ntl records in FS distances from 100yds to 1 mile; nicknamed "Iron Barr"; eventually competed against others who missed '40 Olympics and won 2 gold, 2 silver and 1 bronze in '90 World Masters Games; res. Markham, Ont

BARRÉ, Alexandra (canoeing); b. 29 Jan 1958, Budapest, Hungary; given name: Alexandra Sandor; m. Denis; c. Stephanie, Mylanie; Laval; mem. Hungarian ntl team '75-79; '76 Hungarian Olympic team, '75 jr. worlds, '78 worlds; mem. Cdn ntl kayak team '80-85; 2 ntl K1 500m titles; 2 gold '83 Pan-Am championships; 3 gold Vichy, 1 Zaandam, Duisburg regatta titles; with Sue Holloway silver 500m K2, bronze 500m K4 '84 Olympics; mem. 3 world championship teams; res. Lac Beauport, Que.

BARRÉ, Denis (canoeing); b. 4 Feb 1948, Lachine, Que.; m. Alexandra Sandor; c. Stephanie, Mylanie; TV, film teacher; mem. '72, '76, '80 Olympics; '76 ntl K1 1000m, '80 K2, K4 1000m, K2 500m, Olympic trials, Zaandam regatta K2 500m, 1000m, 10,000m, K4 1000m, 500m, Bydgoszcz regatta K2 1000m, ntl K1 500m; coach Que. Canoe Club; res. Lac Beauport, Que.

BARRÉ, Jean (canoeing); b. 3 Jan 1945, Verdun, Que.; m. Henriette Soucy; c. Carolyne, Jean Francois; Laval, BPhE; fitness consultant; from '59 winner 50 regional canoeing, kayaking titles, 20 times provincial canoeing finalist; twice ntl kayak tandem, 4s titlist; silver '68 NA tandem kayak; ntl canoeing team mem. '68-72; semifinalist kayak tandem, 4s '68, '72 Olympics, Belgrade world championships; silver '62 international school rowing championships; bronze '72 x-country skiing championships, gold 1st NA roller ski race '72; mem. silver medal Swiss interschool hockey champions '63; TV French network canoeing analyst '68, '72, '76 Olympics; res. Quebec City, Que

BARRESI, Jamie (football/coaching); b. 27 Nov 1956, Ottawa, Ont.; given name: James Vito; UofO, BSc, teaching cert., Penn State, MSc, PHd, UFla, MSc; football coach; began football career in HS at Hamilton, UofO, UGuelph; began coaching as asst. UofO '81, '83, Penn State '84-85, '88-92, Florida '86-87, Wake Forest '93-00, Central Fla. '01-03, Hamilton (CFL) '04; participated Orange, Fiesta, Aloha (2), Blockbuster, Holiday bowls, Vanier Cup as coach; ntl championship game vs. Oklahoma '86; coached 1st round NFL draft picks O.J. McDuffie, Rick Nattiel; res. Winter Park, Fla.

BARRETT, Danny (football); b. 18 Dec 1961, Boynton Beach, Fla.; m. Alison; c. Joshua, Zachary, Whitney; Cincinnati; football coach; pro qb CFL Calgary '83-85, '89-91, '96-97, Toronto '85, '87-88, BC '92-93, Ottawa '94-95; USFL New Jersey Generals '86; CFL record: 148g, 33td, 1cvt, 463 carries, 2426yds, 31td, 3029 passes, 1631 completed, 23,134yds, 91int, 132tds, caught 34 passes, 501yds, 2td; 2 Grey Cup finals; set CFL record 601 passing yards single game '93; asst coach Calgary '97-98, BC '99; head coach Sask. '00-04; co-capt Cincinnati '82, hon. mention *AP* all-American; active in Athletes in Action; res. Regina, Sask.

BARRIE, Rachel (hockey); b. 12 Nov 1982, Arnprior, Ont.; given name: Rachel Elizabeth; St. Lawrence U; goalie; began playing competitive hockey age 4; became goalie because brother Nathan required target at which to shoot pucks while playing street hockey; competed in minor hockey ranks; Ottawa West team MVP in major atom '92; top goalie award Sudbury Big Nickel tournament '98; drafted by Smiths Falls (CJHL) becoming first girl to play in league; mem. Team Ont. '99 Canada Games; try out with ntl women's team '97 ranking among top three goalies; goalie ntl women's –22 team; SLU 1st team all-star, female goalie of '03; Sarah Devens Eastern College Athletic Conf. leadership award; res. Arnprior/Ottawa, Ont.

BARRON, Andy (speed skating); b. 2 May 1951, Penrith, Eng.; given name: Andrew James; m. Heather Rendall; UofAlta., BEd.; started as figure skater; Alta. novice men's, pairs, Prairie juvenile titlist; competed ntl swimming, water polo championships; ntl speed skating team mem. '71-76; ntl 1500m title '73; ntl records for 1500m, 3000m, 5000m, 10,000m distances; won 6 ISU international medals; mem. '72, '76 Olympic teams; ntl jr. team coach '81-82; tech. dir. CASSA '83-91; ntl short track coach from '92; Kinsmen Salute to Youth Award '71; PetroCan coaching award; res. Calgary, Alta.

BARROW, John (football); b. 31 Oct 1935, Delray Beach, Fla.; m. Evangelina; c. Gregg, Elaine, Kyle; Georgia Military Academy, Florida; businessman; oe/og/mg, team capt. final year; *Look* all-American, Atlanta TD Club Southeastern Conf. lineman of year, Southeastern Conference *AP, UPI, INS* all-South 1st team; 3rd draft Detroit (NFL); CFL Hamilton '57-70; 9 Grey Cup finals, 4 winners; EFC all-star 12 times, all-Canadian 11 times; 8 Schenley lineman-of-yr nominations, won '62, runnerup 5 times; CFL lineman of century '67; Hamilton all-star team of pro era '50-67; GM Toronto '71-75; radio analyst Hamilton games; mem. Florida, Canadian Football, Florida State Sports halls of fame; res. Missouri, Tex.

BARRY, Cliff (coaching); b. 1 Jun 1946, Montreal, Que.; given name: Clifford Alan; m. Susan Wheeler; c. Carling; Sir George Williams, BA, UWO, BPhed; competitive swim coach; standout water polo player '68-76; mem. ntl Olympic water polo team '72 (capt), '76; mem./capt. '67, '71, '75 Pan Am Games, '71, '75 world championships teams; Canada's outstanding water polo player '68-72; began full-time coaching '76 in Guelph; Region of Waterloo head swim coach '79; head coach Pointe Claire SC '86; coach Etobicoke SC; among protegees were Victor Davis, Mike West; 3 Cdn swim-coach-of-yr awards; coached ntl team titlists '91, ntl women's titlists '90-91; '93 Canada Games coach; swim coach '84, '88 Olympic teams, various Pan-Pac, world, PAG, CG, Canada Games teams; lectured/coached at Cdn, US coaches clinics, Wilfrid Laurier; coached 8 ntl men's, women's, 7 Ont. title teams; 5 top age-group champions; placed 8 swimmers on Olympic, 3 on PAG, Pan-Pacific, 6 Canada Games teams; 3 Cdn, Ont. swim coach-of-yr awards; 2 PetroCan coaching awards; mem. Ont. Aquatic Hall of Fame; res. Mississauga, Ont.

BARRY, Martin (hockey); b. 8 Dec 1904, St. Gabriel, Que., d. 20 Aug 1969, Halifax, N.S.; pro NY Americans '27-28, Boston '29-35, 5 consecutive 20-goal seasons, Detroit '35-39, Montreal '39-40; mem. '36-37 Stanley Cup winners; Lady Byng Trophy '37, all-star ctr '37; NHL record: 195 goals, 192 assists; mem. Hockey Hall of Fame.

BARRY, Michael (wrestling/judo); b. 28 Jun 1954, Saint John, N.B.; given name: Michael Gerard; m. Sharon Shewchuk; c. Quinton, Brianne, Rashon, Castille; UNB, Ryerson, UWO BA, Windsor LLB; lawyer; received early training in judo earning black belt at 17; attended '72 Olympic trials; entering UNB switched to wrestling; represented N.B. in wrestling '71 Canada Games; moved to Ryerson '73 to train under Pat Bolger; competing in 57-62kg class mem. ntl team '75-84; 3 ntl titles, 2 runnerup; 2 OUAA, CIAU titles; shared outstanding wrestler award with brother Sean '79 ntl championships; competed '76 Olympics, 3 World Cups (2 bronze); gold '81, '83 Canada Cup; 1 gold, 2 silver, 1 bronze in 4 intl competitions '75-81; Commonwealth Games silver '78; competed in '77 worlds, '77, '81 FISU Games; nicknamed "Spike"; ret'd. from competition '84; mem. Saint John, N.B. Sports halls of fame; res. London, Ont.

BARTLETT, Don (curling); b. 1 Apr 1960, Gander, Nfld.; given name: Donald Brian; m. Shauna Stewart; c. Stewart, Donald; postal clerk; lead for Kevin Martin Alberta rink '91, '92, '95-97, '00 Briers; all-star '91-92; won Briers '91, '97; silver medal '91 Worlds; competed '92, '02 (silver) Olympics; mem. WCT VO Cup title rink '94, FlexiCoil $60,000 'spiel winner '97; M&M Skins title '01; qualifying event for WCT grand slam bears his name; res. Spruce Grove, Alta.

BARTLETT, Sue Anne (curling); b. 9 Sep 1943, Grand Falls, Nfld.; given name: Sylvie Anne Byrne; m. John Bartlett (d); c. Joanne, John, Russell; insurance agent; began curling age 23; skipped Nfld. rinks to 11 provincial women's championships giving her distinction of appearing in more ntl championships than any other woman curler in Canada; never won a ntl crown but was a finalist three times; won '71 Nfld. mixed; 6 Nfld. sr. women's titles; mem. Cdn Curling Hall of Fame; res. Labrador City, Nfld.

BARTON, Julie (table tennis); b. 25 Sep 1972, Halifax N.S.; athlete, singer; began representing Canada internationally at 14; noted for fast, powerful, aggressive play; mem. ntl team from '87; competed in worlds India '87, Germany '89; 6 ntl junior singles titles; won '88 senior women's title; won Canada Cup title '91; with Caroline Sylvestre silver medal '91 Wiltshire tournament in England; with Michelle Cada '90 ntl jr. girls doubles; won '89 NA jr. singles, doubles; finalist with Lijuan Geng '90 World Cup qualification women's doubles; '91 PAG women's, mixed doubles bronze; coached by Mariann Domonkos; twice NS woman athlete of yr; outstanding Black Cultural Centre athlete in NS; twice Ottawa ACT award winner; mem. Nepean Wall of Fame; res. Nepean, Ont.

BARWELL, Gord (football); b. 6 Sep 1944, Saskatoon, Sask.; d. 22 Apr 1988, Toronto, Ont.; given name: Gordon Keith; m. Nancy Phyliss Schoenhals; c. Jay, Jody; Eastern Canadian dir. Athletes in Action; ntl age-group honors HS t&f; 1 season Sask. Hilltops jrs.; Roughriders '64-73; db/fl; 7 Western Conf. playoffs, 4 Grey Cups; caught 102yd td pass from Ron Lancaster Vancouver '65; mem. Roughriders Plaza of Honor.

BARWISE, Bob (shooting); b. 13 Mar 1937, Charlottetown, P.E.I.; given name: Robert Claude; m. Janet; c. Gail, Joanne, Robin, John; Prince of Wales Coll.; ret'd hotelier, disco, restaurant operator; operates rifle business; former mem. RCMP; 4 Atlantic full-bore titles; pres. PEI Rifle Assn. from '74; 11 times Bisley competitor; commandant '88 team; won Queen's prize 1st stage '80; DCRA Governor-General's silver badge '80, '84; Bisley team adjutant '78; initial winner Burke target rifle award; mem. PEI Sports Hall of Fame; res. Charlottetown, P.E.I.

BARYLUK, Mitch (basketball); b. 20 Jun 1931, Winnipeg, Man.; m. Eileen Brown; c. Marty, Adam; travel agency owner; played/coached varied teams in Winnipeg '43-52, including '50-51 Cdn Jr. champ Stellars; key in rebuilding Thunder Bay men's basketball program; twice pres. TBBA; organized clinics, summer leagues; player-coach Sr. Y Grads '52-55; coached HS, Sr. League teams; won TBBA city men's title with Dinty's Kentuckians '64-68; introduced women's basketball to TB; sponsor TB Oldtimers; Geraldton tournament titles '81-84, Manitoba Master Hoop Classic '86; TB Oldtimers honour award '86; player/coach/sponsor TB Travel slo-pitch team; mem. NWO Sports, Man. Basketball halls of fame; res. Thunder Bay, Ont.

BASE, John (curling); b. 23 Feb 1963, Oakville, Ont.; sales rep.; twice competed in Canadian junior championships, won in '82; won '83 world junior title; 6 time competitor in provincial men's Tankard playdowns; res. Oakville, Ont.

BASS, Danny (football); b. 31 Mar 1958, Lansing, Mich.; Michigan State; owner Hyundai dealership; pro lb Toronto '80-81, Calgary '81-83, Edmonton '84-'91; CFL record: 179g, 22 interceptions, 230yds returned, 1td, 19 fumbles recovered, returned 109yds, 2td, 47 qb sacks; 8 WFC all-star; 6 CFL all-star; 3 Norm Fieldgate trophy awards; twice runnerup Schenley defensive player award; led CFL defensive tackles '88; CFL outstanding defensive player '89; 3 Grey Cup finals, 1 winner; mem. Cdn Football Hall of Fame, Eskimos Wall of Honor; res. Sherwood Park, Alta.

BASSETT, Carling (tennis); b. 9 Oct 1967, Toronto, Ont.; m. Robert Seguso, c. Holden John, Carling, Ridley; tennis player; daughter of sports entrepreneur John F. Bassett; US -12 clay court title; 1st Canadian Orange Bowl jr. title winner, ntl girls' 18-and-under singles; pro at 15; 1st pro victory Ginny of Central Pa. '83; 1st Canadian woman to advance to 4th round Wimbledon '83; at 15 youngest Wimbledon competitor; mem. '83 Federation Cup team; lost to Chris

Evert Lloyd Amelia Island final; Osaka, Japan tournament title '84; ranked 1st Canada '82-84, 2nd world jr. ranking; highest ranking ever by Cdn in WPTA history moving from 169 to 8 '85; *Tennis Magazine* '83 pro rookie of year; Canadian female tennis player of '83; 2 Bobbie Rosenfeld trophies; worked as fashion model, movie actress; mem. Ont. Legends, Canada's Sport, Cdn Tennis halls of fame; res. Boca Raton, Fla.

BASSETT, John Jr. (entrepreneur); b.1939, Toronto, Ont.; d. 14 May 1986, Toronto, Ont.; m. Sue Carling; c. Carling, John, Vicky, Heidi; Upper Can. College, UNB, UWO; eldest son of media magnate John W. Bassett; mem. UNB hockey title team; qb UNB football team; Cdn Open jr. doubles tennis champion at 15; reporter *Victoria Times, Toronto Telegram*; owned WHA Toronto Toros, WFL Toronto Northmen, later Memphis Southmen and USFL Tampa Bay Bandits; shocked establishment by signing NFL stars Paul Warfield, Larry Csonka, Jim Kiick who had played with Super Bowl champion Miami Dolphins; film producer.

BASTARACHE, Clarence (t&f/swimming/wheelchair basketball); b. 27 Sep 1946, Bouctouche, N.B.; m. Oliva Cormier; ret'd. stationary engineer; competed nationally '71-85 amassing 40 gold, 22 silver, 15 bronze medals; competed internationally '72-77, '82; named to but did not compete for Cdn team '71, '78-79; amassed 1 gold, 8 silver, 5 bronze; participated Intl Super Challenge '76-79; held Cdn shotput record '72-74, pentathlon record '75-79, club throw record '72-78, 25m breaststroke (since events discontinued records still in force), Cdn record 50m breaststroke '75-85, javelin '73-82; mem. N.B. Cdn wheelchair volleyball title teams '74-75; pentathlon bronze '76 Toronto Olympiad; 3 best athlete in class awards; Atlantic Disabled Games MVP award; N.B. Wheelchair Sports Assn. Volunteer of '93 award; Eastern Cdn Wheelchair basketball foul shooting champion '83-84; prov., ntl merit awards; mem. Bathurst Wheelchair Basketball title team; all-star award '76; dir. N.B. Wheelchair Sports Assn.; mgr. Bathurst Community Venture Van from '79; chair. Canada Winter Games '03; founding mem./pres. Chaleur Handicap Sports and Recreation Club; mem. Bathurst, N.B. Sports halls of fame; res. North Tetagouche, N.B.

BASTET, Evert (sailing); b. 30 May 1950, Maracaibo, Venezuela; Sir George Williams; sailboat mast mfgr., highway engineer; HS pole vaulter, alpine ski instructor, ski jumper, diver; began competing '60; mem. ntl team from '67; skipper jr. pre-Centennial champion '65; crew FD silver '84 Olympics; alternate '68, crewed with Hans Fogh '73-76, Terry McLaughlin from '78; mem. '72, '76, 80, '84, '88, '92 Olympic teams; won '73, '80 world, '74, '79 NA, '79-81 CORK, '71, '76 S.P.O.R.T., '70 US national, '76 European, '80 Hyeres, '81 Can-Am FD titles; '73 US laser title; sport excellence award '83, Olympic champion award '85, with McLaughlin SFC team of year runnerup '80; Que. Sailing Fed. Outstanding achievement award bears his name; mem. Cdn Olympic Hall of Fame; res. Brome, Que.

BATES, Mark (triathlon); b. 24 Jun 1968, Penticton, B.C.; m. Hilary Watt; Queen's BA; coach/speaker; mem. Queen's swim, x-country teams; competitive swimmer Kingston Blue Marlins 7yrs; worked as lifeguard; made triathlon debut in Belleville; winner of numerous major triathlons such as Niagara, Great Lakes, Muskoka; made world debut '89; silver '95 PAG; 2nd in 1st Ironman '97; 4 ntl triathlon titles; 2 ntl long-course titles; capt. Cdn ntl team '91-96; head coach 321 TriClub, Pacific Spirit Triathlon club; certified personal trainer, fitness consultant; licensed coach; founder, head coach North Shore Xtreme Jr. triathlon club; head coach UBC Masters swim team '94-97; contributing writer *Inside Triathlon* magazine; Kingston athlete of '91; Canada 125 award; res. N. Vancouver, B.C.

BATH, Doc (all-around); b. 9 Mar 1889, Bath, England., d. 19 Sep 1980, Weyburn, Sask.; given name: Leonard Harry; m. Helen; c. Gladys Helen, Valarie Doreen Jean; nurse; Somerset Eng. 440, mile, 6-mile, x-country championships '08; British army Aldershot command '10 6-mile, '11-13 6-mile North and South India champion, emigrated to Canada '25; trainer Weyburn Beaver fastball team 13yrs, also baseball, hockey trainer; coached oldtimers hockey 3yrs; trainer Weyburn Red Wings hockey club '61-75, Comets, Molson's Weyburn Canadians '62-75, Canadian fastball title '72; mem. Sask. Sports Hall of Fame.

BATHGATE, Andy (hockey); b 28 Aug 1932, Winnipeg, Man.; given name: Andrew James; m. Merle Lewis; c. Sandra, Billy; golf driving range operator; capt./rw Guelph Memorial Cup winners '51-52; pro NYR organization '52-53; minor league Vancouver (WHL), Cleveland (AHL); Rangers '54-63, Toronto '63-64, Detroit '65-66, Pittsburgh '67-68, '70-71, Vancouver Canucks (WHL) '68-69, MVP award; played briefly in Switzerland, returned to coach 3 seasons; played briefly Vancouver Blazers (WHA) '74; early exponent of slapshot; among 1st to develop curved banana blade; his shot which struck Jacques Plante in face 1 Nov. '59 led to face masks being used regularly by goalies; scored 1st goal in Penguins franchise history; capt. Rangers; mem. '54 Stanley Cup winners; Hart Trophy '59; twice 1st, 2nd team all-star; scoring co-champion with Bobby Hull '61-62; NHL record: 1069 scheduled games, 349g, 624a, 54 playoff games, 21g, 14a, 8 all-star games; nicknamed "Tubby"; West Side Trophy, Macbeth Trophy, Frank Boucher Trophy; NHL milestone award '82; prominent golfer; mem. Man. Sports, Hockey, Man. Hockey, Switzerland Ambri-Piotta Hockey Club halls of fame; res. Bramalea, Ont.

BATLEY, Jamie (lacrosse); b. 9 Jan 1967, Peterborough, Ont.; Maryland; '86-87 Peterborough Minto Cup champion all-star; known for offensive prowess; leading scorer Ont. jr A league '86-87, MVP '87; led Kenner Rams to 3 Ont. high school field lacrosse titles; mem. midget all-Cdn title team '83; NCAA Div. 1 all-American '93; mem. ntl team from '89; Peterborough athlete of '87; res. Peterborough, Ont.

BASTIEN, Baz (hockey/administration); b. 29 Aug 1919, Timmins, Ont.; d. 15 Mar 1983, Pittsburgh, Pa; given name: Aldege; hockey exec.; goal OHA Sr. Port Colborne, EHL Atlantic City '39-40, OHA Sr., Toronto Marlies '40-42, OSHL Cornwall '42-43; 5 games NHL Leafs '45, AHL Pittsburgh '45-49, 22 games PCHL Hollywood '46-47; eye injury opening day '49 training camp ended career; served as GM Pittsburgh NHL '77-83; 3 AHL 1st team all-star; 2 Hap Holmes trophies; AHL outstanding goalie award bears his name; mem. Hockey Heritage North Hall of Fame.

BATSTONE, Harry (football); b. 5 Sep 1899, Hamilton, Ont., d. 11 Mar 1972, Kingston, Ont.; Queen's, MD; physician; football, baseball, hockey various school, city leagues; in same backfield with Lionel Conacher led Argos to '20 Interprovincial title, lost Grey Cup final to UofT; won Grey Cup '21; with Pep Leadlay, Red McKelvey helped Queen's win 3 consecutive Intercollegiate titles, 3 Grey Cups; Queen's coach on 3 occasions; capt. Argos 1921; mem. Queen's, Canadian Football, Canada's Sports halls of fame.

BATTAGLIA, Frankie (boxing); b. 1910, Winnipeg, Man.; d. 1971, California; chance meeting as teenager with Jack Dempsey fashioned life; began amateur ring career '26; mem. '28 Olympic team; pro '30; top world middleweight contender; KO'd number 1 contender Ben Jeby 1st round '32; rematch after Jeby had claimed title resulted in TKO victory for Jeby in 13, result of eye cut; lost world title bid by decision to Freddie Steel '36; ret'd '38 following 100 amateur, pro bouts; mem. Man. Sports Hall of Fame.

BATTERSBY, Robert (rowing); b. 1 Nov 1948, Vancouver B.C.; given name: Robert Glenn; UBC, BApSc; professional engineer; mem. UBC varsity rowing team '70-72; coxed pairs '71, '75 Pan-Am, '72 Olympic, '74 world championships teams; from '76 coach UBC/VRC women's team; guided 8s to ntl women's, Western sprint titles '79; placed 3 UBC rowers on '81 ntl team; res. Vancouver, B.C.

BATTLE, Greg (football); b. 14 Apr 1964, Long Beach, Calif.; m. Anna; Arizona State; lb NFL Denver '86; joined CFL Winnipeg '87-93, '97-98, Las Vegas, Ottawa '94, Memphis '95, Saskatchewan '96; CFL record (through '98): 189gp, 812 def. tackles, 26 qb sacks; 3 Eastern, 2 CFL all-star; 3 James McCaffrey trophies; outstanding CFL defensive player '90, '91, runnerup '89; 3 Grey Cup finals, 1 winner; Grey Cup def. star '90; set CFL record with 14 def. tackles '93 Grey Cup game; def. MVP '85 Holiday Bowl; res. Phoenix, Ariz.

BAUCK, Dean (t&f); b. 16 May 1954, Vancouver, B.C.; given name: Dean Evan; m. Kim Tebbutt; c. Cara, Dalli; UBC, BSc., MBA; real estate broker; high jump specialist; mem. ntl team '74-81; silver vs. France (indoors), gold vs Britain, Greece, West Germany, Wales '74; bronze '78 CG; ntl jr. record with 1st jump over 7'; gold '81 Pacific Conf. Games; 5th '79 PAG; mem. '80 Olympic team; PB: 2.21m outdoors, 2.19m indoors '81; coached briefly; participated in slo-pitch softball, basketball; res. Delta, B.C.

BAUER, Bobby (hockey); b. 16 Feb 1915, Waterloo, Ont.; d. 16 Sep 1964, Kitchener, Ont.; given name: Robert Theodore; m. Marguerite Bauer; c. Bobby, Bradley; St. Michael's College, UofT; jr. Kitchener-Waterloo; rw with Woody Dumart, Milt Schmidt to form Sauerkraut line; trio joined Boston (NHL) '36 season, as Kraut Line helped Boston finish 1st 4 successive seasons, 2 Stanley Cups; coached K-W Dutchmen '56 Olympic bronze; final Boston Gardens appearance '51-52 season scoring goal, assist in special game as Kraut Line honored; among NHL leading scorers 3 times; 4 times NHL all-star, 3 times Lady Byng Trophy; NHL record: 327 scheduled games, 123g, 137a, 48 playoff games, 11g, 8a; mem. Waterloo County, Hockey halls of fame.

BAUER, David (hockey); b. 2 Nov 1924, Waterloo, Ont.; d. 9 Nov 1988, Goderich, Ont.; given name: David William; St. Michael's College, UofT, OCE, Notre Dame U; Basilican priest, teacher; brother Bobby mem. famed Kraut Line; jr. Toronto, Oshawa, Windsor; football, jr., sr. baseball K-W region; managed, coached St. Michael's Majors, won Memorial Cup; coached UBC hockey team; '64 conceived National Team plan which became basic concept for Canadian international hockey participation evolving into Hockey Canada; Hockey Canada director; coached Austrian national team '73 world tournament; assisted with Japanese ntl team development; Officer Order of Canada '67; UCalgary arena bears his name; mem. Waterloo County, Hockey, IIHF, Cdn Olympic, UBC, Canada's Sports halls of fame.

BAUER, Lyle (football); b. 22 Aug 1958, Saskatoon, Sask.; Weber State Coll. BA; football exec., realtor; 38th overall draft pick Saskatchewan '79; pro guard Winnipeg '82-91; CFL record: 161g; EFC all-star '90; 3 Grey Cup finals, 3 winners; AGM Blue Bombers from '92; res. Winnipeg, Man.

BAUER, Steve (cycling); b. 12 Jun 1959, Grimsby, Ont.; given name: Steven Todd; m. Elayne; c. Kohen; Waterloo, Brock hon. LLD; operates Steve Bauer bike tours; ntl pursuit team mem. '77-84; ntl points race titles '79, '81-83; mem. '78, '82 CG, '79 PAG, '77, '80, '82-83 world championship, '84, '96 Olympic teams; silver sr. road race '82 CG; 190km road race silver '84 Olympics; bronze world pro road race championships '84; 2 30km national Madison, 4 men's 4000 team pursuit titles; 10,000 mass start winner, 2nd 30,000 mass start Barbados '82; 2 Lowenbreau, 1 Tour of Somerville, Tour of Texas, 2 Carlsberg Light, Hull Festival, Zurich, Dienze GP, Grand Prix of Americas road race titles; won 1st stage and retained yellow jersey 5 consec. days '88, led 10 consecutive legs '90 Tour de France; nicknamed "Silent Warrior" on European pro circuit '84-95; acquitted of assault charges brought by Belgian cyclist Claude Criquielion following '88 race crash; mem. 7-Eleven racing team; ret'd '96; Governor-General's meritorious service medal; res. Beamsville, Ont.

BAULD, Donald (all-around); b. 14 Jun 1914, Halifax, N.S.; d. 4 Jul 1996, Halifax, N.S.; m. Evelyn Conrad; c. Donald, Brian; Dalhousie; sporting goods agency owner; versatility encompassed tennis, badminton, basketball, rugby, curling; 2 NS, 3 Halifax County jr. tennis titles; 5 NS, 2 Eastern Cdn men's singles tennis titles; 10 NS #1 rankings, 5th ntl rankings '49; 6 NS, 2 Eastern ntl men's doubles, 1 NS mixed doubles titles; Bermuda men's singles title '59; Ottawa District men's singles '45; 2 NS sr. men's singles titles; twice invited to compete on ntl Davis Cup team but never participated; mem. 2 Gordon Cup teams; with brother Gordon helped Canada claim 1st Gordon Cup in 12 tries '62; 4 Maritime badminton singles, 5 men's doubles, 1 mixed doubles titles, 1 Windsor-Detroit area singles title; capt. Maritime jr. rugby champion Tigers; flying half Wanderers '35-39, 2 Maritime titles; twice capt., leading scorer; mem. Dal Grads, Wanderers Maritime champion basketball teams, team capt., scoring champion; mem. '35 NS champion Grads, 5 consec. city title teams; twice MVP; skip runnerup NS, Maritime jr. title curling rinks; mem. NS entry '58 Brier; winner numerous major bonspiel titles; NS table tennis titlist; mem. NS Sports Hall of Fame.

BAUMANN, Alex (swimming); b. 21 Apr 1964, Prague, Czechoslovakia; given name: Alexander Sasha; m. Tracy Taggart; Indiana, Laurentian; CEO Queensland swimming; ED Sport Development Consul, Queensland, Australia; mem. ntl team '78-87; 200m, 400m individual medley, 1500m FS specialist; 34 ntl titles; 32 ntl FS sprint, IM 4 world 200m, 2 world 400m IM, CG, Olympic 400m IM records; 9 gold Canada Cup meets, 4 gold 4 Nations Cup meet, 3 gold NZ Games, Australian Open meet, CIAU championships, 2 gold FISU, CG; 400m IM gold World Cup; 1st Cdn Olympic swimming gold medal in 72yrs with 400IM WR 4:17.41 Los Angeles 30 Jul '84; added gold 200IM in WR 2:01.42 4 Aug '84; mem. '80, '84 Olympic, '79 PAG, '83 FISU Games teams; 40 Ont., 24 ntl age-group records; Viscount Alexander award '84; Lionel Conacher trophy '84; 3 ntl male swimmer-of-yr awards; 2 CIAU male swimmer of yr; 3 Ont. sports awards; 3 Sudbury athlete of year; '81 Sudbury municipal medallion, award of distinction; with Steve Podborski, Ont. amateur athlete of '81; fed. govt. world record awards '82-84, excellence awards '84-85; flag-bearer '83 FISU, '84 Olympic Games; hon. capt. '94 CG team; 2 Seagram 5 Star awards; Officer Order of Canada '84; mem. Laurentian U Sports Wall, Cdn., Ont. Aquatic, Cdn Olympic, Canada's Sports halls of fame; res. Brisbane, Australia.

BAUN, Bobby (hockey); b. 9 Sep 1936, Lanigan, Sask.; m. Sallie Krohn; c. Jeffrey, Gregory, Brian, Michele, Patricia; insurance salesman, donut franchise owner, dir. Professional Hockey Alumni; jr. Marlboros, 2 Memorial Cup winners; pro Toronto '56-67, '71-73, Oakland '67-68, Detroit '68-70; mem. 4 Stanley Cup winners; pres. NHL Players' Assn; coach Toronto (WHA) '75; NHL record: 964 scheduled games, 37g, 187a, 96 playoff games, 3g, 12a; authored *Lowering the Boom*; res. Claremont, Ont.

BAWDEN, Betty (basketball); b. 22 Dec 1917, Edmonton, Alta.; m. Robert Bowen (d); c. Rowena, Robert; ret'd dept. store buyer, library technician; competitive diver, swimmer ages 10-16; mem. famed Edmonton Grads '39-40; mem. Canadian Basketball, Alta. Sports halls of fame; res. Oakville, Ont.

BAWN, Bev (hockey/baseball); b. 17 Aug 1937, Fredericton, N.B.; given name: Beverly; m. Margaret; safety & training co-ordinator; mem. Eastern Memorial Cup Moncton Beavers '62; with Fredericton Capitals '66 Eastern Cdn Intermediate, '64 NB, '67 Maritime titles; with Campbellton Tigers '72 Hardy Cup; bronze '75 ntl sr. baseball finals; NB titles with Chatham Ironmen, Marysville Royals; coached Mirimichi Gagnon Packers to Hardy Cup title '87; 6 North-South all-star, '71 MVP; governor NB Sports Hall of Fame; mem. NB, Fredericton Sports halls of fame; res. Newcastle, N.B.

BAY, Jason (baseball); b. 20 Sep 1978, Trail, B.C.; given name: Jason Raymond; m. Kristen; N. Idaho CC, Gonzaga; competed for Trail LL World Series; only Cdn to compete in LLWS and major leagues; drafted by Montreal Expos '00; dealt to San Diego '02, Pittsburgh '03; batting .282, 26hr, 82rbi named NL rookie of '04, 1st Cdn, 1st Pirate to win ML top rookie award; 28 rbi games; players choice, SN rookie-of-yr awards; ML record (through '04) 150g, 498ab, 76r, 141h, 31db, 5tr, 30hr, 96rbi, 7sb, .283ba; Tip O'Neill award '04; sister Lauren pitcher ntl women's softball team; res. Phoeniz, Ariz.

BAY, Lauren (softball); b. 9 Aug 1981, Trail, B.C.; Oklahoma; pitcher; brother Jason NL rookie of '04 with Pittsburgh; uncle Gerry Moro 3 time Olympic decathlete; competed '02 worlds; made Olympic debut '04; OSU female student athlete of '03; NCAA Oklahoma woman of '04; res. Trail, B.C.

BAYDOCK, Donna (volleyball); b. 28 Aug 1957, Winnipeg, Man.; given name: Donna Anne; UMan., BPhE, UBC, MPhE; teacher, coach UMan; volleyball at provincial level '74; mem. ntl jr. team Mexico zone championships; mem. UMan Bisonnettes '75-77, twice capt. MVP; mem. silver medal Man. team '75 Canada Games; all-star mem. Bisonettes ntl jr. champions 1976; 3-year mem. ntl jr. team; sr. team '77-81; Vancouver Old Time Ladies' '80 ntl sr. title team; mem. '79 Pan-Am, '80 Olympic teams; UMan female athlete of '77; CIAU coach-of-yr award; res. Winnipeg, Man.

BAYER, Jim (administration); b. 1938, Charlottetown, P.E.I.; d. 1985, Wolfville, N.S.; UNB, BPhE, Springfield Coll., MSc.; educator; PE supervisor NS dept. of ed. '65-72; dir. NS dept. of rec. '72-77; AD Acadia '78-85; p-pres. Atlantic branch CAHPER, AUAA; NS div. Cdn Red Cross Society; p-chair. Interprov. council for sport & rec; board chairman NS Sport Heritage Centre; Cdn Red Cross Society award, Queen's Jubilee medal, Cdn Parks & Rec. Assn. award of merit; hon. life mem. Sport NS, Rec. Assn. of NS.

BAYTOR, Terry (softball); b. 8 Jul 1952, Montreal, Que.; m. Barbara Razniewski; c. Chris, Alexandra; UofT, BA, BEd, MEd; high school principal; Level 5 Softball Canada, Level 3 BC, Elite Calgary coaching credentials; asst. coach ntl sr. men's team '82-89, head coach from '89; has guided ntl team to gold medals in '89 PAG qualifier, '90 Challenge Cup, '91, '95, '99 PAG, '92 ISF worlds, silver '96 worlds; PetroCan coaching award; mem. Softball Canada, Brampton Sports halls of fame; res. Brampton, Ont.

BEACH, Ormand (football); b. 28 Oct 1910, Ponca City, Okla., d. 20 Sep 1938, Sarnia, Ont.; m. Marguerite Booth; Kansas, McGill; engineer; all-state fb '25-28; all-American; described by Dr. James Naismith as "an outstanding anatomical example of the perfect man" helped Kansas tie Notre Dame 0-0 to give Jayhawkers 1st Big 6 title, twice team capt.; listed by Grantland Rice as one of all-time defensive greats in US football; as flying wing and linebacker helped Sarnia Imperials win 4 ORFU titles; 3 Grey Cup appearances, 2 winners; all-league, all-Canadian each year he played; Imperial Oil Trophy as ORFU MVP; died in refinery explosion at Sarnia; HS stadium named in his honor; mem. Sarnia-Lambton Sports, Canadian Football halls of fame.

BEACH, Pete (administration); b. 1906, England; d. Mar 1984, Toronto, Ont.; given name: Nathaniel Allworth; UWO.; educator; received early training Toronto West End Y '20-30; standout wrestler, competed in football/t&f at UWO; coached UWO t&f team; chair. PE comm. Cdn YMCA; operated summer camps; taught at Albert Coll.,

Belleville '35-57 (excluding war years); YMCA War Services dir. England, Italy; made major contributions to AAU of C (t&f), CSF (boxing); credited with rebirth of Cdn boxing in post-war period; exec. dir. OFSAA '58-71; guiding force in founding CFSAA; worked with CAHPER/ COA; ret'd "sort of" '71; OFSAA award for educators for services and contributions to young people through school sports bears his name.

BEAN, Gladys (builder); b. 17 Jun 1918, Montreal, Que.; d. 18 Dec 1986, Montreal, Que.; given name: Mabel Gladys; McGill, BA, BPhE; educator; developed, directed McGill's Royal Victoria Coll. aquatic program '60-65; dir. women's athletics from '66; mem. Que. Sports administration council; when McGill's men's, women's athletic programs merged in '76 became asst. AD; CIAU delegate, rep to CIAU women's athletic comm.; recipient CAHPER Tait McKenzie award '78, CIAU Austin-Matthews award '83; award bearing her name given annually to McGill female athlete who has brought most credit to the university; mem. McGill Sports Hall of Fame.

BEARPARK, Bob (soccer/administration/coach); b. 15 Mar 1943, Berwick-on-Tweed, Eng.; d. 18 Nov 1996, Victoria, B.C.; educator, sports administrator; as youth played Bristol Rovers, Bath City; moved to Canada '76; tech. dir. Ont. Soccer Assn 4yrs; coach Team Can. '84 China tour; head coach Team Canada FIFA world youth championships '84; asst. Cdn Olympic '84, World Cup '86 teams; head coach Team Canada '87; dir. BC Rec. & Sport branch from '90.

BEATON, Bob (boxing/officiating); b. 19 Jun 1912, Port Hood, Cape Breton, N.S.; m. Bertha MacDonald; c. Graham, John, Anita, Cyril Robert, Bernard; ret'd insurance co. branch mgr.; lost sight of one eye at 3; award winning runner, jumper, cyclist, boxer, hockey player; with brother Joe pioneered hockey in Britain in mid-'30s; highly-regarded hockey coach in Maritimes; competed in Maritime Big Four Sr. HL; 12 pro boxing bouts in mid-'30s, winning all, 9 by KO; ring referee '35-83; officiated 40 ntl, 5 Commonwealth, 1 world title bouts; referee-in-chief NS Boxing Authority from '78; introduced 3-judge system to boxing '54; mem. Cdn Boxing, NS Sports halls of fame; res. Pictou, N.S.

BEATON, Ewan (judo); b. 13 Jul 1969, Winnipeg, Man.; UMan., Concordia.; Judo Saskatchewan coach; competing at 60kg won 5 consecutive ntl titles; gold '95, silver '91 PAG; Dutch Open gold '93; 3rd degree black belt; competed '92, '96 Olympics; res. Regina, Sask.

BEATTY, Lou (golf); b. 10 Apr 1918, Woodstock, N.B.; given name: Louis Edgar; educator; mem. 3 NB-PEI Willingdon Cup teams; twice runnerup NB-PEI amateur; 5 NB Srs titles; 6 consecutive Maritime Srs. titles '80-85; mem. 12 NB Srs. teams; PEI Srs. title; 30 Woodstock golf club titles; 6 Old Home Week titles; 3 NB Legion titles; set all-time Woodstock GC record '61; Fredericton Open medallist; only golfer to shoot his age (63) at Woodstock Club '81; nicknamed "Sweet Lou"; mem. NB Sports Hall of Fame; res. Woodstock, N.B.

BEAUDRY, Paul (fencing); b. 11 May 1958, Sherbrooke, Que.; Montreal, BSc., McGill, MBA; sabre specialist; ntl jr. titles '75, '77-78; silver '75 Canada Games; won Ottawa Shield '77; 4 times Eastern Canadian, Que. titlist; won

Governor-General's Cup, Que. Cup, Cornell tournament, Heinneken Cup, Terre des Hommes; mem. silver medal team '78 CG; '77 Que. fencer of year, athlete par excellence Championnats Sportifs Quebecois; res. Sherbrooke, Que.

BEAUDOIN, Andre (t&f); b. 10 Sep 1958, Cowansville, Que.; competed in wheelchair rugby several yrs before being inspired by Andre Viger, Rick Hansen to shift to wheelchair racing; won Boston Marathon '99; competed 5 Paralympics; 2 gold, 5 silver, 5 bronze medals in races covering 100m, 200m, 400m, 800m; WR 100m, 200m; res. Montreal, Que.

BEAUPRE, Don (hockey); b. 19 Sep 1961, Waterloo, Ont.; goalie Sudbury (OHA), Nashville, Birmingham, Salt Lake (CHL), Kalamazoo (IHL), Baltimore (AHL), NHL with Minnesota '80-88, Washington '89-94, Ottawa '94-95, Toronto '96; drafted by Minnesota '80; OHA 1st team all-star '80; 2 NHL all-star games; NHL record: 667 scheduled games, 268-277-75, 37,396min, 17so, 70 playoff games, 33-31, 3,923min, 3so; res. Minnesota.

BECK, Ross (all-around); b. 14 Aug 1928, St. Thomas, Ont.; given name: Ross William; m. Annalee Bernice Voaden; c. Judith, Joanne, David, Alan; UWO., hons. BA, PHRE; ret'd. HS principal; played jr. OBA baseball prov. finals '49; sr. baseball St. Thomas (IC), Nickel Belt League '50-52; tryouts with St. Louis, Brooklyn, Toronto Maple Leaf organizations; standout football/basketball player UWO '48-52; mem. '49 football title team claimed by coach John Metras as "one of best I ever coached"; held ntl rating as basketball official more than 20yrs working all games in '58 ntl sr. men's title series in Ottawa; coached football/basketball at several Ottawa area HS; throughout teaching career played active role in OFSAA as regional rep., prov. principal rep., member of board of dir.; initial recipient Pete Beach award; res. Stittsville, Ont.

BECKETT, Norman (shooting); b. 28 Apr 1909, Hamilton, Ont.; d. Oct 1990, Hamilton, Ont.; m. Alice; c. Susan; accountant; began shooting in teens and developed into one of Canada's top marksmen; anchorman Royal Hamilton Light Infantry Gold team 6 decades; rejected for overseas duty WW2 for poor eyesight but it was never a problem on the range; qualified 18 Bisley teams, competed 9 times; Bisley Queen's Prize '61; 2nd Bisley grand agg. '59; 2 Bisley Imperial Tobacco Cups; 3 DCRA Governor-General's agg., 1 Macdonald Stewart grand agg.; mem. 2 Kalapore teams; more than 40 individual, unit, team prizes during 60-plus yrs of DCRA competition; received DCRA 60yr badge '89.

BECKMAN, Jim (all-around); b. 13 Aug 1935, Halifax, N.S.; m. Donna Guptell; c. Todd, Daina, Tina; welder; outstanding minor hockey career at rw; mem. Fairview juvenile Maritime champions; signed by Boston organization; junior Metro Toronto Lakeshore Bruins 2yrs; all-star 2yrs; all-Ont. title; Estevan Sask. Jr. HL; declined Providence AHL invitation to play Sr. hockey Windsor Maple Leafs, NSHL 6yrs; Sherbrooke Sr. Beavers 4yrs; mem. Bunny Ahearne Trophy winners in Sweden; competed in 5 Allan Cup finals; Grand Falls, Nfld. rec. dir., player-coach Nfld. title team; ret'd as player at 34; outstanding, versatile baseball player Halifax Cardinals H&D League; player-coach Hantsport Shamrocks, batting champ hitting .340 '60, MVP, league champs; tryout

with Atlanta (NL) '61; mem. 2 Hantsport Maritime Sr. champs; 1yr Jonquiere, 4yrs Thetford Mines, Que.; played in Grand Falls league '70-74; 2yrs Sr. softball Alberta Brake & Clutch; level 6 softball official; low handicap golfer; mem. NS Sports Hall of Fame; res. Calgary, Alta.

BÉDARD, Bob (tennis); b. 13 Sep. 1931, St. Hyacinthe, Que.; m. Anne Stacey; c. Mark, Paul, Michael, Peter; Loyola, BA, Sherbrooke, BEd; headmaster, St. Andrews College; semipro hockey, MVP honors Quebec Senior League '55-56; No. 1 Canadian tennis '55-65; mem. '53-61, '67 Davis Cup teams; ntl Open singles champion '55, '57, '58, sharing native record Dr. Jack Wright; 8 Que. Open titles; at least one victory over every No. 1 player from France, Sweden, Denmark, India, US, Mexico, Cuba, Belgium, England, Brazil, Italy '54-59; silver '59 PAG, gold '69 Canada Games; with Don Fontana 3 ntl men's doubles; with Mariette Laframboise '59 ntl mixed title; mem. Canada Fitness Council 2yrs; 3yrs PQLTA v-p., pres., 4 yrs v-p. 2 yrs hon. secty CLTA; with son Peter won 2 ntl father-son titles; mem. Loyola College, Cdn Olympic, Que, Canada's Sports, Cdn Tennis halls of fame; res. Aurora, Ont.

BÉDARD, David (diving); b. 23 Oct 1965, Montreal, Que.; m. Cheryl Watson; coach Pte. Claire; began diving age 10; coached by Don Webb; joined ntl team '83; 29 ntl platform, springboard titles; silver 10m '86, 1m, 10m '90 CG; bronze 10m '87, 3m '95 PAG; 3m semifinalist '89 FINA Cup; semifinalist 3m, 10m '91 World Cup; gold 10m '88 Swedish Cup; mem. '84, '88, '92, '96 Olympic, '86, '90, '94 CG '83, '87, '91, '95 Pan-Am Games teams; set Cdn 3m record '89; University Cup 10m, 3m gold '88, Pan Am Invitational '90; res. Pointe Claire, Que.

BÉDARD, Eric (speed skating); b. 17 Dec 1976, Shawinigan, Que.; short track specialist; mem. ntl team from '97; with Marc Gagnon, Derrick Campbell, Francois Drolet '98 Olympic gold in 5000m relay; individual Olympic 1000m bronze; relay silver '97 worlds; world short track 1500m, 0verall silver 2000; 2 ntl championship gold, 1 silver, 3 bronze; competed '97, won gold '98 world team championships; res. Montreal, Que.

BÉDARD, Héléne (table tennis); b. 8 Apr 1968, Ascot Corners, Que.; twice ntl junior champ; undefeated in team match play '89 world championships; mem. women's bronze medal teams '87 PAG, '89 CG; scored major upset beating top-seeded Thanh Mach in '87 Canadian championships; '89 ntl mixed doubles titlist, finalist women's doubles; mem. Canadian team '89 world championships; twice Quebec female table tennis athlete of year; Canadian junior athlete of year '85; res. Sherbrooke, Que.

BÉDARD, Myriam (biathlon); b. 22 Dec 1969, Ancienne-Lorette, Que.; div. Jean Paquet; c. Maude; TV show host, former marketing VIA Rail; abandoned figure skating as youngster; learned to shoot as Val Cartier cadet; began competing in biathlon at 16; mem. ntl team '87-98; 2 ntl jr., 3 ntl sr., 3 world cup gold; world championship 7.5km title '93; 1st-ever Cdn Olympic biathlon medalist with bronze '92; 2 gold '94 Olympics; competed '98 Olympics; switched to speed skating '98; Biathlon Canada athlete of '90-93; Biathlon Canada female athlete '93-94; Bobbie Rosenfeld, Lou Marsh, Velma Springstead trophies '94;

fed. govt. meritorious service award '93; intl biathlon union development comm.; Val Cartier biathlon training center bears her name; mem. Canadian Olympic, Canada's Sports, Cdn Skiing halls of fame; Olympic Order; res. Quebec City, Que.

BÉDARD, Nancy (synchro swim); b. 11 Nov 1961, Quebec City, Que.; Champlain Regional College; coach; provincial, ntl, international competitor '73-80; 4 Que. jr. team titles; 1sts figures, solo, duet, team Eastern Div. jr. championships, runnerup figures, solo, duet ntl jrs '74; 4 Que. sr., Eastern Div. team titles; 3 ntl sr. team titles; team bronze '78 world championships, silver World Cup, gold Pan-Pacific; silver '80 American Cup; jr. team coach from '80; all-Cdn coach '81; res. Quebec City, Que.

BEDECKI, Tom (administration); b. 4 May 1929, Glace Bay, N.S.; d. 31 Dec 1993, Ottawa, Ont.; m. Ann McDonald; c. Ginni, Bruce, Dayna, Clint; St. Francis Xavier, BA, Springfield College, Ohio State, PhD; ret'd ED Canadian Association for Health, Physical Education and Recreation; mem. McCurdy Cup rugby team, Maritime baseball champions; coached baseball, hockey Colorado College ('57 NCAA champions), hockey Ohio State; HS athletic dir., staff mem. UofOtt, UofFla, Ohio State; mem. SFC exec., CG Assn. of Canada, Canada Sports Awards, International Council for Sport and Physical Education; former dir. Sport Canada, instrumental in initiating, developing international hosting policy, sport exchange programs with USSR, China, Cuba.

BEECROFT, Lynne (field hockey); b. 9 May 1957, Comox, B.C.; UVic, BA MEd; coach UVic, mem. BC HS title team '73; BC jr. team '75-76, '75 ntl title; defence BC sr., ntl team '77-85, 58 intl matches; 4 times World Cup competitor, silver medal team '83; bronze '81 European indoor championships; mem. '84 Olympic team; Cowichan HS athlete of year; Nancy Greene scholarship recipient; BC Premier's athletic award; fed. govt. excellence award '83; accorded Master coach status; 20yrs UVic FH coach earning 10 CIAU gold; prov. coach '85-92; ntl program regional coach; ntl team asst. coach '02; Victoria coach of '02; 4 Canada West coach-of-yr awards; field hockey 3M elite coach of '00; Victoria sportswoman of '95; YM-YWCA Woman of Distinction award '03; BC Women in Sport Leaders & Legends; mem. BC Sports Hall of Fame; res. Victoria, B.C.

BEEDELL, John (canoeing); b. 14 Feb 1933, Wellington, N.Z.; given name: John Leslie; m. Ann Borland; c. Michael, Jeffrey, David; Carleton, BA; ret'd. teacher; ntl jr. K2, C2 champion '56; sr. C2, C4 '57, '59, C2 '61; NA C2, C4 '59; mem. '58 worlds, '60 Olympic teams; res. Ottawa, Ont.

BEERS, John (t&f); b. 17 Aug 1952, Netherlands; given name: John William; m. Angela Elsaesser; UBC, BC Institute of Technology; hj specialist; ntl team '70-76; ntl, Commonwealth record '73; Viscount Alexander award '72; mem. '72 Olympic, '74 CG teams; silver '75 PAG; res. Port Moody, B.C.

BEERS, William George (lacrosse); b. 5 May 1843, Montreal, Que.; d. 26 Dec 1900, Montreal, Que.; Lower Canada College; dentist; outlined 1st laws modern lacrosse; formed National Lacrosse Assn. 1867; toured UK with 1st Canadian lacrosse team to play in Britain 1876, played before Queen Victoria at Windsor; prominent in formation MAAA; several books including *Lacrosse, the National Game of Canada* (1869); founder *Canada Journal of Dental Science* (1868), a Canadian 1st; mem. Canadian Lacrosse, Canada's Sports halls of fame.

BEESTON, Paul (administration); b. 20 Jun 1945, Welland, Ont.; m. Kaye Doherty; c. Aimee, David; UWO, BA, CA, Fellow of Inst. of Chartered Accountants of Ont.; baseball exec.; initial employee Toronto Blue Jays '76; rose to v-p administration, business operations, COO '89, CEO '91; dir. *Toronto Sun Publishing*, Stratford Festival; selected by *Sporting News* as 20th most powerful person in sports '94; pres./CEO Toronto Argonauts '94; COO major league baseball '97-02; mem. Cdn Baseball Hall of Fame; res. Toronto, Ont.

BEGIN, Terry (curling); b. 6 Mar 1938, Port Arthur, Ont.; m. Kathryn Naismith; Carleton, BSc.; curling equipment supplier, patent agent, freelance broadcaster, writer; mem. exec. Ottawa Granite, Navy Curling Clubs, CCA public relations comm., statistician ntl championships; twice skipped, 3 times winner City of Ottawa Grand Aggregate Shield; competed 5 Ont. Consols; mem. organizing comm. '74 Canadian Schoolboy, '77 Montreal Brier; chairman media comm. '79 Ottawa Brier; senior instructor rating, Curl Canada coaches development program instructing at clinics throughout Ontario, Quebec; Scotty Harper Memorial Award for Radio/TV reports '79; res. Ottawa, Ont.

BEHRENS, Norman (canoeing); b. 20 Dec 1956, Lachine, Que.; m. 1. Kathy Bobula, 2. Lorna Peters; c. Veronika; Concordia, BA; ntl jr. C1 1000m '75-76, C2 1000m, C2 500m '77, C4 1000m '78; gold C1, C2 1000m, C1 500m Sr. America Cup '78, C2 500m Continental Cup '79, C1, C2 1000m, C2 500m '80 Olympic trials, C2 1000m, 500m 1980 Zaandam Holland Invitational regatta, C2, C4 1000m, C2 500m '80-81 ntl championships; ntl sr. record 4:21.1 winning '80 ntl C4 1000m; mem. 2 world championships teams; res. Lery, Que.

BEILER, Egon (wrestling); b. 28 Mar 1953, Linz, Austria; given name: Egon Henry; m. Carol; c. Mark, Matt; Waterloo, UWO, BSc, Lakehead, BPHE, DDS; dentist; 3 OFSAA titles; 8 ntl titles classes 136 1/2-149 1/2 lbs; 3 CIAU titles; mem. '72, '76, '80 Olympic, '74, '77-79 world, '74, '78 CG, '75, '79 PAG teams; gold '74 New Zealand, '78 CG, '75 PAG, '76 Toledo World Cup; bronze '73 European championships; mem. St. Jerome's Kitchener HS soccer title team, 3rd in Ont.; 3 St. Jerome's, 2 Waterloo outstanding-wrestler awards; athlete of year St. Jerome's '71, City of Kitchener '73, Waterloo '74, Lakehead U '76; mem. Waterloo County, UWO W-Club, Cdn Amateur Wrestling, Cdn Olympic Sports halls of fame; res. Flesherton, Ont.

BELANGER, Babe (basketball); b. 8 May 1911, Edmonton, Alta.; d. 8 Jan 1999, Osoyoos Lake, B.C.; given name: Noilla; m. Ian MacLean (d); c. Heather, Neil; ret'd secretary; t&f competitor; mem. famed Edmonton Grads '29-37, 136 games, 1441 points for 10.5 avg.; organized sr. citizen's honky tonk band; mem. Cdn Basketball, Alta. Sports halls of fame.

BÉLANGER, Bertrand (harness racing); b. 17 May 1944, St. Michel de Bellechasse, Que.; launched career with Miss Nomer at 17; raced at Quebec Raceway before shifting to Saratoga, N.Y.; a catch-driver for numerous trainers he's rated as a smart tactician; Saratoga Harness Horseman of '81; won driving titles at Saratoga, Green Mountain Park, Monticello Raceway; res: Sarasota Springs, N.Y.

BELANGER, Frenchy (boxing); b. 17 May 1906, Toronto, Ont.; d. 27 May 1969, Toronto, Ont.; given name: Albert; m. Ivy; c. Gerald, Leilani; pro-fighter, waiter; impressive amateur, early pro record '25-26; beat Frankie Genaro in 10 to win vacant NBA world flyweight title '27; defended successfully against Ernie Jarvis '27, lost to Genaro '28, lost rematch; 2yrs ntl champion losing to Steve Rocco '28; regained title beating Rocco '29; lost bid for US flyweight title to Izzy Schwartz '29; final pro bout '32, 7th-round KO by Frankie Wolfram; pro record: 52 bouts, 13 won by KO, 24 by decision, 7 draws, 15 lost decisions; 1 by foul, 2 KO's; nicknamed, "Canadian Wolverine, Canadian Tadpole"; stroke '64 left him paralyzed, speechless but with aid of friend Murphy Blandford spent final years involved with Belanger's Aces softball team; mem. Canada's Sports, Boxing halls of fame.

BELANGER, Josée (soccer); b. 14 May 1986, Coaticook, Que.; forward ntl -19 team; earned 1st intl cap '04 vs. Germany; mem. Cdn '03 Pan-Am Games team; mem. Montreal Xtreme W-League '04; res: Coaticook, Que.

BELCHER, Val (football); b. 6 Jul 1954, Houston, Tex.; m. Terri Lea; c. Layne, Ashton, Megan; Houston; restaurateur; og Houston '73-76; tri-capt. '76 Southwest Conf., Cotton Bowl champions; 3rd round pick Dallas (NFL) '77; saw NFL exhibition game action for Patriots vs. Rams; CFL Ottawa '79-82, Winnipeg '83-84; CFL all-Eastern '79-82; all-Cdn '80-82; Schenley outstanding lineman ntl finalist '80-81; named to 2nd unit Southwest Conf. all-decade team of '70s; organized Texas Shootout Skins Game golf event at Rideau View Country Club to aid Ottawa Civic Hospital fund-raising; restaurateur-, business-person-of-'94 awards; owns Lone Star, Big Daddy's Crab Shack chain; res. Toronto, Ont.

BELCOURT, Tim (curling); b. 4 Jul 1962, Penetanguishene, Ont.; m. Ellen Beck; c. Alicia, Kelly, Nicole; sporting goods store owner; skipped rink Ont. Jr.; mem. Ont. Governor-General's trophy winner '85; second Russ Howard rink 3 Briers; mem. Cdn, world champions '87; mem. 3 Canada Challenge Cups Japan; participated in '87 Olympic trials; runnerup Moncton 100 'spiel; Dick Ellis team award '87; mem. Cdn Curling Hall of Fame; res. Elmvale, Ont.

BÉLEC, Jacques (football); b. 13 Sep 1931, Timmins, Ont.; given name: Joseph Jean Jacques; m. Carolyn; c. Liane, Danielle, Philip; UWO, BA; regional mgr. London Life Ins. Co.; hockey, football UWO; Mustang football MVP '53; pro Montreal '54-56; Grey Cup finalist each year; competitive squash player, golfer; level 3 ski instructor; mountain climber, Mt. Everest, Kalopatai; dir. QGA; capt. Summerlea G&CC; dir. QGA 9yrs, pres. '91; mem. Montreal Badminton & Squash Club; consultant in behavioral science, training, organization, motivation; res. Montreal, Que.

BELFOUR, Ed (hockey); b. 21 Apr 1965, Carman, Man.; m. Rita Marie; c. Dayn, Reaghan; North Dakota; goalie Winkler (MJHL) '85-86; UND '86-87, NCAA title, Saginaw (IHL) '87-89, NHL Chicago '88-97, San Jose '97, Dallas '97-02, Toronto '02-03; IHL rookie of '88; Calder Memorial Trophy '91; 3 Vezina, 4 Jennings trophies, Crozier Saving Grace award; Upper Deck all-rookie team; *Hockey News* rookie of '91, all-star; Trico award for lowest save percentage '91; set NHL record of 11 consecutive playoff victories; reached 400 wins '03; mem. '99 Stanley Cup winner; mem. Team Canada '89-90, '04 (withdrew due to injury); mem. Cdn Olympic gold medal team '02; 5 NHL all-star games; NHL record: (through '04) 856 scheduled games, 435-281-111, 49,510m, 75so, 154 playoff games, 9413m, 335ga, 14so, 85-64; nicknamed "Eagle"; active with Make-A-Wish Foundation; active triathlete; res. Downers Grove, Ill.

BELIVEAU, Jean (hockey); b. 31 Aug 1931, Trois-Rivieres, Que.; m. Élise Couture; c. Héléne; UofOtt, Acadia hon. LLD; ret'd hockey exec.; jr. Que. Aces; Montreal Canadiens '53-71, team capt. '61-71; NHL record: 1125 scheduled games, 507g, 712a, 162 playoff games, 79g, record 97a; 10 Stanley Cup winners; 6 times 1st, 4 times 2nd team all-star; 25 or more goals in 13 seasons, 80 game-winning goals, 3 4-goal, 18 3-goal games; Art Ross trophy '56; Hart Trophy (MVP) '56, '64; Conn Smythe Trophy playoff MVP '65; record 16 consecutive years in playoffs; French-speaking athlete of '67 (Julien Trophy); Lionel Conacher trophy '56; record 16 assists '70-71 playoffs; sr. v-p corporate affairs Canadiens to '93; nicknamed "Le Gros Bill"; jersey 4 ret'd by Canadiens; subject of biography *My Life in Hockey*; Canadiens special ambassador rejected appointment as Governor-General '94; Officer Order of Canada '69 upgraded to Companion '98, mem. Canada's, Que. Sports, Cdn Walk, Hockey halls of fame; res. Longueuil, Que.

BELKIN, Mike (tennis); b. 29 Jun 1945, Montreal, Que.; Miami; teaching pro; with Ron Seifert '57 ntl -13 doubles; -15 singles '59, US ntl jr title '60, US -18 nationals (10th place in US tennis ranks), Canadian -18 singles '62, US Interscholastic singles '63; mem. '67-73 Davis Cup teams; quarterfinalist '68 Australian championships; 3 ntl men's closed singles; top Canadian '71 winning Virginia Slims Masters, semifinalist River Oaks Open, Tanglewood Classic; runnerup Florida championships '72; mem. Cdn Tennis Hall of Fame; res. Miami, Fla.

BELL, Bobby (coaching/administration); b. 13 Aug. 1903, Westmount, Que.; d. 21 Mar 1948, Montreal, Que.; given name: Robert Blagrave; McGill, BA, DDS; dentist; played inter-faculty football; asst. mgr. rugby team, cheerleader; 7yrs McGill hockey; coached McGill hockey '29-37, '42-43, '44-45; 137-58-25 record, 6 Queen's Cup titles, 1 International Intercollegiate title, 2 Que. Sr. HL titles; pres. CIHU, CIRU, Cdn Davis Cup comm., Que. Squash Racquets Assn.; Bobby Bell Memorial trophy awarded annually to Redmen hockey MVP; mem. McGill Sports Hall of Fame.

BELL, George (baseball); b. 21 Oct 1959, San Pedro de Macoris, Dominican Rep.; given name: George Antonio; m. Marie Louisa Beguero; c. Christopher, George Jr., Kevin Antonio; baseball coach; pro Philadelphia organization '78; played in minors at Helena, Spartansburg, Reading,

Oklahoma City, Syracuse; drafted by Blue Jays '80; ML debut with Toronto '81; erratic fielder but powerful hitter; signed as free agent with Chicago Cubs '91; Chicago White Sox '92-93; only player to clear LF roof in 76-yr history of old Comiskey Park, twice in one series '85; Toronto career marked with frequent run-ins with team officials, fans; AL MVP '87; 3 times all-star; set several Toronto records, received numerous awards including AL Silver Slugger; ML record 1587 games, 6123ab, 814r, 1702h, 308db, 34tr, 265hr, 1002bi, 67sb, .278ba; roving hitting instructor Blue Jays '98; made managerial debut with Dominican Winter League team '02; mem. Blue Jays Wall of Distinction; res. San Pedro de Macoris, DR.

BELL, Jane (t&f); b. 6 Feb 1910, Toronto, Ont.; d. 1 Jul 1998, Ft. Myers, Fla.; given name: Florence Jane; m. J. Bert Walker (d); c. John, Judith; m. Doane; Margaret Eaton School; ret'd. PE dir.; standout swimmer, basketball player, hurdler, sprinter; mem. Toronto Ladies, Parkside, Margaret Eaton championship swim teams; set 100yd hurdles record; mem. '28 Olympic team; with Bobbie Rosenfeld, Ethel Smith, Myrtle Cook won Olympic relay gold; Guelph Country Club golf champion; Myrtle Beach mixed two-ball champion '73; mem. 1st Can-Am women's curling team to tour Scotland '55; competed women's world curling Scotland '64; mem. Cdn Olympic, Canada's Sports halls of fame.

BELL, Marilyn (swimming); b. 19 Oct 1937, Toronto, Ont.; m. Joseph DiLascio; c. Lisa, Michael, Janet, Jodi; Loretto College School, McGill, BA, Rider College, MA; teacher; coached by Gus Ryder, began swimming as sprinter age 9; at 15 standout 26-mile Atlantic City marathon swim; greatest achievement '54 when she became first person to conquer Lake Ontario; swam 32 miles from Youngstown, N.Y. to Toronto in 20:58; 1st woman to conquer Straits of Juan de Fuca '56; youngest to swim English Channel '55, conquered other bodies of water before retirement; Barker Bread trophy '52, Lou Marsh Trophy '54, 2 Bobbie Rosenfeld trophies, Cliff Lumsdon award; award in her honor presented annually at CNE to athlete in water-oriented sport; Toronto park bears her name; subject of TV mini-series *Heart: The Marilyn Bell Story*; mem. Order of Ont., Etobicoke, Canada's Sports, US, Ont. Aquatic halls of fame; res. Southampton, N.J.

BELL, Max (horse racing); b. 1912, Regina, Sask.; d. 1972, Calgary, Alta.; given name: George Maxwell; div Suzanne; c. Chester, Diane, Paul, Gretchen; m. Agnes McKeown McMahon; McGill, BComm.; publisher, oilman; purchased 1st horse, Mac Aurelius, from Johnny Longden '36; with Frank McMahon established Golden West Farms; dominant force in NA, European racing circles 36yrs, with victories in Irish Sweeps derby, Queen's Plate, Hollywood Derby; prominent breeder; pres. Balmoral franchise Chicago; dir. Tanforan, Calif.; UMan./Lethbridge arenas, Calgary theatre bear his name; mem. Canadian Horse Racing Hall of Fame.

BELLOWS, Brian (hockey); b. 1 Sep 1964, St. Catharines, Ont.; m. Tracey; c. Kieffer; lw Kitchener Rangers '81-82; OHL 1st team all-star '82; George Parsons award (Memorial Cup most-sportsmanlike player) '82; 1st choice Minnesota '82 draft; pro Minesota '82-92, Montreal '92-95, Tampa Bay '95, Anaheim '96, Vancouver '97, Washington '98-99; played in Germany '97-98 before returning to NHL; mem.

Spengler Cup title team '97; scored 55g '89-90; NHL 2nd team all-star '90; played 3 NHL all-star games; mem. 1 Stanley Cup winner; Team Canada '84; NHL record: 1188 scheduled games, 485g, 537a, 143 playoff games, 51g, 71a; res. Gulf Sport, Fla./Edina, Minn.

BELSHER, Don (touch football); b. 8 Jul 1950, Ottawa, Ont.; given name: Donald Charles; m. Cathy Ritchie; c. Lindsay, Kevin; Algonquin Coll.; truck driver; Jr. A hockey Ottawa 67's '68, M&W Rangers '68-69; MVP CJHL '69; qb/db Ottawa Dan Kelly's '73-83, Ottawa Skemers '84, ntl all-star touring team '74; mem. 3 ntl touch title teams; ntl Touch Bowl MVP '75, '80, '83; minor hockey coach; 3 Ottawa ACT awards; res. Ottawa, Ont.

BELYEA, Arthur (rowing/skating); b. 31 Aug 1885, Saint John, N.B.; d. 6 Jan 1968, Albany, N.Y.; given name: Hilton Arthur; provincial, Maritime, ntl, international awards in sculling, skating; starred as single sculler '04-27, skater '05-21; 35 silver cups, trophies, 33 medals; during '24 Olympics special bronze medal from Olympic committee for good sportsmanship in single sculls; mem. NB Sports Hall of Fame.

BEND, Olive (softball/baseball); b. 7 May 1917, Poplar Point, Man.; d. 2 Feb 1987, Poplar Point, Man.; given name: Olive Elizabeth; m. George Little; c. Roberta, Frances; ret'd teacher; pitched for Winnipeg sr. women's teams 1937-40; authored numerous no-hitters, averaged 13 strikeouts per game; unique distinction of pitching Man., Sask. teams to provincial titles same year; set personal record 22 strikeouts as mem. Moose Jaw team; pro baseball Rockford, Ill. Peaches of AAGPBL; pitched 4 no-hitters, named to all-American girls' baseball team which played at Wrigley Field, Chicago '42; ret'd '45; Man. softball award bears her name; honored Cooperstown, Cdn Baseball halls of fame; mem. Canadian, Man. Softball, Man. Sports halls of fame.

BENEDICT, Clint (hockey); b. 1894, Ottawa Ont.; d. 12 Nov 1976, Ottawa, Ont.; given name: Clinton Stevenson; c. Graham; goalie; Ottawa Senators (NHA, NHL) '13-24, Montreal Maroons '24-30; habit of flopping on ice to block shot forced rule changes to make action legal; NHL record: 364 scheduled games, allowed 874g, 57so for 2.37 avg., 49 playoff games, 87g, 15so, 1.78 avg.; forced into retirement at 34 after stopping two bullet-like Howie Morenz shots, 1st shot shattered his nose, 2nd injured his larynx; because of initial shot, vision was impaired and he became one of first goalies to wear face mask; mem. Ottawa Sports, Hockey halls of fame.

BENEFIELD, Daved (football); b. 16 Feb 1968, Los Angeles, Calif.; Glendale Jr. Coll., Cal-State Northridge; conf. all-star Cal State; def. end CFL Edmonton practice roster '90-91, Ottawa '92-94, BC '95, '97-01, Winnipeg '02-03, Sask. '04; NFL San Francisco '96; CFL, Central, West Conf. all-star awards; numerous player-of-wk awards; punishing tackler; CFL record 5 QB sacks 1 game; career record 70 QB sacks; 1 Grey Cup winner; res. Vancouver, B.C.

BENEVOY, Charles (t&f); b. 26 Jul 1910, Montreal, Que.; d. 21 Aug 2002, Ottawa, Ont.; m. Ida Cohen (d), Bess Levinson; c. Shirleyann, Barry, Ernest (d), Arlene,

Leonard; began competing in international walking events at 60; competing in 7 European countries covered 6000+km in 4-month period; 1st known 80+ competitor to participate in Sri Chinmoy 24-hour Ottawa race at 81; set numerous world, ntl age-group records; mem. Ottawa Jewish Sports Hall of Fame.

BENNETT, Bruce (football); b. 13 Dec 1943, Valdosta, Ga.; given name: Lamar; m. Starling; c. Billy, Bobby, Bradley; Florida, BSc, Valdosta State College, MSc; HS athletic director, football coach; all-American safety UFla '65; Saskatchewan '66-72; all-Canadian '69, 6 times WFC all-star; 35 interceptions during 7-year CFL career for 606yds returned; longest single interception return 112yds vs. Calgary at Regina '72; 4 Grey Cup finals, 1 winner; res. Macclenny, Fla.

BENNETT, Douglas (canoeing); b. 13 Sep 1918, St. Lambert, Que.; given name: Douglas Haig; m. Edna White; c. Jeanette, Barbara, Elaine, Dryden; ret'd Bell Canada; '34 intermediate 4s, ntl tandem titles; Eastern div. jr. singles, int. tandem, CCA int. tandem '37; sr 4s '38; ntl intermediate singles '39; qualified for '40 Olympics which were cancelled by war; silver sr. singles, 4th sr. tandem '48 Olympics; ntl 4s '48; mem. St. Lambert HS football title team '35; D'Arcy McGee sr. champions '36; mem. ORFU Montreal Indians, Cubs; St. Lambert HS Mount Royal jr. hockey champions '37-38; class A handicap Beloeil Golf Club '54; Montreal Sportsmen's Assn. sportsman of '47; mem. Cdn Olympic Hall of Fame; res. Hudson Heights, Que.

BENNETT, Paul (football); b. 27 Mar 1954, Scarborough, Ont.; given name: Paul Frederick; div.; c. MacKenzie, Melissa; Missouri, Waterloo, Wilfrid Laurier; info technology specialist Man. Telecom; territorial draft Argos '77; punt/kickoff return specialist, db; CIAU, OQIFC all-star '76; CFL Toronto '77-79, '84, Winnipeg '80-83, Hamilton '84-87; CFL punt return yardage record 6073; CFL single-season punt return record 965yds rookie season; Argos single-game punt return record 185yds on 9 returns '77; 2 EFC, 2 WFC, 3 CFL all-star; 2 Schenley Outstanding Canadian awards; recipient Dr. Beattie Martin, James McCaffrey, Lew Hayman trophies; 3 Grey Cup finals, 1 winner; Blue Bomber radio broadcaster; nicknamed "Badger"; mem. Cdn Football, Blue Bombers halls of fame; res. Winnipeg, Man.

BENNIE, Elsie (basketball); b. 10 May 1908, Sterling, Scotland; d. 15 Jun 1999, Calgary, Alta.; given name: Elsie Norrie; m. Donald Robson; c. Margaret Ruth, Beverley Jean; stenographer; mem. famed Edmonton Grads '24-33; mem. Canadian Basketball, Alta. Sports halls of fame.

BENNING-REID, Denise (figure skating); b. 1 Sep 1967, Windsor, Ont.; m. Paul Reid; c. Kate, Liam; Windsor BA; skating coach, event management; competed in pairs with Alan Kerslake '83-85, Lyndon Johnston '85-88; with Johnston won St. Ivel, Eng. Skate '87; competed 3 worlds, '88 Olympics; skated briefly Champions on Ice tour; coached South Windsor FSC; event mgr IMG organizing Stars on Ice pro tour, Export A Skins golf game; coach Richmond Hill skating; mem. Windsor/Essex County Sports Hall of Fame; res. Markham, Ont.

BENOIT, Chantal (wheelchair basketball); b. 1 Oct 1960, Beloeil, Que.; m. Reg McClellan; UofOtt, BA; competitive diver 9yrs; played 8yrs with Kamikazes's wheelchair basketball squad before joining the Royals, Shooters and Ottawa Jazz of Ottawa-Carleton Wheelchair Sports Assn; mem. ntl team from '84; silver '86 PAG; competed '84, '88, '92, '96, '00, '04 (flag-bearer) Paralympics; gold '92, '96, '00, bronze '04 Paralympics, '91 Stoke-Mandeville World Games; gold Para PAG '03; Gold Cup gold '94, '98, '02, bronze '90; CWBL gold, MVP with Jazz '92, '95 championships; bronze, all-star '93 CWBL finals; silver, all-star '93-94 CWBL finals; silver with Ottawa Royals '92, '94 NWBT final four; mem. Ottawa Shooters ntl title team '95; MMVP world women's title team '98; Que. Sport Merit award '93; Que. basketball female athlete of '98, '00; Gala 3 Sport Que. team athlete awards; MVP LA Sparks '01, '03; Cumberland Council award; Ottawa wheelchair basketball player of yr award; res. Orleans, Ont.

BENSON, Heather (field hockey); b. 4 Jun 1961, Victoria, B.C.; given name: Heather Mary Lovell; UVic, UBC,, BPhE., BEd, MEd (specialist in hearing impaired); Jr. HS teacher, counsellor jr. HS; competitive swimmer, soccer player; badminton player, field hockey mem. Victoria Sandpipers, Spartans, Vancouver Meralomas, UVic team '80-81, UBC '83-86, Vancouver Island -19 team '79-80, sr. '81, BC junior teams '79-81; mem. BC '81 gold medal Canada Games team; BC sr. team '82-83; ntl -21 team '81-82; mem. ntl gold team Toronto International tournament '82; gold team Scottish 4-country tournament '82; World Cup silver team '83; pre-Olympic training '84; coach prov. age-group teams '85-95, school teams (in varied sports) '79-83, '86-99; CWUAA FH all-star, CIAU tournament eleven '82; media liasion jr. WC '88; mem. ntl jr. badminton team '75-78; Level 2 coach, Level 1 coach/co-ordinator; co-chair. BC summer games '88; coach BCIT-UBC player camps; HS outstanding-female- athlete award; major awards 4 sports at HS level; fed. govt. excellence award '83; Vancouver coach-of-yr awards '88-89; res. Victoria, B.C.

BENSON, Lorne (all-around); b. 16 Sep 1930, Riverton, Man.; m. Betty Lane; c. Sherry, Bonnie, Lori, Robert, Linda; pipefitter BC railroad; nicknamed "Boom Boom"; Blue Bombers '52 WFC Canadian rookie of year, Dr. Beattie Martin Trophy; CFL record 6 tds single game '53, matched by clubmate Bob McNamara (since tds valued at 5 points, is one of 4 sharing 2nd spot to McNamara for single game points with 30), all 6 tds gained rushing, also CFL record; hockey def Winnipeg Maroons '54-55, lacrosse '47-48; Manitoba 100lb boxing title '41; rhp Calgary Purity 99ers, Grandview Maroons, 2 games PCL Vancouver Mounties; 3 successive no-hitters Winnipeg jrs.; mem. '67 ntl champion Molson Canadians; coached Churchill, Man. to 28 straight hockey victories, team won 35 of 38 games winning Northern Man. inter. title; mem. curling rink which scored 8-ender in provincial Consols; mem. Man. Softball Hall of Fame; res. Elkford, B.C.

BENTHAM, Lee (motorsport); b. 27 Jul 1970, Richmond Hill, Ont.; racing driver; won 1st race Whitby Kartways '80; race in kart 12yrs winning 19 championships, record 310 podium finishes with 224 wins; competed 5 FIK world championships; NTN Kart series Formula A title '91; ntl sprint grand nationals (kart) title, SKC Challenge

Cup, SKC Mondial series Formula A karting titles '92; competed in Cdn Michelin Enduro Grand Sports class '94; advanced to Player's/Toyota Atlantic series ranks '95 placing 3rd in rookie championship; recipient 2 Hard Charger awards; '98 KOOL/Toyota Atlantic series champ; res. Newmarket, Ont.

BENTLEY, Doug (hockey); b. 3 Sep 1916, Delisle, Sask.; d. 24 Nov 1972, Saskatoon, Sask.; given name: Douglas Wagner; m. Betty Clark; c. Douglas Jr., Elaine, Patsy, Evelyn; wheat farmer; jr. Saskatoon Wesleys, sr. Regina Vics, Moose Jaw Millers; one of 4 Bentley brothers dominating Prairie hockey '38 at Drumheller, Alta.; with brother Max NHL tryout Boston; NHL Chicago '39-53, NYR '53-54; NHL record: 566 scheduled games, 219g, 324a, 23 playoff games, 9g, 8a; with brother Max and Bill Mosienko formed famed Pony Line; NHL scoring title '42-43; 3 times NHL all-star but never on Stanley Cup winner; last minor pro season '61-62; coached Saskatoon Quakers, Long Beach, Knoxville, Edmonton; scout Edmonton Oil Kings; mem. Sask. Sports, Hockey halls of fame.

BENTLEY, Max (hockey); b. 1 Mar 1920, Delisle, Sask.; d. 19 Jan 1984, Saskatoon, Sask.; given name: Maxwell Herbert Lloyd; m. Betty Miller; c. Lynn, Gary; farmer; Chicago (NHL) '40-48, Toronto '48-53, NYR '53-54; with brother Doug, Bill Mosienko formed Pony Line; nicknamed "Dipsy-Doodle Dandy" for stickhandling ability; mem. 3 Stanley Cup winners; brief comeback with Saskatoon, finally ret'd '56; mem. 1st NHL all-star team; NHL record: 646 scheduled games, 245g, 299a, 52 playoff games, 18g, 27a; NHL scoring titles '46, '47; Hart Trophy '46, Lady Byng Trophy '43; tied Busher Jackson's '34 record 4 2nd-period goals '43, tied by Red Berenson '68, Wayne Gretzky '81; mem. Sask. Sports, Hockey halls of fame.

BERENSON, Red (hockey); b. 8 Dec 1939, Regina, Sask.; given name: Gordon Arthur; m. Joy; c. Kelly, Sandy, Gordie, Rusty; Michigan, BSc, MSc.; hockey coach; jr. Regina Pats; all-American, Western Collegiate Hockey Assn. MVP 43 goals in 28-game season Mich; team capt.; led Belleville McFarlands scorers world amateur tournament; pro Montreal organization '61-66; Hull-Ottawa (EPHL), Quebec (AHL) with brief stints with Habs; NYR '66; St. Louis '67-70, Detroit '71-73, St. Louis '74-77; Team Canada '72; NHL record: 987 scheduled games, 261g, 397a, 85 playoff games, 23g, 14a; leader in formation NHL Players' Assn.; nicknamed "Red Baron"; in NHL record book '68 scoring 6 goals in 8-0 St. Louis win over Philadelphia, tying record set '44 by Detroit's Syd Howe vs Rangers; same game tied record 4 goals 2nd period set '34 by Busher Jackson, equalled '43 by Max Bentley, '81 by Wayne Gretzky; NHL Western Division MVP; asst. coach St. Louis '78-79; head coach '79-82; asst. Buffalo Sabres '82-84; coach Michigan from '84 (record through '03 506-241-53); 4 CCHA titles, NCAA title '96, '98; 9 consec. Great Lakes Invitational titles, 1 College Hockey Showcase title; 23-game undefeated streak '96-97; Jack Adams award winner '81; mem. Mich(U) Hall of Honor, Dekers Club, Mich. Sports halls of fame; named to American Hockey Coaches Assn. all-time favorites list; res. Lansing, Mich.

BEREZOWSKI, Barbara (figure skating); b. 5 Sep 1954, Toronto, Ont.; m. John Ivan; c. Brian, Jarrod; Ryerson; public relations; with partner David Porter ntl jr. dance title '71; sr. ice dance champions '75-76; mem. Skate Canada '73-75 winning silver medal; mem. ntl team 4 world championship competition '73-76; mem. Cdn Olympic team '76; won Lake Placid International Invitational '74; bronze Prestige Cutlery Invitational '75; world pro dance champion '77; Miss Toronto '75; Miss Moscow '75-76; Miss Charm on Ice Munich; runnerup Miss Canada '76; Miss Olympics '76; toured professionally with Stars on Ice USA, Shipstad & Johnson Ice Follies, Toller Cranston Ice Show, Tom Collins World Tour of Champions; chair. Etobicoke Sports Hall of Fame; res. Etobicoke, Ont.

BERGER, Mark (judo); b. 3 Jan 1954, Chernovtsy, Russia; m.; UMan; Soviet master of sport in judo, wrestling, sambo; Western Cdn 95+kg titles '78-80; ntl titles '80-81, '83-84, US open '82; gold '83 PAG, '84 Canada Cup; bronze '84 Olympics; competed '81, '85, coach '93 Maccabiah Games; fed. govt. excellence award '84; mem. Man. Sports, Cdn Judo halls of fame; res. Winnipeg, Man.

BERGER, Sam (football); b. 1 Jan 1900, Ottawa, Ont.; d. 24 Jul 1992, Montreal; m. Ilse Marx (div); c. David, Robert, Julia; Osgoode Hall; lawyer; realty co. owner; EFC legal advisor; p.-pres. Ottawa Football Club, CFL; involved as dir. Ottawa 40yrs; purchased Alouettes '69; involved with 7 Grey Cups winners, 3 in Montreal, 4 in Ottawa; put CFL in big money market signing "Ordinary Superstar" Johnny Rodgers for $1 million-plus; sold Als to Nelson Skalbania '80; brought pro soccer to Montreal; mem. Order of Canada; Cdn. Football, Ottawa Sports halls of fame.

BERGERON, Dean (t&f); b. 12 Dec 1969, La Baie, Que.; Laval; actuary; wheelchair racer in distances from 100m to 1500m; finished 1st '99, 2nd '04 Boston Marathon; 2 silver '98, 2 silver, 1 bronze '02 worlds; 200m gold, 400m, 800m, 1500m silver, 100m bronze '96, 200m, 400m bronze '00, 800m , bronze '04 Paralympics; world 400m record '96; res. St-Augustin-de-Desmaures, Que.

BERGERON, Jean François (boxing); b. 26 Jul 1973, St. Jérome, Que.; store clerk; three ntl 91+ kg titles; gold '94 Copenhagen Cup, '95 Finland Tammer tournament, bronze '96 Bulgaria Strandzata tournament; silver '95 PAG; mem. '96 Olympic team; res. St. Jerome, Que.

BERGEY, Kim (wrestling); b. 7 Aug 1972, Regina, Sask.; m. Kaip; UReg; early training in judo helped escalate rise in women's wrestling ranks; competes at 68kg level; won 3 ntl '62kg, 1 ntl 70kg titles; competed 3 world women's championships; 3 Sunkist Invitational gold; res. Regina, Sask.

BERGMAN, Gary (hockey); b. 7 Oct 1938, Kenora, Ont.; d. 8 Dec 2000, Rochester, Mich.; given name: Gary Gunnar; mem. champion Kenora Rowing Club junior heavy fours; mem. *Tribune* Trophy winning United College curling team; played Jr. football, attended Blue Bombers '59 training camp; intermediate hockey Kenora Thistles, jr. Winnipeg Braves Memorial Cup champions; pro Winnipeg (WHL) '57-60; Buffalo (AHL) '60-61; Cleveland (AHL) '61-63; Springfield '63-64; Memphis (CPHL) '65-66; NHL with

Detroit '64-73, '74-75, Minnesota '73-74; WHA Kansas City '75-76; 3 times most valuable def with Detroit; mem. Team Canada '72 series vs. Russia; mem. NWO Sports Hall of Fame.

BERMEL, Lynne (triathlon); b. 13 Dec 1960, Trenton, Ont.; div. Joe McAllister; Queen's, BA; marketing, public relations; strong swimmer and runner; winner of numerous 5km, 10km races; made ironman triathlon debut '92 posting 9:53:18 for one of fastest debut times in Cdn ironman history; competed on World Cup circuit '93-95 posting 12 top-5 finishes in 15 races; won Niagara International marathon '95; 3rd world ironman rankings '99; Cdn Ironman of yr, 3 Cdn Forces female athlete of yr, Ottawa ACT multi-sport awards; mem. Cdn Forces Sports Hall of Fame; res. Ottawa, Ont.

BERNIER, Sylvie (diving); b. 31 Jan 1964, Quebec City, Que.; m. Gilles Cloutier; c. Catherine, Annabelle, Florence; College Andre-Grasset, UQue BA; TV analyst, financial, pharmaceutical co. spokesperson; mem. ntl team '78-84; 6 gold ntl 3m, 1 gold, silver 1m; 1 bronze 10m; 3m gold Dive Canada, Mex. Intl, all-American, Rostock International, Can-Am-Mex; silver 3m '82 CG; bronze 3m '83 FISU, PAG; bronze '81 FINA WC, '82 world championships, Commonwealth, '83 FISU Games, '83 PAG teams; 3m gold '84 Olympics; ret'd from competition '84; Elaine Tanner, Bobbie Rosenfeld trophies '84; fed. govt. champion award '85; FAS ambassador '85 World Youth year; Seagram 5 Star award '84; tech. advisor Diving Canada '85-86; Sainte-Foy pool bears her name; COA dir. from '88; mem. Order of Canada, Order of Quebec; Intl Swimming (1st Cdn diver so honored), Cdn Aquatic, Olympic, Que., Laval U, Canada's Sports halls of fame; res. Rosemere, Que.

BERNIER, Trista (t&f); b. 22 Jul 1971, North Bay, Ont.; York, B.Sc., BPE; management consultant; pole vault specialist; 2 ntl titles; ntl indoor/outdoor record holder; bronze '98 CG; competed '99 PAG; mem. North Bay Sports Hall of Fame; res. Toronto, Ont.

BERRETT, Tim (t&f); b. 23 Jan 1965, Tunbridge Wells, Eng.; m. Tara Croxford; Oxford BA, Queen's MA; sport/rec. consultant; came to Canada '87 on Canadian Rhodes Foundation scholarship; racewalk specialist; Cdn record 1:22:27 for 20km walk '96; ntl indoor 5km record 18:47.56 '93; 3:56.14 for 50km walk '91; 2 ntl indoor 5km, 1 10km, 3 ntl outdoor 20km titles; US 50km title '90; British Invitational 3km '92; competed '92, '96, '00, '04 Olympic, '93 FISU, '94 Francophone, '94, '98, '02 CG, '95, '99 PAG teams; '91, '93 world championships, '93 World Cup of race walking; silver '94 CG 30km walk, bronze '02 CG 50km; 3 Dr. Fred Tees outstanding university athlete awards; 2 Fred Begley marathon 50km walk awards; res. Edmonton, Alta.

BERRY, Bob (hockey); b. 29 Nov 1943, Montreal, Que.; given name: Robert Victor; m. Lynn Mirach; c. Jina, Cori; Sir George Williams, BA; semipro football; rejected baseball offers Houston Astros; ntl hockey team; pro Montreal organization '68; LA '70-77; NHL record: 541 scheduled games, 159g, 191a, 26 playoff games, 2g, 6a; coach Springfield Indians (AHL) '77-78, LA '78-80; Montreal '81-84, Pittsburgh '84-87; asst. St. Louis '88-91; AGM Blues '92-93, '96-97; AGM/coach Blues '93-96; asst. coach San

Jose '98-99; Western Canada Senators scout; nicknamed "Crease-Line"; res. San Jose, Calif.

BERRYMAN, Tim (football, administration); b. 21 Dec 1954, Hamilton, Ont.; given name: Timothy James; m. Cynthia Fox Hughes; c. Peter James, Sarah; UofOtt, BA; ex-stockbroker, Xerox exec., v-p America's Research Group; all-star mlb UofOtt '74-75; co-capt. undefeated CIAU College Bowl Gee-Gees title team '75; 7 CFL seasons with Edmonton, Hamilton, Ottawa, Toronto; part owner/founder Louisiana Icegators; co-founder/owner/GM Arkansas River Blades; arena football Arkansas Twisters, GM XFL Birmingham; res. Birmingham, Ala.

BERTIE, Gordon (wrestling); b. 20 Aug 1948, St. Gabriel de Brandon, Que.; given name: Gordon William; m. Joan Elizabeth Goldfinch; c. Graham, Laila, Shauna; UofAlta, BSc., BEd., Lakehead U; realtor; 3 CIAU 118-lb titles; 1 ntl 105.5lb FS, 4 114.5lb FS, 1 114.5lb GR titles; silver '74 CG bronze '74 worlds, gold '75, silver '76, bronze '74 Toledo World Cup; mem. '71, '75 PAG, '72, '76 Olympic teams; mem. Alta Sports, Cdn Amateur Wrestling halls of fame; res. Edmonton, Alta.

BERTOIA, Reno (baseball); b. 8 Jan 1935, St. Vito, Udina, Italy; given name: Reno Peter; div.; c. Carl, Ruth, Gina; m. Joan Daly; sc. Beth, Chris, Jennifer; Assumption College, BA; ret'd. HS history department head; Mic Mac League, Windsor, Class D&E Detroit Sandlot League; bonus contract Detroit (AL) '53; spring training '56 earned him starting spot 3B, farmed to Charleston later in season; Tigers '57-58, Washington-Minnesota '59-61, Kansas City, Detroit '61-62, Syracuse '63, Japan '64; AL record: 612 games, 27 HRs, 171 RBI, .244 BA; dir. Windsor/Essex County Sports Hall of Fame; mem. Windsor/Essex County, U Windsor Sports, Cdn Baseball halls of fame; res. Windsor, Ont.

BERTUZZI, Todd (hockey); b. 2 Feb 1975, Sudbury, Ont.; m. Julie; c. Jaden, Tag; center Sudbury (NOHA, OJHL) '90-91, Guelph (OHL) '91-95; all-star '95; 1st draft NYI '93; NHL NYI '95-98, Vancouver '98-04; IHL Utah '97; NHL record: (through '04) 628 scheduled games, 198g, 260a, 24 playoff games, 6g, 8a; drew major suspension '04 for cheap shot which broke neck of Colorado's Steve Moore;Sodertalje Sweden during '04-05 labor dispute; mem. Hockey Heritage North Hall of Fame; res. Sudbury, Ont.

BESSETTE, Lyne (cycling); b. 10 Mar 1975, Knowlton, Qué.; given name: Lyne Hélène; Sherbrooke College; full-time athlete; ntl team from '97; road race gold, TT bronze '97 Canada Games; gold '98 CG road race; '99 PAG silver individual TT; competed '00, '04 Olympics; gold '00 Fitchburg-Longsjo Classic, Tour de 'Toona (USA), '01 Tour de l'Aude (FRA), HP Women's Challenge and Fitchburg-Longsjo Classic (USA); '02 CG bronze individual TT; gold '02 Sea Otter Classic, Fitchburg Longsjo Classic; '03 Cdn TT champion, '04 Cdn elite title; competed '03 worlds; Québec cycling athlete of the '03; *VeloNews* NA female cyclist of '01; res. Knowlton, Qué.

BEST, Bob (shooting); b. 12 Jan 1952, Vancouver, B.C.; given name: Robert Gordon; m. Khirsty Gourlay; UBC, BA; teacher; mem. ntl -20 fencing team '72 world championships; Western Canada épée title '72; mem. cadet

Bisley team '67; 7 times qualified DCRA Bisley team, competed 3; ntl open, closed target titles '82; Canadian Target Rifle Bisley Aggregate titles '82-83; Governor-General's prize Connaught '81; Des Burke Trophy '81; res. Richmond, B.C.

BETKER, Jan (curling); b. 19 Jul 1960, Regina, Sask; m. Frank Macera; c. Steven; admin. asst.; began curling age 13; lead Randy Woytowich '84 ntl mixed title rink; 4 Sask, 3 Scott Tournament of Hearts, 3 world title rinks (3rd for Sandra Peterson Schmirler); gold '98 Olympics; res. Regina, Sask.

BETTY, Trevino (t&f); b. 10 Oct 1971, Portland, Jamaica; UTexas; ntl lj title '96; competed lj '97 FISU Games; 4x100 relay silver '98 Commonwealth, '99 Pan-Am Games; CGF athlete rep. '03; res. Austin, Tex./London, Ont.

BEVAN, Eddie (football); b. 28 Sep 1924, Hamilton, Ont.; d. 29 May 1988, Hamilton, Ont.; given name: Edward Charles; m. Ernestine Pallante; c. Marguerite; truck sales mgr; juvenile to sr. Big Four football Hamilton Tigers '45-48; Wildcats '49; when Tigers, Wildcats amalgamated '50 to become Tiger-Cats, played dg with some offensive duties through '59; capt. '53, '55 teams; 4 Grey Cup finals, 2 winners; asst. coach '60-61; line coach McMaster '62-65; 5 times EFC all-star, 2 East-West Shrine Games; mem. Hamilton's Fabulous Forties team, team of century.

BEVAN, Marv (football); b. 7 Jun 1935, Hamilton, Ont.; m. Cathy Leblanc; c. Leanne, Lisa; Dircom Advt. sales, ret'd. truck sales mgr; 4yrs jr. Tiger-Cats; pro lineman Rough Riders '56-57, '59-65; K-W Dutchmen '58; dir. Hooked on Kids, organized to take under-privileged kids fishing; with Frank Fraser coached Eastview jr. team; res. Kanata, Ont.

BEVERIDGE, Bill (hockey); b. 1 Jul 1909, Ottawa, Ont.; d. 13 Feb 1995, Toronto, Ont. given name: William Stanley; m. Louise McCabe; c. Judith, Bill, Jenny; real estate broker; goaltender Ottawa jr. Shamrocks; after 5 games promoted to sr. club; after 2yrs shifted to New Edinburgh; while attending Glebe HS served as spare goalie Ottawa Shamrocks, attended Chicago training camp; without knowledge was promoted to full-time pro hockey and dealt to Detroit Cougars who doubled salary to $4,000; mem. Cougars '29-30, Ottawa '30-34; shifted to St. Louis with Senators then dealt to Montreal Maroons '35-38; following '39-41 minors stint closed pro career with NYR '42-43; in 296 NHL games allowed 883 goals, posted 17 shutouts and 2.98 goals-against avg.; in youth catcher Glebe juveniles Ont. champions '26; Ont. basketball champions '27.

BEWS, Tom (rodeo); b. 2 Nov 1944, High River, Alta.; m. Rosemary; c. T.J., Guy, Dusty, Peter; ret'd. rancher/wrangler/movie industry co-ordinator; saddle bronc, steer wrestling, team roping specialist; qualified in 6 saddle bronc, 4 steer wrestling Cdn finals; 2 saddle bronc ntl final qualifier; Cdn steer wrestling, saddle bronc titles '71; 5 Cdn all-around titles; CPRA rookie of 1964; cowboy-of-'78 award; Guy Weadick award '76; mem. Cdn Pro Rodeo Hall of Fame; res. Longview, mem. Cdn Pro Rodeo Hall of Fame; Alta.

BEYNON, Tom (football); b. 13 Jul 1941, Kitchener, Ont.; div. c. Natasha, Adrian, Michaela; Queen's, UWO; lawyer, pres/CEO Waterloo Micro Systems; mem. Queen's Golden Gaels OUAA champions '63-64; UWO Mustangs ntl CIAU finalists '65; ot CFL Saskatchewan '66-67, Ottawa '68-70; 4 Grey Cup finals, 3 winners; served as legal counsel for numerous Cdn amateur athletic associations 15yrs; mem. Waterloo County Hall of Fame; res. Waterloo, Ont.

BEZIC, Sandra (figure skating); b. 6 Apr 1956, Toronto, Ont.; given name: Sandra Marie; coach, ret'd choreographer, show producer, director; (see brother Val for competitive record) torn ankle ligaments during '75 training forced Sandra to forego '76 Olympics and turn pro; coached by Ellen Burka, Ron Ludington, Bruce Hyland, Brian Foley; coach, choreographer several ntl, international competitors, including Barbara Underhill, Paul Martini, Katarina Witt, Kurt Browning, Brian Boitano, Josée Chouinard; authored *Passion to Skate*; choreographed and/or produced over 20 TV specials for *Disney, CBS, NBC, CBC, CTV, HBO* including award winning *Carmen on Ice, You Must Remember;* '92, '98 Olympic color commentator; co-producer/dir. Stars on Ice; credited with worldwide artistic clout when named by *Globe & Mail* as one of 25 most powerful people in sport; included in *Maclean's* Canadians Who Made a Difference honor roll; fund-raiser Heart & Stroke Foundation; mem. Etobicoke Sports Hall of Fame; res. Willowdale, Ont.

BEZIC, Val (figure skating); b. 8 Dec 1952, Toronto, Ont.; given name: Val Nickolas; real estate agent; with sister Sandra one of Canada's and world's outstanding pairs skaters; ntl novice title '67; mem. ntl team '69-75; ntl sr. pairs titles '70-74; mem. '72 Olympic, '70-74 worlds teams; injury to Sandra shattered dream of '76 Olympic medal; Zagreb Invitational title '73; pro '75; world pro pairs title '80; res. Oakville, Ont.

BIANCO, Scott (wrestling); b. 9 Nov 1967, Kamloops, B.C.; UBC, SFU; began competing age 16; mem. ntl team '90-96; 82kg gold '91 Challenge Cup, '92 Clark Florez, Mexico; 4 ntl 90kg, 1 100kg titles; 90kg gold '94 CG, '95 Canada Cup; competed '95 Pan-Am, '96 Olympics, '94-95 worlds; outstanding wrestler award '91 Commonwealth championships; res. Burnaby, B.C.

BIASATTI, Hank (baseball/basketball); b. 14 Jan 1922, Beano, Italy; d. 20 Apr 1996, Windsor, Ont; given name: Henry Arcado; Assumption College; baseball, basketball standout Gordon McGregor HS, Assumption HS; first attracted attention as slick-fielding, hard-hitting 1st-baseman East Windsor Cubs; SrIC London Majors; 10yrs minor pro baseball plus stint with '49 Philadelphia Athletics; pro basketball Toronto Huskies '46; mem. Cdn Basketball, Windsor Alumni, Windsor/Essex County Sports halls of fame.

BICKELL, J.P. (builder/hockey); b. 26 Sep 1884, Toronto, Ont.; d. 22 Aug 1951, Toronto, Ont.; given name: John Paris; industrialist/mining exec./financier, public servant; silent partner in Toronto St. Pat's; urged by Conn Smythe transfered interests to Maple Leafs '27; played role in building Maple Leaf Gardens during Depression years; 1st pres., later chair. of Gardens board to his death; memory perpetuated by memorial trophy awarded at discretion of directors to standout Leaf; mem. Hockey Hall of Fame.

BIEBER, Ethel (swimming); b. 6 May 1920, Winnipeg, Man.; d. 1988, Winnipeg, Man.; m. Gordon Bieber; c. 3; began competitive swimming age 10; held juvenile, jr., sr. Women's Amateur SC titles '32-38; ntl jr. 200FS title '34; claimed 2 ntl 200FS, 5 ntl 200, 400FS relay titles setting 4 records in 5yrs; Manitoba 1/2mile title '36; Man. jr. 50, 100, 200FS titles in record times; 3 consec. pier-to-pier *Winnipeg Free Press* titles '38-40; mem. ntl record setting 400FS relay title team '39, 200FS relay teams '40-42; Man. mile champion '37-41; Western Cdn mile champion '37-40; leaving competitive ranks participated in synchro swim; exec. mem. Man. Synchro Swim Assn.; taught/judged synchro swim; Royal Life Saving Society champion; mem. Man. Sports Hall of Fame.

BIESENTHAL, Laryssa (rowing); b. 22 Jun 1971, Walkerton, Ont.; UBC; 4th seat on women's quadruple sculls crew; joined crew '95; silver '95 World championships; 4 Cdn, 2 US titles; bronze women's 8s Lucerne '99; mem. '96 Olympic, '99 PAG teams; with Jenn Browett '99 PAG double sculls gold; res. Victoria, B.C.

BIGRAS, Adrien (golf); b. 1 Mar 1938, Laval, Que.; m. Claude Moreau; c. Chantal; golf pro; growing up near 2 golf clubs he began playing while working at them and, never having competed as an amateur, won more than 100 tournaments across Canada as a pro, including 7 Que. pro titles; 2 Canadian club titles; 3 CPGA seniors crowns; 1 CPGA Super Seniors title; authored *Amélior, votre golf*; res. Rosemere, Que.

BIGRAS, Orv (bowling/horseshoes); b. 17 Jul 1927, Ottawa, Ont.; given name: Orville Francis Joseph; m. Rose Helen Giroux (d); c. Steven, Tanya; St. Patrick Coll., BA; ret'd. cartographer; competed as amateur boxer '39-44; began competitive 5-pin bowling '65, horseshoes '67; competing in final yr of counter pin averaged 275 '65; represented Eastern Canada in ntl competition 3 times singles, 4 times team; led field '71; YBC instructor 4yrs, supervisor 3yrs; competed in Ottawa, Que. TV championships; among 13 400+ singles had best 435; among 10 1000+ crosses had best 1065; 4 father-son tournament titles; high avg. 5 straight sr. league seasons; competing in a variety of horseshoe tournaments in Ont., Que., US, claimed 8 singles, 15 men's doubles (mostly with Leo Gagnon). 3 mixed doubles (with wife Rose) championships; won Ont. sr. singles '84, men's doubles '87; Silvershoe marathon singles silver '86; numerous tournament MVP awards; high avg. Ottawa mixed league '90; res. Carlsbad Springs, Ont.

BIGRAS, Sylvie (volleyball/administration); b. 14 May 1957, Ottawa, Ont.; m. Andre Pajot; c. Samuel, Alexandre; UofOtt, BPHE, MBA; sport administrator; mem. UofOtt varsity volleyball team '75-80; asst. team information officer '84 summer, '88 winter Olympics, '87 PAG; press attache '88 summer Olympics, '90 CG; asst. CdM '92 summer Olympics; chief press officer '95 PAG, '98 winter Olympics, '02 CG; *CBC* production staff '00 summer, '02 winter Olympics; Task Force 2000 mem. '87-88; media relations '10 Vancouver Olympic, Hamilton CG bids; dir. Cdn Sport & Fitness Admin. Centre '86-90; dir. Cdn Sport Council (formerly SFC) '91-96; dir. gen. Volleyball Canada '89-98; dean's honor list UofOtt '77; trustee Ottawa Sports Hall of Fame; res. Ottawa, Ont.

BILODEAU, Alain (weightlifting); b. 9 Jun 1966, Ville LaSalle, Que.; teacher; became interested in weightlifting watching '76 Montreal Olympics; coached by brother Jocelyn; competes in 77kg class; mem. ntl team '85-98; competed '90, '94, '98 (2 bronze) CG, '91, '95 PAG; won '98 ntl title; res. St. Isidore, Que.

BINNS, Hilda (t&f); b. 20 Oct 1945, Hamilton, Ont.; given name: Hilda May Torok; div. David Binns; dictaphone typist; contracted polio before 10th birthday leaving her a paraplegic; launched athletic career '68 at Ont. Wheelchair trials where she made winning impression in debut; rep. Ont., ntl wheelchair games; led all competitors with 8 medals, 2 world records; 1st Canadian gold medalist (2) International Stokes-Mandeville Games (disabled Olympics); 5 gold, 1 silver, 4 bronze '69 Wheelchair Pan-Ams; 5 gold, 2 silver, 1 bronze '71 Pan-Ams; 1 gold, 2 silver '72 Stokes-Mandeville Games; chair. Ont. Wheelchair Sports Assn.; last known res. Hamilton, Ont.

BIONDA, Jack (lacrosse/hockey); b. 18 Sep 1933, Huntsville, Ont.; d. 3 Nov 1999, London, Ont.; given name: Jack Arthur James; m. Joanne Mulholland; restaurateur; def; jr. A Toronto Marlboros '51-53; Sr. A Sault Ste. Marie Greyhounds '54; pro Pittsburgh (AHL) '55, Springfield (AHL) '56-58; Providence (AHL) '59; NHL Toronto '55, Boston '56-59; Victoria Cougars (WHL) '60; Portland Buckaroos (WHL) '61-66; Oldtimers hockey Huntsville from '75; mem. 2 Stanley Cup finalists; mem. 2 WHL title teams; lacrosse Huntsville town league '46-48; Ont. Int. A champions '49-50; Ont. Sr. B champions '51; mem. '52 Minto Cup titlists; '55, '57 Victoria Shamrocks Mann Cup champions; New Westminster Salmonbellies Mann Cup champions '58-59, '62; 7 Mann Cup finals, 5 winners; among Canada's finest box lacrosse players; ended active career Portland '68; Mann Cup record 9 3-goal games; twice Mann Cup MVP; 7 BC Sr. A scoring titles, league, playoff MVP awards; best single-season '59 with 70 goals, 74 assists; 4 times 1st team all-star; Max McDonald, Commissioner's Trophy; Huntsville Centennial Centre bears his name; mem. Cdn, BC, Ont. Lacrosse, Canada's, BC, Spokane, Huntsville Sports halls of fame.

BISHOP, Carole (volleyball); b. 2 Dec 1949, Vancouver, B.C.; UBC, BPhE, MA (2), PhD; clinical psychologist; Vancouver sprint champion '64-65, mem. title relay teams '63-64; BC HS volleyball champions '66; at 16 youngest Cdn to play at international level; mem. 10 ntl sr. women's title teams; 4 BC jr. champions; ntl team '67-78; 3 Pan-Am, 2 world championship, 1 World Cup, 1 Olympic, 4 NA NORCECA championships teams; NORCECA silver '73; BC HS volleyball MVP '67; all-Balkan '75 tournament MVP, '76 European Cup MVP, '71, '75 PAG all-star; ranked 4th setter in world '76; coached 4 city volleyball title teams; '80-81 Vancouver gymnastics titlists; 3 BC govt. academic scholarships; adjunct prof. UBC, assoc. prof SFU, co-ordinator graduate clinical psychology Vancouver General Hospital; mem. BC Sports Hall of Fame; res. Vancouver, B.C.

BISHOP, Jim (lacrosse/hockey); b. 14 May 1929, Toronto, Ont.; d. 7 Sep 1998, Bowmanville, Ont.; given name: James Gerrard; div. Lynn Boothby; c. Joe, Jim Jr., John, Anne, Gael; m. Vonnie Tennant; c. Lynn; St. Michael's College; self-employed; played with St. Vincent's, Scarborough '40-45; coached '46-98, winning 24 Ont. MLA titles; founded/coached Huntsville MLA; organizer/coach/GM Oshawa Green Gaels '63-69, '76-80, '95-97; coached 7 jr. A ntl titles 8 Minto Cup winners; coached both Green Gaels, Detroit Olympics '68, guiding latter to Eastern division, National League finals; coached Windsor Warlocks to consec. President's Cups '70-71; coach/GM Toronto Tomahawks NLL '74, Montreal Quebecois '75; played key role in establishing/building Whitby MLA; guided Whitby Warriors to '97 Minto Cup; with Bruce Norris, Morley Kells helped found NLL; v-p internal administration Detroit (NHL) '67-74; career coaching record (all levels) 352-124-3 regular season, 174-55 playoffs; served as exec. Ont., Canada Lacrosse Assns; 1st tech. dir. CLA; L.B. Pearson award for contribution to lacrosse in Canada, Tip Tether, Merv McKenzie OLA awards; mem. Canadian Lacrosse, Oshawa, Huntsville Sporthalls of fame.

BISSETT, David (field hockey); b. 13 May 1954, Vancouver, B.C.; given name: David Robert Russell George; m. Catherine Jean Cookson; c. Russell Douglas; UBC, BComm., LLB.; co-owner development, construction firm; 2 BC ntl title teams; ntl team '73-83; def '75, '79, silver, '83 gold PAG teams; '76, '84 Olympic, '78 World Cup teams; MVP '68 jr. ntl tournament; capt. or v.-capt. ntl team from '77; with more than 110 international matches has competed on international scene more than any other Canadian field hockey player; fed. govt. excellence award '84; res. New Westminster, B.C.

BISSONNETTE, Serge (shooting); b. 12 Apr 1950, St. Jean d'Iberville, Que.; m. Darlene Hagel; c. Céline; RCMP officer; ntl high-power rifle champion '78-79; Des Burke service rifle award; mem. 12 Cdn intl rifle teams; 24 Intl match medals; 63 ntl match medals; 51 ntl team match titles; 14 intl team titles; 28 HPS crosses; 5 bronze crosses; Sask., Que., Lieut.-Gov. medals; more than 100 prov. level individual, 50-plus prov. team medals; 1 silver, 3 bronze Gov.-Gen. medals; 3 Ont., 2 Sask. 1 Intl achievement awards; Jamaican grand agg.; mem. DCRA council from '77, exec. comm. 9yrs; chair. coaching certification comm, service conditions matches, intl team comm., Palma comm.; p.-pres. Sask Rifle Assn; exec. NCRRA, NDHQRA; res. Orleans, Ont.

BITKOWSKI, Bruno (football); b. 29 Nov 1929, Windsor, Ont.; d. 1966, Ottawa, Ont.; Assumption College; starred in football, basketball throughout HS, college; selected by Toronto's *High News* as all-Ont. tackle; pro Ottawa 11yrs; Big Four rookie of year '51; outstanding blocking ctr; mem. '51, '60 Grey Cup winners; from '66 award in his name given annually to WSSA most gentlemanly player; mem. Windsor/Essex County Sports Hall of Fame.

BITTEN, Mike (badminton); b. 2 Jun 1962, Senneterre, Que.; m. Doris Piche; c. William Michael; pro Ottawa RA Centre; began competing age 12; 9 ntl men's doubles titles, 4 with Mike de Belle, 5 with Bryan Blanshard; 16th world doubles ranking; CG team silver '86, '90, doubles bronze '90; mem. '92 Olympic, '86, '90, '94 CG teams; Pan-Am championships men's doubles, mixed doubles gold; Cdn Open mixed (Doris Pich), men's (Blanshard) doubles gold '89; ret'd from competition '94; res. Ottawa, Ont.

BITZ, Ed (softball, officiating); b. 20 Nov 1929, Leipzig, Sask.; m. Helen Lang; c. Leslie, Sheldon, Trent; UofSask,

BA, BEd.; teacher; amateur baseball '46-61; coached Saskatoon men's softball team '62; began umpiring '63; Sask. Amateur Softball Assn. zone umpire '66-69, provincial umpire-in-chief '70-74; Softball Canada umpire-in-chief '72-84; officiated 33 ntl championships, '76, '80 men's world, '78 women's world, '81 world youth championships; instrumental in producing umpiring teaching aids for use throughout Canada; qualified CAHA referee 27yrs; honored by Century Saskatoon; mem. Sask., Saskatoon Sports, Softball Canada halls of fame; res. Saskatoon, Sask.

BJORN, Tyler (sailing); b. 13 Mar 1970, Montreal, Que.; Bishop's, BA; sailing consultant Byte Boats; mem. Bishop's football team '90-94; Que. sailing coach of '94; Que. Laser class rep. '89, '93 Canada Games; training partner '96 Olympics; '96 Finn Class ntl champion; ntl sailing team '97; res. Dorval, Que.

BLACK, David (golf); b. 15 Sep 1883, Troon, Scotland; d. 26 Mar 1974, Vancouver, B.C.; c. Kenneth; golf pro; emigrated to Canada 1905; pro Country Club of Montreal '05-09; Rivermead GC Lucerne, Que. through '10-20; 25yrs pro Shaughnessy GC; runnerup Canadian Open '11; 4 CPGA, 2 BC Open titles; '24 Washington State Open title; '29 Pacific North West Open; with Duncan Sutherland defeated great Walter Hagen and partner in '29 exhibition; noted for putting prowess as touring pros came to him with their putting problems; mem. RCGA, BC Sports halls of fame.

BLACK, Elmer (curling); b. 28 Oct 1937, Howick, Que.; m. Brenda Baskin; c. Steve, Kim; MacDonald College; sales mgr.; softball standout '50s-'70s; Que. schoolboy runnerup '53-55; skipped Que. rink 1964 Brier; curling instructor Montreal Bonaventure Club '63-64; held various admin. roles CBRCCC, including pres.; res. Howick, Que.

BLACK, Fred (football); b. 1 May 1930, Toronto, Ont.; given name: Frederick George; m. Patricia Miller; c. Pat, Chris, Rory, Terry, Laura, Ryan; St. Mike's College; marketing account exec.; mem. Argonauts '49-57, '59-60; CFL record: 132 league, 14 playoff games; mem. '50, '52 Grey Cup title teams; res. Rexdale, Ont.

BLACK, Ken (golf); b. 13 Jul 1912, Vancouver, B.C.; d. Nov 1995, Vancouver, B.C.; given name: Kenneth McKenzie; among Canada's top amateur golfers; national amateur titlist '39, twice runnerup; mem. 11 Willingdon Cup teams; 3 BC amateur titles, Cdn Western Open, BC Closed champion; record closing round 63 at Shaughnessy helped him defeat Byron Nelson, other top US stars in '36 Golden Jubilee tournament; mem. RCGA, BC Sports halls of fame.

BLACKBURN, Frédéric (speed skating); b. 21 Dec 1972, Chicoutimi, Que.; mem. ntl team from '89; NA short-track champion '87; set Cdn jr. 1500, 400m records; NA short-track jr. champion '88; Cdn sr. record '91; world short-track 5000m silver '90; gold '91 Ottawa short-track Friendly Games; Cdn record 5000m relay '91 Albertville international; silver short-track 1000m, 5000m relay '92 Olympics; mem. '94 Olympic team; gold '94 worlds; team gold '95-96, 500m bronze '96 worlds; mem. Cdn Speed Skating Hall of Fame; res. Montreal, Que.

BLACKMAN, Craig (t&f); b. 25 Feb 1951, Toronto, Ont.; given name: Craig Augustus; m. Patricia; c. Sekou, Akeem, Iman; Oregon, BSc.; mgr. rehabilitation, training service for people with disabilities; at least 1 gold medal each year nationals '64-72 ('71 except); PB: 24'7" long jump, 50'1" triple jump, 10.7 100m, 20.73 200m, 45.98 400m, 1:45.93 800m; mem. '71 PAG, '69 Pacific Conf., '72 Olympic Games teams; 44.9 split '71 PAG, 45.5 split 400 bronze NCAA mile relay; silver '72 NCAA mile relay 45.0 split; gold ntl 400m; 45.5 split in mile relay in which Canada set record 3:04.2 '72 Olympics; res. Toronto, Ont.

BLACKWELL, Andrea (basketball); b. 23 Nov 1962, Calgary, Alta.; given name: Andrea Jill; m. Richard Bigelow; Bishop's. BA, BSc; teacher/coach; mem. Eastern Regional '78-79, provincial '78, Ont. Canada Games, ntl title teams '79; 2 Ont., ntl titles; 3 CIAU championships; mem. ntl jr. '78, sr. women's team '79-96; '83, '87, '87 FISU, '82, '86, '90, '94 worlds; '87, '91, PAG, '84, '96 Olympic teams; mem. '82 Jones Cup title team; bronze '86 worlds; QUAA, CIAU all-star; CIAU female player of '83, CIAU MVP '84; 2 CIAU all-Cdn; Bishop's athlete of yr '83-84; Ottawa ACT basketball award; coach women's basketball Bishop's '84-92; played pro Italy, Belgium, Greece; led club team to '94 Belgian title; mem. Bishop's Athletic Wall of Distinction; res. Kingston, Ont.

BLACKWOOD, Marjorie (tennis); b. 1 May 1957, Karachi, Pakistan; m. Peter Schelling; Millfield School, Somerset, Eng., Texas, UBC; tennis pro, operator Whistler Racquets & Golf Resort; ntl jr. singles, doubles '75; consolation winner '75 Forest Hills Jr.; Rothman's Pacific Coast Open sr. title '75, ntl -21 title '75; mem. Soisbois Cup team '75-77; 3rd round Wimbledon '82; Canada's No. 1 player '79-81; Ottawa ACT tennis award '73, '75, Ont. Sports Achievement Award '73-75, Texas tennis scholarship '75; mem. Federation Cup team '77-82, non-playing capt. '83; pro Western Indoor TC Richmond, B.C.; prov. coach BC 2yrs; ntl touring coach 3yrs; mem. Cdn Tennis, Ottawa Sports halls of fame; res. Whistler, B.C.

BLAIR, Don (football); b. 6 Apr 1972, Ottawa, Ont.; m. Linda Johnson; UCal; rcvr; brilliant career with Calgary Dinosaurs '92-95 culminating with Vanier Cup triumph '95; 138 regular season catches for 2,611yds, 26tds; Hec Crighton, Ted Morris trophies '95; CIAU Howard Mackie award; drafted by Chicago (NFL) '96, late training camp cut; CFL Edmonton '96-98, BC '99-01, Calgary '02-03; CFL record 119gp, 26td, 310recept, 4542yds; competed 2 Grey Cups; wife Linda mem. '98 Cdn long-track speed skating team; res. Calgary, Alta.

BLAIR, Wren (hockey); b. 2 Oct 1925, Lindsay, Ont.; given name: Wren Alvin; ret'd. hockey exec.; nicknamed "The Bird"; Ont. Sr. B title Whitby Dunlops; refused Sr. A status by OHA clubs, Blair convinced B league to turn A and challenged for Allan Cup; won league title and beat Kitchener-Waterloo Dutchmen for Ont. crown '57; '58-59 Allan Cup; world title '58 beating USSR 4-2; GM Kingston, '63 EPHL title; Boston (NHL) personnel director, signed Bobby Orr; major role in revival Oshawa Generals OHA jr. A team '62; '65 Memorial Cup; simultaneously GM Clinton Comets (EHL); coached, managed Minnesota (NHL) 8 seasons; GM Pittsburgh (NHL) '75-77; GM Saginaw Gears (IHL) 2 straight Turner Cups; dir.

player personnel, farm club operations Los Angeles (NHL) '80-84; GM Kingston Frontenacs OHL '91-96; co-author *The Bird: Life & Times of Hockey Legend Wren Blair*; mem. Oshawa Sports Hall of Fame; res. Brooklin, Ont.

BLAIS, Thérèse (tennis); b. 20 Jun 1932, St. Jérome, Que.; given name: Thérèse Helie; m. Jacques Blais; c. Richard, Pierre; tennis club pres., teacher; ranked among top 5 Que. players '50-63; 4yrs club pro Ville St.Laurent, 6yrs Laval, from '69 4 Seasons Club Laval, from '70 instructor Brébeuf College; UofQue. instructor '72; Que. Fedn instructor '75-78; authored tennis instruction manuals; conducted TV instruction clinics; TV analyst Jimmy Connors-Ile Nastase match Montreal '77; 1st ranked ntl veterans class; res. Laval, Que.

BLAKE, Rob (hockey); b. 10 Dec 1969, Simcoe, Ont.; m. Brandy Fleming; c. Jack; Bowling Green; def; NHL LA '90-01, Colorado '01-04; NHL all-rookie team; mem. Team Canada '91, '94, '97, '98, '99, '03 (gold) worlds, '96, '04 (withdrew due to injury) World Cup, '98, '02 (gold) Olympics; 4 all-star games; competes in two-man semipro volleyball tournaments in off-season; NHL record (through '04): 903 scheduled games, 186g, 400a, 116 playoff games, 21g, 42a; Norris trophy '98; res. Los Angeles, Calif.

BLAKE, Terry (bowling); b. 6 May 1969, Happy Valley, Labrador; given name: James Gordon; herdsman; 4 Nfld bowler-of-yr awards; '92, '95, '01 ntl 5-pin singles titles; res. Corner Brook, Nfld.

BLAKE, Toe (hockey); b. 21 Aug 1912, Victoria Mines, Ont.; d. 17 May 1995, Montreal, Que.; given name: Hector; c. Mary Jane, Joan, Bruce; ret'd hockey exec.; baseball Nickel Belt, Hamilton leagues, umpired Quebec Provincial League; mem. '32 Memorial Cup winner; on bench as Montreal Maroons won '35 Stanley Cup; Canadiens '36-48; nicknamed "Old Lamplighter"; left wing Punch Line with Elmer Lach, Rocket Richard; NHL record: 572 scheduled games, 235g, 292a, 57 playoff games, 25g, 37a; Hart Trophy '39, Lady Byng Trophy '46, scoring title '39; mem. 2 Stanley Cup winners; 3 times 1st, twice 2nd team all-star; coached Houston to USHL title, Buffalo (AHL), Valleyfield (Provincial) to Alexander Trophy; Canadiens '55-68; 8 Stanley Cups, record 5 in succession '56-60; mem. Order of Canada, Quebec, Canada's Sports, Hockey Heritage North, Hockey halls of fame.

BLANCHARD, Leo (football); b. 12 Mar 1955, Edmonton, Alta.; m. Diane; UAlta; despite standout college career in which he played in '77 Can-Am College Bowl and earned WIFL, CIAU all-Cdn status, was never drafted by CFL; joined Edmonton as ot '79-87, BC '88, Calgary '88-91; noted for durability, had string of 135 consecutive games played; CFL record: 202 games; 6 WFC, 2 all-Canadian all-star ratings; res. Victoria, B.C.

BLANEY, Fred (judo); b. 14 Nov 1955, Sudbury, Ont.; given name: Frederick Murray; m. Mary Winona Christie; c. Alexander, Andrew; UNB, BSc; dir. construction NB Dept. Transport; raised in Nortondale, N.B.; 6th degree black belt; provincial and/or Atlantic champion '74-80; gold '82, silver '83, '85 Pan-Am Judo championships; 12 international competition medals; 4 ntl titles; mem. '84 Olympic team; '84 US Open gold, bronze; '87 PAG bronze; level 2 coach;

IJF Continental referee; mem. Ntl grading bd; Fredericton Judo Club instructor; v-p Judo Canada, Judo NB; mem. Cdn Judo, NB Sports halls of fame; res. Fredericton, N.B.

BLANSHARD, Bryan (badminton); b. 28 Jan 1966, Toronto, Ont.; m. Julie Brouillard; Carleton, BEng.; civil engineer; ntl jr. singles, men's doubles gold '85; 3 ntl singles, 6 ntl men's doubles titles, 1 with Ian Johnson, 3 with Mike Bitten, 2 ntl mixed doubles with Denyse Julien; more than 30 open tournament victories; ranked 16th in world men's doubles, 28th in singles; '90 CG team silver, men's doubles bronze; mem. '92 Olympic, '90, '94 CG teams; 1 Cdn Open mixed doubles gold; res. Greely, Ont.

BLAXLAND, Jody (field hockey); b. 2 Sep 1963, Vancouver, B.C.; given name: Jody Margaret; m. Ian Fitzpatrick; c. Tyson, Reese, Tanner; Vancouver Community College, UBC, BPhE; BC jr. team '80-82; ntl -21 team '82; ntl gold medal -23 team '82; ntl sr. team from '82; mem. '82 World Cup silver medal team; competed '86 World Cup; BC HS, Burnaby community awards, Burnaby outstanding FH player award; 2 CIAU FH all-Cdn; fed. govt. excellence award '83; res. Pitt Meadows, B.C.

BLOUIN, Marc (cycling); b. 13 May 1953, Ste. Foy, Que.; m. Micheline Côté; sales rep.; Que. novice title '69, jr. '70; mem. ntl team '71, '75, PAG '72, '76 Olympic, 3 world championships; '74 ntl road racing title team; res. Cap Rouge, Que.

BOA, Andrew (shooting); b. 1851, St. Laurent, Que.; d. 1928, St. Laurent, Que.; m., c. Andrew Stuart, James, Helen, Marion, Margaret; primarily trap and skeet shooter; launched family shooting dynasty; established competitive rifle, pistol shooting in Quebec.

BOA, Gil (shooting); b. 8 Aug 1924, Montreal, Que.; d. 7 Sep 1973, St. Catharines, Ont.; given name: Gilmour; m. Kay Sillers; c. George, Anne, Victoria; UofT, BSc.; civil engineer; mem. Canadian international smal-bore rifle team age 16; military rifle team '49-52, international pistol team '47; King's medal Connaught Ranges Ottawa '49-51; Governor-General's prize '55 (matching father's '48 performance), gold world championships '54; mem. 5 Olympic teams, bronze '56, 4th '52, '64; flag-bearer '64 summer Olympics; gold '66 CG; two silver, bronze '71 PAG; 12 ntl small-bore rifle titles; mem. Cdn Olympic, DCRA, Cdn Forces, Canada's Sports halls of fame.

BOA, James Sr. (shooting); b. 10 Mar 1888, St. Laurent, Que.; d. 1976, Toronto, Ont.; m., c. Gilmour, James Jr.; ret'd CIL salesman; 2nd generation marksman; Canadian trap champion; mem. 20 Bisley teams '20-53; Governor-General's Prize '48; 1st Canadian shooter to compete in Olympics '20.

BOA, Sandy (shooting); b. 9 Oct 1956, Toronto, Ont.; given name: George Alexander; m. Yvonne Veendaal; c. Andrew Alexander; Ridley College, UWO, BA; banker; son of Gil Boa; raised in family steeped in shooting tradition; Ont. team '73 Canada Games; Ont., ntl jr. titles '74; Canadian cadet Bisley team '75; Ont. champion '76-77, '82; mem. 4 Benito Juarez, '79 PAG, '80 Scandinavian championships teams; 2 gold '79 Western Canada Games; '82 Ont. Olympic prone position title; '82 Palma title team; res. Toronto, Ont.

BOA, Stuart (shooting); b. 1896, St. Laurent, Que.; d. 23 Sep 1944, Montreal, Que.; given name: Andrew Stuart; m. Ethel Louise Beer; c. John Andrew; Westmount Academy; asst. sales mgr. Dominion Ammunitions Div. CIL; 2nd generation marksman; Military Cross WWI; 5 successive ntl trap titles early '20s; initial appearance on Cdn team at Bisley at 18; Governor-General's Trophy DCRA Ottawa matches '24.

BOA, Vicki (shooting); b. 12 Apr 1955, Toronto, Ont.; given name: Victoria; m. Peter Hall; Guelph, BSc.; sales rep.; 4th generation Bisley calibre shooter; mem. 5 Ont. target rifle teams; 2 ntl, 3 Ont. titles; 1s1t woman to qualify for Canadian Bisley team more than once; with husband won Lake Ont. C5 35 sailing title; res. Toronto, Ont.

BOADWAY, Bob (coaching/swimming); b. 31 May 1938, Port Huron, Mich.; given name: Robert Kenton; m. Donna Lee Roberts; c. Robert Gary, Michael William, Dana Kathleen; Cal State (Long Beach), BA, Chapman Coll; HS all-American Downey CA; 2 US records; 3 US jr. ntl titles, 2 swim, 1 water polo; 3 US sr. men's, 2 NCAA water polo titles; water polo ref. '68 Olympics; swim coach; Level III CNCCP, Elite International ASCA/WSCA, Red Cross instructor/aqua leader, Royal Life Saving Society bronze cross/instructor credentials; active swim coach from '69 Downsview, North York, Burlington, Oakville, Ottawa, Gloucester, Kingston, Scarborough, Pickering, Downey, CA, US Naval Base Long Beach, Hacienda Heights, Fontana, CA; Ont. tech dir. '77-78, '85-89; CNCCP instructor 10yrs; 8yrs Swim Ont. dir.; 15yrs Ont. swim coaches assn dir.; 3yrs Cdn swim coaches assn dir.; coached Team Ont. 4 Canada Games; ntl team '75-76; 9 Ont. age-group touring teams; Swim Ont. 20-yr volunteer award; 3 Ont. coach-of-yr awards; 1 ntl championship team title award; Cdn citizen from '76; res. Port Perry, Ont.

BOATENG, Kwabu (t&f); b. 30 Jun 1974, Eastmont, Ghana; m. Dianetia Stewart; c. Kwaden; graphic artist; hj specialist; moved to Canada '94; tied Mark Boswell for '99 PAG gold; silver '01 Francophonie, '02 CG; 3 ntl titles; gold '00 Zagreb GP; competed '00 Olympics, '01 worlds; res. Montreal, Que.

BODASHEFSKY, Larry (softball); b. 9 May 1956, Oshawa, Ont.; given name: Larry James; m. Bev Ross; c. Brock, Blake; Durham Coll.; surveyor; of; began playing age 11 in Oshawa Park League; jr. with Oshawa Falcon TV '76-77; mem. all-star competitive team; Sr. B RH Cabinet '78 Ont. title team; began playing in ISC program '79 with Oshawa Motor Carries; through retirement '91 played for Newmarket, Oshawa, Peterborough, Owen Sound; competed in 7 ISC world tournaments; 4 times all-World; 1st Cdn named to ISC Hall of Fame; res. Oshawa, Ont.

BODNAR, Gus (hockey/coaching); b. 24 Aug 1925, Ft. William, Ont.; given name: Augustus; m. Etta; c. Carolyn, Andrea; ctr Ft. William jrs. '40-43 (2 Memorial Cups); NHL Toronto '43-47, Chicago '47-54, Boston '54-55; AHL Pittsburgh '46-48; NHL totals 667 scheduled games, 142g, 254a, 32 playoff games, 4g, 3a; with Sweeney Schreiner, Lorne Carr formed Leafs' Bacon Line; with Bud Poile, Gaye Stewart formed Chicago Flying Forts line; assisted on all 3 Bill Mosienko goals scored in 21sec; NHL record fastest goal by rookie in 1st career NHL game, 15sec vs.

NYR; Calder Memorial trophy '44; 2 Stanley Cup, 1 Allan Cup, 1 Memorial Cup winners; coach St. Catharines Jr. A '60-61; founder/coach/GM Lindsay Jr. C '60-65; coach Toronto Marlboros '66-70, Memorial Cup '67; coach/GM Salt Lake (WHL) '70-71, Oshawa (OHA) '70-75; instructor St. Andrews (NB) summer hockey school '70-80; co-coach Cdn Jr. worlds team '76-77; OHA coach of '72 award; avid golfer, sr. club champion Lake Placid, Fla.; mem. NWO, Oshawa Sports halls of fame; res. Oshawa, Ont./Lake Placid, Fla.

BODOGH, Marilyn (curling); b. 9 Mar 1955, Toronto, Ont.; given name: Marilyn Catherine Bodogh; div. George Darte III; c. Gregory, Christopher; mgr. Bodogh Lumber, motivational speaker; began curling age 10; playing second for sister Christine mem. 4 SOnt. jr. title rinks '70-73; Ont. Winter Games winner, runnerup Canadians '71; mem. 11 women's dist. titlists, 4 SO titlists, 2 Ont. titlists; competed 2nd on '81, skip '86, '96 Scott Tournament of Hearts winners; skip '86 women's world title; winner numerous major bonspiels; noted for loquacious, animated behavior on ice; Edmonton Grads team trophy '96; Ont. team of '86; with sister Christine St. Catharines athlete-of-'86 award; mem. Cdn Curling, St. Catharines Sports halls of fame; res. St. Catharines, Ont.

BODOGH-JURGENSON, Christine (curling); b. 31 Jul 1953, Toronto, Ont.; given name: Christine Ann Bodogh; m. Enn Jurgenson; account mgr.; nicknamed "Crisper"; as competitive swimmer excelled in backstroke; also standout in HS volleyball, track; began curling age 12; with sister Marilyn and Holly & Heather Graves won 4 SO jr., 1 Ont. Winter Games titles; runnerup Canada Winter Games '71; mem. 10 Ont. women's district, 3 SO, 2 Ont., 1 Alta. title rinks; competed 6 ntl Scott Tournament of Hearts (Lassie), 1 Alta, 2 Ont., 2 BC, 1 TC; 2nd '86 women's world title rink; won '96 Saskatoon Ladies Classic, Battle of Sexes charity match (vs. Ed Werenich), several major bonspiel titles from '85; with sister Marilyn St. Catharines athlete-of-'86 award, Ont. team of '86; mem. Cdn Curling, St. Catharines Sports halls of fame; res. Vancouver, B.C.

BOEHM, Frank (bowling); b. 30 Mar 1934, Regina, Sask.; given name: Frank Michael; m. Annette Weisgerber; c. Frank Jr., Leeanne, Randy, Tracy, Susan; hydraulic technician, machinist; at 24 Regina top avg. 10-pin rookie; ntl title '64; 7th '67 world championships; '68 Canadian World Cup finals, 13th overall world championships; only Canadian to reach World FIQ finals '71; 6 Sask. doubles, 8 team titles, 12 Regina high-average titles; mem. Sask. Sports Hall of Fame; res. Regina, Sask.

BOES, Allan (golf); b. 15 Jul 1910, Winnipeg, Man.; d. 12 May 1995, Winnipeg, Man.; m. Nancy Gibson; c. Don, Allan, Brian, Patricia, Michael; ret. Cdn Wheat Board; began career as caddy age 11; never had a golf lesson; won Man. Open, Amateur '41, '43-44, '48, 3 times Man. Amateur runnerup; 8 times Man. Amateur medalist; 4 Winnipeg & Dist. open titles; 2nd low amateur '40 Cdn Open; set Pine Ridge (63), Kildonan Municipal (60) club records; mem. 12 Willingdon Cup teams; Willingdon Cup medalist '47; mem. '50-51 Canada Cup teams; scored Canada's only points Canada Cup singles play '50; Man. Srs. title '68; 15 Southwood club championships, 10 in succession; life

mem. Southwood; 5 holes-in-one; mem. Man. Sports Hall of Fame.

BOESE, Kurt (wrestling); b. 4 Nov 1929, Bremen, Germany; m. Wilhelmine Lange; c. Christa, Terry; ret'd. plumbing inspector; North German jr. title '44; emigrated to Canada 1952; 5 ntl, 11 Ont. 154-171lb range titles; 3 Michigan, UofGuelph open titles; 3 bronze Eastern US, AAU championships; bronze '62 CG, '63 PAG; mem. '62 Worlds, '58 Commonwealth, '60 Olympic teams; YMCA coached teams won 6 Ont. titles; 5 times convenor Ont. jr. championships; coach Ont. team 1st Canada Winter Games, ntl team '72 Olympics, 4yrs Waterloo Lutheran, UofWaterloo '70-78; 2 OUAA titles; ntl YMCA leadership award '67; FILA silver star for contribution to Canadian wrestling '76; mem. Waterloo County, Cdn Amateur Wrestling halls of fame; res. Kitchener, Ont.

BOETTGER, Bill (lawn bowling); b. 26 Oct 1941, Kitchener, Ont.; teacher; ntl calibre 5-pin bowler; represented Ont. at ntl competitions; 17 intl lawn bowling appearances; 10 medals including gold men's pairs, bronze men's fours '93 Pacific Bowls, silver men's fours, bronze men's pairs '92 worlds; silver men's pairs '86 CG; also competed '90, '94 CG; Bowls Canada award of merit; life mem. MBA; res. Kitchener, Ont.

BOGUE, Glenn (t&f); b. 30 Aug 1955, Toronto, Ont.; given name: Glenn Patrick; Villanova, BA hons, MA, LLB; lawyer, property restoration Villanova; bronze mile relay '73 Pacific Conf. Games; Canadian Interscholastic records 21.1 200m, 46.8 400m; bronze mile relay '75 PAG; NCAA all-American '75; 400m quarterfinalist '76 Olympics; mem. '76 world indoor dist. medley record team; bronze 400m '78 CG; NCAA mile relay title, all-American '78; NCAA academic all-American '76, '78; Rhodes Scholarship finalist '75; listed *Who's Who in American Colleges*; services mgr. CTFA; res. Haverford, Pa.

BOHAY, Gary (wrestling); b. 26 Dec 1960, Burnaby, B.C.; Arizona State; too small for football he began wrestling at 14; 1st international bout at 23; joined ntl team '83; 6 ntl 62kg freestyle titles; '89 world cup silver; '89 world championships bronze; '87 Yugoslavian Invitational gold; mem. '83 PAG, '88 Olympic, '90 Goodwill Games teams; Pac-10 wrestler of '83; Canada's outstanding wrestler award '86, '89; mem. US, Cdn Wrestling halls of fame; res. Tucson, Ariz.

BOILEAU, Art (t&f); b. 9 Oct 1957, Edmonton, Alta.; m. Ranza Clark; Oregon, BA; mgr. Forerunners; distance runner; 2 ntl marathon titles; competed '83, '93 Worlds, 3 Boston Marathons, 2nd '86 in PB 2:11.15; 3rd '84 National Capital Marathon; twice 10th Fukuoka marathon; mem. '84, '88 Olympic, '86 CG teams; won Los Angeles marathon '87, '89; competes at masters level; res. Vancouver, B.C.

BOIVIN, Leo (hockey); b. 2 Aug 1932, Prescott, Ont.; given name: Leo Joseph; m. Patricia Kirkby; c. Mitch, Paul, Danny; ret'd. hockey scout; starred with Inkerman Rockets jr. team; mem. Port Arthur West End Bruins; rugged def noted for bodychecking skills; turned pro Pittsburgh (AHL) '51; promoted to Toronto (NHL) for 2 games same season; dealt to Boston '54-66, to Detroit '66-67, Pittsburgh '67-

69, Minnesota '68-70; NHL record: 1150 scheduled games, 72g, 250a, 54 playoff games, 3g, 10a; capt. Bruins '63-66; played in 3 all-star games; coached St.Louis '76, '77, Ottawa 67's '72-74; scout St. Louis, Hartford '75-93; mem. Ottawa Sports, Hockey halls of fame; res. Prescott, Ont.

BOLAND, Pat (basketball); b. 13 Apr 1943, Ottawa, Ont.; given name: Patricia Pisnook; m. Kevin Boland; UMan, BA; ret'd women's athletic dir. Concordia; UMan athlete of '63; MVP, all-star '65 Canadian women's basketball championships; team bronze '67 PAG; mgr. ntl women's team '73; v-p Quebec Basketball Fed.; mem. National Advisory Council Fitness and Amateur Sport; v-p QUAA, pres. animation research comm.; TV commentator '76 women's Olympic basketball; mem. CWIAU council; chair '73 ntl university championships; res. Montreal, Que.

BOLDIREV, Ivan (hockey); b. 15 Aug 1949, Zranjanin, Yugoslavia; lw Oshawa (OHA) '67-69, Oklahoma City (CHL); claimed in '69 entry draft by Boston; played in NHL with Boston '70-71, California '71-74, Chicago '74-79, Atlanta '79-80, Vancouver '80-83, Detroit '83-85; NHL record: 15 seasons, 1052 scheduled games, 361g, 505a, 48 playoff games, 13g, 20a; res. Detroit, Mich.

BOLDT, Arnold (t&f); b. 16 Sep 1957, Osler, Sask; given name: Arnold William; m. Inga; c. 2; UofSask, UMan; teacher; principal college programs Keewatin Community Coll.; lost leg in grain auger age 3; through determined effort pursued athletic interests in swimming, skiing, volleyball, t&f; gold hj, lj '76 Olympiad for Disabled; hj gold '92 Paralympics; world hj record for one-legged jumper 1.86m; surpassed it same year K of C Games Saskatoon with 1.94m; progressed steadily boosting world disabled hj record to 2.04m and lj to 3.01m Rome '81; Man. indoor hj record (handicapped and able-bodied) 2.08m; 5 Paralympic championships; unbeaten in disabled meets '76-93; Cdn. flag-bearer '92 Barcelona Paralympics; '80 Paralympic record 1.96m hj still stands; *CBC* mini-series *Crossbar* based loosely on his life; mem. Canada's, Sask, Terry Fox Sports, Cdn Paralympic Comm. halls of fame; res. Thompson, Man.

BOLDUC, Alain (boardsailing); b. 3 Aug 1972, Carignan, Que.; UMtl; fitness instructor; began sailing age 4, windsurfing age 14; Eastern Cdn, CYA 23-and-under titles '95; silver fleet bronze '94 world championships; mem. '96 Olympic team; Marvin McDill CYA rookie-of-yr award '93; Que. Sailing Fed. athlete of year '93; res. Longueuil, Que.

BOLGER, Pat (wrestling/judo); b. 31 Jan 1948, Alexandria, Ont.; given name: Patrick John; Okla, Waterloo, hons. BA; educator; began wrestling at 14 and never lost a high school bout; won 2 OFSAA titles, Midwestern US title; 7 ntl wrestling titles; OQAA, CIAU, Canadian open wrestling titlist '69; silver '70 CG, bronze '71 PAG; mem. '68, '72 Olympic, '67 Pan-Am, '70-71 World championships, '69, '73 FISU Games teams; coach ntl team Tel Aviv memorial tournament '75; earned judo black belt at 16; 4 Canadian, 1 US jr. judo titles; 2 Oklahoma state titles; '65 NA judo title; judo silver '67 PAG, NA high school, bronze '67 world, '68 US ntl championships; quit judo team when refused permission to represent Canada in both judo, wrestling '72 Olympics after qualifying for both teams; ret'd '73; 2 Waterloo outstanding-

athletic-career awards; 2 Viscount Alexander Canadian junior-athlete-of-yr awards; mem. Canadian Amateur Wrestling Hall of Fame; res. Toronto, Ont.

BOLL, Buzz (hockey); b. 6 Mar 1910, Fillmore, Sask.; d. 23 Jan 1990, Regina, Sask.; given name: Frank Thorman; m. Leona Volbrecht; c. William; Regina Teachers College; ret'd farmer; def/lw '30 Regina Pats Memorial Cup winner; sr. Weyburn Beavers, Toronto Marlboros; pro Syracuse; Toronto '33-38, NY Americans '39-42, Boston '42-44; NHL regular season record 133g, 130a, playoffs 7g, 3a; mem. Sask. Sports Hall of Fame.

BOLL, Rod (shooting); b. 9 Jul 1952, Fillmore, Sask.; farmer; trapshooting specialist; mem ntl team from '94; 6 ntl titles in single, double, team trap; world double trap title '94; mem. '96 Olympic, '03 PAG; licensed pilot; res. Fillmore, Sask.

BOND-MILLS, Catherine (t&f); b. 20 Sep 1967, Woodstock, Ont.; given name: Catherine Bond; m. David Mills; c. Brendan Robert; UofT. hospital pharmacist; ntl jr.hj silver; ntl team '85-98; CIAU indoor, Canada Games multiple medallist; competed '92, '96 Olympics; '90, '94, '98 CG; 10 ntl heptathlon titles; ntl record 6193 points; achieved PB 6206 points Goetzis, Austria '94; ntl lj title with PB 6.32m '94; heptathlon bronze '94 CG; CTFA Dr. Fred Tees CIAU athlete of '90 award; UofT Past-Pres. Award, athlete of '90; coach UWO; dir. Athletics Canada; mem. UofT Hall of Fame; mem. Woodstock TC; res. London, Ont.

BONK, John (football); b. 27 Aug 1950, Hamilton, Ont.; m. Chris; c. Jessie; div. sales mgr.; jr. Burlington Braves '70-71; CFL ctr Hamilton '72-73, Winnipeg '73-85; 4 WFC, CFL all-star; 2 Becket-Demarco WFC outstanding lineman awards; Schenley outstanding lineman '84; mem. '84 Grey Cup winner; broadcaster '86-91; asst. coach Hamilton '92-93; mem. Blue Bombers Hall of Fame; res. Stoney Creek, Ont.

BONK, Radek (hockey); b. 9 Jan 1976, Krnov, Czechoslovakia; ctr ZPS Zin jrs. '91-93; mem. Czech jr. ntl team age 13; Czech elite league age 16; rep. Czech Republic '96 World Cup; IHL Las Vegas '93-95; IHL rookie of yr at 17 (youngest ever); 1st Ottawa pick, 3rd overall '94 draft; NHL Ottawa '95-04, Montreal '04; NHL record: (through '04) 689 scheduled games, 152g, 247a, 61 playoff games, 9g, 15a; res. Krnov, Czech Rep.

BONNEAU, Stéphane (tennis); b. 8 Dec 1961, Chicoutimi, Que.; teaching pro, mgr. alternative rock band *In This Life*; ntl -18 champion; 3 times mem. Galea, Davis Cup teams; semifinalist '79 US Open; mem. Que., Canadian teams '77-92; 2nd ranked Que., 3rd Canada '81; most-improved Que. jr. '79; with Caroline Delisle '92 Sun Life mixed doubles; Sun Life ntl singles '84-85; with Martin Dyotte men's ntl doubles '84; mem. '80-85 Davis Cup team; ranked among Quebec's top 10 athletes '79; res. Laval, Que.

BONNELLO, Bonny (equestrian); b. 17 Dec 1950, England; given name: Frances Ann; m. Chesson; c. Billy; began riding age 4, in hunter-jumper competitions; at 13 introduced to dressage; campaigned in Europe 1st time

'75; with purchase of Satchmo '78 began to impress in international events; mem. '80 Olympic team; active coach; res. Calgary, Alta.

BONNEY, Wayne (officiating/hockey); b. 27 May 1953, Ottawa, Ont.; m. Claudette Brophy; c. Allyson; ret'd NHL official; played minor hockey, baseball Ottawa/Nepean; began pro hockey officiating in WHA moving to NHL '79-04 as linesman; operates off-season officiating school; NHL officiating record (all as linesman): 1638 scheduled games, 228 playoff games; res. Mesa, Ariz.

BONNYCASTLE, Charles (builder); b. 6 Dec 1904, Winnipeg, Man.; d. 13 Nov 1985, Saint John, N.B.; given name: Charles Humphrey; UNB, hon. LLB.; educator; nicknamed "Hum"; largely responsible for Saint John area rowing revival; formed Kennebecasis Rowing Club '71; chair. Renforth Regatta '71-76; CARA dir. '72; helped form NBRA '73, Fredericton Rowing Club '75; posted victories Royal Canadian Henley '77, '81, Redding, Eng. International '81, Cdn Ntls '82; NB rowing champion '79; freeman village of Renforth; mem. NB Sports Hall of Fame.

BOON, Dickie (hockey); b. 14 Feb 1874, Belleville, Ont.; d. 3 May 1961, Outremont, Que.; jr. Montreal Young Crystals; def Monarch HC 1897, Montreal AAA jrs. '98-00, srs. '01 helping win Stanley Cup vs. Winnipeg Victorias '02; nicknamed "Little Iron Man"; mgr. Montreal Wanderers '03; 3 Stanley Cups before '16 retirement; never played pro hockey; mem. Hockey Hall of Fame.

BORISOFF, Jainie (wheelchair basketball); b. 20 Jun 1970, Surrey, BC; m. Carrie Linegar; UBC BSc, PhD; neural engineer; point guard; began wheelchair basketball career '90 joining ntl team '95; regarded as team leader on court; frequent team capt; 3 ntl championship gold, 4 silver, 4 bronze; 1 Canada Games silver; 1 CWBL gold; competed '96, '00, '04 Paralympics, 2 gold; 2 world cup bronze; 8 all-star teams; UBC Big Block award; BC wheelchair athlete of '99; several academic awards; res. Vancouver, B.C.

BORODOW, Andy (wrestling); b. 16 Sep 1969, Montreal, Que.; given name: Andrew Mark; Concordia; heavyweight; 2 US FILA jr. world GR titles; mem. ntl team from '87; 130kg silver FS & GR '92 Pan-Am championships, bronze Greco-Roman '91, 2 bronze '95 PAG; 6 ntl FS, 2 GR titles; competed '88, '92, '96 Olympics, 5 Maccabiah Games; 130kg FS gold '94 CG, '85, '89, '93 Maccabiah Games; 2 all-Cdn honors; tried Sumo winning silver '96, bronze '93, '95 Sumo worlds; mem. US Wrestling Hall of Fame; res. Montreal, Que.

BOROWY, Janet (field hockey); b. 7 Jan 1961, Toronto, Ont.; given name: Janet Elizabeth; Queen's, hons. BA; Ont. jr. '79-80; Ont. team '81 Canada Winter Games; Ont. sr. '81-82; -21 team '82; silver medal team World Cup '83; fed. govt. excellence award '83; res. Islington, Ont.

BORSHOLT, Lisa (swimming); b. 5 Apr 1962, North Vancouver, B.C.; given name: Lisa Ann; m. Greenwood; Texas; 100m, 200m breaststroke specialist; mem. ntl team '75-84; '76, '84 Olympic, '78, '82 CG, '83 FISU Games teams; gold 200m '78 CG, world championships; gold

100m, 200m '80-81 winter, summer nationals; masters competitor; res. N.Vancouver, B.C.

BORST, Cathy (curling); b. 3 Sep 1959, Winnipeg, Man.; given name: Cathy King; sep; c. Karston, Travis, Kyle; ntl jr. titles '77-78; prov. mixed titles '88, '94; Alta. women's titles '95, '97-98; skip Scott Tournament of Hearts title '98; nicknamed "Snow White"; res. Edmonton, Alta.

BORTHWICK, Gayle (golf); b. 3 Dec 1943, Regina, Sask.; given name: Patricia Gayle Hitchens; m. Robert John Borthwick; c. Julie; UBC, BEd; teacher; only golfer in Canada to win all four ntl titles, jr. '61, women's amateur '62, mid amateur '92, srs '94-95; won USGA sr. women's title '96; runnerup ntl jr. '60, 4 women's amateurs, 3 Ont. amateurs, 2 BC amateurs, 3 ntl srs. mem. 3 Cdn Commonwealth, 4 Cdn world, 1 Cdn British Amateur teams; capt. Cdn team '80 British Amateur, 2 world amateur teams; won '70 Australian 2-ball title; 2 BC jr., 2 BC, Ont. amateur, 2 Ont. mid amateur, 2 Ont. sr. titles; mem. 2 BC jr, 7 BC, 13 Ont amateur, 2 Ont. sr. teams; teams chair. OLGA '81-83; Mississauga dist. exec. course rating '78-80; pres. women's intermediate golf assn '89; 4yrs OLGA, CLGA advisory comm.; dir. Ada Mackenzie Memorial Foundation from '85, pres. '92-93; mem. Mississauga Hospital charity tournament comm. '95-96; mem. BC Golf, RCGA, Mississauga Sports halls of fame; res. Mississauga, Ont.

BOSCHMAN, Laurie (hockey); b. 4 Jun 1960, Major, Sask.; given name: Laurie Joseph; m. Nancy Friesen; c. Brent, Mark, Jeffrey; Ottawa. EO dir. Hockey Ministries International, Man. shoe stores partner; ctr Brandon (WHL) '76-79, New Brunswick (AHL) '80; 1st pick Toronto '79 entry draft; NHL with Toronto '79-82, Edmonton '82-83, Winnipeg '83-90, New Jersey '90-92, Ottawa '92-93; Ottawa capt.; NHL record: 14 seasons, 1009 scheduled games, 229g, 348a, 57 playoff games, 8g, 13a; WHL all-star '79; res. Stittsville, Ont.

BOSHUCK, Wally (speed skating); b.12 Oct 1928, Saskatoon, Sask.; given name: Walter; m. Dorothy Carrick; c. Lori, Ralph, William, Shawn, Kevin; UofSask BPharm; ret'd. pharmacist; began speed skating at 16; competed for 7yrs before arthritis forced him to hang up skates; set provincial 220-, 440yd records; pres. Saskatoon Lions speed skating club at 18; over the years has served as referee, starter, clerk of course, corner judge, finish line judge, recorder, timer and meet co-ordinator; mem. comm. which wrote modern CASSA constitution; organized clubs in North Battleford, Prince Albert, Moose Jaw; 5yrs dir., 3yrs treas., 1yr v-p CASSA; 2 terms pres. SASSA, pres. Saskatoon Lions SSC; developed learn to skate program for youngsters; mgr. Canadian tour for Chinese team; active as coach from '40s; associate life mem. CASSA; '83 Racer award for contribution to sport; CASSA Air Canada official-of-yr nominee twice; Centennial award; CASSA award of merit; Moose Jaw arena bears his name; mem. Sask. Sports, Cdn Speed Skating halls of fame; res. Moose Jaw, Sask.

BOSS, Leonard (baseball); b. 19 Oct 1919, Springhill, N.S.; m. Colette; c. Joann, Gary; ret'd miner; regarded as greatest fireballing rhp in H&D history; while statistics vague indications are he won 75 per cent of games pitched; authored two no-hitters, several 1-hitters; pitched famed

Fence Busters to 4 provincial titles during '40s; mem. Truro Bearcats '47; rejoined Fence Busters '48-49, Halifax Shipyards '50; all-star MVP '50; rejected pro offers from Boston, Philadelphia; mem. NS Sports Hall of Fame; res. Wakefield, RI

BOSSHART, Dominique (taekwondo); b. 7 Oct 1977, Morges, Vaud; given name: Dominique Simone; full-time athlete; ntl heavyweight champion 1993-2003; bronze '95, '99 PAG, '96, '98 Pan Am Championships; silver '99 worlds; gold '99 Pan Am Olympic selection tournament, '00 Pan Am Championships; bronze '00 Olympics, where taekwondo made its first official appearance; the Cdn Taekwondo Assn female athlete of '96; female MVP '96 nationals; Man. female athlete of '00 by the *Winnipeg Free Press*; res. Winnipeg, Man.

BOSSY, Mike (hockey); b. 22 Jan 1957, Montreal, Que.; given name: Michael Dean; m. Lucie Creamer; c. Josiane, Tanya; PR director Humpty Dumpty; jr. Laval Nationals; NYI 1st choice, 15th overall '77 amateur draft; during 4-year jr. career displayed scoring flare with 309 goals; skill carried into NHL as he set '78 rookie scoring record 53 goals; Calder Memorial Trophy; 9 consecutive 50+ goals seasons; 4 60+ seasons; 1st player to reach 200-goal plateau in 4 seasons; equalled Maurice Richard standard 50 goals in 50 games '80-81; NHL record 35 points 1 playoff year '81; only player in NHL history to score Stanley Cup series-winning goals in consecutive seasons; top Stanley Cup goal scorer '85; set single-season hat-tricks record '81; 5 times 1st, 3 2nd team all-star rw; youngest ever to score 500 NHL goals; Conn Smythe Trophy '82; 3 Lady Byng awards; mem. 4 consecutive Stanley Cup winners; chronic back injury forced retirement following '86-87 season; 10yr NHL record: 752 scheduled games, 573g, 553a, 129 playoff games, 85g, 75a; MVP Team Canada '79 Challenge Cup series; competed in '81 (MVP), '84 Canada Cup tournaments; with Bobby Orr, Cassie Campbell operates kids' hockey school; governor Laval Jr.; with Barry Meisel co-authored *Boss - the Mike Bossy Story*; Cdn Society of New York achievement award; featured on Cdn postage stamps; mem. Hockey, QMJHL hockey halls of fame; res. Laval, Que.

BOSWELL, Mark (t&f); b. 28 Jul 1977, Mandeville, Jamaica; UAustin; high jump specialist; moved to Canada '88; 1st Cdn athlete to win gold at jr. worlds; 4 straight NCAA titles; 19 consec. hj titles; gold '99 PAG; silver '99, bronze '03 worlds; bronze '99 ntls; gold '02 CG; competed '00, '04 Olympics; 5 ntl titles; gold '01 Francophonie Games, '03 Millrose Games, Jamaica, Rome, Athens, German meets; competed 5 world championships; competed '01 Goodwill Games; City of Brampton mayor's plaque; Fred Rowell, Cal Bricker t&f awards; res. Brampton, Ont.

BOTT, Punch (skiing); b. 24 Apr 1917, Montreal, Que.; d. 21 Mar 1994, Pt. Coquitlam, B.C.; given name: Percival Christian; began skiing as elementary school student in Côte des Neiges; one of Canada's skiing standouts in late '30s, early '40s; 11 CASA ntl title medals; holds unique distinction of winning both CASA ntl alpine and nordic titles; began ski jumping '27; tabbed as "schoolboy wonder"; self-coached; won inumerable SCM, City of Montreal, Quebec, Ontario titles; set 160' jump record on now defunct Montreal Ski Hill '38; capt. '36 HS football team; mem.

QRFU Westmount Jr. FB title team '37; also played sr. hockey; mem. Cdn Skiing Hall of Fame.

BOTTERILL, Cal (hockey); b. 17 Oct 1947, Winnipeg, Man.; given name: Calvin Bruce; m. Doreen Ann McCannell; c. Jason, Jennifer; UAlta, PhD; professor UWinnipeg, sports psychologist; mem. ntl men's hockey team '67-69; support staff mem. 7 Olympics; sport psychology consultant NHL NY Rangers, Philadelphia, Chicago, Calgary, Los Angeles; Sport Man. award of excellence; award of teaching excellence UWinnipeg, UCalgary; res. Winnipeg, Man.

BOTTERILL, Jason (hockey); b. 19 May 1976, Edmonton, Alta.; given name: Jason Neil; Michigan, BA; hockey player; won 3 world jr. hockey gold '94-96; NCAA title team '96; mem. Saint John Flames '01 AHL Calder Cup winner; AHL all-star '03 Rochester Americans; academic all-American; res. Winnipeg, Man.

BOTTERILL, Jennifer (hockey); b. 1 May 1979, Ottawa, Ont.; given name: Jennifer Lori; Harvard, BA; hockey player; attended ntl jr. basketball selection camp '96; mem. Man. ringette team Canada Winter Games; team capt. Harvard hockey; set U.S. college record '00-01 of at least one point 74 consec. games; capt. ntl U22 '98 Christmas Cup title team; forward ntl women's team; 8 consec world title teams; Olympic silver '98, gold '02; MVP '01 worlds; 2 Patty Kazmaier top player U.S. women's college hockey awards; mem. Toronto Aeros; res. Winnipeg, Man./Toronto, Ont.

BOTTING, Steve (canoeing); b. 5 Dec 1959, Montreal, Que.; Concordia; '76 ntl juvenile C2 500m; '77 NA jr. C1 500m, ntl juvenile C1, C4 500m; '79 Continental Cup C2 500m; '80 Olympic trials C2 500m, 1000m, Zaandam regatta C2 500m, 1000m; '80-81 ntl C2 500m, 1000m, C4 1000m, '82 C2 500m; ntl sr. record 4:21.1 C4 1000m; mem. '80, '84 Olympic teams; res. Westmount, Que.

BOTTOMS, Lynn (football); b. 2 Jul 1933, Edmonton, Alta.; given name: Lynn Anthony; div; c. John Joseph, Lynn Jr, Michael; Washington, BSc, ME; teacher; c/ss Sunnybrook sr. softball team '46-50; ss Forest Lawn baseball club '50-53; HS football, minor hockey '51-53; Calgary jr. Broncs football '52-53; pro Calgary '54-60, Toronto '60-64; mem. sr. softball Cobourg '64-70; HS football coach from '66; international, regional old timers hockey tournaments from '77; Calgary Broncs outstanding player '53; WFC rookie of '54; provincial award as 1 of top 10 athletes in 1st half century Alta. '55; 3 East-West Shrine Game teams; 4 times Stampeders punt-return leader, twice WIFU, Argos; db Calgary 50-year dream team '70; regional hockey referee; res. Cobourg, Ont.

BOUCHARD, Butch (hockey); b. 4 Sep 1919, Montreal, Que.; given name: Émile Joseph Calixte; m. Marie Claire MacBeth; c. Pierre, Jean, Émile Jr., Michel, Suzanne; ret'd. restaurateur; defensive, play-making standout Montreal 41-56; 3 times 1st, twice 2nd team all-star; team capt.; 785 scheduled games, 49g, 145a, 113 playoff games, 11g, 21a; , coach, exec. jr. clubs; dir.-pres. Montreal Royals baseball club; mem. 4 Stanley Cup winners; mem. Que. Sports, Hockey halls of fame; res. Vercheres, Que./Belair, Fla./Montreal, Que.

BOUCHARD, Dan (hockey); b. 12 Dec 1950, Val d'Or, Que.; given name: Daniel Hector; m. Janet Ratcliffe; c. Jordan, Lindsay; v-p SPT Product Development; goaltender; jr. London Knights; pro Hershey (AHL) '70-71, Oklahoma City (CHL) '71-72, Boston (AHL) '71-72, NHL Atlanta, Calgary, Quebec, Winnipeg '72-86; NHL record: 655 scheduled games, 286-232-113, 37,919min, 2061ga, 27s, 43 playoff games, 13-30-0, 2549min, 147ga, 1sho; competed Canada-Russia series '77; played briefly in France; goalie coach Quebec Nordiques 4yrs; Hap Holmes (AHL) trophy '72; underwent brain surgery '90; coach LifeU title hockey team '97-98; res. Marietta, Ga.

BOUCHARD, Rémi (golf); b. 31 Jan 1964, Lasalle, Que.; Indiana; pro golfer; Que jr. title '82; won Duke of Kent '84, Que. amateur '87; mem. '87 all Big-10, Willingdon Cup teams; pro from '87; won '89 India Open, CPGA winter tour, '88 Que. PGA, Cdn. Asst. pro, Bic Open; '87 Que. rookie of yr, asst. pro of yr, Que. pro of yr; won Que. Tour La Sauvegarde Cap-Rouge; competed in Asia, US mini-tours; res. Brossard, Que.

BOUCHARD, Sylvain (speed skating); b. 12 Apr 1970, Loretteville, Que.; Laval; played hockey to age 12; competed in short-track to age 16 then switched to long-track; power-skating teacher; mem. ntl team from '88; 2 ntl juv long-track titles; 3 ntl sprint titles; world record 1000m; competed '94 Olympics; world single distance championship gold '98; 1000m bronze '95, gold '98 world sprints; ret'd. from competition '98; res. Loretteville. Que.

BOUCHER, Alain (t&f); b. 26 May 1963, North Bay, Ont.; given name: Alain Steve; m. Michelle Louise Cournoyer; c. Nathalie; Danielle; U New Mexico, UofOtt, BPhE, Uof T, BEd; teacher; steeplechase, road running specialist; Ont. HS x-country, 2000m steeplechase titles '82; Pan-Am jr. SC, ntl jr. 2000m SC titles '82; OFSAA 2000m SC record 5:37; ntl scholastic 2000m SC record; held ntl jr. 2000m SC record; 1 gold, 5 silver, 2 bronze ntl 3000m SC championships; SC gold '82 Pan-Am championships; competed '82 world jr., '88 world sr. XC, '84 Pan-Pacific SC, '89 FISU, Francophone Games, '90 CG, '91 Ekiden Japan road race; 9 Ont. SC titles; 3 Fergie Dowdal outstanding track athletes awards; '82 North Bay athlete of yr.; dominant road racer '94-98 winning 63 races; 4 NCRA, 3 Ottawa Lions road racer-of-yr awards; Ottawa ACT road racer-of-'98 award; mem. North Bay Sports Hall of Fame; res. Kanata, Ont.

BOUCHER, Bill (hockey); b. 10 Nov 1899, Ottawa, Ont.; d. 10 Nov 1958, Ottawa, Ont.; m. Thérésa Payette; c. Bob, Bill, June; civil servant; pro Canadiens '21-26; top scorer when Habs won '24 Stanley Cup; Boston '26-27, NY Americans '27-28; with Habs rw on line with Howie Morenz, Aurel Joliat; career total 90g, 34a.

BOUCHER, Bob (hockey); b. 23 Mar 1938, Ottawa, Ont.; d. 16 Dec 2004, Ottawa, Ont.; given name: Robert Joseph; m. Anne Marie O'Neill; c. Trisha, Kerri Marie, Robbie; UofOtt, Carleton, St.Mary's; ret'd mgr. Oceanside Equipment, hockey exec.; scoring leader Ottawa-Hull Jr. Canadiens '57-58 Memorial Cup team; played with St. Michael's; pro Hull-Ottawa (EPHL); eye injury ended NHL aspirations; asst. coach N.S. (AHL), head coach Coal Harbour Jrs. (Hardy Cup '90), St. Mary's '69-82, 7

consecutive conference titles, 231-33-4 record; twice CIAU hockey coach of year; asst. coach Philadelphia (NHL) '80-83; coach Windsor (OHL) '83-84; created St. Mary's Hockey Camp of Champions; mem. N.S., St. Mary's Sports halls of fame.

BOUCHER, Denis (baseball); b. 7 Mar 1968, Lachine, Que.; m. Isabelle Fournier; c. Jade, Corentin, Loic-Antoine; Ntl Baseball Institute; PR ambassador Montreal Expos; lhp Team Canada '86 World Youth tourney; '87 PAG; saw ML service Toronto, Cleveland, Montreal; minors Myrtle Beach (A), Dunedin (A), Syracuse (AAA); Colorado Springs, Las Vegas, Ottawa; ML record 6-10; PCL all-star; mem. Cdn Baseball Hall of Fame; res. Montreal, Que.

BOUCHER, Frank (hockey); b. 7 Oct 1901, Ottawa, Ont.; d. 12 Dec 1977, Kemptville, Ont.; m. Agnes Sylvester; c. Earl; hockey executive, farmer; early prominence Ottawa's New Edinburgh region starring in hockey, baseball, football; pro hockey Ottawa Senators '21, Vancouver Maroons '22-26, NYR '26-38, '43-44, coach NY Rovers (EAHL) '38-39, Rangers '39-48; GM Rangers '48-55; centred line of Bill, Bun Cook with Rangers; Lady Byng Trophy 7 times in 8 years gave him permanent possession original trophy; led US div. NHL scorers '34 with 14g, 30a; pro career record 219g, 298a; Western Canada Jr. Hockey commissioner 10 years, deposed over rules dispute; mem. Ottawa, Kingston, Madison Square Gardens, Canada's Sports, Hockey halls of fame.

BOUCHER, Frank (hockey); b. 3 Mar 1918, Ottawa, Ont.; d 11 Dec. 2003, Osgoode, Ont.; given name: Frank George; m. Marguerite Carruthers; c. Diane; accountant; Ottawa midget champions '31; 2 EOSSA jr. titles Lisgar HS; NY Rovers '37-39, league, US titles '38; AHL Providence, Philadelphia; mem. '42 Eastern Canadian finalist Ottawa RCAF Flyers; coach '48 Olympic, world champion RCAF Flyers; playing-mgr. Wembley Lions '49-53, English ntl title '52; coach Belleville srs. '54; playing-coach RCAF teams '55-68; business mgr. Ottawa-based Team Canada '69; son of Hall of Famer Buck Boucher; as mem. '48 Flyers military athletes of 20th century; mem. Olympic Club Canada, Ottawa Sports, Canadian Forces sports halls of fame.

BOUCHER, Gaétan (speed skating); b. 10 May 1958, Charlesbourg, Que.; m. Karin Fliege; c. 2; Montreal, UCal; sprinted into ntl prominence at 15 winning indoor, outdoor titles; jr. ntl all-around titles '74, '77; world indoor 1000m, 500m, all-around '77; NA all-around, swept ntl team trials '79; ntl indoor 3000m, world indoor 1000m, 1500m, 3000m, all-around, ntl 3000m, 500m, 1500m, 5000m, all-around '80; world record 1:13.39 1000m, 148,785 all-around points '81 Swiss International; world short-track 3000m '81; world outdoor 500m, runnerup world sprint all-around, world short-track all-around '82; ntl 3000m record 4:27.01; competed '80, '84, '88 Olympics; silver 1000m '80, gold 1000m, 1500m, bronze 500m '84 Olympics; 1st Canadian Winter Olympic triple medalist '84; world sprint title '84; Que. athlete of '77, 3 times French Canadian athlete of yr; Viscount Alexander award '77; 4 SFC athlete-of-month awards; Dick Ellis Memorial Trophy team mem. '81; CASSA skater of '80; Thompson Trophy fastest Canadian 500m '76-82; Canadian Superstars title '80; fed. govt. sport excellence award '82, champions award '84; flag bearer

'84 winter Olympics; Lou Marsh, Norton Crowe trophies '84; Seagram 5 Star award '84; named Que. athlete of '80s; 1ˢᵗ Cdn recipient ISU Jacques Favart trophy; honorary Montreal Canadien; PR attaché, Dairy Bureau of Canada; Officer Order of Canada '83; mem. Cdn Olympic, Cdn Speed Skating, Que., Canada's Sports halls of fame; res. Rosemere, Que.

BOUCHER, George (hockey); b. 12 Aug 1895, Ottawa, Ont.; d 17 Oct 1960, Ottawa, Ont.; m. Mabel Olsen; c. Earl (d), Frank; hockey coach, farmer; eldest of famed Boucher brothers, nicknamed "Buck"; hb '15-18 Rough Riders; pro hockey Ottawa Senators '15-27, 4 Stanley Cup victories; Montreal Maroons '28-29, Chicago '30-34; 122 career goals; coach Chicago, Ottawa, Boston, St. Louis, Springfield, Noranda, Que.; coached '49 Ottawa Allan Cup winner; helped select, train '48 Ottawa RCAF Olympic, world champions coached by son Frank; mem. Ottawa Sports, Hockey halls of fame.

BOUCHER, Jerry (boxing); b. 24 Aug 1930, Halifax, N.S.; d. 1 Jul 1986, Moncton, N.B.; given name: Gerald Murray; m. Charlene Ann Keirstead; c. Kimberly, Derek; accountant; flyweight boxing career spanned '48-65; Maritime title '49-54; Atlantic Command Forces title '51; Pacific Northwest Golden Gloves '54; competed '54 BEG; BC Golden Gloves, Western Cdn Diamond Belt; beat Hawaiian fly champ '54; Que. Golden Gloves title '56; competed 6 ntl championships reaching 3 finals; ring record 213 bouts, 201 wins, 11 losses, 1 draw; mem. Cdn Boxing, Cdn Forces halls of fame.

BOUCHER, Kelly (basketball); 13 Jan 1968, Calgary, Alta.; UVic, UCal; fwd/gd; mem. ntl team '88-97; jr ntl team '86-87; temporarily ret'd '91-92; competed in '89, '93 COPABA world qualification tournament, '94 Goodwill Games, '94 World championship tournament teams; mem. COPABA gold medal team '95; played pro Italy, Switzerland, Luxembourg, Hungary '92-97; 5 CIAU all-conference, 1 all-Canadian awards; 1ˢᵗ Cdn woman signed to play in WNBA with Charlotte Sting '98; Calgary HS female athlete of '85; participant in COA Adopt-an-athlete program; res. Charlotte, N.C./Calgary, Alta.

BOURASSA, Jocelyne (golf); b. 30 May 1947, Shawinigan, Que.; Montreal, BA, Wisc, BSc; ret'd pro golfer, promotions, PR Houston Group; nicknamed 'Frenchy'; UMtl basketball, volleyball, skiing, track star; Que. jr. title '63-65, ladies' amateur '63, '69-71; ntl ladies amateur title '65, '71; Ont. title '71; Scottish girls title '67; low amateur Supertest championship '69; mem. winning World Cup team '70; NZ amateur '71; ntl women's match title '65; LPGA rookie of '72; La Canadienne LPGA tournament title in playoff '73; twice among top 20 LPGA money winners; LPGA most-colorful-player award '72; Canadian National Advisory Council '73-74; Bobbie Rosenfeld trophy '72, twice French Canadian athlete of year; LPGA treas. '74-75; 2yr stint as sports writer; golf coach Arizona State '80; mem. Simpson-Sears sports advisory council '75-78; PR with Houston Group from '80; ED du Maurier Classic '80-00; RCGA women's tournament advisor '01-03; *Score* magazine lifetime achievment award; mem. Order of Canada, RCGA, Que. Sports halls of fame; res. Montreal, Que.

BOURBONAIS, Roger (hockey); b. 26 Oct 1942, Edmonton, Alta.; lawyer; capt. '63 Edmonton Oil Kings Memorial Cup champs; mem. ntl team '63-69; competed 2 Olympics, 4 IIHF worlds; bronze '68 Olympics; 3 IIHF world bronze; a prolific scorer usually among top scorer in international play; mem. IIHF Hall of Fame; res. Edmonton, Alta.

BOURDEAU, Yvan (t&f); b. 6 Sep 1959, Beauport, Que.; social worker; blind sprint/lj/tj specialist; gold '80 Olympic lj; ntl titles lj '81-83, tj '82-83, 200m, 4x200 relay, 60m '82, 100m '83; res. Quebec City, Que.

BOURGEOIS, Joel (t&f); b. 25 Apr 1971, Grand-Digue, N.B.; c. Naomi; Moncton, B.Mus; musician; steeplechase specialist; began steeplechase at 17; top Cdn finisher '92 world x-country; CIAU x-c gold '94; competed '94, '98 CG, '95, '99 PAG, '96, '00 Olympic, '91, '93, '95, '97, '99 FISU Games; 4 ntl titles; won '96 Penn Relays; set PB 8:20.08 '99; 3000m SC silver '95, bronze '99 FISU Games; SC gold '99 PAG; 6 MonctonU male athlete-of-yr awards; res. Moncton, N.B.

BOURNE, Bob (hockey/coaching); b. 21 Jun 1954, Kindersley, Sask.; c. Jeff, Justin; stockbroker, hockey exec.; regarded as one of fastest skaters in hockey; lw Saskatoon WCJHL '71-74; NHL drafted by Kansas City '74 but dealt to NYI '74-86, Los Angeles '86-88, Team Canada '85 Canada Cup; NHL totals 964 scheduled games, 258g, 324a, 139 playoff games, 40g, 56a; 4 consec. Stanley Cup winners; coach Las Vegas IHL '93-94, Central Texas WPHL '96-97, Utah IHL from '97; 1 Turner Cup title; with son Jeff (born with spina bifida) co-chair '00 world sledge hockey championships; SI man of '88 award; res. Kelowna, B.C.

BOURNE, Munroe (swimming); b. 26 Jun 1910, Victoria, B.C.; d. 11 Jul 1992, Rothesay, N.B.; given name: Frederick Munroe; m. Margaret Fairweather; c. Robert, Richard, Mary; McGill, BA, MD, Oxford, BA, MA; physician; mem. '28, '32, '36 Olympic teams; team capt. '36; bronze 4x200m '28; 3 gold '30 BE Games; 50m '33 international student games; 100m backstroke, relay Dublin Tailteann '28; mem. McGill, Oxford swimming, water polo teams; pres. Oxford SC '34-35; mem. Montreal AAA; mem. London Otters SC, ntl team race title '34-35; represented Oxford Langlauf skiing '34-35, McGill, MAAA, Oxford in T&F; capt. 3 McGill teams leading them to 2 swimming, 4 t&f, 2 water polo titles; 5 intercollegiate, 2 ntl records; coach McGill swim team '38-40; Rhodes Scholar; Commander Order of St. John '75; mem. Cdn Aquatic, Olympic, McGill Sports halls of fame.

BOURNE, Shae-Lynn (figure skating); b. 24 Jan 1976, Chatham, Ont.; mem. ntl team from '92; 32 intl medals; teamed with Victor Kraatz to become top Cdn ice dance duo; 9 ntl, 7 Skate Canada titles; Skate America title; 2 NKH trophy silver; 1 world gold, 1 silver, 3 bronze; gold, silver Championship Series; Nebelhorn Trophy, Grand Prix International, 4 Continents gold; competed '94, '98, '02 Olympics; turned pro '03; severed ties with Kraatz '03; partnered with Peter Tcherynshev '04; opted to retire from ice dancing in favor of show singles '05; res. Lake Placid, N.Y.

BOURQUE, Ray (hockey); b. 28 Dec 1960, Montreal, Que.; given name: Raymond Jean; m. Christiane; c. Melissa, Christopher, Ryan; defence, Sorel, Verdun (QMJHL) '76-79; drafted by Boston '79; team capt. '85-00; traded to Colorado '00-01; mem. '01 Stanley Cup winner; Calder Trophy '80; 5 Norris trophies; King Clancy trophy '92; Lester Patrick award '03; 12 1st, 5 2nd all-star teams; played in 16 NHL all-star games; '96 all-star game MVP; became Bruins' all-time leading scorer Feb '97; Canada Cup '81, '84, '87; mem. '98 Olympic team; NHL record: 1612 scheduled games, 410g, 1169a, 214 playoff games, 41g, 139a; does extensive work for children's charities; Bruins ret'd. jersey 77; featured on Cdn postage stamps; mem. Hockey Hall of Fame; res. Boxford, Mass.

BOWDEN, Bradley (wheelchair basketball, sledge hockey); b. 26 May 1983, Mississauga, Ont.; mem. Cdn sledge hockey team '98, '02 Paralympics, '04 worlds; began playing wheelchair basketball '96; mem. ntl team from '03; gold '04 Paralympics; gold jr. worlds '01; gold '99, bronze '03 Canada Games; bronze '99, gold '00, '01 CWBL jr.; gold '03, '04 ntls with Team Ont.; gold world jr. '01; mem. Burlington Vipers, Michigan Thunderbirds; res. Orton, Ont.

BOWDEN, Lori (triathlon); b. 13 Jun 1967, Fergus, Ont.; given name: Lori Leigh; m. Peter Reid; former XC runner who went from fun-loving amateur to serious triathlete with 3rd in pro field '97 Australian ironman; duathlon world gold '98; won 2 ironman intl races '99 becoming 1st woman to break 3-hour marathon barrier; 1 of 5 women to break 9-hour ironman mark; won world ironman titles '99, '03; 3 Australian, 5 Cdn, 2 Austrian ironman titles; recorded 2nd fastest ironman ever in 8:51:22; Timberman ironman title '03; 3 triathlete-of-yr awards; 4 times ranked world #1 from '99; ranked 6th by *Outside Magazine* in list of 25 super-heroes; with husband Peter dubbed "World's Fittest Couple"; res. Victoria, B.C.

BOWDEN, Norris (figure skating); b. 13 Aug 1926, Toronto, Ont.; d. 9 Apr 1991, North York, Ont.; given name: Robert Norris; m. Joan; c. David, Kathy, Danny; UofT, BSc, MBA; chartered life underwriter; unique in figure skating winning every discipline in Cdn FS, a feat never again equaled; ntl men's jr./sr. singles titles; ntl Fours title; ntl jr. pair title; with Frances Dafoe ntl sr. pairs '52-55, dance '52, waltz, 10-step titles, NA pairs '53-56, world pairs '54-55; silver '56 Olympics; international skating judge; flag-bearer '56, competed '52 winter Olympics; helped establish Cheshire Homes for Paraplegics; founding pres. Centennial Nursery School for handicapped children; Engineering Society Martha Award for volunteer work; mem. Cdn, US Figure Skating, Cdn Olympic, Canada's Sports halls of fame.

BOWEN, Stacy (t&f); b. 17 Dec 1969, Montego Bay, Jamaica; Alabama; social worker; sprint specialist; ntl jr. 200m title '88; Canada Games record 200m, also 100m gold '89; 3 ntl 200m, 1 400m titles; competed in '90, '94 CG, '91 PAG, '92 Olympic, '93 FISU, Worlds; 2 gold '94 Francophone Games; bronze 4x400 '94 CG; PB: 11.45 100m, 23.16 200m, 52.28 400m; mem. Phoenix TC; res. Downsview, Ont./Tuscaloosa, Ala.

BOWER, Johnny (hockey); b. 8 Nov 1924, Prince Albert, Sask; given name: John William; m. Nancy Brain; c. John Jr., Cynthia, Barbara; hockey scout; jr. Prince Albert; Providence, Cleveland (AHL) '45-56, brief stint NYR, Vancouver (WHL) mid-50s; Maple Leafs '58-70; NHL record: 534 scheduled games, 37so, 2.53 goals-against avg., 72 playoff games, 5so, 2.58 avg.; once 1st team all-star; Vezina Trophy '61, with Terry Sawchuk '65; 3 times Bickell Trophy (most valuable Leaf); 5 times AHL all-star, 3 times Hap Holmes Memorial Trophy AHL MVP, 3 times Leslie Cunningham Trophy; leading goaler award Vancouver '55; following playing career remained with Leafs organization as scout, head scout, asst coach; mem. Canada's, Etobicoke, AHL, Sask Sports, Hockey halls of fame; res. Mississauga, Ont.

BOWERING, Ebbie (basketball); b. 24 Mar 1907, Winipeg, Man; d. 1 Sep 1998, Maple Ridge, B.C.; given name: Ebbie William; m. Marguerite Gertrude Marie Marshall (d); c. William David Samuel, Robert Whitney, Kenneth Wayne; UBC BA, BEd; educator; played softball, baseball, basketball, handball; served on several sports governing bodies; pres. Vancouver, B.C., Cdn Basketball Assns; member-at-large COA; mgr '52 Cdn Olympic basketball team; founding mem. Cdn. Pan-Am Games Assn; '71 PAG; coached HS boys basketball; umpired Vancouver amateur softball leagues; commissioner Vancouver Parks Board in '50s, '60s, including term as chair.; mem. Cdn Basketball Hall of Fame.

BOWES, Sharon (shooting); b. 17 Sep 1966, Windsor, Ont.; Waterloo; office administrator Planned Parenthood; ex-facility co-ordinator Kitchener Minor Soccer Assn; small-bore specialist; began competing at club level '78; mem. ntl team '83-02; competed '86, '90, '94, '98, '02 CG, '87, '91, '95, '99 PAG, '84, '88, '92, '00 Olympic Games, 6 world championships; 5 PAG, 4 CG air rifle gold, 3 PAG, 4 CG silver, 1 PAG, 3 CG, 1 World Cup bronze; ntl air rifle title '90; 2 sports excellence awards; 3 Shooting Fed. athlete-of-yr awards; res. Waterloo, Ont.

BOWIE, Mary Jane (luge); b. 3 Mar 1948, Ottawa, Ont.; given name: Mary Jane Dyment Finlayson; m. Paul Bowie; c. David, James, Laura; UofOtt, BSc, McGill; ret'd. fitness consultant; mem. intercollegiate badminton, t&f, x-country, alpine ski teams; 2 ntl luge titles; twice runnerup NA championships; mem. ntl team 5yrs; mem. '74 European championships, 6 worlds, '76 Olympic teams; '71 Zardini Memorial Avila Que. title; '72 Que. champion; bronze International Grenzhandrennan (Austria) '77; 4th Gosser Preis der Stadt (Innsbruck) '77; intl luge judge; trained Calgary Olympic officials; Level 3 FIS judge; res. Ottawa, Ont.

BOWIE, Russell (hockey); b. 24 Aug 1880, Montreal, Que.; d. 8 Apr 1959, Montreal, Que.; weighed only 112lbs when he joined Winnipeg Victorias 1898; remained amateur (CAHL, ECAHA) throughout career; 234 goals in 80 games over 10-year span; one of few to score 10 goals in single game; 38 in 10 games '07, including 8 one game; led league scorers 5 times; perennial all-star; broken collarbone ended career, became referee; mem. Hockey Hall of Fame.

BOWMAN, Gary (shooting); b. 24 Jun 1957, Hamilton, Ont.; given name: Gary Robert; m. Nancy McLean; c. Connor Russell Brian, Dana Catherine; Mohawk Coll,

McMaster, BA; systems planning mgr. Bell Mobility; began shooting as cadet '72; 2 cadet Bisley teams; 2 Ont. grand aggregate titles; qualified 7 Bisley teams, competed once; mem. 3 Palma teams, team silver '92; mem. '94 CG team; res. Mississauga, Ont.

BOWMAN, Scotty (hockey); b. 20 Jun 1911, Winnipeg, Man.; d. 22 Oct 1990, Winnipeg, Man.; given name: Ralph; def 7 NHL seasons '34-40 with Ottawa, St. Louis, Detroit; gained fame by scoring 1st penalty-shot goal in NHL history 14 Nov 1934 vs. Montreal Maroons; NHL record: 274 scheduled games, 8g, 17a, 22 playoff games, 2g, 2a; mem. 2 Stanley Cup winners; mem. Man. Hockey Hall of Fame.

BOWMAN, Scotty (coaching/hockey); b. 18 Sep 1933, Montreal, Que.; given name: William Scott; m. Suella; c. Alicia, David, Stanley, Nancy, Bob; hon. LLD Canisius Coll.; ret'd. hockey coach, *HNIC* analyst; playing career cut short by head injury '51-52 Jr. A season when allegedly struck by J.G. Talbot's stick; asst. to Sam Pollock as mgr/ coach Hull-Ottawa, 1 Memorial Cup winner; coached Peterborough Petes, Montreal Jr. Canadiens (OHA); 3 seasons Eastern Canadian scout for Habs; coach/GM expansion St. Louis (NHL) '66-71, Stanley Cup finals 3 times; coach Habs '71-79, 5 Stanley Cup, 6 Prince of Wales, 2 Clarence Campbell titles, 4 in succession; coached Team Canada '76, '81 Canada Cup series; coach/GM Buffalo '79-87; dir. hockey operations Pittsburgh '87-91, following death of Bob Johnson took over as coach '91-93, 1 Stanley Cup win; coach Detroit '93-02; 3 Stanley Cups; NHL coaching record: regular season 1244-584-313, playoffs 223-130; set NHL all-time coaching victory record '84-85 season; 900th NHL coaching victory '95, 1000 victory '97; coached 2000th NHL game '00; coached most Stanley Cup winners, 9; 3 NHL coach-of-yr awards; *Sporting News* executive of '80; *Hockey News* exec. of '84; Lester Patrick award '01; subject of Douglas Hunter book *Scotty Bowman - A Life in Hockey*; US Hockey Hall of Fame Gretzky award; selection comm. NHL Hall of Fame; mem. *Hockey Night in Canada* team '87-90; mem. Canada's Sport, Hockey halls of fame; res. Sarasota, Fla./Buffalo, N.Y.

BOWNESS, Rick (hockey); b. 25 Jan 1955, Moncton, N.B.; given name: Richard Gary; m. Judy Egan; c. Ricky, Ryan, Kristen; hockey coach, ex-scout, player personnel exec. Nashville Predators; mem. Halifax jr. Blazers, Montreal in QMJHL; drafted by Atlanta Flames '75; Tulsa (CHL) '76; def/fwd NHL Atlanta, Detroit, St. Louis, Winnipeg '75-82; NHL record: 173 scheduled games, 18g, 37a, 5 playoff games, turned to coaching Sherbrooke (AHL) '82-83; asst. Winnipeg '83-86; head coach Moncton (AHL) '87-89; Maine Mariners '89-91; head coach Boston (NHL) ''91-92; expansion Ottawa '93-95; asst. NYI '95-97, head coach '97-98; asst. Phoenix '99-04, interim head coach '04; *ESPN* color commentator '98; mem. NS Sports Hall of Fame; res. Phoenix, Ariz.

BOWSFIELD, Ted (baseball); b. 10 Jan 1935, Vernon, B.C.; given name: Edward Oliver; m. Marilyn Holden; c. Edward Oliver "Ted" Jr., Bradley McDonald; ret'd. dir. Seattle Kingdome; BC basketball all-star '54; pro baseball '54 moving through minors to (AL) Boston '58-60; 3 of first 4 AL victories vs NY earned him "Yankee-Killer" title; Little World Series finalist '59 as mem. Minneapolis Millers;

Cleveland '60; California '61-62, Kansas City '63-65; Vancouver (PCL) '65 where arm troubles forced retirement; 37-39 ML won-lost record; American Assn. all-star '58; several yrs stadium mgr with LA Angels, Seattle Mariners; mem. BC Sports Hall of Fame; res. Monroe, Wash.

BOX, Ab (football); b. 8 Mar 1909, Toronto, Ont.; d. 30 Jul 2000, Toronto, Ont.; m. Dorothy Sowerby (d), Phyllis Malpass; c. Linda, Donald, Gary, Donald, Marilyn; ret'd; Malvern Grads '28-29; protege of Ted Reeve, Balmy Beach '30-31, ORFU, Eastern, Grey Cup titles '30; Argos punter '32-34, '35-38, Grey Cup '33; frequent all-star; Jeff Russel Memorial Trophy '34; mem. ntl baseball, softball title teams; operated Markham children's day camp; mem. Canadian Football, Balmy Beach, Canada's Sports halls of fame.

BOX, Charlie (all-around); b. 26 Dec 1911, Toronto, Ont.; d. 21 Mar 1993, London, Ont.; given name: Charles Venning; m. Catherine Norsworthy; c. David, Ellen Foster, Charles M., Martha Ann; UWO, BA, OCE; ret'd educator; mem. TSSAA jr. rugby titlist '28, sr. rugby '29-30, capt. '30 team; mem. Jr. ORFU Malvern Grads '32 titlists; 4yrs all-star end (outside right), qb/punt returner UWO, capt. '37 team; with brother Ab mem. '38 Balmy Beach team; field lacrosse '27-32; box lacrosse '32-33; 3 intercollegiate lightweight (135lbs) boxing titles; '35 Silver Gloves div. title, Southwestern, Central Ont. titles; organized WWII Canadian Forces boxing shows Reykavik; coached jr. lacrosse, football Upper Canada Coll. league '33; coached Toronto Malvern CI rugby, hockey titlists; mem. UWO W-Club Sports Hall of Fame.

BOYCE, Jim (tennis); b. 22 Jun 1951, Toronto, Ont.; given name: James Niell; div. Dale Bilodeau; c. Katherine; m. Jody McCormack; Mississippi State, BSc; exec. dir. Ont. Tennis Assn., ex-real estate agent; 5 age-group titles; 5 ntl singles titles, including 3 -18 crowns; 3 times all-South Eastern Conf. team; won 105 of 120 college matches; only Cdn jr. to win both ntl and open titles same year ('68); twice ntl men's doubles champion; ranked in Ont. top 8 from jr. days, in ntl top 15 from '71; twice Davis Cup team mem.; touring pro '77-78, pro mgr. Ottawa All Seasons Racquets Club '77-79, club pro Toronto LTC '80-89; chair. '80 Davis Cup tie vs. Mexico; tennis consultant '77-81; dir. ntl tennis camps; NCTA coach '77-79, Eastern Cdn coach '78-80; ntl 45+ singles title '97; pres. JNB Sports Inc.; Pepsi award '67 outstanding Cdn jr, 4 Ont. sport achievement awards; res. Toronto, Ont.

BOYCE, Walter (motorsport); b. 25 Oct 1946, Ottawa, Ont.; m. Leslie Bradbeer; c. Jennifer, Jamie; Colorado, UofOtt; businessman, entrepreneur; with Doug Woods navigating, ntl open rally titles '70-74; only Canadian to hold FIA top-seed international rating, having won such events as Press on Regardless Rally for '73 world title, Rally of Rideau Lakes, Canadian Winter Rally; with co-driver Robin Edwards Cdn Production A titlist '79, '81-82; with Jim Brandt '86 NA, Sports Car Club of Americas Group A FIA title; mem. Cdn Motorsport Hall of Fame; res. Ottawa, Ont.

BOYCHUK, Andy (t&f); b. 17 May 1941, Orono, Ont.; given name: Andrew Harry; m. Darlene Ann MacDonald; Waterloo, BSc; professional engineer; 10th CG marathon '66; gold '67 PAG; 10th '68 Olympics, '70 CG; 4 national marathon titles; marathon PB: 2:16.13 '75; outstanding harrier and track athlete of '67; *Sarnia Observer* citizen of '67; Sarnia area's outstanding man of '67; mem. Cdn Road Racing Hall of Fame; res. Sarnia, Ont.

BOYD, Barry (t&f); b. 12 Jan 1952, Calgary, Alta.; given name: Barry Allan; UAlta, BComm; administrator CG Foundation; lj specialist; who won every indoor, outdoor ntl age-group title from age 17; '69-79 never out of medals in ntl sr. indoor, outdoor competition; ntl jr. indoor lj record 7.41m; sr. indoor record 7.71m; 9th '75 PAG; PB: 7.77m (wind assisted); ntl outdoor title '74, indoor '75; ret'd following bronze '79 nationals; res. Edmonton, Alta.

BOYD, Mike (curling); b. 13 Jul 1947, Ottawa, Ont.; given name: John Michael; div; c. Marcia, Patrick; Waterloo Lutheran; building service contractor; skipped Ont. Schoolboy champions '66; 3rd NO '72 Brier entry, 2nd '75 Ont. Brier entry, 2nd '76 Ont. mixed champions, all-star ranking each time; 1st player to represent Ont., NO in Brier; co-recipient Sault Ste. Marie sportsman-of-'72 award; Sault Ste. Marie Order of Merit '72; scored eight-ender '71; res. Kanata, Ont.

BOYD, Rob (skiing); b. 15 Feb 1966, Vernon, B.C.; ski coach; started competing at 11; mem. ntl development group '84-85, ntl Alpine B team '85-87, ntl A team '87-97; 27 ntl titles; competed world jrs '84; Olympics '88, '92; World Cup circuit '84-97; 1st Cdn to win WC race in Canada with '89 Whistler downhill victory; tied for 1st Nor-Am downhill standings '86, 2nd '87; 27 top 10 finishes in 84 WC races; tied 3rd '88 WC downhill standings; WC circuit record 3-1-2; Fleishmann Cup title '84; *Ski Racing* magazine Cdn Alpine Skier of yr '88; BC Premier's athletic awards '87-88; BC Sports honor roll '86-87; sports excellence awards '87, '89; coach ntl women's team '04; mem. Cdn Skiing Hall of Fame; res. Whistler, B.C.

BOYES, Dave (rowing); b. 26 Aug 1964, St. Catharines, Ont.; m. Cathy; c. Dillon, MacKenzie, Sidney; tool & die maker GM; began rowing age 15; mem ntl team from '85; gold 4 lw 8s, 1 straight pairs, 1 straight 4s US championships; gold lw 8s '93 world championships; with Jeff Lay, Gavin Hassett, Brian Peaker, silver lw 4s '96 Olympics; silver lw 8s Lucerne '99; res. St. Catharines, Ont.

BOYLE, Charlie (administration, hockey, lacrosse, t&f); b. 19 May 1893, Orillia, Ont.; d. 1966, Fort William, Ont.; given name: Charles Joseph; m. Frances (d), Gertrude Hopwood (d); v/-ptrd. Chapples Dept. Store; mem. Cdn lacrosse title team '12; 3 sprint gold Cdn jr. t&f championships '11; relay WR '13; 20yrs exec. mem. TBAHA, 4 terms pres. '35-55; CAHA meritorious award; life mem. TBAHA; mem. NWO Sports Hall of Fame.

BOYLE, Sheryl (canoeing); b. 13 Nov 1965, Renfrew, Ont.; Carleton ; ex-high performance dir., asst. ntl team coach CCA; former National Gallery projects officer, architect; began competing age 19; mem. ntl team from '86; ntl whitewater titles '93-94; only Cdn female to win world whitewater medals, bronze '93, silver '92; competed '92, '96 Olympics; won Olympic art prizes '92, '94; turned to coaching '97; wrote athlete's marketing guide for Cdn Sport & Fitness Centre; design thesis award Carleton. '90; mem. Ottawa Sports Hall of Fame; res. Ottawa, Ont.

BOYLEN, Christilot (equestrian); b. 12 Apr 1947, Djakarta, Indonesia; given name: Christilot Hansen; m. James A. Boylen; c. Christa-Dora, Billie Jeanne; Branksome Hall; writer, coach; 9 ntl dressage titles; at 17 youngest competitor Olympic Grand Prix dressage '64; 5 gold, 1 silver, 1 bronze in PAG competitions;; best showing ever by Cdn individual dressage 7th '76 Olympics; mem. '64, '68, '72, '76, '80, '84, '92 Olympic teams; 2 US ntl titles; 3 1sts '70 Ohio Dressage Derby; twice ntl EFC horsewoman of year; authored *Canadian Entry and Basic Dressage for North America*; tech. advisor Canadian Dressage Owners and Riders Assn. (CADORA); former v-p International Equestrian Sport Services (IESS) Ltd.; res. Rottingen, Germany.

BOYS, Bev (diving); b. 4 Jul 1951, Toronto, Ont.; m. Stephen Jones; c. Lorin, Suzanne; UMan, UofT; sporting goods business owner '85-93; exec. dir. BC Diving Assn.; 34 ntl sr. titles '66-77; mem. '66, '70, '74, '78 CG '67, '71, '75 PAG, '68, '72, '76 Olympic Games teams; 3 gold, silver, 1 bronze Commonwealth, 2 silver, 1 bronze PAG; US, Russian, Italian, Hungarian, British championships; brief pro diving career; rep. Speedo Canada; BC chair. Cdn Officials Program; 2 Bobbie Rosenfeld trophies; Cdn athlete-of-decade award; Cdn official-of-'00 award; FINA international diving judge, Olympic judge '92, '00, '04; mem. Cdn Olympic, Cdn, Ont. Aquatic, Canada's Sports halls of fame; res. Surrey, B.C.

BRABENEC, Hana (tennis); b. 21 Jun 1928, Prague, Czechoslovakia; given name: Hana Veverka; m. Josef Brabenec; c. Josef Jr.; tennis coach; from 12-27 ranked among top 10 Czech women tennis players; twice runnerup Czech ntl singles; 4 times Czech ntl doubles titlist; '77 coach-mgr. BC tennis team Canada Summer Games, 2 gold, 1 silver, bronze; head coach Vancouver Jericho TC '75-93; res. Vancouver, B.C.

BRABENEC, Josef Jr. (tennis); b. 24 Apr 1957, Ostrava, Czechoslovakia; with John Picken all-Cdn jr.-16, -18, -21 doubles titles, 2 indoor sr. doubles titles; ntl indoor singles '79; mem. '78-79, '82-83 Davis Cup teams; 4th mixed doubles '79 PAG; silver '77 Canada Summer Games; competed French Open, Wimbledon; mem. Jericho TC; res. Surrey, B.C.

BRABENEC, Josef Sr. (tennis); b. 29 Jan 1929, Prague, Czechoslovakia; m. Hana Veverka; c. Josef Jr.; tennis coach; among top Czech jrs.; Belgian jr. title '47; with wife Hana founded Prague youth tennis school '63; capt. Czech ntl teams '64-69; coach Czech ntl jr. team Florida Cup, Orange Bowl '67; head coach Jericho TC Vancouver '70-75; ntl tennis coach '75-84; coached BC team to 2 gold, 2 bronze '73 Canada Summer Games; introduced uniform teaching program throughout Canada; Davis Cup team capt. '77-82, Federation Cup capt. '77-82; with Ken Sinclair ntl 35+ doubles '78, 45+ doubles '80, Monte Carlo international veterans title '78; authored four tennis books; international secty. Czech LTA '63-69; mem. management comm. ILTF '69-71; dir. ITF Continental Training Centre from '93; res. Vancouver, B.C.

BRACK, Bill (motorsport); b. 26 Dec 1935, Toronto, Ont.; given name: William Andrew; automotive dealer; Players' Challenge Series, ntl championships '73-75; drove in 2

Canadian GP Formula 1 events posting highest finish to that time — 8th '69; strong Formula 5000 series contender '69-72; 1st ntl title at 37; won 3 Formula Atlantic races; operates Bill Brack Racing Enterprises and sought to build racing stable '76, included in fold was Jacques Villeneuve '79; Wayne Kelly Trophy '75 for driver best combining sportsmanship with ability; mem. Cdn Motorsport Hall of Fame; res. Toronto, Ont.

BRADLEY-KAMELI, Sue (t&f); b. 17 Sep 1956, Toronto, Ont.; given name: Susan Elaine Bradley; m. Freidoun Kameli; c. Taraneh Christine; UofT, BPHE, San Diego State, UWO., BEd; teacher; hurdles specialist; ntl jr. 100m hurdles record 13.5; juv 80m record 11.1; 3 ntl 100m outdoor, 5 50m indoor titles; mem. '75, '83 PAG '76, '80 Olympic, '79, '83 FISU, '81 Pacific Conf., '82 CG teams; bronze 100m hurdles with PB 13.1 '82 CG; SDSU most valuable track athlete '80; res. London, Ont.

BRAFIELD, Leslie (swimming); b. 7 Feb 1960, Toronto, Ont.; given name: Leslie Ann; Arizona State, UofT; 4th 800m FS '79 PAG; 800m FS title, 2nd 400m FS '80 Canada-West Germany meet; 1st 200m FS, 2nd 200m butterfly, 400m FS '80 CIAU championships; won 400m, 800m FS '80 Japan nationals; mem. '80 Olympic team; res. Bramalea, Ont.

BRAIN, Karen (equestrian); b. 26 Apr 1970, Victoria, B.C.; given name: Karen Ann; part-time research assistant Parkwood Hospital, equestrian coach, trainer; 2 bronze with mare Dasskara '04 Paralympics; won Cdn Open '98 with Double Take; accomplished rider, coach, trainer in 3-day event, representing Canada '98 World Equestrian Games, where she finished in the top-half and secured Canada individual spot '00 Olympics; short- or long-listed for both '99 PAG, '00 Olympics, but could not compete because her horse was injured; riding accident Sept. '01 left her partially paralysed with spinal cord injury; spent 3 months in hospital, almost 2 more yrs rehab as outpatient; started riding again 8 months after accident; could not put feet in stirrups so rode without them using 2 whips to signal horse; attained new goal to represent Canada at the '04 Parlaympics; BC Premier's Athlete of the Year award '98; won Horse Trials Canada scholarship '97; motivational speaker; nationally certified Level II coach; achieved "A" level (highest level) in Pony Club; Greater Victoria Ken Dobson Trophy in recognition of outstanding courage, overcoming adversity and returning to competition; res. London, Ont.

BRAIN, Marilyn (rowing); b. 14 Apr 1959, Halifax, N.S.; m. Howard Campbell; c. Luke, Jefferson; UVic BEd; teacher/coach; with husband operates West Coast Rowing; sweep 2 Canadian Henley, 1 ntl, 3 Head of the Charles, 3 CIAU 8s titles; 1 CIAU coxed 4s title; mem. silver coxed 4s crew '84 Olympics; mem. 6 world championships teams; ret'd. from competition '86; res. Victoria, B.C.

BRAKNIS, Robert (swimming); b. 8 Jan 1973, Montreal, Que.; Florida State; 50m, 100m freestyle, 100m, 200m backstroke specialist; mem. ntl team from '91; bronze 4x100 FS relay '93 Pan-Pacific championship; silver 4x100 medley relay '94 CG; silver 100m back '90 Eight Nations youth meet; gold 100m FS, 100m back, silver 200m back, bronze 50m FS '96 Olympic trials; gold 100m back, 50m FS (tie), silver 100m FS, 200m back '96 Canada Cup; silver

200m back '96 US Grand Prix; competed '96 Olympics; res. Mississauga, Ont.

BRANCATO, George (football); b. 27 May 1931, Brooklyn, N.Y.; m. Barbara Thomson; c. Cindi, Wendy, George Jr., Alicia; Louisiana State, BSc, CalState, MA; offensive, db Chicago Cardinals (NFL) '53-54; CFL Alouettes '55, Rough Riders '56-62; led EFC pass interceptions '57; EFC all-star '61; defensive asst. to Jack Gotta '70; head coach Ottawa '74-84; asst. Saskatchewan '85-89; head coach Cape Breton '90; asst. coach Carleton '92; coaching consultant Rough Riders '93, asst. coach Shreveport Pirates '94; coach Arena Football Charlotte, Las Vegas; coach/GM Ottawa Omega NA Indoor football; mem. 4 Grey Cup finalists, 3 winners, 1 as player; Annis Stukus Trophy CFL coach of '75; International Italian of year in football '76; mem. Ottawa Sports Hall of Fame; res. Nepean, Ont.

BRANCH, Cecilia (t&f); b. 14 Jan 1957, Halifax, N.S.; m. Mark Hayes; c. Jessie, Bridget; Dalhousie, Nevada, BSc; HS teacher; HS basketball MVP '73; bronze 100m '73 ntl championships; pentathlon silver '73 Canada Games; hurdles specialist; mem. '79 PAG, '80 Olympic teams; bronze '79 AIAW championships, all-American; most outstanding athlete, t&f athlete St. Patrick's HS '75; most outstanding t&f performer Nevada '77, '79; dean's list '77; Cdn Masters 400m hurdles record '92; res. Nepean, Ont.

BRANCH, David (administration/hockey); b. 27 Nov 1948, Bathurst, N.B.; hockey exec.; pres. CHL; secty-mgr. OHA '73-77; exec.dir. CAHA '77-79; commissioner OMJHL, now OHL, '79-98; pres. CHL '96-98; res. Toronto, Ont.

BRANCHAUD, Mike (softball/hockey); b. 30 Aug 1965, Cornwall, Ont.; given name: Michael Joseph Lorenzo William; m. Nancy Ann Pearce; UofOtt BSS; Canadian Adult Recreational Hockey Assn. program co-ordinator; mem.Stittsville 56ers jr/sr teams, Turpin Pontiacs, Fingal; silver '93 ntl championships; played as mem. famed Eddie Feigner King and His Court 4-man exhibition team '93-98; mem. King of Diamonds fast-pitch organization specializing in player development '99; played Jr. B hockey CharLan, Morrisburg; assumed CARHA post '98; res. Cornwall, Ont.

BRASSARD, Jean-Luc (skiing); b. 24 Aug 1972, Valleyfield, Que.; motivational speaker Ntl Speaker's Bureau; freestyle moguls specialist; mem. Cdn skiing "Air Force"; began competing age 13; mem. ntl team '90-02; 20 world cup gold, 27 WC silver/bronze; 2 overall world titles; competed '92, '94, '98, '02 Olympics; moguls gold '94 Olympics; 2 World moguls titles; with sister Anne-Marie saved 16-year-old from drowning at Valleyfield, Que. '93; FIS freestyle rookie of '91; 1st Cdn to win Blackcomb WC event '98; co-winner (with Kate Pace) John Semmelink award '94; flag-bearer '98 Olympics; Gillette World Champions award; ret'd from competition '02; res. Grande-Ile, Que.

BRASSEUR, Isabelle (figure skating); b. 28 Jul 1970, Kingsbury, Que.; m. Rocco Marval; c. Gabriella; began competing at 7; mem. ntl team '85-94; with partner Pascal Courchesne '82-86, won ntl. jr pairs title '85; hooked up with Lloyd Eisler '87 scoring '89 Skate Electric, '88, '90 Skate Canada victories; 5 ntl sr. pairs titles (with Eisler);

4 world silver; bronze '92, '94 Olympics; competed '88, '92, '94 Olympics; pro '94; Cdn pro pairs title '97; Cdn Meritorious Service award; with Eisler produced Dreams on Ice show; 2 books devoted to their careers; mem. Cdn Olympic, Canada's Sports, Cdn Figure Skating halls of fame; res. New Jersey.

BRATTY, Gary (weightlifting); b. 15 Jun 1956, Hamilton, Ont.; given name: Gary Ross; McMaster; coach; Hamilton & District, CANUSA Games trials titles '71; silver '71 CANUSA Games; ntl Jr. Olympics 67.5kg title '75; all ntl jr. records, Commonwealth jr. snatch 59.9kg '76; 23 class records Ont. jr., sr., ntl Commonwealth jr.; gold Can-US '76 meet; ntl jr. snatch, clean & jerk records 67.5kg class '76; Ont., ntl sr. lightweight title '77; mem. '78 CG team; PB: 262.5kg total lift '77; best lifter major meet awards '73, '76; res. Halifax, N.S.

BRAUNSTEIN, Terry (curling); b. 18 Apr 1939, Winnipeg, Man.; m. Andrea Greenberg; c. Lisa, Danny; UMan, BComm clothing wholesaler; at 18 won Man. Consols to become youngest Brier skip, forced playoff before bowing to Matt Baldwin 10-6; forced rules revision which prohibited schoolboys from competing for Canadian men's title; rep. Man. '65 Brier; 3 Man. bonspiel grand aggregate titles; 3 carspiel titles; mem. Winnipeg Granite Club, Man., Cdn Curling halls of fame; res. Winnipeg, Man.

BRAY, Shirley (curling); b. 12 Sept 1929, Brandon, Man.; given name: Shirley Elizabeth Walker; m. Richard Merton Bray; c. Reginald, Sandra; all-star 3rd '68 Macdonald Lassie; 3rd Man. Seagram Mixed champion '75; skip Man. entry '85 sr women's nationals; CLCA delegate '77-82; Curl Canada Level II instructor, Level III umpire; pres. MLCA '80-81, hon. life mem. MLCA from '83; 1st woman recipient Gordon McGunigal Memorial Medal for contribution, dedication to game; Curl Canada Herb Millham Award '83; CLCA Appreciation award '85; twice Westman Sportsman of year award nominee; YMCA Woman of Distinction award '90; Brandon Sportsman of year '90; served in executive capacity for varied ntl championships and at club, provincial level; mem. Man., Cdn Curling halls of fame; res. Brandon, Man.

BRAZLEY, Carl (football); b. 5 Sep 1957, Louisville, Ky; m. Jan; c. Sunni Rose, Nicholas; Western Kentucky; pres/CEO Mo' Better Marketing; football player, film business exec.; db; pro Montreal '80-81, Ottawa '81-82, Toronto '83-86, '88, San Diego, Minnesota '87; 5 times EFC all-star; CFL all-star '83; 2 Grey Cup finals, 1 winner; defensive award '83 Grey Cup final; governor Louisville U; res. Louisville, Ky.

BRECK, Ian (football/coaching); b. 11 Aug 1947, Renfrew, Ont.; given name: Ian Ewart; m. Kathryn Barnard; c. Erika, Bridget, Elizabeth; Springfield Coll. BSc, Queen's BEd; football coach; joined Bishop's coaching staff as asst. '84; head coach from '88; through '96 coaching record 56-22-4, 5 regular season titles, 3 playoff championships, appearances in 3 ntl College Bowl championships; OQIFC, CIAU coach of '92; res. Lennoxville, Que.

BREEN, Joe (football); b. 23 Apr 1897, Toronto, Ont.; d. 13 Oct 1978, Montreal, Que.; given name: Joseph Melville;

m. Winnifred Westman; c. Melwyn Joseph; UofT BSc; civil engineer; capt. UofT '19-20, Grey Cup winner '20; capt. Toronto Argos, Parkdale Canoe Club '21, '24; coach UWO football '29-34; 1 Intercollegiate title; mem. UofT, UWO W-Club, Canadian Football, Canada's Sports halls of fame.

BREMNER, Janice (synchro swim); b. 15 Jul 1974, Burlington, Ont.; began competing age 9; mem. ntl team from '90; team gold '96 French Open; team silver '95 PAG '96 Olympic Games, '94 World Aquatic championships; Petro-Canada Cup team gold '92. 2 ntl jr team gold, one duet gold; Petro-Canada Olympic Torch scholarship '94; res. Lynn Valley, B.C.

BRENNAN, Bernie (football/harness racing); b. 1 Oct 1927, Desoronto, Ont.; given name: Bernard Francis; m. Grace Lunney; c. Maureen, Mike, Anne, Paul, Peter, Patrick, Laurie; Guelph, DVM; ret'd. veterinarian; went directly from St. Pat's HS where he won Doran award to Ottawa Rough Riders as halfback '46, Gruen Big 4 rookie of yr trophy; standout at Guelph (OVC) '47-51; rejoined Riders Grey Cup winner '51; standout defenceman Kemptville Royals, Brockville Magedomas hockey clubs; dir. Rideau Carleton Raceway; track veterinarian appointed by ORC responsible for drug testing and soundness; trained many horses on farm near Kemptville; competed on Ottawa, Toronto, Montreal and U.S. tracks; part-owner famed Cam Fella; operated Alta Vista Animal Clinic; mem. Ont. Racing Commission; mem. U Guelph, Ottawa Sports halls of fame; res. Kemptville, Ont.

BRENNER, Veronica (skiing); b. 18 Oct 1974, Scarborough, Ont.; freestyle aerials specialist; 5 ntl titles; worlds bronze '97; ranked 2nd '95, 1st '97 World Cup standings; 8 WC race gold, 5 silver, 1 bronze; mem. ntl team '94-02; competed '98, '02 Olympics; Olympic aerials silver '02; res. Sharon, Ont.

BRETON, Skip (broomball); b. 18 Apr 1964, Mattice, Ont.; given name: Yvan Eugene; m. Julie Ryan; c. Ryanne Hailey, Olivia Michelle; carpenter; competed for Embrun Plumbing 9 time ntl champion; mem. '91 world title team; 6 ntl championship MVP awards; 3 Ottawa ACT broomball, ball hockey awards; 2 Ont., ntl ball hockey championships; ntl silver, bronze; centre 3 ntl all-star teams; res. Kanata, Ont.

BREWER, Carl (hockey); b. 21 Oct 1938, Toronto, Ont.; d. 25 Aug 2001, Toronto, Ont.; given name: Carl Thomas; m. Marilyn Rea; c. Christopher, Michael, Anna-Lisa; McMaster, UofT, BA; businessman; Weston Jr. B; Marlboros Jr. A; '56 Memorial Cup, MVP '57-58; pro Toronto '57-65, '79-80; twice NHL penalty leader; mem. 3 Stanley Cup winners; quit following dispute with coach Punch Imlach '65; regained amateur status '66; mem. ntl team '66-67; outstanding def '67 world tournament; player-coach Muskegon (IAHL) '67-68, Finland '68-69; TML sold rights to Detroit but refused to play before '69-70 season; St.Louis '70-72; left retirement '79-80 for limited duty TML; once 1st, twice 2nd team all-star; NHL record: 604 scheduled games, 25g, 198a, 72 playoff games, 3g, 17a; 5 all-star games; TV color commentator WHA games; gained legal ownership of name Toronto Maple Leafs '83; key figure in ret'd player successful legal action against NHL over pension funds; mem. Canada's Sports Hall of Fame.

BREWER, Eric (hockey); b. 17 Apr 1979, Vernon, B.C.; def. Kamloops (BCAHA) '94-95, Prince George (WHL) '95-98, Louisville (AHL) '99-00; NHL with NYI '98-'00, Edmonton '00-04; Team Canada '02, '04 World Cup (gold), '02 Olympics (gold); ntl jr. team '98; Prince George rookie-of-yr award, all-scholastic award; NHL record (through '04) 404 scheduled games, 34g, 79a, 12 playoff games, 2g, 8a; res. Edmonton, Alta.

BREWSTER, Ken (field hockey/soccer); b. 14 Jul 1935, Barbados, W.I.; Carleton, BComm, UofOtt, MBA; teacher; Barbados ntl soccer team '59-60; mem. Barbados and W.I. ntl FH teams '57-62; mem. exec. Ottawa Field Hockey Club '70-76; coached Ottawa team to silver medal ntl jr. field hockey championships '75; development co-ordinator Outaouais FHC '72-75; res. Orleans, Ont.

BRICKER, Cal (t&f); b. 1884; d. 24 Apr 1963, Grenfell, Sask.; given name: Calvin David; UofT, DDS; dentist; all-around champion UofT and individual intercollegiate champion 1905-06; specialist running broad jump (lj), hop, step and jump (tj); won both events '08 Olympic trials setting long jump record 24'1.5" which held 27 years; bronze lj 4th tj '08 Olympics; lj silver '12 Olympics; officer in charge of Cdn athletes '19 Paris Games for service personnel; mem. UofT; Cdn Olympic, Sask., Canada's Sports halls of Fame.

BRIDLE, Wezer (volleyball); b. 29 Jul 1926, Winnipeg, Man.; m. Joyce; c. Charles, Jim, Clancy, Jeff, Jan, Cal; ret'd. CNR; excelled in all aspects of volleyball as player, coach, official and administrator; founded Man. Volleyball Assn., 1st pres.; founded Central Y Kids program to develop game as sport of choice for youngsters; promoted. coached them to Manitoba's 1st jr. ntl championship '65; formed Manitoba's age-class development system; coached UWpg to 1st CIAU title '68; prov., ntl volleyball officials 20-plus yrs, officiating in CIAU, ntl, Pan-Am, Olympic, NORCECA championships; instrumental in forming Man. Volleyball Officials Assn.; ED Wpg men's league; life mem. Sask. Volleyball Assn.; mem. Man. Sports, Volleyball Canada halls of fame; res. Winnipeg, Man.

BRIEN, Alvin (canoeing); b. 12 Jul 1956, Halifax, N.S.; d. 3 Feb 1982, Caribbean Ocean; Dalhousie, BPhE; teacher; 3000m-3-mile distance runner Maritime indoor, outdoor meets '72-79; kayak specialist; ntl junior K2 500m; Continental Cup K4 500m '79; Commonwealth '80 Olympic team; ntl K4 1000m title '80; died in sailing accident.

BRIEN, Don (canoeing); b. 1 Sep 1959, Halifax, N.S.; given name: Donald Michael; Dalhousie, BPhE, UBC; provincial, ntl x-country runner; kayak specialist; NA jr. K2, K4 titles '76; mem. ntl team from '77; NA jr. K1, K2, K4 10,000m titles, ntl juve. jr. K1, K2 titles, gold K1, silver K2, K4 Canada Summer Games '77; ntl jr. K2 500m, sr. C15 titles '78; ntl sr. K4, C15 titles, gold K4 500m Continental Cup '79; gold K1, K2, K4 1000m, K4 500m '83 Pan-Am championships; with Colin Shaw bronze 1000m K2 '85 world championships; mem. '80, '84 Olympic teams; res. Calgary, Alta.

BRIGDEN, William (canoeing); b. 11 Apr 1916, Winnipeg, Man.; d. 16 Jan 2005, Winnipeg, Man.; m. Marion Patton; c. Robert, Anne, Paul; canoe manufacturer; with partner Jim Nickle dominated 2-man competition '51 Olympic trials; mem. '52 Olympic team; with Don Starkell twice won pro Flin Flon canoe derby; competed in 6 Le Voyageur Winnipeg to Lockport races winning '70; at 63 2nd 15-mile Kenora race; mem. Man. Sports Hall of Fame.

BRIGHT, Johnny (football); b. 11 Jun 1931, Fort Wayne, Ind.; d. 14 Dec 1983, Edmonton, Alta.; div.; c. Darrell Michael, Deanie LaDette, Shaughna Darcine, Kandis Denita; Drake, BSc, UAlta, BEd; Jr. HS principal; HS all-state football, track, basketball; pitched Des Moines, Iowa, to state titles; set 20 Drake football, basketball, track records; led all US college ground gainers, all-American; 1st draft '51 Philadelphia (NFL) as rb; CFL Calgary '52-54, Edmonton '54-64; 7 times WFC all-star, 4 times all-Cdn; Schenley Outstanding Player '59; CFL record: 71td, 10,909yds on 1969 carries for 5.5 avg.; 4 times CFL rushing leader; 5 times surpassed 1000yds single season; 3 times led CFL total carries, 5 times surpassed 200 a season; 4 Grey Cup finals, 3 winners; Drake football player of century; Indiana silver anniversary basketball team; pro basketball Harlem Globetrotters; pitched perfect game Iowa State tournament; 74-27 record as HS football coach, 304-46 basketball; coach Edmonton Monarchs pro fastball team, '72 coach of year; Edmonton athlete of '59; mem. Alta., Edmonton, Iowa, Eskimos, Canadian Football halls of fame.

BRILL, Debbie (t&f); b. 10 Mar 1953, Mission, B.C.; m. Doug Coleman; c. Neil Bogart Ray, Katie, Jake; UBC; hj coach; originator reverse jumping style known as Brill Bend; mem. 5 Olympic, 3 PAG, 3 CG, 2 World Cup teams; gold '70, '82 CG, '71 PAG, '79 WC, International Cup, '82 Millrose Games; 8 ntl titles, 28 international meet titles; 1st Canadian, NA woman to clear 6' barrier '71; numerous Canadian records; world indoor 1.99m '82, Commonwealth record 1.96m '79, US outdoor record 1.95m '82; more than decade ranked among world's best female jumpers; 2 Jack W. Davies, 3 Fred Rowell, '67 Myrtle Cook, 9 Dr. Calvin Bricker Memorial Trophies; with Debbie Van Kiekebelt co-winner Rosenfeld female athlete of '71; BC athlete of decade '80, BCTFA outstanding female athlete of '80; fed. govt. sport excellence award; BC master athlete of '97; BC Women in Sport Leaders & Legends award; Officer Order of Canada '83; mem. Cdn Olympics, BC Sports, Ridge Meadows halls of fame; res. Burnaby, B.C.

BRIND'AMOUR, Rod (hockey); b. 9 Aug 1970, Ottawa, Ont.; m. Kelle; c. Briley Olivia; Notre Dame Coll, Michigan State; ctr/lw; CCHA freshman of '88-89; drafted from Notre Dame Jr.A by St. Louis; NHL St. Louis '89-91, Philadelphia '91-99, Carolina '00-04; NHL all-rookie team '90; Bobby Clarke trophy '92; mem. Team Canada '92-94 worlds, '97 World Cup, '98 Olympics; NHL record (through '04): 1109 scheduled games, 351g, 560a, 116 playoff games, 38g, 51a; Queen's Golden Jubilee medal for support of Cdn Cystic Fibrosis Foundation; res. Marlton, N.J.

BRISSON, Thérése (hockey/ringette); b. 5 Oct 1966, Dollard-des-Ormeaux, Que.; Concordia PhD; ex-prof. Kinesiology UNB, interim ED Athletics Canada; Concordia female rookie of '87, female athlete of '88, '89; def MVP Ferland 4-Glaces Que. champs '93; mem. Team Quebec '94, '95 women's sr. ntl champs; def MVP '95; mem.

NB Maritime Sports Blades ntl bronze team '96; mem. Team Canada from '93; Olympic gold '02, silver '98; 7 world, 2 Pacific Rim, 3 3-Nations Cup titles; with ntl team won '00 4-Nations Cup; capt. '99-01 world title teams; mem. WWHC all-star team; mem. Mississauga Ice Bears, Montreal Wingstar; competed in '90 world ringette championships; NCCP ringette course conductor; mem. ringette ntl coaching comm.; mem. Concordia Sports Hall of Fame; res. Mississauga, Ont.

BRITTON, Bill (football); b. 15 Dec 1935, Kirkland Lake, Ont.; given name: William Leonard; m. Linda Susan Menzies; c. Christopher, Angela, Daniel, Jane; UWO, BA, UBC, LLB; lawyer; 3 times all-star, sr. year MVP UWO; 1st pick BC '58 CFL college draft; fb/lb/punt returner Lions '58-61, Calgary '62-65; 4yrs commentator Calgary football radio broadcasts; 7yrs dir. Stampeders, pres. '83-84; UWO W-Club Sports Hall of Fame; res. Calgary, Alta.

BRKOVICH, Mike (basketball); b. 6 Apr 1958, Windsor, Ont.; given name: Milan; Michigan State; real estate landlord, developer; led W.D. Lowe HS to prov. titles '76-77; 2 1st team all-city; mem. MS Spartans '77-81 winning Big 10 title '78-79, NCAA title '79; among teammates was Magic Johnson; 1st Cdn to start in an NCAA championship game '79; most improved player award as freshman; team assists leader '79-80; co-capt. '80-81; nicknamed "Golden Arm" for outstanding perimeter shooting; mem. ntl team '79 PAG; drafted by and last cut Milwaukee Bucks '81; mem. CBA Milwaukee Flyers '81-82 averaging 18 points per game; competed at sr. men's level '82-92 vs. NCAA schools; mem. Windsor-Essex County Sports Hall of Fame; res. Windsor, Ont.

BROADBENT, Punch (hockey); b. 13 Jul 1893, Ottawa, Ont.; d. 6 Mar 1971, Ottawa, Ont.; given name: Harold Lawton; m. Leda; c. Sally Ann; RCAF officer; amateur New Edinburgh Cliffsides; pro Senators '10-15, '18-23, '27-28, Montreal Maroons '24-27, NY Americans '28-29; 110 NHL goals; 3 Stanley Cup winners Ottawa, 1 Montreal; '21-22 goal-scoring leader with 32; scored 1 or more goals 16 consecutive games (record still stands) '21-22; mem. Ottawa, Canadian Forces, Hockey halls of fame.

BROCHU, Claude (administration); b. 29 Oct 1944, Quebec City; given name: Claude Renaud; m. Michelle; UofOtt, BA, McMaster, MBA; former pres./general partner Montreal Expos; exec. v-p. Seagram, Adams Distillers prior to suceeding John McHale as CEO of Expos '86; mem. ML exec. council, ML Baseball Enterprises Inc., Baseball Operations, Professional Baseball Agreement, ML restructuring comm.; Canada's Baseball Man of Year '90; authored *My Turn at Bat*; mem. Order of Canada; res. Montreal, Que.

BROCK, Dieter (football); b. 12 Feb 1951, Alabama; given name: Ralph Dieter; m. Jamie; c. Jake, Haley, Kaleb; Auburn, Jacksonville State; coach/qb; NFL tryouts with Buffalo, Green Bay, Cleveland; pro Winnipeg (CFL) '74-83, Hamilton '83-84; erased Sam Etcheverry's 25-year-old record with 4796yds passing (topped by Warren Moon) '82; single-season pass attempt record 566 '81, 41 single-game completions vs. Ottawa '81; 4 times WFC passing leader; all-Canadian '81; Jeff Nicklin Trophy, Schenley Outstanding Player '80-81; contract dispute led to trade

to Hamilton for Tom Clements '83; Grey Cup finalist '84; LA (NFL) '85-87; asst. UAlabama-Birmingham '91-94; asst. Hamilton '95, Ottawa '96, Edmonton '99-'00; asst. Alabama State '97; HS coach/AD '98; asst. Tusculum Coll. from '00; mem. Cdn, Blue Bombers Football, Jacksonville State, Alabama halls of fame; res. Greeneville, Tenn.

BROCK, Henry (administration); b. 14 May 1859, Oakville, Ont., d. 26 Aug 1933, Toronto, Ont.; given name: Henry Thompson; standout equestrian, shooter, cricketer, football player; mem. Argonaut Rowing Club; bravery award for rescue near-drowning victim; 1st secty AAU of C 1883, v-p 1887-88, pres. 1889, 1900; mem. Cdn Olympic Sports Hall of Fame.

BROCKWAY, Dot (all-around); b. 28 Nov 1901, Milltown, N.B., d. 10 Sep 1981, Milltown, N.B.; given name: Dorothy; 6 gold, 1 bronze 1st Maritime ladies track meet '26; mem. NB sr. ladies' basketball title team '25-26; St. Croix golf league Dr. Gray trophy ladies title '48, '51-52, '56; prov., international club tennis competition titles '28-29; mem. NB Sports Hall of Fame.

BRODA, Turk (hockey); b. 15 May 1914, Brandon, Man.; d. 17 Oct 1972, Toronto, Ont.; given name: Walter; m. Betty Williams; c. Barbara, Bonny, Betty; goalie/coach; Brandon juv/jrs, Winnipeg Monarchs jrs '33-34; IHL champion Detroit Olympics '34-35; sold to Toronto for then-record $8,000; pro career spanned 16 seasons, 2 out for WW2 service; Vezina Trophy '41, '48, shared '51 with Al Rollins; 62 regular season shutouts, 13 in playoffs; considered money player, excelled in playoffs posting 1.99 goals-against avg. 101 games; mem. 5 Stanley Cup winners; coached Toronto Marlboros to 3 league titles, 2 Memorial Cups; coached London Nationals, Moncton jrs, Quebec Aces; mem. Man. Sports, Man, Cdn Hockey, Royal Cdn Legion halls of fame.

BRODERICK, Kathleen (field hockey); b. 16 Jan 1947, Calgary, Alta.; given name: Kathleen Evann; UMan, BPhE, UAlta, MA; coach Mt. Allison '68-69, UAlta '73-78, Alta jrs '78; asst coach York from '79, associate coach ntl team from '78; mem. '69 Canada Games silver medal team, 3 ntl title teams; mem. ntl team '76-77; asst. coach '78 World Cup, '79 world championships, '81 World Cup, '83 silver medal World Cup, silver '91, bronze '87, '95 PAG teams; coached in '84, '88, '92 Olympics; 3M coach of '89; res. Toronto, Ont.

BRODEUR, Martin (hockey); b. 6 May 1972, Montreal, Que.; div. Melanie; c. Anthony, William, Jeremy, Anabelle Antoinette; followed in footsteps of photographer father Denis who played goal on Canada's '56 Olympic bronze medal team; moved from Montreal midget to St. Hyacinthe jrs; minor pro Utica '92-93; NHL with New Jersey from '92; Calder Trophy, NHL all-rookie team '93-94; 2 Vezina, 4 William Jennings trophies; mem. Team Canada '98, '02 (gold) Olympics; competed '96, '04 World Cup; 3 Stanley Cup winners; 1st goalie in NHL history to post 4 40-win seasons; unprecedented 8 straight 30-win seasons; NHL record 43 wins '97-98, repeated '99-00; NHL record 4433 minutes played single season '95-96; NHL record (through '04): 740 scheduled games, 403-217-105, 43,511min, 1584ga, 75so, 144 playoff games, 84-60, 9029min, 280ga,

20so; hosts Montreal charity golf tournament annually; ESPY award '95; competed 5 NHL all-star games; scored goal vs. Montreal '97 playoffs; res. Montreal, Que.

BRONFMAN, Charles (builder/baseball); b. 27 June 1931, Montreal, Que.; given name: Charles Rosner; m. Andrea Morrison; c. Stephen Rosner, Ellen Jane, Jeremy, Pippa, Tony; Trinity Coll., McGill; 6 hon. doctorates; chair. KOOR Industries; dir. Vivendi Universal; ex-co-chair. Seagram Distillery; key figure as principal shareholder in bringing NL baseball to Canada with inception of Montreal Expos; board chair. '69-90; served vital roles on various ML committees; although he played a hands-off role with club management he enjoyed suiting up in his uniform 83 (a big Seagram brand) at spring training; deeply involved with cultural and philanthropic life in Canada through CRB Foundation; mem. Order of Canada, Cdn Baseball Hall of Fame; res. New York, N.Y.

BRONSON, Pat (all-around); b. 22 Oct 1947, Peterborough, Ont.; given name: Patricia Pauline; Sir Sanford Fleming Coll.; administrator SSFC; although not large in stature, speed, agility, natural talent enabled her to play leading role in several sports, particularly hockey, softball, basketball; 3 HS t&f titles; founding mem. Ont. Women's HA '75; mem. '83 Ont. Sr. D title hockey team, ntl C titlists; coach '90 Ont. Sr. B team; mem. '92 Ont. Sr. A title team; mem. 5 Peterborough city softball title teams '64-68; PWSA Int. B title '66, 4 Int. A title teams; Ont. Tier II titlists '80; leading batter award; mem. Ont./Eastern Cdn basketball title team '68; MVP Peterborough Women's Basketball Assn. '69-70; mem. 5 consec. Peterborough title teams; mem. 3 slo-pitch title teams; most dedicated player award '87; Peterborough female athlete of '76; YMCA woman of '80; hockey sportsmanship/citizenship award '84-85; basketball dedication award; pres. PWBA '71-93; volunteer coach/administrator Special Olympics; tech. sports chair. '98 Ont. Winter Games; mem. Peterborough Sports Hall of Fame; res. Peterborough, Ont.

BROOK, Tom (builder); b. 27 Jan 1908, Pelham, N.Y.; d. 2 Aug 1981, Calgary, Alta.; moved to Calgary '41 and reorganized Stampeders organization; pres. Stampeders '48-51; club dir. '56-58; hired Les Lear as coach '48 and, personally guaranteeing players' salaries, brought in such stars as Woody Strode and Chuck "Sugarfoot" Anderson; team went on to win Grey Cup with undefeated season then won first 10 the following year; booster of interlocking schedule but staunch supporter of single championship game rather than home-and-home series; mem. Cdn Football Hall of Fame.

BROOKER, Todd (skiing); b. 24 Nov 1959, Waterloo, Ont.; m. Lisa Uffelman; c. Zoe, Samantha, Elle; Tim Horton franchise owner; ski lodge operator; father mem. '56 Olympic hockey team; 1st downhill, 2nd slalom, 3rd GS '75 ntl junior; European Cup circuit '78-79, '81; World Cup tour '78-79, '81-84; 3rd downhill '81 NZ championships; broke into winners' circle WC tour Kitzbuhel Austria, Aspen Colorado '83, Furano Japan '85; WC record 3-3-1; fed. govt. excellence award '85; mem. '84 Olympic team; injuries forced retirement from competition '87; *CBS TV* skiing color commentator; mem. Cdn Skiing Hall of Fame; res. Thornbury, Ont.

BROOKS, Lela (speed skating); b. 7 Feb 1908, Toronto, Ont.; d. 11 Sep 1990, Owen Sound; given name: Lela Alene; m. Russ Campbell (d); c. Art, Carol, Donna, Dorothy; m. Clifford Bleich; began collecting Ont., ntl titles, records '21; by end '25 had broken 6 world records; won 3 of 4 races and overall women's title '26 world competition; continued to add to ntl, NA honors, several world records including 1/2-mile indoor, outdoor, 3/4-mile outdoor; mile record Detroit Mardi Gras Festival '28; NA indoor title '35; qualified '36 Olympics but opted for retirement; 1st woman admitted to Old Orchard Skating Club, Toronto; from outset of career to retirement won all titles available to women speed skaters, Ont. indoor, outdoor, all-Canadian, international and world; mem. Cdn Speed Skating, Canada's Sports halls of fame.

BROPHY, John (hockey/coaching); b. 20 Jan 1933, Antigonish, N.S.; m. Nancy White; ret'd coach; def. Halifax (MMHL) '50-51, Troy (IHL) '52-53, Milwaukee (IHL) '52-53, Charlotte (EHL) '55-60, New Haven (EHL) '59-61, '68-70, Long Island (EHL) '61-72, Philadelphia (EHL) '62-64, Jersey Devils (EHL) '71-73; coaching Long Island (NAHL) '73-74, Hampton Gulls (SHL/AHL) '74-78, Birmingham (WHA/CHA) '78-81, Nova Scotia (AHL) '81-84, St. Catharines (AHL) '85-86, Toronto (NHL) asst. '84-85, head coach '86-89, Hampton Roads (ECHL) '89-00, Wheeling (ECHL) '01-03; 3 ECHL, 1 SHL titles; WHA, SHL coach of yr awards; pro coaching record 1027 victories, 2nd in pro ranks to Scotty Bowman's 1244; ECHL coach of yr award bears his name; res. Forest, Va.

BROSSEAU, Eugene (boxing); b. 1895, Montreal, Que.; d. 1968, Montreal, Que.; post office employee; ntl amateur welterweight titles '15-16, US welter title '16, middleweight '17; fought series of San Francisco exhibitions on behalf of Red Cross '17; blow to neck in '19 bout with George Chip caused left arm paralysis; brief comeback '20; pro record: 27 bouts, won 17 by KO, 7 by decision, 1 no-contest, lost decision to Jack Bloomfield and was KO'd by Mike McTigue; instructor '24 Olympic team; only Canadian to win 2 US amateur ring crowns and be selected to halls of fame in both amateur, pro ranks; mem. Cdn Olympic, Canada's Sports, Cdn Boxing halls of fame.

BROTHERS, Tanya (t&f); b. 2 Jul 1963, Thunder Bay, Ont.; UMan; sprint specialist; ntl jr. 50m indoor title '80; jr. outdoor 100-, 200m '81; Canada Games 100-, 200m titles; ntl indoor 200m '82; 3 CIAU titles; mem. '83 FISU, PAG teams; silver 4x100m relay '83 FISU Games; bronze 4x100m relay '83 PAG; PB: 100m 11.70, 200m 23.45; CIAU female indoor t&f athlete-of-yr award; res. Winnipeg, Man.

BROUILLARD, Lou (boxing); b. 23 May 1911, St. Eugene, Que.; d. 14 Sep 1984, Taunton, Mass.; given name: Lucien Pierre; dog breeder; 4 successful amateur years; beat Jack Thompson for world pro welterweight title '31; lost crown to Jackie Fields '32; KO'd Ben Jeby in 7th '33 to win NY Commission middleweight title; lost title to Vince Dundee '33; lost 2 title bids on fouls to Marcel Thil; barred from ring 1 year; mgr. received life suspension; won 60 of 1st 64 bouts, 44 by KO; pro record: 140 bouts, won 64 by KO, 43 on decision, 1 on foul, 3 draws, lost 25 decisions, 3 on fouls, once KO'd (Tiger Jack Fox); mem. Canada's Sports, Canadian Boxing halls of fame.

BROWN, Bobby (hockey); b. 2 Apr 1933, Windsor, Ont.; given name: Robert Clyde; m. Elizabeth Schmidt; c. Suzann, Cheryl, Michael; supervisor estimating C.H. McInnis; mem. Lowe HS Ont, WSSA champs, Windsor Bearcats Jr, champs, 2 OHA Sr. A champs; Windsor Spitfires leading scorer '52; signed by Detroit Red Wings '52 and sent to Sherbrooke; 10yrs Windsor Bulldogs, all-time leading scorer (377g); joined Galt for silver medal '62 worlds; mem. Windsor Bulldogs Allan Cup champs '63; toured Europe with Bulldogs; invited to join KW Dutchmen for '56 Olympics but ruled ineligible because of pro background; player/mgr. Red Wings alumni many years; standout baseball pitcher in youth; several hockey scoring awards; MVP, Most Popular Player awards; avid golfer; mem. Windsor/Essex Sports Hall of Fame; res. Windsor, Ont.

BROWN, Cara (ringette); b. 15 Sep 1965, Edmonton, Alta.; consulting economist; competed 16 ntl championship, 8 gold, 3 silver, 2 bronze '80-00; 3 world championship gold; 6 time ntl championship all-star ctr; scholarship bears her name; ret'd from competition '01; mem. Cdn Ringette Hall of Fame; res. Calgary, Alta.

BROWN, Clayton (rowing/football); b. 16 Sep 1940, St. Catharines, Ont.; given name: Clayton Wayne; m. Lynn Crozier; c. David, Matthew, Susan; Guelph, hons BSc; teacher; mem. 3 SOSSA football title teams; all-Ont. tackle '60; t/punter Guelph '63-65; rejected Montreal pro bid; HS coach from '69; Ont. heavyweight jr. 8 rowing title team, NA Intermediate heavy 8s '59; mem. 3 Cdn Henley heavy 8s title teams; NA sr. 8s title; mem. '60, '68 Olympic teams; HS rowing coach '69-76; mem. Ont. Coaches Assn., rowing, football; res. St. Catharines, Ont.

BROWN, Colin (shooting); b. 28 Jul 1924, Ancaster, Ont.; m. Shirley Bray; c. Charles, Susan, Becky; major (ret'd) Cdn Forces; employed Hamilton Golf & Country Club; began shooting as cadet '39; competed as "Canloan" officer 2Bn Argyll & Sutherland Highlanders WW2; mem. 2 Cdn Forces Bisley teams; '56, '58 Cdn Forces service rifle champion; mem. '62, '65 DCRA Bisley teams, adjutant '66, commandant '73; Bisley Alexander match title '59, 3rd grand aggregate '60; mem. 2 Palma teams; 4 top DCRA F-Class competitor awards; 2 terms exec. v-p DCRA; deputy chair. DCRA council; DCRA 60-year badge '98; res. Ancaster, Ont.

BROWN, D. Wes (football); b. 1894, Ottawa, Ont.; d. Apr 1962, Ottawa, Ont.; began 37yr association with football as ticket manager for Rough Riders '25; held various exec. roles with that club; secty IRFU '41-42, '45, '47-61; appointed permanent secty of what would become Eastern div. of CFL '48; CFL outstanding service award; mem. Ottawa Sports, Cdn Football halls of fame.

BROWN, Dale (boxing); b. 15 Dec 1971, Calgary, Alta.; m. Anne; dock laborer; light heavyweight; mem. Bow Waters Amateur BC, coached by father Bob Brown; mem. ntl team '87-94; 3 ntl titles; Puerto Rico Invitational tournament '89; silver '90 CG; bronze '91, '93 Worlds, PAG, Canada Cup; 81kg gold '94 CG; mem. '92 Olympic team; amateur record 210-40; pro '95; NABF cruiserweight title '97-00, CPBF title '01; pro record 22-2-1, 16kos; res. Montreal, Que.

BROWN, Dick (football); b. 9 May 1925, Cleveland, Ohio; d. 20 May 2000, Dundas, Ont.; given name: Richard Anthony; m. Anne Peetsalu; c. Mark Anthony, Melanie Louise; UofT, BA; asst. football coach, athletics facilities supervisor Guelph; all-city HS end, punter; CIAU all-star tb pro Hamilton '50-54, Toronto '55-57, Montreal '57; mem. '54 Grey Cup winner; punt return specialist; '53 Eastern all-star hb, all-pro safety; '56 all-star; cb Ticat Fabulous Fifties stars ('50-60), Ticat dream team ('50-70), punt returner ('45-73) all-Argos team; coached Burlington Braves, Oakville ORFU Black Knights, Hamilton Hurricanes, U of Guelph.

BROWN, Doug (harness racing); b. 11 Sep 1955, Oshawa, Ont.; harness race driver; began driving at 18, winning just 3 races in initial season; reached 7,000 career victories '98; dominated '90 Greenwood/Mohawk circuit; set world record with Town Pro; Cane Pace, Prix d'Été, Stewart Fraser Memorial with Topnotcher; swept '97 Toronto Pacing series with Riyadh, Cam Fella Pacing Series with Tillys Sam; single-season record 443 victories; 1st in OJC history to reach $6M single season winnings; 25 consec. yrs among NA top 20 in races won; 24 consec. seasons $1M+ in winnings; 8 O'Brien driver of yr, 1 HTA Messenger awards; through '03 7898 wins, $82m+ in purses; res. Bowmanville, Ont.

BROWN, George (rowing); b. 1839, Herring Cove, N.S.; d. 8 Jul 1875, Halifax, N.S.; fisherman; Cogswell Belt race title 1864-68, permanent possession of belt; '71 competed Halifax 4s, single sculls vs. Scottish, British, US rowers; challenges issued world pro champion Joseph Sadler were avoided but Brown turned pro '73; defeated Robert Fulton of famed Paris Crew, US champion John Biglin '73, US singles champion Bill Scharff '74; Brown bet entire life savings on himself against Scharff and won by six seconds; defeated Evan Morris of US '74; while preparing for '75 match with Sadler suffered fatal stroke; mem. NS, Canada's Sports halls of fame.

BROWN, Gord (curling); b. 27 Jul 1918, Manor, Sask.; m. Jean Busby; c. Michael, Denise, Frances; ret'd civil servant; Sask. jr. tennis title '34; pres. Sask. Tennis Assn. '61-62; 3 Sask., 2 Cdn Legion, 2 Regina Grand Aggregate curling titles; pres. Regina Caledonian Club '61-62; exec. mem. Sask CA '61-64; skipped Ottawa entry to 3rd place '66 Ont. Consols; Canadian Branch Governor-General's double rink winner '66, '72; rep. Ottawa Curling Club Ont. Consols playdowns 7 times 8yrs; competed Ont. Srs.; mem. BCsrs. champions '79, runnerup nationals; res. Red Deer, Alta.

BROWN, Hal (t&f/coaching); b. 2 Dec 1917, Meaford, Ont.; given name: William Harold; m. Mildred Eleanor Hoskin; c. Gerry, Susan; Victoria Coll/Coll of Education, BA, teacher's degree, MA; ret'd HS teacher; set Cdn HS javelin record '35; Ont. HS lj champ '36; gold lj, Commonwealth record '38 BE Games; Intercollegiate 100, 220, javelin gold '39; Maritime lj record '43; set British Army lj record, won interservices lj gold '45; ntl lj,tj, javelin titles '46; Jack Davies outstanding athlete of '46 award; pitcher Meaford OABA intermediate baseball champs '37; mem. UofT intercollegiate intermediate basketball title team '39-40; UofT t&f coach '48-70; mem. '59 PAG coaching staff; coach ntl team '60 Olympics; OFSAA 50yr (at North Toronto CI) coaching (basketball/t&f) award; with twin brother Wally elected UofT Athletic Hall of Fame; res. Toronto/Clifford, Ont.

BROWN, Larry (t&f); b. 14 Feb 1952, Sudbury, Ont.; given name: Larry James; Texas, BSc, MEd; underground mine sampler; long distance specialist; twice all-Ont. indoor 2-mile champion; '73 2-mile indoor Houston Astrodome, WAC x-country; '75 WAC 6-mile title, El Paso international marathon; mem. NCAA outdoor track title team '75; American Statesman 10k title '80, 9th in 12,000 field Bloomsday race Spokane Wash.; mem. world x-country team Limerick, Ireland; res. Elliot Lake, Ont.

BROWN, Lisa (ringette); b. 24 Feb 1967, Edmonton, Alta.; mental toughness training consultant; operates Ringette Retreat training school; ctr. ntl team '82-01, capt. '96-01; 8 ntl titles; 3 world title teams; 8 ntl championship all-star ctr; '96 world final MVP; twice scored world title winning goals; sister Cara also ntl team mem.; nicknamed "Star Maker"; 1st player to receive intl achievement award from Finnish Ringette Assn.; res. Calgary, Alta.

BROWN, Louise (tennis); b. 19 Nov 1922, Dunnville, Ont.; d. 25 Nov 2003, Mississauga, Ont.; given name: Louise Cook; m. Ross Brown (d); c. David, Chareen; ret'd insurance agent; '57 ntl women's singles title, with Hilda Doleschell doubles; with Ann Barclay '62 ntl women's doubles; ntl women's sr. singles '70-71; capt. Canada's 1st Federation Cup team '63, player '64, non-playing capt. '66-67, '69; gold '69 Canada Games; 27 consecutive years among nation's top 10; women's rep. Players' Assn.; mem. Cdn Tennis, Canada's, Mississauga Sports halls of fame.

BROWN, Mae (basketball); b. 15 Aug 1903, Minnedosa, Man.; d. 7 Apr 2000, Edmonton; m. Bruce Webb; c. Gary Bruce, Margaret Jane; Alta. Coll.; ret'd; mem. famed Edmonton Grads '27-31; mem. varied Vancouver teams; mem. Cdn Basketball, Alta. Sports halls of fame.

BROWN, Robert (baseball); b. 5 July 1876, Scranton, Pa.; d. 1962, Vancouver, B.C.; Notre Dame; following brilliant career at Notre Dame turned pro Spokane Indians and led club to PCL title; moved to Vancouver and over 45-year period earned title "Mr. Baseball;" instrumental in leading Vancouver to numerous pennants; key role in bringing modern PCL baseball to Vancouver; twice saw stadiums he had built burn down; promoted construction Capilano Stadium; mem. Cdn Baseball, BC Sports halls of fame.

BROWN, Selina (karate); b. 21 Aug 1992, Ottawa, Ont.; student; began karate age 5; ntl, world (WKA) 12 & under traditional kata titles '02-04; ntl, world (WKA) 40kg 12 & under kumite (sparring) titles '03-04; competed in world championships Italy, Switzerland; mem. Pro-Style Martial Arts & Fitness Club; res. Kanata, Ont.

BROWN, Sophie (basketball); b. 21 Sep 1916, London, Eng.; d. 5 Jul 1986, Victoria, B.C.; m. Frank Drake (d); c. Barbara, Bill; accountant; mem. famed Edmonton Grads '35-40, 103 games, 551 points, 5.1 avg.; competitive softball player; mem. Canadian Basketball, Alta. Sports halls of fame.

BROWN, Ted (curling); b. 4 Oct 1937, Kingston, Ont.; given name: Edward James; m. Kathy Deroche; c. Jeff, Tim, Mike; self-employed furniture upholsterer; Ont. Governor-General's, Whitby Dunlop titles '69; Toronto Royals carspiel '71; 3 times competed Ont. Consols, twice as skip; 3rd Dr. Alex Scott-skipped Ont. Consols winner '75; competed Fredericton Brier; skipped Ont. ntl mixed championships '76; invented Brownie broom; res. Kingston, Ont.

BROWN, Tom (football); b. 5 Dec 1936, Albert Lea, Minn.; div.; c. Susan, Tracy, Steven; UMinn; all-American interior lineman; Knute Rockne Award US Coaches' top lineman '61; runnerup to Navy's Joe Bellino Heisman Trophy; mem. Rose Bowl, Hula Bowl, 1st American Football Coaches All-American Game teams; pro BC Lions '62-67; 3 times WFC all-star, twice all-Canadian; 2 Schenley lineman of year awards; Jeff Nicklin Trophy '64; neck injury in '65 game led to retirement '67; mem. 2 Grey Cup finalists, 1 winner; mem. Cdn Football, BC Sports halls of fame; res. New Westminster, B.C.

BROWN, Wally (t&f/coaching); b. 2 Dec 1917, Meaford, Ont.; d. 26 Feb 1971, Haliburton, Ont.; given name: George Wallace; m. Patricia Doreen Gilday; c. Gary, Robert, Virginia, Kathryn; Victoria Coll/Coll of Education, BA, teacher's degree; teacher; Ont. midget lj title '32; Intercollegiate lj title '36; set Commonwealth records, competed in '38 BEG; Intercollegiate champ '38-39 setting records in lj/shotput; Interservices gold lj/tj, Shot, Discus, 2 relay teams; ntl lj/tj champion, competed '48 Olympic trials; outfielder Meaford Intermediate OABA title team '37; fb Victoria Coll. intramural UofT football champs '39; coached t&f/ football Parkdale and Bloor CI '46-71; with twin brother Hal mem. UofT Athletic Hall of Fame.

BROWNE, Cec (all-around); b. 13 Feb 1894, Winnipeg, Man.; d. 13 Aug 1985, Winnipeg, Man.; teenage hockey, track, soccer, swimming sensation; at 22 coached Man. juvenile hockey title team, played on jr. title team same year; with Flying Corps WW1 claimed t&f medals, starred in English rugger league; mem. 3 Allan Cup finalists; Sask. all-around t&f champion; football Regina Roughriders '22; starred for Dick Irvin's Dominion Express baseball team; charter mem. Chicago Black Hawks '26; dealt to Seattle (PCL), 2 scoring crowns; dealt to Boston '30 but ret'd; coach Elmwood juniors Western Canadian finalists '36; Man. Athlete of Century (1870-1970); mem. Man. Hockey, Sports halls of fame.

BROWNE, Ed (basketball); b. 3 May 1934, St. John's, Nfld; d. 14 Feb 1983, St. John's. Nfld; given name: Edward Patrick; Loyola Coll, Memorial, UNB BPE, UPacific MA; educator, coach; competed St. John's regatta as rower '50; Ottawa St. Pat's Ont. HS football champs '51; St. Bonaventure basketball team '52-55; supervisor Cdn. Red Cross water safety '56-58; rec. supervisor Metz, France '60-62; joined Memorial PE staff '62; asst. coach Memorial Boyle Trophy champs '64-65; pres. St. John's, Nfld/Labrador Amateur Basketball Assns. '65; founded Russell tournament '65; coach Nfld Canada Winter Games men's team '66-67, '70-71, '75; prov. coach '70-75; coach Memorial Eastern Cdn champs '73; mgr. Cdn ntl men's team '74, mgr./asst. coach '76 Olympics; dir. PE Sir Wilfred Grenfell (Corner Brook); founded 1st Nfld Masters tourney;

Nfld bkbll recognition award; mem. Nfld, Cdn, St. John's Basketball, Nfld. Sports halls of fame.

BROWNE, Less (football); b. 7 Dec 1959, East Liverpool, Ohio; Colorado State.; db drafted by Pittsburgh Maulers (USFL) '84; joined CFL with Hamilton '84-88, Edmonton, Winnipeg '89, Ottawa '92, BC '93-94; 5 all-Eastern; 5 all-Canadian; 3yrs CFL interception leader; CFL record most interception return yds 14 for 273yds '90; CFL record most interceptions and return yds '92; CFL record: 174g, 7tds, 1 2pt cvt., 87 interceptions for 1,508yds, 4tds; mem. 3 Grey Cup finalists, 2 winners; asst. coach Hamilton '97; TV football analyst from '96; mem. BC Lions Wall, Cdn Football Hall of Fame; res. Hamilton, Ont.

BROWNING, Kurt (figure skating); b. 18 Jun 1966, Rocky Mountain House, Alta.; m. Sonja Rodriguez; c. Gabriel; novice ntl singles title '83, ntl jr title '85, won '88 Skate Electric, Skate Canada, '89-91 ntl, world championships; '90 Goodwill Games, Skate Canada, Nation's Cup, Lalique Trophy France titles; 8th '88, 6th '92, 5th '94 Olympics; plagued by back injury prior to '92 Olympics; 1st skater to execute quadruple toe loop in competition ('88 worlds); 1st Canadian to win three consecutive world titles; 4 time world champion; Lou Marsh trophy '90; 2 Lionel Conacher, 4 Norton Crowe trophies; Cdn Sports Council athlete of '93; ISU Jacques Favart award '97; pro from '94; world '95, Cdn '95, '97 pro titles; flag-bearer '94 winter Olympics; mem. Order of Canada, Cdn Walk, Cdn Olympic, Canada's, Alta Sports, Cdn Figure Skating halls of fame; res. Caroline, Alta.

BRUCE, Ian (sailing); b. 7 Jun 1933, Jamaica, BWI; m. Barbara Brittain; c. Tracy, Tobi; McGill, Syracuse, BID; industrial designer, company pres.; capt. Trinity College hockey team '50-51; McGill squash team '51-53; mem. Olympic yachting team '60 Finn Class, '72 Star Class; team capt. '67-68 International 14ft dinghy world team championships titlists; Canadian International 14ft dinghy titles '67, '75, US title '58; major role in design, development high performance Tasar lightweight dinghy; mem. Royal St. Lawrence Yacht Club; res. Dorval, Que.

BRUCE, Lou (football); b. 16 Jul 1933, Toronto, Ont.; d. 16 Jan 1985, Ottawa, Ont; given name: Lou Alexander; div.; c. Heather, Wendy, Jennifer; Queen's, BA; plastics manufacturer; Toronto all-star football, basketball '50-52; mem. Queen's Golden Gaels, CIAU all-star '54-55; pro Ottawa '56-61; 3 times all-star de; mem. Queen's Sports Hall of Fame.

BRUCE, Winston (rodeo); b. 27 Oct 1937, Stettler, Alta.; div.; c, Christie, Laurence; rodeo mgr. Calgary Stampede; learned the rodeo business from father Laurence who produced rodeos from '20-58 including 1st-ever indoor rodeo in Camrose '46; produced his 1st pro rodeo at age 12; spent 15yrs as pro winning 2 ntl novice saddle bronc titles; 2 pro saddle bronc titles; Calgary Stampede championship, rookie of '59 award, world rookie of year award '59, world championship '61; asst. arena dir. at Stampede '69; rodeo mgr. '70-79, div. mgr from '80; mem. board Pro Rodeo Cowboys Assn,; dir. Assn Rodeo Committees; noted for riding appaloosas exclusively; active minor hockey coach; mem. US, Cdn Rodeo, Alta. Sports halls of fame; res. Calgary, Alta.

BRUMPTON, Jerry (coaching/basketball); b. 25 Jun 1938, Windsor, Ont.; given name: Gerald Preston; m. Helen Ruth French; Guelph BSc; ret'deducator; standout HS football player; mem. Guelph basketball team; 36yr HS coaching career in basketball, football, t&f; began coaching career Essex HS '62-63, W.D. Lowe HS '64-98; sr. basketball coaching record 734-260; 15 WSSAA city titles; 8 OFSAA all-Ont. AAA final four appearances; 8 U of Windsor Invitational titles; record 7 consec WSSAA titles; 2 OFSAA AAA gold, 4 silver, 1 bronze; organizer/head instructor St. Clair Coll. summer basketball camps '78-00; instructor/coach basketball camps Laurier '70-75, Michigan State '78-03, Ont. Olympic sports camps '70's-'90's; head coach Team Ont. silver medal Canada Games '81; Windsor Kinsmen sportsman of '81; mem. Windsor/Essex County Sports Hall of Fame; res. Windsor, Ont.

BRUNET, Caroline (canoeing); b. 20 Mar 1969, Quebec City, Que.; Laval; kayak specialist; PR Home Depot; began competing '84; mem. ntl team from '88; competed '88, '92, '96, '00, '04 Olympics; 9 world championships; 10 ntl K1, 5 K2, 5 K4, 3 International K1, 2 K4 gold; silver K1 '96 Olympics; 1 gold, 2 silver '95 world championships; 1st Cdn to win 3 world K1 gold, 1000-, 500-, 300m '97, repeat '99; 1st Cdn woman ever to win world K1 title; K1 200m, 500m gold, 1000m silver '98 worlds; 200m K1 gold, 500m K1 silver '03 worlds; 4 gold '99 Duisburg regatta; Cdn flag-bearer '00 Olympics; Edmonton Grads team award '95; Lou Marsh '99, Velma Springstead '99, '00 awards; res. Dollard des Ormeux, Que.

BRUNETEAU, Mud (hockey); b. 28 Nov 1914, St. Boniface, Man.; d. 26 May 1982, Omaha, Neb.; given name: Modere; rw; jr. Winnipeg KofC; pro Detroit Olympics (IHL) '34-35; Red Wings '35-36; scored lone goal as Wings defeated Montreal Maroons 1-0 in longest game in NHL history '36; except for brief stint with Pittsburgh (AHL) '37-38 remained with Detroit '45-46; best season '43-44, 35g in 39 games; NHL record 139g, 138a; 3 Stanley Cup winners; after leaving NHL, played for Indianapolis (AHL), Omaha (USHL); mem. Man. Hockey Hall of Fame.

BRUNO, Al (football/coaching); b. 28 Mar 1927, West Chester, Pa.; given name: Alberto Pavalone; m. Marie Giosio; c. Mike, Maria, Lisa; Kentucky, BA; football coach; end Bear Bryant's Kentucky football teams '47-50, forward Adolph Rupp's Kentucky NCAA basketball title teams '48-49; '50 Orange Bowl, '51 Sugar Bowl; US record 10 td passes, 4 in single game from Babe Parilli '50; mem. 1st Kentucky Southeastern Conf. title team '50; all-conf., 3rd team all-American '50; Philadelphia Eagles draft; Toronto '52-54, Winnipeg '55-56; mem. '52 Grey Cup winner; coaching from '57; guided Toronto De La Salle CI to football, basketball titles; player-coach London Lords '58-60, ORFU title '60; taught, coached Pennsylvania HS '61-66; asst. Ottawa '66-67, Hamilton '68-70, '82, Harvard '71-81, Ivy League titles '74-75; head coach Hamilton '83-90; Grey Cup finalist '84-85, winner '86; head coach McMaster '94-96; res. Florida/Hamilton, Ont.

BRYANT, Deborah (rhythmic gymnastics); b. 7 Sep 1957, Moncton, N.B.; given name: Deborah Jane; UMoncton BSc, dip. Health sciences; exec. coach, business management consultant; introduced to sport '71; ntl team '75-84, 1st

non-Ont. selectee; NB sr. champ '73-83; ntl sr. gold '81, silver '80, 3 bronze; competed 4 world, 3 4-continent championships; all-around sr. 4-continents gold '78; Princess Grace all-around title Monaco '81; Canada-China all-around gold '82; role model for NB athletes, helped coach, assisted at clinics; coached in Ont., Sask.; tech., high performance dir. Cdn Rhythmic Gymnastics Fed. mgr. Team Can. '88 CG; ret'd age 27; 2 UdeM female athlete-of-yr awards; NB female athlete of '82; mem. Moncton Sports Wall, NB Sports Hall of fame; res, Gloucester, Ont.

BRYDEN, Rod (builder/hockey); b. 13 Mar 1941, Port Elgin, N.B.; Mount Allison BA, UNB LLB; past-pres./CEO World Heart; at 27 was business prof. UofSask.; served as federal deputy minister; founded Systemhouse, 9 other technology- related companies; entrepreneurial drive, analytical skills and forceful approach to business gave him reputation as masterful wheeler-dealer; became involved with Ottawa Senators '91, eventually taking ownership and waging on-going battle to keep team afloat until he sold it to Eugene Melnyck '03; had key role in construction of Corel Centre; Canada's High Tech Man of Year award; res. Ottawa, Ont.

BRYDSON, Gordie (hockey/golf); b. 3 Jan 1907, Toronto, Ont.; d. 4 Feb 2001, Mississauga, Ont.; m. Dorothy Beamish; ret'd golf pro; flying wing, kicker Toronto Argos '22-23; pro hockey rw Toronto, Chicago, Detroit '24-38; golf pro from '30; 2 Ont. Open, Millar Trophy, CPGA, Rivermead Cup; 1 CPGA Srs., Que. Open titles; runnerup Canadian Open; 4 Ont. PGA Srs titles; club pro Mississauga Golf and Country Club '31-72; pres. OPGA, CPGA; life mem. CPGA; mem. RCGA, Mississauga Sports halls of fame.

BUCHAN, Ken (curling); b. 9 Apr 1940, Harriston, Ont.; given name: Kenneth Donald; m. Deanne Catharine Girodat; c. Christine, Margaret; Waterloo Lutheran, BA, Waterloo, BPhE; teacher; 3rd for Bob Mann 3 Ont. Consols, 2 Briers; skipped own rink 7 Ont. Consols; skipped Ont. entry '69 Brier; Ont. Silver Tankard '72; skipped rink in 3 Ont. mixed championships, '81 ntl mixed Ont. entry; '93, '96 Ont. Srs; active Curl Canada coaching program; res. Kilworth, Ont.

BUCHBERGER, Kelly (hockey); 2 Dec 1966, Langenburg, Sask.; m. Carla; c. Madison, Keeton; rw Melville (SJHL)'83-84; Moose Jaw (WHL) '85-86, Nova Scotia (AHL) '86-88; Edmonton draftee '85; Team Canada '93, '94 (gold), '96 (silver) worlds; NHL Edmonton '87-99, Atlanta '99-00. Los Angeles '00-02, Phoenix '02-03, Pittsburgh '04; Edmonton, Atlanta capt.; 3 Stanley Cup winners; NHL record: (through '04) 1182 scheduled games, 105g, 204a, 97 playoff games, 10g, 14a; nickname Bucky; res. Edmonton, Alta.

BUCHBERGER, Kerri Ann (volleyball); b. 23 Jun 1970, Russell, Man.; UReg; middle blocker; mem. ntl team from '91; competed '93 FISU, '91, '95 PAG, '96 Olympic Games, '91, '95 World Cup; gold '96 Continental Cup; bronze '95 PAG; Canada Cup game star award; 3 GPAC all-star awards; played in Belgium '92; res. Langenburg, Sask./Winnipeg, Man.

BUCKBORO, Dean (swimming); b. 3 Sep 1953, Grande Prairie, Alta.; given name: Dean Kelvie; m. Carole Wade; c. Vikki Lynn; Foothills Jr. College; truck driver; ntl team

'68-73; Alberta 200-, 400-, 800-, 1500m FS; 200-, 400-, 800-, 1650yds FS records; ntl 200-, 400m FS records; silver 400m FS, 800m FS relay '69 Canada Games; shoulder injury forced him to miss '71 PAG; mem. '72 Olympic, '73 world championships teams; res. Calgary, Alta.

BUCKINGHAM, Michelle (judo); b. 1 Sep 1968, Los Angeles, Calif.; Concordia; moved to Canada '71; began competing age 9; mem. ntl team from '87; 1 ntl -52kg, 4 -61kg, 1 57kg titles; 61kg title '97 Pan-Am judo championships; silver '94 Francophone Games, '95 PAG; gold '93 Dutch Open; 3rd degree black belt; competed '92, '96, '00 Olympics; achieved PB placing 5th '97 worlds; Ottawa ACT judo award '97, '01; res. Montreal, Que.

BUCKNA, Mike (hockey); b. 5 Sep 1913, Trail, B.C.; d. 6 Jan 1996, Trail, B.C.; given name: Mike Matthew; m. Aloise (Lola) Frolik (d); c. Mike Joseph; hotelman; 42 medals, numerous 1st, 2nd place trophies HS t&f; mem. 2 BC title jr. hockey teams; Trail Smoke Eaters '32-35, '46, '49; player-coach Prague Lawn & Tennis Club hockey team '36; coach Czech ntl team to '39; considered father of modern Czechoslovakian hockey; guided Czech nationals to European, world titles '47, 1st European team to claim that honor; mem. '50 Western Canadian Intermediate title team; coach Rossland Warriors '54 BC finals; Trail sportsman of '78; honored by Czech, Swedish governments for contribution to European hockey; mem. BC Sports, IIHF halls of fame.

BUCYK, John (hockey); b. 12 May 1935, Edmonton, Alta; given name: John Paul; m. Anne Smith; c. 3; hockey exec.; jr. Edmonton; pro Edmonton (WHL); rookie scoring record, rookie of year award; Detroit '55-57, Boston '57-78; NHL record: 1540 scheduled games, 556g, 813a, 124 playoff games, 41g, 62a; mem. 2 Stanley Cup winners; once 1st, 2nd team all-star lw; surpassed Dit Clapper's 20-season same-club record, Milt Schmidt's club career point mark; 1st Bruin to score 250g; NHL's 7th 500-plus goal scorer '75; joined select circle of 50-goal scorers with 51 '70-71; twice Lady Byng, Dufresne (Bruins MVP) awards; Conacher, Lester Patrick trophies; remained with Bruins in exec. capacity; did some broadcasting; dir. Bruins alumni assn.; chair. Massachusetts State Heart Fund more than decade; jersey 9 ret'd. by Bruins; nicknamed "Chief"; mem. Hockey, Alta Sports halls of fame; res. Boxford, Mass./B.C.

BUDAY, Attila (canoeing); b. 28 Jun 1974, Budapest, Hungary; UofT BPE; brilliant junior career winning C2 1000 gold, C1 1000 bronze '92 Junior Worlds; ntl team mem. from '91; gold C2 1000, C4 500 '92 jr World Cup; C1 500, C2 1000 silver '95, '99 PAG; 16 intl medals; competed '96, '00 Olympics; brother Tamas Jr. also ntl team mem., father Tamas Sr. (Montreal Olympics double medallist for Hungary) is coach; res. Mississauga, Ont.

BUDAY, Tamas Jr. (canoeing); b. 23 Apr 1976, Budapest, Hungary; Sheridan Coll.; mem. ntl canoe team from '93; 2 gold, 1 silver in C1 events '94 Junior Worlds; C4 500 jr World Cup gold; PAG '95, '99 C2 1000 silver; competed '96, '00 Olympics; brother Attila, father Tamas Sr. also involved with ntl team; Viscount Alexander award '94; res. Mississauga. Ont.

BUDDO, Don (all-around); b. 6 Oct 1886, Montreal, Que.; d. 27 Jul 1965, London, Ont.; mem. Montreal Wanderers, Wolverines hockey clubs; standout baseball, lacrosse player early 1900s; football Edmonton Western Football League; ran 400m, 800m '08 Olympics; provincial, ntl t&f 100yds, 3-mile, all field event titles except hammer and shot; mem. '08 Emerald Snowshoe Club which set world 1/4-, 1/2-mile records; Golden Swastika award for work in Boy Scout movement; mem. Cdn Olympic Sports Hall of Fame.

BUDGE, Ervin (snooker); b. 15 Jan 1940, Maniwaki, Que.; m. Corinne Lépine; c. Larry, Tracie, Jon; ret'd snooker executive; 11 KofC, 8 Western Que. snooker titles; US Open title '78; Cdn team capt. '74-91 winning 6 gold, 4 silver in Bermuda, England, USA, Canada; 2 individual international snooker league titles; 3 ACT snooker awards; won more than 50 tournaments 1959-91; founding dir. Cdn Snooker Control Council '74; PR director CSCC '75-84; founding dir. International Snooker League '74; organized Cdn championships '74-80; organized first seniors snooker Olympics '77; organized senior citizen's snooker league for Ottawa, Nepean, Vanier, Kanata, National Capital area; founding dir. Elvis Sighting Society; founder Ottawa Snowsuit Fund gala dinner; founder Blacktie Beanfest charity dinner; fund-raiser Success By Six program; res. Aylmer, Que.

BUDGE, Susan (orienteering); b. 2 Jun 1961, Montreal, Que.; given name: Susan Jane; m. Ian Lowe-Wylde; c. Jamie, Briar; Waterloo, BA., Queen's MA; exercise consultant; ntl -14 title '72; jr. '73-74; NA jr. '75; ntl sr. '76-79, '83; NA sr. '77; 2nd Danish intl 3-day '75; 3rd sr. Canadian intl 6-day '78; 2nd jr. Canadian intl 5-day '76; mem. 5 consec. world championships teams; at 15 youngest ever world championship competitor; ret'd '84; won '80 Karrimor intl mountain marathon Switzerland; mem. Waterloo x-country running, ski teams; Class A Laurentian Zone alpine ski racer; Ont. sports achievement award; res. Terra Cotta, Ont.

BULAU, Horst (ski jumping); b. 14 Aug 1962, Ottawa, Ont.; given name: Horst Hardy; m. Kerry Lennard-White; auto leasing mgr.; entered 1st major competition at 12; ntl jr. 90m title at 16; joined Ont. team '78; 1st Canadian gold medalist at world level '79 70m world jr. title; 13 WC victories; 3rd overall WC standings '81-82, runnerup '83; ntl 70m, US 70m, 90m titles '81, ntl 70m, 90m '83-84; mem. '80, '84, '88, '92 Olympic teams; twice Ottawa ACT athlete of year; Ont. athlete of '83; fed. govt. excellence awards '82-84; John Semmelink Memorial award '79, '83; ret'd. to coaching '88; brief comeback '90; *CTV* color commentator '94 Olympics; mem. Cdn Olympic, Cdn Skiing, Ottawa Sports halls of fame; res. Sharon, Ont.

BULLARD, Mike (hockey); b. 10 Mar 1961, Ottawa, Ont.; m. Linda; c. Kaylie; centre Brantford OHA '78-81; drafted by Pittsburgh '80; remained with Penguins to '86; traded to Calgary '86-88, St. Louis '88, Philadelphia '89-90, Toronto '91-92; played 2 yrs Switzerland, 11 Germany; scoring champion German league '97; NHL record: 727 scheduled games, 329g, 345a, 40 playoff games, 11g, 18a; reached 50-goal plateau with 51 '84; OHA 2nd team all-star '80; res. Landshut, Ger.

BULLOCH, Jim (basketball); b. 23 Feb 1920, Winnipeg, Man.; d. 21 Apr 1991, Winnipeg, Man.; m. Fran Blower; c. Judy, Jim Jr., Dan, Garry; real estate broker; Man. sr. fastball league all-star catcher; coach Western Canadian title winning Legion 141 fastball team; coach St. Andrew's Jr. men, UMan Bisons basketball; '48-55 coach Winnipeg Paulins, '54 ntl champions, world tournament competitors; St. Andrew's Sr. men's coach '59-64, '68-69, 3 ntl titles; Glenlawn CHS 3 consecutive provincial titles; coach '79 ntl champions, '81 Nicollet Inn Sr. men ntl finalists; founder 9-team McGregor Armouries jr. men's league; organized basketball for disabled athletes; instrumental in founding Winnipeg Paraplegic Sports League, Golden Ramblers Wheelchair team; key role in Pan-Am Paraplegic Games '67; Manitoba HS coach of '78; 8 times Winnipeg Sr. men's coach of year; mem. Man. Basketball, Man. Sports halls of fame.

BULLOCK, Bruce (shooting); b. 10 Oct 1969, Burlington, Ont.; given name: Bruce Larsen; Carleton, hons. BA; following footsteps of father Jim and grandfather Don began earning full-bore shooting reputation qualifying for Bisley cadet team '86; mem. 1 Palma world team; 3 -25 ntl teams; mem. 4 men's Bisley teams; res. Cheltenham, Ont.

BULLOCK, Jim (shooting); b. 15 Feb 1944, Victoria, B.C.; given name: James Charles; m. Carol Larson; c. Jason, Bruce; Sir George Williams; pres. Independent Life Brokers of Canada; began shooting age 10; .22 rifle as cadet; full-bore from age 15; Caribbean championship Barbados '78; competed Bisley 10 times; Bisley Grand Aggregate award '84; proficient pistol shooter; father Don ranked among nation's top long range marksmen; res. Mississauga, Ont.

BULMER, Eryn (diving); b. 1 Aug 1976, Edmonton, Alta; m. Barrett; c. 1; Mount Royal Coll.; former gymnast who took up diving after suffering knee injury; competed in both sports '85-89; coached by Hui Tong Dive Calgary club; mem. ntl team '95-03; springboard specialist; 3m gold '96 Olympic trials; '97 FINA World Cup; 1m, 3m gold '98 FINA Grand Prix; 12 ntl titles, 21 intl medals; competed '96, '00 Olympics; '94 Goodwill Games; 3m gold, 1m bronze '98 CG; 3m gold '99 PAG; with Blythe Hartley operates high performance camp; 2 Aquatics Fed. Cdn female athlete-of-yr awards; res. Calgary, Alta.

BUNBURY, Alex (soccer); b. 16 Jun 1967, Plaisance, Guyana; given name: Alexander; m.; c. Kylie, Teal; pro athlete; began play age 12 St. Léonard Bourassa Montreal; striker Hamilton Steelers '87-90, Toronto Blizzard '90, Montreal Supra '91, West Ham United (English 1st div.) '92-93, FC Maritimo Portugal '93-00, Kansas City (MSL) '99-00; mem. ntl -16, -19, Olympic A, B teams; mem. ntl team '86-00; scored 3 goals vs. Bermuda in 4-2 Cdn '92 World Cup qualifier victory; Portugese foreign player of '95; twice Cdn player of yr; 55 international caps; res. Minnesota.

BUNKOWSKY, Barbara (golf); b. 13 Oct 1958, Toronto, Ont.; m. Mark Scherbak; Palm Beach Jr. Coll., Florida State; pro golfer; began playing golf age 10; '81 Ont. match, amateur titles; 2nd ranked ntl amateur '80-82; mem. ntl team '80 world team championships, '82 UK tour; mem. Ont. ntl team champions '80-82; AIAW ntl title '81; pro from '83;

tied 4th '84 Freedom Orlando Classic while posting 1st career low 65 (matched '90); Chrysler-Plymouth Charity Classic title '84; 3rd Mazda LPGA championship '93, Sprint Classic '94; best earning season $167,039 '94; *Score Magazine* Cdn female pro golfer of '91; featured in '87 *Fairway* fashion spread; 1 career hole-in-one; res. West Palm Beach, Fla.

BUONO, Wally (football); b. 7 Feb 1950, Potenza, Italy; m. Sande; c. Amy, Dana, Christie, Michael; Idaho State; football coach; CFL lb/punter Montreal '72-81; club record 90yd punt; CFL record: 358 punts, 14,510yds, 40.5avg, 12 singles; noted for durability, 152 consecutive games; in 5 Grey Cup finals, 2 winners; def. co-ordinator Jr. Concordes '82; asst. coach Concordes-Alouettes '83-86; asst. Calgary '87-89, GM,/head coach '90-02, BC '03; 3 Annis Stukus CFL coach-of-yr awards; hon. chair. Cdn Cancer Society '95; active in Children's Cottage Fund program; res. Calgary, Alta.

BURCH, Billy (hockey); b. 20 Nov 1900, Yonkers, N.Y.; d. Dec 1950,; pro Hamilton Tigers '23; centred line of Green brothers, Redvers (Red), Wilfred (Shorty) and carried team to 1st place NHL '25; Hart Trophy '25; transferred with team to NY where he became capt.; '27 Lady Byng Trophy; dealt from NY Americans to Boston '32; with Chicago '33 broke leg and ret'd; 5 times team scoring leader; 135g, 42a in 390 games; mem. Hockey Hall of Fame.

BURCHUK, Mike (volleyball/coaching); b. 18 Nov 1949, Weiden, Man.; m. Ruth Klassen; c. Evan; UMan BEd; operates Volleyball Experience, coach; began coaching at HS level '69 Beaumont Jr. HS, Selkirk '71-79 guiding teams to prov. level competition; coached Team Man, '79 Canada Winter Games'; Man. coach-of-yr award; coach UWpg women '80-89; 6 consec CIAU titles; 4 CIAU coach-of-yr awards; Man. Volleyball Assn., Man. HSAA female player-of-yr awards bear his name; asst. coach jr. ntl team '80, sr. '82-88; head coach from '89; asst. UMan '03-04; appearances '84, '96 Olympics, '91, '95 (bronze) PAG, 4 WC, 3 worlds, 3 FISU; 1 silver, 3 bronze NORCECA, 4 silver Canada Cup; mem. Man. Sports Hall of Fame; res. Winnipeg, Man.

BURDEN, Willie (football); b. 21 Jul 1951, Longwood, N.C.; given name, Willie James; m. Velma Stokes; c. Willie Jr., Freddie; NC State BA, Ohio MA, Tenn. State EdD; prof. Georgia Southern U.; standout college career; rb drafted by NFL Detroit'74; CFL Calgary '74-81; played 103 CFL games; best yr '75 when he set CFL record 1896yds on 332 carries, 5 consec 100yd games, total 10 for season, 238yds on 34 carries tied Lovell Coleman single-game record; Schenley Outstanding Player, Eddie James, Jeff Nicklin awards '75; 2 WFC, 1 CFL all-star awards; numerous Calgary club awards; Calgary ret'dhis jersey 10; mem. Stampeder Wall, Cdn Football Hall of fame; res. Statesboro, GA.

BURE, Pavel (hockey); b. 31 Mar 1971, Moscow, Russia; right wing; Soviet league rookie award CSKA '89; mem. 3 world jr. title teams; drafted by Vancouver '89; Vancouver '91-99, Florida '99-2001, NYR '02-03; Calder Memorial Trophy '92; 1st team all-star '94; topped 50-game plateau with 60 '93, '94, 51 '98, 58 '00, 59 '01; played 3 NHL all-star games; NHL record: (through '03) 702 scheduled games, 437g, 342a, 64 playoff games, 35g, 35a; nicknamed "Russian Rocket"; competed '98, '02 Olympics; father Vladimir represented Soviet Union as swimmer in '68, '72, '76 Olympics; Rocket Richard award '00-01; right knee surgery '03 threatens playing career; rock singer; res. Moscow/L.A.

BURE, Valeri (hockey); b. 13 Jun 1974, Moscow, Russia; m. Candace; c. Natasha, Lev, Maksim; rw CSKA Moscow '90-91; Spokane (WHL) '91-94, twice all-star; drafted by Montreal '92; stint with Fredericton (AHL) '94-95; NHL Montreal '95-98, Calgary '98-01, Florida '01-03, St. Louis '03-04, Dallas '04; NHL all-star '00; Team Russia '98 (silver), '02 (bronze) Olympics, '94 Worlds, '96 World Cup, '94 world jr bronze; NHL record: (through '04) 621 scheduled games, 174g, 226a, 22 playoff games, 0g, 7a; twice WHL all-star; with brother Pavel holds NHL record total goals by brothers single season; res. Moscow, Russia.

BURELLE, Jacques (administration); b. 8 Jul 1948, Ottawa, Ont.; UofOtt, BA, Ohio, MA; Indiana, PhD; pres. Ottawa Tourism & Convention Authority; ex-sports administrator, marketing consultant; standout football player UofOtt; site and service co-ordinator Montreal Olympics '75-76; deputy GM Montreal Olympic stadium '77; deputy ED Katimavik (Canada's national volunteer youth service program) '77-81; exec. v-p/GM Montreal Manic soccer club '81-84; dir. gen. world gymnastic championships '84-85; co-ordinator Que. Society for Crippled Children Telethon '86; dir. gen. Molson (F1) GP '86-87; ntl dir. Molson sports promotions '87-89; v-p business development Molstar group '89-90; v-p event marketing Everest group '91-92; pres. Eventcorp '92-96; commissioner CPGA tour '97-02; res. Ottawa, Ont.

BURGESS, Blair (harness racing); b. 27 Sep 1961, Toronto, Ont.; began as groom age 11; learned training skills from Stew Firlotte, Gary Bourgon, Paul Radley before moving out on his own '85; although noted as a trainer he did some catch-driving including guiding Amity Chef to NA record; same horse established training credentials winning 3-yr-old colt-of-yr honors; CTA trainer of '87 award; several horses he trained, like Real Desire, Road Machine, On The Road Again, Driven By Design, American Premier and Road To Broadway produced major victories; res. Milton, Ont.

BURGESS, Tim (baseball); b. 1 Sep 1927, London, Ont.; given name: Thomas Roland; div.; c. Thomas, Cynthia; UWO.; ret'd. baseball exec.; mem. several Ont. age-group title teams; pro Hamilton '46; left pro to star in outfield, at 1st base Sr. IC London Majors '48-51; resumed pro career '52 spending much of next decade Triple A Rochester, Columbus with brief ML stints St. Louis, Pittsburgh, California before '62 retirement; 3 silver gloves for fielding excellence; pro lifetime .300 BA; *Look* AAA all-star '53; Sally League MVP '52; Columbus Jets RBI record 96 '59; mgr. London Pontiacs (Sr IC) '63-64; rejoined pros as coach, mgr. '69; won 2 pennants; mgr. of year Modesto (Cal League) '72, Johnson City (Rookie League) '75; ML coach NY Mets '77, Atlanta '78; mgr. Richmond (IL) '79, Charleston (IL) '80, Tulsa (TL) '81-82 (TL title '82), Oklahoma City (AA) '83-84; batting coach ntl jr. team '99-00; mem. Cdn Baseball Hall of Fame; res. Sarasota, Fla./Lambeth, Ont.

BURGESS, Tom (football); b. 6 Mar 1964, Newark, N.J.; Colgate; *AP* all-American hon. mention '85; qb; joined CFL Ottawa '86, '92-93; Saskatchewan '87-89, '94-95, Winnipeg '90-91; 2 all-Eastern; CFL record (through '95): 172 scheduled games, 19tds, 2118 completions on 4034 attempts for 30,308yds, 190tds, 528 carries for 2240yds, 19tds; mem. 2 Grey Cup finalists, 1 winner; Grey Cup offensive star award '90; res. Regina, Sask.

BURKA, Ellen (coaching); b. 11 Aug 1921, Amsterdam, The Netherlands; c. Petra, Astra; figure skating coach, choreographer; Dutch champion; emigrated to Canada 1951; became one of Canada's most respected coaches and choreographers; coached 7 Cdn Olympic and 24 World championships; with Toller Cranston brought new style to figure skating; among students at various stages of their careers were Cranston, Christopher Bowman, Dorothy Hamel, Elvis Stojko and daughter Petra; choreographed 1st Netherlands ice shows, TV specials, Palace Theatre, NY, Radio City Music Hall, NY ice shows; mem. Order of Canada, Etobicoke, Canada's Sports, Cdn Figure Skating halls of fame; res. Toronto, Ont.

BURKA, Petra (figure skating); b. 17 Nov 1946, Amsterdam, The Netherlands; TV commercial producer; coached by mother Ellen; ntl jr. title '61, sr. '63-65; bronze '64 Olympics; gold NA, world '65; pro Holiday on Ice '66-69; consultant Sport Canada '70-74; *CBC* production co-ordinator '75; Lou Marsh Trophy '65; 2 Bobbie Rosenfeld trophies; hon. mem. Toronto Cricket, Skating Club; mem. Cdn Olympic, Ont. Sports Legends, Canada's Sports, Cdn Figure Skating halls of fame; res. Toronto, Ont.

BURKA, Sylvia (speed skating/cycling); b. 4 May 1954, Winnipeg, Man.; div. Jocelyn Lovell; m. David Hogg; from initial ntl speed skating title '67, dominated competitive scene through '80, winning 5 ntl titles (conflicting world events prevented competition 9 other years); more than 40 ntl records '67-80; mem. '72, '76, '80 Olympic teams; 4th '76 100m; competed 22 world championships, winning '73 jr., '76 senior, '77 sprint; world sprint points records (2x500m, 2x1000m) '73; world record all-around points (500m, 1000m, 1500m, 3000m) '76; 6 times Cdn. skater of year; 5 times Man. sportswoman of year; with Sue Nattrass shared Velma Springstead award '77; Order of Buffalo Hunt '73; Governor-General's award, City of Winnipeg award '73; began competitive cycling '75; 12 ntl sprint, 100m, pursuit, time trial, road race events titles; 3 gold '79 Western Canada Games; stage winner Coors international bike classic '80; 4th 300m pursuit '77 world championships; unofficial world record 1000m time trial '80; competed '96 Chicago marathon; Manitoba female amateur athlete of century; mem. Cdn Speed Skating, Cdn Olympic, Man., Canada's Sports halls of fame; res. Toronto, Ont.

BURKE, Brian (administration/hockey); b. 30 Jun 1955, Providence, R.I.; m. Jennifer; c. Katie, Molly, Patrick, Brendan; Providence Coll BA, Harvard LLB; lawyer, hockey exec., broadcaster; adjunct prof. UBC law school; mem. Maine (AHL) Calder Cup winner '77-78; practiced law Boston 6yrs; joined Vancouver Canucks front office '87-92; GM Hartford Whalers '92-93; sr. vp/dir. hockey operations NHL '93-98; pres./GM Canucks '98-04; TV broadcaster '04; mem. Ntl Sports Law Institute, Sports

Lawyers Assn.; dir. Canuck Place; spokesperson Ducks Unlimited; SN NHL exec of '01; res. Vancouver, B.C.

BURKE, Des (shooting); b. 5 Dec 1904, Ottawa, Ont.; d. 11 Apr 1973, Oakville, Ont.; given name: Desmond Thomas; m. Marcella Frances Simpson; c. William Desmond; Queen's, radiologist; childhood illness prevented strenuous sports so aided by father, teacher, became proficient marksman; placed in charge of cadet shooting training; youngest ever to win King's Prize Bisley '24, lost '29 shootoff for same prize; qualified for 23 Bisley teams, able to compete 12 times; amassed more prizes and awards (14 1sts, 11 2nds) than any other Canadian marksman; mem. 5 Kolapore, 3 MacKinnon teams; mem. King's Hundred 7 times; grand aggregate gold cross twice; published *A Practical Rifleman's Guide* ('32), *Canadian Bisley Shooting: An Art and Science* ('70); mem. Canadian Forces, Ottawa, Canada's Sports halls of fame.

BURKE, Jack (boxing); b. 8 Nov 1942, Saint John, N.B.; nicknamed "Golden Boy"; 3 Golden Boy trophy victories; prov., Maritime, ntl bantamweight titles; silver '64 PAG; ret'd undefeated; mem. NB Sports Hall of Fame; res. Saint John, N.B.

BURKE, Larry (weightlifting); b. 15 Jul 1950, Toronto, Ont.; given name: Lawrence David; Dalhousie, UofOtt; plumber; rugby provincially for NS, wrestled at intercollegiate, ntl levels; 82.5kg lifting title '77 Aalborg Cup; 90kg silver '78 nationals, gold '79; bronze '79 PAG 90kg; bronze 90kg '80 Pan-American championships, Canadian nationals; res. Vancouver, B.C.

BURKE, Sean (hockey): b. 29 Jan 1967, Windsor, Ont.; m. Leslie; c. Andie, Brendan; hockey player; goalie Toronto Marlboros '84-86, San Diego IHL '92; Team Canada periodically '86-97; silver world jr. '86; Izvestia tourney gold '87; competed '87, '89, '91, '97 (gold) worlds, all-star '91; Canada Cup '92, '88, '92 (silver) Olympics; NHL New Jersey '88-91, Hartford/Carolina '92-97, Vancouver '98, Philadelphia '98, '04, Florida '98-00, Phoenix '00-04; 1 NHL all-star game; NHL totals: 762 scheduled games, 43,419 minutes, 304-321-101, 70 shutouts, 35 playoff games, 2042 minutes, 12-22-0, 0 shutouts; res. Sylvan Lake, Alta.

BURKHOLDER, Dave (football); b. 21 Oct 1936, Minneapolis, Minn; m. Audrey Hewitt; c. Heidi, David Matthew; UMinn, BA; international sales rep.; 3 football letters as UMinn tackle, 2nd Big 10 team, hon. mention all-American; '57 Blue-Grey, East-West games; pro Winnipeg '58-64; 3 times WIFU all-star; Bombers most valuable lineman '62; mem. 4 Grey Cup winners; res. Hopkins, Minn.

BURLEY, Kris (gymnastics); b. 29 Jan 1974, Truro, N.S.; York U; TV production asst.; all-around competitor; began competing age 5; 1st Nova Scotian named to ntl team '89-02; 1st Cdn to successfully execute Yurchenko entry vault; ntl jr. all-around title '90; 2 gold, 2 silver, 1 bronze '90 Pan-Am jr.; Cdn jr. elite all-around title '91; competed '91, '95 PAG, '93 FISU, Worlds, '94, '98 CG, '96 Olympic Games; 1 gold, 3 silver '94, 1 silver, 1 bronze '98 CG; 3 bronze '95 PAG, team gold, vault bronze '99 PAG; 6 ntl sr, 4 ntl jr, 1 ntl novice, tyro titles; twice NS athlete of yr; recipient 3 academic scholarships; coached in Fredericton; v.-chair Athletes Can. advocacy group; res. Toronto, Ont.

BURNHAM, Barrie (rugby); b. 1 Mar 1938, Vancouver, B.C.; div.; c. Diane, Ricky; salesman; West Vancouver Barbarians and Rowing Club; Meraloma Club '61-81; adept kicker with both feet; scum-half/off. half ntl team '62-71; UK '62, Wales '71 tours; Japan '70 with BC team; 4 BC title teams; "capped" 4 times in Canada; 26 Feb '66 recorded rare feat by scoring in every possible way in a game (try, convert, dropped goal, penalty goal, goal from a mark) earning listing in *Guiness Book of Records*; Howie McPhee Trophy, Vancouver rugby's premier individual award; softball player-coach; mem. BC Sports Hall of Fame; res. Vancouver, B.C.

BURNHAM, Faye (basketball); b. 2 Jun 1920, Vancouver B.C.; m. James Ecclestone; c. Glenn, Brian; UBC; ret'd phys ed teacher; mem. 6 ntl sr. women's basketball teams; Hedlund's BC women's softball title teams; 3ʳᵈ base '44 Neons world title team; rejected pro offers Chicago Glamour League; cf HS, BC women's field hockey teams, Pacific Northwest titles; coached basketball, field hockey, t&f, softball, volleyball Magee HS Vancouver, Hudson Bay track team; former pres. BC branch women's AAUofC, CAHPER; v-p Canadian Camping Assn.; former dir. Vancouver YWCA; mem. National Advisory Council for Fitness, Amateur Sport; mem. BC Sports Hall of Fame; res. Vancouver, B.C.

BURNS, Chris (football); b. 2 Dec 1972, Greenwich, Conn.; Vancouver Coll, Shasta Jr. Coll, Portland State; broadcaster; 2 BC prov. All-star, Jr. coll., NCAA Div II, *USA Today* all-American awards; off.guard drafted by Sask. '94; CFL Ottawa '95-96, '03-04, Calgary '97, Hamilton '98-01; 2 East div all-star; 2 Grey Cups, 1 winner; res. Ottawa, Ont.

BURNS, Leo (administration); b. 20 Oct 1884, Montreal, Que.; d. 5 Sep 1965, Montreal, Que.; average athlete basketball, snowshoeing, distance running; mem. St. Pat's AAA; mgr. '36 Olympic boxing team; ring general '36 ntl championships; track official AAUofC competitions; registrar, pres. Que. branch AAUofC; v-p AAUofC; pres. St. Pat's AAA, Shamrocks AAA, QAHA; dir. Que. Lacrosse Assn.; CAHA merit award; mem. Cdn Olympic Sports Hall of Fame.

BURNS, Pat (coaching/hockey); b. 4 Apr 1952, St. Henri, Que.; m. Line; hockey coach; ex-policeman; coach Hull Olympiques '83-87, 1 QMJHL title; coach Sherbrooke '87-88; Montreal (NHL) '88-92, 1ˢᵗ-place finish rookie year; Toronto '92-96, Boston '97-00, New Jersey '02-03; asst. Canadian Canada Cup gold medal team '91, '86 world junior championships; joined Dick Irvin Sr. as only persons to coach both Montreal and Toronto; also with Irvin lone person to coach three of Original Six teams; NHL coaching record: (through '04) 1019 scheduled games, 501-367-151, 149 playoff games, 78-71; 1 Stanley Cup winner; 1ˢᵗ to win Jack Adams NHL coach of yr award with 3 different teams '89, '93, '98; passed 1000 coaching wins '04; *HN* coach of '93; hockey radio/TV analyst '96-97; res. Lynnfield, Mass.

BURNS, Tommy (boxing); b. 17 Jun 1881, Hanover, Ont.; d. 10 May 1955, Vancouver, B.C.; given name: Noah Brusso; m., c. 1; ordained minister; under Sam Biddle launched ring career Detroit at 19; 7 straight KO's before adopting name Tommy Burns borrowed from jockey friend; 1ˢᵗ loss to Philadelphia Jack O'Brien; when Jim Jeffries ret'd Marvin Hart claimed vacant world heavyweight crown; Burns, O'Brien filed counter claims; only Canadian to hold world heavyweight title '06; defended successfully 11 times including draw, win over O'Brien; lost title to Jack Johnson '08; ended ring career '20 with 36 KO's, 9 decision wins, 4 decision losses, 8 draws, 1 no-contest, once KO'd; 1 minute 28 second KO victory over Jem Roche '08 shortest heavy title bout on record; at 5'7" shortest ever to hold heavy title; authored *Scientific Boxing* '08; mem. Canadian, US Boxing, Canada's Sports halls of fame.

BURROWS, Bob (softball); b. 10 Mar 1947, Victoria, B.C.; given name: Robert John; m. Joette Mason; c. Brady, Lanny, Amanda; Spokane Comm. Coll, Seattle Pacific; insurance adjuster; multi-talented athlete excelling in softball, baseball, basketball; mem. '67 Cdn basketball team PAG; BC champion, MVP Oak Bay '65; attended Seattle Pacific on dual baseball-basketball scholarship; drafted by NBA Seattle SuperSonics but opted for baseball with Kansas City organization; 5 minor league seasons ended with serious injury in exhibition game '72; playing coach Victoria Scorpions (Data Tech) sr. A basketball team; ntl championship MVP, finalist '76; mem. Victoria Bates (Budgets) 4 successive ntl title softball teams '75-78; 1 MVP, 3 all-star awards; 15hrs in 6 ntl finals and *Guiness Book of World Records* inclusion for 4 world tournament HRs and 14 rbi; player-coach Victoria ntl title teams '82-83; Greater Victoria male athlete '74, twice runnerup; 3 team-of-yr awards; competed '76 world tournament which, due to weather, ended with Canada, US, NZ sharing title; began refereeing basketball '80; Victoria Little League pres.; mem. Cdn, BC Softball, South Hill Vancouver, Greater Victoria Sports halls of fame; res. Victoria, B.C.

BURROWS, Pat (field hockey); b. 5 Nov 1959, Barrie, Ont.; given name: Patrick David; m. Dr. Susan Wood; Miami (Ohio), UofT, BPHE, Queen's BEd; teacher; attended Miami on ice hockey scholarship; mem. ntl field hockey (outdoor) team '80-90, '94; ntl indoor FH team '91-93; competed '86, '90, '98 world outdoor, '91 indoor World Cup, '84, '88 Olympics, '81, '85, '89 Intercontinental Cup, gold '83, '87, silver '89, '95 PAG; MVP '89 Intercontinental Cup; team capt. '85-86, '89-90, indoor '91-93; PetroCanada scholarship; ret'd from competition '98; 225 international games; asst. coach ntl men's, Stanford '00; mem. Nepean Sports Wall of Fame; res. Mountain View, Calif.

BURTNYK, Kerry (curling); b. 24 Nov 1958, Reston, Man.; given name: Kerry Grant; m. Patti; c. Rachel, Laura; Red River Comm. Coll.; investment advisor; Man. jr title '78; skipped '79 Canada Winter Games gold medal rink; 8 time competitor Man. finals; at 21 youngest ever to skip Brier winner '81; bronze medal Silver Broom (world) '81; skip '95 Brier, Worlds winner; MCA grand aggregate champion '85-86; skipped Man. rink '81, '88, '95, '01 Briers; organized $250,000 Manitoba cashspiel circuit; nicknamed "Bubba"; res. Winnipeg, Man.

BUSCOMBE, Lisa (archery); b. 15 Dec 1956, Hamilton, Ont.; sep. David Bertoncini; Mohawk Coll., McMaster, hons BComm, UofT, MIR; administrator United Steelworkers; world field archery title '84; Olympic team alternate '84; field archery World Games champion '84, '85; 7 Ont., 6 ntl outdoor titles; 2 OCAA gold; outstanding female athlete award; Dr. Mitminger award; mem. Mohawk Coll., Brampton Sports, Cdn Olympic halls of fame; res. Toronto, Ont.

BUSH, Carmen (coaching/baseball); b. 26 Oct 1912, Toronto, Ont.; d. 5 Dec 2001, Toronto, Ont.; given name: Carmen Bucchiarello; ret'd. Columbus Boys Club dir.; a gifted student thwarted in bid to enroll at U of T because he was under 18; became athletic dir. K. of C. boys club '38; club dir. '63; inner-city icon and legendary coach; nicknamed Baron of Christie Pits; extraordinary contribution to baseball as builder and founder of several leagues; secty Toronto Baseball Assn. 50yrs; mem. Cdn Baseball Hall of Fame.

BUSH, Eddie (hockey); b. 11 Jul 1919, Collingwood, Ont.; d. 31 May 1984, Collingwood, Ont; given name: Edward Webster; m. Mabel Owens; c. Eddie Jr., Sandra Louise; salesman; Jr. A Guelph Biltmores; minor pro seasoning Pittsburgh, Kansas City; joined Detroit (NHL) '41-43; in 3rd game '43 Stanley Cup final scored once, assisted 4 others while playing def as Wings beat Toronto 5-2; post-WW2 Cincinnati scoring record for defencemen; player-coach Collingwood '51-53, 3 Ont. Intermediate A finals, 2 titles; coached Collingwood Jr. C consecutive titles '51-53; coached Guelph, Hamilton, Pittsburgh, Memphis, Kitchener, Richmond, NHL Kansas City Scouts '76; coach Hamilton '62 Memorial Cup winner; OHA jr. coaching record: 17yrs, 401-378-114; mem. Collingwood Sports Hall of Fame.

BUTLER, Barry (table tennis/tennis/basketball/fencing/administration); b. 29 Jul 1946, Ottawa, Ont.; given name: Barry George; m. Barbara Jean; Carleton; consultant; CWSA ntl singles, doubles (with Leslie Lam) table tennis champ '75-80; mem. '76 Paralympic team; 2 US Open silver '01; 2 CTTA wheelchair singles titles; CTTA dir. From '77; initiated Ottawa ACT disabled athlete-of-yr award, wheelchair table tennis program in Ottawa; coached Ottawa, ntl teams; founded Ottawa Paralympic TT team; NA rep. American Paralympic TT comm.; chair CTTA Paralympic advisory comm.; mem. Ottawa Royals wheelchair basketball team '76-96; starting point guard Royals' ntl title team '89, all-star '90; competed 2 NA championship tournaments, 1 silver; '95 ntl title team; Royals' co-founder '75; coach/mgr/GM CWBA tournament dir. '75-96; 2 CWSA fencing silver medals; finalist '95 Southern Regional tennis championships Fla.; founder, dir. NCWTA; Capital City Classic tourney dir. '90-05; co-founder Nepean Disabled Advisory Council; introduced wheelchair rugby to Ottawa area; introduced sledge hockey to Ottawa region; pres. NC Sports Council of disabled from '96; 1 ACT award; res. Ottawa, Ont.

BUTLER, Kathy (t&f); b. 22 Oct 1973, Edinburgh, Scotland; Wisc; 5000m runner; moved to Canada age 11; gold 5000m '95 Big-10 championships, '95-96 NCAA 3000m; ntl title '95; Cdn, NCAA x-country champion '95; mem. '96 (Cdn) '04 (UK) Olympic teams; NCAA x-country runner of yr '96; riled by perceived treatment of Cdn athletes by govt. switched allegiance to Britain to compete from '00; Scotland's female athlete of '01; res. Scotland.

BUTLER, Mike (badminton); b. 9 Mar 1961, Gander, Nfld.; given name: Michael Gerald; m. Rolyne Guzman; c. Michael Roger, Sarah Elizabeth; UNB; Air Canada customer service agent; ntl −16 mixed doubles, 4 ntl intermediate titles (1 singles, 2 men's, 1 mixed doubles), 9 ntl sr titles (5 singles, 3 mixed, 1 men's doubles); 1 triple crown season; US open singles, mixed douibles titles; 4 NB male athlete of yr. Awards; mem. Saint John, N.B. Sports halls of fame; res. Saint John, N.B.

BUTT, Mark (figure skating); b. 25 Apr 1980, Montreal, Que.; given name: Mark Edward; Ashbury Coll., Delaware BSc Ed, Penn MA; musician; pro skater; principal oboist UDel orchestra; Pi Sigma Phi ntl honor fraternity; Golden Key honor society; Stegner scientific research award; outstanding-male-senior award; skating gold novice '97, silver jr. '98; mem. UDel FS team '99-03; US ntl jr. team; ntl coll, jr, men's bronze '00; competed 3 sr. ntl intercollegiate championships; toured 32 cities with Beauty and the Beast ice show '03-04; numerous academic honors; res. Orleans, Ont.

BUTT, Susan (tennis); b. 19 Mar 1938, Vancouver, B.C.; given name: Dorcas Susan; div; c. Tara Susan, Donal Lee Finn; UBC, BA, MA, UChi, PhD; psychologist, associate prof.; more than decade among Canada's leading tennis players, winning singles, doubles, mixed doubles titles BC, Ont., Que., Can., Western Can., Pacific Northwest, US Intercollegiate; top ranked ntl women's tennis '60-61, '67; 3rd round Wimbledon '61; capt. '70-72 Federation Cup teams; v-p CLTA '71-72; author *A Psychology of Sport*, numerous research publications on psychological motivation in sport; clinical psychologist consultant for many athletes, teams, clubs from local to elite levels; mem. Cdn Tennis Hall of Fame; res. Vancouver, B.C.

BUTTERFIELD, Jack (builder/hockey); b. 1 Aug 1919, Regina, Sask; days as player cut short by injury so he turned to role as PR exec./trainer for AHL New Haven Eagles owned by uncle Eddie Shore; later business mgr. Fort Worth (USHL), Oakland (WHL); jack-of-all-trades Springfield (AHL) from concessions mgr to GM; became AHL pres. '66; twice rewrote AHL constitution; key role in keeping minor pro hockey alive as NHL went on expansion binge following conflict with WHA; AHL MVP trophy bears his name; mem. Hockey Hall of Fame; res. Springfield, Mass.

BUTTERFIELD, Joe (rodeo); b. 15 Sep 1961, Calgary, Alta.; farrier, Christmas tree dealer; calf roping, steer wrestling specialist; ntl calf roping title '90; Alta. circuit high point title '93; 2 BC circuit calf roping titles; Skoal pro rodeo circuit CR title '91; owner Cdn CR horse of yr (Vance) '91, (Jake) '95; Dodge, Skoal pro tour, Calgary Stampede SW titles '92; res. Red Deer, Alta.

BUTTERWORTH, Arnie (curling/hockey/golf); b. 7 Jun 1911, Ottawa, Ont; d. 21 May 1999, Ottawa, Ont; given name: Peter Arnold; m. Margaret Geraldine Hughes; Clarkson Coll; ret'd Treasury Dept.; played hockey New Edinburgh Jrs. '27; top scorer Glebe CI jrs. '28; Memorial Cup Eastern Cdn. Finalist Rideau Canoe Club '30; Maritime champion, Allan Cup finalist Dalhousie NB Rangers '32; 4yrs leading scorer Clarkson Coll '34-37; signed to C form by Ottawa Senators; joined Glebe CC '49, Ottawa CC '50; as skip guided rink to numerous City of Ottawa bonspiel honors; CBRCCC Jubilee, Governor-General's trophies; p-pres OCC, CBRCCC; broadcaster CBC radio curling news, CBC-TV Roaring Game show '63-67; mem. Rivermead GC from '40, pres. '64-65; chair ODGA.

BUXTON, Noel (curling); b. 26 Aug 1910, Sheffield, Eng; d. 26 Dec 1988, Winnipeg, Man.; given name: Noel Robert; m. Audrey; c. Noel, Beverley; banker; pres. Deer Lodge CC '61-62; mem. MCA council '62-63, pres. '71-72; instrumental in formation Manitoba Curling Hall of Fame; hon. life mem. CCA, MCA, Deer Lodge CC; mem. selection comm. MSHOF; mem. Cdn Curling Hall of Fame.

C

CADA, Petra (table tennis); b. 2 Feb 1979, Prague, Czechoslovakia; UofO, BSc; works World Health Org.; at 14 youngest to represent Canada at world championships; simultaneously held ntl -14, -17, -21 titles '93, only female ever to do so; women's team gold '95 PAG, '02 CG; English junior open title '95; singles bronze '93 world youth championships; '02 Finnish women's doubles, team gold, singles silver; plays in French league; mem. '96, '04 Olympic, '02 CG teams; gold ntl Top 9 tourney '04; turned pro '04; res. Ottawa, Ont./ Brussels, Belgium.

CADIEUX, David (boxing); b. 25 Nov 1974, St. Jean sur Richelieu, Que.; c. Eden; Trois-Rivieres; special ed.; super heavyweight; judoka 7yrs; began boxing at 17; ntl team from '01; through Jan '04 55-25 record; '01 Francophonie games, Felix Stamm tournament bronze; ntl title '02; CG silver '02; competed '03 PAG; res. Trois-Rivieres, Que.

CAETANO, Errol (table tennis); b. 8 Aug 1953, Georgetown, Guyana; cable engineer; joined ntl team '71; 5 ntl singles, 7 men's doubles, 6 mixed doubles titles; Caribbean singles, men's, mixed doubles '72; Scandinavian Open '75; Eastern Canadian Open '78; mem. '71, '73, '75 world, Commonwealth championships teams; res. Pickering, Ont.

CAFFERY, Jack (t&f); b. 21 May 1879, Hamilton, Ont.; d. 2 Feb 1919, Hamilton, Ont.; given name: John Peter; m. Jane Campbell; c. 3 boys, 3 girls; shoe merchant; Boston Marathon victories '00-01; Hamilton Around the Bay marathon '98, '00; reduced own BM record by 10 minutes '01; ret'd from racing '03; comeback bid '08 failed to produce big results; forced from Olympic trials by foot injury paid own way to '08 Games, finished 11th; running coach from '09; mem. Cdn Road Running Hall of Fame.

CAHILL, Leo (football); b. 30 Jul 1928, Utica, Ill.; div. Shirley; c. Steven, Christy Lee, Terry, Lisa Ann, Betty Lynn; Illinois, BSc,Toledo, MA; football executive; all-state ctr HS sr.; mem. Illinois Rose Bowl titlist; all-Midwest gd, hon. mention all-American, Catholic all-American; Blue-Grey Game; coached Japan, freshman coach Illinois '53; Lewis College line coach '54-55; asst. Toledo '56-57; South Carolina off. coach '58-59; asst. Alouettes '60-64; head coach Toronto Rifles (Continental League) '65, won div. title, tied for title '66; coach Argos '67-72, '77-78, GM '86, goodwill ambassador '04; '71 Grey Cup finalist; GM Memphis Southmen (WFL) '74; league official as league folded '75; TV-radio sports commentator '87-85; v-p Ottawa '96; mem. Etobicoke Sports Hall of Fame; res. Sarnia, Ont.

CAHOON, Ben (football); b. 16 Jul 1972, Orem, Utah; m. Kimberley; c. 3 daughters; Brigham Young; sb/wr; recruited by Utah State, Yale, New Mexico, Idaho but opted for BYU; 1st draft choice Montreal '98; CFL record (through '04) 126 scheduled games, 492 receptions, 6929yds, 36tds; 2ce CFL outstanding Cdn; GC '03 outstanding Cdn award; 4 East div., 1 CFL, CFLPA all-star; 3 Grey Cup finals, 1

winner; under CFL rules given Cdn status after spending 5 of 1st 15yrs in Canada (Edmonton, Calgary, Montreal); res. Cedar Hills, Utah.

CAIN, Jim (football); b. 30 Jun 1938, Toronto, Ont.; m. Pam Mountenay; c. Pam; Detroit, BSc; consultant, ret'd. Stats Can. statistician, economist; among 1st Canadian HS grads sent to US college on CFL team recommendation; pro Ottawa '61-69, playing all line positions except ctr; launched pro career on offence and finished on defence; dt as Riders won consecutive Grey Cups '68-69; asst. coach UofOtt '70-72; mem. UD Sports Hall of Fame; res. Nepean, Ont.

CAIN, Larry (canoeing); b. 9 Jan 1963, Toronto, Ont.; McMaster; teacher/coach/motivational speaker; ntl jr. record 2:08.59 C1 500m '79; 1st Cdn canoeist in 46 years to win at world level claiming 2 golds '81 jr. worlds; '80 Bydgoszcz regatta jr. C1 500m, 1000m; '80 Pan-Am championships C1 1000m; '82 Nottinghamshire regatta C1 1000m; gold C1 1500m '83 Brandenburg regatta, silver C1 500m; gold, silver '83 Sofia regatta; gold 500m C1, silver 1000m C1 '84 Olympics; ntl titles: 8 C1, 2 C2 500m, 4 C1, 2 C2, 1 C4 1000m; competed 3 Olympics; runnerup Viscount Alexander Trophy '81; Canadian Sport Manufacturers Assn. award '81; fed. govt. world champion award '82; coach, Burloak Canoe Club; pres. FAST; mem. Order of Canada, Cdn Olympic, Canada's Sports halls of fame; res. Oakville, Ont.

CAITHNESS, Charlie (soccer/builder); b. 7 Nov 1907, Carnoustie, Scotland; d. 19 Aug 1985, Winnipeg,Man.; player/coach/manager/administrator; managed ANAF Scottish '47-65, Tatra '70-82; 16 Man. championships, including unbroken streak of 12; Scottish won 2 ntl titles; coached Winnipeg Blues in Western Canada League; mgr. ntl champion Manitoba Selects '70; keen interest in youth soccer and development of young players; mem. Man. Sports Hall of Fame.

CALDER, Frank (administration, hockey); b.17 Nov 1877, England; b. 4 Feb 1943, Montreal, Que.; m Amelia Cope; secty Ntl Hockey Assn.; became 1st pres. when NHL formed '17 remaining as such until '43 death; AHL championship trophy, NHL rookie-of-yr trophy bear his name; mem. Hockey Hall of Fame.

CALDER, Marty (wrestling); b. 25 Jan 1967, St. Catharines, Ont.; Brock; m. Tanya; c. Cameron, Alexa; coach; began competing age 14; freestyle and Greco-Roman; competes at 68, 63kg level; competed '91 (bronze), '95, '99 (bronze) Pan-Am, '92, '96 Olympic, '94 CG, '91 (bronze), '93, '97 Worlds, gold '92 Sunkist International Open, '93 Polish GP, '92 Canada Cup, '90 Clansman International; ntl 62kg title '94; gold 62kg '94 CG; 4 CIAU, 5 ntl sr. titles; CIAU outstanding-wrestler award '92 championships; asst. coach Brock, ntl team '01; standout lacrosse player; mem. Cdn jr. title team; drafted by pro Buffalo Bandits; 3 Brock athlete-of-yr awards; mem. St. Catharines, Brock sports halls of fame; res. Thorold, Ont.

CALDWELL, Earl (shooting); b. 27 Oct 1912, Heward, Sask.; given name: Earl Grove; m. Edith Nicol; c. Robert, David; pres. Caldwell Industries; mem. 9 BC skeet, 12 BC. trap all-star teams; '53-73 numerous BC. skeet titles in all gauges; mem. ntl team that broke 498x500; ntl record 9 times PITA all-star; BC. record 7 times all-Canada trap team; 11 provincial titles including all-time 6 doubles crowns; 2 consecutive ntl doubles titles; ntl singles with 494x500; more than 300 titles; mem. '56 Olympic team; res. N. Vancouver, B.C.

CALKINS, Michelle (synchro swim); b. 3 Oct 1958, Calgary, Alta.; m. Douglas DeFilippi; c. Anna, Paul; coach; ntl jr. solo title '73; with Helen Vanderburg won world aquatic duet title '78; '76 PAG team silver; '77 Pan-Pacific duet gold; ret'd to coaching '78 with Calgary Aquabelles, working with several world, Olympic champions; ntl team asst.coach '89-93, head coach '94-04; ntl title teams '73-78; with Vanderburg shared Elaine Tanner award '77; PetroCan coaching award; mem. Alta Sports, Cdn, Intl Aquatic halls of fame; res. Calgary, Alta.

CALLAGHAN, Helen (baseball); b. 18 Mar 1923, Vancouver, B.C.; d. 8 Dec 1992, Santa Barbara, Calif.; div. Bob Candaele; c. Ricky, Rocky, Kelly, Kerry, Casey; m. Ron St. Aubin; home care supervisor; cf; played in All-American Girls Professional Baseball League with Minneapolis '44, Fort Wayne '45-48, Kenosha '48; sister Marg also played in league; BC. jr. 100yd sprint champion; played basketball, lacrosse, softball; son Casey played ML baseball; Lompoc. Calif. scholarship bears her name; honored by Cooperstown, Cdn Baseball halls of Fame.

CALLAGHAN, Margaret (baseball); b. 23 Dec 1921, Vancouver, B.C.; d. Sep 2000, Delta, B.C.; div. Merv Maxwell; c. Guy, Dale; care giver; versatile athlete who played for Cdn champion Vancouver Eilers '51 ntl basketball champions; 8 seasons at 3rd base in AAGPBL with Minneapolis '44, Fort Wayne '45-48, South Bend '49, Peoria '50-51, Kalamazoo '51; competed in '43 women's world amateur softball championships; played 3yrs lacrosse; sister Helen also played AAGPBL; mem. Softball City Surrey Walk of Fame, South Memorial Hall of Fame; honored by Cooperstown, Cdn Baseball halls of fame.

CALLAGHAN, Pius (builder); b. 2 Sep 1914, Charlottetown, P.E.I.; d. 31 Jul 1990, Charlottetown, P.E.I.; m. Winnie; c. 3; St. Dunstan's BA, LLB; journalist, educator; associated with Maritime AHA 20yrs; pres. PEIJHL '68-69; mem. PEI Sports and Racing Commission '82-87; Callaghan Cup awarded annually to Atlantic Canada Jr. A titlists; chair. Charlottetown Gold Cup & Saucer 3yrs; CAHA meritorious award; mem. PEI Sports Hall of Fame.

CALLES, Ada (curling); b. 12 Oct 1920, Lancashire, Eng.; d. 12 Apr 1996, Kimberley, B.C.; given name: Ada Davies; m. Samuel Calles; c. Dan, Sam; Trail business college; rep. Kootenay Dist. at BC. championships 9 consecutive years; BC., ntl titles '62, runnerup ntl final '63, title '64; defeated men's Brier champion Lyall Dagg in special match; following 7-year break teamed again with Ina Hansen to win BC title and tie for 1st, losing playoff in ntl final '71; with Hansen at 3rd skipped BC to 1st ntl srs title '73; mem. BCLCA exec. '60-67 from zone convenor to pres.; CLCA

delegate; chaired '76 BC girls' provincial championship comm.; mem. Canadian Curling Hall of Fame.

CALLURA, Jackie (boxing); b. 1 Jan 1914, Hamilton, Ont.; d. 4 Nov 1993, Hamilton, Ont.; ntl amateur featherweight title '31; mem. '32 Olympic team; pro '36; US National Boxing Assn. featherweight title beating Jackie Wilson in 15 at Providence '43; defended twice before KO loss to Phil Terranova '43 New Orleans; last pro bout Miami '47; fought 100 pro bouts winning 13 by KO, 43 by decision, one on foul, 10 draws, 27 lost decisions, KO'd 6 times; mem. Canada's Sports, Canadian Boxing, Copps Coliseum halls of fame.

CALVILLO, Anthony (football); b. 23 Aug 1972, Los Angeles, Calif.; m. Alexia; Utah State; qb; lettered 2 seasons Utah State; set Utah State record 3260yds total offence '93; threw for 5624yds '92-93; surpassed 6000yd season passing plateau '04; CFL record (through '04) 186 scheduled games, 478 carries, 2347yds, 19tds, 2645 completions on 4478 passes, 39,172yds, 129 int, 214tds; 1stoverall Hamilton pick Las Vegas dispersal draft '95; CFL Las Vegas '94, Hamilton '95-97, Montreal '98-04; 1 Grey Cup winner, Eastern div. all-star '00; CFL outstanding player '03; res. Montreal, Que.

CAMERON, Bev (rowing); b. 17 Jun 1953, Ottawa, Ont,; '75 Canadian Henley, ntl championships single sculls; with sister Trice '75 Canadian Henley double sculls, US women's double sculls; with Cheryl Howard 6th double sculls '76 Olympics; closed competitive career with 4th double sculls (with Howard) '77 world championships; res. Toronto, Ont.

CAMERON, Bob (football); b. 18 Jul 1954, Hamilton, Ont.; m. Louise; c. Brett, Shane; Acadia; ret'd football player; radio color analyst; qb/kicker Acadia; Hec Crighton Award '77; 1st round draft, 6th overall Edmonton '77; signed by Winnipeg as free-agent punter '80; ret'd after 23 CFL seasons '02; all-time CFL, Blue Bomber punting leader; CFL record: 394 scheduled games, 4cvts, 130s, 134pts, 3129punts, 134,301yds; 2 Western, 4 Eastern, 4 CFL, 1 Northern all-star; 2 CFL records; 6 Grey Cup finals, 3 winners; plays with Blue Bombers hockey team; mem. Blue Bomber, Acadia Sports Hall of Fame; res. Winnipeg, Man.

CAMERON, Doug (curling); b. 18 Aug 1933, Charlottetown, P.E.I.; given name: Douglas Allison; m. Barbara Rupert; c. Marilyn, Nancy, Angus, Gordon; Queen's; ret'd deputy minister, accountant; won provincial titles spanning 6 decades '49-91; played in 2 ntl schoolboy, runnerup '50; 7 Briers, 5 as skip; skipped PEI '73 ntl mixed, 2 ntl srs; runnerup '64 Tournament of Champions; competed 3 tournament of champions tournaments; runnerup '64 *CBC Curling Classic*; skipped '70 City of Ottawa grand aggregate winner; dir. PEI Sports Hall of Fame; mem. Cdn Curling, PEI Sports halls of fame; res. Charlottetown, P.E.I.

CAMERON, Fred (t&f); b. 11 Nov 1886, Advocate Harbor, N.S.; d. 18 Mar 1953, Vancouver, B.C.; given name. Frederick; m. Blanche Moffat; tire vulcanizer; began competing '07 meeting with quick success despite lack of training; caught attention of prominent trainer

Tom T. Trenholm and career took off; set Maritime, Cdn 10-, 5-mile records; won '10 Boston Marathon; 1st Boston Marathon winner honored by Mayor of Boston with luncheon, establishing a tradition; beat Clarence DeMar, Walter Hackett, Cliff Horne in series of 5- and 10- mile challenge races Amherst, N.S.; turned pro '11; ran for Illinois AC several years; ret'd '19; won over 100 trophies, 60 cups during career; mem. NS Sports, Cdn Road Running halls of fame.

CAMERON, Harry (hockey); b. 6 Feb 1890, Pembroke, Ont.; d. 20 Oct 1953, Vancouver, B.C.; given name: Harold Hugh; among 1st offensive defencemen; believed 1st player to curve a shot without aid of curved stick; scored 171 goals in 312 games over 14yr pro career Blueshirts (NHA) '13-17, Montreal Wanderers (NHA) '17, Toronto Arenas '18, '20-24 (3 Stanley Cups), Ottawa Senators '19, Canadiens '20; left NHL '24, played in Vancouver, Saskatoon, Minneapolis, St. Louis; coach Saskatoon Sheiks Prairie League '32; mem. Hockey Hall of Fame.

CAMERON, Jack (all-around); b. 3 Dec 1902, Ottawa, Ont.; d. 29 Dec 1981, Danville, Va.; m. Margaret Jane Grant; St. Andrews College, McGill; goal; Toronto Granites Allan Cup champions '21-23; Olympic gold medal '24; rejected pro offer from Montreal Canadiens; NHL referee '32-36; Que. Open golf champion '28; Que. amateur titles '32-33; qualified 9 US amateurs, once quarterfinalist; mem. Ont., Que. Willingdon Cup teams; ntl amateur finalist '32, 3 times semifinalist; cricket wicketkeeper ntl champion Toronto Yorkshire Cricket Club; partnered Jack Purcell England international badminton matches; with Rod Phelan ntl doubles; 4 times Ont. team mem.; with Bill Stewart Ont. doubles; Ont. sports achievement award; mem. Kingston International Hockey Hall of Fame and as mem. Olympic champion Granites Cdn Hockey Hall of Fame Toronto.

CAMERON, Michelle (synchro swim); b. 28 Dec 1962, Calgary, Alta.; m. Al Coulter; c. Alissa, Jacqueline; UCal; motivational speaker; dir. *Rogers Broadcasting*; teamed with Carolyn Waldo to win '86 CG, '88 Olympic duet gold, '85-87 world duet titles; also earned duet gold '85 Rome, Spanish Opens, '85, '87 FINA Cup; Pan-Pacific; Spanish Open team gold '84; ntl duet, team gold, figures bronze; Spanish Open figures silver '85; sport excellence award '86; Dick Ellis award '85; athletes service officer '96 Olympics; mem. Cdn Coaching Assn, Cdn Sports Council, Cdn Athletes Assn.; mem. Order of Canada, Alta Sports, Cdn Aquatic, Intl Swimming, Olympic, Canada's Sports halls of fame; res. Calgary, Alta.

CAMERON, Trice (rowing); b. 23 Feb 1952, Ottawa, Ont.; given name: Patrice Gail; UofOtt; Sport Canada policy analyst; mem. ntl x-country B ski team '73-74; Olympic rowing teams '76, '80; with sister Bev '75 Cdn Henley, US women's double sculls; ntl single sculls '77; Cdn Henley singles '79; Cdn quad, Henley quad titles '80; mem. women's committee FIS '75-77, '85-95; chair. women's adhoc rowing comm. '81; silver Coureur de Bois ntl ski marathon; partner Old Chelsea seasonal x-country ski shop; Level II x-country instructor, Level I coach; res. Gleneagle, Que.

CAMPBELL, Angus (builder/hockey); b. 19 Mar 1884, Stayner, Ont; d. 1976, Toronto, Ont.; given name: Angus Daniel; UofT, BSc; mining engineer; mem. UofT hockey, lacrosse title teams; played hockey Cobalt, Ont '09-14; after playing days ended played key role in amateur hockey development in Northern Ontario; 1st pres. NOHA '19; served as OHA exec.; mem. Hockey Hall of Fame.

CAMPBELL, Cassie (hockey); b. 22 Nov 1973, Brampton, Ont.; Guelph hons. sociology; motivational speaker; soccer/basketball/hockey player; OWIAA all-star def '96; mem. Ont. Canada Winter Games team '91; silver Esso Nationals with North York Aeros '96; mem. ntl team from '94; ntl team capt.; 8 world, 2 Pacific Rim titles; silver '98, gold '02 Olympics; WWHC all-star def. '97; Guelph sportswoman of '96; spokesperson HIP program smoking prevention for young girls; with Bobby Orr, Mike Bossy operates kids' hockey school; mother Eunice played 9 pro football games '69; TV CIAU color commentator; gold Team Alta. '01 Esso ntls; top forward '00 Esso ntls, gold Beatrice Aeros, silver '99 OWIAA 1st, 2nd team all-star; related to Anne of Green Gables author Lucy Maud Montgomery; operated PEI hockey school; res. Calgary, Alta.

CAMPBELL, Clarence (administration); b. 7 Jul 1905, Fleming, Sask.; d. 24 Jun 1984, Montreal, Que.; given name: Clarence Sutherland; m. Phyllis Loraine King; UofAlta, BA, LLB, Oxford(Rhodes Scholar), MA; hockey exec., lawyer; hb Edmonton Eskimos Provincial League, eventually owned club; at 17 organized Edmonton District HA; baseball c/of; designed, built Renfrew Park, Edmonton; at Oxford capt. hockey team; refereed '28 Olympic lacrosse final; Canadian Branch of Royal Caledonian Curling Club event titles; refereed amateur hockey '29-40, NHL '36-40, officiated 155 scheduled, 12 playoff games; Lt.Col. with Canadian War Crimes Investigation unit WW2; NHL pres. '46-77; prominent role in establishing NHL players' pension plan, expansion program; Lester Patrick trophy '72; Centennial Medal '67; NHL created division in his name; MBE, QC; mem. UofAlta., Canada's Sports, Cdn, US Hockey halls of fame.

CAMPBELL, Colin (curling); b. 17 Jan 1901, Shedden, Ont.; d. 25 Dec 1978, Toronto, Ont.; m. Vera Smith; c. 2 sons, 2 daughters; Queen's; engineer, soldier, politician; mem. Ont. rink '51 Macdonald Brier; capt. Cdn Strathcona Cup team Scotland '60, '70, Switzerland '67; mem. Dominion (now Cdn) Curling Assn. from '38, pres. '47-48; chairman International comm. '48-76; Macdonald Brier trustee from '65; Canadian rep. Scotch Cup advisory comm. '64-67; helped organize International Curling Fed. '66; Canadian rep. ICF '67-78, pres. '69-78; life mem. Hamilton Thistle Club, MCA, QCA, OCA, CCA, PCCA, Grand National CC of NA, German CA, Royal Caledonian CC; mem. Canadian Curling Hall of Fame.

CAMPBELL, David (basketball/lacrosse); b. 11 Sep 1925, Vancouver, B.C.; given name: David Hector; m. Joan Jarvis; c. Margot, Craig; UBC, LLD; county court judge; basketball BC. int. champion Arrows '44; Vimy Camp RC Signals '45; UBC Thunderbirds '46-49; mem. '48 ntl champions, Olympic team; mem. '51 ntl champion Cloverleafs; lacrosse BC. juv A champions '41-42; Sr. A Richmond Farmers '43-

50; Ed Bailey Trophy Intercity League outstanding rookie '43; res. Vancouver, B.C.

CAMPBELL, Debbie (t&f); b. 2 Jul 1958, Halifax, N.S.; given name: Deborah Joy; m. Graeme Fell; c. Glory Ann; UVic; early years spent in figure skating; mem. NS t&f team Canada Summer Games '73; Victoria girls city champion 400m, 800m '74; silver 400m Canada Summer Games '78; ntl 800m, indoor 400m titles '78; 400m Portland, Ore., 800m Eugene, Ore. (PB 2:04) '78; bronze 4x400 relay team '78 CG; bronze Ottawa Indoor Games '82; res. Victoria, B.C.

CAMPBELL, Derrick (speed skating); b. 18 Feb 1972, Cambridge, Ont.; coach; former hockey player, figure skater who began speed skating age 12; mem. ntl team from '89; alternate '92, relay team/individual '94, with Marc Gagnon, François Drolet, Éric Bédard relay 5000m gold '98 Olympics; world championship 500m gold '97; 3 world championship silver, 3 bronze; world team championship overall gold '96, '98; short-track coach Olympic oval; mem. Cambridge Sports Hall of Fame; res. Calgary, Alta.

CAMPBELL, Dorothy (golf); b. 1883, Edinburgh, Scotland; d. 1946, New York; m. Hurd (d); m. Howe (d); began competitive career in Scotland with North Berwick 1904-09; emigrated to Canada '10 joining Hamilton club '10-12; mem. Merion Cricket Club, NY from '13; British women's title '09, '11; US titles '09-10, '24; Cdn titles '10-12; mem. Cdn Golf Hall of Fame.

CAMPBELL, Garnet (curling); b. 11 Jan 1927, Avonlea, Sask.; given name: William Garnet; m. DeVerne; c. Vern, Cassandra; farmer; rep. Saskatchewan 10 Briers from '47; skipped '55 winner; skipped Sask. ntl mixed finals '76-77; 6 carspiels, 7 Moose Jaw grand aggregates, 5 Regina titles, Weyburn, Ottawa, Vancouver Totem 'spiels once each; Quebec International, Windsor Invitational, Toronto Canada Life, Calgary Masters titles; twice *CBC Keen Ice* champion; mem. Governor-General's CC, Canadian Curling Hall of Fame; res. Avonlea, Sask.

CAMPBELL, Hugh (football); b. 21 May 1941, Spokane, Wash.; m. Louise; c. Robin, Jill, Rick, Molly; Washington State, BSc, MEd; football executive; all-American end WSU '60-62; drafted San Francisco; Saskatchewan '63-69; CFL record: 321 receptions, 5425yds, 60 tds; 3 times WFC all-star, twice all-Cdn flanker; shares CFL single season td receiving record 17 with Terry Evanshen; coached Whitworth College, Edmonton (CFL) '77-82, USFL LA Express '83, NFL Houston Oilers '84-85; GM Eskimos from '86; guided Eskimos to 6 consecutive Grey Cup finals unprecedented 5 wins in succession; NAIA Dist. 1 coach of '72, '75, CFL coach of '79; mem. Cdn Football Hall of Fame, Sask. Roughriders Plaza of Honor, Edmonton Eskimos Wall of Honor; res. Edmonton, Alta.

CAMPBELL, Jennifer (swimming); b. 26 Apr 1966, Sudbury, Ont.; m. Bruno Michel; c. Kyra, Cassia; Louisiana State BSc, Laurentian, BPhEd; teacher, coach; began career with Copper Cliff SC age 8; joined Laurentian SC at 15; competed annually in Europe from '78; set 1st ntl 50 FS age-group record '75; mem. ntl team '81-85; unprecedented 7 gold '81 Canada Games; competed '82 Commonwealth, '85, '87 FISU games; 3 ntl high point trophies; 32 ntl

championship individual medals (13 gold, 10 silver, 9 bronze); athletic/scholastic all-American; teaches aquatics, coaches Laurentian women's swim team; competes in masters swimming, triathlon events; mem. Ont. Aquatic Hall of Fame; res. Sudbury, Ont.

CAMPBELL, Jerry (football); b. 14 Jul 1944, Spokane, Wash.; div. Betty Ellis; m. Kim Kneeshaw; Idaho, BSc; bartender Capt. Jack's Pub; nicknamed "Soupy"; Idaho lineman of year; all-Skyline team '65; pro Calgary '66-68, '76, Ottawa '68-'75; og/lb; mem. 3 Grey Cup winners; all-Eastern, all-Cdn 7 times; Washington state HS lineman-of-yr; Washington pro athlete of '72-73; Idaho pro athlete of '72-74; mem. Spokane, Wash., Idaho, Ottawa Sports, Cdn Football halls of fame; res. Toronto, Ont.

CAMPBELL, John (harness racing); b. 4 Aug 1955, London, Ont.; m. Paula; horseman; more than 200 victories Windsor-Detroit tracks; moved to Grand Circuit mid-'70s; 15 times NA leading money winning driver; 1st driver to top $6 million in purses single season '83, $14 million '01; 1st-ever to record $100M US in earnings; through '03 9265 victories, $219M in purses; drove 7 winners in 8 starts Meadowlands '83; 1st driver to score 5 times in one card on consecutive nights at Meadowlands; more than 2500 sub-2-minute miles; winner 16 $1M races; drove Willow Weeper world record 1:55.1 Freehold '82; 5 Hambletonian (a record), 3 Little Brown Jug, 7 Messenger Stakes, 3 Maple Leaf Trot, 4 Cane Pace, 6 NA Cup, 2 World Trotting Derby, 4 Cdn Pacing Derby, 47 Bluegrass Stakes, 2 Yonkers Trot, 40 Breeders Crown victories; winner of more than 700 major stakes races; with Mack Lobell, OK Bye, Franconia, Nadia Lobel, Stonebridge Skipper, Run the Table, Miss Easy, Save Fuel, Tagliabue, Muscles Yankee, Real Desire and others shattered numerous track, world records; twice guided Mack Lobell to Harness-Horse-of-Yr awards; also handled Miss Easy, Central Park West, 2yr-old filly-pacers-of-yr; Peace Corps, 2yr-old trotting filly of year; Totally Ruthless, Artsplace, 2yr-old pacing colts of year; piloted Pine Chip to trotter-of-yr honors '93-94; Cdn meritorious service award; nicknamed "Merlin"; founder Standardbred Retirement Foundation; mem. London Sports, Cdn Horse Racing, Harness Racing Living halls of fame; res. River Vale, N.J./Ailsa Craig, Ont.

CAMPBELL, R.D. (coaching); b. 12 Apr 1892, Ottawa, Ont.; d. 4 Dec 1970, Ottawa, Ont.; given name: Robert Duncan; m. Annie Laurie McLaren (d), m. Minnie Constance Currie (d), m. Helen Mary Docksteader; c. Bruce; McMaster, BA, OCE; educator; intercollegiate hj record; '30-53 coached 16 sr., 11 jr. Glebe CI basketball title teams; nearly 50 titles at all levels; coached Glebe Grads '38 ntl sr. title; ntl jr., juve. titles; coached Glebe t&f athletes Arthur Currie Trophy honors 8 times '33-48; established physical culture courses Toronto Hart House, Lake Couchiching for Dept. of Education; introduced team eligibility rules, forward pass, down-field blocking in HS football resulting in Canadian football rules changes; rejected coaching offers McMaster, Rough Riders; Ottawa sportsman of year; Ottawa HS stadium bears his name; mem. Ottawa, McMaster Sports halls of fame.

CAMPBELL, Rachelle (t&f); b. 30 Oct 1956, Guelph, Ont.; given name: Rachelle Mary Angela; m. Bill Clausen;

c. Erika, Elyse, Shaun; Connestoga Coll.; day care teacher; 400m, 800m specialist; gold 400m Canada Games '73; gold 400m, silver 800m '74 jr. Olympics; ntl jr. record 52.6 for 400m; gold 4x400m relay team '75 PAG; mem. '76 Olympic team; bronze 4x400m relay team '78 CG; ntl 400m title '78; competes at masters level; assists Peter Manning as coach Guelph TC; Guelph sports merit award '77; mem. UGuelph Sports Hall of Fame; res. Guelph, Ont.

CAMPBELL, Shirley (swimming); b. 21 Sep 1935, Fergus, Ont.; given name: Shirley Marguerite; m. William Richard Campbell; c. Gary, Sandra; real estate agent; ntl 400m record; qualified for '52 Olympics but illness forced her out; ntl mile Ross Gold Trophy; CNE pro 3-mile race title '52-53; twice fell short in bids to beat Marilyn Bell's Lake Ont. swim record; won Egyptian 3-mile swim; competed in Sportsman's Shows swims; res. Mississauga, Ont.

CAMPO, Danielle (swimming); b. 4 Jan 1985, Windsor, Ont.; UCalgary; 3 gold, 1 silver, 2 world records '00, 1 silver, 2 bronze '04 Paralympics; bronze '02 CG; Ont. jr. citizen of yr, Order of Ont. awards; nicknamed "Golden Girl"; active motivational speaker; res. Tecumseh, Ont./Calgary, Alta.

CANTIN, Diane (horseshoes); b. 30 Jul 1947, St. Raymond, Que.; given name: Diane Par ; m. Réal Cantin; c. Nathalie, Caroline; 6 Que. women's doubles titles; 11 Que. women's singles titles; 8 ntl women's singles titles; records for high-ringer percentage for complete tournament: ntl 88% '89, Que. 84% '93; shot only perfect game in Cdn championship history 24x24 '89; perfect 36x36 '89 Que. championship; 3 world records '87, 54 consec. ringers, 1023 ringers, 448 doubles for complete tournament; 7 top-5 finishes in world tournaments, 3 times runnerup; mem. Cdn Horseshoe Hall of Fame; res. St. Raymond, Que.

CAPOZZI, Herb (racquetball); b. 24 Apr 1925, Kelowna, B.C.; given name: Harold Peter; div.; c. Paula, Greg, Sandra, Sheena; UBC, BA, BComm., UofItaly, education degree; owner, operator men's athletic, recreation centre; football UBC, rejected offers from NY Giants; CFL Calgary, Montreal; GM BC '57-66, Grey Cup '64; chairman CFL, WFC GM's comm.; briefly operated NHL Vancouver; principal owner Vancouver Whitecaps NASL, league title '79; chair. Soccer Canada; with Bob Pickell '73 ntl Masters doubles racquetball champion; ntl Masters singles title '74; ntl Golden Masters title '81; Socred MLA '66-72; mem. Lions Wall, UBC Sports Hall of Fame; res. Vancouver, B.C.

CARBONNEAU, Guy (hockey); b. 18 Mar 1960, Sept Iles, Que.; m. Line; c. Anne-Marie, Kristina; hockey exec.; ctr Chicoutimi (QJHL) '76-80, Nova Scotia (AHL) '80-82, NHL Montreal '80-94, St. Louis '94-95, Dallas '95-00; former capt. Canadiens; 3 Frank Selke trophies; 4 Stanley Cup finals, 3 winners; became supervisor player personnel Mtl '00, asst coach '01-02; exec. role Dallas '02-03; NHL record: 1318 scheduled games, 260g, 403a, 231 playoff games, 38g, 55a; mem. QMJHL Hall of Fame; res. Dallas, Tex.

CARDINAL, Marc (weightlifting); b. 9 May 1956, Kingston, Ont.; given name: Donald Jean-Marc; m. Margaret Newton; c. Jacqueline, Andraya, Jennifer,

Michelle, Sarah, Michael, Stephen (d); UofOtt, MD; radiologist; teenage track, football standout; 18 ntl jr., 1 Commonwealth jr. records; only teenager to clean and jerk 400lbs in Commonwealth competition; class titles '74 Ont. Winter Games, '75-76 ntl jrs., '76, '78, '80 ntl srs. titles; gold '78 CG, 3 silvers '79 PAG; bronze '79 world super-heavyweight championships; best-lifter award '80 nationals; 8 Commonwealth, 9 ntl sr. records; PB: snatch 167.5 kilos, C&J 220 kilos, total lift 387.5 kilos; mem. Ottawa Sports Hall of Fame; res. Blackfoot, Idaho.

CAREY, Jim (bowling); b. 24 Feb 1933, St. John's, Nfld.; m. Beverley Chapman; c. Lisa, Jennifer, Nancy; fish merchant; 5-pin specialist; 13 times bowled 400-plus singles, PB: 448; 16 games 1000-plus triple, PB: 1091; 3 seasons 290-plus average, 298, 293, 291; mem. Nfld. Bowling Hall of Fame; res. St. John's, Nfld.

CARLYLE, Randy (hockey); b. 19 Apr 1956, Sudbury, Ont.; given name: Randy Robert; m. Corey; c. Derek, Craig, Alexis; hockey exec.; def Sudbury jr. '74-76, Dallas (CHL) '76-77; 1st choice Toronto '76 amateur draft; played in NHL with Toronto '76-78, Pittsburgh (capt. 3yrs) '78-84, Winnipeg '84-93; NHL record: 17 seasons, 1055 scheduled games, 148g, 499a, 69 playoff games, 9g, 24a; OHA all-star '76; 4 NHL all-star games; James Norris Memorial trophy '81; 3yrs Winnipeg Jets management team; coach/pres./GM AHL/IHL Manitoba Moose '96-02, '03-05; IHL GM of '99; twice IHL all-star coach; asst. Washington '02-03; mem. Hockey Heritage North, Man. Hockey halls of fame; res. Winnipeg, Man.

CARNEGIE, Herb (hockey/golf); b. 8 Nov 1919, Toronto, Ont.; m. Audrey May Redman; c. Goldie, Dale, Bernice, Rochelle; financial advisor; highly gifted centre who forged brilliant career in Quebec sr. league but was denied play in the NHL due to race; semi-pro Sherbrooke; 3 QHL MVP awards '47-49; with brother Ossie and Manny McIntyre formed Black Aces line; excellent golfer winning 2 Cdn, 1 Ont. srs titles; 2 Ont. Srs Champion of Champions titles; mem. 4 Ont. ntl sr. golf title teams; with Rochelle OGA father-daughter title '66; 4 Summit & Whitevale club titles; launched 1st hockey school in Canada; wrote Future Ace creed '56 then established foundation which awards scholarships to deserving athletes; recipient of countless awards including Harry Jerome, Harmony, B'Nai Brith; Cdn Commerative medal, Metro Toronto Canada Day medal, Ont. Good Citizenship medal, Queen's Silver Jubilee medal, Toronto Onyx Lions Community recognition, North York volunteer, board of ed. Awards; Summit GC trophy bears his name as does Centennial Centre; featured in several TV documentaries; mem. Investors Syndicate Millionaires Club; mem. Order of Ont.; Canada's, Owen Sound, Intl Afro-American Sports, Investors Group, Pride, Summit G&CC halls/walls of fame; res. Toronto, Ont.

CARNEY, Laurie (curling); b. 1 July 1956, Edmonton, Alta.; given name: Laurie Anne; m. Thomas Henry Carney; UBC, BEd; teacher; BC Dist. 1 title rinks skipped by Lindsay Sparkes '82-83; BC title rink '84; with skip Linda Moore Cdn, World titles '85, runnerup Cdn championships '86; all-star lead '84, '86 Cdn, '85 World championships; res. N. Vancouver, B.C.

CARNWATH, Jim (badminton); b. 11 Feb 1935, Woodstock, Ont.; given name: James Dalziel; m. Lianne Darou; c. Sarah, David Fowler, Drew; UofT, BA, LLD; Regional Sr. Justice, Central West Region Superior Court of Justice; 6 Ont singles, 3 mem's, mixed doubles titles; mem. 4 Thomas Cup teams; ntl mixed doubles titles '63-64; CBA pres. '77-78; 8 srs. singles, 4 men's. 1 mixed doubles titles; 2 US srs, masters singles, 2 men's. 3 mixed doubles titles; Cdn open masters title; UofT Bronze T award; pres. UofT badminton club; men. UofT Hall of Fame; res. Toronto, Ont.

CARPENTER, Keith (tennis); b. 3 Aug 1941, England; given name: Alan Keith; m. Judith Dianne; Sir George Williams, BSc; tennis court constructor; with Derek Penner -18 doubles '58; ntl Open doubles with Mike Carpenter '66; ntl Open mixed doubles with Eleanor Dodge '62, with Vickie Berner '63; Open singles runnerup '63; ntl Closed singles '73, Closed doubles '74; mem. Davis Cup teams '62-68, '71; mem. Cdn Dübler Cup, Fred Perry Cup teams; won 2 ntl over-45 doubles, Martini Masters '93 titles; mem. Cdn Tennis Hall of Fame; res. Mississauga, Ont.

CARPENTER, Ken (football); b. 26 Feb 1926, Carlyle, Wash.; given name: Kenneth Leroy; m. Doris Jacobson; c. Kimberly, Kenneth Jr.; Oregon State, BA; recreation dir.; hb Cleveland Browns '50-53, Saskatchewan '54-59; runner/passer/kicker/receiver; '55 Sask. single-season td record with 18, WFC MVP, scoring title; 3 times WFC all-star; 6 year CFL total 55 tds; head coach Sask. '60; US East-West Shrine, college all-star, NFL all-pro, CFL East-West Shrine games; mem. Roughriders Plaza of Honor; res. Indianapolis, Ind.

CARPENTIER, Patrick (motorsport); b. 13 Aug 1971, Joliette, Que., m. Anick Dunn; racing driver; indoor speed skating champion before competing in jr. karting; won Que. jr. 4-stroke karting titles '84-85; Spenard/David F-2000 series title '89; won '90 NA Enduro Kart Racing title; competed in ntl Formula 2000 races '90; ntl Player's Atlantic series title '92; Vancouver Molson Indy Atlantic title '92; steadily moving up through Player's/Toyota Atlantic championship series from '93; record 7 straight victories in '96 series; series champion '96; moved into IndyCar ranks '97; CART rookie of '97; joined Players racing team with fellow Cdn Greg Moore, '98; with Paul Tracy formed all-Cdn Player's-Forsythe racing team; CART victories Michigan '01, Cleveland '02 (runnerup '03), mid-Ohio '02, Monterey '03, '04; res. Las Vegas, Nev.

CARRICK, Donald (golf); b. 18 Sep 1906, Thunder Bay, Ont.; d. 1997 Toronto, Ont.; given name: Donald Day; UofT BA, Harvard LLD; lawyer; U.S., Western jr. title '24; youngest male (18) ever to win ntl amateur title '25, repeat '27; Ont. jr. title '23; Ont. amateur titles '26, '33; Ont. open runnerup '25; intercollegiate boxing title '27; competed as light-heavyweight Olympic boxer '28; runnerup to Lionel Conacher for Canada's male athlete of half century; OBE award; mem. Uof T, RCGA, Ont. Golf halls of fame.

CARRIER, Lyna (synchro swim); b. 29 Apr 1961, Quebec City, Que.; m. Claude; works travel agency; ntl team mem. '77-80; with twin sister Lyne 3 ntl duet titles; 3 ntl team titles; Pan-Pacific team title '79; team bronze '78 worlds,

'79 FINA World Cup; Que. Inst. of Sports synchro athlete of '77-80; mem. Canadian Aquatic Hall of Fame; res. Charny, Que.

CARRIER, Lyne (synchro swim); b. 29 Apr 1961, Quebec City, Que.; m. Serge Chabot; c. Guillaume, Thomas, Maude; secretary; ntl team '77-80; Canada Games solo title '75; with twin sister Lyna 3 ntl duet, team titles; team gold '79 Pan-Pacific Games; team bronze '78 worlds, '79 FINA World Cup; Que. Inst. of Sports synchro athlete of '77-80; mem. Canadian Aquatic Hall of Fame; res. Dolbeau, Que.

CARRUTHERS, Bob (curling); b. 5 Aug 1950, Charlottetown, P.E.I.; m. Joan Marie; c. Robin, Katrina; marketing rep.; skipped PEI entry Seagram Mixed '74; all-star 2nd '77 Seagram Mixed; 3rd for Peter MacDonald's PEI entry '81 Brier; 3rd Bryan Wight's NB entry '85 Brier; res. Riverview, N.B.

CARRUTHERS, Liz (diving); b. 14 Sep 1951, Edmonton, Alta.; given name: Elizabeth Ann: m. John Tweedle; Santa Monica College, CalState; real estate sales rep.; ntl 11-12 100yd butterfly record '63; Alta., Sask. novice, jr., sr. gymnastics titles; ntl diving team '67-76; 10 gold, 25 silver, 10 bronze in 1m, 3m springboard, ntl, International 10m tower; mem. '70 Commonwealth, '71, '75 PAG, '72 Olympic teams; twice ntl champion; Russian, Czechoslovakian, South African International competitions titlist; gold 3m '71 PAG, silver 3m '75 PAG; as mem. CalState diving team 1st woman in history in any sport chosen all-American; recovered from serious '72 auto accident with '75 comeback '75; radio-TV diving events commentator in both English, French; head diving instructor Klondike Diving Club Edmonton '76-79; mem. Alta. Sports Hall of Fame; res. Edmonton, Alta.

CARSCALLEN, Susan (figure skating); b. 5 Mar 1955, Sudbury, Ont.; div. Tim Fallon; m. Vance Rodewalt; c. Vale, Quinn; skating teacher; cashier; with Eric Gillies ntl jr. ice dance title '74, sr. ice dance '77, Skate Canada bronze '77, 6th '77 world ice dance; competed '75-77 worlds, '75-77 Skate Canada, '76 Olympics; silver ntl sr. dance '75-76; pro 1 season Stars on Ice, 2 Ice Capades; one of torch bearers '88 Olympics; res. Calgary, Alta.

CARSTAIRS, Kent (curling); b. 9 Jun 1947, Toronto, Ont.; m. Helen; c. Lesley, Stephanie; accountant; as lead for Russ Howard appeared in 4 Briers, winning '87 and adding world title '87; won Brampton cashspiel '85; runnerup Moncton 100; 1 Canada Challenge Cup victory in Japan; participated in numerous clinics, exhibitions in Canada, Europe, Scotland, Japan; participated Calgary Winter Olympic curling trials; mem. Ontario team of year '87; Dick Ellis award '87; mem. Cdn Curling Hall of Fame; res. Victoria Harbour, Ont.

CARTER, Gary (baseball); b. 8 Apr 1954, Culver City, Calif; given name: Gary Edmund; m. Sandy Lahm; c. Christy, Kimberly, D.J.; catching instructor/broadcaster; capt. HS baseball, basketball, football teams; skipped college for pro career; Orange County baseball player of year, HS athlete of '72; mem. National Honor Society '68-72; drafted Montreal '72; minor leagues '72-74; Expos catcher '74-84, '92, NY Mets '85-89, SF '90, LA '91; *Sporting News* rookie of yr; 4 times Expos player of yr; *Topps, Baseball Digest* rookie all-star; 8 times NL all-star, MVP '81, '84 games, tied record 2 all-star home runs single game; 4 Golden Glove, 2 Silver Bat awards; NL record 7 consec. seasons league leader games caught; Gillette Trophy top fan vote-getter '82 all-star game; 1000th ML hit '82; mem. '81 NL Division title team; '86 Mets World Series champions; ML record: 19 seasons, 2296g, 2056 caught, 1025r, 2092h, 371db31tr, 324hr, 1225rbi; jersey #8 ret'd by Expos; *ABC Superstars* competitor '80-81; nicknamed "Kid"; '85 Joan Payson, '86 Good Guy, '88 Danny Thompson, '89 Roberto Clemente, Volunteer of year awards; author *A Dream Season*; runs annual Leukemia Society charity golf tournament; Florida Marlin TV analyst '93-96; Expos TV analyst '97-99; NY Mets catching instructor '03-04; mem. Baseball, Cdn Baseball, Expos halls of fame; res. Palm Beach Gardens, Fla.

CARTER, Joe (baseball); b. 7 Mar 1960, Oklahoma City, Okla.; given name: Joseph Chris; m. Diana; c. Kia Kionne, Ebony Shante, Jordan Alexander; Wichita State; TV baseball analyst; of All-Missouri Valley Conf.; NCAA all-district 5 1st team, All-American 2nd team '79-80; *Sporting News* college player of '81; played in minors with Midland, Iowa, '81-84; American Assn. rookie of '83; majors from '84 with Chicago (NL), Cleveland (AL), San Diego (NL), Toronto (AL), Baltimore (AL), San Francisco (NL); 1st Cleveland player to record 30hrs and 30sb in single season '87; mem. 2 World Series champions; his 3-run HR in ninth won '93 title for Toronto; reached 2000 hit plateau '97; *Sporting News* Silver Slugger award '91; 12 consec. seasons 20 or more HRs; 10 of 12, 6 consec., 100 or more RBI seasons; MBL record: 2189 scheduled games, 8422ab, 1170r, 2184h, 432db, 53tr, 396hr, 1445rbi, 231sb, .259ba; *ESPN* analyst '98 post-season; Blue Jays TV analyst '99; mem. Blue Jays Wall of Distinction, Cdn Baseball Hall of Fame; res. Leawood, Kan.

CARTER, Mo (motorsport); b. 25 May 1924, Winnipeg, Man.; d. 28 Mar 2002, Pincher Creek, AB; given name: Maurice Charles; div. Lois Tweed; c. Lesley, Susan, Kelly, Steven, Bradley; m. Sheran; sc. Charlotte, Maurice, JoAnne, Curtis, Todd, Cia; St. John's College; automobile dealer; former broadcaster; began career in rallies, 2nd '64 Shell 4000; moved into racing '69 winning ntl sedan title; only Canadian to win major US races plus many on Canadian tracks; ntl A Production title '71-72; IMSA American Sedan & GT champion '72-73; CRCA driver of '70; ntl race driver of '71-72.

CARTER, Vince (basketball); b. 26 Jan 1977, Daytona Beach, Fla.; given name: Vincent Lamar; m. Ellen Rucker; c. 1; North Carolina; pro basketball player; mem. US jr. ntl team '95 worlds; 2 NCAA final four appearances; drafted by Golden State '98; dealt to Toronto '01 becoming franchise player; traded to NJ Nets '04; Schick all-rookie team '99; NBA slam dunk titlist '00; scored 51 points vs. Phoenix '00; 4 NBA all-star games; nicknamed "Showtime"; through '03 NBA record: 310 games, 2809fg, 442 (3 pointers), 1398ft for 8342 points; funded sports facilities Toronto, Daytona Beach; established Embassy of Hope Foundation; Vince Carter celebrity all-star charity game held annually in Toronto; initiated Vince's Hoop Group; Toronto Dixon Park basketball court bears his name; goodwill ambassador Big Brothers/Big Sisters of America; plays sax, drums and was offered Bethune-Cookman music scholarship; Ont. athlete of '01; res. Toronto, Ont.

CARTER, Wendy (badminton); b. 11 Mar 1956, Glasgow, Scotland; given name: Wendy May Clarkson; m. Greg Carter; c. Ryan, Scott, Christie, Curt; UCal; coach/administrator; ntl jr. singles champion '75; with Tracey Vanwassenhove ntl jr. girls' doubles; with Cam Dalgleish mixed doubles; with Lorraine Thorne doubles runnerup; Devlin Cup singles title '80; 5 ntl singles, 4 ladies' doubles, 5 mixed doubles titles; 2 ntl Open titles; all-England quarterfinalist '77, semifinalist '78; team silver, individual bronze '78 CG; Level 4 coach; v-p Badminton Canada; res. Gig Harbor, Wash.

CARTER-ERDMAN, Kelly Ann (cycling); b. 12 May 1964, Edmonton, Alta.; given name: Kelly Ann Carter; m W. Erdman; UCal; nutritionist Canadian Sport Centre Calgary; began racing '83; mem. ntl team '85-92; Olympic team alternate '92; set Cdn sr. record 3,000m individual pursuit of 3:47.69 while placing 4th at worlds; 6 ntl gold, 1 silver; 1 Goodwill Games bronze; silver 3,000m IP '87 PAG; Alta. achievement award '88; mem. Alta. Sports Hall of Fame; res. Banff, Alta.

CARTWRIGHT, Ethel Mary (builder); b. 1 Oct 1880, Clapham, Eng.; d. 18 Sep 1955, Magog, Que.; educator; appointed instructor McGill's Royal Victoria Coll. '06-27; instrumental in creating McGill school of phys ed '19; devised eligibility, playing rules for women's basketball; organized women's intercollegiate league; coached RVC team; established Bronze Baby trophy '21-22; recipient Tait McKenzie CAHPER award '48; mem. McGill Sports Hall of Fame.

CARTY, Hank (shooting); b. 6 Sep 1925, Birch River, Man.; given name: Henry; ret'd; began shooting in militia '51; mem. Man. Rifle Assn council from '57, exec. from '58; mem. shooting comm. '67 PAG; dir. MPRA centennial prize meeting '72; chair. rifle events SFC nationals '93; exec-v-p MPRA '79-83; pres. '84-93; 25yrs DCRA council mem.; MPRA PRO '57-82; Man. v-p DCRA from '84; militia team coach, capt. '53-57; army cadet coach '74-84; Man. Lt.-Governor's gold medal '89; ISU certificate of merit '67; hon. life mem., life governor MPRA; outstanding MPRA volunteer award '91; res. Winnipeg, Man.

CARVER, Julie (shooting); b. 8 Jul 1974, Charlottetown, P.E.I.; given name: Julie Lynn; m. Alfred Dickey; UPEI; began shooting age 13; progressed from small-bore to full-bore competition posting perfect 105 in Inter-maritime shoot becoming 1st junior, 1st female and 4th Islander to accomplish feat; '93 Nova Scotia champion; mem. mini-Palma, Inter-maritime, Atlantic championship, British, provincial, -25 ntl teams; '93 DCRA small-bore title; 3 Governor-General's medals; res. Pownal, P.E.I.

CARVER-DIAS, Claire (synchro swim); b. 19 May 1977, Burlington, Ont.; given name: Claire Rhiannon Carver; m. Douglas Oliver Dias; UofT BA, McGill, MA; communications co-ordinator COC; ntl team '97-02; won more than 12 Cdn titles; '99 PAG, Swiss Open duet, team titles; team gold, solo silver, duet bronze '99 Rome Open; duet silver '00 Japan Open; team bronze '00 Olympics; duet, team bronze '01 worlds; solo bronze '01 French Open; solo, duet gold '02 CG; '96 Petro Canada Olympic Torch scholarship recipient; Mississauga athlete of '00; Cdn aquatic athlete of '02; res. Oakville, Ont.

CASANOVA, Bruno (baseball/football); b. 28 Mar 1927, Windsor, Ont.; m. Audrey; c. Jayne, Kim, Barbara, Susan, Lynn; arena manager; all-city tackle Lowe VHS '44; softball, baseball Windsor before turning pro St. Louis Cardinals organization '58; hit .301 Lawrenceville, Va. .313 Hamilton (Pony League) '59, all-star 2nd baseman; closed pro career Duluth '60; 5yrs St. Thomas Elgins Sr. IC; mem. '54 IC title team; baseball supervisor Chatham '57-62, 15 OBA titles; mem. Windsor-Essex Sports Hall of Fame selection comm.; res. Amherstburg, Ont.

CASANOVA, Willie (baseball/football); b. 15 Nov 1930, Windsor, Ont.; given name: William Anthony; m. Connie Kerhoulas; c. Patti Rose, Anne Marie; UWO, BA, UAlta, BEd; ret'd. exec.-asst. Alberta Teachers' Assn.; mem. 1 football, 4 basketball, track HS title teams; Ont. HS football player of '48; set WOSSA discus record '47 (stood 20yrs); mem. Windsor Cardinals jr. baseball champions '48, Mic Mac baseball, softball title teams; pro baseball NY Yankee organization '51-53, '56; Sr. IC baseball St. Thomas, London; coached minor baseball Chatham, Ont.; mem. '54 St. Thomas IC champions; mem. UWO Mustangs football (basketball) teams '54-58 including undefeated '57 title team; drafted by BC, traded to Calgary '58; cut before season's opener but remained in Calgary to play semi-pro baseball Western Canada League through '62; coached St. Mary's Boys School football '59-63, 2 titles, only 2 games lost in 4 years, coached track team to 3 consecutive titles; asst. grid coach Mt. Royal Jr. Coll. '60-62, head coach '63, Alta. jr. title '60; asst. coach UCal '65-67; avid 4-handicap golfer; mem. Windsor/Essex Sports Hall of Fame; res. Calgary, Alta.

CASEY, Tom (football); b. 1924, Ohio; d. 10 Oct 2002, Bethel, Conn.; m. Mary Fuller; c. Geraldine, Martin, Thomas; Hamilton Institute Virginia, UMan, MD; v-p company medical dir. General Electric Co.; 1 year pro football NY Yankees all-American Conf.; Hamilton Wildcats '49, Blue Bombers '50-55; nicknamed "Citation" while achieving all-star status 7 times; led WIFU rushers '50; excelled as off/def back; gained 100yds single play '52 vs. Saskatchewan; same season gained 205yds in pass interception returns, WIFU single- season td record with 16; Winnipeg citizen of '55; mem. Man. Sports, Cdn, Blue Bombers Football halls of fame.

CASHMAN, Wayne (hockey); b. 24 Jun 1945, Kingston, Ont.; m. Lyn; c. Scott, Becky; hockey coach; jr. Oshawa; pro Boston '67-83; capt. '77-83; lw; 1 2nd team all-star; career record: 1027 scheduled games, 277g, 516a, 145 playoff games, 31g, 57a; 5 Stanley Cup finals, 2 winners; Team Canada '72; scout NYR '86-87; asst. coach NYR '88-92. Tampa Bay '92-96, San Jose '97; Philadelphia '98-00; head coach Philadelphia '97-98; asst. coach Team Canada '97 worlds, '98 Olympics; head coach/dir. hockey operations ECHL Pensecola Ice Pilots '00-01; asst. Boston '01-04; mem. Oshawa Sports Hall of Fame; res. Ocala, Fla.

CASS, Eddie (baseball); b. 12 Jul 1893, Winnipeg, Man.; d. 23 May 1985, Winnipeg, Man.; Georgetown, UMan, LLB; lawyer; college ball Georgetown, Manitoba; all-star 1st baseman; coach '23 Man. jr. titlists, '24-26 intermediates; ret'd as player when called to bar '26 but continued coaching jr. teams through '50s, several provincial titles; with Shorty

Kennedy formed Winnipeg HS football league; with Syd Halter inaugurated annual Catholic field day; Manitoba's Mr. Baseball; noted orator; mem. Man. Sports Hall of Fame.

CASSAN, Gerry (speed skating); b. 5 Dec 1954, Ottawa, Ont.; given name: Gerard; div. Gisele Tasse; Air Canada station attendant; 9 Ont. indoor, 22 outdoor, 4 ntl indoor, 7 outdoor, 3 international indoor, 16 outdoor titles, many records; fastest 500m (40.19) by Cdn skater; mem. '72 Olympic team; gold 500m '74 jr. worlds; Kitchener Oktoberfest indoor title '78; 2 gold, 2 bronze Lake Placid srs competition '83; mem. '63-70 Ont. lacrosse title teams; Ont. jr. open cycling title '72; competed '81 National Capital Marathon; speed skater of '71-72; won 50 km Lake Placid speed skating marathon '91; Cdn sr. masters titles '75, '92; set Cdn Masters record; mem. Ntl Capital Runners Assn.; capt. AC Sunseekers Running Club from '84; Daoust Trophy (Ottawa Valley French Canadian amateur athlete of year) '66, '68; at 8 youngest ever Ottawa ACT award winner; 5 Ont., 3 City of Ottawa sports achievement awards; mem. Ottawa Sports, Cdn Speed Skating halls of fame; res. Ottawa, Ont.

CASSATA, Rick (football); b. 17 Nov 1946, Buffalo, N.Y.; given name: James Rick; m. Diane Then; c. Dana, Justin, Brett; Syracuse BPE; restaurateur; strong-armed qb Tonawanda HS; led team to Niagara Frontier league titles, undefeated season; earned all league honors, all-Western NY, all-American citations; also standout in basketball, baseball claiming league titles, major awards in both; scouted by Miami U, Notre Dame but opted for Syracuse where he teamed with Larry Csonka to appear in Gator, Hula Bowls winning MVP honors in latter; despite baseball offers (he was pitcher/shortstop) from NY Yankees, Washington Senators opted for football in CFL with Calgary, Hamilton, Ottawa; won Grey Cup with Ottawa '73; mem. Greater Buffalo, Ottawa Sports halls of fame; res. Tonawanda, N.Y.

CASSELMAN, Bruce (softball); b. 11 Sep 1964, Williamsburg, Ont.; m. Janet Crain; costal engineering technician; catcher; played with Ottawa Turpin Pontiacs, Carp Valley Pride, Kemptville Thunder, Stittsville 56ers; mem. ntl title Toronto Gators fastball team '93-95, 1st Cdn team to win ISC world title '93, repeat '95; PAG gold '95; defensive standout with reputation of possessing a game-breaking bat; ISC all-world team '93-94; ntl, NA all-star catcher '92; Ottawa ACT fastball player of 1994; res. Ottawa, Ont.

CASSELS, Andrew (hockey); b. 23 Jul 1969, Bramalea, Ont.; m. Tracey; c. Cole, Scout; ctr Ottawa 67's OHL '86-89; Team Canada '89, '96; Sherbrooke AHL '89-90; NHL Montreal '89-91, Hartford '91-97, Calgary '87-99, Vancouver '99-02, Pittsburgh '00-01, Columbus '02-04; OHL MVP '88, 2 OHL all-star; NHL totals: 1020 scheduled games, 204g, 531a, 39 playoff games, 7g, 14a; Hartford, Vancouver Unsung Hero awards; nicknamed "Cass"; res. Brampton, Ont.

CASSIDY, John (speed skating); b. 7 Jun 1952, Montreal, Que.; given name: John Philip; m. Jocelyne Coutu; Loyola; fireman; ntl indoor titles '68, '72, outdoor '70; mem. '72 Olympic, '70, '73, '75 world championships teams; 2nd Que., 4th ntl championships '80; res. Lachine, Que.

CATHERALL, Robin (rowing); b. 20 Oct 1955, Vancouver, B.C.; given name: Robin William; m. Helen Wilkinson; UBC, BSc, MA; teacher; mem. '77 Western NA collegiate champion UBC 8s; gold 8s Henley, ntl championships '77; won Western sprints UBC 8s, 3 golds VRC 8s ntl championships; gold VRC 8s '78 Canadian Henley; silver 8s PAG, 3 golds VRC 8s ntl championships '79; mem. ntl team '77-80; twice world championship competitor; res. Parks, B.C.

CATHERWOOD, Ethel (t&f); b. 28 Apr 1908, Hannah, N.D.; d. 26 Sep 1987, Grass Valley, Calif.; given name: Ethel Hannah; div. James McLaren; div. Byron Mitchell; raised in Saskatoon; excelled in baseball, t&f; brought to Toronto by mining millionaire Teddy Oke, she was coached by Walter Knox and soon was challenging world hj standards; her grace and beauty won her nickname "Saskatoon Lily"; set world record '28; won '28 Olympic gold with leap of 5'2.7 ; embittered by treatment of women athletes by Canadian officials she married and moved to US never again to compete; rejected movie contract offers; mem. Sask, Cdn Olympic, Saskatoon, Canada's Sports halls of fame.

CATTARINICH, Joseph (builder/hockey); b. 13 Nov 1881, Levis, Que.; d. 7 Dec 1938, New Orleans, La; excelled in lacrosse/hockey; goalie Montreal Nationals; a man of few words he was dubbed "the Quiet One" ; a selfless athlete he convinced Montreal mgr. to sign Chicoutimi goalie Georges Vézina, thus putting himself out of a job; played important, but frequently unnoticed, role in development of NHL; with Leo Dandurand and Louis Létourneau purchased Montreal club and established Flying Frenchmen; under his management the Habs won 3 Stanley Cups; sold franchise '35; mem. Hockey Hall of Fame.

CAVALLIN, Isabell (builder/coach/administration); b. unknown; d. 21 Jan 1994, Burnaby, B.C.; m. Roy; c. Timmie; spurred by needs of severely mentally handicapped son, she and Roy became pioneers in providing physical activities for disabled; formed Burnaby Athletic Club '73; formed non-profit BC Sports for Retarded '70; instrumental in bringing Special Olympics program to BC '80; raised funds to provide athletes with equipment, travel, uniforms, accommodation and food; always placing needs of athletes before all else; as a coach she trained them to bring out their potential; constantly challenged system, breaking down barriers faced by mentally-challenged athletes; advisor for Burnaby People First; life mem. Burnaby Assn. for Mentally Handicapped; Burnaby Chamber of Commerce coach/mgr. of '82 award; over 15yr span served as volunteer in excess of 1200 hours annually; an unpaid social worker always available to athletes with special needs; honoured by BC Women in Sport Leaders & Legends; Langara Coll. legacy fund bears her name; mem. BC, Burnaby Sports halls of fame.

CAVALLIN, John (lacrosse); b. 31 Oct 1915, Vancouver, B.C.; d. 6 Sep 2002, Burnaby, B.C.; m. Dorothy; c. Bonnie, Georgia; ret'd trucking co. mgr.; played minor lacrosse Bayley's Province Bluebirds '30-34; sr. Richmond Farmers, New Westminster '35-37; 1st box player to wear protective helmet (to protect his job in social club); 5 Mann Cup finals; Vancouver Burrards to '49 when he turned to coaching that team; guided them to Mann Cup title; 14yr competitive sr.

career produced 454g, 636a; sweater ret'd by Burrards; moved from coaching to varied administrative roles with Burrards; key role in revival of recreational field lacrosse during '50s; spearheaded Mainland Field Lacrosse League, served as commissioner 4yrs; served as governor Cdn Lacrosse Hall of Fame; also excelled in soccer, basketball, golf; mem. Cdn Lacrosse Hall of Fame.

CAVALLIN, Roy (lacrosse); b. 15 Sep 1919, Vancouver, B.C.; given name: Roy Fred; m. Isabell (d); c. Timmie; 16 years sr. lacrosse; mem. 4 Mann Cup finalists, 3 winners; sr. soccer New Westminster Royals; Sr. A basketball Lauries '38; trainer 1st Cdn soccer team World Cup competition; 2yrs lacrosse referee; trainer BC. Lions '58-76; nicknamed "Fritzie", "Rocky"; p.-pres. BC Athletic Trainers' Assn.; pres. BC Sports for Retarded; mem. Canadian Lacrosse Hall of Fame; res. N.Burnaby, B.C.

CERESIA, Mike (racquetball); b. 3 Nov 1962, Sarnia, Ont.; UWO, BA; began playing '83; ntl team mem. from '88; world team gold '88, singles silver '94; ntl singles title '92, 5 ntl doubles titles; team silver '95 PAG; ranked 2nd world singles '94; gold worlds '96; competed '02 worlds; res. Burlington, Ont.

CHABOT, Lorne (hockey); b. 5 Oct 1900, Montreal, Que., d. 10 Oct 1946, Montreal, Que.; in era when diminutive goalies were the vogue, Chabot, at 6'1", stood out; helped Port Arthur win Allan Cup then turned pro NYR '26; posted goals-against averages of 1.56, 1.79 in 2 seasons with Rangers; Maple Leafs '28-33, Canadiens '33-34, Black Hawks '34-35, Montreal Maroons '35-36, NY Americans '36-37; helped Rangers win '28 Stanley Cup; '35 Vezina Trophy, 1st team all-star.

CHALLIS, Terry (softball); b. 29 Dec 1963, Toronto, Ont.; m. Lisa Hope; c. Kyler; sheet metal worker; ISC world championships MVP '93; 1st team all-world of '93-94; all-Canadian '94; mem. Toronto Gators 2 ntl, 1 world title; Green Bay All-Car '97, Owen Sound '98, Oshawa Gators '99; Team Canada '04; res. Whitby, Ont.

CHALMERS, Angela (t&f); b. 6 Sep 1963, Brandon, Man.; m. E. Espinoza; BrandonU; motivational speaker; middle distance specialist; began competing age 9; 1 ntl 3,000, 4 1,500, 1 800 gold; competed '85 FISU, '87 Pan-Am (silver), '88, '92 Olympic, '90, '94 CG, '94 World Cup teams; '92 Olympic 3,000 bronze; 3 CG gold; 1 WC silver; numerous victories in meets throughout world; 1st woman in CG history to win both 1,500 and 3,000 races '90, only woman to successfully defend 3,000 title '94; won Millrose Games mile '95; ntl 3,000m record 8:32.17 '94; ret'd from competition '97; Cdn flagbearer '94 CG; Phil Edwards CFTA athlete of '90; Man. female athlete of '90; Athletics Canada athlete of yr award '94; ntl Aboriginal achievement award '95; Brandon athletic award bears her name; BC Women in Sport Leaders & Legenda award; mem. Man. Sports Hall of Fame; res. Victoria, B.C.

CHALUPKA, Ed (football); b. 23 Feb 1947, Peterborough, Ont.; m. Rosemary; c. Christine, Paul; given name: Edward Stephen; N. Carolina, BA; CFL v-p football operations/ secty-treas from '93; former managing dir./curator Cdn Football Hall of Fame; all-Atlantic Conf., *AP* all-American;

academic all-American; og Hamilton '70-76; 3 times all-Eastern; 4 time Schenley nominee; mem. '72 Grey Cup winner; pres. CFL Players' Assn. '81-85; res. Stoney Creek, Ont.

CHAMBERLAIN, Murph (hockey/coaching); b. 14 Feb 1915 Shawville, Que.; d. 8 May 1971, Woodstock, Ont.; given name: Erwin Groves; c. Peter; ctr Ottawa Primrose, New Edinburgh '32-34, NOHA Noranda, South Porcupine, Sudbury '34-37; NHL Toronto '37-40, Montreal '40-42, '43-49, Brooklyn '41-42, Boston '42-43; NHL totals 510 scheduled games, 100g, 175a, 66 playoff games, 14g, 17a; coached Sydney CBHL '49-50, Charlottetown '52-53, Windsor NOHA '58-59, Sudbury EPHL '60-63; 2 Stanley Cup winners; nickname "Murph", "Old Hardrock".

CHAMBERS, Carlton (t&f); b. 27 Jun 1975, Brampton, Ont.; Clemson; sprinter; Ont. HS 100m title '92; gold 4x100 '94 CG; ntl jr 100m record 10.30, mem. record-setting jr relay team which won bronze World jr championships '94; running 1st leg in preliminaries helped Cdn men's 4x100 relay team claim gold '96 Olympics; NCAA All-American with Clemson. '95; res. Mississagua, Ont.

CHAMBERS, Dave (coaching); b. 7 May 1940, Toronto, Ont.; m. Irene; c. Lori, Linda; UofT, BPhE, UBC, MPhE, Ohio State, PhD; AD York; played Jr. A with Guelph Biltmores/St. Michael's Coll. '56-60; mem. Guelph '57 OHA title team; coach Ohio State '70-72, York '72-77, '84-90, Toronto Marlboros '79-80, Italian ntl team '81-83, Quebec (NHL) '90-92, Team Canada '88; won IIHF B title Italy '81; authored hockey drill book; res. Newmarket, Ont.

CHAMBERS, Mike (administration); b. 21 July 1949, Ottawa, Ont.; m. Joan Altmas; c. Andrew, Jack; UofO Bcom, LLB; lawyer; played hockey Ottawa East; football St. Pat's HS, UofO; paddled Rideau Canoe Club to ntl, NA championship level; engaged in cross-country, downhill skiing; played role in long term lease between City of Ottawa and Rideau Canoe Club; dir, RCC '81-83, '89-90, '96; commodore RCC '91-94; CCA exec. comm.from '83; commodore (Pres.) CCA '86-88; hosted Intl Canoe Fed. World Congress; sr. world canoe racing championships; mem. legal affairs comm. COA; assisted '89 world jr. canoeing championships; mem. COA anti-doping comm.; assisted '89 Pan-Am canoe championships; held varied exec. roles with COA becoming pres. '01; CdM '96 Olympics; RCC executive trophy; accredited ICF official, judge; course umpire '97 world, '99 PAG canoe championships; dir. '10 Olympic, Paralympic organizing comm.; CCA Gilbert award; chair. Ntl Capital Dragon Boat Race Festival; res. Ottawa, Ont.

CHAMBUL, Borys (t&f); b. 17 Feb 1953, Toronto, Ont.; given name: Borys Michael; m. Trudy Marian; c. 1 daughter; Wash, BA, Canadian Memorial Chiropractic College Toronto; doctor of chiropractic; dir. Chambul Chiropractic Group; discus specialist; mem. ntl jr. team '73-74; Pacific 8 discus title '76; NCAA champion; ntl, Commonwealth record 65.40m '76 pre-Olympic meet; NCAA record; mem. '76, '80 Olympic teams; gold '78 CG; ntl title '82; capt. UW track team '73-74; Wash most- inspirational award '76; Fellow of Intl Academy of Clinical Acupuncture; mem. Chinese medicine & Acupuncture Assn of Canada; mem. Sri Lanka

Medicinal Alternative; chiropractic consultant World t&f, basketball games; res. Thornhill, Ont.

CHAMPAGNE, Chantal (hockey/officiating/administration); b. 14 Jun 1965, North Bay, Ont.; Algonquin Coll.; graphic designer; mgr. Cdn sledge hockey for Hockey Canada; active referee NWHL, boys midget AA levels; 1st female to officiate Tier 2 Jr. A game in Ont.; volunteer asst. ref-in-chief for female officiating program Ottawa 9yrs; attended Level VI seminar, highest level for ref. in hockey; rep. Canada 8 ntl women's championships, 2 women's worlds, TSN Challenge Cups, pre-Olympic training camp, 5 4-Nations Cups, 3 3-Nations Intl. championships, Canada Winter Games, numerous prov. championships; OWHA instructor/supervisor 3yrs; ODHA instructor/supervisor 8yrs; res. Calgary, Alta.

CHAMPAGNE, Ed (skiing); b. 12 Jul 1927, Ste. Anne, Man.; given name: Edouard; pharmaceutical rep, skiing administrator; from '45 involved in skiing, alpine in particular, with Puffin/Winnipeg SC holding varied administrative roles; pres. Man. Ski Div. 3yrs; played role in launching Mt. Agassiz, Falcon Lake ski areas in Manitoba; managed Yellowstone, Montana ski area 1yr; ntl alpine ski team exec 21yrs; founder/1st pres. Winnipeg Cycling Club; chair. Man. Cycling Assn '64-68; mem. '67 PAG organizing comm.; hon. mem. Cdn Ski Assn.; life mem. Winnipeg Ski Club; mem. Cdn Skiing Hall of Fame; res. Ottawa, Ont.

CHAMPION, Tony (football); b. 19 Mar 1963, Humbold, Tenn.; Tennessee-Martin; wr; joined CFL Hamilton '85-92; 2 all-Eastern, 1 all-CFL; Jeff Russell Memorial Trophy '89; runnerup CFL most-outstanding player '89; CFL record: 85 scheduled games, 37tds, 340 receptions for 5,498yds; mem. 2 Grey Cup finalists, 1 winner; last known res. Humbold, Tenn.

CHANG, Albert (tennis); b. 27 Feb 1971, Vancouver, B.C.; Harvard; made pro debut '92; had 1st taste of Davis Cup play beating Carlos Drada 6-2, 6-3 as Canada swept Colombia 5-0; won '94 Celle Challenger, France; combined with Leander Paes of India to win Manila Challenger; has recorded victories over Michael Stich and Arnaud Boetsch; competed Wimbledon '95-96; res. Calgary, Alta./Boston, Mass.

CHAPMAN, Art (basketball); b. 28 Oct 1912, Victoria, B.C.; d. 4 Feb 1986, Victoria, B.C.; given name: Arthur St. Clair; m. Kathleen; c. Lyn Arthur, Jim; salesman; HS aggregate t&f title '31-32 in 5 events, high jump, long jump, hop, step & jump (triple jump), shot put, 120yd hurdles; mem. '33 BC. softball champions; at 16 batted .399 sr. baseball league; mem. 5 ntl basketball title teams, '36 Olympic silver medal team; mem. '46 Victoria Dominoes (BC basketball team of half century), ntl title without losing league or playoff game; player-coach-mgr. Vancouver Hornets pro basketball '47-48; helped Canadian army unit win '45 overseas basketball, volleyball, soccer titles; various Little League, Connie Mack baseball exec. positions; '36 team inducted Canada's, '46 team BC Sports halls of fame; with brother Chuck mem. Cdn Basketball, BC, Greater Victoria Sports halls of fame.

CHAPMAN, Chuck (basketball); b. 21 Apr 1911, Vancouver, B.C.; given name: Charles Winston; m. Eily Margaret; c. Clara Mary, Janet Kathleen, Fern Ruth; Victoria

College; ret'd; mem. BC sr. A softball, lacrosse, soccer title teams; mem. 6 BC basketball title teams, capt. 5; mem. '36 Olympic silver medal team; capt. '46 undefeated Victoria Dominoes (BC. team of half century); '36 team Canada's, '46 team BC Sports halls of fame; mem. Cdn Basketball, BC, Greater Victoria Sports halls of fame; res. Victoria, B.C.

CHAPMAN, Currie (skiing); b. 7 May 1947, Montreal, Que.; div. Judi Leinweber; m. Dale Ryan; c. Christie, Jordan; Notre Dame, BA, T.Cert.; ret'd sport administrator; mem. ntl team '64-69; Vail GS, Jackson Hole downhill, slalom titles '68 Can-Am circuit; 8th '68 World Cup Alpine Meadows, Calif.; coached HS volleyball, soccer, basketball '70-78; head coach ntl women's ski team '78-89; pres. Cdn Sports and Fitness Marketing Council '91-94; v-p program operations Alpine Canada from '94; TV skiing color commentator; fed. govt. coach of '86; mem. CPCA from inception, v-p from '96, acting pres. '98; PetroCan coaching award; mem. Cdn Skiing Hall of Fame; res. Sydney, B.C.

CHAPMAN, John (harness racing); b. 25 Nov 1928, Toronto, Ont., d. 2 May 1980, Toronto, Ont.; m. Janice Feldman; c. Cynthia, Wendy, Cheryl, John Jr.; harness driver, trainer; capt. St. Michael's hockey team; 1st harness race win Dufferin Park '47; 3915 career victories, purses totalling more than $21 million; 34 sub-2-minute miles; drove 4-year-old pacing mare Tarport Hap to world record 1:56.3; drove Delmonica Hanover to successive Roosevelt International triumphs '73-74, trained '75 winner, horse of year Savoir; mem. Cdn Horse Racing Hall of Fame.

CHAREST, Isabelle (speed skating); b. 3 Jan 1971, Rimouski, Que.; m. Steve Charbonneau; UMtl; switched from figure to speed skating; mem. ntl team from '87; silver 3000m short-track relay '94 Olympics; mem. '98, '02 (relay bronze) Olympic team; 1 Cnd sr., 3 world records; 2 Goodwill Games gold '94; 2 World short-track 3000m relay, 1 overall gold; 500m gold, 1000m bronze '96 worlds; overall ntl title '95-96; world team championship bronze '98; switched from short- to long- track '98; res. Montreal, Que.

CHARETTE, Agnés (curling); b. 6 Jul 1942, Buckingham, Que.; given name: Agnes Charette; m. Jean St. Pierre; c. Normand, Éric; Hull Teachers' Coll.; teacher; 3 times Outaouais region tennis rep. Quebec Games; National Capital intermediate title '74; skip Outaouais region business girls title rink '81; skip Que. women's title rinks '83-84, '89, '92-94; 5th mem. '91 Que. Tournament of Hearts rep; Cinzano Cup Que. '82; mem. 3 Que. mixed title rinks; Ottawa women's major league title rink '83; skip 8 Que. Srs title rinks, ntl titles '97, '99, '00; record 62 wins; mem. Curling Hall of Fame; res. Buckingham, Que.

CHARETTE, France (curling); b. 8 Apr 1958, Masson, Que.; m. Pierre Charette; c. Duff, Kim; golf pro shop administrator; began curling age 23; with Agnés Charette, Chantal Osborne representing Buckingham CC won 5 Que. Women's titles, competing in 5 Scott Tournament of Hearts; competed 3 ntl mixed championships; res. Rockland, Ont.

CHARETTE, Pierre (curling/golf); b. 23 Jun 1955, Masson, Que.; m. France; c. Duff, Kim; golf pro; 1st to play every position, including 5th man, in Brier competition; skipped

Que. entry '89, '93 Brier, lead for Don Westphal '96 Brier semifinalists, 2nd '97 Brier, 3rd for Guy Hemmings '98, '99 Brier. '98, '99 finalists; all-star 3rd '99; skipped Que. entry '91, '92, 2nd '86 ntl mixed championships; 3rd for Hemmings '97 McCain East title; 3rd for Peter Corner '01 Ont. Nokia Cup; rejoined Hemmings for '03-04; skipped WCT ntl trophy winner '03; pro Buckingham GC, Outaouais GC, Royal Papineau GC; res. Rockland, Ont.

CHARETTE, Richard (t&f); b. 8 Nov 1967, North Bay, Ont.; given name: Richard Allan; m. Elizabeth Ivany; c. Benjamin Wylie; UofOtt, BEd, BPhE; teacher; x-county specialist; mem. CIAU X-C title teams '86-87, '90; individual CIAU title '89; 1500m bronze Pan-Am jrs '86, ntl t&f championships '91; ntl X-C titles '91, '92; res. Ottawa, Ont.

CHARLAND, Jacques (ski jumping); b. 6 May 1930, Trois-Riviéres, Que.; m. Nicole Ebacher; c. Manon; electrician; 8 ntl, 3 US, several NA championships; mem. '52, '56, '60 Olympic, '54, '58, '62, '66 world teams; coach ntl team '68-70; resumed competition '71-75; won more than 400 trophies, cups, medals; mem. Cdn Skiing Hall of Fame; res. Trois-Rivieres, Que.

CHARLEBOIS, Bob (hockey); b. 27 May 1944, Cornwall, Ont.; given name: Robert Richard; m. Maureen Delaney; c. Rob, Joy; UofOtt, BSc, MA, Harvard Business School, PMD; dir. corporate training centre Algonquin Coll.; Montreal jr. '60-64, Omaha, Houston, Memphis CHL '64-68, Minnesota NHL '67-68, Phoenix WHL '68-72, Tulsa CHL '71-72, Ottawa WHA '72-73, New England WHA '73-76; shifted to coaching UofOtt '80-82; Ottawa South Canadian major bantam '91-92, league champion Ottawa Golden Knights major bantam '92-93, Gloucester Rangers Tier II Jr. A '93-95, league title '94; scouted for Hartford NHL, Gloucester CJHL, St. Michael's OHL; owner-teacher hockey school '64-72; taught PE UofOtt '80-82; mem. Ottawa Senators NHL alumni board, Harvard business club Ottawa, Ottawa Board of Trade, American Society for Training and Development; mem. Cornwall Sports Hall of Fame; res. Ottawa, Ont.

CHARLEBOIS, Vera (golf); b. 24 Apr 1930, Smiths Falls, Ont; given name: Vera Anita Donaldson; m. Albert Gilbert Charlebois; c. Owen Arthur, Dennis Joseph Edward; teaching golf pro; scored 1st win in Ottawa dist. '63; 22 Chaudiére Ladies' club titles; 4 Ottawa Dist. Ladies' titles (Ahearn Trophy); mem. 4 Quebec interprovincial women's teams, 7 Quebec Rose Bowl teams; 5 O&D 4-ball best-ball titles; 3 Eastern provinces titles; 4 Allie Jones trophies; 2 Mina Denison Shield teams; 2 Que. seniors titles; 3rd '84 ntl sr women's; 6 O&D sr women's titles; 2 Daytona Beach club titles; winner varied Ottawa Valley invitationals '70-85; set Chaudiére women's club record 72; club pro Emerald Links GC; mem. Russ Taylor OVCA mixed curling title rink; mem. Smiths Falls Recreation Hall of Fame; res. Ottawa, Ont.

CHARLTON, Ken (football); b. 16 Apr 1920, Regina, Sask.; d. 1 May 2004, Burnaby, B.C.;.m. Belle; c. Jim, Tom, Catherine; Regina Westend jrs '38; Regina Western champion jr. Dales '39-40; joined Regina Roughriders '41 but WW2 intervened; played with '42 Winnipeg RCAF team reaching Grey Cup final; '43 All-Service

Roughriders; declined Cleveland Rams tryout '45 opting to stay in Canada; with Regina briefly before joining Ottawa 3 seasons; rejoined Regina '48-54, 4yrs capt.; 2 Grey Cup finals; reached all-star status as flying wing '41, '45-46, rb '48-49; all-Western hb '51; standout punter averaging 38.7yds on 182 punts; could fill in at qb if needed; punishing tackler; among top WIFU rb/punt returners; pres. St. James Winnipeg sr. ntl champs '63; also excelling in baseball/ hockey; mem. Sask. Sports, Roughriders Plaza of Honor; Cdn Football halls of fame.

CHARLTON, Nancy (field hockey); b. 8 Oct 1962, Victoria, B.C.; given name: Nancy Margaret; m. Ian Mollennhauer; c. Arden; UVic, BEd; PE teacher; mem. UVic team '81-85; mem. BC team '80-84; competed '81 Canada Games; ntl team '82-88; mem. World Cup silver medal team '83; mem. '84, '88 Olympic, '86 World Ccup, '87 PAG teams; flag-bearer '87 PAG; jr. HS athletic, sportsmanship awards; '81 Vancouver Island Women's FH award for ability, leadership; fed. govt. excellence awards '83, '88; UVic female athlete of '83-84; Victoria athlete of '89; 5yrs Vancouver Women's FH League MVP; res. Victoria, B.C.

CHARRON, Al (rugby); b. 27 Jul 1966, Ottawa, Ont.; given name: Alan John; m. Annette Saikaley; Carleton, BA; pro rugby player, ex-civil servant; lock or back row Ottawa Irish RC, 7 league titles; mem. 5 Ont. 7-a-side title teams, 2 McCormick Cup winners; '90-94 earned 60 caps as mem. ntl team; capt. ntl team '96; scored try vs. NZ '91 World Cup; scored decisive try vs. Wales '93; played for British Barbarians vs. French Barbarians in '94 game celebrating 50th anniversary of liberation of Paris; competed '91 World Cup (quarterfinalist), '93 World Cup of Sevens; turned pro with Moseley in UK '96, Bristol '97-99, Pau (France) '00; mem. 3 Ottawa men's basketball title teams; 4 Ottawa ACT rugby awards, '93 Ottawa ACT amateur athlete of yr; Ont. Excellence award; named Western England's best rugby player; Bristol player of '98 award; v.-capt. ntl world cup '99 team (all-star); Cdn player of '00 award; record 76 intl caps; announced retirement after '03 World Cup in New Zealand; nickname "Blade"; mem. Twin Elm Wall of Fame; res. Ottawa/ Bristol, Eng.

CHARRON, Guy (hockey); b. 24 Jan 1949, Verdun, Que.; m. Denyse; c. Renee, Erik; centre NHL '69-81 Montreal, Detroit, Kansas City, Washington; NHL record: 734 scheduled games, 221g, 309a; mem. 3 Cdn teams world championships '77-79, bronze '78; player/coach Arosa Swiss League '81-82 champs; EV Landshot, Germany; GM/head coach Que. Remparts '83-85; coach ntl jr world gold '90; asst. GM/coach Team Canada 5yrs, 4 Izvestia, 2 Spengler Cups, '88 Olympics; head coach '90 Cdn jr. world title team; asst. Calgary Flames '90-95, NYI '95-97; head coach Grand Rapids IHL '98-00; IHL coach of '00; asst./interim head coach Anaheim '00-02; asst. coach Montreal '02-04; Commissioner's Trophy '99-00; res. Montreal, Que.

CHARTERS, Harvey (canoeing); b. 8 May 1912, Toronto, Ont.; d. 17 Jul 1995, North Bay, Ont.; given name: Harvey Blashford; m. Margaret Helen Whitham; c. Kent, Craig, Douglas, Kimberley, Elaine; UofT; ret'd engineer; ntl intermediate tandem '31, sr. 4s '34, sr. tandem '35, mile war canoe '30, '37; silver 10,000m tandem, bronze 1000m

tandem '36 Olympics; competed International 14' dinghy sailing regattas.

CHASE, George (shooting); b. 19 Jan 1941, Saint John, N.B.; given name: George Ernest; m. Carla Roberta; c. George Bradley Paul, Michelle Lynne; ret'd.; full-bore specialist; won 8 NB Lt-Governors, 7 times runnerup; 9 NB grand agg titles; 2 Cdn Masters gold, 2 silver; 1 DCRA Macdonald Stewart grand agg; 1 Des Burke Trophy; DCRA Governor-General's bronze; qualified 15 Cdn Bisey teams; big game bow hunting guide specializing in moose, deer, black bears; highly respected artist specializing in wildlife, caricatures; also noted sculptor; res. Saint John, N.B.

CHATEL, Sigrid (fencing); b. 26 Apr 1940, Frankfurt, Germany; given name: Sigrid Gazzera; m. Gilles Chatel; c. Dominique, Mark; Geneva, BA; PR consultant, convention services; moved to Canada '64; twice ntl champion; bronze '67 PAG; mem. '67 worlds, '70 CG, '71 PAG teams; lone Cdn female fencer '68 Olympics; asst. CdM '72 Olympics; mem. COA from '76; chief hostess COJO '73-77; deputy CdM Canadian team '80 Winter Olympics; taught PE Bois-de-Boulonge College Montreal '71-72; 3 times Lévesque Trophy winner Montreal's female athlete of year; res. Montreal, Que.

CHEATER, Millie (t&f); b. 20 Nov 1927, Winnipeg, Man.; given name: Millicent; m. Everett Cousins; c. Kim, Shelley, Kerry; ret'd. school board secretary; inter-HS 50, 100yd sprint titles '43-45; ntl record 75yd sprint title '46; ntl 60m, 100yds, 100m titles '47; quarterfinalist 100, 200m '48 Olympics; 50, 75yds, 400m relay records; mem. Beta Sigma Phi; res. W.Vancouver, B.C.

CHEEVERS, Gerry (hockey); b. 7 Dec 1940, St. Catharines, Ont.; given name: Gerald Michael; m. Betty; c. Craig, Cheryl, Robby; St. Michael's College; hockey scout; jr. A St. Mike's Majors; pro Toronto '61-62; minor pro '62-67; Boston regular goalie '67-72, '75-80; WHA Cleveland Crusaders '73-74; mem. Team Canada '74, '76; twice WHA all-star; Hap Holmes Trophy (AHL top goaler) '65; CPHL top goalie '67; WHA top goalie '73; NHL record: 12 seasons, 26so, 2.89 goals-against average; mem. 2 Stanley Cup winners; coach Bruins '80-84; scout Boston since 85; thoroughbred horse owner; mem. Hockey Hall of Fame; res. North Andover, Mass.

CHELIOS, Chris (hockey); b. 25 Jan 1962, Chicago, Ill.; m. Tracee; c. Dean, Jake, Kiley, Tara; Wisconsin; def. Moose Jaw (SJHL) '79-81, Wisconsin '81-83, Team USA '83-84; NHL Montreal '84-90, Chicago '90-99, Detroit '99-04; mem. NHL all-rookie team; 4 1st, 2 2nd team all-star; played 10 all-star games; Team USA '91 Canada Cup, '96 World Cup (gold), '84, '98 Olympics; 3 Norris trophies; 3 Stanley Cup winners; NHL record (through '04) 1395 scheduled games, 178g, 736a, 222 playoff games, 30g, 107a; made bid for U.S. bobsled team '04; res. Chicago, Ill.

CHENIER, Georges (snooker); b. 14 Nov 1907, Hull, Que.; d. 16 Nov 1970, Toronto, Ont,; m. Bernadette Corrilla; c. Cecile; NA snooker champion '47-70; twice runnerup to England's Fred Davis world championships; world record match play break 144 vs. Walter Donaldson, England '50; world record 6 century breaks vs. Montreal's Leo Levitt '55

NA title matches; world record run 150 for pocket billiards vs. world champion Irving Crane '63; later duplicated feat; '66 stroke paralyzed left side restricting use of left arm; mem. Ottawa, Canada's Sports halls of fame.

CHERNOFF, Mike (curling); b. 21 Dec 1936, Kamsack, Sask.; m. Dorine Dennison; c. Cathy, Bruce; Queen's, BSc; geological engineer; began curling as mem. Kamsack CC, '52; competitor Kingston, Edmonton, Calgary, Medicine Hat, N. Vancouver, Richmond, B.C.; 11 Association zone titles; 7 provincial finals, 3 winners, 2 runners-up; 3rd stone '64, '78, '83 Alta. Brier entries; semifinalist '78 world championship; skip Ont. Jr. Tankard titlist '57; all-star Brier third '78; skipped 12 major 'spiel winners including 2 Kingston, 1 Ottawa city titles; top shooting percentage '78 Silver Broom (world); played key administrative roles with Calgary CC '67-77, Southern Alberta CA '80-83; mem. '80 Calgary Brier organizing comm.; v.-chair. CCA ICF committee '83-85; Canadian delegate ICF '83-85; v-p Vancouver men's world comm. '87; highly successful oil field developer in Ecuador; with son Bruce made $11M endowment to Queen's for chemistry building; funded Chernoff family awards program at Queen's; board mem. Alta. Energy Co.; trustee Queen's; res. Vancouver, B.C.

CHERRY, Don (hockey); b. 5 Feb 1934, Kingston, Ont.; given name: Donald Stewart; m. Rose (d); c. Cindy, Timothy; m. Luba; hockey TV commentator, restaurateur; def Jr. Barrie Flyers; pro Boston organization spending much of career in minors with Hershey, Springfield, Rochester (AHL), Trois-Riviéres, K-W, Sudbury (EPHL), Spokane (WHL); 1 playoff game with Boston (NHL) '55; coach Boston Bruins '74-79, Colorado Rockies '79-80; nicknamed "Grapes"; outspoken, often controversial, colorfully-attired TV commentator on *HNIC Coach's Corner*; ex-owner, coach Mississauga Ice Dogs OHL franchise; with Bobby Orr coach OHL top prospects teams; res. Mississauga, Ont.

CHEVREFILS, Real (hockey); b. 2 May 1932, Timmins, Ont.; d. 8 Jan 1981, Timmins, Ont.; noted for quick skating, deft puck handling; lw Barrie OHA '48-51, 1 Memorial Cup; NHL Boston '51-55, '56-59, Detroit '55-56; saw duty with Hershey, Springfield, Providence, Quebec, Sudbury, Kingston, Winnipeg, Los Angeles, San Francisco before retiring '64 after alcoholism severely erroded his skills; NHL totals: 387 scheduled games, 104g, 97a, 30 playoff games, 5g, 4a; nicknamed "Chevy".

CHIARELLI, John (all-around); b. 5 May 1938, Ottawa, Ont.; given name: John Ross; m. Diane Gervais; c. Kimberly, Stephanie; St. Patrick's Coll., Rensselaer Polytechnic Institute, BEng; patent examiner; jr. B hockey St. Pat's '53-56, jr. A Ottawa Shamrocks '56-57, US Tier 1 RPI '58-62, sr. A Ottawa Montagnards '62-65, Hull Mustangs '65-95; midget end/db Big 4 football St. Pat's '52, St. Pat's HS jrs '53-54, srs '55-56, St. Pat's Coll. '57; touch football Ott. sr. Valiquette Alouettes '68-70; fastball McNab Phillies '49-56, St. Anthony's, Village Sports Club, Hugh Grant '57-65, Hull Volants '66, Ott. sr. Wajax '67-69, Champagne Electric '69-71; player/coach Metro League Turpin Pontiacs '72-78, GM/coach Turpin '79-94; baseball Ott. sr. league '62-64; mem. Ottawa Curling Club from '67; won 2 City of Ottawa bonspiel grand aggregate titles, 2 Kingston Little Canuck, Fisherman's bonspiels, Gord Perry bonspiel, OCA Governor-General's, Ottawa Masters,

CofO srs. grand aggregate; runnerup OCA mixed; coached jr. hockey, football; dir. '81 ntl fastball, 3 Ont. men's, 3 ISC Eastern Cdn championships; chair. Ottawa Masters bonspiel 15yrs, chair. Gord Perry bonspiel 2 yrs, dir. OCC 11yrs; Doran trophy St. Pat's HS, Ottawa ACT sportsman of '86, Softball Canada award of merit, Perth Shootout contributor to game award; Level 2 softball coaching certificate; Ott. RCSSB trustee 6yrs; leading hitter/3b Hull Volants '66; coached teams in 2 ISC world, 2 Cdn men's fastball championships; res. Ottawa, Ont.

CHIBI, Tony (bowling); b. 31 Jan 1936, Punnichy, Sask.; given name: Anthony Joseph; m. Peggee Hillier; c. Tammy Lynne, Carrie Lynn; electrician; 5 Essex County, 5 Ont., 3 ntl 10-pin singles titles; 2nd in 1st tournament of America's '63 averaging 200; Molson Masters titles; world invitational tournament '60-61, '63; qualified 3 ABC masters tournaments; mem. Brunswick advisory staff; perfect sanctioned 300 league play 16 Mar '66; runnerup Canadian Bowling Classic Montreal; high avg. 200 Windsor Major Classic League '62-63; mem. McCallum Challenge Cup winner '64; drafted Detroit pro league '61; award of merit Leamington Dist. Chamber of Comm.; Ont. Athletic Commission merit award; mem. Windsor-Essex County, Greater Miami Sports halls of fame; res. Leamington, Ont.

CHICK, John (builder); b. 21 Jan 1892, Windsor, Ont.; d. 13 Apr 1961, Windsor, Ont.; given name: John Digby; construction co. owner; instrumental role in construction of Windsor Arena; sponsored Ontario Baseball Assn. champion Walkerville Chicks '29; exerted strong influence in bringing pro hockey to Windsor; part-owner, GM Windsor Bulldogs, IHL titles '29, '31; WW2 liaison officer between US-Cdn federal authorities for all NHL, AHL players; considered saviour of wartime hockey; more than 25yrs executive officer AHL; mem. Windsor-Essex Sports Hall of Fame.

CHILD, John (volleyball); b. 4 May 1967, East York, Ont.; Centennial College; beach volleyball specialist; teamed with Ed Drakich to win '92, '93 Cdn pro beach, '92 Jose Cuervo NA titles; with Mark Heese (nicknamed Crazy Defenders) '95 Cdn pro beach title; 1g, 5s, 9b FIVB world championship series through '03; voted best defender, MVP '92; mem. '86 Scarborough Solars ntl indoor champions; competed '96, '00 Olympics; res. Toronto, Ont.

CHIPMAN, A.U. (administration); b. 2 Oct 1902, Winnipeg, Man.; d. 14 Dec 1993, Winnipeg, Man.; given name: Arthur Uniake; m. Louise Arnold; c. Arthur U II, Warwick (d); wholesale food co. chairman; pres. Blue Bombers '44-47; had taste of coaching '41 Grey Cup when Reg Threlfall was ill; pres. CRU, WIFU; 1st trustee Schenley Awards; pres. Winnipeg Rangers '43 Memorial Cup winners; pres. Winnipeg Assiniboine Downs Turf Club; v-p '67 PAG comm.; dir. Winnipeg Goldeyes baseball club; mem. Cdn Football, Blue Bombers halls of fame.

CHIPPER, Eric (football); b. 29 May 1915, Ottawa, Ont.; d. 18 Jan 1996, Ottawa, Ont.; given name: Eric Trevor; m. Frances Newell; c. Diane, Marnie; sheet metal worker; jr. football Ottawa Strathconas '35; mem. Ottawa Trojans WW2; Rough Riders '38-50; Walker Trophy '47, Jeff Russel Memorial Trophy '48; capt. Rough Riders '48; Eastern all-star tackle, standout kicker; basketball Ottawa Tech, Int. Diamonds, sr. Barrett Sailors, '45 MVP; twice scoring champion Ottawa Falcons soccer team; sr. softball, hockey Ottawa Car; operated swim, ski schools for Ottawa Westboro Kiwanis; coached Kiwanis peewee hockey, Ottawa Seconds int. football; mem. Ottawa Rowing Club.

CHIU, Barbara (table tennis); b. 14 Jul 1964, Canton, China; began playing age 8; regarded as blocker who capitalizes on opponent's errors; ntl team from '88; '92 NA open doubles gold, singles silver; '96 NA women's doubles gold; with Johnny Huang won Canada's 1st Commonwealth championships mixed doubles gold '94, women's team bronze '94; best international showing '89 worlds winning 13 of 14 matches; team, women's doubles gold, singles, mixed doubles bronze '95 PAG; partnered with Lijuan Geng won '96 NA women's doubles gold; mem. '92, '96 Olympic teams; res. Vancouver, B.C.

CHIU, Bryan (football); b. 16 Aug 1974, Vancouver, B.C.; m. Carlee; Coll. of Pacific, Washington State; guard/centre; drafted Montreal '97; CFL Montreal '97-04; 4 East, CFLPA all-star; CFL outstanding lineman '02; 3 Grey Cup games, 1 winner; active in community programs, particularly Chinese community, Alouettes jr. FB camp; res. Montreal, Que.

CHOMYC, Lance (football); b. 2 Mar 1963, Edmonton, Alta.; m. Rasa; c. Larissa; UofT; teacher; mem. Edmonton Wildcat Jrs '81-82; led OUAA punters, scorers '83, runnerup '84; OUAA 1st team all-star '83; 6th round draft choice Ottawa '85; 21-day trial with Saskatchewan before joining Argos as free agent '85-93; through '91 led Argos scorers 7 straight yrs; 3rd player in CFL history to top 200 points in single season; set Argos single game FG record with 7 twice in '88; set several Argos place-kicking records; set CFL convert record with 76 straight; twice EFC all-star, once all-Canadian; res. Alliston, Ont/ Edmonton, Alta.

CHOQUETTE, Jean (gymnastics); b. 2 Apr 1956, Montreal, Que.; Quebec, BA; teacher; mem. ntl team '75-82; 2 PAG, 1 CG, 3 FISU, 2 world championships teams; 2 silver '79 PAG, gold, bronze '78 CG, gold, silver '81 NZ Games; twice Que. athlete of month '81; Que. artistic gymnast of '77-78, '80-81; Que. athlete of '80; res. St. Bruno, Que.

CHORNOBRYWY, Lynn (modern pentathlon); b. 16 Sep 1962, Ottawa, Ont.; given name: Janet Lynn; div.; c. 1; fencing coach; ntl titles '79, '81-83; scored 5000+ points 1st time '81; '83 women's world title, record 5328 points; '83 Nordic Cup; fed, govt. world champion award '84; Velma Springstead Trophy '83; res. British Columbia.

CHOUINARD, Guy (hockey); b. 20 Oct 1956, Quebec City, Que.; given name: Guy Camil; jr. Que. Remparts '71-74; 1st Atlanta pick '74 amateur draft; CHL rookie of year Omaha '74-75; NHL Atlanta '74-80, Calgary '80-83, St. Louis '83-84; minor league stints in Nova Scotia (AHL), Peoria (IHL); 50-goal plateau '79 season; NHL record: 578 scheduled games, 205g, 370a, 46 playoff games, 9g, 28a; coach Victoriaville, Laval, Sherbrooke, Quebec '89-02; mem. QMJHL Hall of Fame; res. Quebec City, Que.

CHOUINARD, Jean-Marc (fencing); b. 6 Nov 1963, Montreal, Que.; m. Marie-France Lalibert,; c. Vincent,

Simon; urban planner; began fencing at 15; épée specialist; silver jr. worlds; silver World University Games; 4th '84 Olympics; mem. '84, '88, '92 Olympic, '83 (2 silver) '87 PAG teams; 2 gold '90 CG; mem. Canada's best-ever team which placed 6th '91 Worlds; best ever individual Canadian performance placing 7th '86 Worlds; 3 WC gold; 1st Canadian fencer to rank in world's top 8 5yrs; res. Montreal, Que.

CHOUINARD, Josée (figure skating); b. 21 Aug 1969, Rosemont, Que.; m. Jean-Michel Bombardier; College Francais; ret'd professional skater; began skating age 7; mem. ntl team '88-94; gold '90, bronze '92 Skate Canada; 3 ntl sr. women's titles; 3 Sears Cdn Open titles; competed 4 worlds, '92, '94 Olympics; coached by Louis Stong; pro Stars on Ice '94-97; Cdn women's pro champ '97; res. Toronto, Ont.

CHRISTIE, Alan (t&f); b. 14 Jun 1905, Hamilton, Ont.; d. 9 Jan 2002, West Plains, N.Y.; given name: Alan Thomas; m. Kathleen Aggett; c. Janet, Susan, Carol Anne; UofT, BComm.; ret'd investment consultant; mem. Penn Relays HS mile titlist '22; ntl interscholastic 440yds champion '23; Ont. open indoor 300yds title '23; Ont. open 440yds '23, '25; Ont. open 400m, silver Penn US interscholastic championships 440yds '24; Cdn intercollegiate 440yd titles '24-27; in qualifying for '24 Olympic team set 400m record; quarterfinalist Olympic 400m, mem. 4th place 1600m relay team; mem. UofT intercollegiate record setting mile relay team '26; mem. '28 Hamilton 1600m AAUofC title, ntl record relay team.

CHRISTIE, Steve (football); b. 13 Nov 1967, Oakville, Ont.; given name: Geoffrey Stephen; m. Alison; c. Alexandra Laine; William & Mary; standout HS soccer/ football player; mem. ntl jr World Cup soccer team; set numerous W&M pk records including most points (279), most FGs (57 of 83), most cvts (108 of 116), longest FG (53yds 3 times), drafted by Tampa Bay (NFL), Edmonton (CFL); standout rookie season with Tampa Bay earned selection to all-Rookie team; set several Tampa Bay records; to Buffalo '92-01, San Diego '01-03, NY Giants '04; continued setting NFL records; became most accurate kicker in NFL history with 100 of 124 for 80.65 per cent '95; personal best 59yd FG '93; accomplished painter; major involvement with Buffalo and Erie County Historical Society; res. St. Petersburg, FL.

CHRISTOFOROU, Chris (harness racing); b. 17 Oct 1971, Toronto, Ont.; father Chris Sr. prominent Woodbine trainer; scored 1st victory with Delias Star at Flamboro '90; OJC rookie of yr; 3 O'Brien Cdn driver-of-yr awards; drove Astreos to '00 Little Brown Jug; through '03 4019 wins, $50+M in purses; top single season win total 642 '99; 42 major stakes victories; 3 Breeders crown wins; 3 Des Smith Classic titles; res. Campbellville, Ont.

CHURSKY, Tony (soccer); b. 13 Jun 1953, New Westminster, B.C.; m. Donna; c. Ian, Alex; Simon Fraser; soccer player; amateur soccer Vancouver Croatia, Spartans; pro Seattle Sounders '76-78; led NASL goalies with 0.91 goals-against average rookie season; California Surf, Chicago Sting '79; Toronto Blizzard from '80; '77 Soccer Bowl finalist; international debut ntl team '72; res. Toronto, Ont.

CHUVALO, George (boxing); 12 Sep 1937, Toronto, Ont.; m. Lynne (d); c. Mitchell, Steven (d), George Jr. (d), Jesse (d), Vanessa; m. Joanne; St. Michael's Coll.; runs Fight Against Drugs program, promotions, TV productions; ntl amateur heavyweight title '55; pro '56; beat James J. Parker for ntl heavyweight title '58; defended vs. Yvon Durelle then lost to Bob Cleroux '60; regained it then lost again to Cleroux; reclaimed title beating Jean Claude Roy '68; defended successfully through '79; fought Muhammad Ali, Joe Frazier, Floyd Patterson, Ernie Terrell, George Foreman; never knocked off feet; career total 97 bouts, won 68 by KO, 9 on decision, 2 draws, lost 15 decisions, 1 DQ, 2 TKOs; TV boxing commentator, occasional movie actor; mem. Order of Canada; Cdn Boxing; Rochester Boxing; Canada's, Etobicoke, Ont. Legends Sports halls of fame; res. Weston, Ont.

CHYNOWETH, Ed (hockey/builder); b. 14 Dec 1941, Dodsland, Sask.; given name: James Edward; m. Linda Lindsay; c. Jeff, Dean; pres./owner Kootenay Ice (WHL); 1st full-time pres. WHL '72; organized Cdn Major Junior Hockey League (CHL) '73; pres. '75-96; key role in getting CHL and CHA to form policy comm. to oversee/operate Canada's world jr. team program; p-pres. Sask MHA; 2 CHL distinguished service awards; fed. Fair Play award; CHA order of merit; mem. Intl Centre of Excellence/hockey development comm. '87; mem. Hockey hall of fame selection comm.; mem. Alta Sports Hall of Fame; res. St. Albert, Alta.

CICCARELLI, Dino (hockey); b. 8 Feb 1960, Sarnia, Ont.; m. Lynda; c. Jenna, Kristen, Ashley; rw London Knights '77-80; OHL 2nd team all-star '78; pro Oklahoma City (CHL) '80-81; Minnesota '80-89, Washington '89-92, Detroit '92-96, Tampa Bay '96-98, Florida '98-99; topped scored 55g '81-82, 52 '86-87; topped 1,000 point mark '94, 600g plateau '98; NHL record: 1232 scheduled games, 608g, 592a, 141 playoff games, 73g, 45a; played 4 NHL all-star games; co-owner Motor City Mustangs roller hockey team; co-owner Sarnia Sting jrs. (OHL); res. Kalamazoo, Mich.

CLAIR, Frank (football/coaching); b. 12 May 1917, Hamilton, Ohio; d. Apr 2005, Sarasota, Fla; m. Pat Bausman; c. Robin, Holly (d); Ohio State, Miami of Ohio, BSc; ret'd football exec., scout; all-Big 10 end Ohio State '38; drafted Washington Redskins; asst. coach 71st Infantry Div. in Europe WW2; asst. Miami of Ohio '46, Purdue '47; head coach UofBuffalo '48, Argos '50-54; asst. Cincinnati U '55; head coach Rough Riders '56-69; CFL coaching record: 172-125-7, .579 percentage; made playoffs 17 times 18yrs, league finals 12 times; 6 Grey Cups, 5 winners; twice Annis Stukus Trophy CFL coach of year; nicknamed "The Professor"; GM Rough Riders '70-78, Grey Cup champions '73, '76; scout Argos '82-86; Rough Rider advisor '87-90; Ottawa stadium bears his name; mem. Butler County; Ottawa Sports, Cdn Football halls of fame.

CLANCY, King (hockey); b. 25 Feb 1903, Ottawa, Ont.; d. 10 Nov 1986, Toronto, Ont.; given name: Francis Michael; m. Rae (d); c. Terry, Carol, Ann, Judy, Tom; hockey exec.; amateur hockey Ottawa St. Brigid's; pro at 18 Ottawa Senators; reputation as rushing def; sold to Maple Leafs '30 for unprecedented $35,000+two players; led Leafs to 1st Stanley Cup '31-32; twice 1st, 2nd all-star teams; ret'd following '36-37 season; coached Montreal Maroons half

'37-38 season then switched to refereeing; coach Leafs '50, Cleveland, Pittsburgh (AHL); asst. GM, v-p; also v-p Hamilton CFL club; Bickell Cup for contribution to Leafs; 2 'nights' in his honor Maple Leaf Gardens; noted raconteur; mem. Ottawa, Hockey, Canada's Sports halls of fame.

CLAPPER, Dit (hockey); b. 9 Feb 1907, Newmarket, Ont.; d. 20 Jan 1978, Peterborough, Ont.; given name: Aubrey Victor; m. Lorraine Pratt; c. Donald, Marilyn; accountant, office mgr.; jr. Oshawa at 13; Parkdale Canoe Club, CAHL Boston Tigers; Bruins '27-47, 1st NHL player 20 seasons same club; 9yrs rw, 11 def; NHL record: 833 scheduled games, 228g, 246a, 86 playoff games, 13g, 17 assists; best season '29-30, 41 goals 44-game schedule; mem. 3 Stanley Cup winners; 3 times 1st, 2nd team all-star; Buffalo (AHL) after leaving NHL; coached Bruins 2 seasons, Buffalo '60; sweater No. 5 ret'd by Bruins; mem. Hockey, Peterborough, Canada's Sports halls of fame.

CLARE, Lou (football); b. 13 Mar 1953, Mississauga, Ont.; UMinn; standout hockey player Dixie Beehive organization; jr. St. Catharines Black Hawks; although being groomed for NHL with Chicago accepted UMinn athletic scholarship and shone as db/lb/pk; boyhood dream of playing for Toronto vanished when Argos traded his CFL rights to Hamilton '73; db/cb with Ticats until dealt to Saskatchewan '75; rejoined Hamilton '79-80, Montreal '81; 2 Grey Cup finals; mem. Mississauga Sports Hall of Fame; res. Brampton, Ont.

CLARIDGE, Pat (football); b. 12 Jul 1938, Chilliwack, B.C.; m. Anne Louise Hanna; Wash; stockbroker; mem. 2 Rose Bowl winners; all-Coast split end BC '61-66; mem. Calgary '68 Grey Cup winner; CFL record: 198 receptions for 2497yds; WFC all-star '64, CFL top Canadian nominee; football broadcast color commentator; mem. Lions Wall of Fame; res. Edmonton, Alta.

CLARK, Bud (skiing); b. Jul 1910, Ottawa, Ont.; d. 2 Jan 1975, Ottawa, Ont.; St. Pat's Coll.; sporting goods mgr.; standout skier, paddler; mem. New Edinburgh Canoe Club; international intercollegiate all-around ski champion, Lake Placid combined champion '31; mem. '32, '36 Olympic teams; ntl nordic combined, Que. x-country title '35; built, operated Skiskule Lodge; charter mem. Cdn Amateur Sports Advisory council; dir. COA; 7yrs pres. CASA; initial curator Cdn Ski Museum; mem. Cdn Skiing Hall of Fame.

CLARK, Jim (coaching); b. 22 Mar 1942, St. Thomas, Ont.; given name: James Richard; m. Barbara Jeanne Cook; c. James Robert; Acadia, BA; football coach; asst. coach Acadia '68-69, Tennessee '69-71, Clearwater, Fla. HS '71-75; head coach St. Mary's '76-79; asst. coach UofOtt '79-82, head coach '83-84; scout BC (CFL) '85-91, Calgary '95-98; asst. coach Ottawa '92-93, '04-05 Hamilton '94, Birmingham Barracudas '95; res. Ottawa, Ont.

CLARK, Karen (synchro swim); b. 9 Apr 1972, Montreal, Que.; m. Chris LePoole; UCal BA; journalist *Calgary Herald, CBC*, motivational speaker; introduced to synchro swim by older sister Cathy; mem. ntl team '88-99; 20 ntl titles; solo, duet, team silver world jrs. '89; team silver '91, '94 world aquatic championships; 4 team silver, 1 bronze world cups; solo silver '95 PAG, team silver '96 Olympic Games; team gold '96 French Open, '90 Swiss Open, '91

Petro-Canada Cup, '94 Titrex Cup; solo silver '97 world cup; Helen Vanderburg synchro swim award '87; 3 Calgary Aquabelle achievement awards; 3 Petro-Canada Olympic Torch scholarships; Dale Carnegie achievement award; Mississauga athlete of '97; res. Calgary, Alta.

CLARK, Keith (harness racing); b. 19 Mar 1953, Saskatchewan; following in footsteps of father Lorne, a breeder and trainer, scored 1st win with pacer Billy Quill at 18; 1st driver to win more then $1M in purses exclusively in Western Canada; '83 Western Canada horseman of yr; '87 Cdn horseman of yr; 24 100+ victory seasons, 4737 wins $19+M in purses through '03; 7 Western Canada Derby, 5 Northland Filly Stakes titles; among priminent horses As Promised, That'll Be Me, Disagreement, Flavor of the Day, Expensive Return; res. Dewinton, Alta.

CLARK, Ken (football); b. 26 May 1948, Southampton, Eng.; given name: Kenneth Lawrence; div. Grayce Palmisano; c. Devon, Garrett; m. Terri; sc. Ryan, Jesse; St. Mary's, BA, George Brown College, Sheridan College; printing co. owner; HS athlete of '68, George Brown athlete of '70, St. Mary's athlete of '74; Ted Morris Memorial award '73; pro punter Portland Storm (WFL) '74-75, Hamilton '75-77, Toronto '78-79, LA Rams (NFL) '79-80, Saskatchewan '80-83, Ottawa '83-87; 7 times top CFL punter, 2 EFC, 1 WFC, 3 CFL all-star; LA kicker Super Bowl XIV; all-Canadian, all-WFC '82; CFL record: 12 seasons, 1592 punts, 72,520 yds, 45.6 avg (league record), 2 tds, 23 cvts, 10 fg, 90 singles; res. Barrie, Ont.

CLARK, Paul (t&f); b. 13 Dec 1957, Woodstock, Ont.; optometrist; 3 world, 7 ntl, 1 Pan-Am wheelchair records in distances from 100m to 10km; 15 Ont. Games, 9 Canada Games, 5 Regional Games gold; mem. '80, '84 Olympic, '82 PAG for Disabled teams; res. Woodstock, Ont.

CLARK, Ranza (t&f); b. 13 Dec 1961, Calgary, Alta.; m. Art Boileau; Oregon BA; employed Chapters, owns greeting card co.; BC 1500m title '83; gold 1500m, silver 800m '83 PAG; silver NCAA '84 championships; mem. '84 Olympic, '90 CG teams; '89 ntl 800m title; fed. govt. excellence award '84; res. Vancouver, B.C.

CLARK, Wendel (hockey); b. 25 Oct 1966, Kelvington, Sask.; m. Denise; c. Kylee Lee, Kassidy; lw Saskatoon Jr. '83-85; WHL East 1st team all-star '85; mem. Cdn gold medal world jr. team '85; drafted by Toronto 1st overall '85; NHL Toronto '85-94, '96-98, '00, Quebec '94-95, Colorado '95, NYI '95-96, Tampa Bay '98, Detroit '99, Chicago '99; TML capt.; NHL all-rookie team '86; *Sporting News* rookie of '86; frequent injuries shortened career; NHL record: 793 scheduled games, 330g, 234a, 95 playoff games, 37g, 32a; res. Hopewell Junction, N.Y.

CLARKE, Bill (football); b. 25 Nov 1932, Regina, Sask.; m. Geraldine Bloomer; c. Jim, Tara, Debbie, Peter, Rob; UofSask.; jr. Regina Dales; ctr/dt Roughriders '51-65; twice all-star; mem. '50 Cdn schoolboy curling title rink; ntl sr. men's curling title '88; mem. Cdn Football, Sask Sports halls of fame; res. Regina, Sask.

CLARKE, Bobby (hockey); b. 13 Aug 1949, Flin Flon, Man.; given name: Robert Earle; m. Sandy; c. Wade,

Jody, Lucas, Jakki; hockey exec.; jr. Flin Flon Bombers; Philadelphia's 2nd choice, 17th overall 1969 amateur draft; mem. Flyers '69-84; 2 Stanley Cups; Flyers capt. '72-79, '82-84; at time youngest NHL team capt.; played 1000th game 23 Oct '82; twice 1st, 2nd all-star team ctr; 9 NHL all-star games; mem. Team Canada '72, '76; Hart Trophy '73, '75-6; Bill Masterton Trophy '72; Lester B. Pearson Award '73; Lionel Conacher, Lou Marsh trophies '75; Lester Patrick award '80; Frank J. Selke Trophy '83; Pa. sports writers athlete of '74, Good Guy award '83, most courageous award '80; played entire career suffering chronic diabetes; 1st to win *Sporting News* rookie, player, executive awards; 2 *Sporting News, Hockey News* exec. of yr.; 1st to win *HN* exec award in consec. yrs with different teams; NHL record: 1144 scheduled games, 358 goals, 852 assists; 136 playoff games, 42g, 77a; v-p, GM Philadelphia Flyers '84-90, sr. v-p '92-93; GM Minnesota North Stars '90-92; VP/GM Florida Panthers '93-94; pres/GM/partner Philadelphia '94-03; relinquished pres. Role '03; GM Team Canada '87 Canada Cup title team, '98 Olympic team; jersey 16 ret'd by Flyers; Officer Order of Canada '81; mem. Man. Sports, Flyers, Man, Cdn Hockey halls of fame; res. Moorestown, N.J.

CLARKE, Christine (rowing); b. 11 Aug 1960, Scarborough, Ont.; sweep ntl champion 8s '77, pairs '80; Canadian Henley 8s '77, Head of the Charles '83; mem. '84 Olympic Games, 2 world championships teams; sister Heather also ntl team mem.; res. Vancouver, B.C.

CLARKE, Heather (rowing); b. 25 Jul 1958, Stouffville, Ont.; sweep 8s '77, '80-82 Canadian Henley title crews; 2nd coxed 4s '81 English Henley; 2 ntl 8s titles; mem. '84 Olympic team; sister Christine also ntl team mem.; mem. Cdn Athletes Assn. board; res. Victoria, B.C.

CLARKE, Karen (t&f); b. 7 Oct 1971, Montego Bay, Jamaica; sprint specialist; emigrated to Canada '82; began competing '85; ntl jr. 200m title '89; semifinalist world jr. '90; ntl 100, 200m titles '91; competed '91 worlds, PAG, '92 Olympics, '94 CG; ntl indoor 60m titles '92, '93, 200m indoor title '92; gold *Times-Colonist* 100m '94; PB: 11.40 100m, 23.47 200m; res. Calgary, Alta.

CLARKE, Nig (baseball); b. 15 Dec 1882, Amherstburg, Ont.; d. 15 Jun 1949, River Rouge, Mich.; given name: Jay Justin; Assumption Coll; ret'd Ford Motors; catcher; 8 consecutive homers Jul '02 as Corsicana thumped Texarcana 51-3 in Texas League game; Detroit (AL) '05, Cleveland (AL) '05-10, St. Louis (AL) '11, Philadelphia (NL) '19, Pittsburgh (NL) '20; ML record: 506 scheduled games, .254ba; mem. Cdn Baseball, U Windsor, Windsor-Essex, Canada's Sports halls of fame.

CLARKE, Richard (sailing); b. 20 Nov 1968, Toronto, Ont.; Trent U. rugby coach; following in footsteps of father Alan who won bronze in '67 PAG and who competed in '72 Olympics, he moved from Laser and Flying Dutchman to Finn Class '89; bronze Finn Gold Cup (worlds) '93; CORK gold, NA silver '95, bronze '94; silver '86 IYRU world youth championships; member '96, alternate '92 Olympic teams; Finn gold '99 PAG; CYA male athlete of '93, Ont. sailor of '93; 2 Ont. all-star rugby awards; res. Peterborough, Ont.

CLARKE, Stephen (swimming); b. 21 Jul 1973, Sutton Coldfield, Eng.; Florida; began racing age 6; butterfly specialist; silver 4x100m FS relay '91 Pan-Am, '98 CG; bronze 4x100m medley relay '92 Olympics; bronze 4x100m FS relay '93 Pan-Pacific championships, 4x100 medley relay '98 CG; gold 100m FS, silver 100m fly, 4x100m medley relay '94 CG; 5 Canada Cup gold, 2 silver '96; 8 ntl titles; with Marcel Gery, Ont. swim athlete of '92; masters '01 Ont. championships; res. Brampton, Ont.

CLARKSON, Candy (basketball); b. 30 Nov 1958, Hamilton, Ont.; given name: Candace Leah; div. Kevin Lohr; m. David Bruce Jirik; c. Ashleigh Elizabeth, Alexis Victoria, Tyler Phillip Bradley; Guelph, BSc, Brock, BEd; teacher; mem. OFSAA title teams '75-76; ntl jr. title team '76; ntl sr. women's team '77-80, '82-84; ntl title team '85; all-Cdn university 1st team '77-80, '82-83; tournament MVP '77 ntl sr. women's championship; OWIAA single game record 49 points; bronze worlds, FISU, PAG; competed '84 Olympics, '79, '83 PAG, 2 world championships; Guelph female athlete of '79, Brock co-athlete of yr '82-83; mem. Brock, Guelph, Ancaster HS Sports halls of fame; res. Unionville, Ont.

CLARKSON, Reg (all-around); b. 19 Aug 1925, Victoria, B.C.; given name: Reginald Louis; m. Peggy McCarthy; c. Mary, Rita, Clare, Joan, Greg, Reg Jr., Peggy, Kevin; UBC, BA, BSW, MSW, Victoria Normal School, TCert.; ret'd. prison service social worker; mem. BC HS soccer, basketball title teams; mem. '46 Western Conf. college football champions; pro baseball Vancouver Capilanos '46; contract sold to Brooklyn Dodgers; lf under Walter Alston Ft. Worth batting .337, named all-star; arm problems '48; batted .281 Mobile; semipro Edmonton '49 batting .381, leading league all off. departments; .327 Vancouver Capilanos '50; pro basketball Vancouver Hornets '46-47; football Edmonton '49-50; traded to Calgary for Normie Kwong '51; Vancouver athlete of '46; Island Open golf title; mem. Greater Victoria, UBC, BC Sports halls of fame; res. Vancouver, B.C.

CLASS, Harry (builder/diving); b. 1 Mar 1916, Berlin (Kitchener), Ont.; m. Helen Hirons (d); c. Duncan, Philip; ret'd. pres. frozen food co.; began diving career late '20s; won Western Ont. Jr./Sr. 3m titles '32; 5 Cdn sr 3m, 1 1m titles; 3m bronze '34 BEG; won '36 Olympic trials but CASA chose not to add him to team; while serving in army WW2 engaged in English diving exhibitions for Red Cross; served on CASA exec. 10yrs; diving chair. 4yrs; CNE sports comm. 25yrs; chief referee world pro high diving championships '62-63; editor/publisher *Canadian Aquatic News* '58-59; Swim Ontario Friend of Swimming award; dir. Swim Ontario (Ont. Aquatic) Hall of Fame; master swimmer; French Open gold; mem. Ont. Aquatic Hall of Fame as both athlete and builder; res. Kitchener, Ont.

CLAYTON, Harold (lawn bowling); b. 10 Jun 1916, Lang, Sask.; given name: Harold Wright; ret'd. provincial civil servant; from '45-60 among Saskatchewan's top curlers; 5 Sask., 2 ntl singles lawn bowling titles; mem. '70 BEG team; mem. Sask. Sports Hall of Fame; res. Regina, Sask.

CLAYTON, Juanita (softball); b. 10 Jan 1969, Manitou, Man.; Utah State; social worker; catcher; ntl jr team '85,

'87; competed jr. worlds, '91, '95 PAG, '96 Olympics, '94 worlds; 4 yrs NCAA Div. 1 with Utah State, 2 MVP awards; all-star '95 ntl championships; mem. Man. Softball Hall of Fame; res. Kaleida, Man.

CLEEVELY, Bill (canoeing); b. 23 Oct 1908, Montreal, Que.; d. 26 Nov 1990, Ottawa, Ont; given name: William Gerald; m. Margaret Grace Forbes (d); c. Susan, Lynn, Billy; ret'd CNR; mem. Otterbrun Boating Club '24-28, both tandem and 4s; ntl sr. tandem title with J.O.Mason '27; coach, capt. OBC '35, '47-48; OBC exec., commodore '37; Eastern Div. CCA flag officer, secty. '43, '53-60; commodore CCA '46, secty.-treas. '58-64; mgr. canoe team '60 Olympics; Voyageur Canadian canoeing award '72.

CLEGG, Robin (biathlon); b. 11 Aug 1977, Edmonton, Alta.; full-time athlete; ntl team from '99; ntl jr. title '97; 2 gold '99 ntls, 2 silver '00, 4 gold '01; bronze CISM '02-03; 3 consec. gold '05; competed 4 worlds, '02 Olympics; res. Canmore, Alta.

CLEGHORN, Odie (hockey); b. 1891, Montreal, Que.; d. 13 Jul 1956, Montreal, Que.; given name: Ogilvie; unique distinction of playing major hockey as both forward and goalie, later referee; mem. Canadiens '18-25; 2 seasons Pittsburgh Pirates; 9yr NHL record 96 goals, 29 assists; played 1 game in goal allowing 2 goals; brother Sprague.

CLEGHORN, Sprague (hockey); b. 1890, Montreal, Que.; d. 11 Jul 1956, Montreal, Que.; forward NY Crescents; Renfrew (NHA) '09-10; teamed with Cyclone Taylor on def; once scored 5 goals single game; 6 seasons Montreal Wanderers; Ottawa Senators '19-21, briefly Toronto St.Pat's then Canadiens '22-25, Bruins '26; in 17 seasons (missed '18 with broken leg) 163 goals, 296 games; mem. 2 Stanley Cup winners; brother Odie; mem. Hockey Hall of Fame.

CLEMENS, Roger (baseball); b. 4 Aug 1962, Dayton, Ohio; given name: William Roger; m. Debra Lynn Godfrey; c. Koby Aaron, Kory Allen, Kacy Austin, Kody Alec; Texas, San Jacinto JC; rhp; helped Legion team win State title '79; all-district football de, basketball ctr; drafted NY Mets '81 but didn't sign; 3yrs all-American; NCAA world series title '83; 1st Texas baseball player to have number (21) ret'd.; made pro debut Winter Haven (Fla. St.) '83, New Britain (EL) '83, Pawtucket (EL) '84; Boston (AL) '84-96, Toronto '97-98; New York (AL) '99-03, Houston '04-05; nicknamed "Rocket Roger"; competed 6 world series; AL MVP '86; record 7 Cy Young awards; Joe Cronin award '98; three times led AL in strikeouts single season; 5 ERA titles; 2 20k games; MBL record: 607 scheduled games, 4278.2ip. 310-160w/l, 4099k, 46sho, 1379bob, 3677h, 3.18era; '86 all-star game MVP, recorded 21 victories in initial season with Toronto '97, 20 (15 in succession) in '98; ESPY comeback of '98 award; set ML record running '01 mark to 20-1 all-time AL strikeout leader (3510) '01; surpassed 4000 strikeout, 300 victory levels 13 Jun '03; ranked 2nd to Nolan Ryan (5714) on ML all-time strikeout list '04; active in community charity programs in Boston; created K for Kids program; 2 Ont. athlete of yr awards; mem. ML all-century team; res. Houston, Tex.

CLEMENT, Diane (t&f); b. 27 Sep 1936, Moncton, N.B.; given name: Diane Elaine Matheson; m. Doug Clement;

c. Jennifer, Rand; Sir George Williams; food consultant, restaurant owner, cookbook author; ntl 100m, 200m records '54-55; mem. '56 Olympic team; bronze 4x100 relay '58 CG; pres. CTFA '74-76; co-founder Richmond Kajaks t&f club; mgr. '84-88 ntl t&f team; mem. 2010 Olympic bid comm.; mem. NB Sports Hall of Fame; res. Vancouver, B.C.

CLEMENT, Doug (t&f); b. 15 Jul 1933, Montreal, Que.; given name: Douglas Bruce; m. Diane Matheson; c. Jennifer, Rand; Oregon, BSc, UBC, MD; sports physician; 400m, 800m specialist; mem. '52, '56 Olympic, '54, '58 CG teams; silver 4x440yds relay '54; John Davies award '53, Vanier award '69; physician '70 CG, '71 PAG, '76, '84 Olympic Games; coach '88, '92 Olympic, '86 CG, '91, '93 (head) world championship teams; co-dir. Allan McGavin sports medicine centre; prof. UBC faculty of medicine; team doctor Vancouver Canucks; Geoff Gowan award; PetroCan coaching award; mem. Order of Canada; UBC, BC Sports halls of fame; res. Vancouver, B.C.

CLEMENTS, Tom (football); b. 18 Jun 1953, McKee's Rocks, Pa.; given name: Thomas Albert; m. Kathleen Ann Brady; c. Stephanie Alice, Tom Jr.; Notre Dame; lawyer/coach; qb coach Notre Dame '92-95, New Orleans Saints '97-99, KC '00, Pittsburgh '01-03, Buffalo '04; HS basketball all-American (recruited by N.Carolina); ND qb, all-American 3 of 4 years; mem. '74 ntl championship team, Sugar Bowl winner; Heisman Trophy nominee sr. year; pro Ottawa '75-78; Saskatchewan, Hamilton '79; NFL Kansas City '80; Hamilton '81-83; traded to Winnipeg for Dieter Brock '83; ret'd after '87 season; CFL record: 12 seasons, 4657 attempts, 2807 completions, 39041 yds, 60.3 pct, 252 tds, 214 interceptions; Schenley rookie of '75, Grey Cup winner '76, '84; 6 times EFC all-star; CFL all-star '84; '76, '84 Grey Cup MVP; 5 times EFC passing yardage leader; twice Ticats MVP, Jeff Russel Trophy winner '81; runnerup Schenley outstanding player '81; CFL star of year award '84; mem. Blue Bombers, Ottawa Sports, Cdn Football halls of fame; res. Pittsburgh, Pa.

CLEMONS, Mike (football); b. 15 Jan 1965, Clearwater, Fla.; m. Diane; c. Rachel; William & Mary; football exec., business owner; as college rb gained 4778 all-purpose yds, 31tds '83-87; NCAA Div 1-AA all-American, Virginia major colleges offensive player of '86; 8th round draft KC Chiefs '87; attended Tampa Bay NFL camp '88; made Argos debut 27 Jul '89; quickly earned nickname "Pinball" for exciting, elusive running style; 1st CFL td vs. Ottawa 9 Oct '89; shattered own single-season pro football record for combined yds with 3840 in '97; EFC, CFL all-star as special teams player; CFL record: 185gp, 1107 carries, 5341yds, 85td, 3cvts, 682recept., 7015yds, 46td; 3 Eastern, 2 CFL all-star; Jeff Russel Memorial award '90, 2 CFL records; 4 Grey Cup finals, 2 winners (as player) 1 as coach; CFL outstanding player award '90; head coach Toronto Argos '00, '02-04; Argos pres. '01-03 active in charitable work in Toronto; mem. Argos basketball team; mem. Athletes in Action; Tom Pate Memorial award '94; CFLPA sportsman award; 2 ALS Ironman awards; John Candy Memorial award '95; Order of Ontario; res. Mississauga, Ont.

CLERMONT, Jason (football); b. 24 May 1978, Regina, Sask.; URegina; slotback; CIS all-Cdn, Can-West outstanding player; CFL BC '02-04; CFL rookie of '02,

outstanding Cdn '04, outstanding Cdn Grey Cup '04; CFL record (through '04) 51 scheduled games, 170 receptions, 2570yds, 20tds; active in MS, Heart & Stroke Foundation charities; spokesperson for Lions in United Way, Lions in the House school skills program; res. Vancouver, B.C.

CLEVELAND, Jon (swimming); b. 19 Dec 1970, Fresno, Calif.; UCal, broadcaster; began competing age 9; mem. ntl team '87-96; breaststroke specialist; 23 ntl titles; mem. 3 4x50, 1 4x100 Cdn record relay teams, 1 4x100 world record team; 1st '88, '92 World Cup breaststroke rankings; CIAU 100, 200, 4x100 medley relay short course records '90; 5 CIAU titles; CG gold 200m, 4x100 medley '90, silver 4x100m medley relay, bronze 100, 200 '94; silver 100m, bronze 4x100 medley relay '95 PAG; mem. '88, '92, '96 Olympic teams; 2 CIAU male swimmer of yr; 3 Swimming Canada male athlete of yr awards; 2 masters records; res. London, Ont.

CLEVELAND, Reggie (baseball); b. 23 May 1948, Swift Current, Sask.; given name: Reginald Leslie; m. Kathleen Kubicki; c. Michelle Annette, Michael David, Todd Joseph, Tim, Jon; car salesman; HS athlete of '65 starring in curling, t&f; 2 Alta. javelin records; Babe Ruth League no-hitter '61; pro St. Louis organization '66, Cardinals '69-73, Boston '74-78, Texas '78, Milwaukee '79-81; rh starter/reliever; *Sporting News* NL rookie pitcher of yr, St. Louis chapter BBWA rookie of year; Red Sox Man of '76; 1st Cdn to start ALCS playoff game '75; World Series finalist '75; ML record: 428 scheduled games, 1809ip, 57cg, 930k, 543bob, 105-106, 25sv; 12so, 4.01era; mem. Cdn Baseball Hall of Fame; res. Calgary, Alta/Mansfield, Tex.

CLIFF, Leslie (swimming); b. 11 Mar 1955, Vancouver, B.C.; m. Mark Tindle; c. Scott, Lisa; Arizona State BCom (finance); portfolio mgr.; 15 ntl, 4 British, 1 US titles; 3 gold, 2 silver '71 PAG, 2 gold '74 CG, silver '72 Olympics; specialist 200m, 400m, 800m FS, 200m backstroke, 400m IM; 16 ntl long-course, 12 short-course records; ntl jr. athlete of '72; 2 BC Jr., 3 sr. swimmer-of-yr awards; hon. capt. '94 CG team; earned 33 ntl championship medals; helped initiate Zajac swim camps; Elaine Tanner trophy '72; Officer Order of Canada '71; mem. Cdn Aquatic, Olympic, Canada's, BC Swimming, Sports halls of fame; res. Vancouver, B.C.

CLIFFORD, Betsy (skiing); b. 15 Oct 1953, Ottawa, Ont.; m. Dale Higgins; c. Blake, Carly, Jolene, Roseanne; Algonquin College; *Fleet News* publication asst.; ntl jr. title age 12, women's crown at 13; 8 ntl slalom, GS titles through '75; at 14 youngest Canadian skier ever in Olympics ('68 Grenoble); at 16 youngest world championship winner with GS gold Val Gardena, Italy '70; at 17 women's special slalom title Val d'Isere, France, slalom Schruns, Austria, 2nd overall WC slalom '71; freak accident resulted in 2 broken heels '72 WC downhill; overall Can-Am team title '73; silver '74 WC downhill St. Moritz, bronze WC downhill Pfronten, Germany; WC record 3-3-4; ret'd '76; twice Ottawa ACT athlete of year; mem. Ottawa, US, Cdn Skiing, Cdn Olympic, Canada's Sports halls of fame; res. Almonte, Ont

CLIFFORD, Harvey (skiing); b. 18 Sep 1926, Oak Point, N.B.; d. 13 Jan 1982, N. Palm Beach, Fla.; m. Ellen Vera Kaarsberg; c. Christian, Heidi; Queen's; ski resort owner, operator; brother John Clifford; major ski honors included Taschereau Cup, Canadian Kandahar; US downhill '48; 16th place Olympic downhill finish best ever by Cdn skier to '48; coach, capt. ntl ski team '50 worlds; coach '52 Olympic team; ski school instructor Banff, Laurentians, NZ; chief examiner Canadian Ski Instructors Alliance; 8yrs pres. Mount Snow, Vt. ski development; 7yrs pres. Stratton Mountain, Vt.; owner, operator Glen Ellen, Vt. resort to '79 retirement; mem. Cdn Skiing, Ottawa Sports halls of fame.

CLIFFORD, John (skiing); b. 13 Feb 1923, Ottawa, Ont.; d. 6 Jun 2002, Almonte, Ont.; m. Margaret Phillips; c. Betsy, Joanne, Stephen (d), Susanne; ski area developer, operator; despite schoolyard accident which left him almost blind in right eye, became alpine/water skiing champion; hitch-hiked to Chile to represent Canada Ski Union of Americas (Pan-Am) meet, won overall title; 3 ntl, 2 Que. titles; '48, '52 Olympic team alternate; mem. ntl team '50 world championships; ntl water ski title '55; 4 Que. titles; 9th world water ski finals '55; involved in development Camp Fortune, Carlington Park, Mt. Ste. Marie, Mt. Tremblant, Mt. Cascades, Calabogie Peaks, Mt. Pakenham ski areas; autobiography *White Gold, The John Clifford Story*; mem. Cdn Skiing; Ottawa Sports halls of fame.

CLIFFORD, Shanty (baseball); b. 16 Jan 1924, Clairton, Pa.; d. 4 May 1990, Brantford, Ont.; given name: Luther; m. Lorraine Saunders; ret'd Brant County Bd. of Ed. supervisor; Pa. state discus, shot put champion '41; c-1b baseman Homestead Grays, Indianapolis Clowns Negro National League; mem. '49 Grays pennant winners; Sr. IC Galt, Brantford throughout '50s; batting title '56 with .397; frequent all-star; RBI co-leader '58.

CLIFFORD, William (shooting); b. 1878, Brampton, Ont.; d. 1917, France; cabinet maker; mem. 10th Royal Grenadiers; mem. Cdn Bisley teams '10-11; mem. MacKinnon Cup winning team '10; claimed Bisley King's, Prince of Wales prizes '11 and subsequently honored by Toronto parade on return from England; during WW1 QMS in charge of Ross rifle div.; discovered Ross rifle didn't perform well in battle conditions and urged its withdrawal from service; subsequently got into a dispute with inventor Sir Charles Ross and, knowing he had no hope of winning argument, switched to Royal Flying Corps where he died over France; built ceremonial chair still in use at DCRA Connaught Range in Nepean.

CLIMIE, Jock (football); b. 28 Sep 1968, Toronto, Ont.; sb Queen's, LLB; lawyer; *TSN* football analyst; led OQIFC receivers '88-89; 1st team all-Canadian '88-89; set CIAU receiving record 1091yds '88; CIAU record: 121 receptions for 2130yds, 18tds; CFL Toronto '90, '95, Ottawa '90-94, Montreal '96-01; CFL record: 12 seasons, 627recept., 9619yds, 56td, 1cvt, 338pts; 1 Grey Cup final; res. Ottawa, Ont.

CLINE, Paddy (rowing/basketball); b. 2 Feb 1899, Hamilton, Ont.; d. 13 Mar 1993, Hamilton, Ont.; given name: George; m. Alice Isabel McKenzie; Firestone Co. employee; mem. ntl Int. title basketball team '27, Ont. YMCA sr. champions, OBA semifinalists '29; coached Hamilton Y, guided Livingstone Church girls '39 Ont. jr.

church title; began rowing '20; stroked Leander Boat Club's lightweight 8s '27 ntl title; coached '30-60 producing 40-plus Canadian Henley winners including 4 Hanlan Memorial Cups for sr. heavyweight crews; coached 3 Olympic crews; trophy in his name presented annually by CARA to Canadian Henley lightweight race winners; launched McMaster rowing program; instrumental in founding Eastern Cdn college rowing program; life mem. YMCA; mem. Copps Coliseum Hall of Fame.

CLOUTIER, Guylaine (swimming); b. 1 Oct 1971, Levis, Que.; UMtl; breaststroke specialist; began competing age 7; mem. ntl team '85-96; 10 ntl titles; mem. '88, '92, '96 Olympic, '90, '94 CG, '91, '93 FISU Games, '91, '94 worlds teams; competed in 28 World Cup races winning 3g, 11s, 4b; gold Monte Carlo, Italian, French events; twice 2nd in world breaststroke rankings; silver 100, 200 breaststroke '90 CG; 2 '95 PAG silver; 2g, 1s, 2b FISU Games; 1 CIAU female swimmer of yr, 3 Swim Canada female athlete-of-year awards; res. St-Constant, Laprairie, Que.

CLYDE, Ian (boxing); 15 May 1956, Verdun, Que.; given name: Ian Nathanial; div. Gail Nolan; c. Heather; div. Annette Wahl; c. Amanda; ex-insurance broker; ntl light-flyweight title '72; qualified '72 Olympic team but barred because of age; mem. ntl team 8 years, '76, '80 Olympics, '78 CG, '79 PAG, 3 NA championship, 1 world teams; quarterfinalist '76 Olympics; silver '78 CG; bronze '79 PAG; 1st Cdn medalist (bronze) Cuban invitational '79; Canadian flyweight title '73-80; won 115 of 130 amateur bouts; 27-7-1 pro record; 5 Que. Golden Glove, Eastern Canadian titles; pro '80; managed by Angelo Dundee; Continental flyweight title '83; bit-part Sting II movie; some TV work; res. Verdun, Que.

COAFFEE, Cyril (t&f); b. 14 Feb 1897, Winnipeg, Man.; d. 3 Jul 1945, Winnipeg, Man.; mem. North End Amateur Athletic Club; ran 11.2 for 100m '20 Olympic trials but funding allowed for only 9 competitors and he was 10th-ranked; Winnipeg supporters paid for his trip to Antwerp where he finished 3rd in qualifying heats but didn't reach semifinals; tied Charlie Paddock's world record 9.6 for 100yd dash '22 ntl championships; resulting ntl record stood more than 25 years; ntl 220yd title, teamed with Laurie Armstrong, Billy Miller, Peavey Heffelfinger for ntl record 1:30 in 4x220yd relay; ran for Illinois AC Chicago '23-24; tied 100yd Olympic record 10.8 to qualify for Paris Games; capt. '24 Olympic team but failed to live up to expectations; following games faced many of world's top sprinters in series of British meets and registered frequent victories; ended career losing to Percy Williams '28 Olympic trials; mem. Cdn Olympic; Man., Canada's Sports halls of fame.

COBEN, Muriel (softball/curling); b. 17 Feb 1921, Gelert, Ont.; d. 8 Jun 1979, Saskatoon, Sask.; given name: Muriel Eleanor; dispatcher; rhp; led Tessier Millionaires to undefeated season '36; played for Saskatoon Pats '38-42, '44-45; with Rockford Peaches in AAAGPBL '43; joined Saskatoon Ramblers '46; helped Edmonton Mortons win ntl title '51 posting 2-1 record in final; ret'd '59; mem. Joyce McKee title curling rink '60; mem. Sask., Saskatoon Sports, Alta. Softball halls of fame; honored by Cooperstown, Cdn Baseball halls of Fame.

COCHAND, Louis (skiing); b. 5 Jan 1917, Ste. Marguerite Station, Que.; d. (circa 2000), St. Sauveur des Monts, Que.; given name: Louis Emile; div; c. Josette, Louis Pierre, Heidi, Charles, Antoinette; Lower Canada College; ret'd. hotelier; Que. Kandahar slalom '36-37, downhill, combined '38; Que., Ont., NO combined, downhill, slalom titles '38; gold Austrian downhill '39; founder Canadian Ski School and Instructors' Alliance; 10yrs pres. CSSIA; authored 1st Canadian Ski School manual; mgr. '48 Olympic team; organized 1st Laurentian midget ski meet '53; installed 1st Eastern Canadian double chairlift Chalet Cochand '59; 9yrs pres. Laurentian Resort Assn.; founder, pres. Canadian Area Lift Assn.; British gold Kandahar pin with pearl, diamond Tremblant ski pin, French Croix de Guerre with star, American Air Medal; active skeet shooter; 2nd 12 gauge C Class world championships; McMartin Skeet trophy Montebello '62; mem. Cdn Skiing, Tremblant Ski halls of fame.

COCHRANE, Nigel (sailing); b. 12 Nov 1961, Toronto, Ont.; began sailing age 12; ntl team mem. from '85; with Gord McIlquham enjoyed success in 470 competition '85-88, capped by 4th '88 world championships, 8th '88 Olympics; teamed with Jeff Eckard '89 winning skipper '89 ntl title, '90 Goodwill Games, '91 PAG; competed '88, '92 Olympics; noted coach; mem. Royal Hamilton Yacht Club, Macdonald Sailing Academy; res. Vancouver, B.C.

COCKBURN, Karen (trampoline); b. 2 Oct 1980, Toronto, Ont.; York; competitive gymnast, diver; began trampolining age 11; 9 indiv. ntl titles; 2 WC medals; '00 Olympic bronze; bronze '01 Hannover WC; competed '01 worlds, Goodwill Games; indiv. gold, with Heather McManus synchro silver '02 Canada Cup, Jersey City Holiday Cup; WC gold Greensboro USA '02; 3 WC bronze '03; world gold '03, a Cdn gymnastics first; 10 WC synchronized trampoline medals; 2 Gymnastics Can. trampoline/tumbling athlete of yr awards; mem. COA athletes council; res. Toronto, Ont.

CODY, Della (synchro swim); b. 4 Apr 1917, Plaster Rock, N.B.; d. 22 Sep 1986, Fredericton, N.B.; given name: Della Howlett MacFarlane; m. Norman Cody; UNB; educator; pioneered synchro swim in NB; taught 1st synchro swim credit course UNB '58; helped form NB branch CASSA, 1st pres. '66; coached NB Canada Winter Games team '67; served varied prov. exec. roles and was sport's historian; judge local, prov., divisional, ntl, int'l levels '66-80; 1st NB accredited ntl level judge '68; NB synchro swim trophy bears her name; mem. NB Sports Hall of Fame.

CODY, Harry (speed skating); b. 6 Sep 1887, Ireland; d. 22 Aug 1936, Toronto, Ont.; given name: Robert Henry; c. 2 sons; NA outdoor champion '16; co-founder, coach Toronto Speed Skating Club; coach Old Orchard Speed Skating Club; mem. Cdn Speed Skating Hall of Fame.

COE-JONES, Dawn (golf); b. 19 Oct 1960, Campbell River, B.C.; m. Jimmy Jones; c. James Richard; Lamar U, BSc; pro golfer; BC jr titles '78-79; BC women's amateur titles '82-83; Cdn amateur tile '83; as collegian won Dick McGuire, Husky invitationals; all-American; pro '83; joined LPGA tour '84 qualifying in 1st attempt; career low round 64; capped steady improvement on tour

with victory '92 Kemper Open, '94 Palm Beach Classic, '95 Tournament of Champions; with Dave Barr won Cdn Airlines International Mixed team title '89; '92 LPGA match play title; sponsors jr. tourney at home BC club; *Score* Magazine Cdn. female golfer of '94; mem. inaugural Cdn Nations Cup team '99, winner '02; mem. RCGA Hall of Fame; res. Tampa, Fla.

COFFEY, Paul (hockey); b. 1 Jun 1961, Weston, Ont.; given name: Paul Douglas; m. Stephanie; c. Savannah, Blake; jr. Sault Ste. Marie, Kitchener; twice OHA all-star; Edmonton 1st pick, 6th overall '80 draft; def Edmonton '80-87, Pittsburgh '87-92, Los Angeles '92-93, Detroit '93-96, Hartford '96, Philadelphia '96-'98; Chicago '98-99, Carolina '99-01, Boston '01; special teams consultant Phoenix '02-03; NHL record: 1409 scheduled games, 396g, 1135a, 194 playoff games, 59g, 137a; reached 1500 points '99; 1st NHL def to earn 1000 assists; 4 1st, 4 2nd team all-star; gold Team Canada Canada Cup '84, '87, '91, Worlds '90; 3 James Norris trophies; mem. 4 Stanley Cup winners, 14 all-star games; annual Mississauga Jets Christmas hockey tourney bears his name; mem. Hockey Hall of Fame; res. Toronto, Ont.

COFFEY, Tommy-Joe (football); b. 18 Nov 1936, Amarillo, Tex.; m. Joan Best; c. Connye, Tommy Joe Jr., Ronny, Randy; West Texas State, BSc; employment agency owner; rcvr/pk; outstanding lineman '59 Copper Bowl; 8th round draft Baltimore Colts (NFL) '59; Edmonton (CFL) '59-60, '62-66, Hamilton '67-72, Toronto '73; CFL record: 971 points, 65 tds, 204 converts, 108 field goals, 53 singles, 650 pass receptions, 10,320yds, 63 tds; CFL single-season scoring record (since broken by Dave Cutler) 148 points '69; 3 times WFC, 4 times EFC all-star, 8 times all-Cdn; 3 EFC, 1 WFC scoring titles; WFC record 81 receptions (since broken) '64-65; 7 nominations, 3 times runnerup Schenley outstanding player; 3 Grey Cup finals, 2 winners; 1st in NA pro football with more than 10,000 career receiving yds; only player with name on two stadium walls, Hamilton and Edmonton; chosen #26 on list of best players in CFL history; among top 100 West Texas athletes for 20th century; mem. Eskimos Wall of Honor, Cdn Football Hall of Fame; res. Burlington, Ont.

COGGLES, Susan (ringette/softball); b. 8 Feb 1979, Edmonton, Alta; UAlta, Tennessee; '95 Canada Winter Games gold; 4 ntl championship gold; 3 ntl championship all-star fwd awards; mem. ntl ringette team '98-00 European Summit Series, final game MVP; cf Team Alta. 3 ntl softball championships, '98 all-star fielder; silver '97 Summer Games team Alta.; competed for Team Canada vs. Japan; mem. ntl team reserves; Softball Alta. player of '98; res. Edmonton, Alta./Chatanooga, Tenn.

COGHILL, Sandi (bowling); b. 2 Oct 1961, Winnipeg, Man.; accounting clerk; joined competitive 5-pin ranks '85; 9 ntl open medals, ntl women's singles title, 3 ntl team titles; 6 ntl masters medals, 2 women's team gold; twice ntl tournament all-star; res. Winnipeg, Man.

COHEN, Laurie (t&f); b. 1904 Winnipeg, Man.; d. 27 Nov 1995, Winnipeg, Man.; established sprinting credentials as Winnipeg high schooler '23-28; won Manitoba, Western Canada 100-, 220yd titles '23-24 setting records in each instance; competed in ntl championships '26-27; from '23-

31 won every race he entered in Man. championships except 1, a loss to Cyril Coaffee; coached with Winnipeg Amateur Athletic Assn. '32-41; 40yrs official with Man. t&f Assn.; mem. Man Sports Hall of Fame.

COLE, Andrea (swimming); b. 29 Jan. 1984, Thunder Bay, Ont.; given name: Andrea Jennifer; student, UWO; won 4 medals at 2 Paralympic Games: 4x100m free relay (world record) gold, 100m fly silver '00, 4x100m free relay silver, 100m fly bronze '04 Paralympics; 4x100m medley relay silver, 200m IM bronze '02 IPC Swimming World Championships; 15 ntl championships medals '98-04; 10 ntl, 7 Pan-Am records; 6 Joanne Baker Performance Awards (top ntl level female at Thunder Bay Thunderbolts swim club) '98-03; Team Spirit Award Thunder Bay Thunderbolts '98; Ontario Cerebral Palsy Sports Association's senior athlete of '99; Citizen of Exceptional Achievement Thunder Bay '00 (Southern Cross track '99) '01 (Sydney '00 Paralympics); Pride, Discipline, Excellence Award Thunder Bay Thunderbolts; mem. Victoriaville Centre Walk of Fame Thunder Bay; res. Thunder Bay, Ont.

COLE, Betty (golf/curling); b. 21 Sep 1937, Calgary, Alta.; given name: Betty Stanhope; m. Gordon Cole; c. Jacqueline, Robert; 5 Alta. jr. golf titles; 20 Edmonton City Opens, 14 Alta. Opens; '56 ntl jr., '57 Canadian Open, '67 Canadian Closed; '64 Eastern Provinces, '66 Saskatoon Open; mem. 22 Alta., 2 Ont., 2 Sask. interprovincial teams; mem. 2 Commonwealth, 3 World teams; top ranked Cdn player '74, '76; from '70 ranked among Canada's top 10 10 times; skipped 3 Alta. curling champions; ntl Lassies runnerup '78; 4 Edmonton city titles, 4 Northern Zone titles; Edmonton's outstanding athlete '57; mem. CLGA ntl exec. '80-83; mem. RCGA, Alta. Sports halls of fame; res. Edmonton, Alta.

COLEMAN, Lovell (football); b. 9 May 1938, Hamtramck, Mich.; m. Maureen Denise; Western Mich.; contractor; lettered as college fb '57-59; mid-west conf. all-American '58; turned pro CFL Roughriders but immediately dealt to Calgary for Jack Gotta; 11 CFL seasons with Calgary, Ottawa, BC; 3 times rushed for more than 1000yds single season; 3 times more than 200 carries single season; scored 62 CFL career tds, 42 rushing, on 1135 carries for 6566yds; best single season '64 with 260 carries for 1629yds, 10tds; same season had best single game with 238yds vs. Hamilton; 3 CFL rushing titles; Schenley outstanding player, Calgary athlete of '64; mem. Western Mich Hall of Fame; res. Richmond, B.C.

COLEMAN, Mel (rodeo); b. 7 Dec 1955, Islay, Alta.; m. Theresa; c. Jake; feed store owner; mem. Cdn Professional Rodeo Assn from '74; CPRA rookie of '74; 5 ntl AA all-around championships; 7 ntl saddle bronc titles; Bud pro tour saddle bronc champion '91; holds Cdn Finals Rodeo (CFR), Ntl Finals Rodeo (NFL) saddle bronc qualifications records; mem. Cdn Pro Rodeo Hall of Fame; res. Phoenix, Ariz.

COLISTRO, Peter (t&f/basketball); b. 26 Nov 1952, Vancouver, B.C.; m. Regina Girard; c. Michael, Marianne, Anthony, Paul; Rogers Cablevision; 1st person to break 6-minute mile in a wheelchair; represented Canada in track, basketball 4 Paralympics; mem. 4 Cdn Gold Cup basketball teams; 11 ntl titles with Team BC; mem. Cdn Wheelchair Basketball Hall of Fame; res. Burnaby, B.C.

COLLINS, Doug (football); b. 18 Feb 1945, London, Ont.; given name: Douglas Clement; m. Shirley Joyce Rietveld; c. Douglas, Tari, Peggy, Kristine, Jodie; Detroit, Cincinnati BA, UofT MEd; ret'd educator; standout football, basketball, t&f Windsor Patterson winning WSSA title, all-star honors; several WSSA shot, discus, javelin gold; WOSSA shot record; ntl jr. javelin title '60; linebacker/guard UD, def tackle UC 3yrs; pro CFL Ottawa 8yrs; 3 Grey Cup titles; off. tackle from '71; dealt to Hamilton '75; coached basketball South Carleton HS, football I.E. Weldon SS Lindsay, 2 titles; weight trainer Lindsay swim club; girls basketball coach; Olympia Sports Camp instructor; with brother Ted mem. Windsor/Essex Sports Hall of Fame; res. Little Britain, Ont.

COLLINS, Merv (football); b. 10 Aug 1933, Toronto, Ont.; given name: Mervyn Douglas; m. Christine Salvenmoser; c. David, Natalie, Steven; UAlta, BEd, UofOtt, MEd; ret'd. personnel mgr.; og-lb; Balmy Beach ORFU finals vs Sarnia Imperials '52; only rookie to crack starting lineup Grey Cup champion Argos '53, Hamilton '55, Ottawa '56-65, Edmonton '66; ret'd '67; mem. '60 Grey Cup champions; frequent CFL all-star; founding mem. CFL Players' Pension Fund; res. Ottawa, Ont.

COLLINS, Steve (ski jumping); b. 13 Mar 1964, Fort William, Ont.; given name: Stephen Clark; ntl team '79-84; world jr. 90m title '80; Lahti WC 90m, Big Thunder International 70m '80; ntl jr. 70m title '81; world record 99.5m off 70m, 120.5 off 90m Thunder Bay '80, Finnish record 124m Lahti '80; Czech ski-flying title '80; mem. '80, '84 Olympic teams; Thunder Bay athlete of '80; SFC athlete of month March '80; Ont. achievement award; Tom Longboat award '79; Viscount Alexander Trophy '80; mem. Cdn Skiing, NWO Sports halls of fame; res. Thunder Bay, Ont.

COLMAN, Ann (figure skating); b. 18 Apr 1936, Toronto, Ont.; given name: Ann Johnston; div. Jeremy Colman; c. Dale Ann, Robin Jeremy, Courtney Susannah; UofT, BA; mem. '56 Olympic, '54-56 world championship teams; taught skating Toronto Cricket and Skating Club, Town of Mount Royal '57-60; regained amateur status and served as judge '72-99; children were all ranked provincially, nationally in squash; res. Don Mills, Ont.

COLMAN, Frank (baseball); b. 2 Mar 1918, London, Ont.; d. 19 Feb 1983, London, Ont.; given name: Frank Lloyd; m. Anne; c. Frank, Jerry; Sr. IC batting title, MVP award '36 with London led to pro offers; lhp but sore arm led to switch to 1b/of; ML service Pittsburgh '42-46, NY Yankees '46-47; standout minor league career; batted .363 Willmington, Del. '40, .319 with 18 HRs, 98 RBI Seattle (PCL) '49; .310 Seattle '50; player-coach Toronto (IL) '51-53; owned, operated London franchise Sr. IC '55-57, '59; Great Lakes-Niagara League '58; managed London to IC title '56, Great-Lakes Niagara crown '58; instrumental in formation London's Eager Beaver Baseball Assn., pres. several years; mem. Cdn Baseball Hall of Fame.

COLVILLE, Neil (hockey); b. 4 Aug 1914, Edmonton, Alta.; d. 26 Dec 1987, Vancouver, B.C.; given name: Neil MacNeil; ctr younger brother Mac, Alex Shibicky NYR Bread Line '36-42; capt. TCAF (Ottawa) Flyers Allen

Cup champions '42; Rangers '46-49; switched to def with Frankie Eddolls '48-49; coached '50-51 NYR; 6 yrs Rangers capt., 1 league champion, 1 Stanley Cup; 3 times all-star; mem. Alta Sports, Hockey halls of fame.

COLVILLE, Nelson; b. 11 Nov 1905, Port Perry, Ont.; d. 1988, Vancouver, B.C.; m. Eunice Voss (d); c. Louise; optician; Ont. Rifle Assn. tyro title '21; 1st of 63 Connaught Matches, Ottawa appearances '21; won Walker Match, Connaught '22; Gov.-Gen. Match title '57; mem. 11 Bisley teams, twice commandant; 2ce named to Bisley team after age 70; Connaught 60-yr award '81; mem. Alta Sports Hall of Fame.

COMBE, Harvey (golf); b. 1860, Guilford, Eng.; d. 1922, Victoria, B.C.; m. Charlotte Margaret Wray; c. Nora; BC Supreme Court registrar; first-class tennis player, self-taught golfer; 9 BC amateur titles; inaugural Seattle Open titlist; helped form Victoria GC '93; co-founder Pacific North West Golf Assn. '95; held Victoria GC course record 72 many years; wife won 5 BC women's titles; daughter won 3 Victoria city, 2 Pacific Northwest titles; considered father of BC golf; secty. Victoria GC 1900, '05-18.

COMTOIS, Philippe (diving); b. 25 Aug 1976, Montréal, Qué.; m. Christiane; c. Charlotte; student/coach; 22 ntl titles (14 age-group, 8 sr.); '96, '04 Olympic, '98 CG, '99 PAG, 2 worlds teams; silver 1m '99 FISU; tragic injury Mar. '00 while diving at an England GP meet threatened diving career (tore three ligaments, broke the fibula and suffered nerve damage when his left leg hit the board), but returned to board Oct. and learned to dive again using his right leg for take-off (nerves in left leg never grew back) earning 3m bronze '01 winter ntls; competed '02 CG; medal haul with synchro partner Alexandre Despatie '03 included 3m silver China GP, 10m bronze Australia GP, 3m gold Canada Cup, double silver Mexico GP, 10m bronze FINA Super Final GP, double gold PAG; hole in right eardrum from landing on his side in the water early June '03 prevented summer ntls competition; res. Laval, Qué.

CONACHER, Brian (hockey); b. 31 Aug 1941, Toronto, Ont.; given name: Brian Kennedy; m. Susan Davis; c. Sean; UWO, BA; pres./CEO NHLPA; ex-v-p. building operations Maple Leaf Gardens; Jr. A Toronto Marlboros; UWO hockey; ntl team mem. '64 Olympic, '65 World championships; pro Leafs organization, AHL Calder Cup champion Rochester Americans '66, NHL with Toronto '67 Stanley Cup winners; also played with NHL Detroit, WHA Ottawa; licenced real estate salesman; author *So You Want to Be A Hockey Player*; sports dir. *CKLW-TV* '70; color commentator '69 World championship, '71 CIAU, '72 Canada-Soviet series, 1st WHA game, '76, '88 Winter Olympics; made coaching debut Cortina '64; GM/coach Mohawk Valley Comets (NAHL) '73-76; GM Indianapolis Racers (WHA) '76-77, Edmonton Oilers (WHA) '77-78; marketing mgr. Edmonton Northlands '79-84, CEO Hamilton Entertainment/Convention Facilities '85-89, CEO Royal Agricultural Winter Fair '89-92; NAHL GM of '75; res. Toronto, Ont.

CONACHER, Charlie (hockey); b. 10 Dec 1909, Toronto, Ont.; d. 30 Dec 1967, Toronto, Ont.; given name: Charles William; m. Sonny; c. Peter (Charles William Jr.), Brad,

Scott; brother Lionel; began in goal but shifted to wing; capt. Marlboros '26 Memorial Cup; Toronto Maple Leafs '29-38, Detroit '38-39, NY Americans '39-41; coach Chicago '48-50; scoring titles '34, '35; 3 times 1st, twice 2nd team all-star; originally on line with Joe Primeau, Baldy Cotton, when Busher Jackson replaced Cotton, became known as Kid Line; NHL record: 460 scheduled games, 225g, 173a, 49 playoff games, 17g, 18a; coached Oshawa '44 Memorial Cup winner; annual humanitarian award bears his name; mem. Canada's Sports, Hockey halls of fame.

CONACHER, Lionel Jr. (football); b. 8 Jan 1936, Toronto, Ont.; m. Judith Wilson; c. Lionel III, Duff, Bryce; UWO; Cdn Tire dealer; versatility as high schooler led to numerous awards in football, x-country running, boxing, hockey, t&f; son of Lionel sr; Cdn water ski jumping titles '50-54; wrestled, played football at Western; football MVP award '59; 2 seasons CFL with Montreal '60-61; in '80s mem. Cdn Hobie sailing team in world championships; res. Toronto, Ont.

CONACHER, Lionel Sr. (all-around); b. 24 May 1901, Toronto, Ont.; d. 26 May 1954, Ottawa, Ont.; given name: Lionel Pretoria; m. Dorothy Kennedy; c. Connie, Deanne, Lionel Jr., David, Brian; Duquesne; pro athlete, politician; nicknamed "Big Train"; at 12 Toronto City Rugby League; at 16 Ont. 125lb wrestling title; at 18 middle wing Toronto Central Y Ont. rugby title team; ntl light-heavyweight boxing title '20 in first bout, later fought exhibition with Jack Dempsey; same year senior city rugby, baseball, lacrosse; mem. '26 Toronto Maple Leafs Triple A pro baseball champions; mem. '21 Argos title football team scoring record 15 points in 23-0 Grey Cup victory over Edmonton; NHL def Pittsburgh '25-26, NY Americans '27-30, Montreal Maroons '30-33, '34-37, Black Hawks '33-34; NHL record: 500 scheduled games, 80g, 105a, 35 playoff games, 2g, 2a; mem. 2 Stanley Cup winners; MLA (Lib), MPP (Lib); Ont. Athletic Commissioner; Canada's athlete of half century '50; trophy honoring Canada's outstanding male athlete bears his name; mem. Canada's Sports, Cdn Football, Boxing, Lacrosse, Hockey, Ont. Sports Legends halls of fame.

CONACHER, Pete (hockey); b. 29 Jul 1932, Toronto, Ont.; given name: Charles William Jr.; m. Shirley Ann Randle; investment rep.; jr. Galt '49-51; NHL Chicago '51-54, NYR '54-56, Toronto '57-58; reinstated amateur, mem. '59 World Champion Belleville MacFarlands; minor pro ranks St. Louis, Hershey (AHL) '60-65; Buffalo '65-66; NHL record: 229 scheduled games, 47g, 39a, 7 playoff games, 0g, 0a; res. Etobicoke, Ont.

CONACHER, Roy (hockey); b. 5 Oct 1916, Toronto, Ont.; d. 1984, BC; m. Fran; c. Roy Jr., Mark, Candace; 1 of 10 siblings in family which included twin brother Bert, brothers Charlie and Lionel; early athletic interest in softball but following older brothers turned attention to hockey, playing Marlboro bantam, midget; mem. '36 Memorial Cup winner West Toronto Nationals; all-star mem. OHA sr. champ Dominion Breweries '37; played sr. NO league then attended Boston Bruins camp at 22; considered most naturally talented of hockey playing Conachers; led NHL with 26 goals '39; played 11 NHL seasons with Boston, Detroit, Chicago; NHL record: 490 scheduled games, 226g, 200a, 42 playoff games, 15g, 15a; 2 Stanley Cup winners;

Art Ross trophy '49; following '52 retirement coached Midland to 2 Ont. Jr. C titles; mem. Hockey Heritage North, Hockey halls of fame.

CONDON, Eddie (tennis/skiing); b. 18 Jul 1901, Ottawa, Ont.; d. 30 May 1985, Ottawa, Ont.; given name: Edmund; UofOtt; federal govt. auditor; x-country skier, runner specializing in 1500m, mile; 3ʳᵈ both events '20 Olympic trials; City of Ottawa, Eastern Ont, ntl interscholastic titles both events; ntl, NA Intercollegiate, Eastern US, Ottawa x-country titles; officiated '32 Olympics, '50 World competitions; chair. US Olympic ski trials, NA championships; 9 Ottawa tennis singles titles, NB, P.E.I. provincial titles; organized 1ˢᵗ ntl jr. tennis championships, 25yrs chair; co-chair '38-68 International Kate Smith Trophy ski meet; mem. CLTA jr. development comm. 20yrs; mem. '49 Gordon Trophy team; variety of exec. roles OLTA, CLTA '25-75; CLTA exec.-dir.; editor CLTA manual, record book; founding mem. ntl ski museum; life mem. Rideau LTC, Ottawa Ski Club; Governor's award 75ᵗʰ anniversary Lake Placid Ski Club; Ont. govt. achievement award; mem. Cdn Tennis, Ottawa Sports halls of Fame.

CONDREN, Stephen (harness racing); b. 6 Jul 1957, St. Catharines, Ont.; harness race driver; began driving on OJC circuit '77; won only 12 races in 1ˢᵗ 3yrs; posted 401 wins '87; 200 or more winners 12 consec. seasons '81-92; 21 Dec '87 snapped Ron Waples' '79 single-season Greenwood track victory record with 365ᵗʰ win; with Goalie Jeff won '89 NA Cup; '95 Cadillac Breeders Crown with Armbro Officer; '95 Cdn Trotting Classic with Trustworthy; drove Live or Die to world record equaling 1:51.4 at Lexington Red Mile; through '03 5853 career victories, $79M in purses; O'Brien driver-of-'97 award; res. Milton, Ont.

CONDY, Buddy (baseball); b. 21 Nov 1922, Springhill, N.S.; d. 2 Sep 1993, Halifax, N.S.; given name: William; c. Suzanne, Sheilagh, Patricia; Dalhousie, BSc, MD, CM; physician; made sr. baseball debut at 14 with grand slam homer in 1ˢᵗ plate appearance for Springhill Fence Busters '38; mem. Fence Busters '38-39, '45-46, Halifax Arrows '47, Halifax Capitals '48-51, Saint John Boosters '52, Halifax Cardinals '55; mem. 4 championship teams; recognized premier slugger H&D League; lifetime H&D BA .356; twice batting champion; best season '51 batting .409 but finishing 2ⁿᵈ to Stellarton's Joe Fulgham; led H&D in hits, HR, RBI rookie season '47; MVP award; career BA as Fence Buster .445; regarded by peers as "best player ever to have played in NS"; Halifax mayor's award '48; Dalhousie award '83; mem. NS Sports Hall of Fame.

CONE, Mac (equestrian); b. 23 Aug 1952, Memphis, Tenn.; m. Brenley Carpenter; c. 2 daughters; Southern Ways stable operator; mem. US ntl team; moved to Canada '82; mem. Cdn ntl team from '82; only rider to compete on both US, Cdn ntl teams; competed 10 Nations' Cups; qualified for '95 PAG but injury to horse Elute forced withdrawal; won '94 NY Autumn Classic, Roots Speed Classic, '92 Coupe des Ameriques; mem. '96 Olympic team; ntl show jumping title with Elute '98; res. King City, Ont.

CONGALTON, Jim (curling); b. 26 Sep 1879, Guelph, Ont.; d. 9 Oct 1947, Winnipeg, Man.; m. Blanche Hildegarde Dyson; c. Helen, Frances; salesman; at 12 youngest mem.

in history of Guelph Curling Club, presented to Governor-General as youngest curler in Canada at the time; skipped '27 Winnipeg Granite rink which lost to Ossie Barkwell of Yellow Grass, Sask. for right to rep. West '27 inaugural Brier; mem. 2 Brier winners, '30 as third, '32 as skip; mem. Cdn, Man. Curling halls of fame.

CONGALTON, William (baseball); b. 24 Jan 1875, Guelph, Ont.; d. 16 Aug 1937, Cleveland, Ohio; given name: William Millar; m. Harriet; public utilities employee; nickname "Bunk"; of Chicago Cubs '02, appeared in 42 games; following minor league stints played with Cleveland (AL) '05-07 before being dealt to Boston '07; ML record: 309 games, 6hr, 95rbi, career .293ba.

CONN, Michelle (field hockey); b. 17 Sep 1963, Edmonton, Alta.; UCal, BSc, Mount Royal Coll, BA, Dean's list; financial analyst, pres. MCC consulting; centre for non-profit consulting; 93 International caps; carded athlete '83-92; ntl team asst, capt '89-92; competed '88, '92 Olympics; PAG bronze '87, silver '91; competed '86 (bronze), '90 World Cup; 2 Champions Trophy, 1 Wembley competition; ntl outdoor championship gold '86, silver ;90, bronze ;84; 3 gold, 1 bronze ntl indoor championships; ntl ball hockey bronze '96, silver '97; competed '95 ntl triathlon championships; 1 Alta Achievement award; CIAU all-Cdn 1ˢᵗ team '85; 2 Calgary Booster Club, 2 UCal merit awards; athlete-of-yr nominee; asst. coach UCal '86-89; asst. coach Alta. -16 women '89, Alta. Sr. men indoor team '95; UCal, Alta. Sports halls of fame; res. Calgary, Alta.

CONNELL, Alex (hockey); b. 8 Feb 1900, Ottawa, Ont.; d. 10 May 1958, Ottawa, Ont.; m. Kay Muir; c. Bettianne; fireman; mem. '21 Allan Cup Ottawa Cliffsides; pro goalie Senators '24; mem. '27 Stanley Cup winner; ret'd '33 but made '34 comeback Montreal Maroons Stanley Cup winner; NHL record 6 successive shutouts; ret'd again and coached St. Patrick's College, Senators (QHL) until illness forced him out '49; noted for black cap he always wore while playing goal; catcher St. Brigid's City, interprovincial baseball teams; lacrosse with brother Charlie '20 Ottawa Senators Eastern Cdn champions; mem. Ottawa Sports, Hockey halls of fame.

CONNELL, Charlie (all-around); b. 4 Dec 1897, Ottawa, Ont.; d. 30 Apr 1980, Ottawa, Ont.; m. Ruth Edmonson; c. Frances, Elaine; photo engraver; mem. '27-28 Mann Cup winners; capt. Woodroffe '22 Ottawa title team; ret'd from box lacrosse at 35; Val Cartier army camp middleweight boxing crown '15, Canadian Service Corps title Thorncliffe, Eng.; national amateur middleweight title '19-20; 20yrs mem. Rough Riders; mem. 4 Ottawa district basketball title teams; refereed, coached football, lacrosse; mem. Ottawa Sports, Ottawa CSRA Sports, Cdn Lacrosse halls of fame.

CONNELL, Grant (tennis); b. 17 Nov 1965, Regina, Sask.; m. Sarah Cooper; Texas A&M; Tennis Canada consultant; twice all-American; NCAA player of '85; left-hander; ntl -18 singles, with Glenn Michibata ranked #1 doubles team in world '87-92; ranked #1 Cdn singles 4yrs; ranked #1 IBM/ATP doubles '91 (Michibata), '93 (Patrick Galbraith); mem. Cdn Davis Cup team '84-97; turned pro '86; mem. Cdn Olympic team '88, '96; 22 career doubles titles; Tennis Canada player of '87, '90, '95; Team Canada most improved player '89; with Galbraith world doubles title '95, twice Wimbledon finalists; with Byron Black of Zimbabwe won Italian Open, Wimbledon finalists '96; ATP tour doubles team of yr '93; ret'd from competition '97; non-playing capt. Cdn Davis Cup team '00-04; N. Vancouver tennis center bears his name; mem. Cdn Tennis Hall of Fame; res. Vancouver, B.C.

CONNELLAN, Peter (coaching); b. 17 Jul 1937, Regina, Sask.; m. Elizabeth Wilson; c. Karen, Heather; UAlta. BPhE, BEd., Oregon MSc; teacher; played hockey UAlta '56-58, '60; HS teacher '61-68; principal '61-76; UCal sr. lecturer, football coach '77, '83-95, off. co-ordinator '03; 8 conf. titles, 4 Vanier Cup winners; conf. regular season record 70-32-2; prof. emeritus UCal '93; pres. CIAU Coaches Assn. '94-95; 2 Frank Tindal CIAU coach-of-yr awards; 3M Cdn male coach of '90; CFL, Football Canada award of merit '98; mem. Alta. Sports Hall of Fame; res. Calgary, Alta.

CONNERTY, Doug (bowling); b. 23 Dec 1929, Kemptville, Ont.; given name: Douglas Eric; m. Barbara Eleanor Haddow; c. Jane Patricia, Michael Eric, Kelly Rosemary; ret'd. Bell Canada; competitor/volunteer in game of 5-pins in Ottawa area more than 32yrs; mem. OVFPBA exec. 18yrs, OFPBA 6yrs; OMBA 20yrs, YBC 25yrs; involved as course conductor for Level I & II technical coaching certification pgms; represented Ottawa in 17 prov. championships '69-95; coached Ont. team to prov. title '88, 4ᵗʰ in ntls; won 2 Smiths Falls Open titles; posting tournament record 3088 pinfall for 10 games; recorded perfect 450 game '89; mem. Ont. title team '72, runnerup ntls; Preston Lanes dedicated service award; Zone MBA delegate of yrs award; life mem. OVFPBA; Ottawa-area bowlers-appreciation award '91; YBC recognition award '92; Ont. achievement award '94; OFPBA Zone pres. of '96 award; special plaque as founding mem. Ottawa Zone & YBCA '98; res. Nepean, Ont.

CONNOLLY, Edward (boxing); b. 16 Nov 1876, Saint John, N.B., d. 1932, New York, N.Y.; BE lightweight title 1896; world welterweight title 1900; ret'd age 24 due to poor health; mem. NB Sports Hall of Fame.

CONNOLLY, Perry (sailing); b. 24 Jun 1927, Vancouver, B.C.; given name: Perry Roe; div. Patricia Davidson; c. Brian, Shelagh, Charlotte; Ryerson Institute of Technology; ret'd contractor, marine, export business; followed father's footsteps as mem. Port Credit YC entering competitive ranks in early '60s; with sloop Red Jacket won 11 or 13 Lake Ontario starts '66; competed on Southern Ocean Racing Circuit '67 winning Lipton Cup; 1ˢᵗ non-American to win SORC title '68; part of '69 syndicate (Gordon Fisher, David Osler, George Cuthbertson) which built/raced sloop Manitou to 1ˢᵗ successful defence of Canada's Cup title by vessel designed and built in Canada; res. West Linn, Ore.

CONNOR, Earle (t&f); b. 30 Jul 1976, Castlegar, B.C.; given name: Earle William Campbell; full-time athlete; lost left leg, above knee, at 3 months; growing up in rural Sask. developed keen interest in sports; competed for Sask. tennis team; led HS team to 3ʳᵈ place in prov. rankings; helped hockey team achieve elite level; 1ˢᵗ amputee drafted into jr. hockey; became intrigued with Paralympic t&f competition '96; moved to Hamilton to hone sprint skills Hamilton Olympic Club; competed '98 Goodwill Games, US ntl t&f

championships, Optis Australia GP series, Cdn ntls, '00 Paralympics, dq from '04 Paralympics for drug infraction; 100m gold, 200m silver '00 Paralympics; held world outdoor 100m, 200m, 400m (since beaten), indoor 60m records; runnerup Laureus (Monaco) award '03; coached by Les Gramantik; 3 Cdn disabled-athlete-of-yr awards; mem. Calgary Sports Hall of Fame; res. Calgary, Alta.

CONROY, Jim (football); b. 18 Oct 1937, Vancouver, B.C.; m. Carol Ann Henry; c. Jennifer, Joan, Julie, Debby; SoCal, BSc, Carleton, PEng; small business owner; played football/baseball USC '55-59; football team co-capt. '57; mem. NCAC baseball title team '58; drafted by Buffalo (NFL) '59; pro with Ottawa CFL '60-67, Winnipeg '68; 4 CFL all-star lb; asst. coach UofOtt '69-72; mem. Ottawa Sports Hall of Fame; res. Ottawa, Ont.

CONYD, Magdy (fencing); b. 22 Jun 1939, Alexandria, Egypt; AachenU, W. Germany; physical fitness consultant, director; ntl foils titles '64, '71-72, '82; highest foil rating in Canada '68-70, '72-73, '75; Governor-General's international open foils titles '65-70, '72; Ont. titles '64-65, Quebec '66, BC '68-75, '82-84; mem. 4 world, 2 Olympic teams; team bronze '70 CG; ret'd from competition '76-82; res. Vancouver, B.C.

COOK, Bill (hockey); b. 8 Oct 1895, Brantford, Ont.; d. 5 May 1986, Kingston, Ont.; given name: William Osser; early hockey Kingston, Sault Ste. Marie; pro Saskatoon Sheiks '22-26; 3 WCL scoring titles; '24-25 season 31 goals in 30 games; with demise of WCL, he and brother Bun purchased by NYR '26 playing through '37; rw with Bun and Frank Boucher; 2 scoring titles; 3 1ˢᵗ, 1 2ⁿᵈ team all-star; NHL record: 452 scheduled games, 229g, 138 assists, 46 playoff games, 13g, 12 assists; mem. 2 Stanley Cup winners; Rangers Alumni Assn. award '86; mem. Canada's Sports, Hockey, Kingston District halls of fame.

COOK, Bun (hockey); b. 18 Sep 1903, Kingston, Ont.; d. 19 Mar 1988, Kingston, Ont.; given name: Frederick Joseph; m. Mary Rheaume; c. 3 sons, 2 daughters; farmer; jr. Soo Greyhounds; mem. Allan Cup champions; pro Saskatoon Sheiks '22-26, NYR '26-36, Boston '36-37; NHL record: 473 scheduled games, 158g, 144a, 46 playoff games, 15g, 3a; mem. Hockey, Kingston District halls of Fame.

COOK, Murray (administration); b. 6 Dec 1940, Sackville, N.B.; given name: George Earl Murray; m. Jan; c. Cheryl, Brian, David; Ohio, BS; baseball exec.; attended college on basketball scholarship; ss Pittsburgh organization Batavia (A) '62, Gastonia (A) '63-64; GM Gastonia '65; joined Pirates front office '66; asst. farm dir. '68, dir. minor leagues, scouting '76-82; dir. player development NY Yankees '83, GM '83-84; v-p. GM Montreal '85-87; GM Cincinnati '88-89; scout Florida; mem. South Atlantic League Hall of Fame; res. Florida.

COOK, Myrtle (all-around); b. 5 Jan 1902, Toronto, Ont.; d. 18 Mar 1985, Elora, Ont; given name: Myrtle Alice; m. Lloyd McGowan (d); c. Kenneth, Donald; sportswriter; excelled in t&f, paddling, softball, tennis, ice hockey, speed skating, cycling, basketball, lawn bowling; 400m relay gold '28 Olympics; 100m world record; 100m gold Paris, Philadelphia '28 meets; indoor 60yds winner NY, Chicago,

Philadelphia, Montreal; with Brendan Macken international mixed tennis titles, Que. mixed, ladies' doubles; during 40yr journalistic career had major impact on Cdn women's sport; Governor-General's medal for track, '67 Centennial medal; mem. Cdn Olympic, Que., Canada's, MAAA Sports halls of fame.

COOK, Tommy (hockey); b. 17 May 1907, Ft. William, Ont.; d. 21 Oct 1961, Thunder Bay, Ont.; St. John's College; played junior Ft. William Dominions; college Winnipeg's St. John's College; senior Ft. William Thundering Herd; pro Tulsa Oilers '28; AHA scoring title; NHL Black Hawks, Montreal Maroons '29-38; NHL record: 311 scheduled games, 77g, 98a, 24 playoff games, 2g, 4a; mem. 1 Stanley Cup winner; on retirement coached hockey, baseball in Thunder Bay region; mem. NWO Sports Hall of Fame.

COOKE, Graham (golf); b. 11 Sep 1946, Belleville, Ont.; given name: Leonard Graham; m. Sally; c. Erin, Leigh; Michigan State BSc LA; pres. Graham Cooke & Associates; golf course architect; Ont. jr., medalist ntl jr. '65; NCAA all-American; quarterfinalist Western Amateur bowing 2 and 1 to Ben Crenshaw; participated twice US Amateur; mem. 26 Willingdon Cup teams, '91 champions; 5 Duke of Kent, 4 Alexander of Tunis, '78 Eastern four-ball; runnerup '79 ntl amateur; 2 ntl sr. titles; 4 Que. amateur, 5 times runnerup; 7 ntl mid-amateur titles; mem. '77 Nations Cup, '78 World Pairs, '80 Morocco Invitation, 2 Eisenhower Cup teams; 4 times Que. golfer of year; winner inaugural Graham Cooke Cup OGA tournament players championship '01; res. Hudson, Que.

COOKE, Jack Kent (entrepreneur); b. 25 Oct 1912, Hamilton, Ont.; d. 6 Apr 1997, Upperville, Va.; div. Barbara Jean Carnegie; c. John Kent; div. Jeanne Maxwell Williams; c. Ralph (d); div. Suzanne Martin; c. Jacqueline; m. Marlene Romallo Chalmers; business exec., publisher; mem. Ted Reeve's Malvern CI football title team; acquired substantial piece of Toronto Maple Leafs (IL) baseball team, 4 pennants in 7yrs; *Sporting News* Minor League exec. of '52; unsuccessful bids to purchase Toronto Argos, Detroit Tigers; chair., chief operating officer Washington (NFL) from '60, Super Bowl winner '83; pres. California Sports Inc. (Lakers, Kings) '65-79; pres. Forum of Inglewood, Calif. '66-79; pres. Boxing Forum '72-79; trustee Little League Foundation; dir. National Athletic Institute; with Branch Rickey sought unsuccessfully to launch Continental Baseball League '58; mem. Canadian Baseball Hall of Fame.

COOKE, Stan (all-around); b. 18 Oct 1914, Port Arthur, Ont.; d. 1989, Thunder Bay, Ont.; c. Gordon, William, Stanley Jr., Philip, 1 daughter; real estate agent; jr. hockey Ft. William '32-34; sr. Port Arthur '35-36, St. Moritz, Switzerland '36-38, Ft. William Forts '39-40; mem. jr. title Hornets baseball team '31; rowing gold medallist St. Paul '33, Winnipeg '34, Minneapolis '35; competed in Cdn Henley regatta '31; district men's FS swimming champion '31; 2 holes-in-one, Strathcona GC McGolrick trophy; mem. Westfort Alleymen '45, Northern Engineering Nescoes '46 softball title teams; Ft. William CC curling titles '53-55. 2 sr. zone titles; scored 8-ender '84; Bell-Fast trophy Cdn Elk's bonspiel '84; 1st event winner NWO 60+ bonspiel; qb Ft. William CI jr. football title team '32-33; sr. team '34-35; Dynamiters district sr.

champs '36; hb '37 Flamingoes district sr. champs; Ft. William CI sr. basketball team '34, YMCA Leaders title team '35, Canadian Car AA title team '45; mem. NWO Sports Hall of Fame.

COOMBE, Eldon (curling); b. 8 May 1941, Kingston, Ont.; given name: Eldon James; m. Lynda Ann Jeffrey; c. Jeffrey James, Laurie Lynn; ret'd. legal survey technologist; 1st of 10 Ont. Consols playdown appearances '63 as lead for Bob Knippleburg; Coombe-skipped quartet (Keith Forgues, Jim Patrick, Barry Provost) won Div. 1 OCA titles 7 successive years; rep. Ont. '72 St. John's, Nfld. Brier after winning Consols in 4-way playoff; 3 Canadian Branch Royal Caledonian Curling Club Royal Victoria Jubilee titles; 7 Red Anderson Memorial Trophy titles; '72 *CBC Curling Classic*, Whitby Dunlop 'spiel; swept major branch title honors '66 winning Jubilee, Colts, Governor-General's titles; 3 times Ottawa ACT curler of year; mem. Ottawa Sports Hall of Fame; res. Ottawa, Ont.

COOMBES, Cy (lacrosse); b. 24 Oct 1938, Peterborough, Ont.; d. 4 Dec 1999, Peterborough, Ont.; given name: Cyril Maxwell; m. Gloria; c. Cheryl, Patti; ex-sporting goods owner, auto salesman; mem. '53 Ont. Bantam A hockey titlists; known for speed/scoring ability; 15yrs sr./pro lacrosse player; 1062g, 612a, including playoffs, placed him atop all-time OLA scorers list; Sr. A/major series schedule record 113g '69; in 10yr span among top 10 OLA scorers 9 times; mem. 2 Mann Cup title teams; coached Hastings Minto Cup winner '61, runnerup '62, Mann Cup finalist '83; mem. Cdn Lacrosse, Peterborough Sports halls of fame.

COOPER, Barbara Ann (squash); b. 8 Oct 1949, Brighton, Eng.; began playing age 19; 2 ntl women's doubles, 1 mixed doubles titles; ntl 40+ hardball title '94; won British open/closed singles '86, world 40+ masters singles '92-93; won '93 NA open, Ont closed, '94 Ont. masters 40+, women's, mixed doubles; mem. ntl women's team '94; res. Toronto, Ont.

COOPER, Ralph (football/builder); b. 3 Nov 1908, Hamilton, Ont.; d. 31 Aug 1994, Burlington, Ont.; given name: Ralph William; m. Evelyn Joanna McArthur; c. Kathleen Joanna, Barbara Evelyn, William Press; successfully amalgamated Hamilton Tigers of ORFU and Hamilton Wildcats of IRFU into Hamilton Tiger-Cats '50; pres. '50-52, director to '72, governor '73-77; varied IRFU (Big Four) exec. roles through '50s; helped establish university player draft system; Big Four pres. '55 played key role in developing working agreement with NFL re player movements; chair. newly-formed Cdn Football Council '56; v-p CFL '59, pres. '60; devised East-West interlocking schedule; mem. Cdn Football Hall of Fame.

COOPERBAND, Mary (softball/t&f); b. 16 May 1915, Winnipeg, Man.; m. Clifford Rusen (d); c. David Mark, Vivian Carla; UMan. BA; pitcher; mem. New Method Laundry Int. girls title team '29; Sr. Tigerettes '30-32, MVP '32, Ramblers '33-35. all-star '33; primary school 185'11", HS 208', unofficial world 217'6" ball throw records; played university basketball, volleyball; res. Winnipeg, Man.

COPELAND, Jim (football/administration); b. 2 Jan 1939, Windsor, Ont.; ret'd football exec.; gained early recognition as softball pitcher City Merchants (I title) '57-59, Regina Royals '62-64; def, back Windsor Kennedy CI '52-55 (I city, 1 WOSSA title); capt. Windsor Mic-Mac jr. hockey team; attended Montreal Canadiens tryout camp; leading rusher as halfback with Windsor Jets '56 Detroit A league; rb, db, kick returner Windsor AKO jrs '57-58, ORFU title '58; sr. ORFU rookie of '59 K-W Dutchmen; 9yrs CFL as db, kick returner Montreal '60, Sask. '61-64, Toronto '65-68; as rehab from injury rb Bramalea (ORFU) '67 scored 20tds 8 games; team won ntl title but he had been recalled by Argos; shared CFL record 14 punt returns single game; ret'd to serve as asst. coach/pres./GM Bramalea '65-74, 2 ntl titles; chief Cdn scout Argos '74-81; Cdn talent coordinator Calgary '82; special assignment NFL scout Montreal Concordes '83; 2 Ont achievement awards; CIAU recognition award; all-Argo team '74, modern era '45-73; mem. Windsor/Essex Sports Hall of Fame; res. Windsor, Ont.

COPELAND, Royal (football); b. 12 Oct 1924, North Bay, Ont.; given name: Royal Hayward; m. Barbara Ann; c. Nola Jean, Cindy Ann; CalState, BA, Azusa Pacific College, MA; ret'd. teacher, avocado farmer; mem. Teddy Morris coached RCN team '44; hb Argos, Stampeders '45-49, '52-56, Calgary '50-51; with Joe Krol became Toronto's Gold Dust Twins; won special '49 100yd match race to determine fastest runner in CFL; CFL record: 111 scheduled games, 14 playoff contests, 42 tds; EFC scoring leader '45; tied Argos single-game td record with 4 (all on passes from Krol) vs. Montreal '45, 3 interceptions vs. Hamilton '45; 3 times EFC all-star; Jeff Russel Memorial Trophy '49; mem. 4 Grey Cup winners; mem. Cdn Football Hall of Fame; res. Oxnard, Calif.

COPP, Bobby (hockey); b. 15 Nov 1918, Port Elgin, N.B.; given name: Robert Alonzo; m. Mary MacMillan; c. Judith Ann, Bonnie Lynn; Mount Allison, BA, UofT, DDS; dentist; rugby '36-37, track '38, hockey '34-38 Mount A, '38 Maritime Intercollegiate hockey title; mem. Amherst St. Pat's '37 Maritime jr. champions; UofT intercollegiate titlists '40-41; sr. Marlboros '40-42; pro Maple Leafs '42-43; Canadian Army Dental Corps '43, mem. Maritime title RCAF Flyers Halifax, Ottawa Commandos; coached Ottawa Senators (QHL) 2 months before amateur reinstatement '46; Allan Cup finalist '48, winner '49; excluding 2 games '50 with Leafs, 3 months Smiths Falls Bears '52, mem. Senators '49-55; mem. NB Sports Hall of Fame; res. Ottawa, Ont.

CORAZZA, John (t&f); b. 27 Feb 1954, Quebec City; given name: Giovanni Daniele; m. Adrienne Allard; c. Katerina, Alesandro; UofOtt, BA; salesman; javelin specialist; 3 NB javelin titles; ntl team '77-80; bronze '77 Pacific Conf. Games; silver '77 World Cup trials; competed '78 CG; gold '79, silver '80 ntl outdoor championships; silver International Cup '80; gold '80 Olympic alternate competitions West Germany, England, Norway, bronze France; PB 84.34m; mem. 2 NB teams ntl team handball championships; mem. UofOtt volleyball team; mem. NB Sports Hall of Fame; res. Moncton, N.B.

CORAZZIN, Carlo (soccer); b. 25 Dec 1971, New Westminster, B.C. given name: Giancarlo; mdfld/fwd; 6yrs Metro Ford; BC –15, Cdn –16 teams; 4+ yrs Italy;

Cdn Olympic team '92; pro debut '92 with Winnipeg Fury CSL title team; CSL all-star; Vancouver 86ers '93; Cambridge United '93-94, top team scorer '95-96; mem. ntl team '94-00; mem. '00 Cdn Gold Cup winner; Plymouth 2yrs, Northampton 2yrs, Oldham 3yrs; Apa De Oro '03; Vancouver Whitecaps '03; 2 Worthington, 2 FA Cup teams; res. New Westminster, B.C.

CORBETT, Ed (softball); b. 25 Jan 1917, Calgary, Alta.; d. 10 Apr 2001, Calgary, Alta.; m. Lila Foss; c. Penny, Wendy; played for various Calgary teams including '42 Western Cdn title team; ret'd as player to become umpire, hockey, baseball official; organized Calgary Softball Umpires Assn, serving in several exec. capacities; founding mem. Calgary District ASA, Alta. ASA, Cdn ASA, serving each in varied exec. capacities; pres. Calgary Minor SA, Minor Sports Assn., Alta. Fastball Assn., Western Canada SA; Alta. Softball commissioner '60-65; v-p NA Intl Softball Fed.; co-chair AASA Hall of Fame comm.; Calgary sportsman of '66; life mem. Softball Calgary; Calgary park bears his name; mem. Alta. Sports, Cdn, Alta. Softball halls of fame.

CORDUKES, Don (golf); b. 16 Jun 1925, Ottawa, Ont.; given name: Donald John; m. Helen Donna (d); c. Donna, Norma; Carleton, BComm; ret'd. RCAF; 6 Ottawa C&D match, 3 medal titles; 2 Chaudiere, 7 Ottawa Hunt club titles; course records Royal Ottawa 66, Outaouais 68; 2 RCAF European titles, 2 RCAF ntl titles; 6 Collie Cup, 3 ODGA best ball, 2 CBOT best ball, 12 OVGA field day wins; 2 Cornwall, 1 Molson, 1 Glen Lawrence Opens, 1 Queen's U, Renfrew Invitation titles; 2 OVGA seniors titles; Alexander of Tunis titles '66, '68; Ottawa ACT golfer of '68; mem. 1 Que. Willingdon Cup team, competed '48 Cdn Amateur; res. Ottawa, Ont.

COREY, Ron (administration); b. 13 Dec 1938, Montreal, Que.; m. Danielle Grégoire; c. Stéphanie, Frédérick; hockey exec., former journalist; pres. Montreal Canadiens '82-99; pres. Molson Centre, a structure he was instrumental in making a reality; dir. numerous major corporations; involved in numerous community fund-raising projects; mem. NHL exec. comm.; mem. Order of Canada; res. Montreal, Que.

CORKEY, Joe (baseball/curling); b. 4 Oct 1913, Kingston, Ont.; d. 24 Sep 1994, Kingston, Ont.; given name: Joseph Frederick; m. Stella Irwin; c. Steven Joseph; ret'd store owner; c Collins Bay '32, Kingston Ponies '36; drew 4yr suspension for 'professionalism' (later reduced to 2yrs); played 'outlaw' baseball Quebec 2yr; on reinstatement '38 helped organize Kingston City League; ret'd from active play at 37; exec. mem. Goodyears sr. hockey club '52-56; OHA sr. B titlists; mem. '60 Ont. Brier entry; sponsored stock car racing '57-77.

CORMIER, Rheal (baseball); b. 23 Apr 1967, Moncton, N.B.; Rhode Island Community Coll; lhp relief specialist; drafted by St. Louis '88 he made ML debut '91 primarily as starter (108 games) until arm trouble sidelined him; after undergoing tendon transplant he rebuilt career as reliever with Philadelphia; career record (through '04): 556 games, 65-59, 1183.1ip, 283bob, 706k, 4.01era; res. Philadelphia, Pa.

CORNER, Peter (curling); b. 20 May 1968, Brampton, Ont.; given name: Peter John; Ont. Police Coll.; constable Halton regional police; began curling age 12; finalist '87 Pepsi Jr.; lead for Russ Howard 4 Briers, '93 Cdn, world titlists; all-star lead '93-94 Briers; skip Ont rink '00 Brier; '93 VO Cup champion; 3 *TSN* Skins Games; res. Burlington, Ont.

CORNISH, Geoffrey (golf); b. 1914, Winnipeg, Man.; m. Carol Burr Gawthrop; UBC, Mass; golf course architect; protégée of Stanley Thompson; designed more than 200 courses including Halifax New Ashburn, Montreal Summerlea, Toronto York Downs; with Brian Silva, Mark Mungean formed CSM course designers; pres. American Society of Golf Course Architects '71; co-author *The Golf Course* and *Architects of Golf*; Golf Course Superintendents Assn. of America distinguished service award; US National Golf Foundation distinguished service award; mem. RCGA Hall of Fame; res. Amherst, Mass.

CORNISH, Ray (badminton); b. 11 Jan 1932, Stratford, Ont.; given name: Rayfield Philip; m. Ruth Marie Schlotzhauer; c. Janine, Judith, Peter; UofT, BSc Phm.; pharmacist; with Bev Chittick Ont. mixed doubles title '64; with Bill Parkes Michigan open men's doubles '61; Tor. Granite men's singles '58, with Joan Hennessy mixed doubles '59; with Jim Poole '83 Cdn men's 50+ doubles; 2 WO men's singles, 10 men's doubles, 6 mixed doubles; ranked #1 veterans 35+ WO tennis '73; Stratford Sportsman of '80; res. Stratford, Ont.

CORRIGALL, Jim (football); b. 7 May 1946, Barrie, Ont.; m. Marybeth; c. Jimmy, Amy; Kent State; football coach; all-Mid-American Conf. 1ˢᵗ team all-star 3yrs; *AP* all-American hon. mention; Kent State's most efficient dl; most valuable sophomore awards; 1ˢᵗ jr. Kent State capt.; NEA all-American '69, first Canadian; competed '69 North-South Shrine Bowl; 2ⁿᵈ round NFL St. Louis Cardinals draft '70; pro Argonauts '70-81; EFC Gruen Trophy '70 rookie of year; James P. McCaffrey Trophy '75 EFC outstanding defensive player; '75 Argos' Shopsy Award; all-EFC de 7 times; 4 times CFL all-star; '75 Schenley outstanding dl award; played 146 CFL games; dl coach Miami of Ohio '83-94, head coach Kent State '94-'97; mem. Canadian Football, Barrie Sports, Mid-America Conf, Kent State halls of fame; res. Rootstown, Ohio.

CORSIGLIA, Robin (swimming); b. 12 Aug 1962, Kirkland, Ohio; given name: Robin Marie; m. David Scholefield; c. 2; SouthernCal PhD; USC staff psychologist; breaststroke specialist; youngest mem. '76 Canadian Olympic swim team, bronze 4x100 medley relay; 200m breaststroke, broke own Canadian, Commonwealth record for 100m '76 national championships; national short course 200m medley record 2:05.20 '76; ntl record 100m breaststroke 1:12.60 '77, 200m 2:33.27 '78; gold 100m '78 CG; mem. '79 World championships, PAG teams; Governor-General's silver '76; res. Malibu, Calif.

CORSON, Shayne (hockey); b. 13 Aug 1966, Barrie, Ont.; m. Kelly; c. Shelby, Dylan, Summer; ret'd;. lw OHL Brantford '83-84, Hamilton '84-86, NHL Montreal '86-92, '96-00, Edmonton '92-95, St. Louis '95-96, Toronto '00-03; resigned from Leafs '03; Dallas '04; mem. Team Canada jr. worlds '85, '86, Canada Cup '91, worlds '93, '94, Olympics '98; 2 world gold, 1 silver medals; competed 2 NHL all-star games; capt. St. Louis '95-96; NHL record: 1156 scheduled games, 273g, 420a, 140 playoff games, 38g, 49a; mem. Barrie Sports Hall of Fame; res.Port Carling, Ont.

COSENTINO, Frank (football); b. 22 May 1937, Hamilton, Ont.; m. Sheila McHugh; c. Tony, Mary, Teresa, Peter; UWO., BA, McMaster BPhE, UAlta, MA, PhD; ret'd. educator, dept. head York U.; 4yrs qb UWO Mustangs; mem. 2 CIAU title teams; capt. 1ˢᵗ CIAU championship team '59; 10 years CFL, 7 Hamilton (5 Grey Cup finals, 2 winners), 2 Edmonton, 1 Toronto; 5yrs head coach UWO, 2 CIAU titles; head coach York '78, '84; Frank Tindall CIAU coach-of-'70 award; rhp Hamilton Sr. IC team; authored *Canadian Football: The Grey Cup Years; Passing Game; Ned Hanlan; Not Bad, Eh?; The Renfrew Millionaires; Almonte's Brothers of the Wind*; with M.L.Howell *A History of Physical Education in Canada*; with Glynn Leyshon *Olympic Gold. Winter Gold*; with Don Morrow *Lionel Conacher*; mem. UWO W-Club, OUAA Football Legends Sports halls of fame; res. Eganville, Ont.

COSTELLO, Les (hockey); b. 10 Feb 1928, South Porcupine, Ont.; d. 10 Dec 2002, Toronto, Ont.; given name: Leslie John Thomas; St. Michael's Coll., St. Augustine's seminary; parish priest; strong skater/body-checker; helped St. Mike's win 2 Memorial Cups; joined Leafs in '48 playoffs winning Stanley Cup; 3yrs minor pro Pittsburgh; quit pro hockey '50 to enter priesthood; ordained '57; co-founder famed Flying Fathers charity hockey team which during his time raised more than $4M for varied charities; noted raconteur; brother Murray former NHLer, pres, CAHA; suffered head injury on ice at Kincardine charity game and died week later; mem. Hockey Heritage North Hall of Fame.

COSTELLO, Murray (hockey); b. 24 Feb 1934, South Porcupine, Ont.; given name: James Murray; m. Denise Marie Lancop; c. Michelle, Dan, Jennifer, Jim, Elizabeth, Mary; Windsor, BA, UofOtt, LLB; ret'd hockey administrator; pres. CAHA, ret'd '98; ctr Junior A St. Mike's '50-53; pro '53-58 Chicago, Boston, Detroit in NHL, Hershey (AHL), Edmonton (WHL); 6yrs PR dir. WHL; 4yrs exec. dir. Seattle Totems; 2yrs exec. dir, GM Totems; mem. Ottawa Old Pros; appointed to IIHF exec. council '98; mem. Hockey Heritage North, IIHF halls of fame; res. Ottawa, Ont.

COSTELLO, Ralph (golf); b. 7 Apr 1923, Saint John, N.B.; d. 19 Apr 2001, Saint John, NB; m. Frances; journalist, publisher; NB-PEI Golf Assn v.p. '60-61, pres. '61-62; pres. Riverside GC '65-66; governor RCGA '74, v.p '80, pres. '81; pres. Cdn Golf Foundation '86-89; wrote book *The First Fifty Years*; instrumental in bringing CPGA, 3 ntl amateur tournaments to NB; past chair NB Sports, RCGA halls of fame; Toastmasters' Intl. award '81; NBGA trophy bears his name; hon. gov. RCGA from '85; hon. life mem. NBGA from '88; Sport NB award '89; Rotary Club Paul Harris Fellowship; mem. NB, Saint John Sports halls of fame.

CÔTÉ, Benoit (harness racing); b. 22 Mar 1934, Quebec City, Que.; m. Pierrette; c. Alain, Marc, Lucie, Éric; horseman; highly rated by peers as catch driver in important stakes races in Montreal; most racing in Montreal area; drove Delmonica Hanover to world record 2:00.1 '72 Que.

Grand Circuit Trot; operates public stable; trained, drove for Drummond, Richelieu Farms; mem. Canadian Horse Racing Hall of Fame; res. Anjou, Que.

CÔTÉ, Gérard (t&f); b. 28 Jul 1913, St. Barnabé, Que.; d. 13 Jun 1993, St. Hyacinthe, Que.; m. Lucille Lemoine; c. 3 girls, 1 boy; advertising salesman; developed running stamina while training to be boxer; champion roller skater; world snowshoe racing record '38; 1st Boston Marathon bid 1936 but over-trained by running course 2 days before race; record 2:28.28 1940 winning first of 4 Boston Marathons; other victories '42-43, '48; 2nd 5 Yonkers Marathons before winning 1st of 3 '40; 3 US AAU marathon titles; career record 264 races, 1st 112, 2nd 56, 3rd 26; leg cramps led to 17th '48 Olympics; mem. '50, '54 BEGames teams; ret'd from running '56; record 46 minutes snowshoeing 8-mile event St. Paul, Minn. '58; Ste. Rosalie recreational facility bears his name; Lionel Conacher, Lou Marsh trophies '40; mem. Order of Canada; Canada's, Que. Sports, Cdn Olympic, Cdn Roadrunning halls of fame.

COTE, Kirby (swimming); b. 29 Apr 1984, Winnipeg, Man,; given name: Kirby Ann Lorraine; UWpg; Home Depot; born with visual impairment; from age 7 active gymnast, swimmer; devoted full attention to swimming age 8 and rapidly emerged as a force in the pool; 2 gold (world records), 2 silver (ntl records) '00, 5 gold, 2 silver '04 Paralympics; holds 200m breaststroke, 800m FS world records; Man. female-athlete, female-jr.-athlete-of-'00 awards; res. Winnipeg, Man.

COTTON, Harry (football/boxing); b. 28 Jul 1909, Vancouver, B.C.; d. 2 May 1989, Ottawa, Ont.; given name: Henry Ferguson; m. Olive Eve Wootton; c. Peter Ross (d), John Miles; Royal Military College; real estate agent, ret'd soldier; football RMC '28-29; BC champion Vancouver AC '30-31, Winnipeg '34-35; English rugby Vancouver Rowing Club '29-31; Garrison Football Club Winnipeg '32-34, Man. all-stars '33-34; runnerup British army middleweight boxing title '37; Canadian army western div. middleweight title '32-33; founded Little League baseball Rivers, Man. '50; district administrator Little League Eastern Ont. '60-64; mem. winning curling rink Royal Victoria Jubilee '63.

COUGHLAN, Angela (swimming); b. 4 Oct 1952, London, Eng.; given name: Angela Denise; div. Toomas Arusoo; c. Jessica, Lee, Kate; registered massage therapist; ntl team '67-72; competed '67 (1 silver, 3 bronze), '71 (1 gold, 3 silver, 1 bronze) PAG, '68 (1 bronze) Olympic, '70 (1 gold, 2 silver, 1 bronze) CG; 24 ntl gold, 2 silver; set 1 world record; coached Oakville Aquatic Club '73-76, Pointe Claire '77-78; head of pre-school aquatics St. John's, Nfld '78-79; Velma Springstead Trophy '70; Canadian female swimmer of '70; Burlington pool bears her name; mem. Cdn Olympic, Cdn, Ont. Aquatic halls of fame; res. Toronto, Ont.

COULON, Johnny (boxing); b. 12 Feb 1889, Toronto, Ont.; d. 29 Oct 1973, Chicago, Ill.; boxing coach; age 19 won vacant world bantam title, defended 12 times before losing to Kid Williams '14; title matches twice within 3 week period, later 3 times in month; ret'd following loss to Williams; comeback '16-18; nicknamed "Chicago Spider"; 96 pro bouts, 24 won by KO, 32 by decision, 4 draws, KO'd twice, lost 2 by decision, 32 no-decision bouts; boxing

coach to age 73; mem. US, Canadian Boxing, Canada's Sports halls of fame.

COULSON, Evelyn (basketball); b. 28 Jan 1912, Calgary, Alta.; d. 11 Feb 2001, Edmonton, Alta.; m. Alfred Cameron; c. James, Verna; ret'd stenographer; mem. legendary Edmonton Grads '31-35; mem. Canadian Basketball, Alta. Sports halls of fame.

COULTER, Art (hockey); b. 31 May 1909, Winnipeg, Man.; d. 14 Oct 2000, Spanish Fort, Ala.; given name: Arthur Edmund; m. Gertrude Schneitzer (d); c. Art Jr, Patty; ret'd; Pilgrim AC '24; pro Philadelphia '29; NHL def Chicago '31-35, NYR '35-42; followed Bill Cook as Rangers capt.; mem. 2 Stanley Cup winners; 4 times 2nd team all-star; NHL record: 11 seasons, 30 goals, 82 assists; nicknamed "Trapper" because of penchant for talking hunting, fishing; mem. Man., Cdn Hockey halls of fame.

COULTER, Bruce (football/coaching/administration); b. 19 Nov 1927, Toronto, Ont.; given name: Bruce David; m. Joyce Marilyn Brown; c. Susan, Bruce Jr., Douglas, John; UofT, BA, Bishop's hon. DCL; ret'd. Bishop's athletic dir.; HS all-star football, basketball, t&f; pro db/qb Alouettes '48-57; nicknamed "Bones"; head coach McGill Redmen '58-61, Bishop's Gaiters '62-87; Bishop's AD to '91 retirement; CIAU coach of year '87; winningest CIAU coach 137-80-3 (beaten by Tuffy Knight '96); Frank Tindall award '86; p.-pres. Canadian Assn. of University Athletic Directors, QUAA; p.-dir. CIAU; Bishop's Stadium bears his name; mem. Bishop's Wall, Cdn Football Hall of Fame; res. Lennoxville, Que.

COULTER, Carl (football); b. 14 Nov 1966, Lindsay, Ont.; Carleton BA; centre; Ravens off. player/lineman-of-yr, special teams player-of-yr awards; OQIFC all-star; CFL B.C. '90-92, '96, Ottawa '93, '02, Toronto '94-95, Sask. '97, Hamilton '98-01, '03-04; CFL, East Div all-star awards; 3 Grey Cup finals, 1 winner; CFL record (through '04) 246 scheduled games; res. Ottawa, Ont.

COULTER, Tex (football); b. 2 Oct 1924, Smith County, Tex.; given name: Dewitt; m. Ruth; c. David, Ann, Jeff, Dena; West Point, Texas Christian; artist, writer; all-Texas HS honors '40-42; twice West Point all-American; pro NY Giants (NFL) '46-52, 3 times all-pro; Alouettes '53-56; 3 times all-Cdn; Schenley lineman of '55; mem. Texas Football Hall of Fame; res. Austin, Texas.

COULTHARD, Bill (basketball); b. 29 Dec 1923, Buffalo, N.Y.; given name: William Sanderson; m. Irma Vivian Shultz; c. Carol, Christopher, Bruce, Elizabeth, David; Assumption BA; ret'd. personnel mgr.; all-city Windsor HS '41; all-state Detroit Tech '44; played in CABA finals for Windsor Patricks, Assumption; 6yr mem. Tillsonburg Livingstons, ntl title '52; mem. '52 Olympic team; ret'd following '52-53 season; mem. Windsor-Essex Sports, UWindsor halls of fame; res. Tillsonburg, Ont.

COURNOYER, Yvan (hockey); b. 22 Nov 1943, Drummondville, Que.; given name: Yvan Serge; m. Ginette; c. Marie-France, Yannick, Melanie; businessman; Montreal Jr. Canadiens; pro Montreal '64-79 (4yrs capt.); NHL record: 968 scheduled games, 428g, 435a, 147 playoff games, 64g, 63a; 40

or more goals 3 successive seasons '71-74; 9 3-goal games; 7 points (5g, 2a) as Montreal beat Chicago 12-3 '75; 4 times 2nd team all-star; Smythe Trophy '72 playoffs; mem. Team Canada '72; mem. 10 Stanley Cup winners; coached Montreal Roadrunners Roller Hockey team; asst coach Canadiens '95-97; nicknamed "Roadrunner"; Canadiens special ambassador; mem. Hockey Hall of Fame; res. Blainville, Que.

COURTNALL, Geoff (hockey); 18 Aug 1962, Duncan, B.C.; given name: Geoffrey Lawton; lw Victoria '80-83, AHL Hershey, Moncton '83-86, Team Canada '91; NHL Boston '83-88, Edmonton '88, Washington '88-90, St. Louis '90-91, '95-00, Vancouver '91-95; NHL totals: 1048 scheduled games, 367g, 432a, 156 playoff games, 39g, 70a; brother Russ also played in NHL; mem. BC Hockey Hall of Fame; res. Vancouver, B.C.

COURTNALL, Russ (hockey); b. 2 Jun 1965, Duncan, B.C.; strong, fast skater who received early grounding Notre Dame midgets '80-82; rw Victoria '82-84; Team Canada '84 Olympics, jr. worlds also '91, '92; NHL Toronto '83-88, Montreal '88-92, Minnesota '92-93, Dallas '93-95, Vancouver '95-97, NYR '97, Los Angeles '97-99; 1 NHL all-star game; NHL totals: 1029 scheduled games, 297g, 447a, 129 playoff games, 39g, 44a; mem. BC Hockey Hall of Fame; res. Vancouver, B.C.

COURTWRIGHT, Jim (t&f); b. 16 Dec 1914, North Bay, Ont.; d. 21 Feb, 2003, Kingston, Ont.; given name: James Milton; m. Mary Nora Roche (d); c. Joseph, James, Patricia, Stephen, John, Mary Ellen, Anthony, Frank; UofOtt, BA; Queen's, BSc, Columbia; ret'd v-p Queen's; excelled in t&f (javelin), basketball, football; mem. '36 Olympic team; gold '38 CG; best individual performance BE vs. US relay and team match London, Eng., '36; 12 competitive basketball seasons; mem. '42 ntl finalist Montreal Oilers; HS, college football; Jenkins Trophy Queen's '41 best combined athlete-student; Ames Trophy Glebe CI '34 best student-athlete; Fink Trophy '37 UofOtt best student-athlete.

COUSINEAU, Alain (skiing); b. 28 Jul 1953, Montreal, Que.; m. Helene Ouellette; c. Emelie, Julien; pro skier, restaurateur; Laurentian zone ski team '69-70, Que. team '70-71, ntl team '71-75; pro '75-76 season; 2 Que. Kandahar, ntl GS titles; World Pro Ski circuit '77-81, 7th overall '77, 6th '78; Volvo Cup '78; res. Lachute, Que.

COVINGTON, Grover (football); b. 25 Mar 1956, Monroe, N.C.; Johnson C. Smith; def. end; began CFL career '81 when dealt by Montreal to Hamilton '81-91; CFL sack leader '88 with 25; career CFL QB sack record 157; 7 Eastern, 4 CFL all-star; Schenley def. player award '88; James McCaffrey, Gord Barwell awards; 4 Grey Cup finals, 1 winner; Charlotte Simmons humanitarian award; mem. Cdn Football Hall of Fame; res. Delta, B.C.

COWAN, Gary (golf); b. 28 Oct 1938, Kitchener, Ont.; m. Elaine Koebel; c. Rob, Todd, Jamie, Suzie; ret'd insurance exec.; Ont. juv., jr., ntl jr. titles; only Canadian to twice win US Amateur '66, '71; Canadian amateur '61, 5 times runnerup; Ont. Open '68, 3 times runnerup; 9 Ont. amateur titles; NZ Centennial Invitational, Porter Cup, US North-South titles; individual low scorer world amateur '62, low amateur US Masters '64, low amateur Canadian

Open '60; mem. 22 Ont. Willingdon Cup teams, 5 winners; mem. 6 America's Cup teams, 8 world amateur teams, 5 Commonwealth teams; qualified for seniors pro tour '90; won 1st seniors pro tour title Dotham, Ala. '94; *CTV* golf color commentator; Can male amateur golfer of century; mem. Waterloo County, RCGA, Ont. Legends, Canada's Sports halls of fame; res. Waterloo, Ont.

COWAN, Jack (soccer); b. 6 Jun 1927, Vancouver, B.C.; d. 10 Dec 2000, Vancouver, B.C.; given name: John Lawrence; m. Margaret; c. Gael Isobel, Lynn Jacqueline; UBC, BSc, St. Andrews College, Scotland; electrical engineer B.C. Hydro & Power Authority; UBC Big Block '45-49; Vancouver Coast League '48-49, '55-56; BC all-stars vs. touring Newcastle United team; pro '50 Dundee Scottish League 1st div., twice league cup winners, runnersup '52 Scottish Cup; returned to Canada '55, mem. ntl champion Vancouver Canadians; mem. BC Sports Hall of Fame.

COWDREY, Jim (softball); b. 6 Dec 1957, Toronto, Ont.; given name: James Michael; div. Margaret Reynolds; m. Wendy McDougall; c. Shannon, Amanda, Michael, Erin; private investigator; from '69 one of game's foremost rhps and above-average hitters; through '83 more than 50 no-hitters; wide array league, tournament most-valuable-pitcher, -player awards; mem. '74 Ont. midget, '77 jr. title teams; rookie of year, MV pitcher Ont. Fastball League '80; mem. '80, '84 silver medal world championships teams, '83 gold medal PAG team; MV pitcher, player '81 national championships, '82 Ont. fastball tournament; perfect game leading Agincourt to '82 Ont. title; remained with Agincourt through '94, with New Jersey Windmillers '95-99; res. Brampton, Ont.

COWLEY, Bill (hockey); b. 12 Jun 1912, Bristol, Que.; d. 31 Dec 1993, Ottawa, Ont.; m. Jessie; c. Jill, Jane, John, Dan; ret'd hotel owner; mem. Primrose juniors, Shamrocks, Ottawa all-stars '32 European tour; Halifax Wolverines '34; pro ctr St. Louis Eagles (NHL) '34, Boston '35-47; NHL scoring title '41, Hart Trophy '41, '43; mem. 3 NHL title, 2 Stanley Cup winners; NHL record: 195 regular season goals, 353 assists, 12 playoff goals, 34 assists; 4 times 1st, once 2nd team all-star; 3yrs pres. Smiths Falls Rideaus; part owner Ottawa 67's jrs. '67-75; mem. Ottawa, Smiths Falls Sports, Hockey halls of fame.

COX, Bobby (baseball/coaching); b. 21 May 1941, Tulsa, Okla.; given name: Robert Joseph; m. Pam; c. Keisha, Kami, Skyla; Reedley (CA) jr. coll.; manager; 3b; playing career, mostly in minors with Reno, Salem, Panama City, Albuquerque, Salt Lake City, Tacoma, Austin, Richmond, Syracuse, Ft. Lauderdale and 2 seasons NY Yankees extended '60-71 before injury forced retirement; *Topps* mgr. Ft. Lauderdale '71, West Haven (EL pennant) '72, 4yrs Syracuse (IL Governor's Cup '76); coach Yankees '77; mgr. Atlanta '78-81, '90-04, Toronto '82-85 (AL East title '85); GM Atlanta '85-90; ML mgr. record (through '04) 3536 scheduled games, 2002-1531; 13 div. titles; 4 NL pennants; 2 World Series titles; 2 *SN* mgr-of-yr awards; 2 *AP* mgr-of-yr awards; 3 BBWA mgr-of-yr award; res. Marietta, Ga.

COX, Doug (wrestling); b. 8 Oct 1957, Fergus, Ont.; carpenter, wrestling coach Guelph; Greco-Roman, freestyle competitor at 90kg; mem. ntl team from '85; 4 ntl GR, 2

FS titles; World Cup bronze '80; CG silver '86; PAG FS gold, GR bronze '87; competed '88, '96 Olympic Games; res. Guelph, Ont.

COX, Ernie (football); b. 1894, Hamilton, Ont.; d. 26 Feb 1962, Hamilton, Ont.; m. Cecilia Gibbs; c. Donald, Mrs. Ralph Hammel; firefighter; from Hamilton sandlots to Hamilton Tigers; following WW1 rejoined Tigers '19; played 16 seasons; perennial league, Cdn all-star; inaugural winner Jeff Russel Memorial Trophy '28; mem. 3 Grey Cup winners; nicknamed "Iron Fireman"; mem. Canada's Sports, Cdn Football halls of fame.

COX, Kathy (parachuting); b. 27 Jul 1951, Brampton, Ont.; given name: Kathleen; m. Sutton; jumped into ntl sports limelight winning '73 Cdn overall parachuting title; 4 ntl style, overall, accuracy titles; mid-East US women's title; capt. ntl women's sport parachuting team 5th place overall Yugoslavia world championships; accuracy title '79 Rossignol pro para-ski championships; individual world title for precision landing '80; overall China tournament title; 3rd Cdn woman to earn diamond wings with 2000 freefall jumps; mem. CSPA competition, coaching comm.; *CBC* athlete of '80; Ont. Sports Achievement awards '78-80; mem. Order of Canada; res. Terrace Bay, Ont.

COY, Eric (t&f); b. 16 May 1914, Nottingham, Eng.; d. 28 Oct 1985, Winnipeg, Man; m. Margaret Helen Claudia Hindson; c. John, Rick, Judy; technical services superintendent; NA snowshoe sprint title '33-41 (except '38); 1st ntl javelin title '35; mem. '38 BEG team; ntl discus, javelin, shot put crowns '38; gold discus, silver shot put '38 BEG; AAUofC athlete of year; mem. '40, '48 Olympic, '50, '54 BEG teams; football Winnipeg Wanderers, Lew Hayman's RCAF Hurricanes; coached t&f, wrestling, hockey; mem. Man., Cdn Olympic, Canada's Sports halls of fame.

COZZARIN, Sharon (shooting); b. 5 Oct 1956, Fergus, Ont.; given name: Sharon Hewitson; m. Leo Cozzarin; c. Kayla; financial planner; launched shooting career '85; handgun specialist; mem. ntl team '89-96; set ntl record winning air pistol '90 Cdn world trials; set world record winning air pistol gold '91 PAG; added team silver; competed '92 Olympics; gold '93, silver '94, bronze '92 Crossman air gun championships; sport pistol gold '94 World Cup, also competed '93 World Cup, '96 pre-Olympic World Cup (silver sport pistol); silver air pistol team, bronze individual air pistol '94 CG; sport pistol finalist '95 PAG; female shooting athlete-of-'91 award; res. Fergus, Ont.

CRAIG-EATON, Betty (rowing); b. 26 Sep 1957, Brockville, Ont.; given name: Marion Elizabeth Craig; m. Bruce Eaton; Carleton, BA; insurance adjuster; mem. '76, '80, '84 Olympic teams; ntl titles: 1 8s, 2 pairs; Canadian Henley titles: 1 8s, 3 pairs, 1 coxless 4s; silver '78, '81, bronze '82-83 world championships pairs; pairs titles: 3 Rotsee, 2 West German, 1 Bosbaan, 1 Moscow regattas; with Tricia Smith silver women's pairs '84 Olympics; fed. govt. sports excellence awards '82-84; owner, trainer show jumping horses; res. Aldergrove, B.C.

CRAIG, John (t&f); b. 2 Sep 1953, Toronto, Ont.; given name: John Henry; m. Gael Carol Joyce Robertson; c. Noah,

Joshua; Texas, BSc; sports administrator OTFA; ntl jr. 800m '73, sr. '74; mem. '78 CG, '79 PAG, '80 Olympic, '81 World Cup teams; competes in Masters races; ntl outdoor 1500m champion '79-80, indoor 1500m '80-81; PB: 1500m 3:38.6, mile 3:58.05, 800m 1:49.4; twin brother Paul; published track book for juveniles; res. Thornhill, Ont.

CRAIG, Paul (t&f); b. 2 Sep 1953, Toronto, Ont.; given name: Paul Frederick; m. Judith May Johnson; c. Brydon, Lindsay; Texas; teacher; ntl sr. 1500m title '73, '77; US South-West Conf. mile '73-74; ntl record 3:38.0 '76 Olympic 1500m; mem. '78 CG, '79 World Cup, '80 Olympic teams; competes in Masters events; ntl 3000m record 7:49.6; twin brother John; res. Agincourt, Ont.

CRANHAM, Scott (diving); b. 8 Sep 1954, Toronto, Ont.; Indiana, Texas, BA; family therapist; mem. university, Pointe Claire diving teams under coach Don Webb; from '71-80 won 30 ntl diving titles (feat surpassed by only Bev Boys); mem. '72, '76, '80 Olympic, '73, '78 Worlds (finalist each time), '74, '79 CG, '75, '79 PAG teams; silver 3m, bronze 10m '74, '78 CG; 1st to record inward 3 1/2 tuck, arm-stand triple tuck in '78 Berlin world competition; 5th '80, 2nd '81 world pro cliff-diving championships; Ont. coach Canadian Amateur Diving Assn. '81; res. Pte. Claire, Que.

CRANSTON, Toller (figure skating); b. 20 Apr 1949, Hamilton, Ont.; Ecole des Beaux Arts Montreal; skater, artist; '64 ntl jr. title; '67 Que. Winter Games; 5 ntl sr. singles titles; '73 Skate Canada; mem. 6 Worlds, '72 Olympic teams, ISU winter, summer tours '71-74; launched own short-lived pro ice show '76; 3 Labatt pro skate titles; performed frequently with ice shows and on TV specials; '84 Olympics TV color commentator; German FSA award of decade; '95 Olympic Order; Norton Crowe trophy '74; mem. Order of Canada, Cdn Olympic, Canada's Sports, Ont. Sport Legends, World, Cdn Figure Skating halls of fame; res. Mexico.

CRAVEN, Murray (hockey); b. 20 Jul 1964, Medicine Hat, Alta.; m. Sheri; c. Haley, Sara; jr. Medicine Hat '80-84; NHL with Detroit parts of 2 seasons, Philadelphia '84-91, Hartford '91-93, Vancouver '93-94, Chicago '94-97, San Jose '97-00; NHL record: 1071 scheduled games, 266g, 493a, 118 playoff games, 27g, 43a; served as capt. or alternate capt. with Hartford, Chicago, San Jose; Flyers Class-Guy award; mem. Medicine Hat Wall of Fame; res. Whitefish, Mont.

CRAWFORD, Judy (skiing); b. 22 Dec 1951, Toronto, Ont.; given name: Judith MacPherson; m. Kim Rawley; c. Kristin, Shawn, Leanne, Andrea; UofT, BA; ski coach, examiner; ntl ski team '68-75; ntl titles '71, '73, US title '71, European Cup race France '73; 3rd WC slalom Grindelwald, Switzerland '73; 4th slalom '72 Olympics, '70 world downhill, '74 world combined; John Semmelink Trophy for skiing achievement, sportsmanship; Cdn coach-of-yr award; Camp Fortune coach; examiner Canadian Ski Coaches Federation; mem. Cdn Skiing Hall of Fame; res. Ottawa, Ont.

CRAWFORD, Marc (hockey/coaching); b. 13 Feb 1961, Belleville, Ont.; m. Helene; c. Dylan, Kaitlin; hockey coach, ex-TV analyst; jr. with Cornwall (QMJHL) '79-81; CHL Dallas '81-82; AHL Fredericton '82-86; NHL Vancouver '81-87; NHL playing record: 116 scheduled games, 19g, 31a, 20 playoff games, 1g, 6a; playing asst. Fredericton (AHL) '87-88, asst. coach Milwaukee (IHL) '88-89, coach/GM Cornwall (OHL) '89-91, St. John's (AHL) '91-94, Quebec (NHL) '94-95, Colorado (NHL) '95-98, Vancouver '99-03; 1 Stanley Cup winner; NHL coaching record (through '02): 659 scheduled games, 326-221-93; 3 div., 2 conf. titles; AHL coach of '92; Jack Adams trophy '95; asst. Team Canada (WC silver) '96; head coach Team Canada '98 Olympics; *HNIC* analyst '98-99; mem. 2 Memorial Cup winners; Mem. Cup all-star; res. N. Vancouver, B.C.

CRAWFORD, Rusty (hockey); b. 7 Nov 1884, Cardinal, Ont.; d. 19 Dec 1971; given name; Samuel Russell; amateur 3 seasons Verdun, 2 seasons Prince Albert, Sask., 1 season Saskatoon; Quebec Bulldogs '12-18; mem. Ottawa, Toronto Arenas; 3 Stanley Cup winners; Saskatoon '20, Calgary '21-25, Vancouver '26; closed career at 45 with Minneapolis '29; through 21-yr pro career never missed game due to injury; greatest single game accomplishment was playing entire 112 minutes of Quebec vs. Toronto Stanley Cup final and scoring winning goal; mem. Sask. Sports, Hockey halls of fame.

CREANEY, Doreen (lawn bowling); b. 20 Nov 1935, Toronto, Ont.; given name: Doreen Ann; c. Sandra; exec. asst.; Ont. singles title, silver medal ntls '92; Ont., Cdn pairs champion '95; ntl singles title '99; res. Toronto, Ont.

CREBER, Bill (curling); b. 30 Nov 1935, Toronto, Ont.; m. Carol Anne Ward; c. Brad, Jill; sales rep.; best known for marathon loss to London's Ken Buchan '69 Ont. Consols; led Ont. Silver Tankard titlists '64-65; skipped '74 Tankard winner; skip 3 Toronto Curling Assn. title rinks, 3 Southern Ont. all-star titlists; skipped winners Whitby, Peterborough, St. Catharines, Orillia, Royals Classic, Avonlea Beef O'Rama, Parkway Open, Canada Life 'spiels; runnerup '67, '77 Ont. Tankard; OCA Intermediates title '81; res. Markham, Ont.

CREELMAN, Sharon (field hockey); b. 27 Apr 1964, Windsor, Ont.; given name: Sharon Grace; UNB, York; coach Waterloo; mem. NB provincial teams from '80-83; ntl teams '82-92, UNB team '82-83; 3 CIAU FH all-Cdn; 1 CIAU FH coach-of-yr award; 4 World Cup (silver '83, bronze '86) medal teams; mem. '84, '88, '92 Olympic team; 2 PAG teams; 139 intl caps; fed. govt. excellence award '83; mem. NB Sports Hall of Fame; res. Waterloo, Ont.

CREIGHTON, Dale (baseball/football); b. 12 Jun 1934, London, Ont.; m. Marion Thompson; c. Matthew, Paul, Lyndsey; UWO, BA; ret'd. sr. v-p. individual marketing London Life; 1b/c/of; mem. 6 Ont. baseball title teams '48-58; capt. 3 title teams; sr. baseball Great Lakes-Niagara, Intercounty League London Majors; '58 2nd team all-star; mem. PS, HS basketball title teams, leading scorer twice, all-city twice; mem. HS, WOSSA, Red Feather tournament title football teams; 3 times all-conf. scoring leader, all-star; standout fb UWO Mustangs '54-57; twice OUAA

all-star; all-star, leading rusher ORFU London Lords '56; team MVP, ORFU all-star mlb K-W Dutchmen '58; mem. UWO W-Club Sports Hall of Fame; res. London, Ont.

CRICHLOW, Renn (canoeing); b. 9 May 1969, Ottawa, Ont.; SFU, BSc (kinesiology), Harvard; kayak specialist; began kayaking at 12 as mem. Rideau Canoe Club; mem. ntl team '85-96; ntl midget K1 500m title '85; solid junior career winning gold or silver in 14 of 16 major events including Paris International where he claimed K1 500- and 1000m titles '87; earned bronze K1 1000m '87 junior worlds; 4 gold '88 Continental Cup; 9 ntl senior titles; gold K1 500m '91 Duisburg International, '93 Paris regattas; 1st Canadian to win world championship at senior level with K1 500m title '91; competed '88, '92, '96 Olympics; mem. Burnaby Canoe & Kayak Club; Harry Jerome award; Ottawa ACT Athlete of Year '91; life mem. Rideau Canoe Club; mem. Nepean Wall, Cdn Olympic, Ottawa Sports halls of fame; res. Nepean, Ont./Brookline, Mass.

CRIGHTON, Hec (diving/football); b. 2 Apr 1900, Toronto, Ont.; d. 17 Apr 1967, Toronto, Ont.; given name: Hector Naismith; c. Ronald; UofT, BA, Wisc, MSc; educator; ntl diving title '20; refereed 16 Grey Cup finals through '50; authored 1st CIAU football rule book; trophy in his honor awarded annually to outstanding football player CIAU; mem. UofT Sports, Cdn Football halls of fame.

CRIPPS, Ken (baseball/bowling/darts); b. 4 Dec 1938, Chatham, N.B.; given name: Kenneth Joseph; m. Joan Kingston; c. Angela, Jacelyn, Ken Jr., Michael, Paula, Stephen, Ralph; ex-barber, school bus driver. Miramichi Ice co. owner; pitcher Chatham Ironmen '54-74; mem. NB sr. title team '67-68; mem. Napan Braves Maritime champions '75; coach Chatham jr. Ironmen '70-84; 2 NB titles; ntl darts singles title '75; Maritimes 5-pin singles bowling title '93; coached jr. bowlers, curlers, baseball players; Town of Chatham achievement award '75; mem. Chatham Sports Wall of Fame, NB Baseball Hall of Fame; res. Miramichi, N.B.

CRISP, Terry (hockey/coaching); b. 20 May 1943, Parry Sound, Ont.; m. Sheila; c. Tony, Jeff, Caley; cntr OHA Niagara Falls '61-63; CHL Minneapolis '63-65, Oklahoma '65-67, Kansas City '68; AHL Buffalo '69-70; NHL Boston '65-66, St. Louis '67-72, NYI '72-73, Philadelphia '73-77; NHL record: 536 scheduled games, 67g, 134a, 110 playoff games, 15g, 28a; began coaching as asst. Philadelphia '77-79; head coach Sault Ste. Marie (OHA) '79-85, 3 div., league titles, 2 coach of yr awards; coach Moncton (AHL) '85-87; NHL Calgary '87-90, Tampa Bay '92-98; 3 Stanley Cup winners, 1 as coach; mem. Hockey Heritage North Hall of Fame; res. Tampa, Fla.

CRISTOFOLI, Ed (hockey); b. 2 Jan 1939, Trail, B.C.; given name: Edmund Luciano; m. Shirley Clark; c. Cheryl, Eddie Jr., Dean, Randy; Cominco foreman; ctr/d; Melville, Sask. jrs '57-58; Trail Smoke Eaters '59-63; mem. '61 World, '62 Allan Cup title teams; coaching from '63, guiding juveniles to BC title; coached peewee teams to 4 provincial titles; level 3 CAHA coach; res. Trail, B.C.

CRITELLI, Chris (basketball); b. 5 Dec 1956, St. Catharines, Ont.; given name: Christine Ann; Winnipeg,

Laurentian, Old Dominion, BSc, BEd; athletic dir., coach; all-Cdn 3yrs; academic all-American Old Dominion '81; ntl team '74-80; mem. 2 Laurentian ntl titlists, 2 Old Dominion US championship teams; mem. '76, '80 Olympic, '75, '79 (bronze) PAG, world championships, FISU Games teams; MVP International Cup '79; pro New England Gulls, Chicago Hustle '81-82; women's AD, varsity coach Brock from '83; posted 300th career coaching victory '04; mem. Ont., Cdn Basketball, St, Catharines Sports hall of fame; res. Thorold, Ont.

CROCKER, Willard (tennis); b. 1898, Quincy, Mass.; d. 1964, Montreal, Que.; Tuft's, McGill; teamed with Jack Wright to form outstanding intercollegiate doubles team; one of first players of his era to work with/encourage juniors; won '25 ntl open singles; mem. Cdn Davis Cup team '23-30; posted only two Cdn victories vs. Cuba '24, sole victory over Japan '28; best performances came on clay courts; with Wright 3 ntl open doubles titles; mem. Cdn Tennis, Olympic halls of fame.

CROMBIE, Jamie (squash); b. 13 Sep 1965, Morrisville, Vt.; UWO, BA (econ/polisci); squash pro Cincinnati Country Club; moved to Calgary with family as a child; began play age 13; won 1st tournament he entered Brae Glen Club; mem. 6 ntl world championships teams '85-00; mem. '94 Pan-Am tournament silver medal team, individual gold; Man., Ont., Que., Alta. open titles '94; turned pro '89; team gold '99 PAG; ranked 4th in Cda '00; res. Cincinnati, Oh.

CRONIE, Ab (hockey); b. 29 Jan 1915, Calgary, Alta; d. 1996, Trail, B.C.; given name: Thomas Albert; m. Mary Gripich (d), Iva Stefani; c. Mervyn Allan; ret'd Cominco; mem. Alta. school soccer title team; 4 provincial age-group hockey title teams; Trail Smoke Eaters '34-43; playing-coach '38 Allan Cup, '39 world title teams; pro tryouts NY Americans, Rangers, Detroit; MVP, Sportsman awards '50-51; BCAHA outstanding- player award '52; mem. BC Seniors' Curling Assn.

CRONIN, Carl (football); b. 18 Oct 1908, Chicago, Ill.; d. 13 Sep 1983, Vancouver, B.C.; given name: Carl Michael; m. Ruth Harmon; c. Michael, Pat (d), Dennis (d), Thomas (d); Notre Dame; ret'd electrical business; HS football, pv/jav standout; hb/qb Notre Dame '29-31; 1st US import Winnipeg '32 as player-coach; guided Winnipeg to '33 Western title, losing Grey Cup bid to Toronto; Calgary Broncos coach '35-40; mem. Canadian Football Hall of Fame.

CROOK, Jan (field hockey); b. 9 Oct 1956, Edmonton, Alta.; given name: Janice Maureen; UVic, BA, UofSask.; academic consultant Cdn Sport Centre Calgary; ex-pres. CWUAA; 8yrs competitive age-group swimmer; mem. BC softball team '73 Canada Games; ntl field hockey team '74-81; mem. 4 World Cup tournament teams, twice placing 5th; 3 European tour teams; team capt. '79-81; twice HS athlete of year; HS sportsmanship award; 3 times jr. HS athlete of yr; asst. AD UCal '94-95; res. Calgary, Alta.

CROOKALL, Dot (lacrosse); b. 6 Feb 1899, Toronto, Ont.; d. 31 May 1965, Snug Cove, Bowen Island, B.C.; given name: John; outstanding field lacrosse star with Vancouver teams '11-25; mem. 5 Minto Cup winners, 4 in succession with Vancouver AC '11-14; pro '19; several years baseball umpire; mem. Cdn Lacrosse, BC Sports halls of fame.

CROOKS, Charmaine (t&f); b. 8 Aug 1961, Mandeville, Jamaica; m. Anders Thorsen; Texas, BA; pres./founder NGU consultants; child psychologist, sport/media consultant; moved to Canada '66; ntl jr. 400m '79; 11 ntl 400m, 800m titles; ntl jr. 400m record 52.33 '80; gold Pan-Am jr. championships, 2 Francophone Games silver; 4x400m relay gold '82, '86, bronze '94 CG; 1st Cdn woman to break 2min barrier in 800m with ntl sr. record 1:38.52 '90; gold Buchanan Invitational '82, Tokyo International '83, Harry Jerome Classic 400m '94, Seattle 800m gold '94; 400m silver '82 NCAA championships; gold 400m '83, silver 4x400 relay '87 PAG; 800m silver, 4x100 relay bronze '94 CG; 4x400 silver '84 Olympics; 4x400 World Cup gold '89, '92, 400m silver '92; mem. '80, '84, '88, '92, '96 Olympic, '83 FISU, '83, '87 PAG teams; flag-bearer '96 summer Olympics; ret'd from competition '98; COA dir. Intl. Relations '01; 4 fed. govt. sport excellence awards; 2 UTEP, 2 BC t&f female-athlete-of-yr awards; John F. Bassett Memorial award '91; Olympic champion award '95; Bruce Kidd athletic leadership award '96; Governor-General's community service award '92; dir. '10 Olympic organizing comm.; mem. Cdn Athletes Assn., several other boards; co-host CBC Cycle show '94; creator/producer *No Laughing Matter* breast cancer fund raiser; mem. IOC ethics committee; honored by BC Women in Sport Leaders & Legends; mem. BC Sports Hall of Fame; res. N.Vancouver, B.C.

CROSBY, Andy (rowing); b. 5 Nov 1965, Bella Coola, B.C.; UVic, Memorial; began rowing at 17; mem. ntl 8s '85-92, '96; 1 jr, 3 sr Canadian Henley titles; silver '90-91 worlds; gold '90 US Nationals, Amsterdam International; 2 gold Duisburg International regatta '91; gold '92 Olympics; competed '86 CG, '88, '92, '96 Olympic, '89 FISU Games, 6 world championships; UVic's male rower of yr '89; mem. Cdn Olympic Hall of Fame; res. Hamilton, Ont./St. John's, Nfld.

CROSBY, Sidney (hockey); b. 7 Aug 1987, Cole Harbour, N.S.; made skating debut age 3, playing hockey from age 5; ctr; scored 72g in 57 games with Shattuck-St. Marys prep school in Minnesota '02-03; at 14 MVP, leading scorer Air Canada silver medal team '02; drafted by Rimouski (QMJHL); through '05 amassed 120g, 183a in 121 scheduled QMJHL games earning frequent league, CHL player of week/month/year awards; QMJHL rookie scoring record 135pts in 57 games, several other league reords; QMJHL rookie of yr, scoring champ awards; youngest ever to score goal in world jr. championships '03; touted as budding superstar in mould of Wayne Gretzky, Mario Lemieux; eligible for '05 NHL draft which was cancelled by labor dispute; res. Dartmouth, N.S.

CROSS, Jay (sailing); b. 15 Feb 1953, Toronto, Ont.; engineer; 470 class sailor; 3 ntl, 2 NA, 1 CORK, 1 Hyeres titles; mem. '76, '80, '84 Olympic, '79 PAG, 6 world championships teams; res. Toronto, Ont.

CROSSAN, Errol (soccer); b. 6 Oct 1930, Montreal, Que.; given name: Errol Gilmour; m. June Heafeald; c. Gary,

Deb; ret'd Canada Forest Products; noted for devastating speed he honed his skills on the Isle of Man from age 8; returned to Canada '47 to play with New Westminster Royals winning '53 ntl title; signed by Manchester City '54 and subsequently played with Gillington, Southend United, Norwich City, Layton Orient, Toronto City; achieved stardom during Norwich City '58-59 FA Cup run; competed in 241 football league games scoring 61 goals, including one each in 7 successive games '59; scored 4 goals in 12 FA Cup games; nicknamed Cowboy; returned to Canada '61 to play with Toronto City; mem. Cdn Soccer Hall of Fame; res. Langley, B.C.

CROTHERS, Bill (t&f); b. 24 Dec 1940, Markham, Ont.; given name: William Frederick; m. Morven Johnston; c. Margaret Grace, Andrea Lynn, William Rognvald; UofT, BScPh; ret'd. pharmacist, school board chair.; OFSSA sr. 440yd, ntl jr. 440 titles '59; '61-68 competed regularly both indoor, outdoor Canadian, US, European meets; leading field 440, 880yd events; at one time held all ntl records from 440- to 1500m; world indoor 880yds record; 65 wins in 75 indoor meets; mem. '64, '68 Olympic, '65 FISU, '62, '66 CG, '67 PAG teams; 800m silver '64 Olympics, 800m, 4x400m silver '66 CG; gold '65 FISU Games; ranked 1st '65, 2nd for decade behind Peter Snell for 800m by *Track and Field News*; US 880yd title record 1:46.8 '63, same year posted two fastest 880s in world; ntl sr. 440, 880 titles '61-65; PB: 400m (45.9), 800m (1:45.6), mile (4:02.4); Lou Marsh trophy '63; Lionel Conacher trophy '64; Tennis Can. distinguished service award; mem. National Sports Advisory Council; mem. UofT, Cdn Tennis, Cdn Olympic, Canada's Sports halls of fame; res. Markham, Ont.

CROWE, Norton (administration); b. 6 Jul 1877, Ridgeville, Ont.; d. 14 Sep 1929, Toronto, Ont.; given name: Norton Hervey; one of most prominent sports executives Canada has produced; instrumental in stabilizing Canadian amateur sport; AAUofC secretary 19yrs; standout baseball player in youth, mem. Toronto city title teams; 1st secty. OHA; mgr. ntl swim team '11 Festival of Empire Games; mem. '24 Olympic exec. comm.; trophy in his name awarded annually to Canada's top amateur male athlete; mem. Cdn Olympic Sports Hall of Fame.

CROWELL, Eddie (golf); b. 2 Feb 1925, Halifax, N.S.; given name: Edwin Harvey; Dalhousie, BComm.; played in NS amateur as jr. '39; won 20 titles '46-56, including 3 Abercrombie, 4 Ashburn, 4 NS amateur, 3 Halifax City & District, 1 Brightwood Goodwill, Halifax Bicentennial, Maritime Amateur, NS Open, Truro Invitational; quarterfinalist Cdn Amateur; served term as pres. NSGA; took hiatus from competitive golf '56-82; won 2 Maritime srs. titles; mem. NS Sports Hall of Fame; res. Halifax, N.S.

CROWLEY, Maureen (t&f); b. 26 May 1953, Brampton, Ont.; given name: Maureen Adele; m. Ted de St. Croix, SFU; teacher; 800m, 1500m specialist; ntl team '71-79; 6th 800m, team bronze 4x400m relay '74 CG; Canadian 400m title '74; silver 150m, 800m NZ Games; injuries removed her from '76 Olympic team contention but recovered to compete in world x-country '77, '79; 5 Cdn masters x-country titles; x-country, 2km steeplechase gold, 800m silver '95 world masters; 1500m gold, x-country silver, 800m bronze '99

world masters; gold 8km x-country, 1500m, 800m '01, '03 world masters; women's 4x400m relay gold '03; 3 women's 50+ WR; set ntl women's master indoor mile record 4:49.44; res. Surrey, B.C.

CROZIER, Roger (hockey); b. 16 Mar 1942, Bracebridge, Ont.; d. 11 Jan 1996, Barrie, Ont.; goalie; St. Catharines OHA '59-62, St. Louis, SSM EPHL '61-63, Buffalo, Pittsburgh AHL '61-64, NHL Detroit '64-70, Buffalo '70-76, Washington '76-77; NHL totals 518 scheduled games, 206-197-70, 28,567min, 30sho, 32 playoff games, 14-16, 1789min, 1sho; AHL Red Garrett, Hap Holmes awards, 1 all-star; NHL Calder Memorial, Conn Smythe trophies, 1 all-star; Buffalo Wayne Larkin MVP award; GM/interim coach Washington '81; Roger Crozier Saving Grace award to NHL save percentage leader; nicknamed "Roger the Dodger"; mem. Buffalo Sabres Hall of Fame.

CRUMMER, Keith (t&f); b. 29 Jun 1911, Wallaceburg, Ont.; d. 20 Jun 1990, Chatham, Ont.; given name: Charles Keith; m. Frances Bevan; c. Richard, Diane, Jane, Joan; Ohio State; Union Gas employee; excelled in pole vault, shot put, javelin, discus; 7 WOSSA records '27-31, 2 sr. overall titles; 3 Ont. Athletic Commission meet records; Kent County pv mark 11'8" '29; 15 ntl interscholastic medals while setting 4 records; javelin silver '30 ntl championships; 4th javelin '30 BEG; shared all-around title Canadian Legion meet Cornwall and tied '32 Olympic gold medalist Duncan McNaughton in hj '30; 53 t&f medals, 30 silver cups and John McMartin Memorial Cup, 2 WOSSA sr. title shields, 2 Kennedy CI trophies and wide array of ribbons; def '30-31 OHA finalist Chatham Maroons.

CRUTCHFIELD, Linda (skiing/water-skiing/luge); b. 3 Apr 1942, Shawinigan, Que.; div. Robert Bocock; Sir George Williams, Burke Mountain Academy; ski school director, relator; winner by 11 seconds 1st major ski race Mt. Tremblant Taschereau; invited by Vic Emery '67 to test luge (one-man toboggan), made 4 runs, won ntl title; 10th '68 Olympics; mem. ntl teams in skiing, luge, water skiing; ntl alpine team '60-65, including '64 Olympics; asst. CdM '76 winter Olympics; 14 water ski titles, several jump records; 1st Cdn woman to clear 100' water ski jump; mem. 4 world water ski championships teams; ski school, water ski school dir.; twice ntl alpine, luge, once NA luge champion; Level 3 instructor, Level 4 examiner CSIA; numerous snow, water ski school roles as coach, administrator; John Semmelink Memorial Trophy '64; real estate agent of '91 award; twice Velma Springstead Trophy; mem. Cdn, Laurentian, St. Maurice Valley Skiing, Cdn Ski Instructors' Alliance, Quebec Water Ski halls of fame; res. St. Sauveur des Monts, Que.

CRYSDALE, Jamie (football); b. 14 Dec 1968, Mississauga, Ont.; m. Adrienne; c. Thomas, Grace; Cincinnati BA; pres. Grid Iron Drilling Services; centre; John Pease outstanding lineman '92; trial with NFL NY Giants; drafted BC '92; CFL Calgary '93-04; several CFL lineman-of-wk awards; 1 West all-star award; 4 Grey Cup finals, 2 winners; 205 consec. games; res.Calgary, Alta.

CULLEN, Ronald (coaching); b. 19 Oct 1915, Toronto, Ont.; priest, educator; coached football, hockey, baseball at Windsor Assumption HS for more than 40 years producing numerous athletes who advanced to NHL, NFL, CFL and major league baseball ranks; Windsor baseball stadium bears his name; mem. Windsor/Essex County Sports, Cdn Baseball halls of fame; res. Windsor, Ont.

CULVER, Diane (skiing); b. 14 Sep 1952, Montreal, Que.; given name: Diane Mary; m. William John Grey; McGill; ski coach, examiner; Pontiac Cup '69; mem. ntl alpine team '70 world championships, World Cup team '70-72; 8th GS WC final '70; coached women's Can-Am ski team '75-76; instructor Mt. Tremblant, examiner for Canadian Ski Instructor's Alliance; only female selected on 10-member Canadian demonstration ski team Inter-Ski (International reunion of ski schools) Italy '83; res. New Zealand.

CUMMING, George (golf); b. 20 May 1879, Bridge of Weir, Scotland; d. 26 Mar 1950, Toronto, Ont.; golf pro; rose from caddy ranks to pro Dumfries GC; emigrated to Canada 1900; pro Toronto GC 50yrs; Cdn Open title 1905, 4 times runnerup; tied lowest 18-holes, 8th place '05 US Open; CPGA title '14, 3 times runnerup; pioneered CPGA organization, initial capt., 4yrs v.-capt., 6yrs capt. CPGA; considered Dean of Canadian golf pros; mem. RCGA Hall of Fame.

CUMMINGS, Bruce (football); b. 26 Mar 1927, Ottawa, Ont.; d. 16 Jun 1991, Ottawa, Ont.; given name: Bruce Fredrick; m. Mary Gardner; c. Lynn, David (d); UofT, BSc; engineer; Varsity Blues '47-49; Johnny Copp Memorial Trophy UofT '47; pro Ottawa '50-53; EFC all-star '51; Ottawa MVP, Hiram Walker Trophy winner '50; EFC Jeff Russel Memorial Trophy winner '51.

CUMMINGS, Dave (wrestling); b. 24 Sep 1948, Ottawa, Ont.; d. 30 Apr 1985, Calgary, Alta; given name: David Harold; m. Susanne Ferrier; construction equipment operator; ntl freestyle titles '73-74, Greco-Roman '69, '74; mem. '74 world championships, '75 PAG, '76 Olympic Games teams; asst. coach ntl GR team '76 European tour, Olympic Games; coach UCal wrestling club '77-81; killed in ultra-light aircraft accident.

CUNNEYWORTH, Randy (hockey); b. 10 May 1961, Etobicoke, Ont.; given name: Randy William; m. Marie; c. Jenny, Gregory, Cameron; lw Ottawa 67's (OHL) '79-81; Rochester (AHL) '80-85, '98-00 Springfield '91; claimed by Buffalo '80 entry draft; played in NHL with Buffalo '80-81, '98, Pittsburgh '85-89, Winnipeg '89, Hartford '90-94, Chicago '94, Ottawa '94-98; NHL record: 866 scheduled games, 189g, 225a, 45 playoff games, 7g, 7a; mem. Calder Cup winner Rochester '81; capt. Ottawa '96-98; player/coach Rochester '98-05; res. Pittsford, N.Y.

CUNNINGHAM, Keith (shooting); b. 11 Feb 1950, London, Ont.; given name: Keith Allan; div. Arlene Clancy; c. Jason Wesley, Jesse Robert; Colorado School of Trades; ret'd. Cdn Forces infantry officer, Chief Operations Officer MilCun Marksmanship Complex; served in US Army '70-72, Cdn Army '75-95; began shooting competitively age 20; mem. 8 Cdn Forces Bisley teams; 11 ntl Bisley teams; 7 combined service/target rifle titles; 8 Cdn Forces target rifle, 5 Ont sniper rifle, 5 Ont sniper pairs, 3 Ont service rifle titles; 1 ntl sniper rifle, 3 ntl sniper rifle pairs titles; Ont. Lt.-Governors silver '97; 2 Palma, 8 Commonwealth teams;

2 Des Burke awards; team silver '92 Palma; mem. '94 CG team; coached 4 Cdn Forces Bisley teams, 6 individuals to Queen's medal; Level 3 ntl coach; mem. Cdn Forces Sports Hall of Fame; res. Burnt River, Ont.

CUNNINGHAM, Les (hockey); b. 4 Oct 1913, Calgary, Alta.; d. 9 Apr 1993, Calgary, Alta; mem. Calgary Memorial Cup team '32; Regina Memorial Cup team '33; played 1 season Saskatoon then IHL Buffalo '34-36; brief stints in NHL with NY Americans '36-37, Chicago '39-40; speedy, prolific scorer with Cleveland (AHL) '36-47; San Francisco (PCHL) '47-49; coached Brandon (MJHL) '49-50; brief tenure as scout; led AHL scorers '41; 4 AHL all-stare; AHL MVP award bears his name; mem. Cleveland Sports Hall of Fame.

CURRAN, Randy (baseball); b. 23 Feb 1967, Kitchener, Ont.; Miami Dade Jr. College; city employee; mem. Kitchener jr. Dodgers; Cdn Olympic team '88; rejected Montreal Expos offers '87; pro ball in Verona, Italy '92-94; mem. Kitchener Panthers Sr. (IC) '84-91, from '95; IC rookie of '85, MVP '93, '96, Commissioner's Trophy '96; 1 1st team, 3 2nd team all-star 1b selections; set IC single-season HR record 17 '93; 3 league HR, 2 total bases, 2 RBI, 2 runs scored, 1 walks titles; all-time IC HR leader with 85 (through '96); also through '96 260 lifetime RBI, 334 hits, 57 doubles; brother Kevin standout IC lhp with Kitchener; res. Kitchener, Ont.

CURRIE, Andy (football); b. 5 Jun 1911, Brandon, Man.; d. 14 Aug 1990, Winnipeg, Man.; m. Thelma Wright; c. David, Roger; UMan, BA; deputy minister; coached HS, UMan., Regina Pats; refereed 15yrs Winnipeg area; at 17 Sask. Roughriders '28 Grey Cup, week later helped Pats win ntl jr. title; UMan '29, '31, Roughriders '28, '30, St.John's Srs '32, Winnipeg football club '33; PE dir. for Winnipeg schools '51; provincial dir. PE & R '57; dir. P & R greater Winnipeg '61; 20yrs WIFU official, 14yrs supervisor of officials; mem. Canadian Football Hall of Fame.

CURRIE, Gordon (coaching); b. 20 May 1923, Seamans, Sask.; m. Shirley Clarke; c. Bob, Doug, Jim; Notre Dame College, BA, Mt. Allison, BEd; ret'd. pvcl politician; served as Minister of Science & Technology, Telephones, Education & Manpower '82-86; coached Balfour Tech to 8 prov. football crowns, 6 in succession, 3 prov. hockey titles; 4 Regina Red Sox baseball title teams; coached Regina Rams '65-76 winning 108 of 135 games, 6 ntl, 8 Man.-Sask., 7 Western Jr., 1 Alta. Jr. league titles; ntl amateur coach of '75; CFL, CAFA service-to-the-game awards; mem. Order of Canada, Cdn Football, Sask. Sports halls of fame; res. Regina, Sask.

CURRIER, Doug (bobsleigh); b. 25 Aug 1967, Brockville, Ont.; nationally-ranked shotputter who switched to bobsleigh '89 and became ntl team mem. in rookie year; with Chris Lori, John Graham, Ken Leblanc won 2 ntl 4-man titles, 2 World Cup 4-man races, both at Calgary; finished 1st in world rankings '90, 3rd 4-man, 2-man (with Lori) '91; competed '92 Olympics; res. Prescott, Ont.

CURRY, Floyd (hockey); b. 11 Aug 1925, Chapleau, Ont.; given name: Floyd James; m. June Howie; c. Dawn, Candice; hockey exec.; jr. Oshawa Generals '41-43; '43

Memorial Cup; 2 seasons Montreal Royals (QSHL); mem. '46-47 Alexander Trophy (Allan Cup) champions; pro Buffalo (AHL), Canadiens '47-58; NHL record: 601 scheduled games, 105g, 99a, 91 playoff games, 23g, 17a; mem. 4 Stanley Cup winners; honored by fans with 'night' '57; 5 times all-star; playing-coach Montreal Royals (QSHL) '58-59, EPHL coach '59-61, Que. Aces (AHL) '61-64; dir. advertising sales Canadiens from '65; nicknamed "Busher"; mem. Hockey Heritage North Hall of Fame; res. Montreal, Que.

CURTIS, Crystal (horseshoes); b. 27 Oct 1978, Blairmore, Alta.; nursing assistant Crowsnest Pass health centre; began pitching horseshoes age 9; 4 Alta. jr. girls titles; 6 ntl jr. girls titles; 2 ntl jr. girls records; world jr. girls champion '93; Alta. player of '93; res. Bellevue, Alta.

CURTIS, Ulysses (football); b. 10 May 1926, Albion, Mich.; m. Katherine; c. Carol, Sylvia, Warren; Florida A&M, BA, BPHE, McMaster; ret'd. HS teacher; Negro all-American '48-49; pro Toronto '50-54; 3 times Argos scoring leader; single season td record 16 in 12 games '52; 235 CFL points in 5 seasons, 47 tds; mem. 2 Grey Cup winners; twice EFC all-star; nicknamed "Crazy Legs"; coached 3 Eastern Cdn Toronto jr. title teams; 3yrs backfield coach York; 5yrs teacher-counsellor, program co-ordinator Ont. Athletic Leadership Camp; res. Willowdale, Ont.

CUSTIS, Bernie (football); b. 23 Sep 1929, Philadelphia, Pa.; given name: Bernard Eugene; m. Lorraine DeFoe; Syracuse, BEd, Niagara, MEd; ret'd. educator; football, baseball on Syracuse scholarship; drafted as qb by Cleveland Browns; qb/hb Hamilton '51-54, Ottawa '55; coach Oakville Black Knights (ORFU) 6yrs; Burlington jrs 8yrs, 3 ntl finals; Sheridan Community College '71-80; McMaster from '81; CIAU coach of '82; scout Argos '89-96; scout/player personnel dir. Hamilton '97; mem. McMaster, Canadian Football halls of fame; res. Burlington, Ont.

CUTHBERT, Linda (diving); b. 20 May 1956, Toronto, Ont.; given name: Linda Joanne; m. Andrej Markes; c. Sonia, Jamie; George Brown College; sports marketing, communication; mem. ntl team '73-80; 4 ntl titles, '77 Canada Cup, overall '79 Canada Cup, springboard '77 European invitational; CG gold, 2 PAG bronze, silver jr worlds; mem. '74, '78 CG, '75, '79 PAG, '80 Olympic teams; suffered serious concussion striking head on board during '80 Olympic trials but recovered to close career with tour of Orient '80; pres. CADA Ont.; '92 Olympics TV commentator; FINA international A judge; pres. Cdn Diving Assn.; mem. Cdn Aquatic Hall of Fame; res. Toronto, Ont.

CUTLER, Dave (football); b. 17 Oct 1945, Biggar, Sask.; given name: David Robert Stuart; m. Barbara Justice; c. Rob, John, Scott; SFU BA, PDF; radio time salesman; NAIA Dist. 1 all-star, hon. mention Little All-American lb; 2 team inspiration awards; NFL trial with Green Bay; Edmonton (CFL) '69-84; pk; 8 WFC, 7 CFL scoring titles; set CFL single season records (since surpassed) for scoring, most converts, field goals; runnerup '73 Schenley outstanding Canadian; surpassed George Blanda's 2002 all-time pro points record (since topped by Lui Passaglia); CFL record: 16 seasons, 254 scheduled games, 627 of attempted record 650 converts, 464 of attempted record 790 field goals, 218

singles, 2237 points; played record 253 consecutive games; 9 Grey Cup finals, 6 winners, including 5 in succession; mem. Eskimos Wall of Honor, Greater Victoria, Cdn Football halls of fame; res. Victoria, B.C.

CUTLER, Wes (football); b. 17 Feb 1911, Toronto, Ont.; d. 10 Jun 1956, Toronto, Ont.; UofT; standout end, tackler, blocker, exceptional receiver who starred with UofT '31-32, Argos '33-38; mem. 3 Grey Cup winners; *CP* all-star '33-38; Jeff Russel Memorial Trophy '38; Varsity Bronze T; mem. Cdn Football, Canada's Sports halls of fame.

CUTRONE, Angela (speed skating); b. 19 Jan 1969, St. Léonard, Que.; UMtl; short-track specialist; ntl team from '88; 3 ntl, 2 world. 1 NA, 1 Ottawa short-track titles; mem. 3000m short-track relay team '92 Olympic record, gold; 3 world records; world short-track team gold '91, '94, 3000m relay gold '91, '92, '93; res. St. L onard, Que.

CUTTING, Flo (bowling); b. 26 Dec 1904, Toronto, Ont.; d. 23 Oct 2002, Toronto, Ont.; m. Percy Cutting (d); business college; mem. Toronto playground softball, basketball, t&f title teams early '20s; mem. Lakeside-Olympia Ont. softball title team; league secty-treas. 12yrs; began bowling '30; initial pres. Toronto Ladies' Major League '37; charter mem., secty. CBA; secty at inception of union between Ont.-Western Cdn. bowlers and launching of Cdn 5-pin championships '53; secty. Second Mile Srs. league 10yrs; only Easterner made hon. life mem. WCBA; life mem. OBA, CBA; 2 Ont. achievement awards; mem. Ontario Bowling Hall of Fame.

CYNCAR, Marco (football); b. 13 Apr 1958, Edmonton, Alta.; UAlta.; pro football player; played HS, minor football in Edmonton; jr with Edmonton Wildcats; Edmonton territorial exemption; turned pro Eskimos then dealt to Hamilton '80; reacquired by Edmonton '81; sb Eskimos '81-90; CFL record: 177 games, 276 receptions, 4167yds, 10tds; 6 Grey Cup finals, 3 winners; res. Edmonton, Alta.

CYR, Alain (judo); b. 21 Sep 1955, Quebec City, Que.; construction inspector; bronze '74 jr. worlds; 4 Que., 4 ntl, 2 Eastern Cdn. 2 Que. Cup, 1 Canada Cup, 1 NY, Que., Dutch Open titles; placed in top 8 '81 world championships, top 6 '83 PAG; mem. '80 Olympic team; res. Montreal, Que.

CYR, Louis (weightlifting); b. 1863, St. Cyprien de Napierville, Que.; d. 1912, St. Jean de Matha, Que.; m. Melina; legend that at 17 he pulled loaded wagon from mud by lifting it on his back and decided to become travelling strongman; challenged David Michaud, Canada's strongest of the period, to rock lifting contest; Cyr won lifting 480lb boulder; at 22 joined Montreal Police Force but ret'd when attacked on beat with an axe; signed by promoter Richard Fox and billed as world's strongest man; accepted all challenges and never lost; toured Europe 23 months becoming household name in Western world; tour highlight '89 London's Royal Aquarium Theatre when he lifted a 551lb weight with one finger, 4100lbs on platform stretched across his back, 237.25lbs with one hand to shoulder level then above head and with one hand raised 314lb barrel of cement to shoulder; Marquis of Queensbury (father of modern boxing rules) offered him horse if he could hold pair of horses tied to his arms to a standstill, Cyr won horse; most astounding feat 1895 in Boston when he lifted 18 fat men on plank on his back in what is claimed to be the greatest lift ever made by man, 4337lbs; died at 49 of Bright's disease; mem. Canada's Sports Hall of Fame.

CZAJA, Mitch (basketball/curling); b. 4 Aug 1935, Winnipeg, Man.; given name: Mitchell Peter; m. Mary Gail Langdon; c. Clinton, Aaron, Ainsley; UMan; mechanical engineer; provincial schoolboy curling champion, lost ntl title to Bayne Secord on last rock; curled with Bruce Hudson, reached Man. Consols, lost '56 semi-finals; 2nd Ken Buchan's Ont. Brier entry '69; 4 times Ont. Consols competitor; mem. Ont. Tankard winner, '93 Ont. Srs champs; HS basketball '51-52, ntl jr. finals Winnipeg Light Infantry team '53; sr. Winnipeg Kodiaks, lost '57 ntl final to Montreal; mem. Tillsonburg Livingstons '60; mem. '59 PAG team; Ont. Masters title teams '80-81; res. London, Ont.

CZICH, John (badminton); b. 17 Jan 1953, Renfrew, Ont.; given name: John Mironko; m. Daniele Gallichand; c. Emilie, Marie Chantale; Royal Military College; ret'd. Canadian Forces air engineering officer, computer firm official; RMC light-heavyweight boxing title; Ont. jr. badminton singles '72; finalist national men's closed '76; Boulevard Club doubles '77, singles '80; gold men's doubles '77 Pan-Am championships; mem. '78 silver medal CG team; '78 Scotland Open men's singles, doubles, silver Eastern, Western singles; mem. '79 Thomas Cup, '80 Devlin Cup teams; '80 Pepsi-Cola series singles; ret'd from competition '83; ntl team coach from '90; RMC outstanding-athlete award; mem. Cdn Forces, Ottawa CSRA Sports halls of fame; res. Nepean, Ont.

D'AMICO, John (officiating/hockey); b. 21 Sep 1937, Toronto, Ont.; given name: John David; m. Dorothy Gordon; c. Anthony, Jeffrey, Tina, Angelo; hockey exec.; made NHL officiating debut '64; mostly as linesman but did some refereeing; worked more than 1700 scheduled games, more than 250 playoff games in career which extended through '88; worked more than 20 Stanley Cup finals, 7 all-star games; officiated 4 Canada Cup, '79 Challenge Cup, '87 Rendez-Vous series; NHL officiating coach since retirement; mem. Hockey Hall of Fame; res. Mississauga, Ont.

D'AMOUR, Frenchy (curling); b. 10 Oct 1912, Rossland, B.C.; d. 7 Sep 1995, Trail, B.C.; given name: Théophile; m. Neathlea (Nettie) Templeton; ret'd; skip runnerup '47 Brier; skip '48 Brier winner; 2nd for Reg Stone '62 Brier; skip '49 winner, '50 finalist Edmonton carspiel; hon. life mem. Trail Curling Club; '48 Brier champs inducted into BC Sports Hall of Fame.

D'AMOUR, Léo (shooting); b. 27 Jul 1929, Rigaud, Que.; m. Monique Bastien; c. Danielle, Lyette, Paul, Jean, Louise; Loyalist Coll.; ret'd. Cdn Forces, Rolls Royce Can.; mem. 8 Cdn Bisley teams; 2 ntl teams to Australia, 1 Palma team, 1 Ont. Goodwill Bisley team, 1 BC California long-range championship team; Lt.- Gov. medals Que., NB; won varied Ont., Que., Maritime match titles; Atlantic champion; DCRA grand aggregate title '78; served various exec. roles in DCRA, including pres.; res. Laval, Que.

DACEY, Mark (curling); b. 22 Jun 1966, Saskatoon, Sask.; m. Heather Smith; golf professional; began curling age 11; 3rd for Sask. '95 Brier; skip NS '00 ntl mixed, '01, '03 (runnerup), '04 Brier winning after snapping Alta's Randy Ferbey triple Brier winning streak; res. Halifax, N.S.

DACYSHYN, Anna (diving); b. 10 Jul 1969, Edmonton, Alta.; m. Jeff Hirt; c. Madeline, Karyn; UofT, BSc; switched from gymnastics to diving age 12; mem. ntl team from '86; 10m gold '88, '90 Winter Ntls, '89 Summer Ntls, CG trials, '90 CG, '88, '89 University Cup, Mastercard trials, '88 Pan-Am Invitational, '90 world trials; semifinalist 10m '89 Fina World Cup; 10m silver '89, 91 Winter Ntls, '89 Vienna Volksbank Intl; res. Toronto, Ont.

DAFOE, Frances (figure skating); b. 17 Dec 1929, Toronto, Ont.; div. Norman Melnick; c. Blake, Adrian; m. Paul Bogin; NYV Parsons School of Design; costume designer *CBC-TV*, freelance theatrical, dance, film designer; with Norris Bowden ntl pairs titles '52-55, dance title '52, 4 ntl waltz, 2 10-step titles; NA pairs '53-56, world pairs '54-55; mem. '52, '56 Olympic teams; silver '56 Olympics; introduced 6 new pair elements; international, world, Olympic FS judge; devised, wrote 1st world tech. program for pairs; Order of Ont., Confederation medal, Golden Jubilee medal; dir. Associated Designers of Canada; San Francisco Golden Gate award; *Home Box Office* Ace award; 2 Prix Anik awards; 4 Gemini nominations;

designed '88 Olympic closing ceremony costumes, creator spectacular *Art Forms of Skating — a History of Skating* exhibit; mem. Order of Canada, Cdn Olympic, Cdn, US, World Figure Skating, Canada's Sports halls of fame; res. Jupiter, Fla./Toronto, Ont.

DAHLSTROM, Clint (shooting); b. 30 Jul 1925, Saskatchewan; m. Phyllis (d), Patricia Page; c. Bruce, Susan, sc Jane; UofSask, MSc, Princeton, PhD; ret'd geologist; began competitive small-bore rifles career Calgary '54; bronze free-rifle, team silver '63 PAG; set US small-bore prone record 400 '76; mem. ntl small-bore team '66-78; competed '62 worlds; in full-bore competition mem. 14 Cdn Bisley, 5 Cdn Palma teams; Canada Winter Games team gold; ntl air rifle, 4 ntl gallery rifle, ranked high master in US, Canada; winner numerous club, provincial awards; proficient with crossbow; commissioner Olympic Rifle Club, coach Bisley, CG teams; Lieut.-Gov. awards Sask., BC; res. Victoria, B.C./ Sun City West, Ariz.

DAHLSTROM, Patricia (shooting); b. 11 Jul 1931, England; given name: Patricia Page; m. Clinton Dahlstrom; c. Jane, sc Bruce, Susan; ret'd speech therapist; emigrated to Canada '56; began small-bore shooting Calgary '60; ntl women's sporting rifle title '65; began full-bore shooting '80; mem. Cdn Goodwill team to Australia '88; mem. Ont. Bisley team '94; 1st Cdn woman to reach Bisley Queen's Prize final; adjutant '95 Cdn Bisley team; qualified/competed '96-97 Bisley teams; mem. '96 Cdn Palma team; Tess Spencer award, Women's pairs title '97 DCRA shoot; avid tennis player; res. Victoria, B.C./Sun City West, Ariz.

DAIGLE, Alexandre (hockey); b. 7 Feb 1975, Montreal, Que.; ctr Victoriaville (QMJHL) '91-94; twice QMJHL all-star; CMJHL rookie of '92; 1st Ottawa draft pick '93; signed by Senators for headline-grabbing $12.3M; Viscount Alexander Award '93 but through '96-97 a notable under-achiever and traded to Philadelphia '98, Tampa '99, NYR '99, Hartford (AHL) '99; cut loose by NYR played in LA rec. league; comeback Pittsburgh '02-03, farmed to Wilkes Barre-Scranton (AHL); Minnesota (NHL) '03-04; NHL record (through '04): 570 scheduled games, 124g, 175a, 12 playoff games, 0g, 2a; res. Montreal, Que.

DAIGLE, Nora (boxing); b. 18 Nov 1961, Richibucto Village, N.B.; given name: Nora Marie-Louise; NB Community College, civil engineering technologist dip.; ex-tech. support officer fed. public works; after trying hockey, broomball, softball, began kickboxing age 23; won NA featherweight, super featherweight titles 11-3-1, 6ko record; turned attention solely to boxing age 32 achieving #2 world ranking by Women's International Boxing Federation; pro record through '00 6-3-1; has competed at Caesar's Palace, Trump Taj Mahal (Atlantic City), Corel Centre, Montreal Forum, Montreal Molson Centre; suffered severe beating in world lightweight title loss to Tracy Boyd of Flint, Mich., '97; res. Quebec City, Que.

DAIGLE, Sylvie (speed skating); b. 1 Dec 1962, Sherbrooke, Que.; UMtl; intending to play hockey was hooked at 9 on speed skating session at arena when she arrived; mem. ntl team from '80; 10 ntl, 2 NA, 3 Canada Games, 7 world titles; world records 3000m (5:32.31), 1000m (1:43.66), 500m (49.54) '83, short-track 500m (46.72), 2 Cdn short-track records; mem. '80, '84, '88, '92, '94 Olympic teams; gold 1500m, silver 3000m, 1000m '88 Olympics; gold 3000m relay '92 Olympics; world short-track gold '83-84, '88-90; Thompson Trophy fastest Cdn 500m '81; 2 Elaine Tanner, 1 Velma Springstead trophies; Que. Sports Institute skater of '79; French Cdn athlete of yr (Eugene Lavoix award) '83; fed. govt. world champion awards '83, '89; Thompson Trophy for fastest Cdn 500m '81; CASSA female short- track athlete of yr '88-89, '91; flag-bearer '92 winter Olympics; mem. Que. women's hockey team; mem. Cdn Olympic, Que. Sports, Cdn Speed Skating halls of fame; res. Outremont, Que.

DAIGNAULT, Michel (speed skating); b. 25 Jun 1966, Montreal, Que.; UQue (Montreal); mem. ntl team '84-94; mem. '88, '92 Olympic teams; 2 silver, 2 bronze Olympic short-track medals; 5 world short-track gold; '85 FISU Games gold; set world record 2:25.25 '88 Olympic 1500m; 4 Cdn senior records; 4 NA championships; Que. athlete of yr '89; CASSA male athlete of yr '88-89;sport excellence award '85; world champion award '87; brother Laurent also ntl team mem.; mem. Cdn Speed Skating Hall of Fame; res. Montreal, Que.

DAIGNEAULT, Doug (football); b. 4 Aug 1936, Montreal, Que.; given name: Douglas John; m. Jane DeCoste; c. Betsy, Debbie, Lois, Vickie, Julie; Franklin Academy, Clemson, BSc; salesman; former associate athletic dir., basketball coach Concordia; all-state, hon, mention all-American football, basketball sr. year Franklin; mem. league champion baseball, basketball, football teams; leading scorer freshman basketball Clemson; mem. Orange, Sugar, Bluebonnet Bowl teams; coach basketball South Carolina Textile League; mem. Ottawa (CFL) '60-64, '60 Grey Cup champions, Montreal '64-66; coach Concordia basketball 328 wins, including 66 consecutive league games, 178 losses, 9 league titles, participated 7 ntl championships; football coach '71-75, '72 league title; res. Chateauguay, Que.

DAIGNEAULT, Julie (swimming); b. 25 Jun 1965, Montreal, Que.; freestyle specialist; 10 ntl titles, 1 Canada Cup title; mem. '82 CG, '83 FISU, PAG, '84 Olympic Games teams; bronze 400-, 800m FISU, 200-, 400-, 800m PAG; 3 ntl records; res. Pierrefonds, Que.

DAIGNEAULT, Réjean (harness racing); b. 19 Feb 1948, St. Damase, Que.; harness race driver; began career as groom for Hervé Filion at 16; went on his own after 7yrs; began driving 1973; noted for patented rocking style in sulky; best season '86 when he won 312 races including his 2000th victory; res. Yonkers, N.Y.

DAINES, Duane (rodeo); b. 15 Oct 1958, Innisfail, Alta; m. Cheryl; c. Jennifer, Bailey, Sydney; auctioneer; specialized in saddle bronc/calf roping; mem. CPRA from '79; 3 ntl all-around (AA) titles; 1 ntl SB title; 2 Copenhagen/Dodge tour SB titles; 1 Coors Chute-Out series SB title; 1 Calgary Stampede SB title; 2 Brahma Boot tour SB titles; 1 Sask.,

BC circuit SB titles; 1 Wrangler Jeans Rodeo Showdown SB title; 1 BC/Sask. circuit AA titles; CPRA cowboy of '95 award; paralyzed in Armstrong, BC rodeo accident '95; dir. CPRA; res. Innisfail, Alta.

DALES-SCHUMANN, Stacey (basketball); b. 6 Sep 1979, Collingwood, Ont.; m. Chris Schumann; Oklahoma BA; pro basketball player; 2 all-American; 2 Big 12 player of yr awards; team capt. Oklahoma; '02 Final Four all-star; WNBA Washington Mystics '02-05; ntl team '99-04; competed '99 PAG, '00 Olympics; Brockville award of merit; town declared Stacey Dales day; 2 Brockville sports person of yr awards; *ESPN* radio analyst; *USA Today* rookie analyst award; *ESPN Magazine* point guard of '02; *TSN* TV sideline reporter; academic honors 4 Dean's List, 3 President's Honor Roll; animal protection activist; res. Washington, D.C.

DALEY, Gail (gymnastics): b. 5 Apr 1946, Saskatoon, Sask.; m. Richard Bakker; c. Brian, Kerri; Southern Illinois, BSc, Montclair State MA, Kean Coll MA; speech language pathologist; spotted by coaches Mike Matich, Chuck Sebestyen during tumbling demonstration age 11; Sask. jr gymnastics title '59; Alta., Western Canada jr titles '60-61; mem. Cdn World Games team; 4 ntl sr. titles; mem. '63 (team silver, 2 individual bronze) PAG, '64 Olympic Games teams; moved to US winning several collegiate titles, 3 all-American honors; turned to coaching, officiating; coached Rutgers, Montclair State; officiated 2 International Special Olympics; volunteer Calgary '88 Olympics; Cdn female athlete of '64; Fed. of International Gymnastics pin; mem. Sask., Saskatoon Sports halls of fame; res. Washington, N.J.

DALEY, Jim (coaching): b. 15 Jul 1954, Ottawa, Ont.; m. Diane Hilko; Carleton, BA, Queen's, BEd; football coach; de jr. Ottawa Sooners '70-73, capt. '73 ntl finalists; lb Queen's '74-75; level 4 coaching cert.; began coaching St. Pat's HS Ottawa '76; asst. Carleton '79-81, St. Pius HS '78-82; head coach Sooners '82-84; UofOtt '85-90; asst. Ottawa (CFL) '91-93, Saskatchewan '94-95, head coach '96-98, asst. Calgary '00-03, Winnipeg '04, head coach '04-05; led Sooners to '84 ntl title; 2 OFC coach of yr, North East Regional Assn. coach of '84; 2 OQIFC coach-of-yr awards; res. Calgary, Alta./Winnipeg, Man.

DALLA RIVA, Peter (football); b. 11 Dec 1945, Fanzolo, Treviso, Italy; m. Carol; c. Mark, Lisa; ambassador Molson-O'Keefe; emigrated to Canada age 8; jr. Burlington Braves; sr. ORFU Oakville Knights; entire CFL career as te Montreal '68-81; 3 all-East, 3 all-Cdn te; twice nominee Outstanding Cdn, 1 Outstanding player nomination; Alouettes' leading receiver 5yrs; CFL record: 197 games, 450 receptions, 6413yds, 54tds, 340pts; all-star game MVP '73; 6 Grey Cup finals, 3 winners; jersey 74 ret'd by Alouettes; mem. Cdn Football Hall of Fame; res. Beaconsfield, Que.

DALTON, Chuck (basketball); b. 1 Sep 1927, Windsor, Ont.; given name: Charles Harwood; m. Marcia Lawton; c. Karen Ann, Charles Scott; UWO; ret'd. sales manager, real estate; of London Majors Sr. IC 3yrs, St. Thomas (IC), Frood (NO) 1yr each; basketball UWO, 2yrs Tillsonburg Livingstons; mem. '52 Olympic team; knee injury ended playing career; coach London Intermediates 1 season; pres. London Curling Club; res. London, Ont.

DAMPHOUSSE, Vincent (hockey); b. 17 Dec 1967, Montreal, Que.; centre Laval (QMJHL) '83-86; 2nd team all-star; played in '84 Memorial Cup; NHL Toronto '86-91, Edmonton '91-92, Montreal '92-99, San Jose '99-03, Colorado '04; played briefly in Germany '94-95; capt. Canadiens ('96-99); played in 4 NHL all-star games; all-star MVP '91; mem. '93 Stanley Cup winner; played in '89 worlds; reached 1000 points '00; NHL record: (through '04) 1378 scheduled games, 432g, 773a, 140 playoff games, 41g, 63a; scored 1st Molson Centre goal; mem. Team Canada '96 World Cup; 4-handicap golfer, scored ace '00; active in Shoot for Cure organization; res. Blainville, Que.

DANCEVIC, Frank (tennis); b. 26 Sep 1984, Niagara Falls, Ont.; tennis player; '94 -14 outdoor singles champ; '99 ntl indoor/outdoor doubles titles; 2 -16 indoor singles; '01 -18 indoor singles, doubles; in capturing '01 Wimbledon boy's doubles with Giovanni Lapentti, became only 5th Cdn. to win the Jr. Grand Slam title; ranked as high as 21 Jr. ITF singles, 3 doubles '02; 1st Cdn. teenager to qualify for ATP event when he made it through qualifying draw at Legg Mason Intl; won 1st pro title, 1st doubles trophy '03; 1st Cdn. to win $50,000 Granby Challenger title; 2nd straight $50,000 title at Fifth-Third Bank tourney; reached career-high 196 ranking on ATP Entry System; defeat of Brazilian Flavio Saretta advanced Canada to World Group 1st time in 11 years; 3-3 singles record in Davis Cup play; 10 ntl titles; Tennis Canada Excellence Award '02; res. Niagara Falls, Ont.

DANDURAND, Leo (entrepreneur); b. 9 Jul 1889, Bourbonnais, Ill.; d. 26 Jun 1964, Montreal, Que.; given name: Joseph Viateur; emigrated to Canada age 16; refereed in NHA; administrator Montreal minor hockey; among founders CAHA '14; part owner Montreal Canadiens '21 (team won 3 Stanley Cups); highly respected by sports, business peers; instrumental in introducing deferred penalty rule; governor IIHF Hall of Fame from '47; active in horse racing; among group who owned 17 race tracks including Montreal's Blue Bonnets; with Lew Hayman developed Montreal Alouettes; dir. Montreal Royals baseball club; promoted boxing, wrestling in Montreal area; governor Notre Dame Hospital; mem. Montreal Chamber of Commerce; pres. Montclair-Richelieu Springwater

DANEYKO, Ken (hockey); b. 17 Apr 1964, Windsor, Ont.; m. Jonna Lyn; c. Taylor Lyn, Shane; defence St. Albert (AJHL), Spokane (WHL) '80-81, Seattle (WHL) '82-83, Kamloops (WHL) '83, Maine (AHL) '84-86; New Jersey 2nd draft choice '82; NHL New Jersey '84-03; NHL record: 1283 scheduled games, 36g, 142a, 162 playoff games, 5g, 17a; 2 Stanley Cup winners; had 388 consec. games streak; awarded 2000 Bill Masterton trophy; record 256 games without scoring goal; works with Children's Miracle Network; missed bulk of '97-98 season after voluntarily entering NHL/NHLPA substance abuse program; res. Cherry Hill, N.J.

DANIAR, Stephen (wrestling); b. 18 Jul 1955, Ft. William, Ont.; m. Leslie Bell; Laurentian, Lakehead, BEd, MEd; educator; 1 ntl jr., 5 sr. titles; mem. '76, '80 Olympic, '77-78 World Cup teams; gold 197lbs '78 CG, bronze '79 PAG, '77, '79 Cerra Pelado Cups, '78 World Cup; mem. '78 Mexico world championships team; 4 Thunder Bay achievement awards; most valuable NWO wrestler '78;

Thunder Bay male athlete of '79; mem. '81 Northwestern Ont. indoor soccer title team; coached Lakehead wrestlers '82-85, teams won 4 GPAC titles; named jr. coach of '82, GPAC coach of year '84-85; came out of retirement to win Commonwealth Wrestling Championship gold '85; mem. NWO Sports, Cdn Amateur Wrestling halls, Lakehead U Sports Wall of Fame; res. Thunder Bay, Ont.

DANIEL, Babe (basketball); b. 30 May 1917, Camrose, Alta.; d. 4 Oct 1995, Edmonton, Alta.given name: Muriel; m. George Lineham (d); c. Susan, Marilyn; ret'd hospital supervisor; competitive golfer, bowler, softball player; mem. famed Edmonton Grads basketball team '37-39; mem. Canadian Basketball, Alta. Sports halls of fame.

DANIELS, Danny (t&f/builder): b. 11 Jan 1929, Greater Yarmouth, Norfolk, Eng.; given name: Edwin Robert; m. Marjorie Joyce Gillings; c. Kristi Jane, Kent Jonathan; UAlta, BEd, PhD; consultant/actor; running specialist; '45-51 won varied UK jr/sr titles 440yds-mile distances; moved to Canada winning variety of road running/race walking/ LJ/HJ/pentathlon titles at regional/ntl/world levels; 12 ntl, 4 NA, 1 Pan-American masters titles; Level 3 NCCP coach; Nigerian ntl distance program head coach '73-75; Team Yukon head coach '89-90; meet dir. Pan-Am, NA, Cdn, US International t&f meets; ntl Run Canada comm. '79-96; pres. Cdn Masters Athletic Assn '83-85; pres. Athletics Yukon '86-90; v-p. BC Athletics '95-96, pres. '97-98, BC Seniors Games Society from '96; curator Cdn Road Running Hall of Fame '91-96; 3M coaching award '96; Edinburgh Harriers Outstanding Athlete award '48; mem. Cdn Road Running Hall of Fame; res. Sidney, B.C./Green Valley, Ariz.

DANN, Etta (basketball): b. 9 Mar 1914, Edmonton, Alta.; d. 1978 High River, Alta.; m. Leland Sodererg; c. Eddie; ret'd. secretary; standout softball player; mem. famed Edmonton Grads women's basketball team; mem. Alta. Sports, Cdn Basketball halls of fame.

DANYCHUK, Bill (football); b. 29 Aug 1940, Timmins, Ont.; given name: William D'Arcy; m. Audrey Ann Dawdy; c. Maria Deanna, William Clayton; Tenn, BA; ret'd. pres. D'Arcy Enterprises, v-p. Bazaar & Novelty Co.; all-star basketball, football, track, MVP basketball, football Niagara Dist. HS; og Tennessee '62-64; mem. Tiger-Cats '65-75; 10 times all-star; Ticat MVP '68; mem. Hamilton best team of century; v-p. CFL Players' Assn. 7yrs; ex-dir. World Bingo League; mem. Ukranian Sports Hall of Fame; res. Oakville, Ont.

DANYLUK, Terry (volleyball/coaching); b. 1960, Tofield, Alta.; m. Lori; UAlta. volleyball coach; setter ntl team '78, '81-84, UAlta '78-81; competed '82 Worlds, '84 Olympics; mem. UAlta CIAU title team '81; pro Japan's Suntory Club, Japan Cup title '85; Mulhouse, France '86; Leysin, Switzerland '88-91, 4 Swiss Cup titles; 4 Swiss, 1 Japan, 2 CIAU player-of-yr awards; 1 CIAU, ntl tournament MVP awards; '81 CIAU all-Canadian, UAlta outstanding-male-athlete-of-yr awards; began coaching UAlta '91, 2 CIAU, CWUAA coach-of- yr; 1 ntl title; mem. UAlta Sports Wall of Fame; res. Edmonton, Alta.

DARCH, Art (football); b. 15 Oct 1931, Niagara Falls, Ont.; given name: Arthur Clifford; m. Joyce Sharp; c. Kelly, Jay,

Shannon, Darcy; insurance co. pres.; standout HS football, basketball, track; athlete-of-yr awards '51-52; rejected Mich track scholarship for pro football Hamilton; 1ˢᵗ string og '52-58, missed '59 with injury, Toronto '60-62; mem. 4 Grey Cup finalists, 2 winners; Dominion HS t&f titles '50-51; Ont. jr. shot put, discus, OFSSA discus titles '51; pres. Tiger-Cats QB Club '66-72; freelance radio-TV sportscaster from '63; active in Niagara region minor football program; mem. Brantford Sports Hall of Recognition, Stamford CI, NF Sports walls of fame; res. Burlington, Ont.

DARLING, Dora (golf); b. 11 Aug 1904, Montreal, Que.; d. 19 Nov 1997, London, Ont.; given name: Dora Jean Virtue; m. Arthur Balfour Darling (d); c. Judy, Mary, Brian; women's Canadian Open, runnerup Closed '36; 3 Quebec women's, 3 ntl sr. women's titles.

DARLING, Judy (golf); b. 6 Oct 1937, Montreal, Que.; given name: Judith Kathleen; div. John Douglas Evans; c. Kathy, Cindy, Tracey, Daphne; McGill, BSc; nurse; Quebec Ladies titles '57-61, '72; ntl jr. '57; ntl women's closed '60; ntl women's open '60-61; res. Boca Raton, Fla.

DARRAGH, Jack (hockey); b. 4 Dec 1890, Ottawa, Ont.; d. 28 Jun 1924, Ottawa, Ont.; given name: John Proctor; m. Elizabeth; c. Aileen, Frances, Marion; accountant, poultry breeder; amateur Fort Coulonge, Ottawa Cliffsides; pro Ottawa '11 Stanley Cup champions; mem. Super Six, capt. several Ottawa teams; mem. 4 Stanley Cup winners; on line with Frank Nighbor, Cy Denneny; shifted to lw when Punch Broadbent joined line; brother Harold also played in NHL; career total 195 goals including 24 in one 22-game season; mem. Ottawa Sports, Canadian Hockey halls of fame.

DARWIN, Howard (entrepreneur); b. 10 Sep 1931, Ottawa, Ont.; given name: Howard Joseph; m. Constance Goudie; c. Kim, Nancy, Jack, Jeff; ret'd. jeweller; 30-35 amateur bouts Beaver Boxing Club; switched to refereeing, promoting fights, managing fighters; promotions included wrestling, closed-circuit TV boxing matches; invested in jr. A hockey with formation Ottawa 67's, part-owner; purchased London Gardens, London Jr. A hockey team; remained in hockey through '98; brought Triple A baseball Lynx to Ottawa '93; IL exec. of '95; sold Lynx '00; 1 Memorial Cup, 1 IL championship team; Ottawa ACT Earl Bullis Achievement award '98; ex-trustee Ottawa Sports Hall of Fame; mem. Ottawa Sports Hall of Fame; res. Ottawa, Ont.

DASOVIC, Nick (soccer); b. 5 Dec 1968, Vancouver B.C.; coach; midfielder; 2yrs North York (CSL); '92 CSL all-star; mem. APSL Montreal Impact title team '94; played with Saint-Brieuc (France) '95, FC Treleborgs (Sweden) '96, Vancouver 86ers '96, St. Johnston Scottish 1ˢᵗ div. '96-98, Scottish League finalists '98; player/asst. coach Vancouver Whitecaps '02-03; asst. coach ntl -20 team '03; made ntl team debut '92; 57 international caps; res. Burnaby, B.C.

DATTILIO, Gerry (football); b. 11 Jun 1953, Chomedy, Que.; Northern Colorado; Verdun jrs.; coll. career record more than 4000yds total offence; pro Montreal '75-81, '84, Calgary '82-83; lb/sb/db/receiver before becoming starting qb Alouettes '78; 2 Grey Cup finals; Schenley outstanding Canadian award '80; CFL record: 684 completions on 1246 attempts for 9825yds, 75int, 53tds; 187 carries for 996yds,

8tds; 7 receptions for 113yds, 0tds; 4 fumble recoveries for 1yd, 1td; res. Montreal, Que.

DAVID, Tracy (soccer/coaching); b. 21 Jan 1960, Tomslake, B.C.; UAlta, BPHE, BEd; soccer coach UAlta; played with Tomslake Strikers girls team at 15; rfbAjax -18 ntl championships team '78; statistician UAlta Golden Bears '78-79; with Heather Rennebohm organized university women's club team (Edmonton Angels) winning 6 ntl club titles in 10yrs, 5 in succession '82-86; team capt. 8yrs; fb ntl women's team '86-90; began lobbying for UAlta women's soccer program '82; capt. 1ˢᵗ UAlta women's team '83; helped in organization of women's university league; head coach UAlta '85-00; 4 conference, 2 ntl CIAU titles; 3 CWUAA, 1 CIAU coach-of-yr award; joined Edmonton Azzure team as a player in '91; pres. CIAU women's Soccer Coaches Assn '87-95; asst. coach ntl -17 team '01-03; BC -17 head coach '02; mem. UAlta Sports Wall of Fame; res. Edmonton, Alta.

DAVIDSON, Bob (hockey); b. 10 Feb 1912, Toronto, Ont.; d. 26 Sep 1996, Toronto, Ont.; given name: Robert Edgar; m. Tanis; c. Bob, Jim, Tom; ret'd hockey executive; Jr. A Toronto Canoe Club '29-32; sr. Marlboros '32-33, Toronto All-Stars '33-34; pro Maple Leafs '34-46, capt. '45; mem. 2 Stanley Cup winners; coached Leafs' Pittsburgh farm club '47-50; chief Leafs scout '51, dir. player personnel; J.P. Bickell Leafs' outstanding service award '95; soccer several years Toronto East End club.

DAVIDSON, Chris (rowing); b. 24 Oct 1971, Toronto, Ont.; Queen's, BSc, Victoria, MSc; x-country runner who turned to rowing in high school; won ntl straight pair, 4s titles '95; gold US lightweight 8s '93; bronze lightweight straight 4s '93 world university, straight pair '94 CG; silver straight 4s '95 PAG; competed '96 Olympic Games; ntl team from '93; res. Victoria, B.C.

DAVIDSON, Scotty (hockey); b. 1892, Kingston, Ont.; d. 6 Jun 1915, France; given name: Allan; learned hockey under game's originator James T. Sutherland in Kingston; led Kingston Frontenacs to OHA title '10-11; pro Toronto Blueshirts (NHA) '12-14; 19 goals 20 games '12-13, 24 goals '13-14 leading Toronto to Stanley Cup; killed in action WW1; mem. Hockey Hall of Fame.

DAVIES, Bill (football); b. 1916, Montreal, Que.; d. 28 May 1990, Montreal, Que.; m. Chris; c. Patricia (Trish); starred in football, hockey, lacrosse, softball, baseball; backfielder Montreal noted for two-way play, toughness; Jeff Russel Trophy '39; softball, baseball MVP awards, batting titles; hockey jr., sr. Royals; def Sr. Royals '39 Allan Cup finalists; mem. Canadians, Verdun lacrosse league teams; co-founder NDG Maple Leafs jr. football team; 13yrs coach Lakeshore Flyers, Cdn intermediate champions '53.

DAVIES, Jack (administration); b. 1897, Paris, France; d. 22 Jul 1978, Montreal, Que.; m. Winnifred Hurdman; c. John Bruce; businessman, soldier; more than 300 trophies, medals, prizes in t&f, swimming, water polo, badminton, tennis, table tennis, boxing, equestrian, sailing from childhood to '63; 20yrs mem. Cdn t&f comm, officiated '34 BEG; mem., dir. mgr. numerous CG, PAG, Olympic teams '34-76; 14 times official Canadian delegate BE, CG

Fed.; v-p. Que. Branch AAUofC 17yrs; co-founder, life mem. QTFA; pres., life mem. AAUofC; only Canadian ever elected to IAAF; 1st Canadian v-p. CG Fed. '70-76; pres. Canadian CGA from '53; mem. advisory board, life mem. COA; chairman Commonwealth records comm. from '52; 1st Canadian, charter mem., world t&f Statisticians Assn. from '50; life mem. CTFA, ILTC, QLTF, UKOA, AAU, Canadian Bobsleigh and Luge Assn., SFC, CAWA; chairman Canadian Amateur Sports Hall of Fame; honored by numerous provincial, national, world sports bodies; co-founder MAAA mixed badminton club, KofC badminton club, owner, coach Notre Dame de Grace badminton club; Officer Order of Canada '71; mem. Cdn Olympic Sports, Cdn Aquatic, Helms halls of fame.

DAVIES, Jim (cycling); b. 8 Jan 1906, London, Eng.; d. 11 Jul 1999, Vancouver, B.C.; given name: James Arthur; m. Vera Beatrice Newport; c. Shirley Edith, Diane Estelle; ret'd sales rep.; BC bicycle champion '25-28, ntl champion '27-28; equalled world record '28 Olympics; *Vancouver Province, Victoria Colonist* cups; rode in last competitive race at 43; co-chair cycling comm. '54 BEG; ran China Creek track 5yrs; numerous exec. positions BC Track Cycle Assn.; mem. BC Sports Hall of Fame.

DAVIES, Rod (sailing): b. 17 Nov 1969, Ajax, Ont.; York; Only Cdn to win gold at world youth championships; twice Cdn youth titlist; Canada Games gold '89; CORK gold '90; competed Flying Dutchman class '91 PAG, 4 world championships; won 6 regatta titles '94 before suffering major back injury which recovered to qualify in Laser class for '96 Olympics; brother Ray also Laser sailor; Town of Pickering recognition award '94; 2 Ont., ntl, 1 world achievement awards; res. Pickering, Ont.

DAVIS, Clark (wrestling); b. 15 May 1957, Calgary, Alta.; Concordia; ntl jr. 82kg freestyle, Greco-Roman title '76; ntl jr. GR 90kg '77; Pan-Am jr. 82kg FS, 90kg GR '76; bronze '77 jr. world 82kg FS, silver '79 PAG 82kg FS, silver '81 FISU Games 90kg FS; 10 ntl sr. FS titles; '81 82kg FS Skopje tournament; '82 90kg World Cup title; silver 90kg worlds, gold 90kg CG '82; mem. '84 Olympic team; Que. athlete of '82; fed. govt. excellence award '83; mem. Cdn Amateur Wrestling Hall of Fame; res. Montreal, Que.

DAVIS, Pat (coaching); b. 15 Jan 1936, Windsor, Ont.; given name: Patricia Ann; UofT, BPHE, North Carolina, MEd, OCE; ret'd. phys ed teacher; varsity basketball UofT, softball, basketball in Windsor; dir. women's athletics Waterloo; coach Athena volleyball team; coach Waterloo AA senior women's '75 Ont. title team; Windsor W.F. Herman CI volleyball, basketball, track, gymnastics teams '58-66; CVA coaching comm. chair. '75-78; past coaching chair. Ont. Volleyball Assn.; OWIAA pres. '79-80; chaired comm. which led to amalgamation of OQWCIA and WIAU to form OWIAA; CIAU constitution comm. chair. '80-81; res. Waterloo, Ont.

DAVIS, Penny (sailing); b. 2 Mar 1968, Carlisle, Eng.; given name: Penny Jane Stamper; m. Scott Davis; UBC; 3 consecutive Cdn youth Laser II titles; Canada Games gold '95; with partner Sarah McLean competed '92 Olympics in 470 class; joined with Leigh Pearson '93; gold '95 PAG; competed '96 Olympics; BC sailor of '94; CYA female athlete of '92; res. Vancouver, B.C.

DAVIS, Victor (swimming); b. 10 Feb 1964, Guelph, Ont.; d. 13 Nov 1989, Montreal, Que; splashed onto international aquatic scene at 17 winning '81 NZ gold; 30 ntl titles in 100m, 200m breaststroke, 200m butterfly, 200m, 400m IM; NZ 100m butterfly, 200m breaststroke, 2 US, 2 Canada Cup, 1 Swedish 200m breaststroke, 1 US, Canada Cup 100m breaststroke titles; 7 Cdn, 4 world, 1 CG records; gold '82 worlds, CG, '84 Olympic Games 200m breaststroke, silver 100m breaststroke '82 CG, '84 Olympic Games; WR 2:13.34 200m breaststroke '84 Olympics; silver 4x100 medley relay '84, '88 Olympics; 3 Swim Canada athlete of yr awards; Ont. excellence award, fed. govt. world champion award '83; killed in hit-and-run accident; mem. Order of Canada, Cdn, Ont, International Aquatic, Cdn Olympic, Waterloo County, Ont. Legends, Canada's Sports halls of fame.

DAWSON, Andre (baseball); b. 10 Jul 1954, Miami, Fla.; given name: Andre Nolan; m. Vanessa Turner; c. Daries, Amber; Florida A&M; drafted Montreal '75; outfield regular Expos '77-88, Chicago Cubs '89-92, Boston '93-94, Florida '95-96; ML record 2627 scheduled games, 9927ab, 1373r, 2774h, 503db, 98tr, 438hr, 1591rbi, 314sb, .279ba; NL rookie of year, *Sporting News* rookie of year; Expos' all-time run, triples leader, 2nd to Gary Carter home runs; 3 Silver Bat, 8 Gold Glove awards; NL MVP '87, twice runnerup; *SN* NL player of '81; 3 Expos player of year awards; shared ML record 2 HRs single inning, club record 19-game hitting streak, 3 doubles 1 game, 2 triples 1 game, 6 hits doubleheader; mem. '81 div. title team; 8 all-star games; hampered by knee surgery following '83 season; uniform #10 ret'd by Expos (2nd time since same number worn by Rusty Staub also ret'd); nicknamed "Hawk"; 1 of only 4 ML players with 300 or more hrs, sbs; mem. Cdn Baseball, Expos halls of fame; res. Miami, Fla.

DAWSON, Bob (football); b. 4 Feb 1932, Windsor, Ont.; m. Louise Bennett; c. Debbie, Lori; consulting firm owner; leading scorer AKO Windsor 3 consecutive years including ntl jr. title '52; Tiger-Cats '53-59, rookie of '53; coached Burlington Braves to jr. league title '60; coached McMaster 4 league titles '61-65; res. Ancaster, Ont.

DAWSON, Earl (administration); b. 17 Dec 1925, St. Boniface, Man.; d. 28 Mar 1987, Winnipeg, Man.; m. Madeline O'Callaghan; c. William, Patrick, Nancy, Donald, Randall; regional rep. Fitness & Amateur Sport; pres. MAHA '59-63; chair. CAHA rules comm. '63-66; v-p minor hockey CAHA '66-67; v-p junior hockey CAHA '67-68; pres. CAHA '69-71; chair. Centennial midget hockey championship '67; initiated, chaired 1st ntl referee's clinic '63-64; initiated congress for all levels of hockey in CAHA '69; left international hockey scene '70 to assume duties with Fitness & Amateur Sport; *Brandon Sun* sportsman of '62; USAHA citation '70; life mem. CAHA; mem. Man. Hockey Hall of Fame.

DAWSON, Eddie (basketball); b. 10 Oct 1907, Alford, Lincolnshire County, Eng.; d. 1968, Windsor, Ont.; Detroit; outstanding gd, floor leader; mem. Cdn champion Windsor Alumni '28, Windsor Ford '36 teams; mem. Cdn Olympic silver medal team '36; coach Windsor Patterson CI 36yrs coaching such standouts as Bill Rogin, Jimmy Farmer, Fred Thomas, Bob Simpson, Tommy Grant and Zeno Karcz;

coached Patterson '35 championship track team; mem. Windsor-Essex Sports Hall of Fame.

DAY, Hap (hockey); b. 14 Jun 1901, Owen Sound, Ont.; d. 17 Feb 1990, St. Thomas, Ont.; given name: Clarence Henry; UofT; pharmacist; jr. Midland, Ont.; sr. Hamilton; pro Toronto St. Pat's '24; 33 years involved with hockey as player, coach, referee, GM; teamed with King Clancy on Maple Leafs def; record 4 goals single game by def '29, broken '77 by Leafs' Ian Turnbull; capt. 1ˢᵗ Toronto Stanley Cup winner '32; NHL record: 581 scheduled games, 86g, 116a, 53 playoff games, 4g, 7a; coached West Toronto Nationals '36 Memorial Cup; closed competitive career NY Americans '38; refereed 2 seasons then rejoined Leafs as coach, 5 Stanley Cups, 3 in succession; Toronto mgr. '50-57; mem. Hockey Hall of Fame.

DAY, James (equestrian); b. 7 Jul 1946, Thornhill, Ont.; div.; c. Catherine, Richard; farm manager, horse trainer; operates Day by Day racing stable at Woodbine; mem. ntl team '64-77; individual gold '67, team silver '75 PAG; team gold '68 Olympics; tied world puissance record 7'3" NY '66, Toronto '68; mem. winning world Prix des Nations team '70; NA 3-day title '73; '66-68 horseman of yr; mem. '68, '72, '76 Olympic teams; turned to horse training working primarily for Sam-Son Farms 20yrs; trained Dance Smartly, Sky Classic to Breeders' Cup, Eclipse awards; 5 Labatt Woodbine Oaks titles; 4 US trainer-of-month awards; 4 Sovereign trainer awards; mem. Cdn Olympic, Canada's Sports halls of fame; res. Everett, Ont.

DAZE, Eric (hockey); b. 2 Jul 1975, Montreal, Que.; m. Guylaine; lw/rw Laval Regents (QAAA)'90-92, Beauport (QMJHL) '92-95; 5ᵗʰ choice Chicago '93 draft; NHL Chicago '95-04; NHL record (through '04) 600 scheduled games, 226g, 172a, 37 playoff games, 5g, 7a; twice QMJHL 1ˢᵗ team all-star; CHL Most Sportsmanlike Player of '95; gold Team Canada '95 world jr.; Viscount Alexander award '95; *SN* rookie of yr award; NHL all-rookie team '96; Frank Selke trophy '95; res. Chicago, Ill.

de ROUSSAN, Hugues (handball); b. 23 Mar 1955, Montreal, Que.; m. Annie Blanc; c. Vincent; Montreal, BSc; journalist; ntl team '74-80; Que. team '74-80; Latine Cup '75; mem. '76 Olympic, '76, '77, '80 Americas Cup, '78 world championships; coached variety Que. handball teams; mem. Cdn delegation '82 Olympic Academy; res. Montreal, Que.

de ST. CROIX, Ted (orienteering); b. 30 Aug 1957, Vineland, Ont.; m. Maureen Crowley; Trent, BSc, Carleton; computer programmer; boys -14 Ont. title; 2ⁿᵈ NA boys 15-16 '71; Ont. boys 15-16 '72; NA jr. men '73; men's 17-18 Goteborg Sweden '74; Swedish men's 17-18, Ont. elite '75; US elite '76; 18yrs in top 3 in elite category '74-91; 13 ntl elite (11 in succession) '76-87, 4 NA elite titles; competed 9 worlds; best-ever finish by non-European 10ᵗʰ worlds '85; 2ⁿᵈ Asia-Pacific championships '84; res. White Rock, B.C.

DEACON, Bruce (t&f); b. 5 Dec 1966, Ottawa, Ont.; m. Rosemary; c. Robbie, John; SFU; B.C. Independent Schools coordinator; long-distance runner; ntl team from '91; represented Canada 10,000m '91 FISU Games; gold '95, silver '92 10,000m ntls; silver '03 PAG; competed '94

CG, '96, '00 Olympics marathon, 4 world championships; qualified for '98 CG but withdrew due to injury; won '00 ntl capital/Cdn marathon titles; 2ⁿᵈ '02 NC marathon; marathon silver '03 PAG; res. Victoria, B.C.

DEACON, Tom (all-around); b. 21 Dec 1917, Ottawa, Ont.; d. 20 Jul 1993, Ottawa, Ont.; m. Irene Rich; c. Judy, Tom, Doug; jr. hockey Ottawa; RCAF Flyers '39-43; Service League all-star RCAF Rockcliffe; playing-coach RCAF Uplands '50-52; mem. interior BC, Yukon title teams '52-53; coached RCAF Downsview '54-55; mem. Ottawa Old Stars, Sr. Olympics (over 55) title team '78; from '53 officiated English pro league, ODHA; conducted officiating schools Canada, Europe; mem. RCAF service football title teams '40-41; Ottawa Combined ORFU '43; soccer Corinthians, United Ottawa Sr. City League; highly-rated amateur welterweight boxer '35-39; gold over 55 class '76, 60+ class '80 National Capital marathon.

DEADMARSH, Adam (hockey); b. 10 May 1975, Trail, B.C.; m. Christa; c. Alexis, Madison; forward Beaver Valley (KIJHL) '90-91, Portland (WHL) '91-94; 2ⁿᵈ choice Quebec '93 draft; NHL Quebec '94-95, Colorado '95-01, Los Angeles '01-03; NHL record 567 scheduled games, 184g, 189a, 105 playoff games, 26g, 40a; mem. '96 Stanley Cup winner; '98, '02 (silver) U.S. Olympic team; organized charity golf tournament; dual citizenship; res. Trail, B.C.

DEAKIN, Bobby (baseball/football); b. 15 Dec 1934, London, Ont.; given name: Robert John; m. Danoise Dianne Simpson; c. Rob, Jamie; ret'd. fireman; ss Ont. peewee, bantam, midget all-star title teams; scouted by several ML teams and was signed by Boston Red Sox only to have contract voided under a rule prohibiting signing high school players; at 16 became youngest to play in Sr. IC; played short with London Majors Sr. IC '51-54; all-star '53-54; Majors MVP award; signed by NY Yankee organization '54; played with Birmingham (Southern Assn.)'55; broken back ended '56 season but came back to play with Binghampton (Eastern) '57; Richmond (AAA) '58-59; broken hand suffered in '59 ended career; part-time coach London Majors '60-74; scout Montreal Expos '76, Toronto Blue Jays '77-79; from '80 conducted baseball clinics for Blue Water Baseball Assn.; a standout football all-conf. running back; mem. unbeaten London Central WOSSA Purple Bowl title team '52; res. London, Ont.

DEALY, Wendy (softball); b. 4 Sep 1955, Chatham, N.B.; given name: Wendy Winnifred Marion; St. John Community Coll.; group home counselor; dabbled in recreational curling, golf but softball was big love; played competitively '68-87; attended 14 ntl sr./jr. championships, '73 Canada Games; HS female athlete of yr award; MVP, top pitcher award '75 ntl jr. silver winner; top pitcher '76 jr. ntls; several top pitcher/MVP trophies at provincial level; 19yr career record 607 games played, 542 pitched with 489-49-4 record; 13 of her losses were to men's teams; N.B Softball Assn. Awards '75-76; Governor-General's Celebrations '88 medal; mem. N.B. Sports, Softball halls of fame; res. Miramichi, N.B.

DEAN, Bob (football); b. 17 Dec 1929, Pittsburgh, Pa.; given name: Robert Wadsworth; m. Shirley Anne Donaldson; c. Geoffrey, Matthew, Clayton; Maryland, BSc, UAlta, BEd,

MEd; school administrator; contributed field goal, game-winning convert Edmonton's 26-25 '54 Grey Cup victory over Montreal; Ted Reeve's all-Canadian rating '55; 5yrs mem. Alta. volleyball team; res. Edmonton, Alta.

DEAN, Geordie (lacrosse); b. 8 Dec 1960, New Westminster, B.C.; firefighter; mem. Coquitlam Jr. A '78-81, Richmond Woodies from '82, New Westminster Salmonbellies from '82, ntl team from '85; 2 Mike Kelly Mann Cup MVP awards, 8 league all-stars; 2 Labatt/CP Air awards; 2 Maitland, 1 Huddleston scoring title trophy; 3 Commissioner's trophy Western Lacrosse Assn. MVP, 2 Ellison trophy WLA playoff MVP awards; res. New Westminster, B.C.

DeBENEDETTI, Tania (wrestling); b. 30 Dec 1972, Hamilton, Ont.; m. David Mair; McMaster CPed; certified trainer, Bio-Ped Foot Care Centre, wrestling coach; competes at 46kg level; 2 ntl sr. titles; gold '96 NYAC open; res. Hamilton, Ont.

DeBLONDE, Clare (curling); b. 8 Jan 1943, Swan Lake, Man.; m. Irene Yackel; prov. govt. accountant; runnerup Man. schoolboy title '59; youngest skip Man. bonspiel winner '66; Man. 'spiel winner '72; skip '76 Man. Consols winner, Brier runnerup; 3rd for Earle Morris '80 Man. Brier entry; coach '84 Brier champion Mike Riley rink; res. West St. Paul, Man.

DeBLONDE, Garry (curling); b. 28 Jun 1940, Swan Lake, Man.; m. Diana Wookey; c. Joel, Riley, Karen; UMan, hons. BSc, MSc, PhD; teacher; mem. 4 Man., 2 ntl mixed title rinks; 2 Man. Brier entries; twice mem. Man. bonspiel title rink; '75 Man. carspiel title; twice mem. Ont. Labatt Tankard playdown rinks; pres. Winnipeg Heather CC '72; 8yrs mem. MCA exec. council; v.-chair. CCA Pepsi Jr. championships '80-81; technical dir. Curl Canada '80-86, '88-90; developed, supervised '88 Olympic curling program '87-88; res. Winnipeg, Man.

DÉCARIE, Al (boxing); b. 22 Apr 1916, Montreal, Que.; d. 1996, Montreal, Que.; m. Rita Couture; c. Joan, Dennis; office mgr., purchasing agent; active boxer '28-35; coach Montcalm Boxing Club '36-41; pro referee '38-51; coach Palestre Nationale '45-51; v-p QABA '51-60, pres. '61-64; chair. CABA '61-67; dir. COA '61-67; dir. Palestre Nationale, Paul Sauve Centre '55-71; mgr/coach ntl boxing team '63 PAG, '66 CG, '68 Olympics; media liaison '76 Olympic boxing; v-p Old Timers Boxing Group Inc; boxing event whip '78 CG; pres. Montreal Region ABA '76-82; AAUofC citation '54; Montreal Sportsmen's Assn. award of merit '57; O'Keefe award, US Navy appreciation certificate '67; BCABA exec. of decade award '70; life mem. BCABA.

DECKERT, Merv (handball); b. 9 Mar 1949, Winnipeg, Man.; m. Shirley (d); c. Kelly, Paul, Christine; m. Colleen; c. Jesse; UMan., BSc, BEd; ret'd. teacher, ED Man. Handball Assn.; excelled in baseball, volleyball, hockey, basketball, badminton, soccer and golf; turned attention to handball while at UMan; 10 ntl open/closed titles; '84 world title; '91, '97 world masters (40+); world golden masters (50+) '00; Manitoba male athlete of '84; mem. Man. Order of Buffalo, provost of hunt '94; mem. Man. Sports Hall of Fame; res. Winnipeg, Man.

DECSI, Laszlo (shooting); b. 22 Dec 1934, Budapest, Hungary; m. Donna; c. Sharon, Cindy, Michael; became an amputee '72; without benefit of a coach began pistol shooting '74; mem. ntl SFC hand gun team '75-99, ntl disabled team from '88; ntl titles, 1 air pistol, 1 standard, 3 centre-fire, 1 Cdn 1800 .22 cal., 3 centre-fire, 1 grand aggregate titles; 3 Benito Juarez gold; 4 Australian, 1 British, 5 European Masters, 3 Windsor indoor, 5 Cdn masters; twice high visitor US nationals; represented Canada 4 Paralympics; official '76 Montreal Olympics; competed in 1st world air gun championships for disabled '84; sport pistol world record '93 wheelchair worlds; ntl indoor centre-fire record 594/600; 2 world amputee records; chair. International Sports Organization for Disabled 8yrs; proficient archer; res. Tweed, Ont.

DEGLAU, Jessica (swimming); b. 27 May 1980, Vancouver, B.C.; UBC BA; butterfly specialist; mem. ntl team '95-98; competed '96, '00 Olympics, '98 CG, '99 PAG; Canada Cup 200m fly gold '96; 100m, 200m fly gold Rio de Janiero '95; silver '95 Summer nationals; 2 gold '98 Winter nationals; World Cup short-course 200m fly gold '98; 2 indiv., 2 team bronze '98 CG; 2 individual, 2 relay gold, 2 silver '99 PAG, 2 Cdn records; academic all-Cdn; res. Vancouver, B.C.

DeGRUCHY, John (football); b. 15 Dec 1860, Toronto, Ont.; d. 1940, Toronto, Ont.; exec. with Toronto AC, Toronto Rugby and Athletic Assn.; organized Toronto city football series among Argos, Balmy Beach, Varsity and donated Reg DeGruchy Memorial trophy for the competition; promoted Thanksgiving Day Classic between Sarnia Imperials and Balmy Beach; driving force behind 6-man football which would become popular at senior level during '40's; served Cdn football in various capacities for 50yrs; charter mem. Cdn Football Hall of Fame.

DEKDEBRUN, Al (football); b. 11 May 1921, Buffalo, N.Y.; given name: Allen Edward; m. Corinne Scoones; c. Gregory, Rick; Cornell, BSc; ret'd. chair. Niagara Frontier Transportation Authority; all-American qb Cornell '45; Coffman award '46 East-West Shrine Game MVP; mem. '46 college all-star team; 3yrs US All-American Conf.; 6rs CFL Toronto, Hamilton, Ottawa; mem. '50 Argos Grey Cup winner; coached Canisius College, UofBuffalo; potentate Ismailia Shrine Temple Buffalo; only man to have won both Coffman, Hollingbery awards; res. Williamsville, N.Y.

DELAHANTY, Megan (rowing); b. 24 Mar 1968, Edmonton, Alta.; UBC; Cdn Henley coxless 4s, 8s gold '90; US Ntl 8s gold '91; world championships 8s gold '91; CARA Centennial medal '91; 2 Dick Ellis Memorial awards; mem. Cdn Olympic Hall of Fame; res. Vancouver, B.C.

DELAHEY, Wally (football/coaching); b. 23 Sep 1932, Toronto, Ont.; given name: Wallace Allan; m. Patricia Ann Fowler; c. Karen, Diane, Jill, Brian; UWO, BPHE, OCE; ret'd AD Waterloo; entire Humberside CI football career on undefeated team; excelled at basketball, t&f, gymnastics, swimming; 4yrs varsity football, 1yr swimming; 6yrs HS coach; Waterloo coach '64-81, AD '89-94; pres. K-W branch CAHPER '63-64; pres. Canadian Football Coaches Assn. '69; mem. all-Canadian Football Selection Comm. '72-76; v-p CIAU '89-90, pres. '90-92; CIAU dir. '90-94; asst. CdM '87 FISU Games, CdM '91; chair. Canadian Red Cross

Society water safety services Kitchener branch '64-69; secty.-treas. Twin Cities HSAA '62-66; waterfront dir. Camp Tawingo Huntsville '69-76; v-p Canadian Universities Football Coaches Assn. '79-81; mem. CAFA rules comm. '77-78; Waterloo honor award; mem. Waterloo Sports Hall of Fame; res. Waterloo, Ont.

DELAMARRE, Victor (weightlifting); b. 1888, Lac St. Jean, Que.; d. 1955, Montreal, Que.; m., c. 4 sons, 6 daughters; pro strongman/wrestler/policeman; following footsteps of idol Louis Cyr joined Montreal Police Force despite size, 5'6", 145lbs; lifted world record 309.5lbs one hand '14; with 1 finger lifted 201lbs; lifted platforms with 60 people weighing 7000lbs; pro wrestler from '31, reported to have had 1500 bouts; mem. Canada's Sports Hall of Fame.

DELANEY, Jack (boxing); b. 18 Mar 1900, St. Francis, Que.; d. 27 Nov 1948, Katanah, N.Y.; given name: Ovila Chapdelaine; pro at 19 adopting name Delaney when ring announcer had difficulty pronouncing Chapdelaine; lost to Paul Berlenbach '25 for world light-heavyweight title; beat Berlenbach for title '26 but never defended; last bout, as heavyweight, '32; in 86 pro bouts won 42 on KO, 27 decision, 1 foul, 3 draws, 7 decisions lost, 3 times KO'd, 2 no decisions, 1 no-contest; beat many top names including Tommy Loughran, Tiger Flowers; mem. Canadian Boxing, Canada's Sports halls of fame.

DELASALLE, Philip (gymnastics); b. 18 Jul 1958, Victoria, B.C.; given name: Philip Lawrence; UVic; instrument technician; began gymnastics career at 6; 1st all-around '73, '76-80 ntl championships; mem. '76, '80 Olympic, '78 CG teams; gold all-around, team '78 CG; 15 gold, 8 silver, 2 bronze ntl, intl competitions; Viscount Alexander award '75; Sports BC overall athlete, male athlete of '78; Victoria Transcendental Meditation Society Best Gymnast award '79; with Owen Wastrom operated Prince George gymnastics club '81-85; mem. BC, Greater Victoria Sports halls of fame; res. Victoria, B.C.

DELGADO, Carlos (baseball); b. 25 Jun 1972, Aguadilla, Puerto Rico; given name: Carlos Juan; 1st baseman; turned pro with Toronto organization '89; St. Catharines (NY-P) '89-90, Myrtle Beach (Sally) '91, Syracuse (IL) '91, '94-95, '98, Dunedin (FSL) '92, '98, Knoxville (Sou) '93; Toronto (AL) '93-04; Florida (NL) '05; noted for prodigious homers early in career but spent time seasoning in minors until permanent call-up '96; 29th player to clear Tiger Stadium with home run; set Jays club records '99 with 44hr, 134rbi; 2 Neil MacCarl Jays player-of-month awards; 3 Howard Webster Jays' minor league player-of-yr awards; *USA Today* baseball weekly minor league player of '92; 2 silver slugger awards; MVP awards in 6 leagues; Southern, AL all-star; mem. ML all-star Japan tour '98; *Baseball America* winter league player of '94; 15th player in ML history to hit 4HRS single game 25 Sep '03; ML record (through '04): 1423 scheduled games, 5008ab, 889r, 1413h, 343db, 11tr, 336hr, 1058rbi, 9sb, .282ba; res: Aguadilla, PR.

DELMAGE, Al (curling); b. 16 Jan 1940, Regina, Sask.; m. Dora Scott; c. Gail, Sharon, Sandra, Ron; ret'd. govt. finance officer; skip NWT entries '80, '84-85, '87, '89, 5th man '93 Briers, '72, '84, '86 ntl mixed, '91 ntl senior men's; 5 ntl Elks championships, '89 winner; participant, organizer

Arctic Winter Games '70-96, 3 curling gold medals; exec. mem. NWTCA '68-96; exec. mem. Sport North Fed. '76-82, '85-86, pres. 83-85; NWT curling technical co-ordinator '75-81, '89-96; NWT curling instructor '75-96; NWT government curling co-ordinator '86-96; exec. mem. Ft. Smith CC '66-68; exec. mem. Yellowknife CC '68-96, pres. '88-89; Elks exec. mem. '71-96; 3 times Yellowknife athlete of year; mem. Sport North team of year '85; mem. Cdn Curling Hall of Fame; res. Emerald Park, Sask.

DELVECCHIO, Alex (hockey); b. 4 Dec 1931, Fort William, Ont.; given name: Alexander Peter; m. Teresa De Guiseppe; c. Kenneth, Janice, Corrine, Alex Jr., Leonard; owns Alex Delvecchio Enterprises; jr. Ft. William, Oshawa; pro Detroit '50-73; lw on line with Gordie Howe, Norm Ullman; NHL record: 1549 scheduled games, 456g, 825a, 121 playoff games, 35g, 69a; team capt. '61-73; coached Wings '73, GM '74-77; twice 2nd team all-star; active with Red Wings alumni; 3 Lady Byng trophies; Lester Patrick award; mem. Michigan, NWO Sports, Canadian Hockey halls of fame; res. Orchard Lake, Mich.

DeMARCO, Ab (hockey); b. 27 Feb 1949, Cleveland, Ohio; m. Susan Rendell; c. Marina, Lucia, Micaela; consultant; def. North Bay (NOHA) '66-67, Kitchener (OHA) '67-68, Ottawa Nationals (OHA Sr.), Team Canada '68-69, Omaha (CHL) '69-71; NHL NYR '69-73, St. Louis '73-74, Pittsburgh '74, Vancouver '74-76, LA '76-77, Boston '78-79, Edmonton (WHA) '77-78, Ambri Pioata (Switzerland); NHL record: 344 scheduled games, 44g, 80a, 25 playoff games, 1g, 2a; mem. Hockey Heritage North Hall of Fame; res. North Bay, Ont.

DEMERS, Jacques (coaching/hockey); b. 25 Aug 1944, Montreal, Que.; m. Debbie; c. Mylene, Brandy, Stephanie, Jason; ex-hockey coach; began coaching in Que. jr. ranks; moved into pro ranks with Chicago, Indianapolis, Cincinnati (WHA) '72-79; made NHL debut with Quebec '79-81; coach/GM Fredericton (AHL) '81-83; returned to NHL with St. Louis '83-86, Detroit '86-90, Montreal '92-96, Tampa Bay '97-99; Minnesota '03; NHL coaching record: 1006 scheduled games, 409-467-130, 98 playoff games, 55-43; 1 Stanley Cup winner; 1st coach to win back-to-back Adams trophies; AHL coach/exec.-of-yr awards; radio-TV hockey analyst; res. New Tampa, Fla.

DEMERS, Jacques (weightlifting); b. 27 Jul 1960, Greenfield Park, Que.; Oceania championships 75kg title '81; 4 ntl sr. titles; 1 Ont. title; bronze '82 CG; gold C&J, silver total, bronze snatch '83 PAG; silver 75kg '84 Olympics; 6 ntl sr., 8 Commonwealth records; French, Austrian titles '84; played Wagubu tribesman movie *Quest for Fire*; charged with drug trafficking; fed. govt. excellence award '84; res. Brossard, Que.

DEMONTE, Denise (orienteering); b. 4 Dec 1954, Toronto, Ont.; given name: Denise Maria; m. Ron Lowry; c. Stephen, Eric; McMaster, BPhE, UWO., MA, Cdn Coll Naturopathic Medicine ND; x-country skier; 30km Muskoka Loppet, silver 55km '80 Riviere Rouge Loppet, bronze 160km Canadian Ski Marathon; ntl team '79-87; Canadian champion '81, US, New England titles '79; competed in 4 world championships; 18th '85 worlds, best finish by Cdn woman in world competition; res. Vernon, B.C.

DEMPSTER, Ryan (baseball); b. 3 May 1977, Sechelt, B.C.; given name: Ryan Scott; rhp; drafted by Texas Rangers '95; Triple A Calgary; made ML debut 2000 with Florida Marlins; dealt to Cincinnati '02-03, Chicago Cubs '04; threw 1-hitter vs. NY Mets '00; made all-star game appearance '00; ML record (through '04): 184 scheduled games, 51-56, 984ip, 516bob, 796k, 4.28era; res. Sechelt, B.C.

DENG, Si-An (badminton); b. 25 Jun 1963, Shanghai, China; m. Yong Jaing Liu; c. Joshua; part-time coach; began competing at 17; mem. Chinese ntl team; moved to Canada '88; '93 ntl single, doubles titles; ntl doubles '95; represented Canada '94 CG, silver women's singles, bronze (with Denyse Julien) women's doubles; doubles gold (with Julien), silver singles, mixed doubles '95 PAG, mem. '96 Olympic team; res. Richmond, B.C.

DENNENY, Corb (hockey); b. 25 Jan 1894, Cornwall, Ont.; d. 16 Jan 1963, Toronto, Ont.; given name: Corbett; m. Mary Hellewell; c. Dorothy; played sr. hockey with Cornwall, Cobalt, O'Brien Mines before he moved with brother Cy into NHA ranks with Toronto '14-16, Ottawa '17; joined Toronto Arenas in NHL '17-22, '26-27, Hamilton '23-24, Chicago '27-28; PCHA Vancouver, Saskatoon, AHL Minneapolis, Chicago, Newark (Can-Am); ret'd following '31 season; twice all-star; NHL totals 176 scheduled games, 103g, 41a, 16 playoff games, 7g, 3a; one of 7 in NHL history to score 6 goals single game (feat matched by brother Cy) '21; centred line with Reg Noble, Babe Dye; 2 Stanley Cup winners.

DENNENY, Cy (hockey); b. 23 Dec 1891, Farran's Point, Ont.; d. 10 Sep 1970, Ottawa, Ont.; given name: Cyril Joseph; m. Malvina K. Eastman (d), m. Isobel Clark; c. Kathlyn, Janet, Alma (d); civil servant; early hockey Cornwall County League, Russell, Ont. '12, O'Brien Mine team; pro Toronto Shamrocks '14-15, Ottawa Senators '16-28; on line with Frank Nighbor, Punch Broadbent; mem. 5 Stanley Cup winners; coach, asst. mgr. 1yr Boston Bruins; refereed 1yr NHL; coach jr., sr. amateur teams Ottawa '31-32; coach Senators '32-33; NHL record: 12 seasons, 246 goals, 20 3-goal games, 5 4-goal games, 1 6-goal game; 12 consecutive game goal-scoring streak '17-18; exponent of curved stick; mem. Ottawa, Cornwall Sports, Canadian Hockey halls of fame.

DENONCOURT, Sonia (soccer/officiating); b. 25 Jun 1964, Sherbrooke, Que.; Sherbrooke, BPhE, UofOtt, MSA; soccer administrator, merchant, educator; began soccer officiating at 13; refereed in ntl women's championships '81; lineswoman CSL '87-92; officiated Canada Games '93, APSL from '93, CIAU men's championships '94, women's ntl, world, Chiquita Cup championships from '83, received FIFA referee badge '94; men's CONCACAF championships '94; appointed 1 of 12 referee for '95 FIFA women's worlds; refereed 3 World Cups; 1st woman to referee an Olympic game; officiated '96, '00 Olympics; 1st female referee in Brazilian pro soccer; ret'd as on-field official '04; CSA Ray Morgan Memorial award; Breakthrough award '99; Ottawa lifetime achievement award '04; mem. Cdn Soccer Hall of Fame; res. Gatineau, Que.

DEPIERO, Mary (diving); b. 14 May 1968, Fort William, Ont.; m. Geller; Lakehead U; coach; excelled as gymnast before turning to diving at 14; 1m silver '85 Canada Summer Games; mem. ntl team '88-94; 14 ntl sr. titles; '91 5th place finish 1m best-ever for Cdn at Worlds; 4g, 3b ntl 3m, 4g, 1s, 1m championships; 1m gold '90, bronze '94 CG; *CBC* color commentator '00 Olympics; diving coach Thunder Bay, St. John's, Nfld; mem. NWO Hall of Fame; res. St. John's, Nfld.

DESABRAIS, Paul (softball); b. 24 Sep 1924, Hull, Que.; given name: Joseph Paul Ernest; sep.; c. Guy, Andre; ret'd. construction engineer superintendent; perfected pitching skills with RCAF '43; introduced windmill delivery to Ottawa area but played of until pitch legalized '49; through '50s, '60s National Capital region's premier pitcher; 12 consecutive seasons Oscar-Lambert Hull Commercial League; ret'd. from competition '78; in 35-year career 255 wins, 57 losses; in '55 appeared in 73 games in 4 leagues; pitched 4 complete games, 1 5-inning match single day '51; 11 consecutive victories, including 7 shutouts '58; 2 perfect games among 12 career no-hitters; 3 times Gil O. Julien, twice Ottawa ACT Trophy candidates; mem. Softball Canada, Ottawa Sports halls of fame; res. Vanier, Ont.

DESCHAMPS, Claude (softball); b. 7 Aug 1934, Ottawa, Ont.; d. 22 Sep 1983, Ottawa, Ont.; m. Dolorese Seguin; c. Marc, Lucie, Louise; LaSalle Academy; exec. dir. Softball Canada; 2nd baseman Hull; helped organize Hull Volants team '71, Atlantic Seaboard Major Fastball League, '73 ntl men's sr. softball championships Hull; major role sr. fastball Ottawa area with organization Metro Major League; 6yrs secty.-general Hull International Softball tournament; Softball Canada exec.-dir. '75-83; key role in formation Softball Canada Hall of Fame; mem. Softball Canada, Ottawa Sports halls of fame.

DESCHATELETS, Richard (wrestling); b. 4 Apr 1954, Sturgeon Falls, Ont.; m. Suzanne Rochon; Guelph, BSc; AD Brock; '73 ntl jr. 82kg FS title; bronze 74kg '73 jr. worlds; 7 ntl sr. FS, 1GR titles; 4 CIAU FS titles; Cerro Pelado 82kg '78, 90kg '80, '84; gold 82kg '78 CG; bronze 90kg '79 PAG, '77, '80 World Cup, 100kg '82 World Cup; silver 82kg '75, 100kg '83 PAG; gold 100kg '82 CG; scored upset victory over USSR Olympic gold medallist at worlds; competed 3 PAG, 2 CG, 1 Olympic team; Sturgeon Falls HS athlete of '72, Guelph athlete of '76-77; established Azilda wrestling club where he coaches; coach Brock, 2 CIAU, 1 OUAA coach-of-yr awards; fed. Govt. excellence award '83; mem. Guelph, Cdn Wrestling halls of fame; res. St. Catharines, Ont.

DESCLOUDS, Rick (coaching); b. 3 Apr 1951, Montreal, Que.; c. Danny, Dwain; St. Pat's Coll BA, Ottawa Teachers Coll; teacher; coached community hockey 8yrs winning 2 Ntl Capital titles with Westboro Kiwanis; 31yrs minor baseball coach, 25 as major div. tournament coach; reached prov finals 8 times, winning 3 consec. titles; twice ntl championship finalists; coached 91 Ottawa Board title teams in 8 different sports including 12 basketball titles in 15yrs, 26 volleyball crowns in 30yrs; coached Glashan Spikers volleyball team to 14 Ont. titles, 7 elementary, 6 bantam; Glashan team had 61-0 streak through 5 Feb. '05; 2 Ottawa ACT Little League team awards; ACT sportsman of '88; Hudson Sargeant Ottawa School Board award '93; board chairman's achievement award '02; named to

Ottawa Citizen top 100 sportsmen of 20th century; Pinecrest baseball diamond bears his name; res. Stittsville, Ont.

DESJARDINS, Éric (hockey); b. 14 Jun 1969, Rouyn, Que.; m. Manon Bouthiller; c. Jakob; def Granby (QMJHL) '86-88, Sherbrooke (AHL) '88, NHL Montreal '88-94, Philadelphia '94-03; QMJHL Butch Bouchard trophy; 2 Pa. humanitarian awards; 6 Barry Ashbee trophies; capt. Flyers from '00; mem. Team Canada '88-89 (gold) world jr., '91 Canada Cup. '96 worlds, '98 Olympics; mem. 1 Stanley Cup winner; *Hockey News* 2nd team all-star '95; 1 NHL all-star game; NHL record: (through '04) 1098 scheduled games, 132g, 419a, 162 playoff games, 22g, 54a; active CF Foundation, Children's Miracle Network; res. St-Adolphe-D'Howard, Que.

DESJARDINS, Gerry (hockey); b. 22 Jul 1944, Sudbury, Ont.; given name: Gerard Ferdinand; m. Michelle Parenteau; c. Daniel; sales rep./part owner Canada Steel; jr. Toronto Marlboros; minor pro '65-68; NHL Los Angeles, Chicago, NYI, Buffalo '68-78, excluding '74-75 Baltimore (WHA); 10yr major pro record 331 games, 12 shutouts, 3.29 goals against average; goaltending consultant Buffalo; Red Garrett Memorial Trophy with Cleveland (AHL) '68; mem. Hockey Heritage North Hall of Fame; res. London, Ont.

DESJARDINS, Larry (all-around/builder); b. 15 Mar 1923, St. Boniface, Man.; given name: Laurent Louis; m. Bernice McGuire (d); c. Carolyn, Patricia (d), Suzanne, Michelle (d); m. Mel Langevin; sc. Christopher; St. Boniface Coll, St. Paul's Coll, Cincinnati Coll. Of Embalming; ret'd. funeral dir., ret'd politician; baseball lhp/1b St. Boniface juves, St. Paul's Coll, Norwood srs, RCN, St. Boniface Native Sons, semipro Cincinnati, Winnipeg Rods (ManDak League); football 2-way tackle St. Paul's, UMan, Blue Bombers; coached Isaac Newton HS, St. Paul's Coll., Winnipeg Rods; exec. mem. Blue Bombers; hockey def St. Boniface jrs, Esquires; pres./GM St. Boniface jr. Canadians; area (NHL) scout for Montreal, Boston; among 1st to scout European talent '68 Olympics; entered political arena '50; held numerous prov. portfolios through '87 retirement; ED Man. Health Organizations '87-90; mem. Man. Sports, Man. Hockey halls of fame; res. Winnipeg, Man.

DESJARDINS, Paul (football); b. 12 Sep 1943, Ottawa, Ont.; given name: Paul Robert; m. Vona Elizabeth Freeman; c. Michelle, Steven, Jason; UofOtt, BSc, UMan, MSc, PhD; v-p GM Biovail Corp.; mem. UofOtt Gee-Gees '60-65; pro Winnipeg '65-70, Toronto '71-73; CFL all-star ctr (East) '71-73, all-Cdn '73; '68 Winnipeg MVP; best all-around athlete UofOtt '63-64; top volleyball player UofOtt '64-65; Gil O. Julien Trophy French Canadian athlete of '65; mem. UofOtt Football Hall of Fame; res. Toronto, Ont.

DESJARLAIS, Robert (fencing); b. 26 Aug 1907, St. David Yamaska, Que.; d. (circa 1993), Westmount, Que.; m. Laurette Douvet; c. Mirielle, Lorraine, France; St. Laurent Coll., St. Paul's Academy; fencing equipment supplier; mem. '48 Olympic, '50, '54 BEG, '58 World championships teams; fencing secty., prov. pres.; fencing chairman AAUofC; Baron de Coubertin award '78; OUA men's épée trophy bears his name; mem. Que. Sports Hall of Fame.

DESLAURIERS, Mario (equestrian); b. 23 Feb 1965, Venise-en, Que.; div.; c. Sari; 5th generation show horse rider; outstanding foreign, international rider Madison Square Garden '83; 2nd Spruce Meadow '83; spare '83 PAG team; gold aboard Aramis '84 World Cup; mem. '84, '88 Olympic teams; fed. govt. world champion award '84; won Bryhar Futures Stakes aboard Fiezal '95; ntl show jumping title aboard Amistad '97; Hudson Valley Resort GP aboard Big Sir '02; Ocala GP aboard Kathleen '03; res. Kingston, N.H.

DESMARTEAU, Étienne (t&f); b. 1877, Montreal, Que.; d. 1905 Montreal, Que.; policeman; at 6'1", 225lbs smallest of 5 brothers; with brother Zacharie competed annually Toronto, NY, Montreal, Boston Police Games; specialized in 56lb weight toss, like today's hammer throw; sponsored by MAAA became 1st Canadian Olympic gold medalist '04 winning weight toss; event discontinued following '20 games; world record 15'9" height and 36'6.5" distance; '76 Olympic facility named in his honor; mem. Cdn Olympic, Que., Canada's Sports Hall of Fame.

DESPATIE, Alexandre (diving); b. 8 Jun 1985, Montreal, Que.; began swimming/diving age 5; coached by Michel Larouche; ntl jr. records on all 3 boards; electrified international diving by earning '98 CG 10m gold at 13; gold 1m, 3m, bronze 10m '02 CG; world jr. gold 1m, 3m, 10m '02; world 10m gold '03; 2 gold, 1 bronze '03 PAG; competed '00, '04 Olympics; through '03 18 ntl titles; mem. CAMO club; 3 Viscount Alexander awards; Cdn Amateur Diving Assn male athlete '00; res. Laval, Que.

DESSUREAULT, Michel (fencing); b. 11 Mar 1957, Bouchette, Que.; given name: Michel Daniel; m. Anne Marie Viau; c. 2 daughters; Carleton BA.; dir. Caron Training Centre, French teacher, coach, operator Gatineau fencing club, fencing equipment co. owner; began fencing at 13; ntl status fencer '75-94, épée, foil specialist; mem. '75, '79, '83, '87 PAG, '76, '84, '88 Olympic, '77, '79, '81 FISU, '78, '82 Commonwealth Championships teams; 7 ntl jr. titles, 4 épée, 3 foil; ntl sr. épée title '80, foil '81; mem. 3 RA ntl foil title teams; 4 Governor-General's foil, 2 épée titles; team foil bronze '78, silver '82 Commonwealth championships, épée gold '86 CG; épée team gold, individual silver '83 PAG; best Cdn Olympic fencing showing 10th '84; mem. COA advisory council; mem. '91 Sports Canada task force on policy review; mem. Ottawa CSRA Sports Hall of Fame; res. Gatineau, Que.

DEVAL, Gordon (fishing); b. 18 Jan 1930, Winnipeg, Man.; m. Britta; c. Ronald, Randall, Connie, Wendy; UofT, Shaw Business School; insurance agent; all ntl distance-casting records from '55; all-around champion from '55; 1st represented Canada world championships '57 and annually from '75; world title runnerup '75; Commonwealth champion '77-80; NA salmon fly title '79; 2-hand spinning distance title '80; world record anglers' fly distance 174', 1-ounce spin distance and 3/8-ounce unrestricted bait distance 531' and 384' respectively; from '75 established more than 40 records; res. Scarborough, Ont.

DeVENNEY, Sandra (all-around); b. 7 Mar 1946, Fredericton Junction, N.B.; given name: Sandra Lea Davenport; m.; admin. officer prov. govt.; competing in wheelchair t&f, table tennis, basketball, swimming won 24 gold, 24 silver, 8 bronze medals, 6 records Cdn wheelchair games '71-78; founding mem. NB Wheelchair Assn; competed 2 Stoke-Mandeville Games (3 silver, 2 bronze), 2 Olympiads for Disabled, '75 Pan-Am Wheelchair Games (1 gold, 1 silver, 3 bronze); mem. ntl women's wheelchair basketball team '76-77, 6 NB wheelchair basketball teams; 2 best female athlete awards; Fredericton athletic achievement awards '73-78; mem. NB Sports Hall of Fame; res. Fredericton Junction, N.B.

DEVINE, Jack (administration); b. 22 Feb 1919, Toronto, Ont.; d. 28 Apr 1989, Belleville, Ont.; given name: William John; m. Minnie Woodman; c. Bruce, Nancy, Stephen; sports broadcaster; pres. OHA '67-69, CAHA '73-75; dir. IIHF '75-78; pres. Ont. Sports Writers, Sportscasters Assn.; commander Bay of Quinte Power Squadron; life mem. OHA, CAHA, Prince Edward Power Boat Racing Club; hon. mem. Metro Toronto HL; OHA Gold Stick award; SFC broadcasting award '67; CBF award of decade '70-80; City of Belleville award '76; mem. Belleville Sports Hall of Fame.

DEVLIN, Alex (basketball); b. 12 Dec 1949, Edmonton, Alta.; given name: Alexander Joseph; m. Dianne Linda Gillies; c. Jeremy, Kelly Anne; SFU, BA; HS coach, ex-lumber salesman; ctr SFU '69-73; hon. mention all-American NAIA '73; mem. ntl team '72-76; missed '72 Olympics due to injury; mem. '76 Olympic, '74 world, '75 Pan-Am, '73 FISU, '74 America vs. world teams; res. Port Moody, B.C.

DEVLIN-HASHMAN, Judy (badminton); b. 1935, Winnipeg, Man,; given name Judy Devlin; m. Hashman; trained by father Frank, a 6-time English titlist, from age 7; during 15yr competitive career won 6 ntl jr., 56 ntl sr. titles US (12 singles), Canadian (3 singles and, with sister Sue, 3 women's, 1 mixed doubles), English (10 singles, 12 women's, 8 mixed doubles), Dutch, German, Irish, Jamaican, Scottish, Swedish; authored *Beginning Badminton;* res. Wooton. Abongdon, Oxon, Eng.

DEVONISH, Nicole (t&f); b. 24 Aug 1973, Toronto, Ont.; Texas; gold lj silver 200m '92 ntl jr championships; silver lj '92 world jr.; mem. '93 FISU, '94 Commonwealth, '96 Olympic teams; lj gold '95-96 SWC championships; silver lj Penn Relays, NCAA championships '96; Cdn lj record 6.66m '96; Cal Bricker Memorial Trophy '92; Myrtle Cook trophy '89; res. Newtonville, Ont.

de VOS, Jason (soccer); b. 2 Jan 1974, London, Ont.; defender Ipswich Town (Eng. 1st div.); mem. Cdn -20 team 2 games '91; Olympic -23 team '94-96; competed '94 Francophonie Games; made World Cup team debut '97; 46 WC intl caps, 14 -23 caps, 2 -20 caps; capt. ntl men's team Gold Cup tourney all-star; broken foot sidelined him 3 months '03; played with Dundee United '98, Darlington, capt. Wigan '02-03, Ipswich '04; res. London, Ont.

DEWAR, Phyllis (swimming); b. 5 Mar 1916, Moose Jaw, Sask.; d. 8 Apr 1961, Toronto, Ont.; m. Murray Lowery (d); c. Judith, Joanne, Wayne, Frank; 3 Sask., 1 ntl 1-mile titles; gold 100yd, 400yd FS, 300yd medley, 400yd relay '34 BEG; set 5 ntl records '35; qualified '36 Olympic team

but flu bout produced poor performance; gold 400yd FS '38 BEG; Bobbie Rosenfeld Trophy '34; mem. Canadian Aquatic, BC Swimming, Olympic, Sask., Canada's Sports halls of fame.

DeWARE, Mabel (curling); b. 9 Aug 1926, Moncton, N.B.; given name: Mabel Keiver; m. Ralph Baxter DeWare; c. Kimberly, Peter, Michael, Joanne; politician; skip ntl women's '63 title team; p.-pres. Moncton YM-YWCA, Beaver Curling Club, NB Ladies Curling Assn; mem., minister NB Legislature '78-87; summoned to Cdn Senate '90; mem. NB Sports, Cdn Curling halls of fame; res. Shediac, N.B.

DEWIS, Karen (tennis); b. 19 Sep 1962, London, Ont.; UCLA BA magna cum laude, UofT LLB, Georgetown LLM; law firm partner; held ntl age-group singles, doubles titles from -12 through -18; twice runnerup ntl women's singles; mem. AIAW ntl title team; Que. Open Alcan singles '81; Ont. singles, doubles (Sue Black) '82; mem. 1 jr. Wimbledon, 2 jr. Italian Open, 1 Soisbault Cup teams; played some events on women's pro circuit; ret'd. from competition '88; res. Washington, D.C.

deWIT, Willie (boxing); b. 13 Jun 1961, Three Hills, Alta.; given name: William Theodore; m. Suzan Ayers; c. Ashley, Sarah, Len, Caitlyn; UAlta LLB; lawyer; sought as qb by UAlta; became hooked on boxing with initial bout which he won in 20 seconds; Alta. 81kg heavyweight titles '79-80; BC Golden Gloves 81kg title '80, Alta. Golden Gloves 91kg title '81; ntl 91kg title '81, '83, super-heavyweight '82, Alta. 91kg title '81; '80 Mayor's Cup; 91kg gold '81 NZ Games; 1st Cdn to win NA 91kg title '82, repeat '83; 91kg gold '82 CG, '83-84 world championship challenge; silver '84 Olympics; Alta. Golden Boy award 1981; Canada's "best prospect" '81; outstanding service to Canadian amateur boxing award '80; fed. govt. world champion award '83; Calgary athlete of '83; turned pro '84; won Cdn heavyweight title '86; subject of book *Lord of the Ring;* ret'd. from ring '88; mem. Alta Sports Hall of Fame; res. Grande Prairie, Alta.

DEWITTE, Marcel (curling); b. 27 Nov 1927, Belgium; given name: Marcel George Maurice; div. Joan Ann Newell; ret'd. arena, parks mgr., refrigeration engineer; ice maker Simcoe Curling Club '58-60, Sarnia G&CC '61-62; ice superintendent 16-sheet Ivanhoe CC London '63-76; Ont. Legion Zone A rep. '68; rated as one of Canada's most competent curling ice makers; conducted clinics under OCA auspices; mem. '74 London Brier, '81 Silver Broom (world) steering comms; chief ice maker '74, '86, '91-95 Briers, '78 Cdn Lassie, '86 Tournament of Hearts; '80 men's jr. worlds; '81 Silver Broom (world), '82-83 Ont. Labatt Tankard; '93-94 Worlds; CCA '95 achievement award; res. Norwich, Ont.

DEXTER, Glen (sailing); b. 1 Nov 1952, Lunenburg, N.S.; given name: Glen Vincent; m. Jane Filbee; Dalhousie, BSc, LLB; lawyer; with Andreas Josenhans, Sandy MacMillan Olympic class world soling champion '77, '80; prov. titles '74-76; youngest soling crew '76 Olympics; 1st Maritime Olympic sailors; NS achievement award, Moosehead sports award; mem. NS, Canada's Sports halls of fame; res. Tantallon, N.S.

DIACHUN, Jennifer (gymnastics); b. 14 Aug 1953, Toronto, Ont.; given name: Jennifer Marie; m. Peter Palmer; c. Michael; UofT, UBC, BSc; physiotherapist, assists husband in marketing business; ntl sr. title '69-72, '74; Canadian Intercollegiate title '73, '76; mem. '68, '72 Olympic, '70, '74 world tournament, '73 FISU Games teams; 2 bronze '71 PAG; coach Phoenix Gym Club '77-78, Thompson GC '79-80; Ont. Gymnastics Fed. outstanding person in gymnastics '75; res. Burlington, Ont.

DIBBEN, Hugh (all-around); b. 13 Jun 1930, Peterborough, Ont.; d. 4 Apr 2001, Peterborough, Ont.; given name: Hugh Ernest; m. Catherine Toole; CGE engineering technologist; played cricket Peterborough Whitaker CC '48-67; mem. Matthews Cup Ont. title team '48; excelled as tennis doubles player with Quaker Park TC; with Don Little '68, Tony Bigg '73 Kawartha League title; singles title '72; mem. 2 Quaker title teams; competed 35yrs in volleyball; mem. all-Ont. Int. title team '61; 20yr basketball career included HS, Ont. Int. B title teams; Peterborough table tennis title '53; mem. Peterborough Sports Hall of Fame.

DICKENSON, Dave (football); b. 11 Jan 1973, Great Falls, Mont.; m. Tammy; Montana; qb; led Montana to 1st NCAA Div. 1-AA ntl title '95; 3 Big Sky Conf. player-of-yr/MVP awards; CFL Calgary '97-00, B.C. '03-04; NFL San Diego '01, spent some time with Seattle, Detroit, Miami; Jeff Nicklin, CFL outstanding player '00 award; 3 Grey Cup finals, 1 winner; CFL record (through '04) 1083 completions on 1645 attempts, 15,724yds, 108tds, 35int, 161 carries, 1011yds, 11tds; res. Calgary, Alta./ Vancouver, B.C.

DICKESON, Jean (golf); b. 19 Sep 1922, Baker Brook, N.B.; d. 6 Jun 2004, Fredericton, N.B.; given name: Jean May; m. Hugh Dickeson; administrative skills led to 9yrs NB Ladies Golf Association jr. development chair, v-p, secty-treas '63-71; 10yrs ntl executive from '71 becoming ntl pres. '78-79; CLGA delegate to World Council '78, Commonwealth Council '79; 2yrs v-p Great Britain Ladies Golf Union; NB Ladies Curling Assn. dir./pres. '84-'88 Sport NB Volunteer of '90; Jubilee medal '77; mem. NB, Edmundston Sports halls of fame.

DICKIE, Bill (hockey); b. 20 Feb 1916, Campbellton, N.B.; d. 23 Dec 1997, Ste. Jolie, Que; given name: William Rufus; m. Shirley MacDonald (d); c, Brian, Ronald, Lee; Mount Allison; ret'd. chemical co. mgr.; mem. '32 NB, Maritime HS title teams; '34 NB Sr. B, Maritime titles, NB, Maritime intercollegiate titles with Mount A. '35; capt, coach, goalie Mount A NB undefeated title team '36-37; with John Beavers '38-39 Sydney Millionaires '40-41 Maritime Sr. A titles; Montreal Pats '41-42; 1 game Chicago Blackhawks '42; *Hockey News* most-popular amateur player '42; Valleyfield outstanding citizen plaque '74; mem. NB, Campbellton Sports Hall/Wall of Fame.

DICKINSON, William (lacrosse); b. 22 Sep 1918, Vancouver, B.C.; d. 31 May 1979, Vancouver, B.C.; during 17yr box lacrosse career scored 611 goals, 330 assists in 398 games; mem. 1 Mann Cup, 4 provincial winners; league MVP '46 Salmonbellies; 5yrs referee; 6yrs league commissioner; 2yrs coach; mem. Canadian Lacrosse, BC Sports halls of fame.

DICKSON, Gordon (t&f); b. 2 Jan 1932, Calgary, Alta.; m. Sheilah MacKenzie; c. Kevin, Craig; Drake, BA, NYU, MA; accountant; ntl 10,000m title '58; ntl x-country '57-59; ntl marathon titles '57-60, '64; mem. '58, '62 CG, '59 PAG, '60 Olympic Games teams; bronze '59 PAG marathon; 3 times in top 10 Boston Marathon, 3rd '59; won 5 Around the Bay races; pres. Hamilton Athletic Club; Norton Crowe award '59; mem. Cdn Roadrunning Hall of Fame; res. Burlington, Ont.

DIDUCK, Judy (hockey/ringette): b. 21 Apr 1966, Edmonton, Alta.; owner specialty advertising sales co.; competed in every ntl women's championship with Edmonton Chimos from '85; '92 ntl title; defensive MVP '94; played '90-91 season in Switzerland; def 4 Team Canada world, 2 Pacific Rim, 1 3-Nations Cup titles; mem. '98 Olympic team; capt. 3-pete UAlta Pandas women's university champs '04; ret'd from competition '04; mem. Team Alberta '90 world ringette champions; brother Gerald played in NHL; res. Sherwood Park, Alta.

DIETIKER, Judy (speed skating/cycling); b. 5 Mar 1956, Manchester, Eng.; m. Peter Davison; c. Chris, Jenny, Natalie, Paul, Anthony; fitness consultant; began speed skating age 8; 2 Ont. Bantam titles; 6 Ont. sr titles; Lake Placid Diamond Trophy; ntl team '70-94 competing in European, China tours, Olympic trials, world championships; 2 silver, 1 bronze '71 Canada Winter Games; set numerous ntl rcords; competed 1st-ever ntl women's cycling track/road championships; claiming track gold '72, '74, road gold '73, '75; mem. ntl team '74 worlds; Ont. track title '80; broke women's 1000m world record '80; represented Canada numerous US events '81; 1st woman president in 108-yr Ottawa Bicycle Club history '85; competing at Masters level claimed gold Ont. championships '91, Canada's Capital and ntl Masters '94; coach in speed skating, cycling; CASSA roll of honor; mem. Ottawa Sports Hall of Fame; res. Manotick, Ont.

DIFFIN, Charlie (officiating/basketball); b. 13 Jan 1930, Ottawa, Ont.; given name: Charles Hazen; m. Joan Lawruk; c. Donna; ret'd. mgr. E.B. Eddy; refereed 1st game at 14 when assigned ref failed to show for HS game; that launched career which would span 55yrs; worked at all levels from youth to CIAU ntl championships; officiated in ntl sr, Eastern Cdn and jr. championships; did 1st CIAU game at 17 and ret'dfrom CIAU after 36yrs; refereed games involving Harlem Globetrotters, Chinese ntl team; supervisor of OUAA officials and continued to evaluate and assign CIAU, Community College officials through '99; 4yrs v-p, pres. OVBABO 28yrs; fellow Ottawa and Carleton HS Athletic Assns.; Wink Willox award from CABO; Ottawa ACT volunteer of 2000; mem. Ottawa Sports Hall of Fame; res. Ottawa, Ont.

DILIO, Frank (administration); b. 12 Apr 1912, Montreal, Que.; d. 26 Jan 1997, Montreal, Que.; m. Lillian Desmarais; c. Frederick, Elizabeth, Patricia, Francis; ret'd city clerk; '31-38 secty. St. Anne's Young Men's HL, league title; secty. '39-41 QJAHA, pres. '41-44; registrar, secty QAHA '44-63; pres. QMJHL '69-71; Montreal Sportsman of '43; CAHA merit award '63; division of QMJHL bears his name; mem. Canadian Hockey Hall of Fame.

DIMITROFF, Tom (football); b. 6 Jun 1936, Barberton, Ohio; d. 20 Jan 1996, Strongsville, Ohio; m. Helen; c. Randy, Sharon, Tom Jr.; Miami of Ohio; football exec.; qb Ottawa (CFL) '57-58, Boston Patriots (AFC); HS coach Barberton; asst. coach Miami of Ohio '69-72, Kansas State '73, Ottawa '74-77, '84-86; head coach Hamilton '78, Guelph '79-83, Rough Riders '86; scout Cleveland (NFL) '87-96; mem. Guelph Sports Hall of Fame.

DINEEN, Bill (hockey); b. 18 Sep 1932, Arvida, Que.; given name: William Patrick; m. Patricia Sheedy; c. Shawn, Peter, Rose, Gordon, Kevin, Jerry; St. Michael's Coll; hockey scout; '53-58 in NHL with Detroit, Chicago; mem. 2 Stanley Cup winners with Detroit; NHL record: 323 scheduled games, 51g, 44a, 37 playoff games, 1g, 1a; minor league stints '58-70 with Buffalo, Cleveland, Rochester, Quebec, Seattle, Denver; coached Houston WHA '72-78, 2 Avco Cups; coached Adirondack AHL '83-90, 2 Calder Cups; GM Adirondack; several coach-of-yr honors WHA, AHL; coach Philadelphia NHL '91-93, 60-60-20 record; mem. Ottawa Sports Hall of Fame; res. Lake George, N.Y.

DINEEN, Gord (hockey/copaching); b. 21 Sep 1962, Toronto, Ont.; m. Alexandra; c. Molly; hockey coach; def. SSM (OHL) '80-82, Indianapolis (CHL) '82-84, Springfield (AHL) '84-86, NHL NYI '82-88, '95, Minnesota '87-88, Pittsburgh '88-91, Ottawa '92-94, IHL Muskegon '88-92, San Diego '92-94, Denver '94-95, Utah '95-99, '99-00, Chicago '99; capt. 3 IHL Turner Cup winners; mem. 1 Stanley Cup winner; NHL totals 538 scheduled games, 16g, 90a, 695pim, 40 playoff games, 1g, 7a, 69pim; trophy bearing his name awarded annually to Utah top defenceman (he won it 3 times); only Utah player to have jersey (2) ret'd; Bobby Orr, Bob Gassoff trophies; player-coach Utah '99-00, asst. coach '04-05, Louisville (AHL) '00-01; head coach ECHL Macon '01-02, Richmond '02-03; father Bill, brothers Kevin, Peter all played in NHL; res. Utah/Lake George, N.Y.

DINEEN, Kevin (hockey); b. 28 Oct 1963, Quebec City, Que.; m. Ann; c. Hannah, Emma; UDenver; hockey exec.; rw St. Michael's Jr. B; Denver '81-83; Team Canada '83-87; mem. '84 Olympic, '85, '89, '93 Worlds, Canada Cup, Rendez-Vous '87 teams; drafted by Hartford; brief minor league stints with Birmingham, Houston; NHL Hartford '84-91, '95-97, Philadelphia '91-95, Carolina '97-99, Ottawa '99-00, Columbus '00-03; capt. Flyers, Whalers, Hurricanes 2yrs; played 1000th game Ottawa '99; NHL record 1188 scheduled games, 355g, 405a, 2229 PIM; 59 playoff games, 23g, 18a; 2 NHL all-star games; *SN* 2nd all-star team '87; True Grit award, 3-Star award of excellence, Mark Kravitz, Hartford Booster Club MVP awards, Bud Light/NHL man-of-'91 award, Philadelphia Media Class Guy award '92; res. Columbus, Ohio

DINSLEY, Tom (diving); b. 25 Jun 1941, Regina, Sask.; given name: Thomas Edward; m. Patricia Venini; c. Sean; Indiana, BSc, UBC, LLB.; lawyer; mediator B.C. Insurance Corp; dominated BC diving scene '58-65 winning 7 consec. titles; ntl champion '62-65; 3m silver '62 CG, gold '63 PAG; mem. '64 Olympic team; CIAU title '68; mem. top ranked Indiana aquatic team 4yrs; '62 Indiana state champion; throughout career never lower than 2nd ntl championships; mem. BC Sports, Ridge Meadows, Cdn Aquatic halls of fame; res. Pitt Meadows, B.C.

DION, Michel (shooting); b. 30 Jun 1959, Pont Rouge, Que.; m. Anita; c. Anna Maria, 1 son; Laval; teacher; rifle specialist; began shooting '70; ntl team '80-98; team silver small-bore prone, full-bore 3-positions '83 PAG; competed '92, '96 Olympics, '83, '91, '95 PAG, '86, '94, '98 CG; team silver '86 CG; gold ind. small-bore '86, 3-position pairs (with Wayne Sorensen) '86, '98; Games record '86; bronze ind. small-bore rifle prone '94 CG; world cup prone gold '92; SFC athlete of '95; res. Paris, France.

DION, Yves (gymnastics/administration); b. 29 Apr 1959, Québec, Qué.; c. Jean-Philippe, Nicolas, Laura; Laval, École polytechnique de Montréal, B.Eng.; civil engineer; pres./founder Dynetsys Technologies Inc., teacher École polytechnique de l'U. de Montréal; v-p/partner, BGH-Planning Inc. '84-99; guest prof. Lausanne, Tunisia '98-00; Qué. gymnastics team '75-85; ntl team '79-85; 3 gold, 1 silver, 1 bronze '79 Canada Games; competed '81, '83 worlds, '84 Olympics; team gold '82 Commonwealth championships; team bronze '83 PAG; 2 Laval athlete-of-yr awards, Centre Immaculée Conception Montreal, '85; mem. Gymnastics Canada's men's elite planning comm. '80-85, various COA comms '84-92, Athletes' Council chair. '88-92), anti-doping, team selection comms; mem. Fair Play Commission '88-92; chaired 'Sport – the 3rd Millennium' intl symposium '90; mem., COA annual congress org. committee '96; res. Chambly, Qué.

DIONNE, Deidra (skiing); b. 5 Feb 1982, North Battleford, Sask.; given name: Deidra Rae; UAthabasca BA; aerials specialist; ntl team from '01; bronze '99 in 1st-ever world cup, silver following weekend world cup event; 2 WC silver '00-01 season; bronze '01, '03 worlds; bronze '02 Olympics; 3rd overall '01-02 season; 2 WC bronze to Jan. '04; WC female rookie of '00; res. Red Deer, Alta.

DIONNE, Marcel (hockey); b. 3 Aug 1951, Drummondville, Que.; given name: Marcel Elphege; m. Carol Gaudet; c. Lisa Lee, Garrett; ret'd. realtor/dry cleaning/plumbing business owner; jr. A Drummondville, St. Catharines; twice led OHA jr. scorers; Detroit's 1st pick, 2nd overall '71 amateur draft; NHL rookie record to that time 28 goals, 49 assists, 77 points '71-72; Detroit '71-75, Los Angeles '75-87, NYR '87-89; 6 50+ goal seasons, 5 in succession; 1 Art Ross, 2 Lady Byng, 2 Lester B. Pearson awards; 2 1st, 2nd team all-star ctr; mem. Team Canada '76, '81, '82, Canada Cup '76; NHL record: 1348 scheduled games, 731g, 1040a, 49 playoff games, 21g, 24a; Drummondville arena bears his name; ex-partner/pres. Carolina Stingrays (ECHL); plays OT hockey; mem. Greatest Legends of Hockey touring team; mem. Hockey, Canada's Sports halls of fame; res. Buffalo, N.Y.

DiPIETRO, Rocky (football); b. 30 Jan 1956, Sault Ste. Marie, Ont.; m. Patty Stamps; c. Joseph, Daniel; UofOtt, BA, Brock BPE, B.Ed; HS teacher; wr/sb, all-Cdn UofOtt; mem. '75 Vanier Cup winner; number one protected player Hamilton '77 draft; played entire CFL career with Hamilton '78-91; all-time leading Tiger-Cat, CFL receiver with 706 receptions; career total 9762 reception yds, 45tds; surpassed 1000yds in receptions 3 times; 3 Lou Hayman awards; Schenley outstanding Canadian award '82, '89; 4 EFC, 2 CFL all-star; 4 Grey Cup finals, '86 winner; mem. Tiger-Cat Walk of Fame; UofOtt, Cdn Football halls of fame; res. Ridgeville, Ont.

DISTELMEYER, Wally (figure skating/coaching); b. 14 Jul 1925, Kitchener, Ont.; d. 23 Dec 1999, Oakville, Ont.; given name: Wallace William; m. Bette Wrinch; c. Jane, David; 1942 jr. ntl pairs with Floraine Ducharme; 3 ntl pairs titles '46 Joyce Perkins, '47-48 Suzanne Morrow; '47 NA champion, '48 Olympic, world bronze (with Morrow); 3rd men's singles '47 NA Championships; won 5 of 6 disciplines (sr. pairs, waltz, singles, 10-step, dance) '48 ntls, a first in FS history; with Morrow 1st team to perform the acclaimed "death spiral" in international competition; 1st Cdn pair to win Olympic or world medal; turned pro and started coaching '48; founded Stamford Summer Skating School '50; taught at Toronto-area and Buffalo clubs until Alzheimer's forced him to retire '96; coaching rep. CFSA; pres. Professional Skating Association of Canada; mem. Mississauga, Olympic, Cdn Figure Skating halls of fame.

DIXON, George (boxing); b. 29 Jul 1870, Halifax, N.S.; d. 6 Jan 1909, New York, N.Y.; nicknamed "Little Chocolate"; at 16 KO'd Young Johnson; claimed vacant world bantam title 1888; defended twice; beat Cal McCarthy in 22 rounds 1891 to win featherweight title; defended 3 times before losing to Solly Smith 20 rounds 1897; regained crown beating Dave Sullivan in 10 1898; lost to Terry McGovern 1900 then, when McGovern couldn't make weight, fought Abe Attel for title losing in 15 1901; final fight 1906; pro record 158 bouts (estimated he fought some 800 times including barnstorming), won 30 by KO, 55 by decision, 1 on foul, 38 draws, 21 decisions lost, 4 times KO'd, 9 no decisions; longest fight 70 round draw with McCarthy; mem. US, Canadian Boxing, NS, Canada's Sports halls of fame.

DIXON, George (football); b. 19 Oct 1933, New Haven, Conn.; d. 6 Aug 1990, Montreal, Que.; m. Carol Grant; c. Kirk, Eric; UofBridgeport; promotions; Green Bay (NFL) draft; pro Montreal '59-65; 7yr CFL record 59 tds, including 18 '60 season, 896 carries for 5615yds, 6.3 avg.; best single season '62 216 carries for 1520yds, 7.0 avg., 11 tds; with Willie Fleming shared CFL mark longest single play gain 109yds '63; '62 Schenley outstanding player, Jeff Russel Memorial Trophy; Lord Calvert Trophy; frequent EFC, all-Cdn all-star hb mem. Cdn Football Hall of Fame.

DIXON, Stephanie (swimming); b. 10 Feb 1984, Brampton, Ont.; UVictoria; born without right leg she competed 2 Paralympics; 4 gold, 2 silver, 4 WR '00, 1 gold, 6 silver, 1 bronze, 1 WR '04; 3 gold, 1 WR '02 worlds; 1 WR '03 ntls; Swim Canada female swimmer with disability '01 award; King Clancy award '01; res. Caledon, Ont./Victoria, B.C.

DOAN, Shane (hockey); b. 10 Oct 1976, Halkirk, Alta; m. Andrea; c. Gracie, Joshua; ctr. Kamloops (WHL) '92-95, Springfield (AHL) '97-98; NHL Winnipeg '95-96, Phoenix '96-04; Team Canada '99 worlds, '04 World Cup (gold); 2 Memorial Cup titles, MVP, all-star '95; Kamloops Diamond in Rough award; NHL record (through '04) 648 scheduled games, 142g, 209a, 32 playoff games, 6g, 6a; scored WC title winning goal; res. Kamloops, B.C.

DOCHERTY, Alexander (t&f); b. 6 May 1904, Scotland; d. 3 Nov 1973, Montreal, Que.; m. Gwendolyn Mullins; c. Doreen, Gilbert; McGill; Northern Electric installation superintendent; middle distance runner; mem. Montreal AAA; ntl 1500m record; ntl mile champion; mem. '28

Olympic team; scored several victories on pre-, post-Olympic UK tour; Montreal Forum indoor meet title; rejected invitation to attend Notre Dame.

DOCKERILL, Sylvia (swimming); b. 17 Sep 1951, Vancouver, B.C.; given name: Sylvia Elizabeth; div. Christopher Dodd; m. Preston; UBC, BHE; home economics teacher; mem. ntl team '69-72; '70 CG, '71 PAG, '72 Olympic teams; gold 100m breast stroke '71 PAG, 7th medley relay '72 Olympic Games; active masters swimmer; res. Victoria, B.C.

DODGE, Ann (canoeing); b. 26 Mar 1958, Halifax, N.S.; given name: Ann Marie; div. Frederick Cooper; m. Mark Smith; c. Jasmine; Dalhousie, BPhE, Miss Murphy's Business College; kinesiology teacher Acadia; 3 gold '73 Canada Games; mem. ntl team '74-79; mem. '75 jr. worlds, '74, '77-78 worlds, '76 Olympic teams; specialized in singles, K2 (with Sue Holloway); mem. Dalhousie volleyball team '77; NS athlete of '73; mem. NS Sports Hall of Fame; res. Coldbrook, N.S.

DOEY, Jennifer (rowing); b. 9 Jan 1965, Scarborough, Ont.; m. Richard Doey; teacher; started rowing in HS '80; mem. Ntl team from '83; 2 Cdn 4s w/c, 1 8s title; 3 Head of the Charles 8s; '86 CG gold coxed 4s; 2 Amsterdam International coxed8s; 1 US Nationals coxed 4s, 2 8s, 2 coxless 4s; '89 FISU Games coxless 4s silver; '90 Vienna International pairs gold; '91 world coxless 4s, 8s gold; sport excellence award, '91 CARA Centennial Medal, Dick Ellis Memorial senior team of year '91 trophy; res. Vancouver, B.C.

DOHERTY, James (harness racing); b. 27 Sep 1940, Saint John, N.B.; trainer/driver/owner; drove 1st race and won '56; worked Milton Downey stable '60s; raced at Montreal, New England tracks; on NE circuit '66-76 winning NA driving title '72; one of only four drivers to win a race at Meadowlands each year since it opened in '76; best season 270 wins '76; through '03 4506 career victories, over $36M in purses; guided Green With Envy to aged pacing-mare-of-yr honors '84-85; with Sunbird Groovey set world record for aged trotting mare on half-mile track; wins include Alexander Memorial, New Jersey Classic, American National; mem. NE Harness Writers, NB, Saint John Sports, Horse Racing Living halls of fame; res. Saint John N.B./Clifton, N.J.

DOHERTY, Kevin (judo); b. 6 Nov 1958, Toronto, Ont.; Concordia; coach, ntl team '76-84; 1 ntl 71kg, 3 78kg titles; 1 US, Ont. Canada Cup 71kg title; 2 Canada Cup, International German, 1 Hungarian, Dutch 78kg titles; mem. '79, '83 PAG, '77, '82 Pan-Am championships, '81 world championships, '84 Olympic teams; gold 71kg '77, silver 78kg '82 Pan-Am championships; silver 71kg '79 PAG; bronze 78kg '81 worlds; fed. govt. excellence awards '82; Judo Can. tech. comm.; mem. Cdn Judo Hall of Fame; res. Notre Dame de Grace, Que.

DOIRON, Phillip (hockey/baseball); b. 7 May 1941, Moncton, N.B.; given name: Phillip Joseph; div. Betty Ann Deware; c. Patricia Joanne; ret'd fireman; c/lw Maritime midget, jr. A champs; played with Eastern Cdn champion Moncton Beavers '60 Memorial Cup; tryout Barrie

Memorial Cup champs '61; played in '63 Eastern Cdn Allan Cup playdowns; invited by Wren Blair to Minnesota North Stars training camp but did not report due to new job with fire dept.; won N.B. sr. HL scoring title '65; mem. Saint John Hardy Cup title team; ss/c with 2 Maritime sr. baseball title teams; set Maritime sr. batting avg. record .538 '64; insisted on wearing number 5 in every sport; N.B. athlete of decade '60-70; 1ˢᵗ Maritimer to participate in Pan-Am Games baseball '67; mem. Saint John, Battleford, Sask walls, Man. Baseball, N.B., Moncton Sports halls of fame; res. Moncton, N.B.

DOJACK, Paul (football); b. 24 Apr 1917, Winnipeg, Man.; given name: Paul Stanley; m. Ellen Annie Dawson; ret'd boys' school director; co-founder Dales Athletic Club; softball p, qb city juv football title team; coached Dales 4 consecutive Western Canadian football titles, '38 ntl jr. title; WIFU official, supervisor '47-73; officiated 546 games, including 15 Grey Cups, 9 as head referee; syndicated sports column on football rules; chair. '67 ntl jr. championships, Regina Centennial bantam football tournament; 36yrs youth correctional services; v-p Sask. Sports Hall of Fame '81, chair. selection comm. '76; mem. Cdn Football, Canada's, Sask. Sports halls of fame; res. Regina, Sask.

DOLAN, Paul (soccer): b. 16 Apr 1966, Ottawa, Ont.; promotion mgr. Umbro Canada; goaltender Vancouver Whitecaps NASL, Hamilton Steelers CSL, Vancouver 86ers A League; '88 CSL all-star; keeper for ntl -20 team '85 World Cup; youngest keeper to compete in World Cup game; participant 4 World Cup campaigns; mem. ntl team from '84; competed in '86 World Cup; 48 international caps; res. Vancouver, B.C.

DOLEGIEWICZ, Bishop (t&f); b. 8 Jul 1953, Toronto, Ont.; Texas; discus, shot put specialist; 3 all-American; 3 US titles; 1 ntl jr., CG discus, sr. shot put records; 8 ntl shot put titles; gold shot put '75 FISU Games, silver shot put '75, '79 PAG, bronze shot put '78, discus '82 CG; mem. '76, '80, '84 Olympic, '79, '81 World Cup teams; competed '00 *NBC* strongest men event; ntl team coach '85-90; head field events coach Southern Utah; PB: 20.85m shot, 65.12 discus; PetroCan coaching excellence award; res. Saskatoon, Sask.

DOMBROSKI, Ben (shooting); b. 31 Mar 1959, Orsainville, Que.; car dealership employee; full-bore rifle specialist; won Ont. grand aggregate; 2 Ont. Lt-Gov's. awards; qualified 8 Bisley teams; DCRA Gov-Gen's, Macdonald-Stewart Grand Aggregate, Bisley Aggregate titles '98; res. Angus, Ont.

DOMIK, Bernard (roller skating); b. 27 Sep 1933, Montreal, Que.; m. Rosemary Byard; c. Virginia Suzanne, Kenneth Bernard; cartage co. owner; ntl novice 4s champion '55; Eastern regional 4s titles '55, '57; ntl intermediate 4s '59; 2ⁿᵈ NA 4s '59; represented Canada in Roller Skating Rinks of America; ret'd '59; res. Toronto, Ont.

DOMIK, Bob (softball); b. 8 Jun 1942, Duparquet, Que.; m. Ann Purdy; c. Dawn Darlene, Sunday Rozalee; Davita Dorothy; partner cartage business; mem. '72 world-title team, pitched no-hitter, voted world's best pitcher with 0.00 ERA; 7 ntl championships from '68, 2 titles; 14 consecutive

strikeouts, 18 of 21 outs one '75 7-inning game; designed pitching program available through Softball Canada; pres.-founder Canadian International Softball Ambassadors; res. Cameron, Ont.

DOMONKOS, Mariann (table tennis); b. 12 Feb 1958, Budapest, Hungary; m. Adam Sharara; Concordia, UofOtt; coach; 9 Que. singles, 11 women's doubles, 7 mixed doubles titles; 10 ntl singles titles (in succession); mem. ntl team from '72; 4 ntl jr. girls, 1 NA jr. girls titles; NA women's doubles '72; gold medal sweep, singles, women's, mixed doubles, team '79 PAG; with Gloria Hsu gold '85, with Joe Ng silver '91 Commonwealth championships doubles; competed '88 Olympics; competed as amateur in West German pro league '81-82 ranking 3ʳᵈ overall; '82 ntl Open women's singles titles (1ˢᵗ Canadian); certified Que., Cdn. table tennis coach; Que. team athlete of '78; Southwest Que. athlete of '78, '80; ntl team coach '88-98; mem. Que. Sports Hall of Fame; res. Ottawa, Ont.

DONAGHEY, Sam (soccer/administration); b. 2 Feb 1922, Londonderry Co., Northern Ireland; m. Margaret Henderson; c. Alison Yvonne, Glynis Margaret, Samuel, Motra Elaine, Kery, Derryn; ret'd. policeman, cartographer; excelled in soccer, boxing, coached t&f in youth; emigrated to Canada '52; founder/player/mgr. Edmonton Police Soccer Team; coached youth soccer; anchor Edmonton Police Tug-O-War team '53-55; exec. Edmonton Dist. SA, ASA from '55; wrote 1ˢᵗ Alta soccer handbook; founder/editor *Alberta Soccer Bulletin; Cdn Soccer News;* upgraded soccer officiating in Alta.; Edmonton District HA exec '60-61; founder/exec. Western Canada SL, CSA; ntl team mgr. '67 PAG, '68 Olympics; clubhouse chair./assoc. dir. Edmonton International Speedway; key role in '78 Edmonton CG; liasion dir. '73 Brier; Intl ambassador '83 FISU Games; founder/pres. CSA Alumni Assn. from '97; ASA outstanding contribution award; Carling award '60; Edmonton sport leadership award; Edmonton Sportsman of '69; 2 United Way sportsman awards; hon. Chief 7 Cree, 1 Blackfoot, Ojibawa, Metis bands; life mem. Club Stardust Edmonton; recipient 1 of 7 Royal Bank jr. Olympic ring; Klondike Days silver tankard award; Royal Irish award; Northern Ireland sports council award; Edmonton mayor's award; 3 Alta awards; CG award; CSA Aubrey Sanford award; Kidney Foundation award; Editor's Choice award for poetry; Defence of Britain medal; War Service medal; Centennial medal '67; Cdn 125 medal '92; Cdn, Alta police long-service medals; Masonic medal of merit; mem. Order of Canada, Edmonton Sports, Historical halls of fame; res. Edmonton, Alta.

DONAHUE, Jake (t&f): b. 6 Apr 1940, St. Stephen, N.B.; given name: John Edward; m. Theresa; wheelchair t&f, table tennis; won 6 gold, 16 silver, 12 bronze in ntl wheelchair competitions '73-83; 3 silver, 5 bronze in 4 Pan-Am Wheelchair Games; ntl shotput record 6.14m '84; bronze '76, '80, silver, bronze '84 Olympics for Physically Disabled; St. Stephen's athlete of '76; NB merit award '76; NB outstanding athlete '78, CWSA most improved athlete '78; Greenough Sports Person of '79; 2 *St. Stephen's Courier* athlete-of-yr awards; mem. NB Sports Hall of Fame; res. St. Stephen, N.B.

DONATELLI, Eden (speed skating); b. 19 Jul 1970, Mission, B.C.; m. Julian Green; McGill; coach; mem. ntl team from '86; set Cdn short-track midget 300m record '83; 1st overall '86 Cdn jr. championships; mem. '86 world record short-track 3000m relay team; set Cdn long-track junior 5000m record; 8 world short-track gold medals; '88 Olympic 500m silver, 3000m relay bronze; set Cdn sr. record placing 6th '88 Olympics 1000m; 2 Cdn junior, 1 Cdn intermediate, 6 Cdn senior records; 2 Pacific Rim team short-track titles; world champion award '87, '89; BC jr. athlete of '87; mem. Athletes motivating excellence group; mem. BC Sports Hall of Fame; res. Mission, B.C.

DONISON, Butch (wrestling); b. 29 Sep 1938, Avonlea, Sask; given name: Sebastien; m. Patricia Greenaway; c. Mike, Diana; Denver, BSc; engineer; youngest of three wrestling brothers; 15yr wrestling career during which he competed in every weight class at provincial level winning titles in all but one; 3yrs all-Rocky Mountain Conf.; 13 provincial titles '53-67; 3 ntl titles; CG middleweight silver '66; coach Regina WC '65-67, UofRegina wrestling team '68-69; mem. Sask. Sports Hall of Fame; res. Regina, Sask.

DONISON, Danny (wrestling); b. 12 Aug 1932, Avonlea, Sask.; m. Marilyn Sedman; c. Lori, Lisa; UofRegina; administrator; 6 Sask. light, welter-,middleweight titles '53-68, 5 times runnerup; ntl lightweight title '55; Man. lightweight title '58; coach Regina WC '54-65; chair. wrestling comm. Sask. branch AAUofC '55-60; 2yrs secty. Regina Caps hockey club; secty.-treas. Regina Boxing & Wrestling Club '55-68; Man. outstanding wrestler award '58; mem. Sask. Sports Hall of Fame; res. Regina, Sask.

DONISON, Lee (wrestling/boxing); b. 9 Mar 1928, Avonlea, Sask.; m. Joan Peterson; c. Brian Lee, Garan-Loren, Ross Normand, Joanne Betty; Purdue; ret'd. insurance exec.; Sask. heavyweight wrestling titles '53-56; Sask. light-heavyweight boxing title '52, '63, heavyweight '53-57; ntl light heavy boxing title '63; alternate '54 BEG team; only Canadian athlete to win provincial, ntl boxing, wrestling titles 4 successive years '53-56; chairman Sask. boxing & wrestling '53-54, boxing '55-58, '62-63; Sask. championship outstanding- wrestler award '54; mem. Sask. Sports Hall of Fame; res. Regina, Sask.

DONNELLY, Sharon (triathlon); b. 29 Jul 1967, Scarborough, Ont.; given name: Sharon Lynn; m. David Rudnicki; Royal Military College, BComm; PE teacher; sports consultant; triathlete, reserve officer; specialist in Olympic distances; began competitive career as swimmer; competed in '84 Olympic trials; mem. '84 ntl record 4x100 medley relay team; held ntl, prov. 100m fly records; mem. Cdn Forces running team '90-95, CF winter biathlon team '94-95; launched, coached Petawawa running club '93-95, swim coach; ntl triathlon title '97; competed on WC circuit from '97; Cdn female WC triathlete of '97; CF female athlete of '95; 2 Ont. achievement awards; Ottawa ACT triathlete of '96-97; World Military Games fair play award '95; 2 Ont. international elite female triathletre awards; 10th in world rankings '96; honored by city of Gloucester '98; gold '99 PAG; silver '00 WC triathlon; mem. '00, '04 Olympic teams; turned to coaching '05; Ont. Assn of Triathletes elite Olympic award; mem. Cdn Forces Sports Hall of Fame; res. Kingston, Ont.

DONOHUE, Jack (basketball/coaching); b. 4 Jun 1931, New York, N.Y.; d. 16 Apr 2003, Kanata, Ont.; m. Mary Jane Choffin; c. Carol, John Joe, Kathy, Mary Beth, Bryan, Maura; Fordham, BA, NYU, MA; consultant Vancouver Grizzlies; began coaching St. Nicholas of Tolentine NYC '54, shifted to Power Memorial NYC; HS coaching record 250-46 including 71 consecutive victories due largely to efforts of Lew Alcindor (Kareem Abdul Jabbar); coach Holy Cross '65-71 compiling 106-65 record; Eastern region coach of '70; Cdn ntl team coach '72-90; guided team to 4th '76 Olympics; gold '83 FISU Games; qualified team for '80, '84, '88 Olympics; noted raconteur, TV commentator, business consultant; conceived popular *Donohue's Legends* TV series; CIAU championship tourney MVP award bears his name; spokesman for yr-of-the-coach-in-Cda; Cdn Coaching Assn. Geoff Gowan award; King Clancy award for work with disabled; Coach Mac award; Kanata, Ont. school bears his name; mem. Ont., Cdn Basketball; Ottawa, Canada's, Cdn Olympic Sports, NYC Coaches, Cdn Assn. of Public Speakers halls of fame.

DORATY, Ken (hockey); b. 23 Jun 1906, Stittsville, Ont.; d. 4 May 1981, Moose Jaw, Sask.; given name: Kenneth Edward; m. Dorothy; c. Saundra, Curtis; billiard parlor chain owner; raised in Rouleau, Sask.; mem. '25 Regina Pats Memorial Cup winners; diminutive size earned him variety of nicknames "Mighty Atom, Little Poison, Mighty Mite, Midget, Mighty Molecule" and one which stuck"Cagey"; brief stint Chicago '26-27; Toronto '33-35; gained reputation as money player with knack for scoring big goals like one at 4:46 of 6th overtime period as Toronto nipped Boston 1-0 in 5th game best-of-five '33 Stanley Cup semifinal; '34 accounted for fastest 3 goals in regulation play as Toronro beat Ottawa 7-4; frequently at odds with Conn Smythe, he closed NHL career with Detroit '37-38; coached Moose Jaw Canucks to '46 Memorial Cup finals; key role in Metro Prystai signing with Chicago; mem. Goulbourn Wall, Sask. Sports Hall of Fame.

DORE, David (figure skating/administration); b. 9 Aug 1940, Etobicoke, Ont.; given name: David Michael Dore; m. Carol Ann Massari; c. Christopher, Jeffrey Paul; Windsor, BA; UofT, BEd; C.A.E.; ret'd; introduced to skating as a child for therapy against polio; went on to become ntl level competitor; '64 Cdn fours title; ISU judge. officiating 7 worlds, '84 Olympics; Skate Canada pres.'80-84, youngest person to serve as pres. and only successive two-term pres; Skate Canada Dir.-Gen. '85-02; during his tenure he founded Ntl Team program, created Athlete Trust, wrote many technical programs, served as administrator '90, '96 worlds, spearheaded development of Events Trust, was CEO '01 worlds; at community level club administrator Toronto Cricket, Skating and Curling Club, Minto Skating Club; judges chair. Central Ontario Section; COA dir. '80-84, chair. Seneca Coll. Coaching Advisory Board '79-85, George Brown College Advisory Board '80-84; started management consulting upon retiring from Skate Canada, but give it up when elected v-p figure skating for the ISU '02-06; chair. ISU Development Commission, exec. mem. ISU Grand Prix Commission; Queen's 25th year medal, Ontario Special Achievement Award, Air Canada exec. of '83 award, Canada 125 Medal, American Express Cdn Sport Administrator of '93, award of excellence Ont. Bursary Comm. (longstanding contribution to figure skating);

named as one of 25 most influential people in world figure skating by *International Figure Skating Magazine*; Olympic Order; *Toronto Globe & Mail* one of 25 most influential Canadians in sport community (amateur and professional); res. Ottawa, Ont.

DORSCH, Henry (football); b. 11 Nov 1940, Weyburn, Sask.; m. Helen Patricia Kalb; c. Douglas, Natalie, Debra; Tulsa, BSc; annuity broker; 2yrs Regina Rams before starring at fb Tulsa; db/fb Saskatchewan '64-73; 4 Grey Cup finals, 1 winner; mem. Roughriders management comm. '75-80; GM Roughriders '78-80; res. Regina, Sask.

DORSEY, Dean (football); b. 13 May 1957, Toronto. Ont.; m. Lee McArthur; c. Paul, Thomas, Matt; UofT BPhE; bartender, ex-v-p Impac Golf, ret'd. football coach; punter, place kicking specialist; played jr Scarborough Rams '77; Jr A hockey Sault Ste. Marie '76-77; special teams award UofT; pro CFL Toronto '82; USFL Washington Federals '83; CFL Ottawa '84-87, '89-90; NFL Philadelphia '88; CFL Edmonton '91 tied Mark Mosley's all-pro record 23 consecutive field goals '87; all-Eastern '87; head coach Jr. Riders '97-98, QMJFL '98 champions; res. Kanata, Ont.

DOTY, Frederick (football); b. 25 Oct 1924, Toronto, Ont.; m. Beverley Brown; c. Cole, Tobin; UofT, BSc; ret'd civil engineer, pres. Dufferin Concrete Products; jr. Calgary '44; basketball Calgary RCAF '43-44; pro football Toronto '45-49; played both Argos, Varsity '46; 3 Grey Cup champions; mem. Mississauga Sports Hall of Fame; res. Mississauga, Ont.

DOUCET, Everard (builder/hockey); b. 29 Dec 1911, Bathurst, N.B.; d. 2 Oct 1971, Bathurst, N.B.; m. Betty; coached all levels juv through sr.; 3 Maritime titles; coached Bathurst Papermakers to North Shore titles '49-52; inagurated Bathurst minor hockey, baseball programs; Centennial medal; mem. NB, Bathurst Sports halls of fame.

DOUCET, Paul (boxing); b. 9 Oct 1917, Bathurst, N.B.; d. 8 Oct 1939, Bathurst, N.B.; nicknamed "Kid Lulu"; following standout amateur career turned pro '35; held Maritime lightweight title '38, Cdn jr. welterweight '39, Eastern Cdn lightweight '40; from '36-38 fought 37 times posting 30 wins, 5 losses, 2 draws, 15 KOs; ranked 3rd contender for Cdn lightweight title; fought Maurice Arnault (French welter champion), Dave Castilloux (Cdn lightweight titlist); killed in auto accident; mem. NB Sports Hall of Fame.

DOUCETTE, Gerry (football); b. 18 Sep 1933, Toronto, Ont.; d. 7 Apr 2001, Oakville, Ont.; given name: Gerald David; m. Mildred Ruth Grosse; c. Mike, Steve, Jill, Sue; salesman; led Etobicoke Rams to TDIAA title; Balmy Beach ORFU '53; Argos '54-59; qb/p/pk; CFL record: 75 scheduled games, 366 passes, 180 completions, 14 tds, 158 kickoffs, including 62 '56 season, 8458yds, 180 punts, 6691yds; dir. Argos ticket sales '78-79.

DOUGLAS, Jason (boxing); b. 6 Feb 1980, St. Ann, Jamaica; given name: Jason Bernard Douglas; full-time athlete; 91 kg heavyweight; started boxing age 13; 6 Ont. titles; silver '98 Pan Am Jrs; '98 Cdn. intermediate champion; '00 Jamaican ntl champion; '00 Olympic alternate; 3 Cdn. Sr. titles; gold '02 CG; bronze '03 PAG; 101-15 record to Jan. '04; Ont.

Best Boxer award '01; rookie of '02 award in first year as ntl. sr. champion; res. Kitchener, Ont.

DOUGLAS, Jim (lacrosse); b. 12 Mar 1919, New Westminster, B.C.; d. 24 July 2003, New Westminster, B.C.; m. Marg; c. 2; plywood industry exec.; considered one of best box lacrosse players in his era; competed for Adanacs at 17 scoring 31 goals in 15 games in rookie season; set Sr. A one-game record 12 goals, 4 assists '39 (record still stands); mem. 2 Mann Cup winners, 5 league champions; league MVP '39; 466 career goals, 182 assists, 218 games in 11 years with New Westminster, (Adanacs & Salmonbellies); mem. Canadian Lacrosse, BC Sports halls of fame.

DOUTHWRIGHT, Joyce (basketball/field hockey); b. 25 Apr 1950, Moncton, N.B.; given name: Joyce Anne; m. Dick Slipp; c. Shanda, Tyler; UNB, BPhE, BA; teacher, coach, coaching co-ordinator NBFHA; mem. ntl women's basketball team '69-76, NB team from '71; NB ntl title team '80, player-coach; 4 times ntl tournament all-star; mem. NB field hockey team '69-74; MVP UNB field hockey team '70-71; coached basketball, field hockey UNB; 2 CIAU FH coach-of-yr awards; tech. dir. NBABA '74-76; mem. '76 Olympic team; coach NB team '79 Canada Games; coached NB women's basketball Francophone Games bronze medal team '97; 2 CIAU FH coach-of-yr awards; mem. UNB phys ed dept. '76-80; selector ntl field hockey team; UNB athlete of '73-74; CIAU FH rookie-of-yr trophy bears her name; mem. NB Sports, Cdn Basketball, Olympic halls of fame; res. Fredericton, N.B.

DOWDING, John (figure skating); b. 27 Apr 1957, Oakville, Ont.; given name: John Stuart; m. Diane Doris; pro skater; with sister Debbie ntl jr. dance title '74; teamed with Lorna Wighton from '75; ntl titles '76-79; mem. '80 Olympic, world teams; only Cdn Oberstdorf title winners; 1st Cdn dance team to join Ice Capades; pro dance title '83; res. Fresno, Calif.

DOWDS, Maureen (t&f); b. 3 Jul 1948, Whitehorse, Yukon; given name: Maureen Joan; UMan, UWO.; ED Manitoba Special Olympics, ex-HS phys ed teacher; shot put specialist; twice top HS, UMan female athlete; Red River shot put title '64; ntl jr. '67; bronze, ntl jr. record 47'1" '67 PAG; ntl title '68; CWIAA title '72; runnerup ntl championships '74-75; 4th '75 PAG with PB 16.46m to tie record; injury forced her from '76 Olympics into retirement; mem. Man. Sports Hall of Fame selection comm.; mem. Man. Sports Hall of Fame; res. Winnipeg, Man.

DOWELL, Hanson (administration); b. 14 Sep 1906, Stewiacke, N.S.; d. 23 Sep 2000, Middleton, N.S.; given name: Hanson Taylor; m. Marjorie Alice Mosher; c. Charles Hanson, Roy Francis Mosher, Judith Helen, Edgar Douglass, Janet Marjorie; Dalhousie, LLB; ret'd judge; Central Valley HL officer '35-36; pres. Maritime AHA '36-40; v-p CAHA '40-45, pres. '45-47; pres. CVHL '52-53; treas. MAHA '68-74; NSHA '74-81; USAHA citation '50; CAHA merit award '62; life mem. CAHA, Middleton CC; mem. NS Sports Hall of Fame.

DOWNEY, Raymond (boxing); b. 23 Sep 1968, Halifax, N.S.; c. Tyler Flint, Raya Flint; pro boxer; son of Dave Downey former Cdn middleweight champion; became Cdn jr featherweight champ at 14; at 17 won Cdn intermediate light middleweight title; at 18 became Cdn senior light-middleweight king; mem. Citadel Amateur Boxing Club coached by Taylor Gordon; bronze '88 Olympics; silver '90 World Cup, CG; gold '89 Canada Games, '90 President's Cup in Indonesia; SFC Viscount Alexander trophy '89; Olympic champion award '89; turned pro '93; pro record: 13-1-1, 9kos; res. Philadelphia, Pa.

DOWNS, Darcy (skiing); b. 26 Aug 1968, Regina, Sask.; m. Jane Mather; freestyle specialist; Nor-Am aerials champion '91-92; 10 WC medals; 4 straight ntl combined titles '92-94; ntl ballet title '95; world combined gold '97; ntl aerials silver '98; Ottawa ACT FS skier of '97; res. Vancouver, B.C.

DOYLE, Jimmy (golf); b. 28 Feb 1933, Winnipeg, Man.; d. 6 Apr 1991, Sandy Hook, Man.; given name: James Arthur; m. Beverly Byron; c. Drew, Byron, Pat, Maureen; Man. jr. title '51; mem. ntl jr. basketball champion Winnipeg Light Infantry team '51; Sask. Open title '61; runnerup Man. Open '57; ND State Open, Thunder Bay Open titles; won '75 Man. Amateur; 2 Man. Srs titles; '88 age group sr. A title; '89 medalist sr. interprovincial team championships, 3rd individual;11 Man. Willingdon Cup teams; Cdn amateur title, low medalist '68; mem. '68 Eisenhower Cup team; Man. athlete of '68; mem. Man. Sports Hall of Fame.

DRAFFIN, Ernie (soccer); b. 21 Sep 1909, Winnipeg, Man., d. 19 Dec 1982, Winnipeg, Man.; m. Louise; c. Arlene; politician; goalie '23-24 Welton Cup HS team, '25-26 Man. HS title team, '27, '30 Man. jr. title teams, '31 Westbrook John Queen Cup winner, '33 2nd div. United Weston team; '34 Man. title team; assisted in formation National League; Man. FA pres. '55-61; tech. dir. soccer '67 PAG; MFA registrar; founding dir., hon. life mem. Man. Sports Fed.; life mem. MSA; CCF MLA Assiniboia; mem. Man. Sports Hall of Fame.

DRAKE, Clare (coaching/hockey/football); b. 9 Oct 1928, Yorkton, Sask.; given name. Clare James; m. Dolly Claire Carlson; c. Debbie Clare, Jami Lee; UBC, BPhE, UAlta, BEd, hon. LLD, Washington, MSc, Oregon, EdD; ret'd. prof., hockey coach; jr. A hockey Regina, Medicine Hat, sr. Yorkton; semipro baseball; basketball, football, hockey UBC, hockey team capt. sr. year, hockey UAlta; began coaching minor hockey, football, basketball, t&f '51, football, baseball '55; coach German ntl HL '54-55; UAlta head hockey coach from '58 (excluding '69-70, '75-76, '79-80); coach Edmonton Oilers (WHA) '75-76; asst. coach Winnipeg (NHL) '88-91; special assignments coach San Jose from '92; UAlta head football coach '62, '67-68; rare feat of guiding UAlta to Vanier Cup football title '67, CIAU hockey title '67-68; winningest univ. hockey coach NA history, 1st Cdn univ. hockey coach to record 500 victories; through '87 guided UAlta to 622 wins, 16 conference, 6 ntl titles; coached Lacombe Rockets '65 Ahearne Cup; ntl team '72, '81, '87 FISU Games, gold '81; co-coach '80 Olympic team; coached first-ever Cdn team Spengler Cup winner '84; ntl novice singles racquetball title '71; Edmonton sportsman of year '67, '75; CHA Juckes award '92; hon. life mem. Alta. Football Coaches Assn.; 2 CIAU hockey coach-of-yr awards; active

administrative role football, hockey; authored numerous hockey articles; UAlta arena bears his name; mem. UAlta Sports Wall, Ualta Alumni wall of recognition, Canada's, Alta., BC Sports halls of fame; res. Edmonton, Alta.

DRAKE, Dallas (hockey); b. 4 Feb 1969, Trail, B.C.; m. Amy; c. Jackson, Delaney, Darby Ann; North Michigan; rw Rossland (KIJHL) 84-87, Vernon (BCHL) '87-88, North-Michigan '88-92; 6th choice Detroit '89 draft; NHL Detroit '92-94, Winnipeg '94-96, Phoenix '96-00, St. Louis 2000-04; NHL record (through '04) 822 scheduled games, 166g, 267a, 68 playoff games, 13g, 16a; NCAA all-American '92; WCHA player of '92 award; WCHA all-star '92; mem. NMU Sports Hall of Fame; nickname "Dally"; res. St. Louis, Mo.

DRAKE, Maureen (tennis); b. 21 Mar 1971, Toronto, Ont.; tennis player; Cdn. Fed Cup team from '91; reached 4th round '99 Australian Open; defeated first top-10 player (Patty Schnyder) '99; career high ranking 47 on WTA Tour '99; 3rd round Wimbledon '02; 6 ITF Women's Circuit singles titles; 8-3 singles record in Fed Cup play; Tennis Canada Excellence Award female player of '02; res. Toronto, Ont.

DRAKICH, Ed (volleyball); b. 30 Sep 1962, Windsor, Ont.; UofT; 2 CIAU all-Cdn; represented Canada in 120 international indoor matches '85-88; pro with Munich '88-89; played beach volleyball from '85 winning 4 ntl titles; sister, mother both played on ntl teams; with Jose Cuervo NA champion '92; competed 6 world beach championships; res. Toronto, Ont.

DRAPER, Kris (hockey); b. 24 May 1971, Toronto, Ont.; m., c. 2; ctr Don Mills (MTHL) '87-88; Team Canada '88-90; Ottawa 67's '90-91; 4th Winnipeg choice '89 draft; AHL stints in Moncton, Adirondack; NHL Winnipeg '91-92, Detroit '93-04; NHL record (through '04) 724 scheduled games, 108g, 128a, 148 playoff games, 18g, 20a; 1 Selke trophy; mem. 2 Stanley Cup winners; mem. Team Canada '04 World Cup (gold); res. Detroit, Mich.

DRAXINGER, Kevin (swimming); b. 16 Mar 1967, Vancouver, B.C.; UBC; backstroke specialist; mem. ntl team from '87; 2 Canada Games gold; 9 ntl titles; 4 CIAU titles; 6 World Cup competitions gold medals; bronze '90, silver '94 CG 200m backstroke; mem. '91 FISU, '92 Olympic team; ntl 200m record holder; 1 CIAU male swimmer of yr award; res. Richmond, B.C.

DRAYTON, Jerome (t&f); b. 10 Jan 1945, Kolbermoor, W.Germany; given name: Peter Buniak; UofT, McMaster, BA; ret'd. govt. fitness consultant; 12 ntl titles, 13 records at varied distances; 1st of 4 ntl 10,000m titles '68; ntl record for distance 28:25.8 '70; ntl 5000m title '70; ntl marathon champion '72; 3 Fukuoka Japan marathon titles; Boston marathon '77; world record indoor 3-mile 13:06.0 '75, 10-mile track record 46:37.6 '73; mem. 3 CG, '68, '76 Olympic teams; silver '78 CG; '79 National Capital, '80 Maryland International marathon titles; ret'd from competition '84; Norton Crowe trophy '77; Mimico HS, Lakeshore Etobicoke, Ont. athlete-of-yr awards; Cdn runner-of-'75 award; names Canada's top male marathoner of century; mem. Cdn Roadrunners, Etobicoke, Canada's Sports halls of fame; res. Toronto, Ont.

DRILLON, Gord (hockey); b. 23 Oct 1914, Moncton, N.B.; d. 23 Sep 1986, Saint John, N.B.; given name: Gordon Arthur; m. Barbara Alice Lee; NB govt. consultant; jr. Moncton Athletics, Wheelers, Toronto Young Rangers, Lions, sr. Pittsburgh '35; pro Maple Leafs '36-42, Canadiens '42-43; NHL record: 155g, 139a, playoffs 26g, 15a; twice 1st, 2nd team all-star; NHL scoring title, Lady Byng Trophy '37-38; chosen by fans as most popular NHL player '39; with Bob Davidson, Syl Apps Sr. formed Leafs' DAD line; southpaw softball pitcher Toronto Danforth Aces, Maritime CNR; competed Eastern Cdn tennis championships; honored by City of Saint John; mem. Canada's, Saint John, NB Sports, Canadian Hockey halls of fame.

DRINKWATER, Graham (hockey); b. 22 Feb 1875, Montreal, Que.; d. 26 Sep 1946, Montreal, Que.; given name: Charles Graham; McGill; jr. MAAA 1892-93 title team; McGill jr. football, int. hockey champions; Montreal Victorias 4 Stanley Cup winners, team capt. 1898-99; never turned pro; mem. Hockey Hall of Fame.

DRISCOLL, Mary Ellen (golf); b. 30 Dec 1937, Saint John, N.B.; ed. dir. St. Joseph's Hospital; 6 NB, 3 Maritime jr. titles '53-58; lost ntl jr. title in playoff '57; 25 NB women's amateur, 6 NS ladies, 12 (10 consec.) NB sr. ladies titles; mem. 38 NB ladies amateur teams; runner-up Cdn amateur '65; 27 Riverside Club titles; nominated as alternate to 3 Commonwealth teams; dubbed "Queen of NB Golf"; twice broke 70 barrier; mem. NB, Saint John Sports halls of fame; res. Rothesay, N.B.

DROLET, François (speed skating); b. 16 Jul 1972, Ste-Foy, Que; Laval; short-track specialist; 2 bronze '95 Universiade; 2 world championship relay silver; 2 world team championship gold '96; with Marc Gagnon, Derrick Campbell, Éric Bedard gold '98 Olympic 5000m relay; gold '98 world team championships; noted for superstitions; res. Montreal, Que.

DROLET, Nancy (hockey); b. 2 Aug 1973, Drummondville, Que.; m. Nathalie Allaire (same sex ceremony); orthotherapist/massotherapist; owner Team Spirit Enterprises; standout softball player mem. ntl team '90-91; PAG silver '91; competed '89 Canada Summer Games in softball, '91 Canada Winter Games in hockey; began playing hockey age 5; ntl team '92-02; fwd world, 7 ntl, 2 Pacific Rim, 3 3-Nations Cup title teams; silver '98 Olympics; 112 goals in 108 intl games; mem. Vancouver Griffins title team, top scorer; MVP '99 Esso Cup ntls; outstanding-player award '94 ntls; Elaine Tanner Trophy '92; operates summer hockey school; res. Repentigny, Que./Vancouver, B.C.

DRYDEN, Dave (hockey); b. 5 Sep 1941, Hamilton, Ont.; given name: David Murray; m. Sandra Bailey; c. Debra, Greg; Waterloo, Wilfrid Laurier, BA, York, (hons) BA, Niagara Falls, MA; ret'd. PS principal; goaltender Galt Jrs.; 9 NHL seasons with NYR '61-62, Chicago '65-69, Buffalo '70-73, Edmonton '79-80; WHA with Chicago '74-75, Edmonton '75-70; minor league stints with Rochester, Buffalo (AHL), St. Louis (CPHL), Dallas (CHL), Salt Lake (WHL); NHL record: 203 scheduled games, 48-57-24, 10,424min, 9so, 555ga, 3 playoff games, 0-2, 137min, 9ga; WHA record: 242 scheduled games, 13,920min, 8so, 808ga, 19 playoff games, 958min, 63ga; asst. coach Edmonton '79;

mgr./coach Peterborough OHL '79-81, goalie coach Detroit '85-91, goalie consultant Nippon Paper Crane, Japan from '96; WHA MVP award '79; res. Oakville, Ont.

DRYDEN, Ken (hockey); b. 8 Aug 1947, Hamilton, Ont.; given name: Kenneth Wayne; m. Lynda; c. Sarah, Michael; Cornell, UMan, McGill, LLB., hon LLD, Windsor, UBC, York; hockey executive, politician, lawyer, author; jr. B Etobicoke; Boston 3rd choice, 14 overall '64 amateur draft; opted for Cornell; 3 times all-American, ECAA tournament MVP; BostonU outstanding-opponent award '69; ntl team; pro Montreal Voyageurs '70-71; Canadiens '71-79; sat out '73-74 to complete law studies; Calder Memorial Trophy, 5 Vezina Trophies, 1 Conn Smythe Trophy; 5 1st team, once 2nd team all-star goalie; mem. Team Canada '72, '76; NHL record: 397 scheduled games, 46so, 2.24 avg., 112 playoff games, 10 so, 2.40 avg., 338-89-74 win-loss-tie record; mem. 6 Stanley Cup winners; authored *The Game*, with Roy MacGregor *Home Game*, 2 other books; Ont. Youth commissioner '84-86, Yukon youth consultant '87; pres./CEO/GM Maple Leafs '97-04; *ABC-TV* color commentator 3 winter Olympics; initiated Ken Dryden scholarships; resigned as TML GM to enter politics; mem. Etobicoke, Canada's Sports, Hockey halls of fame; res. Toronto, Ont.

DRYDEN, Nikki (swimming); b. 4 May 1975, Calgary, Alta.; Brown; backstroke, FS specialist; began competing age 10; 16 ntl titles; mem. ntl team from '91; 3 silver '91 PAG, bronze '94 CG; mem. '92, '96 Olympic Games teams; competed '93 Pan-Pacific championships; Victoria jr athlete of '91; res. Gainesville, Fla.

DUBE, Ajay (field hockey); b. 10 Oct 1960, Paris, France; Humber College, York; owns sports apparel co.; emigrated to Canada age 11; goalkeeper Ont., Cdn -21, senior teams; ret'd from ntl outdoor team '89 but returned '94; mem. Outaouais, Ookpik clubs; mem. '87 gold medal PAG team; mem. '88 Olympic team; competes in both outdoor, indoor events; varied exec. roles with Ookpik, FH Ont.; competed '93 Ottawa marathon; mem. Big Brothers organization; mgr. Cdn Pan-Am Cup team '02; res. Toronto, Ont.

DUBÉ, Danielle (hockey); b. 10 Mar 1976, Vancouver, B.C.; pro hockey player; played 13yrs Grandview MHA; Jr. B with BC champion Grandview Steelers '94, Abbotsford Pilots '95; Jr. A Penticton Panthers '94; goaltender Central Texas Stampede Western Pro League '96-97; plays roller hockey with Vancouver Voodoos; mem. Team Canada from '93; 6 world, 2 Pacific Rim, 3 3-Nations Cup titles; silver '98, gold '02 Olympics; 3rd woman to play in men's pro hockey league as goalie WCHL Long Beach; mem. BC '01 Canada Winter Games team; BC female athlete of '96; res. Vancouver, B.C.

DUBLINSKI, Tom (football); b. 8 Aug 1930, Chicago, Ill.; m. Jo Ann Hurley; c. Michael, Karen, William, Mary Jo, Richard; Utah, BSc ret'd. insurance exec.; pro Detroit '52-54, Toronto '55-57, '62, NY Giants '58, Hamilton '59, '61, Denver '60; all-conf. HS baseball, football, college football; offensive player of week US college ranks, hon, mention all-American qb; 4th in US total offence sr. year, 2yrs conf. offensive leader; mem. Detroit NFL title teams '52-53, div. champs '54; only pro qb to play entire college all-star game offensively and defensively '54; mem. '58

Giants' div. champs; completed CFL record 16 of 18 passes for Argos vs Ticats '55 season opener; mem. '59, '61 EFC Hamilton title teams; played in inaugural Cdn East-West all-star game; res. Fountain Hills, Ariz.

DUBNICOFF, Tanya (cycling); b. 7 Nov 1969, Winnipeg, Man.; UMan.; cycling coach Olympic oval; ntl jr. development cycling coach; played ringette from age 7; mem. Team Canada '90 Worlds; BMX racer from age 12 winning ntl age-group title; began sprint cycling age 18; 4 PAG, 2 CG gold; competed '91, '95, '99 PAG, '94, '98 CG; 1st Cdn woman to win world sprint championship '93; 10 ntl sprint titles, 6 ntl 500 titles; 1 PAG, CG, 1 world, 2 ntl records; 3 World Cup race victories; ITT 500m silver, sprint bronze '98, '99 worlds; competed '92 (6), '96 (8), '00 (7) Olympics; flag-bearer '99 PAG; also excelled in hockey; mem. Man. Sports Hall of Fame; res. Calgary, Alta.

DUBOIS, Luc (skiing); b. 19 Jun 1946, Ste. Agathe, Que.; m. Line Marcoux; c. Olivier, Elise, Magalie; Montreal, BA, UofOtt, BPhE; ski event producer; distributor health supplements; ex-hotelier; broken leg during '65 ntl jr. championships ended promising competitive career; coaching '66-76; Level IV CSIA certificate; Que. team coach '70-71; asst. coach men's WC team '71-72; asst. program dir. CSA '72-73; program dir. '73-76; p.-pres. Canadian Ski Coaches Fed.; v-p CSIA; mem. ntl tech. comm. CSCF, CSIA; demonstrator '79 Interski; jr. college athlete of '64; competitive water skier '60-64, Que. champion, masters champion; res. St. Jovite, Que.

DUBOIS, Theo (rowing); b. 19 May 1911, Brussels, Belgium; given name: Theo Alfred; UMan, BArch; ret'd. architect, Wpg planning examiner; ntl jr. singles '38, CAAO singles, sr. doubles '39; qualified for cancelled '40 Olympics; NAAO sr. doubles with Albert Riley '40; US singles '40-41, '47; ntl singles '41-42; Eastern Rowing Assn. singles '42; ntl doubles '47; failed to qualify '48 Olympics despite posting time faster than Olympic winner; ret'd from major competition '48; veteran's trophy '76-77 North Western Rowing Assn. regatta; outstanding cyclist; twice defeated US champion Adolph Velthuysen '34; representing Ottawa YMCA won EO light-heavyweight boxing title '43; Lou Marsh Trophy, Canadian athlete of '41; mem. Man. Sports Hall of Fame; res. Winnipeg, Man.

DUCEY, John (baseball); b. 31 Aug 1908, Buffalo, N.Y.; d. 12 Sep 1983, Edmonton, Alta.; m. Grace Jay Mungull; c. Brant, Duane; real estate broker; batboy Edmonton Western pro league '21; 1b Edmonton Yeomen jrs.; umpire Calif., N.E. '31-45; co-founder Intercity Big 4 League Alta. '46; mgr. class A Western International league '53-54, Eskimos semipro club (WCL) '55-61; mgr. ntl team National Baseball Congress global world series runnerup '57; formed Edmonton Oldtimers BA '64; hon. dir. Edmonton Trappers AAA club; trustee Carling-O'Keefe award of merit; mem. Edmonton, Alta. Sports, Canadian Baseball halls of fame.

DUCHESNAY, Isabelle (figure skating); b. 18 Dec 1963, Hull, Que.; div. Christopher Dean; c. Paul; UofOtt; pro skater, coach; with brother Paul formed ice dance team which earned ntl jr. silver '82, bronze Cdn sr. championships '84-95; feeling they were being ignored by Cdn skating officials took advantage of dual Canadian-French citizenship to compete

for France where they claimed ntl titles '85-92; world bronze '89, silver '90, gold '91; competed '88, '92 Olympics winning silver '92; 1 silver, 2 bronze European championships; turned pro and toured with varied ice shows from '90; appeared in TV/film productions; did some TV/radio announcing in France, Germany, Canada; organized/managed own skating tours in Europe; conducted leadership/stress seminars; hon. pres. Pavillon du Parc Foundation '96; hon. pres. Star 97 ballroom and competitive dancing '96; back injury to Paul led to retirement from competition '97; thwarted by CFSA in getting coaching certification left Canada again to teach with Kerry Leitch at JP Igloo Ice & Inline Sports Complex; rinks in France, Aylmer, Que. bear their name, also street in Aylmer; awarded French Legion of Honor; mem. Ottawa Sports Hall of Fame; res. Aylmer, Que.

DUCHESNAY, Paul (figure skating); b. 31 Jul 1961, Hull, Que.; UofOtt, BSc; pro figure skater; dual Canadian-French citizenship; with sister Isabelle formed ice dance team which won world championship; (see Isabelle for competitive record); back injury led to retirement from competition '97; thwarted by CFSA in getting coaching certification left Canada again to teach with Kerry Leitch at JP Igloo Ice & Inline Sports Complex; rinks in France, Aylmer, Que. bear their name, also street in Aylmer; awarded French Legion of Honor; mem. Ottawa Sports Hall of Fame; res. Aylmer, Que.

DUCHESNE, Gaétan (hockey); b. 11 Jul 1962, Les Saulles, Que.; m. Gina DeRico; c. Jeremy, Chloe; Dutech Architect Supply; lw Quebec (QJHL) '79-81, Hershey (AHL) '83, NHL Washington '81-87, Quebec '87-89, Minnesota '89-93, San Jose '93-95, Florida '95; NHL record: 1028 scheduled games, 179g, 254a, 84 playoff games, 14g, 13a; res. St. Augustine, Que.

DUDLEY, George (builder/hockey); b. 19 Apr 1894, Midland, Ont.; d. 8 May 1960, Midland, Ont.; UofT, LLD; lawyer; played hockey in Midland; after earning law degree turned to executive roles; mem. CAHA exec. '25, pres. '40-42, secty '45, secty-mgr.; major role in early visits to Canada by Russian teams; treas. OHA; pres. IIHF; head hockey section '60 Olympic Games at time of death; mem. Hockey Hall of Fame.

DUDLEY, Rick (hockey/coaching/administration); b. 31 Jan 1949, Toronto, Ont.; given name: Rick Clarence; m. Ja Hee; lw OHA St. Catharines '68-69, CHL Iowa '69-70, IHL Flint '70-71, AHL Cleveland '70-71, Cincinnati '71-73, Fredericton '81-82, NHL Buffalo '72-75, '78-81, Winnipeg '80-81, WHA Cincinnati '75-77; NHL totals 307 scheduled games, 75g, 99a, 25 playoff games, 7g, 2a; WHA totals 270 scheduled games, 131g, 146a, 4 playoff games, 0g, 1a; WHA all-star; wore jersey 99 with Jets; part-owner/v.-pres Belleville OHL; ECHL league pres. '83-86; GM/coach Carolina ECHL; coached Carolina ACHL '82-86, 4 league, 2 playoff titles; coach IHL Flint '86-88, San Diego '92-93, Phoenix '93-94, Detroit '94-96 (1 Turner Cup); New Haven AHL '88-89; Buffalo NHL '89-92, Florida '03-04; GM Tampa Bay, 2yrs, Ottawa, 1yr, Florida 2yrs; commissioner's trophy '88, Fred Huber trophy '97; res. Florida.

DUFF, Alexander (coaching); b. 12 Apr 1887, Scotland; d. 16 Dec 1952, Toronto, Ont.; given name: Alexander Robert; UofT, BSc; chemical engineer; hon. coach High

Park Club; formed Dolphinets SC teaching aquatic skills for girls and women; guided Jean Kirkpatrick 1st Cdn woman to medal in US competition; coached Dorothy Prior 1st Cdn female swimmer to compete in Olympics '28; coached Cdn swimming/diving team '34 BEG; asst coach '36 Olympics; Toronto pool bears his name; mem. Ont. Aquatic Hall of Fame.

DUFF, Dick (hockey); b. 18 Feb 1936, Kirkland Lake, Ont.; given name: Richard Terrance; St. Michael's College, Assumption College, BA; ret'd hockey scout; jr. St. Mike's; pro Toronto '54-63; lw line with Tod Sloan, George Armstrong; NYR '64, Montreal '65-69, Los Angeles '70, Buffalo '71-72; asst coach Leafs '79-81, head coach 2 games; scout '81-93; NHL record: 1030 scheduled games, 283g, 289a, 114 playoff games, 30g, 49a; mem. 6 Stanley Cup winners; mem. Hockey Heritage North Hall of Fame; res. Mississauga, Ont.

DUFF, Mike (motorsport); b. 13 Dec 1939, Toronto, Ont.; given name: Michael Alan; m. Carol Sullivan; c. Christopher, Jacqueline, Tony; Ministry of Labor; launched Cdn motorcycle racing career '55; European circuit road racer '60; 5th 350cc class, 3rd 250cc class '63 worlds; 2nd 250cc '65 worlds; 9th person in world to lap Isle of Man at 100 mph avg.; 1st to lap Belgian GP course on 250cc at 125 mph avg.; Belgian GP title '64, Dutch TT 125, Finnish GP 250cc '65; 2nd Isle of Man '65; major injury sustained '65 led to '68 retirement following US, Cdn circuit races; changed name to Michelle following gender change operation '85; mem. Cdn Motorsport Hall of Fame; res. Coldwater, Ont.

DUFFY, James (t&f); b. 1 May 1890, Sligo County, Ireland; d. 23 Apr 1915, Ypres, Belgium; stone cutter; emigrated to Canada '11; 5th marathon '12 Olympics; Ward marathon, Hamilton Around-the-Bay marathon titles '12; Boston marathon '14; pro with limited success '14; killed overseas WW1.

DUFRESNE, Coleen (basketball); b. 15 Feb 1953, Halifax, N.S.; m. Kim Stewner; c. Nicholas; UofOtt, BPhE, McGill; AD UMan.; NS, Que. shot put, javelin, triple jump records; led OUAA basketball scorers 4yrs; ntl team '74-76; mem. '75 world, PAG, '76 Olympic teams; mem. Que. team '71, '75 Canada Winter Games teams; all-Cdn '75; Ottawa region basketball athlete of '74-75; coached sr. basketball Que., NB, Que. provincial jr. team; asst. coach '79 Canada Games gold medal team; taught HS phys ed Pte. Claire '76-79; mem. UNB phys ed staff '80-84; UMan basketball coach '84-01; 3 CIAU titles; 3 CIAU coach-of-yr awards; res. Winnipeg, Man.

DUGAN, Arnie (lacrosse/hockey); b. 9 Jan 1928, Windsor, Ont.; given name: Arnold Lee; m. Adele Gardiner; c. Lorraine, Arnie Jr., Alex, Cathy, Christine; ret'd. B.C. Hydro; jr. hockey Lakefield, Peterborough, Stratford, Toronto Young Rangers; pro Washington (AHL), Akron (IHL), Lake Placid (EL), Milwaukee (IHL), Detroit (IHL), Peterborough Srs.; baseball, football with jr. teams; lacrosse Ont. Sr. B champs '47-48; set Cdn box lacrosse Sr. A record 10g, 8a single game '50 while leading Ont. league scoring; mem. 5 Mann Cup finalists, 3 titles; 2 1st team all-star; capt. Nanaimo Clipper to 2 Coy Cup (BCHA sr. div.) titles; mem. Cdn. Lacrosse, Peterborough Sports halls of fame; res. Ucluelet, B.C.

DUGAN, Jackie (boxing); b. 28 Apr 1926, Peterborough, Ont.; d. 31 Jan 2005, Peterborough, Ont.; given name: John Edwin; m. Gail O'Heggerty; c. Patty, Melanie; ret'd. youth worker; won 95 of 105 amateur bouts; lost only 2 of 46 pro bouts; armed forces middleweight title '44-45; Cdn middleweight title '47; ret'd. as unbeaten title holder; dir. Toronto St. Alban's Boys Club; mem. Peterborough Sports, Cdn Boxing halls of fame.

DUGGAN, Herrick (sailing); b. 1862, Toronto, Ont; d. 1946, Toronto, Ont.; given name: George Herrick; Upper Canada College, UofT; construction engineer; assisted in formation Toronto Yacht Club 1880, Lake Yacht Racing Assn.; as mem. Royal St. Lawrence YC Montreal 1896 challenged for Seawanhaka Cup; designed 5 of 18 challengers and skippered Glencairn I to cup victory; defended successfully vs. US, UK challengers; designed unusual yacht Dominion, claimed as single hulled with two waterlines although rivals said it was double-hulled catamaran; in his time considered best designer of small boats in world; designed, built total of 142 boats; mem. Canada's Sports Hall of Fame.

DUGGAN, Keltie (swimming); b. 7 Sep 1970, Edmonton, Alta.; UAlta; breaststroke specialist; mem. ntl team from '87; 8 Ntl, 5 CIAU, 1 Pan Pacific titles; '87 PAG gold 100m breaststroke, silver 4x100 medley relay; '90 CG gold 100m breaststroke, bronze 4x100 medley relay; '90 worlds 50m bronze; Swimming Canada's female athlete of year '89; 2 CIAU female swimmer of yr; UAlta Bakewell trophy female athlete of year '89-90; sport excellence award; res. Edmonton, Alta.

DUGUAY, Ron (hockey/coaching); b. 6 Jul 1957, Sudbury, Ont.; m. Kim Alexis; c. Nora, Amber, Shay, (sc) Jamie, Bobby; hockey exec.; ctr OMJHL Sudbury '73-77, Team Canada '77, '81; NHL NYR '77-83, '86-88, Detroit '83-86, Pittsburgh '86-87, Los Angeles '88-89, IHL Colorado '87-88, San Diego '90-92, WCHL San Diego '95-98, Mannheimer Ger. '89-90, ACHL Jacksonville '98-99; NHL totals: 864 scheduled games, 274g, 346a, 89 playoff games, 31g, 22a; 1 NHL all-star, 1 Stanley Cup final; reputation as Broadway playboy; coach/GM Jacksonville ACHL; active in HMI; nickname "Doogie"; mem. Hockey Heritage North Hall of Fame; res. Ponte Verda Beach, Fla.

DUGUID, Don (curling); b. 21 Oct 1935, Winnipeg, Man.; div.; c. Terry, Dale, Dean, Randy, Kevin, Jill Staub; ex-*CBC* curling commentator; 6yrs mem. Terry Braunstein rink; mem. Howie Wood Jr. '57 Man. Brier entry; third for Braunstein '65 Brier winner; skipped Brier, Silver Broom (world) winners '70-71; 3 times Man. bonspiel grand aggregate winner; popularized youth curling schools, use of microphones on curlers for live broadcasts; '72-00 *CBC* curling commentator working '94 CG, '92, '98 Olympic Games; chair. '98 Brier; mem. Canada's, Man. Sports, Cdn, Man. Curling halls of fame; res. Winnipeg, Man.

DUHAIME, Greg (t&f); b. 11 Aug 1953, Espanola, Ont.; d. 28 Oct 1992, Port Elgin, Ont.; distance runner; ntl 3000m steeplechase record 8:36.3 '79; ntl indoor 3000m title '80; 3 ntl steeplechase, 1 5000m titles; Pacific Conf. Games steeplechase title '81; bronze steeplechase '82 CG, '83 PAG; ntl steeplechase, x-country records; mem. '79

PAG, '84 Olympic Games teams; mem. North Bay Sports Hall of Fame.

DUHAMEL, Miguel (motorsport); b. 26 May 1967, Lasalle, Que.; pro racer; with brother Mario raced mini-bikes before graduating to bigger machines; turned road race pro '88; AMA Superbike (1st Cdn), 600 SuperSport titles '95; 23 Superbike wins, 6 win streak; 40 SuperSport wins, 10 win streak; 3 Daytona 200, 4 AMA 600 SuperSport titles; won FIM world endurance team title with Team Kawasaki '92; won 2nd 600cc SuperSport series title with 7 race wins '93; rode Harley-Davidson debut of VR 1000 Superbike '94; AMA rookie of yr '90, pro-athlete-of-'95 award; res. Los Angeles, Calif./Sarasota, Fla./Montreal, Que.

DUHAMEL, Yvon (motorsport); b. 17 Oct 1939, Montreal, Que.; m. Sofia Cecchino; c. Mario, Jina, Miguel; businessman; 7 times White Trophy winner, highest award in Cdn motorcycling; '67-68 Daytona Classic 250cc class; ntl '81 GP 750cc; 1st rider to lap Daytona at more than 150mph; '71-72 AMA ntl titles at Tallegada, Ala., AMA 125 miler at Atlanta; '73 250-mile Ontario, Calif. title; top point scorer English match race series; 10th stock car grand ntl '73; world 750cc title '73; European 750cc title '74; world snowmobile title '70; only winner 500-mile Winnipeg-St. Paul snowmobile race title '72; ntl speed records both motorcycles, snowmobiles; '77 ntl GP 250cc title; ret'd '77 but returned to racing '82 to add to legend; at 58 won Vintage Daytona race; runnerup '01 Vintage race; mem. Que. Sports Hall of Fame; res. LaSalle, Que.

DUKESHIRE, Kelly (basketball); b. 23 Feb 1960, Kimberley, B.C.; UVic; policeman; mem. 4 time CIAU champion Vikings; ntl team from '80; forward gold medal '83 FISU Games team; ankle injury kept him from '84 Olympic team; CIAU Jack Donohue MVP trophy; fed. govt. excellence award '84; res. Victoria, B.C.

DUMART, Woody (hockey); b. 23 Dec 1916, Kitchener, Ont.; d. 19 Oct 2001, Needham, Mass.; given name: Woodrow Wilson Clarence; m. Phyllis; c. Bruce, Jeff, Judith; mem. OHA champion Kitchener jrs. '34-35; brief minor pro stint then became Boston (NHL) regular '37-54 (excluding '42-45 service in RCAF); with Milt Schmidt, Bobby Bauer formed famed Kraut Line; NHL record: 771 scheduled games, 211g, 218a, 82 playoff games, 12g, 15a; mem. 2 Stanley Cup winners; mem. Waterloo County, Hockey halls of fame.

DUMELIE, Larry (football); b. 7 Dec 1936, Lafleche, Sask.; given name: Lawrence; m. Karen Marie Mitton; c. Michele, Bobby, Sherrie, Doug, James; Arizona, BA, BSc; Cdn GM Computer Systems Corp.; db Saskatchewan '60-68; 3 times led Sask. in interceptions; 2 Grey Cup finals, 1 winner; coach Saskatoon Hilltop jrs '69; pres. Saskatoon Handball Assn., doubles champion '69; minor hockey coach London, Ont. '73-74; active in Oldtimers hockey; mem. Sask. Roughriders Plaza of Honor; res. Osgoode, Ont.

DuMOULIN, Seppi (football); b. 1878, Montreal, Que.; d. 25 Mar 1963, Hamilton, Ont.; given name: Septimus; exceptional kicker, backfielder; mem. 6 ntl title teams; mem. Hamilton Tigers '94-06; instrumental in formation Saskatchewan FL, Western Canada RFU; hon. coach Tigers '10, Winnipeg '19; only man to hold chief offices in 3 major football unions, IRFU, WCRFU, ORFU; pres., life mem. Tigers; CFL outstanding service award; charter mem. Cdn Football Hall of Fame.

DUNBAR, William (curling); b. 3 Aug 1895, Kinmount, Ont.; d. 14 May 1974, Vancouver, B.C.; m. Gladys Dougan; c. Verna Doreen; UofSask; farmer; honed curling skills in US; skipped Sask. Brier entry '40; won '54 Saskatoon carspiel; Sask. football club '21; Saskatoon prov. rugby champions '23; Sask. high jump, broad jump, shot put, 100yd dash, discus titles '22; baseball Western Cdn pro league; mem. Sask. Sports Hall of Fame.

DUNCAN, Cecil (administration); b. 1 Feb 1893, Ottawa, Ont.; d. 25 Dec 1979, Ottawa, Ont.; c. Beryl; public servant; lacrosse, baseball player, boxer in youth '10-20; key role in formation Ottawa sr. city hockey league; managed Ottawa all-stars on successful European tour '32-32; governor/v-p AAUofC '34-36; pres. CAHA '36-38; 1st Cdn rep./v-p Ligue internationale de hockey sur glace; championed hockey at all international levels; managed Sudbury Wolves on world title-winning tour of Europe '38; managed Ottawa Tigers sr. ORFU team '45-46; v-p Quebec Rugby Union; secty-treas/registrar ODHA 51yrs; secty Eastern Ont. Baseball Assn., Ottawa jr. Football league; US Amateur Hockey Assn citation of honor/gold shield '50/life mem.; Ont. Sport Achievement Award '75, special Ont. citation '76.

DUNCANSON, Albert (hockey); b. 2 Oct 1911, Winnipeg, Man.; d. 27 Mar 2000, Cowansville, Que.; given name: Albert Gordon; m. Violet Burr; c. Judith, Mary Jane; ret'd oil co. administrator; mem. Elmwood Millionaires '31 Memorial Cup winner; mem. '32 Olympic gold medal team; mem. '37 Ont. senior champion Dominion Brewery team Toronto.

DUNDERDALE, Tommy (hockey); b. 6 May 1887, Benelia, Australia; d. 16 Dec 1960 Winnipeg, Man.; centre; 5yrs sr., pro Winnipeg '05-09; Montreal Shamrocks (NHA) '10; Que. Bulldogs '11; Victoria, Portland (PCHA) '12-23; Saskatoon, Edmonton (WCHL) '24; twice scoring champion; during 12 PCHA seasons scored more goals than any other player in league; scored in each of Victoria's 15 games '14; league all-star ctr; career total 225 goals in 290 league games plus 6 goals in 12 playoff games; coached, managed teams in Los Angeles, Edmonton, Winnipeg; mem. Man., Cdn Hockey halls of fame.

DUNHAM, Steve (rodeo); b. 18 Jul 1956, High River, Alta; horse trainer; bareback/calf roping specialist; CPRA mem. from '76; 2 ntl AA titles; 5 ntl BB titles; 1 ntl high-point title; 2 Calgary Stampede BB titles; 1 Cowboy-of-yr award; 1 Coors Chute-out BB title; 2 Alta. circuit AA titles; 1 Alta., 2 BC circuit BB titles; 1 Skoal pro rodeo tour BB title; 1 Dodge pro rodeo tour BB title; mem. Cdn pro Rodeo Hall of Fame; res. Turner Valley, Alta.

DUNIGAN, Matt (football); b. 6 Dec 1960, Lakewood, Ohio; m. Kathy; c. Dane, Dolan, Madison; Louisiana Tech; football exec., ex-TV color commentator; ret'd. qb; broke Terry Bradshaw's LTU record with 7010 career yards offence; all-Southern Conf. 1st team '82, 2nd team '81; state MVP, Kodak/*AP* all-American; pro Edmonton '83-87, BC

'88-89, Toronto '90-91, Winnipeg '92-94, Birmingham '95, Hamilton '96; CFL record: 194 scheduled games, 850 carries, 5031yds, 77tds, 2cvts, 5476 passes, 3057 completions, 43,857yds, 306tds, 211int, 14 playoff games, 3tds, 50 carries for 324yds, 4tds, 321 pass attempts, 175 completions, 2679yds, 16tds, CFL record 713 passing yds 1 game '94; set/tied 3 CFL records; 2nd only to Ron Lancaster in career passing yds; 2 all-WFC, 2 all-EFC, 1 all-Southern, 4 all-Cdn; 3 times outstanding player nominee, ntl runnerup '93; Tom Pate Memorial Award '89; Jeff Russel award '93; 5 Grey Cup finals, 2 winners; 12 concussions in 14yr CFL career led to retirement; Valdosta State off. co-ordinator '97-98; *TSN* football commentator '99-03; coach/GM Calgary Stampeders '04; mem. Winnipeg Blue Bombers Hall of Fame; res. Birmingham, Ala.

DUNKERLEY, Jason (t&f); b. 21 Aug 1977, Newtonards, N. Ireland; GuelphU; moved to Canada '91; blind distance runner; gold '98 world blind games, '99 800m Cdn blind games, '02 IPC 1500m worlds, '03 IBSP 800m, 1500m worlds; silver 1500m '00, '04 Paralympics, bronze 800m '00 Paralympics; works with guide Greg Dailey; Ottawa male athlete of '04 award; res. Hamilton, Ont.

DUNLAP, Frank (football/hockey); b. 10 Aug 1924, Ottawa, Ont.; d. 26 Sep 1993, Ottawa, Ont.; given name: Frank Egan; m. Mary Kathryn Heney; c. David, Michael, Patrick, Daniel; St. Patrick's College, BComm, Osgoode Hall, LLB; county court judge; hockey St. Mike's Majors '42-44, brief '43 stint Toronto Maple Leafs; Ottawa Commandos (QSHL) '44, Hull Volants (QSHL) '45, Ottawa Senators (QSHL) '36, Pembroke Lumber Kings '47; football Ottawa Trojans '42, Ottawa Combines '43, pro Ottawa(CFL) '44-47, '50-51, Toronto '48-49; all-Cdn qb '46; mem. '51 Ottawa Grey Cup champions; mem. Canada Fitness Council '67-69.

DUNLAP, Jake (football); b. 18 Aug 1926, Ottawa, Ont.; given name: John; m. Dena Morrison; c. John, Joanne; UofOtt, Osgoode Hall LLB; ret'd. lawyer, prov. govt. appointee; lineman Ottawa '43-48, '51, '53-54, Toronto '49-50, Hamilton '52; hockey Ottawa Senators '45-46; football radio color commentator; dir. Rough Riders; GM '78-82; Ont. agent-general to US; gifted raconteur, master of ceremonies; mem. Ottawa Sports Hall of Fame; res. Ottawa, Ont.

DUNLAP, Moffatt (equestrian); b. 31 Mar 1941, Toronto, Ont.; div. c. Louise, John; UWO, BA; real estate broker; mem. Canadian Equestrian team '58-76; bronze medal Nations' Cup team '67 PAG; gold team '70 world championships; dir. Canadian Equestrian Team; v.-chair., administrative comm. Royal Winter Fair; past dir. Canadian Pony Club, Canadian Horse Shows Assn. Canadian Horse Council and Horseman's Benevolent and Protective Assn. (Ont. region); res. King, Ont.

DUNN, James (builder/hockey); b. 24 Mar 1898, Winnipeg, Man; d. 7 Jan 1979, Winnipeg, Man.; became involved with hockey on return from WW1 where he received Military Medal for bravery; local league secty/convenor/timekeeper; when his league was taken over by MAHA '27 he turned his talents to that organization; MAHA v-p '42; served 6yrs as pres MAHA; v-p/pres. CAHA; convenor '67-68 world tournaments; also held exec. offices in baseball, softball,

football, lacrosse, speed skating, basketball, boxing, t&f; mem. Hockey Hall of Fame.

DUNN, Marc (volleyball); b. 9 Sep 1965, North Bay, Ont.; m. Kristine Drakich; UofT; fireman, coach; CIAU indoor volleyball standout winning all-Canadian, MVP awards; mem. ntl indoor team '88-91; ntl masters team from '01; turned to beach volleyball as partner with brother-in-law Ed Drakich '95; mem. '96 Olympic team; 2 world police/firemen games beach volleyball champs; '01 indoor 6's, 2's gold; asst coach UofT '92-01; head coach Bronte jr. beach team '99-01, 1 prov. gold, silver; res. Toronto, Ont.

DUNN, Mary (basketball); b. 6 Mar 1902, Hamilton, Scotland; d. 4 Aug 1996, Calgary, Alta.; m. Robert Dickson; c. Mary, Bruce, Joan, Jean; secretary; mem. legendary Edmonton Grads '22-26; mem. Canadian Basketball, Alta. Sports halls of fame.

DUNSMORE, Fred (all-around); b. 30 Mar 1929; m. Margaret Manley; c. Jeff, John, Danny; chartered accountant; all-star HS qb age 15; 2 seasons Streatham English hockey league, rookie of yr; at 17 mem. Brandon Wheat Kings jrs.; star fwd capt. Winnipeg Maroons Red Wreckers Allan Cup champions '64; appeared in 5 ntl finals; mem. ntl team '65 world championships; serious eye injury tarnished his ability but did not detract from it; bbll p/3b Rosedales, St. Boniface Natives '45-54; rejected Philadelphia Athletics pro offers; trial with Winnipeg Goldeyes '54 but opted to retain amateur status; finalist for Man. athlete of century '70; mem. Man. Hockey, Man. Sports halls of fame; res. Winnipeg, Man.

DUPERE, Denis (hockey); b. 21 Jun 1948, Jonquiere, Que.; div.; c. Rachelle; shipper Tournament Sports; played road hockey as a child but did not acquire first skated until age 14; lw Kitchener (OHA) '66-68, all-Ont. 2yrs; Ottawa Nationals (OHA Sr.), CHL stints Omaha, Tulsa; AHL Rhode Island, Hampton, Philadelphia; NHL Toronto '70-74, Washington '74-75, St. Louis '75, Kansas City '75-76, Colorado '76-78; NHL record: 421 scheduled games, 80g, 99a, 16 playoff games, 1g, 0a; mem. '75 NHL all-star game; played Senior Intercounty baseball with champion Kitchener Panthers '68-69; res. Kitchener, Ont.

DUPREY, Donalda (t&f); b. 1 Mar 1967, Fredericton, N.B.; Lousiana State; teacher; hurdler; began competing age 11; 2 ntl jr. 400m, 1 100m hurdle titles; mem. 4x400m jr. record relay team; gold 400m, 100mH '94 Harry Jerome Classic, 400mH '94 Francophone Games; ntl 100m, 400mH titles '94; Texas Relays 100mH, ntl indoor 400m titles '93; mem. '86, '90, '94 CG, '92 Olympic, '94 Francophone, '95 PAG, 3 world championships teams; silver 400mH '86 CG; bronze 4x400 '94 CG; silver 100mH '95 PAG; Athletics Canada athlete of '94; res. Port Elgin, Ont./Baton Rouge, La.

DUPUIS, Lori (hockey); b. 14 Nov 1972, Cornwall, Ont.; UofT, hons. BA; runs hockey school with teammate Jayna Hefford; forward; UofT Blues '91-97, team capt. 3yrs; 4 OWIAA gold; ntl women's team from '95-04; 3 world titles; Olympic silver '98, gold '02; 2 PacRim gold teams, 3 gold, 1 silver 3-Nations Cups teams, 2 gold, 1 silver 4-Nations Cup teams; 2 NWHL Western Division 2nd all-star teams; played minor hockey Cornwall; with NWHL's Brampton

Thunder from '98; res. Williamstown, Ont.

DUREPOS, Dave (wheelchair basketball); b. 14 Jul 1968, Fredericton, N.B.; given name: David Roger; m. Monique Cormier; c. Chelsie Beckett; cartographic technician; motorcycle accident at age 20 left him a paraplegic; ardent pre-accident basketball player, his determination to continue earned him the Atlantic wheelchair basketball rookie award '90; 2 Atlantic League MVP, all-star, conference titles; mem. ntl team from '94; 2 ntl championship all-star; 5 NB wheelchair-athlete-of-yr, all-star, 2 MVP awards; NB male athlete of '01; 2 World Gold Cup bronze; competed '96, capt. Team Canada '00 Paralympic gold, '04 gold; all-star, MVP awards with Milwaukee Bucks 2 NBWA finals; set ntl team foul-shooting record 86 in row, 16 consec. 3-pointers; scored career high 50 points vs. Moncton '00; 2 Nashville Lightning tournament MVP awards; Investors Group bursary recipient; mem. Cdn Wheelchair Basketball Hall of Fame; res. Charters Settlement, N.B.

DURELLE, Yvon (boxing); b. 14 Oct 1929, Baie Ste. Anne, N.B.; m. Thérèsa Martin; c. Geneva, Yvon Jr., Paul, Françine; rted. fisherman, club owner, museum operator; nicknamed "Doux"; first recorded bout '47; ntl middleweight title 4 May '53 (KO'd George Ross in 12th), light-heavyweight title 9 Sep '53 (12-round decision over Gordon Wallace), lost crown 17 Nov '53 to Doug Harper in 12, regained it 7 Jul '54, defended twice; BE light-heavyweight title '57 stopping Wallace in two; defended once; challenged Archie Moore for world light-heavyweight title '58, losing on KO in 11; KO'd in 3rd '59 rematch; challenged George Chuvalo '59 for ntl heavyweight crown but was KO'd in 12; ret'd to try wrestling '61; brief boxing comeback '63; pro boxing record 105 bouts, 44 won by KO, 38 by decision, 10 lost on decision, 3 on fouls, 9 by KO, 1 no contest; cleared on manslaughter charge after fight with bar patron; mem. NB, Moncton, Canada's Sports, Cdn Boxing halls of fame; res. Baie Ste. Anne, N.B.

DURRELL, Jim (builder); b. 15 Dec 1946, Montreal, Que.; given name: James Allan; m. Carolyn; c. Melissa, Michael; Acadia B.Comm.; pres, Capital Dodge Chrysler Jeep; played varsity fb, team capt Axemen '64-68; coached minor fb in '70s; mayor of Ottawa '85-91; highly involved in Ottawa sports scene; put together community ownership group to purchase Rough Riders from Alan Waters; brought Grey Cup to Ottawa '88; helped bring Triple A baseball (Lynx) to Ottawa; instrumental in bringing Ottawa Senators back to Ottawa '85-90; 1st pres. Senators '90-92; pres. Rough Riders '96; trustee Ottawa Sports Hall of Fame from '82, chair. '90-95; governor Canada's Sports Hall of Fame from '99; res. Ottawa, Ont.

DURNAN, Bill (hockey); b. 22 Jan 1915, Toronto, Ont.; d. 31 Oct 1972, Toronto, Ont.; m. Amanda; c. Deanna, Brenda; goaler Sudbury jrs '33-35 OHA finalists; 3 seasons NOHA contenders; Kirkland Lake Allan Cup winners '40; ambidextrous brilliance attracted Montreal scouts; Vezina Trophy '43-44 rookie season; 7 seasons with Habs 6 Vezina Trophies; 1st team all-star 6 times; mem. 4 league champions, 2 Stanley Cup winners; '48-49 established modern NHL record 4 consecutive shutouts, playing 309 minutes 21 seconds shutout hockey record broken '04 by

Brian Boucher (Phoenix); career 2.36 goals against avg. in 383 scheduled games, 34 shutouts; standout softball pitcher with at least 14 no-hitters; once fanned 24 in 9-inning game; pitched Montreal to 4 successive provincial titles; featured on Cdn postage stamps; mem. Canada's Sports, Hockey Heritage North, Hockey halls of fame.

DUSSAULT, Jacques (coaching/football); b. 4 May 1950, Montreal, Que.; div.; c. François, Jean-Michel; McGill, BPhE, Miami of Ohio, MPhE; football coach; asst. coach Albany State '80-81, Montreal (CFL) '82-85, '97-99, Acadia '87-88; head coach Mount Allison '89-90; Montreal Machine (WFL) '91-92; asst. McGill '92, St. Leonard, Que./Eastern Cdn jr, champs '94-95; head coach Que. elite team which won Cdn title '93-94, Cannes Iron Masks (WFL) '96; has served as guest coach with NFL Buffalo, Philadelphia, NY Giants, NY Jets, Pittsburgh, New England, WFL Frankfurt Galaxy, also BostonU, Michigan State; TV football analyst, *RDS*; res. Montreal, Que.

DUTHIE, Carol Ann (water skiing); b. 18 Feb 1937, Toronto, Ont.; d. 14 Aug 2001, Toronto, Ont.; m. Donald MacDonald; c. Gavin, David, Meridith; U Toronto, B.Ed; teacher; with family serving as support group (her father was CNE director of sports), she demonstrated dedication to sport as youngster and earned 1st of five Ont. women's titles at age 14; world jr. title, Mexican ntl, U.S. Open titles '53; ntl women's title '54; competed in shows at Cypress Gardens, Fla.; active fund raiser; Etobicoke outstanding citizen award; mem. Cdn Amateur, Etobicoke Sports, Etobicoke HS halls of fame.

DUTHIE, George (administration); b. 25 Oct 1901, Fraserburgh, Scotland; d. 9 Mar 1968, Toronto, Ont.; c. Lorne, Donald, Carole Anne; CNE staff mem.; marathon swim organizer; mem. National Advisory Council Fitness, Amateur Sport; responsible for RCAF sports, entertainment WW2; M.B.E.; mem. Cdn Olympic, Canada's Sports halls of fame.

DUTTON, Mervyn Red (hockey); b. 23 Jul 1897, Russell, Man.; d. 15 Mar 1987, Calgary, Alta.; given name: Norman Alexander; m. Mary McDonald; c. Joseph, Alexander, Norman, Beryl; St. John's College; ret'd construction exec.; intercollegiate Winnipeg '14-15, overseas '15-19; hockey Winnipeg '20-22; pro Calgary (WCHL) '23-26, NHL Montreal Maroons '26-30, NY Americans '30-37, player-coach '36-37; coach, mgr. Americans '36-42; succeeded Frank Calder NHL president '43-46; pres. Calgary Stampeder Football Club '56-58; NHL playing record on def 29 goals, 67 assists; mem. Order of Canada; mem. Cdn, Man. Hockey, Man. Sports halls of fame.

DVORAK, Tom (equestrian); b. 25 Jul 1965, Braunschwieg, Germany; m. Ellen Rumball; c. Alexandra; began riding friend's pony and acquired 1st horse age 12; turned attention to dressage age 14; moved to Canada '82; mem. ntl team '90-03; young riders team silver '85; 17 Grand Prix victories; won '94 Cdn League Volvo World Cup aboard Asanti; team gold '93 NA regional challenge; competed '90 world equestrian games, '96 Olympics, world cup '98; dominant figure at Devon with 2 gold '02, 1 gold '03; res. Hillsburgh, Ont.

DWYER, John (boxing); b. 15 Aug 1847, St. John's, Nfld.; d. 19 Mar 1882, Brooklyn, N.Y.; county court clerk; raised in Brooklyn; at 5'9 1/2", 163lbs small for heavyweight but packed powerful punch; beat Jim Elliott in 12 rounds 9 May '79, Long Point, Ont., to claim world heavyweight title; ret'd undefeated.

DYE, Babe (hockey); b. 13 May 1896, Hamilton, Ont.; d. 3 Jan 1962, Chicago, Ill.; given name: Cecil Henry; foreman contract paving firm; hb Toronto Argos, baseball Toronto; jr. hockey Ont. champion Aura Lee '17; Toronto St. Pat's '19-26; Chicago (NHL) '26, missed '27 with broken leg, NY Americans '28, 4 times NHL scoring champion; twice scored 5 goals single game; 2 11-game scoring streaks; mem. 1 Stanley Cup winner; highest goals-per-game record in NHL with 200 in 225 games; coached Chicago Shamrocks (AA), refereed 5 NHL seasons; mem. Hockey Hall of Fame.

EAGLE, Don (gymnastics); b. 23 Mar 1944, Halifax, N.S.; given name: Donald Gordon; m. Jean Adams; c. Heather, Doug; UNB professor, asst. AD; Atlantic Intercollegiate all-around champion '65-66; coach, official, administrator from '67; founded Fredericton Eagles gym club '68; founded NB gymnastics assn. '67; chair. NBGA '72-74; served various roles at provincial, ntl, intl, levels; officiated at '75, '87 Pan-Am, '78, '82, '90 CG, '92 Olympic Games; mgr. Cdn gym team '88 Olympics; has earned highest rating possible for gymnastics official; life mem. Cdn Gymnastics Fed.; mem. NB, Fredericton Sports Hall of Fame; res. Fredericton, N.B.

EAGLES, Kim (shooting); b. 15 Dec 1976, Montréal, Qué.; given name: Kimberley-Anne; Malaspina U. BSc nursing; Saskatchewan Institute of Applied Science and Technology, perioperative nursing diploma; operating room nurse; retd from tetrathlon to focus on shooting after taking silver '94 Intl. Tetrathlon championships; coached young tetrathletes at the '95, '96, '97, '01 ntl championships; ntl shooting team member '95-04; air pistol gold, sport pistol bronze at 1st intl shooting competition '96 NA championships; sport pistol bronze '98 CG; air pistol gold '99 PAG; air pistol gold '00 Crosman Grand Prix; competed '00 Olympics, '03 USA world cup; multiple ntl championships; SFC's female shooter of '96; 3 BC Premier's athletic awards; res. Maple Ridge B.C.

EAGLESON, Alan (administration/hockey); b. 24 Apr 1933, St. Catharines, Ont.; given name: Robert Alan; m. Nancy Elizabeth Fisk; c. Trevor Allan, Jill Anne; UofT, BA, LLB; disbarred lawyer, player agent; ex-dir. Hockey Canada; arranged '72 Summit series; organized 5 Canada Cup series; exec.-dir. NHL Players' Assn. '67-91; twice Etobicoke outstanding-young-man award; Vanier award 1 of Canada's 5 outstanding young men '68; University College bronze award, Arts Trophy for athletics '57; following FBI investigation, US grand jury indicted on 32 counts of fraud, embezzlement, racketeering, receiving kickbacks and obstruction of justice '94; subsequent RCMP investigation led to criminal charges; guilty pleas in US, Canada and plea bargaining result in minimal 18-month prison sentence '98; paroled after serving just 6 months; criminal activities led to expulsion from Canada's Sports, Hockey halls of fame, also stripped of the Order of Canada he had received in '89; res. Toronto, Ont.

EARLEY, Ted (basketball/officiating); b. unknown. Toronto, Ont.; d. Nov 1978, London, Ont.; m. Grace; rec. director; baseball umpire Man., Ont.; basketball official '40-73; ntl. chair/, 1st pres. CABO; pres. London Boards Approved Basketball, Football Officials; pres. OABA; exec-secty Ntl Assn Basketball Coaches Can,; co-ordinator world seminar approved basketball officials; owner/GM London Pontiacs Sr. IC baseball team (succeeding Bob Ferguson); rec. dir. Dryden, London Jewish Community Centre; 11yrs London PUC rec. dept.; London

sports centre bears his name; Basketball Can. memorial award bears his name; mem. Cdn, Ont Basketball halls of fame.

EATHORNE, A.J. (golf); b. 12 Jul 1976, Calgary, Alta.; given name: Anna-Jane; New Mexico State; BC women's amateur titles '95-97; Cdn women's amateur title '97; mem. 5th ranked New Mexico State team '88; 3 college titles, 2 Big West titles, NCAA 1st team all-American '97-98; turned pro '98; won 2 Futures Tour events; earned LPGA tour card and exempt status as co-medalist '98 final qualifying tournament; 3 top-10 finishes in rookie '99 season; mem. '01 Nations' Cup title team; 2 Big West Conf. player of yr, NCAA New Mexico woman of '98; mem. NMU Hall of Fame; res. Penticton, B.C.

EAVES, John (skiing); b. 8 Apr 1953, Montreal, Que.; given name: John Ironside; m. Brigitte Callory; Bishop's College; pro skier, promoter; son of former ski champion Rhoda Wurtele; freestyle specialist; 3 world combined FS titles; 3 world aerials titles; won Challenge of Sexes Superstars rowing competition, 5th overall '79; Challenge of Sexes, Challenge of Superskiers titles '80; Australian FS titles '79-80; movie stuntman *For Your Eyes Only, The Soldier;* composed, recorded music in Nashville for ballet skiing; Laurentian zone alpine skier; advanced wind surfer; mem. Cdn Skiing Hall of Fame; res. Calgary, Alta.

EBBELS, Bill (tennis); b. 20 Jul 1922, Saskatoon, Sask.; given name: William Dennis; m. Ruth Hutchison; c. Harold, John, James, William, Virginia, Andrea; UofSask, BComm; investment dealer; Sask. -13 title '35; UofSask singles '41; jr. A hockey Saskatoon Chiefs; basketball UofSask Huskies; hockey UofSask '46-47; Halifax Naval College tennis title '42; 8 Sask. men's singles (record); 7 Sask. men's doubles; 4 Regina singles, doubles titles; Regina Civil Service TC champion; 9 Sask. veterans singles, 7 veterans men's doubles titles; only player to win provincial men's, veteran's singles same year '67; at 49 oldest competitor '69 Canada Summer Games posting 7-5 singles record; Regina squash champion '67-68; hip replacement operations ended competitive career '80; 2 terms pres. SLTA; Regina B'nai B'rith Sportsman's Award '72; mem. Sask., UofSask Sports halls of fame; res. Regina, Sask.

EBEN, Mike (football); b. 29 Jan 1946, Zatec, Czechoslovakia; given name: Michael Christopher; m. Nancy Marsden; c. Lhara, Christopher; UofT, BA, MA, PhD; housemaster, teacher Upper Canada Coll; ex-prof. York; initial winner Hec Crighton Trophy; 4yrs all-star, OUAA MVP, led UofT to inaugural Vanier Cup triumph; pro Toronto '68-69, '71-77, Edmonton '70, Hamilton '77, Ottawa '77; CFL record: 341 receptions, 4752yds, 24tds; WFC, EFC all-star; Schenley outstanding-Cdn nominee; 37 consecutive pass catching games; 1 Grey Cup final; asst. coach York '84; mem. UotT Sports, OUAA Football Legends halls of fame; res. Toronto, Ont.

ECKARD, Jeff (sailing); b. 18 Dec 1965, Pietermaritzburg, R.S.A.; sailmaker; skipper 470 crew; teamed with Nigel Cochrane won ntl championships '89-91; gold Goodwill Games '90, PAG '91; mem. Royal Victoria YC; res. Victoria, B.C.

ECKEL, Shirley (t&f); b. 3 Feb 1932, Toronto, Ont.; given name: Shirley Gretchen; m. Dr. William H. Kerr (d); c. Gretchen, Christopher, Elizabeth, Thomas; UofT, BA; ranked 4th internationally 50m hurdles age 12; gold '45-46 jr. Olympics; at 20 ntl 80m hurdles title, record, ranked 8th in world; mem. '52 Olympic, '54 BEG teams; ntl 80m titles '52-53, '55; throughout career NA champion; res. Islington, Ont.

ECUYER, Al (football); b. 1937, New Orleans, La.; Notre Dame; stockbroker; capt. ND, twice all-American guard; drafted NY Giants (NFL); Edmonton (CFL) '59-65, co-capt. '64, Toronto '66, Montreal '67-68; twice nominated outstanding player, outstanding lineman; twice coaches all-Canadian (2nd team); *Vancouver Sun* all-star ilb; twice Blue Bombers' all-opponents team; res. New Orleans, La.

EDDIE, Arden (baseball); b. 4 Aug 1947, Wallaceburg, Ont.; m. Shelley Lane Gill; c. Ashley Lane; realtor/home renovator; knee injury playing as sea cadet in Nova Scotia reduced his pro prospects but not his enthusiasm for game; mem. '68 Cdn jr. champion Sarnia Drawbridge Inn; mem. London Sr. Intercounty team from '67; became London Majors club owner '76; mem. '69, '75 Intercounty champs, 5 div. winners; 2 IC exec. of yr, 1 Commissioners Trophy; 1 1st team, 6 2nd team all-star selections; led IC in triples twice, stolen bases 3 times, walks 4 times; set numerous IC records '67-00 [including 832 games, 34 seasons, 764h, 180sb, 382rbi, 660bob]; instrumental in keeping sr amateur baseball alive in London; signed Fergie Jenkins for '84-85 seasons; his team has played key role in community affairs and has led league in attendance since '67; has served Majors as pres./GM/mgr./player; mem. Wallaceburg Sports Hall of Fame; res. London, Ont.

EDDOLLS, Frank (hockey); b. 5 Jul 1921, Lachine, Que.; d. 13 Aug 1961, Ridgeway, Ont.; given name: Frank Herbert; def. minor hockey with Verdun '37-39, Oshawa '39-41, Hershey (AHL) '41-42, Buffalo '45-47, '52-54, Cincinnati '51-52, Montreal RCAF, Canada Car, Services '42-44; NHL Montreal '44-47, NYR '47-52 (capt.); coached Saskatoon '51-52, Buffalo (AHL) '52-54, '55-57, '60-61, Chicago (NHL) '54-55; NHL totals 317 scheduled games, 23g, 43a, 31 playoff games, 0g, 2a; Lady Byng trophy '43; 4 Memorial Cup finals.

EDEH, Rosey (t&f); b. 16 Aug 1966, London, Eng.; Rice; c. Lisha; TV sports reporter; emigrated to Canada '69; began competing age 13; hurdles, sprint specialist; 1 ntl jr., 6 ntl sr. records; 3 jr. ntl, 4 sr, ntl, 1 Que., 10 international invitational meet golds; competed '88, '92, '96 Olympic, '89 Francophone, FISU, '90 CG, '95 PAG, '91 world indoor, '92 World Cup, '93 world outdoor teams; top Que. female athletic prospect award '88; res. La Salle, Que.

EDEY, Marjorie (golf); b. 8 Dec 1913, Winnipeg, Man.; d. 27 Mar 1981, Winnipeg, Man.; given name: Marjorie Isobel; m. William Edey; mem. St. Charles G&CC; world

record 36 club titles; won Man. women's amateur '46-51, Winnipeg & Dist. titles '48-51, Man. Srs. titles '62-65; mem. 20 interprovincial teams, 3 Srs. teams; gained permanent possession Alcrest Cup emblem of St. Charles club title; Edey Cup became replacement; mem. Man. Sports Hall of Fame.

EDWARDS, Betty (swimming); b. 22 Feb 1911, Toronto, Ont.; given name: Elizabeth Alberta; m. Frank Tancock (d); c. Brian Frank, Beverley Elizabeth; UofT BA; post grad work Toronto Hospital for Sick Children; ret'd asst. to chair. dept. philosophy York; FS, backstroke specialist, ornamental (synchronized) swimmer; mem. '32 Olympic, '30, '34 BEG teams; won '30 Detroit River swim; 2 ntl titles; 2 ntl records; 6 Ont. titles, 1 record; 1 Que.title; won '29 1/2 mile Dominion Day, Brulé Lake, CNE titles, '34 Hamilton Bay swim; 2 CNE 1 mile titles; 1 Toronto HS 100yd FS title; 3 Granite Club long-plunge titles, 3 ornamental titles; UofT jr./sr. T awards; special gold medal for 440yd FS ntl record '27; Gale trophy '39; starred in two *Associated Screen News* films; mem. UofT Sports, Ont. Aquatic halls of fame; res. Islington, Ont.

EDWARDS, Jake (curling); b. 7 May 1921, Kingston, Ont.; d. 6 Aug 1978, Kingston, Ont.; given name: Jack Leisk; m. Lois Smith (d); c. Sandra, Tracy; m. Joan Whalen; auto dealer; knuckleball pitcher with various Kingston-area baseball teams; rejected pro contract Jersey City Giants; mem. Canadian Army overseas baseball titlists WW2; twice Amherstview Club golf champion, twice srs champion; Alcan Srs title '76; OCA Gov-Gen's, Silver Tankard titles, twice Burden, *Globe & Mail* trophies; 6 times Ont. Consols competitor; rep. Ont. '60 Brier; 2 Ont. Srs titles; 10 consecutive wins 2 straight years City of Ottawa bonspiel, 1 grand aggregate title; mem. National Fitness Council '64-67; mem. Kingston Dist. Sports Hall of Fame.

EDWARDS, John (canoeing); b. 1 Jul 1954, Almonte, Ont.; m. Susan Gifford; c. Bliss, Chantry; UBC, SFU, Architectural Assn. School, Carleton, BArch; architect; competitive paddler '67-78 collecting variety of gold, silver, bronze medals ntl/intl, international competitions; mem. ntl team '72-78; mem. '72, '76 Olympic, '75 PAG, '75, '78 world championship teams; gold 1000m, 500m C1, 1000m C2, silver 500m C2 '75 Pan-Am regatta; commodore CPCC '88-93; consultant Pantages Theatre restoration; Canada 125 medal; res. Carleton Place, Ont.

EDWARDS, Phil (t&f); b. 13 Sep 1907, Georgetown, British Guiana; d. 6 Sep 1971, Montreal, Que.; given name. Philip Aron; NYU, McGill, MD; physician; capt. track teams NYU, McGill; ntl middle-distance titles Canada, US, Ireland, Poland, Latvia; 4th 800m, relay bronze '28 Olympics, bronze 800m, 1500m, 4x400 relay '32 Olympics, capt., 800m bronze, beat world record but finished 5th 1500m '36 Olympics; 880yd gold representing British Guiana '34 BEG; led McGill to 6 consec t&f titles, 5 as capt.; part-time coach McGill track team; sole 4-time winner US indoor ntls 600yd titles; held 13 ntl records; initial winner Lou Marsh Trophy '36; Lionel Conacher trophy '36; AAUofC top athlete '36; trophy bearing his name awarded annually to Canada's outstanding t&f athlete; mem. Cdn Olympic, McGill, Canada's Sports halls of fame.

EDWARDS, Ted (football/basketball); b. 20 Dec 1915, Ottawa, Ont.; d. 24 Oct 2003, Ottawa, Ont.; given name: Frederick; m. Doris Margaret Irvine; c. Ted Jr., Peggy, Pat, Penny; UofOtt, Queen's; ret'd civil servant; hb Rough Riders '37, '39-40; mem. 2 Grey Cup finalists, 1 winner; gd ntl finalist Glebe Grads basketball team '37; coached jr. football Queen's '38; qb Montreal Bulldogs '41; all-star hb intermediate service league '42; playing coach, all-star hb QRFU finalist Verdun '43; hb/capt. Ottawa Trojans ORFU '44-46; coach UofOtt football '45-54; fastball Snowden Junction League '41-42; gd Montreal Oilers basketball team '42-43, capt. '43, ntl finalists '42; guard, capt. UofOtt ntl intermediate finalists '44; sr. city basketball '44-46; basketball coach, college, city league clubs '47-55; coached 3 NORFU league titlists Sudbury '55-57; mem. Ottawa CSRA Sports Hall of Fame.

EGERTON, Stan (t&f); b. 2 Oct 1925, Toronto, Ont.; given name: Stanley Harris; m. Dollie Olphert; c. George, Carolyn, Stan Jr., James; fire dept. capt.; Toronto city pole vault title '39-40; Cdn army 2nd Div. 100-, 220yd spring title '43; pv silver '50 BEG; joined Masters program '74; pv bronze '75, gold '77, '79 World Masters Games; Ont., Cdn pv, 100-, 200m masters titles '80-85; Cdn, world 60m record for 60-year-olds '86; res. Toronto, Ont.

EHRLICK, Allan (equestrian); b. 4 Apr 1946, Toronto, Ont.; given name: Allan Howard Lincoln; m. Linda Lowe; UofT; farm manager; 3-day event specialist; mem. ntl team '66-76; 3 ntl 3-day event titles; '73 NA title; mem. '67, '71 Pan-Am, '68, '72, '76 Olympic Games teams; polo player Toronto Polo Club; res. Campbellville, Ont.

EIRIKSON, Tom (rodeo); b. 5 Feb 1954, Innisfail, Alta; m. Candy; c. Wyatt, Josh, Rebecca-Jo; movie stuntman/co-ordinator; saddle bronc, calf roping, steer wrestling, team roping; qualified for 7 ntl finals; 4 ntl all-around titles; 3 Linderman awards; res. Okotoks, Alta.

EISLER, Laurie (volleyball/coaching); b. 3 Sep 1964, Regina, Sask.; given name: Laurie Baber; m. Terry Eisler; c. Clayton, Jenae; UofSask, BEd, MSc; coach UAlta; concentrated on volleyball at university after successful HS career in t&f, basketball, volleyball; setter Sask. Huskiettes '82-87; 4 CWUAA all-star awards, CIAU 2nd team '87; switched to coaching assisting Mark Tennant '87-91, 1yr stint as head coach; shifted to UAlta as head coach '91-92; 5 ntl CIAU championship appearances, 12-3 record; 3 CIAU women's volleyball titles; 4 CWUAA, 1 CIAU coach-of-yr awards; 3M coach-of-'96 award; coached ntl women's beach volleyball team '96 Olympics; res. Edmonton, Alta.

EISLER, Lloyd Jr. (figure skating); b. 28 Apr 1963, Seaforth, Ont.; given name: Lloyd Edgar; McMaster; nicknamed "Herbie"; part-owner Action Sport Fitness; Western Ont. sectional juv men's title '75; partner Lorri Baier '73-82, Katherina Matousek '82-86; Isabelle Brasseur '87-94; Ont. Winter Games pairs gold '76; ntl novice pairs '77; ntl jr. pairs '79; bronze '79 jr. worlds pairs; ntl novice singles '80; runnerup jr. world pairs '80; 5 ntl pairs titles; 2 Skate Canada gold; 4 worlds silver; '92, '94 Olympic pairs bronze; mem. '84, '88, '92, '94 Olympic teams; turned pro '94; Cdn pro pairs title '97;

Cdn meritorious service award '95; mem. Canada's Sports, Cdn Figure Skating, Cdn Olympic halls of fame; res. Hamilton, Ont.

ELDER, Jim (equestrian); b. 27 Jul 1934, Toronto, Ont.; m. Marianne; c. Michael, Mark, Elizabeth, Erin; Upper Canada College, UofT, BA; company pres.; mem. ntl team '50-84, individual international champion Royal Winter Fair 3 times; 4 Eastern Canadian titles; team development series champion '65-66; mem. 8 Olympic '56-84, 7 PAG '59-83; jumping team gold '68 Olympics, '80 Olympic alternate, '59, '71 PAG '70 worlds; individual, team silver '83 PAG; team bronze '56 Olympic, '67 PAG; mem. '82 Nation's Cup team; Rothman's Montreal Grand Prix title '82; Officer Order of Canada '83; mem. Cdn Olympic, Canada's Sports halls of fame; res. Aurora, Ont.

ELFORD, Gear (football); b. 4 Apr 1902, Hamilton, Ont.; d. (circa 1990), Hamilton, Ont.; given name: Harold Norman; m. Alice; c. Estelle; ret'd; mem. CRU int. champion Hamilton Tigers '21; outstanding lineman '22-30 Tigers ORFU, IPRU; '23 ORFU title Hamilton Rowing Club; 5 IPRU titles, 2 Grey Cups; basketball Hamilton city, church leagues; recorded Hamilton's 1st perfect 450 in 5-pin bowling '37; lineman best-of-century Tiger team '67.

ELGAARD, Ray (football); b. 29 Aug 1959, Edmonton, Alta.; m. Gina; c. Linnea, Myles; Utah (criminology); financial planner; rcvr, drafted 2nd round '83 Sask.; ret'd '96; CFL record: 220 scheduled games, 78tds, 2 2pt conversions, 830 receptions for 13,198yds; 6 all-Western, 4 all-CFL all-star; 3 Dr. Beattie Martin trophies; 3 outstanding Cdn; set/tied 3 CFL receiving records; mem. 1 Grey Cup winner; nicknamed "Harley"; active in Sask. chapter Children's Wish Foundation; mem. Cdn Football Hall of Fame; res. Las Vegas, Nev.

ELIOWITZ, Abe (football); b. 15 Nov 1910, New York, N.Y.; d. 19 Nov 1981, Livonia, Mich.; m. Ida Lachman (d); c. Susan, Linda, Samuel; Michigan State, BSc; teacher; all-American MSU '32-33; southpaw passer/punter Ottawa (CFL) '33-35, Montreal '36-37; baseball Ottawa Crains St. Lawrence League; fb/hb/ flying wing; Big Four scoring leader '35; 4 times all-star; Jeff Russel Trophy '35; coached football, baseball, x-country running Detroit Cooley, Redford HS; 2 city football, 3 baseball titles; mem. Canadian Football Hall of Fame.

ELLEFSON, Steve (all-around); b. 16 Oct 1954, Edmonton, Alta.; given name: Stephen John; Lethbridge U; realtor; partial paraplegic; excelled in skiing, basketball, tennis, road racing; mem. ntl disabled ski team; world combined champion '86-88; forced to quit skiing due to back injury '88; Paralympic downhill bronze '88; began wheelchair track, road racing '89; Alta. 10km title '91; Alta. tennis title '89-91; gold '92 Calgary Police 1/2 marathon, Mother's Day 10km, Calgary Stampede marathon, Oz Day Masters 10km '96; silver *Vancouver Sun* 10km, Alta. 36.7mile marathon '92; competed '96, '00 Paralympics; mem. Calgary Grizzlies basketball team, '89 ntl wheelchair titlists; Toronto Spitfires tournament all-star '91; res. Calgary, Alta.

ELLETT, Dave (hockey); b. 30 Mar 1964, Cleveland, Ohio; given name: David John George; m. Annie Bianco; c.

Sierra; Bowling Green; ret'd def, mounted cowboy shooter; played minor hockey in Ottawa; father Bob played in AHL and coached in OHA; CCHA all-star, NCAA all-tournament team as BGU won NCAA championship '84; drafted by Winnipeg '82 entry draft; played in NHL with Winnipeg '84-90, Toronto '90-97, New Jersey '97, Boston '97-99, St. Louis '99-00; NHL record: 1129 scheduled games, 153g, 415a, 126 playoff games, 11g, 46a; played 2 all-star games; with Garry Galley owned All-Star Saloon in Almonte, Ont.; wife Annie noted mounted pistol shooter known as "Outlaw Annie", rodeo star, kick boxer; res. Cove Creek, Ariz.

ELLIFF, Jim (lawn bowling); b. 30 Nov 1935, Toronto, Ont.; m. Julia Price; c. David (d), Laura; UofT; sales agent; skipped '77 Ont. Colts triple title team; won Ont. men's singles '80, '98; vice Ont. fours title teams '89, '97; skipped US Open trebles title team '93, singles '94, '95, pairs '95; ntl silver medals singles '80, fours '89; 2 bowler-of-week awards; mem. ntl team '80-83; mgr. ntl team '98 CG; res. Aurora, Ont.

ELLINGSON, James (football); b. 18 May 1963, Calgary, Alta.; m. Kathleen; c. Alexanne, Rachel; salesman, ex-sports broadcaster; nicknamed "Duke"; sb Richmond Raiders Jrs; CFL Sask. '86-90, Ottawa '90-96; CFL record: 169g, 19tds, 1cvt, 255recept., 3502yds, 8 playoff games, 14rcpt., 201yds, 1td; mem. 1 Grey Cup winner; res. Kanata, Ont.

ELLIOTT, Allen (administration); b. 6 Feb 1922, Manitoba; m. Dagmar; c. Terry, Joann, James; ret'd sales mgr.; from '64 dir. Babe Ruth Baseball International; pres. Baseball BC '72-90; 5yrs dir. Sport BC; pres. Baseball Canada '90-92; life mem. Western Canada Baseball; life mem. BC Babe Ruth Baseball; mem. BC Baseball honor roll BC Sports Hall of Fame; res. Surrey, B.C.

ELLIOTT, Bob (all-around); b. 29 Mar 1910, Kingston, Ont.; d. 21 May 1970, Kingston, Ont.; given name: Robert Fawcette; m. Sarah Delia "Deed" Whitney; c. Robert Whitney, Elizabeth Mae; Queen's, BA; purchaser aluminum co.; son of Hockey Hall of Famer Chaucer Elliott; hb/oe/cb Queen's; mem. 2 intercollegiate title teams; 5 athletic letters; lost eye playing football '34; sr. ORFU football Balmy Beach '35; football coach Garrison, RMC, Queen's WW2, guided Garrison Ont. Int. title '40; 5yrs intercollegiate official; mem. '29 Queen's intercollegiate, 2 Kingston YMCA Ont. Int. basketball title teams; semipro baseball Brockville, Smiths Falls, Delora Srs, Creighton Mines, Kingston Ponies '24-38; coached 3 Kingston jr., juve. title teams, '67 OBA title team; mem. 3 OCA Gov-Gen's Trophy, 2 Silver Tankard curling rinks; mem. '60 Ont. Brier rink; life mem. Kingston Curling Club; honored by peers with appreciation day '68; Wally Elmer Memorial Trophy (Kingston sportsman of year); Kingston distinguished achievement award; Ont. achievement award; mem. Queen's Football, Kingston Dist. Sports halls of fame.

ELLIOTT, Chaucer (hockey/football); b. 1879, Kingston, Ont.; d. 13 Mar 1913, Kingston, Ont.; given name: Edwin Smith; m. Elizabeth Montague; c. Robert Fawcette; played point, capt. Queen's; capt. '99 Granites ntl title football team; Toronto baseball team '03; coach Toronto Argos football team, '06 Hamilton Tigers title team; mem. Montreal AAA; organized semipro baseball league; owned,

organized, managed St. Thomas Canadian Baseball League; hockey referee '03-13; mem. Hockey Hall of Fame.

ELLIOTT, Geoff (t&f); b. 7 Apr 1931, Ilford, Eng.; given name: Geoffrey Michael; m. Pamela Seaborne; c. Ann, Carol, Yvonne; London, BSc, California, MA; ret'd asst. dean PE UAlta.; rugby player in England; mem. English international t&f team '50-59; pv gold '54, '58 CG; mem. England's '52 Olympic team; mem. RAF Fighter Command basketball team; Canadian citizen '70; chair. sports div., venues co-ordinator '78 CG; authored several articles on gymnastics, kinesiology, t&f, 5 books; *CBC* color commentator; dir. SFC; trustee O'Keefe Sports Foundation; CTFA dir.-gen. '78-81; part-time consultant UCal Olympic oval; life mem. Cdn Gymnastics Fed.; res. Calgary, Alta.

ELLIOTT, Stewart (horse racing); b. 1 Mar 1965, Toronto, Ont.; div.; following footsteps of father Dennis, a jockey for 22yrs, before becoming Ocala, Fla. trainer; mother also a horse trainer; began riding '81 at Keystone Park (now Philadelphia Park); leading rider Atlantic City, Suffolk Downs; competed regularly on such secondary circuits as Rockingham, Monmouth, Maryland before riding Smarty Jones to Kentucky Derby, Preakness victories and missing elusive Triple Crown with loss by a length at '04 Belmont Stakes; breakthrough year '04 with 1,363 mounts, 262 wins, 211 seconds, 177 thirds; brushes with law, alcoholism; res. Washington Crossing, Pa.

ELLIS, Craig (football); b. 26 Jan 1961, Los Angeles, Calif.; m. Linda; c. Brittany, Jasmyne; San Diego State.; pro rcvr San Francisco (NFL) '82, Winnipeg (CFL) '82, Calgary '83, Saskatchewan '84-85, Toronto '86, '93, Miami '86, LA Raiders '87, Dallas (NFL) '88, Edmonton (CFL) '89-92; 3 times leading CFL receiver; 3 all-WFC, 2 CFL all-star; Jeff Nicklin award 90; runnerup CFL outstanding player '90; set CFL record 8yrs catching passes all games; 1 Grey Cup final; CFL record: 121 scheduled games, 88tds, 493 carries for 2,095yds, 30tds, 580 receptions for 7,757yds, 58tds; res. California.

ELLIS, Phyllis (field hockey); b. 11 Nov 1959, Oakville, Ont.; m. Stewart Gavin; c. Max, Taylor; UofT; mem. Ont. team '75-84, ntl -21 team '80, -23 team '82, ntl team '80-84; defence World Cup silver medal team '83; mem. '84 Olympic team; fed. govt. excellence award '83; mem. UofT Sports Hall of Fame; res. Toronto, Ont.

ELLIS, Ron (hockey); b. 8 Jan 1945, Lindsay, Ont.; given name: Ronald John Edward; m. Janis Eveline; c. Ron Jr., Kathleen; York; resort owner; influenced by father Randy, mem. '48 RCAF Flyers Olympic champions, peewee North Bay, Ottawa Cradle League; Weston Dukes Jr. B at 15; Jr. A Marlboros; mem. '64 Memorial Cup winner; pro Maple Leafs '64-81; NHL record: 1034 scheduled games, 332g, 308a, 70 playoff games, 18g, 8a; began Leafs career wearing No. 8 but at Ace Bailey's request wore No. 6 which had been ret'd with Bailey '34; mem. 1 Stanley Cup winner; Team Canada '72, '77; mem. Lindsay Sports, Mississauga Hockey halls of fame; res. Collingwood, Ont.

ELMER, Ken (t&f); b. 24 Apr 1948, Vancouver, B.C.; given name: Kenneth Mark; m. Janet Neufeld; c. Jonathon, Shannon; UBC, BA; teacher; mem. UBC soccer team '67-

71; middle-distance specialist; mem. '72 Olympic, '73 Pan-Pacific, '74 CG '75 PAG teams; 5th 800m '75 PAG; PB: 3:58.5 mile, 3:40.5 1500m, 1:48.2 800m; major role BC elementary school participation championship program; Bobby Gaul UBC outstanding-athlete award '73; organized Henry Jerome Classic, Vancouver Sunkist meets; mem. UBC Sports Hall of Fame; res. New Westminster, B.C.

ELMER, Wally (hockey/coaching); b. 1898, Kingston, Ont.; d. 28 Aug 1978, Kingston, Ont.; given name: Wallace Druce; m. Inez Tucker; service station, dry cleaning operator; standout jr. with Kingston Frontenacs '18; St. Paul, Minn. '22; pro Saskatoon Sheiks '23-24; Victoria Cougars '25 Stanley Cup champions; also played with teams in Windsor, Philadelphia, New Haven before returning to Kingston to coach Queen's hockey team '29; coached Kingston Jr. B, Sr. B OHA titlists; original mem. International Hockey Hall of Fame comm.; Kingston Ponies baseball club dir.; Central Ontario baseball league dir.; Kingston youth centre named in his honor; name inscribed in Kingston Book of Honorable Achievement; trophy bearing his name awarded annually to Kingston sportsman of year; mem. Kingston Sports, Queen's Coaches halls of fame.

ELRICK, Elizabeth (basketball); b. 15 Jan 1901, Glasgow, Scotland; d. 29 Jun 1984, Winnipeg, Man.; m. Rex Murray; c. Maureen, Rhoda; mem. famed Edmonton Grads '22-23; mem. Canadian Basketball, Alta. Sports halls of fame.

ELSBY, Ted (football); b. 3 Jan 1932, Galt, Ont.; d. 5 Nov 1984, Beaconsfield, Que.; given name: Edward Ernest; m. Pauline Patricia Pepper; c. Elaine, Paul, Steven, Gary; salesman; jr. Brantford Indians; pro dt Alouettes '54-65; mem. '56-57 East-West Shrine Game teams; EFC all-star '64; 1st-ballot nominee '64 3 Schenley Awards, best Canadian, best lineman, best player, winning none; football coach UofMtl 4yrs, Sir George Williams 1yr, Beaconsfield HS 2yrs; mem. Cambridge, Waterloo County halls of fame.

EMBULDENIYA, Herb (boxing/officiating/administration); b. 18 Dec 1931, Sri Lanka; USri Lanka; flyweight gold at university; emigrated to Winnipeg '68; highly regarded as judge at prov., ntl, intl levels; recipient of numerous honors from governing bodies throughout world; 1st Cdn elected to Intl Exec. Comm. of Boxing '92; judge IABA '69 Toronto tournament; chair. '88 Winnipeg PAG advisory bid-comm.; chair. PAG boxing; dir. Man. Sports Fed.; hon. life mem. CABA; mem. Cdn Boxing, Man. Sports halls of fame; res. Winnipeg, Man.

EMERSON, Eddie (football); b. 11 Mar 1892, Cordeil, Ga.; d. 27 Jan 1970, Ottawa, Ont.; m. Heasley Parker; c. Marilyn; automobile salesman; flying wing on offence, inside wing on defence '09-37, unpaid, with Ottawa; 3 Grey Cup finals, 2 winners; twice club pres., '30 while playing, '47-50; Big Four pres. '48-49; noted auto racer; mem. Canada's, Ottawa Sports, Canadian Football halls of fame.

EMERY, John (bobsleigh); b. 4 Jan 1932, Montreal, Que.; m. Debbie; c. Allison, John David; Trinity College School, Queen's, MD; ret'd plastic surgeon; Stubb's Trophy RCN(R) best all-around athlete; with brother Victor formed Laurentian Bobsleighding Assoc. '57; with Victor, Doug

Anakin, Peter Kirby '64 Olympic gold; won 190lb+ 13-mile California mountain race (Double Dipsea) '70; swam across Golden Gate Bridge entrance '75; triathlon ('80 Hawaii Ironman), marathon ('79 Boston) competitor; Centennial Medal; mem. Cdn Olympic, Canada's Sports halls of fame; res. San Francisco, Calif.

EMERY, Victor (bobsleigh); b. 28 Jun 1933, Montreal, Que.; div. Jenifer Wontner; c. Vanessa, Samantha, Alistair; Trinity College School, UWO, BA, L'Alliance Française, Harvard, MBA; dir. Foundation for Formation Hoteliere; ex-dir. Savoy Hotels chain; ex-chair Lake Louise ski area; competed internationally Olympic Finn Class sailing, class A 4-way skiing; pilot '64 Olympic, '65 world championship gold medal bobsleigh teams; mem. COA, chef de mission-adjoint '68 winter Olympic team; from '70 TV commentator bobsleigh, luge, x-country skiing during world, Olympic competitions; helped in Cdn bid '88 Calgary Winter Olympics; '80 Olympic fund-raiser; active masters x-country skier; mem. Viking Internationals '03 Cdn Ski Marathon Ottawa Ski Club trophy winning team; chair. Great Britain's National Byway leisure cycling program; mem. Cdn Olympic, Canada's Sports halls of fame; res. London, Eng.

EMMS, Hap (hockey); b. 12 Jan 1905, Barrie, Ont.; d. 23 Oct 1988, Niagara Falls, Ont.; given name: Leighton; m. Mabel Hill; c. Paul; standout baseball pitcher, soccer, hockey player; rejected pro baseball offers; scoring leader OHA Jr. B Barrie Colts; mem. Allandale CNR Apprentice League champs, Ont. Jr. finalist Midland, Brantford intermediates; pro Montreal Maroons '26; farmed to Stratford (CanPro), 1 title in 2 seasons; 2yrs Windsor (IL); acquired by NY Americans '30; Detroit '32-34; Americans '34-37; Boston '38; NHL record: 320 scheduled games, 36g, 53a, 14 playoff games, 0g, 0a; gained reputation as rugged defender, tenacious checker; 2yrs Pittsburgh, playing-coach Omaha Knights, 1 American Assn. title; coached Barrie Colts, Juveniles; coach St. Louis '45-46; Barrie Flyers Jr. A '47-61; Niagara Falls Flyers '61-74; jr. coaching record 15yrs, 362-355-67; 5 OHA, 4 Eastern Cdn titles, 4 Memorial Cups; OHL division named in his honor; founded Barrie Flyers Minor Hockey Assn.; mem. Barrie Sports Hall of Fame.

EMPRINGHAM, David (motorsport); b. 28 Dec 1963, Toronto, Ont.; m. Sue; UWO, BEc; began racing at 22 when parents presented him with Spenard/David Racing School course as graduation gift; competed in Player's/GM series, Firestone Firehawk Endurance series (GS class), Porsche Turbo Cup series before stepping up to Atlantic series machines; claimed Toyota Atlantic series titles '93-94, runnerup '95; advanced to Indy Lights '96 claiming 3 poles and 3 victories; series rookie-of-yr award; Gilles Villeneuve award; '96 series title; joined Stewart team '98 as coach; Hylton Motorsports team driver development program '01; movie stunt driver; res. Toronto, Ont.

EMSLIE, Bob (baseball); b. 27 Jan 1859, Guelph, Ont.; d. 26 Apr 1943, St. Thomas, Ont.; given name: Robert Daniel; umpire; amateur pitcher Waterville Kansas, London, Harriston, St. Thomas; pro Camden N.J.; ML Baltimore (AA) '83-85, Philadelphia (AA) '85; ML record: 44-44w-l, 3.19era; best season '84, 32 victories; 1st Cdn to pitch ML shutout; injured arm barnstorming; turned to umpiring

'87, back in ML '90 Amer. Assn.; Western League '91, NL '91-24; WL advisory board on retirement; nicknamed "Blind Bob" by John McGraw for involvement in famed Fred Merkle boner play (failure to touch 2nd base); mem. Baseball Hall of Fame honor roll of umpires, Cdn Baseball Hall of Fame.

ENNIS, Peter (basketball/coaching); b. 6 Apr 1946, Sudbury, Ont.; d. 14 Jan 1997, Sudbury, Ont.; given name: Peter Lawrence; m. Gail Ainslie; c. Liam, Kelly; Laurentian, BA; educator, basketball coach; coached Lady Vees '79-96, posting 248-48 record, including 189-14 in regular season play; 2 CIAU titles, 2 CIAU silver, 3 bronze medals; 7 OWIAA titles; 4 OWIAA coach-of-yr awards; twice CIAU coach of yr; his Lady Vees qualified for ntl tournament 17 consecutive yrs; 7 yrs chair Interuniversity Athletics at Laurentian; asst. coach ntl women's team '89-94, head coach ntl women's team '96 Olympics; coach '95 Canada Games gold medal team; women's team coach '93 FISU Games; mem. Laurentian Sports Wall of Fame.

ENOS, Ed (football); b. 30 Jun 1934, Boston, Mass; given name: Edmund Francis; m. Janice McCluskey; c. Edmund III, Michael, Laurie; Connecticut, BSc, Boston, MEd, PhD, Munich, German College (Leipzig), Swiss Research Institute; ret'd chair. Bio-PE dept., athletic dir., Concordia; Connecticut football '53-57; pro lb NY Giants '57, '59, BC '57-59; coach HS '60, NorwichU '61-62, Montreal '63-64; AD Loyola College '65-74; '74-90 Bio-PE dept. chairman, AD Concordia; from '79 supervisor Montreal Expos conditioning program; founder Bio-PE dept., International Institute Comparative PE, Sports; dir. Lakeshore General Hospital sports medicine symposium, Olympic PE, Sports symposium; NYR research, fitness consultant; Tau Kappa Epsilon fraternity alumnus of year; US Sports Academy distinguished service award; mem. Loyola College Senate, Connecticut, Alouettes Alumni Assn. Sports halls of fame; res. Baie D'Urfe, Que.

ENRIGHT, Jim (wheelchair basketball, t&f): b. 28 Apr 1964, Gatineau, Que.; civil servant; mem. Ottawa-Carleton Wheelchair Sports, Cdn Amputee Sports Assns. from '79; ntl high jump record 1.66m; Ont. javelin 40m record; Stoke-Mandeville World Games gold '89, '91; mem. Ottawa Royals NWBT silver medal team '92, bronze '94; CWBL gold with Royals '89; ntl championship MVP '94; 2yrs sports administrative liaison officer '92 Cdn Winter Games for disabled; competed '92, '96, Paralympics; mgr. '00 Paralympic men's wheelchair basketball team; v-p OCWSA '85-87, '91-92; res. Gatineau, Que.

EON, Suzanne (synchro swim); b. 19 Feb 1924, Montreal, Que.; d. 23 Jan 1994, Lac St. Charles, Que.; St. Mary's Academy, Bart's Business School; synchronized swimming coach '50-78 guiding competitors to 124 ntl open/closed titles; coached 5 PAG entries '55-75, 4 international invitationals '57-76, 3 worlds '73-78, 2 Pan-Pacific Games, 3 Canada Games; international coaching record '55-78: 10 gold, 18 silver, 7 bronze medals; Dick Ellis trophy team '75, Swedish Best-Nation-in-World trophy team '76; coached Sylvie Fortier to int-jr.-athlete-of-'75 award; Quebec City media coach of '63, Confederation medal '67; mem. Order of Canada; CASSA distinguished service award, Canadian council for co-operation in aquatics award, Que. coach of

yr, Sports and Fitness coach-of-month award '74, Standard Brands award '75; runnerup Air Canada amateur coach of '73; mem. Order of Canada.

ERDMAN, Wayne (judo); b. 3 Feb 1952, Kitchener, Ont.; given name: Wayne John; judo instructor; Ont. 160lb title '67; Eastern Cdn. jr. 154lb title '68; ntl 70k '71, '73, '75, '76; 78k '80; ranked world's top 16 holding '72 Olympic gold medalist, '73 world champion Nomura of Japan to points draw '73 worlds; Pan-Am 70k gold '74; PAG 70k gold, ranked world's top 8 '75; mem. '76 Olympic team; Canada Cup 78k bronze '80; runnerup ntl amateur athlete of '74; res. Don Mills, Ont.

ERVASTI, Ed (golf); b. 13 Jan 1914, Minneapolis, Minn.; given name: Edward Walker; m. Jane Bradshaw; c. Thomas, John, David; Wayne State; ret'd general manager; finalist '43 Salt Lake City, Utah amateurs; '47 Michigan amateur, St. Louis district titles; only Michigan qualifier '53 US Amateur; twice low amateur Erie, Pa., Open; London District title '66; 3 Sunningdale, 1 London Hunt club titles; 6 ntl srs titles; Cdn Sr. Amateur title '76; 2 North/South sr. amateur titles; intl sr. title '79; Rankin Memorial Trophy winner once; 3 Ont. srs titles; 4 US srs titles; world super sr. title '94; nen, Cdn team 23 Triangular Cup matches; Ervasti Cup competed for annually; pres. CSGA '86-87; London sportsman of '01; mem. Michigan, Ont. Golf, High Point, NC halls of fame; res. London, Ont.

ESMIE, Robert (t&f); 5 Jul 1972, Kingston, Jamaica; mem. Speaker's Bureau; sprinter; emigrated to Canada '84; began competing at 16; gold 100m, 200m Canada vs. Ireland '92; silver 100m '94 Harry Jerome Classic; bronze 100m '94 NY Games; silver 100m, gold 200m '94 ntl championships; PB: 10.18 100m, 20.70 200m; mem. 4x100 gold relay team '95-97 world outdoor championships, '96 Olympic Games; mem. '94 CG, '96 Olympic Games teams; 2 Cdn men's team-of-yr awards; resigned from relay team '97 citing personality conflicts; nicknamed "Blast Off"; mem. Canadian Olympic Hall of Fame ('96 Oly gold 4x100 relay team); res. Surrey, B.C.

ESPOSITO, Phil (hockey); b. 20 Feb 1942, Sault Ste. Marie, Ont.; given name: Philip Anthony; div. Donna; c. Laurie, Carrie, Cherise; radio/TV hockey analyst, ex-hockey exec.; Sarnia Jr. B, St. Catharines Jr. A; pro Sault Ste. Marie, St. Louis; NHL winger Chicago '63-67, ctr Boston '67-75, NYR '75-81; NHL record: 1282 scheduled games, 717g, 873a, 130 playoff games, 61g, 76a; 1st player NHL history 100+ points single season; 1st player 70+ goals single season with 76 '70-71; tied Frank Mahovlich most Stanley Cup playoff points single season with 27; 50+ goals 5 consec. seasons; 5 consec. 100+ point seasons; 1st player 150+ points (152) '70-71; 27 3-goal, 5 4-goal games; 3rd in career goals, points; standout with Team Canada '72, '76; mem. 2 Stanley Cup winners, 6 1st, 2 2nd all-star teams; 5 Ross, 2 Hart, 2 Lester Patrick, 2 Lester Pearson, 1 Lou Marsh, 2 Lionel Conacher trophies; founder Phil Esposito Foundation, Masters of Hockey OT game; NHL milestone award; jersey No. 7 ret'd by Bruins; TV color commentator; v-p/GM NYR '86-90; instrumental in organizing successful Tampa Bay Lightning NHL franchise expansion bid for '92-93 season; pres./GM Lightning '92-98; wrote *Thunder & Lightning;* minority owner Cincinnati

Cyclones (ECHL); Officer Order of Canada '72; mem. Canada's Sports, Hockey Heritage North, Hockey, SSM Hockey halls of fame; res. Tampa, Fla.

ESPOSITO, Tony (hockey); b. 23 Apr 1943, Sault Ste. Marie, Ont.; given name: Anthony James; m. Marilyn; c. Mark, Jason; Michigan Tech, BSc; ex-hockey exec.; pro Vancouver (WHL) '67, Houston (CHL) '68; NHL goalie Montreal '68-69, Chicago '69-84; NHL record: 886 scheduled games, 52,585 min. 2563 goals, 76so, 2.92 avg.; 3 1st team, 2 2nd team all-star; 6 NHL all-star games; Calder Memorial Trophy '70; mem. 1 Stanley Cup winner; won/ shared 3 Vezina Trophies; US citizen; mem. Team Canada '72, Team USA '81 Canada Cup series; pres. NHLPA; v-p/GM Pittsburgh '88-90; dir. hockey dev./scout Tampa Bay Lightning '95-98, fired mid-season '98; jersey No. 35 ret'd by Blackhawks; nickname "Tony 0"; mem. Hockey Heritage North, Hockey, SSM Hockey halls of fame; res. St. Petersburg Beach, Fla.

ESTABROOKS, John (builder/administration/golf); b. 12 Oct 1939, Saint John, N.B.; NB-PEI jr. title '57; 2 NB-PEI amateur titles; rep. NB-PEI, NS, Nfld. 4 Willingdon Cup teams; gov. Grand Falls GC; chair. Nfld jr. development program 3yrs; chair NB course rating, handicap comm. '72-74; gov. Moncton GC '75-79; NB jr. development chair 6yrs; pres. NBGA '81-83; gov. RCGA 10yrs; chair. 4 sucessful ntl tournaments; hon. life gov. NBGA; Estabrooks Cup competition bears his name; mem. Moncton Sports wall, NB Sports hall of fame; res. Riverview, N.B.

ESTAY, Ron (football); b. 22 Dec 1948, Raceland, La.; given name: Ronnie James; m. Debbie Lewis; c. Brannon Michael, Angela; Louisiana State, BS; football coach; d-tackle LSU team of century; d-capt. Hula Bowl '72; played in '71 Orange Bowl. East-West Shriner's game, Sun Bowl; 3 varsity football letters; *AP/UPI* all-American; Chris Schinkel all-American award; 1st team coaches all-American '71; numerous other college athletic/academic awards; drafted by BC Lions, Denver Broncos, to Edmonton '73-82; d-capt. Eskimos '73-76; also saw service with New York (WFL), Washington (USFL), Jacksonville; retd from pro play '94; 9 Grey Cup finals, 6 winners; 4 Western Conf., Cdn all-star; 2 CFL all-pro; Western Conf. dl of '77; Schenley award nominee '75; Edmonton Eskimos Giver award; mem. varied professional organizations; entered coaching ranks Jackson HS 1yr, Christian Life Academy 4yrs, Evangel U 12yrs, Liberty U 1yr, d.-line coach Saskatchewan Roughriders from '01; coached '96 #1-ranked nationally defence NAIA Div. II; 3 #1 Heart of America Conf, defensive awards; mem. LSU, Alta. Sports, Cdn Football halls of fame; res. Regina, Sask.

ESTWICK, Leslie (t&f); b. 20 Dec 1960, Goderich, Ont.; computer consultant; mem. Athletics Canada bd dir.; ntl hj title, runnerup heptathlon '87; 5 gold hj Jesse Owens Invitational; bronze hj, silver 60mH '87 CIAU championships; silver 60mH Belgium, 100mH, hj Italy '88; bronze hj '89 Francophone Games; 3 ntl hj titles; gold 100mH '92 Provo Invitational; gold heptathlon '93 Ohio Relays; competed '90, '94 CG, '91 PAG, world championships; mem. Ottawa Lions TC; mem. Ottawa Athletic Club racing team '99; 1 gold, 3 silver '97, 2 gold '99 world masters; 3 gold '98 Caribbean Masters; 4 gold

'01 US masters; 3 gold, 40-44 age group records Cdn masters, 2 gold, 1 bronze world masters '03; age-group WR 80m hurdles, hj silver, lj bronze '01 world veterans championship; turned attention to bobsleighing '01; res. Gloucester, Ont.

ETCHEGARY, Gus (soccer); b. 28 May 1924, St. Lawrence, Nfld.; given name: Augustine Alexander; m. Kay Diab; c. Glenn, Grant; ret'd exec. v-p Fishery Products International, chair. Fisheries Council of Canada '81-82; mem. 3 St. Lawrence soccer title teams; pres. Burin Peninsula, St. John's, Nfld. soccer assn.; v-p CSA; soccer referee; St. Pierre-Miquelon service-to-soccer award; mem. Burin Peninsula, Nfld. Sports, Soccer, St. Lawrence, St. John's Soccer halls of fame; res. Paradise, Nfld.

ETCHEVERRY, Sam (football); b. 20 May 1930, Carlsbad, N.M.; m. Juanita Louise Mulcahy (d); c. Steve (d), Mike, Nancy, Jennifer; Denver, BA; investment advisor; qb '50 Pineapple Bowl; pro Montreal (CFL) '52-59, St. Louis Cardinals (NFL) '60-61; nicknamed "The Rifle"; CFL record '54 (when league began keeping records) to '59: 1630 completions on 2829 pass attempts for 25,582yds, 163int, 174tds; single season EFC passing yardage record 4723yds '56; shares CFL record longest completed pass 109yds to Hal Patterson '56; 3 Grey Cup finals; traded to Hamilton '60 but opted for NFL; coach Que. Rifles (UFL), Alouettes '70 Grey Cup winner; 6 times EFC all-star; Schenley outstanding player '54; Jeff Russel Memorial Trophy '54, '58; pres. Montreal Concordes '82-83; mem. Que. Sports, Cdn Football, MAAA halls of fame; res. Nun's Island, Que.

EVANS, Clay (swimming); b. 28 Oct 1953, El Bagre, Colombia; given name: Thomas Clayton; UCLA BArch; coach; butterfly, backstroke specialist; mem. '72, '76 (silver) Olympic, '79 PAG teams; 100m butterfly bronze '79 PAG; ntl 100m backstroke, 200m IM titles '72, 100m butterfly '76; silver 100m butterfly, bronze 50m FS '80 Four Nation Cup; ret'd '80; ntl 200m IM record '72; mem. UCLA water polo team; Gov-Gen's medal '76; competitive masters swimmer holding 40+ US, world records; US masters coach of '92-93; dir. SoCal Aquatics; lifetime achievement award Master Aquatic Coaches Assn.; res. Huntington Beach, Calif.

EVANS, Eddie (rugby); b. 15 Sep 1964, Terrace, B.C.; UBC; IBM business planner Japan; jr. football Victoria, Vancouver; prop Cdn jr. rugby team, ntl sr team '85-98; competed 3 World Cups; Canada's most capped player; earned 1st of 48 caps vs. USA '86; mem. IBM Tokyo team; res. Tokyo, Japan.

EVANS, Jodi (basketball); b. 16 Aug 1968, Calgary, Alta.; UCal, BComm, Oxford (Rhodes Scholarship) PhD; guard HS provincial title team '86; mem. UCal team that went 69-0 and won '88-89 CIAU titles; mem. jr. ntl team '87, sr. team '88-96; mem. '91 FISU Games bronze medal team; competed '90, '94 world, Goodwill Games, '91 PAG, '96 Olympic Games; COPABA gold '95, bronze '93; played on Oxford men's '93 title team; pro with English, German, Greek teams; CIAU all-Cdn '90-91; Nan Copp player-of-'91 award; HS female athlete-of-'86 award; res. Norway/Calgary.

EVANS, Mark (rowing); b. 16 Aug 1957, Toronto, Ont.; Oxford; gold coxed 4s, pairs Nottingham International; coxed, coxless 4s, pairs Canadian Henley, ntl championships; mem. 8s gold crew '84 Olympics; Dick Ellis award '84; twin brother Michael; res. Toronto, Ont.

EVANS, Michael (rowing); b. 16 Aug 1957, Toronto, Ont.; given name: John Michael; Princeton, AB, Oxford; ntl, Ont. pairs, 4s, 8s champion '75-83; bronze FISA world youth championships '75; stroke '77 8s, '79, '81, '83 pairs world championships; gold Nottingham International coxed 4s, pair; mem. gold 8s crew '84 Olympics; 9 Canadian Henley titles; finalist English Royal Henley, mem. '80, '84 Olympic teams; stroke Princeton IRA regatta freshman champions '76; stroke varsity heavy 8s '77-81; capt. varsity heavyweight program '79-81; Dick Ellis award '84; res. London, Eng.

EVANSHEN, Terry (football); b. 13 Jun 1944, Montreal, Que.; given name: Terrance Anthony; m. Lorraine Galarneau; c. Tracy Lee, Tara, Jennifer; Utah State; ex-sales mgr. motivational speaker; Portland Seahawks (Atlantic Coast Conference) '64; hb/wr Alouettes '65, '70-74, EFC rookie of yr; Calgary '66-69, Hamilton '74-77, Toronto '78; twice Schenley top Canadian; twice EFC, 4 times WFC all-star, once all-Cdn; 600 CFL career receptions for 9697yds, 80tds, only 3 fumbles; shares longest pass reception record with Hal Patterson 109yds from Jerry Keeling '66; twice led EFC, WFC receivers single season; with Hugh Campbell shares single-season td pass receptions with 17; CFL record most games catching passes 181; 3 times 1000+ reception yards single season; CFL record 10 consecutive games catching td passes; 61 games catching td passes; caught 4td passes vs. Ottawa 7 Sep 1975; mem. 3 Grey Cup finalists, 1 winner; *CBC-TV* football color commentator 2yrs; awarded $1.6M in damages from '88 auto accident which severely affected his memory; conducts speaking tours; subject of June Callwood book *Man Who Lost Himself*; mem. Cdn Football Hall of Fame; res. Brooklin, Ont.

EVILLE, Vern (t&f); b. 21 Dec 1910, Brandon, Man.; d. 9 Nov 1973, Halifax, N.S.; given name: Vernon Drew Millidge; m. Joyce Whitney Favin; c. Drew; Acadia; standout basketball, rugby, t&f performer; mem. Acadia Axemen ntl sr. cage finalists; standout half for Acadia in English rugby; Maritime jr. discus/lj titlist '28; led Ken Wo squad to team title '29 winning 440, 880 dashes, hj, 120yd high hurdles; named to Cdn team for '30 Empire Games but polio terminated career; mem. NS Sports Hall of Fame.

EVON, Russ (all-around); b. 15 Aug 1917, Windsor, Ont.; d. 9 Nov 1998, St. Thomas, Ont.; given name: Russell Phillip; m. Hellen; c. Donna, Ron; ret'd owner laundry, dry cleaning business; outstanding teenage fastballer; Border Cities Softball Federation '38; fanned record 25 consecutive batters, several no-hitters; 3 world tournaments, coached 4th, winning one; 18 Sr. IC baseball seasons London, St. Thomas '43-60; career .345 batting avg., twice batting champion; led each league in which he played at least once, including strong Detroit Class A League '39; mem. 3 Ont. basketball title teams; OHA Int., International HL; outstanding-player award IHL

'40-41; 35yrs hockey referee; strong swimmer; involved in more than 30 rescues of potential drowning victims; top-ranked 10-pin bowler; mem. Windsor-Essex Sports Hall of Fame.

EWERT, Elmer (archery); b. 19 Sep 1934, St. Catharines, Ont.; m. Beverely Smith; c. Lorraine, Kevin, Trevor; Notre Dame(BC), Waterloo; laboratory technologist; '67 ntl champion; mem. Ambassador's Cup, world championships teams, '72 Olympic team; '74 Ont. champion; res. Wellesley, Ont.

EWING, Walter (shooting); b. 11 Feb 1878, Montreal, Que.; d. 1927, given name: Walter Hamilton; m. Ethel Raeburn McIntyre; c. Morris, Marguerite, Walter James, David Russell; pres. Lackawanna Coal Co.; began trapshooting '05; won '08 Olympic gold with score of 72 of possible 80; declined invitation to defend title '12 Olympics; won Clarendon Cup in 1st annual Canadian Indians tournament in Montreal '06; won ntl championship, Grand Canadian Handicap, Brewers and Maltsters Cup, provincial individual titles; also competed in DCRA rifle events winning 8-man Dominion, 10-man provincial, 5-man international, 6-man provincial and 5-man Lansdowne Cup team titles in same year; mem. Cdn Olympic, Canada's Sports halls of fame.

EXELBY, Clare (football); b. 5 Nov 1937, Toronto, Ont.; given name: Clare Douglas; m. Maureen Girvin; c. Julie Lynn, Randy Allan; UofT, BA; teacher Erindale Coll; mem. ntl finalist Parkdale Jr. Lions '56, ntl title '57; pro Toronto '58-59, '61-63, Calgary '60, Montreal '64-65; WFC all-star db, league interception leader; all-Canadian db '64; coached 5 Toronto city HS title teams; def. coach York '68-72; def. co-ordinator jr. Argos '78-79; res. Toronto, Ont.

EYNON, Bob (swimming); b. 16 Aug 1935, North Bay, Ont.; given name: Robert Barrie; m. Mary Ellen Thompson (d); c. Susan, Robert, Patrick; UWO, BA, Illinois, MSc; ret'd assoc-prof., swimming coach; successful competitive career led to coaching ntl women's swim team '67 PAG, UK touring team '73-74; CIAU swim coach of '66, '75; treas. CASA '60-72; chair. Ont. Swimming Coaches Assn. '66-73; chair. CIAU Swimming Coaches Assn. '73-75; Ont. merit award '70; Cdn Red Cross Society merit award '71; works Buck Dawson summer camp; res. London, Ont.

EZINICKI, Bill (hockey/golf); b. 11 Mar 1924, Winnipeg, Man.; nicknamed "Wild Bill" for his love of body contact; a free-wheeler, he was noted for violent body checks which frequently put opponents out of game; carried insurance policy which paid him per stitch taken in on-ice battles; jr. 1yr Winnipeg Rangers, mem. Oshawa Generals Memorial Cup team '44; pro '44-55 with Toronto, Boston, NYR; played in 2 NHL all-star games; mem. 3 Stanley Cup winners; NHL record: 368 scheduled games, 79g,105a, 40 playoff games, 5g, 8a; ret'd '55 to pursue career as pro golfer; spent time on PGA tour; mem. Man. Hockey Hall of Fame; res. Bolton, Mass.

FABRE, Édouard (t&f); b. 21 Aug 1885, Ste. Geneviéve, Que.; d. 1 Jul 1939, Montreal, Que.; m. Blanche; c. Marcelle, Marie-Blanche, Édouard; construction worker; in 30 years of competition ran 315 match races, won hundreds of trophies, medals; in one 24-hour event was pitted against horse to see who could run furthest, Fabre won; competed '06 Athens marathon, '12 Stockholm Olympics; entered 1st Boston marathon '11; won on 5th try '15; won 200-mile, 6-day snowshoe marathon Quebec to Montreal, averaging just under 6 mph; mem. Canada's Sports Hall of Fame.

FABRIS, Lucio (badminton); b. 7 Nov 1957, Sudbury, Ont.; given name: Lucio Mario; m. Judy Humphry; c. Kristina; UofT BSc (Pharm); pharmacist, owner Med-I-Well Services; from '73-81 dominant force on Ont., ntl scenes; ntl jr. men's doubles '73-74; swept Ont., ntl jr. singles, men's, mixed doubles '75; ntl mixed doubles '76; silver '78 CG; OUAA men's singles, doubles '79; Ont., municipal sport achievement awards; 2 ntl healthcare awards; CPha Innovative Practice award; res. Creighton Mine/Sudbury, Ont.

FABRO, Sam (builder); b. 8 Dec 1920, Udine, Italy; m. Anne Marie Temple; c. James; UWO; ret'd board chair. W.G. McMahon Ltd.; accomplished hockey, baseball, football player; mem. Winnipeg Rangers Memorial Cup champs '41; sr. Reo Flyers; fl/fw/hb Winnipeg Blue Bombers '42; chair. baseball competition '67 PAG; pres. Man. Baseball Assn. '68-69; chair. Man. Games '74-78; among founders Man. Hockey Players Assn., chair. '66-80; mem./chair. Winnipeg Enterprises '67-83; launched Man. marathon and canoeathon; chair. of same; chair. Man. Hockey Hall of Fame; chair. Man. Sports Hall of Fame; v-chair. Man. Wildlife Foundation; day declared in his honor in Winnipeg; nickname "Slippery Sam"; mem. Order of Canada; Man. Order of the Buffalo; Man. Sports, Hockey halls of fame; res. Winnipeg, Man.

FAIRBANKS, Lloyd (football); b. 28 Apr 1953, Raymond, Alta.; m. Jackie; c. Kelly, Todd, Kathy; Brigham Young; ol Calgary '75-82, '89-92; Montreal '83-86, Hamilton '87-89; 3 times WFC, 3 EFC, 2 CFL all-star; Schenley ol finalist '82; Beckett-DeMarco (outstanding WFC lineman) award '82; mem. Stampeders Wall of Fame; res. Raymond, Alta.

FAIRS, Jack (football/baseball/tennis); b. 22 Aug 1923, Toronto, Ont.; given name: John Russell; m. Peggy Duncan; c. Nancy, Kimberly, John; UWO, BSc, Columbia, MA; prof.; football UWO '42-46; backfield coach UWO '48-62; catcher minor pro baseball '39-54, London Sr. IC, Welland Atlas Steel; '48 Sandlot World Series title; part-time scout NY Yankees; coached 5 Ont. Bantam A title teams; tennis coach '48-62; UWO squash coach '59-96; US intercollegiate squash titles '77, '80; UWO no lower than 2nd CIAU squash from '72; Squash Canada distinguished service award; 3M 50yr coaching award; mem. UWO W-Club, London Sports halls of fame; res. London, Ont.

FALARDEAU, Johanne (badminton); b. 2 Mar 1961, Montreal, Que.; given name: Marie Johanne Lucille; Laval; coach, Que. Badminton Fed.; 2 Que. singles, 1 doubles titles; 2 ntl singles, 3 doubles, 2 mixed doubles titles; 3 singles, 4 doubles, 2 mixed doubles Pan-Am championships titles; 1 French doubles, mixed doubles titles, 1 US doubles title; team silver '78, '82, doubles gold '82 CG; fed. govt. excellence award '83; res. Quebec City.

FALONEY, Bernie (football); b. 15 Jun 1932, Carnegie, Pa.; d. 14 Jun 1999, Hamilton, Ont.; m. Janet Wallace; c. Bernie Jr., Wally; Maryland, BSc; pres. construction machinery, industrial products company; football, baseball, basketball Maryland '50-53; rejected pro baseball offers; all-American, Atlantic Coast Conf. player of year, all-American Scholastic team; qb, co-capt. Maryland undefeated season, ntl title '53; '52 Sugar Bowl, '53 Orange Bowl; SF 49ers 1st draft '53; pro Edmonton '54; Bolling AFB Generals 2 service titles '55-56; Hamilton '57-64, 1st qb to lead both Eastern, Western team to Grey Cup victories ('54, '57); Montreal '65-66, BC '67; CFL record: completed 1493 of 2876 passes for 24,264yds, 151td, 201 interceptions, .519 percentage; *CBC* color commentator '68; 9 Grey Cup finals, 4 winners; Dapper Dan award Washington, DC Touchdown Club '53; CFL Schenley outstanding player '61, Jeff Russel '65; Maryland man of '71/distinguished- sports-alumnus award '72; twice Ted Reeve all-Cdn team; coached '73 CFL all-stars over Grey Cup champions; mem. Cdn Football, Canada's Sports, Copps Coliseum halls of fame.

FALOON, Joanna (canoeing); b. 1 Jun 1955, Ottawa, Ont.; given name: Joanna Patricia; m. Wally Kaczkowski; c. Kenneth; UAlta., Illinois Coll. of Podiatric Medicine; podiatrist; top athlete Notre Dame HS '72; mem. UAlta water polo team '75-76; mem. Rideau Canoe Club '71-73; ntl jr. K4 title; ntl women's C2 title '85; world, US C2 women's title '91; world, ntl C1 women's title '92; competed '91-97 Hawaii outrigger world championships; 5 gold NA marathon canoe racing championships '97; 2 gold, 1 silver US marathon canoe/kayak championships '98; retained NA C1 marathon title '99; C1 12-mile women's world pro title; built reputation as one of world's top marathon canoe/kayak paddlers; also competes in triathlon, running events; mem. Nepean Sports Wall of Fame; res. Merrickville, Ont.

FANNING, Jim (baseball); b. 14 Sep 1927, Chicago, Ill.; given name: William James; m. Marie; c. 2; Buena Vista College, BPhE, Illinois, MA; baseball exec.; pro ball at 22 catcher Chicago Cubs organization; 64 ML games Cubs '54-57; mgr. Tulsa (TL) '58, Dallas (AA) '59-60, Eau Claire, Wisc. '61, field and GM; Braves' special assignment scout '63-64; AGM '64-66; dir. scouting, farm operations '67; dir. ML scouting bureau commissioner's office '68; mem. numerous baseball organizational comm.; with Montreal at Expos '68 inception; GM through '76; v-p from '73; dir. player development '77-81, from '83; field mgr. '81-82, '84, advisor to GM, broadcaster; scout Colorado '92-00; special asst. to Gord Ash Toronto '01; charter mem. Buena

Vista sports hall of fame; '72 Buena Vista Alumni Assn. outstanding-service award; Hartley, Iowa, baseball park named in his honor; mem. Cdn Baseball Hall of Fame; res. Dorchester, Ont.

FARLEY, Phil (golf); b. 27 Mar 1912, Toronto, Ont.; d. 10 Apr 1974, Toronto, Ont.; m. Ruth; c. Maureen, Michael, Diane, Philip Edward; stockbroker; Ont. jr. title '30; 6 Ont. amateurs, 2 Ont. Opens, 1 Que. amateur; runnerup 3 ntl amateurs; low amateur 5 Cdn Opens; 3 times Cdn amateur finalist; with Phil Brownlee '61 Ont. best ball; mem. 12 Ont., 3 Que. Willingdon Cup teams; 6 G.S. Lyons team titles; 1 Duke of Kent, 3 Ont. srs, 2 RCGA srs, 2 CSGA titles; pres. OGA '49; RCGA governor '50-74; RCGA pres. '67; mem. RCGA Hall of Fame.

FARMER, Jim (football); b. 28 Nov 1916, Glasgow, Scotland; d. 5 Jan 1988, London, Ont.; given name: James Gordon; m. Joan; c. Brian, Peter, Sarah; Assumption College, UWO, OCE; salesman; undefeated distance swimmer 4yrs; all-star HS football, basketball; sr. individual t&f honors '34; Windsor Patterson CI all-time all-around athlete; mem. '35 jr. A baseball champions; pitched sr. A softball; with Assumption mem. ntl basketball finalists '36; capt. CIAU '37-38 basketball champions; OQAA all-star fb '38; pro Toronto Argos '39; dir. Windsor Rockets (ORFU) '47; mem. CIAU football rules comm. '59-75; 7yrs referee-in-chief OQAA, 10yrs editor, rules interpreter OQAA, OUAA, CIAU; mem. Windsor-Essex County, UWO W-Club Sports halls of fame.

FARMER, Ken (hockey); b. 26 Jul 1912, Westmount, Que.; d. 12 Jan 2005, Westmount, Que.; given name: Kenneth Pentin; m. Mildred Larayne Strachan; c. Howard, Ian, Cynthia, Pamela; McGill, BComm, CA; ret'd chartered accountant; hockey McGill '31-34; mem. '36 Olympic silver medal team; CIAU tennis doubles champion; pres. COA '53-61; chair. Ntl Advisory Council on Fitness, Amateur Sport '62-65; pres. CG Assn. of Canada '78-84; dir. Montreal Olympic organizing comm.; active in charity work; mem. Order of Canada, Cdn Olympic, McGill Sports halls of fame.

FARNSWORTH, Terry (judo); b. 27 Aug 1942, Portland, Me.; given name: Terry Allen; m. Heather Higgins; c. Lanisa Dawn, Joshua George; SophiaU (Tokyo), BEc; manufacturing co. pres.; ntl 93k titles '72-73; gold '69, double silver '73 Maccabiah Games; mem. ntl team '71-73; competed '72 Olympics, '73 PAG, '71-73 worlds; mem. selection comm., judo chairman Canadian Maccabiah Games Comm.; res. Bois des Filion, Que.

FARRELL, Neil (t&f); b. 13 Feb 1915, Arthur, Ont.; given name: Neil John; m. Isabel Couper; ret'd Ont. govt.; average distance runner; chair. ntl t&f comm. '56-60; secty. AAUofC '61-66; mem. ntl records comm. '56-67; mem. AAUofC Hall of Fame Comm. '61-67; t&f rep., dir. COA '57-60; mem.-at-large COA '61-64; p.-pres., secty Southwestern Ont. branch AAUofC, Hamilton Olympic Comm.; mgr. Canadian BEG t&f team '58, Olympic t&f team '60; asst. mgr. Canadian CG teams '66, '74; mgr. '70, GM '78 CG teams; hon. secty. CCGA from '63; mem. SFC citations comm. '65-67; deputy ref. '76 Olympic marathon; v-p America Zone CG Fed.; Ont. sport achievement award '68; mem. Cdn Olympic Sports Hall of Fame; res. Hamilton, Ont.

FARROW, Brad (judo); b. 5 Oct 1956, Vancouver, B.C.; given name: Brad William; m. Laurel King; c. Taylor, Kristen; Concordia, BSc, UWO, MBA; management consultant; 5th degree black belt; 11 Canadian 63kg and/or 65kg titles; gold 63kg '75, 65kg '79 PAG; mem. '76, '80, '84 Olympic teams; gold '79, '81 Dutch Open, '80 German Open, '83-84 Canada Cup; silver '79 Hungarian Cup; bronze '77 British Open, '80 Pacific Rim, Cuban Open, '81 Pacific Rim, German Open; mem. ntl team '75, '79, '81 world championships; bronze '83 FISU Games; mem. Cdn Judo Hall of Fame; res. Calgary, Alta.

FAUL, Adam (boxing); b. 18 Apr 1929, Regina, Sask.; m. Marjorie Evelyn Shaw; c. Kevin Darrell, Cheryl Lynn, Mark Perry, Gregory Shaw; municipal secty-treas.; '45-47 Sask. light-heavyweight title; ntl light-heavyweight title '47; Western Diamond Belt, 1 Sask., 2 ntl heavyweight titles, Olympic trials '48; mem. '48 Olympic team; ring record 60-4; football Regina Eastend jr. Bombers, Sask. Roughriders '44; mem. Sask. Sports Hall of Fame; res. Spy Hill, Sask.

FAULKNER, Alex (hockey); b. 21 May 1936, Bishop's Falls, Nfld.; given name: Selm Alexander; m. Doris May Reid; c. Shawn, Alexandra, Tammy Sue; owner, operator sr. citizen's home; mem. Nfld title teams all levels; 6 times all-Nfld sr.; NHL TML '61, Detroit '62-64; twice Stanley Cup finalist; Allan Cup semifinalist Galt '72-73; mem. Nfld Sports Hall of Fame; res. Bishop's Falls, Nfld.

FAULKNER, John (swimming); b. 12 Dec 1923, Kingston, Ont.; given name: John Arthur; m. Margaret Isabelle Rowntree; c. Laura Megan, Melanie Anne; Queen's, BA, BPhE, Michigan, MSc, PhD; professor, director UofM Institute of Gerontology; intercollegiate football '46-50, basketball '46-47; football, basketball coach Ottawa Glebe CI '52-56; coached Ottawa Ski Club ntl jr. title team '53; coach UWO swim team '56-60, OQAA titles '59-60; coached swimming, diving teams '60 Olympics; active American College of Sports Medicine from '60, trustee '63-75, pres. '71-72; published myriad papers on research on physiological responses to sport; twice competed National Ski Marathon; UofM Burke Aaron Hinsdale scholar award '62, American College of Sports Medicine citation '78; res. Ann Arbor, Mich.

FAUQUIER, Harry (tennis); b. 28 Aug 1942, Toronto, Ont.; given name: Henry Edmund; m. Lindsay Smith; c. Sarah; Michigan, BA; partner tennis court construction co.; ntl jr. title '59-60; Big 10 title '61-62; capt. Michigan team '63-64; mem. '63 PAG team; mem. 10 Davis Cup teams, twice capt.; with John Sharpe ntl Open men's doubles '68; among Canada's top 5 10yrs; 5yrs No. 1 Ont.; won international tournaments North, South America, Europe; competed at Forest Hills, Wimbledon; assisted Ken Sinclair in organizing ntl Open tournaments Toronto, Montreal; mem. Cdn Dübler Cup, Fred Perry Cup teams; 4 ntl srs doubles titles; mem. Cdn Tennis Hall of Fame; res. Aurora, Ont.

FAUST, Lisa (field hockey); b. 9 Nov 1966, Vancouver, B.C.; given name: Lisa Elaine; m. Rick Roberts; SFU, BA; level II certified coach; coach Douglas College; mem. ntl team from '94; capt. during '02 European tour; through '02 played in excess of 105 international matches; played 3yrs with teams in Germany; competed '95 Olympic qualifier, '97, '01 World Cup qualifier; '98, '02 C G; bronze '95, '99 PAG, '01 Pan-Am Cup; 12yrs field hockey coach SFU; BC player-of-yr award; Vancouver Premier League MVP; 2 coach of yr awards; mem. Burnaby Sports Hall of Fame; res. Vancouver, B.C.

FAWCETT, Mark (snowboarding); b. 17 Jan 1972, Saint John, N.B.; ardent windsurfer who has excelled on World Cup pro snowboarding circuit; 2 WC gold, 1 silver, 2 bronze; 2 ISF World Series gold, 2 ISF Masters gold; ntl slalom title '98; competed '97 world championships, '98 Olympics; equipment breakdown ruined Olympic slalom hopes at Nagano; ISF surfboarder of '95; nicknamed "Fuzzy"; res. East Riverside, N.B./Hood River, Ore.

FEAGAN, Ron (harness racing); b. 10 Mar 1942, Goderich, Ont.; d. 12 Jan 1979, Dundas, Ont.; m. Susan; c. Blair; 1st Cdn to drive 200 winners single season; Cdn co-horseman of '65; youngest driver to reach 1000 victories '68; Canada's leading race winner '66, '69-70; top Cdn money winner '68, '70; Golden Horseshoe Circuit dash, money leader '72-76; 3000 win plateau '78; purses exceeded $6M; drove H.A. Meadowland '66 Queen City Pacing Stakes, Canadian Pacing Derby, Canadian Harness Horse-of-yr honors; mem. Cdn Horse Racing Hall of Fame.

FEAR, Cap (football); b. 11 Jun 1901, Old Sailbury, Eng.; d. 12 Feb 1978, St. Catharines, Ont.; given name: Alfred Henry John; m. Gertrude Lilian Farr; construction superintendent; outside wing Toronto Argos '20-27, 3 league titles, 1 Grey Cup; mem. team which lost only one game '21-22 seasons; Hamilton Tigers '28-32, 2 league titles, 2 Grey Cups; hockey Aura Lee sr. OHA, Ont. Hydro Toronto Mercantile League; runnerup NA welterweight boxing title; stroke Argonaut Rowing Club lightweight 8s, 4s same day Canadian Henley victors; Lachine, Detroit, Dominion Day regatta titles; mem. Hamilton best-of-century (1867-1949) amateur era all-star football team; mem. Canada's Sports, Cdn Football halls of fame.

FEDERKO, Bernie (hockey); b. 12 May 1956, Foam Lake, Sask.; given name: Bernard Allan; m. Bernadette; c. Jordan, Dustin, Drew; hockey broadcaster; ctr Saskatoon (WHL) '73-76, Kansas City (CHL) '76-77; 1st pick St. Louis '76 amateur draft; played in NHL with St. Louis '77-89, Detroit '89-90; jersey #24 ret'd by Blues; 1st player NHL history 50+ assists 10 consec. seasons; NHL record: 14 seasons, 1000 scheduled games, 369g, 761a, 91 playoff games, 35g, 66a; WHL all-star '76; WHL MVP '76; played in 2 NHL all-star games; GM/head coach St. Louis Vipers roller hockey team '93-95, club pres. '95-98; mem. Hockey Hall of Fame; res. St. Louis, Mo.

FEDORUK, Sylvia (all-around); b. 5 May 1927, Canora, Sask.; UofSask, BA, MA, FCCPM; ret'd physicist, prof., ex-Lieut.-Gov. Sask.; 2 gold, 1 silver, 1 bronze, T. Eaton Trophy top individual performer '47 Dominion t&f championships; mem. Saskatoon Ramblers '48 provincial women's, '54 Regina Gorins, '55 Saskatoon Ramblers Western Canada softball champions; 12 inter-varsity title teams (5 basketball, 2 t&f, 3 volleyball, 2 golf) '46-51; inter-varsity individual golf title '51; Gov.-Gen.'s gold medal UofSask '49; Queen's Jubilee medal '77; coached university volleyball, curling

teams 2yrs; 3rd for Joyce McKee 3 provincial, 2 ntl curling championships; pres. CLCA '71-72; pres. SLCA '59; pres. Women's Athletic Board UofSask '49; dir., mem. Order of Canada, Cdn Curling, Sask. Sports Halls, UofSask Sports Wall of Fame; res. Regina, Sask.

FEDOSA, Bob (curling); b. 14 Dec 1945, Saskatoon, Sask.; given name: Robert William; m. Sandra Jean; York, BA; ret'd educator; 7 times Ont. men's finalist; skip Ont. entry '79 Brier; skip 2 Ont. Silver Tankard winners; Cdn srs. finalist '02; res. Brampton, Ont.

FEE, Earl (t&f); b. 22 Mar 1929, Elstow, Sask.; given name: Earl William; div.; c. Tyler, Curtis, Melanie Suttar; UofT, BSc, MSc; ret'd nuclear engineer; early track exposure '46-53 then took 33yr hiatus from sport '53-86; began training North York TC '86 then shifted to Saugeen TC and Credit Valley Marathon Club; from '86-98 broke more than 25 age-group world records in 300-, 400m hurdles, 400, 800, 1500, mile runs; through '98 held 17 existing world masters, 7 Cdn masters track records; 6 ntl x-country age-group titles; 4 Cdn Masters athlete-of-meet awards; 4 Ont. Masters male t&f athlete-of-yr awards; 3 Mississauga Master athlete-of-yr awards; authored *Secrets of a World Masters Champion - How to be a Champion 9-90*; res. Mississauga, Ont.

FELICIEN, Perdita (t&f); b. 29 Aug 1980, Oshawa, Ont.; Illinois; hurdles specialist; 10 all-American, 3 NCAA, 4 Big 10 titles, 3 Drake Relays outstanding female athlete honors, 6 Drake Relays titles; '01 Big 10 outdoor t&f athlete-of-yr; '01, '03 ntl outdoor t&f athlete-of-yr awards; Illini, Big 10 record holder; ntl jr. hurdles champ '99; competed '00, '04 Olympics; startled world in Paris '03 claiming world 100m hurdles gold; added world indoor 60m hurdles title '04; PB 12.46; turned pro '03; awarded key to city of Pickering; *Daily Illini* female athlete of '00; crashed on 1st Olympic final hurdle '04; brother Sam tae kwando pro; Bobbie Rosenfeld, Velma Springstead awards '03; shared Athletics Canada award with Chantal Petitclerc (who refused award) '04; res. Pickering, Ont./ Champagne, Ill.

FELL, Graeme (t&f); b. 19 Mar 1959, Romford, Eng.; m. Debbie Campbell; c. Cori-Ann Jill, Taylor John; athletic consultant; 3,000m steeplechase, 3000m specialist; began competing age 11; as mem. GB ntl team won '82 CG silver; emigrated to Canada from San Diego '84; 6 ntl titles; 2 Cdn sr. records; competed '86, '90, '94 CG, '88, '92 Olympic Games; CG gold '86, bronze '94; World Cup bronze '85; 2 CIAU all-Cdn; Tribute-to-Champions award '87, Athletics Canada athlete of '94; BC male athlete of '85; res. Vancouver, B.C.

FELL, Jeffrey (horse racing); b. 20 Jun 1956, Hamilton, Ont.; jockey; riding Winter's Tale became 1st winner Suburban, Brooklyn, Marlboro Cup, NY state's 3 richest handicap races single season; Hialeah, Gulfstream, Belmont riding titles; shares NY state record 6 consec. race victories '80; with Norcliffe '76 Prince of Wales, Queen's Plate; '79 Whitney Stakes, '81 Wood Memorial; through '83 victories exceed 2300, earnings exceed $30M; mem. Cdn Horse Racing, Copps Coliseum halls of fame; res. Hallandale, Fla.

FELLOWS, Ron (motorsport); b. 28 Sep 1959, Windsor, Ont.; given name: Ronald Charles; m. Lynda Stewart; c.

Lindsay, Samuel, Patrick; pro racer; received racing license '78; raced on Ont./Que. region club circuit; competed in Formula 1600 series; competed in Players-GM series from mid '80s winning series title '89; drove in SCCA Trans-Am series '91-96 posting 19 victories at Watkin's Glen; won Chev Mfrs title '95; became 2nd Cdn driver (Earl Ross was 1ˢᵗ) to claim a NASCAR title winning Parts America 150 truck race with record performance Watkin's Glen '98; same season, teamed with Rob Morgan to drive world Ferrari to victory at Watkin's Glen; became 1ˢᵗ non-American to win Busch Grand National Lysol 200 race '98; made Winston Cup debut '98; won Rolex 24-hour Daytona sports car race; 2 24-hour of LeMans GTS titles; Bud Pole award NASCAR Busch series '99; 3 GNC Live Well 200 titles Watkin's Glen; '02 ALMS GTS series title; founded Sunoco Ron Fellows Karting championship as Huntington's disease fund-raiser; mem. Earnhardt Winston Cup team '03; res. Mississauga, Ont.

FENNELL, Dave (football); b. 4 Feb 1953, Edmonton, Alta.; NDak, UAlta, LLD; lawyer; jr. Edmonton Wildcats; dt Edmonton '73-83; nicknamed "Dr. Death"; mem. 9 Grey Cup finals, 6 winners, 5 in succession; outstanding Cdn, def. player '82 Grey Cup final; top def. player '83 all-star game; 5 times all-WFC, all-Cdn; Schenley outstanding-Cdn award '79, runnerup '80; Schenley best-defensive-player award '78; Norm Fieldgate Trophy '78-79; Dr. Beattie Martin Trophy '78-80; mem. Cdn Football, Alta Sports Halls, Eskimos Wall of Fame; res. Edmonton, Alta.

FENNELL, Neil (builder/softball); b. 9 Jul 1948, Picton, Ont.; given name: Neil Harold; m. Connie Ellen Conboy; c. Melissa Ann; UNB; OPP officer; all-consuming interest in fast-pitch softball and a strong commitment to details led to establishment in '90 of Perth Shootout, a world-class, alcohol free, family oriented fastball tournament which continues to grow in reputation; Canadian, US, New Zealand, Australian, Danish teams have participated; tournament proceeds (in excess of $100,000) have assisted local charities; mem. Intl Softball Congress Hall of Fame; res. Perth, Ont.

FENNELL, Pat (boxing); b. 7 Jun 1957, Toronto, Ont.; given name: Patrick William; m. Sandee Phillips; c. Ryan, Sean, Egan, Connor; UofT; teacher; Ont. 81kg, Golden Gloves titles '77, '79; ntl amateur 81kg '77, '79-80; NY State Golden Gloves '79; bronze '79 US Golden Gloves; gold '78, bronze '79 Tammer Turnaus international; gold '79 AAU championships; gold '79 Tour of France; bronze '79 PAG; 2yrs jr. hockey; mem. volleyball team Ont. Winter Games '75; mem. '80 Olympic team; res. Aurora, Ont.

FERBEY, Randy (curling); b. 30 May 1959, Edmonton, Alta; m. Wendy Bain; c. Cody, Spencer, Taylor; customer service printing industry; skip '85-86 ntl mixed; all-star '86; competed 5 Briers, 5 winners; 3rd for Pat Ryan '88-89 Brier, '89 world title rinks; all-star '88, world all-star '89; skipped (but threw 3rd) '01, '02, '03 Brier winners; world title '02, '03; McCain/*TSN* Skins Game '03; established record 23g undefeated Brier streak Mar 14 '02 to Mar 10 '04; 2 Alta Achievement awards; runnerup '87 Olympic trials; Dick Ellis Memorial trophy '89; mem. Cdn Curling Hall of Fame; res. Sherwood Park, Alta.

FERGUS, Bert (badminton); b. 1 Nov 1932, Trail, B.C.; given name: Robert Miles; m. Cordiet Veritege; BC Normal School teaching cert., UBC BEd, Special Ed., Western Wash. MEd; ret'd school administrator; semifinalist in 1ˢᵗ ntl jr. championships '50; with Daryl Thompson ntl men's doubles title '55; mixed doubles gold, and with Dave McTaggart men's doubles silver '57 Mexican Open; with world champion Eddy Choong of Malaysia took US Open men's doubles silver '59; with Wayne Macdonnell ntl men's doubles title '63; 15 gold medals in singles, men's, mixed doubles in ntl masters championships; world masters '86 bronze men's singles, doubles, '94, '98 men's singles, doubles silver, '98 team silver, mixed doubles bronze; numerous BC jr, sr, masters titles; mem. Thomas Cup teams '58-64, team mgr. '67; Vancouver achievement award '66; Queen's Jubilee medal; life mem. Badminton BC, Vancouver Racquets Club; res. Richmond, B.C.

FERGUSON, Arnold (lacrosse); b. 28 Jul 1922, Anyox, B.C.; d. 27 Jan 1981, Victoria, B.C.; given name: Cecil Arnold; m. Floss Ray; c. Diana, Dale, Barbara; BC Liquor Control Board; active role lacrosse, soccer; mem. '43 New Westminster, '55 Victoria Mann Cup champions; Vancouver Adanacs; R.L.Maitland Sportsmanship award '50, Sid Thomas Memorial Trophy '51; initial recipient Laurie Dillabough Trophy as mem. Shamrocks; refereed lacrosse several years; mem. Cdn Lacrosse Hall of Fame.

FERGUSON, Bruce (shooting); b. 10 Apr 1958, Charlottetown, P.E.I.; given name: Athol Bruce; UPEI, BSc; computer technician; began small-bore shooting as a cadet; moved into full-bore ranks '88; won DCRA Gooderham match '92; mem. variety of mini-Palma, provincial, Maritime teams; mem. '93 Cdn Bisley team; cadet shooting instructor from '83; res. Charlottetown, P.E.I.

FERGUSON, Dorothy (baseball); b. 17 Feb 1923, Virden, Man.; d. 8 May 2003, Rockford, Ill.; given name: Dorothy Blanche; m. Donald Key; c. Douglas, Dona; operated painting/decorating business; set 220/mile records as speed skater with Winnipeg club 6yrs; 2b St. Vital Tigerettes intermediate softball champs '41-42; helped St. Vital win sr. women's titles '43-44; blessed with strong arm, good legs, joined Rockford Peaches in AAGPBL '45-54, helping win titles '45, '48-50; in 950 games collected 716 hits in 3216 at bats, 520 runs, .223 BA, 91hbp; husband mem. Cdn Olympic t&f team; nicknamed "Dottie" or "Fergy"; mem. Man. Baseball Hall of Fame; honored by Cooperstown, Cdn Baseball halls of fame.

FERGUSON, John (hockey); b. 5 Sep 1938, Vancouver, B.C.; given name: John Bowie; m. Joan; c. Christina, Catherine, John Jr., Joanne; hockey exec.; stick boy Vancouver Canucks (WHL); jr. Melville Sask., sr. Ft. Wayne; pro Cleveland Barons (AHL); lw Montreal '63-71; team's "policeman;" NHL record: 500 scheduled games, 145g, 158a, 85 playoff games, 20g, 18a; mem. 5 Stanley Cup winners; asst. coach Team Canada '72, GM '81; GM WHA all-stars who beat Russians 3 straight games '79; coach, GM NYR '75-79; GM Winnipeg Jets WHA Avco Cup winners '79; GM Jets (NHL) '79-87; GM Cdn world silver medallist '89; dir. player personnel Ottawa '92-95; pro scout San Jose '97-02. consultant to GM '02-03; 3 *Sporting News,* 2 *Hockey News* exec. of yr; pres. Windsor Raceway 3yrs; operated Montreal

Québécois Pro Lacrosse League; mem. BC Hockey, Sports, Hockey halls of fame; res. Amherstberg, Ont.

FERGUSON, Ken (shooting); b. 24 May 1952, Springhill, N.S.; given name: Kenneth Earl; m. Elizabeth Yvonne D'Orsay; c. Alan, David, Edward; correctional services officer; rifle specialist; 4 NS district titles; 5 Maritime titles; 6 DND Queen's medals; Des Burke, Helmer aggregate awards; 5 ntl service rifle, regional, 8 CSC institutional titles; 5 NS service rifle titles; represented Cdn Forces at 11 international competitions in England, Scotland, US, Australia; res. Springhill, N.S.

FERGUSON, Larry (lacrosse); b. 4 Jan 1939, Peterborough, Ont.; given name: Larry Sidney Gordon; div. Denise Forbes; c. Warrren, Kent, Brad; m. Lynda Moore; furniture salesman; ex-owner Home Brew Wine store, sporting goods store; graduate of Peterborough minor lacrosse, hockey ranks winning Ont. titles at peewee, bantam, midget levels; mem. Brampton Minto Cup winner '57; as jr. won sr. OLA scoring title '58; also scoring title '65; mem. 3 Mann Cup champions; 63 points scored in 34 Mann Cup games; noted for accurate underhand shot; in 18 seasons played 544 games scoring 750g, 718a; played/coached pro lacrosse with Philadelphia Wings, Boston Bolts; coached Peterborough Lakers '87 after which he ret'd from game; mem. Cdn, Ont. Lacrosse, Peterborough Sports halls of fame; res. Peterborough, Ont.

FERGUSON, Lorne (hockey); b. 26 May 1930, Palmerston, Ont,; given name: Lorne Robert; m. Irene Johnson; c. Lorne Jr., Robert, Kimberlee, Lori, Timothy; ret'd Labatt's sales rep.; sr. baseball, jr. B hockey Kingston; jr. A Guelph Biltmores; NY Rovers; Tulsa USHL; NHL Boston '49-55, Detroit '55-57, Chicago '57-59; NHL record: 422 scheduled games, 82g, 80a; led '53-54 Hershey Bears (AHL) in goals with 45; with Red Sullivan, Dunc Fisher set AHL points record for one line; minor hockey coach Kingston; mem. Kingston Dist. Sports Hall of Fame; res. Kingston, Ont.

FERGUSON, Merv (administration); b. 1 Jul 1909, London, Ont.; m. May; notary public; polio terminated promising versatile athletic career; directed efforts to administration; secty. BC Lacrosse Assn.; 8yrs mem., chairman Vancouver Athletic Commission; governor Pacific National Exhibition Sports Comm.; mem. BC branch AAUofC '48; 10yrs BC amateur boxing commission; 9yrs treas. amateur sports council; chairman BC Sports Hall of Fame; pres. AAUofC '63-65; secty-treas AAUofC ntl boxing comm.; 10yrs exec. mem. PAG Assoc.; mem.-at-large British CG Assn.; 3yrs pres. Canadian Amateur Sports Federation; asst. mgr. '67, mgr. '71 PAG teams; mem. Canada Games council; chairman technical advisory board Canada Summer Games '73; mem. COA; pres. BCLA '43-58, CLA '62-63; CLA liaison officer to International Amateur Lacrosse Federation '67-72; mem. BC Sports Advisory Council; BC Sportsman award '67-68, Air Canada amateur sports exec. of year; mem. Cdn Olympic, BC Sports, Cdn Lacrosse halls of fame; res. Galiano, B.C.

FERGUSON, Reid (curling); b. 16 May 1953, Toronto, Ont.; given name: William Reid; Wilfrid Laurier, BA; restaurateur, advt. mgr. *Ontario Curling Report*; Toronto HS hockey all-star; Laurier golf team; East York Ont.

junior baseball champions; lead with Paul Savage '77 Ont. champion rink, competing in Brier; Thunder Bay cashspiel winner '76; res. Vancouver, B.C.

FERGUSON, Rich (t&f); b. 3 Aug 1931, Calgary, Alta.; d. 24 May 1986, Rancho Mirage, Calif.; div. Kathleen Mavis McNamee; c. David, Jeanne, John; Iowa, BSc, BComm., UWO, MBA; businessman; 3rd to Roger Bannister, John Landy '54 BEG miracle mile Vancouver in 4:04.6; equalled that time '55 NCAA championships; Lionel Conacher trophy '54; former pres. Spalding Canada.

FERGUSON, Skit (baseball); b. 16 Oct 1925, Reserve Mines, N.S.; given name: Philip; m. Helen Charlton; c. Karla, Stephen, Elaine, Brenda; St.FX, BSc., TechUof NS, BSc (mech. eng.); ret'd engineer, operations mgr. Imperial Oil; lhp/1b/of; mem. '44 Maritime jr. champion Dominion Hawks (struck out 19 in title final); '45 Cape Breton sr. league champion Dominion Hawks; posted 18-1 w-l record, won Halifax & District League batting title with .468 as mem. '46 Truro Bearcats; mem. '45-46 St. FX intercollegiate title teams; mem. semipro Drummondville Cubs (Que. Prov. League) '47; mem. HDL Halifax Shipyards team '48-49; coached minor baseball '55-60, Maritime midget titlists '57; returned to active play Dartmouth Arrows, Halifax Mets '62-66; mem. 2 Maritime sr. title teams; overall sr. pitching record 50-5; rejected pro offers; jr. hockey Cape Breton '43; 2 intercollegiate scoring titles, 1 Halifax Industrial HL scoring crown; twice skipped rink to NS consols playdowns; mem. '63 NS mixed title rink; skipped 2 Atlantic Oilmen's 'spiel winners; mem. St. FX, NS Sports halls of fame; res. Dartmouth, N.S.

FERGUSON, Tracey (t&f/wheelchair basketball): b. 7 Sep 1974, Richmond Hill, Ont.; Illinois MA; consultant Sport Canada; motivational speaker; born with Spina Bifida; standout wheelchair basketball, track athlete; basketball gold '92, '96, '00, bronze '04 Paralympic Games; 3 world championship gold medal basketball teams; Ada MacKenzie Memorial Foundation bursary twice; res. Ottawa, Ont.

FERGUSON, Vince (baseball/hockey); b. 11 Feb 1906, Halifax, N.S.; d. 29 Aug 1984, Halifax, N.S.; given name: Vincent de Paul; m. Gertrude Butler; c. Carol, Sheila, Paul; electrical inspector; excelled in baseball, hockey, rugby, soccer, t&f; participated in baseball as player, coach '19-45; sometime pitcher but mostly if/of; jr. baseball Halifax Socials '24-26; mem. NS, Maritime champion St. Agnes team '30; noted as clutch hitter and capable of big play under pressure; '31-39 with Willow Park Casinos, Halifax Capitals, Cardinals, frequently leading teams to provincial finals with his bat and speed; batted left, won 5 batting titles, one with .449 average; playing coach Halifax Shipyards team during WW2; played senior hockey '27-35 with Crescents, Wolverines; mem. 2 NS title teams, '35 Allan Cup champion Wolverines; noted as playmaker, he won two league scoring titles; rejected pro offers from Montreal Maroons; honored by NS Amateur Baseball Assn., City of Halifax; mem. NS Sports Hall of Fame.

FERGUSSON, Layton (baseball); b. 8 Sep 1908, Port Morien, N.S.; d. 27 Feb 1994, Windsor, N.S.; given name: Neil Layton; m. Grace Edith Avery; c. William; McGill, MCL; ret'd lawyer; early association with baseball Port

Morien jr., int. sr. leagues; pitched for Reserve Miner Boys in Cape Breton Colliery League, 1ˢᵗ Cape Breton team to reach NS finals; mem. Sydney sr. amateur team 1yr; pro Glace Bay Miners, '36 Cape Breton Collier League finalists; pres. Cape Breton jr. league; secty-treas. Colliery sr. league several years; MLA Glace Bay; mem. NS Sports Hall of Fame.

FERNANDEZ, Tony (baseball); b. 30 Jun 1962, San Pedro de Macoris, DR; given name: Octavio Antonio; m. Clara; c. Joel Octavio, Jonathan David, Abraham Antonio; essentially a shortstop but played second or third; turned pro with Kinston (Carolina) '80; Syracuse (AAA) '81-83, '84; Toronto (AL) '83-'90, '93, '98-99, '01, San Diego (NL) '91-'92, NY (NL) '93, Cincinnati (NL) '94, NY (AL) '95, Cleveland (AL) '97, Japan '00, Milwaukee '01; in World Series with Toronto '93, Cleveland '97; 5 all-star games; 4 Gold Glove awards; reached 2000 hits '98; MBL record: 2158 scheduled games, 7911ab, 1057r, 2276h, 414db, 92tr, 94hr, 844rbi, 246sb, .288ba; DR Little League bears his name; res. Boca Raton, Fla.

FERRARO, John (football/basketball); b. 18 Dec 1910, Buffalo, N.Y.; d. 28 Sep 1981, Bridgewater, N.J.; given name: John James; m. Edna Winifred Letts; c. John Jr., Robert Letts, Linda Joan; Cornell, BSc; oil co. sales supervisor; all-NY state basketball team '28-29; mem. undefeated Cook Academy '29-30 Eastern States basketball title team; mem. US all-star basketball team which introduced sport to Venezuela '30; capt. '33 Cornell football team; all-American '31-33; capt. Cornell basketball '33-34, Ivy League scoring title, Eastern Intercollegiate all-star; playing-coach Hamilton Tigers '34-35; Orm Beach trophy '34; Grey Cup finalist '35; Montreal '36-40; 7 times all-Cdn; qb Hamilton best-of-century (1867-1949) amateur era team; Lew Hayman's best-of-'30s dream team; Cornell 30-year ('12-42) all-intercollegiate team; Eastern Intercollegiate 50-year ('01-51) all-star team; mgr.-player, scoring leader Dominion Douglas '36-37 Eastern Canadian basketball title team; coach Queen's basketball '37-38; player, leading scorer McGill Grads '39-40 ntl title basketball team; mgr.-player-coach ntl finalist Oilers basketball team '41-42; mem. Cornell Athletic, Cdn Football halls of fame.

FERRARO, Ray (hockey); b. 23 Aug 1964, Trail, B.C.; div. Tracey; c. Matthew, Landon; m. Cammi Granato; ctr Penticton '81-82; Portland '82-93; Brandon '83-84; Binghampton (AHL) '84-85; NHL Hartford '84-90, NYI '90-95, NYR '95-96, LA '96-99, Atlanta '99-02, St. Louis '02; Team Canada '89, '96 worlds; reached 400g plateau '02; NHL record 1258 scheduled games, 408g, 490 a, 68 playoff games, 21g, 22a; *ESPN, TSN* playoff analyst; established foundation to assist disadvantaged Southern California youngsters; mem. Cdn Little League Trail baseball title team '76; mem. BC Hockey Hall of Fame; res. Trail, B.C./San Diego, Calif.

FERRONE, Dan (football); b. 3 Apr 1958, Oakville, Ont.; m. Barbara; c. Matthew, Marco, Danielle; SFU; operates Ferrone Ventures Inc., ex-football exec.; NAIA Div. 1 all-star gd; pro Toronto '81-88, '90-92, Calgary '89; 5 all-EFC, 1 all-WFC, 3 all-Cdn selections; twice runnerup Schenley outstanding-offensive-lineman award; Leo Dandurand outstanding EFC offensive-lineman award twice; 5 Grey

Cup finals, 2 winners; nicknamed "mayor of Oakville"; pres. CFLPA '94-00; asst. Toronto Argos 2001; v-p Toronto Argos '02-03; made unsuccessful bid for political office '00; res. Oakville, Ont.

FIELDGATE, Norm (football); b. 12 Jan 1932, Regina, Sask.; given name: William Norman; m. Doreen Caughlin; c. Carey, Lesley, Janine; ret'd automotive parts distributor; from Sask. junior ranks, joined original BC Lions team '53; last original to retire '66; co-capt. Lions several seasons; oe/de/clb; 37 career interceptions; 3 time WFC all-star, once all-Cdn; 3 times Lions' MVP; most popular Lion '65; one of two Lions (with By Bailey) honored by fans with 'day' '62; mem. BC Place Wall, BC Sports, Cdn Football halls of fame; res. North Vancouver, B.C.

FILANE, Domenic (boxing); b. 17 Mar 1969, Schreiber, Ont.; given name: Domenic Figliomeni; sport wear designer, boxing club owner; began competing '83; Schreiber '88 Olympic torch athlete of yr; 3 Detroit Golden Gloves titles; 9 ntl 48kg titles; bronze '90, '94 CG; competed '92, '96 Olympic, '95 PAG; bronze '94 Copenhagen Cup; gold '96 Stockholm Box Open; bronze '96 Multi-Nation (Liverpool) tournament; res. Schreiber, Ont.

FILCHOCK, Frank (football); b. 10 Aug 1916, Crucible, Pa.; Indiana; ret'd; all-around HS athlete capable of sprinting 100yds in 10 sec; pro Pittsburgh (NFL), Washington, NY Giants; suspended over gambling charge; subsequently cleared but chose Cdn football with Hamilton, Montreal; coached, qb'd Hamilton Tigers to '48 final vs. Ottawa but lost when he broke wrist early in game; led Alouettes to Grey Cup '49; player-of-yr award; Imperial Trophy ORFU MVP; head coach Edmonton '52 guiding them to WIFU title but Grey Cup loss; coach Saskatchewan '53-57, reached playoffs 4 consec. years; 1ˢᵗ head coach Denver Broncos; Lionel Conacher trophy '49; res. Portland, Ore.

FILION, Henri (harness racing); b. 22 May 1941, Angers, Que.; d. 9 Apr 1997, Aylmer, Que.; m. Ginette Martel; c. Henri Jr., Andrée, Alain, Chantal; one of 8 racing Filion brothers; drove Blue Bonnets track at 19; US circuit mid-'60s; while campaigning at Foxboro '72 swamp fever claimed 11 of his horses; joined brother Hervé, in NY; 7 consecutive $1 million seasons; 3318 victories, $21 million in purses; classic victories include Sheppard Pace, Westchester Trot, Reynolds Memorial, Goshen Cup; died in track accident in Aylmer, Que.

FILION, Hervé, (harness racing); b. 1 Feb 1940, Angers, Que.; m. Barbara Ann; c. 4; harness race driver; standardbred racing's most prolific race winner; 1ˢᵗ driver in world with more than 400 (407) wins single season '68; boosted own record to 605 '72 then 637 '74, 798 '88, 814 '89 (broken '92 by Walter Case Jr.); 16 USTA driving titles; 7 times season leading money winner; through '03 15,017 victories with purses exceeding $86M; won 110 major stakes races including 2 Little Brown Jugs, 2 Cane Pace, 2 Breeders Crowns; world champion '70; international drivers' stakes winner Australia '71; 8 winners one day Hinsdale, N.H. '78; 5 winners clocked at 1:59.4 or less one day Brandywine '70; twice French Canadian athlete of yr (Julien Trophy); '71 Lou Marsh Trophy; Hickok pro athlete of month Nov '71; Proximity Award '73; 10 Harness Tracks of America driver-of-yr awards; French-athlete-of-world award; charged with race fixing (never proved) '95; returned to racing 25 Jun '02 in Delaware; Officer Order of Canada '71; mem. Canada's, Ottawa Sports, Cdn Horse Racing, Living Horsemen's halls of fame; res. Albertson, N.Y.

FILION, Sylvain (harness racing); b. 7 Feb 1969, Angers, Que.; hails from one of harness racing's greatest families; father Yves won NA Cup '88, uncle Herve has won more races than any other driver in world; began competitive driving '87; through '03 3636 wins, over $28M in purses; spent most of time racing in Montreal before shifting to Ontario circuit '98; has enjoyed some success outside Canada; brought Canada '99 World Driving Championship in Australia; drove Goliath Bayama to US Pacing title, Breeders Crown '01; other top horses driven include Goodtime Bayama, Ring of Life, High on Emotion; res. Saint-Andre-D'Argent, Que.

FILION, Yves (harness racing); b. 23 Dec 1946, Angers, Que.; given name: Yves Léo; c. Sylvain; horse trainer; campaigned on small Cdn tracks to '66 when he moved into fast lane at Montreal tracks; worked for a time with brother Hervé before branching out on his own; from '75 has based activities at Blue Bonnets; through '95 3554 victories, $18M in purses; drove Runnymede Lobell to '88 Cane Pace, Prix d'Ete, NA Cup, Confederation Cup victories; leading Blue Bonnets driver '76, '85, '88; ret'd dir. Que. region Standardbred Canada; res. Lachute, Que.

FILTEAU, Nancy (judo); b. 3 Apr 1962, Swift Current, Sask.; given name: Nancy Jewitt; m. Ron Filteau; c. Tyler, Justin; meat inspector; began judo career '73 earning '83 PAG silver, '86 CG gold; ret'd '87 to raise family; returned to competition '94; bronze '95 PAG; silver '94 CNE, US Open; competed '96 Olympics; 3rd degree black belt; res. Moose Jaw, Sask.

FINDLAY, Dave (canoeing); b. 13 Nov 1927, Almonte, Ont.; m. Betty Asseltine; c. David, Janet, Steven, Laura, Allison; UofT, BSc; ret'd engineer; coach Ottawa Valley clubs '56-80; commodore ntl assn. '63; mgr, ntl team '74-78, Olympic team '76; Carleton Place Citizen of '80; res. Carleton Place, Ont.

FINDLAY, Dick (boxing); b. 23 Mar 1945, Vancouver, B.C.; div; c. Ricky; Molson's Brewery employee; moved through weight-class ranks from 85lb-139lb '57-66 claiming 2 Emerald, 6 Golden Gloves titles; ntl amateur 139lb title '66-68; mem. ntl team '66 BEG, '67 US Nationals, PAG, '68 Olympics; 2 BC Golden Boy, 1 Diamond Boy awards; BC outstanding boxer '68; refereed 5yrs; res. Vancouver, B.C.

FINDLEY, John (harness racing); b. 2 Sep 1924, Braeside, Ont.; m. Mary Jane Chateauvert; Ont. Veterinary College; ret'd veterinarian, horse breeder, driver, trainer; won 1st race age 13; 8 consec. Ont. Golden Horseshoe Circuit driving titles; leading NA driver '69, runnerup '70; leading NA percentage driver 200-300 drives category '75; 13 individual driving titles; more than 1500 career victories, $2 million in purses won; operated Madawaska Farms; among outstanding horses he has bred, trained and/or raced are Dalyce Blue (only Cdn sired filly to win open stake race in US, 1st Canadian-bred 3-yr-old trotter to better 2:05 mile),

Peaches Atom (champion Canadian-bred trotting mare '63-65), Autumn Frost, Crimson Duchess (2-year-old Canadian trotter of year), The Black Douglas, Canny Choice, Moon Magic (1:58 fastest mile by Findley-bred pacer); mem. Cdn Horseracing Hall of Fame; res. Arnprior, Ont.

FINE, Jack (bowling); b. 28 Jul 1925, Toronto, Ont.; m. Valerie Simmonds (d); c. Janet, Harry, Joanne, Walter; UofT, BA; bowling exec.; founder Bowling Proprietors' Assn. of Ont. '54, serving as pres, treas, dir. 25yrs; co-founder BPA of Canada, serving in varied exec. roles, including pres.; dir. BPA of America; mem., promotion chair Multi-unit Bowling Information Group; founder Builders of Bowling Industry annual awards dinner '73; founder, pres. Bowlerama Ltd., Canada's largest bowling chain with 17 Southern Ont. centres; pres. Bowling Sales of Canada; mem. Ont. interprovincial squash team; veterans-class club squash champion '66; recipient Ont. govt. recognition certificate, Ont. corporate sports citation; mem. Ont. 5-pin bowling Hall of Fame, builders' div., Greater Toronto 10-pin Hall of Fame; res. Toronto, Ont.

FINK, Hardy (builder): b. 8 May 1947, Hof, Germany; given name: Hartmut Walter; m. Cynthia Fay Bonesky; c. Heidi Marion, Jennifer May; Hamilton Teacher's Coll., McMaster BPhE, BA, UAlta. MSc, UBC, MPhE; gymnastics consultant; began competing age 16; mem. Ont. jr. team '66-67, sr. '69-71; Alta. sr title '74; capt. McMaster team '69-73; head coach Hamilton Germania Gym Club '68-74; part-time coach Edmonton's Bounder Gym Club '73-75; gym instructor McMaster '72-73, UBC '83-98; ntl men's FISU Games team '70; Ont. coaching chair. '72; mem. ntl coaching certification pgm '75-84; part-time coach Port Alberni Parks '76; established, owned, operated Port Alberni Gymnastics Academy '76-83, accumulating 143 BC, 4 ntl, 38 Western Cdn titles; conducted coaching clinics throughout NA, coached Cdn girls team on European tours '82-83; established UBC gym club '84; held various exec. roles locally, provincially, nationally; 6 times ntl team CdM; at 21 youngest international judge; judged at Olympic, Worlds, PAG, CG '74-87; conducted numerous judging courses; chaired variety of ntl, prov. judging comms.; ntl high performance coach '88-98; authored numerous gymnastics publications, *CBC-TV* gymnastics analyst; CGF builder of '78; IOC recognition award '80; BCGA coach of '80; CIAU coach of '85; pres. FIG men's tech. comm.; res. Vancouver, B.C.

FINLAY, Robert (t&f); b. 3 Aug 1943, London, Eng.; m. Eleanor Young; c. Katherine Anne, Jennifer Margaret; Waterloo; tech/account rep computer services; OFSAA x-country title team '61, OQAA 1, 3 mile titles '66, OQAA 3mile '67, OQAA x-c titles '66-67; competed in PAG '67, CG '70, Olympics '68, '72, Pan-Pacific '69; Inter. x-c champ '69; Victoria, Australia 10mile road champ '71; mem. Toronto Olympic Club; Waterloo athlete of year '66-67; ntl indoor records 2mi, 3mi, 5000m, outdoor 2000m, 3000m, 5000m, 2mi; res. Scarborough, Ont.

FINN, Ron (officiating/hockey); b. 1 Dec 1940, Toronto, Ont.; m. Sheilagh Roach (d); c. Sean, Shannon, Tara, Theresa; NHL linesman '69-96; worked 2 NHL all-star games, Rendez-Vous '87, Canada, Challenge Cup series; officiated 1st Montreal vs. Chicago exhibition in London,

Eng.; set NHL record working 252nd career playoff game '91; worked 1980 scheduled games, 291 playoff games; worked final NHL game at 55; instructor various Ont. hockey officiating schools; with David Boyd authored *On the Lines*; res. Brampton, Ont.

FINNAMORE, Arthur (baseball); b. 13 Dec 1882, Fredericton, N.B.; d. 23 Feb 1978, Saint John, N.B.; m. Althea Sallaws MacLean; UNB; dept. of agriculture; nicknamed "Flying Frederictonian" for performances in 100-, 220yd track events; at 14 received $5 per game to play baseball for Doaktown, Boisetown teams thereby becoming pro; officially joined pro ranks at 23 catching for Glace Bay in Cape Breton League; later played in Western Canada; captained, coached Glace Bay to league title '13; became highly-respected umpire; university rugby star; as mountain climber scaled Bald Mountain, Mount Carleton; mem. NB Sports Hall of Fame.

FINNIGAN, Frank (hockey); b. 9 Jul 1903, Shawville, Que.; d. 25 Dec 1991, Shawville, Que.; given name: Frank Arthur; m. Maye Horner, c. Joan, Norma, Frank Jr., Ross; UofOtt; rw UofOtt, Ottawa Coll., Montagnards '21-24; NHL Ottawa Senators '23-34, St. Louis '34-35, Toronto '31-32, '35-37; played '34 all-star game; NHL totals 556 scheduled games, 115g, 88a, 11 playoff games, 0g, 3a; nicknamed "Shawville Express"; with return to NHL of Senators in '90 he became key link to past glory; jersey 8 ret'd by modern Senators.

FIRBY, Howard (coaching); b. 18 Sep 1924, Montgomery, Ala.; d. 30 Mar 1991, Vancouver, B.C.; given name: Howard Baldwin; div.; c. Louise, Grant, Joanne; Vancouver school of art; freelance commercial artist, pro swimming coach; HS track champion; afflicted by polio '45; coach Vancouver SC '47-56; founding coach Canadian Dolphins SC '56-67; coach Winnipeg Cardinal SC '67-69; tech. dir. '70-72; coach Coho SC Victoria '73-80; asst. coach '55 PAG; starter '54 BEG; ntl team coach '58 BEG, '64 Olympic Games; coach-mgr. ntl team South Africa tour '67, Russia tour '69; coached swimmers, including Helen Hunt, to 11 world records, Games' gold in all strokes, more than 100 individual ntl sr. titles, more than 300 ntl sr. records; 6 ntl team titlists; Centennial medal '67; mem. BC, Canada's Sports, Cdn Aquatic, International, BC Swimming halls of fame.

FIREMAN, Jack (builder); b. 9 Feb 1939, Toronto, Ont.; div.; c. Belinda, James; UofT, BA, Osgoode Hall LB, NYU, LLM; lawyer, QC; a litigation lawyer with a great passion for fastpitch softball, he financed and founded Toronto Gators team '93; in initial season won ntl men's sr. title, became 1st Cdn team to win ICS World championship '94, repeat '95; gold medal PAG qualifier; res. Toronto, Ont.

FIRESTONE, Bruce (builder); b. 4 Dec 1951, Montreal, Que.; given name: Bruce Murray; m. Dawn Marie MacMillan; c. Andrew, Rachel, Miriam, Matthew, Jessica; McGill BEng (civil), New South Wales MEng (Sci), Australian National U PhD, Harvard (finance), UWO (econ), Laval (French); adjunct research prof. Carleton School of Business; founder NHL Ottawa Senators, Corel Centre; former NHL governor; exec. advisory comm., marketing/pub. relations comm.; annual atom invitational hockey tourney bears his name; Kanata city econ. dev. task force; Ottawa intl airport planning comm.; Ottawa 67's advisory board; former majority owner CFL Ottawa Rough Riders; founding dir. Ottawa Art Gallery (housing Firestone family Group of Seven collection); former publisher *Ottawa Business News;* intl business dev. consultant for companies/governments world-wide author of wide array of business, finance books; res. Ottawa, Ont.

FIRLOTTE, Stewart (harness racing); b. 1 Jul 1940, Noranda, Que.; m. Joanne; c. 2; trainer; following above-average junior hockey career pursued pro aspirations with Quebec Aces in AHL; after falling short in NHL bid moved to Moncton NB to play sr. hockey and work for industrial finance firm; promotion led to Toronto but investing in a horse drew him to work with Ben White stables in Florida as groom '70; returned to Canada '76 to open public stable and invest in horses including Triple Crown winner Ralph Hanover; gained national attention campaigning Town Pro '89 winning Breeders Crown at Pompano, Fla.; strong showings with Digger Almahurst, Historic and Headline Hanover, Daylon Trooper, Articulator secured his place among NA's top trainers; res. Orlando, Fla.

FIRTH, Doug (skiing); b. 11 Aug 1911, Toronto, Ont.; d. 4 May 2001, Toronto, Ont.; given name: Douglas Ernest; m. Jean; c. Suzanne, Edward; UofT BSc, DO; osteopathic surgeon; amateur skiing pioneer; fou8nded Canadian Ski Patrol System; served as chair. 10yrs; wrote and rewrote Red Cross First Aid manual; active as volunteer Big Brothers of Toronto, Red Cross, Toronto Ski Club, Shaw, Stratford Festivals, Canadian Opera Guild, National Ballet, Canadian Osteopathic Assoc. & Aid Society; life mem. Toronto Ski Club, Cdn Ski Patrol; Dr. Doug ski run Collingwood Blue Mountain resort named in his honor; mem. Order of Canada, Canadian Skiing Hall of Fame.

FIRTH, Sharon (skiing); b. 31 Dec 1953, Aklavik, N.W.T.; given name: Sharon Anne; civil servant; with twin sister Shirley one of Canada's premier x-country skiers; ntl jr. champion '68-9; mem. ntl team from '70; mem. '72, '80, '84 Olympic teams; 4 ntl 3x5km relay, 2 5km, 1 each 10km, 17km, 20km titles; 2 NA 10km, 1 each 3x5km relay, 5km titles; gold 3x5km relay '80, 5k '81 Gitchi Gami Games, 20km '81 Dannon series; 29th '81-82, 35th '82-83 World Cup circuit; John Semmelink Memorial award '72; mem. Order of Canada, Cdn Skiing Hall of Fame; res. Yellowknife, N.W.T.

FIRTH, Shirley (skiing); b. 31 Dec 1953, Aklavik, N.W.T.; given name: Shirley Anne; m. Jan Larsson; PR officer; with sister Sharon among Canada's premier x-country skiers; '69 junior 5km title; mem. ntl team from '70; mem. '72, '76, '80, '84 Olympic teams; 5 consecutive ntl 10km, 4 5km, 3 20km, 2 3x5km relay titles; 2 NA 3x5km relay, 1 5km titles; 10km gold '76 Canada Cup, '76, '80, '81, 3x5km relay '80 Gitchi Gami Games; 5km, 10km, 20km gold '80 Dannon series; best WC finish ever by Canadian placing 4th 10km Czechoslovakia '81; 11th '81-82, 25th '82-83 World Cup circuit; John Semmelink Memorial award '72; mem. Order of Canada, Cdn Skiing Hall of Fame; res. St-Etienne de Crossey, France.

FISHER, Frank (football/hockey); b. 1 Jan 1901, Barlieboro, Ont.; d. 23 Apr 1983, Toronto, Ont.; given name: Franklin; m. Dorothy Smith; c. Franklin Stewart, Ellenora;

RMC, Osgoode Hall, BA, LLB; lawyer Q.C.; mem. '20-21 Varsity Blues intercollegiate football champions, '20 Grey Cup winner; mem. Varsity Grads Allan Cup hockey titlists '27, Olympic gold medalists '28; life mem. Royal Canadian Yacht Club, Toronto University Club; mem. Toronto Golf Club.

FISHER, Hugh (canoeing); b. 1 Oct 1955, New Zealand; SFU, MD; physician; kayak specialist; mem. '76, '80, '84 Olympic, '77, '79, '82, '83 world championships teams, silver K2 1000m '82, bronze K2 500m '83 worlds; 7 ntl K2, 4 K4, 1 C4 titles; 3 Zaandam K2, 2 K4 titles; Vichy K1, Bydgoszcz, Poland K1, K2, Tata K2 titles; silver K2 1000m Moscow, Brandenburg '83; with Alwyn Morris gold 1000m, bronze 500m K2 '84 Olympics; coach BC team '81 Canada Games; world outrigger champion '79-80; fed. govt. excellence awards '83-84; coach Cdn jr. dragonboat crew; mem. Order of Canada, Cdn Olympic, Canada's, BC Sports halls of fame; res. Penticton, B.C.

FITCH, Ed (shooting); b. 28 Mar 1949, Montreal, Que.; given name: Edward; m. Sharon Paul; c. Rena, Leora; RMC, BEng. (civil); CF Command and Staff Coll; National Securities studies course; Major-General; marksmanship training began with archery and evolved into small-bore rifles with Queen's Own Rifles and HS cadets; mem. RMC rifle/pistol teams; competed frequently in BCRA, PQRA, DCRA matches; CFSAC pistol tyro title '81; mem. 2 DCRA Black Powder, Bisley teams; major interest ISU pistol; active role in Long Range Black Powder competition from '78; liaison officer BCRA '78-81, v-p PQRA '83-84; mem. DCRA council '83-84; dir. DCRA Black Powder pgm, '88-93; DCRA council/exec. comm from '88; mem. 2 Cdn Maccabiah Games ISU pistol teams, 1 silver, 5 bronze; instrumental in involving CF in CISM-Pistol; commandant DCRA Bisley rifle team '98; mem. Cdn team 1st World Military Olympics (CISM) '95; CF patron of shooting from '01; res. Ottawa, Ont.

FITZGERALD, Billy (lacrosse); b. 1888, St. Catharines, Ont.; d. 1926, at 19 mem. Sr. Athletic Lacrosse Club St. Catharines, Globe Shield '05-12; mem. undefeated '07-08 teams; mem. Conn Jones team Vancouver, Minto Cup; Toronto Lacrosse Club; following WW1 played briefly in Vancouver; helped organize St. Catharines team Ont. semipro league; coached Hobart College of Geneva, N.Y., Swathmore College, West Point; refereed OALA sr. division; mem. Canada's Sports, Lacrosse halls of fame.

FITZGERALD, Marie (speed skating); b. 12 Apr 1946, St. Paul, Alta.; given name: Marie Louise Phyllis; ntl outdoor mass-start champion '64; ntl outdoor mass-start records 220-, 880yds, 3/4 miles, 1 mile; ntl indoor mass-start champion '63-70; ntl indoor mass-start records   440-, 880yds, 3/4, 1 mile; ntl open indoor title '65; mem. Alta. outdoor team inaugural Canada Winter Games; ranked among best indoor skaters ever developed in Canada; mem. Cdn Speed Skating Hall of Fame; res. Rocky Mountain House, Alta.

FITZGERALD, Mel (t&f); b. 20 Jul 1953, Trepassey, Nfld.; m. Jane; printer; wheelchair athletics; ntl 1500m, 800m titles '78-79, 10,000m title '83; PAG gold 1500m '78, 800m '78, '82, 5000, '82, silver 100m '78, 1500m, 400m '82; Olympic gold 800m, silver 1500m '80; Rome invitational gold 1500m '81; 800m world record '82; Norton Crowe award '80; mem. Order of Canada; res. St. John's, Nfld.

FITZGERALD, Tom (hockey); b. 28 Aug 1968, Billerica, Mass.; Providence Coll; rw Austin prep school, Providence Coll., Team USA; AHL Springfield, Capital District; NHL NYI '88-93, Florida '93-98, Colorado '97-98, Nashville (capt.) '98-02, Chicago '02, Toronto '02-04; NHL totals: 1026 scheduled games, 135g, 184a, 78 playoff games, 7g, 12a; res. Toronto, Ont.

FITZPATRICK, Allan (soccer/badminton); b. 29 Jun 1909, Montreal, Que.; d. 12 Oct 1990, Pierrefonds, Que.; given name: Daniel Allan; m. Edna Heazel (d); Sir George William; asst. purchasing agent; mem. ntl title soccer teams '34-35; frequent all-star; 2yrs Stelco team coach; 2yrs dir. Que. FA; helped launch Murray Badminton League; held varied exec. roles over 35yr period; coached, played major role in promoting badminton nationally; known throughout Que. as "Mr. Badminton"; active in game's administration provincially, nationally; CBA pres.'71-72; ntl team mgr. '66, '70, asst. GM '74, '78, GM '82 CG; CBA rep. Canadian CG Assn. '66-70, treas. '70-86, hon. v-p from '87; past sports dir. MAAA; CCGA rep. on Sports Fed. of Canada; mem. Canadian Amateur Sports Hall of Fame selection comm. '71-80; Queen's Jubilee medal '77; H.I. Evans Memorial award for contributions to Canadian badminton; QBA awards '64, '78; New England BA award '71.

FLACK, Herb (speed skating); b. 29 Jun 1913, Penetanguishene, Ont.; d. (circa 1995), Stroud, Ont.; given name: Herbert Samuel; m. Norma Heagle; c. Victor, Elinor; DeLaSalle College; ret'd; Toronto, Ontario, NA indoor, outdoor, ntl outdoor champion '29; Diamond Trophy international outdoor title '29; ntl int. outdoor titles '30-31; NA sr. indoor champion '35; mem. '32 Olympic team.

FLAMAN, Fern (hockey); b. 25 Jan 1927, Dysart, Sask.; given name: Ferdinand Charles; hockey scout; def; mem. Boston Olympics (EL); Bruins (NHL) '44-51, '54-61, Maple Leafs '51-54, Providence (AHL) '61-64; player/coach/GM Rhode Island Reds '63-64; smooth-skating, hard-hitter who broke into pro ranks as teenager during WW2; won league titles in AHL, WHL, CHL as coach; coached Northeastern Huskies '70-89 winning several championships including 4 Beanpot trophies, Hockey East title '89; US college coach of '82; more than 250 career collegiate victories; NHL record: 17 seasons, 910 scheduled games, 34g, 174a, 63 playoff games, 4g, 8a; scout NJ '90-03; mem. 1 Stanley Cup winner; 3 2nd team all-star; mem. Rhode Island, Sask. Sports, Hockey halls of fame; res. Westwood, Mass.

FLANAGAN, Flin (football);b. 27 Sep 1897, Thorne, Que.; d. 12 Mar 1994, Ste-Anne-de-Bellevue, Que.; given name: James Cyril; McGill, DDS; dentist; surviving serious WWI battlefield wounds he starred for McGill football/hockey teams '19-23; mem. Yates Cup champion '19 team; capt. hockey team '22-23; noted for stick-handling, prolific scoring; declined Montreal Canadiens pro overtures; coached McGill '28 title team; mem. McGill Sports Hall of Fame.

FLANAGAN, Pat (wrestling); b. 31 Aug 1918, Toronto, Ont.; d. 10 Jun 1985, Toronto, Ont.; given name: Winnett

Wallingford Watson; m. Evelyn; c. Warren, Dennis; prominent in jr. football with jr. Argos, Balmy Beach, wrestling in high school; launched pro career in England adopting name of Flanagan to avoid confusion with Whipper Billy Watson; active competitor until he reached mid-50s then turned to refereeing in '70s; active in community activities; highly respected by peers, fans.

FLEMING, Joe (football); b. 5 Dec 1971, Wellesley, Mass.; m. Stacy; c. 3; New Hampshire; real estate/insurance broker; dt; attended NFL Cleveland camp '95; CFL BC '96-97, Winnipeg '98-99, '03-04, Calgary '00-01, '03; ret'd following '01 Grey Cup victory; returned for '03 season; 1 East, West, CFL all-star; CFL outstanding defensive player '03; res. Boston, Mass.

FLEMING, Sean (football); b. 19 Mar 1970, Burnaby, B.C.; Wyoming, BA; Price, Waterhouse-Coopers; kicker; CFL Edmonton '92-04; CFL record (through '04); 461fg, 609cvt, 160d, 2152pts, 920 punts, 39,309yds; 2 Grey Cup finals, 1 winner; outstanding Cdn award '93 GC; hon. chair Alta. Diabetic Research Foundation golf tourney; res. Edmonton, Alta.

FLEMING, Vic (harness racing); b. 1887, Dundas, Ont.; d. 1955, Lexington, Ky.; m., c. Bill, Charlie, Jim; horseman; 35yr racing career; recorded 1st 2-minute mile '20 with Louie Grattan; 3 $25,000 events single week '28 with Grattan Bars, 2 in identical 1:59.5 mile clockings; drove Billy Direct to fastest mile (to that time) in 1:55 '38; same day steered The Widower to 1:59.5 mile; during career drove 8 pacers, 4 trotters to sub 2-minute miles; injured in Delaware, Ohio, spill, ret'd to work as racing official Saratoga, N.Y.; mem. Hall of Fame of the Trotter, Canadian Horse Racing Hall of Fame.

FLEMING, Willie (football); b. 2 Feb 1939, Detroit, Mich.; m. Arlene McDaniels; c. Eric, Anthony; Iowa; sales manager; all-city HS hb '56; *AP* all-Big 10 '57, tied single season 11 td record; starred '59 Rose Bowl; pro BC '59-66; nicknamed "Willie-the-Wisp"; twice surpassed 1000yd rushing mark single season; twice teamed with Joe Kapp for 106yd td pass; shares CFL single-play record 109yds; CFL record: 86td, 1 convert, 517 points, rushing 6125yds, 868 carries, 7.1 avg, 37td, 231 receptions, 4480yds; single-season yardage record 2027 - 1234 rushing, 639 on pass receptions, 154 on kickoff returns '63; scored decisive td '64 BC Grey Cup victory over Hamilton; 3 times most popular Lion, WFC all-star; once all-Cdn; mem. BC Sports, Cdn Football halls of fame; res. Detroit, Mich.

FLEMONS, Wade (swimming); b. 26 Aug 1960, Regina, Sask.; m. Michelle Bogaard; Stanford, BSc, IE, UWO, MBA; corporate finance; backstroke specialist; Canada Cup 100m gold; 4 Nation Cup 100m, 200m, 4x100 medley relay gold; Japanese nationals 100m, 200m gold; mem. '78, '82 CG, '79, '83 PAG, '80 Olympic, '83 FISU, '78, '82 world teams; bronze 100m '82 CG; NCAA 200m breaststroke gold, 100m silver '81; BC achievement award; res. Vancouver, B.C.

FLETCHER, Bill (curling); b. 16 May 1954, Kingston, Ont.; given name: William Stanley; m. Pamela; c. Kate, Jess, Maddy; biology researcher; mem. Ont. entry '71-72 ntl

schoolboy; all-star lead Earle Morris Ont. rink '85 Brier; 2nd '95 Ont. Intermediate title rink; res. Ottawa, Ont.

FLETCHER, Cliff (hockey/administration); b. 16 Aug 1935, Montreal, Que.; div; c. Chuck, Kristy; m. Linda; hockey exec; began hockey career with Junior Canadiens serving 10yrs as scout; Eastern Cdn scout St. Louis (NHL) '67; AGM St. Louis '69-72, 3 Stanley Cup finals, 2 West div titles; joined Flames in Atlanta as GM '72; organized franchise shift to Calgary '80; in 11 seasons under his guidance Flames won 1 Stanley Cup, 2 President's trophies, 2 Campbell Conference, 2 Smythe div. titles; *HN* man of yr, exec of yr '93; pres/CEO/GM Maple Leafs '91-97; advisor to GM Tampa Bay '97-99; mgr. Team Canada '00 worlds; sr. v-p hockey operations/GM (briefly) Phoenix Coyotes '00-04; ex-mem. Hockey Hall of Fame selection comm.; mem. Hockey Hall of Fame; res. Longboat Key, Fla.

FLETCHER, Douglas (all-around); b. 18 Nov 1892, Leicester, Eng.; d. 6 Aug 1976, Victoria, B.C.; m. Ethel Maud; c. Dorothy, Joan; hotel, meat market proprietor; 9yrs Albion Cricket Club scoring numerous centuries; active to age 50; pres. Greater Victoria League '42-68; organized minor lacrosse '44; coached and/or managed 35 provincial champions; pres. BCLA '48; v-p CLA '57; active player to age 40; refereed several years; with late Ivan Temple organized Victoria MHA '43; pres. Vancouver Island Sr. HL; 12 consecutive pitching victories Sons of England '34 softball league champions; 2 holes-in-one during golf career which began '29; 5yrs Uplands GC pres.; BCAHA Diamond Stick award '64, Sid Thomas Memorial Trophy '52, Memorial Arena plaque '60, Centennial Medal '67, Victoria Sportsman of '68, *Sport Magazine* plaque '68; life mem. Greater Victoria LA; mem. Cdn Lacrosse, Greater Victoria, BC Sports halls of fame.

FLETCHER, Pat (golf); b. 18 Jun 1916, Clacton-on-Sea, Eng.; d. 23 Jul 1985, Victoria, B.C.; m. Dorothy Fraser; c. Patricia Ann, Allan Hugh, Edward Michael; golf pro; 3 Sask. Open titles; CPGA title '52; low Canadian '53 Canadian Open; 1st Canadian since '14 to win Canadian Open '54; former golf pro Saskatoon G&CC, Royal Montreal; Que. Spring Open title '56-57; mem. 4 Hopkins Trophy match teams; CPGA pres. '62-65; mem. RCGA, Greater Victoria, Sask., Canada's Sports halls of fame.

FLETT, Bill (hockey); b. 21 Jul 1943, Vermillion, Alta.; d. 13 Jul 1999, Edmonton, Alta.; m. Doreen; c. Cody, Dean, Shane; raised on a ranch in Okotoks, Alta. he rode in youth rodeos as a teenager; father C. M. played pro hockey; rw Melville (SJHL) '60-63, Rochester (AHL), Charlotte (EHL), Denver (WHL) '63-64, Victoria (WHL) '64-65, Tulsa (CHL) '64-67; NHL Los Angeles '67-72, Philadelphia '72-74, Toronto '74-75, Atlanta '75-77, Edmonton '79-80, WHA Edmonton '76-79; *SN* NHL West div. rookie of '67 award; 1 Stanley Cup winner; scout Edmonton following retirement; NHL/WHA totals 884 scheduled games, 305g, 299a, 67 playoff games, 12g, 20a; nicknamed "Cowboy".

FLEURY, Lionel (hockey); b. 25 Dec 1912, Quebec City, Que.; d. (circa 1998), Ste. Foy, Que.; m. Raymonde Doyon; c. Louise, Jacques, Denyse, Alice, Marc, Charles; ret'd personnel advisor; active golfer, hockey player; referee/ coach/mgr/ jr. A hockey, baseball; regional, provincial, ntl hockey pres.; IIHF executive mem.; life mem. QAHA, CAHA; involved in conception of Canada Games; founder Que. region minor hockey organization; coach/mgr/secty/ pres. Jr. A hockey league simultaneously; US AAHA citation, Centennial Medal, Laval sportsmanship award.

FLEURY, Theoren (hockey); b. 29 Jun 1968, Oxbow, Sask.; div. Veronica; c. Josh, Tatum, Stephanie, Alexa, Beaux; ctr/rw; mem. '87-88 world jr title teams; Turner Cup (IHL) winner '88; at 5-5 smallest player in NHL in '90s; jr. Moose Jaw (WHL) '84-88; 201 jr. goals; 9th draft choice Calgary '87 entry draft; pro Salt Lake (IHL) '88-89, Calgary (NHL) '89-99, Colorado '99, NYR '99-01, Chicago '02-03; 51 goals in 79 games '90-91; *Hockey News* jr player of '88; mem. Team Canada '90-91 worlds, silver '91, Canada Cup '91 (gold), world cup '96; 1 Stanley Cup; mem. '98, '02 (gold) Olympic team; shared Alka Seltzer plus award with Marty McSorley '91; 1st team NHL all-star '95; played in 5 NHL all-star games; NHL record: (through '03) 1084 scheduled games, 455g, 633a, 77 playoff games, 34g, 45a; became all-time Flames scoring leader '99; Juvenile Diabetes NA man of yr '92; erratic behavior due to drinking led to frequent disciplinary problems; suspended 6 months sans pay for substance abuse; waived by Chicago '03; res. Calgary, Alta.

FLEWWELLING, Larry (diving); b. 8 Sep 1965, Kentville, N.S.; m. June Sasano; UAlta; coached by father Herb won 3 ntl 1-metre, 1 3-metre titles; mem. '88 Olympic, '87 PAG, '90 CG teams; 3-metre silver '90 CG; competed FINA World Cup '89, world aquatic championships '91; res. Edmonton, Alta.

FLOOD, Lisa (swimming); b. 1 Aug 1971, Scarborough, Ont.; Villanova, BA (psychology); P&G human resources; ex-membership services Ont. Coll of Teachers; coach; breaststroke specialist; began swimming age 1 in YMCA infant swim program; 2 gold, 1 silver '95 PAG, 2 bronze '91 PAG, 2 bronze '94 CG; competed '92, '96 Olympic, '93, '95 Pan-Pacific championships; ntl 4x100 medley relay record '95; '91 Villanova female athlete of yr; '91-92 all-American, Big East outstanding female athlete; Eastern women's swimming athlete as outstanding swimmer '91 Princeton meet; NCAA top 8 award '94; coach Pickering SC '97-98; athlete rep Swimming Canada bd.; mem. Villanova Swimming Wall of Honor, Ont. Aquatic Hall of Fame; res. Pickering, Ont.

FLOREAL, Edrick (t&f); b. 5 Oct 1966, Gonaives, Haiti; m. LaVonna Martin; c. Edrick Jr., Mikaielle Gisele; Arkansas; head coach women's track team Stanford; emigrated to Canada age 8; 1st athlete to win 3 consec. NCAA, 10 consec. ntl tj titles; 1st Canadian to exceed 17m in tj both indoor/ outdoor; 20 ntl, 5 NCAA tj/lj titles; 7 times all-American; ntl tj/lj records jr. and sr.; mem. '88, '92 Olympic, '86, '90, '94 CG, 3 world championship teams; bronze tj '90 CG; 8.20m ntl lj, 17.29 tj records; coach Nebraska, Georgia Tech, Kentucky, Stanford; 5 NCAA titles; res. Palo Alto, Calif.

FLUTIE, Darren (football); b. 18 Nov 1966, Manchester, Md.; m. Terri; c. Taylor Amanda, Troy; Boston College; wr; BColl. single-season record 111 catches for 1731yds, 8tds '84; career leader BColl. 134 recept. for 2000yds, 14tds; pro NFL San Diego '88-89, Phoenix '90, CFL BC

'91-95, Edmonton '96-97, Hamilton '98-02; CFL career reception leader 972 (regular season), 85 (playoff); 2nd all-time receiving yds 14,359; 4 Grey Cup finals, 2 winner; 4 all-Western, 2 CFL all-Cdn; also used as punt, kickoff returner; 9yrs 1000yd plus receiving; shared league record 4 games 100+yds receiving single season; plays guitar in Flutie Brothers band; res. Franklin, Mass.

FLUTIE, Doug (football); b. 23 Oct 1962, Manchester, Md.; m. Laurie; c. Alexa, Doug Jr.; Boston College, BSc; qb; gained fame for 50yd Hail Mary td pass in last minute of BColl 47-45 win over Miami '84; Heisman Trophy '84; all-American, *UPI, Sporting News*, Kodak, ECAC player of '84; all-time NCAA passing leader at graduation; selected/ signed by USFL New Jersey Generals '85; spent '85 season on NFL Rams development squad; traded to Chicago '86, New England '87-89; joined CFL BC '90-91, Calgary '92-95, Toronto '96-97, Buffalo (NFL) '98-00, San Diego '01; named to '98 Pro Bowl team; CFL record: 117 scheduled games, 61tds, 612 carries for 4118yds, 2545 completions on 4854 attempts for 41,355yds, 270tds, 131int; 4 Jeff Nicklin, 1 Jeff Russel, 6 CFL outstanding player, 2 Grey Cup MVP, 4 all-Western, 1 all-Eastern, 5 all-CFL all-star, 1 Terry Evanshen awards; set/tied 2 CFL passing records; mem. 3 Grey Cup finals, 2 winners; brother Darren mem. Eskimos/ Tiger-Cats; street (Flutie Pass) in Natick, Mass. bears his name; avid musician (drummer), he and Darren (guitar) have touring group known as the Flutie Brothers, released CD entitled *Catch This* '96; cereal *Flutie Flakes*, candy bar bearing his name introduced '98; res. Natick, Mass.

FLYNN, Chris (football); b. 17 Nov 1966, Buckingham, Que.; m. Sandy Brassard; c. Chelsea; St. Mary's; teacher, coach; led SMU Huskies to 4 straight AUAA titles while amassing 83-8 record; set CIAU career record 87 td passes; played in 2 Vanier Cup finals; the most acclaimed qb in Canadian college history, awarded Hec Crighton Trophy unprecedented three times; despite brilliant college career was only token CFL draft by Ottawa; opted for WLAF Montreal Machine but saw little action behind undistinguished American players; played semipro Montreal Voyageurs, Ottawa Bootleggers of Empire League, Empire League player of '92; coach Montreal CEGEP, Philemon Wright HS; semipro team in France; 3 time Ottawa ACT football award winner; ACT athlete of year '91; 4 Buckingham athlete-of-yr awards; made '94 headlines with rescue of drowning woman from river in France; res. Buckingham, Que.

FLYNN, Clarke (bobsleigh/weightlifting); b. 8 Jul 1959, Jever, Germany; m. Laurie Graham; c. Kylie Grace, Taylor Michela; UofOtt, BAdmin; marketing; v-p Bobsleigh Canada; mem. ntl bobsleigh team '80-88; competed 6 world championships, '84 Olympics; competitive Olympic-style weight lifter '79-84; competed in ntl weightlifting championships '82-84; WC bobsleigh commentator *TSN Winter Speed, US Prime Sports*, '94, '98 Olympics; '97 worlds; res. Ottawa, Ont.

FOGH, Hans (sailing); b. 8 Mar 1938, Copenhagen, Denmark; m. Kirsten Andersen; c. Morten, Thomas; gardener, sailmaker; Danish Pirate class title at 19; European Flying Dutchman title '60; FD silver '60 Olympics; FD world title '62; Kiel Week FD title, 4th

'64 Olympics; Danish 505 titles '65-66; Scandinavian FD titles '65, '67; emigrated to Canada '69, Canadian citizen '75; US nationals FD '70, soling '81-82; crewed for Paul Elvstrom world soling title '74; skippered soling bronze '84 Olympics; British Open FD, NA FD, soling, Great Lakes, Atlantic Coast soling titles; mem. 7 Olympic teams; 4 CORK soling titles; ranked among world's top 10 competitive sailors; author *Sailor's Manual*; mem. Order of Canada, Etobicoke, Cdn Olympic, Canada's Sports halls of fame; res. Etobicoke, Ont.

FOLEY, Jim (football); b. 27 Oct 1947, Ottawa, Ont; m. Lesley Cheryl Scharf; c. Rodney James, Tara; UPEI, BA; human resources officer Regional Municipality of Ottawa-Carleton; pro rb/wr Montreal '71-72, Ottawa '73-77; EFC rookie of year; Hiram Walker Trophy '74 as players' player; Schenley top Canadian award '75, Lew Hayman trophy '75; mem. 2 Grey Cup winners; asst. coach Carleton '79, UofOtt '90; res. Ottawa, Ont.

FOLEY, Joe (boxing); b. 19 Jul 1938, Badger, Nfld; m. Lorraine Amos; c. Raymond Carl, Dwayne Joseph; ret'd Cdn Forces; light-middleweight; fought competitively '57-66; nicknamed "Punchey"; NB area light-middle title '58-59, Eastern Cdn, CF titles '59; Cdn Infantry Brigade Group titles '59-61, '63-65; Eastern command, tri-services titles, runnerup CF title '60; tri-services title '63; mem. Black Watch boxing team '62-65; competitive record 49 bouts, 46 wins (35 by KO), 3 losses; established Oromocto BC '78; coach Oromocto Pioneer BC '88; 3 Mr. Boxing Canada awards; played key role in bringing Cdn Boxing Hall of Fame to Oromocto; Royal Cdn Legion appreciation award; Oromocto recognition award; mem. Oromocto Sports Wall, World, Cdn, Rochester Boxing halls of fame; res. Oromocto, N.B.

FOLIGNO, Mike (hockey); b. 29 Jan 1959, Sudbury, Ont.; given name: Mike Anthony; m. Janis; c. Cara, Lisa. Nicholas, Marcus; coach; rw Sudbury (OHA) '75-79; 1st team all-star '79; 1st pick Detroit '79 entry draft; played in NHL with Detroit '79-81, Buffalo '81-90, Toronto '90-93, Florida '93-94; NHL record: 15 seasons, 1018 scheduled games, 355g, 372a, 57 playoff games, 15g, 17a; launched coaching career in Toronto organization '95-96 as asst. St. John's (AHL), Toronto; pro scout Leafs '96; asst. coach Colorado '97-98; head coach Hershey Bears (AHL) '99-03; coach/GM Sudbury Wolves '03-05; mem. Hockey Heritage North Hall of Fame; res. Sudbury, Ont.

FOLK, Rick (curling/golf); b. 5 Mar 1950, Saskatoon, Sask.; given name: Richard Dale Basil; m. Elizabeth Short; c. Kevin, Andrea; UofSask; sporting goods store owner; skipped '68 Sask. HS champions, runnerup nationals; skip Sask, jr. title rink '71; Western Canada university champion '70; 5 Sask. mixed titles; '74, '83 ntl mixed titles, twice runnerup; skipped Sask. 3 Briers, '80 title, twice runnerup; BC 4 Briers, twice runnerup, '94 winner; '80, '94 world champion; mem. Sask. jr. golf team '66-68; Sask. jr. golf title '67-68; mem. 6 Sask. Willingdon Cup teams; Sask. men's champion '71-72; asst. golf pro '74-75; elected to Sask. provincial govt. '82-86; Minister Culture & Recreation '83-86; Dick Ellis trophy '80; mem. Cdn Curling, Saskatoon Sports and with '80 rink Sask Sports, with '94 rink BC Sports halls of fame; res. Kelowna, B.C.

FONSECA, Peter (t&f); b. 5 Oct 1966, Lisbon, Portugal; m. Christina Yaremczuk; Oregon, BA, Windsor BEd; politician, management consultant, owner import business; marathon specialist; moved to Toronto '68; made marathon debut '90 with bronze LA; Pac 10 10,000m titlist '90; x-country all-American '90; silver Rheims, Houston Tenneco, Toronto marathons '94; gold '95 Houston, Toronto marathons, Kelowna half-marathon '96; competed '94 CG, '96 Olympic Games; CTFA Fred Begley Memorial trophy '90; elected MLA '03; res. Toronto, Ont.

FONTAINE, Lucien (harness racing); b. 4 Dec 1939, Pointe Aux Trembles, Que.; nicknamed "Loosh"; received early training working for Keith Waples, Clint Hodgins; Big Apple driving titles '68, '77-78; best year '77 with 245 victories; Messenger Stakes with Valiant Bret '73; more than 3300 victories, $20 million in purses; res. Tarrytown, N.Y.

FONTAINE, Nicolas (skiing); b. 5 Oct 1970, Magog, Que.; freestyle specialist; mem. ntl team from '90; 5 ntl aerials titles; competed '92 (demonstration), '94, '98 winter Olympics; world championship gold '97; World Cup aerials gold '96-99; 6 World Cup race gold, 2 silver, 1 bronze; 4 WC overall gold; 4 world FS titles; res. Magog, Que.

FONTANA, Don (tennis); b. 18 Jun 1931, Toronto, Ont.; given name: Donald Anthony; UCLA; tennis consultant; 2 Ont. Open singles titles; with Bob Bedard Que. Open doubles, 3 ntl men's doubles; finalist '56 ntl men's singles; mem. 10 Davis Cup teams, 3 non-playing capt.; played Wimbledon twice, Forest Hills 11 times, French Open once; organized ntl championships for CLTA; chief consultant Rothmans Cdn Grand Prix tournaments; TV tennis color commentator; res. Toronto, Ont.

FONTEYNE, Karen (synchro swim); b. 29 Jan 1969, Calgary, Alta.; given name: Karen Denise; UCal, BComm, UWO, MBA; economic analyst Amoco Canada; switched from gymnastics to synchro with Calgary Aquabelles at age 11; mem. ntl team '87-96; with Cari Read won '93 ntl duet championship; known for innovative style; team gold '96 French Open; team silver '95 Pan-Am, '96 Olympic Games, '94 Worlds, French, German Opens; team gold '94 Titrex Cup, '90 Swiss Open; Petro-Canada Olympic Torch scholarships '90-92; res. Calgary, Alta.

FONTINATO, Lou (hockey); b. 20 Jan 1932, Guelph, Ont.; c. Nancy, Louie, Roger; farmer; jr. Guelph Biltmores; pro '52-53 Vancouver, Saskatoon (WHL); NHL defenceman NYR '54-61, Montreal '61-63; career terminated by neck injury; NHL record: 536 games, 26 goals, 78 assists, 1247 penalty minutes, 21 playoff games, 0g, 2a; ; reputation as 'policeman', one of league's tough guys; res. Guelph, Ont.

FOOT, Fred (t&f); b. 28 Oct 1916, Folkestone, Kent, Eng; d. 23 Oct 2002, Toronto, Ont.; given name: Frederick Albert; m. Mary Betty Reid; c. Angela, Deborah; ret'd Metro Toronto police; from late '40s one of Canada's top track coaches; coached East York TC 25yrs, UofT 15yrs, '56 Olympic, '62 CG teams; 3 CIAU x-country coach-of-yr awards; prominent athletes coached included Bill Crothers, Dave Bailey, George Shepherd, Jackie McDonald, Bruce Kidd, Sue Bradley.

FOOTE, Adam (hockey); b. 10 Jul 1971, Toronto, Ont.; m. Jennifer Cook; c. Callan, Nolan; def Whitby (OMHA), Sault Ste. Marie (OHL) '88-91, Halifax (AHL) '91-92, NHL Quebec '91-95, Colorado '95-03; OHL 1st team all-star '91; mem. '96, '01 Stanley Cup winners; mem. Team Canada '96, '04 World Cup (gold), '98, '02 (gold) Olympics; NHL record (through '04): 799 scheduled games, 55g, 179a, 154 playoff games, 7g, 34a; also plays a good game of lacrosse, sponsors 2 teams; nicknamed "Footer"; res. Newcastle, Ont./Colorado.

FORBES, Bruce (golf); b. 18 Apr 1922, Chatham, Ont.; d. 4 Oct 2001, Brantford, Ont.; pres. Brantford G&CC '58; pres. OGA '62; pres. RCGA '65; ED RCGA '70-78; key role in RCGA move to Glen Abbey GC; capt. victorious Cdn team '65 America's Cup; capt. 4 Cdn teams world amateur championships; capt. Cdn team '71 NZ Centennial (formerly Commonwealth matches); hon. life governor OGA, RCGA; hon. mem. CPGA; mem. Cdn, Ont. Golf halls of fame.

FORBES, Pansy (synchro swim); b. 8 Mar 1898, England; d. 16 Sep 1989, Peterborough, Ont.; given name: Pansy Evelyn Louise; c. Iris Mary; led Peterborough Ornamental Swim Club to world fame as coach throughout '40s, '50s, '60s; recognized world leader in her sport, a pioneer in training methods and innovative procedures; Peterborough Citizen of '53; Cdn Centennial Medal; Ont. Citizenship medal '73; Ont. Synchronized Swimming Assn. Achievement award; mem. Cdn Aquatic, Peterborough Sports halls of fame.

FORBES, Sarah (field hockey); b. 11 Jan 1973, Victoria, B.C.; given name: Sarah Jean; York U., hons kinesiology & health sciences, paramedicine diploma; paramedic; goalkeeper; started playing '88, gold for NB Canada Summer Games; mem -18 ntl team ; competed '93 Jr World Cup, '94 World Cup, '95 Olympic qualifier; mem. '98, '02 CG teams; bronze '99 PAG, '01 Americas Cup; NB ice hockey team capt. '91 Canada Winter Games; 3 CIAU All-Cdn; 4 OUA 1st team all star; 4 OUA indoor 1st team all star; '97 Gail Wilson Award (CIAU); York U. athlete of '98; res. Toronto, Ont.

FORD, Alan (football); b. 2 Jul 1943, Regina, Sask.; given name: Robert Alan; m. Sally Ann; c. Tracy, Robert, Jill; UofPacific, BA; football exec.; accepted UP basketball scholarship then switched to football; pro se/hb/fl/db/cb/te/p. Roughriders '65-76; set Sask. record 207 consecutive games played (regular season and playoffs); handled bulk of Sask. punting over 12 seasons kicking ball 1041 times for 41,880yds, 40.23yd avg., 23 singles, 6647 career receiving/rushing yds; twice Canadian Schenley award nominee; Grey Cup record 87yd punt '67; 4 Grey Cup finals, '66 winner; ass't coach, admin dir, AGM, GM, CEO. Roughriders '79-99; interim GM Hamilton '03; trustee CFLPA pension fund; mem. Roughriders Plaza of Honor; res. Regina, Sask.

FORD, Albert (swimming); b. 21 Dec 1904, Redding, Eng.; d. 24 Nov 1988, Winnipeg, Man.; m. Ruth Kosar; c. Betty, Carol, Leon; UMan, PEng; standout swimmer '24-36; freestyle specialist; 3 Cdn, 11 YMCA, 18 Man., 1 Sask. titles in distances from 50yds-3 miles; held Man. records in all but 50yd FS; named to '36 Olympic team but work/family committments kept him home; pres. Man. section CASA '42-44, '51-52; ntl pres. '53-54; meet referee BE & CG '54;;

chair. '67 PAG aquatic committee; Man. swimmer of half century; life mem. Winnipeg Winter Club, Winnipeg Canoe Club; mem. Man. Sports, Cdn Aquatic halls of fame.

FORD, Bruce (rowing); b. 18 Sep 1954, Victoria, B.C.; given name: Bruce Singleton; UVic, UBC, BSc; fisheries technician, BC Fish & Wildlife Branch; mem. UVic varsity 8s '72-73, jr. varsity, varsity 8s '73-74; began sculling as mem. Victoria City RC '76; Canadian Henley jr. single sculls '77; sr. single, double sculls '77-78, '82, quadruple sculls '77-78; gold double sculls '79 PAG, bronze coxless quad sculls '84 Olympics; 3 ntl single, double sculls, 1 quadruple sculls titles; Royal Henley double sculls challenge cup '80; mem. '80, '84 Olympic teams; co-winner Victoria athlete-of-yr award, BC team-of-yr award '79; res. Richmond, B.C.

FORD, David (canoeing): b. 23 Mar 1967, Edmonton, Alta.; one of top kayakers in world; ntl team mem. from '83. 7 ntl titles; competed 4 Olympics; won Canada's first-ever gold medal World Cup '92; world title '99; 9 career medals on World Cup circuit; gold Brazil '02; overall gold, whitewater slalom silver, K1 bronze '03 World Cup; world whitewater slalom champ '03; Norton Crowe award '03; res. Cultus Lake, B.C.

FORD, Russ (baseball); b. 25 Apr 1883, Brandon, Man.; d. 24 Jan 1960, Rockingham, N.C.; given name: Russell William; hotel mgr, draftsman, banker, mill shipper; followed older brother Gene (who played briefly with Detroit '05) to majors with NY Highlanders (later Yankees) '09; rh spitball pitcher who became author of emery ball in Southern Assn. '08; 26-6 record '10, 1.65era, 1 1-hitter, 1 2-hitter, 3 3-hitters; 22-11 in '11 then slipped to 13-21 in '12; asked to take pay cut from $5,500 to $3,500 so jumped to Buffalo, Federal League where he posted 21-6 record '14; his career ended when emery ball pitch outlawed '15; ML record 99-71, 2.59era; mem. Man. Sports, Cdn Baseball halls of fame.

FORDER, Anna (figure skating); b. 25 May 1951, Oshawa, Ont.; given name: Anna Louise; m. Murray McLaughlin; c. Brooke Kimberly; Durham College; figure skating coach; teamed with Richard Stephens in pairs competition '63-68; mem. '68 Olympics, '69 Worlds teams; from '70 taught and coached all levels from novice through world, Olympic calibre; mem. Oshawa Sports Hall of Fame; res. Blackstock, Ont.

FORGERON, Mike (rowing); b. 24 Jan 1966, Main-A-Dieu, N.S.; racing shell repairs; made debut on ntl team '91 PAG winning silver men's pairs, bronze men's 8s; '92 Olympic gold men's 8s; FISU Games double sculls silver '93; gold straight 4s '94 Amsterdam International; with Todd Hallett double sculls '96 Olympics; NS athlete of '93; Rowing Can. Centennial medal; mem. Cdn Olympic Hall of Fame; res. Mississauga, Ont.

FORGUES, Keith (curling); b. 17 Sep 1942, Vulcan, Alta.; m. Carole Pender; c. Lisa, Michael; UAlta, BSc; chemist; 3rd '63 Edmonton zone Consols winner; 7 consec. years Ottawa Dist. Consols titlist '68-74, skip '71; 3rd Eldon Coombe '72 Ont. Brier rink; 4 Canadian Branch Royal Victoria Jubilee titles, 1 as skip; 2 Branch Gov.-Gen.'s trophies, 1 as skip; 2nd for Terry Begin City of Ottawa grand aggregate title '71-72;

CBC cross-country curling series winner '72, runnerup '73; Whitby invitational '72; Northern Ont. CA bonspiel title '75; Branch Colts '66; 7 Red Anderson Memorial Trophies; mem. Ottawa Sports Hall of Fame; res. Ottawa, Ont.

FORHAN, Bob (hockey); b. 27 Mar 1936, Newmarket, Ont.; m. Sandra O'Rourke; c. Bobby, Michael, Scott, Joe; UBC, BPhE; ret'd teacher, politician; OHA jr. B champion Weston Dukes '52-53; leading scorer jr. A Guelph Biltmores '53-56; sr. A Sudbury Wolves; mem. Kitchener-Waterloo Dutchmen '60 Olympic silver medal Trail Smoke Eaters '64 world tournament team, ntl team '64 Olympics, '65 worlds; Municipality of York regional chair. '79-84, CAO to '95; res. Newmarket, Ont.

FORREST, Craig (soccer); b. 20 Sep 1967, Vancouver, B.C.; TV soccer analyst; goalkeeper; began play age 12 Bel Aire City, Coquitlam '79; mem. BC -16 ntl title team; mem. ntl -20 B, World Cup teams, 37 international caps; mem. ntl team '88-01; 19sho 56 ntl team appearances; pro Ipswich '88-97, Chelsea '97, West Ham United '97-02, Upton Park Hammers; English 1st div. champions '92; Cdn player of '94 award; TV analyst World Cup; MVP Cdn Gold Cup gold medal team '00; diagnosed with testicular cancer '01; ret'd from competition '02; res. Ipswich, Eng./Vancouver, B.C.

FORREST, Robin (lawn bowling/field hockey); b. 10 Mar 1946, Vancouver, B.C.; given name: Robin Mary Stewart; m. Steve; c. Christopher, Jennifer; civil servant; active participant/official field hockey from teens; selected to Vancouver Island ladies' FH rep list '79-81; 1st Cdn woman to qualify to umpire men's FH matches '77; co-founder Victoria Rebels Sports Club '71, Vancouver Island jr. boys FH league '73; competes for Rebels Renegades VILFHA Div. 3; coach BC -16 girls FH champions '86; life men. VILFHA; began lawn bowling '87; BC women's pairs champion '92; mem. ntl team '95-96; ntl women's singles title '96; res. Victoria, B.C.

FORRESTER, Nicole (t&f); b. 17 Nov 1976, Toronto, Ont.; given name: Nicole Wendy; UMich, BSc, BA, UTex, MA; high jump specialist; ranked #1 in Canada, '99-01; bronze '99 PAG, ntl championship; silver '01 FISU, Francophone Games; '02 ntl champion, bronze '02 CG competed '02 World Cup, '97, '99 FISU, '98 CG, '99 PAG, '99 worlds; 5 all-American; Big Ten athlete of the year; 2nd highest indoor jump (1.93m/6'3"), 4th highest outdoor jump (1.94m/6'3") for a Canadian female; mentor for young female adults making the transition to high school; volunteers coaching young athletes; motivational speaker; res. Aurora, Ont.

FORRESTER, Ron (jiu-jitsu); b. 3 Jun 1927, Durham, Eng.; m. Ethel Moore; mgr. technical services, welder; 8th degree black belt jiu-jitsu, 2nd degree black belt karate; martial arts prof.; founder-pres. Canadian Jiu-jitsu Assoc. Inc., World Council Jiu-jitsu Organizations; black belt of '68 award CJA; coach ntl team, title winners international tournaments Hawaii '77, Toronto '78; American JI distinguished service award '75; Ont. special achievement award '78; pres. Cdn Jiu-jitsu Council; mem. Black Belt Hall of Fame; res. Oakville, Ont.

FORSHAW, Sheila (field hockey); b. 28 Jun 1958, Toronto, Ont.; York, BSc; managerial positions York 20+yrs; ex-ED

OWIAA; mem. Ont. jr. team '74-77, Ont. sr. team from '76, York team '77-82, Nomads club from '77, ntl team '78-84; mem. '83 World Cup silver medal team, '84 Olympic team; 2 Yeowomen-of-yr awards; fed. govt. excellence award '83; OWIAA communications officer; OUA, Fox 40 honor award '03; mem. York, Mississauga Sports halls of fame; res. Willowdale, Ont.

FORSYTH, David (soccer); b. 15 Dec 1852, Perthshire, Scotland; d. 13 Sep 1936, Beamsville, Ont.; m. Augusta Miglius (d); c. Otto; UofT; HS principal; considered father of Canadian soccer; raised in Berlin (Kitchener); capt. Berlin Lacrosse Club; mem. Berlin Cricket Club; canoeist, lawn bowler, cyclist; ctr UofT football (soccer) team; organized Western Football Assoc., NA's 1st league '80, remained involved through '19, 5yrs secty.; hon. life pres. Dominion FA; secty.-treas. OFA 5yrs; King's Silver Jubilee medal '35; UotT math silver medal; chairman Berlin Board of Health; mem. Waterloo County Hall of Fame.

FORT, Neal (football); b. 12 Apr 1968, Warner Robins, Ga; m. Darla; c. 2; Brigham Young; tackle; 2ce Western Conf coll. All-star; played Sr. Bowl, Japan Bowl; NFL LA Rams '91, Atlanta camp '92; CFL Baltimore '84-85, Montreal '86-04; ret's '00 then changed mind and returned to Als; 5 Grey Cup finals, 2 wins; 1 CFL, South Div, 3 East all-star; Montreal player assn. rep.; res. Houston, Tex.

FORTIER, Sylvie (synchro swim); b. 31 Aug 1958, Quebec City, Que.; BA, public relations; 24 gold, 4 silver, 2 bronze at ntl level '73-76; 12 Que. titles; 2 silver Pan-Pacific Games '74; 8 golds mid-Canada regionals '75-76; solo silver '75 PAG; 3 silver '75 world championships; 2 gold, 1 silver '76 international championships; 2 golds, 1 silver '76 Pan-Pacific Games; world champion '76; Elaine Tanner Trophy '76; mem. Cdn Aquatic, Canada's Sports halls of fame; res. Quebec City, Que.

FOSTER, Norma (karate'coaching/officiating); b. 17 Oct 1952, Edinburgh, Scotland; given name: Norma Anne; Aberdeen Tech. Coll., biologist; medical scientific editor, Guseikai Karate Club operator; competitive swimmer who began karate career at 17; became 1st woman to earn karate black belt in Aberdeen; 6th degree black belt; 2 ntl kata, kumite titles; strong advocate of equal rights for women in karate world; key role in formation of women's div. Canada '83; worked hard to get women judges approved internationally for both gender events; 1st woman granted judging status by WKF; 1st woman appointed to WKF referee council; chair. WKF women's comm.; trained in Scotland, Japan, Canada; taught karate in Iran '03; Sport BC official-of-'04; BC Women in Sport Leaders & Legends; mem. Burnaby Sports Hall of Fame; res. Burnaby, B.C.

FOSTER, Red (administration); b. 1 Mar 1905, Toronto, Ont.; d. 18 Jan 1985, Toronto, Ont.; given name: Harry; m. Kathryn; Ridley College; advertising exec., humanitarian; hockey Toronto Canoe Club jrs., St. Mary's, Marlboros srs.; organized, coached, played for Sr. OHA Sea Fleas; hb jr. Argos, capt. Ont. title team; Argos srs.; Sr. ORFU Balmy Beach '28-30, Grey Cup '30; lacrosse Maitlands Sr. OALA; ss Toronto Garrison Officers' League Machine Gunners softball team; won 1st official outdoor hydroplane (sea flea) outboard race in Canada; runnerup world international championships, earning reputation as one of NA's most daring and capable drivers; pioneered sports broadcasting; established charitable foundation for mentally challenged; chair/CEO Canadian Special Olympics; chair. Canada's Sports Hall of Fame; mem. Lou Marsh Trophy selection comm., CNE Sports Comm.; Ont. special achievement award; many community awards for charitable works; mem. Order of Canada, Canada's Sports Hall of Fame.

FOULDS, William C (football); b. 1888, Toronto, Ont.; d. 1954, Toronto, Ont.; UofT; qb Toronto Varsity '09 Grey Cup win; coached Argos '11, '14-15; won Grey Cup '14; held various exec. posts with Argos, CRU; pres. CRU '21, '37; chair. rules comm.; referee-in-chief IRFU; instrumental in establishing East-West Grey Cup final '21; personally financed Eskimos travel costs to assure ntl final would be held; charter mem. UofT, Cdn Football halls of fame.

FOURNIER, Lionel (t&f); b. 19 Mar 1917, Pincher Creek, Alta.; d. 3 Sep 1993, Canmore, Alta.; given name: Lionel Joseph; m. Rita May Lorden; c. Robert, Ellen, Paul, Anne; UBC, BA, BComm, McGill, BSc, UAlta, MA; prof.; 2nd hj, lj '37 BEG trials; 3 track, 2 football letters UBC; capt. McGill t&f team '47-48; intercollegiate discus record; Canada's 1st international decathlon competitor '48 Olympics; t&f coach UAlta; among initiators of sports competitions for Canada's handicapped athletes '67; ntl team coach '67 PAG for wheelchair athletes, '68 paralympics, Alta. team '69 ntl wheelchair championships; co-ordinator '68 ntl wheelchair championships; founder Canadian Wheelchair Sports Assn., Edmonton Paralympics Assn.; mgr. ntl wheelchair team '69 PAG; administrator-coach ntl t&f training centre for Canadian Legion Edmonton '68-69; chair. rec. div. CAHPER '67-69; initiated, developed t&f, football, basketball, volleyball programs Quebec's Saguenay region '47-62; chair. 1st playground Olympics for greater Montreal '52; Paralympic award winner; mem. Alta Sports Hall of Fame.

FOUTS, Dick (football); b. 7 Aug 1933, Omaha, Neb.; d. 5 Aug 2003, Pebble Beach, Calif.; given name: Richard Lee; Missouri, Kansas; HS all-American; drafted by LA Rams; DE Toronto '57-61, '67, BC Lions '62-66, '68-69; 94 CFL games played; 3 all-Cdn, all-Western; mem. '64 Grey Cup winner; DeMarco-Beckett Memorial trophy '65; named to BC all-time dream team; mem. BC Lions Wall of Fame.

FOWLER, Dick (baseball); b. 30 Mar 1921, Toronto, Ont.; d. 22 May 1972, Oneonta, N.Y.; given name: Richard John; m. Joyce Howard; c. Tom (d); rhp, began pro career Cornwall, Batavia, Oneonta in Can-Am League; moved to Toronto (IL) '41; 10 seasons with Philadelphia Athletics (NL) amassing 66-79 record, 4.11era, 221games, 1303ip, 382k, 578bob, 11sho; pitched 1-0 no-hitter for Connie Mack's Athletics vs. St. Louis Browns 9 Sep 1945, his lone win that season following return from WW2 service; returned to minors with Charleston '53-54; mem. Cdn Baseball Hall of Fame.

FOWLER, Frank (golf); b. 31 Mar 1932, Edmonton, Alta.; ret'd golf pro; won '49 Edmonton jr. title; 2 Edmonton amateur titles; began career as club pro '55 Grand Prairie, Alta.; later pro Red Deer, Canyon Meadow, Fairmont, Drumheller, North Battleford clubs; won Sask. PGA title '66, runnerup Alta., CPHA; with George Knudson rep. Canada World Cup of Golf; 5 prov. sr. crowns, CPGA sr. title '86; mem. North

Battleford Sports Hall of Fame; res. North Battleford, Sask.

FOWLER, Pete (swimming/sports medicine); b. 25 Sep 1938, London, Ont.; given name: Peter John; m. Elizabeth Ann (Libby) McAskile; c. Timothy John, Megan Elizabeth, Cameron McAskile, Peter Ian; UWO hons. BA, MD; orthopaedic surgeon; swimming silver '59 PAG; interned UMich; resident UMich., London Victoria, UWO hospitals; fellow Duke U Medical Centre; surgery prof. UWO; medical dir. Fowler-Kennedy Sport Medicine Centre, London Health Science Centre; Cdn team orthopaedic consultant '75 PAG, '80 Olympics, CMO '84 Olympic, '90, '98 CG teams; pres. Cdn Academy Sport Medicine (CASM) '80-81; pres. ISAKOS '95-97; chair. FIMS '90-98; pres. AOSSM '02-03; Claude Brown UWO award; Cdn Sports Medicine & Science Council, Bay Area Knee Society lifetime achievement awards; UWO Alumni Professional Achievement award; Cdn Orthopaedic award of excellence; mem. Woodstock Sports Wall, UWO W-Club Sports, London Sports halls of fame; res. London, Ont.

FOWLIE, Jim (swimming); b. 26 Jul 1956, Prince George, B.C.; given name: James Kenneth; m. Barbara Lynn Bengston; c. Carrie Ann, Johnathan; swimming coach; 400IM silver, 200m butterfly bronze '73 Canada Games; bronze 4x200 FS relay '74 CG; ntl 400IM record '74; 400IM gold, Commonwealth record '75 world trials; mem. '75 worlds team; 400IM gold PAG trials '75; gold, ntl record 4:26.25 (fastest in world that year) '76; failed to qualify for '76 Olympic team; ret'd to coaching Prince George SC '77, Lions Gate SC '78, UCal '79-80; coached Alberta '81 Canada Games; coach Manta Aquatic Club Winnipeg, North York Aquatic Club; mem. CASA apprentice coaching program; coached men's team '81 long-course western nationals; mem. ntl coaching staff '81 youth championships Sweden; numerous ntl team appointments '81-91; asst. coach '90 CG; sr. coach AIS '92-02; coached Australian teams 3 world short-course championships, '96, '04 (Canada) Olympics, 2 World Cups; head coach Pacific Sport ntl swim center from '02; ntl team interim head coach '04; res. Vancouver, B.C.

FOX, Fred (t&f/hockey); b. 18 Jan 1914, Lunenburg, N.S.; d. 3 Jan 2003, Lunenburg, N.S.; given name: Fred Gordon Stephen; m. Jacqueline; c. Michael, Patricia, Pamela; Mount Allison; ret'd firefighter, public servant; NS 220yd sprint title '30, Maritime titles 100-, 200yd dashes '31; 100yd record stood 28 years; Maritime sprint champion jr. '33, sr. '34-35; Highland Games sprint titles '34-35; competed '32, '36 Olympic, '34, '38 BEG trials; mem. '37 Coronation, '40 Armed Forces track teams; mem. 15 Maritime Firemen title track teams; mem. Lunenburg Falcons, Chester Ravens hockey teams '30s-'50s, 6 league titles, 1 scoring title; mem. Berwick Apple Kings; top scorer Mount A Maritime intercollegiate title teams '32-33; mem. NS finalist Lunenburg HS baseball team '31; mem. 3 NS finalist Lunenburg Bluenosers softball teams; following WW2 turned to hockey administration; pres. South Shore HL '48-51; pres. MAHA '59-61, '70-74; pres. NSHA '74-79, '81-84; mem. NSFAS advisory council 5yrs; dir. Sport NS to '83; mem. NS Sports Hall of Fame selection comm.; NS sport exec. of '83; Royal Canadian Legion meritorious award, King's Coronation, Queen's Coronation, Jubilee medals, Centennial medal, CAHA outstanding, meritorious service awards, Toronto Metro, NOHA, OMHA, NS Metro Valley plaques, MAHA long service pin; Lunenburg honoured him with Fred Fox Day '80; 1ˢᵗ life mem. NSHA; life mem. Royal Cdn Legion Lunenburg branch; life mem. national POW Assoc.; hon. life mem. Lunenburg Fire Dept.; mem. NS Sports Hall of Fame.

FOX, Jim (hockey); b. 18 May 1960, Conistron, Ont.; m. Susie; broadcaster; rw North Bay '75-76, Ottawa '77-80; Team Canada '80, '86 (bronze); NHL Los Angeles '80-90; missed entire '88-89 season following knee surgery; OHA all-star, MVP, leading scorer awards '80; NHL record: 578 scheduled games, 186g, 293a, 22 playoff games, 4g, 8a; dir. community relations Kings '90-94; played himself in *Mystery Alaska* movie; dir. Kings Care Foundation; 1ˢᵗ King's community award recipient; Kings TV color commentator from '90; mem. Hockey Heritage North Hall of Fame; res. Redondo Beach, Calif.

FOX, Rick (basketball); b. 24 Jul 1969, Toronto, Ont.; given name: Ulrich Alexander; m. Vanessa L. Williams; c. 1; North Carolina; basketball player/actor; moved with family to Bahamas at age 2; moved to Warsaw, Indiana, at 14; from '87-91 appeared in 140 North Carolina Tarheels scheduled games scoring 1703 points; *Sporting News* 3rd team all-American '91; Boston 1ˢᵗ round NBA draft pick (24th overall) '91; small forward 6-7, 231; NBA all-rookie 2nd team '92; played with Boston '91-97, LA '97-04; NBA record: ('91-03) 892g, 8783pts; playoffs 95g, 711pts; mem. Team Canada '89, '94 world championships; left foot injury '03 led to '04 retirement; had cameo role in movie *He Got Game*; mother Dianne Gerace high jumper Cdn team '64 Olympics; res. Salem, Mass.

FOX, Terry (t&f); b. 28 Jul 1958, Port Coquitlam, B.C.; d. 28 Jun 1981, New Westminster, B.C.; given name: Terrence Stanley; SFU; active HS basketball player; lost right leg to cancer at 18; indominatable spirit provided inspiration to entire nation as he sought to run across Canada to raise funds for cancer research; Marathon of Hope raised $23.5 million; launched run 12 Apr '80 in Newfoundland; covered 5342km before illness in Thunder Bay (cancer had spread to lungs) forced him to quit 2 Sep '80; ntl day of mourning declared on his death; subject of '83 movie; '80 Lou Marsh Trophy; Companion of Order of Canada '80; Order of Dogwood, *CP* man of year '80; SFU established gold medal in his memory and communities throughout country named parks, sports facilities, streets, halls of fame in his honor; hon. mem. Canada's Sports Hall of Fame.

FOXCROFT, Bob (fencing); b. 17 Aug 1934, London, Ont.; given name: Robert Samuel; salesman; 12 times Ont. foil, épée, sabre champion; 5 ntl sabre titles; mem. '59, '67, '71 PAG teams; bronze team foil '59, team sabre '67; mem. '62, '66, '70 CG teams; bronze team sabre '66; mem. '74 Commonwealth fencing championships sabre team silver medalists; mem. '64, '72 Olympic, '58, '67 world championships teams; ret'd after 25 competitive seasons '79; fencing coach Seneca College, London Sword Club, UWO, Toronto Jewish Community Centre; v-p AAUofC at its dissolution; pres. Ont. Fencing Assn.; Ont. special achievement award '65, '71; res. North York, Ont.

FOXCROFT, Ron (officiating/basketball); b. 5 Nov 1945, Hamilton, Ont.; given name: Ronald Lewis; m. Marie Louise Grant; c. Steven, David, Ronnie; pres. Fluke Transport, Fox 40 International Inc.; under tutelage of Kitch MacPherson launched 35yr basketball officiating career '63 at high school level, 29 consec. yrs CIAU referee; achieved international and NCAA Div. 1 status officiating in more than 30 countries including the '76 Olympics gold medal game and NCAA Sweet 16 '98; lone Cdn to referee in NCAA from '80; 1ˢᵗ Cdn elected to NASO, 2 terms as chair.; refereed 6 Ont. HS title, 7 CIAU title, 15 OUAA West title games; worked OUAA West playoffs 23yrs, 10 NIT, 4 NCAA tournaments, title finals Sun Belt, Atlantic 10, Metro Atlantic Conference; OUAA West officials panel supervisor from '93; international events included Olympic, Pan-Am, World, FISU, Continental Cup, Goodwill Games, Japan Classic; inventor of award winning Fox 40 pealess whistle now used by sports officials throughout world; dir. Hamilton Tiger-Cats from '93; chair. '94 World championship of basketball Hamilton organizing comm.; co-chair '96 Hamilton Grey Cup; pres./CEO Hamilton-Brantford 2001 Canada Summer Games bid comm.; chair. '98 CIAU basketball championship bid comm.; plays active role in community affairs serving on boards of numerous organizations; pres. Hamilton Chamber of Commerce '95; named by *Profit* magazine among top 10 Cdn entrepreneurs of decade; Stoney Creek Citizen of '91; B'Nai Brith Canada award of merit '95; Hamilton Distinguished Citizen of '97 award; appointed NBA game observer; mem. Ont., Cdn Basketball halls of fame; res. Burlington, Ont.

FOYSTON, Frank (hockey); b. 2 Feb 1891, Minesing, Ont.; d. 19 Jan 1966, Seattle, Wash.; given name: Frank Corbett; mem. '11-12 OHA sr. title Toronto Eaton team; pro '12 Toronto (NHA); ctr '13-14 Stanley Cup winners; Seattle '15-24; guided 1ˢᵗ US Stanley Cup winners '16-17; Victoria '24-26; mem. '25 Stanley Cup winner; Detroit '26-28; 6 Stanley Cup finals, 3 winners; mem. Hockey Hall of Fame.

FRACAS, Gino (football); b. 28 Apr 1930, Windsor, Ont.; given name: Gino Mark; m. Leona Deck; c. Mark, Michael, Gina, Paul, Donna; UWO, BA, UAlta, BEd, UMich, MA; ret'd prof., football coach; fb/lb UWO '51-54, 3 times all-star, twice OQAA scoring champion, '55 MVP; pro fb/lb Edmonton (CFL) '55-62; co-capt. def. signal caller '61-62; 3 Grey Cup finals, 2 winners; head coach UAlta '63-66, 3 league titles, '63 Golden Bowl, beginning of ntl College Bowl play; met UotT 1ˢᵗ official College Bowl '65; head coach Windsor Lancers '68-86; '69 western div. CCIFC titlists, '75 OUAA west div. champions; head coach CIAU all-stars '79 Can-Am Bowl; 2 OUAA West coach-of-yr awards; v-p Canadian Football Coaches Assn. '69-70; mem. CAFA ntl working comm. for football certification; life mem. Alta. FCA; ntl wrestling drawmaster '67-78, '76 Olympics, '78 CG, Worlds; FILA award of merit; authored *Basic Football Fundamentals*; CIAU trophy awarded annually to top assist. football coach bears his name; Football Canada-CFL award of merit '87; ret'd from teaching '95; coaches HS football; dir. Windsor-Essex Sports Hall of Fame; mem. UWO W-Club, Windsor-Essex Sports, Windsor Alumni, OUAA Football Legends halls of fame; res. Windsor, Ont.

FRANCIS, Bob (coaching/hockey); b. 5 Dec 1958, North Battleford, Sask.; m. Deborah; c. Kelley, Kristine, Ryan; New Hampshire; hockey coach; played 4 seasons New Hampshire (ECAC); signed as free agent by Calgary then dealt to Detroit; played most of career in minors; 14 NHL games with Detroit '82-83; player/coach Salt Lake City (IHL) '86-89; coach Salt Lake '89-93, Saint John (AHL) '93-95, Providence (AHL) '95-97, Phoenix (NHL) '99-03; asst. Boston '97-99; IHL title, Turner Cup '87; with father Emile became 1st father-son combination to win Jack Adams trophy; res. Scottsdale, Ariz.

FRANCIS, Emile (hockey); b. 13 Sep 1926, North Battleford, Sask.; given name: Emile Percy; m. Em; c. Rick, Bob; ret'd hockey exec.; 14 pro seasons with 12 clubs including parts of 6 as goalie NHL Black Hawks, NYR; nicknamed "The Cat"; ret'd '60, managed Western Canada baseball clubs; coach Guelph jr. A '61; GM, 3 stints as coach Rangers '61-76; exec. vp/GM St. Louis '76-83; pres., GM Hartford '83-89; NHL playing record: 3.74 goals per game avg., in 95 games; coaching record: won 393, lost 273, tied 112 regular season, won 40, lost 53 in playoffs; *Sporting, Hockey News* hockey exec-of-yr awards; Lester Patrick Trophy '82; mem. Hockey Hall of Fame selection comm.; mem. Hockey, Sask., AHL, North Battleford Sports halls of fame; res. Palm Beach, Fla./Glastonbury, Conn.

FRANCIS, Ron (hockey); b. 1 Mar 1963, Sault Ste Marie, Ont.; m. Mary Lou; c. Kaitlyn, Michael, Connor; ctr SSM jr. '80-82; 1st Hartford draft pick '81; NHL Hartford '81-91, Pittsburgh '91-98, Carolina '98-03, Toronto '04; reached 1000a '98; Selke, Alka-Seltzer plus award '95; 3 Lady Byng, 1 King Clancy trophies, 4 Whalers MVP awards; 4 NHL all-star games; mem. 2 Stanley Cup winners; NHL record: (through '04) 1731 scheduled games, 549g, 1249a, 171 playoff games, 46g, 97a; reached 1700p '02; NHL Foundation player award for charity work with children; chair. SSM Special Olympics summer games; mem. Board Carolina Kids 'n Community Foundation; mem. Hockey Heritage North Hall of Fame; res. Pittsburgh, Pa.

FRANK, Bill (football); b. 13 Apr 1938, Denver, Colo; given name: William Jr.; div. Barbara; c. Jeffrey, Kari-Lynn; m. Carole; San Diego Jr. College, Colorado; ret'd businessman; award winning college wrestler; West Coast and jr. college all-American; mem. Colorado all-time all-star team; pro BC '63-64, tryout Denver (NFL) Toronto '65-68; Winnipeg '69-76; tremendous strength earned him offensive captaincy, nickname "Head Hog"; 7 times all-Cdn ot; 3 all-East, 4 all-West; Blue Bombers lineman of '70-75; 2 Dr. Bert Oja awards; 6 times Schenley Award nominee; mem. Argos quarter-century team '74, Winnipeg all-time dream team; played '63 Grey Cup; mem. Athletes in Action; player rep. Canadian Football Players' Assn.; mem. Blue Bombers, Cdn Football halls of fame; res. White Rock, B.C.

FRANK, Chris (bobsleigh); b. 6 Feb 1949, Banger, N. Wales; m. Nancy Keyes; c. Elizabeth, Graham; Carleton, BComm; broadcasting consultant; mem. ntl team '74-78, Diamond Trophy race winner; competed '75, '77, '78 world championships, '76 Olympics; 2nd '78 NA championships; best world title finish 12th 4-man sled '78; active canoeist, '80 Olympic team alternate; res. Ottawa, Ont.

FRANKS, Lisa (t&f); b. 6 Apr 1982, Moose Jaw, Sask.; UofSask, mechanical engineering; highly motivated athlete as child; mem. HS Little League team '96; Ateriovenous Malformation (AVM) age 14 left her quadriplegic; inept medical attention almost cost life; but after months of intense

and painful therapy at Wascana Rehab Centre in Regina she regained use of upper body and directed energy to wheelchair rugby 2yrs before switching to wheelchair racing; mem. Team Sask. '97 Canada Games; earning 4 gold, 1 silver '00, 2 gold '04 Paralympics; set world 400m, 1500m, 5000m records; received Moose Jaw key to city; 2 Sask. youth athlete of yr, YM-YWCA youth women of distinction, Cdn Foundation for Disabled, Cdn Wheelchair Sport, Sask., Moose Jaw female athlete of yr, Bob Adams, King Clancy, Athletics Can. outstanding athlete, Cdn Wheelchair basketball spirit & fair play, Cdn Paraplegic youth leadership, Peacock Pride awards; recipient of numerous bursaries/scholarships; res. Saskatoon, Sask.

FRASER, Alexa Stirling (golf); b. 5 Sep 1897, Atlanta, Ga.; d. 15 Apr 1977, Ottawa, Ont.; m. Dr. Wilbert A Fraser; c. Sandra, Alin Robert, Richard Douglas; women's southern championships '.15-16, '19; US women's amateur '14, '19-20, 3 times runnerup, semifinalist twice; Cdn women's amateur '20, '34, twice runnerup; 8 Ottawa City & District women's titles; teamed with Bobby Jones on '18 Red Cross fund-raising tour; mem. Ottawa, RCGA halls of fame.

FRASER, Anna (skiing); b. 25 Jul 1963, Ottawa, Ont.; m. Rob Sproule; c. Kate; marketing, communications consultant; freestyle specialist; daughter of former House of Commons Speaker John Fraser; member Ont. team before joining ntl team '84-88; won 5 World Cup series gold medals; 4th in aerials '88 Olympics; had best year '86 winning ntl ballet, aerials titles, 4 of 8 aerials events on WC circuit; 37 individual WC medals on Grand Prix circuit; World Cup aerial GP title '86; ret'd from competition following '88 Olympics; TSN *Women in Sport* interviewer; CBC '92, '98 Olympic FS color commentator; motivational speaker FAME; COC Education 2010 program; mem. Ottawa Sports, Cdn Skiing halls of fame; res. Toronto, Ont.

FRASER, Bud (basketball/t&f); b. 16 Oct 1923, Bridgewater, N.S.; given name: Arthur; m. Ella Thomson; c. Geoffrey, Robin, Judy, Terry, Jill, Scott; McGill, BSc, Minnesota, MA; ret'd educator; NS hj title '40; Armed Forces hj title '42-43; Southeast Asia Armed Forces champion 6 events '45; CIAU basketball all-star '48-50; Montreal city basketball all-star '48-50; capt. McGill basketball team; silver award McGill Athletic Council, 3 track letters; coached Maritime int. champion Brookfield Elks '50-51, Western Canada Intercollegiate basketball champion UMan '54-57, Minnesota freshman basketball team; Winnipeg basketball coach of '53-54; sr. consultant Sport Canada; athletic dir. UofT; res. Brampton, Ont.

FRASER, Cam (football); b. 16 Feb 1932, Hamilton, Ont.; given name: Cameron Donald; m. Betty Robertson; c. Donna Sandra; ret'd steel company employee, businessman; kicking specialist; Tiger-Cats '52-62, '69; career total 101 singles; 10yr totals (CFL records only kept from '54) 987 punts, 44,287yds, 44.9 avg.; CFL record most punting yds single season 7222yds on 157 punts '57; quit 7yr retirement to fill in for injured Joe Zuger '69; from '73 coached champion Ancaster girls' softball team; punter Tiger-Cats pro era ('50-67) team; res. Mississauga, Ont.

FRASER, Frank (football); b. 26 Oct 1935, Montreal, Que.; d. 17 May 2004, Ottawa, Ont.; div. Janet Beers; c.

Gregory, Natalie, Nathan, Wannita; m. Donna Coates; sc. David; Ohio State, Tennessee A&I BSc; ret'd mechanical engineer; jr. A hockey Que. Frontenacs, Jonquiérre; jr. baseball Laval Ahuntsic Montreal league; Montreal HS, US college football; CFL hb '56-63 with Montreal, Ottawa, Regina, Edmonton, Winnipeg; mem. '62 Grey Cup winner; led Canadian receivers '59-60; capt. Ottawa Beavers rugby team; with Marv Bevan coach Eastview jr. team.

FRASER, George (football); b. 2 Feb 1911, Stanley, Scotland; d. 9 Dec 1992, Ottawa, Ont; given name: George Henry; m. Violet May Jay; c. Andy; ret'd Canada Post; Ottawa Gladstone jrs '31; flying wing, end, guard, kicker Rough Riders '32-47; until '39 had never kicked a football, when regular kicker was injured he filled in and booted 3 field goals; interim coach '46; asst. coach '47; 3 Grey Cup finals, 1 winner; Jeff Russel Trophy '45; 6 times all-star; highly durable player missing only one game in entire CFL career; mem. Ottawa CSRA Hall of Fame.

FRASER, Gord (cycling); b. 19 Nov 1968, Ottawa, Ont.; m. Caryn Isom; c. Angus Ian; pro cyclist; began racing '86; specialized in track several years before switching to road racing; broke kneecap during '91 Canada Cup race; competed '90, '94 CG, '96, '00, '04 Olympic Games; competed in Canada with Control Data Systems; amateur in Europe with ASPTT team, winning 18 races '94, including Tour of Basque Country title, Robert Gauthier trophy, Paris-Troyes; exceptional sprinter; pro Motorola Cycle team '94-96, Mutuelle de Seine-et-Marne team '97, Mercury Cycle team '98-02, Health Net '03-04 competing mostly in NA; won 4th stage '97 French GP du Midi Libre; competed, failed to complete 1st Tour de France '97; won 1st stage Spain's Tour of Austurias '98; 3 medals '98 Fresno races; '99 PAG road race silver; GP de Rennes Coupe de France event '00; won opening stage Malaysian tour de Langkawi '00; won '02 Manhattan Beach GP; Cdn elite title '04; nicknamed "Flash Gordon"; with Linda Jackson co-winner '95 Ottawa ACT athlete of yr; Cdn cycling male road athlete '99; mem. Nepean Sports Wall of Fame; res. Tucson, Ariz.

FRASER, Hugh (t&f); b. 10 Jul 1952, Kingston, Jamaica; given name: Hugh Lloyd; div. Ann Kennedy; c. Robin, Curtis, Mark; m. Alexandra Reid; Queen's, BA, UofOtt, LLB; lawyer, prov. court judge; sprinter; ntl team '71-78; mem. '75 PAG, '76 Olympics, '78 CG teams; ntl 100m, 200m title holder; ntl indoor 300yd record 31.0; ntl automatic timing 200m 20.86 '75 PAG beating Harry Jerome's '68 Olympic 21.22; 15th world '75; mem. 4x100 bronze relay team '75 PAG setting Cdn record 38.86; football UofOtt '76, drafted by Toronto (CFL) but did not play; Bobby Kerr Memorial Trophy '71; dir. CTFA '81-83; CdM inaugural world athletics championships '83; pres. Sports Federation of Canada '85-90; v-p '90-94, pres. '92-94 CG Assn.; chair. Dubin sports advisory council '88-90; chair. Cdn Human Rights Commission; mediator varied sports disputes '90-93; guest lecturer on sports and the law Carleton, Concordia '76-93; mem. international court of arbitration for sports from '95; arbitrator '96 Olympics, '98 CG; res. Ottawa, Ont.

FRASER, Iain (soccer); b. 3 Apr 1964, Gedburgh, Scotland; m.; Hartwick Coll; player/coach Sacramento (WISL); honed skills in Scotland; all-American Hartwick Coll. '84; def Hamilton Steelers, Toronto Blizzard, Montreal Supra (CSL)

'87-90; 13 CSL goals; Colorado Foxes (APSL) '93-94; Knights (CISL) '95; New England Revolution (MLS) '95-97; indoor Milwaukee (NPSL) '98; Cdn ntl team '94-97; 30 international caps; WISL title '03; WISL def, coach-of-'03 award;; res. Burlington, Ont.

FRASER, Kerry (officiating/hockey); b. 30 May 1952, Sarnia, Ont.; given name: Kerry Hilton; div Mattie Spencer; m. Kathy McVeigh; c. Marcie, Ryan, Jessica, Matthew, Ian, Jaime, Kara; NHL referee/PR for financial institution; played minor hockey; attended NHL officiating school '72; refereed 8 Stanley Cup finals, World Cup series, '98 Olympics; broke Andy Van Hellemond record for scheduled games officiated with 1476; NHL record as referee through '03: 1476 scheduled, 223 playoff games; works with amateur hockey officials groups in off-season; res. Voorhees, NJ.

FRASER, Martin (canoeing); b. 14 Apr 1959, Deep River, Ont.; given name: Martin Roy; m. Jane Sues; UofT, BSc; accountant; with Steve Wilson ntl juv tandem canoe titles '74-76; ntl juv singles '74-76; ntl jr. 500m, 1000m singles '78; 3rd 500m singles, tandem, 1000m tandem '78 NA championships; with Ivan Charalambij 2nd 500m, 1000m tandem Mexico Cup '78; 2nd 1000m tandem, 3rd 500m singles (top NA finisher in each) '79 Canada Cup; jr. ntl C2 500m title '79; C1 500m, 1000m titles '81 Continental Cup; C4 1000m ntl title '82; ntl canoe team mem. from '76; mem. '80 Olympic team; PS, HS outstanding student awards, Ont. scholar; res. Mississauga, Ont.

FRASER, Sherry (curling); b. 26 Jun 1967, Lethbridge, Alta; data co. administrator; began curling age 11; 2nd Kelley Law (Owen) BC women's title rink '95, '97; 4 times runnerup; bronze '97 Olympic trials; BC mixed title finalist '93; mem. '93 Richmond 'spiel, '96 Saskatoon Ladies Classic title rinks; winner STOH Ford Hot Shots competition '97; media relations World Curling Classic '03; res. Vancouver, B.C.

FRAZER, Gerry (shooting); b. 18 Jun 1939, Edmonton, Alta.; given name: Gerald; m. Lili Kopala; c. Richard, Lynn, Tracy, stepchildren Dorothy, Rachel; UBC, BSc; ret'd mechanical engineer; began shooting competitively age 9; full-bore rifle specialist; 2 BC Lieut.-Gov.s titles; qualified 6, competed 4 Cdn Bisley teams; mem. '88 Palma team; v-p BCRA, mem. DCRA exec. council; res. Powell River, B.C.

FRÉCHETTE, Sylvie (synchro swim); b. 26 Jun 1967, Montreal, Que.; m. Pascal Van Strydonck; c. Emma; UMtl BPHE; aquatic designer, asst. artistic co-ordinator Cirque du Soleil water show; learned to swim age 7; switched to synchro at 8; swept Cdn jr titles '81-82; mem. Ntl B team '82, Ntl A team '83-96; Canada Games solo gold '86; won ntl solo, duet (with Nathalie Guay); world aquatic championship solo gold '91 with highest score (201.013) ever recorded at worlds, awarded 7 10s; 2 world, 4 ntl solo titles; 25 intl competition gold among 65 medals; assisted figure skaters Isabelle Brasseur-Lloyd Eisler with pairs routine '92 Olympics; scoring error by Brazilian judge resulted in Olympic solo silver '92 but appeal launched by IOC exec-v-p Dick Pound finally resulted in change to gold in special ceremony '93; team silver '96 Olympics; sport excellence award '86; world champion award '87; Elaine Tanner Trophy '86; Aquatic Federation of Canada female athlete of year '89-91; Grace Under Pressure award; pool at Montreal's Claude Robillard Centre named in her honor; Luso Fraternities trophy from Intl. Assn. for Non-Violent Sports; 10 Quebec Sport merit awards; Maurice Richard, Pat Sellers, Helen Vanderburg awards; fed. govt. meritorious service award '93; Cdn Olympic Order; Cdn Meritory Service Cross; variety of other achievement awards; CSF award bears her name; published autobiography *Gold at Last* mem. Cdn Aquatic, Intl Swimming, Canada's, Que. Sports halls of fame; res. Las Vegas, Nev.

FREDRICKSON, Frank (hockey); b. 11 Jun 1895, Winnipeg, Man.; d. 28 May 1979, Toronto, Ont.; UMan; insurance agent; capt. UMan team; mem. Allan Cup, '20 Olympic champion Winnipeg Falcons; scored both goals in 2-0 gold medal victory over US; Victoria Aristocrats, later Cougars; 2 Stanley Cup winners; half season Detroit, Boston '27-30; twice led PCL, WCL scorers; 1st NHL player-coach-mgr. Pittsburgh '30; knee injury ended playing career '31; coach hockey, lacrosse Winnipeg '31-32, hockey Princeton '33-35, UBC 7yrs; 1st player to write instructional articles on hockey for newspaper (*Toronto Star*) '32; mem. BC, Man. Sports, Cdn, Man. Hockey halls of fame.

FREEMAN, John (coaching/t&f); b. 17 Nov 1916, Toronto, Ont; d. 8 Feb 1990, Vancouver, B.C.; given name: John David; m. 1. Shirley Eastham, 2. Joan Jelinski; c. Hugh; UBC, CGA; federal government auditor; pioneer in innovative training techniques, especially for women sprinters; among his trainees were Patty Loverock, Margo Howe, Maureen Crowley, Jean Sparling; Loverock and Howe part of '76 Olympic 4x100 relay team which placed 4th setting Cdn record; training techniques included strength training for enhanced performance (before US used weights in training sprinters) over distance training, scientific testing for athlete fitness level; moved resolution with AAU in early '60s that removed 400m restrictions on women's ntl x-c events; created/organized/assisted with numerous track meets; pioneered coaching clinics like Cdn Legion Jr. Olympic Training Plan; pioneered prov./ntl certification programs; ntl sprints/relays coach '71-90; CTFA Western Can. Sprint co-ordinator '71-90; ntl team event co-ordinator; ntl team selection comm. member; delegate Athletics Can. AGM '73-87; numerous local/prov. Awards; CTFA Cdn Amateur coach of '76; Air Canada amateur sports award; Bourges France certificate of honor.

FRENCH, Joan (softball); b. 11 Dec 1935, Calgary, Alta; given name: Joan Grace Irene Jorginson; m. Bernie French (d); c. Jeffrey Warren, Bernie Grant (d); Calgary Business Coll.; realtor; participated in t&f, basketball, curling, softball; 3b Hillhurst Sunnyside Sr. A Alta. champions '56-62; named to Cdn team for world championships in Australia '63 but trip cancelled due to lack of funding; mem. Calgary Comets Sr. A team '63-68; 4 provincial titles; coach Calgary Timac Tires Sr. A '69-74, 4 provincial titles, Canada Games silver '69; coached Cdn Sr. A championships '69-74, 2 silver medals; Western Cdn Masters gold '87; pres., dir. Sport Alta. 8yrs; Calgary Booster Club leadership award '79; mem. Alta. Sport, Cdn Softball halls of fame; res. Calgary, Alta.

FRICK, Tim (coaching/wheelchair basketball); b. 23 Nov 1952, Aldershot, Eng.; given name: Timothy John Charles; m. Geraldine May Phillips; UBC BPE, Med, Dip Ed; PE instructor Douglas Coll.; NCCP master course conductor;

coached Douglas Coll. to 96 ntl club team titles (through '04); coach BC Breakers women's team from '97; coach VCC Langara men's volleyball team '80 CCAA gold; coached Rick Hansen in wheelchair volleyball '77-84 and on Man in Motion tour; coached Terry Fox wheelchair volleyball, track '77-79; 6 Cdn Coaching Assn. excellence awards; Canada 125 medal; Order of BC medal; Sport BC coach of yr '98; BC Wheelchair Sports coach-of-millennium award; international coach-of-yr award; 3M male coach of '01; Queen's Jubilee medal; Promotion Plus leadership award; res. Port Coquitlam, B.C.

FRIESEN, Ron (diving); b. 13 Feb 1949, Saskatoon, Sask.; given name: Ronald George; UofSask, BPHE, UVic, LLB; lawyer; CIAU 3m title '69, 1m, 3m '70-71; bronze 3m '70 CG; ntl 1m, 3m, 10m tower titles '71, 3m, 10m tower '72; mem. '69 FISU, '71 PAG, '72 Olympic teams; most distinguished US phys. ed. graduate '71; rec. dir. Oak Bay, B.C. '75-78; res. Vancouver, B.C.

FRIPP, John (skiing, football); b. 11 Feb 1921, Ottawa, Ont.; m. Lizabeth Drolet; c. Jay (d), David, Kim, Robert, Renee; insurance broker; ski school director; standout hockey, football player Glebe CI; Gatineau zone ski champion at 17 but deemed too young to receive trophy; flying wing Ottawa Rough Riders '41-42, '46; rookie of yr '41; served in RCAF '42-45; played for Montreal Hornets '45; Ottawa Trojans '47; directed Mont Tremblant ski school '46-48; won 4 Quebec Kandahar (open class) titles; numerous major ski event titles across NA; mem. Cdn Ski, Ottawa Sports, Laurentian Ski halls of fame; res. Ottawa, Ont.

FRIPP, Kim (skiing); b.31 Oct 1952, Ottawa, Ont.; given name: Peter Kemp; c. Jonathon, Dana, Dakota; insurance broker; ski jumping specialist; ntl jr. champ '69; 2nd ntl championships '73; mem. '76 Olympic team; chair ntl capital div. Ski jumping from '77; level 2 ski jump coach from '77; FIS judge (ski jumping, Nordic combined) from '95; res. Ottawa, Ont.

FRIPP, Shaun (skiing/coaching); b. 9 Sep 1936, Ottawa, Ont.; m. Patricia Ann Doig; c. Brett, Judson, Tara; St. Pat's Coll.; ret'd IBM marketing rep.; played football with St. Pat's city champs '55; excelled in x-c, jumping, downhill, slalom; as jr. 3 Que. div., 2 ntl team titles, indiv. ntl jumping gold '52, bronze downhill '53; claimed wide array of zone, div., ntl honors; won ntl sr. slalom title '56; attended 1st ntl training camp winning men's special slalom (Anne Heggtveit won women's title); ntl team '58; competed '58 FIS worlds; downhill silver 1st Commonwealth winter games '58; career plagued by injuries; 6 major event wins '59; OSC alpine combined title, Christopher Klotz Memorial GS title '59; 7 major race titles '62-65; raced in Cdn masters series in '80s-'90s; Eastern masters slalom, GS titles; certified Level II coach; Gatineau zone head coach '60-70; coached prov. jr/juv teams; alpine chair. Gatineau zone; dir. Cdn Ski Museum from '00; co-founder Ottawa Masters Assn.; served varied roles in Pontiac Cup, Sealtest, FIS races; St. Pat's Rector's ski trophy, Jackrabbit gold pin; res. Ottawa, Ont.

FRITZ, Bill (t&f); b. 14 Aug 1914, Ferry Bank, Alta.; d. 14 Oct 1995, London, Ont.; given name: William Duncan; m. Kathleen Nickell; c. David, Jim, Barbara; Queen's,

BSc; ret'd engineer; WOSSA int. 1/4-mile, bj, mile relay champion, sr. 220yd, 1/4-mile setting Windsor, WOSSA records; intercollegiate 1/4-mile, 220 titles; 4th '34 BEG 1/4-mile; ran for Toronto Beaches, West End Y; mem. '36 Olympic, '38 BEG teams; Glasgow 1/4-mile, Munich 400m titles; silver 1/4-mile, gold relay '38 BEG; Victoria State record 47.4 winning Melbourne, Australia, 1/4-mile handicap race '38; Millrose, Boston indoor 600m titles '38; Queen's Jenkins Trophy for athletic-scholastic excellence; mem. Windsor-Essex Sports Hall of Fame.

FRITZ, Bob (football); b. 29 Jul 1909, International Falls, Minn.; d. (circa 1990), Fargo, N.D.; given name: Robert Francis; m. Phyllis Marcille; Concordia College, BA, Minnesota; ret'd sporting goods business; all-conf. fb '31-34; *UPI* all-American '34; head coach/qb/fb Winnipeg Rugby Club '35-37, '42; all-Cdn qb; player-coach Bombers '37; player-coach Edmonton Eskimos '38-40; mem. '42 Grey Cup finalist Western Canada Air Force team; 3 Grey Cups, 1 winner; life mem. Blue Bomber Alumni Assn.; Blue Bomber certificate of merit '70.

FRITZ, Bud (harness racing); b. 15 Jul 1935, Walkerton, Ont.; given name: William; made driving debut at Elmira Raceway at 14; enjoyed great success with Apaches Fame '90-91 winning NA Cup, Prix d'été, and several other major stakes races; with 1:51.4 mile Apaches Fame became fastest Canadian-sired horse of all time; Cdn Horseman of '86; leading driver/trainer in Ont. Sires Stakes '86; mem. Cdn Horse Racing Hall of Fame; res. Walkerton, Ont.

FROBEL, Doug (baseball); b. 6 Jun 1959, Nepean, Ont.; given name: Douglas Steven; m. Barbara Ann Ambrose; self-employed; moved through Ottawa Nepean Canadians system to pro ranks with Pittsburgh organization '77; saw minor league action at A level with Charleston, Shelby, Auburn, Salem, AA with Buffalo, AAA with Portland, Hawaii, Indianapolis, Vancouver; ML with Pittsburgh '82-85, Montreal '85-86, Cleveland '87; pinch-runner for Willie Stargell in his final major league game; ended pro career with White Sox farm in Vancouver Triple-A '89; ML record 268 games, 542ab, 70r, 109h, 21db, 4tr, 20hr, 58bi, 13sb, .201ba; teacher of youth baseball, lecturer on sports/mental excellence; mem. Ottawa, Nepean Sports hall/walls of fame; res. Nepean, Ont./ Pittsburgh, Pa.

FROST, Barclay (t&f); b. 6 Jun 1941, Pembroke, Ont.; given name: Barclay William; m. Janet Small; c. Kendra, Kevin, Kirk; Carleton, BA; teacher; mem. '60 HS football champions; HS hj/lj records; Ottawa HS boys' singles badminton title '61; outstanding HS athlete award '61; active basketball, softball, hockey player; pv coach Ottawa Harriers; twice competed ntl t&f championships, 3rd '62 lj; coach 8 consecutive x-country t&f PS title teams; jumping events official Olympics, PAG, *Ottawa Citizen* Indoor Games, Canada Games; co-chairman Ont. t&f oficials council '80-81; mem. Goulbourn Sports Wall of Fame; res. Munster, Ont.

FROST, Stan (shooting); b. 2 Sep 1939, Montreal, Que.; given name: Stanley Edward; m. Anne; Queen's, BSc; health physicist, v-p environment & safety Cameco; began shooting '53; ntl small-bore team '65-83; gold master's badge '70 world English match rifle championships; team bronze '73

300m free- rifle Benito Juarez (World Cup); 3-position Ont. indoor title '73, prone title '74; silver master badge English match '74 worlds; full-bore gold '88 worlds; DCRA 2 Ottawa Regiment, Gooderham, 1 Des Burke, Gibson match titles; several Ont. small-bore prone, standard rifle titles; competed '75 PAG, 2 ISU Worlds; won Ont. Lieut.-Gov. '87, Sask. Lieut.-Gov., Sask. grand agg., PPRA grand agg. '91; 2 ntl 556/.222 titles; 2 Pershing trophy team titles; SFC exec. mem. '68-69, v.-chair. match rifle section '70-75; mem. 10 Bisley teams; DCRA exec. v-p '96-98; res. Saskatoon, Sask.

FROSTAD, Mark (horse racing); b. 19 Jan 1949, Brantford, Ont.; m. Pam; c. Kate, Justine; Princeton, BA, UWO, MBA; horse trainer; began working summers at father George's Bo-Teek Farm; ran own bloodstock business for several yrs before becoming a trainer '90; guided Bruce's Mill to Sovereign Award champion 3-yr-old male '94; principal client Sam-Son Farms; trained Cdn 3-yr-old male champion Victor Cooley, Chief Bearhart to Cdn turf male titles '96; Sovereign Award top trainer finalist '96; won '96 Queen's Plate with Victor Cooley, Breeders' Stakes with Chief Bearhart; with Cryptocloser won Prince of Wales Stakes '97; served term as pres. Cdn Thoroughbred Horse Society; trustee OJC; res. Toronto, Ont.

FRY, Barry (curling); b. 21 Dec 1939, Winnipeg, Man.; given name: Barry William; m. Judith Marjorie; c. Ryan Bennet; sales agent; skipped 2 Man. 1 ntl mixed, 1 Man title rinks; skipped '79 Macdonald Brier (last under their sponsorship); 3 Man. senior men's title rinks; 4 carspiel titles; skip Cdn masters title rink 2001; mem. Man. Curling Hall of Fame; res. Winnipeg, Man.

FRY, Gladys (basketball); b. 26 Feb 1907, Kitscoty, Alta.; d. 17 Mar 1991, Calgary, Alta.; given name: Gladys Alberta; m. William Jackson Douglas; c. Robert John, James Gordon; UAlta; lab technician; 4yrs UAlta team; mem. Tipton Tigers, Narsconas; mem. legendary Edmonton Grads '27-36; part of Grads team which played exhibitions in conjunction with '28, '32, '36 Olympics; 161 games, 1679 points, 10.4 avg.; HS t&f champion; twice Edna Bakewell Trophy for highest t&f points UAlta; mem. Canadian Basketball, Alta. Sports Halls, U Alta Sports Wall of Fame.

FRY, Harry (rowing); b. 13 Sep 1905, Dundas, Ont.; d. 1985, Dundas, Ont.; given name: Harry Brittain; m. Elsie Mason; c. Stephanie, Gary, Brian (d); Park Business College; Union Gas employee; began rowing '30 Leander Boat Club; 3rd seat bronze medal crew '30 BEG; 8s bronze '32 Olympics; ret'd following '36 Olympics; Hamilton YMCA handball champion '41, '43-45.

FRY, Jay (football); b. 23 Mar 1929, Hamilton, Ohio; given name: Jay Charles; m. Phyllis Anne Burna; c. Jay T, Elizabeth, Julie; Miami, BA, MA; coach; played football, wrestled Miami 50-52; competed Salad (now Fiesta) Bowl title team; mem. MAC title team, all-MAC; coached Celina HS 52-53; player/coach K-W Dutchmen 53-55, all-ORFU 3yrs; coached OAC (now GuelphU) 3yrs; college football/wrestling titles; head wrestling/asst football coach Miami '56-62; guided 1 MAC wrestling, 2 MAC football title teams, Tangerine (now Citrus) Bowl winner; asst football/wrestling coach York '62-63; head wrestling/asst.

football coach Indiana only Indiana team to compete in Rose Bowl '68, Big 10 title '67; asst. coach Ottawa (CFL) '70-73, Grey Cup title '73; coach Memphis Southmen (WFL) '74-75, won division title; asst. NY Giants (NFL) '76-78; initiated, operated Can-Am sports camps near Oxford, Ohio, many years; mem. Guelph, Miami, Indiana Football, Butler County Sports halls of fame; res. Oxford, Ohio.

FRYATT, Dave (soccer); b. 24 Jul 1921, Chilliwack, B.C.; given name: David Mark; m. Verona Lucille Nicholson; c. Richard, Marcia; accountant; active competitor 21yrs; from '52 administrator provincial, ntl, international levels; BC Soccer Commission secty '52-54, chair. '55-61, '75-81, treas. '52-67; Cdn Soccer Assn. dir. 25yrs, v-p '62, pres. '63-64, p.-pres. '65-67, treas. '69-71; Pacific Coast SL v-p-treas. '57-58, auditor '59-62; secty-treas BC youth soccer 34yrs; CSA exec. '57 World Cup team; founding mem. *Vancouver Sun* tournament of champions '52; founding mem./dir. West Coast Soccer Society from '86; mem. '73 Canada Summer Games comm., Soccer Canada World Cup comm. '76-77, '79-81; v-p/treas. CSA Alumni Assn '87-98; life mem. BC Youth Soccer Assn., CSA; PCSL appreciation award; 2 Aubrey Sanford meritorious service awards; Kaizen lifetime achievement award; CSA president's outstanding service award; Sport BC dedication to sport award; CSA 50 AGM award; Centennial medal; mem. BC, Burnaby Sports, Cdn Soccer halls of fame; res. Burnaby, B.C.

FRYER, Brian (football); b. 16 Jul 1953, Edmonton, Alta.; m. Barbara Brady; c. Colin, Jason; UAlta BPhE; exec. dir. Football Alta.; set city, Alta. lj,tj records, Cdn hurdles record; receiver, mem. Western Jr. champion Edmonton Huskies '71; 3 times all-conf., all-Cdn, '75 Hec Crighton Trophy winner Alta. Golden Bears; mem. College Bowl champions '72; Eskimos territorial draft '76; 1st Cdn collegian to be drafted by and play for NFL team; only rookie to make Washington NFL lineup '76; 10 games before returning to Canada and CFL; mem. Eskimos '78-85; 5 Grey Cup titles; mem. UAlta Sports Wall of Fame; res. Edmonton, Alta.

FUHR, Grant (hockey); b. 28 Sep 1962, Spruce Grove, Alta.; div. Corrine, Jill; c. Janine, Rachelle, R.J.; m. Candice; c. Kendy; hockey coach; jr. Victoria (WHL) '79-81; twice all-star, '80 rookie of year; 1st choice Edmonton '81 entry draft; NHL's 1st black goalie; Edmonton (NHL) '81-91 with brief minor stints in Moncton, Cape Breton; traded to Toronto '91, LA '95, St. Louis '95-99, Calgary '99-00; 6 NHL all-star games; twice NHL all-star; backstopped Oilers to 5 Stanley Cups; Vezina Trophy '88; shared Jennings trophy '94; NHL record most games by goalie single season 75 ('87-88); twice mem. Team Canada, mem. Team NHL Rendez-Vous '87; served 55 game suspension for cocaine use start '90-91 season; goalie coach Phoenix '04; NHL record: 868 scheduled games, 403-295-114, 48,945min, 25so; 150 playoff games, 8834min, 92-50, 6sho; jersey 31 ret'd by Oilers; above average golfer; mem. Hockey Hall of Fame; res. Ladue, Mo.

FUHR, Heather (triathlon); b. 19 Jan 1968, Edmonton, Alta.; given name: Heather Sherry; m. Roch John Frey; triathlete; UAlta, BComm; track, x-country runner UAlta; competed in initial triathlon '89; raced professionally from '91; 3 consec. Japan ironman triathlon titles '95-97; Alabama, Brazil, Cdn powerman titles; won '97 Pacific Grove triathlon; won world ironman triathlon title '97; won '99 Isuzu, '00 German, 3

US Ironman women's title; Cdn triathlete of '97; *Triathlete Magazine* long-distance triathlete of '97; performance of '97 competitors award; through '03 13 Ironman titles; res. San Diego, Calif.

FULLER, Debbie (diving); b. 24 Jun 1966, Montreal, Que.; given name: Debbie Lynne; Ohio State.; gold 3m, 5m, silver 1m '80 Norway Cup; 2 ntl 10m, 1 3m, 1m titles; gold 10m, 3m '86 CG; bronze 3m '87 PAG; mem. '80, '84, '88 Olympic, '82, '86 CG, '83, '87 PAG, '86 worlds, '85 FISU, NZ Games, Australian Open teams; '87 sport excellence award; mem. Cdn Aquatic Hall of Fame; res. Pte. Claire, Que.

FULLER, Rose (softball); b. 17 Mar 1954, Vancouver, B.C.; given name: Rosemary Ann; UVic, MEd; Nikken distributor, therapist, ex-teacher; began playing organized softball at 14; at 16 mem. Victoria Vicettes Sr. B team; with catcher Joanne Mick developed series of intricate hand codes to communicate; rhp whose fastball was clocked at 120 km/h; mem. silver-medal Canada Games team; joined Sr. A Green & Louis team (later Doc's Blues/Alpha Sports) '74; played key role 10 consecutive provincial, 6 ntl championships; competed '77 Tokyo Friendship Games; mem. silver-medal '78 world championships team; during '78 season posted spectacular 52-1-2 record; mem. 6 intl. tours teams; named one of top 3 female pitchers in world; frequent MVP, top pitcher, all-star awards; rejected US pro offers; ret'd from competition '83 but continued conducting free pitching, coaching clinics; Victoria female athlete of '75; mem. Greater Victoria, BC Sports, BC, Vancouver, Cdn Softball halls of fame; res. Cobble Hill, B.C.

FULLER, Wendy (diving); b. 8 Jan 1965, Montreal, Que.; given name: Wendy Marie; div. Scott Reich; m. Jay Leru; Miami; 3yrs competitive gymnast; mem. ntl diving team '79-88; sister Debbie also on team; 10m gold, 1m, 3m silver Germany, 10m gold, 3m silver Switzerland '80 European tour; silver 10m Dive Canada '81; silver '87 PAG; mem. '81 NZ Games, '83 CG teams, '85 FISU Games, '87 FINA World Cup, PAG teams; mem. '88 Olympic team; res. Miami, Fla.

FULTON, Greg (administration); b. 8 Dec 1919, Winnipeg, Man.; d. 8 Decd 2003, Toronto, Ont.; m. Angela Bombardier (d); c. Robert, Byrne, Rebecca; UAlta, BComm; hon. CFL secty-treas; developed play-by-play summaries as student newspaper reporter; statistician Stampeders '50-66; compiled 1st CFL official record manual '66; mem. CFL rules comm. from '64; editor *Official CFL Playing Rules* from '67; CFL hon. secty-treas. from '67; helped organize CFLPA pension plan '67; 1st recipient Commissioner's Award '90; mem. Cdn Football Hall of Fame.

FULTON, Jack (lacrosse); b. 30 Jul 1926, New Westminster, B.C.; m. Jean Kemp; c. Craig, Jackie; Marine College; ret'd deputy fire chief; mgr. New Westminster Salmonbellies '56-66; exec.-mem. Cdn Lacrosse Assn. '67-74, pres. '71-72; GM ntl team '74 world championships; governor Cdn Lacrosse Hall of Fame '67-73, chair. '74-81; treas. jr. Salmonbellies '75-78; mem. Cdn Lacrosse Hall of Fame; res. New Westminster, B.C.

FULTON, Ken (golf); b. 8 Dec 1943, Prince Rupert, B.C.; given name: Kenneth William; m. Sheila Ross Fairty; c. Stacey, Kari, Erin, Katherine, Jennifer; Ariz. State, BSc;

golf centre owner/operator; Arizona State amateur title '65; played on PGA tour '68-73; 2 ntl club pro titles; CPGA Seniors title '96; mem. European Seniors tour '97; res. Port Hope, Ont.

FUNG, Lori (rhythmic gymnastics); b. 21 Feb 1963, Vancouver, B.C.; m. J.D. Jackson; c. Alexander; coach UBC, co-owner/coach Elite Club; judge; ntl all-around titles '82-83; mem. 4-Continent club title team '82; gold all-around '84 Olympics as sport became part of Olympic program 1ˢᵗ time; turned to coaching following '88 retirement; BC Women in Sport Leaders & Legends award; hon. chair. Cdn Cancer Society; mem. Order of Canada, Cdn Olympic, Canada's, BC Sports halls of fame; res. Vancouver, B.C.

FURNEAUX, Karen (canoeing); b. 23 Dec 1976, Halifax, N.S.; given name: Karen Allison; Dalhousie U., BSc kinesiology, MSc candidate; kayak sprint specialist; world champion, K2 200m '98, K1 200m '01; silver K2 500m '99 worlds; 5ᵗʰ K2 500m '00 Olympics; 4 NS female athlete-of-yr awards; Queen's Jubilee medal '02; res. Waverley, N.S.

FUZESI, Mary (rhythmic gymnastics); b. 21 Feb 1974, Budapest, Hungary; m. Newton; Seneca Coll BSc, Cdn Therapeutic Coll RMT; communications; moved to Canada age 3; began rhythmics at 9; mem. ntl team from '86; spurred by success of Lori Fung, scored first international victory in Greece '89; Cdn elite title '90; 3 gold, 1 silver, 1 bronze '90 CG; gold, silver, bronze medals in '90 French competitions; 3 bronze medals in Bulgaria '90, 3 gold 4-Continents competition Japan, bronze world cup Belgium; 2 gold, 2 silver, 2nd overall '91 PAG; '88 Elaine Tanner trophy; res. Thornhill, Ont.

GABLER, Wally (football); b. 9 Jun 1944, Royal Oak, Mich.; given name: Wallace Gabler III; m. Jacqueline Bescoby; c. Wallace IV, Tamara, Melissa; New Mexico Military Institute, UMich, BA; investment dealer, v-p Nesbitt Burns; HS all-state db; jr. college all-American NMMI; Michigan qb'65 Rose Bowl champions; pro Toronto '66-68, '72, Winnipeg '69-70, Hamilton '71; CFL career record: 854 completions, 1690 attempts, 13,080yds, 61tds; res. Burlington, Ont.

GABRIEL, Brian (shooting); b. 5 Aug 1956, Kitchener, Ont.; given name: Brian Bruce; licensed electrician; skeet specialist; ntl team '79-89; mem. '80 Olympic, '82 CG, '83 PAG; ntl title '82; team gold '82 CG; silver PAG '83; 50th anniversary all-Cdn title '82; Cambridge athlete of '80; fed. govt. excellence award '83; res. Kitchener, Ont.

GABRIEL, Tony (football); b. 11 Dec 1948, Hamilton, Ont.; given name: Tony Peter; m. Diane Ellen Gaudaur; c. Benjamin Daniel, Laura Daniele, Shane Bradley; Syracuse, BSc; stockbroker; se, broke most of Syracuse major receiving records; NCAA record 2 tds in just over 2 minutes; pro Hamilton '71-74; 3 last-minute catches set up Hamilton 13-10 Grey Cup victory '72; CFL playoff record 15 receptions vs. Ottawa '74 semifinals; Ottawa '75-81; 3 Grey Cup finals, 2 winners; 5 times EFC leading receiver; 5 times 1000+ yards in receptions single season; caught passes in 161 games including pro record 138 consecutive games; CFL record 8 seasons catching passes every game; CFL career record: 614 receptions for 9841yds, 69tds; 11 times EFC all-star, 8 times all-Cdn; 4 Schenley Canadian player-of-yr awards; Jeff Russel Memorial Trophy '78; Schenley Outstanding Player award '78; 3 Lew Hayman EFC outstanding Canadian awards; Canadian player of game '76 Grey Cup; caught Grey Cup winning td pass from Tom Clements; Shopsy award '76; *Canadian Superstars* TV series winner '76; mem. Ottawa, Canada's Sports, Cdn Football halls of fame; res. Oakville, Ont.

GADSBY, Bill (hockey); b. 8 Aug 1927, Calgary, Alta.; given name: William Alexander; m. Edna Anne Marie; c. Brenda, Judy, Donna, Sandy; ret'd P.R., sales rental crane co.; golf range dir.; as a child survived sinking of Athenia '39; jr. hockey Edmonton; pro Kansas City (USHL), Chicago '46-54, NYR '54-61, Detroit '61-66; coach Detroit '68-69; 3 times 1ˢᵗ, 4 times 2nd team all-star def; collected close to 600 stitches during 20yr NHL career; never on Stanley Cup winner; while Chicago capt. '52 stricken by polio but returned to become 3rd player in NHL history to play 20 seasons; with Pierre Pilote shared record most assists by def single season and led NHL def 437 lifetime assists (both later topped by Bobby Orr); NHL record: 1248 scheduled games, 130g, 437a, 1539pim, 67 playoff games, 4g, 23a, 92pim; 2yrs coach Edmonton Oil Kings, '67 league title; biography *Grateful Gadsby;* mem. Red Wing Oldtimers team; mem. Alta Sports, Hockey halls of fame; res. Southfield, Mich.

GAERTNER, Travis (wheelchair basketball); b. 16 Jan 1980, Winnipeg, Man.; actuary; began wheelchair basketball career '91; mem. ntl team from '98; gold jr. worlds '97, '01; bronze '98, '02 worlds; gold '00, '04 Paralympics; 1 silver, 1 bronze ntl championships; 2 gold, 1 silver, 1 bronze CWBL; 4 all-star teams; mem. Milwaukee Bucks, Winnipeg Thunder; res. Chicago, Ill.

GAGE, Bob (builder); b. 1 Jan 1920, Smithville, Ont.; UWO (Assumption Coll.), BA, UofT, BSW; ret'd sports writer; active in promoting amateur sport at high school, university levels; key role in compiling history of HS sport in London; Fred Sgambati media award; Doug Gilbert media award; Cdn Sports Advisory Council award; initial recipient CIAU media award; OFSAA outstanding contribution to t&f award; CIAU Football Coaches Assn. award; Cdn Amateur Wrestling Assn. media award; Ont. Achievement award; Ntl. Assn., Basketball Coaches merit award; federal govt. Tribute to Champions award; hon. life mem. CIAU Information Directors; life mem. Basketball Hall of Fame; UWO basketball award bears his name; mem. UWO W Club, OUAA Football Legends, London Sports halls of fame; res. London, Ont.

GAGNÉ, Eric (baseball); b. 7 Jan 1976, Montreal, Que.; given name: Eric Serge; Seminole (OK) jr. coll.; rhp, relief specialist; Los Angeles Dodgers '99-04; ML record: (through '04) 24-21, 282games, 530.0ip, 413h, 214r, 194er, 60hr, 179bob, 604k, 152sv, 48 starts; set ML record 55 consec. saves single season '03, 84 consec. over 2 seasons; 3yrs all-star; NL Cy Young award '03; MLPA outstanding NL pitcher award; Tip O'Neill award '02 (shared with Larry Walker), '03; res. Montreal, Que.

GAGNÉ, France (t&f); b. 18 Oct. 1962, L'Ascension, Lac St-Jean, Qué.; m. Yohamma Ricardo; c. Laurie; full-time athlete; mem. 4 world championship, Paralympic Games teams; Paralympics silver discus '92, javelin '96, '00, bronze discus '00, javelin '04; world javelin champion '03, silver '02; javelin, discus gold '03 PAG; Cdn. javelin, discus champion '04; "Bronze Memoris" at the Quebec Gala of Sport; public motivational speaker for businesses and schools; res. Québec City, Qué.

GAGNÉ, Maurice (cycling/speed skating); b. 2 Dec 1936, Amqui, Que; competitive cyclist '58-67; mem. '58, '62 CG, '58 world championships teams; competitive speed skater '58-72; ntl indoor mass start champion '70-71; ntl indoor mass start records; NA, ntl outdoor titles '66; Canada Games title '67; Que. skater-of-year award; honored by CASSA for participation in development of sport in Que.; mem. Canadian Speed Skating Hall of Fame; res. Charlesbourg, Que.

GAGNÉ, Simon (hockey); b. 29 Feb 1980, Ste. Foy, Que.; lw QMJHL Beauport '96-97, Quebec '97-99, NHL Philadelphia '99-04; Team Canada '99 world jr. silver; '02 Olympic gold, '04 World Cup (gold); QMJHL all-star; jersey 12 ret'd by Remparts; Pelle Lindbergh Memorial trophy '01;

NHL all-rookie team; 1 NHL all-star game; NHL record (through '04) 354 scheduled games, 113g, 132a, 59 playoff games, 17g, 10a; holds annual charity golf tournament; nicknamed "Gags"; initial player selected (by Quebec) in WHA '04 draft; res. Ste. Foy, Que.

GAGNIER, Ed (gymnastics); b. 1 Feb 1936, Windsor, Ont.; m. Carolyn; c. Bonnie, Becky; UMich, BSc, MA; ret'd gymnastics coach; Canadian jr. athlete of '54; mem. '56 Olympic team; Big 10 all-around champion '57; Mich Yost honour award '57-58; Iowa State gymnastics coach '63-85; 3 times NCAA coach of year; coach US FISU games team '70, 10 Big-8 conf. champions, 3 NCAA ntl title teams; gymnasts he coached won 16 individual NCAA, 71 Big 8 titles, 53 all-America honours; mem. US Olympic gymnastics comm., chair. NCAA Gymnastics rules comm.; mem. US Gymnastics Foreign Relations Comm.; pres. National Assn. College Gymnastics Coaches; varied ISU athletic dept. admin. roles; mem. US Gymnastics, ISU Sports halls of fame; res. Ames, Iowa.

GAGNON, Marc (speed skating); b. 24 May 1975, Chicoutimi, Que.; following brother Sylvain and coaching parents; is regarded as the best short-track speed skater in the world; mem. ntl team '91-02; overall gold '90 Canada Winter Games, NA short-track championships '92, Lake Placid International '92; 8 gold, 6 silver, 1 bronze world short-track championships; overall, relay gold '95, '98 world team, 1500m, 3000m, overall world individual '98 championships; 4 '95, 2 '94 Bormio Cup gold; 1000m bronze '94 Olympics; with Derrick Campbell, François Drolet, Éric Bédard '98 Olympic 5000m relay gold; '02 Olympic 500m, 1500m relay gold, 1500 m bronze; serious back injury in '93 competition but rebounded to winning form; 2 gold, 1 silver '96 China Challenge; set world 1000m, tied 500m world short-track records; 7 Cdn Speed Skating athlete-of-yr awards; res. Montreal, Que.

GAGNON, Sylvain (speed skating); b. 30 May 1970, Dolbeau, Que.; began speed skating to improve hockey skills; numerous ntl, NA age-group titles; mem. ntl team '89-98; 2 Cdn senior 5000m relay records; silver short-track 5000m relay '89 worlds, '92 Olympics; 2 gold world team championships '95; 3 gold, 1 silver '95 Bormino Cup; Korea Challenge match relay gold '93; world short-track 1500m gold '93; 2 Cdn International Challenge gold; Speed Skating Can, short-track male athlete '90; res. Montreal, Que.

GAINES, Gene (football); b. 26 Jun 1938, Los Angeles, Calif.; given name: Eugene Carver; m. Marion Backstrom; c. Ellen Courtney, Eugene Jr., Elaine Carla; UCLA, BSc; football coach; pro Montreal '61, Ottawa '62-69, Montreal (player-coach) '70-76; outstanding db; 42 career interceptions returned 683yds; returned kickoff 128yds in playoff vs. Hamilton '64; Jeff Russel Memorial Trophy '66; 6 Grey Cup finals as player, 4 winners; 5 all-EFC, 3 all-CFL; asst. coach Montreal '77-80, '96-98, Edmonton '81-82, Los Angeles (USFL) '83, Houston (NFL) '84-85; Winnipeg '86-90, '01-03, BC '91-95; mem. Cdn Football Hall of Fame; res. Winnipeg, Man.

GAINEY, Bob (hockey); b. 13 Dec 1953, Peterborough, Ont.; given name: Robert Michael; m. Cathy (d); c. Anna, Stephen, Laura, Colleen; hockey exec.; hon. degree Trent;

jr. Peterborough Petes; 1st Montreal pick, 8th overall '73 amateur draft; defensive forward; Team Canada '76, '81; NHL playing record: 1160 scheduled games, 239g, 262a, 182 playoff games, 25g, 48a; NHL coaching record: 376 scheduled games, 154-171-51, 44 playoff games, 23-21; 8yrs team capt. Canadiens; coach Epinol, France, '89-90; Minnesota North Stars/Dallas Stars '89-96, GM '92-01, v-p/GM Montreal '03; mem. 6 Stanley Cup winners; 4 Frank Selke Trophies; 1 Conn Smythe Trophy; Cdn Society of NY achievement award; AGM Team Canada '96 World, '98 Olympic teams; mem. Canada's, Peterborough Sports, Hockey halls of fame; res. Peterborough, Ont./ Montreal, Que.

GAIRDNER, Bill (t&f); b. 19 Oct 1940, Oakville, Ont.; given name: William Douglas; m. Jean Donalda Sparling; c. Christine, Emilie, Ruthann, Billy, Franklin; Colorado, BA, Stanford, MA, PhD; former pres. Fitness Institute; operates York Flyers TC; decathlete; mem. '63 PAG, '64 Olympic, '66, '70 CG teams; decathlon silver '63 PAG; PB: 7147 decathlon points '64 Olympics, 14.2 in 110 hurdles, 51.3 in 400 hurdles, 10.9 100m, 22' lj, 49'2" sp, 5'10" hj, 48.8 400m, 156' discus, 12'6" pv, 196'8" javelin, 4:24.5 1500m; ran PB 400 hurdles age 32; varied exec. roles municipal, provincial, ntl t&f, skiing associations; pres. Canadian Masters X-Country Ski Assn.; 4th ntl Masters 30k x-country '80; 1st degree judo black belt; TV color commentator '76 Olympics, '77, '79 t&f World Cup, '78 CG; res. King City, Ont.

GAIT, Gary (lacrosse); b. 4 Apr 1967, Victoria, B.C.; m. Nicole Black; c. Taylor, Braeden; Syracuse; pro coach/player; with twin brother Paul helped Syracuse win 3 NCAA titles '88-90; mem. ntl team from '89; mem. Mt. Washington Wolfpack '92-93, Philadelphia Wings, Detroit Turbos '93-97, Baltimore Thunder '98-00, Washington Power '00-02; 2 Enners awards as NCAA Div. 1 player of yr; 2 McLaughlin awards as NCAA Div. 1 midfielder of yr; 3 1st team all-American; Brine Award NCAA Div. 1 title game MVP '90; 2 NCAA playoff scoring titles; set US Intercollegiate Lacrosse Assn. season goal scoring record; mem. 4 Cdn, 1 US field lacrosse title teams, 2 major indoor league titles, 1 Minto, 1 Mann Cup title teams; mem. '94 World Cup team; res. Syracuse, N.Y.

GAIT, Paul (lacrosse); b. 4 Apr 1967, Victoria, B.C.; Syracuse; tech. dir. Manchester, Eng., team; with twin brother Gary helped Syracuse win 3 NCAA titles '88-90; mem. ntl team '89-98; competed '90 North-South game; mem. NCAA 25th anniversary team; mem. ntl team 3 World games; mem. Detroit Turbos, Mt. Washington Wolfpack, Pittsburgh, Rochester, Philadelphia Wings, Syracuse Smash, Washington Power teams; also played on OLA, WLA teams; '89 Brine award; 1 NCAA playoff scoring title; 3 1st team all-American; mem. 4 Cdn, 1 US field titles, 2 major indoor, 1 Minto, 1 Mann Cup titles; 3 major indoor league, 2 Minto Cup, 1 Mann Cup MVP awards; 2nd team NLL all-star '98; 1 MILL scoring title; 1 NLL scoring title, MVP award; ret'd '02; mem. '94 World Cup team; res. Manchester, Eng.

GALBRAITH, Clint (harness racing); b. 22 Jul 1937, Tara, Ont.; sc. Don; campaigned on Buffalo/Batavia circuit from '57; dominated NY Sire Stakes with Nick Kash, Top Freight, Bye Bye T, Pastabyrd; time-trialed trotter ABC Freight in 1:57.1 as 2-year-old; campaigned legendary Niatross, harness horse of '79-80, winning Woodrow Wilson Pace,

Kentucky Pacing Derby '79, Little Brown Jug, Messenger Stakes, Meadowlands Pace, Prix D'été, Oliver W. Holmes, Gaines Memorial, Cane Pace, Dancer Memorial, Battle of Brandywine; set world records with Niatross, Call For Rain; more than 2900 winners, $19 million in purses; mem. Cdn Horse Racing Hall of Fame; res. Scottsville, N.Y.

GALBRAITH, Sheldon (figure skating); b. 24 May 1922, Teulon, Man.; given name: Sheldon William; m. Jeanne Schulte; c. Jeannie, Brian, Kathy, Barbara Jane, Mary Louise; figure skating teacher; California Pacific Coast jr., sr. champion '37-40; US ntl titles '39-40; pro Ice Follies '40-43; pro Ottawa Minto Club '46-47, Seattle '48-49, Toronto skating club '49-97; Olympic team coach '48, '56, '60; pupils include world champions Barbara Ann Scott, Frances Dafoe, Norris Bowden, Barbara Wagner, Bob Paul, Donald Jackson; key role in founding Cdn. Pro Skaters Assn.; mem. Order of Canada; Cdn, US Figure Skating, Cdn Olympic, Canada's Sports halls of fame; res. Aurora, Ont.

GALE, Bill (harness racing); b. 18 Oct 1948, Toronto, Ont.; m. Janice Johnston; c. Jason, Jennifer; introduced to driving by Morris MacDonald; dominated dash winning, UDR titles Windsor Raceway; Wolverine, Hazel Park throughout '80s; became a key figure on OJC circuit in '90s despite variety of injuries; through '03 won 78 major stakes races including 2 Frank Ryan Memorial; Maple Leaf Trot with Program Speed; through '03 6318 career victories, $41M in purses; res. Eden Mills, Ont.

GALLANT, Georgie (t&f); b. 4 Dec 1928, Shediac, N.B.; given name: Georges Joseph; 5 Boston Marathon runs, top Cdn '52 placing 20th overall; successive Dartmouth Natal Day 6-mile race victories '56-62; 5 8-mile Halifax Natal Day race titles; 3 New Glasgow 5-mile race titles; res. Cap Pele, N.B.

GALLANT, Peter (curling); b. 20 Dec 1958, Charlottetown, P.E.I.; m. Leanne; c. Brett, Christopher; salesman; began curling age 13; skipped PEI 4 ntl mixed championships winning Cdn title '87; 2nd for Peter Jenkins '82 Brier; 3rd '91, '93, '95, '97, '99, '01 PEI Brier representatives; res. Charlottetown, P.E.I.

GALLEN, Winnie (basketball); b. 4 Jul 1917, Mawer, Sask.; d. 5 Feb 1996, Sherwood Park, Alta.; m. William John Reid; c. Ian, Suellen, Melanie; mem. HS basketball title team; mem. famed Edmonton Grads '36-37, '39-40; 6 prov. shot put, discus medals; mem. 3 prov. title softball teams; 1yr pro softball Chicago; mem. Muttart Lumber hockey team; 4 Northern Alta. zone curling titles, '71 Alta sr. ladies' titlist; mem. Canadian Basketball, Alta. Sports halls of fame.

GALLEY, Garry (hockey); b. 16 Apr 1963, Montreal, Que.; m. Terry-Lynn Callaghan; c. Shaylynn, Wyatt; Bowling Green (communications major); broadcaster; 3G Hockey pres.; played minor hockey in Ottawa; CJHL Gloucester; def; BGU CCHA '83-85 div., '84 NCAA champs; 2 1st team CCHA all-star, NCAA all-American '84; drafted by Los Angeles '83; brief AHL stint in New Haven; played NHL Los Angeles '84-87, '97-99, Washington '87-88, Boston '88-92, Philadelphia '92-95, Buffalo '95-97, NYI '00; NHL record: 1023 scheduled

games, 110g, 440a, 85 playoff games, 7g, 23a; topped 1000 penalty-minute mark '97; 2 Barry Ashbee top Flyers def, 1 Punch Imlach awards; competed 1 Stanley Cup final, 2 all-star games; mem. Team Canada '93, '97 (silver) worlds; with Dave Ellett owned Almonte saloon; minor hockey coach (level 2); res. Ottawa, Ont.

GAMBLE, Dick (hockey); b. 16 Nov 1928, Moncton, N.B.; given name: Richard Frank; mem. Moncton Bruins Maritime Jr. champions '45, Que. sr. all-star team '51; NHL Montreal '51-53, '55-56, Chicago '54-55, Toronto '65-67; mem. '52 Stanley Cup winner; 11 AHL seasons Buffalo, Rochester; 4 AHL all-star teams; mem. 3 Calder Cup champions; coach Rochester Americans '68-71; NHL record: 195 scheduled games, 41g, 41a, 14 playoff games, 1g, 2a; AHL Les Cunningham, John Sollenberger awards '66; AHL record 4 seasons 40+ goals, 11 seasons 30+ goals, most goals (131) 3 consecutive seasons '64-67; mem. Rochester Americans, NB Sports halls of fame; res. Leroy, N.Y.

GARAPICK, Nancy (swimming); b. 24 Sep 1961, Halifax, N.S.; given name: Nancy Ellen; USC, UAlta, Dalhousie.; teacher; mem. ntl team '74-83; 14 ntl gold, 15 silver, 13 bronze; 1 world championship silver, bronze; 2 Canada Cup gold, 1 silver, 2 bronze; 1 4-Nations Cup gold, bronze; 1 Japanese nationals gold; 1 Australian nationals bronze; 1 PAG silver, 3 bronze; 2 Olympic bronze; 3 CIAU gold plus a wide array of gold, silver and bronze won in numerous ntl, international competitions; world record 2:16.33 200m backstroke '75, 100m backstroke 1:03.28 (during heat) '76 Olympics; 5 ntl records; mem. '76, '80 Olympic, '79 PAG, '78 CG teams; Bobbie Rosenfeld Trophy '75; with Diane Jones (Konihowski) shares '75 Velma Springstead award; seriously injured cycling accident '83; Gov.-Gen.'s silver medal '76, all-American '80; AUAA swimmer of '82; mem. Cdn Olympic, NS Sports halls of fame; res. Halifax, N.S.

GARDINER, Charlie (hockey); b. 31 Dec 1904, Edinburgh, Scotland; d. 13 Jun 1934, St. Boniface, Man.; given name: Charles Robert; emigrated to Canada age 7; excelled in baseball, rugby, hockey; goaltender Selkirk intermediates at 14; with Winnipeg Maroons APHL '26-27; Chicago (NHL) '27-34; NHL record: 316 scheduled games, 112 victories, 2.02 GA avg; 21 playoff games, 1.37 GA avg.; 47 career shutouts; Vezina trophy '32, '34; 3 1st team, 1 2nd team all-star; 1 Stanley Cup winner; mem. Man. Sports, Man., Cdn Hockey halls of fame.

GARDINER, Herb (hockey); b. 8 May 1891, Winnipeg, Man.; d. 11 Jan 1972, Winnipeg, Man.; given name: Herbert Martin; played with Winnipeg Victorias '08-09, Bankers League '10-11; served Cdn Army overseas '15-18; Calgary Tigers '19-26; joined NHL at 35 with Montreal '26-29; player/coach Chicago '29 returning to Canadiens for playoffs; dealt to Boston then Philadelphia Arrows of Can-Am league; mem. Man. Hockey Hall of Fame.

GARDINER, Tyrone (boxing); b. 2 Apr 1939, Sydney, N.S.; m. Floria MacKeigan; c. Jamie; correctional officer; began boxing '54; Maritime lightweight, Eastern Cdn titles '61; Cdn lightweight title '63; ret'd undefeated '66; mem. Cdn Professional Boxing Assn., Cape Breton Boxing

Comm.; pres. Venetian Gardens Boxing club; mem. NS Sports, Cdn, World Boxing halls of fame; res. Mira, N.S.

GARDNER, Cal (hockey); b. 30 Oct 1924, Transcona, Man.; d. 10 Oct 2001, Toronto, Ont.; given name: Calvin Pearly; m. Mary Malone; c. David, Paul; ret'd account exec., Telemedia; ctr CUAC, Winnipeg Esquires; Winnipeg Rangers '43 Memorial Cup champions; leading scorer, MVP NY Rovers (EHL); NYR '45-48, Toronto '48-52; Stanley Cup winning goal '49; mem. '51 Stanley Cup winner; Chicago '52-53, Boston '53-57; NHL record: 696 scheduled games, 154g, 238a, 61 playoff games, 7g, 10a; playing-coach, MVP Springfield (AHL); leading scorer Providence; playing-coach Kingston (EPHL); leading scorer Cleveland Barons (AHL); both sons played in NHL; color commentator 3yrs Bruins, later Leafs network; son Paul (ass't coach Nashville Predators) had 10-yr NHL career; Man. Hockey Hall of Fame.

GARE, Danny (hockey); b. 14 May 1954, Nelson, B.C.; given name: Daniel Mirl; sports broadcaster, ex-coach; jr. Calgary Centennials; 2nd Buffalo choice '74 amateur draft; Buffalo '74-81, Detroit '81-86, Edmonton '86-87; twice scored 50+ goals, 50 '76, 56 '80; 2nd team all-star rw '80; Team Canada '76, '81; NHL record: 827 scheduled games, 354g, 331a, 64 playoff games, 25g, 21a; color analyst Tampa Bay '92-93; asst. coach Tampa Bay '93-96; Sabres broadcaster '89-92, '97-03; operates summer hockey school; mem. Buffalo Sabres, BC hockey halls of fame; res. Nelson, B.C./Buffalo, N.Y.

GAREAU, Jacqueline (t&f); b. 10 Mar 1953, L'Annonciation, Que.; m. Gilles; c. Yannick; respiratory technician, operates sporting goods store; marathon specialist; l'Ile d'Orleans, Montreal International, Skylon, National Capital, Los Angeles marathon titles; competed 5 Boston marathons winning '80 race after Rosie Ruiz sham discovered; ntl 10km road race, 10,000m titles '85; 5th '83 world championships; 2 ntl sr. records; mem. '84 Olympic team; Canada's female marathoner of century; mem. Que. Sports, Cdn Road Running halls of fame; res. Boulder, Colo.

GARNEAU, Louis (cycling); b. 9 Aug 1958, Quebec City, Que.; m. Monique Arsenault; c. William, Edouard, Victoria; Laval, BA; pres./designer sport apparel mfr. co.; 4 ntl titles, 3 road race, 1 time trial; 1 Que., Hamilton GP, GP du Carretour, Montreal GP, Beauport GP titles; mem. '84 Olympic, '78, '82 CG, '83 FISU, '82-83 world championships teams; res. St-Augustine de Desmaires, Que.

GARROW, Alex (basketball); b. 3 Jan 1937, St. Regis, Que.; d. 6 Aug 1997, Fort Erie, Ont.; given name: Alexander Edwin; m. Carol Harris; c. Terrence, Kathryn, Patrick; Alabama, Algonquin College; nickname "Chief"; all-Catholic Buffalo HS basketball; Alabama on basketball scholarship '57-58; Tillsonburg Livingstons '60-61; mem. national title team '60; plan to turn pro Elmer Ripley's Washington ABA team scrapped through injury which sidelined him '62 season; mem. '63 Yvon Coutu team Montreal, sr. league MVP '63-64; capt. 1st Que. team '67 Canada Winter Games; coached Nepean bantam basketball.

GARSIDE, Bert (bowling); b. 16 Aug 1931, Toronto, Ont.; given name: Bert Kenneth; m. Hester MacDonald; c. Brian,

Tracy, Caron, Michael; ret'd managing dir. Ontario 5-Pin Bowler's Assn.; bantamweight who backed boasts with actions; standout pool player, bowler; once tied Russian chess master while still in HS; 4 perfect 450 games; lifetime 255 average; record 15 consecutive TV appearance victories; won every major tournament except O'Connor Open during competitive days; mem. Scarborough record-setting ntl championship men's team; moved into bowling administration '59; dir. Canadian Bowling Congress '62-66; exec. dir. CBC, OBC from '66; instrumental formation 1st Toronto bowlers' assn., Master Bowlers' Assn.; founder, pres. Scarborough Proprietors', Scarborough Bowlers' Assn.; created bowling equipment (shoes); syndicated newspaper instruction column, several instruction manuals; invented instant average calculator; collated, rewrote 5-pin rule book; key role establishing bowling as recognized sport on Ont., ntl scene; helped unify East-West standard scoring system, equipment standards; life mem. MBA; Scarborough Sports and Recreation Assn. award; Builders of Bowling Industry award '79; mem. Ont. 5-Pin Bowling Hall of Fame; res. Pickering, Ont./Florida.

GARTNER, Mike (hockey); b. 29 Oct 1959, Ottawa, Ont.; given name: Michael Alfred; m. Colleen; c. Joshua, Natalie, Dylan; hockey exec.; jr. Niagara Falls '76-78; OHA rookie of year '76-77, all-star '78; mem. Team Canada world jr. team '78; Washington 1st pick, 4th overall '79 draft; pro Cincinnati WHA '78-79, rw Washington NHL '79-89, Minnesota '89-90, NYR '90-94, Toronto '94-96, Phoenix '96-98; NHL record: 1432 scheduled games, 708g, 627a, 122 playoff games, 43g, 50a; scored 50g '85; 30 or more 15 consecutive seasons; with 611th career goal 9 Mar '94 moved into 5th place on all-time list; passed 700g '97; 7 NHL all-star games; mem. Team Canada for 4 Canada Cup, 2 World tournaments; 2 NHL fastest-skater awards; *ESPN TV* analyst; pres. NHLPA;, dir. NHLPA business operations; active in varied charitable organizations, Hockey Ministries Intl.; mem. Hockey Hall of Fame; res. Toronto, Ont.

GARVIE, Clarence (coaching); b. 1912, Saskatoon, Sask.; d. 22 Jan 1993, Saskatoon, Sask.; given name: Clarence Harry; m. Vi Woods; c. Marion, Gordon (d), Neil, David; UofSask, BA, BSc; HS principal; standout swimmer, football, hockey player at college, mem. 8 title teams; coached football, t&f, swimming various levels in Sask.; established Saskatoon, Riverdale TC; established SHSAA '50, pres. '52-53; pres. Saskatoon Hilltop jr. football club '68; wrestling chairman '71 Canada Games; officiated pv event '76 Olympics; mem. Sask., Saskatoon, UofSask. Sports halls of fame.

GARVIE, Gord (wrestling); b. 25 Oct 1944, Saskatoon, Sask.; d. 6 Aug 1988, Saskatoon, Sask.; given name: Gordon Taylor; m. Joan Katherine Willness; c. Trona Lee, Lana Katherine, Carla Vi, Barton Minor; UofSask, BA, BEd, MSc, UAlta, PhD; asst. professor, wrestling, football coach; football Nutana Blues '59-61, Saskatoon Hilltops '62-65, Saskatchewan Huskies '66-69, 7 times all-star, MVP Blues, Hilltops; Western Canada Hec Crighton award nominee '69; hockey to jr. A level; CIAU wrestling titles '67-69, ntl amateur title '69; UofSask. athlete of '66-69; mem. '68 Olympic, '69 world championships teams; player-coach Thunder Bay Mustangs football club '70-71; LakeheadU wrestling coach '70-75; coached 5 ntl open titlists; mgr.

'73 FISU Games team, asst. coach Toledo World Cup team; coach '74 CG, '74-76 World Cup, '76 Olympic teams; mem. Cdn Wrestling, Sask., Saskatoon, LakeheadU, UofSask. Sports halls of fame.

GASSIEN, Reg (harness racing); b. 11 Aug 1949, Lindsay, Ont.; began competitive driving career on fairground circuit before graduating to OJC circuit '81; equalled Greenwood track record with 6 consecutive race victories on one card; involved in 2 triple dead heats; believed to be only driver to have participated in a pair of triple ties; through '03 won 3,383 races and totalled more than $20M in purses; several Kawartha Downs driving titles; among most frequent winners were Jo Car Lyn, Treecoscious, Cathedra, Our Jude and Lantern Light; res. Lindsay, Ont.

GASTON, Cito (baseball); b. 17 Mar 1944, San Antonio, Tex.; given name: Clarence Edward; m. Denise; c. Adrian, Carly; baseball exec.; of minors with Binghamton, Greenville, West Palm Beach, Batavia, Austin, Richmond ('64-68) Santo Domingo, Leon Mexico ('79-80); major leagues '67-78 with Atlanta, San Diego, Pittsburgh (NL); ML playing record 1026 scheduled games, 3120ab, 314r, 799h, 106 2b, 30 3b, 91hr, 387rbi, .256ba; turned to coaching Atlanta '81, Toronto '82-89; mgr. Blue Jays '89-97; 2 World Series winners; 4 div. Titles; Jays batting coach '00-01; ML managerial record 1319 scheduled games, 683-636; 1st Afro-American to manage WS winner; Canada's baseball man of '89; mem. Blue Jays Wall of Distinction, Cdn Baseball Hall of Fame; res. Dunedin, Fla.

GATE, George (swimming/coaching); b. 11 Dec 1924, Carlisle, Cumberland, Eng.; given name: George Frederick; div.; c. Richard, Diane, William, Brenda; aquatic dir. Pointe Claire; coach Ocean Falls, B.C., '50-63, Pte. Claire from '65; coached '54 CG, '63 PAG, '68 Olympic, '73 world championships, '77, '81 Maccabiah Games; Swim Canada special recognition award; dir. Swim Canada; mem. Cdn Aquatic, Swim BC, Olympic, Que., BC, Canada's Sports halls of fame; res. Pointe Claire, Que.

GAUDAUR, Jake Jr. (football/administration); b. 5 Oct 1920, Orillia, Ont.; given name: Jacob Gill Jr.; m. Isobel Grace Scott; c. Jacqueline Gaye, Diane Ellen, Janice Arlene; ret'd football exec.; son of former world pro rowing champion; '38 NA schoolboy rowing singles, ntl jr. singles; ntl sr. mile rowing title '41; mem. '39 ntl jr. lacrosse champion Orillia Terriers; 1st pro football at 19 Hamilton; Toronto '41; mem. '42 Grey Cup champion RCAF Hurricanes; mem. 8-player group who purchased, operated ORFU Toronto Indians '45-46; simultaneously played pro lacrosse Hamilton Tigers; co-capt. '47 Montreal Alouettes, lacrosse Que. Montagnards; capt. '48-49 ORFU champion Hamilton Tigers; capt. '50-51 Tiger-Cats; ret'd to become Hamilton club dir.; reactivated '53 to centre Hamilton to Grey Cup victory; club pres. '54; pres.-GM '56-68; EFC pres. '59; CFL pres. '62; dir. Canadian Football Hall of Fame '63-84, mem. selection comm. '68-84, chair. '78-84; CFL commissioner '68-84; chair. CFL players pension advisory board, rules comm.; chair. CFL management council '81-84; governor Canada's Sports Hall of Fame; Officer Order of Canada; mem. Cdn Football, Canada's, Orillia, Copps Coliseum Sports halls of fame; res. Burlington, Ont.

GAUDAUR, Jake Sr. (rowing); b. 3 Apr 1858, Orillia, Ont.; d. 11 Oct 1937, Orillia, Ont.; given name: Jacob Gill; m. Cora Coons (d); Ida Harris (d); Alice Grace Hemming (d); c. 6 sons, 6 daughters; pro oarsman, boat livery, fishing guide; 1st race at 17; 3rd to Ned Hanlan, James Riley; 1st significant race in shell '79 Barrie regatta; challenged Hanlan's conqueror, William Beach, losing by length; '87-97 set records nearly every time he rowed; from '92 world's best oarsman; 3-mile record 19:6 Austin, Tex., '93; lowered mark '94 to 19:1.5 (still stands); beat Jim Stanury for world's pro title '96, defended '98 vs. Robert Johnson of Vancouver; ret'd following loss to Australia's George Towns '01; mem. Canada's, Orillia Sports halls of fame.

GAUDET, Benoît (boxing); b. 18 Dec 1979, Drummondville, Qué.; full-time boxer; 57kg 1st Québec boxer to win 10 ntl championships ('94-95 int., '96-97 jr., '99-04 sr.); lone Cdn. boxer to have beaten a Cuban at major competition; gold '95 Canada Games; '96 jr. worlds bronze; '99 worlds bronze; '99 pre-Pan Ams silver; bronze '02 CG; competed '99, '03 PAG; 3 gold, 2 silver in 6 intl. '03 competitions; 115-45 record to Jan. '04; res. Drummondville, Qué.

GAUDET, Oscar (hockey); b. 27 Oct 1941, Moncton, N,B,; m. Peggy; Labatt's sales rep.; helped Moncton Bears '75 and Moncton Hawks '79 win Hardy Cup; pro with Chicago (NHL) organization; league titles with Buffalo AHL '64, Dallas CHL '69, Portland WHL '71; CHL scoring title '67-68; never fewer than 20 goals a season during pro career; 482 points in 447 pro games; Dallas MVP '68-70; Maritime sr. league assist record '62-63 with 110; AHL rookie of '64 award; mem. Moncton, NS, NB Sports halls of fame; res. Moncton, N.B.

GAUDETTE, Cecelia (bowling); b. 31 Jul 1941, North Battleford, Sask.; d. Jan 2002, North Battleford, Sask.; given name: Cecelia Coons; m. Maurice Gaudette; began 5-pin bowling career '56; rep. N. Battleford '66 Cdn Proprietors singles championships; in 12-game roll off averaged 280; competing in '66 Cdn Western 5-pin women's singles rolled 8-game series 2182 pins, 273 game avg., to claim title; won ntl women's 5-pin crown beating nearest rival by 140 pins; mem. North Battleford Sports Hall of Fame.

GAUTHIER, Gérard (officiating/hockey); b. 5 Sep 1948, Montreal, Que.; m. Shirley Williams; c. Michael, David; 2yrs officiating at jr. level; attended 1st NHL training camp '71; made NHL debut as linesman 16 Oct '71; reached 2000g '98; worked 2 NHL all-star games, 2 Canada Cup series, 6 Stanley Cup finals; '98 Olympics; NHL record: 2345 scheduled games, 244 playoff games; res. Dollard des Ormeaux, Que.

GAUTHIER, Paul (boccia); b. 25 Nov 1970, Vancouver, B.C.; given name: Paul Joseph; pres. PACT Consulting & Enterprises Ltd.; consultant for Community Reintegration project; while cerebral palsy affects mobility his competitive nature has helped him excel in varied sports; shifted from motorized wheelchair soccer to boccia; mem. ntl team from '92; competed '96, '00, '04 Paralympics; 2 bronze '00, gold, bronze '04; individual silver, doubles gold '03 World Cup; ntl title '04; res. Vancouver, B.C.

GAUTHIER, Pierre (administration/hockey); b. 28 May 1953, Montreal, Que.; m. Manon Roberge; c. Catherine,

Vincent; Syracuse, BSc, Minn, MSc; hockey exec.; scout Quebec Nordiques '83-85, asst. dir. scouting '86-88, chief scout '89-93; AGM Anaheim '93-95, GM Baltimore Bandits (AHL); GM Ottawa Senators '95-98; pres./GM Anaheim '98-01; dir. pro scouting Montreal '03; GM Team Canada world championship silver medal team '96; with Bob Clarke, Bob Gainey helped assemble '97 world championship gold medal, '98 Olympic teams; res. Montreal, Que.

GAUTHIER, Sébastien (boxing); b. 15 Apr 1982, St-Jérôme, Qué.; gym trainer; 48kg; started boxing '98; jr. champion 51kg in initial ntls '00, 4 ntl sr. titles 1 at 48kg, 3 at 51kg; '01 Francophonie Games 48kg silver; '02 Acropolis Cup 51kg silver, CG bronze; gold '03 Mayaguez tournament, quarter-finalist '03 PAG; dropped back down to 48kg '04; 46-20 record to Jan. '04; Boxing Canada rookie of '01; 1st-ever recipient Arturo Gatti Award (for determination) '02; res. St-Jérôme, Qué.

GAVILLUCCI, Angelo (wheelchair basketball/sledge hockey/t&f); b. 3 Jul 1960, Melbourne, Australia; federal pensions adjudicator; shot put, discus, javelin specialist; wheelchair basketball player; mem. Ottawa Lions TFC; world shot put record; ntl shot put, discus records; Ont., EO shot put, discus, javelin records; mem. ntl team from '90; competed '94 worlds; '98 Paralympics sledge hockey team; ntl sledge hockey team '98-04; Trination Cup gold '99; Ottawa Lion's TFC President's award '94; res. Ottawa, Ont.

GAY, Mary (golf); b. 16 Sep 1931, Toronto, Ont.; ret'd supervisor payroll and records; Ont. Open '52, 3 times runnerup; 5 times runnerup Canadian Open, 3 times runnerup Cdn Closed; mem. Cdn ladies' team 2 UK tours, 3 Ont., 2 Alta. interprovincial teams; skip '62-63 Ont. Business Girls curling champions; mem. Waterloo County Hall of Fame; res. Waterloo, Ont.

GAYFORD, Tom (equestrian); b. 21 Nov 1928, Toronto, Ont.; m. Martha West; c. Margaret, Mary, Janet, Virginia, Elizabeth; UofT; ret'd stockbroker. co. dir.; began competing age 8; with father, Major Gordon Gayford, first father-son combination to compete internationally; mem. '59, '67, '71 PAG, '70 world, '52, '60, '68 Olympic teams; coached ntl equestrian teams '72, '80 Olympic, '78 world, '79, '83 PAG teams; mem. '59 3-day gold team, capt. '71 PAG; mem. '68 Olympic gold Prix des Nations team; Rothman modified GP, ntl horse show jumping titles '72; US Horse Show, NY puissance titles 3 successive years; set NA puissance record '63; when horse Big Dee mysteriously beaten in stall ret'd from competition '72; CdM Cdn ntl jumping team 5 Nations Cup gold, 2 PAG silver; designed Montreal '76 Olympic jumping course; international team coach '78-96; Cdn horseman of '62; founding dir. Toronto Polo Club; competed in polo; licensed owner-trainer OJC steeplechase circuit; helped reorganize Ntl Hunt & Steeplechase Assn '50; branched into thoroughbred training through '84; dir., exec. Cdn Hunter Society; bred War Life Gov.-Gen.'s Cup winner RWF '57; ntl dir. Cdn Pony Club 5yrs; chair. equestrian div. Coaching Assn.; ntl chair. Level 3 jumping program; founding dir. CEF '77. exec. through '98; qualified intl jumper judge, course designer; founding dir. OEF, dir. best-ever program; mem. Cdn Olympic, Canada's Sports halls of fame; res. Stouffville, Ont.

GEIGER, Marla (curling); b. 19 Dec 1970, Nanaimo, B.C.; Industry Canada co-ordinator; BC HS girls, prov., ntl jr. title rinks '87; world jr. title rink '88; BC jr. champion, runnerup ntls '89, BC mixed fnalist '92; 3rd 2 Kelley Law (Owen) BC STOH title rinks, 2 runnerup; won Saskatoon Ladies Classic '96; bronze '97 Olympic trials; res. Vancouver, B.C.

GELINAS, Martin (hockey); b. 5 Jun 1970, Shawinigan, Que.; lw Hull (QMJHL) '87-89; QMJHL all-star; CHL rookie award; George Parsons Memorial Cup sportsmanship award; drafted by LA '88; dealt to Edmonton; NHL Edmonton '88-93, Quebec '93-94, Vancouver '93-97, Carolina '97-02, Calgary '02-04; NHL record (through '04) 1052 scheduled games, 269g, 286a, 147 playoff games, 23g, 33a; earned nickname "Eliminator" by scoring 3 series-winning goals '04 Stanley Cup playoffs; res. Calgary, Alta.

GELINEAU, Jack (hockey); b. 11 Nov 1924, Toronto, Ont.; d. 12 Nov 1998, St. Bruno, Que.; McGill, BComm; ret'd seniors home mgr.; goalie RCAF team during WW2; played with Jr. Canadiens '44-45, McGill '45-49 posting 48-21-2 record; intermediate basketball, football, varsity baseball; tryout with Boston (AL); capt. McGill '46 Queen's Cup title; while still attending university was called up to Boston (NHL); Calder Trophy '50; dealt to Chicago following salary squabble with Jack Adams; NHL record: 143 scheduled games, 46-64-33, 8580min, 447ga, 7so, 4 playoff games, 1-2, 7ga, 1so; ret'd '54; hon. pres. Redmen hockey team; McGill male athlete of '48; British Empire Medal for wartime bravery; mem. McGill Sports Hall of Fame.

GELLARD, Kim (curling); b. 6 Nov 1974, Toronto, Ont.; UWO, BA; admin. asst. Scotia McLeod; skip ntl jr. title rink '93, world jr. '94; 3rd for Marilyn Bodogh '96 STOH, world title rink; competed as Team Canada mem. '97 STOH; competed '97 Olympic trials; skipped Ont. '99 STOH; Cdn female team of '96 award; res. Markham, Ont.

GELLER, Mitch (diving/coaching); b. 30 Sep 1961, Montréal, Qué.; given name: Mitchell Arthur; m. Bobbiann Mcpherson; c. Chloe; UofTex; ntl team coach; mem. ntl team '78-'82; moved into professional diving, managing, performing in high dive shows in Canada, US, Europe; Cdn. high diving record '84 with reverse double somersault from height of 125'; began coaching '86 Thunder Bay; club won age group, sr. ntl team titles; moved to Victoria founding Pacific Coast Diving Club, now known as "Boardworks", only club based on private enterprise model; appointed Canada's first ntl team head coach '97; elevated Canada to one of the top 3 diving nations; participated 3 Olympic Games: as a coach '92, '00, *CBC* commentator '96; coached 3 CG, 3 aquatic worlds, 2 Goodwill Games; res. Carp, Ont.

GENDRON, Francine (t&f); b. 16 Nov 1955, Montreal, Que.; UofQue (Mtl); teacher; ntl jr. 800m, 500m titles '75; sr. 800m '77, 1500m '79; sr. 400m hurdles '75, '77; ntl outdoor 1000m record 2:36.9, 400m hurdles 58.23, indoor 600m 1:30.8, 1000m 2:45.3; ntl sr. indoor 800m, 1500m titles '78; gold 800m Canada vs, Italy '78; mem. '77 FISU,

'78 CG, '79 PAG, FISU, World Cup, '80 Olympic teams; '81 Que. university 600m, 1000m, 300m, ntl 800m titles; res. Laval, Que.

GENDRON, Gilles (harness racing); b. 20 Jan 1945, Quebec City, Que.; sep; turned to pro driving '67; trained by Marcel Dostie; NA record 232 victories Blue Bonnets '72; twice Cdn rep. world driving championships, 3rd '79; 13 consecutive 200+ victory seasons racing almost exclusively Blue Bonnets until he was expelled in '85 for reasons never explained; continued racing exclusively in US; among top 10 NA 7 times; winner 10 Blue Bonnets driving titles; became 9th NA driver to surpass 4000 victories '85; res. Hudson, Que.

GENEREUX, George (shooting); b. 1 Mar 1935, Saskatoon, Sask.; d. 10 Apr 1989, Saskatoon, Sask.; given name: George Patrick; m. Lee; c. Andrea, George; UofSask, BA, McGill, MD; diagnostic radiologist; trap specialist; at 13 1st major competition title; 3 successive Man.-Sask. jr. titles; NA jr. championship, Sask. title, tied 2nd world finals, gold '52 Olympics; Lou Marsh trophy '52; ntl jr. athlete of year; rheumatoid arthritis ended sporting career at age 20; Saskatoon citizen of year; mem. Saskatoon, Cdn Olympic, Canada's, Sask. Sports halls of fame.

GENG, Lijuan (table tennis); b. 15 Jan 1963, Hebel, China; m. Horatio Pintea; c. James Ross; Carleton; pizza business owner; began playing age 8; won '85 world doubles, silver in singles, while representing China, under name He Zhili; mixed doubles world gold '87; double gold Czech Open, 1st ever for Cdn table tennis athlete; '89 English Open, '90 German, Hungarian, '91 Czech, '92 French, Italian Open, '95 US, '95-96 NA singles titles; with Julie Barton finalist women's doubles '90 worlds; undefeated during '89-90 Canada Cup season; 5 gold '95 PAG. mem. '96 Olympic team; '02 CG women's team bronze; through '02 12 consec ntl women's singles, mixed doubles, 11 women's doubles titles; 1st Cdn woman to win World Cup medal with bronze '97; 1st ranked female player Canada, NA, 10th world; with husband played professionally in Germany '90-94; Ottawa ACT table tennis award '97; res. Ottawa, Ont.

GENGE, Ronald (archery); b. 4 Aug 1922, Camaru, New Zealand; m. Rose; c. Lois Daphne, Colin Leslie, Christopher Ian, Gregory Floyd; ret'd cabinet maker; made own bow, other equipment and launched archery career '36; 15 competitive years all branches of sport, target, field, hunting, flight; moved to Canada '57; made/repaired archery equipment, conducted instruction classes; mem. organizing comm. ntl coaching program; ntl level archery coaching co-ordinator '66-79; '72 Olympic coach, archery official '76 Olympics; conducted 1st ntl training camp '72; international judge candidate to world governing body (FITA) '72-76; Canada's technical lecturer to Olympic solidarity seminars '77, '80; mem. Alta. advisory comm. ntl coaching development program; lecturer IOC coaching seminar '78; hon. life mem. Federation of Canadian Archers; Scoula Centrale Dello Sport of Rome award, Queen's jubilee medal, Australian Archery Assoc. award; level 4 coaching status; res. Edmonton, Alta.

GENOIS, Réjean (tennis); b. 30 Dec 1952, Quebec City, Que.; given name: Joseph George Réjean; m. Marie Falardeau; c. Annie, Maxime; Florida State.; tennis pro, accountant; '71 jr. Davis Cup title; pro tour '75; leading player '76 Rothman Grand Prix tour; mem. 7 Davis Cup teams; top seed Canada '76-78; 84th world rankings '78; ntl indoor title '81; led 3-2 Davis Cup qualifying round victory over Colombia '83; Quebec City athlete of '73; pres. Quebec Tennis Fed. '89-98; Tennis Can, distinguished service award; mem. Cdn Tennis, Que. Sports halls of fame; res. Loretteville, Que.

GEOFFRION, Bernie (hockey); b. 14 Feb 1931, Montreal, Que.; m. Marlene Morenz; c. Linda, Robert, Danny; business exec.; nicknamed "Boom Boom"; pro debut '50-51 Montreal; Calder Memorial Trophy rookie of year '51-52; 2nd player to score 50 goals single season '60-61; ret'd '64; coached Quebec City 2 consecutive pennants; drafted by NYR '66-68; ret'd due to ulcers; Rangers coach briefly, coach Atlanta '72-75, Canadiens briefly '79; NHL record: 883 scheduled games, 393g, 429a, 132 playoff games, 58g, 60a; Atlanta TV color commentator, publicity dir.; 2 Ross, 1 Hart trophies; mem. 7 Prince of Wales Trophy, 6 Stanley Cup winners; mem. Canada's Sports, Hockey halls of fame; res. Marietta, Ga.

GEORGE, Ed (shooting); b. 27 Jul 1904, Miami, Man.; d. 29 Mar 1988, Winnipeg, Man.; given name: William Edison; m. Aurora Johnson; c. Ronald, Rae, Beverly, Linda; UMan, dairy dip.; ret'd Cominco sales mgr.; internationally renowned target rifle shooter, coach; with son Ron dominated Sask. shooting scene '51-71; St. George's Cross (top 25 in Commonwealth); 15 prov. titles, 15 Gov.-Gen.'s silver medals; mem. 1st Cdn team to win all international team prizes '69 Bisley matches; qualified 6 Bisley teams, competed 5; '58 Bisley grand aggregate, City of Ottawa match; hon. life mem. Sask., Man. rifle, fish & game assoc.; secty. SPRA '57-64; mem. Sask. Sports Hall of Fame.

GEORGE, Ron (shooting); b. 1 Oct 1937, Winnipeg, Man.; given name: Ronald Edison; m. Leni Mayer; c. Mark, Shari, Scott; UofSask, MEng, MSc, Waterloo, PhD; consultant, ex-pres. ACTC Technologies Inc.; with father Ed dominated Sask. shooting scene '51-71; St. George's Cross, 15 prov. titles, 15 Gov-Gen.'s Silver medals; mem. 18 ntl, 20 prov. teams; mem. 1st team to win all international team prizes '69 Bisley; Queen's gold badge (3rd) Bisley; pres. SPRA '64-71; exec. mem. Alta. football assn., Sport Alta.; mem. Sask. Sports Hall of Fame; res. Calgary, Alta.

GERARD, Eddie (hockey); b. 22 Feb 1890, Ottawa, Ont.; d. 7 Aug 1937, Ottawa, Ont.; given name: Edward George; m. Lillian Mackenzie; c. Ailsa, Margaret; printer; active hockey, baseball, cricket, canoeing as teenager; with Don Mackenzie Dominion canoe tandem title at 15; backfielder Rough Riders '09-13; def Senators '13-24; team capt. '20-21; mem. 4 Stanley Cup winners, 1 on loan to Toronto St. Pat's; coached Montreal Maroons to '26 Stanley Cup; managed NY Americans '30-32; rejoined Maroons '33; St. Louis Eagles '34 but illness forced him to retire mid-season; mem. Canada's, Ottawa Sports, Hockey halls of fame.

GERELA, Ted (football); b. 12 Mar 1944, Powell River, B.C.; Washington State; fireman; played soccer as youth but was conventional style place kicker Washington State; discovered Gogolak brothers NFL success with soccer-style kicking so altered own style; pro rb/pk BC '67-73; Dr. Beattie Martin Trophy; twice 5 field goals single game; CFL record: 132 converts, 123 field goals, 69 singles, 570 points; CFL scoring leader '68; World Police/Fire Games flag football silver '01; res. Powell River, B.C.

GEREIN, Clayton (t&f); b. 24 May 1964, North Battleford, Sask.; given name: Clayton Ross; m. Ruth Van Der Koot; c. Jasmine, Zoe; horseback riding accident at 18 left him wheelchair-bound; ntl wheelchair racing team from '85; numerous intl, world medals; world 5000m record (13:32 '92); Cdn. 5000m record '04; PB marathon time 1:54 Hiedlberg; 13 medals 5 Paralympics; 800m, 5000m gold, 1500m silver, marathon bronze '88; gold 5000m, marathon, bronze 800m, 1500m '92; gold 5000m, silver marathon, bronze 1500m '96; marathon gold '00, bronze '04; 12 Peach Tree Road Race titles; 125th Anniversary Commemorative Medal; 3 Sask athlete-of-yr awards; '01 Athletics Canada Fred Begley award; Sask. Sports Medicine Council Speaking Bureau; volunteer Cdn. Paraplegic Assn.; board mem., athletics co-ordinator Sask. Wheelchair Sports Assn.; board mem. Ntl Sports Centre Saskatchewan; coaches wheelchair athletics; mem. North Battleford Sports Hall of Fame; res. Pilot Butte, Sask.

GERIS, Harry (wrestling); b. 22 Nov 1947, Netherlands; given name: Harry Ted; m. Jo-Anne Kathleen Knight; c. Jason Scott, Shawn Joseph, Ryan Alexander; Oklahoma State, BSc; insurance broker; Ont. HS titles '66-67; 5 ntl Open FS, 3 GR unlimited class titles; US ntl jr. college heavyweight title '68; heavyweight silver '72 AAU, USWF championships; bronze '75 PAG; AAU heavyweight title '76; mem. '66 CG, '73 FISU, '72 NCAA, '72, '76 Olympic teams; pres. Ont. Olympic Wrestling Federation '77-79; pres. London Wrestling Club; mem. Cdn Wrestling, Ntl Junior College Wrestling halls of fame; res. London, Ont.

GERVAIS, Hec (curling); b. 4 Nov 1933, St. Albert, Alta; d. 19 Jul 1997, St. Albert, Alta.; given name: Hector Joseph; m. Helen Bowman (d); c. Janet, Sandy, Hector Jr., Stanley, Kim; farmer; football Edmonton Wildcats, '53 tryout with Eskimos; 9 times Northern Alta. provincial curling playdown rep, 4 titles; 2 Brier titles, '61 world title; Toronto Tournament of Champions, 2 Calgary Masters titles; known for push shot; freelance broadcaster at major curling events; mem. '87 Edmonton Brier comm.; Curl Canada Brier MVP award bears his name; mem. Cdn Curling, Alta. Sports halls of fame.

GERY, Marcel (swimming); b. 15 Mar 1965, Smolenice, Czechoslovakia; m. Michaela; c. Nathaniel, Nolan; Seneca College; real estate broker, owner Markham private school; began swimming age 8; mem. Czech ntl team; defected to Canada '86; mem. Cdn ntl team '87-94; freestyle, butterfly specialist; 20 ntl titles; Cdn records 100, 200 FS, 100 fly; held world short-course 100 fly record '90-94; 1 Commonwealth record; 2 Rome Seven Hills, 1 France International, 11 World Cup races, 2 Fina Cup, 1 Quebec Cup, 1 Monte Carlo gold medals; '90 CG 4x100 medley relay gold, 100m fly silver, 4x100m FS relay bronze; Olympic 4x100 medley relay bronze '92; ranked 1st World Cup butterfly '90-91; Ont. athlete of '91; 3 Swim Ont athlete-of-yr awards; mem. Ont. Aquatic Hall of Fame; res. Aurora, Ont.

GETLIFFE, Ray (hockey/golf); b. 3 Apr 1914, Galt, Ont.; m. Lorna; c. John, Lorna; ret'd textile co. executive; pro hockey Boston '36-39, Montreal '39-45; mem. 2 Stanley Cup winners; 5 goals for Habs vs. Bruins '43; NHL record: 393 scheduled games, 136g, 137a, 45 playoff games, 9g, 10a; mem. Ont. Willingdon Cup winner '38; pres. QGA, '60, RCGA '69; governor RCGA '61-75; hon. life gov. '78; mem. Canadian Srs GA, American Srs GA, US Eastern GA, Southern Srs GA; res. London, Ont.

GETTY, Don (football); b. 30 Aug 1933, Westmount, Que.; given name: Donald Ross; m. Margaret Inez Mitchell; c. Dale, David, Darin, Derek; UWO, BA; ret'd politician, investment firm owner; qb'd to 2 Eastern titles; starting gd OUAA basketball title teams; teamed with Jackie Parker, Johnny Bright, Normie Kwong in Edmonton backfield '54; led Eskimos to '56 Grey Cup victory over Montreal; topped WIFU in yds-per-completion '59, runnerup to Russ Jackson Cdn player of year; WIFU passing leader '61; 10yr CFL completion avg. .536; dir. Eskimos football club; Alta. MLA '67-80, 2 ministerial portfolios; Premier Alta. '85-92; hon. Chief Whitefish Lake Cree band; past dir. Derrick Golf and Winter Club; officer Order of Canada '99; mem. Eskimos Wall of Honor, UWO W-Club, OUAA Football Legends halls of fame; res. Edmonton, Alta.

GIACOMIN, Ed (hockey); b. 6 Jun 1939, Sudbury, Ont.; ex-goaltender; after failing to stick with Jr A, Detroit Red Wings clubs returned to Sudbury to play 2 seasons Midnight Industrial League; joined EHL Washington Presidents '69, advanced to Providence AHL; spent 7 seasons in minors before joining NHL NYR '65-75; 9 shutouts in 2nd season led Rangers to playoffs; 5 time all-star; traded to Detroit '75-78; NHL record: 289w, 54so, 2.82 goals against avg.; jersey #1 ret'd by NY; mem. AHL, Hockey Heritage North, Hockey halls of fame; res. Ft. Myers, Fla.

GIARDINO, Wayne (football); b. 7 Nov 1943, Peterborough, Ont.; given name: Wayne Maurice; m. Nancy Von Fielitzsch; c. Nicole, David; Florida State, BA; prov. court official; ret'd football exec.; capt. FSU, all-state rb; rejected Dodgers baseball invitation for football scholarship; college baseball world series '65; lb/fb Ottawa '67-76; Gruen Trophy (EFC rookie of year) '67; Hiram Walker Trophy; Schenley outstanding Canadian nominee '71; frequent all-star; mem. 3 Grey Cup winners; dir. player personnel Ottawa '83-87; asst. coach '84; asst. coach UofOtt '90; coach Ottawa Sooners '94; asst coach, dir. player personnel Hamilton '95-96; ass't coach, Orlando, AFL '97; res. Almonte, Ont.

GIBBONS, Pops (softball); b. 24 Aug 1916, Nevis, St. Kitts; d. 2 Jul 1998, Scarborough, Ont.; given name: Percy Walston; m. Irene McGregor; c. Ginger, Nancy, Percy Jr., Shane, Lori, Scott; employed Champion Team Ware; active player in youth; interest in coaching and training remained throughout his life; exceptional coach of young players and was known as "Pops" to all; served as usher Maple Leaf Gardens more than 25yrs; trainer NA Fastpitch Assn. World Series champion Scarborough Royals '96; trainer Toronto Gators '93 ISC world title team; subject of *YTV* special '97; a familiar figure at tournaments throughout Ontario and country working with wide array of teams; to his death he reported daily for duty at Champion Team Ware.

GIBEAU, Marie-Josée (canoeing); b. 2 Nov 1972, Lachine, Que.; m. Ouimet; mem. ntl team '88-91, '93-96; bronze '89 Junior Worlds; gold K-4 500, silver K-2 500 '95, K2, K4 gold '99 PAG; world K-2 200m, K-4 200m champion '95; gold K-2 '98 worlds; competed '96, '00 Olympics; Edmonton Grads team award; res. Lachine, Que.

GIBSON, Bryan (boxing); b. 10 Nov 1947, Kentville, N.S.; given name: Bryan Richard; m. Teresa Ann Dorey; c. Curtis, Chad; stationary engineer; Montreal Expos tryout camp '69; Que. Golden Gloves middleweight champion '71-76; Eastern, ntl titles '74-75; NA light-heavyweight title '75; middleweight bronze '74 East German championships; '76 Eastern ntl middleweight title; mem. '75 PAG, '76 Olympic teams; res. Kentville, Kings Co., N.S.

GIBSON, Cheryl (swimming); b. 28 Jul 1959, Edmonton, Alta.; given name: Cheryl Ann; m. Ralph Brokop; c. Andrew, Lindsay; Arizona State, BSc, CA; UofT LLB; lawyer, accountant; mem. ntl swim team '74-82, '76, '80 Olympic, '75, '79 PAG, '78, '82 CG teams; silver 200m butterfly, 400m IM, bronze 200m backstroke, 200m IM '75 PAG, silver 100m, 200m backstroke, 400m medley relay '79 PAG, silver 400m IM with PB ntl record 4:48.10 '76 Olympics, gold 200m backstroke, bronze 100m backstroke, 400m IM '78 CG; 4 1sts, 1 2nd '77 Canada Cup meet; 2 silvers '78 worlds, setting Commonwealth record 2:14.23 200m backstroke; 2 1sts US ntls '76; 3 1sts, 1 2nd '81 US Intercollegiate; 4 1sts '81 ntls; gold 4x100 medley relay, silver 200m IM '82 CG; 11yrs dir. Swimming Canada; 4yrs Alta. Sport Council Tech Comm.; mem. sponsor comm. '96 World Figure Skating championship; co-chair Swimming World Cup Society; chair. unsuccessful bid by Edmonton to hold '99 World Swimming championship; Alta. Premier's award '77, Velma Springstead Trophy '76, Gov.-Gen.'s silver medal '76, Edmonton athlete of '77, Arizona State female athlete of '81, female swimmer of '76, '78; Edmonton YWCA woman-of-distinction award '98; mem. Cdn Aquatic, Cdn Olympic, Alta., Ariz. State Sports halls of fame; res. Edmonton, Alta.

GIBSON, Doug (hockey/softball); b. 28 Sep 1953, Peterborough, Ont.; given name: Douglas John; 3yrs Peterborough Jr.A, breaking Mickey Redmond's goal-scoring mark; Memorial Cup finalist '72; ctr AHL Rochester Americans '73-80 with NHL stints with Boston Bruins, Washington; mem. Garmisch-Partenkirchen '81 German title team; twice AHL MVP, 1st team all-star; '75 AHL scoring champion; *Hockey News* minor league player of '75; softball standout at 2b and pitching; Peterborough player of '78; mem. Rochester Americans, Peterborough Sports halls of fame; res. Peterborough, Ont.

GIBSON, George (baseball); b. 22 Jul 1880, London, Ont.; d. 25 Jan 1967, London, Ont.; m. Margaret McMurphy; c. Marguerite, George Jr., William; pro baseball player, bricklayer; round face earned him nickname "Mooney"; moved from semi-pro to pro ranks Eastern (later IL) League Buffalo, Montreal; catcher Pittsburgh (NL) '05-16, NY Giants '17-18; ML career record: 1213 games, 3776ab, 295r, 893h, 142db, 49tr, 15hr, 345rbi, 40sb, .236ba; best season '14 batting .285 in 102 games; considered among game's best handlers of pitchers; strong arm made him one of few catchers with 200 assists in single season; 1st player

to catch 150 games single season '09; mgr. Pirates '20-22, '32-34, Chicago Cubs '25; coach Washington '23, Toronto (IL) '34; World Series winner '09, finalist '17; Canada's baseball player of half century '50; all-time all-star catcher with Pirates; mem. Canada's, London Sports, Cdn Baseball halls of fame.

GIBSON, Jack (builder/hockey); b. 10 Sep 1880, Berlin (Kitchener), Ont.; d. 7 Oct 1955, Calgary, Alta.; Detroit Medical School; dentist; outstanding player with OHA intermediate champs '97; instrumental in organizing Portage Lake team '02, capt., leading scorer; recognized for organizing 1st pro league in world, the International League '04 with teams from Houghton, Calumet, Sault Ste. Marie, Mich., and Pittsburgh and Sault Ste. Marie, Ont.; Portage Lakes team, considered one of finest ever assembled challenged Ottawa Silver Seven and Montreal to championship series but were refused; when star players were lured back to Canada he set up dental practice in Calgary; mem. Hockey Hall of Fame.

GIBSON, Jack (builder); b. 27 May 1931, Peterborough, Ont.; given name: John William; served as coach, manager, convenor, pres. PCCHL '61-62; 9yrs mgr. Peterborough Jr. B team; with Neil Thompson operated Peterborough softball teams '61-66; mgr. Mann Cup title teams '66, '73; helped organize semipro league '68, won title '69; mgr. Maryland Arrows in pro league '74-75; 1st team to play in Landover Cap Centre; mgr. Canada's field lacrosse team '67 world championships; mem. Peterborough Sports Hall of Fame; res. Peterborough, Ont.

GIFFORD, Heather (water polo); b. 24 Mar 1956, Ottawa, Ont., m. Shaun Seaman; c. Eben, Logan, Hannah; Queen's, BPhE; goaltender; introduced to water polo Canterbury HS '72; mem. Team Ont. '74-82; mem. Ottawa Water Polo team '73-82; ntl team '77-82; key role in Canada's world championship title '81; made major contribution to sport coaching City of Ottawa jr. women '80-82; v-p Ont. Water Polo Assn. '81-82; player rep. Ont. Water Polo Coaches Comm. '77-81; v-p/dir. responsible for ntl women's team development Water Polo Canada '83-85; commissioner Cdn Water Polo League '83; mem. Ont. Aquatic Hall of Fame; res. Kanata, Ont.

GIGUERE, Nathalie (swimming); b. 16 Jan 1973, Quebec City, Que.; Laval; freestyle, breaststroke specialist; 6 ntl titles; competed '89, '91, '93 Pan-Pacific championships, '91 world, '92 Olympic, '90, '94 CG; gold 200m breaststroke '90 CG; res. Charlesbourg, Que.

GILBERT, Don (curling); b. 28 Jun 1930, St. Thomas, Ont.; d. 4 Oct 1998, St. Thomas, Ont.; given name: Donald Alexander; m. Patricia Marie Anderson; c. Michael, David, Stephen, Jeffrey; UofT, DDS; dentist; 2nd on Ont. Colts title rink '59; skipped Dunker Trophy winner '63 OCA Colts competition; 3rd '61 OCA Gov.-Gen.'s trophy winner; 2 OCA Silver Tankard winners; skip '68 Ont. Brier entry, 6-4 record Kelowna; hon. life mem. St. Thomas CC.

GILBERT, Don (football/coaching); b. 6 Oct 1943, Buffalo, N.Y.; given name: Don Alan; m. Patricia Gale Tananbaum; c. Eric Jonathon, Kara Ann; Buffalo, BEd, MEd; real estate agent; 12 major HS athletic letters, various community awards, 6 major college letters while starring in football, basketball, baseball; Dom Grossi Award (outstanding BuffaloU athlete) '65, Penn State Award (outstanding student-athlete) '65; db/qb Ottawa (CFL) '66-67, Winnipeg '68; head football coach UofOtt '71-75, 5 consecutive conference titles, Canadian College Bowl title '75; CIAU football coach of '75; coach Rough Riders '74 CFL all-star game victory; TV color commentator Buffalo Bills '80; mem. UofOtt Football Hall of Fame; res. East Amherst, N.Y.

GILBERT, Glenroy (t&f/bobsleigh); b. 31 Aug 1968, Port of Spain, Trinidad; m. Syreeta Barnett; c. Ella-Grace; Louisiana State; ntl t&f coach; moved to Canada '76; began competing lj/tj 15; won tj silver '85 jr. ntls; lj gold, tj silver '86; shifted attention to sprints winning PAG 100m gold '95; 2nd to Donovan Bailey's sub-10 second 100 '95 LSU Invitational; 4x100 relay gold '94 CG, '96 Olympics, '95-97 worlds; '93 world silver; 100m PB 10.04 '95, 20.37 in 200 '93; competed '88, '92, '96, '00 summer Olympics, '90, '94 CG, '95, '99 PAG, '89, '94 Francophonie, '93 FISU Games; '99 PAG 4x100 relay silver; mem. 4-man bobsleigh team '94 Olympics; 2 Cdn sr. records; 2 Dick Ellis team awards; Ottawa ACT athlete of '96, athletics award '97; Canadian Olympic Hall of Fame ('96 Oly gold 4x100 relay team); ret'd from competition '01; res. Ottawa, Ont.

GILBERT, Greg (hockey/coaching); b. 22 Jan 1962, Mississauga, Ont.; m. Tammy; c. Lauren, Brenden, Dylan; coach; lw Toronto Marlies '79-81; NHL NYI '82-88, Chicago '88-93, NYR '93-94, St. Louis '94-96; NHL record: 837 scheduled games, 150g, 228a, 133 playoff games, 17g, 33a; 3 Stanley Cup winners; AHL stints with Indianapolis, Springfield; coach Worcester AHL 3yrs; asst. Calgary '00, head coach '01-03; Mississauga (OHL) '03-05; AHL coach of '97; *SN* minor league coach of '97; res. Mississauga, Ont.

GILBERT, Rod (hockey); b. 1 Jul 1941, Montreal, Que.; given name: Rodrigue Gabriel; m. Arunee Leeaphorn; hockey exec.; jr. A Guelph; OHA scoring leader, Red Tilson Memorial Trophy; pro NYR farm system; Rangers regular '62-78; 1st, 2nd team all-star once each; Team Canada '72; with Jean Ratelle, Vic Hadfield formed GAG (goal-a-game) line; NHL career record:1065 scheduled games, 406g, 615a, 79 playoff games, 34g, 33a; West Side Assoc. Trophy NYR MVP; Bill Masterton Memorial Trophy '76; NHL milestone award '82; Lester Patrick trophy '91; NY mgr. community relations; youth hockey clinic instructor; jersey #7 ret'd by NY; mem. Hockey Hall of Fame; res. New York, N.Y.

GILBEY, Janice (water polo); b. 10 Oct 1957, Ottawa, Ont.; d. 7 Feb 1984, Toronto, Ont.; Algonquin Coll.; launched competitive career Canterbury HS '72; joined Ottawa league '73; Team Ont. '75-79, ntl team '79-82; world championships gold '81; mem./asst. coach Toronto Golden Jets '83; v-p women's development Ont. Water Polo Assn. '83; diagnosed with leukemia '83; mem. Ont. Aquatic Hall of Fame.

GILES, Peter (canoeing); b. 18 Apr 1970, London, Ont.; given name: Peter Mark; m. Kate Latham; c. Adam; Dalhousie BSc, SFU, Stanford PhD; systems engineer; mem. ntl team from '88; '91 PAG bronze K-1, K-2, K-4 1000; gold

K-4 500, silver K-4 200 Milano World Cup '96; competed '96 Olympics; res. Halifax, N.S.

GILES, Steve (canoeing); b. 4 Jul 1972, St. Andrews, N.B.; m. Angela Julien; c. Macy; Dalhousie, BEng.; electrical engineer; mem. ntl team from '89; mem. '92, '96, '00 (bronze C-1 1000), '04 Olympic teams; silver C-2 1000, C-1 500, 200 '96 Milano World Cup; competed 7 World championships earning bronze C-1 500m '93, '02, gold C-1 1000m '98; C-1 1000m gold, 500m silver '99 PAG; '99 Duisburg regatta C-1 1000m gold; res. Dartmouth, N.S.

GILL, Nicolas (judo); b. 24 Apr 1972, Montreal, Que.; Quebec; began competing age 6; mem. ntl team '89-05; 10 ntl titles; 86kg bronze '92 Olympics, gold '94 US Open, '95, '99 Pan-Am, Hungarian Open '95, Belgian Open '96, Francophone 100kg '01, '02 CG; swept 5 -100kg gold Budapest '03; gold '02 Pan-Am judo championships; competed '89, '01 Francophone, '90, '02 CG, '91, '95, '99, '03 (silver) PAG, '92, '96, '00, '04 (flagbearer) Olympic Games, '91, '93, '95 worlds; 1st Cdn to win worlds silver '93, bronze '95; 4th degree black belt; Viscount Alexander trophy '92; res. Montreal, Que.

GILL, Todd (hockey); b. 9 Nov 1965, Cardinal, Ont.; m. Krista; c. Chloe, Madeline; def. Windsor (OHL) '82-85; AHL St. Catharines '85-86, Newmarket '85-88, Cincinnati '00-01, Springfield, Norfolk '02-03, Lausitzer, Germany '03-04; NHL Toronto '84-96, San Jose '96-98, St. Louis '98-99, Detroit '98-00, '01, Phoenix '99-00, Colorado '01-02, Chicago '02-03, Florida '04; NHL totals 1007 scheduled games, 82g, 270a, 1214pim, 103 playoff games, 7g, 30a, 193pim; res. Germany.

GILLETT, George (softball); b. 21 Feb 1934, Hoyt, Sunbury Co. N.B.; m. Anna; CFB truck driver; coach/mgr./prompter/exec. more than 40yrs; coached 37 provincial, 14 interprovincial title teams; zone dir. Softball NB; organized '84 Eastern Cdn intermediate championships; Joe Garagan award for contribution to greater Fredericton area softball; Softball NB Charlie O'Brien Memorial award; mem. NB Sports Hall of Fame; res. Hoyt, N.B.

GILLICK, Pat (baseball/administration); b. 22 Aug 1937, Chico, Calif.; m. Doris Sander; c. Kimberley; SouthernCal, BSc; baseball exec.; mem. USC college world series titlists '58; semipro Edmonton '58; 5ys lhp Baltimore farm system, 45-32 record; asst. farm dir., scouting dir. Houston '64-73; co-ordinator player dev., scouting NY Yankees '74-76; v-p player personnel Toronto '76; exec. v-p baseball operations '77-94; GM Baltimore '95-98, Seattle '99-03; Canada's baseball man of '83; 2 ML baseball exec-of-yr awards; mem. Cdn Baseball Hall of Fame; res. Seattle, Wash.

GILLIES, Clark (hockey); b. 7 Apr 1954, Moose Jaw, Sask.; stockbroker; played minor baseball 3yrs in Houston organization; lw 3yrs Regina Pats, 1 Memorial Cup, WCHL 1st team all-star; drafted NYI with Bryan Trottier, Mike Bossy formed Trio Grande line; capt. NYI at 22 served 21/2 yrs; tied NHL record 3 consec. game-winning goals vs. Buffalo '77 playoffs; 2 1st team all-star; competed '79 Challenge Cup series, silver '81 Canada Cup; 4 consec. Stanley Cup winners; noted for great 2-way play as power forward, hard work, leadership; NHL NYI '74-86, Buffalo '86-88; NHL totals 958 scheduled games, 319g, 378a, 164 playoff games, 47g, 47a; NYI ret'd jersey 9; ardent golfer; nickname "Jethro"; mem. Hockey Hall of Fame; res. New York, N.Y.

GILLIS, Duncan (t&f); b. 3 Jan 1883, Cape Breton, N.S.; d. 1965, Vancouver, B.C.; policeman; silver 16lb hammer throw '12 Olympics; BC hammer record unsurpassed until '67; ntl heavyweight wrestling title; flag-bearer '12 summer Olympics; mem. Cdn Olympic, BC Sports halls of fame.

GILLIS, Eddie (baseball); b. 6 Oct 1916, New Waterford, N.S.; given name: Eddie Martin; Dalhousie; ret'd teacher, baseball coach; Triple A rated Cape Breton Colliery pro league at 17; 5'5.5", 135lb 2b; all-star rookie season; outstanding player awards '35, '48 all-star games; player-coach Waterford Strands '39, 2 Cape Breton titles; coached New Waterford Maritime bantam champs '70, int. champs '38, NS juvenile champs '60, bantam champs '45; Halifax ntl jr. champs '76, Kentville ntl jr. finalists '62-63, NS ntl jr. finalists '64, NS entry '77 Canada Games; NS juve. title '61, sr. '60, '63, Maritime midget '60, 7 NS HS title teams; Maritime jr. '53, NS sr. '80, runnerup ntl championships '81; pro scout Milwaukee Braves, St. Louis Cardinals; baseball dir. Cooper Sports Camp '70; conducted successful boxing clubs Cape Breton, Kentville, Halifax 20yrs producing numerous amateur, pro titlists at provincial, ntl levels; mem. famed Caledonia rugby team; mem. NS Sports Hall of Fame; res. Kentville, N.S.

GILMOUR, Billy (hockey); b. 21 Mar 1885, Ottawa, Ont.; d. 13 Mar 1959, Montreal, Que.; given name: Hamilton Livingstone; m. Merle Woods; c. Germaine; McGill, engineer; Ottawa Silver Seven '02-06, rw 3 consecutive Stanley Cup winners; 10 goals 7 games, 5 in 4 playoff contests rookie season; Montreal Victorias Eastern Canada Amateur HA '07; Ottawa Senators '08-09, won Stanley Cup, 11 goals 11 games; ret'd 6 seasons; tried '15-16 2-game comeback with Senators, sccored against George Vezina, then ret'd; mem. Ottawa, Hockey halls of fame.

GILMOUR, Bob (skiing/coaching); b. 1 Jan 1935, Rosemere, Que.; given name: Robert; m. Gloria Glen; c. Steve, Rodney, Brenda; pres. Gilmour Sport; began competing at 11; mem. Nordik Ski Club; won Laurentian zone, Que, Cdn jr., sr. race titles; Taschereau downhill '53, foreran course '03; won Que. Kandarar '56; mem. '60 Olympic team; ntl team '58-62; coached ntl, prov, zone clubs '62-72; raced pro/masters '60-96; served varied exec. roles ntl ski team, alpine ski assn., Que., Laurentian zone; coached Nancy Greene program; rookie instructor award '94, instructor of ;'03 award; level 111 CSIA, level 1 CFSA as mem. Cdn Ski Instructors Alliance; spent life in ski supplies/service industry; mem. Laurentian, Cdn Ski halls of fame; res. Mont. Tremblant, Que.

GILMOUR, Buddy (harness racing); b. 23 Jul 1932, Lucan, Ont.; given name: William; m. Gwen Harner; c. 4; ret'd harness race driver; drove first race '52 Dufferin Park; first win with Money Maker same year; Batavia Downs fire '61 destroyed almost entire stable; Roosevelt Raceway dash winning record 1:56 '73; through '95 5380 winners with purses totalling more than $44 million; more than 40 sub-2-min. miles; twice Al B. White Trophy Roosevelt dash winner; Roosevelt Futurity with Strike Out '71; as trainer had greatest success with George Campos-owned pacer Myakka Prince

'73 tying Roosevelt track record for aged geldings with 1:59 mile, $166,980 in winnings; 2nd driver in history to top $1.8 million single season winnings '73 (other Hervé Filion); more than 50 major stakes race victories, including 12 in '84-85 with On The Road Again; mem. Cdn Horse Racing Hall of Fame; res. Westbury, N.Y.

GILMOUR, Doug (hockey); b. 25 Jun 1963, Kingston, Ont.; m. Amy Pavel; c. Jake, Maddison, Tyson; ctr Cornwall Jr. '81-83; OHL 1st team all-star, MVP '83; MVP '97 Canada Cup gold medal Team Canada; drafted by St. Louis '82; NHL with St. Louis '83-88, Calgary '88-91, Toronto '92-97, '03, New Jersey '97-98, Chicago '98-99, Buffalo '00-01, Montreal '01-02; Selke trophy '93; 2 NHL all-star games; NHL record: 1474 scheduled games, 450g, 964a, 182 playoff games, 60g, 127a; cameo appearance in movie *Bogus*; res. Toronto, Ont.

GIRARD, Hugo (powerlifting); b. 20 Dec 1971, Ste-Anne-de-Portneuf, Que.; given name: Hugo Joseph; m. Nadine Tremblay; police officer; considered one of strongest men in world; holds many ntl. world powerlifting records in super-heavyweight category; ntl strongest man title '99; 3 world power muscle titles; competed 4 world's strongest man competitions placing 2nd '01; 2 NA titles; won Strongman super series title '02; North Bay, Finnish GP titles; 5 ntl titles; competition advisor for 2 Cdn. championships; competition organizer for the '01 Gatineau Hot Air Balloon Strongman; preparation for a major competition featured in '02 documentary *Strongman*; Canada's Economic Development Ambassador '03; pres. Cdn Fed. Of Strength Athletes; competitions organizer and major promoter of sport; excellent orator; res. Gatineau, Que.

GIRARD, Ken (golf/hockey); b. 18 Dec 1936, Toronto, Ont.; given name: Kenneth John; m. Vivian Spencer; c. Lori Ann, Brian; golf pro London Hunt; won Ont. PGA title '68; 2 Ont. PGA titles; won both jr., sr. div. Bermuda titles; 3yrs jr. hockey Toronto Marlboros; mem. 2 Memorial Cup teams; played 7 NHL games with TML '56-60; res. London, Ont.

GIRLETZ, Wilf (rodeo); b. 28 Sep 1928, Dewinton, Alta; d. 17 May 1995, Hanna, Alta.; given name: Wilfred Gordon; m. Maxine; c. Kevin, Ray, Glenda, Randy; rancher; began rodeo career age 15; 5 ntl bull riding titles; 3 ntl all-around (AA) titles; became stock contractor from '84 raising rodeo bulls at Youngstown, Alta., ranch; died of injuries suffered in riding accident; mem. Cdn Rodeo Hall of Fame.

GISIGER, Michelle (lacrosse); b. 17 Aug 1960, Winnipeg, Man.; given name: Michelle Marie Lynne; UMan, BPhE, BEd; teacher; with Roger Dawes cycled Winnipeg to PEI on tandem bicycle '84; mem. Man., ntl women's FH team '79-84; UMan on FH scholarship '80-85; Man. soccer player '85; div. A sr. women's soccer, basketball player; mem. Man. sr. women's field lacrosse team '85-92; competed with ntl team '89, '93 World Cup, '92 William & Mary tour, Scotland, England, Wales tour; spent summer '91 teaching phys ed Mali as part of CTF special project to help developing countries; res. Winnipeg, Man.

GLADSTONE, Jim (rodeo); b. 18 Nov 1942, Cardston, Alta.; c. 5; Lethbridge Coll., UAlta, LLB; lawyer; grandfather James 1st Alta. native senator; father Fred ntl calf roping champion; competed in 1st rodeo age 11; turned pro '60 establishing reputation on Indian semi-pro circuit; Indian Rodeo Cowboy Assn. calf roping titles '63, '65, added steer wrestling, all-around titles '68; 3 ntl calf roping titles; qualified for 8 ntl rodeo finals, 4 NA finals; scored Canada's 1st world victory in timed event '77; surpassed Kenny McLean's 10yr record for career earnings '61; Indian Rodeo's man of yr '78; mem. Cdn Pro Rodeo, Alta. Sports halls of fame; res. Alderside, Alta.

GLASSER, Red (bowling); b. 5 Feb 1931, Regina, Sask.; given name: Anton; m. Clotilde Brown; c. Gerald, Barry, Janyce, Anthony, Donald, Douglas, Cathy; ret'd auto body-man; 10-pin bowler; 6 Sask. singles, doubles titles; ntl singles '62, doubles '64; perfect 300 game '62; Cdn rep. ABC Masters '62, World Invitational '63, World FIQ tournament '71; instructor, v-p Regina Men's 10-pin Assn.; tackle '40 ntl jr. Navy title football team; mem. Sask. Sports Hall of Fame; res. Regina, Sask.

GLASSER, Sully (football); b. 25 Oct. 1922, Regina, Sask.; d. 1 Aug 1986, Regina, Sask.; given name: Sullivan John; m. Terry Hier; c. Donna, Brenda, Sullivan, Jill, Marsha, Grant; chartered life underwriter; backfielder. Roughriders '46-57; WFC all-star 1946; scored td vs. Ottawa '51 Grey Cup; 6yrs sr. baseball, jr. hockey.

GLAZIER, Lori (snowboarding); b. 19 Sep 1971, Oshawa, Ont.; began snowboarding age 19; 2 ntl championships; placed 5th US Open; mem. '98 Olympic team; silver '02 Whistler WC; res. Courtice, Ont./Whistler, B.C.

GLEN, Kathy (synchro swim); 9 Jan 1966, Madison, Wisc.; introduced to synchro age 10; 1st mem. Vancouver Aquasonics to achieve ntl team status '84; with Christine Larsen '90 CG duet gold; with Lisa Alexander '91 world championship duet bronze; res. Port Moody, B.C.

GLENN, Steve (football); b. 4 May 1971, Ottawa, Ont.; m. Janna; c. Brianna, Mackenzie, Connor; Ottawa BA; played peewee/bantam in Victoria, Richmond, B.C. (prov. title); East Gloucester bantams; Cairine Wilson HS; 3yrs capt. UofO; 3 OQIFC all-star, Gee-Gees def. player-of-yr/MVP awards; CFL long snapper/linebacker Montreal '96, BC '96-98, Winnipeg '99-01, Ottawa '02-04; 1 Grey Cup final; Ottawa special team player of '02; res. Orleans, Ont.

GLESBY, Tom (boxing); b. 17 Jul 1969, Winnipeg, Man.; mem. Napper's Boxing Club; Cdn amateur heavyweight champion '88, '91; '88 Bulgarian tournament title; '91 Canada Cup champion; mem. '88, '92 Olympic, '91 PAG teams; pro record 20-1-1; stripped of Cdn heavyweight title '97 for failure to defend title in 3yrs; res. Welland, Ont.

GLOAG, Norm (basketball); b. 9 Jul 1919, Vancouver, B.C.; d. 11 Jun 1997, Vancouver, B.C.; given name: Norman Grainger; m. Elizabeth Jones; c. John, Mary; ret'd airline sales mgr.; sr. men's basketball Vancouver '38-48 excluding '42-45; mem. Cloverleafs Sr. A team Philippines tour, '48 ntl titlists; mgr. ntl team '56 Olympics, '59 '62 world tournament; Cdn basketball rep. '60, '64, '68, '72, '76, '80 Olympics; chair. Van. ABA '51-85, 2 terms pres. CABA '70-74; dir. Basketball Canada; mem. PAG committee; dir. COA, Vancouver-Garibaldi Olympic comm.; mem. women's commission FIBA; v-p Central Board FIBA '76-

80, mem. Central Board '80; Air Canada Amateur Sports Exec. of '75; mem. Cdn Basketball, Cdn Olympic, BC Sports halls of fame.

GLOVER, Fred (hockey/coaching); b. 5 Jan 1928, Toronto, Ont.; d. 16 May 2001, Cleveland, Ohio; given name: Frederick Austin; ctr Galt OHA '45-47, Omaha USHL '47-48, Indianapolis AHL '48-52, Cleveland '52-68, player-coach '62-68, NHL Detroit '48-52, Chicago '52-53; coach Cleveland '68-70, California Seals '70-74, Los Angeles NHL '71-72; AHL coaching record 96-207-53; twice led AHL scorers; held AHL records games played 1201, goals 520, assists 914, points 1334, 16 20-goal seasons, 120 playoff games; 6 AHL all-star games; 5 Calder Cup titles; 3 Les Cunningham, 2 John Sollenberger awards; Cleveland ret'd jersey 9.

GLOVER, Penny (squash); b. 18 Aug 1942, Cardish, Wales; Welsh Inst. of Advanced Technology; labor relations mgr.; Ont. open title '71; 7 Ont. closed titles; mem. ntl women's squash team Australian tour '75; ntl veterans (40+) '83-84, (45+) titles '89-90; Level A official; Ont. Sports Achievement award '83; res. Ottawa, Ont.

GLYNN, Hugh (administration); b. 26 Jul 1925, Richard, Sask.; m. Joan Penfold; c. Michael, Sheryl, Kelly; ret'd sports exec.; refrigeration, heating mechanic, coached baseball, minor hockey and competed in figure skating; served in various executive capacities at club, Ntl levels; exec. mgr. CFSA '66-74; v-p, pres. National Sport & Recreation Centre '74-92; key role in design, establishment of NSRC on Naismith Dr., Gloucester; res. Nepean, Ont.

GMOSER, Hans (skiing/mountaineering); b. 7 Jul 1932, Braunau, Austria; given name: Johann Wolfgang; m. Margaret Grace MacGougan; c. Conrad, Robson; attended Harvard Business School; mountain guide, businessman; 1st ascent of 16,525ft. Mt. Blackburn, Alaska; 1st ascent Wickersham Wall on Mt. McKinley; 2nd ascent East Ridge Mt. Logan (19,850ft. Canada's highest); developed alpine ski touring Western Canadian mountains, helicopter skiing Bugaboos, Cariboos, Monashees; hon. pres. Association of Cdn Mountain Guides; hon. mem. International Federation of Mountain Guides Association; mem. Order of Canada, Cdn Skiing Hall of Fame; res. Banff, Alta.

GODBOUT, François (tennis); b. 10 Apr 1938, Montreal, Que.; m. Sibylla Hesse; c. Louis, Christian; Sherbrooke, BA, Montreal, LLB; lawyer; Que., ntl jr. titles '56; mem. '59-64, '69 Davis Cup teams; pres. QTF '69-71; secty. Que. Athletic Fed. '72-77; v-p COA from '78; mem. Air Canada Awards selection comm. from '78; v-p Tennis Canada '80; mem. Calgary Olympics comm., '86 soccer World Cup bid comm.; mem. Que. Sports, Cdn Tennis halls of fame; res. Montreal, Que.

GOERMANN, Elfriede (gymnastics/coaching); b. 30 Oct 1937, Rastenburg, Germany; given name: Elfriede Wolff; m. Wolfgang Goermann; c. Monica, Jens; Ntl, Man. team coach '77-86; head coach, program dir. Winnipeg Gymnastics Centre '77-87; chair Man. Coaches Assn. '82-83; chair Man. provincial judges '67-72; served as international gymnastics judge '74-80, including judge at '76 Olympics; mem. high performance judges assembly; judge Western Cdn championships '84-87; life mem. Canadian Gymnastics

Federation; brevet judge of women's gymnastics, top international judging award; mem. Man. Sports Hall of Fame; res. Winnipeg, Man.

GOERMANN, Monica (gymnastics); b. 1 Sep 1964, Winnipeg, Man.; m. Michael Tomlinson; c. Maija Danielle; Man. BPhE; gym teacher, operates dance studio; coached by mother Elfriede; silver all-around '77 junior nationals; all-around silver '78 CG; gold all-around, team, uneven bars, silver floor exercises, bronze beam '79 PAG; mem. '80 Olympic team; '79 ntl all-around, beam, floor exercises, uneven bars titles, '80 Swiss invitational team gold, all-around, floor exercise bronze; tied for gold floor exercises '81 UK vs. Canada meet; Vince Leah Memorial award '99; subject *NFB* documentary; Man. Gymnastic Assn. Sports excellence award; mem. Man. Sports Hall of Fame; res. Winnipeg, Man.

GOFF, Ken (boxing); b. 2 Mar 1910, Bournemouth, Eng.; d. 26 Jan 1993, Regina, Sask.; given name: Kenneth Horace George; m. Margaret Dobson; c. Beverly, George, Kenneth James (d), Peggy, Penny; Paragon Business College; accountant, Regina deputy treasurer; fought as featherweight, lightweight '30-34; Sask. champion, ntl semifinalist '34; began coaching '36 Regina Olympic Club, Regina City Police Club '44-49; asst. coach '48 Olympic, mgr.-coach '56 Olympic teams; trained ntl champions Claude Warwick, Adam Faul; Regina father of '60; pres. Regina Boxing Club '73; Regina B'nai B'rith sports personality of '81; known as Mr Boxing in Sask; mem. Sask. Sports Hall of Fame.

GOLAB, Tony (football); b. 17 Jan 1919, Windsor, Ont.; given name: Anthony Charles; wid.; c. Michael, Keri-Ann; UofPuget Sound; ret'd RCAF Wing Cdr., Sport Canada official; basketball Dominion champion Windsor Alumni, Ottawa Glebe Grads; football Sarnia Imperials '38 ORFU champions; fb Rough Riders '39-41, '45-50; '41 Jeff Russel Trophy (Big Four MVP); '41 *CP* award Canada's outstanding athlete; 9 times all-Cdn; 4 Grey Cup finals, '40 winner; coached Hamilton ORFU Panthers '52-53, RMC '54-57, 3 successive titles; Atlantic Football Conf. v-p '59; GM Alouettes '68-69; consultant Sport Canada '72-84; nicknamed "Golden Boy"; Lionel Conacher trophy '41; mem. Order of Canada, Ottawa, Cdn Forces, Cdn Football, Canada's, Royal Cdn Legion, Windsor-Essex Sports halls of fame; res. Aylmer, Que.

GOLD, Otto (coaching); b. 18 May 1909, Prague, Czechoslovakia; d. Apr 1977, Toronto, Ont.; Prague novice '19, jr '20 figure skating titles; won 1 novice, 5 jr, 1 sr singles, 1 pairs European titles; ret'd from competition '30; began teaching in Switzerland '32; taught in Prague '34-35; moved to England '36 joining Coliseum skating show '37; emigrated to Canada '38; professional Minto Skating Club Ottawa '38-46; pioneered summer skating schools in Kitchener '40; taught at Vancouver/New Westminster '44-50; taught in Toronto from '50; helped launch career of Dorothy Hamill at Norwalk, Conn.; students included: Donald Jackson, Donald Gilchrist, Frances Dafoe, Norris Bowden, Barbara Ann Scott and Mary Rose Thacker; mem. Cdn Figure Skating Hall of Fame.

GOLDEN, Shira (wheelchair basketball); 2 Jan 1971, Toronto, Ont,; Waterloo BSc, SFU MRM, UBC MLA; land

planner; ntl team from '98; gold worlds '02, bronze '04 Paralympics; with BC Breakers CWBL silver '98, bronze '04; res. Vancouver, B.C.

GOLDHAM, Bob (hockey); b. 12 May 1922, Georgetown, Ont.; d. 6 Sep 1991, Toronto, Ont.; given name: Robert John; m. Elinor Platt; c. Patricia, Susan, Barbara; def Toronto Marlboros jrs.; pro Hershey, Washington, Pittsburgh (AHL), Toronto '41-46 (excluding '42-45 Navy WW2); Black Hawks '48, Red Wings '51-56; mem. 5 league champion, 5 Stanley Cup winners; 2nd team all-star def; NHL record: 650 scheduled games, 28g, 143a, 66 playoff games, 3g, 14a; coached St. Michael's Majors 3yrs; mem. Minto Cup lacrosse title team Orillia Terriers '41; mem. Hamilton Tigers lacrosse team '41-46.

GOLDSWORTHY, Bill (hockey); b. 24 Aug 1944, Kitchener, Ont.; d. 24 May 1996 Minneapolis, Minn.; given name: William Alfred; c. Tammy Lynn, William; rw Niagara Falls OHA '62-65 1 Memorial Cup winner; Oklahoma CHL, Buffalo AHL '66-67; NHL Boston '65-67, Minnesota '57-76, NYR '77-78; stints with Memphis CHL, Team Canada '72 Summit series, New Haven AHL, Indianapolis, Edmonton WHA to retirement '79; NHL totals 771 scheduled games, 283g, 258a, 40 playpff games, 18g, 19a; turned to coaching San Antonio CHL; introduced Goldy Shuffle move after scoring goal; died of complications from AIDS; Minnesota ret'd jersey 8.

GOMEZ, Avelino (horse racing); b. Oct 1928, Havana, Cuba; d. 21 Jun 1980, Toronto, Ont.; m. Patricia; c. Avelino Jr., Matthew, Jackie; jockey; several victories in US, Canada through '58, returned to Cuba investing in business, real estate; lost all in Castro revolution; Canadian citizen '64; 6 ntl racing titles; led NA riders with 318 victories '66 with .32 highest percentage ever for NA champ; 1st Cdn. jockey to win 300 races single season; 4 Queen's Plate winners, Lyford Cay '57, Victoria Park '60, Tilted Hero '66, Jumpin' Joseph '69; flamboyant crowd pleaser nicknamed "Go Go Gomez, El Perfecto, Cuban Hawk"; defied death threats riding Victoria Park '60 Queen's Plate; at time of death, (of injuries in 3-horse Woodbine spill), ranked 7th among race-winning jockeys on world list with more than 4000 winners; mem. Etobicoke, Canada's Sports; Canadian Horse Racing halls of fame.

GOOD, Norah (t&f); b. 10 Jun 1957, Ottawa, Ont.; m. Brent Broughton; c. Jared, Neal, Matthew; health care worker; visually challenged athlete; 400m, 800m, 1500m, 3000m running titles, 3000m walk title '83 Canadian Games for Physically Disabled; ntl 3000m run record; 3000m run title '84 international Games for Disabled, silver 1500m; mem. East Ottawa Lions TC; participated in '87 Olympic torch run; res. Ottawa, Ont.

GOODFELLOW, Ebbie (hockey); b. 9 Apr 1906, Ottawa. Ont.; d. 10 Sep 1985, Sarasota, Fla.; given name: Ebenezer Ralston; m. Rosalind Sloan (d); c. Ebbie Ramsey, Douglas, Margaret; all-star ctr Ottawa Montagnards; pro Detroit organization; all-star Olympics International League '28-29; ctr/def Red Wings '29-43; coached Wings during '42 Stanley Cup finals vs. Toronto; coach Black Hawks '50-52; Hart Trophy (MVP) '40; twice 1st team, once 2nd team all-star; mem. 3 Stanley Cup winners; NHL record: 575 scheduled games, 134g, 190a, 45 playoff games, 8g, 8a; led American Div. scorers '30-31; mem. Hockey Hall of Fame selection comm.; mem. Ottawa, Michigan, Hockey halls of fame.

GOODINGS, Thomas (builder); b. 20 Apr 1964, Montreal, Que; given name: Thomas John Talbot; Algonquin Coll, Intl Academy of Design; graphic designer; co-coach McGill women's hockey '87-89; asst./head coach Ottawa Sledge-hammers '90-98; dir. of coaches Sledge Hockey Canada '93-98; asst./head coach Cdn Sledge Hockey team '92-02; from '02 board mem. IPC sledgehockey comm.; involved in prov., world, paralympic, invitational competitions '92-02; 6 gold, 2 silver, 3 bronze; res. Kanata, Ont.

GOODMAN, Russell (skiing); b. 5 May 1953, Montreal, Que.; c. Anna, Geoffrey; McGill ; chartered accountant, managing partner Price Waterhouse; international alpine status '73, best international slalom ranking among Canadians Feb '73-May '75; 10th '74 slalom world championships St. Moritz, best finish to that time by Canadian male skier in Olympic, World Cup or world championship competition; runnerup '72 ntl slalom final, '74-75 GS; '75 Can-Am GS, ntl spring slalom Rossland, B.C., Hunter Mountain Can-Am GS, Waterville Valley Can-Am dual slalom; 3rd Can-Am overall '75; mem. European Cup team '73-74; 4th Andora slalom '73, 7th Caspoggio, Sella Nevea, Czechoslovakia, slaloms '73; 6th Sella Nevea GS, 9th slalom '74; pres. Red Birds Ski Club Mt. Tremblant; mem. Canadian Ski Instructors Alliance; res. Pointe Claire, Que.

GOODYEAR, Scott (motorsport); b. 20 Dec 1959, Toronto, Ont.; given name: Donald Scott; m. Leslie; c. Christopher, Michael, Haley; race driver, driving school owner, operator; began kart racing age 9; won 14 Ntl, NA karting titles '69-76; entered Formula Ford circuit '80 winning series title, Cdn Drivers Assn driver-of-year; Cdn Formula Ford titles '81-82; competed on Formula 2000, Trans Am circuit '83-84; placed 4th '85 Pro Sports 2000 series championships; drove in '86 Rothman's Porsche Turbo Cup series, earned 2nd RDA driver of year title; won 5 of 9 starts, series championship in Formula Atlantic series for Houston-based Tom Mitchell team; passed CART rookie test '87, placed 8th Toronto Molson Indy, earned $119,479 in 7 CART races; 3rd in GTO div. of Daytona 24hrs; won 3 of 8 races and Rothman's Porsche Turbo Cup championship '88; successful '89 Formula Atlantic series led to inclusion on McDonnell Racing team; joined Budweiser/King team; lack of sponsor left him sidelined '95 season; Walker team '96; joined IRL '97 with Treadway team; '98 Panther Racing team owned by NFL qb Jim Harbaugh; Team Cheever '01; qualified for 1st Indianapolis 500 race '90, runnerup '92, '97; won '92, '94 Michigan 500, '99 Phoenix 200; won fastest race in IRL history with record speed avg. 175.276mph '00; res. Newmarket, Ont./Carmel, Ind.

GOOLD, Billy (hockey); b. 16 Mar 1930, Ottawa, Ont.; given name: William Frederick; m. Joyce; c. Greg, Jeffrey, Amy; ret'd Sears-Roebuck; excelled in football/hockey Ottawa Tech title teams; played jr. Ottawa Montagnards, Senators (city title); center 12yrs Montreal organization with Memorial Cup champ jr. Canadiens '50, sr. Royals, Halifax Atlantics ('53 Atlantic Cup); Cincinnati Mohawks, capt, player-coach, all-star center, coach '53-58; twice team scoring leader; 4 straight IHL Turner Cup titles; IHL record:

302 scheduled games, 111g, 255a; mem. Cincinnati Hockey Hall of Fame; res. Cincinnati, Ohio.

GOPLEN, Henrietta (speed skating); b. 14 Jul 1932, Saskatoon, Sask.; given name: Henrietta Barbara Flora Ann Mackay; m. Bernard Peter Goplen; c. Gary Bernard, Craig Eldon, Gordon Robert, Barbara Lynn (d); UofSask BSc; home economist; participated in basketball, t&f, volleyball; began speed skating age 10; city titles '43-46; Alta indoor/ outdoor title '48; set Sask 3000m record; heavy involvement in community activities; served on UofSask., senate '79-84; active role in varied capacities with Saskatoon Lions, Saskatchewan, Cdn Amateur Speed Skating Assn '42-83; Level II coaching certificate; coach Saskatoon Lions '75-83; judge '88 Olympics, '87 world short-track championships; active mem. Participaction Saskatoon '73-80; delegate to Participaction conference Sweden '79; mgr. '83, '87, CdM '86 Winter Games; pres. Sask Sports Hall of Fame '88; v-p CASSA '88-92, pres. '94; chair. awards comm. '97-98; hon life mem. Saskatoon Lions SSC; '82 Sask SS coach of yr; Century 100 sports award, CASSA Centennial medal, Dairy Producers merit award; John Hurdis award; authored *Saskatchewan's Sportsman Gourmet Guide* cook book; mem. UofSask Sports Wall, Saskatoon Sports Hall of Fame; res. Saskatoon, Sask.

GORBUS, Glen (baseball); b. 8 Jul 1930, Drumheller, Alta.; d. 12 Jun 1990, Calgary, Alta.; given name: Glen Edward; c. Kriston, Kari, Kandis; sales mgr. catering co.; pro Brooklyn Dodgers organization '49; Class D Medford, Ore., Class C Bisbee-Douglas, Class A Pueblo, AA Fort Worth '49-54; drafted by Cincinnati '55, traded to Philadelphia same season; split '56 between Phillies, Triple A Miami; traded to St. Louis '57, spent part of season Triple A Omaha; sold to L.A. Dodgers '58, spent season Triple A Spokane; tired of life in minors, ML record 117 games, 277ab, 29r, 66h, 13db, 1tr, 4hr,29bi, 0sb, .238ba; ret'd '59; world record longest baseball throw 445'10" Omaha '57; mem. Alta Sports Hall of Fame.

GORDON, Frances (basketball); b. 1915, Red Deer, Alta.; d. 14 Apr 2004, Red Deer, Alta.; given name: Frances Marie; m. Oswin Clifford Mills (d); c. Brian Arthur, Gerry Douglas; Edmonton Normal School; ret'd teacher; mem. famed Edmonton Grads '36-37; mem. Canadian Basketball, Alta. Sports halls of fame.

GORDON, Jackie (hockey); b. 3 Mar 1928, Winnipeg, Man.; given name: John; ret'd hockey exec.; 17yrs player/ coach/mgr Cleveland (AHL), 4 Calder Cup winners; New Haven (AHL) '49-50, Cincinnati (AHL) '50-51, brief stints NYR '48-51; 4yrs. asst. GM Rangers; coached Minnesota 3 seasons, part of 2 others, some scouting, GM '74-78; AGM Vancouver '79-84, GM '85-86, sr. v-p '87, sr. advisor '87-91; NHL coaching record: 290 league games, 116-124-50 ties, 25 playoff games 11-14 ; mem. Man. Hockey Hall of Fame; res. Vancouver, B.C.

GORDON, Megan (diving); b. 12 Apr 1971, West Vancouver, B.C.; m. Mike Parker; c. Madelaine; UBC, BComm, French immersion; agent NSB; competitive swimmer '78-82; competitive gymnast '78-84; began competitive diving age 9; mem. jr. ntl team '81-86, sr. ntl team '89-96; 5 sr. ntl 10m silver medals; bronze Volksbank Intl, silver Bolzano

Intl '93; 5th '91 PAG silver '93, 6th '95 FISU games, 5th '94 Goodwill Games; Olympic alternate '92; BC athlete award '85-92; BC govt passport to education scholarship '86-89; Nancy Greene scholarship '89, '92; BC best-ever athlete '88; BC flag bearer Western Canada Games '87; motivational speaker BC Esteem Team; coaching at all levels; res. Vancouver, B.C.

GORDON, Paige (diving); b. 25 Apr 1973, N. Vancouver, B.C.; m. Eddie Parenti; UBC; gymnast, began diving age 8; mem. ntl jr team; medalled at jr. worlds, jr Can-Am-Mex series; swept 3 Canada Games title '89; mem. ntl sr team '90-96; bronze '90, silver '94 CG, silver '91 PAG, '93 FISU Games; mem. '92, '96 Olympic, '90, '94 CG, '91 PAG teams; 4 ntl 10m, 3 ntl 3m titles; 4th ranked 3m in world; sole Cdn invited to participate in '94 Goodwill Games; 2 Italian outstanding-diver awards; BC jr athlete of '89; Elaine Tanner award '91; BC sr athlete of '93; with sister Megan, mem. BC Esteem Team; res. Palo Alto, Calif.

GORDON, Taylor (coaching/boxing); b. 16 Sep 1931, Melfort, Sask.; m. Greta Marina Blackmore; c. Dwain Keith, Ann Marina, Wayne Ephraim; boxing coach; ret'd as CPO after 25yr RCN career; coached ntl team 5 Olympic, 4 PAG, CG, 4 world championships; head coach and/or mgr. Team Canada 5 NA championships, 1 Goodwill, Australian Games, 5 Canada, 4 President's, 2 King's, 2 World Cups, 13 major international tournaments; asst. tech. dir. '67 PAG; coaching instructor Colorado Olympic training centre '82; tech. dir. Olympic qualification tournament '96; field supervisor '96 Olympics; coached Chris Clarke to '75 PAG gold; son Wayne Olympic team capt '84, asst. coach '92 providing 1st father-son combinations in such roles in Cdn Olympic boxing; successful in placing an athlete from his own Citadel Amateur Boxing Club on ntl team in 8 Olympic Games; mem. exec. comm. CABA; PetroCan coaching excellence award; res. Lower Sackville, N.S.

GORDON, Wayne (coaching/boxing); b. 30 Mar 1963, Victoria, B.C.; given name: Wayne Ephraim; m. Treva Tucker; c. Ann Kathleen, Rachael Amelia, Taylor Jesse; boxing coach; 4 Cdn amateur boxing titles; competed welterweight class '83 PAG, '84 Olympic Games; coach ntl team '88 world jr. championships, '92, '96 Olympics, '98 CG; PetroCan coaching excellence award; banned 4yrs by CABA; res. Beaverbank, N.S.

GORING, Alison (curling); b. 15 Nov 1963, Toronto, Ont.; given name: Alison Dawn; automotive accounts clerk; mem. Bayview CC; began curling age 12; skipped '83 Cdn jr. title rink; skipped ntl women's title rink '90; skipped 3 Ont. women's title rinks, 1 Team Canada rink in Scott Tournament of Hearts; Level I official; res. North York, Ont.

GORING, Butch (hockey); b. 22 Oct 1949, St. Boniface, Man.; given name: Robert Thomas; m. Cathy; c. Shannon, Kelly; hockey coach; jr. Winnipeg Rangers, Jets, Dauphin Kings; mem. ntl team '68; 4th LA pick '69 amateur draft; pro Springfield '69-70, LA '69-80, NYI '80-84, Boston '84-85; mem. 4 Stanley Cup winners '80-83; NHL record: 16 seasons, 1107 scheduled games, 375g, 513a, 134 playoff games, 38g, 50a; playing-asst. NYI '81; coach Bruins '84-86, Spokane (WHL), Capital Dist. Islanders '90-93; IHL Las Vegas Thunder '93-94, Utah Grizzlies '94-98, NYI '99-01;

coached in Germany '02-04; 2 IHL titles; IHL coach-of-'96 award; Bill Masterton Trophy '78, Lady Byng Trophy '78, Conn Smythe Trophy '81; mem. Man. Hockey, Sports halls of fame; res. Huntington, NY./Dusseldorf, Germany.

GORMAN, Charles (speed skating); b. 6 Jul 1897, Saint John, N.B.; d. 12 Feb 1940, Saint John, N.B.; given name: Charles Ingraham; gas station operator; p/of, led NB baseball league batters .450, MVP '25; rejected NY Yankee pro offers; ntl outdoor titles '24-26; NA indoor titles '26-28; NA outdoor title '24; mem. '24, '28 Olympic teams; beat '24 Olympic champion Clas Thunberg of Finland for '26 world title, retained title breaking 1/6-mile record, shaving second from own 440yd standard '27; 7th 500m 1928 Winter Olympics when another skater fell in his path; denied another heat, left games in protest; NA record 220yd indoor, 400yd indoor, outdoor, 1/6-mile times still stand; once won 16 events in 11 days. mem. Cdn Speed Skating, NB, Cdn Olympic, Canada's, Saint John Sports halls of fame.

GORMAN, T. P. (Tommy) (entrepreneur); b. 9 Jun 1886, Ottawa, Ont.; d. 15 May 1961, Ottawa, Ont.; given name: Thomas Patrick; m. Mary Elizabeth Westwick; c. Betty, Frank, Joe; sportswriter, coach; at 22 youngest mem. '08 Olympic lacrosse gold medal team; 1 of 5 men involved '17 birth of NHL; introduced hockey to NYC with Americans; coach/owner Senators title teams '20-21, '23, Black Hawks '34, Montreal Maroons '35, Canadiens '44, '46; coached and/or managed 7 Stanley Cup winners; left NHL '46 to take over Ottawa Auditorium; Ottawa Senators (QSHL) pres., '49 Allan Cup winners; asst. GM Aqua Caliente race track Mexico '29-32, acquired Connaught Park '40s; introduced harness racing to National Capital area; involved Ottawa entry International baseball league; mem. Ottawa, Hockey, Cdn Horse Racing halls of fame.

GORRELL, Miles (football); b. 16 Oct 1955, Calgary, Alta.; UofOtt; football exec.; ot; jr. Calgary Mohawks; CIAU all-Cdn, MVP; CFL Calgary '78-82, Ottawa '82, Montreal '82-85, Hamilton '85-91, '96, Winnipeg '92-95, '97-98; 5 all-Eastern, 1 all-CFL all-star; 2 Leo Dandurand trophy; 2 runnerup CFL outstanding offensive lineman awards; 1st CFL position player to play 300 scheduled games; 4 Grey Cup finals, 1 winner; hon. Commissioner Cdn Sr. Football League; dir. Cdn personnel Calgary Stampeders '04; res. Winnipeg, Man.

GOSS, Sandy (swimming); b. 2 Oct 1966, Amherst, N.S.; m. Judy; c. Riley; Florida; stockbroker; began competitive swimming age 8; mem. Ntl team from '83-89; FS, BS specialist; 33 ntl championship medals, 8 gold, 8 silver, 17 bronze; 11 intl meet medals; 8 Cdn Sr., 3 Commonwealth records; 200m backstroke gold, 4x100 FS relay silver '86 CG; '84 FS, '88 4x100 medley relay Olympics silver; '87 NCAA 200m back silver; 6 Ntl championships; 2 Olympic champion awards; '87 Sport excellence award; '88 Ont. aquatic athlete of year; mem. Ont. Aquatic Hall of Fame; res. Toronto, Ont.

GOSSET, John (basketball/softball/administration); b. 7 May 1963, Almonte, Ont.; given name: Jean; div.; Algonquin Coll; ED Naismith Foundation; established athletic/recreational program for aboriginals in northern Quebec; recognized authority on James Naismith; contributor to numerous books/publications on subject and basketball history; played sr. fastball Stittsville 56ers, Turpin Pontiacs, Carp Valley Pride; jr. Smiths Falls Redmen; MVP '82 Ont. championships; top batter '83 Ont. championships; Metro Major Fastball League rookie of '85; small bktbll fwd Algonquin Thunder '85; lettered in football, basketball, volleyball, badminton, t&f Almonte HS; v-pres. Canadian Association for Sport Heritage; mem. Ottawa Sports, Cdn Basketball hall of fame selection comm.; mem. Smiths Falls Sports Hall of Fame; res. Almonte, Ont.

GOTELL, Chelsey (swimming); b. 20 Feb 1986, Antigonish, N.S.; student; visually impaired; mem. Antigonish Aquanauts SC; ntl 50m FGS title '04; competed 2 Paralympics; 1 silver, 2 bronze '00, 1 gold, 3 bronze '04; 2 world backstroke records; res. Antigonish, N.S.

GOTFREDSEN, Leif (rowing); b. 28 Jun 1934, Herning, Denmark; m. Betty Carol Walsh; c. Signe, Erik; George Brown College, Ryerson PTI; ret'd electrician; competed Denmark '52-57 winning coxed 4s title, 2nd Nordic coxed 4s championships '53, sr. 8s Great International Berliner regatta title '55; mem. Toronto Argonaut Rowing Club '60-70; ntl sr. double sculls '62, jr. single sculls '63, sr. single sculls '64; mem. '64 Olympic team; silver PAG double sculls '67; oarsman, exec., coach Victoria City RC '74-79; director BCRA '74-81, v-p '81; ntl team coach '78-80, jr. team coach '86-87; CARA coach of '78; dir. CARA '81-85; Greater Victoria Sports Council sportsman-of-year; '79-80 CARA Centennial award; res. Victoria, B.C.

GOTTA, Jack (football); b. 14 Nov 1931, Ironwood, Mich.; m. Joan Patterson; c. Jeff, Tony, Jake, Gia; Oregon State; realtor, ret'd football executive; receiver, Oregon State; service football Hamilton AFB; capt. '55 USAF team, all-service all-star, league MVP; caught 44 passes for 8tds; last cut Cleveland (NFL)'56, Calgary (CFL) for final 7 games; '57 Shrine Game; Saskatchewan '60-63; Montreal '64; CFL playing record: 253 receptions, 4317yds, 20tds; WFC all-star; asst. coach Sask. '65-66; asst. Ottawa '67-69, head coach '70-73; Grey Cup '73; twice Annis Stukus Trophy CFL coach of year; coach Birmingham (WFL) '74; GM and/or coach Stampeders '77-79, '82-83; coach Sask. '85-86; 11yr CFL coaching record (including playoffs): 89-87-5; TV football color commentator '84; res. Cochrane, Alta.

GOULDING, Bev (administration); b. 29 Jun 1912, Toronto, Ont.; d. 23 Aug 1998, Kitchener, Ont.; given name: George Beverley; m. Kathryn Currie; c. George David, Nancy Kathryn; UofT, BA; ret'd teacher; coached HS football, basketball winning 6 assn. football, 3 assn., 1 CABA juv basketball titles; exec.-dir. Ont. Federation of School Athletic Associations '71-77; mem. Peterborough Sports Hall of Fame.

GOULDING, George (t&f); b. 16 Nov 1884, Hull, Eng.; d. 31 Jan. 1966, Toronto Ont.; given name: George Henry; div.; c. Verna, Bev; sporting good business owner; mile walker, marathon runner; mem. '08 Olympic team; 300 career race victories at distances from 1-40 miles; gold '12 Olympics 10,000m race in record 46:28.4; twice world mile records including 6:25.8 Toronto '11; many stunt races; 10 miles against man driving horse and buggy; defeated 4 man US relay team in 4 mile NY walk; 8 1/4 miles 1 hour

walk around Toronto Varsity oval; '16 record for 7 miles 50:40 Rutgers; mem. Cdn Olympic, Canada's Sports halls of fame.

GOULET, Joanne (golf); b. 5 May 1935, Melville, Sask.; UofReg; administrative officer; 30 Regina, 6 Sask. Women's. 3 srs. titles; at 16 youngest golfer ntl women's championships; mem. '64 world championships team; Commonwealth Trophy semifinalist '64 British Open; course records Regina GC, Wascana G&CC, Saskatoon Riverdale GC; numerous provincial teams; national jr. chairman; Regina golf course named in her honor; mem. Sask. Sports Hall of Fame; res. Regina, Sask.

GOULET, Michel (hockey); b. 21 Apr 1960, Peribonka, Que.; m. Andrée; c. Dominique, Vincent, Nicolas; hockey exec.; lw Quebec jr. Remparts'76-78; Birmingham (WHA) '78-79; 1st-round pick Quebec '79 draft; NHL Quebec '79-90, Chicago '90-94; topped 50g with 57 '83, 56 '84, 55 '85, 53 '86; 3 1st, 2 2nd all-star; competed 5 all-star games; mem. Cdn '83 world championship bronze team; Team Canada '84, '87 Canada Cup titlists; NHL record: 1089 scheduled games, 548g, 604a, 92 playoff games, 39g, 39a; jersey #16 ret'd by Nordiques; v-p, dir. player personnel Colorado Avalanche '95-03; scout San Diego; mem. Hockey Hall of Fame; res. Highlands Ranch, Colo.

GOURLAY, Jean (field hockey); b. 29 Sep 1957, Kapuskasing, Ont; m. Steve Major; UofT, BPHE, BEd; teacher; mem. Ont. jr. team '74-76, int. '76-80, sr. '78-83; UofT team competing in tours throughout world; mem. '78, '81, '83 World Cup, '79 world championships teams; World Cup silver '83; ntl team capt. '79, co-capt. '82-83; named to World 2nd all-star team '83; T-Holders female athlete-of-yr award; bronze, silver T awards; mem. UofT Sports Hall of Fame; res. Burlington, Ont.

GOWAN, Geoff (administration); b. 2 Nov 1929, Ravenglass, Cunbira, Eng.; given name: Geoffrey Russell; m. Rhoda Tyson; c. Susan Elizabeth, Simon Russell; Loughborough Coll. of Ed. Dip. PE, Purdue, MSc, Wisconsin, PhD; ret'd pres., tech. co-ordinator Coaching Assn. of Canada; lj/tj specialist college, county levels; rugby footballer college, club levels; major coaching role Royal Canadian Legion t&f clinics, Guelph; coached 4 Olympic track finalists; key role development comprehensive coaching programs for Canadian sport; author numerous articles, lecturer, TV color commentator national, international t&f competitions; mem. Order of Canada, Cdn Olympic, Canada's Sports halls of fame; res. Halifax, N.S.

GOWANLOCK, Ab (curling); b. 14 Dec 1900, Glenboro, Man.; d. 27 Sep 1988, Dauphin, Man.; given name: Albert Adam; m. Esther Kemp (d); c. Gail; skipped Manitoba rinks to Brier titles '38, '53; scored 4 8-enders; ardent golfer; life mem. Manitoba Curling Assn., Dauphin and Glenboro Curling Clubs; mem. Man, Cdn Curling, Man. Sports halls of fame.

GOWSELL, Paul (curling); b. 5 Sep 1957, Squamish, B.C.; given name: Christopher Paul; m. Kathi Ostrom; c. Sam, Sophie; waterworks inspector; skipped 2 world jr. title rinks; '80 Alta. Brier rep.; twice topped $65,000 rink earnings '77-78; official spare '88 Olympics; res. Calgary, Alta.

GOYETTE, Danielle (hockey); b. 30 Jan 1966, Ste-Foy, Que.; Home Depot plumbing supplies; began playing hockey at 16; fwd Team Que. '94-96 women's sr. ntls; gold '95, '96 Esso ntls; most-valuable forward '96 ntl championships; leading scorer '92, '94 world championship tournaments, all-star awards; 7 world, 2 Pacific Rim, 1 3-Nations Cup gold; attends Olympic Oval high performance female hockey program; mem. '98 Olympic silver, '02 gold medal teams; mem. Team Canada world fastball championships 3yrs Oval X-Treme, gold '01 Team Alberta; res. Calgary, Alta.

GOYETTE, Phil (hockey); b. 31 Oct 1933, Lachine, Que.; ctr Montreal QJHL '50-54, Cincinnati IHL '54-55 (all-star), Montreal QHL '55-57; NHL Montreal '56-63, NYR '63-69, '72, St. Louis '69-70, Buffalo '70-72; NHL totals 941 scheduled games, 207g, 467a, 94 playoff games, 17g, 29a; 4 Stanley Cup winners; James Gatschene Memorial, George Wilkerson trophies; Lady Byng trophy '70; nicknamed "The Professor"; coached NYI part of '72-73 season; res. Montreal. Que.

GRACE, John (football); b. 10 Feb 1977, Okeechobee, Fla.; Marshall BA, MA; lb; 2 Marshall defensive MVP awards; 2 MAC conf. all-star; Motor City Bowl MVP '98; CFL Montreal '00-01, Ottawa '02-03, Calgary '04; Renegades outstanding player award '03; CFL all-star; also t&f standout; res. Calgary, Alta.

GRACE, Maureen (all-around/coaching/sports medicine); b. 4 Sep 1958, Fort William, Ont.; given name: Sharon Maureen; Lakehead BSc, MSc, MD; physician; competing in 400m, 800m, 1500m, 10mile events '72-78 accumulated numerous medals, records; CIAU championship swimming gold, 2 most-valuable-swimmer awards; mem. Thunder Bay rowing club '79-86 claiming gold, silver, bronze medals in Cdn Henley, Cdn championships; single sculls bronze '83 PAG; asst. coach Thunderbolt swim club '78-81; coach TBRC '84-86, Team Ont. '85; team physician Cdn Women's ice hockey team '94, ntl rowing team '95; mem. NWO Sports Hall of Fame; res. Thunder Bay, Ont.

GRAHAM, Barbara (figure skating/coaching/officiating); b. 17 Oct 1936, Toronto, Ont.; d. 9 May 2004, Edmonton, Alta.; given name: Barbara Aldwynne Bourne; Toronto Teachers College; teacher/figure skating consultant; with Tom Moneypenny '56 ntl jr. pairs title; intl judge '67-72; CFSA tech. dir. '72-91; clinician leader NZ, Russia, South Africa '85-95; state coaching dir. Queensland, Australia, '94-97; skater development, talent ID advisor Skate Canada's Alta-NWT/Nunavut section from '97; Canada 125 Commemorative Medal; Skate Canada bursary bears her name; mem. Skate Canada Hall of Fame.

GRAHAM, Charles (boxing); b. 13 Mar 1896, Carlisle, Eng.; d. circa 1980s, m. Ivy; c. 2 daughters; boxed, coached in England as amateur, pro; coached Edmonton '54-73; guided champions in every division from flyweight to heavyweight except light- middleweight; coached Marv Arneson '68 Olympics, '70 CG gold, 5 ntl titles; mem. Alta. Sports Hall of Fame.

GRAHAM, Gail (golf); b. 16 Jan 1964, Vanderhoof, B.C.; m. Terry Graham; Lamar, BSc; golf pro; began playing golf at 13 in Winnipeg; 2 Man. amateur titles; mem. Cdn Commonwealth title team '87; mem Canada's inaugural Nations Cup team '99; low amateur '87 LPGA du Maurier Classic; won LPGA Fieldcrest-Canon Classic '95; won Alpine Australian Ladies' Masters title '97; NCAA academic All-American; 1 career hole-in-one; low career round 66; *Score* magazine Cdn female golfer of '96; res. Kelowna, B.C.

GRAHAM, Hugh (equestrian); b. 10 Feb 1949, Georgetown, Ont.; m. Cindy Firestone; c. Laurel; self-employed; tutored by Olympic gold medallist Jim Day; launched show-jumping career in '70's; mem. ntl team from '82; 7 GP jumping titles; 2 Cdn titles; team gold '87, silver '83 PAG; aboard Sirocco won '89 NA title; mem. '84, '96 Olympic, '83, '87, '95 PAG teams; competed in world championships, 4 World Cup finals; won 2 Queen Elizabeth II Cup titles; 2 Rothman's equestrian-of-year awards; res. Schomberg, Ont.

GRAHAM, John (bobsleigh/t&f); b. 20 Nov 1965, Moose Jaw, Sask.; UCal, BA; real estate developer; competitive hurdler who was '88 Olympic semifinalist; 3 CG bronze medals; 7 Cdn titles, 3 in 400m sprints, 4 in 400m hurdles; mem. ntl bobsleigh team '87-92; with Chris Lori, Ken LeBlanc, Allan Cearns ntl 4-man title '88; with Lori, Leblanc, Doug Currier ntl 4-man crowns '90, '92, world cup gold '91, 1st place WC ranking '90; competed '92 Olympics; res. Seattle, Wash.

GRAHAM, Laurie (skiing); b. 30 Mar 1960, Orangeville, Ont.; given name: Laurie Jean; m. Clarke Flynn; c. Kylie Grace, Taylor Michela; UofT Schools; downhill specialist; mem. Southern Ont. ski team '74-77; ntl ski team '77-87; ntl downhill champion '80, super GS '84; WC '79-86 record 6-4-5; WC super GS France, downhill title Mt. Tremblant '83, downhill Val d'Isere, Banff '85; downhill bronze '82 world championships; NA Ski Trophy series downhill title '83; mem. '80, '84, '88 Olympic teams; ret'd from ntl team '88; tournament of champions challenge gold NZ '95; won 3 legends of skiing downhill titles; Jeep Eagle tournament of champions title '95; MCI relays gold '96, Sprint world ski challenge as mem. Team NA '98; athletes liaison '94 Olympics; *Ski Racing International Journal* Cdn alpine-female-skier-of-'83 award; Bobbie Rosenfeld award '86; fed. govt female-athlete-of-'86 award; fed. govt. excellence awards '82-87, '89; mem. Order of Canada, Cdn Skiing, Olympic, Brampton, Canada's Sports halls of fame; res. Ottawa, Ont.

GRAHAM, Milt (football); b. 28 Jul 1934, Watervliet, N.Y.; given name: Milton Russell; m. Gertrude Engle; c. David, Mark, Laurie; Colgate, BA; ret'd FBI agent, Cape Cod inn owner; played football/basketball in college; hon. mention football all-American; drafted by both NFL, NBA; pro football Ottawa '56-61; mem. '60 Grey Cup champions; CFL all-Canadian '58; mem. Boston Patriots AFL '61-63; '62 Unsung Hero award; res. Yarmouth Port, Mass.

GRAHAM, Phil (rowing); b. 16 Jul 1970, Halifax, N.S.; Trent, BA; began competing in x-country skiing age 8; attended Canada Games as skier; raced for Nfld team '85-91; spent summers '84-86 canoeing in Northern Ont.; began rowing at Trent; mem. ntl rowing team from '93; 2 PAG '95 silver; FISU Games straight pairs gold, quadruple sculls silver '93; 2 ntl straight pairs titles; gold straight pair '94

Amsterdam International; competed 2 world championships, '96 , '00 Olympics; res. Cornerbrook, Nfld.

GRAHAM, Sally (shooting); b. 12 Oct 1953, Lakefield, Ont.; mem. Lakefield Rifle Club; 8 consec. Cdn Women's small-bore titles; Cdn expert class grand aggregate title '72; Masters class grand aggregate '74; mem. 3 Ont. 4-member Cdn title teams; 5yrs mem. ntl team; mem. Peterborough Sports Hall of Fame; res. Peterborough, Ont.

GRAND'MAITRE, Josée (racquetball); b. 28 Jul 1961, Montreal, Que. UofOtt, BSc, Quebec, admin. certificate; 8 Que. titles; 3 ntl doubles, 1 ntl singles titles; 3 world doubles silver; competed '95 PAG; coach ntl espoir team from '94; ntl team rep. Racquetball Canada bd. of dir.; mem. COA athletic council; Level 3 coaching cert.; technical course conductor; asst. coach Montreal development centre; res. Longueuil, Que.

GRANDI, Thomas (skiing); b. 27 Dec 1972, Bolzano, Italy; m. Sara Renner; moved to Canada age 2; began skiing in Nancy Greene program age 9; slalom, GS specialist; mem. ntl team from '92; US GS title '93; 5 ntl GS titles; competed '94, '98 Olympics; World Cup GS bronze '97, silver '04; became 1st Cdn male to win GS gold in 38yr history of World Cup, Italy '04, followed with WC GS gold Austria 3 days later; John Semmelink award '04; res. Canmore, Alta.

GRANEY, Jack (baseball); b. 10 Jun 1886, St. Thomas, Ont.; d. 20 Apr 1978, Louisana, Mo.; given name: John Gladstone; m. Pauline Perry; c. John (d), Margot; automotive dealer, sportscaster; early baseball as pitcher Western Ont.; minor pro Rochester, Wilkes-Barre, Portland; Cleveland (AL) as outfielder '10-22; ML record 1402 games, 4705ab, 706r, 1178h, 219db, 79tr, 18hr, 420bl, 148sb, .250ba; mgr. Des Moines (WL) '22; as leadoff 1st batter to face Babe Ruth when he appeared with Boston Red Sox as pitcher '14 (Graney singled); mem. '20 Cleveland World Series champions; 1st player to move to broadcast booth, voice of Indians '33-54; 1st player to wear number on uniform scheduled '16 league game; Cleveland branch SABR bears his name; trophy for outstanding media contribution to Cdn baseball bears his name; mem. Cdn Baseball Hall of Fame.

GRANT, Benny (hockey/golf); b. 14 Jul 1908, Owen Sound, Ont.; d. 30 Jul 1991, Owen Sound, Ont.; given name: Benjamin Cameron; m. Phyllis Dare Pratt; c. Carole Anne, Benny, Robert; Imperial Oil employee; mem. '27 Memorial Cup champion Owen Sound Greys; pro London '28; Toronto '29-34, loaned to NY Americans '30, '34; stints in minors Boston Cubs, Syracuse, Philadelphia, Springfeild, St Paul; sold to Chicago '42, ret'd; returned to Toronto '43, Boston '44; Charlie Gardiner Trophy top goalie St. Paul '42; 3 times AHL all-star; MVP Syracuse '32, Springfield '37; Owen Sound golf club men's champ '53, 5 srs titles.

GRANT, Bud (football/coaching); b. 20 May 1927, Superior, Wisc.; given name: Harry Peter. m. Pat; c. 5; Minnesota; ret'd football coach; 2 seasons pro basketball Minneapolis Lakers; pro football Philadelphia Eagles; oe Blue Bombers '53-56, topped WFC pass receivers 3 of 4yrs; 3 time WFC all-star; WFC single-season 68 reception record; coach Winnipeg '57-66, 112 wins, 66 losses, 3 ties .647 percentage; 8 league finals, 6 Grey Cup finals, 4 winners; coach Minnesota (NFL) '67-83, '85; only coach to win 100+ games in both CFL, NFL; NFL coaching record: 168 wins, 87 losses, 5 ties; 4 Super Bowl appearances; UofMinn athlete of 1/2 century '51; mem. Man. Sports, Cdn, US Football, Blue Bombers halls of fame; res. Kewadon, Minn.

GRANT, Danny (hockey); b. 21 Feb 1946, Fredericton, N.B.; prov. sports consultant, hockey coach; jr. Peterborough Petes '62-66; pro Montreal '66-68, Minnesota '68-74, Detroit '74-78, Los Angeles '78-79; set Minnesota club record for consecutive games (442); 50g Detroit '75; Calder Memorial trophy '69; AHL Golden Skate award '86; won NHL showdown competitions '75-76; scoring titles Original Six Hockey Heroes tounament '84-85; instrumental in acquiring AHL franchise for Fredericton; pres/player/asst coach Fredericton Express; Express jersey 16 and NHL jersey 21 ret'd; coached Fredericton Capitals to NB intermediate titles '80-81, Eastern Cdn Hardy Cup '80; coached Fredericton Boldons Red Wings to Atlantic midget crown '89; coach UNB '95-97; Halifax Mooseheads (QMJHL) '97; director of scouting Halifax from '98; governor Canada's Sports Hall of Fame; NHL record: 736 scheduled games, 263g, 272a, 43 playoff games, 10g, 14a; mem. NB Sports Hall of Fame; res. Nasonworth, N.B.

GRANT, Duncan (parachuting/administration); b. 29 Jul 1950, Whitehorse, Y.T.; m. Ginette Vanasse; c. Marc, Nicole; Algonquin Travel; sport administrator; tech. dir. Canadian Sport Parachuting Assn '80-85, Fitness Canada '86, Cdn Archers '86-93, Baseball '93-98; 1st 10-way '74; 2nd 10-way '75-76; 2nd 8-way '77, '79; 3rd 4-way '76, '78-79; instructor examiner, instructor rigger, CAC coach; aerial photographer; more than 3300 jumps, 37 hours free fall time; exec. dir. Baseball Canada; res. Ottawa, Ont.

GRANT, Fred (harness racing); b. 23 Jan 1951, North Sydney, N.S.; while playing junior hockey, was thrust into standardbred scene as a track announcer when regular announcer died; received his driver's license and won the first race; worked for Stanley Dancer, Billy Haughton training the likes of Silent Majority, Handle With Care; branched out on own developing Senor Skipper, Ella Hanover and Major Knight; became leading trainer at Meadowlands '84; trained world record holder Wholesale, free-for-all pacer Cambest; his major impact on sport came as trainer although he drives occasionally winning 323 races and more than $1M in purses; res. East Rutherford, N.J.

GRANT, Martha (swimming/equestrian); b. 22 Oct 1954, Saskatoon, Sask.; given name: Martha Stina Nelson; m. Donald James Grant; Uof Sask, BSc, BEd; competitive swimmer '63-72; 43 provincial records, ntl age-group standards 200m IM; '71 sr. girls 100m backstroke mark; mem. Dolphins SC; men. '72 Olympic team; 1st 200m backstroke, 200m IM '72 Warsaw meet; became involved in equestrian sport attaining B1 National Pony Club standard before age eligibility excluded her; continues to show horses, judge at volunteer level; coach HS volleyball; level 1 t&f coaching certificate; active x-country skier; mem. Sask., Saskatoon Sports halls of fame; res. Saskatoon, Sask.

GRANT, Mike (hockey); b. 1870s, Montreal, Que.; d. 1961 Montreal, Que.; capt. Montreal Victorias, Stanley Cup '94, '96-98; mem. Victorias (CAHL) '99-1900, '02, Shamrocks '01; ret'd to refereeing following '02 season; mem. Hockey Hall of Fame.

GRANT, Otis (boxing); b. 23 Dec 1967, St. Anns, Jamaica; UMontreal; pro boxer; middleweight; launched pro career '88; through '04 35 wins (17kos), 2 losses, 1 draw; won WBA Intl, Cdn middle crown '91; retained Cdn title '92; NABF middle title '92-98; won WBO middle crown '97-98; lost WBA, WBC light-heavy titles to Roy Jones Jr. '98; injury received in car accident kept him out of ring almost 5yrs; returned to claim Cdn Super middleweight, vacant WBC Intl Super middleweight titles '04; nicknamed "Magic"; res. Montreal, Que.

GRANT, Tommy (football); b. 9 Jan 1935, Windsor, Ont; m. Ida Gagnon; c. Colette, Lisa, Tommy Jr, Michelle; ret'd car salesman; outstanding HS jr. (AKO) football career led to pro ranks Hamilton '56; won EFC rookie-of-yr Gruen Trophy; hb 4 seasons Hamilton, Winnipeg; caught 329 passes for 6542yds, 19.9 avg., 51tds; most productive season '64, 44 passes for 1029yds; 105yd kickoff return vs. Montreal '62; frequent all-star; 1yr pro outfielder Detroit Tigers chain; mem. Cdn Football Hall of Fame; res. Burlington, Ont.

GRASSICK, Greg (football/coaching); b. 1900, Regina, Sask.; d. 4 Apr 1983, Regina, Sask.; m ; c. Janet, Marion, Jim, Geordie; McGill; hb under coach Shag Shaughnessey McGill; hb/coach. Roughriders '27-32, 5 Grey Cup finals; introduced huddle to Western football as coach Regina Dales '33; coached Roughriders '34; helped introduce forward pass to Cdn. game '29 Grey Cup; accomodations mgr. Roughriders '48-50; mem. Sask. Sports Hall of Fame.

GRATTON, Paul (volleyball); b. 8 Nov 1958, Ottawa, Ont; m. France Fouquette; UofOtt, BPhE; athlete representative, pres. Sim Gratton Inc.; mem. ntl jr. team '77; ntl sr. team '78-85, capt. '82-85; competed '84 Olympics; pro volleyball Osaka, Japan, '84-87; 3 championship MVP awards; 3yrs best hitter, all-star in championships, 2 best-server awards, 1 best blocker award; pro Treviso, Italy '91; Frejus, France, '87-92; 3 French titles, 3 French Cup; 2 runnerup French championship, 1 silver, bronze European championships; MVP/best hitter several tournaments; pro Bordeaux, France, '93; pres. Sport International Management '94; part-time volleyball teacher UofOtt from '95; volleyball consultant conducting clinics for players/coaches from '92; mem. Ottawa Sports Hall of Fame; res. Orleans, Ont.

GRAVELLE, Gérard (ski jumping); b. 15 Dec 1934, Hull, Que.; m. Rita Guertin; c. Michel, Rosane; blacksmith; mem. '60 Olympic, '62 world championships, '55-57 Que. Games teams; Gil O Julien trophy as French athlete of '61; Ont. athlete-of-yr. nominee '62-63; res. Hull, Que.

GRAVELLE, Red (hockey); b. 7 Dec 1927, Aylmer, Que.; d. 18 Jan 1997, Trenton, Ont.; given name: Orval; m. Jeanne Perrier (d), Phyllis Sprowl; c. Suzanne, John, Paul, Phil, Rebecca; superintendent works, engineering Solicitor General of Canada; Jr. B Ottawa '45-47; pro tryout NYR '47; mem. RCAF Flyers Olympic title team '48; Sr. A Ottawa,

Smith Falls, Pembroke, Quebec City, Belleville, Trenton, P.E.I.; hockey referee '55-75 working Allan, Memorial Cup finals; '66 anniversary medallion for Jr. A playoff officiating; ret'd RCAF '70; active in Old Timers hockey; as mem. '48 Flyers mem. Ottawa Sports Hall of Fame.

GRAVES, Adam (hockey); b. 12 Apr 1968, Toronto, Ont.; m. Violet; c. Madison (d), Montana, Logan; TV hockey analyst; ctr Windsor (OHL) '85-87 (capt OHL titlist), Adirondack (AHL) '87-88 (title), Team Canada '87; drafted by Detroit '86; lw NHL with Detroit '87-89, Edmonton '89-91, NYR '91-00, San Jose '01-03; 2nd team NHL all-star '94; NHL record 1152 scheduled games, 329g, 287a, 125 playoff games, 38g, 27a; mem. 2 Stanley Cup winners; 52g '94; King Clancy Memorial trophy '94; mem. Team Canada '88 World jr. title team; capt. Team Canada '93; played organized soccer 12yrs; celebrity chair. NYC Family Dynamics; 3 Players' Player, 10 NYR club awards; active in charitable work; res. Tecumseh, Ont.

GRAVES, Richard (ski jumping); b. 22 Apr 1955, Montreal, Que.; given name: Richard MacFarlane; Guelph; at 14 jr. B alpine racer, mem. Ottawa jr. x-country team; switched to jumping '70; mem. ntl jumping team '72, jr. titlist '72-73; runnerup US jrs, 3rd srs, 37th world ski flying championships, 20th world jr. '73; 7th Garmisch International '74; 2nd NA plastic jumping championships '75; ntl 70m title '75-76; O'Keefe international '76; res. Ottawa, Ont.

GRAY, Clyde (boxing); b. 10 Mar 1946, Windsor, N.S.; m. Evelyn Coates; c. Tony, Jennifer, Clyde Jr, Jeremy; 30 wins, 2 losses, 32 amateur bouts; 2 NY State Golden Gloves titles; managed by Irv Ungerman, 69 wins, 10 losses, 79 pro bouts; victories included 49 by KO; ntl, Commonwealth welterweight titles simultaneously; unsuccessful 3 world title bids; ntl welter title '71 beating Donato Paduano; '73 Commonwealth title beating Eddie Blay; defended ntl crown 7 times; lost title to Guerra Chavez regained it within 12 months; defended Commonwealth crown 7 times; lost title to Chris Clark '79 regained it within 4 months; only Cdn to retire as reigning ntl, Commonwealth champion; mem. fed. govt. task force to improve safety in boxing '80-81; supervisor Ont. boxing '80; Ont. Athletic Commissioner '81-88; introduced passport system of boxer ID & licencing; fight judge; boxing instructor Regent Park BC from '91; mem. Cdn Boxing, NS Sports halls of fame; res. Scarborough, Ont.

GRAY, George (t&f); b. 1865, Coldwater, Ont.; d. 1933, Sault Ste. Marie, Ont.; at '85 Canadian Amateur Athletic Assn. meet Toronto put shot 41'5.5" to win title with initial toss in 1st competition, held it 17yrs; acclaimed world champion; eldest brother John twice won 2-oared rowing title of America; 2 cousins were rowers Jake Gaudaur Sr., all-round athlete, track coach Harry Gill; world shot put record 43'11" '87, held it through '02, broke own record several times; at retirement had won 188 medals, trophies for shot put; mem. Canada's Sports Hall of Fame.

GRAY, Gerry (soccer); b. 20 Jan 1961, Glasgow, Scotland; given name: Gerard; m. Michelle Rafferty; c. Shannon, Daniel, Justine; Business Succession Planning; hb; received initial taste of soccer in Scotland and on moving to Canada pursued his soccer education with Malton minor program;

served international apprenticeship with ntl youth team; played key role in helping Canada win CONCACAF zone title; competed '79 FIFA world championships; pro Vancouver Whitecaps '80-82, Montreal Manic, NY Cosmos, Chicago Sting (NASL title '84), Ottawa Intrepid, San Francisco Golden Bay, Tacoma Stars, Hamilton Steelers, Toronto Blizzard; earned 1st international cap in rookie season; competed in 11 Olympic tournament contests including run to '84 Olympic quarter-finals; played 33 full sr. international games; with Whitecaps in indoor play scored 29 goals in 32 games '80-81; Mississauga pro athlete of '80; mem. Cdn Soccer, Mississauga Sports halls of fame; res. Tacoma, Wash.

GRAY, Herb (football); b. 12 Jun 1934, Baytown, Tex.; given name: Herbert William; m. Maureen Ann Fitzgerald; c. James Kevin, Stephen Craig, Bryan David; Texas, BSc.; ret'd building supply co. v-p; 3 all-district, 1 all-state HS awards, all-Southern, all-American sr. year; Texas all-Southwestern Conference 3 years, lineman of year, all-American sr. year; pro Winnipeg '56-65; all-star guard-end 7 times, frequent all-Cdn; defensive capt. 9yrs; played Sr. Bowl, Can-US Shrine Games; 6 Grey Cup finals, 4 winners; '60 Schenley Award Outstanding lineman (1st def. player); '65 Dr. Bert Oja most-valuable-Bomber-lineman award; Winnipeg defensive player of 1st 1/2 century; CFL all-time all-star; mem. Longhorn Hall of Honor, Cdn, Blue Bombers Football, Blue Bombers Alumni Alley, Man. Sports halls of fame; res. Canyon Lake, Tex.

GRAY, Rob (t&f); b. 5 Oct 1956, Toronto, Ont.; given name: Robert John Kelly; Southern Methodist, Osgoode Hall; lawyer; discus specialist; Toronto HS champion '73-75; Ont., ntl jr. title '76; ntl sr. title '79, '83; silver '82, bronze '78 CG; mem. '79 PAG, '80, '84 Olympic, '79, '83 FISU Games teams; steroids use resulted in banishment from '86 CG team, indefinite CTFA suspension; last known res. Downsview, Ont.

GRAY, Robert Jr. (golf); b. 16 Apr 1909, Fraserborough, Scotland; d. 31 Oct 1966, Scarborough, Ont.; became youngest head pro in Canada '28; represented Canada vs. US pros '37; defeated US open champ Ralph Guldahl 4&2; 2 Ont. open titles; 4 Que. open, 1 Southern Ont. open title; 4 CPGA Millar trophy, 3 runnerup; 5 CPGA runnerup; Cdn Open runnerup to Sam Snead '41; 4 low Cdn at Cdn Open; participated 2 US Opens; head pro Chatham '26-28, Colony Club Algonac, Mich '28-29, Hawthorne Valley, Detroit '30-34, Windsor Essex '35-37, Scarborough '38-66; mem. Ont. Golf Hall of Fame.

GRAY, Steve (rugby); b. 19 Jul 1963, Ottawa, Ont.; given name: Stephen Douglas; Algonquin Coll.; customer acct. rep. BC Hydro; Jr. A hockey Ottawa Senators; wing/ctr ntl -19s vs. Japan '82; earned 1st of 47 caps vs. US '84; ntl record 3 tries vs. US '87; competed '87, '91, '95 World Cup, '93 World Cup of 7s, 6 Hong Kong 7s tournaments; ret'd '97; nicknamed "Kats"; res. Vancouver, B.C.

GREAVES, Joe (baseball/curling); b. 23 Nov 1914, Port Arthur, Ont.; d. 3 Sep 2002, Thunder Bay, Ont.; given name: James George; m. Dorothy Benson; c. Elaine, John, Jim, Bernard; ret'd printer, hall of fame curator; earned nickname "Two-bagger Joe" during standout 28yr baseball career as

player, coach, organizer, umpire; organized Port Arthur Little League '52; coached, umpired LL 16yrs; softball organizer, fund-raiser, umpire '33-47; chair. Legion sports comm. '46-50; formed Legion Boxing Club; organized, managed Green Rivers sr. football club '37; mgr. Packers football team '38-40; exec. mem. Port Arthur Mustangs sr. football team '46-47; organized Port Arthur sr. basketball team '39; had key role in Thunder Bay minor hockey program; exec. mem. Port Arthur Curling & Athletic Club; exec. mem. Northwestern Ont. CA 10yrs; key role in promoting youth curling; mem. Port Arthur stadium building comm; mem. Port Arthur Parks & Civic Recreation comm; developer, curator Northwestern Ont. Sports Hall of Fame; mem. NWO Sports Hall of Fame.

GREAVES, Sandra (judo/coaching); b. 17 Jun 1963, Winnipeg, Man.; operated Judo World Ottawa; introduced to judo '77; ntl, US jr. titles '79; ntl team '84-92; 6 ntl sr, Canada Cup titles; competed 3 worlds; silver '89 Francophonie Games; 2 Pan-Am championships silver; gold 66kg '87 PAG; bronze '88 Austrian Open; competed '88, '92 Olympics; ret'd from competition '94; considered trailblazer in her sport; 1st degree black belt; coach Thunder Bay, Montreal ntl training centre, Judo Ont., Judo Canada; Sask prov. coach '90-92; Judo Ont. Sandra Greaves Cup awarded annually to best female waza (technique); mem. NWO Sports, Judo Can. halls of fame; res. Thunder Bay, Ont.

GREEN, Donald (sailing); b. 8 Oct 1932, Hamilton, Ont.; given name: Donald MacKenzie; m. Marion Alexandra Little; c. Sharon, Stephen; Ryerson PTI, UWO, McMaster; chair., chief exec. officer Tridon Cos.; at 12 captained Royal Hamilton Yacht Club's 3rd-place entry '46 international jr. regatta Toronto, '47 won same event; at 19 sailed around world aboard brigantine Yankee skippered by Capt. Irving Johnson; authored book *White Wings Around the World*; '78 skippered Evergreen to Canada's Cup victory; yacht destroyed '79 Fastnet disaster; new Evergreen built '81; past-commodore RHYC; governor Olympic Trust of Canada; dir. Cdn National Sportsmen's Shows; chairman True North Syndicate; Burlington young man of '69; 1 of 10 outstanding Ont. young men '69; Ryerson Fellowship '79; Ryerson alumni achievement award; mem. Order of Canada; res. Burlington, Ont.

GREEN, Gary (hockey); b. 23 Aug 1953, Tillsonburg, Ont.; given name: Gary Lee; m. Sharon Causyn; c. Jennifer; Guelph, BA; *TSN* hockey color commentator; minor pro def WHA Vancouver Blazers chain before turning to coaching; CEO Tam O'Shanter Hockey School at 21; 3yrs asst. to Roger Neilson Peterborough Petes; coach Petes at 24, Memorial Cup finals 2 straight years, championship '79; co-authored 3 hockey books; merged Tam O'Shanter, Can-Am hockey schools; launched series of intl pro hockey symposiums; coach Hershey Bears to start '79-80; elevated to Washington 14 Nov '79 becoming youngest coach in NHL history at 26; 5 Nov '81 fired; NHL record: 50-78-29; OMJHL coach of '79; head coach Cdn team Swiss Challenge, Deutchland Cup '02, Spengler Cup '04; res. Riva, Md.

GREEN, Peter (rowing); b. 15 Feb 1920, South Wellington, B.C.; given name: Peter Valentine; m. Sylvia Pearl Isnor; c. David, Valerie; McNaughton Hall Hamilton; ret'd DND;

stroke oar for Leander club heavy 4s '43, stroke heavy 8s following year; scored several US, Canadian regatta victories; mem. Olympic 8s semifinalists '48; lost to Vancouver crew '52 Olympic trials; res. Victoria, B.C.

GREEN, Roland (cycling); b. 19 Jul 1974, Victoria, B.C.; full-time athlete; mountain bike x-c, road ITT, road racer; ntl team from '91; burst onto world competitive stage with '92 Tour d'Abitibi title; ntl ITT title '95; earned medals in Hawaii, Malaysia; 3 ntl x-c titles; 3 NORBA short track USA titles; relay bronze world mountain bike '99, silver '00; gold MTB x-c '02 CG, 1st ever CG gold in mountain biking; '01-02 WC, world champion; competed '00 Olympics; allergy to pollen can effect performance; 3 Cdn cyclist-of-yr. awards; mem. Trek/Volkswagen, US Postal teams; NA male cyclist of '01; *Cycling News* male MTB racer of '02; 2 Norton Crowe awards; 2 CCA president's trophies; 2 PacificSport Ntl Cycling Centre elite male athlete awards; res. Victoria, B.C.

GREEN, Ron (curling); b. 11 Apr 1947, Toronto, Ont.; given name: Ronald Lawerence; div. Carol; c. Leslie; m. Linda; c. Lindsay, Robyn; pres. Gratham Industries; with Paul Savage Ont. jr. title '66; with Bill Creber runnerup to Ken Buchan '69 Consols; with Savage Ont. Brier entry '73, '74, '77; won '73-74 Royals carspiel; competed *CBC Curling Classic* '73-74, won '77-78; won '75 Century Curling Classic Calgary; skipped own rink to Canada Life title Toronto; all-star lead '73-74 Briers; only player from Eastern Canada named to Brier all-time all-star team for 1st 50yrs; res. Toronto, Ont.

GREEN, Shawn (baseball); b.10 Nov 1972, Des Plaines, Ill; given name: Shawn David; of, standout HS career Tustin, Calif. Led to scholarship offer from Stanford; drafted by Toronto '91; donated portion of signing bonus to Metro Toronto Housing Authority Breakfast Club for needy children; minor league stops in Dunedin, Knoxville, Syracuse (MVP) before joining Blue Jays as regular '95; gold glove fielder with strong arm; left-handed batter with power; became 1st Blue Jay to post 30hr/30sb in single season '98; belted 42hr, 123rbi, club record 28 game hitting streak '99 earning all-star status; gold glove award '99; LA '99-04; Arizona '05; hit 4HR, 2B, 1B for ML 19 total-base record vs. Milwaukee '02; IL rookie of '94, IL, Florida State all-star, IL batting title '94; ML record (through '04): 1514 scheduled games, 5525ab, 907r, 1560h, 347db, 27tr, 281hr, 885rbi, 139sb, .282ba; res. Newport Beach, Calif.

GREEN, Shorty (hockey); b. 17 Jul 1896, Sudbury, Ont.; d. 19 Apr 1960,; given name: Wilfred Thomas; Sudbury Intermediates NOHA '14-15; after WW1 joined Hamilton Tigers, '19 Allan Cup; returned to Sudbury to '23; pro Hamilton Tigers '23, league title '25; as capt. spokesman for players who refused to participate in playoffs unless club paid $200 per player; club owners refused and Toronto-Montreal were forced to meet for title; Hamilton franchise shifted to NY; Green scored 1st goal in Madison Square Garden 19 Dec '25; coached through '33 before retiring; mem. Hockey Heritage North, Hockey halls of fame.

GREEN, Ted (hockey); b. 23 Mar 1940, Eriksdale, Man.; given name: Edward Joseph; m. Pat; c. 3; hockey exec.; St. Boniface jrs, Winnipeg (WHL) Memorial Cup winners,

Kingston (EPHL), NHL Boston 60-72; mem. '72 Stanley Cup winner; stay at home def; NHL record: 620 scheduled games, 48g, 206a, 31 playoff games, 4g, 8a; played in WHA with New England Whalers '72-75, Winnipeg Jets '75-79 winning 4 Avco Cups; playing career and life seriously threatened when his head became target of Wayne Maki stick assault at Ottawa Civic Centre, 3 brain operations followed; returned for 9 more seasons but his aggressive nature was subdued; turned to coaching Carmen Hornets (Man. intermediate champs) '79-80; asst. Team Canada '84 Canada Cup; asst. Edmonton '81-85, '86-89, '97-00, head coach '89-93; ass't to Oilers president '93-'97; asst. coach NYR '01-04; 5 Stanley Cup winners; mem. Man. Hockey, Sports halls of fame; res. Edmonton, Alta.

GREENE, Nancy (skiing); b. 11 May 1943, Ottawa, Ont.; given name: Nancy Catherine; m. Al Raine; c. Charles, William; Cahilty Lodge co-owner; ntl team '59-68; mem. '60, '64, '68 Olympic teams; GS gold, slalom silver '68 Olympics; mem. world championships team '62-66; 7 ntl, 3 US titles; '67-68 World Cup; FIS, WC combined golds '68; WC record 14-2-4; ret'd following '68 Olympics; Order of Canada silver medal '67, Order of Dogwood, Lou Marsh, Bobbie Rosenfeld trophies '67-68; B'nai B'rith woman of '68; 17th winner Halva intl. Skiing award; hon. chair. Nancy Greene Ski League; BC female athlete of century; mem. '68-69 fed. Task Force on Sport for Canadians, FIS WC comm.; prominent as sports ambassador; TV color commentator; Toni Sailor summer ski camp; dir. ski racing Blackcomb Mountain; ski dir. Sun Peaks resort; special rep. Rossignol Skis; active mem. Cdn Ski Team alumni; flag-bearer '68 winter Olympics; Officer Order of Canada '67; Order of B.C.; named Canada's female athlete of century '99; BC Women in Sport Leaders & Legends award; mem. Cdn, US Skiing, Cdn Olympic, Canada's, BC, Ont. Legends Sports halls of fame; Cdn Walk of Fame; res. Sun Peaks, B.C.

GREENFELD, Sherman (racquetball); b. 3 Jun 1962, Winnipeg, Man.; UMan. BEd; racquets pro; began playing age 16; record 10 ntl titles; unbeaten 13 consecutive yrs in Man. tournament play; bronze '79 Canada Winter Games; gold '95 PAG qualifier; silver, bronze '95 PAG; gold men's singles '94, '98, with Mike Ceresia silver men's doubles '94 world amateur championships; mem. 2 ntl men's title teams; won tournament of Americas title; twice Man. YMHA Jewish athlete of yr; mem. Man. Sports Hall of Fame; res. Winnipeg, Man.

GREENIDGE, Ricardo (t&f/bobsleigh); b. 12 Feb 1971, Ottawa, Ont.; Blinn College; 200m specialist; 1st international appearance vs. US '89; silver 100, 200m vs. Ireland '92; ntl jr. 200m title '90; competed world jr. championships '90; ntl indoor 200m title '93, outdoor title '94; competed in '93 world indoor championships, '94 CG; silver 200m '94 Francophone Games; PB: 10.44 100m, 20.87 200m '92; mem. ntl bobsleigh team from '96; as brakeman for Pierre Lueders WC gold '97; competed '98 Olympics; ntl 2-man title '99; mem. Ottawa Lions TC; HS soccer standout; res. Calgary, Alta.

GREENOUGH, Gail (equestrian); b. 7 Mar 1960, Edmonton, Alta.; m. Neil Runions; sc. Jeff, Derek; UAlta. BA; freelance coach; began riding age 11; competed in dressage before shifting to show jumping; won individual dressage bronze Alta summer games; ntl team '83-93; mem. Nations Cup title team '84; riding Mr. T became 1st women/North American to win world title '86; qualified but did not compete 3 World Cup , competed '03 PAG; *CBC-TV* color commentator '88 Olympics, '97 World Cup; honored by Alta. Sports Writers, Metro Toronto Convention Centre Women's Show; *TSN* female athlete of '86; finalist ntl female athlete of '86; subject of TV special; produced show jumping clinic video; mem. Order of Canada, Cdn Olympic, Alta Sports halls of fame; res. Bend, Ore.

GREENWAY, Tom (judo); b. 28 Sep 1956, Lethbridge, Alta.; given name: Thomas Myers: UofLethbridge; 95kg victories CNE, jr. Olympics '74; 4 provincial, 2 ntl titles; 3 gold Western Canada Games; mem. '76, '80 Olympic, '79 PAG, '78, '80 Pan-American championships teams; victories '77 US Youth championships, '80 Takahama Cup, '80 Pan-Am championships, '81 Czechoslovakian, Desert Opens; UMan. title '81; silver '79, bronze '80 US Open; demo bronze '86 CG; 4yr suspension for banned substance use '92 overturned on appeal '96; prov. Officials certification; sensi Hoodoo Martial Arts; res. Lethbridge, Alta.

GREGG, Randy (hockey); b. 19 Feb 1956, Edmonton, Alta.; given name: Randall John; m. Kathy Vott; c. Jamie, Ryan, Jessica, Sarah; UAlta., BSc, MD; general practitioner; def. UAlta '75-79, Team Canada '79-80, '84, '87-88, competed '84 Canada Cup, '80, '88 Olympics; player-coach Kukuda, Japan, '80-82; NHL Edmonton '82-90, Vancouver '91-92; NHL totals 474 scheduled games, 41g, 152a, 137 playoff games, 12g, 40a; 5 Stanley Cup winners; Can-West CIAU outstanding player award '79, Red Dutton award '79; *TSN*-Dr. Randy Gregg award presented annually by CIS to athlete displaying outstanding athletic/academic/ community service standards; with Bob Steadward founded FunTeam hockey program to provide affordable hockey for youngsters; pres. 13yrs; mem. UAlta Sports wall, Cdn Olympic hall of fame; res. Edmonton, Alta.

GRÉGOIRE, Hélène (water skiing); b.10 Mar 1953, Hull, Que.; given name: Héléne Madeleine; div. Robert Langevin; c. Joelle, Michelle; Montreal, DMD; dentist; dominated girls division ntl championships '69-70, gold slalom, jumping, tricks; ntl team '70-77; 10 ntl titles; 6 gold Can-Am competitions; mem. 1 World Cup, PAG, 3 world championships teams; Gil O Julien Trophy French Canadian amateur athlete of '70; Que. Sports Federation water skiing sports merit award '74; as alpine skier ntl jr. GS gold '69; mem. elite development comm. CAWSA; supervisor Que. Games water skiing '81; mem. Ottawa Sports Hall of Fame; res. Hull, Que.

GRENDA, Ed (snowshoe/soccer/hockey); b. 11 Jan 1942, Vancouver, B.C.; given name: Edward Ronald; m. Helen Elizabeth Andrascik; c. Bradley, Adam; UBC, BA, MA, London School of Economics; university lecturer, social science consultant; competitive snowshoer racing in Canada, US, France '74-92; won 400m title Lewiston, Me., '81, 8km race walk Ottawa '83, Lewiston '85; ntl 8km race walk titles '83, '85; 3 Ont./West Que. 8km titles; 4 race-walker-of-yr awards; dir. Cdn Snowshoe Assn. '91-97, head coach '91-97, co-chair. International Snowshoe Comm. (France) '92-94; dir. Ont. Soccer Assn. '91-95, v-p '95, pres. '95-97; dir. Cdn Soccer Assn. '96-98; pres/dir. International Hockey Hall of

Fame and Museum Kingston '80-95; secty IIHFM '95-97; v-p Ont. Assn of Triathletes; res. Kingston, Ont.

GRENIER, Louis (speed skating); b. 20 Jul 1960, Toronto, Ont.; computer technician; ntl indoor all-around titles '72-73, '79; NA indoor title '79; 2nd 500m, 4th 1000m, 3000m world indoor '79; 2nd 1500m, 3000m, all-around '80 world indoor; Caltex Cup, Australia '79; world short-track 500m, 1000m, 3000m, all-around '83; world record 500m; Norton Crowe Trophy '83; fed. govt. world champion award '83; short-track team leader '94 Olympics; 2 short-track male athlete-of-yr awards; mem. Cdn Speed Skating Hall of Fame; res. Lac Beauport, Que.

GRESCHNER, Ron (hockey); b. 22 Dec 1954, Goodsoil, Sask.; div. Carol Alt; restaurateur, hockey school dir.; def. New Westminster WHL '71-74 (all-star '74), Providence AHL '74; NHL NYR '74-90; NHL totals 982 scheduled games, 179g, 431a, 84 playoff goals, 17g, 32a; Rangers Crumb Bum, Good Guy awards; played 1 NHL all-star game; involved in charity work; res. New York, N.Y.

GRETSINGER, Bert (curling); b. 7 Apr 1951, Winnipeg, Man.; m. Carmel; c. Kristine, Matthew; businessman; 6 Brier appearances, played 3rd for Bernie Sparkes '76, Rick Folk '89, 2nd Folk '93-94, skip '99 Brier; winner '94; mem. '94 world title rink; res. Kelowna, B.C.

GRETZKY, Wayne (hockey); b. 26 Jan 1961, Brantford, Ont.; m. Janet Jones; c. Paulina Mary Jean, Ty Robert, Trevor Douglas, Tristan Wayne, Emma Marie; UAlta hon. LLD; hockey exec.; jr. Peterborough, Sault Ste. Marie; OHA rookie of year '77-78; pro WHA Indianapolis '78-79 (rookie of year), Edmonton (WHA, NHL) '79-88, Los Angeles '88-95, St. Louis '95-96, NYR '96-99; nicknamed "Great One"; scoring prowess rewrote record book; at retirement held/shared 61 NHL records; 9 50+ goal seasons; 4 times topped 200-point single season 212 '81-82, 205 '83-84, 208 '84-85, 215 '85-86; record 92g single 80-game season '81-82; 163a '85-86; youngest player to achieve 1000pts (in 424th game '84-85 season); surpassed Gordie Howe's all-time NHL goal record of 801 '94, assist record of 1850 '97; 9 Hart Trophies, 8 in succession, '80-87, '89; 10 Ross Trophies, 7 in succession, '81-87, '90-91, '94; 4 Lady Byng Trophies, 5 Lester B Pearson awards; 2 Conn Smythe trophies, '94 Lester Patrick award; 3 Emery Edge; 3 performer-of-yr awards; 8 1st team, 7 2nd team all-star ctr; 4 NHL plus/minus titles; 18 NHL all-star games; 3 NHL all-star game MVP awards; Lou Kaplan WHA rookie-of-'79 award; mem. '78 jr. worlds, '82 worlds, 4 Canada Cup teams (3 titles), capt. '96 World Cup team, mem. '98 Olympic team; NHL record: 1487 scheduled games, 894g, 1963a, 208 playoff games, 122g, 260a; mem. 4 Stanley Cup winners; 51-game consecutive point scoring streak '83-84; fastest 50 goals 39 games '81; 6 Lionel Conacher, 4 Lou Marsh trophies; *SI* Sportsman of '82, Hickox Pro athlete of '83; 3 successive Seagram's 7 Crowns hockey-player-of-yr awards; 4 *Sporting News*, 5 *Hockey News* awards; *AP*, Ont. athlete-of-year awards; *AP* male athlete of decade '89; *Hockey News* Greatest-Player-of-All-time award '98; *CP* Cdn male athlete of century; *AP* hockey player of century; *SI* Cdn athlete of century list; jersey 99 ret'd by NHL; co-owner, pres. Belleville Bulls Jr.A OHA '82-84; owner Hull Olympiques QMJHL '85-92; co-owner with Bruce McNall, John Candy of CFL Argos

'91-93; co-owner Phoenix Coyotes; GM Team Canada '02 Olympic gold, '04 worlds; partner restaurant chain, Windsor Rec. complex; Brantford Rec. complex, Edmonton street bear his name; Officer Order of Canada '84; initial recipient US Hockey Hall of Fame award bearing his name; Olympic Order; Wayne Gretzky Fantasy Camp launched '03; Wayne Gretzky Foundation; active in community charitable programs; participated in successful Cdn bid for 2010 winter Olympics; mem. Canadian Walk, Brantford Wall, Alta., Canada's Sports, Hockey, IIHF halls of fame; res. Thousand Oaks, Calif.

GRIBBIN, Chris (administration/skiing/golf); b. 20 Aug 1921, Montreal, Que.; given name: Christopher Howard; m. Yvette Gerin-Lajoie; c. Christine, Michael, Philip; Loyola, BA, McGill, Montreal; ret'd exec.-dir. Quebec Golf Assn., professor Montreal; Cdn Ski Instructors Alliance secty-treas, Level IV examiner '48-63; 12yrs Montreal alpine, nordic ski coach; Intl Assn Golf Administrators pres. '78-79; began QGA association as tournament dir. '54, exec. dir '66-90; instrumental in translation of golf rules to French '60s; established Que. provincial qualifying system; initiated most favorable "Greenbelt" legislation '70s; stimulated prov., district annual golf symposiums; co-ordinated turfgrass referral service subsidized by QGA, bilingual club handbook; developed training program to improve candidates for Willingdon Cup team; promoted modernization QGA constitution; res. Pte. Claire, Que.

GRIFFIN, Audrey (swimming); b. 16 Jun 1902, Burgess Hill, Sussex, Eng.; d. 28 Aug 1995, Victoria, B.C.; given name: Audrey Mildred; m. John Russell Kieran; St. Anne's Academy; ntl, Pacific Northwest titles; never lost a BC women's championship entered '15-30; tireless competitor, swam every distance from 50yds to 3 miles, never losing a 220-, 440- or 880yd event; nicknamed "Mike"; 5 ntl championships, twice runnerup; 9 Victoria mixed 3 mile swim titles in 12 attempts, beating both men, women; mem. BC, Greater Victoria Sports halls of fame.

GRIFFIN, Pat (wheelchair basketball); b. 14 Nov 1960, Alberton, P.E.I.; given name: Patrick Emmett; m. Barbara Jean Lalor; c. Craig Patrick; St. Mary's, BComm; senior inquiries agent Revenue Canada Taxation; began playing wheelchair basketball '79; mem. Edmonton Raiders, 4 ntl titles, 4 championship MVP awards; mem. Team Canada from '84, capt. '86-92; co-capt. '92 Paralympic team; gold Stoke-Mandeville Games '89-91; competed '96 Paralympics; high scoring performer; 4th '86 ntl wheelchair 10km road race; mem. ntl bronze medal sledge hockey team '94 Paralympics, Norway; res. Edmonton, Alta.

GRIFFING, Dean (football); b. 17 May 1915, St George, Kan.; d. 1998, Sandwich, Ill.; div. Bea Metcalfe; c. Barbara, Doug; m. Ann Dockendorf; c. Christopher, Susan; Kansas State; ret'd restaurateur; ctr Chicago Cardinals '35; helped Regina win '36 WIFU title but CRU ruled club had broken eligibility rules so Grey Cup challenge rights were forfeited; nicknamed "Bad Man"; 5 times all-Cdn ctr; Sask. player-coach through '43; Toronto Balmy Beach player-line coach '44; owner-coach Stampeders '45-47; mgr. Roughriders '54-57; operated all-America Bowl Game Tucson '58-59; mgr. Denver (AFL) '59-63; scout Detroit, Chicago to '70; mem. Cdn Football Hall of Fame.

GRIFFIS, Si (hockey); b. 1883, Onaga, Kansas; d. Jul 1950, Kenora, Ont.; given name: Silas Seth; rover, def Rat Portage (Kenora) Thistles '03-07; ret'd following '07 season, returned '12-18 Vancouver Millionaires (PCHA); helped Kenora claim league titles '00-04, Stanley Cup '06; capt. Millionaires Stanley Cup final '15; nicknamed "Sox"; stroked jr. 4s '05 Canadian Henley title; excelled as southpaw golfer, 10-pin bowler; mem. NWO Sports, Hockey halls of fame.

GRIFFITH, Cal (baseball/administration); b. 1 Dec 1911, Montreal, Que.; d. 20 Oct 1999, Melbourne, Fla.; given name: Calvin; Staunton Military Academy, George Washington U; baseball executive; following father's death '20, he and sister Thelma adopted by uncle Clark; Washington Senators batboy '22; gained baseball club operation experience Chatanooga, Charlotte, AL Senators; on death of uncle '55, co-owner (with sister), pres. Senators; transferred club to Minnesota '60, renamed Twins; under his regime '65 AL pennant, World Series loss to LA 4-3, 2 div. titles ('69-70); sold club '84.

GRIFFITH, Harry (coaching); b. 19 Sep 1878, Hamilton, Ont.; d. 9 Dec 1960, Toronto, Ont.; given name: Henry Crawford; m. Ethel Clare Wright; c. 1 son, 1 daughter; Ridley College, Trinity College, BA, MA; educator; qb varsity football team; coached Trinity '07-10, 2 consecutive Grey Cups; Ridley rugby, cricket coach '11-49; mem. Canada's Sports, Cdn Football Hall of Fame.

GRIFFITHS, Frank (builder/hockey); b. 17 Dec 1916, Burnaby, B.C.; d. 7 Apr 1994, Vancouver, B.C; UBC, FCA; founded/developed Northwest Sports Enterprises '74 and purchased Vancouver hockey club; fostered relations with Vancouver-based club and province; NHL governor '74-94; vice-chair. NHL, mem. audit comm. '79-87; assisted numerous clubs in solidifying finances; mem. Hockey Hall of Fame.

GRIFFITHS, Joe (coaching); b. Mar 1885, Swansea, Wales; d. 22 Jul 1967, Saskatoon, Sask.; m. Mary Elizabeth Byers; c. Betty, Patricia; UofSask. hon. LLD teacher; 32yrs t&f, swimming coach UofSask.; coached each sport in separate Olympics '36, '48; UofSask. swim team unbeaten 11 straight years; organized 1st annual Sask. HS t&f meet; Griffiths's Trophy awarded annually to western collegiate swim title team; Regina Stadium named in his honor; life mem. Royal Life Saving Society; CAHPER honor award; Saskatoon Citizen of Year; mem. Sask., Saskatoon Sports halls of fame.

GRIMSLEY, Ross (baseball); b. 7 Jan 1950, Topeka, Kan.; given name: Ross Albert III; m. Byrd Worrell; c. Patrick; Jacksonville State Community Coll.; baseball coach; all-conf., J.C. all-American; drafted by Cincinnati '69; minors with Sioux Falls (A), Indianapolis (AAA); ML lhp with Cincinnati '71-73, Baltimore '73-77, '82, Montreal '78-79, Cleveland '80-81; ML record: 345 games, 124-99, 3.52era, 2039ip, 559bob, 750k, 79 complete games; became 1st 20-game winner in Expos history '78 with 20-11 record, 2.05era, earned all-star status; 2-1 record '72 World Series; minor league pitching coach for Mariners '84-89, '90-93, Braves '89; dir. baseball operations Amarillo Dillas '94-95; pitching coach Rochester (AAA) '96, Reading (AA) from '97; nicknamed "Skuz"; res. Timonium, Md.

GRINER, Wendy (figure skating); b. 16 Apr 1944, Hamilton, Ont.; given name: Wendy Elizabeth; m. Dr. Donald Peter Ballantyne; c. Peter, Rob, Karen; Branksome Hall; registered medical technologist; '59 ntl jr. champion; sr. title '60-63; NA title '63; silver '62 world championships; mem. '60, '64 Olympic teams; res. Thunder Bay, Ont.

GRINNELL, Rae (skiing); b. 24 Apr 1921, Toronto, Ont.; m. Betty Heron; c. Eric, Jane, Douglas, Sheila; UNB, BScF; ret'd forest economist; zone, provincial, CIAU titles; developed ski clubs several areas in Canada; Ont. zone, div. pres. CASA 12 years, ntl pres. '61-64; 1st Cdn, 2nd NA on FIS Council '63-71; mem. FIS eligibility comm. '62-73; COA dir. '63-73; chairman National Ski Museum; 8yrs exec. mem., v-p Canadian Amateur Sports Federation; mem. Cdn Skiing Hall of Fame; res. Manotick, Ont.

GROFF, Doug (canoeing/skiing); b. 16 Sep 1912, Winnipeg, Man.; d. 1993, Winnipeg, Man.; m. Florence Kieper; c. Judith, Geraldine, Susan, Nancy; ret'd wholesale sporting goods; mem. Winnipeg Canoe Club; 6 sr. singles titles; 5 65-mile Les Voyageurs race titles; won Cdn intermediate fours '35, singles '36, tandem '37, Sr. tandem, singles '37; cox Cdn quarter-mile war canoe titlist '38; won American Canoe Assn. 6-mile singles, single blade 4s, double blade 4s, Sr. singles '38; qualified for '40 Olympic team winning 10,000m tandem '39; won Man. Sr. 4s '46; rear-commodore WCC '38, vice-commodore ACA '38; chair. WCC 85th reunion '78, pres. WCC past commodores assn, hon. commodore WCC '80; mem. 3-man team making 1st ski ascent Mt. Athabasca '40; chief ski mountaineering instructor Cdn army '43-44; chair. Manitoba Zone CASA '48; chair. CASA Central div.; Man. downhill title '35, slalom '35-36, '38-39, jumping '36, '38, x-country '37-40, Srs. slalom '79; life mem. WSC; won 141 International dinghy sailing title Red River '39; won Labatt's Pro-Am golf title Pine Ridge '62; chair., v-p organizing board '67 PAG committee; mem. Man. Order of Buffalo Hunt; honored by Winnipeg Police Commission, PAG Assn., Man. Good Citizenship award; mem. Man. Sports Hall of Fame.

GROSS, George Jr. (water polo); b. 8 Mar 1952, Toronto, Ont.; Yale, BSc; UofT, BEd; owner G-Squared Promotion Ltd., G-Squared Productions Ltd.; competitive swimmer, mem. '73 FISU Games team; ntl water polo team '75-87; averaged goal-per-game 170 consec. intl games; def 2 Olympic, 5 PAG, 2 FISU, 3 world championships teams; bronze '79, '83 PAG; competed ntl championships '77-94, 14yrs all-star, MVP '81, '86; 2 UofT MVP awards; men's ntl team coach '87-91, '94-96; founder/coach Toronto Golden Jets '81-91, 2 titles, Phantoms '93-95, 1 title; 5 Eastern WP League (US) all-star awards; International referee; accredited Level 1 clinic conductor; Sport Canada consultant '77-79; pres. Golden Jets, Phantoms, mem. Ont. WP board; deeply involved at administration level of sport; columnist for now defunct *Aquatics* magazine; founded/folded *Inside Water* magazine; masters swimmer; mem. Yale Wall, Ont. Aquatic Hall of Fame; res. Thornhill, Ont.

GROUT, Cameron (swimming); b. 23 Oct 1939, Montreal, Que.; given name: Robert Cameron Lundy; m. Marsha Leigh Beaton; c. Christi, Robin; McGill, BSc; investment dealer; 21 ntl titles; medalist '58 BEG, '59 PAG; finalist '60 Olympics; coach MAAA '63-64, Que. all-star team

'64; dir. CASA Que. section '64-65, NS section '73-75; pres. NS section CASA '70-72; ntl dir. CASA '73-75; 1st pres. Sport NS '70-73; dir. Olympic Club Canada '73-75, pres. '73-74; dir. COA '74; dir. SFC '72-73; chair. NS Kinsmen Special Olympics '73; chair. Oakville Parks, Recreation Commission '76-90; chair. Canadian Council for co-operation in aquatics '77-78; NS award for sport, recreation administration '75; hon. life mem. Sport NS; Canadian swimmer of year '58-59; Montreal athlete of '58-59; outstanding McGill athlete '58; mem. McGill, MAAA Hall of Fame; res. Oakville, Ont.

GROUT, Glen (diving); b. 31 May 1952, N.Vancouver; B.C.; SFU; ntl jr. 1m, 3m springboard titles '69; gold 3m winter nationals '72; bronze 2m, silver 10m '73 summer nationals; silver 10m '73 winter nationals; gold 10m '75 winter nationals; mem. '73, '75 worlds, '74 CG, '76 Olympic teams; res. Vancouver, B.C.

GROVES, Kristina (speed skating); b. 4 Dec 1976, Calgary, Alta.; given name: Kristina Nicole; UCalgary, kinesiology; mem. sr. ntl team from '97; 3000m, 1500m gold '98, all-around '04 ntls; competed '02 Olympics; ranked 9th overall 1500m, 3000m '02-03 world cup standings; 4th overall at '03 world all round championships; competed '03 world single distance championships; won 1st ever world cup medal in '03 at Baselga di Piné (team pursuit event); 2 Petro Canada Olympic Torch Scholarship, Dairy Farmers of Canada Pure Determination Fund; 6 Ottawa Sport Media Award long-track speed skating awards; Ottawa female amateur athlete of '03, '04 awards; YES Program public speaker for elementary, junior high and high school students; res. Calgary, Alta.

GRUNDY, Art (shooting); b. 1 Dec 1933, Windsor, Ont.; given name: Robert Arthur; m. Sue; c. Gloria, Angela, Arlene; ret'd GM supervisor; began competitive shooting '48; ntl small-bore champion '64; mem. '80 Olympic team; qualified 11 Bisley, 4 Palma teams; Ont. Games gold '73; 2 Indiana State prone titles; mem. North Shore, Cedar Springs Rifle Clubs, Livonia Sportsman Club; active hockey, slow-pitch softball player; mem. '70-71 ntl Sr. B lacrosse champion Windsor Warlocks; NRA distinguished marksman award '94; nicknamed "The Grunt"; res. Belle River, Ont.

GUAY, Lucie (canoeing); b. 12 Dec 1958, Montreal, Que.; m. Yvon Robert; c. Francis, Simon; ex-electrical supply co. employee, fitness dir.; kayak specialist; ntl jr. K1 500m record; 5 ntl K4 500m, 2 K2, 1 K1 titles; 12 500m, mostly K4, titles international regattas; mem. bronze 500m K4 crew '84 Olympics; mem. ntl team '79, '81, '82, '83 worlds, '80, '83 Pan-Am championships, '81 Commonwealth Cup, '80, '84 Olympic Games; res. Blainville, Que.

GUDEREIT, Marcia (curling); b. 8 Sep 1965, Moose Jaw, Sask; given name: Marcia Schiml; m. Kerry Gudereit; c. Colin; systems analyst; began curling age 15; lead for Sandra Schmirler's STOH, world title rinks '93-94, '97, gold '98 Olympics; res. Regina, Sask.

GUDWER, Doug (skiing); b. 22 Jun 1956, Prince George, B.C.; given name: Douglas Wade; Ft. Lewis College, Durango, Colo.; park ranger; x-country specialist; 3rd '72 ntl jr. championships; ntl team '72; US jr. title '73; ntl jr. '74;

all-American '75-76; spare '76 Olympics; Canadian 50km title; mem. world championships team '78; 3 1sts '80 ntl championships; Mark Warber scholastic award '75; mem. Prince George Hall of Fame; res. Calgary, Alta.

GUELLY, Debbie (rodeo); b. 13 Oct 1968, Fort St. John, B.C.; m. Gord Renger; barrel racing specialist; NRA pole bending title '84; 2 NRA steer-undecorating titles; NRA cowgirl of '89; joined CPRA ranks '90; Alta LBR Futurity ('91), Derby ('92) titles; Bud pro tour LBR title '95; 3 SK circuit LBR titles; 3 Alta circuit LBR titles; holds LBR single-season money-winning record; Wrangler circuit LBR title '96; 4 ntl LBR titles; res. Okotoks, Alta.

GUERIN, Bill (hockey); b. 9 Nov 1970, Worcester, Mass.; m. Kara; c. Kayla, Grace, Liam; Boston Coll; rw Boston Coll '89-91; AHL Utica '91-93; Team USA '89, '90 world jr., '96 world cup, '98. '02 (silver) Olympics; NHL New Jersey '91-97, Edmonton '97-00, Boston '00-02, Dallas '02-04; NHL record (through '04): 879 scheduled games, 315g, 308a, 91 playoff games, 25g, 19a; 1 Stanley Cup winner; Edmonton team MVP; NHL '01 all-star game MVP; in Sweden during '04-05 labor dispute; res. Wilbraham, Mass.

GUERRERO, Vladimir (baseball); b. 9 Feb 1976, Nizao Bani, Dominican Republic; given name: Vladimir Alvino; of; joined pro ranks '93 playing in minors with developmental, rookie, Albany, West Palm Beach (A), Harrisburg (AA) before joining parent Montreal '96-03, Anaheim '04; established himself as a franchise player with prodigious home runs; set franchise record 42 homers, 131rbi, 84 extra-base hits, .600 slugging percentage, 31-game hitting streak (tops in ML) in '99; 1st Expo to top 30hr, 100rbi, 100r 2 consec. seasons; hit for cycle '03; ML all-star; brother Wilton (infielder) Montreal teammate; 3 silver-slugger awards; 4 Expos player-of-yr awards; *Baseball America's* AA player of '96, Eastern League MVP, rookie of yr, all-star, Rawlings rookie of yr, *SN* minor league player of '96; EL batting title '96; 9rbi game vs. Boston '04; AL MVP '04; ML record (through '04) 1160 scheduled games, 4375ab, 765r, 1421h, 265db, 36tr, 273hr, 828rbi, 138sb, .325ba; res. Nizao Bani, DR.

GUEST, Jack (rowing); b. 28 Mar 1906, Montreal, Que.; d. 12 Jun 1972, Toronto, Ont.; given name: John Schofield; m. Mary Macdonald; c. John Jr., Donald; business exec.; jr., assn. singles '27; mem. Argonaut jr. 8s under coach Joe Wright Sr., twice lost Diamond Sculls titles to Joe Wright Jr. '28-29; with Joe Jr. silver double sculls '28 Olympics; ntl single sculls title '29; defeated German champion by nearly 200yds to win world Diamond Sculls '30; ret'd from competition '30; pres. Don RC '38-52, Dominion Day Regatta Assn. '46-56, CAAO '55-56; dir. COA '60-68; mgr. '56 Olympic rowing team; asst. mgr. BEG rowing teams '62, '66; 1st Cdn elected to world rowing governing body (FISA) '69; mem. Cdn Olympic, Canada's Sports halls of fame.

GUILBAULT, Michele (golf); b. 7 Jan 1960, Montreal, Que.; Florida State; ntl reduction in handicap award '74, dropping from 26 to 9; 3 Que. amateur titles; Que., ntl jr. '78; low amateur '79 Peter Jackson Classic; mem. Que. jr. team '76-78; Que. amateur team '79-81; ntl jr. team '77-78; sr. team '79-80; Commonwealth team '79; FSU team '79-81; 5 intercollegiate victories '79-80; all-American '81, all-state

'79-81, all-region '80-81; mem. AIAW title team '81; 8 course records; Canada's top jr. golfer '77; Que. athlete of '78; HS athlete of '77; mem. Canada's 1st Commonwealth title team '79; res. Pte Claire, Que.

GUINN, Tom (shooting); b. 1 Sep 1944, St. Catharines, Ont.; electrician; pistol specialist; mem. ntl team from '74; free-pistol gold, air pistol bronze, team bronze '83 CG; free-pistol team gold, air pistol silver '86 CG; free-pistol gold, team gold '79 PAG; ntl air pistol title '81; Benito Juarez air pistol gold '78; mem. '76, '80, '84 Olympic, '75, '79, '83 PAG, '82, '86 CG; 9 Benito Juarez, 6 Worlds championships teams; SFC Golden Anniversary Award '82; fed. govt. award '83; res. Fonthill, Ont.

GUNELL, Roy (water polo); b. 28 Aug 1943, Hamilton, Ont.; given name: Roy Richard; m. Patricia; c. Lisa, Joel; UofT, Teachers' College; teacher; competitive swimmer Hamilton Y, Aquatic Club '56-63; mem. 7 ntl title water polo teams '58-72; Ont., ntl referee from '71; v-p Water Polo Canada '74-77; FINA referee, 7 world, 3 PAG, 3 Olympic, 5 FISU Games, more than 125 international events; founded, coached, administered Stoney Creek Water Polo Club '84-94, 3 Ont. titles; chair. coaches comm. OWPA '93; HS coach from '70; McMaster Friends of Distinction, Ont. Special achievement awards; FINA officiating plaque; chair. Water Polo Can. Officials comm.; mem. exec. comm. International Referees Assn. of Water Polo; mem. Ont. Aquatic Hall of Fame; res. Stoney Creek, Ont.

GUNNLAUGSON, Lloyd (curling); b. 18 Dec 1929, Cypress River, Man.; d. 5 Jun 1988, Winnipeg, Man.; given name: Lloyd Harold; m. Jeanette Collins; c. Darryl, Derrick, Lynette, Alanna; plasterer; began curling Man. jampail ranks; part owner Valour Rd. CC; Man. seniors titles '82-85, Ntl seniors '82-84, runnerup '84; skipped '83 Man. men's title rink, a rare title double; won 4 MCA bonspiel events, 6 Valour Rd. CC club titles; Man. athlete-of-year nominee '84; p-pres. Valour Rd. CC; club rep. to MCA; life mem. MCA, Valour Rd. CC; nicknamed "Gunner"; mem. Canadian Curling, Man. Sports halls of fame.

GUNTER, Andy (shooting); b. 5 Sep 1892, Lower Queensbury, N.B.; d. 4 Jul 1986, Saint John, N.B.; given name: Andrew George; m.; c. Doug; educator; mem. Cdn Bisley team '33; adjutant Cdn Bisley team '48; placed in Queen's 100 '48; secty-treas. Saint John Rifle Assn. '28-31, NB Rifle Assn.; City of Ottawa gold medal '32; Bostock trophy '32; Ntl Rifle Assn medal '33; Donegal medal (Bisley) '33; hon. life mem. DCRA; mem. NB Sports Hall of Fame.

GURNEY, Helen (coaching); b. 16 Oct 1918, Whitby, Ont.; UofT, BA, BEd; ret'd educator; coached Windsor Forster Spartans to 8 city, WOSSA basketball, 8 volleyball, 7 overall t&f titles and 16 divisional track titles '44-58; officiated women's basketball on international level 22yrs; formed 1st women's board of officials Windsor '45-46; editor women's basketball rule book '62-67; founding mem. OFSAA, mem. of OFSAA '52-77; Cdn rep. to American Physical Education Assn.; authored several books including history of girls sports in Ont and history of CAHPER; recognized authority in youth leadership development; key role in founding Cdn. Women's Interuniversity AA; UofT honor award; Tait

McKenzie award; OFSAA citation; Bing Caswell award; Sport Canada coach-of-yr award; Thomas Louden award; YWCA Women of Distinction award; UofT Arbor award; Toronto Life Fashion award; Queen's silver, golden jubilee medals; Herstory Award; fellow NA Society; life mem. OEA, OPHEA; mem. UofT, Windsor Essex Sports halls of fame; res. Don Mills, Ont.

GURNEY, Jack (football); b. 9 Apr 1923, Brantford, Ont.; d. 27 Nov 2004, Ottawa, Ont.; given name: John Thomas; m. Doreen Melba Shaw; c. Diane Charlene (d), Elisabeth Ann; McMaster, BA; ret'd Bell Canada; refereed basketball, soccer, baseball all levels to college '42-73; minor football official '44-52, all leagues through college '52-73; OUAA referee-in-chief '73-89; amateur football case book editor '72-90; secty. Canadian Football Officials Assn. '69-78, rules interpreter '79-90; editor, rules interpreter Canadian rule book for amateur football '76-90; Air Canada amateur-official-of-'86 award; mem. McMaster Sports, Cdn Football halls of fame.

GUROWKA, Joe (curling); b. 28 Apr 1933, The Pas, Man.; m. Shirley Young (d); c. Jim, Kim; UMan, BComm.; UWO, MBA; ret'd civil engineer, co. pres.; rep. Dixie Curling Club in provincial play 18 years earning nickname "Dixie Joe"; 10 Ont. championships appearances, twice winner; runnerup '66 Brier; mem. 3 Ont., 3 Cdn sr. title rinks; Cdn Masters title '00; Canada Life bonspiel title '69, '79; pres. OCA '83-84; CCA '88-89; chair. Curl Canada development comm.; chair. Curl Ont.; active provincial, ntl coach; mem. Gov.-Gen.'s Curling Club; mem. Cdn Curling Hall of Fame; res. Mississauga, Ont.

GURR, Donna-Marie (swimming); b. 18 Feb 1955, Vancouver, B.C.; taxi driver; 5 gold '69 British nationals; mem. '70, '74 CG, '71 PAG, '72 Olympic teams; 3 PAG gold, 2 CG, 1 PAG silver, 3 CG, 1 Olympic bronze medals; ntl backstroke titlist '69-72; 5 Canada Summer Games, 10 ntl titles; mem. Order of Canada; mem. BC Sports, Swimming, Cdn Aquatic halls of fame; res. Vancouver, B.C.

GURUNLIAN, Varouj (basketball); b. 1 Mar 1955, Alexandria, Egypt; m. Sylvia Stepanian; c. Christopher, Lisa, Christine; Dawson College, Laurentian, St.FX, BSc, BEd; HS teacher; soccer, basketball in Egypt; moved to Montreal age 14; HS basketball, soccer MVP awards '69-73; 3yrs Dawson basketball all-star; top scorer Que. '75 Canada Games gold medal team; mem. Dawson ntl title team, all-Canadian, MVP, college athlete of '76; St.FX rookie of '77; AUAA all-star '78-81; 2nd all-time St.FX scorer; all-Cdn, athlete of '81; St.FX foul shooting percentage record '81; mem. ntl team '76-84; gd '80, '84 (alternate) Olympic, '77, '79, '81 FISU, '83 PAG teams, gold '78 Commonwealth championships; coached HS, 3yrs Dawson. ntl gold, silver, bronze, Que. team to gold '85 Canada Games; university level referee; listed in *Armenian American Who's Who in Sport*; mem. Dawson College Hall of Fame; res. Montreal, Que.

GUTNICK, Paul (shooting); b. 7 Jun 1927, Winnipeg, Man.; given name: Paul Eugene; m. Terrence Elizabeth Nydis; c. Raymond Charles, Bernard Lyndon; office mgr., accountant; began competitive shooting at 16; among

finest marksmen in Man. history winning virtually all major match titles over span of more than 40yrs; rep. Man. in DCRA competition 25 consec. yrs; mem. '62 Bisley team; while shooting in '70 Manitoba summer matches won unprecedented six titles including grand aggregate; 1st Manitoban to win Calgary Frost on Pumpkin shoot; mem. 1st militia team to beat Cdn Forces regulars and Americans; active in shooting administration; exec. council mem. MPRA, DCRA; conducted hunter safety programs; Queen's Jubilee medal '78; res. Winnipeg, Man.

GUZZO, Patrick (hockey/softball/baseball); b. 14 Oct 1917, Ottawa, Ont.; d. 19 Jan 1993, Ottawa, Ont; m. Mary; c. Patrick, Barry, Donnie, Meri-Lee; county court officer; sr. softball pitcher at 15; mem. Eastern Ont. title teams; among leading pitchers, hitters 12 seasons '30s-'40s; mem. Ont. baseball title teams, 3 Hull, Que. title teams; mem. 2 int., 2 interscholastic hockey title teams; 3 Allan Cup Eastern Cdn finals; mem. '48 Olympic, RCAF Flyers world title teams; numerous hockey MVP awards; nicknamed "Patsy"; mem. Cdn Forces, Ottawa Sports halls of fame.

GWYNNE, Lefty (boxing); b. 5 Oct 1912, Toronto, Ont.; d. 16 Apr 2001, Toronto, Ont.; given name: Horace; m. Henrietta Aisbitt; c. John, Gordon, Larry; ret'd rec. centre employee; 118lb gold '32 Olympics; pro bantamweight boxer '35-39; Canadian pro bantamweight title '38-39; ret'd undefeated '39; 26yrs jockey, trainer, jockey's agent; mem. Cdn Olympic, Canada's Sports, Boxing halls of fame.

H

HACKNER, Al (curling); b. 18 Jul 1954, Nipigon, Ont.; given name: Allan; m. Margaret Nicol; c. Andrew, Graham; railway switchman; skipped Alta. mixed title winner '77; men's NOnt. titles '80-82, '85, '88-89, '92, '95, '01; Brier runnerup '80-81; skipped Rick Lang, Bob Nicol, Bruce Kennedy ('82), Lang, Ian Tetley, Pat Perroud ('85) to Brier, World championships; 5 Thunder Bay, 3 Longlac, 2 Regina, 1 St. John's, Edmonton, Sault Ste. Marie, Saskatoon, Kelowna, Kamloops major cashspiel titles; fed. govt. world champion award '82; mem. Cdn Curling, (team) NWO Sports halls of fame; res. Thunder Bay, Ont.

HADFIELD, Vic (hockey); b. 4 Oct 1940, Oakville, Ont.; given name: Victor Edward; driving range operator; lw; jr. St. Catharines Teepees; pro AHL Buffalo '60-61, Baltimore '62-63, NHL NYR '61-74, Pittsburgh '74-77; 2nd team all-star '72; mem. Team Canada '72; mem. NYR GAG Line; plodding digger with tough guy reputation; scored 50g '72; capt. Rangers '71; scout Rangers '78-79; NHL record: 16 seasons, 1002 scheduled games, 323g, 389a, 74 playoff games, 27g, 21a; res. Burlington, Ont.

HADLOW, Terry (weightlifting); b. 13 Nov 1957, North Bay, Ont.; UofOtt; strength coach, trainer; gold 67.5kg '75 Canada Games; 90kg '78, '80-81 national championships; gold, national sr. record 90kg '80 Pan-Am championships; bronze 90kg '77 Queen's silver jubilee; silver 90kg '78 CG, '79 PAG; mem. '80, '84 Olympic teams; received absolute discharge following conviction for importing anabolic steroids '84; expelled from '84 Olympics for failure to pass steroids test; trainer ntl men's volleyball team '99; coach Man. High Performance Centre, Dakota Ringette, UMan. Volleyball, Winnipeg MJHL Blues; res. Winnipeg, Man.

HAFEY, Art (boxing); b. 17 Jan 1951, Stellarton, N.S.; given name: Arthur Douglas; m. Cathy Marie MacKenzie; self employed; former number 1 contender for world featherweight title; lost title bid on TKO to multi-titlist Alexis Arguello '74; split matches vs. Reuben Olivaries, winning by TKO, losing by decision; KO'd former world jr. lightweight champion Alfredo Marcano; stopped in 7 by future world featherweight champ Danny Lopez in final pro bout; forced into early retirement by eye injury; turned briefly to coaching in PEI; mem. Stellarton Hearts Wall, NS, Pictou County Sports, Cdn Boxing halls of fame; res. Trenton, N.S.

HAHN, Robin (equestrian); b. 19 Jun 1933, Regina, Sask.; m. Maureen; c. Apryl, Amber, Jaysen; UBC; farmer; began showing horses Western Canada age 17; mem. 3-day event team '67, '71 PAG, '68, '72, '76 Olympics; 5th '67 PAG 3-day aboard Warden; 9th '68 Olympics aboard Taffy; '70, '72 ntl 3-day titles; capt. '71 PAG gold team; capt. '76 Olympic 3-day team; active in sport's exec. branch provincially, nationally; qualified show judge; conducts horsemanship clinics in US, Canada; mem. Sask. Sports Hall of Fame; res. Lumley, B.C.

HAIG, Cathy (field hockey); b. 22 Feb 1957, Montreal, Que.; John Abbott College, McGill; teacher, fitness instructor; mem. Que. sr. team, ntl team '77-81; mem. bronze medal team European Zone indoor championships '81; Montreal West HS athlete of '70-74; John Abbott College athlete of '76; Que. field hockey player of '77, '81; res. St. Pierre, Que.

HAIGHT, Deedee (skiing); b. 28 Apr 1964, Trail, B.C.; given name: Diana Catherine; m. Thomas Arn; ntl juv title '78; overall Europa Cup title '81; FIS slalom title '83; 2 top 10 WC finishes through '83-84; mem. '84 Olympic team; ntl downhill title '84; chair. Alpine Can. high performance advisory comm.; res. Armstrong, B.C.

HAIGHT, Jim (hockey); b. 2 Jun 1913, Humboldt, Sask.; given name: James Oscar; m. Anna Nova Bannantyne (d); c. Barbara Gale, James Wilson; Nutana College; ret'd Cominco; mem. '30 Saskatoon Wesleys provincial midget, '31 juv, '32 Western Cdn jr. titlists; mem. Nelson Maple Leafs '34; Trail Smoke Eaters '35-40; reputation as hard-rock def; mem. '38 Allan Cup, '39 world champions; grand-daughter Deedee ntl ski team; as mem. '38-39 Smoke Eaters mem. BC Sports Hall of Fame; res. Rossland, B.C.

HAINE, Audrey (baseball); b. 9 May 1927, Winnipeg, Man.; given name: Audrey May; m. Austin Daniels; c. Marilyn, Craig, Cheryl, Kathryn, Scott, Douglas; ret'd secretary; rhp; played in AAGPBL, with Minneapolis '44 winning title despite team losing home park; shifted to Ft. Wayne '45, Grand Rapids '46-47. Peoria '47-48, Rockford '51; career record 72-70; 493k, 3.48 ERA; avid bowler, golfer; mem. Man. Baseball Hall of Fame; honored by Cooperstown, Cdn Baseball halls of fame; res. Bay Village, Ohio.

HAINEY, Tom (swimming); b. 6 Nov 1965, Atikokan, Ont.; Brock; co-owner Barrier Breakers Outfitting; coach; born with spina bifida he began swimming age 11, racing age 12; mem. ntl team 11yrs; 22 ntl wheelchair games gold; 14 Stoke-Mandeville Games gold; 8 world wheelchair games gold; 3 gold intl physically disabled games; 4 PA wheelchair gold; competed '84 (5 gold, 3 WR), '88, '92 Paralympics, '94 CG; swam entire 97km width of Quetico Provincial Park in tribute to late mother; athlete rep. Canada Sport Council '96; coach Atikokan, Selkirk, Winnipeg; coach '00 Paralympic swim team; Man. Masters Aquatic Club '97-04; mem. Ont. Aquatic, Terry Fox, NWO Sports halls of fame; res. Winnipeg, Man.

HAINSWORTH, George (hockey); b. 26 Jun 1895, Toronto, Ont.; d. 9 Oct 1950; goal Kitchener jrs, Allan Cup '18; pro Saskatoon '23-24; Canadiens '26-33, '37, Maple Leafs '33-37; stopped first-ever NHL penalty shot Nov. 10 '34 Leafs vs. Canadiens; Vezina trophy 1st 3 seasons with Montreal; allowed 43 goals in 44 games '28-29 with 22 shutouts as team won 22 games; traded to Toronto for Lorne Chabot; died in auto accident; NHL record: 2.02 avg., 91so, 465 scheduled games, 2.15 avg., 8so, 52 playoff games; mem. Hockey Hall of Fame.

HAIST, Jane (t&f); b. 1 Mar 1949, St. Catharines, Ont.; York, Tennessee; mem. '74 CG, '75 PAG, '76 Olympic teams; gold, Cdn, Commonwealth records shot put, discus '74 CG; bronze discus '75 PAG; ntl discus record 61.70m '75 vs. Sweden; best shot performance Cardiff, Wales, '74 16.12m; 11th discus '76 Olympics; gold discus Adelaide International meet, Pacific Conf. Games, Perth International meet '77, Tom Black Classic '79; Rowell Trophy outstanding Cdn amateur athlete in jumping, weight events '74; res. Fenwick, Ont.

HALDER, Wally (hockey/tennis); b. 15 Sep 1925, Toronto, Ont.; d. 27 Oct 1994, Toronto, Ont.; given name: Wallace Edwin; m. Joyce; c. Gregory, Christina, Matthew; UofT, BA, OCE; p-pres. Olympic Trust; capt. UofT hockey team; mem. '48 Olympic gold medal team; swimming, diving instructor Ont. Athletic Commission; coach UotT, Trinity College hockey teams; ntl sr. doubles tennis champion; mem. Gordon Trophy tennis teams; Biggs Trophy UofT; mem. UofT, Ottawa Sports (as mem. 48 Flyers) halls of fame.

HALEY, Andrew (swimming); b. 16 Jan 1974, Moncton, N.B.; Dalhousie BA, UofOtt MA; works for Toronto Blue Jays; began competing age 15 at Sydney, N.S.; 6 ntl, 6 world records; bronze 400m FS '92, 2 bronze '96, gold, bronze, WR '00 Paralympics; 5 gold '93 Cdn Foresters championships; gold 100m FS '94 CG; world gold '98, '02; male athlete-of-yr award; res. Toronto, Ont.

HALL, Chris (lacrosse/coaching); b. 17 Sep 1950, Victoria, B.C.; human resources mgr., coach; mem. 2 Western Lacrosse Assn. title winners, coached 2 others; mem. '79 Mann Cup winner, coached another '83; player/coach 6 Cdn field lacrosse title teams; mem. '82 bronze, '86 silver lacrosse world cup; played professionally Ntl Lacrosse League Boston Bolts '75; ntl team coach '89-94; coached '90 World Cup silver medallists; coach Victoria, Calgary (NLL) lacrosse teams; res. Calgary, Alta.

HALL, Glenn (hockey); b. 3 Oct 1931, Humboldt, Sask.; given name: Glenn Henry; m. Pauline Patrick; c. Patrick, Leslie, Tammy, Lindsay; farmer, hockey coach; goal Windsor Spitfires jrs, MVP; pro Indianapolis AHL '52; Edmonton '53-55 with brief stints at Detroit; 12 shutouts led NHL '56-57; Chicago '57-67, St. Louis '67-71; mem. '61 Stanley Cup winner; 5 times led NHL in shutouts; 3 Vezina trophies; Calder Memorial rookie of year; Conn Smythe Trophy; King Clancy award '93; 7 times 1st team, 4 times 2nd team all-star; NHL record: 896 scheduled games, including 552 in succession (502 started & finished in row), 407-326-163; 2239ga, 2.51 avg., 84so, 115 playoff games, 32ga, 2.79 avg. 6so; 13 all-star games, 27 periods, 22ga, .81 avg.; goaltending consultant Calgary; jersey #1 ret'd by Blackhawks; mem. Sask,, AHL, Hockey halls of fame; res. Stony Plain, Alta.

HALL, Joe (hockey); b. 3 May 1882, Staffordshire, Eng.; d. 5 Apr 1919, Seattle, Wash; given name: Joseph Henry; mem. Winnipeg Rowing Club, Rat Portage until turning pro '05-06 with Kenora; Que. Bulldogs '10-16, 2 Stanley Cups; finished career Montreal Canadiens winning NHA title '18-19; influenza epidemic ended Stanley Cup series in Seattle and Hall's life; mem. Man., Cdn Hockey halls of fame.

HALL, Peter (sailing); b. 5 Jun 1949, Montreal, Que.; given name: Peter William; m. Margot McFarlane; c. Krista, Nicholas, William; Queen's, BA, McGill., BCL.; business developer, lawyer; helmsman in soling, lightning competitions; mem. ntl yachting team from '75; mem. '77 World Cup champion soling crew; '89 Lightning world champion; gold '77, '79, silver '76, '78, '80-81, '94 CORK championships; silver '77, bronze '78 Kiel Week competition; bronze '83 NA, '78 European championships; Lightning silver '87 PAG; competed '91, '95 PAG; Masters world title '01; Royal St. Lawrence Yacht Club titles '00-01; 3 Que., 1 ntl-sailor-of-yr awards; 1 Que team-of-yr award; res. Westmount, Que.

HALLADAY, Del (lacrosse); b. 17 Nov 1972, Victoria, B.C.; given name: Delbert Andrew; m. Miranda Griffith; c. Rex; Loyola College, BA communications; co-owner Elephant Island Orchard Wines; played for Loyola College, '92-95, full lacrosse scholarship, 2 all-American; mem. '92 -19 ntl team; '98 ntl field lacrosse team (silver World Games); 7 yrs WLA; '95 WLA rookie of yr, 3 1st team all-star; Mann Cup '97, '99 Victoria Shamrocks, led Shamrocks in scoring '98; 6yrs NLL; Syracuse Smash, '98-00; capt., top scorer Ottawa Rebel '01; Washington Power '02; asst. capt. Colorado Mammoth; res. Naramata, B.C.

HALLAS, Kory (basketball); b. 23 Apr 1969, Ottawa, Ont.; m. Helene; c. Ashley, Chance; Eastern Mich; policeman; mem. OFSAA champion Almonte HS; NCAA all-star; mem. ntl team '91-98; 3 NBA tryouts; 4yrs pro Europe with Italy, Spain, Lebanon; annual Almonte 3 on 3 charity tournament bears his name; res. Windsor, Ont.

HALLDORSON, Dan (golf); b. 2 Apr 1952, Winnipeg, Man.; given name: Daniel Albert; m. Pat; c. Angie; golf exec., pro golfer; '69 Man. jr.; '71 Man. PGA; 4 Man. Opens; '77 Sask. Open; '80 Que. Open; mem. 6 Cdn World Cup teams, winner (with Jim Nelford) '80, (with Dave Barr '85); twice qualified for pro tour '74, '78, regular '78-00; Pensacola Open '80, Colorado Open '82, Deposit Guaranty Classic '86; CPGA title '86; *Score* magazine outstanding Cdn pro of '82; twice CPGA player of year; Canadian Tour Order of Merit '83; competed on USPGA, Asia, Ben Hogan tours, PGA Srs. Tour '02; overcame hand and back ailments which threatened career; deputy dir. Cdn golf tour from '05; mem. Cdn Golf Hall of Fame; res. Cambridge, Ill.

HALLETT, Todd (rowing); b. 12 May 1970, Shelburne, N.S.; m. Emma Taylor; Dalhousie BA; teacher; at urging of friend decided to "give rowing a try" with almost instant success; gold singles, doubles '88 jr. ntls; mem. ntl team '91-02; US straight 4s title '94; competed '92, '96, '00 Olympics; '94-95 worlds; single sculls bronze '91, silver 8s '95 PAG; Rowing Canada junior-sculler-of-'88 award; res. Victoria, B.C.

HALLIDAY, Milton (hockey); b. 21 Sep 1906, Ottawa, Ont.; d. 16 Aug 1989, Ottawa, Ont.; m. Hilda Joad; c. Barry Milton, Marion Hilda, Carolyn Mary; body shop owner; mem. Stewarton AC, Gunners Int. Club; pro Ottawa Senators '26-28; mem. '27 Ottawa Stanley Cup winner, backup ctr to Frank Nighbor; minor pro London, Hamilton, Boston Cubs, Cleveland; nicknamed "The Blond Flash".

HALPENNY, Rachelle (all-around); b. 9 Nov 1950, Hull, Que.; given name: Rachelle Marengere; m. James Halpenny; c. Charles, Justin; St. Lawrence, Algonquin Coll.; sports consultant; gold slalom, rifle shooting, table tennis, bronze archery, track '78 international games for cerebral palsey; gold table tennis, slalom, silver soccer, bronze club (shot put) '82 CP Games; active in community affairs dealing with awareness of needs or persons with disabilities; res. Rockland, Ont.

HALTER, G. Sydney (football/administration); b. 18 Apr 1905, Winnipeg, Man.; d. 24 Oct 1990, Winnipeg, Man.; UMan, BA, LLB; lawyer QC; treas. Winnipeg football club '35, pres. '42; pres. Winnipeg Amateur Athletic Assoc. '30-45; pres. Man. branch AAUofC '35-38, pres. AAUofC '38-46; WIFU commissioner '53-57; initial CFL commissioner '58-66; chair. Man. Horse Racing Commission '65-71, '78-81; Manitoba Sports Hall of Fame honored members gallery bears his name; Officer Order of Canada '77; mem. Cdn Horse Racing, Cdn Olympic, Canada's, Man. Sports, Cdn Football halls of fame.

HALVORSEN, John (t&f); b. 17 Aug 1966, Oslo, Norway; m. Susan Elizabeth Ferguson; c. Tove, Mats, Britt; UofOtt, BSc, MBA; production mgr. Nortel; long-distance running specialist; 4 Norwegian 10,000m, 2 5000m championships; represented Norway '88, '92 Olympics; competed in world x-country races from '85 (as junior); landed immigrant Canada '94; 4 CIAU x-country titles; 3 CIAU x-country all-Cdn; competed '87 FISU Games; won OFSAA sr boys x-country title '89; won several ntl x-country, Timex road race titles; Nordion National Capital 10km title '95; 2 Gasparilla Tampa 15km, 1 Orlando Red Lobster 10km, Spokane Bloomsday 12km, Boston 10km milk run, Jacksonville River Run, titles; competed '91 NY Marathon; set several course records; Runners World road racer of '89; 2 UofOtt athlete-of-yr awards; Nordion race dir., NCM board '00, race dir. '01; res. Kanata, Ont.

HAM, Tracy (football); b. 5 Jan 1964, High Springs, Fla.; m. Valarie; c. Tracy II, Caleb; Georgia Southern (sports management); coach Clark Atlanta '03-04; asst. Bulloch Academy; qb; led GSC to 2 Div 1-AA titles; only player in US college history to rush for more than 3000yds and pass for over 5000yds; turned pro CFL Edmonton '87-92, Toronto '93, Baltimore '94-95, Montreal '96-99; CFL record: 12 seasons. 4945 passes, 2670 complete, 40,534yds, 164int, 284td, 1015 carries, 8043yds, 59td, 354pts.; Jeff Nicklin trophy '89; CFL outstanding player '89; 1 all-Western, 1 all-CFL all-star; set 2 CFL qb rushing records; mem. 3 Grey Cup finals, 1 winner; '95 Grey Cup MVP; nicknamed "Hambone"; active in Athletes in Action; made acting debut in *Raisin in the Sun* '94; res. Statesboro, Ga.

HAMBLY, Fraser (bowling); b. 14 Mar 1943, London, Ont.; m. Hope McBride; York, BA; teacher; began bowling five-pins age 12 quickly stamping himself a natural; won ntl jr. singles, team '57; 2 ntl open singles, 2 Masters team titles; 4 Ont. open singles, 2 open team titles; more than 40 career tournament victories including $10,000 Cdn invitational singles '74, 7 MBA victories; won high tournament average, ntl titles through 5 decades; career avg. 260, 16 perfect 450 games, 2 sanctioned; career-high triple 1162, high five 1654, high 10 3087; proficient golfer; coach 2 Toronto slo-pitch

softball title teams; bowling coach; Toronto Major Bowling League exec.; mem. Ont. 5-pin Bowling Hall of Fame; res. Toronto, Ont.

HAMBROOK, Sharon (synchro swim); b. 28 Mar 1963, Calgary, Alta.; m. Ben Boreyko (d); c. Kelsey, Micaela; with Kelly Kryczka world duet championship '82; silver solo '83, team gold '83, silver '79 PAG, duet silver as sport introduced to '84 Olympic Games; 1 ntl duet, 3 team titles; duet gold Scandinavian Open, Mazda invitational; team gold Scandinavian Open, America Cup; Pan-Pacific solo, figures, duet, 2 team gold; Aquatic Fed. swimmers of '82; fed. govt. world champion award '83, excellence award '84; mem. Cdn Aquatic, Olympic halls of fame; res. La Jolla, Calif.

HAMES, Dick (softball); b. 12 Oct 1935, Windsor, Ont.; given name: Richard Franklin; m. Sherry Kim; c. Richard Alan; pres. Cdn Home Remodelling Group Inc.; WOSSA badminton singles title while attending Kennedy CI; also shone in soccer, basketball; mem. Windsor AKO basketball jrs '53-57; Sarnia Drawbridge '67 Canada Winter Games gold; mem. Team Ont. Cdn sr. A tournament; pitcher Windsor & Dist. Softball '56-59, Providence, RI '60, Windsor sr. OASA champs '61, St. Thomas Memorials '62-67 ('65 OASA Sr A champs, competed provincials '67), London TV Cable '68-71 (CASA champs '70), silver with Winnipeg ISF Worlds '68, Richmond Hills Dynes '71 CASA title, '72 ISF World champs; virus contracted in Phillipines in '72 virtually ended career although he didn't officially retire from Sr.A ranks, with Oshawa Tony's '78; co-founder Ont. Fastball League '73; mem. '94 Oakville A's National Oldtimers Baseball Federation champions; mem. Cdn Softball, Sarnia, Windsor/Essex, Canada's Sports (as member of '72 Dynes) halls of fame; res. Burlington, Ont.

HAMILTON, Doug (rowing); b. 19 Aug 1958, Toronto, Ont.; m. Lynn Polson; c. Frederick, Douglas; Queen's, LLB; lawyer; Cdn Henley jr. pairs title '78; Cdn Henley single sculls, 2 double sculls titles; 2 US ntl single sculls titles; ntl single, double sculls titles; 2 world university single sculls titles; mem. bronze coxless quad sculls crew '84 Olympics; mem. men's gold medal quad '85 worlds (1ˢᵗ Cdn gold at modern world rowing championships); quad sculls bronze '86-87 worlds; quad sculls gold Royal English Henley (course record) '87; mem. '88 Olympic team; v-p high performance Rowing Canada '89-97; COA dir., chair. sports & venues comm. '08 Toronto Olympic bid; chair. Toronto High Performance Centre; Cdn team-of-yr award '85; Kingston athlete of '82; Queen's Jenkins Trophy top male graduating student '83; res. Toronto, Ont.

HAMILTON, Douglas (harness racing); b. 20 Mar 1947, Port Elgin, Ont.; followed grandfather Lambert and father Irwin onto county fair circuit but at 17 elected to pursue bigger purses at Windsor Raceway; after stints with Gerry Bookmyer and the late Ron Feagan he went on his own; through '95 had 3321 victories and purses exceeding $18M; operated from Northlfield Park, Ohio, before shifting to Chicago area; claimed varied driver titles Sportsman's Park, Balmoral; drove Nite Strike to world record for aged pacing mares '86; mem. Northfield Park Hall of Fame; res. Beecher, IL.

HAMILTON, Gar (golf); b. 26 Aug 1949, Toronto, Ont.; given name: Garned Frederick; m. Nancy Hatfield; New

Mexico State, Indiana BSc; head pro Mississauga Golf & Country Club; Ont. Jr champ '66; represented Canada Dominican Intl Amateur '71; all Big-10 team '72; turned pro '73; CPGA tour school champ '73; Ont., Alta., Man. Open titles; 4 Space Coast pro tour titles; qualified for PGHA tour '76-77, '80; exempt status Asian, Australian, European tours '78-80; 5 Ont. PGA player of yr.' 4 CPGA club pro titles; '02 CPGA srs. title; low Cdn AT&T Cdn sr. open '01-02; Ont. PGA '00 pro of yr (administrative) award; res. Oakville, Ont.

HAMILTON, Jack (administration); b. 11 Jun 1886, Caledonia, Ont.; d. 5 Aug 1976, Regina, Sask.; given name: John Welch; m. Elsie White Greason; c. Donald, Hugh; GM lumber co.; organized construction 3500-seat hockey rink Saskatoon '18; coached Regina Vics hockey club '20s, later club pres.; SAHA pres. '25-27; CAHA pres. '30; secty Regina Roughriders football club '23-27, pres. WIFU '28; pres. Sask. branch CAAU, ntl pres. '37; COA exec 17yrs; pres. Sask Amateur Basketball Assn. '33-34, AAUofC '37-38; headed Queen City Gardens Co. which raised funds to install artificial ice in Regina hockey rink, operated rink 11 years; headed operation to construct 3500-seat Moose Jaw rink '57; numerous honors from sport, business community, nation; King George VI coronation medal for work on behalf of athletics; Jack Hamilton rink in Regina; Regina Optimist sportsman of year; CAHA medal of merit; honorary life mem. SAHA; mem. Sask., Cdn Olympic, Canada's Sports halls of fame.

HAMMOND, Alvin (hockey/t&f); b. 18 Dec 1891, Rolla N.D.; d. 11 Mar 1979, Regina, Sask; given name: Richard Alvin; m. Grace Wood; c. Richard Alvin Jr., Margery; salesman; all-around t&f athlete, Sask. 100m, 220-, 440yds sprints, running broad jump, hop, step & jump titles; won these events 3 times in Saskatoon, Regina, Moose Jaw, once Swift Current; represented Sask. 3 times in Olympic trials; hockey Victoria club, '14 world amateur title Regina; mem. Sask. Sports Hall of Fame.

HAMMOND, Gord (lacrosse); b. 5 Mar 1926, Toronto, Ont.; d. Aug 2002, London, Ont.; m. Yvonne Burnie; c. Bob, Joanne, Abbie, Nola, Steve, Ken; Ryerson PTI; ret'd buildings mgr.; mem. Mimico OLA midget title team; Sr. A Mimico/Brampton '43, Mimico '44, Orillia '46, '52-53; Ont. title '43, Eastern Canada '52; Int. Orillia '47, '49, Midland '48, Alliston '50-55; referee '56-64; varied OLA executive roles '65-67; secty-treas. CLA '67-82; gov. Lacrosse Hall of Fame; helped reactivate international competition dormant from '28 with '67 world tournament Toronto; hockey Toronto Navy jrs '43-44, Orillia Terriers Sr. B '47-49; OHA referee '50-60; Alliston lacrosse MVP '50; OLA Mr. Lacrosse award '67; CLA Lester B. Pearson award '76; mem. Cdn Lacrosse Hall of Fame.

HAMPTON, Richard (shooting); b. 12 May 1914, England; d. 23 Dec 1997, Nepean, Ont.; m. Veronica Garvin; c. Ralph; ret'd Cdn Forces major; qualified for Bisley team 21 times; 5 ntl high-powered titles; mem. 4 Cdn Army Bisley teams; gold rifle award; authored regulations, conditions for Cdn Forces rifle competition; top 50 Bisley aggregate DCRA shoot 26 times, top 40 23 times, top 30 21 times, top 20 17 times, top 10 10 times, top 5 5 times; 6 individual DCRA match titles; Bisley Queen's Prize '66; coached Bisley cadet

teams; Desmond Burke Trophy; mem. Canadian Forces Sports Hall of Fame.

HANLAN, Ned (rowing); b. 12 Jul 1855, Toronto, Ont.; d. 4 Jan 1908, Toronto, Ont.; m. Margaret Gordon Sutherland; c. 2 sons, 6 daughters; pro oarsman, politician; US Centennial singles 1876; beat Wallace Ross '77 for Canadian title; beat Eph Morris '78 for US title; by '79, "Boy in Blue" nickname referred to rowing outfit, NA rowing king; 1st oarsman to master sliding seat; world rowing title 6yrs before losing to Australian William Beach '84; ret'd from racing 1901; one end of Toronto Island re-christened Hanlan's Point; town in Australia named in his honor; 20-foot statue erected in his memory CNE '26; lost only 6 of more than 350 career races; Toronto alderman; mem. Ont. Legends, Canada's Sports Hall of Fame.

HANLEY, Bill (builder/hockey); b. 28 Feb 1915, Balleyeast, Northern Ireland; d. 17 Sep 1990, Toronto, Ont.; given name: William; Ont. Agricultural Coll.; became involved with hockey as timekeeper jr., Maple Leafs games; became asst. to George Panter, OHA business mgr.; became secty-mgr. OHA '74 to his death; mem. Hockey Hall of Fame.

HANNIBAL, Frank (builder); b. 23 Sep 1892, Bristol, Eng.; d. 27 Mar 1959, Winnipeg, Man.; joined Winnipeg football exec. '34; helped build club which in '35 would become 1st Western Canadian club to win Grey Cup; became club pres. '41 and was rewarded with another Grey Cup; held many exec. offices, including pres. WIFU; CFL outstanding contribution award '53; mem. Cdn Football Hall of Fame.

HANSEN, Ina (curling); b. 7 Nov 1920, Boissevaine, Man.; d. 20 Oct 2001, Kimberley, B.C.; given name: Georgina Rutherford; m. Alvin Hansen; c. Lynn Vernon, Joanne Candace; UofSask; city clerk; represented Kootenays in BC provincial women's play 18 times, 12yrs in succession; 7 provincial, 3 ntl titles; skipped '62, '64 women's title winners; 3rd for Ada Callas '73 Srs title; East Kootenay zone convenor; mem. BCLCA exec. '55-57, pres. '57; jr. delegate '58, sr. delegate '59 to WLCA; BC voice in establishment of Cdn championships; mem. Canadian Curling Hall of Fame.

HANSEN, Lars (basketball); b. 14 Sep 1954, Copenhagen, Denmark; given name: Lars Erik; Washington, BA; businessman; mem. ntl team '72-77; '76 Olympic, '75 PAG, '73, '77 FISU Games teams; drafted NBA Chicago Bulls; played briefly '80 champion Seattle Supersonics; tryout Kansas City; pro basketball Italy, Spain; res. Coquitlam, B.C.

HANSEN, Rick (all-around); b. 26 Aug 1957, Port Alberni, B.C.; given name: Richard Marvin; m. Amanda Reed; c. Emma Kathleen, Rebecca, Alana; UBC, BPhE; disability consultant, pres./CEO Man in Motion Foundation; truck accident at 15 left him paralyzed both legs; HS most inspirational athlete award; initiated, capt. BC wheelchair volleyball team '76, 3 ntl titles; 7 ntl wheelchair basketball title teams; track sprint, marathon competitor; ntl marathon record, 5 world track records, 1 PAG record; 12 track gold BC Games, gold 800m, silver 1500m, bronze 4x100m relay '80 wheelchair Olympics; 6 gold '82 wheelchair PAG; 7 marathon victories; BC wheelchair tennis singles titles '81-82,

Hawaii Games singles, doubles titles; coached able-bodied volleyball, basketball HS level; Man in Motion 40,000km world tour '87 raised $20M which led to establishment of Rick Hansen Institute at UBC funding research into spinal cord injuries; goodwill ambassador, fund raiser; fed. govt. excellence award '83; BC physically-disabled-athlete-of-yr awards '79-80, '82; outstanding Canadian athlete award; 3 UBC special achievement awards; BC Sports Hall of Fame W.A.C. Bennett award; '94 Royal Bank award; Canada's man of yr '87; Companion Order of Canada '87; co-author 2 books; mem. UBC Sports, Terry Fox, Cdn Road Racing halls of fame; res. Richmond, B.C.

HANSEN, Warren (curling); b. 15 Feb 1943, Edmonton, Alta.; given name: Warren Richard; Northern Alberta Institute of Technology; marketing, public relations; mem. Edmonton Huskies football club 3 consecutive titles '62-64; 2nd Hec Gervais' '74 Brier winner; with Jim Pettapiece launched Silver Broom (world) Curling School '72; 1st tech. dir. Curl Canada '76; responsible for compilation, writing Curl Canada manuals, instructor certification program; CCA, CLCA, Curl Canada dir. marketing, from '80, P.R. '80-90; media attache '92 Olympics; author *Curling: The History, the Players, the Game*; res. Vancouver, B.C.

HANSON, Fritzie (football); b. 13 Jul 1912, Perham, Minn.; d. 14 Feb 1996, Calgary, Alta.; given name: Melvin; m. Maxine; c. Trudy, Marilyn, Paula, Alix; North Dakota State; insurance broker, v-p Reed Stenhouse; brilliant HS career included single game in which he scored 11 tds, 9 converts; Little All-American NDS; WIFU Winnipeg '35-46, Calgary '47-48; elusive running skills earned him nickname "Twinkle Toes"; 8 Grey Cup finals, 4 winners; vs. Hamilton '35 gained 300-plus yards on punt returns, including 78-yarder for td, on muddy field; 5 times WIFU all-star hb, '38 WIFU scoring title, Dave Dryburgh trophy; Lionel Conacher trophy '39; mem. Cdn Football, Man, Canada's Sports halls of fame.

HARDING, Dick (t&f); b. 9 Feb 1934, Chatham, Ont.; given name: Richard; m. Gilliam Bastian; c. Beverley, Wendy, Geoffrey, Timothy, Christopher; UofT, BSc; marketing mgr.; sprint specialist; mem. '54 BEG (440yds), '55 PAG (200m, 400m, relays), '56 Olympic (100m, relay) teams; pres. Que. TFA '62; mgr. t&f team '66 CG; mem. at large COA; Hec Phillips CIAU t&f trophy '54; res. Markham, Ont.

HARE, Dorothy (shooting); b. 16 Jan 1979, Renfrew, Ont.; m. Cameron Ludwig; Augustana Coll., BA; greenhouse worker; following footsteps of 3-time Olympian father Bill she began competitive shooting age 11; competed Canada Winter Games; competed '98, '02 CG earning 10m air pistol doubles gold, singles silver; '99 PAG air pistol gold; 2 Crossman GP air pistol gold; res. Langley, B.C.

HARE, William (shooting); b. 14 May 1935, Ottawa, Ont.; d. 15 Jan 2005, Irricana, Alta.; given name: William Edward; m. Frances Green; c. John, Lorna, Dorothy, Lynda; Carleton, BA, Queen's, BD, St. Paul's U, MA; ret'd United Church minister; pistol specialist, mem. '62, '70, '74 world, '63, '67, '71 PAG, '64, '68, '72 Olympic, '74 CG teams; team silver '63, '71 PAG; 4th overall '67 Canada Winter Games; Ont. handgun title '70; mem. ntl team '62-83; team

mgr. '78-83; competed ntl handgun finals '55-80; gold team standard pistol, silver team air pistol '73 Confederation of Americas shoot; gold rapid fire '74 CG; chair. SFC handgun officials section '69-72, SFC dir. '73-76, ntl handgun team manager '78-83; coach '78 world, CG, '79-80 Karelia matches Finland, '03 PAG.

HARGREAVES, Doug (coaching); b. 20 Dec 1931, Sault Ste. Marie, Ont.; given name: John Walter Douglas; m. Norma Frances; c. Vicki, Gayle, Lynn; Queen's, BA, Dalhousie, UWO, MSc; ret'd football/basketball coach, ret'd Cdn Forces; og Queen's; coached at HS level Kingston, Moose Jaw, Sault Ste. Marie, college level Queen's, RMC, US Coast Guard Academy, Dalhousie, Shearwater, N.S., RCAF flying instructor, HS teacher; AD Dalhousie '72-75; assoc. prof./head coach Queen's '76-94; played major role in running NA-style football clinics in Europe; guided Gaels to league semifinals 16 consec seasons, 9 league titles, 3 Vanier Cup finals, 2 winners; became ntl career leader CIAU football games coached '94; key role in establishing Queen's Football Hall of Fame; lifetime CIAU coaching record 128-103-3; mem. Queen's Football, Coaches, Kingston Sports halls of fame; res. Kingston, Ont.

HARMEN, Wendy (baton twirling); b. 6 Sep 1957, Regina, Sask.; UofReg, BEd; civil servant; capt. Optimist Buffalo Gals world corps, dance twirl champions '76, '78; 5 ntl twirling titles; former ntl Miss Majorette; 1st world hoopbaton, world duet (Pam Wilson Price) '76; tech. chairman Sask.; coach, judge; res. Regina, Sask.

HARNETT, Curt (cycling); b. 14 May 1965, Toronto, Ont.; given name: Curtis Melvin; competitions co-ordinator IMG; drafted London OHL Jr. A but opted for competitive cycling at 15; track specialist; 30 ntl titles; ntl team '83-96; 1000m silver '84, sprint bronze '92, '96 Olympic Games; gold 1000m, bronze sprint '87 PAG; silver sprint '90, '94 CG; gold sprint '90 Goodwill Games; silver '90, '95 (WR) World sprints; ntl jr. sprint, points race, team pursuit titles '83; 6 ntl sprint titles; PB: 1:06.06 ('84); mem. '83, '87, '93 PAG, '84, '88, '92, '96 Olympic, '86, '90, '94 CG teams; world cup 200m match sprint gold '96; 1st sub 10-sec. 200m world sprint record 9.865; Russ Copeland (ntl top jr. cyclist) trophy '82; *CBC* color commentator, motivational speaker; mem. NWO Sports Hall of Fame; res. Toronto, Ont.

HARPELL, Winnifred (all-around); b. 3 Oct 1929, Owen Sound, Ont.; given name: Winnifred Marie; m. Richard Bocking; c. Michael, Douglas, James, Christopher, Stephen, Patrick; RN; active in figure skating, t&f, tennis; mem. Thunder Bay FS Club '38-48; sr. champion '45; jr., sr. t&f titles '43-49; Port Arthur sr. women's doubles '44-45; jr. women's singles Port Arthur, Duluth '46; 1st Cdn to compete in US women's tennis championships '46; Ont. Jr. women's title '46; 1st girl to win ntl title after only 2 1/2yrs in game; 1st to win all 3 titles 1 tournament; mem. NWO Sports Hall of Fame; res. Victoria, B.C.

HARPER, George (shooting); b. 21 Sep 1936, New Glasgow, N.S.; given name: George Ross; m. Azul Annis Nickerson; c. Stephen, Jamie; ret'd major, logistics officer DND; high-powered rifle specialist; mem. ntl cadet Bisley team '55; 7 times qualified ntl Bisley team, competed 5 times; mem. 2 Palma match teams, 1 Kalapore match winner; top Canadian, 14th overall, Bisley '72; recipient Commandant's Prize; Bisley record 100 14Vs '72 MacKinnon Team match; mem. 3 Bisley Overseas match title teams; Alexander Graham Bell match title team '55; recipient 2 Donnegal medals, 3 Queen's badges at Bisley; ntl Tyro, Connaught match titles; mem. Cdn team Australian match '92; Lieut.-.Gov. gold PEI, 2 bronnze NB; capt. 2 NS, 1 Maritime rugby title teams mid-'50s; also excelled in gymnastics; took up marathon running as conditioner at 35; participated in 15 major marathons in Ottawa, Montreal, Halifax; v-p NCRRA/NDHQRA from '90; mem. Cdn Forces, NS Sports halls of fame; res. Gloucester, Ont.

HARPER, Glenn (football); b. 12 Sep 1962, Edmonton, Alta.; div. C. Nicole, Ryan; m.Lisa; c. Jenna, Daniel; Washington State; qb at WSU, punter; drafted by Sask (CFL) '86; played in CFL with Calgary '86-88, Toronto '89-90, Edmonton '91-96, Ottawa '02-03; 2 Western all-star; CFL record: [171g, 2cvts, 42s, 1404 punts for 57,641yds,] completed 12 of 17 passes for 199yds, 3tds; 13 playoff games, 2 Grey Cup finals, 1 winner; res. Edmonton, Alta./Ottawa, Ont.

HARPER, Ted (cycling); b. 14 Jul 1917, Sherbrooke, Que.; d. 9 Jan 1998, Barrie, Ont.; given name: Edward Arthur; m. Margaret Fraser Murray (d), Brenda Deen; c. Edward William, Ross (d), Patricia; sports columnist, advertising salesman; pro 6-day bike racing specialist competing throughout NA during '30s; with WW2 popularity of sport waned and he ret'd to work in munitions factory; charter-mem. Stroud Optimist Club; p-pres. Barrie Optimists; authored *Six-Days of Madness*.

HARPER, Terry (hockey); b. 27 Jan 1940, Regina, Sask.; given name: Terrance Victor; m. Gladys Piluk; c. Terrence Gregory Peter, Jeffrey Todd, Brigitte Dawn; UBC, SFU, Loyola, McGill; real estate broker, hockey coach; '56 Olympic track team tryout; mem. Regina Rams football club '57-60; Sask. Roughriders tryout '60; mem. Regina Pats hockey club '57-60; mem. Memorial Cup finalists; picked for '60 Olympic hockey team but couldn't get release from Pats; pro Montreal Royals '60; Hull-Ottawa Canadiens (EPHL) '61-62, Montreal (NHL) '62-72, LA '72-75, Detroit '75-79, St. Louis '80; mem. 5 Stanley Cup winners; designed, developed 1st plastic hockey skate boots; asst. coach Colorado Rockies '81; GM Sacramento (RHIL) '94-97; NHL record: 1066 scheduled games, 35g, 221a, 112 playoff games, 4g, 13a; res. Birmingham, Mich.

HARRINGTON, Dave (highland games); b. 12 Jan 1945, Fresno, Calif.; div. Janet Hogg; c. Brenna, Joanna, Andrew; m. Margaret Barrie; sc. Nathan, Rachel Barrie; Stanford, BA, BEd; international management consultant; ntl discus title '71; ntl t&f team '73; ntl Highland Games champion '78-84; most-travelled Cdn competitor; more than 800 individual competition victories, fewer than 20 losses; all Cdn records, 3 NA records; world sheaf toss record '83; US champion '83; '81-84 ranked among world's top 10; active as games builder; avid art collector; res. Ottawa, Ont.

HARRINGTON, Ed (football); b. 8 Feb 1941, Speer, Okla.; given name: Edison Dean; div.; c. Wendy, Dusti Kia; Langston, BSc; patient advocate North Bay psychiatric hospital; Oklahoma state weightlifting titles '60-62;

nicknamed "Hercules"; pro Houston (NFL) '62; Toronto (CFL) as og '63; EFC all-star '64; Toronto Rifles Continental League '65; rejoined Argos '67-70; 3 times all-eastern, all-Cdn; quarter-horse breeder; plays, writes Bluegrass music; res. Field, Ont.

HARRIS, Lesley (badminton); b. 18 Oct 1954, Kuala Lampur, Malaysia; given name: Lesley Elizabeth; m. R.K. Bercuson; McGill, BA; project, systems analyst; ntl jr. singles, doubles badminton titles '73-74, ntl ladies' singles finalist '75, doubles finalist '76-77; mem. '75 Uber Cup semifinalists; bronze ladies singles '71 Canada Winter Games; with Mila Zaruba Horak '70 girls -18 ntl tennis doubles; res. Town of Mount Royal, Que.

HARRIS, Merelynn (basketball); b. 28 Apr 1969, Toronto, Ont.; given name: Merelynn Lange; m. Harris; c. Deja Sabine, Kassandra Nicole; UNLV; standout ctr, winner 2 HS MVP awards; UNLV freshman of '89, leading scorer, rebounder '91-92, all-Conference '92, 2 Big West titles; made Cdn ntl team age 16; mem. '86, '90, '94 world championship, '90 Goodwill, '91 FISU, '85 world junior championship, '96 Olympic teams; bronze '93, gold '95 COPABA championships; pro France, Germany '92-94; WNBA Phoenix Mercury '99; res. Las Vegas, Nev.

HARRIS, Mike (curling/golf); B. 6 Sept 1961, Georgetown, Ont.; golf pro; skip Ont. jr. curling title '86, Ont. mixed '89; skip 5 Ont. Tankard rinks, '92, '93 runnerups, winner '04; skip 3 Welton Beauchamp titles; defeated Alberta's Kevin Martin 6-5 to earn right to represent Canada in '98 Olympics; after placing 1st in round robin and breezing through semifinal fell victim to flu and a hot Swiss rink to settle for Olympic silver '98; *CBC-TV* curling analyst; set course record 66 winning '92 Aurora pro-am; former head pro Donalda GC; head golf instructor Pischelsdorf, Austria; res. Oakville, Ont.

HARRIS, Susan (gymnastics, synchroswim, canoeing); b. 2 Dec 1941, Toronto, Ont.; given name: Susan Brown; m. Peter Harris; c. Todd Peter, Shannon Suzanne; UWO, BA; teaching certificate; teacher; founder Mississauga gymnastics club '69, dir. 14yrs; pres. Ont. Gymnastics Fed. 4yrs; dir. CGF 6yrs; chair Gymnastics Canada awards comm. 12yrs; chair Gymnastics Mississauga 25th anniversary celebration; chair Gymnastic Challenge 2000; dir. Olympium Synchronized Swimming Club 2 yrs; mem. Mississauga sports award comm. 9yrs, Hall of Fame comm.; artistic gymnastic judge '00 Olympics, '87, '95, '99 PAG, '78, '94, '98 CG, '79, '83 FISU Games; chair. OFSAA gymnastics championships 8yrs; chair host comm. '80 WC; chair. ntl championship '84; regional judge from '68, ntl judge from '70, intl judge '77-00, brevet judge '85-00; judged 32 consec. ntl championships; officiated 2 Olympics, 3 worlds, 3 PAG, 3 CG, 1 FISU, 1 all-African gymnastics championships, intl competitions in Germany, Yugoslavia, Romania, Japan, Italy, France, US and Canada; coached HS gymnastics 10yrs, volleyball 6yrs, competitive masters paddler; multimedalist kayak '98 world masters games; life mem. Gymnastics Canada, Ont.; Mississauga volunteer award, Ont. Govt, OGF special achievement awards, Canada 125 medal; mem. Mississauga Sports Hall of Fame; res. Caledon East, Ont.

HARRIS, Wayne (football); b. 4 May 1938, Hampton, Ark,; given name: Carrol Wayne; m. Anne Dearth; c.

Wayne Jr., Heather Wynelle, Andrew Cooper; Arkansas; v-p, mgr. field operations drilling, exploration co.; lb/gd Eldorado Jr. HS, all-state '52-53; HS all-state '55-56, all-Southern, all-American '56; Arkansas HS all-star game outstanding lineman '56; Arkansas scholarship '57-60; all-Southwest Conference '59-60; all-American '60; *Houston Post* award outstanding Southwest Conference player; Arkansas, Louisiana, Texas athlete of year '60; '59 Gator, '60 All-American, Cotton Bowls; Arkansas Association Neil Gibson Martin Victory Trophy '60; drafted by Boston Patriots; pro Calgary '61-72; all-Western Conference 11 times, all-Cdn 9 times; 4 times Schenley outstanding lineman, once runnerup; 3 Grey Cup finals, 1 winner; outstanding player '71 Grey Cup; Demarco-Becket Trophy winner; Calgary athlete of '67; 2 most-popular-player awards; twice Stampeder president's award; sweater #55 ret'd by club on Wayne Harris Day '73; roasted by CFL Player's Assn. '76; coached jr. football '73, HS football '75-76; named to all-century Arkansas team; mem. Canadian Football, Alta., Ark. Sports halls of fame; res. Calgary, Alta.

HARRISON, Herm (football); b. 29 Sep 1939, Rocky Mountain, N.C.; given name: Herman Austin; c. Tamara; Arizona State, BA; sales *CKMX/CJAY* radio; conf, all-star, hon. mention all-American; pro end Calgary '64-72; CFL record: 443 receptions for 6693yds, 43tds; best season '68 1306yds; best game vs. Sask. 29 Sep '68 12 receptions 237yds; 3 WFL , 2 CFL pass reception titles; 4 td receptions single game vs. Winnipeg '70; 3 1000-plus yards seasons; 60 consecutive game reception string '68-72; 16 100-plus yards games; 5 times WFC all-star, 4 all-Cdn; 2 most-popular-player awards; nicknamed "Ham Hands"; Stampeders club dir. '75-81; jersey ret'd by Duquesne HS; Penn. House of Reps. citation; active in Stampeder community affairs, fund raisers; mem. Cdn Football Hall of Fame; res. Calgary, Alta.

HARRISON, Neil (curling); b. 23 Jan 1949, Peterborough, Ont.; given name: Neil Gordon; m. Jane Clune; c. Amber, Sean; firefighter; began curling age 12; mem. Ed Werenich's Ont., ntl firefighters title rinks '78-80,'82-84; mem. Werenich's Ont. Labatt Tankard title rink '81, '83-84; competed 6 Briers total, 1 winner; mem. Werenich's Ont., ntl, World title rink '83; CCR all-star '83-84, '88; normally plays lead; Dick Ellis team award '83; fed. govt. world champion award '83; mem. Canadian Curling Hall of Fame; res. Pickering, Ont.

HARRISON-TUCKER, Ardin (t&f); b. 14 Mar 1974, Edmonton, Alta.; given name: Ardin Renee Harrison; m. Ben Tucker; c. Nathan; Fresno State ; pole vault specialist; husband Ben played for the San Francisco Giants 5yrs and now works for *CBS* in Phoenix; brother Justin is a pilot in Winnipeg and brother Trevor is a member of the US rugby team; dad Jim played in the NHL (Edmonton, Toronto, Chicago and Boston) 12yrs; mom Liz was mem. ntl equestrian team; Liz passed away from breast cancer in 1999; Ardin spokesperson for thebreastcancersite.com; ran 400m hurdles and 4x400m relay at Fresno State; '00 Cdn ntl champion; competed '01 Francophonie Games; '02 CG team mem.; silver '02 Sky Athletics Invitational Phoenix; second highest jump ever by a Cdn female pole vaulter (4.25m '02 Los Angeles Invitational); res. Peoria, Arizona.

HART, Bret (wrestling); b. 2 Jul 1957, Calgary, Alta.; m. Julie; c. Jade, Dallas, Alexandra Sabina, Blade; Mount Royal Coll.; pro wrestler; won city/prov. titles in 3 weight categories; following college became film director but lure of wrestling ring took over; nicknamed "The Hitman"; noted for accurate textbook execution of every manoeuver; signature move The Sharpshooter; developed interest in sport from father Stu, former CFL football player and wrestling gym operator; has made guest appearances as actor in TV series *Lonesome Dove, Mad TV* and animated role in *The Simpsons*; writes column for *Calgary Sun*; accomplished cartoonist; WHL Calgary Hitmen, of which he is former co-owner, named after him; res. Calgary, Alta.

HART, David (water polo); b. 6 Dec 1951, Hamilton, Ont.; given name: David Andrew; m. Francesse Kopczewski; c. Jesse, Kasia; McMaster., BA, BPhE; coach; owner Oyate Native Gallery; as competitive swimmer set 7 Ont., 6 ntl records; mem. ntl jr men's water polo title team '69, runnerup '70; mem. 4 ntl sr. men's title teams, 5 OUAA titles; mem. '72, '76 Olympic, '71, '75 PAG, '75 world aquatic championships; coached Hamilton Aquatic Club to ntl sr. men's title '77, jr. men's gold medal team '77 Canada Games; Ivor Wynne Trophy as McMaster outstanding athlete of year; 13yrs tech. dir. Water Polo Canada; coach Carleton '94-99; OUAA coach of '94; coach ntl men's team '96-02; innovator who launched Cdn Water Polo League, Legacy coaching program, Cdn Dream Team '99, men's ntl team alumni; coach Brazil ntl women's team; Jimmy Thompson Memorial award; Ottawa ACT Trivett award; mem. McMaster Sports, Ont. Aquatic halls of fame; res. Ottawa, Ont.

HART, Gaétan (boxing); b. 9 Nov 1953, Buckingham, Que.; div. Line Charboneau; c. Denis, Melanie, Mathieu; m. Ghyslaine; hardware trucker; ret'd pro boxer; 7 amateur bouts, won all; 91 pro bouts, 60 wins, 27 losses, 4 draws; 26 KOs; 3 times ntl lightweight titlist; beat Cleveland Denny for title '78, defended 3 times; lost title to Nicky Furlano '79, regained it from Furlano '80; stripped of title for failure to defend within designated time; regained title from Michel Lalonde '81; lost title to Johnny Summerhayes; fought 5 world champions including Aaron Pryor, Claude Noel; Denny died following beating by Hart '80, Ralph Racine in coma several weeks following Hart beating '80; ret'd from ring '84; made brief, but unsuccessful comeback bid '90-92, '00; Buckingham street named in his honor; subject of NFB film *Le Steak*; res. Buckingham, Que.

HART, Nelson (lawn bowling/administration); b. 11 Jun 1888, Opa Twp., Ont.; d. 7 Dec 1959, London, Ont.; pres. UWO; mem. Ont. doubles lawn bowling title team '39; pres. OLBA, CLBA; 6yrs lawn bowling umpire; represented UWO on CIAU board; CIAU pres. '50-51; co-founder Western Ont. Secondary School Athletics (WOSSA), 10yrs hon. secty.; hon. secty. COA '38-49; chef de mission Cdn Olympic team '48; 25yrs AAUofC secty; variety of other AAUofC exec. offices, pres. '48; mem. BE, CG Assoc. of Canada advisory board '49-59; mem. Cdn Olympic Sports Hall of Fame.

HART, Stu (wrestling/builder/coaching); b. 3 May 1915, Saskatoon, Sask.; d. 16 Oct 2003, Calgary, Alta.; m. Helen Smith (d); c. Smith, Bruce, Keith, Wayne, Dean (d), Elizabeth, Georgia, Bret, Allison, Ross, Diana, Owen (d);

wrestling coach, promoter; standout ctr Edmonton Eskimos; standout amateur wrestler denied opportunity to compete in '40 Olympics due to WW2; began pro wrestling career under tutelage of Toots Mondt and competed 4 decades; began promoting wrestling founding Stampede Wrestling '48; formed Foothills Athletic Club in Calgary home with wrestling training center known as The Dungeon; gained renown as trainer of young talent including sons Bret (Hitman) and Owen (Blue Blazer) who gained considerable repute on pro circuit; mem. Order of Canada; Canadian Wrestling Hall of Fame.

HARTL, Gus (shooting); b. 1954, Austria; municipal employee; handgun specialist; began shooting competitively '78; competed in PPC, Bullseye, ntl standard, centre-fire, air pistol events claiming a myriad of titles; set ntl PPC record 600 47x '86 then improved on it with 600 50x '95; holds PPC aggregate 1198 97x of possible 1200; 2 NRA, 1 Canton, Detroit regional PPC titles; mem. only 2 Cdn teams to win world PPC titles; mem. Bullseye competition Mayleigh Cup title team '89; 1 ntl standard pistol, 3 ntl 1800 (2700) .22cal, 4 centre-fire, 2 .45cal, 3 grand aggregate titles; Ont. Handgun Assn. award; mem. NRA 1490, 2600 clubs; ntl PPC titles '02-03; NRA distinguished revolver award; numerous president's 100 medals; res. Toronto, Ont.

HARTLEY, Blythe (diving); b. 2 May 1982, Edmonton, Alta.; USC; earned numerous Cdn age-group titles; 1m, 10m gold '99 jr. worlds; ntl jr. female athlete of yr; 10m silver, 3m bronze '99, 3m, 3m synchro gold, 10m bronze '03 PAG; 1m silver, 10m bronze '02 CG; won 1st World Cup crown 10m '01 Fukuoka, Japan; '03 world aquatics 1m bronze; competed '00 Olympics; 2 NCAA 1m, 10m titles; 1st woman ever to win NCAA 1m, 10m titles same competition; '02 NCAA, Pac-10 female diver-of-yr award '02; with Eryn Bulmer operates Calgary high-performance camps; res. N. Vancouver, B.C.

HARTLEY, Bob (coaching/hockey); b. 7 Sep 1960, Hawkesbury, Ont.; m. Micheline; c. Kristin, Steve; begam coaching career with CJHL Hawkesbury '87-91; 2 league titles; Laval (QMJHL) '91-93; Memorial Cup '93; asst. Cornwall (AHL) '93-94, head coach '94-96, Hershey (AHL) '96-98; Calder Cup '97; Colorado (NHL) '98-02; Atlanta '03; Stanley Cup '01; asst. NA team '01 NHL all-star game; NHL coaching record (through '03) 698 scheduled games, 212-133-53, 80 playoff games, 49-31; noted for summer hockey camps, community involvement; res. Hawkesbury, Ont.

HARTLEY, Errol (field hockey); b. 16 Mar 1940, Allahabad, India; given name: Errol Patrick: m. Patricia Ann; c. Adrian Christopher, Lorraine, Nicole; London, P Eng, MIEE, BSc; engineer; rep. BC 4 consecutive interprovincial title-winning teams '68-71; coached BC '72 interprovincial champions; coached Canada's bronze medal team '71, silver '75 PAG; coached ntl team '70-79; 10th '76 Olympics; res. Trinidad.

HARTMAN, Barney (shooting); b. 2 Nov 1916, Swan River, Man.; m. Joahanna Carr; c. Shelley Jo-Anne; ret'd sales promotion; considered world's greatest skeet shooter; capt. 10 NSSA all-American skeet team; 4 perfect 100x100 410 gauge; nearly 30 world records in 12, 20, 28, 410 gauge, all-around categories; world record .9875 avg. with 395x400

with 410 gauge '66; world record .9991 avg. with 1049x1050 12 gauge '68 (mark broken '71 by US shooter with perfect 1.000); 28 gauge .9980 record '69 with 499x500, 20 gauge .9983 record avg. '71 with 599x600; '66-73 avg. .99038 all-around category; once broke 2002 clay targets without miss; silver, 4 bronze world international competition '61-63; 9yrs industry pro shooter with highest overall standard 12, 20, 28, 410 gauge; author '67 instruction book *Hartman on Skeet*; mem. Order of Canada, Ottawa, Ottawa CSRA, Canadian Forces, US National Skeet Shooting Assn., Canada's Sports halls of fame; res. Orleans, Ont.

HARTSBURG, Craig (hockey); b. 29 Jun 1959, Stratford, Ont.; m. Peggy; c. Chris, Katie; coach; def Sault Ste. Marie (OHL) '76-78; pro Birmingham (WHA) '78-79; Minnesota (NHL) '79-89; capt. North Stars 6 seasons; NHL playing record: 570 scheduled games, 98g, 315a, 61 playoff games 15g, 27a; competed 3 all-star games; launched coaching career as asst. Minnesota '89-90, Philadelphia '90-94, '02-03; head coach Guelph (OHL) '94-95, Chicago '95-98, Anaheim '98-99, SSM '01-02, '04-05; NHL coaching record: regular season 184-190-69, playoffs 8-12; mem. Team Canada 3 world tournaments; Canada Cup gold '87; Canada Cup best def '87; OHL coach of '95, '02 awards; mem. North Stars 25th anniversary dream team; res. Sault Ste. Marie, Ont.

HARTZELL, Irene (swimming); b. 19 Oct 1922, Winnipeg, Man.; div. Dr. George D. Athans; c. George Jr., Greg, Gary; during '40s Man. breaststroke titlist, ntl record holder; 4 consec. Man. synchronized swimming titles; returned to competitive swimming in masters category '88; won prov., ntl titles and established numerous records; mem. BC world record mixed medley relay team '95; silver, 2 breaststroke bronze World Masters, setting ntl records in each instance; res. Kelowna, B.C.

HARVEY, Buster (hockey); b. 2 Apr 1950, Fredericton, N.B.; given name: Frederick John Charles; engine machine shop; began career Halifax jr. Canadiens '67 Maritime title team; NB title Fredericton Jr. Red Wings '68; Hamilton Jr. Red Wings OJHL '68-70; drafted by Minnesota NHL '70-74, Cleveland AHL '71-72, Atlanta NHL '74-75, Kansas City NHL '75-76, CHL '77, Detroit NHL '76-77, Philadelphia AHL '77-78; NHL record: 7 seasons, 407 scheduled games, 90g, 118a, 14 playoff games, 0g, 2a; mem. Kansas City CHL title team '77; OJHL rookie of '69, scoring leader; 2nd team AHL all-star '72; coached Fredericton Jr. Red Wings to NB title '80; mem. NB Sports Hall of Fame; res. Fredericton, N.B.

HARVEY, Doug (hockey); b. 19 Dec 1924, Montreal, Que.; d. 26 Dec 1989, Montreal, Que.; given name: Douglas Norman; m. Ursula; c. 5; employee Connaught Park; mem. Ottawa Border Baseball League team 2 years; led league hitters one season with .351 BA; rejected Boston Braves pro offers; mem. Montreal Royals Allan Cup winner; pro hockey Montreal '47-61, NYR '61-64, Detroit '66-67, St. Louis '68-69; coach Rangers '61-62; mem. 6 Stanley Cup winners; 7 Norris Trophy; 10 1st team, 1 2nd team all-star def; jersey #2 ret'd by Canadiens; mem. Hockey Hall of Fame.

HARVEY, Florence (golf); b. 1878 England; d. 1968 South Africa; took up golf around 1900 in Hamilton and quickly became one of top players; 4 Ont. Ladies' titles; 2 Cdn Ladies' Open (twice runnerup); semifinalist US women's amateur '10; after serving as a Red Cross ambulance driver in WW1 participated in British Ladies' championship '20; mem. Cdn, Ont. Golf halls of fame.

HARVEY, Nancy (golf); b. 2 May 1962, Swift Current, Sask.; m. Glen "Doc" Harvey; Arizona State; psychologist, pro golfer; mem. Sask jr. team '77-80; Sask ladies amateur title '80; mem. international jr. team '80; mem. Sask amateur team '81-84; turned pro '88; 3 CPGA women's titles; career low round 66; scored LPGA ace; with husband manages public golf course; mem. Canada's inaugural Nations Cup team '99; res. Mesa, Ariz.

HARVEY, Pierre (cycling/skiing); b. 24 Mar 1957, Rimouski, Que.; m. Mireille Belzile; Laval; engineer; competitive swimmer age 12-15; competitive cyclist at 15; mem. ntl team '75-80, '84; mem. '76 Summer, '84 Winter, Summer, '88 Winter Olympic teams; competitive x-country skier at 17; ntl team '80-88; ntl 15km titles '81-83, '85-88, 30km '82, '85-88, 50km '83, '86-88; NA 3x10km relay '81, 15km, 30km '83; Sett Internationale Del Fondo 30km '82; ntl 3x10km relay '82, 25.5km '83; won '87 WC 30km race Sweden; twice 4th WC 15km events; 14 times among WC top 8; mem. Order of Canada, Cdn Skiing, Que. Sports halls of fame; res. St-Ferreol-Les-Neiges, Que.

HARVEY, Scott Jr. (baseball/hockey); b. 17 Apr 1949, Fredericton, N.B.; given name: Laurence Melvin; NB Power Commission; pro baseball with LA Dodgers Ogden, Utah, Pioneer League farm club '67; St. Louis Cardinals' St. Petersburg, Fla. State League, Lewiston, Me., Northwestern League farm clubs '69-70; mem. several NB title teams; mem. NB team '69 Canada Games; record 13 appearances with ntl title teams, 2 jr., 11 sr., winning gold '81, '82, 2 silver, 2 bronze; pitched losing 1-0 decision vs. Cuban world amateur titlists '76; set NBSBL batting avg. record with .552 '77; pro hockey AHL Boston Braves; Frederiction athlete of '65; mem. Fredericton Sports Wall, NB Baseball, NB Sports halls of fame; res. Fredericton, N.B.

HARVEY, Scott Sr. (baseball); b. 30 Mar 1926, Grand Manan, N.B.; d. 19 Dec 2000, Fredericton, N.B.; m. Joan Estey; c. Scott Jr., Jane; Mt. Allison; ret'd exec.-secty. NB Mutual Insurance Assn.; mem. '47-48 NB champion Marysville Royals, Brooklyn Dodgers tryout '48, Black's Harbour Brunswicks '49-54, Marysville Royals '55-64; coached Royals 6yrs; 11yrs mem. NB Federation of Amateur Baseball, 7 as pres.; v-p Baseball Canada 7yrs; mem. NB Sports Hall of Fame.

HASLAM, Eleanor (t&f); b. 1939, Saskatoon, Sask.; m. Ole Jensen; c.4;UofSask; UBC; cancer researcher; mem. Nutana Kiwanis TC under coach Bob Adams; Sask. HS 50-, 75yd dash, ntl juv 100yds, 220yds, sr. 220yds records; mem. '56, '60 Olympic, '58 BEG teams; set Olympic 800-, world 60yd indoor records; 3 ntl titles; ntl juv 220yd record 24.5, 5 golds '57 Western Canada championships; twice broke ntl women's 100yd-dash record, lowered 220 yd mark to 24.1; relay team bronze '58 BEG; 1st female winner Dr. Fred Tees Trophy Canada's outstanding university athlete '58; Gov.-Gen.'s academic medal; mem. Sask., Saskatoon Sports halls of fame; res. Denmark.

HASLAM, Phyllis (swimming); b. 24 May 1913, Dharmsala, India; d. 23 Aug 1991, Toronto, Ont.; given name: Phyllis Georgie; UofSask, BSc, UofT, social work dip., Trinity College, DSLitt; exec.-dir. Elizabeth Fry Society; ntl 100-, 220yd breaststroke records '32; world record 1:18.3 100yd breaststroke '32 (unrecognized as standard, again lowered before time registered); BEG 200yd breaststroke mark 2:52.6 in heats; BEG 200yd silver, team gold 3x100yd relay; mem. UofSask. swim team '31-34, UotT swim team '35-36; received Varsity T; volunteer swim coach several years; officer Order of Canada '78; mem. Cdn Aquatic, Cdn Olympic, Sask. Sports halls of fame.

HASSETT, Gavin (rowing); b. 13 Jul 1973, Saint John, N.B.; UVic; began rowing '89; mem. ntl team '93-03; competes lightweight men's straight 4s; competed '91 Canada Games; gold jr. worlds '91 8s, men's light 8s '93 worlds, straight 4s Amsterdam '94, US championships '95; bronze straight 4s '93 FISU Games; (silver lw 4's) '96, '00 Olympics; res. Victoria, B.C.

HATANAKA, Bill (football); b. 3 May 1954, Bathurst, N.B.; given name: William Harry; m. Janet Christine Daly; c. William Robert, Ryan James; York, Hon BA, Harvard Business School; COO Royal Investments; 1st-round draft Rough Riders '76; CFL Ottawa '76-78, Hamilton '79; mem. '76 Grey Cup title team; set Grey Cup record longest punt return 79yds; York Hall of Fame; res. Toronto, Ont.

HATSKIN, Ben (builder); b. 30 Sep 1917, Winnipeg, Man.; d. 18 Oct 1990, Winnipeg, Man.; given name: Benjamin; m. Cecelia Rashcovsky; Oklahoma; real estate exec.; among first Canadians offered US college football scholarship; pro Winnipeg '36-41; Grey Cup winners '39, '41; jr. hockey Kildonan Stars '36; formed Jets hockey club in WCHL '66; instrumental in formation World Hockey Assn. with Winnipeg Jets as members; signed Bobby Hull to give WHA credibility; maintained jr. entry in WHL; chair. WHA, owner Honolulu franchise WFL '73; involved in International Basketball Assn. for Winnipeg '86; Manitoba Man of Year, *Sporting News* executive of year '73; mem. Man. Sports, Hockey halls of fame.

HATTIN, Heather (rowing); b. 15 May 1961, Windsor, Ont.; given name: Heather Carlyle; m. Robert Ridpath; c. Jenna Carlyle; Guelph, BSc, UofT, MSc; rehabilitation specialist; began rowing in HS; joined Don Rowing Club '76; international competitive debut '83 PAG winning heavyweight doubles silver; alternate '84, competed '88 Olympics; competed '84-86 worlds; lightweight singles bronze '86 CG; Mississauga female amateur athlete of '87; mem. Athletes Resource Group, Cdn Rowing Athletes' Council, UofT, Guelph Athletes' councils; mem. Mississauga Sports Hall of Fame; res. Guelph, Ont.

HAUCH, Paul (swimming/administration); b. 27 Dec 1903, Tokyo, Japan; d. 21 Mar 1981, Orlando, Florida; m. Marion Louise Bole; c. Guy, Jon, Bill; Northwestern, UWO, MD, Royal College of Physicians, Surgeons, DMR(D); radiologist; capt. UWO football '31; initial recipient G. Howard Ferguson Award UWO outstanding athlete, scholar; capt. UWO basketball '29, swim team '32; runnerup freshman tennis championships Northwestern

'25; founder/swim coach London YMCA Aquatic Club '46-73; pres. Ont. section CASA '45-59, secty. '59-68; v-p ASUA '59; dir.-v-p COA, chairman medical advisory comm. '60-69; mem. COA '69-76; mem. technical swim comm. FINA '56-68, mem. FINA bureau '68-72, hon. secty. FINA '72-76; successfully defended rights of foreign-born Canadians to represent Canada in Olympics; introduced Swim-A-Thons; Air Canada amateur sports exec. of '67; Ont. Athletic Commission award '68; mem. National Fitness Advisory Council '65-66; mgr./physician 3 Olympic teams; Centennial medal '67; mem. W-Club, London Sports, Cdn Olympic, Cdn, Ont. Aquatic halls of fame.

HAWCO, Sherry (gymnastics); b. 17 Feb 1964, Cambridge, Ont.; d. 26 Oct 1991, Cambridge, Ont.; given name: Sherry Louise; m. Mark Delanty; c. Brandon Hawco; team gold, all-around silver '78 CG; gold team, beam '79 PAG; mem. '80 Olympic team; ntl title '81; ntl gymnastics championship choreography award bears her name; mem. Cambridge, Waterloo County Sports halls of fame.

HAWERCHUK, Dale (hockey); b. 4 Apr 1963, Toronto, Ont. m. Crystal; c. Alexis, Eric; horse breeder; ctr Cornwall Royals '79-81; CMJL, QMJHL player of year '81; Memorial Cup most sportsmanlike player '80, MVP '81; 1st overall '81 draft; pro Winnipeg '81-90, Buffalo '90-95, St. Louis '95-96, Philadelphia '96-97; Calder Memorial Trophy '82; mem. Team Canada '87, '91 Canada Cup; MVP, Star of Stars award '91; scored 53g '85; NHL record: 1188 scheduled games, 518g, 891a, 97 playoff games, 30g, 69a; Hockey, QMJHL halls of fame; res. Orangeville, Ont.

HAWKINS, John (t&f); b. 8 Jun 1949, Kelowna, B.C.; given name: Francis John Alexander; UBC, BPhE, MPhE; fitness centre instructor; hj specialist; BC midget title '64, juv '65, jr. '67; switched from scissor jump to Fosbury Flop and '71 became 1st Cdn to clear 7'; mem. '70, '74 CG, '71 PAG, '72 Olympic, '70, '73 FISU Games teams; silver '70 CG, bronze '73 FISU Games; ntl indoor record '72; WCIAU, Pan-Pacific titles '73; mem. CIAU basketball champions FISU Games team '70, BC men's '77 volleyball titlists; BC athlete of '71; res. Vancouver, B.C.

HAWLEY, Sandy (horse racing); b. 16 Apr 1949, Oshawa, Ont.; given name: Sanford Desmond; div. Sherry; div. Vicky Beck; m. Lisa John; c. Russell, Bradley; PR ambassador OJC, ex-jockey; runnerup Ont. HS 96lb wrestling title; began riding under Duke Campbell '68; top NA apprentice '69; NA leading race-winning jockey '70, '72; competed Southern California circuit '79-88; 515 victories '73 eclipsed Bill Shoemaker's '53 mark of 485 (subsequently beaten by Chris McCarran's 547 '74); 4 Queen's Plate, 8 Canadian Oaks titles; at 27 youngest jockey to reach 3000 victories '76; topped 6000 wins '92; underwent 2 skin cancer operations '87, lung cancer surgery '93; injured '95 Woodbine spill; LA (NHL) penalty box official; 2 Lou Marsh trophies, George Woolf award, US racing's Eclipse award, Avelino Gomez award, 2 Sovereign awards; Joe Palmer award; ret'd '98; career record: 6449w, 4825p, 4158s, with 31,454 mounts, career earnings $88,666,071; mem. Order of Canada, Ntl Museum of Racing, Canadian Horse Racing, Canada's, Oshawa, Mississauga Sports halls of fame; res. Mississauga, Ont.

HAY, Bill (hockey); b. 8 Dec 1935, Saskatoon, Sask.; given name: William Charles; m. Nancy; c. Pam, Penny, Donald; Colorado College, BSc; hockey exec.; Calgary (WHL)'58-59, Chicago (NHL) '59-67; Calder Memorial Trophy; with Bobby Hull, Murray Balfour formed Chicago's Million Dollar Line; NHL record: 506 scheduled games, 113g, 273a, 70 playoff games, 18g, 37a; mem. '61 Stanley Cup winner; chair. Hockey Canada development comm., chair Saddledome Foundation; v-p Bow Valley Industries, '81-90; created International Hockey Centre of Excellence '85; Centre of Excellence planning advisor for CHA; mem. Hockey Canada International comm. '82-90; mem. Hockey Hall of Fame selection comm, Special Olympics Advisory Board; dir. Hockey Hall of Fame, chair. from '98; pres/alternate governor Calgary; mem. Sask Sports Hall of Fame; res. Calgary, Alta.

HAY, Charles (builder/hockey); b. 28 Jun 1902, Kingston, Ont.; d. 24 Oct 1973, Calgary, Alta.; c. Bill; UofSask; ret'd oil exec.; goal; finalist '21 Allan Cup with UofSask; major role in negotiating first international series involving Canada-Russia '72; helped organize Hockey Canada; HC pres.; key role in formulation of ntl team program; mem. Hockey Hall of Fame.

HAY, Denny (rodeo); b. 6 Nov 1967, Stony Plain, Alta; m. Susan; c. Amber, Rebekka, Kennedy; rancher; saddle bronc, calf roping specialist; ntl novice saddle bronc title '87; CPRA rookie of yr '89; 2 BC circuit SB titles, Coors Chute Out, Skoal pro rodeo titles '91; APRC AA, SB titles '94; CFR SB average leader '96; 3 ntl SB titles; co-champ Pikes Peak or Bust rodeo; Stampede SB champ '98; gold '02 Olympic saddle bronc demo sport; res. Mayerthorpe, Alta.

HAY, George (hockey); b. 10 Jan 1898, Listowel, Ont.; d. 13 Jul 1975, Stratford, Ont.; given name: George William; Winnipeg Jr./Sr. Monarchs '15-16, Regina Vics '20-21; pro Regina Caps '20, 87 goals, 57 assists 4 years; Portland Rosebuds, 18 goals before '26 sale to Chicago; Detroit Cougars '27-33; NHL career record: 73 goals, 54 assists; lw coaches' dream team; mem. Man., Cdn Hockey halls of fame.

HAY, Rod (rodeo); b. 5 Jan 1969, Stony Plain, Alta.; m. Shellee; c. Logan, Dawson; rancher; saddle bronc specialist; joined CPRA '89; world SB rookie of '89; 3 Stampede SB titles; 7 ntl SB titles; 5 CPRA SB season leader titles; 1 world SB season-leader; 4 Alta, 1 SK circuit SB titles; res. Wildwood, Alta.

HAYDENLUCK, Greg (t&f/bobsleigh); b. 7 Jul 1958, Emerson, N.B.; m.; UofT; South Dakota; teacher; NCAA Div II all-American decathlete; ntl decathlon champion '85, '87; competed as decathlete '82 CG; turned to bobsleigh at 26; mem. ntl team '84-92; 3 ntl 2-man, 4-man titles; competed '88, '92 Olympics; USD Hall of Fame; res. Toronto, Ont.

HAYES, Bob (football/coaching); b. 29 Mar 1933, Perth, Ont.; given name: Robert Gerald; m. Heather Robbins; c. Robert, Thomas, Jordan, Holly, Laurel; St.Mary's, BA; ret'd athletic dir.; jr. A hockey London Nationals '51; rb Stadacona, Shearwater; 3 MVP awards, 2 scoring titles; 4 Purdy Cup title teams; 1st Maritime Football Union player to top 1000yds rushing single season with 1265 on 133 carries Shearwater '57; coach/AD St. Mary's; introduced single pillar football goalpost to Maritime game '67; coached SMU hockey '58-60; CAFA profile award; mem. St. Mary's, NS Sports halls of fame; res. Halifax, N.S.

HAYES, George (hockey); b. 7 Sep 1920, Montreal, Que.; d. 19 Nov 1987, Beachville, Ont.; given name: George William; m. Judy; c. Bill, George Jr., Susan; hockey official, freelance writer; jr. hockey Ingersoll, Woodstock; baseball outfielder, of/1b Stratford, Ingersoll, Woodstock, Tillsonburg; football Woodstock provincial jr. champions '36; pushed into hockey refereeing '40 when handed life suspension from amateur sport after brawl in Tillsonburg baseball game; NHL linesman '46-64; 1549 league, 149 playoff games; OHA, AHL referee, worked Memorial Cup finals '46; officiated more than 3000 games all leagues; mem. Hockey Hall of Fame.

HAYES, Jay (equestrian); b. 14 Jun 1957, Hartford, Conn.; m. Shawn Carpenter; c. Lauren, Ainsley, Regan; Connecticutt,. BSc; horseman, North Ridge stables operator; raised on dairy farm; began riding age 12; played intercollegiate polo; Cdn citizen, mem. ntl team from '85; mem. 23 Nations Cup teams, 5 World Cup finals, '90 World championships; mem. '92 Olympic team (leading qualifier); won Tropicana GP '94-'96; res. Cheltenham, Ont.

HAYES, John (soccer); b. 25 Mar 1913, Belfast, N. Ireland; d. 3 Sep 1974, Saskatoon, Sask.; given name: John Fielding; m. Doris Roegele; c. Faye, Brian, Cheryl; railway carman; 40 years active soccer goaler; 6 Saskatoon Shields; faced various visiting UK clubs; indoor soccer to age 59; coached 3 provincial jr., HS, 1 midget, 3 Saskatoon HS title teams; goaler Saskatoon United broomball team '54-73, 7 successive city titles; honored by Saskatoon SA for contribution to game; trophy bearing his name awarded by Saskatoon United to city HS soccer titlists from '75; mem. Sask. Sports Hall of Fame.

HAYHURST, Tom (shooting); b. 1868, England; d. 1948, Toronto, Ont.; emigrated to Canada 1892; while still in England won Prince of Wales prize at Bisley 1889; Pte. 13th Battalion Cdn Light Infantry; became 1st Cdn marksman to win Queen's Prize at Bisley (in shootoff) 1895; mem. DCRA Hall of Fame.

HAYMAN, Lew (football/coaching); b. 30 Sep 1908, Paterson, N.J.; d. 29 Jun 1984, Toronto, Ont.; given name: Lewis Edward; m. Joan; New York Military Academy, Syracuse; football exec.; came to Canada '32 to join Warren Stevens at UotT; considered Canadian football's greatest architect; coached 5 Grey Cup winners, '33, '37-38 Argos, '42 RCAF Hurricanes, '49 Alouettes; coach Argos '33-40, RCAF Hurricanes '41-45; part-owner, coach, GM Alouettes '46-54; Argos exec. officer from '57; CFL pres. '49-50; responsible for several CFL firsts, televised games, night games, Sunday games, break in color bar; managing dir. Argos '79-81; hon. chair. from '81; mem. Canadian Football Hall of Fame.

HAYMAN, Ron (cycling); b. 31 Aug 1954, Camosie Glen, Scotland; given name: Ronald Leslie; BC Institute of Technology; v-p sales/marketing Tacars; ntl jr. track title

'72, team pursuit '72-75, individual pursuit '79, 10-mile title '75-76, road race title '77, '79; mem. '72, '76 Olympic, '73-75, '77-78 world, '78 CG teams; 3 seasons Belgian pro circuit winning 15 6-day events; '79 Tour of Ireland title; 3 Vancouver Gastown GP titles; pro '79 scoring several major victories; sport dir. 7-Eleven pro team; level 3 coach, level 2 course conductor; TV analyst '96 Olympics; mgr. Kona pro mountain bike team; organizer Action Quest; dir. Ntl racing program CCA; Olympic solidarity coaching course conductor; res. Summerland, B.C.

HAYTER, Ron (baseball/boxing/administration); b. 30 Jul 1936, Regina, Sask.; m. Jacqueline Bacon; c. Sparkle, Sandra, Nevin; semi-ret'd journalist, politician, mem. ntl parole bd., operates own news & PR firm; worked with a variety of weeklies before becoming a reporter with *Edmonton Journal*, correspondent for *Time Magazine*; promising southpaw boxer in youth and played competitive baseball to age 44; p-pres., life mem., dir. IBA; past exec. WBA; life mem. WCBA; mem. selection comm. Cdn Baseball Hall of Fame; exec. dir. Edmonton Boxing & Wrestling Commission; chair. Edmonton Intl. Baseball Foundation, organizers of World Youth AAA baseball championships in Edmonton; played key role in baseball acceptance as Olympic sport; founding dir. '78 CG; Edmonton city alderman '71-95; hon. dir. Crystal Kids Youth Centre; instrumental in Edmonton disabled adults transportation system; p-pres., life mem. Alta. Urban Municipalities Assn.; hon. life mem. Fed. Cdn Municipalities; Vanier award as one of Canada's five outstanding young Cdns '74; life mem. Yellowhead Highway Assn.; AUMA award of excellence, distinguished service award; FCM roll of honor; Alta. achivement award; mem. Alta., Nicaragua, Cdn Boxing, Edmonton Sports halls of fame; res. Edmonton, Alta.

HAYWARD, Bob (speedboat racing); b. 27 Oct 1928, Embro, Ont.; d. 10 Sep 1961, Detroit River, Mich.; mechanic Miss Supertest hydroplane crew '57; as driver '59 St. Clair international trophy; upset Maverick '59 in record 104.098 mph to snap 30-year US hold on Harmsworth Trophy; defended title '60-61; record 116.464 mph '60; killed driving Miss Supertest II Detroit River Silver Cup race; Union of International Motor Boating sport medal of honor '60; mem. Canada's Sports Hall of Fame.

HAZZARD, Elmer (water skiing); b. 18 Mar 1932, North Battleford, Sask.; m. Evelyn; c. Greg, Blaine, Arlene; transmission co. owner; Regina Beach open trick, Stoney Lake overall title '70; Sask. sr. overall title '72-73; national sr. tricks title '73-74; from '72 11 gold veterans class tricks; 3 national veterans records; 8 Western Canada tricks titles; judge, coach; v-p Sask. WSA, Regina WSC; 3 Sask. water-skier-of-yr awards; mem. Sask Sports Hall of Fame; res. Regina, Sask.

HEADLAND, Martin (motorsport); b. 7 Jul 1950, Beckenham, Eng.; given name: Martin George; m. Elizabeth Shaughnessy; aeronautical engineer; GM Skyservice Toronto; rally driver; with Jean-Paul Pérusse won ntl, NA co-driver Class A titles '87; with Tim O'Neill won ntl, NA co-driver titles '88-89; with O'Neill only outright win by production car in US rally '89; with Walter Boyce, Pérusse, Taisto Heinonen won several US, Cdn ntl titles; with Jeff Zwart 2nd overall in 25-day Panama to Alaska rally '97; won

'03 Rocky Mountain rally; 3 NA rally cup awards; mem. Toyota, Volkswagen, Nissan, Suzuki factory teams; mem. Suzuki world title class team '87-88 Olympus, Wa.; avid interest as trainer, participant in equestrian show jumping events; res. Schomberg, Ont.

HEADLEY, Ron (boxing); b. 22 Jun 1908, Ottawa, Ont.; d. 7 Feb 1983, Ottawa, Ont.; given name: Ronald Kenneth; m. Carmel Corr (d); pro boxer; standout school athlete starring in soccer, basketball, baseball, hockey; became addicted to boxing at 14 winning Ottawa District, Eastern Ont. titles; turned pro at 19; more then 100 welterweight pro fights winning most of them largely by knockouts; beat former world welter champion Sammy Mandell; headlined numerous boxing cards across Canada, northern NY State, England drawing rave reviews but little money; noted as a clever boxer and hard hitter who never acknowledged defeat; thwarted in bid to claim U.K. welter title by losing decision to Jack Hood; knockout by Gordon Wallace eliminated him from contention for Canadian title; boxing instructor UofT; trainer Ottawa Senators QSHL, Ottawa Rough Riders.

HEANEY, Brian (basketball/coaching); b. 9 Mar 1946, Brooklyn, N.Y.; given name: Brian Patrick; m. Liana Hynes; c. Pamela Jane, Jennifer Christine, Brian Niles; Acadia, BSc, Central Mich, MA; financial services, TV analyst; ex-coach.; 8 all-time Acadia scoring records including 74 points single game, 52 in one half, single season scoring avg. 34.5; pro NBA Baltimore Bullets '69-70, EPBL Sunbury Mercs '70-71; coach St. Mary's '71-79, UAlta '80-82, UofT '83-86; 3 CIAU titles; 1st person to win CIAU titles as player, coach; 1 CIAU coaches '78-79; mem. '78 Halifax CABA men's sr. A titlists, coached ntl women's team '75 PAG, worlds, '76 Olympics; TV color commentator '83 FISU, '84, '00 Olympics, '98 worlds; *TSN* NBA analyst '97-03, Raptors *NBA-TV* '02-03; analyst CIAU/CIS ntl championships '80-03; color analyst CBA Toronto Tornadoes '85, world league Hamilton Skyhawks '92, OUAA men's game of yr '94-98; Kitch McPherson award; chair. '02 Final 8 tourney; mem. Acadia, St. Mary's, OUAA men's officials, NS Sports, Canadian Basketball halls of fame; res. Oakville, Ont.

HEANEY, Geraldine (hockey); b. 1 Oct 1967, Belfast, Ireland; rec. programmer North Toronto Community Centre; def 18yrs Toronto Beatrice Aeros 2 ntl sr titles; competed annually in ntl championships '87-02; MVP '92, most valuable def '93, '97. '01 sr. ntls; 3 MVD Sr AA OWHA titles; mem. 7 Team Canada world champions, '98 Olympic silver, '02 gold medal teams; MVD, all-star '92, MVD '94 worlds; silver '97, gold '96 3-Nations Cup teams; gold '96 Pacific Rim; 125 intl games, 27g, 66a; mem. '92 women's world champion roller hockey team, silver '94; Cdn citizen '90; only woman featured in *HNIC* top 10 goals for '89-90 season (world champ game-winner); ret'd from ntl team '02; res. Weston, Ont.

HEAP, Alan (table tennis); b. 10 Mar 1947, Bolton, Eng.; m. Cathy Roccasalva; Hull, BA, McMaster, MA; teacher; British universities champion '66, '68-69; Lancashire Open '72; mem. Ont. team '74-80; National Capital Open '73, '76; Que. Open, Ont. closed '78; Montreal, Toronto, Ont., Eastern Canada Opens '79; res. Markham, Ont.

HEARN, Eugene (speed skating/softball); b. 8 May 1929, Odessa, Sask.; c. Debbie, Jeff, Kathy; charter mem. Saskatoon SSC '42; competitor/coach '56-66; club pres. '50-52; SASSA pres. '57-59; coach Sask. team 1st Canada Winter Games '67; 1st CASSA ntl coach '67; began officiating '70, first as referee then as starter; starter Cdn indoor '71, 4 ntl championships; chief starter NA, intl championships '80-88; official '88 Winter Olympics; active in Special Olympics program; hon. life mem. Saskatoon Lions SSC; Sask. sport volunteer award; softball distinguished service award; Dairy Producers Foundation volunteer award; CASSA award of excellence; Speed Skating Canada official '94 award; mem. Sask. Sports, Cdn Amateur Speed Skating halls of fame; res. Saskatoon, Sask.

HEATH, Jeff (baseball); b. 1 Apr 1915, Ft. William, Ont.; d. 9 Dec 1975, Seattle, Wash.; given name: John Geoffrey; m. Ann; became US citizen '36; learned baseball fundamentals in Seattle HS; began pro career Zanesville (Mid-Atlantic) '36, Milwaukee (AA) '37; of Cleveland '36-45, Washington '46, St. Louis '46-47, Boston (NL) '48-49; 3 times topped .300 single season, .343 '38, .340 '41, .319 '48; runnerup to Jimmy Foxx '38 AL batting race; twice all-star team mem.; led AL in triples '41; 3 career grand slams; with Boston Braves mem. .300 of '48 World Series finalists, but broken leg kept him out of series; led NL in fielding; led player revolt vs. mgr. Oscar Vitt '40; career record 1383g, 1447h, 887rbi, 777r, 102t, 279d, 194hr, 56sb, .293ba; color commentator Seattle Rainiers telecasts, wrote WS stories for *Seattle Post-Intelligencer*; mem. NWO Sports, Canadian Baseball halls of fame.

HEATLEY, Dany (hockey); b. 21 Jan 1981, Freibourg, Germany; UWisc.; lw Calgary Doyle Cup title team; CHL player of '99; top scorer/MVP '98 Air Canada Cup; UWisconsin '99-01, WCHA title '00; drafted by Atlanta '00; Team Canada '02 worlds, '04 World Cup (gold); bronze '00, '01 world jr.; NHL Atlanta '01-04; Calder Memorial trophy '02; *SN* rookie of yr.; *HN* co-rookie of yr award (with teammate Ilya Kovalchuk); driver of car in which teammate Dan Snyder was killed in '03 accident; NHL record (through '04) 190 scheduled games, 80g, 101a; played in Switzerland during '04 labor dispute; res. Atlanta, Ga.

HEBENTON, Andy (hockey); b. 3 Oct 1929, Winnipeg, Man.; given name: Andrew Alex; m. Gael; c. Clayton, Theresa; jr. Winnipeg Canadians '48-49; Montreal sr. Royals; pro Cincinnati (AHL), Victoria Cougars (PCHL, WHL), Portland, missed only 3 of 280 games, 3 PCHL titles; NYR '55-63, Boston '63-64; NHL record 630 consecutive game (broken by Garry Unger); NHL record: 189g, 202a; frequent all-star; played 1000th consec. pro game '66; 26yr pro career comprised 1735 games; 5 Fred J. Hume trophies (WHL most gentlemanly player); runnerup NHL rookie of '56; Lady Byng Trophy '57; Rangers Players' Prize; player/coach Portland (WHL) '74-75; mem. Man. Hockey Hall of Fame; res. Portland, Ore.

HÉBERT, Jacques (harness racing); b. 22 Aug 1942, Drummondville, Que.; started career with father Joseph and uncle Cyprien in Trois-Riviéres; worked 3yrs with Jean Jodoin before striking out on his own '66; one of most consistent drivers on Montreal circuit winning 100 or more races 32 consec. seasons; has built reputation of winning with long shots and other troubled animals; among top horses Carissa, Electric Stena, Excitante, McCooeye, Beardmore, Magoo; through '03 5551 wins, $34+M in purses; res. Montreal, Que.

HEDBERG, Anders (hockey); b. 25 Feb 1951, Ornskoldsvik, Sweden; m. Gun-Marie; c. Mattias, Johan, Hanna; Stockholm Institute PE teaching diploma; hockey exec.; rw on line with Bobby Hull and fellow countryman Ulf Nilsson, proved a proficient sniper with WHA Winnipeg Jets '74-78 playing 286 scheduled games with 236g, 222a; 50+ goals in each of 4 seasons, 70 '77, 63 '78, 53 '75, 50 '76; played in NHL with NYR '73-85 posting record of 465 scheduled games, 172g, 226a, 58 playoff games, 22g, 24a; on retirement became 1st European to secure top management position in NHL as AGM NYR '85-86; managed Stockholm AJK team; full-time scout TML '91-96; AGM TML '97-99; Edmonton dir. European scouting briefly; Swedish ntl program GM '00-02; dir. player development Ottawa '02-04; res. Ottawa, Ont./Lidingo, Sweden.

HEDDLE, Kathleen (rowing); b. 27 Nov 1965, Trail, B.C.; UBC BA; sport administrator; began rowing '85; gold straight pair '87 PAG, 8s & straight pair '92 Olympic Games, '91 worlds; Cdn Henley 4 gold 8s, 3 coxed 4s, 1 single sculls; International regatta gold 3 straight pairs, 2 8s, 1 straight 4s, double sculls; 1 ntl 8s gold; ret'd '93 season but came back to take world double sculls (McBean) gold '95, Olympics '96, also bronze quad sculls; ret'd '96; Tribute of Champions '89 sport excellence award; BC athlete of yr, Vancouver merit awards; CARA '91 centennial award; Dick Ellis Memorial sr. team award '91-92; Thomas Keller award '99; BC Women in Sport Leaders & Legends award; Order of BC; mem. UBC, Cdn Olympic, BC, Canada's Sports halls of fame; res, Vancouver, B.C.

HEDGES, Brian (football); b. 2 Aug 1952, Fort Churchill, Man.; given name: Brian Robie; m. Kathryn Elizabeth Eadie; c. Trisha, Andrea; Carleton, hons BComm; chartered accountant, sr. v-p, CFO Russel Metals; honed football skills with Ottawa Bel-Air Lions city title team '64; mem. Laurentian Lions '66-69, Ott. HS champs '68; mem. Carleton Ravens '70-74; 2 conf. all-star, 1 all-Canadian awards; Doug Banton '73, Jack Vogan '74 awards; dt Rough Riders '76-80; mem. Grey Cup champions '76; played on last Riders team with winning season record '79; Carleton Sports Hall of Fame; res. Etobicoke, Ont.

HEDGEWICK, Mike (football); b. 22 Oct 1916, Montreal, Que.; d. Sep 2003, Windsor, Ont.; given name: Michael; m. Margaret Clinansmith; c. Michael, Robert; ret'd accountant; half, safety, qb W.D. Lowe jr./sr. HS champs; 2 all-city awards; scored 2tds as Sarnia Imperials won '36 Grey Cup; Eastern semifinalists 3yrs; mem. Hamilton Tigers '40, '45, Hamilton Wildcats (ORFU) '41-42; 2 outstanding player awards Cdn Navy Halifax team; player/asst. coach Windsor Rockets (ORFU) '46; 15yrs referee-in-chief Windsor HS league; set 100yd sprint record in service t&f meet '43; excelled in softball, baseball, hockey, lacrosse, winning several city, county titles; golf club champion '66; recorded 2 holes-in-one; with wife won husband-wife golf tournaments; mem. Sarnia-Lambton, Windsor-Essex Sports halls of fame.

HEENEY, Walter (bowling/builder/administration); b. 27

Mar 1944, Toronto, Ont.; m. Catherine Ryan; c. Sheila, David, Jan; ED Ont. Master Bowlers Assn, tech-dir. Ont. 5-pin Bowling Assn; Ont. singles title '77, ntl runnerup; bowled 2000 games on MBA tour (more than any other bowler); 6 MBAO titles; ranked 23rd among 20th Century 5-pinners; competed 29 prov championships; won '72 Ace Invitational, '81 Snow Bowl Open, '87 Hamilton Survival, '95 Masters Srs. Tour tourney titles; personal highs: 448 single, 1090 triple, 1682 5-game score, 2940 10-game score; lifetime avg. 250; designed Mark Ten masters skills program; launched MBA Ont. Special Olympics doubles tourney '90; ntl tech. advisor for 5-pin bowling Cdn Special Olympics '91-96; plays leading role in Ont. 5-pin BA annual bowling school; program dir. '74-77, tech. dir. '79-99 Ont. 5-pin BA; v-p. marketing Pro Bowling Ltd. '77-79; wrote bowling column, covered minor hockey for *Toronto Star* '74-81; introduced Hiram Walker to 5-pin sponsorship '81-96; pres. MBAO '72-74, Cdn MBA from '78; dir. Ont. Sport Legends Hall of Fame; life mem. MBA; mem. (builder/player divs.) 5-pin bowling Hall of Fame; res. Pickering, Ont.

HEES, George (football); b. 17 Jun 1910, Toronto, Ont.; d. 12 Jun 1996, Toronto, Ont.; m. Mabel Dunlop; c. Catherine Mabel, Martha Ann, Roslyn Georgia; Royal Military College, UofT, Cambridge; soldier, politician; mem. Argos '34, '38 Grey Cup title team; Progressive Conservative MP '50-62, '65-94; mem. Privy Council; Min. Transport '57-60, Min. Trade & Commerce '60-63; Min. Veteran's Affairs '84-94; dir. Montreal World Fair '64; pres. Mtl., Cdn. stock exchanges; mem. Order of Canada.

HEESE, Mark (volleyball); b. 15 Aug 1969, Toronto, Ont.; McMaster; played indoors with McMaster '88-92; focused talents on beach volleyball '90 competing in Barcelona Olympic exhibition; 4 ntl titles; teamed with John Child '95-03 winning bronze '96 world, gold '97 ntl pro championship series; through '03 107 games on pro circuit, 1g, 5s, 10b, $382,090 prize money; noted for defensive skills; bronze '96 Olympics; best digger/setter '97 Labatt Blue pro beach tour award; res. Toronto, Ont.

HEFFORD, Jayna (hockey); b. 14 May 1977, Trenton, Ont.; UofT; OWIAA rookie of '97; fwd Brampton Thunder; capt. Team Ont. Canada Games gold '95; Team Ont. u-18 ntls gold; ntl team from '97; 5 world gold; Olympic silver '98, gold '02; 3 gold, 1 silver 3-Nations Cup; 2 gold, 1 silver 4-Nations Cup; top scorer '99-00 worlds; participated '01 Can-Am foot hockey championship; co-owner (with Lori Dupuis) Olympic Bound hockey school; female spokesperson CHA Initiation program; hon. chair. Greater Kingston For Kids Forever campaign; Kingston amateur athlete of '98; nickname "Heff"; res. Kingston, Ont.

HEGAN, Larry (football); b. 14 Feb 1908, Wetaskwin, Alta.; d. 9 Oct 1994, Calgary, Alta.; given name: Robert John; m. Elga Muriel "Mike" Stayner; c. Dick, Mary, Jim, Roger, Tom; UofSask; ret'd GM Eatons; 5yrs football UofSask, 2yrs team capt., 2yrs university hockey; unable to secure job in engineering in '30s played pro football Roughriders '34-39; mem. '34 Grey Cup finalists; '36 WFC all-star; mem. winning 4s '36 international rowing regatta Ft. William.

HEGGTVEIT, Anne (skiing); b. 11 Jan 1939, Ottawa, Ont.; m. Ross Hamilton; c. Timothy, Christianne; retail stores chain comptroller; father Halvor former x-country champion, uncles Bud Clark, Bruce Heggtveit former Olympic skiers; age 7 Gatineau Zone sr. women's slalom, combined titles; by '52 had won all Ottawa area major competitions; 1st international success '54 Holmenkollen GS Norway, at 15 youngest winner in event's 50-year history; 15th combined '56 Olympics; '59 St.Moritz, Arlberg-Kandahar, Que. Kandahar, ntl alpine titles; '60 US slalom, GS, swept Roch Cup events; Canada's 1st Olympic skiing gold medalist, 1st non-European FIS world alpine combined gold medalist '60; 3.3 second Olympic victory greatest margin by woman in Games history; *CP* female athlete of '59-60; Lou Marsh Trophy '60, 2 Bobbie Rosenfeld awards; mem. Order of Canada, US Ntl, Cdn Skiing, Ottawa, Cdn Olympic, Ont. Sports Legends, Canada's Sports halls of fame; res. Grand Isle, Vt.

HEGGTVEIT, Halvor (skiing); b. 16 Mar 1907, Leland, N.D.; d. 18 Jan. 1995, Clinton, Ont.; m. Dorothy Clark (d); c. Alexander, Anne; raised in Saskatchewan; began x-country skiing Ottawa '20s; 4 Lady Willingdon Trophy wins; silver ntl championships '30, '33; won every '34 race entered, including Ottawa, Que., ntl x-country titles; coached daughter Anne until she'd won ntl jr. ladies' downhill, slalom, combined titles at 13; occupational conflict prevented him from participating '32 Olympics although named to team; mem. Olympic Club of Canada; life mem. Ottawa Ski Club; mem. Ottawa CSRA Sports Hall of Fame.

HEIKKILA, Bill (t&f); b. 17 Aug 1944, Toronto, Ont.; m. Patricia Hunnakko; c. Kirsti, Kaarina, Liisa, Leila; Oregon, BSc, MPhE; Sport Canada consultant; 5 ntl sr. javelin titles; gold '69 Canada Games; ntl juv, sr. javelin records; mem. '67 PAG, '68 Olympic Games teams; Oregon all-American, 2nd '67 NCAA championships; coached several of Canada's top javelin throwers; hon. life mem. Cdn Gymnastics Fed.; res. Nepean, Ont.

HEIL, Jenn (skiing); b. 11 Apr 1983, Edmonton, Alta.; given name: Jennifer Adele; full-time athlete; moguls specialist; mem. ntl team from '01; exploded onto scene at 16 as mem. Cdn. development team, winning '00 ntls in both single, dual moguls; repeated wins '01 ntls; silver, bronze '00-01 WC events; 3 WC medals '01-02, including 1st-ever gold; missed '02 Olympic bronze by 1/100 of point; spent '02/-03 season on rehab, strengthening after several seasons dealing with shin pain, lower back problems; silver in 1st WC '03-04 season, first race since returning from a 1 year lay-off; podium results continued with 5 gold, 2 silver in 9 WC events to Feb. '05; res. Montréal, Qué

HEIMRATH, Ludwig Sr. (motorsport); b. 11 Aug 1934, Munich, Germany; m. Brigitte Wlochowitz; c. Ludwig Jr., Karin; auto dealer; 3 ntl driving titles; 7 Ont. driving titles; began racing career on motorcycles Germany '52; competed 1st Players' 200 race '61 Mosport; more than 200 Mosport victories; represented Canada USAC, USRRC, Can-Am events; runnerup to Trans-Am champion Peter Gregg '74; res. Scarborough, Ont.

HELLARD, Rick (triathlon); b. 23 May 1966, Ottawa, Ont.; sports consultant, endurance coach; in 16yr period competed 241 triathlons; victories in 3 OAC, 4 Mt. Tremblant (course

rec.), 3 Sharbot Lake, varied races in France, Switzerland, US; 2nd Nogoya, Japan; 3rd Embrun, France, ironman; competed in Australian Worlds; ntl team mem. 4yrs; raced in France 3yrs; accomplished at all distances; won Kingston 1/2 marathon '98, Husky Howl 5k '04; 3 Ottawa ACT awards; res. Ottawa, Ont.

HELLEUR, Kay (golf); b. 1 Feb 1921, Kenogami, Que.; given name: Katherine; 2 Ont. sr. ladies' amateur titles, twice runnerup; ntl sr. ladies' title '74, 3 runnerup; instrumental in developing 1st CLGA sr. women's amateur championships '71; personally designed, supervised construction Woodbridge G&CC; owned, operated Woodlands G&CC '53-69; founder, dir. Ada Mackenzie Memorial Foundation' capt. Cdn team '66 World Cup matches; mem. 9 Ont. sr. prov. teams; dir. Summerlea (now Humber Valley) '45-52; 15 Rosedale GC ladies' club titles, 8 srs; '40 St. Andrews women's title; 8 Oshawa ladies, 1 sr. club titles; mem. Ont. Golf Hall of Fame; res. Toronto, Ont.

HELLIWELL, David (rowing); b. 26 Jul 1935, Vancouver, B.C.; d. 30 Dec 1993, Vancouver, B.C.; m. Margaret Adam; c. Kerby, Wendy, Cathy, Marnie, John; UBC, CA; company pres.; mem. UBC jr. varsity crew '55; Olympic silver UBC varsity 8s '56; CG silver UBC varsity 4s '58; coach silver medal '59 PAG 8s; pres. Vancouver Rowing Club '62; coach Alta. Canada Games '69; rowing chair. Canada Games '73; v-p Canadian Assn. of Amateur Oarsmen '71; trustee BC Sports Hall of Fame '80; hon. v-p Vancouver RC; mem. Cdn Olympic, BC, Canada's Sports halls of fame.

HEMMINGS, Guy (curling); b. 10 May 1962, Saint-Jean sur Richelieu, Qué.; m. Josée Plamondon; c. Frédérique, William; UMtl., BA; owner of 'Les Serres St-Tomat' (greenhouses); started to curl '84 Outremont CC; 4 Québec men's, mixed titles 2 McCain's East titles; competed *TSN* Skins Game; 4 Labatt Briers, runnerup '98, '99; recruited by CCA to heighten awareness of the sport and recruit new players; Guy Hemmings Rockin' the House Tour has visited over 100 Cdn. communities since the fall '01, conducting clinics, speaking at receptions, visiting sick kids' wings at hospitals, giving interviews and signing autographs; 2 Que. Sport Fed. team-of-year awards; res. Saint-Aimé, Qué.

HENDERSON, Gil (shooting); b. 5 Sep 1926, Toronto, Ont.; given name: Gilbert James; m. Molly (d); ret'd mechanical contractor; converted golf course to farm then to wildlife sanctuary then to Tim Horton Onondaga children's camp; trapshooting specialist, mem. '60 Olympic, '66, '74 world championships, '71 world moving target championships, '75 Championship of Americas teams; pres. Canadian Trapshooting Assn.; v-p Shooting Federation of Canada; coach-mgr. shotgun team '72 Olympics, CG team '74; mgr. shotgun events '76 Olympics; res. St. George, Ont.

HENDERSON, Paul (hockey); b. 28 Jan 1943, Kincardine, Ont.; given name: Paul Garnet; m. Eleanor Alton; c. Heather, Jennifer, Jill; account exec., evangelist; jr. A Hamilton Red Wings '60-63; mem. Memorial Cup titlists '62; 1st all-star team; Max Kaminsky Trophy; Detroit (NHL) '63-68, Toronto '68-74; WHA Toronto Toros '74-76, Birmingham (WHA, CHL) '76-81; briefly returned to NHL Atlanta '79; major pro record: 1067 scheduled games (NHL-WHA), 376 goals, 384 assists, 61 playoff games, 12 goals, 15 assists;

mem. '71-72 NHL all-star game teams; mem. Team Canada '72, '74; achieved hockey immortality with goal at 19:26 of final period in deciding game which gave Team Canada 6-5 victory over Soviets 28 Sep '72; series MVP; active in Campus Crusade for Christ; mem. Canada's, Etobicoke, Mississauga Sports halls of fame; res. Mississauga, Ont.

HENDERSON, Paul (sailing); b. 17 Nov 1934, Toronto, Ont.; given name: Paul Franklin; m. Mary Katherine Lynn McLeod; c. John, Martha; UofT. BSc; engineer; 4 Aphrodite Cup jr. team race titles; mem. Royal Canadian Yacht Club; jr. club champion, fleet capt. '50; 2 CIAU titles; English, US, Bermuda, world, Alexander of Tunis International 14' dinghy titles; Dutch, US, 2 Canadian Flying Dutchman Olympics Class titles; 2 ntl Finn Olympic Class single-handed titles; US Midwest Tempest Olympic Class keel boat title; US Atlantic Coast Soling Olympic Class keel yacht title; NA Fireball title; mem. '64, '68 Olympic teams; coach '72 Olympic yachting team; founding dir. Water Rat Sailing Club; 3rd world '74 FD; ntl Soling titles '75; dir. ntl sailing team '70-71; Ont. squash open doubles semifinalist '73; Ont. yachtsman of '74; mem. National Fitness Advisory Council '74-76; dir. CYA, International Yacht Racing Union, Ont. Sailing Assn., Canadian Squash Racquets Assn.; ex-IOC dir.; key role in Toronto's failed '96 Olympics bid; organized bid to bring world basketball championships to Toronto; dir. '10 Olympic organizing comm.; mem. Cdn Olympic Sports Hall of Fame; res. Toronto, Ont.

HENDERSON, Roy (wheelchair basketball); b. 14 Oct 1955, Peterborough, Ont.; Home Depot; began playing '84 with Toronto Spitfires; also played with Kitchener Twin City Spinners '88-93, Ottawa Royals '92-95; mem. Ont. team from '87, ntl team from '88; competed '88, '92, '96, '00 (gold), '04 (gold) Paralympics; 1 Stoke-Mandeville gold; 9 gold, 3 silver ntl championships; 1 CWBL gold; 1 NWBT bronze; 4 World Cup bronze; 2 all-star teams; res. Otonabee Twp.

HENDERSON, Scott (skiing); b. 15 Apr 1943, Calgary, Alta.; given name: George Scott Robert; div. Patricia Pitt, m. Barbara Ferries; sc. Kathryn, Misty, Mark; independent sports equipment sales; ntl alpine ski team '62-69; 3 ntl, US alpine titles; '67 international race winner Australia; top 10 Europe several times '68-69; turned pro; Lange racing director '70-72; ntl men's alpine coach '72-78, produced World Cup race winners '75-76, mem. Cdn Skiing, Alta Sports halls of fame; res. Nederland, Colo.

HENDRICKSON, Lefty (football); b. 27 Apr 1943, Squamish, B.C.; given name: Lynn Alfred; m. Carol Anne; c. Craig Stephen, Scott Patrick; Oregon, BSc; auto dealer; HS basketball all-star '59-62; jr. football all-star '60-63; Pacific 8 hon. mention te '67-68; pro BC '68-73, ol/receiver; CFL record: 123 receptions for 1669yds, 13.5yd avg. 7tds; WFC all-star '73; all-star softball 1b Brandon '76, '78; v-p '79 Canada Winter Games; res. Alexander, Man.

HENDRIE, George (horse racing/administration); b. 10 Jun 1906, Hamilton, Ont.; d. 14 Oct 1988, Toronto, Ont.; given name: George Campbell; m. Elizabeth Olmsted; c. George Muir, Anthony Olmsted; Upper Canada College; cartage co. owner, horseman; followed footsteps of grandfather William, father William Jr., as pres. OJC '63-71; hon.

pres. from '71; racing steward OJC '30s; dir. OJC '43-52, managing dir. '53; charter mem. Ont. Racing Commission; mem. Canadian Horse Racing Hall of Fame.

HENDRIE, George Jr. (horse racing/administration); b. 28 Jul 1930, Toronto, Ont.; given name: George Muir; m. Elizabeth "Betsy" Bartlett; c. George C II, Geoffrey, Jane; Ridley Coll, UWO, BA; ret'd family transportation co.; carried on family racing tradition begun by great-grandfather William; raced a stable in partnership with father and from '88 has enjoyed moderate success with own racing stable; chair. Board of Trustees Ontario Jockey Club from '92; magnificent E.P. Taylor turf course opened in '94 and highly successful '96 Breeders' Cup at Woodbine rank high on his list of accomplishments as OJC chair.; res. Toronto, Ont.

HENDRY, Joan (t&f); b. 14 May 1945, Glasgow, Scotland; given name: Joan Lynn; UofOtt, BA; teacher; lj/sprint specialist; mem. '67 PAG, '68, '72 Olympic, '69 Pan-Pacific, '70 CG teams; relay silver '69 Pan-Pacific, 2 bronze '70 CG; ntl lj/relay records; Canada's top sprinter over 100m '72 with 11.4sec best time; injury forced withdrawal '72 Olympics; began running again '75; co-holder ntl indoor 50m 6.2sec record; '67-71 ntl women's lj record holder; formed Ottawa Super P.I.T.S. (participants in track) club '79; res. Osgoode, Ont.

HENLEY, Garney (football); b. 21 Dec 1935, Elgin, N.D.; m. Phyllis Diekmann; c. Pamela, Lori, Jody, Garney Kyle; Huron College, BA; ret'd university AD/football exec.; most prolific scorer in history of US college football with 394 points 31-game, 4yr career; drafted Green Bay Packers (NFL), NY (AFL) '60; part of '60 season with Packers before joining Hamilton (CFL); shone def/off '60-75; 59 interceptions for 5tds, record 916yds; caught 4td passes single game; career total 364 punts returned for 2844yds including 83 in '66 season; 10 times EFC all-star, all-Cdn; 6 times Schenley outstanding player nominee, winner '72; Jeff Russel Memorial Trophy twice; Ticats best-of-century team '67; 7 Grey Cup finals, 4 winners; Ticats asst. coach '76; AD Mount Allison '77; 10 years basketball coach Guelph, '74 CIAU titlists; AD, basketball coach Brock '78-94; dir. FB operations Rough Riders '95; mem. Guelph, Cdn Football, US College Football, South Dakota Sports halls of fame; res. Huron, S.D.

HENNESSEY, Walter (harness racing); b. 4 Oct 1956, Charlottetown, P.E.I.; in early stages of career rewrote Maritimes record books posting standards for victories and earnings; made initial foray out of Maritimes '83 winning Canadian Ice Racing Classic; ranked among top drivers at Saratoga, Pompano Park in '90s; piloted America's Pastime to world record-equaling 1:51.4 '92; won 7 New York Sires Stakes at Buffalo Raceway, including track record 6 in succession, '92; piloted My Dolly, Catch As Catch Can to Breeders Crown titles '97; through '03 5875 victories for purses totaling more than $40M; 118 major stakes titles including 25 W.N. Reynolds Memorial and with Moni Maker 14 titles;; res. Coconut Creek, Fla.

HENICK, Ed (builder/football); b. 10 Dec 1927, Saskatoon, Sask.; d. 24 Nov 2000, Saskatoon, Sask.; playing HS football whetted appetite for game; joined prov. jr. champion Saskatoon Hilltops '47; turned to coaching

'48; worked way up administrative ladder to pres. '63-64; helped form Saskatoon Minor Flag Football League '57-80; commissioner Kinsmen tackle league '62-82; pres, Football Saskatchewan '73-74, secty-treas. '75-00; pres. Prairie Jr. Football Conf. '84-85; Sask. Amateur football recognition award; Sask sport voluntary service award; Kinsmen Sportsman of '81; honored by BC, Regina Rams, Football Canada, Sask. Roughriders; life mem. Hilltops, CJFL; meritorious service award CJFL, Sask. HS all-star game bear his name; mem. Saskatoon Sports, Cdn Football halls of fame.

HENNIGAR, Carl (speed skating); b. Feb 1926, Halifax, N.S.; given name: Carl Austin; McGill, B Eng; ret'd engineer; mem. KW Sertoma SSC '66-97, club pres. '72-76; pres. Ont. ASSA '75-79; com. mem. training institute for sport administrators '80-81, co-chair. '82-83; active organizational role in club, provincial, ntl, NA events; avid cyclist, x-country skier, basketball, tennis player in youth; maintains ham radio license and holds private pilot's license; very active in community affairs; mem. Cdn Amateur Speed Skating Hall of Fame; res. Kitchener, Ont.

HENNING, Cam (swimming); b. 24 Nov 1960, Edmonton, Alta.; given name: Cameron John; m. Anastazia Shelenko; c. Oscar Wylie, Laszlo John; Alabama, UAlta. BA; mgr. Loomis; backstroke specialist; ntl team '76-84; 5 ntl titles, 6 ntl, 2 CG records; mem. '78, '82 CG, '79 FISU, '80, '84 Olympic, '83 PAG teams; 200m gold, 100m silver '82 CG; 3 Canada Cup gold, 3 Four Nation Cup gold; Southeastern Conf. 200m backstroke champion '81; gold 400m FS, 100m, 200m backstroke '83 CIAU championships;1 CIAU male-swimmer-of-yr award; bronze 200m backstroke '84 Olympics; fed. govt. excellence award '83; 3 Alta jubilee awards; mem. Alta Sports Hall of Fame; res. Calgary, Alta.

HENNYEY, Donna (fencing); b. 10 Apr 1942, New York, N. Y.; given name: Donna Jean Atkinson; m. Alex Richard Hennyey; c. Mark Alexander, Allison Marijke; UofT, BA, MA; nutrition consultant; mem. ntl fencing team '67-77, mem. 4 world, 3 PAG, 2 Olympic teams; team silver '75 PAG; 5 Italian Martini Rossi, 3 NY Martini Rossi, 1 German international, London De Beaumont Cup, Austrian international titles, 2 Ont. women's titles, 6 times runnerup; 2 Eastern Canadian, 3 ntl, 5 Heroes International, 3 Gov.-Gen.'s, 4 Harmonie International titles; winner Golden Foil, Dell Open events; mem. 3 Ont., 5 ntl title teams; Norman Craig award Ont. female athlete of '68; res. Toronto, Ont.

HENNYEY, Imre (fencing); b. 14 Jul 1913, Cattaro, Yugoslavia; d. 6 Sep 1989, Toronto, Ont.; m. Ilona Szelecsenyi; c. Alex, Sheilah; Ludovika Academy, UofT, BSc; teacher; world university épée title '39 Vienna; Hungarian épée title '41, '43, '47; mem. Hungarian '48, '52 Olympic teams; coached '53-54 Hungarian modern pentathon fencing team; coached UotT fencing team '61-80; coach '68 Canadian Olympic, '70 CG teams.

HENRY, Camille (hockey); b. 31 Jan 1933, Quebec City, Que.; d. 11 Sep 1997, Quebec City, Que.; given name: Camille Wilfrid; div. Aimée Sylvestre (Quebec actress Dominique Michel); c. Martine, Nathalie; diminutive 5-7, 138lbs; rejected baseball for hockey; stickboy with father's

Sherbrooke Saints Que. sr. team; 3yrs Que. Citadel jrs.; pro NYR '53-55, '56-64, '67-68, Chicago '65, St. Louis '68-70; Calder Memorial Trophy '54; nicknamed "The Eel"; hosted Montreal radio show; coached NY Raiders-Golden Blades-Jersey Knights WHA '72-74; Lady Byng Trophy '58; 2nd team all-star lw '58; NHL record: 817 scheduled games, 279g, 249a, only 88 penalty minutes; 48 playoff games, 6g, 12a; 3 all-star games.

HENRY, Daryl (parachuting); b. 25 Apr 1935, Cranbrook, B.C.; given name: Daryl Arthur; m. Carol Warner; UofT, B.Arch.; screenwriter; 1st jump '58; 4 ntl overall titles, team leader '60 world championships; mem. overall title team world's 1st paraski championships '62; ntl team capt. '62, '64, '66 worlds; 1st world accuracy record ever established in competition '62; 1st overall Massachusetts Governor's Cup '62, Las Vegas international '63; NA record 3 consecutive dead centers in competition; 1st overall California pro championships '65; ntl group of 3 altitude record (22,500') '66; coached US Marine team to gold Brazil '65; Cdn team leader Adriatic Cup Yugoslavia '69; judge, TV commentator, coach, exec. in all phases of sport; several ntl, US, UK records; Confederation Medal; author variety of parachuting articles; res. Santa Barbara, Calif.

HENSELWOOD, Jill (equestrian); b. 1 Nov 1962, Ottawa, Ont.; given name: Jill MacAngus; m. Bob Henselwood; Uof Ott, BPHE; co-operator Juniper Farms; t&f athlete in university; certified t&f coach, level 3 jumper coach; entered grand prix competition '89; mem. ntl team from '91; aboard Canadian Colors mem. '92 Nations Cup title team; 9 grand prix victories; mem. '95, '99 PAG teams, team bronze '99; won 3 World Cup qualifiers; competed '02 World Cup; earned berth on '96 Olympic team but declined because her mount Aerial was unavailable to travel to Atlanta; won '92 Mexico GP, '95 Seoul GP, '96 Indio, Calif., GP, '03 Ocala GP; res. Oxford Mills, Ont.

HENTGEN, Pat (baseball); b. 13 Nov 1968, Detroit, Mich.; given name: Patrick George; m. Darlene; c. Taylor Renee, Hannah; rhp; played HS baseball/football; capt. baseball team; rejected scholarship offer Western Mich; originally ss; made pro debut St. Catharines (NYP) helping them win A league title '86, Myrtle Beach (SAL) '87, Dunedin (FSL) '88-89; Knoxville (Sou) '90, Syracuse (Int) '91-92, Toronto (AL) '91-99, '04; St. Louis (NL) '00-02; Baltimore '03; ML record: (through '04) 344 scheduled games, 2075.1ip, 2111h, 1076r, 775bob, 1290k, 131-112w/l; 3 all-star games; mem. '93 World Series winner; 1st Blue Jay to win Cy Young award '96; res. Palm Harbor, Fla./Michigan.

HEPBURN, Doug (weightlifting); b. 16 Sep 1926, Vancouver B.C.; d. 22 Nov 2000, Vancouver, BC; given name: Douglas Ivan; health food/gym equipment distributor; born with clubbed foot which never healed; went on body building program, put 300lbs on 5'10" frame, earned title of strongest man in history; turned competitive '48 pressing ntl record 300lbs; US jr./sr. ntl titles; world heavyweight title '53 with lift of 1030lbs; '54 BEG gold; at age 70 issued challenge to any man in world, without use of drugs, to match his lifting feats, no one ever responded; considered himself as poorest best- known man in Canada; Lou Marsh, Lionel Conacher trophies '53; BC man of '54; mem. Cdn Olympic, BC, Canada's Sports halls of fame.

HERBERT, Michael (equestrian); b. 4 Oct 1932, Oxford, Eng.; given name: Michael Towner; riding instructor; pro. horseman from age 20; trained horses, riders for 3-day events Great Britain; horse/rider combinations have won 8 gold, 2 silver in national, European, Olympic competition; coached '71 Cdn PAG team gold, individual silver, '78 world championships team gold; Martini & Rossi Horseman of '78; Fellowship of the British Horse Society '70; res. East Ferry, Ireland.

HERLEN, Ossie (boxing); b. 26 Nov 1918, Star City, Sask.; d. 9 Jun 1944, Europe; given name: Ernest Osborne; mem. Saskatoon Tech '37 title football team; started boxing at 15; used ring name Biff Bapp briefly; lost initial Sask. amateur title bid '36; stopped Sask. lightweight titlist Billy Moore in 2nd round '37; Sask. welterweight title '38; Cdn welterweight title '39; boxed in service winning Toronto Garrison welterweight title; ring record: 33 fights, 12 won by TKO, 12 by decision, 3 TKO, 1 draw, lost 5 by decision; never KO'd in 9yrs of boxing; v-p Saskatoon Golden Gloves Boxing Club at formation '38; mem. Sask. Sports Hall of Fame.

HERLINVEAUX, Louise (curling); b. 3 Oct 1958, Nanaimo, B.C.; UVic; sr. systems analyst BC ministry of finance; 2nd for Pat Sanders' '87 Scott Tournament of Hearts/World women's titlists; lead Steve Skillings' '85 ntl mixed title rink; mem. BC Sports Hall of Fame; res. Victoria, B.C.

HERMAN, Wally (t&f); b. 11 Nov 1925, Winnipeg, Man.; m. Marie; c. Robert, Christine, Richard; UMan B.Comm.; Oxford BA, MA; ret'd civil servant; participated in Canadian Ski Marathon; became enamored with marathon running at age 49; ran 1st of (through '04) 630 marathons in 97 countries in '75; set goal of competing in every country in alphabet (A-Z); only X not done since no country begins with that letter; ranks among world's top mega-runners; completed all but 10 races he started; competed in 144 untra-marathons; PB 3:37.40 in race 242 in Spain '87; res. Ottawa, Ont.

HERMANN, Tiny (curling/football); b. 25 Aug 1906, Halifax, N.S.; d. 30 Nov 1966, Metcalfe, Ont.; given name: Charles Bismark; m. Loretta Hutchingame; c. Phyllis, Carolanne; insurance agent, ret'd RCMP; from his youth exhibited exceptional strength and athletic ability; mem. NS champion Kings Collegiate HS rugby, prov. champion basketball team; starred for Halifax Wanderers AC in rugby, softball, baseball; BEG discus silver, shot put bronze '30; grand aggregate gold cup Cdn Legion field day Cornwall '33; played football 8 seasons with Rough Riders earning frequent all-star status as inside wing/pk; mem. 5 Big Four champions; competed 2 Grey Cup finals, 1 winner; despite size was regarded as one of cleanest players in the game; received only one penalty during his career; honored by *MacLean's, Canadian Press* '39; ret'd '40 to serve in navy WW2; mentioned in dispatches for rescues at sea; 1st football coach Carleton; coached Ashbury Coll. srs 10yrs; had 2 consec. undefeated seasons; mem. Ottawa Curling Club, Gov.-Gen.'s CC; launched schoolboy curling in Ottawa; trophy bearing his name competed for by schoolboy curlers 30yrs; '56 Ottawa curler-of-yr award; instrumental in formation OVCA, served as 2nd pres.; chair.

City of Ottawa bonspiel '60; won grand aggregate title '63; chair. '67 Brier comm.; died in plane crash while on Brier business; Outaouais golf club initiated cup, Ashbury Coll scholarship in his memory; mem. NS, Ottawa Sports halls of fame.

HERMANSON, Myrna (synchro swim); b. 1 May 1963, Montreal, Que.; given name; Myrna Jean; div.; c. Caleb; m. Harry Kruger; sc. Eric, Blaine, Rachel; Southern Alberta Institute of Technology; mem. Calgary YWCA Aquabelles '73-81; mem. ntl jr. gold medal teams '77-78; mem. silver medal team '78 Canada Winter Games; silver team '80 sr. nationals; ntl team mem. '80; team gold Swedish International competition; began modelling '81; Alta. Achievement awards '77-78; res. Cochrane, Alta.

HERMITAGE, Robbyn (badminton); b. 22 Apr 1970, Montreal, Que.; Atwater Club pro; ntl team from '94; quarterfinalist '94 Cdn, Welsh, US, '95 Scottish Opens doubles; gold '99, silver '95 PAG doubles, bronze '95 PAG singles; gold doubles '97 Pan-Am championships; competed '95, '98 Worlds, '00 Olympics; 7 ntl doubles titles; res. Montreal, Que.

HERN, Riley (hockey); b. 5 Dec 1880, St. Mary's, Ont.; d. 24 Jun 1929, Montreal, Que.; given name: William Milton; c. Al (d); business exec.; goaltender hometown OHA jr. team; London ints., srs; 7 title teams 1st 9yrs; pro Portage Lake team Houghton, Mich., '04; Montreal Wanderers '06-11, 3 Stanley Cups; referee, goal judge several years; twice Rosemere golf club champion; pres. St. Rose Boating Club; mem. Hockey Hall of Fame.

HERSCHMILLER, Tom (rowing/skiing/swimming); b. 6 Apr 1978, Comox, B.C.; given name: Thomas Alan; Princeton, BA; student Sydney Medical School; '03 world champion in fours; silver fours '04 Olympics; mem. sr. eights '98, '99, '01 worlds, '00 Olympics; after a year away from ntl team '02, competed men's fours '03 Lucerne world cup, Henley Royal, worlds, gold '04 Duisburg Regatta, Munich world cup, silver Lucerne world cup, Olympics; started x-country skiing age 2; won Cypress BC Cup race; also competitive swimmer, winning BC provincial FS relay title; while rowing at Princeton lost only 1 regular season race during 4 years; 3 Eastern sprints titles, 1 ntl championship; Richard Challener Cdn. Studies Senior Thesis Prize at Princeton; res. Comox, B.C.

HERSHFIELD, Leible (all-around); b. 30 Aug 1909, Winnipeg, Man.; d. Jun 1999, Winnipeg, Man.; m. Babe; c. Joel, Susan, Myron; gold '24 Winnipeg HS t&f championships; cf 27 consecutive years Winnipeg softball teams, playing entire career without glove; mem. Western Cdn, Ukraine Cdn, vets title teams; soccer '24-45; Winnipeg dist. amateur football league gold medal '30; 40yrs Winnipeg recreational 10-pin league; Royal Life Saving Society instructor; PE dir. YMHA '36-42, '52-74; Centennial medal; life mem., governor YMHA; best Jewish athlete of 1/2 century '19-69; author *The Jewish Athlete, a Nostalgic View*; mem. Man. Softball, Sports halls of fame.

HERST, Alison (canoeing); b. 7 Mar 1971, Toronto, Ont.; Laurentian, UofT; m. Ivano Lussignoli; c. Zoe (adopted); mem. Cdn ntl team '90-96, Italian ntl team from '98;

competed '92, '96 Olympics; gold K-4 200 '95 Worlds, K-2, K-4 200, silver K-2 500 Milano, Italy; Edmonton Grads team award; mem. North Bay Sports Hall of Fame; res. North Bay, Ont./Cremona, Italy.

HETHERINGTON, Jill (tennis); b. 27 Oct 1964, Brampton, Ont.; m. Hultquist; Florida; tennis coach; 4 time all-American; 5 ntl jr. titles; 2 gold FISU Games; record 9 ntl women's doubles, 1 mixed doubles titles; mem. '81-82 Continental Cup teams, Federation Cup team from '83; ranked among world's best doubles players; best WTA tour ranking (with Patty Fendick) #1 '89; Australian Open finalist '89; 1st Cdn to reach Wimbledon doubles semifinals '86; played World Team Tennis for Tampa Bay '92-93; mem. '84 (demonstration sport), '88, '96 Olympic teams; Tennis Canada player of '88, most improved '89, with Carling Bassett doubles team '86, '88, Helen Kelesi '87, Mandy Wilson '89, Patricia Hy '90-91; With Kathy Rinaldi '92 WTA Tour doubles-team-of-year nominee '92; WTA sportsmanship award '92; TC top female doubles player '93; mem. WTA drug testing comm, WTA Special Olympics comm.; ret'd from competition '98; asst. women's coach Washington; 11 TC excellence awards; mem. Cdn Tennis Hall of Fame; res. Woodinville, Wash.

HEVENOR, George (golf); b. 4 Aug 1904, Saint John, N.B.; d. 24 Nov 1991, Toronto, Ont.; m. Martha; c. George Jr.; ret'd stockbroker; mem. Balmy Beach (ORFU) football team '25-26; canoe racer Island Aquatic Paddling Assn.; mem. Toronto Central Y basketball teams 5 years; 3 Ont. srs, 1 CSGA golf titles; 5 Ont. parent-child titles; golf exec more than 30 years; pres. OGA '59, RCGA '73; life governor each assn.

HEWITSON, Bobby (officiating); b. 23 Jan 1892, Toronto, Ont; d. 9 Jan 1969, Toronto, Ont.; sportswriter, curator; despite diminutive stature became standout lacrosse player, football qb, hockey official; mem. '12 Maitlands Ont. lacrosse, Capitals ntl jr. football champions; sports writer *Toronto Globe*, *Telegram*, ret'd as sports editor '57; referee lacrosse, football, hockey; 10yrs officiated NHL; 25yrs secty. CRU; closely associated with horse racing; charter mem. *CBC Hot Stove League*; 1st curator Canada's Sports, Hockey halls of fame; ret'd '67; mem. Hockey Hall of Fame.

HEWITT, Foster (hockey); b. 21 Nov 1903, Toronto, Ont; d. 21 Apr 1985, Toronto, Ont; given name: Foster William; m. Joan; c. Wendy, Bill, Elizabeth, Ann; Upper Canada College, UofT; sportscaster; intercollegiate 112, 118lb boxing titles; received Varsity T; editor *Toronto Star* radio page '22; broadcast 1st-ever complete hockey game '23; through career of more than 50yrs broadcast numerous sports, feature news events; with father, Hockey Hall of Famer W.A.Hewitt, broadcast '25 King's Plate, world's 1st airing of horse race; accomplished yet another broadcasting 1st '27 combining with father, who wired running results, to dramatize Allan Cup play between UotT Grads and Ft William from Vancouver; MC offical opening Maple Leaf Gardens '31; frequent international hockey game coverage throughout world earned him title "The Voice of Hockey"; Canada's 1st TV commentator in '33 experiment; when TV became viable medium acted as play-by-play man 15yrs; author several sports books; dir. numerous companies;

Canadian broadcaster-of-year award; NY Hockey Writers award; *CTV-CBS* special award for Canada-Russia '72 hockey series coverage; Ont., Toronto achievement awards; B'Nai Brith sportsman of year; Charlie Conacher Research Fund citation, award of merit; Upper Canada College athletic complex named in honor of Foster and Bill Hewitt; officer Order of Canada; mem. Ont. Sports Legends, Hockey, Canada's Sports halls of fame.

HEWITT, W.A. (administration); b. 15 May 1875, Cobourg, Ont.; d. 8 Sep 1966, Toronto, Ont.; given name: William Archibald; ret'd sports editor; 41yrs newspaper man *Toronto News*, *Toronto Star* (31yrs sports editor); secty. OHA '03-61; registrar, treas. CAHA 39yrs; mgr. 3 Olympic title teams; helped form Big Four football league '07; served terms as pres., secty. CRU; patrol judge Woodbine racetrack from '05; presiding steward Ont. tracks 14yrs; conceived 1st goal nets; 1st attractions mgr. Maple Leaf Gardens '31; with son Foster participated in hockey, horse racing broadcasting 1sts; mem. Hockey Hall of Fame.

HEWLETT, Karen (field hockey); b. 4 Oct 1959, Toronto, Ont.; given name: Karen Lynn; Sheridan College, UofT; animal technician; mem. Toronto Gopher's FH team from '77, 4 prov. titles; mem. Ont. jr. team '75-79, Ont. -23 team '78-82; mem. Ont. silver Canada Games team '81, Ont. sr. team '78, '80-82; mem. national team '81-96; World Cup silver team '83; mem. '84 Olympic team; 2 HS athlete-of-yr awards; fed. govt. excellence award '83; res. Mississauga, Ont.

HEWSON, Joanne (skiing); b. 23 Aug 1930, Montreal, Que.; given name: Joanne Selden; div. Robert Dewar Staniforth; c. Mariel Hewson, Lisa Dewar; m. Henry Maynard (Mark) Rees Jr.; McGill, Concordia, BFA; artist; McGill ski team '49-51; top girl '51 Olympic ski trials; top Cdn (8th downhill), (13th slalom) '52 Olympics; Alberg Kandahar pin with 3rd downhill; '53 Que. Kandahar title; broke leg in training prior to '54 world championships; coach McGill women's ski team '58-62; co-founder Ski Jay club for girls 8-17, active with group '58-68; active golfer, ladies' pres. Kanawaki GC '82; publicity chairman, jr. development chairman QLGA; res. Westmount, Que.

HEXTALL, Bryan Sr. (hockey); b. 31 Jul 1913, Grenfell, Sask.; d. 25 Jul 1984, Poplar Point, Man.; given name: Bryan Aldwyn; m. Gertrude Lyon; c. Bryan Jr., Dennis, Richard, Heather, Randy; lumber, hardware business; mem. Poplar Point, Man. juv titlists; jr. Winnipeg Monarchs, Portage La Prairie; MJHL scoring title; pro Vancouver Lions '34-36, WHL title '36; Philadelphia Ramblers '36; NYR '36-48; NHL record: 449 scheduled games, 187g, 175a, 37 playoff games, 8g, 9a; NHL scoring title '42 with 56 pts.; 20 or more goals 7 of 12 NHL seasons; scored winning overtime goal '40 Stanley Cup final vs Toronto; 3 times 1st, twice 2nd team all-star; mem. Man. Sports, Man., Cdn Hockey halls of fame.

HEXTALL, Ron (hockey); b. 3 May 1964, Brandon, Man.; m. Diane; c. Kristin, Brett, Rebecca, Jeffrey; goalie Brandon Wheat Kings (WHL); 6th pick Philadelphia '82 draft; Brandon '81-84, Hershey (AHL) '84-86, '89, Kalamazoo (IHL) '84-85; Philadelphia (NHL) '86-92, '95-99, Quebec '93, NYI '93-94; scored goal vs Boston '87, playoff goal vs. Washington '89; NHL record: 608 scheduled games, 296-214-69, 34,750 min, 23so, 93 playoff games, 47-43, 5456min, 276ga, 2so, AHL rookie of '86; Vezina trophy '87; Conn Smythe trophy '87; Bobby Clarke trophy '87; 1 Class Guy award; mem. Team Canada '87; res. Voorhees, N.J.

HEYDENFELDT, Bob (football); b. 17 Sep 1933, Santa Monica, Calif.; given name: Robert Marshall; m. JoAnn Good; c. Linda Jo, Robert Tad, Richard Daniel, Dina Marie; UCLA, BSc; furniture wholesaler & jobber; top college punter in US '54; Rose Bowl, North-South Shrine game as UCLA jr. '54; refusal to play Sunday football led to NFL shunning him in draft; pro Edmonton winning WFC punting title '55; mem. Grey Cup winner; kicked single which provided 6-6 tie 1st Cdn East-West all-star game '55; res. Lafayette, Calif.

HEYMANS, Emilie (diving); b. 14 Dec 1981, Brussels, Belgium; Antoine de St. Exupery; 21 ntl titles; 18 intl medals; platform gold '97 jr. worlds; 10m gold '99 PAG; 3m bronze '99 jr. worlds; 3m silver '99 FINA world cup; with Anne Montminy 10m synchro silver '00 Olympics; 10m, 3m silver '02 CG; 1st Cdn to win 10m gold '03 worlds; 10m individual, with Marie-Eve Marleau platform synchro gold, with Blythe Hartley 3m synchro, 3m silver '03 PAG; holds several Cdn records; Diving Canada female athlete of '02; res. St. Lambert, Que.

HIBBERD, Ted (hockey); b. 22 Apr 1926, Ottawa, Ont.; given name: Thomas Edward; m. Anna Armstrong; c. Lesley, Wendy, Nancye, Jeffrey, Laurie; ret'd underwriting supervisor; jr. hockey New Edinburgh, Ottawa Montagnards, Hull; intermediate Senators; mem. '48 world, Olympic champion RCAF Flyers; CHA Olympic award; with Flyers team mem. Ottawa Sports Hall of Fame; res. Ottawa, Ont.

HIBBERT, Curtis (gymnastics); b. 9 Feb 1966, St. Andrew, Jamaica; York.; gymnastics instructor; began competing age 7; mem. ntl team '83-92; 1st Cdn gymnast to win medal at world championships with horizontal bars silver '87; 1st Cdn gymnast to make 3 Olympic event finals '88; 5 consecutive ntl all-around titles '88-92; mem. '83 PAG, '87 FISU, '85, '87, '89, '91 worlds, '88, '92 Olympic, '90 CG, '90 World Cup teams; ntl sports excellence award '89; 5 CG gold, 1 silver, 1 bronze '90; PAG silver '83; life mem. Cdn Gymnastics Fed.; res. Toronto, Ont.

HICKOX, Mac (canoeing); b. 2 Sep 1946, Boston, Mass.; m. Adrienne Dunn; c. Marin, Randi; McMaster BA, BPHE, UofT, BEd; HS teacher; family moved to Mississauga when he was an infant; lw Jr. B Dixie Beehives, St. Catharines Jr. A Black Hawks, Hamilton Red Wings, CIAU McMaster, Toronto; helped Toronto win '71 CIAU title; with Dean Oldershaw won ntl juv C2 at 15; won 25 ntl, 2 NA titles; represented both Can. and US in Olympic competition, Can, as alternate '64, coach '76, US in pairs '68; coached Mississauga to 6 ntl titles; coached John Wood to '76 Olympic silver; Cdn coach of '76 award; coached Glenforest HS sr. boys x-country team to OFSAA gold '88; ret'd from coaching '94; earned 11 gold in canoeing/x-country skiing as master athlete '87; founded Cdn Assn. of Coaches in Canoe & Kayak '94; Port Credit HS athlete of '66, Mississauga most-valuable member '88-89, volunteer of '90, 2 civic recognition awards; CCA Gilbert award '96; mem. Mississauga Sports Hall of Fame; res. Mississauga, Ont.

HIELTJES, Ben (lacrosse); b. 12 Apr 1963, New Westminster, B.C.; given name: Bernard John; m. Dawna Nelson; c. Benjamin, Hanna; Whittier Coll. BA; sales mgr.; mem. Whittier College Poets '85-86, North Shore Indians '85-86, New Westminster Salmonbellies '86-92, '95, Richmond field team from '86; ntl team '89-94; came out of retirement to join Vancouver Ravens (NLL) '01; competed 2 world championships; mem. 3 Mann Cup winners; '85 President's Cup titlists, MVP; '89 Mike Kelly Mann Cup MVP award; mem. Cdn Lacrosse Hall of Fame; res. New Westminster, B.C.

HIGGINS, Robina (t&f); b. 28 Apr 1915, Winnipeg, Man; d. 31 Dec 1990, Winnipeg, Man.; m. G.D."Pud" Haight; c. Dee, Dorlene, Fred; T.Eaton Co. employee; dominated Cdn t&f scene '35-40; ntl shot put titles '35-36, javelin '39-40, discus '36, ball throw '36, '39-40; javelin gold '38 BEG; Bobbie Rosenfeld award '37; basketball standout with Man. champion Dominion Business College 10yrs; mem. Western Canada finalists; mem. Man. Basketball, Cdn Olympic, Man. Sports halls of fame.

HIGGINS, Tim (hockey); b. 7 Feb 1958, Ottawa, Ont.; div. Jane Forrest; c. Laureen, Kristen, Kelly; hockey scout Chicago Black Hawks; rw Ottawa West Golden Knights midgets, Ottawa 67's Jr. B; Ottawa 67's Jr. A '74-78, amassing 217 points in 197 scheduled games; played in '77 Memorial Cup final; 1st Chicago choice, 10th overall '78 amateur draft; NHL Chicago '78-84, NJ '84-86, Detroit '86-89; AHL New Brunswick '79, Adirondack '89; developed into premier defensive player twice leading team in plus/minus figures; NHL record: 708 scheduled games, 154g, 198a; 65 playoff games, 5g, 8a; mem. Ottawa midget team which held touring Russians to 4-4 draw; scout Ottawa Senators '92-96, Chicago from '97; res. Ottawa, Ont.

HIGHBAUGH, Larry (football); b. 14 Jan 1950, Indianapolis, Ind.; given name: Larry Eugene; m. Pat; c. Monica, Angela, Tara; Indiana; sporting goods store operator; t&f all-American; world record 60yd dash (6.8); Dallas Cowboys draft '71; pro BC (CFL) '71-72, Edmonton '72-83; CFL record most career interceptions 66; 770yds on returns; 6 WFC, 4 all-Cdn selections; Eskimos MVP '77 playing db/wr; 9 Grey Cup finals, 6 winners, 5 in succession; volleyball star; mem. Eskimos Wall of Fame, Cdn Ftbll Hall of Fame; res. Snellville, Ga.

HIGSON, Allison (swimming); b. 13 Mar 1973, Mississauga, Ont.; Stanford; sports media rep.; mem. Cobra SC age 6; 10yrs mem. Etobicoke SC; breaststroke specialist; 4 gold, 1 record '85 Canada Games; mem. ntl team '85-92; won 1st of 14 ntl titles at age 12; 2 gold, 1 silver '86 CG; at 13 youngest ever to win CG gold; bronze '86, youngest ever to medal in worlds; gold, 2 silver, bronze '87 Pan-Pacific; 1 world, 2 Cdn records '88 Olympic trials; relay bronze '88 Olympics; silver, bronze '89 Pan-Pacific; relay silver '90 CG; competed '92 Olympics; 2 Swim Canada jr., 3 sr. female-athlete-of-yr awards; ntl/prov. achievement awards; lone female to win Esso Cup; Olympic champion medal; Ont., Swim Ont. team-of-yr awards; mem. Ont. Aquatic Hall of Fame; res. Palo Alto, Calif.

HILDEBRAND, Ike (lacrosse/hockey); b. 27 May 1927, Winnipeg, Man.; given name: Isaac Bruce; m. Barbara Mae

Park; c. Isaac Jay, Jody Ann, Daniel, Heidi, Melanie; ret'd structural engineer; sporting goods manufacturer's rep.; at 15 mem. '43 New Westminster Salmonbellies Mann Cup winner; 16 seasons sr. lacrosse New Westminster, Mimico, Peterborough; more than 900 goals, 700 assists while playing 7 successive Mann Cup finalist, 5 winners with Peterborough; at 17 youngest player ever to win Mike Kelly Mann Cup MVP award; MVP, twice scoring champion both East, West leagues; sr. hockey at 17 Seattle Ironmen; OHA jr. A Oshawa Generals '45-47; sr. Toronto Marlboros; 9yrs pro, parts of 3 NHL seasons NYR, Chicago; US League scoring champion Kansas City '51, AHL top scorer Cleveland '53; mem. Cleveland AHL Calder Cup champions '52-53; 1st team all-star rw US League '51, AHL '53; leading scorer Belleville McFarlands Allan Cup, world champions '59-60; pro career record: 185g, 209a; coached Peterborough Mann Cup winner '54; McFarlands '59 Allan Cup, '60 world championship; twice Green MVP Trophy; jr. A hockey coach 6yrs Peterborough, London, Oshawa; sr. hockey 6yrs Pembroke, Belleville, Orillia; Allan Cup Orillia '69; Toronto NHL Oldtimers; mem. Canada's Sports, Canadian Lacrosse halls of fame; res. Marana, Ariz.

HILL, Harvey (weightlifting); b. 16 Dec 1897, Shaw's Lane, Eng.; d. circa 1985; m. Elsie; competitor '25-27 then switched to coaching, officiating, administration; coached Verdun Weightlifting Club '28-42, South-Western YMCA Verdun '42-53; mgr.-coach '47 world championships, '48 Olympics, '50 BEG teams; refereed NA championships '36-58, Fédération Halterophile Canadienne '27-54, variety regional, prov., ntl, international meets '27-58; founded Que. Weightlifters Assoc. '36, secty. '36-58; introduced weightlifting to AAUofC '36; organized secretarial weightlifting contests '36-58; founded CWA, secty. '48-58; AAUofC ntl weightlifting chair. '50-52; chair. at founding of BE Weightlifting Federation, v-p '48; mem. Cdn Olympic Sports Hall of Fame.

HILL, Jim (all-around); b. 26 Jan 1914, Kenora, Ont.; standout in hockey, football, basketball, softball, t&f, soccer, golf; goalie Port Arthur Eskimos '28 Intercity midget champions; '30 Port Arthur Tech HS champs, '36-37 TB-Man. senior champs (MVP); played for Duluth, Minn., '38-39; Western Cdn champion PASCOL team '43-44; pro Omaha, Witchita (AA) '39-40, Portland (PCL), Fort Worth (AHL) '40-41; of/ss variety of title softball teams '32-45; hb/punter Port Arthur Collegiate/Seniors '31-36, 2 title teams; forward 5 HS basketball title teams '32-36; fb CNR Regina Sask. title soccer team '39; champion HS pv/discus/3-mile runner '31-33; began playing golf in '40s winning 2 Duluth tournaments; coached Navy jr. hockey title team '43; mem. NWO Sports Hall of Fame; res. Duluth, Minn.

HILL, Norm (football); b. 8 Nov 1928, Winnipeg, Man.; given name: Norman Charles; m. Elizabeth Anne Murdoch; c. Averie, Kym, David, Shauna; UMan MD, MSc, Royal College of Surgeons FRCS, American College of Surgeons FACS; ret'd neurosurgeon; played hockey Winnipeg Excelsiors '40-43, Western Can. Midget title '43; off/def end Winnipeg city champs '45; UMan '46-47; Calgary Stampeders '48-50, '54, Winnipeg Blue Bombers '51-53; 3 Grey Cup finals, 1 winner; post grad training Mayo Clinic; professor, head of neurosurgery UMan '86-96; mem. Alta. Sports Hall of Fame; res. Winnipeg, Man.

HILL, Stewart (football); b. 16 Mar 1962, Seattle, Wash; Washington; de; turned pro Edmonton '84-90, BC '91-92, Saskatchewan '93; CFL record: 164 scheduled games, 6tds, 5 interceptions, 12 fumble recoveries, 126 qb sacks, 231 defensive, special teams tackles; Jackie Parker Trophy '84; Norm Fieldgate Trophy '90; 5 all-Western, 2 all-CFL all-star; CFL top rookie runnerup '84; CFL outstanding defensive player runnerup '90; res. Seattle, Wash.

HILLER, John (baseball); b. 8 Apr 1943, Scarborough, Ont.; given name: John Fredrick; m. Janis Patricia Baldwin; c. Wendy Louise, Joseph Scott, Danielle Patricia; farmer, ex-policeman; lhp Toronto minors; pro Detroit organization '62; minors Jamestown, Duluth, Knoxville, Montgomery, Syracuse, Toledo; Detroit '65-80; relief specialist; career threatened by '71 heart attack but made came back to extend ML career 8 more years; '73 Hutch Award, AL comeback player of year, ML fireman of year, Tiger of year, King Tiger award, 4th Cy Young, MVP voting; tied AL record for victories by relief pitcher with 17 in '74, ML record 31 decisions for fireman '74 (17-14); missed much of '75 with arm injury, 12-8 won-lost record, 2.38era '76; ML career record: 87-76, 545 games, 125sv, 1036k, 2.83era; ML record most consecutive strikeouts, start of game, 6 '68, AL record most intentional walks season 19 '74, ML record 38 saves '73 (broken '83 by Dan Quisenberry); following 215 consecutive relief appearances made 1st start a 4-hit shutout over Milwaukee; mem. '68 World Series winner, '74 AL all-star team; saved child from drowning in Anaheim pool '73; mem. Canada's Sports, Cdn Baseball halls of fame; res. Felch, Mich.

HILLMAN, Larry (hockey); b. 5 Feb 1937, Kirkland Lake, Ont.; given name: Lawrence Morley; sep. c. Laurie, Valerie, Darryn, Peter; ret'd hockey coach, businessman; jr. Windsor, Hamilton; NHL Detroit '54-57; Boston '57-60, Toronto '60-68, Minnesota, Montreal '68-69, Philadelphia '69-71, Los Angeles '71, Buffalo '71-73; WHA Cleveland '73-75, Winnipeg '75-76; AHL Eddie Shore Award as top def '60; NHL record: 790 scheduled games, 36g, 196a, 579pim, 74 playoff games, 2g, 9a, 30pim; mem. 6 Stanley Cup, 1 Calder Cup winners; AHL all-star; with Ralph Backstrom, Wilf Paiement operates summer fishing camp; mem. Hockey Heritage North Hall of Fame; res. Beamsville, Ont.

HILTON, Alex (boxing); b. 20 Dec 1964, Ville LaSalle, Que.; given name: Alexander Stewart; div. Olga Grecco; c. 2; m. Lynda Mark; c. Holly, Phoebe; ret'd pro boxer, cook, restaurant mgr.; lost only one of 104 amateur bouts; 7 Que. Golden Gloves titles, 3 ntl amateur, 2 jr. Olympic titles; to '83 unbeaten in pro ranks; ntl middleweight title, Continental champion; ranked 15th in world; Cdn Pro Boxing Council middleweight title '92; 37-11 pro record, including 23kos; out-of-ring behavior led to frequent criminal charges, 5yr prison term; res. Verdun, Que.

HILTON, Dave Jr. (boxing); b. 9 Dec 1963, Port Credit, Ont.; given name: David Stewart Jr; div. Ann-Marie Gatti; c. Jeannie, Anna-Marie; pro boxer; lost only 2 of 132 amateur bouts; 4 ntl, 3 Jr. Olympic, 9 Que. Golden Gloves, '80 Winter Games titles; pro at 17; pro record (through '99) 37-1-3, 25kos; ntl welterweight title '84, stripped of same '85 for failure to defend in specified time; ranked 16th in world; ntl middleweight title '98-99; WBC super-middleweight title

'00, stripped of title '01; out-of-ring behavior led to frequent criminal charges; convicted of sexual assault charges against minors '01; res. Montreal, Que.

HILTON, Dave Sr. (boxing); b. 29 Aug 1940, Edmunston, N.B.; given name: David Stewart; m. Jean Mills; c. Jo-Ann, David Jr., Alex, Matthew, Stewart, Jimmy; boxing trainer; won all 72 amateur bouts; '66 Tennessee Golden Gloves, '67 Texas Golden Gloves, '68 Kentucky Golden Gloves titles; 138 pro bouts, lost 15; ntl featherweight title 10yrs, jr. middleweight crown; ret'd undefeated; boxing coach; 9 ntl titles in family; res. Montreal, Que.

HILTON, Geordie (golf); b. 17 Jan 1952, Ottawa, Ont.; d. 18 Sep 1990, Oakville, Ont.; given name: George Richard; UWO, hons. BA; exec. dir. RCGA; standout amateur golfer Ottawa area; 3 athletic letters UWO; asst. amateur tournament co-ordinator RCGA '74-75; Canadian Open co-ordinator RCGA '76-77; asst. exec. dir. RCGA '77-78, exec. dir. '78-90; exec. dir. Canadian Golf Foundation '79-81; dir. American Golf Sponsors '80-90; mem. handicap procedure comm. USGA '81-90; board chair. Glen Abbey GC '81-90; treas. CGF '81-90.

HILTON, Matthew (boxing); b. 27 Dec 1965, Cooksville, Ont.; middleweight; won all 106 amateur bouts, 97 by KO; 4 ntl, 1 Jr. Olympics, 8 Que. Golden Gloves titles; to '84 won all 12 pro bouts, 10 by KO; 4th ranked in Canada; out-of-ring behavior led to frequent criminal charges; res. Montreal, Que.

HILZINGER, Karl (football/skiing); b. 7 Sep 1932, Montreal, Que.; d. 15 Dec 1988, Seattle, Wash.; given name: Karl Hans; Sir George Williams, BA, UCLA; manufacturer, sports consultant War Amps Canada; hb Montreal '52, Sask. '53-54, '59, Ottawa '55-58; pro ski instructor Canadian Ski Alliance 20yrs; level 4 rating; pro skin diver 10yrs; lost both legs 20 Jun '64 auto accident; active in teaching skiing, golf, other sports to handicapped youngsters.

HIND, Terry (builder); b. 23 Jul 1920, Winnipeg, Man.; given name: Terrence John; m. Evelyn Carey; c. Richard; ret'd Red Cross; pitched for jr. Rosedales, sr. CUAC Blues, St. Boniface Native Sons, Carman; pitched several 1-hitters; in one tournament pitched 27 innings in single day allowing 1 run; in 27yrs in amateur-pro hockey was mgr. juv Winnipeg Monarchs, exec. mgr. Man. Jr. Hockey League, helped build Winnipeg Maroons '64 Allan Cup winner, helped Ben Hatskin launch Winnipeg Jets and WHA, helped Ed Rutherford start Man. Major Jr. HL, mgr. Charleswood Hawks; significant 5yr role in football evolution, business mgr. Blue Bombers '65-66, GM '67, promotions mgr. '68-69; involved with baseball 36yrs as player, GM Winnipeg Goldeyes '54-65, GM AAA Winnipeg Whips '71-72, active role in formation of group seeking return of Triple A baseball to Winnipeg '86; mem. Man. Hockey, Baseball, Sports halls of fame; res. Winnipeg, Man.

HINDMARCH, Robert (hockey); b. 27 May 1930, Nanaimo, B.C.; given name: Robert George; m. Jean; c. Robert Bruce, David Stephen; UBC, BPhE, Oregon, MSc, DEd; ret'd prof.; dir. UBC external relations; college football, hockey player; Dr. Gordon Burke football award UBC '52; Bobby Gaul trophy UBC outstanding athlete

'53; asst. coach UBC football '55-62; UBC hockey coach from '65; mgr. '64 Olympic hockey team; chair. Hockey Development Council; dir. CAHA; asst. dir. COA; CdM '84 Winter Olympics; v-p COA; 1 CIAU Austin-Matthews award; mem. UBC Hall of Fame; res. Vancouver, B.C.

HINDS, Sterling (t&f/football); b. 31 Oct 1961, Toronto, Ont.; m. Antoria Henry; c. Chanelle Antoria Joyce; Washington BA; Re/Max real estate broker, Rogers cable services; sprint specialist; silver 4x100m relay '83 FISU Games, bronze '84 Olympics; with brothers Doug, Jerry ntl t&f team mem.; mem. Washington Huskies '83 Rose Bowl, 2 Aloha Bowl Games football teams; rb Argos '84; career curtailed by knee injury; mem. Mississauga Sports Hall of Fame; res. Mississauga, Ont.

HINTON, Tom (football); b. 19 Mar 1936, Ruston, La.; given name: William Thomas; m. Patsy Nelson; c. Steve, Janet, Terry; Louisiana Tech, BA; GM; all-state t&f (shot put, discus), football; all-American HS football; 3yrs college all-Conf. gd; Gulf State Conf. athlete of year; 1st from conf. to play North-South game, all-American; drafted NFL Chicago Cardinals; pro BC '58-66, 136 CFL games; WFC all-star 5 times, all-Cdn twice; several times Lions' fans most popular; several times Lions Schenley nominee; became Cdn citizen '63; 6yrs Lions' dir.; mem. Cdn Football Hall of Fame; res. Ruston, La.

HISTED, Jack (t&f); b. 9 May 1903, Hamilton, Ont.; d. 14 Jun 1988, Hamilton, Ont.; given name: John Henry; m. Ora Eileen Myles; c. John Allan, Betty Ora; ret'd sales mgr. Domtar, 10yrs Wood Gundy; football 3yrs jr. Tigers; 4 Ont. running hj titles; runnerup ntl championships; US ntl jr. champion '24; pres. Hamilton Olympic Club; pres. Southwestern Ont. Branch AAUofC; pres. AAUofC '59-60; COA mem.-at-large 10yrs; t&f team mgr. '52 Olympics; chair. constitution, by-laws comm. PAG; BE, CG Assn. mem.-at-large 6yrs; v-p ntl sports advisory council 2yrs; chair. PE comm. National Council YMCA '58-64; mem. YMCA ntl exec. comm. '58-64; dir. Greater Hamilton Downtown YMCA '63-64, chair. PE comm. '44-58; Ont. Achievement Award; Hamilton Downtown YMCA citation.

HITCHCOCK, Dean (volleyball); b. 13 May 1956, Plaster Rock, N.B.; m. Deborah Lee Phillips; UCal; distributor Richard McDonald Corp; power hitter; sister Monica was mem. women's ntl team; mem. '79, '81, '83 FISU Games, '77, '80-83 Canada Cup, '79, '83 PAG, '78, '82 world championships teams; gold team '80, '82 Canada Cup, '81 Commonwealth championships; ret'd '85; Sport NB male athlete of '79; mem. Saint John Sports Hall of Fame; res. Calgary, Alta.

HITCHCOCK, Ken (coaching/hockey); b. 17 Dec 1951, Edmonton, Alta.; m. Nancy; c. Emily, Alex, Noah; UAlta.; hockey coach; coached Sherwood Park midget AAA team 10yrs with 575-69 record; 2 Alta. MHA coach-of-yr awards; head coach WHL Kamloops Blazers with 291-125-15 record; 2 WHL, 1 CHL coach-of-yr award; asst. coach Team Canada '87, '04 worlds. '02 Olympic gold; asst. coach NHL Philadelphia '90-93, head coach '02-03; head coach IHL Kalamazoo '93-94, 1 div. title; head coach NHL Dallas '96-02; Stanley Cup '99; head coach world all-stars '98; NHL record ('03) 322-186-73-10; twice NHL, IHL all-star team coach; *Sporting News, Hockey News* coach-of-yr awards; res. Coppell, Tex.

HITCHCOCK, Monica (volleyball); b. 26 Feb 1958, Plaster Rock, N.B.; given name: Monica Joan; m. Claude Moore; UNB, York., Memorial, BPhE; sales rep. Valley Graphics; mem. ntl jr. title team '74-75; power hitter; mem. '75 Canada Winter Games, '77, '81, '83 FISU Games, '77 Canada Cup, '79, '83 PAG '84 Olympic Games, '81 CIAU championships teams; ret'd '85 but returned to game '86 playing Sr. A club team which won 9 NB, 1 Eastern Cdn titles; Sport NB female athlete of '83; brother Dean was mem. men's ntl volleyball team; mem. NB, Saint John Sports, Volleyball NB halls of fame; res. Saint John, N.B.

HITCHCOCK, Rob (football); b. 28 Oct 1970, Hamilton, Ont.; m. Michelle; c. Ava; Weber State BA; NCAA Div. 1-AA all-American; all-Big Sky conf. all-star; CFL Hamilton '95-04; 166 scheduled games; 3 CFL, East Div. all-star; 2 Grey Cup finals, 1 winner; res. St. Catharines, Ont.

HNATIUK, Glen (golf); b. 15 May 1965, Selkirk, Man.; m. Julia; c. Aileen Caitlin, Morgan Mary; Southern Miss; turned pro '90; played on Nike, Canadian, US PGA tours; mem. Cdn WC team '00; earned PGA tour card placing 8th Nike tour money list '99; won Nike Tri-Cities Open, South Carolina, Utah Classics; annual charity tourney in support of Man. KidSport program bears his name; elbow surgery '04 disrupted career several months; res. Homosassa, Fla.

HOBKIRK, Alan (field hockey); b. 7 Nov 1952, Vancouver, B.C.; given name: Alan Arthur; m.; UBC, BA; LLB, Oxford, MA; lawyer; Rhodes Scholar; mem. BC jr. team '66-70, 2yrs capt., 1 v.-capt.; BC srs '70-73; 5 ntl title teams; capt. Oxford '75-76; capt. Folkstone International Festival winner '76; mem. ntl team '71-79, 55 caps; bronze '71, silver '75 PAG; mem. UBC Hall of Fame; res. Vancouver, B.C.

HODGE, Ken (hockey); b. 25 Jun 1944, Birmingham, Eng.; rw St. Catharines jrs; pro Buffalo '64-65, Chicago '64-67, Boston '67-76, NYR '76-78; NHL record: 881 scheduled games, 328g, 472a, 97 playoff games, 34g, 47a; 2 Stanley Cup winners; scored 50g '74; AHL Eddie Powers Memorial trophy; res. Lynnfield, Mass.

HODGES, Bob (speed skating); b. 30 Dec 1943, Saskatoon, Sask.; USask, BSc, UAlta, PhD, RockefellerU; educator UAlta; began competitive skating in elementary school; competed 15yrs; won ntl bantam, 2 intermediate, 5 sr. titles '53-69; competed internationally '65-72; mem. '68, '72 Olympic Game, '68, '70-71 world championship teams; 2 bronze 1st Canada Winter Games; coached ntl team level '73-76; mem. Olympic development comm. '73-76; CASSA dir., v-p '76-83; mgr '80 Olympic team; race dir. '90 women's world, '94 world sprint; recipient of numerous academic awards; mem. Sask., Saskatoon Sports halls of fame; res. Edmonton, Alta.

HODGINS, Clint (harness racing); b. 18 Jun 1907, Clandeboye, Ont.; d. 21 Oct 1980, London, Ont.; driver, trainer, breeder; drove more than 2000 winning races US, Canada; led US dash winners '49 with 128, money winners with $184,108; 42 sub 2-min. miles; won Little Brown Jug,

Messenger Pace, Kentucky Futurity, Cane Pace (twice); drove Adios Butler to 1:59.2 mile, 1st sub 2-min. clocking in Little Brown Jug history '59; co-holder world record 11 victories single program Dufferin Park '39; among best he bred, trained, drove were Bye Bye Byrd (horse of '59), Elaine Rodney, Skipper Thorpe, Sing Away Herbert, Pat's Bye Bye, Terry Parker, Acrasia, Proximity; mem. Cdn Horse Racing, Horseman's halls of fame.

HODGSON, George (swimming); b. 12 Oct 1893, Montreal, Que.; d. 1 May 1983, Montreal, Que.; given name: George Ritchie; m. Edyte Harrower (d); c. George H., Thomas; m. Hilda Birch; McGill.; investment counsel; competed in swimming, water polo at McGill; Festival of Empire Games London '11, defeated world mile record holder Sid Battersby of Britain; only Cdn to win individual Olympic swimming gold 400m, 1500m FS events in record times '12; also 1000m, mile records, all broken by Johnny Weismuller; competed '20 Olympics; mem. Que., Cdn Olympic, International, Cdn Aquatic, Canada's, McGill Sports halls of fame.

HODGSON, Paul (baseball); b. 14 Apr 1960, Montreal, Que.; given name: Paul Joseph Denis; m. Kimberley; *CBC* sportscaster; began baseball career Marysville age 12; at 16 joined sr. Marysville Royals; all-star lf Cdn sr. championships '76; turned pro Blue Jays '77; minor league stints in Utica, Dunedin, Knoxville, Kingston, N.C.; briefly on Jays' ML roster '80-81; injuries forced retirement '84; mem. '84 Marysville Royals NB sr. title team; trial with Montreal '85; mem. Fredericton Cardinals, Moncton Mets Atlantic Sr. champions; all-star 3b; associate scout for Blue Jays; mem. NB Baseball, Fredericton Walls, NB Sports halls of fame; res. Fredericton, N.B.

HOFFMAN, Abby (t&f); b. 11 Feb 1947, Toronto, Ont.; given name: Abigail; UofT, BA, MA; dir. gen. Women's Health Bureau; dir. Sport Canada '81-91; at 11 def Toronto boys' team peewee hockey tournament; represented Canada internationally '62-76 competing 4 Olympic, 4 PAG, 2 CG, 3 FISU, 1 Maccabiah Games; 8 ntl 800m titles; ntl record holder 800m '62-75 cutting time from 2:10.8 to 2:00.2, 440yd '63-76 with 54.4, indoor 1500m 4:13.3; gold '66 CG 880yds, '63, '71 PAG 800m, '69 Maccabiah 400m, 800m; silver '75 PAG 800m, '67 FISU 800m, bronze '67 PAG 800m, '75 PAG 1500m, '65 FISU 800m; finalist 800m '68, '72 Olympics, Commonwealth record 2:00.2 in latter; flag-bearer '76 summer Olympics; mem. IAAF council from '95; City of Toronto Civic Award of Merit '76, Ont. Award of Merit '75; Herstorical Award '92; mem. Canada's all-time women's outdoor t&f team; hon. life mem. Cdn Gymnastics Fed.; Officer Order of Canada; mem. UofT, Canada's Sports, Cdn Olympic halls of fame; res. Ottawa, Ont.

HOGARTH, Malcolm (gymnastics); b. 15 Feb 1934, Toronto, Ont; d. 30 Oct 2001, Winnipeg, Man; from '69 active in development of gymnastics in Canada at local, rgnl, pvcl, ntl, intl levels; played key role in formation/growth of Gymnastics Canada; developed military security plan '76 Olympics; active in staging of '85 World Artistic Gymnastics championships Montreal; Cdn voting delegate FIG World Congress; chair. FIG rules of order comm.; 1st v-p Pacific Alliance of Ntl Gymnastics Federations; rewrote PANGF constitution; pres. Man. Gymnastics Assn. 78-82;

dir. Gymnastics Canada '78-01; pres. Gymnastics Canada '83-90; life mem. Gymnastics Canada; Donald King Memorial (volunteer) award.

HOGG, Wendy (swimming); b. 15 Sep 1956, Vancouver, B.C.; given name: Wendy Elizabeth Cook; m. Douglas Hogg; c. Melissa, Sarah; UBC, UAlta, BPhE; teacher; backstroke specialist; mem. ntl team '71-78; mem. 2 Olympic, 1 CG, 2 world championship teams; gold 100m, 200m back, 4x100m medley relay '74 CG; world record 1:04.78 4x100m medley relay; 200yd US short course, 200m long course titles '74; bronze 4x100 medley, 4th 100m back '76 Olympics; 5 1sts '76 nationals; ntl records '76 400m FS relay 3:52,98, 200m medley relay 1:59.16, 400m medley relay 4:18.80; BC jr. athlete of '73; BC, Bobbie Rosenfeld, Velma Springstead awards '74; Gov.-Gen.'s silver medal '76; coach Edmonton Southside SC '76-78, Cranbrook Triton SC '80-82; mem. BC Sports, BC Swimming, Cdn Aquatic halls of fame; res. Cranbrook, B.C.

HOHL, David (wrestling); b. 25 Mar 1966, Winnipeg, Man.; UMan.; v-p technical Wrestling Can.; began wrestling age 14; mem. ntl team from '86; 3 CIAU titles; 2 CIAU wrestler-of-yr awards; competes freestyle at 74kg; 1 jr, 3 sr ntl titles; silver '95, bronze '91 PAG; gold '94 CG; competed '92, '96 Olympic Games; gold '87 Challenge Cup, '92 Czech Grand Prix, '95 Trophco Milone GP; UMan. athlete of '90; res. Winnipeg, Man./St. Catharines, Ont.

HOHL, Elmer (horseshoes); b. 16 Jan 1919, Wellesley, Ont.; d. 5 Sep 1987, Wellesley, Ont.; m. Hilda Seyler; c. Sandra, Susan, Richard, Karen, Steve; carpenter; from '56 held 15 ntl, 19 Ont., 6 world titles; 1 of 2 in World Horseshoe Pitching Assn. history (formed '03) to pitch perfect game of 30 consecutive ringers in competition; pitched 69 consecutive ringers, 3 short of world mark held by Ted Allen, Boulder, Colo., with whom he shares perfect game record; best performance '68 world tournament scoring 572 of maximum 600 to break world record 571 set by Harold Reno, Sabrina, Ohio; ringer percentage of 88.5 broke '69 standard 87.5 set by Casey Jones, Waukesha, Wisc.; 5-pin bowler with 260 avg.; Ont 4-game men's record 1376 posted '71; frequent ntl 5-pin championship competitor; mem. Waterloo County, Intl., Cdn Horseshoe halls of fame.

HOHL, Steve (horseshoes); b. 21 Nov 1962, Kitchener, Ont.; div.; construction estimator/project mgr.; son of world champion Elmer Hohl; 5 Ont. jr. men's titles; 5 Ont. men's singles titles; 4 ntl jr. men's titles; '83 ntl men's title; world jr. men's title '78; competed 3 men's world championships; 2 ntl, 1 world record; res. Kitchener, Ont.

HOLLETT, Flash (hockey); b. 13 Apr 1912, North Sydney, N.S.; d. 20 Apr 1999, Mississauga, Ont.; given name: Frank William; m. Florence; c. 2; stockbroker, fruit farmer; standout lacrosse player; def. Syracuse, Buffalo (IHL) '32-36; NHL Ottawa ''33-34, Toronto '34-36, Boston '36-44, Detroit 43-46; Toronto Staffords (TIHL) '46-47, Kitchener OHA Sr. '47-48, Toronto Marlboros '48-50, 2 Allan Cup finals, 1 winner; 2 NHL all-star; 1st NHL defenceman to score 20 goals single season, a mark which stood 24yrs before beaten by Bobby Orr; NHL totals 562 scheduled games, 132g, 181a, 79 playoff games, 8g, 26a; coached with Pittsburgh AHL.

HOLLIMON, Joe (football); b. 5 Nov 1952, Truman, Ark.; given name: Joseph Julius; m. Glenda; c. Terry, Tony, Trenton; Arkansas State; all-Southland Conf. '74; Minnesota draft '75; pro Edmonton from '76; cb/punt return specialist; led WFC 9 interceptions '82; 3 all-WFC, 1 all-Cdn selections; numerous team records; CFL Players' Assn. top d/b award; mem. 6 Grey Cup finalists, 5 consec. winners; res. Sherwood Park, Alta.

HOLLOWAY, Condredge (football); b. 25 Jan 1954, Huntsville, Ala.; div.; c. Jasmine; m. Courtney Haralson; c. Condredge III; Tennessee; asst. AD Tenn.; rejected baseball offers from Montreal Expos; 12th round NE Patriots NFL draft; pro qb Rough Riders '75-80, Argos '81-86, Lions '87; CFL record: 1710 completions on 3013 pass attempts, 25,193yds, 155tds, 94int; Jeff Russel Memorial Trophy '82; 3 EFC all-star; all-Cdn '82; Carlsberg player of '82; Schenley outstanding player '82; 3 Grey Cup finals, 2 winners; Argos ret'd his jersey; mem. 125th CFL anniversary team; all-time qb UT football 1st century; so popular at Tenn. his exploits were put to music "Go Condredge"; former exec CHL Huntsville Channel Cats; nickname "Huntsville Houdini" or "Artful Dodger"; active in Big Brothers of America; mem. Cdn Football, Ottawa, Tenn. Sports, Tenn. Baseball halls of fame; res. Knoxville, Tenn.

HOLLOWAY, Sue (canoeing/x-c skiing); b. 19 May 1955, Halifax, N.S.; m. Greg Joy; c. Sarah, Alexandra; SFU, UBC, BPhE; dir. operations Go for Green, motivational speaker; ntl jr. x-country ski title '72; qualified for both skiing, canoeing ntl teams '73; through '83 1 ntl jr. K1, 6 sr. K1, K2, 3 sr. K4, 1 war canoe title; 2 NA K1, K2, 1 K4, 1 K1 6,000m titles; competed 9 world championships; 3 golds Canada Cup, Continental Cup, 4 golds Continental championships; 5 1sts '80 European tour; gold K2, K4 500m '83, bronze K1 500m '75 Pan-Am championships; with Alexandra Barre, silver 500m K2, bronze 500m K4 '84 Olympics; gold K2, K4 '83 Vichy regatta; represented Canada x-country skiing Winter Olympics, K1, K2 Summer Olympics '76; 1st woman to participate in previously all-male Molokai-Oahu outrigger race Hawaii '79, placed 3rd; 4th '81 Hawaii women's race; mem. '76, '80, '84 Olympic teams; named flag-bearer for boycotted '80 summer Olympics; x-country ski coach; mem. SFU swim team '77-80; UBC x-country track team '83; ret'd from competiton '84; *CBC* Olympic commentator '88, '92, '94, '02 Olympic team support staff; with husband Greg operates motivational speaking bureau 'Raising the Bar"; Ottawa ACT amateur athlete of '73; nominated for Velma Springstead, Elaine Tanner trophies; trustee Ottawa Sports Hall of Fame; mem. Cdn Olympic, Ottawa Sports halls of fame; res. Ottawa, Ont.

HOLMAN, Sam (builder/baseball); b. 16 Mar 1945, Kansas City, Missouri; École de Commerce (Neuchatel, Switzerland), USoDak, Carleton; baseball bat maker, owner of the Original Maple Bat Corporation; founder of Sam®Bat, who successfully introduced sugar maple to the game of baseball in 1977; sugar maple was quickly established as the premier wood for baseball bats, and Sam®Bat shares the world homerun record of 73 with Barry Bonds – as Barry says, "it is my record, it is Sam's bat"; the first maple Sam®Bats are in the Museum of Science and Technology (Ottawa, Ont.), the Baseball Hall of Fame and Museum (Cooperstown, N.Y.) and the

Smithsonian Museum of American History (Washington, D.C.); res. Ottawa, Ont.

HOLMES, Derek (hockey); b. 15 Aug 1939, Kemptville, Ont.; m. Louise Cornu; c. Sean, Katherine; St. Michael's College, Carleton, BA; European players agent; jr. hockey St. Mike's, Ottawa Montagnards; college hockey Carleton; '65 best player award Spengler Cup; capt. Eastern Ntl Team '67-70; player-coach teams in England, Austria, Switzerland; ntl coach Finland '61-62; Olympic, ntl coach Switzerland '72-74; GM Team Canada '77, '78 World championships; tech. dir. Hockey Canada '74-80; mem. Hockey Club Ambri-Piotta Switzerland, IIHF halls of fame; res. Ottawa, Ont.

HOLMES, Hap (hockey); b. 1889, Aurora, Ont.; d. 1940, Florida; given name: Harry; star goalie National HA, Pacific Coast HA, Western Canadian HL, Western HL, NHL; pro '12-13 Toronto, 15 seasons Toronto, Seattle, Victoria, Detroit during which he posted a 2.90 goals-against avg. 409 games; mem. 7 league title teams, 4 Stanley Cup winners; Holmes Memorial Trophy presented annually to best goaltender AHL; mem. Hockey Hall of Fame.

HOLNESS, Bob (softball); b. 4 Nov 1952, Victoria, B.C.; m. Susan Crowther; c. Jennifer, Rebecca; civic employee; ss Victoria Bates BC, Western Cdn title team '69; 10 BC title teams; '76 world champion, '79 PAG teams; ntl championships MVP, 4 BC MVP awards; 2nd world championships batting '76; coach sr. softball; res. Victoria, B.C.

HOLZSCHEITER, Herb (golf); b. 8 Jan 1946, West Hill, Ont.; given name: Herbert; m. Mary Scheepers; c. Kelly, Christi; CPGA business school; golf professional; TDIAA HS title '64; Scarborough GC caddy champion '63; worked part-time for Bob Gray Scarborough GC '63-65, asst. pro '65-67; playing pro Thunderbird GC '68-76; asst. '78-86, head pro Weston Golf Club from '87; conducted April golf school for GM employees '73-76; BIC Open '70; runnerup Nfld. Open '72; third Alta. Open '69, Ont. Open '73-74; won Molson-Spec Invitational '73-74; Ont. PGA '75, '78, '80, '82; Hunt Trophy OPGA scoring avg. 67.3 '75; course record 66 Spruce Needles (Timmins) '69, 66 Brockville '74, 64 Thunderbird (old) '72, (new) '74, 63 Board of Trade CC '76; tournament player's rep. Peter Jackson golf tour; Peter Jackson golf tour tournament dir. '77-78; competed '79 US Open; Ont. Assistants title '82; mem. Ont.-Que. matches team '80, '89; runnerup Srs CPGA title '96; dir. CPGA '75-76; res. Mississauga, Ont.

HOMENUIK, Wilf (golf); b. 30 Dec 1937, Kamsack, Sask.; div. Jean Young; c. Gwen, Scott, Jason; golf pro, teacher; Sask. jr. '54; Sask. amateur '53; Man. amateur '56-57; mem. Man. Willingdon Cup team; pro '58; US tour '66; Man. Open '61, '72, Alberta Open '61, '65, CPGA '65, '71, Peru Open '65, Panama Open '66, Millar Trophy '67, '68, East Ridge '71, Labatt Invitational '73, Lake Michigan Classic '73; Dauphin pro-am '75; mem. Canada's World Cup team '71, '74; head pro London Highlands '76-78; mem. Yorkton Sports Hall of Fame; res. Toronto, Ont.

HOMER-DIXON, Marjorie (canoeing); b. 10 Aug 1945, Indochina; McMaster, BPhE; supervisor women's fitness center, kayak coach; ntl K2 title '67-68, bronze '67 PAG; ntl record K1 '68; mem. '68, '72 Olympic teams; silver K2 NA championships '69; mem. 1st Cdn girls K4 NA gold team '69; semifinalist '71 worlds; turned to coaching '72; guided 4 paddlers to age-group ntl titles, 2 to jr. world competition; Mississauga Jaycees most-outstanding-young-person award '72; TV color commentator '76 Olympics; mem. Mississauga Sports Hall of Fame; res. Surrey, B.C.

HONG, Al (bowling); b. 14 Dec 1940, Winnipeg, Man.; div. Sharon Potts; c. Kelly, Robert; m. Cathy Munro; exec-dir. Ont. 5-pin Bowling Assn.; began competitive bowling Saskatoon '62; highest season avg. 278 in Saskatoon '72; rolled perfect 450 game '72; mem. '76 Calgary ntl champion men's team; ntl championship all-star; won '69 Man. Open singles; began coaching high school teams '66; Calgary city champion '75; coach ntl women's team Manila worlds '80; won Cornwall open singles '88; res. Pickering, Ont.

HOOD, Bruce (hockey/officiating); b. 14 Mar 1936, Wentworth County, Ont.; given name: Bruce Melvin; m. Daphne; York; mediator, arbitrator; referee in NHL '63-84; 1st referee to work 1000 NHL games; last ref to wear sweater #1; last ref to officiate in all original six arenas; refereed 3 NHL all-star, 156 Stanley Cup playoff games; officiated in Canada Cup, world championships, Spengler Cup; operated intl schools of refereeing 18yrs; res. Hillsburgh, Ont.

HOOD, Graham (t&f); b. 2 Apr 1972, Winnipeg, Man.; Arkansas, BSc; exercise psychologist, full-time athlete; middle distance specialist; ntl jr. 1500 title '91; US x-country ntl jr. title '91; competed '90 world jr., world x-country; '92, '96 Olympics, '94, '02 CG; NCAA 1500 silver '92. indoor mile '95; Pan-Am jr. 1500 gold, 800m bronze '91; won Millrose Games mile '95; won Harry Jerome Classic 1500m '96; 1500m gold '99 PAG; Cdn sr 1500m record 3:33.94, 1000m record 2:16.88, mile record 3:51.55; 1500m gold '98 Robin Tait Classic NZ, Sydney GP, Waikiki mile; 3 ntl 1500m titles; competed '01, '03 worlds; mem. Burlington Legion Optimist TC; res. Victoria, B.C.

HOOGEWERF, Simon (t&f); b. 11 May 1963, Beaver Lodge, Alta.; given name: Simon Edward Charles; m. Sarah Chritchley; UBC, BSc, MD; physician; 800-, 1000m specialist; BC HS 800m champion '80-81; mem. ntl jr. team '81; ntl sr. team '82-91; UBC team '81-86; 3 CIAU 100m, 1 600m indoor titles; ntl 800m titles '83-88; set CIAU, ntl 800/1000m records; competed '84, '88 Olympics, '87 PAG, '86, '90 CG, '83, '87, '91 worlds; indoor 800m bronze '91 worlds; 5 Big Block awards; Bobby Gaul trophy; mem. UBC Sports Hall of Fame; res. Victoria, B.C.

HOOPER, Charmaine (soccer); b. 15 Jan 1968, Georgetown, Guyana; m. Chuck Codd; North Carolina State BSc; pro soccer striker; began play age 12 with Nepean Hotspurs; moved to Lynwood Spirits; NCAA finalist; 3 time all-American; 1st ntl appearance CONCACAF championships Haiti '91; mem. ntl team '86-03; all-CONCACAF qualifying tournament team '98; led ntl team in scoring '94; played with club teams Norway, Italy; pro with Tokyo Shidox, Chicago, Atlanta; named to intl. all-star team for '99 women's World Cup; CSA female soccer player of '94-95; MVP Chicago Cobras '98; Algarve Cup '01, '02, '03; Gold Cup '00 4th, '02 silver; World Cup '03 4th (scoring two goals in six games to earn all-star selection); inaugural WUSA all-star team; 1st woman mem. USL Hall of Fame; thru '04, 116 caps, 63 goals; res. Wheaton, Ill.

HOOPER, Lyndon (soccer); b. 30 May 1966, Georgetown, Guyana; m. Jennifer Beckford; Wilfrid Laurier, BA; began play age 10 in Zambia; minor soccer Nepean; pro National Capital Pioneers '87, Montreal Supra '88, Toronto Blizzard '89-93, Birmingham City 2yrs, Cinci Silverbacks (NPSL), Montreal Impact A League champs '95-98, also played for A-League Hampton Roads '99, Toronto Lynx '00; mem. ntl -20 team; mem. '92 Olympic team; 66 international caps; res. Willowdale, Ont.

HOOPER, Tom (hockey); b. 24 Nov 1883, Rat Portage (now Kenora), Ont.; d. 23 Mar 1960, Thunder Bay, Ont.; given name: Charles Thomas; with Tommy Phillips helped Kenora Thistles win '01 Man., Northwestern League titles; Thistles challenged for Stanley Cup '03, '05, '07 achieving success latter year but 2 months later lost Cup to Montreal Wanderers; played final season with Wanderers '07-08 again winning Stanley Cup; mem. NWO, Hockey halls of fame.

HOPE, Gord (wrestling/goal ball); b. 12 Aug 1954, Red Deer, Alta.; given name: Gordon Fred Kellock Luke; m. Erin Anne Kelly; c. Michelle, Kathleen, Christina; UofOtt, BA, MA, Carleton, PhD; human & management consulting services, G. Hope Enterprises; v-p Brantford Tournament Capital of Ont.; class B1 blind wrestler; silver 57kg '84 world games for blind; ntl wrestling records '76-77, '84; lj record '78; mem. Ont. ntl goal ball title team '80; mem. ntl goal ball team '78; US ntl blind wrestling title '85; co-ordinator ntl indoor games for blind '79, Cdn marathon for blind '84, Cdn goal ball championships '85; inaugurated annual National Capital invitational goal ball tournament '86; res. Brantford, Ont.

HORGAN, Fred (basketball); b. 22 Jan 1942, Saint John, N.B.; given name: Frederick Gerard; m. Barbara Shideler; c. Kimberly, Cheryl, Lee, Michelle; St.FX, BA, UNB, BEd; ret'd teacher; mem. NB basketball officials assn. '67-99; founding mem. CABO '74; 3 time nominee Air Canada exec. award; CABO council of interpreters '74-99; co-edited CABO-FIBA rules casebook; author/editor CABO officials handbook; mem. CABO board of evaluators '80-99; mem. IAABO (NB Branch) '69-99; IAABO exec. '83-94, pres '93, only non-American to hold this post; IAABO approved clinician; tech. advisor FIBA rules instructional films; co-clinician FIBA certification/recertification clinics; one of 10 clinicians worldwide certified to certify/recertify international officials '92-99; COPABA, FIBA technical commissions '98-99; basketball tech. commissioner '00, '04 Olympics; FIBA official rules interpreter; Ted Early Memorial Award; Basketball NB exec. of '85; hon. life mem. Basketball NB, IAABO; mem. NB, Saint John, Cdn Basketball halls of fame; res. Saint John, N.B.

HORN, Alf (fencing); b. 6 Jan 1913, Spjelkavik, Norway; d. 1991, St. Laurent, Que.; m. Lavinia; c. Carl, Allan (d); ret'd *Montreal Star*; Que. épée champion '38-40, '48-49, foil '40, sabre '40; ntl épée title '48-49; pres. Que. Fencing Assoc.; chair. AAUofC Fencing Comm.; mem. COA Fencing Comm.; BE & C Games Fencing Comm.; coached fencing Central YMCA; mem. '48 Olympic team; mgr. BE & CG fencing

team '54; qualified, but unable to attend '50 BE & CG; Que. Branch AAUofC plaque for contribution to fencing.

HORNE, Stan (golf); b. 4 Jan 1912, Ripon, Eng.; d. 1995, Nun's Island, Que.; given name: Stanley; m. Suzanne Marcoux; Nun's Island golf dir., pro; CPGA champion '36-38; low Cdn Canadian Open '37, '39; 8 Que. Open titles; 1st Cdn to go on complete US pro golf tour '39-40; low Cdn $10,000 PGA Open Islesmere '45; 4th Miami Open '37; 2nd Lake Placid Open '38; competed Masters '37, '38 (finished stroke ahead of Bobby Jones in latter); 5th Pinehurst Open, Thomasville Open '40; 3rd St. Petersburg Open '40; won Ont. Millar Trophy twice; Que. Spring Open title '60; CPGA Srs title '62; Que. PGA match play champion 10 times; played in 1st Canada Cup matches; partnered with Jules Huot to beat Ben Hogan, Lawson Little in Miami International 4-ball match; playing with Ed Furgol, Jules Huot at Dubsdread in Orlando '46 set 9-hole record 26 with 7 birdies, 1 eagle, 1 par; 8 holes-in-one; 29yrs Islesmere Golf Club pro; mem. QGA Hall of Fame.

HORNER, Red (hockey); b. 28 May 1909, Lynden, Ont; given name; George Reginald; def Toronto Marlboros, Brokers' League before joining Maple leafs '28-40; led NHL in penalty minutes 8 successive seasons; record 167 penalty minutes in 43 games during '35-36 season stood 20 years; career total 1254 penalty minutes; capt. Leafs '37-38; NHL record: 42g, 110a; mem. Hockey Hall of Fame; res. Toronto, Ont.

HORN-MILLER, Waneek (water polo); b. 30 Nov 1975, Montréal, Qué.; given name: Waneek Karakwinionta Sunshine Onakarakete Miller; Carleton BPSc; public/ motivational speaker; full-blooded Mohawk from Kahnawake Mohawk Territory; was behind the lines during the '90 Oka crisis and was stabbed by soldier at the end of siege (she turned this life-changing experience into a way to empower her on road to dream of competing in Olympics, as she had seen fellow Mohawk Alwyn Morris do in '84); began playing water polo at age 13 following 6yr competitive swimming, running career; ntl jr. team '94; 9yr ntl team career; '99 PAG champion; co-capt. '00 Olympic team; bronze '01 FINA world championships; '92-93 Sacred Run participant; 3 Carleton U. athlete-of-yr awards; MVP '99 sr. women's ntls; competed 5 NA Indigenous Games; res. Kahnawake, Qué.

HORTON, Tim (hockey); b. 12 Jan 1930, Cochrane, Ont., d. 21 Feb 1974, Toronto, Ont.; given name: Myles Gilbert; m. Dolores Michalek (d); c. Jeri-Lyn, Kim, Kelly, Tracey; St. Michael's College; hockey player, franchise donut chain owner; jr. A St. Mike's Majors where he was OHA penalty leader 1st year; pro Maple Leafs '49, spent much of next 3yrs Pittsburgh Hornets AHL, won Calder Cup, all-star def. berth; Toronto regular '52-70; NYR '70-71, Pittsburgh '71-72, Buffalo '72-74; twice 1st, 3 times 2nd team all-star; mem. 5 Stanley Cup winners; NHL record: 1446 scheduled games, 115g, 403a, 1611pim, 126 playoff games, 11g, 39a, 183pim; killed in single-car accident; jersey #2 ret'd by Sabres in his memory; J.P. Bickell trophy TML MVP '69. mem. Hockey Heritage North, Hockey, Canada's Sports halls of fame.

HORVATH, Bronco (hockey); b. 12 Mar 1930, Port Colborne, Ont.; given name: Bronco Joseph; m. Dolly

Tonelli; c. Mark, Barbara; ret'd hockey exec.; made NHL debut at 25 with Vic Stasiuk and Johnny Bucyk to form Boston's famed Uke Line; missed NHL scoring title '60 by single point to Bobby Hull; NHL '55-68 with NYR, Montreal, Boston, Chicago, Toronto, Minnesota; stints in minors with Rochester, Tulsa; NHL record: 434 scheduled games, 141g, 185a, 36 playoff games, 12g, 9a; played in 2 all-star games; coached London Knights (OHA), Cape Cod Cubs; res. South Yarmouth, Mass.

HORWOOD, Don (basketball/coaching); b. 30 Aug 1946, Carbonear, Nfld.; m. Jill Chipman; c. Chris, Kelly; Memorial. BPhE, BEd, UAlta MA; basketball coach UAlta; small forward Memorial '63-68, capt. '68; coached Victoria Oak Bay HS '69-78; 3 BC titles; asst coach UAlta '78-79, head coach Victoria Spectrum HS '79-83, UAlta; '83-04; UAlta record (through '03) 466-263; 3 CIAU titles; coached ntl jrs. '98; *CBC-TV* basketball color commentator '96 Olympics; 3 CIAU coach-of-yr awards; res. Edmonton, Alta.

HOSSA, Marian (hockey); b. 12 Jan 1979, Stara Lubovna, Slovakia; rw Dukla Trencin Slovak jr. '95-97; Team Slovakia '97, '98 world jr, '96-99, '01 worlds, '02 Olympics; Portland (WHL) '97-98; western conf rookie of yr; Memorial Cup winner '99; 1st round pick, 12th overall Ottawa '97 draft; NHL record (through '04): 467 scheduled games, 188g, 202a, 51 playoff games, 13g, 21a; Calder rookie trophy '99; nickname "Hoss"; with Mora Sweden, Dukla Trencin during '04-05 labor dispute; res. Trencin, Slovakia.

HOUBREGS, Bob (basketball); b. 12 Mar 1932, Vancouver, B.C.; m. Ardis Olson; c. Bob Jr., Todd, Jol, Guy; Washington; ret'd salesman Converse, GM Seattle Sonics '69-73; moved to Seattle age 6; 3yr letter winner UW; NCAA player of '53; all-district '52, all-American '53; 3 Pacific Coast titles; led team to Final-Four appearance '53; numerous UW records; career high 1774pts; single-game record 49pts; 30 or more points in game 9 times; 3 all-PCC selections; 1st pick NBA draft Milwaukee '53; played with Baltimore '54, Boston '55, Ft. Wayne '55-57, Detroit '57-58; deadly hook shot earned him nickname "Hooks"; mem. US, Cdn Basketball, UW Husky Sports (both player/coach) halls of fame; res. Penn Valley, Calif.

HOUCK, Norm (curling); b. 4 Feb 1934, Winnipeg, Man.; given name: James Norman; UMan, BSc, BEd; ret'd; skipped Man. entry '62 Brier, losing title in playoff to Richardson rink; 3 ntl Srs. titles, one as skip, 2 as 3rd for Jim Ursel; hon. life mem. Man. Curling Assn.; mem. Man. Curling Hall of Fame; res. Winnipeg, Man.

HOULD-MARCHAND, Valerie (synchro swim); b. 29 May 1980, Riviere-du-Loup, Que; followed lead of synchro swim coach mother Chantal Hould and at at 15 youngest to become ntl A team member; team silver '96 Olympics, team gold '95 jr worlds, '96 French Open; '98 CG solo gold; solo bronze, team gold '99 Roma Synchro Open; res. Quebec City, Que./Edmonton, Alta.

HOULDEN, Jim (shooting); b. 15 Feb 1904, Hamilton, Ont.; d. 19 Nov 1994, Milton, Ont.; given name: James Walter; m. Rita Andrea; c. Anne; Queen's, BSc; ballistic engineer; began small-bore shooting as cadet '19 progressing through HS ranks to military rifles on outdoor ranges; ballistician

CIL ammo div.; chief ballistician CIL Defence Services WW2; Western sales mgr. CIL, mem. pro shooting staff following WW2; competed at Ottawa's Connaught ranges when opened in '21 and received 60yr award for annual competition (excluding war years) '81; 15 times Bisley team mem., commandant '65; declared best shot in Cdn Armed Forces '32-34; King's silver Bisley '32; in addition to high-powered rifle also ranking shooter in pistol, small-bore, trap and skeet; life mem. GBNRA; life gov. DCRA; mem. Man. Sports Hall of Fame.

HOULE, Réjean (hockey); b. 25 Oct 1949, Rouyn, Que.; m. Micheline Côtes; c. Sylvain, Jean-François, Annie; hockey exec.; l/r wing Montreal Jr. Canadiens; 1st overall draft pick by Canadiens '69; played in NHL with Montreal '69-73, '76-83; in WHA Quebec '73-76; mem. 5 Stanley Cup winners; NHL record: 635 scheduled games, 161g, 247a, 90 playoff games, 14g, 34a; PR dir. Molson Breweries '86-95; v-p/GM Canadiens '95-00, PR ambassador Canadiens from '00; res. Ville Lasalle, Que.

HOULT, Billy (bowling); b. 18 Jun 1932, Toronto, Ont.; given name : William George; m. Shirley Baker; c. William Jr., David (from 1st marriage), Karen, Vicki, Debbie, Sherry; Dominion Business Coll.; trophy mfr.; youngest bowler ever to win Cdn Bowling Congress all-events tournament by winning singles, doubles, mixed doubles at 14 (in rubber boots); Eastern, ntl singles '65; only triple Eastern singles champ '70; won 1st Master Bowlers tourney on TV '64; Master Bowlers mixed triples '66; Ont., ntl MB of '67-68; MB 10 percent tourney '70; MB CNE tourney '74; MB pro bowling tourney; mem. '66 Ont. men's title team that placed 2nd to Winnipeg as both teams topped national pinfall record; mem. Ont. mixed title team '73; rolled sanctioned perfect 450 game in major league play Spadina Bowl; competitive career average 260; mem. Ont. 5-Pin Bowling Hall of Fame; res. Agincourt, Ont.

HOUSLEY, Phil (hockey); b. 9 Mar 1964, St. Paul, Minn.; m. Karin; c. Taylor, Reide, Avery, Wilson; def. St. Paul's USHL, HS '80- 82; drafted by Buffalo '92; NHL Buffalo '82-90, Winnipeg '90-93, St. Louis '93-94, Calgary '94-96, '98-01, New Jersey '96, Washington '96-98, Chicago '01-02, Toronto '02-03; Zurcher (Swiss) '94; Team USA 9 intl tournaments, WC gold '96, Olympic silver '02; 7 NHL all-star; NHL record: 1495 scheduled games, 338g, 894a, 85 playoff games, 13g, 43a; res. St. Paul, Minn.

HOUSTON, Heather (curling); b. 4 Feb 1959, Red Rock, Ont.; Lakehead, HBA; visual artist; Northwestern Ont. jr. champion '74, '76; Ont. Winter Games participant '76; NO mixed champion '84; NWO women's champion '86; Scott Tournament of Hearts titles '88-89; world champion '89; skipped inaugural JVC *TSN* women's skins game '96; Velma Springstead award '89; Tim Ryan course scholarship Lakehead '83; Dean's drawing medal '84; mem. NWO Sports, Cdn Curling halls of fame; res. Thunder Bay, Ont.

HOUSTON, Neil (curling); b. 19 Jan 1957, Calgary, Alta.; given name: Neil William; m. Beverley Karen Bakka; c. Katherine, Andrew; SAIT, hotel/restaurant admin, UCal, BPhE, Concordia, sports admin.; CCA dir. championship services & special programs; ntl badminton, soccer, 3rd

Paul Gowsell Schoolboy curling titles '75; world jr. curling title '76; mem. 4 Alta. men's curling title teams; 2ⁿᵈ for Ed Lukowich '86 Brier, Worlds championships; '88 Olympic bronze medalist; Calgary athlete of '76; res. Orleans, Ont.

HOWARD, Dick (soccer/builder); b. 10 Jun 1943, Bromborough, England; given name: Richard James; m. Anne Martin; Chester College (England), Diploma in PE, Brockport State (USA), BSc (PE); consultant; pro soccer player in NASL (Detroit, Rochester, Toronto), '68-75; coaching staff member, Cdn ntl teams (-16, -20 world cups); '75-92; technical director, CSA, '86-92; FIFA coaching instructor, '88-present; member of FIFA technical committee since '98; chairman, CONCACAF coaching committee since '00; first person in Canadian soccer to have played, coached and managed in ntl program; longest serving NA coach in FIFA; soccer commentator and analyst (print, radio and television); author 2 books on game; mem. Cdn Soccer Hall of Fame; res. Toronto, Ont.

HOWARD, Gerry (softball/officiating); b. 11 Sep 1939, Neepawa, Man,; given name: Milton Gerald; m. Lois Lorraine Johnson; c. Calvin, Leanne; life insurance agent; grew up playing softball Kelwood, Man., but series of back operations forced retirement at 22; turned to umpiring; Softball Man. umpire-in-chief '68-71; Softball Can. deputy umpire-in-chief '84-86, umpire-in-chief '86-94; officiated 14 ntl, 12 world, 2 PAG, 1 Olympics; officials selection comm. 3 Olympics; co-chair softball '99 PAG; officials comm. 7 ISF congresses; deputy roles interpreter ISF '89-03; certified ISF instructor conducting clinics around world; mem. Man. Sports, Softball, Can., Man halls of fame; res. Winnipeg, Man.

HOWARD, Glenn (curling); b. 17 Jul 1962, Midland, Ont.; given name: Glenn William; m. Judy; c. Scott, Carly; mgr. Brewer's Retail; began curling at 11; skip 3 Ont. Pepsi jr. competitions; 3ʳᵈ for brother Russ, won Gov.-Gen.'s Ont. title '85; competed 7 Briers, 2 winners; world titles '87, '93; 4 *TSN Skins Game* titles; 1 VO Cup title; attended '87 Olympic trials; 3 Canada Challenge Cups in Japan; Ont. team of '87; participated in numerous clinics, exhibitions in Canada, Europe, Japan; Dick Ellis team award '87; skipped rink to '01 McCain Superspiel, '02 WCT National trophy, '03 Don Bartlett Classic; mem. Cdn Curling Hall of Fame; res. Coldwater, Ont.

HOWARD, Kid (boxing); b. 9 Oct 1928, Terrace Bay, N.S.; d. 4 Jan 1975, Halifax, N.S.; given name: Richard; c. 1 daughter (d), 1 son; plumber, liquor store clerk; 1ˢᵗ pro bout at 15; of 108 bouts during 7 year span won 77, lost 26, drew 5; never knocked out; in only 4 did he fail to go distance; Maritime lightweight title '49; ntl title '54-60; campaigned internationally as featherweight; ranked 6ᵗʰ in world by *Ring Magazine*; at 5'2" considered short even for featherweight; noted for aggressive style and considered "crowd pleaser", met some of ring's top contenders including Kenny Lane, Teddy "Red Top" Davis, Willie Toweel, Orlando Zulueta, Ray Famechon; fought Toweel for BE crown but lost decision; health deteriorated following death of daughter and marriage breakup; mem. Canadian Boxing, NS, Canada's Sports halls of fame.

HOWARD, Russ (curling); b. 19 Feb 1956, Midland, Ont.;

m. Wendy; c. Steven, Ashley; dir. golf & real estate Royal Oaks GC; began curling at 13; won '76 Ont. Colts; competed 11 Briers, 2 winners; record 100 Brier game victories; with brother Glenn, Tim Belcourt, Kent Carstairs won '87 Brier, worlds; with brother Glenn, Wayne Middaugh, Peter Corner won '93 Brier, worlds; Ont. team of '87; 4 *TSN Skins Games* titles; 1 VO Cup title; 3 McCain Superspiel titles; attended '87 Olympic trials; 2 WCT Players championships; 3 Canada Challenge Cup titles in Japan; '85 Ont. Gov.-Gen.'s title; skipped Ont., NB in Brier play; 2 8-enders; played key role in free-guard zone rule, other innovations; at frequent odds with CCA over sponsorship rules; suspended by WCT for ignoring CCA event ban; participated in numerous clinics in Canada, Europe, Japan; Dick Ellis team award '87; *TSN* analyst '01; mem. Cdn Curling Hall of Fame; res. Moncton, N.B.

HOWARD, Tom (t&f); b. 20 Sep 1948, Vancouver, B.C.; given name: Thomas George; div. Cheryl Lynne Spowage; UBC; transit operator; mem. '73 FISU, '75, '79 Pan-Am, '76 Olympic teams; ntl marathon title, 2ⁿᵈ ntl outdoor 10,000m '74; 4ᵗʰ '75 Boston Marathon 2:13.24; bronze '75 PAG marathon; 30ᵗʰ '76 Olympics marathon; 3 Seattle marathon titles; mem. Cdn Road Running Hall of Fame; res. Surrey, B.C.

HOWE, Bruce (rugby); b. 13 Mar 1941, Palm North, N.Z.; given name: Bruce Leslie; m. Janice Marilyn Franklin; c. Carolyn Anne, Jonathan Bruce; Dunedin Teachers College, PE dip., Oregon, BSc, MSc, PhD; dean faculty of Ed. UVic; played cricket, boxed, competed in track, rugby at NZ HS, college levels; cricket at club level; rugby club, college levels; represented NZ provincially in rugby; toured UK with Oregon team '66; capt. BC '72 vs All Blacks; coached rugby HS, college level, asst. coach NZ provincial team '75; coached Vancouver Island Reps '75-78; 2 McKechnie Cups; coached BC team on '78 Samoa, Fiji tour, won ntl title, beat Australian State Champion Queensland; ntl rugby team coach '79-82; UVic rugby coach; res. Victoria, B.C.

HOWE, Dan (canoeing); b. 31 Dec 1970, Kingston, Ont.; Queen's; engineer; mem. ntl team '89-98; C-4 gold Duisburg Regatta '93; C-2 500 gold, C-1 1000 bronze '95 PAG; C-2 1000 silver Milano '96; C-4 200 silver Szeged '96; gold (with Steve Giles) C-2 1000, C-2 500 Hemispheric '96 Olympic qualifier regatta; competed '94, '95, '97 worlds, '96 Olympics; res. North Bay, Ont.

HOWE, Gordie (hockey); b. 31 Mar 1928, Floral, Sask.; given name: Gordon; m. Colleen Joffa; c. Marty, Mark, Murray, Cathleen; hon. LLD Regina; hockey exec., restaurateur; 1ˢᵗ pro contract '45 Omaha Knights (USHL); 32 seasons major hockey; 26 NHL, Detroit '46-71, Hartford '79-80, 6 WHA Houston '73-76, New England '77-79; regarded as one of game's greatest rw; NHL record: 1767 scheduled games, 801g, 1049a, 157 playoff games, 68g, 42a; major trophies: 6 Hart (MVP); 6 Art Ross (scoring); 1 Lester Patrick, 1 2ⁿᵈ team all-star, all-star selectee 15 consecutive years; played in 22 all-star games scoring 10 goals, 8 assists; co-holder all-star points in single-game mark of 4 '65; following '71 retirement 2yrs Red Wings v-p before joining sons Marty, Mark with Houston '73-74; despite age, 45, WHA MVP '74; helped Aeros win 2 Avco Cups, all-star each season; major hockey's 1ˢᵗ playing club pres.

'75-76; WHA record: 419 scheduled games, 174g, 334a, 78 playoff games, 28g, 43a; at 69 with 40 sec. cameo shift for Detroit Vipers (IHL) 3 Oct '97 became only athlete to play pro hockey over six decades; jersey #9 ret'd by Red Wings, Whalers; Lionel Conacher Trophy '63; *Sport Magazine* hockey player of quarter century '71; *SI* Cdn athlete of century list; dir. player development Hartford Whalers; Hartford advisory board; Officer Order of Canada; mem. Canada's Walk of Fame, Whalers, Hockey, Canada's, Sask. Sports halls of fame; res. Traverse City, Mich.

HOWE, Syd (hockey); b. 28 Sep 1911, Ottawa, Ont.; d. 20 May 1976, Ottawa, Ont.; given name: Sydney Harris; m. Frances Sullivan; c. Shirley; civil servant; mem. 1st Ottawa Memorial Cup finalist losing '28 to Regina; pro Ottawa Senators (NHL) '29-30, '32-34, Philadelphia Quakers '30-31, St. Louis '34; Detroit '35-46; NHL record: 237g, 291a; modern record '44 scoring 6 goals in game vs Rangers, mark since equalled by Red Berenson, Darryl Sittler; mem. 3 league champions, 3 Stanley Cup winners; mem. Ottawa Sport, Ottawa CSRA Sports, Hockey halls of fame.

HOWELL, Harry (hockey); b. 28 Dec 1932, Hamilton, Ont.; given name: Henry Vernon; m. Marilyn Gorrie; c. Danny (d), Cheryl; hockey exec.; jr. Guelph Biltmores; pro NYR '52-69; Ranger record more than 1000 games; Oakland '69-70, L.A. '71; WHA NY Raiders (then Golden Blades), Jersey Knights, San Diego Mariners, player-coach '74-75; AGM Cleveland Barons (NHL) '76, GM '76-77; coach Minnesota '77-78; scout Minn., Edm.; NHL record: 21 seasons, 1411 scheduled games, 94g, 324a, 38 playoff games, 3g, 3a; James Norris Memorial Trophy '66-67; 1st team all-star once; NHL milestone award '82; mem. Hockey, AHL halls of fame; res. Hamilton, Ont.

HOWELL, Ron (football/hockey); b. 4 Dec 1935, Hamilton, Ont.; d. 16 Mar 1992, Ancaster, Ont.; given name: Ronald John; m. Ruth Jean Moore; c. Robin, Lisa, Cathy, Tracey; ret'd furrier; Guelph Biltmores OHA jr. A, Tilson Award '55-56; sr. Kitchener-Waterloo; pro Rochester AHL; minors Vancouver (WHL), Long Island (EHL), ret'd '64; pro football Hamilton '54-62, BC '62, Toronto '64-65, Montreal '66; CFL record: 13 seasons, returned 458 punts for 2742yds, 6.0 avg., 5tds; 4 Grey Cup finals, 1 winner; Gruen EFC rookie of '54; Schenley outstanding Canadian '58.

HOWES, Bob (football); b. 4 Jan 1943, Kirkland Lake, Ont.; given name: Robert Alexander; m. Mary Padden; c. Chris, Beau; Queen's, Waterloo, UAlta; ret'd football coach, teacher; mem. basketball, football teams Queen's, football Waterloo; drafted '66 by Calgary; pro BC '69-72, Edmonton '72-81; CFL all-star ctr '74; also ot; capt. Eskimos '75-77; mem. 8 Grey Cup finalists, 5 winners; asst. coach Queen's '84-95, head coach '96-99; asst. UofT '03; OQIFC coach of '96; mem. Queen's Coaches Hall of Fame; res. Toronto, Ont.

HOWIE, Al (t&f); b. 16 Sep 1945, West Kilbride Ayershire, Scotland; given name: Allan; m. Claudia Cole; c. Gabe, Dana; Androssan Academy; stonemason; began racing '79; averages 15-20 marathons, 5-10 ultra marathons annually; NA 24-hour race record; ran 350-mile race '79; world record longest non-stop race 187.5 miles in 37h, 57min.; noted

for quick recovery ability, ran 150-mile 24-hour race and 6 days later won 50-mile race '82; x-Canada 72-day record run '91; res. Victoria, B.C.

HOWKINS, Mark (shooting); b. 17 Jun 1953, Brisbane, Australia; given name: Patrick; m. Danielle Perrot; c. Christine, David; self-employed; handgun specialist; mem. ntl team '79-95; 7 ntl rapid-fire titles; competed '84, '88 Olympics, '87, '91 PAG, '86, '90, '94 CG, '85, '89 Championship of Americas, '86, '90 worlds; numerous World Cup competitions; 2 bronze '86, silver '90 CG; gold, silver '85 Championship of Americas; res. Calgary, Alta.

HOWSON, Barry (basketball); b. 17 Jun 1939, London, Ont.; given name: Barry Franklin; div.; c. Micheline, David, Bryan; UWO, BA, Wayne State, MEd; HS teacher, PE department head; mem. all-Ont. HS champions '57-58, OQAA champions Western '60; Tillsonburg Livingstons-London Fredricks Eastern Cdn sr. A titlists '61; Montreal Yvan Coutu Huskies Eastern Cdn titlist '62; London 5B Sports '63; mem. '64 Olympic team, Toronto Dow Kings sr. A champions; Sarnia Drawbridge '66-68, Ont. sr. title '68; gold '66 Canada Winter Games; mem. '67 PAG team; London Host-Rent-A-Car team '69-70; national team world championships '71; Ont. sr. A champion London Celtics '72-73; Sarnia Trader Bryan int. A Bullets '75; Sarnia Northgate Bowl int. '76; twice MVP Windsor Masters (40+) tournament; 3 35+ Sarnia Tennis Club titles; coach St. Patrick's HS basketball, football, track, tennis, Lambton College basketball; mem. Sarnia-Lambton Sports, Cdn Basketball halls of fame; res. Sarnia, Ont.

HRITZUK, Eugene (curling); b. 12 Oct 1949, St. Walburg, Sask.; m. Joanne Seltenrich; c. Trina, Valene; UofSask, BA, BEd, MEd; farmer/real estate salesman; standout HS athlete; competed in 19 university sports; coached Sask. basketball, t&f finalists; played sr. baseball Sask., Man., Alta; 3 time Sask softball finalist; Northern Sask. HS curling finalist '66-67; tied for runnerup ntl firefighters '80; amassed more than $100,000 in cashspiels '83-86 seasons; top money winner cashspiel circuit '85-86 with $60,000; won Calgary carspiel '85, Saskatoon Nutana Pot of Gold unprecedented 3 consec. yrs.; twice won Saskatoon Super League; 3 time prov. tankard finalist; posted undefeated record winning Sask. Tankard '85; skip semifinalist '85 Brier, 5th man, coach '86 Brier rink; competed '87 Olympic trials; skip Sask. '02 ntl srs.; Saskatoon athlete-of-yr nominee '86; res. Loreburn, Sask.

HRUDEY, Kelly (hockey); b. 13 Jan 1961, Edmonton, Alta.; given name: Kevin Stephen; m. Donna; c. Jessica, Megan, Kaitlin; broadcaster; goalie Medicine Hat (WHL) '78-81; NYI 2nd pick '80 draft; Indianapolis (CHL) '81-84; mem. Team Canada '84; Islanders '84-89; Los Angeles '89-96, San Jose '96-98; shared 2 Terry Sawchuk (CHL top goalie) trophies; Tommy Ivan (CHL MVP) trophy '83; NHL record: 677 scheduled games, 271-265-88, 38,084min, 17so, 85 playoff games, 5163min, 283ga, 36-46; *HNIC* color analyst; coach CHL Top Prospects team; res. Redondo Beach, Calif./Calgary, Alta.

HSU, Gloria (table tennis); b. 7 Oct 1956, South Africa; asst. animator Atkinson Film-Arts; 2 ntl woman's closed doubles titles; mem. ntl team from '75; national Top 12 title '80; CNE Open women's singles, doubles, mixed doubles, Ont. closed singles title '8l; mem. Ont. title team, woman's singles finalist Cdn. closed championships '80; gold women's doubles world student championships '80, team silver '80, '82; team silver '82 CG team bronze '83 PAG; ntl, US Open team semifinalist '8l; mem. '79-83 CG, worlds teams; res. Toronto, Ont.

HUANG, Johnny (table tennis); b. 5 Oct 1962, Canton, China; m.; coach; began competing age 9; mem. Chinese ntl team winning '85 singles, '86 doubles, '85 Scandinavian open titles; emigrated to Canada '87; undefeated in NA Feb '90-Mar '91; 1st Cdn to win medal (bronze) at World Cup '93; gold, 2 bronze '91, triple gold '94 Commonwealth championships; competed '96 Olympic Games; 2 ntl singles, 1 doubles, 1 team titles; 2 Japan Open, 3 US Open, 5 CNE International, 4 Commonwealth championships, 4 NA titles; '02 CG singles silver; ntl jr. team coach from '90; pro Germany '92-93, France '93-95, Japan from '95; res. Toronto, Ont.

HUARD, Camille (boxing); b. 29 Oct l95l, St. Francois de Pabos, Que.; div. Connie Murray; c. Nicolas; m. Suzanne Dernier; c. Christine Marie, Marie-Pier, Noemie; Laval, BA; youth consultant/educator; Que., Eastern Cdn featherweight (57kg) titles '70, '73-76; Que. Open class bronze '7l; Que. lightweight (60kg) title, silver Eastern Cdn.; Eastern Cdn. 57kg title '73; lost '74 NA final to Wilfredo Benitez, later world pro champ; mem. ntl team '74 world championships; silver '75, gold '76 ntl championships; mem. '76 Olympic team losing split decision to Poland's Lazlek Kosedowski; coach Que. team '79 Canada Games, ntl team Finnish International tournament; coach Grande-Riviere boxing club '80-82; res. Gaspe, Que.

HUBAND, Deb (all-around); b. 5 Sep l956, Ottawa, Ont.; given name: Deborah Ellen; John Abbott College, Concordia, Bishop's., hons. BA, UBC,MSc; coach, speech-language pathologist; mem. Oakville Jays softball team '69-72; Oakville swim club '68-72, Oakville HS swimming, track, volleyball, basketball teams '69-72, Beaconsfield HS basketball, volleyball teams '72-76, Que. softball, basketball teams '74-75, college basketball '76-80, field hockey '76-77; co-capt. ntl women's basketball team '78-84; basketball all-Que. '77-80, all-Cdn '78-80, softball all-Que., all-Cdn '74-75; MVP, all-star awards CIAU championships '77-80; guard '80 Jones Cup gold team; shares CIAU women's single-game 50 points record with Carol Turney; mem. '84 Olympic team, 2 world championship bronze; 7 school athlete-of-yr awards; Softball Canada jr. catcher-of-yr award; Concordia rookie of '76-77; Hon. Howard Ferguson academic award Bishop's '77-79; asst. women's basketball coach UBC '88-91, head coach '95-99; asst. coach women's ntl team '99; coached BC regional girls team '95 BC summer games; coached '03 Cdn FISU Games team; CIS coach of yr (basketball) '04; mem. Nepean, Bishop's Walls, Cdn Basketball, Ottawa Sports halls of fame; res. Nepean, Ont./Vancouver, B.C.

HUCK, Fran (hockey); b. 12 Apr 1945, Regina, Sask.; brilliant major jr. career Regina Pats scoring more than 135 points in each of 2 full seasons; mem. Ottawa Nationals OHA Sr. '67-68, ntl team '65-69; 2 IIHF world, 1 Olympic bronze; 2 tourney all-star awards; pro NHL Montreal '69-

70, St. Louis '70-73; AHL Montreal '69-71; WHL Denver '71-72; WHA Winnipeg '73-74, '76-78, Minnesota '74-76; Leader Cup (WHL MVP) '72; mem. IIHF Hall of Fame; res. Regina, Sask.

HUDDY, Charlie (hockey); b. 2 Jun 1959, Oshawa, Ont.; m. Karen; c. Amanda, Ryan; hockey coach; def Oshawa (OHA) '77-79, Houston (CHL) '79-80, Wichita (CHL) '80-82, NHL Edmonton '80-91, Los Angeles '91-94, Buffalo '94-96, '97, St. Louis '96; NHL plus/minus leader '83; Team Canada (gold) '84; 5 Stanley Cup winners; Emery Edge award; NHL record: 1017 scheduled games, 99g, 354a, 183 playoff games, 19g, 66a; player/asst coach Rochester (AHL) '96-97; head coach/dir. hockey ops Huntington (ECHL) '97-98; asst. NYR '98-00, Edmonton '00-03; res. Edmonton, Alta.

HUDON, Joe Jr. (harness racing); b. 30 May 1951, Teulon, Man.; m. Shirley; c. John, Patrick, Phillip; premier driver Cloverdale, B.C. track 15yrs; ntl UDR title '80; 4th '78 world driving championships; moved to OJC circuit '91; Cdn horseman of '94; through '02 scored 3670 victories with purses topping $13 million; res. Rockwood, Ont.

HUDSON, Bruce (curling); b. l3 Nov 1928, Winnipeg, Man.; m. Verla Scott; c. Diane, Gordon, Elaine, Scott; UMan; ret'd Manitoba Queen's Printer; 11 men's provincial championships, finalist 4 yrs in succession '64-67 matching Ken Watson record; Man. rep. '64, '67 Brier, '80-8l Seniors; Man. bonspiel title '6l; catcher '46-55 Rosedales juv & jr., St. Boniface Native Sons baseball teams; hon. life mem. Strathcona (scty-treas 20yrs, p.-pres), Pine Ridge CC (p.-pres), Man. Curling Assn.; mem. Man. Curling Hall of Fame; res. Winnipeg, Man.

HUDSON, Gordon (curling); b. 5 Jan 1894, Kenora, Ont.; d. 10 July 1959, Winnipeg, Man.; m. Flora MacLean; c. Bruce, Margaret; manufacturers agent; catcher sr. baseball; 5 Man. Bonspiel titles; skipped Brier winners '28-29, winning 18 of 20 games played; pres. Strathcona CC '25-27, later secty; pres., hon. life mem. Kenora, Strathcona CC, Man., Dominion Curling Associations; mem. Man. Sports, Curling, Cdn Curling halls of fame.

HUDSON, John (t&f); b. 15 May l936, Belfast, N. Ireland; div. Melissa Louise Harvey; c. Saundra Lynn, Lisa Marie; m. Linda Diane Smith; Dubuque, BSc; sports TV consultant; all-Ireland youth x-country champion '54; Iowa Conf. x-country titles '57, '59-60, 1-mile champion '59, 2-mile champion '58-59; 1st ntl t&f coach '69; exec. dir. Coaching Assn. of Canada '7l-75; dir. *CBC Sports*, '78-80; dir. media properties Labatt breweries '79-82; exec. producer Blue Jays baseball '81-96; with Ken Twigg co-founder Maple Leaf Indoor Games Toronto '63; res. Mississauga, Ont.

HUFF, Bruce (builder); b. 22 Jun 1934, Morpeth, Ont.; given name: Bruce Eberle; m. Carolyn Elsie Deline; c. Kelly, Tim; UWO; retd journalist; active as amateur athlete, coach, administrator baseball, hockey, lacrosse, softball; key role in development of oldtimer hockey from '75; played in 1st world cup '77; seniors game activist, participant all levels; founding chair. London Sports Hall of Fame; Western Fair assn. Sport archivist; founder London

Oldtimers SA; London sportsperson of '02 award; reporter, sports editor *London Free Press*; numerous media awards, citations; mem. Cdn Adult Recreational Hockey Assn., Dresden Sports halls of fame; res. London, Ont.

HUFNAGEL, John (football); b. 13 Sep 1951, Corapolis, Pa.; m. Peni; c. Neely, Lindsay, Cole; Penn State; football coach, real estate broker; all-American qb Penn State; competed in Cotton Bowl, Sugar Bowl, Hula Bowl; pro Denver (NFL) 3 seasons; CFL Calgary '76-79, Saskatchewan '80-83, '87, Winnipeg '84-86; player/coach Saskatchewan '87; assisted UCal 2 seasons; off.co-ordinator/qb coach Calgary '90-97; head coach/GM New Jersey Red Dogs (Arena FL) '97-98; asst. BC '98, Cleveland Browns '99-00, Indianapolis Colts '01, New Orleans '02, New England '03; NY Giants '04; mem. 1 Grey Cup winner; res. New Orleans, La.

HUGHES, Billy (all-around); b. Jul 1888, Durham, Eng.; d. 14 Nov 1975, St. Anne's, Man.; m. Marjorie; c. Vivian, Pat, John; athletic trainer; outstanding boxer losing only 9 of 189 bouts over 14yrs; held Cdn feather, bantam, lightweight titles; ret'd from ring '24; began coaching Montreal Westmount HS, interscholastic title; coached Montreal Winged Wheelers '19-22, Queen's '22-26 (26 consec. victories), Hamilton Tigers '32-33, Rough Riders '35-36, RCAF Manning Pool, WW2; 4 Grey Cup titlists, Queen's '22-24, Hamilton '32; coached IRFU title winners with Ottawa, Manning Pool; trainer Cdn t&f, boxing teams '24 Olympics; numerous pro, amateur hockey teams including Chicago; Winnipeg, Calgary, Regina football clubs; trainer/ coach numerous amateur football, rugby, boxing, track teams; coached/trained world speed skating titlist Everett McGowan; YMCA AD/instructor/health unit dir. '42-57; life mem. YMCA, Blue Bombers; mem. Queen's Coaches, Cdn. Football, Man. Sports halls of fame.

HUGHES, Clara (cycling/speed skating); b. 27 Sep 1972, Winnipeg, Man.; m. Peter; competitive speed skater from '88; began cycle racing at 17; 3000m individual pursuit specialist; 10 ntl titles; competed '91, '95, '99, '03 PAG, '94, '02 CG, '96, '00 summer, '02 winter Olympics; '93, '94 worlds; 3 PAG silver, 2 bronze, 1 CG gold, 1 silver; 3 bronze '96 Olympics; 5000m long-track Olympic bronze '02; Tour de L'Aude silver '93; world Road Individual Time Trial silver '95; Sea Otter Classic '98 gold; Canada Games '93 speed skating 3000m gold; world 5000m long-track title '04; YTV Youth Achievement Award '92; Cdn long-track female skater of '04; mem. Cdn Speed Skating Hall of Fame; res. Hamilton, Ont.

HUGHES, George (football); b. 19 Aug 1925, Norfolk, Va.; given name; George Samuel; m. Kate Parker; c. George Jr., Kathy, Susan; William and Mary, BSc, MA; ret'd football coach, hardware store owner; ctr/gd in college appearing in '48 Dixie, '49 Delta bowls; all-state, all-Southern, all-American; participant Blue-Grey, College all-star games; 5yrs pro Pittsburgh, twice all-Pro; 4yrs HS coach, 12yrs coach Norfolk Neptunes Continental, Atlantic Coast Football League; Rough Rider line coach '74-80; mem. Virginia Sports Hall of Fame; res. Norfolk, Va.

HUGHES, Karen (coaching/hockey); b. 28 Oct 1963, Scarborough, Ont.; St. Michael's Coll, UofT BComm., MSc;

economist, sr. advisor Ont. management board, coach; mem. 5 OWIAA title teams, 2yrs capt.; 3 CIAU finals; soccer standout earning 3 Ont. all-star honors, 1 CIAU all-star; began coaching hockey UofT '91, head coach from '93; 2 OUAA, 1 CIAU titles; ntl team asst. '98-00, head coach '02-04; 3 world, 2 3-Nations, *TSN* Challenge Cup titles, 1 4-Nations Cup title; asst. '02 Olympic gold, 3 IIHL world gold; head coach ntl -22 team '01; accredited Level 4 coach; 2 3M coaching awards; CIAU coach of '01; mem. UofT Sports Hall of Fame; res. Agincourt, Ont.

HULL, Bobby (hockey); b. 3 Jan 1939, Pointe Anne, Ont.; given name: Robert Marvin; div. Judy Learie; c. Terry; div. Joanne McKay; c. Bobby Jr., Blake, Brett, Bart, Michelle; ret'd hockey player, cattle farmer; jr. B Hespeler, Woodstock, Galt; jr. A St. Catharines Black Hawks '55-57; pro Chicago (NHL) '57-72, Winnipeg Jets (WHA) '72-79; Team Canada '76; NHL record: 1036 scheduled games, 604g, 549a, 116 playoff games, 62g, 67a; WHA record: 411 scheduled games, 303g, 335a, 60 playoff games, 43g, 37a; 5 50+goal seasons Chicago; 1st team all-star NHL 10 times, WHA 5 times; 2nd team NHL twice; 3 Art Ross, 2 Hart, 1 Lady Byng, Lester Patrick Award; 2 Gary Davidson Trophies (WHA MVP); nicknamed "Golden Jet"; jersey #9 ret'd by Chicago, Winnipeg; fastest left-handed slap shot 118.3 mph, fastest skater 29.7 mph; 2 Lionel Conacher awards; USHHOF Gretzky international award; TV hockey commentator; wrote 2 hockey books; commissioner new WHA '03; owner grand champion hereford bull '94 Royal Winter Fair; mem. Officer Order of Canada; Canada's Sports, Hockey halls of fame; res. Ashville, N.C.

HULL, Brett (hockey); b. 9 Aug 1964, Belleville, Ont.; m. Allison; c. Jude, Jayde, Crosby; UMinn (Duluth); son of Hockey Hall of Famer Bobby Hull; played with Minn.-Duluth WCHA '84-86, freshman-of-yr award; drafted by Calgary '84; Moncton AHL '86-87; WCHA 1st team all-star '86, AHL 1st team all-star '87; Red Garrett Memorial trophy '87; NHL Calgary '86-87, St. Louis '88-98, Dallas '98-00, Detroit '01-04, Phoenix '04; 50+ goals '90 72, '91 86, '92 70, '93 54, '94 57; achieved 700g '03; moved into 3rd all-time NHL goal list (732) '04; NHL record (through '04): 1264 scheduled games, 741g, 649a, 202 playoff games, 103g, 87a; 3 1st team all-star; 1 Lady Byng, 2 Dodge Ram, 1 Hart, 1 Pearson, 1 ProSet player-of-year awards; capt. Blues '92-95 played 7 NHL all-star games, '92 MVP; *Hockey News* minor league player-of-yr award; scored '99 Stanley Cup final winner in 3rd overtime of game 6 vs. Buffalo; mem. '02 Stanley Cup winner; mem. Team USA '86 Worlds; mem. Team USA '98, '02 Olympics; res. Duluth, Minn.

HULL, Dennis (hockey); b. 19 Nov 1944, Pointe Anne, Ont.; given name: Dennis William; m. Mary Sue; c. Martha, John; Brock, BA; ret'd athletic dir. Illinois Institute of Technology; jr. St. Catharines; lw Chicago '64-77, Detroit '77-78; Team Canada '72; NHL record: 959 scheduled games, 303 goals, 351 assists, 104 playoff games, 33 goals, 34 assists; 2nd team all-star '73; 1 40-goal, 3 30-goal seasons; noted raconteur; res. Welland, Ont.

HUMBER, Bruce (t&f); b. 11 Oct 1913, Victoria, B.C.; d. 18 Aug 1988, Vancouver, B.C.; m. Anne Barry; c. Richard, Lezlie Anne; Washington, BA; sales manager; all-time Seattle prep school records of 9.9, 21.8 in 100-, 220yds; at university ran 9.6 and 20.8; mem. 4th place Cdn. Olympic relay team '36; coach '50 BEG track team, '52 Olympic team; mem. Washington, BC, Greater Victoria Sports halls of fame.

HUME, Fred (lacrosse/hockey/soccer); b. 2 May 1892, Sapperton, B.C.; d. 17 Feb 1967, Vancouver, B.C.; given name: Frederick; player, later pres. New Westminster Salmonbellies; pres. 3-time ntl champion New Westminster Royals soccer team; helped form Western Hockey League; owned, operated New Westminster Royals, later Vancouver Canucks in WHL; major role in bringing BEG to Vancouver '54; mem. BC Sports, Hockey, Lacrosse halls of fame.

HUME, Ian (t&f); b. 20 Aug 1914, Foster, Que.; given name: Ian Knowlton; m. Melita Jean Fraser; c. Edward, Margaret, Heather, Laurel, Vicki; Bishop's; BA; Macdonald College; ret'd teacher; 1st t&f gold medal '29; competed prov., ntl level 4 jumping events, 110m high hurdles, javelin, relay through '55; numerous Cdn sr. hj, javelin titles; mem. '54 BE&CG team; mem. prov. finalists baseball team '40s, prov. Sr. B titlist; 8 gold, 8 silver, 4 bronze world Masters t&f competitions '75-81; 14 world, 40+ Cdn Masters t&f records; t&f coach from '37; coach '66, mgr. '70, referee '78 CG; field coach '59 PAG; pres. CTFA '68-71; former mem. COA, rep. several IAAF Congresses; mem. IAAF Comm. for women's athletics from '72; technical official field events from '42; developed new procedures for '76 Olympic decathlon; pres. FAQ, Que. Basketball Assoc.; chair. tech. comm. World Veterans Assoc.; various offical capacities '76 Olympics, '78 CG, '79 World Cup, '79 Russia-US-Canada meet, '80 Pan-Am jr. championships; Lieut.-Gov.'s Medal for French specialists studies '40; mem. Order of Canada, Bishop's Wall, Cdn Olympic Sports Hall of Fame; res. Melbourne, Que.

HUMPHRY, Jay (figure skating); b. 28 Jul 1948, Vancouver, B.C.; m. Cheryl Frost; v-p operations & bookings VEE Corp.; ntl jr. men's singles title '63; sr. men's '68-69; world competitor '65-69; silver '69 NA; 7th '68 Olympics; 7yrs Ice Follies; operated NY Babes in Toyland 1yr; mgr. Sesame St. road show 10yrs; res. Ham Lake, Minn.

HUNGERFORD, George (rowing); b. 2 Jan 1944, Vancouver, B.C.; given name: George William; m. Jane Knott; c. Geordie, Michael, Andrew, Jane; UBC, BA, LLB; lawyer, QC; with Roger Jackson pairs gold '64 Olympics; Lou Marsh Trophy winner with Jackson '64; founding dir., v-p Olympic Club Canada; trustee, p-pres-chair. BC Sports Hall of Fame; mem. Vancouver Athletic Commission; mem. COA PAG comm.; BC jr. athlete of '64; UBC Big Block award; gov. Olympic Trust; dir. Vancouver 2010 Olympic bid; Canada 125 medal, Queen's Golden Jubilee medal; UBC alumni award of distinction; Knight Commander of Grace Sovereign Order St. John of Jerusalem; Salvation Army recognition award; Officer Order of Canada; mem. Cdn Olympic, Canada's, BC, UBC Sports halls of fame; res. Vancouver, B.C.

HUNT, Claudia (canoeing); b. 12 Mar 1950, Montreal, Que.; m. Sebastian Cardarelli; c. Alea, Luisa, Arom; UofOtt, BSc, MSc; partner information technology co.; flat water kayak specialist; mem. ntl team '66-75; mem. '67 PAG, '68, '72 Olympic teams; ntl K1 title '69-70, K4 '68-69, '73-75; NA K4 title '70; res. Navan, Ont.

HUNT, Helen (volleyball/swimming); b. 28 Dec 1938, Vancouver, B.C.; given name: Helen Stewart; m. Ted Hunt; c. Shelley; UBC, BEd, MEd; teacher; silver '54 CG , 4x100 medley relay; 100m freestyle gold, 2 relay silver '55, silver 4x100 FS relay '59 PAG; competed '56 Olympics; held world 100yd FS record 3 weeks '56; Canada's outstanding female swimmer '55-56; BC athlete of '55; mem. ntl women's volleyball team '67-73, BC ntl championship team '64-74, '77; mem. '67, '71 PAG teams; mem. Cdn Aquatic, BC Sports halls of fame; res. Vancouver, B.C.

HUNT, Lynda Adams (diving); b. 4 Jun 1920, Vancouver, B.C.; d. 26 Feb 1997, Halfmoon Bay, B.C.; m. Harold Hunt (d); c. Brian; Western Washington Coll.; at 14 youngest performer '34 BEG; overcame acrophobia (fear of heights) to excel in tower, springboard diving events; mem. '36 Olympic, '34, '38, '50 BEG teams; 2 silver '38, springboard bronze '50; ntl high-tower titles '34, '39; coach Vancouver Amateur SC 20yrs, UBCSC 5yrs; judge '54, chaperone '58 BEG; exec. mem. Cdn Diving Assn.; mem. BC Sports Hall of Fame.

HUNT, Ted (all-around); b. 15 Mar 1933, Vancouver, B.C.; given name: Edmund Arthur; m. Helen Stewart; c. Shelly; UBC, BPhE, MPhE, EdD, Washington, MA; ret'd school administrator; short story author; capt. BC in rugby victories over Australia '58, Japan '61; mem. British Lions '67 McKechnie Cup winner; mem. Burrards Mann Cup lacrosse team '61, '64; BC (CFL) hb '57-58; Lions' rookie of '57, candidate for CFL top Canadian award '58; mem. '52 Olympic ski jumping team, '54 FIS team, 8th '54 Swedish ntl championships; UBC light-heavyweight boxing title 4yrs; BC athlete of '57; Bob Gaul Memorial Award '58; Howie McPhee Memorial Award '61; *Telefilm Can.* Fellowship; mem. BC, UBC Sports Hall of Fame; res. Vancouver, B.C.

HUNTER, Dale (hockey); b. 31 Jul 1960, Petrolia, Ont.; m. Karynka; c. Dylan, Shalen, Tucker; hockey exec./coach; lw/ctr Kitchener, Sudbury (OHA) '77-80, drafted by Quebec '79; NHL with Quebec '80-87, Washington '87-99, Colorado '99; Washington team capt. '94-99; only player in NHL history to log 300g, 3000pim; reached 1000-point plateau '98; NHL record: 1407 scheduled games, 323g, 697a, 186 playoff games, 42g, 76a; played in 1 NHL all-star game; joined Washington front office '99; with brother Mark co-owner OHL London Knights; London coach '01-05; guided Knights to CHL record 29-0-2 record '04 before bowing to Sudbury; OHL coach of '04; res. London, Ont.

HUNTER, Gord (orienteering); b. 20 Jan 1946, Montreal, Que.; div. Anne Marie Cartile (d); c. Dierdre, Philip; Dalhousie, BA; ret'd teacher; muni. politician; mem. '70 Ottawa Sooners (Sr. ORFU); Ottawa Indians rugby team '69-73, '79-81; orienteering competitor from '70; Ont. elite title '75, Que. '76, ntl '72-74; twice 2nd, once 3rd NA championships; 8 Ntl titles, 3 elite, 3 masters (35-40), 2 masters (40-45); represented Canada 7 world championships; gold (45-49) '94, gold, silver (50-54) '98, bronze men's 40-54 gold '98 World Masters Games; editor *Orienteering Canada* '76-80; dir. COF from '77; mem. intl' Orienteering Federation Council '80; mem. Nepean Wall of Fame; res. Nepean, Ont.

HUNTER, Jim (skiing); b. 30 May 1953, Shaunavon, Sask.; given name: James Mark; m. Gail Jespersen; c. Anna, Heidi, Maria, Gail, Sterling; motivational speaker; nicknamed "Jungle Jim"; mem. ntl team '70-77; mem. '72, '76 Olympic teams, bronze combined '72; 6 ntl GS titles; US GS title '72; WC record 0-1-1; pro circuit '77-81; 3ʳᵈ in world pro ranks '77-78, 4ᵗʰ '78-79; author, film script writer; subject of NFB film *The Sword of the Lord*; with Marshall Shelley wrote *Man Against the Mountain*; TV color commentator '84 Winter Olympics; mem. Cdn, US Ski halls of fame; res. Calgary, Alta.

HUNTER, Malcolm (skiing); b. 23 May 1950, London, Eng.; given name: Malcolm Wesley; m. Theo Palmer; c. Shawn, Chelsea; Carleton, BA; chartered accountant; sports exec.; x-country specialist; ntl jr. title '68; sr. 15km '69-70, 30km '71; mem. '70 world Nordic ski championships, '72 Olympic teams; dir. Ont. ski council '84; coach Ont., NWT '73-76; chair. Ont. Cross-Country '90-95; exec. dir. Cross-Country Canada '84-90, from '95; Ont. Special Achievement award; res. Manotick, Ont.

HUNTER, Rod (curling); b. 24 Aug 1943, Norwich, N.Y.; given name: Roderick George McLean; m. Patricia Gail Karman; c. Onalee, Charlene; UWpg, BSc; corporate secretary; 3ʳᵈ for Don Duguid '70-71 Man. Consols, Brier, Silver Broom (world) title rink; 3ʳᵈ on '73, skip '75 Man. Brier entry; *CBC-TV* curling series winner '70-72, runnerup '76; '70 Heather carspiel, International Crystal Trophy Zurich, Switzerland; Man. bonspiel grand aggregate '70, '75; Man. Open '78; 4 times Man. bonspiel Birks Trophy winner; mem. Man. Sports, Canadian Curling halls of fame; res. Edmonton, Alta.

HUNTLEY, Gordon (horse racing); b. 6 Nov 1919, Queensville, Ont.; d. 25 Jul 1998, Toronto, Ont.; m. Phyllis; c. Lynn; horse trainer; became interested in horses '44 moving to California to hone his skills; returned to Toronto late '40s to train more than 1000 race winners including Ramblin Road which dominated Ont. racing scene '63-64 winning Grey, Vandal, Bison City, Seaway Stakes and Silver Ship winner of Victoria, Bison City, Friar Rock, Queenston Stakes during '50s; mem. Cdn Horse Racing Hall of Fame.

HUOT, Benoit (swimming); b. 24 Jan 1984, Longueuil, Que.; student, Home Depot; born with "club foot"; extensive surgery and therapy has improved condition; an avid swimmer he tried out and made ntl team '98; building massive collection of international honors including 6 world titles, 14 world championship medals, 10 world records; 3 gold, 3silver '00 Paralympics; 5 gold, 1 silver, 3 world records '04 Paralympics; Commonwealth male elite athlete with disability '03; Swimming Canada swimmer of '03 award; res. Longueuil, Que.

HUOT, Jean-Pierre (shooting); b. 21 Oct 1951, Thetford-Mines, Que.; m. Johanne Beaulieu; c. Stephanie, Cyndia, Amélie; Thetford-Mines Coll, BA (psychology); florist; handgun specialist; shot recreationally several years before going competitive at 35; mem. ntl team '85-99; 3 ntl free-pistol, 5 ntl men's air pistol, 3 Crossman ntl indoor titles; competed 5 world championships, 15 World Cups, 2 Championship of Americas; air pistol gold, air pistol pairs (with John Rochon) silver '94, 2 bronze '98 CG; free team gold '91, team air bronze '95 PAG; ntl air pistol record 581; Que. Shooting Fed. athlete of '95; special ambassador Thetford-Mines 100ᵗʰ anniversary; res. Pontbriand, Que.

HUOT, Jules (golf); b. 7 Jan 1908, Boischatel, Que.; d. 2 Feb 1999, Montreal, Que.; m. Simone Bolduc; c. Louise, Jeannine, Lucie, Robert; 1ˢᵗ Canadian to win USPGA sanctioned tournament '37 General Brock Open Fonthill, Ont.; among Canada's premier tournament golfers '30s-50s; 3 CPGA titles, 4 times runnerup; 5 QPGA, 3 Que. Open titles; twice top Canadian Cdn. Open; played inaugural Masters Tournament, 2 others; mem. 4 ntl Hopkins Cup teams; club pro Lake St. Joseph, Kent, Laval sur le Lac clubs; pres. CPGA '39, '46; pres. QPGA '67-68; wrote book *Le Golf*; mem. RCGA, Canada's Sports halls of fame.

HUPP, Howie (baseball); b. 18 May 1936, Neudorf, Sask.; m. Heather Hammel; c. Cathy, Darren; salesman Johnson & Johnson; rhp Ont. champion Kitchener Jr. Dodgers, Waterloo Jr. Siskins, Kitchener Sr. Panthers '58-66; 2ⁿᵈ team Senior Intercounty all-star '62; Sr. IC record: 69 games, 375.1ip, 22-21, 341h, 168r, 120bb, 239so, 2.79era; played hockey with Galt (OHA Sr.) Hornets; 5yrs scout Detroit Tigers; res. Kitchener, Ont.

HURD, Alex (speed skating); b. 21 Jul 1910, Montreal, Que.; d. 28 May 1982, Tampa, Fla.; m. Maxine Lieberstein (d); c. Alexis, Pamela; business exec.; Ont. title '26; ntl 1 mile outdoor titles '29-30; NA 5 mile titles '30-31, 3 indoor titles; world record 10,000m. silver 1500m, bronze 500m '32 Olympics; mid-Atlantic Joseph Donaghue 3-mile trophy '33; 2 St. Louis silver skate titles; international outdoor title '34; world indoor 2 mile record '35; world 500m backwards race record 55.3; pro International Ice Follies '38-40, NY Radio City Music Hall ice show '41-43; mem. Canadian Speed Skating Hall of Fame.

HURDIS, John (speed skating); b. 27 Apr 1927, Birmingham, Eng.; m. Mary Kathleen Powell; c. Lynda, Janette, John; ret'd asst. dir. professional development services; club skater '43 Eng., South Africa '47; secty. National Ice Racing League of National Skating Assn. of Great Britain; GBNSA judge '49-50; instrumental in formation Grenadier Toronto, Sertoma Kitchener clubs; sec.-tres. Ont. Amateur Speed Skating Assn. '61-64; v-p Cdn. Amateur Speed Skating Assn. '62-64, exec.-sec. '64-67, pres. '64-69, '72-76, dir. '69-70, '72-78, '80-82; co-ordinator several Cdn indoor, outdoor title meets, Barrie Winter Carnival '60-65; mem. COA '72-78, governor National Sports, Recreation Centre '74-76, Sports Ont. dir. '69-71; major role in upgrading, organizing sport; mem. ISU short-track tech. comm. '77-80, chair. '80-84; editor *The Racer*, Canada's official speed skating publication; editor Ont. *Skater's Edge* journal; author variety of articles, books on speed skating; Centennial Medal '67, Queen's Silver Jubilee Medal '78; life mem. Birmingham Ice Racing Club, US amateur Skating Union; hon. mem. ISU; historian, chair. CASSA Hall of Fame committee '79-82; managing editor, production mgr. *The Short Trackers*, international short-track speed skating newspaper; mem. Cdn Amateur Speed Skating Hall of Fame; res. Mississauga, Ont.

HURLEY, Bill (cycling); b. 8 Nov 1967, Halifax, N.S.; given name: William Joseph; m. Annie Létourneau; UofOtt, Intl MBA, St. Mary's, BComm; cyclist/entrepreneur; '97 ntl cyclocross champion; twice world masters champion; '01 Pan -Am mountain-bike champion; '02 Canada Cup series champion; numerous provincial titles; represented Canada 11 world championships (mountain-bike and cyclocross); over 50 intl race wins; has done more than 400 days of racing over 16yrs; active sport builder from '87: public relations and marketing, athlete development; developed numerous cycling teams in Canada and Europe; mem. West Quebec Wheelers Cycling Club; twice athlete of year; res. Chelsea, Que.

HUSHAGEN, Earle (curling); b. 27 Jan 1928, Lampman, Sask.; given name: Donald Earle; m. Wyn Elliott; c. Sandra, Christine, Signe; ret'd mgr. Humber Highland CC; 2nd Andy Grant's Ont. Brier entry '55; skipped Ont. entry ntl mixed '67, '70, Ont. entry ntl srs '84, '86; ntl srs. title '86; 2 Ont. Masters titles; major bonspiel titles include Toronto Royals, Whitby, Canada Life; active in administration OCA; hon. life mem. OCA; res. Peterborough, Ont.

HUSHAGEN, Sandra (curling); b. 15 Jul 1953, Toronto, Ont.; m. Randy Baker; c. Eric; Guelph, Wilfrid Laurier, MBA; mgr. business dev. London Health Sciences Centre; gained early repute in track as hurdler; 2nd 100m hurdles Eastern Cdn championships '72; competed Ont dressage championships '81-82; skipped Ont. jr. women's title rinks '72-73; Ont. business women's SOLCA title rink '82; competed at provincial level in women's, mixed events; made Ont. curling history as first female skip at provincial mixed championships '86, placed 3rd; skipped rink '90 Ont. STOH championships; renewed interest in equestrian sport '97; res. Sparta, Ont.

HUTCHINS, Jack (t&f); b. 8 Jun 1926, Vancouver, B.C.; given name: John William; m. Joan Kappel (d); c. Judith, Jill, Jaffrey; Oregon, BSc; ret'd Sears manager; runner; ntl 880yds titles '46-47, '51 (shared Cdn record with Bill Parnell), 440yd '51 (Cdn open/BC native record); won 800m, 2nd 1500m '48 Olympic trials; competed '48, '52 Olympics, '50 (880yd silver), '54 BEG; mem. B.E. 2-mile relay team vs. US '48, '52 (silver); won mile run titles Oregon AAU championships '49 (Oregon record), BC '49, Northern Div. Pacfic Coast Conf '50; silver Compton Relays '50; 440yd gold '50 BC Caledonian Games (BC record), '50 Victoria Highland Games, '51 BC police; 880yd gold '50 Victoria Highland, PC North Div., '51 BC police, Victoria Y, '52 PC Conf, '52 NCAA 800m; undefeated in local meets mile & 880yd '52; Cdn record '51 Olympic Club 1500m; all-American '51-52; Dr. Jack Davies award '48; Oregon Emerald Award '52; AAU outstanding-Canadian-t&f-athlete award '52; res. West Vancouver, B.C.

HUTCHISON, Jim (speedboat racing); b. 10 May 1909, England; d. 1 Jan 1995, Vancouver, B.C.; given name: James Hay; built enviable competitive record over 2 decades; racing his Teasers, broke every record, regularly out-performing European, US rivals '46-64; set 3 Cdn 1-mile class records '52-54; 1st Cdn to design, build, race 3-point hydroplane; instrumental in popularizing hydroplane racing in BC; won 4 consecutive Pacific Northwest Gold Cups, '55 Challenge Cup, Western Canada high-point awards '55-56; ret'd from competition '64 but continued to design/build hydroplanes; designed, built legendary "War Canoe" which won '70 US ntl power boat title; mem. BC Sports Hall of Fame.

HUTCHISON, Patti (all-around); b. 11 Oct 1958, Lockeport, N.S.; given name: Patti Lynne Langille; m. Archibald Hutchison; c. Wendy Elaine; Acadia, Dalhousie, BPhE, Public Administration; Miss Murphy's Business Coll, hons medical secty. diploma; Sports History dev. co-ordinator NS Sport Hall of Fame & Museum; 2 NS AA HS basketball, soccer titles; 3 Lockeport HS female athlete-of-yr awards; 2 AUAA all-conf. all-star; Acadia basketball MVP '77; capt. NS Canada Games bronze medal team; CIAU silver with Dalhousie; capt. NS Red Fox ntl women's title team '81; played sr. women's basketball '81-96; mem. Dalhousie women's team '96-97 setting 3 AUAA records; mem. 9 NS touch football title teams; 4 MVP awards; 2 Sport NS football player-of-yr awards; mem. NS jr. field hockey teams '73-75, NS sr. team at ntls '76, NS masters at ntls '97; HS softball '73-76, NS champions '74-75; Amherst NS slow pitch title team '94; res. Halifax, N.S.

HUTTON, Bouse (hockey/football/lacrosse); b. 24 Oct. 1877, Ottawa, Ont.; d. 27 Oct 1962, Ottawa, Ont.; given name: John Bower; goal hockey, lacrosse, fb football; mem. 3 ntl title teams '07 (Minto Cup, Grey Cup, Stanley Cup); lacrosse Ottawa Capitals, won Minto Cup, toured Eng.; Rough Riders, Silver Seven; Ottawa int. hockey champions '98-99; Silver Seven 6 seasons posting 2.90 goals-against avg. in 36 games; registered league's only 2 shutouts '01-02 season; allowed 28 goals 12 playoff games; helped Silver Seven win 2 Stanley Cups; coach jr., sr. hockey Ottawa several years; mem. Ottawa Sports, Hockey halls of fame.

HUTTON, Ralph (swimming); b. 6 Mar 1948, Ocean Falls, B.C.; div. Karen Morison; c. Kyle, Courtney; m. Robin Russell; Colorado State, Foothills College; policeman; nicknamed "Iron Man"; freestyle, backstroke specialist; 32 ntl records, world mark 4:06.5 700m FS; mem. '64, '68, '72 Olympic, '63, '67, '71 PAG, '66, '70 CG teams; won medals in all but '64, '72 Olympics, record 12 CG medals; best showing '66 CG 1 gold, 5 silver, 2 bronze, '67 PAG 1 gold, 5 silver; silver 400m FS '68 Olympics; total 24 medals in intl games greatest ever by Cdn athlete in any sport; 5 Beatty, 3 ntl high-point awards; masters competitor; mem. International, BC Swimming, Cdn Aquatic, Cdn Olympic, BC, Canada's Sports halls of fame; res. Lion's Bay, B.C.

HY, Patricia (tennis); b. 22 Aug 1965, Phnom Penh, Kampuchea; m. Yves Boulais; Bradenton Academy, UCLA; pres./owner Simply Soft Inc.; tennis pro; all-American; mem. Hong Kong Federation Cup team '81-82, '85, '87, Olympic team '84; ranked #1 Hong Kong '87-88, Canada '92-96; best WTA ranking 28th '93; Cdn citizen from '91; ended Helen Kelesi's 4yr Cdn title reign '91; 4 Tennis Canada female player-of-yr awards, comeback player of '91; mem. Cdn Fed. Cup team from '91; led Canada to Fed. Cup victory over Italy '95; recorded victories over Jennifer Capriati, Helena Sukova, Jana Novotna, Magdalena Makeeva, Katerina Maleeva, Helen Kelesi; Wimbledon jr. doubles title (with Patty Fendick) '83; 4 ntl singles titles; mem. WTA Special Olympics comm.; mem. '92, '96 Olympic teams; mem. Cdn Tennis Hall of Fame; res. Richmond Hill, Ont./Hilton Head, S.C.

HYLAND, Bruce (figure skating/coaching); b. 7 Jun 1926, Toronto, Ont.; given name: Bruce Leonard; m. Margaret

Wilson Roberts; c. Jacquelyn, Douglas, Michael; coach, rink owner; competitive swimmer; roller skating champion; with partners Margaret Roberts, Joyce Perkins won ntl sr. ice dance, 2nd in pairs; produced numerous roller, ice skating shows; weekly *Hyland and Sports* TV show in Toronto; introduced power skating for hockey players at Tam O'Shanter hockey school; started Professional Skating Assn. of Canada with Sheldon Galbraith, Helmut May, Osborne Coulson; coached such Cdn skaters as Maria/Otto Jelinek, Debbi Wilkes/Guy Revell to Olympic/world honors 18yrs; broadcast international skating competitions for Cdn radio; joined Ice Capades organization San Diego as coach '77; remained 7yrs before purchasing rink in Clearwater, Fla. where he and his wife teach skating; mem. Cdn Figure Skating Hall of Fame; res. Clearwater, Fla.

HYLAND, Harry (hockey); b. 2 Jan 1889, Montreal, Que.; d. 8 Aug 1969, Montreal, Que.; m. Anna Harvey (d); early hockey Montreal Gaelics, St. Ann's, Shamrocks; pro with latter '08-09 although still jr. age; scored twice 1st pro game; joined Wanderers in time to play rw on Stanley Cup winner; New Westminster (PCHL) '11-12 16 goals 12 games as team won league title; rejoined Wanderers '13 scoring 8 goals in game vs Que. 28 for season; joined Ottawa '18; mem. Hockey Hall of Fame.

HYLAND, Margaret (figure skating/coaching); b. 21 Mar 1923, Toronto; given name: Margaret Wilson Roberts; m. Bruce Leonard Hyland; c. Jacquelyn, Douglas, Michael; coach, rink owner; with Peter Killam runnerup ntl jr. pairs; with Bruce Hyland runnerup ntl sr. pairs, won ntl sr. ice dance '47; over 18yr span coached the likes of Maria/Otto Jelinek, Debbi Wilkes/Guy Revell and numerous other skaters to world/Olympic honors; joined Ice Capades in San Diego as coach 7yrs before purchasing rink in Clearwater; with husband Bruce mem. Cdn Figure Skating Hall of Fame; res. Clearwater, Fla.

HYNDUIK, Ollie (bowling); b. 8 Nov 1928, Winnipeg, Man.; as teenager gained prominence as CUAC senior women's softball catcher; switched attention to 5-pin bowling; won ntl women's singles crowns '55, '58; from '54-64 won 5 City of Winnipeg women's singles titles; '53-62 held top women's average 8 seasons capped by 256 avg '58-59; rolled perfect 450 game '52; coached Winnipeg to world women's team title '73; 10yrs head bowling pro Winnipeg Winter Club; Man. Order of Buffalo award '73; mem. Man. 5-Pin, Man. Sports halls of fame; res. Dundas, Ont.

I

IACOVELLI, Orlando (wrestling); b. 7 Dec 1939, Ithaca, N.Y.; m. Helen Okros; c. Sheila, David; Ithaca Coll. BSc, MSc, Iowa State; self-employed/landlord; asst. coach Ithaca HS '87-88, head coach '88-91; supervisor men's intercollegiate athletics, wrestling coach '65-86 Guelph; asst. football coach Guelph; coached Guelph to 12 OUAA wrestling titles; dir. Ont. Wrestling School '71-82, 3 ntl titles; ntl team coach 4 world championships, '76 Olympics; v-p CAWA '72-74, acting pres. '72-73; meet dir. 2 CIAU x-country championships; instituted ntl wrestling coaches clinics; mem. OAWF '68-72; 2 OUAA coach of yr, ntl wrestling title '69; CIAU coach of '76; wrestling all-American '64; mem. Ithaca Coll, Guelph, Cdn Amateur Wrestling, NY State Section IV Athletic halls of fame; res. Ithaca, N.Y.

IGALI, Daniel (wrestling); b. 3 Feb 1974, Eniwari, Bayelsa State, Nigeria; given name: Baraladei Daniel; Douglas Coll., SFU, BA; youth ambassador CAWA '01-03; grew up wrestling which was part of village culture; as part of large family (21 children) had no shortage of wrestling opponents; began freestyle wrestling '90 winning 1st ntl title; competed in 1st African championships '93; won '94 62kg title; attended CG in Canada '94 and decided to remain in Canada; under coaches Dave Mckay and Mike Jones won 116 consec. matches; placed 4th '98 Worlds, disputed 2nd '98 World Cup; PAG bronze '99; claimed 1st world title '99; CG 74kg gold '02; Cdn flag-bearer '02 CG; Lou Marsh trophy 2000, 2 Norton Crowe awards; mem. B.C., Burnaby Sports Hall of Fame; res. Burnaby, B.C.

IGINLA, Jarome (hockey); b. 1 Jul 1977, Edmonton, Alta.; rw St. Albert jr. '91-93; Kamloops (WHL) '93-96; WHL player-of-yr award; WHL West, Cdn Major Jr. 1st all-star teams; 2 Memorial Cup winners; Memorial Cup George Parsons Trophy; 1st pick Dallas '95 draft; dealt to Calgary '95; NHL Calgary '96-04; capt. Flames '03-04; scored 52g '01-02 season; NHL record: (through '04) 626 scheduled games, 250g, 253a, 28 playoff games, 14g, 10a; NHL all-rookie team '97; world jr. gold '94, '96, most-outstanding-forward award; mem. Team Canada '92 ntl jr., '97 worlds (gold); Olympic gold '02; *Sporting News* player of '02; 1 Ross, 2 Richard, 1 Pearson trophies, 2 Molson Cup, Scurfield Humanitarian awards; played 1 NHL all-star game; Farjestad, Sweden, during '04-05 labor dispute; res. St. Albert, Alta.

IGOROV, Metodi (shooting); b. 11 Mar 1959, Sofia, Bulgaria; m. Kamelia Igorova; c. Christina; Quebec BSc, Coll. Edouard Montpetit; corrections officer; rapid-fire pistol specialist; 3 Bulgarian, 1 Balkans Games, 1 French Cup, 7 Quebec, 3 Cdn championships; 2 Cap-de-la-Madeleine grand aggregate titles; 1 Bouche-du-Rh™ne, 1 C™te d'Azur France titles; set Cdn record '96; won gold medal and set rapid-fire record '98 CG; also added CG silver in centre-fire pairs with John Rochon; gold 25m rapid-fire pistol '02 CG; res. St. Laurent, Que.

IKEDA, Richard (gymnastics): b. 26 Nov 1974, Kamloops, B.C.; Fraser Valley Coll.; began competing age 9; both parents

were ntl level gymnasts; all-around competitor; competed '96, '04 Olympics, '91, '95, '99 PAG, '94, '98, '02 CG; '93, '01 FISU Games, '93 Worlds, '93 world gymnastics challenge; 1 ntl jr, 6 ntl sr titles; 1 gold, 1 silver, 2 bronze '94, 2 silver, 1 bronze '98, team silver '02 CG; 2 bronze '95. team bronze '99 PAG; '99, '00 Elite Can. Gold; Gymnastics Fed. athlete of '93; father Mits ntl team coach; res. Abbotsford, B.C.

ILESIC, Hank (football); b. 17 Sep 1959, Edmonton, Alta.; given name: Henry; m. Jeri Fedunec; advertising/printing business; punter Eskimos while still high school student '77-81, Argos '82-93; Ti-Cats '95; signed by San Diego, Los Angeles (NFL) '90 but released before playing any league games; 8 all-CFL, 4 all-WFC, 4 all-EFC; 6 CFL punting average titles; 9 Grey Cup finals, 7 winners; CFL record 9 singles on kickoffs, Argos team scoring record 159 points '84; 22 Argos records; CFL record: 256g, 98cvts, 59fg, 183s, 2049 punts, 91,753yds, 44.8 avg; res. Islington, Ont.

IMLACH, Punch (hockey); b. 15 Mar 1918, Toronto, Ont.; d. 1 Dec 1987, Toronto, Ont.; given name: George; m. Dorothy; c. Brent, Marlene; hockey executive; Young Rangers Jrs, Toronto Marlboros, Toronto Goodyears srs.; earned name "Punch" with Goodyears when he was knocked out in a game and swung punches at his team trainer; led army team scorers 1 season as ctr; brief trial Detroit (NHL) following WW2; 11yrs player, coach, mgr., eventually part-owner, Que. Aces; joined Bruins organization 1yr mgr.-coach Springfield Indians; mgr.-coach Maple Leafs '58-69, 4 Stanley Cups; sports columnist 5 seasons *Toronto Telegram, Toronto Sun;* coach/ GM Buffalo '70-78; GM Toronto '80-81; mem. Hockey Hall of Fame.

INGALDSON, Fred (basketball); b. 9 Feb 1932, Winnipeg, Man.; given name: Fred Einer; m. Jane Gray; c. Kris; Montana State, BSc; owner/operator wholesale vending corp.; HS standout, team capt., top scorer; mem. Harlem touring team; coach jr. varsity city champs; mem. Winnipeg Light Infantry ntl jr. title team '52; Man. Jr. all-star, MVP award, leading scorer; HS athlete-of-'52 award; 1st Cdn awarded basketball scholarship to major university (Montana State) '52-56; also offered McGill basketball/ football scholarship; 4yrs varsity 1st string; 2 MVP awards; 3 NAIA titles; Morgen award; 2 all-conference; named in *Who's Who in American Universities;* rookie of yr, capt. St. Vital Bulldogs '57; mem. Tillsonburg Livingstons '58-60; 1 Eastern, 1 ntl titles; playing-coach, capt., top scorer; named to ntl team for '58 worlds, '59 Pan-Am Games, '60 Olympics; leading scorer, MVP, all-star Winnipeg Carling title team '61; playing-coach, top scorer IPAC sr. men's team '62-64; 2 Western Cdn titles; mem. '60 Olympic team; capt., all-star St. Andrews team '65-72; silver Que. Winter games '66; sr. A MVP '67; mem. '67 Pan-Am team; perennial all-star, frequent league, tournament MVP; ntl men's sr. title team; asst. coach Manitoba Bisons, coach ntl team Cuba tour; basketball rep at numerous sports award functions in Manitoba; Ukranian athlete of '68; Mike Spack award for contribution to basketball in Man.; Order of

Buffalo Hunt achievement award; 5yrs *CBC* basketball color commentator; instructor basketball; athletic versatility saw him play soccer 20yrs in sr, div; mem. '52 ntl jr. title team; St, Vital sr. ntl football, champs, HS all-star; competed in curling, t&f; mem. Man., Cdn, Tillsonburg Basketball, Man. Sports halls of fame; res. Winnipeg, Man.

INGARFIELD, Earl (hockey); b. 25 Oct 1934, Lethbridge, Alta; given name: Earl Thompson; m. Grace Nelson; c. Rae-Ann, Jean Marie, Earl Jr.; hockey scout; ctr Lethbridge jrs; NHL NYR '58-67, Pittsburgh '67-68, Oakland '68-70, California '70-71; NHL record: 746 scheduled games, 179g, 226a, 21 playoff games, 9g, 8a; coached Regina Pats Jr. 1yr; interim coach NYI '72-73 (record: 30 games, 6-22-2); owner/AGM/coach Lethbridge Broncos 3yrs; Western scout Islanders '72-75, from '82; res. Lethbridge, Alta.

INNES, Cam (coaching); b. 30 Sep 1946, Windsor, Ont.; given name: William Campbell; m. Lynda Quinton; c. James; Queen's, BA, BPHE, Windsor, MPhE, UWO, MBA; dir. people management RLG International; twice OUAA all-conf. ctr, once all-Cdn; 1st round draft Edmonton Eskimos; 5 seasons, 4 head coach, St.FX, head coach UofOtt '78-81; asst. coach UWO '82-83, 2 conference titlist, 1 OQIFC, Atlantic Bowl champion, 1 College Bowl finalist; Atlantic Conference coach of '77, OQIFC coach of '79-80, CIAU coach of '80; mem. CFL-CIAU liaison comm.; mem. CAFA rules comm.; pres. CIAU Football Coaches Assn. '81-82; ex-marketing dir. UCal; Churchill Bowl chair. '95; res. Burnaby, B.C.

INNES, Marjorie (sailing); b. 11 Jan 1947, Hamilton, Ont.; given name: Marjorie Newton; m. Derek Innes; c. Greg, Sandra; UWO, BPHE, Queen's Teachers College, Fanshawe College; respiratory therapist; lone women competing in male field won 4 ntl Hobie Cat titles; 1st woman to qualify for Hobie Cat world championships '75; also competed '79, '81, '86 worlds placing 3rd in field of 36 in '81; with son Greg, Sue Slocum won 3 consecutive ntl Dart 18 catamaran titles; won 3 solo Dart 18 titles; crewed for husband Derek for '95 ntl Dart title; athlete-of-yr honors in both public/high school, competing in badminton, curling, tennis; taught phys ed '66-69 Dorchester HS; res. London, Ont.

INNIS, Jessie (basketball); b. 16 Jan 1911, Edmonton, Alta.; d. 7 Aug 1987, Edmonton, Alta.; m. Edward Maloney (d); c. William Edward; stenographer; mem. Edmonton Gradettes, famed Edmonton Grads '32-35; prov. runnerup silver div. golf; mem. Toddies baseball team; mem. Canadian Basketball, Alta. Sports halls of fame.

ION, Mickey (hockey/lacrosse); b. 25 Feb 1886, Paris, Ont.; d. 26 Oct 1964, Seattle, Wash.; given name: Frederick; standout lacrosse, baseball player in youth; pro lacrosse Toronto Tecumsehs, Vancouver, New Westminster; refereed amateur hockey, attracted attention of Frank Patrick who moved him into pro ranks '13; top official Pacific Coast League, NHL; refereed Howie Morenz Memorial game Montreal Forum '37; ret'd '41; mem. Hockey Hall of Fame.

IRELAND, Mike (speed skating); b. 1 Mar 1974, Winnipeg, Man.; UCal; long track specialist; competed '94, '02 Olympics; 3 WC silver, 3 bronze; world overall sprint title '01, runnerup '00; mem. Cdn Speed Skating Hall of Fame; res. Calgary, Alta.

IRELAND, Sean (speed skating): b. 14 Nov 1969, Mississauga, Ont.; UCal; coach Olympic Oval; mem. ntl team '88-94; competed '92, '94 Olympics; 2 ntl jr. records; 3 ntl. jr. long-track titles; 1 sr long-track, 2 sprint titles; mem. ntl team coaching staff; 4 PetroCan coaching-excellence awards; res. Calgary, Alta.

IRVIN, Dick Sr. (hockey/coaching); b. 19 Jul 1892, Limestone Ridge, Ont.; d. 16 May 1957, Montreal, Que.; given name: James Dickenson; m. Bertha Helen Bain; c. Dick Jr., Fay; Winnipeg Strathcona jrs., int. Monarchs; scored all 9 goals vs. Toronto in 9-1 Winnipeg victory, won 5 Man. scoring titles; mem. '15 Allan Cup winner; pro Portland Rosebuds (PCHL) '15-16; reinstated amateur Regina Vics after WW1; turned pro again Regina Caps (WCHL), Portland; when club became Chicago Black Hawks '26 went with them at age 34; in initial NHL season finished point behind Rangers' Bill Cook in scoring race; ret'd as player after skull fracture '27 season; coach Chicago '30-31; Toronto '32-40, Montreal '41-55; coaching innovator, 1st to rotate 3 intact lines, employ goalie shuttle system; coach 4 Stanley Cup winners; mem. Man., Cdn Hockey halls of fame.

IRWIN, Al (football); b. 16 Mar 1943, Toronto, Ont.; given name: Alan Lyness; div.; c. Thomas Alan, Jane Anne; McMaster, BA, UAlta, LLB; lawyer, real estate developer; mem. Richview CI TdIAA football titlist, Ont. t&f champions; football, varsity basketball McMaster; pro football 1st draft choice Alouettes, EFC rookie of '64; Toronto '66-68, Edmonton '69, Hamilton '70; end/db; scoring leader Toronto touch football champions '76; res. Willowdale, Ont.

IRWIN, Art (baseball); b. 14 Feb 1858, Toronto, Ont.; d. 16 Jul 1921, Atlantic Ocean,; given name: Arthur Albert; married; simultaneously had wives in Boston, New York, a fact revealed following his mysterious drowning death; ss Aetna 1873-74, Amateurs of Boston 1875-79; pro Worcester 1880-82, Providence 1883-85, Philadelphia 1886-89, 1894, Washington 1889, Boston 1890-91; 1010 ML games, .241 lifetime avg.; ss 1st "World Series" between Providence and New York Metropolitans 1884; playing mgr. Washington 1889, Boston 1891, Philadelphia 1894; non-playing mgr. Washington 1892, 1898-99, Philadelphia 1895, NY 1896; ML mgr. record: 416-427; inventor of infielder's glove 1885; soccer team mgr. 1894; owner Toronto IL team; scout Highlanders '08-12; brother John also played inf/of in majors; nicknamed "Doc", "Sandy", "Cut Rate".

IRWIN, Bert (skiing); b. 1 Oct 1917, Princeton, B.C.; given name: Albert Keith; m. Leila Margaret Colloton; c. Albert Richard "Bert", Marsha Leanne, Thomas Russel; ret. realtor; during '30s, '40s Class A competitor jumping, x-country, downhill, slalom; Western Cdn., Pacific Northwestern downhill, slalom titles; '47 Que. Kandahar, Cdn slalom; mem. '48 Olympic ski team; coach '50 women's World Cup team; awarded DFC WW2; res. Kelowna, B.C.

IRWIN, Cathy Lee (figure skating); b. 4 Sep 1952, Vancouver B.C.; m. Bruce Jacobs; Seneca College; figure skating teacher; ntl jr. singles '66; gold '67 Que. Winter Games; ladies' singles St.Gervais, France, Grand Prix '70; mem. '72 Olympic team; '72 Moscow Skate; competed '73 world pro with Holiday on Ice; Centennial medal '67; res. Toronto, Ont.

IRWIN, Dave (skiing); b. 12 Jul 1954, Fort William, Ont.; given name: David Benjamin; m. Lynne Harrison; c. Caitlin, Dean; SFU; self-employed; ntl team '71-82; World Cup downhill victory Dec. '75 Schladming, Austria; 8th '76, 11th '80 Olympics; US ntl title '80; WC record 1-0-1; Europa Cup gold '79; Thunder Bay athlete of '73, '75; Ont. athlete of '75; runnerup Cdn athlete of '75; flag-bearer '76 winter Olympics; certified Level 4 CSIA, Level 3 CSCF coach; dir. Masters ski camps; competed Golden Gate Productions ski events '97; dir. Fels Cdn Ski Co.; active in Legends ski competitions; seriously injured in skiing accident '01; nickname "Kamikaze Canuck"; 2 Gerald Ford American Ski Classic titles; mem. BC, NWO Sports, Cdn Skiing halls of fame; res.Canmore, Alta.

ISBISTER, Robert Jr. (football); b. 27 Oct 1914, Hamilton, Ont.; d. 19 Aug 1971, Hamilton, Ont.; m. Hazel Kroeber; c. Betty, Janet, Susan; UofT; noted for booming punts as kicking backfielder Delta CI, Toronto Varsity; mem. Argos '37-38; Eastern all-star '38; punted for 1167yds vs Ottawa 27 Nov '37, averaging 55.6 yds per punt.

ISBISTER, Robert Sr. (football); b. 9 Jun 1885, Hamilton, Ont.; d. 29 Apr 1963, Hamilton, Ont.; m. Madlan Grace Darling (d); c. Robert Jr. (d), Allan (d), Phillip, Donald; flying wing, various line positions Hamilton Tigers '05-19; cited for all-around ability '19; refereed intercollegiate ranks several years; pres. Big 4 '20; mem. Hamilton club board of governors '33; mem. Canada's Sports, Canadian Football halls of fame.

ISHOY, Mark (equestrian); b. 1 Apr 1955, Toronto, Ont.; m. Penny Tulk; c. Claire, Matthew; Guelph, hons. BSc; CEO MGI Packers, partner Maple Freezers, Banner Rendering; gained riding experience foxhunting in Caledon Hills; began showing horses at 18; mem. gold medal team FISU Games, NA jr. 3-day title team '75; open int. 3-day Eastern Canada title '77; Cdn international 3-day title, gold world 3-day '78; capt. 3-day event team '80 Olympics; coached Alta to NA Young Riders title '88; mem. Cdn Equestrian Team selection comm. '86-92; chair. 3-day event team '92-94; recipient '79 Dick Ellis Memorial Trophy; res. Rockwood, Ont.

ISSAJENKO, Angella (t&f); b. 28 Sep 1958, Jamaica; m. Tony Issajenko; c. Sacha, Natasha, Dimitri, Sophia; York; fitness trainer; mem. Scarborough Optimists TC; sprint specialist; '79 ntl 100m, 200m outdoor champion; Colgate Games meet record 400m (52.20) '80; 5th 100m, 200m WC '79, 4th '81; 12 ntl sr. records with best 100m (11.00), 200m (22.19), 4x100m relay (43.01); Cdn open 50m (6.18); silver 200m, bronze 100m '79 PAG; gold 100m, 4x400m relay, silver 4x100m relay, bronze 200m '82, gold 200, silver 4x100, bronze 100 '86 CG; silver 4x100 relay '84 Olympics; mem. '78 CG, '80, '84, '88 Olympic, '83 PAG teams; ntl outdoor 100m, 200m champion '79-82, 100 '88; indoor 50m '80-81, 200m '83; Ont. athlete of '80; SFC female athlete of year; CIAU female athlete of '81; 2 CIAU indoor records; outstanding female athlete '82 ntl sr. championships; 2 Velma Springstead trophies; Ont., fed. govt. excellence awards '83; mem. Order of Canada; res. Toronto, Ont.

ITO, Don (water skiing); b. 16 Aug 1937, Ocean Falls, B.C.; given name: Donald Masato; div.; c. Donald Chadwick, Kimberley Dawn; ret'd construction, spool manufacturing;

won 6 drag racing trophies '62-63; barefoot water skier in '60s; introduced to kite flying skiing in early '60s he became dominant force in that sport winning 10 tricks gold, 1 silver, 7 slalom gold, 1 silver, 8 overall gold, 2 silver, 1 bronze in international competition '66-72; he so dominated US flyers that they restricted participation to US citizens from '71; he taught many young hopefuls the art but interest in that phase of sport waned dramatically in '70s; competed in Cdn Oldtimers Hockey in '80s; mem. Belleville Sports Hall of Fame; res. Baltimore, Ont.

IUS, Chris (boxing); b. 14 Jan 1954, Vancouver, B.C.; given name: Christopher Anthony; m. Patricia Scanlon; c. Natalie; carpenter; competitive boxer '61-76 at weights from 50lb-119lb; Emerald Gloves titles '62-66, '68-70; Wash. State Jr. Golden Gloves title '65; BC Tournament of Champions titles '67, '69; Pacific Northwestern title '67; Pacific Coast Jr. title '69; Western Cdn jr. titles '67, '70; Silver Gloves champion '68-69; national sr. titles '70-73, '76; BC '71, Vancouver '72, Tacoma '71, Portland '76 Golden Gloves titles; BC Winter Games title '71; BC senior titles '71-72; Western Cdn. titles '71, '75-76; silver '71 NA championships; bronze '71 Scandinavian Tour; silver '72 Holland International; silver '73 European championships; silver '75 AAU Internationals; mem. '72, '76 Olympic teams; Emerald Award '68-70; Jimmy Syme Memorial Award '70-72; North Vancouver amateur athlete of '73; res. Maple Ridge, B.C.

IVAN, Tommy (hockey/coaching); b. 31 Jan 1911, Toronto, Ont.; d. 24 Jun 1999, Lake Forest, Ill; m. Dorothy (d); ret'd hockey exec; coach Omaha Knights (USHL) '45-46, Indianapolis (AHL) '46-47, Detroit '47-54; guided Wings to 6 consecutive NHL titles (Prince of Wales Trophy), 3 Stanley Cups in 7 seasons; GM Black Hawks '54-77, credited with building Hawks into strong club through farm system; under his management Hawks won 1 Stanley Cup, 6 division titles; responsible for many NHL rule changes; pioneered in tapping college ranks for talent; co-mgr. team USA '76 Canada Cup series; v-p, asst. to pres., v-p/alternate governor Black Hawks '77-98; NHL coaching record: 610 scheduled games, 302 wins, 196 losses, 112 ties, .587 percentage, 67 playoff games, 36w, 31l, .537 percentage; Lester Patrick Award '75; *Hockey News/Itech* King Clancy Memorial award '94; chair. US Hockey Hall of Fame; mem. Hockey Hall of Fame selection comm.; mem. Hockey Hall of Fame.

IVES, Charles (squash); b. 10 Nov 1915, London, Eng.; given name: Charles William; m. Mollie Irene Beard; c. Barbara; squash pro; began career as ball boy at Queen's Club, London; jr. pro age 18; moved to Canada '33 as teaching pro Winnipeg Winter Club; Carleton Club pro from '77; Cdn Queen's Jubilee medal; hon. citizen of Winnipeg '84; Manitoba Squash Assn bronze plaque; Cdn Squash Racquets Assn distinguished service award; mem. Man. Sports Hall of Fame; res. Winnipeg, Man.

IVORY, Clifford (football); b. 1 Aug 1975, Thomasville, Ga; Troy State; db/wr; drafted by NFL San Diego; played with Scottish Claymores NFL Europe '99; CFL Hamilton '00-01, Toronto '02-04; 2 East Div, CFL all-star; 1 Grey Cup winner; res. Toronto, Ont.

IVY, Pop (football/coaching); b. 25 Jan 1916, Norman, Okla; d. 19 May 2003, Norman, Okla; given name: Frank;

UOkla; ret'd football coach; end/kicker, all-American UO '39; played NFL Pittsburgh '40, AFL Chicago Cardinals '40-47; launched coaching career as asst to Bud Wilkinson UOkla ('50 ntl title); head coach Edmonton Eskimos '54-57 winning consec. Grey Cups '54-56; 4yrs head coach Chicago Cardinals, 2yrs Houston Oilers; lifetime coaching record 82-56-2, 12-5 in playoffs; asst. coach/scout NY Giants; ret'd '84; renowned as offensive innovator; only man to serve as head coach in NFL, AFL and CFL.

J

JACKART, Dan (rugby); b. 4 May 1960, Natal, B.C.; m. Trudy Hopman; UBC Langara Coll.; firefighter; mem. UBC Old Boys RC; made intl debut '91 vs. Japan; standout tight head '91 World Cup; mem. '92 Cdn team in CANZ series; ret'd '96; res. New Westminster, B.C.

JACKES, Arthur (t&f); b. 26 Jun 1924, Toronto, Ont. given name: Arthur Mortimer; m. Charlotte Haultain; c. Norman, Rosemary, Malcolm, Hugh; UofT, BSc; ret'd; hj champion '48-49; mem. '48 Olympic (6th), '50 BEG teams; US citizen '56; res. Greenbank, Wash.

JACKS, Sam (ringette); b. 23 Apr 1915, Scotland; d. 14 May 1975, North Bay, Ont.; given name: Samuel Perry; m. Agnes McKrell; c. Barry, Bruce, Brian; NB rec. dir.; an innovator who began recreation career in Toronto '35; organized Toronto Boys' Club; 1st North Bay rec. dir. '48; developed game of floor hockey and wrote initial rules '36; developed 1st NO playground HA; coached ntl jr. Olympic floor hockey bronze medal team; asst. dir. Toronto West End YMCA '34-40; conceived game of ringette '63 and refined rules '65; presented Sam Jacks Trophy to winning Tween A champion West Ferris in 1st Ladies Recreational Ringette tournament; pres. Ont. society municipal rec. directors '63; Ont. achievement award '71; outstanding contribution and dedication to recreation citation; fellowship American Institute of Park exec., Ont. Society Municipal rec. dirs.; mem. North Bay, Ringette Canada halls of fame.

JACKSON, Busher (hockey); b. 19 Jan 1911, Toronto, Ont.; d. 25 Jun 1966, Toronto, Ont. given name; Harvey; Toronto Marlboros jrs., pro Maple Leafs '30-39; with Charlie Conacher, Joe Primeau formed original Kid Line; mem. 3 league champions, 1 Stanley Cup winner; 4 times 1st, once 2nd team all-star; NHL scoring leader '32-33; NY '39-42, Boston '42-44; NHL record: 633 scheduled games, 241 goals, 234 assists, 72 playoff games, 18 goals, 12 assists; mem. Canada's Sports, Hockey halls of fame.

JACKSON, Don (archery); b. 25 Oct 1932, Lindsay, Ont.; given name: Donald Arthur; m. Rose Ann Coulas; c. Nancy; archery business operator; self-taught archer, began shooting '65, ntl field archery title '66; runnerup field, target grand aggregate '67; ntl, Ont. indoor, 9th world target '67; Ont. indoor, ntl target, field, aggregate '68-69, 6th world field, 9th target; ntl target, runnerup field '70; Ont. indoor '70-71; 6th '72 Olympics; numerous ntl records; pro '73-80; reinstated amateur, '80 ntl field, Ont. target, field titles; '81 Ont. indoor, '82 Ont., ntl indoor; res. Lindsay, Ont.

JACKSON, Donald (figure skating); b. 2 Apr 1940, Oshawa, Ont; div. Joanne Diercks; c. Donald Jr., Derek, Michael, Jeannine, Stephanie; m. Barbara Fryer; sc. Rosalie, Richard; exec.-dir. Minto Skating Club; 5 ntl, 2 NA, 1 world title '55-62; bronze '60 Olympics; 1st skater ever to perform triple lutz in competition Prague '62; pro Ice Follies '62-68; world pro champion '70; 1st to execute arms-folded triple salchow ('77), a feat filmed for UK TV show *Record*

Breakers; from '78 has marketed Jackson skating products; Minto Club rink bears his name; Lou Marsh Trophy '62; mem. Order of Canada, US Figure Skating, Cdn Olympic, Ont. Legends, Canada's Sports halls of fame; res. Nepean, Ont.

JACKSON, Glen (football); b. 5 Apr 1954, Vancouver, B.C.; m. Barbara; c. Tessa, Marguax; SFU, BA; Dist. 1, all-Northwest all-star '73-75; ranked as one of finest SFU products ever; territorial protection BC; lb Lions from '76; noted for durability, never missing game; ranked high among CFL interception ranks; 6 times WFC all-star; B.C. Lions Wall of Fame; res. Vancouver, B.C.

JACKSON, Linda (cycling): b. 13 Nov 1958, Montreal, Que.; m. Kevin Deierling; UWO, hons BA, Stanford, MBA; CFO San Francisco internet co.; competitive swimmer in youth before dropping out of sport for 15yrs during which she carved out a highly lucrative business career as v-p investment banking; despite an opportunity for highly-paid job she opted to pursue her dream as a top-flight competitive cyclist at 32; bronze medals in Cdn road race championships '92-93 led to ntl team, 6 titles; competed on '93 European tour; standout on '94 European tour including 5th women's Tour de France; 3rd overall California Tour of Redlands, tour of NZ; silver 93.6km women's road race '94, 28km road race '98 CG; competed '95 PAG, '96 Olympics; won '97 Tour de L'Aude, ntl time trial, road racing titles; 3rd '97 women's Tour de France; runnerup Tour of Italy '97-98; won Hewlett-Packard International women's challenge '98; with Gord Fraser co-winner '95 Ottawa ACT athlete of yr; NA, ACT cyclist award '97; Cdn female cyclist of '97; ret'd from competition '00; mem. Nepean Sports Wall of Fame; res. Los Altos Hill, Calif.

JACKSON, Roger (rowing/administration); b. 14 Jan 1942, Toronto, Ont.; given name: Roger Charles; m. Linda; c. Christopher, Alex, Geoffry; UWO BA, UBC, MPhE, Wisconsin, PhD; ex-dean faculty of PE UCal; mem. '60-63 university ntl rowing 8s champions; with George Hungerford gold pairs '64 Olympics; with R. Fieldwalter '65 Scandinavian pairs; flag-bearer, finalist single sculls '68 Olympics; mem. '72 Olympic team; dir. Sport Canada '76-78, co-ordinated '76 Olympics Game Plan; v-p COA '81-82, pres. '82-90; chairman advisory board Calgary Olympic Development Assoc.; founder/dir. UCal sports medicine clinic; special advisor UCal Raising our Sights academic plan; gov. Olympic Trust; with Hungerford, Lou Marsh Trophy '64; hon. life mem. Cdn Gymnastics Fed.; Officer Order of Canada '84; mem. Cdn Olympic, Canada's Sports halls of fame; res. Calgary, Alta.

JACKSON, Rose Ann (archery); b. 15 Jun 1952, Barry's Bay, Ont; given name: Rose Ann Coulas; m. Don Jackson; c. Nancy; medical laboratory tech.; ntl indoor women's amateur champion '79-82; outdoor women's amateur unlimited target field, aggregate champion '79-81; 19 open, 14 closed ntl amateur women's records; tied professional men's 60m, 30m, records, men's amateur unlimited hunter record; 1st woman in Canada to break 1300 of possible 1440 points barrier in FITA round; PB: 1322; topped 1300 points 3 times; res. Lindsay, Ont.

JACKSON, Russ (football); b. 28 Jul 1936, Hamilton, Ont.; given name: Russell Stanley; m. Lois Hendershot; c. Kevin, Suzanne, Nancy; McMaster, BSc; ret'd HS principal/educational consultant; Sr. IC baseball Hamilton; pro football Ottawa '58-69, starting qb from '63; CFL record: completed 1341 of 2511 passes for 23,341yds, 125 intercepted, 184tds; led EFC passers 6 times; carried 738 times for 5045yds, 6.6yd avg., scored 55tds, 330 pts; 4 Grey Cup finals, 3 winners; 3 Schenley outstanding-player awards, 4 top Canadian; 2 Jeff Russel Memorial Trophy; Lou Marsh Trophy '69; 2 Lionel Conacher awards; CFL commissioner's award '04; coached Toronto '75-76; TV color commentator several seasons; CIAU student-athlete annual award bears his name; educational consultant Missisauga Ice Dogs '98; *SI* Cdn athlete of century list; Officer Order of Canada; mem. Ottawa, McMaster, Ont. Sports Legends; Canada's Sports, Cdn Football halls of fame; res. Burlington, Ont.

JACOBS, Dave (skiing); b. 1 Oct 1933, Montreal, Que.; given name: David Lloyd; div.; c. Bernard, William, Kelly, Tracey; m. Susan Hellie; c. Lara; St. Lawrence, B S., MIT; corporate exec.; jr, B hockey player; won Que. Kandahar '56; ntl downhill champion '57; mem. ntl team '57-61; Val David ski school dir. '62-63; designer/mgr. Talisman ski area '63; head coach ntl alpine team '64-67; sr. mem. Cdn. Ski Instructors Assn; mem. National Coaches Assn.; 2nd '80 veterans super 40 World Cup slalom, GS, downhill, combined; mem. Cdn, Colorado. Laurentian Skiing halls of fame; res. Boulder, Colo.

JACOBS, Jack (football); b. 1920, Holdenville, Okla.; d. 12 Jan 1974, North Greensboro, N.C.; Oklahoma; nicknamed "Indian Jack"; NFL Cleveland Rams, Washington, Green Bay; led NFL punters with Packers '47; qb Winnipeg '50-54; CFL record: 709 of 1330 passes for 11,094yds, 41.0 avg, 104tds, 57 singles; prolific passer, completed 31 of 48 vs. Hamilton '53; 6 td passes vs. Calgary '52; scout Bombers '55; coach London Lords (ORFU) 2 seasons; asst. Hamilton, Montreal, Edmonton; Jeff Nicklin Memorial Trophy (MVP) '52; twice Grey Cup finalist; twice all-star; mem. Canadian Football Hall of Fame.

JACOBSEN, George (equestrian/skiing); b. 20 Sep 1912, Vienna, Austria; d. 28 Sep 1994, Montreal, Que.; m. Peggy McCulloch; McGill, DSc, Zurich, PEng, Clermont (France); arctic consultant; jr. ski jump, downhill competitor '28-33; equestrian jumping, dressage competitor '28-50; CdM '56 Olympic team; joint master Lake of Two Mountains Hunt '58-94; pres. Cdn Horse Show Assn, which became Cdn. Equestrian Fed. '63-76; chair. CEF '77-84, hon. chair. to death; international equestrian dressage, jumping judge; mem. executive FEI; dir. COA, American Equestrian Federation; dir. Sir Edmund Hillary Foundation; mem. Order of Canada; recipient Royal Swedish Olympic Medal; CEF gold medal; CEF equestrian-of-yr trophy bears his name.

JAMANI, Aysha (soccer); b. 28 Jun 1987, Calgary, Alta.; forward heralded as budding superstar while appearing in

5 CONCACAF Olympic qualifying matches '04; made ntl -19 debut '04 China Four Nations tourney; 7 intl caps; 14 goals in 15 intl games; mem. Edmonton Aviators W-League '04; res. Calgary, Alta.

JAMES, Angela (hockey); b. 22 Dec 1964, Thornhill, Ont.; rec. co-ordinator Seneca Coll; mem. '91, '93 sr ntl champion Toronto Aeros; 3 COWHL all-star, MVP '91, 3 scoring titles; mem. 4 Team Canada world champions; 3 world all-star; top player award '94; Pacific Rim, 3-Nations Cup gold; Level IV official, intermediate hockey coach; participated world roller hockey championships winning gold '93, silver '94; ret'd from competition '00; res. Thornhill, Ont.

JAMES, Eddie (football); b. 30 Sep 1907, Winnipeg, Man.; d. 26 Dec 1958, Winnipeg, Man.; given name: Edwin; m. Moria Kathleen FitzGerald; c. Don, Gerry; nicknamed "Dynamite"; hb/db Winnipeg, Regina Pats, Winnipeg St. John's, Regina Roughriders through '20s, early '30s; trophy in his honor awarded annually to WFC leading rusher; charter mem. Canadian Football Hall of Fame.

JAMES, Gerry (football/hockey); b. 22 Oct 1934, Regina, Sask; given name: Gerald Edwin; m. Margaret Petrie; c. Debra, Tracy, Tara, Kelly, Brady; ret'd hockey exec., hotelier, storekeeper, property mgr; HS football to youngest in CFL at 17; CFL Winnipeg, Sask. '52-64; 63tds, 143cvts, 40fg, 21s for 645pts; 995 carries for 5554yds (5.6yd avg), 57tds; twice rushed for 1000+ yds single season; record for tds scored rushing with 18 '57; scored 1 other on pass same season to tie Pat Abbruzzi; twice Dave Dryburgh Trophy as WFC scoring leader, once runnerup; twice WFC all-star; twice Schenley top Canadian award; offered contract by NY Giants (NFL); at 16 mem. Winnipeg Monarchs '51 Memorial Cup finalists; Toronto Marlboros '55 Memorial Cup champions; rw Maple Leafs '54-59; 149 scheduled games, 14g, 26a, 15 playoff games, 1g; competed in 2 major ntl finals within 6 months '59 Grey Cup, '60 Stanley Cup; mem. 6 Grey Cup finalists, 4 winners; coached in Switzerland '63-64; owner/coach/player Yorkton Terriers, Sask. Jr. HL (Tier 2) '66-69, 4 consec. Sask. titles; coached 3 all-star teams; 2 coach-of-yr awards; coached SJHL, WHL teams 19yrs; 2 Sask. titles; 7 all-star coach awards; organized/coached Weyburn Special Olympics floor hockey team; nickmaned "Kid Dynamite"; election to Canadian Football Hall of Fame provided grid shrine with (Eddie "Dynamite" James) 1st father-son combination; mem. Cdn Football, Man., Blue Bombers, Sask, Yorkton Sports halls of fame; res. Nanoose Bay, B.C.

JAMES, Jeff (harness racing): b. 17 Jan 1952, Brantford, Ont.; Guelph; while studying to become veterinarian decided to pursue racing from sulky seat '75; driving debut with 2nd place in Matron Stakes; one of most consistent drivers on Michigan main circuit from '80 winning 4466 races for purses totalling $18M through '97; posted 11-race win streak with Jerry's Cadet '95; res. Farmington Hills, MI.

JANI, Louis (judo): b. 6 Dec 1957, Montreal, Que.; m.; Sport Canada consultant; 6 ntl 86kg titles; PAG gold '79, '83; 3 Que. Open gold; gold Pan-Am championships, Canada Cup, East Coast; silver US Open, Pacific Rim, Kano Cup, German, Paris championships; 16 ntl, intl bronze; competed '80, '84, '88 Olympics, '79, '83 PAG,

'82, '84 FISU Games, '79, '83, '85 worlds; fed. govt. sport excellence award '84; res. Ottawa, Ont.

JANS, Edward (shooting); b. 17 Aug 1946, Medicine Hat, Alta.; m. Irene Roso; draftsman; began shooting as hobby '67; handgun specialist; mem. ntl team from '69; mem. '70, '80 worlds, '71, '75, '79 PAG, '72, '80 Olympics, '78 CC teams; bronze team free-pistol '75, '78 Benito Juarez International; silver team standard-fire '78 Benito Juarez; silver centre-fire, gold team free-pistol '79 PAG; free-pistol silver '78 CG; res. Calgary, Alta.

JANS, Melanie (squash); b. 3 Jul 1973, Montreal, Que.; UofT, BPHE; pro squash player; 5 ntl jr. titles; 3 ntl sr. titles in 4yrs; mem. 4 ntl women's teams; competed 2 jr., '92, '94 worlds; won '94 Barrie Pro-Am, Hi-Tec Curzons Classic; mem. '94 Pan-Am championships 2 silver medal team; 2 gold '95, '99, 2 silver '03 PAG; Petro-Can Olympic Torch scholarship '94; res. Georgetown, Ont.

JANSE, Roy (sailing): b. 4 Jun 1971, Edmonton, Alta.; Tornado class sailor; crew for skipper Marc Peers; former ntl judo team mem.; hooked up with Peers in HS; NA, Cdn championships '93; SPORT gold '96; competed '96 Olympic Games; Edmonton City salute-to-excellence award '94; res. Edmonton, Alta.

JANSSENS, Sandy (horseshoes); b. 9 Jul 1971, Wallaceburg, Ont.; given name: Sandy McLachlin; m. Dale Janssens; c. Britney; certified general accountant; 68 Ont. women's singles titles; runnerup ntl championships '87; several perfect games; set world record (since surpassed) for complete world tournament average 88.2% '87; world jr. women's title '86; only Cdn to win world women's title '87, 3 times runnerup; 3 consec. Silver Shoe titles; played at White House inauguration of George Bush Horseshoe Court '89; 5 Elmer Hohl Ringer Classics titles; mem. Intl. Horseshoe Players Assn. Hall of Fame; res. Wallaceburg, Ont.

JANUSKOVA, Eva (tennis); b. 27 May 1978, Tabor, Czechoslovakia; emigrated to Canada age 5; through '95 won 15 ntl indoor, outdoor, singles, doubles titles; ranked No. 1 Ont. -14 '90; mem. World Youth Cup -16 team '92; played Virginia satellite circuit '94; ntl -18 title '95; mem. Nepean Sports Wall of Fame; res. Nepean, Ont./Montreal, Que.

JANZEN, Henry (football); b. 7 Jun 1940, Winnipeg, Man.; m. Judy Munro; c. Dean, Joanne; North Dakota, BSc, Northern Colorado, MA, PhD; dean of men, AD UMan.; Blue Bombers '59-65; Dr. Beattie Martin Trophy as WFC rookie of year; outstanding Canadian Winnipeg '62, '65; all-Cdn '65; 3 Grey Cup winners; led WFC in punt return yards 394, best avg. runback 7.3yds; coached UMan. Bisons to College Bowl championship '69-70; CIAU coach of '69; res. Winnipeg, Man.

JARDIN, Anne (swimming); b. 26 Jul 1959, Montreal, Que.; given name: Anne Elizabeth; m. Jim Alexander; c. Kevin, Ian, Claire; Houston, BPhE, BSc; tech. program co-ordinator CASA '82-89; freestyle (FS), butterfly specialist; ntl team '74-81; gold 4x100 FS relay '74 CG; silver 4x100 FS relay, bronze 200m FS '75 PAG; bronze 4x100 FS relay

'75 world championships; bronze 4x100 FS, 4x100 medley relays '76 Olympics; silver 4x100 FS relay '79 PAG; mem. '80 Olympic team; asst. mgr. '84 Olympic swim team; PB: 100m FS 56.75, 200m FS 2:02.5, 400m FS 4:20; mem. Houston swim team; Gov.-Gen.'s silver medal '76; mem. Que. Swimming, Sports halls of fame; res. Ottawa, Ont.

JARVIS, Doug (hockey); b. 24 Mar 1955, Brantford, Ont,; m. Linda; c. Laura, Landry; hockey coach; ctr Brantford (OJHL) '71-72, Peterborough (OHA) jrs '72-75; drafted by Toronto '75 then dealt to Montreal where he played '75-82; Washington '82-85, Hartford '85-87; NHL record: 964 scheduled games, 139g, 264a, 105 playoff games, 14g, 27a; mem. 4 Stanley Cup winners; Selke trophy '84, Masterton trophy '87; established NHL record of playing 962 consec. regular season games; player/asst./head coach Binghamton (AHL) '87-88; asst. coach Minnesota, Dallas '88-02; head coach Hamilton (AHL) '03-05; asst. Cdn Spengler Cup team '03; res. Hamilton, Ont.

JASIAK, Andrew (shooting); b. 4 Jul 1962, Ottawa, Ont.; OPP officer; mem. numerous Ont. small-bore teams '81-86; '78 cadet Bisley team; '84, '96 Cdn Bisley teams; coach '85-86 cadet Bisley teams; runnerup DCRA grand agg. '95; mem. '85 Palma team; res. Smiths Falls, Ont.

JAUCH, Ray (football); b. 11 Feb 1938, Mendota, Ill.; m. Sarah; c. 4 sons; Iowa, BSc; football executive; mem. '59 Iowa Rose Bowl team; pro Winnipeg '60; turned to coaching after leg injury '61; coach Winnipeg jr. Rods '62, Iowa '64; asst. to Neill Armstrong Edmonton '66-69, head coach '70-76; Annis Stukus CFL coach-of-yr trophy '70, '80; guided Eskimos to WFC title '73-76, Grey Cup '75; mgr. football operations Edmonton '77; head coach Blue Bombers '78-82; guided Winnipeg to Western final '80, '82; coach USFL Washington Federals '83-84; commissioner Arena Football League; head coach St. AmbroseU '90; asst. Saskatchewan '91-93, head coach '94-95; CFL coaching record (including playoffs): 15 seasons, 134-107-4; res. Regina, Sask.

JELINEK, Maria (figure skating); b. 16 Nov 1942, Prague, Czechoslovakia; m. Paul Harrington; c. Mark, Michael, Matthew; Michigan; teamed with brother Otto in pairs competion (see Otto Jelinek for record); pro skater '63-69 Ice Capades; mem. Cdn Olympic, Cdn Figure Skating, Canada's Sports halls of fame; res. Toronto, Ont.

JELINEK, Otto (figure skating); b. 20 May 1940, Prague, Czechoslovakia; m. Leata; c. Misha, Jamie; Appelby College, Swiss Alpine Business College; pres. Jelinek International; ret'd politician, real estate broker, sporting goods mfr.; with sister Maria '55 ntl jr. pairs title; 3rd '57-58 world, 4th '59, 2nd '60; 4th '60 Olympic pairs; '61 NA, ntl pairs titles, '62 ntl senior, world pairs; pro skater Ice Capades '63-69; Lake Placid pro pairs title '64; MP (PC) for Halton '72-93; cabinet min. PC govt.; TV color analyst '84 Winter Olympics; dir. Sparta Prague hockey team; mem. Czech Olympic Assn.; mem. Cdn Olympic, Cdn Figure Skating, Canada's Sports halls of fame; res. Prague.

JELTKOV, Alexander (gymnastics); b. 25 Feb 1978, Tbilissi, Georgia; following year in Israel moved to Canada '90; mem. ntl team from '94; 4 gold, 4 silver '95 Grand Prairie Canada Games; 1 gold, 1 silver '96 jr. Pan-Am championships; competed '98 (high bar gold, team bronze), '02 (team silver, all-around, horizontal bars bronze) CG; high bar gold, individual silver, team bronze '99 PAG; 1 worlds silver, bronze; competed '00, '04 Olympics; 2 gold, 2 bronze '03 Elite Canada; res. Montreal, Que.

JENKINS, Bill (curling); b. 19 Feb 1957, Charlottetown, P.E.I.; given name: William Kenneth; m. Sheila Dianne Matheson; c. Lindsay Dianne; Dalhousie, UPEI, BA; asst. v-p W.F. Moreau & Associates; skip 3 prov. junior titles; ntl jr. title '76; ntl jr. player of '76; prov. Legion title '78; world jr. title '77, highest percentage ever in international competition final; Dick Ellis team award '77; mem. PEI Sports Hall of Fame; res. St. John's, Nfld.

JENKINS, Fergie (baseball); b. 13 Dec 1943, Chatham, Ont.; given name: Ferguson Arthur; div. Katherine Henson; c. Kelly, Delores, Kimberley; m. Maryanne (d); c. Samantha (d), Raymond; baseball exec.; ex-pitching coach; rhp; 1st pro contract '62 Philadelphia Phillies organization; 4 seasons in minors 43-26 record; Phillies '65-66, Chicago Cubs '66-73, '82-83, Texas '74-75, '78-81, Boston '76-77; ML record 284-226, 49sho, 3192k (6th all-time); 7 20-plus victory seasons, 6 in succession Cubs '67-72, 1 with Texas '74; only pitcher with more than 3000k, less than 1000bob; 4th pitcher in history with 100 or more victories in each league; 3 NL all-star teams; led ML pitchers in putouts with 363; NL Cy Young Award (24-13) Cubs '71; AL comeback player of '74 Texas (25-12); led NL 3 times, AL once complete games; tied ML record with 5 1-0 losses '68 season; 4 Lionel Conacher awards; Lou Marsh Trophy '74; 2yrs pitching coach Oklahoma City AAA, roving instructor Cincinnati organization '93-94, pitching coach Cubs '95-96; hon. capt. NL all-star game team '95; granted absolute discharge following drug charge conviction '80; pitched London Sr. IC '84; made unsuccessful bid for Ont. legislature seat; 1st Canadian elected to BBHOF; 1st commissioner Cdn Baseball League; mem. Order of Canada, Cdn Walk, Cdn, Major League Baseball, Chicago, Ont. Legends, Canada's Sports halls of fame; res. Anthem, Ariz.

JENKINS, Peter (curling); b. 19 Dec 1959, Charlottetown, P.E.I.; skip '77-79 PEI jr. title rinks; 2nd '80-81 PEI mixed title rinks; skip Alpine Super League, Charlottetown title rinks '81-82; mem. runnerup rink ntl mixed '80; skip '82 PEI Brier entry; res. Charlottetown, P.E.I.

JENKINS, Shorty (curling); b. 27 Sep 1935, Hanna, Alta.; given name: Clarence William; m. Johanna Elisabeth Geertje-Willemsen; c. Kitty, Kiet; golf course superintendent/ice maker, ret'd Cdn Forces; initial experience in golf club maintenance at Cold Lake, Alta., '59-62; greens-keeper Trenton Golf/Curling Club '68-76, Bay of Quinte Golf/Country Club '76-90, Kingston Cataraqui Golf/Country Club from '91; 28yrs mem. Cdn, 18yrs America, 19yrs Ont. Golf Course Superintendents Assn.; 5yrs mem. Ottawa Valley, 6yrs Ont. Turfgrass Assn.; began making curling ice '68; through '97-98 icemaker/consultant 3 Briers, 3 Scott Tournament of Hearts, 4 Worlds, 1 ntl juniors, 1 ntl mixed, 1 Olympic trials, 2 WCT VO Cups, 12 *TSN* Skins Games, 30 Ont. men's/women's/mixed/jr championships; icemaker Swiss tournament of champions, Las Vegas Desert 'spiel, Scottish jr., 9 Ottawa Classic/Welton Beauchamp and various other major bonspiels; Level III ice technician, Level I technical coach, 23yrs coaching various teams; has conducted ice-

making clinics throughout Canada/Scotland; served on exec. comm. for several OCA/OLCA competitions; life mem. Bay of Quinte GCC, Ennismore CC; 10 Labatt, 1 Ont., Las Vegas, Bay of Quinte GCC, OCA, Scott Paper Appreciation Awards; CCA Achievement Award; Ont. Tankard Sportsmanship trophy bears his name; mem. Cdn Curling Hall of Fame; res. Kingston, Ont.

JENSEN, Al (golf); b. 24 Jan 1938, Montreal, Que.; given name: Allan Howard; div; c. Allan Jr., Jim; m. Ann Darbyshire; c. Andrew Scott, Erin; ret'd golf pro, Cdn Forces; runnerup ntl asst. championships '75; won 4 pro tournaments '76, Earl Stimpson Shield for best overall tournament performance among Ottawa Valley pros '76, '78, '84; 3 competitive course records: 59 Poplar Grove, 70 Petawawa, 64 Hylands South course; Ottawa zone CPGA champion '78; 2 zone asst. titles; runnerup '88 ntl CPGA Seniors; 3 holes-in-1; son Allan Jr. Que. juv champion '78, Jim mem. Ont. jr. title curling rink '83; res. Ottawa, Ont.

JERANT, Martina (basketball); b. 30 Jan 1974, Windsor, Ont.; Brown, BA; centre Ivy League titlists '92-94; mem. ntl jr team '92, sr team from '93; bronze '93, gold '95 COPABA tournaments; competed '94 Goodwill, '94-95 Jones Cup, '95 FISU, '96 Olympic Games; pro Zagreb, Croatia; Brown freshman athlete of '92, Ivy League rookie of '92, IL player of '93; competed '94 NCAA tournament; res. Grosse Point, Mich.

JEROME, Harry (t&f); b. 30 Sep 1940, Prince Albert, Sask.; d. 7 Dec 1982, Vancouver, B.C.; given name: Henry Winston; div.; Oregon, BSc, MA; sports consultant; shared world record 10 seconds for 100m dash '60 with Germany's Armin Hary; tied world 100yd sprint record 9.3 Corvallis, Ore., '61; tied Bob Hayes' world record 9.1 Edmonton '66; '62 NCAA 220yd title in 20.8; anchored Oregon team that equaled world 440yd relay record of 40.00 on course with 2 turns; mem. '60, '64, '68 Olympic teams; bronze medal 100m in 10.1 '64; repeated time '68 but finished 7th; gold 100m '67 Winnipeg PAG in 10.2; held 6 world sprint records; for several years Sport Canada consultant; Officer Order of Canada; mem. Canadian Walk, BC, Cdn Olympic, Sask., Canada's Sports halls of fame.

JEROME, Valerie (t&f); b. 28 Apr 1944, St. Boniface, Man.; given name: Valerie Jerome; div. Ronald Parker; c. Stuart; UBC; teacher; ntl sr. 60m, 100m, long jump titles, mem. BC champion 4x100 relay team '59; relay bronze '59 PAG; mem. '60 Olympic, '66 CG; chief judge '76 Olympics; distance jumps referee '78 CG; PB: 100m 11.6 '68, 200m 24.2 '68, hj 1.55m '71, lj 5.64m '67, 100m hurdles 15.3 '73; BC Athletics longstanding service award; res. Vancouver, B.C.

JESPERSEN, Eric (sailing); b. 18 Oct 1961, Port Alberni, B.C.; m; c. Emma Elizabeth, Ross Campbell; boat builder; began competing at 12; mem. ntl team from '91; with Ross MacDonald became 1st all-Cdn team to win Star Worlds in 83yr history of class '94; Star class Olympic bronze '92; competed '96 Olympics; ntl titles '93-94; with MacDonald CYA male athlete of '94, Rolex Canadian sailor of '92; sister Julie mem. ntl rowing team; res. Sidney, B.C.

JESPERSEN, Julie (rowing); b. 18 Sep 1969, Sidney, B.C.; UVic, BSc; began rowing in HS; mem. ntl team from '88; 5

ntl, 2 US, 4 international regatta titles; gold straight 4s, silver straight pairs '91 PAG; spare '92 Olympic Games; World straight 4s bronze '93; brother Eric Olympic yachtsman; res. Sidney, B.C.

JEYASEELAN, Sonya (tennis); b. 24 Apr 1976, New Westminster, B.C.; tennis player; Cdn. Fed Cup team from '94; defeat of world #6 Venus Williams at Amelia Island '99 was biggest upset on WTA Tour in 2yrs (Sonya was qualifier ranked #140); scored another big upset '00 Grand Slam Wimbledon with career-best win over 4th ranked former champion Conchita Martinez to reach 3rd round; reached 3rd round of Australian Open '00; mem. '00 Olympic team; career-high ranking #48 in '00; 10-5 singles, 15-2 doubles record Fed Cup play; no Cdn. has won more Fed Cup doubles matches; 3 ITF Women's Circuit singles titles; 2 WTA Tour doubles titles; returned to Tour '02 after having surgery to remove tumours from behind her eyes; Tennis Canada Excellence Awards female player of '00, female doubles player of '01; res. Toronto, Ont.

JMAEFF, Peter (shooting); b. 31 Aug 1937, Regina, Sask.; m. Gladys; c. Leslie, Karen, Lisa; UofSask. BSc, MSc; mechanical engineer, systems dir. Sask. Medical Care Insurance Branch; full-bore specialist; mem. 5 Cdn Bisley teams; adjutant '83, team commandant '87, vice-commandant '90; SPRA Lieut.-Gov.'s title '75, grand aggregate '75, '92; SPRA pres. '75-85, small-bore pres. '88-92; Sask Sports Federation pres. '85; SFC dir. '82-92; CdM SFC Benito Juarez '90, Los Angeles '91; ISU International B official; jury mem. 2 world cups; res. Regina, Sask.

JOBIN, Marcel (t&f); b. 3 Jan 1942, Parent, Abitibi, Que.; m.; race walker; 13 ntl 20km, 1 30km titles; silver 30km '82 CG; gold 30km, silver 50km Marcel Jobin International races; mem. '71, '75, '79, '83 PAG, '76, '80, '84 Olympic, '78, '82 CG, '81 World Cup, '83 world championships teams; world indoor mile walk record 5:55.8 '79, NA, ntl 20km, ntl 5km, 10km records; ntl, CG 30km records; QTFF male athlete of '83; ret'd from competition '84; mem. Que. Sports Hall of Fame; res. St. Boniface, Que.

JOE, Peter (table tennis); b. 15 Dec 1959, Vancouver, B.C.; given name: Peter Gordon; UBC; ntl jr. title '76-77; BC champion '78-80; ranked ntl top 5 from '78; 3rd ntl men's singles '78-79, '81; extensive international experience with ntl team; res. Vancouver, B.C.

JOHL, Yogi (wrestling); b. 3 Jan 1970, Vancouver, B.C.; competes at 125kg level; wrestled internationally from '89; 2 ntl sr. Greco Roman, 1 sr. freestyle titles; competed '94 Francophone, '96 Olympic Games, '95 World championships; mem. Burnaby Mountain Wrestling Club; res. Vancouver, B.C.

JOHNSON, Ben (t&f); b. 30 Dec 1961, Jamaica; Centennial College; personal trainer; sprint specialist; 4 ntl 50m, 1 4x200m relay titles; mem. '82, '86 CG, '83 PAG, FISU, '84 Olympic Games teams; 2 gold, 1 bronze '86, 2 silver '82 CG, silver 4x100 relay '83 FISU Games, bronze 100m, 4x100m relay team '84 Olympics; ntl indoor 4x200m, ntl sr. 50m, 100m records; world indoor 60m record; earned world's fastest human title beating triple Olympic gold medalist Carl Lewis, world record holder Calvin Smith in

'86 Zurich race; PB 9.95 for 100m '86 in Moscow; won '85 World Cup 100m title; won '88 Olympic gold in Seoul with 9.79 run but failed steroid test and was stripped of Olympic gold and world record; suspended from competition 2 years and actions sparked Dubin Inquiry into drug use in sports, subsequent failed drug test led to lifetime suspension from t&f; turned attention briefly to soccer; became personal trainer for soccer star Diego Maradonna '97; 3 Norton Crowe, 2 Lionel Conacher, Lou Marsh trophies; mem. Order of Canada, Cdn Olympic Sports Hall of Fame; res. Toronto, Ont.

JOHNSON, Cari Lynne (shooting); b. 22 Feb 1977, Campbell River, B.C.; sales representative; first made ntl team '93; double bronze '91 Canada Winter Games; double gold, B.C. flag bearer '95 Canada Winter Games; 1st lady in air rifle/3-position rifle at ntl championships/Crossman Cdn GP air gun championships, '98-'01; 7th in air rifle '99 PAG; '00 Olympian; '02 CG bronze; shooting team mgr '03 Canada Winter Games; numerous prov., ntl awards in air , small-bore rifle '92-02; 2 Ed Shaske awards as top junior in all shooting sports; res. Campbell River, B.C.

JOHNSON, Ching (hockey); b. 7 Dec 1897, Winnipeg, Man.; d. 16 Jun 1979, Tacoma Park, Md.; given name: Ivan Wilfrid; d Winnipeg Monarchs '19; 3yrs Eveleth, Minn., Miners; 3yrs Minneapolis Millers; NYR '26-37, 2 Stanley Cups; NY Americans '37-38; continued to play in minors to age 46; player-coach Hollywood Wolves; Helms Award; NHL record: 463 scheduled games, 38g, 48a, 60 playoff games, 5g, 2a; represented Rangers 1st NHL all-star game '34; 3 times 1st team, twice 2nd team all-star; mem. Man., Cdn Hockey halls of fame.

JOHNSON, Chris (boxing); b. 8 Aug 1971, Manchester, Jamaica; middleweight; came to Canada '80; mem. Jamestown Amateur AC, coached by Arnie Boehm; mem. ntl team from '89; brother Greg also boxer; gold '89, '91 Canada Cup, '90 CG, '89, '90, '91 ntl championships; silver '91 PAG; bronze '90 Goodwill Games; mem. '92 Olympic team; res. Kitchener, Ont.

JOHNSON, Daisy (basketball); b. 16 Mar 1902, Jumping Pound, Alta.; d. Aug 1978, Edmonton, Alta.; given name: Margaret; Camrose Normal School; teacher; mem. famed Edmonton Grads '20-27; competed 1st ntl, international championships; sister Dorothy also mem. Grads; until death involved in compiling history, memorabilia of Grads; mem. Canadian Basketball, Alta. Sports halls of fame.

JOHNSON, Danny (harness racing): b. 11 Jan 1950, Windsor, Ont.; Windsor, BSc; broke into sport as groom with Greg Wright stables; won trainer titles at Hazel Park, Wolverine '76; shifted to Meadowlands adding trainer titles '77-79; won driving titles at Hazel Park, Windsor Raceway; driving Stir Fry won '88 US pacing championship; through '03 4392 victories with purses exceeding $20M; res. Windsor, Ont.

JOHNSON, Dave (swimming); b. 2 Aug 1951, Montreal, Que.; given name: David Michael; m. Wendy Quirk; c. Michael, Rosemary; swim coach; freestyler '70 FISU, '71 PAG; asst. coach '75 PAG, '76 Olympic teams; head coach women's swim team '78 CG, world championships; head coach men's team '79 PAG; Olympic team coach '76-04; head coach Pointe Claire SC '76-78, Edmonton SC from '78; 2 CIAU swim-coach-of-yr awards; res. Calgary, Alta.

JOHNSON, Don (t&f/skiing); b. 17 Aug 1942, Petrolia, Ont.; given name: Donald Hugh; m. Carole Cunningham; c. Michael, Christopher, Paul; Queen's, MD, FRCS (C), FACS; orthopedic surgeon, dir. Carleton sports medicine clinic; Jr. B hockey; competitor 30 marathons, 6 ultra marathons, 12 ntl ski marathons, '82 Hawaii Ironman, Western States 100 mile run '83; 5 Rideau Lakes cycle tours; 4 Liévre canoe marathons, 5 Colonel By triathlons; team physician Carleton, Sooners, Rough Riders football 10yrs, Senators hockey, ntl x-country ski, t&f team; medical officer '76 winter, summer Olympics; attempted Mt. Everest climb '81; initiated Don Johnson Fitness Awards; res. Nepean, Ont.

JOHNSON, Don (administration); b. 25 Mar 1930, Halifax, N.S.; given name: Donald Stewart; m. Florence Helen Harris; c. Peter, Michael, Cathy; St. Mary's College; ret'd civil servant; pres. '75-77, life mem. CAHA; pres. NAHA; commissioner Southern Shore HL; treas. Softball Nfld.; prov. delegate CASA; pres. St. John's Sr. SL; chair. carnival comm. St. John's Figure Skating Club; governor ntl YBC; commodore Terra Nova Yacht Club; dir. SFC; treas. Nfld., & Lab. Amateur Sports Fed.; hon. life mem. Softball Nfld.; dir. NSRC; chair. interprov. S&R Council; mem. Canada Games council; dir. Hockey Canada; hon. life mem. SFC; ADM Nfld. Parks, Rec. & Youth, dept. of culture, Rec. & Youth; mem. Nfld. & Lab. Sports Hall of Fame; res. St. John's, Nfld.

JOHNSON, Donnie (baseball); b. 8 Apr 1926, Marysville, N.B.; given name: Donald Walter; m. Mae; ret'd; Marysville Maroons NB jr. titlists '43; NB sr. titles Marysville Royals '47-48, '55; NB batting titles .443 '52, .415 '57; twice NBSBL all-star 3b; pro trial Brooklyn Dodgers Vero Beach camp '49; playing coach Marysville Royals '59; turned to umpiring '60; officiated NB sr finals '66, Canada Summer Games '69; coached Marysville bantams to Fredericton city crowns '78-79; mem. NB Baseball (charter), NB Sports halls of fame; res. Fredericton, N.B.

JOHNSON, Dorothy (basketball); b. 22 Jan 1906, Jumping Pound, Alta.; m. Ronald Sherlock; c. Elizabeth Ann; at 15 youngest mem. famed Edmonton Grads '21-27; mem. 1st ntl, international, world title teams; organized women's, mixed bowling leagues Vancouver; sister Daisy also mem. Grads; mem. Canadian Basketball, Alta. Sports halls of fame; res. Vancouver, B.C.

JOHNSON, Greg (boxing); b. 18 Oct 1967, Montreal, Que.; welterweight; gold '90, '91 ntl championships, '90 Indonesia President's Cup; silver '90 CG; res. Montreal, Que.

JOHNSON, Jenny (field hockey); b. 9 Jan 1979, Duncan, B.C.; given name: Jenny Elizabeth Zinkan-McGrade; m. Jeff Alan Johnson; UAlta, BPE/BEd (minor biology); teacher; competed for BC ntl championships from '91; mem. jr. ntl team '94, sr. ntl team '98; silver '97 jr. World Cup qualifier; mem. '98, '02 CG team; bronze '99 PAG; bronze '01 Americas Cup; 81 intl caps; '97 BC Sport's Hall of Fame; female HS athlete of yr; res. Duncan, B.C.

JOHNSON, Joey (wheelchair basketball); b. 26 Jul 1975, Winnipeg, Man.; given name: Joey Cameron; m. Mellissa Christina Dyson; c. Owen Elias; UWisc (Whitewater); pro athlete; became involved with wheelchair basketball at age 8; competed at sr. level from '83; mem. ntl team from '95; played for Winnipeg Thunder, Wollongong Hawks (Australia), RSL Lahn-Dill (Germany); competed '96, gold '00, '04 Paralympics; 2 World Cup bronze; 3 gold, 1 silver CWBL; 1 NWBA gold, 1 bronze; 1 NWBL gold; 2 X-Treme, 1 Blister Bowl gold; 1 ntl gold, silver, 2 bronze; 7 all-star teams; 7 MVP awards; res. Lorette, Man./Giessen, Germany.

JOHNSON, Julia (table tennis); b. 28 Aug 1963, Montreal, Que.; given name: Julia Carol; Carleton.; from '74 earned string of age-group titles including Montreal Open '75-76, Que. Open '76, '81, Toronto Open '77-78, '80, Ont. Open '77-78, '81, Ont. Closed '77-78; ntl jr. '77, '79-81; Eastern US Open -15, -17 singles, doubles; gold medal team Canada vs US jr. tournament '79; jr. miss singles CNE '80; most improved jr. award '81; mem. ntl team from '81; res. Brampton, Ont.

JOHNSON, Marian (swimming); b. 6 Dec 1954, Montreal, Que.; given name: Marian Lee Stuart; m.Thomas Francis Johnson; c. Matthew, Hailey, Mark, Tracy; McGill, BEd; swim coach; Olympic trials gold in 100m, 200m breaststroke resulted in participation in '72 Olympics; also '73, '75 worlds; gold 4x100 medley relay, silver 100m breaststroke '74, gold 4x100 MR, bronze 100m breaststroke '78 CG; bronze 100m breaststroke '75 PAG; gold 100m breaststroke '77 FISU Games; res. Delta, B.C.

JOHNSON, Moose (hockey); b. 1886 Montreal, Que.; d. 25 Mar 1963, White Rock, B.C.; given name: Ernest; lw/def Montreal MAAA '02-03; pro Montreal Wanderers; mem. 4 Stanley Cup winners; New Westminster Royals '12; 11yrs PCL with Portland, Victoria Maroons, Los Angeles, 123 goals, 270 games; all-star 10 consecutive years; PCL staged special Moose Johnson night in his honor; mem. Hockey Hall of Fame.

JOHNSON, Tom (hockey); b. 18 Feb 1928, Baldur, Man.; given name: Thomas Christian; m. Doris; c. Tom, Julie; hockey exec.; Winnipeg jr. Monarchs '45, Montreal sr. Royals '47; '48-50 Buffalo (AHL); def. Montreal Canadiens '50-63; Boston Bruins '63-65; NHL record: 978 scheduled games, 51 goals, 213 assists, 111 playoff games, 8 goals, 15 assists; mem. 6 Stanley Cup winners; 1st team all-star '59, 2nd team '56; Norris Trophy (top NHL def) '59; coached Boston to 1st Prince of Wales trophy in 30 years '70-71, repeated '71-72 winning Stanley Cup; asst. GM/v-p '73-89; v-p from '89; mem. AHL, Man. Sports, Hockey halls of fame; res. Concord, Mass.

JOHNSON, Tom (swimming/coaching); b. 2 Aug 1951, Montreal, Que.; given name: Thomas Francis; m. Marian Lee Stuart; c. Matthew, Haylee, Mark, Tracy; McGill BComm; swim coach Pacific Dolphins, UBC; Olympic coach '80, '84, '88, '92, '96; CG coach '78, '82, '86, '90, '94, '98; PAG swim coach '75, '79, '83, '87; coached 4 world championships; BC swim-coach-of-yr awards '92-98; 5 CIAU coach-of-yr awards; Omega coach of yr '97; 3 PetroCan coaching excellence award; res. Delta, B.C.

JOHNSON, William (football); b. 4 Dec 1964, Munroe, La.; Northeast Louisiana; drafted by Chicago (NFL) '87-88, New Orleans '89, Calgary from '89; 5 Western, CFL, 1 Northern all-star, Norm Fieldgate trophy '91; led CFL qb sacks '91 with 16; CFL record: (through '95) 115g, 251 def. tackles, 90 qb sacks; mem. 3 Grey Cup finals, 1 winner; res. Calgary, Alta.

JOHNSTON, Bob (rowing); b. 6 Apr 1868, Charlottetown, P.E.I.; d. 9 Aug 1951, Vancouver, B.C.; considered greatest sculler Vancouver Rowing Club, Pacific Northwest ever had; moved west '88, began rowing '89; dominated rowing scene winning BC, Pacific Coast, ntl sculling titles; as pro '98 lost world title to Jake Gaudaur Sr.; coached by legendary Ned Hanlon; turned to coaching mid-'20s, developed dynasty of excellent oarsmen; coached Ned Pratt, Noel de Mille to '32 Olympic bronze pairs medal; always coached from rowing float, never coach boat; several years VRC dir.; hon. v-p VRC; mem. BC Sports halls of fame.

JOHNSTON, Cynthia (basketball): b. 11 Oct 1968, Calgary, Alta.; Bishop's, BA, SAIT (photo journalism); forward Bishop's '86-91, 2 CIAU ntl championship tournament appearances; mem. NB silver medal team '94 Francophone Games; bronze medal team '85 Canada Games; mem. ntl jr team '85-86, sr team '87-99; competed '87, '91 FISU, '90 Goodwill, '91 PAG, '94 World, '96 Olympic Games; COPABA bronze '93, gold '95; pro Belgium '92-96, Switzerland '97; HS athlete of '86; Bishop's female athlete of '88-91; Que. university female athlete of yr twice; won -14 NB tennis singles title; res. Calgary, Alta.

JOHNSTON, Ed (hockey); b. 24 Nov 1935, Montreal, Que.; given name: Edward Joseph; m. Diane; c. Michele, E. J. Jr., Joseph; hockey exec.; goaltender Johnstown Jets (EHL) '56-57; minor pro Winnipeg, Edmonton, Spokane, Shawinigan, Los Angeles, Hull-Ottawa '57-62; NHL Boston '62-73, Toronto '73-74, St. Louis '74-77, Chicago '77-78; NHL playing record: 592 scheduled games, 234-257-81, 34,216min, 1855ga, 32so, 18 playoff games, 7-10-0, 1023min, 57ga, 1so; last NHL goalie to play every minute of a season, 70g '63-64; mem. 2 Stanley Cup winners; made coaching debut New Brunswick (AHL) '78-79; head coach Chicago (NHL) '79-80, 1 div. title; head coach Pittsburgh '80-83, '93-97; GM Pittsburgh '83-88, AGM '88-89, '97-99; GM Hartford '89-92; EPHL leading-goalie award, record 11so '60-61 season; res. South Hills (Pittsburgh), Pa.

JOHNSTON, John (golf); b. 19 May 1925, Vancouver, B.C.; m. Elizabeth; c. Gregory, John, David; ret'd real estate salesman; '53 New Westminster, '59 Canadian amateur beating Gary Cowan one up; Mexican amateur, Penticton Open, BC Open '67; mem. '67 Commonwealth team; 6 times BC Willingdon Cup team mem.; 4 times America's Cup team; mem. BC Sports Hall of Fame; res. Vancouver, B.C.

JOHNSTON, Marshall (hockey/administration); b. 6 Jun 1941, Birch Hills, Sask.; m. Barbara; c. Jill, Amy; Denver; hockey exec.; jr. SJHL Prince Albert '57-59; UDenver '59-63; Team Canada '63-68; SSHL Winnipeg '65; OHA sr. Ottawa '67; pro NHL Minnesota '68-71, California '71-74; AHL Cleveland, CHL Iowa "68-71; Eddie Shore AHL def. award '71; AHL all-star '71; competed '64, '68 (bronze) Olympics; 3 IIHF worlds; asst. coach Canada '78

worlds, head coach '79, '82 worlds; coached Team USA inaugural IIHL world jr. championships; coach California Golden Seals '74-75; head coach Denver 4yrs, WCHA title, coach-of-yr. award; AGM, interim coach Colorado Rockies '81-82; dir. player personnel NJ '83-93; 2yrs ED CIPRO (hockey scouting group); scout NYI '95-96; dir. player personnel, GM Ottawa Senators '96-02; dir. player evaluation Chicago Black Hawks '02-03; mem. IIHF Hall of Fame; res. Chicago, Ill.

JOHNSTON, Percy (speed skating); b. 21 Feb 1903, Orillia, Ont.; d. 24 Jul 1988, Oshawa, Ont.; given name: Henry Percy; m. Kathleen; c. Carl, Aileen; maintenance engineer; began collecting mass of medals '16 at Kitchener Winter carnival; 4 Ont. indoor, 1 outdoor titles; ntl outdoor title '28; NA indoor '29; NA indoor 3/4 mile, 3 mile, 5 mile US records; mem. Cdn Speed Skating Hall of Fame.

JOHNSTONE, Charlie (all-around); b. 10 Aug 1873, Montreal, Que.; d. 25 Jan 1945, Winnipeg, Man. first reached prominence in lacrosse; cover point for 90th Lacrosse Club '91-95; named to all-Winnipeg team which played world champion Montreal Shamrocks '95; hockey rover '97-1902 Winnipeg Victorias; '02 Stanley Cup winner; rowing crew mem. '96 Minneapolis International regatta; singles champion American, Cdn ntl regattas; won singles, doubles '97 American ntl regatta; '01-03 mem. victorious crews US ntl regattas; capt./coach Winnipeg Rowing Club '03-07; coached sr crews in '30s; won 7 American sweep oar championships, feat equalled only by Conrad Riley; accomplished curler, gymnast; mem. Man. Sports Hall of Fame.

JOHNSTONE, Chris (football); b. 12 Dec 1963, Kingston, Jamaica; Bakersfield Jr. Coll.; rb, joined CFL as free agent Edmonton '86-92, Winnipeg '93-95; 1 Eastern all-star; mem. 4 Grey Cup finalists, 1 winner; res. Winnipeg, Man.

JOHNSTONE, Lori (racquetball); b. 14 Oct 1967, Oromocto N.B.; given name: Lori Anne; m. Jean Pierre Cantin; c. Melina; Concordia, BA, specialization in applied social science; Ecole de langue Française et de culture Québécoise, UQuébec à Chicoutimi, intensive French immersion program; UCal, UofOtt; sport administrator; helped set up the Ntl Sport Centre (Atlantic Canada) '99 as their first athlete services manager; special advisor Secretary of State for Amateur Sport, '99-01; racquetball primary sport from age 13; also competed in volleyball and athletics (high school level, 4A provincials); '82 Alberta Winter Games gold at 14; Alberta prov. champ, women's open singles and doubles '88-89; ntl team '89-91 espoir, '91-96 sr.; placed 1st/2nd in singles and/or doubles at roughly 30 tournaments in Canada and US; team silver '91 World Cup Challenge; serious ankle injury '94 ntls and three weeks later long-term injury to right elbow led to corrective surgery/rehabilitation; competed left-handed while in rehabilitation for right elbow/left ankle and won singles, femmes A '94 Quebec provs; placed 4th '95 ntls (women's A); retd from ntl team '96 due to ongoing problems with right elbow; Racquetball Canada's athlete rep, '93-96; chair. ntl team comm.'98-99; dir. Athletes CAN '94-99, v-chair. '95-97), chair. '97-99); mem. COA's Athletes Council, '97-99; named one of most influential women in sport by CAAWS '00; named by *Globe & Mail* one of Cdn sport's top 10 "Behind the Scenes" leaders '00; Johnny F. Bassett Memorial

Award '01; Ivan Velan Award, Racquetball Canada's most prestigious award, '01; mem. Oromocto & Area Sports Wall of Fame; res. Waterville-Sunbury County, N.B.

JOLIAT, Aurel (hockey); b. 29 Aug 1901, Ottawa, Ont.; d. 2 Jun 1986, Ottawa, Ont.; given name: Aurel Emile; m. Berthe (d), m. Yvette; sc. Nicole, Luc, Maurice Emard; railway employee; kicking fb New Edinburgh (Ottawa), Rough Riders, Regina Wascana Boat Club before turning to hockey; mem. New Edinburgh, Iroquois Falls, Saskatoon Sheiks; acquired by Canadiens for Newsy Lalonde '22; lw for Canadiens to '38 retirement; nicknamed "Mighty Atom", "Little Giant"; 270 goals over 16 NHL seasons; mem. 3 Stanley Cup winners; Hart trophy '34; 1st all-star team once, 2nd team 3 times; active mem. Ottawa Old Pros '80-85; mem. Ottawa, Canada's Sports, Hockey halls of fame.

JOLIN, Yvon Jr. (barrel jumping); b. 30 Apr 1958, Montreal; Hydro-Quebec employee; world indoor champion '80-86, '88-91; Canadian champion '80-86, '88-'90; 2 world records: clearing 18 barrels and distance of 28'6"; listed in *Guiness Book of Records*; instrumental in bid to make barrel jumping an Olympic sport; mem. US National Winter Sports Hall of Fame; res. Le Guardeur, Que.

JONAS, Don (football); b. 3 Dec 1938, Scranton, Pa.; given name: Donald Walter; m. Rosemary Eisman; c. Jaudon, Jennifer; Penn State, BSc; ret'd sales rep.; football coach; all-American; pro rb Philadelphia (NFL) '62; cut after 1st game; Atlantic Coast League qb/kicker/MVP; Newark Bears, Orlando Panthers Continental League, MVP 3 consecutive seasons; led Panthers to 4 pennants, 2 league titles; Continental single-game record 63 pass attempts, 25 completions; single season record 41 td passes, kicked 56 straight converts '68-69; CFL Toronto '70, Winnipeg '71-74, Hamilton '74; CFL record: 1930 passes, 997 completions, 15,064yds, 130 interceptions, 98tds; Jeff Nicklin (WFC MVP), Dave Dryburgh (WFC scoring), Schenley (CFL outstanding player) awards '71; twice WFC all-star, once all-Canadian; PR dir. city of Orlando '76-79; football coach Central Florida from '79; mem. Scranton Sports Hall of Fame; res. Casselberry, Fla.

JONES, Candy (figure skating); b. 20 Mar 1955, Kingston, Ont.; given name: Candace Lynne; m. Donald Fraser; c. 2; McGill, BSc, MD; physician, teacher UVermont; ntl gold medals freestyle, figures at 13; added gold in dance, pairs; US gold figures, FS; began pairs skating with Don Fraser '73; ntl sr. pairs titles '75-76; mem. worlds '75-76, Olympic teams '76; pro '76, toured with Toller Cranston's Ice Show; appeared at Broadway's Palace Theater; world pro pairs titles '77-79; made appearances on TV in Stars on Ice, Battle of the Ice Stars, Challenge of the Sexes, Headline Hunters; coach Laval; res. Vermont.

JONES, Chris (softball); b. 19 Apr 1967, Oshawa, Ont.; given name: Christopher; Durham Coll.; law clerk; mem. ntl fastball team '94-04; PAG gold '95; gold '91 Ont, silver '91 ntl championships, '91, '94 ISC worlds; bronze '92, '94 ntl championships; all-Canadian ss '93-94; res. Oshawa, Ont.

JONES, Colleen (curling); b. 16 Dec 1959, Halifax, N.S.; given name: Colleen Patricia; m. Scott Saunders; c. Zach, Luke; *CBC* sports/weather announcer; began curling age 15;

mem. 2 NS jr., 7 NS mixed, 15 NS women's title rinks; 3rd husband Scott's ntl mixed title team '93, Paul Flemming's ntl mixed title rink '99; skipped '82, '99, '01-04 Scott Tournament of Hearts title rinks, '01, '04 world titles, silver '03; mem. Cdn Curling Hall of Fame; res. Halifax, N.S.

JONES, Debbie (curling); b. 23 Mar 1953, Winnipeg, Man.; given name: Deborah Anne; m. Stan Walker; legal secty; all-star lead Man., Cdn. mixed title rinks '77; 2nd BC women's title rink '84; all-star 2nd BC women's, Cdn, world title rinks '85; mem. 1st women's carspiel winning rink Kelowna '85; 2nd Team Canada, runnerup '86 Scott Tournament of Hearts; from '77-90 competed 5 prov. mixed, 8 prov. women's championships; 3rd for Janet Harvey '97 STOH; fed. govt. champions award '85; 2nd '88 Olympic gold medal team; mem. '88 *TSN* Skins title rink; v-p special events '88 men's world curling championships; mem. '85 BC team of year; hon. life mem. North Shore Winter Club; mem. BC Sports, Canadian Curling halls of fame; res. Winnipeg, Man.

JONES, Jim (softball); b. 15 Nov 1959, Conquest, Sask.; given name: James William; m. Lynne Ledingham; c. Cory Benjamin, Jordy Jonathon; USIU San Diego, Kelsey Inst., Camrose Lutheran Coll; exec. dir. Softball Alberta; ex-recreation dir.; played Jr. A hockey Humboldt '78-80; hockey scholarships USIU San Diego, Camrose Lutheran; mem. ntl men's softball team '82-88; PAG gold '83, '87; world championship silver medal '84; ntl title team '87; ntl championships all-star '82, '83, '84; Saskatoon athlete of year '83; mem. Cdn Softball, Saskatoon Sports halls of fame; res. Delisle, Sask.

JONES, John (motorsport); b. 19 Oct 1965, Thunder Bay, Ont.; given name: John Bradley; Henry Ford U; at 15 worked as bull cook at arctic gold mine to raise money for 1st race car; racing career began as birthday present when he attended Mosport Racing School; competed in go-kart racing at 14; won Western ice racing title at 16; 1st Cdn and youngest racer ever to win IMSA GTO title at 19; 7 wins included 24-hour Daytona, 12-hour Sebring; lone North American on European Formula 3000 circuit '86-87 seasons; 7 top-10 finishes earned him IndyCar series rookie-of-year title; res. Thunder Bay, Ont.

JONES, Tom (motorsport); b. 13 Sep 1941, Belfast, N. Ireland; c. John; construction co. owner; emigrated to Port Arthur age 7; began auto racing age 16; turned pro at 19 racing '57 Corvette or '63 Jaguar; in '60s began driving Cdn rally circuits; strong showings led to ranking as Canada's 1st FIA-graded rally driver; dominated International ice racing circuit '73-78; Prairie regional road racing GT-2 class champion '79-80; Sports Car Club of America, Cdn Auto Sports Club titles, 6 track records '80; 1st Cdn to win both GT1, GT2 Western Cdn Sports Car championships same day '80; several top finishes GT3 class '81; US Nationals title '81; signed as #1 Ford driver in Canada; ret'd from racing '84; Thunder Bay Jaycees NWO outstanding young person award '80; Thunder Bay athlete of '81; mem. NWO Sports Hall of Fame; res. Thunder Bay, Ont.

JONES, Tyrone (football); b. 3 Aug 1961, St. Mary's, Ga.; Southern; lb turned pro CFL Winnipeg '83-87, '89-91, Saskatchewan '92, BC '93; NFL Phoenix Cardinals '88; 3 all-Western, 4 all-CFL, 2 all-Eastern all-star; Norm Fieldgate trophy '85; Schenley outstanding defensive player '85; CFL record: 151 scheduled games, 3tds, 15 interceptions, 15 playoff games; mem. 2 Grey Cup winners; res. Georgia.

JONKER, Karel (rowing); b. 5 Jul 1949, Amsterdam, Netherlands; given name: Karel Anton Johan: m. Karen Farstad; c. Erik; UBC, BA; district sales mgr. GMC; UBC-VRC intercollegiate Western Sprints '70-73; ntl team '70-73; mem. 8s which won Hanlon Cup '70 St. Catharines; coxed 4, pairs, 8s '70 ntl trials; bronze '71 PAG; competed European championships '72-73, English Henley '72, world championships '70; mem. '72 Olympic team; UBC Big Block Club, Olympic Club of Canada; res. Surrey, B.C.

JOSENHANS, Andreas (sailing); b. 12 Sep 1950, Germany; m. Kathryn Ritchie; Dalhousie; sports administrator, sailmaker; with Glen Dexter, Sandy MacMillan won NS Soling titles '74-76; mem. '76, '84 Olympic teams; world soling titles '77, '80; also won world Star class title; NS achievement award, Moosehead sports award; mem. NS, Canada's Sports halls of fame; res. Milford, Conn.

JOSEPH, Curtis (hockey); b. 29 Apr 1967, Keswick, Ont.; m. Nancy; c. Tristan, Taylor, Madison; goal Notre Dame Coll. (SJHL) '87-88, Wisc.; (WCHA) '88-89, Peoria (IHL) '89-90, Las Vegas '95-96, NHL St. Louis '90-95, Edmonton '95-98, Toronto '98-02, Detroit '02-04; WCHA 1st team all-star '89; competed '94, '02 NHL all-star games; Team Canada gold '96 World Cup, silver '96 worlds; mem. '98, '02 (gold) Olympic teams; NHL record (through '04): 798 scheduled games, 396-289-90, 46,396min, 2124ga, 43sho, 130 playoff games, 62-66. 8027min, 326ga, 16sho; 1st yr Oiler Chrysler Canada award; Oiler MVP, Most Popular player, Molson Cup awards '97; King Clancy trophy '00; nicknamed "Cujo"; res. Edmonton, Alta.

JOSEPH, Darren (football); b. 29 Aug 1968, Ottawa, Ont.; UofOtt BA; rb, OQIFC, all-Cdn all-star; Panda Game MVP; 3yrs Ottawa Sooners; set Cdn jr. football season rushing record 1413yds '90; rushed for 295yds, 2tds vs. Oshawa '90; CFL Ottawa '90, '92-94, '03, Sask. '95-98, Toronto '99-00, '01, Montreal '00; noted as punishing tackler; res. Ottawa, Ont.

JOVANOVSKI, Ed (hockey); b. 26 Jun 1976, Windsor, Ont.; m. Kirstin; c. Kylie, Kyra; father pro soccer player Yugoslavia; did not start playing hockey until age 11; def. Windsor (OHL) '91-95; 1st pick overall '94 NHL draft; 1 1st, 2nd team all-star; 1st overall draft pick Florida '94-99, Vancouver '99-04; NHL all-rookie team; *HN* rookie of yr; 2 NHL all-star games; Team Canada '96, '04 World Cup, '98 Worlds, '02 Olympics (gold); Babe Pratt award; NHL record (through '04) 643 scheduled games, 78g, 206a, 58 playoff games, 10g, 18a; res. Florida.

JOY, Greg (t&f); b. 23 Apr 1956, Portland, Ore.; given name: Gregory Andrew; m. Sue Holloway; c. Sarah, Alexandra; Texas, UofT BPhE; motivational speaker; ex-food bank exec-director; hj specialist; 2 NCAA titles; ntl interscholastic record 2.12m; ntl team '73-82; silver '76 Olympics with 2.23m; PB, world indoor record 2.31m College Park, Md., '78; gold '78 Oslo Games (2.24m); silver '78 CG; several intl titles; 4 ntl titles; OUAA, CIAU titles '83; Gov.-Gen.'s silver medal '76; Lou Marsh, Norton Crowe trophies '76; with wife Sue operates motivational speaking bureau Raising the Bar; mem.

Cdn Olympic, BC Sports halls of fame; res. Ottawa, Ont.

JUCKES, Gordon (hockey); b. 20 Jun 1914, Watrous, Sask.; d. 1 Oct 1994, London, Ont.; given name: Gordon Wainwright; m. Clara Thompson; hockey exec.; mem. Sask. AHA '48-60; pres. CAHA '59-60; exec. dir. CAHA '60-78; life mem. IIHF, CAHA, SAHA; CAHA trust established in his memory; mem. Order of British Empire (MBE), Order of Canada (OM), Canada Decoration (CD), Sask., Canada's Sports, Hockey halls of fame.

JUDD, Oscar (baseball); b. 14 Feb 1908, Rebecca, Ont.; d. 27 Dec 1995, Ingersoll, Ont.; given name: Thomas William Oscar; lhp; played amateur Ingersoll, Guelph; minor pro Springfield, Columbus, Ohio, Columbus, Ga., Rochester, Sacramento, Decatur, Iowa, Toronto; ML pitching Boston (AL) '41-45, Philadelphia (NL) '45-48; ML record: 161 games, 99cg, 771ip, 744h, 399r, 334er, 25hr, 304k, 397bob, 40-51, 4so, 7sv, 3.90era; better than average hitter he frequently saw service in pinch-hitting role; hit inside-the-park homer Ebbetts Field '46; ML batting record: 206 games, 317ab, 83h, 11d, 5t, 3hr, 36r, 19rbi, 37k, 27bob, .262ba; won 20 games in each ML; at 37 pitched finest ML game for Philadelphia blanking NY Giants 2-0 in 11 innings allowing just 1 hit through 10 innings and 3 for game; pitched Yankee Stadium season opener '42; mem. '43 All-Star team; mem. Cdn Baseball Hall of Fame.

JULIEN, Denyse (badminton); b. 22 Jul 1960, Rouyn, Que.; began competing age 14; mem. ntl team from '81; ntl jr doubles title '79; 12 ntl singles, 5 women's doubles, 5 mixed doubles gold; through '96 competed 13 Cdn Open, 6 worlds, 6 US Opens, 4 CG, 1 Olympic, 3 PAG, 2 Pan-Am championships, various international opens; 3 CG silver, 3 bronze; has represented Canada in Uber, Sudirman Cup team competitions; turned in brilliant performance in '95 PAG winning singles, women's doubles (with Si-An Deng) and mixed doubles (Darryl Yung); Wimbledon Open, Welsh Open singles titles; mixed doubles (Iain Sydie) gold, women's doubles (Charmaine Reid) silver '99 PAG; mixed doubles (Philippe Bourrett) gold '03 PAG; accomplished golfer; res. Calgary, Alta.

JUNOR, Daisy (all-around); b. 10 Jul 1920, Regina, Sask.; given name: Daisy Knezovich; m. David Junor; ret'd secty; among top Regina t&f athletes '30-35; mem. Regina all-star basketball squad who played vs. famed Edmonton Grads; mem. Sask. champion Regina Caps women's softball team '45; power-hitting outfielder with South Bend '46-49, Fort Wayne '49 in AAGPBL; competed in 3 ntl 5-pin bowling championships; 5 club, 2 Regina, 1 Sask. sr. golf titles; mem. 5 Sask. interprovincial golf teams; served various administrative roles in Sask. Ladies' Golf Assn., particularly jr. development; honored by Cooperstown, Cdn Baseball halls of fame; mem. North Battleford Baseball, Sask. Sports halls of fame; res. Regina, Sask.

JURASIN, Bobby (football); b. 26 Aug 1964, Wakefield, Mich.; Northern Mich; de; signed as free agent by Sask; in CFL '86-97, Toronto '98; 181 games, 360 tackles, 132 qb sacks, 3tds, 2 on pass receptions; 5 Western, 3 CFL all-star awards; 7 playoff games; 5 Hardest Hitter awards; CFL Hardest Hitter of '90; mem. '89 Grey Cup champions; res. Regina, Sask.

KABAT, Greg (football); b. 21 May 1911, Wisconsin; d. 1985, Weisir, Idaho; m. Faye Besant; Wisc., BSc; teacher, coach; football, track, 1st team all-Big 10 '30-32; hockey star at Wisc.; pro Winnipeg '33-40; qb/fb/pk/gd/flying wing; Bomber line coach initial season; mem. 2 Grey Cup finalists; key role 1st-ever Grey Cup victory by western team '35; entire '38 Grey Cup game with broken toe; playing coach Vancouver Grizzlies '41; taught, coached football LA area following retirement; coached St. Paul's HS, St. Paul's jrs while playing for Winnipeg; mem. Canadian Football Hall of Fame.

KABEL, Todd (horse racing); b. 7 Dec 1965, McCreary, Man.; as a teenager rode young steers/quarter-horses; under trainer Clifford Grey launched career as jockey '84; top Cdn apprentice '86; moved to OJC circuit '90 and won 2 outstanding-jockey Sovereign awards; rode Regal Discovery to '95 Queen's Plate; leg injury '96 deprived him of consecutive top-jockey awards; 1st jockey in Cdn history to win $10M in single year '03; winner of recorrrrd 36 stake races; res. Toronto, Ont.

KADATZ, Dennis (football); b. 1 Nov 1938, Edmonton, Alta.; given name: Dennis Melvin; m. Denise Esper; c. Karen, Kim, Kurt; UAlta, BPhE, MA, Oregon; former assoc. prof., assoc. dean of PE UCal; mem. Edmonton jr. Huskies '56-56, UAlta Golden Bears '59-60; coach Strathcona HS 3yrs; head coach Huskies '61-63, ntl jr. title '62-63; head coach UCal '64-68; UCal AD. '66-85; asst. FB coach '69-77; Alta. jr. football all-star player, coach; v-p Stampeders '86-88; GM CODA '88-99; Alta. Football Coaches Assn. coach of year; UCal male/female athlete-of-yr awards bear his name; res. Calgary, Alta.

KAILL, Bob (orienteering); b. 12 Dec 1942, Liverpool, N.S.; given name: Robert Douglas; m. Kristina Eriksson; c. Erik; Waterloo, BA, UofGothenburg, Sweden; coach, criminology reseacher; top Cdn. ntl championships '71; Cdn titles '79, '99; never beaten by North American in major competition; top Cdn. world championships '72, '74; former editor *National Orienteering*; coach Atlantic Youth orienteering team; coached in Australia, Sweden; res. Molndal, Sweden.

KALAILIEFF, Bette Jean (softball); b. 11 May 1932, Welland, Ont; given name: Bette Jean Hannell; m. Edward Kalailieff; c. Dawn Eileen, Edward Joseph; Welland Business Coll.; newspaper editor/film librarian; founded Port Colborne Comettes Ladies Fastball Club '58 serving as player/coach/mgr through '97; 4 Ont. titles; Ont. Women's Softball Assn treas. '62-70, v-p. '71-75, pres. '75-88, dir. from '88; Ont. softball commissioner '77-85; mem. Softball Ont. exec. council '68-96; Softball Canada v-p. '85-87; dir. Softball Canada from '87; only woman to serve on Port Colborne rec. comm.; player/mgr Port Colborne ladies basketball club '57-78, leading scorer at 45; obtained city grant to start minor girls softball program '62; coached as many as 3 teams simultaneously while still playing; won

Ont. squirt '73, bantam '71, midget '72 titles; business mgr. Port Colborne Operatic Society from '51; Sports Council builder-of-sport award; Ont. achievement award; Ont. Corps d'Elite award; YWCA Niagara Region Sports Woman of '88; mem. Cdn Softball Hall of Fame; res. Port Colborne, Ont.

KALLOS, Garry (wrestling); b. 5 Mar 1956, Budapest, Hungary; Concordia, insurance agent; 3 ntl FS, 2 GR titles; gold FS '77, '81, GR '81 Maccabiah Games; gold FS '78 CIAU championships; gold 90kg Sambo '83 PAG; mem. '80, '84 Olympic teams; mem. Concordia Sports Hall of Fame; res. Montreal, Que.

KANCHANARAPHI, Raphi (badminton); b. 6 Nov 1936, Bangkok, Thailand; m. Suda; c. Rangsiman, Baisri; badminton pro; 4 Thailand ntl titles; mem. 4 Thomas Cup teams; undefeated over 3 years Thomas Cup play; moved to Canada '69; 4 times Ont., Cdn. champion; won Cdn Open twice, mixed doubles, men's doubles once each; res. Willowdale, Ont.

KANE, Frank (hockey/baseball); b. 4 Aug 1932, Chatham, N.B.; m. Carole; St. Thomas; public utilities board; mem. Chatham All-Stars '49 NB juvenile hockey champs; St. Thomas NB-PEI intercollegiate title '50-51; Miramichi Braves Maritime sr. champs '54-55; Chatham Ironmen NB intermediate champs '60-61; baseball with Chatham Ironmen 17yrs; coached minor hockey/baseball many yrs, winning NB midget title; mem. Chatham Sports Wall of Fame; res. Chatham, N.B.

KANE, Lorie (golf); b. 19 Dec 1964, Charlottetown, P.E.I.; Acadia; pro golfer; mem. Cdn international team '89-92; Commonwealth team '91; world amateur team '92; Mexican amateur title '91; turned pro '93; participated Central Fla. challenge tour, du Maurier series titles '94-95; competed in 9 LPGA events '96 earning $28,585; recorded career low 69 Youngstown-Warren LPGA Classic '96; gained exempt status '97; 8 top 10 finishes '97, 11 in '98 tour; lost '97 LPGA championship title, '01 Takefuji Classic to Annika Sorenstam in playoff; lost 2 tour events in playoffs '99; posted best-ever money earnings on tour by Cdn with $475,249 '98; 5 consec Cdn LPGA titles; 1st LPGA victory Michelob Light Classic '00; won New Albany Classic, Mizuno Open '00; Takefuji Hawaii Classic '01; with Janice Moodie (US) won 2 Hyundai team match titles; posted career low 63 '02 Takefugi Classic; Bobbie Rosenfeld Trophy '97; LPGA Heather Farr award '98; William & Mousie Powell award '00; through '04 had 17 2nd place tour finishes; mem. Canada's inaugural Nations Cup team '99, gold '01; res. Charlottetown, P.E.I.

KANGAS, Kathy (parachuting); b. 18 Mar 1944, Lautakylla, Finland; given name: Kathy Krystina; div.; c. Zachary Kangas-Sainsbury; UWO, BPHE, Illinois, MSc; ret'd part owner, CEO Kangas Food & Sauna Ltd.; asst. AD Lakehead '68-70, asst prof., gym coach Buffalo State '70-71; mgr. Norwester Fitness Centre '91-98; sports dir *CBQ* radio '87-88; mem. Finnish, Cdn. t&f teams early '60s; mem. Eastern College volleyball title teams '63-67; 10-pin bowling champ; ski patroller; MVP Finnish-Cdn baseball title team; ntl parachuting team mem. '70-85; competed 6 world championships; only person in world to compete in 8 worlds and be ntl team mem. 11 years; for 10yrs ranked ntl top 4, worlds top 21; 1st Cdn woman to pass 3000 free-fall jumps earning double diamond wings; at retirement had most jumps by Cdn woman 3191; Cdn women's accuracy landing record; coached US college gymnastics champion '71; pres. UWO gymnastics club '63-67; UWO athlete of '67, Thunder Bay female athlete of '71, distinguished citizen award '81, Ont. sports achievement award '83; Wieben parachuting sportsmanship award; coach US ntl coll. Champ Kathy Gleason '71; mem. NWO Sports Hall of Fame; res. Thunder Bay, Ont.

KANJEE, Hashmuk (field hockey); b. 27 Dec 1950, Salisbury, Zimbabwe; UAlta, BPhE; coach; outdoor store buyer; mem. Zimbabwe prov. schoolboys team '67-69; ntl schoolboy team '69; prov. sr. t&f team (lj) '68-71; Zimbabwe armed forces field hockey team '71-72; UAlta t&f team '72-76; Alta. field hockey team '72-77, capt. '77; ntl team mem. '77-94; mem. '79 PAG team; coach UBC women's team; res. Vancouver, B.C.

KANT, Hari (field hockey): b. 23 Aug 1969, Ottawa, Ont.; Carleton, BSc; software engineer; goal; bronze '88 jr. PAG; competed '93 Inter-continental Cup, '98 CG; silver '95, gold '99 PAG, Australian Cup, '95 Indo-Pan-American Gold Cup, '00 Olympics, '03 indoor world cup; silver '00 America's Cup, gold '02 indoor Pan-Am Cup; mem. ntl team '87-03; competed in English premier league '98-99; res. Gloucester, Ont.

KAPP, Joe (football); b. 19 Mar 1939, Stockton, Calif.; given name: Robert Joseph; m. Marcia; c. J.J.; Calif. (Berkeley); bar & grill owner; business development co. mgr., actor; HS football, baseball, basketball standout; Berkley on football, basketball scholarship; qb '59 Rose Bowl loss to Iowa, MVP award; in Hula Bowl; drafted by Washington but opted for CFL Calgary '60-61; following knee surgery dealt to BC '62-67; guided Lions WFC titles '63-64; Grey Cup victory '64; CFL record: completed 1476 of 2709 pass attempts for 22,725 yds, 137tds; twice all-Cdn., '64 Grey Cup MVP, runnerup '63 Schenley Outstanding Player Award; following salary impasse dealt to Minnesota (NFL) '67-70; led Vikings to '67 div. title, '70 Super Bowl; tied NFL record with 7 td passes as Vikes drubbed Colt's 52-14 28 Sep '69; Boston Patriots '70-71; only player to qb in Rose Bowl, Super Bowl and Grey Cup; acted in several movies, TV shows; coach Berkeley '82-86; PAC-10 coach of '82; Dec '69 Hickok pro-athlete-of-month award, '69 Vince Lombardi dedication award; '63 Bob Bourne Memorial Trophy Lions most popular player; Roberto Clemente award '03; nicknamed "Injun Joe"; founder TD! Inc.; pres./GM Lions '89-90; mem. Cdn Football Hall of Fame; res. Los Gatos, Calif.

KARCH, Karla (basketball); b. 26 Aug 1964, Vancouver, B.C.; div. Jeff Gailus; UCal, UVic; asst. coach Mount Royal Cougars; gd '86 bronze medal world championship, '87 PAG, '91 FISU Games, '93 COPABA world qualification teams; mem. CIAU title team '86-87;

competed '94 Goodwill Games, world championships; gold '95 COPABA Olympic qualifing tournament; pro Germany, Hungary; mem. Hungarian Cup title, '96, '00 Olympic teams; CIAU all-Canadian '87-88; 2 HS athletic awards; active in COA Adopt-an-athlete program; res. Vancouver, B.C.

KARCZ, Zeno (football); b. 16 Mar 1935, Toronto, Ont.; given name: Zenon Peter; m. Ethel Cullen; UMich, BA; sales mgr; baseball Detroit Federation League; 2 seasons Windsor AKO; football scholarship UMich; pro Hamilton '56, became regular '58; equally adept as hb/end/clb; EFC all-star 3 times; *Globe & Mail* all-Cdn. lb 5 times; Schenley Cdn. Award '65; 8 Grey Cup games, 3 winners; coach Windsor minor hockey, AKO football, Hamilton minor hockey, football; res. Burlington, Ont.

KARIYA, Paul (hockey): b. 16 Oct 1974, Vancouver, B.C.; given name: Paul Tetsuhiko; Maine; lw Penticton (BCJHL '90-92), Maine '92-94; Team Canada Jr. '91-93; Team Canada '94 (silver), '98, '02 (gold) Olympics, 3 World championships; 1st ever Anaheim draftee; NHL Anaheim '94-03. Colorado '03-04; recorded 50 goals '95-96 season; team capt. from '96; 6 NHL all-star games; 2 Lady Byng trophies; 2 1st team NHL all-star; Hobey Baker (NCAA outstanding player); Hockey East rookie, player-of-yr awards; reached 500 points in 417th game; Maine ret'd jersey 9; NHL record (through '04): 657 scheduled games, 311g, 394a, 36 playoff games, 14g, 16a; active in children's charities; res. Orange County, Calif./Vancouver, B.C.

KARPUK, Pete (football/baseball); b. 1927, d. 4 Mar 1985, Toronto, Ont.; played pro baseball Toronto (IL), Ottawa (Border), Galt (Sr IC); pro football db Ottawa, Hamilton, Montreal '48-56; CFL record: 12tds, 8 interceptions; caught key td pass to help Ottawa win '51 Grey Cup; best remembered for coming off bench to tackle Ulysses Curtis to prevent td following interception in season's final game '51; also noted for dropping lateral pass and giving up on it after thinking he heard officials' whistles before Woody Strode scooped up ball and set up winning td by Calgary '48 Grey Cup final; mem. 3 Grey Cup finalists, 1 winner.

KARRYS, George (curling); b. 15 Feb 1967, Toronto, Ont.; m. Jeanette Lee; Ryerson, BA journalism; COA fund raiser/marketer; played second for Mike Harris ntl jr. rink '86; 5 Ont. championship appearances; mem. World Curling Tour money leading rink, Olympic trials champion '97; played lead on silver medal Harris rink '98 Olympics; res. Toronto, Ont.

KARRYS, Steve (football); b. 20 Jun 1924, Montreal, Que.; m. Helen Bazos; c. Anita Elaine, Steven James; UofT; wholesale distributor; mem. Argos '45-46, '51-52, UotT '47, Rough Riders '48-50; 4 Grey Cup finals, 3 winners; db, Argos modern era all-stars ('45-73); res. Willowdale, Ont.

KASTING, Robert (swimming); b. 28 Aug 1950, Ottawa, Ont.; Yale, BA, Stockholm, Dip. Social Science, McGill, LLD; lawyer; all-Ivy honors Yale swim team '70-72; all-American '70, '72; capt. Yale '72; ntl team '67-75; silver 400m FS, 800m FS relays '67 PAG; capt., bronze

400m medley relay '72 Olympic team; silver 400m FS, 800m FS relay '66, '70 CG; gold 400m medley relay '70 CG; bronze 100m FS, silver 400m FS, 800m FS, 400m medley relays '71 PAG; dir. Olympic Club of Canada; res. Yellowknife, NWT.

KAUL, Anil (badminton): b. 25 Dec 1964, Amritsar, India; coach; moved to Canada '73; mem. ntl team from '87; 2 men's doubles, 3 mixed doubles ntl titles; competed '92, '96 Olympics; gold men's doubles, silver mixed doubles '95 PAG, men's, mixed doubles gold, team silver '94 CG; competed '91, '93 Worlds; 2 Grand Prix men's, mixed doubles bronze; res. Victoria, B.C.

KAWAJA, John (curling); b. 27 Apr 1961, Chandler, Que.; given name: John Warren; m. Laura; c. Kristyn; York, BA; Adidas business unit mgr.; mem. ntl jr. championship runnerup rink '80; 2nd Ed Werenich '83-84 Ont. title rinks, winner '83, '90 (3rd) Labatt Brier, world title winners; all-star 2nd '83 Brier; competed 5 Briers, 2 winners; fed. govt. world champion award '83; Dick Ellis team award '83; mem. Cdn Curling Hall of Fame; res. Agincourt, Ont.

KAWASAKI, Mitch (judo/wrestling); b. 4 Mar 1950, Hamilton, Ont.; given name: Mitchell Akira; div. Darlene Spencer; c. Stephanie, Becky, Katie; Lakehead, hons. BPHE, McGill; company v-p; twice ntl 193lb judo champion; world competition '71.'73; 4th Pan-Am judo championships; 5th degree black belt; 4 ntl wrestling titles; 4th '75 PAG; 2nd Hungarian Freedom Cup; 6th '76 Olympics; gold '74 CG; knee injuries forced him from freestyle to Greco-Roman style wrestling '75; mem. '76 Olympic team; judo teacher Onteora Japanese Community Center; chief instructor Kawasaki Rendokan; mem. Ont. grading board; head coach Judo Ont.; also successful gymnast; Thunder Bay, Lakehead male- athlete-of-yr awards; Hamilton Civic Diamond Ring award; res. Hamilton, Ont.

KAY, Jack Jr (golf); b. 14 Jul 1964, Montreal, Que.; m. Christie; Furman, BAdm; followed father into pro golf ranks; Ont, Jr., New Eng. Jr., Cdn. jr. titles '82; capt. Furman golf team, 3 college titles, all-American status; semifinalist US Amateur; 2nd '86 Cdn. Amateur; mem. '86 world amateur title team; low amateur BC Open; played in '86 Masters, Cdn. Open; pro '87; competed on Cdn., USPGA, Australian, Asian, US mini-tours; won '91 Singapore Open; res. Markham, Ont.

KAYSMITH, Henry (rowing); b. 3 Nov 1904, London, Eng.; d. circa 2000, Toronto, Ont.; given name: Henry Ernest; m. Jean McGill; c. Beverley; rowed from '23-33 both sculls, sweep oar; capt., coach Argo rowing club '47-56; 2 ntl lightweight titles; coach Olympic rowing team '52; when Canadian boats were wrecked in storm, Canadian crews rented Stockholm RC shells and 8s set record with 1st photo finish in Olympic history by tieing Swedish crew; pres. Argo Rowing Club.

KAZANOWSKI, Gerald (basketball); b. 12 Oct 1960, Nanaimo, B.C.; m. Claudia Solorzano; c. Sarah; UVic, BA; certified financial planner; fwd 4 UVic CIAU title teams; mem. BC HS title team '78; ntl. team '81-92; mem. Cdn world jr. team '79; gold team '83 FISU Games; ntl team runnerup '82 Jones Cup; mem. 4 FISU Games, 3 World

championships, '83 PAG, '84, '88 Olympic teams; 7th round draft NBA Utah Jazz '83; pro stops in Spain, Sweden, Finland, Switzerland, Argentina, Mexico '83-92; Leon, Spain, all-star '87-88; 1 CIAU all-Cdn; fed. govt. excellence award '84; BC HS player of '78; mem. Cdn Basketball Hall of Fame; res. Sidney, B.C.

KAZIENKO, Linda (archery); b. 29 May 1955, Grimsby, Ont.; Guelph DVM; veterinarian; FITA star tournament target title '78; Arizona State target title '82; 3 ntl target titles; mem. ntl team '79, '83 PAG, '82 CG, '79, '81, '83 world championships, '84 Olympics; PAG team silver '79, '83; mem. Guelph Sports Hall of Fame; res. Burlington, Ont.

KEANE, Mike (hockey); b. 29 May 1967, Winnipeg, Man.; m. Tammy; c. Jackson, Olivia; lw Winnipeg (MAHA, WHL) '83-94; Moose Jaw (WHL) '84-87; Sherbrooke (AHL) '87-88; non-drafted free agent; NHL Montreal '88-95, Colorado '95-97, '01-03, NYR '97-98, Dallas '98-01, Vancouver '03-04; NHL record (through '04) 1161 scheduled games, 168g, 302a, 220 playoff games, 34g, 40a; 5 consec. Western Conf. finals; mem. Stanley Cup winners with Montreal, Colorado, Dallas; capt. Montreal '95; res. Denver, Colo.

KEAST, Brian (cycling); b. 27 Nov 1953, Vancouver, B.C.; given name: Brian Scott; salesman; ntl team pursuit titles '72-73, '75; ntl 10-mile title '72; BC road race '75, track titles '75, '78; ntl 180km road race title '75; '75, '78 Gastown GP, '75 ntl road race title, '73 Tour de l'Est Que., '78 Stage 5 Dolux, N.Z.; mem. '72 Olympic, '74 CG, '73-75 World championship teams; res. Vancouver, B.C.

KEATING, Jack (baseball/hockey); b. 12 Feb 1908, Newcastle, N.B.; d. 5 Jun 1985, Saint John, N.B.; given name: John Richard; surveyor; led NB sr. league in batting with .389 '27; hockey Hawkins Academy, Chatham Ironmen, Saint John Fusiliers; pro New York Americans, Buffalo, Providence, Syracuse, St. Paul; coached St. John Beavers to Maritime sr. title '46; nicknamed "Miramichi Flash"; mem. NB, Saint John Sports halls of fame.

KEATING, Murray (t&f); b. 28 May 1952, Manning, Alta.; given name: Kenneth Murray; m. Sheila Punshon; c. Ryan, Allison; SFU, BA; pres/CEO International Parkside Products Inc.; hammer throw specialist; BC HS, ntl juv. titles '70; 2nd ntl jr. '71; ntl jr. title with record 59.22m (194'3"), 2nd NAIA nationals '72; ntl sr. record 64.30m, NAIA title, mem. '73 FISU Games team; ntl title with 67.46m record, 4th '75 PAG; ntl record 68.30m mem. '76 Olympic team; ret'd from competition '78; res. South Surrey, B.C.

KEATS, Duke (hockey); b. 1 Mar 1895, Montreal, Que.; d. 17 Jan 1972, Victoria, BC; given name: Gordon Blanchard; standout baseball player; at 17 pro Toronto (NHA); returned to amateur briefly with Peterborough then rejoined Toronto; amateur with Edmonton, pro '19-20 with Patricks; led WCL scorers '22-23; sold to Boston (NHL), transferred to Detroit midway through season, joined Chicago '27; scoring champion Tulsa American Assn.; remained in hockey several more seasons with various WCL teams; scored 119 goals in 128 games prior to playing in NHL where he added 30 goals in 2 seasons; mem. Hockey Heritage North, Hockey Hall of Fame.

KEELING, Butch (hockey); b. 10 Aug 1905, Owen Sound, Ont.; d. 12 Nov 1984, Toronto, Ont.; given name: Melville Sidney; m. Winnifred Hulse (d); UWO; sales rep.; mem. Owen Sound Greys '21-25, Memorial Cup champs '24; London Srs '25-26; Toronto St. Pat's '26; pro Maple Leafs '27-28, NYR '28-38; mem.'33 Stanley Cup winners; NHL record: 157g, 63a plus 11g, 11a, 47 playoff games; asst. coach Philadelphia Ramblers '39-40; mgr.-playing coach Kansas City (AHL) '40-41; refereed AHL '41-46, 3 seasons NHL; thoroughbred horse owner '31-37.

KEELING, Jerry (football); b. 2 Aug 1939, Enid, Okla.; m. Vella; c. Tina, Terry, Tucker; Tulsa; football coach; twice all-Missouri Valley qb; CFL Calgary '61-72, Ottawa '73-75; def standout early in pro career; CFL record fumble return 102yds '64; CFL career record: 2477 pass attempts, 1302 completions, 18,239yds, 158 interceptions, 119tds; 4 Grey Cup finals, 2 winners; 5 all-Western, 3 all-Cdn selections; Hiram Walker Trophy '73; shares CFL record 109yd td pass (to Terry Evanshen '66); twice Calgary MVP, most-popular player; began coaching Northwestern Oklahoma State '80; asst. Ottawa '81, '95, Calgary '82-83, Saskatchewan '84; mem. Cdn Football Hall of Fame; res. Tulsa, Okla.

KEENAN, Bill (skiing); b. 10 Oct 1957, Port Arthur, Ont.; UCal, BComm; commercial real estate developer; solid grounding in alpine competition led to membership on ntl jr. freestyle team; considered Canada's outstanding moguls skier; accomplished gymnast, water skier; 2nd mogul grand prix, freestyle rookie of year World Cup circuit '80; 5th WC GP '81, 3rd '82; gold, silver Australian international championships '82; world moguls title '83; mem. Cdn Skiing Hall of Fame; res. Boca Raton, Fla.

KEENAN, Mike (hockey/coaching); b. 21 Oct 1949, Bowmanville, Ont.; given name: Michael Edward; div. Rita; c. Gayla; m. Nola; c. Grant, Reed; St. Lawrence, BSc; UofT, MEd; hockey exec., TV color commentator; began coaching at jr B level winning back-to-back Metro Toronto league titles; Peterborough Memorial Cup winner '80, Rochester (AHL) Calder Cup '83, UofT '84 CIAU title; coached 3 NHL all-star games; coached ntl jr. team '80; 3 Team Canada, 2 Canada Cup winners; head coach Philadelphia '84-88, Chicago 88-91 (GM '89-92), coach NYR '93-94, coach/GM St. Louis '94-97; coach Vancouver '97-99; coach Boston '00-01, Florida '01-03, (GM '04-05); 6 div. titles; 3 president's trophies, 3 Stanley Cup wins; 3 50+win, 5 100+point seasons; *Hockey News* coach of '91; NHL Jack Adams coach-of-yr trophy '85; coached 3 NHL all-star teams; NHL coaching record (through '03) 1207 scheduled games, 579-463-145-20, 160 playoff games, 91-69; res. Vancouver, B.C.

KEENAN, Roy (boxing); b. 26 Aug 1930, Montreal, Que.; m. Irma Joan Draycott; c. Wayne, Glenn; Sir George Williams; buyer, supervisor; golden gloves 135lb title '49-50; Montreal open 135lb title, ntl title '50; golden gloves 139lb title '52; ntl 139lb title '52; competed '52 Olympics, lost only bout & ret'd from ring; ring record (all amateur): 58 bouts, won 39, 7 by KO, 15 by TKO, 17 by decision, lost 19, 1 by TKO, 18 by decision; res. Montreal, Que.

KEEPER, Joe (t&f); b. 17 Jan 1886, Walker Lake, Man., d. 29 Sep 1971, Winnipeg, Man.; given name: Benjamin

Joseph; c. 4 sons, 3 daughters; carpenter, Hudson's Bay Co.; mem. Norway House Cree band; 2nd in 1st race '09 Brandon indoor mile; joined Winnipeg North End AC, won 7 mile road races '10-11; set Cdn 10-mile record 54:50 Ft. William '11; top Cdn placing 2nd ntl 3 mile race Montreal '11; 2nd 5,000, 10,000m heats '12 Olympics, 4th 10,000m final, didn't compete in 5,000m final due to foot injury; competed in exhibition races vs. Tom Longboat in Europe during WWI; Joe Keeper Memorial Run staged annually by Man. Runners' Assn.; recipient Military Medal; mem. Cdn Olympic, Man. Sports, Cdn Road Running halls of fame.

KEFFER, Karl (golf); b. 1882 Tottenham, Ont.; d. 1950, Toronto, Ont.; honed his golf skills as caddie; later asst to George Cumming Toronto GC; lone Cdn-born player to win Cdn Open ('09, '14), runnerup '19; 1 Que., Man. open titles; helped found CPGA '11; hon. sect-treas CPGA '14-28; capt. CPGA '34-37; pres. CPGA '38-40; head pro Royal Ottawa '11-43; mem. RCGA, Ont. Golf halls of fame.

KEHOE, Rick (hockey); b. 15 Jul 1951, Windsor, Ont.; given name: Rick Thomas; m. Peg; c. Karrie; hockey coach; rw; London Knights, Hamilton Red Wings Jrs.; pro Tulsa CHL '71-72; NHL Maple Leafs '71-74, Penguins '74-85; NHL record: 14 seasons, 906 scheduled games, 371g, 396a, 39 playoff games, 4g, 17a; scored 55g '81; Lady Byng trophy '81; played in 2 all-star games; scout Pittsburgh '85-86, '95-99; asst. coach Pittsburgh '87-01; head coach '01-03; NHL record 55-81-14-10; mem. Penguins, Western Pa. halls of fame; res. Pittsburgh, Pa.

KEITH, Harold (curling); b. 30 Sep 1939, Moncton, N.B.; given name: Harold Chester: m. Sylvia Irene McEwen; c. Rick, Derrick, Kelly, Abbey; company pres.; mem. NB rink '57 ntl Schoolboy championships, '60, '62, '64, '69-70 Briers; above average performer t&f, baseball, softball; res. Riverview, N.B.

KEITH, Vicki (swimming); b. 26 Feb 1961, Winnipeg, Man.; m. John Munro; sc. Bruce, Cory; Queen's; motivational speaker, creator Reach for Your Dreams workshops; strength and endurance placed her among most successful marathon swimmers in history; swam butterfly stroke for 12 miles setting 1 of 17 world records; among remarkable achievements are 129 hours, 45 minutes continuous swimming '86; 1st double crossing Lake Ont. '87; 1st to swim all of the Great Lakes '88; crossing Fuca Strait in 14 hours doing butterfly stroke; greatest number of Lake Ont. crossings; covered 43.067 miles in 24hrs '90; among other bodies of water conquered: Lake Winnipeg, Catalina Channel, English Channel, Sydney (Australia) Harbor; has worked as lifeguard, coach both swimming, gymnastics; dir. Ont. Place '89-91, Sport Ont. '93-94; mem. Ont. Sports awards selection comm '96, Terry Fox Hall of Fame induction comm. '97-98; raised hundreds of thousands of dollars for charity, particularly disabled children; has written several children's books; 2 Kiwanis athlete-of-yr, Kingston athlete-of-yr, Ont. , Man., Cdn achievement awards; Gus Ryder, King Clancy, Dr. Robert Jackson, Vanier, Trillium, Rosemary George, Heart, Women-Who-Make-A-Difference awards; honored by cities of Toronto, Kingston, Winnipeg, Ottawa, Los Angeles, Goderich, Ont., Harbor Beach, Mich., state of Mich.; Ont., International Variety Clubs; B'Nai Brith woman of '89; mem. Order of Canada, Ontario; mem. Terry Fox, Ontario Aquatic, Kingston Sports halls of fame; res. Kingston, Ont.

KELESI, Helen (tennis): b. 15 Nov 1969, Victoria, B.C.; nicknamed "Hurricane Helen"; turned pro at 15; mem. Cdn Federation Cup teams '86-94; twice French Open quarterfinalist; best WTA ranking 13 in '89; 2 Bobbie Rosenfeld awards; with Monica Seles won '90 Italian Open doubles; unprecedented 4 straight Cdn women's singles titles '87-90; 3 TC player of yr, TC most improved '85; 2 Cdn doubles team-of-yr awards; mem. '88 Olympic team; brain tumor operations '95, '97; returned to tour briefly '97; mem. Cdn Tennis Hall of Fame; res. Vancouver, B.C.

KELLAND, Kelly (softball): b. 1 Nov 1962, London, Ont.; Ohio State. BSc; child care worker; mem. ntl team 10yrs; 1b '90, '94 worlds, '87, '95 PAG, '96 Olympics; 2 silver, 1 bronze ntl championships; bronze '87 PAG; MVP, top batter Vancouver sr. women's league '92; asst. ntl team coach '01; res. Kamloops, B.C.

KELLAR, Becky (hockey): b. 1 Jan 1975, Hagersville, Ont.; Brown., BA, teaching certificate; WLU MBA; def; '93 ntl -18 champion with Team Ontario, MVP award; played with Brown Bears '93-97, 20g, 29a in 23 games '94-95; ntl women's team from '97; 4 world titles; Olympic silver '98, gold '02; 3 gold, 1 silver 3-Nations Cup teams, 2 gold, 1 silver 4-Nations Cup teams; with Team Ont. gold '00, bronze '01 ntls; MVP Brown, several all-Conf. awards, academic all-Ivy '97; 4yrs 2nd base Brown softball team; minor hockey Glanbrook, Ont.; mem. NWHL Beatrice Aeros from '98; res. Hagersville, Ont.

KELLS, Morley (lacrosse): b. 26 Jan 1936, Midland, Ont.; given name: Morley Cecil; m. Gloria Pellegrin; c. Christine, Bradley, Terrence, Louise; from '81, MPP Humber Riding, Etobicoke-Lakeshore; mem. Long Branch Monarchs '55 Minto Cup winners; coached Brantford Warriors to '71 Mann Cup; coach, GM Rochester Griffins winning '74 Nations Cup; with Jim Bishop, Bruce Norris, helped create National Lacrosse League '73; CLA Lester B. Pearson Award for contribution to game '73; mem. Etobicoke Sports, Cdn Lacrosse halls of fame; res. Etobicoke, Ont.

KELLY, Brian (football): b. 27 Mar 1956, Los Angeles, Calif.; m. Kim; c. Ryan, Katelyn, Alanna; Washington State; all-Pac 10 wide receiver '77; CFL Edmonton '79-87; 6 WFC, CFL all-star selections; Schenley CFL rookie of year '79; mem. 5 Grey Cup winners; CFL record 575 receptions, 11,169yds, 97tds, 586pts; led WFC pass receptions 104 in '83; 5 times surpassed 1000yds single season; 18td catches set CFL record '84; nicknamed "Howdy Doody"; res. Edmonton, Alta.

KELLY, Con (football/speed skating): b. 15 Jan 1934, Edmonton, Alta.; m. Marlene McDermott; c. Con Jr., Vincent, Nancy Lee; plumber; nicknamed "Shipwreck Kelly"; all-star HS basketball '51; Sask., Alta. jr. speed skating titles '46-47; jr. football Edmonton Wildcats '52 Little Grey Cup finalists; fb Eskimos '55-56 Grey Cup finals; res. Edmonton, Alta.

KELLY, Ellison (football): b. 17 May 1936, Lake City, Fla.;

given name: Ellison Lamar; m. Sheila Clarke; c. Claudette, Jude, Claire, Jerry, Catherine, Karen; Mich. State BA; ret'd Ont. recreation supervisor; attended MSU on full scholarship excelling in football, t&f (shot & discus), boxing; *Look* all-American team '58; all-Big 10 team '57-58; scholastic all-American '58; solid lineman with NY Giants (NFL) '59; to CFL Hamilton '60-70, Toronto '71-72; usually gd/t but versatility enabled him to play de/lb; played 175 consec. regular-season games; 4 all-East gd; 4 all-East tackle; 1 all-Cdn gd; 2 all-Cdn tackle; mem. 7 Grey Cup finals, 3 winners; CFL stars-of-week panel of judges; mem. Cdn Football Hall of Fame; res. Hamilton, Ont.

KELLY, Henry (builder/softball): b. 18 Jan 1922, Stilesville, N.B.; given name: Henry Burton; m. Pearl; from 1938 softball player, coach, official, administrator; played 35yrs Moncton District Softball League, coached 29 of those 35yrs; led teams to 1 Jr., 2 Sr. A Maritime titles; pres. Moncton City League 12yrs; exec. NBSA 18yrs; commissioner CASA '68-77; coach NB all-stars '73, '77 Canada Games; coached Moncton Rebels to 15 NB women's titles, 8 ntl appearances and '75 silver medal; active umpire 12yrs; helped form NB Softball Umpires Assn.; chair. 2 ntl women's championships; refereed/coached amateur hockey; mgr. Moncton Hawks '78 Hardy Cup winner; Moncton softball field bears his name; named City of Moncton ambassador; nicknamed "Hawk"; mem. Moncton Wall, NB Sports Hall of Fame; res. Moncton, N.B.

KELLY, Janis (volleyball): b. 20 Mar 1971, Winnipeg, Man.; UWpg.; twice Canada Cup all-star; gold '93 CIAU championships; CIAU nationals all-star '93; twice GPAC all-star; silver '93 Canada Cup; competed '91, '93 FISU, '96 Olympic Games; bronze '95 PAG; gold, MVP '96 Continental Cup; silver '93 Canada Cup; UWpg female athlete of '92; res. Winnipeg, Man.

KELLY, Jim (motorsport): b. 1929, Hamilton, Ont.; d. 5 Oct 1997, Hamilton, Ont. given name: James Edward; m. Muriel; accountant Revenue Canada; began riding motorcycles age 20; despite diminutive 5-6, 130lb frame developed effective, if unorthodox, driving techniques; became highly proficient as road racer, hill climber, speedway, trial, enduro, motocross, ice racer; 4 ntl ice racing titles; set x-country record on Yamaha 650, Sydney, N.S., to Vancouver in 92h22m '72; helped establish Canada as force at international 6-day enduro championships; rated by *Off Road News* as Canada's No. 1 motorcyclist.

KELLY, Joanne (wheelchair basketball): b. 23 Jun 1964, Toronto, Ont.; div.; c. Kyle James; sport administration/customer service; born with spina bifida; launched wheelchair basketball career at 27; with Calgary Rollers 5 ntl titles; with Western Grizzlies 1 US ntl title; '00 Paralympic gold; 2 world titles; '97 Cdn all-star; 4 Calgary Booster Club/City of Calgary recognition awards; Queen's Golden Jubilee Commemorative medal; mem. Cdn Wheelchair Basketball Hall of Fame; res. Calgary, Alta.

KELLY, Patrick (speed skating): b. 23 Jun 1962, Toronto, Ont.; McGill; consultant; son of NHL Hall of Famer Red Kelly and former NA speed skating titlist Andrea McLaughlin; sister Kitty Ice Capades soloist; played hockey McGill '81-83, Toronto Metro Jr. B champions

'81; career threatened by leg fracture '84 but rebounded to begin racing '85 and join ntl team '88; long-track specialist; competed '92, '94 Olympics; ntl overall, sprint titles '93; res. Calgary, Alta.

KELLY, Pete (hockey); b. 22 May 1912, St. Vital, Man.; given name: Peter Cameron; ret'd educator; NHL St. Louis Eagles '34-35, Detroit '35-39, NY Americans '40-41, Brooklyn Americans '41-42; mem. 2 Detroit Stanley Cup winners; AHL scoring record '41-42 season; AD UNB 25yrs; mem. NB Sports Hall of Fame; res. Fredericton, N.B.

KELLY, Red (hockey); b. 19 Jul 1927, Simcoe, Ont.; given name: Leonard Patrick; m. Andrea McLaughlin; c. Andrea Catherine (Casey), Leonard Patrick Jr., Conn Lawrence, Christina Frances (Kitty); St. Michael's College; pres. C.A.M.P. Systems Canada Ltd., pres., board chair. McLaughlin Enterprises Ltd., NYC, pres. Leonard P. Kelly Ltd.; St. Michael's midget champions '43-44; Jr. B champions '44-45; Jr. A Memorial Cup finalists '45-47; Detroit '47-59, Toronto '59-67; ret'd to coach Los Angeles '68-70; Pittsburgh '70-73, Toronto '73-77; NHL record: 1316 scheduled games, 281g, 542a, 164 playoff games, 33g, 59a; mem. 9 Prince of Wales Trophy, 8 Stanley Cup winners; 4 Lady Byng, 1 Norris Trophy; 6 times 1st team, twice 2nd team all-star; *Hockey News* NHL coach of '70; MP (Lib) York-West '62-65; *Encyclopaedia Britannica* Achievement-in-Life award '80; manufacturer of ankle bracelets for Ont. govt. to monitor convicts; mem. Ont. Legends, Canada's Sports, Hockey halls of fame; res. Toronto, Ont.

KELLY, Steven (shooting); b. 24 Aug 1952, Ottawa, Ont.; given name: Steven Thomas; Algonquin Coll., Dip Chem. Tech., Carleton, BSc; chemist; hand gun specialist; Ont., Que. titles; ntl -21 champion '72; ntl team '71-85; bronze standard pistol '74 nationals; gold team air pistol, rapid-fire pistol '77-78, free pistol '78, silver individual rapid-fire pistol '78-79, bronze air pistol '81 nationals; mem. '74, '78 world championships, '75-77 Benito Juarez, '76 Olympics, '75, '79 PAG, '77 Shooting Championships of Americas teams; team silver standard pistol '76, team bronze rapid-fire pistol '76-77; team silver centre-fire pistol '79 PAG; Civil Service RA athlete of '76-77; Ottawa ACT shooting award '75; res. Ottawa, Ont.

KELSALL, Karen (gymnastics); b. 11 Dec 1962, Nanaimo, B.C.; given name: Karen Barbara; California; chiropractor; ntl jr. champion '76; 3 sr. titles; 13th '75 PAG, 27th '76 Olympics, 4th '78 CG, 10th '78 Worlds; all-around Coca-Cola International, Elite Zone, Bulgaria-Canada Invitational, Pacific Rim '78; mem. US championships title team '80; New Westminster *Columbian* athlete-of-year award '76-77; BC jr. athlete of '77; res. Portland, Ore.

KEMKAREN, Heather (figure skating); b. 2 Aug 1958, Winnipeg, Man.; UofT; '75 Vienna Trophy; 3rd '76 Richmond Trophy; 2nd ntl championships, 3rd Skate Canada '77; ntl women's singles titles '78, '80, runnerup '79; mem. '80 Olympic team; boardroom decision which bypassed her for world competiton led to retirement; res. Guelph, Ont.

KEMP, Nigel (swimming); b. 8 Jul 1944, Southampton, Eng.; m. Pauline Quixley; c. Carolyn, Stuart; Loughbrough, DLC, Oregon, BSc, MSc; asst. prof. Dalhousie; competitive

swimmer in England; head coach Halifax Trojan Aquatic Club '71-80; ntl teams coach; world, CG, Olympic, FISU competition; dir. Cdn. Swimming Coaches Assn.; chair. CIAU SCA; tech. advisor CASA Ed. Services Div.; mem. National Coaching Development Comm.; most famous protegee Nancy Garapick; ntl swim coach of '75; CIAU swim coach of '74, '80; head swim coach Dalhousie.; res. Halifax, N.S.

KEMP, Sally (coaching); b. 15 Sep 1939, Montreal, Que.; given name: Sally Elizabeth; MacDonald College, Sir George Williams, BA, SUNY (Cortland), MSc; phys ed teacher, asst AD Waterloo; mem. MacDonald basketball team 2 years, MVP soccer, hockey; basketball YMCA Blues '64-68, Harmony, Jackson 5 teams Kitchener winning frequent city titles; coach women's volleyball, basketball, badminton SGW '65-68, basketball '68-82, field hockey '68-77, Waterloo, basketball, volleyball YM-YWCA Leadership camps, Camp Cuyaga; pres. Montreal Women's Basketball League '66-68, East-West Conference intercollegiate athletics '67-68; pres. Ont. Women's Intercollegiate Athletic Assn.; mem. exec. comm. OLBA '72-74, pres. '74-75; v-p. Waterloo regional sports council from '74; res. Waterloo, Ont.

KEMPSTER, Ray (lawn bowling/curling); b. 21 Aug 1909, Winnipeg, Man.; d. 16 Jul 1995, Ottawa, Ont.; given name: Raymond Francis Edward; m. Astrid Victoria Olsen; RCAF staff college; ret'd W/C RCAF; HS rugger, track; badminton, tennis, golf, lawn bowling, curling RCAF Saskatoon; RCAF Trenton badminton singles champion '36, RCAF Saskatoon pairs title '43; 2nd Ont. gold medal team '73 Canada Games lawn bowling rinks competition; pres. PLBA of Ont. '78; pres. Rockcliffe CC '54; mem. Ottawa Valley Curling Assoc. exec.; mem. Gov.-Gen.'s Curling Club.

KENNAWAY, Joe (soccer); b. 25 Jan 1905, Pointe St. Charles, Montreal, Que.; d. 7 Mar 1969, Johnston N. Providence, RI; given name: James; m. Loretta Murphy; c. 3 sons, 2 daughters; began career as fb but injury forced him to play goal where less running was involved; played jr. with Silver Fox, St. Matthews, Woodhall, Sons of Scotland before moving to sr. ranks with Montreal CPR '25-26, Providence '27-30, Fall River '31, New Bedford '31, Glasgow Celtics '31-39; 2 Scottish titles, 3 Scottish FA Cup winners; twice played for Scottish League vs. Irish League; player-mgr Montreal Vickers; coach Brown '46-59; became US citizen '48; mem. N.E., Cdn. Soccer halls of fame.

KENNEDY, Bill (swimming); b. 26 Oct 1952, London, Ont.; given name: William Ray; div. Deborah Stock; c. Richard, Heather; m. Patricia Peters; c. Janelle, Nicklaus; Michigan, UWO, BA, UofOtt, LLB; lawyer; backstroke specialist; at 14 youngest mem. '67 PAG team placing 7th 100m backstroke; 3 gold Canada Games '69; 2 gold '70 CG; bronze 100m backstroke '71 PAG; mem. '72 Olympic team; 3 CIAU titles; mem. Cdn Aquatic Hall of Fame; res. Grand Bend, Ont.

KENNEDY, Bruce (curling); b. 23 Jun 1948, Port Arthur, Ont.; m. Tracy Lynn Wark; c. Lisa, Philip; CP rail engineer; lead Al Hackner's '82 Brier, Silver Broom (world) winner; mem. 3 NO Brier entries; '79-80 Thunder Bay GP, '80 World Open, '81 Sault Ste. Marie cashspiel champions; fed. govt. world champion award '82; res. Thunder Bay, Ont.

KENNEDY, Corrina (canoeing): b. 30 Nov 1970, Saskatoon, Sask.; UofSask; engineer; 1st woman from Saskatchewan to qualify for ntl canoe team; 2 gold, 1 silver '91 PAG; gold K-2, K-4 200 '95 World championships; gold K-4 500 pre-Olympic regatta '95; 3 gold, 1 silver Szeged '96; gold K-4 200 Milano '96; gold K-2 500 '96 Olympic team trials; Edmonton Grads team award; res. Saskatoon, Sask.

KENNEDY, Louise (swimming): b. 16 Aug 1949, London, Ont.; given name: Helen Louise; div. James Glen Cross; c. Cameron James, Graham, John Conway Kennedy, Karlie Jean Kennedy; m. Bruce Casler; UWO, BA; ntl team '64-67; mem. '64 Olympic team; mem. world record 440yd freestyle relay team CG '66; mem. Cdn Aquatic Hall of Fame; res. London, Ont.

KENNEDY, Sheldon (hockey): b. 15 Jun 1969, Elkhorn, Man.; m. Janna Coakwell; c. Ryan; jr. Swift Current (WHL) playing 159 scheduled games, 134g, 153a; mem. '89 Memorial Cup winner, named tournament all-star; mem. Team Canada '88 world jr. title team; drafted Detroit '88; dealt to Winnipeg '94; claimed by Calgary on waivers '95; signed as free agent by Boston '96; saw AHL action with Adirondack Calder Cup team '92; NHL record: 56 scheduled games, 8g, 10a; sent shock waves through hockey world by charging veteran coach Graham James with sexual assault over a period of 6yrs; resulting investigation put James in prison after pleading guilty to 300 counts; established Sheldon Kennedy Foundation to assist victims of child abuse; following path of Terry Fox, Rick Hansen, did cross-Canada fund-raising tour on roller blades '98; launched hockey comeback with Man. Moose (IHL) '98; joined German league '99; res. Calgary, Alta.

KENNEDY, Ted (hockey): b. 12 Dec 1925, Humberstone, Ont.; given name: Theodore; m. Doreen Belfort; c. Mark Ayre; ret'd Ft. Erie race track security official; nicknamed "Teeder"; juv., sr. Port Colborne Ont.; joined Maple Leafs at 17, capt. at 22; 5 Stanley Cup victories; Hart Trophy '54-55 season; led Leafs scorers '46-47 with 28g, 32a, 60pts in 60 games; NHL record: 696 scheduled games, 231g, 329a, 74 playoff games, 28g, 28a; ctr Leafs' 2nd Kid Line, later known as KLM Line, of Vic Lynn, Howie Meeker; ret'd '55, returned briefly '57 to help injury-riddled Leafs; coach Upper Canada College, Peterborough Petes(OHL); twice J.P. Bickell Memorial Trophy as Leaf's MVP; jersey #9 honored by Leafs; mem. Hockey Hall of Fame; res. Port Colborne, Ont.

KENNEDY, Tracy (curling): b. 4 Nov 1963, Fort William, Ont.; given name: Tracy Lynn Wark; m. Bruce Kennedy; c. Lisa, Philip; competed 4 STOH tournaments, 2 winners; played lead for Heather Houston's '88 Ont., '88-89 Cdn title rinks, '89 world champion, '88 world runnerup; mem. Ont. team of '89; mem. NWO Sports, Cdn Curling halls of fame; res. Thunder Bay, Ont.

KENNERD, Trevor (football): b. 23 Dec 1955, Edmonton, Alta.; m. Caroline; UAlta; pk; CFL Winnipeg '80-91; shared CFL record 7 FG 1 game; tied CFL single-game convert record with 9 vs Ottawa '84; set single-season CFL scoring record (since eclipsed) with 198 '85; 2 all-CFL, 3 all-WFC; 2 CFL scoring titles; twice led CFL in field goals; CFL record: 188g; 509cvts, 394fg, 149s, 1840 points; 3 Grey Cup winners; pres. Blue Bomber Alumni; mem. Blue Bumber Hall of Fame; res. Winnipeg, Man.

KENNY, Clayton (boxing): b. 21 Dec 1928, Ottawa Ont.; given name: Clayton Orten; m. Helene Anna Dunlop; c. Jamie, John, Bill; ret'd civil servant; Que. Golden Gloves lightweight title '46; several years Ont. lightweight titlist; ntl lightweight title '52; mem. '52 Olympic team; capt. ntl boxing team '54 BEG; in 103 bouts won 89, drew 4, lost 9; Ottawa outstanding-athlete award; Ottawa Boys Club example-to-youth award; mem. Ottawa CSRA, Ottawa Sports, Canadian Boxing halls of fame; res. Carleton Place, Ont.

KENT, Chris (skiing): b. 12 Oct 1961, Calgary Alta; given name: George Christopher; UCal; fence builder; '77 ntl juv. downhill, giant slalom titlist; '79 jr. downhill; mem. ntl team from '80; Mt. Hutt, NZ, FIS downhill '80; 4th World Cup downhill Val D'Isere, France, '81; silver '83 FIS GS, ntl super GS '84; Alta. achievement awards '77, '79; res. Calgary, Alta.

KENYON, Jack (basketball/coaching): b. 26 Aug 1935, Calgary, Alta.; d. 19 Sep 1994, Calgary, Alta.; given name: John Charles; m. Joena Carole Hampton; c. Jay (d); UAlta BSc, UCal MSc; educator/coach Mount Royal Coll.; played basketball both universities; coached Mount Royal Coll. '62-82, 2 ntl titles; coached ntl jr. men's team '75-79, competed jr. worlds; coached ntl men's B team Cuba tournament; coached Alta. jr. men's team '84-85, silver Canada Games '84; son Jay all-Cdn; asst. coach Calgary 88's (WBL) '89; Calgary Booster Club leadership award; ACAC coach-of-yr award; Percy Page leadership award '83; Jack Kenyon memorial scholarship fund established; center court Mount Royal athletic complex named Kenyon Court; ACAC men's title trophy bears his name; mem. Alta Sports, Cdn Basketball halls of fame.

KEON, Dave (hockey): b. 22 Mar 1940, Noranda, Que.; given name: David Michael; div. Lola; c. David, Anne, Marie, Kathleen, Tim; m. Jane Bloomer; c. Holly, Jody; business executive; Noranda Mines juv.; tryout at 15 with Detroit; 3 years Toronto St. Mikes; Maple Leafs '60-75; Minnesota, Indianapolis, New England WHA '75-79; returned to NHL with Hartford '79-82; Calder Memorial Trophy; twice Lady Byng Trophy; Conn Smythe Trophy '67 playoffs; twice 2nd team all-star ctr; NHL record: 1296 scheduled games, 396g, 590a, 92 playoff games, 32g, 36a; WHA record: 301 scheduled games, 102g, 189a, 36 playoff games, 13g, 23a; mem. Team Canada '77; Rouyn-Noranda arena bears his name; mem. Whalers, Hockey halls of fame; res. West Palm Beach, Florida.

KEPLEY, Dan (football): b. 24 Sep 1953, Albemarle, N.C.; given name: Danny Ray; div. Terry Lynn; c. Michael; East Carolina. BPE; football coach; MVP freshman college year, all-conf., all-state 3yrs, all-American honorable mention twice, *AP, NEA* all-American '74; MVP as sr.; pro Dallas '75; lb Edmonton '75-84; asst. coach Eskimos '85, '02-03, UAlta '01; 7 Grey Cup finals, 6 winners; 5 all-WFC, all-CFL awards; Schenley defensive player '77, '80-81; Edmonton radio, *CBC, ESPN* TV color commentator '89-99; 1 CFLPA western conf. top lb, top def. player, 3 Norm Fieldgate awards; mem. East Carolina, Cdn Football halls of fame; res. Edmonton, Alta.

KER, Michael (swimming); b. 21 Jul 1957, Vancouver, B.C.; given name: Michael Gordon; m. Paula Joan Whisenand; c. Jessica, Justin; pres. Web Plan Inc., dir. Pattern Recognizer.com Inc.; 4 gold, 1 silver '73 Canada Games; ntl sr. records 400m, 800m, 1500m, 500yd, 1650yd FS events; ntl 1500m titles '73, '75; mem. '73, '75 world championships, '76 Olympic teams; 4 gold, 1 bronze '75 Western Canada Games; 4th 400m FS '77 FISU Games; masters competitor; res. Stittsville, Ont.

KERCKHOFF, Claudia (canoeing, skiing); b. 24 Jan 1961, Toronto, Ont.; given name: Claudia Annette; m. Dirk Van Wijk; c. Katrina, Stefani; Carleton, BComm.; owner/dir. Madawaska Kanu Centre; OWL rafting; ntl women's kayak slalom champion '74-85; NA title '76; Europa Cup gold '77; competed '80 (6th), '82 (bronze), '83 (5th) world championships; distance skier; 1st/youngest woman to finish gold course Cdn Ski Marathon '76; won 3 50km class world loppet events; avid painter; res. Ottawa, Ont.

KERCKHOFF, Hermann (canoeing); b. 27 Dec 1937, Berlin, Germany; given name: Hermann Walter; m. Christa Ottenberg; c. Claudia, Annette, Ina; camp dir.; 4 ntl kayaking titles '69-73; mem. Olympic team '72; from '73 owner-operator Madawaska Kanu Camp; launched Ottawa Whitewater Leaders (OWL) rafting division of school '81; res. Don Mills, Ont.

KERN, Ben (golf); b. 11 Aug 1946, Rolandia, Brazil; d. 14 Oct 2002, Caledon, Ont.; m. Janet; c. Shandy, Tobin, Jordan; New Mexico Col.; golf pro; runnerup '65 Ont. amateur, '67 Ont. Open; '68-69 New Mexico intercollegiate, '69 New Mexico college invitational titles; 1st Cdn named 1st team all-American '68; won New Mexico Open '68, '74; pro '69; 4th San Antonio Open; low Canadian '74 Cdn. Open; New Mexico PGA '74, Ont. PGA '77, Cdn Shrine tournament '79; tied 2nd Sun City Open, 6th Sea Pines Open on satellite tour; twice mem. Canadian World Cup team; head pro National Club Woodbridge, Ont.; *Score* Magazine Cdn club professional of year '91; golf dir. Devil's Pulpit from '96; mem. Mississauga Sports Hall of Fame; res. Brampton, Ont.

KERN, Laurie (t&f); b. 6 Feb 1957, Vancouver, B.C.; UBC, BA; teacher; javelin specialist; ntl jr. titles '73, '75; sr. outdoors '79-80; mem. ntl team '74-81; mem. '75, '79 PAG, '78 CG, '79 FISU, '80 Olympic, '81 Pan-Pacific Games teams; ntl bantam, midget, jr., sr. records; bronze '78 CG, gold '79 FISU, '80 Colgate Games; '80 Philadelphia Olympic alternative with Canadian record 57.44m; res, Richmond, B.C.

KERN, Stan (softball); b. 17 Apr 1942, Edmonton, Alta.; given name; Stanice Frederick; m. Joan Roth; c. Trevor, Michelle, Rhonda; mem. Alta. jr. champions '61; Edmonton Playboys '65-67; Edmonton Beta-Well Riggers '68-69; Edmonton Sun Life Red Sox '70-72; Victoria Bate '73-77; mem. title winning teams Hull, Calgary, Montana, Edmonton Klondike, Yakima, Victoria, Seattle tournaments; mem. 7 league, 3 Northern Alta., 3 Alta, 6 BC title teams; mem. 10 ntl championships teams; mem. ntl champion Victoria Bate teams '75-78; 9 top pitcher, 5 Most Valuable Pitcher, 5 MVP, 1 all-star pitcher award; mem. '76 Victoria Bate team, co-holders World Softball championships; 4

BC Sports Council, 2 city of Victoria, 1 *CFAX* awards; on retirement from game 9 Jun '79 honored with plaques from Victoria Bate, Victoria Budget teams, for contribution to softball in Edmonton, by Edmonton teammates, opponents, fans; nicknamed "The Colonel"; coached '80 BC peewee A softball champions; mem. Cdn Softball hall of Fame; res. Victoria, B.C.

KERNAGHAN, Marty (softball); b. 9 Aug 1958, Grafton, Ont.; given name: Martin Arthur; m. Beverley Macklin; c. Jennie, Abby; corporate pilot/hockey exec.; 3b; Oshawa Tonys, Camrose, Alta, Calgary Dome Petroleum, Alta Brake & Clutch, Sioux City; mem. 4 Cdn, 4 US, 4 world title teams; mem. Team Canada PAG '83, ISF '92 title teams; 8 times all-world, MVP '86 worlds; won ISC worlds with Sioux City Penn Corp '88-89, National Health Care Discount '91-92; ret'd '95; v-p/dir. hockey operations Sioux City Musketeers (USHL); mem. ISC Hall of Fame; res. Sioux City, Iowa.

KERR, Barbara (equestrian); b. 20 Jul 1947, Winnipeg, Man.; given name: Barbara Mary Simpson; m. Dr. Barney Kerr; c. Tara, Kelly, Barbara, Patrick Jackson; UAlta., BPhE; UBC, teacher's cert.; business mgr.; competitive figure skater to age 17; 1st woman on Western Canada ski patrol '66; 1st equestrian breakthrough '69 winning Aachen (Ger.) Stake Trophy; 1st, 2nd place ribbons Dublin Ladies' championships; 1st Harrisburg GP '70; mem. bronze medal team '71 PAG; mem. '72 Olympic team; leading rider (foreign) NY National Horse Show '72; bronze ladies' world championships '74; '75-78 concentrated on training young horses, raising family; returned to ntl competition '79; mem. winning Western Team Rothmans East-West Challenge Cup; res. Langley, B.C.

KERR, Bill (golf); b. 14 Jan 1911, Belfast, Ireland; d. 27 Jan 1997, Pointe Claire, Que.; given name: William Henry; m. Constance Daniels; c. William Daniels, Robert John; golf pro; twice PGA champion ('45, '60); 5 times CPGA match play champion; 4 times Que. Open winner; 2nd Canada Cup matches; 5th '55 Greater Greensboro Open; competed '60 Mexican Open, '61 Masters, Caribbean tour; won initial pro tournament Mid Ocean GC, Bermuda; 9 holes-in-one; twice ntl Srs winner; hon. mem. Beaconsfield (Pointe Claire), Palm Beach National Golf Clubs (Lake Worth, Fla.).

KERR, Bobby (t&f); b. 1882, Ireland, d. 1963, Hamilton, Ont.; won 100yd, 440yd, 880yd races Hamilton Coronation Games '02 and '02, '04 ntl 100yd titles; mem. '04, '08 Olympic teams; ntl 100yd, 220yd titles '07; ntl 100yd (9.4), 50yd records; gold 200m, bronze 100m '08 Olympics; '08 British Stamford Bridge meet 100yd, 220yd titles, Harvey Gold Cup as meet's outstanding athlete; defended both titles '09 Dublin, became Irish champion; selected for '12 Olympics but chose retirement; during competitive career won nearly 400 awards, trophies, set 6 Cdn records; mem. Canada's Sports, Canadian Olympic halls of fame.

KERR, Cay (swimming); b. 25 Jan 1921, Edinburgh, Scotland; given name: Catherine Ross Gordon; m. Donald Kerr; c. Gordon, David, Donald, Deborah, Andrea, Laura; began swimming early '30s; won first provincial age-group title '33; 1st ntl title '35, 1st Cdn record '37; set 2 Cdn, 5 Man. records, won 4 ntl titles '39; 5 ntl titles, 3 Cdn records '40, Cdn female-athlete-of-yr nominee; continued to compete at ntl level through '58; devoted attention solely to synchronized swimming '59; set 5 ntl, 11 Manitoba records; won 13 Cdn, 4 Western Canadian, 56 Manitoba titles; 5 Manitoba solo synchronized swim titles; early competitive career spanned '33-'59; returned to pool in masters competition 17 provincial titles, including 5 consecutive solo, 2 duet titles '59-63; 16 provincial Masters age-group records; 1 gold, 4 silver, 2 bronze medals World Masters championships '84; more than 35yrs in synchronized swimming as competitor, coach, judge, administrator; helped organize Canadian Aquatic Hall of Fame; served term as pres. Winnipeg Synchro Swim Club, founding pres. Man. section CASSA; Ntl pres. CASSA '57-60; mgr. synchro swim team '59 PAG; meet official '54 BEG, '59 PAG; master meet official for swimming, diving, synchro swim judge, coach; pres. Ladies Aquatic Hall of Fame; mem. Red Cross water safety advisory board; Royal Life Saving instructor, examiner; mem. Man. Sports Hall of Fame, Order of Canada; res. Winnipeg, Man.

KERR, Jane (swimming); b. 12 May 1968, Mississauga, Ont.; Florida, BAdm; employee Anderson Consulting; team capt.Fla., 5 Southeast Conf. titles, 24 all-American awards; FS sprint specialist; launched competitive career age 8; 8yrs ntl team; 32 ntl titles; 4 ntl championship high point titles; ntl 200FS record; 3 silver '83 PAG, 2 gold, 2 silver, 2 bronze '86 CG, silver, 2 bronze '87 Pan-Pacific championships; mem. '84, '88 Olympic teams; 4x100 medley relay bronze '88 Olympics; 3 Mississauga female- athlete-of-yr awards; Ont., Swim Ont. team-of-yr awards; mem. Mississauga Sports, Ont. Aquatic halls of fame; res. Mississauga, Ont.

KERR, John (sailing); b. 9 Aug 1951, Toronto, Ont.; m. Heather McNevin; Upper Canada College, UWO, BSc; v-p. marketing Kerrwil Publications; ntl Soling class titles '73-78; European Soling title '78; NA, US title '77, '82; CORK title '81-82; 3rd worlds '78; 5th worlds '79; French World Cup title '78; Kiel Week '78; 3rd NA '80; mem. ntl sailing team; mem. '84 Olympic Soling bronze crew; gold, silver Duke of Edinburgh awards; res, Mississauga, Ont.

KERR, Randy (harness racing); b. 9 Jun 1956, Kitchener, Ont.; worked for father Palmer, brother Terry as teenager; began driving Western Fair Raceway at 18 then moved to Windsor with Terry; branched out on own '80 winning driving titles Windsor, Leamington; topped century mark 16 consecutive years; through '97 2860 victories and purses exceeding $10M; res. Amherstburg, Ont.

KERR, Terry (harness racing); b. 23 Dec 1953, Kitchener, Ont.; given name: Terence; became entranced with standardbred racing age 11 when father Palmer purchased first horse; learned driving techniques from the late Ron Feagan; shifted base of operations from OJC circuit to California, BC and Pompano Park, Fla.; with trotter Dapper Dillon represented Canada in Roosevelt International '77, finishing 3rd; guided pacer Quite A Sensation to world record '86; regularly drove Red Bow Tie '96 season; through '03 6223 victories with purses exceeding $19M; res. Sarnia, Ont.

KERR, Tim (hockey); b. 5 Jan 1960, Windsor, Ont.; m. Kathy Hafer (d); c: Kayleigh, Kimberley; m. Margaret Wilson; c. Garret, Wesley, Tanner; owner real estate,

insurance, construction cos; rw Windsor Spitfires '76-77, Kingston Canadians '77-80, Maine Mariners '79-80; not drafted but joined NHL Philadelphia '80-91, NYR '91-92, Hartford '92-93; scored 54g '84, '85, 58 '86, '87; set NHL powerplay single-season record with 34 '85-86; Bill Masterton Trophy '89; NHL record: 655 scheduled games, 370g, 304a, 81 playoff games, 40g, 31a; p-pres. Flyers Alumni Assn.; mem. Windsor/Essex County Sports, Flyers hockey halls of fame; res. Avalon, N.J.

KERRIGAN, Mike (football): b. 27 Apr 1960, Chicago, Ill.; Northwestern; qb, signed as free agent by New England (NFL) '82; joined Toronto CFL '84; Hamilton '86-91, '95-96, Toronto '92-94; 2 Eastern all-star; set CFL playoff game passing record with 35 vs. Toronto '86; CFL record: 154 games, 5tds, 305yds on 134 carries, completed 1534 of 2870 passes for 21,714yds, 126tds, 163int; 6 playoff games, 2 Grey Cup finals, 1 winner; Grey Cup offensive star '86; res. Hamilton, Ont.

KERWIN, Gale (boxing); b. 9 Jan 1935, Ottawa, Ont.; d. 19 Sep 2001, Ottawa, Ont.; given name: Gale Allen; m. Joyce Payne; c. Allen, Kathleen, Shawn, Christine; politician, real estate broker; competed as amateur '47-53 attaining finals twice in Olympic trials; pro '54; KO'd Bobo Fiddler in 12th for ntl welterweight title '58; lost world lightweight title bid to Joe Brown '59; lost middleweight title bid to Ralph Dupas '60; lost jr. welter title bid to Dulio Loi '61; British Empire welterweight title, ranked 10th world welterweight divison; ret'd from ring following 1st round TKO of Frank Marvin '62; pro record: 47 bouts, won 12 by KO, 21 by decision, 3 draws, lost 3 by TKO, 8 by decision; launched Gale Kerwin Boxing Club '97; mem. Ottawa Sports, Canadian Boxing halls of fame.

KERWOOD, Tony (harness racing): b. 26 May 1958, Scarborough, Ont.; given name: Anthony; with urging of father Frank began to impress as driver age 17; spends some time training horses at father's farm near Bowmanville; one of leading drivers on OJC circuit winning 9 UDR titles; drove Pacific Rocket to USTA/USHWA Older Horse Pacer of '95 title; through '03 3629 victories and purses exceeding $41M; res. Campbellville, Ont.

KESLER, Reg (rodeo); b. 16 Oct 1919, Lethbridge, Alta; d. 16 May 2001, Stirling, Alta.; m. Elizabeth (Liz); c. Greg, Mark (d), Pat, Janet, Leanne, Jeanie; rancher, ret'd stock contractor; bucking horse specialist; began rodeo career age 11; 3 ntl all-around (AA) titles; 2 Cdn all-around awards Calgary Stampede; produced 1st rodeo Cranbrook, B.C., '51; with Harry Vold supplied much of the rodeo stock in Alta. in the '50 and '60s; nickname "The Colonel"; mem. Cdn Rodeo Historical Assn.; Western Heritage Centre; mem. Order of Canada, Alta. Sports, Cdn Rodeo halls of fame.

KEYES, Carole (luge); b. 2 Sept 1952, Woodstock, N.B.; given name: Carole Maxine; asst. spa co-ordinator Grey Rocks Inn; mem. ntl luge team '74-84; 3 ntl, 2 NA, 1 Empire State singles titles; mem. '76, '80, '84 Olympic teams; competed world championships '77, '79; head coach ntl team '84-87; chief athletic therapist ntl women's basketball team '80-84; Cdn Athletic Therapists Assn. service award; mem. NB Sports Hall of Fame; res. St. Jovite, Que.

KEYS, Eagle (football); b. 4 Dec 1923, Turkey Neck Bend, Ky.; m. Joyce White (d); c. Betty, Eagle Jr. "Buddy", Dale, Janice, Karen; Western Kentucky State College, BSc, Kentucky, MA; ret'd International Steel & Pipe exec., football coach; pro ctr Alouettes '49-51; Eskimos '52-54; all-Western '52-54; following '54 Eskimos Grey Cup win ret'd to coaching; head coach Eskimos '59-63, guiding them to Grey Cup final '60; Saskatchewan asst. '64, head coach '65-70, Grey Cup victory '66, finals '67, '69; head coach BC '71-75; Annis Stukus Trophy CFL coach of '68; mem. Canadian Football Hall of Fame; res. Langley, B.C.

KEYTE, Lawrence (modern pentathlon); b. 11 Sep 1963, Boston, Mass. given name: Lawrence Edgar; Queen's; teacher; ntl tetrathlon champion '78, '80-81 (shooting, running, swimming, riding); ntl junior champion '82; 1ˢᵗ individually '79, capt. 1ˢᵗ place Canadian team '79 US tetrathlon championships; 1ˢᵗ overall '80, champion jr. '81 West Point Academy triathlon (delete riding); mem. modern pentathlon (add fencing to tetrathlon) team jr. worlds '80-83; shared Bell HS athlete award '80-81; Ottawa ACT awards '79-80; PB: 4963 points world jr. '83; res. Ottawa, Ont.

KHAN, Sharif (squash); b. 10 Nov 1945, Peshawar, Pakistan; m. Jacqueline Taylor; Millfield School, Eng.; squash pro; Somerset county champion at 13; British jr. champion Drysdale Cup at 16; 12 ntl, NA open titles from '69; 9 NA pro, 5 Boston Open, 4 Boodles Gin Open, 4 MAAA Open titles; twice world invitational racquets champion; Mennan Cup world invitational title '79; mem. world-renowned Khan family of squash champions; NA Open Trophy dating back to '54 won by Khan family members 22 times, ret'd to Sharif's permanent possession '81; Squash Canada distinguished service award; res. Toronto, Ont.

KIDD, Bruce (t&f); b. 26 Jul 1943, Ottawa, Ont.; m. Phyllis Berck; UofT, BA, Chicago, MA; prof./UofT athletic dir.; Commonwealth 6-mile title '62; ntl 1 mile '61, '63, 3 mile '61, '62, '64, 6 mile '62, '64, x-country '60, '61, '63; US 3 mile indoor '61-62, 6 mile '62, x-country '61, '63; British 2 mile indoor '64; mem. '64 Olympic, '62 CG teams; Lou Marsh Trophy '61; Lionel Conacher trophy '61-62; authored '83 study on athletes rights in Canada; '93 Bryce Taylor award for contribution to amateur sport; mem. advisory bd. women's sport intl.; mem. UofT, Cdn Olympic, Canada's Sports halls of fame; res. Toronto, Ont.

KIDD, James (sailing); b. 28 Jul 1953, London, Eng.; given name: James Michael; UofT, hons. BSc; chartered accountant; mem. Royal Cdn Yacht Club jr. sailing program to age 16; ntl, international titles in Albacore, International 14, Fireball classes; mem. ntl team; Flying Dutchman silver '75 PAG; 6ᵗʰ FD world championships '76; mem. '76 Olympic team; world International 14 class champion '77; ntl FD titlist, 4ᵗʰ worlds '78; throughout career teamed with younger brother Hugh; res. Toronto, Ont.

KIEFER, Eniko (diving); b. 12 Aug 1960, Montreal, Que.; McGill; 3 US International 1m, 3m titles; 7 ntl age-group 1m, 3m, one 10m titles; '71 world age-group 3m title; 5 ntl sr. 1m titles; 2 Can-Am-Mex jr. titles; CIAU 1m, 3m titles '81; mem. '76, '80 Olympic, '78 CG, World teams; 3m bronze '78 CG; outstanding female diver '81 CIAU

championships; mem. McGill Sports Hall of Fame; res. Dollard des Ormeaux, Que.

KIELTY, Terry (football/builder); b. 28 Jun 1923, Wakefield, Yorkshire, Eng.; given name: John Terrence; m. Jacqueline Beaubien; c. Kimberly, Kristen, Mark; Ryerson; ret'd broadcaster; attended Ont. Athletic Commission camp '38, '40 as student t&f athlete; ctr Toronto Indians (ORFU) '40, RCAF '41-46; joined *CRFA* radio Ottawa '46 remaining in varied roled to '92; founding mem. Football Reporters of Canada; pres. '67; toastmaster '67 Grey Cup dinner; MC Schenley awards '68-80; broadcast voice Ottawa Rough Riders several yrs; club pres. '77-86; mem. CFL (media section), Ottawa Sports halls of fame; res. Ottawa, Ont.

KIERSTEAD, Bob (shooting/coaching/administration); b. 31 Jan 1945, Saint John, N.B.; given name: Robert Douglas; m. Brenda Marie Gilbert; c. Stacey Marie, Graham Edison; UNB BA, MEd; project exec. NB govt.; NCCP Level 5 coach; Charter Professional Coach, Intl shooting coaches school Weisbaden, Germany; head coach Marysville Shooting Club '80-99; head coach NB pistol team '84-00; head coach ntl pistol team '86-01, Cdn Army CISM pistol team '95-00, ntl Paralympic rifle/pistol team from '95; coached shooters 2 Olympics, 3 Paralympics, 2 CG, 2 PAG, 5 worlds, 4 Canada Games, numerous competitions throughout world; mem. world Paralympic shooting governing body from '00; ntl v-p SFC target shooting '99-04; dir. SFC from '92; NB firearms advisory comm. from '00; v-p NB Firearms Alliance '93-96; mem. Assessions comm. NB Sports Hall of Fame '99-01; hon. life mem. O'Dell Collectors & Shooters Fraternity '03; Cdn coaching-excellence award '98; 2 NB Sports coach-of-yr awards; mem. Fredericton Sports wall, NB Sports hall of fame; res. Fredericton, N.B.

KIHN, Richard (gymnastics); b. 15 Aug 1935, Alzenau, West Germany; m. Tina; c. Markus, Britta; accountant, hospital controller; ntl men's champion '59, '61, '63-64; qualified for worlds '62, PAG '63 but was ineligible on citizenship grounds; treasurer Ont., Cdn. Gymnastics Federations, World Cup '80; meet dir. annual Ont. Milk Meet; judge men's gymnastics; rhythmics team mgr.; Ont. special achievement award; life mem. Cdn Gymnastics Fed.; res. Etobicoke, Ont.

KIKUCHI, David (gymnastics); b. 27 Dec 1979, Truro, N.S.; given name: David Taro; Dalhousie, statistics; full-time athlete; 5ᵗʰ in rings, 11ᵗʰ in team '01 FISU Games; 12ᵗʰ in team, 15ᵗʰ in rings '01 worlds; silver '02 ntl championships; 11ᵗʰ in parallel bars '02 worlds; competed '04 Olympics; Gymnastics Canada's athlete of yr, '01-02; res. Fall River, N.S.

KILBURN, Joey (bobsleigh); b. 27 Apr 1949, Ottawa, Ont; given name: Joseph William; Sheridan College; coach; began bobsleighing '74 as brakeman 4-man sled; 2ⁿᵈ ntl 2-man, NA 4-man '74; NA 4-man title '75; driver 2-man sled '76, '80 Olympics; drove ntl 2-man title sled '77-79, 4-man '79; mem. '79 world championships team; ret'd '81 but came back to compete in 2-, 4-man events '82; coach/tech. dir. Bobsleigh Can '85-90; development coach '90-92; coached '92 Olympic team; coached US program '93-95; FIBT international coach from '96; res. Ottawa, Ont.

KILLINGBECK, Molly (t&f); b. 3 Feb 1959, Jamaica; given name: Molly Elizabeth; m. Liam O'Connor; York, BA; Athlete Service mgr. CSCO coach; ntl indoor 200m title '80, 400m '80-81; 16 gold, 13 silver, 7 bronze medals at both 200m & 400m distances in international competitions; mem. 4x400m gold, 4x100m silver medal relay teams '82 CG, 4x400 silver relay team '84 Olympics; mem. ntl sr. record 4x100m relay '82, 600m record, 4x400 relay '83; CIAU 600-, 300-, 60m gold '85; gold, silver, bronze '81 Pacific Conference Games; 3 silver '83, 1 silver '85 FISU games; mem. '80 (boycotted) '84, '88 Olympic Games teams; ret'd from competition '89; 1 CIAU indoor t&f female athlete of yr; 1 CIAU indoor record; coach Phoenix TC, Windsor Legion TC, Windsor, York; part-time Athletics Can. coach; guest coach People's Republic of China '90; head track coach '93 world deaf games; sprint coach '93 indoor worlds, FISU Games, '94 CG, '96 Olympic Games (men's 4x100m gold medal relay); OTFA sprint coach '90-95; head coach/GM Windsor Legion T&FC '93-95; 3 OWIAA, 1 OUAA, 1 CAC, 1 Wittnauer coaching-excellence awards; Athletics Canada ntl relay co-ordinator, chair ntl women's sprint development prgm, mem. board Toronto '08 Olympic bids comm.; 10 Ont. sport excellence awards, 3 fed. govt sport excellence awards, 2 York female-athlete-of-yr awards; Harry Jerome award '84; PetroCan coaching excellence award; mem. York Hall of Fame; res. Toronto, Ont.

KILREA, Brian (hockey/coaching); b. 21 Oct 1934, Ottawa, Ont.; given name: Brian Blair; m. Judy Ringer; c. William, Dianne, Linda; hockey exec.; nicknamed "Killer"; Ottawa minor ranks to Troy Sr. Bruins; pro Edmonton (WHL) '57-58; Vancouver (WHL), Rochester, Springfield (AHL), Tulsa (CHL) through '68-69 season; brief NHL appearances with Detroit '57, LA '67, 3 goals, 5 assists; scored 1st goal in LA Kings franchise history; 9 seasons Springfield (AHL), 3 Calder Cups; coach-mgr. Ottawa 67's '73-84, '87-94, '95-04, GM only '94; through '03 won 11 East div. titles; Memorial Cup '84, '99; became winningest Cdn jr coach 17 Jan '97 with 742nd victory; reached 1,000 victories '03; OHL coach-of-yr awards; coach ntl jr. team '83; asst. coach NYI '84-86 (1 win as interim head coach); Ottawa declared day in his honor; trustee Ottawa Sports Hall of Fame; named CHL all-time team coach '99; Ottawa arena bears his name; CHA coach-of-yr (which he won once) trophy bears his name; City of Ottawa amateur coach award bears his name; mem. Ottawa Sports, Springfield, Cdn Hockey halls of fame; res: Ottawa, Ont.

KILREA, Hec (hockey); b. 11 Jun 1907, Navan, Ont., d. 8 Oct 1969, Detroit, Mich.; given name: Hector Joseph; m. Lois Shannon; Detroit Ford; pro Ottawa Senators '25-31, '32-33, Detroit '31-32, '35-39, Toronto '33-35; ranked among fastest skaters in NHL; beat Howie Morenz in match race at Montreal; assisted on Mud Bruneteau goal which ended longest game in NHL history; mem. 3 Stanley Cup champions; NHL record: 176g, 129a; in US Army WW2 received Distinguished Service Cross, Croix de Guerre, 3 Purple Hearts.

KILREA, Wally (hockey); b. 18 Feb 1909, Ottawa, Ont.; d. 3 Jul 1992, London, Ont.; given name: Walter Charles; m. Marie Pratt; c. Wally Jr. (d); ctr Ottawa Montagnards '27-29; AHL stints with London '30, Windsor '34, Detroit '35-36, Pittsburgh '37-38, Hershey '38-44; 1 AHL all-star, led AHL scorers '43; NHL Ottawa '29-30, '32-33, Philadelphia '30-31, NY Americans '31-32, Montreal Maroons '33-34, Detroit '34-38; NHL totals 329 scheduled games, 35g, 58a, 25 playoff games, 2g, 4a; 2 Stanley Cup winners; coached AHL Fort Worth, Grand Rapids; 1 AHL title; nicknamed "The Pest"; brothers Hec, Ken, nephew Brian all played in NHL.

KIMBALL, Norm (football/administration); b. 29 Jun 1930, Edmonton, Alta.; m. Sharon; c. Douglas, Brian, Robert; football executive; joined Eskimos organization '61 as minor football co-ordinator; moved through organization serving as office mgr., asst. GM, to GM '64; exec. mgr. '76-85; instrumental in developing Eskimos dynasty which resulted in 9 Grey Cup appearances in 10yrs, 6 successive titles; developed superior scouting system; strong impact on CFL growth working on various committees; Edmonton Sportsman of yr; pres./CEO Alouettes '86, folded team on eve of '87 season; mem. Cdn Football Hall of Fame; res. Calgary, Alta.

KING, Dave (hockey/coaching): b. 22 Dec 1947, North Battleford, Sask.; m. Linda; c. Jennifer, Scott, Andrew; UofSask, BAPE, BEd; hockey scout, coach; mem. UofSask Huskies 4yrs; coached 2 Sask. jr. B titlists; asst coach Huskies '72-73, head coach Billings, Mont., WHL '77-79, UofSask. '79-83, CIAU title '83; ntl jrs '81-83, world gold '82; asst Team Canada bronze '82, head coach '83-92; head coach '84, '88, '92 (silver) Olympic teams, Izvestia silver '86, gold '87; coach Team Canada '03; coached ntl jr team to world gold '82, bronze '83; coached Japan '98 Olympics; coached Calgary (NHL) '92-95 (109-76-31); asst. Montreal '97-99; European pro scout for Montreal '99; coach Columbus (NHL) '00-03; NHL record (thru '03) 188-215-56-14; CIAU title '83; 3 world silvers; Dunc McCallum Memorial Trophy '78; WHL coach of '78; CIAU coach of '80, 3 Canada West coach of year, Cdn Coaching Assn. coach of '92 award; *Hockey News* International Sportsman of '91; 3 Colb McEown UofSask awards; PetroCan coaching-excellence award; Father David Bauer award; consultant Japanese IHF mem. Order of Canada, Cdn Olympic, Intl Ice Hockey halls, UofSask Wall of Fame; res. Calgary, Alta.

KING, Don (football/officiating): b. 23 Mar 1919, Regina, Sask.; d. 28 Jun 1986, Regina, Sask.; accomplished in softball, hockey and particularly football; 3yrs Regina intercollegiate ranks before joining Regina Jr. Dales; Western Cdn champions; '39; encouraged by Piffles Taylor played key role in keeping Roughriders alive during '40s as lineman, secty-treas, mgr, asst. coach; began officiating '46; worked more than 1100 games from peewee through pro; pres. Regina football officials assn. 7yrs; instrumental in organizing similar groups throughout country; officiated 4 Grey Cup finals, 2 all-star games, 3 jr finals; 25yrs on-field, 11yrs officiating supervisor; mem. Sask. Sports Hall of Fame.

KING, Donald (cricket); b. 18 Oct 1916, Naramata, B.C., d. 2 Oct 1977, Toronto, Ont.; Pannal Ash Coll. Harrogate, Eng.; achieved rare English schoolboy double academic head boy, athletics capt.; school colors in cricket, racquet sports, track; 440yd, 1-mile, rugby records; earned cap as schoolboy international in rugby; helped organize school teams in France; secty. Ont. Cricket Assn. '47-52; instrumental in restructuring OCA, reorganizing Cdn. CA; re-established international series between US-Canada; Cdn. rep. International Cricket Conference; authored several articles on cricket in domestic, international publications; hon. life mem. Mid-Ulster Cricket group; hon. life mem. Emu Club New South Wales; hon. Old Boy Upper Canada Coll.; hon. v-p. U.K. Assn. of Cricket Umpires; dir. Sports Federation of Canada; MBE.

KING, Mike (football); b. 13 May 1925, Toronto, Ont.; m. Allisen Allan; c. Glen, Gary; company mgr.; Toronto Indians Beaches '44-49; fb/dg Eskimos '50-57; 201 carries for 910yds '51, WFC all-star fb '50-51; East-West Shrine game '55; mem. 3 Grey Cup winners; res. West Vancouver, B.C.

KING, Peter (rowing): b. 25 Oct 1940, Glasgow, Scotland; given name: Peter Charles; McGill, BEng, UWO, MBA; dir. office of Auditor-General; served in Royal Navy '57-74, achieved rank of Lieut. Cmdr., Cnd naval reserve '75-82; dir. CARA from '67, ORC '68-94, pres. '95; life mem. Ntl Assn. Amateur Oarsmen, ORC; mem. Assn. Professional Engineers of Ont., Royal Cdn Military Institute; authored *Art and a Century of Canadian Rowing*; authored numerous briefs, articles pertaining to rowing; holds international rowing umpire's license. Level II coaching certificate; coached local, rgnl, pvcl, ntl levels; managed university fencing teams; chaired NCD x-country skiing; mgr. officials '76 Olympics; ME *Catch* magazine; as student won Que., Ont. sabre, foils titles, various rowing crowns; bronze Cdn. Ski Marathon; silver Masters singles '83 ntl rowing championships; City of London, Ottawa, ORA, CARA Centennial, President's awards; SFC Doug Gilbert award '80; Air Canada Sports Executive of '80; Ottawa ACT Sportsman of '84; mem. Cdn Forces Hall of Fame; res. Ottawa, Ont.

KING, Vivian (swimming); b. 4 Apr 1930, Winnipeg, Man.; m. Alex Thompson; c. Wayne, Lorne; Winnipeg juv titlist '41; Man. Jr. 1/2 mile title '44; Man. 50-, 100-, 220yds, l/2 mile FS, 50-, 100yds backstroke titles '45; swept all Man. jr titles, added Cdn jr. 100yd FS title '46; 23 Man., 4 Western Cdn, 5 Cdn, 10 Ont., 4 Watertown, N.Y., titles '47-51; ntl mile (Ross Gold Cup) champion '49-51; Cdn record 400m FS '48; mem. '48 Olympic team; turned pro '52; won world pro 3 mile title, 4th 26 mile Atlantic City race, swam Lake Winnipeg (18 miles) in record 8:30:00; ardent curler; mem. Man. Sports Hall of Fame; res. Winnipeg, Man.

KINGSMITH, Ray (curling); b. 28 Jun 1927, Queenstown, Alta.; d. 3 May 1988, Calgary, Alta.; m. Nancy Holoboff; c. Marlene, Doug, Joan, Don; Calgary business coll.; sales mgr. Cominco; pres. Glencoe CC '62; pres. SACA '66-67, secty-treas. '70-79; CCA exec. from '79, pres. '83-84; v-p Canadian Curling Reporters; baseball player, umpire; organizer, commissioner Calgary Little League; assoc. dir. Calgary Stampeder Football Club; Calgary Sportsman of '80; CCA exec.-of-yr. award bears his name; mem. Canadian Curling, Alta. Sports halls of fame.

KINISKI, Gene (wrestling/football): b. 23 Nov 1928, Edmonton, Alta.; given name: Eugene Nicholas; m. Marion Kay Weller (d); c. Kelly Eugene, Nicholas Clayton; Arizona;

ret'd bar owner; played football/wrestled Arizona; Alta heavyweight wrestling champion '48-50; AAU champion '51; drafted by LA Rams '52 but better offer brought him home for 3 CFL seasons as Eskimos lineman; 41yrs pro wrestling; def. Lou Thesz for world heavyweight title; held title '66-69; nickname "Big Thunder"; mem. Pro, Cdn Wrestling halls of fame; res. Blaine, Wash.

KINNEY, Margaret (basketball); b. 1 Feb 1912, Edmonton, Alta.; d. 9 Sep 1995, Montreal, Que.; m. Fred Howes; UAlta, BA; ret'd supervisor public affairs Que. region *CBC* (English); mem. UAlta women's basketball, track teams '28-29, '30-32; mem. famed Edmonton Commercial Grads '28-30; mem. Canadian Basketball, Alta. Sports halls of fame.

KINSELLA, J.J. (builder); b. 12 Apr 1908, Regina, Sask.; given name: John Joseph; m. Joyce Gwynneth Mathie; c. Bruce Michael Stephen, John Dermott Andrew; St. Pat's Coll., Carleton; fed. govt. management analyst; 4-letter HS athlete starring in baseball, football, hockey, boxing; mem. Ottawa Montagnard Jr., Montcalm hockey clubs winning Ott. Dist. Int. title '31; mem. Banker's HL; Ott. Dist. featherweight boxing title '31; organized minor baseball, football, hockey programs; conceived, built Silver Stick hockey tournaments into international event which have flourished from 1957; Ottawa ACT sportsman of '69; res. Ottawa, Ont.

KINSELLA, Ray (builder); b. 27 Jan 1911, Ottawa, Ont. d. 29 Apr 1996, Ottawa, Ont. m. Callista Ryan (d); c. Stephen; played briefly in NHL with Ottawa Senators; Eastern Cdn. welterweight boxing champion; boxing instructor Ottawa Boys Club; founding mem. Civil Service RA, major fund raiser for massive all-purpose complex; 3 terms pres. Ottawa RA Centre; RA Centre arena bears his name; life mem. Ottawa CSRA; mem. Ottawa CSRA, Ottawa Sports halls of fame.

KIRBY, Bruce (sailing); b. 2 Jan 1929, Ottawa, Ont., m. Margo Dancey; c. Janice, Kelly; yacht designer; mem. '56, '64 Finn class, '68 Star class Olympic teams; International 14 titles '63-64; mem. 3-boat world International 14 class team titlists '58, '61; '78-79 NA Tempest class champion; designed own craft for Admiral's Cup, Fastnet races Eng.; designed Laser, world's most popular sailboat, '69; designer Canada I, Canada's 1st America's Cup challenger since 1800s; mem. Ottawa Sports, Sailing halls of fame; res. Rowayton, Conn.

KIRBY, Peter (bobsleigh/skiing); b. 17 Dec 1931, Montreal, Que.; given name: Peter Murray; m. Lynnette Castonguay; c. Gillian, Martha; Dartmouth College,. BA, McGill; pres. Northsport Ltd.; ntl jr. alpine ski title '53; mem. ntl FIS team '54; capt. Dartmouth ski team '56; bobsled competitor '61-66; mem. '64 Olympic gold 4-man team, 4th 2-man team; mem. '65 world title 4-man team; mem. Cdn Olympic, Canada's Sports halls of fame; res. Beaconsfield, Que.

KIRKCONNELL, Herb (badminton); b. 6 Sep 1925, Toronto, Ont.; div. Lois, m. Peggy; Durham Coll., UofT; ret'd; 7 ntl, 8 Ont. sr. men's doubles, 3 Ont. men's doubles titles; mem. Thomas Cup team '61; pres. Ont. Badminton Assn. '76-78; pres. Cdn. Badminton Assn. '79-81; mgr. Cdn team '74, '78, '82, '86 CG; mem. Durham Coll. Athletics Hall of Fame; res. Whitby, Ont.

KIRZINGER, Dave (football); b. 1 Mar 1956, Victoria, B.C.; m. Pam; c. Erin Elizabeth; SFU, UBC; sales rep.; HS athlete of '73; BC 1st team HS basketball all-star; starred in basketball SFU 1 season; football starting og UBC, top lineman '77; 1st draft pick '78; CFL Calgary '78-86; Stampeders player rep.; res. Calgary, Alta.

KISS, Kristina (soccer); b. 13 Feb 1981, Ottawa, Ont.; Carleton; program dir., head coach Ont. Youth Soccer League -15 team; ntl jr. judo title (44kg) '95; midfielder 2 Nepean United ntl club title teams; mem. W-League Ottawa Fury; messy signing incident with Oklahoma State prevented her playing NCAA soccer; mem. Ont. -17, -19 teams; competed '00, '02 Gold Cup, capt. '03 Pan-Am Games; scored 1st intl goal '00; made WC team debut Algarve Cup '00; 60 intl caps; ret'd from ntl team '04 to join Floya of Norwegian Premier League; res. Kanata, Ont.

KISSICK, Myrna (horseshoes); b. 9 Dec 1936, Stauffer, Alta.; given name: Myrna Taylor; m. Jim Kissick (d), Wilf Donald; sc. Kenneth; ret'd farmer/rancher; began horseshoe pitching '72; earned bronze Alta. Summer Games '72; 12 Alta. women's titles; 4 ntl women's titles; competed 8 world championships; Alta high-ringer record; with Sylvianne Moisan involved in best game ever thrown by women (126 shoes) '95 ntl championships; 2 Alta. achievement awards; mem. Alta. HPA, Horseshoe Canada halls of fame; res. Caroline, Alta.

KLASSEN, Cindy (speed skating/hockey/lacrosse); b.12 Aug 1979, Winnipeg. Man.; competed '94 CG field lacrosse; mem. ntl women's jr. hockey team '96; tried speed skating '97 and was named to ntl team '99; gold 1000m, bronze 500m '99 world jrs.; bronze '01 world 1500m single distance race; 3 bronze '01 worlds; WC bronze '01, silver '02; Olympic 3000m bronze '02; women's all-around title '03; 4 WR; shared Speed Skating Canada female skater of '01 with Catriona Le May Doan; res. Winnipeg, Man.

KLIMPEL, Carol (swimming): b. 30 Mar 1963, Toronto, Ont.; given name: Carol Henny; m.; Texas; freestyle specialist; bronze 100m FS '77 Canada Games; gold 100m FS, 4x100 FS relay, 400 IM '78 CG, gold 4x100 FS relay '79 Canada-Russia dual meet; 2 bronze '79 Canada Cup; ntl 50m 100m, 200m, 4x100 FS relay records; 100m FS gold World Cup '80-81; Speedo world sprint award '80; 21 ntl championship medals; 9 ntl, 4 4-nation, 1 Swedish, 1 Japanese titles; 4 ntl, 2 CG, 1 Commonwealth records; silver 4x100 FS relay '79, '83 PAG; mem. '80, '84 Olympic teams; active masters swimmer; mem. Ont. Aquatic Hall of Fame; res. West Hill, Ont./Nashville, Tenn.

KNIGHT, Courtney (t&f); b. 20 Jan. 1976; 100 Mile House, B.C.; given name: Courtney Marie; Simon Fraser, BA; full-time athlete; Cdn. Blind sports record holder pentathlon, discus, shot put, 100m, 800m, lj.; ntl from '92; 1st Cdn. athlete with disability to qualify for able-bodied provincial team (Team BC '95 Western Canada Games, Cdn. Jr. t&f championships); four-time Paralympian: 4th in discus in '92, silver discus, 4th pentathlon in '96, silver pentathlon, 4th discus '00, bronze discus '04; silver discus '94, '02,

'03, pentathlon '98, '03, bronze shot put '03 worlds; 1st athlete-with-disability to win BC HS event ('95 discus); gold pentathlon '97 European championships; gold discus, pentathlon '99, 01 PAG; Sport BC athlete with disability award '95; BC Athletics female-athlete-with-disability awards '96-03; Cdn Olympic Academy delegate '97; BC Premier's Sport Award '98-03; athletes' rep., BC, Cdn Blind Sports Assns. '98-00, Athletics Canada '02-04 athletics team capt. '02-03 worlds, '04 Paralympics; youth motivational speaker; res. Burnaby, B.C.

KNIGHT, Lee (football); b. 8 Feb 1965, Wallesey, Eng.; m. Lisa; c. Kathy Lee, Sam, Connor; correctional officer; fb/sb Burlington jr Tiger-Cats (Braves); signed as free agent Hamilton '87; selected by Montreal '96 equalization draft; claimed on waivers by Ottawa '96; traded to Hamilton '96; 1 Grey Cup final; res. Burlington, Ont.

KNIGHT, Pete (rodeo); b. 1904, Philadelphia, Pa.; d. May 1937, Hayward, Calif.; shared championship honors 1st Calgary Stampede '24; world rodeo championships '26, '35-36; '30 reserve championship American Rodeo Assn; thrown, killed defending title '37; mem. Cdn Pro Rodeo, Alta. Sports halls of fame.

KNIGHT, Tuffy (coaching); b. 17 May 1936, Clarksburg, W.Va.; given name: David; m. Connie Rose Audia; c. Timothy Allen, Brian David; Fairmont State Coll., BA, West Virginia, MA; football coach; 5ys head football, track, 3yrs basketball coach Crooksville, Ohio, HS; Class A Ohio state HS grid title '63; AD/head football coach Wilfrid Laurier '65-83; OIAA football titles '66, '68; OUAA titles '72-73, '78, '97; CIAU College Bowl finalist '66, '68, '72; CIAU coaching record (through '96) 138-80-5; overtook Bruce Coulter as CIAU winningest coach in '96 season; 3 CIAU Frank Tindall coach-of-yr awards; OUAA coach of '79, '80; Southeastern Ohio FB coach of '62-63; dir. player personnel Argos '84-88; head FB coach Waterloo '88-97; res. Waterloo, Ont.

KNOX, Swede (officiating/hockey); b. 2 Mar 1948, Edmonton, Alta.; m. Maureen Baldwin; c. Ryan, Brett; Athabaska, BBA, Alya. Inst. Tech.; NHL linesman; played jr. hockey Alta. jr. league; joined NHL '71 appearing in initial game 14 Oct '72; worked 1500th game '91; 1 NHL all-star game, 5 Stanley Cup finals; NHL record 2000+ scheduled games, 200 playoff games; res. Edmonton, Alta.

KNOX, Walter (t&f); b. 1878, Listowel, Ont.; d. 3 Mar 1951, St. Petersburg, Fla.; Beloit Coll., Illinois; athlete, coach; '96-33 recorded 359 1sts, 90 2nds, 52 3rds in formal competition; '07 won 5 ntl titles in single meet beating Cdn world class athletes Ed Archibald (pv), Dr. Cal Bricker (bj), Bobby Kerr ('08 Olympic sprint champion) in their own specialties while each was at his peak; ntl records 100yd dash (tieing 9.8 world record), 22.8 for 220yd, 46'5" shot put, 12'6" pv, 24'2" running bj, 10'7.5" standing bj; 128' discus; British tour '11 won 57 1sts, 23 2nds, 31 3rds; coach Olympic team Stockholm Games; American all-pro '13 defeating US champ John A. MacDonald in match contest Hanlan's Pt. Toronto; competed vs. BE champion F.R. Cramb for world all-around title '14 winning 6 of 8 events; coach '16 British Olympic but WWI cancelled games; coach '20 Olympic Games; chief coach Ont.

Athletic Commission several years; mem. Cdn Olympic, Canada's Sports halls of fame.

KNUDSON, George (golf): b. 28 Jun 1937, Winnipeg, Man.; d. 24 Jan 1989, Toronto, Ont.; given name: George Alfred Christian; m. Shirley; c. Kevin, Paul, Dean; golf pro; Man. jr. title '54-55, ntl jr. '55; mem. Man. Willingdon Cup teams '56-57; Man. Open '58-60, Ont. Open '60-61, '78, Atlantic Open '76; 5 CPGA titles; 12 PGA tour titles '61-72; individual low, International Trophy '66 World Cup; with Al Balding won '68 World Cup; tied 2nd US Masters '69; won Australian Wills Masters '69, runnerup '70; winner in playoff with Stan Leonard Shell Wonderful World of Golf '63-64, in playoff with Balding '64-65, runnerup to Gene Littler '65-66, Al Geiberger '67-68; Peter Jackson Cup '76; CPGA golfer of 20th century; mem. Order of Canada, RCGA, Ont. Sports Legends, Canada's Sports halls of fame.

KOHARSKI, Don (officiating/hockey): b. 2 Dec 1955, Halifax, N.S.; given name: Donald Nicholas; m. Susan Anderson; c. Jamie, Kevin; hired as WHA official at 18; joined NHL as linesman '77 becoming referee after 163 games; gained international experience in Canada Cup '87, '91; worked 15 consec. conf. finals, 7 Stanley Cup finals, 1 NHL all-star game; NHL record (as linesman/referee) through '03: 1477 scheduled, 212 playoffs games; res. St. Louis, Mo.

KOIVU, Saku (hockey): b. 23 Nov 1974, Turku, Finland; m. Hanna; ctr TPS Turku '90-95; Finnish ntl team "92-95; Team Finland '94 (bronze), '98 (bronze) Olympics; Finnish player of '95; gold '95 worlds, best-forward award; silver '99 worlds; NHL Montreal '95-04; NHL record (through '04): 497 scheduled games, 120g, 278a, 40 playoff games, 13g, 21a; capt. Montreal from '99; missed much of '01-02 season while battling cancer; 2 NHL all-star games; res. Turku, Finland.

KOLAR, Stan (golf): b. 1 Nov 1922, Czechoslovakia; d. 22 Dec 2002, Ottawa, Ont.; m. Ethel Marie Barlow; c. Terence, Lynn, Tracey; ret'd golf pro; runnerup Man. jr. '29; won Thunder Bay amateur '41; Lachute Open twice, Rawdon Open, Que. Open; runnerup CPGA Seniors twice; Canada's 3rd master pro '77.

KOLBOVIC, Renata (tennis): b. 30 Jul 1976, Brno, Czech Republic; UCal Berkeley; tennis player; all-American; runner-up 4 ITF events in Mexico, 2 ITF events at Hilton Head, 1 each Montréal, Edmonton; 1st pro title '95 ITF event Mexico City, not dropping a set until final; Fed Cup member from '99; def. Marlene Weingartner 6-2, 6-2 to reach 2nd round '99 Cdn. Open; mem. '99 PAG team; res. Vancouver, B.C.

KOMONEN, Dave (t&f): b. 16 Dec 1898, Kakisalmi, Finland; d. 19 Apr 1978, Helsinki, Finland; given name: Taavi; div. c. Patti, Unto; m. Elsa Hamalamen; c. Elia; carpenter; emigrated to Canada '29; ntl, US marathon titles, 2nd Boston Marathon '33; mem. Sudbury Frood Mines AC; unsuccessful bid Finnish Olympic team '32; won '34 Boston Marathon; failed to qualify '34 BEG team; returned to Finland '51; Lionel Conacher award '33.

KONANTZ, Gordon (skiing/sailing): b. 12 Oct 1932,

Winnipeg, Man.; given name: Gordon Edward; m. Gail Macdonald; c. Leslie, Donald, Erin; UWpg, Queen's, BComm; GM North American Lumber; competed nationally alpine, x-country championships; Norwegian Birkenbeiner '77, '79, US Birkenbeiner '75, Cdn masters x-country '80-81; pres. Loch Lomond Ski Club, Thunder Bay '56; pres. Puffin SC '61-62; chair. Man. div. CSA '67-68; with Gary Coopland formed Man. jr. Jackrabbit program '57; pres. Man. Cross-Country Ski Assn. from '76; chair. ntl ski team comm., dir. Cross-Country Canada '80-81; commodore Royal Lake of Woods Yacht Club '65, '71; pres. Man. Sailing Assn. dir. CYA '74-76; mem. Winnipeg PAG comm. '67; pres. Winnipeg Squash Racquet Club '73-74; dir. Man. Sports Fed. '81-83; chair. Man. Foundation for Sports; level 2 x-country ski instructor; instructor examiner CYA; mem. Man. Sports Hall of Fame; res. Winnipeg, Man.

KONCHALSKI, Steve (basketball): b. 11 Apr 1945, New York, N.Y; given name: Stephen; m. Charlene MacFarlane; c. Christopher, Julianne, Maria; Acadia, BA, Dalhousie, LLB; basketball coach St. FX; mem. Acadia Axemen team '62-66; twice all-conf.; 4 scoring records leading team to ntl title '65; title tournament MVP; Acadia career record 1479pts; coached St. FX to 9 CIAU title tournament appearances, 3 titles; 6 AUAA championships; CIS coach of '01; ntl team asst. coach '73-88, head coach '95-99; mem. Acadia Sports, Cdn Basketball Hall of Fame; res. Antigonish, N.S.

KONIHOWSKI, Diane (t&f): b. 7 Mar 1951, Vancouver, B.C.; given name: Diane Helen Jones; m. John Konihowski; c. Janna Lee, Alana; UofSask, BPhE; mgr. Calgary ntl sports centre; ntl pentathlon champion '69, '72-78; jr. titlist '70; ntl sr. indoor lj title '74; mem. '70, '74, '78 CG, '73 FISU, '72, '76, '80 Olympic, '75, '79, '83 (coach) PAG teams; pentathlon gold '75 PAG, bronze '73 FISU, '78 CG; Polish, Czechoslovakian pentathlon titles '74; world indoor record 4540pts '75 ntl championships; PB (outdoor) 4673 winning '75 PAG; ntl records indoor 50m hurdles 7.1m, lj 6.37m, shot put 16.23m; ranked 3rd world pentathlon '77-78; team leader Olympic services '94; co-holder Velma Springstead trophy '75 (Nancy Garapick), '78 (Cathy Sherk); 2 Bobbie Rosenfeld awards; '78 ntl lj title; *CBC* radio commentator; COA v-p; mem. Canada's Sports Hall of Fame selection comm.; CdM '00 Olympics; mem. Order of Canada, Cdn Olympic, Sask. Sports Halls, UofSask Sports Wall of Fame; res. Calgary, Alta.

KONIHOWSKI, John (football): b. 6 Jan 1950, Moose Jaw, Sask.; given name: John William; m. Diane Jones; c. Janna Lee, Alana; Brigham Young, UofSask; operates sports surface co.; 5 ntl age-class tj titles; Sask. HS lj, tj, high hurdles records; ntl indoor tj record 49'10"; won '72 Olympic trials 400m hurdles; ntl record 300m (34.7) '72; football UofSask '71, '73; all-CIAU wr '73; drafted Stampeders '72; mem. Eskimos '74-80; Edmonton nominee '75 rookie of year; mem. 5 Grey Cup finalists, 4 winners; active mem. Prairie Golden Canadian TC; mem. UofSask Sports Wall of Fame; res. Calgary, Alta.

KOONER, Andrew Singh (boxing): b. 11 May 1979, Kettering, England; full-time athlete; 54kg; emigrated to Canada age 3; began boxing age 13; 1st ntl title age 14 at '93 jr. ntls with only 7 fights under his belt; 10 ntl titles, 3 jr.,

2 int., 5 sr.; silver '96 jr. worlds; bronze '98, silver '00 CG; competed '00 Olympics, '01, '03 worlds; bronze '03 PAG; record 100-18 to Jan. '04; 2 Kersi Awards for contributions to community through sport; res. Tecumseh, Ont.

KOOTNEKOFF, John (basketball): b. 10 Aug 1935, Canora, Sask.; given name: John Lee; m. Mary Katherine Farrell; c. J.C., Kurtis, Karolyn Marie; Seattle, BEd, Washington, MSc; facilitator of positive information; mem. Seattle NCAA finalist team '58; mem. '60 Olympic team; player/coach 7 Sr. A ntl title teams; coached several ntl team players during '70s; named 1 of 100 most physically fit 40+ Canadians '76; film dir. radio, TC personality; authored *From Kooty with Love*; pres. dir. Horizon Positive Self Image Institute; listed *American Coll. Who's Who* for academic, athletic achievements; mem. BC Sports Hall of Fame; res. Burnaby, B.C.

KOPAS, Jack (harness racing): b. 16 Oct 1928, Lumsden, Sask.; m. Alice; c. John, Roger; horseman; developed racing interest working for Jim Kealey farm; became Gibbs brothers trainer; active driver from '64; Cdn horseman of '69, '76; protégée of Clint Hodgins; among top horses Super Wave, Jade Prince, Shadow Star, Nat Lobell, Super Clint, Areba, Armbro Bramble; 21 classic race victories including 6 Reynolds Memorial, 2 Sheppard Pace, 1 Cane Pace; mem. Harness Racing Hall of Fame; res. Ilderton, Ont.

KOPAS, Ron (baton twirling): b. 2 Oct 1941, Toronto, Ont.; m. Heather Rand; c. Paul, Steven; twirling coach; 5 ntl men's titles; world duet (Isabel Wright) title '59; led ntl champion Ticat corps; WBTF clinic co-ordinator throughout world; WBTF judge; coach Ont., ntl, world corps champions '79-82; tech. chair. Twirl Canada, tech. v.-chair WBTF; res. Bramalea, Ont.

KORN, Alison (rowing): b. 22 Nov 1970, Ottawa, Ont.; Carleton, MJourn., UWO; journalist; mem. ntl team '95-00; Head of Charles coxed 4's gold '95; silver women's 8's '96, bronze '00 Olympics; pairs gold (with Emma Robinson), silver 8's '97, pairs gold '98, bronze women's 8's worlds; made coaching debut UWO; Ottawa ACT rowing award '97; joined all-female ski trek to North Pole '01; mem. Ottawa Sports Hall, Nepean Sports Wall of Fame; res. Nepean, Ont./Toronto, Ont.

KOSANOVIC, Zoran (table tennis): b. 1956, Yugoslavia; d. 4 Feb 1998, Toronto, Ont.; m. Darinka Jovanov; c. Tanya, Sasha; mem. Yugoslavian ntl team placing 2nd in world play at 18; emigrated to Canada '79; 5 Yugoslavian, 5 Cdn ntl men's singles titles; at one stage of career ranked 7 in world; coached Cdn ntl, Ont. provincial teams several yrs.

KOSKIE, Corey (baseball); b. 28 Jun 1973, Anola, Man.; given name: Cordel Leonard; UMan.; pro baseball player; 3b Minnesota Twins '98-04, Toronto Blue Jays '05; ML record (through '04): 816 scheduled games, 2788ab, 438r, 781h, 180db, 13tr, 101hr, 437rbi, 66sb, .280ba; played hockey as youth; res. Minneapolis, Minn.

KOSMOS, Mark (football): b. 28 Oct 1945, Baltimore, Md.; given name: Markus Michael; m. Nikki Marie Zaharis; c. Markus Michael Jr., Nicole; Oklahoma, BA; restaurateur; all-league football Eastern Oklahoma Jr. Coll; twice all-

league; mem.'69 Pottstown Firebirds (ACFL) title team; pro Montreal '70-71, Hamilton '72, Ottawa '73-77; all-Cdn., Eastern Schenley lineman-of-yr. nominee '71; all-Eastern '75-76; mem. 4 Grey Cup champions, 3 different teams; radio football show host; mem. Rough Riders advisory board; mem. CFL all-time all-stars; res. Nepean, Ont.

KOUZMANIS, Tom (soccer): b. 22 Apr 1973, North York, Ont.; UofT; midfielder; 1st draft expansion Nova Scotia Clippers '91; mem. Canada's Olympic -23 team; 1st Cdn player in 110yrs to score two goals in 1st 2 intl games for Canada; played with Nova Scotia Clippers, Montreal Supra CSL; mem. Montreal Impact A League '96, Toronto Shooting Stars indoor league, Vaughan (CPSL), Toronto Olympians; UofT forfeited '03 season when he was judged ineligible because of pro background; res. North York, Ont.

KOVITS, Herman (rowing): b. 20 Jan 1933, Lashburn, Sask.; given name: Joseph Herman; m. Brenda; c. Carolyn Andres, Eric.; UBC, BA, McGill, DDS; dentist; UBC Big Block award for rowing; mem. '54 BEG gold medal 8s crew; mem. Class B BC fastball champions '56; mem. BC Sports Hall of Fame; res. Chilliwack, B.C.

KOWALSKI, Killer (wrestling): b. 13 Oct 1926, Windsor, Ont.; given name: Wladek; c. Walter; operater Institute for Pro Wrestling; competed in estimated 8000 matches over 26yr career; involved in 1st Cdn televised match with Yukon Eric; remembered for accidentally ripping off Eric's ear during '54 Montreal match; 8 AWA/IWA world heavyweight titles; NWA US heavy title; with Gorilla Monsoon WWF US tag-team crown; 4 IWA world tag-team titles; 7 Montreal Intl. titles; battled such stars as Whipper Billy Watson, Nature Boy Buddy Rogers, Georgeous George; protégées include Luna Vachon, Chyna; mem. Windsor-Essex Sports, WWF, TRC Pro Wrestling halls of fame; res. Andover, Mass.

KOZAK, Chelan (equestrian): b. 16 Jan 1969, Revelstoke, B.C.; m. Jason Koningen; began competitive career at 14; mem. ntl team from '91; youngest mem. Canada's three-day event team '94 World Equestrian Games; riding Soweto; competed '96 Olympics, '99 PAG; res. Abbotsford, B.C.

KRAATZ, Victor (figure skating): b. 7 Apr 1971, Berlin, Germany; mem. ntl team from '92; with Shae-Lynn Bourne formed outstanding Cdn ice dance duo from '91; 10 ntl, 6 Skate Canada titles; Skate America title '02; 4-Continents title '03; 2 NHK trophy silver; 1 Worlds gold, 1 silver, 4 bronze; Championship series gold, silver; Neblehorn trophy gold; 32 intl medals; competed '94, '98, '02 Olympics; '03 world title; turned pro '03; severed ties with Bourne, ret'd from competition '03; res. W. Vancouver, B.C.

KRAEMER, Bob (football): b. 31 May 1950, Winnipeg, Man.; m. Beverly; c. Robbie, Danny; UMan, BPhE; ntl dir. Athletes in Action; conference all-star team, twice conference MVP; guided UMan to College Bowl titles '69-70; outstanding player '69 College Bowl; 1st round draft Blue Bombers, WFC rookie of '71 as wr; caught 43 passes '73 while setting single-game Bombers record with 11 catches; ret'd '75; res. Abbotsford, B.C.

KRAUSE, Willi (coaching): b. 11 Dec 1909, Pasewalk, Germany; m. Eva Jordan; c. Christa, Axel; ret'd master pattern maker; limited success as bj, javelin competitor; instrumental in developing Erika Fish as German champion, top international competitor; major role in developing Trail T&FC into one of Canada's best; supervised Trail indoor track construction; coached BC track team ntl championships, '64 Olympic trials; within 1st decade in Trail his athletes had won numerous ntl titles, set 6 Cdn, 1 world record while harvesting silver, bronze medals at PAG, CG; several of his trainees earned US university scholarships; Jim Morris award Trail sportsman of '77; Trail citizen of '79; National Recreation Assn award '84; BC certificate of merit '81; mem. BC Sports Hall of Fame; res. Burnaby, B.C.

KREINER, Kathy (skiing): b. 4 May, 1957, Timmins, Ont.; m. Dave Phillips; c. Nelson Phillip, Liam, Michaela; Utah, BA, UofOtt, MA; sport psychology consultant, motivational speaker; home schooler; at 12 youngest ever to win Mt. Tremblant Taschereau downhill; at 14 joined older sister Laurie on ntl World Cup team; mem. '72 Olympic team; gold WC GS Pfronten, WGermany, '74; 6 ntl titles, 4 times runnerup '74-81; gold GS '76 Olympics, 4th combined '80 Olympics; 2 WC silver, 1 bronze medals; 2 Pontiac Cup bronze; FIS gold GS '75; downhill silver '81; 4th overall WC GS '76-77; WC record 1-1-3; raced '80-81 as independent; Bobbie Rosenfeld award, Ont. athlete of '76; with freestyle skiing husband Dave operated ski program Blackcomb Mt., B.C.; competitive water skier; active in Youth for Christ program; mem. Cdn Skiing, Cdn Olympic, Ont. Legends, Canada's Sports halls of fame; res. N. Vancouver, B.C.

KREINER, Laurie (skiing): b. 30 Jun 1954, Timmins, Ont.; given name: Lauren Margaret; sep. Ron Vaillancourt; c. David William, Angela, Russell; municipal employee; ex-ski resort mgr., owner; ntl downhill title '69; mem. '70 FIS, '72, '76 Olympic, '69-76 ntl teams; US ntl GS title '71; 4th GS '72 Olympics; '75 Roch Cup title; overall downhill title '75 Can-Am series; ntl sport tech. advisor alpine skiing from '94; minor soccer administrator; director Timmins Ski Racers; active in Cdn Special Olympics; Ont. Achievement award, Timmins Sportswoman of '72; res. South Porcupine, Ont.

KREMPIEN, Jennifer (wheelchair basketball); b. 19 Feb 1975, St. Albert, Alta.; UAlta BSc, Capital Health Authority Dietetic Internship; registered dietician; 3 Paralympic, world gold; 2 world all-star; gold '99 tournament of Americas, silver '02; competed 12 ntl finals with Edmonton Aurora Lights 3 ntl gold, 4 silver, 3 bronze; 4 ntl all-star; mem. Cdn Wheelchair Basketball Hall of Fame; res. Richmond, B.C.

KRISTMANSON, Alan (basketball): b. 5 Nov 1961, Vancouver, B.C.; m. Danielle Cosens; SFU.; golf pro; basketball coach; 3rd team Cdn HS all-star '79; fwd ntl team '87-92; WBL '90-91 scoring leader; mem. '87 PAG, FISU, '88 Olympic teams; pro New Zealand '86, avg. 42pts per game; asst. coach SFU; played golf as jr.; turned pro '93; dir. golf Whistler GC; res. Whistler, B.C.

KROEKER, Tim (t&f): b. 25 May 1971, Chilliwack, B.C.; SFU; hurdler; ntl jr. 110m title '89; 5 ntl titles; bronze '94 Francophone Games; mem. ntl team from '90; competed '91 PAG, '91, '93 FISU, '94 CG, '96 Olympic Games, '93, '95 worlds; gold '95 Harry Jerome, Fresno relays, '94 Flagstaff, '93 Provo, Utah, relays; bronze '95 Nurnberg

Grand Prix; BC athlete of '93; Sr. male athlete of '93; res. Surrey, B.C.

KROL, Joe (football): b. 20 Feb 1919, Hamilton, Ont.; m. Pat (d); c. Richard, Peter; UWO, BA; ret'd insurance exec., govt. consultant; nicknamed "King"; runner, passer, kicker; helped UWO win '39 intercollegiate title, Hamilton Wildcats ntl finals '43; with Argos '45-52; mem. 6 Grey Cup winners; with Royal Copeland formed Gold Dust Twins; Jeff Russel trophy '46; Lionel Conacher trophy '46-47; Lou Marsh trophy '46; Grey Cup record 30 points; named to all-time Argos team '96; mem. UWO W-Club, Ont. Sports Legends, Cdn Football, Canada's Sports halls of fame; res. Toronto, Ont.

KROLL, Horst (motorsport); b. 16 May 1936, Germany; m. Hildegard Schmelzle; c. Birgit; operates auto service business; ntl -2 litre title '67-68; ntl driving title '68; Germany's Algemeiner Deutscher Automobil Club gold medal with diamonds for distinguished service to international autosport '68; raced in Formula 5000 series in Canada, US; twice runnerup to ntl champion Eppie Sietzes Sr.; 3 ntl Formula Vee titles; mem. Cdn Motorsport Hall of Fame; res. Scarborough, Ont.

KROMM, Bobby (hockey): b. 8 Jun 1929, Calgary, Alta.; given name: Robert David; m. Geraldine Louise DeRosa; c. David, Robin, Richard, Michelle; manufacturing rep.; amateur hockey Kimberly Dynamiters, North Sydney Victorias, Trail Smoke Eaters; mem. '61 world champion, '62 Allan Cup champion Smoke Eaters; coached Smoke Eaters 4yrs, Nelson Maple Leafs 2yrs; pro coaching ranks Seattle (WHL) 1yr, St. Louis Braves (CHL) 1yr, Dallas Black Hawks (CHL) 9yrs, Winnipeg Jets (WHA) 2yrs, Detroit (NHL) 3yrs; coached 3 CHL champions, 1 Avco Cup WHA champion; CHL, WHA, NHL coach-of-yr awards; res. Livonia, Mich.

KROUSE, Bob (football): b. 21 Feb 1943, Hamilton, Ont.; given name: Frank Robert; m. Marjorie Hughes; c. Robert Joseph, Paul Edgar, John Henry; McMaster, BA, BPhE, Buffalo, MA; ret'd HS phys ed teacher; Olympia Sport Camp instructor; twice all-city HS fb/db; mem. 1st Cdn HS mile relay team to post sub-3:30 indoor mile (3:27.9); pro Hamilton '63-75; fb/db/cb; capt. Ticats '73, player-coach '75; EFC all-star '67; defensive co-ordinator McMaster '80; head coach Sheridan College from '82; Cdn scout Tiger-Cats; res. Grimsby, Ont.

KRUGER, Harry (football): b. 11 Mar 1954, Calgary, Alta.; div. c. Eric, Blaine, Rachel; m. Myrna Hermanson; sc. Caleb; UCal, BComm; Paintball field owner, Calgary indoor arena, Cochrane outdoor field; CIAU all-Canadian '77; CFL db with Calgary, Winnipeg, Ottawa '78-84; res. Cochrane, Alta.

KRUPP, Charlie (builder): b. 1906, Winnipeg, Man.; d. 21 Jan 1958, Winnipeg, Man.; YMHA baseball, softball catcher with strong defensive skills; soccer standout; also participated in basketball, football, hockey, lacrosse, 10-pin bowling, curling; while his athletic skills were considerable his major impact came as a builder serving as a coach, executive, sponsor and liberal contributor to many sporting organizations; coached several outstanding sr. men's softball teams '40s-'50s; exec Winnipeg Blue Bombers, Esquires jr.

hockey club, Maple Leaf curling club; operated Winnipeg Monarchs jr. hockey club, horse racing stable; sponsored numerous teams including Winnipeg Dominoes women's basketball team; Teeni-League baseball, women's softball, Man. Olympic basketball players all benefitted from his generosity and support; softball park bears his name; mem. Man. Sports Hall of Fame.

KRYCZKA, Joe (administration): b. 4 Jun 1935, Coleman, Alta.; d. 11 Jan 1991, Calgary, Alta.; UAlta. BL; lawyer, judge; mem. '49-50 Alta midget hockey champs; capt. Alta. juveniles; def with UAlta Golden Bears '53-56; 3 Western Canada Intercollegiate titles; shoulder injury ended playing career; turned to coaching/refereeing' elected to AAHA exec. '63; pres. CAHA '72; instrumental in organizing 1st Canada-Russia series; dir./v-p Calgary Olympic Development Assn. '79; nicknamed "Justice Joe"; life mem. AAHA, CAHA, CODA; Canada's Sports Exec. of '72; Alta. outstanding-sport-achievement award '72; mem. AAHA, Alta, Canada's Sports halls of fame.

KRYCZKA, Kelly (synchro swim): b. 8 Jul 1961, Calgary, Alta.; given name: Kelly Marie; m. William Irwin; c. Stephanie, Kristine, Scott (d); Jennifer, Nicole; UCal, BPhE; mem. Calgary YWCA Aquabelles; ntl jr. solo title, figures, duet, team aggregate '76; ntl sr. team title '77, '81, '83; ntl sr. duet title '79, '82, solo '80-83, figures '80-82; mem. '84 Olympic, '79, '83 PAG, '79, '81 Pan Pacific, '79, '82 World championships team; duet gold '79, '82 World Cup, '79 PAG, '80 Scandinavian Open, Mazda Invitational; solo gold '80 Mazda, Swiss Open; solo silver, duet, team gold '82 Worlds, '83 PAG; figures bronze '83 PAG; duet silver as sport introduced to Olympics '84; teamed with Sharon Hambrook for most duet victories; 5 Alta. achievement awards; Calgary Booster Club outstanding-athletic-performance award; with Hambrook Aquatic Fed. top swimmers '82; fed. govt world-champions award '83, excellence award '84; coach in masters program; mem. Alta. Sports, Cdn Olympic, Cdn Aquatic halls of fame; res. Calgary, Alta.

KUBINEC, John (builder): b. 26 Jun 1933, Fort William, Ont.; d. 2 Aug 1995, Thunder Bay, Ont.; given name: John Peter; fwd Fort William bantam, jr. teams '42-53; tryout Montreal Canadiens; Sydney (MMHL) '54; Port Arthur int. '56; referee TBAHA '56-82; officiated variety of ntl events including Allan Cup, Memorial Cup, Centennial Cup, college, USHL championships; voted best referee '68 Olympics; conducted numerous officiating clinics; referee-in-chief Thunder Bay non-contact league '85-93; TBAHA most-valuable-employee award '69; sportsmanship award bears his name; mem. NWO Sports Hall of Fame.

KUEBER, Philip (rowing): b. 17 Nov 1934, Galahad, Alta.; given name: Philip Thomas; m. Eleanor Kepper; c. Kathryn, Philip Jr., Heidi, John; UBC, BComm, LLB; barrister & solicitor, QC; mem. UBC rowing crew '54-57; gold crew '54 BEG; silver Royal Henley '55, Olympics '56; gold Western sprint championships '55; gov. Olympic Trust; mem. Cdn Olympic, Alta Sports halls of fame; last known res. Calgary, Alta.

KULAI, Dan (soccer): b. 10 Nov 1907, Ladysmith, B.C.; d. 22 Aug 1980, Vancouver, B.C.; m. Margaret; c. 1 son, 1 daughter; fire chief; mem. New Westminster Royals ntl

soccer title teams '27-28; fwd, later goalie, with BC Select teams several seasons; refereed 25yrs; officiated in World Cup, PAG, most of world's top soccer matches; several years Vancouver city handball singles, doubles champion; mem. BC Sports Hall of Fame.

KULEZA, Kasia (synchro swim): b. 29 Aug 1976, Warsaw, Poland; Vanier Coll.; emigrated to Canada age 7; became involved with synchro swim age 10; team gold '96 French Open, '93 jr worlds, '92 jr ntls; silver '96 Olympic, '95 PAG, World Aquatic championships; ntl senior solo, duet (with Stephanie Bissonnette), figures gold 1993; Helen Vanderburg synchro swim award 1993; ruled ineligible for Polish '00 Olympic team under residency rules; res. Laval, Que.

KULKA, Glenn (football): b. 3 Mar 1964, Edmonton, Alta.; div.; m. Mariko Marsters; c. Laura, Faith, Jaxon; Bakersfield Coll. BA; ex-auto sales mgr.; radio football analyst; played major jr. hockey Medicine Hat, Spokane (WHL), pro ECHL '96; signed as free agent de Edmonton '86 but released and joined Montreal '86; Toronto '87-89, Ottawa '90-94, Sask. '95-96; 1 Eastern all-star; mem. '87 Grey Cup finalist; turned to pro wrestling '97-01; blown knee ended ring career; worked in fitness industry; res. Kanata, Ont.

KURRI, Jari (hockey): b. 18 May 1960, Helsinki, Finland; m. Tina; c. Joonas, Ville; coach; rw Jokerit, Finnish league '77-80, '94; Edmonton (NHL) '80-90, Milan, Italy, '90-91; Los Angeles '91-95; Anaheim '96; Colorado '97-98; 2 1st team, 3 2nd team all-star; Lady Byng Trophy '85; traded to Philadelphia then to Los Angeles same day '91; scored 71g '84-85 and followed up with 68 and 54 in subsequent years; NHL record: 1251 scheduled games, 601g, 797a, 200 playoff games, 106g, 127a; achieved 600g '97; played 7 NHL all-star games; mem. 5 Stanley Cup winners; won Bermuda Cup tennis tournaments in Helsinki '83-85; 2 Kings outstanding-defensive-player awards; '91 World championships 1st team all-star; competed for Finland '98 Olympics; asst. Finnish ntl team '03; mem. Hockey Hall of Fame; res. Calabasas, Calif./Helsinki, Finland.

KURTENBACH, Orland (hockey): b. 7 Sep 1936, Cudworth, Sask.; ctr Prince Albert, Saskatoon, Flin Flon ('58 Memorial Cup); pro '58-74 WHL Vancouver, San Francisco, AHL Buffalo, Springfield, Providence, CHL Omaha, NHL NYR '60, '66-70, Boston '61, '63-65, Toronto '65-66, Vancouver '70-74; NHL record: 639 scheduled games, 119g, 213a, 19 playoff games, 2g, 4a; WHL rookie-of-'58 award; coach Seattle, Tulsa; CHL coach of '76 award; coach Canucks '76; active with Canucks Alumni over 20yrs; mem. BC hockey Hall of Fame; res. Delta, B.C.

KUTROWSKI, Linda (wheelchair basketball): b. 20 Jun 1958, Deep River, Ont.; given name: Linda Denovan; m. Ed Kutrowski; Carleton (computer science), Ryerson (chemical technology); civil servant; regarded as one of the most patient and methodical players in Cdn wheelchair basketball annals; mem. 2 ntl title teams with Ottawa Jazz; also competed nationally with Ottawa Royals, Jazz; mem. '92, gold '96, '00, bronze '04 Paralympics, '94, '98, '02 World gold medal teams; res. Ottawa, Ont.

KUZMICH, Heather (golf): b. 18 Jul 1968, Port Arthur, Ont.; Georgia; all-SEC '87-88; pro golfer; 4 Ont., 4 ntl jr.

titles; mem. 4 ntl jr. title teams; 1ˢᵗ international section jr. worlds; longest driving champion '83 women's Western US jr. championships; 3 successive Barcoven club titles; mem. 4 Ont. title teams; 5 course records; ranked #1 Cdn jr. '81-84; *Score* magazine Cdn jr. golfer of '83; resident pro Silver Spring GC; res. Mechanicsburg, Pa.

KWASNYCIA, Don (shooting): b. 30 Apr 1952, Toronto, Ont.; self-employed; mem. ntl team '77-98; ntl skeet record 382/400 '77; ntl skeet titles '77-78; won '81 ntl team trials, '80 Olympic trials; sr. record 434 winning team gold Grand Prix Von Lippe; mem. '78, '86, '94 CG, '77-78, '81, '85 '90, '93 Worlds, '79, '87, '91 PAG, '88 Olympic Games; '79-82, '85, '87 Benito Juarez International teams; record 394/400 '79 US nationals; Cdn grand prix gold '92; res. Downsview, Ont.

KWONG, Normie (football): b. 24 Oct 1929, Calgary, Alta.; given name: Norman Lim Kwong; m. Mary; c. Gregory, Bradley, Martin, Randy; Mount Royal College; Lt. Govenor Alta, real estate broker, sports exec.; nicknamed "China Clipper"; Calgary North Hill Blizzard Jrs; 13yrs fb Calgary, Edmonton; in 10yrs recorded statistics (from'51) 74tds, 9022yds rushing, 5.2yds per carry; Eddie James Memorial trophy as WFC leading rusher 3 times; mem. 4 Grey Cup title teams including 3 consecutive with Edmonton '54-56; 5 times all-star; twice Schenley outstanding Cdn award '55-56; at '60 retirement held over 30 CFL records, including 134 playoff games; Lionel Conacher trophy '55; pres./GM Calgary '88-92; GM BC '96; noted raconteur; prominent in ntl, regional affairs; part owner NHL Calgary Flames; mem. Alta., Canada's Sports, Football halls of fame; res. Calgary, Alta.

KYLE, Doug (t&f): b. 22 Jul 1932, Toronto, Ont.; given name: Douglas Haig; m. Carol Hemmings; c. Suzanne, Bobby; UBC, BA, Michigan, MA; economist; 4 ntl 3-mile, 6 6-mile titles; 1 10-mile, marathon, 3 ntl x-country titles; 10 ntl records in distances from 2-15 miles, 3000-25,000 metres; 9 Alta. records from 1-10 miles, US 6-mile record; mem. '54 BEG, '56, '60 Olympic, '59, '63 PAG teams; silver 10,000m, bronze 5000m '59 PAG; silver 7000m Sao Paulo Brazil '59; Fred Tees award outstanding coll. athlete '54; Jack Davies award outstanding track athlete '56, '59; Norton Crowe award outstanding amateur athlete '56; ntl track team coach '67 PAG, '68 Olympic Games; Calgary athlete of '68; mem. Cdn Roadrunners Hall of Fame selection comm.; mem. Alta., Cdn Amateur Sports halls of fame; res. Calgary, Alta.

KYVELOS, Hercules (boxing): b. 25 Feb 1975, Montreal, Que.; pro boxer; competed at 67 kg.; 1 ntl amateur title; '95 PAG bronze; competed '96 Olympics; Cdn welterweight title; to Feb. '02 5ᵗʰ ranked in world 21-0-0, 11kos; res. Montreal, Que.

L

LABIGNAN, Italo (fishing); b. 26 Dec 1956, Yugoslavia; m. Rhonda Armstrong; c. Amanda, John, Jessica, Patricia; Sir Sanford Fleming Coll.; fish/wildlife technician; TV personality/producer; pro fisherman from age 28; won *Fish & Stream* 64th annual fishing contest '74, Labatt Loyalist smallmouth bass tournament '84; Garcia fishing award '74, Fenwick Master Angler award '78; co-host *Canadian Sport Fishing TSN* series; writer/partner ntl fishing magazine *Canadian Sport Fishing*; authored more than 10 books on fishing; res. Freelton, Ont.

LABINE, Leo (hockey); b. 22 Jul 1931, Haileybury, Ont.; d. 25 Feb, 2005; given name: Leo Gerald; rw OHL St. Michael's '49-50, Barrie '50-51, AHL Hershey '51-53, NHL Boston '51-61, Detroit '60-62, WHL Los Angeles '62-67, EPHL '61-62; NHL totals: 643 scheduled games, 128g, 193a, 60 playoff games, 12g, 11a; 2 NHL, 1 WHL all-star; pioneer in art of trash talk who used every trick, foul or tool to terrorize and needle opponents; above average scoring touch and ferocious sense of team spirit; 3 goals, 3 assists in '54 game earned him nickname "Haileybury Hurricane"; mem. Hockey Heritage North Hall of Fame.

LABLANCHE, George (boxing); b. 17 Dec 1856, Point Levi, Que., d. 10 May 1918, Lawrence, Mass.; KO'd in 13 by Jack (Nonpareil) Dempsey in middleweight title bid '86; '89 rematch saw Dempsey disqualified for illegal punch despite 32nd round KO; Lablanche title claim disallowed; record: 69 bouts, won 17 by KO, 18 by decision, 6 draws, 10 decisions lost, 14 times KO'd, 2 lost on foul, 1 no decision, 1 no-contest.

LACELLE, Ron (boxing): b. 7 Apr 1929, Ottawa, Ont.; m. Yvonne Emily Cust; c. Ronald, Harvey, Robert, Coleen, Laura; ret'd RCAF; began boxing Ottawa Boys Club age 9; followed Mel Swartzman to newly-formed Beaver Boxing Club; won 112lb Golden Gloves '42; 118lb Cdn bantamweight champion '46; 126lb Olympic trials finalist '48 vs. Eddie Haddad; mem. Ottawa Sports Hall of Fame; res. Smiths Falls, Ont.

LACH, Elmer (hockey); b. 22 Jan 1918, Nokomis, Sask.; given name: Elmer James; m. Kathleen Louise Fletcher; c. Ronald James; dir. ntl accounts Maislin Transport; jr. Regina Abbotts, sr. Weyburn Beavers, Moose Jaw Millers; pro '40-55 Canadiens; missed '41-42 season when broken arm, 1st of several major injuries, which earned him nickname "Elmer the Unlucky", sidelined him; teamed with Maurice Richard, Toe Blake on wings to form Punch Line; NHL record: 646 scheduled games, 215g, 408a, 76 playoff games, 19g, 45a; 3 time 1st, twice 2nd team all-star; mem. 3 Stanley Cup winners, 4 league champions; Hart trophy '45; Ross trophy '45, '48; coach Loyola Jr. Canadiens, Montreal Royals (QHL); mem. Sask. Sports, Hockey halls of fame; res. Pte. Claire, Que.

LACHANCE, Jason (t&f); b. 29 Dec 1980, Ottawa, Ont.; full-time athlete, communications rep.; sprint specialist; 200m gold, 100m, 400m silver '00 Paralympics; bronze 4x400m relay '02 worlds; 5 ntl, 1 world record; 5 gold CP-ISRA worlds '01; 1 gold, 1 silver, 2 bronze '01 Metro Toronto challenge; gold, bronze ntl paralympic championships; competed Swedish, Swiss, Dixie (silver) games, IPC worlds; competed '00, '04 Paralympics; res. Australia.

LACHANCE, Michel (harness racing): b. 16 Dec 1950, St. Augustine, Que.; c. Patrick; followed brothers Gilles, Pierre and Andre into business; was winning country fair races age 12; won 1st pari-mutuel race age 18; won leading driver awards at Blue Bonnets, Brandywine, Batavia, Foxboro, Yonkers, Roosevelt; driving night and day eclipsed Hervé Filion's single-season victory record with 770 wins '86, later surpassed by Filion; led all NA drivers 4yrs; through '03 9475 victories, including 433 major stakes races, for purses exceeding $155M; drove 5 Little Brown Jug, 3 Cane Pace, 2 Messengers Stakes, 2 Prix d'Ete, 1 Canadian Trotting Classic, 2 World Trotting Derby, 3 Yonkers Trot, 2 US Pacing Championship, 7 Matron Stakes, 2 Kentucky Futurity, 3 NA Cup, 4 Hambletonian winners, 23 Breeders Crown, 31 Bluegrass; drove Matt's Scooter to Harness Horse of '89 title, setting Cdn, world records; drove Western Dreamer to Little Brown Jug record 1:51 1/5 '97 and harness racing's Triple Crown; mem. Cdn Horse Racing, Living halls of fame; res. Englishtown, N.J.

LACY, Irene (gymnastics): b. 30 Aug 1946, Nipawin, Sask.; given name: Dorothy Irene Haworth; m. William Gerald Lacy; c. William Guy, William Greg; Southern Illinois, BSc; ret'd teacher; Cdn all-around title '66; NCAA all-around title '66; mem. Cdn Olympic team '64; mem. '61, '65 World Games team; silver balance beam '63 PAG; *Sports Illustrated* award of merit '66; mem. Southern Illinois, Sask., Saskatoon Sports halls of fame; res. Quesnel, B.C.

LADIK, Oleg (wrestling): b. 18 Sep 1971, Kiev, USSR; 100kg freestyle; moved to Canada '92; competes at 125kg level; mem. ntl team from '95; 3 sr. ntl 100kg titles; gold '93 World Cup, '93, '97 Maccabiah, '94 Francophone Games; competed '96 Olympic Games, 3 Cerro Pelado, 2 Canada Cup, 2 world championship tournaments; 3 USSR jr, 2 sr. titles; res. Montreal, Que.

LAFLEUR, Guy (hockey); b. 20 Sep 1951, Thurso, Que.; given name: Guy Damien; m. Lise Barre; c. Martin, Mark; restaurateur; Canadiens team ambassador; 233 goals with Que. Remparts juniors; 130g, 79a in final season; Montreal 1st choice, 1st overall '71 amateur draft; rw Canadiens '71-84, NYR '88-89, Quebec '89-91; 6 consecutive seasons 50 or more goals; reached 500g 20 Dec '83; became Canadiens' all-time scoring leader 9 Feb '84; NHL record: 1126 scheduled games, 560g, 793a, 128 playoff games, 58g, 76a; mem. 5 Stanley Cup winners; 6 times 1st team all-star; Art Ross Trophy '76-78; Lester B. Pearson Trophy '77; Hart Trophy '77-78; Conn Smythe Trophy '77; Lou Marsh, Lionel Conacher trophies '77; jersey #10 ret'd by Canadiens; mem. Team Canada '76, '81; *Sport Magazine* playoff MVP award '77; named to CHL all-time team '99; Officer Order of Canada '80; mem. Canada's, Que. Sports, Hockey halls of fame; res. Ile Bizard, Que.

LAING, George (all-around); b. 20 Oct 1892, Windsor, Ont.; d. 23 Oct. 1963, Windsor, Ont.; given name: George Frederick; m. Agnes Dewar; c. Joyce Edith Benson, George Dewar, Charles Alexander; Trinity Coll, McGill, MD, CM; surgeon; versatile athlete who shone in football, cricket, hockey, tennis, badminton, golf; capt., outside wing, ctr half McGill Redmen whose skills prompted coach Frank Shaughnessy to call him "the finest athlete I ever had anything to do with, the fastest, easiest runner I had ever seen"; intercollegiate tennis singles/doubles titles, Que. singles '14; Detroit singles finalist '15; Mich. open badminton doubles title '30; while in England during WW1 took up golf and went on to win 7 Essex G&CC titles, 1 international, 5 Cdn Srs titles; Devonshire, Triangular Cup matches; mem. Windsor/Essex County, McGill U Sports halls of fame.

LAING, John (cricket); b. 1874, Toronto, Ont, d. 1 Nov 1947, Toronto, Ont.; lawyer; fast bowler, capable batsman; 9 international matches vs US, avg. 10.83, best effort to time by Cdn; considered world class by peers; NA record 313 runs '03; registered Canada's 1st international hat-trick.

LAIRD, Stu (football): b. 8 Jul 1960, Assiniboia, Sask.; UCal, BA; fireman; dl; played 4yrs with Dinosaurs; signed as free agent by Sask. '83; released and joined Montreal Concordes; again released and signed with Calgary; mem. Stampeders '85-96; CFL record: 170 games, 219 tackles, 72 qb sacks; 13 playoff games, 3 Grey Cup finals, 1 winner; 1 Western all-star; Calgary Lord Beaverbrook HS outstanding male athlete '78; jersey #75 ret'd by Stamps; pres CFLPA; res. Calgary, Alta.

LALIBERTE, Connie (curling): b. 21 Oct 1960, Winnipeg, Man; given name: Connie Augustine; m. Charlie Salina; c. Cody; UMan. BA; computer analyst, programmer; excelled in t&f, volleyball, basketball, hockey, bowling, broomball, baseball, field hockey, handball, curling in teens; mem. GPAC field hockey title teams, -23 Western Canada Games title field hockey team; named to ntl FH team '81; competed '81 American Cup; capt. UMan. FH team; holds Level II FH umpiring, Level I coaching certificates; mem. Man, jr, women's title rink '76-77; lead Man, women's title rink '80; began skipping '81 meting with considerable early success; Level 1 Curl Canada instructor's cert.; 4 Man. women's titles; skipped ntl women's title rink '84, '92, '95, Worlds '84gold, '92bronze, '95silver; mem. Man. Sports, Man., Cdn Curling halls of fame; res. Winnipeg, Man.

LALIME, Patrick (hockey); b. 7 Jul 1974, St. Bonaventure, Que.; m. Marie-Helene; c. Liliana, Rosemary; goalie Shawinigan (QMJHL) '92-94; Hampton Roads (ECHL), Cleveland (IHL) '94-96, Grand Rapids (IHL) '97-98, Kansas City (IHL) '98-99; NHL Pittsburgh '96-97, Ottawa '99-04, St. Louis '04; set NHL rookie record 14-0-2 to start NHL career; NHL all-rookie team; NHL record (through '04): 322 scheduled games, 167-112-32, 18,553min; 738ga, 33sho, res. St. Bonaventure, Que.

LALLY, Joe (lacrosse); b. 1868, Cornwall, Ont., d. 1956, Cornwall, Ont.; given name: Patrick Joseph; player, referee,

equipment manufacturer; instrumental in establishing Canadian Lacrosse Assn. '25; donated Lally Perpetual Trophy '30 to be awarded annually to teams representing Canada & US; mem. Cornwall, Canada's Sports, Lacrosse halls of fame.

LALONDE, Bernie (skiing/canoeing); b. 14 Dec 1945, Ottawa, Ont.; given name: Bernard Georges; UofOtt, MD; sports medicine physician; x-country skier Cdn ski marathons; ntl masters kayak titlist '81, 6th ntl srs '83; asst. coach '72-76, head coach '76-78 ntl women's alpine ski team; head ntl alpine ski team medical group from '78; coach whitewater slalom '81-85; ntl whitewater kayaking slalom team '83 world championships; asst. coach '92 Olympics; medical officer 7 Olympics; res. Ottawa, Ont.

LALONDE, Donny (boxing); b. 12 Mar 1960, Victoria, B.C.; accomplished minor hockey player; an average amateur boxer; failed in bid for '80 Olympic team; promoted by Jay Coleman fought Roddy MacDonald for CPBF light-heavyweight title which he won '83 and held through '85; earned nickname "Golden Boy"; won vacant WBC Continental Americas light-heavy title '87; under mgr. David Wolf beat Eddie Davis for vacant WBC title; defended vs. Leslie "Tiger" Stewart; subsequently lost to Sugar Ray Leonard '88; pro record 41 wins (33kos), 5 losses, 1 draw; ret'd from ring '03; mem. Man. Sports Hall of Fame; res. Winnipeg, Man.

LALONDE, Lally (hockey/football/lacrosse); b. 13 Nov 1926, Ottawa, Ont.; given name: Jean Paul; m. Marjory Rocheleau; c. Tina Tracey; UofOtt; ret'd postal employee; CFL Rough Riders '48-50, Alouettes '51-52; various sr., minor pro teams over 22yr span; lacrosse 25yrs; mem. '51 Mann Cup champion Peterborough Timbermen; coached sr., jr. A hockey 10yrs; coached Hull Beavers to Eastern Cdn jr.A title '69; QJHL coach of '69; PR dir. Rough Riders '69-71; frequent radio sports show host, guest; mem. Gloucester Wall, Ottawa Sports Hall of Fame; res. Ottawa, Ont.

LALONDE, Newsy (hockey/lacrosse); b. 1888, Cornwall, Ont., d. 21 Nov 1971; given name: Edouard; reporter, printer; from 16-28 travelled country with various lacrosse clubs; pro hockey at 18 Sault Ste. Marie, International League; 38 goals in 11 games Renfrew Millionaires '10-11; mem. Canadiens '13-22; 4 times scoring champion; mem. 2 Stanley Cup winners; 4 years player-mgr. WHL Saskatoon Sheiks; concluded career '26 in Vancouver; career total 441g, 365 games; coached NY Americans, Montreal Canadiens, Ottawa Senators; mem. Cornwall, Canada's Sports, Lacrosse, Hockey halls of fame.

LAMAZE, Eric (equestrian): b. 17 Apr 1968, Montreal, Que.; m. Megan Johnston; Torrey Pines stables operator; grew from rough districts of Montreal to one of Canada's leading show jumpers; successful jr., hunter rider; natural eye for distance enhanced effectiveness in grand prix ring '92; mem. ntl team from '93; 2nd Cdn World Cup League standings '94; won '95 Shell Cup Derby, ntl show jumping title; mem. champion Cdn Nations' Cup team; only show jumper to qualify two horses (Rio Grande, Cagney) for '96 Olympics; failure to pass drug test cost him '00 Olympics shot and led to 4yr ban; expulsion rescinded and he returned to competition '97; team bronze '99 PAG; cocaine use led to ban from '00 Olympics; res. Schomberg, Ont.

LAMB, Joe (hockey); b. 18 Jun 1906, Sussex, N.B., d. 21 Aug 1982, Ottawa, Ont.; given name: Joseph Gordon; m. Marguerite Gillis (d); c. Joanne Isobel, Margot Elizabeth; ret'd Lt. Col.; Sussex Dairy Kings sr. '22-25, winning NB, PEI championships, Maritime title '24; Montreal Bankers League '25-27; NHL Montreal Maroons, Ottawa, NY Americans, Boston, Canadiens, St. Louis, Detroit '27-38; 108g, 101a; only player to appear in NHL's 2 longest games; led NHL with 119 PIM in 44 games with Ottawa; Ottawa District class A golf champion '49; secty-mgr. Ottawa Valley Curling Assn.'68-76, Ottawa District Golf Assn. '65-76; mem. Gov.-Gen.'s Curling Club; mem. NB Sports Hall of Fame.

LAMB, Willie (golf); b. 15 Dec 1902, Montrose Angus, Scotland, d. 28 Jan 1969, St Petersburg, Fla.; asst. pro Toronto GC '24-28; pro Monterey GC Mexico (winter months) '25-30; head pro Toronto Uplands '29-33, Lambton Golf Club '34-64; 5 times CPGA champion, runnerup once; winner Ont. Open '32, 3 times runnerup; Que. Open '31-33; won Millar Trophy '30; capt. CPGA '29; pres. Ont. PGA '48-50; on '64 retirement made CPGA life mem., mem. Canadian Golf Hall of Fame.

LAMBERT, Claude (boxing): b. 16 Feb 1969, Repentigny, Que.; competes at 54 kg; '94 ntl champion; bronze '95 PAG; competed '94 CG, '96 Olympic Games; res. Repentigny, Que.

LAMBERT, Laurie (field hockey); b. 18 Nov 1960, Lachine, Que.; given name: Laurie Jean; UNB, UBC, York; mem. Que. jr. team '73-79; mem. Que. Sr. team from '76; mem. '77 Canada Games, '78-82 CIAU championships; mem. national team from '80; mem. World Cup silver medal team '83, '84 Olympic team; fed. govt. excellence award '83; res. Downsview, Ont.

LAMBERT, Nathalie (speed skating); b. 12 Jan 1963, Montreal, Que.; Montreal BA, MA; communications; began skating age 12; mem. ntl team from '81; competed despite genetic osteoarthritis; relay bronze '88, relay gold '92, silver '94 Olympics; world champion '91, '93, '94; world 1,000m record 1:32.70; CASSA female short-track athlete of '91 (co-winner), '92, '93, athlete of '84-85, '86-87 (indoor), '85-86 (outdoor), '89-93; dream of competing in '98 Olympics shattered with broken ankle in '97 short-track meet; hon. capt./TV analyst '98 Olympics; asst. CdM '04 summer Olympics; mem. Canada's, Cdn Olympic Sports halls of fame; res. Ville d'Anjou, Que.

LAMMENS, Hank (sailing/hockey): b. 21 Feb 1966, Brockville, Ont.; hockey player, sailor; coached by brother Mark made competitive sailing debut age 11; only Cdn sailor to win 3 ntl youth championships in 2 different events; Ont. male athlete of '90; switched from Laser to Finn class '88; world Finn titles '90, '91; NA, ntl Finn titles '93; disqualified for forgetting life jacket '92 Olympics; competed '87 PAG; CYA Rolex sailor of '90-91; def St. Lawrence ECAC '84-88; drafted NYI '85; AHL Springfield '88-90, Capital Dist AHL, Kansas City IHL '90-91; Team Canada '92-93; NHL Senators '93-95; AHL PEI '93-95; mem. Team Canada '93 worlds; 2 ECAC all-star 2nd teams, 1 NCAA East 2nd all-star team; mem. Cdn Olympic Sports Hall of Fame; res. Brockville, Ont.

LAMY, Gaetan (harness racing): b. 23 Feb 1947, Trois-Rivieres, Que.; c. Yannick; made pro debut at 18 driving father's pacing mare Miss Direct; Hippodrome Trois-Rivieres driving champion 19yrs; Cdn driver of '92; represented Canada '92 World Drivers Championship in Moscow; home construction accident '93 almost cost him his life, but he rebounded to resume competitive career '94; through '03 6177 victories with purses topping $27M; res. Riviere Beaudette, Que.

LANCASTER, Ron (football); b.14 Oct 1938, Fairchance, Pa.; m. Beverly Vaughan; c. Lana, Ronald David, Robert Lee; Wittenberg (Ohio) Coll., BEd; football exec.; pro Ottawa '60-62; Saskatchewan '63-78; CFL record: 3384 pass completions, 6233 attempts, 50,535yds, 396 interceptions, 333tds; Sask. single-season record 3869yds on 297 completions '76; tds single season (28 '66); qb'd Sask. to 5 Grey Cup finals, 1 winner; mem. '60 Ottawa Grey Cup winner; 6 times WFC all-star, 4 times all-Canadian; 5 times Jeff Nicklin Memorial Trophy as WFC MVP; Schenley outstanding-player award '70, '76, runner-up '66; coach. Roughriders '79-80, Eskimos '91-97, Tiger-Cats '98-03; CFL head-coaching record: 266 scheduled games, 138-127-1, 3OT losses; 21 playoff games, 12-9, 4 Grey Cups, 2 wimmers; GM Ticats '04; 2 Annis Stukus CFL coach-of-yr. awards; *CBC TV* football color commentator; mem. Canada's, Sask. Sports, Cdn Football halls of fame; res. Hamilton, Ont.

LANCE, Jackie (softball); b. 9 Jun 1974, Grande Prairie, Alta.; given name: Leona Jacoba Van Hooydonk; m. John A. Lance; Crowder College softball scholarship '92-93; New Mexico, BCrim, BPsych; firefighter; Team BC silver '90 Western Canada Summer Games; gold '92 Cdn midget championships; Team BC bronze '93 Canada Games; ntl team '97-00, '03; bronze, most popular player '97 Haarlem (Netherlands) tourney; bronze '97 Pan-Am qualifier; competed '98 worlds; '99 PAG silver; all-star 2B '00 Cdn sr. championships; 8th '00 Olympics; '01 Women's Professional Softball League gold team mem.; UWest Florida asst. coach, '97-98; MVP '92 Cdn women's fast-pitch championships; Phi Theta Kappa (Academic Honor Society), student ambassador scholarship Crowder College'93-94; outstanding female graduate, homecoming queen, *Who's Who in America Jr. Colleges*, UNM of '94-97; MVP, top offensive player '96-97; Award of Distinction '01; contribution to promotion of girls/women in physical activity and sport '01; mem. Albuquerque Sports Hall of Fame; res. Cedar Crest, New Mexico.

LANCIA, Adam (wheelchair basketball); b. 17 Jan 1980, Toronto, Ont.; Illinois; began playing wheelchair basketball '89; earned gold jr. worlds '97, '01; mem. ntl team from '02; bronze worlds '02; gold '04 Paralympics; mem. Team Ont., 3 ntl titles; 1 CWBL all-star team; mem. Variety Village, Illinois teams; res. Toronto, Ont.

LANDERS, Pete (softball): b. 3 Jan 1947, South Porcupine, Ont.; given name: Peter Michael; m. Patricia Morris; c. Michael, Julie, Paul; laborer; Jr. B hockey Oshawa '76, Sr. A Whitby; lhp; Int. A at 16 South Porcupine; Jr. A Oshawa '66-67; all-Ont. title '67; Sr. A Oshawa Tonys '68-70; mem. Ont. team '69 Canada Summer Games; won Cdn title with London '70; with Campbell River, B.C., '71, picked up by

Victoria Bates for ntls; '72 ntl title with Weyburn, Sask., beating world champ Richmond Hill Dynes in final; Toronto Globals '73-74; enjoyed career year '74 with Ont. record 27 wins, 13 shutouts, 394 strikeouts, 4 perfect games; picked up by Oshawa Tonys to win ntl title '74; played with Oshawa '75 losing ntls to Victoria Bates who picked him up for worlds in which they wound up in 3-way title tie due to rain; arm problems restricted play with Oshawa '76-77; won Western Major Fastball League title with Red Deer '78; credited with all 21 put-outs in '69 2-hitter as he fanned 19 and made 2 put-outs on grounders; 2 ntl championships MVP awards; mem. Cdn Softball Hall of Fame; res. Orono, Ont.

LANDRY, Denis (t&f); b. 16 Apr 1948, Iroquois Falls, Ont.; m. Maureen Ann Commerford; c. Sean, Craig; Windsor, BPHE, UofOtt, MEd; teacher; mem. OFSAA x-country sr. boys title team '66-67; convenor '73, '78 OFSAA x-country championship North Bay; exec. co-ordinator CAHPERD ntl office, coached with Ottawa Kinsmen Harriers, UofOtt; mem. OTFA exec. from '74 serving as v-p '78, '98, pres. '79-83; dir. 1st Pan-Am jr. t&f championships '80; CdM Cdn team '82 jr. PAG; coaching development mgr. CTFA '83-88; Ottawa elementary school athletic assn. pres. '95-96; coached such champions as Alain Boucher, Bob Rice, Richard Charette, OFSAA medalists; coached UofOtt x-country team '84-95 winning 3 OUAA, CIAU titles; also coached basketball, soccer; Ont. govt. special achievement award '82, 2 CIAU x-country coach-of-yr awards; OBE coaches award '97; res. Ottawa, Ont.

LANDRY, Robert (horse racing): b. 18 Sep 1962, Toronto, Ont.; persistence his strong suit as he struggled through more than a decade of disappointments, injuries and bad luck before putting together his 1st 100-victory season '92; claimed his niche in Cdn horse racing history winning consec. Sovereign top jockey awards '93-94; best season '94 winning 175 races; more than 1,300 career victories; res. Mississauga, Ont.

LANDS, Ben (basketball); b. 22 Feb 1921, Montreal, Que.; m. Rita Jodhan; c. Michael, Larry, Michelle; owner specialty printing co.; mem. 15 title teams, 5 ntl, '37-55; mem. '48 Olympic team, nominated to '52 team; 3 times mem. Maccabiah Games team; coached 2 Que. sr. B title teams '46-48; coached sr. basketball '56-67; played jr. football '38; 35 years recreational softball; commissioner Cote St. Luc Lob Ball League from '79; 6 YM-YWHA sr. MVP awards; YM-YWHA outstanding athlete of '56; mem. YM-YWHA Jewish Hall of Fame; res. Cote St. Luc, Que.

LANDY, Frank (football): b. 24 May 1950, Fort William, Ont.; given name: Francis; m. Jan; c. Alicia, Jorden; North Dakota; radio advertising sales; versatile athlete; standout in hockey, baseball, wrestling, basketball, football as a youth; received early football grounding with Ukes bantams, Selkirk Rams; attended Regina HS; rights held by Roughriders; received UND scholarship where he played dt making all-conference; capt. Fighting Sioux '71-74; MVP in Camelia Bowl '72; pro in CFL with Sask. '72; mem. '76 western champs; dealt to BC '77; all-star dt '77-78; returned to Sask. then dealt to Toronto '80; ret'd '81; asst. coach Richmond (BC) Raiders '84; mem. NWO Sports Hall of Fame; res. Richmond, B.C.

LANE, Ken (canoeing); b. 16 Aug 1923, Toronto, Ont.; given name: Kenneth; m. Madge Wilson; c. Christine, Laurel, Robin, Lisa; UofT, hons. BA; ret'd corporate GM Simpson-Sears; 19 Cdn C1, C2, C4, War Canoe titles '46-56; silver 10,000m C2 '52 Olympics; secty-treas. Balmy Beach Canoe Club '46-49; editor *The Canadian Paddler* '53-59; mem. CNE sports committee '55-81; Dominion Day Regatta Assn. exec. '55-81, pres. '61-65; Western Ont. Div. Canada Canoe Assn. secty. '50-54, exec.-flag officer '55-56, flag officer '57-60, treas. '62-81; CCA dir. '56-58, '61-76, v.-commodore '59, commodore '60, hon. commodore '80-81, mem. financial comm. '80-81, Olympic, International committees '69-72; mgr '67 PAG, '72 Olympic canoe teams; mem. St. Catharines national canoe championships organizing comm. '68; NA Canoe Racing Assn.; key role in promoting/developing sport throughout career; Ont. Sr. squash title '74, ntl doubles finalist '78; mem. Simpson-Sears curling league title rink '81; Queen's Golden Jubilee medal; mem. Cdn Olympic Hall of Fame; res. Scarborough, Ont.

LANE, Sharon (t&f); b. 24 Oct 1958, Hamilton, Ont.; given name: Sharon Marie; UWO., hons BA, MA; hurdles specialist; ntl sr. 100m title '78-79, '81; ntl 100m hurdles record 13.43 '79 FISU Games; silver '79 PAG; mem. '78 CG, '80 Olympic Games teams; res. Ancaster, Ont.

LANG, Dale (ballooning); b. 18 Aug 1951, Calgary, Alta.; given name: Dale Frederick; m. Diane McMurry; c. Jeffrey, Mark; Anglican Church priest; professional balloonist; ntl champion '79; co-pilot 1st balloon over North Pole; ntl sales dir. Barnes Sport Balloon; pres. Balloon Adventures Calgary; youth minister St. James Anglican Church; res. Calgary, Alta.

LANG, Kara (soccer); b. 22 Oct 1986, Calgary, Alta.; def/mdfld/fwd; mem. ntl -19 FIFA worlds gold medal team; at 15 youngest ever to score 1st intl goal; made intl debut '02; scored 4 goals vs. Jamaica '02; made WC team debut Algarve Cup '02; 64 intl caps; 31 intl match goals; switched to defence, captain of ntl -19 team at '04 Worlds in Thailand; mem. Vancouver Whitecaps W-League team; res. Oakville, Ont.

LANG, Lorraine (curling); b. 8 Oct 1956, Port Arthur, Ont.; given name: Lorraine Edwards; m. Rick Lang; c. Adam, Sarah; X-ray technician; third for Heather Houston '88-89 Scott Tournament of Hearts title, '89 world title; also won Ont. women's titles '83, '88, '91; mem. '81 NO, ntl mixed title rinks; mem. Cdn Curling (team), NWO Sports halls of fame; res. Thunder Bay, Ont.

LANG, Rick (curling); b. 12 Dec 1953, Fort William Ont.; given name: Richard Porter; m. Lorraine Edwards; c. Adam, Sarah; Lakehead, hons BA social work; services mgr. Children's Aid Society; 3rd for Doug Smith '71 ntl jr. runnerup; 3rd or skip in 10 Brier appearances; with Bill Tetley '75 Brier, with Al Hackner '82, '85 Brier, World titles; skipped '81 Seagram Mixed ntl champions; recipient '81 ntl mixed congeniality award, '82 Silver Broom Colin Campbell Award most-sportsmanlike player, '91 Brier Ross Harstone award for sportsmanship/ability; capt. NA team '03 Continental Cup of Curling; mem. Cdn Curling (team), NWO Sports halls of fame; res. Thunder Bay, Ont.

LANGDON, Jeff (figure skating); b. 13 Aug 1975, Smiths Falls, Ont.; mem. ntl team '90-01; gold Nebelhorn, bronze International Grand Prix '93; competed jr. worlds '93; silver '97 ntl championships; competed '97 worlds; coached by Doug Leigh, Robert Tebby; competed '98 Olympics; res. Barrie, Ont.

LANGFORD, Harry (football); b. 6 Dec 1929, Winnipeg, Man.; m. Muriel Robertson; c. Glen, Carol; ret'd v-p Prudential Steel; began career Daniel MacIntyre CI '45-46; two-way player, all-star, team capt; jr. football Weston Wildcats, O & D all-star, capt '47-49; MVP award, Tessler Memorial award from MFL; pro Calgary '50-58, BC '59; 8yrs Calgary capt.; og/lb/de/mg/ctr, 1st player to record 158 consec. games; ended career with 164 league, exhibition, playoff, all-star games; earned title of "Iron Man" missing just one game in entire career from HS to retirement; 7 all-star honors; twice Schenley nominee; asst. coach MacIntyre prov. title teams 3yrs; coached Drumheller 3yrs, 1 Alta title; founder/coach Calgary Colts jrs 3yrs; lineman of decade ('42-51) Winnipeg high schools; Calgary footballer of '57; off. right guard Calgary quarter and half-century teams; hon. life mem. Alta Automotive Retailers Assn.; mem. Calgary Grey Cup comm.; p-pres. Stampeders Alumni; hon. life dir. Calgary Exhibition and Stampede; avid golfer; helped organize CFL Old Boys golf tournaments '95-96; mem. Stampeder wall of fame; res. Nanaimo, B.C.

LANGFORD, Sam (boxing); b. 12 Feb 1880, Weymouth, N.S., d. 12 Jan 1956, Cambridge, Mass.; nicknamed "Boston Tar Baby"; fought almost 300 bouts, many not recorded; among opponents were Jack McVey, Jack Johnson, Stanley Ketchel, Joe Jennette, Young Peter Jackson, Joe (the original) Walcott, Jack Blackburn; held "Negro" heavyweight title losing it '19 to Harry Wills; won/lost Mexican heavyweight title '23; ranked by *Ring Magazine* among top 10 all-time heavyweights; stood 5'5" with 84" reach: 252 recorded bouts, 99 won by KO, 37 by decision, 1 on foul, 31 draws, 19 lost on decision, 4 by KO, 59 no decision, 2 no contest; tied 9th *AP* boxers of century rankings; mem. Canadian, US Boxing, NS, Canada's Sports halls of fame.

LANGLOIS, Al (curling); b. 4 Aug 1915, Winnipeg, Man. given name: Allan David; ret'd; skipped inter-HS champions '34; winner variety of events Manitoba Bonspiel; 3rd for Billy Walsh Sr. winning Man. Consols, Brier '52, '56; mem. Man., Cdn Curling halls of fame; res. Winnipeg, Man.

LANGLOIS, Jocelyn (shooting/coaching); b. 28 May 1947, Granby, Qué.; given name: Jocelyn Remarc; m. Nicole Patenaude; c. Nicolas; self-employed; SFC technical director, '90-'96; NCCP certified level 5 pistol coach; Québec rapid-fire pistol champion, indoor '80, outdoor '81; won several medals ntl pistol championships, air gun grand prix '82-86; Cdn international pistol team '85-86; ntl pistol team asst. coach, '87-00; pistol team coach '88 Olympics, '90 worlds, '91 Canada Games (for Québec), '91 world air gun championships; '95 PAG, '98 CG; '91 graduate intl shooting coach German Shooting School; '98 NATO military pentathlon gold team pistol coach; team leader at '99 PAG, '00 Olympics, '01 Championship of the Americas; '94 CG jury member; '95, '03 Canada Games technical advisor; mem. COA staging team '96 Olympics; '89 coach of the year, all disciplines, Richelieu Yamaska

Region; has participated in over 25 world cups from '88; res. Hull, Qué.

LANGLOIS, Lloyd (skiing); b. 11 Nov 1962, Sherbrooke, Que.; freestyle aerials specialist; began competing age 16; mem. ntl team "Cdn Air Force" from '85; 47 World Cup gold; '85, '93 World Cup champion; '86, '89 world champion; bronze '88, '94 Olympics; twice ret'd to recover from injuries, ret'd permanently '98; world champion awards '85, '86; Tribute to Champions sports excellence awards '87, '89; mem. Cdn Olympic, Cdn Ski halls of fame; res. Magog, Que.

LAPALME, Denis (wheelchair basketball); 29 Apr 1959, Timmins, Ont.; given name: Denis Orval; m. Catherine Anne Mallette; c. Jennifer, Michelle; Waterloo, hons BA; media analyst Transport Canada; mem. ntl wheelchair basketball team '86-92; 5 times ntl championship all-star; MVP '87 ntls; mem. 4th place Barcelona Paralympics team; mem. Ottawa Shooters ntl champions '95; res. Nepean, Ont.

LAPERRIÉRE, André (hockey); b. 12 Jun 1925, Montreal, Que.; given name: Henry André; m. Marthe Sabourin; c. Josée, Luc; Montreal, BA; ret'd printer; fwd/def Maple Leaf jrs 2 yrs; UMtl 5yrs; mem. '48 Olympic gold medal Flyers; Que. league srs with Sorel, Drummondville 3yrs; played in Montreal commercial league; 10yrs OT hockey; as mem. Of '48 Flyers named military athletes of century; mem. as mem. of '48 Flyers Ottawa Sports Hall of Fame; res. Outremont, Que.

LAPERRIÉRE, Jacques (hockey); b. 22 Nov 1941, Rouyn-Noranda, Que.; m. Elaine; c. Martin, Daniel, Michele; hockey coach; def Montreal Juniors; turned pro with Hull-Ottawa (EPHL) '59-63; Montreal '62-74; Calder Memorial Trophy '64; Norris Trophy '66; playing career ended due to knee injury; mem. 6 Stanley Cup winners plus 2 as asst. coach; 5 times all-star; NHL record: 691 scheduled games, 40g, 242a, 88 playoff games, 9g, 22a; coached junior hockey; asst. coach Canadiens '81-97, Bruins '97-01, NYI '01-03, NJ from '03; mem. Hockey Hall of Fame; res. Montreal, Que.

LAPOINTE, Guy (hockey); b. 18 Mar 1948, Montreal, Que.; given name: Guy Gerard; m. Louise; c. Guy Jr., Stephanie, Jordan; hockey scout; def. Montreal Jr. Canadiens; played in NHL with Montreal '68-82, St. Louis '82-83, Boston '83-84; mem 6 Stanley Cup winners; 4 all-star games; 1 1st, 3 2nd team all-star; NHL record: 884 scheduled games, 171g, 451a, 123 playoff games, 26g, 44a; asst. coach Quebec '84-85. '87-90; GM/head coach Longueuil (QMJHL) '85-87; 1 QMJHL title; scout Calgary '90-95, from '97; asst. coach Calgary '95-97; mem. Hockey Hall of Fame; res. Montreal, Que.

LAPORTE, Paul (shooting); b. 9 May 1928, Edmundston, N.B.; m. Irene Blais; c. Sonia, Richard; restaurateur; ntl high-avg. titles all-around '69-70, 12 gauge '69, '73, 20 gauge '70, '72, 28 gauge '69-70; 34 high overall avg., 36 12ga, 17 20ga, 17 28ga, 13 410 bore titles '67-73; 12 world records; world tuna fishing record 1160lbs; mem. National Skeet Shooting Assn. Hall of Fame; res. Montreal, Que.

LAPPAGE, Ron (judo/wrestling); b. 27 Jun 1945, Dryden, Ont.; c. 3; Queen's, UAlta. PhD; educator, AD Lakehead;

started judo age 12; capt. Queen's judo team, OUAA light-heavyweight title; capt. UAlta judo team, 5 WCIAA heavyweight titles; CIAU heavy, open champion '67; 5 Alta. light-heavy black belt titles; ret'd from judo with 3rd degree black belt '74; began wrestling age 22; 2 WCIAA 190lb titles; 4 Alta. titles; 1 ntl 198lb Greco-Roman title; mem. ntl team '70 worlds; ret'd from competition '74; in youth also active in football, road running, x-country skiing; Queen's letterman '65; UAlta. male athlete of '67-68; UAlta Block A ring, numeral 4 awards; 2 Edmonton, 1 Thunder Bay awards; 1 Alta. achievement award; wrestling, judo coach Lakehead.; varied exec., comm. roles as associate PE prof. Lakehead; mem. LakeheadU Hall of Fame selection comm.; mem. NWO Sports Hall of Fame; res. Thunder Bay.

LAPRADE, Edgar (hockey); b. 10 Oct 1919, Mine Centre, Ont.; given name: Edgar Louis; m. Arline Whear (d); c. Diane (Bonnie), Judith, Marcia; ret'd sporting goods store owner; nicknamed "Beaver"; fluid skater and expert stick handler; joined NHL NYR '45-55; NHL record: 500 scheduled games, 108g, 172a, 18 playoff games, 4g, 9a; played in 4 NHL all-star games; Calder trophy winner '46; alderman Port Arthur/Thunder Bay 15yrs; ret'd from politics following unsuccessful bid for mayor's job; helped found NWO Sports Hall of Fame; mem. NWO Sports, Hockey halls of fame; res. Thunder Bay, Ont.

LAPTHORNE, Whitey (baseball); b. 1 Apr 1942, London, Ont.; given name: David James; m. Mary Jane McDonald; c. Andrea, Heather, Joseph; UWO, BA, Wayne State, MEd; OCE; ret'd PS principal; infielder London Majors (Sr. Intercounty) '60-78; .275 lifetime avg.; best season '63 with .346; twice 1st team all-star 3b; once 2nd team all-star 1b; active in slo-pitch softball; mem. Ont., ntl baseball championships, PAG playdowns teams '70; res. London, Ont.

LAREAU, Sebastién (tennis); b. 27 Apr 1973, Montreal, Que.; ntl -12, -16, -18, senior singles, doubles titles; career record (since '90) 11-9 in Davis Cup play; with Sebastién LeBlanc won '90 French Open, Wimbledon junior doubles titles, first Canadians to win a Grand Slam title; turned pro '91; scored victory over 6th ranked Michael Stich '94 European championships; twice ranked #1 in Canada; 2 ATP Tour doubles titles; with Leblanc shared Viscount Alexander award '90; with Daniel Nestor won '98 Japan Open, '00 Olympics, Masters series doubles; mem. '98-02 Davis Cup teams; teamed with Alex O'Brien (US) to become 1st Cdn to claim grand slam victory with men's doubles US Open and ATP Tour world doubles title '99; with Nestor won Wilson-McCall award '00; res. Boucherville, Que.

LARGE, Bert (lacrosse); b. 12 May 1907, Brampton, Ont.; m. Alice Gibson; c. Alberta, Margi-Fay; ret'd plumber, apt. superintendent; mem. Brampton Amateur Lacrosse Assn. sr. champions '26; mem. Mann Cup winner '30; pro Toronto Maple Leafs '31, Toronto Tecumsehs '32; mem. Mimico-Brampton Combines Mann Cup winner '42, Mike Kelly Memorial Medal Mann Cup playoff MVP; mem. Ont. champion Mimico-Brampton Combines '43; mem. Cdn Lacrosse Hall of Fame; res. Brampton, Ont.

LARIVIÉRE, Chelsea (t&f); b. 23 Dec 1983, Toronto, Ont.; given name: Chelsea Frances; full-time athlete; class T34

cerebral palsy; wheelchair sprint specialist; excels at skiing, sledge hockey, jiu-jitsu (green belt); mem. Ottawa Lions TC from '96; 6 gold '97 jr. Orange Bowl; 5 gold '97, 3 gold, 2 silver '98 Ont. Games for physically disabled; 2 gold, 3 silver Windsor indoor, 4 gold Ont. Summer Games; 4 silver, 1 bronze '99 Southern Cross Games (Australia); competed '00 Paralympics; 1 gold, 3 silver '01 CP-ISRA worlds; 1 silver, 2 bronze '02 IPC worlds; ntl, prov. sprint records; Ont. CP jr. athlete of yr '97; Burlington Disabled Sports, Easter Seal, Carl Hiebert personal achievement, VON awards; extensive volunteer work, speaking engagements; res. Mountain, Ont.

LARMER, Steve (hockey); b. 16 Jun 1961, Peterborough, Ont.; m. Rose Drake; c. Bailey Rose; Sanford Fleming Coll.; NHLPA player consultant; rw Peterborough (OHA) '77-78, Niagara Falls '78-81, New Brunswick (AHL) '81-82; drafted by Chicago '80; NHL with Chicago '81-93, NYR '93-95; OHA, AHL all-star; NHL all-rookie team '83; Calder Memorial Trophy '83; 2 NHL all-star games; 1 Stanley Cup winner; ironman streak of 884 consecutive games ended '93; scored series clinching goal vs. US '91 Canada Cup; nicknamed "Grandpa"; NHL record: 1006 scheduled games, 441g, 571a, 140 playoff games, 56g, 75a; p-pres. PPHAA; res. Peterborough, Ont.

LaROCHE, Alain (skiing); b. 20 Sep 1963, Quebec City, Que.; impressive record in alpine events from '77 led to competition as mem. national jr. freestyle team; competed at World Cup level from '82; 6 WC combined, 2 aerials titles; 2 ntl combined, 1 moguls, 1 ballet, 1 aerials titles; 1 NA combined, aerials titles; world title '84; fed. govt. excellence '83, world champion awards '84; mem. Cdn Olympic Sports Hall of Fame; res. Lac Beaufort, Que.

LaROCHE, Philippe (skiing); b. 12 Dec 1966, Quebec City, Que.; c. 1; freestyle aerials specialist; began competing age 12; mem. ntl team "Cdn Air Force" from '87; 17 World Cup gold; 3 World Cup championships; 3 ntl titles; '92 Olympic gold, '94 silver; brothers Yves, Alain Dominic, all freestylers, sister Lucie, alpine skier; Tribute to Champions sports excellence award '89; res. Lac Beauport, Que.

LaROCHE, Yves (skiing); b. 7 Jun 1959, Quebec City, Que.; aerials specialist; mem. ntl team '82-86; 4 1sts, 2 2nds 8 World Cup events '84; WC aerials titlist '84, '86; near fatal para-gliding accident '89 ended competitive career; ntl team aerials coach '94 Olympics; fed. govt. excellence award '84; mem. Cdn Skiing Hall of Fame; res. Lac Beauport, Que.

LAROCQUE, Bunny (hockey); b. 6 Apr 1952, Hull, Que.; d. 29 Jul 1992, Hull, Que.; given name: Michel Raymond; m. Helene Legris; c. Stephane, Philippe, Mathieu; pro hockey player; goalie Ottawa 67's jrs.; 2nd pick Montreal 6th overall '72 draft; Canadiens '73-81, Maple Leafs '81-83, Philadelphia '83, St. Louis '83-84; shared Vezina Trophy Ken Dryden '77-79, Denis Heron, Richard Sevigny '81; mem. 4 Stanley Cup winners; NHL record: 312 scheduled games, 17,615min, 160-89-45, 978ga, 17so, 3.33 ga avg, 14 playoff games, 6-6, 759min, 37ga, 1so, 2.92 ga avg.

LAROCQUE, Dominique (cycling/skating); b. 29 Dec 1962, Sturgeon Falls, Ont.; UofOtt, BA; athletic consultant, owns mountain bike training school, holistic psycho therapy;

ntl mountain bike team mem. '91; represented Canada at world championships; '93 10km in-line skating record holder NY Central Park race; won 145km Athens-to-Atlanta in-line skating marathon '93; Cdn in-line skating title '96; gold 25km, silver 100km Kuopio, Finland, Ice Marathon speed skating competition '94; silver 100km elite women's in-line event at New York; developed Creative Wheel Consulting; res. Ottawa, Ont.

La ROCQUE, Penny (curling); b. Yarmouth N.S.; given name: Penny Wilson; m. Guy La Rocque; Dalhousie, MSc; dir. Athletics East Assn.; mem. NS rink ntl women's championship '74, '78-79, '83, '86; skipped '83 ntl title rink; mem. NS rink ntl mixed championships '79, '81-82. '84; 6ᵗʰ in Canada Gillette Fitness Challenge '79; Fitness & Amateur Sport athletic scholarship (curling) '79; mem. Canadian Curling Hall of Fame; res. Halifax, N.S.

LARODA, John (karate); b. 8 May 1963, Haiti; owner Pro-Style Martial Arts & Fitness; emigrated to Canada '75; began karate career '79; achieved black belt status '86; numerous tournament triumphs; gold, bronze '02, 2 bronze '03 worlds; 5ᵗʰ degree black belt; res. Dunrobin, Ont.

LAROSE, Bob (football/basketball); b. 6 Mar 1946, Toronto Ont. given name: Robert Alexander; m. Marianne Jorgenson; c. Karen, Jennifer; UWO hons. BPhE, MPhE; asst. football coach UWO '84-92, '93-03, head coach '92; football, basketball star UWO; grid team capt. '69; wr Winnipeg '70-77; Bombers 1ˢᵗ draft choice; CFL record; 227 receptions, 4209yds, 18.5 avg., 29tds; asst. coach UMan. '77, UWO '79, UofOtt '81, '83; *Toronto Telegram* HS athlete of '65; UWO athlete of '70; All-Cdn wr CFL '72; Blue Bombers Cdn athlete of '75; color commentator CFL games *CBC* '78; tech. dir. CAFA '80-83, exec. dir. '83-84; mem. W-Club Sports Hall of Fame; res. London, Ont.

LAROSE, Gilbert (gymnastics); b. 13 Sep 1942, Montreal, Que.; m. Terri; c. Gil Jr., Glenn; UMich, BSc; professor, businessman; ntl gymnastic champion '65, '68; mem. ntl team '62 World championships, European tour, '64, '68 Olympics; Big-10 all-around titlist; NCAA all-around, 4 events titlist '62-63; capt. Mich team; Mid-West, Flint Open titles; 7yrs pres. Que. Gymnastics Fed.; 7yrs gymnast, ntl judge, coach; res. Longueuil, Que.

LAROSE, Simon (tennis); b. 28 Jun 1978, Cap-de-la-Madeleine, Qué.; Mississippi State; tennis player; all-American; Davis Cup team from '98; 6-7 singles record in Davis Cup, 1-1 doubles; doubles semifinalist (with American partner Jan-Michael Gambill) '01 Tennis Masters Canada; jumped 376 spots to #206 on ATP Entry System; came from behind to take Australia's Lleyton Hewitt to third set in 1ˢᵗ round, centre court action of '01 Tennis Masters Series Canada; qualified for 1ˢᵗ ATP event (Legg Mason Tennis Classic in Washington '03) and won 1ˢᵗ round match; reached 3ʳᵈ round Tennis Masters Canada '03, defeating Brazil's Gustavo Kuertin in 1ˢᵗ round; career-high #204 on ATP Entry Rankings; #1 in Canada several months '03; res. Cap-de-la-Madeleine, Qué.

LAROUCHE, Pierre (hockey); b. 16 Nov 1955, Taschereau, Que.; m. Cindy; product spokesman; ctr, Quebec, Sorel Jr. Black Hawks '72-74; NHL Pittsburgh in '74 amateur draft;

Pittsburgh '74-78, Montreal '78-'82, Hartford '82-83, NYR '83-88; scored 53g '76, 50 '80; NHL record: 812 scheduled games, 395g, 427a, 64 playoff games, 20g, 34a; mem 1 Stanley Cup winner; active in community charity work; res. Pittsburgh, Pa.

LARSEN, Christine (synchro swim): b. 15 Dec 1967, Coquitlam, B.C; began career '74; mem. ntl team '76-92 and again from '95; with Kathy Glen won '90 CG, Swiss Open, '91 Petro-Canada Cup duet gold; team gold '96 French, '90 Swiss Opens, '88 Petro-Canada Cup; silver '91 worlds, '96 Olympics; sister Karen ntl team mem; ret'd from competition to coach Nanaimo Diamonds Club '93-94; returned to competition to qualify for '96 Olympics; res. Coquitlam, B.C.

LASHUK, Mike (football); b. 9 Dec 1938, Edmonton, Alta.; UAlta., BPhE Southern Illinois, MSc; assoc. prof.; Edmonton City jr. golf, prov. HS shot put titles; jr. A hockey Edmonton Oil Kings; pro Eskimos '57-63; Dr. Beattie Martin Trophy WFC rookie of '57; clb, twice selected by teammates top Cdn player; coached HS football 5yrs; head coach UCal Dinosaurs from '70 leading team to National College Bowl final '75, losing to UofOtt; res. Calgary, Alta.

LASKIN, Mark (equestrian); b. 19 Oct 1956, New York; UAlta; farm mgr.; dominated '79 Rothman's Grand Prix circuit winning 1ˢᵗ place ribbons in 9 of 11 events including Vancouver, Toronto World Cup competitions; Rothman's equestrian of '78-81; mem. ntl team; mem. gold medal Nations Cup, Olympic alternate team '80; res. Santa Fe, N.M.

LATULIPPE, Phil (t&f); b. 16 Mar 1919, Cabano, Que.; ret'd Cdn Forces; ultra runner; began running age 48 to lose weight, quit smoking; at 50 covered 100miles in Ottawa Miles for Millions charity walk; 3 *Guinness Book of Records* marks for world's longest non-stop runs; longest 300miles '72; completed documented across-Canada run '81; also ran Alaska to Shawinigan, Que., ran 65-69 age-group world 48hr 150miles, 1689yds record '89; 1ˢᵗ Cdn 70+ ultra-marathoner; crossed Canada Vancouver to Halifax in 134 days '89; Foundation Phil Latulippe bears his name; mem. Order of Canada; res. Loretteville, Que.

LAUMANN, Silken (rowing): b. 14 Nov 1964, Mississauga, Ont.; m. John Wallace; c. William Laumann; operates Silken & Co., motivational speaker; gave up competitive running to concentrate on rowing '82; mem. ntl team '83-98, competing single, double and quadruple sculls; 5 Cdn Henley, 3 Amsterdam, 2 ntl, 1 San Diego gold; '87 PAG single gold; competed '84, '88, '92, '96 Olympics winning silver '96, bronze '84 and '92, in amazing display of grit after serious training accident; overall women's World Cup single scull gold '91; won single scull gold '95 PAG but stripped of quadruple gold when she inadvertently consumed banned substance in cough medicine; 2 fed. govt. meritorious service awards; Lou Marsh, Velma Springstead trophies '91; 2 Bobbie Rosenfeld awards; BC female athlete of '91; CARA Centennial award; 2 ORA athlete-of-yr awards; Mississauga athlete of '84; Olympic champion award '85; Olympic Order '95; hon. Dr. of Laws degree UVic '94; subject of film feature '96; special Cdn citizen's gold medal '92; Grace Under Pressure award '96; BC Women in Sport Leaders & Legends award; Thomas Keller award '99; ntl child day award '03; Vancouver Island award of excellence; mem. Cdn Olympic, Canada's Sports halls of fame; res. Victoria, B.C.

LAURIN, Lucien (horse racing); b. 1915, Montreal, Que.; d. 26 Jun 2000, Key Largo, Fla; m. Juliette; c. Roger; horse trainer; moderately successful career as jockey (161 wins) '29-42; ruled off track at Narragansett '38 when battery was found in pocket; with aid of Alfred Vanderbilt reinstated '41; joined Reg Webster and career as trainer blossomed; trained Quill juv. filly of '58, Amberoid Belmont Stakes winner '66; replaced son Roger at Meadow Stable '71; brought Riva Ridge to title honors at 2, double classic winner at 3, champion handicapper at 4; trained Triple Crown winner Secretariat; trained 34 major stakes winners; mem. Saratoga Springs, Canadian Horse Racing halls of fame.

LAURIN, Roger (horse racing); b. 11 Sep 1935, Montreal, Que.; m. Nina; c. Robert, Ricky; horse trainer; followed father Lucien's footsteps and established reputation as one of NA's top trainers; moved from Meadow Stable to Phipps family string; enjoyed best success with Numbered Account '71-72, Pearl Necklace '76-79, Miss Cavendish '64, Drumtop '70-71; res. Garden City, N.J.

LAUSCHER, Regan (luge); b. 21 Feb 1980, Saskatoon, Sask.; Mount Royal College; ntl team from '99; 4th '00 jr. worlds; 12th '02 Olympics; six top-10 results on '02-03 WC circuit; silver '03 NA Championships; 4 ntl titles; track record holder Canada Olympic Park; Red Deer's female athlete of the '01; res. Calgary, Alta.

LAVIOLETTE, Jack (hockey/lacrosse); b. 27 Aug 1879, Belleville, Ont., d. 10 Jan 1960, Montreal, Que.; amateur hockey '89 Montreal Overland jrs.; CP Telegaphs '00 then Nationals of Federal League in both hockey, lacrosse; with formation of IHL (1st pro league) '04 played 4 seasons Sault Ste. Marie, Mich., team, capt. '06; when league disbanded '07 played with Montreal Shamrocks, lacrosse with Nationals; with Newsy Lalonde mem. '10 team which lost Minto Cup to New Westminster; with formation '09 of NHA involved in recruiting, managing Montreal Canadiens, oldest pro hockey team still in existence in Canada; fwd Canadiens 1st Stanley Cup win '16; became referee after injury '17; mem. Canada's Sports, Hockey halls of fame.

LAVOIE, Marc (fencing); b. 29 Apr 1954, Ottawa, Ont.; m. Camille Lafortune; c. Jerome, Adrien, Christopher; Carleton, BA, UofParis, PhD; professor, UofOtt; won French team handball, baseball, class B team golf titles while attending HS in Paris; ntl jr. sabre champion '73-74; sr. sabre '75-79, '85-86; mem. '73-75, '78, '81-82 world championships, '76, '84 Olympic, '75, '79, '83 PAG, '74, '78, '82 Commonwealth championships teams; team bronze '74, silver, sabre silver '78 Commonwealth championships, team bronze '83 PAG; ntl team capt. '78; ret'd from competition '84; authored 2 hockey-related books; Carleton athlete of '74-75; Ottawa ACT fencer of '74; res. Hull, Que.

LAW, Kelley (Owen) (curling); b. 11 Jan 1966, Burnaby, B.C.; given name: Kelley Atkins; m. Bruce Law; c. 3;

conveyancer law corp; runnerup '87 BC Schoolgirl, jr. championships; skipped rink in 9 BC STOH competitions, 5 titles; bronze '92 ntl STOH; gold '00 STOH, worlds; bronze '97, gold '01 Olympic trials; skip '02 Olympic bronze rink; Kamloops, Richmond, Saskatoon major bonspiel titles; rink awarded '00 Edmonton Grads team title; BC Women in Sport Leaders & Legends award; res. Coquitlam, B.C.

LAWES, Keith (curling); b. 15 Oct 1937, Montreal, Que.; given name: Leslie Keith; m. Judith Anne Northey; c. David Keith, Judith Andrea, Christopher Charles; Lower Canada Coll., McGill; ret'd trust co. mgr.; twice Newfoundland, Ontario provincial finalist Brier playdowns; 3rd '69 Nfld. Brier entry; earned nickname "Super Broom" as substitute sweeper for Nfld 7 games '71 Brier, 4 games with NB '74 Brier; won '72 OCA Challenge Round; '73 OCA Silver Tankard with St. Thomas; sr. instructor Curl Canada; res. Winnipeg, Man.

LAWSON, Smirle (football); b. 1888, Guelph, Ont., d. 22 Dec 1963, Toronto, Ont.; given name: Alexander Smirle; m. Pearl Forsyth; c. Elizabeth, Amy, Isobel; UofT, MB, MD hons., MRCP (London), MRCS (Eng.); medical doctor; hard-charging hb; led Varsity Blues to '09 Grey Cup; mem., capt. Argos '11-14; Canada's original "Big Train"; medical officer WWI; taught surgery UofT; mem. Toronto General Hospital staff; chief coroner of Ont. '37-62; gained international rep. as coroner; 1st white man admitted to Ojibway tribe at Moose Pt. Indian Reserve; mem. UofT, Ottawa, Cdn Football, Canada's Sports halls of fame.

LAY, Jeff (rowing); b. 6 Oct 1969, Ottawa, Ont.; UWO, BSc; varsity rowing coach; started rowing in HS; mem. ntl team from '93; gold light 8s '93 worlds, US championships, straight 4 '94 Amsterdam, '95 US championships; 2 silver '95 PAG; silver light 4s '96 Olympics; silver lw 8's Lucerne; involved in coaching at all levels; res. London, Ont.

LAY, Marion (swimming); b. 26 Nov 1948, Vancouver, B.C.; given name: Marion Beverly; CalState Poly., BA, CalState, MA; tech. chair. ntl sports ctr Greater Vancouver; ntl 100m FS title '64-68, mem. '64, '68 Olympic, '66 CG, '67 PAG teams; British Open 100m FS record '65 Blackpool, Eng.; team capt., won 2 gold, set world record 4x110yd FS relay '66 CG; team capt., 4 silver '67 PAG; bronze 100m FS US long-course nationals '67; South African open 100m FS record '68; capt. '68 Olympic swim team, 4th 100m FS, bronze 4x100m FS relay; coached UWO '71-72 swim team to 4th place '72 CWIAU championships; *CBC* swimming color commentator; asst. coach Ottawa Kingfish SC; dir. institute for study of sport in society '71-75; acting mgr. tech. programs Sport Canada; founding mem. CAAWS; IOC Women and Sport award; Carol Anne Letheren Intl sport leadership award; v-chair. 2010 Olympic bid comm.; pres 2010 Legacies Now Society; COA exec. comm.; ntl task force for sport; founder/chair. Pacific Sport ntl sports ctr; founding mem. Women Sport intl; Bryce Taylor, Herstorical, Vancouver YWCA awards; authored several cook books; mem. BC Swimming, Cdn Aquatic Hall of Fame; res. Vancouver, B.C.

LAYTON, Athol (wrestling); b. 20 Aug 1920, Surrey, Eng.; d. 18 Jan 1984, Toronto, Ont.; given name: Athol Alfred; m. Leah Emma Kett; c. John Gordon, Christopher Thomas;

pro wrestler, TV sports commentator; moved to Australia at 13; Australian amateur heavyweight boxing champion '38-43; began pro wrestling career Singapore '49; began NA wrestling career Toronto '50; given nickname "Lord"; with Lord James Blears won NWA world tag team title '53; began career as TV wrestling commentator Buffalo '59; with Ilio Dipaulo won world tag team title '59; noted raconteur; promotions mgr FBM Distillery '78-84; noted for charitable work with Shriner's Hospitals, Variety Club of Ont., St. Alban's Boys & Girls Club, Easter Seals; Ont. citizenship medal '83.

LEA, Mary (shooting): b. 15 Sep, Alexandra, P.E.I.; d. 19 Jan 2002, Crapaud, P.E.I.; given name: Mary MacLennan; m, Crilly Lea; ret'd teacher, creamery mgr.; 1st female to qualify for Cdn Bisley team; capt. Cdn Kalapore title team Bisley '51; mem. PEI, DCRA Sports halls of fame.

LEACH, Al (all-around): b. 12 Jul 1917, Richmond, Ont.; d. 26 May 2000, Ottawa. Ont.; given name: Alvin Douglas; m. Valerie Evelyn Bennett; c. Douglas John, Patricia Gail; ret'd chief mechanical inspector, plan examiner; HS swim champion '35-37; Kiwanis jr. Big 4 football champions '37; Oakwood Indians ORFU intermediate titlists '38-39; Toronto Sr. Commercial HL '38-40; Ottawa football (Combines, Trojans, Rough Riders) '41-47; Ottawa District Football (soccer) Assn. '43-48; ODFA title '48; Ottawa Mercantile Softball League '43-46, Eastern Ont. title '45; Ottawa Valley Curling Assn. dir., p-pres.; mem. Gov.Gen.'s Curling Club; mem. '81 Ont. Masters title rink; Curl Canada Level 1 instructor.

LEACH, Reg (hockey): b. 23 Apr 1950, Riverton, Man.; given name: Reginald Joseph; jr. Flin Flon, set scoring record, league MVP; 1st pick Boston '70 draft; Bruins '70-72, California '72-74, Philadelphia '74-82, Detroit '82-83; topped scored 61g '76, 50 '80; Stanley Cup playoff record 19 goals '76; Team Canada '76; NHL record: 934 scheduled games, 381g, 285a, 94 playoff games, 47g, 22a; 2nd team all-star rw '76; Conn Smythe trophy '76; mem. '75 Stanley Cup winner; nicknamed "Riverton Rifle"; mem. Man. Hockey Hall of Fame; res. Sewell, NJ

LEADER, Al (builder/hockey/baseball): b. 4 Dec 1903, Barnsley, Man.; d. 8 May 1982, Rancho Mirage, Calif; given name: George Alfred; m. Alice Segerstrom; c. Albert, Ruth, Raymond, Dawn; organized, played for Sask. jr. title team '24; semipro baseball Northern Sask.; helped organize Seattle city HL '32; organized defence league Seattle, Portland '43-44; helped organize Pacific Coast HL '44; PCHL pres. '44-49 (name changed to Western HL '51); served in hockey as player, coach, mgr., referee, owner, pres.; v-p USAHA; naturalized US citizen '33; pres. Rainier G&CC Seattle; v-p Desert Island CC, Rancho Mirage, Calif., '79-81; Lester Patrick award '76; mem. Man., Cdn Hockey halls of fame.

LEADLAY, Pep (football): b. 7 Mar 1898, Hamilton, Ont.; d. 8 Sep 1984, Hamilton, Ont.; given name: Frank Robert; m. Vera Esther Rymal; Queen's, BSc; ret'd civil engineer; great exponent of drop kick; Hamilton Tigers intermediate ntl champions '15; Hamilton Tigers Interprovincial Union '19-20; Queen's '21-25 winning ntl coll. titles, Grey Cup '22-24, OQAA titles '22-25; Hamilton Tigers '26-30,

league title '27; ORFU ntl title '30; capt. Queen's, Hamilton teams; mem. Golden Gaels team which scored 26 consec. victories; mem. Queen's, Cdn Football, Canada's Sports halls of fame.

LEAH, Vince (builder): b. 29 Nov 1913, West Kildonan, Man.; d. 9 Aug 1993, Winnipeg, Man.; m. Mary; c. Donald; journalist; began sports writing *Winnipeg Tribune* '30; operated 1st soccer, hockey teams at age 13; authored 9 books on local history; hon. doctorate (LLD) UMan. '85; hon. chief Winnipeg Fire Dept. for work with Fire Fighters Historical Society and Fire Fighters Burn Fund; honored by Cdn Amateur Hockey Assn., Cdn Soccer Assn., Cdn Parks & Rec. Assn., Cdn Amateur Sports Federation; US ntl Rec. Assn.; mem. Order of Canada, Man. Sports, Hockey halls of fame.

LEAR, Les (football): b. 22 Aug 1918, Grafton, N.D.; d. 1979 Hollywood, Fla.; m. Betty Louise Neill; mem. Winnipeg Deer Lodge Jrs.; Blue Bombers '37-42; all-star lineman 3 times; helped Bombers win WIFU titles '37-39, Grey Cup '39; Cleveland Rams (NFL) '42-45, LA Rams '46-47; 2nd team US pro all-star '45; traded to Detroit '47 but ret'd to coach CFL Stampeders; guided Calgary to Grey Cup '48; following season won west but lost Grey Cup final to Montreal; mem. Cdn Football Hall of Fame.

LEARN, Ed (football): b. 30 Sep 1935, Welland, Ont.; given name: Harry Edward; div.; c. Billy, Paul, Janice; m. Bernadee; sc. Christopher, Kimberley; automobile dealer; dh ORFU champion K-W Dutchman '56-57; 12yr dh Montreal, Toronto; punt return specialist; CFL record: 508 punt returns, 3091yds, 6.1 avg., 578yds returning 51 pass interceptions; all-Eastern 3 times, All-Cdn once; Montreal nominee Cdn player of '61; EFC leading 7 interceptions '68; dh modern era Argo all-star team ('45-73); nicknamed "Spider"; res. St. Catharines, Ont.

LEARY, George (shooting): b. 19 Nov 1957, Newmarket, Ont.; ntl parts mgr., toolmaker; trapshooting specialist; ntl team from '73; European jr. Grand Prix '77; team gold, individual bronze '78 Benito Juarez; silver '78, 2 silver '94 CG; team, individual gold '91, bronze '79, '99 PAG; mem. 5 Olympic, 4 CG, 3 PAG teams; 3 ntl, 8 Ont., 5 Que., 3 Benito Juarez, 1 European, 1 Welsh, 1 British trap titles; head ref. trap shooting '76 Olympics; SFC Golden Anniversary award '82; SFC male shooter of '91; res. Newmarket, Ont.

LEBEL, Bob (hockey): b. 21 Sep 1905, Quebec City, Que.; d. 20 Sep 1999, Longueuil, Que.; given name: Robert; m. Lucile Begin; c. Jean-Marc; Que. City Commercial Academy; ret'd Bennett Inc.; jr., sr., Que. City; coached int. teams Montreal; 11yrs amateur hockey referee; founder, pres. ISHL '44-47; pres. QAHL '55-57, CAHA '57-69; pres. IIHF '60-63; trustee George T. Richardson Memorial Trophy (Eastern Jr. championship), W.G. Hardy Cup (ntl int.); QMJHL div. bears his name; life mem. QAHA, CAHA; 17yrs mem. governing board Cdn Hockey Hall of Fame; former Chambly, Que., mayor; Kent GC, Sherbrooke Opens, Bank of Montreal golf titles; Confederation medal; mem. Cdn Hockey, IIHF, Que. Sports halls of fame.

LeBLANC, Eugene (baseball/hockey): b. 29 Jan 1929, College Bridge, N.B.; d. 31 Dec 2001, Moncton, N.B.; exec.

dir. Memramcook Institute; coached Memramcook Rovers to '61, '65 Maritime Int. A, NB sr. baseball titles; founder/dir. minor baseball league operations in Memramcook Valley '61-65; sub-commissioner NBABA '63-64; helped create baseball facilities Memramcook Valley '68-70; coached Moncton Beavers to Maritime juvenile '58-59, Maritime junior '59-60 hockey titles; founder/dir. Memramcook Valley minor hockey league '68-70; exec. NBAHA '75-76; UMoncton recognition award '88; mem. NB Sports Hall of Fame.

LeBLANC, Guillaume (t&f): b. 14 Apr 1962, Sept-Iles, Que.; Montreal; engineer; race walker; ntl 3km, 10km, 20km, 5000m titles; Swedish 20km title; Cdn records 10km 39:26.02 '90, 30km 2:04.56 '90; PB: 20km 1:21.12 '86, 50km 3:56.46 '92; 30km gold '90, silver '86, bronze '82 CG, gold '83, bronze '85 FISU, gold '89 Francophone Games; mem. '84, '88, '92 Olympic, '83 PAG; fed. govt. excellence award '84; Rimouski sports complex bears his name; res. Rimouski, Que.

LeBLANC, Ken (bobsleigh): b. 13 Feb 1968, Ottawa, Ont.; crewman 4/2-man teams; ntl team '85-92, '97-02; competed '88, '92, '98, '02 Olympics; 3 WC 4-man, 1 2-man race titles; mem. 4-man crew which claimed '89-90 WC series championship; 2-man world bronze '01; Ottawa ACT award; res. Calgary, Alta.

LeBLANC, Louise-Marie (fencing): b. 8 Jan 1958, Ottawa, Ont.; UofOtt, BA; computer programmer analyst; ntl jr. foil champion '74-78, sr. '76-78, '81; Ottawa Shield '78-81; team silver '75, '79 PAG; Gov.-Gen.s Cup '79; team silver '78 CG; silver foil '83 Commonwealth championships; brief '92 comeback winning ntl épée title; winner, at least once, every major competition in Canada; represented Canada World Youth, World University, Worlds, Ramon Fonst International, Michel Alaux, Debeaumont, NY Open tournaments; Cornell Open titles '77-79; D'Aoust Trophy French Cdn amateur athlete of '75; res. Ottawa, Ont.

LEBLANC, Vicky (softball): b. 16 May 1973, Ste-Anne, N.B.; div. Bastarache; Dieppe Community Coll.; rhp; pitcher ntl team '97-00; competed 3 ntl championships claiming silver '97; hurled perfect game vs. Denmark '98 worlds; silver '99 PAG; competed '00 Olympics; top batter, player '88, '99 ntls, top pitcher '91 ntls; NB Softball female athete of '98; res. Notre Dame, N.B.

LECAVALIER, Vincent (hockey): b. 21 Apr 1980, Ile Bizard, Que.; ctr. Notre Dame (SJHL) '95-96, Rimouski (QMJHL) '96-98; Team Canada '98 world jr., '01, '04 World Cup (gold), tourney MVP; gold -18 3-Nations tournament; participated '97 Top Prospects game; Que. male athlete of yr; CHL, QMJHL all-star, rookie of yr; drafted 1st overall by Tampa Bay '98; NHL record Tampa Bay through '04 467 scheduled games, 146g, 181a, 34 playoff games, 9g, 7a; 1 Stanley Cup winner; played in Russia during '04 labor dispute; res. Montreal, Que.

LeCLAIR, John (hockey): b. 5 Jul 1969, St. Albans, Vermont; m. Christina; c. MacKenzie, Cal, Jagger; Vermont; lw Bellows Academy HS'85-87, Vermont '87-91; ECAC all-star; Fredericton (AHL) '91; NHL Montreal '91-95, Philadelphia '95-04; Team USA '89 world jr., '96 World Cup, '98, '02 (silver) Olympics; 1 Stanley Cup winner; 5

NHL all-star games; 3 1st, 2 2nd team NHL all-star, 1 *HN* 1st, 2nd team, 1 *SN* 1st team; reached 50-goal plateau '96 51, '97 50, '98 '51; 2 Bobby Clarke, 1 Pelle Lindbergh, 2 Bud Ice plus-minus, 1 *SN* Good Guy awards; active role in John LeClair Foundation, Greater Philadelphia Food Bank; NHL record (through '04) 873 scheduled games, 382g, 379a, 154 playoff games, 42g, 47a; res. Voorhees, N.J.

LECLERC, Andre (horseshoes): b. 13 Dec 1964, St. Hyacinthe, Que.; m. Sylvianne Moisan; c. Sandra; administrator; Que. jr. singles title '79; 9 Que. men's singles titles; 7 Que. men's doubles titles; 8 ntl men's singles titles; 2 recognized perfect games; men's record for high ringer percentage complete tournament '87 Que. championship 81%, ntl 95.8% '85; 3 top 10 finishes in world tournament; Horseshoe Canada player of decade '80s; wrote *Historique du lancer de fers au Quebec 1958-88*; editor *Canadian Horseshoe Pitchers Yearbook* '91-96; men. Cdn Horseshoe Hall of Fame; res. Chertsey, Que.

LEDDY, Jack (golf): b. 27 Oct 1912, Saskatoon, Sask.; d. 27 Nov 1990, Saskatoon, Sask.; given name: John Edward; m. Rita Wilkinson; c. Mary, Joanne, Jennifer, Michael; UofSask., McGill, MD; surgeon; runnerup '30 Sask. jr., '68 sr. championships; pres. RCGA '62; non-playing capt. Cdn 2nd place team world amateur tournament '62; mem. Sask. Sports Hall of Fame.

LEDERHOUSE, Phil (golf): b. 23 Nov 1915, Prince Albert, Sask.; d. 15 Aug 1991, St. Boniface, Man.; given name: Philip Edward; m. Ruby Rankin; c. Bryan, Grant, Lynda; merchant; lost sight at age 19; at 34 took up golf and with no prior experience and 6 months coaching won Cdn title and placed 3rd in International Blind Golfers' championship; from '50 won 17 Sask, 16 Western Cdn, 5 ntl blind golfers titles; twice world runnerup; held world record '66-67 with round of 89; recorded hole-in-one '89; a threat in every tournament he entered due to natural technique; sponsored by Lions Club and played with the likes of Jack Nicklaus, Walter Hagan, Bob Hope, Ed Sullivan; Sask athlete-of-'90; life mem. Lions Club; mem. Sask., Prince Albert Sports halls of fame.

LEDUC, Mark (boxing): b. 4 May 1962, Kingston, Ont.; construction worker, set builder film industry; competed as light-welterweight (63.5kg); 3 ntl titles; 2 gold, 1 silver, 1 bronze Canada Cup; President's Cup bronze '91; competed '91 PAG, '92 Olympics, '92 Worlds; gold '92 NA intl tourney; appeared in Gemini winning documentary on gays & lesbians in sport, *CBC's Last Closet*; mem. Kingston Amateur BC; 6yr sentence Collins Bay for armed robbery; res. Kingston, Ont.

LEE, Knotty (baseball): b. 12 May 1877, Toronto, Ont.; d. 5 Sep 1962, Smiths Falls, Ont.; given name: George Joseph; m. Eva Hammer; c. Herbert, George, Louis, Raymond, William, Donald, Laurence; pro baseball player, hotel owner; in late '90s he possessed awesome, then legal, spitball pitch and was regarded as best amateur pitcher in Toronto; 6 decade relationship with baseball; played for 11 minor league teams, managed 10 more; scout for legendary Connie Mack's Philadelphia Athletics 2 decades; worked for Joe McCarthy's Yankees; business mgr. Toronto Maple Leafs (IL) 7yrs; team owner/founder 6 leagues including

1st Cdn pro league '11, Mich.-Ont., Can-Am, Pony and Border leagues; during minor league centennial celebration at Cooperstown Baseball Hall of Fame '39 represented Abner Doubleday, alleged baseball game inventor, in special ceremonies; uniform he wore that day displayed at Cdn Baseball Hall of Fame in St. Mary's; mem. Cdn Baseball Hall of Fame.

LEE, Peter (hockey): b. 2 Jan 1956, Chester, Eng.; given name: Peter John; m. Judy Perry; c. Christopher, Jeremy, Joshua; coach; scored most OHA jr. A career goals (215), points (451) and in '75-76 most goals single season (81) as mem. Ottawa 67's; OHA MVP, Tilson Trophy, highest-scoring rw Mahon trophy '76; honored with Peter Lee Day Ottawa Civic Centre '76; twice Ottawa ACT hockey player of yr; pro Nova Scotia AHL '76-77; Pittsburgh NHL '77-83; played Dusseldorf, Germany, '83-93; NHL record: 431 scheduled games, 114g, 131a, 19 playoff games, 0g, 8a; jersey ret'd by 67's; asst. coach 67's '93, head coach '94-95; player-coach EC Wolfsburg, Germany, '95-04; CHL outstanding player '76; res. Germany.

LEE, Scott (canoeing): b. 15 Mar 1949, Saskatoon, Sask.; given name: Thomas Garfield Scott; m. Mary Jane Lynch; c. Nicole, Christopher; McMaster, BA, Ont. Teachers Coll., BEd; teacher; age-group ntl titles '63-68; with John Wood ntl, NA C2 '69-70; ntl C2 '72-73, C1 '73; trained in Budapest '70-71; mem. ntl team '68 Olympics, '70-72 world championships; ret'd from competition '73; coach Mississauga Canoe Club 3yrs; active distance runner; res. Acton, Ont.

LEE, Tae Eun (taekwondo): b. Kwangju, South Korea; m. In Soon Shin; c. Chi Yong Lee, Chi Hoon Lee; National University of Chun Nam BA, MA; Taekwondo Grandmaster Instructor (since 1977); Ottawa Bureau Chief, *Korea Times* daily newspaper (from '78); Korean army '63-65; instrumental in development of taekwondo nationally, internationally: secretary general '80-86, pres. '88-01 WTF Taekwondo Assn Can.; technical advisor DND Can. , CISM from '87; dir. COC, '88-03; hosted '88 Olympic team trials; auditor, exec. council World Taekwondo Fed. from '93; mem. promotion comm. for takewondo Olympic status '94-95; presidential advisor Pan Am Taekwondo Union from '97; intl. relations ambassador Toronto '08 Olympic bid comm.; chair., hosting/org. comm. '99 Commonwealth Games; pres./founder of Cdn. Special Needs Taekwondo Assn. '01; author *Mastering Taekwondo – A Korean Martial Art, Mastering Taekwondo Sparring – The Basics and Grandmaster Tae Eun Lee Comic Book*; Korea-Canada intl. culture, trade and academic co-ordinator '81-97; founder of the UofOtt Tae Eun Lee Scholarship, the Special Needs Taekwondo Program Foundation and Carleton's Korean Language course; volunteer advisor for DARE (Young Offenders Program '84-86); RCMP SWAT team training instructor for ERT (Emergency Response Team) '88; volunteer translator Languages of Life from '80; Merivale High School Advisory Council community rep., life mem.; numerous civic, prov., ntl, Korean, Hong Kong, US, world awards, citations, medals and commendations; mem. Ottawa Sports Hall of Fame; res. Ottawa, Ont.

LEE-GARTNER, Kerrin (skiing): b. 21 Sep 1966, Trail, B.C.; given name: Kerrin Lee; m. Max Gartner; c. Riana, Stephanie; owner/operator Snow Creek Lodge & Fernie Alpine Resort; mem. alpine development group '83-84, C

team '84-86, B team '86-88, A team '88-94; 3 ntl downhill, 2 GS titles; WC record 3silver, 4bronze; 2 Fleishman Cup, 2 NA Cup, 4 FIS, 2 Nor-Am gold; competed '88, '92, '94 Olympics; '92 Olympic DH gold; *CBC, TSN* skiing analyst from '95; fed. govt meritorious service award '93; Velma Springstead award '92; Order of BC; Calgary female-athlete-of-yr award; BC Women in Sport Leaders & Legends award; mem. Cdn Olympic, Cdn Skiing; Alta., BC, Canada's Sports halls of fame; res. Fernie, B.C.

LEEMAN, Gary (hockey): b. 19 Feb 1964, Toronto, Ont.; operates hobby farm; rw; jr. WHL Regina '81-82; drafted by Toronto '82; NHL Toronto '83-91 with brief stints in AHL with St. Catharines '85-86, Fredericton '94, Gardena, Italy, '95, Worcester (AHL), Utah (IHL) '96-97, Hanover, Germany, '97-99; NHL Calgary '91-93, Montreal '93-94, Vancouver '95-96, St. Louis '97; 1 Stanley Cup winner; NHL record: 667 scheduled games, 199g, 267a, 36 playoff games, 8g, 16a; scored 51g '90; helped organize Hockey for Homeless charity tournament; res. Caledon, Ont.

LEEMING, Marjorie (tennis): b. 4 Jun 1903, Kamloops, B.C.; d. 10 Jun 1987, Victoria, B.C.; UBC, BA; teacher; BC-16 title '15-18; Victoria clay court ladies singles, doubles '22-24, '26, mixed doubles '22-23; BC singles '23, '25-26, ladies, mixed doubles '25; ntl singles '25-26, doubles '25, '30, '32, mixed doubles '25, '30; Oregon State singles '26; Eastern Cdn singles, doubles '32; competed Forest Hills '32; tennis, badminton, golf instructor UBC '47-59; 2nd seeded nationally badminton '29; 6 times outstanding BC tennis player; BC Women in Sport Leaders & Legends award; mem. BC, Greater Victoria Sports halls of fame.

LEETCH, Brian (hockey): b. 3 Mar 1968, Corpus Christi, Tex.; m. Mary Beth; c. Jack; Boston Coll.; standout HS pitcher with live arm; def. HS, Boston Coll.; 3 yrs US ntl jr. team; Team US '88-89; 3 Olympics, '89 worlds, '91 Canada Cup; capt. '96 World Cup gold team; named to all-time US team; drafted NYR '88; NHL NYR '88-04, Toronto '04; 12 NYR team awards, several NYR team records; Calder Memorial, 2 Norris, 1 Conn Smythe awards; played 10 NHL all-star games; 1 Stanley Cup winner; frequent all-star selectee; does extensive charitable work; NHL record (through '04): 1144 scheduled games, 242g, 754a, 95 playoff games, 28g, 69a; res. New York, N.Y.

LEFAIVE, Lou (administration): b. 13 Feb 1928, Windsor, Ont.; d. 4 Jul 2002, Ottawa, Ont.; given name: Louis Ernest; m. Winnifred; c. Louise, Michelle, Maria, Jacqueline; UofOtt, St. Patrick's Coll.; ret'd sports administrator; football, basketball, semipro softball Windsor; coached basketball UofOtt, St. Pat's; dir. Sport Canada '68-75, '78-80; pres. Ntl Sport Recreation Centre '75-78; pres. Hockey Canada '80-82; exec-dir. Cdn Figure Skating Assn. '83-85; exec-dir. Sport Marketing Canada '86-92; founding mem. Hockey Canada, Coaching Assn of Canada, Canada Games Council; dir. COA; hon. life mem. Cdn Gymnastics Fed.

LEFRANÇOIS, Charles (t&f): b. 19 Dec 1972, Montreal, Que.; Ahuntsic Coll.; hj; began competing age 14; Que. jr. indoor/outdoor, ntl indoor jr. titles '91; Canada Games hj gold, tj bronze '93; competed '94 CG, '95 PAG, '96 Olympic Games, '95 world outdoor championships; ntl title '95; res. Montreal, Que.

LEGACE, François (weightlifting): b. 13 Oct 1971, St. Hyacinthe, Que.; began competing age 12; competed '91 PAG, '93 Worlds; 54kg bronze snatch, overall total '94 CG; res. Ste-Rosalie, Que.

LEGGATT, Art (baseball): b. 29 May 1941, Chatham, N.B.; given name: Arthur Michael; m. Carol; millworker; pitcher; began career with Chatham Ironmen age 14; 2 NB, 2 Maritime titles; signed pro contract Cleveland Indians; minor pro stops with Dubuque A, Salinas AA making all-star with latter; returned to Ironmen '66-81; arm trouble brought shift to 1st base; 7 NB sr., 5 Atlantic championships; mem. NB Baseball, Chatham Wall, NB Sports halls of fame; res. Chatham, N.B.

LEGGATT, Ian (golf): b. 23 Sep 1965, Cambridge, Ont.; m. Lori; c. Mia Riess; Texas Wesleyan; former prov., ntl level speed skater; honed golfing skills at Texas Wesleyan; twice NAIA all-American; turned pro '90; competed Buy.Com, South Africa, Australia, South America, Cdn, US PGA tours; mem. 3 Cdn WC teams; won Buy.Com Dayton Open '00, PGA Tucson Open '02; 7 career Cdn tour runnerup honors '90-99; TaylorMade staff player from '00; eye surgery disrupted playing career '01; active in children's charities; res. Scottsdale, Ariz.

LEHMAN, Hughie (hockey): b. 27 Oct 1885, Pembroke, Ont.; d. 8 Apr 1961, Toronto, Ont.; given name: Frederick Hugh; nickname "Old Eagle Eyes"; goalie Pembroke '05, Sault Ste. Marie (international pro league) '06, Pembroke semipro '07, Berlin (Kitchener) Ont. pro league '08-10, New Westminster Royals '11-13, Vancouver Millionaires (PCL) '14-25, Chicago (NHL) '26-27; mem. 8 Stanley Cup challengers, won with Vancouver '14-15; with Percy LeSueur shares record for playing on 2 Stanley Cup challengers within 2 months (Galt vs. Ottawa, Berlin vs. Wanderers '09-10); mem. Hockey Hall of Fame.

LEHMANN, Ken (football): b. 13 Jan 1942, Louisville, Ky.; m. Bonnie Roos; c. Eric, Heidi, Bridget; Xavier, BSc; newspaper exec.; capt/MV lineman 2ys in coll.; Xavier legion of honor; lb Rough Riders '64-72; Schenley lineman of '68, runnerup '66; 6 times EFC all-star, 5 times all-Cdn; mem. 3 Grey Cup finalists, 2 winners; asst. coach UofOtt 1 season; mem. Ottawa Sports Hall of Fame; res. Ottawa, Ont.

LEIBEL, Allan (sailing): b. 28 Feb 1945, Montreal, Que.; m. Barbara Nemoy; UofT, BComm, LLD; lawyer; won '72 Olympic Dragon trials, 8th in games; 8th Tempest world championships '75; won '76 Olympic Tempest trials, 5th in Games; NA Star class title '79; CORK Star title '81; won '80 Olympic Star trials, missed Games due to boycott; res. Toronto, Ont.

LEIGH, Doug (coaching/figure skating): b. 4 Apr 1950, Huntsville, Ont.; m. Michelle; c. Dustin; professional skating coach; silver medal ntl jr. men's championships '66 but lack of confidence in own skating ability led to coaching Orillia '68; opened Mariposa School of Skating in Orillia at 24; coached Brian Orser to 8 ntl titles, 2 Olympic silver medals, 1 world title; has coached 26 ntl, 14 international titlists; coached at 16 worlds, 5 Olympics; coached Elvis Stojko to 4 ntl, 3 world titles, 2 Olympic silver medals; 3M coaching award; 9 Longines-Wittnauer coaching awards;

Paul Harris Fellowship award; Ont. coach-of-yr award; Ont, world achievement award; Air Canada award; 9 PetroCan coaching excellence awards; mem. Cdn Figure Skating Hall of Fame; res. Barrie, Ont.

LEINEMANN, Conrad (volleyball); b. 2 Apr 1971, Kelowna, B.C.; m. Jane Roos; UBC, human kinetics; beach volleyball player; '99 PAG champion; '01 Francophone Games champion; competed '00 Olympics; 2 ntl titles; UBC athlete of '94; UBC Canada West player of '94; res. Toronto, Ont.

LEITCH, Kerry (figure skating/baseball): b.5 Mar 1941, Woodstock, Ont.; given name: Thomas Kerry; div.Barbara Still; m. Kathryn Stewart; c. Kristi Lee, Christine, James; Detroit; pro skating school owner, coach; catcher jr. IC age 15-18, sr. London Pontiacs, Guelph age 17-24; began skating age 10, teaching age 17; trained by Otto Gold, Marcus Nikkanen; passed 7th figures test, competed jr. nationals; level 3 certified coach; coached Cdns in worlds, Olympics, internationally in England, Australia, Finland, Holland, France, US, Belgium; among his students Sheri Baier, Robert Cowan, Lloyd Eisler, Lyndon Johnston; NCCP master rated pro; dir. ntl Pairs Centre, champions training centre, ntl ice skating centre; pres. Intl. Pro Skating Union from '91; dir. NA training camp Lake Placid; dir. Preston FSC 30yrs; dir. J.P. Igloo FSC; ex-board mem. CFSA; FS coach-of-yr award; 2 PetroCan coaching-excellence awards; mem. Waterloo Region Hall of Fame; res. Ellenton, Fla.

LEITHAM, Bobby (boxing): b. 25 May 1906, Perth, Scotland; m. Ethel Gordon (d); c. Joyce, Doreen; m. Celine Pinet; ret'd Cdn Freight Assn inspector; juv football Verdun, jr. Grand Trunk Railways; won several 5-mile road races; 2nd to Edouard Fabre in 1 major race; won several major distance swim events; ntl level diver; ntl amateur flyweight boxing title '25-27, Que., Montreal titles '26-27; 4 international titles; ranked 3rd pro bantamweight div.; lost 20-round decision to Johnny King in '33 BE title bid; Verdun city key '79; GT-CN Old Boys plaque; mem. Cdn Boxing Hall of Fame; res. Montreal, Que./St. Petersburg, Fla.

LEMAIRE, Jacques (hockey): b. 7 Sep 1945, LaSalle, Que.; given name: Jacques Gerard; m. Mychele; c. Patrice, Danyk, Magalie; hockey coach.; jr. Montreal Canadiens; NHL Canadiens '67-79; NHL playing record: 853 scheduled games, 366g, 469a, 145 playoff games, 61g, 78a; coaching record: 229 scheduled games, 117-80-32, 67 playoff games, 44-29; mem. 8 Stanley Cup winners as player; player/coach Europe '80-81; asst. coach SUNY College '81; coach Longueuil QMJHL '82-83; coach Canadiens '83-85; asst. GM Canadiens '86-92, '98-99, 2 more Stanley Cups; managing dir. Verdun Jr. Canadiens '88-89; managing dir. Fredericton '91-93; coach New Jersey '93-98; Stanley Cup '96, scout NJ '98; 1st coach Minnesota Wild '00-04; NHL coaching record (through '03) 721 scheduled games, 340-276-104-15; playoff 57-44; 2 Adams trophies; 2 *Hockey News* coach-of-yr awards; mem. Hockey Hall of Fame; res. Vaudreuil sur la Lac, Que./Sarasota, Fla.

LEMAY, Lucille (archery): b. 20 Jul 1950, Montreal, Que.; given name: Lucille Goyette; m. Roger Lemay; c. Michele; secretary; competed in all ntl outdoor championships '76-84 winning titles '76-79; 5th '76 Olympic target competition;

Championship of the Americas field bronze '75-77; bronze US nationals '77; PB international showing 5th Double FITA Star tournament, replacement for boycotted '80 Olympics; bronze '82 CG; res. Boisbriand, Que.

LEMAY, Roger (archery): b. 9 Apr 1950, Montreal, Que.; m. Lucille Goyette; c. Michele; policeman; competed all ntl outdoor championships '74-84, winning target, field titles '79, runnerup '74; 1st 9yrs of competition shot lefthanded, switched to righthand shooting '78; mem. 5 Championship of the Americas, 4 world championships, 3 US nationals teams; 1st '80 Olympic trials; competed '80 Olympics alternative Double FITA tournament; silver '82 CG; res. Boisbriand, Que.

LE MAY-DOAN, Catriona (speed skating); b. 23 Dec 1970, Saskatoon, Sask.; given name: Catriona Le May; m. Bart Doan; c. Greta; UCal; soccer, ringette player who followed sister Ailsa into speed skating; competed in t&f as heptathlete for Sask. '93 Canada Games; skating long-track specialist; World Cup 500m bronze '92; competed '94, '98 (gold, bronze), '02 (gold) Olympics; 6 ntl sprint titles; 8 World Cup medals '96 including gold, silver World championships; spectacular '98 season earning Olympic, World Cup overall, world sprint, world single distance gold; 9 WC gold '98; 6 gold, overall title '99 WC; mem. ntl team '88-03; set 2 world records '97; silver '99 worlds; '99, '01 world single distance champ; 9 gold, overall WC title '01; WC sprint title '02; 7 consec. WC race wins '02; Olympic flag-bearer '02; lowered world 500m record unprecedented 6 times; 4 ntl outstanding-skater awards; 3 Bobby Rosenfeld awards; Lou Marsh award '02; ret'd from competition '03; dir. '10 Olympic organizing comm.; Calgary female athlete of yr award; res. Calgary, Alta.

LEMELIN, Reggie (hockey/coaching); b. 19 Nov 1954, Sherbrooke, Que.; given name: Rejean; m. Rona; c. Stephanie, Brian; coach; goalie; QMJHL Sherbrooke '72-74; AHL Philadelphia '74-79 with brief stops at Richmond, Springfield; CHL Birmingham '79-81; Team Canada '84 Canada Cup gold; drafted by Philadelphia NHL, Chicago WHA; NHL Atlanta '78-80, Calgary '80-87, Boston '87-93; NHL totals: 507 scheduled games, 28,006 minutes, 236-262-63, 24sho, 59 playoff games, 3119 minutes, 23-25-0, 2sho; 1 AHL, NHL all-stars; 3 Stanley Cup finals; goalie coach Philadelphia from '77; with Andy Moog shared '90 Jennings award; Calgary athlete of '84 award; res. Peabody, Mass.

LEMIEUX, Claude (hockey): b. 16 Jul 1965, Buckingham, Que.; m. Deborah; c. Christopher, Michael, Brendan, Claudia; rw Trois-Rivieres, Verdun (QMJHL), Nova Scotia, Sherbrooke (AHL); drafted by Montreal '83; NHL with Montreal '83-90, New Jersey '90-95, '99-00, Colorado '95-99, Phoenix '00-02, Dallas '02-03; mem. 3 Stanley Cup winners (with 3 different teams); Conn Smythe trophy '95; competed in Rendez-Vous '87; Team Canada '85 world jr., '97 Worlds, '88, '96 World Cup; brother Jocelyn also in NHL; reached 300g '98; NHL record 1197 scheduled games, 379g, 406a, 233 playoff games, 80g, 78a; QMJHL all-star, '85 Guy Lafleur QMJHL playoff MVP trophy; nickname "Pepe"; mem. QMJHL Hall of Fame; res. Parber, Colo.

LEMIEUX, Gerald (boxing): b. 1 Feb 1909, Levis, Que.; d. 26 May 1959, Edmundston, N.B.; nicknamed "Biff" or "Flying Frenchman"; career spanned '28-37; Maritime featherweight titles '30, '35; 226 pro bouts in bantam, featherweight classes; fought world champions Harry Jeffra, Joey Archibald; mem. NB Sports Hall of Fame.

LEMIEUX, Lawrence (sailing): b. 12 Nov 1955, Edmonton, Alta.; boat builder; began competing age 9; Finn specialist; mem. ntl team from '78; competed '84, '88 Olympics, 8 worlds; 1 US National, 5 Midwinter, 1 European, 2 CORK gold; NA Finn title '94; PAG gold '91; best remembered for courageous and sportsmanlike act in '88 Olympics when he rescued another competitor whose boat had capsized; ntl Finn Assoc. secty.; res. Edmonton, Alta.

LEMIEUX, Mario (hockey): b. 5 Oct 1965, Montreal, Que.; m. Nathalie Asselin; c. Lauren Rachel, Austin, Stephanie, Alexa; hockey exec., player; standout jr. ctr Laval Titan '81-84; QMJHL MVP '84 with 133g, 149a; Cdn jr record: 247g, 315a, 562pts; Cdn major jr. player of '84; Pittsburgh's 1st pick, 1st overall '84 draft; Calder Memorial Trophy '85; mem. all-rookie team '85; 4 L.B. Pearson, 2 Conn Smythe, 1 Masterton, 6 Ross, 3 Hart, 2 Dodge performer of yr, 1 Dodge Ram Tough trophies, 1 Pro Set NHL player-of-yr award, 1 Alka Seltzer plus award; *Hockey News* player of '93; 5 1st team, 3 2nd team all-star; played in 9 NHL all-star games; mem. 2 Stanley Cup winners; mem. Team Canada '90 Canada Cup, capt. '02 Olympic gold winners, '04 World Cup; 50 goals in 50 games '96; topped 50-goal plateau '87 (54), '88 (70), '89 (85), '93 (69), '96 (69), '97 (50); prolific scorer plagued by chronic back ailment; diagnosed with Hodgkin's disease '93; nicknamed "The Savior" by Pittsburgh fans; Lou Marsh Trophy '93; 2 Lionel Conacher awards; NHL record (through '04): 889 scheduled games, 683g, 1018a; 107 playoff games, 76g, 96a; tied single-period goal scoring record with 4 in 3rd period vs. Montreal '97; reached 600g '97, 1000a, 1700pts '03; ret'd following '96-97, made comeback '01; named to CHL all-time team '99; key figure in purchase of Penguins '99; Pittsburgh street bears his name; founder/chair Cancer research foundation; mem. Cdn Walk, Hockey, Canada's Sports halls of fame; res. Sewickley, Pa.

LEMMERMAN, Bruce (football): b. 4 Oct 1945, Los Angeles, Calif.; m. Brigitte Jaeger; c. Lisa Nicole, Jennifer Leigh; San Fernando Valley State Coll., BA, Cal State Northridge; football exec.; 3yrs HS baseball, football, all-conference, all-city baseball sr. yr.; 3yrs baseball, football SFVS, all-conf. 2yrs each sport; athlete of sr. yr; all-American hon. mention; qb Atlanta (NFL) '69-71, Edmonton (CFL) '71-78; 6 Grey Cup finals, 3 winners; traded to Hamilton, ret'd '80; asst coach Edmonton '81-82, LA Express (USFL), Houston (NFL) '84-85, Winnipeg '87-88; dir. ops. Edmonton '90-93; dir. college scouting New Orleans Saints from '94; mem. Cal State Hall of Fame; res. Destrehan, La.

LENARD, Al (football): b. 6 Jan 1921, Windsor, Ont.; given name: Aldon Lewis; m. Jean Louise Bidwell; c. James Aldon; Queen's, BA, BPHE, UMich, MA, Illinois, PhD; ret'd prof. AD; Silverwood trophy, WOSSA t&f MVP '38; ORFU football Hamilton Wildcats '40-42, '45, Imperial Oil trophy '41; Eastern Cdn scoring leader '41-42; qb Queen's '46-49; 1st Queen's capt. chosen twice '47-48; asst. coach '54-70; pres. ntl AD's Assn '72; v-p CIAU '73; chair.

CIAU admin. comm. '73-74; chair. OUAA admin, council '74-76, pres. '82-88; coached intercollegiate champions in curling, golf; '57 Kingston golf champion; mem. Kingston Sports, Queen's Coaches, Football halls of fame; res. Kingston, Ont.

LENARDON, Norman (hockey): b. 20 Oct 1933, Trail, B.C.; m. Eugenia Kennedy; c. Therese, Jim, Elizabeth, Maria; bricklayer, restaurateur; HS baseball, basketball, volleyball; sr. softball, jr. baseball; minor, jr. hockey Trail, sr. Trail, Rossland; peewee hockey MVP award, 6g, 5a in 10 games for Seattle vs. New Westminster '58 playoffs; rejected pro offers '59; mem. '61 world champion Trail Smoke Eaters; scored title clinching goal vs. Soviets in final game; mem. '62 Trail Allan Cup champions; with entire Trail team mem. BC Sports Hall of Fame; res. Trail, B.C.

LENARDUZZI, Bob (soccer): b. 1 May 1955, Vancouver, B.C.; given name: Robert Italo; m. Deanne Veitch; soccer exec.; at 15 mem. Vancouver Spartans in now-defunct Western Canada SL; 5ys Reading of English 3rd div.; loaned by Reading to Vancouver Whitecaps '74-75; contract purchased by Whitecaps '76; through '83 only original Whitecap still on team; became all-time Whitecap scoring leader '81; ntl team '73-86; represented Canada internationally more than 30 times; mem. '84 Olympic, '86 World Cup finals teams; 47 international caps; mem. '79 NASL Soccer Bowl champions; as midfielder scored 10g, 17a, named NA player of '78; NASL 2nd team all-star as defender '79; mem. Tacoma Stars MISL '84-85; playing coach Vancouver 86ers '86-92, 5 titles, GM '98-02; ntl team coach '92-97; GM/dir. soccer operations Vancouver Whitecaps from '03; mem. CSA board '98; 1st Cdn named NA player of yr '78; only player to play all 11 positions on field; CSL coach of yr '88-89, CSL GM of '91; Lou Marsh trophy nominee '78; ranked among top 30 CONCACAF players of century; Italo-Cdn of '02; Jack Diamond Vancouver Sport Personality of '02; TV soccer analyst; mem. BC Sports, Cdn, US Ntl, NA Soccer halls of fame; res. N. Vancouver, B.C.

LENARDUZZI, Sam (soccer): b. 19 Dec 1949, Udine, Italy; rejected Reading, Eng., pro offers; mem. ntl team '67-78; represented Canada internationally close to 50 times, including '67 PAG; pro def Vancouver Whitecaps '74-78; traded to Toronto Blizzard '79-81; polished raconteur, dir. PR Whitecaps '78; coached Blizzard reserves '82; mem. Cdn, Ont. Soccer halls of fame; res. Vancouver, B.C.

LENOVER, Max (t&f): b. 27 Aug 1918, Chatham, Ont.; given name: Roy Maxwell; m. Ruth Ione Maxwell; c. Ruth Ann, Robert Maxwell; Loyola, PHB; ret'd corporate industrial engineer; mem. Chatham Queen's AC int. OHA hockey team; Ont. int. schoolboy 440yd recordholder; champion miler, capt. Loyola t&f team; in 4yrs at Loyola never lost a dual competition race; established numerous school, state, ntl records; Illinois x-country titlist; nicknamed "Legs"; mem. '38 BEG team; mem. Loyola Sports Hall of Fame; recognized in *US Colleges Who's Who*; res. Jacksonville, Fla.

LEONARD, Stan (golf): b. 2 Feb 1915, Vancouver, B.C.; m. Chris Main; c. Linda; ret'd golf pro; won 1st tournament he entered, '32 BC Amateur, repeat '35; semifinalist Cdn

Amateur '36-37; mem. 6 BC Willingdon Cup teams; touring pro '55-63; included among 44 pro victories were '57 Greater Greensboro Open, '58 Tournament of Champions, '60 Western Open; twice low individual World Cup ('53-59), with Jules Huot '53 runnerup; 8 CPGA titles, 5 times runnerup; 9 Rivermead Cups as low Cdn in Cdn Open; 5 BC, 9 Alta., 2 Sask. Open, 1 Millar Trophy titles; mem. 9 Canada Cup, 6 Hopkins Cup teams; 3rd US Masters '58-59; ntl sr. pro title '75; golfer of '59; head pro Desert Island CC Rancho Mirage, Calif., '74-81; emeritus dir. of golf from '81; mem. RCGA, BC Golf, BC, Canada's Sports halls of Fame; res. Rancho Mirage, Calif./Vancouver, B.C.

LEPAGE, Carolyne (judo): b. 9 Jun 1975, Montreal, Que.; competes at 48 kg; 1st degree black belt; began competing age 15; bronze '94 Francophonie Games 4 ntl titles; silver '95, '99, '03 PAG; competed '96 Olympics, '02 (gold) CG, '03 World Cup; missed '01 WC, Francophonie Games due to doping suspension which was lifted on appeal; res. Boucherville, Que.

LESCHYSHYN, Curtis (hockey); b. 21 Sep 1969, Thompson, Man,; m. Laura; def. Sask Blades '85-88; NHL Quebec '88-95, Colorado '95-96, Washington '96, Hartford '96-97, Carolina '97-00, Minnesota '00-01, Ottawa '01-04; 1 Stanley Cup; reached 1000 game '05; NHL record (through '04) 1033 scheduled games, 47g, 165a, 68 playoff games, 2g, 6a; res. Littleton, Colo.

LESPI, Leo (hockey): b. 24 Feb 1915, Ft. William, Ont.; nicknamed "Flying Finn", Kusti; played Jr. Port Arthur West Ends, Sudbury Cub Wolves; turned pro Boston organization 1 season Boston Cubs; loaned to AHA Minneapolis Millers where he played 10yrs; mem. 1 AHA title team; set rw record with 35 goals; played in inaugural AHA all-star game '41; ret'd from pro ranks '47 returning to Nipigon to coach Flyers to '52 North Shore title; active many yrs with Nipigon Old Timers; day in his honor held in Nipigon '65; Celebration '88 award; mem. NWO Sports Hall of Fame; res. Nipigon, Ont.

LESSARD, Lucille (archery): b. 26 May 1957, Quebec City, Que.; m. R. Hutchinson; 5 ntl titles; '74 world field title; Pacific Coast field title '74; Champion of the Americas '75; mem. '80 Olympic team; Que. athlete of '74; Elaine Tanner award; mem. Cdn Olympic, Canada's Sports Hall of Fame; res. Waterloo, Ont.

LeSUEUR, Percy (hockey): b. 18 Nov 1881, Quebec City, Que.; d. 27 Jan 1962, Hamilton, Ont.; m. Georgia Steele; c. Steve Douglas; hockey exec.; nicknamed "Peerless Percy"; jr. Que. Victorias, sr. Que.; Ottawa Silver Seven '06-13; mem. 2 Stanley Cup winners; 3yrs team capt.; mgr., coach '13-14; Toronto Arenas '14; career spanned 50yrs as player, coach, mgr., referee, equipment designer, arena mgr., broadcaster, columnist; designed gauntlet type goalie gloves, net used by NHA, NHL '12-25; original mem. radio's *Hot Stove League*; ret'd '46; mem. Ottawa Sports, Hockey halls of fame.

LESWICK, Tony (hockey); b. 17 Mar 1923, Humboldt, Sask; d. 1 Jul 2001, Vancouver, B.C.; given name: Anthony Joseph; c. 2 sons, 2 daughters; winger with reputation as speedy skater with poor shot; SJHL Saskatoon '39-40;

SSHL Saskatoon '41-44; AHL Cleveland '42-43; Victoria City '43; PCHL New Westminster '44; Winnipeg City '44-45; NHL NYR '45-51, Detroit '51-55, '57, Chicago '55-56; WHL Edmonton '56-59, Vancouver '59-60; NHL totals 740 scheduled games, 165g, 159a, 59 playoff games, 13g, 10a; played 6 NHL all-star games; 3 Stanley Cup winners; overtime goal game 7 gave Detroit '54 Stanley Cup; nicknamed "Mighty Mouse"; brothers Jack, Pete both played in NHL; mem. Saskatoon Sports Hall of Fame.

LETHEREN, Carol Anne (administration): b. 27 Jul 1942, Toronto, Ont.; d. 2 Feb 2001, Toronto, Ont; m. Michael Murnaghan; c. Dan Letheren; UofT, BPhE, BA; York, MBA; CEO/Secty Gen. COA; assoc. prof Uof T '63-70; York '70-77; Cdn. Govt. consultant '77-79; sr. partner/co-owner marketing planning and consultant co. '79-94; active role in ntl, international affairs particularly concerning women/athletics; IOC mem. in Canada '90; press commission IOC '92-94; served on variety of IOC, Ont., COA, educational committees from '81; coached archery, gymnastics, volleyball university varsity level; ntl women's gymnastics team '70 FISU Games; officiated international gymnastics '76, '84 Olympic, '78, '82 CG, '74, '79, '81, '83, '85 World, '73, '83 FISU Games, '77, '79 European championships, '78, '80 World Cup; won intercollegiate badminton titles in '50s, varsity volleyball player; masters marathon, 10km runner; varied admin roles ntl volleyball assn., Ont. Cdn, Itnl gymnastics fed.; pres. COA '90-94; CdM Cdn team '88 Olympics; Air Canada official of '78; McCain's volunteer of '88; Cdn Gymnastics Fed. gold service pin '85; YMCA woman of distinction '92; York public contribution award '92; hon. LLD UofT '93; hon. life mem. Cdn, Intl Gymnastics Feds.; mem. UofT Sports Hall of Fame

LETOURNEAU, Fanny (synchro swim); b. 24 Jun 1979, Quebec City, Qué.; UofT, sciences student; '95 jr. world champion; '96 ntl solo, team titles; best athlete overall all categories of age groups; '99 Pan-Am champion duet (Claire Carver-Dias), team; '00 Olympic team bronze; '01 world team, duet bronze; '02 CG duet gold; 2 silver '03 PAG (partnered with Courtenay Stewart); given title "Ambassador of the city of Deux-Montagnes" by mayor '98; medal of Deux-Montagnes citizenship '00, one of 15 medals given in 75 years; Deux-Montagnes municipal pool is called the "Fanny Letourneau Pool"; res. Deux-Montagnes, Qué.

LETTERI, Tino (soccer): b. 27 Sep 1957, Italy; goaler Minnesota Strikers (NASL) '80-81, '84, Vancouver Whitecaps '82-83, Hamilton '87; leading NASL goalie '83 with 0.86 goals against avg.; 2 NASL all-star; NASL NA player of '83; mem. '76, '84 Olympic, '86 WC teams; mem. Cdn Soccer Hall of Fame; res. N. Vancouver, B.C.

LEUSZLER, Winnie Roach (swimming): b. 3 Feb 1926, Pt. Credit, Ont.; d. 1 May 2004, White Rock, B.C.; given name: Winnie Roach; m. Morris Leuszler; c. Frances, Sharon, Phyllis, Norman, Michael; won 1st medal in Pt. Credit River swim age 9; frequent Trent Canal, Etobicoke distance swim victories; at 18 became 1st Cdn to win US AAU 2.5-mile swim; 1st Cdn woman to swim English Channel '51; competed in '54 Lake Ontario swim which brought fame to Marilyn Bell; competed in varied Toronto-area sports; one day in '44 won 4 t&f races at distances from 50-440yds

then won 5-mile St. Clair River swim; served in Cdn Armed Forces '44-45; 1st woman hired as YMCA swim coach in Kitchener; in each centre in which career soldier husband posted played active role in establishing recreational programs; established Calgary Stampeders swim club; set up athletic programs in Kingston, Calgary women's prisons; toured one season with Cypress Gardens water ski show; 1st official woman baseball/softball umpire; active in Canada-France student exchange programs; presented with keys to Toronto, Kitchener, North York, Marshfield, WI; ; mayor for a day Vancouver; mem. Ont. Aquatic, Cdn Forces Sports halls of fame.

LEVANTIS, Steve (football): b. 28 Jul 1916, Montreal, Que.; m. Lillian; Assumption Coll.; sales & marketing; mem. 3 TDIAA champions; Ont. sr. baseball title team; Toronto Argos '36-41, '45-49; mem. 5 Grey Cup champions; EFC all-star '45; tackle all-Argos '21-41 team; res. Ancaster, Ont.

LEVER, Don (hockey); b. 14 Nov 1952, South Porcupine, Ont.; given name: Donald Richard; m. Karen; c. Michael, Sarah, Caitlin; hockey coach; ctr/lw Niagara Falls OHA '70-72; drafted by Vancouver '72; NHL Vancouver '72-80, Atlanta '80, Calgary '80-81, Colorado '81-82, New Jersey '82-85, Buffalo '85-87; player/coach Rochester AHL '90-92; NHL record: 1020 scheduled games, 313g, 367a, 30 playoff games, 7g, 10a; head coach Rochester '91-92; 2 Calder Cup finals, 1 winner; asst./assoc. coach Sabres '87-88, '92-02, St. Louis '02-04; AHL coach of '91; mem. Hockey Heritage North Hall of Fame; res. Amherst, N.Y.

LEVESQUE, Jean-Louis (horse racing): b. 13 Apr 1911, Gaspe Peninsula, Que.; d. 29 Dec 1994, Montreal, Que.; m. Jeanne; c. Andree, Suzanne, Pierre; Gaspe Coll., St. Dunstan's., Laval., BA; hon. degrees Laval, Montreal, Moncton, St. Dunstan's; investment broker; with '56 purchase of 2 trotters became racing devotee; purchased Blue Bonnets Raceway '58; later owned Richelieu, Windsor Raceways; re-introduced thoroughbred racing to Montreal; further involved with purchase of racing stock, including 6 horse-of-year winners, '75 Queen's Plate winner L'Enjoleur; MonctonU PE complex bears his name; horse racing's man of '83; Eleanor Roosevelt award for world peace; trustee OJC; mem. Order of Canada, Cdn Business, Cdn Horse Racing, Canada's Sports halls of fame.

LEVY, Marv (football/coaching): b. 3 Aug 1928, Chicago, Ill; m. Mary Francis; Coe College, Harvard, MA; ret'd coach, TV/Radio analyst; rb Coe Coll '48-50; 2yrs HS coach; coach Coe Coll. '53-55; asst. New Mexico '56-57, head coach '58-59, California '60-63, William & Mary '64-68; began pro coaching career as asst. with Philadelphia '69, LA '70, Washington '71-72, 1 Super Bowl; head coach Montreal '73-77 posting 50-34-4 record, 2 Grey Cup victories; head coach Kansas City '78-82; following 2yr hiatus from game became head coach Chicago Blitz (USFL) '84; Buffalo Bills '86-97; 6 AFC titles, coached 4 consecutive Super Bowl finalists; pro career coaching record 144-113; Phi Beta Kappa at Coe; mem. NFL Hall of Fame; res. Chicago, Ill.

LEWIS, Bill (curling): b. 8 Feb 1921, Angusville, Man.; given name: William Morris; div. Avis Slitch; c. Patricia,

Dale, Guy; div. Carol Devereaux; m. Helen McDonald; ret'd CF, taxi co. owner; winner 2 Ont. Silver Tankards, 2 Burden Trophies; twice competed Ont. Consols, once runner-up; Ont. Mixed finalist; won Ont. Legion title; City of Ottawa grand aggregate champion, runnerup once; 3rd stone for Jake Edwards (delivering final rocks each end) 3 Ont. Srs. title rinks; res. Saskatoon, Sask.

LEWIS, Bryan (officiating/hockey); b. 10 Sep 1942, Alliston, Ont.; given name: Bryan Howard; m. Elaine Margaret Pallett; c. Janelle Lynn, Duane Howard, Alyson Megan; ret'd dir. officiating NHL; played Jr. C Georgetown, Jr. B Dixie, Burlington; worked OHA Jr. A, 2 Canada-Russia international exhibitions; founder/ referee-in-chief Georgetown Ref's Assn. '57-66; joined NHL staff '67 working 3yrs WHL, CHL, AHL before appearing in initial NHL league game 6 Jan '70; NHL record: 1031 scheduled games over 19 seasons; worked '81 all-star, '84 Canada Cup; ret'd '86 to join supervisory staff; dir. officiating '89-01; OHA referees' honor roll; res. Georgetown, Ont.

LEWIS, Dave (hockey); b. 3 Jul 1953, Kindersley, Sask.; given name: David Rodney; m. Brenda; c. Ryan, Meagan; coach; def Saskatoon Blades Jr '71-73; drafted by NYI; Islanders '73-80, Los Angeles '80-83, Minnesota '83, New Jersey '83-86, Detroit '86-87; NHL record: 1008 scheduled games; 36g, 187a, 91 playoff games, 1g, 20a; joined Detroit coaching staff '87 as asst.; assoc. coach '97-02, head coach '02-05; 3 Stanley Cup winners; actively involved in Make-A-Wish Foundation; res. Detroit, Mich.

LEWIS, Herbie (hockey); b. 17 Apr 1907, Calgary, Alta; d. 20 Jan 1991, Indianapolis, Ind.; m. Ceverene Adams; c. Gerald, George; lw; with Calgary Jr. Canadians; nicknamed "Duke of Duluth" for 4yr stint with Duluth Hornets where he was undisputed chief drawing card in AHL; spent 11 seasons in NHL '28-39 with Detroit Cougars, Falcons, Red Wings; on line with Cooney Weiland, Larry Aurie; named Red Wings capt. '33; started in 1st-ever NHL all-star game '34; participated in longest game in NHL history; mem. 2 Stanley Cup winners; NHL record: 484 scheduled games, 148g, 161a, 38 playoff games, 13g, 10a; brought hockey to Indianapolis as player/coach AHL Indianapolis Capitols claiming Calder Cup '42; ret'd from hockey '43; mem. Hockey Hall of Fame.

LEWIS, Lennox (boxing): b. 2 Sep 1965, Stratford, Eng.; raised in Kitchener, Ont. from age 12; Canada Games 81kg heavyweight title '83; jr. world 91kg super heavyweight title '83; Stockholm Open, Canada vs. US, ntl 91kg titles '84; mem. '84, '88 Olympic teams; super-heavyweight gold '86 CG, '88 Olympics; turned pro, returned to UK '89; won British, European heavyweight titles, Commonwealth title '92, WBC title '93 (lost '94, regained '97); fought Evander Holyfield in title unification match '99 and, although considered by most observers as winner, was deprived of titles when match ruled a draw sparking fix investigation; unanimous decision in '99 rematch gave him WBC, WBA, IBF titles; lost titles on KO by Hasim Rahman '01; reclaimed titles in rematch; KO'd Mike Tyson '02, Vitali Klitschko to retain world title '03; gave up IBF title '03; ret'd '04; pro record: 42-2-1, 32 kos; Viscount Alexander Trophy '83; Norton Crowe award '88; fed. govt excellence award '84; BWAA Edward J. Neil award '99;

mem. Order of Canada, Cdn Olympic Sports, Waterloo County halls of fame; res. London, Eng.

LEWIS, Leo (football): b. 4 Feb 1933, Des Moines, Iowa; given name: Leo Everett Jr.; m. Doris Marie; c. Leo III, Marc, Barry; Lincoln, BSc, Missouri, MEd; ret'd instructor, coach Lincoln; all-city St. Paul, Minn., HS football, basketball; all-Midwest Athletic Assn. 1st team all-star rb '51-54; *Pittsburgh Courier* all-American 3 times; *AP* Little all-American twice; Philip Morris all-American '53; 4457yds rushing in 4 seasons, including 245yds single game, 1239yds single season, 623 carries for 7.15yd avg., 64 career tds, 22 single season, 4 times scored 4 in one game, 132 scoring points 1 season, all Lincoln records; dubbed "the Lincoln Locomotive"; pro Blue Bombers '55-66; CFL record: 8856yds rushing, 1351 carries, 6.57 avg., 48tds; twice rushed over 1000yds single season; 234 passes caught for 4251yds, 26tds; CFL leader career kickoff returns 187 for 5444yds, 1td; 450 points on 75tds, 5 converts, 1 single; 6 times CFL all-star; mem. all-decade Blue Bombers team of '60s; 6 Grey Cup finals, 4 winners; head football coach Lincoln '73-75; dir. intramural sports, golf coach, women's basketball coach Lincoln; jersey #30 ret'd by Lincoln; mem. Cdn Football Hall of Fame; res. Columbia, Mo.

LEWIS, Loyd (football): b. 23 Feb 1962, Dallas, Tex.; Texas A&I; dt; drafted by Houston Gamblers (USFL), by Minnesota Vikings (NFL) '84; played 1 season Houston; joined Ottawa (CFL) as free agent '85; played in CFL with Ottawa '85-91, '95-96, Edmonton '92, Winnipeg '93-94; CFL record: 180 games, 245 tackles, 83 qb sacks; 4 Eastern, 1 Western all-star; 7 playoff games, mem. '93 Grey Cup finalists; res. Ottawa, Ont.

LEWIS, Ray (t&f): b. 8 Oct 1910, Hamilton, Ont.; d. 14 Nov 2003, Hamilton, Ont.; given name: Raymond Gray; m. Vivienne; c. Larry; ret'd govt chauffer; HS 100yd, 220yd, 440yd, mile relay titles; twice ntl 440yd title; bronze 1500m relay '32 Olympics; silver '34 BEG mile relay; 5 ntl 600yd indoor titles; lit torch opening ceremonies '00 Intl Children's Games in Hamilton; mem. Order of Canada.

LEWIS, Stanley (roller skating/canoeing): b. 29 Feb 1888, Ottawa, Ont.; d. 18 Aug 1970, Ottawa, Ont; m. Pearl Brooks; c. Elda; hon. LLD UofOtt; ntl roller skating titles '09-10; mem. Ottawa Harrier hockey club; mem. Britannia ntl champion war canoe team '15; active with Ottawa football club '12-14; mem. Ottawa branch exec. AAUofC; mayor of Ottawa '36-48; mem. OBE.

LEYSHON, Glynn (wrestling); b. 2 Aug 1929, Hamilton, Ont.; given name: Glynn Arthur; m. Judith; c. Sian, Gar, Rhysa, Tal; UWO, PhD; ret'd asst dean, AD; prof. Emeritus twice intercollegiate wrestling champion; referee '67 PAG; coach UWO '64-80; 8 league champions; coach ntl team 4 world championship tournaments, 2 FISU Games, 3 World Cup of Wrestling, '79 Pan-Am, '80 Olympic teams; CIAU coach of '76; Silver Star Award, F dration Internationale de Lutte '76; co-author (with Frank Cosentino) Olympic Gold; author *Of Mats and Men, Judoka*; Ont. special achievement award; UWO wrestling trophy bears his name; mem. Cdn Amateur Wrestling, W-Club Sports halls of fame; res. London, Ont.

L'HEUREUX, Bill (hockey/football): b. 28 Feb 1918, Port Arthur, Ont.; given name: Willard Joseph; m. Viola M. Suitor; c. Susan, Mary, Bill Jr.; Assumption Coll, BA, UMich. MA, UNB, LLD; professor; college hockey Assumption '34-36, sr. Windsor '40, Cornwall Flyers Que. sr. '41-43; Arnprior, Hull, Renfrew, Cornwall, Alexandria ODHA '45-49; coach Maxville HS '39, Cornwall CIVS '40-43, Ottawa Tech '45-48, Ottawa St. Patrick's '49-50, UWO Mustangs '50-55, '63-65; coach women's intercollegiate hockey UWO ; football Assumption '34-37; coached Cornwall '40-43, Galt CIVS '43-45, Ottawa Tech '45-50. asst. UWO '50-56; chair. Ntl Advisory Council on Fitness, Amateur Sport '66-69; CAHPER Tait McKenzie honor award '67; Hockey Canada development comm. '75-76; wrote several books on hockey; OUA, UWO outstanding-hockey-player award bears his name; mem. W-Club Sports Hall of Fame; res. Toronto, Ont.

LIBERTY, Jeff (diving): b. 5 Feb 1978, North Bay, Ont.; given name: Jeffrey Ryan Liberty; m. Nicole Podoleski; youth shelter peer counsellor; couldn't do the required lengths at the public pool to be allowed in the deep end where he really wanted to be, so he took up diving to get around it; ntl team '97-03; 14 ntl titles (9 sr., 5 jr.); competed '00 Olympics '99 PAG, '99, '00 world cup, '02 CG; Gov.-Gen.'s Award, Calgary Fire Department's Medal of Honour, Calgary EMS (Emergency Medical Services) Citizen's Award for swimming to rescue pregnant woman trapped in car in icy Bow River '01; ret'd from competition following US GP '03; res. Calgary, Alta.

LICHTY, Kathy (rowing): b. 16 Oct 1957, North Bay, Ont.; m. David Boyes; sweep ntl team from '76; 2 Cdn Henley 8s, 1 coxed 4s titles; 1 ntl, Holland Cup coxed 4s titles; mem. '77-79, '82-83 world championships, '84 Olympic teams; res. St. Catharines, Ont.

LIDSTONE, Dorothy (archery): b. 2 Nov 1938, Wetaskiwin, Alta.; given name; Dorothy Carole Wagar; div.; archery equipment manufacturer; 3 prov., 4 Pacific Northwest titles; ntl, world championships '69; variety of records including 2361 points in world championships; ret'd from competition '70; FCA female-athlete-of-yr award bears her name; mem. Cdn Olympic, Canada's, BC Sports halls of fame; res. Abbotsford, B.C.

LIEBERMAN, Moe (football): b. 16 Jun 1891, Toronto, Ont.; d. 2 May 1984, Edmonton, Alta.; given name: Moses Isaac; m. Emily Sereth (d); c. Ethel, Samuel; UAlta., BSc, MSc, UofT, LLB; lawyer, QC; qb Alta. '15-18; mem. Eskimos '19-21; helped raise funds to finance 1st western challenge for Grey Cup '21; mgr. Eskimos '22; several yrs. offical in Western Canada; active in organizational aspect of game; p.-pres. Western Canada Rugby Football Union; mem. Eskimos directorate from late 30s to late 50s; v-p/pres. Eskimos; mem. Edmonton board of governors '58-84; active in formation Eskimos Alumni Club; mem. Alta. Sports, Canadian Football halls of fame.

LIEBROCK, Chuck (football): b. 24 May 1943, Windsor, Ont.; m. Michele Hanson; c. Kristen, Cara, Mike; St. Mary's, Hillsdale Coll., BSc; mgr. Petro-Canada; played football, basketball, t&f, weightlifting; all-city football honors at Patterson CI; og; CFL drafted by Toronto '68, dealt to

Winnipeg '70-77; Tommy Lumsden Memorial trophy (Most Valuable Canadian on Bombers) '77; mem. Windsor-Essex Sports Hall of Fame; res. Sudbury, Ont.

LIEPA, Ingrid (speed skating): b. 24 Mar 1966, Ottawa, Ont.; UCal, LLB; lawyer; novice level figure skater; switched to speed skating as means of stress management when she moved to Calgary to pursue law studies '90; began competing age 24; long-track specialist; ntl team from '92; ntl all-around title '95; 2 ntl records; competed '94, '98 Olympics, '96, '97 worlds; res. Calgary, Alta.

LIFFORD, Johnny (boxing): b. 19 Jan 1911, Fredericton, N.B.; d. 13 Aug 1972, South Boston, Mass.,; ring career spanned '24-44; Maritime lightweight, welterweight, middleweight titles; won 222 of 235 bouts; mem. NB Sports Hall of Fame.

LIMNIATIS, John (soccer): b. 24 Jun 1967, Athens, Greece; midfielder; mem. ntl team program from '83; made ntl team international debut '87; played in CSL with Ottawa Intrepid '87-88; Greek 1st div. Aris; Montreal Impact A League from '93-98, player-coach '00-03; Charleston Battery A-League '99; indoor with Kansas City Attack NPSL '95-96; res. Montreal, Que.

LIMPERT, Marianne (swimming): b. 10 Oct 1972, Matagami, Que.; UofT, UNB; father was ntl heavyweight boxing titlist '64-65; 10 ntl titles, 6 ntl records; mem. ntl team '92-03; world short-course 4x200 FS gold '95; 2 gold, 1 silver '93 FISU Games; silver, 4 bronze '94, 1 gold, 1 bronze '98, '02 CG; 5 silver, 1 bronze '95, 2 gold, 2 bronze '99 PAG; 2 gold, 2 bronze '96 Canada Cup; 2 gold, 1 silver, 3 bronze '93 CIAU championships, 3 world cup gold '95; 200IM silver '96 Olympics; competed '92, '96, '00 Olympic Games, '93 Pan-Pacific championships; Goodwill Games 01 silver; world short-course 100IM silver, 200IM bronze '00; Cdn flag-bearer '98 CG; res. Vancouver, B.C./Fredericton, N.B.

LINDEN, Trevor (hockey): b. 11 Apr 1970, Medicine Hat, Alta.; m. Cristina; ctr/rw Medicine Hat (WHL) '86-88; 2 Memorial Cup winners; NHL Vancouver '88-98, '01-04; NYI (capt.) '98-99, Montreal '99-01, Washington '01; became youngest capt. in NHL at 20; youngest to play in NHL all-star game; 1st Canuck rookie to win Cyclone Taylor team MVP trophy; *Hockey News* rookie-of-yr award; mem. '88 world jr. gold medal team, Team Canada '91 worlds, '96 World Cup, '98 Olympics; NHL all-rookie team; competed 2 NHL all-star teams; NHL record: (through '04) 1161 scheduled games, 349g, 465a, 112 playoff games, 32g, 60a; King Clancy Memorial trophy '97; Gillette world champion award; very active in community, charitable work; hon. spokesperson Canuck Place; developed Captain's Crew program; active Youth Against Violence program, Ronald McDonald House, Cancer Society's Lottery for Hope; has done some *BCTV* commentary work; pres, NHLPA; res. Kitsilano, B.C.

LINDLEY, Earl (football): b. 13 Mar 1933, Wellsville, Utah; given name: Earl Leishman; m. Marilyn Jensen; c. Greg, Teresa, Lance, Corey, Wade; Utah State, BSc, MSc; teacher, football coach; 11 HS football, basketball, t&f, baseball letters; HS all-state 2yrs; led US scorers sr. year; lb, drafted by NFL Chicago, joined Edmonton '54-57; all-star '56; mem. 3 Grey Cup winners; head coach Idaho Falls HS 3yrs; asst. coach Brigham Young 7yrs; from '68 head coach Sky View HS, Logan, Utah; res. Smithfield, Utah.

LINDQUIST, Vic (hockey/officiating); b. 22 Mar 1908, Gold Rock, Ont., d. 30 Nov 1983, Winnipeg, Man.; given name: Carl Victor; m. Gertrude Anderson; c. Marlene, Vicki, Susan, Randall, Rodney; mem. Western finalist Kenora jrs.; Winnipeg Allan Cup team '31; mem. '32 Olympic, world champion gold medal teams; mem. '35 world champion Winnipeg Monarchs; coached Swedish ntl team '35-36; rheumatic fever terminated playing career '39; began officiating '41; refereed 35 years Pacific, Western pro leagues; CAHA referee-in-chief; officiated 9 Memorial, Allan Cup, 1 Alexander Cup final, 2 world championships, 1 Olympics; rejected offers to officiate in NHL; avid golfer, 2 holes-in-one, several club championships; mem. NWO Sports, IIHF, Man. Hockey halls of fame.

LINDROS, Eric (hockey): b. 28 Feb 1973, London, Ont.; ctr; played jr. Det. Compuware, Oshawa Generals '89-92; mem. 2 Team Canada world jr. gold medal teams; mem. Memorial Cup team Oshawa '90; OHL 1st team all-star '91; competed '91 Canada Cup, '93 worlds, '96 world cup, '92, (capt.) '98, '02 (gold) Olympic teams; Cdn major jr. player of '90, '91; Memorial Cup all-star '90; 1st pick overall by Quebec '91 entry draft but refused to play for Nordiques as he had earlier with Sault Ste. Marie, which led to Lindros Rule in OHL; traded to Philadelphia; considered franchise player; after suffering numerous concussions relieved of captaincy and sought trade '00; dealt to NYR '01-04; mem. NHL Upper Deck rookie team '93; 1st team '95, 2nd team '96 all-star; played in 6 NHL all-star games; NHL record (through '04): 678 scheduled games, 356g, 461a, 50 playoff games, 24g, 33a; 3 Bobby Clarke, 1 L.B. Pearson, Hart trophies; Viscount Alexander award '91; charity golf tourney bears his name; res. Muskoka, Ont.

LINDSAY, Ted (hockey); b. 29 Jul 1925, Renfrew, Ont.; given name: Robert Blake Theodore; m. Joanne; c. 3; auto equipment sales; jr. St. Mike's Majors, Oshawa's '44 Memorial Cup winner; Detroit '44-57, '64-65 (out of retirement), Chicago '57-60, lw on Wings' Production Line with Sid Abel, Gordie Howe; mem. 7 straight NHL league titles, 4 Stanley Cup winners; frequent penalty leader; nicknamed "Tempestuous Ted", "Terrible Ted", "Forever Furious"; 8 times 1st, once 2nd team all-star; NHL record: 1068 scheduled games, 379g, 472a, 1808pim, 133 playoff games, 47g, 49a; 5g, 5a in 11 all-star games; pres. NHL Players' Assn.; GM. Detroit '77-81; coach '79-80; *THN* exec. of '77; jersey #7 ret'd by Red Wings; 1 of 4 official ambassadors of hockey NHL 75th anniversary; mem. Hockey Heritage North, Hockey, Canada's Sports halls of fame; res. Rochester Hills, Mich.

LINSEMAN, Ken (hockey); b. 11 Aug 1958, Kingston, Ont.; m. Pam; c. Kyle, Holly Rae; real estate; OHA jr. ctr Kingston '74-77; turned pro WHA Birmingham '77-78; joined Philadelphia (NHL) '78-82 with brief stint in Maine (AHL); dealt by Flyers to Hartford who traded him to Edmonton same day '82; with Edmonton '82-84, Boston '84-90, rejoined Flyers '90, Edmonton '90-91, Toronto '91-92; played in Italy briefly '91-92; ctr'd line of Brian Propp

and Paul Holmgren which was dubbed Rat Patrol and was nicknamed "The Rat"; OHA all-star '77; NHL record: 860 scheduled games, 256g, 551a, 113 playoff games, 43g, 77a; WHA record: 71 scheduled games, 38g, 38a, 5 playoff games, 2g, 2a; 1 Stanley Cup winner; landmark court case lowered NHL draft age to 18 from 20; instructor Deron Quint hockey operations; res. Hampton Beach, N.H.

LINTON, Keith (harness racing); b. 5 Dec 1947, Regina, Sask.; nicknamed "Mighty Mite from Moose Jaw"; UDR titles '73, '76; moved from Regina-Saskatoon fair circuit to Assiniboia Downs '67; later shifted to BC's Cloverdale-Sandown circuit; more than 2000 victories, all in Canada; res. Moose Jaw, Sask.

LIPARI, Michel (weightlifting); b. 18 Dec 1933, Montreal, Que.; m. Antoinette Eusanio; c. Mickeal Angelo, Anne-Marie, Mark Anthony, Catherine; North Carolina State College; owner Lipari Moving & Cartage; Que. bodybuilding champion '51; Montreal lightweight wrestling champion '53; competed as light-heavyweight weightlifter '58-63; flagbearer Cdn team '59, bronze '63 PAG; mem. '58 BEG, '60 Olympic, '62 World championships teams; ntl press record 299lbs, clean & jerk 358lbs '60s; res. Baie d'Urfe, Que.

LISCOMBE, Carl (hockey); b. 17 May 1915, Perth, Ont.; d. 23 Feb 2004, Wailuku, Hawaii; given name: Harold Carlyle; c. Susan; lw OHA Sr. Hamilton '34-35, '51, Chatham '52-54; AHL Detroit '35-36, Pittsburgh '36-38, Indianapolis '39-41, St. Louis-Providence '46-50; IHL Sarnia-Detroit '50-52; NHL Detroit '37-46; all-star status 1 NHL, 2 AHL, 1 IHL; mem. 1 Calder, 1 Stanley Cup winner; NHL totals 373 scheduled games, 137g, 140a, 59 playoff games, 22g, 19a; 2 Les Cunningham MVP, 1 John Sollenberger awards; AHL scoring title trophy bears his name; nicknamed "Lefty".

LISKE, Peter (football); b. 24 May 1941, Plainfield, N.J.; m. Debbie Hackwith; c. Kim, Tucker; Penn State, BSc, MBA; AD Toledo; Penn baseball star leading Nittany Lions to College World Series '63; led Penn to Gator Bowls '61-62, Hula Bowl (MVP) '63; qb/db NYJets AFL, Toronto (CFL) '65, Calgary '66-68, '73-74, Denver (NFL) '69-70, Philadelphia '71-72, BC Lions '74-75; capt. Broncos, Eagles, Stampeders; 3 times CFL passing leader; single season CFL td pass record 40 '67; CFL record: 1449 completions, 2571 attempts for 21,266yds, 133int, 130tds; Schenley outstanding-player award '67, Jeff Nicklin WFC MVP award '67; Western Athletic Conf. referee '77-83, NFL referee '82-89; assoc. AD UWash '85-92; AD Idaho '93-96; noted for placing high emphasis on academics; res. Holland, Ohio

LISTER, Ralph (all-around); b. 30 Jul 1908, Harvey Station, N.B.; d. 31 Oct 1990, Moncton, N.B.; given name: Ralph William; Mount Allison; nicknamed "Bull"; mem. NB sr. rugby/football title teams '26, '28; 6 intercollegiate, sr. basketball title teams, Eastern ntl finalists '28; NB sr. baseball titlists '28; AD Mount Allison '31-36, coached 26 NB, Maritime title teams; skipped Beaver Curling Club rink to Ganong Cup, berth in '56 Brier; mem. NB Sports Hall of Fame.

LITTLE, Ken (all-around); b. 30 Jul 1929, Winnipeg, Man.; given name: Gordon Kenneth; m. Shirley Adams; c. Gordon, Karen, Glenda, Laura; UMan., BComm, Inst.

Man. Chartered Accountants, CA; ret'd partner Deloitte & Touche; achieved high competitive level in hockey, baseball, football, t&f, curling; in hockey West End AC Man. Bantam B, Midget title, Man. Jr,, Sr, English HL Autumn Cup with Streatham '52; knee injury suffered in jr. football ended hockey career '54; set Winnipeg, Man. Sprint records; placed 2nd in bid for '48 Olympic team; all-star rb Weston Wildcats Man. Jr. football champs '49; all-star outfielder greater Winnipeg juv., jr. Rosedale baseball title teams; St. Boniface Native Sons sr. champs; tryout with Philadelphia Athletics, played a few games with Winnipeg in Mandak league; above average contact hitter with outstanding base running skills; played on 2 Winnipeg HS soccer, 1 basketball title teams; competed 2 Briers as 2nd for Bruce Hudson; competed 10 prov. playdowns, 2 winners, '64 all-star 2nd; 3rd for Hudson in winning 18 consec. games and grand agg. Manitoba bonspiel; claimed 8 varied event titles in that competition plus numerous other curling event titles; runnerup BC srs. '98; wife Shirley mem. 3 time ntl sr. champion Evelyn Krahn rink; HS athletics/academics award '47; finalist '00 Man. male athlete of century; mem. Man. Baseball, Man. Sports halls of fame; res. Kelowna, B.C.

LITTLE, Laura (diving); b. 25 Jul, 1907, Toronto, Ont.; d. (circa 1995) Toronto, Ont.; m. Miller; at 17 became 1st Cdn women's diving champion, both high and low boards '24; won 3 ntl titles; only Toronto girl to dive from 33-foot tower; officially opened Toronto Sunnyside pool '25 by diving off high tower with Cdn flag held aloft in each hand.

LITZENBERGER, Eddie (hockey); b. 15 Jul 1932, Neudorf, Sask.; given name: Edward Charles John; m. Doreen (d); m. Gayle Marie Goschen; c. Dean, Kelly Lynne, John; Regina Coll; ret'd; rw Regina Pats 3yrs, 2yrs capt., 2 Memorial Cup finals; Montreal Royals, 2 championships; NHL Montreal '52-55, Chicago '55-61, Detroit '61-62, Toronto '62-64; AHL Rochester '65-66; Calder Memorial Trophy '55; team capt Chicago 4yrs; mem. 6 successive championship teams 4 Stanley Cups, 2 Calder Cups; res. Etobicoke, Ont.

LIUT, Mike (hockey); b. 7 Jan 1956, Weston, Ont.; m. Mary Ann Donnewald; c. Justin, Blake, Jenna; Bowling Green, BSc (business), Detroit Coll. of Law, Mich State, JD; lawyer; became hockey devotee at 15 playing jr. B Markham, Dixie; played goal for Bowling Green; drafted by St. Louis (NHL) '76 but opted for 2 seasons in WHA with Cincinnati; joined NHL St. Louis '79-84, Hartford '84-89. Washington '89-92, mem. '81 Canada Cup; NHL record: 663 scheduled games, 294-271-74, 38,155 min, 2219ga, 25so, 67 playoff games, 29-32, 2so; NHL all-star game MVP '81; *Hockey News* player of '81; Lester B. Pearson trophy; Norris div. title '81, Adams div. title '87; 1st team all-star '81, 2nd team '87; did some hockey broadcasting; collective bargaining/other labor related issues with NHLPA; volunteer asst. coach Mich '95-98; res. Bloomfield Hills, Mich.

LIVINGSTON, Emilie (rhythmic gymnastics); b. 4 Jan 1983, Toronto, Ont.; given name: Emilie Isabelle Natasha; motivational speaker; '97 ntl jr. title; team silver '98 CG; indiv. gold '99 PAG, Elite Can., Coupe d'Opale; competed '00 Olympics; hoop bronze Bulgaria '01; ntl team capt. '02-03; PAG '03 group silver; spokesperson KidSport Ont.; res. Markham, Ont.

LIVINGSTON, Gerry (builder/basketball); b. 16 Jun 1915, Smith's Falls, Ont.; d. 18 Oct 1988, London, Ont.; given name: Gerald Vincent; m. Violet Anne Demaine; c. Marnie, Michael, Gerald (d), Patrick, Peter, Jane, Sally; Assumption Coll., BA; manufacturer; signed pro baseball contract with Cleveland Indians '37 but ruptured appendix thwarted his career; purchased small box mfg. co. in Tillsonburg and created financial empire; sponsored intermediate basketball team and built it into reknowned Tillsonburg Livvies; 2 ntl titles; formed nucleus of '52, '60 Olympic teams; mem. Cdn Basketball Hall of Fame.

LJUBISIC, Lilo (t&f); b. 17 Dec 1960, Beograd, Yugoslavia; given name: Ljiljana; m. Robert Andersen; UBC; motivational speaker; blind athlete who has competed in goalball, discus, shot put at world, paralympic levels achieving 19 intl podium finishes; competed 5 paralympics earning 6 medals including '92 gold; 4 gold, 2 silver, 2 bronze in 6 IPC worlds; has parlayed 2 decades of paralympic competition ('84-04) into lifetime commitment to sports for athletes with disabilities; chair. Intl Paralympic Athletes comm., mem. IOC Athletes Commission; mem. AthletesCan board; CAAWS board; past Cdn Blind Sports Assn. tech. officer; held world discus, shot records; 2 BC disabled athlete-of-yr awards; BC Women in Sport Leaders & Legends, CAAWS most-influential-women-in-sport awards; 2 Investors Griup bursaries; Sport Canada, Cdn govt. recognition awards; Canada 125 medal; TriCity Chamber of Commerce, Vancouver city awards; res. Coquitlam, B.C.

LLEWELLYN, Jaret (water skiing); b. 27 Jul 1970, Innisfail, Alta.; m. Britta Grebe; c. Dorien; pro water skier; ntl team from '86; gold team, individual tricks, jumps '95, tricks gold, jumps silver '99, '03 PAG; 5 US Masters overall, 3 world jump, 3 WC jump, 7 Moomba Masters overall titles; 3 British Masters jump gold; '00 French Masters jumps & tricks gold; 4 gold '02 Pan-Am championships; gold US open, pro tour competitions '00-03; pro tour sky fly season title '01; won jump titles '95, '96 Paddy Classic, '97 Portland pro tour; '96 Pan-Am championship overall, jump titles; overall silver '03 worlds; set world jump record '92; PB: buoys 51 (slalom), tricks 10,820 points (ntl record), jump 67.5m (ntl record); mem. '91, '93 '95 (bronze), '97 (bronze), '01 (gold) world championships teams, mem. Alta. Sports Hall of Fame; res. Innisfail, Alta./Florida.

LOARING, John (t&f/swimming); b. 3 Aug 1915, Winnipeg, Man., d. 20 Nov 1969, Windsor, Ont.; given name: John Wilfrid; m. Ellen Selina Ruston; c. Mary Ellen, David John (d), George Robert John, David Charles, Esther Ann; Huron College; pres. construction co.; sprint, hurdles specialist; high hurdles titlist, anchored winning mile relay team '34 Inter-Empire schoolboy games; silver low hurdles '36 Olympics; gold 440yd hurdles, 440yd relay, mile relay '38 BEG;. '35 sr. intercollegiate 100yd, 220yd low hurdles, 440yd titles; Ont. 440 hurdles '36; 4th 400m '37 PAG; 4 ntl sr. intercollegiate swim titles; mem. '39 int. intercollegiate harrier title team; ntl 400m hurdles record; equalled British 440yd hurdles record '42; helped form Windsor Swim Club, pres. '47-52; officiated many Windsor track meets, CG '66; exec. mem. CG Assn., AAUofC, COA, Windsor recreation commission; coached Windsor Swim Club water polo team; athletic co-ordinator Windsor-Detroit Freedom Festival '63;

J.W. Davies track trophy '38; Windsor Boy Scout exec. award '58; Windsor SC award '69; trophies bearing his name awarded annually by UWindsor to HS swim champions, Kennedy relay 400m dash winners; numerous swimming pool design awards; mem. Cdn Olympic, Windsor-Essex, W-Club Sports halls of fame.

LOBEL, Art (curling); b. 13 May 1935, Virden, Man; m. Shirley Pollock; c. Rob, Steven; UMan, BSc; mechanical engineer; skipped Que. '66 ntl mixed title rink; lead on Que. Brier entry '70, 3rd '72, '75-77; won '77 Brier, runnerup Silver Broom; won '75 *CBC* curling classic; all-star 3rd '77 Brier; 3 Ont., 3 Cdn seniors titles; mem. Canadian Curling Hall of Fame; res. Thornhill, Ont.

LOCKETT, Donna (t&f): b. 26 Apr 1965, Montreal, Que.; given name: Donna-Marie; Carleton, PhD; researcher; duathlon specialist; 2 Ont. 5km, 1 10km road racing titles; cyclist Ont. triathlon team relay titlist '92; 3 Eastern Cdn, 1 Ont, 2 ntl duathlon titles; mem. ntl elite team '93-94; competed '93 world championships; won '91 Gloucester half-marathon, '90 Cdn international duathlon; '94 car accident threatened duathlon career but extensive therapy put her back on track as she turned attention to marathons; won '97 Marathon by the Sea in Saint John, N.B., in record time; res. Ottawa, Ont.

LOCKHART, Gene (swimming/football); b. 18 Jul 1891, London, Ont., d. 31 Mar 1957, Santa Monica, Calif.; m. Kathleen Arthur; c. June; St. Michael's Coll., De LaSalle Inst., Brompton Oratory School, London, Eng.; actor; capt St. Mike's hockey team; football for Toronto Argos; Canadian mile swimming title '09; appeared in about 300 movies, numerous stage plays.

LOCKING, Norm (hockey); b. 24 May 1911, Owen Sound, Ont.; d. 15 May 1995, Port Elgin, Ont.; m. Beth Daniel; c. Fred; ret'd salesman; Owen Sound Greys '28-31; pro Chicago (NHL) '31-32; Pittsburgh, Tulsa '32-34; brief service with Chicago '34-36; sold to Toronto organization, played in Syracuse through '38; Cleveland '39-44; led Syracuse, AHL scorers, earned MVP award.

LOGAN, Freddie (speed skating); b. 28 Feb 1884, Gondola Point, N.B., d. 12 Feb 1962, Ottawa, Ont.; given name: Frederick William; m. Hannah Elizabeth Murphy; c. Gertrude, Willie, Valentine, Bessie, Francis, Dorothy; store mgr.; NB, Maritime jr. champion '05-11; Maritime 440yd champion '05; international outdoor 220, 880, 3-mile titles, US, ntl outdoor 220yd, 880yd, mile titles '07; US outdoor 220, international mile, ntl 1-, 3-mile titles '08; world indoor 220, 440 records, 3 Maritime titles, records '10; mem. Canadian Speed Skating, NB Sports halls of fame.

LOGAN, Tip (football); b. 30 Nov 1927, St. Thomas, Ont.; given name: John Robert; m. Helen Marie Batt; c. Timothy John, Claudia Marie; Queen's, BA; ret'd; amateur football St. Catharines jr. Rams, Queen's; pro Hamilton '50-55; twice CIAU all-star; led Big 4 scorers '51; pk specialist, CFL record (since surpassed) 85 consecutive conversions; Big 4 all-star 1yr.; mem. '53 Grey Cup champions; intercollegiate football official, 8 College Bowls; minor, intermediate baseball Fort Erie, pro Brooklyn Dodger chain in class D Flordia State, Pony Leagues; mem. Welland sr. OBA

champion '49; mem. COSSA basketball champions '48; officiated HS basketball 10yrs.; runnerup '73 Ont. Colts curling championship; skipped Hamilton City title rink '75-76; won *CHCH-TV* bonspiel 1st 3yrs of competition; founder, pres. Hamilton minor football assnn.; pres. Lakeshore Football Officials Assn; pres. Ont. Amateur Football Assn; former exec.-dir. OAFA; former mem. amateur football rules comm.; dir. Hamilton football trust fund; mem. Queen's Sports Hall of Fame; res. Hamilton, Ont.

LOGAN, Willie (speed skating/rowing); b. 15 Mar 1907, Saint John, N.B., d. 6 Nov 1955, Sackville, N.B.; given name: William Frederick; m. Dorita Gould; c. Sylvia; plumbing store mgr.; competitive skater '20-36, oarsman '23-33; ntl skating titles '22-23, '25; Maritime titles '24-36; international champion '25; 2nd overall '26 worlds; mem. '28, '32 Olympic teams, capt., 2 bronze '32; mem. Canadian Speed Skating, NB Sports halls of fame.

LOHNES, Rita (golf); b. 4 Aug 1938, Riverport, N.S.; given name: Rita Leone; m. Gary Haines; c. Dorothy Ann, Sandra Leone; Bridgewater Commercial; competitive golfer '51-69, from '83; 4 NS, 2 Maritime jr. titles; 5 NS, Maritime women's titles; 12 club titles (Lunenburg Bluenose 4; Whitby 1; Daytona Volusia 1, Riviera 1; Thornhill Uplands 3; Burlington Indian Wells 2); Peterborough Invitational title '64; low net Ont. PGA pro-lady '64; ntl jr. runnerup '58; mem. 8 NS interprovincial teams; mem. ntl jr. team titlists '54; mem. NS Sports Hall of Fame; res. Oakville, Ont.

LOISELLE, Claude (hockey); b. 29 May 1963, Ottawa, Ont.; m. Jo-Anne Sipowicz; c. Brenly, Realyng, Bron, Majorlaing; McGill LLB; lawyer, hockey exec.; spoke limited English as child but worked hard to master language as he pursued hockey career; def/ctr Orleans minor hockey system; jr. A Gloucester Rangers; OHL Windsor Spitfires (capt.); drafted by Detroit '81 splitting career between Detroit, Adirondack '81-86; mem. Adirondack Calder Cup winner; NHL New Jersey ; '86-89, Quebec '89-91, Toronto '91-92, NYI '92-94; career cut short by knee injury; noted as checker, strong faceoff man; mem. Team Canada '82; NHL record: 616 scheduled games, 92g, 117a, 41 playoff games 4g, 11a; D'Aoust award Hull midget tourney MVP; Ed Wood award Rhode Island bantam tourney MVP; Belleville peewee tourney MVP award; 3 Molson Cup jr. A awards; accepted as mature student at McGill and graduated in law in 3yrs; passed US bar exams; assoc. dir. NHL hockey operations; res. Ridgewood, N.J.

LOMBARDO, Guy (speedboat racing); b. 19 Jun 1902, London, Ont., d. 5 Nov 1977, Houston, Tex; m. Lilliebelle Glenn; band leader; won '46 International Gold Cup, ntl sweepstakes for unlimited hydroplanes with his Tempo boats; US ntl champion '46-49; secty. American Power Boating Assn.; began racing '38, winning every major trophy in Gold Cup unlimited class for 20-40' propellor-driven boats; set then speed record 119.7mph '48; ret'd '52, returned '55-56 winning ntl titles; mem. US Speedboat Hall of Fame; Canadian Walk of Fame.

LONEY, Don (football); b. 16 Nov 1923, Ottawa, Ont.; d. 19 Jun 2004, Sherbrooke, N.S.; given name: Donald John; North Carolina State.; ret'd school administrator; jr., service football Montreal, Halifax; pro Montreal, Toronto,

Ottawa, Calgary; capt. Ottawa 3yrs.; mem. 3 Grey Cup finalists, 2 winners; ret'd '55; Jeff Russel Memorial trophy '50; frequent Eastern all-star, once all-Canadian; coached 3yrs Ottawa HS, 3yrs Navy, 17yrs college football; won 3 service league, 9 college conference titles, '66 ntl college crown; St.FX football '57-74 coaching record: 133 wins, 31 losses, 2 ties; 6 Atlantic Bowl finals, 4 winners; '74-76 with Devco; '77 National Defence consultant; '78 Fitness, Amateur Sport consultant; '78-82 alumni dir. St.FX; CAFA-CFL plaque, NS recognition award '73; Centennial Medal '67; CIAU trophy bearing his name presented annually to Atlantic Bowl MVP; former pres. Canadian Football Coaches Assn.; noted artist; regarded as "Godfather" of Cdn football in Maritimes; mem. NS, Ottawa, Canada's Sports, Canadian Football, Cdn Forces halls of fame.

LONG, Bill (hockey); b. 2 Jan 1918, Barrie, Ont.; given name: William Edwin; m. Dorothy Catharine Wiles; c. Terry; ret'd hockey exec.; Jr. B Barrie, sr. Port Colborne; pro Pittsburgh, Kansas City; Jr. B coach '50-51, Jr. A 'Sunday coach' before moving to Niagara Falls '60; coach Ottawa 67's '67-71; coach London Knights '72-80, GM '72-84; OHA jr. A coaching record: 15yrs, 439-383-100; coach jr. B champions '51, juv champions '54, Memorial Cup finalists '63, Memorial Cup champions '65; res. London, Ont.

LONG, Warren (gymnastics); b. 16 Apr 1956, Victoria, B.C.; Calif.,UofSask; mem. ntl team '77-84; gold medals parallel bars '77 Pacific championships, ntl vault '77, '79, '82-84, floor exercises '79, parallel bars '82; vault Chunichi Cup '80; mem. '79, '83 FISU, '80, '84 Olympic, World Cup, '81, '83 World championships teams; 3 silver, 2 bronze '79 PAG; silver vault '83 FISU Games; res. Saskatoon, Sask.

LONGBOAT, Tom (t&f); b. 4 Jul 1886, Brantford, Ont., d. 9 Jan 1949, Brantford, Ont.; given name: Thomas Charles; m. Lauretta Maracle (d); m. Martha Silversmith; c. Ted, Clifford, Tom Jr., Phyllis; outran horse over 12-mile course '06; 3 consecutive 15-mile Toronto marathons; set Boston marathon record '07; as pro beat Italian champion Dorando Pietri, Britain's Alf Shrubb several times; competed '08 Olympics; last major race '12; victim of exploitation by promoters; mem. Cdn Olympic, Canada's Sports, Ont. Sports Legends, Cdn Roadrunners halls of fame.

LONGDEN, Johnny (horse racing); b. 14 Feb 1907, Wakefield, Eng.; d. 14 Feb 2003, Banning, Calif.; given name: John Eric; div. Helen; c. Vance (d); m. Hazel Tarn (d); c. Andrea, Eric; m. Kathy; jockey, trainer; because Wakefield to Southhampton train was late missed inagural voyage of Titanic; raised in Taber, Alta.; summer cowboy age 10; left school age 13 to work in mines; '25 worked for Spud Murphy ranch competing in country fairs; began thoroughbred racing Salt Lake City '27; unconventional riding style earned him nickname "The Pumper"; until retirement to become trainer '66 rode then-record 6032 winners, 4914 seconds, 4273 thirds with $24,665,800 in earnings; 3 Sep '56 broke Sir Gordon Richards' existing record with 4871; scored 5000th victory '57; ntl champion jockey '38,'47-48; rode Count Fleet to Triple Crown (Kentucky Derby, Preakness, Belmont Stakes) '43; frequent accident victim, 5 times told racing career was over but each time battled back to win more races; instrumental in founding Jockey's Guild '41; ret'd as trainer '89; Woolf Memorial award '52; special Eclipse

award '95; mem. Alta., Canada's Sports, Horse Racing, US National Jockey's halls of Fame.

LONSBERRY, Ross (hockey); b. 7 Feb 1947, Humboldt, Sask.; given name: David Ross; lw Estevan SJHL '62-66; CHL Minneapolis '65, Oklahoma City '67-69; AHL Buffalo '67-69; NHL Boston '66, Los Angeles '69-72, Philadelphia '71-78, Pittsburgh '78-81; NHL totals: 968 scheduled games, 256g, 310a, 100 playoff games, 21g, 25a; 2 Stanley Cup winners; res. Humboldt, Sask.

LOOMER, Lorne (rowing); b. 1937, Penticton, B.C.; given name: Lorne Kenneth; m. Elisabeth Baess; c. Lise-Lotte, Anne-Lise; UBC, BA, BSc, PhC; pharmacist; gold '56 Olympics coxless 4; gold 8s '58 BEG; silver '60 Olympics; built UVic rowing program; mem. UVic, Greater Victoria, Cdn Olympic, BC, Canada's Sports halls of fame; res. Victoria, B.C.

LORD, Herv (t&f/wheelchair basketball/sledge hockey): b. 3 Mar 1958, St. Pamphile, Que.; m. Kelly-Anne; govt. staffing asst.; versatile wheelchair athlete competing in track, road racing, sledge hockey, sledge racing, basketball; 4 gold, 2 silver, 1 bronze ntl championships; 3 world gold; world record 4x100m Berlin '94; gold '95 National Capital marathon; 4 ntl sledge hockey title teams; 2 World Cup title teams; bronze '94 Paralympics; competed '98 (silver), '02 Paralympics sledge hockey team; bronze '96, gold '00 world sledge hockey championships; gold '99 Paralympic commerative; 2 Ottawa Lions TC outstanding-wheelchair-athlete awards, OLTC president's award; 3 Ottawa ACT awards; 3 sledge hockey MVP awards, World Cup, ntl all-star; OWSA athlete of '93; Cdn, Ont. achievement awards; res. Ottawa, Ont.

LORD, Lovel (curling); b. 29 Sep 1942, Trenton, Ont.; m. Joan; c. Wendy, April; insurance broker; began curling Moose Jaw age 12; mem. Winnipeg Westwinn CC title rink '66; skipped Sault Ste. Marie 'spiel winner, NO playoff entry '70; mem. Bill Lewis Kingston rink '72-74, winner Ottawa Masters, *Whig-Standard* 'spiels; 2nd Earle Morris Ottawa Navy rink which lost provincial final in playoff vs. Joe Gurowka '76; 8 Ont. finals, 1 as skip; 3rd Morris Brier rink '85; mem. 2 OCA Silver Tankard title rinks; res. Ottawa, Ont.

LORD, Margaret (administration); b. 2 Oct, Hamilton, Ont.; d. Sep 1993, Burlington, Ont.; given name: Mary Margaret; Hamilton Teachers Coll.; teacher; active in amateur sports from '29; v-p British Commonwealth Games Assn. '54-76; from '76 hon. v-p; only woman in Commonwealth to serve as officer; only woman elected to AAU exec.; chair. AAUofC honors, awards comm. 15yrs.; only woman elected pres. AAUofC branch; dir. COA; mgr. '36, '52 Cdn. Olympic t&f teams; mgr. '54, '62 Cdn. CG teams; secty. '58 Cdn. CG team; 1 of 2 women mem. 1st Ntl Advisory Council for Fitness, Amateur Sport; Sports Federation of Canada award; Centennial Medal '67; life mem. Hamilton Olympic Club; mem. Cdn Olympic Sports Hall of Fame.

LORD, Tom (t&f); b. 26 Apr 1910, Hingham, Mass.; m. Helen Gzowski; c. Tom Jr., John; McGill, Sir George Williams; financial planner, Investors Syndicate Ltd.; ntl 880yd title '35; founding secty. QATFA '34-38; chair. ntl t&f comm. AAU of C '48-54; AGM., mgr. ntl t&f team, mem. jury of appeal '50, '54 BE&CG; chair. jury of appeal BE Commonwealth Games '66, '70, '74, '78; pres. QATFA, meet dir., Europe vs Americas Expo '67 Montreal; dir. CFTA '69-71; dir. Fed. d'Athletisme du Que. '70-75; CTFA ntl officials chair. '72-79; track ref. '75 PAG; mgr. athletics officials '76 Olympics; chair. CTFA rules comm. '80-90; Air Canada sports official of '77; Queen's Jubilee Medal; MBE; mem. COA; mem. Cdn Olympic Hall of Fame; res. Kitchener, Ont.

LORI, Chris (bobsled): b. 24 Jul 1962, Windsor, Ont.; Royal Roads Military College, MBA; began competing age 22; driver ntl team '85-98; competed 10 world championships, '88, '92, '94, '98 Olympics; 1 CODA Cup 2 man, 3 ntl 2-man, 3 ntl 4-man, 2 World Cup 4-man gold; finished 1st '90 World Cup overall 4-man standings; bronze '91 World Cup 2,4, combined; 22 World Cup medals; mem. Windsor/Essex Sports Hall of Fame; res. W. Vancouver, B.C.

LORION, Guy (shooting): b. 23 Mar 1953, Montreal, Que.; m.; mem. small-bore rifle teams '79, '83 Pan-Am, '78, '81-82 world, '82 CG, '84 Olympic, 8 Benito Juarez Games; 1 gold, 1 silver, 3 bronze PAG, silver, bronze CG; SFC golden anniversary award '82; res. Longueuil, Que.

LOVE, Drew (administration/basketball): b. 16 May 1952, Ottawa, Ont.; given name: Garnet Andrew; m. Leslie Ogilvie; c. Derek, Kathryn; Carleton, BA, MA public admin.; Concordia, Graduate Dip. sports admin.; UofOtt, MBA; AD Carleton; mem. Carleton Ravens basketball team '70-74, '77-78; capt. '74; MVP Memorial U tourney '73; exec. EXPO '05 bid omm. '92-95; exec. Ottawa-Carleton '01 Canada Summer Games bid comm. '96; finance comm., bd mem., CIS from '96; treas., exec. comm. OUA '97-00; pres. OUA '01-02; pres. CIS '03-05; CdM '03 Winter Universiade; res. Ottawa, Ont.

LOVE, Jon (basketball): b. 10 May 1954, Ottawa, Ont.; given name: Jonathan Courtney; m. Joanne Elizabeth Maguire; c. Kyrie Elizabeth, Jenna Louise; Carleton hons BA, UofOtt BEd; estate planning specialist CIBC Wood Gundy; 5 Lisgar HS title teams; Ottawa Bantam, 2 jr., 2 sr. title teams; also volleyball standout, 3 city HS titles, '71 OFSAA title; OFSAA badminton mixed doubles bronze; hj/tj HS medalist; leading scorer/rebounder Carleton 5yrs; with York's Dave Coulthard only players to be named OUAA East all-star 5yrs, 3 Ravens MVP, 1 OUAA championship tourney all-star; 3yrs Ravens capt.; Olympic team trials; 2 Carleton male athlete-of-yr awards; Jack Vogan graduating male athlete-of-yr award; honored by university with Jon Love night '78; only Carleton athlete to have jersey (#25) ret'd; at retirement leading scorer (2100+), rebounder (1942) in school history; frequent tournament all-star, MVP; founding mem./p-pres. CURBAA; asst. coach Carleton varsity basketball 10+yrs; mem. Carleton Sports Hall of Fame; res. Ottawa, Ont.

LOVELL, Jocelyn (cycling): b. 19 Jul 1950, Eng.; given name: Jocelyn Bjorn; div. Sylvia Burka; m. Neil Annie Francis; pres. Spinal Cord Society of Canada; 38 ntl championships '63-83; mem. 3 PAG; 3 Olympic; 9 world championships; 3 CG teams; gold, silver, bronze '70, 3 gold '78 CG; gold '71, '75; held PAG 1000m record

28yrs; 2nd world 1000m '78; silver '78 ntl speed skating championships; Norton Crowe award '75; paralyzed in truck-bike collision '83; often called "Bad Boy of Cdn Cycling"; mem. Cdn Olympic, Cdn Cycling, Canada's Sports halls of fame; res. Mississauga, Ont.

LOVEROCK, Patty (t&f): b. 21 Feb 1953, Vancouver, B.C.; given name: Patricia Elaine; m. Neil Ayers; c. Jessica; UBC, BRE, UWO, MA; former journalist. teacher; ntl record holder 4x100 (43.63); bronze 4x100 CG '70; silver 100m, bronze 4x100 '75 PAG; bronze 100m '75 FISU; semifinalist 100m, 200m '76 Olympics; silver 4x100 CG '78; ret'd from competition '78; coached Div. 2 Lee County girls track title team; mem. BC Sports Hall of Fame; res. Fort Myers, Fla.

LOVETT, Claire (all-around): b. 24 Oct, Regina, Sask.; given name: Clara Louise Ehman; m. Robert Frederick Lovett (d); ret'd secty.; ntl badminton singles titles '47-48, ladies' doubles '47-48, mixed open doubles '63, sr. ladies' doubles '73-76, 6 US state, 18 prov., 20 city championships; mem. '57 Uber Cup team; runnerup '82 Cdn., US Grand Masters ladies' doubles; '46-67 won 16 Vancouver Lawn Tennis & Badminton Club tennis titles, Western Canadian grass court mixed doubles '52, ntl singles '66; Vancouver srs singles '78, ladies' doubles '77, ntl ladies' doubles '81; mem. numerous basketball title teams in Regina, numerous scoring records, lone Canadian chosen to join all-star quintet; HS ice, field hockey, baseball, t&f; top-rated bowler leading Regina Ramblers 5-pin team scoring; once engaged famed Mildred 'Babe' Zaharias in friendly afternoon of competitive matches in tennis, 5- & 10-pin bowling and upstaged US athletic great in each instance; active in badminton coaching, administration; '77 formed BC Tennis Assn. for Sr. Ladies; mem. Cdn Olympic, BC, Sask. Sports halls of fame; res. Vancouver, B.C.

LOWE, Kevin (hockey): b. 15 Apr 1959, Lachute, Que.; m. Karen Percy; c. Devyn Jean, Darby, Keegan, Karly; hockey exec.; def Quebec (QJHL) '77-79; only anglophone capt.; 1st Edmonton pick '79 draft; NHL with Edmonton '79-92, '96-98, NYR '92-96; asst. coach Edmonton '98-99; head coach '99-00; GM '00-04; mem. 6 Stanley Cup winners; 7 all-star games; 1st NHL player to claim both Bud man-of-yr, King Clancy Memorial awards in 1 season '90; scored 1st-ever Edmonton NHL goal; Edmonton capt. '90-91; holds Oilers' record regular and post-season games played; mem. Team Canada '82, '84; asst. ED '02 Olympic (gold), '04 world teams; NHL record: 1254 scheduled games, 84g, 347a, 214 playoff games, 10g, 48a; NHL coaching record: 82 scheduled games, 32-34-16; active Edmonton Christmas Bureau; mem. QMJHL Hall of Fame; res. Edmonton, Alta.

LOWERY, Ron (orienteering): b. 29 Nov 1955, Halifax, N.S.; given name: Ronald William; m. Denise DeMonte; McMaster, BA BPhE, UWO, MA; fitness consultant; 4 ntl jr., 1 NA championships; mem. ntl team from '74; competed 4 world championships; best international performance 30th '79 worlds, 8th team relay '78 worlds; ntl champion '75, runnerup 4 times; NA champion '77, runnerup once; US title '76, runnerup 3 times; New Eng. title '79, runnerup once; bronze Coureur de Bois Canadian Ski Marathon; Ont. Athletic Achievement award; res. Hamilton, Ont.

LOWRY, Dave (hockey); b. 14 Feb 1965, Sudbury, Ont.; m. Elaine; c. Sarah, Joel, Adam; played minor hockey Nepean, Ont.; lw jr. London (OHL) '82-85; 1st team all-star; drafted by Vancouver '83; minor pro Fredericton (AHL) '87-88, Peoria (IHL) '88-89; NHL Vancouver '85-88, St. Louis '88-93, Florida '93-97, San Jose '97-00, Calgary '00-04; NHL record (through '04) 1084 scheduled games, 164g, 187a, 111 playoff games, 16g, 20a; mem. Hockey Heritage North Hall of Fame; res. Vancouver, B.C.

LUCAS, Eric (boxing); b. 29 May 1971, Montréal, Qué.; c. Alyssa, Melodie; pro boxer, co-owner Granby, Sherbrooke restaurants; 65-19 amateur record; '87 Cdn. jr. featherweight champion; silver 67kg welterweight '88 int. ntls; bronze '89 Canada Cup; 75 kg middleweight bronze '91 sr. ntls; pro debut Dec. '91 vs Errol Brown; '93-94 Cdn. super-middleweight title; '94 Cdn. light-heavyweight title; WBC super-middleweight title '01 beating Glenn Catley; lost title '03 to Markus Beyer; pro record of 36-6-3 (13 KOs); res. Magog Qué.

LUCAS, Joe (rodeo); b. 10 Jan 1959, Olds, Alta; m. Sheona; c. Rickey Joe, Kyle, Kaitlyn; Cross Fire Rope Co.; calf roping, steer wrestling specialist; joined CPRA ranks '80; NFR rookie of '83; 4 ntl, 3 Sask.; 3 Alta. CR titles; Calgary Stampede CR title '87; Bud pro tour, BC circuit CR titles '90; 3 ntl, 2 Alta. circuit high-point titles; Coors Chute Out, Brahma Boot CR titles, Skoal pro rodeo tour SW crown '96; cowboy-of-year award '96; res. Carstairs, Alta.

LUCE, Don (hockey); b. 2 Oct 1948, London, Ont.; given name: Donald Harold; m. Diane; c. Scott, Kim, Kelly, Kristin; hockey exec.; ctr Kitchener Rangers jrs; pro Omaha (CHL) '68-70; NHL NYR '69-70, Detroit '70-71, Buffalo '71-80, Los Angeles '81, Toronto '82; NHL record: 894 scheduled games, 225g, 329a, 71 playoff games, 17g, 22a; record 8 short-handed goals single season, incredible +61 plus/minus ranking; Masterton trophy '75; standout penalty-killer; head coach Pinebridge Bucks (ACHL) '83-84; joined Buffalo front office '84 as scout, asst. coach '85-87, dir. player personnel '87-04; key role in bringing Alexander Mogilny to America '89; mem. Buffalo Sabres, Greater Buffalo Sports halls of fame; res. Williamsville, N.Y.

LUCHT, Edward (basketball); b. 6 Nov 1931, Jeffrey, Alta.; m. Lyla May Ford; c. Gregory, Duane, Karen, Sandra; UAlta., BSc; CIL projects mgr.; ctr UAlta Golden Bears '50-54; Edmonton Townhallers '54-56; ntl finalists '56; mem. Montreal Snowdon Y ntl championship team '57; playing coach Lakeshore Flyers '58; ret'd from competitive basketball '60; mem. 2 WCIAU title teams, ntl CIAU finalists '52; ntl intercollegiate single-game scoring record 88 points '53-54 season vs. UofSask.; ntl Sr. B title with Lakeshore Flyers '58; mem. '58 PAG team; mem. team which defeated Soviets in intl play '58; res. Etobicoke, Ont.

LUDTKE, Frank (cycling/speed skating); b. 12 Jan 1936, Cologne, Germany; given name: Frank Martin; m. Kay Robinson; c. Robert; graphics, communications art instructor; mem. 3 world championships speed skating teams; alternate '68 Olympics; ntl title '68; mem. '67, '71 PAG, '70 CG, World championships, '72 Olympic cycling teams; specialized in individual, team pursuit; coach '78 ntl cycling track team; asst. ntl coach '79-80; res. Pt. Moody, B.C.

LUDWIG, Craig (hockey/coaching); b. 15 Mar 1961, Rhinelander, Wisc.; c. Trevor; UNDak; def. UND '79-82, Team USA '80; NHL '82-90, NYI '90-91, Minnesota '91-93, Dallas '93-99; NHL totals: 1256 scheduled games, 38g, 184a, 177 playoff games, 4g, 25a; 2 Stanley Cup winners; pro scout Dallas '99; asst. coach Michigan IHL ;00, Utah IHL '00-02; 3 Montreal Jacques Beauchamp awards; res. Wisconsin.

LUEDERS, Pierre (bobsleigh); b. 26 Sep 1970, Edmonton, Alta; given name: Pierre Fritz; UAlta; switched career aspirations from t&f to bobsleigh on suggestion from German cousin; mem. Alta Bobsleigh Assn; driver jr. ntl team '90; ntl men's team from '93; among premier drivers in world; became 1st driver to earn WC gold in debut race; 1st driver to win 2/4/combined titles in single season; 27 WC medals; 4 WC 2-man titles; 2 WC combined (2/4-man) titles; competed '94, '98, '02 Olympics; with brakeman Dave MacEachern Olympic 2-man gold '98 (actually finishing in tie with Italian team); won 3 world 2-man titles; set world push record; ntl 2, 4-man titles '03; WC 4-man gold, silver, 2-man silver '05; res. Calgary, Alta.

LUFTSPRING, Sammy (boxing); b. 14 May 1916, Toronto, Ont,; d. 27 Sep 2000, Toronto, Ont.; given name: Yisrael; m. Elsie Goodman; c. Brian, Orian; travel agent; lost just 5 of 105 amateur bouts '32-35 resulting in Gold Gloves titles from bantam to welterweight; protesting Germany's treatment of Jews, rejected '36 Olympic team trials; under guidance of Harry Sniderman began Spanish tour but was stopped by civil war; launched pro career '36; met Gordon Wallace for ntl welterweight title '37 losing split decision; under mgr. Al Weill won Cdn. welterweight title in 13th round TKO over Frank Genovese '38; world-ranked '38 beating 3rd-ranked Salvy Saban; while prepping for title bout with Henry Armstrong lost left eye in bout vs. Steve Belloise, terminating career at 24; won 50 of 56 pro bouts; turned to refereeing, licensed by Ont. Athlete Commission; officiated more than 2,000 amateur, pro bouts including world heavyweight title match George Chuvalo-Ernie Terrell, 3 British Commonwealth, 20 ntl pro championship bouts; author *Call Me Sammy*; mem. Canada's Sports, Ont. Sports Legends, Cdn Boxing, Cdn Jewish halls of fame.

LUKANOVICH, Karen (canoeing); b. 22 May 1960, Montreal, Que.; given name: Karen Leigh; UofOtt; pres. Simon River Sports; competitive skier '72-76; raced on jr. circuit '73; mem. Viking Ski Club, ranked among best jr. x-country skiers Que. '74-78; ntl juvenile K1, K2, K4, sr. K2, K4 paddling titles '77-78; sr. K4 '80-81; swept every kayak event in midget, juv, sr. classes '76 Que championships; at 16 youngest Cdn. Olympic competitor '76 Olympics; mem. '80 Olympic team, ntl team '77-79; res. Morin Heights, Que.

LUKANOVICH, Louis (canoeing); b. 5 Dec 1930, Zagreb, Yugoslavia; m. Jean Alnes; c. Karen, Julianne; Concordia, BSc; MDCC Systems pres.; K4 Yugoslavian ntl team mem. '50 world championships; moved to Canada '51; mem. ntl canoe team '53-68; 21 ntl titles; 7 NA titles; mem. '60 Olympic team; coach Cartierville, Que., Lachine canoe clubs; ntl team coach; Olympic coach '72, '76; pro ski instructor '63-73; founder/chief designer Simon River Sports; mem. Order of Canada; Jubilee Medal; res. Beaconsfield, Que.

LUKE, Michael (rugby); b. 10 Oct 1946, Penzance, Cornwall, Eng.; m. Arlene McCann; Bristol, BA, Bordeaux, SFU, MA; French prof.; mem. Stade BordleaisU Club French 1ˢᵗ div., Penzance, Newlyn teams; with Tony Evans, Mick, Tom, Noel Browne instrumental in formation of St. John's, Nfld., rugby club; standout hooker, later club pres.; Maritime title '72; mem. regional, ntl teams vs. international opponents from '73; capt. Canada's tour to Wales, Eng., France '79; invited to play with UK teams; coach, administrator; original mem., dir. CRC; capped 13 times for Canada; res. St. John's, Nfld.

LUKOWICH, Ed (curling); b. 1 Mar 1946, North Battleford, Sask.; given name: Edward Richard; m. Judy Marie Mayer; c. Pamela Ann; UofSask. BEd, BPhE; US Curling Assn. Development dir. from '00; personal investor; 3ʳᵈ on brother Mike's Sask. Cdn HS title rink '62; competed in 5 Briers; skip '78, '86 Alta. Brier winners, '83 runnerup; world champion '86; topped curling's Gold Trail money winners '89-90 ($175,000), '87-88 ($101,250); founder Canadian, World curling pro tours; founder Seagram's VO Cup championship; founder WCT Players Assn.; skipped Canadian rink in '88 Olympics (demonstration sport); innovator of rock testing method; founder *TSN* Skins Game; exec. dir. WCT; won 3 Western Intercollegiate titles, *CBC* Curling Classic '78. *TSN* Skins '87, Moncton 100 '90, 4 carspiels, authored six books on curling; instructional videos; operated curling supply business; coached Team USA '03 FISU Games; nicknamed "Fast Eddie"; mem. Cdn Curling, UofSask Sports halls of fame; res. Calgary, Alta.

LUMLEY, Harry (hockey); b. 11 Nov 1926, Owen Sound, Ont.; d. 13 Sep 1998, London, Ont.; m. Frances Buckley; c. Kerri Ann, James, Frank, Harry Jr.; ret'd livestock auction mgr.; goal Owen Sound intermediates, Barrie jrs.; pro Indianapolis (AHL) '43-44, Detroit (NHL) '45-50, Chicago '51, Toronto '52-56, Boston '57-61; Vezina Trophy (TML) with 1.85 avg.; J.P.Bickell Memorial Gold Cup as Leafs' MVP, 1ˢᵗ team all-star '54-55; NHL record: 803 scheduled games, 2210ga, 71so, 2.75 ga avg., 76 playoff games, 199ga, 7so, 2.62 ga avg., mem. 1 Stanley Cup winner; Owen Sound arena bears his name; mem. Owen Sound Sports, Hockey halls of fame.

LUMSDEN, Bill (curling/administration); b. 27 May 1907, Brandon, Man.; d. 5 Apr 1982, Winnipeg, Man.; m. Eve Wall; c. William (d), Jean, Patricia; insurance co. partner; mem. Winnipeg Parks Board 7yrs; held varied executive positions Elmwood CC 50yrs; hon. life mem. from '53; hon. secty MCA '46-47, pres. '47-48, hon. life mem. from '52; chair. '70 Brier comm.; secty MCA life members assn. 25yrs; life mem. Civic Caledonian, Charleswood, Deer Lodge, Maple Leaf, West Kildonan, Rossmere Curling Clubs, Winnipeg Clubs Secretaries Assn., Past Presidents of Manitoba Clubs Assn.; won Hudson Bay ('64), Ganong ('54) trophies MCA bonspiel; pres. DCA '66-67, hon. life mem. from '69; 4yrs chair. curling hall of fame selection comm.; 1ˢᵗ chair. DCA schoolboy championship comm.; negotiated Seagram sponsorship of sr. men's curling championships; v-p RCCC '67; life mem. Ont., Que., BC curling assocs.; dir. Winnipeg Silver Broom '78; 3yrs mem. Air Canada exec. of yr selection board; Air Canada exec. of '68; Man. govt. Buffalo award, Man. Sports Fed. merit certificate,

Centennial Medal; hon. citizen St. Boniface; mem. Canadian Curling, Man. Sports halls of fame.

LUMSDEN, Jesse (football); b. 3 Aug 1982, Edmonton, Alta.; given name: Everett James; McMaster; son of former CFL star Neil Lumsden; set CIS single-season rushing record 1816yds in 178 carries over 8 games, 21 single-season tds; 1ˢᵗ NA running back to average 10yrs (10.20) per carry with minimum 150 carries; became CIS career td leader with 47; Ont. conf. career rushing record 4238yds; single-game record 344yds on 24 carries, including 3tds, one of 108yds another OUA record; equaled father's career day record (set '75 vs. Queen's) with 5tds vs. UWO; 4 Yates Cup titles; Hec Crighton trophy '04; OUA player of yr; standout performance '05 East-West Shrine game; res. Burlington, Ont.

LUMSDEN, Neil (football); b. 19 Dec 1952, London, Ont.; given name: Neil James; m. Donna Warner; c. Jesse, Kristin; UofOtt, BA; biz. exec., broadcaster; athlete of year at every school he attended; brilliant college career capped by '75 Yates Cup, Vanier Cup triumphs, produced CIAU record 410 career points, OUAA record 148 points single season, 36 career field goals, 41 single-season converts, 15 single-season tds (equalled record of Eric Walter of McGill, Toronto); league all-star 4 times, all-Cdn. 3 times, 3 times Omega Trophy (OUAA MVP); Ted Morris Trophy (MVP) '75 College Bowl; all-time UofOtt offensive records including 3111yds rushing; outstanding rb 4 times, MVP 3 times; athlete of '75; ACT (Ottawa) athlete of '75; pro Toronto '76-77, Hamilton '78-79, Edmonton '80-85; EFC, runnerup CFL rookie of '76; mem. 3 Grey Cup champions; following stint in real estate joined Ottawa Rough Riders front office '91-92, Hamilton Tiger-Cats '93-00 (GM); GM/COO '03 world cycling championships; conducts TV sports show; pres. True Gravity Sports & Entertainment Consulting; mem. UofOtt Football, OUAA, Ottawa Sports halls of fame; res. Burlington, Ont.

LUMSDON, Cliff (swimming); b. 13 Apr 1931, Toronto, Ont.; d. 31 Aug 1991, Toronto, Ont.; sep.; c. Kim; Humber College; parks & recreation supervisor; 5 world marathon swim championships; 1ˢᵗ to conquer Straits of Juan de Fuca '56; regarded as king of pro swimmers; coached by Gus Ryder; coached daughter Kim, Diane Nyad; manager Lakeshore Swim Club; Lou Marsh Trophy '49; mem. Order of Canada, Cdn, Ont. Aquatic, Etobicoke, Canada's Sports halls of fame.

LUMSDON, Kim (swimming); b. 3 Feb 1957, Toronto, Ont; m. Robert Ian Young; Branksome Hall; swimming teacher, coach; 6ᵗʰ AAU long distance (3-mile) nationals '73; 1ˢᵗ woman, 5ᵗʰ overall, Rio de la Plate Argentina 5-mile swim '74; 2ⁿᵈ woman, 5ᵗʰ overall, Lac St. Jean 5-mile swim '75; cold water, exhaustion ended '75 Lake Ontario bid; 3ʳᵈ woman, 10ᵗʰ overall, Lac St. Jean 25-mile swim '76; conquered 32-mile Lake Ont. in 21hrs, 27 min., despite 4-6' waves '76; 3ʳᵈ best women's marathon swimmer in world '76; open water swim coach; head coach Normac Masters SC; won Gus Ryder, Borough of Etobicoke awards for Lake Ont. swim; res. Etobicoke, Ont.

LUND, Pentti (hockey): b. 6 Dec 1925, Karijoki, Finland; div.; c. Patricia, Judy, Joanne; ret'd sports ed. *Times-News*;

emigrated to Port Arthur age 6; learned hockey skills Port Arthur minor program; TBJHL jr. scoring titles '43-45; sr. EAHL Boston Olympics '45-47, 1 scoring title; ntl US amateur title '47; pro AHL Hershey Bears '47-48; NHL NYR '48-51; Calder Memorial Trophy (rookie of yr); Boston '52-53; lost use of right eye 13 Nov 1951 hockey accident leading to voluntary retirement from pro game with Victoria WHL '53; played sr. amateur hockey with Sault Ste. Marie '54-55 before retiring from game; coached Ft. William sr. Beavers '58, Thunder Bay Oldtimers late '60s; NHL record: 259 scheduled games, 44g, 55a, 18 playoff games, 7g, 5a; scoring champ '50 Stanley Cup playoffs 6g, 5a; mem. NWO Sports Hall of Fame; res. Thunder Bay.

LUNSFORD, Earl (football); b. 19 Oct 1933, Stillwater, Okla.; m. Margot; c. Brenda, Lamar; Oklahoma State, BA, MA; ret'd football exec.; all-American fb '55; drafted by Philadelpha (NFL) but turned pro with Calgary (CFL) '56 leading club in scoring 1st season; 1034yds, 10tds on 183 carries '59 seasons; single-game WFC rushing record 211yds '60; 1st player to gain more than a mile rushing single season '61 with 296 carries for 1796yds; twice Eddie James Trophy winner as WFC leading rusher; CFL record: 1199 carries, 6994 yds., 56tds; 5tds vs Edmonton Sep '62; 5 times 1000-plus yds seasons, 3 times 200-plus carries in season,; GM Winnipeg '67-82, Calgary '85-87; mem. Cdn Football Hall of Fame; res. Ft. Worth, Tex.

LUONGO, Roberto (hockey); b. 4 Apr 1979, St. Leonard, Que.; goal QMJHL Val d'Or '95-98, Acadie-Bathurst '98-99; AHL; twice Memorial Cup finalist; Lowell '99-00, Louisville '00; Team Canada '01, '04 World Cup (gold); highest-ever goalie drafted '97 by NYI; dealt to Florida '00; NHL NYI '99-00, Florida '00-04; NHL record (through '04) 267 scheduled games, 14,828min, 80-138-33, goals against 653, so 23; guest instructor Florida Panthers goaltending school; launched Louie Saves Lives community charity program; res. Sunrise, Fla.

LUSTER, Marv (football): b. 27 Nov 1939, Shreveport, La.; UCLA; db; competed '61 East-West game, all-America Graduation Bowl (outstanding player award); drafted by LA Rams; CFL Montreal '61-64, '73-74, Toronto '64-72; 9 all-star berths in 13 seasons; 6 all-Canadian; began career at oe before moving to def where he shone as lb/db; CFL record: 113 receptions for 1963yds, 11tds, 26 interceptions 312yds; 2 Grey Cup finals, 1 winner; mem. Cdn Football Hall of Fame; res. Los Angeles, Calif.

LUZZI, Don (football): b. 20 Aug 1935, North Branford, Conn.; Villanova; co-capt. '57 Villanova team; Catholic College all-American '56-57; played in '58 Senior Bowl, East-West Shrine Bowl; pro Calgary '58-69; ot/dt; Grey Cup finalist '68; 5 all-Western dt, 2 all-Western ot awards; 4 all-Canadian dt awards; Schenley outstanding-lineman award '58; Scott-Mamino Calgary athlete of yr '58; Becket-DeMarco outstanding-WFC-lineman award '58; mem. Cdn Football Hall of Fame; res. Cakgary, Alta.

LYLE, Dulcie (golf); b. 25 Mar 1918, Allan's Corners, Que.; given name: Dulcie Isabella Jessie Logan; m. Robert Lyle; Notre Dame Ladies Coll.; ntl HS javelin record; equalled ntl 100yd breaststroke mark during BEG trials; with Marian Macdonald won 3 MAAA, Montreal District badminton

doubles titlest; MAAA squash titlist; began golf age 31, reduced handicap to 4 in 2 yrs; 14 Kaniwaki club titles, 10 Montreal & Dist., 14 provincial titles; '60 ntl Closed, '71 Srs., '73 US Srs. titles; mem. 14 Que. ladies', 5 srs. interprov. teams; non-playing capt. ntl World Cup team '68; semifinalist Doherty '62; 3rd US North-South '72; res. Montreal, Que./Delray Beach, Fla.

LYON, Don (skiing): b. 4 Oct 1944, Ottawa, Ont.; m. Jacqueline Rouvier; c. Pascal, Olivier; travel agent; mildly successful competitive career including 3 seasons on world pro tour; began coaching Mt. Tremblant late '60s; coached Ntl Capital Div.; joined ntl women's program '70-95; head coach Outaouais Development ski team '99-01; among skiers he coached were Judy Crawford, Betsy Clifford, Kathy Kreiner, Kerrin Lee-Gartner, Kate Pace, Karen Percy, Laurie Graham, Gerry Sorensen, Deedee Haight; 3 Longines-Wittenauer, 3 PetroCan coaching-excellence awards; mem. Ottawa Sports, Cdn Ski halls of fame; res. Ottawa, Ont.

LYON, George (golf); b. 27 Jul 1858, Richmond, Ont., d. 11 May 1938, Toronto Ont.; given name: George Seymour; m. Annette M. Martin; c. George S. Jr., Fred M.; ntl pv record 1876; with Toronto Rosedale vs. combined Peterborough-Toronto cricket team carried bat for ntl record 238; began golf at 38, 8 ntl amateurs, runnerup twice; at 46 only person in history to win Olympic gold in golf beating US champion Chandler Egan 3 & 2 St. Louis '04; mem. Goulbourn Wall, RCGA, Cdn Olympic, Canada's Sports halls of fame.

M

MABEY, Hap (curling); b. 25 Oct 1939, Saint John, N.B. given name: Harold Arthur; m. Lina Petrea Andersen; c. Joy, Kim, Nathalie, Tanya, Adonica, David, Peter; ret'd sporting goods agent; mem. '53 Maritime midget, '55 NB juv., '59 Maritime jr., '60 Maritime sr. A baseball title teams; Maritime Sr.A fastball title '60; NB Schoolboy curling title '57; 5 times NB Brier representative, NB srs. curling title '00; mem. Oldtimers hockey team; res. Riverview, N.B.

MABEY, Harold (curling); b. 27 Mar 1904, Tryon, P.E.I.; d. 30 Sep 1994, Riverview, N.B.; given name: John Harold; m. Gladys Burden; c. Harold (Hap), Roger; Prince of Wales Coll.; ret'd; played coll. football, all-star hockey goalie; associated with minor baseball Moncton region several years, serving as assn. pres., dir.; 3 times teamed with son Hap, Harold Keith to win NB men's curling title, compete in Brier; 3 NB Srs. titles; 2 NB Diamond Srs.(over 60); pres., hon. mem. Moncton Curlers Assn.; pres. NBCA; coached 2 jr. men's, 1 jr. women's rink to NB title; mem. Canadian Curling Hall of Fame.

MacADAM, Lane (administrator); b. 13 May 1960, Ottawa, Ont.; given name: Joel Lane; m. Susan Jackson; c. Kali, Kirsten, Laurel; Laurentian hons B.Comm,; sport exec./administrator, dir.-gen. Sport Canada from '02; 20+yrs serving at highest levels of Cdn. amateur sport and fitness; special advisor, exec. asst. 4 federal ministers of Fitness & Amateur Sport '84-91; pres./CEO Canada Games Council '91-02, presiding over 5 successful sets ntl games (Kamloops '93, Grande Prairie '95, Brandon '97, Cornerbrook '99, London '01); began process for Bathurst-Campbellton Games '03; mem. organizing comm. Classic Moments in Canadian Sport, '91-93; v-p. CSFAC '96-98; researcher/writer/consultant, Parliamentary sub-comm. on Study of Sport in Canada '98; managing partner Canadian Sport Awards '97-00; board mem., Spirit of Sport Foundation '00-01; mem. Sport Matters Working Group, '00-01; awarded Secretary of State Fellowship for Advanced Study in French '79; capt. Laurentian soccer ntl. title team '83; all-Cdn; Laurentian Voyageur athletic excellence award; volunteer coach (NCCP Level 2) in local ringette and soccer; mem. Laurentian Hall of Fame; res. Ottawa, Ont.

MacASKILL, Klari (canoeing); b. 31 Dec 1964, Budapest Hungary. m. Neil MacAskill; former mem. Hungarian ntl team; moved to Canada '88; ntl team from '89; competed '92. '96 Olympic Games; K-4 200 bronze '94 World championships; gold K-4 500, bronze K-2 500 '95 Pre-Olympic regatta; gold K-4 200 Szeged '96; 2 gold, 1 silver Milano '96; 4 ntl titles; Edmonton Grads team trophy '95; res. Renfrew, Ont.

MacBETH, Donald (horse racing); b. 29 Aug 1949, Red Deer, Alta.; d. 1 Mar 1987, Ocala, Fla.; m. Joanne; c. Tiffany, Heather, Don, Christina; won with 1st mount, Walking Box, '67; leading apprentice rider Ak-Sar-Ben Omaha; leading rider Atlantic City '73, Hialeah '79, Monmouth Park '78-80, Aqueduct '81; more than 2000 winners, $20 million in purses; 13 major stakes race victories; mem. Alta. Sports Hall of Fame.

MacCULLOCH, Todd (basketball); b. 27 Jan 1976, Winnipeg, Man.; given name: Todd Carlyle; m. Jana; Washington BA; pro basketball player; hon. mention all-American; 2 all-Pac 10; drafted by Philadelphia '99-00, '02-03, New Jersey '01-02; participated Schick rookie game '00; NBA community assist award '02; foot injury (neuropathy) '03 led to '04 retirement; res. Philadelphia, Pa.

MacDONALD, Byron (swimming); b. 23 Jul 1950, Chicago, Ill.; given name: Arthur Byron; div. Paula Thomson; m. Lisha Van Leeuwen; c. Troy, Shane, Kenzie; Michigan, BComm, MA; university lecturer, coach; as polio therapy began swimming age 6; capt. HS, Mich. swim team; gold 100m butterfly, 4x100 medley relay, leading 1st ever Cdn 1-3 international sweep of medals '70 CG; bronze 100m fly, silver 4x100 medley relay '71 PAG; silver 100m fly '73 FISU, '74 CG; mem. '72 Olympic team; ranked among top 15 butterflyers in world '70-75; 4 Commonwealth 100m fly records; ntl 100m fly record, 200m fly record; numerous prov. records; all-American 3yrs Mich., NCAA finalist; all-Cdn, 3 gold CIAU championships '73; coach men's team FISU Games '79, '81, '93; coach '92 Olympic team; coach York, UofT, North York; 9 CIAU coach-of-yr awards; *CBC-TV* swimming color commentator; 2 PetroCan coaching excellence awards; mem. Cdn Aquatic Hall of Fame; res. Toronto, Ont.

MACDONALD, Daniel (builder/gymnastics); b. 12 Jun 1946, Noranda, Que.; NB; phys ed. prof. Moncton; 2 AUAA titles; rep.NB '67 Canada Winter Games; affected all levels of gymnastics (local, prov., ntl) as administrator, coach, official, educator; founded Moncton Gymnastic club; instructor/coach UdeM; NBGA from '72, pres. '75-80; nationally-certified judge; course conductor NCCP, Centre for NB Coaching Education dir. '95-02; dir. Gymnastics Can. 17yrs, v-p '92-95; mgr. ntl team '76 Olympics, '79 worlds; organized ntl, CIAU championships; Gymnastics Can. service award; life mem. NBGA, NBGA volunteer award; mem. NB Sports Hall of Fame; res. Moncton, N.B.

MacDONALD, Gary (swimming); b. 15 Dec 1953, Mission, B.C.; given name: Gary Wayne; SFU; mem. Dolphins Swim Club; mem. '73 FISU, '74 CG, '75 PAG, '76 Olympic teams; gold, 2 bronze '74 CG, silver 400m FS '75 PAG; silver 4x100m medley relay '76 Olympics; 4 gold '76 ntls; 1 CIAU male-swimmer-of-yr award; PB: 100m FS 53.31, 200m FS 1:38.51; ntl records 400m FS relay 3:33.42, 400m medley relay 3:55.69; Gov.-Gen.'s silver medal '76; mem. BC Swimming Hall of Fame; res. Mission, B.C.

MacDONALD, Irene (diving); b. 22 Nov 1933, Hamilton, Ont. d. 20 Jun 2002, Delta, B.C.; given name: Irene Margaret; ret'd prov. diving development co-ordinator;

coach to '88; 15 ntl titles '51-61, 6 US ntl '57-60, 2 Mexican titles '58-59; bronze 3m springboard '54, silver '58 CG; bronze '56, 6th '60 Olympics; Ont. 3m titles '51-55, BC '61, Que. '56; Velma Springstead Trophy '57; dir. BC Sports Fed.; chair. Diving for Canada '62-66; diving coach CG team '66, European tour team '71, world championships team '73-75; trustee BC Sports Hall of Fame; CADA tech. dir. '67-69; *CBC* analyst 2yrs; BC Women in Sport Leaders & Legends award; mem. Order of BC, BC Sports, Cdn Aquatic, Canada's Sports, Cdn Olympic Sports halls of fame.

MacDONALD, Jackie (t&f); b. 12 Oct 1932, Toronto, Ont.; m. Bill Gelling; c. Andrew, Steven; Carleton, BA, Montreal MA; ret'd teacher; Ont. jr. diving title '48; mem. Toronto Globetrotters jr. basketball champions '49-50; ntl shot put title '53; ntl shot put record, silver '54 BEG; 5th discus '55 PAG; beat own record placing 10th shot put '56 Olympics; only Cdn rep. Moscow World Youth Games '57; bronze '58 CG; res. Gloucester, Ont.

MacDONALD, Kilby (hockey); b. 6 Sep 1913, Ottawa, Ont.; d. 14 May 1986, Florida; m. Mary Hayes (d); c. Kilby-Ann, Terry, Allan; ret'd Labatts regional sales mgr.; mem. UofOtt, HS ntl title football team; hockey Lasalle jrs. '26-27, Montagnard jrs. '28-32, Kirkland Lake srs. '34-35, Noranda Copper Kings '35-36; pro NYR organization '36, with Rovers, Philadelphia Ramblers; Rangers regular '39-40 winning Calder Memorial Trophy as rookie of year; except for '42-44 when he played with Montreal army during service stint WW2, remained with Rangers through '44-45 campaign; mem. Stanley Cup champions '39-40; 5 yrs Rangers Eastern Ont. scout; coach at West Point. Arvida, Baltimore, Quebec; Memorial Cup finalist vs. Barrie '51; helped with Ottawa Cradle League; coach St. Anthony srs.; mgr.-coach Babe Ruth baseball teams winning Ont., Cdn titles, competing in Washington, D.C., world championships; mem. Ottawa Sports Hall of Fame.

MacDONALD, Noel (basketball); b. 23 Jan 1915, Mortlach, Sask.; given name: Noel Marguerite; m. Harry Robertson; c. Donald, Dale Jean; business school; mem. Edmonton Grads '33-39, capt. '36-39; in 135 games scored 1874 points for 13.8 points-per-game avg., best in club's history; softball Gyro Pats, Muttart Pats; coached HS, UAlta. girls basketball; coached Libyan teams during 13 yr stay in country; Bobbie Rosenfeld award '38; mem. Cdn Basketball, Alta., Canada's Sports halls of fame; res. Qualicum Beach, B.C./Sun City W, Ariz.

MacDONALD, Ross (sailing); b. 27 Jan 1965, Vancouver, B.C.; m. Marcia Pellicano; production mgr.; began competing '82; Star class sailor; with Bruce MacDonald 3 ntl, 1 PAG gold '87, with Pat Dion '95 NA title; with Eric Jespersen 2 ntl, 1 worlds titles; with Jespersen '92 Olympic bronze, '93 NA, '94 ntl, world, '95 European championship gold; competed 5 Olympics, '87, '95 PAG; with Jespersen 1st all-Cdn crew to win world Star title; with Mike Wolfs '04 Olympic Star silver; Tribute to Champions sport-excellence award '89; CYA sailor of '87, '94; Rolex Cdn sailor of '90, '92; BC sailor of '89, '92, '93; res. Vancouver, B.C.

MACDONALD, Wen (curling); b. 20 Dec 1908, Charlottetown, P.E.I.; d. 20 Apr 2000, Charlottetown, P.E.I.; given name: Wendell Leigh; m. Elizabeth Matthew; c.

Patricia Jane, Janet Leigh, Kenneth, Debra; Prince of Wales Coll., Dalhousie, Edinburgh, MD; radiologist; rep. PEI '46, '54-56 Brier; 13 prov. srs. titles; skip ntl srs. champions '72, '76-77; skip PEI entry '68 ntl mixed; pres. PEI curling assn.; CCA dir.; mem. Gov.-Gen.'s CC; mem. Canadian Curling (inducted as curler and builder), PEI Sports halls of fame.

MacDONELL, Paul (harness racing); b. 29 Jan 1963, Oshawa, Ont.; launched career at 18 working with Doug Brown stable; has since emerged as one of top drivers on tough OJC circuit; scored major upset '90 by driving longshot Bay's Fella to victory over Topnotcher to record longest mutuel price in Breeders Crown history, $140,600, for a $2 wager; piloted Bay's Fella '90, Billyjojimbob '91, Lifetime Dream '93, Village Jiffy '94, Village Jasper '97, Duke of York '01 Breeders Crown triumphs; leading driver Charlottetown Driving Park '87-88; piloted Village Jiffy to '94 top-older-pacer honors, Lifetime Dream to top-aged-trotting-mare honors '93, Billyjojimbob '91 aged trotting horse; through '03 3254 victories, including 81 major stakes titles, and purses exceeding $47M; res. Orono, Ont.

MacDONNELL, Wayne (badminton); b. 28 June 1940, Vancouver, B.C.; given name: Wayne Barry; m. Gil Semadeni; c. Brian, Leanna; exec. officer Sears Ltd.; record 6 ntl men's singles titles '62-67; ntl doubles champion '63; 6 BC singles, 5 BC doubles, 7 Vancouver singles, 3 Oregon State, 14 Washington State singles; 4 NS singles, 2 NS men's doubles, 3 NS mixed doubles, '66 US mixed doubles, '71 Irish Open singles titles; record 6 times mem. Cdn Thomas Cup team; men's ntl record for international appearances; pres. CBA; res. Oakville, Ont.

MacDUFF, Alan (broomball); b. 25 Jun 1949, Hawkesbury, Ont.; m. Elaine Carol Arthurs; c. Erin Dawn, Emily Alanna; dairy farmer; played competitive ball-hockey '83-93; began playing broomball '65; ntl gold '82 Pop Shoppe, '91-95 Embrun Plumbing, '96 Embrun Sport; ntl silver '86 Independent Radiator, '90 Embrun Plumbing; ntl bronze '79 Sun Life team; world gold '91 Embrun Plumbing; 6 MVP, 2 sportsmanship, 7 best-def awards; ntl championship 2nd team all-star '86; official EOBA Ottawa Nationals; EIBA official of '00; Canada Celebration award '88; res. St. Eugene, Ont.

MacEACHERN, Dave (bobsleigh); b. 4 Nov 1967, Charlottetown, P.E.I.; brakeman ntl team '90-2000; brakeman for Pierre Lueders winning Olympic 2-man gold '98 (actually tied with Italian team); also competed '92, '94 Olympics; 9 World Cup 2-man gold, 5 silver, 3 bronze; 1 WC 4-man gold, 1 silver, 4 bronze; 2 final WC standing 2-man gold, 1 silver, 1 combined silver; 1 world championship 2-man silver; ret'd from competition '00; res. Calgary, Alta.

MacEACHERN, Shanyn (gymnastics); b. 17 Feb 1980, Brampton, Ont.; LSU; all-around performer; mem. ntl team '95-99; competed '95 worlds, PAG, '96 Olympics; 1 ntl jr., 2 ntl elite titles; res. Brampton, Ont.

MacFARLANE, Gus (basketball); b. 19 Feb 1925, Montreal, Que.; d. 22 Feb 1991, Charlottetown, P.E.I.; given name: Angus McKechnie; McGill., BA, BEd; War Veterans Allowance Board mem.; playground supervisor, basketball statistician, referee, coach, football coach, Montreal region exec. '49-56; guided Verdun to Que. Boy's Brigade basketball title, jr. hockey title '49; coached Verdun Pats to Que. juv football title '50; coached Verdun to Que. int. YMCA basketball title '52; coached Verdun HS sr. football titlists '54-55; athletic dir., coach Mount Allison '57-69, 2 NB football, 2 NB, PEI basketball titles; lifetime coaching record in basketball, football, hockey, softball, 326 wins, 122 losses, 3 ties; GM ntl basketball team '69-70; dean of men McMaster '71; resource asst. National Administrative Centre for Sport, Recreation Ottawa '70; MP (Lib) Hamilton Mountain '74-79; key role in creation of offices of Ministers of State for Fitness & Amateur Sport and Federal-Provincial relations; life mem. CAFC, hon. mem., pres. CAUAD, National Assn. of Basketball Coaches of Canada merit award.

MacGOWAN, Margaret (t&f); b. 21 Sep 1954, Waterford, Ont.; given name: Margaret Eleanor; div. Bryan Stride; c. Christopher; m. Ross Hendershot; c. Kyle; Brock, BPhE. BEd; teacher; mem. '74, '78 CG, '76 Olympic, '77 FISU, '75, PAG, World Cup teams; team bronze 4x400 relay '74, '78 CG; team gold 4x400 relay '75 PAG; finalist 4x400m relay '76 Olympics; PB: 100m (11.4), 200m (23.4), 400m (52.8); 2 ntl masters records; masters world gold, 2 bronze '91; Brock Hall of Fame; res. Mildmay, Ont.

MACH, Gerard (coaching); b. 16 Sep 1926, Poland; speed coach consultant; ret'd CTFA ntl program dir., ntl team coach '73-92; sprinter '52 Polish Olympic team; Polish ntl sprints, hurdles coach '52-72; under his guidance Polish t&f team emerged as one of Europe's most powerful in '50s and '60s; Cdn team coach '76, '80, '84 Olympic, '78, '82 CG, '79 PAG, '81 World Cup; res. Ottawa, Ont.

MacINNES, Bob (curling); b. 23 Sep 1932, Lochiel Twp., Ont.; m. Marie Cutbush; c. Brenda, Kent, Neil, Elizabeth; Fanshawe College; personnel officer; as third with Bob Knippelberg (Ottawa) twice runnerup Ont. Consols; with Bill Lewis (Trenton) won City of Ottawa bonspiel grand aggregate beating Kingston's Jake Edwards in playoff '66; with Lewis runnerup '67 Ont. Consols, won Ontario Tankard '67; skipped Trenton rink to '69 Ont. Tankard, competed in Ont. Consols; represented Canada in international matches in Scotland, Europe, res. Schumacher, Ont.

MacINNES, Kent (curling); b. 15 Feb 1938, Kirkland Lake, Ont.; given name: Errol Kent; m. June Quick; c. Deborah, David, Katherine; senior buyer mining operations; runnerup Ont. junior men's '56; with Jack Polyblank represented Northern Ont. 3 Briers; NO runnerup '62; Brier all-star 2nd '64; NO mixed title '67, twice runnerup; v.-chair. CCA mixed committee '78-80, chair. '81-82; CCA award of merit '84; res. Timmins, Ont.

MacINNIS, Al (hockey); b. 11 Jul 1963, Inverness, N.S.; given name: Allan; m. Jackie; c. Carson, Ryan, Riley, Lauren;; def Kitchener (OHA) '80-83, Colorado (CHL) '84; OHL Max Kaminsky top-def. award '93; 1st Calgary pick '81 draft; NHL with Calgary '81-94, St. Louis '94-04; 4 NHL 1st team, 3 2nd team all-star; Conn Smythe trophy '89; Norris trophy '99; played 11 all-star games; mem. 1 Stanley Cup winner; noted for booming slap-shot, 7 hardest-shot titles;; competed '90 worlds, '91 Canada Cup; mem.

'98, '02 (gold) Olympic teams; NHL record: (through '04) 1416 scheduled games, 340g, 934a, 177 playoff games, 39g, 121a; nickname "Chopper"; res. Town & Country, Mo./Calgary, Alta.

MACKAY, Craig (speed skating); b. 1 Apr 1927, Banff, Atla.; given name: Craig Innis; m. Gwen Bibbey; c. Kim, Heather, Terri, Craig Jr. Cam, Tom; road building contractor; mem. Saskatoon Lions Speed Skating Club; 25yr competitive career; Saskatoon, Sask. titles '44-45; '47 Alta. sr. men's 220yd record, gold '47 ntl sr. men's 3-mile; *Star-Phoenix* road race 3-mile mark '48; Alta. champion '51; mem. '67 Canada Winter Games team; mem. '48, '52, alternate '56, '60 Olympic, '50 world championships teams; helped institute Olympic trials for skaters; key role '57 NA outdoor speed skating championships; mem. ISA; 2yrs pres. Saskatchewan branch CASA, 2yrs v-p CASA; chair '68 ntl outdoor, '73 indoor championships; chair Canada Winter Games Speed Skating comm. '70-71; chair CASA Hall of Fame comm. from '68; mem. Sask., Saskatoon Sports, Canadian Speed Skating Halls of fame; res. Saskatoon, Sask.

MacKAY, Elizabeth (diving); b. 9 May 1960, Chicoutimi, Que.; given name: Elizabeth Hugette; Laval; mem. '78 CG, World Games, '79 PAG, '80 phantom Olympic team; silver 3m, bronze 10m Vienna International, silver 10m, bronze 3m, Bolzano Internations '80; silver 10m '78, bronze 10m '81 Canada Cup; gold 1m, 3m Norway Cup '80; 5 ntl championships '77-80; all-around ntl champion '79, '81; res. Cap Rouge, Que.

MACKAY, Gerry (baseball/builder/curling); b. 19 Feb 1930, Kenton, Man.; joined ManDak League Brandon Greys at 19; 3 strong seasons earned contract with Chicago Cubs organization; with Northern League (Class C) Sioux Falls hit .349 '52, .337 '53; split '54 between Visalia (Calif. League) and Brandon Greys then moved to El Paso (B League) playing inf/of and batting .371 while earning all-star status; joined Yankee organization '56; returned to Brandon to stay '57 hitting .394; played/coached Brandon sr. Cloverleafs to consec. Man. sr. league titles; chosen mgr. 1st ntl team '67; competed in '67, '71 PAG, '72 World championships; dir. Cdn Fed of Amateur Baseball '67-74; instrumental in establishing Old Timers baseball in Man.; talented curler reaching Man. sr. men's finals '87; skipped Man. masters title rink '97; mem. Man. Sports Hall of Fame; res. Brandon, Man.

MacKAY, Mickey (hockey); b. 21 May 1894, Chesley, Ont., d. 21 May 1940, Nelson, B.C.; given name: Duncan McMillan; nicknamed "Wee Scot"; sr. hockey Edmonton, Grand Forks, B.C., Vancouver Millionaires (PCL) '15, 33 goals rookie season missing scoring title by single point; remained with Vancouver through '25-26 season, three scoring titles, 202 goals, 242 games; Chicago team's leading scorer '27-28; played half of '28-29 season in Pittsburgh then joined Boston Bruins, mem. 2 Stanley Cup winners; Boston business mgr. '30; mem. BC Hockey, Hockey halls of fame.

MacKAY, Sherraine (fencing): b. 21 Jun 1975, Brooks, Alta.; given name: Sherraine Schalm; m. Geordie MacKay; UofOtt; teacher; began fencing at 14; excelled at all age categories; won ntl cadet, 2 junior épée titles; UofOtt MVP awards '94-95; ranked #1 sr. nationally; 4ᵗʰ (best ever by Cdn) in world cup épée; competed '95 (team bronze), '99 (team silver) PAG; mem. ntl women's épée team from '94; Ottawa Shield women's épée title '98; Elite Circuit, French Circuit gold, 2 World Cup bronze '99; NA Cup silver '98; 6ᵗʰ world sr. championships '99, best ever by Cdn fencer; competed '00, '04 Olympics; 1ˢᵗ Cdn woman to win WC fencing event in Spanish épée '00; won WC events Havana, Puerto Rico (2), Austria; 1ˢᵗ Cdn to win 3 consec. WC medals; added 5ᵗʰ WC win of season in Australia; 2ⁿᵈ in world épée rankings '03; res. Budapest, Hungary.

MACKELL, Fleming (hockey); b. 30 Apr 1929, Montreal, Que.; given name: Fleming David; div. Kathleen O'Brien; c. Rosemary, Kathy, Michael, Jo-Anne, Shaun, Maureen, Sheilagh, Fleming Jr.; St. Pat's Coll, St. Mike's Coll.; auto sales; qb football teams at St. Pat's, St. Mike's; at 15 played jr. Quebec; 2yrs jr. St. Mike's Coll.; Toronto (NHL) '47-52, Boston '52-60; at 18 youngest to that time ever to play in NHL all-star game; NHL record: 665 scheduled games, 149g, 220a, 80 playoff games, 22g, 41a; competed 4 all-star games; with father Jack, whose name was mispelled McKell on Stanley Cup while member of Ottawa Senators, one of few father-son combinations to play for two Stanley Cup winners each; coached Quebec (AHL) 1yr; 5 GM Grand Master salesman awards; res. Verdun, Que.

MACKEN, Brendan (tennis); b. 21 Jan 1923, Montreal, Que.; given name: Brendan Hubert; m. Elizabeth Gillam; c. Nancy, Ginny, Peggy, Helen, Bren Jr.; William and Mary, BSc; owner chemical co., lawn bowls distributor; mem. '46-52 Davis Cup teams, capt. '54; only Cdn to beat Australian in Davis Cup play (Billy Sidwell '49); one of two Cdns to beat US player in Davis Cup action (Bob Perry '52); Cdn men's singles title '50; with brother Jim ntl men's doubles '47, repeat '51 with Lorne Main; ntl mixed doubles (with sister Patricia) '47; Que., Ont. singles, doubles, mixed doubles titles '52; ret'd '54; 1ˢᵗ chairman CLTA junior development; '67 chairman Davis Cup selection comm.; 2yrs pres. QLTA; ntl veteran squash doubles title with late Paul Ouimet '68-69, US runnerup each year; A ranked squash singles player; ranked #1 over 55 category in tennis '82; active role in annual Gordon Trophy srs. matches; instrumental in arranging US scholarships for Cdn tennis players; pres. MAAA; life mem. Toronto Cricket & Skating Club; mem. Cdn Tennis Hall of Fame; res. Richmond Hill, Ont.

MACKEN, Jim (tennis); b. 29 July 1925, Montreal, Que.; m. Audrey Maureen; c. Gerald, Kathy, Chris, Patrick, Tony; William and Mary, BA; ret'd distributor; capt. W&M tennis team '49; NCAA champions '47-48; playing mem. Davis Cup team '46, non-playing capt. '63, '65; with brother Bren ntl men's doubles champion '46; ranked in Canada's top 10 '46-58; NS, Que., Ont., BC titles; BC, Pacific Northwest, Pacific Coast squash titles; ranked #2 nationally over 55 bracket tennis '82; pres. BC Tennis Assn.; promoted first BC Umpires Assn. '81; TV color commentator regional, ntl jr. tennis championships; umpire Davis Cup, WCT matches; chair. '71 Davis Cup comm.; Centennial medal '67: avid golfer, scored hole-in-one '98; Tennis Can. distinguished service award; mem. NCAA Tennis Hall of Fame; res: Richmond, B.C.

MACKEN, Patricia (tennis); b. July 1928, Montreal, Que.; div. Eldon Smart; c. Jennifer, Sheila; William and Mary; jr. provincial titles Que., Ont. '43-45; Vermont State ladies' singles, doubles, mixed doubles (with Clark Taylor) '48; 5 Que. sr. ladies' singles, doubles; 7 Montreal City, District ladies' singles, doubles; ntl ladies' open singles, doubles, mixed doubles (with brother Brendan) '47; mem. Wightman Cup team vs Britian '48; Alberta, Manitoba ladies' doubles, mixed titles; '50 *CP* poll female tennis player of half century; res. W. Vancouver, B.C.

MacKENZIE, Ada (golf); b. 30 Oct 1891, Toronto, Ont., d. 25 Jan 1973, Richmond Hill, Ont.; Havergal College; 5 ntl ladies' open, closed, 8 seniors, 9 Ont. ladies, 2 seniors, 10 Toronto, district titles; 3 successive Havergal Cups; instrumental in formation Toronto Ladies' Golf Club '24; twice reached semifinals US women's amateur; 2 Bermuda titles; competed internationally for Scotland and Canada; last seniors title '69 at age 78; from '71 ntl seniors have competed for Ada MacKenzie Trophy; Bobbie Rosenfeld award '33; mem. RCGA, Cdn Olympic, Ont. Legends, Canada's Sports halls of fame.

MacKENZIE, Barry (hockey); b. 16 Aug 1941, Toronto, Ont.; UBC; player dev. co-ordinator Minnesota Wild; jr. Toronto St. Mike's '60-62; UBC '62-63; Team Canada '63-68; competed '64, '68 (bronze) Olympics; Ottawa Nationals (OHA Sr.) '67-68; NHL Minnesota '68-69; CHL Memphis '68-69; playing coach Seibu Japan '75-78; IIHF World '64 (bronze), '65, '66 (bronze), '67 (bronze); mem. IIHF Hall of Fame; res. Minnesota.

MacKENZIE, Bill (baseball); b. 27 July 1946, Pictou, N.S.; given name: William Roy; m. Janet Eldridge; St. Clair Community College; salesman; ex-dir. Canadian scouting for Expos;; catcher; pro Detroit organization '66; minor ball at Lakeland, Fla.; Erie, Pa.; Statesville, N.C.; Dubuque, Iowa; West Palm Beach, Fla.; broken shoulder ended playing career; minor league instructor Bristol, Tenn.; coached Bristol, Lakeland, Rocky Mount, N.C., West Palm Beach; 7yrs Expos administrative assistant, scout, player development co-ordinator; signed David Palmer and recommended Tim Raines to Expos; tech. dir. Baseball Canada '79-89; managed '83 PAG gold medal team; sales rep. Holman bats; res. Ottawa, Ont.

MacKENZIE, Eric (baseball); b. 29 Aug 1932, Glendon, Alta.; given name: Eric Hugh; m. Gail McNaughton; c. Christine, Coleen, Lee; recreation dir.; pro baseball as catcher in Athletics' organization '51-58, brief major league service Kansas City A's '55; coach ntl amateur baseball team '78, '80 World Games, '79, '83 PAG; '81,'83 Intercontinental Cup; son Lee mem. Kitchener Memorial Cup champions '81; res. Mooretown, Ont.

MacKENZIE, Shanty (football); b. 27 Aug 1920, Scotland; d. 6 May 2001, Agincourt, Ont.; given name: Donald; m. Audrey Lock; c. Mary Louise, Catherine, Marion, William Hugh; building superintendent; Toronto Argos '40-41, '50-53; Toronto Balmy Beach (ORFU) '46-49, player-coach '49; capt. '50 Grey Cup champions; mem. 2 Grey Cup champions; line coach Parkdale Lions '57 jr. champions, North York Knights, Scarborough Rams '55-63.; Jimmy Keith Memorial Trophy.

MACKIE, Baz (football); b. 8 Mar 1932, Weston, Ont.; given name: Clarence; m. Marilynn Ellins; c. Douglas, Jo-Anne, Stephen; UofT, BPHE, BA, BEd; secondary school principal; football, lacrosse, hockey, t&f Weston CI Ironmen; only player to make 1st and 2nd TDIAA all-star teams in history of league, '51 1st team tackle, 2nd team fb; dg UofT Varsity Blues '52-55; mem. '54 OUAA champions; pro Argos '55-57; mem. Big Four all-Cdn team '56; res. Rexdale, Ont.

MACKIE, Gordie (builder); b. 17 Jan 1922, Winnipeg, Man.; m. Marguerite; c. Heather, Holly, Bonnie, Craig; certified physiotherapist; boxing instructor Winnipeg YMCA '49; owned/operated St. Boniface-Madison Boxing/Wrestling Club '55-60; Cdn Olympic team therapist '72, '76; chief therapist Blue Bombers '59-69; 5 times CFL all-stars therapist; therapist '70 Cdn Davis Cup, '74 Team Canada hockey Summit Series teams; UMan. therapist; founding mem. Cdn Athletic Therapists Assn. '66; mem. Man. Sports Hall of Fame; res. Winnipeg, Man.

MACKIE-MORELLI, Anne (t&f); b. 18 June 1955, Calgary, Alta.; given name: Anne Mackie; m. Claudio David Morelli; UBC, BPhE, SFU, MA; 2nd fastest 400m in Canada '74; while touring Europe with ntl team '75 sustained foot fracture which cost her berth on PAG, Olympic teams; '76 ntl 400m title, '79 400m, 800m indoor, 800m outdoor titles, '80 800m ntl outdoor title; mem. Pacific Conference, World Cup, FISU, '78 CG, '79 PAG, '80 Olympic teams; bronze '77 Berlin 800m, Melbourne 400m, silver 800m World Cup trials; bronze 4x400m relay '78 CG; silver 4x400m, bronze 4x100m relay '78 Pacific Conference Games; semifinalist 800m '77, '79, 400m '79 FISU Games; bronze 4x400m relay '79 PAG; gold 800m '79, silver 800m '80 *Edmonton Journal* Games; fastest 800m in Canada '77, 3rd fastest ever with 2:01.6; UBC athlete of '76-77; mem. Alta. Sports Hall of Fame; last known res. Vanderhoof, B.C.

MacKINNON, Dan (harness racing/all-around); b. 12 Nov 1876, Highfield, P.E.I.; d. 24 Dec 1964, Charlottetown, P.E.I.; c. Morris; pharmacist, fox farmer, publisher; Maritime mile running titles 1897-99; DCRA, Gov.-Gen.'s medals for shooting '20; during 12-day period '15 won 15 of 16 starts with pacer Helen R; his horse Volo Rico upset previously unbeaten US-owned Eula H. '31; world ice racing record Mt. Clemens, Mich., '23 with The Yank; Eastern harness racing promoter '30; USTA director, promoter '30-61; pres. Provincial Exhibition Assn.; DSO, Croix d'Guerre WW1; mem. Canadian Horse Racing, PEI, Canada's Sports halls of fame.

MacKINNON, Zoe (field hockey); b. 5 Oct 1959, Toronto, Ont.; given name: Zoe Elizabeth; UofT, BPHE; physical educator; mem. Ont. team from '75; ntl team '81-84; UofT team '78-83; goaltender World Cup silver medal team '83; mem. '84 Olympic team; fed. govt. excellence award '83; res. Bramalea, Ont.

MacLACHLAN, Alan (bobsleigh); b. 2 May 1957, Toronto, Ont.; given name: Alan William; m. Jill Henry; Upper Canada College, UWO, BA; investment analyst; t&f competitor Toronto region as youth; mem. ntl bobsleigh team from '78; attained driver status '80; mem. 4-man crew

which crashed in '80 Lake Placid Olympics; mem. '84 Olympic team; res. Bolton, Ont.

MacLAGGAN, James (administration); b. 10 Aug 1923, Blackville, N.B.; d. 30 Oct 2003, Bathurst, N.B.; given name: James Coburn; v-p '68-71, pres. '71-75 NBAHA; mem. sr., int. CAHA councils; dir. NB Baseball Assn. '68-71; dir. NB Sports Fed. '72-74; chair. NB Sports Hall of Fame '79-80; CAHA service citations '65, '67; NB sports exec. of '82; Air Can. Cup '02 organizing comm.; mem. NB Sports Hall of Fame.

MacLEAN, Allan (jiu jitsu); b. 7 Feb 1953, Exeter, Ont.; given name: Allan John; Waterloo, BSc; pharmaceutical salesman; South Huron DHS most valuable male athlete '71; began jiu jitsu training Waterloo '71; 1st degree black belt '75, 2nd degree '78; organized Kitchener jiu jitsu club '77; mem. ntl team '78; instructor Kitchener club; res. Kitchener, Ont.

MacLEAN, John (hockey/coaching); b. 20 Nov 1964, Oshawa, Ont.; m. Adrienne; c. John Carter; rw Oshawa jrs. '81-84; Memorial Cup all-star '83; NHL New Jersey '83-91, '92-97 (missed '91-92 season due to injury), San Jose '97-98, NYR '98-01, Dallas '01-02; asst. coach NJ '02-03; NHL record 1194 scheduled games, 413g, 429a, 104 playoff games, 35g, 48a; 2 NHL all-star games; 1 Stanley Cup winner; mem. Team Canada '84 jr. worlds, '89 worlds; wife former golf pro; res. Montclair, N.J.

MacLEAN, Lucella (baseball); b. 3 Jan 1921, Lloydminster, Sask; given name: Lucella Katherine; m. George Mervyn Ross; ret'd TV factory inspector; active in hockey, basketball; began playing softball Lloydminster sr. team; prov. champ Saskatoon Pats; catcher in AAGPBL with South Bend '43-44 playing 101 games .204ba, .953fa; following season of sr. ball in Edmonton returned to US National League finishing career with Chicago '46-52; hon. chair. Cdn jr. A women's title tourney '83; in later years active in lawn bowling, curling; mem. Sask. Baseball Hall of Fame Battleford; honored by Cooperstown, Cdn Baseball halls of fame; res. Lloydminster, Sask.

MacLEISH, Rick (hockey); b. 3 Jan 1950, Lindsay, Ont.; given name: Richard George; m. Carolyn; c. Danielle; Jr. A Peterborough '68-70; Boston's 2nd pick, 4th overall '70; Oklahoma (CHL), Richmond (AHL); NHL Philadelphia '70-81, '83-84, Hartford '81, Pittsburgh '81-83, Detroit '84; scored 50g '72-73; NHL record: 846 scheduled games, 349g, 410a, 114 playoff games, 54g, 53a; mem. 2 Stanley Cup winners; mem. Flyers Hall of Fame; res. Philadelphia, Pa.

MacLEOD, Tammy (diving); b. 3 Aug 1956, Vancouver, B.C.; given names Tammy Donna; m. John Percy; c. Matthew, Tia; sc. Gavin Logan; UBC, hons. Econ.; realtor;; gold 1m '71 ntls 13-14 age-group; bronze 3m '72 winter ntls; bronze 10m '74 summer ntls; silver 10m '71 world age-group finals; silver 3m, 10m '71 Bolzano competition; gold 1m, 3m '73 Australian jr. ntls, silver 10m, bronze 1m '73 Australian sr. ntls; bronze 3m '74 USSR; bronze 10m '75 NZ Games; mem. '76 Olympic team; ret'd from competition '76; swimming, diving instructor, lifeguard; res. Vancouver, B.C.

MacMARTIN, Andrew (triathlon); b. 23 Jul 1972, Montreal, Que.; given name: Andrew Christopher; triathlete; bronze Cdn ski marathon '88; Que. triathlon title '89; jr. Commonwealth silver '90; 2 ntl men's titles; 5 world cup victories; mem. '92 gold medal team world championships; gold Tampa International '94; ranked #1 world ITU ratings '92; awarded Juan Antonio Samaranch trophy, *Triathlete Magazine* rookie of '92; res. Tucson, Ariz./Westmount, Que.

MacMILLAN, Billy (hockey); b. 7 Mar 1943, Charlottetown. P.E.I.; given name: William Stewart; m. Marjorie Linkletter; c. John, Anne, Susan; UMan, BPhE; hockey exec.; mem. ntl team '66-70; pro Toronto '70-72, Atlanta '72-73, NYI '73-77; NHL playing record: 446 games, 74 goals, 77 assists, 53 playoff games, 6 goals, 6 assists; coached Fort Worth '77-79 winning '78 CHL title; asst. coach Islanders '79-80; coach Colorado '80-81, GM '81; New Jersey coach-GM '82-83; CHL coach of the year '77-78 season; coach UPEI; mem. PEI Sports Hall of Fame; res. Charlottetown, P.E.I.

MacMILLAN, Sandy (sailing); b. 1 Jul 1952, Lunenburg, N.S.; Dalhousie; sailmaker; teamed with Glen Dexter, Andreas Josenhans to win world Soling titles '77, '80; mem. '74-76 NS title crews; '76 Olympic team; NS achievement award '77, Moosehead Sports award '80; mem. NS, Canada's Sports halls of fame; res. Tantallon, N.S.

MacNEIL, Al (hockey); b. 27 Sep 1935, Sydney, N.S.; given name: Allister Wences; m. Norma; c. Allison, Alister; def Toronto Marlboros jrs.; NHL '55-68 Toronto, Montreal, Chicago, NYR, Pittsburgh; NHL record: 524 scheduled games, 17g, 75a, 37 playoff games, 0g, 4a; mem. 2 Stanley Cup winners; coach Houston Apollos; Canadiens, Stanley Cup rookie season '70; GM/coach NS Voyageurs (AHL) '71-77, 4 1st place finishes, 3 Calder Cups; asst. Team Canada Canada Cup teams '76, '81; head coach Calgary '79-92 (interim '03); NHL coaching record: 138-113-55; AGM Calgary '82-89; dir. hockey operations Calgary from '90; mem. Sydney, NS sports halls of fame; res. Calgary, Alta.

MacPHERSON, Kitch (basketball); b. 11 June 1916, Hamilton, Ont.; d. 17 Oct 1998, Hamilton, Ont.; given name: Herbert Horatio Kitchener; m. Jessie Park; c. Catharine, Edward; ret'd stereotyper; officiated 27 years, 1st Canadian to hold international referee card; officiated PAG '59, Russian ntl team tour of US '60, '62, Manila world games '62, PAG '67, Philadelphia World Cup '68; supervisor Western Division OUAA referees; CIAU Coaches award, Ont. service to basketball award; OUA championship MVP trophy bears his name; Fox 40 Kitch MacPherson award of excellence Sports Officials Canada award; OUA men's basketball award bears his name; mem. Ont., Cdn Basketball Hall of Fame.

MacPHERSON, Michelle (swimming); b. 11 May 1966, Toronto, Ont.; m. John Hojnacki; c. Zachary, Dylan; Cincinnati; began swimming at Pointe Claire, Que.; 5 ntl butterfly, 6 IM titles; 2 Canada Cup butterfly, 3 IM titles; 2 ntl, 1 CG records; gold 4x100 medley relay, bronze 100m butterfly, 400m IM '82 CG; silver 4x100 MR, 200m IM, 100m butterfly, bronze 400m IM '83 PAG; mem. 4x100 bronze medley relay '84 Olympics; 4yrs all-American; asst. swim coach Cincinnati; Ont. achievement award '81, Metro Toronto recognition award '82, fed. govt. excellence award '83; mem. Ont. Aquatic Hall of Fame; res. Chandler, Ariz.

MacRITCHIE, Kay (basketball); b. 22 Jan 1922, Saskatoon, Sask.; m. Donald Ross MacBeth; c. Donald Malcolm, Kerry; mem. Edmonton, Vancouver softball title teams '34-51; HS hj/lj/swimming titles; basketball with variety of Edmonton, Vancouver teams '37-50; most notable was '38-40 tenure with famed Edmonton Grads, one of only 38 women to play on team during its 25yr history of unparalleled success; as mem. of prov., Western Cdn title Vancouver Hedlunds '40-46, mem. BC Sports Hall of Fame; as Grad mem. Canadian Basketball, Alta. Sports, Softball halls of fame; res. Comox, B.C.

MacTAVISH, Craig (hockey); b. 15 Aug 1958, London, Ont.; m. Debbie; c. Nathan, Sean; US college hockey Lowell, Mass.; coach; ctr Binghamton, Springfield, Erie (AHL); drafted by Boston '79; NHL with Boston '79-84, Edmonton '85-94, NYR '94, Philadelphia '94-96, St. Louis '96-97; mem. 4 Stanley Cup winners; 1 NHL all-star game; team capt. Edmonton '93-95; last player to play entire NHL career without helmet; asst coach Rangers '97-99, Oilers '99, Oilers head coach '00-04; NHL record: 1093 scheduled games, 213g, 267a, 193 playoff games, 20g, 38a; NHL coaching record (through '03) 245 scheduled games, 113-89-35-16; res. Edmonton, Alta.

MACVICAR, Don (powerlifting); b. 10 Jun 1956, Glace Bay, N.S.; given name: Donald Frank; m. Carole; purchasing dept. Dofasco Steel; began lifting career '78; a diminutive 4-11, 114 pounds he lifted 10 times his body weight and in '82 was judged strongest man in Canada; 4 ntl, 5 Ont. titles; never defeated in Canada; 38 ntl records; 2 NA titles; 1 Eastern Cdn title; World Cup silver '80; World Games silver '81; competed throughout Canada and US and in England, India, Sweden; ret'd '83; organized church youth group, floor hockey league; basketball coach; plays flute in church band; NA weightlifting drug marshal; nicknamed "Mighty Mite"; mem. Copps Coliseum Sports Wall, Nova Scotia Sports Hall of Fame; res. Stoney Creek, Ont.

MADDIN, Janet (t&f); b. 4 May 1949, Winnipeg, Man.; m. Allan Neale; c. Heather, David; SFU, BA, UMan, BEd; teacher; sprinter; set 6 ntl, 16 Man. records, won 4 ntl championship gold '64; 2 ntl age-group, 1 ntl open, 4 ntl championship gold '66; competed '66 BEG; silver '67 PAG; set ntl age-group 400m record '68; mem. Cdn CG team '70; set world indoor 300m record '70; Olympic team alternate '64; Man. jr. athlete of '64; Daniel McIntyre CI outstanding athlete, Gov.-Gen.'s medal '66; mem. Man. Sports Hall of Fame; res. Winnipeg, Man.

MAGNUSON, Keith (hockey); b. 27 Apr 1947, Wadena, Sask.; d. 15 Dec 2003, Vaughan, Ont.; given name: Keith Arlen; m. Cindy White; c. Kevin, Molly; Denver, BSc; sales exec. Coca-Cola; Denver '64-69, co-capt. Pioneers to 2 NCAA titles; def Chicago '69-79; NHL record: 589 scheduled games, 14g, 125a, 68 playoff games, 3g, 9a; mem. '69-70 league title team; chronic knee injury led to retirement '79; asst. coach Black Hawks '79-80, head coach '80-81; NHL coaching record: 132 scheduled games, 49-57-26; mem. Ill. AHA board; p-chair. NHL Alumni Assn.; p-pres. Chicago alumni assn.

MAGNUSSEN, Karen (figure skating); b. 4 Apr 1952, North Vancouver, B.C.; m. Tony Cella; c. 1 son; SFU.; skating teacher; ntl jr. singles '65, sr. '68, '70-73; mem. '68, '72 Olympic teams; NA title '71; silver '72 Olympics; world championship '73; pro Ice Capades to '73-77; BC junior athlete of '67; BC sports merit award '70; Bobbie Rosenfeld award '73; BC athlete of '72; 2 Velma Springstead awards; Officer Order of Canada '73; taught skating Boston area four years then ret'd to raise family; flag-bearer '72 winter Olympics; hon. head figure skating coach Special Olympics Assn.; BC Women in Sport Leaders & Legenda award; N.Van. rec. centre bears her name; mem. BC, Canada's Sports, Cdn Olympic, Cdn Figure Skating halls of fame; res. N.Vancouver, B.C.

MAH, Sy (t&f): b. 2 Aug 1926, Bagshaw, Alta; d. 7 Nov 1988, Toledo, Ohio; given name: Thian; Alta BA, McMaster BPHE, UofT BEd, MEd; physiology prof.; ran 1st marathon 6 May 1967 at Toronto; broke existing world marathon record with 198th '81; 200th marathon '81, 300th '83, 400th '86; at time of death had completed in world record 524 marathons; founder cardiac rehabilitation program Toledo; regarded by marathoners/ultramarathoners as outstanding competitor and inspiration to many distance runners; ultramarathon award bears his name; Toledo statue erected in his honor.

MAHER, Peter (hockey); b. 11 Nov 1946, Campbellton, N.B.; m. Nancy; hockey broadcaster; played minor hockey from age 13; conceived/promoted idea of NB North-South All-Star hockey game to raise funds for children/adults with intellectual disability; became voice of Maple Leafs '78, Flames from '80; Campbellton sportsman-of-yr awards '67, '88; mem. NB, Campbellton Sports halls of fame; res. Calgary, Alta.

MAHER, Peter (t&f); b. 30 Mar 1960, Ottawa,Ont.; m. Brenda; c. Kevin, Louise; radio station owner; investment consultant; marathon specialist; lived in Ireland '62-86 holding joint Cdn/Irish citizenship; Irish 800m, 1500m, 3000m titles; Irish road runner series title '86; 4 Around the Bay 30km titles, record 1:33.00; gold 2 Man., 1 Calif., Montreal, National Capital, Barbados, Hamilton; competed '88, '92 Olympics, '91, '93 Worlds, '95 Boston marathons; 3 Fred Begley Memorial trophies; marathon PB 2:11.46 '91; res. St. Petersburg, Fla.

MAHEY, Diane (field hockey); b. 20 Jan 1960, Victoria, B.C.; given name: Diane Lea; m. Shiaz Virjee; c. Arif; UVic; mem. UVic team '78-82, BC jr. team '78-80, BC sr. team '80-83; mem. ntl team '80-86 representing Canada in European competitions '80-82, World Cup competitions '80, '83; mem. '83 World Cup silver medal team; mem. '84 Olympic team; BC prov. team '80-92; UVic female athlete of '82; res. Vancouver, B.C.

MAHONY, Bill (swimming); b. 16 Sep 1949, New Westminster, B.C.; given name: William Victor; m. Fran Cruise; c. Cole, Laurel; UBC, BSc; investment research; bronze 200m breast stroke '66 CG silver 4x100 medley relay '67 PAG; semifinalist 100m breast stroke '68 Olympics; 3 gold in 100m, 200m breast stroke, 4x100 medley '70 CG; 4x100 medley relay silver '71 PAG; bronze 4x100 medley, semifinalist 100 breast stroke '72 Olympics; gold 4x100

medley '74 CG; numerous ntl sr. records '66-74; 1st Cdn to break 2:40 and 2:30 breast stroke barriers; worked with handicapped children; helped establish BC Cerebral Palsey Sports Assn.; mem. BC Sports, BC Swimming, Cdn Aquatic halls of fame; res. Surrey, B.C.

MAHORN, Atlee (t&f); b. 27 Oct 1965, Clarendon, Jamaica; California (Berkley); sprinter; moved to Canada '80; began competing age 16; competed '88, '92 Olympic, '86, '94 CG, '85 FISU Games; gold 200m, 4x100 relay '86 CG; gold 100m ntl outdoor jr., sr., BYU relays, 200m ntl outdoor jr, 3 sr., 2 Nice France, 1 *Victoria Times-Colonist*, Harry Jerome, 400m Arizona State, 300m Great Britain; 1 ntl jr, 5 ntl sr records; Phil Edwards Memorial Trophy '91; '87 sport excellence award; PB 10.16 100m, 20.17 200m; res. Montreal, Que.

MAHOVLICH, Frank (hockey); b. 10 Jan 1938, Timmins, Ont.; given name: Francis William; m. Marie; c. Michael, Nancy, Teddy; St. Michael's College, Assumption College; Senator, ret'd travel agent; jr. St. Michael's College; OHA junior all-star, Red Tilson Memorial Trophy (MVP) '56-57; baseball talents attracted pro offer Boston Red Sox; strong competitive swimmer; pro Maple Leafs '57-68; Calder Memorial Trophy NHL rookie of year; Red Wings '68-71, Canadiens '71-74; Toronto (later Birmingham) WHA '74-78; 3 times NHL first team, 6 times 2nd team all-star lw; tied Phil Esposito for Stanley Cup playoff points 1 yr with 27, including record 14 goals; NHL record: 1181 scheduled games, 533g, 570a, 137 playoff games, 51g, 67a; best single season '68-69 with Detroit scoring 49 goals; played with brother Pete while with Montreal; mem. Team Canada '72; appointed to Cdn Senate '98; featured on Cdn postage stamps; mem. Order of Canada, Order of St. Michael's, Ont. Legends, Canada's Sports, Hockey halls of fame; res. Toronto, Ont.

MAHOVLICH, Pete (hockey); b. 10 Oct 1946, Timmins, Ont.; given name: Peter Joseph; div.; c. Peter Jr., Jeffrey, Margaret-Ann; m. Elise; broadcaster, hockey coach, scout; ctr jr A Hamilton Red Wings; second overall '63 amateur draft; with brief stints at Pittsburgh (AHL), Fort Worth (CPHL) mem. Detroit '65-69; Montreal '69-78, Pittsburgh '78-79, Detroit '79-81, Adirondack (AHL) '80-83; NHL record: 884 scheduled games, 288g, 485a, 88 playoff games, 30g, 42a; mem. Team Canada '72, '76, 4 Stanley Cup winners; TV broadcaster New Jersey; area scout San Jose '92-94; GM/coach Ft. Worth (CHL); scout NYR '86-87; coach Toledo (IHL); coach/GM Adirondack; coach Cape Breton (AHL) '94-95; scout Edmonton '95-97, Tampa Bay '97-99, Atlanta from '99; res. Bolton Landing, N.Y.

MAIN, Lorne (tennis); b. 9 Jul 1930, Vancouver, B.C.; given name: Lorne Garnet; m. Ivy Malloy (d); c. Kelly, Kevin, Kristine, Kasey; California (Berkeley); tennis pro; ntl jr. singles '46, '47, '48; US jr. hardcourt title '47; with Jim McGregor '46 jr. doubles; ntl men's doubles (with Brendan Macken) '51, (Luis Ayala) '54; ntl mixed doubles (Barbara Knapp) '50; playing mem. Davis Cup team '49-55 (10-11 record), non-playing capt. 5 times; ranked #1 '51-54; with Bob Bedard defeated Chile, Australia and US team of Vic Seixas, Hugh Stewart to win '76 Stevens Cup; victory over Ayala, Belgium, Monte Carlo titles '54 career highlights; from '75-98 won 18 srs singles titles in 45, 55, 60, 65, 70 divs. mem. 20 Gordon Cup teams; competed 17 world srs. championships winning 5 singles titles; with Ken Sinclair 4 consec. Austria Cup 55+ team titles, Von Cramm Cup (60), Britannia Cup (65), 6 world doubles titles; ITF world singles/doubles (for 70-75) titles '99; with Sinclair won '99 Jack Crawford Cup; proficient squash player; teamed with David Pemberton-Smith for 4 consec ntl titles '60-63; suffered effects of alcoholism; mem. Cdn Tennis Hall of Fame; res. Aurora, Ont./Florida.

MAKOLOSKY, Randy (t&f); b. 26 Jul 1953, Calgary, Alta.; given name: Randall Samuel; m. Tina Maureen Groszko; UCal; Bay dept. mgr.; ntl jr. 800m record 1:48.9 ('70); with Bill Crothers shared sr. 800m indoor record 1:49.5 ('74); 3 times ntl sr. indoor 800m champion; mem. ntl team '73-75; last known res. Calgary, Alta.

MAKOWSKY, Gene (football); b. 17 Apr 1973, Saslatoon, Sask.; USask; t/g; mem. 2 Hardy Cup title teams; Can-West conf. all-star; lineman of '93 award; drafted Saskatchewan Roughriders '95; through '04 163 scheduled games, including 32 in succession; played 1 Grey Cup final; CFL outstanding-lineman award '04; res. Regina, Sask.

MALAR, Joanne (swimming); b. 30 Oct 1975, Hamilton, Ont.; m. Mike Morraele; UCal; coach Hamilton-Wentworth Aquatic Clmade intl debut '90 CG; 4 silver, 1 bronze '91, 2 gold, 3 silver, 1 bronze '95, 3 gold, 1 silver, 1 bronze '99, 1 gold, 1 silver, 1 bronze '03 PAG; competed '92, '96, '00 Olympics, '93, '99 (2 gold) Pan-Pacific, 3 world short course championships, bronze '94, 1 gold, 2 silver, 2 bronze '98 CG; 2 CIAU female-swimmer-of-yr awards; 3 CIAU records; ret'd briefly '01 with total of 71 intl medals; made '03 comeback to win ntl 400m title; invitational swim meet bears her name; res. Hamilton, Ont.

MALCOLM, Andrew (all-around); b. 15 Sep 1901, Saint John N.B.; d. 23 Jan 1986, Saint John, N.B.; m. Jean Harding; c. Jean, Bruce; wholesale merchant; capt. Saint John HS rugby, basketball teams, co-captained t&f team; intermediate basketball through '21, sr. Trojans through '32, capt. 11yrs, 9 NB, 8 Maritime, 1 Eastern title; beat Windsor, Ont., for '32 Eastern title but lost international title to Winnipeg Toilers; led scorers in each series they played; coached Saint John HS basketball team '28-33; refereed basketball several yrs including Cdn Interscholastic championships '33. ntl sr. championships '30; Maritime shot put record '24, ntl title '24, '27; 3 gold, 1 silver, 2 bronze '25 ntl championships; led city league baseball batters '22; nicknamed "Beef"; nominated '50 *CP* poll athletes of half century; Andrew Malcolm Trophy awarded annually by YMCA to Saint John male athlete of year; mem. NB Sports Hall of Fame.

MALONE, Joe (hockey); b. 28 Feb 1890, Quebec City, Que., d. 15 May 1969, Montreal, Que.; tool maker; began organized hockey '07 Crescent jrs; pro Waterloo '09, Quebec '10-17, '19-20, Montreal Canadiens '17-19, '22-24, Hamilton '20-22; NHL scoring record 7 goals in single game with Que. Bulldogs vs Toronto St. Pats '20; '17-18 season 44 goals in 22-game schedule; '19-20 scored 39 goals, 6 assists in 24-game schedule; pro career record 379 goals; capt.-coach 2 Que. Stanley Cup winners; "Phantom Joe"; 9 goals vs. Sydney Millionaires '13 Stanley Cup playoff

game, 8 goals one game vs. Wanderers '17; mem. Hockey Hall of Fame.

MALONEY, Don (hockey); b. 5 Sep 1958, Lindsay, Ont.; given name: Donald Michael; m. Toni; c. Donald Jr,; hockey exec.; lw Kitchener jrs '75-77; minor pro New Haven (AHL); NHL with NYR '79-89, Hartford '89-90, NYI '90-91; NHL record: 765 scheduled games, 214g, 350a, 94 playoff games, 22g, 35a; played in 2 NHL all-star games, MVP '84 game; AGM Islanders '92-95; Eastern pro scout San; '96-97; AGM Rangers '97-04 (simultaneously GM Hartford AHL); coached Hartford (AHL) to Calder Cup '00; scored with initial shot in NHL vs. Boston '79; set record (since broken) for rookie point scoring (20) in Stanley Cup playoffs '79; Rangers Crumb Bum, Good Guy awards, 3 Rangers Players' Player awards; mem. silver medal Team Canada world championship team; AGM Cdn '03 IIHL world gold medal team; res. Rye, N.Y.

MALONEY, Phil (hockey); b. 6 Oct 1927, Ottawa, Ont.; given name: Philip Francis; m. Patricia Ludlow Drake; c. Pippa, Shelagh, Maggie, Robyn; St. Pat's Coll; ret'd hockey exec., equipment sales; raised in Sandy Hill region where he wass on several school title teams; played center Que. Sr. league with Shawinigan Falls; turned pro with Hershey (AHL) '48; saw other AHL duty with Pittsburgh '50-54, Buffalo '59-61; NHL Boston '49-51, Toronto '51-53, Chicago '58-60; QHL Ottawa '53-55; WHL Vancouver '54-59, '61-70; through 23 pro playing years amassed 1392 scheduled games, 505g, 916a, 112 playoff games, 42g, 68a; 1 AHL, 2 WHL MVP awards; 1 Stanley Cup; 2 WHL Patrick Cup teams; 1 WHL scoring title; 3 Fred Hume; 1 Les Cunningham award; co-holder 2 WHL scoring records; WHL playoff scoring record 25pts 11 games; 5 WHL all-star; Vancouver held "night" in his honor; on retirement as player became Vancouver scout before turning to coaching with WHL Seattle; coached Vancouver NHL '73-76; also Canucks GM '74-77; mem. BC Hockey Hall of Fame; res. Ladysmith, B.C.

MALTBY, Kirk (hockey); b. 22 Dec 1972, Guelph, Ont.; rw Owen Sound (OHL) '89-92, Cape Breton (AHL) '92-93, '95; NHL Edmonton '93-96, Detroit '96-04; OHL rookie of '90, 2 MVP awards 1yr capt. Owen Sound; CHL all-star game '92; with Cape Breton '93 Calder Cup; Team Canada '04 World Cup (gold); NHL record (through '04) 717 scheduled games, 102g, 109a, 113 playoff games, 13g, 11a; 2 Stanley Cup winners; res. Cambridge, Ont.

MANAHAN, Cliff (curling); b. 11 Oct 1888, Fort William, Ont., d. 20 Mar 1970, Edmonton, Alta.; given name: Clifford Ross; m. Elizabeth Ann Jones, (d), m. Mary Watson McAndrew Eckert; c. Ross (d), Robert, Donald, Doris, Kathleen, June, Marjorie, Dawn; civil servant; 8 Alberta, 9 Northern Alta. titles; mem. 5 Brier entries, '33, '37, winners; 7 Alta. CA and grand aggregate, 8 Edmonton grand challenge titles; winner 65 major championships; life mem. Alta. CA, Royal Glenora CC, Granite CC of Edmonton; mem. Edmonton, Alta. Sports, Canadian Curling halls of fame.

MANDARICH, Tony (football); b. 23 Sep 1966, Oakville, Ont.; Michigan State; owner/GM Century Pines GC; NFL tackle Green Bay '89-92, Indianapolis '96-98; 1st round draft

Green Bay '89; nickname "Incredible Bulk"; hosts annual celebrity charity gold tournament; res. Flamborough, Ont.

MANIAGO, Cesare (hockey); b. 13 Jan 1939, Trail, B.C.; goalie St. Mike's OHA, Sudbury, Hull-Ottawa EPHL, (1 all-star), Vancouver, Spokane WHL, Quebec, Buffalo, Baltimore AHL, Omaha, Minneapolis CPHL, 1 all-star; NHL Toronto '60-61, Montreal '62-63, NYR '65-67, Minnesota '67-76, Vancouver '76-78; NHL totals: 568 scheduled games, 32,570 minutes, 189-259-96, 30sho, 36 playoffs, 2245 minutes, 15-21-0, 3sho; asst. coach Vancouver '88-89; CHL Tommy Ivan MVP award '65; Terry Sawchuk trophy; allowed Bernie Geoffrion's 50th goal '61, Bobby Hull's 51st goal '66; recognized as superb team player/inspirational leader; mem. BC Hockey Hall of Fame; res. Trail, B.C.

MANLEY, Elizabeth (figure skating); b. 7 Aug 1965, Belleville, Ont.; given name: Elizabeth Ann; coach; initial 1st place finish pre-novice ladies '74; 1st Eastern Ontario sectionals victory juv B ladies '75; EO sectional novice ladies '77; EO sectionals, eastern divisionals jr. ladies '79; 2nd ntl jr. ladies '80; 3rd eastern divisionals, ntl sr. ladies, jr. worlds '81; 2nd ntl sr. singles '84; mem. '84 Olympic, world championship teams; 1st woman in Canada to land a triple combination in competition; silver '88 Olympics; US Open pro title '97; Orleans, Ont. arena, park, pool named in her honor; authored *Thumbs Up*; co-owner skating tour; coach with Kerry Leitch in Ellenton, Fla '00; mem. Order of Canada, Cdn Olympic, Ottawa Sports, Cdn. Figure Skating halls of fame; res. Ellenton, Fla.

MANN, Avard (curling); b. 18 Sep 1894, Elgin, N.B., d. 8 Apr 1984, Truro, N.S.; m. Mable; c. Lloyd (d), Bob (d), Phyllis; ret'd; class AA Maritime skeet title '38; 3 NS junior curling titles; 3 times NS Brier rep.; NS seniors title '65, Maritime Johnson senior championship; mem. NS Sports Hall of Fame.

MANN, Bob (curling); b. 5 Jan 1922, Truro, N.S.; d. 1995, Mississauga, Ont. m. Lena (d); c. Bob, Susan, Patricia, Sandy; ret'd regional sales manager; mem. NS jr. hockey champions '39-40; 6yrs sr. hockey Truro Bearcats; refereed Big Six League '50-51; NS class A skeet title '48; 3 times NS Consols finalist, 5 times Ont. finalist; rep. NS '60 Brier, Ont. '63-64; OCA Silver Tankard '68., OCA intermediate '72, finalist OCA srs '75-76; 3rd Tournament of Champions, Maple Leaf Gardens '64.

MANN, Dave (football); b. 6 Feb 1932, Berkeley, Calif; given name: David Carl; div. Gail; c. Angela, Melissa, David; m. Susan; Oregon State; salesman, actor, restaurateur; Chicago Cardinals 3yrs; Argos '58, '60-70; rb, carried ball 107 times for 556 yds, caught 33 passes for 319 yds; appeared in 155 league, 13 playoff games; 2nd in Argos all-time scoring records with 435 points (33td, 73c, 22fg, 98s); punter '60-70 with 1261 punts for 55,745yds including 1 for 102 yds; twice scored tds on punt returns; handled 139 kickoffs for 7862yds and as returner carried 36 for 755 yds; EFC all-star team '45-73; nicknamed "Superman"; res. Mississauga, Ont.

MANN, David (archery); b. 1 Oct 1957, Vancouver, B.C.; given name: David Lorne; m. Wendy Killick; UBC, BPhE, UAlta, MSc; medical doctor; Vancouver target champion '72-73; mem. ntl team '75-78; mem. '75, '77 world target championship, '76 Olympic (7th), world field championship, '76, '78 Tournament of the Americas teams; 4 of 5 ntl records for single-round international (FITA) competition; CAC coaching scholarship '79; level 4 coaching certificate; res. Calgary, Alta.

MANNING, Peter (t&f); b. 6 Apr 1931, Romford, Essex, Eng.; given name: Peter George; m. Myra Laycock; c. Helen Jane, Gillian Claire, Sarah Louise; London, Man; ret'd sports management co. owner; dir. Manitoba CTFA '67-70, CTFA coach of '74, runnerup Air Canada award '74; coached 1600m relays '76 Olympics; coached '76, '84, '88, '92 Olympic, '78, '90 CG, '79 PAG teams; ntl co-ordinator sr. sprints, relays '89-96; res. Guelph, Ont.

MANTHA, Sylvio (hockey); b. 14 Apr 1903, Montreal, Que., d. Aug 1974, Montreal, Que.; Notre Dame de Grace jrs. '18-19; moved through intermediate, sr ranks to QSHL Nationals before turning pro; fwd as amateur, def as pro Montreal Canadiens '23-36, Boston '36-37; mem. 9 Prince of Wales Trophy, 3 Stanley Cup winners; player-coach with Habs '35-36; 2 seasons as NHL linesman, AHL referee; coach jr., sr. teams several years; twice 2nd team all-star; NHL record: scored 63g, 72a; mem. Hockey Hall of Fame.

MARA, George (hockey); b. 12 Dec 1921, Toronto, Ont.; given name: George Edward; m. Margaret Roddick; c. George Jr., Diane; Upper Canada College; chair. Jannock Ltd.; Jr. B at 15, Jr. A Toronto Marlboros '41; mem. Toronto Navy team '42; rejected pro offers from Toronto, NYR, Detroit; mem. '48 RCAF Flyers Olympic champions; founded Olympic Trust '71; gov. Olympic Trust; Canada Medal, Cdn Olympic Order; mem. Order of Canada, Cdn Olympic, Ottawa Sports, Canada's Sports halls of fame; res. Don Mills, Ont.

MARANDA, Veronique (soccer); b. 18 Aug 1986, Saint Lambert, Que.; midfielder ntl -19 team, WC team, W-League Montreal Xtreme; mem. '03 Pan-Am Games team; made WC debut '03; 18 intl caps; res. Saint Lambert, Que.

MARCH, Bill (mountaineering); b. 14 Dec 1941, Chelmsford, Eng.; d. 8 Sep 1990, Inverness, B.C.; given name: William Joseph; m. Karen Louise Kreutzweiser; c. Anthony James; King's Coll, London, Lougnborough Coll, Idaho State; prof.; began climbing UofLondon '59; deputy dir. Glenmore Lodge national outdoor training centre '67-74; dir. UK mountaineering centre '76-77; co-ordinator outdoor pursuit program UCal '77-83; 80 1st ascents Scotland, Canada, Ecuador, US; 4 Himalaya expeditions; leader '82 Mt. Everest expedition which placed 2 Cdns, 4 Sherpas on summit; author 3 mountaineering books; ashes scattered atop Mt. Everest '98 by Tom Whittaker, 1st disabled person to reach summit; mem. International Assn. of Mountain Guides; Alta Sports Hall of Fame Special Award.

MARCHAND, Claude (parachuting); b. 20 Nov 1954, Quebec City, Que.; m. Louise Poitras; aviation mechanic; began skydiving '74; more than 1500 jumps; won ntl 8-way '78-80; 4-way '80; mem. Cdn 2nd place 8-way, alternate 1st place 4-way team France '79, 2nd place 4-way team China '80; res. Abbotsford, B.C.

MARCHILDON, Phil (baseball); b. 25 Oct 1913, Penetanguishene, Ont.; d. 10 Jan 1997, Toronto, Ont.; given name: Phillip Joseph; m. Irene Patience; c. Dawna, Carol; St. Michael's College; ret'd hospital furnishing co. employee; pitched Penetang intermediates to Ont. finals '30's, Creighton Mines to Nickle Belt title and provincial finals '38; 2 seasons with Toronto Maple Leafs (IL), part of one with Cornwall (Can-Am) before joining Connie Mack's Athletics '40; 17-14 record with A's '42; honored by fans with Marchildon night Philadelphia '45; 19-9 record '47 with 1-hitter, 2 2-hitters; closed pro career Boston '50; Senior Intercounty Guelph, Waterloo; ML record: 185 games, 68-75, 481k, 6so, 3.93era; spent 9mos German POW camp WW2; co-authored *Ace, Phil Marchildon*; mem. Canadian Baseball, Etobicoke, Canada's, Ont. Legends Sports halls of fame.

MARECHEK, Bill (lacrosse); b. 12 Jun 1955, Kitchener, Ont.; department mgr.; began playing age 13; mem. McDonald's Bread Jr. A '74, Nepean Lumbermen Jr. '75-76, Victoria Payless '76-81, '92, Victoria Royal Waxmen '80-92, ntl team '81-96; 7 Cdn field lacrosse title teams; Victoria Shamrocks '79 Mann Cup winner; noted for strong stickhandling ability, deft scoring touch; named to '90 all-world team; res. Victoria, B.C.

MARECHEK, Tom (lacrosse); b. 25 Aug 1968, Kitchener, Ont.; Syracuse; coach; mem. Victoria Royal Waxmen '85-88, Esquimalt Jr. Legion '85-89, Syracuse Orangemen '89-92, Philadelphia Wings '94-00, Baltimore Bayhawks '01-03; ntl team '89-98; 6 1st team, 2 2nd team all-pro; 2 NLL all-star, 2 NLL title teams; mem. 2 NCAA, 4 ntl field title teams; top scorer '88 Minto Cup winner; 4 all-American; 4th all-time NCAA goal scorer; 2 runnerup NCAA attackman-of-year; mem. '90 Mann Cup winners; MILL rookie of '94; res. Baltimore, Md.

MAREK, Deb (ringette); b. 8 Mar 1962, Winnipeg, Man.; Manitoba B.Comm; coach; information-marketing officer Lethbridge leisure services; versatile athlete who played and coached both field and ice hockey as well as ringette at national level; as goalie claimed ntl ringette gold '82, '83, '85-87 with Team Man., '90, '92, '94 with Team Alta.; coached Team Alta. to gold '96-97; goaltender '90, '92, coach '96 Cdn world gold medal teams; coach ntl team to '00; res. Lethbridge, Alta.

MARIN, Violaine (shooting); b. 5 Apr 1956, Montréal, Qué.; m. Marcel J. Rheault; c. Geneviéve, Guillaume; Cégep Ahuntsic, graphic design; medical secretary; named to Qué. pistol team '91, ntl pistol team '92; Qué. air and sport pistol winner in almost all Qué. championships from '94; placed in the top positions for air and sport pistol at every ntl championships from '95; Cdn record '96 ntl air pistol championships; mem. '95, '99 PAG; '98, '02 CG teams; SFC 25th anniversary female pistol shooter award '03; res. St-Léonard, Qué.

MARINKO, Max (table tennis); b. 30 Sep 1916, Ljubljana, Yugoslavia; d. 26 Aug 1975, Toronto, Ont.; teacher; only player to represent 3 countries, Yugoslavia (1), Czechoslovakia (2), Canada (1), world Swaythling Cup (men's team) championships; mem. 2 title winners Czechoslovakia; moved to Canada '54; 9 ntl men's closed singles, '58 men's open singles, doubles, '57 mixed open doubles; finalist '58 US men's open singles; mem. ITTF Swaythling Cup Club; mem. 30 Cdn international team competitions; Perc McLeod Memorial Award for contribution to table tennis.

MARION, Alain (shooting); b. 23 Dec 1946, Pointe Gatineau, Que.; div.; c. Karine; ret'd police officer; 22 Que. small-bore prone-rifle, 2 free-rifle titles; mem. 4 ntl small-bore title teams; through '04 qualified Bisley teams record 36 times, competed 24 times; 14 Bisley Queen's finals; Queen's Prize Bisley '80, '83, '96 (Cdn record), silver medal '72, 3rd '87, '90; Bisley grand aggregate '90, silver cross '73-80; Cdn record 8 ntl (CTR Bisley Agg.) championships; 10 Macdonald Stewart grand aggregate titles; Gov.-Gen.'s prize '85, '96, '00, 5 times runnerup; gold, silver '86, silver '98 CG; mem. '74, '86, '98 CG team; mem. 8 Cdn Palma teams; team gold '72, '82, silver '92 Palma matches; mem. DCRA council, executive; mem. Order of Canada, Ottawa Sports Hall of Fame; res. Hull, Que.

MARKER, Gus (hockey); b. 1905, Wetaskiwin, Alta.; d. 7 Oct 1997, Kingston, Ont.; given name: August Solberg; m. Lillian Malroney; owner building supply, concrete co.; didn't begin skating until he was 14 but proved a natural; began pro career Tulsa (AHA) '28; forward NHL '32-42 with Detroit, Montreal Maroons, Toronto, Brooklyn; mem. 1 Stanley Cup winner; mgr./coach Tulsa 2yrs; NHL record: 322 scheduled games, 64g, 69a; 46 playoff games, 5g, 7a.

MARKLE, Jean (horseshoes); b. 22 Jul 1938, Clapham, London, Eng.; given name: Jean Palmer; m. Larry Markle; c. Dawn; exec. secty; emigrated to Canada '61; asst. to ntl assn. pres. George Schummer '69-73; secty-treas. Horseshoe Canada '73-84; treas./tournament director Horseshoe Canada '79-91; asst. to rgnl. dir. Jack Adams NHPA from '73; authored tournament manual; conducted numerous seminars; life mem. Horseshoe Canada; mem. '97 world championships org. comm.; charter mem. Horseshoe Canada, mem. Cdn, Ont. Horseshoe halls of fame; res. Hamilton, Ont.

MARKLE, Larry (horseshoes); b. 8 Apr 1919, Napanee, Ont.; m. Jean Palmer; c. Dawn; carpenter; began pitching horseshoes age 14; military service interrupted play and he didn't return to game until '53; Hamilton champion '61; 8 Ont., Cdn senior men's titles; ntl intermediate men's title '82; competed 12 world tourneys; dir. Horseshoe Ont.; mem. Cdn., Ont. Horseshoe halls of fame; res. Hamilton, Ont.

MARLEAU, Patrick (hockey); b. 15 Sep 1979, Aneroid, Sask.; ctr Seattle (WHL) '95-97; NHL San Jose '97-04; Team Canada '04 World Cup (gold); NHL record (through '04) 558 scheduled games, 153g, 174a, 51 playoff games, 19g, 12a; with Trent McCleery established foundation to assist needy children; res. San Jose, Calif.

MARQUETTE, Ulla (t&f); b. 28 Jun 1958, Edmonton, Alta.; m.; c. Maianna; teacher; long distance runner; 2 CIAU 1500m titles; '85 ntl 3000m title; CIAU 1500m record; competed world cup, x-country, FISU Games; 3 CIAU x-country all-Cdn; ntl 10km titles '91-92, 3000m title '92; gold 10,000m Harry Jerome Classic '94; ntl 10,000m title '94; res. Sooke, B.C.

MARSH, Brad (hockey); b. 31 Mar 1958, London, Ont.; given name: Charles Bradley; m. Patty Quaile; c. Erik, Patrick, Victoria, Madeline; restaurateur, hockey exec.; def London (OHA) '74-78; with Rob Ramage co-winner Max Kaminsky trophy '78; twice all-star; claimed by Atlanta '79 expansion draft; played in NHL with Atlanta '78-80, Calgary '80-81, Philadelphia '81-88, Toronto '88-91, Detroit '91-92, Ottawa '92-93; NHL record: 15 seasons, 1086 scheduled games, 23g, 175a, 97 playoff games, 6g, 18a; res. Kanata, Ont.

MARSH, Lou (builder); b. 1878 Campbellford, Ont., d. 4 Mar 1936, Toronto, Ont.; given name: Lewis Edwin; journalist; defeated Bobby Kerr in 100yd race; hockey, boxing referee; 43yrs *Toronto Star* sports dept., editor; trophy in his name awarded annually to Canada's outstanding athlete.

MARSHALL, Blake (football); b. 17 May 1965, Guelph, Ont.; UWO; fb; pro Edmonton '87-93; CFL record: 88 scheduled games, 65tds, 523 carries for 2,449yds, 54tds, 143 receptions for 1,467yds, 11tds, 9 playoff games, 5tds; 3 all-Western, 3 all-CFL all-star; GMC outstanding Canadian '91; Dr. Beattie Martin trophy '91; tied CFL record 20tds single season '91; mem. 3 Grey Cup finalists, 2 winners; mem. UWO W Club Hall of Fame; res. Edmonton, Alta.

MARSHALL, Don (hockey); b. 23 Mar 1932, Verdun, Que.; given name: Donald Robert; m. Betty; c. 4; lw Cincinnati Mohawks (IHL), Montreal Royals (QHL), Buffalo (AHL); NHL Montreal '51-52, '55-63, NYR '63-70, Buffalo '70-71, Toronto '71-72; Red Garrett Memorial trophy (AHL) '54; mem. 5 Stanley Cup winners; NHL record: 1176 scheduled games, 265g, 324a, 94 playoff games, 8g, 15a; res. Stuart, Fla.

MARSHALL, Dru (field hockey/coaching); b. 2 Mar 1958, Winnipeg, Man.; given name: June Dru; UMan, BPhE, UAlta, MSc, PhD; assoc. prof/coach; father Tom played def for Allen Cup champion Winnipeg Maroons; ctr-half UMan '76-79, UAlta '80-81; twice shared scoring titles; coach UAlta Pandas '81-96; 2 CIAU ntl tournament bronze; 4 CWUAA, 2 CIAU, 1 3M Canada coach-of-yr awards; head coach ntl jr. women's team 9yrs; head coach ntl sr. women's team from '96; bronze '99 PAG, '01 Americas Cup; mem. UAlta Sports Wall of Fame; res. Edmonton, Alta.

MARSHALL, Greg (football); b. 9 Sep 1956, Beverley, Mass.; m. Cindy; c. Christine, Bryan, Caitlin, Kelsey; Oregon State; coach, teacher; PAC-10 all-star '77; drafted Philadelphia, played briefly NFL Baltimore '78; Ottawa '79-87; de; Schenley outstanding defensive player '83; *CBC-TV* coaches all-star, Ottawa def. MVP, Bill Smyth Memorial Trophy, Rothman lineman of year '83; 4 Eastern, 2 CFL all-star; James McCaffrey Memorial Trophy '83; CFL all-time all-star team; coach Ottawa Bootleggers '90, Ottawa Sooners '91-93; Cdn. Junior coach of year; asst. Saskatchewan '94-01, Edmonton '02-04, Ottawa '05; 1 Grey Cup winner; res. Ottawa, Ont.

MARSHALL, Jack (hockey); b. 14 Mar 1877, St. Vallier, Que., d. 7 Aug 1965, Montreal, Que.; mem 3 Caledonia Cup soccer winners '90s; '97 Britannia rugby title team; hockey fwd/def. 17yrs 7 different teams, 5 Stanley Cup winners; Winnipeg Victorias '01, Montreal Victorias '02-03, Wanderers '04-05, '07, '10-12, '16-17, Montagnards '07, Shamrocks '08-09, Toronto Arenas '13-15, twice led league scorers; player-mgr. Arenas '13-14, guided club to '14 Stanley Cup; 99 career goals in 132 league games, 13 in 18 playoff games; scored 6 goals in 1 game, 5 goals in two others; mem. Hockey Hall of Fame.

MARSHALL, Neal (speed skating); b. 13 Jun 1969, Victoria, B.C.; long-track sprint coach Olympic Oval; following with 3 brothers, great grandfather Klaas Hanje, a Dutch champion, and uncle Joe Janje, former Cdn ntl team mem; long-track specialist; competed '94 Olympics; 1st Cdn to win a World Cup overall title '95; 2nd overall for '96 WC circuit; 3 ntl records; 4 ntl distance skating awards; 3 outstanding Cdn-male-skater awards; ret'd from competition '98; *CTV* commentator; PetroCan coaching-excellence award; res. Calgary, Alta.

MARTEL, Marty (bowling); b. 1887, Cape Breton, d. 1958, Halifax, N.S.; given name: Wilbert; world candlepin record for single string 213, total 496 for three strings; helped form NS Wolverines, Allan Cup winners; mem. NS, Canada's sports halls of fame.

MARTELL, Henry (golf); b. 1913, Edmonton, Alta., d. 12 Jun 1984, Edmonton, Alta.; policeman, golf pro; 14 Edmonton City Open, 12 Edmonton City amateur, 9 Alta. amateur, 4 Alta. Open, 4 Sask. Open, 1 Ont. Open, '49 Cdn Amateur, '53, '58 CPGA, '66, '71 CPGA Seniors titles; 1st Albertan to win major ntl title; mem. 3 ntl teams; pro Edmonton Highlands GC '48-79; Edmonton junior tennis champion, mem. basketball title team; mem. Alta. Sports, RCGA halls of fame.

MARTENS, Camille (rhythmic gymnastics); b. 1 Jun 1976, Vancouver, B.C.; m. Patrick Yam; c. Micah Daniel Patrick, Anastasia Elyse; owner/operator/coach Okanagan Rhythmics gym club; began competing age 10; ntl jr '91, sr all-around title '94; competed '93 worlds, '94 CG, '96 Olympics; team gold, 4 individual silver '94 CG; BC novice title '86; Miss Elegance trophy '91 France international; res. Vernon, B.C.

MARTIN, Carol (t&f); b. 19 Apr 1948, Toronto, Ont.; given name: Carol Lynne; SFU, York, BA; track coach; bronze discus '66 CG 159'3"; silver '67 PAG 156'3"; silver '69 Pan-Pacific Games; bronze '70 CG 158'10"; won '72 Olympic trials; ntl record 55.45m '72; unexpectedly dropped from '72 Olympic team; gold '73 Pan-Pacific Games; bronze '74 CG, PB 56.60m; ret'd '76; discus, shot put coach UofT Track and Field Club; res. Palgrave, Ont.

MARTIN, Doug (swimming); b. 14 Dec 1955, Windsor, Ont.; given name: Douglas William; m. Laurie March; c. Brad, Jessica; SFU BA; management consultant; began competitive swimming age 7; variety of WSSA, OFSAA records; 5 ntl FS records; # NAIA all-America, title teams; 5 NAIA gold, 3 records; 2 Ont. Games gold '73; 1g, 1s, 3b Canada Games '73; ntl 1500 FS record; mem. ntl team '74-76; competed '75 PAG, worlds, '76 Olympics; ret'd from competition '77; diagnosed diabetic '80; Windsor Kinsmen athlete of '76; Ont. achievement award; chair. Ont. Olympians '88; chair. BC Olympians '03; mem. Windsor/Essex Sports Hall of Fame; res. Vancouver, B.C.

MARTIN, Flora Greenwood (curling/softball); b. 21 Jun 1916, Treherne, Man.; given name: Flora Mae Greenwood; m. Geoff Martin; c. Bill; mem. Treherne softball team which won 8 of 9 Manitoba tournaments '38-39; won 9 Vancouver Island ladies' curling titles; 6 Vancouver Island Sr. ladies' titles; skipped BC ntl entries in both Macdonald Lassie, Srs '74-75; ntl srs titles '74-75, '79-80, runnerup '81; mem. Vancouver Island O'Keefe mixed title rink '64; in lawn bowling Vancouver Island novice title '69; Vancouver Open singles '74, runnerup '75; runnerup BC pairs championships '74-75; master-athlete-of-yr finalist BC Sports Federation '74-75; hon. life mem. Victoria Curling Club; mem. Canadian Curling, Greater Victoria halls of fame; res. Victoria, B.C.

MARTIN, Frank (boxing); b. 25 Feb 1908, Montreal, Que.; m. Margot; c. Robert, Brian, Thelma; Strathcona Academy; ret'd fur trader, mechanic, hotelman; Montreal junior flyweight (112 lbs) champion '27; senior provincial, ntl titles '28; mem. '28 Olympic team; Montreal city, provincial bantamweight (118 lb) titles '29; pro '29 winning ntl bantam title and ranking 3rd in world; when top 2 ranked bantams refused to fight he moved into featherweight (126 lb) ranks and won ntl title to hold 2 crowns simultaneously; fought professionally 10yrs; while living in NWT 20yrs did some competitive dogsled racing; res. Atikokan, Ont.

MARTIN, Fritz (golf); b. 15 Sep 1869, York, Ont.; d. 19 May 1934, Hamilton, Ont.; with brother-in-law George S. Lyon engaged in numerous legendary matches; Cdn amateur titles '02, '10, twice runnerup; 1st lefthander to win Cdn. Amateur; Cdn Srs. title '27; pres. Hamilton G&CC '10, 5 times club capt.; 9 HG&CC titles, 5 times runnerup; 3 Hamilton Dist. titles; 3 times runnerup Niagara Invitation; Lambton Invitation title '06, twice runnerup; international cricketer, prominent curler, rugby football hb; mem. RCGA Hall of Fame.

MARTIN, Jacques (hockey/coaching); b. 1 Oct 1952, St. Pascal, Ont.; sep.; c. Angela, Nathalee; St. Lawrence Coll.; coach; began coaching career at St. Lawrence '76; coached at Algonquin Coll, Brockville, Hawkesbury in CJHL; asst./scout Peterborough; head coach Guelph (OHL) '86; won Memorial Cup; OHL coach of '86; head coach St. Louis (NHL) '86-88 winning 1 Norris div. title; asst. Chicago '88-90, Quebec '90-93; GM/head coach Cornwall (AHL) '93-94 winning Southern div. title; asst. Colorado '94-96 (Stanley Cup); head coach Ottawa '96-04, Florida '04-05; 3 Northeast div. titles, '03 President's Cup; Adams Trophy nominee '97, '01, '03 winner '99; Gordon Juckes award; *SN* coach of '99; head coach world team '00, East '03 all-stars; asst. '02 Olympic gold team, world '04 team; NHL coaching record (through '04) 852 scheduled games, 364-296-109-14; founder/operator Jacques Martin hockey school; res. Stittsville, Ont.

MARTIN, John (bowling); b. 30 Nov 1919, Toronto, Ont.; given name: John Martyn; sep.; c. Patricia, Wayne (d), Calvin, Michael, Ronald, Randall, John Jr., Kevin; bowling proprietor; 5-pin bowler, entered business with opening of O'Connor Bowl, Toronto, '51; major role in elimination of counter pin and adoption of new scoring system; through his efforts bowling became regular *CBC-TV* feature 9 yrs; annual O'Connor Open among country's top competitions

from '57; staged attractions such as ntl Invitational Singles, Rotary '50' Marathon; founding mem. Bowling Proprietors Assn. of Ont, Canada, p.-pres. of each; Builders of Bowling Industry Award '74; mem. Ont. 5-pin Bowling Hall of Fame; res. Toronto, Ont.

MARTIN, Kevin (curling); b. 31 Jul 1966, Killam, Alta.; m. Shauna; c. Karrick, Kalycia; owner Kevin's Curling Supplies; operates Kevin Martin's curling academy; skipped Alberta 6 Briers, winning twice; CCR 1st team all-star '96; silver '91 world championship; finalist '98 Olympic team qualifier bowling 6-5 to Ontario's Mike Harris; skipped '02 Olympic silver rink; won '97, '01 *TSN* Skins' Game, '03 M&M Skins title; 3 WCT titles; head World Curling Players Assn.; hosts annual jr. bonspiel; res. Edmonton, Alta.

MARTIN, Peter (football); b. 20 Oct 1940, Toronto, Ont.; given name: Peter Thomas Ross; m. Wendy Warwick; c. Cindy, Kristi, Peter James, Jennifer; UWO, BPhE; ret'd phys ed teacher, adult program leader Peel Board; co-capt., MVP UWO Mustangs '63; first college draft choice Ottawa '64; mem. East York Argos ntl sr. champions '64; CFL Argos lb '65-72; 103 league, 10 playoff games; radio commentator Argos games '77-94; SkyDome PA announcer for Argos games; pres. Argos alumni; res. Mississauga, Ont.

MARTIN, Pit (hockey); b. 9 Dec 1943, Noranda, Que.; given name: Hubert Jacques; m. Pat Gurniss; c. 4 daughters; McMaster; owns Windsor Pool Service; ex-restaurateur; mem. '58 NOHA title team; OHA Hamilton jrs.; 2 seasons Pittsburgh (AHL); ctr Detroit '63-65, Boston '65-67, Chicago '67-77, Vancouver '78-79; NHL record: 1101 scheduled games, 324g, 485a, 100 playoff games, 27g, 31a; Bill Masterton Memorial Trophy '70; licensed pilot; res. Tecumseh, Ont.

MARTIN, Rick (hockey); b. 26 Jul 1951, Verdun, Que.; given name: Richard Lionel; m. Martha; c. 3 sons; computer consultant; hockey coach; lw; Montreal Canadiens jrs.; 1st Buffalo draft '71; mem. Sabres '71-81, Los Angeles '81-82; with Rene Robert, Gil Perreault formed Buffalo's French Connection line; twice 1st, 2nd team all-star; scored 52g in both '74-75; Team Canada '76; retirement forced by injury; following lengthy court action was awarded $2.5M in medical malpractice suit '94; jersey #7 ret'd by Sabres; skill development coach Buffalo '03-04; NHL record: 685 scheduled games, 384g, 317a, 63 playoff games, 24g, 29a; res. Buffalo, N.Y.

MARTIN, Robert (t&f); b. 23 Jul 1950, Paris, Ont.; given name: Robert John; m. Mary Kerr; c. Nicole Ann; St. Andrew's College, Oregon, BSc; pres. Marco Sales, Incentives Ltd.; mem. Hamilton Spartan TC; track scholarship Oregon '70-74; ntl jr. outdoor 100m, 200m titles '69, indoor 50m '70; NCAA all-American Oregon '71; ntl sr. 100m, 200m champion '72; Pan-Pacific finalist, ntl 200m titlist '73-74, '77; mem. '74 CG, '74-75 European tour, '75 PAG, '76 Olympic, '77 FISU Games teams; bronze, Cdn record PAG 4x100m relay, double silver medalist US Games, 4th NZ Games '75; national sr. indoor 50m title '76; ntl record 4x200m relay team '77; res. Brantford, Ont.

MARTIN, Seth (hockey); b. 4 May 1933, Rossland, B.C.; m. Beverley Linn; c. Lynne, Patti, Susan; ret'd fireman;

Lethbridge jrs. '49-52; goalie Trail Smoke Eaters '52-63, '68-69, '70-72, Rossland Sr. Warriors '63-66, St. Louis NHL '67-68; Spokane Jets WIHL '69-70, '72-73; coach Spokane PCHL '78-79, Trail '82-84; best goalie '61 World Cup gold Smoke Eaters; ntl team '64, '68 Olympics, 5 world championships (1 gold, 4 bronze); most valuable goalie awards '61, '63, '64, '66; mem. 3 Allan Cup winners; PCHL coach of '79; BCAHA outstanding player of '65; mem. BC Hockey, Sports, IIHF halls of fame; res. Trail, B.C.

MARTINEZ, Dennis (baseball); b. 14 May 1955, Granada, Nicaragua; given name: Jose Dennis; m. Luz Marina Garcia; c. Dennis, Erica, Gilberto, Ricardo; represented Nicaragua '72-73 amateur World Series; turned pro '74 playing in minors with Miami (A), Asheville (AA), Rochester, Indianapolis (AAA), in majors with Baltimore (AL) '76-86, Montreal (NL) '86-93, Cleveland (AL) '94-96, Seattle (AL) '97, Atlanta (NL) '98; ML record: 692 scheduled games, 245-193, 122cg, 30sho, 3999.2ip, 1165bob, 2426k, 3.70era; post-season 3-3. 19k, 2.74era, 0-2 WS, 6k, 3.86era; one of 7 pitchers to post 100 victories in both AL/NL; pitched perfect game for Montreal vs. Los Angeles '91; 4 all-star games; 2 World Series; nicknamed "El Presidente"; founder Dennis Martinez Foundation for under-privileged children; res. Miami, Fla.

MARTINEZ, Pedro (baseball); b. 25 Oct 1971, Manoguayabo, D.R.; Ohio Dominican Coll.; rhp; signed by Dodgers as amateur free agent '88; played with Los Angeles '92-93, Montreal '94-97, Boston '98-04, NY Mets '05; 1 World Series winner; ML record: (through '04) 182-76; 388 scheduled games, 42cg, 2296ip, 1746h, 766r, 615bob, 2653k, 2.71era; recorded banner year with Montreal '97 pitching 1-hitter vs. Cincinnati, becoming 1st Latin pitcher to record 300k single season, 1st pitcher with 300k (305) and sub-2.00era (1.90) since Steve Carlton '72, 1st rhp since Walter Johnson '12; NL all-star; Montreal, *Sporting News* NL pitcher of yr, 3rd ML pitcher to win Cy Young awards both leagues NL '97, AL '99; 3 Cy Young awards; 2 ESPY awards; '99 all-star MVP; res. Santo Domingo, D.R.

MARTINI, Paul (figure skating); b. 2 Nov 1960, Woodbridge, Ont.; given name: Paul Lloyd; m. Elizabeth Wallace; c. Kate Emily, Robert; York, BA; figure skating, hockey coach; with Barbara Underhill 5 ntl jr. & sr. titles; jr. world pairs title '78; St. Gervais Grand Prix (France), Nebelhorn Trophy (Germany) '78; Ste. Ivel, (England), NHK Trophy (Japan) '80; mem. world championships teams '79-84, Olympics '80, '84, Skate Moscow '79; bronze '83, gold '84 worlds; pro '84-98; 7 pro world pairs titles; *CBC* '92, '98 Olympic, 3 world, 1 European championships color commentator; coach Arc Skating Academy; mem. Canada's Sports, Cdn Olympic, Cdn Figure Skating halls of fame; res. Bradford, Ont.

MARTITSCH, Karl (builder); b. 19 Nov 1917, Ratnitz, Austria; d. circa 2000, Bahamas, m. Beverly Ann Westman (d); c. Nicholas, Francesca; Graz. MSc; Munich, Vienna; m consulting engineer; mem. Austrian ntl ski team 12yrs; participated in all four disciplines, downhill, slalom, x-country, jumping; in 25 competitive yrs earned 360 trophies/prizes; Austrian jr. slalom title '36; Austrian nordic, academic nordic combined, 3-way, 4-way combined titles '46; earned medals in competitions in Austria, Italy,

Switzerland; competed '48 Olympics, '50 worlds; won NA 4-way title '50; academic rep. ski sports in Austria '46-49; moved to Canada '51Canadian rep. FIS from '63; FIS jumping judge; mem. FIS Council '79-92; played key role in construction of ski-jumping/recreational facilities Lake Placid, Calgary, Revelstoke, Thunder Bay, Banff, Mont Ste. Anne, Ironwood/Iron Mountain, Mich, Anchorage, Alaska; Austrian Olympic medal for contribution to '76 Innsbruck winter games; Cdn commemorative medal; mem. Cdn Ski Hall of Fame.

MARUK, Dennis (hockey); b. 17 Nov 1955, Toronto, Ont.; given name: Dennis John; m. Joni; c. Jonathan, 2 daughters; Creative Concepts marketing, hockey coach; 113 goals 2 seasons ctr London Knights Jr. A; 2nd draft pick California '75; Cleveland '76-78, Minnesota '78, '83-89, Washington '78-83; scored 50g '81, 60 '82; NHL record: 888 scheduled games, 356g, 522a, 34 playoff games, 14g, 22a; nicknamed "Peewee"; HS hockey coach; head coach Minnesota (RHI) '94-95, Lake Charles (WPHL) '97-98, Baton Rouge (ECHL) '01-02; res. Eden Prairie, Minn.

MASCOE, Patrick (judo); b. 9 Dec 1960, Ottawa, Ont.; given name: John Patrick; m. Louanne Tee; UofO BA (2), BEd; teacher; introduced to martial arts age 11; enjoyed some success as FS wrestler; trained in Japan; became 1st non-Japanese HS judo head coach; serious knee injury '90 threatened career; tech advisor, coach Singapore ntl team '97-00; 2 Am-Can intl open gold, 1 bronze; Japan Hamura Cup, Hitotsubashi Open; Atlantic Open title; 2 Cleveland Open intl; 4 Eastern Cdn, US open titles; 2 Rocky Mountain Open silver; Furukawa Open silver; CNE Open silver; 2 Cdn Open bronze; 6 Ont. Titles; Ont. Open kata title; Ont. Courage Award; res. Nepean, Ont.

MASON, Janice (rowing); b. 23 Nov 1959, Edmonton, Alta.; West Coast Coll. of Massage Therapy; 7 ntl, Cdn Henley, 1 US title; gold double sculls '81 Royal Henley; mem. '79, '82, '83 world championships, '80, '84 Olympic teams; bronze double sculls '82 worlds; res. Vancouver, B.C.

MASON, Susan (swimming); b. 3 Jun 1960, Halifax, N.S.; given name: Susan Marguerite; m. Donald Allan MacLeod; Dalhousie, BSc; teacher, physiotherapist; mem. Halifax Trojan Aquatic Club; ntl team mem. '77-84; 3 gold, 1 silver, 1 bronze '77 Canada Games; freestyle specialist in 100m to 1500m; 2 bronze Coca Cola Inter-nations '78, bronze 400m FS relay FISU Games '79; CIAU championships 200m FS '79, 400m, 800m FS '79-80; mem. '78 CG team; AUAA outstanding-female-swimmer awards '79-81, CIAU outstanding-female-swimmer award '79, Dalhousie outstanding-female-athlete award '79; mem. NS Sports Hall of Fame; res. Halifax, N.S.

MASOTTI, Paul (football); b. 10 Mar 1965, Hamilton, Ont.; m. Vivi; c. Andrin, Athena; Acadia; football exec.; wr; 2 AUAA, 1 CIAU all-star; drafted by Toronto '88; attended Washington NFL camp '88; with Argos '88-99; GM Argos '00-01; v-p./dir. player personnel '02-03; asst. coach Argos '03; CFL record: 190 games, 44tds, 1cvt, 556 receptions for 8772yds, 306pts; 3 Grey Cup finals, 3 winner; 2 Eastern, 1 CFL all-star; Dick Suderman trophy '97; Stoney Creek community award; res. Stoney Creek, Ont.

MASTERS, Wally (football/baseball); b. 28 Mar 1907, Pen Argyl, Pa.; d. 12 Jul 1992, Ottawa, Ont.; given name: Walter Thomas; m. Ruth Anna Newman; c. Walter Thomas Jr.; Pennsylvania; public relations; all-American college baseball rhp '31 winning 15 in row, 28-3 record; Knute Rockne football all-American team '31; pro baseball 1yr each Washington, Philadelphia (AL), Philadelphia (NL), Ottawa Nationals Border League '47; pro qb Philadephia, Chicago-Pittsburgh combined teams; all-Cdn Ottawa '32; coached Riders '33-34 (simultaneously managed Ottawa Crains Can-Am baseball league), St. Patrick's College '35, Ottawa Trojans ORFU '47, Rough Riders '48-50; coached Wilmington, Del., Clippers in American Assn. '37-39; overall football coaching record 88 wins, 22 losses, 2 ties; ORFU title '47; guided Riders to '48 Grey Cup bowing to Calgary 12-7; mem. Ottawa Sports Hall of Fame.

MASTERTON, Bill (hockey); b. 13 Aug 1938, Winnipeg, Man.; d. 15 Jan 1968, Minneapolis, Minn.; given name: William; Denver, MB; ctr St. Boniface Jrs., Man. champions '56; when NHL expanded '67-68 he joined Minnesota playing 38 games scoring 4g and adding 8a before disaster struck; on 13 Jan after being checked he struck his head on the ice and died 2 days later; NHL created Bill Masterton trophy in his memory; mem. Man. Hockey Hall of Fame.

MATHER, Eddie (archery/t&f); b. 4 Aug 1895, Hyde, Cheshire, Eng.; d. 16 Sep 1983, White Rock, B.C.; m. c. Marion; track star, archer, gunsmith and accomplished musician, machinist, violin-maker; emigrated to Saskatoon with parents '06; following WW1 service supervisor municipal swimming pool '28-39; competed in '24 Olympic trials but did not go to Games; master archer he played role in formation of Saskatoon, Bedford Road, RCAF Archery Clubs; helped found Western Development Museum, several bands in Saskatoon; lifetime and founding mem./asst. conductor Saskatoon Symphony Orchestra; at 88 swam 88 lengths of pool, about 1 mile.

MATHERS, Frank (builder/hockey); b. 29 Mar 1924, Winnipeg, Man.; d. 9 Feb 2005, Hershey, Pa.; given name: Frank Sydney; m. Pat Killey; NHL with Toronto '48-52, 23 scheduled games, 1g, 3a; became AHL star def with Hershey Bears, 5 consec. all-star teams; both player/coach with Hershey; ret'd as player '62; 3 Calder Cup titles; pres/GM Bears '73-91; 3 more Calder Cups; honored with Frank Mathers night by Bears; Lester Patrick Trophy '87; mem. Cdn, Man. Hockey halls of fame.

MATHESON, Dan (wrestling/boxing); b. 11 Jul 1893, Emerald, P.E.I.; d. 9 Feb 1950, Regina, Sask.; given name: Donald John; m. Katie Belle McKenzie; c. James (d), Earl, Donald, Agnes; Regina police sergeant; gold '23-25, '31, silver '22, '32 AAUofC ntl heavyweight wrestling championships; Sask. boxing champion; mem. Regina boxing/wrestling commission; proficient in hammer throw, discus, shot put, pole vault events; trained numerous wrestling champions including Earl McCready; mem. PEI, Sask. Sports halls of fame.

MATHIEU, Wilfrid (speed skating/cycling/snowshoeing); b. 11 Sep 1910, Ottawa, Ont.; d. 16 Nov 1984, Ottawa, Ont.; m. Germaine Raizenne; c. Henri, Therese, Jacques (d), Madeleine, Louise, Rolande, Gilles; painter; won ntl men's 10-mile cycling title; won 120-mile Montreal to Ottawa world snowshoeing title; won ntl men's speed skating title; served as lifeguard Champlain Bath; swimming, skiing instructor, dir. l'Oeuvre de la jeunesse d'Ottawa; volunteer coach, official Ottawa speed skating events; sportscaster, analyst Ottawa French language radio; final competition age 72 placing 3rd world senior speed skating championship '82.

MATIOWSKI, Buck (builder/hockey/boxing); b. 31 Mar 1936, Winnipeg, Man.; responsible for many firsts in Man, hockey from organizing 1st-ever women's prov. tourney '55 to founding Western Man. 1st summer hockey school in Brandon '67; chair. Man. Boxing/Wrestling Commission '80-95; dir. Cdn pro boxing 10yrs; inspector/co-ordinator Man. Boxing Commission; involved in organization, promotion, development of broomball, figure skating, t&f, sailing; coached/organized women's hockey in Shoal Lake, Bisset as early as '54; authored *Task Force on Hockey Violence* report for CAHA; toured Soviet Union as part of CAHA coaches' study '74; MAHA pres.; introduced plan to divide Man. into minor hockey regions; mem. Man. Sports Hall of Fame; res. Winnipeg, Man.

MATOBA, Tom (baseball); b. 19 Sep 1898, Vancouver, B.C.; d. (circa 1990) Weston, Ont.; m. Hideko Yieno; c. Raye, Clara, Rumi, Eri; gardener; at 16 one of dominant players Japanese Cdn Archis team; united with Nippon Club '18; mem. Vancouver Sr. Terminal League pennant team '26; noted for home run power at Vancouver Athletic Park; never lost enthusiasm for game despite relocation ordeals inflicted on Japanese Canadians WW2; coach Niagara to Fruit Belt Softball League title; mem. Canadian Baseball Hall of Fame.

MATTHEWS, Don (coaching/football); b. 22 Jun 1939, Amesbury, Mass.; div. c. Mike, Mark, Pat; Idaho; football exec.; served in US Marine Corps; arrived at Idaho as walk-on; left 4yrs later as team capt.; began coaching as asst Idaho; successful HS coach Nevada, Washington, Oregon; 2 state titles; joined CFL as Edmonton asst. '77-82, '89; head coach BC '83-88, Toronto '90, '96-98, Edmonton '99-00, Montreal '01-04; Orlando Thunder (WLAF) '91, Saskatchewan '91-93, Baltimore (CFL) '93-95; 7 Grey Cup finals, 5 titles; surpassed Frank Clair's 147 regular season victory total '97 to become CFL's winningest coach; 6 Annis Stukus coach-of-yr awards; became Cdn citizen '04; res. Montreal, Que.

MATTHEWS, John (bowling); b. 2 May 1948, Winnipeg, Man.; given name: John Clifford; m. Phyllis Gail Jeske; c. Dorelle Dawn Lenore, Joel John Llewelyn; UMan, BA, BEd; teacher; 5-pin specialist; mem. Man. mixed title team '77, men's title team '78; coach Alta. mixed team titlists '80; mem. Alta. Masters men's team titlists '80; representing Man. won '81 ntl Masters singles title; 4-handicap golfer; hole-in-one '70; Southwood Club match title '77; mem. Man. Colt (17-18) championship baseball team '77; Sr. B fastball league all-star '72; mem. Man. team handball champions '75; Winnipeg club singles, men's doubles tennis titles '77; coached several jr. HS basketball, volleyball, soccer teams; res. Winnipeg, Man.

MATTHEWS, Tam (sailing); b. 8 Oct 1955, Peterborough, Ont.; m. Janet Orgill; c. Geoffrey, Alison; UofT BA; head master Ashbury Coll.; 470 sailor; 2 ntl, 1 CORK, 1 Hyeres, 2 NA titles; gold Bongard Cup Ont. Intl-14 '84; 2 NA Flying Scot titles; mem. '79 PAG, '78-81 world championships, '80, '84, '96 (team leader) Olympic teams; res.Ottawa, Ont.

MATTHIAS, Brendan (t&f); b. 12 Aug 1969, Toronto, Ont.; UofT; long-distance runner; began competing age 10; Ont. HS champion '83-84; ntl jr. 1500m titlist; competed world jr. championships '88; ran 3:58.03 indoor mile; ntl indoor 1500m title '90; CIAU 10km title; won *Victoria* Times-Colonist 1500m '91; won Toronto 10km '92; ntl indoor, UofT Classic 3000m title '93; competed in world indoor meet '93; ntl 10,000 title '94; ntl indoor 3000m record 7:30.90 '93, 5000m record 13:41.73 '94; mem. UTTC; res. Thornhill, Ont.

MATTSON, Dale (shuffleboard); b. 24 Feb 1955, Victoria, B.C.; given name: Dale Christopher; m. Diane Weger; computer operator supervisor; mem. Man. champion, runnerup basketball, baseball, fastball, volleyball, football HS teams; capt. basketball, fastball title teams; highest winning percentage shuffleboard league play '78-84; won Man. singles, runnerup Cdn '78; mem. Man. title teams '78-84; Cdn men's doubles title '84-85; runnerup Cdn mixed doubles '84-85; Man. mixed champion '84-86; res. Winnipeg, Man.

MAUCH, Gene (baseball); b. 18 Nov 1925, Salina, Kan.; given name: Eugene William; m. Nina Lee Taylor; c. Leanne; ret'd baseball manager; pro Brooklyn Dodgers organization '43; minor clubs Durham, Montreal, St. Paul; Indianapolis, Milwaukee, Atlanta, Los Angeles, Minneapolis, ML Brooklyn, Pittsburgh, Chicago (NL), Boston (NL), St. Louis (NL), Boston (AL) through '59; 1st managerial assignment Atlanta (Southern) '53; managed Minneapolis (A.A.) '58-59; Philadelphia '60-68; 1st Montreal Expos manager '69-75; Minnesota '76-80, California '81-82, '85; ML managerial record: 3942 scheduled games, 1902-2037; guided Angels to AL Western div. title '82; 3 times NL mgr. of yr.; *Sporting News* ML mgr. of yr.; Canada's baseball man of '73; 1 mgr, 3 coach NL all-star team; res. Rancho Mirage, Calif.

MAUGHAN, George (boxing); b. 8 May 1910, Toronto, Ont.; d. 16 Jun 2003, Guadalajara, Mex.; given name: George Burwell; m. Joan Brais; c. Marilyn, G.B. Jr., Walter, David, Joanne, Carol; McGill, MD, MSc, FACS, FRCOG, FRCS(C); ret'd professor emeritus McGill; intercollegiate football '28; intercollegiate shot put, swimming, water polo '30; began boxing '29, competed at college level '30-34; 2 ntl titles; flag-bearer, semifinalist 79.38kg '32 Olympics; Canada Medal; mem. McGill Sports Hall of Fame.

MAUNDER, Maria (rowing); b. 19 Mar 1972, St. John's, Nfld.; women's 8s; learned to row at Ridley College; mem. ntl team from '92; gold 8s '93 FISU Games; silver 8's '96 Olympics; res. London, Ont./Victoria, B.C.

MAURICE, Paul (coaching/hockey); b. 30 Jan 1967, Sault Ste. Marie, Ont.; m. Michelle; c. Sydney, Jake, Luke; coach; eye injury ended playing career at young age; mem. Compuware hockey organization 16yrs; guided Detroit (OHL) to Memorial Cup playoffs '95; asst./later head coach Hartford '95-97 and shifted with team to Carolina '97-03; at time of appointment youngest head coach in

NHL; coached '97 NHL all-star game; guided Hurricanes to Stanley Cup finals '02; NHL coaching record: (through '03) 644 scheduled games, 260-279-91-9, 35 playoff games, 17-18; res. Cary, N. C.

MAURICE, Pauline (softball); b. 17 Dec 1967, Welland, Ont.; Kent State, BSc; telephone customer service rep.; of; Kent State career batting avg. .397; competed '90, '94 world championships; '91 (silver), '95 PAG; '94 South Pacific Classic; '96 Olympics; semipro Saronne, Italy '92; Kent State female athlete of decade '92; 1st team all-region, 2nd team all-American NCAA Div. 1 '90; 2 ntl championship all-star awards; Welland Sportsman of '85; 3 Welland female-athlete-of-yr awards; nickname "Turbo"; Kent State Sports Hall of Fame; res. Welland, Ont.

MAWHINNEY, Bill (golf); b. 7 May 1929, Vancouver, B.C.; d. 26 Jan 1995, Abbotsford, B.C.; given name: William Cecil; m. Jess; c. Chris, Jocelyn, Marilyn; golf pro; defeated Stan Leonard 1-up for 1st of 2 BC match titles '47; 2 BC jr., '52 Pacific Northwest Amateur titles; ntl jr. '48, ntl amateur title '50; mem. Willingdon Cup, Morse Cup, Hudson Cup, America's Cup teams; semifinalist '52 US Amateur; Seattle, Tacoma Open titles before turning pro; Millar Trophy CPGA match champion '57; BC Open title '57; mem. BC Sports Hall of Fame.

MAXWELL, Brian (t&f); b. 1953, London, Eng,; d. 19 Mar 2004, San Anselmo, Calif.; m. Jennifer Biddaulph; c. Alex, Justin, Christopher, Julia, James, Andrew; UCal Berkley, B.Arch.; entrepreneur; raised in Toronto; competed in marathon events throughout world winning many; 2 NC marathon titles; '75 ntl marathon title; competed several Boston marathons; 3rd in world marathon rankings '77; qualified for boycotted '80 Olympics; coached UCal x-country team; invented Power Bar energy supplement '83 subsequently selling company to Nestle for reported $375M '00; UCal sports facility bears his name; UCal Brutus Hamilton student athlete award; chair Game Ready; dir. Active Network; featured in articles in *People, Forbes, Business Week, Fast Company* magazines.

MAXWELL, Doug (builder/curling); b. 13 Jan 1928, Toronto, Ont.; given name: Douglas Dean; m. Shirley Ann Ward; c. Douglas Ward, Gordon Dean, Janet Louise, William James; UofT, BComm, MComm; ret'd editor/publisher; earned school letters in variety of sports; part-time work at *CBC* during school days evolved into staff position on both radio/TV working in sports/children's program areas; utilized marketing skills with Ont, Centennial Commission; had role in establishment Ont. Sports Fed., and Ont. Sports Centre; business mgr. for Nancy Greene '68; special researcher fed, govt, task force on sports '68-69; consultant COA '69-77; chef de communications COA 3 Olympic Games; began curling '49; 1 of 4 founding mem. Humber Highlands CC, served as secty/pres.; Toronto CA pres. '69; OCA mem.-at-large '67; exec. dir. Air Canada Silver Brooms '68-85; exec.dir. Hexagon world curling championships '86-88; consultant world curling championship comm. from '89; key role in obtaining Labatt's as Brier sponsor replacement for Macdonald Tobacco; exec.dir OCF '88-93; undistinguished playing career but did score an 8-ender; radio/TV curling commentator *CBC/BBC* many years; helped in developing *TSN* Skins Game; editor/publisher

Canadian Curling News from late '70s; charter mem. secty-treas Canadian Curling Reporters; authored 3 curling books, Labatt draw book; inaugurated/organized Toronto, later ntl, mixed championships; organized/directed Tournament of Champions at Maple Leaf Gardens mid-60s; innovator who had hand in introduction of time clocks, baseball-style scoreboards and varied other game upgrading features; initiated international standardization of game rules; chief umpire Silver Brooms '68-72; organized Moncton 100, Las Vegas Desertspiel; Scotty Harper Memorial award; TCA curler of '74; hon. life mem Sask. CA; OCA media award; CCA achievement award; honored by Swedish, German, Italian, French, Swiss, Royal Caledonian CC; mem. Cdn Curling Hall of Fame; res. Markdale, Ont.

MAXWELL, Gavin (canoeing); b. 28 Aug 1970, Mississauga, Ont.; McMaster; ntl canoe team mem. '90-96; 2 PAG bronze '91; silver C-4 200 Szeged '96; gold C-4 200 Milano '96, C-1 1000 Hemespheric Olympic Qualifier '96; 3 ntl C-4 titles; competed '96 Olympics, gold C1 1000, bronze C2 1000 '93, gold C1, C4 1000 '94 worlds; res. Oakville, Ont.

MAXWELL, Steamer (hockey); b. 19 May 1890, Winnipeg, Man., d. 11 Sep 1975, Winnipeg, Man.; given name: Fred; skating prowess earned nickname "Steamer"; began playing '10; received several pro offers during playing career but chose to remain amateur; rover Winnipeg Monarchs Allan Cup champions '14-15; ret'd as player '17, coach Monarchs 2 seasons; coached Winnipeg Falcons to '19 Allan Cup, '20 Olympics, world championships, Winnipeg Rangers to Manitoba title '25-26, Winnipeg Maroons (APHL) '26-28; guided Elmwood Millionaires to junior, senior Manitoba titles '29-30; Monarchs to world title '35; officiated many games, amateur and pro '10-40; mem. Man., Cdn Hockey halls of fame.

MAYER, Alfons (shooting); b. 1 Feb 1938, Weiler, Germany; div.; c. Anita, Linda; m. Irngard; mechanical foreman; several ntl, Ont. rifle championships; gold English Match '67 PAG setting world record perfect 600; 4th world English Match competition; '68 NY State title; Ont. free-rifle, sporting rifle, prone titles '82; team silver '79, '83, bronze '71, '79, '83 PAG; mem. '68, '72, '80 Olympic, '66, '74, '78, '82 world teams, '77, '79, '81, '83 Benito Juarez teams; res. Kitchener, Ont.

MAYERS, Wallace (basketball); b. 5 Nov 1908, New Westminster, B.C., d. 3 Aug 1976, Vancouver, B.C.; UBC; university soccer star; '26 BC jr. claycourt tennis champion; 3rd '27 ntl swimming championships; mem. 4 ntl men's basketball title teams; led New Westminster Adanacs to BC's first ntl cage crown '29; mem. BC Sports Hall of Fame.

MAYES, Rueben (football); b. 6 Jun 1963, North Battleford, Sask.; Washington State; ret. pro football player; set NCAA, WSU rb records while leading Pac-10 rushers '84-85; twice Pac-10 player of year; all-American '85; 10th in Heisman voting '85; played in Senior, East-West Shrine, Blue-Gray Bowl games; twice Pac-10 all-conference; *UPI*, Football Writers of America 1st team, *AP*, *Football News* 2nd team all-star; pro New Orleans '86-90, Seattle Seahawks '91-93 *UPI* NFC rookie of '86; Football Writers NFL rookie of '86; Harry Jerome Award (Canada's

outstanding black athlete) '84; Sask. male athlete of year '84-85; res. Pullman, Wash.

MAYNES, Billy (t&f); b. 1902, Saint John, N.B.; d. 4 Aug 1966, Saint John, N.B.; c. Douglas; Oxford, Rhodes Scholar '25; journalist; NB outdoor relay '21, 440yd '22 titlist; Maritime outdoor quarter-mile champion '22-23; described as "fastest quarter-miler Maritimes have produced"; despite 3yd penalty lost '23 AAUC 440yd title by mere inches; mem. '24 Olympic team; mem. NB Sports Hall of Fame.

MAYOTTE, Roger (harness racing); b. 9 Aug 1956, Thunder Bay, Ont.; apprenticed with Gary Crowe, Keith Waples, Bill Troy, Percy Robillard before branching out on own '81; meteoric rise has ranked him among top reinsmen on OJC circuit; with Kingsbridge, That'll Be Me won Breeders Crown titles; Maple Leaf Trot with Earl '94; Take A Look one of his best horses; through '03 2841 victories with purses exceeding $34M; res. Mississauga, Ont.

MAZINKE, Harvey (curling); b. 6 Apr 1937, Sewell, Man.; m. Marian Dickson; c. Scott, Dietta; UMan, BSc; engineer; 3rd for Bruce Hudson '64 Man. Brier entry; skipped 11 Sask. finalist rinks, including mixed, '73, '75 Sask. men's titles, '73 Brier title, lost in Silver Broom (World) final; all-star Brier skip '73; Ross Harstone award '75; Regina B'nai B'rith Sportsman of '73; coach '82 Sask. jr. title rink; pres. CCA; dir. Sask. Sports Admin. Centre, governor UofSask; mem. Cdn Curling, Sask. Sports halls of fame; res. Kelowna, B.C.

MAZUR, Eddie (hockey); b. 25 Jul 1929, Winnipeg, Man.; d. 3 Jul 1995, Winnipeg, Man.; given name: Edward Joseph; nickname "Spider"; lw with Winnipeg Monarchs winning prov. titles at all minor levels as well as juv and jr.; a proven winner he also played with '51 PCHL champion Victoria, '53 Stanley Cup champion Montreal and '56 WHL titlist Winnipeg; NHL record: 6 seasons with Montreal, Chicago, 107 scheduled games, 8g, 20a, 25 playoff games, 4g, 5a; overall pro record 1086games, 391g, 461a; on retirement tireless hockey volunteer; mem. Man. Hockey Hall of Fame.

MAZURAK, Steve (football); b. 25 May 1951, Regina, Sask.; given name: Steven Lee; m. Heather Thomson; c. Lee, Jacklyn, Andrew; North Dakota; radio color commentator; mem. Regina Rams '71-72; Roughriders '73-81; td '76 Grey Cup final; 2 all-star games; Schenley outstanding Cdn nominee; led wrs in catches '77; CFLPA exec. dir. '82-87; res. Regina, Sask.

McARTON, Cheryl (swimming); b. 25 Apr 1966, Ottawa, Ont.; given name: Cheryl Ann; m. Peter Ward; c. Rebecca Lynn, Rachel; Arkansas, BSc; ntl 800m FS relay record '81; 3 silver, 1 bronze '84 winter ntls; gold, 2 bronze '87 winter ntls; mem. '82 CG, '84 Olympic, '87 FISU, '87 PAG teams; 2 silver, 1 bronze '87 PAG; 4 NCAA all-American '85-88; 3 academic all-American; North York female athlete of '86; sister Jennifer ntl team diver; res. Indiana, Pa.

McARTON, Jennifer (diving); b. 2 Feb 1968, Ottawa, Ont.; m. Jeff Wright; c. Justin, Nicolas; Uof T, BPHE, BA, BEd; HS teacher; 2 ntl 10m, 1 world age-group 3m title; silver 10m '82 CG; mem. '82, '86 CG teams; finalist '82 World

Aquatic Games, '83 World Cup; performed 20m high diving exhibitions Canada's Wonderland '89; avid skier, canoeist; sister Cheryl mem. ntl swim team; competes at masters level; res. Orleans, Ont.

McBEAN, Marnie (rowing); b. 28 Jan 1968, Vancouver, B.C.; UWO; public speaker/coach; launched career with Toronto Argonaut RC '85; mem. ntl jr. team '86, sr. team from '89; switched from sweep specialty to sculling '93; mem. '91 world, '92 Olympic straight pair (with Kathleen Heddle), 8s gold medal crews, '96 Olympic double sculls gold (Heddle), quad sculls bronze; 3 World Cup titles; CG single sculls gold '94; mem. '89, '93 FISU, '88 (spare), '92, '96 Olympic, '95, '99 PAG teams; after winning double sculls gold, stripped of '95 PAG quadruple sculls gold when teammate Silken Laumann tested positive for mistakenly taking illegal decongestant; 1st woman to reach Olympic/world podium 6 different boat classes; 11 medals '98 worlds; 7 international regatta gold, 8 US, 2 Cdn titles; single sculls gold '99 PAG; back injury forced her from '00 Olympic team; ret'd from rowing competition '01; began mountain climbing '97; certified snowboard instructor; turned attention to triathlons '01; Dick Ellis Memorial trophy for sr. team of '91-92; ntl spokesperson Kids Help Phone; Cdn meritorious service award; UWO, ORA female athlete of '89; CARA centennial medal '91; FISA Thomas Keller medal; mem. Cdn Olympic, Canada's Sports Hall of Fame; res. Toronto, Ont.

McBLAIN, Liz (t&f); b. 30 Jan 1948, Bandung, Indonesia; given name: Elizabeth Vanderstam; m. William McBlain; Lethbridge, UAlta, BPhE; teacher; pentathlon specialist; ntl team '73-81; PB: 3,951 pentathlon points, 400m hurdles 61.2, 400m 54.9, 53.88 in relay leg; outstanding Calgary athlete '67, outstanding Lethbridge athlete '71; competitor masters circuit from '78; competed world masters (age-group) championships '83-97; WR masters (35+) tj '84, 40+ indoor 200, 400m, hj '88; ntl record masters javelin, 100m, 400m hurdles '84; bronze world pentathlon '03; volunteer every major intl event in Edmonton from '78; co-dir. '94 masters PAG; res. Edmonton, Alta.

McBRIEN, Harry (football); b. 1910, Toronto, Ont., d. 31 Aug 1976, Toronto, Ont.; m. Kathleen; c. Derek, Scott; pres. Sterling Coffee Co., L.L. Garr Enterprises; football official '26-50; seriously injured officiating '50 national jr. final; organized Toronto District Board of Football officials; secty.-treas. Toronto Dist. Interscholastic AA; secty. CRU '51-66; mem. 3-man comm. which streamlined rules '67; governor, mem. Canadian Football Hall of Fame selection comm. '67-76; major role in developing Grey Cup into ntl festival; mem. Canada's Sports, Canadian Football halls of fame.

McBURNEY, Margaret (basketball); b. 10 Apr 1909, Fernie, B.C.; m. Victor Vasheresse (d); ret'd secretary; 1st baseman Edmonton Toddies baseball team; mem. Monarch ladies hockey team, 3 championships; longest playing mem. legendary Edmonton Grads '26-36; played in 164 games amassing 2079 points for 12.6 avg.; world champion free throw artist 61 in succession '31; twice mem. team which claimed world title honors during exhibition tournaments staged in conjunction with Olympics; coached jr. girls basketball Edmonton, Vancouver; 5-pin bowling

champion; mem. Canadian Basketball, Alta. Sports halls of fame; res. Edmonton, Alta.

McCAFFREY, Janice (t&f); b. 20 Oct 1959, Etobicoke, Ont.; given name: Janice Leslie Turner; m. Bill McCaffrey; c. Scott, Jamie; psychologist, workshop facilitator; pres. Success Coaching; began career as middle distance runner then switched to race walking to compete in '81 Canada Summer Games where she won bronze; 10 ntl titles; mem. '87, '95 PAG, '90, '94, '98 CG, '92, '96, '00 Olympic Games, 5 World championship teams; 10km RW bronze '94 CG, gold '94 Francophonie Games; 3 Athletics Alta. female-athlete-of-yr awards; '89 Alta. achievement award; ranked among top 10 marathoners in Canada; top Cdn woman, 20th overall '97 NY marathon; set '00 world 20k record 1:34.50; race walking coach; res. Calgary, Alta.

McCAFFREY, Jimmy (football); b. 1895, Alexandria, Ont., d. 29 Oct 1966, Alexandria, Ont.; m. Ella Krock (d); c. Patricia; government registrar of trademarks; managed St.Brigid's hockey club; pres. Ottawa Senators Que. Sr. League; mgr. Rough Riders '23-59, 7 Grey Cup finals, 4 titles; Big Four pres. '40, '56; helped form Eastern Football Conference; Schenley award trustee '55; mem. Ottawa, Canadian Football halls of fame.

McCALL, Robert (figure skating); b. 14 Sep 1958, Halifax, N.S.; d. 15 Nov 1991, Toronto, Ont.; Dalhousie; ice dance specialist; teamed with Marie McNeil '75-81, Tracy Wilson '81-84; 7 ntl, 1 Skate Canada titles; jr. world bronze '77; mem. '84, '88 (bronze) Olympic, '80-84 world championships (2 bronze) teams; pro with Wilson Stars on Ice '88, world pro title '89; mem. Order of Canada, Cdn Olympic Sports, Skate Canada halls of fame.

McCANCE, Ches (football); b. 19 Feb 1915, Winnipeg, Man.; d. 8 May 1956, Winnipeg, Man.; given name: Chester William; m. Frances Elizabeth Carson; c. William Robert, Margaret Elizabeth; wine salesman; CFL with Winnipeg, Montreal; 8 Grey Cup finals, 3 winners; 2 field goals, 2 singles as Bombers edged Ottawa 18-16 '41 final; field goal, 3 converts, 1 single as Als beat Calgary '49 final; 3rd Ken Weldon's Que. entry '52, '53 Briers; lost title playoff '53; coached Isaac Newton jr. HS to Man. football title '40; asst. coach Blue Bombers '43; mem. Canadian Football Hall of Fame.

McCANN, Dave (football); b. 5 Feb 1889, Ottawa, Ont.; d. 27 Mar 1959, Ottawa, Ont.; m. 1. Florence Wilson (d), 2. May Stafford; c. Lenore, June; civil servant, insurance exec.; mem. Ottawa Senators (renamed Rough Riders) '07-20; credited with originating flying wing position '10; mem. '09 Interprovincial title team; intercollegiate football referee '21-24; coach Rough Riders (Senators) '26-27, 2 Grey Cups; pres. CRU '27; mem., chairman CRU rules comm. '27-58; prominent paddler New Edinburgh Canoe Club; Canadian Branch Gov.-Gen.'s, Royal Victoria Jubilee curling trophies; mem. Ottawa CC '18-58; mem. Gov.-Gen.'s CC; mem. '09 YMCA Eastern Cdn basketball, city baseball, ntl war canoe titlists; mem. Ottawa Sports, Canadian Football halls of fame.

McCANNELL, Don (speed skating); b. 11 Dec 1918, Minto, N.D.; d. 25 Apr 1985, Winnipeg, Man.; given name:

Donald Grant; m. Florence Esler; c. Joan, Doreen, Donna; instrumental in Sargent Park skating track expansion to Olympic standards; liaison Winnipeg Parks & Rec and Man. SSA '63-82; mem. Winnipeg SSC from '58, serving various exec. roles; exec. mem. MSSA; dir. CASSA, chair. Olympic development comm.; coached Man. team Canada Winter Games '67, '64 Olympic, '65, '67 ladies' world teams; tech. advisor, color commentator *CTV* '76 Winter Olympics; WSSC volunteer award bears his name; mem. Canadian Speed Skating Hall of Fame.

McCANNELL, Donna (speed skating); b. 20 Feb 1950, Winnipeg, Man.; m. Bob Keating; c. Kim, Andrea; UMan, BPhE; teacher; Man. mass start titles: midget '62, juv. '63-64; sr. indoor titles '69, '71; ntl mass start titles: juv. '63, jr. '66; intermediate indoor titles '67-68, sr. '71; mem. jr. Olympic team '66; mem. '72 Olympic team; res. Winnipeg, Man.

McCANNELL, Doreen (speed skating); b. 29 Jul 1947, Winnipeg, Man.; given name: Doreen Ann: m. Calvin Bruce Botterill; c. Jennifer, Jason; UMan, BPhE, Ed. Cert.; ret'd teacher; 8 Man., 6 ntl titles; NA, US Olympic style champion '66; mem. '64, '68 Olympic, '65, '67, '68 world championships teams; 5 gold Canada Winter Games '67; Man. jr. athlete of '61; Man. athlete of '65; Man. female athlete of '66; mem. Man. Sports, Cdn Speed Skating halls of fame; res. Winnipeg, Man.

McCARTHY, Scott (weightlifting); b. 17 Mar 1972, Grand Falls, Nfld.; given name: Scott Edward; m. Erin Steele; c. Matthew, Tijana; retail; 4 Canada Games, 2 as athlete, 2 as coach; mem. '98, '99 worlds teams; '02 Cdn 77kg title; double bronze '02 CG; certified Level 3 coach; '03 world jr. title team coach; pres Yukon Weightlifting Association from '02; res. Whitehorse, Yukon

McCASKILL, Kirk (baseball); b. 9 Apr 1961, Kapuskasing, Ont.; given name: Kirk Edward; m. Dana Metzger; c. Riley, Reese, Bennett; Vermont; ret'd; hockey all-American, Hobey Baker runnerup '81; rw drafted by Winnipeg Jets '82 but after part of minor league season opted for baseball; rhp; drafted by California '82; 10 seasons in California organization and at ML level '85-91; joined White Sox as free agent '92-96; ML record: 380 games, 242 started, 30 complete games, 1729ip, 1748h, 876r, 154hr, 665w, 1003k, 72wp, 9bk, 106-108 w/l, 11so, 7sv, 4.12era; 0-2 in LCS; 1st pitcher in ML history to surrender back-to-back homers to a father/son combination (Ken Griffey Sr/Jr); played '97 season in Italy; mem. Cdn Baseball Hall of Fame; res. Rancho Santa Fe, Calif.

McCAW, Doug (bowling); b. 26 Nov 1954, Regina, Sask.; given name: Douglas Ronald; m. Wendy Shewchuk; c. Ashley, Taylor; letter carrier; mem. 2 YBC Sask., 1 ntl title teams; '86 Sask. mixed, '93 men's title teams, '93 singles; made ntl history rolling perfect 450 game during '93 Cdn championships for which he received $50,000; ntl men's open singles gold '94, silver '98, '00; 3 ntl open team silver; twice ntl championship all-star; level 2 coach guiding numerous YBC teams at prov. level; mem. Regina 5-pin Assn. exec. 15yrs; chair. Coca-Cola Classic cash tournament; coached Sask. open all-stars '90, '93; sr. hockey referee to '91; level B basketball official; mem. 2

Sask. sr. men's B title fastball teams; res. Regina, Sask.

McCLEERY, Alan (canoeing); b. 13 Jun 1929, Montreal, Que.; m. Joan Louise Hart; c. Colin, Colleen, Gail, Shawn; Sir George Williams; ret'd mgr. Bell Canada; 5yrs water polo Montreal Concordia; 8yrs football to sr. level; competed at 175lb class in Golden Glove boxing; competed nationally, internationally in canoeing; mem. 1000m kayak tandem team '60 Olympics; mem. Cdn Ski Instructors Alliance from '66; alpine skiing teacher Mont. Ste. Sauveur, Gray Rocks, Morin Heights, Vorlage; res. Ottawa, Ont.

McCLELLAN, Reg (wheelchair basketball); b. 2 Apr 1954, Pierceland, Sask.; m. Chantal Benoit; consultant; ED Cdn Wheelchair Basketball Assn. '88-99; significant role in development of wheelchair basketball throughout Canada; founding ED Cdn Wheelchair Basketball Fed. '94; mem. Intl. Wheelchair Basketball Fed. '87-00; gold classifier from '90; founding pres/CEO RGK Wheelchairs Inc. '02; began career in Edmonton; founded Northern Lights organization; played with clubs in Vancouver, Calgary, Toronto, St. Hyacinthe, Halifax, Ottawa; player/coach various teams including ntl team '74-94; multiple all-star, MVP awards; mem. 10 ntl title teams; competed 4 Paralympic Games, 6 world championships; capt. '91 Stoke-Mandeville World Games gold medal team; CWBL gold '87 Calgary Grizzlies, '89, '95 Ottawa Royals; player/coach Gold Cup silver '86, bronze '90; silver '92, bronze '94; with Alta. Northern Lights, Ottawa Royals 4 NWBT final four; capt. Cdn team '92 Barcelona Paralympics; ntl tourney MVP trophy bears his name; res. Orleans, Ont.

McCLINTOCK, Joel (water skiing); b. 9 Oct 1960, Mississauga, Ont.; given name: Joel Scott; m. Michelle; c. J.D., Justin; coach ntl jr. team, program dev. dir.; mem. ntl team '77-85; 1st intl. competition '76; ntl jr. title '76; ntl boys title '77; skied in 1st world championship '77; won 1st intl. medal, gold, '78; ntl open overall titles '78-80; world overall title '79; California Intl.Cup, Pan-Am Group titles '80; ntl trick record 7300 points; he & sister Judy only siblings ever to win overall world titles; ntl slalom record; author *Complete Instructional Book of Waterskiing*; Viscount Alexander award '79; 3 PetroCan coaching-excellence awards; mem. Cdn Olympic, Cambridge, Mississauga Sports halls of fame; res. Florida.

McCLINTOCK, Judy (water skiing); b. 6 Sep 1963, Mississauga, Ont.; given name: Judith Louise; m. Perry Messer; c. Jamie, Jenna, Jay; fitness club co-owner; pro water skier; ntl jr. girls tricks title age 9, jr. girls overall titlist '74, '76-77; alternate '77 world championships team; 3rd slalom 1st intl. appearance '78 Group One championships; '85 (women's tricks gold), '91, '93 (team gold) world championships; '81 British Masters overall title; 3rd jumping, 4th overall '81 world championships; women's overall world title '95; jr. girls slalom, tricks, girls slalom, tricks, jump, open women's tricks, jumps records; with brothers Jim, Joel, Jeff, Lions Club citizens of '77; mem. Cdn Olympic Sports Hall of Fame; res. Northampton, Mass.

McCLOY, Paul (t&f); b. 6 Nov 1963, St. John's, Nfld.; Memorial; teacher; distance runner; ntl jr. 10,000m titlist; CIAU titlist; ntl x-country champion; PAG, Canada Games bronze; ntl x-country title '90; silver 5000m ntls, Cdn

Airlines; gold 10,000m Harry Jerome Classic; National Capital, Boston Milk Run 10km titles; competed '90, '94 CG, '94 world x-country; 3 CIAU x-country all-Cdn; 1 CIAU indoor t&f record; mem. Mount Pearl TC; brother Bill mem. ntl water polo team, sister Cora ntl rowing team; res. St. John's, Nfld.

McCOMB, Bill (hockey); b. 14 Dec 1920, Newmarket, Ont.; given name: William Eugene; m. Janet Allan; c. David, Bill Jr.; owner McComb Heating; Jr C, B Aurora '36-38; St. Catharines Jr B '39; Toronto Hockey League Major Sr. '40-42; army teams '42-44; pro Providence '45-46; St Louis '47-49; Indianapolis '50; AHL record fastest goal after start of period (6 sec.) '46; mem. Owen Sound Mercurys '51-54, Meaford '55-57; coached several Western Ont. teams, Owen Sound Old Timers; res. Owen Sound, Ont.

McCONACHIE, John (football/hockey); b. 18 Jul 1941, Montreal, Que.; given name: John Alexander; m. Diane Gregory; c. Sean, Ryan; Sir George Williams, BA; ret'd dir. marketing, communication CIAU; HS male athlete of '58-60; mem. Rosemount Bombers '60 ntl jr. football titlists, '61 ntl finalists; mem. '63-64 SGW ntl finalists hockey team; 3yrs head coach South Shore Colts juv football team; interscholastic gymnastics, badminton (singles, doubles titles), soccer (team capt. 2 seasons), volleyball (team capt.); pres. South Shore Colts football club 2 yrs; outstanding-def award South Shore intermediate HL '66-67; Frank Ratcliffe Sport Canada award '98; res. Stittsville, Ont.

McCONKEY. Jim (skiing); b. 12 Jun 1926, Barrie, Ont.; m. Paule Deschenes; c. Susan, George, Shane; ret'd ski school dir./retailer; began skiing age 6; instructor Gray Rocks '47-48, '52-53, Yosemite, Calif. '48-51, Alta, Utah '53-63; mgr. Banff chairlift corp '51-52; ski school dir. Park City '63-64; Tod Mt. (now Sun Peaks) ski school dir./shop owner '64-68; coach Franz Gabl summer ski race camps '64-68; dir/retailer Whistler Mt. '68-86, goodwill promoter Whistler '86-96; from '50 appeared in numerous ski films and subject of varied magazine articles; active in archery, shooting, canoeing, kayaking, golf; mem. Cdn Ski Hall of Fame; res. Borrego Springs, Calif/Denman Island, B.C.

McCONNELL, Russ (hockey/football); b. 7 Jan 1918, Montreal, Que.; d. 7 Sep 1942, Gulf of St. Lawrence; given name: Russell Henry; McGill.; while attending McGill mem. 3 Queen's Cup CIHU, 3 Alex Thompson Trophy IIHL title hockey teams, 2 football teams; 2 IIHL scoring crowns; 12 McGill hockey records; capt. '39 squad; set career (94 games) records for goals (116), assists (95), points (211) which stood 4 decades; most points single game (10) in '39, accomplishing feat twice; rejected NYR pro offers; died in WWII when ship torpedoed; Ken Stewart Cup as QSHL MVP '39; mem. McGill Sports Hall of Fame.

McCORMACK, Mildred (basketball); b. 21 Jun 1909, Buffalo, N.Y.; d. Mar 1991, New Westminster, B.C.; m. Walter Wilkie (d); c. Maurice, Jack; ret'd secretary; catcher 3 Edmonton Toddies baseball title teams; forward famed Edmonton Grads '26-32, 94 games, 924 points, 9.8 avg.; husband mem. '28 Olympic lacrosse team; mem. Canadian Basketball, Alta. Sports halls of fame.

McCORMICK, Frank (shooting); b. 14 Sep 1924,

Montreal, Que.; given name: Frank McLeod; m. Lillian Johnson; c. Brian, Theresa, Kathleen; Sir George Williams; dir. marketing, Information Science Industries Ltd.; sporting rifle, match rifle, handgun, trap, skeet shooting '48-74; ntl pro skeet champion '59, '61-62, '67, Que. '59-63, '67, Ont. '60; Can-Am '67; mem. ntl skeet team '59 PAG, all-American team '62, all-Canadian trap team '65; mgr. ntl team '58, '62 world championships, '60, '64 Olympic, '59 PAG; COA dir.; CASF dir., v-p; Cdn PAG comm. secty; Cdn BEG Assn. dir.; Shooting Federation of Canada secty, treas, exec.-dir.; Cdn, Que. Skeet Shooting Assn. founding dir.; Que. Rifle Assn. dir.; Ont. Skeet Shooting Assn. secty; Cdn delegate International Shooting Union; conducted financial campaigns, arranged travel, participation for 12 Cdn intl. shooting teams; tournament dir. NSSA world skeet championships '63-65; tournament dir. ntl skeet championships more than 20yrs; ISU Jubilee Medal '57; Confederation Medal '67; Que. Safety Award; res. Beaconsfield, Que.

McCOURT, Dan (officiating/hockey); b. 14 Aug 1954, Falconbridge, Ont.; m. Betty Behm; c. Lisa, Shari; oficiated at minor levels until joining NHL '79; appeared in initial NHL game as linesman 27 Dec '80; worked '90 all-star game; through '03 linesman 1525 NHL scheduled, 56 playoff games; active with Easter Seals Society; brother Dale played in NHL; res. Detroit, Mich./Garson, Ont.

McCRAE, Don (basketball/coaching); b. 14 Apr 1935, Guelph, Ont.; given name: Donald Glen; m. Judith Ann Moore; c. Susan, Kate; UWO, BA, McMaster, BPhE; coach Waterloo; jr. B hockey Guelph '53-55, sr.A Kingston '57; basketball Tillsonburg Livingstons '58-60; mem. '59 PAG, '60 Olympic teams, intercollegiate titlists '61; coached 6 Kitchener HS basketball, 4 football title teams; coach Waterloo from '71; 8 consec. league titles; 3rd ntls 3 times; only undefeated team CIAU history '75; 1 CIAU coach-of-yr award; coach ntl women's team '77-84; bronze '79 worlds, PAG, FISU Games; dispute with Basketball Canada exec. led to firing '83 but when players revolted was reinstated; OUA J.S. McManus coaching award; mem. Ont., Cdn Basketball Hall of Fame; res. Waterloo, Ont.

McCRAE, John (curling); b. 26 Apr 1940, Lindsay, Ont.; given name: John Duncan Sinclair; m. Eleanor; c. Carol, Scott, Steve; OCA GM from '88; mem. Lindsay recreation commision '74-83, chair. '79-83; began curling '53; Ont. schoolboy finalist '57-59; 3 Gov.-Gen.'s zone winner; Consols prov. finalist '71; Consols zone winner '73; Silver Tankard zone winner '75; pres. Lindsay CC '71, life mem. from '92; CCA award of merit '87; club rep., zone rep., chair. competitions comm. OCA in '70s; pres. OCA '82-83; promotions dir. OCA '84-88; res. Oshawa, Ont.

McCRAE, Judy (field hockey); b. 24 Apr 1947, Sarnia, Ont.; given name: Judith Ann Moore; m. Don McCrae; c. Susan, Kate; WMich, BA, NCarolina, MSc; teacher, coach; Waterloo athletic dir., coach women's field hockey, badminton, curling; co-ordinator WO women's summer games Kitchener '74; 3yrs regional rep. OFHA; 4yrs publicity officer, exec. mem. OWIAA; mem. advisory council, 3yrs dir. Waterloo regional sports council; instructor ntl coaching development program; '76 pres. OWFHA; v-p CWFHA from '77; mem. steering comm. Ont. Sportplan '76;

Ont. rep CWIAU; chairman Cdn team development comm. CWFHA; *CBC-TV* color commentator '84 Olympics; res. Waterloo, Ont.

McCREADY, Earl (wrestling); b. 6 May 1905, Lansdowne, Ont., d. 6 Dec 1983, Seattle, Wash; m. Margaret; Okla. A&M, BPhE; masseur; launched wrestling career Regina CI, attending first tournament New Westminster, B.C., '26; lettered in A&M football, all-state gd; mem. varsity wrestling team '28-30 winning all matches in 30 major college meets over 3yrs; capt. '30 team; 4 Cdn heavyweight titles; 3 Dodder (top points) wrestling awards, 1 Curtis Cup (outstanding scholar-athlete), Roberts award (outstanding athlete), dean's honor roll 2 successive semesters; mem. '28 Olympic team; gold '30 BEG as Canadians swept all 7 wrestling categories; by '30 had won every amateur wrestling honor available in Cdn, US, Commonwealth; wrestled as pro throughout world; BE pro title, defended it several times; ranked 2nd in world to Jim Londos, to whom he lost in world title bid '32; 1st wrestler to give demonstration on television; mem. US, Cdn Wrestling, Helm's, Okla., Calgary Stampede, Cdn Olympic, Sask., Canada's Sports halls of fame.

McCREATH, Ralph (figure skating); b. 27 Apr 1919, Toronto, Ont., d. 2 May 1997, Toronto, Ont.; div.; c. Jim, Martin, Paul, Michelle; UofT, LLD; lawyer, QC; 19 ntl, NA singles, pairs, fours championships; nominated to '40 Olympic team but games not held due to WW2; from '56 intl, Olympic judge, referee; chair./secty exec. comm/ gov. Olympic Trust; mem. Cdn Figure Skating Hall of Fame.

McCREDIE, Nancy (t&f); b. 5 Feb 1945, Belleville, Ont.; animal groomer; shot put, discus specialist; ntl shot record placing 5th '64 Olympics; gold shot '63, '67, discus '63 PAG; bronze shot '66 CG; ntl female track athlete of '63; PB: discus 169'31/2", shot 52'61/4"; mem. Brampton, Cdn Olympic Sports halls of fame; res. Shawville, Que.

McCRIMMON, Brad (hockey); b. 29 Mar 1959, Dodsland, Sask.; def Brandon (WHL) '77-79; 2 WHL 1st team all-star; drafted by Boston '79; NHL with Boston '79-82, Philadelphia '82-87, Calgary '87-90, Detroit '90-93, Hartford '93-96, Phoenix '96-97; NHL plus/minus leader '88; NHL 2nd team all-star '88; asst coach NYI '97-99, Calgary '00-03, Atlanta '03-04; asst. Cdn '03 Swiss Cup, -18 world championships teams; mem. 1 Stanley Cup winner; NHL record 1222 scheduled games, 81g, 322a, 116 playoff games, 11g, 18a; res. Dodsland, Sask.

McCUBBINS, Chris (t&f); b. 22 Nov 1945, Enid, Okla.; Okla. State; steeplechase specialist; NCAA Div. 1 champ '67; competed '67 PAG; moved to Winnipeg '70 and dominated long-distance running at pvcl level winning majority of races from steeplechase to 20km to '89; ntl steeplechase title '72, 2 ntl x-country titles, won 10,000m '76 Olympic trials but injuries, as they had in '68, prevented him from competing; from '71-77 set 7 Man records, dominated Cdn distance-running scene; ranked 4th master runner by *Runner's World* '93; mem. Man. Sports Hall of Fame; res. Winnipeg, Man.

McCULLOCH, Jack (speed skating); b. 15 Aug 1872, Perth, Ont., d. Jan 1918, Winnipeg, Man.; c. Marguerite;

skate manufacturer; mem. Winnipeg Victorias who won 9 of 11 hockey games on Eastern tour and outscored rivals 76-36, '90; Man. cycling champion '92; Western roller skating titlist; ntl speed skating titles '93, '97; US nationals '96, world title '97; pro '98 and barnstormed several yrs; made possibly 1st pair of tube skates in Canada; mem. Canadian Speed Skating, Canada's Sports halls of fame.

McCUSKER, Joan (curling); b. 8 Jun 1965, Yorkton, Sask; m. Brian McCusker; c. Rory, Christina, 1 other; UofSask BEd; ret'd teacher, motivational speaker; began curling age 12; mem. '92 Sask. mixed title rink; 3 Sask. women's title rinks; 2nd Sandra Schmirler's 3-time STOH, world title rinks; gold '98 Olympics; *CBC-TV* curling analyst; *TSN* Skins title '98; *CP* team of '98 award; mem. Canada's Sports Hall of Fame; res. Regina, Sask.

McDADI, Hatem (tennis/coaching); 10 Jan 1964, Beirut, Lebanon; m. Jennifer Lynne Lennedy; McGill BEd; dir. player dev. Tennis Canada; co-founder Trivett-McDadi Tennis Academy, dir. part-owner CMG Tennis Inc.; former Cdn champ, Davis Cup team mem.; coach '00 Olympic women's team; Sunshine Cup capt.; Tennis Can. touring coach; 7 yrs Fed. Cup coach; certified Level 4 coach; coaching excellence award '97; res. Mississauga, Ont.

McDERMID, Heather (rowing); b. 17 Oct 1968, Calgary, Alta.; Rice; business owner; NCAA all-American track star '89-90; mem. ntl rowing team from '95; mem. women's 8s silver medal crew '96, bronze '00 Olympics; Rice track MVP award '90; res. Calgary, Alta.

McDIARMID, Don (tennis); b. 21 Nov 1915, Ottawa, Ont.; d. 3 Feb 2002, Lac Carling, Que.; given name: Donald Stuart; m. Janet Scanlon; c. Kimberley, Margo; ret. public servant; numerous Ottawa, Eastern Cdn, Que. doubles, singles titles; ntl open men's singles title '40; mem. '46 Davis Cup team vs. Mexico; with Jean Marois rep. Canada Pan-Am championships; twice played at Forest Hills; life mem. Rideau Tennis & Squash Club; mem. Ottawa Sports Hall of Fame.

McDONALD, Dennis (hockey); b. 10 Apr 1937, Flin Flon, Man.; given name: Dennis Francis; m. Valdeen Bremwell; c. Andrew, Marcia, Michelle; NDak, BSc, Mich. State, MSc; hockey administrator; football letterman UND '57; mem. St. Vital Bulldogs, Manitoba '58-60, ntl champions '60; coached football Winnipeg Kelvin HS, Man. title '62; hockey 20yrs from minor through college ranks; pres. Cdn Hockey Coaches Assn. '74; Winnipeg city sports, athletics supervisor 6yrs.; Scarborough Centennial College AD 7yrs.; Percy Genser HS sportsmanship award '64; UND football scholarship '64; St. Vital most valuable lineman '58; chair. IIHF coaches comm. '76; AGM/dir. hockey operations Winnipeg Jets, GM Moncton Hawks; Gordon Juckes award; mem. Man. Hockey Hall of Fame; res. River Heights, Man.

McDONALD, Doug (rowing); b. 11 May 1935, Thorsby, Alta.; given name: Douglas John; m. Diane Louise Wyma; c. Donald Andrew, Dustin Allan; UBC, BSF; corporate mgr.; 8s specialist; mem. '54 BEG, '55 Royal Henley, '56 Olympic teams; mem. Cdn Olympic Hall of Fame; res. Garibaldi, B.C.

McDONALD, Joan (archery); b. 23 Feb 1943, Toronto, Ont.; given name: Joan Frances Gallie; div.; c. David, Christopher; computer trainer; ntl FS target '62, '64-67, '92-93, FS field '64-66, '89, '91, '93-94; grand champion '64-66; mem. 6 world teams; team silver, individual bronze '79 PAG; team gold '79 field Championships of Americas; FCA female athlete of '89; team leader '95 Olympic trials, world championships, '96 Olympics; head coach '99 PAG; FCA coach of '92; figure skating judge; mem. Cdn Olympic Sports Hall of Fame; res. Toronto, Ont.

McDONALD, Lanny (hockey); b. 16 Feb 1953, Hanna, Alta.; given name: Lanny King; m. Ardelle Moyer; c. Andra, Leah, Barrett, Graham; hockey exec., marketing exec.; jr. Lethbridge, Calgary, Medicine Hat; Toronto's 1st choice, 4th overall '73 amateur draft; Leafs record for rw 93 points '75-76; mem. Team Canada '76, '81; mem. '78 NHL Challenge Series; Colorado '79-81; Calgary '81-89; 4 NHL all-star; scored 66g '83; NHL record: 1111 games, 500g, 506a, 117 playoff games, 44g, 40a; co-capt. '89 Stanley Cup winner; v-p/marketing dir., corporate development Flames '90-00; GM Team Canada '01, dir. player personnel '04 IIHF worlds; Bill Masterton Memorial Trophy '83; King Clancy Memorial trophy '88; NHL man of '89; 2 Ralph Scurfield Humanitarian awards; active in charitable work Special Olympics, Ronald McDonald House, Children's Miracle Network telethon; jersey 9 ret'd by Flames; mem. Hockey, Alta. sports halls of fame; res. Calgary, Alta.

McDONALD, Les (triathlon/builder/administration); b. 30 Apr 1933, Gates Head-on-Tyne, Eng.; m. Monique Richer; c. Ian, Helen, Daniel; ret'd electrician; intl alpine, x-country ski competitor; made major mountaineering ascents in Europe, America; coached Whistler, BC alpine teams; creator 1st Whistler downhill course; founder Triathlon Canada, Pan-Am Triathlon Confed.; instrumental in achieving program status for triathlon PAG, Central Amer, Caribbean Games; pres/founder Intl Triathlon Union from '89; key role in helping triathlon earn Olympic status; similar role in CG, Goodwill Games; council mem Intl Sports Feds; mem. IOC sub-comm; 5 age-group world triathlon titles; played role in successful Vancouver 2010 Olympic bid; Nice, France civic award; mem BC Sports Hall of Fame; res. N. Vancouver, B.C.

McDONALD, Vern (basketball); b. 5 Jul 1910, Winnipeg, Man.; d. 1999, Hamilton, Ont.; given name: Vern Henry; m. Ethel Fines; ret'd; coached basketball teams to 5 city, 3 Ont. 1 ntl championship; secty-treas. Basketball Ont. 16 yrs.; treas. CABA '72-76; lacrosse coach; honored by Ont. government for contribution to sport, Cdn Coaches Assn. for contribution to basketball, International Assn. of Approved Basketball Officials for work on behalf of basketball in Canada; life mem. Basketball Ont.

McEACHERN, Archie (cycling); b. 1874, Woodville, Ont., d. 13 May 1902, Atlantic City, N.J.; ntl amateur welterweight boxing title 1898; fought briefly as pro; 25-mile Boston indoor cycling title '00; world record 5-mile race, Chicago 6-day title '02; rapidly developing into one of most popular riders of his day, he died of injuries suffered in training accident.

McEACHERN, Ken (football); b. 14 Jan 1953, Regina, Sask.; m. Charlotte; Weber State Coll.; CFL Sask. '74-82, '84, Toronto '83; CFL rookie of '74; 3 WFC, 1 EFC, 1 all-Cdn safety selections; CFL interception leader with 10 '80; all-time Sask. interception leader; Schenley outstanding-Cdn nominee '83; mem. '83 Grey Cup champions; Tom Pate award '81; res. Regina, Sask.

McELROY, Walter (golf); b. 11 Jul 1927, Vancouver, B.C.; given name: Walter Grassie; m. Jean Engbaum; c. Walter Jr., Bradley, Whitney, Robert; pres. Grassie Jewelers Ltd.; ntl jr. runnerup '46; quarterfinalist '46 ntl men's match play championships, semifinalist '48; ranked top amateur in Canada '49; ntl amateur title '51; twice defeated Frank Stranahan to rank as top amateur in world '52; mem. America's Cup team '52, '54; 2nd '54 America's Cup; top amateur, 7th overall Canadian Open '54; 2nd '54 Commonwealth matches; quaterfinalist '54 British Amateur; mem. 7 BC Willingdon Cup teams, 3 winners; 2 Vancouver city jr. titles; '48 Vancouver city men's closed champion; 2 BC jr. titles; '51 BC men's closed champion; ret'd from competitive golf '54; mem. BC Sports Hall of Fame; res. Vancouver, B.C.

McEWEN, Bill (builder/football/hockey); b. 29 Nov 1918, Ottawa, Ont.; d. 17 Jun 2004, West Vancouver, B.C.; given name: William Livingston; m. Irene; c. Terry, Ellen; Guelph BSc; ex-sales mgr. Atomic Energy; part-owner/pres. Ottawa Rough Riders '62-69; co-founder/pres. CAFA '65-66; dir./pres. B.C. Lions '72-75; part-owner/dir. Vancouver Canucks '74-94; pres. SFC '73-77; v-p/dir. Commonwealth Games Assn.; chair Ntl Advisory Council on Fitness & Amateur Sport; mem. Canada Games Council; hon. pres. Cdn Parks & Rec. Assn.; dir. Old Timers HA; co-founder/dir. Ottawa Nationals (WHA); co-founder NHL Alumni Assn.; chair. Canada Safety Council; established Interprovincial jr. football league; dir. Northwest Sports Enterprises; pres. B.C. Liberal Party; mem. Capilano G&CC; Bryce Taylor Memorial award for volunteer leadership.

McEWEN, Cam (builder/curling); b. 1890, Schreiber, Ont.; d. 18 Feb 1970, Thunder Bay, Ont.; given name: Cameron Willard; pioneer in the sport competing in myriad of bonspiels; mem. Fort William CC '05-70, pres. '22-23; originating mem. Dominion HS Curling Assoc.; chair. NO school curling comm. '48-60; ret'd from competition '53; chair. 1st ntl HS championship '56; life mem. MCA, Ft. William CC, Cdn School Curling Assn., Kakabeka Falls CC, NOCA; mem. Cdn Curling, NWO Sports halls of fame.

McEWEN, Don (t&f); b. 27 Aug 1928, Montreal, Que.; given name: Donald Scott; m. Amber Jean Clark; c. Scott Cameron, Anna Maria; UMich, BBA, MA; sales rep, educator; Cdn jr/sr mile champion; set HS mile record 4:18.8; attended UMan on athletic scholarship; capt. UMan t&f team '52; Big-10 4-mile x-country champion, record holder '49, 2 mile, indoor mile titles '50; NCAA 2 mile champion/record holder/all-American; Big 10 4-mile, 1-mile titles/records; world indoor dirt track 2-mile record; anchored indoor/outdoor distance medley relay world records '51-52; anchored US record 4-mile relay team '51 Drake relays; Cdn/BE 2-mile indoor/outdoor records; ntl mile/2-mile records; anchored world distance medley relay record team '52; held Cdn scholastic mile/2-mile records several yrs; ret'd from competition '52; coached UofT track team '53-54; coach UMan track '55-83; Big-10 medal for outstanding athletics/academics '52; Jack Davies trophy '51; mem. Mich. Hall of Honor; res. Ann Arbor, Mich.

McFARLAND, Packy (football/basketball); b. 25 Sep 1934, Bangor, Me.; given name: John; m. Irene; c. John Jr., Mike, Kathleen, Patricia, Joe, Debbi, David, Danny; St. Francis Xavier, BA, BEd, Springfield College, MPhE, DPhE; ret'd assoc. prof., phys ed chair. St.FX; mem. St.FX football, basketball teams '52-56, capt. both teams '56; head basketball coach '60-74; NSSFL off/def all-star teams '55; *Halifax Herald* outstanding-lineman trophy '55; pres. Cdn Assn. Basketball Coaches '72-73; honor award CABC '76; pres. Antigonish Minor Basketball Assn. '75-77; mem. St.FX Sports Hall of Fame; res. Antigonish, N.S.

McFARLANE, Bob (t&f/football); b. 28 May 1927, London, Ont.; given name: Robert Malcolm: m. Patricia Jean Henderson; c. Janie, Wendy, Laurie; Ridley College, UWO, MD; ret'd plastic surgeon, professor of surgery; backfielder UWO team which won CIAU titles '45-47, '49-50; mem. intercollegiate, Eastern Cdn all-star teams; ran 880yd relay 1:27.1, 440yd 47.5, mile relay 3:17.1 '47, ran 400m 47.3 '48; ran 500yd 48.00, 1000yd 2:18.1, mile relay 3:32.4, 300yd 30.00, 880yd 1:53.2 '50; flag-bearer '48 summer Olympics, mem. 4x100m relay team which placed fifth; harness race horse owner, breeder; Lou Marsh Trophy '50; John W. Davies trophy (AAUofC) '47, '50; mem. UWO W-Club Sports Hall of Fame; res. London, Ont.

McFARLANE, Brent (t&f, coaching); b. 2 May 1945, Winnipeg, Man.; given name: Allyn Brent; c. Christopher, Andrea; gc. Bryce; Waterloo, hons kinesiology; taught grade school phys ed 25yrs; full-time coach; mem. UW t&f teams '68-70: 2 OUAA title teams; 2 varsity record setting relay teams; 4x200m relay record stood 20 years before broken '89 by team he coached; head coach KW t&f club 23yrs served on exec. 25yrs; wrote, established jr. club program, head coach, Waterloo x-country team '89-96, t&f team from '89; coached nationally unranked UW women's x-country team to upset OWIAA provincial and CIAU ntl title '96; Waterloo's first ntl title in 20yrs; ntl hurdle coach over 28yrs; level IV NCCP certified coach in sprints and hurdles and a level III middle- and long-distance coach; has studied and visited coaches in over 50 countries; knowledge of biomechanics, speed, strength and current world trends has resulted in publications of over 550 articles; author Canada's NCCP Level II Sprints, Hurdles, Relay and Level III Hurdles, 4 hurdle books; 4 editions of *'The Science of Hurdling'* have sold over 12,000 copies worldwide; Cdn clinician for hurdle and sprint clinics throughout world; over 35yrs intl coaching experience, including 33 ntl teams; head coach '00 hurdle coach '80, '84 '88 Olympics; coached 4 worlds, 3 CG, 2 PAG; head coach 3 ntl jr. teams vs USA; head coach, '93 Pan Am jr., '94 jr. worlds; 2 coach of yr. awards, 3M Coaching Award of Excellence '93; OWIAA/CIAU x-country coach of '96; 3 OWIAA women's t&f coach-of-yr awards; 1st annual Special Recognition Award from KW Big Brothers '02; mem. UW Athletic Hall of Fame; res. Waterloo, Ont.

McFARLANE, Brian (hockey); b. 10 Aug 1931, New Liskeard, Ont.; m. Joan; c. Michael, Lauren, Brenda; St.

Lawrence; hockey historian, broadcaster; capt. Inkerman Rockets Jr. A hockey team; attended St. Lawrence on hockey scholarship; 3yrs class pres; 1st to score more than 100 career goals for school; as ctr/capt. led team to 2 NCAA finals; all-American; 17yrs mem. NHL Oldtimers (only amateur); sports commentator *CFRA* Ottawa, *WRGB-TV* Schenectady, *CFRB* Toronto; 1st Cdn to work network hockey for *CBS* '60; sports dir. *CFCF-TV* Montreal, *CFTO-TV* Toronto; 26yrs *Hockey Night in Canada*; 3yrs *NBC* hockey; introduced animated Peter Puck character to hockey telecasts; author of more than 40 books on hockey; comes by writing skills honestly as his father Leslie (aka Franklin W. Dixon) authored first 23 books in famous Hardy Boys series; hon. pres. Society for International Hockey Research; editorial consultant Total Sports Raleigh, N.C.; operates hockey museum in Niagara Falls, Ont.; popular public speaker/MC; mem. Hockey (media section), St. Lawrence, Ottawa sports halls of fame; res. Willowdale, Ont.

McFARLANE, Don (football/t&f); b. 18 May 1926, London, Ont.; given name: Donald Cecil; m. Frances Smith (d); c. David, Donald, Karen, Joanne; m. Llynda Hinds; Ridley College, UWO, MD; ret'd ocular surgeon; with brother Bob mem. UWO Mustangs powerhouse backfield '44-50; ntl titles '45-47, '49-50; intercollegiate, Eastern Cdn all-star; George McCullough MVP Trophy; mem. UWO track team '46-49 specializing 200m, 400m, 800m events; competed Eastern Canada vs Eastern US track meets '46-47; mem. 4x100m 5th place relay team '48 Olympics; qualified '50 BEG team but did not compete due to final year medical student obligations; mem. UWO W-Club Sports Hall of Fame; res. London, Ont.

McFATER, Allan (boxing); b. 6 Jan 1931, Mimico, Ont.; given name: Allan James; m. Joan Constance Allen; c. Bradley, Cheryl, Barbara, Grant, Jeffrey; Meisterschaft Coll.; ret'd sales/marketing Molson Breweries; welterweight; began boxing age 10 Mimico Boys Club; fought 90 amateur bouts, winning 86, losing decisions to Norm Thompson, Ron Lacelle, Carl Zoba and drawing with Clayton Kenny; defeated each in rematches; fought 40 pro bouts, winning 34; held Cdn welterweight title '54-55; lost decision to world lightweight champion Jimmy Carter '52; mem. Cdn Boxing, Mississauga sports halls of fame; res. Mississauga, Ont.

McGEE, Doug (football/t&f); b. 6 Sep 1954, Ottawa, Ont.; m. Patricia McQuay; c. Raquel; Richmond, BA.; insurance exec. RBC Dominion Securities; 4 HS shot put titles; set records which stood for 17yrs; Ont. HS shot put title '73; mem. Ottawa Uplands Kinsmen Harriers TC '67-73; co-capt. Glebe HS jr. football titlists '69; ol Ottawa Sooners '72; attended Richmond on football scholarship '73-77; Southern Conf. title '75; co-capt. sr. year; played all five ol positions Rough Riders '77-81; coached o-line Carleton '91, UofOtt '82, '85, ntl jr. champion Sooners '84; active in PR activities for Rough Riders and with MD Assn; p.-pres. Mississauga chapter Cdn Life Underwriters; res. Scarborough, Ont.

McGEE, Frank (hockey); b. 1882, Ottawa, Ont.; d. 16 Sep 1916, Courcelette, France; given name: Francis; ctr/rover Ottawa Silver Seven '03-06; mem. 3 consecutive Stanley Cup winners; 71 goals, 23 regular season games; 22 playoff games, 63 goals, including 14 in single game vs. Dawson City '05 as Ottawa won 23-2, 8 consecutive goals in span of

8 minutes, 20 seconds; 7 times 5 goals single game; mem. Ottawa Sports, Hockey halls of fame.

McGILL, Frank (all-around); b. 20 Jun 1894, Montreal, Que., d. 2 Jul 1980, Montreal, Que.; given name: Frank Scholes; m. Margaret Williamson; c. Isabel, Nancy, John; McGill; ret'd Air Vice-Marshall; qb'd Montreal Big Four '19 title team calling signals in French; ntl 100yd outdoor record '12; capt. MAAA water polo team, 3 ntl titles; mem. George Hamilton international sailing crew; pres. Interprovincial Football Union, MAAA Football Club; Sir Vincent Meredith Trophy as best all-around MAAA athlete; CFL Schenley awards trustee; Companion of Bath, Haakon VII Cross of Liberation, Order of Lafayette; mem. Canadian Football, Canada's Sports halls of fame.

McGILLIVRAY, David (figure skating); b. 30 Sep 1949, Sarnia, Ont.; given name: David Lachlan; UofT, MD, FRCPS, FAAP; pediatrician. assoc. dir Montreal Children's Hospital, assoc. prof. pediatrics McGill; '66 ntl jr. men's title; '70 sr. men's title; mem. worlds teams '68-70, '69 NA championships, '68 Olympics; turned to marathon running late '70's; competed Montreal marathon '79, Ottawa '80, Boston '81; best time 2:45.41 Boston '81; res. Montreal, Que.

McGIMSIE, Billy (hockey); b. 7 Jun 1880, Woodsville, Ont., d. 28 Oct 1968, Calgary, Alta.; given name: William George; ctr Kenora Thistles 10yrs; entire major league career with one club; mem. 4 Stanley Cup finalists, 1 winner; dislocated shoulder in Ottawa exhibition contest ended career; mem. Hockey, NWO Sports halls of fame.

McGOWAN, George (football); b. 10 Mar 1948, Bethesda, Md; m. Jo; Glendale Jr. College; Kansas; began career as youth in Glendale; rcvr/db Kansas earning Orange Bowl MVP honors; drafted by NFL Atlanta; joined CFL Edmonton '71-78; 3 CFL all-star; 5 Grey Cups, 2 winners; CFL career record 8yrs, 424 catches for 6356yds, 42tds; set CFL single-game reception record of 15 (since broken), 98 single-season receptions (since broken); had 48 consec. games with one or more receptions; '73 Schenley Outstanding Player award following 81 catches for 1123yds, 9tds; Jeff Nicklin award; worked as male model in off-season; mem. Cdn Football Hall, Edmonton Eskimos Wall of Fame; res. California.

McGRATH, Larry (curling); b. 14 Jun 1940, Dodsland, Sask.; given name: Larry Martin; m. Agnes Heit; c. Grant, Daryl, Scott; dir. Hec Gervais Academic & Curling Scholarship Foundation, farmer; baseball, softball standout several years; 14 time competitor Northern Sask. Brier playdowns; 4 times prov. finals, twice runnerup; skip Sask entry to runnerup spot '74 Brier; skip '67-68, '71 Sask., Cdn mixed title rinks posting 28-2 record at nationals; 3 Edmonton carspiel titles; mem. Sask. Sports, Canadian Curling halls of fame; res. Dodsland, Sask.

McGRATH, Seamus (cycling); b. 3 May 1976, Mississauga, Ont.; given name: Seamus Patrick; Guelph; professional athlete; ntl team from '96; Ont. champ '95; '98 espoir x-country ntl champion; competed '98, '02 MTB worlds; overall gold '99 Cactus Cup (USA); 5th x-country '99 PAG; bronze '01 MTB ntls; silver '02 CG, MTB x-country; overall gold NORBA short-track championship, Canada Cup; res. Victoria, B.C.

McGUIRE, Pierre (hockey, coaching); b. 8 Aug 1961, Englewood, N.J.; given name: Regis Pierre; m. Melanie Labonte; c. Justine Rose, Ryan Pierre; Lower Canada Coll, Hobart Coll. BA; hockey broadcaster; 4yrs hockey, football, baseball Hobart Coll.; played pro in Europe; attended NJ Devils training camp '84-85; coach Hobart Coll, Babson Coll., St. Lawrence U '84-90; special assignment scout, asst. coach Pittsburgh Penguins '90-92, 2 Stanley Cups; asst. coach, asst. GM, head coach Hartford Whalers '92-94; at 32 youngest NHL head coach '94; head pro-scout, asst. coach Ottawa Senators '94-96; head coach Baton Rouge (St. Louis farm team) '96-99; hockey broadcaster *CJAD, TSN* from '97; writer *SI*; numerous daily radio shows coast-to-coast; res. Westmount, Que.

McHALE, John (baseball); b. 21 Sep 1921, Detroit, Mich.; given name: John Joseph; m. Patricia Cameron; c. John Jr., Kevin, Brian, Cam, Anne, Mavie; Notre Dame.; ret'd baseball exec.; city, state baseball, basketball, football all-star; ctr Fighting Irish early '40s; 1b Detroit (AL) organization '41-48; with ML club '45 pennant drive, parts of '47-48 seasons; Detroit farm director, AGM, GM '48-58; v-p, GM Milwaukee '59-60; pres. '61-66; incumbent when Braves moved franchise to Atlanta '66; administrator, asst. to commissioner '67; simultaneously advisor to city of Montreal in campaign for ML franchise; part-owner Expos; pres., CEO '68-91; GM '78-84; NL rep. exec. council of government of organized professional baseball; NL v-p '70-84; mem. baseball playing rules comm., joint drug comm.; dir. Baseball Hall of Fame; mem. Cdn Baseball Hall of Fame; res. Palm Beach, Fla.

McINNIS, Andy (t&f/coaching); b. 16 Mar 1954, London, Ont. given name: Andrew Stuart; c. Emily Edith; UWO, BA, MA, Louisiana State.; coach; asst. t&f coach UWO '78-83; head coach London-Western TFC '80-84; asst. coach LSU '84-87; head coach Ottawa Lions TFC '88-96; program dir. Ntl Capital t&f ctr '88-96; ntl sr. events co-ordinator Athletics Canada '92-96; head coach Athletics Canada speed/power events '97-99; head coach Cdn Olympic team '96, world jr. team '92; consultant '99-01; assoc. coach UHawaii from '01; has served in coaching capacity 5 Olympic, 4 CG, 9 world championships, 2 FISU Games; conducts frequent clinics for athletes/coaches; has coached 11 major international Games medallists, 48 Games representatives; coached Mark McKoy, Sheldon Blockburger to world records; coached 8 SEC, 2 NCAA title teams; LSU-coached teams 1st-ever men's/women's NCAA title teams same year; 3 CIAU, 6 OWIAA title teams; coached 22 ntl sr. outdoor/indoor championships, 51 ntl medallists; 96 Ont. title athletes; 5 Ont. club championship teams; 3M coaching award '92, Wittnauer coaching-excellence award '96; training consultant Bobsleigh Canada; res. Manoa, Hawaii.

McINTOSH, Bob (harness racing); b. 11 Aug 1952, Windsor, Ont.; standardbred trainer; raised in the business with father Jack and brother Doug, he began working with brother's stable at 19; 5 yrs later developed his own stable and success followed rapidly; 7 Cdn trainer-of-yr awards; Cdn Horseman of '93 after leading Staying Together to horse-of-'93 award; experienced similar result with Artsplace '92 and earned Glen Garnsey trainer-of-yr award from US Harness Writers Assn; Artiscape, Allamerican

Ingot, Lady Graceful other noted horses he has trained and driven; res. LaSalle, Ont.

McINTOSH, Pam (orienteering); b. 23 Mar 1949, Beaverlodge, Alta.; given name: Pamela Jean; Guelph BSc, UofT, BEd; phys ed teacher; Ont. elite ladies' title '72, 2nd ntl finals, '73 Ont., Ohio titles; '74 Ont. title; mem. ntl team, 35th (top Cdn) world championship; ntl elite title '75; Ont. Athletic Commission Award; last known res. Ridgeway, Ont.

McINTYRE, Jack (hockey); b. 8 Sep 1930, Brussels, Ont.; d. 16 Mar 1998, London, Ont.; given name: John Archibald; m. Donna; c. Randy, Rick, Robbie, Roger, Ronanye; auto salesman; def. St. Catharines jrs; pro Hershey, Buffalo (AHL), lw Boston '49-53, Chicago '53-58, Detroit '58-60; NHL record: 499 scheduled games, 109g, 102a, 29 playoff games, 7g, 6a; scored overtime goal which beat Detroit in '53 Stanley Cup semis; beat Toronto single-handedly scoring 4g, 2a in 6-2 Chicago victory; 1st head coach London Nationals; played London Oldtimers, Old Indians, London Huff 'N Puff; hon. chair. Great Lakes Cup tourney.

McISAAC, Tim (swimming); b. 10 Jan 1959, Winnipeg, Man.; UWpg BEd; ScotiaBank; born blind, his introduction to swimming was at Ross MacDonald school for blind; 5 gold Ont. Games '75; mem ntl team from '76; 1 gold, 2 silver, 2 bronze '76 disabled Olympics; 1st blind swimmer to master tumble turn; amassed 19 Canada Games gold, 12 Cdn indoor games gold, 28 summer ntls gold, 28 Cdn Foresters Games gold, 10 Cdn Paralympic trials gold; ruled pool internationally '79-88 claiming 14g, 4s, 5b in 3 Paralympics, 5g, 4s, 8b 2 worlds; 1st blind student to graduate from UWpg with BEd degree; 1st blind ScotiaBank employee; Man. male athlete of '82; Viscount Alexander Cdn jr. male athlete of '76; exec. Man. Sports & Rec. Assn. for Blind, Cdn Blind Sports Assn.; treas. Council of Cdns with Disabilities; mem. Winnipeg Access Advisory Commission, ScotiaBankers for Universal Access; chair. MLPD (Manitoba League of Persons with Disabilities); mem. Man Sports Hall of Fame; res. Winnipeg, Man.

McKAY, Dave (baseball); b. 14 Mar 1950, Vancouver, B.C.; given name: David Lawrence; m. Lene Brondum Yjord; c. Cody Dean; Columbia Basin Junior College, Creighton; baseball coach; mem. '70 PAG team; pro Wisconsin Rapids (Midwest) '70, Lynchburg (Carolina) '72-73, Orlando (Southern) '74, all-star 3b, Tacoma (PCL) '75, all-star ss; Minnesota (AL) '75; home run in first major league plate appearance; hit safely in first 5 games and 21 of 22; acquired by Toronto '76 expansion draft; Oakland '80-82; coach Oakland, St. Louis; ML record: 645 scheduled games, 1928ab, 191r, 441h, 70db, 15tr, 21hr, 170rbi, 20sb, .229ba; mem. Cdn Baseball Hall of Fame; res. Vancouver, B.C.

McKAY, Heather (squash/racquetball); b. 31 Jul 1941, Queanbeyan, New South Wales, Australia; given name: Heather Pamela Blundell; squash, racquetball instructor; Australian women's squash champion 14 consecutive years '60-73; British women's world champion '76, '79; mem. Australian women's ntl field hockey team '67, '71; US ntl amateur racquetball champion '79; women's pro racquetball assn. US ntl champion '80-81; Toronto, ntl racquetball titles '82; *Australian Broadcasting Commission* sportsman

of '67; Squash Canada distinguished service award; MBE '69; Order of Australia '79; mem. WISPA Hall of Fame; res. Australia.

McKAY, Roy (baseball); b. 1 Aug 1933, London, Ont.; d. 25 Dec 1995, London, Ont.; given name: Roy Alexander; m. Ruth McPherson; c. Alex, Rosemary (d), Jim (d); specifications writer; lhp; signed with Detroit organization following '52 trial with Dodgers; Douglas, Ga., Idaho Falls parts of '53, '55 seasons; Sr. IC, Great Lakes-Niagara Leagues with London, most valuable pitcher '57; best season '58 with 10-6 record, 2.79 ERA; led in complete games '58 with 13; topped circuit in hit batsmen '58 with 16; mgr. London '69-72, '74-76, '81-82; three-time IC all-star mgr.

McKAY, Willie (t&f/football); b. 30 Mar 1930, Toronto, Ont.; d. 20 Oct 2000, Ottawa; given name: William Earl; m. Barbara Ethel Askew; c. Robin, Paul; UofOtt, OCE; HS art teacher; football to semipro 15yrs; coached HS 14, officiated 7; pres. Oakville Black Knights '58-60; ran 100yds (10.2), 220yds (22.4) jr. Olympics; chair. Ont. t&f officials council '76; mem. OTFA exec. '76-77; comptroller ntl officials comm. CTFA '77-80, chair. '81; throws ref. '78 CG, '79 World Cup, '77, '81 Canada Games, '80 Pan-Am jr. championships; OFAS achievement award '64; Oakville award of merit '68; Alan Klarer Trophy for leadership in sports (Oakville Rec. Dept.).

McKEAN, Jim (baseball/officiating); b. 26 May 1945, Montreal, Que.; given name: James Gilbert; m.; Sir George Williams., Concordia, BEd; pro baseball umpire; qb/k NDG Maple Leafs; pro Alouettes '64; 3 seasons Als, 2 Sask.; mem. '67 Grey Cup finalists; qualified OHA official working numerous junior games, 1 Memorial Cup championship series; baseball umpire from '70; AL from '74; worked AL playoff series '77; World Series '79; all-star games '80-82; off-season basketball coach; Fla. state doubles racquetball champion; Larry Smith Award '70; mem. Cdn Baseball Hall of Fame; res. St. Petersburg, Fla.

McKECHNIE, Walt (hockey); b. 19 Jan 1947, London, Ont.; given name: Walter Thomas John; great stickhandler and playmaker; ctr OHA London '65-67, WHL Phoenix '67-69, CHL Iowa '69-70, Salt Lake '83-84, AHL Cleveland '70-71, Team Canada '77; NHL Minnesota '67-71, California '71-74, Boston '74-75, Detroit '74-77, '81-83, Washington '77, Cleveland '77-78, Toronto '78-80, Colorado '79-81; NHL totals: 955 scheduled games, 214g, 392a, 15 playoff games, 7g, 5a; WHL rookie award '68; active in old timers hockey, golf; res. Haliburton, Ont.

McKEE, Jamie (badminton); b. 11 Aug 1951, Toronto, Ont.; given name: James Keating; m. Linda Mason; c. Tommy, Fiona; York, hons BSc; chemist; Ont. men's singles champion '73-78; twice Ont. men's doubles champion; ntl men's singles titles '77-78; PAG men's singles titlist '78; 3 PAG doubles titles; 2 Eastern, Western Opens singles titles; mem. silver medal team '78 CG; mem. '79 Thomas Cup team; twice Pepsi-Cola doubles champion; high performance dir. Ont. Badminton Assn.; res. Markham, Ont.

McKEE, Joyce (curling); b. 29 Oct 1933, Asquith, Sask.; d. 29 Dec 1999, Saskatoon, Sask.; given name: Helen Joyce;

stock control operator; mem. several Sask., Western Canada softball title teams early '50s; 8 Sask. ladies curling titles, 5 as skip, 3 as second; 6 ntl titles, 3 as skip, 3 as second, runnerup '62 ntl finals; Cdn sr. women's title '92; Saskatoon sportswoman of '69; Curl Canada outstanding-contribution award '84; Gov.-Gen.'s award; mem. Sask. Sports, Canadian Curling halls of fame.

McKEE, Walt (football/soccer/coaching); b. 28 Jun 1949, Belfast, N. Ireland; given name: William Walter Jeremiah; m. Terry Louise Schroeder; c. Darcie, Kathleen; UMan, BPhE, MEd; AD UMan. '93-01, PE&R studies faculty head from '01; mem. 2 CIAU Vanier Cup winners; k/p Winnipeg '72-75, Edmonton '75; founding mem. Winnipeg Fury CPSL team; Level V soccer coach; mem. ntl soccer team '71; asst. coach ntl team '86; mem. ntl champion all-star soccer team '70; coached soccer at amateur/pro levels; pres. Great Plains Athletic Conference from '95; dir. CIAU from '95; dir. Manitoba Special Olympics '94-96, Sport Manitoba from '96; dir. soccer coaching '84-87; dir. player personnel Winnipeg Fury SC '86-90; dir. UMan high performance ctr '93-96; co-chair. practice facilities '99 PAG; res. Winnipeg, Man.

McKEGNEY, Tony (hockey); b. 15 Feb 1958, Montreal, Que.; entrepreneur; product of Sarnia minor hockey program; lw Kingston OHA '74-78, 2 OHA all-star; Team Canada '78, AHL Hershey '79; NHL Buffalo '78-83, Quebec '83-85, '89-91,Minnesota '84-86, NYR '86-87, St. Louis '87-89, Detroit '90, Chicago '90-91; NHL totals: 912 scheduled games, 320g, 319a, 79 playoff games, 24g, 23a; owner Sarnia Bluewater, 12 other sports domes; established Deerhurst NHL alumni hockey camps; res. Buffalo, N.Y.

McKENZIE, Johnny (hockey); b. 12 Dec 1937, High River, Alta.; given name: John Albert; div.; c. Betty, Jacqueline, Lori, Amy, Megan; BMW salesman; at 15 mem. Calgary jrs followed by Medicine Hat, St. Catharines; pro Chicago (NHL) '58-59, '63-65, Detroit '59-61, NYR '65-66, Boston '66-72; jumped to WHA Philadelphia, Vancouver, Minnesota, Cincinnati, New England '72-80; saw minor league duty with Calgary, Hershey, Buffalo, St. Louis; set AHL playoff scoring record; NHL record: 691 scheduled games, 206g, 268a, 69 playoff games, 15g, 32a; spent off-seasons as calf roper in rodeos; mem. 2 Stanley Cup winners; on retirement in bid to help athletes operated full-service bank to '85; plays hockey, slo-pitch softball with Boston alumni; nicknamed "Cowboy" or "Pie"; res. Stoneham, Mass.

McKENZIE, Ken (builder/hockey); b. 19 Aug 1923, Winnipeg, Man.; d. 9 Apr 2003, Mississauga, Ont.; journalist; midget-aged dfcman with jr. St. James Canadians; began journalistic career *Winnipeg Free Press;Montreal Gazette* following WWII; hired to organize NHL stats; became NHL PR dir.; saw realization of dream of hockey publication by launching *Hockey News* '47; produced 1st NHL press/radio guides and NHL official Guide & Record Book; mem. Hockey, Man. Sports halls of fame.

McKENZIE, Merv (all-around); b. 1 Dec 1920, Moose Jaw, Sask.; d. 23 Jan 1977, Mississauga, Ont.; given name: Lawrence Mervyn; m. Jean Elizabeth Trimbee; c. Marilyn, Kerry, Janis; Ontario Athletic Commissioner; raised in Orillia, Ont., he excelled in t&f, football, hockey, swimming, lacrosse; won 100yd backstroke CNE '39; capt. Orillia Minto Cup ntl jr. lacrosse title team '40; sr. lacrosse with Mimico, Hamilton, Peterborough; mem. Hamilton Mann Cup ntl sr title team '48, Peterborough Mann Cup title team '51; played lacrosse, hockey RCAF '41-46; set Trenton AFB 50yd backstroke record; played hockey Toronto Mercantile league; Ont. Athletic Commissioner '52-77; Ont. lacrosse commissioner '54-77; coached Long Branch Ont. jr. lacrosse title team '55; pres. Cdn Boxing Assn. '59-61, World Boxing Assn. '64; Cdn Confederation medal; 2 trophies honoring his name awarded annually by Ont. Lacrosse Assn.; mem. Mississauga Sports, Cdn Lacrosse halls of fame.

McKENZIE, Tait (builder); b. 26 May 1867, Almonte, Ont., d. 28 Apr 1938, Philadelphia, Pa.; given name: Robert Tait; m. Ethel O'Neil; McGill, BA, MD, hon LLD, Springfield College, MPhE; developed own frail frame through exercise establishing foundation upon which he developed programs leading to recognition as father of NA phys-ed programs; won Wickstead silver medal as '87 intercollegiate jr. gymnastics champion, gold medal as sr. champion '89; college hj title; succeeded James Naismith as McGill gym instructor '90; instrumental in forming McGill's 1st basketball team; 1st McGill medical dir., among forerunners in orthopaedic surgery '92; British army medical corps WWI; contributions to sport art through sculpting without peer; among best known works which exemplified perfection in physical development are *The Onslaught*, *Brothers of the Wind*; many of his works used in design of Olympic Medals; also noted for war memorials; wrote books on physical education, sports medicine; twice pres. American Physical Education Assn.; chair. Penn PE; mem. American Academy of Physical Education, Philadelphia St. Andrews Society; instrumental in development Philadelphia playground system, Boy Scout movement; York athletic ctr bears his name; mem. Cdn Olympic, McGill Sports halls of fame.

McKENZIE, Tom (baseball); 11 Apr 1942, London, Ont.; m. Cheryl MacDonald; c. Kerry-Sue, Tommy-Jay; UWO, BA, Oregon, MA, teacher; all-Ont. honors as hockey goalie, in track, football; minor baseball London; London Majors Sr. IC team '60-65, Kitchener '66-80; 21yr IC batting average .314; twice batting champion; 438 IC games played, 570 career hits, 383 runs scored, 155 stolen bases; managed Kitchener '66-67, '80, '96; 16 times all-star ss or manager; IC MVP '70; men. 4 Kitchener IC title teams; mem. Ont. team '70, '76 national championships, '67, '71, '79 PAG teams, '70, '71 world amateur championships teams; coach Kitchener minor baseball, HS football, basketball; mem. Man. Baseball Hall of Fame; res. Kitchener, Ont.

McKEOWN, Bob (football); b. 10 Oct 1950, Ottawa, Ont.; given name: Robert Duff; div. Alice Ramo; c. Robert III; m. Sheilagh D'Arcy McGee; c. Alexander, D'Arcy, Liam; Yale, BA; TV journalist; *CBC Fifth Estate; CBS* news; *NBC* news correspondent; ntl age-group discus title '65; varsity football Yale; ctr Rough Riders '71-76; EFC all-star '74; mem. Grey Cup champions '73; 1 US Emmy, 2 Cdn Gemini awards; res. New York, N.Y.

McKERLICH, Bill (rowing); b. 2 Dec 1936, Vancouver, B.C.; given name: Willian Alister; m. Gail Turland; c.

Ian, Ross, Leigh, Sarah; UBC, BEd, Oregon, MSc; asst. superintendent of schools; pulling #6 oar Cdn 8s crew won '56, '60 Olympic silver, '58 BEG gold; CRA referee, FISA international rowing official; consultant Vancouver '10 Olympic bid; mem. Cdn Olympic Hall of Fame; res. White Rock, B.C.

McKIBBON, John (basketball); b. 14 Sep 1939, Sudbury, Ont.; div. Patricia; c. Jeffrey, Tommy, Patti-Lyn, Susan; m. Joanne McClory; Laurentian, BA, UofT, MDiv; United Church minister; mem. ntl team '59 PAG, '60, '64 Olympics, '72 China tour; head basketball coach Laurentian '67-69; Laurentian athlete of '70, '72; mem. Laurentian Sports Wall, Cdn Basketball Hall of Fame; res. Uxbridge, Ont.

McKILLOP, Bob (baseball/hockey); b. 1 Jun 1942, Toronto, Ont.; given name: Robert Commings; m. Margaret; c. Robert Jr., Barbara; Waterloo, BA, BPhE; ret'd phys-ed teacher, ret'd ED Ont. Baseball Assoc. '95-03; rhp/c Toronto People's Jewellers jr. team '59; pro White Sox organization '60-64; Kitchener Sr.IC '66-76; lifetime IC record: .342 BA, 31-11 w-l record, 2.37 ERA; managed Kitchener '68-69, '71, 56-24 record, '71 pennant; 3 IC home run, 5 RBI, 2 total bases leader titles; led IC hitters '69 with .381, pitchers '66 with 0.93 ERA; 7 times 1st team all-star catcher, once 1st team rhp, manager; 4 times MVP; mem. Ont gold medal team '69 Canada Games, ntl team '67 PAG; hockey, football coach Waterloo; pres. Kitchener Minor Baseball Assn.; mem. Man. Baseball, Waterloo County Hall of Fame; res. Kitchener, Ont.

McKINLEY, Harold (harness racing); b. 24 Dec 1921, Sault Ste. Marie, Ont.; d. 22 May 1998, Georgetown, Ont.; given name: Harold Andrew; m. Audrey (d); m. Myrna Noecker; sc. Janice, Lori, Tracy, Andrew Termano; horseman; raised in Peace River, Alta., he developed love of horses and built a life-long reputation as a harness driver and trainer; trained and drove horses for Armstrong Bros. stable '54-69 then with wife Audrey established Butterball Farm at Norval, Ont.; won numerous major races, including '72 Queen City Pace and '60 Maple Leaf Trot; winner of close to 1000 career races, several Greenwood dash titles; among his top horses were Lynden Bye Bye, Armbro Express, Vandella and Norbeth Hanover; mem. Cdn Horse Racing Hall of Fame.

McKINNON, Archie (all-around); b. 19 Aug 1896, Glasgow, Scotland, d. 25 Dec 1984, Victoria, B.C.; m. Dorothy Bell Aird; c. Dorothy Joan, Isabel Ann, Heather Anne; Washington, YMCA School Sealbeck, Wash.; phys ed dir.; competed and/or coached CG teams '28-61; '28 Olympic competitor, '32 diving coach, '36 t&f coach, '48 diving, swimming coach, '52 swimming coach; various awards including naming of Victoria YM-YWCA pool, UVic athletic complex in his honor; Freeman City of Victoria '61; CAPHER Tait McKenzie award '81; mem. Greater Victoria, Cdn Amateur, BC Swimming, BC Sports halls of fame.

McKINNON, Frank (all-around); b. 16 Jun 1934, Wellwood, Man.; m. Bonnie Lynn Cachran; c. Jeffrey, Kevin; Brandon College, BSc, BPaed, UMan, BPhE; school principal; mem. divisional HS t&f title team '51; jr. hockey Brandon Wheat Kings; mem. 3 Man. sr. baseball title teams; 2 Western fastball title teams; '55 WIAU hockey scoring title; 10yrs MAHA exec., 5yrs pres; 5yrs dir. CAHA; chair. CAHA

awards comm. '77-78; mem. CAHA restructing comm.; 2yrs v-p CAHA sr., int. hockey; 2yrs CAHA v-p development; mem. Man. Hockey Players Foundation; 4yrs v.-chair. Man. advisory council FAS; mem. ntl advisory council COTHA; mem. organizing comm. 1st world jr. hockey tournament; mem. Carman baseball comm. '67 PAG; chair. '78 Pembina Valley winter games; 2yrs pres. Carman-Dufferin MHA; Centennial Cup trustee; coached provincial title basketball, baseball, hockey teams; also t&f, volleyball, soccer coach; dir., v-p SFC; v-p COA; mem. IIHF congress '79-81; chair. CAHA '79-81; CAHA award for contribution to minor hockey '77; Hockey Can. order of merit; life mem. Hockey Can. ntl appeals comm.; mem. Man. Hockey, Sports halls of fame; res. Winnipeg, Man.

McKOY, Mark (t&f); b. 10 Dec 1961, Georgetown, Guyana; York., Louisiana State; m. Yvette Grabner; c. 2; pres/CEO United Family Martial Arts, owner/operator Gold Medal Enterprises; hurdle specialist; 4 ntl 110m hurdles, 2 50m hurdles, 1 4x200m relay titles; CIAU 50m, 50m hurdles, 4x200, 4x400 relay titles; gold 110m hurdles '82, '86, gold 4x100m relay '86, silver '82 CG; bronze 110m hurdles '83 FISU Games; world indoor 60m hurdles bronze '91; gold '92 Japan meet; Cdn 110m hurdles record 13.11 '92; mem. '83 Pan-Am, '84, '88, '92 Olympic Games teams; 7 ntl, 2 CIAU indoor t&f, 1 Commonwealth, CG, world records; outstanding male athlete '82 ntl outdoor championships; fed. govt. excellence award '83; 3rd international superstars competition '82; suspended 2yrs for leaving '88 Olympic team without notice; 1 CIAU indoor t&f male-athlete-of-yr award; became Austrian citizen '94; mem. Cdn Olympic Sports Hall of Fame; res. Traun, Austria/Toronto, Ont.

McLAREN, Grant (t&f); b. 19 Aug 1948, Paris, Ont.; m. Janet Manley; c. Christopher, Heather; Guelph, BSc, UWO, PhD; dairy farmer; CWOSSA 2-mile title '65, ntl jr. x-country '67, OQAA 3-mile '68, Canada Games steeplechase, 5000m '69, OQAA 1500m, 5000m, steeplechase '70, Philadelphia 2-mile, Drake Relays 3-mile '72, Pan-Pacific Games 5000m '73, Montreal France-Canada dual meet 3000m '74; mem. Toronto Olympic Club; Guelph athlete of '68-69; outstanding CIAU track athlete '70; UWO athlete of '72-73; ntl records indoor 2-mile, outdoor 3-mile, 3000m, 5000m, steeplechase, 2000m; 3:59 mile '72; mem. '71, '75 PAG, '70, '74 CG, '72, '76 Olympic teams; mem. Guelph, W-Club Sports halls of fame; res. Drumbo, Ont.

McLAREN, Robert (t&f); b. 19 Apr 1945, Victoria, B.C.; m. Nancy Oldfield; c. Lindsay, Brian; Oregon State, BSc; supervisor BC Telephone; equalled ntl HS 100yd record 9.8; 3-yr letterman Oregon State track team; '66 ntl indoor 300yd title; silver 1600m relay, ntl record 3:04.8, bronze 400m hurdles, ntl record 51.4, '67 PAG; reduced 400m mark to 50.7 '68; mem. '68 Olympic team; res. N. Vancouver, B.C.

McLARNIN, Jimmy (boxing); b. 19 Dec 1907, Belfast, Ireland; d. 28 Oct 2004, Richland, Wash.; m. Lillian Cupit; c. Grace Ellen, Jean, Nancy, Jim; ret'd chromium plating business; began boxing age 12, pro at 16; unbeaten 19 straight bouts; protégée of Pop Foster who guided him through success and left him a fortune; lost world lightweight title bid in 15 to Sammy Mandell '28 NYC; KO'd Young Corbett III in 1st for world welterweight crown

'33 LA; lost title in 15 to Barney Ross '34 NYC; regained title beating Ross in 15 same year; again lost title to Ross in 15 '35 NYC; ret'd from ring '36; pro record 77 fights winning 20 by KO, 42 on decision, 1 on foul, 3 draws, 10 losses on decision, 1 on TKO (due to cut under eye); nickname: "Baby Face"; Canada's boxer of half century '50 *CP* poll; mem. US, Canadian Boxing, IBHOF, BC, Canada's Sports halls of fame.

McLAUGHLIN, Dean (horseshoes); b. 7 Mar 1921, Oshawa, Ont.; m. Wilma; c. Steven Brant, Dale Mary; ret'd store owner; 6 Ont. men's singles titles; 13 ntl men's singles titles; NA champion '60, runnerup '67; twice placed in top 16 world tournament; set world record 91.6% avg. 5 consec. games; 1st Cdn to qualify in championship division at World tournament; manufactured own brand of horseshoes; mem. NHPA. Horseshoe Canada, Oshawa Sports halls of fame; res. Oshawa, Ont.

McLAUGHLIN, Frank (sailing); b. 15 Apr 1960, Toronto, Ont.; UofT; lawyer; began sailing age 9; ntl jr. Fireball champion '77; mem. ntl team from '82; 3 ntl 420 titles; Ont. Laser titles '80-81; 470 bronze '83 PAG; mem. '84, '88, '92 Olympic teams; '88 Olympic Flying Dutchman bronze with John Millen; CORK FD titles '89-90; worlds bronze '86; father Paul 2 time Olympian; brother FD skipper Terry McLaughlin; res. Toronto, Ont.

McLAUGHLIN, Jack (golf): b. 31 Dec 1933, Ottawa, Ont.; d. 23 Jan 1991, Palm Springs, Calif.; m. Marilyn; c. Jim, Mike, Kelly, Ed; St. Mike's Coll; jr. Scarborough G&CC; 2nd Ont. jr.; won Ont. jr. best ball; capt. St. Mike's golf team; turned pro '53; pro Cedar Brae '56-60, Bayview CC (Toronto) '61-73, Shaughnessy (Vancouver) '74-91; quarterfinalist Millar match; personal low 67 Brantford; served on numerous CPGA, Ont., BC committees; head coach CLGA ntl team '88-91; launched jr.-jr. golf programs for ages 4-11; helped start UBC golf program; 1st Cdn pro invited to teach US pros at their business school '73-74; ranked as one of Canada's top teaching pros; CPGA, BC golf awards bear his name.

McLAUGHLIN, Sam (horse racing); b. 8 Sep 1871, Enniskillen, Ont., d. 6 Jan 1972, Oshawa, Ont.; given name: Robert Samuel; m. Adelaide Louise Mowbray (d); c. 5 daughters; York, LLD; chair. GMC; many cycling awards as youth; as sailor won '25 Richardson Cup and championship of Great Lakes; entered first horse show '26 with jumpers; won 1500 ribbons, 400 trophies on Canada, US circuit; concentrated on breeding, racing thoroughbreds with his Parkwood Stables; produced King's/Queen's Plate winners Horometer '34, Kingarvie '46, Moldy '47; v-p, dir. Jockey Club, Ltd.; mem. Canadian Horse Racing, Canada's, Oshawa Sports halls of fame.

McLAUGHLIN, Terry (sailing); b. 24 Jul 1956, Toronto, Ont.; stockbroker; national, NA, Can-Am, 2 CORK Flying Dutchman titles; skipper Clipper Xerox Challenge Cup series; skipper Canada 1 America's Cup series; gold FD '80, bronze '83 world championships; mem. '80, '84 Olympic team; with Ev Bastet FD silver '84 Olympics; 6 York Cup match-race titles; won '01, '03 Canada Cup series; mem. runnerup SFC team of '80; fed. govt. excellence award '83; Knickerbocker Cup title '03; res. Toronto, Ont.

McLEAN, Arnold (golf); b. 4 Jun 1928, Montreal, Que.; m. Lavina Jean Matheson; c. Arnold Jr., Brian, Donna; Sir George Williams.; golf dir., master pro; junior hockey, baseball; Que. jr. golf title '41; Que. PGA '54, Spring Open '61; runnerup Que. Open '54; pres. QPGA '59-60, CPGA '76-77; life mem. CPGA master pros; designer/GM/head pro Club de Golf Lorraine; mem. Cdn Golf Superintendent's Assn., Professional Golf Club Repairman's Assn.; res. Lorraine, Que.

McLEAN, Kenny (rodeo); b. 17 May 1939, Penticton, B.C.; d. 13 Jul 2002, Taber, Alta.; m. Penny Wise; c. Guy, Tracey, Steven, Jill; rancher; v-p. PRCA; 5 ntl saddle bronc, 1 calf roping, steer wrestling, 4 all-around titles, 2 high-point titles; world sr pro calf roper '01; US rodeo circuit rookie of '61; world saddle bronc title '62; 3 times winner of competition limited to participation by world's top 15 saddle bronc riders; twice winner Bill Linderman award (open only to winners of $1,000 in three events); remodeled ancestral homestead to provide area in which he trained horses and conducted school for team roping; competed on Indian rodeo circuit; rodeo series created in his honor '03; mem. Order of Canada, Ntl Pro Rodeo, Canada's, Okanagan, BC Sports halls of fame.

McLEAN, Kirk (hockey); b. 26 Jun 1966, Willowdale, Ont.; honed goal tending skills with Don Mills TMHL; OHL Oshawa '83-86, AHL Maine '86-87, Team Canada '90; NHL New Jersey '85-87, Vancouver '87-98, Carolina '98, Florida '98-99, NYR '99-01; NHL totals: 612 scheduled games, 35,090 minutes, 245-252-72, 44sho, 68 playoff games, 4189 minutes, 34-34-0, 0sho; played 2 NHL all-star games; avid golfer; res. Vancouver, B.C.

McLELLAND, Ivan (hockey); b. 15 Mar 1931, Campbell's Bay, Que; m. Faye Amos; c. David, Bonnie, Rhonda; GM Okanagan Mfgrs. Ltd.; goalie South Porcupine jrs. '45-47; NO jr. title '47; mem. St. Catharines TeePees '47-48; South Porcupine Porkies '48-50; NO sr. title '49-50; Penticton Vees '50-56; Western Cdn sr. title '52-53, Allan Cup '53-54, World championship '55; from 14 Mar '55 to 15 Aug '81 was only goalie to shut out Russians in international competition; res. Pentiction, B.C.

McLEOD, Barbara (t&f); b. 20 Oct 1937, Timmins, Ont.; given name: Barbara Caswell; m. Bill McLeod; began running age 43 to "get in shape" and evolved into veritable running machine; ultramarathon specialist; women 50-54 world 6day 393miles, 48hours 177miles, indoor 24hours 113miles records; women 55-59 world 50mile, 50km road/track records; 9 NA age 50-59 records; 27 Cdn Masters Women 40+ records; has run throughout world in such locales as Greece, China, Spain, US and Canada; ran 4 ultras in '96 placing 1st woman, 4th overall in 3; competing in 60-64 age group 64 races, 8 ultras winning 1; women's 65-69 NA record Houston '04; 4NA, 14 ntl age-group records; ran Cdn Intl marathon on 65th birthday; 9 Gloucester Sports awards; 2 Gloucester outstanding achievement awards; Breakthrough award '90; Ottawa ACT award '89; 4 Ont. sports awards; mem. Cdn Road Running, Ottawa Sports halls of fame; res. Gloucester, Ont/ Corpus Christi, Tex.

McLEOD, Jackie (hockey/baseball); b. 30 Apr 1930, Hazlet, Sask.; given name: Robert John; m. Beverly Evans; c. Don,

Patti; Notre Dame College; hockey exec., chief pilot Concorde Group; jr. ND Coll. '45-47; jr. Moose Jaw Canucks '47-49; pro NYR '49-55; Saskatoon, Vancouver, Calgary (WHL) '55-60; world champion Trail Smoke Eaters '61; sr. Saskatoon, Moose Jaw '62-65; coach/GM ntl team '65-70; coach/GM/ owner WHL Saskatoon Blades '70-80; silver medal, scoring title, all-star rw '61 World Cup; bronze '66 worlds; Centennial tournament champions '67; coached Canada to bronze '67 worlds, '68 Olympics; in youth star p/1b; mem. Sask. jr. champ Gull Lake Lakers, North Battleford Beavers 4 titles; player/coach/mgr. Swift Current Indians 10yrs; developed Swift Current minor baseball system; ret'd from baseball '66; offered minor league contract by Chicago Cubs; mem. Sask. Baseball, IIHF halls of fame; res. Saskatoon, Sask.

McLOUGHLIN, Mark (football); b. 26 Oct 1965, Liverpool, Eng.; South Dakota; ex-football exec.; kicker; CFL with Calgary '88-03; CFL record: 278gp, 664fg, 815cvts, 146s, 2953pts; 5 Western, 1 Northern, 3 CFL all-star; 3 CFL scoring titles; 4 Dave Dryburgh Memorial trophies; Tom Pate Memorial award '95; 6 Grey Cup finals, 3 winners; USD athlete/academic-of-yr award; implemented Calgary "Stay in School" program; involved in Calgary Educational Partnership Foundation; briefly served as pres/ GM, consultant Stampeders '03; res. Calgary, Alta.

McMAHON, David (biathlon); b. 6 May 1964, Middleton, N.S.; div. Michelle; c. Caitlin, Christopher; m. Lise Meloche; RMC, B. Eng.; computer engineer, XC Zone. TV film co. owner; elite competitor in biathlon, x-country skiing, mountain running; 2 Canada Cup biathlon series titles; 5 ntl biathlon championship medals; ntl title '93; once ranked 3rd in world summer biathlon; top North American '97 world Loppet ski racing circuit; 7th world masters '98; coach at Olympic level; conducts masters ski camps; wrote biathlon tech. manual; res. Chelsea, Que.

McMAHON, Gary (shooting); b. 25 Feb 1932, Roland, Man.; given name: Garfield Walter; m. Ruby Bertha Fulton; Brandon, BSc, UBC, MSc; research scientist; 1st of 3 ntl open handgun titles '58; NS handgun title '59-66; mem. '60, '64 Olympic, '62 (5th free-pistol), '66 world, '59, '63, '67, '71 PAG, '66 CG teams; bronze individual centre-fire, team free-pistol '59 PAG; 3 silver, 1 bronze indiviual centre-fire '63 PAG; bronze free-pistol '66 CG silver centre-fire team '72 PAG; best international performer '62 worlds; res. Stewiacke, N.S.

McMAHON, John (kickboxing); b. 8 Jun 1971, Ottawa, Ont.; given name: John Harold Moran; m. Carianne Pelletier; Carleton BA, CDI College, computer programmer analyst; owns Nomad Kickboxing, a web intelligence and software business Knowledge First, speaking & coaching business Progressive MindWorks; 3 WKA ntl titles, continuous boxing light-heavyweight; 3 WAKO Intercontinental titles, team 2 indiv. titles '98; WKA, WPKA world titles '00, WKA world bronze '99, ntl team coach (WKA, WPKA federations) from '99; peak performance/mental management specialist; res. Orleans, Ont.

McMAHON, John (soccer/administration); b. 9 Apr 1922, Glasgow, Scotland; m. Ivy; c. Bill, Marilyn; ret'd sports administrator; immigrated to Watrous, Sask., '23 but returned to Scotland during Depression where he played

Glasgow jr. league; joined Scottish FA as referee '46; officiated Scottish pro league; returning to Canada officiated in Toronto '51-54; dir. Toronto Church SL; 1st pres. TDMSA '59; introduced minor soccer to Toronto boroughs; dir. OMSA; exec. Toronto City Eastern Canada pro team '61-82; had role in formation NASL; mgr. ntl team '71-82, GM '74-82; life mem. CSA; v-p CSA Alumni; gov. Soccer Hall of Fame & Museum to '99; mem. OSA Heritage comm.; mem. Cdn Soccer Hall of Fame; res. Toronto, Ont.

McMANN, Chuck (football); b. 11 May 1951, Toronto, Ont., m. Margaret; c. Kristin, Jeffery, Jonathan; Wilfrid Laurier BA, McGill BEd; teacher, football coach; 2 CIAU all-star teams, team MVP '75; rb 10 CFL seasons Alouette/ Concordes, 1 Grey Cup winner; asst. coach Coll. Viau '86, Vanier Coll. '87, Waterloo '88-91; guest coach Calgary '90-91; asst. Calgary '92-00, 2 Grey Cup winners; head coach Montreal '01; head coach McGill Redmen '02-03, Frank Tindall CIS coach-of-yr trophy '02; res. Montreal, Que.

McMANUS, Danny (football); b. 17 Jun 1965, Dania, Fla.; m. Kim; c. Kelsey; Florida State; qb, distribution business owner; '88 Fiesta Bowl MVP; FSU player of yr '86-87; drafted by Kansas City (NFL) '88; joined CFL with Winnipeg '90-92, BC '93-95, Edmonton '96-97, Hamilton '98-03; CFL outstanding player '99; CFL record (through '04): 247 scheduled gp, 7297passes, 3421comp., 50,431yds, 260int, 247tds, 144 carries, 418yds, 17tds; 6 Grey Cup finals, 3 winners; all-Eastern, CFL all-star '99; res. Indianapolis, Indiana.

McMANUS, Heather (trampoline); b. 3 Sep 1973, Etobicoke, Ont.; given name: Heather Janet Ross; m. Sean McManus; Lakehead B.Sc, UNorthern B.C., BEd, Algonquin Coll; coach, co-owner Spring Action trampoline & circus group; competed '01 world championship, '02 world cup, '04 Olympics; with partner Karen Cockburn 2nd 3 WC synchronized trampoline events '02, Canada Cup gold '03; ntl singles, synchro gold '03; trampolinist-of-decade ('90s) award; 2 Cdn-trampolinist-of-yr awards; res. Almonte, Ont.

McMILLAN, Leigh (football); b. 8 Nov 1935, Edmonton Alta.; given name: Herbert Leigh; m. Aline Baril; c. Linda, Karen, John; Denver, BSc, UAlta, BEd, graduate dip. vocational guidance; HS teacher, counsellor; hb/safety Edmonton '56-58; averaged 5.4yds per carry on 66 punt returns '56 Grey Cup champions; Edm. club record 93 punt returns '58; mem. Alta. champion Lacombe Rockets Intermediate A hockey team '60-61; UAlta Golden Bears CIAU hockey champions '63-64; coach minor hockey, soccer, fastball, sr. football Austin O'Brien HS; disabled fitness ctr bears his name; res. Edmonton, Alta.

McMILLAN, Roy (curling); b. 1 Apr 1893, Stratford, Ont. d. 28 Nov 1983, Ottawa, Ont.; m. Helen Belyea; c. Jean, Dorothy, Catherine, Donald; UofT; chemical engineer, teacher; won Royal Victoria Jubilee, Royal Caledonia; Branch Gov.-Gen.'s 3 times, runnerup 4 times, srs. twice; twice reached Ont. srs. playdowns; mem. Gov.-Gen.'s CC; life mem. CBRCCC, OCA, Rideau CC.

McMURRAY, Mary (curling); b. 6 Mar 1896, Newcastle, N.B.; d, 1986, Bathurst, N.B.; m. Andrew M. McMurray (d); c. Betty; through 41 consec. yrs played major role in spreading curling through Maritimes; 1st pres. NB Ladies Curling Assn.; hon. mem. Bathurst CC, Que. City Cambrai CC; hon. life mem. NBLCA; mem. Canadian Curling Hall of Fame.

McNAB, Peter (hockey); b. 8 May 1952, Vancouver, B.C.; given name: Peter Maxwell; div. c. Shannon, Robyn; Denver; hockey broadcaster; son of 47-yr hockey exec. Max McNab, brother Dave Anaheim AGM; ctr Denver '71-73; pro AHL Cincinnati, NHL Buffalo '73-76, Boston '76-84, Vancouver '84-85, New Jersey '85-87; NHL record: 954 scheduled games, 363g, 450a, 107 playoff games, 40g, 42a; began broadcasting *NJ Sports Channel* '87-95; moved into similar role Colorado '95; highly involved in community affairs, charitable works; res. Littleton, Colo.

McNAMARA, Bob (football); b. 12 Aug 1931, Hastings, Minn.; m. Annette; c. Anne, Suzy, Bobby; Minn., BSc; owner McNamara's Irish Sports Bar; all-American hb Minn. '54; Winnipeg (CFL)'55-58; Denver (NFL) '60-61; all-Cdn '56 with 1101yds rushing on 178 carries for 17 tds; CFL record 36 points single game at Vancouver tying Lorne Benson for most tds single game (6); 1 Grey Cup winner; US paddleball doubles title '58, singles '70; US International, Canadian masters racquetball champion '76; res. Minneapolis, Minn.

McNAMARA, George (hockey); b. 26 Aug 1886, Penetanguishene, Ont., d. 10 Mar 1952, Sault Ste. Marie, Ont.; major hockey debut with Michigan Sault; Montreal Shamrocks (ECL) '08-09, Halifax Crescents (MPL) 3 seasons, Toronto Tecumsehs '12-13, Toronto Ontarios '13-14 season; Cdn Army 228th Sportsman's Battalion team NHA; coached Sault Greyhounds to '24 Allan Cup; mem. Hockey Hall of Fame.

McNAMEE, Kathleen (swimming); b. 8 Jan 1931, Vancouver, B.C.; given name: Kathleen Mavis; div. Rich Ferguson; c. David, Jeanne, John; UBC, UofT, SFU; dir. volunteer personnel, Vancouver YWCA; competed 10yrs at VASC; mem. '48, '52 Olympic, '50 BEG teams; ntl 200yd, 400yd FS records; organized, coached 1st competitive swim club Burlington, Ont. '69-75, guiding 5 swimmers to ntl team status, 1 to Olympic level; Beatrice Pines Trophy as Canada's outstanding female swimmer '52; last known res. N. Vancouver, B.C.

McNAUGHTON, Don (builder); b. 18 Jul 1926, Montreal, Que.; given name: Donald William; m. Barbara Ann Little (d); c. Tim, John, Susan, Ann; m. Erin Leah Shannon; Sir George Williams, Loyola Coll, Concordia; ret'd pres./CEO Schenley Canada; average athlete in youth earning swimming, mile running medals; co-ordinated CFL Schenley awards 1963-89; dir. Lions '69-70; mem. Alouettes council '64-67, chair. '69; mem. Alouettes Alumni Assn; served varied roles with Loyola, Sir George Williams, Concordia alumni organizations, St. Mary's hospital; mem. bd. Cdn Safety Council '73-93; has served as mem/officer Irwin Swangaard Stadium Vancouver, Que. Society for Disabled Children, Cdn Arthritis Society and host of other humanitarian efforts; Confederation 125 medal; Queen's Golden Jubilee medal; CFL Outstanding Service award; Save the Children Fund award; Loyola medal; Humberto

Santos award; life mem. St. Patrick's Society; mem. Cdn Football Hall of Fame; res. Westmount, Que.

McNAUGHTON, Duncan (t&f); b. 7 Dec 1910, Cornwall, Ont.; d. 1998, Austin, Tex.; given name: Duncan Anderson; m. Eileen Frances Garrioch; c. Diane, Sheila, Ellen; SoCal, BA, PhD, CalTech, MSc; consulting geologist; capt., coach '29 provincial basketball champs; individual titles '29 Vancouver HS track meet, BC HS Olympiad; mem. USC track team; disqualified for illegal jumping techniques '30 BEG; change to conventional Western roll resulted in California state title, State hj record; US intercollegiate hj title '33; gold '32 Olympics clearing 6'6"; mem. Cdn Olympic, Cornwall, BC, Canada's Sports halls of fame.

McNEIL, Gerry (hockey); b. 17 Apr 1926, Quebec City, Que.; d. 17 Jun 2004, Montreal, Que.; given name: Gerard George; ret'd Seagram Distillers; goal Montreal Royals (jr & sr) QHL '43-49, '55-57, EPHL '59-66; AHL Cincinnati '49-50, Rochester '57-59, Quebec '60-61; NHL Montreal '48-54, '56-58; 3 QSHL all-star, MVP, 1 QHL Vezina, 1 AHL all-star; 2 Stanley Cup winners; coach Jonquiere QJHL '54-55; 3 NHL all-star games; NHL record: 276 scheduled games, 119-105-52, 28so, 35 playoff games, 17-18, 5so; best remembered for yielding Bill Barilko goal which gave Toronto Stanley Cup title over Montreal '51.

McNEIL, Jay (football); b. 20 Aug 1970, London, Ont.; m. Tara; c. Cuyler; Kent State; salesman; ol MAC all-American; CFL Calgary '94-04; 2 CFL, West all-star; 4 Grey Cup finals, 2 winners; res. Calgary, Alta.

McNENEY, Arley (wheelchair basketball); b. 15 Nov 1982, New Westminster, B.C.; UVictoria; began playing wheelchair basketball '97; bronze Canada Games '99; mem. ntl team from '01; gold ('02), silver ('04) Roosevelt Cup World Challenge; gold World championships '02; bronze '04 ntls, Paralympics; 2 Gov.-Gen.'s academic awards; T.S. MacPherson scholarship; Rosalind Petch writing award; res. New Westminster, B.C.

McNICHOL, Doug (football); b. 29 Mar 1930, St. Catharines, Ont.; given name: Douglas Stewart; m. Clara MacFarlane; c. Scott, Cameron, Clara; UWO, BA; ret'd company pres.; basketball UWO '49-53, team capt. '51-52; football UWO '49-53, all-star status 3yrs; pro Montreal '53-60, 4yrs all-star de; de/t Toronto '61-63; twice *Weekend Magazine* all-star; asst. coach ntl sr. champion East York Argos '66, Bramalea Satellites '67; pres. Ont. Midget Football League '79-80; mem. UWO Sports Hall of Fame; res. Mississauga, Ont.

McNICOLL, Bruce (triathlon); b. 29 Aug 1958, Bern, Switzerland; m. LeeAnne; c. Mallory; Carleton, BA, UofOtt, BEd; teacher; victor in more than 50 triathlons '82-91; 5 Ntl Capital, 4 OAC-Gatineau triathlon titles; mem. Ntl Elite '86, Ont. Elite teams '89-90; ntl age- group team '90; competed in Canada, US, Japan; 3 all-American status awards by *Triathlon Today* magazine; PB 1:51.59 for certified Olympic distance triathlon Boston; res. Gloucester, Ont.

McNIE, Murray (t&f); b. 17 Nov 1902, Glasgow, Scotland; d. 27 Nov 1982, London, Ont.; Glasgow Coll. of Electro-Therapy, Medical Massage; ret'd trainer, track coach; asst.

t&f coach, trainer '36, '48 Olympic teams; coach, trainer UWO '34-68; CIAU, UWO citations for contribution to football over 35yrs.; mem. UWO Sports Hall of Fame.

McPHEE, Barry (curling); b. 24 Mar 1947, Kamloops, B.C.; m. Karen; c. Erin, Nicole, Spencer, Angela; golf professional; skipped BC 4 Briers; lost extra-end semifinal to Russ Howard '86 Brier; res. Kamloops, B.C.

McPHEE, Dennis (football/coaching); b. 3 Mar 1958, Hamilton, Ont.; given names: Dennis Aeneas; m. Joanne Evans; c. Macklin, Caelan, Catherine; St. Mary's BA; football coach; all-time sack leader Oakville jrs.; Hamilton Wildcats '84-88; 5yr starter, 2yrs capt. St. Mary's, also 3yrs hockey; CFL Toronto '82 exhibition season, Edmonton '84; 8yrs Northern Football Conference, all-star 5yrs; 2 def-player-of-yr awards; NFC lineman of '88; asst. coach McMaster '84-88; asst. Guelph '90-94, 1 Yates Cup; asst. Hamilton Tiger-Cats '95-01, '04; 1 Grey Cup winner; head coach St. Francis Xavier '02-03; Atlantic Conf coach of '02; mem. NFC Hall of Fame; res. Hamilton, Ont./ Truro, N.S.

McPHERSON, Don (builder); b. 1918, Regina, Sask.; d. 1973, Regina, Sask.; dir. Sask. Roughriders '49-73; pres. CFL '59, CRU '63, WFC '65; on invitation chaired comm. which reorganized BC Lions; life mem. BC Lions; mem. Cdn Football Hall of Fame.

McPHERSON, Donald (figure skating); b. 20 Feb 1945, Windsor, Ont.; d. 24 Nov 2001, Munich, Germany; given name: John Donald; skating teacher; Western Ont. novice title '57, sr. '58-59, ntl jr. '59; 1st Canadian to win ntl, NA, world amateur titles in single year ('63) without having won any of them; at 18 youngest to win world title; world pro title '65; 10th '60 Olympics; 11yrs mem. Holiday on Ice show; mem. Cdn Figure Skating, Cdn Olympic, Canada's Sports halls of fame.

McPHERSON, Gary (wheelchair basketball/administration); b. 28 Jun 1946, Edson, Alta.; given name: Gary William Wilcox; m. Valerie June Kamitono; c. Keiko Janet, Jamie Robert; Alta Correspondence School Branch, UAlta. hon. LLD; ED Cdn. Centre for Social Entrepreneurship at UAlta school of business; adjunct prof. Phys Ed UAlta.; small-business partner/owner Wise Village Inc.; ED, treas., pres. Cdn. Wheelchair Sports Assn. '72-93; GM Alta. Northern Lights Wheelchair Basketball Society '79-87; mgr. Cdn. Men's Wheelchair basketball team '79, '83 worlds; Robert Fertile, Donald King, King Clancy, Robert Jackson, CAHPER, Queen's Golden Jubilee, Alta. achievement awards; Edmonton Jaycees Citizen of '86; Cdn Occupational and Physical Therapist Assn award; Edmonton sportswriters/ sportscasters award; mem. Order of Canada; mem. Alta., Edmonton Sports halls of fame; res. Edmonton, Alta.

McQUARTERS, Ed (football); b. 16 Apr 1943, Tulsa, Okla.; given name: Eddie Lee; m. PaulElla Ann "Bunny" Durant; c. Ed Jr., Mike; Okla., BPE; ret'd SaskPower Corp.; HS discus, shot put records; dl all-city, academic football teams; state wrestling title; UO wrestling scholarship; 2nd Big 8 wrestling tournament '62; switched scholarship to football; competed '62 Orange Bowl; mem. '63 Gator Bowl team; 2 OU game star awards; drafted by Dallas but dealt to St. Louis (NFL) '64-65, Sask. (CFL) '66-74; returned

recovered fumble for td to put Sask. In '66 Grey Cup vs. Ottawa; 2 Grey Cup finals, 1 winner; Schenley lineman of '67; all-Cdn 3yrs; WFC outstanding lineman twice; coach's all-pro team '69; CFL team of decade, *Canadian Magazine* best of '60s dl '69; lost left eye '71 home workshop accident; named to Roughrider 75th anniversary all-star team; 2 Beckett-DeMarco trophies; mem. Cdn Football Hall of Fame, Sask. Football Plaza of Honor; res. Regina, Sask.

McRAE, Ed (cycling); b. 13 Apr 1953, Kamloops, B.C.; given name: Edward Renner; SFU, BA; industrial sales rep.; NA jr. title '70; 5 times BC road racing champion; mem. '71 PAG, '72 Olympic, '73 world championships teams; only Canadian to win gold medal in international Grand Prix (US '73); res. Vancouver, B.C.

McREAVY, Pat (hockey); b. 16 Jan 1918, Owen Sound, Ont.; d. 13 Nov 2001, Owen Sound, Ont,; given name: Patrick Joseph; m. Evelyn Baker Burns; St. Michael's Coll.; auto service mgr.; jr. Owen Sound, St. Mike's Majors, Coppercliff Redmen, Sudbury Wolves; mem. '38 world title team; pro Boston '39-42; mem. '41 Stanley Cup winners; Detroit '42; closed pro career with St. Louis AHL; mem. Owen Sound Mercurys Allan Cup champions '51; coached Mercurys 2yrs; oldtimers hockey to retirement age 62; annual trophy awarded OHL Owen Sound Attack unsung hero bears his name.

McSORLEY, Marty (hockey); b. 18 May 1963, Hamilton, Ont.; given name: Martin James; coach; def. Cayuga, Hamilton jrs. '79-81, OHL Belleville '81-83, AHL Baltimore '83-85, Nova Scotia '86-87, IHL Grand Rapids '01; NHL Pittsburgh '83-85, '93-94, Edmonton '85-88, '98-99, Los Angeles '88-94, '94-96, NYR '95-96, San Jose '96-98, Boston '99-00; NHL totals: 961 scheduled games, 108g, 251a, 116 playoff games, 10g, 19a; 2 Stanley Cup winners; NHL career virtually terminated with suspension following assault on Donald Brasheer's head with stick; shared '91 Alka Seltzer Plus award with Theoren Fleury; coach Springfield AHL '02; res. Springfield, Mass.

McTAGUE, Mike (football); b. 31 May 1958, Toronto, Ont.; NDak State; all-conf. wr/pk '78-79; capt. NDS Bisons '79, MVP, hon. mention all-American; 7 school scoring, receiving records; 3 conf. records; all-time leading scorer; numerous HS tj/lj records; territorial draft Toronto '78; CFL punter Calgary from '79-84, Montreal '85-86; mem. NDS Hall of Fame; res. Calgary, Alta.

McTAVISH, Bill (curling); b. 13 Jul 1917, Winnipeg, Man.; d. 7 Feb 1988, Winnipeg, Man.; given name: William Boyd; m. Ann; c. Jamie, John, Gordon, Billy; UMan, BSc, MD; ret'd general practitioner; 22 consecutive victories '50 Winnipeg bonspiel, winning Brinks, Eatons, grand aggregate, British Consols trophies; runnerup '50 Brier, Man. srs. titles '73-74, ntl srs. '73; with sons John, Gordon, Billy competed in '76 Perth, Scotland, Invitational Master's.; mem. Man, Curling Hall of Fame.

McWHIRTER, Cliff (boxing); b. 19 Apr 1913, London, Ont.; given name: Clifford Gilbert; m. Mary Warbeck; c. Lloyd Gary, David Clifford; Wells Business Academy; ret'd insurance co. supervisor; Western Ont. featherweight title age 14; several Golden Gloves titles before turning pro '32; campaigned under ring name of Babe La Varre; on 1st boxing card ever staged at Maple Leaf Gardens; career total: 157 bouts, won 136, lost 17, 4 draws; never KO'd; trainer, mgr., promoter; handled Bob Flannigan, Jackie "Spider" Armstrong, Teddy Swain, Gil Geekie, all of Toronto; mem. Canadian Boxing, London Sports halls of fame; res. London, Ont.

MEAGHER, Aileen (t&f); b. 26 Nov 1910, Edmonton, Alta.; d. 2 Aug 1987, Halifax, N.S.; given name: Aileen Alethea; Dalhousie, BA; ret'd teacher; qualified '32 Olympics as sprinter but severe charley horse prevented participation; gold 660yds relay, silver 440yd relay, 220yd sprint '34 BEG; bronze 400m relay, 100m semifinalist '36 Olympics; silver 440yd, bronze 660yd relay, 4th 220yd finals '38 BEG; Bobbie Rosenfeld Trophy '35; annual Halifax intl track meet bears her name; mem. Cdn Olympic Sports Hall of Fame.

MEAGHER, Kathy (golf); b. 14 Feb 1947, Chatham (Miramichi) N.B.; given name: Kathy Whitty; m. John Meagher; c. Kathryn; UNB, BPE; ED N.B. Sports Hall of Fame; 2 NB jr. titles; 2 NB amateur titles; 3 NB srs. Titles; with daughter Kethryn 2 NBGA mother-daughter titles; NBLGA player of '01 award; mem. 21 NB prov teams; res. Hanwell, N.B.

MEAGHER, Robyn (t&f); b 17 Jun 1967, Antigonish, N.S.; UVic; research officer; middle distance specialist; started competing age 12; ntl jr. 1500 title '84; ntl indoors 1500m title '86; silver '88 CIAU championships; won '89 NY Games mile, '01 Oregon 1500; ntl 3000m title '91; CIAU, ntl indoor 1500m title '90; competed '90, '94 CG, '91, '99 Worlds, '92, '96 Olympics; silver 3000m '94 CG; President's Cup UVic '90, Athletics Canada athlete of '94; res. Victoria, B.C.

MEEKER, Howie (hockey); b. 4 Nov 1923, New Hamburg, Ont.; given name: Howard William; m. Grace Vera Hammer (d); c. Jane, Peggy, Kim, Howie Jr., Michael, Andy; m. Leah Marshall; corp. pres.; Maple Leafs '46-54; part of 2nd generation Kid Line with Vic Lynn, Teeder Kennedy; scored 5g single game; NHL Calder Trophy '47; mem. 4 Stanley Cup winners; coached Stratford '52, Pittsburgh (AHL) to '54 Calder Cup victory; at 32 youngest Maple Leafs coach '56-57; 5 months Leafs GM before being fired by Stafford Smythe; NHL coaching record: 70 scheduled games, 21-34-15; operates boys' hockey schools Parksville, B.C., Potsdam, N.Y., Vancouver; *CBC Hockey Night in Canada* color commentator, analyst; ret'd as *TSN* hockey analyst '98; author several hockey instruction books; autobiography *Golly Gee - It's Me*; MP (PC) Waterloo South '51-53; Parksville arena bears his name; mem. Hockey, BC Sports, Hockey, Waterloo County halls of fame; res. Parksville, B.C.

MEHLENBACHER, Jack (harness racing/officiating); b. 14 Mar 1922, Nelles Corners, Ont.; d. 31 Mar 1999, Cayuga, Ont.; given name: Jack Leslie; m. Geraldine Austin; c. Jack Jr., Jerry, Jane, Joanne; seed merchant/farmer/standardbred horse breeder; catcher Ont. champion Hagersville Int. B baseball team '39; referee OHA in '40s officiating in Memorial, Allan Cup finals; referee NHL '50s; driving Vanduzen won Toronto Maple Leaf trot at Thorncliffe

Raceway '53; through '50s and '60s among leading drivers at Thorncliffe, Batavia Downs, Buffalo Raceway.

MEISSNER, Ernie (diving); b. 29 May 1937, Belgrade, Yugoslavia; UMich; pres. travel bureau chain; all-American; 11 ntl titles '58-68; 3m bronze '62 CG; 5th 3m '60 Olympics; mem. Waterloo County Hall of Fame; res. Kitchener, Ont.

MEISZTER, Ernst (coaching); b. 18 Apr 1921, Cluj, Romania; accredited fencing master; 1st class water polo player; began fencing '39; mem. Romanian national team '46-58, capt. '52 Olympic team; coach Romanian team '49-62, Brazil national team '64-65; emigrated to Canada '66; coach Cdn team '75 PAG, '76 Olympic Games; fencing instructor Humber Coll., Brock, Toronto Unicorn Club; operates Meister Fencing Academy Willowdale; res. Willowdale, Ont.

MELDRUM, Jenny (t&f); b. 12 Apr 1943, Northampton, Eng.; given name: Jennifer Anne Wingerson; div.; c. Samantha, Gregory; m. Stewart Madill; secretary; hurdles, pentathlon specialist; hurdles silver '63 PAG, bronze '66 BEG; pentathlon silver '67 PAG, bronze '70 CG; mem. '63, '67, '71 PAG, '66, '70 BE&CG, '64, '68 Olympic teams; qualified for '72 Olympics but opted for retirement; national pentathlon, hurdles, lj records; asst. mgr. '75 PAG t&f team; *CBC* t&f color commentator; res. Coquitlam, B.C.

MELESCHUK, Orest (curling); b. 11 Apr 1940, St. Boniface, Man.; m. Patricia Frances McSherry; c. Sean, Karin; United Coll.; engineering tech.; nicknamed "Big OO"; Man. university champion, Charleswood carspiel, *CBC* televised series; '74 Grey Cup 'spiel Toronto; competed 8 prov. championships winning Man. Consols, Brier, Silver Broom '72; Sudbury Superspiel '76; Cdn Open Masters title '02; mem. Man. Curling Hall of Fame; res. St. Boniface, Man.

MELLANBY, Scott (hockey); b. 11 Jun 1966, Montreal, Que.; m. Susan; c. Carter, Nicholas, Courtney; Wisc.; began skating at 3; rw Don Mills (MTHL) '82-83; Henry Carr (OJHL-B) '83-84; UWisc. '84-86; NHL Philadelphia '86-91, Edmonton '91-93, Florida '93-01, St. Louis '01-03; 1 NHL all-star game; only NHL player to score 300 career goals without scoring a hat-trick; capt. Florida '97-01; Mayers Cup. Good Guy awards; founded Mellanby Autism Foundation; NHL record: (through '04) 1291 scheduled games, 340g, 430a, 132 playoff games, 24g, 29a; res. St. Louis, Mo.

MELLWAY, Dean (all-around); b. 26 Oct 1949, Shediac, N.B.; given name: Byron Dean; m. Amanda Griffiths; c. Robin, Darin, Taylor, Frank, Kristina, Gillian, Marty, Carly; Waterloo BA, Laurier MA; career services Carleton; has represented Canada in various events from '76; mem. Cdn Wheelchair Basketball team '76-84; snooker gold '76 Olympiad for physically disabled; silver '87, gold '89 ntl, bronze world wheelchair tennis, became prime organizer Cdn sledge hockey as intl entity; 3 world sledge hockey gold, 1 bronze, capt. Paralympic silver '98, bronze '94 teams; has played key roles in administrative aspect of sport/recreation for disabled; founding mem. Central Ont. developmental riding program; founding mem/pres. Twin Cities (Kitchener-Waterloo) Spinners Wheelchair Sports

Club; chair Ont. Wheelchair Sports Assn. '75-77; v-chair. Cdn Wheelchair Sports Assn. '78-79; convenor Oktoberfest Wheelchair Basketball tourney '78-80; organized 1st ntl wheelchair basketball championship '79; ED Ont. '79-81, Cdn '81-90 Wheelchair Sports Assn.; founding mem. Fitness Can. advisory comm. for Cdns with disabilities '86; vital roles in Rick Hansen Man in Motion tour, creation Ntl Access Awareness Week; convenor '88 intl sledge hockey tourney; pres. OAC Rolling Racquets wheelchair tennis club; mem. Active Lifestyles Alliance for Cdns with disabilities; ED Cdn winter games for physically disabled '92; co-founder Canwin Sports Ltd., sledge hockey equipment; res. Ottawa, Ont.

MELOCHE, Gilles (hockey); b. 12 Jul 1950, Montreal, Que.; m. Sophie; c. Eric, Annie; coach/scout; goal Verdun jrs, Flint (IHL); NHL Chicago '70-71, California '71-76, Cleveland '76-78, Minnesota '78-85, Pittsburgh '85-88; NHL record: 988 scheduled games, 270-351-131, 45,401min, 2756ga, 20so, 45 playoff games, 21-19-0, 2464min, 143ga, 2so; turned to coaching '89-99; goalie coach/scout Pittsburgh; res. Rosemere, Que.

MELOCHE, Lise (biathlon); b. 19 Apr 1960, Ottawa, Ont.; m. David McMahon; sc. Caitlin, Christopher; UofOtt, BSc, BEd; teacher, exercise physiologist, XC Zone.TV film co. co-owner; 2 time Olympian, one of best technical skiers in country; mem. ntl biathlon, x-country ski teams '84-94; competed 200 WC races placing top 10 21 times; 7 WC medals; 3rd overall WC ranking '86; WC gold '91; pioneer in women's biathlon; won ntl, US, Swiss titles; competes as pro elite skier; coaches high performance athletes; helped write biathlon tech. manual; res: Chelsea, Que.

MELVIN, Doug (administration/baseball); b. 8 Aug 1952, Chatham, Ont.; m. Ellen; c. Ashley, Cory; baseball exec.; standout HS athlete starring in football, basketball, hockey Chatham Kent ss; mem. *CKSS* athletic Hall of Fame; credits Ferguson Jenkins with helping him decide to pursue pro baseball career; pitched 6yrs Pittsburgh, Yankee organizations; worked in Yankee organization '79-85, scouting dir. '85; 9yrs Baltimore organization serving in such varied roles as dir. player personnel/asst. GM '86-94; GM Texas '94-01, exec.v-p '96; scout Boston '01-02; GM Milwaukee '02-03; *Sporting News* ML exec. of '96, Baseball America AL exec. of '96; mem. Texas Baseball Hall of Fame; res. Milwaukee, Wisc.

MERAW, Ann (swimming); b. 23 Feb 1917, Powell River, B.C.; given name: Barbara Annabelle Mundigel; m. Joseph Meraw (d); c. William; Pittman Business College; ret'd aquatic dir.; established reputation for swimming endurance by negotiating 10 miles across Howe Sound and back age 10; after claiming all available amateur honors turned pro at 17 and established 7 world speed and distance records, including 42 miles in 25 hours 1 minute, 55 miles in 32 hours 12 minutes; became Canada's 1st registered female life guard; known as "Queen of the Polar Bears", the hardy group of swimmers who brave Vancouver's icy English Bay on New Year's Day; organized 1st water babies program; conducted courses for military, civilian personnel in hazardous jobs and physically challenged; examiner/instructor Royal Life Saving Society `40-70; swim instructor Vancouver parks board `58-70; swim coach `58-82; with husband

Joe trained field dogs; coached swimming, field hockey, skiing, basketball, tennis, synchronized swimming, diving, badminton, gymnastics, 1st Vancouver women's baseball team; tech. advisor *Beachcombers* TV series; Canada 125 commemorative medal; hon. life mem. Royal Life Saving Society; recognized in *BC Who's Who*; organized Ridge Meadows Hall of Fame; BC Women in Sport Leaders & Legends award; mem. BC Sports, Ridge Meadows halls of fame; res. Maple Ridge, B.C.

MERCIER, Michel (weightlifting); b. 2 Oct 1954, La Sarre, Que.; Laval, BPhE; phys ed teacher; Que. 60kg titles '73, '75; ntl 60kg '77-78, '80; Canada Games gold '75; Ottawa International silver 67.5kg '78; CG gold 60kg '78; gold 67.5kg silver, bronze 60kg Commonwealth championships; bronze 60kg Pan-Am championships; Que. weightlifter-of-year award; res. La Sarre, Que.

MERETSKY, Toots (basketball); b. 17 May 1912, Windsor, Ont.; given name: Irving; m. Eleanor; c. Warren, Lynn, Rodd (d); Assumption Coll.; ret'd furniture store owner; began playing basketball in public school; established reputation as deadly shooter and strong court general; mem. '36 silver medal Olympic team; 2yrs playing coach Port Alberni; versatile athlete who qb'd HS football team, played ss with Windsor Olympics baseball team; mem. Cdn Basketball, Windsor-Essex Sports halls of fame; res. Windsor, Ont.

MERKLINGER, Anne (swimming/curling); b. 15 Nov 1958, London Ont. given name: Anne Lousie; m. Don Michie; c. Meagan, Connor; South Carolina, BSc; swim coach, sports administrator; mem. prominent curling family; curling: bronze '75 Canada Winter Games; silver ntl jr. ladies '76; silver Ont. jr. ladies '78; fifth mem. Alison Goring Ont. title rink '90; skip Ont. women's title rink '93-94, '98, '00; semifinalist '93, finalist '98 Scott Tournament of Hearts; became involved in swimming for therapeutic reasons following injury; East. Cdn. 100m, 200m breaststroke titles '76; silver 200m breaststroke '77 FISU Games; mem. ntl swim team '77-79; finalist Coca-Cola intl '79; capt. UofSC swim team '81; all-American 8 events '79-81; dean's list UofSC '78-81; Ottawa ACT swimming awards '77, '79; Breakthrough leadership award '97; Johnny F. Bassett award '98; Marj Mitchell STOH award '00; exec. dir. Cdn Canoe Assn.; res. Metcalfe, Ont.

MERKLINGER, Bill (curling); b. 30 May 1956, Montreal, Que.; given name: William Arthur; UofOtt, BPhE; federal government management consultant; competitive swimmer prior to turning attention to curling; Ont. jr men's curling champion '73; rep. PEI '75 Canada Winter Games; competed '75, '82 Maritime men's championships; 3rd for brother Dave '81 Ont. men's Tankard playdowns; skipped PEI to 3rd place with 8-5 record '82 Seagram Mixed; res. Ottawa, Ont.

MERKLINGER, Dave (curling); b. 14 Mar 1955, Montreal, Que.; given name: David Michael; m. Janet Davies; c. Michael, Jennifer; curling ice maker; Ont. jr. tankard '73; Ont. Silver Tankard '76-77, '79; 8 Ont. Tankard (Consols) appearances, 6 as skip; 1 Ont. mixed competition; lead for Earle Morris '85 Ont. Brier rink; skip McCain East Superspiel winner; icemaker ntl STOH '98; res. Vancouver, B.C.

MERRICK, Wayne (hockey); b. 23 Apr 1952, Sarnia, Ont.; given name: Leonard Wayne; m. Carol Lee Moore; c. Courtney, Andrew; financial planner; Silver Stick midget tournament MVP '69; jr. Ottawa 67's '69-71; 1st pick St. Louis '72 draft; Denver (WHL) '72; NHL St. Louis '72-75, California '75-76, Cleveland '76-78, NYI '78-84; NHL record: 774 scheduled games, 191g, 265a, 102 playoff games, 19g, 30a; 4 Stanley Cup winners; scored final game winner vs. Minnesota '81 Stanley Cup; overtime winning goal vs. Quebec '82 Stanley Cup playoffs; res. Lindenhurst, NY/London, Ont.

MERRILL, Horace (canoeing/hockey); b. 30 Nov 1884, Toronto, Ont.; d. 24 Dec 1958, Ottawa, Ont.; given name: Horace Jefferson; m. Phyllis May Parker; c. Bill. Dorothy, Audrey, Lois; ret'd printing co. pres., school board trustee; standout paddler, hockey, football, soccer, basketball player; backbone of YMCA basketball, soccer, rugby teams '04-08; frequent MVP awards; 3 ntl sr. single-blade canoe, 3 sr. war canoe, 1 sr. tandem canoe titles; def Allan Cup champion Cliffsides '09; 7 seasons with Ottawa Senators; 3 Stanley Cup finals, 1 winner; mem. Glebe Curling Club Gov.-Gen.'s Cup winner '24; secty-treas. Cdn Canoe Assn.; mem. Ottawa Sports Hall of Fame.

MERVYN, Glen (rowing); b. 17 Feb 1937, Vancouver, B.C.; given name: Glen Alexander; m. Christina Maclean; c. Tyler, Sasha; UBC, BSc, Harvard, MEd; pres.-GM ski lift importing, installation bus.; #6 seat '58 BEG gold medal crew, #6 seat '59 PAG silver medal crew; stroke '60 Olympic Games silver medal crew; coached UBC crews '63-64; coached ntl crews '64 Olympics, including gold medal pairs Roger Jackson, George Hungerford; mem. 8s crew Cdn championships '58-60; unofficial 2501 full-twist situps record '58 while testing effect of vitamin E on athlete's diet; as mem. '60 Olympic 8s silver medalist inducted into BC Sports Hall of Fame; res. Kelowna, B.C.

MESSIER, Mark (hockey); b. 18 Jan 1961, Edmonton, Alta.; given name: Mark Douglas; c. Lyon; ctr Portland (WHL) '77-78, Indianapolis, Cincinnati (WHA) '78-79, Houston (CHL) '79-80; Edmonton's 2nd choice '79 draft; NHL Edmonton '79-91 (capt.), NYR '91-97, '00-04 (capt.), Vancouver '97-00; mem. 3 Canada Cup teams, Team Canada '89 Worlds, '87 Rendez-Vous team; 4 1st team, 1 2nd team all-star; 2 Hart, 2 Pearson, 1 Conn Smythe trophies; mem. 6 Stanley Cup winners; 15 all-star games; *Sporting, Hockey News* player of '90; NHL record: (through '04) 1756 scheduled games, 694g, 1193a, 236 playoff games, 109g, 186a; joined Wayne Gretzky, Gordie Howe, Marcel Dionne, Phil Esposito on 1500 point plateau '96; reached 1800pts '01; moved into 2nd place on all-time NHL point list at 1851 '03; proficient golfer; very active in children's charities; mem. Madison Square Gardens Walk of Fame; res. Hilton Head, S.C.

MESSNER, Joe (water skiing); b. 1 Mar 1924, Solbad Hall, Tirol, Austria; m. Linda Ohm-Meier; c. Peter, Bill (d), Patricia; Ferdinand FranzensU. Innsbruck, Handelsakademie, Austria; ntl exec-dir Friends of SOS, ex-exec-dir Children's Aid Society; 42 prov titles; 12 gold, 8 silver, 10 bronze in ntl competition; 4 golds Ont. Games, European srs. title '72, 43 other international medals; competitive record includes 102 1sts, 20 2nds, 9 3rds, variety of prov., ntl records; operator

Mesle Sport; 14 special awards, 5 Ont. achievement, 8 Ont. sports achievement, 1 Command Sports award; mem. Cdn Hang Gliding Assn. holds special pilots license for paragliding; res. Ottawa, Ont.

MESSNER, Pat (water skiing); b. 17 Mar 1954, Hamilton, Ont.; given name: Patricia Marilyn; McGill, Carleton; Waterloo BA, UofOtt, BEd, Algonquin Coll.; musician, HS teacher; '64-81 dominated ntl water skiing scene; 15 ntl, 45 Ont. titles; '72 Carl Fisher Cup, '78 US Masters slalom (1st Cdn woman), '76 Western Hemisphere slalom, Aquaba international champion '79, world slalom champion '79 (1st Cdn woman), 44 other tournaments; bronze '69 Canada Summer Games; bronze '72 Olympics (only Cdn); silver '72 Western Hemisphere slalom; bronze '75 world championships (1st Cdn woman); silver '77 world championships (only Cdn); silver '80 World Cup; 10 Ont., 7 Ottawa ACT sports-achievement awards, Ottawa ACT athlete of '79, SFC '79 intl-achievement award; Level 3 master coach; mem. athletes advisory comm. on ntl sports, ntl coaching '76-79; chief instructor Mesle Sport (recreational, competitive instruction for water skiing, windsurfing, kayaking, hang gliding) from '72; OCRAS academic-excellence award '85; mem. ntl medical/science comm.; WSC disabled skiing comm.; returned to competition '04 winning Eastern Cdn, ntl masters titles, set 2 slalom records; mem. Order of Canada, Cdn Waterski/Wakeboarding, Ottawa Sports halls of fame; res. Carleton Place, Ont.

METRAS, John (coaching); b. 8 Apr 1909, Dowagiac, Mich., d. 13 Apr 1982, Naples, Fla.; given name: John Pius; m. Shirley Goodheart; c. John Jr., Robert, Mary Lynn; Detroit, hon. LLD UWO; coach, AD UWO; all-state HS hb; all-American mention as ctr UDet; with St. Mike's Coll. starred in ORFU '33-34; all-Cdn ctr '34; joined Bill Stern as asst. coach UWO '35, head coach '39-69; football coaching record: 106 wins, 76 losses, 11 ties, 9 league titles; teams once had undefeated run of 29 games; basketball coach '45-64, teams won or shared 14 titles, 24 league-game winning streak; UWO athletic dir. '45-72; nicknamed "The Bull"; various offical capacities in football, basketball rules-making bodies Canada, US; hon.-pres. Assn. of Cdn. Intercollegiate Football Coaches; trophy in his honor awarded to Cdn. coll. football lineman of year; mem. Cdn Football, Cdn Basketball, UWO, London Sports halls of fame.

METZ, Nick (hockey); b. 16 Feb 1914, Wilcox, Sask.; d. 24 Aug 1990, Wilcox, Sask; Notre Dame Coll, St. Michael's Coll; farmer; began hockey career under Fr. Athol Murray; mem. '34 Memorial Cup winner; signed with Maple Leafs; following stint with Syracuse farm team rejoined Toronto for playoffs; spent 12 seasons with Leafs scoring 131g, 119a while playing lw/ctr; 9 Stanley Cup finals, 4 winners; record 3 assists 1 period '41 Stanley Cup semifinals vs. Boston; while serving in army WW2 mem. Victoria team which lost to Ottawa in Allan Cup finals; mgr. Wilcox Cardinals sr. baseball team; also proficient curler, baseball, lacrosse player; mem. Sask. Sports Hall of Fame.

MEYER, Bill (water polo); b. 4 Nov 1958, Hamilton, Ont.; m. Cathy; c. Kayla; UofOtt; recruiter/trainer Keller Williams Realty, financial consultant, ex-branch mgr. Canada Trust

'85-01; gold '77 Canada Games; mem. jr. ntl team '76-77, ntl sr. team '77-85; bronze '79, '83 PAG; mem. '82 world, '83 FISU, '84 Olympic teams; mem. '01 Ont. Sr. men's title team; competed over 200 international games; res. Ottawa, Ont.

MEYER, Cynthia (shooting); b. 6 Oct 1965, New York; given name: Cynthia Barbara; m. Robert F. Cranshaw; c. Olivia; URichmond, BSc, New York Law School, JD cum laude, The American College, ChFC, CLU; financial consultant; mother a Canadian; following father's lead began trap shooting age 22; 4 Cdn. woman's trap titles; 6 Cdn. woman's double trap titles; '96, '00 Olympics; bronze double trap '96 World Cup; silver double trap '97 worlds; bronze double trap '02 Suhl world cup; 4 medals, including individual gold, bronze '02 CG; 2 silver '03 PAG; 2 Cdn female-shooter-of-yr awards; 8 Amateur Trap Assn. All-American; volunteer New York Junior League; res. Bowen Island, B.C./ New York, NY

MICHEL, Yvette (swimming/t&f); b. 26 Aug 1965, Chilliwack, B.C.; blind swimmer, shot put/lj specialist; 13 prov., 7 ntl, 23 world/Olympic Games for Disabled swimming records; res. Vancouver, B.C.

MICHIBATA, Glenn (tennis); b. 13 Jun 1962, Toronto, Ont.; m. Angie; Pepperdine; coach USC '97-00, Princeton from '00, ex-tennis club dir.; Cdn -12 singles '74, -18 singles, doubles '78, '80; ntl jr singles '80; ntl jr. indoor title '81; with Martin Wostenholme ntl -18 doubles '78, '80; ntl sr singles titles '81-82, doubles '85, '89; 1st Cdn to win all-American ranking 3 straight years; NCAA '82 finalist; mem. 9 Davis Cup, '79-81 Galea Cup teams; won USTA Hawaiian Satellite singles, San Francisco, Springfield doubles '85; teamed with Grant Connell '88 to produce formidable doubles combination; semifinalist French Open; Wimbledon '91; 9 Tennis Canada excellence awards, twice player of yr, 5 doubles team of yr; ret'd from competition '94; mem. Tennis Can. Hall of Fame; res. Whistler, B.C.

MICHIENZI, Peter (wrestling); b. 22 Feb 1934, Curinga, Italy; m. Margaret Dixon; c. Peter (Piero), Marina, Mario; printer; 10 ntl FS titles, 5 Greco-Roman titles (15 titles a ntl record); Jewish Invitational Buffalo, Mich. State titles; silver '62 BEG; bronze '66 CG; mem. '62 world, '63, '67 Pan-Am, '68 Olympic Games teams; capt. ntl team '66-68; outstanding wrestler '66 ntl championships; Ont. Fitness, Sport Awards '66, '69; Ont. medallion of excellence in sport '67; Italo-Cdn. sports award '73; London Jaycees young man of '67; volunteer coach from '57 guiding London Y to 3 prov. titles, Ont. team to Canada Games gold '71; coach London Amateur Wrestling, Athletic Club, UWO to OQAA runnerup honors '70-71; A1 status as international amateur wrestling referee; dir. Olympic Club of Canada; silver medal '76 World Wrestling Assn.; mem. Cdn Amateur Wrestling, London Sports halls of fame; res. London, Ont.

MICKOSKI, Nick (hockey); b. 7 Dec 1927, Winnipeg, Man.; d. 13 Mar 2002, Winnipeg, Man.; lw CUAC, St. James jrs., NY Rovers; minor pro New Haven, Cincinnati (AHL), NHL NY '47-60 season playing with NYR, Chicago, Detroit, Boston; NHL record: 703 scheduled games, 158g, 185a, 18 playoff games, 1g, 6a; played '63 season with San Francisco Seals winning WHL title; standout golfer;

2 Man. Amateur, 1 Sr., 2 Grey Owls titles; mem. Man. Hockey Hall of Fame.

MIDDAUGH, Wayne (curling); b. 20 Sep 1967, Brampton, Ont.; div. Pam; m. Sherry; c. Kelly; golf pro/icemaker, M&M meat shop franchise owner; finalist '87 Pepsi jr.; 2nd for Russ Howard '91-94 Labatt Briers; '93 winner, '93 World champion; '91-94, '03 *TSN* Skins; '93 VO Cup; skipped own rink from '95; won *TSN* Skins Game '95-96; skipped '98 (winner), '01 Ont. Brier entries; won Ford Worlds '98; skipped WCT '98, '02 top money winner; WCT title '99-02; Telus Cdn Open title '01; res. Victoria Harbour, Ont.

MIDDLETON, Rick (hockey); b. 4 Dec 1953, Toronto, Ont.; given name: Richard David; m. Karen; c. Claudine, Jarret, Brett; broadcaster, owner/operator Rick Middleton Enterprises; jr. Oshawa Generals; 1st draft NYR '73; rw Rangers '74-76; Boston '76-88; Garrett Memorial Trophy (AHL rookie of year) '73-74; Lady Byng '82; 2nd team all-star '82; 51g '81-82; Team Canada '81, '84; NHL record: 1005 scheduled games, 448g, 540a, 114 playoff games, 45g, 55a; played in Europe; coach US '02 Paralympic gold sledge hockey team; res. Boston, Mass.

MIDGLEY, Arnold (skiing); b. 28 Apr 1935, Ottawa, Ont.; given name: Philip Arnold Samuel; m. Caroline Morris; c. Eric, Adam; Carleton, Queen's, BSc; electrical engineer; mem. Ottawa Night Riders, Camp Fortune; OQAA Alpine title '57-58; won Robertson Kandahar, alpine races vs. ntl team '58; mem. ntl team '59-63; coach Que.-div teams Camp Fortune '60-64; admin. FIS '63-79; tech delegate FIS; ntl alpine titles '60, '62; FIS Congress mem. '75-79; chair. Cdn Ski Museum; mem. Cdn Ski, Ottawa Sports halls of fame; res. Ottawa, Ont.

MIGAY, Rudy (hockey); b. 18 Nov 1928, Fort William, Ont.; all-around athlete who excelled in baseball and hockey; player/coach sr. baseball teams in Port Arthur, Fort William; dimunitive (5'6") but quick ctr Port Arthur, St. Mike's jrs., 2 Memorial Cup titles; pro AHL Pittsburgh '48-52 (Calder Cup winner), Rochester '58-60, '62; NHL Toronto '49, '52-59; NHL record: 418 scheduled games, 59g, 92a, 15 playoff games, 1g, 0a; WHL Denver '63-64; CHL Tulsa '64-66; coach Port Arthur '60-62, winning Ahearne Cup '62; coached in AHL, CHL through '71; scout Buffalo Sabres; AHL all-star, Les Cunningham MVP award '59; played 1 NHL all-star game; mem. NWO Sports Hall of Fame; res. Thunder Bay, Ont.

MIKAWOS, Stan (football); b. 11 May 1958, Gdansk, Poland; NDak;dt; territorial exemption Blue Bombers; with Winnipeg '82-97; 5 Grey Cup finals, 3 winners; 1 Eastern all-star; res. Winnipeg, Man.

MIKI, Fuji (curling); b. 20 Sep 1941, Vancouver B.C.; given name: Fuji Roy; m. Mary Anne Uyele; c. Tracey Anne, Bryan; auto parts salesman; mem. '60 Pacific Coast hockey champions; mem. 3 Pacific Coast Zone 3 curling champions; mem. '79 BC Brier entry; prov. men's finalist '80-82; 2nd on '82 ntl Seagram Mixed title rink; mem. '77 Japanese Cdn. curling title team; res. Burnaby, B.C.

MIKITA, Stan (hockey); b. 20 May 1940, Sokolce, Czech.; given name: Stanislas Gvoth; m. Jill; c. Scott, Meg, Jane,

Christopher; hon. LLD Brock; restaurateur; nicknamed "Stash"; jr. St. Catharines TeePees; 3 times OHA all-star, MVP once, '58-59, scoring title; Black Hawks '59-80, NHL's 1st triple crown winner, (Ross, Hart, Lady Byng trophies) in single season '66-67, repeated '67-68; 4 Ross (scoring), 2 Hart (MVP), 2 Lady Byng (most gentlemanly); Lester Patrick Trophy '75-76; 6 times 1st, twice 2nd team all-star ctr; Team Canada '72; NHL season record: 1394 games, 541g, 926a, 155 playoff games, 59g, 91a; inventive player, developed suspension helmet, curved stick; with Ab McDonald, Ken Wharram formed Scooter Line; record 21 playoff points in 12 games, record 15 assists; jersey #21 ret'd by Hawks; featured on Cdn postage stamps; Hockey Hall of Fame selection comm.; mem. Slovak, NHL Hockey halls of fame; res. Oak Brook, Ill.

MIKOWETZ, Rudy (racquetball/tennis/golf); b. 30 May 1922, Rudig, Czechoslovakia; given name: Rudolf Karl; div. Terry Seguin; c. Lisa; div. Grace Lam; m. Bonnie Erickson; ret'd businessman; life threatening pleurisy age 9; outdoor activities prescribed as therapy; became polished soccer player attracting pro offers despite youth; tennis became his passion at 17; '39 Czech jr. grenade-throwing champion with 84m throw; forced into German army WW2 serving on Russian front; taught tennis, skiing for US army in Austria; won '51 Salzburg tennis title and named to Austrian Davis Cup team but emigrated to Canada before Davis Cup play began; NCTA singles titlist; began racquetball play at 45; ntl 55+ title '80; world finalist, Northeastern US title '79, Florida champion '77; ODGA srs title '79, Que. srs. golf title '80; Bedard Trophy '82, Rivermead GC srs. title '83; Ottawa ACT racquetball awards '79-80; ex-partner Queensview Racquet Club, La Sporteque de Hull; res. Galax, Va.

MILES, Barron (football); b. 1 Jan 1972, Roselle, N.J.; m. Jennifer Bazate; c. Raven, Barron Jr., Eva; Nebraska; db; signed by NFL Pittsburgh '97 and assigned to Frankfurt (NFL Europe); CFL Montreal '98-04; East div rookie of '98; East div. outstanding def. player '02; 3 CFL, 4 East Div., CFLPA all-star; Tom Pate Memorial award; spokesperson Royal Victoria Hospital neonatal intensive care unit through Cuddles program; created Reaching Out to Children Alouettes School is Cool basketball program; res. Montreal, Que.

MILES, Johnny (t&f); b. 30 Oct 1905, Halifax, Eng.; d. 15 Jun 2003, Hamilton, Ont.; m. Elizabeth Connon; ret'd mfr. co. mgr.; ntl 5-mile, Halifax Herald 10-mile titles '25, Boston Marathon '26, '29; ntl 10,000m '28; bronze '30 BEG; mem. '28, '32 Olympic teams; mem. Order of Canada; Cdn Roadrunners, NS, Canada's Sports halls of fame.

MILES, Kay (swimming); b. 28 Jul 1931, London, Ont. sep. Bob Easun; c. David, Jeff, Susan; UWO, hons BA; teacher; Central CI basketball, volleyball, t&f standout; mem. BEG swim team '50; excelled in coll. swimming, basketball, volleyball; Claude Brown Trophy for contribution to UWO sport '54; coached UWO women's swim teams to 2 intercollegiate titles '54-56; active Masters swimmer from '77, setting group ntl records; chair. Ont. Masters Swim Assn.; 1st woman elected to UWO W-Club Sports Hall of Fame; res. Thornhill, Ont.

MILES, Rollie (football); b. 16 Feb 1928, Washington, D.C.; d. 17 Aug 1995, Edmonton, Alta; m. Marianne; c.

Rolanda, Tony, Monica, Mario, Michelle, Rollie Jr., Brett; St. Augustine Coll., BA, Ariz., MEd; phys ed supervisor; all-American '50; 10 athletic letters basketball, baseball, t&f; Class A baseball Boston's Regina farm team '51; hb Eskimos '51-62; CFL record: 278 punts returned 2085yds, 7.5 avg., 88 kickoff returns 2131yds, 24.2 avg., including 100yd td, 38 interceptions returned 547yds; 8 times WFL all-star, 4 times all-Cdn; 3 times club MVP; variety of club records; most tds 1 season, most yds gained single game, most interceptions 1 season; mem. Edmonton, Alta. Sports, Canadian Football halls of fame.

MILES, Wiff (officiating); b. 9 Nov 1931, Fredericton, N.B.; given name: William Boddington; c. Wendy, Susan, Allan; accounting officer; officiated every level hockey from schoolboy to sr. '47-89; formed NB referees assn.; pres./chief official '68-80; at request of Soviet Sports Fed., officiated in Leningrad game '69; Charles Daigle top NB hockey exec.; Fredericton area MHA award; mem. NB Sports Hall of Fame; res. Fredericton, N.B.

MILFORD, Jake (hockey); b. 29 Jul 1914, Charlottetown, P.E.I.; d. 24 Dec 1984, Vancouver, B.C.; given name: John Calverley; standout junior Winnipeg Columbus, Kenora Thistles; rejected pro offers Detroit, NY to play 3yrs in England; minor pro Cleveland, Springfield, Buffalo (AHL); traded by Eddie Shore from Springfield to Buffalo for 2 sets used Art Ross nets; 14yrs Rangers system; Central League coach-of-yr trophy bears his name; GM LA '73-77, Vancouver '77-84; mem. Man., Cdn Hockey halls of fame.

MILLAR, Ian (equestrian); b. 6 Jan 1947, Halifax, N.S.; m. Lynn Doran; c. Jonathon, Amy; horseman, businessman; mem. ntl team from '71; mem. '72, '76, '80, '84, '88, '92, '96, '00, '04 Olympic, '71, '75, '79, '83, '87, '95, '99, '03 PAG, 5 World Show Jumping teams; 2 individual, 1 team gold, 3 team silver, 1 individual, 1 team bronze PAG; team gold '80 alternative Olympics; world's most successful GP/derby riders, with Big Ben his most successful mount, unprecedented 130 victories; personal record 11 GP wins single season '92; 1st rider to lead World Cup League 9 times; 1st ever to successfully defend World Cup title '88-89; twice ranked #1 in world; competed in 84 Nations Cups; mem. 14 Nations Cup title teams; numerous ntl, NA, European titles; 9 ntl GP champion rider titles; Ottawa ACT equestrian of '75; ret'd Welcome Stakes Class Trophy NY International with 3rd straight win '80; riding Big Ben won 4 Fleischmann World Cup, 5 Smirnoff Cup, 2 du Maurier (world's richest GP) titles; with My Girl won Big Ben GP Challenge Toronto '96; ntl equestrian of '84; Ont. male athlete of '89; seriously injured in water jump spill '95; competed on European circuit '98-99; flag-bearer '99 PAG; co-authored *Riding High*; nicknamed "Captain Canada" by peers; mem. Order of Canada, Cdn Olympic, Canada's, Ottawa Sports halls of fame; res. Perth, Ont.

MILLAR, Torchy (equestrian); b. 20 Aug 1945, Calgary, Alta.; given name: Terrance; m. Elizabeth Wiebe; c. Jessica Anne; Carleton, BA; farm manager; initial international competition '67; mem. '68, '72 Olympic, '71, '83 PAG teams; individual bronze, team gold '71, team silver '83 PAG; Rothman's NA GP '71, '73; NA, Eastern Cdn jumper titles '67; mem. '71 prix de nations title teams NY, Toronto horse shows; NY show jumping title '73; ntl show jumping title '73; ntl jumping derby '77; sole Cdn qualifier '79 WC finals; '80 jumper stakes title; res. Kettleby, Ont.

MILLEN, Greg (hockey); b. 25 Jun 1957, Toronto, Ont.; TV hockey analyst; goalie; OHA jr. Peterborough '74-77, SSM '77; IHL Kalamazoo '77, San Diego '92; NHL Pittsburgh '78-81, Hartford '81-85, St. Louis '85-89, Quebec '89-90, Chicago '90-91, Detroit '91-92; AHL Maine '91-92; NHL record: 604 scheduled games, 216-284-89, 17sho, 59 playoff games, 27-29; mem. Team Canada '82; p-pres. PPHAA; color commentator Hockey Night in Canada, Fox Sports, Molstar Communications, Ottawa Senators; res. Bridgenorth, Ont.

MILLER, Clayton (shooting); b. 7 Oct 1977, North York, Ont.; given name: Clayton Alexander; UBC, BSc, BEd; working on an LLB, UofSask.; skeet specialist; started shooting age 10; when he first started shooting gun was taller than he was; competed '96 Olympics; silver '97 Atlanta World Cup; bronze '99 PAG; double skeet silver '98 worlds; gold '02 CG; Kelowna athlete of '03; res. Kelowna, B.C.

MILLER, Colin (soccer); b. 4 Oct 1964, Lanark, Scotland; given name: Colin Fyfe; coach; honed skills in Vancouver; mfld Hamilton Steelers CSL '88-90; Glasgow, Doncaster, Hamilkton Academicals, Hearts, Dunfermline (Scottish League); mem. ntl team from '83; capt. team Canada in Gold Cup play '92-96; 13 WC qualifying matches; 61 International caps; Abbotsford head coach '00; interim ntl team coach '03; mem. Cdn Soccer Hall of Fame; res. Abbotsford, B.C.

MILLER, Colleen (rowing); b. 12 Dec 1967, Matlock, Man.; Comcheq services; former competitive swimmer who began rowing '89; bow for Wendy Wiebe lightweight double scull; mem. ntl team '89-99; 4 world championship, 2 International regatta, 2 US championship golds; competed '96 Olympics; Man. female athlete of '95; Dick Ellis team award '90; mem. Man. Sports Hall of Fame; res. Winnipeg, Man.

MILLER, Dave (sailing); b. 18 Sep 1943, Vancouver, B.C.; given name: David Sidney; m. Susan Jean; UBC, BComm; sailmaker; with crew Colin Park, Kenneth Baxter '60 NA jr. sailing title, Sears Cup; at 19 skipper '64 Olympic Star; crew mem., tactician 4th place Dragon '68 Olympics; bronze medal skipper Soling Class '72 Olympics; res. Victoria, B.C.

MILLER, Doug Jr. (bowling); b. 25 Nov 1927, Peterborough, Ont.; given name: James Douglas; m. Colleen Smith; c. Douglas, Carol, Dan, Dave, Anne Marie; ret'd tool designer, product mgr., exec., fund raiser; minor, intermediate, sr. B lacrosse; jr., int., sr. football, hockey, boxing; lacrosse Toledo, Ohio, '49;, Peterborough Sr. B '50, Windsor Webster Motors '51; coached Peterborough, Ont., juv lacrosse titlist '52; built Allencourt Lanes Richmond Hill, mgr. '60-62; conceived, founded Youth Bowling Council (YBC) '62; launched world bantam tournament; key role in eliminating counter pin from 5-pin game; formed Bowling Proprietors Assn. of Canada; exec. dir. BPAO, BPAC '62-69; owned, operated Newmarket Redman hockey team '75-78; led Can-Am lacrosse league in penalties 2 seasons; model

shipbuilder of note; pioneer in development of facial, eye protection for hockey players with CCM '75-78; Ont. achievement award, Builder of Bowling Industry award; grand marshall Variety bike-a-thon Toronto '81; BPAO 50th anniversary award; mem. Ont. 5-pin Bowling Hall of Fame; res. Peterborough, Ont.

MILLER, Doug Sr. (lacrosse); b. 1904, Peterborough, Ont.; d. 8 Mar 1986, Seminole, Fla.; given name: Thomas Douglas; m. Alice Mary Ebbs; c. Douglas, Adele, Marilyn; ret'd contractor; mem. champion Crescents Peterborough sr. city league; sr., jr., Oshawa '23, Wallaceburg '24; competitive career lasted 27yrs.; final game marked beginning of sr. play for son Doug as both appeared on field the same day; as contractor dominant force behind construction of 4000-seat Miller Bowl (named in his honor) by Peterborough Lacrosse Club; mem. Canadian Lacrosse, Peterborough Sports halls of fame.

MILLER, Esther (skiing); b. 10 Sep 1957, Edmonton, Alta.; given name: Esther Ruth; x-country specialist; ntl jr. title '73; mem. ntl team '74-82; BC 5km champion '73; NA 3x5km '78-79; ntl 5km, 1st overall Dannon series '80; Ont. 5km, 10km, national 5km, 3x5km, NA 4x5km relay titles '81; mem. '76, '80 Olympic; '79, '81 Swedish Ski Games, '79, '81 Finland World Cup teams; res. Burns Lake, B.C.

MILLER, James (harness racing); b. 13 Sep 1945, Saint John, N.B.; after stints as commercial pilot and serious shot at professional hockey settled on horse training; from $250 purses at Paterson Park, B.C., he's graduated to Grand Circuit racing; first major acquisition was Invincible Shadow which earned Aged Pacer of '74; he also makes the occasional catch drive which, through '95, have produced 953 wins and purses exceeding $6M; among star horses he's trained are former world champion Brisco Hanover, million-dollar winner J.D's Buck, Tijuana Taxi, Brace Yourself and Cheery Hello; winter-trains at Ben White Raceway; res. Clarcona, Fla.

MILLER, Leigh (t&f); b. 17 Aug 1905, Elmsdale, N.S.; d. 24 May 1998, Halifax, N.S.; m. Helen Oliver; c. James, Evan; Dalhousie, BComm; ret'd production mgr.; Maritime sprint champion '25-31; Ont. sprint champion '28-31; ntl, NA indoor sprint titles '30; 3 world 100yd, 1 world 100m, 60m (indoor), ntl indoor 40yd record; mem. '30 BEG gold medal relay team; 25yrs t&f coach Toronto, Montreal, Halifax; head t&f coach '54 Empire Games; subject of S. M. Parker poem; Dalhousie gold medal, sports plaque; '30 BEG president's medal; mem. NS Sports Hall of Fame.

MILLER, Linda (shooting); b. 5 Jul 1952, Noranda, Que.; given name: Linda Karen; sep. Szulga; Ryerson, BA; management consultant/entrepreneur; initial target shooting experience '85; moved to Olympic events '89; qualified for ntl small-bore rifle team '90; won World Cup medals '92-95; CG pairs (with Christina Ashcroft) bronze '94; switch to full-bore competition '96; 3 Que., 4 Ont., 3 ntl championships; nationally certified coach; founding mem. SFC ntl coaching comm.; mgr/head coach Ont. rifle team '91-94; dir. ORA '97, Ont. small-bore fed. '89-91; conducts coaching seminars; founder/editor *CoachNet*; dir./mgr./administrator varied sports organizations; res. Toronto, Ont.

MILLER, Russ (curling/darts); b. 13 Sep 1918, London, Ont.; given name: Russell Edward; m. Frances Elizabeth Blakey (d); c. Bonnie Jean; ret'd sheet metal worker; 26 London Curling Club championships,; Ont. Silver Tankard '48, '54, numerous City of London bonspiel titles; with wife Fran, won Auld London mixed, Tillsonburg Tobacco Belt; 3 8-enders; Ont. Points championship '58-59; 6 times competed Ont. Consols; 12 Royal Cdn Legion zone titles, provincial '59, 4th nationals; *London Free Press* sportsman of '59; mem. Ont. champion dart teams '55, '74, several city titles; numerous perfect 180 scores with either hand; flag-bearer '74 London Brier; life mem. LCC; ranked in London's top 10 5-pin bowlers '62; res. London, Ont.

MILLER, Shannon (hockey/coaching); b. 1964, Melfort, Sask.; UofSask, BPhE; coach; ex-police officer; played in 1st-ever women's ntl championship '82, also competed '83-85; ended competitive playing career '89; refereed university level women's hockey '82-85; moved from Sask. to Calgary to become police officer '88; started 1st-ever girl's minor hockey team in Calgary '89; began ntl coaching career '91 as asst. leading Alta women's team to Canada Games gold; asst. '92, '94 Cdn women's world gold medal team coached Canada to gold at 2 Pacific Rim championships; coached Calgary Classics to '95-96 Alta provincial gold; ntl bronze; chair. female hockey in Sask.; pres. Southern Alta Women's HL; mem. Cdn hockey's female council '85; hired by Olympic Oval '95 to lead 1st-ever international high performance female hockey program; coached ntl team to '97 women's world title; coach '98 Cdn women's silver medal Olympic team; head coach UMinn-Duluth women's hockey; Breakthrough award '98; PetroCan coaching excellence award; res. Duluth, Minn.

MILLER, Tommy (curling); b. 18 Oct 1943, North Bay, Ont.; given name: Thomas James; m. Marlene Marsh; c. Shawna; ret'd banker; competitive curling record included *Ottawa Journal* trophy '65 City of Ottawa bonspiel; OCA Gov.-Gen.'s, Whitby Dunlop titles '69; OCA Silver Tankard '70; Royals cashspiel '71; competed 3 Ont. Tankards; with Alex Scott, Ted Brown, Mike Boyd won '75 Ont. Tankard and competed in Brier; also competed in '65 *CBC* Rotating Game, '75 *CBC* Curling Classic; avid golfer; res. Ottawa, Ont.

MILLER, Zan (t&f); b. 26 Jan 1899, Sussex, N.B., d. 19 Mar 1957, Sussex, N.B.; given name: Andrew; Maritime hj champion '20; ntl hj,bj titles '22-23; mem. '24 Olympic team; mem. NB Sports Hall of Fame.

MILLIKIN, Hugh (curling); b. 4 Jul 1957, N. Vancouver, B.C.; given name: Hugh Ronald Alexander; m. Sara Waller; c. Carlee; Algonquin Coll.; managing dir. JetForm; following mother Alma's lead curling in Ottawa area; all-star third '81, all-star second '88 Ontario Tankard; second for Dave Van Dine's Ottawa RCMP Canadian mixed title rink '86; skip Australia rink '92-99 Worlds, '92, '98 Winter Olympics, '92-96 Pacific titles; Colin Campbell award '93 Worlds; res. Sydney, Australia/Ottawa, Ont.

MILLINGTON, Sean (football); b. 1 Feb 1968, Vamcouver, B.C.; SFU; TV producer, commentator, actor, businessman; rb; 1st overall pick by Edmonton '90 CFL draft; tryout NFL NY Giants '90; released by Eskimos, joined BC '91-97,

'00-02. Winnipeg '98-99, Edmonton '99; CFL record: 186 scheduled games, 1105 carries for 5058yds, 307 receptions for 3166yds, 85tds, 9 playoff games, 3tds; Dr. Beattie Martin award; 4 all-Cdn, 5 Western all-star; 2 CFL outstanding-Cdn awards; 2 Grey Cup finals, 1 winner; GC outstanding Cdn award; accomplished pianist; operated video game store, nightclub; TV acting stints *X-Files, Outer Limits, Stargate*; exec. producer Centre Aisle Productions; *CBC-TV* host; res. Delta, B.C.

MILLS, Bob (rowing); b. 9 Dec 1958, Halifax, N.S.; sculling specialist; double sculls gold, quad 4s gold '83 PAG; single sculls bronze '84 Olympics; mem. NS Sports Hall of Fame; res. Dartmouth, N.S.

MILLS, James (football); b. 24 Sep 1961, Vancouver, B.C.; Hawaii; ot; drafted by Baltimore NFL '83; dealt to Denver '86; joined CFL Lions '86-93, '95-98, Ottawa '94; 5 Western, 3 CFL all-star; 2 CFL outstanding ol awards; 2 Becket-DeMarco Memorial awards; 7 playoff games; res. Vancouver, B.C.

MILNE, Howie (all-around); b. 1903, Park River, N.D.; d. (circa 1990) Weyburn, Sask.; given name: Howard; m. Violet Benallick Bartlett; ret'd; hockey Regina jrs., Vic's 2 seasons, Pat's 2 seasons; 4 prov. jr. champions; mem. losing Pat's '22 Memorial Cup series; ctr/def sr. Vic's '23-24; replaced Al Ritchie as coach Monarchs '27 winning Memorial Cup; reorganized sr. Vic's, coached 1 season; officiated '33 Western Canada jr. final series; jr. football YMCA Regina '18-20, 2 prov. titles; 4 seasons player/coach Roughriders; 1st Western offical to work Grey Cup final '31; Cdn football all-star '23; ss/3b with Y Regina North Side Baseball League int., sr. divisions; mem. Champ's Hotel team '19-27; best season '23 leading Southern Baseball League batters with .423; pro offer from Minneapolis Millers of American Assn.; basketball Moose Jaw, Saskatoon, Regina, 2 prov. titles, lost ntl finals to Winnipeg Toilers '25; 1 of few to play, coach in Memorial Cup final, play, officiate in Grey Cup final; pres. Regina Juv Baseball League '26; Regina outstanding athlete '23, '24; mem. Sask. Sports Hall of Fame, Roughriders Plaza of Honor.

MIMBS, Robert (football); b. 6 Aug 1964, Kansas City, Mo.; Kansas; rb NFL with NY Jets, Dallas, Phoenix '86-89; CFL Winnipeg '90-92, BC '92-93, Sask. '95-97; CFL record: 81 games, 40tds, 1cvt, 1244 carries for 6162yds, 36tds, 178 receptions for 1726yds, 4tds; 2 Eastern, 1 Western, 3 CFL all-star; Jeff Russel Memorial Trophy '91, Jeff Nicklin Memorial Trophy '96; runnerup CFL outstanding player '91, '96; 3 playoff games, mem. '90 Grey Cup champion; res. Regina, Sask.

MINDORFF, Philip (swimming); b. 13 Jul 1963, Stratford, Ont.; m. Anne; c. Leah; Brock; computer programmer; class S8 swimmer; competed Ont. Games '77; mem. Ont. team Games for Physically disabled; competed '78 ntls, '79 Stoke Mandeville Games (100m backstroke bronze); '80, '84. '88 Paralympics; 2 silver '84, bronze '88; 3 Canada Games gold '83; 3 ntl records; Ont. Amputee Sport Assn. male athlete of '84; ret'd following '90 international disabled championships; also competed in triathlons/t&f/volleyball; mem. Ont. Aquatic Hall of Fame; res. North York, Ont.

MINER, Hazel (administration); b. 6 Apr 1935, Outlook, Sask.; given name: Hazel Jean Hopkins; m. William Manning Miner; c. Debbie, Max, Diana, Michael; secretary; formed Nepean Amateur Basketball Assn. '70, pres. '70-83; founded Ottawa Rookies League '73; Eastern Ont. pres. OABA '74; launched Ont. jr. development program '77; pres. National Capital BA '79; dir. Ont. player development OABA '83; operated annual summer basketball training camps '76-88; Ottawa ACT Sportswoman of '83; res. Nepean, Ont.

MINOR, Ron (t&f/wheelchair basketball); b. 13 Oct 1957, Magrath, Alta.; fed. govt claims officer; wheelchair athletics; world records at 400m, 800m, 1000m, 1500m distances; gold 100m, 800m, 1500m '78, 2 silver, 2 bronze '82 PAG for Disabled; 1 gold, 2 silver '79 Stoke-Mandeville Games; gold 1500m Superchallenge '79; 2 gold, 2 silver, 1 bronze '83 ntl championships; mem. 5 Paralympic teams, 2 Gold Cup basketball teams; Alta. provincial award '79; CWSA athlete of '78; mem. Alta. Sports, Cdn Wheelchair Basketball halls of fame; res. Edmonton, Alta.

MINSHALL, Barbara (horse racing); b. 6 Nov 1953, Montreal, Que.; given name: Barbara Stracey; m. Aubrey Minshall (d); sc. Shawn, Patrick; horse trainer; began riding as pony club mem.; dressage specialist; earned gold, silver in AHSA dressage events '73; gold, silver Cdn International dressage show '74; reserve Ont. advanced champion, silver with ntl dressage team '75 PAG; GP silver Ont. dressage championships 4th with ntl team '76 Olympics; encouraged by husband developed into topnotch thoroughbred trainer; became licensed trainer '95 posting 23 race wins; 1st woman to saddle a Cdn triple crown race winner with Kiridashi in Prince of Wales Stakes; with 139 mounts claimed 40 wins, 25 seconds, 34 thirds '96; 15 stakes race winners, including 2nd Prince of Wales with Stephanotis, $2.1M in winnings brought Minshall Farms 15 Sovereign Award nominations; Mt. Sasafrass named horse of yr, champion older horse; Minshall Farms received outstanding breeder and owner Soverign awards; 1st female to win Sovereign trainer-of-yr award; res. Hillsburgh, Ont.

MINTENKO, Mike (swimming); b. 7 Nov 1975, Moose Jaw, Sask.; UNLV BSc; butterfly specialist; mem. Dolphins SC; 2 WC gold '99, '00; competed '00, '04 Olympics, '01 worlds, silver 100m fly '02 CG; 2 gold '00 ntls; res. Vancouver, B.C.

MITCHELL, Bill (builder); b. 30 Oct 1914, Berlin, Ont.; d. 10 May 2000, Guelph, Ont.; given name: William; m. Eleanor Hales; c. William Jr.; Ont. Agricultural Coll.; ret'd AD Guelph; HS all-around t&f champion all levels; rugby, basketball, boxing standout at college level; recipient football Wildman trophy; mem. Guelph Sports Hall of Fame.

MITCHELL, Dale (soccer/coaching); b. 21 Apr 1958, Vancouver, B.C.; given name: Dale William; m. Dianne Grace; c. Danielle, Kristina, Jakob; coach; ntl team '76-93; Vancouver Whitecaps, Portland Timbers, Montreal Manic NASL '77-83; MISL '83-93; Vancouver 86ers CSL '88-94; 5 CSL all-star; 5 MISL all-star; rep. Can 54 Intl A games; all-time Cdn goal scoring leader with 19; mem. '84 Olympic, '86 World Cup teams; coached Can. to best-ever 5th place

World Youth championships '03; res. Port Moody, B.C.

MITCHELL, Doug (administration); b. 19 Feb 1939, Calgary, Alta.; m. Lois; c. Shelley, Steven, Sue Ann, Scott; Colorado Coll, UBC, LLD; lawyer (QC); attended Colorado on hockey scholarship; football UBC, CFL BC, Hamilton '60-61; general counsel Calgary Flames, rep. Flames NHL governors; chair. advisory comm. ntl Olympic hockey team; credited with re-birth of hockey in Calgary; dir. Calgary Olympic Development Assn.; legal counsel '88 winter Olympics; color commentator Stampeder football broadcasts 9yrs; sponsored NBA exhibitions Calgary, Edmonton; established Willie deWit trust; CFL commissioner '84-89; chair. SAIT governors; ntl co-chair., regional managing partner Borden Ladner Gervais LLP; res. Calgary, Alta.

MITCHELL, Doug (coaching); b. 14 Jul 1942, Windsor, Ont.; m. Irana Bellringer; c. Christina, Stacy, Todd; UWO, BA; football coach; HS, college football standout; pro Hamilton '67-74, Montreal '74; mem. 3 Grey Cup winners; OUAA heavyweight wrestling title '65, '67, Ont. amateur champion '65-67; coach NB wrestling team '83 Canada Winter Games; CIAU coach of '81; coached football 3yrs Burlington HS, 5yrs Mount Allison, UofT '83-85; UWO athlete of '67; mem. UWO W Club Hall of Fame; res. Toronto, Ont.

MITCHELL, Kurt (shooting); b. 19 Nov 1951, Lethbridge, Alta.; given name: Kurt Davison; Waterloo, BSc; electronic engineer; mem. bronze 300m team '73 Western Hemisphere championships; mem. '74, '79 World championships, '76, '80 Olympics, '75, '79 PAG teams; individual 10m air rifle bronze '79 PAG; unofficial world record 400/400 40 shots prone '80, 599/600 60 shots prone '81; ntl 3 position small-bore record 2308 '80 Olympic trials; ntl overall champion '76, prone champion '76-77, '80; res. Stratford, Ont.

MITCHELL, Pinky (boxing); b. 29 May 1930, Ottawa, Ont.; given name: Frederick John; m. Evelyn Mildred Lavigne; c. Dawn, Susan, Holly; ret'd RCAF; made ring debut at age 6 in Ottawa; final bout of more than 100 (of which he won 93) was in Baden Baden, Germany; golden gloves novice div. title (147lbs) '43, open div. (160lbs) '45; enlisted in RCAF '46 fighting when postings permitted; defeated British navy champ '48; won Cdn middle title '50; scored victories over Al Baldwin, Billy Pinkus; lost decision to Yvon Durelle '52; KO'd Manitoba champ Ray Bohemier '52; scored decision over Cdn light-heavy champ Al Sparks '53; defeated ntl champ Jerry Buchanan by KO, ntl heavy champ Jim Saunders by decision '53; lost to BE champ Wilf Greaves '54; posted victories over German Olympic champ '59, USAF all-worlds champ '60; res. Ottawa, Ont.

MITCHELL, Ray (bowling); b. 22 Mar 1931, Peace River, Alta.; given name: Raymond Harold; m. Mari Dillon; c. Adrienne, Jocelyn; engineering mgr.; several UK regional swimming, boxing titles; '51 mem. Toronto Bell men's 5-pin league; started 10-pin bowling early '60's; '67-68 Southern Ont. singles, 3rd ntl singles; mem. Scarborough league champs who established ntl 3-game, 5-man record 3385; '72 SO, ntl singles titles, world 10-pin title Hamburg, Germany; mem. world team medal chams; 37 sanctioned tournament titles; tech. co-ordinator Cdn 10-pin Federation, ntl coach; coached in Japan, Philippines, South America, Canada; bowling columnist *Globe & Mail*; pres. American Zone World Bowling Writers Assn. from '81; mem. Canada's Sports, Cdn 10-Pin Bowling halls of fame; res. Scarborough, Ont.

MITRUK, Steve (gymnastics); b. 17 Jan 1947, Hamilton, Ont.; given name: Stephen Frederick; m. Brigitte; c. Terry, Christopher; McMaster, BA, UofT, BEd; HS teacher; mem. '67 Winter Games, '68, '72 Olympic, '69 Cup of Americas, '71, '73 FISU, '71 PAG, '70, '74 world teams; Werry Cup, OUAA gymnast-of-yr award record 5 consec. yrs. '69-73; McMaster athlete of '72; mem. McMaster Sports Hall of Fame; res. Burlington, Ont.

MITTON, Randy (officiating/hockey); b. 22 Sep 1950, Fredericton, N.B. m. Maureen Loblaw; c. Michael, Jeffrey; working through minor ranks spent 2 seasons as linesman WHL, AHL; moved into NHL '72 appearing in initial game 26 Dec '73; gained international experience '87 Canada Cup; officiated '88 NHL all-star game; NHL record through '03: linesman 2044 scheduled, 159 playoff games; conducted officiating schools in off-season; res. Leduc, Alta.

MOBBERLEY, Herb (all-around); b. 18 Oct 1904, Dudley Staffordshire, Eng.; d. 26 Jun 1988, Winnipeg, Man.; m. Marcella; c. Terry, Dale (d), Patrick, Janet; ret'd machinist CNR, superintendent TCA; nicknamed "Mighty Atom"; mem. original Blue Bombers, 2 Grey Cup titles; baseball with Winnipeg Nifties; hockey with Winnipeg Maroons; credited with saving drowning swimmer; avid hunter, fisherman; inventor in both aeronautical, fishing fields; designed Flatfish Lures; noted gunsmith; mem. Man. Sports Hall of Fame.

MOBERG-PARKER, Tine (sailing); b. 4 Jun 1969, Honefoss, Norway; given name: Tine Moberg; m. Dave Parker; SFU BA; sailing coach/consultant, owns West Coast Race Clinics training/consulting firm; Europe class sailor; competed in first Optimist world championships age 12; mem. Norwegian ntl team '85-93, Cdn ntl team from '93; World title '91; World Cup titles '90-92; since joining Cdn team has claimed gold in 8 regattas; mem. '96 Olympic team; brother Peer Moberg Laser sailor Norwegian Olympic team; coach Royal Vancouver YC; Norwegian YA female athlete of '91; Canadian YA female athlete of '94; BC Premier's athletic award '95; coaching excellence award; ntl team coach Vancouver Sports Centre; res. Vancouver, B.C.

MOBILIO, Domenic (soccer); b. 14 Jan 1969, Vancouver, B.C.; d. 13 Nov 2004, Vancouver, B.C.; coach; mem. ntl -20 team '87 World Youth championships; striker, ntl -17 team; prolific scorer who in 6 CSL campaigns was all-time leading scorer with 81g in 121 scheduled games; 6 CSL all-star awards; 3 CSL records; '91 CSL scoring title with record 25g; CSL MVP '91; 4 league titles; notched 170 career goals in 286 games with 86ers '87-01; hamstring injury hampered play '95; comeback with Vancouver 86ers A-League '96; mem. ntl team '86-98; 25 international caps; NPSL Edmonton Drillers '96-99, Philadelphia Kicks '99-01; asst. coach Whitecaps '02; tech. dir. Coquitlam City Soccer Assn.

MOFFATT, Rich (curling); b. 8 Mar 1959, Ottawa, Ont.; given name: Richard John; m. Denise Allan; Algonquin Coll.; rec. management; following in footsteps of grandfather Roy MacMillan and mother Kay, scored impressive victories in college championship ranks; competed in 9 Ont. men's championships, semifinalist '98, winner '99; skip runnerup rink '96 ntl mixed champioonship; skip runnerup McCain. *TSN* Skins game '89; skipped 3 OCA Silver Tankard title rinks, 2 Shorty Jenkins Classic, Toronto Royals, Welton Beauchamp, City of Ottawa 'spiel titles; res. Ottawa, Ont.

MOGILNY, Alexander (hockey); b. 18 Feb 1969, Khabarovsk, Russia; m. Natalia; c. Alex, Anna; rw; joined Central Red Army team at 17; mem. Soviet '88 Olympic gold medal team, youngest ever Soviet player; top fwd '88, gold '89 jr. worlds; mem. Russia's World Cup team '96; selected by Buffalo '88 NHL entry draft; NHL Buffalo '89-95, Vancouver '95-00, New Jersey '00-01, Toronto '01-04; scored 1st NHL goal 20 seconds into initial game; scored 76g '93, 55 '96; NHL record: (through '04) 956 scheduled games, 461g, 546a, 124 playoff games, 39g, 47a; recipient Buffalo's Frank Eddolls Memorial trophy, Vancouver's Cyrus McLean trophy, Lady Byng trophy '03; 1 Stanley Cup winner; mem. 4 all-star teams; became US citizen '00; res. Point Roberts, Wash.

MOHNS, Doug (hockey); b. 13 Dec 1933, Capreol, Ont.; given name: Douglas Allen; m. Tabor; def./lw Barrie Jr. Flyers; NHL Boston '53-64, Chicago '64-71, Minnesota '71-73, Atlanta '73-74, Washington '74-75; NHL record: 1390 scheduled games, 248g, 462a, 94 playoff games, 14g, 36a; 7 NHL all-star games; founder, v-p Advantage Health Corp.; co-founder Dianne De Vanna Centre for abused children; Capreol park bears his name; nicknamed "Diesel"; res. Bedford, Mass.

MOIR, Darrell (football); b. 15 Aug 1958, Calgary, Alta.; m. Donna; c. Sean; UCal; fitness dir. Edgemont Racquet Club; 3 times HS athlete of year; sr. prov. 110m low hurdles record; qb UCal; CFL db CFL Stampeders '79-85; res. Calgary, Alta.

MOISAN, Sylvianne (horseshoes); b. 21 Jul 1966, St. Raymond, Que.; m. Andre LeClerc; c. Sandra; secretary; 5 Quebec women's doubles titles; twice runnerup Que. women's singles; 8 ntl women's singles titles; with Sue Snyder involved in best game ever thrown by women (130 shoes) '95 World tournament, with Myrna Kissick (126 shoes) '95 ntl championship; record 25 consec. doubles; 5 world records, shares 2 others, 4 consec. world gold, 3 silver, 2 bronze; perfect 26/26 ringer game '01, 24/24 '02; mem. Horseshoe Can. Hall of Fame; es. Chertsey, Que.

MOLITOR, Paul (baseball); b. 22 Aug 1956, St. Paul, Minn.; given name: Paul Lee; m. Linda; c. Blaire; Minn.; nicknamed "Molly" or "Ignitor"; all-state in baseball, basketball, 2 all-conference awards; participated Montreal International Games '75; drafted by St. Louis (NL) '74; pro Milwaukee '77; played with Burlington in minors '77; in major leagues with Milwaukee '78-92, Toronto '93-95, Minnesota '96-98; ML record: 2683 scheduled games, 10,835ab, 1782r, 3319h, 605db, 114tr, 234hr, 1307rbi, 504sb, .306ba; mem. 2 World Series champions, winning World Series MVP award with Toronto '93; 5 AL all-star teams; career played with various injuries; Midwest League prospect of yr, MVP award, batting title '77; AL rookie of '78; 2 Harvey Kuenn hitting-excellence awards; Milwaukee distinguished citizen award '90; 2 *Sporting News* Silver Slugger awards; Adults for Youth Good Guy award '86; Brewers' comeback player of '85; reached 2000 hits '91, 3000 '96; moved into 9th place on all-time ML hit list with 3309 27 Aug '98; Branch Rickey award '98; very active in community charitable projects; mem. Baseball Hall of Fame; res. Mequon, Wisc.

MOLLE, Bob (wrestling/football); b. 23 Sep 1962, Saskatoon, Sask.; m. Karen; c. 3; SFU; sales mgr.; wrestling coach; Saskatoon, provincial HS heavyweight titles; NAIA 100+kg FS title '83; 4 ntl FS titles; bronze '83 PAG; bronze World Cup '84; back surgery three weeks before '84 Olympics threatened participation but came through to win silver medal; became 1st heavyweight to win 4 straight American Ntl Amateur Intercollegiate titles; coach UMan.; with Ned Brigante shared 2 CIAU coach-of-yr honors; mem. 4 Evan Hardy football teams, '80 provincial champions; 1 season Saskatoon Hilltops; all-American og honors at SFU '85; pro Blue Bombers '85-92; capt. '90 team; mem. '88, '90 Grey Cup title teams; mem. Saskatchewan Sports, Cdn Amateur Wrestling, NAIA halls of fame; res. Winnipeg, Man.

MOLNAR, Bill (shooting); b.21 Feb 1937, Brooks, Alta.; given name William Julius; m. Anne Bedford; c. Deborah, Leslie; Royal Roads MC; Lt. Col. Cdn Armed Forces; military rifle team '58-80, 4 Bisley teams; Queen's medal; ntl pistol team '75-78; silver free-pistol '75 PAG, free-pistol team bronze Benito Juarez Games Mexico; mem. NB sporting rifle team Canada Winter Games '66; CISM competitions Chile, Nigeria, USA, Sweden, Italy; men. Cdn Forces Sports Hall of Fame; res. Kanata, Ont.

MOLSON, Hartland (hockey); b. 29 May 1907, Montreal, Que; d. 1 Oct 2002, Montreal, Que.; given name: Hartland deMontarville; m. 1. Maria Magdalene Posner; c. Zoe Anne; m. 2. Margaret de Lancey Meighan (d); Royal Military Coll., LLd; senator from '55, dir. Molson Ltd., Bank of Montreal, CIL; flew 60 combat missions during Battle of Britain; mem. Kingston jr. OHA champion, Memorial Cup finalists '26; mem. RMC hockey teams '24-28; RMC Intermediate Intercollegiate football champions '27; coach Chamonix, France, hockey club '29; also active in t&f, soccer, cricket; pres./chairman Montreal Canadien's hockey club '57-68; v.-patron Que. Rifle Assn.; from '54 hon. pres. Cdn CG Assn.; gov. Palestre Nationale; ex-pres. Cdn Arena Co.; hon. dir. Cdn Fed. of Silent Sports, Cdn Paraplegic Games; hon. mem. QMHA; life mem. AAUofC, Montreal Flying Club; hon. patron Olympic AC; patron Que. Rugger Union, Cdn Olympic Training Regatta (CORK); mem. advisory comm. COA; winter sports fair comm. Laurentian Ski Zone; hon.v-p Golden Glove tournament; hon. dir. QRCA; patron Little Grey Cup ntl jr. football championships; hon. pres. International Bantam hockey tournament; mem. advisory council Atlantic Salmon Assn., dir., mem. International advisory group IASF; OBE; hon. degrees Montreal, Calgary, Bishop's, RMC; Knight Order of St. John's of Jerusalem, Priory of Can.; officer Order of Que.; mem. Order of Canada, Hockey Hall of Fame.

MOLSON, Percy (all-around); b. 14 Aug 1880, Cacuona, Que.; d. 5 Jul 1917, Vimy Ridge, France; given name: Percival; McGill, BA; shone in t&f, hockey, tennis, badminton, golf, cricket, billiards, aquatics, football at McGill 1898-01; at 16 mem. 1896 Stanley Cup champion Montreal Victorias; brilliant rb, exceptional kicker, capt. MAAA Winged Wheelers 1902-06; set world lj record 1900; epitomy of sportsmanship with unique distinction of never having been penalized for unfair play in any sport in which he participated; youngest mem. McGill bd of governors; served with distinction (Military Cross) as capt. in WWI until killed in action; left bequest to McGill which led to Molson Memorial Stadium; 3 McGill athlete-of-yr titles; mem. Cdn Football, McGill Sports halls of fame.

MONCKTON, Philip (rowing); b. 8 Apr 1952, St. Boniface, Man.; given name: John Philip; div. Deborah Holmes; m. Tracey Black; c. Geoffrey, Gillian; UWO, BA, MA; product mgr. Scepter Corp; mem. UWO Mustangs '71, '74 CIAU football title teams; all-Cdn de '74; mem. straight 4s '76, single sculls '80 Olympic, '77, '79 World championships teams; silver '79 PAG, mem. bronze coxless quad sculls crew '84 Olympics; 1st Cdn in 50yrs to advance to semifinals diamond sculls '80 Royal Henley Regatta; UWO male athlete of '76; coaching from '88; Rowing Canada high perf. v.-pres; res. Toronto, Ont.

MONEY, Ken (t&f); b. 4 Jan 1935, Toronto, Ont.; given name: Kenneth Eric; m. Sheila Donelly; c. Laura; UofT, BA, MA, PhD; ret'd research scientist, astronaut; 5yrs ntl hj champion; ntl record 6'7 3/4" set while placing 5th '56 Olympics; mem. '58 BEG team; candidate for possible space mission '85 but never into orbit; teamed with Mark Grantham to win US international badminton 60+ masters men's doubles title '98; mem. UofT, Cdn Forces Sports halls of fame; res. Willowdale, Ont.

MONNOT, Ray (basketball); b. 24 May 1932, Pittsburgh, Pa.; d. 6 Feb 1999, Ottawa, Ont.; div.; c. Christopher, Sandra, Susan; UWO, BA; PMO mgr. finance personnel/admin.; mem. Toronto Nortown Tri-Bells, ntl sr. champions '53-54; UWO intercollegiate titlists '54-55, '55-56, capt. UWO '55-57; UWO record 44pts 1 game '56-57; UWO single season 530, career 1278 scoring records; mem. Tillsonburg Livingstons ntl champions '59-60, '59 PAG, '60 Olympic Games teams; UWO outstanding athlete '57; former bar owner; mem. Ottawa Dildo pickup football/basketball teams; accomplished singer; mem. UWO W-Club Hall of Fame.

MONOD, Peter (skiing); b. 7 Jan 1957, Banff, Alta.; part owner sporting goods store; mem. Alta. Ski Team '74-76; ntl team '77-81; slalom, GS specialist; Can-Am circuit '75-77; Europa, World Cup series '77-81; mem. '78 world title team; Alta. Cup champion '74-75, 1st FIS GS France '78; overall ntl Spring series titlist '78; 2nd Europa Cup GS France '79; US GS title '80; 6 ntl, 1 US titles; Alta. sports achievement awards '78-80; res. Banff, Alta.

MONROE, Jessica (rowing); b. 31 May 1966, Palo Alto, CA; moved to Canada '72; mem. ntl '88-92 and again from '95; gold 8s, straight 4s '92 Olympics, '91 Worlds, silver 8s '96 Olympics; 2 International regatta titles; 2 Dick Ellis team awards; res. Victoria, B.C.

MONSON, Walter (hockey); b. 29 Nov 1909, Winnipeg, Man.; d. 9 Jan 1988, Winnipeg, Man.; given name: Walter George; m. Mary Alderdice; c. Walter, Gail; ret'd machinist; amateur hockey Elmwood Millionaires ('28 Man. jr. title), Jack King Srs., Selkirk Fishermen; 2. Man. sr. titles, 2 scoring crowns; pro Pittsburgh Yellow Jackets (AHL), Moncton (Maritime League), Harringay Racers (Eng.); coached Winnipeg Jr. Monarchs Memorial Cup winner '46; ctr '32 Olympic gold medal team; mem. Man. Hockey, Sports halls of fame.

MONTABONE, Monty (t&f); b. 26 Aug 1903, Grand Rapids, Mich.; d. 27 Sep 1999, Nepean, Ont.; given name: Warren Joseph; m. Jean Margaret Collins (d); c. Sue-Ann, Carol Jane, Robert; Loyola Coll.; electrical engineer; ret'd owner electrical supply bus.; US jr. ntl hurdles champion; mem. '24, '28 Canadian Olympic teams; ntl hurdles titles '24-28; competitive snowshoer, world record 120yds; dog sled racing gold medalist; hon. mem. CG Assn. of Canada; coached at YM-YWCA 2yrs; 38yrs mem. Kiwanis club; key role in creating Manotick Mini Run Heart Institute fund raiser; Kiwanian of '86 award for Eastern Canada, Caribbean; Illuminating Engineering Society of North America distinguished service award '86.

MONTFORD, Joe (football); b. 30 Jul 1970, Beauford, N.C.; m.; South Carolina State; fb/de/lb 1st team all-MEAC, def. player of yr, all-American; attended Cleveland NFL camp '94; Charlotte (Arena League) '95; trial with Amsterdam (WLAF); CFL Shreveport '95, Hamilton (in dispersal draft) '96-01, '03-04, Toronto '02; 4 Eastern, CFL def. player awards; 3 CFL outstanding-def.-player awards; 2 Grey Cups, 1 winner; res. Beaufort, N.C.

MONTGOMERY, Carol (triathlon); b. 24 Aug 1965, Sechelt, B.C.; 10,000m runner; represented Canada World x-country championships, CG '94, '02 (gold); silver 10,000m, bronze 5,000m '95 PAG; silver '91 World triathlon championships; bronze '99 PAG; WC triathlon gold '00, '02; competed '00, '04 Olympics; won numerous triathlons throughout world; 1st Cdn woman to qualify for 2 events (triathlon, 10,000m) same summer Olympics '00; '93 triathlete and duathlete of year; 6 ntl titles; res. N. Vancouver, B.C.

MONTGOMERY, Ken (football); b. 8 Jan 1907, Wetaskiwin, Alta., d. 17 May 1981, Edmonton, Alta.; m. Evelyn Wright; c. Douglas, Lawrence; McTavish Business Coll.; businessman; mem. '23 Central Alta. hockey champions; pres., exec. officer Edmonton Athletic Club '34-40; associated with 2 jr. hockey clubs, 2 Memorial Cup finals '34-39; co-founder, road secty. Eskimos football club '38-39; pres. '52-54, Grey Cup '54; pres. CRU '56, WIFU '57; co-founder CFL; mem. CRU Shrine Comm. initiating East-West Shrine charity games '54-56; v-p Eskimos football alumni '62; trustee Schenley Awards '58-63; v.-chair Alta., Sask. Thoroughbred Racing Society '60-62; chair Eskimos Football Club board of inquiry '63; mem. Canadian Football Hall of Fame.

MONTGOMERY, Willie (broomball/coaching); b. 25 May 1947, Cornwall, Ont.; given name: Wilson; m. Irene St. Louis; c. Deborah Anne, Darryl; float driver; coached Embrun Plumbing/Sports to 10 ntl, 1 world broomball titles;

2 Eastern, 3 I-Tech, 1 Russell Twp, 1 ntl coach-of-yr awards; 1 ntl all-star team coach award; 1 ntl, Ont. achievement awards; Federation of Broomball Assn. of Ont. Hall of Fame award; res. Embrun, Ont.

MONTMINY, Anne (diving); b. 28 Jan 1975, Montreal, Que.; m. Daniel Sachs Goldman; John Abbott College, UMtl LLB, NYU LLM; lawyer; began competitive diving age 8; age-group competitor '85-89; ntl team '90-00; gold 10m, team silver '93 FISU Games; 10m bronze '99 FISU Games; competed '92, '96, '00 Olympics; gold 10m '94 CC, '95 PAG; ntl 10m title '98, '99; Cdn flag-bearer '93 FISU Games; bronze 10m, silver (with Emelie Heymans) 10m platform synchro '00 Olympics; silver 10m FINA WC '00; ret'd from competition '00; Aquatic Fed. Of Canada, Cdn. Amateur Diving Assn. female athlete of '00; Elaine Tanner award '93; res. Pointe Claire, Que./San Francisco, Calif.

MOOG, Andy (hockey); b. 18 Feb 1960, Penticton, B.C.; given name: Donald Andrew; m. Karla Ziegler; c. Alyssa, Arielle, Abby; goalie consultant; Tier 2 hockey Kamloops Braves, Penticton Vees; Tier 1 Billings Bighorns; drafted Edmonton '80; pro Wichita Winds '80; called up to NHL Oilers for Stanley Cup playoffs '81, turned in standout performance; 6 Stanley Cup finals, 3 winners; 3 President's winners; 2nd team all-star Billings (WHL) '80, Wichita (CHL) '82; Edmonton '81-87; Cdn Olympic team '88; Boston '88-92; Dallas '93-97, Montreal '97-98; shared Wm. Jennings trophy with Rejean Lemilin '90; 3 NHL all-star games; reached 300 victory milestone '94; NHL record: 713 scheduled games, 372-209-88, 40,151min, 28so, 132 playoff games, 7452min, 68-57, 4so; part owner Ft. Worth Brahmas (WPHL); goaltending consultant NHL Atlanta '99, Vancouver '99-02, Dallas '02-04, Cdn Olympic team '02, '01, '02 world jrs & worlds; financial interest in hockey equipment mfg. co.; mem. BC Hockey Hall of Fame; res. Coppell, Tex.

MOOG, Don (hockey); b. 7 Oct 1932, Regina, Sask.; d. 16 Jun 1993, Penticton, B.C.; given name: Donald Ernest; m. Shirley Reading; c. Jan, Kelly, Mike, Andrew, Darrell; Greyhound bus driver; 4yrs backup goalie Penticton Vees; mem. '54 Allan Cup, '55 World title teams; mem. Kamloops Sr. Elks '55-56, Medicine Hat Intermediates '56-57; ntl intermediate finalist Penticton '60; mem. Penticton Old Timers.

MOON, Warren (football); b. 18 Nov 1956, Los Angeles, Calif.; m. Felicia; c. Joshua, Chelsea, Jeffrey; Washington; pro football player; HS MVP, all-American; Pac-8 player of '77; qb, MVP '78 Rose Bowl winner; pro Edmonton '78-83, Houston (NFL) '84-93, Seattle '97-98, Kansas City '99-00; CFL record: 2382 passes, 1369 completions for 21,228, 144tds, 77 interceptions; 5648yds '83 all-time single- season record, topping own 5000yd mark set '82 which eclipsed all-pro standard 4802yds set by Dan Fouts, San Diego '81; effective ball carrier with 330 carries, 1700yds, 16tds; 5 Grey Cup victories; Schenley outstanding player '83; NFL record: 208g, 3988 completions in 6823 attempts for 49,325yds, 291tds, 233int; 9 time Pro Bowl; NFL man of '89; formed foundation to assist disadvantaged youngsters and homeless in Houston; mem. Edmonton Eskimos Wall of Honor, Cdn Football Hall of Fame; res. Houston, Tex.

MOORE, Bob (t&f); b. 11 Nov 1940, Doveridge, Eng.; given name: Robert William; m. Barbara Jane McVicar; c. Fiona, Jennifer; Leeds, BSc, PhD,UofT, Dip. Clinical Chemistry; clinical biochemist; ntl 10-mile title '69-73; competed 4 Boston Marathons, 5th once, 7th 3 times; mem. '70 CG, '71 PAG; PB: 3km 8:09, 5km 14:22, 10km 29:49, 10 miles 48:49, 1 mile 4:19, 3 miles 13:40, marathon 2:16.45; National Capital marathon '77; 40+ ntl marthon title '81; former pres., Toronto Olympic Club; co-founder, pres. Metro Toronto Road Running Assn.; res. Toronto, Ont.

MOORE, Buzz (rugby); b. 20 Apr 1921, Regina, Sask.; given name: Douglas Lorne; UBC athletic dept. bus. mgr.; mem. Meralomas '37-63; mem. almost every Vancouver ntl representative team in that period; capt. BC team Japan tour '59, ntl team UK tour '62; invited to join famed Barbarian team; 1st Cdn made honorary Barbarian, rugby's most coveted honor; played/coached representitive teams against opponents from 9 countries; Jack Patterson Memorial Trophy, BCRU's premier individual trophy; pres. VRU '54-66; mem. BCRU 12 yrs; mem. BC, UBC Sports halls of fame; res. West Vancouver, B.C.

MOORE, Curt (baseball); b. 10 Oct 1920, Marysville, N.B.; given name: Curtis; m. Dorothy; ret'd; won NB jr. title with Marysville Maroons '37, 4 NB sr. titles with Devon, Marysville; 4 league all-star; batting titles '53, '56; acknowledged as one of outstanding pitchers/clutch hitters starring in era of US imports; team leader and role model for younger players; ret'd '58; mem. NB Baseball, Sports halls of fame; res. Fredericton, N.B.

MOORE, Dickie (hockey); b. 6 Jan 1931, Montreal, Que.; given name: Richard Winston; m. Joan; c. John, Lianne, Richard (d); property rentals; led Montreal Royals, Jr. Canadien's to Memorial Cup victories; mem. Royals (QSHL) '51-52; Canadiens '52-63, Toronto '64-65, St Louis '67-68; Art Ross Trophy '58, '59; twice 1st team all-star lw, once 2nd team; NHL record: 719 scheduled games, 261g, 347a, 135 playoff games, 46g, 64a; mem. 6 Stanley Cup winners; mem. Hockey Hall of Fame; res. Ville Mount Royal, Que.

MOORE, Gail Harvey (golf); b. 13 Jun 1943, Toronto, Ont.; d. May 1993, Coquitlam, B.C.; given name: Gail Harvey; m. Dr. James B. Moore; c. Dana, Julie, James; UofT, BPHE; ntl jr. titles '58-60; ntl Closed '64-65; runnerup '63 Canadian Open, Closed; '70 ntl Open, BC titles; mem. 4 women's world teams, 2 Commonwealth teams; mem. Ont interprovincal team '58-66, BC team '68-72, '74-75, '83; mem. Cdn Golf Hall of Fame.

MOORE, Greg (motorsport); b. 22 Apr 1975, Maple Ridge, B.C.; d. 31 Oct 1999, Fontana, Calif.; began racing career with go-karts '86; NA Enduro go-kart title '90; Esso Protec Formula 1600 rookie of '91; USAC Formula 2000 West championship, rookie of yr '92; youngest at 18 to win IndyCar sanctioned race in Phoenix '94; mem. Player's Ltd. team winning 10 Indy Lights, 5 in succession, to run victory total through '95 to 13; PPG-Firestone IndyLights champion '95; youngest at 22yrs, 1 month, 10 days to win CART race with victory in '97 Miller 200; made it two in row Detroit; won '98 Rio De Janiero, US 500 CART races;

Miami CART GP '99; killed in California Speedway crash; racing number 99 ret'd by CART; charitable foundation bears his name; mem. Ridge Meadows Hall of Fame.

MOORE, Harry (baseball); b. 8 Dec 1914, Camlachie, Ont.; d. 1986, Sarnia, Ont.; m. Margaret Harriet Bayly; c. Sylvia Elaine; justice of the peace; at 15 mem. Detroit Triple A sandlot team but father's death brought him home to stay; pitched with above average control; competed 23yrs; 3 walks in 26 games 1 season; began coaching at 23; Detroit Tigers scout '58; dir. Sarnia baseball coaches '58-70; guided Sarnia teams to several OBA, 2 ntl sr. titles; coached Sarnia to Michigan Outstate title; had hand in development of such players as Ferguson Jenkins, Dick Drago, Jim Gosger, Jim Northrup; signed former Baseball Canada tech. dir. Bill MacKenzie to Det. pro contract '66; special asst. instructor ntl team from '77; hitting instructor Wes Rinker Fla. Baseball Schools; scout Expos from '72; operated baseball school from '80; author several hundred poems, some published, noted raconteur; nicknamed "The Old Bear"; Ont. Centennial Achievement award '67; Canadian championship award '68; Sarnia-Lambton Sports Hall of Fame builders award.

MOORE, Linda (curling); b. 24 Feb 1954, Vancouver, B.C.; given name: Linda Tweedie; m. Allan Moore; UBC, BHE, MBA; exec-dir Curl BC, *TSN* curling commentator/analyst, former teacher; began curling at 13; twice skipped BC entry Cdn Jr championships; CIAU title '74; BC women's title '84, 3 times runnerup; Scott Tournament of Hearts bronze '84, gold '85; team became 1st Team Canada with direct entry into '86 Cdn women's title tourney where they placed 2nd; '85 world champions; named BC team of year; all-star skip '85 Worlds, '86 STOH; skipped team to Olympic (demonstration) gold, *TSN* Skins title '88; Level II CCA certified coach; business of curling seminar facilitator; UBC Big Block award; hon. life mem. North Shore Winter Club; BCLCA Janette Robbins appreciation award; Vancouver YWCA Woman of Distinction award; CCA achievement award; mem. CCA marketing comm; mem. BC Sports, Cdn Curling halls of fame; res. N. Vancouver, B.C.

MOORE, Quip (baseball); b. 15 Sep 1904, Saint John, N.B.; d. 20 Oct 1994, Saint John, N.B.; given name: Clarence Francis; played amateur, semipro Saint John, Milltown, Salem, Reading, Mass., '21-41; set Maritime record 9 rbi 1 game '24; led league in triples, doubles, batting, stolen bases '24; offered St. Louis (NL) tryout '25; batted .300 or better throughout career; called greatest cf to come out of NB; mem. NB Sports Hall of Fame.

MOORE, Travis (football); b. 5 Aug 1970, Santa Monica, Calif.; m. Erika; c. Travis, Tyvon; Santa Monica Comm. Coll, Ball State; wr CFL Calgary '94-'02, Sask. '03-04; XFL San Francisco '01; 2 CFL, West Conf. all-star; 4 Grey Cup games, 2 winners; CFL record (through '04) 146 scheduled games, 615 receptions, 9503yds, 75tds; res. Phoenix, Ariz.

MORAN, Paddy (hockey); b. 11 Mar 1877, Quebec City, Que., d. 14 Jan 1966, Que. City, Que.; given name: Patrick Joseph; 2yrs. Que. Dominion jrs.; Crescent intermediates 1895-01, ntl intermediate title; standup goalie; Que.

Bulldogs '01-02, except for '09-10 seasons with Haileybury, remained with Bulldogs 16 season posting 5.4 avg., 201 games; successive Stanley Cups '12-13; mem. Hockey Hall of Fame.

MORAND, Jim (harness racing); b. 30 Sep 1964, Windsor, Ont.; began as groom for stepfather Gerry Bookmyer at 15; won Ohio Harness Horsemen's Assn. youth driving title '81; moved from Ohio fair circuit to Rosecroft where he established himself as a top driver; with Kiev Hanover won '90 Messenger, Bluegrass, Cleveland Classic, Tattersalls and Bret Hanover stakes; through '03 6289 victories with purses exceeding $34M; res. Dover, Del.

MOREAU, Lucette (t&f); b. 17 Jan 1956, Pte. Cascades, Que.; McGill, BPhE; national discus titles '76, '80-81, shotput '76; bronze shotput '75 PAG; bronze discus '77 Adelaide International, shotput Pacific Conference Games; bronze discus '78 CG; silver discus '80 Colgate Games, Philadelphia Olympic alternative; mem. '75, '79 PAG, '76, '80 Olympic, '78 CG teams; res. Pte. Cascades, Que.

MORENZ, Howie (hockey); b. 21 Sep 1902, Mitchell, Ont., d. 8 Mar 1937, Montreal, Que.; given name: Howarth; m. Mary McKay; c. Howie Jr., Donald (d), Marlene; nicknamed "Stratford Streak", "Mitchell Meteor"; Stratford OHA jrs.; Canadien's '23-34; briefly with Chicago, NY then returned to Habs '36; died after hockey injury; NHL record: 550 scheduled games, 270g, 197a, 47 playoff games, 21g, 11a; Art Ross Trophy '28, '31; Hart Trophy (MVP) 3 times; mem. 5 league championship teams, 3 Stanley Cup winners; Canada's hockey player of 1/2 century '50 *CP* poll; jersey #7 ret'd by Canadiens; mem. Que. Sports, Hockey halls of fame.

MORGAN, Colin (judo); b. 12 Nov 1973, Calgary, Alta.; competes at 78 kg; Ntl title '93; bronze '95 PAG; competed '96 Olympics; twin brother Keith also ntl team mem.; res. Calgary, Alta.

MORGAN, Keith (judo); b. 12 Nov 1973, Calgary, Alta.; competes at 92 kg; 2nd degree black belt; 3 ntl titles; gold '95, bronze '99, competed '02 PAG; competed '96, '00 Olympics; 90kg FISU Games gold '99; '02 CG 90kg silver; twin brother Colin also ntl team mem.; res. Calgary, Alta.

MORNEAU, Marie-Josee (judo); b. 4 Dec 1969, Longueuil, Que.; competes at 56 kg having moved up from 51 kg; 3 ntl sr titles; Canada Cup gold '91-92; competed '96 Olympics; res. Longueuil, Que.

MOROZ, Evelyn (baseball); b. 11 Nov 1924, Tyndall, Man.; given name: Evelyn Wawryshyn; m. 1. John Litwin (d), 2. Henry Moroz; c. Linda, Gregory, Dawn, Sheryl, Penny, Tammy; ret'd teacher/Winnipeg Aquatics dept.; sprinter/jumper Man. t&f sr. champion '40; ss Man. women's softball title teams '41, '45; MVP Koman trophy; top scorer Winnipeg Sr. women's ntl champion hockey team '50; played 2b/of in AAGPBL with Kenosha '46, Muskegon '46-47, Springfield '48, Ft. Wayne '49-51; hit .266 in 544 games; not noted for power but good clutch hitter driving in 193 runs; honored by Cooperstown, Cdn Baseball halls of fame; mem. Man. Baseball, Man. Sports halls of fame; res. Winnipeg, Man.

MORRIS, Alwyn (canoeing); b. 22 Nov 1957, Montreal, Que.; Capilano Coll.; public servant; mem. ntl team '77-87; '77 ntl jr. K1 500m, 1000m; '79 Continental Cup K1 1000m; '79-80 Zaandam regatta 4K 500m, '80 K1 1000m; '80 Olympic trials K1 1000m; ntl '80-83 K1 1000m, '81, '83 K1 500m; '82 Tata regatta K2 500m with Hugh Fisher; Moscow K1 10,000m '83; silver K2 1000m '82, bronze 500m '83 worlds; gold 1000m, bronze 500m K2 '84 Olympics; mem. 7 world championship, 3 Olympic teams; 6 ntl K1 titles; world K2 silver, bronze; commodore Onake Canoe Club; coach '87 FISU Games; '77, '85 Tom Longboat award (top NA Native athlete); fed. govt. excellence awards '83-84; John F. Bassett Memorial award for community works '92; award bearing his name recognizes community service involvement, educational excellence, athletic prowess; youth ambassador for Canada during international youth year; mem. Order of Canada, Canada's Sports, Cdn Olympic, Que. Sports halls of fame; res. Kahnawake, Que.

MORRIS, Chris (football); b. 13 Sep 1968, Scarborough, Ont.; m. Stacy; c. Trevor, Tyler; Toronto; teacher; tackle; CFL Edmonton '92-04; Edmonton outstanding rookie award; CFL record (through '04) 222 scheduled, 18 playoff games; 2 Grey Cup finals, 1 winner; coach north team annual Edmonton HS camp; res. Edmonton, Alta.

MORRIS, Earle (curling); b. 16 Aug 1945, Rosthern, Sask.; given name: Earle Harold Clifford; m. Maureen Phelan; c. Marie, Sarah, John; RMC, BSc; Canadian Forces sports consultant; skip '69-70 CFB title rinks; Ottawa Navy CC '76 Ont. Consols finalists; '78 Winnipeg Super League titlist; '79 Man. ACC points champion; '81 Montreal Super League titlist; lone curler to represent 3 provinces in Brier play, skip Man. '80 Brier entry; 3rd Que. '82 Brier entry; skip '85 Ont. Brier entry; finalist 3 City of Ottawa bonspiels; son John skipped ntl, world jr. men's title rinks '98-99; inventor Stabilizer broom handle; mem. Cdn Forces Sports Hall of Fame; res. Gloucester, Ont.

MORRIS, Frank (football); b. 14 May 1923, Toronto, Ont.; m. Dorothy Broad; c. Marsha, William, Frank Jr., Steven, Peter, David; football executive; lineman Toronto Navy '42, Halifax Navy '43-44, Argos '45-49, Eskimos '53-58; frequent all-star; coach UAlta '59-64; rejoined Eskimos organization '70; dir. player development; involved in 16 Grey Cup games, 12 winners; as player mem. 6 Grey Cup champions; key role in scouting of Canadian players for Edmonton dynasty of '70s and '80s; mem. Eskimos Wall of Honor, Alta., Canadian Football halls of fame; res. Edmonton, Alta.

MORRIS, Fred (ski jumping); b. 1 Aug 1917, Toronto, Ont.; d. 18 Feb 1994, Ottawa, Ont.; given name: Frederick George; m. Helen McSweeney; c. Patrick, Ted, Caroline, Gayle, Mary-Ann; ret'd Canada Packers; began skiing, jumping recreationally mid-'20s; became involved in administrative end of sport Ottawa Ski Club '55; National Capital Division jumping chair. '63-76; v-chair. CSA jumping comm. '64-68, chair. '69-70, '76-80; Olympic comm. jumping rep. '80-82; mgr. ntl jumping team '79, pre-Olympics, '80 Olympics, World Cup team '79-80; mgr., coach ntl jr. team '74, World jr. Nordics '79-80; v-chair. CSA jumping; chair. NCD, OSC jumping comm. '82; ntl ski jumping judge, ntl coach numerous international competitions; Ottawa ACT Sportsman of '79; Ont. special-achievement award '84; mem. Canadian Skiing, Ottawa Sports halls of fame.

MORRIS, Greg (baseball/hockey); b. 27 Oct 1943, Saint John N.B. given name: Clifford Gregory; m. Linda; St. ThomasU; HS principal; played hockey with NB Bantam champs '58 and baseball NB Midget '57, sr. '67-68; began coaching baseball teams to NB titles '61 winning in leagues from mosquito to sr.; several Maritime, Atlantic titles; coached sr. teams to 1 silver, 3 bronze at Cdn championships; coached gold '90, silver '88 medal teams ntl midget finals; coached ntl team at '78 worlds; coached hockey teams to 10 prov. titles; St. Thomas athlete of '63; Moosehead coach of '78; 2 Baseball NB team-of-yr awards (Chatham Midget Ironmen); mem. Chatham Sports Wall, NB Sports Hall of Fame; res. Chatham, N.B.

MORRIS, Jim (all-around); b. 15 Dec 1911, Tacoma, Wash.; d. 27 Nov 1995, Trail, B.C.; given name: James Henry; m. Mary Isabel Wright; c. Gary Wayne, James Thomas; ret'd personnel officer; excelled in t&f, baseball, lacrosse, hockey, basketball, swimming, softball, soccer, speed skating, curling, golf; mem. 27 BC championship teams, including 8 hockey titlists; mem. '38 Trail Allan Cup winners, '39 Smoke Eaters world championship team; began hockey career Trail Jrs., Smoke Eaters '32-46; mem. 3 Blaylock Bowl soccer title teams; pitched no-hitter, batted .400 1yr, struck out 18 batters 1 game; coached Smoke Eaters 3 seasons; coached/managed various other Trail teams in varity of sports; 8yrs hockey ref.; Jim Morris Award presented annually to Trail sportsman of year; mem. BC Sports Hall of Fame.

MORRIS, John (curling); b. 16 Dec 1978, Ottawa, Ont.; SWU BKin.; pro curler; skipped 3 Ont. jr. title rinks, 2 ntl, world titles; 2 all-star skip awards at worlds; runnerup Nokia Brier '02, 2nd team all-star skip; coached by father Earle, a 3-time Brier competitor; res. Calgary, Alta.

MORRIS, Price (weightlifting); b. 22 Oct 1941, Frankford, Ont.; given name: Ernest Price; m. Louise Mills; c. Jacqueline, Price Jr.; Guelph; farmer; competed 17yrs; 5 ntl titles; 4th '67 PAG; 1st Cdn to lift 400lbs; bronze '70 CG; 4 bronze '71 PAG; mem. '72 Olympic team; ntl records all categories; PB: clean & jerk 413lbs, press 382 1/2lbs, snatch 308lbs, total lift 1085lbs; 1st Cdn to unofficially total 1102lbs, to that time had lifted 400lbs more times than any other Cdn in history; res. Frankford, Ont.

MORRIS, Sid (all-around); b. 22 Aug 1928, Toronto, Ont.; m. Sheila Mellor; c. Shawn, Katrina; York; financial exec.; sport involvement ranged from participant to coaching to administration and included minor hockey, softball, baseball, football, basketball, paddling, billiards, t&f and 5-pin bowling; signed to Class D pact as pitcher in Phillies chain but injuries kept him in Canada with Rogers Fuels team; set pins at Towne Bowl where he honed bowling skills and competed at major level; instrumental in developing Ont. Sports Lottery to finance amateur sport; major sponsor of numerous amateur sports teams/programs; served as bowling columnist, exec., coach; competed in Sportsman's Masters championship; Toronto zone pres.; 6yrs treas. Master Bowlers Assn.; mem. Ont. champion Balmy Beach

canoe team; competed in 1st intl masters t&f championships in Europe at 45; mem. Ont. Sports Legends advisory board; Golden Jubilee medal; life mem. MBA; mem. Ont. 5-Pin Hall of Fame; res. Newmarket, Ont.

MORRIS, Teddy (football); b. 1910, Toronto, Ont., d. 5 Sep 1965, Toronto, Ont.; career spanned 3 decades as football player, coach; at 16 softball Toronto Industrial League, hb with brother Gord's jr. team; capt. Winnipeg Native Sons to Western jr. title, lost ntl title to jr. Argos; mem. Argos '31-41; backfield coach last 2 seasons; coach HMCS York WW2 winning '44 service title; coach Argos '45-49; 3 Grey Cups as player, 3 as coach; Jeff Russel Memorial Trophy '37; CIAU College Bowl MVP award bears his name; mem. Canadian Football Hall of Fame.

MORRISON, Arnie (football); b. 30 Oct 1907, Northfield, Que.; d. 16 Mar 1976, Ottawa, Ont.; given name: George Arnold; m. Isobel Margaret Asher; c. Margot; fed. govt. accountant qb'd Rideau jrs., Rangers (QRFU), Ottawa Rough Riders during '30s; Jeff Russel award '36; catcher Davidson's Eastern Ont. baseball champs '30; played hockey with Shamrock jrs., New Edinburgh, Rideaus; Rivermead golf club champion '57; active curler Ottawa Curling Club; coached Carleton Ravens football in late '40s; football broadcaster; nickname "Mighty Atom" or "Little General"; mem. CSRA Hall of Fame

MORRISON, Bernie (football); b. 25 Mar 1955, Winnipeg, Man.; m. Debbie; c. Annie, Carly, Marshall; UMan, BA; sales rep.; capt. Bisons '77; CIAU all-star lb '76-77; all-Cdn; mem. '78 Can-Am Bowl team; Winnipeg territorial draft '78; CFL lb Winnipeg '78, Calgary '78-88; noted for pass coverage ability; res. Calgary, Alta.

MORRISON, Lee (softball/curling); b. 14 Oct 1938, Regina, Sask.; given name: Lenore Pickrell; m. Larry Morrison; c. Lance, Layne; UofT, BPhE, UofSask, BEd, Oregon, MSc; asst. prof.; softball '58, '60 Regina Lexiers, '64 Saskatoon Imperials prov. titlist; mem. UofT women's ice hockey team '60, UofSask. volleyball team '61-62; mem. winning rinks Saskatoon ladies' bonspiel '65-69; prov., ntl title rinks '69 (2nd Joyce McKee), '71-73 (lead Vera Pezer); coach UofSask. women's team '62-73, 6 conference titles; coached '72-73 ntl girls' champions; coach UofSask. women's field hockey team '67-70, 1 conference title; coached Sherry Sherick rink '96-98; Sask. srs title (3rd Sheila Rowan) '94; sr. T award UofT; mem. Sask., Saskatoon Sports, Cdn Curling halls of fame; res. Saskatoon, Sask.

MORRISON, Roland (fencing); b. 13 Mar 1951, Toronto, Ont.; UNB, BA, LLB; investigator, coach Lightning Fencing Club; began fencing '69 CMR de St. Jean, Que.; mem. '71 NB Canada Winter Games fencing team; variety of NB foil, épée, sabre titles '72-81; Lieut.-Gov.'s foil champion '76, sabre titlist '79-81; variety of executive positions with NB, Cdn Fencing Assn. '72-81; coach NB Winter Games fencing teams '75, '79; level II foil coach; res. Dartmouth, N.S.

MORRISON, Scotty (administration/officiating); b. 22 Apr 1930, Montreal, Que.; given name: Ian; m. Joan Perry; c. Ian, Perry (d), Donald, Cameron, Katharine, Karen, Joanne, Carolyn; ret'd Hockey Hall of Fame administrator; jr. hockey Canadiens organization; turned to refereeing in

QAHA, Que. Sr. League, WHL; at 24 youngest referee (to that time) to work NHL '54-56; entered sales field with Goodyear, Yardley '57-64; returned to NHL as referee-in-chief '65; NHL v-p officiating '81-86; appointed v-p, project development, pres. Hockey Hall of Fame '86-91; chair. Hockey Hall of Fame '91-98; served term as pres. Assn. of Sports Museums and halls of fame (ASMHF); mem. Hockey hall of fame; res. Etobicoke, Ont.

MORRISSEY, Janet (figure skating); b. 12 Oct 1959, Ottawa, Ont.; given name: Janet Katherine; Carleton, BA; broadcast journalist; Eastern Ont. juvenile ladies title '70; EO pre-novice '72; EO jr. '76-77, sr. '77-79; Eastern Canada jr. '77, sr. '79; ntl sr. champion '79; competed internationally St. Gervais GP (bronze), Nebelhorn Trophy (bronze), Skate Canada, Venna Worlds, Lake Placid pre-Olympics, Richmond Trophy; CFSA Bursary Award '79, Ont. achievement awards '75-80, Ottawa ACT figure skating award '79-80; mem. Nepean Wall, Ottawa Sports Hall of Fame; res. New York, N.Y.

MORROW, Al (rowing/coaching); b. 28 Dec 1949, Hamilton, Ont.; given name: Alan George; m. Julia Eutemia Santavicca; c. Claire, Gregory, Stefan, Marisa; UWO, BA; UBC, BPhE; rowing coach; through '97 rowed or coached with ntl team 33yrs; rowed or coached 7 Olympic, 5 PAG, 1 CG, 2 FISU Games, 11 world championships; his crews earned 12 medals (9 gold) at world championships '92-96; head coach ntl women's team, UWO women's team; dir. ntl rowing ctr; fed. govt meritorious service award; FISA coach of '99 award; 9 PetroCan/Wittenauer/Longines Wittenauer coaching-excellence awards; Geoff Gowan coaching award; mem. Cdn Olympic, UWO W Club halls of fame; res. London, Ont.

MORROW, Brenden (hockey); b. 16 Jan 1978, Carlyle, Sask.; m. Anne-Marie; lw Portland (WHL) '95-99; Michigan (IHL) '00; NHL Dallas '99-04; Team Canada '98 world jr. (silver), '04 World Cup (gold); 2 WHL all-star games, 1 Memorial Cup final; best pro prospect award; NHL record (through '04) 370 scheduled games, 97g, 107a, 48 playoff games, 5g, 13a; res. Dallas, Tex.

MORROW, Carol (diving); b. 6 Apr 1946, New Westminster, B.C.; given name: Carol Ann; m. Maurice Wright; c. Sean Cameron, Kerry Michael; UBC, BEd; ret'd teacher; several BC jr. backstroke, synchronized swimming, diving titles; ntl jr. 100yd backstroke title; '63 ntl open tower diving title, '64 1m title; bronze '64 US ntl 3m championships; mem. '64 Olympic diving team; res. Surrey, B.C.

MORROW, Suzanne (figure skating); b. 14 Dec 1930, Toronto, Ont.; div.; c. Kristen Lyn Francis; Ont. Veterinary Coll.; veterinarian; only woman in Cdn figure skating history to hold sr. ntl titles in singles ('49-51), pairs ('47-48) and dance ('48); NA pairs champion with Wally Diestelmeyer '47; bronze Olympic pairs, world championships '48, '50-52; 5th singles '52 Olympics; international judge from '64, judging Olympic, world competitions; dir. CFSA; Doberman Pinscher breeder; mem. Skate Can., Cdn Olympic halls of fame; res. Toronto, Ont.

MOSCA, Angelo (football/wrestling); b. 13 Feb 1937, Waltham, Mass.; m. Gwen (d); c. Jolene, Angelo Jr., Gino;

Notre Dame; ret'd wrestling promoter; lineman; played 15 CFL seasons with Hamilton, Ottawa, Montreal; 9 Grey Cup finals, 5 winners; 5 all-Eastern, 8 all-Cdn awards; runnerup Cdn defensive-lineman-of-yr award '63-70; wrestled professionally 25yrs; occasional actor; goodwill ambassador for CFL; raconteur; mem. Cdn Football Hall of Fame; res. Niagara-on-the-Lake, Ont.

MOSES, Paul (football/t&f); b. 11 Dec 1953, Almonte, Ont.; given name: Paul David; m. Waheeda Khan; c. Mikayla Justine; Carleton BA; sales mgr. MDS Nordion; set HS 200m (lasted 23yrs), lj records; received 4 t&f top athlete awards; co-capt. 3yrs undefeated Almonte HS football seasons; set single-season ko return for tds record with 6 '70; ORFU Ottawa Sooners '71-75; 3 Eastern Cdn finals; co-capt., def. MVP ntl jr. champions '74; set Sooners ko returns for tds record with 4 '74; CFL Ottawa Rough Riders '76; asst. coach Earl of March HS football Ottawa finalists; res. Ottawa, Ont.

MOSIENKO, Bill (hockey); b. 2 Nov 1921, Winnipeg, Man.; d. 9 Jul 1994, Winnipeg, Man.; m. Wanda; c. Billie, Brian, Wendy; bowling proprietor; Winnipeg Monarchs jrs.; pro Providence, Kansas City; Chicago '41-55; rw on Pony Line with Max, Doug Bentley; Lady Byng Trophy '45; 2 2nd team all-star; record 21 seconds fastest 3 goals one game vs. NYR Mar '52; NHL record: 711 scheduled games, 258g, 282a, 22 playoff games, 10g, 4a; in 1030 pro games over 20yrs accumulated only 129 penalty mins.; with Alf Pike launched pro hockey Winnipeg; their Warriors won Edinburgh Trophy inaugural season '56; mem. Warriors through '59, coach '60; mem. Man. Sports, Man., Cdn Hockey halls of fame.

MOSS, Joe (football/coaching); b. 9 Apr 1930, Elkins, W.Va.; div.; c. Joe Jr., Nancee Gay; m. Yvonne; c. 2 stepsons; Maryland, BSc; football coach, ret'd Lt.Col. USAF; ol Maryland, 2yrs univ. basketball; mem. '49 Gator Bowl, '51 Sugar Bowl, '52 College All-Star Game teams; tackle Washington (NFL) '53; player-coach Bolling AFB service title team '53-54; all-service team; lineman Rough Riders '55; asst. coach Maryland '56, Texas Tech '57-59, West Texas State '60, USAF Academy '61-68, Philadelphia (NFL) '69-72, Argos '73-76, '83-84, '87-89, '93-96; Roughriders '77, Rough Riders '78-81, '96, Tiger-Cats '90-92, '97; asst. coach Toronto Phantoms Arena FB team '01; head coach Argos (interim) '74, UofOtt (7-0 record) '82, Ottawa '85-86; res. Ancaster, Ont.

MOSS, Judy (diving); b. 7 Jun 1916, Winnipeg, Man.; d. 6 Oct 2001, Vancouver, B.C.; m. Kennedy; UMan; '32 Man. springboard title; '34 ntl title; 4th '34 BEG trials, with backing of Winnipeg Winter club included on ntl team; 3m springboard gold '34 BEG; ret'd following '35 ntl championships; mem. Man. Sports, Cdn Aquatic halls of fame.

MOSS-LOVSHIN, Shona (sailing); b. 12 Apr 1969, Kitchener, Ont.; m. Steve Lovshin; c. Devlin; UofOtt, BSc; UAlta MSc, WLU MBA; considered pursuing career as world class x-country skier but changed mind in late teens; began sailing age 8; won CORK Laser title '88; women's division Laser II gold '89 world championships; Radial women's world title '90; CORK Europe class bronze '90; PAG Radial gold '91; mid-winter regatta Radial gold '91;

top Canadian '91 women's world championships; competed '92 Olympics; top IYRU world ranking 14; top IYRU women's world ranking 12; switched to 505 class '93; CYA female athlete of '91; res. Chelsea, Que.

MOST, Joe (bowling); b. 17 Nov 1926, Regina, Sask.; given name: Joseph Matthew; m. Betty Bellerby; c. Jack, Cathy; optician; with Red Glasser ntl 10-pin doubles title '64; mem. 4 Sask., numerous Sask., Regina singles, doubles title teams; co-founder Regina youth 10-pin program, coach, instructor; 4yrs dir. ntl 10-pin fed.; secty. Sask. 10-pin fed. 10yrs; secty. Regina 10-pin assn. more than 20yrs; mem. Sask. Sports Hall of Fame; res. Regina, Sask.

MOTZEK, Peter (field hockey); b. 1 Jun 1957, Vancouver, B.C.; m. Candy; c. Reese, Deanna; Remax sales agent; mem. ntl team '72-81; represented Canada on tours of Great Britian, New Zealand, Malaysia, Australia, Holland, Germany; mem. '75, '79 PAG (2 silver), '76 Olympic; '77, '81 International Cup, '78 World Cup teams; coast guard volunteer; res. Ladner, B.C.

MOUAT, Michael (field hockey); b. 20 Mar 1954, Vancouver, B.C.; given name: Michael Malcolm; UBC, BSc; electrical engineer; fwd ntl champion BC team '72; mem. ntl team '71-82; mem. '71 PAG (bronze), '76 Olympic, '77 International Cup, '78 World Cup; mem. tour team in Great Britian, Argentina, Chile, Malaysia, Germany, Holland, Australia; res. Vancouver, B.C.

MOUNTIFIELD, Eleanor (basketball); b. 1902, Fort Yukon, Alaska; d. 8 Feb 1985, Lewiston, Idaho; m. Charles D. Vogelsong; c. Charles M.; nicknamed "Tattie"; mem. famed Edmonton Commercial Grads '20-24; mem. Canadian Basketball, Alta. Sports halls of fame.

MOYER, John (baseball/bowling); b. 4 Jan 1913, Waterloo, Ont.; d. 13 May 1987, Waterloo, Ont.; given name: Edward John; m. Isabelle Eadie; ret'd painter; pitched Waterloo Tigers to OBA Sr. B title hurling 13 successive playoff games, winning 10; mem. Waterloo '34-35 Intermediate B, '36 Intermediate A title teams; 24 strikeouts single games; pitched '39 OBA playoff no-hitter vs. Port Credit then ran no-hit string to 16 innings; in 7 '39 OBA games struck out 71, 217 for season; earlier in '39 campaign pitched no-hitter vs. Kitchener; as 5-pin bowler won '59 O'Connor Open, ntl men's singles title; 2 Eastern Cdn singles crowns '58-59; mem. 3 Ont. title teams; ret'd from competitive bowling '76; Elmira, Ont. srs. golf champion '80; mem. Ont. 5-Pin Bowling, Waterloo County halls of fame.

MOYNIHAN, Kerry (administration); b. 26 Jul 1956, New Westminster, B,C.; m. Helene St. Denis; c. Caroline, Dana; Laurentian, hons B Comm; ED dept. External Affairs Olds (Alta.) Coll.; ED Ont, Cycling Assn. '79-80; tech. dir. Canadian Hostelling Assn. '79-80; ED Shooting Fed. of Canada ;81-85; asst. product mgr. American Express Canada '85-86; ED Ont. Gymnastics Fed. '86-89; ED Canadian Canoe Assn. '89-93; GM '95 Canada Games '93-95; GM '97 Canada Games; CEO CIAU '97-99; pres. Alpine Can. '99-02; res. Calgary, Alta.

MUCKLER, John (coaching/hockey); b. 3 Apr 1934, Midland, Ont.; m. Audrey; c. John, Cindy, Karen, Tracy, Jenny; hockey exec.; launched coaching career '59 serving in minors as coach and/or GM with NY Rovers, Long Island (EHL), Memphis, Dallas, Wichita (CHL), Cleveland, Jacksonville, Providence, Rhode Island (AHL) over a span of 14 seasons; EHL, AHL coach–of-yr awards; 1 CHL title; NHL head coach Minnesota '68-69, Edmonton '89-91, Buffalo '91-95, NYR '97-99; pro scout 2yrs with Vancouver; GM Ottawa Senators '02-04; has served in roles from scouting to asst., co-coach, head coach, GM with several organizations; had role in 5 Stanley Cup winners, 3 NHL all-star games; co-coach Team Canada '84, asst. coach '87 Canada Cup title teams; NHL coaching record: 648 scheduled games, 276-288-84, 67 playoff games 36-31; 1 Stanley Cup; 2 *Hockey News* coach/exec-of-yr awards; mem. Brantford Wall of Distinction, Paris (Ont.) Sports Hall of Fame; res. Buffalo, NY/Kanata, Ont.

MUENZER, Lori-Ann (cycling); b. 21 May 1966 Toronto, Ont.; full-time athlete, legal secretary; sprint specialist; plagued by injuries throughout career but perseverance produced some excellent results; 3 Que. Cup, 2 Que. road titles; ntl team from '94; began track career winning '94 Cuban title; 11 ntl titles, 9 WC medals; 3 Que. titles; 2 Que. road & track awards; competed '98 (bronze), '02 CG silver, 2 bronze, CG record; '00, '04 (gold match sprint) Olympics; '99, '03 PAG; gold, silver '99 PAG; 2 silver, bronze worlds; double gold Malaysia, bronze Poland, Mexico '01 World Cup; bronze '03 WC; silver '01 Goodwill Games; 3 gold, 1 silver, 2 ntl records '02 Pan-Am road & track championships; 3 Alex Steida, 3 Jennie Longo, 2 Eddie Merckx, 1 Steve Bauer awards, Bobbie Rosenfeld, *Canadian Cyclist* female-cyclist-of-yr awards '04; res. Edmonton, Alta.

MUIR, Debbie (synchro swim); b. 12 Jun 1953, Calgary, Alta.; given name: Debbie Humphrey; m. Neil Muir; UCal, BEd; sports consultant; formed Performax Training & Development; ex-synchronized swimming coach; mem. ntl team '71-73; silver team medal '71 PAG, gold team '73 world aquatic championships; began coaching '73; ntl team coach '76-95; coached 1st ntl duet (Helen Vanderburg, Michelle Calkins) to win international competition vs. top US swimmers '77 Pan-Pacific Games; coached gold medalists in duet, solo '78 World Aquatic championships, duet, solo '79 PAG, FINA Cup; coached '79 PAG silver medal team; '79 Pan-Pacific gold medalist solo; coached Kelly Kryczka to sweep of individual ntl sr. titles '80; Kryczka, Sharon Hambrook to titles in solo, duet British tri-meet; ntl all-stars Pan-Pacific Games '81; Canada's World champions '82; consultant several ntl teams throughout world; Air Canada coach of '86, runnerup '77; 3 PetroCan coaching excellence awards; YWCA women of distinction award; mem. Canada's, Alta. Sports, Cdn Olympic, Cdn Aquatic halls of fame; res. Calgary, Alta.

MUIR, Lela (archery); b. 4 Nov 1934, Duncan, B.C.; given name: Lela Viola Yetman; div.; c. Ian William Muir; UVic; archery shop owner; local level championships in swimming, t&f, baseball, tennis, badminton '40-52; mem. BC jr. basketball champions '49-51, Sr. A champions '54, ntl runnerup '54; mem. ntl ladies archery team champions '70; ntl team '71 Ambassador Cup; '72 Olympic team; mem. BC team '70-71, '73-74, '77, '79; archery judge; res. Victoria, B.C.

MULLEN, Cary (skiing); b. 2 Oct 1969, Calgary, Alta.; champion gymnast in youth; allergy to cows, horses precluded pursuit of real love, rodeo; began competing age 5; mem. ntl team from '90; 2 FIS slalom, GS gold; WC downhill gold, silver '94; WC record 1-2-0; competed '90 PAG Winter Games, '92, '94, '98 Olympics; ret'd from competition '00 following serious injury; mem. Cdn Ski Hall of Fame; res. Banff, Alta.

MULLER, Kirk (hockey); b. 8 Feb 1966, Kingston, Ont.; m. Stacey; c. Brittney, Kourtney, Bryelle, Kira; lw Kingston '80-82; Guelph '82-84; Team Canada '84 Olympics, '03 worlds (gold) ; NHL New Jersey '84-91, Montreal '91-94, NYI '95-96, Toronto '96-97, Florida '97-99, Dallas '99-03; capt. Devils '87-91, Canadiens '94-95; NHL record 1349 scheduled games, 357g, 602a, 127 playoff games, 33g, 36a; 2 Stanley Cup winners; 6 NHL all-star games; asst. coach Kingston Frontenacs '03-04; ardent triathlete; res. Kingston, Ont.

MULLINS, Joe (t&f); b. 18 Oct 1937, Glace Bay, N.S.; m. Sally Kennedy; c. Patricia, Kathy; Nebraska, BSc, Maine, BEd; teacher; established numerous NS, Maritime 440-, 880yd standards mid-'50s; considered ntl king of the 880; frequent Big 8 Conf. titles '57-60; set world indoor record 1:11.4 for 600yds '56; mem. '58 BEG, '60 Olympic teams; Nebraska athlete of '60; Viscount Alexander trophy '55-56; mem. NS Sports Hall of Fame; res. Sydney, N.S.

MULLINS, Peter (basketball); b. 9 Jul 1926, Sydney, Australia; Washington State, EdD; assoc. professor; 6th decathlon '48 Olympics; mem. ntl basketball team '59 world tournament; coached ntl basketball team '69-71; coached UBC basketball, t&f; CIS basketball rookie award bears his name; mem. UBC Sports Hall of Fame; res. Vancouver, B.C.

MUMFORD, Peter (builder/figure skating); b. 1920, Ottawa, Ont.; d. 1986, Ottawa, Ont.; m. Mary; c. Ted, Blaize; ret'd Brig. Gen.; regarded as one of the administrative giants of local, ntl figure skating; chair. '78 world championships; advisor jr. worlds '84; chair. '76 Skate Canada; pres. Nepean Figure Skating Club; v-chair, secty Eastern Ont. section '71-75; 4yrs exec/ dir. Sport Medicine Council of Canada; mem. Cdn Figure Skating Hall of Fame.

MUNDINGER, Karin (golf); b. 9 Nov 1959, Toronto, Ont.; c. Kasey; Ohio State; twice Cdn jr. runnerup; 2 Ont. titles; runnerup '81 Doherty Cup; 6 college titles, including Big-10 crown; shot round of 65 at 17; joined pro tour '85; res. Toronto, Ont.

MUNRO, Bruce (curling); b. 23 Mar 1947, Hanover, Ont.; m. Sandra Joan Ross; c. Mark, Lyndsay; Ryerson PTI; publisher.; ranked among top shotmakers in prov.; competed Ont. Consols 7 times, won title '82, runnerup twice; won Whitby Dunlop 'spiel '71; 4 times OCA Challenge round, winner '70, '75, '82, runnerup '74; won 2 Toronto Royals carspiels; '75 Royals cashspiel; won '70 Whitby Dunlop cashspiel, 3 times runnerup; 4 Toronto Major League titles; 2 Guelph cashspiel titles; ret'd from competition '86; res. Komoka, Ont.

MUNRO, Johnny (football); b. 27 Sep 1913, Toronto, Ont.; d. 26 Oct 1994, North York, Ont.; given name: John McCulloch; m. Bette Gilmour; c. Michael John, Elizabeth

Anne, Brian Gilmour; Queen's, BA, UofT, Cambridge; ret'd sr. v-p life assurance co.; mem. numerous Toronto baseball teams; 3yrs HS all-star, 1yr all-Cdn with Queen's; mem. '33-38 Argos, 3 Grey Cup champions; hockey Marlboro jrs, 4yrs Queen's, leading coll. scorer; EFC referee 14yrs; past Schenley Award trustee; gov. Canada's Sports Hall of Fame from '84; mem. Queen's Sports Hall of Fame.

MUNTON, Mabel (basketball); b. 30 Mar 1914, Edmonton, Alta.; d. 16 Jan 1994, Edmonton, Alta.; m. Jack McCloy; c. Patricia, Robert; ret'd secretary; mem. famed Edmonton Grads '32-40, 148 games, 852 points, 5.7 avg.; mem. 2 Alta. ladies curling title teams; mem. Canadian Basketball, Alta. Sports halls of fame.

MURCHISON, Cliff (curling); b. 20 Oct 1896, Souris, Man.; d. 30 Dec 1987, Ottawa, Ont.; m. Grace Masterman; c. Kenneth, Grace Mary, Angus Clifford; UofT, BA, UMan, LLB; ret'd Unemployment Ins. Commissioner; wounds sustained during WW1 curtailed some early athletic activities but not his enthusiasm; pres. Man. Baseball Assn. '21-22; co-founder, v-p Memorial Cup champion St. Boniface Seals '38; began curling in Man., brought interest in game to Ottawa '44; key role in formation Ottawa Valley Curling Assn., City of Ottawa Bonspiel, Granite Club of West Ottawa; pres. OVCA '59-60; chair. City of Ottawa bonspiel '61; King's Counsel '41; mem. Gov.-Gen.'s Curling Club; mem. Ottawa Sports, Canadian Curling halls of fame.

MURPHY, Cal (coaching); b. 12 Mar 1932, Winnipeg, Man.; m. Joyce; c. Carol, Michael, Barbara, Erin, Shannon, Brian, Kelly; UBC, BA, Eastern Washington, MA; football executive; coached in HS by CFL Hall of Famer Greg Kabat; qb/lb UBC; brief stint db CFL Lions '56; HS/college coach '56-64, asst. EWU '65-67, Hawaii '68-72, San Jose State '73, Lions '74-75; head coach Lions '75-76, asst. Montreal '77, Edmonton '78-82; head coach Winnipeg '83-86, '92-96; GM Winnipeg '87-96; asst. Sask. '97-98, head coach '99; asst. Frankfurt (GER) Galaxy Football Europe '00; coach briefly Chicago (XFL) '01; scout Indianapolis NFL '01; Annis Stukus Trophy winner '83-84; involved in 11 Grey Cup finals, 9 winners; underwent heart transplant '92; mem. Cdn Ftbll, UBC Sports halls of fame; res. Regina, Sask.

MURPHY, James (football); 10 Oct 1959, Deland, Fla.; Utah State; restaurateur; outstanding receiver Utah State; dreafted by Minnesota, cut and joined Kansas City as kick returner; joined Winnipeg CFL '82-90 (fractured ankle ended career); all-time leading Winnipeg receiver; set 2 club records (116 receptions for 1746yds; most yds gained receiving 9036); 4 Eastern, 2 CFL all-star; Schenley outstanding player '86; Jeff Nicklin award '86; 2 Ken Ploen team MVP awards; Grey Cup MVP '88; mem. 3 Grey Cup winners; mem. Winnipeg, Cdn Football halls of fame; res. Winnipeg, Man.

MURPHY, Larry (hockey); b. 8 Mar 1961, Scarborough, Ont.; m.; c. 3; def Peterborough (OHA) '78-80; 1st LA pick '80 draft; NHL with LA '80-83, Washington '83-89, Minnesota '89-90, Pittsburgh '90-95, Toronto '95-96, Detroit '97-01; OHA 1st team all-star, 3 NHL 2nd team all-star; mem. 1 Memorial Cup, 2 Canada Cup, 4 Stanley Cup winners; 2 NHL all-star games; set NHL record for games played by defenceman (1447) '99; passed 1200pts '00; NHL record: 1615 scheduled games, 287g, 929a, 215 playoff games, 37g, 115a; mem. Hockey Hall of Fame; res. Peterborough, Ont.

MURPHY, Pat (cycling); b. 7 Nov 1933, South Norwich Twp, Ont.; given name: James Patrick; m. Marlene; sales exec.; ntl amateur track title '52, pursuit '53; mem. '54, '58 BEG, '56 Olympic teams; winner, record holder '56 Que.-Montreal road race; res. Schaumburg, Ill.

MURPHY, Ron (football); b. 13 Jun 1932, Hamilton, Ont.; m. Betty; c. Paula Jane, Douglas Paul, Gregory Ronald; McGill, BSc, MEd; educator; outstanding HS football career '46-52; MVP, most-sportsmanlike awards; Red Feather HS tournament title team, MVP '51; twice league all-star; mem. jr. Tiger-Cats '52, Grey Cup champion Ticats '53; McGill Redmen '54-58, MV lineman '54; 3 seasons sr. Redmen, all-star; joined McGill athletic staff '58-64; pro Alouettes; ret'd following '61 campaign; asst. coach McGill '62, OUAA title; UofT phys ed staff, asst. coach Blues '64; head football coach Toronto Varsity '66-82; Old Crow Society CIAU coach of '74; res. Toronto, Ont.

MURPHY, Ron (hockey); b. 10 Apr 1933, Hamilton, Ont.; given name: Robert Ronald; m. Carole Audrea Gorrie; c. Ronald, Kimberley, Linda; hotel owner; jr. Guelph Biltmores '47-51; pro NYR '52-56, Chicago '57-63, Detroit '63-65, Boston '66-70; ret'd due to shoulder injury; mem. '61, '70 Stanley Cup winners; mem '65 league champions; NHL record: 889 scheduled games, 205g, 274a, 53 playoff games, 7g, 8a; coached Kitchener jr. Rangers '71-73; res. Hagersville, Ont.

MURRAY, Albert (golf); b. 3 Sep 1887, Nottingham, Eng.; d. 7 Jun 1974, Montreal, Que.; golf pro; emigrated to Canada '02; asst. Toronto GC, Westmount GC; head pro Plains of Abraham Que. City, Outremont, Kanawaki, Montreal CC, Royal Que., Beaconsfield; at 20 youngest winner Canadian Open '08, repeat '13; launched Canada's 1st indoor golf school Montreal; CPGA title '24, 3 times runnerup; '30 Que. Open title; 3 times CPGA capt.; pres. CPGA '41; renowned architect of more than 30 clubs, many in Que.; mem. RCGA Hall of Fame.

MURRAY, Bob (hockey); b. 26 Nov 1954, Kingston, Ont.; given name: Robert Frederick; m. Betsy; c. Kevin, Amanda, Andrew, Kathleen; hockey exec.; def. Cornwall Royals jrs. '72-74; pro Dallas (CHL) '74-75; Chicago (NHL) '75-90; NHL record: 1008 scheduled games, 132g, 382a, 112 playoff games, 19g, 37a; played in 3 all-star games; pro scout Chicago '90-95, dir. player personnel '91-95; asst. GM '95-97; GM '97-99; res. Chicago, Ill.

MURRAY, Bruce (golf); b. 29 Dec 1938, Ft. William, Ont.; given name: Robert Bruce; m. Nance Kirkland; c. Pam, Craig, Heather, Kirk; golf pro; Alta. jr. titles '56-57; club pro 2yrs Kitchener Rockaway, 13yrs St. Catharines GC, 6 yrs Royal Montreal; 2yrs CPGA educational chair.; CPGA capt., v-p, pres.; 3yrs dir. CPGA; founded Bill Burgoyne Memorial tournament for mentally retarded St. Catharines; chair. 1st CPGA PAG Classic, Las Vegas; res. Hudson, Que

MURRAY, Bryan (coaching); b. 5 Dec 1942, Shawville,

Que.; given name: Bryan Clarence; m. Geraldine Sutton; c. Heide, Brittany; McGill; hockey exec.; 4yrs AD/coach McGill; coached Pembroke CJHL; coached at college, minor pro level; guided Regina Pats to '80 WHL title; coached Hershey Bears AHL '80-81; Washington (NHL) '81-90; coach/GM Detroit '90-93; GM only '93-94; v.p./GM Florida Panthers '94-00, coach '97; Anaheim coach '01, vp/GM '02-03; coach Ottawa Senators '04; *Hockey News* minor league coach of '81; NHL coach of '84; div. titles '89, '92; GM Team Canada '99 worlds; NHL coaching record: 1057 scheduled games, 513-413-131, 78 playoff games, 34-44; res. Ft. Lauderdale, Fla.

MURRAY, Charlie (golf); b. 1880, Birmingham, Eng.; d. Jun 1939, Montreal, Que.; c. Ken; golf pro; teenage golf sensation; asst. Toronto GC; head pro Royal Montreal '06-39; twice Cdn Open titlist, once runnerup; 10 Que. Open titles; mem. RCGA Hall of Fame.

MURRAY, Dave (skiing); b. 5 Sep 1953, Montreal, Que.; d. 23 Oct 1990, Vancouver, B.C.; given name: William David; m. Stephanie Sloane; c. Julia; skier, instructor; mem. ntl World Cup team '73-82, '74, '78 world championships, '76, '80 Olympic teams; 2nd WC downhill Chamonix, France '78, Schladming, Austria '79, 3rd Lake Placid pre-Olympic '79; ranked 3rd world downhill '79; overall ntl champion '79; Europa Cup downhill Artesina, Limone '78; BC athlete of '79; mem. BC Sports, Cdn Skiing halls of fame.

MURRAY, Eddie (football); b. 29 Aug 1956, Halifax, N.S.; Tulane; pk specialist; 7th round NFL draft choice Detroit '80; played in NFL with Detroit '80-91, '99, Kansas City/Tampa Bay '92, Dallas '93, Philadelphia '94, Washington '95, '00, Minnesota '97, Dallas '99; NFL record: 240g, 337FG, 521cvts, 1532pts; set NFL record 237 consec. cvts 12 Oct. '97; res. Minneapolis, Minn.

MURRAY, Glen (hockey); b. 1 Nov 1972, Halifax, N.S.; given name: Glen John; m. Katie; c. Hunter; rw 3 seasons Sudbury (OHL), Providence (AHL) '92-93; Team Canada '98 worlds; NHL Boston '92-94, '01-04, Pittsburgh '95-97, Los Angeles '97-01; NHL record (through '04) 823 scheduled games, 268g, 255a, 87 playoff games, 20g, 22a; res. Boston, Mass.

MURRAY, Ken (administration); b. 28 Nov 1911, Montreal, Que., d. 16 Oct 1979, Ottawa, Ont.; given name: Kenneth George; m. Evelyn Eileen Henderson; c. Glenn Andrew, Donna Lynn; Sir George Williams, McGill.; sport administrator; mem. 3 Allan Cup hockey champions, Montreal Big 4 football team; coached jr. B hockey 3yrs, jr. A 2yrs, McGill hockey 3yrs.; dir. MAAA; pres. Canadian Amateur Swimming Assn.; v-p British CG Assn. of Canada; mem. Institute of Assn. exec.; Cdn Diving Advisory Council; pres. Beaver Oil Co.; program assn. co-ordinator COA '71-79; mem. Canada's Sports Hall of Fame.

MURRAY, Pere (administration/coaching); b. 9 Jan 1892, Toronto, Ont.; d. 15 Dec 1975, Regina, Sask.; given name: Athol; Laval, BA, Osgoode Hall, UofOtt, hon. PhD, UAlta., hon LLD; ordained priest; following brief stint as newspaper reporter, law student entered seminary, ordained secular priest '18; brief stays in Orillia, Penetanguishene, Ont.; chancellor Regina diocese '23-27; organized predominantly

Protestant group of boys into Regina Argos AC which in 8yrs gained renown as hockey, football, baseball, lacrosse powers; with boys from his Argo club forming nucleus, established Notre Dame Coll. at Wilcox, Sask. '27, degree-granting institution affiliated with UofOtt, now known as Athol Murray College of Notre Dame; man of vast energy, determination, he shepherded college through depression years; produced such noted alumni as Nick, Don Metz, Jackie McLeod, Garth Boesch, Gus Kyle of NHL fame, Gordon Currie of football repute; Hounds of Notre Dame rank among best-known names in Canadian sport; mem. Order of Canada; honored by Ottawa, Alta. educational institutions; testimonial dinner in his honor Regina '65; mem. Sask., Hockey, Canada's Sports halls of fame.

MURRAY, Scott (shooting); b. 1 Mar 1946, Guelph, Ont.; given name: David Scott; m. Eleanor Closs; Carleton, BA, UofOtt, LLB; lawyer; full-bore rifle specialist; with various victories in DCRA, Bisley competitions, including '94 DCRA Gov.-Gen.'s trophy, '96 Macdonald Stewart Grand Aggregate, ranked among top marksmen in Canada; 16 consec. Bisley team qualification, competed each time; mem. Cdn winning teams in Kolapore, MacKinnon, Empire, Canada, Commonwealth matches; res. Arnprior, Ont.

MURRAY, Terry (hockey); b. 20 Jul 1950, Shawville, Que.; given name: Terry Rodney; m. Linda; c. Megan, Lindsey; hockey coach; def Pembroke (CJHL) title team, Ottawa 67's (OHL); pro Providence, Baltimore, Boston, Richmond, Maine (AHL), Oklahoma City (CHL), Salt Lake (WHL), Cincinnati (IHL), NHL California, Philadelphia, Detroit, Washington '72-82; NHL playing record: 302 scheduled games, 4g, 76a, 18 playoff games, 2g, 2a; mem. 2 Calder Cup winners; turned to coaching Baltimore '88-90; asst. to brother Bryan at Washington 6yrs, head coach '90-94, Philadelphia '94-97, Florida '98-01; advance scout Flyers '01, asst. coach '03; NHL coaching record: (through '03) 737 scheduled games, 360-288-89; 89 playoff games, 46-43; scout Philadelphia '97, '01-04; coach Team USA '99 worlds; res. Coral Springs, Fla.

MYDEN, Curtis (swimming); b. 31 Dec 1973, Calgary, Alta.; UCal; began racing age 7; mother Barbara master level swim official; competed '92, '96. '00 (bronze) Olympics, '93 FISU, '91, '93, '95 (bronze), '97 (2 silver), '99 (2 silver) Pan-Pacific championships; gold 400m IM, bronze 200m IM '93 world short-course championships; 2 silver '94 CG; 2 gold, 2 bronze '95, 1 gold '99 PAG, 2 bronze '96 Olympics; competed '02 CG; ret'd '02 with 28 ntl titles, 68 intl medals; ntl 200IM, 400IM records; 1 CIAU record; CIAU Howard. Mackie award; Cdn Aquatic Fed. male athlete '97; mem. UCal Sports Hall of Fame; res. Calgary, Alta.

NADEAU, Daniel (shooting); b. 28 Feb 1954, Quebec City, Que.; Laval, BSc; Que. government biologist; mem. ntl team '74-78; running-bore title '75 pre-Olympic match; rep. Canada world moving-target matches '75, Puerto Rican championships '75, twice Benito Juarez matches, Championship of the Americas '76; ntl running-bore champion '75-77; ret'd from competition '78; res. Beaudry, Que.

NADIN, Robert (officiating/hockey); b. 15 Mar 1933, Toronto, Ont.; m. Nancy Wood; c. Kenneth, Janice; UofT, BPHE; mem. UofT hockey team; refereed OHA from '56; refereed more than 100 intl hockey games in Canada, Europe, Asia including '72 Olympics, '74 Leningrad world jr.; supervisor of referees '76 Canada Cup series; referee-in-chief CAHA; mem. IIHF rules & referee comm.; conducted referee clinics China, Japan '77; runnerup '81 Air Canada referee award; res. Weston, Ont.

NADON, Chantal (kickboxing); b. 25 Feb 1971, North Bay, Ont.; given name: Chantal Marie; m. Michael McNamara; c. Brigitte; Canadore Coll.; kickboxing instructor; at 14 became intrigued with martial arts after watching movie *Karate Kid*; began training at Elite Twin Dragon club; struck gold winning Ont. Amateur Boxing title '94; advanced to kickboxing and engaged in 1st pro bout '94; petite build, delicate features fooled most opponents to underestimate her talents, much to their chagrin; she won FFKA Cdn, world featherweight titles '97; ISKA NA bantam, world flyweight, super-flyweight, WKN world flyweight titles; through '04 15-3-2 record; nicknamed "North Bay Assassin"; Kid Sport Ont. ambassador; res. Toronto, Ont.

NAGURSKI, Bronco (football/wrestling); b. 3 Nov 1908, Rainy River, Ont.; d. 7 Jan 1990, Chicago, Ill.; given name: Bronislau; m. Eileen Kane; c. Bronco Jr.; Minn.; all-American '27-29; only player in US coll. history to be all-star fb/t '30; symbol of power and ruggedness in pro football; a bulldozing runner and bone-crushing lb; rushed for 4031yds in 9 pro seasons with Chicago '30-37, '43; 3 times all-NFL; 2tds helped Bears win '33 title; after 6yr retirement returned to help Bears claim '43 crown; asst. coach Sask.'35-36; wrestled professionally '33-60; held 3 world titles; son played 8yrs CFL Hamilton; charter mem. NFL Hall of Fame.

NAGY, Imre (fencing); b. 7 May 1941, Kolozjvar, Hungary; sep.; c. Nataley, Gregory; administrator Dominion Textile; mem. ntl sabre team '70-79; team silver '74 CG; mem. '74 Worlds, CG, '75, '79 PAG, '76 Olympic teams; 5 Que. prov. sabre titles, '75 Eastern Cdn champion; 3 times Gov.-Gen.'s, Terre des Hommes tournament champion; Cupe du Que., Ottawa Shield tournament titles; res. Ville Lasalle, Que.

NAIMARK, Barry (curling); b. 1 Jul 1932, Regina, Sask.; m. Dell-Jean Miller; c. Benjamin, Carmella; lumberman; proficient trapshooter; mem. Cdn '65, '69 Maccabiah Games team; as lead, third, skip 4 BC Consols titles, 1 runnerup;

lead '64 Brier, World title rinks; Brier runnerup '77; BC mixed title '69; BC seniors title '83, runnerup '84; res. Richmond, B.C.

NAIRN, Bill (football); b. 16 Nov 1912, Winnipeg, Man.; d. 1986, Winnipeg, Man.; m. Stella Patricia King; c. Herbert Gordon; ret'd regional mgr.; Deer Lake jrs. '31-33; gd/pk Blue Bombers '34, '36-40; Winnipeg Victorias '35; officiated '41-70 including 20 Western finals, 18 Grey Cups; mem. Howie Wood curling rink 20yrs.

NAISMITH, James (basketball); b. 6 Nov 1861, Almonte, Ont.; d. 28 Nov 1939, Lawrence, Kan.; m. Maude Sherman; c. Margaret, Hellen, John, Maude, James Jr.; McGill, BA, DD, Presbyterian Theological Coll., Springfield Coll., Gross Medical School, MD, Kansas; 11 academic degrees; played football under Amos Alonzo Stagg at Springfield; top McGill gymnast; McGill's 1st phys-ed dir.; inventor of basketball Springfield, Mass., '91 using soccer ball, pair of peach baskets; also credited with designing 1st leather football helmet to protect players' ears; Naismith Memorial Basketball Hall of Fame, Springfield, Mass., completed '68; Cdn Basketball Hall of Fame in Almonte bears his name; ntl amateur sports ctr in Gloucester, Ont., on street which bears his name; mem. US, Cdn, Ont. Basketball, Cdn Olympic, Canada's, Ont. Legends, Ottawa, Kansas, McGill. Sports halls of fame.

NAKAMURA, Hiroshi (judo); b. 22 Jun 1942, Tokyo, Japan; m. Keiko Maruyama; c. Emi, Yumi, Karen; ChuoU, BEc, Kodokan Judo Institute (7th dan); judo coach; tech. dir. Que. Judo Assn. '76-84; mem. Japanese ntl team '62-67; silver all-Japan middleweight championships '66; coached Chuo to all-Japan university title '66; among top 16 Japanese Open championships '64, '66; coach Montreal judo club '70-73, from '89; head coach QJA '68-70; ntl team coach '73-76, '84-89; coach Cdn '75, '87, '95 PAG, '76, '88, '96 Olympic teams, 5 world championships teams, 2 FISU Games teams; level 3 ntl coaching certificate; international referee from '75; 4 PetroCan coaching-excellence awards; res. Pierrefonds, Que.

NANNE, Lou (hockey); b. 2 Jun 1941, Sault Ste. Marie, Ont.; given name: Louis Vincent; m. Francine Yvette Potvin; c. Michelle, Michael, Marc, Marty;Minn., BSB; exec. v-p/ntl sales mgr. asset management co, hockey exec.; US citizen, capt./MVP/scoring champ/all-American Minn.; capt. '68 US Olympic, '75-77 world championships teams; def./rw North Stars '67-78; player rep/v-p NHLPA '72-78; NHL record: 635 scheduled games, 68g, 157a, 32 playoff games 4g, 19a; coach North Stars '78; GM '78-88, pres. '88-90; NHL governor '74-91; GM Team USA '81, '84, '87 Canada Cup, '94 worlds; broadcaster Minn. State HS tournament from '64, active in hockey broadcasting for *HNIC, NBC, CBS, ESPN, CFAN* radio from '78; served on numerous NHL committees; wrote document for NHL-WHA merger; chair. CHL governors, NHL GMs comm.; liaison NHL-NCAA; mem. US hockey international comm.; Cdn Hockey Hall of Fame board; North Stars most-popular player, most-valuable-def awards; Lester Patrick award '89; Hockey Hall of Fame heritage award; 50yr WCHA team award; highly active in community affairs chairing many charitable events; mem. Minn. Sports, US Hockey, IIHF halls of fame; res. Edina, Minn.

NANSEN, Derek (officiating/hockey); b. 12 Jun 1971, Ottawa, Ont.; given name: Derek Kaare; div; c. Ashley Karen Brooks; Algonquin Coll.; refereed Ottawa District minor hockey; linesman jr. hockey (ODHA), major jr. hockey (OHL), AHL; worked Sr. A pool world championships Germany '01, '02 Winter Olympics, '02 Memorial Cup, AHL Calder Cup final; became NHL linesman '03; res. Kanata, Ont.

NANTAIS, Red (basketball); b. 1913, Windsor, Ont.; d. 26 Jan 2004, Windsor, Ont.; given name: Stanley Alphonse; m. Jean Mahoney; c. David, Peter, Clare, Charles, Dan; Assumption; all-city gd Assumption HS '33 title team; led "Five Fighting Freshmen" to ntl sr. men's final '35; mem. Windsor Ford V8s who formed nucleus of '36 Olympic silver medal team; turned to coaching; 13yrs Assumption Coll; 201-146 record; mem. Cdn Basketball, Windsor Alumni, Windsor/Essex County Sports halls of fame.

NAPPER, Jason (diving); b. 12 Feb 1972, Thunder Bay, Ont.; Lakehead; began competing age 11; 4yrs jr. ntl team; sr. ntl team from '90; bronze 1m '91 Cuba invitational; team bronze '91 FISU Games; gold 3m '93 PAG invitational; silver 1m Rostock international '93; gold 1m, bronze 3m '94 CG; res. Thunder Bay, Ont.

NARCISSE, Donald (football); b. 26 Feb 1965, Port Arthur, Tex.; m. Cassandra; c. Donald Jr., 1 daughter; Texas Southern; wr; pro Sask. '87-99; eclipsed Ray Elgaard's CFL career reception record of 830 with 833 '98; all-pro record of 216 consecutive games with at least 1 reception; CFL record (through '99): 198gp, 872 recep., 12,366yds, 74td, 4cvt, 452pts; 3 Western, 1 Northern, 3 CFL all-star teams; mem. '89 Grey Cup winner, '86 Freedom Bowl; res. Regina, Sask.

NASH, Jack (golf); b. 18 Dec 1911, London, Ont.; d. 4 Jan 1993, London, Ont.; m. Kelly; c. Becky, John, Rob, David; UofT, UWO; jeweller; runnerup Ont. jr. '29-30; 3 Ont. amateur titles; with father John A. Ont. father-son title '35; same crown 5 more times, twice each with sons Rob, David, once with John C; mem. 12 Ont. Willingdon Cup teams; l3 London Hunt & Country Club championships; 1 Ont., ntl Srs. title; quarterfinals British Amateur '33; US Amateur '35; mem. London Hunt George S. Lyon Trophy team '60; 3 Ont. men's doubles badminton titles; ntl finalist; 2 Ont. Silver Tankards with London CC; competed 4 Ont. Consols playdowns.

NASH, Rick (hockey); b. 16 Jun 1984, Brampton, Ont.; lw Toronto Marlboros (OHF) '99-00, London (OHL) '00-02; Team Canada '01 6 Nations -18 gold, '01 -17 world challenge bronze, '02 world jr. silver, '04 World Cup (gold); OHL rookie of yr; London capt. rookie yr.; OHL, CHL all-rookie team; CHL top-prospects game; 1st overall draft pick '02; NHL Columbus '02-04; Richard Trophy '04; NHL record: 154 scheduled games, 58g, 38a;

standout lacrosse, volleyball player ; played with Davos, Switzerland, during '04 labor dispute, won Spengler Cup; res. Brampton, Ont.

NASH, Steve (basketball); b. 7 Feb 1974, Vancouver, B.C.; Santa Clara; given name: Steven John; West Coast conf. player of '95-96; Santa Clara all-time assists (510), free throw percentage (.861) leader; 2 West Coast Conf. player-of-yr awards; 1st freshman named WCC tourney MVP; FISU Games silver Team Canada '93; Team BC Canada Games bronze '93; father John, brother Martin both played pro soccer in England; excelled at lacrosse, soccer, hockey; NBA Phoenix Suns '96-98, '04-05, Dallas Mavericks '98-04; NBA record: (through '04) 102 scheduled games, 4 playoff games; 1st NBA player to record 10 or more assists in 11 consec. victories surpassing Magic Johnson mark '04; 2 NBA all-star; recorded 1st triple double '03; mem. Cdn team '00 Olympics; subject of Jeff Rudd book *Long Shot: Steve Nash's Journey to the NBA*; participated '97 NBA rookie game, 2 all-star games; hon. chair. Canada Games; purchases block of tickets for each game for distribution to local charities; Lionel Conacher award '02; res. Dallas, Tex.

NASLUND, Markus (hockey); b. 30 Jul 1973, Ornskoldsvik, Sweden; m. Lotta; c. Rebecca, Isabella, Alex; rw Ormskoldsviks (Sweden 3) '88-89, McDo AJK (Sweden jr. & sr.) '90-93; Cleveland (AHL) '93-94; NHL Pittsburgh '93-95, Vancouver '95-04; capt. Vancouver from '00; Team Sweden '92-93 world jr., silver '93 world sr., '95-96 World Cup, '02 Olympics; 3 world all-star team selections; Lester B. Pearson award '03; 4 Cyrus McLean, 2 Molson Cup, 3 Cyclone Taylor awards; nickname "Nazzy"; NHL record (through '04) 790 scheduled games, 290g, 339a, 33 playoff games, 9g, 19a; Modo Sweden during '04-05 labor dispute; res. Kitsilano, B.C./Ornskoldsvik, Sweden.

NATTRASS, Sue (shooting); b. 5 Nov 1950, Medicine Hat, Alta.; given name: Susan Marie; UAlta, BA, MA, PhD; medical research assn., ex-athletic dir., journalist; mem. ntl trapshooting team '69-02; 6 world titles; 4 world records; 1st woman trapshooter to compete in Olympics '76; mem. 5 Olympic teams; silver '95 PAG; 2 bronze '02 CG; 3 gold Benito Juarez International; gold '73, silver '81 Championship of the Americas; ntl women's title '68-83; capt. women's all-American trap team '73-78; 1st woman to win both high-overall, all-around honors from 27yds; only woman to score perfect 200 three times; top woman all-around NA standing '73-77; won '77 European Grand Prix; coached skiing Cornell, McMaster, Blue Mountain; Order of Delta Gamma Rose Award '76; Canada's female athlete of '77, '81; Ont. athlete of '77; Edmonton outstanding-contribution-to-sport awards '68-76, '79, '81; Alta. achievement awards '69-77, '80; Ont. achievement awards '75-78; Shooting Fed. golden anniversary award '82; fed. govt. world champion award '82, excellence award '84; Edmonton Sports Reporters award; mem. Canada's Sports Hall of Fame selection comm.; amateur athlete of '81; Lou Marsh Trophy '81; 2 Velma Springstead awards; hon. Edm. Big Sister '79; mem. FAS ntl advisory council '81-83; SFC dir. '80; 2 WC doubles titles; AD St. Mary's.; Officer Order of Canada '81; mem. World Amateur Trapshooting, Cdn Olympic, Alta., Canada's Sports halls of fame; res. Seattle, Wash.

NAYLER, Thomas (entrepreneur); b. 29 Apr 1904, West Bromwich, Eng.; d. 8 Feb 1981, Toronto, Ont.; equipment mgr, trainer, skate-sharpener; emigrated to Canada '11; for 59yrs master skate sharpener/equipment mgr. for Toronto Maple Leafs; earned recognition as inventor/innovator of wide variety of equipment improvements such as better elbow, shin, ankle pads, goalie trappers, boot protectors which are standards today; also designed special equipment which made skate sharpening for types of blades an art; as salaried employee at Maple Leaf Gardens he never received royalties for creations, which included; portable skate-sharpening machine; involved with all 11 Leafs Stanley Cup winners, '72 Summit Series; NHL gold plaque for service to sport '67; mem. Cdn Athletic Trainers Assn. Hall of Fame.

NEALE, Cynthia (equestrian); b. 19 Jun 1952, Edmonton, Alta.; m. Neil Ishoy; c. Kahla, Zachary; intl debut as youngest mem. '71 PAG gold medal dressage team; youngest mem. '72 Olympic team; Ont. medium dressage title '73; high-point title Detroit Horse Show '74; reserve rider '76 Olympic dressage team, mem. '80, '88 Olympic teams; 11 ntl, intl 1sts; 1st Cdn to compete world dressage championships '78, impressive 8th place finish; Martini & Rossi horseman of '78-79; mem. '88 Olympic bronze medal dressage team; res. Jerseyville, Ont.

NEALE, Doris (basketball); b. 26 Jun 1911, Ottawa, Ont.; d. 26 Feb 1992, Edmonton, Alta.; given name: Doris Edwina; m. Edward Chapman (d); c. Peter, Judith, Randall; ret'd secretary; mem. famed Edmonton Grads '29-36, 116 games, 607 points, 5.2 avg.; mem. Canadian Basketball, Alta. Sports halls of fame.

NEALE, Harry (hockey); b. 9 Mar 1937, Sarnia, Ont.; given name: Harry Watson; UofT, McMaster, Ohio State; *Hockey Night in Canada* TV analyst; jr. Toronto Marlboros '55-58; mem. '55-56 Memorial Cup winners, all-star def; sr. Galt Terriers '60 Allan Cup winners; Hamilton Hillpark SS, Westdale SS coach '60-66; Ohio State coach '66-70; Hamilton Red Wings coach '71, Hartford (WHA) '75-78, Vancouver (NHL) '78-82, '84, GM Canucks '82-85; Detroit '85-86; coach Team USA '76 Canada Cup; NHL coaching record: 442 scheduled games, 150-212-80; *CBC* hockey analyst '98 Olympics; res. East Amherst, N.Y.

NEDOHIN, Dave (curling/water skiing); b. 20 Dec 1973, Winnipeg, Man,; given name: David Neill; m. Heather Arlene Godberson; c. Halle, June, Kristine; UMan. BSc; geo-environmental engineer, owner CT & Associates Engineering Inc.; playing 3rd but throwing final rocks for Randy Ferbey won consec, Briers '01-03, worlds '02-03; Continental Cup, *TSN* Skins Game, M&M Skins titles '02; 2 Canada Cup titles; twice top money winner WCT; among top 10 WCT money winners '95-04; mem. ntl barefoot water ski team '91-98, '04; bronze '94, '98, '04 ntls; numerous medals individual events '86-03; res. Sherwood Park, Alta.

NEELY, Cam (hockey); b. 21 Jun 1965, Comox, B.C.; rw; jr with Portland (WHL); drafted '83 by Vancouver; played with Canucks '83-86, Boston '86-96; scored 55g '90, 51 '91, 54 '94; NHL record: 726 scheduled games, 395g, 299a, 93 playoff games, 57g, 32a; Bill Masterton trophy '94; 4 2nd all-star team; frequent injuries curtailed even greater production and degenerative hip condition dictated retirement prior to '96-97 campaign; opened Martha's Vineyard restaurant '92; established Cam Neely Foundation, Neely House for families of hospitalized cancer patients; Boston ret'd jersey #8; mem. Ridge Meadows, BC Hockey halls of fame; res. Winchester, Mass.

NEIL, Andrea (soccer); b. 26 Oct 1971, Vancouver, B.C.; UBC, BSc; midfielder; made ntl WC team debut '91 CONCACAF title; 2nd Cdn to earn 100 intl caps; competed 3 WC, 2 CONCACAF tournaments; scored all three goals as Canada beat Scotland in Algarve Cup '00; mem. Vancouver Whitecaps (W-League); res. Vancouver, B.C.

NEILL, Cliff (softball); b. 8 Feb 1926, Ottawa, Ont.; given name: Clifton; m. McCaffrey (d); c. Bonnie, Bill; m. Coyne; c. Craig, Shelley; ret'd Ont. Hydro; above average hockey player; outstanding softball pitcher; 7 Eastern Ont. sr. titles; numerous no-hitters including 2 perfect games '56; all-Ont. sr. title team '56; lifetime BA .290; 24k's single Eastern Ont. playoff game; mem. Ottawa Sports Hall of Fame; res. Nepean, Ont.

NEILL, Susan (administration); b. 17 May 1944, Toronto, Ont.; UofT, BPhE, UofOtt, PhD; educator, sport administrator; pres. Alta. WFHA '70-74; coach Alta. team '72-78; coach ntl women's field hockey team '74; pres. CWFHA; dir. Coaching Assn. of Canada from '79; assoc. professor of phys-ed UAlta; dir. policy planning/evaluation Sport Canada; mem. UofT Sports Hall of Fame; res. Ottawa, Ont.

NEILSON, Roger (coaching); b. 16 Jun 1934, Toronto, Ont.; d. 20 Jun 2003, Peterborough, Ont.; given name: Roger Paul; McMaster, BPhE, hon. LLD; hockey coach; ex-HS teacher; former baseball coach; coach Peterborough jr. A 10yrs, 1 OHA title; Dallas (CHL) '76; Toronto '77-79; asst. Buffalo '79-80, head coach '80-81; Vancouver '81-83, Stanley Cup finalists '82; LA '83-84; asst. Chicago '84-87; scout/broadcaster Blackhawks '87-88; coach NYR '89-93; coach Florida '93-95; coach Philadelphia '98-99; Ottawa (2 games) '02 to run career total to 1000; NHL coaching record: 460-381-159; dir. CJHL Pembroke '95; asst. coach St. Louis '97, Ottawa '00-03; 3 NHL div. titles; 1st NHL coach to use video as training tool, hence name "Captain Video"; hockey school operator; experimented with bunji jumping in NZ '93; diagnosed with cancer '99; Senators Foundation established Roger's House to assist in care of kids with cancer; Gordon Juckes award; Peterborough street bears his name; mem. Order of Canada; Hockey Hall of Fame.

NEILSON, Scott (t&f); b. 31 Jan 1957, New Westminster, B.C.; given name: Robert Scott; Washington, BC, UBC; ntl records juv 12lb hammer throw 72.34m, jr. 16lb hammer 67.06, sr. hammer 72.74m; NA HS 12lb hammer throw; bronze '75, gold '79 PAG; silver '78 CG; NCAA hammer titlist '76-79; mem. '80 Olympic team; Washington most valuable t&f performer '79; BCTFA male athlete of '80; last known res. New Westminster, B.C.

NEILSON, Terry (sailing); b. 2 Nov 1958, Toronto, Ont.; insurance agent; 3 ntl, 1 European laser titles; CORK, mid-winter regatta, US Finn class titles; world laser title '82; Finn bronze '84 Olympics; Norton Crowe award '82; fed. govt. world champion award '82; Ont. excellence award '83; res. Islington, Ont.

NEJEDLY, Jana (tennis); b. 9 Jun 1974, Prague, Czech Republic; tennis player; Cdn. Fed Cup team from '94; competed '96 Olympics; career-best Grand Slam showing was 3rd round '99 Australian Open, '01 US Open; career-high #64 on WTA Tour '00; biggest win of career over world #12 Barbara Schett Hilton Head '00; Cdn. record most Fed Cup singles victories with 19 (19-6 record, with only two losses coming after '98; 8 ITF Women's Circuit singles titles, including three in '03; ret'd '03; most-improved-female-player award '95; Tennis Canada female player of '01; res. Boston, Mass.

NELFORD, Jim (golf); b. 28 Jun 1955, Vancouver, B.C.; given name: James Cameron; m. Linda; c. Blake; Brigham Young; pro golfer; outstanding jr, college career; '75-76 Canadian amateur, '77 Western amateur titles, French Nation's Cup; pro from '77; mem. 3 World Cup teams, with Dan Halldorson won '80 WC title; 1st PGA victory '84 Essex International; runnerup '83 Heritage Classic; lost '84 Crosby title to Hale Irwin in playoff; righthander who putts lefthanded; *Score* magazine Cdn pro of '83; boating accident threatened playing career but he bounced back; golf analyst *ESPN*; res. Phoenix, Ariz.

NELSON, Donald (coaching); b. 23 Sep 1928, Saint John, N.B.; m. Margaret Lewis; c. Kathy, Wendy, Linda; Springfield Coll. B.Sc, Okla. M.Ed; ret'd prof./coach; athletic dir. Trois-Rivieres HS '52-56; coach/prof. phys ed. UNB '56-91; coach UNB football '56-67, basketball '56-88; mem. N.B. Sports Hall of Fame; res. Fredericton, N.B.

NELSON, Roger (football); b. 8 May 1932, Brady, Okla.; d. 29 Jul 1996, Houston, Tex.; given name: Roger Dean; m. Barbara Anne; c. Dianna, Mark, Carol, Michael; Oklahoma, KC Western Dental College; oil executive; guard/tackle/centre; HS all-American; Big 7 Conf. all-American '51-53; co-capt. Oklahoma Sooners; drafted by Washington (NFL) '54 but opted for CFL with Edmonton; mem. Eskimos '54, '56-68; all-Western ot '57-60; offensive playing-line coach '62-63; Schenley outstanding lineman award '59; mem. Grey Cup winners '54, '56; became Cdn citizen '62; mem. Cdn Football Hall of Fame.

NEMESVARY, Mike (skiing/trampoline); b. 3 Mar 1961, Glasgow, Scotland; education assn. co-ordinator disability awareness and prevention program; mem. Ont. jr. lacrosse title team '71; freestyle ski specialist; Ont. Winter Games aerials title '76; 3 ntl jr, 5 int., 2 sr. titles; 1 NY State, Vermont titles; 4 Que., WC, 3 Europa Cup, 2 European, 5 British, 1 Scottish titles; European water ramp title; world record for skiers performing most black flips; ntl jr. trampoline title; injured in trampoline accident mid '80s and rendered a quadraplegic; recipient Perry medal for outstanding contribution to British skiing; 2 European TV documentary awards; 2 Ottawa ACT skiing awards; Celebrity Guild of Great Britain award; conducted around-the-world fund raising tour; awarded key to city by Ottawa council; mem. Nepean Wall of Fame; res. Ottawa, Ont.

NESBITT, Keith (skiing); b. 14 Jan 1930, Montreal, Que.; m. Linda Miller; c. Karen, Brian, Christopher, Krista, Andrea; Sir George William; sport administrator, real estate agent; competitive skiing through '52; Laurentian ski zone official '53, pres. '56; pres. Que. Div. 2 terms; National

Alpine chair. '63-65; 1st full-time mgr. CSA '67; helped create permanent ntl ski team '58; instrumental in bringing intl ski racing to Canada through '66 du Maurier series; created coaching certification program, official suppliers program for ntl ski team, athletic grading or classification system, 1st officials courses; active SFC, COA; exec. dir. Canadian Ski Assn. '67-77, Canadian Weightlifting Assn. '78-85, Cdn Ski Museum from '96; mem. Cdn Skiing Hall of Fame; res. Ottawa, Ont.

NESTERENKO, Eric (hockey); b. 31 Oct 1933, Flin Flon, Man.; given name: Eric Paul; div. Barbara; c. Melanie, Donna, Paul; UofT, UWO; ski instructor; rw; jr scoring star with Toronto Marlboros; turned pro with Leafs at 18; played 21 NHL seasons — with Toronto '51-56, Chicago '56-72; NHL record: 1219 scheduled games, 250g, 324a, 124 playoff games, 13g, 24a; mem. 1 Stanley Cup winner; on loan to Winnipeg Warriors '55-56 from Toronto won WHL title/Edinburgh Cup; player/GM Trail Smoke Eaters at 43; learned to ski while coaching in Lausanne, Switzerland; dabbled in stockbroking, journalism; ran recreational hockey program Aspen; joined Aspen ski patrol '78; hockey consultant, actor in movie *Youngblood*; became ski instructor at Vail, Colo., from '81; guest lecturer Guelph; plays occasional oldtimers hockey games; mem. Man. Hockey Hall of Fame; res. Vail, Colo.

NESTOR, Daniel (tennis); b. 4 Sep 1972, Belgrade, Yugoslavia; lefthanded, two-handed backhand; moved to Canada '76; won ntl -16, -18 outdoor singles titles; -12, -14, -16, -18 doubles titles; Orange Bowl -16 doubles '88; 3 Cdn international doubles; 2 SunLife nationals doubles; attained #1 ntl doubles ranking in -12, -14, -16 categories; mem. world champion Sunshine Cup -18 team '89; turned pro '91; mem. ntl Davis Cup team '90-03, 7-5 in singles, 5-2 doubles; scored major victories over world #1 Stefan Edberg '92 Davis Cup, top-seed Thomas Muster '96 duMaurier Open; mem. '96, '00 Olympic team; teamed with Mark Knowles of Bahamas '94 for doubles; won Bogota '94, New Zealand, Indianapolis titles, finalists Australian Open, Wimbledon semifinals '95, German Open doubles '96, Mason, Ohio, ATP doubles '98; Mexican Open doubles '03; with Sebastien Lareau won '98 Japan Open, '00 Olympics, Masters series gold; reached '99 Wimbledon 4th round before bowing to Pete Sampras; with Sandon Stolle won Adidas Intl doubles '01; claimed 1st tennis grand slam victory '02 winning Australian Open doubles, with Knowles ranked #1 in world, won 5 Intl men's doubles titles including US Open '04; with Lareau Wilson-McCall award; res. North York, Ont.

NESUKAITIS, Violetta (table tennis); b. 28 Mar 1951, Toronto, Ont. m. Josip Turcinovic; c. Carlo, Julio; bank data center clerk; among 28 jr. titles won Ont. midget girls, Ont. Open, Closed, girls -15; won more than 100 ntl, US titles in singles, women's, mixed doubles including 10 ntl singles; finalist Commonwealth mixed doubles '75; trained in Europe, Japan; made promotional instruction film for Prudential Life; top-ranked Canada, 6th Commonwealth; ret'd '77; res. Toronto, Ont.

NETTLES, Ray (football); b. 1 Aug 1949, Jacksonville, Fla.; given name: Ernest Ray; div; Tennessee; trucker; coll. all-star; BC '72-76, Toronto '77-78; Ottawa '79; '73 WFC, CFL Schenley Award outstanding lineman; 4 times WFC all-star; HS coach Fla.; asst. coach UofOtt '82-84; mem. Cdn Football Hall of Fame; res. Jacksonville, Fla.

NEUFELD, Chris (curling); b. 21 Apr 1957, Winnipeg, Man; m. Pearl; c. Denni, B.J., Michael; baker; began curling age 12; second for Vic Peters '92, '93, '97 Briers; winner '92; res. Gimli, Man.

NEUMANN, Peter (football); b. 10 Aug 1931, St. Catharines, Ont.; m. Edia Schellenberg; c. Peter, Kristine, Denise, Jimmy, Nancy; employee GM; de/lb Hamilton '51-63; 7 Grey Cup finals, 3 winners; mem. Canadian Football Hall of Fame; res. St. Catharines, Ont.

NEWHOUSE, Ian (t&f); b. 25 Dec 1956, Calgary, Alta.; m. Donna; c. Joseph, Dougie; UAlta BSc, MSc, UBC PhD; dean professional schools Lakehead; mem. Edm. Olympic Club; 3 ntl indoor 400m, 2 800m titles, 3 outdoor 400m hurdles titles; mem. '79, '83 PAG, '80, '84 Olympic, '82 CG, '79, '81, '83 FISU Games teams; ntl record 400m hurdles (49.80), 500yds (57.7), 500m (1:03.6), 400m (47.63); fastest electronic time in world 600m (1:17.52) '81 CIAU championships; world record 300m hurdles (37.0) '81 Vandal International; male athlete of '81 CIAU championships; 2 CIAU indoor t&f male-athlete-of-yr awards; res. Thunder Bay, Ont.

NEWMAN, Al (coaching/football); b. 2 Apr 1912, Detroit, Mich.; d. 23 Nov 2003, Windsor, Ont.; m. Enid; c, Alan, David; during 40-year career at Windsor Patterson CI won 30 titles in football and other sports; one of 20 student coaches invited by German Olympic Committee to attend '36 Berlin Olympics; most successful coach in Windsor AKO football team's history with 10 consec. league, 4 Eastern Cdn, 2 ntl titles; coached 8 t&f title teams; coached ntl title gymnasts; OFSAA director; mem. Canadian Fitness Council 3yrs; mem. Windsor-Essex County, UWindsor Sports halls of fame,

NEWMAN, Bernard (coaching); b. 4 Aug 1914, Windsor, Ont.; d. 6 Nov 1995, Windsor, Ont.; m. Lee Werbowecki; c. Bernard Jr., Leeann, Jane, Gary, Patricia; Assumption Coll.; teacher, politician; as Windsor teacher '34-58 gained reputation as gymnastics coach; among protégées ntl champions Ernestine Russell, Ed Gagnier; coached more than 170 individual titlists; only coach to guide ntl jr. male, sr. women's athlete of year same year; ntl chair. of gymnastics AAU '55-56; coach ntl gymnastics team '56 Olympics, '58 world, '59 PAG; Windsor alderman '55-60; MLA (Lib) Windsor; mem. Windsor-Essex County Sports Hall of Fame.

NEWMAN, Pat (rowing); b. 7 Aug 1963, St. Catharines, Ont.; men's 8s.; mem. ntl team from '87; competed '92, '96 Olympics; 2 Cdn, 3 US, 2 International regatta, 1 World championship gold; res. St. Catharines, Ont.

NEWSHAM, David (soccer); b. 21 Nov 1928, Saskatoon, Sask.; m. Pearl Hoogeveen; c. Stephanie, Noel, Andrea; UofSask, BA, LLB, QC; lawyer; 25yrs competitive soccer; mem. 3 prov. title teams; competed vs. 3 touring European teams; founder Saskatoon United Soccer Club; founding mem. Western Canada Soccer League; served at all levels of administration; 25yrs. Saskatoon Soccer Assn. exec., 20yrs prov. exec.; 5yrs CSA exec.; 5 terms pres., 10yrs secty. prov. SA; pres. Saskatoon SA; coach Arsenal Youth team; mem. Sask. Sports Council; res. Saskatoon, Sask.

NEWTON, Jack (football); b. 2 Jan 1887, Sarnia, Ont., d. 23 Dec 1967, Sarnia, Ont.; m. Eleanor Watson; c. John, Fred; UofT; educator; mem. '09 UofT Grey Cup winners, all-star; coached Varsity to 2 interprov. titles, '14 Grey Cup; head coach Sarnia CI, several Ont. championships; coached Sarnia intermediates 8yrs. numerous Ont., ntl championships; head coach Sarnia Imperials; mem. Cdn Football Hall of Fame.

NEZAN, Andy (golf); b. 10 Nov 1926, Ottawa, Ont.; d. 5 Feb 1997, Ottawa, Ont.; given name: Joseph André Rodolphe; m. Rose Sydor; c. Diane, Greg; engraver; 2 Que. amateur titles; 4 ODGA match, 2 ODGA medal, with Glen Seely 2 ODGA best-ball titles; 2 Collie Cups; 8 Rivermead, 1 Chaudiere club titles; mem. '69 Que. Willingdon Cup team, '83 ntl triangular matches team; 2 O'Keefe Open, Renfrew, Buckingham Invitationals; 2 Ottawa ACT golf awards; ACT amateur athlete of '64; Charles Daoust French-speaking amateur athlete of '65; hon. life mem. Rivermead Golf Club; mem. Ottawa Sports Hall of Fame.

NG, Gideon Joe (table tennis); b. 15 Nov 1963, Toronto, Ont.; Seneca Coll., UofT; optician; mem. ntl team from '79; 1 US singles title; 1 CNE International mixed doubles title; overcame battle with cancer in '80s to win PAG gold '87; mem. '88, '96 Olympic, '82, '94 Commonwealth championships, NA, world universities championships, '83, '87 PAG teams; team silver '83 PAG; won '90 Western Japan open; Canada Cup gold '91; NA singles titles '88-89, '91, men's doubles '93, '96; ntl men's singles '85, '89; ntl triple crown winner '89; with Johnny Huang doubles gold '94 Commonwealth championships; res. Toronto, Ont.

NICHOLAS, Cindy (swimming); b. 20 Aug 1957, Toronto, Ont.; given name: Cynthia Maria; m. Roy LeGrow; UofT, Windsor, LLB; lawyer; record 15h10m conquest of Lake Ont. 16 Aug '74; record 9h 46m English Channel swim from France to England '75; record 1st 25km Syrian Jablak to Lattakia swim; women's division '76 Chibougama single-day 3-swim competition (10, 5, 1 1/2 miles), women's div. 25-mile Lake St. John swim; 1st woman to complete 2-way English Channel swim '77; 2-way record 19h12m '79; 1st person to complete 3, 2-way crossings 1yr '81; 1st woman to swim Chaleur Bay from Grand Anse, NB, to Paspebiac, Que., '77; 2-way Chaleur Bay swim '78; women's div. International Cross-Channel Race in record 10h10m '79; repeat '81; crowned "Queen of the English Channel" with 19 crossings, including 5 2-way trips; World Federation of Swimming world's women's international swimming champion '76; Scarborough, Toronto, Ont. Cdn govt. awards; Capt. Webb Silver award; Sotiraki Trophy; Athletic Club of Columbus trophy; Ont., Bobbie Rosenfeld award '77; Vanier Award; recognized in *Guinness Book of World Records*; mem. Order of Canada; UK swimming, US International, Ont. Aquatic, Ont. Legends, Canada's Sports halls of fame; res. Scarborough, Ont.

NICHOLL, Jimmy (soccer); b. 28 Dec 1956, Hamilton, Ont.; m. Sue; c. Kate; mdfld N. Ireland Schoolboy Team; pro Manchester United '72; shifted to fb, initial 2nd Div.

English League game '75; club moved into 1st Div. '76; 1st Canadian-born player in FA Cup final; more than 200 games for Manchester United 1st team; on loan to 1st Div. Sunderland '82; sold to Toronto Blizzard '82; mem. N. Ireland World Cup team '82; Irish Ntl team asst. mgr.; mgr. Millwall '96-97, Raith '97-99, Dumfermline '99-04; res. Belfast, N.I.

NICHOLLS, Bernie (hockey); b. 24 Jun 1961, Haliburton, Ont.; given name: Bernie Irvine; m. Heather DeBrouwer; c. McKenna, Flynn, Jack (d); hockey exec.; ctr Kingston (OHA); drafted by LA '80; New Haven (AHL) '81-82; Kings '81-90, NYR '90-91, Edmonton '91-93, New Jersey '93-94, Chicago '94-96, San Jose '96-98; 3 NHL all-star games; NHL record: 1117 scheduled games, 475g, 732a, 118 playoff games, 42g, 72a; scored 70g '89; joined San Jose front office '98; proficient golfer, competes on celebrity tour; part-owner New Mexico Scorpions (WPHL); res. San Jose, Calif.

NICHOLSON, Bob (hockey/administration); b. 27 May 1953, Penticton, B.C.; m. Lorna; c. Mandi, Marijean, Grant; Providence Coll.; pres. Hockey Canada; capt. BC Midget AAA, 2 BCJHL title teams; development co-ordinator BCAHA '79-89; instrumental in coaching, officiating clinics; v-p CAHA '89; key role in developing coaching, youth skill programs; headed up ntl team programs for both men and women; became Hockey Canada pres. '98; during his ntl watch has seen teams earn 22 gold, 6 silver, 1 bronze on intl. scene; res. Calgary, Alta.

NICKS, Frank (t&f); b. 7 Feb 1914, Halifax, N.S.; given name: Frank Stanley; c. Barry William; ret'd career soldier, exec. secretary; began competitive running age 10 and quickly emerged as standout sprint star setting records which stood for several decades; Maritime junior sprint champion; mem. '34 BEG team; injury ended career '35; posted 80 1sts, 14 2nds, 7 3rds in races '24-35; also standout in rugby, soccer, badminton, tennis; 40yrs in Boy Scout movement; life mem. Kiwanis; NS athlete of '33; awarded OBE, Coronation medal; mem. NS Sports Hall of Fame; res. Halifax, N.S.

NICOL, Helen (baseball); b. 9 May 1920, Ardley, Alta.; given name: Helen Margaret; div. Gordon Fox; ret'd Motorola Corp; rhp; began playing softball at 13; advanced to sr. women's league at 15; scouted by former hockey star Johnny Gotsleig and joined AAGPBL '43 remaining with Kenosha to '46 before shifting to Rockford; '46-52; during 10yr pro career appeared in 313 games with 163-118 w/l record, 2382ip, 1076k, 1.89era; also standout ice hockey player, helping team to Western Cdn, Banff Winter Carnival titles; speed skater; competed in t&f, 7yrs club golf champion, has a hole-in-one to her record; honored by Cooperstown, Cdn Baseball halls of fame; mem. Alta. Sports Hall of Fame; res. Tempe, Ariz.

NICOL, Robert (curling); b. 10 Sep 1952, Ft. Frances, Ont.; m. Marion; plumbing assn. co-ordinator; mem. '79-80 Thunder Bay grand prix 'spiel title, '80 World Open, '81 Soo cashspiel; 2nd for Al Hackner rink 4 NO Brier reps; mem. '82 Brier, Silver Broom (World) title rink; res. Thunder Bay, Ont.

NICURITY, Bryan (basketball); b. 21 Sep 1936, Regina, Sask.; given name: Bryan Lee; div.; c. Leslee, Jason; Regina, admin/human resources; ret'd Sask. Power Corp; ED Basketball Saskatchewan; competed '51-64; officiating from '62; builder/administrator from '58; officiated 6 CIAU men's & women's championships; 8 men's. women's CCAA, jr. ntls; 2 Canada Games; internationally '66-77 working '67 Pan-Am Games, '68-69 World Cup, '76 Olympics, '75 women's worlds; '70-75 men's, women's tours to China, Mexico, Cuba, Europe, South America; founding mem. CABO '72, v-pres 7yrs, pres. 4yrs; helped develop 1st case book, mechanics manual; ntl evaluator, clinician, chair. officials selection comm. for ntl championships, selection comm. for intl assignments; mem. Cdn basketball tech., development comm.; Cdn rep COPABA technical comm.; CABO Ted Early Memorial award; Basketball Canada president's award (1st for official); 4 scholarships for officials attending university bear his name; mem. Sask. Sports, Cdn Basketball halls of fame; res.Regina, Sask.

NIEDERMAYER, Rob (hockey); b. 28 Dec 1974, Cassiar, B.C.; ctr Medicine Hat jr. '90-95; Team Canada World jr. gold '93, '04 worlds; WHL East all-star '93; WHL top prospect award; NHL Florida '93-01, Calgary '01-02, Anaheim '02-04; NHL record (through '04): 696 scheduled games, 129g, 207a, 52 playoff games, 11g, 11a; brother Scott with N.J.; res. Vancouver, B.C.

NIEDERMAYER, Scott (hockey); 31 Aug 1973, Edmonton, Alta.; m. Lisa; c. John Logan, Jackson Robert; def. Kamloops jr. '89-92; Team Canada '90-92, '97, '04; NHL New Jersey Devils '91-04; NHL record (through '04): 892 scheduled games, 112g, 364a, 146 playoff games, 17g, 47a; 1 Norris trophy; 2 Stanley Cup winners; 1 all-star game; mem. Muscular Dystrophy Assn, Muscle Team from '98; res. Cranbrook, B.C.

NIELSEN, Ken (football); b. 10 May 1942, Hanna, Alta.; m. Marsha Murray; c. Alana, Jennifer, Grant, Keith; UAlta, DDS; dentist; hb/e Blue Bombers '65-70; Western Conference all-star 3 times; '68 Schenley outstanding-Cdn Award; caught CFL record-tying 109yd td pass from Kenny Ploen at Calgary '65; career total 280 passes for 4340yds (15.5 avg), 31tds; Man. male athlete of '67; completed Vancouver marathon '81; res. Winnipeg, Man.

NIEMEYER, Frederic (tennis); b. 24 Apr 1976, Campbellton, N.B.; Middle Tennessee State; tennis player; Davis Cup team from '98; lifted Canada to a historic 3-2 win over Mexico with a five-set singles victory in Davis Cup play '01; won 3 consec. doubles Challengers '02; qualified for 1st ever ATP event June '03 ($800,000 Gerry Weber Open Halle, Germany); qualified for Wimbledon 1st Grand Slam '03; ranked #1 in singles in Canada '02-03; ranked career high #170 on ATP Entry System '03; 2 wins over top-20 players (Mantilla, Gonzalez); 5-5 singles, 4-1 doubles record in Davis Cup; Tennis Canada singles player of '02; res. Deauville, Qué.

NIEUWENDYK, Joe (hockey); b. 10 Sep 1966, Oshawa, Ont.; m. Tina; c. Jackson Johannes, Tyra; Cornell; ctr Cornell (ECAC), ntl team '84-87; 2 NCAA East All-American, 2 ECAC 1st team all-star; ECAC rookie of '85; Cornell MVP '87; 2nd Calgary pick '85 draft; NHL with Calgary '86-95 (capt.), Dallas '95-99, New Jersey '02-03, Toronto '03-04; Calder Memorial trophy '88; NHL all-rookie team '88; Dodge Ram Tough award '88; King Clancy trophy '95; Conn Smythe trophy '99; mem. 2 Stanley Cup winners; 4 NHL all-star games; competed worlds '90, world jr. '86; mem. '98, '02 (gold) Olympic team; scored 51g '88, '89; 400 career goals '98; NHL record: (through '04) 1177 scheduled games, 533g, 529a, 158 playoff games, 66g, 50a; hon. chair Capital Campaign for SPCA of Texas; res. Toronto, Ont.

NIGHBOR, Frank (hockey); b. 26 Jan 1893, Pembroke, Ont., d. 13 Apr 1966, Pembroke, Ont; m. Dorothy Slattery (d); c. Frank Jr.; m. Ann Heney (d); c. Patrick, Pauline, Catharine; insurance exec.; Port Arthur '10-11 season; pro Toronto '13; Vancouver Millionaires Stanley Cup winners '14-15, Ottawa Senators '15-29, Toronto '29; with Senators 4 Stanley Cup winners; nicknamed "Flying Dutchman", "Pembroke Peach"; tied for '17 scoring lead 41 goals in 20 games; 233 goals in 281 regular season games, 16 in 33 playoffs; 1st recipient Lady Byng Trophy '25, repeat '26; 1st recipient Hart Trophy '24; noted for popularizing poke check; mem. Ottawa Sports, Hockey halls of fame.

NIGHTINGALE, Lynn (figure skating); b. 5 Aug 1956, Edmonton, Alta.; m Bob Connor; c. Jessica; UWO; journalist, coach; EO sr. titles '70-72, ntl jr. '72, sr. '74-77, Skate Canada '73-74, Prague Skate '73, Moscow Skate '74; 9th '76 Olympics; mem. '73-77 worlds teams; pro Ice Capades '77-82; Cdn Ladies pro champion '81; skating double in movies *Youngblood* and *Skate*; City of Ottawa awards '72-74; Ottawa ACT athlete of '74; mem. Ottawa Sports Hall of Fame; res. Kanata, Ont.

NILSSON, Kent (hockey); b. 31 Aug 1956, Nynashamn, Sweden; c. Robert; hockey scout; ctr AIK Sweden '76-77; WHA Winnipeg Jets '77-79; WHA record: 158 scheduled games, 81g, 133a; NHL Atlanta Flames '79-80, Calgary Flames '80-85, Minnesota '85-86, Edmonton '86-87, '94-95; NHL record: 553 scheduled games, 264g, 422a, 59 games, 11g, 41a; mem. 1 Stanley Cup winner; became Edmonton scout '94 and, except for 6-game comeback bid '94-95, has remained as scout; brother Ulf also played in WHA/NHL; res. Stockholm, Sweden.

NOBLE, Reg (hockey); b. 23 Jun 1895, Collingwood, Ont.; d. 19 Jan 1962, Alliston, Ont.; given name: Edward Reginald; Collingwood jrs '15 OHA group titlist, prov. semifinalist; Toronto Riversides OHA sr. title team '16; pro Toronto '16-17, when team disbanded joined Montreal Canadiens; Toronto Arenas at inception of NHL '17-18, 28 goals in 22 games, Stanley Cup winner; St. Pat's '21-22 Stanley Cup winners; Montreal Maroons '24-26, '33, Stanley Cup winner '26; Detroit Cougars '27-32; 170 NHL goals; 1 season Cleveland (IHL); refereed 2yrs NHL; mem. Hockey Hall of Fame.

NOEL, Leo (boxing); b. 14 May 1940, Cocagne, N.B.; given name: Leo Joseph; Moncton city works supervisor; amateur record 19-0, with 16 KOs; Maritime Golden Gloves title '62; turned pro, won NB-PEI lightweight title '63; Maritime lightweight title, 5th ranked Canada '66; Eastern Cdn title '67; ranked #1 Cdn title contender '69-71; lost 8th round TKO to Al Ford in ntl title bout '71; ret'd from ring '72; secty, chair. Moncton Boxing Commission; secty

boxing/wrestling commission '81-84; Moncton city award '69, Moncton citizenship award '86; mem. Moncton Wall, Cdn Boxing, NB Sports halls of fame; res. Moncton, N.B.

NOGA, Arleene (baseball/softball/curling/bowling); b. 1 Jan 1924, Ogema, Sask; given name: Arleene Cecelia Johnson; m. Ronald Noga (d); c. Carol Lee, Robert Craig; ret'd admin. asst.; 3b All-American Girls Professional Baseball League '45-48; only player to play all league games over 2 seasons; set 3b fielding record; played 1st organized softball '44 in Regina sr. league; played 9 provincial championships, 5 Western Cdn championships, '53 amateur softball world championship; 2 batting titles, 2 MVP awards, 1st team all-star; competitive curler '51-77; skipped Regina Ladies 'spiel grand aggregate winner '60; participated 5 Sask, 1 BC district playdowns; mem. Vics B mixed league 5-pin team '53; league organizer/administrator; held ladies high avg. several years; dir. AAGPBLPA from '87; mem. Sask. Baseball, Sask Sports halls of fame; honored by Cooperstown, St. Mary's Baseball halls of fame; res. Regina, Sask.

NOLAN, Frank Jr. (boxing); b. 24 Jan 1961, Sault Ste. Marie, Ont.; steelworker; Ont. 60kg title '78, ntl 60kg title '79; runnerup 60kg '78, US Golden Gloves, '79 NY State Golden Gloves; bronze 67kg '80 Acropolis Cup; quarterfinalist 60kg '78 CG; mem. '78 CG, '79 PAG teams; res. Sault Ste. Marie.

NOLAN, Frank Sr. (boxing); b. 4 Oct 1932, Garden River, Ont.; d. 8 Mar 2003, Sault Ste. Marie; m. Charlotte Gingras; c. Stephen, Frank Jr., Brien, Michael; steelworker; competitive boxer '42-58; began coaching '72; ntl team coach '78 CG, '79 PAG, '78 Finnish International competition, '78 US Golden Gloves.

NOLAN, Owen (hockey); b. 12 Feb 1972, Belfast, N. Ireland; m. Diana; restaurateur; raised in Thorold, Ont.; played baseball, soccer in youth; began skating age 9; rw Cornwall jr. OHL '88-90; AHL Halifax '90; Team Canada '97; NHL Quebec '90-95, Colorado '95, San Jose '95-03, Toronto '03-04; NHL record (through '04): 915 scvheduled games, 349g, 386a, 58 playoff games, 18g, 16a; capt. San Diego '98-00; 4 NHL all-star games; Hap Emms OHL rookie award; OHL 1st team all-star; Jim McMahon Memorial trophy; "Buster"; res, San Jose, Calif.

NOLAN, Steve (boxing); b. 10 Feb 1960, Sault Ste. Marie, Ont.; given name: Stephen; m. Dory Lacasse; c. Deborah; steelworker; '74-75 jr. Olympics 57kg titles; ntl int. 57kg title '76-77, sr. '81-83; NA 57kg title '76; Tour de France 57kg title '79; Stockholm open 60kg title '84; bronze 57kg '80 NZ Games; mem. '80, Olympic, '82 CG, '83 PAG teams; res. Sault Ste. Marie, Ont.

NOLAN, Ted (hockey/coaching); b. 7 Apr 1958, Garden River Reserve, Ont.; given name: Theodore John; m. Sandra; c. Brandon, Jordan; Lake Superior State; hockey coach; full-blooded Ojibwa; ctr/lw jr. NOHA Kenora '75-76, OMJHL SSM '76-78; drafted by Detroit '78; pro CHL Kansas City '78-79, AHL Adirondack '79-84 (1 Calder Cup), Rochester '84-85, Baltimore '85-86; NHL Detroit '81-84, Pittsburgh '85-86; NHL record: 78 scheduled games, 6g, 16a; asst. coach SSM '87-88, head coach '88-94 (2 league titles), '93

Memorial Cup; asst. coach Hartford (NHL) '94-95; head coach Buffalo '95-97; Jack Adams trophy '97; SSM medal of merit; Order of Ont.; ntl aboriginal achievement award; hon. LLP Algoma Coll; launched Ted Nolan Anishinabe hockey school '86; dir. hockey operations/head coach Indigenous Hockey Corp.; pro sports consultant Assembly of First Nations; res. Garden River Reserve, Ont.

NOLET, Alan (gymnastics); b. 17 Dec 1967, Toronto, Ont.; McMaster; m. Tamara; began competing age 12; mem. ntl team from '86; all-around competitor; his high bar routine considered one of most difficult in world; competed '90, '94 CG, '94 University Cup, '91, '94 Worlds, '88, '92, '96 Olympic, '87, '95 PAG, '93 FISU Games; 2 gold, 2 silver '90, 1 gold, 1 bronze '94 CG, 1 bronze '95 PAG; 6 gold, 1 silver '94 University Cup; all-around gold '95, 2 gold '94 World Challenge; CIAU gold '94; 3 ntl sr titles, 8 ntl elite titles; res. Hamilton, Ont.

NOONEY, John (gymnastics); b. 21 Jun 1921, Bendon, Ireland; d. 2 Aug 2003, Credit Valley, Ont.; m. Patricia Phelan; Christian Brothers Coll., Ireland; ret'd sr. civil servant Ont.; 14yrs PTI (all sports) RAF; emigrated to Canada '50; pioneer Ont. Gymnastics Assn.; wrote 1st gymnastics handbook for YMCA; coach Etobicoke; international judge PAG; tech. dir. Ont. men's gymnastics; Ont. judging chairman; exec. mem. OGF; historian OGF, CGF; Cdn reporter *Modern Gymnast* mag.; mem. British Olympics Comm.; considered father of Ont. gymnastics; life mem. Cdn Gymnastics Fed.

NORD, Dennis (coaching); b. 8 Apr 1945, Winnipeg, Man.; m. Patricia; c. Christie, Lana, Danny; UWpg; teacher, coach; mem./coach numerous prov. volleyball, basketball title teams; coached Man. jr. men to 3 ntl volleyball titles; coached UWpg men to 3 ntl volleyball titles; coach ntl men's volleyball team '73 FISU games; asst. coach '67 men's Olympic team; head coach ntl team '77; *CBC-TV* ntl trivia champion '79-80; dir. Canadian Volleyball board from '82; res. Winnipeg, Man.

NORDHAGEN, Christine (wrestling); b. 26 Jun 1971, Valhalla Centre, Alta; m. Leigh Vierling; UCal; teacher; competes in 68kg, 75kg class; gold (68kg) 6 world championships (3 in succession), 1 PAG, 1 German ntl, 1 Gilbert Schaub, 1 France International tournaments; 1 world 75g, 5 ntl, world 68kg titles; Canada's female wrestler of yr '93-96; International female wrestler of '97; '04 Olympic team; res. Valhalla Centre, Alta.

NORMAN, Clint (taekwon-do); b. 21 Jul 1955, Hamilton, Ont.; head instructor Norman's Taekwon-Do Centres; began taekwon-do training '73; pioneered ITF taekwon-do in Sask. '84; founding mem. Sask. Taekwon-Do Fed. International; level 3 coach; ITF Sask. tech. dir; head coach, trainer for Sask.; 2 ntl heavyweight titles; West Cdn sparring title; capt. ntl team '86-92; NA team gold '86; Intercontinental Cup, European championships team gold '86; individual patters silver, sparring bronze, '86 European championships; 2 gold, 2 silver, 1 bronze PAG championships; 4 silver, 2 bronze world championships; active in conducting coaching/technical seminars; v-p ITF, chair. PAG championships; v-p Western Cdn ITF; trainer/ instructor more than 42 ntl champions; ITF outstanding

instructor award; mem. Sask Sports Hall of Fame; res. Regina, Sask.

NORMAN, Larry (canoeing); b. 5 Apr 1966, Toronto, Ont.; UBC; kinesiologist; began paddling age 10; mem. ntl team '86-98; competed '92, '96 Olympic Games; 5 ntl C-1 titles; res. Ottawa, Ont.

NORMAN, Moe (golf); b. 10 Jul 1929, Kitchener, Ont.; d. 4 Sep 2004, Kitchener, Ont.; given name: Murray; pro golfer; ntl amateur title '55; pro '58; tied Stan Leonard low Cdn '57 Cdn Open; 3 Alta., 2 Sask., 3 Man. 1 Ont, Atlantic, Que. Open titles; Millar Trophy; 2 CPGA, 7 CPGA Sr. titles; record 9-hole 28 back 9 CPGA final Old Ashburn, Halifax; mem. numerous Ont. Willingdon Cup, ntl America's Cup teams; Rockway's George S. Lyon team matches, '71 World Cup team; 33 course records, 17 holes-in-one; twice recorded rounds of 59; 13 Cdn tour wins; considered by peers most proficient shotmaker despite impatient behavior; popular with fans due to running repartee throughout round; mem. RCGA, Waterloo County halls of fame.

NORMAN, Percy (swimming/coaching); b. 14 Mar 1904, New Westminster, B.C.; d. May 1957, Vancouver, B.C.; began career as marathon swimmer but found greater satisfaction as coach; head coach Vancouver Amateur Swim Club '31-55; coached '36 Olympic, '54 BE&CG teams; among top students were: Helen & Mary Stewart, Jack Pomfret, Howard Firby, Lynda Adams, George Athans Sr.; Vancouver pool bears his name; mem. BC Sports, Swimming halls of fame.

NORMANDIN, Pierre (table tennis); b. 11 Oct 1959, Montreal, Que.; given name: Pierre Gerard; McGill, BSc; with Marc Lesiege ntl jr. boys' doubles, with Mariann Domonkos jr. mixed doubles; twice Que. -17 champion; final jr. year swept prov. singles, both doubles; silver singles, team gold Israel Hapoel Games; twice mem. English Open, once Italian Open teams; mem. bronze team '79 PAG, bronze team World Student table tennis championships '81; 2nd ntl Top 12 tournament '80; mem. New Zealand Games, world championships teams '81; twice Ottawa Open titlist; res. Westmount, Que.

NORRIS, Edgar (rowing); b. 23 Dec 1902, Evesham, Eng.; d. (circa 1990), Toronto, Ont.; given name: Cyril Edgar; m. Renee Vielete; ret'd Toronto city clerk; mem. Argonaut bronze-medal 8s '28 Olympics; mem. ntl champion 140lb Don Rowing Club 8s, jr. 8s Argos crew, open-championship Argos 8s; Argos 8s who finished in dead heat in English Henley then lost in row-over; Toronto Civic Award; pres. Ont. Municipal Assn., Scarborough Golf & Country Club.

NORTHCOTT, Ron (curling); b. 31 Dec 1935, Innisfail, Alta.; given name: Ronald Charles; m. Gerry McKay; c. Karen, Greg; steel production co. owner; launched curling career Vulcan jr. HS; skip Alta. entry '63-64, '66-69 Briers, won 3; 3 times world champion; nicknamed "The Owl"; mem. Gov.-Gen.'s CC; mem. Order of Canada, Alta., Canada's Sports, Curling halls of fame; res. Calgary, Alta.

NORTHUP, Helen (basketball); b. 16 Mar 1916, Arcadia, Fla.; m. Harry Arthur Alexander; c. James Barrie, Robert Keith; ret'd secretary; softball Edmonton Gyro Pats; avid curler, golfer; mem. famed Edmonton Grads '34-40, 105 games, 1019 points, 9.7 avg.; mem. Canadian Basketball, Alta. Sports halls of fame; res. Edmonton, Alta.

NORTON, Ross (wheelchair basketball); b. 20 Apr 1973, Calgary, Alta.; banker; began wheelchair basketball career '88 playing 6yrs Red Deer Rebels, 8 Alberta Northern Lights; mem. Ntl team from '99; Canada Games gold '95; 2 ntl championship silver; America's tourney silver '98; world championship bronze '02; Paralympic gold '00, '04; res. Edmonton, Alta.

NORTON, Wayne (baseball); b. 12 Nov 1942, Winnipeg, Man.; given name: Wayne Lester; m. Trudy Drake; c. Steve, Elizabeth; Whitworth Coll., Howard.; prov. baseball development co-ordinator; pro '61-70 NY Yankees, Kansas City, Oakland organizations; rec. dir. Vancouver Jewish Community Center '66-74; BC Rec. & Fitness Branch assn. co-ordinator '75-80; BC Amateur Baseball assn. co-ordinator; Montreal Expos Western Canada scout '75-80; part-time tech. dir. Cdn Fed. of Amateur Baseball 2yrs; CFAB ntl technical comm. '75-82; mem. BC mission staff '77 Canada Games; coached ntl team international competition Italy, Nicaragua, US, Canada; '75 PAG; conducted x-Canada clinics for O'Keefe Sports Foundation; scout Seattle Mariners; res. Port Moody, B.C.

NOSEWORTHY, Mark (curling); b. 3 Nov 1959, St. John's, Nfld.; m. Carol Power; c. Matthew, Nicole; Memorial, BA; exec. officer; silver '72 Canada Games; skipped Nfld. rink '82, '87, '94 Brier; total Brier record 21-12; 2 Ross Hartstone awards; 2nd team all-star skip '87; res. St. John's, Nfld.

NOWOSIELSKI, Dan (fencing); b. 16 Nov 1966, Montreal, Que.; m. France Lamoureux; c. Jessica, Audrey; Princeton, BA, McGill, MSc; high performance dir. CFA; began fencing age 12; mem. ntl team from '84; épée specialist; competed '88, '92, '96 Olympic, 5 FISU, '87, '91, '95, '99 PAG, 12 world championships; 13 ntl titles in both épée, foil; épée team gold '92 ntls; individual, team bronze '91 PAG; equalled best-ever Cdn placing 7th men's épée Netherlands '95; bronze '96 World Cup; 2 Commonwealth championship team gold; named top fencer '87 FISU Games; flag-bearer '91 FISU Games; brother Leszek also ntl team mem.; res. Ottawa, Ont./Laval, Que.

NOWOSIELSKI, Leszek (fencing); b. 12 Sep 1968, Montreal, Que.; m. Julie Tessier; Notre Dame, MacDonald Coll.; Nortel instructor; began fencing age 11; 4 time all-American; mem. ntl team '91-00; sabre specialist; Commonwealth championship gold '94; mem. '95 PAG team; res. Ottawa, Ont.

NUGENT, Andrea (swimming); b. 1 Nov 1968, Montreal, Que.; McGill, UCal; 8 ntl titles; ntl record 50m FS; bronze 4x100 MR '88 Olympic Games; silver, bronze '93 FISU Games; relay gold '86, FS bronze '90 CG; competed '94 CG, '92 Olympic Games; 2 CIAU records; '87 sports excellence award, '89 Olympic champions award; res. Calgary, Alta.

NUNNS, Brenda (tennis); b. 13 Sep 1945, Toronto, Ont.; m. John Michael Shoemaker; c. Adam, Alexandra, John, David, Victoria; Trinity Coll.,UofT, BA, UofOtt, MHA;

father Gilbert 7 times Davis Cup team mem., mother Beatrice Eastern Cdn champion; with Faye Urban ntl girls -15 doubles '60, girls -18 doubles '61-63; with variety of partners Ont., Que., BC, Washington State -18 doubles; with Urban '64 Tennessee, Tri-State doubles; ntl women's open doubles '65; intercollegiate women's singles '63-66, Ont. -18 singles '62; with Cynthia Nowlan National Capital women's doubles '75; mem. Fed. Cup team '66; mem. Rockcliffe Lawn Tennis Club; teaching pro '78-81; mem. Intl. Lawn Tennis Club; res. North Saanich, B.C.

NUNNS, Gilbert (tennis); b. 30 Jun 1907, Leeds, Eng.; d. d. 16 Jul 2001, Toronto, Ont.; m. Beatrice Symons; c. Mary, Margot, Ruth, Brenda; Lower Canada Coll., UofT, BA; ret'd advertising agency v-p; at 15 Que. boys' champion; won both Ont., Que. jr., sr. titles; 7 times Davis Cup team mem., capt. '34; No. 1 Canada '30; 2 ntl jr. open titles; mem. UofT, Cdn Tennis halls of fame.

NUTTER, Janet (diving); b. 2 Apr 1953, Montreal, Que.; m. Chris Rudge; c. Diane, Ryan; UMan, BA, Queen's, BEd; ED. OWIAA; *CBC-TV* sports commentator; bronze 1m, gold 3m '73 Canada Games; gold 3m CIAWU '73 championships; bronze 3m '73 summer ntls; silver 10m '75 USSR, Mexico; mem. '73 New Zealand, FISU Games, Canada Cup teams; gold 3m, bronze 10m '78 CG; 6th 3m '78 World Aquatic championships; silver 3m '79 FINA World Cup; bronze 3m '79 PAG; mem. '80 Olympic team; '76-80 ntl 3m champion; mem. Cdn Aquatic Hall of Fame; res. Thornhill, Ont.

NYE, Barry (wrestling); b. 3 Jul 1936, Toronto, Ont.; given name: Barry William; m. Valerie Sampson; c. Stacey, Kimberley; comm. affairs mgr. Air Canada; Toronto 125.5lb titles '56-57; mem. Toronto Central YMCA Ont. Y title team '56; coach Scarborough Police Youth Club '57-60, Montreal Boys & Girls Club '61-67, Sir George Williams '68-69, Vanier Coll. '71-72, North Island WC '72-74, Pierrefonds WC '74-77, Riverdale WC '77-80; officiated '67 PAG, '69 World jr., '70 World championships; coach, mgr. '70 jr. ntl team; mgr. '72 Olympic team; headed Cdn wrestling delegation '74 world championships, '78 CG, '79 PAG; pres. Montreal pre-Olympic competitions '75; wrestling chair., host pres. Montreal Olympics; sec. QAWA '68-70, pres. Que. Olympic WA '70-72, v-p CAWA officials assn. '70-71, v-p CAWA '72-73, pres. '73-80; v-p CGA Canada from '78, chair. '94; dir. COA from '73; mem. world wrestling body; hon. citizen Winnipeg '75; World Wrestling Fed. gold star, diploma '76; Air Canada merit award for contribution to wrestling '77; Queen's Medal '78; finalist '80 Air Canada sport exec. of year; mem. Cdn Amateur Wrestling Hall of Fame; res. Mississauga, Ont.

NYSTROM, Karen (hockey/soccer); b. 17 Jun 1969, Scarborough, Ont.; Northeastern; account supervisor Nike Canada; HS soccer/hockey MVP '84-89; mem. Scarborough United Ont. Cup soccer champs '83-88; Central Ont. WHL scoring title '92, twice runnerup; COWHL all-star '89-97; mem. OWHA Scarborough Firefighters '85-91; Ont. Winter Games gold '85-87; coached Scarborough Girls' Bantam A team 2yrs; forward 3 world title teams, '96 Pacific Rim, 3-Nation's Cup gold medal teams; '98 Olympic silver; res. Scarborough, Ont.

OAKLEY, Alex (t&f); b. 26 Apr 1926, St. John's, Nfld.; given name: Alexander Harold; auto worker; race walking specialist; mem. '60, '64, '72, '76 Olympic teams, 6ᵗʰ '60; gold 20km '63 PAG, World Masters 5km, 25km titles '75; mem. 2 CG teams; Ont. athlete of '60; mem. Cdn Olympic, Oshawa, Nfld. Sports halls of fame; res. Hastings, Ont.

OATES, Adam (hockey/lacrosse); b. 27 Aug 1962, Weston, Ont.; Rensselaer Polytechnic Institute; ctr RPI '82-85; drafted by Detroit '85; Adirondack (AHL} '85; NHL Detroit '85-89, St. Louis '89-92, Boston '92-97, Washington '97-02, Philadelphia '02, Anaheim '03, Edmonton '03-04; NHL totals: 1337 scheduled games, 341g, 1079a, 163 playoff games, 42g, 114a; reached 1000pts '97, 1000a '02; NHL record most assists 1 period (4); 4 time finalist for Lady Byng trophy; standout lacrosse player jr./sr./major Etobicoke, Port Elgin, Owen Sound, Brampton '79-84; lacrosse record: 120 scheduled games, 305g, 409a, 34 playoff games, 65g, 90a; record most assists (19), points (29) single jr. game '81; 3 Dennis McIntosh MVP awards; *Advertiser* top scorer trophy '81; res. Palm Beach, Fla.

OBECK, Vic (football); b. 28 Mar 1921, Philadelphia, Pa., d. 21 Apr 1979, New York, N.Y.; Springfield Coll., BSc, Columbia, MA, NYU, PhD; owner public relations firm; coll. letters football, track, wrestling, swimming, lacrosse, boxing; pro football 3yrs Chicago Cardinals, Brooklyn Dodgers; coach, athletic dir. McGill '47-55; GM Alouettes 2yrs; athletic dir. NYU 12yrs. authored book on fitness, isometric exercises; public relations officer '76 Olympics.

OBERLANDER, Fred (wrestling/builder); b. 1913 Vienna, Austria; d. 1996, Montreal, Que.; c. Philip; considered one of the outstanding wrestlers to compete on world stage; 2 European, 6 French, 8 British championships; represented Britain '48 Olympics; moved to Canada '49; 2 ntl titles; with Joey Richman was driving force behind Cdn, NA Maccabi movement; high standards as wrestler, coach, leader were catalyst which produced many YMHA champion wrestlers; Maccabiah Games titles '50, '53; declared world's greatest Jewish athlete '53; dir. world Maccabiah Games comm. '65-75; pres. Cdn Amateur Wrestling Assn. '65-69; dir. CG '65-75; dir. Cdn Amateur Sports Fed. '65-69; dir. COA '65-73; FILA wrestling rep. '76 Olympics; hon. pres. Maccabi Can.; trustee Montreal YM-YWHA; recipient Olympic Order '84; mem. Cdn Olympic, Montreal YM-YWHA, CAWA halls of fame.

OBERLANDER, Phil (wrestling); b. 17 Aug 1939, London, Eng.; given name: Philip Mordechi; div.; c. Anthony, Joel, Karen; Cornell; sales rep; 5 ntl welterweight titles '60-65; gold Greco-Roman welterweight div. '61 Maccabiah Games; silver '62 CG; 5ᵗʰ welterweight FS '63 Toledo World Cup; 6ᵗʰ FS welterweight '64 Olympics; res. Ithaca, N.Y.

OBEY, Arthur (coaching/hockey/baseball); b. 25 Nov 1931, Piapot Reserve, Sask.; m. Yvonne Adams; c. 9; Notre Dame Coll.; school supervisor; coach Lebret Indians jr. B hockey champions '57-58; Lebret Indians juv C, midget C champs '58-59; coach Lebret Indians HS basketball B champs; competitively he pitched baseball and recruited players for Notre Dame Hounds, Balcarres Braves, Fort Qu'Appellle Sioux; mem. Fort Qu'Appelle Sioux Indians Sask. Int. C hockey champs '56-57; 2 Tom Longboat awards; mem. Sask. Indian First Nations Sports Hall of Fame; res. Fort Qu'Appelle, Sask.

O'BILLOVICH, Bob (football/basketball/coaching); b. 30 Jun 1940, Butte, Montana; m. Judy Ristow; c. Tracey, Jodi, Coy; Montana, BA; football exec.; lettered in football, basketball, baseball Montana, all-Skyline Conference in each; twice Grizzly award for combining academic-athletic excellence; Dragstedt award, basketball MVP, '60-61; all-American football hon. mention; led US coll. pass interceptions '60; Earhart award best defensive basketballer Montana '61-62; Montana athlete of decade '60-70; St. Louis (NFL) draftee; late cut AFL Denver; all-star db United League Indianapolis, led league in interceptions '62; Ottawa db/backup qb '63-67; twice EFC all-star; twice led EFC interceptions, CFL once; basketball coach Eastern Ont. Institute of Technology (later Algonquin) '65-69; football coach UofOtt '70 guiding team to Coll. Bowl; basketball coach, sports info. officer Carleton '71-73; basketball coach, asst-co-ordinator intercollegiate athletics UofOtt '73-77; asst. coach Rough Riders '76-81; head coach Argos '82-90, '93-94, '95, Lions '91-92; GM Argos '93-95; player-personnel dir. Sask. '98-99, Calgary '00-02 (also AGM), dir. player personnel BC '03; 3 Grey Cup finals, 1 winner; CFL coaching record: 113-112-3; CFL coach of '82, '87 (Annis Stukus trophy); TV football analyst '96-97; only head coach in Canada to guide teams to CIAU basketball, football championships, CFL Grey Cup; mem. Montana Grizzlies Basketball, Butte Sports, UofOtt Football halls of fame; res. Mississauga, Ont.

OBODIAC, Stan (all-around); b. 7 Feb 1922, Yorkton, Sask.; d. 5 Nov 1984, Toronto, Ont.; m. Emma; c. Erin, Hadley; publicity dir., author; Sask. midget, juv hockey; mem. Winston Churchill Cup winning team; leading scorer (12 goals) '51 world hockey Lethbridge Maple Leafs title team; coach Swiss ntl hockey team '52-53; mem. Sask. softball title team '39; mem. Regina Western Canada softball champions '42; Sask. sand greens golf titles '48-49; Eastern Sask. Open, Yorkton City Open, Melville City Open, Tisdale Open, Maple Leaf Gardens Open; author several sports books including *No Substitute for Victory*, *Red Kelly*, *The Leafs, the 1ˢᵗ 50yrs*; hon. dir. Timmy Tyke hockey tournament; publicity dir. Maple Leafs 25yrs; mem Sask., Yorkton Sports, British Ice Hockey, Canadian Hockey, Boxing halls of fame.

OBST, Herbert (fencing); b. 26 Jun 1936, Striegan, Germany; m. Elisabeth Hullay; c. Gregory; self employed sales agent; 10 Que., 3 ntl foil titles; mem. '66 CG, '67, '71, '75 PAG, '72 Olympic teams; finalist men's foil '71 PAG; res. Beaconsfield, Que.

O'BRIEN, J. Ambrose (hockey); b. 27 May 1885, Renfrew, Ont., d. 25 Apr 1968, Ottawa, Ont.; m. Mary Adele Gorman (d); c. Lawrence (d), Brian, Barry, Justin, Gerald; UofT; jr., intermediate, sr. hockey Renfrew, UofT; organized National Hockey Assn.; with father, Sen. M.J. O'Brien, financed 4 clubs including Renfrew Millionaires, Montreal Canadiens; mem. Ottawa Sports, Hockey halls of fame.

O'BRIEN, Joe (harness racing); b. 25 Jun 1917, Alberton, P.E.I.; d. 29 Sep 1984, Shafter, Calif.; m. Ilene Dyer; sc. Stanley, Channing Bayless; driver, trainer; Maritimes circuit with father, 4 brothers to '35; operated own stable in Nova Scotia; '43-47 led all Maritime drivers in victories; US circuit '47; more than 4,500 winners, $20 million in purses; 3 Little Brown Jug, 2 Hambletonian winners; more than 500 sub 2:00 min. miles; in winning '55 Hambletonian drove Scott Frost to world's 1st 2 min. mile for a 2yr old; drove Steady Star to 1:52 mile for fastest clocking ever by a standardbred '71; drove world record 44 sub 2 min. miles, 32 2 min miles single season '75; drove Flower Child to 1:58.4 for 1st European sub 2 min trotting mile Sweden '75; instrumental in developing 2 Horse of Year winners, Scott Frost ('55-56), Fresh Yankee ('70); drove Scott Frost to '55 Hambletonian, Yonkers Futurity, Kentucky Futurity, 1st horse in history to claim harness racing's triple crown; with Clint Hodgins co-holder world record 11 wins single program (Truro, NS '42); USTA dir.; mem. PEI, Canada's Sports, Canadian Horse Racing, US Hall of Fame of the Trotter, Bob Elias, California Sports halls of fame.

O'BRIEN, John (baseball); b. 13 Jul 1866, West Saint John, N.B.; d. 13 May 1913, Lewiston, Me.; nicknamed "Chewing Gum"; NL '91-99, .254 lifetime avg., 229rbi, 501 games; played with Brooklyn, Chicago, Louisville, Washington, Baltimore, Pittsburgh; minor league umpire; mem. NB Sports Hall of Fame.

O'CONNOR, Buddy (hockey); b. 21 Jun 1916, Montreal, Que.; d. 24 Aug 1977, Montreal, Que.; given name: Herbert William; m. Jennie; ctr; standout minor career gaining reputation as a master playmaker, smoothly deceptive skater and brilliant stick handler; with Montreal Royals ctr'd one of hockey's all-time great amateur forward lines, the Razzle Dazzle line of O'Connor, Pete Morin and Gerry Heffernan; NHL with Canadiens '41-47, NYR '47-51; NHL record: 509 scheduled games, 140g, 257a, 53 playoff games, 15g, 21a; mem. 2 Stanley Cup winners; Hart, Lady Byng, Lionel Conacher trophies '48; mem. Hockey Hall of Fame.

O'CONNOR, Larry (t&f); b. 22 Sep 1916, Toronto, Ont.; d. 6 Sep 1995, Chatham, Ont.; given name: Lawrence Gerard; m. Helen Elizabeth Conway; c. Lawrence Jr., Thomas, Jane; UofT, Osgoode Hall, LLB; lawyer; ntl intercollegiate 120yd high hurdles '35-37; mem. '36 Olympic, 5th 110m hurdles, '38 BEG teams, silver 120yd high hurdles, gold 440yd relay; world record 60yd indoor hurdles '37; Norton Crowe Memorial Trophy '39; mem. UofT, Cdn Olympic Sports halls of fame.

O'CONNOR, Zeke (football); b. 5 Feb 1926, New York, N.Y.; given name: William; m. Nancy Jean Seffing; c. Cathie, Karen, Christopher; Notre Dame, BSc, Columbia, MA; ret'd business exec.; all-American '44; capt. Great Lakes Naval football team under Paul Brown, mem. Great Lakes basketball team under Weeb Ewbank '45; pro Buffalo Bills '48, Cleveland Browns '49, NY Yankees '50-51, Toronto Argos '52-53, Grey Cup champions '52; head coach Balmy Beach ORFU '54-56; active mountaineer, mem. Sir Edmund Hillary foundation; radio football commentator '58-81; pres. Sports Fed. of Canada '82-84; founder Nepal Special Olympics; Nepal Bhakta award; hon. life governor Canada's Sports Hall of Fame; res. Islington, Ont.

O'DONNELL, William (harness racing); b. 4 May 1948, Springhill, N.S.; given name: William Arthur; m. Barbara Lynn McGregor; c. Faith, Christopher, Megan, Sean; entered business as second trainer for Jim Doherty in New England; became licensed driver at 24; moved to Saratoga to go head-to-head with J.P. Morel; set single- season record 269 victories '79 (since broken) at Saratoga before moving to Meadowlands and Grand Circuit; broke old money winning standard by 50% with more than $9M '84 season in which he posted 422 victories then in '85 became sport's 1st $10M man with earnings of $10,207,372; drove Nihilator to '84 world record 1:49.2, later same day won Hambletonian with Prakas in record time; won 2 Little Brown Jug, 1 Hambletonian, 1 Cane Pace, 1 Yonkers Trot, 2 Cdn Pacing Derby, 12 Breeders Crown, 2 World Trotting Derby, 3 Kentucky Futurity, 2 Messenger Stakes among more than 200 major stakes titles; tabbed by NY racing fans as "Magic Man"; drove `93 Horse of Year Staying Together; through `03 5579 victories and purses exceeding $95M; lived in US '70-01 before returning to Ontario; mem. Hall of Fame of the Trotter, Cdn Trotting, NS, Canada's Sports halls of Fame; res. Acton, Ont.

O'DOWDA, Ernie (builder); b. 1916, Elmwood, Man.; d. 25 Jun 1985, Winnipeg, Man.; following average athletic career was instrumental in revival of lacrosse in Winnipeg; coached/managed Elmwood Terriers, Elmwood Pats; pres. Man. Lacrosse Assn.; driving force behind establishment of Cdn Little League group during '50s; avid curler; hon. life mem. Elmwood CC; with Alex Irvin operated amateur boxing/wrestling cards; 1st Cdn recipient American National Recreation Assn. award '56; City of Winnipeg Community Service award '64, '72; Winnipeg park bears his name; mem. Man. Sports Hall of Fame.

OGDEN, Steve (curling); b. 21 Jun 1953, Moncton, N.B.; given name: Stephen Gerald; Dalhousie., BComm; investment advisor; runnerup NB Schoolboy '71; runnerup NS Tankard '82; winner 4 NS mixed, 2 ntl mixed titles; skip NS '83 Brier; NB 800m running championship '71; res. Halifax, N.S.

OGILVIE, Peter (t&f); b. 2 May 1972, Vancouver, B.C.; SFU; ntl jr.100, 200m titles; competed world jr. championships '88, '90, PAG jr. '89, '91, CG '90, '94, PAG, Worlds '91, Olympics '92, '96, FISU Games '93, Francophone Games '94; relay silver '91 PAG; bronze 200m '94 Harry Jerome Classic; gold 60m, silver 300m Cargill Indoor Games, Winnipeg, '94; silver ntl 200m '94; PB: 10.29 100m, 20.46 200m; 3 Burnaby athlete of yr, 2 BC HS athlete of yr, BC t&f male athlete of '92; mem. Vancouver Olympic Club; res. Burnaby, B.C./Brisbane, Australia.

O'GRADY, Diane (rowing); b. 23 Nov 1967, North Bay, Ont.; Queen's; former fencer she captained OWIAA team champions '87; began rowing age 21; captained Queen's team '91-92. 2nd seat women's quadruple sculls; mem. ntl team from '94; 3 Cdn, 2 US titles; FISU Games gold '93; PAG gold '95; Olympic bronze '96; CARA, Ontario female sculler of year awards '94; res. Victoria, B.C.

OGRODNICK, John (hockey); b. 20 Jun 1959, Ottawa, Ont.; given name: John Alexander; m. BettyAnne Leonelli; c. KelseyAnne, Breanne; investment consultant; lw; jr. New Westminster WHL '77-79; drafted by Detroit '79; Adirondack AHL '79-80; Detroit NHL '79-86, '92-93, Quebec '87, NYR '87-92; NHL record: 14 seasons, 928 scheduled games, 402g, 425a, 41 playoff games, 18g, 8a; shared WHL rookie of '78 award with Keith Brown; 1st NHL all-star '85; 5 all-star games; scored 55g '85; *Fox TV* hockey analyst; res. Farmington Hills, Mich.

OHAMA, Kendra (wheelchair basketball); b. 1 Jun 1965 Brooks, Alta.; m. Tom Walsh; Alta Coll. Of Art; jewellery metalsmith; mem. Rocky Mountain Rollers, Calgary Grizzlies, Aurora Lights; in youth played baseball, judo, volleyball; began wheelchair basketball career '90; ntl team from '91; made intl rookie debut Stoke-Mandeville '91; 3 gold, 1 bronze Paralympics; 2 Gold Cup world, 1 world, 1 America's tourney gold; 6 CWBL gold, 3 silver, 1 bronze; 1 MVP, 2 all-star awards; Alta, Calgary achievement awards; fed. govt. recognition award; mem. CWBA, NWWBA halls of fame; res. Calgary, Alta.

O'HARA, Jane (tennis); b. 24 Jul 1951, Toronto, Ont.; given name: Jane Ellen; UofT, BA; journalist; ntl girls -12 closed singles '63; through '69 won girls -14, -16, -18 (twice) closed singles, Open girls -18 singles, doubles (with Karen Will); 4 times Wimbledon competitor reaching quarterfinals mixed doubles '70; 6 times mem. Fed. Cup team; 1st ntl women's rankings '75; ret'd '76; ex-sports editor *Ottawa Sun;* employed *MacLean's*; mem. Cdn Tennis Hall of Fame; res. Toronto, Ont.

OKEKE, Uzooma (football); b. 3 Sep 1970 Beaumont, Tex; m. Tracey; c. Cayla, Lauren; Southern Methodist; guard/tackle; CFL Shreveport '94-95, Ottawa '96, Montreal '97-04; NGL Chicago camp '00; 5 CFL, East div., 4 CFLPA all-star; CFL lineman of '99 award; 3 Grey Cup finals, 1 winner; nicknamed "Uzo"; active with School is Cool basketball program, Alouettes jr. fb camp; res. Montreal, Que.

OLAFSSON, Shirley (t&f); b. 10 Apr 1927, Vancouver, B.C.; given name: Shirley Gordon; m. Herbert Olafsson (d); c. Heather Sigrid, David Herbert; overcame club foot birth defect to excel in basketball, t&f, field hockey; mem. BC champion Int. A basketball team; '44-45 ntl sr. women's title basketball team; Sr. B, Cagett League, BC League, Vancouver City, Cdn Underwood trophies; '50 ntl hj title; mem. '48 Olympic, '50 BEG teams; capt. '50 BEG t&f team; numerous ntl, international field hockey matches; coached basketball, t&f several yrs; husband Herb mem. 2 Cdn basketball title teams, '55 world, '59 PAG teams; level 3 curling coach; mem. BC Sports Hall of Fame as mem. '44-45 Hedlunds team; res. Richmond, B.C.

OLAND, Erick (cycling); b. 18 Mar 1924, Winnipeg, Man.; m. Rita; c. Janice, Lynda, Judy, Erick Jr.; Man. juv champion '36-38; jr. title '38-40; 5 sr. titles; prairie overall jr. champ

'40, sr. '43; 3 ntl titles; top ntl mile racer '47, '49; ntl 100km title '50; mem. '50 BEG team; set Cdn 100km, Man 5mile records; ret'd from competition at 27; 2 terms pres. Man. Cycling Assn.; dir. Cdn Cycling Assn.; mem. Man. Sports Hall of Fame; res. Winnipeg, Man.

OLDERSHAW, Bert (canoeing); b. 10 Nov 1921, Toronto, Ont.; m. Marcelle; c. Dean, Reed, Scott, Lee, Lynn; ret'd sales promotion; several ntl titles; only Cdn paddler to reach finals 3 successive Olympics; 5th 10,000m tandem canoe '48; 7th 1000m kayak '52; 5th 1000m tandem canoe '56; founded Mississauga Canoe Club '57; 12yrs dir. COA; dir. South Peel Red Cross Water Safety program; organized Mississauga Water Safety canoeing course; formed Canamtur Ltd., to assist in amateur sport funding; from '71 Canamtur has raised more than $1 million from private sector; dir. US International Swimming Hall of Fame; designed crests for CTFA, CASA; res. Burlington, Ont.

OLDERSHAW, Dean (canoeing); b. 7 Aug 1946, Toronto, Ont.; m. Diane Panet Raymond; c. Adri, Dana, Craig; Guelph, BSc-PE, UofT, BEd; teacher; 48 1st place finishes in all events (K1,K2,K4,C1,C2,C4) '62-78; 15 1st all events NA championships '66-77; 6 victories '69 Ottawa CCA championships; mem. 8 World Championships, '72, '76 Olympic teams; Ont. coaching certification asst.-co-ordinator '78-81; head coach Mississagua Canoe Club '70, Mohawk Canoe Club '73, Oakville CC '80-81, Ont. team '80-81, Canada Games team '81; res. Burlington, Ont.

OLDERSHAW, Scott (canoeing); b. 23 Feb 1954, Toronto, Ont.; m. Connie Lee Tipping; c. Adam; Sheridan Coll.; coach; 23 ntl, 8 NA championships '67-83; 16yrs ntl team; mem. '84 Olympic, 12 world championships teams; semifinalist K1 500m, 1000m '81 worlds; gold 500m K4 '79-80 Zaandam intl regatta; ntl kayak coach '90; Team Ont. coach '90-03, 5 ntl titles; PetroCan coaching excellence award; res. Burlington, Ont.

OLERUD, John (baseball); b. 5 Aug 1968, Seattle, Wash.; given name: John Garrett; m. Kelly; c. 2; Washington State; 1b/lhp US ntl team Intercontinental Cup '88; lettered in 3 sports in HS; all-state baseball MVP; Baseball America's NCAA player of yr '87-88; set Washington State baseball records; drafted by Yankees '86 but opted to continue education; never played in minors; 1b Toronto '89-96, Mets '97-99, Seattle '00-04, NY Yankees '04; ML record (through '04): 2147 scheduled games, 7419ab, 1121r, 2189h, 493db, 13tr, 248hr, 1193rbi, 11sb, .295ba; made serious run at .400ba '93 finally winning AL batting title with .363; runnerup to Larry Walker '98 NL batting race with .354; Hutch Award '93; hit for elusive cycle vs. Montreal '97; mem. 2 World Series champions; nickname "Big Rude"; res. Phoenix, Ariz.

OLESEN, Marc (t&f); b. 13 Oct 1964, Ottawa, Ont.; given name: Marc Christian; Stanford; 1500m, 3000m, 5000m, x-country specialist; 9 Ont., 7 OFSAA, 2 Legion, 2 ntl, 1 Ont. Summer Games titles; Ont. midget outdoor 3000m record (8:53.1); ntl midget indoor 3,000m record (8:36.6); '81 *Ottawa Citizen* Indoor Games HS 1500m; ranked 2nd in world for age-group '81 world championships; '82 Ont. 8000m x-country title, Mitel l0k road race; 1st Cdn high schooler to break 4-min. mile barrier 3:58.08 Burnaby, BC,

16 Jun '83; mem. '83 FISU Games team; mem. Ottawa Kinsmen Harriers; Ottawa ACT t&f award, Confederation HS Cardinal award; mem. Cdn HS Hall, Nepean Wall of Fame; res. California.

OLIN, Ralf (speed skating); b. 12 Apr 1925, Seattle, Wash.; given name: Ralf Emil; rep. Canada 5 Olympic Games, competitor '52, '56, '60, '64, flag-bearer '64; coach '68; mem. '56 world championships team; ntl metric champion '62-63, '66; variety ntl metric records; ntl mass start mile record; key role in promoting Olympic style competition which established Cdn strength in world outdoor events; mem. Alta. Sports, Canadian Speed Skating halls of fame; res. Ladysmith, B.C.

OLIVER, Al (baseball); b. 14 Oct 1946, Portsmouth, Ohio; given name: Albert Jr.; m. Donna; c. Aaron, Felisa; Kent State; baseball coach; of/1b; Pittsburgh '68-77, Texas '77-81, Montreal '82-83, San Francisco '84, Philadelphia '84, LA/Toronto '85; only player in history to combine 200 hits, 100 RBI single season both AL, NL; 8 consec. .300-plus seasons; 1st Expos NL batting champion with .331 '82; Expos player of '82, 2 Expos player-of-month awards; NL player of month, week awards; *Sporting News*, *UPI* all-star; mem. 5 NL, 2 AL all-star teams; AL record total bases doubleheader 21 '80; ML record: 18 seasons, 2368 scheduled games, 9049ab, 2743h, 1189r; 529db, 77tr, 219hr, 1326rbi, 84sb, .303ba; mem. '71 World Series finalists, 3 Silver Slugger awards; Canada's baseball man of '82; college baseball coach Portsmouth, Ohio; res. Portsmouth, Ohio.

OLIVER, Harry (hockey); b. 26 Oct 1898, Selkirk, Man.; d. 16 Jun 1985, Winnipeg, Man.; given name: Harold; Selkirk Fishermen, Man. jr. champions '17-18; Selkirk Srs. Western Cdn champions, Allan Cup finalists '18-19; pro Calgary '21-26; Western Canada champions, Stanley Cup finalists '23-34; Boston (NHL) '26-34; mem. '29 Stanley Cup winners; Rangers '34-37; with Calgary scored 91 goals, 49 assists; in 11 NHL campaigns scored 127 goals, 95 assists; pro record: 218g, 144a; mem. Cdn, Man. Hockey halls of fame.

OLIVER, Murray (hockey); b. 14 Nov 1937, Hamilton, Ont.; given name: Murray Clifford; m. Helen Marie Murray; c. Michael, Susan; hockey scout; baseball ss Hamilton, Galt (Sr. IC) pro tryout Cleveland Indians '57; Tilson Trophy as mem. Hamilton Tiger-Cubs Jr.A hockey team '58; pro Edmonton Flyers '58-59, 2nd in top rookie vote; Boston '61-66; Toronto '67-69; Minnesota '70-75; NHL record: 1127 games, 274 goals, 454 assists; asst. coach/scout Minnesota, '78-88, interim head coach '82-83; coaching record: 41 scheduled games, 21-12-8; dir. pro scouting Vancouver '88-98; pro scout Toronto '02-04; res. Edina, Minn.

OLIVER, Roy (t&f); b. 1909 Linden, N.S.; d. Jan 1991, New Glasgow, N.S.; m. Helen Rankin; CNR conductor; 1st race was 3-miler '27; won 9 *New Glasgow Evening News* 10-mile races; competed regularly in Canada, England and USA; won 4 *Halifax Herald* modified marathons; mem. Cdn Empire Games teams '34, '38; pushed Cy Bricker to Cdn record '32 Olympic trials; set ntl records for 5000m, 10,000m, 6miles; won 27 of 36 races '31-33, 6 2nds, 1 3rd; ret'd from competition '39; NS 10,000m record stood 39yrs; key role in inauguration of Johnny Miles marathon

in New Glasgow; mem. NS Sports, Cdn Road Running halls of fame.

OLIVIER, Caroline (skiing); b. 22 Dec 1971, Quebec City, Que.; Laval; freestyle aerials specialist; began competing at 18; mem. ntl team '91-99; 2 ntl silver; competed '94, '98 Olympics, '95, '97 worlds; 3 World Cup race gold, 4 bronze; ranked 3rd WC finals standings '95, '97; res. Cap Rouge, Que.

OLMSTEAD, Bert (hockey); b. 4 Sep 1926, Sceptre, Sask.; given name: Murray Bert; m. Nora Jean Moffatt; c. Dennis, Bonnie; ret'd farmer; jr. Moose Jaw; pro Kansas City, Milwaukee (USHL); NHL Chicago '49-50, Montreal '50-58, Toronto '58-62; NHL record: 848 scheduled games, 181g, 421a, 115 playoff games, 16g, 43a; mem. 5 Stanley Cup winners; earned reputation as hardnosed player and team motivator; 2 2nd team all-star; twice led NHL in assists; scout for Rangers; coach 2yrs Vancouver (WHL); 1st coach Oakland expansion team '67; NHL coaching record: 64 games, 11-37-16; mem. Hockey, Sask. Sports halls of fame; res. Calgary, Alta.

OLMSTED, Barbara (canoeing); b. 17 Aug 1959, North Bay, Ont.; Queen's BA, BPhE, BEd, UWO, MA; teacher; kayak specialist; '77 Canada Games K2, K1, K4 500m titles; semifinalist '77 jr. worlds K2 500m; ntl sr. record 2:03.2 winning '79 K2 500m title; '81 Commonwealth Cup K2 500m, 1000m; '82 Vichy regatta K4 500m; '83 PAG championships K4 500m; mem. 500m K4 bronze crew '84 Olympics; competed '88 Olympics, '81-83, '85-87 worlds; 2 ntl K2 500m, 1 K4 titles; ret'd from competition '88; coach North Bay club '89-92, club exec. '93-96; sister Nancy ntl team mem.; res. North Bay, Ont.

OLMSTED, Nancy (canoeing); b. 25 Feb 1966, North Bay, Ont.; Queen's, BA, BPhE, Nipissing, BEd, McMaster, BSc; physiotherapist; kayak specialist; sister Barbara ntl team mem.; 5 ntl K1 500m, 4 K2 500m, 2 K4 500m titles; 1 K1, 2 K2, 2 K4 500m PAG championships titles; mem. '84, '88 Olympic teams; ret'd from competition '92; res. North Bay, Ont.

OLSEN, Phil (t&f); b. 31 Jan 1957, Nanaimo, B.C.; given name: Philip Einar; m. Anne Robinson; Tennessee; teaching asst, strength coach; ntl team '73-86; world javelin record for 16-19 yr-olds; holds oldest standing BC javelin record (71.46) from '74; 9 ntl sr. javelin titles; 4yr Tennessee letterman; 4 times all-American; NCAA javelin champion '76; gold '73 Canada Games, '78 CG; Commonwealth, ntl, junior world javelin record 87.72m '76 Olympic qualifying round; triple crown '77 Melbourne International, gold '77-79 Dogwood Relays, '80 France Olympic alternatives, '80 Tom Brown Classic, '81 Pacific Conf. Games; Viscount Alexander amateur athletic award '73; mem. '76, '80, '84 Olympic, '78, '82 CG, '75, '79, PAG teams; 2 Tennessee outstanding-athlete awards; named by *Athletics* magazine to Canada's all-time men's t&f team; res. Nanaimo, B.C.

OLSON, Betty (speed skating/t&f); b. 19 Sep 1928, Winnipeg, Man.; given name: Betty Mitchell; m. Robert Olson; c. Nancy, Karen, Barbara; business coll.; secty/real estate agent; 5 women's NA speed skating titles '46-50; represented Canada world championships '49; ntl 200-metre t&f champion '47; mem. Manitoba, Cdn Speed Skating halls of fame; res. Newport Beach, Calif.

OLSON, Billy (snooker); b. 14 Jan 1922, North Battleford, Sask.; d. 11 Feb 1995, Ottawa, Ont.; Dominion Wide photo processing co. owner; photographer; processed photographs for *Ottawa Journal, The Canadian Press, Globe & Mail, Toronto Telegram*, motion films Rough Riders, Alouettes, *CBC*; shift to video forced closure of film processing operation '86; became involved in snooker as hobby '64 after watching Joe and Fred Davis in UK; owned Karrys Bowling & Billiards, Century Club '64-85; mem. Ottawa team which competed 13 times in International Snooker Players amateur team championships, winning six titles; also claimed individual championship '84 in Bermuda; nicknamed "Mr. Death" for intense approach to competition.

OLSON, Greg (golf); b. 21 Feb 1954, Bitburg, Germany; given name: Gregory Glenn; m. Tracy Miller; c. Samantha + 1; Florida Junior College, AA, Florida, BA, BSc; Apple USA advertising agency account exec.; mem. Que. jr. team '71-72, Que.-Ont. team '71-72, Que. Willingdon Cup team '74, '76, '80; mem. Fla. colleges all-state team '74-75; Fla. State colleges district champion '75; Cape Coral, Fla., Intercollegiate Invitational champion '78; mem. Florida golf team '77-78; '82 Que. Amateur title, runnerup '72, 3 Alexander of Tunis trophies; low amateur '77 Quebec Open; 4th Cdn amateur '79, won Cdn amateur '80; alternate Cdn world best-ball team '79; top-ranked Que. player '80; low individual '80 Que. Willingdon Cup champions; low Cdn, 13th overall '80 world amateur; CPGA tour card '83; '78 presidential recognition award Florida; Ottawa ACT athlete of '80; Que. golfer of '82, res. San Jose, Calif.

OLSON, Scott (boxing); b. 26 Feb 1968, Edmonton, Alta.; m. Fiona; c. Ava, Hannah; ret'd pro boxer; 48kg (flyweight) boxer; competed in '85 World Cup, '86 World championships, CG, '87 President's Cup, PAG, '88 Olympics; gold CG, President's Cup; turned pro '88; nicknamed "Bulldog"; twice broken right hand cost him world title bout shots; defeated Roger Espanola 10 Dec 1994 to claim International Boxing Organization world flyweight title; lost IBA world light-flyweight title on 10th round KO to Michael Carbajal '97; lost Cdn super-bantamweight title bid to Steve Molitor '02; pro record 34-4-2, 25kos; Egerton Markus mgr.; organized charitable foundation; res. Edmonton, Alta.

O'MALLEY, Terry (hockey); b. 21 Oct 1940, Toronto, Ont.; m. Deborah Suzanne Hindle; c. Kathleen, Frank, Bridget; UBC, UMan; educator; St. Michael's College '61 Memorial Cup team; ntl team Olympic program '63-70; capt. '66; player-coach Japan '71-78, 5 MVP awards; competed 3 IIHF worlds; 1st Cdn to play on 3 Olympic hockey teams; at age 39, 124 days oldest Cdn to play on Olympic hockey team '80; coach Notre Dame Coll. Hounds ntl midget finalists '84; mem. IIHF Hall of Fame; res. Wilcox, Sask.

O'NEILL, Brian (administration); b. 25 Jan 1929, Montreal, Que.; m. Jean Yates; c. Sean, Darcy, Nancy, Patrick, Sandra; Loyola College, BA, McGill, BComm; consultant, former exec.-v-p National Hockey League; hockey, football Loyola College; varsity hockey McGill; junior B Montreal Winged Wheelers; mem. Montreal MAAA, Hockey halls of fame;

res. Montreal, Que.

O'NEILL, John (rowing); b. 1877, Ketch Harbor, N.S., d. 1967, Halifax, N.S.; '04 Halifax harbor sculling title; Middle States regatta singles title '05, '07; US Assn. singles '08; US single sculls '09; mem. NS, Canada's Sports halls of fame.

O'NEILL, Kay (curling); b. 7 Dec 1926, Stratford, Ont.; given name: Catherine; m. Joe O'Neill; c. Michael, Kathy; launched curling career '67; competed 11 Eastern Ont. ladies championships, 10 as skip; skipped 3 EOLCA sr. finals; skipped 2 Lady Tweedsmuir titlists; won Southern Ont. silver tankard '72, runnerup '73; scored 8-ender '73; won EOLCA int. title '85; skipped in 5 Ont. ladies finals; rep. prov. '70 ntls; 3 mixed zone titles, 2 Ont. mixed finals; 3rd ntl mixed finals '76; 2 Kingston CC, 4 Cataraqui G&CC titles; Kingston Kiwanis outstanding achievement award '80; res. Kingston, Ont.

O'NEILL, Tip (baseball); b. 25 May 1858, Woodstock, Ont.; d. 31 Dec 1915, Montreal, Que.; given name: James Edward; restaurateur; early baseball Ont. leagues, pitched amateur ball Harriston, Woodstock, leading latter to ntl title '80; semipro Detroit; major leagues NY Metropolitans, St. Louis, Chicago, Cincinnati as p/of; with John Humphries formed 1st all-Cdn battery '83; 10yr big league record of 16-16 as pitcher and .326ba through 1054 games; 38 World Series games; in '87 compiled all-time record .492 single-season avg. (walks were treated as hits that season), with walks removed avg. recalculated to .435; only batter to lead league in doubles, triples, homers same season; competed Players' League '90; ret'd to Montreal where he played key role in bringing pro baseball to that city; pres. Montreal (EL) team; served as umpire; mem. Windsor-Essex Sports, Cdn Baseball, Canada's Sports halls of fame.

ONESCHUK, Steve (football); b. 22 Nov 1930, St. Catharines, Ont.; d. 20 Apr 1996, Hamilton, Ont.; m. Marilyn McIntosh; c. Douglas, James; UofT, BPHE; HS principal; mem. St. Catharines jr. Athletics ('48 Minto Cup lacrosse finalist), sr. Athletics '49, '50; UofT football all-star 4yrs; Johnny Copp Memorial Trophy '54; George M. Biggs Trophy '53-54; Hamilton (CFL)'55-60, co-capt. 3yrs; 2 East-West Shrine games; EFC, *Globe and Mail* all-star 3 times; led Ticat scorers '57 as hb/pk; 3 Grey Cup finals, 1 winner; asst. coach Ticats '61; mem. UofT Sports Hall of Fame.

OPSAL, Frank (shooting); b. 18 Nov 1928, Vancouver, B.C.; given name: Frank Edward; div.; c. Laura Louise, Frank Matthew, Cynthia Marie; financier; trap and skeet specialist; 6 BC skeet titles; 3 ntl, 10 BC trap titles; twice posted BC record perfect 200x200 trap singles in prov. competition; Western Zone singles trap champion '57; mem. 7 Pacific International Trapshooting Assn. all-star teams; mem. '62 Sports Afield all-American trap team, 4 *Sports Afield* all-Canada trap teams, *Hunting and Fishing in Canada* all-star team '60-64; *Rod and Gun in Canada* '66 all-star team; winner more than 300 tournaments; mem. BC combined trap and skeet all-star teams '54-67; 7 times capt.; capt. ntl team '62 world championships; mem. ntl trap team '56 Olympics; mem. BC Sports Hall of Fame; res. Vancouver, B.C.

O'QUINN, Red (football); b. 7 Sep 1925, Bluett Falls, N.C.; d. 21 Apr 2002, Ottawa, Ont.; given name: John William; m. Dorothy Brown; c. Kathy, John III; Wake Forest, BSc, MA; ret'd marketing manager; all-Southern receiver; pro Chicago (NFL) 2yrs; te Montreal (CFL) '52-59, combined with Sam Etcheverry for 377 receptions, 5679yds, 24tds (from '54 when EFC records were kept); frequent all-East, all-Canadian; honored by Montreal fans with 'day' '59; 3 Grey Cup finals; Grey Cup records '54 with 13 receptions, 316 yds, longest pass and run 90 yds.; best season '55 with 78 receptions; GM Ottawa '62-69, Montreal '70-71; with Etcheverry Montreal sportsman of year for '70 Grey Cup victory; mem. Wake Forest, North Carolina Sports, Canadian Football halls of fame.

ORBAN, Bill (football/hockey/builder/sports medicine); b. 21 Apr 1922, Regina, Sask.; d. 18 Oct 2003, Ottawa, Ont.; given name: William Andrew Robert; m. Virginia Krasuin; c. Bill, Jim, Dan, Jerry, John, Patricia, Victoria; Campion Coll., California (Berkeley), McGill BSc, hon. DSc, Illinois MSc, PhD, Regina hon. LLD; ret'd public servant, scientist; jr. A hockey Regina earned scholarship offer to Berkeley; earned nickname "Wild Bill"; played CFL football Regina, Winnipeg; joined military as PT instructor; with DND developed 5BX fitness program for RCAF; aside from international recognition received no monetary reward for idea which became universally accepted; AD Loyola Coll '49-53; fitness consultant RCAF '56-58; dir. PE USask '58-66; dean human kinetics UofO '66-76, prof. '68-92; researcher Elisabeth Bruyere Centre from '93; wrote, edited several works pertaining to active physical science; fitness pioneer, developer PESE; fellow American Coll. of Sports Medicine, service award; CAHPER honors award; Cdn Assoc. Sports Sciences, Fitness Can. achievement, research awards; mem. Loyola Coll., Sask Sports halls of fame.

O'REE, Willie (hockey); b. 15 Oct 1935, Fredericton, N.B.; given name: William Eldon; NHL dir. Youth development; NHL/USA dir. Diversity Task Force; pro debut Que. Aces '56; became 1st black man to play in NHL 18 Jan '58; played 45 NHL games with Boston '58-61; 13yrs WHL with Los Angeles, San Diego '61-74; New Haven (AHL) '73; San Diego (semipro) '74-76, PHL '79; led WHL scorers '64 with 38 goals; ret'd '79; baseball Fredericton Tigers, Milwaukee Braves tryout '53; subject of TV documentary *Echoes in the Rink* '93; jersey #20 ret'd by San Diego Gulls; hon. doctorate Saint Thomas U '92; Lester Patrick award; mem. San Diego, NB Sports halls of fame; res. La Mesa, Calif.

ORGAN, Gerry (football); b. 4 Dec 1944, Cheltenham, Eng.; m. Lore Oser; c. James, Leah; Guelph, BSc; pastor, ed. dir. Christian Business Ministries; all-Cdn Guelph Gryphons; pk Rough Riders '71-83; 4 EFC, 1 CFL scoring titles; 2nd only to Dave Cutler CFL all-time scoring; 6 FG single game '73, '80; shares CFL record 4 FG single quarter; PB 154 consec. converts '74-79; Schenley outstanding Canadian award '73, runnerup '72; CFL record: 2 tds, 391 converts, 318 field goals, 105 singles, 1462 points; 1st EFC player to pass 1000 pts; sweater #71 ret'd '84; mem. Athletes in Action; mem. Guelph, OUAA football, Ottawa Sports halls of fame; res. King City, Ont.

O'ROURKE, Frank (baseball); b. 28 Nov 1894, Hamilton, Ont.; d. 14 May 1986, Chatham, N.J.; given name: James Francis; nicknamed "Blackie"; spent 70yrs involved with baseball; began ML career at 17 as shortstop with Boston Braves; minor league stints with Bridgeport (Conn. League), Lawrence (New England League), Wilkes-Barre (NY State League) before joining Brooklyn Dodgers as 3b '17-18; back to minors with New London (EL), Birmingham (IL), Toronto (IL) before joining Washington (AL) as ss '20-21; dealt to Red Sox '22; back to Toronto '23-24 then claimed by Detroit to play 2b '24-26; dealt to St. Louis Browns he played 3b '27-31; player/mgr. Milwaukee (AA) '31-33, Montreal (IL) '34, Charlotte (Piedmont) '35, El Dorado (Cotton States) '36-39; minor league managerial record 536-534; scout Cincinnati '41-51, NY Yankees '52-83; ML record: 1131 games, 4069ab, 1032h, 196d, 42t, 15hr, 547r, 430rbi, 101sb, .254ba.

ORR, Bobby (hockey); b. 20 Mar 1948, Parry Sound, Ont.; given name: Robert Gordon; m. Peggy; c. Darren; North Eastern (Boston), hon. doctorate in humanities; hockey exec., player agent, pres. Orr Hockey Group; ss MacTier Ont. provincial champion jr. baseball team '63; Oshawa Generals OHA Jr. A club at 14; led team to '66 OHA title; with help of Alan Eagleson signed reported $70,000 pro contract Boston Sep '66; deal considered cornerstone for NHL Players' Assn.; Calder Memorial Trophy NHL rookie of '67; 2 Art Ross scoring, 3 Hart MVP, 2 Conn Smythe, 8 James Norris Memorial Trophies; 8 times 1st team, once 2nd team all-star def; NHL regular season assist record 102 '70-71; record point total for def 139 same season; playoff assist record 19 '71-72; playoff point record for def same season with 24; regular season goals record for def 46 '74-75; 2 Stanley Cups; played out option, signed by Chicago '76; 6 knee operations led to retirement '78-79; asst. coach Chicago '76-77; MVP Canada Cup '76; NHL record: 657 scheduled games, 270g, 645a, 74 playoff games, 26g, 66a; asst. to NHL pres. '78-82; Lou Marsh, Lionel Conacher trophies '70; *Sport Magazine, Sports Illustrated* athlete-of-yr awards; jersey #4 ret'd by Bruins; Jean Beliveau award '97; named to CHL all-time team '99; co-owner Lowell, Mass., AHL franchise '95; with Mike Bossy, Cassie Campbell operates hockey school; with Don Cherry coach OHL Top Prospects teams; OHL conf. title trophy bears his name; *SI* Cdn athletes of century list; Parry Sound Hall of Fame bears his name; Officer Order of Canada '79; mem. Ont. Sports Legends, Oshawa, Canada's Sports, Hockey halls of fame, Canada's Walk of Fame; res. Weston, Mass.

ORR, Lindsay (karate); b. 27 Oct 1987, Ottawa, Ont.; rhythmic gymnast age 5-9; active in karate, snowboarding, weightlifting, fencing, rugby; 5 months after starting karate at age 9 competed in initial tournament as yellow belt; participant in 3 disciplines, sport karate, kata, weapons; jr. black belt age 12; 1st degree black belt at 13; began competing internationally age 11; competed in WKA worlds from '99; 4 ntl titles; 3 gold, 1 silver, 6 bronze in world competition '99-03; res. Kanata, Ont.

ORSER, Brian (figure skating); b. 18 Dec 1961, Belleville, Ont.; given name: Brian Ernest; bottling co. rep.; began skating age 6; ntl novice singles title '77; jr. '79; Vienna Cup '79; Canada Games gold '75; '80 International Grand Prix title, 2nd Nebelhorn Trophy; ntl senior champion '81-84; '81 St. Ivel singles; gold Skate Canada '83; bronze '83, silver '84 worlds; silver '84 Olympics, Sears Open title '01; fed. govt. excellence award '83, world champion award '84; flag-bearer '88 winter Olympics; *CTV* skating color commentator '93; Officer Order of Canada '88; mem. Cdn Olympic, Canada's Sports, Cdn Figure Skating halls of fame; res. Ottawa, Ont.

ORTON, George (t&f); b. 10 Jan 1873, Strathroy, Ont., d. 25 Jun 1958, Meredith, N.H.; m. Edith Wayne Martin; UofT, BC, Pennsylvania, MA, PhD; educator; middle-, long-distance runner; competing for Toronto Lacrosse Club won both Cdn, US mile titles '92-93; captained Penn track team, mem. NYAC; regarded as most consistent runner and student of the sport; by '00 had accumulated 121 victories, including 15 US titles; although Cdn by birth was invited to join US team for '00 Olympics; as Canada did not compete he entered 2500m steeplechase for US; won gold medal and bronze in 400m hurdles to become 1st Cdn to strike Olympic gold; authored several articles and book on running; dir. Philadelphia Municipal Stadium '26; founded children's sports camp in New Hampshire; mem. UofT, Cdn Olympic, Canada's Sports halls of fame.

ORYSZCYN, Eugene (gymnastics); b. 14 Oct 1914, Lwiw, Poland; d. 17 Aug 1997, Toronto, Ont.; Warsaw, LLD, BPhE; established solid reputation as gymnastics competitor, coach, judge in Europe before emigrating to Canada '60; chief trainer Polish Wlokniar Assn. training camp tech. dir. '49-54; trainer Gymnastic Centre of Technical Training, Krakow '54-59; accepted as international judge '59; judged in 5 world championships, 2 Olympic, 1 PAG, FISU Games; coached Etobicoke Jaycees; chair Ont. judges comm; mem. ntl judges comm.; chair. Ont. coaching comm.; co-author ntl men's technical manual; life mem. Cdn Gymnastics Fed.

OSBALDISTON, Paul (football); b. 27 Apr 1964, Oldham, Eng.; m, Leigh-Anne; Western Montana; punter/kicker; learned fundamentals at Kamloops, B.C., HS; mem. Richmond, B.C., jr. Raiders title teams; drafted by BC '86, dealt to Winnipeg '86, Hamilton '86-03; CFL record (through '03): 289 scheduled games, 648fg, 654cvt, 254s, 2853pts, 1241kickoffs, 70,831yds, 17s, 2100punts, 87,542yds, 84s; 3 Eastern, 1 CFL all-star; set CFL single season points record with 233 '89 (later tied by Dave Ridgway); tied Ridgway with 8FG single game '96; Lew Hayman trophy '90; 7 Easters, 3 CFL outstanding Canadian runnerup '90; Dick Suderman trophy '86 Grey Cup; 4 Grey Cup finals, 2 winners; Tiger-Cats Charlotte Simmons humanitarian award '90; 27 Hamilton club records; nicknamed "Oz"; res. Beamsville, Ont.

OSBORNE, Bob (administration/basketball); b. 10 Apr 1913, Victoria, B.C.; d. 8 May 2003, Vancouver, B.C.; given name: Robert Freer; m. Dorothy Beatrice McRae; c. Wayne McRae (d), Robert David; UBC, BA, BEd, hon LLD UWO, SouthernCal, Oregon State, Washington; ret'd professor; mem. UBC ntl title team '31; played 11yrs Sr. A basketball; mem. '36, coach '48 Olympic basketball teams; mgr. '56 Olympic t&f team; 33yrs UBC professor, dir. school of Phys Ed and Rec.; coached t&f, basketball; coached UBC '48 title basketball team; AGM '54, GM '58 CG, '59, '63 PAG teams; liaison mem. '67, CdM '71, '75 PAG; pres AAUofC '50-51; chair. BC sports council '67-70; pres. Vancouver Field Sports Fed., dir/v-p COA, exec. mem. PAG sports organization, hon. v-p Cdn CG Assn.,

trustee BC Sports Hall of Fame; founding mem. varied BC sport organizations; mem. National Advisory Council on fitness and amateur sport '61-62; dir. Cdn Sports Medicine Council; recipient of myriad of sports related awards; Olympic Order, CAHPER honor award, National Assn. of Cdn Basketball Coaches merit award, Confederation medal '67, Queen's Jubilee medal '77; UBC athletic complex bears his name; mem. Order of Canada, UBC, Cdn Basketball, Cdn Olympic, BC Sports halls of fame.

OSBORNE, Mark (hockey); b. 13 Aug 1961, Toronto, Ont.; solid two-way lw Niagara Falls (capt.) '78-81; AHL Adirondack '81 Calder Cup; IHL Cleveland '95-98; NHL Detroit '81-83, NYR '83-86, '86-87, '94-95, Toronto '86-87, '87-90, '90-92, '92-94, Winnipeg '90-91, '91-92; NHL totals: 919 scheduled games, 212g, 319a, 87 playoff games, 12g, 16a; noted for checking prowess, winning corner battles; nicknamed "Ozzie"; res. Toronto, Ont.

O'SHEA, Michael (football); b. 21 Sep 1970, North Bay, Ont.; m. Richere; c. 2; Guelph; restaurateur; mem. ACTRA, commercial pilot; linebacker; LB/long snapper Guelph '89-92; OUAA, CIAU all-star; Yates Cup title team; OUAA def-player-of-yr award; competed East-West Shrine game; drafted by Edmonton '93; NFL tryout Detroit; CFL Hamilton '95-93, '00, Toronto '96-99, '01-04; 2 Grey Cup winners; 4 div., 1 CFL all-star; CFL outstanding-rookie award, Toronto FRC outstanding Cdn award; res. Milton, Ont.

O'SULLIVAN, Shawn (boxing); b. 9 May 1962, Toronto, Ont.; UofT; '78 ntl jr. light-middleweight (71kg) title; Ont. Golden Gloves '78-79, Ont. jr. 71kg '78, NY State Golden Gloves '79; Ont. Intermediate 71kg titles '80-81; ntl Intermediate 71kg '80; NZ Games 71kg '81; ntl sr. 71kg '81, '83; World Cup '81; silver '80 Finnish International meet; enroute to '81 Cordova Cardin tournament bronze defeated world, Olympic champion; NA light-middleweight title '83; world championship challenge title '83; CG gold '82; silver '84 Olympics; outstanding boxer awards '81 NZ Games, '80 Finnish International; CABA outstanding service award '80, SFC athlete of month (Nov '81) award, fed. govt. world champion award '82-83, Ont. excellence award '83, Viscount Alexander award '81; brief pro career '84-88; launched brief comeback bid '91, again in '96; ret'd for good due to eye injury '97; res. Toronto, Ont.

OTTENBRITE, Anne (swimming); b. 12 May 1966, Whitby, Ont.; m. Marlin Muylaert; c. Cameron, Quinn; Guelph, BComm, USC; coach Pickering SC; breaststroke specialist; USC all-American '85; gold 100m, 200m '81 Canada Games, Canada Cup; 8 ntl sr., 5 Commonwealth, 3 CG records; 3 ntl 100m, 4 200m breaststroke titles; silver 100m, bronze 200m '82 world championships; gold 200m, 4x100 medley, silver 100m '82 GG gold 100m breaststroke, silver 4x100m medley relay '83 PAG gold 200m, silver 100m breaststroke, bronze 4x100 medley relay '84 Olympics; CASA swimmer of '82, Cdn Aquatic Fed. female athlete of '83; hon. capt. '94 CG team; coached Guelph '93-97; OWIAA coach of '96; mem. Order of Canada, Cdn Olympic, Aquatic, Intl Swimming, Canada's Sports halls of fame; res. Port Perry, Ont.

OTTEY, Milt (t&f); b. 29 Dec 1959, Jamaica; Texas; hj specialist; operates Over the Top TC Scarborough; ex-coach Kent State.; mem. Scarborough Optimists TC; ntl team mem. from '78-86; 6 ntl, 1 US, 20 international titles; mem. '79 PAG, '80, '84 Olympic, '82 CG, '83 FISU Games teams; bronze '79 PAG, gold '82 CG; '82 NCAA title; ntl, Commonwealth records; Ont. athlete of '82; *Track and Field News* top hj in world '82; runnerup '82 Norton Crowe award; Jack Davies (top athlete), Cal Bricker (top jumper), Fred Rowell (top field athlete) awards '82; fed. govt. excellence award '83; res. Toronto, Ont.

OTTO, Joel (hockey); b. 29 Oct 1961, Elk River, Minn.; given name: Joel Stuart; Bermidji State; ctr 4yrs Bermidji State; 2 all-American; AHL Moncton; Team USA '84, '90 worlds, '88, '92 Canada Cup, '96 WC gold, '98 Olympics; NHL Calgary '84-95, Philadelphia '95-98; NHL totals: 943 scheduled games, 195g, 313a, 122 playoff games, 27g, 47a; 2 all-star games; 1 Stanley Cup winner; asst. coach UCalgary '99; scout San Diego '02-03; res. Calgary, Alta.

OUELLETTE, Bert (tennis); 17 Aug 1916, Toronto, Ont.; given name: Herbert; ret'd postman, tennis teacher; began teaching tennis following WW2; pro, pres. La Boheme TC; teaching pro Brooklyn Park TC St. Lambert, club dir., shareholder 20yrs; tech. dir. jr. programming QLTF; 20yrs Montreal playgrounds teaching pro; master teacher; tech. advisor Quebec Games; pres. Que. chapter Cdn Assn. of Tennis Instructors and Counselors; taught game to more than 10,000 players; Centennial Medal '67; res. Montreal, Que.

OUELLETTE, Caroline (hockey); b. 25 May 1979, Montréal, Qué.; Concordia BA, Minnesota, National Police Academy Québec; fwd; bronze Team Que. '95 Canada Games, gold '97 jr. ntls; gold, named top forward '99 ntls, silver. MVP '01 ntls; national women's team from '99; 4 world titles; '02 Olympic gold; 2 gold 3-Nations Cup; gold '02, silver '03 4-Nations Cup; mem. Québec fastball team '97 Canada Games; Minnesota-Duluth (WCHA) 2yrs; res. Montréal, Qué.

OUELLETTE, Gerry (shooting); b. 14 Aug 1934, Windsor, Ont.; d. 25 Jun 1975, Windsor, Ont.; given name: Joseph Raymond Gerald; m. Judith; c. Mark; auto tool designer, teacher; ntl junior and cadet service rifle titles '51; Lieut.-Gov.'s medal '52; small-bore prone gold '56 Olympics with perfect 600 score; ntl service pistol title '57; gold, 2 silver '59 PAG, silver '67 PAG; 6th '68 Olympics; mem. 13 ntl Bisley teams; 8 Queen's finals, finished in top 25 12 times; with wife Judy became 1st husband-wife team to represent Canada at Bisley '71; 3 CTR Bisley Agg. titles, 4 DCRA Macdonald Stewart grand aggregate titles; 7th world masters '58; Canada Post honored him with postage stamp '96; mem. Cdn Forces, DCRA, Canada's, Cdn Olympic, Windsor-Essex County Sports halls of fame.

OUELLETTE, Luc (harness racing); b. 22 Jul 1965, St. Augustin, Que.; m. Anita; c. Luc; received grounding in sport with grandfather Gideon and uncle Michel Lachance from age 11; as Michel's own driving career blossomed, Luc earned his A driving license and began campaigning his own 3-horse stable at Monticello Raceway; his stable grew as other owners grew to trust his training/driving skills; operated at Roosevelt '87, made Yonkers home base '88; became full-time catch driver '90 disposing of his

own stable; drove free-for-all pacing sensation Riyadh on '95 five-race win string; HTA driver of '95 title; USHWA Rising Star award; set record 9 wins on single card Yonkers '95; 174 major stakes titles including Little Brown Jug with Million Dollar Cam '02; moved to Milton '03 driving for such trainers as Blair Burgess, Mark Ford, Ned Varty; through '03 6699 victories with purses exceeding $87M; res. Campleville, Ont.

OUELLETTE, Red (hockey/baseball/golf); b. 1 Nov 1938, Grand Falls, N.B.; given name: Gerald Adrian; ret'd Campbellton sports dir.; Jr. B hockey OHA Waterloo Siskins '58-59; 12yrs pro hockey with EPHL Kingston Frontenacs '59-60, Boston NHL '60-61, Buffalo AHL '65-70, capt. Calder Cup champions '70, Omaha CHL '70-71, capt. Adams Cup titlists; prolific scorer; coached Campbellton Tigers to 3 Hardy Cups; amateur baseball Grand Falls Cataracts, NB title '62; mgr/player/coach Cabano Braves, 2 league titles; 6 batting titles '60-68; rookie-of-yr award '59; 3 Que.-NB sr. baseball league MVP/coach-of-yr awards; CHL MVP '71; avid golfer; scored 7th career hole-in-one '04; mem. NB, Campbellton Sports halls of fame; res. Grand Falls, N.B.

OVEREND, Alan (speed skating); b. 22 Dec 1951, Abbotsford, B.C.; given name: Alan Howard; m. Shirley Inkster; c. Andrew, Christopher; UBC, BSc, UAlta., MSc; consulting engineer; 7 BC age-group titles; 9 Alta. sr. titles; ntl jr. '67, intermediate '68 short-track titles; Alta master men's '89 short-track title; exec. officer Calgary SSC '77-81; v-p AASSA '83-88; volunteer asst.-coordinator '88 Olympics; officials asst-co-ordinator '86 NA Short-Track, '87 pre-Olympic World Cup, '88 Olympics; revised ntl officials certification program; developed officials manuals; Alta skater of '80, Calgary SSC master skater of '91-93; res. Calgary, Alta.

OVEREND, Bill (speed skating); b. 28 Oct 1959, Abbotsford, B.C.; given name: William Ernest; m. Patricia; UofOtt, BA, King's College, BJ, UCal, MBA; print media specialist, Parks Canada; 4 BC age-class titles; mem. BC team '74-80, Ontario '80-82; BC team 2 Canada Winter Games; Ottawa, Abbotsford, Mission, Halifax/Dartmouth coach; co-organizer/participant clinics in Hythe, St. Paul, Jasper, Anchorage, Whitehorse, Dawson Creek, Mission, Abbotsford; media liaison short-track '88 Winter Olympics; published World Cup bulletins '96; res. Calgary, Alta.

OVEREND, Clara (speed skating); b. 13 Mar 1926, Kelowna, B.C.; given name: Clara Johanna Spall; m. William Howard Overall; c. Alan Howard, Thomas James, Laura Jean, William Ernest; UBC, UofT; occupational therapist; club coach Dawson Creek '65-72, Mission '72-77, Abbotsford '74-81, Whitehorse '81-85, Team BC '71, '75 Canada Winter Games; Yukon team coach '84 Arctic Winter Games; co-ordinator BC summer skating school; certified coach; founded skating clubs Mission, Abbotsford/Matsqui, Sardis, Maple Ridge, Surrey in BC and Haines Junction, YT; formed Yukon Territorial Speed Skating Assn,; BCSSA exec. '68-80; v-p CASSA '71-76, '82-86; chaired various CASSA comms.'71-86; CASSA pres. '77-81; asst. team mgr. '76 Olympics; CASSA rep. '80 Olympics, World Short Track, '81 NA short-track championships; runnerup Air Canada sport administrator of '82; John Hurdis CASSA outstanding volunteer of '86 award; mem. Cdn Amateur Speed Skating Hall of Fame; res. Salmon Arm, B.C.

OVEREND, Howard (speed skating); b. 27 Feb 1917, Toronto, Ont.; given name: William Howard; m. Clara Johanna Spall; c. Alan Howard, Thomas James, Laura Jean, William Ernest; UofT, BA, BLS; ret'd librarian; creator, 1ˢᵗ editor CASSA's *The Racer* '65; pres. Dawson Creek SSC '65-66, BC SSA '68-69; v-p CASSA '70-72; meet asst.-co-ordinator ntl outdoor championships '66; active in BC Seniors Games t&f; CASF award '68, John Hurdis award '73; mem. Cdn Amateur Speed Skating Hall of Fame; res. Salmon Arm, B.C.

OVEREND, Tom (speed skating); b. 30 Apr 1953, Abbotsford, B.C.; given name: Thomas James; m. Leslie Joy Post; c. Halley, Gregory; UAlta, BPhE, UWO MA, PhD; professor UWO; 1000m gold '71 Canada Winter Games; mem. ntl team '71-78; mem. '76 Olympic, '755, '77 world championship teams; CASSA tech. dir. '78-82; dir. CASSA '86-87, '88-91; *CTV* color commentator '80 Lake Placid Olympics; mem. National Capital Runners Assn.; competed in National Capital Marathon; alumni gold medal as top graduating PE student '78; John Hurdis award '94; OSSA award of merit '93; family recipients Gagne Family award; res. London, Ont.

OVERLAND, Kevin (speed skating); b. 8 Jun 1974, Toronto, Ont.; long-track specialist; mem. ntl team from '92; sister Cindy also ntl team mem.; 2 WC 1000m, 1 500m bronze; set Cdn 1500m record; competed 2 world sprint, 1 single-distance championships; 500m bronze '98 Olympics; mem. Cambridge Sports Hall of Fame; res. Kitchener, Ont./Calgary, Alta.

OWEN, Jon (baseball); b. 19 Jun 1958, Leatherhead, Eng.; m. Cathy Hesselman; c. Jesse, Travis; Southern Miss; Ont. ministry of transportation; pitcher London Majors, Sr. IC '76-97; 994 ip in 166 games, 67 wins, 758k; 4 times league all-star; res. London, Ont.

OXENBURY, Noel (swimming); b. 25 Dec 1918, New Westminster, B.C.; given name: Noel Gertrude; m. James William Morrow; c. Carol Ann; ntl jr. girls 50yd FS record '33, 50yd FS, backstroke, 100yd FS '34, jr. world 50m FS, 150yd IM '34; 6 ntl 100yd backstroke titles; ntl jr. 100yd FS champion '35; mem. '34, '38BEG, '36 Olympic teams; gold 400yd FS relay '38 BEG; NZ 100yd backstroke record '38; ntl records 200yd, 100yd backstroke, world record 300yd medley relay; Pacific Coast international, Pacific Northwest 100yd backstroke champion; Crescent Beach SC coach '42-43, '49-54; coached BC synchronized swim champions Frances Lett, Carol Ann McPherson, ntl champion Allan Brew, jr. diving champion Margaret Mary Leeson; Vancouver Y swim club coach '44-46; founder, coach Kah-Mi Synchronized SC '54-60; UBC synchronized SC coach '57-58; chaperone '60 Olympic team; life mem. Crescent Beach SC, BCSSA; mem. BC Sports, BC Swimming halls of fame; res. Surrey, B.C.

OYE, Moe (judo/coaching); b. 1 Apr 1937, Ucluelet, B.C.; given name: Mamoru; m. Mildred Boberg; c. Steven; UMan BEd; ret'd educator; learned craft from Tommy Mutani at RCMP barracks and YMCA in late '40s; earned coaching reputation with UMan club over 30yrs; coached Olympians Mark Berger, Ewan Beaton, Niki Jenkins and other ntl team members such as Steve Oye, Kevin McIver; played major role in judo growth throughout prov.; mem. Judo Canada, Man. Sports halls of fame; res. Winnipeg, Man.

OYLER, Don (curling); b. 8 Mar 1907, Kentville, N.S.; d. 1990, Kentville, N.S.; given name: Herbert Donald; m. Dorothy Harris; c. Marilyn, John; ret'd fuel merchant; established Brier record skipping '51 ntl men's title winner to 10-0 mark; performance made possible by addition of Newfoundland to Brier field; mem. NS Sports Hall of Fame.

P

PACE, Kate (skiing); b. 13 Feb 1969, North Bay, Ont.; m. Dr. Mark Lindsay; 3rd youngest 10 children; began competing age 6; mem. ntl alpine development group '86-88, ntl team '88-98; won world championship '93; 3 ntl downhill, 1 combined, 1 FIS downhill, 2 slalom, 2 World Cup downhill gold; WC record 2-1-2; plagued by injuries throughout career but rebounded to claim major victories; 5th downhill '94 Olympics; competed '98 Olympics; North Bay athlete of yr '87, '91; Cdn Sports Council athlete of '93; Ont. female athlete of '93; Bobbie Rosenfeld, Velma Springstead, John Semmelink trophies; Kid Sport Ont., ambassador; mem. Cdn Skiing Hall of Fame; res. White Lake, Ont.

PACHAL, Vern (hockey); b. 4 Nov 1930, Yorkton, Sask; given name: Vernon Jack; m. Marilyn Kay Lowenberger; c. Kent, Kurt, Jane, Jill; UAlta, BA, BEd; teacher; Western Cdn jr. scoring champ '50-51; 3 UAlta scoring titles; mem. 3 Western Cdn college title teams; MVP Sask. Sr.HL '62; UAlta athlete-of-'60 award; played pro hockey Syracuse AHL; pitcher Yorkton Man-Sask baseball league '52; chair. Yorkton Sports Hall of Fame; res. Yorkton, Sask.

PACHL, Carole (figure skating); b. 23 Nov 1938, Prague, Czechoslovakia; given name: Carole Jane; div.; c. Natalie, Kim Lerch; public relations; silver medal ntl jr. '51 only to have CFSA retract it and give her bronze instead; bronze '53 national championships; ntl title '55-57, only Que. skater to that time to reign as ntl champion; runnerup NA '57, 3rd '55; 4th worlds '57; 6th '56 Olympics despite suffering broken vertebrae in practice 2 days before competition; rep. Canada 4 times worlds, twice North Americans, once Olympics; ret'd '57; last known res. Montreal, Que.

PADDOCK, John (hockey); b. 9 Jun 1954, Brandon, Man.; m. Jill; c. Jenny, Sally, Anna, Alyssa; coach; rw Brandon (WCJHL) '72-74, Richmond, Springfield, Maine (AHL) '74-84, NHL stints with Washington '75-76, Philadelphia '76-77, '79-80, 82-83, Quebec '80-81; turned to coaching '83-85 Maine (AHL); head coach Hershey (AHL) '85-89, Binghamton '90-91, '02-05; NHL Winnipeg Jets '91-95, Hartford (AHL) '99-02; reached 500 AHL victory playeau '04; asst. Ottawa Senators '05; 3 Calder Cup titles; HN minor pro coach '00; res. Sandow, Sask./Simsbury, Conn.

PAGE, Andrea (t&f); b. 4 Sep 1956, Windsor, Ont.; given name: Andrea Rose; m. David Lee Steen; c. Kory, Jordan, Jacey, Jack; McMaster, BA, MSc, MD, CCFP, Windsor hon LLD; physician; 3 ntl 400m hurdles titles; ntl 400m hurdle record '82; mem. ntl team '81-86; competed '82, '86 CG, '83 PAG, '83 FISU, '84 Olympics (semifinalist); competed '83 Worlds; mem. Windsor/Essex Sports Hall of Fame; res. Tecumseh, Ont.

PAGE, Fred (hockey, administration, builder); b. 29 Sep 1915, Port Arthur, Ont.; d. 23 Dec 1997, Vancouver, B.C.; given name: Frederick; m. Ethel Willianen; c. Elizabeth, Judith; ret'd manager; Port Arthur Jrs. '33-34, Srs. '34-35,

Nipigon Intermediates '35-36; coached, managed teams in Fort William MHA '43-46; exec. mem. FWMHA '47-48, pres. '50-54; dir. Thunder Bay AHA '54-58, pres. '59-62; v-p CAHA '63-65, pres. '66-68, p.-pres to '71; v-p IIHF '69-72; mem. hockey directorate '68, chair. '72 Olympics; pres. Pacific Junior A League '73-78; exec.-mgr. Central Div. BCJHL '81-90; life mem. CAHA, Fort William MHA; Centennial Medal; CAHA, AHAUS, IIHF, FWMHA citations; mem. Hockey, BC Hockey, BC, NWO Sports halls of fame.

PAGE, Percy (coaching); b. 14 May 1887, Rochester, N.Y., d. 2 Mar 1973, Edmonton, Alta; given name: John Percy; m. Maude Roche; c. Patricia; Queen's, hon. LLD UAlta; teacher, politician; coached Edmonton Grads '15-40, team played 522 games, won 502 for 96.2 percentage; attended Olympics Paris '24, Amsterdam '28, Los Angeles '32, Berlin '36, won 27 consecutive exhibition games constituting world championships; coached team to 23 of 24 prov. titles, 15 of 15 Western Canadian titles, 29 of 31 ntl championships games, 18 of 18 Underwood Trophy tournaments vs. US; during team's 25-year existence recorded victory streaks of 147 and 78 games; missed attendance at only 3 games in club's history, once while skipping Alta. rink to prov. title and twice while campaigning politically; MLA (PC) '52-59; Lieut.-Gov. Alta. '59-66; Edmonton recreation facility, high school bear his name; mem. Alta., Canada's Sports, Cdn Basketball, Naismith Memorial Basketball halls of fame.

PAGÉ, Pierre (hockey); b. 30 Apr 1948, St. Hermas, Que.; m. Donna; c. Lauren; hockey coach; Dalhousie, MPHE; coach/lecturer Dalhousie '72; Maritime title '79; consultant Halifax Voyageurs 7yrs; guest coach Cdn Olympic team '80; asst. Team Canada '81, '95; served in several capacities with Calgary (NHL) organization '80-88; GM/coach Denver, Moncton; head coach Minnesota '88-90, Quebec '91-94, Calgary '95-97, Anaheim '97-98; NHL coaching record: 636 scheduled games, 253-301-82; 22 playoff games, 6-16; pro scout Toronto '94-95; res. Tustin, Calif.

PAICE, Terry (wrestling); b. 22 Feb 1953, Whitewood, Sask.; given name: Terrence Ephraham; m. Lidia Pistillo; Lakehead, BPHE; contractor; initial major victory '71 Canada Winter Games; ntl jr. title '73; won '72, '74 CIAU titles; 2 ntl sr. FS, 4 sr. Greco-Roman titles; CG gold '74, PAG bronze '75, 5th '76 Olympics; 2 World Cup bronze; USAAU championship bronze '76; 2 CAWA outstanding wrestler awards; Lakehead athlete of yr '72; Thunder Bay athlete of '74; accumulated 20 gold, 2 silver, 6 bronze in major competitions; 1st Sask. provincial wrestling coach; mem. Saskatchewan Sports, Cdn Amateur Wrestling halls of fame; res. Moose Jaw, Sask.

PAJACZKOWSKI, Tony (football); b. 31 May 1936, Verdun, Que.; regarded short on finesse and polish but long on desire, strength and brute ability as he shone in CFL with Calgary '55-65, Montreal '66-67; played de/gd; 5 all-Western, 1 all-Eastern, 4 all-Canadian gd awards;

1 all-Western de award; Schenley outstanding Canadian award '61, runnerup '60; mem. Cdn Football Hall of Fame; res. Naples, Fla.

PALMASON, Diane (t&f); b. 15 Mar 1938, St. Catharines, Ont.; given name: Florence Diane; div. Hutton; c. Leanne, Craig, Eric, Tracy Hutton; m. Ben Johns; Queen's, BA; sports programmer; 220yds sprinter '54 BEG team; silver marathon World Veterans t&f championships '79; silver 10,000m World Veterans, ntl Masters record 39.10; bronze 5000m World Veterans '79; ntl Masters (40 plus) records, 1500m 4:53, 5000m 18:36.7, 10km 37:38:98; NA, ntl Masters records 800m 2:20.9, marathon 2:49.14; Masters (60-64) WR mile '03; Ont. sports achievement award; asst. ed. *CMA Journal*; res. Engelwood, Colorado

PALMER, Alison (field hockey); b. 21 Aug 1960, Vancouver, B.C.; given name: Alison Gail; UBC; mem. UBC varsity team '80-83, BC -23 team '80, '82; ntl -23 team '82; mem. World Cup silver medal team '83; UBC female-athlete-of-yr co-winner '83; res. Vancouver, B.C.

PALMER, David (baseball); b. 19 Oct 1957, Glens Falls, N.Y.; given name: David William; m. Beverly Richey; c. John Brandon; rhp picked by Montreal '76 amateur draft; ML debut '78; Florida State League record 37 consec. innings without issuing a walk; in ML rookie season set club mark 8 consec. victories; elbow surgery appeared likely to shorten promising career and he saw limited action '81-83; returned to starting rotation '84 and hurled 5-inning perfect game (shortened by rain); ML record: Montreal '78-85, Atlanta '86-87, Philadelphia '88, Detroit, Cleveland '89; 212 games, 64-59, 1085ip, 748k, 434bb, 3.78era; res. Cordova, Tenn.

PALMER, Doug (curling); b. 9 Mar 1944, MacGregor, Man.; given name: Douglas Cyril; m. Margaret Phillips; c. Scott, Christine; insurance adjuster; jr. A, B hockey MacGregor, Winnipeg; sr.A fastball Portage La Prairie, Man., titlists '66; curled in '66 Man. Consols, 9 Ont. Consols (Tankards); winner every major 'spiel title Niagara Peninsula, record 6 Banana Belt titles; only skip to win every event in Whitby Sunlife; OCA Challenge Round winner; res. Welland, Ont.

PALMER, Lillian (t&f); b. 23 Jun 1913, Vancouver, B.C.; given name: Lillian Emily; m. Charles Collingwood Alderson (d); c. Donald, Blake; PS, HS 50, 100yd dash, hj/bj records; as ineligible 15-year-old beat '28 Olympics seniors, set world record 50yd 5.4; mem. '32 Olympic silver medal relay team; with Hilda Strike, 2 British runners beat US gold medal team in post-Olympic match; '32, '34 BC women's 200m title; mem. gold medal relay team BEG; capt. ntl team, 4th 200m, flag bearer '34 Women's World Games; hole-in-one Point Grey Club '72; active in organizing junior women's golf McCleery GC; mem. Cdn Amateur, BC Sports halls of fame; res. Vancouver, B.C.

PALMER, Marilyn (golf); b. 17 Dec 1946, Vancouver, B.C.; m. Don O'Connor; c. Ryan, Sean; UBC, BEd; ret'd teacher; daughter of golf pro she began winning with Interior Ladies crown at 14; BC jr. titles '63-65, '66 ntl ladies' Closed, Open runnerup twice; ntl Open medalist '69, Pacific Northwest Golf Assn. title '73, medal '66, '72; low amateur LPGA Bluegrass, Titleholders; Doherty Cup medallist; qualified 4 US, 1 British Amateurs; with Joycelyne Bourassa NZ Foursomes title '71; with Dale Shaw ntl Foursomes '76, International Fourball '72; mem. 4 ladies' Commonwealth ('79 title), 6 World Cup teams; 1 B.C. jr. team, 33 Alta./BC interprovincial teams; 7 Alta. Western Cdn team; won '79 Sask 8 Alta Amateur, 2 Alta Srs.; 9 BC women's, 1 Cdn women's amateur, close; low Canadian '81 ntl ladies; *Score Magazine* Cdn ladies' amateur golfer '81; 2 Henry Viney awards; 2 Calgary Booster Club honors; hon. life mem. Elks Lodge & GC; CLGA ntl advisory panel from '93; honored as Cdn outstanding female amateur golfer '81, top Cdn female sr. golfer '97; mem. Marine Drive Legends, Kamloops Sports, Cdn, BC Golf halls of fame; res. Calgary, Alta.

PALMER, Sue (cycling); b. 27 Jan 1967, Collingwood, Ont.; m. Christopher Komar; c. Trinity; McMaster BPHE, Windsor BEd; road racing specialist; began cycling as XC ski training in HS and became highly competitive at university; following 3yrs on ntl team almost ret'd after broke leg '91 criterium race but returned to take silver in individual road race, team time trial gold '92-93 ntl championships; competed '94-95 Tour de France, '94, '02 (silver) CG, '96 Olympic Games, '00, '01 worlds; ntl road racing title '96; Golden Horseshoe athlete of '02; 24+ mountain competition victories; res. Hamilton, Ont.

PANASIK, Bob (golf); b. 20 Oct 1941, Windsor, Ont; div. Dolores; c. Melissa; pro golfer; Ont. jr., best ball, ntl jr. '58, at 15 youngest to make a cut on PGA tour at '57 Cdn Open; Ont. amateur '59, Ont. jr. '60; pro '60; 2 Brooks Bursary awards; pro from '59; Que. Open '74, Alta. Open '74-75, Sask. Open '74, Nfld. Open '73, Atlantic Open '75, NO PGA '66, CPGA '72-73, Cdn Tar Sands tournament of champions '76, Cdn TPC, Man Open '86; '88-89 CPGA Winter Tour; top money winner CPGA Winter Tour '89; Peter Jackson Cup order of merit '75; limited success 1 yr US pro tour; 3 CPGA Seniors titles; mem. World Cup team '72-74; ntl golfer of '74; mem. Windsor/Essex Sports Hall of Fame; res. Tecumseh, Ont.

PANASIS, Rita (basketball/softball); b. 29 Mar 1921, Vancouver, B.C.; d. 17 Mar 2003, Coquitlam, B.C.; given name: Marietta; m. Samuel William Bell; c. Suzanne, Richard; Duffus Business School; mem. BC Intermediate A basketball title team '38-39, Senior B '39-40, Senior A '40-41; mem. ntl Senior A champion Hedlunds '42-46, Nut House '47, Eilers '53-54; 11 provincial, 8 ntl title teams; offer from Abe Saperstein to play with ladies' pro team; ctr Percy Page personal all-Canadian all-star team; mem. several Vancouver city softball title teams; ntl team '44 World amateur softball championships; mem. '46 BC champion Ballards team; '49 Western Cdn champion Western Mutual team; rejected pro offers Chicago Bluebird team; mem. Eilers '55 PAG team but didn't compete due to injury; mem. Cdn Basketball, BC, Maple Ridge Sports halls of fame.

PANGMAN, Arthur (skiing); b. 1 Jul 1905, Montreal, Que.; d. 25 Jun 1996, Senneville, Que.; given name: Arthur Henry; m. Lois Martin; c. Peter, Jill; McGill, BSc; ret'd engineer; mem. McGill ski team; intercollegiate snowshoe title '28; mem. McGill rowing team Cdn Henley 140lb 4s, 8s titlists '29; mem. '32 Olympic team; mgr., coach, spare

'36 Olympic ski team; mem. McGill '32 international intercollegiate relay title team; Que. Kandahar downhill title '32; chair. Laurentian Ski Zone '30-32; v-p CSA '36-37; founder, later pres., Red Birds SC '28; Mt. Tremblant peak bears his name; mem. Laurentian, Cdn Skiing halls of fame.

PANTING, Bill (speed skating); b. 6 Apr 1925, Winnipeg, Man.; given name: Arthur William; ntl jr. records '41; ntl outdoor champion '51; 1ˢᵗ commissioner CASA; mem. CASA rules comm.; asst. coach ntl team '73; ISU referee; exec. mem. Winnipeg Speed Skating Club; mem. Man. Centennial Commission; mem. Cdn Speed Skating Hall of Fame; res. Winnipeg, Man.

PAOPAO, Joe (football, coaching); b. 30 Jun 1955, Honolulu, Hawaii; m. Dottie; c. Tyler, Andrew, Kristin, Carson; Mira Costa Jr. Coll, Long Beach State; football coach; from '78 QB 11 seasons CFL, BC Lions, Saskatchewan, Ottawa, Winnipeg; 1721 completions in 3008 attempts for 22,474yds, 117tds; turned to coaching '89 BC before returning at QB Lions '90; returned to coaching with BC '91-93, Edmonton '94-95; BC head coach '96; asst. Winnipeg '97, San Francisco (XFL) '98, BC '99-00; head coach Ottawa Renegades '02-04; coack/GM '05; nicknamed "Throwin' Samoan"; set CFL record with 18 consec. completions '79; res. Ottawa, Ont.

PAPASIDERIS, Peter (shooting); b. 19 Feb 1935, Greece; m. Lydia; c. Dimitrios, Diane; hair stylist; began shooting '67 winning 3 medals in first shoot; won numerous BC, Sask., Alta., provincial championships; City of Victoria medal; City of Ottawa gold watch (subsequently stolen); Hayhurst, Patron's DCRA matches; Sask. Lieut.-Gov.'s, grand aggregate; 3 Alta. Lieut.-Gov.'s, 2 ISU titles; tied for St. George's medal Bisley, losing shootoff; Bisley Queen's Silver medal '83, runnerup '84; qualified for 13 Cdn Bisley, 3 Cdn Palma teams; 2 Des Burke awards; Booster Club achievement award; Alta., Calgary achievement awards; mem. DCRA Hall of Fame; res. Calgary, Alta.

PAPROSKI, Steve (football); b. 23 Sep 1928, Lwow, Poland; d. 8 Dec 1993, Smiths Falls, Ont.; given name: Steven Eugene; m. Mary Elizabeth Coburn; c. Patrick Steven, Peter John, Annamarie, Alexandra, Elizabeth; North Dakota, Arizona, Banff School of Advanced Management; sales mgr., politician; college football ND, Arizona; pro Edmonton '49-54; Alta. HS heavyweight wrestling champion '43, runnerup ntl championship '43-44; MP (PC) '68-93; min. of state for multiculturism, fitness and amateur sport in Joe Clark government.

PARÉ, Mark (officiating/hockey); b. 26 Jul 1957, Windsor, Ont.; m. Debbie Glos; c. 2 daughters, 1 son; moved through Windsor minor hockey to OHA Major Jr. A (as referee) 2yrs; initial NHL game as linesman 11 Oct '79; made NHL all-star game debut '92; NHL record through '03: 1721 scheduled, 25 playoff games as linesman; res. Windsor, Ont.

PARENT, Bernie (hockey); b. 3 Apr 1945, Montreal, Que.; given name: Bernard Marcel; m. Carol Wilson; c. Chuck, Bernie, Kim; company v-p, ex-hockey coach; jr. Niagara Falls Flyers; goalie Boston '65-67, Philadelphia '67-71, '73-79, Toronto '71-72, Philadelphia (WHA) '72-73; NHL

record: 608 scheduled games, 1493ga, 55so, 2.55ga avg., 71 playoff games, 174ga, 6so, 2.43ga avg.; WHA record: 63 games, 220ga, 2so, 3.61ga avg.; won/shared 2 Vezina Trophies; 2 Conn Smythe Trophies; twice 1ˢᵗ team all-star; mem. 2 Stanley Cup winners; playing career terminated 17 Feb '79 when Ranger defenceman Jimmy Watson's stick struck him in right eye; goaltending coach Philadelphia '82-96; jersey #1 ret'd by Flyers; named to CHL all-time team '99; mem. Board of Advisors Schcio Eye Institute; mem. Flyers, Hockey halls of fame; res. Cherry Hill, N.J.

PARENTI, Eddie (swimming); b. 26 Jun 1971, Montreal, Que.; m. Paige Gordon; Stanford; junior engineer; 200m, 400m freestyle, 100m, 200m butterfly specialist; mem. ntl team '90-97, 4yrs team capt.; 7 ntl titles; ntl record 4x200m FS relay 7:22.74 set in '91; silver 4x200 FS relay '89 Pan-Pacifics; silver 4x200 FS relay '90 CG; silver 4x50m FS relay '91 Worlds; bronze 4x200m FS relay '91 Pan-Pacifics; bronze 4x100m medley relay '95 PAG; mem. '92, '96 Olympic teams, '94 CG; ret'd from competition '97; mem. Nepean Sports Wall of Fame; res. West Vancouver, B.C.

PARFITT, Adam (rowing); b. 22 Apr 1974, Victoria, B.C.; UVic; Victoria City RC mgr.; began rowing in high school '89; mem. ntl team '94-00; 2 ntl HS, 1 US 2 ntl junior, 2 ntl senior, 1 International regatta golds; 2 silver '95 PAG; competed '96, '00 Olympics; Rowing Canada jr sculler of '91; coach VCRC jrs. '97-99; res. Victoria B.C.

PARK, Brad (hockey); b. 6 Jul 1948, Toronto, Ont.; given name: Douglas Bradford; m. Gerry George; c. Jamie, Rob, Alexa, Kelly, Ben; consultant, partner Amesbury Sports Park; juvenile Scarborough Lions; jr. Toronto Marlboros; 1ˢᵗ choice NYR '66 amateur draft; denceman Buffalo (AHL) '68, Rangers '68-75, Boston '75-83, Detroit '83-85; mem. Team Canada '72; 5 times 1ˢᵗ team, 2 2ⁿᵈ team all-star; NHL record: 1113 scheduled games, 213g, 683a, 158 playoff games, 35g, 90a; NHL career regular season assist record for def; TV hockey broadcaster '85; coach Detroit '85-86; '83 Charlie Conacher Memorial Trophy, '84 Bill Masterton Trophy; mem. Hockey Hall of Fame; res. Lynnfield, Mass.

PARKER, Jackie (football); b. 1 Jan 1932, Knoxville, Tenn.; given name: John Dickerson; m. Peggy; c. Jere Jo, Peggy Mae, Jack Jr.; Mississippi State; ret'd football coach; all-American, '52-53 Southeastern Conference MVP, scoring record 120 points '52; qb/hb/wr/pk/p Eskimos '54-62; 3 Grey Cup titles; Argos '63-65; coach Toronto Rifles Continental League '66; Lions' asst. '68, head coach '69, GM '70-75; head coach Eskimos '83-87; 7 Jeff Nicklin Memorial Trophies (WFC MVP), 3 times WFC, CFL all-star; CFL record: 88tds, 103c, 40fg, 19s, 750 points, 5210yds rushing, 135 receptions 2308yds, 2061 passes, 1089 completions, 16,476yds, 88tds; CFL player of quarter-century; mem. Alta., Canada's Sports, Football, Edmonton, Mississippi halls, Eskimos wall of fame; res. Edmonton, Alta.

PARKER, James (football); b. 1 Jan 1958, Philadelphia, Pa.; Wake Forest; outside linebacker, def. end; all-conf all-American, alumni player of yr award; nose guard '76 Blue-Gray game; CFL Edmonton '80-84, B.C. '84-89, Toronto '90-91; 6 Western all-star, 5 CFL all-star; 4 CFL

QB sacks titles; single season sack record 26.5 '84; 139,5 career sacks; 3 Norm Fieldgate trophies; 3 Schenley def. player of yr. Awards; Grey Cup def. player '85; competed 5 Grey Cup finals, 4 winners; nicknamed "Quick"; mem. Cdn Football Hall of Fame; res. Burnaby, B.C.

PARKER, Ken (builder); b. 22 Jun 1941, Armstrong, Ont.; m. Diane; company owner; active mem. Ottawa sports community from '74; founding mem./ex-race dir. Ntl Capital Marathon, Nordion 10k road races (Ntl Capital Race Weekend); host 2 Olympic, 1 CG trials; operated monthly marathon information clinics; NCM 1st NA race to use on-line computers for race timing; strong promoter women's running; brought both Bonnie Bell, Avon women's races to Ottawa; race dir. many running events including '81 Avon Intl worlds focusing world-wide attention on Ottawa; race dir. CHEZ/Osaga 10k and variety lesser events; founding coach (East) Ottawa Lions TC '75-81; founded OAC racing team, a women's road racing and triathlon club, continues to coach there; displayed versatility coaching youths 9-17 in Gloucester Basketball Assn.; won Ont, silver; as athlete competed in marathons 13yrs with PB 2hrs, 42min "81 NCM; several duathlons including '99 world age group championships; ran leg of '76 Olympic torch relay; operates not-for-profit web site (Runner's Web); throughout career played key role in fund-raising to support amateur athletes; his company SIRIUS sponsors triathlete Sharon Donnelly, midget boys basketball, cross-country ski event, school scholarship programs; city lifeguard program, atom hockey teams; active lobbyist for indoor training facility; involved with "See You in Athens" fundraiser to support Cdn Olympians; Queen's Jubilee medal; ACT sports volunteer of '02; res. Ottawa, Ont.

PARKIN, Lorne (football); b. 3 Oct 1919, Toronto, Ont.; m. Ella Grace; c. John, Robert; ret'd policeman; Toronto Indians '47, Toronto Indians Beaches ORFU '48; pro Argos '49-55; mem. '50, '52 Grey Cup winners; coached Toronto police tug-of-war team to NA titles '60-73; res. Toronto, Ont.

PARKS, Arnold (shooting); b. 14 Jun 1930, Saint John, N.B.; given name: Alfred Arnold; m. Zola Sypher; c. Victoria, Sonya Jane; certified general accountant; ntl cadet small-bore outdoor title '48; 4 NB Prince of Wales, Governor's Cups; NB, Atlantic Rifle championships; mem. 10 Bisley teams, adjutant '68 team, 3 Palma teams, 19 NB inter-Maritime, coach 3 times, titles twice; mem. 22 NB DCRA Ottawa shoot teams; won Gov.-Gen.'s match twice; Bisley Century match '67, Clock Tower '69, St. George's Silver Cross '73, Queen's prize '68, in Queen's Hundred 5 times; mem. several Kolapore, MacKinnon match teams, several winners; NB indoor small-bore champion several times; DCRA small-bore title '70; life mem. DCRA, NBRA; pres. NBRA, Saint John Garrison Military Rifle Assn.; various exec. roles DCRA, NBRA; coached juniors, cadets; mem. DCRA Cdn Forces, NB Sports halls of fame; res. Saint John, N.B.

PARNELL, Bill (t&f); b. 14 Feb 1928, Vancouver, B.C.; given name: Comer William; m. Joan Mary; c. John, Leslie, Keith, Jacquelyn; Washington State, BSc, BPhE, UBC, teacher's certificate; educator; all-American WSU miler; mem. '48, '52 Olympic, '50, '54 BEG; gold with 4:11 mile

'50 games, capt. '52, '54 teams; several ntl titles, records; flag-bearer '52 summer Olympics; Norton Crowe Memorial Award, Canada's male athlete of '49; mem. Cdn Olympic, BC Sports halls of fame; res. N. Vancouver, B.C.

PARNELL, Paul (lacrosse); b. 28 Mar 1938, Peterborough, Ont.; given name: Paul Arthur; m. Joan Cundell; c. Randy, Penny; captain fire prevention office; int. football Peterborough '58-59, Victoria Drakes '60; Jr. B hockey Peterborough, int. Lakefield, Victoria, New Westminster; sr. lacrosse Peterborough '58-59, Victoria '60, New Westminster '61-75; mem. 9 Mann Cup, 2 World championship finals; record 441 league games, record 912 goals, 865 assists; league scoring title '65; twice Mann Cup MVP (Mike Kelly medal); 13 times all-star, 7 1st team; Commission Trophy '65 league MVP; Ellison Trophy '72 playoff MVP; playing-coach New Westminster Salmonbellies '71-72; jr. Salmonbellies '77; chair, treas. Canadian Lacrosse Hall of Fame '81-85; commissioner WLA '83-86; mem. Canadian Lacrosse, Peterborough Sports halls of fame; res. New Westminster, B.C.

PARRIS-WASHINGTON, Christine (softball); b. 23 Jan 1967, Truro, N.S.; given name: Christine Parris; m. Robert Washington; Crowder Jr. Coll, UNLV BSc; asst. coach Bowling Green, ex-asst. UNLV; 3 NCAA all-American; Big West Conf. player of '91; 3b/ss '90, '94 world championships, '91 (silver) PAG, '94 South Pacific Classic; with Redding Rebels 4 Canada Cup championships, 2 titles, '96 Olympics; 3 NCAA all-American awards; 3 NCAA all-American awards; 3 ASA ntl titles; 2 ASA all-American awards; Canada Cup batting title '93, MVP award '96; Big West Conf. player of '91; res. Bowling Green, Ohio

PARRISH, Larry (baseball); b. 10 Nov 1953, Winter Haven, Fla.; given name: Larry Alton; m. Jennifer Leigh Wetzel; c. Jessica, Joshua, Amanda; baseball exec.; Seminole Jr. Coll; all-conf. baseball/basketball Haines City HS '71; baseball coach; primarily 3b but also played other infield/outfield positions; swung with such force batting helmet fell off his head and he would catch it; Montreal '74-81, Texas '82-88, Boston '88; ML record: 1891g, 6792ab, 850r, 1789h, 360 db, 33tr, 256 hr, 992rbi, 30sb, .263ba; 2 seasons in Japan leading in home runs with 42 '89; coached/managed Detroit farm system '92-96; bench-coach Detroit '97-98, mgr. '98-99; guided Niagara Falls to NY-Penn title '93, Jacksonville to AA title '96; 2 NL all-star teams; Expos player of '79; hit 3 grand slams in single week '82; 4 career 3-homer games; mem. Montreal Expos Hall of Fame; res. Haines City, Fla.

PARRY, Jack (all-around); b. 8 Jun 1922, Windsor, Ont.; d. 14 Dec 1990, Chatham, Ont.; given name: John Clayton; m. Anne Huffman; c. Jann, Jay, Jill, Jon; UWO., MD; anaesthesiologist; Windsor Forster CI, WOSSA, Ont. records in sprints, field events (lj/tj) several years; 2yrs Windsor all-city football; '42 Grey Cup with Toronto Hurricanes; UWO Mustangs football MVP, t&f team '47-49; mem. Cdn record relay team '47; mem. '48 Olympic team but injury kept him from competing; ntl 100m, 200m champion '48; outfielder London Majors (Sr. IC), sr. baseball Windsor, signed by Cleveland (AL) but WW2 interfered; served as bomber pilot RCAF; awarded DFC; John Davies trophy Canada's top track athlete '48, Dr. Claude Brown

Memorial trophy, George McCullogh trophy; mem. UWO W-Club, Windsor-Essex Sports halls of fame.

PART, John (darts); b. 29 Jun 1966, North York, Ont.; given name: John Eric; div. Holly Jean Boynton; Upper Canada Coll, UofT; ex-real estate broker, pro darts player; 3 Ont, 2 ntl singles, 4 Hamilton Power Point Open, 2 Cleveland Extravaganza, 1 Chicago Windy City Open, Laurel (UK) Open Southwest Regional titles; Embassy world professional title '94, finalist '01; world title '03; World Cup international open title '95, '03; with Carl Mercer of Regina won '93 World Cup pairs, '94 Pacific Cup pairs; with Patricia Farrell '94 Pacific Cup mixed pairs; with Doug Scanlon 2, John Verwey 1 ntl pairs titles; ranked #1 in Canada from '93; nicknamed "Darth Maple"; *BBC* darts commentator; res. Oshawa, Ont.

PASCAL, Jean (boxing); b. 28 Oct 1982, Port-au-Prince, Haiti; CollPge Ahuntsic police tech student; 75 kg; started boxing age 14; '98 cadet ntl champion; '99-00 int. ntl titles; 4 ntl sr. titles; gold '99 Canada Games; gold '01 Francophonie Games, 5th '01 worlds; gold '02 CG; bronze '03 PAG; gold '03 Multi-Nations Tournament, Ireland; bronze '03 Copenhagen Cup; in 113 amateur bouts 98-15 record (to '04); 3 Boxing Canada boxer-of-yr awards; res. Laval, Qué.

PASHBY, Tom (builder); b.23 Mar 1915, Toronto, Ont; given name: Thomas Joseph; m. Helen Audrey Verna Christie (d); c. William Thomas, Robert Christie, Jane Elizabeth; UToronto, MD, CRCS; ophthamologist; coached house league hockey, MTHL, baseball teams in Leaside many years; served as medical officer RCAF WW2; served on staff Toronto Western Hospital, Hospital for Sick Children, Scarborough Centenary Hospital; pioneered facial protectors and lobbied CAHA to make them mandatory; chaired comm. to set standards for hockey, lacrosse facial equipment; key role in making helmets mandatory in hockey; served on comm. to prevent spinal cord injuries and concussions; considered authority in sports medicine; respected at every level of sport; created eye protection for racquet sports; Dr. Tom Pashby sports safety fund sponsored helmets for cyclists; CSA award of Merit, John Jenkins award; COS eye safety award; OHA distinguished service award; CAHA Gordon Juckes award; Toronto Civic award of merit; East York Bulldog award; Ont. Sports citation; Cdn Commerative award; Canada sports safety award; Standard Council of Can. J.P. Carriere award; American Academy Ophthalmology honor award; Toronto Ophthamological sports prevention award; Ont. Hockey development center recognition award; Cdn Academy of sports medicine award; Academy of medicine Toronto award; Cdn orthopaedic Assn. Award; MTHL Chamandy award; Hockey News man of yr '90; Ont, Recreation Facilities Assn, award of merit; Cdn delegate to ISO tech comm. for hockey equipment; dir. US Institute for preventitive sports medicine; mem. Cdn Standards Assn sports comm.; mem. Cdn Ophthalmological Society; sr. mem. CMA; mem. American Academy of Ophthalmological ; mem. Order of Canada; Canada's Sports Hall of Fame; res. Toronto, Ont.

PASQUALE, Eli (basketball); b. 24 Aug 1960, Sudbury, Ont.; m. Karen Graham; c. Isiah, Emanuel; UVic, BA; auto sales mgr., sports camp operator; gd 5 UVic CIAU title teams; mem. ntl team '78-92, '97; competed 3 FISU, 2 Pan-Am, 4 world championships, 2 Olympic Games teams; gold '82 worlds fair tournament, '83 FISU Games; bronze '85 FISU Games; CIAU player of '82-83; NBA tryout Seattle (NBA) '84, Chicago '85; CIAU 2 MVP Jack Donohue trophies, 1 Mike Moser Memorial trophy; 2 CIAU all-Cdn; played pro ball in Argentina, Germany, Switzerland; BC athlete of '82; ntl sports excellence award '84; Victoria athlete of decade ('80-90); coaching, camps in 20 cities; mem. Cdn Basketball Hall of Fame; res. Victoria, B.C.

PASSAGLIA, Lui (football); b. 7 Jun 1954, Vancouver, B.C.; m. Loa; c. Lea, Loren; SFU, BA; dir. BC Lions community relations; qb/rcvr SFU, Dist. 1, all-Northwest all-star twice; top Lions draft '76; played with BC '76-00; CFL record: 408gp, 875fg, 1045cvts, 321s, 3991pts, 133,826 punting yds; among most consistent place kickers in CFL history; only 2 misses in 1047 career convert tries, converting 511 consecutively in one stretch; CFL record 90.9 fg success rate; scored 2 career tds including 1 in final scheduled game; 6 WFC, 3 all-CFL; 3 CFL scoring titles; 12 CFL records; all-time CFL leader in 6 categories; 5 Grey Cup finals, 2 winners; kicked winning FG '94, '00 Grey Cup games; 2 Dick Suderman trophies; mem. Cdn Ftbll, SFU Sports halls of fame; res. Vancouver, B.C.

PATAKY, Bill (basketball); b. 12 May 1930, Windsor, Ont.; given name: William Andrew; m. Joan Monaghan; c. Maureen, Joanne, Monica, Margaret, Jane; Windsor, UWO, OCE; ret'd educator; Windsor all-city football backfielder, basketball fwd '48-49; ss Windsor jr. Ont. finalist '48-49; hb Assumption College (Windsor) jr. ORFU all-Ont. finalist; varsity basketball Assumption Coll. '49-50; ss Frood Mine team Sudbury '51; UWO Mustangs basketball all-star '51-52; mem. Tillsonburg Livingstons '52 Olympic basketball team; football Sarnia Imperials ORFU '53; sr. basketball '53-65 Sarnia-Port Huron area; res. Sarnia, Ont.

PATERSON, Gord (football/curling); b. 7 Sep 1950, Winnipeg, Man.; m. Judy; c. Lyndsey; UMan; stockbroker; te Winnipeg '74-79, Hamilton '79-81; WFC Schenley top Canadian candidate '77; 2nd Man. entry '83 Brier; res. Winnipeg, Man.

PATON, Brian (softball); b. 17 Sep 1959, Woodstock, Ont.; given name: Brian Kenneth; m. Susanne Michelle; c. Lindsay, Bryan, Brittany, Jordan, Brendan; self-employed printer; played AHL hockey Detroit organization; mem. Team Canada fastball '87-99; mem. ISC world, ntl champion Toronto Gators '93, '95; PAG gold '87, '91, '95, '99; mem. Green Bay All-Car '97, Tampa Bay (ISC Worlds) '98, Ballston Lake '99; res. Woodstock, Ont.

PATON, Jim (shooting); b. 24 May 1957, Newcastle, N.B.; given name: James Andrew MacMillan; m. Anna Huis; UVic, BA; liquor store mgr. BC govt.; ranked among nation's top full-bore marksmen; DCRA Gov.-Gen.'s trophy triumphs '86, '95, '97, '99; Australian grand aggregate '88; mem. 3 Palma teams; mem. Cdn Bisley team 14 consec. yrs from '85; gold, silver '98 CG; once runnerup DCRA grand agg.; BC target rifle title '95; '97 Commonwealth championships individual gold; Bisley Aggregate (Cdn Match Rifle) title '99; 3 ISU match titles; 2 President's, Short Range Agg., Gov.-Gen.'s qualifier match, 1 Letson match titles; Bisley

George's Cross silver, Century, Wimbledon match titles; mem DCRA Hall of Fame; res. White Rock, B.C.

PATRICK, Frank (hockey); b. 23 Dec 1885, Ottawa, Ont., d. 29 Jun 1960, Vancouver, B.C.; m. Catherine Porter; c. Joseph, Gloria, Frances; McGill; hockey exec.; refereed MSL at 18, Stanley Cup playoffs at 20; def Montreal Victorias (CAHL) '04, Westmount (CAHL) '05, Montreal Victorias (ECAHA) '08, Renfrew Millionaires (NHA) '10, Vancouver Millionaires (PCHA) '12-18, Vancouver Millionaires (WCHL) '25, coach Bruins '34-36; created Vancouver Millionaires, owner, coach, mgr.-capt. '15 Stanley Cup team; mgr. Canadiens; innovative genius put 22 pieces of legislation on NHL rule books, including origination of blue line; with brother Lester established Pacific Coast League, later sold entire league to eastern interests; managing-dir. NHL; mem. BC Hockey, Sports, Hockey halls of fame.

PATRICK, James (hockey); b. 14 Jun 1963, Winnipeg, Man.; given name: James Allan; m. Deborah Vervoort; c. Brandon, Quinn; U North Dakota; top defenceman award St. James Canadians at 14, winning Kelly Cup Western Canada title; top defenceman '80 Notre Dame Air Canada Cup midget champs; outstanding Cdn Jr. B player (Chapstick award) '81 Prince Albert Centennial Cup champs; gold Team Canada '82 world juniors; rookie of yr, all-star '82 UND NCAA title team; bronze Team Canada '83 world jrs; U.S. college all-American; gold Team Canada '84, '87 Canada Cup, '03 worlds; mem. Cdn Olympic team '84; NHL NY Rangers '84-93, Hartford '93-94, Calgary '94-98, Buffalo '98-04; NHL record: (through '04) 1280 scheduled games, 149g, 490a, 117 playoff games, 6g, 32a; res. Williamsville, N.Y.

PATRICK, Lester (hockey); b. 31 Dec 1883, Drummondville, Que.; d. 1 Jun 1960, Victoria, B.C.; m. Grace Victoria Linn; c. Lynn, Murray; McGill; hockey exec.; def Brandon, Man. '03, Westmount (CAHL) '05, Montreal Wanderers (ECAHA) '06-07, capt. 2 Stanley Cup winners; capt. Nelson, B.C., '08-09; Renfrew Millionaires '10; formed Victoria Aristocrats, helped establish Pacific Coast League, organized clubs and built artifical ice arenas in all league centres; played Victoria '12-16, '19-26, Spokane '17, Seattle '18; NYR mgr.-coach, player '26-39, GM through '46; 7 times NHL all-star coach; with Aristocrats defeated Que. for '13 world title although Stanley Cup not at stake; won Stanley Cup '24 with Victoria Cougars ; 3 Stanley Cups Rangers; trophy in his memory for service to US hockey from '66; division of NHL given his name '74; nicknamed "Silver Fox"; mem. BC Hockey, BC, Greater Victoria Sports, Hockey halls of fame.

PATRICK, Lynn (hockey); b. 3 Feb 1912, Victoria B.C.; d. 26 Jan 1980, St. Louis, Mo.; given name: Joseph Lynn; div. Dorothy Davis, m. Bernice Pachal (d.); c. Lester Lee, Craig, Karen, Glenn, Dean; hockey exec.; mem. ntl champion Blue Ribbons basketball team, BC Reps rugby team, Winnipeg Blue Bombers; NYR '35-43, '45-46; 1st team all-star '42; mem. '40 Stanley Cup winner; coached Rangers '50 Stanley Cup finals, Boston '50-53, coach-GM to '65; coach-GM St. Louis '66; exec. v-p '67-77; mem. B C Hockey, BC, Greater Victoria Sports, Hockey halls of fame.

PATRICK, Muzz (hockey); b. 28 Jun 1915, Victoria, B.C.; d. 23 Jul 1998, Riverside, Conn; given name: Frederick Murray; m. Jessie Farr; c. Lynda, Richard, Paul, Lori; def NYR '37-41, '45-46; coach Rangers '54-55, GM '55-64, later v-p; ret'd from hockey scene '73; mem. Victoria Dominoes ntl basketball champions; ntl amateur heavyweight boxing title '36; with Art Coulter became one of Rangers' toughest defensive units; following WW2 US army duty, coached, managed in minors; competing for Victoria Y under coach Archie MacKinnon won city interscholastic mile, half-mile same day; mem. BC Hockey, BC, Greater Victoria Sports Hall of Fame.

PATRICK, Steve Jr. (hockey); b. 4 Feb 1961, Winnipeg, Man.; given name: Stephen Gary; m. Kerry Chornomen; c. Nolan, Madison, Amy; UWinnipeg; real estate co. CEO; excelled in baseball, basketball, volleyball, hockey; hockey with Woodhaven Community Club ages 7-10; 36 goals in 30 games St. James AAA '75-76; joined St. James jrs at 15 winning MVP award; MJHL all-star '78; mem. Brandon Wheat Kings Memorial Cup finalists '79; mem. Brandon '79-80; 1st round pick NHL Buffalo Sabres '80; NHL Buffalo, NYR, Quebec '81-86; Rochester (AHL); NHL record: 250 scheduled games, 40g, 68a, 12 playoff games, 0g, 1a; res. Winnipeg, Man.

PATRICK, Steve Sr. (football); b. 24 Mar 1932, Glenella, Man.; given name: Stephen Clifford; m. Marjorie June Mathieson; c. Kim, Carolyn, Sandra, Stephen, James, Lisa, Tara; pres. Patrick Realty/Insurance; mg Winnipeg '52-64; 290 CFL games; twice all-star, Bombers' top lineman '58, Schenley best Cdn nominee '59; twice CFL all-star game participant; most valuable Cdn '57; captained Bombers '61-64; mem. 6 Grey Cup , 4 winners; competed briefly on pro wrestling circuit having trained at Y under famed Stu Hart; mem. Man. legislature (Lib.) '62-77; regarded as champion of all resolution makers; sons James, Steve Jr. both played in NHL; mem. Man. Sports Hall of Fame; res. Winnipeg, Man.

PATTEMORE, Claude (golf); b. 1927 Athens, Ont.; d. 24 Apr 2004, Hamilton, Ont.; dynamite explosion on road construction project at 21 cost him his eyesight; following rehab in Toronto, Hamilton took job with CNIB; 3yrs after accident was introduced to golf and following yr claimed ntl title; dominated visually impaired golf scene for 2 decades winning '63 U.S., Intl blind golf titles; 12 Cdn, 14 Ont. blind golf titles; represented Canada in team matches vs. U.S.; mem. Ont. Blind curling title rink '01; annual Village Green tournament bears his name.

PATTERSON, Hal (football); b. 1933, Rozel, Kansas; given name: Harold; div.; c. 1 son; Kansas; road builder; nicknamed "Prince Hal"; Kansas all-star baseball, basketball, football; Montreal '54-60, Hamilton '61-67; began pro career as db, switched to rcvr; CFL record: 460 pass receptions, 9473yds, 20.6 avg., 64tds, returned 105 kickoffs, 2871yds, 27.3 avg., 3tds, scored total 75tds, 432pts; best single season '56, 88 passes, CFL record 1914yds; best game 29 Sep '56 CFL record 338yds in receptions; longest single gain 109yds; longest kickoff return 105yds; Lord Calvert Trophy (Montreal MVP) 3 times; Jeff Russel Memorial Trophy '56; Schenley outstanding player award '56, runnerup '57; 8 times EFC all-star, twice all-Canadian;

9 Grey Cup finals, 3 winners; mem. Canadian Football Hall of Fame; last known res. Hanston, Kansas.

PATTERSON, Joe (softball); b. 6 Feb 1936, Regina, Sask.; given name: Joseph James; m. Marylou Burton; c. Bradley, Angela; fire fighter; perennial all-star 1b/of Victoria '59-68; mem. 2 BC Sr. B title teams; Victoria Bate '69-74; 8 BC Sr. A titles; 3 ntl titles; coached Bate to co-world title '76; twice ntl softball coach of yr; mem. Canadian Amateur Softball, Greater Victoria Sports halls of fame; res. Victoria, B.C.

PAUL, Chuck (officiating/football); b. 16 Aug 1930, Ottawa, Ont.; given name: Charles William; m. Elizabeth Leclerc; c. Susan, David, Greg; ret'd EMR; St. Pat's Little Big Four League; 5 titles Ottawa Tech; Gerry Boucher Memorial OHSAA best football player, Mayor's Trophy top athlete awards; John David Eaton gold watch Red Feather tourney MVP; Peterborough Orfuns intermediates '50-51; Ottawa Seconds Intermediates '52-53, 2yr all-star, Beesley MVP award; Montreal Verdun Intermediates '64; began refereeing minor football '56; CFL official '63-91, 480 games, 8 Grey Cups; CFL supervisor '92-01; college supervisor '94-02; CFL 25yr service plaque; OMFA distinguished service award; CFL, amateur football awards of merit; hockey Ottawa Tech 4 title teams; top def., all-star 2yrs jr. Montagnards; Army, Hull Volants teams ECHL '50-53; 12yrs with varied Ottawa Valley7 teams; on-ice official Ottawa Cradle League '60-63; coached Nepean, South Ottawa minor hockey '68-87; played minor baseball Ottawa East; Sudbury Nickel Belt League '46-49; pro Border League Ottawa, Cornwall '50-51; 3 Gatineau Club B golf titles; 5 Royal Victoria Jubilee curling titles; mem. Ottawa Sports Hall of Fame; res. Nepean, Ont.

PAUL, Donald (builder); b. 5 Mar 1933, Hamilton, Ont.; m. Joan; c. Margo, Gordon, Douglas; UofT; p-pres. Collingwood Shipbuilders HC; p-pres./charter mem. Collingwood Blue Mountain Golf & Country Club; played key exec. role in '91 Ontario Winter Games; exec./charter mem. Collingwood Sports Hall of Fame '74-90; mem. exec. comm. Collingwood YMCA '78; p-chair. Collingwood Recreation Board; player/coach/mgr. Christie's Men's Wear Slo-pitch all-Ont. finalists '78, '90, 3 Summerfest tournament titles, 3 league titles; chair Summerfest slo-pitch tourney '85-90; recipient Order of Collingwood '91; mem. Collingwood Sports Hall of Fame; nickname "Doc"; res. Collingwood, Ont.

PAUL, Robert (figure skating); b. 2 Jun 1937, Toronto, Ont.; m. Sally Ann Welsh; skating choreographer, coach; 5 ntl, 2 NA, 4 world titles; '60 Olympic gold; Ice Capades '61-64; from '65 coached US world and Olympic competitors; choreographer '68 Olympic gold medalist Peggy Fleming; with Barbara Wagner shared '59 Lou Marsh Trophy; flag-bearer '60 winter Olympics; mem. Cdn, US Figure Skating, Cdn Olympic, Canada's Sports halls of fame; res. Beverly Hills, Calif.

PAULETTO, Bruno (t&f); b. 21 Jan 1954, Portogruaro, Italy; Central Michigan, B.Sc, Tennessee, MSc; teacher, author, coach; runs Power Systems Inc.; shot put specialist; recognized authority on strength & conditioning education; mem. ntl jr. team '73-75, sr. team '76-84; 5th '77 World Cup; 4th '77 FISU Games; silver '77 Pacific Conference Games;

gold '78 NCAA indoor, silver outdoor championships; 4 ntl titles; gold '79 Dogwood Relays, Florida Relays, '80 Tom Black Classic; silver '78 CG, '80 Copenhagen Games, Dogwood Relays; bronze '78 Helsinki Games, '79 Canada-Russia dual meet, *Edmonton Journal* Games, PAG; 5 gold, 3 silver, 2 bronze '80 Olympic alternative meets; gold '82 CG; mem. '84 Olympic team; 3 times all-American; 3 times Mid-American Conference titlist and record holder; '78 university scholar-athlete of year; fed. govt. excellence award '83; p-pres. US ntl strength & conditioning assn.; res. Knoxville, Tenn.

PAULSON, Jamie (badminton); b. 26 Apr 1948, Calgary, Alta; m. Clair Wilson; c. Julie, Christopher, Daniel; UCal, BComm, UWO, MBA; investment broker; 4 ntl jr., sr. singles titles; with Yves Pare 5 ntl men's doubles; twice singles, doubles champion Jamaican, Mexican Opens; led Canada to 1st NA title over US '69; bronze Singapore world championships; gold singles, bronze doubles '70 CG; silver '74 CG; twice Thomas Cup team mem.; among top 5 singles players in world 5 consecutive years; mem. Alta. Sports Hall of Fame; res. Calgary, Alta.

PAVELICH, Matt (hockey/officiating); b. 12 Mar 1934, Park Hills Gold Mines, Ont.; began officiating minor hockey at 14; referee-in-chief Northern Michigan Int. League; personally worked Michigan Tech home games; following impressive performances in AHL games '55-56 he made NHL debut 11 Oct. '56; remained as linesman in NHL through '79 working 1727 scheduled games, 245 Stanley Cup playoff games, 11 NHL all-star games; NHL supervisor of officials; USHL supervisor of officials '96-04; 1st linesman elected to Hockey Hall of Fame; res. Sault Ste. Marie, Mich.

PAYNE, Marita (t&f); b. 7 Oct 1960, Barbados; m. Mitchell Wiggins; c. Mitchell, Stephanie, Nicholas; Florida State; sprint specialist; mem. Scarborough Optimists TC; mem. bronze medal 4x400m relay team '79 PAG; silver 4x100m relay '82 CG; 200m, 4x400m, 4x100m relay silvers '83 FISU, silvers 4x100, 4x400 relays '84 Olympics; ntl outdoor 4x100m relay title '80; silver 100m, 200m '80 Colgate Games; ntl outdoor 400m '81; '82 NCAA 400m title; 4 ntl sr. records; fed. govt. excellence award '82; mem. Cdn Olympic Hall of Fame; res. Concord, Ont.

PAYTON, Elfrid (football); b. 22 Sep 1967, Gretna, La; Grambling; teacher; dl; CFL Winnipeg '91-93, Shreveport '94, Baltimore '94-95, Montreal '96-99, Winnipeg '00, Toronto '01, Edmonton '02-04; 3 CFL, 1 West, 4 East div. all-stars; CFL outstanding def. player '02, runnerup '93; 2 Grey Cup finals, 1 winner; CFL record (through '04) 472 def. tackles, 154 qb sacks; res. Louisiana.

PEACOSH, Walter (hockey); b. 16 Sep 1935, The Pas, Man.; given name: Walter Nickolas; m. Alice Allen; c. Debra, Ricky, Carrie, Yvonne, Robert, David; millwright; jr. Flin Flon Bombers '53-55; mem. Penticton V's '56-58; MVP '58; Vancouver Canucks (WHL) '58-59, Western Cdn title '58; Spokane Comets '60; mem. Trail Smoke Eaters world title team '60-61; ntl int. finalist Summerland, B.C., '62; Trail Smoke Eaters '62-63, 4th in world championships; Kimberley Dynamiters '64-70; MVP, scoring champion '66-68; picked up by Allan Cup finalist Nelson Maple Leafs '66; coach Kimberley '70-72; mem. Trail Smoke Eaters Old Timers Sweden tour '73-74; East Kootney Old Timers from '75; ntl titles '77, '79; mem. BC Sports Hall of Fame with '61 Trail team; res. Kimberley, B.C.

PEAKER, Brian (rowing); b. 26 May 1959, London, Ont.; UWO; financial advisor; lightweight men's straight four stroke; began rowing age 16; mem. ntl team '85-86, '89, from '92; straight four bronze '86 CG, silver '96 Olympics; 3 US, 1 world championship; res. London, Ont.

PEARCE, Bobby (rowing); b. 30 Sep 1905, Sydney, Australia, d. 20 May 1976, Toronto, Ont.; m. Velma Hilda; c. Jon Robert, Jill Elizabeth, Robert Ernest; salesman; Australian army heavyweight boxing champion '26; world amateur sculling champion, gold '28, '32 Olympics; sculling gold '30 BEG; '31 diamond sculls Henley Eng.; competed for Australia '32 Olympics although Cdn resident; pro world title CNE '33; lost only 2 races in pro career; Lou Marsh Trophy '38; Australia's athlete of past 200 years '70; second only to Joe Wright Sr. as Canada's outstanding oarsman of half century '50 *CP* poll; mem. Cdn Olympic, Canada's Sports Hall of Fame.

PEARCE, Dave (softball); b. 10 Jul 1937, Montreal, Que.; given name: David Albert; div.; c. Karen, Kevin, Kyle; m. Jane Haigh; sc. Susan; ret'd RCMP superintendent; softball ambassador; pitched at Sr. A level, 4 ntl, 1 world championships; playing career extended more than 30yrs; coached more than 20yrs at sr. level; 3 world tournaments, Italian men '78, Cdn women '82, Cdn men '84; mgr. Cdn men's ntl team '82-89; coached Italian women's European titlists '79, Canadian men's PAG gold '83, Sask. Boys Canada Games gold team '93; authored 10 softball instruction books; organized Regina Gold program operating softball, baseball instruction camps for kids and sponsoring teams to ntl, intl events; in 10 intl events his teams won 4g 2s, 1b medals; conducts clinics throughout the world; coached Australian ntl team; competed judo 15yrs; 2nd degree black belt; coached community baseball, hockey in Ottawa, Regina; mem. Cdn Softball Hall of Fame; res. Regina, Sask.

PEARCE, John (equestrian); b. 3 May 1960, Toronto, Ont.; m. Cathy; Forestview Farm operator; spent many yrs in amateur/owner jumper class before launching Grand Prix career '90; mem. ntl team from '92; competed '92 World Cup final; '00 Olympics; '98 World Equestrian Games; winning Cdn Nations' Cup teams '92, '95; expert carpenter; 4 GP victories '96, 2 '97; rode Champagne to Big Ben Memorial GP '03; leading Cdn rider award; won '98 Jump Canada series; res. Stouffville, Ont.

PEARN, Perry (coaching/hockey); b. 6 Jun 1951, Stettler, Alta; given name: Perry Douglas; m. Cindy Lee Beerwart; c. Kristy, Alexis, Lacey, Daryl; U Alta, BPE, ed. Dip, master of coaching, U Calgary; hockey coach; mem. Centennial Cup champion Red Deer '71; 6 NAIT ntl title teams; asst. coach ntl under 18 team '85, head coach '86; asst. ntl jr team 90-92, head coach '93; 3 world gold; head coach Ambri-Piotta (Swiss Elite) '94-95, Medicine Hat '95-96; asst. Winnipeg Jets '96-97, Ottawa Senators '97-04, NY Rangers '04; res. St. Albert, Alta.

PEARSALL, Shane (hockey/administration); b. 19 Jan 1958, Barrie, Ont.; given name: Shane Andrew; UofT, UCal; CEO Bobsleigh Can.; formerly worked in oil/gas industry; def./lw Barrie ntl midget title team '75; Ottawa 67's '75-78; CIAU all-Cdn; Team Canada '78-80; drafted by Pittsburgh but never played in NHL; CIS Red Dutton award '83; coached Calgary minor hockey, UCal; chair. COA athlete council '97-01; mission staff '98 Olympics; Cdn Olympic Committee exec. from '01; asst. CdM '02 Olympics; CdM '06 Olympics; served on Athletes Can. board; res. Calgary, Alta.

PEARSON, Mike (football/hockey/baseball); b. 23 Apr 1897, Toronto, Ont.; d. 27 Dec 1972, Ottawa, Ont.; given name: Lester Bowles; m. Maryon Moody; c. Geoffrey Arthur Holland, Patricia Lillian; Victoria College, BA, St. John's College, Oxford, BA, hon. degrees 48 universities; statesman; Prime Minister of Canada '63-68; interfaculty rugby, basketball, football, hockey, lacrosse at Oxford; coach sr. hockey '26-27, sr. football, lacrosse '26-27, sr. ORFU football '27-28; OBE '35, Nobel Peace Prize '57; trophy in his name presented annually by CIAU, NHL; mem. UofT Sports, Cdn Baseball halls of fame.

PEARSON, Paul (football); b. 15 Jun 1957, Campbell River, B.C.; m. Shan Williams; c. David, Michael; College of the Siskiyous, UBC, BA; deli operator; drafted by Calgary '78; sb Toronto Argos '79-87; ranked among CFL's premier receivers; CFL record 424 receptions for 5867yds; 3 Grey Cup finals, 1 winner; Schenley outstanding Canadian nominee '81-83; co-chair. Metro Toronto Big Brothers Bowl for Millions; res. Kelowna, B.C.

PECA, Michael (hockey); b. 26 Mar 1974, Toronto, Ont. m.Kristen; c. Trevor; ctr Toronto Nats (MTHL), '89-90, Sudbury (OHL) '90-92, Ottawa 67's (OHL) '92-94, Hamilton, Syracuse (AHL); NHL Vancouver '94-95, Buffalo '95-00, NYI '01-04; capt. Sabres, Islanders; Frank Selke trophy '97, '02; Olympic gold '02; capt. Team Canada '01 Worlds, gold '94 jr. worlds; NHL record: (through '04) 622 scheduled games, 151g, 220a, 69 playoff games, 9g, 14a; res. Toronto, Ont.

PEDEN, Doug (all-around); b. 18 Apr 1916, Victoria, B.C.; given name: James Douglas; m. Trudy; ret'd sports editor; competed professionally bicycle racing, basketball, baseball; rode 37 international 6-day races, won 7, 2nd 9 times; ntl pro sprint title '39; mem. House of David baseball team; player, manager minor league teams Pittsburgh organization; runnerup class B Interstate League batting .357 York, Pa., '46; guard 3 Victoria Dominoes ntl basketball title teams; top Canadian scorer, silver medal '36 Olympic team; pro Buffalo Bisons, Vancouver Hornets; BC, regional jr. tennis titles; BC rugby fb/p/pk; all-around t&f performer; zone sr. golf champion '77; also competed in swimming, soccer, cricket, softball; mem. Cdn Basketball, BC, Greater Victoria, Canada's Sports halls of fame; res. Victoria, B.C.

PEDEN, Sandy (shooting); b. 3 May 1934, Edmonton, Alta.; m.; ret'd; cyclist '54 BEG; Man. full-bore title '63; BC titles '72, '74; ntl title '81; mem. '82 CG team; CTR Bisley aggregate gold cross '81; 5 individual DCRA aggregate titles; coach Malaysian ntl team 3yrs; coach Cdn CG team '98; res. Victoria, B.C.

PEDEN, Torchy (cycling); b. 16 Apr 1906, Victoria, B.C., d. 26 Jan 1980, Chicago, Ill.; given name: William John; m. Annamae; c. 4; retail sporting goods; competed '28 Olympics after winning ntl titles at 1, 5 miles, tying for all-around ntl amateur title; 5 ntl amateur indoor titles, records in 4, '29; English 103-mile record 1h39:39; pro '29-48, 38 wins in 148 6-day races; US record for mile 73.5 mph '31; mem. Canada's, BC, Greater Victoria Sports halls of fame.

PEEL, Ann (t&f); b. 27 Feb 1961, Ottawa, Ont.; div.; c. Michael, Andrew; UofT, BA (hon), LLB; lawyer; dir. corporate social responsibility dept. Magna International; race walking specialist; Pan-Am jr. gold '80; 5ᵗʰ '81 World Cup, 7ᵗʰ '83, 10ᵗʰ '85, 7ᵗʰ '87, 16ᵗʰ '89; Americas Cup gold '84, '88, silver '86; PAG silver '87; Universiade 4ᵗʰ '85, bronze '87; world indoor championship bronze '85, '87, 6ᵗʰ '89; competed '90 CG; 18 ntl titles; ntl records 1500m, 3000m (indoor), 3km, 5km, 10km; 1ˢᵗ chair./founding mem. Athletes CAN (formerly Cdn Athletes Assn.) '93; mem. Canada's all-time women's t&f team '93; '99 Breakthrough award; ED FAST; mem. Ottawa Sports Hall of Fame; res. Toronto, Ont.

PEERS, Danielle (wheelchair basketball); b. 24 Apr 1978, Edmonton, Alta.; given name: Danielle Lorraine; m. Tamara Leigh; UofA, BA Sociology; investor relations; diagnosed with muscular dystrophy at age 24; captained Grant MacEwan College "stand up" team to #1 ntl. ranking '98; academic-athletic all-Cdn. '98; started playing wheelchair basketball '00; ntl team from '03; bronze medalist, all-star '01 CWBL women's finals; bronze '02 CWBL women's finals; silver, MVP '03 CWBL women's finals; silver, all-star '03 US women's finals; gold, all-star '04 CWBL women's finals, leading Edmonton Inferno with 23 points, 11 rebounds in title game; gold, MVP '04 CWBA Int'l. Invitational; bronze '04 Paralympics; brother Marc mem. '96 Cdn. Olympic sailing team; res. Edmonton, Alta.

PELCHAT, Ann-Marie (skiing); b. 30 May 1974, Levis, Que.; freestyle moguls specialist; mem. ntl team '94-98; 4 ntl titles; competed '98, '02 Olympics, '97 worlds; res. Levis, Que.

PELECH, Jack (builder); b. 21 Jun 1933, Hamilton, Ont.; given name: John; McMaster, BA; Osgoode Hall LLB; lawyer; played football, basketball, handball in youth; turned to coaching/administration; asst. fb coach McMaster '62-66; dir. Hamilton YMCA boards from '55, pres. '77; active as administrator in varied Hamilton sports/recreation/ university organizations; chair. PAG/CG bids committees; 8yr mem. National Advisory Council on Fitness & Amateur Sport; 7yrs governor ntl Youth Bowling Council; chair. ntl Canada Games council '71-99; 3yr chair. Fred Sgambati charity golf tournament; ntl. handball doubles champ '75; mem. Hamilton Copp's Coliseum Wall of Fame comm. '87-99; trustee Tiger-Cats trust fund for amateur sports '86-99; Ont. sport volunteer citation; '87 Hamilton citizen of yr; dir. McMaster Friends of Football group; mem. McMaster Sports Hall of Fame; res. Hamilton, Ont.

PELKEY, Arthur (boxing); b. 27 Oct 1884, Chatham, Ont., d. 18 Feb 1921, Ford City, Ont.; given name: Andrew Arthur Peletier; fought Tommy Burns, Jess Willard, Jim Coffey to

no decisions; KO victory '13 resulted in death of opponent Luther McCarty, Pelkey never again won a bout; KO'd by Gunboat Smith in lone title challenge '14; in 50-bout career won 12 by KO, 9 by decision, 4 draws, lost 1 decision, KO'd 13 times, 11 no decisions.

PELLETIER, Annie (diving); b. 22 Dec 1973, Montreal, Que.; College Andre-Grasset; mgr. COA community relations; competitive swimmer age 6-8; gymnast 8-13; began diving age 13; mem. Montreal CAMO Club; jr ntl 3m title '91; sr ntl 3m title '93; won 1m, 3m summer ntl sr. titles '94, 1m winter ntls '94, '95; 1m, 3m gold '94 CG, 3m gold, 1m silver '95 PAG, 1m bronze '94 worlds, 3m bronze '96 Olympics; competed '91 PAG, '93 FISU Games; 2 bronze '95 Dive Canada; Bev Boys outstanding diver awards '91, '93; 3 Que. female-diver-of-yr awards; ret'd from competition '96; noted for charitable work; mem. Cdn Olympic Hall of Fame; res. Montreal, Que.

PELLETIER, David (figure skating); b. 22 Nov 1974, Sayabec, Que.; with partner Julie Laporte (later killed in an auto accident) competed in '92 world jrs.; teamed with Allison Gaylor '95, Caroline Roy '98 before partnering with Jamie Sale from '98 to make Cdn figure skating history; undefeated Nov. '00 through '02 Olympics; see Sale for competitive details; given gold medal made by fans from across Canada; a made-for-TV movie is in the works; turned pro after '02 Winter Olympics and signed a four year contract with Stars On Ice; Lou Marsh, team or yr. trophies; Queen's Golden Jubilee Award; hon. mem. Edmonton Rotary Club; Paul Harris Fellow award from Rotary International '03; res. Edmonton, Alta.

PELLETIER, Leo-Charles (boxing); b. 26 Jan 1952, Eel River Crossing, N.B.; RCMP officer; mem. ntl team '72-78; Maritime Golden Gloves titles '68-78; Eastern Cdn Golden Gloves '72-76; Cdn amateur welterweight title '73-74; 39 international bouts, 34 wins; overall record 112 wins, 20 losses; 3 international gold medals; silver '73 NA championships; bronze '75 pre-Olympic tournament; NB boxer of '71-73; mem. NB Sports Hall of Fame; res. Balmoral, N.B.

PELLS, Leah (t&F); b. 9 Nov 1964, Vancouver, B.C.; m. John Turenne; c. Luke; SFU BA; full-time athlete, ex-child care counsellor; middle-distance runner; ntl jr. 1500m titlist '83; NAIA 1500, 3000m titles '83, '88; ntl 3000m titles '90, '93, 1500m '95; competed '90, '94, '98 CG, '92, '96, '00 Olympic Games, '99 PAG, '88, '90, '92, '94 world x-country; won '94 *Victoria Times-Colonist* 1500m; silver 1500m '99 PAG; displayed essence of Olympics with amazing, albeit non-medal, performance '96; SFU female athlete, Burnaby outstanding athlete of '88; SFU Sports Hall of Fame; res. Coquitlam, B.C.

PELYK, Mike (hockey); b. 29 Sep 1947, Toronto, Ont.; given name: Michael Joseph; m. Sarah MacLean; c. Kimberley, Christopher, Leah, Stacy, Robert; UofT, BA, York, MBA; real estate development and acquisition; jr. def Toronto Marlboros; Maple Leafs 3ʳᵈ choice, 17ᵗʰ overall '63 amateur draft; NHL record: 441 scheduled games, 29g, 88a; 2 seasons Vancouver Blazers, Cincinnati Stingers WHA; capt. Stingers; mem. Toronto NHL Old Stars; res. Weston, Ont.

PERCIVAL, Lloyd (all-around); b. 3 Jun 1913, Toronto, Ont., d. 23 Jul 1974, Montreal, Que.; m. Dorothy Macdonell; c. Janet; physical educator; nicknamed "Ace"; ntl jr. tennis finals at 16; ntl bantam Golden Gloves boxing title, qualified for Olympics but too young to participate; high scorer '36 Cdn cricket team touring England; coached '32 National Sea Flea midgets to undefeated hockey season; launched Sports College '41, at peak of program 800,000 students were registered; began Canadian Amateur Sports and Physical Fitness Development Service '56; founder Fitness Institute; t&f coach; formed Don Mills TC; Coronation medal from Queen Elizabeth.

PERCY, Karen (skiing); b. 10 Oct 1966, Edmonton, Alta.; given name: Karen Lynne; m. Kevin Lowe; c. Dervyn Jean, Darby, Keegan; alpine specialist; silver WC downhill Zinal, Switzerland, '88; bronze WC downhill Banff '86; WC record 0-2-3; 2 bronze '88 Olympics; mem. Order of Canada, Cdn Skiing, Cdn Olympic, Alta., Canada's Sports halls of fame; res. Edmonton, Alta.

PEREIRA, Ken (field hockey); b. 12 Jul 1973, Unionville, Ont.; given name: Kenneth; Centennial Coll.; quick, adept stick handler with accurate shot; 162 ntl team caps; represented Canada '95 (silver), '99 (gold) PAG, '00 Olympics, '02 CG; silver '00 America's Cup; gold '02 indoor Pan-Am Cup; gold '99 world indoor classic, Australia Cup; mem. Cdn team which posted best-ever sixth place finish '98 World Cup; res. Unionville, Ont.

PEROWNE, Ron (football); b. 5 Feb 1950, Montreal, Que.; given name: Ronald Grant; m. Gail Elizabeth Murphy; c. Charles; Bishop's., BA, McGill,BTheology; football, hockey coach; football, hockey Lower Canada College, 4yrs Bishop's, 1yr hockey McGill; pro football 2Ω seasons Alouettes; coach Bishop's football, hockey teams; mem. Bishop's Sports Wall of Fame; res. Lennoxville, Que.

PERREAULT, Annie (speed skating); b. 28 Jul 1971, Windsor, Que.; office clerk, gym owner; followed tradition set by family members such as sister Maryse who claimed world title honors and several world championship medals earlier; competed in age-class events from '84 earning gold at midget, junior, intermediate, senior levels; 3 Canada Winter Games gold '87; 2 Pacific Rim gold '91; 2 world short-track team/relay gold; '92 Olympics relay gold; Bormio Cup 1500m, relay gold '95, 500m, 1000m, 1500m relay gold '94; world championships 500m silver '96; Cdn open overall bronze '96; Cdn International Challenge 500m gold '94; short-track 500m gold, 3000m relay bronze '98 Olympics; world team bronze, relay silver '98; silver '99 worlds; ret'd from competition '03; played women's pro soccer; Que. athlete of '98; res. Rock Forest, Que.

PERREAULT, Gil (hockey); b. 13 Nov 1950, Victoriaville, Que.; given name: Gilbert; Sabres PR ambassador from '97; Montreal Jr. Canadiens; twice OHA 1st team all-star ctr; 1st Buffalo pick, 1st overall '70 amateur draft; Calder Memorial Trophy '71; Lady Byng Trophy '73; twice NHL 2nd team all-star; NHL record '70-87: 1191 scheduled games, 512g, 814a, 90 playoff games, 33g, 70a; mem. 5 Team Canada Canada Cup teams; jersey #11 ret'd by Sabres; mem. Hockey Hall of Fame; res. Buffalo, N.Y.

PERRIER, Ross (officiating/football); b. 26 Jun 1934, Toronto, Ont.; d. 29 Oct 1999, Scarborough, Ont.; m. Joan Halloran; c. Joanne, Karen, Michele, Michael; ret'd fireman; officiated in CFL 18 seasons including 335 regular season and playoff games; worked 7 Grey Cup finals; ret'd after '90 season to become officiating supervisor; when league expanded into US he returned to active duty for '94 season; 1 of 2 CFL officiating supervisors to '95 when he was promoted to dir. of officiating.

PERROUD, Pat (curling); b. 31 Dec 1962, Thunder Bay; given name: Patrick Charles; m. Jane Hooper; c. Gabriel; software engineer; began curling as jr. in TB; competed 4 Briers, 2 winners; lead Al Hackner '85, Ed Werenich '90 Brier, world title rinks; with Werenich 1, Wayne Middaugh 2 *TSN* Skins Games titles; CCR 1st team all-star lead '90; mem. Ont. team of '85; ntl mixed finalist '95; mem. Cdn Curling Hall of Fame; res. Bradford, Ont.

PERRY, Gordon (football/curling); b. 18 Mar 1903, Moncton, N.B.; d. 19 Sep 2003, Ottawa, Ont.; m. Jessie Keith (d), c. Gordon Jr., Marilyn, Patricia; m. Betty Bywater Thomas (d); m. Muriel Taggart; ret'd Bank of Canada; Montreal city league baseball, hockey, Westward football intermediates '26-27; Montreal Winged Wheelers '28-34, capt. '31 unbeaten, untied (14 games) team to Grey Cup title; Jeff Russel Memorial Trophy '31; all-Eastern 4 times; Royal Victoria Jubilee in both irons ('53), granites ('56); Branch Gov.-Gen.'s '61; hon. chair. '93 Ottawa Brier; hon. capt. '03 Montreal Alouettes; p-pres, life mem. OCC; mem. Gov.-Gen.'s CC; bonspiel named in his honor by Ottawa CC; mem. Ottawa, NB, Que., Canada's Sports, Cdn Football halls of fame.

PERRY, Nellie (basketball); b. 4 Feb 1903, London, Eng.; d. Apr 1991, Victoria, B.C.; given name: Ellen; m. Gordon McIntosh; c. Tim, Bud, Alan, Ron, Barbara, Carol, Wendy; mem. famed Edmonton Grads '21-24, 40 games, 242 points, 6.5 avg.; mem. Canadian Basketball, Alta. Sports halls of fame.

PERRY, Norm (football); b. 1 Jun 1904, Sarnia, Ont., d. 17 Nov 1957, Sarnia, Ont.; m. Marie McPhail; c. Don, Dick; safety supervisor; hb 8 seasons jr., intermediate football; 8 seasons sr. ORFU Sarnia Imperials, 7 titles, 1 Grey Cup; capt. '34 Grey Cup champions, MVP that season; perennial all-star; ORFU exec. officer several years; CRU pres. '53; term as mayor of Sarnia; mem. Canadian Football Hall of Fame.

PESCHISOLIDO, Paul (soccer); b. 25 May 1971, Scarborough, Ont.; m.; c. 1 daughter; striker West Bromwich Albion; competed for Cdn -17 team '87 world championships; 1st pick CSL Toronto Blizzard '89; scored 32g during 4yr stint with Blizzard; twice CSL all-star; debuted for ntl sr. team '92 scoring 1st international goal in 3-1 win over Hong Kong; signed with Birmingham (English 1st Div) '92; transferred to Stoke City '94-95 scoring 22g before returning to Birmingham '96; sold to West Bromwich for '96-97, Fulham '97-98, Sheffield United '01-03; represented Canada internationally from '92; Cdn player of '96 award; 45 international caps; res. Pickering, Ont./England.

PETER, Richard (wheelchair basketball); b. 10 Sep 1972, Duncan, B.C.; m. Marni Abbott; program coordinator B.C.

Wheelchair Sports; versatile athlete excelling in racquetball, tennis, athletics, ball hockey, basketball; mem. Cowichan First Nation; began playing wheelchair basketball at 16; mem. BC team from '88, ntl team from '94; 3 ntl titles; numerous MVP, all-star awards; Paralympic gold '00, 3 world bronze; competed 2 Paralympics; board mem. B.C. Wheelchair Basketball Society, B.C. Aboriginal Network on Disabilities; advocate for First Nations people with disability; res. Vancouver, B.C.

PETERS, Vic (curling); b. 24 Mar 1955, Steinbach, Man.; m. Debora; c. Kasandra, Daley, Elisabeth; golf course superintendent/ice maker; eye injury playing hockey forced attention shift to curling at 18; skipped Manitoba entry '92, '93, '97 Brier; won '92 Brier; bronze medal '92 world championships; all-star skip 2 Briers, 1 worlds; Ross Harstone award '97 Brier; holds Rossmere G&CC amateur course record 64; competes on WCT; res. Winnipeg, Man.

PETITCLERC, Chantal (t&f); b. 15 Dec 1969, Ste, Foy, Que.; wheelchair racer; broadcaster; lost use of legs in accident at 13; became competitive swimmer before shifting to wheelchair racing '88, intl competition from '92; 2 bronze '92, 2 gold, 3 silver '96 , 2 gold '00, 5 gold, 3WR '04 Paralympics; gold '04 Olympic "demonstration"; 800m gold '02 CG; 2 gold '94 Francophone Games; 5 gold '95 Stoke-Mandeville Games, Ian Hume Invitational; 2 gold '94 IPC World Athletic championships. 2 ntl 10km, marathon titles; 3 gold, WR Swiss championships '03; ntl record in 100, 200, 400, 800, 1500, marathon; refused to share Athletics Canada award with Perdita Felicien '04; named *MacLean's* Canadian of '04; res. Montreal, Que.

PETTAPIECE, Jim (curling); b. 7 May 1943, Saskatoon, Sask.; given name: James Kenneth; Nevada; owner International Curling Promotions; Sask. jr., sr. baseball title teams; Nevada baseball scholarship; mem. Don Duguid Man. Consols, Brier, Silver Broom championships rinks '70-71; Brier all-star 2nd '70-71; mem. Dan Fink Man. Consols winner, Brier entry '73; instructor Silver Broom Curling Schools, Curl Canada Clinics '71-75; mem. Man., Cdn Curling halls of fame; res. Langley, B.C.

PETTIGREW, Vern (wrestling); b. 30 Mar 1908, Durham, Ont. d. 29 Oct 2004, Regina, Sask.; given name: John Vernon; m. Jean Saunderson; c. Robert, Heather, Ronald; ret'd stonecutter, firefighter; 5 ntl titles '33-40; 4th featherweight (134lbs) '36 Olympics; wrestling instructor Regina City Police '35-37; referee-in-chief ntl wrestling championships '55; Regina boxing/wrestling commission '56-86; mem. Cdn Olympic, Sask. Sports, Cdn Amateur Wrestling halls of fame.

PETTINGER, Glen (basketball); b. 27 Sep 1928, Toronto, Ont.; given name: Glen Murray; m. Nancy Louise Hayman; c. Wendy, Kim, Jill, Christopher; UofT, UWO, BA; ret'd HS principal; mem. East York CI Ont. Golden Ball champions '46, York Belting ntl junior titlist '47; CIAU all-star UofT '49; UWO Mustangs CIAU winners '52, All-Canadian; mem. Tillsonburg Livingstons '52 Olympics; capt. Nortown Tri-Bells ntl sr. basketball titlist '53; mem. '55 PAG team; Ottawa Fellers '59 ntl finalist; res. Gloucester, Ont.

PETTINICCHI, Sabrina (wheelchair basketball); b. 9 Aug 1972, Montreal, Que; CEGEP Joliette, Vieux-Montreal; interior designer Hydro Quebec; car accident at 17 left her a paraplegic; introduced to wheelchair basketball '91; named to ntl team '96; Paralympic gold '96, '00; World Cup gold '98, '02; res. Montreal, Que.

PEZER, Vera (curling); b. 13 Jan 1939, Melfort, Sask.; given name: Vera Rose; Sask, BA, MA, PhD; ret'd associate v-p. USask., asst. professor; won intercollegiate titles; 3rd Joyce McKee rink '69 ntl ladies' title; skipped ntl title rinks '71-73; coached ntl jr. champions '75; 3 Western intercollegiate champions; mem. Saskatoon Imperials '63-69 provincial women's softball champions, '69 ntl title; mem. Sask. interprovincial golf teams '70-77; Saskatoon sportswoman of '68; team psychologist '92 Olympics; author *Stone Age: Social History of Curling in Prairies;* mem. Sask., Saskatoon Sports, Canadian Curling halls of fame; res. Saskatoon, Sask.

PFEIFER, Alan (football); b. 27 Dec 1928, Newark, N.J.; m. Alva; c. Ross, Judy Ann, Linda, Mary; Fordham, BSc; equestrian equipment sales; HS all-state football 2 years, baseball 1 year; college all-Eastern, all-American '50; 6 years pro football NY Giants, Argos, Rough Riders; all-pro '51, '55; CFL scoring title '55; led EFC pass receivers 3 times; EFC record for most td passes caught 1 season with 15; most receptions single game 13; with Hugh Campbell shares CFL record of catching 3 td passes 1 game 3 times 1 season; Argos record holder most 100yd games 17; most 100yd games single season 8; mem. Fordham Sports Hall of Fame; res. Phoenix, Ariz.

PFEIFER, Scott (curling); b. 5 Jan 1977, St. Albert, Alta.; given name: Scott Michael; m. Chantelle Davison; c. Marlow, Dominic; UAlta BSc, MBA; '94 world jr. champion (as second); '94 Cdn jr. all-star second, sportsmanship award; skip '97 world jr. brone, sportsmanship award; all-star second Randy Ferbey rink '01-03 ntl, '02-03 world title rinks; res. Sherwood Park, Alta

PHIBBS, Bob (basketball); b. 26 May 1927, Windsor, Ont.; given name: Robert James; m. Mary; c. Lizabeth Jean, Christine Louise, Richard James; UWO, BA; company v-p; Ont. discus, javelin titles '46; 3 UWO intercollegiate football title teams, 4 basketball title teams; capt. '52 ntl sr. men's basketball champions, Olympic team; Claude Brown Memorial Trophy '49 as UWO outstanding athlete; res. Calgary, Alta.

PHILIP, Bob (hockey/coaching); b. 15 Apr 1944, Montreal, Que.; m. Linda Carey; c. Matthew; Sir George Williams, BA, McGill, BEd, Concordia, MA; AD UBC; starred with SGW hockey team '67-70, co-capt. '70; coached SGW hockey '72-75; QUAA coach of '73; asst. coach Concordia '75-84; AD Concordia '85-92; AD UBC from '92; mem. CHA advisory group; res. Delta, B.C.

PHILLIPS, Alf Jr. (curling); b. 10 Sep 1938, Toronto, Ont.; given name: Alfred John; m. June Doreen Carnell; c. Cliff, Steve, Wayne; Ryerson business school; v-p Canadian Conklin Shows; Ont. -17 100yd FS swimming title; won Ont. jr. tankard '58; 3 Ont. Silver tankards; skipped Brier winner '67; City of Ottawa champion '75; mem. Gov.-

Gen.'s CC; publisher *Ontario Curling Report* from '74; res. Toronto, Ont.

PHILLIPS, Alf Sr. (diving/curling); b. 27 Jul 1908, Durham, Ont.; d. 28 Jul 1994, Toronto,Ont.; m. Margaret Dobson; c. Alf Jr., Dave; company pres.; Ont. springboard, platform fancy diving champion '26-34, ntl champion '26-34 retiring undefeated; 7th platform '28, 4th springboard '32 Olympics; 1st double winner '30 BEG; 4 Ont. Silver Tankard titles; 2 Canada Life, 5 Canada Life seniors titles; won Toronto International, ntl seniors '69; skip '56 Ont. champions, lost Brier extra-end playoff; mem. Gov.-Gen.'s CC; mem. Cdn Curling, Olympic, Cdn, Ont. Aquatic halls of fame.

PHILLIPS, Bill (baseball); b. 1857, Saint John, N.B.; d. 7 Oct 1900, Chicago, Ill; 1b; 1st Cdn to play in major leagues with Cleveland Blues '79-84; 1st Cdn to hit home run ('80); joined Brooklyn Bridegrooms (AA) '85-87; finished ML career with Kansas City '88; regarded as excellent fielder; ML record: 1038 games, 4255ab, 1130h, 562r, 214d, 98t, 17hr, .266ba.; mem. Cdn Baseball Hall of Fame.

PHILLIPS, Chris (hockey); b. 9 Mar 1978, Calgary, Alta; m. Erin Hancock; c. Benjamin, Zoe;ʃ def. Ft. McMurray (AJHL) 2yrs; capt. Team Alta. '95 Canada Winter Games; WHL Prince Albert Jr. '95-96, Lethbridge '96-97; Memorial Cup finalist '97; WHL rookie of yr, CHL prospects game player of game '96; CHL, WHL all-rookie teams; gold '96, '97 world jr; mem. Team Canada '00 worlds; Ottawa 1st pick, 1st overall '96 NHL draft; versatility has sometimes led to duty on left wing; NHL record (through '04): 467 scheduled games, 31g, 88a, 58 playoff games, 4g, 7a; with Brynas Sweden during '04-05 labor dispute; res. Sylvan Lake, Alta./Kanata, Ont.

PHILLIPS, Jerry (rodeo); b. Dec 1951, Claresholm, Alta.; given name: Patti Jerry Duce; m. Lee Phillips; c. Fallon; horse trainer, movie wrangler, stunt-person; began trick riding with sister Joy age 9; as Flying Duces they toured NA, Eng., Scotland, Bermuda, Japan; made barrel racing debut age 11; 9 ntl women's barrel racing titles; 1st Cdn rider to qualify for ntl rodeo finals; 3 ntl finals appearances; 1st Miss Rodeo Canada; rodeo queen judge Miss Worlds '81; won numerous Southern Circuit titles and awards; mem. Cdn Rodeo Hall of Fame; res. Carseland, Alta.

PHILLIPS, Peter (curling); b. 9 May 1943, Toronto, Ont.; given name: Peter Edward; m. Beverley Johnstone; c. Monica, Ryan; Waterloo, Ryerson PTI; partner printing co.; Ont. men's championship runner-up '72, '80; 2 Ont. Silver Tankard titles; 6 times provincial championship competitor; res. Willowdale, Ont.

PHILLIPS, Tommy (hockey); b. 22 May 1883, Kenora, Ont., d. 30 Nov 1923, Toronto, Ont.; given name: Thomas Neil; m. Ella Gertrude Kilgour; c. Margery Merceline, Mary Margaret, James Kilgour; McGill, UofT; timber merchant; Toronto Marlboros '04, OHA sr. title; capt. Kenora Thistles 2 Stanley Cup challenges '06-07; 13 goals in 6 playoff games as Kenora won Stanley Cup '07; 26 goals in 10 games '07-08 Ottawa Senators; mem. 6 Stanley Cup challengers, 1 winner; closed career with Vancouver Millionaires '12; mem. Hockey Hall of Fame.

PHILLIPS-MAYA, Wendy (t&f, figure skating); b. 7 Jan 1972, Moncton, N.B.; m. Ricardo Maya; Acadia BPE; began skating age 2, t&f age 12; NB skating champ gold test levels '86; NB discus titlist '87-97; ntl midget title '87, jr. '90; bronze '92, '96 Olympic trials; Canada Games gold '93; ntl Espoir team mem. '93; competed '94, '97 Francophone Games; mem. Team Canada vs. Australian Olympic team '96; posted PB 49.58 '97; held all NB women's discus records; res. Ottawa, Ont.

PHINNEY, Gertrude (t&f); b. 18 Jan 1909, Lawrencetown, N.S.; m. Brannon Young (d); c. Bette, Fred, Harold, Carol, Richard; m. Thomas Beattie; Acadia, BSc, BEd; ret'd teacher; trained 2 weeks then entered '27 Maritime t&f championships "to win some points for her team;" by day's end had run 14 races (including heats) winning 5 titles, setting 2 sprint, 1 hurdles, 1 bj records; "some points" amounted to 28, sufficient to single-handedly win meet for her team; added 2 indoor sprint records '27; surpassed performance '28 Maritime meet with 6 titles, 4 records; ntl 220yd title '28; tied world 60yd record; 7 Maritime titles, 1 record '29; dissuaded from competing in '28 Olympics by father on grounds t&f events too strenuous for female anatomy; mem. '26 ntl finalist Ex-Dalhousie basketball team; won numerous srs. tennis titles; 3 *Halifax Chronicle* trophies, Dalhousie Award; mem. NS, Kings County Sports halls of fame; res. Wolfville, N.S.

PHOENIX, Skip (diving); b. 19 Aug 1948, Addis Ababa, Ethiopia; m. Mary Turner; c. Kimberlee, Samantha; Guelph, BSc, BPhE., UWO, BEd, UofT, MEd; clubs supervisor UofT; bronze 3m springboard '73 winter, '74 summer nationals; silver '74 summer nationals, bronze 1m '75 winter nationals; mem. 2 Canada Cup, '76 Olympics; coach from '77-92; coached UofT to CIAU title '81; 4 CIAU diving-coach-of-yr awards; Oly coach '88, '92; coached several divers to Commonwealth, World medals; lettered in t&f; Eastern Cdn lj/tj titles '69; mem. Guelph Sports Hall of Fame; res. Toronto, Ont.

PIASKOSKI, Jim (football); b. 10 Oct 1948, Levack, Ont.; given name: James Peter; m. Nancy Ross; c. Janna, Ross; Eastern Michigan College; PR Hugh Dolan Distribution; Sudbury Spartans juniors to ot/dt Rough Riders '72-82; mem. '73, '76 Grey Cup champions; '76 City of Ottawa grand aggregate curling title rink; res. Manotick, Ont.

PICHE, Doris (badminton); b. 14 Oct 1965, La Sarre, Que.; m. Mike Bitten; c. William Michael; UofOtt; began competing age 15; mem. ntl team from '85; ntl women's doubles title with Si-An Deng '90, Denyse Julien '92; 2 French. 1 Spanish, 1 Irish Open singles gold; 1 PAG championships singles, 2 women's doubles, 1 mixed doubles gold; Cdn Open women's, mixed doubles gold; 1 Welsh Open women's doubles title; team silver '90 CG; mem. 3 worlds, 2 CG, 1 Olympic Games teams; res. Ottawa, Ont.

PICHE, Ron (baseball); b. 22 May 1934, Verdun, Que.; div. Isobel; c. Luc, Christine; rhp; middle reliever; one of 1st Francophones to play regularly in ML baseball; played 134 games through 6 seasons with Milwaukee, California, St. Louis '60-66; ML record, 134 scheduled games, 222.1ip, 10-16, 4.19era, 157k, 12sv; 10yrs in minors including stint with Toronto Maple Leafgs (IL); honored with "day" in

Toronto; worked in Montreal Expos organization from '70 serving in varied capacities from coach to stadium mgr. to public relations; mem. Cdn Baseball, Quebec Sports, Baseball halls of fame; res. Montreal, Que.

PICKARD, Allan (builder/hockey); b. 2 Jan 1895, Exeter, Ont.; d. 7 Apr 1975, Exeter, Ont.; organizer/administrator Regina YMCA League mid-'20s from which grew Regina Parks League, one of largest and best-organized in country; coach/pres/ Regina Aces sr. team; mem. SAHA exec, pres. '41, served 2 terms; pres. Sask. sr. league pres. Western Canada sr. league; governor Sask. jr., Western Canada jr. leagues' pres. CAHA '47-50; life mem. SAHA, CAHA; mem. Hockey Hall of Fame.

PICKARD, LeRoy (softball/basketball); b. 9 Sep 1919, St. Catharines, Ont.; given name: LeRoy Garnet; m. Lillian Louise Lohnes; c. Linda Christine, Laurel Marie; ret'd general supervisor McKinnon Industries, GM Canada; accounting; in his youth won St. Catharines horseshoe, checker, softball titles; capt. 2b/3b '41 OABA Jr. A champions; player/secty-treas. Can-Am basketball assn. '47-50; player/secty. St. Catharines Softball Assn. mem. 2 OASA, 3 OABA title teams; 3 St. Catharines, 1 Ont. Mr. Softball awards; served in varied exec. capacities OASA '55-94; Royal Canadian Legion minor softball/hockey exec./umpire '56-74; OCBA secty '49-51; OASA life mem. from '82; secty. Niagara Olde Tyme Sports Assn. '86-97; secty men's 10-pin league '86-97; active bowler from '90; mem. CASA, St. Catharines Sports halls of fame; res. St. Catharines, Ont.

PICKARD, Vic (t&f); b. 23 Oct 1903, Hamilton, Ont.; d. (circa 1998) Miami, Fla.; given name: Victor; m. Elizabeth Hershberger; c. Jane, Victor Jr., Carolyn Anne; Pittsburgh, BSc; ret'd dept. store exec.; pv, javelin specialist; despite winning '20 Olympic trials was excluded from team; mem. '24, '28 Olympic teams; '24, '28 BE vs US claiming pv silvers each time; gold '24 Irish Olympics; 5 ntl pv titles; ntl record '28; silver US championships '29; '24 Scottish pv title, record; gold '27, silver '28-29 Penn Relays, gold '27, '29, silver '28 Ohio Relays; Pittsburgh pv mark of 13'10" which lasted until advent of fiberglass pole; twice 3rd NC4A championships; pv/javelin titles '24 NA Interscholastic championships; ret'd from competition '31; mem. Pittsburgh, Western Pennsylvania, Cdn Olympic Sports halls of fame.

PICKELL, Bob (basketball); b. 2 Jul 1927, Kovna, Lithuania; d. 8 Aug 1987, Toronto, Ont.; given name: Bernard; m. Wendy; c. Al, Stephen; Portland; v-p TV Bureau of Canada; 4 times Portland all-star, mem. 3 NIT tournament teams; 5 ntl title teams; 5 MVP awards; mem. '59 PAG, '52, '56 Olympic Games teams; football Edmonton '51-52, BC '54; AAU basketball '51 Hawaii; toured Far East with Universal Motors team '52-53; 2 Vancouver City handball singles, doubles titles; with Herb Capozzi ntl Masters racquetball doubles '73; drove in Shell 4,000 rally 4 times.

PICKELL, Stephen (swimming); b. 11 Aug 1957, Vancouver, B.C.; given name: Stephen John; m. Shelley Sanborn; c. Blake, Nicolas, Paul, Cooper; Capilano College, USC, insurance broker; asst. swim coach USC; 39 ntl championships '73-80; mem. ntl team '73-80; gold, silver '74 CG; silver '76 Olympics; silver, bronze '79 PAG; 9 1sts '76 nationals, '75 World trials; 34 ntl sr. records; Viscount Alexander award '74; mem. '80 Olympic team; mem. BC Swimming Hall of Fame; res. Tustin, Calif.

PICKERING, Bob (curling); b. 19 Sep 1932, Regina, Sask.; given name: Robert Hugh; m. Dorothy Somerville; c. Laurie, Pattie, Sheri; ret'd politician; MLA Bengough '78-81, served as minister of Rural Development; Parks & Renewable Resources; nicknamed "Peewee"; 6 times provincial champion, Brier rep., 2nd several times; '64 Massey-Ferguson ntl Farmers' title, Canadian Elks '75; twice winner Canadian Open Carspiel Edmonton; twice Calgary Masters champion; mem. Canadian Curling Hall of Fame; res. Phoenix, Ariz./Regina, Sask.

PIDSKALNY, Diane (t&f/wheelchair basketball); b. 3 May 1948, Ethelbert, Man.; m. Alex Hrychuk; c. A.J.; UMan BA; grain farmer, sports exec.; began competing in variety of sports '68; mem. ntl women's wheelchair basketball team '71-90; mem. Man mixed wheelchair basketball team '68-92, Man women's league '96-97; holds Class V women's discus, shot put, javelin records; with teammate Joanne MacDonald Pan-Am gold table tennis doubles '75, '78; ntl Class V table tennis singles champion; more than 100 medals, 20 in international competition; frequent all-star basketball honors; competed 2 Paralympics, gold, 2 silver, bronze '76; helped Canada claim 1st ever Stoke-Mandeville gold '91; commissioner women's div. CWBA '98; v.-pres. athletes rep. CWBA; active wheelchair curler; res. Fork River, Man.

PIELAK, Casmer (baseball); b. 3 Feb 1939, Candiac, Sask.; m. Lavern Haider; c. Warren; businessman; played baseball, hockey in both Candiac, Regina; coached juv Columbus boys baseball league; pres. Columbus Boys League '69-70; pres. Sask. Baseball Assn. '71-72; v-p Baseball Canada '73-75; pres. Baseball Canada '75-85; chair Sask. Sport '76; chair Sask. Lottery '77; v-p International Federation of Amateur Baseball '76-84; secty-general IBA '84-92; instrumental in baseball being '88 Olympic demonstration sport; founding mem. Sask. Sport; mem. Sask Sports Hall of Fame; res. Regina, Sask.

PIERCE, Glen (curling); b. 19 Sep 1941, Tisdale, Sask.; given name: Glen Arnold; m. Eleanor Vuksic; c. Brent, Shannon; mechanical contractor; 11 times Pacific Coast men's finalist; won 6 major cashspiels; skipped BC entry '79 Brier; provincial Tankard finalist '80-82; skipped BC entry to ntl Seagram Mixed title '82; coach Greg McAuley rink '00 worlds; res. New Westminster, B.C.

PIETRACUPA, Michel (weightlifting); b. 12 Jul 1959, Baie Comeau, Que.; ntl jr. record 232.5kg '78 jr. worlds; broke same record with 262.5kg '79 Canada vs England meet; ntl sr. snatch record 135.0kg '81 then broke own standard with 138.9kg '82; ntl sr., Commonwealth clean and jerk record 178.0kg '82; 60kg title Canada vs US '77, 67.5kg jr. America Cup '79, 75kg Que. championships '80, ntl titles '81-82; ntl sr. lift record 315.0kg '82; mem. '80 Olympic team; res. St-Thomas d'Aquin, Que.

PILCHER, Al (skiing); b. 18 Sep 1964, Toronto, Ont.; x-country specialist; also active in duathlons/triathlons; '91 ntl x-country champion; scored 2 1sts '91 Continental Cup series; NA 10km, 30km titles '90; competed '88 Olympics, '89 world championships; res. Orangeville, Ont.

PILON, Claude (wrestling); b. 13 Jun 1950, Ottawa, Ont.; m. Rosalie Sutherland; c. Jean-Marc, Jeffrey Thomas; UofOtt, hons. BPHE; financial advisor, fed. govt.; ntl jr. discus, hammer titles '69-70; de Ottawa Sooners ntl jr., sr. ORFU finalist '70-71; 1 ntl jr. 5 sr. FS wrestling titles; mem. '71, '75 PAG, '73 FISU Games teams; bronze '70, gold '74 CG; silver World Cup '75; CIAU champion '71-74; alternate Greco-Roman team '76 Olympics; pro football Rough Riders '77; 3rd ntl judo black belt championships '82-83; judo black belt '83; consultant Sport Canada '76-80; mem. Cdn Wrestling Hall of Fame; res. Ottawa, Ont.

PILON, Jacques (t&f); b. 16 Aug 1957, Ottawa, Ont.; Dalhousie, UofOtt; launched competitive career B1 (0 vision to light perception) '75; 5 ntl 800m, 1500m, 2 5000m titles; gold 1500m, silver 10,000m '78 Pan-Ams for disabled; gold 1500m '80 Blind Olympics; 1st blind runner to crack 3 hour barrier 2h58:53 National Capital Marathon '83; world records for totally blind 800m, 1500m, ntl records 800m, 1500m, 5000m; silver 1500m Stoke-Mandeville Games for disabled; 1st blind competitor Ottawa Indoor Games; unbeaten at prov. level 800m, 1500m; pres. Ont. Blind Sports Assn. '77; mem. Ottawa Sports Hall of Fame; res. London, Ont.

PILOTE, Pierre (hockey); b. 11 Dec 1931, Kenogami, Que.; given name: Pierre Paul; m. Ann Greshchyshyn; c. Denise, Pierre, Renee, David; ret'd businessman, farmer; def; began organized hockey career Fort Erie at 16; Jr. B Niagara Falls; Jr. A St. Catharines Tee Pees; pro Buffalo AHL '51-55, Chicago NHL '55-68, Toronto '68-69; 5 1st, 3 2nd team all-star; 3 Norris Trophy; capt. Black Hawks '63-68; 1 Stanley Cup; NHL record: 890 scheduled games, 80g, 418a, 86 playoff games, 8g, 53a; raised German short hair pointers; mem. Hockey Hall of Fame; res. Elmvale, Ont.

PILOUS, Rudy (builder/hockey); b. 11 Aug 1914, Winnipeg, Man.; d. 5 Dec 1994, St. Catharines, Ont.; played jr. hockey Portage La Prairie, Winnipeg Monarchs; sr. Nelson, B.C., Eng., NY Rovers; established jr. club in St. Catharines; scout/promotions assistant Buffalo '46; helped Houston win USHL title ;47; sent by Buffalo to San Diego Skyhawks and helped them win PC title '49; reputation as trouble-shooter/promoter firmly established he went on to become mgr/coach St. Catharines Memorial Cup winners '54, '69; coached Black Hawks to '61 Stanley Cup; mgr./coach WHL champion Denver Invaders '64; mgr. WHA Avco Cup champion Winnipeg Jets '76, '78; scout Detroit, Los Angeles; GM Toronto's St. Catharines farm club; mem. Cdn, Man. Hockey halls of fame.

PINDER, Gerry (hockey); b. 15 Sep 1948, Saskatoon, Sask.; given name: Allan Gerald; m. Kaylene Cloward; c. Matt, Patrick, Brett; UofSask, BComm, UMan; real estate developer; mem. Nutana midgets; jr. Saskatoon Blades '65-67; MVP, scoring champion '67; mem. ntl bronze medal team '68 Olympics, '69 world championships; pro Chicago (NHL) '69-71, California (NHL) '72, Cleveland

Crusaders (WHA) '72-76, San Diego Mariners (WHA) '76-77, Edmonton Oilers (WHA) '77-78; eye injury reduced efficiency; co-owner Regina Pats jr. team; scratch golfer; mem. 4 Sask. Willingdon Cup teams; mem. Sask, Saskatoon Sports halls of fame; res. Calgary, Alta.

PINDER, Herb (hockey); b. 29 Dec 1946, Boston, Mass.; given name: Herbert Charles; m. Madeleine Luiten; c. Scott, Danielle; UofSask, BA, UMan, LLB, Harvard Business School, MBA; businessman, player agent; from junior ranks to ntl team; mem. '68 bronze medal Olympic team; ankle fractured in skiing accident ended playing career; exec. asst. to pres. Calgary Broncs (WHA); became player rep. '73; clients have included Peter McNab, Kevin Maxwell, Mike Rogers, Ryan Walter, Dave Williams, Joe Nieuwendyk, Mike Richter, Trevor Kidd, Bill and Chris Hajt; co-owner Regina Pats jr. team; before injury enjoyed standout golfing career; competed in Sask. jr., Regina amateur; Sask. jr. champion; mem. Sask. Willingdon Cup team; has served on numerous corporate boards; governor Canada's Sports Hall of Fame; trustee Fraser Inst., Manning Awards; chair. PRIDE Canada; mem. Sask., Saskatoon Sports halls of fame; res. Saskatoon, Sask.

PINKNEY, David Sr. (harness racing); b. 16 Nov 1931, South Ohio, N.S.; c. Dave Jr., Greg; following father Kirk's footsteps he began driving '51 with most of his career spent campaigning in the Maritimes; despite 3241 victories won purses totalling only $2.4M; with Team Hanover won '87 Haughton Memorial and Hanover Colt Stakes; former dir. USTA; mem. Cdn Horse Racing Hall of Fame; res. Truro, N.S.

PINTEA, Horatio (table tennis); b. 11 Nov 1962, Oradea, Romania; m. Lijuan Geng; c. James Ross; UofOtt; operates pizza business; team, mixed doubles (Mariann Domonkos) silver '83 PAG; men's doubles (Pradeenan Peter-Paul) bronze '99 PAG, '99 Butterfly Cup; 3 ntl, 1 Lousiana, CNE mixed doubles gold; 1 ntl, NA men's doubles gold; 1 ntl, NA, Louisiana men's singles gold; res. Ottawa, Ont.

PIOTROWSKI, Irene (t&f); b. 9 Jul 1941, Skaudvile, Lithuania; given name: Irena Macijauskas; div.; UBC; jewelry store owner/mgr.; BC x-country title, ntl 100yd record '63; ntl, world record 11.4 for 100m '64; mem. '64 '68 Olympic teams; world indoor 300yd, 300m records; silver 100yd, bronze 220yd '66 CG; 5 first, ntl 220yd 23.5 mark BC vs Oregon meet; silver, bronze '67 PAG; ntl record 11.3 100m '68 Olympics; Yukon Flour Packing title '74 backpacking 500lbs 100ft, 600lbs 50 ft; carried 342lbs 50 ft '75 Powell River Sea Festival; women's '74 European tour manager; PB: 100yd 10.4, 100m 11.3; mem. BC Sports Hall of Fame; res. Vancouver, B.C.

PIPE, Andrew (sport medicine/basketball); b. 28 Feb 1949, Nottingham, Eng,; given name: Andrew Lawrence; m. Mary Elaine Gordon; c. Joshua John Pipe Gordon; Queen's BA, MD, LLD (hon); Brock DSc (hon); physician U of O Heart Institute; played intercollegiate soccer '67-74; team physician women's ntl volleyball team '91-83, ntl alpine ski team from '80, men's ntl basketball team from '78; physician 5 Olympics; chief medical officer '87 PAG, '92 Olympics; p-pres. Cdn Academy of Sport Medicine; trustee American College of Sport Medicine; chair. Cdn Centre for Ethics in

Sport; sr. associate editor Clinical Journal of Sport Medicine; Bryce Taylor award for volunteer leadership; Basketball Canada president's award; IOC Sport Medicine award; IOC award for Sport, Health & Wellbeing; mem. Order of Canada; Cdn Olympic Hall of Fame; res. Ottawa, Ont.

PIRNIE, Bruce (t&f); b. 20 Sep 1942, Boston, Mass.; div. Karen Hayton; c. Elizabeth, Catherine; m. Jane Edstrom; Yankton College, BA, South Dakota State; ex-teacher, CTFA ntl throwing coach, head coach high- performance centre, t&f coach UMan.; college all-conference track, football; all-league de St. Vital Bulldogs, ntl sr. champions '68; competed for US '67 PAG; co-capt. '72, '76 Olympic team; shot put silver '73 Pan-Pacific Games '73; bronze '74 CG; gold '75 PAG; 5 ntl indoor, outdoor shot put titles; began coaching '66; 3 CIAU indoor t&f coach-of-yr awards; ntl Espoir team asst.-co-ordinator '87-98; coach 2 CG, 3 PAG teams; v-p Man Basketball Assn.; pres. Norwood Basketball Club; res. Winnipeg, Man.

PISCHKE, Garth (volleyball); b. 12 Aug 1955, Winnipeg, Man.; m. Cindy Lynn Shepherd; c. Dane, Taylor; UMan, BA; coach; played with UMan Bisons '77-79; 3 CIAU title teams; 3 ntl -20 titles; 5 CVA open, 3 USVBA open titles; mem. 29 ntl title teams including '91 Cdn beach doubles; mem. ntl team '76-90; competed '76, '84 Olympics; played pro IVA El Paso, Denver; IVA rookie of '78, MVP '79; 12 ntl championship all-star teams, 6 MVP awards; all-American at 7 USVBA championships, 1 MVP award; through '97 Bisons coach 20yrs, qualifying for ntls each year; 7 CIAU gold, 9 silver, 1 bronze; has amassed more than 1000 coaching triumphs; 5 CIAU coach-of-yr awards; coached varied developmental/experienced club teams to 3 -18, 4 -20, 4CVA open titles; mem. Cdn Olympic, Man. Sports halls of fame; res. Winnipeg, Man.

PITCAIRN, Bob (shooting); b. 26 Jun 1938, Summerside, P.E.I.; given name: Robert Andrew; m. Kay Reade; c. Lee-Anne, Donald; Prince of Wales Coll.; ret'd airline pilot; began small-bore shooting '52, target rifle shooting '60; 8 BC target rifle titles, BC sub-machine gun title '83, 2 BC service rifle titles; 4 BC Lieut.-Gov.'s prizes; qualified 28 Bisley teams; Bisley grand aggregate gold cross '65, silver cross '81; qualified 9 Cdn Palma Teams; DCRA ntl full-bore titles, Gov.-Gen.'s '62, '64; CTR Agg. '90; Macdonald Stewart grand agg. gold cross '90, silver cross '82;. prov exec. pres. '74-78, '90-98; ntl exec., life-gov. BCRA, DCRA; mem. Cdn Forces, PEI Sports halls of fame; res. Chilliwack, B.C.

PITRE, Didier (hockey/lacrosse); b. 1884, Sault Ste. Marie, Ont., d. 29 Jul 1934, Sault Ste. Marie, Mich.; pro def Nationals of Federal Amateur HL; teamed with Jack Laviolette Shamrocks international pro league '08; mem. Lester Patrick's Edmonton team '09; first player signed when Laviolette formed Montreal Canadiens '09-10 and remained with that club until '23 retirement except '13-14 season with Vancouver; moved to rw '11, teamed with Laviolette, Newsy Lalonde to form top line which led Habs to '16 Stanley Cup, team became known as "Flying Frenchmen"; most productive season '15 with 30 goals; in 19 seasons, 282 games, 240 goals, 27 playoff games, 14 goals; lacrosse player with variety of teams; nicknamed "Cannonball"; mem. Canadian Lacrosse, Hockey halls of fame.

PITTS, Allen (football); b. 28 Jun 1963, Tucson, Ariz; Cal State Fullerton; sb; attended NFL LA Rams camps '86-87; made impressive CFL debut with Calgary '90 catching passes in 17 of 18 regular-season games with 65 receptions; during 11yr CFL career set records for all-time receiving yardage (14,891), all-time receiving tds (117), most games catching a td pass (86), most 100yd plus receiving games (61), most td pass receptions single season (21); through '99 in 149 regular season games, 14 playoff games, 5 Grey Cup finals, 2 winners (through '98); 100yds or more receiving 61 times in regular season play; CFL career receptions record 966; 9 all-star awards; 4 Keith Spaith awards; President's ring award '94; res. Calgary, Alta.

PIZZEY, Blair (bowling); b. 5 Jan 1963, Saskatoon, Sask.; given name: Blair Kenneth; m.; c. Branden; UofSask.; auto sales mgr.; played hockey, baseball provincially, softball, provincially, nationally; five-pin bowler; silver '78 Saskatchewan Winter Games; bronze '83 Canada Winter Games; Saskatchewan, ntl singles titles '86; *CBC* singles title '87; Molson open singles titlist '88; res. Saskatoon, Sask.

PLANTE, Jacques (hockey); b. 17 Jan 1929, Mt. Carmel, Que.; d. 26 Feb 1986, Switzerland; m. Jacqueline; c. Michel (d.), Richard; hockey coach; jr. Quebec City; minor pro Montreal Royals (QHL), Buffalo (AHL); goalie Canadiens '52-63, Rangers '63-65, Blues '68-70, Maple Leafs '70-73, Bruins '73, Edmonton (WHA) '74-75; coach Quebec Nordiques (WHA) '73-74; goalie coach Flyers '79-82; Hart Trophy (MVP) '62, 7 times Vezina Trophy, including 5 in succession '56-60; 3 times 1st team, 4 times 2nd team NHL all-star; revolutionized net-minding methods; pioneered modern-day goalie's masks; Montreal jr league commissioner; asst. coach California Seals '67-68; led Quebec minor pro baseball league hitters several seasons; jersey #1 ret'd by Canadiens; mem. Canada's Sports, Hockey halls of fame.

PLATTS, Robin (horse racing); b. 27 Apr 1947, Leicester, Eng.; father's letter to OJC president John Mooney led to opportunity to learn the jockey's art under famed trainer Lou Cavalaris Jr.; made riding debut '66; as apprentice '68 won 219 races including Cdn International championship aboard Frenetico; evolved into one of Woodbine's top money riders winning 4 Queen's Plates, 3 Prince of Wales Stakes, 4 Breeder's Stakes; Sovereign top jockey award '79; Avelino Gomez Memorial award '92; career totals: 20,409 mounts, 3244 1sts, 2831 2nds, 2567 3rds; ret'd from racing '00; mem. Cdn Horse Racing Hall of Fame; res. Toronto, Ont.

PLAXTON, Hugh (hockey); b. 16 May 1904, Barrie, Ont.; d. 1 Dec 1982, Mississauga, Ont.; given name: Hugh John; m. Grace Livingstone Innes; c. Martha, Catherine, Charles Timothy, John Innes (d.); UofT, BA, Osgoode Hall, LLB; ret'd lawyer; mem. Varsity Grad hockey team; Allan Cup champions '27; Olympic gold '28; MP-Lib Toronto Trinity '35-39; mem. Mississauga Sports Hall of Fame.

PLESS, Willie (football); b. 21 Feb 1964, Anniston, Ala; Kansas; ret'd linebacker; Lombardi, Butkus awards nominee; AP second team all-American; MVP '85 Blue-Grey game; participated Senior, East-West Shrine Bowls; set Big 8 Conf. career tackle record; KU tackle leader award bears his name; pro CFL Toronto '86-89, B.C. '90, Edmonton '91-98, '00. Sask '99; CFL record 1241 regular season, 88 playoff/def. tackles; 11 CFL, 2 Eastern, 9 Western, 1 Northern all-star; Frank Gibson Eastern rookie '86, 5 Norm Fieldgate trophies; 5 CFL outstanding defensive player awards, 1 runnerup; 3 Grey Cup finals, 1 winner; mem. Cdn FB Hall of Fame; res. Lawrence, Kan.

PLOEN, Ken (football); b. 3 Jun 1935, Lost Nation, Iowa; given name: Kenneth Allen; m. Janet Ruth Newcomer; c. Kendra Kay, Douglas Allen, Carol Louise; Iowa, BSc; ret'd Blue Bombers sales/marketing chief; HS, college all-American; all-Big 10 MVP, Midwest player of '56; '57 Rose Bowl MVP; CFL Winnipeg '57-67; as db '59 established club interception record with 10; as qb completed 1084 of 1916 passes for 16,470yds, 119tds, 56.6 completion avg., 106 interceptions; shares CFL record for longest completed pass-109yds to Ken Nielsen '65; 3 times WFC, all-pro all-star; 6 Grey Cup finals, 4 winners; '61 Grey Cup MVP; Notre Dame all-opponent team qb '56; Blue Bomber outstanding offensive player of half-century; mem. Canadian Football, Blue Bombers, Rose Bowl, Iowa HS, Iowa Letterman's, Man. Sports halls of fame; res. Winnipeg, Man.

PLOUDRE, Tony (fencing); b. 2 Feb 1966, Chibougamau, Que.; began fencing age 11; sabre specialist; mem. ntl team '85-98; competed '88, '92, '96 Olympics; NA Cup circuit gold '94, Continental Olympic qualifier team gold '95; 2 team silver PAG; with triumph over former world champion Chris Etropolski of Bulgaria, helped Canada to best-ever sabre team showing at worlds with 6th place '91, also 6th '93; ntl sabre title '96; 2 Petro-Canada fund scholarships; res. Montreal, Que.

PLUMMER, Reg (field hockey); b. 6 Aug 1953, Sudbury, Ont.; given name: Reginald Frederick; m. Gail Dawson; Carleton, UBC, BSc; economist; ntl team '73-92; gold '83, silver '75, '79 PAG; mem. '76, '84 Olympic, '78 World Cup, '80 Intercontinental Cup teams; MVP Lahr, Germany, international tournament '76; mem. BC gold medal team '80 ntl championships; asst coach ntl -21 team to '96; mem. ntl high performance team comm.; mem. Outaouais FHC; fed. govt. excellence award '84; res. Kanata, Ont.

POCE, Paul (t&f/coaching); b. 19 Sep 1929, Toronto, Ont; given name: Paul Francis; div. Ethel McKnight; m. Lorraine Watt; UofT; operates Toronto Olympic TC; one of Canada's top milers in '40s and competitor over all distances up to 6 miles to '56; several prov., US distance- race titles; ntl team coach from '60; coach team '66, '70, '78, '86, '90, '94 CG, '67, '75, '79, '83 PAG, '72, '76, '80, '92 Olympic Games, '68 Scandinavia, '71 Italy, '74 European tour; res. Mississauga, Ont.

POCKAR, Brian (figure skating); b. 27 Oct 1959, Calgary, Alta.; d. 28 Apr 1992, Calgary, Alta.; given name: Brian James; UCal; competed '71 Canada Games; at novice level nationally '72-73, ntl junior level '74-75, bronze world junior '76; silver '77 ntl sr. men's, St. Gervais Grand Prix; bronze '78 Skate Canada, '79 England Rotary; ntl sr. men's champion '78-80; world team mem. '77-81; silver '80 Skate Canada; gold '80 St. Ivel England; bronze worlds '82; mem. '80 Olympic team; ret'd '83; artistic dir. '88 Olympic team; TV color commentator; Alberta achievement awards '76-81;

Calgary Booster Club athlete of '80; pro skating lifetime achievement award; mem. Calgary Olympic advisory comm; mem. Alta Sports Hall of Fame.

POCKLINGTON, Peter (builder/hockey); b. 18 Nov 1941, Regina, Sask.; div. c. 4; chair. Pocklington Financial Corp.; sport involvement began with Edmonton Oilers in WHA '77; played key role in moving team into NHL; 5 Stanley Cup winners; mem. chairman's exec. comm. NHL board of governors; sport interest not confined to hockey; owner Edmonton Trappers (PCL) baseball club, Edmonton Drillers (ntl pro soccer league); involved in Can-Am auto racing with Paul Newman; among world's top jet boat racers; wide array of business interests; sold interest in Oilers '98; res. California.

PODBORSKI, Steve (skiing); b. 25 Jul 1957, Toronto, Ont.; given name: Stephen Gregory; div. Ann Rhomer; m. Cathy Rooney; c. Benjamin, Madelaine; ski instructor; mem. ntl team '73-84; ntl slalom champion '77, downhill runnerup '80; NA jr. downhill champion '75; 8 WC downhill victories moved him to forefront among "Kamikaze Kids" as daredevil Canadian male downhillers were termed on World Cup circuit; '80-81 season runnerup for WC downhill title despite coming off knee surgery previous summer; WC downhill title '81-82; WC record 8-5-7; ranked by FIS as world's top downhiller '80-81 season; bronze '80 Olympics, mem. '84 Olympic team; ntl downhill title '84; Ont. athlete of '80, co-holder with Alex Baumann '81; 2 Norton Crowe awards; CSA John Semmelink Trophy '81; course record 1:55.48 in winning WC downhill Garmisch '81; NBC cycling commentator '04 Olympics; avid snowboarder; Officer Order of Canada '82; mem. Cdn Olympic Sports, Ont. Legends, Cdn Skiing halls of fame; res. Whistler, B.C.

PODIVINSKY, Edi (skiing); b. 8 Mar 1970, Edmonton, Alta.; m. Kim; c. Olivia Grace; UWO; mem. ntl alpine development group '87-89, ntl team '90-02; ntl juv downhill gold '85; 1 ntl, 1 jr. world, 4 FIS, 1 World Cup downhill gold; 1 FIS Super G, 2 FIS slalom gold; downhill bronze '94 Olympics; competed '98, '02 Olympics; won US downhill title '98; WC record 1-0-1; brother Tom rodeo rider; res. Port Credit, Ont.

POILE, Bud (builder/hockey); b. 10 Feb 1924, Fort William, Ont.; d. 4 Jan 2005, Vancouver, B.C.; given name: Norman; c. David; ret'd hockey exec.; began pro career Leafs '42; led team in playoff scoring '43; mem. Toronto Stanley Cup winner '47; played in NHL with Toronto, Chicago, Detroit, New York, Boston '42-50; NHL record: 311 scheduled games, 107g, 122a, 23 playoff games, 4g, 5a; turned to administration; coached minor league title winners in Edmonton, San Francisco; GM Philadelphia, Vancouver in NHL; played key role in building 2 Philadelphia Stanley Cup winners; exec/v-p WHA; commissioner CHL '76-84; during '83-84 season also commissioner IHL; forced to suspend CHL operations and stayed with IHL post through '89; Lester Patrick award '89; mem. Hockey, B.C. Hockey, BC, NWO Sports halls of fame.

POIRIER, Joe (football); b. 30 Jul 1937, Montreal, Que.; given name: John Joseph; m. Geraldine Lavoie; c. Erin, J.J., Noemi, Sam; Loyola, BA; McGill, BSW; UofOtt, MSW;

marketing/sales Cdn Tourism Commission; nicknamed "The Fox"; following standout college career turned pro as db with CFL Rough Riders '59-70; EFC rookie of year '59; annually *Globe & Mail* Eastern all-star from '59; CFL Eastern all-star '60-66; all-Canadian '66; 4 Grey Cups, 3 winners; Loyola sportsmanship award '57; McGill sportsmanship award '58; mem. Ottawa, Loyola Sports halls of fame; res. Aylmer, Que.

POITRAS, Tina (t&f); b. 5 Oct 1970, Thompson, Man.; McGill; race walk specialist; began competing '88; world jr. 5km walk gold '89; 5000m Pan-Am jr. championship gold; won 3000m Japan International; 2 ntl outdoor 10km walk gold; competed '92, '96 Olympics; '91, '93 FISU Games, '94 Francophone Games, 2 world championships; Shell scholarship best Quebec student athlete '91-92; Terry Fox award '92; res. Montreal, Que.

POLINARIO, Anne (swimming); b. 5 Aug 1979, Havana, Cuba; York U; mem. Variety Village SC; reached podium in all ntl competitions for swimmers with disability since inaugural ntl championships '95 where she won 5 gold; competed 2 Paralympics; 3 bronze '00, 2 gold, 3 silver '04; res. Toronto, Ont.

POLLOCK, Lloyd (builder); b. 26 Jul 1909, Pine River, Ont.; given name: Lloyd Thompson; ret'd railroader; secty-tres Windsor City HL; instrumental in bringing OHA Junior A hockey to Windsor with Spitfires '46; pres. OHA '61, CAHA '68; mem. Windsor-Essex Sports Hall of Fame; res. Windsor, Ont.

POLLOCK, Sam (hockey); b. 15 Dec 1925, Montreal, Que.; m. Mimi Kinsella; c. Rachel, Sam Jr., Mary; chair./CEO Toronto Blue Jays; former hockey exec.; coached Junior Canadiens '47-53, 1 Memorial Cup winner; Hull-Ottawa Canadiens (EPHL) '59-62; GM Montreal Canadiens '64-78; 9 Stanley Cup winners; '76 *Sporting News* NHL exec. of year; managing dir. Team Canada '76; elected Great Montrealer in Sport past 2 decades '78; chair. John Labatt Ltd., '91-95; chair. Blue Jays '95-99; Officer Order of Canada '85; mem. Hockey, Canada's Sports halls of fame; res. Toronto, Ont.

POLSON, Lynn (basketball); b. 19 Apr 1962, St. Catharines, Ont.; m. Doug Hamilton; c. Frederick, Douglas; Bishop's, BA, Concordia, sports admin. diploma; gd ntl team '91-88; 2 CIAU title teams; gold Jones Cup '82; mem. '81, '83, '85 FISU, '83, '87 (bronze) PAG, '84 Olympic teams; capt. '86 World championship bronze medal team; mem., all-star German semi-pro league '85-97; ntl tour all-star '88; MVP honors Hungary, Czechoslovakia, Canada-Russia series; 3 Bishop's athlete-of-yr awards; 3 CIAU all-Canadian awards; 2 ntl championship MVP awards; res. St. Catharines, Ont.

POMFRET, Jack (all-around); b. 22 Nov 1922, Vancouver, B.C.; given name: Jack Bradshaw; m. Marilyn Russell; c. Lynne, Penny, Jay; Washington, BA, MSc; prof. Emeritus UBC; ntl age-group, sr. native, open swim records; '41 world record; mem. '40 Wash. world record medley relay team; Pacific Coast Conf. record holder; mem. Wash. conf. title team; NCAA all-American; swim coach White Rock SC, Vancouver SC, UAlta., UBC; '70-71 college coach of year; all-star 4yrs HS rugby title teams; mem.

Meraloma Vancouver, BC title teams; capt. Washington Huskies basketball team; *AP* Pac. Conf. all-star; mem. 1 Meraloma, 3 Cloverleaf ntl title teams; mem. '48 Olympic team; *Daily Province* MVP Trophy; offered pro contract Northwest League; coached UBC juniors to 2 BC titles; coached UBC Thunderbirds 15yrs; asst. coach '56 ntl champion BC all-stars, Olympic team; coached RCAF Western Command service champions, Evergreen Conf. all-stars; football to college level, coached UBC 5yrs; mem. Vancouver, Edmonton sr. softball leagues; Edmonton league batting title; baseball Wash., Vancouver sr. league; pro offers Yankees; mem. Wash. boxing team winning all bouts on KO or TKO; jr. hockey Vancouver Lions; semipro Seattle McGregors; pro offers Vancouver Lions, NYR; mem. Richmond Locarno juvenile, jr. lacrosse title teams; mem. 5 soccer title teams; active in swimming, basketball administration at ntl championship, BE, PAG, Olympic Games levels from '62; meet manager, referee CASA swims more than 25 years; key role CIAU aquatic program development; founder BC basketball coaches assn.; pres. Wash. Big W Club; mem. Wash. Oval Club; considered one of greatest athletes in UW history; mem. BC Sports Hall of Fame selection comm.; mem. UBC, BC Sports halls of fame; res. Vancouver, B.C.

PONTING, Tom (swimming); b. 28 Jan 1965, Montreal, Que.; m.; c. 3; UCal; oil/gas industry, coach; butterfly specialist; ntl sr 200m butterfly record; 2 200m, 1 100m CIAU, 16 ntl titles; silver 4x100 MR '83 PAG, FISU, bronze 100m butterfly '83 FISU games; 1 world, 2 Cdn, Commonwealth, 3 CIAU records; 2 CIAU male swimmer of yr awards; only Cdn swimmer to win medals in 3 Olympics 4x100 medley relay silver '84, '88, bronze '92; 2 CG 4x100 medley relay gold; 2 CG silver, 1 bronze; 3 Pan-Pacific silver, 1 bronze; ret'd from competition '94; mem. Alta. Sports, Cdn Olympic halls of fame; res. Calgary, Alta.

POPLAWSKI, Joe (football); b. 2 Sep 1957, Edmonton, Alta.; m. Darlene Dick; UAlta, BSc, UMan BEd; v-p Ranger insurance; college standout receiver; wr Blue Bombers '78-86; Schenley rookie of '78; Jackie Parker Trophy, Dr. Beattie Martin Trophy '78; Schenley Outstanding Canadian '81; 5 CFL all-Cdn.; 1 Grey Cup winner; radio color commentator; dir. Winnipeg Football Club; mem. UAlta Sports Wall, Cdn Football Hall of Fame; res. Winnipeg, Man.

POPP, Jim (football/administration/coaching); b. 21 Dec 1964, Elkin, N.C.; m. Kimberly Hamilton; c. Hannah Nicole, Hayley Payton, Preston Joseph, Hudson Blake; Michigan State; football exec.; wr/db Michigan State; coached Michigan State '86, North Carolina '87, Citadel '88-90, WFL (now NFL Europe) Raleigh-Durham Skyhawks; helped form Professional Spring Football League, dir. personnel '92; dir. Personnel/asst. coach Sask CFL '92-93; AGM/player personnel dir. CFL Baltimore Stallions (only US Grey Cup winner) '94-95; v-p/GM Montreal '96-04; involved 5 Grey Cup finals, 2 winners; res. Montreal, Que./Mooresville, N.C.

PORTER, Bob (all-around); b. 3 Dec 1913, Toronto, Ont.; d. 14 Mar 1995, Toronto, Ont.; mem. 3 HS sr. football title teams, Balmy Beach '32-48; 6 amateur baseball title teams; pro East Texas League '36, Toronto (IL) '36-39, Springfield (IL), Washington (AL) '41; mem. '35 softball title team;

'31 St. Simons juv lacrosse team; jr. hockey Marlboros, int. champion Toronto Royals; rejected pro offers Maple Leafs, Montreal Maroons; coach St. Andrew's College football title team '39; football referee 10yrs ORFU, CIAU; mem. Canada's Sports Hall of Fame.

PORTER, Derek (rowing); b. 2 Nov 1967, Belfast, Ireland; McGill, Victoria BSc; Cdn Memorial Chiropractic Coll.; chiropractor; mem. ntl team '89-01; stroke for '92 Olympic gold medal 8s crew; switched to single sculls '93 winning gold World championships, '99 PAG; silver '96 Olympics; competed '02 Olympics; 4 Cdn, 2 US, 3 Intl regatta golds; mem. Cdn Olympic Hall of Fame; res. Vancouver, B.C.

PORTER, John (hockey); b. 21 Jan 1904, Toronto, Ont.; d. (circa 1990) Toronto; given name: John Chester; m. Marjorie Reever; c. John Jr., Ruth; UofT, BA; ret'd v.-chair. Simpson's; def '21 UTS jr. OHA team; group finalist UofT OHA jrs. '22; OHA finalist UofT '23; OHA semifinalist UofT seniors '25-26; mem. '27 Varsity Grads Allan Cup champions, '28 Olympic champions; flag-bearer '28 winter Olympics; coached '29-30 Varsity Srs to Intercollegiate, OHA titles; pres. Rosedale Golf Club '51, Toronto Hunt Club '69.

PORTER, Ken (t&f); b. 27 Jul 1948, Montreal, Que.; given name: Thomas Kenneth; UAlta, BPhE; sport administrator, coach; mem. CTFA selection comm. '71-72, chair. '72-73; chair. CG Foundation Edmonton athletics '72-77, competition dir. '77-78, asst. sports co-ordinator '77-78; mem. COJO, Montreal Olympics organizing comm. '75-76; CG Foundation Brisbane '80-82; ntl, international t&f meet director '69-80; coach ntl sprint team from '73; head coach Edmonton Olympic Club '79-80; sr. sprints, hurdles coach Australia '80-81; coaching development asst.-co-ordinator Alta. TFA '79-80; official observer '74 European championships, '75 PAG, '77, '79 World Cup, '81 New Zealand games; BC Athletics official-of-yr., long-standing-service awards; mem. Athletics Can. wall of honor; BC Athletics Hall of Fame; res. Edmonton, Alta.

PORTER, Muriel (curling); b. 1903, Toronto, Ont.; d. (circa 1980s) Vancouver, B.C.; given name: Muriel Kathleen Steen; m. Dr. Alvin B. Porter (d.); c. Robert Thomas, Charles Beverly; UBC; ret'd teacher; organized Vancouver Ladies Curling Club '48, pres. 2yrs; helped organize BC Ladies Curling Assn. '50; gold medal best HS female athlete; mem. Canadian Curling Hall of Fame.

POSCENTE, Vincent (skiing); b. 1 Oct 1962, Edmonton, Alta.; m. Michelle Lemmons; c. Max, Alexia; UAlta. BA; professional speaker; speed skiing specialist; luge racer; began skiing at 25; 2 ntl titles; 5 ntl records; ranked among world's top 10 '90-92; competed in speed skiing '92 Olympics; ntl speed record 135 m.p.h. (216.7 k.p.h.); an adventurer he dove among sharks off Australia's Great Barrier Reef, hang-glided in Rockies, dove off world's largest permanent bungee jump (230'); overcame total malfunction while parachuting; pres. Olympians of Canada Calgary '94-95; chair. Olympic Academy of Can. org. comm. '95; chair./founder Alta. Youth Olympic symposium '87-95; dir. Olympic Hall of Fame '94-95; chair. Lillehammer Olympic team sendoff '93-94; selected to Intl. Cdn. Olympic Academy; host broadcaster media liaison

(luge) '88 Olympics; managing dir. Alta. Luge Assn. '85-88; real estate award winner; owner/operator video production co.; mem. ntl speakers assn.; res. Dallas, Tex.

POST, Sandra (golf); b. 4 Jun 1948, Oakville, Ont.; div.; m. John McDermid; teaching pro golfer; ntl jr. titles '64-66, 3 Ont. jr. 1 Ont. Open, South Atlantic titles; pro from '68; '68 LPGA title, beating Kathy Whitworth in playoff; LPGA rookie of year '68; hole-in-one '68 at Cypress Creek Club Boyton Fla.; 8 LPGA tournament victories through '84; 1 Lou Marsh, 2 Bobbie Rosenfeld trophies; capt. inaugural Nation's Cup team; exec. editor *World of Women's Golf;* CTV, ABC golf color commentator; Cdn female pro golfer of century; mem. *Canada's* Sports, RCGA halls of fame; res. Palgrave, Ont.

POTHIER, Eric (luge); b. 3 Aug 1979, Calgary, Alta.; carpenter/construction; doubles specialist with Grant Albrecht from '02, previous partner Chris Moffat; ntl team from '99; competed 2 worlds; 4 top-10 WC results in '00-01, including 6th Oberhof; 5 top-10 WC results '01-02, including 4th Calgary, 5th '02 Olympics; started '02-03 WC circuit with 2 4th place finishes, 4 more top-10 results; ended season with 9th place WC ranking; 5 ntl titles; res. Airdrie, Alta.

POTHIER, Hector (football); b. 13 Jun 1954, St. Catharines, Ont.; m. Louisa; St. Mary's, McGill; 4 conf. all-star, 1 all-Cdn awards; John Metras Trophy CIAU top lineman; originally drafted by Montreal; rights dealt to Edmonton; Eskimos regular '78-89; ot; WFC all-star, all-Cdn '81; 6 Grey Cup winners (5 in succession); mem. Eskimos hockey team; res. Edmonton, Alta.

POTTER, Billy (hockey/baseball/football); b. 10 Oct 1951, Ottawa, Ont.; given name: William Lorne; m. Linda Walton; c. Bradley, David, Brendan, Jesse; Carleton, BComm; economic analyst; mem. peewee Silver Stick hockey title team; midget league scoring champion; mem. 2 CJHL title teams; capt. Carleton, 2 scoring titles; Doug Canton award for athletic excellence Carleton; Little League, Babe Ruth baseball; mem. Ont. Babe Ruth title team; twice represented Canada vs US; mem. 6 Interprovincial Sr. baseball league title teams; twice led league batters; mem. '80 OBA title team; 4 times league all-star; 3 times Ottawa Senior Touch Football League scoring champion; '80 top sportsman trophy OSTFL; mem. ntl touch fb all-stars '79; mem. '79 Ont. touch football title team; brother Dale former mem. Edmonton Eskimos; res. Nepean, Ont.

POTTER, Dale (football); b. 9 Nov 1949, Ottawa, Ont.; given name: Dale William; m. Janet Mary Stirton; c. Braydon, Kenzie; Lenoir Rhyne College, UofOtt, BPhE; UAlta; teacher; HS football MVP '68; played baseball to age 20; excelled as lb 3 seasons UofOtt team capt. 2 years; MVP, top defensive player '71; missed '72 season due to injury after earning Roy Farran award as top training camp player; drafted Winnipeg '73; Edmonton '74-83, Toronto '84; 8 Grey Cup finals, 6 winners; Western all-star, all-Cdn '80; outstanding Cdn, most valuable defensive player '80 Grey Cup game; Joe Clarke award as Eskimo player doing most for team with least recognition '75-76; CFL Players' Assn. Western Conf. lb of '75; plays touch football; coached minor football 5yrs; mem. UofOtt Football, Ottawa Sports halls of fame; res. Nepean, Ont.

POTTER, John (builder/football/coaching); b. 3 Sep 1921, Winnipeg, Man.; d. 10 Nov 1999, Winnipeg, Man.; c. Gregory; UMan.; educator; mem. St. John's Tech city champs '39-40, UM city jrs. '40-41, UMan Varsity '45-47; officiated during '50s; coach Daniel McIntyre HS '51-65, 5 title teams; coached Elmwood HS 4yrs; volunteer coach River East 10yrs, 1 title; Man. HS coach-of-'50s award; CFA distinguished service award; testimoinial dinner given by former players '70; mem. Man. Sports Hall of Fame.

POTVIN, Denis (hockey); b. 29 Oct 1953, Ottawa, Ont.; given name: Denis Charles; m. Valerie; c. Madeleine, Annabelle, Christian; hockey broadcaster; mem. Ottawa 67's jrs.; twice OHA junior A Max Kaminsky award as top def; 1st pick NYI, 1st overall '73 amateur draft; Calder Memorial Trophy NHL rookie of '74; 3 James Norris Memorial trophies; 5 times 1st team, once 2nd team all-star; mem. 4 Stanley Cup winners; mem. Team Canada '76, '81; Islander capt. '79-80, '86-87; NHL record 25 points by def one playoff year; tied NHL records 3 power-play goals 1 game, 2 in 1 period; NHL record: 15 seasons, 1060 games, 310g, 742a, 185 playoff games, 56g, 108a; hon. chairman Suffolk County United Cerebral Palsy Assn.; jerseys ret'd by 67's, Islanders; named to CHL all-time team '99; mem. Hockey, Canada's, Ottawa Sports halls of fame; res. Lighthouse Point, Fla.

POTVIN, Felix (hockey); b. 23 Jun 1971, Anjou, Que; m. Sabrina; c. Noemie, Felicia, Xavier; goal Montreal-Bourassa (QAAA), Chicoutimi (QMJHL), St. John's (AHL); NHL Toronto '91-98, NYI '98-00, Vancouver '01, Los Angeles '01-03, Boston '03-04; gold jr. worlds '91; mem. Team Canada '98 worlds; nicknamed "Cat"; NHL record: (through '04) 635 scheduled games, 36,765min, 266-260-85, 32sho, 72 playoff games, 4435min, 35-37, 8sho; CHL goalie of '91; Memorial Cup all-star '91; Hap Emms Memorial Cup top goalie award '91; Red Garrett AHL top rookie, Baz Bastien top goalie awards '92; NHL all-rookie team '93; 2 NHL all-star games; res. Montreal, Que.

POTVIN, Jean (hockey); b. 25 Mar 1949, Hull, Que.; given name: Jean Rene; m. Lorraine Paluck; c. Kim, Leslie-Ann; UofOtt; broadcaster, stockbroker; Hull Hawks (CJHL) 2 seasons; mem. national team; 2 seasons Ottawa 67's; pro Springfield (AHL) '69-70; NHL with Los Angeles '70-71, Philadelphia '72-73, NYI '73-78, '79-81, Cleveland '78, Minnesota '78-79; ret'd '81 after teaming with brother Denis on def with Islanders and winning 2 Stanley Cups; NHL record: 613 games, 63g, 224a, 39 playoff games, 2g, 9a; res. Huntington Station, N.Y.

POULIN, Dave (hockey/coaching); b. 17 Dec 1958, Timmins, Ont.; m. Lim; c. Lindsay, Taylor, Kylie; Notre Dame BA (marketing); c/lw Notre Dame '78-82, Rogle Sweden, Maine (AHL) '82-83; NHL Philadelphia '82-90, Boston '90-93, Washington '93-95; NHL record: 724 scheduled games, 205g, 325a, 129 playoff games, 31g, 42a, 1 Stanley Cup winner; 3 NHL all-star games; King Clancy, Frank Selke trophies; capt. Flyers; coach Notre Dame from '95; mem. Hockey Heritage North, Flyers halls of fame; res. South Bend, Ind.

POUND, Richard (swimming/administration); b. 22 Mar 1942, St. Catharines, Ont.; given name: Richard William

Duncan: div. Mary Sherrill Owen; c. William Trevor Whitley, Duncan Robert Fraser, Megan Christy; m. Julie Houghton Keith; McGill, B Comm, BCL., Sir George Williams, BA; US Sports Academy (hon) PhD; Windsor (hon) LLD; lawyer, QC; chartered accountant; mem. Que. bar from '68, Ont. bar from '80; fellow Order of Chartered Accounts of Que.; tax specialist; varied key roles with McGill, Cdn Red Cross, Coaching Assn, Cdn Squash Racquetgs Assn.; p-pres. MAAA; 4 ntl FS, 1 butterfly, 3 relay titles; ntl records 40, 50, 100, 110, 200yd, 100m FS; 6 provincial FS titles, records 40, 50 100, 200, 220yd, 100, 200m; intercollegiate FS champion 5yrs, records 50, 100, 200, 220 yds; mem. '59 PAG team; 6th 100m FS '60 Olympics, 4th 400m medley relay; gold 110yd FS record 55.8 '62 CG, silver 880yd, 440yd FS relays; pres. COA '77-82; mem. IOC from '78, v-p '97-00; ex IOC marketing chief; bid for presidency failed; chair. World Anti-Doping Agency; gov. Olympic Trust; dir. '10 Olympic organizing comm.; authored several books; Officer Order of Canada '92, Order of Que. '93; Intl Swimming Hall of Fame gold medallion; CIAU L.B. Pearson award; Cdn Olympic Gold Order; mem. Canadian Aquatic, Olympic, Que. Sports halls of fame; res. Montreal, Que.

POUNDER, Cheryl (hockey); b. 21 Jun 1976, Montreal, Que.; m. Mike O'Toole; WLU BA; ergonomist; world roller hockey gold '92, silver '94; 3 OWIAA all-star; ntl u-18 title team '93; def. Beatrice Aeros from '98; bronze team Ont. '99, '01, gold '00 Esso Cup; 5 world gold, Olympic gold '02; 4 Nations gold '00, silver '03, 3 Nations 4 gold; Mississauga female athlete of yr., 2 WLU female athlete of yr. awards; grandfather Phil Wimmer GM Montreal jr. Canadiens in '70s; nickname "Pounds"; res. Mississauga, Ont.

POWELL, Bill (boxing/bowling); b. 14 Oct 1921, Moose Jaw, Sask., d. 28 Dec 1978, Thunder Bay, Ont.; given name: William Thomas; m. Treasure Corrigan; c. Bob, Faye, Lorrie, Donna Rae; mem. '38 BEG team; ntl bantam, feather, lightweight titles; '46 ntl welterweight title; organized Thunder Bay Legion 5-pin bowling programs; pres. WCFPBA '72; 4yrs pres. TBFPBA; coach, pres. HS 5-pin tournaments; mem. Winnipeg, Boxing halls of fame; '80 sportsman's award Thunder Bay; George Rowe Memorial Award.

POWELL, Cliff (administration); b. 24 Jul 1899, Westmount, Que.; d. 18 Nov 1987, Montreal, Que.; given name: Clifford Baden; m. Doris Sharples; c. Brian, Tim, Ann; McGill.; company board chair.; capt. St. Lambert war canoe, competed tandem 4s '20-25; European baseball following WWI, also hockey, football, baseball Montreal region '20-25; dir. COA, patron Canadian Canoe Assn., pres. Canadian Bobsleigh, Luge Assn.; mem. Cdn Olympic Sports Hall of Fame.

POWELL, Lori-Jane (racquetball); b. 8 Nov 1971, Saskatoon, Sask.; UofSask, BA, ISNTE; performance consultant Powell Performance Services; numerous medals at ntl, world jr. level; mem. ntl team from '94; women's singles gold '94, doubled gold '02 tournament of Americas; 2 ntl singles, 3 women's doubles, 1 mixed doubles titles; singles silver '94, team gold, doubles bronze '00 worlds; PAG doubles silver '99, singles bronze '03; certified fitness consultant; Level III coach; mem. CMTR; res. Calgary, Alta.

POWER, Dale (tennis/hockey); b. 2 Oct 1949, Toronto, Ont.; given name: Dale Thomas; m. Joan Kathryn Westman: Oklahoma City ; tennis pro; OHA jr. hockey St. Catharines, Peterborough Petes '67-68; 5th pick Montreal '69 draft; pro Fort Wayne Komets (IHL) 1 season; ntl -18 closed tennis title '67; OCU tennis scholarship '70; mem. '72, '76 Davis Cup teams; among Canada's top 10 singles players from '68; ntl men's doubles title '73; top men's singles player '75 Rothman's Summer Grand Prix tour '80; ntl indoor singles, doubles titles '78, outdoor '79; pro circuit '76-81; playing coach Canadian Alcan tennis team '83; Racquet Power touring pro; mgr. Pinecrest TC, Chateau Montebello, Rideau Tennis & Squash Club; switched competitive attention to squash '95; res. Ottawa, Ont.

POWER, Jonathon (squash); b. 9 Aug 1974, Comox, B.C.; m. Sita; ntl jr. titles '85-92; 5 ntl men's titles; mem. ntl jr. men's team '90, '92; team placed 3rd, best ever by Canada, '92 worlds; his 2nd place finish best ever by Canadian; youngest-ever men's ntl team mem. '91; mem. ntl sr. men's team '93-98; individual silver, team gold '95 PAG; silver '98, gold '02 CG; won '95 MAAA invitational, '96 tournament of champions (1st NA player to win major world squash event) German, 2 US pro masters, Val de Loire. 2 Hungarian Open, '97 Qatar Open, finalist '97 worlds; top-ranked in Canada '97; 1st non-European to win Australian Open '98; won Cathay Pacific Open '98; won Flanders Open '99, British Open '99, Pakistan Open '02, US Super Series '03; 1st NA player to win world open title '98; 1st Canadian ranked No. 1 in world '99; through '04 33 tour titles; res. Montreal, Que.

POWLESS, Gaylord (lacrosse); b. 1 Dec 1946, Brantford, Ont.; d. 28 Jul 2001, Haggersville, Ont.; given name: Gaylord Ross; m. Patty Broker; c. Gaylene, Chris; ret'd construction; ctr jr./sr./major/pro Oshawa, Detroit, Brantford, Six Nations, Coquitlam, Syracuse, Montreal, Brampton '64-77; cumulative record: 705 scheduled games, 588g, 914a, 118 playoff games, 207g, 317a; 4 Minto, 1 Mann Cup title teams; Jim McConaghy Minto Cup MVP awards '64, '67; 2 Ken Ross ability/sportsmanship awards; 1 Bucko MacDonald, 2 *Advertiser* top scorer awards; 4 1st team, 1 2nd team all-star ctr awards; mem. Cdn Lacrosse Hall of Fame.

POWLESS, Ross (lacrosse); b. 29 Sep 1926, Six Nations of the Grand River, Ont.; d. 26 May 2003, Paris, Ont.; given name: Alexander Ross; m. Margaret Wilma Bomberry; c. Gaylord (d), Gail, Gary, Audrey, Gregory, Harry, Arlene, Richard, Darryl, Karen, Anthony, Jeffrey, Jacqueline; ret'd construction supervisor/band council mem.; Sr. B Eastern Cdn Huntsville title team '50; mem. Peterborough Mann Cup titlists '51-54; player/coach Lewiston, NY/Tuscarora Indian Reserve Eastern Sr, B champs '55; '58-68 coach Brantford Warriors Ont. Int. A/Sr. B titles, player/coach Hamilton Lincoln Burners Sr. A, coach Six Nations All-Indian sr. team; coach Cdn sr. men's team Expo '67; coach. mgr. Rochester NALA titlists '69; co-coach First Nations silver-medal team '80 Nations Cup; 3 terms Six Nations rec. comm.; pres. Six Nations MHA '66; mem. building comm. Six Nations Sports/Cultural Memorial Centre; Mike Kelly Mann Cup MVP award '53; 2 Tom Longboat awards; Ont. Municipal Rec. Assn. volunteer service award; mem. Cdn Lacrosse Hall of Fame.

PRATHER, Rollie (football); b. 17 Jul 1925, Eureka, Kan.; d. 28 May 1996, Calgary, Alta.; given name: Rollin Wayne; m. Gwyneth Mary Evans; c. Russell Rollin Wayne, Teresa Anne, Candice Louise, Shannon Maureen Kelly, Kathleen Moira Kelly; Kansas State, BSc; geologist; pres., chief exec. officer gas dev. co.; all-American t&f '47-48; pro Edmonton '50-54; all-Cdn '51-52; CFL record most passes caught one game 15 '52; pro-am golf classic champion Willow Park G&CC '71; dir. Eskimos; mem. Kansas State Football Hall of Fame.

PRATT, Babe (hockey); b. 7 Jan 1916, Stoney Mountain, Man.; d. 16 Dec 1988, Vancouver, B.C.; given name: Walter; v-p, public relations asst. Vancouver Canucks; mem. 15 championship teams in 26-year playing career; Man. midget, juv titles Elmwood Maple Leafs; Man. jr. title, scoring title Kenora; def NYR '35-36, Maple Leafs '42-46, Boston '46-47; NHL record: 517 scheduled games, 83g, 209a, 64 playoff games, 12g, 17a; on leaving NHL played with Hershey, New Westminster, Tacoma; Hart Trophy NHL MVP '44, mem. 1st, 2nd all-star teams; mem. '40 Stanley Cup, '42 Prince of Wales Trophy winners; mem. Cdn, Man. Hockey halls of fame.

PRATT, Ned (rowing); b. 15 Jul 1911, Boston, Mass.; given name: Charles Edward; m. Catherine Gordon Lang; m. Peter, Toni; UofT, BArch; ret'd architect; North Pacific junior singles '29, Sir Thomas Lipton Trophy '31; with Noel de Mille '32 North Pacific doubles, ntl championship, bronze doubles '32 Olympics, Pacific Coast title; gymnasium bears his name; mem. BC Sports Hall of Fame; res. West Vancouver, B.C.

PREDIGER, Pete (baseball); b. 1913, Odessa, Russia, d. 4 Feb 1974, Saskatoon, Sask.; given name: Peter John; raised in Macklin, Sask.; mem. Edmonton jrs. '32; mem. Neilberg Monarchs 38yrs, playing in remarkable 34 consec. Saskatoon Exhibition Baseball Tournaments; 5 title teams; semipro North Battleford Beavers '50-55, Lloydminster Meridians '57; ret'd from play at 50; umpired to death from cancer; coached Legion baseball, softball, hockey 20yrs; toured Europe with Krefield Canadians hockey club '36; mem. Canadian Baseball, Sask. Sports halls of fame.

PREFONTAINE, Noel (football); b. 23 Dec 1973, Camp Pendleton, Calif.; Cal-State Fullerton, San Diego State; criminal justice; punter; spent youth in Montreal; standout HS qb; *San Diego Tribune* athlete of yr; WAC all-American; varied US college punting records; pro LA Extreme (XFL) '02; NFL Baltimore, KC '02; CFL Toronto '98-04; CFL record (through '04) 118 scheduled games; 896 punts, 40,866yds; 105fg; 401ko, 23,288yds; 5 East, 4 CFL all-star; 1 Grey Cup title; mem. Argos charity basketball team; res. San Diego, Calif.

PRÉMONT, Marie-HélPne (cycling); b. 24 Oct 1977, Québec, Qué.; Laval BSc kinesiology; pharmacology student; mountain biking specialist; competed '02 CG; '03 Cdn. champ; worlds '03-04; 2nd '04 world cup circuit cumulative; '04 Olympic silver; *Canadian Cyclist* magazine Cdn. female cyclist of '04; res. Chateau-Richer, Qué.

PRENTICE, Bob (baseball); b. 12 Aug 1928, Toronto, Ont.; d. 9 Feb 1995, Toronto, Ont.; given name: Robert

Fergus; m. Nancy Sutherland; c. Jamie Susan, Richard Robert Scott; dir. Cdn scouting Blue Jays; all-star qb '44-46 Riverdale CI football team; mem. Ont. Jr. A Toronto Young Rangers hockey team '46-47; pro baseball Cleveland (AL) organization '48-57; Cdn chief scout Detroit '59-76; dir. Cdn scouting Blue Jays '76-95; freelance sports columnist *Toronto Telegram* '60-63; *CBS TV* broadcaster's asst. PGA golf tournaments '72-76.

PRENTICE, Bruce (administration); b. 31 Jul 1933, Toronto, Ont.; given name: Bruce Leslie; m. Audrey Grace Robertson; c. Brad, Laura, Graham, David; pres. Deamfield International Management Group; mem. OBA juv baseball champions '50, sr. OBA titlists '53; Detroit Tiger prospect; coach/dir. playground baseball program '56-60, '59 Toronto city champions; founder/head coach 1st college/university baseball program in Canada Seneca Coll. '78-82; mem. NJCAA, NY-Penn conference; formed Metro College Baseball League '83; head coach Ryerson '83-84; Blue Jays scout '79-85; founder/pres. Cdn Baseball Hall of Fame '78-93; owner Proway baseball schools '81-84; skip bronze medal novice lawn bowling team '97; skip Balmy Beach Club curling league champions '96; brother Bob Blue Jay scouting dir.; operates Ont. Sport Legends, World Baseball, World Sport Legends, Royal Canadian Legion Sports halls of fame; res. Toronto, Ont.

PRENTICE, Dean (hockey); b. 5 Oct 1932, Schumacher, Ont.; given name: Dean Sutherland; m. June Collier; c. Kelly, Kerry; lw; jr. Guelph Biltmores; played 22 seasons in NHL with NYR '52-63, forming line with Andy Bathgate and Larry Popein, Boston '63-66, Detroit '66-69, Pittsburgh '69-71, Minnesota '71-74; NHL record: 1378 scheduled games, 391g, 469a, 54 playoff games, 13g, 17a; competed 4 NHL all-star games; coach New Haven (AHL) '75-77, Traverse City '77-78; with figure skating coach Kerry Leitch operated hockey school in Galt '64; assisted Glen Sather in Banff hockey school; setup Can-Am Hockey Schools; mgr./parks and rec. dir. Ayr 10yrs; active in Hockey Ministries International; plays old timers hockey; mem. Hockey Heritage North Hall of Fame; res. Cambridge, Ont.

PRESTON, Ken (football); b. 29 Oct 1917, Portland, Ont.; d. 2 Aug 1991, Regina, Sask.; given name: Kenneth Joseph; m. Dorothy Barber (d); c. William, Douglas, Richard, Donna; Queen's, BComm; ret'd football exec.; football Queen's '36-39; pro Sask. '40, '46-48, Winnipeg '41 playing in Grey Cup victory, Ottawa '45; Saskatchewan GM '58-79; mem. Cdn Football, Sask. Sports halls of fame.

PRICE, Harry (administration); b. 6 Apr 1896, Toronto, Ont.; d. 19 Feb 1985, Toronto, Ont.; given name: Harry Isaac; m. Ethel Hilker (d); c. Harry, Ethel Margaret; businessman; sports promoter; key role in establishment Canada's Sports Hall of Fame, chairman bd. of govs. '55-69; key role in establishment of govt. fitness, amateur sport administration; pres. CNE; MP York West; mem. Canada's Sports Hall of Fame.

PRICE, Noel (hockey); b. 9 Dec 1935, Brockville, Ont.; given name: Garry Noel; m. Joann Packota; c. Christine, Joel; ret'd; played minor hockey in Coniston; mem. Falconbridge Jr. A team at 15 where he was offered St. Michael's Coll. scholarship and played 4yrs in OHA Jr.

A; turned pro '56; def. Rochester, Baltimore, Springfield, Quebec, Nova Scotia (AHL), Winnipeg (WHL); NHL with Toronto, NYR, Detroit, Montreal, Pittsburgh, Los Angeles, Atlanta; NHL record: 499 scheduled games, 14g, 114a, 12 playoff games, 0g, 1a; ret'd following '75-76 season; 4 Calder Cups, 1 Stanley Cup; 3 AHL 1st team, 1 2nd team all-star; only player to win 3 Eddie Shore best AHL def awards; named top def Springfield 50th anniversary team; mem. Springfield Hockey, Hockey Heritage North and with '72 Calder Cup title team Nova Scotia Sports halls of fame; res. Kanata, Ont.

PRICE, Steve (softball); b. 24 Dec 1963, Toronto, Ont.; lhp/of; salesman; began as intermediate with Verona; played sr. with Kemptville Thunder, Toronto Gators, Middletown, NY, Heflin Builders Ballston Lake, NY, Decatur Pride, Vancouver Ravens, Green Bay; mem. ntl team; mem. ISC Toronto Gators world title team '93; PAG gold '95, '99; res. Kingston, Ont.

PRIDHAM, Chris (tennis); b. 11 Apr 1965, Toronto, Ont.; ntl -16 singles, doubles titles; ntl -18 doubles; posted singles victories Hawaiian Satellite '87, Sun Life Classic '88, Troia Setubal '89, Bloomfield Hills Challenge '92; doubles victories Sun Life ntls '91, Munich Challenger '92; 3rd round singles Wimbledon '88, Australian Open '89, Player's International '92; Tennis Canada most-improved award '87; pro '85; ranked 2nd Canada '92-93; mem. Cdn Davis Cup team from '88; mem. '88 Olympic team; active spokes-person, fund-raiser CAVEAT (Canadians Against Violence Everywhere Advocating Its Termination); highest ATP ranking 75 in '88; res. Oakville, Ont.

PRIESTLEY, Gladys (swimming); b. 17 Jun 1938, Montreal, Que.; given name: Gladys Jean; m. Ross Watson; c. Ray Allan, Lori Anne; ntl FS relay titles, record times '50-58; mem. '52 (silver FS, medley relay), '56 Olympics; silver 400m FS '54, relay '58 BEG; FS finalist '55 PAG; res. Arundel, Que.

PRIESTMAN, Keith (badminton); b. 21 Jan 1959, Scarborough, Ont.; given name: Keith Jack; m. Patti Bell; c. Ryan, Kelsey; Waterloo, BSc; mgr racquets div. Sportslines Intl.; 11 Ont. titles, including 2 jr. singles, '79 Open singles, 3 OUAA titles; 8 ntl titles; junior doubles with Jeff Goldsworthy; intermediate singles '79, '81; intermediate mixed doubles with Sandra Skillings '80; men's doubles with John Czich '82; mem. Pan-Am championships '80, Canadian Open, Devlin Cup, Am-Can, All-England teams; mem. ntl team '79-85; team silver '82 CG; turned to coaching '82-90; finalist Waterloo County amateur athlete of '78; mem. Waterloo Athletic Hall of Fame; res. Bowmanville, Ont.

PRIESTNER, Cathy (speed skating); b. 27 May 1956, Windsor, Ont.; given name: Catherine Ann; div. Merle Douglas Faminow; c. Leah Colette; m. Todd Allinger; c. Alicia, Colten; Mount Royal College; sr. v-pres. sport VANOC; managing dir. Games Operations '06 Torino winter Olympics; dir. ice events '02 Salt Lake City winter Olympics; ex-asst. AD UCal; 6 ntl titles; gold 400m, silver 500m '71 Canada Games; silver 500m, 1000m '75 junior world; 5th overall world championships '75 with silver 500m, bronze 1000m, 14th 1500m, 3000m; third overall '75 world sprint championships with gold 500m, 4th 1000m, 6th 500m, 1000m; silver 500m, 6th 1000m '76 Olympics; ntl open records 500m, 1000m; fastest 500m award 3 times; '75 Calgary athlete of year; Gov.-Gen.'s silver medal '76; coach ntl jr. team '76; coached Champaign, Ill., speed skating club; with Ken Read torch bearer '88 Olympics opening ceremonies; *CBC* '92, '98 Olympic speed skating analyst; mem. Olympic Order, Alta. Sports, Cdn Speed Skating, Cdn Olympic halls of fame; res. Seattle, Wash./Vancouver, B.C.

PRIMEAU, Joe (hockey); b. 29 Jan 1906, Lindsay, Ont.; d. 15 May 1989, Toronto, Ont.; m. Helen Marie Meagher; c. Joe Jr., Bill, Bob, Anne, Richard; St. Michael's College; hockey coach, businessman; ctr St. Michael's College jrs.; pro Toronto Ravinas '27, league scoring title; Maple Leafs '28-36; ctr'd Kid Line with Charlie Conacher, Busher Jackson; twice runnerup NHL scoring race; Lady Byng Trophy '32; 2nd team all-star '34; coach 23 years, Memorial (2), Allan, Stanley Cup winners; mem. '32 Stanley Cup champions, coached '51 titlist; mem. Hockey, Canada's, Mississauga Sports halls of fame.

PRIMEAU, Keith (hockey); b. 24 Nov 1971, Toronto, Ont.; m. Lisa; c. Corey, Kylie, Chayse; ctr OHL Niagara Falls, AHL Adirondack (Calder Cup) '92, NHL Detroit '90-96, Hartford '96-97, Carolina '97-00 (capt), Philadelphia '00-04; mem. Team Canada '96 World Cup, '97, '98 worlds, '98 Olympics; NHL record (through '04): 900 scheduled games, 265g, 347a, 128 playoff games, 18g, 39a; Pa. Class Guy award; one of founders Hockey's Helping Hands; active with Drug Awareness Resistance Education program, Make-a-Wish Foundation; res. Hartford, Conn.

PRIMROSE, John (shooting); b. 28 May 1942, Ottawa, Ont.; UofAlta, BPhE, MSc., self-employed investor, dir. Pinhead Components Inc.; mem. 13 world championships trapshooting teams, gold '75, '83, 4 silver; mem. '68, '72, '76, '84, '88, '92 Olympics; mem. '74, '78, '82, '86, '90 CG teams winning gold '74, '78; ntl doubles champion '69 Pan-Am championships; mem. '75, '79, '83, '87, '95 (team silver) PAG teams; Benito Juarez title '77; 13 ntl titles; ntl record 386x400 '68, 296x300 '70; mem. Edmonton Gun Club, dir. '64-70; pres. Alberta International Style Trap Assn. '72-99; dir. Shooting Federation of Canada '73-75; chair. shooting tech. comm. '78 CG; flag-bearer '82 CG; founding comm. mem. Alberta Federation of Shooting Sports; mem. COA athletes council '80-92; Golden Anniversary SFC award for contribution to sport '82; fed. govt. world champion award '84; mem. Order of Canada, Alta., UAlta, Edmonton; Cdn Olympic, Canada's Sports halls of fame; res. Edmonton, Alta.

PRINGLE, Mike (football); b. 1 Oct 1967, Los Angeles, Calif.; Washington State; Cal State (Fullerton); personal trainer; rb; led nation all-purpose yds with 2690 '89; NFL Atlanta '90-91, WLAF Sacramento Surge '92, CFL Edmonton '92, '03-04, Sacramento '93, Baltimore '94-95, Montreal '96-02; CFL record: 148tds, 2x2cvt, 892pts, 2962 carries for 16,424yds, 136tds, 396 recep., 3830yds, 12tds; 7 Eastern, 1 Southern, 6 CFL all-star teams; set CFL single-season rushing record 2065yds on 347 carries '98; 67 100+yd games surpassed George Reed career record '03; surpassed Reed all-time rushing record of 16,116yds, tds scored '04; 4 Terry Evanshen trophies; 2 CFL outstanding

player awards, MVP '95 Grey Cup; 11 playoff games, 5 Grey Cup finals, 3 winners; res. Los Angeles, Calif.

PRINTERS, Casey (football); b. 16 May 1981, DeSoto, Tex.; Texas Christian, Florida A&M; qb 2 conf. title winners; *Dallas Morning News* freshman-of-yr award; Mobile Bowl MVP; *SN* freshman all-American; CFL BC '03-04; CFL outstanding player award '04; CFL record (through '04) 494 passes, 325 completed, 5088yds, 35tds, 10int, 82 carries, 469yds, 9tds; res. Dallas, Tex.

PRIOR, Russ (weightlifting); b. 11 Jul 1949, Hamilton, Ont.; m. Barbara Behan; c. Kyle, Scott, Heather; McMaster, Carleton, Queen's, UMan, North Dakota, BA, BEd, BSc; HS teacher; 28 Commonwealth, 74 ntl records, including all Commonwealth, ntl standards 110kg class; ntl, Commonwealth snatch record 172.5kg super heavyweight class; 9 ntl titles, 3 CG gold medals; 3 ntl teenage titles (2 at 82.5kg, 1 at 90kg); '68 American teenage champion 82.5kg; 2 NA 110kg titles; PAG 110kg gold '75; silver Pan-Am championships twice; gold Western Canada Games 110kg '79; mem. '76, '80 Olympic Games, awarded (on paper) snatch bronze '76 Olympics when Bulgarian disqualified for steroid use; '73 world championships teams; 1st Cdn to win gold medals 3 successive CG; ret'd from competition after winning silver '81 NA championships; regarded by many as Canada's strongest man of his time; res. Winnipeg, Man.

PROCHER, Theda (bowling); b. 24 Jun 1917, Chapleau, Ont.; given name: Theda Crowhurst; m. Bill Procher; c. Teddy, Ken; Ont. singles title '69; mem. 3 ntl ladies', 1 ntl mixed title teams; PB: 420 single, 1029 triple; highest season avg. 272 in '69; top level coach, instructor Master Bowlers Assn. program; mem. Ont. 5-Pin Hall of Fame; res. Toronto, Ont.

PROFIT, Mel (football); b. 30 Jul 1941, New York, N.Y.; UCLA; raised in San Jose, Calif.; tight end UCLA; drafted by LA Rams (NFL), Kansas City (AFL); signed with LA but following injury was dealt to Pittsburgh where he spent season on taxi squad; quit game to travel Europe; returned to game with B.C. Lions who dealt him to Toronto Argos; made CFL debut Toronto '66-72; became focal point in 1st CFL players strike '69; released by Argos '72 and became host of City TV talk show, Argos color commentator CFRB radio; East all-star '71; Jeff Russel award '71; mem. all-time Argos dream team; nicknamed "Mousy"; authored *For Love, Money and Future Considerations;* res. San Jose, Calif.

PRONGER, Chris (hockey); b. 10 Oct 1974, Dryden, Ont.; m. Lauren; c. Jack; def OHL Peterborough '91-93; NHL Hartford '93-95, St. Louis '95-03; team capt. from '97; NHL record (through '04): 722 scheduled games, 94g, 306a, 85 playoff games, 10g, 41a; NHL all-rookie team; Hartford Most Valuable Defenceman award '94; CHL def. of '93; Max Kaminsky award '93; Hart, Norris trophies; 1st team all-star '00; played 2 NHL all-star games; mem. Team Canada '98, '02 (gold) Olympics, '92 world jr., '96 worlds; developed Prongers Pack for under-privileged kids; brother Sean with Columbus; part-owner Mississauga Ice Dogs (OHL); res. Dryden, Ont.

PRONOVOST, Jean (hockey/coaching); b. 18 Dec 1945, Shawinigan, Que.; m. Diane; rw Victoriaville QJHL '63-64,

Niagara Falls OHA '64-66, Oklahoma City CHL '66-68; NHL Pittsburgh '68-78, Atlanta/Calgary '78-80, Washington '80-82; NHL totals: 998 scheduled games, 391g, 383a, 35 playoff games, 11g, 9a; scored 52g '76; 4 NHL all-star games; several Penguin team awards including rookie, points leader, 5 players' player, 3 MVP awards; v-p/coach San Diego Seals '92-95, '02-04; active in Hockey Ministries International; res. San Diego, Calif.

PRONOVOST, Marcel (hockey); b. 15 Jun 1930, Lac la Tortue, Que.; given name: Joseph René Marcel; m. Cindy Lapierre (d); c. Michel, Brigitte, Léo; m. Eva; hockey scout; def. jr. A Windsor Spitfires; pro Detroit (IHL) '47-49; Omaha (USHL) '49-50; Indianapolis (AHL) '50-51; Detroit '51-65, Toronto '65-70; player/coach Tulsa (CHL) '70-72, coach of year '71; coach Chicago Cougars (WHA) '72-73; Hull, Que. juniors '75-77, '79-80; Buffalo '77-79; asst. coach Detroit '79-81; Windsor Spitfires (OHL) '81-82; NHL Central Scouting Bureau 5yrs; scout New Jersey from '90; NHL record: 1206 scheduled games, 88g, 257a, 134 playoff games, 8g, 23a; mem. 8 Prince of Wales Trophy (league title), 5 Stanley Cup winners; twice 1st, 2nd team all-star; Jake Milford trophy '69-70; mem. Hockey Hall of Fame; res. Windsor, Ont.

PROPP, Brian (hockey); b.15 Feb 1959, Lanigan, Sask.; m. Kris Vollmer; c. Paige, Jackson; hockey TV color analyst; lw Melville (SJHL) '75-76, Brandon (WCJHL) '76-79; ntl jr. team '79; mem. Team Canada '79, '82, '83, '88, '93; Canada Cup, Spengler Cup winning teams; 1st draft choice Philadelphia '79; with NHL Flyers '79-90, Boston '90, Minnesota '90-93, Hartford '93-94; Lugano (Switz) '93; twice all-star Brandon; 5 NHL all-star games; set several Flyers club records; NHL record: 1016 scheduled games, 425g, 579a, 160 playoff games, 64g, 84a; named to CHL all-time team '99; mem. Sask. Sports, Flyers halls of fame; res: Mount Laurel, N.J.

PROULX, Rita (curling); b. 16 Jun 1919, Quebec City, Que.; given name: Rita Louise Couture; m. Jean Noel Proulx; Montreal.; Cdn Red Cross volunteer; pres. Que. Winter Club '50-53; pres., organizer 1st International ladies' bonspiel '51; pres., organizer Que. Ladies' Curling Assn. '56; won 1st provincial curling title; organized Que. Ladies' Curling Council '68; pres. 1st ntl jr. girls curling championship '73; organized 1st curling school for jrs. in Canada, instructor '75; pres. CLCA '78-79; treasurer La Federation Québécoise de Curling Inc.; Cdn rep. ICF Ladies' Comm.; authored constitution, by-laws for women's curling in Que.; chair. Que. district golf course rating committee; pres. Ladies' Sr. golf championship '74; Cdn Red Cross Service Medal '45, Queen's jubilee medal '77; Quebec sports administrator of '78; mem. Canadian Curling Hall of Fame; res. Quebec City, Que.

PROVOST, Barry (curling); b. 15 Mar 1944, Ottawa, Ont.; given name: Barry Michael; m. Nancy Carol Jeffrey; c. James Warren, Tyler; Gould Business College; branch mgr. insurance group; North Eastern Alta. Schoolboy title '63; lead Eldon Coombe's Ottawa rink, 7 consecutive OCA Div. 1 titles; Ont. Consols title, Brier berth '72; 3 Cdn Branch Royal Caledonian Curling Club Royal Victoria Jubilee titles; 7 Red Anderson Memorial championships; *CBC* Curling

Classic '72; Whitby Dunlop 'spiel '72; 3 Ottawa ACT curler-of-yr awards, rated one of Canada's outstanding leads and sweepers; active in Stittsville minor softball program; mem. Ottawa Sports Hall of Fame; res. Stittsville, Ont.

PROVOST, Claude (hockey); b. 17 Sep 1933, Montreal, Que.; rw Montreal QJHL '51-54, Shawinigan QHL '54-55; NHL Montreal '55-70; NHL totals: 1005 scheduled games, 254g, 335a, 126 playoff games, 25g, 38a; 9 Stanley Cup winners; 1 1st team NHL all-star; competed 11 NHL all-star games; coach Rosemont QJHL '70-71; Bill Masterton trophy '68; res. Montreal, Que.

PROVOST, Mary (all-around); b. 29 Jul 1920, Ottawa, Ont.; given name: Mary Haydon; m. Peter Provost; c. Peter Gerard, Carolyn Anne; Willis Business School; ret'd E.B. Eddy; honored by Boy Scout Assn for leadership role '48-54; among founders of Ottawa track club, fore-runner of Ottawa Lions TC; began competitive high jumping '36; set ntl jr. record '37; also excelled in long, broad jumps setting records in each; recognized by AAU of C as one of finest women athletes; ranked top prospect for '40 Olympics (cancelled by WW2); among first to perfect roll over scissors in HJ; '36-39 won 3 ntl, CCE, Ont, 2 EOSSA, 1 BEG trials HJ titles, 1 EOSSA LJ, BJ, 1 Ont BJ titles; as golfer won 2 Glenlea, several Gatineau ladies club titles; in '40s center ntl women's basketball title team; avid 5-pin bowler for 20yrs; curled Rockcliffe CC; certified track judge working numerous meets including *Citizen* Indoor Games and Cdn t&f championships '82; recipient Ottawa civic crest, Dominion championship crest; mem. Ottawa Sports Hall of Fame; res. Ottawa, Ont.

PRYSTAI, Metro (hockey); b. 7 Nov 1927, Yorkton, Sask.; m. 1. Evelyn Peppler (d), 2. Mavis Evans; c. David, Merrill (d), Karen, Michael, James; ret'd Prystai Insurance Agency owner; Moose Jaw jrs.; NHL ctr for Chicago '47-50, '55-56, Detroit '50-54, '56-58; NHL record: 674 scheduled games, 151g, 179a, 43 playoff games, 12g, 14a; 3 NHL all-star games; 2 Stanley Cup winners; coached Omaha (CHL), Moose Jaw (SJHL) league titles '60-62, Melville (SJHL); 3b/mgr. Yorkton Man-Sask baseball league '52; salesman O'Keefe Brewery; operated International Hockey School, Nelson, B.C.; mem. Sask. Sports Hall of Fame; res. Yorkton, Sask.

PSUTKA, Harry (baseball/hockey); b. 19 Nov 1926, Kitchener, Ont.; m. Joan Rita Kipper; c. David, Thomas, Douglas, Andrew; St. Michael's Coll.; furniture salesman; catcher jr., sr. IC with Kitchener; 4yrs pro in Detroit chain with Jamestown (Pony), Durham (Carolina), Flint (Central), Williamsport (Eastern), Davenport (3I); def Kitchener minor hockey system, St. Mike's Jr. A, Marlboroughs Sr. A; pro Pittsburgh Hornets (AHL), Maple Leafs (NHL), playoff backup '49; mem. Memorial Cup '46, Allan Cup '43, Stanley Cup '49 winners; res. Kitchener, Ont.

PUDDY, Bill (swimming); b. 19 Dec 1916, Toronto, Ont.; d. (circa 2000) Toronto, Ont.; given name: William Albert; m. Eileen Anna Stoneburg (d.), Marion Frances Forlong; c. Susan, John; ret'd company pres.; mem. Toronto Westend YMCA swim team age 10-12; competed international YMCA championships Ann Arbor, Mich., '31; ntl jr. titles ages 14-17; ntl open breaststroke titlist '34-36; gold, bronze

'34 BEG; CNE breaststroke titlist '31-36; declined Michigan athletic scholarship; mem. '36 Olympic team; won 120 medals, trophies '30-36, establishing numerous records; Ont. open breaststroke jr., sr. titles '31-36; mem. Cdn, Ont. Aquatic halls of fame.

PUGH, Bob (football/hockey); b. 29 Oct 1928, Montreal, Que.; given name: Robert Wesley; m. Thora Doreen Sheppard; c. Paige, Stacey, Wesley, Corrie; Springfield Coll., BSc; ret'd exec. v-p CIAU; qb Verdun Bulldogs, Westmount Warriors, '48 Dominion Int. champion HMCS Donnacona; sr. fastball Verdun Crawford Park; jr. B hockey Verdun Maple Leafs; AD14yrs Macdonald Coll., head coach football 14yrs, hockey coach 10yrs.; pres. Ottawa St. Lawrence Athletic Assn. 6yrs.; pres CIAU 2yrs.; dir. Hockey Canada, SFC; dir. school of sports admin. Laurentian; CdM '73 FISU Games; with John McConachie played major role in elevating several intercollegiate sports to ntl championship status; CIAU Austin-Matthews award; res. Pakenham, Ont.

PUGH, Lionel (t&f); b. 1 Apr 1922, Wales; d. 14 Jul 2002, Vancouver; given name: David Lionel; m. Irene Samuel; c. Jane; UofWales, t&f coach UBC; Welsh HS javelin records; colors in rugby, soccer, squash, boxing; capt. boxing team; 1st class rugby for Headingley, Swansea; Great Britain ntl t&f coach '52-62; coach Oxford t&f '62-64; coach UBC '64-87, 4 ntl, 25 Canada West titles; Canadian ntl t&f coach '69-73; coach Nigerian CG team '58, Canadian CG team '70, PAG team '71, Olympic team '72; authored 3 t&f books; coach 45 top international athletes in Britain, Canada; Air Canada coach of '73; mem. UBC Sports Hall of Fame.

PUGLIESE, Dan (administration); b. 7 May 1931, St. Catharines, Ont.; given name: Daniel Joseph; m. Carol Erb; c. 5; McMaster, BA, BPhE, Buffalo, MEd; businessman; coll. letters football, basketball; several yrs. exec-admin National Sports & Recreation Center Ottawa; coach basketball, football, baseball, t&f at community, HS, university levels; designed numerous sports/recreation programs/facilities in Kitchener-Waterloo, Ottawa regions; with Jim Rose wrote *Basketball for the New Coach*; standardbred horse owner; res. St. Catharines, Ont.

PUGLIESE, Rick (water polo); b. 30 Oct 1952, Hamilton, Ont.; given name: Patrick; m. Carol MacCrimmon; c. David, Patrick, Matthew; McMaster, BA, Brock, BEd; HS teacher; mem. Hamilton Aquatic Water Polo Club winning 6 ntl titles; mem. ntl team '69-76; mem. silver medal team '69 Canada Games; mem. '71, '75 PAG, '72, '76 Olympic, '75 World Aquatic Games; coach HS swimming, golf; mem. McMaster Sports Hall of Fame; res. Dundas, Ont.

PUHL, Terry (baseball); b. 8 Jul 1956, Melville, Sask.; given name: Terry Stephen; m. Jacqueline; stockbroker; 4 Sask. sandlot, bantam, midget title teams; MVP Melville Western Cdn bantam champs '71; MVP honors Barrhead, Alta., tournament; rejected by Expos in tryout camp; pro Houston organization '73-90, Kansas City '91; hard-hitting of, noted for def skills, who moved through farm chain with Covington, Dubuque, Columbus, Memphis, Charleston to Astros '77; in 60 rookie season games '77 batted .301; '78 NL all-star team; standout player '80 NL championship series; ML record: 1531 scheduled games, 4855ab, 1361h, 676r, 226db, 56tr,

62hr, 435rbi, 217sb, .280ba, .993 fp (18 errors 2576 chances); Canada's baseball man of '80; mem. Cdn Baseball, Sask Sports halls of fame; res. Missouri City, Tex.

PULFORD, Bob (hockey); b. 31 Mar 1936, Newton Robinson, Ont.; given name: Robert Jesse; m. Roslyn McIlroy; c. Rob, Lindsay, Jennifer; McMaster, BA; hockey exec.; mem. Toronto Marlboros, 2 successive Memorial Cups; Maple Leafs '56-70, LA '70-72; NHL record: 1079 scheduled games, 281g, 362a, 89 playoff games, 25g, 26a; mem. 4 Stanley Cup winners; 6 time all-star; NHL coach of '74-75; coach LA '72-77, coach/GM Chicago '77-90, (interim) '99; GM to '97, (interim '03), sr.v-p '90-04; coach Team USA '76, co-GM Team USA '91 Canada Cup; NHL coaching record: 336-305-130; *Hockey News* coach of '78; 1st pres. NHL players union '67; mem. Brampton ntl jr. lacrosse champions, Weston CI football all-star; mem. Hockey Hall of Fame; res. Chicago, Ill.

PULFORD, Harvey (all-around); b. 22 Apr 1875, Toronto, Ont., d. 31 Oct 1940, Ottawa, Ont.; given name: Ernest Harvey; m. Jean Davison; c. Harvey P., Lawrence Moore; ins. salesman; HS hockey, football, paddling, lacrosse title teams; mem. Ottawa Silver Seven '93-09, 3 Stanley Cup winners; backfielder Rough Riders '93-09, 4 ntl title teams; lacrosse Capitals '96-00, 4 ntl titles; Eastern Canadian light-heavyweight, heavyweight boxing titles '96-98; Eastern Canadian double-, single-blade paddling champion '98; mem. '00 war canoe title crew; ntl, US titles; mem. Hanlan Memorial, Canadian Henley, US International title crews '10; stroked Ottawa 8s to '11 Eng. Henley semifinals; Ottawa squash title '22-24; mem. Ottawa Sports, Ont. Legends, Hockey halls of fame.

PULLEN, Harry (football); b. 26 Dec 1907, Coventry, Eng.; d. 15 Oct 2003, White Rock, B.C.; m. Pansy Horel; (d) c. Frances, Kathleen, Tom; UofSask, BA, UofT, BPaed, EdD, FCIS, FCCT, FOISE; professor, school superintendent; player-mgr. St. Thomas Tigers Junior ORFU champions '27-28; player-coach Saskatoon Quakers '29-33; Sask. sr. softball champions '35; Sask. Varsity Grads sr. basketball champions '35; coach Saskatoon Wesleys '35.

PULLEN, Tom (football); b. 3 Jan 1945, Ottawa, Ont., given name: Thomas Robert; m. Judith Lynn O'Neil; c. Tracey-Lynn, Kevin Thomas; Michigan, BSc, UofOtt; pres. Kiptra Intl Marketing; jr. hockey Ottawa Montagnards; prov, city track meets in hj/hurdles; Golden Ball basketball tournament with Glebe; *Journal* Trophy Ottawa HS lineman of '61; te Ottawa '68-70, '72-74, Montreal '70-71, Toronto '75; asst. coach Carleton '76; mem. 4 Grey Cup winners; mem. Ottawa Old Pros hockey club; res. Nepean, Ont.

PULLEN, Wayne (archery); b. 27 Feb 1945, St. Thomas, Ont.; m. Anne-Marie; c. Jason, Shannon; machinist; ntl men's titles '70-73, '80; mem. '72 Olympic, alternate '76, '80 Olympic, '71, '73, '75, '80, '81 world championships, '79, '80 Championship of Americas teams; bronze '71 world championships; mem. '70 Ambassador Cup winning team; 2 golds field events Championships of America '73; ntl records in field, 1200 '72, broke both '74; FITA record '73; 10 ntl records; res. Dorchester, Ont.

PUNTOUS, Patricia (t&f); b. 28 Dec 1960, Montreal,

Que.; Quebec (Montreal), BPHE; triathlete; with twin sister Sylviane tied 1st Orlando, Tampa, Panama City, Atlanta triathlons, won US triathlon series nl title; 2nd Hawaii Ironman triathlon '83-84; running half marathons '00; res. California.

PUNTOUS, Sylviane (t&f); b. 28 Dec 1960, Montreal, Que.; Quebec (Montreal), BPHE; triathlete; Que. 3000m record '79; hand-in-hand with twin sister Patricia shared 4 US triathlon titles, US triathlon series ntl championship; 1st Hawaii Ironman triathlon '83-84; res. California.

PURCELL, Jack (badminton); b. 24 Dec 1903, Guelph, Ont.; d. 10 Jun 1991, Toronto, Ont. given name: John Edward; m. Helen Colson (d); c. William, Nancy, Peter, Philip; m. June Copland; c. Robbie, Scott, Ian, Jack Fairclough; stockbroker; 5 consecutive Ont. singles titles, numerous men's, mixed doubles titles '27-31; ntl singles champion '29, '30; pro '32, unbeaten world pro champion to '45 retirement; runnerup ntl jr. tennis title '22; outstanding athlete of Ω century miscellaneous sports division '50 *CP* poll; mem. Toronto Stock Exchange '49-60; life mem. RCYC; mem. Rosedale GC, RCYC, Tortuga Club, Fla.; mem. Cdn Olympic, Canada's Sports Hall of Fame.

PURDY, Margaret (tennis/badminton); b. 27 Nov 1907, Saint John, N.B., d. 4 Apr 1972, Saint John, N.B.; given name: Margaret Henderson; nicknamed "Bunny", "Henny"; active tennis player '22-59, 3 NB ladies' singles titles; 2 prov. mixed doubles; Turnbull Cup competition 2 singles, 6 ladies' doubles, 1 Maritime titles; ntl badminton title '31; mem. NB Sports Hall of Fame.

PURNELL, Ashley (t&f); b. 25 May 1983, Ottawa, Ont.; given name: Ashley Cruise; Stanford; '01 Canada Games 100m, 200m, 4x100m titles; '01 jr. ntl 100m hurdles, 100m, 200m titles; gold 100m hurdles, silver 100m, 200m '01 Pan Am jr., competed '02 jr. worlds; 200m silver '02 sr. ntls; '02 ntl HS 100m, 200m titles; broke 20-year HS 100m record held by Angela Bailey '02; 200m title '03 Washington, Boise Sate Invitationals; broke Stanford 200m record '03; ranked #1 200m '03 ntl indoor sr.; Cdn; Ont. HS championships athlete '01; Stanford indoor t&f athlete '03; all-American '04; Ottawa ACT sport award winner; res. Metcalfe, Ont.

PURNELL, Heather (gymnastics); b. 5 Nov 1986, Ottawa, Ont.; given name: Heather Mary; Stanford; ntl team mem. from '99; novice ntl title '99; jr. ntl champion '00; 2nd AA '02 ntls; 1st AA, '02 Elite Canada; team bronze team '02 CG; bronze floor '02 Pacific Alliance Intl.; competed '03 Visa American Cup where only eight women in the world were invited to compete; team capt., bronze '03 USA vs Australia vs Canada (Anaheim); silver '03 PAG; Elite Canada all-around title '03; all-American '04; silver Pacific Alliance meet '04; competed '04 Olympics; 3 Ottawa ACT sport awards; res. Metcalfe, Ont.

PYC, Jack (bobsleigh); b. 17 Jul 1972, Wroclaw, Poland; SAIT industrial instrumentation dip.; m.; emigrated to Canada '81; parents both mem. Polish ntl track team; brakeman ntl team from '91; with Pierre Lueders 1 ntl 2-man, 2 4-man titles; teaming with drivers Lueders, Chris Lori won 55 gold, 3 silver, 1 bronze 2-man medals, 3 gold, 2 silver, 4 bronze 4-man World Cup circuit medals; world

championship 2-man silver '95; competed '92, '94, '98 Olympics; res. Calgary, Alta.

PYLE, Dave (wrestling/coaching); b. 30 Jun 1917, Aberdeen, Scotland; emigrated to Moose Jaw, Sask. as a child; began wrestling as teenager; began coaching '50; over 3 decades guided provincial teams in ntl, international competitions; his charges earned 42 ntl medals, 4 international gold, 2 silver, 2 bronze; 115 prov. champs; among his charges were Olympians Ray Lougheed, Terry Paice; international coach of Canada-US combined wrestling vs, Japan '66; mem. Sask. Sports, Cdn Wrestling halls of fame; res. Moose Jaw, Sask.

PYZER, Doug (football); b. 8 Oct 1923, Toronto, Ont.; m. Noreen; c. Jeannie, Douglas, Ruth Linda; UofT; ret'd mgr; Toronto Indians '42, RCAF Hurricanes '43-44, Toronto Indians '45-46, Argos '47, '49, '51-53, Toronto Beaches Indians '48, Eskimos '50; mem. 2 Grey Cup champions; player-coach Toronto Beaches Sr. A fastball '49-55, 2 titles; mem. Columbus Boy's Club Ont. bantam baseball champions '38, Webber Machinery Ont. jr. titlist '40; 1st in 100yd, 220yd dashes Ont. RCAF t&f championships '40-41, repeat RCAF Eastern Cdn championships '43; mem. Toronto, Ont. midget hockey champions '39; mem. Toronto, Ont. int. A basketball champions '50; res. Toronto, Ont.

Q

QUACKENBUSH, Bill (hockey); b. 2 Mar 1922, Toronto, Ont.; d. 11 Sep 1999, Pennsylvania; given name: Hubert George; m. Joan Kalloch; c. Bruce, Scott, Todd; Northeastern, ACE; athletic administrator, coach; mem. Toronto Native Sons Jr. A team '40-41, OHA champion Brantford Lions '41-42; pro Detroit '42-49, Boston '49-56; Red Wings MVP '44-45; Lady Byng Trophy '48-49 season; 3 times 1st team, twice 2nd team NHL all-star; NHL record: 774 games, 62 goals, 222 assists, 79 playoff games, 2 goals, 19 assists; through 13 seasons drew only 1 major penalty and career total 95 penalty minutes; among game's most effective def, excellent checker; coached hockey, golf Princeton '67-85, 5 men's, 3 women's Ivy League golf titles; mem. Hockey Hall of Fame.

QUANTRILL, Paul (baseball); b. 3 Nov 1968, London, Ont.; given name: Paul John; Wisconsin; rhp Boston (AL) '92-94; Philadelphia (NL) '94-95; Toronto (AL) '96-01); Los Angeles (NL) '02-03, New York (AL) '04; ML record (through '04) 791g, 1186ip, 1349h, 557r, 322bob, 689k, 66-76, 21sv; used primarily as setup relief pitcher; res. Los Angeles, Calif.

QUENNEVILLE, Joel (hockey/coaching); b. 15 Sep 1958, Windsor, Ont.; m. Elizabeth "Boo"; c. Dylan, Lily, Anna; hockey coach; def. Windsor jr. OHA '75-78; AHL New Brunswick "79, Baltimore '90-91, St. John's (player-coach) '91-92; NHL Toronto '78-80, Colorado '80-82, New Jersey '82-83, Hartford '83-90, Washington '90-91; NHL playing record: 803 scheduled games, 54g, 136a, 32 playoff games, 0g, 8a; coach Springfield (AHL) '93-94; asst. coach Colorado 3yrs; head coach St. Louis '97-04, Colorado '04; NHL coaching record (through '04): 593 scheduled games, 307-207-77; coach NA all-stars '01; head coach Team Canada '04 but resigned before world tournament citing exhaustion; active in community charitable affairs; res. St. Louis, Mo.

QUESSY, Marc (t&f); b. 20 Sep 1962, Cap-de-la-Madelaine, Que.; wheelchair racer; mem. ntl team from '86; 2 silver '92, 2 bronze '96 Paralympics; ntl 10km title '93; Athletics Canada 400m, 1500m titles '93; Francophone Games 100m gold '94. IPC 4x100 gold '94; Stoke-Mandeville Games 800m gold '95. 3 Black Top Invitational gold '96; 2 world, 4 ntl records; res. Sherbrooke, Que.

QUIGLEY, Ernest; (basketball, baseball, football, officiating); b. 22 Mar 1880, New Castle, N.B.; d. 10 Dec 1960, New Brunswick; Kansas B.Ed.; coach, official; 4 sport star Kansas; studied under James Naismith; broke hand in baseball game effectively ending career as athlete; officiated 1500+ basketball, 400+ football, 5400 major league baseball games; supervisor NCAA tourney officials '40-42; worked 3 Rose Bowls, 6 World Series (including '19 Black Sox series), '36 Olympic basketball final; mem. NCAA football rules comm. '46-54; coached Central Missouri State, St. Mary's Coll.; often relied on high-pitched voice to control basketball games rather than whistle; AD Kansas '44-50; mem. US, Cdn Basketball, Kansas Sports halls of fame.

QUILTY, Silver (football); b. 8 Feb 1891, Renfrew, Ont., d. 2 Dec 1976, Toronto, Ont.; m. Irene Boyle; c. John (d), Helen (d), Bernadine, Ken, Bob; UofOtt, BA, McGill; insurance exec., civil servant; outside wing UofOtt Sr. Intercollegiate champions '07; Rough Riders '13; coll. football McGill '14; refereed intercollegiate, interprov. football 5yrs; coach Ottawa; pres. CAHA '24-26; mem. Cdn Football, Ottawa, Canada's Sports halls of fame.

QUINN, Pat (hockey); b. 29 Jan 1943, Hamilton, Ont.; given name: John Brian Patrick; m. Sandra; c. Valerie, Kalli; San Diego, Widener, Delaware Law School, LLB; hockey coach; def Knoxville Knights; pro Tulsa, Memphis, Houston, Seattle; claimed in draft by Montreal from Detroit then sold to St. Louis who dealt him to Toronto; NHL '68-77, Toronto, Vancouver, Atlanta; asst. coach Philadelphia '77; head coach Maine (AHL) '78, Philadelphia '78-80, Los Angeles '84-87, coach/GM Vancouver '90-94, coach Toronto '98-04, coach/GM '99-04; coached Team Canada world bronze '86; coach '02 Olympic gold team, '04 worlds team; 2 Jack Adams NHL coach-of-yr awards; *Sporting News, Hockey News* coach/exec. awards; pres./ GM Vancouver '87-97; GM '98 Cdn world championships team; set NHL record 35-game undefeated streak '79-80; NHL playing record: 606 scheduled games, 18g, 113a, 11 playoff games, 0g, 1a; NHL coaching record (through '03): 1154 scheduled games, 571-427-144-15, 170 playoff games, 88-82; Jake Milford award '95; Jack Diamond Sports Personality of '95 award; mem. Hockey Hall of Fame selection comm.; mem. BC Hockey Hall of Fame; res. Toronto, Ont.

QUINTAL, Stephane (hockey); b. 22 Oct 1968, Boucherville, Que.; m. Anick; def. QMJHL Granby '85-87, Hull '87-88; AHL Maine '88-91; NHL Boston '88-92, St. Louis '92-93, Winnipeg '93-95, Montreal '95-99, '01-04, NYR '99-00, Chicago '00-01, Los Angeles '04; reached 1000 game plateau '04; NHL record (through '04) 1037 scheduled games, 63g, 180a, 52 playoff games, 2g, 10a; nickname "Q"; res. Outremont, Que.

QUIRK, Wendy (swimming); b. 29 May 1959, Montreal, Que.; m. Dave Johnson; c. Michael, Rosemary; UAlta, BPHE, Florida; coach UCal SC; FS, butterfly specialist ranging from 100m-1500m; ranked among Canada's finest aquatic competitors with 49 gold, 31 silver, 21 bronze medals; 25 ntl sr., 3 Commonwealth records; mem. '74, '78 CG, '75, '79 PAG, '76, '80 Olympic, '75, '78 World championships, '79, '80 Canada Cup, '80 US, Japanese nationals teams; 3 ntl 100m, 2 200m butterfly, 4 400m FS, 1 200m FS, 4 4x100m FS relay, 2 4x50m FS relay, 1 4x100m medley relay, 1 4x200m FS relay titles; asst. mgr. '83 FISU Games swim team; Aquatic Fed. of Can. athlete of '80; 2 Alta. outstanding swimmer awards; res. Calgary, Alta.

R

RACINE, Moe (football); b. 14 Oct 1937, Cornwall, Ont.; given name: Maurice Joseph; m. Donna Donihee; c. Tom, Scott, Lee Ann, Bruce; ret'd insurance exec.; tackle Ottawa (CFL) '60-74; as pk recorded 176 converts, 62 field goals; 5 Grey Cup finals, 4 winners; 4 times EFC all-star, once all-Cdn; Gil O. Julien, Cornwall outstanding French Cdn athlete, Cornwall outstanding athlete awards; jersey # 62 ret'd; mem. Rough Rider advisory board '82-92; mem. Cornwall, Ottawa Sports halls of fame; res. Metcalfe, Ont.

RADKE, Lori (wheelchair basketball); b 27 Feb 1966, Wetaskiwin, Alta.; c. Connor; UofA BScPT; physical therapist; mem. Red Deer Rebels, Calgary Rocky Mountain Rollers; knee injuries suffered in variety of sports resulted in several surgical reconstructions and eventual decision to compete in wheelchair basketball where she has excelled from '92; mem. ntl team from '94; 6 gold, 3 silver, 1 bronze CWBL; 1 gold, 2 silver, 1 bronze NWWBL; 1 worlds gold; 2 gold, 1 bronze Paralympics; 2 Gold Cup World gold; 4 all-star, 3 MVP awards; res. Calgary, Alta.

RADMORE, Joey (t&f); b. 18 Oct 1978, Ottawa, Ont.; athlete, occasional model; to create active lifestyle this cerebral palsy athlete became involved with disabled sports age 12 focusing on competitive track/road racing; mem. ntl team from '96; competing in CP3/T33 class earned 100m silver, 400m PB '96 Paralympics; has established Cdn records in 100m, 400m, 800m, 1500m, 5000m as well as 10km, 15km road races; world records 200m, 800m; Ont. record 1500m; gold, silver '97 CP-ISRA world championships; world 100m, 200m records '99; mem. Panthers, Ottawa Lions TC; Ont. jr. CP athlete of '93; Ont. sr. CP athlete of '96; Cdn YTV Athletes div. award; 100m gold (record), 400m silver '98 worlds; 5 gold, 2 world records Southern Cross championships Sydney, Australia '99; mem. Order of Ontario; res. Kemptville, Ont.

RAE, Al (basketball/officiating); b. 26 Dec 1932, Weyburn, Sask.; given name: Allen Gordon; m. Edna Beryl Bright; c. Allan Gordon William; Carleton, BA; self-employed; ret'd RCMP '72, Sport Canada consultant '72-82, Basketball Canada exec.-dir. '82-89; officiated '64, '68, '72, '76 Olympics, '67, '71, '75, '79 PAG, 3 FISU Games, 7 Asian, 7 Canadian, 4 CIAU, 1 Indian, 1 Japan, 1 European championships, 2 A.W. Jones Taiwan tournament; mem. FIBA tech. comm. '76-94, v-p. '84-94; mem. tech. comm. '84, '88, '92 Olympics; mem. IAABO from '58; Air Canada sports official of '81 award; 1st NA official to receive FIBA Order of Merit '97; pres. SFC '90-92; founding mem./pres. Sports Officials of Canada '03; mem. Cdn, Man. Basketball halls of fame; res. Ottawa, Ont.

RAFFIN, Romel (basketball); b. 23 Apr 1954, Toronto, Ont.; m. Susan Kay Bergstrom; c Jessica Joan, Kayley Alice; Penn State, BSc, UCal; HS teacher; MVP, mem. all-Ont. HS title team; twice K-W all-star; Penn State on basketball scholarship '72-76; mem. ntl team '74-76, '79-84; mem. '76, '80, '84, '88 Olympic, '75, '79, '83, '87 PAG teams; semipro

Italy '76-78, Venezuela '80; mem. UCal Dinosaurs '79-80, hon. mention all-Cdn; brother Angelo mem. '70 Grey Cup champion Alouettes; Penn State all-time Lion Letterman; mem. Cdn Basketball Hall of Fame; res. Calgary, Alta.

RAFTERY, John (boxing); b. 30 Dec 1956, Bristol, Eng.; m. Anna-Marie Tarrant; c. Julia; UofT, BA, Queen's, LLB; lawyer; 2 NY State Golden Gloves titles; 4 ntl, 5 Ont., 2 Eastern Cdn titles; gold '77 Tamner Turnaus tournament Finland; bronze '78 CG; gold Ireland '79; bronze World Cup '81; represented boxing in official CG film *Going the Distance*; subject of NFB film on boxing; ret'd '83; res. Mississauga, Ont.

RAIKE, Stan (t&f); b. 20 Jan 1923, Hamilton, Ont.; m. Theona Gaudette; c. Denise, Maureen; ret'd Ont. Police Commission; field specialist, hammer, discus, shot put; 7 ntl shot, 3 discus, 2 hammer titles; numerous athlete-of-meet awards annual Toronto police games '52-66; world record 56lb high throw 17'10"; mem. '54, '58 CG teams; ntl records discus, shot put, hammer; Fred Rowell Trophy '55, '60; res. Brampton, Ont.

RAIMEY, Dave (football); b. 18 Nov 1940, Dayton, Ohio; UMichigan; running back; led UM scorers; began pro career Cleveland NFL '63; CFL Winnipeg '65-69, Toronto (def. back) '69-74' mem. 1000yd club Winnipeg '65-66; 4 Winnipeg all-star awards; Eastern Conf., CFL all-star '69; Air Canada award '66; played 2 Grey Cup finals; CFL career: 5528yds rushing on 883 carries, 25 rushing tds, 170 receptions for 2189yds, 12tds; UM Meyer Morton award '61, team MVP '62; mem. Winnipeg, Cdn Football halls of fame; res. Dayton, Ohio.

RAINE, Al (coaching); b. 22 Oct 1941, Dauphin, Man.; m. Nancy Greene; c. Charles, William; ski development co-ordinator; co-owner Cahilty Lodge; coach ntl alpine ski team '68-70; CSA program dir. '70-73; exec.-dir. Whistler Resort Assn. to '82; mem. Canada's WC, Nor-Am comm.; TV color commentator international competitions; mem. Cdn Skiing Hall of Fame; res. Sun Peaks, B.C.

RAINES, Tim (baseball); b. 16 Sep 1959, Sanford, Fla.; given name: Timothy; m. Virginia Hilton; c. Tim Jr., Andre Darrel; standout HS tailback; drafted Expos '77; *Sporting News*, Topps, *Baseball Bulletin* minor league player of '80; Amer. Assn. batting champion, stolen base leader, rookie of year; Montreal '81-90, '01 White Sox '91-95, Yankees '96-98, Oakland '99, Baltimore (with son) '01, Florida '02; ML rookie theft record 71 in 88 games as season shortened by strike; *TSN* rookie of year, *UPI* all-star; switch-hitting infielder/outfielder, ranked among game's premier base stealers; set AL record 37 consecutive steals '95; 3 Expos player-of-yr awards; 7 NL all-star appearances; '86 Silver Slugger award; NL batting title with .334 '86; mem. '96, '98 World Series champion Yankees; nicknamed "Rock"; diagnosed with Lupus disease '99; ret'd '00 then made '01 comeback with Montreal; mgr. Brevard County (Florida

State A league); coach Expos '04, White Sox '05; ML record: 2502 scheduled games, 8872ab, 1565r, 2605h, 430db, 113tr, 170hr, 980rbi, 808sb, .294ba; #30 ret'd by Expos '04; res. Palm Beach Gardens, Fla.

RAINVILLE, Marcel (tennis); b. 1903 Montreal, Que.; d. 1949 Montreal, Que.; McGill; lawyer; regarded as one of most colorful, tenacious and tragic characters in Cdn tennis; nicknamed "Pee Wee"; mem. Cdn Davis Cup team '29-34; played on Florida's Orange Circuit in winter and returned to Canada for summer season; also spent time on French Riviera playing with famed Musketeers; one of 1st players to wear shorts and no socks, constantly changed shoes; while lacking most skill shots he compensated with steadiness and conditioning; won '34 Cdn Open singles; scored some amazing Davis Cup upsets beating Wimbledon champion Sydney Wood and George Lott of US; adequate doubles player winning Cdn open with Jack Wright '31 and Lott '32; drinking problem led to suicide; mem. Cdn Tennis Hall of Fame.

RALEIGH, Don (hockey); b. 27 Jun 1926, Kenora, Ont.; given name: James Donald; m. Janice Pitblado; c. Susan, Jack; Brandon Coll.; ret'd insurance broker; nicknamed "Bones"; at 16 played jr. Winnipeg Monarchs; played 13 games with NYR '43 before broken jaw sent him home; 2 more jr. seasons with Brandon winning MJHL scoring title '46; minor pro stints with Brooklyn, NY Rovers, Saskatoon, St. Paul, Providence; rejoined Rangers '47 later becoming team capt.; scored 2 overtime game winners '50 Stanley Cup final but Rangers lost series to Detroit in overtime in game 7; played 10 NHL seasons with NY appearing in 535 scheduled games, 101g, 219a, 18 playoff games, 6g, 5a; playing coach in WHL '56-58 before retiring; jersey #7 retd by Rangers; mem. BrandonU, Man. Hockey, Sports halls of fame; res. Winnipeg, Man.

RAMAGE, Pat (administration); b. 21 Jun 1922, Vancouver, B.C.; d. 13 Jan 2003, Montreal, Que.; given name: Patricia Marie Doyle; m. Paul Ramage; St. Paul's Academy; involvement with Cdn Ski Assn. began '48 and covered variety of roles including director, comm. chair., hon. secty-treas., fund raiser; mgr. 8 Canadian ski teams in international competition; world ski congress rep. 8 times; mem. international jury of appeal 6 times; FIS technical delegate World Cup races 7 times; 1st Cdn named to an FIS comm. '61; 1st Cdn jury mem. Winter Olympics '64; COA mem. at large '53-64, '66-72; PAG clothing co-ordinator '71, '75, same role '76 Olympics, '73, '77 Maccabiah Games, '78 CG; hon. treas. Cdn modern pentathlon '78-80, co-organizer '79 ntl championships; CSA dir. to COA '72-82; chair. biathlon comm., team mgr. biathlon world championships '81; co-chair. Laurentian Ski Zone; CSA merit award '65; Centennial Medal '67; Ont. Athletic merit award '68; finalist Air Canada Amateur Sport exec. award '70; Queen's jubilee medal '78; mem. Order of Canada; Cdn Skiing, Cdn Amateur, Canada's Sports halls of fame.

RAMAGE, Rob (hockey); b. 11 Jan 1959, Byron, Ont.; given name: George; def. London OHA Jr. '75-78; WHA Birmingham '78-79; 3 Team Canada worlds; NHL Colorado '79-82, St. Louis '82-88, Calgary '88-89, Toronto '89-91, Minnesota '91-92, Tampa Bay '92-93, Montreal '93, Philadelphia '93-94; OHA, WHA all-star; 4 NHL all-star

games; NHL record: 1044 scheduled games, 139g, 425a, 84 playoff games, 8g, 42a; driver of vehicle in which Keith Magnuson died in accident '03; res. London, Ont.

RAMSAY, Craig (hockey/coaching); b. 17 Mar 1951, Weston, Ont.; m. Susan; c. Travis, Jud, Brendan, Summer; hockey coach; lw Peterborough jr. '67-71; Cincinnati (AHL) '71; NHL Buffalo '71-85; NHL record: 1070 scheduled games, 252g, 420a, 89 playoff games, 17g, 31a; Selke Trophy; 1 NHL all-star; had string of 776 consec. games with Buffalo; served 8 seasons with Sabres in roles ranging from interim coach to AGM; asst. coach Florida '93-95; pro scout Dallas '95-96; asst. coach Ottawa '96-98, Philadelphia '98-99, interim head coach '00-01; assoc. coach Tampa Bay '01-04; dir. PPHAA; nickname "Rammer"; res. Peterborough, Ont,

RANDALL, Sam (horse racing); b. 25 Sep 1881, Bruce County, Ont., d. 2 Nov 1961, Vancouver, B.C.; c. William, John, Robert; stove business operator, horseman; entered horse racing '19; key role in developing thoroughbred racing Western Canada; dir. Vancouver Ascot Jockey Club, Vancouver Thoroughbred Assn., Hastings (now Exhibition) Park; constructed Lansdowne Park, Williams Track, Victoria; operated Brighouse Park, Colwood, Vancouver Island; 1st to install photo-finish cameras; backed construction of 1st closed-in electric starting gate '39; instrumental in developing breed in BC; developed Ascot Stock, Dairy Farm; mem. Canadian Horse Racing Hall of Fame.

RANEK, Josh (football); b. 11 May 1978, Tyndall, S.D.; m. Danielle; South Dakota State; rb; set NCAA Div. II rushing records over 4 seasons; wife Danielle ran '03 NYC marathon; attended Dallas NFL training camp; CFL Ottawa Renegades '02-04; CFL East all-star; powerful runner; CFL record (through '04) 395 carries, 2182yds, 15tds, 100 receptions, 1046yds, 6tds; res. San Diego, Calif.

RANGER, Melissa (lawn bowling); b. 16 May 1981, Espanola, Ont.; began lawn bowling age 10; won Ont. -16 junior singles titles '93, '97; won Ont. Summer Games -16 junior singles '94, '96; at 17 became youngest ever to win sr. ladies' provincial singles title '98; standout 5-pin bowler winning Ont. bantam title, ntl bronze '92; Ont. jr. title '96; CG '02 women's team silver; res. Edmonton, Alta.

RANKIN, Callie (harness racing); b. 22 May 1950, North Sydney, N.S.; given name: William; standardbred racing is a way of life for the Rankin family; tested talents one season at Foxboro Raceway before establishing strong presence at Exhibition Park in Saint John; after a decade had 5yr stint at Tartan Downs Sydney before shifting to Flamboro Downs; more than 2800 victories with purses exceeding $5M; Flamboro horseman of year '88-89; Flamboro driving title '90; res. Dundas, Ont.

RANKIN, Frank (hockey); b. 1 Apr 1889, Stratford, Ont., d. 23 Jul 1932, Toronto, Ont.; rover in 7-man hockey era; led Statford jrs. to 3 consecutive OHA titles; capt. Eaton Athletic Assn. to Ont. titles '10-11, '11-12, lost Allan Cup to Winnipeg Victorias each time; with Toronto St. Mike's in OHA finals '12-13, '13-14, lost to Toronto R&AA each time; coached Toronto Granites to '24 Olympic title; mem. Hockey Hall of Fame.

RANKIN, Heather (curling); b. 30 Apr 1965, Halifax, N.S.; given name: Heather Velma; m. Brian Murray Fowlie; Acadia, BSc; computer consultant, pres. Scotia Consulting Inc.; began curling age 9 coached by parents; sister Beth played 3ʳᵈ for her for 20yrs; NS jr title '84; attended Acadia on scholarship; AUAA title '85; all-star ntl STOH skip '90; 3ʳᵈ for Colleen Jones '93 STOH; mem. NS volleyball title team '82; starting setter Acadia volleyball '84-85; goalie undefeated girls HS field hockey team; res. Calgary, Alta.

RANKINE, Scotty (t&f); b. 6 Jan 1909, Hamilton, Scotland; d. 10 Jan 1995, Wasaga Beach, Ont.; given name: Robert Scade; m. Edna May Hodgkiss; c. Ian, Lynne, Craig; ret'd deputy sheriff; 2 ntl marathon titles; competed 3 Boston Marathons, placing 4ᵗʰ, 5ᵗʰ, 7ᵗʰ; 2 US 15km, 1 20km titles; ntl 5000m title to qualify for '32 Olympics, 5000m finalist; mem. '36 Olympic team but leg cramps at 7500m mark of 10,000m race forced him out; silver 6-mile, 4ᵗʰ 3-mile '34, silver 6-mile, bronze 3-mile '38 BEG; Lionel Conacher Trophy '35; mem. Cdn Road Racing Hall of Fame.

RANNELLI, William Jr. (boxing); b. 15 May 1958, Sudbury, Ont.; given name: William Raymond; m. Sue Davlut; contractor; Ont. titles '76-81; ntl titles '76-79, '81; US Golden Gloves silver '77; Tampere, Finland silver '78; bronze CG '78; mem. '79 PAG team; silver Canada vs Ireland '79; bronze East Germany Chemical Cup tournament '81; bronze Greece Acropolis Cup tournament '81; nominee Kinsmen male athlete of '78-80; CABA Hall of Fame; res. Val Caron, Ont.

RANSOM, James (fencing); b. 2 Apr 1971, Toronto, Ont.; UofOtt; teacher; accomplished t&f athlete before switching to fencing; mem. Algonquin First Nation; aspiring film director; jr. ntl épée title '92 sr. '97; ntl men's épée team gold '96; won Can-Am Open epee title '93; mem. OUAA épée title team '93; mem. ntl team from '94; competed 5 sr. World Cup events; mem. '94 CG, '95 world, '96 Olympic teams; Cdn flag bearer '97 FISU Games; res. Nepean, Ont.

RATANASEANGSUANG, Channarong (badminton); b. 26 Apr 1939, Bangkok, Thailand; m. Joyce Rati; c. Paul, David; San Diego City College; badminton pro, coach; Thailand ntl champion '61-62; ranked 2ⁿᵈ in world with 2ⁿᵈ place finish All-England tournament '62; pro teacher Calgary Glencoe Club '67-04; ntl team coach '84-96; under his guidance, such players as Jamie Paulson, Wendy Clarkson emerged as world performers; team mgr. 4 world, 3 CG, '96 Olympic teams; 3 ntl doubles, 4 Mexican ntl titles, US, Scottish, Denmark, Asian, CG titles; Alberta achievement awards '75-76; International Badminton Federation Meritorious Service Award '88; mem. US., Sweden, Thailand, Alta. Sports halls of fame; res. Calgary, Alta.

RATCLIFFE, Frank (administration); b. 11 Sep 1944, Montreal, Que.; d. 3 Apr 1995, Toronto, Ont.; given name: Frank Ronald; m. Kathy MacDonald; c. Tracey, Christopher; communication dir. COA '82-95; info dir NSRC '78-82; PR co-ordinator Coaching Assn. of Canada '77-78; founding editor *Coaching Review* magazine; head Cdn team communication unit '84, '88, '92 summer, winter Olympics, '83, '87, '91, '95 PAG; press attache '82 CG; CCA memorial trophy bears his name.

RATELLE, Jean (hockey); b. 3 Oct 1940, Lac St. Jean, Que.; given name: Joseph Gilbert Yvon Jean; m. Nancy; c. 3 daughters; hockey scout; Guelph Jr. Royals; minor pro Trois-Rivieres, Kitchener-Waterloo (EPHL), Baltimore (AHL); NHL NYR '64-75, Boston '75-81; baseball Guelph Sr. IC, attracted ML offers from Milwaukee, Los Angeles organizations; 2ⁿᵈ team NHL all-star ctr; Bill Masterton Memorial, Lester B. Pearson, 2 Lady Byng trophies; Team Canada '72; NHL record: 1281 scheduled games, 491g, 776a, 123 playoff games, 32g, 66a; asst. coach '81-85, scout Boston '81-99; mem. AHL, Hockey halls of fame; res. Lynnfield, Mass.

RATHGEB, Chuck (all-around); b. 2 Dec 1921, Trois-Rivieres, Que.; m. Rosemary; Upper Canada College, UofT; board chair.; mem. '35 Canadian Commonwealth cricket team; mem. '50-51 team which climbed Mt. Edith Cavell, Mt. Robson; founding mem. Cdn Bobsleigh, Luge Assn.; competed '59-61 world bobsleigh championships; organized, coached '64 Olympic gold medal sledders; mgr.-driver Comstock auto racing team; with late Peter Ryan driving won 1ˢᵗ Canadian Grand Prix; twice won Shell Trans-Canada rally, 3 times ntl winter rally; 1ˢᵗ Cdn to campaign cars at Daytona, Sebring, LeMans in world-class races, at 52 finished 10ᵗʰ '73 Targa Florio road race Sicily; drove '75 Trans-Sahara World Cup rally; founding mem., pres. Balloon Club of Canada; entry Trans-Canada balloon race Calgary to Winnipeg; flew over Alps by balloon from Zurich to Milan '67; entry London-to-Monte Carlo powerboat race '72; won Cdn Handicap Gulfstream Park, Fl., Canada Day '72; 1 of 3 Cdns to have taken the Big Six animals (lion, leopard, elephant, buffalo, rhino, tiger) in big game hunting; Cdn entry international tuna championships; gov. Olympic Trust; mem. Cdn Motorsport Hall of Fame; res. Toronto, Ont.

RATHWELL, Bob (administration); b. 23 Jun 1929, Lachine, Que.; m. Ruth Rawn; c. David, Douglas, Leslie; UWO, hons BA; ret'd computer systems analyst/ programmer/consultant; involved in amateur sport from age 19 as Little League coach; not a particularly gifted athlete; mgr. HS soccer team; 2 terms Ottawa RA exec. mem.; instrumental in creating Riverside Dr. playing fields; coached house-league/inter-club competitive hockey Nepean MHA 10yrs; coached softball and began soccer involvement '70; pres. Lynwood Minor soccer club 10yrs before becoming involved in game at league/district levels; served as chair./secty/statistician Ottawa Carleton SL as well as pres/secty EODSA from '75; 8yrs dir. Ontario SA; developed computerized sports record keeping system; chair United Way campaign; certified Level 1 hockey/soccer coach; Ottawa ACT sportsman of '88; life mem. EODSA; res. Nepean, Ont.

RATUSHNY, Ed (builder); b. 18 May 1942, Kamsack, Sask.; given name: Edward Joseph; m. Lynn Diane Allen; c. Kimberly Anne, Daniel Paul John, Gregory Allen (d); UofSask. BA, LLB, London LLM, Michigan LLM, SJD; law professor, player agent/arbitrator; registered player agent NHLPA; independent adjudicator Cdn Centre for Drug-Free Sport; arbitrator international court of arbitration for sport Lausanne, Switzerland; arbitrator/mediator, ADR program for amateur sport, centre for sport and law; mem. bd of regents Ont. women's HA; mem. bd of regents Sport

Medicine and Science Council of Canada; QC; mem. Order of Canada; res. Ottawa, Ont.

RAU, Richard (t&f); b. 17 Jun 1939, Windsor, Ont.; given name: Richard Frederick; m. Dianne Verrege; c. Robyn; Michigan, Assumption College; salesman; all-Windsor basketball '57-58, leading scorer; ntl HS record 120yd low hurdles (13.2), tj (46'4"); mem. 2 WOSSA soccer, volleyball champions; WOSSA hj/lj/high hurdle records; Ont. lj/tj records; basketball Assumption Lancers '60-61; Mic-Mac baseball batting champion .395 '57; mem. BEG team '58; ankle injury playing football at Mich. '59 ended track career; fastball Hamilton Big Four league '65-67; Royal Arcanum Trophy HS athlete of year '58, Viscount Alexander Trophy Canada's outstanding HS athlete '58; res. Burlington, Ont.

RAUHANEN, Eric (biathlon); b. 3 May 1959, Winnipeg, Man.; div. Shauna Whyte; ret'd Canadian Forces, big game outfitter; mem. ntl team '82-88; ntl 10km title '83, 20km, 4x7.5km relay '84, NA 4x7.5km relay title '84; ntl 20km aggregate titles '85-86; mem. Que. 4x7.5km relay ntl title team '89; mem. Cdn Forces Sports Hall of Fame; res. Edson, Alta.

RAUTINS, Leo (basketball); b. 20 Mar 1960, Toronto, Ont.; div. Maria; c. Michael, Andy, Jay, Sammy; m. Jamie Lawson; Minnesota, Syracuse; basketball announcer; coach 4yrs. St. Michael's College; rated best player in Canada sr. year; at 16 youngest ever to qualify for Olympic basketball team; toured Europe with junior Olympic team because he was too young to play in FISU Games; 150 US college scholarship offers, chose Minnesota; transferred to Syracuse after rookie year in which he received Big-10 honorable mention; all-star '80 Olympic qualifying tournament as team became first Canadian squad to qualify for Olympics through tournament play; with Syracuse '80-81 Big East tournament MVP, all-tournament NIT finalist; at 16 led Cdn scorers vs Yugoslavia, Russia; MVP '78 CG basketball tournament; 2nd top scorer world championships, 2nd team all-world; 2nd team all-star '79 PAG; FISU Games all-star '79; Viscount Alexander Trophy '78; 1st Canadian 1st round pick (17th overall Philadelphia '76ers) '83 NBA draft; subsequently traded to Indiana Pacers, Atlanta Hawks before injuries forced him to broadcast booth; Syracuse basketball broadcaster; comeback with teams in Europe 5yrs; ntl team '92; color commentator Toronto Raptors (NBA) from '95; with Tony House operates annual basketball, golf tournaments in Ottawa; ntl team coach '05; mem. Ont., Cdn Basketball halls of fame; res. DeWitt, N.Y.

RAYMOND, Claude (baseball); b. 7 May 1937, St. Jean, Que.; given name: Jean Claude Marc; m. Rita Duval; c. Natalie, Claude-Marc; Académie Commerciale Catholique, St. Jean; sportscaster, coach; strong right arm led to 17yr pro baseball career, 12 in major leagues; particularly effective as relief pitcher; with Chicago White Sox, Milwaukee Braves, Houston Astros, Atlanta Braves, Montreal Expos; Milwaukee rookie of '62; mem. NL all-star team '66; ML record: 449 scheduled games 46-53, 3.66era, 83sv, 225bob, 497k; 23 saves with Expos '70; honored as Canada's baseball man of '70; 3 times St. Jean athlete of yr; St. Jean man of '70; French radio network baseball broadcaster with Expos; roving coach Expos '02; mem. Cdn Baseball,

Montreal Expos, Que. Sports halls of fame; res. St. Luc and Mt. Orford, Que.

RAYNER, Chuck (hockey); b. 11 Aug 1920, Sutherland, Sask.; d. 5 Oct 2002, Langley, B.C.; given name: Claude Earl; m. Ina Lackey; c. Roberta; ret'd rental business; goalie Saskatoon Jr. Wesleys, Western Cdn jr. finalists '35-36; goalie Kenora Thistles 3 seasons; capt. Memorial Cup finalist '38-39; pro Springfield Indians '39-40; NY (Brooklyn) Americans '40-42; following navy stint WW2 NHL Rangers '45-53; NHL record: 424 scheduled games, 25so, 3.06ga avg., 18 playoff games, 1so, 2.43 avg.; Hart Trophy '50; 3 times NHL 2nd team all-star; coached in Edmonton, Nelson, Kenora; NHL milestone award; mem. Cdn, Man. Hockey, Sask, NWO, Saskatoon Sports halls of fame.

REA, Harold (administration); b. 26 Sep 1907, Kincardine, Ont.; d. 19 Jul 1985, Toronto, Ont; m. Marion Josephine Currie; c. Marilyn, Barbara; Inst. Chartered Accountants, CA, FCA; ret'd business exec.; ntl pres. YMCA '63-65; chair. fed. govt. task force on sport '69; 1st chair. Cdn Coaching Assn.; chair. bd. of governors Canada's Sports Hall of Fame '69-75; mem. Order of Canada, Canada's Sports Hall of Fame.

READ, Cari (synchro swim); b. 4 Sep 1970, Edmonton, Alta.; m. Din; Calgary; coach; began synchro age 9; mem. ntl team from '88; solo, duet gold '92 Loano Cup, '94 German Open; duet gold '93 ntl championship, Optrex World Challenge; team gold '90 Swiss Open, '93 Nationals, '94 Titrex Cup, '96 French Open; figures gold '92 Loano Cup; '95 PAG, '96 Olympic Games team silver; res. Calgary, Alta.

READ, Dee (skiing); b. 21 Jun 1926, Montreal, Que.; d. 8 May 2004, Calgary, Alta.; given name: Dorothy Burden; m. John Read; c. Jim, Ken, Ron, Jan; McGill, BSc; honed skiing skills in Laurentians with Penguin Ski Club; competed ntl championships winning '48 downhill, combined, 3rd slalom; four children all competitive skiers, two members of ntl team; considered matriarch of Cdn Alpine ski racing through 6 decades as participant, organizer, volunteer; chair Alberta Alpine, Alpine Canada; Dee Read Kinder Cup race held annually; Calgary Booster Club sportsman of yr award; avid golfer; mem. Cdn Ski Hall of Fame.

READ, Frank (coaching); b. 1 Mar 1911, Vancouver, B.C.; d. Jan 1994, Mexico; given name: Frank Harold; m. Beatrice Emma Davis; c. Hugh David, Charles Anthony; ret'd hotelman; football Vancouver AC '30-34; rower Vancouver RC '31-34, '39; coached UBC rowing crews to BEG 8s gold '54, Henley Royal Regatta Grand Challenge Cup 8s silver '55, Olympic 4s gold, 8s silver '56, 8s silver '60; Cdn Amateur Assn. of Rowing award of merit; mem. UBC, Cdn Amateur, BC Sports halls of fame.

READ, Ken (skiing); b. 6 Nov 1955, Ann Arbor, Mich.; given name: Kenneth John; m. Lynda Robbins; c. Erik, Kevyn, Jeffrey; UCal, UWO BA; pres. Alpine Canada, Read & Co.; consulting firm IOC athletes commission; mem. World Cup teams '73-83; WC record 5-3-6, Val D'Isere, France, '75-76, Cortina, Italy, '76, Schladming, Austria, '78, Kitzbuhel, Austria, Wegen, Switzerland, '80, twice runner-up, twice 3rd; leader of "Crazy Canucks"; mem. Olympic team '76 (5th downhill), '80; 5 ntl downhill titles, 1 combined title; Lou Marsh Trophy (with Graham Smith) '78; Norton Crowe award '79; Calgary athlete of '80; Premiers' outstanding achievement award '80; *CBC, CBS* Olympic skiing analyst; freelance journalist; '80 winter Olympic flag-bearer; mem. IOC athletes commission from '85; CdM '92 Olympics; ISF Olympic downhill design expert; mem. ISF exec. board from '88; operates Cystic Fibrosis fund-raisers; author *White Circus*; active board mem. several organizations; mem. Order of Canada, Canada's, Cdn Skiing, Cdn Amateur, Alta. Sports halls of fame; res. Calgary, Alta.

REARDON, Ken (hockey); b. 1 Apr 1921, Winnipeg, Man.; given name: Kenneth Joseph; m. Suzanne Raymond; c. Catherine Anne, Donat Raymond, Kenneth Anthony, Anthony Kelly; ret'd hockey exec.; Winnipeg -12 champions, Edmonton jr.; mem. Ottawa Commandos '43 Allan Cup winner; Canadiens '40-42, '45-50, all-star def; mem. 1 Stanley Cup winner; NHL record: 341 scheduled games, 26g, 96a; 3 all-star games; exec. Montreal organization; Field Marshall Montgomery award of merit WW2; mem. Cdn, Man. Hockey halls of fame; res. Montreal, Que.

REAVES, Willard (football); b. 17 Aug 1959, Flagstaff, Ariz.; given name: Willard Sheldon; m. Brenda Skwark; c. Regina, Ryan, Jordan; Northern Arizona U, BA criminology; Sgt Sheriff's office; running back; multi-sport star in HS; 1st non-sr. to rush for 1000+yds in single season; 2 1st team, 1 2nd team all-American; pro Green Bay 2yrs, Winnipeg Blue Bombers '83-88; Western Div. CFL rookie of '83 (Jackie Parker trophy); Schenley outstanding player of '84; helped Bombers win 1st Grey Cup since '62; frequent all-star; set record most 100yds rushing games one season (10), including record 8 in succession; posted record 1733yds on 304 carries '84; tied CFL record 4 tds one game, tied season mark of 18tds; 221yds rushing single game, 44 career tds, 1158 carries club records; had NFL trials Washington '88, Miami '89; Cdn citizen; mem. Blue Bomber, Northern Arizona, Manitoba Sports halls of fame; res. Winnipeg, Man.

REAY, Billy (hockey); b. 21 Aug 1918, Winnipeg, Man.; d. 23 Sep 2004, Madison, Wisc.; m. Clare; c. Adele, Billy Jr.; ret'd hockey exec.; unique among NHL coaches because he coached before he played; player-coach Que. Aces '44-45, Allan Cup winner; coached 1 Memorial Cup winner; ctr Detroit 4 games over 2 seasons '42-44, Montreal '45-53, 2 Stanley Cups; NHL record: 479 scheduled games, 105 goals, 162 assists, 63 playoff games, 13 goals, 16 assists; coached Victoria Cougars (WHL) 2 seasons, Seattle (WHL) 1, Rochester (AHL), Maple Leafs '57-58; replaced by Punch Imalch early following season, joined Chicago organization and coached Sault Ste. Marie (EPHL) 1 season, Buffalo (AHL) 2 seasons; Black Hawks '63-77, Prince of Wales Trophy '67, Clarence Campbell Bowl '71-73; NHL coaching record: 1102 scheduled games, 542-385-175 losses, 170 ties, 116 playoff games, 56-60; NHL milestone award; mem. Man. Hockey Hall of Fame.

REBAGLIATI, Ross (snowboarding); b. 14 Jul 1971, Vancouver, B.C.; m. Renée Schembri; Langers.; consultant/ commentator *Outdoor Life Network*; ret'd pro snowboarder; giant slalom specialist; WC circuit overall gold, silver, 3

bronze; ntl team '96-2000; burst into world prominence winning '98 Olympic gold at Nagano, Japan, as snowboarding made Olympic debut; marginal traces of marijuana in urine sample led to IOC bid to strip him of medal but subsequent COA appeal overturned IOC ruling; resulting publicity led to US talk-show circuit appearances (Jay Leno Tonight Show); res. Whistler, B.C.

REBHOLZ, Russ (football); b. 11 Sep 1908, Portage, Wisc.; d. 2 Aug 2002, Milwaukee, Wisc.; m. June Simonson; c. Ted, James, Tim, Bonnie; Wisconsin, BSc, MSc; ret'd teacher, coach; nicknamed "Doss"; HS standout baseball, t&f, basketball, football; all-conf. basketball 4 years, football 3 years; all-tournament basketball honors as a ctr despite standing only 5'7"; all-state ctr '26; played both off/def in football at Wisconsin; 3 letters each in football, basketball; played '32 East-West Shrine football game; joined Winnipeg in club's initial season '33 and quickly earned reputation as prolific passer, outstanding blocker and kicker and an elusive, shifty runner; threw what is believed longest pass in CFL history (68yds in air) to Lynn Patrick who galloped additional 10yds for td; 5 times all-Cdn; helped Winnipeg win first Grey Cup '35 with 2 td passes and kicking both converts; player-coach '32 Winnipeg St. John's rugby team; 2nd leading scorer '33 Toiler basketball team; following 5yr Cdn grid career coached HS, college athletics in US guiding teams to several regional, state honors; mem. Canadian Football Hall of Fame.

RECCHI, Mark (hockey); b. 1 Feb 1968, Kamloops, B.C.; m. Alexa; rw; jr New Westminster WHL '85-86, Kamloops '86-88; drafted by Pittsburgh '88; NHL Pittsburgh '88-92, '04, Philadelphia '92-95, '99-04, Montreal '95-99; brief Muskeogon IHL stints '89, '90; scored 53g '93; 7 NHL all-star games; '97 MVP; 1 Stanley Cup; 2 Molson Cup player-of-yr awards; 2 Bobby Clarke trophies; 1 Pa. Class Guy award; mem. 2 Team Canada gold medal teams, '88 world jr. gold; reached 1000g '02; 570 consec-game streak; NHL record (through '04): 1173 scheduled games, 456g, 745a, 110 playoff games, 40g, 57a; WHL, IHL, NHL 2nd team all-star; mem. '98 Olympic team; Kamloops male athlete of 20th Century; res. Kamloops, B.C./ Pittsburgh, Pa.

REDDEN, Chrissy (cycling); b. 16 Mar 1969, Hamilton, Ont.; given name: Christina deJonge; U. of Guelph, BSc; full-time athlete; mountain bike XC specialist; ntl team from '94; 3 Canada Cups gold; competed '97, '01 world cup, '98 worlds, '99 cyclocross, 2 ntl XC titles; 7th in '99 UCI ranking; 7th '00 world XC championships; 6th overall, '00 UCI world cup (finished 2nd in the Mont Ste. Anne UCI world cup); 1st, AMBC XC Philadelphia; competed '00 Olympics; gold Napa Valley TT, Mont Ste. Anne XC, silver Grouse Mountain XC; '01 world champion, team relay; '02 CG MTB XC champion; gold Norba #4 Sand Point, Norba #2 West Virginia '03; 2nd overall '03 US ntl mountain bike series; silver '03 ntls; *Canadian Cyclist* female cyclist of '99; Pacific Sport female cyclist of '01; Carole King Sportswoman of '02; Redlands Bicycle Race '02 George Heller Award; Guinness world record holder for quickest ascent of tallest free standing building in the world (CN Tower); res. Victoria, B.C.

REDDEN, Wade (hockey); b. 12 Jun 1977, Lloydminster, Sask.; def. Brandon WHL jr. '93-96; Memorial Cup all-star

'96; Team Canada '95-96 (2 gold) world jr, '99, '01 worlds; drafted by NYI and swapped to Ottawa for Brian Berard '96; NHL Ottawa '96-04; NHL record (through '04): 629 scheduled games, 78g, 208a, 54 playoff games, 6g, 17a; 1 all-star game; scored 1st NHL goal on 1st shot; popular figure in community; purchase of Corel Centre box benefits underprivileged children; res. Lloydminster, Sask.

REDDON, Lesley (hockey); b. 15 Nov 1970, Mississauga, Ont.; UofT BComm., UNB MPHE; co-ordinator female hockey CHA; all-star goaltender 4 OWIAA champion Lady Blues teams '89-93; mem. 2 ntl sr. women's, 4 Ont. Sr. AA title teams; 1st woman to play UNB men's hockey '94-96; mem. Maritime Sports Blades (NB) in 3 ntl women's championship tournaments, silver '95, bronze '96; competitive softball player '90, '94 nationals; goalie '92 world champion roller hockey team, '94 silver medallist; ntl women's hockey team mem. from '94; Olympic gold '02; 2 world, 1 Pacific Rim, 1 3-Nations Cup titles; attends Olympic Oval high-performance female hockey program; res. Calgary, Alta.

REDMOND, Mickey (hockey); b. 27 Dec 1947, Kirkland Lake, Ont.; given name: Michael Edward; div; c. Kelley, Shannon; automotive steel sales rep.; tour business operator; 4yrs OHA Jr. A Peterborough Petes; pro Montreal '67-70, Detroit '70-76; back injury led to retirement; NHL record: 538 scheduled games, 233g, 195a; scored 52g '73, 51 '74; twice NHL all-star; *Hockey Night in Canada* TV analyst; mem. Peterborough Sports Hall of Fame; res. Franklin, Mich.

REED, George (football); b. 2 Oct 1939, Vicksburg, Miss.; given name: George Robert; m. Angelina; c. Keith, Vicky, Georgette; Washington State, BEd; sales promotion mgr.; Saskatchewan fb '63-75; 44 CFL records; 3245 carries for all-pro record 16,115yds, all-pro 137tds; 11 1000yd seasons for career 4.97yd avg; caught 300 passes for 2772yds, 3tds; mem. 1 Grey Cup winner; CFL all-star 11 times; Jeff Nicklin Memorial Trophy (WFC MVP) '66; Schenley outstanding player award '65, runnerup '68, '69; Tom Pate Memorial Trophy '76; City of Regina, Province of Saskatchewan 'day' in his honor '74; pres. CFL Players' Assn. '72-81; mem. Order of Canada; mem. Sask., Canada's Sports, Canadian Football halls of fame; res. Calgary, Alta.

REED, Georgette (t&f); b. 26 Jan 1967, Regina, Sask.; Washington State; marketing advisor Cdn Sports Centre; daughter of CFL Hall of Famer George Reed; throw specialist; Canada Games record '89; shot put gold Oregon International, bronze Pac-10 championships '91; ntl indoor shot title '93; 5 ntl outdoor shot titles; mem. '89, '94 Francophone, '91, '95 PAG, '92 Olympic, '94 CG teams; gold shot '94 Harry Jerome Classic; Athletic Alta. sr. female athlete of '90, Alta. achievement award '91; outstanding sr. female athlete '90-91; NCAA all-American '90-91; coach '03 FISU Games; res. Calgary, Alta.

REES, David (skiing); b. 25 Feb 1943, Barnard Castle, Eng.; div. Gail Fortey; c. Stephanie, Andrew; m.Jean Bristow; Carleton, BSc, MA, UofOtt, PhD; professor; coach, administrator; x-country specialist; mem. ntl team '62-72; 5 gold, 6 silver, 6 bronze at ntl championship level; winner numerous Ont., NA titles; 2 gold, 1 bronze '71 Canada

Games; alternate '64, competed '68 Olympics; won every university x-country ski race entered '61-64; coached at club level Ottawa, North Bay; ntl x-country team coach '74-78; chair. NO Div. 2yrs; v.-chair. CSA 5yrs; 1st pres. Cdn Assn. of Nordic Ski Instructors; v-p Cdn Masters x-country Ski Assn.; authored x-country skiing book, numerous magazine articles, coaching manuals; key speaker Ottawa Ski Symposium '75; Carleton athlete of '62, Ottawa ACT skiing award '62; pres. X-country Canada; coach '92 Olympic team; ski coach NipissingU; x-country volunteer award bears his name; mem. Cdn Skiing, North Bay Sports halls of fame; res. Canmore, Alta.

REES, Gareth (rugby); b. 30 Jun 1967, Duncan, B.C.; Victoria BA, Oxford MA; CEO Rugby Canada; teacher (at Eton Coll.)/pro rugby player; Oxford Blue '93-94; made international debut vs. US '86; mem. London Wasps in John Player Cup as teenager '86; fly-half, capt. Team Canada '95 World Cup, '97 Pacific Rim title teams; at 19 youngest player in inaugural World Cup game '87; lone Canadian to play in all four rugby World Cups; Canada's top all-time scorer 45 tests, 388 points on 7 tries, 7 drop goals, 89pens, 34cvt; scored all the points in tests vs. US, France, Wales '94; English Courage League scoring title '96-97; Pacific Rim scoring title '97; mem. BC Castaway Wanderers, London Wasps (pro) teams, served as asst. coach Wasps; Rugby Union Writers' Club of Britain award; 2 UVic athlete-of-yr awards; mem. UVic Sports Hall of Fame; res. Vancouver, B.C.

REEVE, Ted (lacrosse/football); b. 6 Jan 1902, Toronto, Ont., d. 27 Aug 1983, Toronto, Ont.; given name: Edward Henry; m. Alvern Florence Donaldson; c. Joseph, Susan; sportswriter; nicknamed "The Moaner"; early football Toronto St. Aidan jrs, Argonauts; coach, player Toronto Beaches FC '24-30; ORFU title '27; Grey Cup victories '27, '30; 4yrs lacrosse Brampton Excelsiors; Mann Cup Brampton '26, '30, Oshawa '28; coached Queen's to 3 intercollegiate football titles '33-38; Ont., federal government achievement awards; Fred Sgambati award '82; mem. Queen's Football, Coaches, Canada's Sports, Lacrosse, Football, News halls of fame.

REGAN, Larry (hockey/administration); b. 7 Aug 1930, North Bay, Ont.; given name: Lawrence Emmett; m. Pauline LeBlanc; c. Natalie; UCLA; ret'd sports administrator; played jr. Toronto Marlboros '48-50; sr. Ottawa Senators (OSHL) at 17; Allan Cup finalists '47; MVP Shawinigan Falls '51-52; Quebec Aces '52-55, MVP '54; NHL Boston '56-59, Toronto '59-61; NHL record: 280 scheduled games, 41g, 95a, 42 playoff games, 7g, 14a; Calder Memorial trophy '57; 2yrs Stanley Cup finals; player/coach Pittsburgh Hornets (AHL) '62, Innbruck, Austria '62-65; coach Baltimore (AHL) '65-66; head scout LA Kings '65-66; GM LA Kings '66-74; coach Montreal srs '74-75; NHL coaching record: 88 scheduled games, 27-47-14; pres. Cdn Oldtimers Hockey Assn. '75-95; organized Relive the Dream hockey series; mem. Ottawa Sports Hall of Fame; res. Ottawa, Ont.

REGEHR, Robyn (hockey); b. 19 Apr 1980, Recife, Brazil; def. Kamloops (WHL) '96-99, Saint John (AHL) '99; Team Canada '04 World Cup (gold); drafted by Colorado '98; NHL Calgary '99-04; NHL record (through '04) 364

scheduled games, 12g, 42a, 26 playoff games, 2g, 7a; res. Calgary, Alta.

REGNIER, Claude (skateboarding); b. 30 Dec 1958, Cornwall, Ont.; given name: Claude Emery; m. Ginette Larivierre; c. Richard, Lindsay, Jason; SK8 City consultant; ntl slalom champion '81-98; made pro debut '86; Expo '86, PSL '90 pro titles; coach/instructor from '77; coached minor hockey '91-98; coached minor football '94; coached/ played broomball '81-91; '82-83 coach-of-yr award; in-line skating instructor/coach '92-96; BMX biking coach; 16yrs competitive 5-pin bowler excelling at YBC competitions; designed/built skateboard facilities in various communities; dir. Cdn Amateur Skateboard Assn; res. Ottawa, Ont.

REID, Bobby (soccer/hockey/boxing); b. 13 Sep 1890, Hamilton, Scotland, d. Dec 1982, Saskatoon, Sask.; given name: Robert John; soccer as player, coach, mgr., administrator, trainer '14-51; 8 title teams; key role in developing schoolboy soccer in Sask.; 96th Highlanders boxing title '16; boxing trainer, coach administrator '16-39; coached-managed Ozzie Herlen to '37 Sask. lightweight, '38 welterweight titles; while employed in NYR organization designed team jacket; trainer Western Canadian girls' fastball titlist, '54 Little World Series rep.; trainer Saskatoon Commodores baseball team '58-74; mem. Sask. Sports Hall of Fame.

REID, Bruce (water skiing); b. 23 May 1956, Selkirk, Man.; given name: Alexander Bruce; m. Elizabeth Christine Allan; c. James Brody; UMan, BPE, MD, FRCSC; orthopaedic surgeon; mem. ntl team '70-83; 21 ntl titles, 17 ntl records; 4 Man. barefoot titles; competed 6 Worlds; silver overall, team '82 World Cup, bronze jump '79 world championships, '80 World Cup; mem. Man., Cdn WSA, Man. Underwater Council, Cdn Fencing Assn., CAHPER; Alta., Sask water ski coach '82-83; man. WS pres., tech comm. chair. '76-77; Man. sports excellence award, Queen's Jubilee medal, Winnipeg outstanding sport achievement award; hockey referee, girls basketball coach; mem. Man. Sports Hall of Fame; res. Alton, Ill.

REID, Ian (water skiing); b. 7 Apr 1931, Selkirk, Man.; given name: Ian Livingstone; m. Ruth Elaine Wood; c. Kim, Patricia, Bruce; MD, FRCS; with father William became founding members Selkirk Seals Water Ski Club, Man. Water Ski Assn.; a pioneer and daredevil once reaching speed of 80mph skiing behind an airplane; 8 Man. Open titles; never competed nationally although all three children were ntl team members/champions; mem. prov., ntl, intl water ski associations; instrumental in making helmets/life jackets mandatory jumping equipment; noted historian of sport; established country's only water skiing museum in Selkirk; judge of prov., ntl, intl competitions; PRIDE Canada parent of '89 award; Solicitor-General crime prevention award; Selkirk Citizen of '90 award; Man. Medical Assn. Health & safety promotion award '96; mem. Order of Canada, Man. Sports Hall of Fame; res. Selkirk, Man.

REID, Lefty (softball/bowling); b. 25 Sep 1927, Mersea Twp, Ont.; given name: Maurice Hugh; m. Evelyn Dorothy Wickens (d); c. Dale, Janet, Gary, Scott, Terry; Geo. Brown College; ret'd hockey administrator; fastball lhp with many Ont. teams; Leamington, Ont., HS mile record; mem. Portage

La Prairie, Man., RCAF softball title team '46, Ont. jr. finalist '47, Peterborough city champs '49; active pitcher through '78, Toronto Press League MVP, all-star honors; one of 65 world masters 5-pin finalists '60; numerous city, regional singles, match play, team titles, all-star bowling honors; twice Ont. Legion titlist, singles '58, doubles '60; sports journalist Trenton, Belleville, Chatham, Galt, Peterborough, *Toronto Telegram*; awards for school sport coverage; charter mem. Cdn Bowling Writers Assn.; v.p. Ont. Bowlers Assn.; managed 20-lane bowling house 3Ω years; Jr. B hockey league convener '53-54; sr. OHA statistician '53; asst. to Bobby Hewitson, then curator Canada's Sports, Hockey halls of fame '67; curator both halls '68-74; Hockey only '75-90; mem. Hot Stove Club, Ont. Museum Assn., Cdn Assn. for Sport Heritage, co-founder, v.p. American Society of Museums and halls of fame; volunteer curator Peterborough Sports Hall of Fame; res. Peterborough, Ont.

REID, Pat (coaching/administration); b. 17 Mar 1949, Edmonton, Alta.; given name: Patrick Alexander; div. Brigitte Bittner; m. Beverly McDonald; c. Taylor, Brett; Waterloo, hons. BSc, UWO, MA, Pacific Western, PhD; special sr. marketing mgr. Health Canada; part-time prof. UofOtt; former dir. sponsorship & promotions Corel Corp.; former dir- gen. Sport Medicine & Science Council of Canada, dir. Swimming Canada, CAHA v-p. intl. operations, Sport Canada consultant '74-88; mgr. Best Ever '88 program '83-88, for which he received commendation from IOC pres.; IAABO official '69-79; ntl hj coach; European tour jumps coach '79-81; competed '72 Boston, Cdn marathons; head field event coach Ont. t&f title team '77 Canada Games; coached 16 ntl hj title winners; founder, meet dir. *Ottawa Citizen* Indoor Games 14yrs; hj coach Americas team '81 World Cup; head t&f coach '84 Olympics, hj coach '86 Commonwealth, '87 Pan-Am, '88 world jr. championships; mem. NA Meet Directors Assn. from '78; chair. Ont. T&F Coaches Assn. '78-82; 1st person to direct 3 CAHA consec. world championship ice hockey teams, jr. men '90-91, sr. women '91; coach/tech. consultant/ administrator '72, '76, '84, '88. '92 summer Olympics, '80, '84, '88 '78 CG, '79 Moscow Spartakaide, '81 pre-CG; '87 PAG, '88 World jr. championships; tech. consultant '80 Winter Olympic team; intl. IAAF hj lecturer from '78; key role in facility development Mooney's Bay, Lansdowne Park Coliseum; responsible for name change of Palladium to Corel Centre in Kanata '96; developed sponsorship of WTA tour by Corel; responsible for pitch that led to $1M Alexi Yashin contribution to NAC '98; chair. Ottawa Capital Games organizing comm., '06 Ont. Summer Games bid comm.; dir. Eastern Ont. bantam girls basketball championships '03; active minor hockey coach, plays oldtimer hockey and slow pitch; pres/CEO Balloon View; played key role in reviving Ottawa amateur athlete awards dinner when ACT withdrew; res. Ottawa, Ont

REID, Peter (triathlon); b. 27 May 1969, Montreal, Que.; given name: Peter James; m. Lori Leigh Bowden; Bishop's, BA; professional triathlete; won '97 Ironman Lanzerote; 3 Australian ironman titles; 2 World ironman titles (Hawaii); '99 Austria ironman, 2 Cdn ironman titles; 6 Cdn long distance triathlete of yr. awards; Norton Crowe award '98; res. Victoria, B.C.

REID, Robert (golf); b. 10 Mar 1917, Swift Current, Sask.;d. 29 Dec 1994, Prince Albert, Sask.; given name:

Robert Douglas; m. Eleanor Young; c. Bob, Gordon; UofT, DDS; dentist; back-to-back individual Cdn Intercollegiate titles '37-38; 5 Sask amateur titles; mem. 7 Willingdon Cup Teams; '34 Sask jr. title; 2 Sask. Sr. titles; pres. Sask. Golf Assn. '55; pres. Sask Seniors Golf Assn. '76-77; mem. Sask. Sports Hall of Fame.

REILLY, Keith (curling); b. 2 Sep 1938, Ochre River, Man.; m. Rosemary Lanzarotta; c. Lisa, Chris; Waterloo Lutheran, BA; ret'd teacher, Wheels in Action Co. owner; began curling '48; all-star lead Alf Phillips Jr. rink '67 Brier winner; competed 7 Ont. Consols; twice OCA intermediate champion; mem. 2 Canada Life, 2 Toronto Metro Major League, 1 Whitby Dunlop, 3 Avonlea Beef-O-Rama, 1 Kirkland Lake cash, 2 OCA Challenge Round, 1 Molson Carspiel title rinks; coach 2 Toronto CA Jr. girls, 3 Ont. Jr. women's, 1 Cdn Jr. women's title rinks '81-85; coach Canada Games gold medalists '83, TCA Sun Life winner '83; hon. life mem. OCA; TCA curler of year '84; mem. Phillips rink which forced OCA to rethink code of ethics and paved way for cashspiels in Ont. '68; active in coaching, officiating, supervisory, organizational capacity with Curl Canada from '73; conducted clinics, Japanese curlers in Japan and Canada '97-98; CCA achievement award; res. Rexdale, Ont.

REIMER, Eugene (all-around); b. 21 Jan 1940, Swift Current, Sask.; given name: Eugene Donald; div.; c. Jim, Kevin, Lianne; UCollege Fraser Valley hon. LLD; owner Reimer Enterprises Ltd.; childhood polio left him with minimal leg use but that proved no deterrent as he excelled in variety of wheelchair sports including weightlifting, archery, swimming, basketball, volleyball, t&f; quickly became one of B.C.'s top all-around athletes; from '68 to '80 retirement amassed over 50 ntl, 22 intl medals, 5 gold, 4 silver, 1 bronze Olympics, 2 gold, 3 silver, 2 bronze PAG; 2 WR; Norton Crowe award '72; W.A.C. Bennett award '91; B.C. sports award, middle school bear his name; 1st recipient Reimer award; chair. '02 B.C. Disability Games; Rotary Intl. Paul Harris Fellow; active in promotion of '10 Olympics; mem. Order of Canada; mem. Terry Fox, B.C. Sports halls of fame; res. Abbotsford, B.C.

REISER, Glenda (t&f); b. 16 Jun 1955, Ottawa, Ont.; UofOtt, MD; physician; Cdn native, open record 4:06.7 for 1500m '72 Olympics; 3 ntl 1500m titles; gold '74 CG; Elaine Tanner award '73; mem. Ottawa Sports Hall of Fame; res. Ottawa, Ont.

REMMEN, Ray (harness racing); b. 28 May 1947, Saskatoon, Sask. m. Shirley; c. Kati, Tammy; drove 1st race at 16 at Ladner, B.C.; campaigned with moderate success on Sask., Alta. circuits (won 3 Western Canada pacing derbys) and Windsor Raceway before moving to Meadowlands, N.J., where he ranks among top drivers; posted 1st-ever Western Canada sub-2min. mile with Stormin Stephen '75; with Shiaway Pat won 1st Hambletonian raced at Meadowlands '81; with Dance Spell won '82 World Trotting Derby; with Grade One Woodrow Wilson Stakes '85; drove Beach Towel to Little Brown Jug, horse-of-yr titles '90; 2 Breeders Crown titles; only driver to win Woodrow Wilson, Peter Haughton Memorial, Hambletonian; through '03 2866 victories, $33+M in purses; mem. Cdn, Living Horse Racing halls of fame; res. Lodi, N.J.

RENAUD, Ab (hockey); b. 2 Oct 1920, Ottawa, Ont.; given name: Albert Romeo; m. Lorraine Somers; ret'd public servant; mem. Woodroffe juvs '36; Lasalle jrs. '37-39; Hull Volants Sr. A '40-41; various armed forces teams '41-46; mem. Cdn Forces title team in Eng. '45; mem. Ottawa Senators '46, Ottawa Montagnards '47; mem. gold medal Olympic, World champion RCAF Flyers '48; mem. Flyers in Eastern Canada HL '49-50; mem. Ottawa army team ECHL '51; player-coach Brockville Magedomas NY-Ont. League '52-57; mem. Ottawa Old Pros; CHA Olympic award; with '48 Olympic title team mem. Ottawa Sports Hall of Fame, military athletes of 20th century; res. Ottawa, Ont.

RENAUD, Chris (swimming); b. 29 Aug 1976, Fredericton. N.B.; Mount Royal Coll; head coach MRC '01-04; 100m, 200m backstroke specialist; 17 ntl titles; mem. ntl team '95-00; 1st Cdn to post sub-2min 200 backstroke '96; silver 100m, 200m back '93 Eight nations youth meet; silver 4x100m medley relay '94 CG; bronze 4x100m medley relay '95 PAG; silver 200m back '95 World short course championships; gold 200m back, silver 100m back '96 Olympic trials; gold 200m back, 4x100m medley relay, silver 100m back, bronze 200m IM '96 Canada Cup; silver 200m back, bronze 50m back, 100m back '96 World Cup; competed '96, '00 Olympics; 4 CIAU records; res. Calgary, Alta

RENAUD, Don (golf); b. 17 May 1937, Ottawa, Ont.; m. Teri Bertrand; c. Debbie; golf pro; mem. CPGA/PGA 45yrs; winner 58 pro/pro-am tournaments; low pro Pebble Beach, Scotland world pro-ams; won '57 Rochester Open; 3 OV asst. titles, runnerup OV pro championship; 2 OV seniors titles; ntl asst. title; low pro Bermuda Goodwill; teaching pro averaging 1500 lessons a yr; assoc. pro Ottawa Hunt, Cleveland Oakwood, Rochester Oakhill; served as head pro Ottawa Rideau View, Cedarhill, Peterborough Kawartha; dir. of golf Blockbuster, Ft. Lauderdale, Fla., Eagle Creek, Dunrobin, Ont.; res. Kanata, Ont./Tamarac, Fla.

RENKEN, Brian (wrestling); b. 21 Jun 1955, Ft. William, Ont.; given name: Brian Henry; m. Barbara Jane McComb; c. Andrew, Kayla; UWO, BA, UofOtt. LLB; lawyer; ntl jr. FS, GR champion 74kg '74-75; mem. '75 ntl jr. world team; gold Canada Games '75; men's ntl team '75-82; gold CIAU '76, '78, '80; CIAU outstanding wrestler '80; mem. '76 Olympic team both categories; mem. '80 Olympic team; UWO most valuable wrestler '75-76, '77-78; mem. '77, '81 FISU, '78 '82 world championships teams; bronze '79 PAG, '83 CG, '80 World Cup; ntl sr. GR. 2 FS titles; brother Lloyd ntl team wrestler; UWO George Oliphant trophy; mem. UWO-W Club, NWO Sports halls of fame; res. Meaford, Ont.

RENKEN, Lloyd (wrestling); b. 27 Jun 1957, Dryden, Ont.; UWO, hons. BA, Lakehead, BEd; phys-ed. teacher; freestyle specialist; Pan-Am jr. 62kg title '76; CIAU 68kg titles '79-80; ntl team '80-84; ntl 68kg FS title, outstanding wrestler award '82; bronze 68kg '82 CG, '84 World Cup; competed '81 FISU, '82 world championships; 4 London outstanding wrestler awards; UWO MVP award '80; brother ntl team wrestler Brian Renken; mem. UWO W-Club, NWO Sports halls of fame; res. Thunder Bay, Ont.

RENNEY, Tom (coaching); b. 1 Mar 1955, Cranbrook, B.C.; m. Glenda; c. Jessica, Jamie; North Dakota, BPhE; hockey exec.; began coaching with Kamloops Blazers

(WHL) '90; 2 league titles, 1 Memorial Cup; asst. Team Canada '92 world jrs.; head coach ntl -18 Phoenix Cup winners '92; joined ntl team sr. program '92, head coach '93-96, silver '94 Olympics, bronze '95, silver '96 Worlds; head coach Vancouver (NHL) '96; replaced by Mike Keenan '97; NHL coaching record (through '03): 101 scheduled games, 39-53-9; CHA v-p. '97-00; head coach ntl jr. team '98-99; dir. NYR player personnel '00-03; asst coach NYR '03, head coach '04; asst. Team Canada '04 worlds; 3M Coaches Canada, WHL coach of '91 awards; Sport BC coach-of-'92 award; res. Calgary, Alta

RENWICK, Gordon (hockey/administration); b. 13 Feb 1935, Cambridge, Ont.; pres. Galt Hornets Sr. OHA 7yrs; Allan Cup titles '69, '71; built strong relationship with European teams and earned respect of officials; served as NHL CdM whenever they hosted European teams playing in NA; was key link in holding '72 Canada-Soviet together; pres. CHA '77-79; IIHF v-pres. '86-94; CHA volunteer of '79 award; hon. mem. IIHF; played major role in getting NHL and IIHF into discussions which led to NHL Olympic participation; mem. Cambridge Sports, IIHF Hall of Fame; res. Cambridge, Ont.

RESCH, Chico (hockey/coaching); b. 10 Jul 1948, Moose Jaw, Sask.; given name: Glenn; m. Diane; UMinn-Duluth; broadcaster; goalie Regina Pats '66-67, UMinn '67-71, Muskegon IHL '71-72, New Haven AHL '72-73; represented both Canada, US in Canada Cup; NHL NYI '74-81, Colorado '80-82, New Jersey '82-86, Philadelphia '86-87; 1 Stanley Cup winner; NHL totals: 571 scheduled games, 32,279 minutes, 231-224-82, 52sho, 41 playoff games, 2144 minutes, 17-17-0, 0sho; played 3 NHL all-star games; mem. WCHA, IHL, CHL, 2 NHL all-star teams; goalie coach Philadelphia '82-88, Minnesota '90, Ottawa '92-96; coach/GM WHL Tri City; began broadcasting '88 as Minnesota analyst; FOX sports network from '96; IHL James Norris, Garry Longman trophies; CHL Tommy Ivan MVP trophy; NHL Bill Masterton trophy; res. Emily, Minn./Little Ferry, N.J.

RESTIVO, John (coaching); b. 30 Jul 1946, Winnipeg, Man.; given name: John Phillip; m. Vivian Brown; c. Kevin, Kimberly, Heather; UWpg, BA, UMan, BPhE; sports marketing/promotion; mgr. ntl basketball team '72-73; asst. athletic dir. UMan '71-72; pres. Bison Booster Club '70-72; PR dir. Man. Central Soccer League '71; mgr. Bisons basketball team '70-72; exec. dir. Cdn Amateur Basketball Assn. '73-76; mgr. special programming, exec. asst. to pres. NSRC '76-96; head basketball coach UofOtt '79-88; OUAA coach of '83; res. Kanata, Ont.

RETI, Harvey; (boxing); b. 1 Sep 1937, Paddock Wood, Sask.; given name: Harvey Neil; m. Mabel Martin; c. Douglas, Lawrence, Tyler, Debra Leigh; ret'd soldier, correctional service employee; ntl amateur welterweight title '61; light-welterweight title '62-64; bronze '62 CG; mem. '64 Olympic team; head Yukon Amateur Boxing Assn; mem. Alta. Sports, Canadian Forces Sports halls of fame; res. Whitehorse, Y.T.

REVELL, Guy (figure skating); b. 2 Aug 1941, Newmarket, Ont.; d. 11 Mar 1981, Coquitlam, B.C.; m. Mary; c. Todd, Tammy; formed pair team with Debbi Wilkes '59 and

promptly won ntl jr. title; pair pioneered several techniques including double loop twist; NA title '63; 2 ntl sr. titles; Olympic silver, world bronze; turned pro following '64 retirement; skated with Ice Capades, Ice Follies, Holiday on Ice; taught Coquitlas SC; mem. Skate Can. Hall of Fame.

REVILLE, Ralph (golf); b. 1867, Witney, Eng.; d. 1957, Brantford, Ont.; publisher; emigrated to Canada '82; launched golfing career Brantford '84; sold interests in *Brantford Courier* '13; founder, publisher, managing editor Canada's 1st golf magazine *Canadian Golfer* '15-33; publication recognized internationally as "best golf journal in world;" secty CGA rules comm. '16-21; helped found Canadian Seniors' Golf Assn. '18; secty CSGA '18-26; governor CSGA to death; mem. RCGA Hall of Fame.

REYNOLDS, Shelley (ringette); b. 3 Apr 1975, Edmonton, Alta.; NATE; competed in 10 ntl championships winning gold '90, '03, silver '94, bronze '95; mem. 2 gold, 1 bronze world championships; forward 4 ntl all-star teams; played 8 months in Finland; versatile athlete who excels in volleyball, soccer, hockey; res. Edmonton, Alta.

REYNOLDS, Warren (basketball); b. 26 May 1936, Winnipeg, Man.; given name: Warren Alfred; div.; c. Jeffrey, Jodie; Windsor (Assumption); TDIAA sr. football titlists, all-star '55; 2 TDIAA scholastic basketball title teams with Etobicoke, all-star '55; 2 ntl Jr. A title teams; intercollegiate intermediate title team '59; mem. Tillsonburg Livingstons ntl Sr. A title team '60; competed '59 PAG, '60, '64 Olympic teams; champion Ont. Sr. B Toronto Dow Kings '63, ntl Sr. A '64; ntl 46+ squash title '82; ntl platform tennis sr. title '87; mem, Cdn Basketball Hall of Fame; res. Etobicoke, Ont.

RHEAUME, Manon (hockey); b. 2 Feb 1972, Trois-Rivieres, Que.; m. Gerry St-Cyr; c. Dylan; pro hockey goaltender, coach; began playing hockey at 6; 1st girl to play in annual Que. peewee tournament; made hockey history as 1st female to play in regular season Quebec Major Junior Hockey League game; made NHL history when signed by Phil Esposito to play with Tampa Bay Lightning; appeared in one exhibition game before being sent to Knoxville (ECHL); traded to Nashville Knights, Las Vegas Thunder, Tallahasse Stars; loaned to Austrian team and beat Swiss elite team; mem. NJ Rockin Rollers '95, Ottawa Loggers '96, Sacramento River Rats '97; mem. '92 Team Canada world champions, '98 Olympic team; world all-star; ret'd from ntl team '00; mem. Montreal Wingstars of Ntl women's HL; asst. coach UMinn-Duluth women's team; published book *Manon, alone in front of the net*; res. Santa Ana, Calif.

RIBBINS, Peter (football); b. 31 Aug 1948, Belfast, Northern Ireland; m. Siobhan Flanigan; c. Emily, Taylor; East Carolina., UofOtt, BSc; pres/COO Cayman Water Co.; football East Carolina, UofOtt; 3 years all-conf. dh/fl UofOtt; 1yr all-Cdn; mem. '70 College Bowl finalist; pro Winnipeg '71-76; all-Cdn db '72; Hamilton '73, Edmonton '77; mem. UofOtt Football Hall of Fame; res. Grand Cayman, B.W.I.

RICCI, Mike (hockey); b. 27 Oct 1971, Scarborough, Ont.; m. Beth; c. Jade; pro athlete; cntr Toronto Marlies (MTHL) '86-87, Peterborough (OHL) '87-90 (capt.); 1st choice Philadelphia '90; capt. Team Canada '90 jr. worlds gold; NHL Philadelphia '90-92, Quebec '92-95, Colorado '95-97, San Jose '97-04, Phoenix '04; NHL record (through '04) 1014 scheduled games, 233g, 355a, 110 playoff games, 23g, 43a; mem. Team Canada world gold team '94; 1 Stanley Cup; 2 OHL all-star, OHL MVP '90, CMJHL player of '90; 2 San Jose iron-man awards; Denver fans voted him sexiest athlete '97; talented soccer player; nicknamed "Reech"; res. San Jose, Calif.

RICHARD, Henri (hockey); b. 29 Feb 1936, Montreal, Que.; given name: Joseph Henri; m. Lise Villiard; c. Michélle, Gilles, Denis, France; sports columnist, club owner; 50 goals in single season as jr. before joining Canadiens '55 at 19; ctr'd line with brother Maurice on right, Dickie Moore on left; mem. Habs '55-75, ret'd holding club record for most seasons (20), most games (1256); NHL record: 1256 scheduled games, 358g, 688a, 180 playoff games, 49g, 80a; mem. 11 Stanley Cup winners; one 1st team, 3 2nd team all-star; tied playoff record 3 assists one period vs. Maple Leafs '60; nicknamed "Pocket Rocket"; jersey #16 ret'd by Canadiens; Canadiens special ambassador; mem. Canada's Sports, Hockey halls of fame; res. Montreal, Que.

RICHARD, Jacques (hockey); b. 7 Oct 1952, Quebec City, Que.; d. 7 Oct 2002, Issoudin, Que.; lw Que. jr. Remparts; Memorial Cup '71; QMJHL 1st team all-star '72; 1st Atlanta pick, 2nd overall '72 draft; Atlanta '72-75, Buffalo '75-79, Quebec '79-83; scored 52g '80-81; served drug-related prison sentence; NHL record: 556 scheduled games, 160g, 187a, 35 playoff games, 5g, 5a.

RICHARD, Maurice (hockey); b. 4 Aug 1921, Montreal, Que.; d. 27 May 2000, Montreal, Que.; m. Lucille; c. Hugettte, Maurice Jr. Norman, Andr_, Suzannne, Paul, Jean; ret'd fishing supply company owner; Verdun jrs., Canadiens srs.; NHL Canadiens '42-60; NHL record: 978 scheduled games, 544g, 421a, 133 playoff games, 82g, 44a, record 83 game-winning, 28 game-tying goals; 1st to score 50 goals in 50 games '44-45; record 5 goals, 3 assists Dec '44; 8 times 1st, 6 times 2nd team all-star; nicknamed "Rocket"; Hart Trophy (MVP) '47; never won league scoring title; capt. Habs several seasons; 8 Stanley Cup winners; suspension from playoffs for striking official triggered Montreal Forum riot; coached Quebec Nordiques WHA; 3 Lionel Conacher awards; Lou Marsh Trophy '57; special ambassador Canadiens from '80; jersey #9 ret'd by Canadiens; museum honoring his life in Montreal; NHL top-goal-scorer award bears his name; Officer Order of Canada '67, upgraded to Companion '98; mem. Que., Canada's Sports, Hockey halls of fame.

RICHARDS, Brad (hockey); b. 2 May 1980, Murray Harbour, P.E.I.; Notre Dame Coll.; ctr. Rimouski (QMJHL) '97-00; 1 Memorial Cup title; CHL player of '00; QMJHL, Memorial Cup MVP awards; Team Canada '01 world jr., '04 World Cup (gold); NHL Tampa Bay '00-04; 1 Stanley Cup winner; Lady Byng, Conn Smythe trophies '04; record 7 post-season game winning goals '04; NHL record (through '04) 326 scheduled games, 84g, 193a, 34 playoff games, 12g, 14a; played in Russia during '04 labor dispute; res. Murray Harbour, P.E.I.

RICHARDS, Eileen (speed skating); 13 Apr 1923, Winnipeg, Man. given name: Eileen Whalley; m. Richards; launched career with Grade 9 city championship '38; joined Winnipeg SC club '40; Man int. 3-mile title, 4 sr. ladies man. Open titles; bronze '42 NA championship; 3 Minneapolis Lakes titles; lone Cdn to win *Detroit Times* Harry Carl trophy; Wyandotte, Mich. Gold cup '45; retd '46 after winning Cdn sr. women's outdoor title; set ntl records 440yd, 880yd events; set NY 440yd record; runnerup Lou Marsh trophy '46; mem. Man. Sports Hall of Fame; res. Winnipeg, Man.

RICHARDSON, Arnold (curling); b. 2 Oct 1928, Estevan, Sask.; given name: Arnold Wellington; m. Edna Shirley Fleming; c. Shelley Joanne, Kimbal Brian, Laurie Susan, Nancy Anne; ret'd carpenter; 3rd on Richardson family rink with cousins Ernie, Garnet and Wes; best-known foursome in Canadian curling history winning unprecedented 4 Briers, 4 world championships (Scotch Cup) '59-63; mem. Sask. Sports, Canadian Curling, Canada's Sports halls of fame; res. Silton, Sask.

RICHARDSON, Bert (rowing); b. 25 Nov 1903, Toronto, Ont.; d. 27 Jan 1982, Toronto, Ont.; given name: Herbert Trenchard; m. Betty McPherson (d); sc. John; carpenter, salesman; minor baseball '22-24; Argos jr. football '25; rowing with Argonaut Club from '25; US jr. championship '26; bronze with Argos crew '28 Olympics; mem. '30 BEG team.

RICHARDSON, Blair (boxing); b. 1940, South Bar, N.S., d. 5 Mar 1971, Boston, Mass.; m. Beverly MacDowell; c. Lisa; Canadian, BE middleweight titles, twice vs Gomeo Brennan of the Bahamas for the latter '65, lost 1st, won 2nd; death from brain tumor; mem. NS Sports, Canadian Boxing halls of fame

RICHARDSON, Ernie (curling); b. 4 Aug 1931, Stoughton, Sask.; div. Marcia Carle; c. Don, Judy, Jim; m. Edith Velma Jordan Ricki Eventon; sc. Robin, Lynn; ret'd owner electrical wholesale-retail business; began curling '45 playing lead 1yr then skip thereafter; skipped 5 Saskatchewan title rinks, record 4 Briers, world championships; noted for aggressive takeout style; 3 Brier all-star-skip awards; skipped Cdn Elks title team '61; *CBC* Cross Canada, Calgary Masters, numerous car, cash 'spiels; authored several books on curling; *SI* award of merit '63; life mem. 3 curling clubs; World Curling Fed. Freytag award; avid golfer; mem. Order of Canada; Gov.-Gen.'s CC; Canadian Curling, Sask., Canada's Sports halls of fame; res. Regina, Sask./Scottsdale, Ariz.

RICHARDSON, Garnet (curling); b. 6 Nov 1933, Stoughton, Sask.; given name: Garnet Sam; m. Kay Meronuk; c. Brenda, Robert; ret'd contractor; teamed with brother Ernie, cousins Arnold, Wes, later Mel Perry, to win 5 Saskatchewan men's championships, 4 Macdonald Briers, 4 Scotch Cups (worlds); *CBC* Cross-Canada title, numerous western carspiels; rep. Regina 10 prov. championships, 3 as skip, 7 as 2nd; skipped Sask. mixed title rink '73; catcher with Sask. -18 baseball champions; freelance sportscaster for curling competitions at prov., national levels; mem. Curling Reporters of Canada; mem. Canadian Curling, Canada's Sports halls of fame; res. Regina, Sask.

RICHARDSON, George (hockey); b. 1880s, Kingston, Ont., d. 9 Feb 1916, France; mem. Queen's '09 Allan Cup winner; OHA sr. finals with 14th Regiment team '06-07; killed in WW1 action in France; George Richardson Memorial Stadium is home of Queen's Golden Gaels Kingston; mem. Hockey Hall of Fame.

RICHARDSON, Jillian (t&f); b. 10 Mar 1965, Trinidad; m. William Briscoe; c. Sterling, Paris, Trey; UCal, BA; sprint specialist; gold 4x400m relay '82, '86, silver 400m '86 CG; silver 4x400m relay '83 FISU, PAG; bronze 4x100m relay '83 PAG; silver 400m '91 world indoor championships; 3 ntl 400m, 2 200m titles; Colgate Games 200m, 400m titles; silver 4x400 relay '84 Olympics; competed '88, '92 Olympics; gold 400m '91 IAAF Grand Prix; '93 indoor GP title; 4 ntl jr, 1 sr. records; ranked in top 2 400m, top 3 200 m '86-92; flag bearer '93 world championships; fed. govt. excellence award '83; 1 CIAU indoor t&f female-athlete-of-yr award; 3 Calgary Booster Club, 4 Alta. achievement awards; UCal. female athlete of '87, 2 UCal merit awards, 1 ATFA athlete of '97 award; Cdn HS Hall of Fame award; active in community activities; parade marshal '85 Calgary Stampede; subject of *CBC* documentary; hon. chair. Terry Fox Foundation, '93 run; hon. starter '94 Mayor's Day Stampede runoff marathon; Olympic rep. 3 Stampede parades; seriously injured in '93 auto accident; rebounded to become active coach; res. Calgary, Alta.

RICHARDSON, John (water polo/administration); b. 6 Mar 1937, Toronto, Ont.; d. 5 Jul 1981, Puerto Rico; m. June; c. Cynthia, Suzanne; UofT, BSc, UAlta, MSc, Mich. PhD; professor UWO; competitive swimmer Etobicoke SC; Cdn backstroke record; began playing water polo UofT; founded Alta, Ont. Water Polo Assns; secty '61-67, pres. '67-75 Cdn Water Polo Assn.; 2yrs secty FINA; mem. COA '68-80; instrumental in expanding water polo competition in CIAU; helped develop coaching assn. certification program for water polo; helped create ntl women's team, '81 Canada Games participants; dir., exec. comm. mem. Sport Ontario '70-80; team mgr. '72 Olympics, water polo referee '76 Olympics, '71 PAG, '81 world juv championships; life hon. pres. CWPA; Royal Life award; OUA men's water polo title trophy bears his name; mem. London Aquatic Wall, Cdn, Ont. Aquatic halls of fame.

RICHARDSON, Kate (gymnastics); b. 27 Jun 1984, Vancouver, B.C.; given name: Kate Geraldine; UCLA, '96 ntl novice title '98 jr. ntl title; gold team '99 PAG; competed '99, '01 worlds; '00 Olympics; gold beam '01 American Cup; '01ntl vault, beam, floor titles; '02 CG AA, beam gold; Sport BC comeback of '03 award; res. Coquitlam, B.C.

RICHARDSON, Kathy (swimming); b. 17 Oct 1963, Toronto, Ont.; Brock; bronze 200m breaststroke '82 CG; mem. '80 Olympic, '83 FISU Games teams; 3 CIAU 400m IM, 2 200m breaststroke, 800m FS, 1 400m FS titles; Pan-Pacific, Speedo 400m IM, 4-Nations 400m FS titles; res. Toronto, Ont.

RICHARDSON, Luke (hockey); b. 26 Mar 1969, Ottawa, Ont.; m. Stephanie; c. Morgan, Daron; began playing hockey age 5; father Glen deeply involved in Ottawa minor hockey; def. through Ottawa minor hockey ranks, Peterborough 2yrs; Team Canada '86 jr. worlds silver,

'94 worlds gold, '96 worlds silver; NHL Toronto '87-91, Edmonton '91-97, Philadelphia '97-02, Columbus '02-04. capt. '03-04; NHL record (through '04): 1247 scheduled games, 32g, 147a, 69 playoff games, 0g, 8a; nickname "Rich"; res. Columbus, Ohio.

RICHARDSON, Stephanie (swimming); b. 11 Feb 1977, Toronto, Ont.; Florida; paramedic; 200m, 400m, 800m freestyle specialist. mem. ntl team '95-00; gold 4x100m, 4x200m FS relay '91 Eight Nations youth meet; bronze 4x200m FS relay '94 CG; gold 800m, silver 200m FS '96 Olympic trials; silver 400m FS '96 Canada Cup; competed '96 Olympics; coach Killarney SC 5yrs, Rocky Mountain Masters SC 3yrs; swim coach for triathletes; res. Calgary, Alta.

RICHARDSON, Wes (curling); b. 20 Mar 1930, Stoughton, Sask.; m. Arlene Johnson; c. Kirt, Kathrine, Gregory, Margo; ret'd industrial electrician; played hockey, baseball in his youth; pitcher Regina Red Sox; since youngsters were not permitted to curl on 2-sheet Stoughton club ice his competitive career didn't begin seriously until '57-58 season; did not join cousins Ernie, Sam (Garnet) and Arnold to form famed Richardson rink until '58-59 season; played lead in 4 Briers (3 winners) and world championships; back surgery kept him from '63 Brier which rink won with Mel Perry his replacement; retiring from competition he moved to Hawaii becoming active in marathon running; while in Saskatchewan was active in long distance cycling competing in numerous 100-mile rides and twice in Regina to Saskatoon 1-day races; ran final marathon at age 50; mem. Sask., Canada's Sport, Cdn Curling halls of fame; res. Kailua, Hawaii.

RICHER, Stephane (hockey); b. 7 Jun 1966, Ripon, Que.; m. Sabrina; right wing; jr. Granby, Chicoutimi QMJHL '83-85; drafted by Montreal '84; Sherbrooke AHL '87; Montreal NHL '85-91, '96-97, New Jersey '91-96, Tampa Bay '98-2000, St. Louis '00, Washington '00; scored 50g '88, 51 '90; QMJHL rookie of '84; QMJHL all-star '85; mem. '86, '95 Stanley Cup winners, 1 NHL all-star game; NHL record: 986 scheduled games, 407g, 384a, 131 playoff games, 53g, 45a; res. Montpellier, Que.

RICHMAN, Joey (all-around); b. 25 Apr 1915, Montreal, Que.; m. Roz Shizgai; c. Steve, Mark; ret'd owner sales agency; played, coached basketball '32-57; mem. 4 ntl finalists, 7 Que. titlists as player, 3 ntl champions as coach; frequent league, tournament MVP, all-star, scoring champion; instrumental in making YMHA respected force in Montreal, ntl cage circles; coached YMHA to unblemished 29-0 record, ntl title '56-57 season; end Montreal Cubs '39-41, hb RCAF Hurricanes '41-42, Grey Cup winner '42; played with Lachine, Hamilton, Ottawa Trojans, Alouettes (CFL) through '47; pres. Alouette Alumni Assn. '77-80; without formal training coached RCAF t&f team '42; began competing as sprinter at 27; PB: 100yds 9.7, 220yds 21.9; with Fred Oberlander organized 1st Canadian entry Maccabiah Games; coached '50 basketball team, '53, '57 t&f teams; chair. athletic co-ordinating comm. Maccabiah Games from '57; coach ntl women's t&f team '52 Olympics; mem. HS soccer title team '31; novice 126lb Golden Gloves boxing title '37; semipro baseball Hamilton '44; Que. sr. singles tennis titles '56, '66, 5 Martini masters titles, 5 ntl srs. titles; Montreal outstanding athlete '46; mem. Montreal YM-YWHA Sports Hall of Fame; res. Montreal, Que.

RICHMAN, Ruby (basketball); b. 22 Sep 1934, Toronto, Ont.; given name: Reuben; m. Eileen Young; c. Alana, Jacqueline, Steven; UofT, BComm, LLB, Osgoode Hall; sports administrator; capt. TDHS champions '52; 7 years mem. Varsity Blues basketball team, capt. '56-59, champion '58; player-coach Maccabiah Games teams '61, '65, '69, '73 (bronze), Sao Paulo, Brazil, '66, Olympics '64, '68, '72, PAG '67; player-coach ntl sr. men's champions '63-64; mem. 3 Ont. jr. softball titlists, 2 Toronto sr. titlists, 1 Ont. jr. baseball titlist, 2 Toronto jr. champions, capt. Ont. midget, juv, Jr. B. hockey champions; pres. Basketball Ont., Basketball Canada, Sports Federation of Canada, Sport Ont.; outstanding all-around athlete UofT; W.A. Potter Trophy UofT Blues MVP '58; chair. ntl selection comm. Cdn Maccabiah Games Assn.; mem. Cdn Basketball Hall of Fame; res. Willowdale, Ont.

RICKER, Maelle (snowboarding); b. 2 Dec 1978, N. Vancouver, B.C.; given name: Maelle Daniea; halfpipe specialist, world snowboard cross; began snowboarding '94; ntl team from '96; ISF world jr. gold; '97 ntl champion; mem. '98 Olympic team; missed '02 Olympics due to injury; 3 WC gold, 1 silver, 3 bronze; res. Whistler, B.C.

RIDD, Carl (basketball); b. 17 Aug 1929, Winnipeg, Man.; d. 29 Mar 2003, Winnipeg, Man.; m. Beverley Tozer; c. Laurel, Brian, Karen; UMan, BA, MA, United College, BD., Drew., PhD; ret'd university prof., United Church minister, political activist; mem. 8 consecutive Man. champion basketball teams '48-55, all-star '50-55; mem. 3 Western Canada title teams (UMan Bisons '50, Varsity Grads '52, Winnipeg Paulins '54); latter team won ntl title; mem. '52 Olympic team; 2nd all-star world tournament team '54; '49-50 4th highest college basketball scorer NA; rejected NBA offers; did some coaching at minor level; nicknamed "King Carl"; mem. Cdn, Man. Basketball, Man. Sports halls of fame.

RIDGWAY, Dave (football); b. 24 Apr 1959, Stockport, Eng.; div. Nancy; c. Christopher Dallas, Drew Bradley; Toledo; dir. operations TeleMatrix; kicker; began fb career Robinson HS, Burlington, Ont.; drafted/released by Montreal '81, Saskatchewan '82-95; 7 all-Western, 6 all-CFL all-star; set/tied 8 CFL records; most consec. fg 28 '93; most fg 1 game 8 '88 (tied by Paul Osbaldiston '96); longest fg 60yds; career total 2374 points; 3 Dave Dryburgh Memorial trophies; Dick Suderman outstanding Cdn Grey Cup '89; mem. 1 Grey Cup winner; jersey 36 ret'd by Roughriders; mem. Cdn Football hall of fame; res. Colorado Springs, Colo.

RIGNEY, Frank (football); b. 9 Apr 1936, East St. Louis, Ill.; given name: Frank Joseph; div; c. Mitchell Frank, Lisa Karen, Kathy Dawn; Iowa, BA; investment broker, golf club distributor, TV commentator; played in North-South, Senior Bowl games, Rose Bowl '57; 3rd draft Philadelphia (NFL); ot/dt Blue Bombers '58-67; 5 Grey Cup finals, 4 winners; 7 times all-pro; Beckett-DeMarco Trophy twice; Schenley defensive player of '61; *CBC-TV* football commentator 20yrs; mem. Canadian Football Hall of Fame; res. West Vancouver, B.C.

RILEY, Con (rowing); b. 25 Aug 1875, Atlantic Ocean, d. 20 Nov 1960, Winnipeg, Man.; given name: Conrad Stephenson; m. Jean Isabel Culver; c. 6 sons, 2 daughters; dir. Hudson's Bay Co.; Winnipeg Rowing Club '92-29 as rower, coach, official; WRC pres. '11, hon. pres. '29; Steward's Challenge Cup in 4s as stroke Winnipeg crew '10 Royal Henley regatta; led 14 WRC rowers to 7 NA titles (8s, 4s, sr., int. doubles, singles) '12; last race at age 70; mem. Canada's, Manitoba's Sports halls of fame.

RILEY, Culver (rowing); b. 21 Jun 1907, Winnipeg, Man., d. 1970, Winnipeg, Man.; given name: William Culver; m. Elizabeth Hamilton; c. William Culver Jr., Evelyn Hamilton, Christopher Hamilton; St. John's College, McGill, LLD; bd. chair. Cdn Indemnity Co.; dir. Royal Bank, Great-West Life, Dominion Bronze, Union Oil, *Southam Press*; mem. ntl title crew '27-28; exec. mem. Winnipeg Football Club, pres. '50-51; key role in construction Winnipeg football, baseball, hockey complex; pres. Winnipeg '67 PAG comm.; dir., mem. OBE, National Hockey Foundation, Canada's, Man. Sports halls of fame.

RILEY, Martin (basketball); b. 8 May 1955, Winnipeg, Man.; given name: Martin James; m. June Fick; UMan, BPhE; basketball coach; mem. undefeated Manitoba HS title team; provincial title, MVP, all-star honors; 4 times 1st team, once 2nd team GPAC all-star; all-time points, assists leader; mem. CIAU titlist '76, championship series MVP; 3 times all-Cdn; Mike Moser award '77; 3 CIAU all-Cdn; 1st HS player to qualify for men's ntl team; ntl team mem. '75-82, capt. '78-82; mem. 2 Intercontinental tournament, '76, '80 Olympic, '75, '79 PAG, 2 FISU Games, 2 world championships teams; semipro Argentina 1yr; Man. male athlete of '76; coach UMan men's varsity team '83-84; mem. Cdn., Man. Basketball, Man. Sports halls of fame; res. Winnipeg, Man.

RINKE, Chris (wrestling); b. 26 Oct 1960, Port Coquitlam, B.C.; SFU; freestyle specialist; gold 82kg '82, '86 CG; bronze 82kg '82-83 World Cup, '83 PAG, '84 Olympic Games; 8 ntl FS titles; 1st Cdn gold medalist Freiburg International tournament '84; fed. govt. excellence award '83; mem. Ntl (U.S.), Cdn Wrestling, SFU Sports halls of fame; res. Port Coquitlam, B.C.

RISEBROUGH, Doug (hockey); b. 29 Jan 1954, Guelph, Ont.; m. Marilyn; c. Allison, Lindsay; hockey exec.; jr. Guelph, Kitchener; Nova Scotia (AHL), NHL Montreal '74-82, Calgary '82-87 (capt. 4 yrs); NHL playing record: 740 scheduled games, 185g, 286a, 124 playoff games, 21g, 37a; mem. 4 Stanley Cup winners; asst. Calgary '87-89; head coach '90-92; NHL coaching record: 144 scheduled games, 71-56-17; 7 playoff games, 3-4; 2 President's Cups, 1 Stanley Cup; AGM Calgary; GM '91-95; held various positions with ntl team '95-96; v-p hockey operations Edmonton Oilers '96-99; GM Minnesota Wild '99-04; res. Edmonton, Alta.

RITA, Adam (football/coaching/administration); b. 21 Sep 1948, Kauai, Hawaii; m. Karen; c. Kevin, Harrison; Boise State BPE; football exec.; c/ot Boise State; coached Boise State 9yrs, UNLV 3yrs, Hawaii, UBC; guest coach BC Lions training camp 6yrs; broke into pro coaching ranks as asst. BC '83; varied coaching roles in CFL with BC, Toronto (head coach '91), Edmonton, Ottawa, Memphis; GM BC '00; VP Argos '04; 5 Grey Cup finals, 1 winner as head coach; CFL Annis Stukus coach-of-yr award '91; CFLPA coach of '97; res. Oakville, Ont.

RITCHIE, Alvin (coaching); b. 12 Dec 1890, Cobden, Ont.; d. Apr 1966, Regina, Sask.; given name: Alvin Horace; customs officer; among Canada's coaching greats; nicknamed "Silver Fox"; often called "The Knute Rockne of Canada"; best known for football coaching exploits, also gained prominence in hockey; only coach in Cdn history to guide teams to Little Grey Cup, Memorial Cup titles; asst. coach Regina sr. football club '21; major role in organizing Regina Pats hockey team, coached them to Memorial Cup triumphs '25, '28, '30; instrumental in organizing Sask. Jr. Hockey League; coached Regina Pats jr. football club to Western Cdn titles '25-28, ntl title (Little Grey Cup) '28; head coach Regina Roughriders (he gave them their name), consecutive Grey Cup finals '29-32 but never a winner; football teams he coached recorded 56 consecutive league victories, 9 western titles, 1 ntl crown; ret'd from coaching '36; scouted for NYR hockey club more than 30yrs; strong crusader for Cdn football rule changes trimming from 14 to 12 players, encouraging forward pass 2yrs before East approved it, importing of US players; mem. Canadian Football, Sask., Canada's Sports halls of fame.

RITCHIE, Andy (swimming); b. 6 Dec 1958, Port Arthur, Ont.; given name: Andrew James Allan; Florida, Lakehead, BPHE; ntl team '75-79; mem. '76 Olympic, '77 FISU, '78 CG teams; world 400IM, 200m breaststroke ranking; 2 silvers Florida conf. championships, all-America status; bronze 400IM '77 FISU Games; 3rd 200m breaststroke '78 CG trials; 2nd 400IM European tour meet Paris '79; gold 200m breaststroke, silver 200IM, 100m breaststroke '80 CIAU championships; silver 200m breaststroke '81 CIAU championships; Lakehead male athlete of '79-80; ntl masters record '95; mem. NWO Sports Hall of Fame; res. Thunder Bay, Ont.

RITCHIE, Bill (basketball); b. 6 Apr 1923, Saint John, N.B.; given name: William Struan; St. Francis Xavier; active official '50-72; formed NB Assn Approved Basketball Officials '57; authored basketball coaches manual '63; chair. officials selection comm. for ntl, intl championships '79-85; mem. ntl comm. Cdn Assn. Basketball Officials '74-85; pres. Cdn Assn. Basketball Officials '79-85; pres. Atlantic provinces CAHPER '68-69; dir. Cdn School Sports Fed. '70-82; chair. NB Sports Hall of Fame selection comm. '70-73; chair./governor NB Sports Hall of Fame '77-78; APAHPER honor award; IAABO merit award; CSSF award; NBOA honor award; Basketball NB special award; life mem. IAABO; CABA scholarship bears his name; mem. St. FX, NB Sports, Canadian Basketball halls of fame; res. Fredericton, N.B.

RITCHIE, Dale (ballooning); b. 19 Oct 1952, London, Ont.; m. Cynthia Egbert; c. Michael Dale, Christopher Paul; UCal, UAlta, BSc; operations mgr. Balloon Adventures; competed '81 world hot air balloon championships; 3rd ntl hot air balloon championships; won '81 Foothills Balloon race; res. Calgary, Alta.

RITCHIE, Dave (football); b. 3 Sep 1938, New Bedford,

Mass.; m. Sharon; c. Phyllis, Susan, Dave; Cincinnati; fb/lb at Cincinnati; football coach; coached Fairmount State Coll '78-82, 1 ntl title; coached Marshall, Brown, Cincinnati; asst. coach Montreal '83-86; Winnipeg '90 Grey Cup; Ottawa; head coach BC 3yrs, '94 Grey Cup; head coach Montreal '97-98, coach/GM Winnipeg '99-04; Stukus coach of '01 award; res. Winnipeg, Man.

RITCHIE, Jo-Anne (triathlon); b. 9 Mar 1960, Vancouver, B.C.; given name: Jo-Anne Lynne; m. Blake William Dean; c. William, Jillian, Spencer; SFU, BBA; homemaker, part-time fitness trainer; 9 Cdn Grand Prix titles; gold '91 ITU short-course worl' championship; silver '92 ITU worlds; bronze '93 ITU worlds; ntl women's titles '91-93; mem. Triathlon Canada, B.C. Sports Hall of Fame; res. Kelowna, B.C.

RITCHIE, John (skiing); b. 4 Jul 1948, Port Arthur, Ont.; given name: John Francis Stewart; m. Eileen Grimsgaard; c. Damien, Max; Lakehead, MA; financial officer; mem. ntl team '67-71, Lakehead team '71-73; head coach Kootenay Zone '73-75; head coach women's ntl ski team '75-76; men's ntl team '76-83; Level IV Cdn Ski Coaches Federation; Level III Cdn Ski Instructors Alliance; master coach, Coaching Assn. of Canada; co-authored *Ski the Canadian Way*; v.-chair Rough Riders 2yrs; res. Invermere, B.C.

RITCHIE, Trevor (harness racing); b. 14 Jun 1956, London, Ont.; displayed interest in racing at age 10; began driving London's Western Fair Raceway then shifted to Flamboro and Windsor; 3 dash, 2 UDR titles Windsor; moved on to OJC circuit; with Quite A Sensation won '86 and Frugal Gourmet '87 NA Cup, Prix d'Ete; piloted Ready To Rumble to Cdn Pacing Derby title '94; with Yankee Paco '00 Hambletonian, Cdn Trotting Classic; 71 major stakes victories; O'Brien driver of '00 award; through '03 3147 victories with purses exceeding $45M; res. Acton, Ont.

RIZAK, Gene (basketball); b. 27 Aug 1938, Windsor, Ont.; div. Claire Anna Best; c. John, Anna, Joe, Susan, Samantha, Joshua; Assumption College, BA, McMaster, BPhE, UBC, MPhE; ret'd educator, basketball coach; all-star Windsor HS champions '57; Assumption '57-60, Ont. intercollegiate title '59, co-champions '58; led league scorers, set record 44 points 1 game vs UofT, NA record 26 of 28 free throws; averaged 25 points per game, led McMaster scorers '60-61; mem. Tillsonburg Lvingstons, London Fredericksons, Eastern Cdn title '61-62; Montreal Yvon Coutu Huskies '62-64, '62 Eastern Cdn title; UBC '64-65; 3 ntl titles IGA '65-67; Art Willoughby Trophy, Vancouver men's rookie of '65; mem. ntl team '67 PAG; Vancouver White Spots '68 ntl finalist; coached HS '60-67, SFU '68-70, Regina '70-79; varied administrative roles SABA; wrote Basketball for the Beginning Coach and Teacher; pitched 2 seasons London Senior IC Baseball League; Sask. 55+, Alta. 60+ tennis titles, runnerup ntl 60+ championships; mem. UWindsor Sports Hall of Fame; res. Calgary, Alta.

ROBERGE, Patrick (judo); b. 18 sep 1970, Chicoutimi, Que.; U Quebec; program mgr. Sport Canada; 3 ntl titles; silver '96 European tour, '98 FISU, '97 Francophone Games; bronze '98 U.S. Open; mem. '92 Olympic team; Quebec Judo Assn. Male competitor of '97-98; res. Montreal, Que.

ROBERT, Magli (orienteering); b. 18 Sep 1964, Sherbrooke, Que.; m. Farshad Sepadji; c. Jasmine, Darya; UofOtt, MD; gynecologist; won OFSAA x-country ski titles while attending Gloucester HS; represented Canada in 3 world orienteering championships; 6 ntl, 2 NA elite women's titles; ret'd '01; res. Calgary, Alta.

ROBERT, Yvon Sr. (wrestling); b. 8 Oct 1914, Montreal, Que.; d. 13 Jul 1971, Montreal, Que.; c. Yvon Jr.; pro wrestler; pro career spanned 26yrs ('33-59) in which he emerged as a Quebec sports icon rivaling Rocket Richard in popularity; won 16 Montreal intl titles '36-56; AWA, NWA, British Empire, New England titles; teamed with Whipper Billy Watson for Cdn tag-team title; world tag-team title; noted for agility, strength.

ROBERTS, Gary (hockey); b. 23 May 1966, North York, Ont.; m. Tamara; c. Jordan; standout lacrosse player; mem. Minto Cup jr. title team; lw, capt. Ottawa 67's '82-85, Guelph '86; 2 Memorial Cup winners; 2 OHL 2nd team all-star; silver '86 world jr.; 1st round draft Calgary '84; Moncton (AHL); NHL Calgary '86-96, missed '96-97 with injury, Carolina '97-99, Toronto '00-03; scored 53g '92; 2 NHL all-star games; reached 1000 games '04; NHL record (through '04): 1030 scheduled games, 397g, 408a, 114 playoff games, 28g 57a; Stanley Cup winner '89; Bill Masterton trophy '96; spokesman Alta. Lung Assn.; co-owner Uxbridge golf course; res. Uxbridge, Ont.

ROBERTS, Gordon (hockey); b. 5 Sep 1891, Ottawa, Ont., d. 2 Sep 1966, Ottawa, Ont; McGill, MD; physician; Ottawa Senators (NHA) '10, Montreal Wanderers (NHA) '11-16; Vancouver Millionaires '17 setting PCHA record 43 goals in 23 games; Seattle Metropolitans (PCHA) '18, Vancouver '20; 203 goals in 166 regular-season games but never played on title team; twice scored 6 goals in single games; once scored five; mem. Ottawa Sports, Hockey halls of fame.

ROBERTS, Jay (football); b. 20 Oct 1942, Des Moines, Iowa; div.; c. Jed, Kimberly, Kelley; Kansas, BA; public servant; earned all-state recognition in football, basketball; ntl merit scholarship finalist; 7 varsity letters in football, basketball, t&f at Kansas '61-63; te Ottawa '64-70; 3 Grey Cup finals, 2 winners; son Jed with Edmonton '91-98; res. Ottawa, Ont.

ROBERTS, Jim (hockey/coaching); b. 9 Apr 1940, Toronto, Ont.; given name: James Wilfred; m. Judy; c. Vicki, Corey; coach; def./rw Peterborough Petes jr.; NHL with Montreal '63-67, '71-77, St. Louis '67-'71, '77-78; NHL record: 1006 scheduled games, 126g, 194a, 153 playoff games, 20g, 16a; 5 Stanley Cup winners; began coaching career as asst. Buffalo '79-84; asst. Pittsburgh '84-88; head coach Springfield '88-90 winning 2 Calder Cups; brief stints as NHL head coach Buffalo '81-82, Hartford '91-92, St. Louis '96-97; GM/head coach Worcester Ice Cats (AHL) '94-96; asst. coach St. Louis '96-02; NHL coaching record: 134 scheduled games, 50-60-24, 7 playoff games, 3-4; res. St. Louis, Mo.

ROBERTS, Rick (field hockey); b. 8 Dec 1967, Victoria, B.C.; given name: Richard Arthur Maynard; m. Lisa Faust; UBC, BA, B.Ed; teacher; played ice hockey as youth; began playing field hockey seriously at 18; defence ntl team from

'89; capt/ '02 European tour team; prior to '02 CG had 166 ntl team caps; silver '95, gold '99 PAG; competed '98, '02 CG, 2000 Olympics, '98 World Cup, '01 WC qualifier; active as coach at varied levels from '88; avid guitarist and song writer co-composer '98 CG theme song "The Goose is in Malaysia"; res. Vancouver, B.C.

ROBERTS, Roy (badminton/administration); b. 13 Nov 1931, Solihull, Warwickshire, Eng.; given name: Reginald Roy; div. Mary Pagett; c. David Pagett, Jonathan Charles; m. Nicole Letourneau; Bardsley Coll. Birmingham, Eng. Barch; ret'd sports administrator; emigrated to Canada '66; Cdn citizen from '73; tech dir. Badminton Canada '73-79; high performance dir. '79-96; CEO '86-96; served as exec. officer Scarborough BA, Toronto Inter-Church BA, Toronto District BA, v-p, pres. OBA '66-73; introduced structures athlete development program, coaching, officials certification programs; dir. Badminton Canada, ntl coaching chair. '69-73; introduced ntl coaching clinic program; Cdn delegate IBF council '78-96; IBF sr. consultant on Pan-Am affairs; played major role in enhancing badminton's profile in Olympic community; recipient Confederation 125 medal, 2 Queen's Jubilee awards, Badminton Canada honorary lifetime award, Blouin Special award, IBF distinguished service award; mem. Cdn Olympic, Badminton Quebec halls of fame; res. Ottawa, Ont.

ROBERTSON, Bruce (swimming); b. 27 Apr 1953, Vancouver, B.C.; given name: Bruce Richard; m. Sheila Jocelyn Hurtig Bresalier; c. Andrew Alexander; sc. Michael, Julie Bresalier; UBC, SFU, DGS, CA; management consultant; silver 100m butterfly (55.56), bronze 4x100 medley relay '72 Olympics; gold 100m butterfly (55.67), bronze 4x100 medley relay '73 world championships; gold 4x100 medley relay, 4x100 FS relay, silver 100m FS (53.67), 200m FS (1:57.22), bronze 100m butterfly (56.8), 4x200 FS relay '74 CG;, 4th 100m butterfly (56.31), 4x100 medley relay '75 world championships; silver 4x100 FS relay, 4x100 butterfly (56.8), 100m FS (53.44) '75 PAG; mem. '76 Olympic team; 5 1sts, 1 2nd '77 NAIA championships; 2 world, 8 ntl masters records while claiming 5 gold, silver ntl masters championships '99, 5 gold '03; v-p CGF '03; shared '73 Norton Crowe award with George Athans Jr.; mem. Order of Canada; mem. BC Swimming, Cdn Aquatic, Olympic, BC, Canada's Sports halls of fame; res. Manotick, Ont.

ROBERTSON, Doug (weightlifting); b. 27 Mar 1949, Vancouver, B.C.; given name: Douglas Stewart; m. Peggy Phillips; c. Stewart, Ashton; foreman BC Rail; 2nd 123lb class '69-70 ntl championships; 132lb title '71 Canada Winter Games; 2nd 132lb class '71-72 ntl championships; mem. '73 world championships, '74 CG, '75 PAG teams; ntl 132lb titles '73, '75-76; BC champion '68-76, '78; res. Backendale, B.C.

ROBERTSON, Nancy (diving); b. 25 Dec 1949, Saskatoon, Sask.; given name: Nancy Jean; m. Larry Brawley; c. Kristen, Tara; UMan, exec-dir. Kitchener business development org.; 4th '67 PAG 3m; 8th 10m, 13th 3m '68 Olympics; silver 10m '70 CG; gold 10m '71 PAG; 7th 10m '72 Olympics; ntl team mgr. '86-87; FINA intl judge; mem. Cdn., Ont. Aquatic halls of fame; res. Waterloo, Ont.

ROBERTSON, Sandy (all-around); b. 26 Feb 1923, Vancouver, B.C.; given name: Edward Alastair Sandy; m. Mary Patricia; c. Barbara Joyce, Bruce Richard, Carolyn Patricia; UBC, BSc; ret'd consulting engineer, baseball Vancouver srs. '39-46, Louisville Colonels, Durham Bulls '46-47, Vancouver Capilanos '47-53; basketball UBC Thunderbirds '42-46, ntl champion Vancouver Meralomas '47, Vancouver Clover Leafs '48-53, 4 ntl titles; soccer UBC '46, Vancouver City, Pacific Coast League '52; squash '63-64 Vancouver City, BC, Pacific Northwest titles; semifinalist ntl sr. doubles '75-76; coach UBC, Pony, Babe Ruth, Jr. Pacific Coast baseball teams, Clover Leaf jr. basketball; George Pringle Trophy, rookie of year UBC basketball '43; MVP UBC basketball '46; basketball MVP '47-48; baseball MVP, all-star '50; mem. Vancouver Baseball, UBC, BC Sports halls of fame; res. Vancouver, B.C.

ROBILLARD, Gene (football/tennis); b. 15 Jan 1929, Ottawa, Ont.; given name: Eugene Thomas; div.; c. Matthew Thomas, Timothy John; McGill, BSc; ret'd HS teacher; mayor's trophy Ottawa Tech top athlete; Gerry Boucher Memorial Trophy OHSAA best football player, Kinsmen Shield OHSAA best hockey player 1st player to win both city awards; McGill qb int., sr. football; 3yrs varsity hockey; int. shot put champion '50; intercollegiate all-star db '51; qb'd Ottawa Seconds ORFU '52; pro BC '54; 2 Ottawa int. men's doubles tennis title, with Rick Marshall, Jacques Tamaro; int. men's singles title; Ottawa men's sr. doubles with Murray Wiggins; Ottawa and Rideau Tennis club int., sr. singles, men's doubles, mixed doubles titles; mem. '78 Ottawa team sr. hockey Olympics; chair. '80 ntl tennis championships; mem. Ottawa, Ont.

ROBINSON, Al (baseball, hockey, golf); b. 21 Aug 1931, Hamilton, Ont.; given name: Allan Ross; m. Doreen Cooper; c. Scott, John, Janice; chartered life underwriter (CLU); ret'd regional mgr. London Life; p/of 3 Ont. baseball title teams; convenor Oakridge minor hockey 3yrs; GM Woodstock Sr. A OHA Allan Cup quarter-finalists '77; commissioner OHA Sr. A '82-85; pro entertainer (impressionist); McDonalds sports citation; numerous amateur golf awards; res. London, Ont.

ROBINSON, Bill (basketball); b. 2 Feb 1949, Chemainus, B.C.; m. Susan Ford; c. Ella, Leah; SFU, U of Americas, Mexico, Waterloo; self-employed; HS all-star; NAIA all-American (1st Cdn) at SFU; 3yrs. conf. all-star; sparkplug for Jack Donohue's ntl team '69-76 excluding 2 seasons; frequent all-star gd, tournament MVP; 2 Intercontinental Cup, '74 World, '75 PAG, '76 Olympic Games teams; all-Cdn status SFU, Waterloo; NBA trial with Buffalo, ABA Virginia Squires; semipro Belgium, Mexico; mem. SFU Sports, Cdn Basketball halls of fame; res. Duncan, B.C.

ROBINSON, Bill (football); b. 23 Apr 1951, Toronto, Ont.; given name: William Robert; m. Barbara-Jo MacNeil; c. Kristi-Jo, Billy Jr.; St. Mary's, BComm;UWO; exec.-dir. Sport Heritage Nova Scotia; qb'd undefeated HS team '68-69; Maritime CIAU college MVP '71-73; conf. title winners '71-73; College Bowl title over McGill '73; all-star 4 consec. years; helped UWO win Western Bowl, College Bowl '74; all-Cdn qb; George McCullah UWO MVP award; pro Ottawa '75; mem. '76 Grey Cup champions; mem. Ont. basketball B champions '78, '80; Ont. touch football

champions '79; Ont. sr. baseball champions '80; pres. Senior Interprovincial Baseball League '81; exec.-dir. CAFA '77-83; chair. CIAU final eight basketball tournament; res. Halifax, N.S.

ROBINSON, Bill (harness racing); b. 5 Sep 1946, Hamilton, Ont.; left tire factory to pursue career in standardbred racing; has become one of the finest trainers in business with the likes of Precious Bunny, Cam's Card Shary, Riyadh, Presidential Ball, Pacific Rocket, Panifesto, Rule The Wind, Abbatom, All I Ask, Dream Maker, Lime Time, Topnotcher, Western Dreamer and Silent Spring; USHWA Glen Garnsey Trainer of '93 award; CTA Trainer of '91, '94; Breeders Crown trainer of '95; 4 Cdn. non-driving trainer- of-yr awards; several of his charges have claimed horse- of-yr honors as well as victories in the Little Brown Jug, Messenger Stakes, Cane Pace, Cdn Pacing Derby and varied world records; his Western Dreamer set Little Brown Jug record 1:51 1/5 '97; through '03 1289 victories as trainer with purses exceeding $32M; drew 5yr suspension '03 when pacer Flight Plan tested positive for elevated blood gas reading; res: Hagersville, Ont.

ROBINSON, Blondie (bowling); b. 3 Jan 1928, Kirkland Lake, Ont.; d. 19 Oct 1999, Weston, Ont.; given name: Graydon Ormiston; m. Phyllis Jones; sheet metal mechanic; led Intercounty 5-pin League '49-50 with 245; 3rd Cdn Bowling Assn. singles tournament '46; with Ken Drury of Sarnia 2nd '52 CBA doubles; averaged 265, rolled high triple of 1066 (418) Regina '53-54; '62 10-pin rookie season avg. 189; 2 perfect 300 games (1 sanctioned); 3 299 sanctioned games, 3 unsanctioned, 796 sanctioned triple, 802 unsanctioned; nore than 75 700s; ntl all-events 9 game record 1941 '66; with Ray Mitchell mem. of team which set record 3385 games; twice winner, 3 times runnerup provincial 700 tournament; 3 times winner Toronto 700 tournament; with Ray Mitchell Toronto scratch doubles; 3 times Toronto scratch all-events, twice city singles; Jim Brace ntl all-stars tournament, runnerup twice; CPBA singles champion '66, '78; averaged career high 212 for '80 season; Ont. scratch singles title '80; topped field of 25 to win '69 world 10-pin title; won Osaka Challenge tourney '69; failed in world title defence '70; Toronto bowler of year; mem. Canada's Sports, Greater Toronto 10-pin BA halls of fame.

ROBINSON, Bob (wrestling); b. 10 Sep 1958, Montreal, Que.; UWO; freestyle specialist; 62kg gold '82 CG, bronze '83 PAG; 3 ntl 62kg FS, 1 52kg GR titles; mem. '81 FISU, '83 World Cup, world championships, '84 Olympic teams; silver Freiburg tournament '84; fed. govt. excellence award '83; res. Pierrefonds, Que.

ROBINSON, Bobby (builder); b. 8 Apr 1888, Peterborough, Ont.; d. 6 Jun 1974, Burlington, Ont.; given name: Melville Marks; m. Maribel Fair Hawkins; c. Edna Margaret; editor; organized first Empire (later Commonwealth) Games in Hamilton '30; ntl team mgr. '34, '38; Olympic team mgr. '28, '32; mem. Canadian Amateur Sports Hall of Fame.

ROBINSON, Claude (builder/hockey); b. 17 Dec 1881, Harriston, Ont.; d. 27 Jun 1976, Vancouver, B.C.; mem. Winnipeg Victorias as player/exec. Victorias brought Allan, Stanley Cups to Winnipeg during his tenure; recognizing need he suggested formation of ntl assn. to compete for amateur hockey championships; result was CAHA formed '14 with him as 1st secty.; mgr. Cdn Olympic squad '32; life member CAHA; mem. Man., Cdn Hockey halls of fame.

ROBINSON, Emma (rowing); b. 26 Nov 1971, Montreal, Que.; m. Ken Murray; UofT; started rowing at university; mem. ntl team '93-02; gold World University 8s '93; 2 US titles; women's 8s silver '96 Olympics; with Alison Korn pairs gold '97, '98 worlds; with Theresa Luke '99 PAG pairs gold; with Luke set WR in heat then won gold Lucerne WC regatta; diagnosed with thyroid cancer '99; with Luke won Wilson-McCall pairs team award '00; res. Victoria, B.C.

ROBINSON, Jackie (baseball); b. 31 Jan 1919, Cairo, Ga.; d. 24 Oct 1972, Stamford, Conn.; given name: Jack Roosevelt; m. Rachel Isum; c. Jackie Jr. (d), Sharon, David; UCLA; lettered in baseball, football, basketball, t&f '41; played in African-American Baseball League; broke baseball's color barrier when signed by Branch Rickey to become 1st modern-era African-American to compete in major leagues with Brooklyn Dodgers; made pro ball debut with Montreal Royals 1946; played initial ML game with Dodgers 15 Apr 1947; Rookie of the Year; overcame major racist pressure of time to establish himself as ML standout; with Dodgers played 1b, 2b, ss, 3b, of '47-56 over 1382 games with .311BA; subject of numerous movies, TV specials, books; wife established Jackie Robinson Foundation to assist minority students; UCLA stadium bears his name; special tribute paid on 50th anniversary of his ML debut; Congressional gold medal; mem. Baseball Hall of Fame; hon. mem. Cdn Baseball Hall of Fame.

ROBINSON, Jennifer (figure skating); b. 2 Dec 1976, Goderich, Ont.; m. Shane Dennison; Ryerson; coached by Michelle Leigh; made intl debut German Blue Swords '93; competed '94 jr. worlds; 7 sr worlds, 6 Skate Canada, 3 Skate America, 5 ISU 4 continents, 3 Sears Open (2 silver); competed '02 Olympics; through '03 won 1 ntl jr, 6 ntl sr. women's titles; athletes rep. Skate Canada board; res. Barrie, Ont.

ROBINSON, Larry (football); b. 18 Apr 1942, Calgary, Alta.; m. Donna Dempster; c. Kirk, Tyler, Wesley, Scott; Mt. Royal College; OPI sales rep.; qb Calgary Western Canada HS champions '59; guided Mt. Royal Cougars to '60 Western Cdn jr. finals; rcvr/safety/k Stampeders '61-75, Dr. Beattie Martin WFC rookie-of-yr award; twice Dave Dryburgh WFC scoring title; 3 times WFC all-star; 4 time Schenley outstanding Canadian nominee, twice runnerup; Calgary MVP award '72; at retirement CFL all-time scoring leader; 1st player to gain 1000 pts; CFL record: 9tds, 362 converts, 171 field goals, 101 singles, 1030 pts (record since surpassed); 50 pass interceptions for 717yds, 3tds; returned fumble recoveries for 219yds; mem. 3 Grey Cup finalists, 1 winner; mem. Stampeder Wall, Cdn Football Hall of Fame; res. Calgary, Alta.

ROBINSON, Larry (hockey); b. 2 Jun 1951, Winchester, Ont.; given name: Larry Clark; m. Jeannette; c. Jeffrey, Rachelle; jr. Brockville, Kitchener '69-71; 4th pick Montreal, 20th overall '71 draft; Nova Scotia (AHL) '71-72; def Canadiens '72-89, LA Kings '89-92; James Norris Memorial Trophy '77, '80, Conn Smythe Trophy '78; 3 times 1st team, 3

2nd team all-star; mem. 5 Stanley Cup winners; NHL playing record: 1384 scheduled games, 208g, 750a, 227 playoff games, 28g, 116a; mem. Team Canada '76, '81, '84; asst. coach New Jersey '93-95, '02-04; Stanley Cup '95; head coach Kings '95-99, Devils '99-01; NHL coaching record: 469 scheduled games, 195-210-64, 52 playoff games, 31-21; Brockville CJHL team ret'd his #3 jersey; active polo player; growing interest in thoroughbred racehorse ownership; mem. Hockey, Canada's, Ottawa Sports halls of fame; res. Peterborough, Ont./Sarasota, Fla.

ROBINSON, Larry (rodeo); b. 27 Dec 1957, Innisfail, Alta.; m. Darlene; c. Kirk, Ben, Maria, Renee; farmer; calf roping specialist; CPRA mem. from '75; CPRA Permit award '75; Stampede CR title '86; 6 ntl CR titles; CPRA cowboy of '97 award; res. Innisfail, Alta.

ROBINSON, Morrie (cycling); b. 3 Sep 1911, Vancouver, B.C.; given name: Morris Tremayne; m. Hazel; c. Dawne; ret'd cycle importer; began 23yr competitive career age 17; 1st intl competition '29 winning 66-mile Magnolia Bluff U.S. road race in record time; broken back threatened career '31 but returned to competition '32 and went on to set records in 25-mile Pacific Coast, B.C. 1/10-mile, 1000m Olympic trials, Allan Trophy race, 15-mile Moody Cup, Gen. Clark 54-mile, Blaine Handicap, varied other races; in many instances eclipsed records set by Torchy Peden and Jim Davies; career record 71 1sts, 47 2nds, 27 3rds; won 5 Province Cup, 5 25-mile Pacific Coast championships, 5 B.C. 1-mile, 3 2-mile, 3 5-mile, 2 10-mile titles, 2 Moody Cup, 2 Colonist Cup, 3 Vancouver/Blaine Road Race, 2 Caledonian 2/5-mile titles; qualified '34, competed '38 B.E. Games; qualified but did not compete 1 Olympics; served as pres. Vancouver, Burnaby cycling clubs, v-pres. Cdn Youth Hostels; coached may successful riders; organized post-WW2 Provincial Cup races; officiated '54, '58 B.E.G.; medal presenter '94 Commonwealth Games; grandson is Olympian Laurie Schong; mem. B.C. Sports Hall of Fame; res. Camano Island, Wash.

ROBITAILLE, Daniel (weightlifting); b. 11 Nov 1953, Val d'Or, Que.; m. Claudette Leblanc; UofOtt; ntl jr. featherweight title '70; numerous Ont. jr., sr. records; 3 bronze '75 PAG; ntl 75kg title '77 with 282.5 overall lift; asst. coach jr. world championship team '80; res. Elliot Lake, Ont.

ROBITAILLE, Luc (hockey); b. 17 Feb 1966, Montreal, Que. m. Stacia Rae; c. Steven, Jesse; lw Hull Olympiques '83-86; QMJHL, Cdn major junior player of '86; 9th-round draft choice LA Kings '86; NHL with Kings '86-94, '97-01, '03-04, Pittsburgh '94-95, NYR '95-97. Detroit '01-03; Calder Memorial Trophy '87; NHL all-rookie team; 5 1st, 2 2nd all-star; 6 NHL all-star games; scored 53g '88, 52 '90, 63 '93; reached 1000pts '98; became highest scoring left winger NHL history '04; NHL record: (through '04) 1366 scheduled games, 653g, 717a, 159 playoff games, 58g, 69a; mem. Team Canada World title team '94. Olympic gold '02; 1 Stanley Cup; nicknamed "Lucky"; res. Los Angeles, Calif.

ROBSON, Fred (speed skating); b. 1879, Toronto, Ont.; d. 1944, Toronto, Ont; piano repairman; Toronto jr. champion '97; Ont. champion '97-02; at 19 3 world records; at 22 world records 220yd, 440yd hurdles, 60yd, 75yd sprints; at peak of career '99-16 held 9 world records, shared mile mark of 2:41.2 with Philadephia's Morris Wood; ntl barrel jumping record with 11, running high jump record 4'2"; mem. Cdn Speed Skating, Canada's Sports halls of fame.

ROBSON, Lex (golf); b. 7 Feb 1898, Scotland; d. 27 Jan 1976, Peterborough, Ont.; given name: Alexander Laurie; Cdn match play champion; 6 Millar trophies, 1 runnerup; CPGA title '33, runnerup '34; won Ont. Open '35, 3 times runnerup; 2nd Que. Open '33; head pro Kawartha G&CC '40-64; mem. Peterborough Sports Hall of Fame.

ROCHON, Henri (tennis); b. 12 Mar 1924, Montreal, Que.; given name: Henri Denis; m. Yolande Belisle; c. Danielle, France; insurance salesman; various Que. age-group titles, at 17 Que. jr. crown; ntl men's open singles '49; mem. Davis Cup team '46-53, '55-56, capt. '56; with Dr. Breen Marian ntl sr. men's doubles '72; ntl 60+ outdoor '89, 65+ indoor title '91; 3yrs teaching pro including year as resident pro Ville St. Laurent Indoor Tennis Club; res. Montreal, Que.

ROCHON, John (shooting); b. 11 Dec 1941, Cadillac, Que.; given name: Jean Louis Arthur Joseph; m. Donna Francis Green; c. Christine, Judy, John Jr., Tony; ret'd mechanic, firearms instructor; mem. ntl team '85-98; handgun specialist; 42 ntl titles (all disciplines); gold '91, bronze '95 PAG; competed '90, won silver, bronze '94, silver, 3 bronze '98 CG; competed 5 Crossman air gun championships winning 1 gold, silver, bronze; mem. Elliot Lake Sharpshooters Handgun Club, Algoma Rod & Gun Club; res. Elliot Lake, Ont.

ROCHON, Stephane (skiing); b. 15 Mar 1974, Laval, Que.; freestyle moguls specialist; mem. ntl team 93-03; ntl gold '96, '02, bronze '97; 4 World Cup race gold, 4 silver, 3 bronze; world championship silver '97, bronze '01; ranked 2nd '96 WC final standings; competed '98, '02 Olympics; with Tami Bradley '02 ntl FS dual moguls title; res. St. Saveur, Que.

ROCK, Richard (t&f); b. 6 Nov 1957, Reading, Eng.; given name: Richard Oliver; Southern Illinois; ntl jr. lj champion '75; mem. '76, '80 Olympic, '77 FISU, '78 CG, '79 PAG teams; Missouri Valley Conf. indoor lj record 24'5" '76; bronze NCAA indoor championships '77; Southern Ill. indoor, outdoor lj record holder at 25'3", 26'8" respectively; PB: 26'8"; ntl lj champion '78-80; res. Agincourt, Ont.

RODDEN, Mike (hockey/football); b. 24 Apr 1891, Mattawa, Ont., d. 11 Jan 1978, Kingston, Ont.; given name: Michael James; m. Mildred Alice Wormith; c. William Bernard, Richard John; Queen's, McGill; ret'd sports editor; football, hockey, soccer, lacrosse as player, coach, official, chronicler; 4 football seasons Queen's, 1 McGill, all-star 4 times, each at a different position; 15 Tricolor letters, record never equalled; hockey Queen's, Haileybury, Toronto St. Pat's; coached Queen's football '16; middle wing Toronto Argos '19; coached Argos to '20 Grey Cup final, lost to UofT; Parkdale Canoe Club ORFU titles '21-22; guided Balmy Beach to '24 Grey Cup final, lost to Queen's; won Grey Cup '28-29 as Hamilton coach; coached 42 football teams, 27 league titles, 2 of 5 Grey Cup appearances; coached Toronto de LaSalle, St. Mary's, St. Pat's, UotT

hockey; refereed 2864 hockey games, 1187 in NHL; mem. Canadian Football, Hockey halls of fame.

RODGERS, Johnny (football); b. 5 Jul 1951, Omaha, Neb.; div. Daryl; c. Terry, Latonya, Johnni; m. Jawana; c. Jewel; Nebraska, BA; owner/mgr. Jetware, Champion Productions; all-time leading Nebraska receiver with 143 catches for 2479yds ('70-72); awarded Heisman trophy '72; played in CFL with Montreal '73-76; earned nickname "Ordinary Superstar"; CFL rookie of yr; all-CFL 3yrs; runnerup CFL MVP '76; joined NFL with San Diego '76; remained for 3 injury-plagued seasons; founded 1st weekly cable TV magazine *Tuned In*; key figure in '97 Pro Flag tour; res. Omaha, Neb.

RODNEY, David (mountaineering); b. 27 Jun 1964, Mankota, Sask.; given name: David Anthony; m. Jennifer Adams; USask BA, BEd; Newman Coll MRE; pro speaker, world adventurer & guide, film maker, writer, humanitarian; only Cdn in history to successfully summit Mt. Everest twice '99, '01 despite back broken in 6 places, 4 knee operations, shoulder reconstruction; mem. '97 Can-Am Everest expedition communications coordinator (world's 1st business/education interactive e-mail website of its kind from Everest); climbed Argentina's Cerro Aconcagua '97; numerous other ascents in Asia, Australia, West Indies, Europe, South & North America; key role in spreading world-wide awareness of mountaineering with dozens of TV specials, books, newspaper/magazine articles, documentaries; authored *Heroes With Heart (Canadian Athletes You Can Look Up To),* featured in *Back to Everest: The Dave Rodney* Story (National Geographic TV); active in minor hockey at local, prov, ntl, intl levels; mem. Sask. Winter Games volleyball title team; active in t&f, baseball, football, curling, golf, swimming, cycling, skiing; active as coach several sports; taught PE in 2 provinces, 3 countries; introduced volleyball to St. Vincent WI; hon. chair. USask Presidents' fund raising campaign; role with city, prov. educational/political boards; spokesperson: "Banded Peak Challenge for Kids' Cancer Camp with Dave Rodney"; founder "Top of World Society for Children"; mayor's comm. mem "Turn Off the Violence", "Peace Heroes"; Calgary special achievement award, prov. award of distinction; Yorkton's Rodney Ridge named in his honor; Queen's Jubilee medal; mem. Yorkton Sports Hall of Fame; res. Calgary, Alta.

ROE, Lot (speed skating); b. 2 Sep 1881, Kincardine, Ont., d. 28 Oct 1964, Toronto, Ont.; m. Fannie May; c. John Murray, Arthur Edward, Anna May, Clarice Isabel; compositor; international 220yd sprint titles '10-12, '15-16; ntl all-around indoor titles '10, '13, outdoor '13; competitive skater '97-24; world 1Ω mile record 4:10; New England Ω-mile title '10; developed point system to determine all-around international champions; 2 CNE 100yd-dash (t&f) titles; mem. Canadian Speed Skating Hall of Fame.

ROGERS, Bruce (swimming); b. 4 Jun 1957, Toronto, Ont.; given name: Bruce Hibbert; Miami, UofT, Indiana, BA, UWO, MBA; ntl butterfly champion '74-75, records each time; 2 silver, 1 bronze '63 Canada Games; mem. '74 CG, '75 PAG, worlds, '76 Olympic, '77 FISU Games teams; bronze 200m butterfly '77 FISU Games; 2 Masters records; res. Oakville, Ont.

ROGERS, Chris (horse racing); b. 1924, Hamilton, Ont.; d. 29 Oct 1976, Hamilton, Ont.; jockey; began riding '41; quickly developed into what Eddie Arcaro described as "the complete rider"; 3 Queen's Plate winners, Epic '49, McGill '50, Collisteo '54; 2nd aboard Lincoln Road '58 Kentucky Derby; lifetime totals: 2043 wins, 2127 seconds, 2207 thirds from 21,424 mounts; successfully overcame alchoholism which threatened career; while enjoying good '76 season, sustained broken leg in Woodbine spill 30 Sep; died of lung cancer; mem. Canadian Horse Racing Hall of Fame.

ROGERS, Danny (swimming); b. 19 Sep 1958, Toronto, Ont.; given name: Daniel Clive; Indiana, BA; 3 silver, 1 bronze (backstroke, IM races) '77 winter nationals; silver (100m backstroke), bronze (200m backstroke) '78 summer nationals; 3 gold, 2 silver '77 Canada Games; mem. '79 FISU Games team; res. Mississauga, Ont.

ROGERS, Doug (judo); b. 26 Jan 1941, Truro, N.S.; given name: Alfred Harold Douglas; University in Japan; airline pilot; ntl judo titles '64-72; gold Canada Winter Games '71; silver '64 Olympics; bronze '65 Worlds; gold, silver '67 PAG; flag-bearer '72 summer Olympics; capt. all-Japan university judo team tiltists, 1st Caucasian so named; coached judo UBC, guiding team to Western Canada university titles '75-77; mem. Cdn Amateur, Judo, BC, Canada's Sports halls of fame; res. Vancouver, B.C.

ROGERS, Melville (figure skating/builder); b. 5 Jan 1899, Ottawa, Ont.; d. 26 Sep 1973, Ottawa, Ont.; m. Isobel (Tish) Blyth (d); c. David, Pamela; UofT, BA, Osgoode Hall, LLB; active in hockey, rugby, tennis; 18 sr. ntl figure skating titles in singles, pairs, fours; 5 Cdn, 2NA singles titles; with sister Gladys won '27 ntl pairs and with Margaret Davis '38 ntl dance title; mem. Cdn and 4 NA fours title teams; 1st male to represent Canada in Olympic figure skating '24; mem. '32 Olympic team; International Skating Union gold medal; 4 Royal Ottawa, 2 Rivermead golf club titles; RCGA governor; key role in formation and served 14yrs pres. Cdn Sports Advisory Council (later Sports Federation of Canada); drafted that body's constitution; associated with Minto Skating Club 60yrs; founded Minto Follies; life mem., hon. pres. Minto Club; 2 terms pres. CFSA; chaired international judges comm. 15yrs; Minto FS Club scholarship fund bears his name; COA dir.; mem. Cdn Amateur, Cdn Figure Skating, Ottawa Sports halls of fame.

ROGERS, Shotty (rowing); b. 1887, St. John's Nfld.; d. 1963, St. John's, Nfld.; given name: Levi; coxed more than 300 crews to victory; last victory '62 at age 75; mem. Newfoundland, Canada's Sports halls of fame.

ROGERS, Steve (baseball); b. 26 Oct 1949, Jefferson City, Mo.; given name: Stephen Douglas; m. Barbara Bodnarchuk; c. Colleen, Stephen Jason, Geoffrey Douglas; Tulsa, BSc; 4yr college record 31-5, outstanding amateur athlete US Southwest '71, college world series all-star; pro Montreal organization '71; ML roster '73-85; ML record: 399 scheduled games, 158-152, 129cg, 2837.7ip, 876bob, 1621k, 3.17era; *Sporting News* rookie pitcher of '73, Topps ML rookie all-star team; 100th ML victory 9 Sep '80, 150th 7 Sep '83; 4 1-hitters; 6 NL player of month awards, 5 all-star games; runnerup Cy Young balloting '82; nicknamed "Cy"; Expos player rep.; mem. Cdn Baseball Hall of Fame; res. Springfield, Okla.

ROGIN, Bill (basketball); b. 9 Jun 1915, Windsor, Ont.; d. 7 Mar 1987, Windsor, Ont.; m. Florence Fisher; c. Ann, Steven, Howard; Assumption Coll., BA, UofT, BPHE; ret'd HS principal; nicknamed "Moose"; Windsor HS shot put record '31-50; mem. Assumption Coll. "5 Fighting Freshmen" '33-37; 4yrs top scorer; Eastern Cdn finalists '34, ntl champions '35; NCAA single-game scoring record, world record 16 successive foul shots; mem. Victoria Dominoes '37-38; football, basketball UofT '38-39; semipro basketball Detroit '40-44; named to '36 Olympic team at own expense but did not attend; tryout as catcher with Philadelphia Athletics; coached Sarnia CI '39-44, Toronto YMHA '45-48; refereed basketball '32-65, ORFU football '39-48, EFC, Grey Cup final '47; life mem. Windsor Dist. Football, Basketball Refs., Umpires Assns.; son Steve qb Matt Anthony's unbeaten UofOtt Gee-Gees team, wife Florence mem. Windsor Alumni ntl finalist basketball team vs. Edmonton Grads '35; founding mem./dir. Windsor Essex County Sports Hall of Fame; mem. Windsor Essex County Sports, UWindsor, Cdn Basketball halls of fame.

ROKOSH, Greg (rowing); b. 24 Jan 1942, Flin Flon, Man.; given name: Gregory Joseph; m. Gillian Green; c. Amanda, Jennifer; UofSask, BA, BComm; sport administrator; 5yrs varsity football gd/lb Sask.; 2yrs capt.; founder Sask. Letterman's club; school's top athletic award; capt. wrestling team competing at 191lbs, heavyweight levels; Toronto Open FS title; began rowing as theraphy '68; mem. Toronto Argonaut RC '68-74; 5 ntl titles in pairs, 4s, 8s; several Ont. titles; semifinalist Royal Henley England '70, '72; with Ian Gordon, Karl Jonker, Don Curphey 9th (best by Cdns) '72 Olympics; won '72 Martini-Achter coxless 4s; turned to marathon running '74; PB 2h52min; coached rowing York, UofT, Ottawa; coaching co-ordinator CARA; created *Catch* magazine for CARA; designed ntl team program used by CARA; *CBC-TV* color commentator '84 Olympics; res. Russell, Ont.

ROLLICK, Bruce (badminton); b. 11 Apr 1943, Vancouver, B.C.; given name: Bruce Irwin Alexander; m. Judith Ellen Humber; c. Lisa Jane, Elayne Alexandra; UBC,BSc; consulting actuary; won all age-group prov. jr. titles; ntl men's open singles '68; with wife Judi closed mixed doubles '69, 5 times ntl men's closed singles; with Rolf Patterson '72 men's doubles; with Mimi Nilsson '77 mixed doubles; mem. 4 Thomas Cup, '70 CG, '72 China tour teams; active as coach for jrs., srs.; mem. silver medal team '98 Nike World games; with Patterson formed Badminton Perpetual Excellence Foundation; res. Vancouver, B.C.

ROLLICK, Judi (badminton); b. 17 Aug 1944, Seattle, Wash.; given name: Judith Ellen Humber; m. Bruce Rollick; c. Lisa Jane, Elayne Alexandra; teacher; ntl jr. champion, ladies' closed singles, mixed doubles once each, with Mimi Nilsson ladies' closed doubles twice; mem. 2 Uber Cup, China tour '72, 3 CG teams; twice ntl veteran ladies singles, doubles champion; proficient golfer; mem. Greater Victoria Sports Hall of Fame; res. Vancouver, B.C.

ROLLO, Kathy (diving); b. 30 Oct 1951, Warroad, Minn.; given name: Kathleen Mary; m. Donald Seaman; c. Erin Rae, Rebecca Rollo; Saskatoon, BSc, Central Mich., MA; registered nurse, nursing teacher; Saskatchewan diving champion '65-72; 4th tower '67 PAG, '70 CG; mem. '72 Olympic team; coached 3yrs; FINA International judge from '82; mem. Sask. Sports Hall of Fame; res. Regina, Sask.

ROMANO, Rocco (football); b. 1 Jan 1963, Hamilton, Ont.; Concordia; ret'd og; drafted Calgary '87, from '92-02, Toronto '88, Ottawa '89, BC '90-91; 3 Western, 1 Northern, 3 CFL all-star; Becket-DeMarco Memorial Trophy '94; runnerup CFL outstanding offensive lineman '94; 3 Grey Cup finals, 1 winner; res. Calgary, Alta.

RONEY, Jean (lawn bowling); b. 11 Sep 1945, Nokomis, Sask; given name: Jean Marie Berkan; m. Keith Norman; UofSask, BA; forensic scientist RCMP; skipped Sask women's pairs '87, '90-92 Cdn championships; mem. ntl team from '90; ntl women's singles titles '89, '93; skip 1st Cdn women's gold medal fours in international competition '93 Pacific Bowls; skip women's fours silver '94, gold '95 ntl championships; competed '94 CG women's singles; skip '95 women's fours bronze Pacific Bowls; competed world bowls '96, world women's indoor singles '93; US Open, Asia Pacific singles titles '03; res. Regina, Sask.

RONEY, Keith (lawn bowling); b. 7 Feb 1948, Regina, Sask; given name: Keith Norman; m. Jean Marie Berkan; Regina, BA; curator Royal Sask. Museum; 16 provincial titles; 3 ntl pairs, 2 ntl fours gold; 1 ntl singles, 1 pair silver; 2 ntl singles, pairs bronze; mem. ntl team from '88; represented Canada 2 Hong Kong, 2 Pacific Rim, 1 world indoor singles, 1 world bowls championships; WOBA singles gold '96; 2 Sun City, Fla. triples, 1 LA pairs gold; '93 LA bowler of tournament award; with Michel Larue '03 Asia Pacific pairs gold; res. Regina, Sask.

RONNING, Cliff (hockey); b. 1 Oct 1965, Burnaby, B.C.; given name: Clifford John; m. Ivana; c. Taryn, Kristin, Ty; cntr. New Westminster '82-85; WHL MVP '85; Team Canada '85-87, '01; Peoria (IHL), '89; HC Asiago Italy '89-90; NHL St. Louis '86-89, '90, Vancouver "91-96, Phoenix '96-98, Nashville '98-00, Los Angeles '00-02, Minnesota '02-03, NYI '04; NHL record (through '04) 1137 scheduled games, 306g, 563a, 126 playoff games, 29g, 57a; WHL all-star '85; nicknamed "Ace"; res. Vancouver, B.C.

ROOST, Ain (t&f); b. 5 Dec 1947, Upsala, Sweden; m. Dianne; c. Lindsey Melissa; Minnesota, PhD; psychologist; 5th javelin '66 CG; 4th discus '74 CG; bronze discus '71 PAG; 5th discus '75 PAG; silver discus '73 Pan-Pacific Games; mem. '72 Olympic team; ntl discus title '71-74; res. San Diego, Calif.

ROSE, Bob (golf); b. 19 Apr 1939, Toronto, Ont.; m. Kathy; c. Steven, Ruth Ann; golf pro; qualified in 1st tour school in US '66; played on PGA tour '66; 3 CPGA seniors titles; shot 57 on par 71, 6500yrd Beverly Golf Club course '81; 1 CPGA title; res. Waterdown, Ont.

ROSE, Jimmy (basketball/coaching); b. 1 Dec 1905, Niagara Falls, Ont.; d. 29 Jul 1995, Niagara Falls, Ont.; given name: James Vincent; m. Doreen; c. James Jr. (d); Queen's BA; educator, coach; coached basketball, baseball in church, district leagues; mem. NFCVI faculty '40-71; nicknamed "The Chief"; coached NFCVI teams to all-Ont. titles '51-53, '62-64; teams put together win streaks of 71, 66 games;

coaching record 668-165 with never a losing season; 15 sr., 12 jr., 3 midget titles; avid curler, golfer; NFCVI gym bears his name; mem. NF Sports wall, Cdn, Ont. Basketball halls of fame.

ROSEN, David (squash); b. 14 Mar 1970, Ottawa, Ont.; given name: David Jonathan; m. Kelli Lakis; Franklin & Marshall College; squash pro, sports equipment mfgr.; nicknamed "Duddy"; ranked top 5 in Cdn jr. hardball/softball squash '82-88; gold PAG, Maccabiah Youth Games '86; mem. F&M varsity squash team '88-92, team capt., MVP, all-American '91-92; ranked 12 US softball singles, 6 US men's doubles '93-94; ranked 5 US men's doubles '94-95, mixed doubles '96-97, 21 softball men's singles '95-96; mem. US Maccabiah Games squash team '97; coached Agnes Irwin School girls team to 3 undefeated championship seasons '92-95; coached 20 US nationally ranked jr. players; head squash pro Philadelphia Country Club, Gladwyne, Pa., '95-97; head squash pro/GM Denver Club '98-02; US ntl doubles finalist '98, '01, semifinalist '00, '03; ranked 21 Intl. Squash Doubles Assn. '03; founding investor, dir. sales Harrow Sports; res. Lafayette, Colo.

ROSEN, Goody (baseball); b. 28 Aug 1912, Toronto, Ont.; d. 6 Apr 1994, Toronto, Ont.; given name: Goodwin George; m. Mildred Rothberg; c. John Michael, Cecil Brendan; ret'd sales mgr.; outfielder; Toronto amateur baseball product; pro Louisville (AAA); Brooklyn Dodgers '37-39, '44-46, NY Giants '46; runnerup NL batting race '45 with .325 avg.; ML record: 551 games, 1916ab, 557h, 71d, 34t, 22hr, 197rbi, .291ba; mem. NL all-star team '45; 1st game with NY went 7 for 9 vs. Dodgers in doubleheader, winning RBI each game; ended career Toronto (IL); mem. Canada's Baseball Hall of Fame.

ROSENFELD, Bobbie (t&f); b. 28 Dec 1903, Russia, d. 14 Nov 1969, Toronto, Ont.; given name: Fanny; sportswriter; Canada's female athlete of half century '50 *CP* poll; silver 100m, gold 4x100 women's relay '28 Olympics, record 48.2; co-holder 11.00 100yd world record; '25 world 220yd record 26.00 disallowed when track found to be foot short; during '25 Ont. ladies' t&f championships scored 1st in shot put, discus, running bj, 200yd dash, 100yd low hurdles, 2nd 100yd dash, javelin (all in one afternoon); '24 Toronto grass courts tennis title; Cdn. female-athlete-of-yr award named for her; mem. Barrie, Cdn Amateur, Cdn Jewish, Canada's, Ont. Legends Sports halls of fame.

ROSS, Art (hockey); b. 13 Jan 1886, Naughton, Ont., d. 5 Aug 1964, Boston, Mass.; given name: Arthur Howie; developed nets, pucks still in use in NHL; def 14 years with Westmount (CAHL), Brandon (MHL), Kenora (MHL), Montreal Wanderers (ECAHA), Haileybury (NHA), Wanderers (NHA), Ottawa Senators (NHA); 85 goals in 167 games; best single season '12 with 16 goals in 18 games; mem. Kenora '07, Wanderers '08 Stanley Cup winners; ret'd '18 to referee; mgr. Hamilton Tigers, coach-mgr. Boston Bruins when they joined NHL '24; NHL coaching record: 758 scheduled games, 368-300-90, 65 playoff games, 27-33-5, 1 Stanley Cup; Lester Patrick award; Art Ross Trophy awarded to NHL scoring champion; mem. Hockey, Canada's Sports halls of fame.

ROSS, Betty (basketball); b. Apr 1915, Edmonton, Alta.; m. Ray Bellamy; c. Penny, Betty-Raye, Douglas; ret'd secretary; mem. legendary Edmonton Grads '37-39; mem. Canadian Basketball, Alta. Sports halls of fame; res. Summerland, B.C.

ROSS, Chucker (curling); b. 4 Dec 1934, Montreal, Que.; m. Sheila Peever Seltzer; c. Becki, Brenda, Larry, Karey, Julie; Institute of Chartered Accountants of Ont.; chartered accountant; skipped NO rink '74 Brier; skipped NO entry '82 ntl Seagram Mixed; skipped '81 Bowling Green, Ohio International mixed title winner; NO jr. men's golf champion '53; mem. NOSAA sr. basketball title team '53, national Sr. B title team '56; avid windsurfer; with wife Sheila has achieved official instructor status and has windsurfed as far south as Caribbean; res. Sudbury, Ont.

ROSS, Dave (trampoline/coaching/builder); b. 30 Apr 1950, Canberra, Australia; given name: David Alastair Ross; m. Kathryn Parkin; c. Laura; Queen's U., hons. BSc.; coach/trampoline mfgr.; traveled extensively as youth as father was Cdn diplomat; competitive gymnast who found trampolining more exciting; dedicate life to coaching trampoline; competed, self-taught at ntl., intl. levels; 4 Ont. sr. men's trampoline titles; first in the world to do a 10 triples routine in a bungee; inventor of world's only "Supertramp" (20'x13' bed), "Two-trick Spectacular", "Mixed Synchro", "Four-corner Bungee"; ntl team coach every worlds from '76; personal coach 22 Cdn. athletes who have competed at this level so far; from '80 only 24 non-European athletes have made finals (top 10) at worlds and 11 of these were Canadians, ranking Canada the top non-European country in world; coached 9 of the 11 finalists, including Canada's only medallists John Ross (bronze '82), Karen Cockburn (gold '03); coach '00 Olympic bronze medallists Karen Cockburn, Mathieu Turgeon; current ntl. team dir. trampoline; head coach/owner Skyriders Trampoline Place, the only custom-made trampoline facility in North America; top Ont. trampoline team from '76; intl. level judge from '86, NCCP ntl. master course conductor Levels 1-3; co-wrote NCCP trampoline manuals; has used his insight from physics to become a world leader in the trampoline manufacturing industry; founder and owner of Rebound Products (trampolines and related equipment; CGF lifetime mem. and long-time service award; OGF diamond pin for 25yrs service; PetroCan coaching excellence award; Gymnastics Canada's male coach of '00; Ontario male coach of '00; res. Thornhill, Ont.

ROSS, Earl (motorsport); b. 4 Sep 1941, Charlottetown, P.E.I.; given name: Earl Seymour; m. Yvonne; c. 3 daughters; auto mechanic, racing driver; raced stock cars as hobby Delaware, Nilestown tracks; '72 Export A grand championship; competed in 21 NASCAR races '74, 1st Canadian to win Grand National race, Old Dominion 500 at Martinsville, Va.; 2nd Michigan International Speedway Motor State 400, NASCAR Grand National rookie of '74; Canadian Motorsport's man of '74; res. Ailsa Craig, Ont.

ROSS, George (boxing); b. 22 Mar 1922, Sydney, N.S.; dockworker; ring career spanned '46-53, '57-58; 22 amateur, 52 pro bouts; pro record: 42 wins, 1 draw, 9 losses; ntl middleweight title '48-50; mem. NS Sports Hall of Fame; res. Halifax, N.S.

ROSS, Marie Claire (swimming); b. 21 Nov 1975, Kingston,

Ont.; UWO, Ryerson; B3 blind athlete; standout in all swimming disciplines; mem. London Aquatic Club; 1 silver, 1 bronze '92 Paralympics; 1 gold, 1 silver, 4 bronze IPC World championships '94; 3 gold, 3 silver IPC swim trials '95; 2 gold, 1 silver, 3 bronze Paralympics '96, competed '00 Paralympics; 3 gold, 3 silver World blind championships '98; world records 50-100-, 200m breaststroke; mem. Ryerson Sports Hall of Fame; res. London, Ont.

ROSS, P.D. (rowing); b. 1 Jan 1858, Montreal, Que., d. 5 Jul 1949, Ottawa, Ont.; given name: Philip Dansken; m. Mary Littlejohn; McGill; publisher; Que. single sculls title, twice stroked 4-oared crews to ntl championships; capt. McGill football team '76; standout hockey, lacrosse player; founder several golf clubs; hockey, lacrosse referee; Minto Cup, Stanley Cup trustee; mem. Hockey Hall of Fame.

ROSS-GIFFEN, Jill (t&f); b. 23 Feb 1958, London, Ont.; given name: Jillian Margaret Ross; div. Frank Giffen; UofT; heptathlon specialist; ntl jr. pentathlon title '76; gold pentathlon '77 Canada Games; mem. '78, '82 CG, '79, '83 PAG, '80, '83 FISU, '84 Olympic Games teams; pentathlon bronze '79 PAG; lj gold Tom Black Classic '79; CIAU lj titles '80-81; heptathlon bronze '82 CG; ntl heptathlon record 6110 points '82; ntl pentathlon, lj, heptathlon titles; 1st Cdn woman to win 8 events in 7-event heptathlon '83 winning 200m twice; res. Toronto, Ont.

ROTE, Tobin (football); b. 18 Jan 1928 San Antonio, Tex; d. 27 Jun 2000, Saginaw, Mich; m. Julie; Rice; salesman; all-Southwest Conf. '49; led Rice to '50 Cotton Bowl title; pro NFL Green Bay '50-56, Detroit '57-59, CFL Toronto '60-62, AFL San Diego '63-64, Denver '66; pro record: NFL completed 1082 of 2450 pass attempts for 15,144yds, 119tds, 158int; CFL 662 completions in 1187 attempts for 9872tds, 66tds, 58int; AFL 247 completions on 457 attempts for 3706yds, 30tds, 32int; asst. coach Rice; led Lions to '57 NFL title; considered one of football's most prolific passers; set numerous Argos passing records including 38 completions on 54 attempts single game; mem. Green Bay Packers, San Antonio Sports halls of fame.

ROTHWELL, Nigel (gymnastics); b. 29 Apr 1957, Romford, Essex, Eng.; given name: Nigel Mark; Michigan, BSc, MSc; coach, athlete; mem. ntl team from '75; mem. '75, '79 Pan-Am, '77, '81 FISU, '78 CG teams, numerous major international meets; team silver '79 PAG; gold floor exercises, silver horizontal bar, all around, bronze parallel bars, rings, vault '81 ntl championships; twice runnerup all-around Big-0 Conf.; res. Switzerland.

ROUGHTON, William (speed skating); b. 14 Jan 1883, London, Eng., d. 19 Nov 1963, Montreal, Que.; playing pres. Montreal Soccer Club; founder Montreal Hockey League; pres. Amateur Skating Assn. of Canada '31-58; starter '32 Winter Olympics; life mem. MAAA; mem. Canadian Speed Skating Hall of Fame.

ROUNTREE, Jim (football); b. 21 Apr 1936, Miami, Fla.; m. Nan; c. James Jr., Taren; Florida; construction industry, State Farm Insurance Agency; HS all-state, all-American; all-Southeastern Conf., Gators' MVP '57; hb Toronto '58-67; combined with Tobin Rote 10 Sep '61 for 108yd td pass-run play; all-time Argos interception record 41; all-Cdn

'62; 7 all-Eastern Conf. selections; asst. coach Argos '68-72, '77-78, Memphis Southmen (WFL) '74-75; nickname "Tree"; diagnosed with bladder cancer '03; mem. Florida Sports Hall of Fame; res. Tamarak, Fla.

ROUSSEAU, Bobby (hockey/golf); b. 26 Jul 1940, Montreal, Que.; given name: Joseph Jean-Paul Robert; golf pro; St. Jean jrs. at 15, jr., sr. Hull-Ottawa; mem. '60 Olympic silver medal team; pro Rochester (AHL), Hull-Ottawa (EPHL); rw Montreal '61-70; Calder Memorial Trophy; Minnesota '70-71, Rangers '71-75; one of first to use helmet; mem. 4 Stanley Cup winners; 2nd team all-star '66; twice scored 30 goals 1 season; NHL record: 942 scheduled games, 245 goals, 458 assists, 128 playoff games, 27 goals, 57 assists; 5 goals 1 game vs. Detroit '64; pitched no-hit game for St. Hyacinthe baseball jrs.; Joliette Country Club competitive golf course record 66; res. Sorel, Que.

ROWAN, Sheila (softball/curling); b. 22 Apr 1940, Young, Sask.; given name: Sheila Anne; stenographer; all-star Saskatoon Imperials '68 ntl women's softball championships, ntl titles '69-70; mem. ntl team '70 world tournament, Sask. team '69 Canada Summer Games; coach Saskatoon Baldwinettes 2 seasons, 1 ntl title; 3rd with Vera Pezer ntl women's title rink '71-73; defeated '72 ntl men's champion Orest Meleschuk in televised match; ntl sr. women's title rink '92; mem. Sask Sports, Canadian Curling halls of fame; res. Saskatoon, Sask.

ROWE, Earl (harness racing); b. 13 May 1894, Hull, Iowa, d. 10 Feb 1984, Toronto, Ont.; given name: William Earl; m. Treva Lennox; c. Bill, Jean, Lennox; UofOtt, DSS, UWO, LLD; horseman, business exec., politician; drove harness horses '13-'70; operated Rowelands Farm; 7 Standardbred Horse Society Trotting Futurity titles; '52 Maple Leaf Trotting Classic; with son Bill instrumental in founding Windsor, Barrie Raceways; MLA Ont. '23-25; federal MP '25-35, '37-62; cabinet minister Bennett govt.; Ont. PC leader '36; Ont. Lieut.-Gov. '63-68; pres. CSHS '27-28, '58-61; prominent as breeder/trainer; hon. dir. Ont. Harness Horsemen's Assoc.; mem. Canadian Horse Racing Hall of Fame.

ROWE, Paul (football); b. 25 Jan 1917, Victoria, B.C.; d. 26 Aug 1990, Calgary, Alta.; div.; c. Barry, Robert, Virginia; Oregon; ret'd; all-Canadian as mem. Victoria, BC English rugby teams; t&f with Victoria YMCA; football Oregon, Calgary Bronks '38-40; Canadian Army '44, Stampeders '45-50; named greatest plunging fb in Canadian Football '48; led Calgary to '48 Grey Cup; Western all-star 4 times; Dave Dryburgh scoring champion trophy '39, '48; ret'd due to injuries and served as coach, advisor in minor football; mem. Alta., BC, Greater Victoria Sports, Cdn Football, Canada's Sports halls of fame.

ROWELL, Fred (builder); b. 20 May 1916, Toronto, Ont.; d. 14 Sep 1996, Agassiz, B.C.; given name: Frederick Newton Alexander; active t&f athlete from youth to masters level; founded Vancouver Olympic Club; initiated Vancouver relays '49; asst. track coach UBC '48-53; ED/head coach VOC '49-57, pres. '57-63, dir. to '65, hon. dir '65-96; established selection standards for CTFA teams; dir, COA '46-50, '53-56; mgr t&f team '48 Olympics; AAUofC exec. '47-56, pres. BC branch '55-57; mem. Vancouver

mayor's special BEG comm. '50-51; comm. chair. '54 BEG; established Canada's 1st accredited coaching school at UBC '53; CdM '55 PAG; editor *T&F Digest* and *Around the Track*; dir. BC Amateur Sports Council '64-96; mem. BC Sports Hall of Fame.

ROWLAND, Gordie (football); b. 1 Sep 1930, Montreal, Que.; m. Joan Lloyd; c. Jill, Janet, Gary; ret'd Glidden Paint mgr; football Montreal Orfuns intermediates, soccer Stelco srs., ntl champions '54; Blue Bombers '54-63; 5 Grey Cup finals, 4 winners; 5 times WFC all-star db; leading Canadian WFC '58, Schenley runnerup; returned career total 324 punts for 2395yds, 7.8 avg.; returned 215 kickoffs for 9546yds; intercepted 31 passes, 4 for tds; 4yrs UMan. asst. coach, Vanier Cup '70; coached minor football several yrs; mem. Man. Sports Hall of Fame; res. Winnipeg, Man.

ROXBURGH, Doug (golf); b. 28 Dec 1951, Santo Domingo, Dominion Republic; given name: Douglas Ian; m. Lorna McPherson; c. James, Geordie; Oregon, SFU, BComm; ret'd accountant; dir. RCGA player development from '99; golf range operator; BC junior title '69-70; ntl junior '70; 3 Vancouver city jr. titles; 13 BC amateur, 4 runnerup, 5 Vancouver City sr. titles; 4 ntl amateur titles, twice runnerup; semifinalist British Amateur '79; mem. 19 BC Willingdon Cup, 4 BC jr. teams; 7 Eisenhower World team matches, 2 Commonwealth Trophy matches, '77 Nations Cup Paris, '81 Simon Bolivar Cup Maracaibo; mem. SFU, RCGA, BC Golf, BC Sports halls of fame; res. Vancouver, B.C.

ROY, Aldo (weightlifting); b. 22 Mar 1942, Sudbury, Ont.; given name: Aldo Robert Joseph; Laurentian, BA, UofOtt, MA; HS history dept. head; at 17 ntl sr. titlist, 3 ntl sr., open records; mem. '62 CG, '63, '67 PAG, '65 world championships, '68 Olympics teams; coach from '72; asst. and/or head coach '78 jr. world team, '79 PAG, America's team '80 Pan-Am championships, '80 Olympics, '81 Commonwealth championships; TV colorcaster Olympics, CG, PAG; res. Ottawa, Ont.

ROY, Andy (sailing); b. 3 Jan 1958, Halifax, N.S.; given name: Andrew Martin; m. Danielle Schell; c. Kenneth, Grant; Carleton B.Comm; pres. Odim Spectrum Ltd.; ntl Laser champion '81; Australian ntl Laser title '82; US ntl Laser title '83; silver Laser '82 worlds, '83 Pan-Am Games; crewman Canada II '86 America's Cup competition; helmsman Mumm 30 class '02 NA world championships gold, '02 worlds bronze; fed. govt. excellence award '82; res. Peterborough, Ont.

ROY, Diane (t&f); b. 1 Jan 1971, Lac-des-Aigles, Que.; exec. asst.; 800m, marathon specialist; mem. Que. Wheelchair Athletics from '93; ntl team from '94; gold, silver for Que at Canada Games; frequent marathon competitor placing among top 5 in Boston, Japan marathons; set ntl marathon, 5000m records; ntl 5000m title '00; competed 3 Paralympics; 2 bronze '04 Paralympics; competed Swiss, Swedish, world championships; 2 gold, 3 silver, 2 bronze Toronto Challenge; 3 gold, 1 silver Can-Am '03; res. Hatley, Que.

ROY, Kevin (weightlifting); b. 21 Apr 1963, Sudbury, Ont.; Laurentian; jr. America Cup 90kg title '79; 3 ntl

100kg, 1 Ont. 100kg titles; 9 ntl, Commonwealth jr., 3 ntl, Commonwealth sr. records; bronze 100kg '82 CG, 3 silver 110kg '83 PAG; mem. '84 Olympic team; 2yr drug infraction ban '90; res. Coniston, Ont.

ROY, Patrick (hockey); b. 5 Oct 1965, Quebec City, Que.; m. Michele; c. Jonathan, Frederick. Jana; ret'd hockey player, spa owner; goalie Granby Bisons; 4th round pick Montreal '84 draft; Sherbrooke (AHL), Granby '84-85, Montreal '85-95, Colorado '95-03; 3 Conn Smythe trophies; 5 William Jennings awards; NHL all-rookie team; 3 Vezina trophies; *Hockey News* playoff MVP award '93; 2 Trico goaltending awards; 3 1st, 2 2nd team all-star; played 10 NHL all-star games; mem. 4 Stanley Cup winners, '98 Olympic team; with 17 Oct '00 win became winningest goalie in NHL history with 448 victories; 1st goalie to post 200 victories each with two different teams; 1st goalie to play 1000 NHL scheduled games; 1st to log more than 60,000 minutes in nets; NHL record: 1029 scheduled games, 551-315-131, 60,227min, 66sho, 247 playoff games, 15,206min, 584ga, 23sho, 151-94; Avalanche ret'd jersey 33; part-owner/GM QMJHL Quebec Remparts; active in children's charities; avid card collector; res. Ste-Foy, Que.

ROY, Simon (racquetball); b. 4 Mar 1969, Quebec City, Que.; Southwest Missouri State; marketing; ntl juv, jr. titles; singles silver tournament of Americas '94; men's doubles gold '96, silver '92 world championships; 5 ntl men's doubles titles; 5 ntl singles silver; res. Ste-Foy, Que.

RUBENSTEIN, Louis (figure skating); b. 23 Sep 1861, Montreal, Que.; d. 3 Jan 1931, Montreal, Que.; partner, silverplaters and manufacturers; learned skating at Jackson Haines school; Montreal skating title at 17; ntl title '82-89; US titles '88-89, 1891; world title '90; key role in founding Canadian Amateur Skating Assn. '78; pres. International Skating Union of America '07-09; monument to his memory Montreal '39; 18yrs pres. Cdn Wheelman's Assn.; ranked by some as father of bowling in Canada; mem. US Figure Skating, Cdn Amateur, Cdn Speed Skating, Canada's, Montreal YM-YWHA Sports halls of fame.

RUBES, Jan (tennis); b. 6 Jun 1920, St. Volyne, Czechoslovakia; m. Susan Douglas Burstein; c. Jonathan, Anthony; Prague Academy of Music; actor/singer; claimed several Czech junior club tennis titles, Czech jr. x-country ski champion; immigrated to Canada '48; claimed several Ont. seniors age-group singles/doubles titles; ntl seniors singles title '82; has represented Canada in Crawford Cup play in Australia, France; mem. Cdn team Venice, Fla., tennis league; 3 Ont. athletic excellence awards; opera singer, long association Cdn Opera Co.; active TV/movie actor, director; res. Collingwood, Ont.

RUBY, Martin (football); b. 1922 Waco, Tex; m. Delmar; c. Marsha. Deanna; Texas A&M; competed 3 Bowl Games; SW Intercollegiate Conf. MVP '41; following WW2 service played several seasons with Brooklyn Dodgers, NY Yankees (football); two-way tackle Roughriders '51-57; 4 all-West ot, 3 all-West dt awards; 3 times two-way all-star; mem. Cdn Football Hall of Fame; res. Salmon Arm, B.C.

RUCCHIN, Steve (hockey); b. 4 Jul 1971, Thunder Bay, Ont.; UWO; 2-way cntr, faceoff specialist; 3 OUAA all-star,

player of '94, all-Cdn '94; NHL Anaheim '94-04; NHL record (through '04) 616 scheduled games, 153g, 279a, 33 playoffs, 8g, 8a; capt. Mighty Ducks '03-04; res. Orange County, Calif.

RUCKSTUHL, Sandy (administration/football); b. 29 Feb 1944, Trenton, Ont.; given name: Rexford Alexander; m. Linda Robinson; c. Steve (d), Caine; ret'd Foreign Affairs; played major role in Ottawa, Eastern Ont., minor football programs more than 25yrs; pres. Myers Riders 25yrs; v-p NCAFA 15yrs; pres. Wilson Bowl '92; pres. -17 Eastern Ont. team; res. Ottawa, Ont.

RUEGGER, Silvia (t&f); b. 23 Feb 1961, Ottawa, Ont.; UGuelph BA; Tech. Clothing div. Brooks; mem. Etobicoke Huskies-Striders; National Capital Marathon (1st ever marathon) course record 2:30.37 '84; mem. '84 Olympic team; won '85 Houston (CR 2:28.36), '87 Pittsburgh marathons; 2 CIAU XC titles; 1 CIAU X-C all-Cdn; 2 UGuelph female-athlete-of-yr awards; seriously injured '85 car accident; mem. Guelph Sports Hall of Fame; res. Guelph, Ont.

RUEL, Claude (hockey/coaching); b. 12 Sep 1938, Sherbrooke, Que.; given name: Claude Robert; ret'd hockey exec.; loss of sight in left eye when struck with a stick playing jr. hockey ended his playing career; began working in Montreal organization at 15; coached Jr. Canadiens 5yrs; chief scout Montreal 2yrs; dir. player development '66-68, '81-98; became youngest NHL coach '68; guided Canadiens to Stanley Cup in initial season; replaced as coach '71 by Al MacNeil; asst coach '73, '76-79 Stanley Cup winners; replaced Bernie Geoffrion as head coach '80-81; NHL coaching record: 305 scheduled games, 172-82-51; 27 playoff games, 18-9, 2 Stanley Cups; res. Montreal, Que.

RUFF, Lindy (hockey/coaching); b. 17 Feb 1060, Warburg, Alta.; m. Gaye; c. Brett, Eryn, Brian, Madeleine; coach; def/lw Taber, Lethbridge jrs '76-79; NHL Buffalo '79-89 (capt. From '86), NYR '89-91, AHL Rochester '91-92, IHL (player/asst. coach) San Diego '92-93; NHL record: 691 scheduled games, 105g, 195a, 52 playoff games, 11g, 13a; asst. Florida '93-96; coach Buffalo '97-04; res. Clarence, N.Y.

RUITER, Garth (curling/baseball/basketball); b. 26 Jun 1920, St. Jerome, Que.; given name: Garth George Ward; m. Dorothy Jean Stephen; c. Allan Van, Stephen; UofT; manufacturers' agent; jr. baseball Guelph '35-36; Toronto Viaduct, Beach Leagues '37-39; Navy '43; mem. Snowdon softball league Montreal '56-57; coached Dorval to ntl Little League finals '67; mem. Interscholastic baseball title team Guelph '36-37; West End Y Toronto Sr. League '38-39; mem. Service League titlist Victoria Navy team '41-42; mem. Maritime champion New Waterford Strands Cape Breton, N.S., '43; mem. Halifax Stadacona service, prov. titlist '44-45; mem. East York Grads Ont. Sr. League '46-48; YMHA Toronto Sr. League '49-51; player-coach Orillia Int. Ont. champions '53; mem. Montreal YMHA Que. sr. champions '56; began curling Orillia '53; 2nd Que. rink '62 Brier; skipped City of Ottawa grand aggregate winner '65; skipped Que. rinks to 1 Gov.-Gen.'s Trophy, 4 Royal Canadian Legion ntl finals, title '66; 4 Que. srs titles; 3rd Jim Wilson's Que. ntl srs champions '81; life mem./p-pres.

Lachine CC; club championship trophy bears his name; res. Dorval, Que.

RUMBOLD, Dave (shooting); b. 30 Dec 1934, Guilford, Surrey, Eng.; given name: David William; m. Audrey Florence Solly; c. Yvonne Susan, Joanne Elisabeth, Ian David; aeronautical engineer, ret'd major Cdn Forces; mem. 12 Ont. target rifle teams from '62, capt. '78; Ont. champion '79; mem. 4 RCAF, 12 ntl Bisley teams, adjutant '74, v.-capt. '83, commandant '86; mem. 4 Cdn Palma teams, adjutant '72, coach '85; competed twice US nationals, '80 world championships; 30 individual medals at prov., ntl, international levels; shooter, capt. or coach ntl teams which won 1 Palma, 1 Empire, 3 Kolapore, 5 Overseas, 3 Commonwealth, 6 Canada matches; coached team to WR short-range 1182x1200 vs. Britain '84; mem. council, exec. comm. ORA from '74, DCRA from '69; dir. DCRA support operations '76-78, chair. several committees; organized DCRA ntl matches '76-82; editor *Canadian Marksman* '75-76; DCRA life governor; res. Ottawa, Ont.

RUNGE, Paul (baseball/officiating); b. 20 Oct 1941, St. Catharines, Ont.; given name: Paul Edward; m. Anastasia Mouzas; c. Brian, Renee; Arizona State; umpire, real estate broker; minor ball Houston, California chains; umpired California, Eastern, Pacific Coast Leagues; 1st ML game '73; mem. NL umpiring staff '74-97; father Ed, son Brian also ML umpires; worked 3 all-star, 3 championship series, '79 World Series games; res. El Cajon, Calif.

RUOFF, Bernie (football); b. 12 Oct 1951, Hiedenheim-Wurtemberg, W. Germany; given name: Bernd; m. Colette; Syracuse, BA; sr. yr. MVP; raised in Kitchener; kicking specialist; pro NE Patriots; CFL Winnipeg '75-79, Hamilton '80-87; 4 EFC, 2 WFC scoring titles; 4 div. punting titles; 4 times EFC all-star; 1 Grey Cup winner; kicked 58yd FG '75; Ticats career FG, single season points, all-time scoring records; dog breeder; last known res. Fisherville, Ont.

RUPERTUS, Glenn (biathlon); b. 26 Jul 1964, Wetaskwin, Alta.; given name: Glenn Richard; m. Dorothy Joan Denroche; c. Stephanie Kathryn May; Augustana BA; Cdn Forces, coach Biathlon B.C.; nicknamed "Rockit"; began as x-country skier '77; competitive skier, runner to '80; 17yrs ntl biathlon team; competed '88, '92, '94 Winter Olympics; 6 world championships; 4 world military championships; competed World Cup circuit from '86; 2 NA 10km, 1 20km, 1 relay titles; 6 ntl 20km gold, 2 silver, 2 bronze, 2 10km gold, 2 silver, 3 bronze, 6 ntl relay gold; won 20km, 10km gold '96 Australian championships; Level IV coaching certificate; 4 Biathlon Canada athlete of yr, 9 Alta. Achievement awards, '94 award of excellence; Rudy Setz Memorial award '98; res. Courtenay, B.C.

RUSEDSKI, Greg (tennis); b. 6 Sep 1973, Montreal, Que.; m. Lucy Connor; lefthander; turned pro '91; won 1st major tournament at Newport, R.I., '93; ranked 1 in Canada '93; mem. Cdn Davis Cup team; TC player of '93, most-improved-player award '93; opted to compete for England '95; reached final '97 US Open before bowing to Patrick Rafter; ranked 10 ATP rankings '97; defeated #1 Pete Sampras to win '98 French Open; European Community title '98; *BBC* British sports personality of '97; record

149mph serve speed; cleared Mar '04 of Jul '03 charge he used banned performance-enhancing drug; named British Davis Cup team '04; res. London, Eng.

RUSNOV, Rob (archery); b. 12 Sep 1973, Toronto, Ont.; York, Ryerson; electrical engineer; enjoyed moderate success in hockey, competitive swimming, sailing; archery became focal point of athletic life at 14; won ntl jr. title, 2 ntl sr. crowns; PAG gold '95, silver '99; competed '96, '00 Olympics, '97, '99 worlds; coached by Joan McDonald; res. Richmond Hill, Ont.

RUSSEL, Blair (hockey); b. 17 Sep 1880, Montreal, Que., d. 7 Dec 1961, Montreal, Que.; all-star Montreal Victorias 1889-08; scoring 110 goals in 67 games; once 7 goals in single game, also 6 and 5 goal games; mem. Hockey Hall of Fame.

RUSSEL, Jeff (football); b. 27 Oct 1900, Ouray, Colo.; d. 3 May 1926, Montreal, Que.; given name: Jeffrey Cameron; Lower Canada Coll., RMC, McGill; power co. lineman; starred as hb RMC '17-20, McGill '20-22, Montreal Winged Wheelers '22-25; killed while repairing power lines during a storm; trophy in his honor awarded annually to EFC outstanding player; mem. Cdn Football Hall of Fame.

RUSSELL, Ernest (hockey); b. 21 Oct 1883, Montreal, Que., d. 23 Feb 1963, Montreal, Que.; capt. Sterling hockey jrs., MAAA football jrs. ntl titles same year; sr. hockey Winged Wheelers '05; Montreal Wanderers '06-14; 180 goals in 98 games, 3-goal hat-tricks 5 successive games, 42 goals in 9 games '07; mem. 4 Stanley Cup winners; 2 league scoring titles, once scored in 10 consecutive games; mem. Hockey Hall of Fame.

RUSSELL, Ernestine (gymnastics); b. 10 Jun 1938, Windsor, Ont.; div. John Carter; c. Kelly; div. Jim Weaver; Michigan State, BSc; coach Utah State; ntl women's gymnastic champion '55-60; 4 times NA champion; mem. '56, '60 Olympic teams; 5 golds '58 PAG; competed '59 world championships; Velma Springstead Trophy '55-57; authored several gymnastics books; coach US women's gym team '77 FISU, '80 Olympics; mem. Cdn Amateur, Windsor-Essex County Sports halls of fame; res. Garden City, Utah.

RUSSELL, Jamie (basketball); b. 23 Apr 1952, Niagara Falls, Ont.; given name: James Craig; Colgate, Waterloo, McMaster MD; physician; mem. '71 HS champs; MVP Klondike, Naismith Classics '75; OUAA Lebel plaque, all-star, CIAU all-Cdn, Mike Moser CIAU MVP trophy, UW Hagey-Siegfried team MVP award '76; 9yrs ntl team; 2 FISU, '76 Olympic Games; competed '74, '78 worlds; mem. Cdn Basketball Hall of Fame; res. Burlington, Ont

RUSSO, Erminia (volleyball); b. 24 Jul 1964, Kelowna, B.C.; coach; at 5-8 considered small for sport but compensated with strength, hard work; competed for Canada '90 Goodwill, 2 worlds, 3 World Cups, 2 PAG, 2 FISU, '96 Olympics (co-capt.); also competed in beach volleyball; retd from competition to coach UBC women's varsity team '97, Canada West title; CIS coach-of-yr. award; honored by BC Women in Sport Leaders & Legends; *TSN* commentator '02 CIS championships; res. Montreal, Que.

RUTHERFORD, Jim (hockey/administration); b. 17 Feb 1949, Beeton, Ont.; div.; c. Andrea; hockey exec.; goal Hamilton jrs; pro Fort Worth (CHL) '69-71, Hershey '71-72; NHL Detroit '70-71, '74-81, '82-83, Pittsburgh '71-74, Toronto '81, Los Angeles '81-82; NHL record: 457 scheduled games, 151-227-59; 25,895min, 1576ga, 14so, 8 playoff games, 2-5; 440min, 28ga; 5yrs Detroit player rep. mem. Team Canada '77, '79 worlds; on retirement from play joined Compuware serving as dir. hockey operations; key role in Compuware purchase Windsor Spitfires '84; GM Spitfires '84-89; reached Memorial Cup finals '88; led Compuware efforts to bring Detroit 1st OHL franchise '89; pres./GM Hartford '94; 1st GM Carolina; OHL exec. of '87-88; CHL exec. of '87; helped build Carolina Hurricanes which played in '02 Stanley Cup finals; *HN* exec of '02; res. Raleigh, N.C.

RUTTAN, Jack (hockey); b. 5 Apr 1889, Winnipeg, Man., d. 7 Jan 1973, Winnipeg, Man.; Winnipeg juv title '05-06; St. John's College '07-08 Man. University HL title; Man. Varsity '09-10 Winnipeg Sr. HL title; Winnipeg Hockey Club '12-13, won league title, Allan Cup; coach Winnipeg srs. '19-20, UMan '23; officiated Winnipeg Senior League '20-22; mem. Cdn, Man. Hockey halls of fame.

RUYS, Henk (soccer); b. 27 Jan 1934, Veghel, Holland; m. Riek; c. Ingrid, Robert, Steve, Christene; fire fighter; Dutch 3rd div. before emigrating to Canada '57; mem. several Saskatoon, prov. all-star teams; several scoring titles; coached Saskatoon Hollandia '58; Hollandia rep. Saskatchewan Soccer Assn.; club secty. '59; mem. Saskatoon SA council '59; various administrative roles from local through ntl levels; founding pres. Saskatoon Minor SA '66-74; active referee and referees administrator; Queen's anniversary medal '77; Saskatchewan sport recognition award; Saskatoon and Dist. SA appreciation award; Cdn Youth Soccer Assn. outstanding achievement award; Saskatoon soccer centre bears his name; mem. Sask., Saskatoon Sports halls of fame; res. Coquitlam, B.C.

RYAN, Doc (basketball); b. 30 Jun 1950, Orangestad, Dutch Antilles; given name: Peter; Florida A&M; Quebec (Trois-Rivieres), St. Francis Xavier, Dalhousie; women's basketball coach; mem. CYO titlist '58-59, gold medal team '70 Canada Winter Games; Rutger League all-star '72; mem. Knoxville Coll. SIAC champions '72-73; Florida A&M '75-76; CIAU leading scorer UQTR '76-77; all-Cdn, all-conf. '76-77, AUAA all-conf. '77-79; mem. Olympic teams '76, '80; coach Dalhousie, St. FX; mem. ntl sr. champions '80-81, ntl tournament MVP; '79-80 "Do it with the Doc" international 3 on 3 champion; outstanding NS adult male athlete '81; res. Antigonish, N.S.

RYAN, Doreen (all-around); b. 27 Sep 1931, Edmonton, Alta.; given name: Doreen Delores McLeod; div; c. Ken, Debby, Dave; UAlta, BEd; PE consultant; 39 major speed skating titles include 17 Alta. (indoor, outdoor), 7 Sask., 2 Man. and 10 ntl championships; tied for NA title '52, runnerup '62; ntl jr. '47, intermediate '49, sr. '51, '53-54, '57-59, '62-63; mem. '60, '64 Olympic, '64 Worlds teams; won '59 Olympic time trials, '64 Swiss International time trials; jr. lj/hj/60m Edmonton Highland Games; scholastic 60m, 100m, 60m hurdles, hj; ntl discus, 60m hurdles, 100m, softball throw '47; Myrtle Cook Trophy for highest

aggregate points; sr. 100m,/lj '48 Highland Games, discus, 60m, 100m scholastic meet; sr. 220yds, discus '49 Highland Games; mem. Edmonton HS, prov. title basketball teams; city softball teams; HS badminton singles titles; swam backstroke competitively 1 year; mgr. ntl t&f team '74 CG, '76, '80 Olympic, '79 PAG; administrative duties '78, '82 CG, Alta. Sportswoman of '64; 1st women inducted into Edmonton Sports Hall of Fame; mem. Cdn Speed Skating, Alta. Sports halls of fame; res. Edmonton, Alta.

RYAN, Joe (football); b. 1900, Starbuck, Man., d. 2 Jun 1979, Victoria, B.C.; given name: Joseph Bernard; m. Helen Katherine Killeen; c. Mary Jo, Kathleen, James Timothy, Cynthia Ann; securities officer, football administrator; promoted rugby football Winnipeg '31-35, amalgamated Winnipeg Rugby, St. John's Club '32; imported Carl Cronin from Notre Dame as player-coach and won '33 title, Grey Cup (first for West) '35; developed intercity league '36-40; managed Winnipeg club 7 of first 11 years of operation winning 6 league titles, 3 Grey Cups; 14yrs mem. CRU rules comm.; with Lew Hayman, Eric Cradock, Leo Dandurand helped establish Montreal Alouettes; scouted talent like Frank Filchock, Joey Pal, Pete Thodos, Rod Pantages to help Als win '49 Grey Cup; GM Edmonton 5 years; launched night football Winnipeg; hon. life mem. Winnipeg Football Club, Winnipeg FC Alumni Assoc.; CRU plaque for service to football in Canada; mem. Canadian Football, Canada's Sports halls of fame.

RYAN, Pat (curling); b. 28 Sep 1955, Winnipeg, Man.; given name: Pat John Charles; m. Penny; c. Lynsay; management accountant; Man. jr. men's title '73; 2nd for Paul Devlin '79 Brier; all-star skip, lost title in extra end playoff to Al Hackner '85 Brier; finalist '86 ntl mixed; skip '88-89 Brier winners, 3rd for Rick Folk '93-94 Brier, '94 winner; skip '89, 3rd '94 world title rinks; Dick Ellis team award '89; won WCT Yukon Classic '03; mem. Cdn Curling Hall of Fame; res. Kelowna, B.C.

RYAN, Peter (motorsport/skiing); b. 10 Jun 1940, Philadelphia, Pa., d. 2 Jul 1962, Paris, France; as teenager won major Que. ski titles Taschereau, Ryan Cup, Que. Kandahar; 2nd to Buddy Werner US Nationals; mem. ntl water-ski team, among top 5 2 years; won auto racing Vanderbilt Cup, Canadian Grand Prix; injured while competing for Lotus factory team at Reims, France, and died in hospital; mem. Cdn Motorsport Hall of Fame.

RYAN, Tommy (bowling/builder); b. 1882, Guelph, Ont., d. 19 Nov 1961, Toronto, Ont.; m. Ruth Robins; auctioneer, art gallery owner; credited with inventing 5-pin bowling; opened Toronto's 1st bowling house '05; founded Miss Toronto beauty contest; mem. Ont. 5-pin Bowling, Canada's Sports halls of fame.

RYAN, Vinnie (boxing); b. 1 Jul 1939, Dublin, Ireland; m. Valerie; c. Sean, Jackie; master plumber, mechanical contractor; Irish jr./intermediate boxing titles; schoolboy champion for GB; Irish sr. welterweight champion; dir. coaching, pres. Boxing Ontario; exec mem. Cdn Amateur Boxing Assn.; res. Ancaster, Ont.

RYDER, Gus (swimming); b. 11 Jan 1899, Toronto, Ont.; d. 23 May 1991, Toronto, Ont.; given name: Augustus Joseph;

m. Phyllis Hamilton; customs broker; jr. hockey Auralee; football Excelsiors, Argos intermediates; rowed 4yrs Argos; represented Canada 4 times internationally in handball; swam in several across-the-bay races Toronto; formed 700-mem. New Toronto (later Lakeshore) swim club; taught thousands of crippled children to swim; personally credited with 47 rescues from drowning; coached Marilyn Bell, Cliff Lumsdon; Canada's man of year twice; US Presidental sports award '75; hon. chief Six-Nations Indian tribe; handball award 70-80 age-group sr. Olympics '76; Argo Rowing Club medal; wide array of honors from service clubs for work on behalf of crippled children; Toronto, Victoria awards of merit; Ont. government medal; mem. Order of Canada; mem. Etobicoke, Mississauga, Toronto Playground, US, Ont. Aquatic, Canada's Sports halls of fame.

RYDING, Graham (squash); b. 16 Jun 1975, Winnipeg, Man.; given name: Graham Mark; Uof T, BA; squash professional; 7 ntl jr. titles; ntl team mem. from '95; men's team capt. '99, '01; competed on the PSA World Tour from '95; silver '97 world team championships; 4 ntl titles; '99 PAG double gold, silver '03; '02 CG quarter finalist; PSA dir. '03; res. Toronto, Ont.

RYPIEN, Mark (football); b. 2 Oct 1962, Calgary, Alta.; div. Annette; c. Andrew (d), Ambre, Angela; Washington State; Holiday Inn Express hotels partner; qb; NFL Washington '87-93, Cleveland '94, St. Louis '95, '97, Philadelphia '96, Atlanta '98, Indianapolis '01; NFL record 100g completed 1461 of 2604 attempts for 18,473yds, 115tds, 88int; 1 Super Bowl victory; Super Bowl XXV MVP; played 2 Pro Bowls; HS coach; played sr. men's hockey '02-03; brothers Tim, Dave played for ntl men's baseball team; res. Spokane, Wash.

SABOURIN, Jamie (karate/kickboxing); b. 30 Sep 1967, Toronto, Ont.; given name: Jamie Michael; m. Joanne Leclerc; c. Nickolas, Brittany; Algonquin Coll investigator/ martial arts instructor; became involved age 12; winner of more than 150 tournament titles; competing in 64kg class; 10 ntl kick-boxing titles; WKA world sparring, European FS Forms gold, FS Weapons silver '93; WKA world sparring, FS Weapons gold '95; WKC world FS Forms gold '96; mem. Team Canada '98; 4 Gloucester outstanding achievement awards; res. Nepean, Ont.

SAFTIC, Michael (harness racing); b. 3 Dec 1961, Sudbury, Ont.; from a groom at Sudbury Downs, became 2nd trainer and eventually fill-in driver with Garth Gordon Stables in Toronto; top horse Ellamony won USTA/ USHWA mare pacer of '95 award; other top horses include Rair Earth, Please Me Please, D.M. Dilinger, Sir Luck, Groovie Day; through '03 3287 wins with purses topping $47M; 37 major stakes titles including 1 Breeders Crown; res. Campbellville, Ont.

SAKIC, Joe (hockey); b. 7 Jul 1969, Burnaby, B.C.; given name: Joseph Steve; m. Debbie; c. Mitchell, Chase, Kamryn; part-owner restaurant; ctr Swift Current (WHL) '86-88; drafted by Quebec '87; pro Quebec '88-95, Colorado '95-03; WHL rookie '87, twice player of year; Cdn major jr. player of '88; NHL record: (through '04) 1155 scheduled games, 542g, 860a, 153 playoff games, 78g, 91a; scored 51g '96; passed 500g'03; 11 NHL all-star games; team capt. from '92; mem. Team Canada '88 world jr., '90, '93, '94 worlds, '96, '04 World Cup, '98, '02 (gold) Olympic teams; Conn Smythe Trophy '96; Hart, Lady Byng, Lester Patrick Trophies '01; *SI* player of '01; '96, '01 Stanley Cup champs; active in Food Bank charities; Farjestad during '04-05 labor dispute; mem. Burnaby Sports Hall of Fame; res. Aurora, Co.

SALE, Jamie (figure skating); b. 21 Apr 1977, Red Deer, Alta.; pro skater Stars on Ice; as singles skater won ntl novice, jr. bronze; competed in 1st sr. ntls '95; '92 Cdn. jr. champion, teamed with Jason Turner competed '94 Olympics; after again trying solo teamed with David Pelletier '98; as team undefeated Nov. '00 through '02 Olympics; they claimed 3 Skate America, 3 Cdn, 2 ISU 4 Continents, Sears Open titles; won world pairs '01; became household names when their *Love Story* gold-medal performance placed them second behind Russian skaters Elena Berezhnaya and Anton Sikharulidze in Salt Lake City Olympics pairs final; after ensuing worldwide uproar and exposé of corrupt judging unprecedented second set of gold medals was awarded; media frenzy continued long after Olympic flame was extinguished; the pair has graced covers of *Newsweek, Time* magazines, made countless TV talk show appearances; Lou Marsh, team of yr. trophies; Queen's Golden Jubilee Award; hon. mem. Edmonton Rotary Club; Paul Harris Fellow Rotary International award; featured in Jan. '04 *FHM* magazine; res. Edmonton, Alta.

SALLY, Kevin (archery); b. 12 May 1972, Richmond Hill, Ont.; Ryerson BSc; electrical engineer; mem. ntl team '92-98; ntl outdoor title '95; gold '93 Canada Summer Games; competed '95 PAG, World championships, '96 Olympics, Championship of Americas; res. Pickering, Ont.

SALMING, Borje (hockey); b. 17 Apr 1951, Kiruna, Sweden; given name: Anders Borje; m. Margitta; c. Anders; underwear mfgr.; Swedish ntl jr. team, champion Brynas club Swedish Division 1, Swedish ntl team; all-star '73 world amateur championships; pro Toronto '73-89, Detroit '89-90; ended playing days in Sweden '90-94; NHL record: 1148 scheduled games, 150g, 637a, 81 playoff games, 12g, 37a; 1 1st, 5 2nd all-star teams; with club-mate Inge Hammarstrom became first of European stars to attain NHL stardom; rated one of game's finest defensive defencemen; mem. Hockey Hall of Fame; res. Stockholm, Sweden.

SALTER, Allen (weightlifting); b. 11 Oct 1936, Almonte, Ont.; m. Waveney Morphy; CGA; fed. govt. auditor; ntl bantamweight (123lb) champion '60-63; 280 lb clean and jerk record for that class which stood '63-76; ntl featherweight (132lb) champion '64-66; lightweight champion (148lb) '68; silver bantamweight '62, bronze featherweight '66 CG; mem. 2 World, 1 Olympic Games teams; City of Ottawa crest, Ottawa ACT outstanding amateur athlete award '62; res. Carp, Ont.

SAMIS, John (badminton); b. 15 Nov 1918, Swift Current, Sask.; given name: John Clinton; m. Grace Peggy; c. Page, Julie; ret'd investment dealer; 7 Vancouver City, provincial titles; 3 ntl singles titles; ranked 4th in world '41; mem. Canada's 1st international Thomas Cup team; at 15 youngest ntl sr. singles titlist; while serving in Cdn navy competed in British War Relief exhibition matches; mem. BC Sports Hall of Fame; res. W. Vancouver, B.C.

SAMPLE, Bonnie (canoeing); b. 9 Apr 1948, Port Credit, Ont.; given name: Bonnie Jane Buchanan; m. Tim Sample; c. Kirsten, Tomas, Lindsay; McMaster, BA, BPhE, Oregon, MSc; real estate agent; competitive paddler '62-75; coach Mississauga Canoe Club '70-75, Rideau Canoe Club '75-77; ntl canoeing jr. development/sr. team coach '77-83; ntl canoe team program mgr. '84-87; coached Canadian teams '75 NA, '77, '79, '81 jr. worlds, 3 Continental Cups; coached Ont. team Canada Games; *CBC-Radio* analyst '84 Olympics; Rideau Canoe Club executive-of-yr award; co-chair fencing Ontario winter games; taught program for disabled UofOtt; author *It's Got to be Fun*; res. Barrie, Ont.

SAMPLE, Tim (builder); b. 6 Jul 1947, Barrie, Ont.; m. Bonnie Buchanan; c. Kirsten, Tomas, Lindsay; sports marketing; coached basketball, hockey, soccer to intermediate level '68-97; founder, exec. St. Lambert hockey school; mem. Cdn paddling comm. '78-80; vice-commodore Rideau Canoe Club '78-81; chair. '81 canoe ntls; co-ordinator '93 Ottawa Twining Games; mem. mayor's council '86 Ottawa CG bid; ntl canoe team mgr,

4 world, 2 Olympic Games, 3 Continental Cup, 2 Canada/America Cups, varied international regattas; founder/chair Canada Day international regatta '85-89; fencing chair. '91 Ont. Winter Games; event/volunteer operations chair. '93 world indoor championships; chair. volunteer operations Hockey Canada Cdn Olympic team Ont. tour '93-94; chair. volunteer operations '94 world basketball championships; dir. volunteer operations '97 Special Olympics world winter games; dir. operations review '01 Peterborough Canada Games feasibility study; dir. Barrie Sports Hall of Fame; event mgr. '96 Fr. Bauer Cup hockey tournament; res. Barrie, Ont.

SAMPLONIUS, Anne (cycling): b. 11 Feb 1968, Grand Rapids, Mich.; UAlta, York; moved to Canada '72; began road racing competitively '92; played competitive women's hockey at UAlta and York; mem. Timex Racing Team; claimed yellow jersey for 2 days at '94 women's Tour de France; silver '94 worlds; competed '94, '98 CG, '95 PAG, '93-94 worlds. '03 Tour de L'Aude; res. Brampton, Ont.

SAMPSON, Darryl (football); b. 21 Sep 1963, Scarborough, Ont.; York; m.; c. 3 daughters; coach; db;. CFL Winnipeg '86-98; 1 Eastern, CFL all-star; 4 Grey Cup finals, 2 winners; asst. York '96-98, Winnipeg '01-02, Montreal '03; res. Toronto, Ont.

SAMS, Judy (golf): b. 7 Oct 1957, Toronto, Ont.; m. William Ralph Sams; c. Jennifer; Ohio State; as jr. at Ohio State won '79 Midwest region title; '80 Ontario amateur title; turned pro '82; career low round 67; Cdn amateur golfer of '80; res. Sarasota, Fla.

SAMUEL, Randy (soccer); b. 23 Dec 1963, Trinidad & Tobago; given name: Randolph Fitzgerald; cb; began play age 12 Southam Warriors, Richmond, B.C.; defender Edmonton Eagles '83, Vancouver Whitecaps '83-84, PSV Eindhoven '86-88, Volendam '88-90, Fortuna Sittard '90-96, Stoke City, Port Vale, Harstad, Norway, '96-97, Vancouver 86ers '98-99, Hampton Roads '00, Montreal '01; mem. BC -16, -18 Selects, ntl -18; competed in World Cup '86; mem. PSV Eindhoven Dutch title team; made intl debut '83 with Team Canada vs. Honddouras; Canada's all-time leading intl match performer with 82 caps; res. Richmond, B.C.

SANDERLIN, Don (shooting); b. 26 Feb 1933, Viking, Alta.; given name: Donald Edward; m. Rita Zima; c. Roxanna; electrical construction firm owner; skeet shooting specialist; ntl champion '67-69, '71-72; US champion '68, '73; won Olympic trials '68, '72, PAG trials '75; mem. 3 PAG, 2 Olympic, 9 world championships teams; 4 times all-American; res. Edmonton, Alta.

SANDERSON, Derek (hockey); b. 16 Jun 1946, Niagara Falls, Ont.; v-p Boston Private Bank & Trust; ex-youth counsellor, hockey broadcaster, managing dir. Sports Group; Jr. A Niagara Falls; ctr Boston '65-74, Philadelphia (WHA) '72, Rangers '74-75, St. Louis '75-77, Vancouver '77, Pittsburgh '78; NHL record: 598 scheduled games, 202g, 250a, 56 playoff games, 18g, 12a; Calder rookie of year trophy '68; mem. 2 Stanley Cup winners; highest-paid athlete '73 when he jumped to WHA briefly; earned reputation as bon vivant and addiction to high living, alcohol and drugs led to dissipation of wealth and health; at 38

hired by Boston mayor to work on alcohol and drug abuse commission; underwent 7 hip replacement operations; res. Boston, Mass.

SANDERSON, Geoff (hockey); b. 1 Feb 1972, Hay River, NWT; m. Ellen; c. Ben, Jake; lw Swift Current jr. WHL '88-91; AHL Springfield '91; Hameelinna, Finland '94-95; Team Canada worlds '93, '94 (gold), '97 (gold); NHL Hartford '90-97, Carolina '97-98, Vancouver '98, Buffalo '98-00, Columbus '00-04, Vancouver '04; NHL record (through '04): 928 scheduled games, 316g, 296a, 55 playoff games, 9g, 10a; 2 NHL all-star games; res. Whitefish, Montana.

SANDERSON, Gus (shooting); b. 3 Jan 1929, Ottawa, Ont.; m. Betty Benedict; c. Janet, Jeffrey; ret'd engineer; skeet shooting specialist; Ottawa Valley Club, Ont. titles '55; ntl titles '63-64, '66, '74, '79, '83; world title '79; sub-seniors world title '80; 6 Capital of Canada shoot titles; 6 times all-American skeet team; 3 Ottawa ACT skeet shooting awards; mem. Cdn Skeet Shooting, Ottawa Sports halls of fame; res. Ottawa, Ont.

SANDERSON, Lyle (coaching); b. 8 Nov 1938, Maple Creek, Sask.; given name: Lyle Kingman; m. Carol Wood; c. Michael, Krista; UofSask, BA, MSc; assoc. prof. of PE, UofSask.; middle distance runner; head t&f coach UofSask from '65; 13 conf. team titles; ntl teams coach '76, '80 Olympics, '78 CG; Air Canada amateur-coach-of-yr nominee '77, '79; 1 CIAU X-C coach-of-yr award; chairman CTFA tech. comm. 3 years; CTFA multiple event co-ordinator; pres. CIAU t&f coaches assn. '84-88; dir. NA/Central American/Caribbean t&f from '89; t&f coach UofSask.; Rotary Golden Wheel, Sask. Kinsmen Sportsman, Athletics Can. leadership excellence awards; mem. USask Wall, Saskatoon Sports Hall of Fame; res. Saskatoon, Sask.

SANDHU, Emanuel (figure skating); b. 18 Nov 1980, Toronto, Ont.; full-time athlete; began skating age 8; 8yrs ballet training; coached by Joanne McLeod; Eastern div. Jr. title '97; 3 Cdn sr. titles; competed '02 Olympics, 1 world jr, 4 world srs, 5 4-Continents, 3 Skate Canada (1 gold, silver), 2 Skate America; '01 Goodwill Games; 1st to complete triple-triple (triple toe x 3) combination in competition; upset victor Colorado Springs GP '04; res. Burnaby, B.C.

SANDOR, Akos (weightlifting); b. 11 Dec 1977, Szombathely, Hungary; Centennial Coll.; truck/coach technician; began competing age 9; moved to Canada '90; 2 ntl jr. titles; 6 ntl sr. titles; competed 6 worlds; gold '95 Canada Games; 2nd Cdn male to medal at jr. worlds since they began in '75 (1 silver, 2 bronze '97); 3 gold '98, 3 silver '02 CG; competed '99, '03 PAG; gold '00 Pan-Am Championships; bronze '00 college/university worlds; Cdn. record holder 105kg, 105+kg for snatch , c&j; 2 Mississauga civic awards; coached by father, Steve, mem. Hungarian ntl weightlifting team 10yrs and '84 Olympian; res. Scarborough, Ont.

SANDS, Johnny (speed skating); b. 17 Apr 1933, Saskatoon, Sask.; given name: John Valance; hb Saskatoon Hilltops '51-53; ntl jr title '53; ntl outdoor titles '55, '57-58, shared '53 title with Frank Stack; mem. '56, '60 Olympic teams; ntl 220yds record '56-64, 500m record '56-68; coach

Que. '60s; established Gagne family award '96; mem. Cdn Speed Skating, Saskatoon Sports halls of fame; res. Mississauga, Ont.

SANDULO, Joey (boxing); b. 5 May 1931, Ottawa, Ont.; given name: Joseph Oleg; m. Mary Theresa Lewis; c. Patrick, Mary Jane, Kelly; ret'd cartographer; Ottawa Golden Gloves novice title '46; Que. Golden Gloves 106lb novice, Jack Dempsey Trophy '47; Ont., Eastern Canadian, ntl flyweight titles '48; youngest boxer to represent Canada in Olympics '48; Cdn Forces, BC bantam titles '49; with Gord Montagano operated boxing classes Ottawa '50-53; started Ottawa RA fitness program '59; launched Beaver Boxing Club '74, pres. '75; ring record shows 5 losses in 75 bouts; refereed pro, amateur boxing bouts from '53; Ottawa ACT sportsman of '80; Ottawa Community Builder award; Boxing Ont. Legends award; mem. Canadian Boxing, Ottawa Sports halls of fame; res. Nepean, Ont.

SANDUSKY, Jim (football): b. 9 Sep 1961, Othello, Wash.; m.; c. 2; Nevada, San Diego State; football coach; 1st team all-Western; played in Japan Bowl; MVP Hula Bowl; coach, wr; drafted USFL Philadelphia Stars, NFL Detroit '84; joined CFL BC '84-87, Edmonton '88, '91-96; NFL Seattle '89-90 but sat out with injuries; CFL record: 170 scheduled games, 70tds, 1 2-point convert, 586 receptions for 9737yds, 69tds, 147 punt returns for 1399yds, 1td; 3 Western, 2 CFL all-star; 3 Grey Cup finals, 2 winners; asst. coach BC '97; active in Athletes in Action; res. Vancouver, B.C.

SANFORD, Aubrey (soccer); b. 4 Sep 1905, Nanaimo, B.C.; d. 5 Jan 1985, Vancouver, B.C.; m. Muriel Audrey; c. Judith Ann, Anthony Albert; UBC; ret'd chartered accountant; 45yr involvement with soccer; mem. 3 ntl champions with Westminster Royals '28, '30-31; managed same club to ntl titles '53, '55; CSA pres. '69-72; runnerup Air Canada Amateur Sport Award '72; mem. Cdn Soccer, BC Sports halls of fame.

SANGSTER-DALEY, Rose Marie (soccer); b. 19 Mar 1971, Kingston, Jamaica; UHartford BComm.; accountant; moved to Windsor age 10, adopted by aunt; 3 all-city awards Kennedy CI; '89 city title team; also shone in t&f, basketball, badminton; played club soccer sr Nationals; full scholarship '90-94, 50g, 23a college career; 3 2nd team all-American; 3 all-New England, all-Northeast region, all-North Atlantic Conf. 1st team all-star; twice Hermann trophy ntl player of yr nominee; 3 North Atlantic Conf. titles; mem. ntl team '93 FISU Games; pro Sweden, Japan (all-Japan title team '95; Toronto Rexdale Ont. sr. champs '01; coached in Windsor, Japan; mem. Windsor/Essex Sports, U Hartford halls of fame; res. Toronto, Ont.

SANKEY, Derek (basketball); b. 17 Dec 1948, Vancouver, B.C.; given name: Derek William; m. Irene Sigismund; c. Jordan, Adrienne; UBC, BA, MEd; teacher, ex-mgr. education BC Central Credit Union; HS basketball '60-66, 2 city titles; mem. ntl jr. men's title team '67; UBC Thunderbirds '67-71, 2 ntl champions; asst. coach 6yrs; Vancouver sr. men's Dogwood League '72-79; MVP, all-star '75; ntl team '70-76; mem. '71, '75 PAG, '76 Olympics, '70, '74 World championships, '73 FISU Games teams, '98 World Masters; coached UBC jr. varsity '71-72, '75-77, HS teams '72-75, '77-98; globetrotter whose cage pursuits

encompassed 36 countries; coach all levels 31yrs; dir. Basketball Can. '85-94; exec. Basketball BC '80-84, '93-97; chair. High Hoops '95-03; exec. BC Girls HS basketball '98-01; mem. UBC Block Club, pres. '71; mem. Cdn Basketball Hall of Fame; res. Richmond, B.C.

SAPUNJIS, Dave (football): b. 7 Sep 1967, Toronto, Ont.; UWO, BA; oil co. sales rep.; sb; mem. '90 Vanier Cup winner; CFL Calgary '90-96; CFL record: 120 scheduled games, 47tds, 2 2-point converts, 460 receptions for 6586yds, 46tds, 10 punt returns for 124yds, 1td, 9 playoff games, 3tds; 1 Western, 1 Northern, 2 CFL all-star; Dr. Beattie Martin trophy '93; Jeff Nicklin Memorial trophy '95; Lew Hayman trophy '95; CFL outstanding Cdn '93, '95; most valuable Cdn '91-92, '95 Grey Cup; 9 playoff games, 3tds; 3 Grey Cup finals, 1 winner; mem. Calgary ownership group '05; res. Calgary, Alta.

SARGENT, Frank (builder/hockey/curling); b. 1902, Fergus, Ont.; d. 28 Sep 1988, Thunder Bay, Ont.; mem. Cdn sr. lacrosse title team '20; mem. TBAHA '28-55, 5yrs pres.; Port Arthur GC pres. '39-41; pres. CAHA '42-44; 1st pres. NOCA; pres. DCA '52; founding mem. Port Arthur Curling & Athletic Club; 1st person ever to hold ntl presidency 2 sports (hockey, curling); life mem. Port Arthur, Ft. William Curling & Athletic Clubs, NWOCA, MCA, OCA, DCA, CAHA, QCA; USHA appreciation award; OHA gold stick award; Cdn Legion sportsman award; appreciation for curling contributions award; Centennial medal; curling Grand Prix honor award; Queen's anniversary medal; Gyro Club appreciation award; Cdn Hockey Hall of Fame meritorious award; mem. Governor-General's CC; Cdn Curling, NWO Sports halls of fame.

SASKAMOOSE, Fred (hockey); b. 25 Dec 1933, Sandy Lake Indian Reserve, Sask.; given name: Frederick George; m. Loretta Isbester; c. Algin, Phyllis (d), Garth, Beverley, Kevin, Karen, Derrick, Neil, Ryan; farmer/hunter; learned to skate on bobskates as child; attended St. Michael residential school in Duck Lake age 8; mem. St. Michael provincial midget title team '49; 4yrs with Moose Jaw (WHL); MVP '53; jumped from jr. to Chicago (NHL) at 19 playing in 11 games; 1st Treaty Indian to play in NHL; played in minors with New Westminster, Calgary, Chicoutimi, Kamloops; refusal of Chicago to give him release to regain amateur status cost him opportunity to join Penticton Vees for Allan Cup and World championships; Kamloops paid $10,000 for his release and he remained with that sr. club 7yrs; hon. chief Kamloops Indian reserve; became involved in Native leadership serving as band councilor several years, 7yrs chief; developed Native hockey schools for youth; established Sask. Native bantams travelling team; builder Native Sports/Recreation programs and facilities; nicknamed "Chief Thunder Stick"; mem. Sask. First Nations Sports Hall, Meadow Lake Sask Wall of Fame; res. Shell Lake, Sask.

SATHER, Glen (hockey); b. 2 Sep 1943, High River, Alta.; given name: Glen Cameron; m. Ann; c. Justin, Shannon; hockey exec.; lw Edmonton jrs., Memphis, Oklahoma City; NHL '66-76 with Boston, Pittsburgh, Rangers, St. Louis, Montreal, Minnesota; Oilers (WHA) '76; NHL record: 658 scheduled games, 80g, 113a, 72 playoff games, 1g, 5a; turned to coaching '77; coach Team Canada '84 Canada

Cup; GM Team Canada '94, '96 Worlds; mem. management comm. '87 Rendez-Vous; coach/GM Edmonton Oilers '78-89, pres./GM '89-00, pres/GM NYR from '00, coach '03-04; architect of 5 Edmonton Stanley Cup winners; Jack Adams coach of '86 award; Fr. David Bauer award '97; 1 of only 6 coaches in NHL history to coach 5 all-star games; NHL coaching record: 842 scheduled games, 464-268-110, 127 playoff games, 89-37-1, 4 Stanley Cups; mem. Alta. Sports, Cdn Hockey halls of fame; res. Edmonton/Banff, Alta.

SAUNDERS, Alex (football): b. 20 Apr 1929, Stratford, Ont.; given name: Robert Alexander; m. Beverley Joynt; c. Alex, Julia, Tim, Sheila; CF Staff College; ret'd military officer, public servant; as teenager earned Ottawa all-star gd award, Rough Riders outstanding lineman award; Ottawa, Ontario all-star ctr '48; played gd/ctr/lb with Rough Riders '48, rookie lineman of year nominee; moved into coaching ranks in Ottawa-Carleton MFA '72-81; Football Ont. Northeastern coach of '80; held varied exec. roles with North Eastern Region Amateur Football organization '81-88; mem. '84-85 Camp Olympia coaching staff; offensive line coach, interim GM Ottawa Bootleggers NAMLFA runnerup '89; coach 2 Sir Robert Borden HS jr. National Capital champions; ntl Level III coaching certificate; player/coach Cdn Forces Western Canada basketball title team '56; mem. Rivers, Man., Air Training centre lacrosse team; shot put, relay specialist in t&f; forces rugby '57-62; forces volleyball '65-73; exec. Rough Riders Alumni Assn.; res. Nepean, Ont.

SAUNDERS, Billy (baseball): b. 26 May 1946, Fredericton, N.B.; m. Mary; civil technician; one of NB's most successful coaches in ntl competition (43-30) winning 2 gold, 1 silver, 3 bronze medals; coach/manager/owner Marysville Royals for 3 prov, 3 Atlantic championships; ntl championship silver, bronze medals; coached 1st ever NB Cdn title team '81; instrumental in forming NB jr. baseball league; managed Fredericton Royals to 2 NB jr. titles; founding mem. NB baseball coaches assn.; 9ys part-time NY Yankees scout; 2 Baseball NB coach-of-yr awards; mem. NB, Fredericton, Saint John, NB Baseball halls of fame; res. Fredericton, N.B.

SAUNDERS, Bryan (t&f): b. 9 Jul 1952, Trinidad; div. Andrea Lynch; c. Shannon; m. Metta Gordon; c. Dorice, Blaine; North Platt (Neb), Bishop State (Mobile), Long Beach State Coll.; bakery business; began racing at 21; mem. Scarborough Optimist TC; 400m specialist; ntl sr. record '77; mem. '75, '79, '83 PAG '76, '80, '84 Olympic, '78 CG, '75, '77 FISU Games. '77, '79 World Cup teams; bronze '75 FISU Games; 5 ntl 400m titles; ret'd '84; coached HS girls 3yrs Compton, Calif.; res. Willowdale, Ont.

SAUNDERS, Dyce (cricket): b. 22 Mar 1862, Guelph, Ont., d. 12 Jun 1930, London, Ont.; c. Thomas (d); Trinity College; finest wicket keeper in Canadian history; capt. Trinity Coll.; at 19 mem. ntl team vs. US; mem. 12 international match teams; final international match at 43; starred '87 UK tour; considered "Grand Old Man" of Canadian cricket.

SAUNDERS, Jim (boxing): b. 4 Jan 1932, Winnipeg, Man.; given name: James Allan; m. Marion; c. James, Cole, June; ret'd truck driver; Man. amateur champion, ntl champion '49, '52-53; mem. '52 Olympic team; ret'd from

ring '61; honored by COA '76; nicknamed "Babyface"; res. Winnipeg, Man.

SAUNDERS, Sandy (rowing): b. 25 Jan 1912, Hamilton, Ont.; given name: Thomas Vassar Claude; m. Florence Papps; c. Claude, Lois, Janice; ret'd Stelco; 17yr competitive career; stroked Leander Boat Club jr. 8s to '34 ntl title, Ned Hanlan Trophy; identical honors heavy 8s '35, '39; stroked heavy 8s to Dominion Day, CNE regatta victories '37-38; mem. '36, '48 (alternate) Olympics; won Olympic trials '39 but '40 games cancelled due to WW2; Henley, ntl junior double sculls '40; Henley single sculls '44; ORFU football Hamilton Tiger-Cubs '37; mgr. '60 Olympic crews; mgr. Leander BC '33-38; Leander rowing chair. '39-46, v-p. '48; charter mem. Central Ont. Rowing Assn.; hon. pres. '54-58, secty. '58-66; mem. exec. Cdn Secondary School RA '53-61, pres. '61-62; Leander rep. to CAAO '49-52, v-p. '52-56, pres. '57-58, p-pres. '58-60, hon. pres. from '92; Cdn Henley regatta chair. '52-98; starter, referee '49-98; 1st Cdn international referee '60 Olympics; life mem. Leander BC; Argonaut RC club award; Ottawa RC award; St. Catharines RC award; B'nai B'rith, Shamrock Boystown, CAAO president's awards; 3 Ont. achievement awards; CAAO award of merit; Centennial Medal; life mem., alumni award St. Catharines RC; ORC trust fund bears his name; mem. Order of Canada, Canada's Sports Hall of Fame; res. Hamilton, Ont.

SAUNDERS, William (horse racing): b. 13 Apr 1915, Bozeman, Mont.; m. Marguerite Chisholm; horseman; nicknamed "Smoky"; began riding '32 in Calgary area; after breaking maiden at Tanforan rose rapidly up competitive ladder under Sunny Jim Fitzsimmons; gained prominence riding Omaha to thoroughbred racing's Triple Crown (Kentucky Derby, Preakness, Belmont Stakes) '35; at 17 youngest jockey to achieve this feat; recorded victories in Louisiana Derby, Detroit Derby, Chicago Derby, San Juan Capistrano Handicap, Fashion Stakes, Saratoga Handicap; ret'd from saddle '50 to serve as race steward, placing judge, patrol judge at several US tracks including Washington Park, Hawthorne, Garden State, Tropical, Hialeah, Gulfstream; New York Turf Writers' Man of Year; mem. Canadian Horse Racing Hall of Fame; res. Hallandale, Fla.

SAUVÉ, Gordon (boxing): b. 16 Mar 1906, St. Zotique, Que.; d. (circa 1995), Verdun, Que.; m. Blanche Brisset; c. Laurent; ret'd; gained 1st boxing training through Mike Gibbons correspondence course; 1st novice title MAAA; mem. Palestre Nationale training under Joe Flanagan, Gene Brosseau; 1st-rate amateur in '30s; national amateur bantamweight (118lbs) title; never knocked down or out in his career; retiring from competition he became highly-regarded referee; when Que. boxing commission overruled one of his decisions he quit officiating for QABA; officiated national title bouts for CBF; coach national boxing team '48 Olympics; AAUofC boxing official; citations from AAUofC, Olympic Club; 15yrs chief QABA referee, 10yrs chief judge, 10yrs professional referee.

SAVAGE, Marilyn (coaching): b. 3 Jun 1934, Toronto, Ont.; given name: Marilyn Florence Charters; m. Frederick James Savage; c. Frederick James; UofT, BPHE; teaching master Seneca College; coach ntl women's gymnastics teams '66-70 world championships, '67 PAG, '68, '72 Olympic, '67-

75 Canada Games teams; coach Scarborough Winstonettes gymnastics club '64-78; coached 11 competitors to Olympic status; coached ntl champions Jennifer Diachun, Nancy McDonnell; mem. National Advisory Council on Fitness, Amateur Sport '68-77; founding mem., dir. Coaching Assn. of Canada '70-78; founder Seneca College coaching program, Canada's 1st sports school; runnerup Air Canada coach of '73 award; mem. COA '68-81; Ont. achievement awards '69, '71; Centennial Medal '67; Jubilee Medal '77; Coaching Assn. Honors; Geoff Gowan award '03; life mem. Cdn Gymnastics Fed.; res. Cambridge, Ont.

SAVAGE, Paul (curling); b. 25 Jun 1947, Toronto, Ont; given name: Allin Paul; m. Barbara Lee; c. Bradley, Lisa; Seneca College; partner Sporteck Software, '65 Ont. Schoolboy title; Ont. jr. title '66; 7 times Ont. Brier rep.; skipped winning provincial Consols rinks '70, '73, '74, '77, '87; 3rd with Ed Werenich's '83-84 Ont. Tankard, '83 Brier, Silver Broom champions; won '78 *CBC* Classic; author Canadian Curling Hack to House ('74); mem. Hamilton World Curling comm.; Dick Ellis team award '83; mem. Cdn Curling Hall of Fame; res. Markham, Ont.

SAVAGEAU, Daniele (hockey/coaching); b. 22 Apr 1962, Deux Montagnes, Que.; U Montreal, RCMP Academy; police officer; led Team Quebec to Montreal Gold Cup '96, silver '97 Esso Cup; asst. Montreal Rocket (QMJHL) '99-2000; head coach ntl –19 silver team '96; head coach ntl women's team '98-02, 5 ntl titles; Olympic silver '98, gold '02; 3 Nations gold '98, 4 nations gold '00; Cdn Coaching Assn coach of '99 award; Que. Coach of 2000, YMCA woman of 2000; Cdn female coach of '02; retd from ntl team '02; spokesperson Cdn Coaching Assn.; Eng-French TV analyst HNIC; security officer '76 Olympics; 3 PetroCan coaching excellence awards; res. Deux Montagnes, Que.

SAVARD, Denis (hockey): b. 4 Feb 1961, Pointe Gatineau, Que.; m. Mona; c. Tanya Lee; hockey coach; ctr Verdun Jr; 1st pick Chicago '80 draft; pro Chicago '80-90, '95-97, Montreal '90-93, Tampa Bay '93-95; QMJHL all-star, MVP '80; 1 2nd team NHL all-star; mem. 1 Stanley Cup winner; NHL record: 1196 scheduled games, 473g, 865a, 169 playoff games, 66g, 109a; jersey #18 ret'd by Chicago; Chicago development coach/community relations ambassador; asst. coach Chicago '00, interim head coach '01; mem. Hockey Hall of Fame, Montreal Canadiens wall of honor; res. Chicago, Ill.

SAVARD, Serge (hockey); b. 22 Jan 1946, Montreal, Que.; hockey exec. realtor; jr. Montreal Canadiens; def NHL Canadiens '66-81, Winnipeg '81-83; Team Canada '72, '76; NHL record: 1040 scheduled games, 106g, 333a, 130 playoff games, 19g, 49a; mem. 7 Stanley Cup winners; Conn Smythe Trophy '69, Bill Masterton Trophy '79; once 2nd team all-star; v-p./managing dir./GM Canadiens '83-95; consultant Expos, Alouettes; featured on Canadian postage stamps; Officer Order of Canada '94; mem. Hockey Hall of Fame selection comm.; mem. Hockey Hall of Fame; res. Montreal, Que.

SAVIJARVI, Liisa (skiing); b. 29 Dec 1963, Bracebridge, Ont.; m. Brian Sewell; c. Lily Ray; partner Ski Escape Inc.; ntl GS champion '84-86; ntl DH champion '87; competed '84 Olympics; mem. '88 Olympic team but injury

prevented competition; World Cup Super G title Japan '86; ranked 2nd WC Super G, 5th WC downhill '86; Ski Racing Magazine, Kodak Corp Cdn skier of yr awards '86; ret'd from competition '88 following serious tibia, spinal injuries; mem. Cdn Skiing Hall of Fame; res. Toronto, Ont.

SAWCHUK, Bill (swimming): b. 8 Jan 1959, Roblin, Man.; m.; c. Carlie, Matt; Florida.; hobby farm operator, aquatic supply dealer, ex-swim coach; began competitive swimming Thunder Bay Thunderbolts '73; ntl team '75-82; close to 40 top 3 finishes in ntl, intl competitions; several ntl records; PAG 200 IM bronze '75, 3 silver 2 bronze '79; 7 medals '78 CG, including 2 medley gold; competed '76 Olympics, qualified '80 boycotted Olympics; Southeastern Conf. swimmer of '80; turned to coaching Nashville '82-85, Vancouver Hyack 15yrs; competes at masters level; mem. Cdn, Ont. Aquatic, NWO Sports halls of fame; res. Maple Ridge, B.C.

SAWCHUK, Terry (hockey): b. 28 Dec 1929, Winnipeg, Man, d. 31 May 1970, New York, N.Y.; given name: Terrance Gordon; div.; c. 7; goalie Winnipeg Rangers jrs., Windsor Spitfires jrs; USHL, AHL, NHL rookie-of-yr awards; NHL Detroit '49-55, '57-64, '68-69, Boston '55-56, Toronto '64-67, Los Angeles '67-68, Rangers '69-70; NHL record: 971 scheduled games, 953 complete games, 2401 goals-against, 2.52 avg., 103so, 106 playoff games, 267 goals-against, 2.64 avg., 12 so; mem. 4 Stanley Cup winners; 3 times 1st, 4 times 2nd team all-star; Vezina Trophy 4 times (1 shared with Johnny Bower); died following altercation with teammate Ron Stewart (cleared of guilt); jersey #1 ret'd by Red Wings; Winnipeg arena named in his honor; Manitoba male pro athlete of 20th century; mem. Cdn, Man. Hockey halls of fame.

SAWICKI, Ted (lacrosse): b. 31 Jan 1962, St. Catharines, Ont.; teacher, coach; ntl team goalie from '81; mem. Niagara Warriors '81, St. Catharines Jr. A '82-84, Victoria Payless '84-87, Brooklin Redmen '88-89, Oshawa Blue Knights '88-90, Detroit Turbos '89, St, Catharines OLA, Buffalo MILL '96-99; mem. Niagara Founders Cup winner '81, Brooklin Mann Cup winner '88; 5 ntl field lacrosse titles; record 63 saves single game; 2 silver, 3 bronze ntl team worlds; 2 defensive MVP awards; mem. 3 ntl title teams; 3 ntl championship all-star goalie; mem. MILL '91 title team; 3 MILL 1st team all-star awards; asst. coach '98 worlds; head coach Buffalo '00-02, Burlington, McMaster women; 4 Peel Region women's HS titles; level 4 field lacrosse referee; mem. Ont. Lacrosse Hall of Fame; res. Milton, Ont.

SAWULA, Lorne (volleyball); b. 19 Feb 1947, Edmonton, Alta.; given name: Lorne William; UAlta, BPhE, MA, PhD; coach; ex-hi-performance dir. Australian VBA; mem. '67 Alta. Canada Winter Games volleyball team; mem. UAlta men's volleyball team '64-69; WCIAA all-star '64-69; mem. Alta. champion Edmonton Phoenix, Dalhousie Volleyball Clubs '69-74; coach UAlta men's team '71-73, Dalhousie women's Montreal, Atlantic champions '73-75, UBC Thunderbirds CIAU men's titlists '75-77, UofOtt '78-81; asst. coach women's ntl team '74-75; coach ntl jr. women's ntl team '76; tech. dir. CVA '77-84; ntl women's coach '81-85, from '01; hi-perf. dir. VB Canada '86-90; head coach Swiss women's team '91-93, Australia '94; sole Cdn mem. International Volleyball Assn., Coaches

Commission; appointed master coach '79; authored most of CVA coaching manuals from levels 1-4; has given coaching clinics in more than 40 countries; served on varied FIVB commissions 18yrs; coached UAlta '00 CIAU title team; res. Edmonton, Alta.

SAX, Joe (t&f); b. 5 Nov 1952, Toronto, Ont.; given name: Joseph Anton; UofT, BPHE, UWO, BEd; teacher; ntl record 3000m steeplechase '74 with 8:36.8; mem. '78 CG team; ntl 3,000m title '78; *Toronto Star* Invitational 1500m '79; 3rd Tor. Marathon '80; dir. OTFA, privacy officer '03; res. Toronto, Ont.

SAY, Rick (swimming); b. 18 May 1979, Salmon Arm, B.C.; UCal, UVic; freestyle specialist; competed '98, '02 (bronze) CG, '99, '03 PAG, '99 (2 bronze), '01 worlds, '00 Olympics; 6 gold, 1 silver '01 WC short course circuit; 10 ntl 200/400m titles; '01 swimmer-of-yr award; ntl 100m FS record 48.38; res. Victoria, B.C.

SAZIO, Ralph (football); b. 22 Jul 1922, South Orange, N.J.; given name: Ralph Joseph; m. Rose Louise Matthews; c. Mark, Peggy; College of William and Mary, BSc, Columbia, MA; ret'd football exec.; capt. William and Mary football team; pro Brooklyn Dodgers; tackle, asst. coach Hamilton '50, head coach '63-67; CFL coaching record: 59-25-1, 4 Grey Cup finals, 3 winners; GM, dir. Tiger-Cats '68-72; club pres. '73-81; CFL pres. '75; pres. Argos '81-89; mem. Cdn Football Hall of Fame; res. Burlington, Ont.

SCAPINELLO, Ray (officiating/hockey); b. 5 Nov 1946, Guelph, Ont.; m. Maureen Flaherty; c. Ryan; NHL linesman '71-04; worked 3 NHL all-star games, 17 consec. Stanley Cup finals, Canada Cup, Challenge Cup, Rendez-Vous '87, Olympics '98; NHL record: 2906 games; low handicap golfer; active in Make A Wish Foundation activities; res. Guelph, Ont.

SCHERER, Sue (hockey/softball); b. 27 Aug 1956, Kitchener, Ont.; given name: Susan; Guelph, BA; consultant; mem. Cdn women's softball teams '83 (gold), '87 (bronze) PAG; competed in '82, '86 world softball championships; capt. '90, mem. '92 Team Canada world ice hockey champions; coach Guelph varsity women's hockey team '93-96; Fair Play Canada ambassador '91-98; Ont. mission staff '93, '97 Canada summer games; CIAU planning comm. ntl coaching school for women '93-98; Met. Life foundation for athletic scholarships comm. '94-98; CAAWS board mem. '94-98; Johnny F. Bassett Memorial award '96; program co-ordinator F.A.M.E. '91-95, program consultant '95-96;Women on Move award '98; consultant Scherer Energy Unlimited from '96; res. London, Ont.

SCHLEGEL, Elfi (gymnastics); b. 17 May 1964, Toronto, Ont.; m. Marc Dunn; c.Olivia, Frances; Florida State; operates Schlegel's gym; coach, broadcaster; 3 all-American, 11 NCAA Southeast regional, 4 Southeast Conf. titles; 4 Ont. titles; '78 national, Commonwealth champion; team gold, silver uneven bars, vault, bronze all-around '79 PAG; mem. '80 Olympic, 4 world championships teams; bronze vault '80 World Cup; gold vault, bronze all-around, uneven bars '81 New Zealand Games; 4 gold '81 Canada vs Great Britain; 5 gold Canada vs Norway '81; silver beam '81 Ennia Gold Cup; Cdn FISU Games teams '83, '85;

asst. coach Florida; Olympic games *CTV, CBC, NBC TV* commentator; Ont. Gymnastics Fed. special achievement award '85; co-host *TSN* Gym Rock '01; life mem. Cdn Gymnastics Fed.; res. Toronto, Ont.

SCHLEIMER, Joseph (wrestling); b. 31 May 1909, Austria; d. 23 Nov 1988, Mississauga, Ont.; m. Margaret; c. Ewin; ret'd architectural draftsman, manufacturer wood products and construction; ntl 164lb title '34-36; gold '34 BEG; bronze '36 Olympics; coach ntl wrestling team '59, '63 PAG, '62 CG, world championships, '64 Olympic; chair. AAUofC wrestling comm. '60-64; pres. OAWF '55-60; wrestling coach Broadview YMCA Toronto '50-71; Ont. achievement awards '70-72, '75 for service to sport; dir. CAWA many years; mem. Cdn Amateur Sports, Cdn Amateur Wrestling halls of fame.

SCHMALZ, Tubby (administration); b. 19 Dec 1916, Breslau, Ont., d. 7 Dec 1981, Walkerton, Ont.; given name: Clarence; m. Dorothy Wolfe; c. Marilyn, Susan, Ann, Jacqueline; innkeeper; jr. hockey Kitchener, Brantford; coached, managed Walkerton OHA int. champions '54-55; mem. OHA exec. 25yrs, 3 terms pres.; commissioner OMJHL '74-79; board mem. Hockey Canada; board chairman CAHA; instituted coaching, refereeing clinics in OHA, a program adopted throughout CAHA; OHA Gold Stick award, CAHA meritorious service award; life mem. OHA; 17yrs. mem. Walkerton town council, reeve at time of death.

SCHMIDT, Milt (hockey); b. 5 Mar 1918, Kitchener, Ont.; given name: Milton Conrad; m. Marie Peterson; c. Milton Jr., Nancy; ret'd hockey exec., Boston Madison Square Garden Club mgr.; ctr Bruins '36-55, excluding 3 WW2 seasons RCAF, mem. Allan Cup champion Ottawa Hurricanes; ctr'd famed Boston Kraut Line of Woody Dumart, Bobby Bauer; NHL record: 776 scheduled games, 229g, 336a, 80 playoff games, 24g, 25a; NHL scoring title '40; Hart Trophy (MVP) '52; mem. 2 Stanley Cup winners; 3 times 1st team, once 2nd team all-star; coached Bruins '55-61, '62-66, also GM; coach-GM Washington in NHL expansion program '73-78; NHL coaching record: 770 scheduled games, 250-394-126; 34 playoff games, 15-19; served as corporate season ticket sales chief Bruins; mem. Hockey, Canada's Sports halls of fame; res. Dover, Mass.

SCHMIDT-FOSTER, Angela (skiing); b. 6 Jan 1960, Woodstock, Ont. m. Don Foster; c. Joey, Stephen, Suzanne; self-employed; top Cdn jr. x-country skier '77-79; ntl x-country ski team mem. '76-92; competed 4 Olympic, world championships; 1st Cdn to crack top 3 world cup competition '87; top Canadian in most international competitions; 12yrs on WC circuit; runs Jackrabbit program; Kerri Lotion award of excellence '91; Midland highway junction bears her name; res. Midland, Ont.

SCHMIRLER, Sandra (curling); b. 11 Jun 1963, Biggar, Sask.; d. 2 Mar 2000, Regina, Sask; given name: Sandra Marie Peterson; m. Shannon England Schmirler; c. Sara, Jenna; UofSask. BA; leisure centre supervisor; excelled in swimming, volleyball, badminton; began curling age 13; won '92 Sask. mixed title; 3 Sask. women's championships; skipped Saskatchewan to Scott Tournament of Hearts titles '93-94, '97; 1st to skip 3 world curling title rinks; skipped rink to '98 Olympic gold; skipped *TSN* women's skins game winner '98; subject of *Gold on Ice*, Perry Lefko book; Biggar park named in her memory; mem. Cdn Olympic, Cdn Curling, Canada's, Sask. Sports halls of fame.

SCHNEIDER, Angela (rowing); b. 28 Oct 1959, St. Thomas, Ont.; UofT; asst. dean ethics/equity UWO; sweep 2 Cdn Henley coxed 4s, 8s crews; 1 ntl coxed 4s, 8s; 2 Dominion Day, Head of Charles regatta 8s titlists; mem. silver coxed 4s '84 Olympics; res. London, Ont.

SCHNEIDER, Bert (boxing); b. 1 Jul 1897, Cleveland, Ohio; d. 20 Feb 1986, Stanwood, Wash.; given name: Albert; m. Mary Ellen Henderson (d.); US immigration service; with Montreal Swimming Club water polo team, skier, diver, swimmer and boxer; joined Montreal Casquette Club training under Eugene Brosseau; MAAA welterweight title, 1 city title 2 ntl titles; gold '20 Olympics scoring 4 wins in 3 days; 90 pro bouts; mem. Canadian Boxing, Canada's Sports, Amateur Sports halls of fame.

SCHNURR, Paula (t&f); b. 15 Jan 1964, Kirkland Lake, Ont.; m. Peter Self; McMaster BPHE; teacher; middle distance runner; 25 OWIAA indoor/outdoor medals, 18 gold; 2 CIAU indoor records; represented Canada '92, '96 Olympic, '94 CG; double gold '88 CIAU championships (top athlete award); 2 ntl 3000m, 2 1500m, 1 800m titles; silver 1500m '94 CG; 5 CIAU all-Cdn; McMaster female athlete of 1985; mem. McMaster Hall of Fame; res. Burlington, Ont.

SCHOCK, Ron (hockey); b. 19 Dec 1943, Chapleau, Ont.; given name: Ronald Lawrence; ctr EPHL Kingston '62-63, OHA Niagara Falls '63-643, 1 Memorial Cup, CPHL Minneapolis '64, Kansas City '67, WHL '65-66, AHL Hershey '78-79, Rochester '79-80, NHL Boston '63-67, St. Louis '67-69, Pittsburgh '69-77, Buffalo '77-78; NHL totals: 909 scheduled games, 166g, 351a, 55 playoff games, 4g, 16a; Pittsburgh unsung hero, leading point scorer, 2 Players' Player, 2 MVP awards; brother Dan also played in NHL; res. Pittsburgh, Pa.

SCHOENFELD, Jim (hockey/coaching); b. 4 Sep 1952, Galt, Ont,; given name: James Grant; m. Theresa; c. Justin, Katie, Adam, Nathan; hockey coach; def Niagara Falls Flyers jr; pro AHL Cincinnati, NHL Buffalo '72-81, '84-85, Detroit '81-83, Boston '83-84; NHL playing record: 719 scheduled games, 51g, 204a, 75 playoff games, 3g, 13a; youngest team capt. to that time '74; 2nd team all-star '80; NHL's top rookie def '72; played in 2 all-star games; launched coaching career Rochester (AHL) '84; NHL with Buffalo '85-86, New Jersey '87-90, Washington '93-97, Phoenix '97-99; NHL record: 580 scheduled games, 256-248-78, 57 playoff games, 26-31; *ESPN* hockey analyst; mem. Sabres Hall of Fame; res. Phoenix, Ariz.

SCHOENHALS, Dorenda (curling); b. 14 Jun 1947, Moose Jaw, Sask.; given name: Dorenda Alene Stirton; div. Paul Schoenhals; c. Susan, Ryan, Karyn; m. Bill Bailey; UofSask, BSc; nurse, heart patient educator; skipped HS rink to prov. title at 15; 5 consecutive WCIAA titles '64-69; ntl Intercollegiate title '67; with sister Cheryl playing 3rd skipped ntl Lassies title rink '70; 3rd on Rick Folk mixed provincial title rinks '75, '81-83; ntl title '83, twice

runnerup; mem. UofSask Sports Wall, Sask Sports Hall of Fame; res. Calgary, Alta.

SCHOENHALS, Paul (football); b. 5 Nov 1941, Clinton, Ont.; given name: Paul John; div. Dorenda Stirton; c. Susan, Ryan, Karyn; div. Pat Bugera; UofSask, BEd, MEd; pres. Petroleum Industry Training Service; jr. football Saskatoon; asst. coach Saskatoon Hilltops 7yrs, head coach 6yrs; assisted Al Ledingham in guiding Hilltops to ntl junior title '68; head coach '78 ntl jr. champions; mem. Sask. legislature '82-86 holding various ministerial portfolios; mem. Cdn Srs Golf Assn.; res. Calgary, Alta.

SCHOLES, Louis (rowing); b. 1880, Toronto, Ont., d. 1942, Toronto, Ont; US intermediate singles '01; 2 major sr. sculls events defeating US champion C.S. Titus at '02 Harlem Regatta; with partner Frank Smith won both Canadian, US double sculls titles '03; Dominion Day Regatta, Cdn Henley, USNRA singles titles '03; 1st Canadian to win English Henley diamond sculls in record 8:23.2 '04; brother Jack held ntl featherweight, lightweight boxing titles, '00-01 US amateur featherweight title; mem. Cdn Amateur, Canada's Sports Hall of Fame.

SCHOOLEY, Dennis (baseball); b. 10 Mar 1953, Stratford, Ont.; div.; Wilfrid Laurier, BComm; chartered accountant; played varsity hockey at WLU; 3b Stratford Jr. Optimists; saw 1st Sr. Intercounty action while still jr. age; 1st full sr. season with Stratford Hillers at 1B '72; all-star 2b '75; played half of '83 season in Waterloo; made managerial debut with Hillers '79; managed Hillers to 7 Sr. IC titles, 3 times runnerup; as player competed in 566 games, 444 hits; as mgr. (through '97) 815 career games, 484 wins, both league records; operates top-rated baseball school; brother Pat 12 seasons infielder with Hillers; David Hastings exec. of '89 trophy; res. Stratford, Ont.

SCHOOTMAN, Teddy (administration); b. 28 Aug 1918, Ridgewood, N.J.; m. Mies de Chavonnes Vrugt; c. Anneke, Roel, Joke; Rotterdam Technical College; sr. engineer BC Hydro and Power Authority; moved to Canada '53; mem. Dolphin SC '61-80; chief of officials BC Centennial meet '64; organized officials clinics '65-67; v-p. Dolphin SC '66, pres. '68-73; v-p. BC section CASA '68-73, pres. '74; dir. CASA '75; ntl swim team chair. '70-73; mem., chair. ntl team selection comm.; chair. '67 BC championships, short-course nationals '69, summer nationals '76, winter nationals '78; BC team mgr. '68 nationals; organized, managed Dolphin European tour '69; Olympic aquatic team mgr. '72; deck official '73, '75 worlds; organized West Van. Dolphin SC as Dolphin affiliate, also club at Tsawwassen and Master SC; res. West Vancouver, B.C.

SCHREIDER, Gary (football); b. 21 Apr 1934, Belleville, Ont.; m. Patricia; c. Gary Jr., Ronald, Thomas, Michael, Suzanne; Queen's, BA, UofOtt, LLB; lawyer, QC; mem. 3 Toronto St. Michael's Ont. Catholic Conf. champions; intercollegiate champion Queen's Golden Gaels '55; 9 CFL seasons '56-64 with Ottawa, BC, Hamilton; hb/pk; 3 times all-star; ntl jr. 60yd dash record 6.3 in HS training under Lloyd Percival; 1st pres. CFL Players' Assn. '63; appointed sole arbitrator player salaries, disputes by NHL and NHLPA '76-93; mem. Ottawa, Belleville Sports halls of fame; res. Ottawa, Ont.

SCHRIEWER, Tex (football); b. 30 Sep 1934, New Braunfels, Texas; given name: Menan; m. Sandra Jefferies; c. 6; Texas (Austin), BBA; insurance, real estate exec.; all-South, Western Conf. honors '54-55, hon. mention all-American '55; pro Toronto '56; led Argos in receptions with 43 for 691yds, 1td '57; dealt to Saskatchewan for Cookie Gilchrist '59; rejoined Argos '60-62; all-Eastern with Argos '57; res. San Antonio, Tex.

SCHRINER, Sweeney (hockey); b. 30 Nov 1911, Calgary, Alta.; d. 4 Jul 1990, Calgary, Alta.; given name: David; m. Mary; c. Joanne, Norman; ret'd Fina Petroleum; jr., sr. Calgary; pro Syracuse '33-34; NY Americans '34-39, Maple Leafs '39-46; Calder Memorial Trophy '35; NHL scoring titles '35-36; mem. 2 Stanley Cup winners; once each 1st, 2nd all-star teams; NHL record: 201g, 204a; mem. Alta. Sports, Hockey Hall of Fame.

SCHROETER, Reg (hockey); b. 11 Sep 1921, Ottawa, Ont.; d. 30 Jul 2002, Ottawa, Ont.; m. Norma Elizabeth Thomas (d); c. Thomas, Carol Ann; m. Shirley Luce Howe; sc. Heather, Bill; ret'd Air Transport Board, ret'd dept Indian & Northern Affairs; mem. '48 RCAF Flyers Olympic (12g, 5a), world amateur hockey champions; refereed for 17yrs; as '48 Olympic team mem. Ottawa Sports Hall of Fame.

SCHUETTE, Tom (football); b. 10 Jan 1945, East St. Louis, Ill.; given name: Thomas Paul; Indiana, BSc; realtor associate, restaurateur; all-American coaches 1st team, *Sport Magazine* 2nd team, hon. mention *AP, UPI* as og Indiana; all-Big-10; all-academic Big-10 '66; played in East-West Shrine all-star game '66; Balfour Award Indiana for athletic, academic excellence; pro Ottawa '67-77; mem. 4 Grey Cup champions, 2 all-star games; twice topped East in CFL all-pro countdown series, 2nd, 3rd nationally; res. St. Agustine, Fla.

SCHULER, Laura (hockey): b. 3 Dec 1970, Scarborough, Ont.; Northeastern, UofT BSc; coach; attended 3 ntl soccer championships with Scarborough United; hockey fwd with Toronto Aeros '81-84, Scarborough Firefighters '84-89; Northeastern Huskies '89-94, Toronto Red Wings in COWHL, UofT Lady Blues from '94; ntl team 11yrs; 7 world, 2 Pacific Rim, 1 3-Nations Cup titles; mem. '98 Olympic (silver) team; coach UMass. '03-04; res. Boston, Mass.

SCHULZE, Rudy (shooting); b. 31 Oct 1928, Berlin, Germany; m. Eva; c. Karin, Christina; merchant; began competitive shooting with sporting rifles Woodstock '55; 1st major competition '56 Ont. outdoor championships; organized Norwich Rifle Club; instrumental in formation Ont. Sporting Rifle Assn.; founding pres.; chair. sporting rifle section CCAM '62; mem. '66 world championships, '67 PAG, '68 Olympic, '61, '65 Pershing Trophy teams; ntl sporting rifle champion '65; mem. silver medal teams '67 Canada Winter Games, PAG; mem. Germany's Wiesbadener Schutzengellschaft organization '69-75; German Landesmeister (provincial) champion; v-p., coach Ont. ISU rifle team; res. Waterloo, Ont.

SCHWENDE, Carl (fencing); b. 20 Feb 1920, Basel, Switzerland; d. 30 Dec 2002, Montreal, Que.; m. Claire; c. Heidi, Maria; estimator-designer; competed in Switzerland, France '33-47; competed for Montreal Palestre Nationale from '49; coach Immaculate Conception '56, Notre Dame Centre '59; mem. '54, '58, '62 BE, '59 PAG, '60 Olympic Games teams; gold team sabre, silver team épée, individual épée, bronze team foil '54, silver team épée '58, silver team sabre, bronze team foil, épée '62 BEG; bronze team foil, sabre '59 PAG; flag-bearer '60 summer Olympics; supervisor PQFA '52-56; mem. National Fencing Comm. '53-61; pres. PQFA '56; coach McGill fencing team '59, '66-67; pres. Que. Branch AAUofC '62-67; pres. CFA; pres./dir. Que. Sports Hall of Fame; OUA men's saber title trophy bears his name; mem. Cdn Amateur, Que. Sports halls of fame.

SCHWENGERS, Bernie (tennis): b. 26 May 1880, Surrey, Eng.; d. 6 Dec 1946, Victoria, B.C.; given name: Bernhard Peter; gifted all-around athlete excelling in tennis, baseball, soccer, rugby, t&f, polo, basketball, field hockey, cricket, golf, lacrosse; 3 Vancouver LTC titles; 7 Victoria LTC titles; 6 BC Open, 7 BC Mainland titles; 6 Pacific Northwest titles; Oregon, Quebec singles titles; 2 ntl open singles titles; Middlesex, Eng., all-England singles titles; mem. '13-14 Davis Cup teams; mem. Cdn Amateur, Cdn Tennis, BC, Greater Victoria, Canada's Sports halls of fame.

SCOCCIA, Sam (football): b. 27 Jul 1928, Hamilton; d. 12 May 1996, Hamilton, Ont.; givan name: Samuel Patrick; m. Mary Elizabeth; c. Susan, Debra, Jacqueline; refrigeration mechanic; mg CFL Hamilton '51, Saskatchewan '52-54, Ottawa '55-65; *Globe & Mail* IRFU Cdn all-star '57; all-Cdn '63; mem. '60 Grey Cup champions; line coach Hamilton Hurricanes '69-70; line coach McMaster early '70s; mem. Ticats alumni assn.; McMaster Lettermen's/friends-of-distinction award; mem. McMaster Sports Hall of Fame.

SCODELLARO, Duke (hockey); b. 23 May 1914, Maple Leaf, Alta.; d. (circa 2000), Trail. B.C.; given name: Dulio Joseph; m. Jeanne Marie Lepage; c. Janice, Darrel; ret'd office equipment technician; goalie Bellevue Intermediates '31-35, Coleman Srs. '35-37; mem. Trail Smoke Eaters '37-41, '45-52; Allan Cup, World championship teams '38-39; 7 shutouts in 12 playoff games, acclaimed Western Cdn Amateur Hockey's outstanding goalie; pro tryouts NYR, Vancouver Lions; mem. Toronto RCAF all-Ont. champions '43-45; BCAHA outstanding player award.

SCORRAR, Doug (t&f); b. 9 Sep 1948, Auckland, N.Z.; given name: Douglas Alfred; m. Janis Grace Anderson; c. Brendan Alfred Anderson, Grace Margaret Anderson; Ohio State, BSc, MA; account federal govt.; Sport Canada consultant '80-90; ntl midget mile record 4:24.9 '64; ntl HS 2-mile record 9:16.6 '65, 9:12.3 '67; OFSSA 2-mile title '65-67, jr. international 3-mile title '67; Big 10 Conf. x-country '68, 2 other Big 10 titles, 3-mile runnerup '70; Ohio State records 2-mile indoor, 1, 2, 3, 6-mile outdoor, 2, 4-mile outdoor relay; 6 ntl titles; mem. ntl team '75-76; 10,000m champion '76; Bermuda international marathon '77; distance running coach; dir. NCM '88-00; res. Ottawa, Ont.

SCOTT, Abbie (basketball); b. 6 Oct 1902, Cheyenne, Wyo.; d. 24 Feb 1991, Edmonton, Alta.; given name: Abigail Esther; m. Robert Kennedy (d); c. Lois Anne; Edmonton Business Coll.; ret'd secretary; mem. famed Edmonton

Grads '22-24, 30 games 184 points, 6.1 avg.; mem. Canadian Basketball, Alta. Sports halls of fame.

SCOTT, Barbara Ann (figure skating); b. 9 May 1928, Ottawa, Ont.; m. Thomas V. King; at 10 youngest to pass gold figures test; ntl jr. title '40; sr. champion '44-48; NA titlist '45-48; world champion '47-48; Olympic gold '48; 1st NA to win European, Olympic titles same year; pro '49-54 with Skating Sensation, Hollywood Ice Review; pro skating judge; trained, showed horses as hobby; with Tipper, who died at 34, won more than 400 trophies during 30-year span; Lou Marsh Trophy '45, '47, '48; 3 Bobbie Rosenfeld awards; Officer Order of Canada; named to *SI* Canadian athletes-of-century list; mem. Cdn Figure Skating, Cdn Amateur (Olympic), Ottawa, Canada's Sports Halls, Canada's Walk of Fame; res. Amelia Island, Fla.

SCOTT, Beckie (skiing); b. 1 Aug 1974, Vegreville, Alta.; given name: Rebecca Anne; m. Justin Wadsworth; full-time athlete; competed '98 Olympics; rewrote Cdn record book since first making ntl team '94; 1st NA woman to win Olympic medal in cross-country skiing (pursuit race, '02); original bronze boosted to silver, later to gold, when Russian skiers guilty of drug use; placed in top 10 in each of her other three '02 Olympic events; 3 World Cup sprint medals '02-03 season: bronze Linz AUT, silver Asiago ITA, Borlange SWE; ardent advocate of drug-free sport, in an athletes' petition demanding establishment of independent drug-testing body for all World Cup, Olympic competitions; UNICEF Canada Special representative for challenging fellow athletes at '01 Continental Cup to donate their prize money to Afghanistan relief project; John Semmelink award '03; res. Bend, Oregon.

SCOTT, Debbie (t&f); b. 16 Dec 1958, Victoria, B.C.; m. Ron Bowker; UVic, BEd; teacher; mem. UVRC; BC jr. 3000m, ntl jr. 1500m, 3000m '76; ntl 1500m '77; mem. '77 Pacific Conf., World Cup, FISU Games, '78, '82, '86, '90, '94 CG, '87 PAG, '84, '88, '92 Olympic Games; '79, '81 World Cup x-country, '81-82 European tour teams; CIAU 1500m, 3000m titles '81-82, Sweden International 800m, Oslo Games, ntl 1500m, WC trials 3000m '81; ntl outdoor 1500m, 3000m, 5th Avenue mile '82; ntl sr. 5000m record (15:48.99) '82 Prefontaine Classic; ntl outdoor 1500 title '91; sr. ntl, Commonwealth record (4:29.67) '82 Oslo mile, (4:23.96) '82 5th Ave. mile; ntl record (8:48.85) 3000m Koblenz, Germany '82; 1500, 3000 silver '86 CG, 1500 silver '87 PAG; mem. Greater Victoria Sports Hall of Fame; res. Victoria, B.C.

SCOTT, Mike (canoeing); b. 1 Dec 1930, Ottawa, Ont.; given name: Patrick; m. Lola Lewis; c. Jennifer, David, Judy; Carleton; ret'd asst. product planner; competitive paddler '49-61; x-country ski racer '52-60; mem. RCAF Rockcliffe, YMCA boxing clubs '53-58; coached boxing YMCA, Ottawa Boys Club, Beaver Boxing Club; coach, administrator; commodore Rideau Canoe Club '61-85; organizing chair. 7 ntl championship regattas; coached minor hockey '74-75; competitor several Canadian Ski Marathons; competed annually in National Capital Marathon from inception, '78 Skylon Marathon, '79 NY Marathon; Ottawa ACT Sportsman of '71; National Health & Welfare Operation Lifestyle award '79; author *The Rideau Canoe Club: A Century of Paddling 1902-2002;*

mem. Ottawa Sports Hall of Fame; res. Nepean, Ont.

SCOTT, Norman (hockey/figure skating/golf); b. 19 Mar 1892, Ottawa, Ont.; d. 2 Oct 1981, Montreal, Que.; given name: Norman Mackie; m. Margery Northey; c. Margery Ann; McGill B.Eng; engineer; at 16 mem. Ottawa Cliffsides '08 Allan Cup champions; '10 intercollegiate hockey title; began figure skating Minto Club; won '14 Cdn, US singles, pairs titles; silver '20 ntl singles, fours; Royal Ottawa golf club title '15; 6 Royal Montreal club titles; set Royal Montreal amateur record 69; capt. 3 Cdn Lesley Cup teams; RCGA amateur runnerup '21; partnered with Prince of Wales in '27 golf match; pres. QGA '30; nicknamed "Skinch".

SCOTT, Tom (football); b. 19 Nov 1951, California; m. Susan; c. Carey, Elizabeth; San Mateo Jr. Coll., Washington; Wash. receiving record; all-Pac. 8, 2nd team all-American; drafted Detroit NFL; opted for CFL Winnipeg '74-77, Edmonton '78-83, Calgary '84; CFL rookie of '74; established all-time CFL reception yardage record with 10,837 on 649 catches '84; 6 times 1000yds plus season; CFL record 88 td passes; mem. 5 consec. Grey Cup winners; mem. Cdn Football Hall of Fame; res. Tucson, Ariz.

SCOTT, Vince (football); b. 10 Jul 1925, Leroy, N.Y.; d. 13 Jul 1992, Hamilton, Ont.; div.; c. Joseph, Robert, Vincent Jr., Gail; Notre Dame, BSc; radio sports commentator; 9 athletic letters HS football, track, baseball; twice Western NY State football all-star; mem. '43 Western NY State championship football team; NY State sectional shot put champion '43; mem. '46 ntl football champions; Pitts all-opponents team '45; pro Buffalo (NFL '47-48, title game vs Cleveland '48; Hamilton (CFL) '49-62, Eastern all-star 10 times; Stuke's '54 dream team; twice Ted Reeves' all-Canada team; '55 coaches dream team; Jack Matheson's '67 all-pro team chosen for *US All-Pro Magazine*; Hamilton's Fabulous Fifty's all-star team; Eastern team of century; in 4 all-star games; twice honored by 'day' ('48 Buffalo, Hamilton qb club); Batavia, N.Y., Notre Dame Booster Club outstanding athlete of decade; coached Oakville Black Knights (ORFU) 3yrs, Hillfield College Hamilton 3yrs; mem. 6 Grey Cup finalists, 2 winners; mem. Canadian Football Hall of Fame.

SEAGRAM, Joseph (horse racing); b. 15 Apr 1841, Fisher's Mill, Ont., d. 18 Aug 1919, Waterloo, Ont.; m. Stephanie Urbs; c. Edward, Thomas, Norman, Joseph, Alice; Brant Stratton's Business Coll.; distiller; parlayed business success into horse racing dynasty; his horses claimed 15 Queen's Plate winners; obtaining English broodmares he established a string of Ont.-bred champions on his Waterloo farm; pres. OJC; only Cdn hon. mem. English Jockey Club; mem. Canadian Horse Racing Hall of Fame.

SEARS, John (golf): b. 17 Jan 1936, Fredericton, N.B.; given name: John Patrick; mem. FHS Class L NB basketball title team '53, NB interscholastic rugby title team '53, Fredericton Capitals Maritime Intermediate A '60 title team; Fredericton GC jr. title '51-53, sr. '68; NB-PEI amateur titles '60, '65, Nfld. '72; 4 NB-PEI district titles, 2 Madawaska Invitationals, 2 PEI Opens, runnerup once; low scorer 4 NB-PEI Willingdon Cup trials; mem. 8 NB-PEI Willingdon Cup teams; 4 Frank Robertson trophies; NB jr. golf scholarship program bears his name; mem. NB Sports Hall of Fame; res. Fredericton, N.B.

SECORD, Al (hockey): b. 3 Mar 1958, Sudbury, Ont.; given name: Alan Edward William; m. Tracy Shaw; pilot American Airlines; lw; jr. St. Catharines, Hamilton OHA '76-78; Memorial Cup '76; drafted by Boston '78; minor pro Rochester, Springfield AHL; NHL Boston '78-81, Chicago '81-87, '89-90, Toronto '87-89, Philadelphia '89; NHL record: 12 seasons, 766 scheduled games, 273g, 222a, 102 playoff games, 21g, 34a; scored 54g '83; res. Dallas, TX/Elmhurst, Ill.

SEELY, Glen (golf/baseball); b. 4 Sep 1928, Saint John, N.B.; m. Pauline Rouleau; c. Kim, Jamie, Cindy; merchant; pitcher Ottawa Nationals baseball team '48, '50, Sudbury '48-49, Ogdensburg, N.Y., part of '50 season; lefthander 40-5 record over 2 seasons; mem. Rivermead GC from '63; 3 Alexander of Tunis titles; Que. Willingdon Cup team mem.; res. Nepean, Ont.

SEIBERT, Earl (hockey); b. 7 Dec 1911, Kitchener, Ont.; d. 16 May 1990, Agawam, Mass.; given name: Earl Walter; def. Springfield (AHL) '29-31, NYR '31-35, Chicago '35-45, Detroit '45-46; all-star 10 consecutive seasons, 4 times first team; NHL record: 89g, 187a, plus 11g, 8a in playoffs; following serious concussion became 1st player to wear helmet in AHL; with father Oliver, 1st father-son combination Hockey Hall of Fame.

SEIBERT, Oliver (hockey); b. 18 Mar 1881, Berlin, Ont., d. 15 May 1944, Kitchener, Ont.; goalie, later forward, on team comprised solely of family members; 6 seasons mem. champion Berlin Rangers (WOHA); pro Houghton, Mich., '07; London, Guelph in Ont. pro, Northwestern Mich. leagues; wearing old rocker skates once beat a trotter in one-mile match race on Grand River ice despite fact trotter set mile record 2:13; with son Earl 1st father-son combination Hockey Hall of Fame.

SEILING, Rod (hockey/administration); b. 14 Nov 1944, Elmira, Ont.; given name: Rodney Albert; m. Sharon Bland; c. Michael, Bradley; Wilfrid Laurier, BA; pres. Greater Toronto Hotel Assn., Ontario Hotel & Motel Assn.; former exec.v-p. Racetracks of Canada; def. Rangers '64-75, Toronto '75-76, St.Louis '77-79, Atlanta '79; Team Canada '72; NHL record: 979 scheduled games, 62 goals, 269 assists, 77 playoff games, 4 goals, 8 assists; licensed standardbred owner, trainer; GM Elmira Raceway '79-82; exec. v-p. Racetracks of Canada '82; helped found NHLPA, mem. player-owner council which negotiated 1st collective agreement in NHL; turned Elmira track from losing to profitable operation; former mem. ORC advisory board; dir. Racetracks of Canada, Racing Hall of Fame, Harness Tracks of Ont.; former mem. CTA, USTA, Cdn Standardbred Horse Society, Ont. Standardbred Breeders Improvement Assn.; pres. NHL Oldtimers charity hockey team; ex-co-ordinator ntl Race Against MS harness div.; chair. Team Canada '72 Representation Inc.; v-p. corp. dev. OJC 3yrs; res. Toronto, Ont.

SEITZ, Tyler (luge); b. 13 Aug 1976, Calgary, Alta.; journeyman training, ntl luge team assistant coach/

millwright; ntl team '96-03; bronze '97 jr. worlds; mem. '98, '02 Olympic teams; competed 3 world championships; 4 top-10 WC career results, including bronze '02; 4 ntl titles; res. Calgary, Alta.

SELANNE, Teemu (hockey): b. 3 Jul 1970, Helsinki, Finland; m. Sirpa; c. Eemil, Eetu, Leevi; played with Jokerit, Finland, '87-92, league leading scorer, mem. Finnish ntl. title team; mem. Finnish team '89 world jr., '91 Canada Cup, worlds, '92, '96 (bronze), '02 Olympics, '99 worlds; drafted by Winnipeg '88 but didn't join Jets until '92-96; Anaheim '96-'01, San Jose '01-03; Colorado '03-04; impressive rookie season with 76 goals; also scored 51g '97 52 '98; Calder Memorial trophy '93; *HN, Beckett, SN* rookie of '93; NHL/Upper Deck rookie team; 2 1st team all-star; 7 NHL all-star games, '98 MVP; nicknamed "Finnish Flash", "Salami", "Flying Finn"; active interest in auto racing, car collecting; NHL record (through '04): 879 scheduled games, 452g, 499a, 49 playoff games, 18g, 15a; passed 300g '99; initial recipient Rocket Richard trophy '99; active in children's charities; co-owner Finnish hockey club; res. Helsinki, Finland/Anaheim, Calif.

SELKE, Frank Sr. (hockey/builder); b. 7 May 1893, Berlin, Ont.; d. 3 Jul 1985, Rigaud, Que.; given name: Frank Joseph Aloysius; m. Mary Agnes Schmidt; c. Blanche, Chilton, Evelyn, Audrey, Delphine, Frank, Geraldine; electrician, ret'd hockey exec.; managed first hockey team (bantam) at 13; also managed teams to minor city, provincial softball, baseball, hockey titles; managed 3 Memorial Cup winners; associated with Conn Smythe in early days of Maple Leafs; managed Toronto to 3 Stanley Cups; GM Canadiens '46-64, 6 Stanley Cup champions; also managed 1 Allan Cup champion; founding dir. Hockey Hall of Fame; prominent in construction Maple Leaf Gardens, Cincinnati Gardens, Rochester War Memorial, numerous other arenas; Frank J. Selke Trophy awarded annually to best defensive forward in NHL; mem. Canada's Sports, Hockey halls of fame.

SELKIRK, George (baseball); b. 4 Jan 1899, Huntsville, Ont.; d. 19 Jan 1987, Ft. Lauderdale, Fla.; given name: George Alexander; nicknamed "Twinkletoes"; led Toronto (IL) in HRs '32; mem. Yankees '34-42; became regular replacing Babe Ruth in outfield; ML record: 846 games, 810h, 503r, 576rbi, 49sb, .290ba; GM Washington Senators '64-69; 6 World Series, batting .265 in 21 games; twice drove in 100 or more runs; mem. Canadian Baseball Hall of Fame.

SELLER, Peggy (all-around); b. 23 Jan 1905, Edinburgh, Scotland; d. 31 Mar 1996, Newmarket, Ont.; given name: Margaret Cameron Shearer; m. Dr. Reg Seller; c. Marna, Donald; competing in 1st competition in world sanctioned by a swimming governing body won Que. synchronized swim title '24; all Royal Life Saving Awards '24; 5 Que., ntl 3m diving titles; capt. 3 ntl water polo title teams; helped write rules for Gale Trophy, emblematic of ntl synchro. swim championship; won Gale Trophy 1st 4 times; standout in hockey, basketball, volleyball, baseball, tennis, figure skating, t&f; provincial titles javelin, 100yd dash, bj, relays; first woman secty. FINA, CASA Que. section; secty.-treas. CASA '48-50, Cdn Royal Life Saving Society 10yrs; wrote FINA synchro. swim rules '52; wrote descriptive rule book on sport, co-authored with US champion Beulah

Gundling book on Aquatic Art; v-p. International Academy of Aquatic Art '54; hon. mem. IAAA, CSSA; mem. Pointe Claire SC advisory board; mem. Canadian, US Aquatic, Intl. Swimming, Canada's Sports halls of fame.

SELTZER, Sheila (curling); b. 29 Oct 1938, Iroquois Falls, Ont.; given name: Sheila Evelyn Peever; m. J.R. Chucker Ross; Stratford Teachers' College; ret'd school teacher; from '70-84 curled in 15 Ont. title playdowns in business girls, ladies, srs., mixed; runnerup '75 Ont. Business Girls; skipped '78, '81 Ont. Lassie title rinks; 3rd on NO Seagram Mixed title winner '82; skip 2 ntl sr. women's title rinks; 3rd on Toronto Royals Molson's champions '77; skipped Ottawa Crystal Pebble winner '79, '97, Ottawa Molson's Masters champion '80; 3rd on '81 Bowling Green, Ohio, International mixed title rink; all-star skip NO sr. women's title rink '94; mem. Sudbury Northland AC; Burlington 12-mile relay road race champion, Brantford 6-mile masters road race, 10-mile Hamilton masters road race titles '78; avid windsurfer; with husband has achieved official instructor status and has windsurfed as far south as Caribbean; Sudbury female athlete of '81; res. Subury, Ont.

SELWOOD, Brad (hockey/coaching); b. 18 Mar 1948, Leamington, Ont.; given name: Bradley Wayne; m. Bonnie Murdison; c. Ryan, Kevin; GM car dealership, hockey exec.; catcher Essex jr. baseball title teams '64-65; played baseball to age 18 when he shifted full attention to hockey; played minor hockey in Leamington, Essex systems; mem. Leamington Ont. juvenile champs '66; Jr. B St. Thomas '67; Jr. A Niagara Falls Memorial Cup champs '68; drafted by TML '68; CHL with Tulsa '68-69, '70-71, Houston, Fort Worth '80-81; WHL Vancouver '69-70, rookie of yr; NHL TML '70-72, LA '79-80 (169 scheduled games, 7g, 40a); drafted by New England (WHA) '72-79 (494 scheduled games, 48g, 155a); 3 WHA all-star; Team Canada '75 Summit series; AHL New Haven '81-82; asst. coach LA Kings '82-83; coached hockey, baseball in Toronto region from '84; minor hockey Thornhill '84-93; London Jr. A '96-97; coach/GM Aurora '97-00, Newmarket '00-03; 5 coach of yr awards; minor baseball Thornhill '84-92, Leaside jr. sr. teams '93-99; GM Oshawa Generals OHL from '03; mem. Windsor/Essex Sports Hall of Fame; res. Sharon, Ont.

SENECAL, Jean-François (shooting); b. 29 Jun 1961, Laval, Que.; engineer; mem. '79-83 Benito Juarez, '82, '86, '90, '94 CG, '83, '87, '95 PAG, '84, '88, '92. '96 Olympic, '82-83 world championship teams; 2 gold, 2 silver, 1 bronze CG; 2 gold, 7 silver, 1 bronze PAG; Shooting Fed. golden anniversary award '82; fed. govt. excellence award '83; res. Chomedy, Que.

SENKLER, Harry (rowing); b. 24 Jul 1866, Brockville, Ont.; d. 1926, Vancouver, B.C.; given name: John Henry; m. Margaret Richards; Upper Canada College, Osgoode Hall; lawyer (KC); capt. Argonaut ntl title crews '91-92; rugby star UofT; international cricketer; standout sprinter UofT; standout baseball player; capt. Vancouver Boating Club '95-98, Vancouver Rowing Club '99-1900, '23; mem. Cdn. Olympic Comm.

SENOS, Eddie (boxing); b. 25 Mar 1928, Ottawa, Ont.; given name: Edward; m. Lorraine Lecusson; c. Stephen,

Thomas, James Scott; ret'd auto salesman; Ont. golden gloves title '45, Que. '46; bronze '48 Olympic trials; Ont. middleweight titles '50, '52; bronze '54 BEG trials; mem. Canadian Boxing Hall of Fame; res. Nepean, Ont.

SERVOLD, Clarence (skiing); b. 1927, Camrose, Alta.; m. Marjorie Webster; c. Marty, Connie, David, Luann; Seattle, Denver BSc; ret'd civil engineering consultant; played hockey as youth but became enamoured with Nordic skiing as jr. mem. Camrose SC; 2 US college titles with Denver '56-60; competed '54 ntl championships Sweden, Finland, Norway; won Cdn ntl 15km, 30km. Nordic combined titles '55; mem. '56 (19th in 15km, 22 in 50km was highest finish to that time by any NA X-C skier) '60 Olympic team; ntl seniors 15km X-C title '64; enjoyed considerable success at masters level; involved in coaching Alta. jr., ntl X-C teams; played active role in establishing Nordic Combined skiing popularity across Canada; chair. jumping/Nordic combined '90 Alta. winter games; worked with CODA; 1st Cdn on FIS XC comm.; mem. Alta. Sports, Cdn Skiing halls of fame; res. Camrose, Alta.

SERVOLD, Irvin (skiing); b. 14 Nov 1932, Camrose, Alta.; given name: Irvin Benjamen; m. Eleanor Bernice Vekved; c. Mark, Helen-Marie, Jon, Niel, Ingrid, Daniel; Seattle, UAlta, BEd, BPhE; teacher; learned to ski using barrel staves as skis, poplar trees for poles; Alta. x-country, jumping titles; ntl jr. jumping title '50; 11 ntl sr. Nordic combined titles '53-68; mem. '56, '60 Olympic teams; ntl team coach; conducted officials' clinics for Canada Winter Games '72, '75; UAlta Nordic coach '57-62; coach FISU Games '72; x-country coach Miasama ski games Japan '73; co-founder Devon Nordic Ski Club; ntl x-country ski chairman '68-69, '71, '73; mem. ntl x-country program comm. '68-75; Alta. div. tech. chair. '76-98; UAlta male athlete of '62; International Intercollegiate x-country champion '58-61; Alta. sports service award '80; mem. Cdn Skiing; Alta. Sports halls of fame; res. Devon, Alta.

SEVIGNY, Chantal (speed skating): b. 13 Jul 1975, Sherbrooke, Que.; Ahuntsic Coll.; began speed skating age 8; although deaf she relies on coaches and shadows cast by fellow competitors to help her during competition; 2 gold, 3 silver '95 Canada Games; qualified as substitute on Cdn world team '95; mem. '98 Olympic team; res. Montreal, Que.

SEWELL, Don (shooting): b. 22 Jun 1927, Winnipeg, Man.; given name: Donald Ferrand; m. Doran Westhead; c. Dena, Lori, Gren, Michael, Kip; UMan; ret'd Air Canada; began target shooting age 8; 1st major win Man. Air Cadet League sporting rifle high aggregate '43; joined St. James Rifle Club '47; Man. title '48; won every division indoor, outdoor match '49-60; mem. 4 Cdn Dewar teams; perfect 400 '58; won Red River Valley titles '53-57; final .22 competition '62; switched to full-bore '60; mem. 18 Bisley teams, 3 McKinnon match, 1 Africa, Empire match, St. Georges Cross, *Daily Telegraph* match titles; Cdn Target Rifle title '65, '89, '94; competed '73 Canada Summer Games; 5 Man. Lieut.-Gov. gold medals, 9 Man. target rifle titles; mem. 4 Palma teams, 2 silver medals; Man. Intl Honors Supreme '75; twice missed opportunity to compete in CG due to work/injury; mem. Man. Sports, DCRA halls of fame; res. Winnipeg, Man.

SEWELL, Doran (shooting): b. 26 Dec 1932, Manchester, Eng.; given name: Doran Westhead; m. Don Sewell; c. Dena, Lori, Gren, Michael, Kip; Man. Rifle Assn. Historian, ret'd Revenue Canada appeals officer; developed interest in full-bore shooting while serving with Northern Rhodesia police force '53; 1st woman in Africa to win NRA Donegall medal '56; numerous Rhodesian titles '54-60; served on exec. Northern Rhodesia RA, Chingola RC; moved to Canada '60 after making initial Bisley appearance; represented Alta. provincially, internationally '61-67; wed and moved to Man. '67; 1st woman in world mem. Palma team '67, won gold; mem. 3 Cdn Palma teams, '73 silver; ntl small-bore postal title '71; ntl women's title '90; numerous provincial titles from '68; MPRA team adjutant '73, commandant '76; competed '73 Canada Summer Games; capt. Cdn CG team '84, adjutant '87, commandant '95 Cdn Bisley team; competed 4 Bisley teams; Man. target rifle title '94; Man. Lieut.-Gov gold medal '93, Intl Honors Supreme award '75; exec. MPRA from '68; DCRA exec.; Man. Sports Fed. dir. 2yrs; mem. Man. Sports Hall of Fame; res. Winnipeg, Man.

SHACK, Eddie (hockey): b. 11 Feb 1937, Sudbury, Ont.; given name: Edward Steven Phillip; m. Norma Given; c. Cathy, Timmy; owner Eddie Shack donut shops; jr. Guelph Biltmores; NYR '58-61, Toronto '61-67, Boston '67-69, Los Angeles '69-71, Buffalo '71-72, Pittsburgh '72-75; NHL record: 1047 scheduled games, 239g, 226a, 74 playoff games, 6g, 7a; mem. 4 Stanley Cup winners; dir. NHL Oldtimers Assn.; ref. OT challenge games; nicknamed "The Entertainer"; spokesman Prostate Cancer Foundation; res. Toronto, Ont.

SHAKESPEARE, Shannon (swimming): b. 6 May 1977, Mission, B.C.; Michigan; freestyle, breaststroke specialist; 7 all-American, 5 Big-10 titles; mem. ntl team from '93; 7 ntl titles, 88 ntl records; gold, silver '95 world short-course championships; ntl, Commonwealth 50m FS (sc) record, ntl 100m FS (sc) record; competed '92 eight-nations youth meet, '93, '97 Pan-Pacific, world short course championships; 2 bronze '94 CG; 4 silver '95 PAG; 4 Canada Cup gold '96; mem. '96, '00 Olympic teams; Big-10 swimmer of '00 award; res. Winnipeg, Man.

SHANAHAN, Brendan (hockey): b. 23 Jan 1969, Mimico, Ont.; m. Catharine; c. Jack, Maggie; lw; jr. London OHL '85-87; drafted by New Jersey '87; NHL New Jersey '87-91, St. Louis '91-95, Hartford '95-96, Detroit '96-03; NHL record (through '04): 1268 scheduled games, 558g, 593a, 151 playoff games, 52g, 65a; scored 51g '93, 52 '94; passed 500g '02; 3 Stanley Cup winners; 2 NHL 1st team all-star; 3 NHL all-star games; mem. Team Canada '87 Jr. Worlds, Team Canada '91 Canada Cup, '94 worlds, '96 World Cup, '98, '02 (gold) Olympics; hon. chair. Michigan Alzheimer's Disease Research Centre charity softball game; became US citizen '02; jersey #19 ret'd by London Knights; res. Simsbury, CT.

SHANKS, Vicki (racquetball): b. 14 Feb 1965, N. Vancouver, B.C.; m. Paul; UBC, BPhE; HS teacher; 8yrs ntl team; 4 ntl women's doubles titles; 4 Tournament of the Americas silver; 4 world women's doubles silver; women's doubles (with partner Debbie Ward) silver '95 PAG; active marathon runner; res. N. Vancouver, B.C.

SHANNON, Carver (football): b. 28 Apr 1938, Corinth, Miss.; given name: Carver Beauregard; m. Loraine; c. Michael; Southern Illinois, B.S., UCLA, MA; aircraft co. mgr; numerous Southern Illinois football records including scoring for one game, season and career, best rushing avg. game, season, career; track record 9.4 for 100yds; led US major college scorers '56; twice all-American; voted school's greatest athlete '75; pro Winnipeg '59-61, Hamilton '61; 2 Grey Cup finals, 1 winner; Los Angeles (NFL) '62; led Rams in yardage, best avg. single game on punt returns, most pass interceptions '62; second in NFL kickoff returns, 3rd punt returns '63; all pro dhb '64; pro tennis umpire; Pac-10 football official; res. Los Angeles, Calif.

SHAPKA, Guy (rodeo): b. 23 May 1963, Calgary, Alta; m. Tammy; c. Tanner, Teagan; rancher; saddle bronc specialist; CPRA mem. from '84; CPRA, PRCA rookie of '84 awards; ntl SB title '87; 1 BC, SK SB titles; CPRA cowboy of '02 award; res. Alix, Alta.

SHARPE, Tony (t&f): b. 28 Jun 1961, Jamaica; m. Colleen Taffe; employee Xerox; sprint specialist; York; mem. Scarborough Optimists TC; mem. '79, '83 PAG, '80, '84 Olympic, '82 CG, '83 FISU Games teams; ntl 100m, 400m, 4x200m relay titles; silver 4x100m relay '82 CG; bronze 4x100m relay '84 Olympics; ntl sr. record 200m (20.22), 4x100 relay (38.43); ntl sr. record, world best 4x200m (1:23.97) '83; Dr. Fred Tees Memorial Trophy (top CIAU athlete) '82; res. Pickering, Ont.

SHARPLES, Jim (curling): b. 16 Mar 1936, Oshawa, Ont.; given name: James Douglas; m. Sandra; c. Donna, Grant; UofT, BComm; Cornell, MA; Osgoode Hall, LLB; lawyer; competed 9 Ont. Consols/Tankard; won 3 Labatt Challenge Rounds; 3 Silver Tankard titles; 5 Ont. seniors titles, twice runnerup; Canadian seniors champion skip '89, '92; 45 ntl srs. wins; chair. organization, constitution, rules comm. OCA '87-93; v-p OCA '92-94, pres. '95-96; res. Markham, Ont.

SHASKE, Ed Jr. (shooting): b. 19 Jan 1957, Edmonton, Alta., d. 31 Mar 1982, Edmonton, Alta.; given name: Edward Mark; UAlta; real estate appraiser; above avg. jr. hockey player; offered several US college hockey scholarships; coach midget B team; Industrial HL dir. '79-81; trap shooting specialist; ntl trapshooting team mem. '77-82; 5 international world trapshooting title competitions; officiated '76 Olympics, trapshooting chairman '78 CG; US Pacific Coast champion '77; mem. gold medal team '78 Benito Juarez matches; mem. '80 Olympic team; tied for 1st '80 British Grand Prix; tied 2nd '80 Brazilian Grand Prix; runnerup '81 Cdn International trapshoot; '81 Western Cdn title; organized, coached Edmonton jr. shooting program '79-80; mem. organizing comm. '83 World Moving Target championships; Edmonton achievement awards '77-78, '81; Alta. achievement awards '78, '80; mem. Alta. Sports Hall of Fame.

SHATTO, Dick (football): b. 23 Jun 1933, Springfield, Ohio; d. 4 Feb 2003, New Port Richey, Fla.; given name: Richard Darrell; m. Lynne Garlough; c. Randy, Becky, Cindy, Jay, Kathy; Kentucky; resort exec.; football, track star Kentucky; pro Toronto '54-65; fb/hb/sb/fl; 15 Argos offensive records; most points (career) 542, most tds (career) 91, (game) 4, most carries (career) 1322, most yds gained rushing (career) 6958, most 100yd games (career) 16, most receptions (career) 466, most yds gained receiving (career) 6584, most tds rushing (career) 39, (game) 3, most tds receiving (career) 52, most kickoff returns (career) 83, (season) 25, most yds kickoff returns (career) 1991, (season) 636; twice Jeff Russel Memorial Trophy winner; twice runnerup Schenley outstanding player award; 6 EFC all-star, once all-Cdn; rejoined Argos '74 as marketing mgr., media and public relations; managing dir. '76-79; All-Time Argos team '96; jersey #22 ret'd by Argos; daughter Cindy mem. Cdn ntl diving team '71-79; mem. Canadian Football Hall of Fame.

SHAUGHNESSY, Frank Jr. (hockey/football/golf); b. 21 Jun 1911, Roanoke, Va., d. 12 Jun 1982, Montreal, Que.; Loyola, BA, McGill; Bell Canada; son of Shag Shaughnessy; football all-star McGill '34; mem. McGill intercollegiate hockey champions '34-35, Canadian Olympic hockey team '36; coach freshman football, hockey McGill; v-p. Laurentian Ski Zone '52-55; tech. chair. Que. div. CSA '54-55; ntl ski team chair. '54-55; CdM winter Olympic teams '56, '60, '64, '68, '72; COA v-p. '57-82; dir. QGA '58-64; pres. '64; governor RCGA '65-69, chair. '67; pres. Montreal Sportsmen's Assn. '68-72; chair. Air Canada amateur-sport-exec-of-yr award comm. '68-72; mem. Loyola, Cdn Amateur, Canada's Sports halls of fame.

SHAUGHNESSY, Shag (baseball); b. 8 Apr 1884, Amboy, Ill., d. 15 May 1969, Montreal, Que.; given name: Francis Joseph; m. Katherine Quinn; c. 8 sons, 1 daughter; Notre Dame; capt. Notre Dame football, baseball teams '03-04; pro baseball Washington '05, Philadelphia '08, mgr. Roanoke, Va., Fort Wayne, Ind.; coached football 1yr Clemson; introduced option play to US football while coaching at Yale, Cornell; 1st pro McGill football coach '12-28, won 2 Yates Cups, overall record 32-52-4; introduced forward pass to Cdn university football; coached McGill men's, women's hockey teams; managed Ottawa baseball team to 3 straight pennants; formed Cdn Pro Baseball League with teams from Ottawa, Brantford, Guelph, Kitchener and Peterborough; GM Ottawa hockey club; mgr. Hamilton baseball club '19; coach, scout Detroit Tigers; rebuilt Montreal Royals and won 1st Montreal pennant of century '35; instituted playoff system (adopted from hockey) initiating Little World Series; International League pres. '36-60; broke pro baseball's color bar by signing Jackie Robinson to Montreal Royals '46; appointed by baseball commissioner Happy Chandler to recodify baseball rules '49; mem. McGill, Loyola, Cdn Baseball, Football halls of fame.

SHAVER, Ron (figure skating); b. 16 Jun 1951, Galt, Ont.; Detroit; coach FS Club of Texas; gold Skate Canada '74, '76, silver '73, '75; silver Skate Moscow '73; ntl men's singles title '77; competed 4 world championships, '76 Olympics; pro Ice Capades '77; world pro title '81; choreographer ntl championships; level 3 coach; coached Hamilton SC; worked with Special Olympics; mem. Waterloo County Hall of Fame; res. Houston, Tex.

SHAW, Colin (canoeing); b. 17 Mar 1954, Powell River, B.C.; carpenter; ntl jr. K2, K4, sr. K4 1000m '75; sr. K1, K2 500m, 1000m, jr. 500m (ntl jr. record 1:53.24) '79; Olympic trials, Zaandan regatta K4 1000m, ntl K2 500m,

1000m '80; semifinalist K4 500m '81 world championships; Commonwealth Cup K1 500m, 10,000m, K2 500m, ntl K2 500m, 1000m, K4 1000m '81-83; mem. '84 Olympic team; res. Coquitlam, B.C.

SHAW, Dan (football); b. 18 Dec 1933, Toronto, Ont.; d. 5 Mar 1992, Toronto, Ont.; given name: Dan Ross; m. Beverley Ford; c. Stephen, Susan, Dani; sporting goods salesman; Toronto HS all-star two-way gd/t '48-51; Toronto Balmy Beach sr. ORFU '52-53 winning league title latter year, losing to Winnipeg Grey Cup semifinal; Toronto '54-57; secty.-treas. Argo Old Boys; convenor Ont. Junior Football Conf. '65-72, exec. dir. '72-77; mem. founding comm. Argo Playback Club '67, dir. '67-74; v.-chair. Argo Double Blue Club; chair. founding comm. Cdn Football Hall of Fame Club '76; Ont. achievement award '72; CAFA-CFL award '80.

SHAW, Gerry (football); b. 6 Dec 1942, Hamilton, Ont.; given name: Robert Gerald; m. Norma Inkster; c. Bradley, Keri; Washington State, BA; v-p.,dir., investment dealer; college football '62-64; pro Calgary '65-74; twice mem. Western Conf. champions; mem. '71 Grey Cup champions; twice in CFL all-star games; led CFL receivers in td receptions '72 with 12; caught 65 passes for 1002yds '72 season; CFL record: 310 receptions for 4732yds, 34tds; res. Calgary, Alta.

SHAW, Paul (shooting): b. 20 Jun 1949, Collingwood, Ont.; given name: Ian Paul; m. Beverley Milmire; c. Destiny, Drew; UWO LLB; lawyer; trapshooting specialist in Olympic, ATA style; 3 ntl doubles titles; mem. ntl team from '86; 5 all-American ATA trap team; ntl double trap titles '91-93; competed '87 silver, bronze, '95 team silver, '03 PAG; '96 Olympics, multiple world, world cup teams; '03 Ont. open trap title; pres. SFC from '96, Ont. Olympic Trap Assn. from inception; capt. Ont. all-star ATA style teams; numerous championships at Grand American, satellite Grands, state, prov. tournaments; pres, Ont. prov. assn. '92-94; vocal advocate for sport shooting community; res. Collingwood, Ont

SHAW, Wayne (football); b. 24 Feb 1939, Bladworth, Sask. m. Joan; c. Kimberly; Notre Dame College, UofSask; businessman; football '56-58 Notre Dame College; jr. Saskatoon Hilltops '59-60, all-star mlb '59, ot '60, Man.-Sask. Jr. League MVP '60; ntl jr. championship '60; olb Roughriders '61-72; 5 times WFC all-star, once all-Cdn; club's nominee for Schenley award once; mem. 4 Grey Cup finalists, 1 winner; all-time Sask. all-time all-star team; mem. Sask, Sports Hall of Fame; res. Winnipeg, Man.

SHEA, Stu (shooting): b. 5 Jul 1926, Dartford, Ont.; d. 22 Sep 2000, Peterborough, Ont.; given name Stuart Wallace; m. Helen Thackeray; c. Sheldon, Gary, Allan, Terry, Patti, Cathy, Carolyn; hotelier, entrepreneur; skeet shooting specialist; Ont. open overall title '61; NO title, 1 of 3 tied for world crown '62; Cdn open 28-gauge title '64; Ont title, father/son 12-gauge champion '68; Ont. 410 gauge title '75; Cdn high overall, 28-gauge titlist, Ont. all-star '76; top all-around shooter over 50, open 20-gauge inter-American champion, Ont. all-star '77; NO high overall '78; Cdn Open 2-man, 5-man, sub-senior overall winner '79; 400-target marathon 410-gauge title '81; mem. Peterborough Sports Hall of Fame.

SHEAHAN, Pat (football/coaching): b. 10 Oct 1956, Pembroke, Ont.; given name: Patrick; m. Lee McClure; c. Ryan, Erin, Devan; Concordia, BSc, DSA, MA, McGill, BEd; football coach; qb Brockville HS team '72-75; te/ot/og/ctr Concordia '75-79; 2 tryouts with Edmonton (CFL); O-line coach Montreal Jr. Concordes '82-83; Eastern Cdn title '82; asst. coach McGill '84-88, Vanier Cup '87; head coach Concordia '89-99 (61-44-1), Queen's '00-01; outstanding lineman award '77; OQIFC coach of '90; res. Kingston, Ont.

SHEDD, Marjory (badminton); b. 17 Mar 1926, Toronto, Ont.; given name: Marjory Jean; ret'd lab technician, sport instructor; gd '45 ntl jr. basketball champion Carltonettes; led Toronto Montgomery Maids to '50 ntl sr. title; volleyball '59 ntl champion Broadview Y, '60-62 University Settlement Blacks, '65 University Settlement Rebels; coached UofT Ladies volleyball tean '64-74; mem. '67 PAG volleyball, '70 CG badminton teams; finalist ntl badminton singles '51-52; 6 ntl singles, 5 mixed, 14 ladies' doubles titles; mem. 6 Uber Cup teams; mem. Cdn Amateur, Canada's Sports halls of fame; res. Toronto, Ont.

SHEFFIELD, Cathy (judo); b. 6 Aug 1959, Toronto, Ont.; m. Phil Takahashi; c. Christy, Jenny, Emily; York, BA, UofOtt, BEd; mem. ntl team '76-83; 52kg gold '80 Pan-Am championships; ntl 52kg titles '78-79; 4th degree black belt; res. Kanata, Ont.

SHEPHERD, George (t&f); b. 23 Apr 1938, Port Colborne, Ont.; m. Sylvia Mary; c. Craig Andrew; UWO BPHE; HS teacher; ntl 400m hurdles champion '58-63, ntl record '58-65; mem. East York track club 1-mile relay team '60-68, ntl titles, 3:08.6 record; mem. '60 Olympic team; p.-pres. Olympic Club of Canada; res. Toronto, Ont.

SHEPPARD, Gregg (hockey); b. 23 Apr 1949, North Battleford, Sask; m. Karen; ctr Estevan jr. '65-69, Oklahoma (CHL) '69-72, Salt Lake (WHL), Boston (AHL); 2 CHL all-star, MVP Tommy Ivan trophy '72; NHL Boston '72-78 (1 Stanley Cup), Pittsburgh '78-82; NHL record: 657 scheduled games, 206g, 293a, 82 playoff games, 32g, 40a; mem. North Battleford Western Cdn juvenile champs'65; mem. North Battleford Sports Hall of Fame; res. North Battleford, Sask.

SHEPPARD, Ray (hockey): b. 27 May, 1966, Pembroke, Ont.; m. Lucie; c. Lyndsay, Douglas; rw Cornwall (OHL), Rochester (AHL); Buffalo '87-90, NYR '90-91, Detroit '91-95, San Jose '95-96, Florida '96-97, '99-00, Carolina '97-99; scored 52g '94; NHL record: 817 scheduled games, 357g, 300a, 81 playoff games, 30g, 20a; OHL 1st team all-star; NHL all-rookie team; res. Boca Raton, Fla.

SHERIDAN, Juan (football); b. 2 Feb 1925, Havana, Cuba, d. 7 Oct 1969, Ormstown, Que.; m. Elizabeth Hedrick; c. Martha, Gordon, Bob, Bruce, John; UofT; sales rep.; sports dir. HMCS Donnacona, mem. '44 Grey Cup champions; played with Toronto Balmy Beach, Toronto Indians; Montreal Alouettes '48-59, mem. '49 Grey Cup winner; frequent all-star, all-Cdn ctr; nicknamed "The Pear"; asst. coach Queen's.

SHERK, Cathy (golf): b. 17 Jun 1970, Fonthill, Ont.; div.; c. 1 son; golf administrator; teaching pro Niagara Parks Commission; operates Sherkwood Golf School Ltd.; Ont. amateur titles '76, '78; ntl amateur titles '77-78; US amateur champ '78; North-South Women's amateur title '78; low individual world amateur '78; CPGA championship '88, '90-91; Ont athlete of '78; *Golf Digest* women's amateur golfer of '78; co-winner (with Diane Konihowski) Velma Springstead award '78; CLGA advisor/coach '94-99; player dir. du Maurier series; pro co-ordinator Ont. jr. girls camp; Ont. PGA teaching pro of '02; mem. RCGA Hall of Fame; res. Toronto, Ont.

SHERO, Fred (hockey/coaching); b. 23 Oct 1925, Winnipeg, Man.; d. 24 Nov 1990, Camden, N.J.; given name: Fred Alexander; c. Ray; ntl bantam boxing title as teenager; def; jr. St. James, Winnipeg Rangers, NY Rovers, HMCS Chippawa; 3 seasons NYR; 2 Calder Cups with Cleveland (AHL); mem. '56 WHL champion Winnipeg Warriors; player-coach Shawinigan QHL title team'58; 13yrs coaching in minors piloting IHL St. Paul, CPHL St. Paul, Omaha, AHL Buffalo title teams; AHL coach of yr; coached Philadelphia '71-78; concluded coaching career with Rangers '78-81 and Europe; NHL coaching record: 734 scheduled games, 390-225-119; 110 playoff games, 63-47, 2 Stanley Cups; mem. Man. Hockey , Sports halls of fame.

SHERRING, William (t&f); b. 1877, Hamilton, Ont., d. 1964, Hamilton, Ont.; railway brakeman; at 16 won races at Ont. fairs; at 20 3rd Hamilton's around-the-bay race (about 19 miles); won same race '99, '03; 2nd 1900 Boston Marthon; gold '06 special Athens Olympics; took race lead after 2Ω hours, finished in record 2:51:23.6; accompanied over line by Prince George of Greece; finished race weighing 98lbs, a loss of 14lbs during race; mem. Cdn Amateur, Canada's Sports halls of fame.

SHERWOOD, Liv (sailing); b.27 Nov 1923, Ottawa, Ont.; d.7 Jun 2002, Ottawa, Ont.; given name: Livius Anglin; m. Anne Galligan (d); c. Christopher, Mary; UofT, BA, Osgoode Hall; ret'd provincial court judge; international 14' dinghy champion BYC '54-57; Dragon Class '58-60, Shark Class '64-67; Shark Class ntl '64, NA '65 champion; 3 Severn Trophy dinghy titles; p.-pres. St. Lawrence Valley Yachting Assn.; founded BYC jr. program '56; dir. CYA '57-67, '70-83, councillor from '83; CYA rules committee '70-98, chair. '78-81; mem. CYA appeals comm. '70-98, chair. '70-75; International Yachting Racing Union racing rules comm. '74-98; certified international yachting judge '80-98; jury mem./chair. 7 America's Cup, 1 Canada's Cup, 27 world championships; dir. sailing '76 Olympics; Ottawa citizen of '71; Beppe Croce intl sailing award; Rolex CYA sailor-of-yr award; elected CYA Councillor of Honor; mem. Gov.-Gen.'s Curling Club; mem. Ottawa Sports Hall of Fame.

SHEWCHUK, Tammy Lee (hockey); b. 31 Dec 1977, Pointe-Claire, Qué.; Harvard hons BA, fwd; 1st female to play on her atom, pee wee, bantam, midget boys teams; 1st female, non-goalie, to play in Qué. Intl. Pee Wee Tournament '90-91; Team Qué. '91, '95 Canada Games, leading scorer '95; silver, top scorer Team Qué. '95 ntls; ntl women's team from '97; 2 world titles, '02 Olympic gold, 2 gold 3-Nations Cup, 1 gold 4-Nations Cup; gold ntl -22 team '98 Christmas Cup, leading Cdn scorer, all-star; women's US college hockey title, broke Harvard single-season goal, points record as rookie, broke NCAA goal scoring record with 52, 1st team all-American; registered 258th career point '01 to become NCAA's all-time leading scorer for women's hockey; NCAA record career goals (160), assists (147), points (307); finalist Patty Kazmaier Award (top NCAA women's hockey player) '01; Harvard's John Dooley Award for player who best combines sportsmanship, enthusiasm and devotion to her team and to the game; res. St-Laurent, Que.

SHEWFELT, Kyle (gymnastics); b. 6 May 1982, Calgary, Alta.; given name: Kyle Keith; full-time athlete; competed '00, '04 (floor gold) Olympics; silver floor '00 World Cup; gold vault, high bar, silver floor, bronze all around '02 ntls; gold floor, vault, team silver '02 CG; competed '02 worlds; silver floor '02 World Cup; 1st Cdn gymnast invited to participate in Goodwill Games; Alta Sport, Recreation, Parks and Wildlife jr. male athlete '02; Conacher Trophy Cdn Male Athlete of '04; res. Calgary, Alta.

SHIBICKY, Alex (hockey); b. 19 May 1914, Winnipeg, Man.; given name: Alexis Dimitri; m. Gloria May Aspinall; c. Alex, Kathy, Lori, Nancy, Bill; ret'd; rw jr. Selkirk Fishermen; pro NYR '36-42, '45-46; Providence AHL '41-42; mem. Allan Cup champion Ottawa Commandos '42-43; New Haven Ramblers '46-47; coached WHL New Westminster Royals '47-49, '53-54, Flin Flon Bombers SJHL '49-53, Kelowna Packers '54-55, IHL Indianapolis Chiefs '60-61; mem. '40 Stanley Cup champions; NHL record: 324 scheduled games, 110g, 91a, 39 playoff games, 12g, 12a; mem. Man. Hockey Hall of Fame; res. White Rock, B.C.

SHIELDS, Al (hockey); b. 10 May 1907, Ottawa, Ont.; d. 24 Sep 1975, Ottawa, Ont.; m. Mary Patricia McLewin; c. John, David, Peter, Patti Jane, Carole Ann; began playing days with Ottawa Montagnards '27-28 Allan Cup '28; New Haven (Can-Am) '27-28; NHL Ottawa Senators '28-30, '32-34, Philadelphia Quakers '30-31, NY Americans '31-32, '36-37, Montreal Maroons '34-36, '37-38, Boston Bruins '36-37; NHL record: 459 scheduled games, 42g, 46a, 17 playoff games, 0g, 1a; 1 Stanley Cup winner; New Haven (AHL) '38-41; Washington Lions (AHL) '41-42; Arnprior RCAF '42-44; played '34 NHL all-star game; coached at New Haven; referee AHL '46-48.

SHIELDS, Kathy (basketball/coaching); b. 18 Jan 1951, W.Vancouver, B.C.; m. Ken Shields; Laurentian, BComm, UBC, BPhE; coach UVic; competed as ntl team mem. '70-74; coach jr. varsity '76-77; varsity asst. coach '77-78; head basketball coach '78-99; coached 12 CWUAA, 8 ntl CIAU title teams; 320-50 college coaching record; BC team of '92; groomed 13 UVic athletes for ntl women's team; ntl jr team coach '83; development team coach '86; asst. sr. ntl team '82-84, '88-92; head coach sr. ntl team '92-95; coached '93 America's Zone world qualification bronze medal team '93, '94 world championships team; 3 CIAU, 7 Canada West coach-of-yr awards; 2 Basketball BC, 1 Sport BC, 2 3M coaching awards; master coach ntl coaching institute '86-98; level 4 coaching cert.; dir. CG board '93-94; former UVic AD; coached in Japan; mem. Cdn Basketball, UVic Sports halls of fame; res. Victoria, B.C.

SHIELDS, Ken (basketball/coaching); b. 7 Dec 1945, Beaverlodge, Alta.; m. Kathy; UCal, BA, UBC, BPhE,

MPhE; coach; founding pres. Commonwealth Centre for Sport Development; AD/basketball coach UVic '78-89; 7 consec CIAU ntl titles; coached BC ream, ntl jr, ntl B teams; ntl men's team head coach 5yrs; directed establishment of National Coaching Institute '86; led in creation of high-performance training centres for rowing, soccer, middle-distance running; CCA certified master coach for basketball; 4 CIAU coach-of-yr awards; '81 BC coach of year; George Pearkes Memorial award for leadership in university sports; dir. CCA, NCI; mem. '94 CG bids comm., governor Victoria CG Society; pres. CPCA '93-98; mem. Order of Canada; mem. UVic Sports, Cdn Basketball halls of fame; res. Victoria, B.C.

SHOCKEY-MILANESE, Barbara (swimming); b. 16 May 1962, Saskatoon, Sask.; given name: Barbara Shockey; m. Thomas Jay Milanese; c. Anthony, Jamie, Thomas; Miami, Dowling Coll., BA; art teacher; began swimming age 6; coached by Harry Bailey attained ntl level; at 14 set 2 provincial records; forte 800m FS; coached by Ken Olsen competed '78 CG, World championships; 800m FS bronze '79 PAG; 3 masters gold Empire State Games '93; silver, bronze '95 US ntl masters; mem. Sask, Saskatoon Sports halls of fame; res. Boca Raton, Fla.

SHONG, Laurie (modern pentathlon/fencing): b. 2 Jan 1971, Vancouver, B.C.; Vancouver Community College; actor/model; successful age-group swimmer; only Cdn to win world fencing title jr. épée '88 world cadet championships; silver '91 junior worlds; 5th '91 jr. worlds Modern Pentathlon best-ever result by Cdn male; 1st Cdn to qualify for two sports in same summer Olympics '92; Pan-Pacific MP bronze '91; team épée gold, individual bronze '90 Commonwealth championships; 6 epee gold US circuit; rebounded from near fatal auto accident '93 to win fencing titles NA Cup circuit, Tournoi des Grands Vins, Commonwealth championships '94; Pro Fencing League gold '98; épée bronze '99 PAG; qualified for '96, '00 Olympics; WC men's épée bronze '00; through '00 won 70 gold, 23 silver, 18 bronze; Harry Jerome, 2 Fair Play awards, BC jr.athlete of '88; res. Vancouver, B.C.

SHORE, Eddie (hockey); b. 25 Nov 1902, Ft. Qu'Apelle, Sask.; d. 16 Mar 1985, Springfield, Mass.; given name: Edward William; m. Katie McRae (d.); c. Ted; Manitoba Agricultural College; ret'd hockey exec.; wife mem. famed Edmonton Grads basketball team '24-29; Melville Millionaires '23-24; def. Regina Caps, Edmonton (WCL); Boston (NHL) '26-39, NY Americans '39-40; season; NHL record: 105 goals, 179 assists; 4 Hart Trophy (MVP awards); 7 1st, 1 2nd team all-star; mem. 2 Stanley Cup winners; owned, operated Springfield (AHL) '40-78, excluding WW2 yrs as GM, coach Buffalo Bisons; 3 consec Calder Cup title teams; briefly operated New Haven franchise, owned Fort Worth (USHL), Oakland (PCHL) until sold to California Seals; past v-p. AHL; '70 Lester Patrick Trophy for contribution to US hockey; hon. governor AHL; jersey #2 ret'd by Bruins; mem. Hockey, Canada's Sports halls of fame.

SHORT, George (football/t&f); b. 5 May 1941, Saskatoon, Sask.; given name: George Douglas; m. Margaret Jean Parr; c. Stacey Lynn, Lesley Anne;UAlta, BPhE, UCal, BEd, Windsor, MPhE; ret'd asst. athletic dir.; db '58 Sask. HS champs, '59 ntl jr. champion Saskatoon Hilltops; mem.

WCIAA champion Alta. Bears '62-64, Calgary Dinosaurs '67, CCIFC champion, Prairie Bowl finalist Windsor Lancers '69; ntl jr. sprint champion '59, setting 100yd dash record 9.8 sec.; mem. '59 PAG, '60 Olympic teams; WCIAA all-star, hon. mention all-Cdn '64, CIAU all-Cdn. '69; pres. Cdn Assn. University Athletic Directors '75; Hong Kong delegation Olympic attache '76; pres. Olympic Club of Canada '77; ret'd asst. AD, lecturer Concordia.; mem. Sask. Sports (as '59 Hilltops member), Saskatoon Sports halls of fame; res. Beaconsfield, Que.

SHORT, Robert (field hockey); b. 11 Aug 1972, Maidstone, England; given name: Robert Ian; Uvic., BA geography; web development and outreach for United Nations Environment Programme; silver '95, gold '99 PAG; competed '98 world cup; '98, '02 CG, '00 Olympics; res. Saltspring Island, B.C.

SHOULDICE, Hap (football/officiating); b. 12 Mar 1907, Ottawa, Ont., d. 21 May 1981, Ottawa, Ont.; given name: Hans; m. Lois McCulloch; c. Don, Doug, Drew (d); ret'd chief administrator customer accounting, CFL dir. of officiating; organized, managed, coached, Gowlings to '27 ntl juv basketball title; coach Rideau Aquatic sr. ladies' canoe team; juv lacrosse Strathconas '22-25; catcher Ottawa Hydro Mercantile softball league, Masonic League early '30s; paddled Rideau club '25-35, 5yrs war canoe capt., ladies' war canoe capt.; paddler '30 BEG; coach Shamrock Jr. hockey team '27-29; coach-mgr. Rideau Jr. '30 Memorial Cup semifinalists; began hockey, football officiating '27; worked 9 ntl hockey finals, Memorial, Allan, Alexander Cup; CFL official '35-58, 8 Grey Cup finals; EFC supervisor of officials '58, same role for CFL '72; organized first hockey, football officials assn. in Canada; mem. Ottawa Sports, Canadian Football halls of fame.

SHRUBB, Alf (t&f); b. 1878, Slinfield, Sussex, Eng., d. 23 Apr 1964, Bowmanville, Ont.; tobacconist; dominated world distance running scene 2-20 miles around turn of century; mem. Horsham Blue Star Harriers 1898, 1, 3, 4 mile titles; South London Harriers 1900; Eng. sr. x-country titles '01-04, international x-country titles '03-04, 10 AAA track titles in 4 years; 6 world, 6 GB records; missed Olympic opportunity when Britain failed to send team to '04 Games; pro '05, moving to Boston '05, Toronto '09; competed with and defeated Dorando Pietri, Johnny Hayes, Bill Sherring, Tom Longboat in all races less than 20 miles; lost to Longboat '09 NY marathon; engaged in profitable (reported $3,000 per win, $2,000 per loss) 10-race series with Longboat winning 7 at 10-16 miles, losing 3 at 20 or more miles; fan pleaser with varying running styles; trainer, x-country coach Harvard '15; 1st pro coach Oxford '15-26.

SHUTT, Steve (hockey); b. 1 Jul 1952, Toronto, Ont.; given name: Stephen John; mgr. CIMCO ice making equipment hockey coach; jr. Toronto Marlboros; 1st Montreal pick, 4th overall '72 draft; lw Canadiens '72-84, Los Angeles '84-85; scored 60g+ '76-77 season; once 1st, twice 2nd team all-star; Team Canada '76; NHL record: 935 scheduled games, 424g, 393a, 99 playoff games, 50g, 48a; mem. 5 Stanley Cup winners; color commentator on radio 3yrs; asst. coach Canadiens '93-97; mem. Hockey Hall of Fame; res. Montreal, Que.

SICILIANO, Dave (builder/hockey); b. 7 Jul 1946, Ft. William, Ont.; Lakehead; fwd Ft. William jrs '63-65; 3 intercollegiate all-star; MVP, 2 NAIA scoring titles; Marquette Mich. Rangers '70-71; playing coach Helsinki '71-72, Allan Cup title Thunder Bay '74-75; coach sr. men's, Little League baseball, Thunder Bay jr. hockey, Lakehead U hockey, bantam, midget, jr. A hockey; AD Lakehead '78-79; dir. operations Team Ontario u-17 team; coach/GM USHL Thunder Bay jr. A; coach Cdn u-17, u-18 teams; asst. Team Canada world jr. gold team '92; coach ntl bantam AAA title team; 2 Centennial Cup, 4 USHL titles; HDCO hockey development in Ont. award; Gordon Juckes meritorious award; 3 USHL coach of yr awards; mem. NWO Sports Hall of Fame; res. Thunder Bay, Ont.

SIDDERS, George (boxing); 2 Jun 1907, London, Eng.; d. (circa) 1990, Galiano Island, B.C.; given name: George William; m. 3 times; Sir George Williams, College of Divine Metaphysics, Indianapolis; Que. military dist. lightweight title '25; Montreal, Que. lightweight crowns '26; claimed ntl amateur lightweight, welterweight titles during span of 1 hour on a single night '26; ntl pro welterweight crown '28; British army PT instructor Aldershot, Eng., '40; chief instructor remedial, physical exercise training for Cdn army in England '40-45; active in soccer, baseball, swimming, golf, tennis.

SIDWELL, Pop (builder/swimming); b. 4 Dec 1893, England; d. 5 Mar 1980, Winnipeg, Man.; given name: Arthur; swimming diploma age 11 launched lifetime commitment to aquatics; emigrated to Winnipeg at 27; silver 200yd breaststroke Cdn championships; earned reputation as coach guiding numerous swimmers to international prominence; began coaching career '38 at YMCA; added YWCA to resume '40; UMan. swim coach '42-50; authored several swimming books; honoured by YMCA, Winnipeg city with tribute dinner '60; annual mid-Can. Masters meet bears his name; mem. Man. Sports Hall of Fame.

SIEBERT, Babe (hockey); b. 14 Jan 1904, Plattsville, Ont.; d. 25 Aug 1939, St. Joseph, Ont.; given name: Albert Charles; Kitchener OHA jrs. '22-23; Niagara Falls srs. '24-25, NHL Montreal Maroons '25-32, Rangers '32-34, Boston '34-36, Canadiens '36-39; with Maroons lw 5yrs on Big S line with Nels Stewart, Hooley Smith; 1st team all-star def. 3 successive years; Hart Trophy '37; captain '39 team, signed to coach Canadiens following season but drowned during summer; mem. Hockey Hall of Fame.

SIGFUSSON, Svein (t&f); b. 15 Jul 1912, Lundar, Man.; d. 1993, Winnipeg, Man.; m. Thelma Goodman; c. Skuli Norman, Darlene Sigridur, Linda Gudran, Lois Olive Iris, Charles Svein; owner Sigfusson Transportation Co.; ntl discus record '38 in initial competitive performance; hammer throw gold, discus, shot, tj, javelin silvers '38 ntl championships; won hammer '47-48, silver discus '48 nationals; bronze discus '50 BEG; mem. '54 BEG team; lost records make totals incomplete but it is known he won at least 8 Man., 9 ntl titles '38-54; all-Canada t&f team '54, councilman Cdn CG Assn.; Manitoba Centennial Medal, Order of Canada; mem. Manitoba Sports Hall of Fame.

SILVERBERG, Doug (golf); b. 16 Jan 1933, Red Deer, Alta.; given name: Douglas Howard; m. Carole Barber; c.

Douglas Kirk, Kyle Robert, Scott William; Colorado Coll.; London Life insurance exec.; jr. hockey Port Arthur; all-American, all-Cdn; 2 Alta. juvenile, 2 Alta HS, 3 Alta. jr. golf titles; Cdn jr. '50, runnerup '51; 6 Alta. amateur, 3 runnerup, 1 Alta. Open, lost 2ⁿᵈ in playoff, twice runnerup, 8 times low amateur; 2 Alta match play pro-am; 8 Central Alta amateur, 3 Central Alta Open titles; Sask. Amateur '55, Open '58; mem. 23 Willingdon Cup (3 winners); 5 Commonwealth teams, '71 winner; 4 Americas Cup, 2 World Amateur teams; 3yrs pres. Calgary GA; dir. Edmonton G&CC; mem. RCGA, Alta. Sports halls of fame; res. Calgary, Alta.

SILVERHEELS, Jay (lacrosse/boxing); b. 26 May 1912, Six Nations of the Grand River, Ont.; d. 5 Mar 1980, Canoga Park, Calif; given name: Harry Smith; m. 1. Laura Bailey; c. Sharon; m. 2. Mary; c. Jay Jr., Karen, Pamela, Marilyn; actor; a superb athlete, he played professional lacrosse with Buffalo, Toronto Tecumsehs and semi-pro hockey; won NY State Golden Gloves middleweight boxing title '37; while competing in lacrosse and hockey in California '33 was encouraged by Joe E. Brown and Richard Dix to try acting as film extra; career took off when he earned role of Tonto on Lone Ranger TV series; appeared in numerous movies, three times playing Geronimo in major movies; among movie credits were*: Broken Arrow, Saskatchewan, Captain from Castile*; in later years raised and drove standardbred horses; mem. Brantford Wall of Recognition, Cdn Lacrosse, Western NY Entertainment halls of fame.

SIMARD, Martine (synchro swim); b. 29 Mar 1961, Quebec City; Laval.; competitive diver, swimmer before focusing attention on synchronized swimming '69; mem. Que. 15-and-under team '74; 2ⁿᵈ duet, team '76 ntl championships; ntl title team '78-80; mem. '78 world championships, '80 FINA Cup, American Challenge Cup teams; mem. Pan-Pacific Games gold medal team '79; res. Sillery, Que.

SIMARD, Richard (harness racing); b. 24 Aug 1959, Montreal, Que.; following lead of father and grandfather became racing fan as youngster; began racing ponies age 11; at age 15 had 36 drives behind ponies on single day; launched driving career '81 working part-time for Henri Filion then full-time with Lillian LaPointe; moved to Quebec City and branched out on his own with stops at Rideau Carleton, Blue Bonnets, Trois-Rivieres; moved to Windsor to drive for Luc Borassa; breakthrough came in '96 with 379 wins followed by career high 418 in '97; returned to Quebec circuit '01 splitting time between Que. and Ont.; through '03 4607 wins and in excess of $22M in purses; nicknamed "The Cat"; res. Coteau-Du-Lac, Que.

SIMBOLI, Chris (skiing); b. 18 Sep 1962, Ottawa, Ont.; m. Melanie Palenik; c. Madison; Windsor LLB, Detroit JD; lawyer; freestyle specialist; moved from Ont. to ntl team '84; ntl men's aerials title '86; 1ˢᵗ skier to achieve freestyle grand slam winning world title, World Cup, Grand Prix '89; 3 Ont., 7 ntl titles; won 46 WP, GP medals '84-89; ret'd from competition '89; CSA John Semmelink trophy, 1ˢᵗ FS skier so honored; finalist Cdn male athlete of '89; Ottawa ACT athlete of '89; mem. Nepean Wall, Cdn Skiing, Ottawa Sports halls of fame; res. Nepean, Ont.

SIMMER, Charlie (hockey); b. 20 Mar 1954, Terrace Bay, Ont.; given name: Charles Robert; div.; c. Brittany Ann;

m. Jody,; c. Jake, Austin; sales recruiter, TV-radio hockey analyst; jr. Sault Ste. Marie Greyhounds; 4ᵗʰ California pick, 39ᵗʰ overall '74 draft; lw California '74-76, Cleveland '76-77, Los Angeles '77-84, Boston '84-87, Pittsburgh '87-88; Team Canada '83; 1 season Frankfurt, Germany; asst. coach San Diego Gulls (IHL) '89-90; successive 56 goal seasons Kings '79-81; 2 1ˢᵗ, 2ⁿᵈ team all-star; with Marcel Dionne, Dave Taylor formed LA's Triple Crown Line; played 3 NHL all-star games; NHL record: 712 scheduled games, 342g, 369a, 24 playoff games, 9g, 9a; Bill Masterton trophy '86; radio analyst Anaheim Mighty Ducks, TV analyst Phoenix; dir. City of Hope; active in varied charitable organizations; mem. NWO Sports Hall of Fame; res. Scottsdale, Ariz.

SIMONS, Pop (softball); b. 15 Jan 1894, Penzance, Eng.; d. (circa) 1990, Vancouver, B.C.; given name: Richard Percy; ret'd storekeeper; mediocre playing career as ss failed to dull enthusiasm for game; sponsored 1ˢᵗ team '37; with Cece White arranged for installation of lights Vancouver South Memorial Park, instrumental in formation of BCASA, CASA; treasurer BCASA '48-77; CASA's 1ˢᵗ secty '65, later v-p., dir. to '71; secty BC Amateur Basketball Assn. 5yrs; 1ˢᵗ life mem. CSA '72; mem. Softball Canada Hall of Fame.

SIMPSON, Ben (football); b. 1878, Peterborough, Ont., d. 20 Oct 1964, Guelph, Ont.; Queen's, MA, Normal School; educator; int. football Queen's; Hamilton Tigers '04-10, 2 Ont., 1 ntl titles; captain '10 team; referee 3yrs intercollegiate ranks, 7 interprovincial league; mem. Tiger team which, with Ottawa, demonstrated Cdn game to US fans; mem. Canada's Sports, Canadian Football halls of fame.

SIMPSON, Bill (soccer); b. 13 Sep 1894, Paisley, Scotland, d. 1974, Toronto, Ont.; foreman; mem. Fraserburg team Toronto, Toronto City in National Soccer League, Davenport Albion, Toronto Scottish, '19 league title; 15yrs secty.-treas. Ont. Soccer Assn., 14yrs pres. Toronto District Soccer Assn.; 4yrs pres. CSFA; credited with many innovations in Cdn soccer; mgr. 1ˢᵗ Cdn team to play USSR; launched Canada's soccer coaching schools; mem. Canada's Sports Hall of Fame.

SIMPSON, Bob (football); b. 20 Apr 1930, Windsor, Ont.; div. Cecile; c. Robert John, Gary Lee, Lynn Patricia, Mark Stanley; m. Mary Francis; c. Mary Leigh; Assumption College; ret'd LCBO clerk; forward 2 Ont. HS basketball title teams; 4ys Tillsonburg Livingstons; mem. '52 Olympic team; 1yr Windor Rockets (ORFU); Rough Riders '50-62; CFL record: caught 65 td passes, record surpassed '75 by Terry Evanshan; 386 lifetime points, 12 other defensive tds, 274 receptions 9 recorded seasons, 6034yds (22.0yds-per-catch avg. 2ⁿᵈ only to Whit Tucker 22.4); best single season 47 receptions '56; 6 times EFC all-star, 4 times all-Cdn; outstanding player (Gordon Sturtridge Memorial Trophy) '57 East-West Game; runnerup Schenley outstanding Cdn '56; mem. 2 Grey Cup winners; jersey #70 ret'd by Riders; coach Ashbury College football several years; PR director Ottawa; several years Ottawa sr. basketball league; exec.-dir. National Capital Regional Sports Council; mem. Cdn Football, Ottawa, Windsor-Essex Sports halls of fame; res. Nepean, Ont.

SIMPSON, Bruce (t&f); b. 6 Mar 1950, Toronto, Ont.; div. Joanne; m. Senga Nicholson; c. Colin, Katie; UCLA,

UofT BSc, UofOtt, LLB; lawyer; ntl pv title '65, ntl record 12'6 1/2" (3.81m); ranked among top 6 indoor vaulters in world '68; mem. '70, '78, '82 CG, '72, '76 Olympic, '71, '75, '79 PAG, '75 FISU Games, '77, '79 World Cup teams; bronze '71, gold '79 PAG; gold '78 CG; silver '75 FISU Games; ntl indoor record 17'4 3/4" (5.30m); '77 Adelaide Interntl, Pacific Conf titles; gold Melbourne Interntl, *Etobicoke Guardian*, ntl championships '80; ntl indoor, outdoor titles '81; does some coaching in Toronto area; res. Toronto, Ont.

SIMPSON, Bullet Joe (hockey); b. 13 Aug 1893, Selkirk, Man., d. 26 Dec 1973, Florida; given name: Harold Joseph; compensated for lightweight stature with speed to become great defenceman and earn nickname "Bullet Joe"; amateur hockey Winnipeg Victorias '14-15; mem. Winnipeg 61st Battalion Allan Cup winner; Selkirk Fishermen '19-20; Edmonton Eskimos '21-25, 2 WCHL titles; NY Americans (NHL) '25-31; managed Americans '32-35; New Haven, Minneapolis before retiring; awarded Military Medal; mem. Canada's Sports, Man., Cdn Hockey halls of fame.

SIMPSON, Craig (hockey): b. 15 Feb 1967, London, Ont.; m. Christine Kirkland; c. Dillon; Michigan State; hockey coach, TV hockey color commentator; lw; Mich. State CCHA '83-85; CCHA all-star; NCAA all-American; drafted by Pittsburgh '85-88, Edmonton '87-93, Buffalo '93-95; asst coach Edmonton '93-94; NHL record: 634 scheduled games, 247g, 250a, 67 playoff games, 36g, 32a; res. Edmonton, Alta./Los Angeles, Calif.

SIMPSON, Jimmy (football/builder): b. 1 Nov 1906, Hamilton, Ont.; d. 16 Nov 1975, Hamilton, Ont.; c. Jim Jr.; began football career with Hamilton Tigers '28 and remained affiliated with game as player/official/trainer almost 50yrs; outside wing with 6 Grey Cup finalists, 4 winners; scored 4 Grey Cup Tds; turned to officiating '45-56; joined Tiger-Cats as asst. trainer '57; head trainer '60-75; nicknamed "The Rooster"; affiliated with 19 Grey Cup games, 6 as player, 3 as official and 10 as trainer; mem. Cdn Football Hall of Fame.

SIMPSON, John (equestrian): b. 3 Jul 1949, Calgary, Alta.; m. Tracy Bowman; c. Christy, Luke; rancher; ntl team '73-80; US President's Cup '78; Rotterdam GP title '77; jumping team silver '79 PAG; mem. '76 Olympic, '79 PAG teams; res. Cochrane, Alta.

SIMPSON, Rene (tennis): b. 14 Jan 1966, Sarnia, Ont.; given name: Norine Karen; div. Barry Alter; Texas Christian, BA (business/accounting); Tennis Canada player services mgr. from '98; Ont. Open singles titles '87-90; mem. Cdn Federation Cup team '88-98, coach '99; mem. '88, '92 Olympic team; all-American singles, doubles TCU '88, all-American Southwest Conf. MVP '88, Southwest region sr. player of '88, all-Southwest Conf. academic team; mem. TCU all-decade team; ntl singles title '92; ntl women's, mixed doubles titles '93-94; with Helen Kelesi Tennis Canada doubles team of '92; TC most improved player '88; highest WTA ranking 70 in '89; 3 intl doubles titles; 10yrs pro; asst. coach, non-playing capt. '00-03 Fed. Cup teams; won 35+ women's world title '03; Fed. Cup outstanding sr. female award; res. Toronto, Ont.

SINCLAIR, Christine (soccer); b. 12 Jun 1983, Burnaby, B.C.; UPortland; fwd with scoring touch; led HS team to 3 AAA league titles; selected to BC -14 all-stars at 11; led club teams to 6 league, 5 prov. titles; led Portland to 1st-ever NCAA title; 2 all-American 1st team; Soccer America, West Coast Conf. freshman of '01; top scoring freshman is US 23g, 8a, 54pts; Cdn -19 team '99, ntl sr. team from '00; through Jul '04 amassed 64 intl caps, 49 goals; mem. W-League Vancouver Whitecaps; Golden Ball MVP award '02; res. Burnaby, B.C.

SINCLAIR, Ken (tennis): b. 4 Jan 1930, Toronto, Ont.; given name: Kenneth Donald; m. Elizabeth Stella Aston; c Bill, Bob, Pat, Kelly; insurance broker; 3 world championships for journalists; won 45+ and 55+ indoor, outdoor ntl singles titles; with Lorne Main 9 world srs. doubles titles, 4 consec. Austria Cups, Von Cramm Cup '92, Britannia Cup '98; European indoor singles, doubles '91; chair. Cdn open championships in '70s and '80s. 3 consec. Crawford Cup titles; world 70+ title; mem. Cdn Tennis Hall of Fame; res. Aurora, Ont.

SINCLAIR, Marjorie (curling): b. 25 Jan 1911, England; d. (circa 1995) Edmonton, Alta.; given name: Marjorie Helen; m. Duncan S. Sinclair; c. Jaclyn, John; secty. Western Canada Ladies' Curling Assn. '49-50; delegate for Northern Alta. LCA on WCLCA '50-52; WCLCA secty. '54; pres. Eaton NALCA '55-56; pres. NALCA '57-58; pres. Edmonton LCC '59-60; Western Canada delegate CLCA '61-63; Sinclair Trophy presented annually to NALCA champions; pres. CLCA '63-64; secty. NALCA '61-68, also ALCA twice during that period; mem. 1st women's baseball team Calgary; mem. Canadian Curling Hall of Fame.

SINDEN, Harry (hockey): b. 14 Sep 1932, Collins Bay, Ont.; given name: Harry James; m. Eleanor; c. Nancy, Carol, Donna, Julie; hockey exec.; 5yrs def sr. OHA guiding Whitby Dunlops to '57 Allan Cup, '58 world amateur championship; player-coach Kingston (EPHL), Minneapolis, Oklahoma City (CPHL) 6yrs; CPHL championship '66; never played in NHL; coach Boston '67-70, '79-80, GM '72-03, pres. from '89; coached '60 Team Canada Olympic silver medal team, '72 Team Canada victory over USSR; NHL coaching record:327 scheduled games, 153-116-58; 43 playoff games, 24-19; 1 Stanley Cup; 1st NHL GM to reach 1000 victories during his tenure with same club; Lester Patrick award '99; dir. Hockey Hall of Fame; mem. IIHF, AHL, Hockey halls of fame; res. Winchester, Mass.

SINGLETON, Gordon (cycling): b. 9 Aug 1956, Niagara Falls, Ont.; m. Louann Godak; c. Christopher, James; auto store mgr.; began competitive cycling '74 winning Ont. jr title; ntl sr. sprint titles '75-77; mem. '75-77 World championships, '75, '79 PAG, '76 Olympic, '78 CG teams; gold, bronze '78 CG; 2 gold '79 PAG, silver worlds; within 24-hour span set world 200m, 500m, 1000m sprint records '80, 1st cyclist to accomplish feat in so short a time; NA records 200m, 1000m; mem. ntl team '75-80; pro with AMF Wheel Goods '81; silver world sprints '81; 2 world pro records; world title '82; 1st Cdn cyclist to win coveted rainbow jersey; career ended following '82 track crash; Ont. athlete of '79; twice runnerup Cdn athlete of yr; *CBC-TV* color commentator '84 Olympics, '94 CG; also TV analyst for *CTV, TSN*; does some coaching; mem. selection comm. NF Sports Wall of Fame; mem. Order of Canada; mem. NF Sports Wall, Cdn Cycling Hall of Fame; res. St. Catharines, Ont.

SINGLETON, Harvey (football/basketball/t&f); b. 22 Dec 1932, Chicago, Ill.; m. Sonja Matwichuk; c. Patti-Jo, Todd; Kentucky State, BSc, Eastern Michigan, MSc; teacher, coach; 12 athletic letters Kentucky State; 4yrs all-conf. rcvr, little all-American status; mem. Argos '52; ORFU champion Toronto Balmy Beach; 2yrs all-conf. basketball KSU; mem. Dow Kings Ont. Sr. A champions, YMHA Sr. A champions; played briefly Harlem Globetrotters; vertical jumps referee '76 Montreal Olympics; co-operater, co-director VYTIS basketball camp 5yrs; coach HS, McMaster basketball several years; McMaster Friends of Distinction award; res. Oakville, Ont.

SIPPEL, Lori (softball); b. 16 May 1965, Stratford, Ont.; given name: Lori Anne; Nebraska, BScEd.; coach; rhp; competed '81 World Youth Games; mem. '84 ntl title team; 3 US ntl gold, 1 silver; PAG gold '83, silver '91, bronze '87; college world series silver; competed 4 world championships; mem. ntl team 15yrs; mem. '96, '00 Olympic team; ret'd but came back to help Team Canada qualify for '00 Olympics; most inspirational player award '98 Canada Cup; jersey #16 ret'd by Nebraska; softball coach Nebraska; Academic All-American '88; TV softball analyst '99 PAG; mem. Cdn Softball Hall of Fame; res. Lincoln, Neb.

SISSAOURI, Guivi (wrestling): b. 15 Apr 1971, Tsibilisi, Georgia; m. Grace Abellar; c. Gayle; florist; emigrated to Canada '88 Cdn citizen '95; 3 ntl sr 57kg, 1 62kg titles; gold '94 Francophone Games, silver '95, bronze '97 world championships; gold '95, silver '97 Canada Cup; gold '96 Pan-American championships; '96 (silver), '00, '04 Olympic Games; gold Austrian, Poland GP, NY, Romanian Open, '01 world; 60kg gold '02 CG; res. Montreal, Que.

SITTLER, Darryl (hockey); b. 18 Sep 1950, St. Jacob's, Ont.; given name: Darryl Glen; m. Wendy (d); c. Ryan, Megan, Ashley; hockey exec.; OHA junior A London Knights; 1st pick Maple Leafs, 8th overall '70 amateur draft; Toronto '70-82, Philadelphia '82-84, Detroit '84-85; once 2nd team all-star ctr; NHL record 10-point game Feb '76 vs Boston with 6 goals, 4 assists; 6 goals tied modern NHL mark shared by Syd Howe, Red Berenson; in playoffs vs Philadelphia same season scored 5 goals in single game; 1 league, 5 Toronto club records; mem. Team Canada '76; scored overtime winner vs Czechoslovakia which gave Canada title; Leafs captain '75-'81; NHL record: 1096 scheduled games, 484g, 637a, 76 playoff games, 29g, 45a; hon. chair. McDonald House, prominent numerous charities; special consultant to Toronto pres. Cliff Fletcher '91-96; dir. marketing/community relations '97; fan choice as Leafs all-time team ctr; jersey #27 ret'd by TML; mem. Waterloo County, Ont. Legends, Hockey halls of fame; res. East Amherst, N.Y.

SKILLINGS-HARNEY, Sandra (badminton); b. 29 Aug 1959, Vancouver, B.C.; m. Greg Harney; c. Stewart. Kathleem; Langara Coll; racquets pro; ntl intermediate doubles, mixed doubles, singles titles '80; Pepsi-Cola mixed doubles '80; silver singles, mixed doubles (with Ken

Priestman) '80 Pan-Am championships; ntl doubles (with Wendy Carter) '82; quarterfinalist Scotland '83; mem. '84 Uber Cup team; team silver '82, '86 CG; ret'd '86 and turned to squash, coaching; #1 ranked BC squash 1yr; competitive squash '86-93; coached squash/badminton '89-98; mgr. BC Canada Winter Games badminton team '99; dir. CG Sports Dev. board; res. Victoria, B.C.

SKINNER, Archie (golf); b. 21 Aug 1913, St. Andrews, Scotland; d. 19 May 1989, Fredericton, N.B.; NB, PEI, Maritime Open champion '33-60; course record St. Andrews '41, Digby Pines '36; mem. NB Sports Hall of Fame.

SKINNER, Chris (football); b. 15 Dec 1961, Saint John, N.B.; UNB, Bishop's BA; financial services; product Simonds minor football program jumping directly from peewee to HS football; HS rookie-of-yr at 14; led CIAU in rushing (800yds) '83; OQIFC outstanding player award; drafted by Edmonton, all-rookie team '84; tailback Schenley top Cdn nominee '86; 2 Grey Cup games, 1 winner; rb CFL '84-91 Edmonton, Ottawa, BC; CFL record: 2850yds rushing on 570 carries, 2874yds receiving on 278 catches, 24tds; mem. Saint John, NB Sports halls of fame; res. Safety Harbour, Fla.

SKINNER, Grant (softball); b. 5 Jun 1952, Vancouver, B.C.; given name: Grant Thomas; m. Cheryl Murphy; c. Bryan; Molson Breweries rep.; 2b; mem. ntl team '80-93; ntl championship MVP '80; gold '83 PAG, silver '84 worlds; 4 time all-Canadian playing in 9 ntl championships; mem. '93 Toronto Gators ISC world, ntl title teams; head coach CJHL Ottawa Jr. Senators '98; mem. Nepean Wall of Fame; Softball Canada, Man. Softball halls of fame; res. Kanata, Ont.

SKINNER, Jim (hockey); b. 12 Jan 1917, Selkirk, Man.; given name: James Donald; m. Vivian Reynolds; c. Holly, Karen, Teresa, Jim Jr.; hockey consultant; def with Flin Flon Bombers; pro Indianapolis (AHL); player-capt.-asst. coach Omaha (USHL); ret'd as player '47; 6yrs coach Windsor Spitfires, 1yr Hamilton Red Wings; coach Detroit (NHL) '54-58; NHL coaching record: 247 scheduled games, 123-78-46; 26 playoff games, 14-12; 2 league titles, 1 Stanley Cup; served many roles with Detroit including head scout, dir. farm club operations, asst. GM, dir. hockey operations, GM; mem. Man. Hockey Hall of Fame; res. Windsor, Ont.

SKINNER, Larry Jr. (hockey/softball); b. 21 Apr 1956, Vancouver, B.C.; given name: Larry Foster; m. Laurie McRae; c. Jordan, Angela; newspaper circulation mgr.; Jr. A hockey with Ottawa 67's '75-76; Colorado Rockies (NHL) '76-80; 2yrs Austria, 5yrs France; won French Cup B div. title '82; scored 1st goal in Colorado Rockies franchise history; NHL record: 47 scheduled games, 10g, 12a, 2 playoff games, 0g, 0a; all-star 3b ntl fastball championships '80, '81, '86, '90; batting champion ntl championships PEI; mem. ntl '84 world silver medal team; asst. coach CJHL Ottawa Jr. Senators '98; mem. Nepean Wall of Fame; res. Kanata, Ont.

SKINNER, Larry Sr. (hockey/softball); b. 25 Jul 1930, Keyes, Man.; m. Marjorie Blair; c. Grant, David, Ruth, Larry, Shannon; Oregon; ret'd dir. marketing, communication CAHA; softball player, coach, manager 30yrs; participated in 3 world softball championships, 6 ntl finals; 5yrs Pacific Coast Soccer League; 1 ntl soccer championship; exec.-dir. CASA 3yrs; dir. marketing CAHA '73-95; res. Manotick, Ont.

SKRESLET, Laurie (mountaineering); b. 25 Oct 1949, Calgary, Alta.; m. Monique Viau; c. Natasha; mountain guide/motivational speaker; served stints in Norwegian, US merchant marine; began mountaineering age 20; graduate of Colorado Outward Bound school; 7yrs instructor Cdn Outward Bound School; 1st Cdn to summit Mount Everest; certified mem. Assn. of Cdn Mountain Guides; as mem. '82 Mt. Everest expedition mem. Alta. Sports Hall of Fame; res. Calgary, Alta.

SKRIEN, Dave (football/coaching); b. 1929, Brooten, Minn.; m. Dee; c. Scott, Bruce, Christopher; Minnesota, BSc, MA; ret'd parks and recreation supervisor; fb Sask., Winnipeg '53, Grey Cup finalist; HS coach Minnesota; backfield coach Ball State College, Minn.; asst. coach BC (CFL) '59-60, head coach '61-67; WFC titles '63-64, Grey Cup victory '64; asst. Boise State College '67, Eskimos '68; head coach Roughriders '69-72 losing Grey Cup final to Hamilton '72; asst. WFL Memphis Southmen '73-75; part-time coach '79-81 nationally-ranked Golden Valley Lutheran Jr. College; full time parks and recreation dir. Richfield, Minn., '76-94; Annis Stukus Trophy as CFL coach of '63; BC Lions Wall of Fame; res. Eden Prairie, Minn.

SKUCE, Lou (rowing); b. 6 Jul 1886, Ottawa, Ont.; d. 21 Nov 1951, Toronto, Ont.; given name: Thomas Lewis; div. Dorothy Eddis; c. John Lewis, Nancy, Sandra, 1 other daughter; m. Kipling Fraser; UofT; cartoonist; as youth excelled in variety of sports; mem. Britannia Boating Club for decade distinguishing himself as paddler, oarsman; won title honors in both Canada and U.S.; stroke sr. four; mem. war canoe crew; twice played role in saving boaters whose lives were at risk in Ottawa river rapids; also competed with success for Parkdale Canoe Club; for several years standout football, rugby, hockey player noted for fleetness afoot; an accomplished singer (baritone), playwrite and actor; his artistic skills which were prominent in the *Ottawa Journal, Toronto World, Toronto Star, Globe and Mail, Sunday World;* murals on Toronto City Press Club walls remain today; created cartoonograph machine; chair. Toronto chapter American Guild of Variety Artists.

SLACK, Bill (harness racing/baseball); b. 24 Oct 1929, Toronto, Ont.; given name: William Michael Blakeley; sep.; c. Steven, Michael, Brian; St. Michael's College; ret'd racing secty. Blue Bonnets Raceway; mem. Toronto Marlboros midget hockey champions '46; Ont. jr. baseball championship team '50; pro tryout Brooklyn Dodgers; played briefly Boston Braves farm system; Que. area scout Detroit '72-77, Toronto '77-98; asst. program dir. Thorncliffe Raceway '50; program dir. Dufferin Park Raceway '51; program dir. Richelieu Park, Blue Bonnets Raceways '52-67; racing secty. Blue Bonnets '67-94; feature columnist *Harness World* from '65; TV commentator Que. Derby '60s; developed harness racing charts, past performance program for Que.; res. Anjou, Que.

SLACK, Bill (baseball): b. 3 May 1933, Petrolia, Ont.;

given name: William Henry; m. Patricia; c. Victor, Cindy, Karen, Timmy; baseball coach; mem. Sarnia Jr. B hockey champs '50-51; pitcher, Sr. Intercounty with London; drafted by Chicago (NHL) but opted for baseball signing with Boston (AL) organization; spent 33yrs in Boston organization as player, manager, pitching coach; mgr. Savanah (SAL); Texas Rangers org. minor league pitching co-ordinator; 10yrs Atlanta organization as minor league pitching coach Danville Braves; pitching coach Wilmington (KC org.) '02-04; jersey #37 ret'd By Winston-Salem; mem. Sarnia/Lambton Sports, Winston-Salem, Cdn Baseball halls of fame; res. Winston Salem, N.C.

SLACK, Stan (baseball): b. 2 Jun 1930, Petrolia, Ont.; given name: Stanley Frederick; m. Marnie Marie; c. Linda, William, Lori, Julie, Brian (d); ret'd steamfitter; signed with St. Louis (NL) organization as pitcher age 14; won 1st pro game in Appalachian League before turning 15; 8 seasons with Cardinals, Braves winning 69 games; mem. OBA champion Lou Ball Jrs., London Majors Srs.; coached minor, senior teams in Sarnia area several yrs; mgr. London Majors Sr, IC '91; mem, Sarnia/Lambton Sports Hall of Fame; res. Sarnia, Ont.

SLATER, Bill (swimming); b. 18 Apr 1940, Vancouver, B.C.; m. Carol Picard; c. David, Jamie, Scott, Bradley; Pennsylvania, Bsc (Econ); investment counsellor; ntl jr., sr. records 440, 880, 1650, mile FS, 220, 440 IM; mem. '56 Olympic, '58 BEG teams; bronze men's 4x220yd FS relay '58 BEG; res. West Vancouver, B.C.

SLAVIK, Jerry (t&f); b. 6 Jan 1932, Blenheim, Ont.; m. Helen Hames; c. Carol, John, Brian, Patricia, Mary, Margaret; ret'd businessman; coached Mic-Mac baseball '56-58; began running as form of therapy '66; ran Boston Marathon '70, 3 Detroit marathons; organized Windsor's 1st road running club and organized numerous road races over 30-plus years; co-founder still active WRACE (Walkers & Runners Around County of Essex) '80; dir. YMCA 13yrs, pres. '76-77; organizer/official Windsor St. Clair Rotary Club Automan triathlon 15yrs; helped organize Windsor separate school, public school, high school, university t&f meets for more than a decade; organizer/official variety of city school, college, university cross-country meets for more than a decade; race dir. annual Terry Fox run 16yrs; officiated '76 Olympics, ntl t&f championships '88, Ont. jr. t&f, triathlon, Intl race walk championships '95; numerous awards including '88 sports volunteer, certificate of merit, Windsor U A award; Confederation medal, AKO person of '95, Meda Charitable Trust award, Windsor board partners in education award; St. Clair Booster Club '98 person of yr; Ont. sports award, Windsor Roseland Rotary sports person of 2000; averages about 1200 hours annually on community volunteer work; mem. Windsor/Essex Sports Hall of Fame; res. Windsor, Ont.

SLEEMAN, George (baseball); b. 1841, St. David's, Ont., d. 1926, Guelph, Ont.; businessman, politician; mgr. Silver Creek Brewery team '72; pres. Guelph Maple Leafs '74; imported US players to bolster team; world semipro tournament title '74, ntl championships '74-75; pres. co-founder Canadian Assn. of Ballplayers; rated a petty despot and pioneer of Canadian baseball; key role in formation International Assn. '77; mem. Cdn Baseball Hall of Fame.

SLOAN, Susan (swimming); b. 5 Apr 1958, Stettler, Alta.; given name: Susan Estelle; m. Kelsey; Arizona State; butterfly specialist; Stettler Centennial, Vancouver Dolphins, Etobicoke Olympian swim clubs; medalist nationals '74-80; mem. several ntl record setting relay teams; won 100m butterfly, Olympic trials with Commonwealth record 1:02.41 '76; bronze 4x100m medley relay '76 Montreal Olympics; ntl record 100m butterfly 1:02.0 '77; 4 times all-American; gold 4x100m FS relay, '78 CG; bronze 4x100m relay '78 Berlin World Games; mem. '79 PAG team; last known res. res. Comox, B.C.

SLOAN, Tod (hockey); b. 30 Nov 1927, Vinton, Que.; given name: Aloysius Martin; m. Jean Aird; c. Marilyn, Joanne, Donald; St. Michael's College; salesman; ctr. Jr. A St. Mike's Majors; AHL Pittsburgh '46-49, Cleveland '49-50; Eddie Powers Memorial trophy '46; NHL Toronto '47-58, Chicago '58-61; once 2nd team all-star; mem. 4 Stanley Cup winners; NHL record: 745 scheduled games, 220g, 262a, 47 playoff games, 9g, 12a; played in 3 all-star games; coached minor hockey several years; mem. Toronto Oldtimers hockey team; res. Jackson's Point, Ont.

SMALE, Ted (football): b. 23 Jun 1932, Toronto, Ont.; given name: Fred; m. Dorothea Mary Hoffman; c. Frederick Douglas, Elizabeth Dawne, Karen Lorraine, Randall Scott; UofT, BASc., PEng; ret'd mgr. Nordion International; te/de Humberside CI Toronto HS champions; all-star end engineering faculty title team '51; all-star te Balmy Beach ORFU '52; 3yrs te UofT Blues; '54 intercollegiate champions; co-capt sr. yr; 3yrs all-star; drafted by Toronto CFL but job with AEC in Ottawa led to sale to Ottawa '56-62; 3yrs de, 4 te; mem. '60 Grey Cup champions but knee injury kept him from game; *Globe & Mail* all-Canadian '56-59; mem. Kanata B League badminton title team '79; Kanata golf club champion '68-69; OVGA 2-ball title (with Fred Drummie) '86; res. Kanata, Ont.

SMALL, Sami Jo (hockey); b. 25 Mar 1976, Winnipeg, Man.; Stanford, mechanical engineering; goal/def Team Manitoba '91 Canada Games; played midget AAA. junior "B"; ntl women's team from '97; 4 world titles; '02 Olympic gold; travelled with '98 Olympic team as third goalie; 2 gold 3-Nations Cup; gold, silver 4-Nations Cup; Pac-10 hockey player of '97; top goaltender, all-star '99, '00 worlds; scored goal '01 with NWHL Brampton Thunder; mem. ntl jr. t&f team 4yrs, capt. Pan Am Jr., mem. Stanford track team '94-98; played on men's hockey team Stanford until '99; mem. NWHL Beatrice Aeros; res. Winnipeg, Man.

SMEATON, Cooper (hockey/officiating); b. 22 Jul 1890, Carleton Place, Ont.; d. 3 Oct 1978, Montreal. Que.; a proficient hockey. baseball, football and basketball player with Westmount AAA, he rejected pro hockey offers choosing instead to devote his attention to officiating, first in amateur then from '13 in pro ranks, for more than 25yrs he handled numerous Stanley, Allan Cup games; mgr./coach Philadelphia Quakers '30-31; head NHL referee '31-37; served overseas WW1 earning Military Medal; Stanley Cup trustee '46-78; mem. Hockey Hall of Fame.

SMITH, Adam (softball): b. 29 Dec 1964, Hagersville, Ont.; given name: Adam Jeffery; m. Lauren English; c.

Rachel Marie Bennett, Jon (sc); dairy farmer; mem. Owen Sound Tiremen '89-92, Toronto Gators '93-96, Green Bay All-Car '97, Decatur '98, Oshawa Gators '99; mem. ntl team '89-98; 2 ISC World silver, 1 gold, 1 ISF World gold; 2 ntl title teams; '91, '95, '99 PAG gold; ISC all-world 1st team '94-95; res. Hagersville, Ont.

SMITH, Alfred E. (hockey); b. 3 Jun 1873, Ottawa, Ont., d. 21 Aug 1953, Ottawa, Ont.; mem. 1st Ottawa team (Electrics) to compete in organized hockey 1890 OHA; played 3yrs then ret'd; returned to hockey age 30 helping Ottawa win 2 Stanley Cups; Kenora '07, Ottawa '07-08, Pittsburgh in city pro league; ret'd to coach Renfrew, Ottawa, NY Americans, Moncton, N.B., North Bay; player-coach Ottawa Cliffsides '09 Allan Cup winners; Bully's Acres lacrosse team 1889; coach Ottawa lacrosse club, '22 Eastern Ont. title; qb Rough Riders, '03 Que. titlist; with brother Tommy mem. Ottawa Sports, Hockey halls of fame.

SMITH, Becky (swimming); b. 3 Jun 1959, Edmonton, Alta.; given name: Rebecca Gwendolyn; m. Bruce Wiber; c. Davis; UAlta BEd; teacher; ntl team '73-78; gold, 2 silvers '74, silver, bronze '78 CG; bronze 400IM, 400FS relay '76 Olympics; 2 bronze world aquatic games '78; 2 golds '73 youth team Sweden; 6 gold Coca-Cola meets; 5 gold, 1 silver Canada Summer Games; gold, silver, 2 bronze '75 NZ Games; 3 Commonwealth records; numerous ntl titles; mem. sr. women's water polo team '79-81; asst. coach Olympian Club '79-81; City of Edmonton awards '73-78; Alta. awards '73-78, Edmonton Sport Reporters Assn. award '74, Gov.-Gen.'s medal '76; CWIAU outstanding female swimmer '78; mem. UAlta Wall, Edmonton, Alta. Sports halls of fame; res. Edmonton, Alta.

SMITH, Bev (basketball); b. 4 Apr 1960, Armstrong, B.C.; Oregon; coach/consultant; led Salmon Arms Jewels to 89-game win streak, 3 BCHS titles; forward ntl team '79-88, '92-96; gold Jones Cup '82; bronze 2 PAG, '79, '86 world championships, '79 FISU Games, '82 Federation Cup; mem. '79, '81 FISU, '84, '96 (capt) Olympic Games teams; all-star '79 world championships; 12yrs Vivo Vicenza, Italy, team, all-star each yr; head coach sr. women's div. 1 league Italy 3yrs; I Italian, European Cup titles; level 4 coaching cert.; coach Cdn ntl women's team '97-01, PAG silver '99; '00 Olympics; coach Oregon '01-04, WNIT title '01; BC Women in Sport Leaders & Legends award; mem. Oregon, BC Sports, Cdn Basketball, Cdn Olympic halls of fame; res. Salmon Arm, B.C.

SMITH, Billy (hockey): b. 12 Dec 1950, Perth, Ont.; m. Debbie; c. Chad, Corey; hockey coach; goalie Cornwall jr. Royals; drafted by L.A. (NHL) '70; 2 seasons Springfield (AHL); picked in '72 expansion draft by NYI; NHL record '71-89, 680 scheduled games, 305w, 233l, 105t, 22so, 2031g, 3.17 goal/game avg., 132 playoff games, 88w, 36l, 348g, 5so, 2.73ga; mem. 4 Stanley Cup winners; jersey #31 ret'd by Islanders; 1 Vezina Trophy, shared William Jennings trophy with Roland Melanson; Conn Smythe trophy '83; became 1st NHL goalie credited with goal (vs Colorado) 28 Nov '79, (shot actually made by Colorado player from behind Islanders net and travelling length of ice into empty net); Florida goalie coach 5yrs; asst. coach '98-01; NYI goalie coach '01-04; mem. Hockey, Ottawa Sports halls of fame; res. West Palm Beach, Fla.

SMITH, Bobby (hockey); b. 12 Feb 1958, North Sydney, N.S.; given name: Robert David; m. Elizabeth Robertson; c. Ryan, Megan, Daniel; UofOtt, Minn. Curt Carlson School of Management, BSc, MBA; ret'd hockey exec.; ctr Jr. A Ottawa 67's '75-78; OHA record 192 points, including 123 assists, '77-78; Ottawa, OHA (Red Tilson Trophy) MVP '78; twice OHA all-star; Eddie Powers Memorial Trophy '78; Ontario MVP Labatt Cup international tournament '77; Cdn junior player of '78; mem. Team Canada jr. World Cup '78; 1st pick Minnesota (NHL), 1st overall '78 amateur draft; North Stars '78-83, '90-93, Montreal '83-90; Calder Memorial Trophy; mem. Stanley Cup finalist '81, winner '86; NHL record: 1077 scheduled games, 357g, 679a, 184 playoff games, 64g, 96a; played 4 NHL all-star games; shares NHL single season playoff record of 5 game-winning goals '91; v-p. NHLPA '81-90; v-p. dir. hockey operations Phoenix '96, GM '96-01; consultant Carolina '01-02; 67's ret'd jersey #15; majority owner Halifax Mooseheads QMJHL '03; mem. Ottawa Sports Hall of Fame; res. Scottsdale, Ariz.

SMITH, Brian (hockey); b. 6 Sep 1941, Ottawa, Ont.; d. 2 Aug 1995, Ottawa, Ont.; given name: Brian Desmond; m. Alana Kainz; TV sportscaster; jr. Ottawa Montagnards '57-58, jr. Canadiens '59-61; pro Hull-Ottawa (EPHL) '61-63; Innsbruck, Austria, '63-64; Springfield Indians (AHL) '64-67; Los Angeles (NHL) '67-68; Minnesota '68-69; Denver Spurs (WHL) '69-70; Berne, Switzerland, '70-72; Houston Aeros (WHA) '72-73; victim of random shooting at Ottawa TV station; charitable foundation founded in his honor; mem. Ottawa Sports Hall of Fame.

SMITH, Clint (hockey); b. 12 Dec 1913, Assiniboia, Sask.; given name: Clinton James; m. Ella Keys (d); c. Judith Ella, Virginia Jane; ret'd businessman; mem. Saskatoon Wesley Jrs.; pro at 18 Rangers organization; 6 seasons NY, 4 Chicago '37-47; NHL record: 483 scheduled games, 161g, 236a, 44 playoff games, 10g, 14a, mere 24pim; mem. 1 Stanley Cup winner; 2 Lady Byng trophies, 3 runnerup; 1st player to win Lady Byng with 2 different teams; set NHL record 49a in 50 game schedule '43-44; played 4 penalty-free seasons in NHL; ctr'd line of Bill Mosienko and Doug Bentley which set single-line single-season record 219 points; playing-coach Tulsa Oilers (USHL), league MVP '47-48; coached St. Paul to USHL title '48-49; founder/6ys pres. BC Benevolent HA; mem. Hockey Hall of Fame; res. W. Vancouver, B.C.

SMITH, Connie (basketball); b. 1903, Walsall, Staffordshire, Eng.; d. 9 Jan 1990, Viking, Alta.; m. Lloyd Clark McIntyre; c. Alan Lloyd; ret'd civil servant; mem. famed Edmonton Grads '20-26, 78 games, 637 points, 8.3 avg.; mem. Canadian Basketball, Alta. Sports halls of fame.

SMITH, Dallas (hockey); b. 10 Oct 1941, Hamiota, Man.; given name: Dallas Earl; def Estevan jrs '58-59; pro Boston '60-62, '65-77, NYR '77-78; EPHL Hull-Ottawa, AHL Pittsburgh, WHL Portland, San Francisco, CPHL champion Oklahoma City Blazers '66-67; NHL record: 890 scheduled games, 55g, 252a, 86 playoff games, 3g, 29a, 2 Stanley Cup winners; mem. Man. Hockey Hall of Fame; res. Portland, ME.

SMITH, Darrell K. (football); b. 5 Nov 1961, Youngstown, Ohio; Central State (Ohio); coach Tuskegee; sb; brief NFL stints Dallas '84, Cincinnati '85; CFL Toronto '86-92, Edmonton '93, Shreveport '94; CFL record: 120 scheduled games, 489 pass receptions for 8,427yds, 52tds, 22 carries, 101yds, 1td; 8 playoff games, 34 catches, 640yds, 5tds; 5 all-Eastern, 2 all-CFL all-star; set/tied 2 CFL records; most tds on passes single season 20 '90; mem. 2 Grey Cup finalists, 1 winner; res. Youngstown, Ohio.

SMITH, David (curling): b. 1 Oct 1919 Saint John, N.B.; d. 5 Jan 1984, Saint John, N.B.; given name: David Charles; m. Beryl; mgr. Saint John Harbor Bridge Authority; pres. Lancaster Little League baseball '62-68; pres. NB MHA '62-63; mem. NB Sports Hall of Fame founding comm. '70; secty '77, '85 Canada Summer Games comms.; NB Curling Assn. secty-treas. '61-83, v-p '72-76; CCA pres. '76-77, v-p. Royal Caledonian CC '76; competed for Canada '79 Lord Strathcona matches in Scotland; hon. life mem. CCA, Carleton CC; mem. Cdn Curling, NB Sports halls of fame.

SMITH, Don (coaching/administration): b. 30 May 1921, Port Colborne, Ont.; d. 1 Sep 1976, Edmonton, Alta.; given name: William Donald; m. Gwen Lewis; c. George, Graham, Scott, Lewis, Sandra, Sue, Rebecca, Allison; UofT, BPHE, Columbia MA, Buffalo, DPHE; educator; UofT outstanding athlete award '46; asst. football coach UofT; associated with Red Cross Society 29yrs; chair. ntl Water Safety '71-76; fb, basketball, hockey coach UAlta 10yrs; administrator, coach UAlta swimming '70-76; chair. '78 CG swim comm.; key role in building Kinsmen Aquatic Centre, competitive pool named in his memory; avid outdoorsman; exec. Alta. Camping Assn. '63-67; ntl pres. Cdn Camping Assn.; CAHPER pres. '67-69; pres. Sport Alta. '74-76; CAHPER honor award; Cdn Red Cross badge of service; Cdn Council in co-operation with Aquatics award; mem. UAlta Sports Wall of Fame, Alta., Edmonton Sports halls of fame.

SMITH, Donn (football); b. 3 Sep 1949, Rochester, Minn.; given name: Laton Donn Frederick; m. Pauline Leger; c. Simon, Natasha; Purdue, BSc; football coach; ex-property mgr. Public Works Can., consultant; mem. Nepean HS (Ottawa) city title team '66; mem. Windsor Vincent Massey HS city titlist team '67-68; all-city Windsor '67-68; pro Ottawa '73-80;, 3 times EFC all-star ctr; Schenley nominee top rookie '73; Schenley nominee best ol '76; mem. '73, '76 Grey Cup champions; CFL all-time all-star ctr; 123 CFL games; asst. coach UofOtt '86-90, Ottawa Sooners '91-95, 1 ntl jr. final; coach Carleton Ravens '96-99; OQIFC coach of '96; guest coach Ottawa, Sask., Toronto (CFL); asst. coach Winnipeg '03; res. Chelsea, Que.

SMITH, Ethel (t&f); b. 1907, Toronto, Ont.; d. 31 Dec 1979, Toronto, Ont.; m. Stewart; natural athlete who excelled in basketball, softball; mem. hydro commission-sponsored t&f team at 16; mem. Cdn Ladies' AC, teamed with Bobbie Rosenfeld, Jane Bell to win major meets, including New York's Millrose Games; ntl 220yd champion '28, bronze 100m '28 Olympics, ran 2nd leg with Rosenfeld, Bell and Myrtle Cook of gold medal 400m relay; 1 of 3 Cdn women to win 2 Olympic track medals (Rosenfeld, Hilda Strike); ret'd from competition '29; mem. Cdn Amateur; Canada's Sports Hall of Fame.

SMITH, Frank (builder/hockey); b. 1 Jun 1894, Chatham, Ont.; d. 11 Jun 1964, Toronto, Ont.; at 17 helped organize Beaches HL which evolved into Metropolitan Toronto HL, probably biggest minor league in world today; became 1ˢᵗ secty '11 and held position until he resigned '62; MTHL life mem.; OHA Gold Stick award; top CAHA award; Toronto award of merit; mem. Hockey Hall of Fame.

SMITH, Gary (hockey): b. 4 Feb 1944, Ottawa, Ont.; given name: Gary Edward; div.; c. Marshall, Sunny, Chelsea; race track official; goalie; mem. '64 Toronto Marlies Memorial Cup winner; pro Toronto Maple Leafs '64; earned nickname "Suitcase" as he saw pro service with Rochester, Hershey AHL, Tulsa CPHL, Victoria WHL, Fort Worth CHL, Indianapolis, Winnipeg WHA, Toronto, Oakland, California, Chicago, Vancouver, Minnesota, Washington, Winnipeg NHL in '64-80 pro career; NHL record: 14 seasons, 532 scheduled games, 152w, 237l, 67t, 29,619min, 1675ga, 26so, 3.39 GA avg., 20 playoff games, 5w, 13l, 0t, 1153min, 62ga, 1so, 3.23 GA avg.; shared Vezina Trophy with Tony Esposito '71; father Des, brother Brian both played in NHL; Brian became 1ˢᵗ brother to score goal against his brother in NHL; mem. Ottawa Sports Hall of Fame; res. Vancouver, B.C.

SMITH, George (swimming); b. 20 Nov 1949, Edmonton, Alta.; given name: George Warren; m. Lorraine Powell; c. Warren, Lindsey, Trent, Fraser; Indiana, UBC, BSc, AthabaskaU, MBA; international new franchise owner; 9 ntl age-group records; mem. '67, '71 PAG, '70 CG, '68 Olympic teams; 3 gold New Zealand, England '68; Cdn, Commonwealth records 200m, 400IM '68 Olympics; 2 gold, 2 silver '70 CG; 2 3rds NCAA championships '69; suffered near fatal motorcycle accident '71; attended UBC and swam for remedial reasons; 1ˢᵗ swimmer to win Bobby Gaul Trophy since '30 inception '75; CIAU 200, 400IM titles, CIAU outstanding swimmer award '77; coached swimming '72-74; City of Edmonton awards '60, '67-71; Alta. awards '69-71; CASA outstanding male swimmer '69; CIAU outstanding male swimmer '74; 6 times CASA Alta. section outstanding male swimmer; presented gold medal to brother Graham for 200IM victory '78 CG; ardent sailor; mem. UAlta Wall, Edmonton, Alta. Sports, Canadian Aquatic halls of fame; res. Nanaimo, B.C.

SMITH, Gina (equestrian): b. 11 Nov 1957, Saskatoon, Sask.; began riding age 12; turning attention to dressage; mem. ntl team from '84; reserve rider '84 Olympics; team bronze '88 Olympics; team gold '91 PAG; competed '96 Olympics; ntl dressage title '97, '99; Saskatchewan Horse Federation President's award '85; German Bereiter award '86. Saskatchewan athlete of year '89; suffered serious injury in riding accident '98; mem. Saskatoon Sports Hall of Fame; res. Brockville, Ont.

SMITH, Glen (rowing); b. 5 Aug 1931, Grand Forks, B.C.; given name: Glen William; m. Jean McKerrow; c. JoAnne, Maureen, Gregory; UBC; physician; mem. '54 BEG gold medal 8-oared crew; runnerup Grand Challenge Cup '55 Royal Henley Regatta; '56 Olympic team; silver medal crew '58 BEG; competed '03 FISA tour of Eng. with Commonwealth four; mem. Cdn Amateur, BC Sports Hall of Fame; res. New Westminster, B.C.

SMITH, Graham (swimming); b. 9 May 1958, Edmonton,

Alta.; given name: Donald Graham; m. Linanne Cameron; c. Cameron, Garrett; UCal, Cal. (Berkley), B Comm, MBA; exec. Pitney Bowes; mem. ntl team '73-82; 56 golds, 23 silvers, 8 bronze medals in competition ranging from ntl championships to CG and Olympic Games; in process set 17 Cdn, 5 CG, 3 Commonwealth, 2 world, 2 US Open records; achieved pinnacle of stardom in home town '78 CG with 6 gold (100m, 200m, breaststroke, 200m, 400m IM, 4x100 FS, 4x100 medley relays), set 5 CG, 3 Commonwealth records; 1ˢᵗ Cdn to win NCAA triple crown (3 individual golds, one relay) '79 NCAA championships; 6 CIAU, NCAA titles; 8 city of Edmonton, 7 Alta. awards, CIAU swimmer of yr award, Lou Marsh Trophy, Lionel Conacher award, Canada Sporting Goods Assn. award, Edmonton Sports Reporters Assn. award, Premier's award for performance, Norton Crowe award '78; hon. citizen of Winnipeg '79; fed. govt. excellence award '82; Gov.-Gen.'s medal '76; mem. Order of Canada; mem. Berkley, UAlta Walls, Canada's, Alta., Cdn Olympic, Edmonton Sports, Cdn Aquatic halls of fame; res. Albany, Calif.

SMITH, Gwen (administration); b. 31 Aug 1925, Toronto, Ont.; given name: Lorna Gwendolyn Lewis; m. William Donald Smith (d); c. George, Graham, Scott, Lewis, Allison, Sandra, Sue, Rebecca; UofT, BPHE; 1ˢᵗ women's PE dir. McMaster; dir. PHE Edmonton YWCA; has coached, officiated and supported swimming at all levels; coached competitive swimmers '62-74; officiated '67 PAG, '73 FISU, '78 CG; served in nearly all exec. capacities CASA Alta. section '62-85; 1ˢᵗ master official in Alta.; chair. Alta. swim officials '62-85; dir. Alta Sports Council '84-92; pres. Sports Alta. '81-84; dir. SFC; mem. Ntl Advisory Council on Fitness and Amateur Sport; served on exec. Cdn Council of Provincial and Territorial Sport Federations; chair. Edmonton Salute to Excellence comm. '90-97; mem. McMaster, Alta., Edmonton Sports halls of fame; res. Edmonton, Alta.

SMITH, Helen (shooting); b. 26 Jul 1950, Kirkland Lake, Ont.; given name: Helen Mae Mann; m. Welland "Smokey" Smith; London Teachers' Coll.; ret'd accounting clerk; handgun specialist; began shooting as a form of recreation '84; entered 1ˢᵗ competition same yr; mem. ntl team '86-97; 5 ntl women's sport pistol, 2 ntl women's air pistol titles; team silver '91 PAG; air pistol gold, sport pistol pairs silver (with Sharon Cozzarin) '94 CG; lost to Cozzarin in '92 Olympic qualifying shootoff; res. London, Ont.

SMITH, Hooley (hockey); b. 7 Jan 1903, Toronto, Ont., d. 24 Aug 1963, Montreal, Que.; given name: Reginald Joseph; mem. Granites '24 Olympic gold medal team; pro Ottawa '24-27, Montreal Maroons '27-36, Boston '36-37, NY Americans '37-41; 3 Stanley Cup finals, 2 winners; with Nels Stewart, Babe Siebert formed famed Maroons' Big S line; once 1ˢᵗ, 2ⁿᵈ team all-star; NHL record: 200g, 215a; mem. Hockey Hall of Fame.

SMITH, Kelly (t&f); b. 12 Apr 1965, Amarillo, Tex.; air traffic controller; moved to Kamloops, B.C. '76; active participant in variety of sports; mem. ntl speed skating team on Swedish tour '87; back broken in rock-climbing fall '91 left him a paraplegic; but he rediscovered his passion for sport competition with wheelchair racing; named to ntl team '98; set ntl 800m, 5000m, 10,000m records while posting numerous top-10 performances throughout world; competed in Boston Marathon '03 (bronze), IAAF worlds '01 (1500m finalist), '00 Paralympic marathon (10th), '02 IPC worlds; '04 Paralympics marathon silver; res. Vancouver, B.C.

SMITH, Larry (football): b. 28 Apr 1951, Montreal, Que.; given name: Lawrence William; m. Leesa Clark MacLean; c. Wesley, Ashley, Bradley; Bishop's, BA, McGill, BCL; football exec.; 1st overall '72 CFL draft by Montreal; rb/sb Alouettes '72-80 playing 140 consecutive regular season, 13 playoff games; competed in 5 Grey Cups, 2 winners; 9th CFL commissioner '92-96; instrumental in league expansion into the US.; pres./CEO Alouettes '97-02,'04; p.-pres. Bishop's Alumni Assn.; governor Bishop's; res. Montreal, Que.

SMITH, Mark (softball): b. 27 Jun 1959, Halifax, NS; given name: Robert Mark; m. Ann Dodge; c. Jasmine; Acadia; NS dept. of justice; lhp and strong hitter; competed 18 ntl championships; co-founder Halifax-Windsor Keiths; 4 PAG gold; ISC world titles with Camarillo Kings '81-82; 1 ISF world title with Team Canada; 5 all-world, 2 all-Cdn; top pitcher/hitter ntls; playing coach Halifax Jaguars; pitching coach Team Canada '98-03, head coach '04; coached ISF world gold '00, jr. worlds '01; mem. NS Sports, ISC, Cdn Softball halls of fame; res. Falmouth, N.S.

SMITH, Michael (t&f): b. 16 Sep 1967, Kenora, Ont.; UofT; brokerage firm; under coach Andy Higgins turned full attention to decathlon '85; competed 12 Gotzis; became 1st NA to win gruelling Gotzis decathlon '91 with 8,427 points, won 2nd '96; '91 world silver with Cdn record 8,549 points; gold '90, '94 CG, '89 Francophone Games; bronze '95 worlds, '98 CG; competed '86, '90, '94, '98 CG, '88, '92, '96 (flag-bearer '92) Olympic Games, 4 world championships; 1 Cdn jr., 3 Cdn sr., 1 Commonwealth record; 1 Arizona State, Florida Relays decathlon gold; 3 ntl outdoor decathlon titles, 1 indoor heptathlon title, 1 pentathlon title; 2 Jack Davies outstanding t&f athlete awards; Athletic Canada athlete of '94; 3 Fred Rowell field-athlete-of-yr awards; *CBC TV* athletics analyst; res. Calgary, Alta.

SMITH, Murray (hockey): b. 23 Oct 1945, Thunder Bay, Ont.; given name: Murray Edward; m. Sharon Wilson; c. Shannon Leigh; Lakehead, BA; personnel mgr.; sr. baseball Thunder Bay; coach Little League baseball; all-time Lakehead hockey records in 4-year college career; most career points 226, single-game points 8, career assists 134, single-game assists 5, season assists 39 shared with Rick Alexander, 6 career hat-tricks shared with Dwight Stirrett, 3 season hat-tricks shared with Dave Vaillant; led team scoring 3 seasons, team goals 3 seasons, team assists twice; twice league MVP; 4yrs NAIA all-American; res. Sudbury, Ont.

SMITH, Neil (hockey/administration): b. 9 Jan 1954, Toronto, Ont.; m. Katia; c. Viktor; Western Mich.; hockey exec.; consultant Pittsburgh Penguins; ex-pres./GM NYR; def. Brockville Jr. (CJHL), team capt./all-American WMU; drafted by NYI and spent 2 seasons in IHS; became Islanders scout '80-81; joined Detroit as dir. pro scouting, later dir. entire farm system; dir. scouting/GM/ governor Adirondack (AHL), 2 Calder Cups; became GM Rangers '89, pres. '92-00; 3 div., 2 President's, 1 Stanley Cup titles; *Hockey News* exec. of '94, *Sporting News* hockey exec. of '92, New Jersey

Sports Writers Assn. exec. of '94 awards; owner Johnstown Chiefs (ECHL); mem. WMU Sports Hall of Fame; res. New York, N.Y.

SMITH, Pop (baseball): b. 12 Oct 1856, Digby, N.S.; d. 18 Apr 1927, Boston, Mass.; given name: Charles Marvin; his initial exposure to baseball was probably to rounders, referred to as the Massachusetts game; arrived on ML scene as "elderly" 23-year-old and was tagged "Pop"; referred to as an agile fielder, with sure hands and an accurate arm; never a great hitter but showed flashes of power and was a good base stealer; normally a 2nd baseman he was regarded as a good utility player; joined Cincinnati (NL) '80; played with Cleveland, Worcester, Buffalo '81, Baltimore, Louisville '82, Columbus '83-84, Pittsburgh '85-89, Boston '90, Washington '91; ML record: 1093 games, 4176ab, 935h, 633r, 141d, 87t, 24hr, .224ba; mem. Cdn Baseball Hall of Fame.

SMITH, Robert (coaching/baseball/hockey): b. 1 Sep 1917, Milner Ridge, Man,; d. 11 Oct 1967, Winnipeg, Man.; excelled in baseball with Transcona srs. in '40s; drew interest from St. Louis Cardinals; began coaching '43-49 Morse Place jrs; 3 prov. titles; coached Elmwood all-stars Mandak League; by '50 operated 10-team peewee program; launched Little League in area; several city, prov., ntl titles; coached '53 mid-Canada champs, LL championships Illinois; coached hockey '47-65; 3 Elmwood city peewee, 4 Kelvin prov. juv champs; sports dir. Elmwood Windsor Club; mem. Man. Sports Hall of Fame.

SMITH, Rosaire (weightlifting): b. 9 Jan 1914, St. Rosaire, Que.; m. Auree Cardin; c. Armand, Gaston, Denis, Claire, Marcel, Jacqueline, Line; ret'd; competed at 123lb (56kg) level; ntl title '41; 3rd worlds '47; mem. '48, '52 Olympics; silver '50 BEG; '48 Commonwealth title; St. Jean Bosco trophy best lifter in class Montreal '48; Que. old timers title '59; taught dumbbell manipulation for high schoolers several years; res. Drummondville N., Que.

SMITH, Sandra (swimming): b. 29 Feb 1952, Edmonton, Alta.; given name: Sandra Irene; div. Gordon Osborne; c. Michael Bradley; m. Wayne Harris; c. Christa Lee, Shana Lynn; Montpellier (France), UAlta, BPhE; swim coach; mem. ntl team '67-71; mem. '67, '71 PAG, '70 CG, FISU Games; ntl 50, 100, 200, 400 FS records; only Cdn medalist (bronze 400FS) '70 FISU Games; tied with sister Sue high-point female as mem. UAlta swim team; asst. coach women's team '73-74; head coach '74-77; asst. coach Edmonton Olympic SC '77-81; coach Alta. team Western Canada Games '79; Edmonton awards '69-70; CWIAU outstanding female swimmer '72; Alta. section CASA outstanding-female-swimmer awards '66-67; mem. UAlta Wall, Edmonton, Alta. Sports halls of fame; res. Swift Current, Sask.

SMITH, Shannon (swimming): b. 28 Sep 1961, Vancouver, B.C.; m. Mark Jones; c. Celestina, Wesani; Hawaii, SFU, Guelph, UBC; ex-kayak guide; mem. Hyack Swim Club coached by Ron Jacks; mem. ntl swim team '74–78; mem. '75 world, '76 Olympic teams; bronze 400m FS with PB 4:14.60 '76 Olympics; 4 gold, 4 silver '77 Canada Cup; ntl record 800m FS 8:41.17 '77; BC jr. athlete of '76; Gov.-Gen.'s silver medal; Elaine Tanner award '76; conducted kayak tours in varied areas throughout world from Caribbean to Queen Charlotte Islands, Fiji and Hawaii; mem. BC Swimming, BC Sports halls of fame; res. Whistler, B.C.

SMITH, Sheldon (motorsport); b. 10 Sep 1928, Peterborough, Ont.; given name: Sheldon Louis; div. Joan Dunk; c. Joanne, Derrick; m. Maxine Rawson; ret'd CGE; began motorcycling age 16; 3 ntl 500-mile, 500 cc endurance titles; ntl motocross scrambles champion 500 cc expert class '58; ntl 500 cc jr. dirt bike title '57; Ont. 500 cc expert class road race title '58; held numerous exec. positions at prov., ntl levels of CMA; ntl CMA pres. '59-60; primarily responsible for development of motocross in Ont.; mem. Peterborough Sports Hall of Fame; res. Belleville, Ont.

SMITH, Sid (hockey); b. 11 Jul 1925, Toronto, Ont.; d. 29 Apr 2004, Toronto, Ont.; given name: Sidney James; m. June Millen; c. Scott, Blaine, Megan; ret'd salesman, court officer; Jr. A Oshawa Generals, Stafford srs., Que. Aces; pro Toronto '46-58; mem. 3 Stanley Cup winners; 2 Lady Byng awards; once 1st, twice 2nd team all-star lw; playing coach Whitby Dunlops, '58 World, '59 Allan Cup champions; NHL record: 601 scheduled games, 186 goals, 183 assists, 44 playoff games, 17 goals, 10 assists; 7 NHL all-star games; coached midget, Jr. C hockey briefly; John Sollenberger (AHL) top scorer award; mem. Toronto Oldtimers team; mem. Hockey Hall of Fame.

SMITH, Stanley (administration); b. 18 Jun 1897, Vancouver, B.C., d. 20 Mar 1975, Vancouver; tireless worker in field of amateur sport administration in BC 50yrs; general chair. '54 BEG; freeman city of Vancouver; mem. BC Sports Hall of Fame.

SMITH, Sue (swimming); b. 7 Dec 1950, Edmonton, Alta.; given name: Susan Evelyn; m. Terry Halak; c. Michael, Leslie; Montpellier (France), UAlta, BEd; teacher; mem. ntl team '67-72; alternate '68 Olympic team; mem. '70 CG, '71 PAG, '72 Olympic teams; 6 ntl titles 100m, 200m butterfly, 200IM, 400IM; 2 ntl records; 2 silver, 1 bronze '70 CG; bronze 200 butterfly '71 PAG; 100yd FS, 200yd butterfly titles '69 NZ; CWIAU high-point female mem. UAlta team '72-73; head coach Royal Glenora SC '72-73; Olympian SC '74-75; asst. to husband Olympian SC '76-78; coached sister Becky, brother Graham and Cheryl Gibson to their first Games teams; Alta. team coach Western Canada Games '75; 1st female Cdn coaching staff '75 World Aquatic championships; Edmonton awards '65, '68-71; Alta. awards '68-72; CWIAU outstanding-female-swimmer awards '72-73; CASA Alta. Section outstanding female swimmer 7 times; mem. UAlta Wall, Edmonton, Alta. Sports Hall of Fame; res. Edmonton, Alta.

SMITH, Tommy (hockey); b. 27 Sep 1885, Ottawa, Ont., d. 1 Aug 1966, Ottawa, Ont.; St. Patrick's Lyceum jrs., Ottawa Victorias srs. '06, led scorers; Pittsburgh (IL) '07, led team with 23 goals in 22 games; rover, OPHL scoring champion with 33 goals 13 games Brantford '09; top scorer, league title Galt '11, lost Stanley Cup bid to Ottawa; Moncton Maritime pro league '12, league crown, lost SC bid to Que. Bulldogs (NHA); Que. Bulldogs '13-16, formed line with Joe Malone, Jack Marks; trailed Malone by 4 goals 39-43 in scoring race, won only Stanley Cup; nicknamed "Little Bulldog" (5'4" 150lbs); mem. Canadiens '17, when NHA dissolved

'18 left hockey; returned for 10 games with Que. '19; in 171 recorded games, 239 goals, 15 in 15 playoff games; 5 times led league scorers, during '13 campaign scored in 14 consecutive games; twice scored 9 goals in single game, one 8-goal game, 4 5-goal games, 10 4-goal games, 15 3-goal games; no records for International or Maritime League play; mem. Ottawa Sports, Hockey halls of fame.

SMITH, Tricia (rowing); b. 14 Apr 1957, Vancouver, B.C.; given name: Tricia Catherine; UBC BA, LLB, hon. LLD; lawyer, specialist Intl sports law; mem. athletically-oriented family, father Marshal UBC rugby star, mother Patricia PAG basketball player, sister Shannon Olympic swimmer; ntl coxed 4 titles '74, '80; 8s '75, '80; with Betty Craig '76, '80 pair titles; gold pairs '76 West German, Swiss regattas; silver women's pairs '84 Olympics; mem. '76, '80, '84 Olympic, '77-79, '81-82 worlds teams; bronze 8s Worlds '77, '78; gold pairs '80 Holland, '83 Moscow regattas; bronze pairs '82-83 worlds; BC athletic achievement award '81; fed. govt. athletic achievement awards '82-84; chair. FISA women's commission; mem. Cdn Olympic, UBC Sports halls of fame; res. Vancouver, B.C.

SMITH, Wayne (weightlifting); b. 13 Jul 1955, Halifax, N.S.; self-employed welder; NS jr. 67kg title at 13; Maritime sr. 75kg title at 14; 2 Maritime records; ntl jr., sr. clean & jerk record 162.5kg 110kg class '73; 3rd NA '74; ntl 100kg title '77; 3 ntl jr., 1 Commonwealth jr. records '75; ntl sr. snatch record 140kg in 90kg class '76, sr. C&J record 100kg class '77; mem. '78 CG, '79 PAG, '81 Commonwealth championships; mem. NS Sports Hall of Fame; res. Truro, N.S.

SMITH-JOHANNSEN, Herman (skiing); b. 15 Jun 1875, Olso, Norway; d. 5 Jan 1987, Tonsberg, Norway; m. Alice Robinson (d); c. Alice Elizabeth, Robert, Ella Margaret; Norwegian Military Academy, UofBerlin; ret'd engineer; instrumental in introducing skiing as form of travel to NA; nicknamed "Jackrabbit'" by Cree and Ojibway Indians; opened Maple Leaf Trail Labelle to Shawbridge 30s; from '54 (age 75) confined skiing to x-country; instrumental in setting trail for Lachute-Ottawa National Ski Marathon; at 99 honored by King Olav V of Norway with Medal of St. Olav, first time to non-resident; subject of CBC films *Jackrabbit* and *The Long Ski Trail* and book *Jackrabbit-his first 100 years*; Dubonnet skier of '75; mem. Order of Canada, Cdn Skiing, Canada's Sports halls of fame.

SMREK, Mike (basketball): b. 31 Aug 1962, Port Robinson, Ont.; given name: Michael Frank; m. Sanja; Canisius Coll.; pro basketball player; set single- season/career field goal percentage record at Canisius; *AP* all-American hon. mention; ECAC North Atlantic 1st team all-star; drafted by Portland (NBA), traded to Chicago '85-86, Los Angeles '86-88, San Antonio '88-89, Golden State '89-92, L.A. Clippers; backup ctr to Kareen Abdul-Jabbar '86-88 winning 2 NBA titles; NBA record: 194 scheduled games, 554pts; 21 playoff games, 11pts; mem. ntl team '92; played in Greece '93, Croatia '96; YMCA fitness instructor Port Robinson; mem. Canisius Coll. Sports Hall of Fame; res. Split, Croatia.

SMYL, Stan (hockey); b. 28 Jan 1958, Glendon, Alta.; given name: Stanley Philip; m. Jennifer; c. Jilian, Natalie, Spencer; hockey coach; rw New Westminster jrs '75-78; pro

Dallas (CHL) '78, Vancouver (NHL) '78-91; NHL record: 896 scheduled games, 262g, 411a, 41 playoff games, 16g, 17a; Canucks team capt. '82-90; 3 Canucks MVP awards; described as "heart & soul" of Canucks during playing days; 1st NHL player to lead a team in goals, assists, points, penalty minutes in single season '79-80; asst. coach Vancouver '91-99; coach Syracuse '99-00; jersey #12 ret'd by Canucks; coach Manitoba Moose (AHL) '01-04; mem. BC Hockey Hall of Fame; res. W. Vancouver, B.C./Winnipeg, Man.

SMYLIE, Doug (football); b. 3 Jun 1922, Toronto, Ont., d. 19 Mar 1983, Toronto, Ont.; given name: Douglas John; div.; c. Randy, Cheryl, Craig; Cornell.; insurance agent; junior OHA; rejected pro hockey offers to join RCAF; won RCAF heavyweight boxing title; 5 gold medals RCAF t&f championships; football Cornell, Ottawa Trojan ORFU title team '47; pro Toronto '45, '49-53, Montreal '46, Ottawa '48; mem. 4 Grey Cup champions; CFL kickoff runback record 95yds '51 (broken '81); 4-handicap golfer, frequent club tourney winner; nicknamed "Big Ci".

SMYLIE, Rod Jr. (football); b. 25 Dec 1924, Toronto, Ont.; d. 8 Nov 1991, Toronto, Ont.; given name: Roderick; m. Helen Quebec; c. Catharine, Diane, Kristin, Rod; ret'd commercial traveller; nicknamed "Little Citation" while playing 11yrs in CFL with Argos '45-45, '48-55, Ottawa Trojans ORFU champions '47; captain Argos '51; mem. 4 Grey Cup champions; modern era ('45-73) Argo all-star team as sb.

SMYLIE, Rod Sr. (hockey/t&f); b. 28 Sep 1895, Toronto, Ont.; d. 3 Mar 1985, Toronto, Ont.; given name: Roderick Thomas; m. Mary Black (d); c. Anne (d), Douglas (d), Rod (d); UofT, MD; ret'd physician; capt. UofT track team; ntl 440yd champion '17; mem. Toronto Dentals hockey team '16-20; lw/capt. '20 world amateur champions; pro Toronto St. Pat's '21-22; rw '22 Stanley Cup winners.

SMYTH, Harry (speed skating); b. 21 Feb 1910, Moncton, N.B.; d. 20 Sep 1992, Moncton, N.B.; given name: Charles Henry; m. Marion Sharpe (d); c. Robert, Richard, Ron, Tom; ret'd CNR shop foreman; trained by his father, a former Maritime speed skating champion; world jr. outdoor title '26; all possible NA titles '26; Maritime cycling champion several times over 20yr span; mem. NB, inter-Maritime rifle team several times; mem. '32 Olympic skating team; managed provincial midget hockey title team; received personally autographed silver skates from actress Norma Talmadge for '26 world title win; Moncton city award for contribution to skating; mem. NB Sports Hall of Fame.

SMYTH, Jack (t&f); b. 24 Mar 1936, Winnipeg, Man.; m. Val; c. John, Kathleen; Houston, BSc, UMan, MEd; ret'd school superintendent; ntl jr., juv tj records; mem. '54 BEG, '55 PAG teams; 4 ntl sr. tj records; Mo. Valley Conf. hurdles record; Drake relays tj, sprint relay records; outstanding t&f athlete Houston '58-59; exec. mem. Man. TFA; mem. Man. Sports Hall of Fame; res. Winnipeg, Man.

SMYTH, Ryan (hockey); b. 21 Feb 1976, Banff, Alta.; lw Banff bantams '90-91, Caronport midgets '91-92, Moose Jaw (WHL) '92-95, Cape Breton (AHL) '96; Team Canada '95 world jr., '00, '01, '02 (capt.), '04 World Cup (gold), Olympic gold '02; NHL Edmonton '94-04; NHL record

(through '04) 642 scheduled games, 198g, 232a, 44 playoff games, 15g, 12a; res. Edmonton, Alta.

SMYTHE, Conn (hockey); b. 1 Feb 1895, Toronto, Ont., d. 18 Nov 1980, Toronto, Ont.; m. Irene; c. Hugh, Mariam, Stafford (d), Patricia; UofT; pres. sand and gravel co., hockey exec.; capt. Toronto Varsity '15 Ont. champions; coached Varsity to '27 Allan Cup, Varsity Grads to '28 Olympic title; coach NYR, released after assembling team that went on to win '28 Stanley Cup; purchased Toronto Pats, changed name to Maple Leafs; involved in Maple Leaf Gardens construction '31; managing dir., later pres. of Gardens, ret'd '61 after his team had won 7 Stanley Cups; supervised construction Toronto CNE's Hockey Hall of Fame; his racing stable produced 3 Queen's Plate winners; long involved with Ont. Society for Crippled Children; awarded Military Cross WW1; mem. UofT, Hockey, Canada's Sports halls of fame.

SMYTHE, Don (badminton); b. 27 Apr 1924, Toronto, Ont.; given name: Donald Keith; m. Betty Rennie; c. Rennie, Jackie, Heather, Kelly, Nancy; UWO; ret'd pres. Donsco Adhesives; 5 Ont. singles, 4 doubles titles; 4 ntl singles, with Budd Porter 4 men's doubles titles; semifinalist all-England (World) badminton championships '53, finalist '54; ranked 2nd in world '54; mem. 3 Thomas Cup teams; non-playing capt. '73; mem. 3 Commonwealth teams; mem. Cdn Amateur Sports Hall of Fame; res. Islington, Ont.

SNELGROVE, Karen (softball); b. 12 Mar 1969, London, Ont.; Missouri; sporting goods sales; rhp; NCAA all-American '91-92; academic all-American '91; pitched back-to-back no-hitters Missouri '91; mem. ntl youth team '87, sr. team '90-96; competed PAG '91 (silver), '95; '96 Olympics, NCAA College World Series '91; played for 3 time ntl jr. champion K-W Civitans, '94 ntl sr. champion Dorchester Jesters; posted 0.18era to lead NCAA '91; developed 2 pitching instruction videos; asst. ntl development team '01-02; mem. Waterloo County Hall of Fame; res. Kitchener, Ont.

SNELLING, Charles (figure skating); b. 17 Sep 1937, Toronto, Ont; m. Velma Green; c. Bradley, Lisa, Scott; UofT, MD; plastic surgeon; ntl jr. men's title '52; sr. titles '54-58, '64; NA silver '57; bronze '57 worlds; mem. '56, '64 Olympic teams; res. Vancouver, B.C.

SNELLING, Deryk (swimming); b. 22 Jul 1933, Darwen, Lancashire, Eng.; British Amateur Swimming Assn. Ntl performance dir. '96-04; pro swim coach; British ntl champion; coach Southhampton SC '62; head coach Vancouver Dolphins '67-76, ntl team titles each year; protegees won gold, silver, bronze medals in CG, PAG, Olympic, World Aquatic Games; coached Cdn ntl team '71 PAG, '72, '76, '80, Olympic, '73 world aquatic, '74 CG teams; coach Etobicoke '77-79, UCal '80-96; 7 CIAU coach-of-yr awards; author *All about Individual Medley*, co-authored *Swimming Coaching at Club Level*; mem. Order of Canada, B.C., Intl. Swimming, Cdn Aquatic halls of fame; res. London, Eng.

SNIPES, Angelo (football): b. 1 Nov 1963, Atlanta, Ga.; given name: Angelo Bernard; West Georgia Coll. '81-84; lb; mem. ntl Div. III title team '82; drafted USFL Oakland

Invaders '85, dealt to Memphis Showboats '86; NFL Washington '86, San Diego '87, Kansas City '88-90; CFL Ottawa '91-93, BC '94, Birmingham '95, Winnipeg '96-97; 3 Eastern, 2 CFL all-star; Jeff Russell Memorial Trophy '92; James McCaffrey trophy '92; runnerup CFL most outstanding player, outstanding defensive player '92; mem. 1 Grey Cup winner; res. Winnipeg, Man.

SNYDER, Brad (t&f): b. 8 Jan 1976, Windsor, Ont.; South Carolina; Ont HS shot put champion '94-95; ntl jr champion '94-95; set ntl jr record 17.34-metres '95; gold '95 Canada-US jr dual meet, '96 Gatorade Classic, Gamecock Invitational, LSU Alumni, Midland Walwyn Freedom Festival; javelin gold SEC championships '96; competed for South Carolina in NCAA championships '96-98; mem. '96 Olympic team; bronze '99 PAG; res. Windsor, Ont./South Carolina.

SOBRIAN, Jules (shooting); b. 22 Jan 1935, San Fernando, Trinidad; m. Frances; c. Camille, Glenn; St. Mary's College, Trinidad, UofT, MD; physician; pistol shooting specialist; '63-84 frequent ntl titles; silver free- pistol, bronze rapid fire '66 CG; bronze centre-fire, silver team '67, '71 PAG; silver rapid fire, gold free- pistol '74 CG; gold free-pistol '73 Western Hemisphere championships; bronze free-pistol, silver rapid fire '75 PAG; gold free-pistol, rapid fire '75 pre-Olympic intl; gold rapid fire '78 CG; mem. '68, '72, '76, '80, '84 Olympic teams; Ont. handgun champion '69-73; SFC golden anniversary award '82; life mem. SFC; pres. Responsible Firearms Owners of Ont. from '95; res. Omemee, Ont.

SOLES, Michael (football): b. 8 Nov 1966, Pointe Claire, Que.; m. Catherine; c. Justine (Montreal's 1st baby of '97); McGill; financial broker Nesbitt Burns; Vanier Cup MVP; CIAU rookie of '86; 2 McGill athlete of yr awards; Que. male student-athlete of '88; rb CFL Edmonton '89-95, Montreal '96-98; CFL record (through '98): 177gp, 42tds, 1cvt, 254pts, 568carries, 2961yds, 20tds, 288recpt, 3112yds, 22tds; 1 Northern, 1 Eastern all-star; Lew Hayman trophy '96; runnerup outstanding Cdn '96; 2 Grey Cup finals, 1 winner; res. Montreal, Que.

SOMERVILLE, Sandy (golf/cricket); b. 4 May 1903, London, Ont.; d. 17 May 1991, London, Ont.; given name: Charles Ross; m. Eleanor Elizabeth Lyle; c. Philip, Kenneth; Ridley College, UofT; ret'd life insurance exec.; played in last international cricket match between Canada, US '21; holds highest score for school cricket in Canada, 212 not out; mem. 12th Battery Ont. int. hockey champions '26; 6 Cdn amateur golf titles between '26-39, runnerup 4 times; Man. amateur, 1st of 4 Ont. amateurs '26; 1st Cdn to win US amateur beating Johnny Goodman in Baltimore '32, Lionel Conacher award '32; '38 semifinalist British amateur; *CP* poll golfer of half century '50; 2 Canadian Seniors Golf Assn. titles, shared title twice; pres. RCGA '57, CSGA '69-70; mem. UofT, RCGA, Cdn Amateur, Canada's, London Sports halls of fame.

SONMOR, Glen (hockey); b. 22 Apr 1929, Moose Jaw, Sask.; given name: Glen Robert; m. Marcia Stowe; c. Kathleen; Minnesota, BSc, Ohio State, MPhE; ret'd hockey exec., scout; Cleveland (AHL), New York (NHL); loss of eye as a result of hockey injury terminated playing

career; Minnesota coach '56; subsequently coach Jr. A St. Catharines; pro Springfield (AHL), Minnesota, Birmingham (WHA); chief scout Minnesota (NHL); GM Minnesota (WHA); coach Minnesota (NHL) '78-83, '84-85; scout Minnesota Wild '02-04; NHL coaching record: 417 scheduled games, 174-161-82; 43 playoff games, 25-18; scout Philadelphia '92-96, Phoenix '98-99; res. Hopkins, Minn.

SONNENBERG, Debbie (softball); b. 4 Jan 1971, Edmonton, Alta.; Huntingdon Coll. BA, Delta State, MSc, MEd; asst. softball coach Mercer U; lhp; competed '93 Canada Cup; ntl jr. championship gold '94; NAIA ntl bronze '94; ntl sr. gold '95; competed '94 sr. women's worlds, '95 PAG, '96 Olympics; NAIA all-American '91-94; ntl jr. championships MVP '93-94; top pitcher '94 PAG qualifier; 4 ntl title teams; asst. Keenesaw State, Auburn, Burnside HS NZ, Delta State; res. Leduc, Alta.

SOPER, Alice (golf); b. 6 Mar 1894, Montreal, Que.; d. 8 Oct 1994, Montreal, Que.; given name: Alice Ross; m. Harold Warren Soper; c. Warren, Anne; Bryn Mawr College; active golfer '12-74; 16 club championships; 1 Montreal Dist. title; mem. 3 Interprovincial teams, 2 Que. Srs. titles; ntl Srs. title '51; women's course records Murray Bay, Delray Beach; 3 Kennebunk, Me., titles; 4 Royal Montreal Charles Murray Memorial Trophy titles; competed '37 US women's amateur; CLGU v-p. '38-40, pres. '41-46.

SOPER, Barry (figure skating); b. 2 Jul 1948, Vancouver, B.C.; given name: Robert Barrett; m. Louise Ann Lind; c. Amy, Tiffany, Sean; UBC, BEd; real estate dev. mgr., coach; hockey, jr. tennis to age 15; teamed competitively with future wife '66; ntl ice dance gold medalist '68; US ice dance gold '69; ntl novice dance '67, jr. dance '69; sr. dance '71-74; 4th NA ice dance '71; mem. world championships '71-74; silver Skate Canada '73; silver dance BC '67, gold dance BC '68-69, BC sr. dance '68; taught elementary school phys-ed. '70-72; Hartshorne Memorial Trophy Squaw Valley '69; BC special achievement award (with Louise) '73; organized 35yr CFS reunion '03; with Louise mem. BC Sports Hall of Fame; res. N. Vancouver, B.C.

SOPER, Louise (figure skating); b. 11 Apr 1948, Vancouver, B.C.; given name: Louise Ann Lind; m. Robert Barrett Soper; c. Amy, Tiffany, Sean; UBC; dental hygienist; gold medalist figures, free skating; 1st teamed with future husband '66; (see Barry Soper for competitive record); Hartshorne Memorial Trophy for highest avg. gold dance test Sun Valley '68; mem. BC Sports Hall of Fame; res. N. Vancouver, B.C.

SOPINKA, John (football); b. 19 Mar 1933, Broderick, Sask.; d. 24 Nov 1997, Ottawa, Ont.; m. Marie Ethel Wilson; c. Randy, Melanie; Queen's, UofT, BA, LLB; lawyer, QC Supreme Court judge; hb Queen's Golden Gaels '52-53; hb UofT Blues '53-54; mem. Intercollegiate champions '54; pro hb/def capt. Argos '55-56, Alouettes '57; frequent legal lecturer; authored 1 book, several articles on law; accomplished violinist.

SORENSEN, Arne (shooting); b. 21 Jan 1934, Denmark; m. Rosemarie Monkman; c. Anna-Marie, Wayne, Stephen; drywall finisher; ntl team '71-84; mem. '71, '75, '79 PAG,

'76, '84 Olympic, '78 CG teams; team silver '79, bronze '71, '75 PAG; Benito Juarez small bore air rifle title '77, Championship of Americas air rifle individual, team titles '77; ntl English match (small-bore 3-position) titles '71-75; SFC golden anniversary award '82; mem. DCRA Hall of Fame; res. Calgary, Alta.

SORENSEN, Gerry (skiing); b. 15 Oct 1958, Kimberley, B.C.; given name: Geraldine Ann; m. Brendan Lenihan; c. Jessica, Nicholas; cashier; mem. ntl team '80-84; Pontiac Cup downhill title '80; 3ʳᵈ ntl downhill '80; initial world cup victory Haus downhill Feb '81; ntl, FIS downhill champion '81, '83; successive WC victories Grindelwald, Switzerland, 13-14 Jan '82; WC downhill France '84; WC record 5-0-1; BC athlete of '81-82; Bobbie Rosenfeld award '82; mem. '84 Olympic team; avid golfer, club title '01; snowboarder; mem. Cdn Skiing, Cdn Amateur, Canada's, BC Sports halls of fame; res. Coeur D'Alene, Idaho

SORENSEN, Ole (wrestling); b. 23 Apr 1948, Randers, Denmark; given name: Ole Toft; m. Claude Tellier, c. Cody, Catherine; UWO, BA, UAlta., BPhE; sr. consultant Sport Canada; Ont. HS titles gymnastics, wrestling; bronze W (most valuable wrestler), Claude Brown Memorial Cup (most valuable male athlete) UWO; block A (most valuable wrestler) UAlta; Alta, Ont. provincial sports achievement awards, several aquatic awards; hj/pv/wrestling titles in college; Alta., Ont., Western Canada Open, college, YMCA, 2 ntl FS wrestling titles; mem. '70 world, CG (bronze), '72 Olympics, '73 FISU Games teams; coached wrestling, gymnastics, aquatics; mem. CAWA ntl coaching staff; CAWA tech. dir. '75-77; lecturer Windsor '74-75; Sport Canada consultant from '77; *CBC-TV* color commentator '84 Olympics; res. Ottawa, Ont.

SORENSEN, Wayne (shooting): b. 8 Jul 1963, Calgary, Alta.; financial planner; following father Arne's lead began shooting at 13; rifle specialist; set ntl record in kneeling stage of 3-position event '82; competed 3 Benito Juarez, World Cup competitions, '92, '96, '00 Olympic, '94, '98 CG, '95, '99 PAG; with Michel Dion 3-position small-bore pairs gold, individual 3-position silver '94, '98 CG; air rifle team silver '95, individual air rifle bronze '99 PAG; 50m prone free-rifle silver '99 PAG; Gil Boa Memorial award '88; Alta. achievement award '79; res. Calgary, Alta.

SOSTORICS, Colleen (hockey); b. 17 Dec 1979, Kennedy, Sask.; UCal; def.; Team Sask. '95 Canada Games, '97 ntl -18 championships; capt. Kennedy boys bantams '96; 2 gold, 1 silver, 1 bronze ntl championship play; ntl -22 team '98-01, gold Christmas Cup Germany; ntl team from '01; gold '01, '04 worlds, '02 Olympics; gold '01 3-Nations Cup, '02 4-Nations Cup, silver '03; Sask. provincial fastball tournament MVP '94, '95; prov. fastball, soccer, hockey titles '97; 2 CIAU all-Cdn; street in Kennedy (Colleen Sostorics Avenue) bears her name; mem. NWHL Oval X-Treme from '99; res. Kennedy, Sask.

SOULLIERE, Bernie (baseball/administration); b.6 Jul 1937, Windsor, Ont.; given name: Bernard; m. Carole Jean Maisonville; c. Michael, Laurie, Christopher, Jerry; ret'd Chrysler; 40yrs expereience as player, coach.mgr, umpire, business mgr., organizer, exec.; p-pres. Ont. Baseball Assn, v-pres Baseball Canada; bus. Mgr ntl youth teams; pres.

Mic-Mac Club, sports chair. 30+yrs; Montreal chapter Pro. Baseball Writers '73 man of yr; Intl Baseball Assn. President's award '86; Baseball Ont. volunteer of yr award; Ont. premier's award; Windsor baseball facility bears his name; coach, organizer 3 Ont. Summer Games baseball title teams; mem. '03 hosting comm. Baseball Canada festival; has served on host comm. for 2 ntl midget, 5 midget prov., 4 sr. prov., 3 world youth, 1 ntl sr. championships plus varied ntl team training camps, ntl invitational, Rick Wiseman Memorial, Rev. Ronald Cullen tournaments; mem. Windsor/ Essex Sports Hall of Fame; res. Windsor, Ont.

SOUCHEREAU, Kelsey (squash): b. 28 Jul 1969, Calgary, Alta.; Alberta College of Art; graphic designer; ntl jr. titles '83-85; mem. ntl jr. women's team '85-87; mem. ntl sr. team from '94, team gold '96 ntl championships; 1 individual, 2 team silver '94 Pan-Am championships; 2 team gold, '95 PAG; competed inaugural World Cup '96; res. Victoria, B.C.

SOVRAN, Gino (basketball/t&f); b. 17 Dec 1924, Windsor, Ont.; m. Inger Kathryn Seim; c. Daniel Louis, Victoria Gene, Ralph Edward, Andrew Lars; Assumption Coll,. BA, Detroit, BME, Northwestern, MSc, Minnesota, PhD; ret'd General Motors research engineer; 4yrs jr., 1yr sr basketball Kennedy CI, 1 WOSSA title, all-star, scoring title; capt. Assumption Coll 2yrs, 1ˢᵗ to score 1000 points in 3 seasons; leading scorer Det. '45-46; competed '46 Eastern Cdn championships; pro Toronto Huskies '46-47; mem. Ont. champion Windsor Alumni '48; hj specialist; winning city, WOSSA, Ont. jr., int., sr. titles; set hj, hop, step & jump (tj) records; also claimed bj/pv/relay titles; competed in some t&f meets with Det. but WW2 curtailed normal activity; mem. Cdn Basketball, Windsor Sports hall of fame; res. Troy, Mich.

SOWIETA, Rick (football): b. 16 Jan 1954, Huesden, Belgium; div. Joanne Elizabeth; c. Katie, Sara; Richmond, BA; restaurateur; mem. Glebe HS jr. football champions '69, coaches def. MVP award; Glebe sr. def. MVP '71; Glebe sr. basketball MVP '71; Glebe Don Lewicki, Dick Stewart awards; def. lineman Ottawa Sooners Eastern jr. football finalists, outstanding dl award; attended Richmond on football scholarship, 2 conf. titles; Toronto CFL '77-78, Ottawa '79-86; 4 all-Eastern all-star awards; Ottawa specialt-team award, Schenley top Canadian nominee; '81 Grey Cup finalist; played in '83 CFL all-star game; received Ottawa 100ᵗʰ regular season game award '85; hon. chair. CF 65 Roses Club '86-87; co-chair. '88 Grey Cup breakfast comm.; asst. coach Ottawa Bootleggers '90-91; asst. coach Sooners '92-94; pres. Sooners '01; asst. coach St. Mark's HS, UofOtt; res. Gloucester, Ont.

SPACK, Mike (basketball); b. 5 Mar 1922, Winnipeg, Man.; m. Kathleen Saint; c. Suzanne, Jamie, Catherine; UMan, MEd; ret'd educator; played college, prov. sr. basketball simultaneously (no longer allowed); mem. Winnipeg Paulins prov. title teams; 2 Western Intercollegiate title teams; mem. '54 ntl sr. championship team; '54 World Cup team; ret'd from active play after 47 years; coached several teams including YMHA ntl jr. finalists; Man. HS basketball commissioner; bantam league organizer; officiated several years, Man officials commissioner; racquetball competitor, instructor; mem. BrandonU faculty

'66-87; several basketball awards in his name competed for annually in Man; mem. Man Basketball Hall of Fame; res. Brandon, Man.

SPARKES, Bernie (curling); b. 15 Oct 1940, Claresholm, Alta.; given name: Bernard Leslie; div. Lindsay Davie; c. Christopher, Karen, Lisa, Selena; m. Laura; ret'd salesman; mem. ntl Pony League baseball champions '55, Babe Ruth League champions '56; mem. '58 Alta. HS curling champions; Edmonton world open carspiel title '65; mem. record 11 Brier rinks, 3 winners, 3 world championship rinks; all-star 2nd Ron Northcott's Brier title rinks '66, '68-69; skip 7 BC Brier reps.; Evergreen, Dogwood, Kamloops, Prince George cashspiels '76; Saskatoon cashspiel '77; finalist Edmonton cashspiel '79, Vernon car spiel '80; noted artist; mem. Canadian Curling, Southern Alta., Lethbridge, BC Sports halls of fame; res. Chilliwack, B.C.

SPARKES, Lindsay (curling); b. 8 Jun 1950, N. Vancouver, B.C.; given name: Lindsay Davie; div. Bernie Sparkes; UBC, SFU BEd; teacher/librarian; skipped ntl women's title rinks '76, '79; 3rd for Linda Moore '85 STOH, world title, '88 Olympic (demonstration) gold medal; ntl women's team leader (coach) from '92 at world, Olympic levels; with Linda Moore competed in first women's skins game; level 4 coach; proficient golfer, skier; mem. Cdn, BC Curling, BC Sports halls of fame; res. N. Vancouver, B.C.

SPARLING, Jean (t&f); b. 26 Feb 1955, Vancouver, B.C.; given name: Jean Donalda; m. Bill Gairdner; c. Christine, Emilie, Ruthann, Billy, Franklin; UBC, UofT, BSc; ntl juv 200m hurdles record '72; gold 100m, 100m hurdles, 200m hurdles, silver 4x100 relay '73 Canada Games; 4th '76 Olympic trials 200m; mem. '77 FISU Games team; ntl 60yd hurdles record 6.63 '78; mem. '74 ntl title BC jr. field hockey team; BC high school athlete of year; res. King City, Ont.

SPEERS, Jim (horse racing); b. 1882, Elmbank, Ont., d. 19 Jul 1955, Winnipeg, Man.; given name: Robert James; "Mr. Racing" in Western Canada; key role fostering Man., Sask., Alta., BC thoroughbred racing; built, operated Whittier, Polo, Chinook Parks; also operated summer race meetings for exhibition associations in Regina, Saskatoon, Edmonton, Calgary; 1st Canadian breeder to raise winners of more than $1 million on NA tracks; 6 consec. Cdn breeder-of-yr awards; founder Prairie, Canadian Thoroughbred Breeders Assns.; founded Canadian Derby for 3-year-old foals; introduced pari-mutuel betting to Canada; pioneered daily double in NA; installed 1st closed automatic starting gate in NA Whittier Park '39; launched Red Book of Canadian Racing '30; mem. Canadian Horse Racing, Man., Canada's Sports halls of fame.

SPEIER, Chris (baseball); b. 28 Jun 1950, Alameda, Calif.; given name: Chris Edward; m. Aleta; c. Justin, Erika, Luke, Travis; California (Santa Barbara); baseball coach, mgr.; semipro Stratford Sr. IC '70; SF Giants '71-77, '87-89, Montreal '77-84, St. Louis '84, Minnesota '84, Chicago Cubs '85-86; ML record: 2260 scheduled games, 7156ab,770r, 1759h, 302db, 50tr, 112hr, 720rbi, 42sb, .246ba; helped Giants reach '71 Western Div. title, batted .375 in losing playoff cause; NL all-star ss *Sporting News* poll '72; *AP* ML all-star '73; mem. 3 NL all-star teams; 1 of

2 Expos (other Tim Foli) to hit for cycle in game '78; Expos single-game RBI record 8 '82; batted .400 in Expos' div. series playoff vs. Phillies '81; minor league mgr. Arizona Diamondbacks org. '98; batting instructor Cubs org.; mem. Athletes for Life; res. Phoenix, Ariz.

SPENCER, Jim (soccer); b. 13 Feb 1915, N. Vancouver, B.C.; d. 14 Apr 1990, Vancouver, B.C.; given name: James Haggarty; m. Sheina Kathleen Murray; c. Jesslen Helen; ret'd fire chief; capt. N. Van. HS bantam title team; coach, mgr. 4 consecutive Van. all-star teams vs visiting Europeans; Sr. A basketball with Lauries; rejected '38 offers to play in Eng. League 1st Div., with West Brom, Derby County; refereed juv soccer; dir. chair. BC Juv Soccer Assn. '62-76; 2 ntl titles; mem. every BC all-star team during 1st div. career; 7 goals, 3 games for BC all-stars California World's Fair; secty. Pacific Coast Soccer League; mem. soccer discipline board and referee assessor; life mem. BC Youth Soccer Assn.; mem. Cdn Soccer, North Shore, BC Sports halls of fame.

SPENCER, Victor (rowing); b. 6 Oct 1882, Victoria, B.C., d. 21 Feb 1969, Vancouver, B.C.; Columbia Coll.; Boer War, WW1 vet.; mem. VRC 60yrs; club pres. '24-25, '28, hon. pres. '29-69.

SPIR, Peter (t&f); b. 6 Nov 1955, Manchester, Eng.; given name: Peter Charles Francis; m. Kimberley Conner; Oregon, BSc; BC, ntl jr. mile record 4:02.9 '74, jr. 1500m record 3:41.4 '75; ntl sr. 1500m title '75; ntl jr. 800m title, ntl, BC jr. 3000m steeplechase record 8:53.4, BC sr. 2000m 5:11.4, BC jr. 3000m 8:18 '75; Pac-8 Conf. 1500m record 3:46; mem. '75 FISU, '76 Olympic, '79 PAG teams; res. Eugene, Ore.

SPOWAGE, Cheryl (t&f/rowing); b. 30 Jan 1953, Comox, B.C.; given name: Cheryl Lynne; div. Tom Howard; c. Francine Louise; UBC, BPhE; teacher; competed at 800m, 1500m, 1 mile distances, '67-72; midget all-around athlete Richmond championships, BC midget 800m champion '67; BC juv mile title '68; bronze open 1500m '69; ntl juv 800m title '69; BC HS 1500m titles '70-71; Stanley Park 15- mile road race title '72; ran '81 Vancouver International marathon in 2:58.19; rowing '74-78; with Pam Gilmore BC double sculls title '75; singles, doubles titles '76; with Bev Cameron 6th Olympic double sculls finals '76; with Cameron BC doubles title '77, singles, doubles, quad titles '78; ntl, Royal Henley titles '78; 4 Richmond Outstanding Athletic Achievement awards; top jr., sr. HS track athlete awards; res. Surrey, B.C.

SPRAGUE, Dave (football): b. 11 Aug 1910, Dunkirk, N.Y., d. 20 Feb 1968, Ottawa, Ont.; given name: David Shafer; m. Catherine Anderson; c. David Jr., John, Judy, Peter, James; company v-p.; teamed with Huck Welch to lead Delta CI to ntl HS title; capt. HS t&f team specializing in miile; football Hamilton Tigers '30-32; 2 interprovincial, 1 Grey Cup winner; Ottawa '33-41; twice capt. Riders, 3 Big Four titles, 1 Grey Cup; all-Eastern, all-Cdn almost every year of 10yr career; mem. Ottawa, Cdn Football, Canada's Sports halls of fame.

SPRATLEY, Jim (shooting); b. 9 Nov 1962, York Twp., Ont.; Centennial Coll.; only sponsored shooter in NA;

youngest mem. ntl team; 2nd jr. small-bore prone '84 Benito Juarez; 3rd '84 ntl championships; PB: unofficial world record tie 600x600 sr. men's English match prone; res. Pickering, Ont.

SPRAY, Robert (rugby); b. 22 May 1913, Surrey, Eng.; d. 10 Apr 1991, Vancouver, B.C.; m. Joan; c. Rosemary, Andrew; insurance agent; knee injury cut playing career short, turned to administration; emigrated to Vancouver '47, became referee; chair. Cdn rugby tours committee '60-65; pres. CRU '65-72; Jack Patterson Memorial Trophy; Air Canada Amateur Sport exec-of-year award candidate; mem. BC Sports Hall of Fame.

SPRING, Doughy (lacrosse); b. 24 Jan 1888, Draper, Ont., d. 1974, New Westminster, B.C.; given name: Clifford; baker, mechanic; mem. New Westminster Salmonbellies '05-36, 5 Minto Cup winners; prolific scorer judged by peers as outstanding player of his day; at 49 scored 9 goals single box lacrosse game; mem. Lacrosse, BC Sports halls of fame.

SPRING, Harry (administration); b. 27 Sep 1912, Moose Jaw, Sask.; d. 17 Jul 1988, Vancouver, B.C.; given name: Harry Charles Frederick; m. Constance Hicks; c. Robert, Elaine; UBC, BA, LLB; lawyer; jr. soccer Moose Jaw; qb 2 Meraloma BC sr. football title teams; pres. Meraloma Club '37, hon. life mem. from '81; chair. BC Lions organizing group; exec. mem. Lions '53-60, life mem. from '60; CFL commissioner's Vancouver rep. '61-80; mem. Lions bd. of governors from '61; mem. Roughriders board; CFL contribution to game award '67, Centennial Medal '67; mem. Canadian Football Hall of Fame.

SPRINGSTEAD, Velma (t&f); b. 22 Aug 1906, Hamilton, Ont., d. 27 Mar 1926, Hamilton, Ont.; given name: Velma Agnes; bronze hj, Lord Decies Trophy (meet's best all-around competitor) '25 UK Canada-UK-Czechoslovakia tri-meet; pneumonia victim at 20; trophy in her honor presented to Women's Amateur Athletic Fed. of Canada (later absorbed by SFC) by Alexandrine Gibb '32 to be awarded to nation's outstanding female athlete annually.

SQUIRES, Bert (weightlifting); b. 17 Aug 1954, St. John's, Nfld.; PE teacher; ntl 100kg title '79, 90kg title '82, 110kg title '84; ntl sr. records snatch 156kg, C&J 186kg, total 337.5kg; silver 100kg '80-81, team bronze '80 Commonwealth championships; bronze 100kg Pan-Am championships, Shanghai invitational '80; silver 100kg '81 Pan-Am championships, Cuban invitational; bronze snatch '83 PAG; mem. '79, '83 Pan-Am, '80, '84 Olympic, '82 CG teams; res. Pangnirtung, NWT.

ST. GERMAIN, Val (football); b. 8 Oct 1971, Ottawa, Ont.; m. Heidi; McGill BA; off. guard; bantam/midget fb Myers Riders; CIAU/OQIFC all-star; CIAU all-Cdn; played '94 East-West Shrine game; McGill athlete of '94 award; CFL Hamilton '94-98, Edmonton '99-01, Ottawa '02-04; 1 East, 1 West all-star; 1 Grey Cup game; res. Ottawa, Ont.

ST. GODARD, Emile (dogsledding); b. 15 Aug 1905, Winnipeg, Man., d. 26 Mar 1948, The Pas, Man.; dog breeder, trainer; gained fame in series of races vs Leonard Seppala; 200-mile The Pas race winner '25, '26; beat Seppala

Que. City '27; pair met annually at Que. City over next 6 years with St. Godard winning 4 times, Seppala twice; pair also competed The Pas, Alaska, Minnesota, Laconia, North Conway with St. Godard winning majority of encounters; last meeting '32 Lake Placid as Olympic demonstration sport following which Seppala, 54, conceded St. Godard's superiority; at peak, '25-35, St. Godard and team raced 1500 miles per season; noted for kindness and concern for his dogs; when lead dog was no longer up to rigors of racing St. Godard ret'd from competition; mem. Man., Canada's Sports halls of fame.

ST. LOUIS, France (hockey); b. 17 Oct 1958, St. Hubert, Que.; PE teacher, sports dir.; competed in sr. women's ntl championships '83-94; fwd 6 ntl sr. women's title teams; 3 Sr. A league MVP awards; 2 Sr. A league scoring titles; 3 ntl championship MVP awards; mem. 6 Team Canada world championship teams; Pacific Rim, 3-Nations Cup gold; mem. '98 Olympic silver medal team; ret'd '99; mem. ntl women's lacrosse teams '85-89, 2 world championships; Que. athlete of '86, athlete of decade '80-90; asst. coach Team Quebec '91 Canada Winter Games; res. St. Hubert, Que.

ST. LOUIS, Martin (hockey); b. 18 Jun 1975, Laval, Que.; m. Heather; c. 1 son; Vermont; rw Vermont '93-97, 4 scoring titles, 3 all-American awards, 1 NCAA all-championship tournament team; Cleveland (IHL) '97-98, Saint John (AHL) '97-00; Team Canada '04 World Cup (gold); NHL Calgary '98-00, Tampa Bay '00-04; NHL record (through '04) 364 scheduled games, 109g, 150a, 34 playoff games, 9g, 15a; 1 Stanley Cup winner; Art Ross, Hart, Lester Pearson awards '04; played with Davos Switzerland during '04 labor dispute, won Spengler Cup; played organized youth soccer; res. Tampa, Fla.

ST. MARSEILLES, Frank (hockey); b. 14 Dec 1939, Sudbury, Ont; m. Brenda Jenkins; c. Rob, Christopher, Lizanne, Chris, Jeff; sales; rw with minor league stints in New Haven (EHL), Sudbury (EPHL), Chatham (OHA, IHL), Port Huron (IHL), Kansas City, Fort Worth (CHL), Nova Scotia (AHL) '61-78; NHL St. Louis '67-73, LA '73-77; 1 NHL all-star game; NHL record: 707 scheduled games, 140g, 285a, 88 playoff games, 20g, 25a; mem. Senators Alumni; res. Ashton, Ont.

ST. MARTIN, Pierre (handball); b. 4 Sep 1957, St. Jean sur Richelieu, Que.; teacher; ntl team '75-80; mem. 5 ntl title teams; mem. '76 Olympic team; 2nd '80 Pan-Am handball championships; Que. handball player of '80; res. St. Jean sur Richelieu.

ST. PIERRE, Kim (hockey/softball/soccer); b. 14 Dec 1978, Chateauguay, Que.; Andre Laurendeau Coll., McGill; shortstop Team Que. Softball; 11yrs soccer standout; goaltender; led McGill women's team to CIAU silver '00 (top rookie award), bronze '01; joined men's team '03-04; 3 CIAU all-Cdn; led Que. Team to Esso Cup silver '01, top goalie award; CIAU championship MVP '00; ntl team from '98; 5 worlds (top goalie award '01, '04), 3 gold 4 Nations, 3 Nations Cups; Olympic gold '02; mem. Cdn u-22 team; CIS female athlete of yr award; Laurendeau athlete of '98 award; father Andre played CHL hockey with Omaha; res. Chateauguay, Que.

ST. PIERRE, Martin (t&f): b. 4 Mar 1972, Ripon, Que.; racewalker; represented Canada '91, '93, '95 World Cup of racewalking, '94 CG, '95 PAG, '96 Olympic Games; gold 10km '93 Canada Games; ntl 20km title '95; Cdn male athletic prospect of year '94. Quebec University male athlete of '90; res. Montreal, Que.

STACEY, Nelles (rowing): b. 9 May 1888, Vancouver, B.C.; d. 31 Jan 1968, Vancouver, B.C.; given name: George Nelles; mem. Vancouver Rowing Club from '06; "Mr. Rowing" Vancouver region; mem. '10-11 Miller Cup rugby titlists; rowed in 2 slot '09 NPAAO 4s title Seattle in record 7:49.5 for 1Ω miles; varied exec. roles Vancouver Rugby Assn., Vancouver Rowing Club; chief fund raiser VRC/UBC mid-'50s BE, CG winners; mgr. '55 Henley 8s, '57-59 PAG teams; trophy in his name awarded annually by VRC to jr. coxless 4s; mem. Cdn Amateur, BC Sports halls of fame.

STACK, Frank (speed skating): b. 1 Jan 1906, Winnipeg, Man.; d. 25 Jan 1987, Winnipeg, Man.; m. Edith Nixon; c. Bonnie, Diane; ret'd salesman; competed regularly '19-54 winning varied honors; Western Canada jr. titles '19-23, sr. '24-29; Western Open indoor title '31-33, world 5-mile record 15:42.2; bronze 10,000m, 4th 500m, 1500m '32 Olympics; 6 ntl titles; US outdoor title '31; world indoor 500m record 47.0; rep. Canada 6 Olympics, 3 as competitor, others as official; only Cdn to win 10,000 Lakes championships also Silver Skate competition Minneapolis, set points record; following 12yr retirement, competed ntl indoor championships at age 60, taking 3 2nds, 2 3rds; life mem. St. James Speed Skating Club Winnipeg; Man. Centennial Comm. '70 speed skater of century; mem. Canadian Speed Skating, Man., Canada's Sports halls of fame.

STAIRS, Matt (baseball) b. 27 Feb 1969, Fredericton, N.B.; given name: Matthew Wade; m. Lisa; c. Nicole, Alicia, Chandler; of; signed as free agent with Expos '89; spent several seasons in minors with Rockford, West Palm Beach, Jacksonville, Harrisburg, Ottawa, New Britain; Pawtuckett, Edmonton; brief stints in ML with Montreal; played with Chunichi Dragons of Japanese Central League '93 before returning to Expos; traded to Boston '94; joined Oakland as free agent '95-00, Chicago Cubs '01, Milwaukee '02, Pittsburgh '03, Kansas City '04; ML record (through '03): 1046 scheduled games, 3060ab, 488r, 813h, 175db, 7tr, 176hr, 568rbi, 23sb, .266ba; shunted between majors and minors until '97 when his power blossomed with 27 homers, followed with 26 '98; 1st Cdn to hit 25 or more HRs in successive seasons; won batting titles Mexican Winter, Eastern Leagues; EL MVP with Harrisburg and EL all-star game MVP '94; tied Triple-A record with 6rbi single inning; res. Cardigan, N.B.

STANFIELD, Fred (hockey/coaching): b. 4 May 1944, Toronto, Ont.; given name: Frederic William; c. Dean; furniture store owner; ctr OHA St. Catharines '61-64, CHL St. Louis '65-67; NHL Chicago '64-66, Boston '67-73, Minnesota '73-75, Buffalo '74-78; NHL totals: 914 scheduled games, 211g, 405a, 106 playoff games, 21g, 35a; 2 Stanley Cup winners; player-coach Hershey AHL '78-79, Niagara Falls OHL '79-80; with John Bucyk, John McMenzie formed Boston's Hot Line; brothers Jack,

Jim also played in NHL; operated summer hockey camps St. Catharines/ Weymouth, Mass.; nicknamed "Steady Freddie"; mem. Mississauga Hockey Hall of Fame; res. Buffalo, N.Y.

STANLEY, Allen (hockey); b. 1 Mar 1926, Timmins, Ont.; given name: Allan Herbert; m. Barbara Bowie; owner, operator resort, golf course; Boston Olympics srs.; pro Providence Reds (AHL); def NYR '48-54, Chicago '54-56, Boston '56-57, Toronto '58-69; rejected coaching offer Quebec Aces (AHL); operates successful hockey school; NHL record: 1244 scheduled games, 100g, 333a, 110 playoff games, 7g, 36a; 4 Stanely Cups; asst. coach Buffalo '77; mem. Hockey Hall of Fame; res. Bobcaygeon, Ont.

STANLEY, Barney (hockey); b. 1 Jun 1893, Paisley, Ont., d. 16 May 1971, Edmonton, Alta.; given name: Russell; jr. Paisley; amateur Edmonton Maritimes, Dominions, Albertas '09-15; mem. Vancouver Millionaires '15-19, 1 Stanley Cup; player-coach amateur Edmonton Eskimos '19-20; player-coach pro Calgary Tigers '20-22, Regina Capitals '23-24, Edmonton Eskimos '24-26, Winnipeg Maroons '26-27; coach-mgr. Chicago Black Hawks '27-28; Minneapolis Millers '28-29; coach Edmonton Pooler jrs. 3 years; as pro played every position except goalie; in 216 games, 144 goals; twice 5 goals single game; mem. Hockey Hall of Fame.

STANOWSKI, Wally (hockey); b. 28 Apr 1919, Winnipeg, Man.; given name: Walter Peter; m. Joyce DuBrule; c. Wally Jr., Adair, Adrian, Craig; salesman; jr. football MVP '37; mem. St. Boniface Seals '38 Memorial Cup champions; pro AHL Syracuse Stars '38-39; excluding '42-44 when he served in RCAF, mem. Maple Leafs '39-48; Rangers '48-51; Cincinnati '51-52; all-star NHL def '41; NHL record: 428 scheduled games, 23g, 88a, 60 playoff games, 3g, 13a; mem. 4 Stanley Cup winners; mem. Toronto NHL Oldtimers to '81; mem. Man. Hockey, Etobicoke Sports halls of fame; res. Etobicoke, Ont.

STAPLETON, Pat (hockey); b. 4 Jul 1940, Sarnia, Ont.; given name: Patrick James; m. Jacqueline Prudence; c.Mary, Maureen, Tommy, Susan, Michael, Christopher; nicknamed "Whitey"; farmer; Jr. B Sarnia, Jr. A St. Catharines, all-star OHA def, mem. Memorial Cup winner; minor pro Sault Ste. Marie, Kingston (EPHL), Portland (WHL) '60-65; Boston, Toronto property, Chicago '65-73; player-coach WHA Chicago Cougars; with Ralph Backstrom, Dave Dryden, bought team to become 1st person in major league history to own team, manage, coach and play simultaneously; when Cougars collapsed joined Indianapolis Racers as player; mem. Team Canada '72, WHA Team Canada '74; tied NHL playoff assists record with 13 '71, set standard of 15 '73 playoffs; NHL, WHA record 6 assists single game; Dennis Murphy Award top WHA def '74; 3 times NHL 2nd team, once WHA 1st team all-star; NHL record: 635 scheduled games, 43g, 294a; mem. Oldtimers hockey, ntl advisory council '83; jr. B team GM '02-04; mem. Sarnia/Lambton Sports Hall of Fame; res. Strathroy, Ont.

STARR, Harold (hockey/football); b. 6 July 1906, Ottawa, Ont.; d. 25 Sep 1981, Ottawa, Ont.; given name: Harold William; hotelier; def. jr. hockey Ottawa Gunners, St. Brigid's, Shamrocks; AHL stints with London, Windsor,

Cleveland; NHL Ottawa '29-31, '32-33, Montreal Maroons '31-32, '34, Montreal Canadiens '32-33, NYR '34-36; NHL totals 205 scheduled games, 6g, 5a, 15 playoff games, 1g, 0a; reinstated amateur '36 and played 2 sr. seasons Ottawa '37-39; hard-nosed tackle, end Ottawa Rough Riders football team; mem. 2 Grey Cup winners; owner-operated Carleton Hotel; mem. Ottawa Sports Hall of Fame.

STASIUK, Vic (hockey); b. 23 May 1929, Lethbridge, Alta.; given name: Victor John; m. Mary Ragnfrid Lenning; c. Vanessa, Elsa, Victor Guy, Jae Jae; ret'd farmer/golf course owner; minor hockey Lethbridge Native Sons, jr. Edmonton-Wetaskiwin Canadians; pro Kansas City '48-49; NHL Chicago '49-50, '55-60. Boston '50-55, '60-63; lw Bruins' famed Uke Line with Bronco Horvath, Johnny Bucyk; NHL record: 745 scheduled games, 183g, 254a, 69 playoff games, 16g, 18a; 1 all-star game, 2 Stanley Cup winners; turned to coaching '63-75 with minor league stints in Pittsburgh, Memphis, NJ, Quebec, California, Denver and NHL stops in Philadelphia, Vancouver, St. Louis; NHL coaching record: 307 scheduled games, 88-153-66; 4 playoff games, 0-4; developed Paradise Canyon Golf & Country Club; recipient Elizabeth Dufresne trophy (Boston); res. Lethbridge, Alta.

STASTNY, Peter (hockey); b.18 Sep 1956, Bratislava, Czechoslovakia; m. Darina; c. Katarina, Kristina, Paul-Peter, Yan-Pavol; hockey exec.; special assignments St. Louis; played with HC Slovan Bratislava '73-80, winning ntl title '79; Czech player of '80; defected to Canada '80; NHL Quebec '80-90, New Jersey '90-93, St. Louis '94-95; Calder Memorial Trophy '81; set 1st yr player record 70a, 109pts; capt. Nordiques '85-90; 6 NHL all-star games; NHL record: 977 scheduled games, 450g, 789a, 93 playoff games, 33g, 72a; at '95 retirement was highest scoring European-born and trained player in NHL history; mem. Czech ntl team '75-76 jr. worlds, '76-77 sr worlds, '76 Canada Cup, '80, '94 (Slovak flag-bearer) Olympics, '95 worlds; became Canadian citizen '84; mem. Team Canada '84 Canada Cup; GM Slovak team '02 Olympics; mem. NHL, IIHF, Slovak Hockey halls of fame; res. St. Louis, Mo.

STAUB, Rusty (baseball); b. 1 Apr 1944, New Orleans, La.; given name: Daniel Joseph; ret'd restaurateur/chef; Louisiana Scholastic athlete of '61; $100,000 signing bonus Houston organization; limited minor league seasoning at Durham, Oklahoma City; Colts '63-64, Astros '65-68, Montreal '69-71, '79, NY Mets '72-75, '81-85, Detroit '76-79, Texas '80; ML record: 2951 scheduled games, 9720ab, 1189r, 2716h, 499db, 47tr, 292hr, 1466rbi, 47sb, .279ba; 1st genuine Expos superstar; nicknamed "Le Grande Orange" for his red hair; 6 all-star game appearances; '73 World Series; uniform #10 ret'd by Expos; mem. Montreal Expos Wall of Fame; res. New York City, N.Y.

STAUDER, Zlatica (rhythmic gymnastics/builder): b. 10 Sep 1946, Bratislava, Czechoslovakia; given name: Zlatica Takacova; m. Milan Stauder; c. Zuzanna; U J.A. Komenski, UMan. BPhE; emigrated to Canada '68; joined Man. Gymnastics Assn. exec and introduced rhythmics discipline to province; developed, taught 1st courses for coaches, teachers, judges in Western Canada; created 1st independent rhythmic gymnastics club in Man; founder, head coach Manitoba High Performance Centre for Rhythmic Gymnastics; instrumental in establishing comm. for alternate education of elite athletes in province; Cdn RGF, international judges comm. high-performance coach, official of '89; Man. Sports administrator of '02; mem. Man. Sports Hall of Fame; res. Winnipeg, Man.

STEAD, Ron (baseball); b. 24 Sep 1936, London, Ont.; m. Betty; c. Ron, David, Heather, Jeff; training supervisor Union Gas; minor baseball Toronto Stanley Park, several OBA titles; initially played 1st base and didn't start pitching until he was 13; batboy Toronto (IL) '45-54; London Sr. IC '55; minor pro Toronto organization '56-57; Sr. IC Brantford '58-66, Guelph '67-72; 16-year IC record: 104 wins, 44 losses, 1365 innings pitched, 1231 strike outs, 262 walks, 119 complete games, 2.08 lifetime ERA; IC record lowest ERA 1 season, 0.35 in 77 innings Guelph '67 (since surpassed); 4 times 1st team, twice 2nd team all-star; IC MVP '60, '63, '65, '67; single-season shutout record (7) '67; mem. Ont. gold medal team '69 Canada Summer Games; mem. '67 PAG team; mem. Man. Baseball Hall of Fame; res. Chatham, Ont.

STEADWARD, Robert (builder); b. 26 May 1946, Eston, Sask.; given name: Robert Daniel; m. Laura Thomson; c. Tommi Lynn, Bobbi Jo; UAlta BPE, MSc, U Oregon PhD, hom. Degrees UAH DDL, Leuven Belgium DDL; educator; multi-sport athlete starring jn football, hockey, baseball, t&f; mem. several champion UAlta teams; coached t&f UAlta '69-79, fb, t&f HS '69-76, community baseball (2 ntl titles) '66-68; fitness consultant NHL Edmonton Oilers, Cdn Olympic hockey team; played major role in Cdn Paralympic program; served as ntl coach '66-76, chef de mission '71-80, ntl governor '70-86, treas. '74-76, pres. '86-91; founder/pres. Alta Wheelchair Sports Assn, Cdn Sports fund for physically disabled; pres. IPC '89-01; organizational role with '78 Commonwealth Games, '83 FISU Games; co-chair '98 Edmonton world athletic championship bid; exec 2010 Vancouver/Whistler Olympiuc/Paralympic bid comm.; exec. CIAU; founder/pres. UAlta Green & Gold Society '84-01; mem. IOC commission on reform; chair. Edmonton Sport Institute; pres. TBL Sport Services; agent/mgr. Skaters Jamie Sale/David Pelletier; founder/dir. Steadward Centre (formerly Rick Hansen Centre); prof. emeritus UAlta; mem. COA '02; recipient Golden Jubilee award, UAlta distinguished alumni, Governors award, U Oregon distinguished service award, Alta achievement award, Kappa Sigma Alumnus, Edmonton service citation, Alta. Sports Council volunteer, Bryce Taylor SFC Memorial, Cdn Commerative medal, King Clancy, Robert Jackson Alta. exemplary service, inaugural Steadward award, Senator John Tower distinguished Kappa Sigma, Rutherford award of excellence, UAlta teaching award, Edmonton ambassador award, Rotary International Paul Harris fellow; hon. Life mem. Alta Paralympic Sports, Alta. Wheelchair Sports, Cdn Wheelchair Sports, Cdn Paralympic comm.; hon. Pres. Intl. Paralympic Comm.; mem. Order of Canada; UAlta Sports Wall, Terry Fox, Alta., Edmonton Sports halls of fame; res. Edmonton, Alta.

STECKLE, Bob (wrestling): b. 21 Aug 1930, Waterloo Twp; given name: Robert John; m. Kay Allison Francis; c. David, Jane, James, Susan; Ont. Agricultural Coll. BSA; farmer; Wildman fb trophy '51; OQAA heavyweight champion '50-52; 9 ntl open FS titles; US open Greco-

Roman champion '55-57; mem. 3 Cdn Olympic teams; silver '54, bronze '58 CG; silver '63 PAG; flag-bearer, 4th Greco-Roman '56 Olympics; Cdn 4H achievement award; mem. Cdn Wrestling, UGuelph Sports halls of fame; res. New Hamburg, Ont.

STEELE, David (soccer/hockey/baseball); b. 31 Dec 1914, Muskeg Lake Reserve, Sask.; d. 22 Jul l996, Regina, Sask.; given name: David Greyeyes; ret'd Dept. Indian Affairs; he excelled in soccer and was 3 times Sask. all-star team mem.; represented Sask. vs. Newcastle United '49 following WW2 service; mem. Cdn Machine Gun Reinforcement Unit soccer team which won overseas army title '42; also played in inter-Allied games; player/coach following WW2; mem. Sask. Sports, Sask. Indian First Nations Sports halls of fame.

STEEN, Dave (t&f); b. 2 Jan 1942, Vancouver, B.C.; m. Cassie Gairdner; c. Laura, Heather, Stefan; Oregon, BSc; writer-author; shot put specialist; ntl shot record 53'10" '60, held (with improvements to 63' 1/4") to '72; bronze '62, gold, Games record '66 CG; mem. ntl track team more than decade; ret'd from shot put competition '71; competed '80 Ottawa marathon; mem. Burnaby Sports Hall of Fame; res. Terra Cotta, Ont.

STEEN, Dave (t&f); b. 14 Nov 1959, Burnaby, B.C.; given name: David Lee; m. Andrea Page; c. Kory, Jordan, Jacey, Jack; UofT, Berkeley; fireman; decathlon specialist; father Dan '56 Cdn decathlon champion; uncle Dave CG shot put gold medalist; '77 Canada Games decathlon/lj, ntl outdoor lj; mem. '79, '83 PAG, '80, '84, '88 Olympic, '81, '83 FISU, '82 CG teams; '80 ntl indoor pentathlon, '81-82 decathlon, '84 heptathlon titles; '82 CIAU long jump; '83-84 UofT track classic pentathlon; decathlon gold '83 FISU, PAG, silver '82, '86 CG, bronze '88 Olympics; 1st Cdn to score more than 8000 points in decathlon with record 8019 '82 LSU Invitational; 9 ntl titles, 7 ntl decathlon records; world pentathlon record 4,104 points '83; 4 Fred Rowell trophies; PB: 8205 decathlon points, 4108 pentathlon points; fed. govt. excellence award '84; Canada Games spokesperson; mem. Canada's Fair Play commission; Ont athlete of '88; mem. Order of Canada; Cdn Amateur, Canada's, BC, Burnaby Sports halls of fame; res. Tecumseh, Ont.

STEEN, Thomas (hockey); b. 8 Jun 1960, Crums, Sweden; c. Alexander; ctr varied Swedish teams, including ntl team, throughout playing days; competed 3 world jr., 3 Canada Cup tournaments winning 1 silver, 2 bronze; 1 world silver, 3 world all-star teams; 1 European jr. title; entire NHL career Winnipeg '81-95; NHL totals: 950 scheduled games, 264g, 553a, 56 playoff games, 12g, 32a; finished career in Germany '95-99; scout Minnesota; nicknamed "Swedish Goon"; Jets ret'd jersey 25 when team moved; res. Gothenburg, Sweden.

STEEVES, Ed (curling): b. 17 Oct 1936, Moncton, N.B.; m. Helen; chiropractor; 3rd for Hap Mabey '69-70 Briers; all-star skip '74 ntl mixed; coached 3 NB jr, '70 ntl jr. title rinks; NB curling exec. '76-80; NB pres. '78-79, NB delegate to CCA '78; CCA dir. '85-91; CCA pres. '89-91; Intl Curling Fed. pres. '88; v-p. World Fed. '90-94; key role in amalgamation of ntl. assn into CCA; worked hard to secure Olympic status for curling; CCA exec. of '92; Ross Harstone award '70; mem. Moncton Sports Wall, Cdn Curling, NB Sports halls of fame; res. Gibsons, B.C.

STEGALL, Milt (football); b. 25 Jan 1970, Cincinnati, Ohio; Miami of Ohio; wr, NFL New Orleans '98; CFL Winnipeg '95-04; 4 CFL, East. 1 West all-star; CFL single-season record 23 tds '02; CFL outstanding player '02; CFL record (through '04) 141 scheduled games, 112tds, 3x2pt cvt; 623 receptions, 11,134yds; res. Winnipeg, Man.

STEMMLE, Brian (skiing); b. 12 Oct 1966, Toronto, Ont.; mem. ntl team '85-99; 2 ntl titles; competed '88, '92, '94, '98 Olympics; downhill specialist; sister Karen former ntl team mem.; WC Super G bronze '85, downhill bronze '87, silver '96; career dogged by injuries, near fatal crash '89 but returned to competition '91; won winter Pan-Am gold '91; 11 world top-10 finishes, 3 WC medals; spirit of sport award; accomplished figure skater; mem. Cdn Skiing Hall of Fame; res. Aurora, Ont.

STEMMLE, Karen (skiing); b. 27 Jan 1964, Toronto, Ont.; given name: Karen Jean; m. Julian Keith Brandon; c. Sydney Jean; personal fitness trainer, motivational speaker, ski coach; holds private pilot's licence; Grade 8 Conservatory of Music (piano); downhill specialist; 5yr mem. ntl team; 5 top 9 finishes world downhill competition; ntl jr. DH title '81; NA DH title '82; with Liisa Savijarvi proprietor Ski Escape Inc.; Level 2 Cdn Ski Instructor Alliance; Level 3 Cdn Ski Coaches Fed.; competed '84 Olympics; competed provincially in figure skating, water skiing; avid scuba diver, motorcyclist; volunteer fund-raiser numerous charities; res. Toronto, Ont.

STEPHENSON, Linda (golf); b. 3 Aug 1944, Domville, Ont.; given name: Linda Mae; Algonquin Coll.; Stats Canada programmer analyst; played competitive softball; began golfing '68; left-hander; mem. Prescott GC '68-83, '98, Carleton Golf & Yacht Club '84-97; winner of 26 consec. and 27 in 28yrs club championships; Que. sr. title; Ottawa City & District titles '85, '86, '88; 4 tournament of champions titles; 6 ladies' course records; 2 holes-in-one; 4 consec. Brockville sr. titles, 21 (20 consec) Prescott, 5 Mississippi, 4 Cornwall field day titles; with Jim MacKay teamed to win 19 Prescott, 2 Tecumseh, 11 Smiths Falls, 3 Cornwall (2 more with Jean Lachance), 3 Ottawa Hunt, 1 Buckingham mixed 2-ball titles; res. Nepean, Ont.

STERNBERG, Gerry (football/basketball); b. 18 Mar 1943, Orsk, Russia; given name: Gerald; m. Tania; c. Arlen, Samantha, Zachary, Ryne; UofT, BA, Osgoode Hall, LLB; barrister, solicitor, player agent; OUAA all-star; '65 Vanier Cup MVP; dh/rb all-star each position '63; pro Edmonton '65, Montreal '66-67, Toronto '69-71, '73, Hamilton '71-72; 2nd to Jim Copeland in Argos records for punt returns with 151 for 861yds; mem. Cdn basketball teams world masters silver '94, Maccabiah Games silver; mem. UofT Hall of Fame; res. Toronto, Ont.

STEVENS, Rick (cricket): b. 18 Mar 1945, London, Eng.; given name: Richard John; m. Jane; emigrated to Canada at 14; mem. Ont. interprov. team '62; ntl Colts cap '63; 5 sr. ntl caps; considered all-arounder who utilizes natural skills to fullest degree; mem. Rest of World team vs. Bermuda '73; mem. Eastern ntl XI in victory over Australian WC team; res. Ajax, Ont.

STEVENS, Scott (hockey): b. 1 Apr 1964, Kitchener, Ont.; m. Donna; c. Kaitlin, Ryan, Kara; def Kitchener (OHL) '80-82; Memorial Cup '82; 1st Washington pick '82 draft; NHL with Washington '82-90, St. Louis '90-91, New Jersey '91-04 (capt); NHL all-rookie team '83; 2 NHL 1st team, 3 2nd team all-star; Alka Seltzer Plus award '94; acquired by New Jersey as compensation for St. Louis signing of free agent Brendan Shanahan; played 12 all-star games; mem. Team Canada '83, '85, '87, '89 worlds, '91 Canada Cup, '96 world cup, '98 Olympics; mem. 2 Stanley Cup winners; only player to participate in 600+ games 2 different teams (Wash, NJ); holds record 1616 games played by def; NHL record: (through '04) 1635 scheduled games, 196g, 712a, 233 playoff games, 26g, 92a; Conn Smythe trophy '00; named by *SN* 5th most fearsome NHL player; active in charitable programs; res. Essex Falls, N.J.

STEVENS, Warren (football): b. 1905, Syracue, N.Y., d. 25 Oct 1978, Melbourne, Aust.; m. Charlotte "Chubby" Tickner; c. Jacqueline; Syracuse, BSc; ret'd UofT athletic dir.; reputation as passing qb while leading Syracuse HS to city football title; all-American mention in university sr. year; rejected pro baseball offers Philadelpia Athletics; mem. MAAA Winged Wheelers, McGill backfield coach; made Cdn rugby football history '31 tossing 1st legal forward pass to end Frank Robinson; Wheelers won Grey Cup that year and Stevens completed 1st Grey Cup 40yd td pass to Ken Grant; 1st to score convert on fake placement and run in Grey Cup; 1st AD UofT '32-70; as head coach (roles he yielded '41) 3 Intercollegiate football and basketball championships; mem: UofT Sports Hall of Fame.

STEVENSON, Art (football): b. 30 May 1916, Gothenburg, Neb.; d. 21 Sep 2000, Phoenix, Ariz.; given name: Arthur Clement; m. Dorothy Bowden; c. Sally, Curtis, Gary; Hastings College MD; ret'd obstetrician, gynecologist; Little all-American, hon. mention in basketball; Little all-American football '36, conf. discus championship; pro Winnipeg '37-41; after WW2 coached Bomber backfield; best all-time all-around athlete Hastings College; mem. Canadian Football Hall of Fame.

STEVENSON, Bill (football); b. 20 Aug 1950, Edmonton, Alta.; given name: William George; m. Carol; c. Stephanie, Tanner; Drake; territorial draft Eskimos; NFL draft Miami; opted for WFL Memphis Southmen '74-75; CFL offensive, defensive lineman Edmonton '75-88; mem. 6 Grey Cup winners; 3 WFC, 2 CFL all-star selections; res. Edmonton, Alta.

STEVENSON, Douglas Roy (football); b. 21 Oct 1930, Drumbo, Ont.; m. Barbara Jean St. Pierre; c. Chrystal Ann, Roderick Michael (d), Tevy Joan, Reme Marie, Wendy May; UofT, UAlta, MSc; hydrogeologist, company pres.; mem. UofT boxing team '51-52; football Kitchener-Waterloo Dutchmen '53-54, ORFU title '54 losing Little Grey Cup game to Edmonton Eskimos; mem. Eskimos '55-62, Grey Cup champions '55, '56; line coach UAlta Golden Bears '64-70, CIAU title '67; res. Langley, B.C.

STEVENSON, Forbis (curling/golf): b. 17 Nov 1913, Saint John, N.B.; d. 14 June 1995, Cold Lake, Alta.; given name: Forbis Beatrice McGeouch; m. Otty Stevenson; c. Norman, Nancy; mem. Mable DeWare Dominion Diamond

D title rink; noted for sportsmanship she served as pres. Paragon Ladies Golf Club, Kingston, NS mem. Grand Centre, Paragon, Westfield, Moncton, Amberdale golf clubs, Middleton, Thistle St. Andrews, Moncton Beaver, Mayflower curling clubs; mem. NB, Moncton Sports halls of fame.

STEVENSON, Greg (rowing): b. 27 Feb 1969, Sherbrooke, Que.; McGill; entrepreneur; began rowing age 20; men's 8s; mem. ntl team from '91; bronze coxless 4s '91 PAG; 2 silver '95 PAG; 1 ntl 8s title; competed '92. '96 Olympics; Quebec Rowing Assn. athlete of yr '91; dir. Victoria Community Corp. Rowing Challenge; res. Victoria, B.C.

STEVENSON, Lori (bowling): b. 28 Oct 1965, Neepawa, Man,; given name: Lori Lynne Greider; m. Peter Stevenson; c. Amy, Sarah; Man. research asst.; YBC Man. singles title '83, ntl bronze; Man. record 4 provincial singles titles; ntl gold '93, '95, silver '84-85; ntl all-star '84, '93, '95; repeat ntl title tied record; ntl women's Hiram Walker Special Old Pins Game title '94; pres. Minnedosa bowlers assn.; received early training from father Wilf and brother Bob, both prominent bowlers; holds Level 2 ntl coaching certificate; coach women's team '03 Man. Championships; res. Minnedosa, Man.

STEVENSON, Ross (horseshoes): b. 11 Jun 1948, Kitchener, Ont.; c. William; owns Horseshoe Express courier; 5 ntl jr. boys titles; 1 Manitoba, 8 Alta. men's singles titles; ntl men's singles title '88; world B class crown '72; 1st Cdn to win world title claiming jr. boys title '65; mem. Cdn Horseshoe Hall of Fame; res. Calgary, Alta.

STEVENSON, Victor (football): b. 22 Sep 1960, New Westminster, B.C.; UCal; tackle; CFL Sask. '82-92, BC '93-95, Toronto '96, Winnipeg '97; 2 Western, 1 Northern, 1 CFL all-star; Becket-DeMarco Memorial trophy '92; runnerup CFL outstanding offensive lineman '92; 2 Grey Cup winners; res. Vancouver, B.C.

STEWART, Black Jack (hockey); b. 6 May 1917, Pilot Mound, Man., d. 25 May 1983, Detroit, Mich.; given name: John Sherratt; race track judge; jr. Portage La Prairie; pro '38 Detroit but spent all but 33 games with Pittsburgh (AHL); Detroit regular '39-50, Chicago '50-52; mem. 2 Stanley Cup winners; 3 times 1st, twice 2nd team all-star def; Detroit MVP '42-43; coached Chatham Maroons, sr. OHA teams Windsor, Kitchener, Pittsburgh (AHL); ret'd from hockey '63; NHL record: 503 scheduled games, 30g, 79a; Florida State harness racing commissioner; mem. Cdn, Man. Hockey halls of fame.

STEWART, Brian (motorsport): b. 27 May 1942, Port Glasgow, Scotland; m. Sharon; c. Kimberley; aggressive racer who began motorsports career '65; Cdn Formula Vee title '69; Cdn Formula Ford title '72; 12th Formula Ford world championships '72; turned attention to team ownership fielding cars in FF1600, FF2000, Super Vee, Atlantic; Brian Stewart Racing drivers earned 10 titles before he entered full-time Indy Lights competition '89 as team mgr Landford Racing; BSR team, including Bryan Herta, P.J. Jones, Gualter Salles, Paul Tracy claimed 7 poles, 9 wins '90; most successful owner in Indy Lights history boasting back-to-back titles, 30 victories, '90-91; 6

victories, 2 poles, 2 rookie titles, 3rd place finishes '95-97; res. Pefferlaw, Ont.

STEWART, Gordon (soccer/lacrosse); b. 6 Jan 1929, Vancouver, B.C.; d. 12 May 2003, Coquitlam, B.C.; m. Doris (d); c. Gordon Jr., Brad, Ross, Kirk, Jim; retd pulp mill safety, insurance officer; adept at ball control, clever playmaker with powerful shot; while still in HS joined North Shore '48 winning Ed Bailey rookie of yr award; competed 14 ntl finals, winning 7 in 17yr career; claimed ntl titles North Shore '49, Vancouver City '50, New Westmindter '55, '58, '60, Vancouver Columbus '64, Vancouver Firefighters '65; recruited by Everton, Ebglish Div. 1 '54 and placed on reserve team; helped Canada score two triumphs over U.S. to qualify for '57 World Cup from which Canada was ousted by Mexico; B.C. soccer all-star '49-53, '55-65; mem. Cdn all-star team which toured England, Scotland, Soviet Union '60; mem. 2 Minto, 2 Mann Cup lacrosse titlists; in 211 sr. games scored 215g, 178a; at 15 won 1st of 2 consec. golden gloves boxing titles; HS basketball all-star; played sr. A Vancouver vs. Harlem Globetrotters; on retirement helped organize sr. lacrosse team in Fort St. James; key role in building 100 Mile House rink; nickname "Gogie"; mem. B.C. Sports Hall of Fame.

STEWART, Gordon (t&f); b. 6 Sep 1948, Toronto, Ont.; given name: Gordon William; m. Sandra Maynard; SFU, BA, MSc; fitness consultant, freelance writer, editor; city all-star basketball '67; North Toronto CI athlete of '66-67; Toronto jr. pv/tj records '62-67; ntl midget tj title '64; ntl jr. decathlon title record 6150 points '68; Canada Games decathlon '69; mem. '70 CG, '71 PAG, '73 FISU Games teams; 4 ntl decathlon titles; record 7438 points '72; ntl team '70-76; authored *Every Body's Fitness Book*; res. Victoria, B.C.

STEWART, Mary (swimming); b. 8 Dec 1945, Vancouver, B.C.; m. R.H. McIlwaine;UBC, BE; teacher; coached by Howard Firby; silver 4x100 FS relay '59 PAG team at 13; finalist 100m FS '60, 100m butterfly '64 Olympic teams; gold 110yd butterfly, silver 4x110 medley, FS relays, bronze 110yd FS '62 CG; silver 100m butterfly, FS, 4x100 medley, FS relays '63 PAG; world records 100m, 110yd butterfly '61-62; UK, US, Cdn ntl butterfly, Cdn ntl FS, backstroke titles; 2 Velma Springstead awards; 2 Beatrice Pines Cdn outstanding-female-swimmer awards; mem. '75 PAG headquarters comm.; BC Lions football team mascot '56-63; mem. Cdn Aquatic, BC Swimming, Amateur, BC Sports halls of fame; res. Vancouver, B.C.

STEWART, Nels (hockey); b. 29 Dec 1900, Montreal, Que., d. 21 Aug 1957, Wasaga Beach, Ont.; given name: Nelson Robert; brewery rep.; Montreal Maroons '25-32, 34 goals rookie season; nicknamed "Old Poison"; with Babe Siebert, Hooley Smith formed S Line; 134 goals, 56 assists 5 years on S Line; 1st NHL player to score more than 300 goals (324 goals, 191 assists, 653 league games); Boston '32-35, NY Americans '35-40; twice Hart Trophy; mem. 1 Stanley Cup winner; coach Port Colborne Srs.; mem. Canada's Sports, Hockey halls of fame.

STEWART, Ray (golf); b. 28 Jan 1957, Matsqui, B.C.; m. Maureen; c. Brett, Tyler; UBC; turned pro '80; Cdn tour victories '99 Telus Edmonton Open, Cdn Masters;

with Dave Barr/Rick Gibson won '94 Dunhill Cup; on PGA tour '83, '87-95; runnerup '89 Chattanooga Classic, '87 Bank of Boston Classic; also played Asian, European tours; twice Dunhill Cup team mem.; ranked 2nd '99 Cdn tour McDonald's Order of Merit; mem. Cdn World Cup of Golf team '99; res. Abbotsford, B.C.

STEWART, Ron (football); b. 25 Sep 1934, Toronto, Ont.; m. Wendy Thomas; c. Melissa, Christian; Queen's, BA, BPHE, UofOtt, LLB.; lawyer, ombudsman, Solicitor-General's dept.; mem. Queen's '55-56 Yates Cup winners, league MVP '57, Webster scholarship '58; pro rb Ottawa '58-70, 4 Grey Cup finals, 3 winners; Jeff Russel Memorial Trophy '60, '67; Schenley top Canadian '60; Lionel Conacher award '60; Walker Trophy (Ottawa club MVP) '60, '67; Eastern Conference all-star '60, '64; Ottawa Jaycees young man of year, Ont. Achievement Award '70; sweater #11 ret'd by Rough Riders; CFL record most-yds-gained-single-game (287 Montreal Oct '60) stood as pro football record until broken '03 by NFL's Jamal Lewis with 295yds; 13-season CFL record: 983 carries, 5690yds, 5.8yds-per-carry avg., 41tds; dir. Ottawa Football Club; mem. Canadian Football, Canada's, Queen's, Ottawa Sports, OUAA Football Legends halls of fame; res. Ottawa, Ont.

STEWART, Ron (hockey); b. 11 Jul 1932, Calgary, Alta.; given name: Ronald George; m. Barbara Christie; hockey exec.; fwd Toronto Marlboros, Windsor Spitfires, Barrie Flyers, Guelph Biltmores all in one season helping latter win Memorial Cup '52; pro Toronto '52-65, Boston '65-67, St. Louis '67-68, NYR '68-71, '72, Vancouver '71, NYI '72-73; NHL record: 1353 games, 276 goals, 253 assists, 119 playoff games, 14 goals, 21 assists; coached '73-74 Portland (WHL) team from last place to playoff final, '74-57 Springfield Kings to AHL championship; Ranger coach '75-76, Los Angeles '77-78; NHL coaching record: 119-46-54-19; 2 playoff games, 0-2; NYR player personnel dir. '77; mem. 3 Stanley Cup winners; res. Kelowna, B.C./Surprise, Ariz.

STEWART, Susan (basketball); b. 14 Nov 1969, Toronto, Ont.; Laurentian, BA (law & justice); civilian employee RCMP; mem. 5 OWIAA, 2 CIAU title teams; 5yrs OWIAA all-star; mem. '87 jr., '90-97 sr. ntl teams; 1st team all-Cdn; competed '91 PAG, '96 Olympics, 2 FISU Games; mem. Athletes in Action tournament team; attended WNBA draft camp; Laurentian athlete of '94 award; Nan Copp award '94; mem. Laurentian Sports Hall of Fame; res. Mississauga, Ont.

STICKLE, Leon (officiating/hockey): b. 20 Apr 1948, Toronto, Ont.; given name: Leon Evan; m. Nancy Smith; c. Jayne, Christine, David; NHL supervisor of officials from '03; played minor hockey Milton, Jr. B. Sarnia, Jr. A St. Catharines; 12yrs minor league officiating; joined NHL '69 as linesman working initial game '70; worked 8 Stanley Cup finals, 4 NHL all-star games, '81, '84 Canada Cup tournaments; worked 1967 NHL scheduled games over 27 seasons; 5yrs dir. hockey operations CHL/WPHL; active with Ont., Cdn Special Olympics; coach minor baseball; res. Mt. Forest, Ont.

STIEB, Dave (baseball); 22 Jul 1957, Santa Ana, Calif.; given name: David Andrew; m. Patti Faso; c. Andrew David; Southern Illinois; ret'd baseball player; *Sporting News* college all-American of; semipro Alaska; drafted Toronto '78; among premier AL rhp; Blue Jays regular '79-92, '98; ML record: 443 scheduled games, 2895.3ip, 176-137, 103cg, 1669k, 1034bob, 3.44era; youngest pitcher '80 all-star game; twice AL pitcher of month; Labatt's, Toronto BBWAA MVP '80, 3 Labatt's pitcher-of-month awards; mem. 7 all-star games; pitched no-hitter vs. Cleveland '90; mem. '92 World Series winner; co-author *Tomorrow I'll be Perfect*; ret'd from baseball '93; made brief comeback in Blue Jays organization '98; mem. Blue Jays Level of Excellence, Cdn Baseball Hall of Fame; res. Incline Village, Nev.

STIEDA, Alex (cycling); b. 13 Apr 1961, Belleville, Ont.; given name: Alexander Nicholas Ernst; m.; c. 2; SFU; mem. jr. world pursuit team '79; ntl jr. track champion '79-80, sr. '81; BC, jr. track, road champion '80; won Tour L'Abitibi '80; ntl team '79-92, last 7 as pro; mem. world pursuit team '81; mem. '82 (4000m bronze) CG, '84 Olympic teams; criticism of FISU Games cycling competition '83 led to CCA rescinding Sport Canada B card; reinstated A Card; 1st Cdn to wear Tour de France yellow jersey '86; 3 gold, 2 bronze '82 Trinidad Tesoro Games; bronze 4000m individual pursuit '83 FISU Games; 15yrs pro racing circuit; involved with BMX racing; res. Edmonton, Alta.

STILLWAGON, Jim (football); b. 11 Feb 1949, Mt. Vernon, Ohio; m. Effie; c. Nicole, Angela, Electra; Ohio State; utilities co. employee; interior lineman; mem. Rose Bowl title team; 1st to win Lombardi, Outland trophies same season; drafted by Green Bay Packers but opted for CFL with Toronto '71-75; 1 Grey Cup final; 3 all-Canadian awards; res. Columbus, Ohio.

STIMPSON, Bob (golf); b. 10 Jun 1930, St. Vital, Man.; m. Carol; c. Kerry; sales; won 3 Alexander of Tunis, 1 Duke of Kent titles; mem. 1 Man., 3 Que. Willingdon Cup teams; Ottawa and district medal, match champion; Ottawa ACT athlete of '63; res. Vancouver, B.C.

STIMPSON, Earl (golf); b. 22 May 1914, Ottawa, Ont.; d. 15 Dec 1995, Ottawa, Ont.; m. Cecile O'Hara; c. Beverley Anne, Colleen; golf pro; life mem. CPGA; owned, operated Ottawa region's largest driving range 17 years; '66 taught game to UN troops in Egypt; 28yrs operated winter golf school for YM-YWCA in Ottawa; operated Kiwanis golf school 22 years; 1st pres., only lifetime mem. Manderley Golf Club; trophy bearing name awarded annually to top pro Ottawa Valley; putter league established bearing his name.

STINSON, Wally (administration); b. 2 Jun 1918, Austin, Man.; given name: Edgar Wallace; div.; c. Donna, Allan, Ronald; UMan., BA, UofSask. ret'd educator; ED SHSAA '48-59; branch AAUofC '51-58, pres. '59; pres. AAUofC '63; mem. National Council on Physical Fitness '48-53, National Advisory Council '61; '65-82 v-p. CG Assn. of Canada; dir. SFC, CTFA; chair. tech. advisory board Canada Winter Games '71; asst. mgr. '70 CG team; GM '74 CG team; track referee '67 PAG, Canada Summer Games Halifax; CAPHER award of honor '72; pres. BC CG Comm.; SHSAA merit honor roll; mem. Sask. Sports Hall of Fame; res. Saskatoon, Sask./Gabriola, B.C./Mexico.

STIRLING, Bummer (football); b. 23 Oct 1907, London, Ont.; d. 28 May 1994, Calgary, Alta.; given name: Hugh;

m. Jean; c. Heather, Susan; ret'd dir. employee relations; mem. '28 Dominion jr. football champions, Sarnia Imperials (ORFU) '29; starred with Imperials through '37, all-star '32-37, all-Eastern '34-36, ORFU MVP '36; mem. 2 Grey Cup winners; Lionel Conacher award '38; mem. Cdn Football, Sarnia/Lambton, Canada's Sports halls of fame.

STIRTON, Erika-Leigh (rhythmic gymnastics); b. 8 Aug 1980, Oakville, Ont.; given name: Erike-Leigh Elisabeth; studied ballet as youngster but on suggestion of rhythmics judge Tamara Bompa switched to rhythmics; mem. Etobicoke Olympium Club; mem. ntl team '95-00; ntl jr. title '94; competed '97 worlds; 5 gold, 1 silver '98 CG; competed '00 Olympics; all-around gold '00 NZ, Brazil meets; group bronze '99 PAG; res. Mississauga, Ont.

STOCK, Ed (lawn bowling); b. 25 Nov 1924, Toronto, Ont.; given name: Edward Hodgins; m. Mary Margaret Meikle; c. Margaret Eileen, Gordon Edward;UWO., BSc, Syracuse, MPA; financial administrator; won several trophies while sailing GP-14s Malayasia '69-71; mem. Brockville Yacht Club; mem. numerous club trophy winning rinks with Ottawa RCN Curling Club; regional convenor Ont. PLBA '77-78; past sec.-treas. OPLBA District 16 '72-77; p.-pres. Elmdale LBC Ottawa '76-77; Distict 16 4s champion '75, singles '73; sec.-treas. '76 ntl championship; Level 2 Ont. Coaching program; res. Brampton, Ont.

STOCKTON, Donald (wrestling); b. 22 Feb 1904, Montreal, Que., d. 16 Jun 1978, Montreal, Que.; given name: Donald Parker; m. Margaret Connolly; c. Alan, Barbara, Patricia, Eric; ret'd foreman; at 19 Que. 160lb wrestling title; mem. '24, '28, '32 Olympic teams, silver 174lbs class '28; 11 Que., 6 ntl titles at varying weights 160-191lbs; aside from Olympics, lost only 1 major match in career, '25 ntl 174lb title to Arthur Coleman; defeated Coleman following night in 191lb title match; '30 BE 174lb title; mem. Verdun jr. football team '24; CNR Int. ORFU title '25; Montreal Winged Wheelers '27-29; mem. Verdun AC lacrosse team mid-'20s; coached Montreal juv, int.-city and district title teams; chief ref., chief judge, supervisor of referees and judges for Que.; mem. Canadian Amateur Sports, Wrestling halls of fame.

STOJKO, Elvis (figure skating): b. 22 Mar 1972, Newmarket, Ont.; York; began skating age 5, competing age 9; ntl jr. champ '88; mem. ntl team '90-02; 5 Skate Canada gold; 7 ntl sr. titles, 4 runnerup; NHK Trophy gold '95, silver '92; competed 10 worlds winning gold '94, '95, '97, also 3 silver, 1 bronze; competed 4 Olympics winning silver '94, '98 (despite serious injury); Lalique trophy bronze '90; 1st skater to complete quadruple toe loop in combination with another jump (double axel) '91 worlds; coached by Doug and Michelle Leigh; ended 13-month retirement '03; turned pro '03; turned to competitive martial arts '04; Ont. male athlete of '93; Norton Crowe, Lionel Conacher awards '94; Cdn meritorious service award; mem. Skate Canada Hall of Fame; res. Richmond Hill, Ont.

STONE, Edith (basketball); b. 9 Apr 1910, Edmonton, Alta.; given name: Edith Lucy; m. Elmer Sutton (d); c. Philip, Margaret; ret'd secretary; mem. famed Edmonton Grads '30-34; Alta. mixed doubles badminton playoffs '50; twin sister Helen also mem. Grads; mem. Alta. Sports, Canadian Basketball halls of fame; res. Edmonton, Alta.

STONE, Helen (basketball); b. 9 Apr 1910, Edmonton, Alta.; given name: Helen Cecilia; m. William James Stewart; Langaro Coll.; ret'd secretary; mem. famed Edmonton Grads team '31-34; with sister Edith only twins ever on team; played 61 games, 412 points, 6.7 avg.; mem. Alta. Sports, Canadian Basketball halls of fame; res. Vancouver, B.C.

STONE, Kylie (gymnastics); b. 16 May 1987, Edmonton, Alta.; given name: Kylie-Anne McColl; '99 novice bars ntl title; 3 Elite Canada floor titles; ntl jr. title '01; double bronze (floor & team) '02 CG; silver vault, floor, bronze beam Jr. Pan Ams; silver team '03 PAG; competed '04 Olympics; 2 Alta. women's artistic gymnast of the year awards; 2 Calgary Booster Club Endowments; res. Calgary, Alta.

STONE, Reg (curling); b. 9 Apr 1914, Vancouver, B.C.; d. 6 Oct 1996, Victoria, B.C.; given name: Reginald Elliot; m. Ruby Elizabeth Morton; ret'd Trail Parks & Rec. superintendent; with brother Roy at 2nd, later 3rd 7 BC championships; '45 BC crown but there was no Brier that year due to WW2; competed in 6 Briers; won Saskatoon carspiel '56; with Roy skipping, Reg at 3rd, '73 BC Seniors title, lost ntl title playoff; mem. BC Senior-Seniors (60+) title rinks '77-81; 9yrs golf pro, greenskeeper Rossland-Trail Country Club; dir. BC Golf Assn.; major role in construction of numerous regional golf clubs; hon. life mem. Trail, Kelowna Curling Clubs, BC Curling Assn., BC Golf Assn., Rossland-Trail Country Club; mem. Canadian Curling, BC Sports halls of fame.

STONE, Rocky (football); b. 16 Apr 1923, Moncton, N.B.; d. 19 Jan 1977, Moncton, N.B.; given name: Charles Frederick; c. Richard; founder NB Amateur Football Union, 1st FA in province '66; organized 1st celebrity dinner to raise funds for Moncton MFL '70; CAFA service award; CFL/CAFA award; life mem. Moncton FA; scholarship in his name awarded annually from '77; Moncton park football field bears his name; mem. NB Sports Hall of Fame.

STONE, Roy (curling); b. 21 Jun 1915, Lena, Man.; d. 21 Jun 2003, Trail, B.C.; given name: Roy Hannah; m. Olive Mary Howlett; c. Larry Roy, Ronald Alfred; ret'd golf pro; mem. 7 provincial title rinks; competed in 6 Briers; won Saskatoon carspiel '56; skipped BC sr. title rink '73, lost ntl title playoff; skipped BC Senior-Seniors (60+) title winners '77-81; like brother, a baker by trade but for 30yrs golf pro, club mgr. Rossland-Trail Country Club; BC Senior PGA title; involved in construction of numerous golf clubs in Trail area; mgr. Trail Curling Club several years; hon. life mem. Trail, Kelowna Curling Clubs, BC Curling Assn., Rossland-Trail Country Club; mem. Canadian Curling, BC Sports halls of fame.

STONEBURGH, Norm (football); b. 31 Mar 1935, Toronto, Ont.; given name: Norman Joseph; m. Dolores Joyce Gore; c. Brad, Blake, Charyl-Ann, Terri-Lynn, Dan, James; De LaSalle Coll.; builder, land developer; 2yrs East York, 1 Balmy Beach, 1 Parkdale Lions; ctr Argonauts '55-58, '60-67; missed entire '59 after breaking leg in exhibition game against NFL St. Louis Cardinals; appeared in 155 league, 8 playoff games over 12 seasons; 6 times EFC all-star; named to Argos team of century; res. Etobicoke, Ont.

STONEMAN, Bill (baseball); b. 7 Apr 1944, Oak Park, Ill.; given name: William Hambly; m. Diane Falardeau; c. Jill, Jeff; Idaho, BSc, Oklahoma, MA; all-Big Sky conf. '65-66, all-NCAA '66; baseball exec.; rhp; ML service Chicago Cubs '67-68, Montreal '69-73, California '74; ML record: 245 scheduled games, 54-85, 46cgm 15sho, 1235,3ip, 602bob, 934k, 4,08era; pitched no-hitters vs. Philadelphia 17 Apr 1969, New York 2 Oct 1972; pitched 1 1-hitter, 2 2-hitters; asst. to Expos pres. John McHale '83, v-p. baseball operations '84-99; GM Anaheim Angels from '00; mem. Expos Hall of Fame; res. Anaheim, Calif.

STOQUA, Pat (basketball/football): b. 29 Apr 1956, Ottawa, Ont.; given name: Patrick Charles Joseph; m. Elizabeth Gilmour; c. Jennifer, Sean, Brendan; Carleton, BA; account exec. Dollco Printing; v-p. sales Cepac Technologies; standout basketball/football player Lisgar CI; mem. '74 all-Ont. basketball title team; Lisgar athlete of yr; 4yrs basketball Carleton, 3 all-star, MVP awards; 3yrs football Carleton; OUAA rookie of yr; 2 conf. db, 1 sb all-star; all-Cdn slotback '79; Carleton football MVP '79; 2 Carleton athlete-of-yr awards; Jack Vogan graduating athlete award; Rough Riders CFL territorial exemption '79; played sb/db with Ottawa '79-85; coached Goulbourn team to Ont. Bantam girls basketball title; mem. Carleton Sports Wall of Fame; res. Stittsville, Ont.

STOREY, Bob (bobsleigh/builder); b. 3 Dec 1942, London, Ont.; given name: Robert Hargan; m. Catherine Sullivan; c. Max, Sarah, Ben; investment co. owner; communications co. exec.; mem. ntl bobsleigh team '66-73; mem. Olympic bobsleigh teams '68 (brakeman), '72 (driver, capt.), '76 (coach); v-p. Cdn Amateur Bobsleigh and Toboggan Assn. '77, '80; pres. '81-82; Cdn rep. to Federation International de Bobsleigh et Toboggan '76-77, '80-82, v-p. '84-94, pres. '94-04; FIBT International juror from '76; mem. Cdn Olympic Hall of Fame; res. Ottawa, Ont.

STOREY, Fred (curling); b. 3 Mar 1932, Empress, Alta.; given name: Frederick Lewis; m. Vivian Fullerton; c. Debbie, Wayne, Sandie, Cheryl, Ron, James; Mount Royal College; ret'd administrative supervisor; 2nd Alta. rink '51 ntl schoolboy championships; lead 7 Alta. title rinks, 7 Briers appearances, 3 titles, world championship as lead for Ron Northcott; mem. '61 Edmonton Tournament of Champions titlist; with Northcott *CBC* Cross-Canada curling title Winnipeg '64, Cdn Open Carspiel Edmonton '65, Vancouver Evergreen Tournament of Champions '71, repeat as lead for George Fink '73; Calgary Masters title '72; Brier all-star lead; from '69 hon. life mem. Calgary Curling Club, pres. '74-75; mem. Canadian Curling, Alta. Sports halls of fame; res. Calgary, Alta.

STOREY, Irene (t&f): b. 10 May 1915, Allendale, Ont.; d. 19 Mar 1986, Toronto, Ont.; m. Pat Weber; c. Lee, Lorrie, Gordon, Pamela; overshadowed in Barrie region by brother Red and Bobbie Rosenfeld; encouraged by mother began running competitively age 10; also standout softball, basketball player; gained attention outside Barrie region defeating Grace Morrison, Mary Frizell in 100yd dash at age 13; Ont. -14 girls 100yds title '28; Ont./Cdn 60m jr. titles '30; CNE -18 100yd title '30; impressed observers beating sr. champion Rosa Grosse O'Neill in 60m run '30; ntl intermediate 60m title '32; recruited by Toronto Lakeside Ladies Club to compete for team; competed but insisted on wearing Allendale jacket which became her trademark; teamed with Frizell, Peggy Matheson, Dot Brookshaw to win 32 consecutive relay titles; mem. ntl relay team '34 World Games; in only 2nd 220yd race of career set ntl record 25.5 beating '28 Olympic 100m titlist Elizabeth Robinson; although placing 3rd in trials was bypassed in favor of Aileen Meagher for '34 games, but, with help of Barrie backers trip to games was underwritten; on retirement, late '30s had won 8 cups, 75 medals; mem. Barrie Sports Hall of Fame.

STOREY, Red (football/hockey); b. 5 Mar 1918, Barrie, Ont.; given name: Roy Alvin; m. Helen Saint Pierre (d); c. Bob, Doug; m Bunnie Lyons; public relations; football Argos '36-41 leading team to Grey Cup victories '37-38; record 3 tds in final quarter '38 Grey Cup; offers from NY Giants, Chicago Bears in NFL; officiated 14yrs Que. Football League, 12yrs Intercollegiate, 12yrs CFL; hockey Barrie jrs., RCAF Camp Borden, Altantic City (EHL), Sault Ste. Marie (Michigan League), Montreal Royals (Que. sr.); refereed 7yrs Que. jr., provincial, sr. leagues, 9yrs AHL, 9yrs NHL; 8yrs lacrosse Orillia, Hamilton Tigers, Lachine, Montreal Canadiens; scored 12 goals single game; refereed 10yrs Que. sr. league; with son Bob (Hamilton '67, Montreal '70) only father-son combination Grey Cup history to play on 2 title winners each; autobiography *Red's Story*; mem. Order of Canada, Barrie Sports, Ont. Legends, Hockey halls of fame; res. Montreal, Que.

STORM, Tim (rowing); b. 18 Jul 1956, Rotterdam, Holland; Ridley Coll.; accountant; sculling specialist; mem. 6 ntl jr., sr. 8s, 4s, coxless 4s, pairs, 4-sculls titles; 5 Canadian Henley titles, 2 US titles; gold pairs '79 PAG; mem. '77-78, '82-83 world championships, '84 Olympic Games teams; res. St. Catharines, Ont.

STOTHART, Paul (hockey); b. 17 May 1957, Ottawa, Ont.; m. Karen Colby; c. Sarah, Alex, Julia; Queen's BSc, MBA; federal ministerial policy advisor, Export Development Canada; 2 Sullivan trophies as Canada's Outstanding university hockey player; in 4yrs at Queen's 106g in 82 games; 3 all-Canadian awards; top scorer in OUAA history; led Gaels to Queen's Cup title '81; top graduating Queen's student-athlete '82; competed in Germany '83; mem. Team Canada in Soviet, Czech tournaments; active minor soccer, hockey coach; mem. Ottawa Old Pros hockey team; mem. Queen's Wall of Fame; res. Ottawa, Ont.

STOTT, Arthur (diving); b. 21 Nov 1909, Victoria, B.C.; given name: Arthur Harling; m. Patricia Clare Copeland; c. Gael, Sheridan, Jon; Victoria College; ret'd newspaper editor; jr. boys Pacific Northwest 3-metre title in 1st competition '23; Vancouver Island sr. men's titles, BC sr. championships late '20s; 2 golds, 2 silvers, 1 bronze in 5 ntl championships; bronze '30 BEG; mem. '32 Olympic team; mem. founding board of trustees BC Sports Hall of Fame; mem. Greater Victoria Sports Hall of Fame; res. Victoria, B.C.

STOUGHTON, Blaine (hockey): b. 13 Mar 1953, Gilbert Plains, Man.; hockey exec.; wing; jr. Flin Flon Bombers '69-73; drafted by Pittsburgh '73; minor pro stints Hershey, New Haven AHL, Oklahoma City CHL; WHA with Cincinnati, Indianapolis, New England '76-79; NHL Pittsburgh '73-74, Toronto '74-76, Hartford '79-83, NYR '83-84; 1 WHL,

NHL all-star; scored 52g WHA '77, 56 '80, 52 '82 in NHL; NHL/WHA record: 11 seasons, 745 scheduled games, 347g, 281a; coach Austin Ice Bats '96-97; v-p./GM '97-03; co-owner Arkansas Glacier Cats WPHL; mem. Man. Hockey Hall of Fame; res. Dauphin, Man.

STOUGHTON, Jeff (curling); b. 26 Jul 1963, Winnipeg, Man.; given name: Jeffrey Roy; m. Susan Leone McElrea; c. Riley John, Cole Jeffrey; Air Canada finance system specialist; 5 Man., 2 ntl mixed titles; represented Man. 5 Briers, winning '96. '99 and adding world gold, silver respectively; competed '98 Olympic trials; competing on WCT recorded wide variety of wins including '03 Founders trophy; mem. Man. Curling Hall of Fame; res. Winnipeg, Man.

STOUTENBERG, Chris (wheelchair basketball); b. 13 Sep 1977, Collingwood, Ont.; Guelph, Illinois; station asst./event facilitator dept. leisure services town of Collingwood; former varsity football player UGuelph; began wheelchair basketball career '97; ntl team from '00; 1 CWBL jr. bronze; 1 worlds bronze; 1 Canada Games gold; 4 gold, 2 silver nationals; 6 all-star teams; '00, '04 Paralympic gold; res. Collingwood, Ont.

STOVEL, Peter (t&f/bobsleigh); b. 5 Jun 1963, Port Arthur, Ont.; UMan.; financial planner; 4 HS track athlete-of-yr awards; receiver HS jr./sr. football teams; 200m, 400m specialist; ran anchor leg UMan. 4x200m ntl record '86 Cdn GP indoor meet; proved proficient 400m hurdler earning bronze '87 Trans-American meet; competed '89 Francophonie Games; noted for explosive, powerful starts he joined ntl bobsleigh team '87; competed '87-92 appearing on WC circuit; mem. '88 (alternate), '92 Olympic teams; with Greg Haydenluck overall 2-man silver '90-91 WC circuit; Man. sport excellence award; mem. NWO Sports Hall of Fame; res. Winnipeg, Man.

STOYKA, Darlene (field hockey); b. 30 Nov 1956, Toronto, Ont.; given name: Darlene Anne; St. Mary's, BA; Canada Post; mem. Toronto Gopher's FH club, 4 prov. titles, 4 Bermuda tournament titles; mem. Ont. team '73-83; ntl titles '81-82; ntl team '76-85; mem. '83 World Cup silver, '84 Olympic teams; accomplished squash player; res. Ottawa, Ont.

STRACHAN, Bill (shooting); b. 10 Oct 1912, Ottawa, Ont.; given name: William James; m. Ethelena Burgess (d); c. Bill Jr.; m. Frances Holomon; ret'd Lieut- Col.; mem. 12 Bisley, 4 Palma (capt.'71), 6 Kalapore, 11 MacKinnon teams; 3 times capt. Cdn army Bisley team; Macdonald Stewart grand aggregate title '62, runnerup '61; Bisley aggregate Canadian target rifle titles '61-62; Bisley team commandant '66; only Cdn Commonwealth sniping champion; pres. NDHQRA '47-49; v-p. GBNRA from '60; v-p. Commonwealth RA; past exec. v-p. DCRA; sr. life gov. DCRA; mem. DCRA Hall of Fame; res. Ottawa, Ont./Holiday, Fla.

STRANGE, Michael (boxing): b. 6 Aug 1970, Niagara Falls, Ont.; bar owner; lightweight; competed '90, '94, '98 CG, '92, '96, '00 Olympic, '95 PAG, '93 Worlds; gold 60kg '94, 63.5kg '98 CG; bronze '95 PAG; gold 2 Canada vs. US competitions '93; gold Stockholm Open '93, Tammer Finland '95; best boxer award '90 ntls, '91 Ont.

championships; 9 ntl titles; Team Investors Group Amateur Athlete Fund award '00; res. Niagara Falls, Ont.

STRATTEN, Gaye (swimming/coaching): b. 25 Apr 1943, Toronto, Ont.; given name: Gaye Harold; m. Lynn Sellors; c. Todd, Taryn; UofT BPHE, North Carolina; swim coach McMaster; Level III NCCP theory/practical/ swimming technical, Level II course conductor; ntl 100/200m backstroke titlist '62-65; attended UNC on swim scholarship 64-66; CIAU swimmer of yr '67-69; UofT swimmer of yr (Bickle award), athlete of yr (Biggs award) '69; 9 OUAA, 2 CIAU, 1 Cdn, 3 Ont. swim-coach-of-yr awards; aquatics innovator/developer; PE dir. University Settlement House, Toronto '66; GM/coach Etobicoke Aquatic Club '69-76; asst. coach Olympium SC '76-77; GM/coach Hamilton Wentworth Aquatic Club from '77; aquatic sports co-ordinator/coach McMaster from '78; mem. Cdn/Ont. swimming coaches assn. from '69; mem.Coaching Assn of Cda from '75; dir. Ont. Amateur Swimming Coaches Assn '69-74, Ont. Amateur Swimming Assn. '69-70; pres. CIAU swim coaches assn '79-86; tech. dir. swimming OUAA from '86; FINA tech sub-comm. for swimming '91 FISU Games; developed financial assistance plan for A/B-carded athletes; started 1ˢᵗ masters swim program; trainer of coaches; coached numerous international level swimmers; ntl team coach at varied worlds, Olympic, PAG, FISU Games from '72; PetroCan coaching excellence award; mem. UofT Sports Hall of Fame; res. Burlington, Ont.

STREETER, Val (golf): b. 1895 Duxbury, Mass., d. 7 Jul 1981, Saint John, N.B.; given name: Percival; 3 NB, PEI, 2 Maritime amateur titles; mem. 3 ntl teams; national srs. (over 70) champion '67; mem. NB Sports Hall of Fame.

STREIT, Marlene Stewart (golf): b. 9 Mar 1934, Cereal Alta.; m. J. Douglas Streit (d); c. Darlene Louise, Lynn Elizabeth; Rollins College BA. hon LL.D Brock; began caddying '47, playing '49; 24 CLGA titles, 9 Closed, 11 Open, 4 Sr. titles; 21 OLGA titles; '53 British women's amateur, 5 US ntl mixed foursomes; '56 US women's amateur; US North-South '56, '74, US Intercollegiate '56, won 34 consecutive matches, a feat unequalled; 9 Ont. ladies', 4 Helen Lee Doherty titles; 5 Ione D. Jones/ Doherty sr. div titles; only woman to win Canadian, British, Australian, US ntl amateur titles; 3 US srs. titles. oldest to win USGA sr. women's title at 69; '56 Shell Wonderful World of Golf title beating pro Marilyn Smith, '66 beating Mickey Wright; low amateur 5 LPGA events; participated 14 CLGA intl (world, commonwealth) teams '53-98; mem. 16 Ont. interprov. teams; won 30 ntl or intl titles with at least one title in each decade '51-03 on 3 continents; 5 Bobbie Rosenfeld awards; Lou Marsh Trophy '51, '56; Cdn woman of yr (tied Charlotte Whitton) '53; named Cdn female amateur golfer of century; *Score Magazine* lifetime achievement award; CLGA distinguished service award; jr. chair OLGA '60-62; dir. Ada MacKenzie Memorial Foundation '74-94 (pres. '84-85); CLGA advisory panel '94-98; selection comm. RCGA hall of fame; governor Canada's Sports hall of fame; CLGA established Marlene Stewart Streit awards fund '66 to aid jr. participation outside Canada; Officer Order of Canada; mem. RCGA, World Golf, Canada's Sports, Ont. Sports Legends halls of fame; res. Stouffville, Ont.

STRIDE, Bryan (t&f): b. 9 Feb 1951, Guelph, Ont.; given name: Bryan Alexander; div. Margaret MacGowan; c. Christopher; Brock, BPhE; teacher; middle-distance, x-country specialist; ntl team '74-78; 4ᵗʰ 3000m steeplechase '75 PAG, 2ⁿᵈ 3000m steeplechase '75 ntl championships; OUAA x-country title '75; 2ⁿᵈ Cdn indoor 3000m '76; PB: 800m (1:52), 1500m (3:48), 3000m steeplechase (8:45); res. St. Catharines, Ont.

STRIKE, Hilda (t&f): b. 1 Sep 1910, Montreal, Que.; d. 9 Mar 1989, Ottawa, Ont.; m. Fred Sisson; c. Barbara; Canadian Commercial College; stenographer; spotted '29 by Olympic gold medalist Myrtle Cook while playing softball, joined Cdn Ladies AC Montreal; by '32 Que., ntl sprint champion; finalist '30 BEG; silver 100m sprint losing narrowly to Stella Walsh, who, when murdered '80, was discovered to be a male, anchored silver medal relay team '32 Olympics; ss Murray's AC Montreal Ladies' Softball title team; with Myrtle Cook formed Murray's AC, Mercury Track Club and became coach; silver 100yd, 4x110 relay '34 BEG; Cdn female athlete of '32; life mem. COA; mem. Canadian Amateur, Canada's Sports halls of fame.

STRONACH, Frank (horse racing/entrepreneur): b. 6 Sep 1932, Austria; m. Frieda; c. Andy, Belinda; numerous hon. LLD degrees from varied universities; owns Magna International Inc.; moved to Canada '54; K-W hospital dishwasher before entering tool & die business; formed Multi Matic Investments '57, merged with Magna Electronics '69; Magna International produces automobile components; became involved in horse racing early '60s; operates breeding farms, stallion stations Ont., Kentucky, Fla.; has campaigned more than 100 stakes winners including Touch Gold '97 Belmont Stakes; Red Bullet '00 Preakness, 2 Queen's Plates, 3 Breeders Cups, Glorious Song '80 Eclipse award winner and Canada's horse of yr; 10 Sovereign owner/breeder, 4 Eclipse awards; purchased myriad of race tracks including Santa Anita, Pimlico, Laurel Park, Gulfstream, Bay Meadows; pres. Austrian major soccer league '99; Ernst & Young entrepreneur-of-yr-lifetime-achievement award; mem. Order of Canada; mem. Cdn Business, Horse Racing halls of fame; res. Switzerland/Newmarket, Ont./Fla./ Colo/Ky.

STRONG, Karen (cycling): b. 23 Sep 1953, Toronto, Ont.; given name: Karen Ann Strong; div. Colin Hearth; c. Joel; Brock; life services mgr. Cdn Sport Centre Calgary; coach; 32 ntl all disciplines; represented Canada 5 world 3000m pursuit (2ⁿᵈ '80, 3ʳᵈ '77), 5 world road race championships, best finish 4ᵗʰ '77; mem. '84 Olympic team; ret'd from competition '84; Level IV coach; St. Catharines athlete of '75; ntl women's road coach 5yrs; PetroCan coaching excellence award; res. Calgary, Alta.

STRONG, Lawrence (tennis): b. 17 May 1940, London, Eng.; given name: Lawrence Franklin; m. Vivienne Russel Cox; c. Nicole, Danielle, Suzette; London, BSc; general management; UK schoolboy title, English international honors; with wife ntl mixed doubles title '68, mixed doubles gold '69 Canada games; capt. Davis Cup team '70-71; pres. CLTA '76; Air Canada Sports Exec. of '77; res. Willowdale, Ont.

STRONGE, Stan (soccer/coaching): b. 29 Dec 1910,

Montreal, Que.; d. Aug 1991, Vancouver, B.C.; given name: Stanley Noble; rehabilitation consultant, Cdn Paraplegic Assn.; soccer goalie '23-40 when accident left him paralyzed from waist down; 9 times all-star; mem. New Westminster Royals '35 ntl titlists; ntl rules chair. for Cdn Wheelchair Sports from '75; BC, ntl swim coach for disabled '67-79; coached Canada's paraplegic swimmers and attended all ntl and intl games for disabled; swimmimg pool named in his honor '80; mem. Order of Canada; double inductee into BC Sports Hall of Fame for disabled sports builder and soccer.

STROULGER, Ken (canoeing); b. 9 Feb 1913, Ottawa, Ont.; d. 15 Feb 1990, Ottawa, Ont.; given name: Charles Kenneth; m. Barbara Taylor; Carleton.; ret'd public servant; stroke C4 Rideau Aquatic Club '36 ntl champions; commodore CCA '50; commodore Rideau Canoe Club '50-60; mgr. ntl team '56 Olympics; hon. commodore Rideau Canoe Club '80-81; mem. Ottawa Sports Hall of Fame; Olympic Club Canada.

STRUMM, Gil (all-around); b. 29 Oct 1920, Saskatoon, Sask.; given name: Gilbert Roger; m. Jean Kemp (d.); c. Beverly, Bob; m. Marnie Garbe; ret'd mgr. SaskTel.; softball cf 27yrs; Sr. A coach '43-83; 14 Sask., 6 Western Canadian, 1 ntl title; coached 2 world championship entries; 12yrs mem. Sask. Grads, Navy, Regina Legion basketball teams; 20yrs basketball coach, 8 prov. titles, 1 university crown; refereed basketball 20yrs; 5yrs semipro baseball; 39yrs dir. Saskatoon Hilltops football club; pres. Saskatoon Sr. Men's Softball League '57; Saskatoon sportsman of '69; ntl championships all-star softball coach '70; sr. prov. curling champion '73; skipped srs rink Sweden '79, Switzerland '81, Scotland '83; scout Vancouver Canucks 9yrs; Queen's Medal '77; avid golfer from '81; mem. Sask., Saskatoon Sports halls of fame; res. Saskatoon, Sask.

STUART, Bruce (hockey); b. 30 Nov 1881, Ottawa, Ont., d. 28 Oct 1961, Ottawa, Ont.; m. Irene; shoe store owner; rover, left wing Ottawa Senators '98-99, 12 goals in 6 games; Que. Bulldogs 1900; rejoined Ottawa '01-02 then moved to International pro league with Pittsburgh, Houghton Mich., Portage Lakes; helped Montreal Wanderers win '08 Stanley Cup; returned to Ottawa following season, capt. '11 Stanley Cup winner; in 3 Cup victories scored 17 goals in 7 games; in 45 career scheduled games posted 63 goals including 6 in single game vs Que.; 2 5-goal games; mem. Ottawa Sports, Hockey halls of fame.

STUART, Hod (hockey); b. 1879, Ottawa, Ont., d. 23 Jun 1907, Belleville, Ont.; given name: William Hodgson; mem. Ironsides, Ottawa Senators, Que., Pittsburgh Victorias teams; mgr. Calumet Mich. 2 seasons before joining Pittsburgh, captain '06; Montreal Wanderers '07 Stanley Cup; 16 goals in 33-game career; flying wing 8yrs Rough Riders; mem. Ottawa Sports, Hockey halls of fame.

STUBBS, Lorraine (equestrian); b. 9 Jun 1950, Toronto, Ont.; given name: Constance Lorraine; York, BA, MA; intl equestrian judge; dressage specialist; mem. ntl equestrian team from '71; competed '71, '75, '91 PAG, '72, '76 Olympic teams; silver '75, team gold '91 PAG; 3rd Aachen, W.Germany, international horse show '74; 2nd Norten-Hardenburg, Germany, '75; won Grand Prix, Special, Ont.

dressage championships '76; London dressage title '81; Canada's 1st level 3 equestrian coach; ex-officio chair. Dressage Can.; Cdn Equestrian Council Intl. Comm.; res. Rockwood, Ont.

STUKUS, Annis (football/hockey); b. 25 Oct 1914, Toronto, Ont.; given name: Annis Paul; m. Doris Louise Shannon; c. Suzanne, Sally, Mary Louise; sportscaster; Argos '35-41; Oakwood Indians '42, Balmy Beach '43, Toronto Navy '44, Toronto Indians '45-46; organized Eskimos '49, coach 3 seasons; organized/coached BC Lions '53-55; GM Vancouver Canucks (WHL) '67, Winnipeg Jets '71-74; helped sign Bobby Hull to WHA contract and instigated sorties into Sweden to sign hockey talent; trophy in his honor awarded CFL coach of year annually; promotions dir. Vancouver Whitecaps '74; mem. BC Place Wall, Cdn Football, Football Reporters of Canada, Canada's Sports halls of fame; res. West Vancouver, B.C.

STUKUS, Bill (football); b. 18 May 1916, Toronto, Ont.; given name: William Joseph; St. Michael's College; bookkeeper, camp athletic director; qb/safety Argos '36-41, '47, RCAF Hurricanes '42-44, Toronto Indians '45-46, Edmonton '49-51; mem. 4 Grey Cup winners; coached minor hockey; AD brother Frank's Fenlon Falls summer camp; res. Toronto, Ont.

STUKUS, Frank (football); b. 7 Aug 1918, Toronto, Ont.; m. Anna Havery (d.); c. Frank Jr. (d), Maureen Elizabeth; m. Pauline Audrey Woolings; ret'd resort, camp operator; fb Argos '38-41, Toronto Indians '42, '45; became Indians owner; established 1st-ever summer hockey camp Fenlon Falls, Ont., '61; coached 1 season int. football Oshawa; owner Byrnell Manor '61-75; 13yrs Etobicoke parks & rec. dept.; back-room power in federal Conservative party from '50's through mid-'80s when actions of PM Brian Mulroney soured him on politics; res. Mississauga, Ont.

STULAC, George (all-around); b. 28 Jun 1933, Toronto, Ont.; given name: George William; UofT; teacher; HS gymnastics, diving titles; intercollegiate swimming titles, mem. football, basketball title teams; mem. ntl water polo title team; Ont. Y diving titlist; 9 1st T awards UofT; Hec Phillips t&f trophy; mem. Toronto West End Y, Tillsonburg Livingstons basketball teams; 1st Cdn to qualify for Olympics in 2 sports same year '60; swimming alternate '52 Olympics; mem. '56 Olympic basketball, '60 Olympic basketball, t&f, '64 basketball teams; decathlon bronze '59 PAG; res. Toronto, Ont.

STUMON, Gregg (football): b. 26 May 1963, Plain Dealing, La.; Southern Arkansas; de; joined CFL BC '86-88, Edmonton '89, Ottawa '90-93, Shreveport '94-95; CFL record: 145 games, 1td, 87 qb sacks, 381 tackles; Norm Fieldgate trophy '87; Schenley outstanding def. player '87; 2 all-Western, 2 all-Eastern, 3 all-CFL all-star; mem. 1 Grey Cup finalist; last known res. Shreveport, La.

STUPP, Heather (racquetball); b. 28 Feb 1964, Montreal, Que.; McGill, BComm, Cdn Inst of Chartered Accountants CA, Harvard, MBA; management consultant; Canada Games singles title '79; 6 ntl singles, 4 ntl doubles titles; 2 world singles, 2 world team titles; PAG team silver, singles bronze '87; Torneo de las Americas singles gold '87, silver

'91; Pacific Rim silver '91; Japan open singles gold '89; mem. Montreal YM/YWHA Sports Hall of Fame; res. Montreal, Que.

STUPP, Howard (wrestling); b. 3 May 1955, Montreal, Que.; given name: Howard Michael; McGill, BSc, LLD; lawyer; dir. IOC legal affairs; 3 ntl open jr., 5 sr. FS, GR titles; sr. open GR champion '76, '78-79, '81; won '81, 2nd '79-80 Cdn Open FS championships; 4 Maccabiah Games gold; '78, '81 CIAU FS titles; most-outstanding-wrestler award '78 CIAU championships; mem. '77-79 world championships, 2 PAG gold; '76, '80 Olympic teams; mem. McGill, Montreal YM-YWHA Sports, Cdn Wrestling halls of fame; res. Lausanne, Switzerland.

STYNER, Dale (squash): b. 9 Nov 1961, Lethbridge, Alta.; m. Lori; c. 2; 4 ntl titles; mem. 5 world championships teams; won Sask., Alta., Calgary, Husky, Pacific Coast Open, Calgary Closed titles; Squash Canada distinguished service award; res. Calgary, Alta.

STYNER, Lori (squash): b. 6 Jan 1963, Burlington, Ont.; m. Dale; c. 2; UCal, BN; medical research; began play age 16 in Sarnia; won Alta., Glencoe Open, Calgary Closed, Triumph Tubular titles; mem. '94 ntl women's team; res. Calgary, Alta.

SUGARMAN, Ken (football); b. 16 Jun 1942, Portland, Ore.; given name: Kenneth Lee; m. Carolyn; c. Kenny, Trevor; Whitworth College, BA, SFU; apple rancher, warehouse operator; Little All-American Whitworth '63; 7th draft Baltimore (NFL), last cut '64; BC '64-72; 3 all-star games; capt., Lions' most popular player '69; Laurie Neimi award as outstanding BC lineman '72; res. Tieton, Wash.

SUKUNDA, Eli (fencing); b. 10 Apr 1949, Windsor, Ont.; m. Marie Vielleux; c. Adrienne, Zachary; Wayne State., BA, UofT, MA; teacher; mem. '75, '79, '83 (sabre team bronze) PAG, '76, '84, '88 (capt.) Olympic Games teams; twice mem. 4th place PAG team; 1st '84, 2nd '75, '78, '82 ntl championships; gold '75 Canada Games, Gov.-Gen.'s Cup '79-80, 5 Ottawa Shield, 4 London Heroes gold, Fred Wach Memorial '82; team gold, silver, sabre bronze Commonwealth championships; coach '93 FISU Games team; Windsor Kiwanis Club athlete of '76; fencing coach RA Centre; Schwende-Tully men's sabre trophy; mem. Windsor-Essex Sports Hall of Fame; res. Brockville, Ont.

SULLIVAN, Frank (hockey/football); b. 26 Jul 1898, Toronto, Ont.; d. 8 Jan 1989, Toronto, Ont.; given name: Francis Gerald; m. Ursula Colleran; c. Catharine, John, Frank Jr., Lee, Edward, Michael, Mary, Patsy, Peter; UofT; ret'd; mem. Harbord CI jr. HS football champions '15; UofT Schools Jr. ORFU champions '17; Central YMCA Jr. ORFU champions '18; UofT '19-20 Intercollegiate champions, '20 Grey Cup champions; Argos Big Four, Grey Cup champions '21; mem. Harbord CI sr. HS hockey champions '16; Aura Lee OHA Jr. champs '17; UofT Intercollegiate champs '20-21; Granite Hockey Club OHA Sr. champions '22; 3 Allan Cup winners; Varsity Grads '27 OHA Sr. champs, '28 Olympic gold medalists; mem. 9 ntl title teams in 10yr span; coached UofT jr. hockey '29-30, srs. '31-33, Intercollegiate title '31-32.

SULLIVAN, Joe (hockey); b. 8 Jan 1901, Toronto, Ont.; d. 3 Sep 1988, Scarborough, Ont.; given name: Joseph Albert; UofT, MD; surgeon, senator; mem. UTS '18-19 Memorial Cup champions; goalie Varsity Grads '28 Olympic gold medalists; mem. '50 *CP* poll team of half century; Intercollegiate golf title, Ont. amateur, runnerup '24 ntl amateur; CIAU goalie of year trophy bears his name; hon. Surgeon to Her Majesty; gov. UofT; hon. Fellow Royal Society of Medicine; chief otolaryngology Cdn. Forces; recipient Canada Medal; mem. UofT Sports Hall of Fame.

SULLIVAN, Kevin (t&f): b. 20 Mar 1974, Brantford, Ont.; m. Karen Harvey; Michigan BEng.; asst. coach; middle-distance specialist; began competing age 12; brilliant HS career led to Michigan scholarship; 4 Big 10, NCAA regional XC titles; 14 all-American awards; 3 Big-10 athlete-of-yr awards; Ont. 800m, 1500m titles '89, ntl 800 title '89; ntl jr. 800m, 1500m titles '92-93; bronze 1500m world jr. championships; won jr. ntl x-country, ntl indoor 1500m, gold 800m, 1500m Tokyo Invitational, gold 800m, bronze 4x100 relay Pan-Am jr. championships '93; competed '93 world championships, '94, '02 CG, '96, '00 Olympic Games; ntl sr. 1500m title '94; silver 1500m '94 CG; 1500m gold Gugl IAAF grand prix Austria '99; set Cdn mile record 3:52.25 '95 Zurich GP; NCAA 1500m, 2 indoor, 1 outdoor mile titles; PB: 3:39.07 1500m; Viscount Alexander Trophy runnerup '93; res. Illinois.

SULLIVAN, Red (hockey): b. 24 Dec 1929, Peterborough, Ont.; given name: George James; m. Marion Redmond; c. Danny, Jane, Suzanne, Kate; ret'd hockey exec.; relative lightweight at 152 pounds; sensational jr. career with St. Catharines; pro stints Boston, Chicago, NYR '49-61; starred in AHL with Hershey; set scoring record 30g, 89a '53-54 season; NHL record: 557 scheduled games, 107g, 239a, 18 playoff games, 1g, 2a; 5 NHL all-star games; voted by NHL coaches "hardest worker, hustler" in league; coached Rangers, Pittsburgh, Washington '62-75; NHL coaching record: 364 scheduled games, 107-198-59; scout for Boston, Philadelphia, NHL Central Scouting; power-hitting fastball infielder; active with NYR alumni; mem. Peterborough Sports Hall of Fame; res. Indian River, Ont.

SULLIVAN, Tommy (boxing); b. 29 Dec 1904, Dublin, Ireland; d. 10 May 1990, Chapeau, Que.; m. Claire Carroll; c. Sharon, Deirdre; ret'd; amateur boxer '21-31; Que. 147lb title '31; Lions Newsboy title Toronto '31; finalist US jr. nationals Boston '31; refereed Montreal Athletic Commission '36-56; coach RCAF St. Thomas, Trenton, Moncton '39-45, Grenadier Guards Montreal '48-56; '52 Olympic boxing coach; ntl coach CABA '71-72.

SUNDIN, Mats (hockey); b. 13 Feb 1971, Bromma, Sweden; played with Nacka, Djurgarden, Sweden, '88-90; 1st European drafted 1st overall in NHL entry draft; NHL Quebec '90-94, Toronto '94-; Leafs capt. from '97; highest scoring Swedish player in NHL hictory; NHL record: (through '04) 1086 scheduled games, 465g, 624a, 83 playoff games, 35g, 39a; 7 NHL all-star games; mem. Team Sweden 4 world championships, '98 title team, silver '03 worlds; competed for Sweden '98, '02 Olympics; '01 MAC award for contributions to children's charities; hon.

capt. Street Buds, Leafs youth ball hockey pgm.; active in Swedish charity pgms. for players with debilitating injuries; res. Toronto, Ont./Sweden.

SUNOHARA, Vicky (hockey): b. 18 May 1970, Scarborough, Ont.; UofT, Northeastern; quality control technician; honed skills in Scarborough boys/girls hockey '75-88; all-American forward Northeastern '88-90; NCAA championship rookie of '88; UofT rookie of '90; Scarborough Firefighters/UofT '90-94; Toronto Red Wings '94-96; Newtonbrook Panthers '96-97; silver North York Aeros '96, bronze Beatrice Aeros '99 Esso ntls; 6 world championship, 1 3-Nations Cup gold; mem. '98 Olympic silver, '02 gold medal teams; res. Scarborough, Ont.

SUNTER, Ian (football); b. 21 Dec 1952, Dundee, Scotland; m. Karen; c. Kelly, David; owner CWS Sports; emigrated to Canada age 15; jr. football Burlington '70-71; moved into CFL from HS ranks as placement specialist; among 1ˢᵗ soccer-style kickers; with Hamilton '72-75; NFL trials Detroit, Buffalo, LA Rams; returned to CFL with Toronto '78-79; mem. '72 Grey Cup winner; res. Burlington, Ont.

SURETTE, Ron (shooting); b. 26 Aug 1943, Shediac, N.B.; given name: Ronald Alfred; m. Juliette; c. Michelle, Travis; ret'd Cdn Forces; 6 Queen's medals; 3 Cdn Service Rifle titles; 6 ntl combined rifle titles; 15 CF Bisley teams; 3 DCRA Bisley teams; mem. Bicentennial rifle championship/Palma teams '88; Atlantic Milita Small Arms team '89-98; Cdn Palma team '92; CFCISM team '92, '94; mem. Cdn Forces Sports Hall of Fame; res. Scoudouc, N.B.

SURIN, Bruny (t&f): b. 12 Jul 1967, Au Cap Haitien, Haiti; m. Birinall; c. Kimberley, Katherine; UQuebec; sports marketing; sprinter; came to Canada '75; began competing in lj/tj '84; switched to sprints '89; competed '88 (lj), '92, '96, '00 Olympic, '87 PAG, '90, '94 CG, '87 FISU, '89, '94 Francophone Games, 4 world championships; 1 ntl outdoor TJ, 3 100m titles; 2 ntl 60m indoor titles; Francophone 100m gold '94; 10 ntl, 1 Commonwealth sr. records; PB 9.92 (100m), 20.48 (200m); 100m bronze '90, 4x100 gold '94 CG; gold 100m '94 Francophone Games; silver world 100m '95, '99; world 60m indoor sprint title '95; mem. '96, '00 Olympic, world gold 4x100m relay team; Jack Davies, Phil Edwards awards '93; Que. t&f athlete of '90; Cy Bricker jump events award '88; 2 Dick Ellis team awards; ambassador '03 IAAF world youth championship; Canadian Olympic Hall of Fame ('96 Oly gold 4x100 relay team); res. Pierrefonds, Que.

SUTER, Gary (hockey); b. 24 Jun 1964, Madison, Wisc.; m. Cathy; c. Jacob, Jared; Wisconsin; def. U Wisconsin '83-85; NHL Calgary '85-94, Chicago '94-98, San Jose '98-02; NHL record 1145 scheduled games, 203g, 641a, 108 playoff games, 17g, 56a; Stanley Cup winner '89; NHL all-rookie team; Calder Trophy '86; played 4 NHL all-star games; Team USA World Cup gold '96; res. Madison, Wisc.

SUTHERIN, Don (football); b. 29 Feb 1936, Empire, Ohio; given name: Don Paul; m. Nancy Carolyn Jones; c. Julie Ann, Gail Lynn, Becky Mae, Jill Mae; Ohio State, Malone College, BA, BScPhE; football coach; HS all-American, all-state; 4 seasons Ohio State under coach Woody Hayes; hon. mention all-American; all-Big-10 def; kicked winning field goal '58

Rose Bowl game; drafted NFL New York Giants; 1 year Giants, 1 Pittsburgh; Tiger-Cats '58, '61-66, Rough Riders '66-70, Argos '70; 6 all-star, 3 all-pro honors, 8 Grey Cup finals, 5 winners; 18 CFL records; CFL record: 4tds, 270c, 114fg, 78ss, 714pts; as db intercepted 58 passes for 599yds; shared CFL record 4 interceptions single game; 4 CFL scoring titles; scout Pittsburgh; HS coach '77-80; asst. coach Ottawa '81-84, Edmonton '85-90, Montreal Machine (WFL) '91, Calgary '91-93; head coach Hamilton '94-97, asst. '98-02; 8 Grey Cups as coach, 3 winners; named to Best-of-'60s-Team-of-Decade; Ohio outstanding athlete, alumnus awards; mem. Ohio Valley Athletic (Dapper Dan Club), Toronto, Ohio HS Athletic, Greater Canton Ohio Slow Pitch, Cdn Football halls of fame; nickname "Suds"; res. Stoney Creek, Ont.

SUTHERLAND, Hugh (hockey); b. 2 Feb 1907, Winnipeg, Man.; d. 9 Sep 1990, Winnipeg, Man.; given name: Hugh Robert; m. Cecilia Anderson; ret'd sales mgr. Sask. Wheat Pool; def Elmwood Millionaires Man. midget, jr. champions; mem. league champion Grain Exchange '29; Winnipeg '31 Allan Cup, '32 Olympic title teams; Selkirk HC '33-36; midget, juvenile, jr. baseball Elmwood Giants, sr. Norwood '29-38.

SUTHERLAND, James (builder/hockey); b. 19 Oct 1870, Kingston, Ont.; d. 30 Sep 1955, Kingston, Ont.; often referred to as "father of hockey", Capt. Sutherland coached Kingston Frontenacs Jrs. to several championships and played key role in popularizing sport in Eastern Ont.; became connected with OHA as district rep.; moved through exec. ranks to pres. '15-17; following WW1 service became pres. CAHA '19; life mem. OHA, CAHA; mem. Hockey Hall of Fame.

SUTHERLAND, Mike (football); b. 25 Jun 1971, Ottawa, Ont.; m. Gaby; Northern Illinois; broadcaster; off. guard; Ottawa Colts bantams, Ottawa Trojans midgets, Ottawa Sooners jr.; all-Big West Conf all-star awards; CFL Sask '96, Montreal '96-00, Winnipeg '01-02, Ottawa '03-04; 2 Grey Cup games; active in community charitable work; res. Nepean, Ont.

SUTTER, Brent (hockey); b. 10 Jun 1962, Viking, Alta; m. Connie; c. Merrick, Brandon, Brooke; hockey exec.; ctr Red Deer, Lethbridge (WHL); 1ˢᵗ pick NYI '80 draft; one of six brothers who played in NHL; played in NHL with Islanders '80-91, Chicago '91-98; Team Canada '84; NHL record: 1111 scheduled games, 363g, 466a, 144 playoff games, 30g, 44a; mem. 2 Stanley Cup, 1 Memorial Cup winners; owner/coach.GM Red Deer (WHL); coached Team Canada world jr. gold team '05; res. Chicago, Ill./Sylvan Lake, Alta.

SUTTER, Brian (hockey); b. 7 Oct 1956, Viking, Alta.; m. Judy; c. Shaun, Abigail; hockey coach; one of 6 brothers who played in NHL; lw jr. Lethbridge Broncos (WHL); Kansas City (CHL) '76-77; NHL with St. Louis '76-88; NHL record: 779 scheduled games, 303g, 333a, 65 playoff games, 21g, 21a; 9yrs Blues capt.; coach St. Louis '88-92, Boston '92-95, Calgary '97-00; Chicago '01-04; Jack Adams trophy '91; *SN* coach of '02; 3-time all-star; NHL coaching record (through '03): 946 scheduled games, 431-369-129-12, 68 playoff games, 28-40; jersey 11 ret'd by St. Louis; founding mem. Sutter Foundation; res. Sylvan Lake, Alta.

SUTTER, Darryl (hockey); b. 19 Aug 1958, Viking, Alta.; given name: Darryl John; m. Wanda; c. Jessie, Brett, Christopher; hockey exec.; 1 of 6 brothers who played in NHL; jr. Lethbridge '76-78; pro AHL New Brunswick '78-80, Japan '78-79, Chicago (NHL) '80-87; NHL playing record: 406 scheduled games, 161g, 118a, 51 playoff games, 24g, 19a; launched coaching career Saginaw (IHL) '88-89, Indianapolis (IHL) '89-90 (won Turner Cup), Chicago (NHL) '92-95 (1 div. title); consultant Chicago '95-97, head coach San Jose '97-02, Calgary '03-04 (also GM); NHL coaching record (through '04) 797 scheduled games, 365-308-104-20; 5ys team capt. Chicago; asst.coach Chicago '87-88, assoc. '90-92; AHL rookie of yr '80; IHL coach of '90; Red Garrett Memorial Award; helped launch Sutter Foundation charitable organization; res. Viking, Alta.

SUTTER, Duane (hockey); b. 16 Mar 1960, Viking, Alta.; m. Cindy; c. Darby, Kassie, Brady; hockey exec.; 1 of 6 brothers who played in NHL; nicknamed "Dog"; rw Lethbridge (WHL) jrs '76-80; NHL Islanders '79-87, Chicago '87-90; NHL record: 731 scheduled games, 139g, 203a, 161 playoff games, 26g, 32a; 4 Stanley Cup winners; scout Chicago 2yrs, head coach Indianapolis (IHL) 3yrs; asst. coach Florida '95-98, '03; scout Panthers '98-99; head coach Florida '01-03; dir. player dev. Florida '04; assoc. coach San Antonio (AHL) '04-05; res. Coral Springs, Fla.

SUTTER, Ron (hockey); b. 2 Dec 1963, Viking, Alta.; m. Margo; c. Madison, Reigan; hockey scout; ctr Lethbridge jrs. '80-83; NHL Philadelphia '82-91, St. Louis '91-94, Quebec '94, Islanders '94-95, Phoenix '95-96, Boston '96, San Jose '96-99, Calgary '00-01; NHL record: 1093 scheduled games, 205g, 328a, 104 playoff games, 8g, 32a; active role in Sutter Foundation and other charitable works; res. Whitefish, Mont.

SUTTON, Stephen (parachuting); b. 29 May 1946, Toronto, Ont.; given name: Stephen John; m. Kathy Cox; pres. Sutton Graphics Inc.; hockey goalie, competed in t&f, equestrian events as youth; world parachuting championships on TV sparked his interest at 16 and at 20 made initial jump; began competing '68 helping Cdn team claim 1st ever overall team medal in world competition; ntl team capt.; Cdn men's accuracy title '72; world accuracy silver '72; retd from competition '72 with more than 2200 jumps to his credit including record 200 jumps in one 24-hour period (actually 21:13); a strong promoter of sport parachuting; licensed rigger/instructor; developing better chutes has been an obsession; introduced square chute to Canada '71; holds several international kite patents; part of Cdn team which set high altitude record (22,500 feet); active coach; guest coach Peruvian team; selected to coach Cdn team at Rome worlds '76 but funding lack prohibited trip; enjoys flying ultralight aircraft; Ont. Achievement award; Diamond Wings from Cdn Sport Parachuting Assn in recognition of 2000 jumps; res. Toronto, Ont.

SUTTON, Warren (basketball/coaching); b. 12 Mar 1939, Chester, Pa.; given name: Warren Leroy; Acadia, Sir George Williams; teacher, coach; Little All-American hon. mention Div. 3 schools; mem. SGW ntl champions, MVP title tournament; 1st NBA draftee from Cdn coll. ranks; mem. Montreal, Ottawa, Kitchener club teams, frequent MVP; began coaching '63; coached Ottawa Ont. jr. girls title team

'71, Kitchener sr. women's Ont. title team '81; asst.Waterloo '84-85; res. Waterloo, Ont.

SUTTON-BROWN, Tammy (basketball); b. 27 Jan 1978, Toronto, Ont.; given name: Tamara Kim; Rutgers, BA; professional basketball player; started as a swimmer from 8-10, winning numerous medals; accumulated several awards, medals in basketball, volleyball, shot put and handball at Markham DHS; Harry Jerome female athlete of '97; NCAA Final Four participant during her years at Rutgers; '99 PAG silver; 2000 Olympian; WNBA all-star '02; MVP honors while playing professionally in Korea '01-02; currently playing professionally in Russia; res. Markham, Ont.

SUZUKI, Arthur (basketball); b. 29 Jul 1937, New Westminster, B.C.; m. Marlene Dubrick; c. Robert, William, Karen; UWO; supervisor production, inventory control; mem. 2 London Ont. city title football, 1 basketball teams; mem. Tillsonburg Livingstons, ntl finalists '58, Ont. title '59; Sr. A London Five B's '65; Ont. Int. A champion 3M '66; Ont. Sr. A champion Sarnia Drawbridge Inn '67 Canada Winter Games gold medal team; Ont. Sr. A champion London Celtics '73; basketball official '61-66; Ont. Masters (over 40) champions '80-81; res. London, Ont.

SWARTMAN, Mel (boxing); b. 3 Nov 1896, Arnprior, Ont.; d. 2 Jan 1985, Ottawa, Ont.; m. Irene Riffon; ret'd armed forces, dog breeder; boxed briefly as welterweight in Hamilton; 25yrs military sports sergeant; organized Ottawa Beaver Boxing Club '30s; BEG boxing team coach '50; coached Olympians Joey Sandulo, Harvey Lacelle, Clayton Kenny; boxing instructor Ottawa Boys' Club; breeder miniature long-haired dachshund champions; mem. Ottawa Sports Hall of Fame.

SWEENEY, Don (hockey); b. 17 Aug 1966, St. Stephen, N.B.; given name: Donald Clarke; m. Christine; c. Jarrod, Tyler; Harvard; NCAA East all-American '87-88, all-star award; gold Team Canada '97 worlds; parts of 3 seasons Maine Mariners (AHL); def. Boston (NHL) '88-03, Dallas '03-04; NHL record: (through '04) 1115 scheduled games, 52g, 221a, 108 playoff games, 9g, 10a; res. Lynnfield, Mass.

SWEENEY, Sylvia (basketball); b. 3 Oct 1956, Montreal, Que.; McGill, St. Mary's, Concordia, Sherbrooke, Laurentian, BA, also attended schools in France, Italy, Australia; owner Portal Entertainment Services; TV producer, director, actor, announcer, reporter, host; ntl team '74-84; mem. '76, '84 Olympic, '75, '79, '83 PAG, '77, '79 FISU Games teams; centre '79 CIAU title team; bronze '79 PAG, FISU Games, '82 Federation Cup; gold '82 Jones Cup; MVP '79 world, CIAU championships; flag-bearer '79 PAG; 3 times all-Cdn; Que. athlete of '79; asst. CdM '96 Olympics; worked with group which brought NBA Raptors to Toronto; CIAU-*TSN* award bears her name; mem. Cdn Basketball Hall of Fame; res. Forest Hill, Ont.

SWEENY, Bimbo (rowing); b. 1888, Vancouver, B.C., d. 12 Feb 1966, Vancouver, B.C.; given name: Campbell; m. Violet Pooley; capt., fb Vancouver Rowing Club rugby team '12, Miller Cup champions '10-11; mem. VRC from 1906; stroked NPAAO jr. 4s, sr. champions '08; strokes '09 4s which won Seattle North Pacific title in record time; VRC pres. '33-35, '46-49.

SWEENY, Violet (golf); b. Dec 1886, Victoria, B.C., d. Mar 1965, Victoria, B.C.; given name: Violet Pooley; m. Bimbo Sweeny; unprecedented 7 Pacific Northwest Golf Assn., 9 BC ladies championships; pres. CLGU '33-42; hon. life mem. BC exec.; 2 trophies bearing her name awarded annually for BC junior golf; BC Women in Sport Leaders & Legends award; mem. BC, Greater Victoria Sports, Cdn Golf halls of fame.

SWEET, Don (football); b. 13 Jul 1948, Vancouver, B.C.; m. Marilyn; c. 2; WSU; pro football player, teacher; placement kicker, punter; attended WSU on soccer scholarship; standout baseball player, golfer; signed by BC but traded to Montreal '72; CFL record 21 consecutive field goals '76; CFL record through '84: 325c, 312fg, 72s, 1333pts; 3 EFC scoring titles; 3 times EFC all-star; 2 Grey Cup winners; res. Dollard des Ormeaux, Que.

SWEETNAM, Nancy (swimming): b. 14 Aug 1973, Lindsay, Ont.; Laurentian, Guelph; mother Marian female swimming coach of '90; breaststroke, IM specialist; mem. ntl team '88-97; 11 CIAU, 30 ntl titles; ntl short-course 200m, 400m FS, 200m breaststroke records; ntl 400 IM record; gold 200IM, bronze 4x100 medley relay '90, silver 400IM, bronze 200IM '94 CG; 3 gold, 1 silver '93 FISU Games; competed '91, '94 world aquatic championships, '95 world short-course, '92, '96 (team capt.) Olympics, 4 World Cup gold '96; 1 CIAAU female-swimmer-of-yr award; Swimming Canada female athlete of '90; Gryphon of '97 award; mem. Ont. Aquatic Hall of Fame; res. Sudbury, Ont.

SWIFT, Bob (football); b. 29 Nov 1943, Shawinigan, Que.; m. Sandy; c. Joelle, Jonathan, Bobby; Clemson, Millersville State Coll.; football coach; CFL rb BC '64-65, og Toronto '66-70, ctr Winnipeg '70-78; rushed for 1054yds rookie season; scored BC's 1st td '64 Grey Cup game; nicknamed "Boss Hogg"; 4 all-WFC, CFL ctr selections; 2 Schenley outstanding Cdn, 3 outstanding lineman nominations; launched coaching career Millersville State; asst. coach Saskatchewan '83-84, Ottawa '85-86, '88, '95, Montreal '87, Upsala Coll '87, Edmonton '89, Calgary '90-91; dir. CAFA relations for Sask. '84; res. Mastersonville, Pa.

SWORDS, Shawn (basketball); b. 27 Dec 1973, Ottawa, Ont.; given name: Jeffrey Shawn; m. Shelley Dewar; Laurentian, BA Economics; pro basketball player; '92 ntl champion Ont. team; 2 OUAA East titles; gold '94 Commonwealth Championships; bronze '95, silver '97 FISU Games; competed '99 PAG, '00 Olympics, '02 worlds; '97 CIAU all-Cdn; Laurentian athlete of '97; 33 pts, 10 rbs, 8 a and 6 stl in his first career professional game; played with Kotaja Finnish men's league, Mulhouse of French B pro league; also played Tier II Junior A hockey Cumberland Grads in their inaugural year; 3 star season award; res. Ottawa, Ont.

SYDIE, Iain (badminton): b.12 Nov 1969, Richmond Hill, Ont.; began playing at 13 following footsteps of '65 Scottish singles champion father; '95 PAG singles silver, doubles gold; competed '96 Olympics; '99 PAG men's (Brent Olynyk), mixed (Denyse Julien) doubles gold; res. Calgary, Alta.

SYDOR, Alison (cycling): b. 9 Sept 1966, Edmonton, Alta.; Victoria; pro athlete; began competing as triathlete age 10; Alta. jr. champion; played ice hockey, volleyball, basketball in high school; burst onto ntl cycling scene at age 21 winning 3 gold '87 Western Canada Summer Games; mem. ntl road team '88-98; 1st Cdn to win world title medal with individual road race bronze '91; intl breakthrough came '90 Tour de L'Aude in France as mem. Cdn team time-trial champs; wore leader's yellow jersey 6 days '91 Tour de L'Aude; competed 1st mountain bike x-country '91; turned pro '93; 1st Cdn woman to win world cup gold '94; 17 WC victories; 5 ntl road race, 2 ntl mountain bike, 1 ntl criterium, 1 ntl team time trial gold; silver team time trial, bronze road race '94 CG; competed '92, '96, '00, '04 Olympics, '90, '94 CG, '95, '99 PAG, mountain bike x-country gold '95, silver '99; women's mountain bike silver '96 Olympics, '03 worlds; 3 world mountain bike overall titles; '98 world team gold, x-country bronze; '98 Sea Otter, Cactus Cup gold; 2 Velma Springstead, 1 Bobbie Rosenfeld awards; BC Women in Sport Leaders & Legends award; Canada's female mountain biker of yr.; Order of BC; res. Victoria, B.C.

SYLVAIN, Georges (jiu-jitsu/karate); b. 31 Dec 1935, Hull, Que.; div. Suzanne Lalonde; c. Jean, Claude, Lynn; ret'd military police; 25yr chief defense training instructor for law & security pgm. Algonquin Coll.; began combative arts training during Korean War excelling in judo, jiu-jitsu, karate, weapons, standard police techniques, western boxing; 10th degree black belt jiu-jitsu, 4th degree black belt karate; chief instructor RCMP '54-66; regarded as pioneer/innovator in Kick-boxing; among pupils was world champion Jean-Yves Theriault; tactical training officer with international reputation; 15yrs police officer; author 4 self-defense books; Algonquin Coll. Order of Merit; Dr. Laurent Isabelle teaching award; Pressure Point Control Management System meritorious award; inventor Sure-Grip Scepter baton; lecturer numerous law enforcement seminars throughout NA; founder CAN-RYU system of jiu-jitsu; pres. Cdn Jiu-Jitsu Union; mem. Cdn Martial Arts Hall of Fame; res. Nepean, Ont.

SYLVAIN, Jules (weightlifting): b. 20 Dec 1925, Quebec City, Que.; m. Martha; c. Danielle, Ginette; butcher; competitive lifter 13 years; 10 ntl 60kg titles; mem. '52, '56 Olympic, '50, '54, '58 CG teams; coached 15 years; international referee; res. Charlesbourg, Que.

SYMONS, Bill (football); b. 14 Jun 1943, Nucla, Colo.; given name: William L; m. Connie Willden (d); c. Kellie, Stacie, Curtis, Myles (sc); m. Trish Peacock; Colorado, BEd; ALA forest products owner/farmer; rb; Green Bay (NFL) '64-65, BC '66, Toronto '67-73; 1 EFC rushing title; 11 games 100-plus yards rushing, 6 in 1 season; CFL record: 4280yds, 807 rushes, 44tds, 264 points, 72 kickoff returns for 1878yds; 3 times led Argos KO retruns, 4 times leading rusher; best single game 7 Sep '70 vs Ottawa scoring 4tds, 3 rushing, 1 on pass reception; Argos single-season rushing record 1107yds; CFL all-star '68-70; Jeff Russel Memorial Trophy '70; Schenley Outstanding Player '68; named to all-time Argos team '96; 1 NFL title; mem. Cdn Football Hall of Fame; res. Hockley Valley, Ont.

SZMIDT, Peter (swimming); b. 12 Aug 1961, Montreal, Que.; m. Donna Ross; UAlta, Cal. (Berkeley); auditor

Imperial Oil; freestyle specialist; NCAA team silver '80; AAU FS gold '81; mem. ntl team '77-84; 15 ntl, 1 Commonwealth, 1 world records; ntl titles: 7 400m, 5 1500m, 4 200m, 2 100m, 4x200m FS relay; CG gold 4x100m FS relay '78, silver 4x200m FSR '78, 200m, 400m FS '82, bronze 4x100m FSR '82; PAG silver 4x100 FSR, bronze 400 FS, 4x200 FSR '79; FISU Games bronze 4x200 FSR '83; mem. '78, '82 CG, '80, '84 Olympic, '79, '83 PAG, '83 FISU Games teams; 3 silver '83 CIAU championships; Cdn. Aquatic Fed. athlete of '80; dir. Swim Canada; mem. Quebec Swimming, Cdn Aquatic halls of fame; res. Toronto, Ont.

SZNAJDER, Andrew (tennis): b. 25 May 1967, Preston, Eng.; m. Kathya Ponce; c. Krystof Ernesto; Pepperdine; PageNet Canada sales exec.; NCAA rookie of year; 2 all–American awards; NCAA indoor singles title '88; mem. 2 Sunshine Cup -18 teams; won Bacardi indoor, Sporting Life singles '86; 3 Tennis Canada player-of-yr awards; Tennis Canada most improved player '85; mem. Cdn Davis Cup team '89–93; pro circuit '88–94; wins over Mats Vilander, Bjorn Borg; 6 ntl singles titles; 46 in ATP rankings '89, highest by Cdn male in open era; plays charity fund-raiser exhibitions Royal Bank tour; conducts nation-wide adult clinics; tennis rep COA athletes council; dir. ntl sports centre Toronto; mem. Cdn Tennis Hall of Fame; res. Mississauga, Ont.

SZTEHLO, Zoltan (equestrian): b. 27 Nov 1921, Budapest, Hungary; d. 16 Jun 1990, Guatemala City; m. Rhonda; Royal Hungarian Military Academy, Debrecen, LLD; ret'd lawyer; accredited dressage judge International Equestrian Federation; Hungarian jr. sabre champion; dressage team gold '71 PAG; mem. '68 Olympic team; 3 Western Canadian dressage titles; Western Canada Games dressage gold '75; trainer-coach Alta. modern pentathlon gold team '75 WCG; mem. '67 PAG equestrian jury; award winning course designer; coach jr. riding teams '80-90; organized 1st NA young riders championship in Maple Ridge, B.C., '82; authored book *The Art of Riding* in Hungarian.

T

TAGLIANI, Alex (motorsport); b. 18 Oct 1972, Montreal, Que.; m. Bronte Kok; pro race car driver; Que. 100cc jr. carting champion '87; Que. Karting rookie of yr; top rookie F125 karting Solignum Cup '89; won '90 Cdn F125 Karting title race; BF Goodrich Challenge title at Cdn Ice Racing championship; Que. F125 Karting title '91; 2 Ice racing GP Unipro title Que. Winter Carnival; 2 Cdn. F125 titles; Cdn, Que. Formula A karting crowns; Bridgestone Racing School champion '92; competed 1st open-wheel race Mt. Tremblant '94; runnerup Atlantic series rookie of '96; 2 Atlantic series wins '97-99; made jump to CART Fed-Ex series '00 after 4 campaigns on Player's/Atlantic series; mem. Rocketsports team; runnerup '03 Molson Indy; won Elkhart Lake Champ car title '04; res. Las Vegas, Nev.

TAKAHASHI, Allyn (judo); b. 20 May 1956, Montreal, Que.; given name: Masao Allyn; Waterloo, BA, MA; GM Isuzu Japan; 3 Ont. 120lb, 1 127lb title; winner 30, runnerup 9 of 40 competitions entered 120-139lb categories '69-76; bronze USJA nationals '72; 3 Eastern Cdn, Ont. HS, CNE invitational, 2 Kingston Y Asahi, jr. Olympic, 1 world junior Shiai title; Ottawa ACT award '72-74, Merivale HS phys-ed award '72-73; 3rd degree Shodan black belt; res. Tokyo, Japan.

TAKAHASHI, June (judo); b. 17 Jun 1933, Vancouver, B.C.; given name: June Hayami; m. Masao; c. Allyn, Philip, Ray, Tina; sport administrator; 1st degree (Shodan) black belt '68, 2nd degree (Nidan) black belt '75; 5th degree black belt '97; assists husband Mas in operation of Japanese Martial Arts Centre; North East Region Cdn Judo Assn. secty-treas., dir. of judo for women '75-76; ntl councillor Judo Canada '76-78; regional rep. Judo Ont.; NA referee; ED Judo Canada; Judo Can. constitution, hall of fame comms.; Ont. Achievement Award; res. Nepean, Ont.

TAKAHASHI, Masao (judo); b. 24 Jun 1929, Vancouver, B.C.; m. June Hayami; c. Allyn, Philip, Ray, Tina; judo instructor, operator Japanese Martial Arts Centre; 8th degree black belt; 3 ntl unlimited weight titles; mem. '61 Paris world championships team; pitched Alta. Japanese evacuees (relocated from BC) to baseball league championship '47; RCAF swimming, diving medalist '50; ntl councillor Judo Canada, v-p./councillor/regional dir. Judo Ont., mem. grading committee; p-referee-in-chief Judo Ont.; referee Pan-American Judo Federation; Centennial medal '67; tech. official for judo '76 Olympics; chair. Judo Ont. grading board; Order of Sacred Treasures Gold Rays with Rosette presented by Emperor of Japan; mem. Cdn Forces Sports, Cdn Judo halls of fame; res. Nepean, Ont.

TAKAHASHI, Philip (judo); b. 12 Jun 1957, Toronto, Ont.; given name: Philip Masato; m. Cathy Sheffield; c. Christy, Jenny, Emily; Algonquin College, UofOtt; HS teacher, coach; Eastern Ont. Open 80lb title '69; gold 58kg Sonthofen, Bavaria, Stuttgart, Germany, Ont. Winter Games '74, Canada Games '75, Ont. jr. Olympics (twice), Cdn Youth Games, Ont. HS; 6th degree judo black belt; 4 ntl 60kg, 2 Ont., Que.,

1 Dutch, international teams, Canada Cup titles; bronze '79 PAG; gold Pan-Am championships '80; bronze '81 worlds, '82 FISU Games; silver 60kg Pacific Rim '83; gold '84 Canada Cup; mem. '80, '84 Olympic team; Detroit Mayor's Trophy for outstanding performance '71-72; ACT (Ottawa) sports award for judo '71, '74, '75; Ont. Sports Achievement Award '70-75; fed. govt. sport excellence award '82; mem. Nepean Wall, Judo Canada Hall of Fame; res. Kanata, Ont.

TAKAHASHI, Ray (judo, wrestling); b. 7 Aug 1958, Downsview, Ont.; given name: Raymond Hugh; m. Janet Dick; c. Mariko, Steven; UWO; UWO wrestling coach; gold '72 US jr. nationals; 10 ntl, 1 Pan-Am jr. titles; ntl team from '75; mem. '76, '80, '84 Olympic, '79, '83 PAG, '78, '82 CG, '81, '83 FISU, '81-82 CIAU, '80, '82 World Cup teams; gold 52kg '78 CG, 57kg '80-81 CIAU, 52kg '83 PAG; ACT (Ottawa) amateur sports award for wrestling, Ont. Sports Achievement Award '75, ntl outstanding wrestler award '80; 1 CIAU coach-of-yr award; fed. govt. excellence award '84; also teaches judo; 3rd degree judo black belt; mem. Cdn Amateur Wrestling, UWO, Ottawa Sports Halls, Nepean Wall of Fame; res. London Ont.

TAKAHASHI, Tina (judo); b. 13 Jan 1960, North York, Ont.; given name: Alice Christina; m. Sean MacFadyen; c. Torin, Adam, Liam; UofOtt, BPhE, BEd; teacher, judo instructor; dominated jr. Ont. ranks; 7 ntl, 6 Ont., 3 Que. 2 Pacific Rim, 1 Desert Open, Canada Cup titles; ntl team '78-87; bronze 48kg '83 PAG; silver '84 Canada Cup; 1st Cdn world champion '84; coach ntl team '88 Olympics; 6th degree black belt; mem. Nepean Wall, Judo Canada Hall of Fame; res. Ottawa, Ont.

TALBOT, Jean Guy (hockey); b. 11 Jul 1932, Cap de la Madelaine, Que.; m. Pierette Cormier; c. Carole, Danny, Michel; jr. Trois Rivieres Reds; def Que. Aces '53-54, Shawingan '54-55, Montreal (NHL) '55-67; mem. 7 Stanley Cup winners; Minnesota, Detroit '67, St. Louis '68-70, Buffalo '70; NHL record: 1056 scheduled games, 43g, 242a, 150 playoff games, 4g, 26a; asst. coach NYR '76-77, head coach '77-78; NHL coaching record: 200 scheduled games, 82-90-28; 8 playoff games 2-6; res. Montreal, Que.

TALLON, Dale (hockey/golf); b. 19 Oct 1950, Noranda, Que.; given name: Michael Dale Lee; m. Meg; c. Lauren, Kirsten; Ryerson PTI.; hockey exec., broadcaster, pro golfer; ntl jr. golf championship '69; missed Ont. title same year by single stroke; def jr. OHA Oshawa Generals, Toronto Marlboros; 1st Vancouver choice, 2nd overall '70 amateur draft; Chicago '73-78, Pittsburgh '78-80; played in 2 all-star games NHL record: 642 scheduled games, 98g, 238a, 33 playoff games, 2g, 10a; radio broadcaster, color commentator Leafs hockey '80-82, Hawks '82-98, '02-04; dir. player personnel Chicago '98-02; AGM '04; res. Chicago, Ill.

TALLON, Wayne (curling): b. 22 May 1956, Ottawa, Ont. given name: Wayne William; m. Susan Fleck; c. Anne-

Marie, Mireille; Algonquin Coll., CGA; town manager; competed 5 Ont. men's Tankards, runnerup '86; skip 2 City of Ottawa grand aggregate title rinks; 4 Ont. Silver Tankard titles; 3rd for Russ Howard '99, '00 Briers; 2 hdcp golfer; St. Stephen club champion; res. St. Stephen, N.B.

TAM, Selwyn (wrestling): b. 8 Dec 1968, Vancouver, B.C.; Douglas Coll., SFU BA; HS teacher; began wrestling at 15; all-American '93; competed '90, '92 Canada Cup. '92 Sunkist Intl Open, Clansman Intl, '94 Cerro Pelado; 52km gold '93 Slovak Grand Prix, 2 ntl championships, '94 CG; bronze '95 PAG; asst. coach SFU from '99; res. Vancouver, B.C.

TAN, Taro (judo): b. 13 Aug 1967, Montreal, Que.; Concordia, Montreal, BA; RCMP constable; began competing age 14; mem. ntl team '86-98; 4th degree black belt; 7 ntl 65kg titles; bronze '87 Pan-Am jr., US Open championships; bronze '90, '94 Pan-Am championships; Canada Cup silver '91, gold '92; bronze '95 PAG; US Open title '94; '96 Italian bronze; competed '96 Olympics, 2 worlds; mem. Quebec Judo Hall of Fame; res. Orleans, Ont.

TANNER, Elaine (swimming); b. 22 Feb 1951, Vancouver, B.C.; div.; c. Scott, Shannon Nahrgang; UAlta.; butterfly, backstroke specialist; 17 ntl titles '65-68; PB: FS 61.5 (100m), 2:14.8 (200m), 4:43.8 (400m), backstroke 66.7 (100m), 2:24.5 (200m), butterfly 65.4 (100m), 2:29.9 (200m), medley 2:31.8 (200m), 5:26.3 (400m); most successful woman swimmer '66 CG at 15 with 4 gold, 3 silver, 2 world records; backstroke golds world record times '67 PAG; Cdn, US, UK butterfly sprint titles '65; final competitive appearance '68 Olympics, 1 silver, 1 bronze; Lou Marsh, Bobbie Rosenfeld awards '66; trophy awarded annually to Canada's top jr. female athlete bears her name; Officer Order of Canada '70; nicknamed "Mighty Mouse"; BC Women in Sport Leaders & Legends award; mem. BC Swimming, Cdn, International Aquatic, Cdn Amateur, BC, Canada's Sports halls of fame; res. Toronto, Ont.

TAPP, Jay (swimming); b. 12 Dec 1959, Toronto, Ont.; given name: John Grenville; div.; c. Jake, Charlie; UCal, BComm; owns Tapp Technologies; mem. '77 Canada Games, '78 Worlds, '79 PAG teams; gold 4x100 medley relay, bronze 100m backstroke '78 CG; CIAU backstroke gold; mem. Cdn Aquatic Hall of Fame; res. Langley, B.C.

TAPP, Larry (administration/swimming); b. 6 Oct 1937, Fort William, Ont.; given name: Lawrence; m. Joanne Fuller; c. John (Jay), Jill; McMaster, BA, Kansas, Bus. Dip; dean Richard Ivey school of business UWO; became involved in competitive swimming as dir. Etobicoke Aquatic Club '67-69; chair. finance Ont. section CASA; Ont. dir/ pres. '71-74; CASA pres. '74-76; key role in fund-raising programs for '76 Olympics; master official '76 Olympics, '78 CG, Worlds, '79 PAG; chair. Aquatic Federation of Canada, Amateur Swimming Union of the Americas tech. swim comm., FINA age-group swim comm., Aquatic Trust of Canada; Ont. achievement award; mem. Ont., Cdn Aquatic halls of fame; res. London, Ont.

TASHLIN, Lesley (t&f): b. 27 May 1969, Toronto. Ont.; m. Craig Taylor; c. Emma; hurdler; represented Canada '94

CG, '95, '99 PAG, '96 Olympic Games; ntl 100mH title '95; 5 intl meet titles; res. Ottawa, Ont./Calgary, Alta.

TATARCHUK, Hank (basketball); b. 2 Aug 1930, Vegreville; given name: Waldmar Eli; m. Arlene Hauberg; c. Erik; UAlta, BPhE, UofOtt, MPhE; pres. Triple T Diversified Associates; ret'd RCAF, asst. dean PE&R; PE specialist training, fitness, research, sports programming; coach RMC basketball '63–67; asst. coach, UAlta. basketball '67–68, '79–81, UMan. '68–71, Carleton '71–73, UofOtt '73–78; offficial, PAG '67; dir. basketball competition, '76 Olympics; v-p. sports div. FISU Games comm. '81–83; National Assn. of Basketball Coaches merit award '77; v-p. LA Olympic organizing comm. '83-84; consultant/ evaluator Seoul Olympic organizing comm. '84-88; FISU Games consultant '85, '97, '95; v-p. World jr. basketball championships '91; dir. sports/venues FISU Games '92-93; v.-chair FISU tech. comm. '87-91; consultant du Maurier LPGA Classic '94-96; commissioner/convenor basketball CWUAA '93-99; mem. Cdn Forces Sports, Cdn Basketball halls of fame; res. Edmonton, Alta.

TATHAM, Pat (basketball); b. 14 Apr 1947, Motherwell, Scotland; given name: Patricia Ann MacDonald; div. Tatham; m. James leBlanc; c. Curtis, Matthew, Catherine; Brock, Waterloo; technical trainer; Ont. midget women's title team '61; 13 Ont. sr. A title teams; Ont. winter games gold '70, bronze '74; ntl juvenile champion Hamilton Electras '62; 2 ntl jr. women's titles; sr. A title, MVP '73; Canada winter games silver '67, gold '71; ntl team '69-76, capt. 4yrs; competed 2 PAG, Worlds, varied European, Asian, South American, North American tours; WBA title with Hamilton Athenas '73, masters tourney title '85; named to '76 Olympic team but pregnancy prevented participation; competed varied invitational tournaments '59-76 earning several MVP, all-star awards; Ont. Centennial medal '67, 5 Ont. achievement awards; mem. Cdn Basketball Hall of Fame; res. Hamilton, Ont.

TAVARES, John (lacrosse): b. 4 Sep 1968, Toronto, Ont.; WLU BA; HS teacher; mem. Mississauga Tomahawks '85-90, Vancouver Bandits '91, Brampton Excelsiors, Buffalo Bandits '92-03, Team Canada '93-02; 3 Mann Cup champions; 3 Mike Kelly MVP awards; 2 Major Indoor Lacrosse League titles, 2 playoff MVP awards; MILL MVP '94, league scoring title, 1st team all-star; 1st NIL player to top 100 (115) points single season; Mississauga pro athlete of '93; saw '01 summer play with Akwesasne, Victoria; Team Canada '02 Lacrosse Worlds; regarded as Buffalo franchise player; Gov.-Gen.'s award '93; res. Mississauga, Ont.

TAYLOR, Betty (t&f); b. 22 Feb 1916, Ingersoll, Ont., d. 2 Feb 1977, Ottawa, Ont.; m. William Campbell; c. Margaret, David; McMaster; ntl int. hurdles title '30 in record time; mem. '32, '36 Olympic, '34 BEG, women's world games teams; London, Eng.; final competitive event Berlin Olympics '36 winning bronze when first 4 runners were given same time; Bobbie Rosenfeld award '36; mem. Cdn Amateur, McMaster Sports halls of fame.

TAYLOR, Bobby (football/hockey); b. 5 Mar 1939, Barrow-in-Furness, Lancashire, Eng.; div.; c. Janet Lee, Bobby Jr.; hotel/bar owner; football Mount Royal College Cougars; wr Calgary '61-65, Toronto '66-70, '74, Hamilton

'71, Edmonton '71-73; CFL record: 521 passes caught for 8223yds, 15.8 avg., 50td; WFC record 74 receptions Calgary '63; twice led EFC receivers; all-Eastern '69; 10 years pro hockey in Toronto, Philadelphia chains with Que. City (AHL), Victoria, Seattle (WHL), Long Island, Tulsa, Rochester, Cherry Hill, N.J., Johnstown, Pa. (EHL), South Peace HL; Toronto Oldtimers hockey; operates Black Bull Tavern in Toronto and Banff lodge; res. Toronto, Ont.

TAYLOR, Bryce (administration); b. 14 Nov 1933, Delisle, Sask.; d. 16 Feb 1989, Toronto, Ont.; given name: Bryce Malcolm; div Patricia; c. Deborah, Barbara, Nancy; m. Cheryl; c. Bryche; Springfield College, DPhE, BSc,UBC, MPhE; York professor; pres. Cdn Gymnastics Fed. '74, '78; pres. Coaching Assn. of Canada '76-77, v-p. '75; dir. National Sport and Recreation Centre '76, COA '75; secty-treas. Mission Dome Inc., '71-73; field rep. Ont. Jr. Olympics '73-74; chair. organizing comm. international gymnastics competition Montreal '75; chair. comm. for unification of sport in Canada '75; mem. Task Force on sport, Ont. reasearch council on leisure; CAC scholarship selection comm. '75; chair. Cdn gymnastic seminar '67-89; mem. American College of Sports Medicine '64; dir. intl sport coaches exchange '65; CdM FISU Games '67; involved in study of sports movement, ntl gymnastics development; CAHPER R. Tait McKenzie award of honor '76, Air Canada amateur sports exec. of '76; author gymnastic coaching manuals, several books, articles on gymnastics, tennis, sport studies.

TAYLOR, Cyclone (hockey); b. 23 Jun 1883, Tara, Ont., d. 9 Jun 1979, Vancouver, B.C.; given name: Fredrick Wellington; m. Thirza Cook; c. Fred Jr., John, Mary, Edward, Joan; civil servant; amateur Listowel, Thessalon, Ont., Portage La Prairie, Man.; pro def Houghton, Mich., '06; 2yrs with both Ottawa, Renfrew; Vancouver '12-21; as rover, ctr scored 194 goals in 186 league games, 15 more in 19 playoff games; 5 scoring titles; 32 goals in 18-game '17-18 season, 6 in single game vs Victoria '16-17; nickname "Cyclone" given him at Ottawa CY Arena '07 by Gov.-Gen. Earl Grey; mem. 2 Stanley Cup winners; Ottawa Capitals lacrosse team '08-10, Mann Cup '08; OBE; mem. Hockey, Lacrosse, Ottawa, BC Sports, BC Hockey halls of fame.

TAYLOR, Dave (hockey); b. 4 Dec 1955, Levack, Ont.; given name: David Andrew; m. Beth; c. Jamie, Katie; Clarkson College; hockey exec.; 14th LA pick, 210th overall '75 draft; with Marcel Dionne, Charlie Simmer formed Triple Crown Line; nicknamed "Stitch"; 2nd team all-star rw '81; played entire NHL career with LA '75-94; 4 yrs capt.; NHL record: 1111 scheduled games, 431g, 638a, 70 playoff games, 23g, 28a; 1st player to win Masterton, King Clancy awards same year '91; active mem, Kings' charity golf, softball tournaments; twice Kings' unsung-hero award; jersey #18 ret'd by LA; AGM Kings 3yrs, GM/v-p. '97-03; *HN* exec of '01; mem. Hockey Hall of Fame; res. Tarzana, Calif.

TAYLOR, E.P. (horse racing); b. 29 Jan 1901, Ottawa, Ont.; d. 14 May 1989, Lyford Cay, BWI; given name: Edward Plunkett; m. Winnifred Thorton Duguid; c. Judith Winifred, Mary Louise, Charles; Ashbury College, McGill, BSc; ret'd investment broker, brewer; owner Winfield Farms; owner Northern Dancer '64 Kentucky Derby, Preakness,

Nijinsky II '70 Epson Derby, English triple crown; pres. Ont. Jockey Club '53-73; did much to revitalize and raise standard of racing in Ont.; 9 Taylor horses won Cdn horse of year, 15 Queen's Plate winners; world's leading breeder '70; 10 NA breeder-of-yr awards; Thoroughbred Racing Assoc. man of '73; instrumental in forming Jockey Club of Canada; Woodbine turf course named in his honor; mem. Canadian Horse Racing, Canada's , Ont. Legends Sports halls of fame.

TAYLOR, Gordon (golf/administration); b. 1909, Montreal, Que.; d. 27 Jan 1999, Montreal, Que.; given name: Gordon Baxter; m. Margaret; hockey with Montreal Royals; Que. diving title; considered prospective Olympic diver; Cdn amateur golf title '32; low amateur Cdn Open '35; mem. 1st Cdn golf team to compete overseas '35; capt. Team Canada 1st Commonwealth tourney '54;capt. Team Can. sr. triangular matches '64; 2 Duke of Kent titles; 2 Cdn srs. golf titles; Que. Am title '54, srs. '68; RCGA governor '50-64, pres. '59; RCGA advisory gov. '65-77; hon. life gov. from '78; pres. Cdn Srs. GA '78-79; pres. QGA '49; mem. Que., RCGA halls of fame.

TAYLOR, Graham (parachuting); b. 26 Apr 1949, New Zealand; given name: Graham Michael; m. Melody Hydman; c. Warren, Jason; New Zealand, Capilano College; contractor; rugby '53-73; MVP Trojan Rugby Club Vancouver '73; HS athletic champion award '67; began skydiving '73; 4-way, 8-way ntl titles '77, '79-80; world champion '77, '79; Australian 4-way title '77; French 4-way title, runnerup 8-way '79; 2nd 4-way China '80; more than 2,500 jumps; res. Claresholm, Alta.

TAYLOR, John (skiing); b. 12 Jan 1908, Toronto, Ont.; d. 4 Nov 1989, Ottawa, Ont.; given name: John Pringle; m. Nattalie Skinner; c. Alex, Robert; ret'd; mem. '32 Olympic team; 2nd ntl x-country championships '34; ntl, Ont., x-country titles '35; dir. Ottawa Ski Club; chair. Gatineau Ski Zone; pres. Heron Park Community Assn.; secty-treas. Ottawa Tennis Club; dir. Canadian Ski Museum.

TAYLOR, Piffles (football); b. 1894, Collingwood, Ont.; d. 24 May 1946, Regina, Sask.; given name: Neil Joseph; UofT; played football at UofT, Regina Roughriders '14-16, '19-20, Regina Boat Club '20-21; coached Regina Boat Club '22-23; pres. Roughriders '34-36, WIFU '37, '41-42, CRU '46; considered largely responsbile for development of football in Western Canada; Regina stadium bears his name and CFL Western champions annually receive trophy bearing his name; mem. Cdn Football, Sask Sports halls of fame.

TAYLOR, Ron (baseball); b. 13 Dec 1937, Toronto, Ont.; given name: Ronald Wesley; m. Rona Douglas; UotT, BA, PPSc., MD; medical doctor, operates sports medicine clinic; rh relief specialist Cleveland '62, St. Louis '63-65, Houston '65-66, New York Mets '67-71, San Diego '72; ML record 491 scheduled games, 800ip, 45-43, 72sv, 3.93era; mem. '64 St. Louis, '69 Mets World Series champions; perfect WS record of 7 innings pitched allowing no hits, no runs and recording a save in each series; 1 win, 1 save '69 playoff vs Atlanta; runnerup NL rookie pitcher of year; mgr. Alta. amateur team while awaiting medical school entrance marks; team doctor Blue Jays; mem. Canada's Sports, Cdn Baseball halls of fame; res. Toronto, Ont.

TAYLOR, Russ (curling); b. 27 Oct 1943, Ottawa, Ont.; given name: Gordon Russell; m. Nicole Boily; c. Candy, Russell Jr., James; private investigator; nicknamed "The Hawk"; competed in 4 Ont. men's championships; skipped Gov.-Gen.'s title rink `81; 3 OCA Intermediate, Quebec International titles; won City of Ottawa Grand Aggregate, Eastern Ont. Major League '85; in 2yr span `85-86 reached 2 intermediate (won both), 2 men's, 1 mixed provincial championships; unique distinction of having curled in competitive bonspiels every month for 2yr period; res. Cumberland, Ont.

TEMPLETON, Bert (coaching/hockey); b. 1940, Irvine, Scotland; d. 5 Dec 2003, Sudbury, Ont.; m. Sandi; c. Craig, Lori, Darren; sc. Julie Evans, Jodie Evans; hockey exec.; coached jr. B Hamilton; 26 seasons OHL with Hamilton, Barrie, Niagara Falls, St. Catharines, North Bay, Sudbury amassing 907-678-148 record; AHL Nova Scotia '79-81; won '76 Memorial Cup; silver world jr. '77; 2 OHL coach, exec. of yr awards; CHL coach, exec. of yr awards.

TENNANT, Mark (coaching); b. 22 Jun 1944, Miniota, Man.; given name: James Mark; m. Gail Marie Olver; c. John Darcy, James Derek, Jodie Breanne; UMan., BPhE, UBC, MPhE; assoc. professor UofSask. coached of women's intercollegiate volleyball team '71-98; 3 CIAU ntl titles; 4 CIAU coach of year; coach of '79; pres. CIAU volleyball coaches assoc. '80; mem. master coaches review board CVA '77-98; IVBF instructor world class coaching courses '80-98; author *Volleyball Team Play* '75; chef adjoint secretariat Volleyball organizing Comm. '76 Olympics; mem. tech. comm. for volleyball FISU Games '84-98; mem. FIVB rules of game, sports organizing comms.; CIAU women's volleyball rookie-of-yr award bears his name; AMTEC award '78; life mem. Sask VBA; mem. UofSask Sports Wall, Saskatoon, Sask. Sports halls of fame; res. Saskatoon, Sask.

TERRY, Jackie (shooting); b. 29 May 1954, Owen Sound, Ont.; chemical technologist; mem. '81-83 world championships, '83 PAG, '84 Olympic Games teams; silver ladies air rifle, 3-position teams '83 PAG; Ont. air, standard rifle titles, Benito Juarez, Championship of Americas, Cuban small-bore prone titles; SFC golden anniversary award '82; res. Burlington, Ont.

TESSIER, Orv (hockey); b. 30 Jun 1933, Cornwall, Ont.; given name: Orval Ray; m. Charlotte Chouinard; c. Adele, Andre, Michael, Julie; hockey exec.; leading scorer '53 Barrie Memorial Cup winner; pro '53-63 Montreal Royals (QHL), Canadiens, Bruins (NHL), Hershey Bears, Springfield Indians (AHL), Kingston Frontenacs (EPHL), Portland Buckaroos (WHL); reinstated amateur Clinton (EHL), Jersey Devils; pro scoring record '59-60 Kingston 59g, 67a; league scoring title '61-62 as player-coach Frontenacs scoring 54g, 60a; league MVP, good conduct awards; coached Cornwall Royals to Memorial Cup '72; Que. Remparts '73 Memorial Cup finalists; Kitchener '81 Memorial Cup finalists; Jr. A coaching record: 12yrs 446-304-74; coached NB Hawks to AHL title '81-82; coach Chicago '82-85; scout Colorado '97-98; NHL coaching record: 213 scheduled games, 99-93-21; 18 playoff games, 9-9; NHL, *Hockey News* coach of '83; res. Fraser's Point, Ont.

TETLEY, Bill (curling); b. 11 Jul 1933, Lionshead, Ont.; d. 9 Jul 2003, Thunder Bay, Ont.; given name: William Ross; m. Elaine Lord; c. Ross, Allan, Ian, Tanis; RIA cost accountant; executive; lead '51, skip '71, '75 Brier, '75 winner; semifinalist '75 Silver Broom (worlds); skip NO rinks 2 ntl mixed, 1 ntl srs; Thunder Bay sportsman of '68; mem. NWO Sports Hall of Fame.

TETLEY, Ian (curling); b. 14 Aug 1962, Port Arthur, Ont.; given name: Ian James; m. Sherry; c. Nicklaus; Lakehead, hons BComm; golf sales specialist; lf '75 Cdn Major Little League baseball title team; competed Cdn juv ski championships '78; 2nd stone Al Hackner's Cdn, World championship rink '85; 2nd Ed Werenich's Cdn, World title rink '90; 2nd Wayne Middaugh's Cdn, World title rink '98; competed 4 Briers; '93 VO Cup winner; with Wayne Middaugh '95-96 *TSN* Skins Game titles; father Bill skipped '75 Brier winner; mem. Cdn Curling Hall of Fame; res. Mississauga, Ont.

TEWKSBURY, Mark (swimming): b. 7 Feb 1968, Calgary, Alta.; UCal, BA, New South Wales, hon. LLD UWO; motivational speaker, consultant; backstroke specialist; began competing age 8; mem. ntl team '84-92; competed '86, '91 worlds, '88, '92 Olympic, '86, '90 CG teams; 4 CG gold, 1 Olympic silver, 1 bronze; 35 World Cup gold, 12 winter ntls, 13 summer ntls gold; 3 overall World Cup backstroke titles; 11 Cdn sr., 4 world, 4 Commonwealth records; COA jr. athlete of '85; Calgary athlete of '90; Aquatics Canada athlete of '87, '90; 3 Swimming Canada jr. male athlete, 2 sr. male athlete awards; '87 fed. govt. Sports Excellence award; '89 Olympic champion award; Lionel Conacher, Norton Crowe awards '92; Johnny F. Bassett award '95; Sydney *Morning Herald* academic prize; resigned from COA/Toronto Olympic bid comm. due to ongoing bidding scandal; declared himself openly gay '98; co-pres. Montreal '06 Gay Games organization; ntl spokesperson for AIDS; budding marathon runner; mem. Cdn Amateur, Canada's, Alta., UCal Sports, Intl. Swimming halls of fame; res. Montreal, Que.

THACKER, Mary Rose (figure skating); b. 9 Apr 1922, Winnipeg, Man., d. Jul 1983, Victoria, B.C.; m. Roy Temple; c. 1 daughter; Winnipeg Winter Club champion at 13; Cdn jr. champion at 14; Cdn sr. titles '39, '41-42, NA titles '40-41; Bobbie Rosenfeld Trophy '39, '41; named to '40 Olympic team but WW2 negated participation; turned pro and performed in numerous ice shows; operated skating rink Bremerton, Wash., summer skating school Nelson, B.C.; pro Victoria Figure Skating Club; among protegees was Karen Magnussen; mem. Cdn Figure Skating, Man. Sports halls of fame.

THEISMANN, Joe (football); b. 9 Sep 1949, New Brunswick, N.J.; m. Cheryl Lynn Brown; c. Joey, Amy, Patrick; Notre Dame; ret'd pro athlete; restaurateur, disc jockey, actor, author, TV football analyst *ESPN* from '88; qb'd Notre Dame to consec. Cotton Bowls; runnerup Heismann Trophy; academic/athletic all-American; rejected pro baseball offers; Virginia State racquetball champion; drafted Miami (NFL) '71 but opted for Toronto (CFL) '71-73; competed '71 Grey Cup final; twice led EFC in passing yardage; Washington (NFL); 2 Super Bowls, 1 winner; frequent team MVP awards, NFL MVP

'83; numerous club records; active in Washington, D.C., charity work, Fellowship of Christian Athletes; finalist TV Superstars competition; Redskins NFL man-of-year; Lions International humanitarian award; author *Idiot's Guide to Professional Football;* res. Vienna, Va.

THELEN, Dave (football); b. 2 Sep 1936, Canton, Ohio; m. Bonnie; c. David Jr., Dayna, Lana, John; Miami of Ohio, BA; partner electric fixtures stores; semipro baseball; 17th round draft choice Cleveland Browns; pro Ottawa '58-64, '65-66 Toronto; CFL record: 8463yds in 1530 carries for 5.5 avg., 47tds; best single game Sep '60 Toronto at Ottawa with 209yds in 33 carries; lead CFL with 1407yds on 245 carries '60; 4tds single game '59; rushed ball 87 consecutive games; mem. Ottawa Sports, Canadian Football halls of fame; res. Nepean, Ont.

THEODORE, Jose (hockey); b. 13 Sep 1976, Laval, Que.; goal; midget Richelieu '90-92, jr. St. Jean '92-94, Hull '94-96; led Hull Olympiques to '95 Memorial Cup; playoff MVP; world gold Team Can '96, all-star worlds '00; AHL Fredericton '95-97, 2 player-of-yr awards; NHL Montreal '95-04; NHL record (through '04) 315 scheduled games, 17,940 minutes, 124-143-30, 624ga, 23sho, 28 playoff games, 1652 minutes, 11-15-0, 1sho; Hart, Vezina trophies '02; Roger Crozier Saving Grace award; with Gjurgarden Sweden during '04-05 labor dispute; res. Ile-des-Soeurs, Que.

THERIAULT, Jean-Yves (kick boxing); b. 15 Jan 1955, Caraquette, N.B.; div. Suzanne Anderson; c. Chantal, Brigitte; fitness consultant, coach; world middleweight champion '80-94, world light-heavyweight title '94-95; 23 times world champion; over 15yr span 51 consecutive victories; pro record: 69-6-1, 60kos; lost title Jun '92 to Rob Kaman, regained it Dec. '92 and lost it again to Australian Tesis Petridis '93; ret'd from ring as Cdn lightheavy champion competed '83 Canadian Superstars; 4 times Gil O. Julien Trophy nominee; authored kick boxing book, series of instructional cassette tapes; conducts frequent intl seminars; mem. Ottawa Sports, Black Belt halls of fame; res. Orleans, Ont.

THIBAULT, Jacques (speed skating); b. 13 Feb 1958, Quebec City, Que.; Laval; GM Calgary Olympic speed skating oval; ntl indoor all-around title '78, outdoor 1500m '79; mem. '80, '84 Olympic Games, '78, '80-84 world sprint championships teams; ntl team coach; fed. govt. excellence award '84; res. Calgary, Alta.

THIBAULT, Jocelyn (hockey); b. 12 Jan 1975, Montreal, Que.; honed goaltending skills with Laval QAAA '90-91; QMJHL Trois-Rivieres '91-92, Sherbrooke '92-93, '94-95; AHL Cornwall '93-94; NHL Quebec '93-95, Colorado '94-95, Montreal '95-99, Chicago '98-04; NHL totals: 536 scheduled games, 30,477 minutes, 227-217-68, 36sho, 17 playoff games, 839 minutes, 4-11-0, 0sho; QMJHL all-rookie award; CHL Jacques Plante, Michel Briere, Marcel Robert awards; CHL, QMJHL all-star; res. Hinsdale, Ill.

THIBODEAU, Nick (curling/shooting); b. 28 Apr 1885, Bathurst, N.B., d. 16 May 1959, Janeville, N.B.; given name: Nicholas Joseph; mem. '14 Bisley rifle team; 5 provincial curling titles, skipped NB entry 5 Briers; '31 skipped Bathurst CC rink to victory over champion Man. dealing

Winnipeg rink lone loss; vs Montreal in same competition was victim of first end 'seven'; 3rd place tie '40; mem. Canadian Curling, NB Sports halls of fame.

THIERRY, Nick (swimming/builder); b. 2 Dec 1938, Budapest, Hungary; UofT, B Arch; editor/publisher; swimming coach '61-82; ntl team coach European tour '65, CG '70; founded International Swimming Statisticians Assn. '86; secty ISSA from '86; FINA world statisticians from '92; edits world swimming annual; editor/publisher *Swim News* from '74; served varied admin, roles Swim Ont., Cdn Swim Coaches Assn.; mem. Intl Swim Hall of Fame selection comm.; Ont. Merit award; Doug Gilbert media award '80; Swim Canada service award; mem. Intl Swimming, Ont. Aquatic Hall of Fame; res. Toronto, Ont.

THIVIÉGE, Jojo (synchro swim); b. 10 Oct 1955, Quebec City, Que.; given name: Jocelyne Carrier; m. Jean Thivierge; c. Francois, Vincent; Laval, BA; coach; ntl jr. solo title '66; Que. all-events champion '67-73; bronze solo Copenhagen international, bronze duet, team Osaka international '70; ntl sr. solo champion '71-73, figures, duet '69-73; silver solo, duet '71 PAG, '73 world aquatic games; silver solo, duet '73 World Aquatic championships; began coaching '74; assisted Cuban coach '75 PAG; choreographer, asst. coach Que. YWCA '74-78, head coach '79; guided Que. to team title '79 Canada Games, sr. ntls; coached ntl team FINA World Cup, Coventry Intl '80, Swiss Open '81; head coach Que. Synchro Elite '76-04; Suzanne Eon most promising coach trophy '77; res. Quebec City, Que.

THOM, Linda (shooting); b. 30 Dec 1943, Hamilton, Ont; given name: Linda Mary Alice Malcolm; m. Donald Cullen Thom; c. Samantha, Murray; Carleton, B.J., Cordon Bleu School of Cooking, Paris; operator L'Academie de Cuisine, caterer, real estate agent; pistol specialist; Ntl Handgun postal matches title '69; ntl titles '70-75, '82-83, record '70; mem. ntl handgun team '70-76, from '82; mem. French SA; 2 gold Federation of the Americas championships '73, unofficial world record; 4th overall US International air pistol, match pistol '82-83; mem. 70, '74, '82 world championship teams; gold Zurich International Matchweek '83; silver match, bronze air '83 PAG, 2 silver Cuban International '83; bronze air '83 Benito Juarez; 7th world ranked '84; gold in shootoff, ntl record Zurich, bronze Munich '84; 1st woman to win gold sport pistol '84 Olympics; 2 ntl air pistol records '85; grand marshall '84 Central Canada Exhibition; Velma Springstead Trophy '84; Ottawa ACT athlete of '84; chaired govt. sports medicine, safety comm. from '85; RA President's trophy '84; unsuccessful bid for PC MPP '95; mem. Order of Canada, Canada's, Ottawa, Cdn Amateur, Ottawa CSRA Sports halls of fame; res. Ottawa, Ont.

THOMAS, Fred (all-around); b. 26 Dec 1923, Windsor, Ont., d. 20 May 1981, Toronto, Ont.; m. Arminta; c. Gregory, Tony, Dennis; Assumption College; educator; 2059 Assumption career points at time 3rd all-time NA college basketball scoring list; mem. Harlem Globetrotters; ntl champion Toronto Tri-Bells; 2nd in balloting Canada's basketball player of half century '50; baseball Cleveland Indians chain, Waterloo, Kitchener Sr. IC; MVP; intl-calibre softball player; pro football Toronto '49; Windsor park named in his honor; mem. Windsor-Essex Sports, Cdn Basketball halls of fame.

THOMAS, Howard (wrestling); b. 18 Jan 1905, London, Eng.; d. Mar 1995, Montreal, Que.; given name: Howard Vincent MacKenzie; m. Catherine Ellen Mary Nichol; c. Murray, Sylvia; ret'd; as teenager played soccer, hockey, basketball, tennis; in his 20's turned to boxing and wrestling; '28-34 ntl lightweight (145lbs) wrestling champion; '30 BE lightweight titlist; mem. '32, '36 Olympic, '34 BEG teams.

THOMAS, Jeff (curling); b. 2 Jul 1958, St. John's, Nfld.; given name: Jeffrey Reynold; m. Candy; c. Colin, Mitchell; nicknamed "Stache"; GM Thomas Glass; skipped Nfld. '75 ntl schoolboy, '77-78 ntl jr. men's, '83 Seagram ntl mixed; skip Nfld. entry '79, '84-85, '97 Briers, lead for Glenn Goss '90 Brier; coach '01 world jr. titlist Brad Gushue; res. St. John's, Nfld.

THOMAS, Jim (football); b. 1940, Columbus, Miss.; m. Lillian; c. Sheila, Darryl; Mississippi Industrial; teacher; nicknamed "Long Gone"; pro Dallas (NFL) '62, led Louisville US League farm club scorers; Edmonton '63-71; as rb; frequent WFC, all-Cdn all-star; twice Canada Packers Trophy outstanding Eskimo player on fan's vote; 1006yds rushing 172 carries '67; CFL record: 1111 carries, 6060yds, 5.5 avg., 37tds; longest run 104yds from scrimmage; res. Columbus, Miss.

THOMAS, Misty (basketball): b. 1 Jul 1964, Santa Monica, Calif.; given name. Misty Paige; UNLV, BSc (sports medicine), Arizona State, BSc (fitness programming); dir. Vancouver Night Hoops program for high-risk teenagers; 5 Windsor all-city HS awards; 3 WSSA/SWOSSA title teams; OFSAA silver, bronze medals; leading scorer 4 HS years; also excelled in volleyball, t&f, tennis, badminton; 2 Windsor outstanding-female-athlete awards; mem. '80 Windsor juv all-Ont. basketball champs; Rhodes Scholar nominee at UNLV; career scoring/assists/free throw/field goal leader UNLV; 2 all-American, 4 Big-West conf. awards; 3 academic all-American awards; UNLV athlete-of-yr award; jersey #4 ret'd (1st female athlete so honored); mem. ntl team '82-89 competing in FISU, Olympic, World, Jones Cup, America's Cup; leading scorer, all-star, bronze medal '86 worlds; 9 knee operations aborted her playing career; asst. coach ntl team '90-93; asst. Arizona State '88-89; head coach UBC '89-95; guided UBC to CWUAA title '94; CWUAA coach of '95; mem. Cdn Basketball, UNLV, Windsor-Essex Sports halls of fame; res. Vancouver, B.C.

THOMAS, Paul (basketball); b. 14 Apr 1926, Saint John, N.B.; given name: Paul Ernest; div. Barbara Diane Baker; c. Scott Paul, Misty Paige, Brett Arthur; m. Kerri Lynn Towers; UWO, BA, UofT, teacher's certificate, Michigan, MSc, SouthernCal, PhD; ret'd university prof., basketball coach; pro baseball Chicago Cubs system 1Ω yrs; MVP Greater Niagara Falls Basketball Assn.; all-Cdn guard UWO 4yrs; mem. 4 CIAU title teams; mem. '52 ntl champion Tillsonburg Livingstons; at 24 youngest ever coach '52 Olympic team, not permitted to play because of pro baseball background; mem. 2 Toronto Tri-Bells ntl title teams; coached college level basketball, USask, San Fernando Valley State, California Lutheran, UWindsor, also baseball, tennis; ntl men's basketball team coach '72-74; pres. National Assn. of Basketball Coaches '74-77; coach-of-yr awards; mem. Niagara Falls Sports Wall, Cdn Basketball,

UWO W Club, UWindsor, Windsor-Essex Sports, Ont. Basketball, OUAA, Niagara Falls Sports, OUAA Officians, Cdn Basketball halls of fame; res. Windsor, Ont.

THOMAS, Shirley (equestrian); b. 12 Jul 1936, Ottawa, Ont.; given name: Shirley Laura; m. Donald Prosser; c. Christopher, Laura, Ruth; Elmwood Ladies College; thoroughbred horse breeder; 1st female rider to claim intl-class honors at Madison Square Garden '53; 1st woman named to Canada's 3-mem. intl equestrian team '53; shared Royal Winter Fair puissance title '53; toured UK and Europe winning Ostende intl ladies' jumping, Rotterdam ladies championship; Government of Ireland Trophy; Ottawa ACT athlete of year; Internationl Equestrian Assn. Cup; Montreal Press Assn. woman of '54; thoroughbred horse breeder; mem. Ottawa Sports Hall of Fame; res. Portland, Ont.

THOMAS, Steve (hockey); b. 15 Jul 1963, Stockport, Eng; m. Lori; c. Lauren, Christian; rw Markham (OJHL), Toronto Marlboros (OHL) '80-84; St. Catharines (AHL) '84-86; Red Garrett trophy (AHL top rookie); AHL all-star; mem. Team Canada 4 worlds, '91(silver), '92 worlds, gold '94, silver (capt.) '96; NHL Toronto '84-87, 99-01, Chicago '87-91, '01-03, NYI '91-95, New Jersey '95-98, Anaheim '03, Detroit '03-04; helped Anaheim reach '03 Stanley Cup final; NHL record (through '04) 1235 scheduled games, 421g, 512a, 174 playoff games, 54g, 53a; res. Chicago, Ill.

THOMAS, Ted (coaching/swimming); b. 29 Sep 1919, Taber, Alta.; given name: Edward; m. Hilda Thomas; c. Hilda Ann, Glynis; ret'd regional manager Alta. Govt. Telephones; mgr. YWCA Sharkettes '59-60, coach '61-64; head coach Killarney SC Calgary '64-68; coach Jasper Place SC '68; coached Alta. team to ntls '66-68; coach women's team '68 Olympics, ntl team China tour '74; pres. Alta. Coaches Council 4 years; v-p. National Swim Coaches '71, pres. '72; Calgary sportsman-of-yr nominee '68; Edmonton recreation citation '74; res. Calgary, Alta.

THOMAS, Wayne (hockey); b. 9 Oct 1947, Ottawa, Ont.; given name: Robert Wayne; m. Barbara; c. Gretchen, Abby; Wisconsin, BPhE; goaltender 3yrs Wisc.; pro AHL Montreal Voyageurs '70-71, Nova Scotia '71-72, New Haven '80, NHL Canadiens '72-74 (1 Stanley Cup), Maple Leafs '75-77, Rangers '77-80; NHL record: 243 scheduled games, 193-93-34, 13,768min, 766ga, 10sho, 15 playoff games, 6-8-0, 849min, 50ga, 1sho; asst. coach Rangers '82-85, Black Hawks '87-88, Blues '90-93, Sharks '93-96; head coach Peoria (IHL) '88-90, Salt Lake City '85-87 winning '86 IHL Turner Cup title; San Jose AGM '96-99; GM Kentucky Thoroughblades '00-01; Cleveland '01-03; res. San Jose, Calif.

THOMAS, Willie (football); b. 14 Aug 1955, Calgary, Alta.; m. Joanne; c. Sarah, Landa; UCal; investment co. owner; Calgary Dinosaurs rookie of year; CFL lb/ctr Calgary '77-79, '83-84, Winnipeg '79-82; nicknamed "Bluto"; res. Calgary, Alta.

THOMPSON, Clif (curling); b. 8 Aug 1913, Brandon, Man.; given name: George Clifton; m. Helen Elizabeth; c. Nancy, Ross, Rick; UofSask, BSc; ret'd engineer; mem. prov. baseball title, curling finalist teams; NO jr. development chair. 6yrs; 1st-ever T&NO pres, CCA; chaired

CCA Brier sponsorship comm.; ICF pres.; Claude H. Allard award '84; mem. Gov.-Gen.'s CC; mem. Cdn Curling Hall of Fame; res. Stroud, Ont.

THOMPSON, Dan (swimming); b. 15 Jun 1956, Toronto, Ont.; given name: Daniel David; UofT, BPHE; sports marketing exec.; butterfly, relay specialist; silver 100 fly, 400MR '77 FISU Games; gold 100 fly, 400MR '78 CG; 2nd world 100 fly '78; 13 ntl, 3 intl, 5 CIAU titles; mem. '78, '82 world championships, '80 Olympic teams; silver 100 fly, 400MR '79 PAG; tied world record 100m fly 53.17 winter ntls short-course; 8 ntl, 3 Commonwealth, 3 CG records; gold 100m butterfly '82 CC; capt. ntl team '78-81, UofT swim team '78-80; 2 CIAU male swimmer of yr awards; UofT male athlete of '80; dir. CASA '78-81; mem. '80 Olympic swim trials organizing comm.; 6 ntl masters records; 1st recipient T Holders award; mem. Cdn Athletes Assn. board '93; mem. Cdn, Ont. Aquatic, UofT Sports halls of fame; res. Don Mills, Ont.

THOMPSON, George (lacrosse); b. 3 May 1910, Bowmanville, Ont.; given name: Walter George; m. Margaret McLaren; c. James, Gordon, Wayne, Barbara Jane; machine operator; mem. Brampton OLA jr. champions '30, Brampton Excelsiors Mann Cup winners '30-31, Mimico-Brampton Combines Mann Cup winners '42; coached Brampton Ont. title peewees '47, Brampton Minto Cup finalists '56, Brampton Excelsiors jrs to successive Minto Cups '57-59; pres. Lacrosse Old Timers '69-70; from '75 governor Canadian Lacrosse Hall of Fame; nickname "Mush"; life mem. Brampton Excelsior Lacrosse Club; mem. Ont., Cdn Lacrosse, Brampton Sports halls of fame; res. Brampton, Ont.

THOMPSON, Jim (speedboat racing); b. 18 Dec 1926, London, Ont.; given name: James Gordon; m. Beverly Smith; c. Adair, Leslie, Ann, Robin, Gordon; Ridley Coll., Royal Roads, UofT, BSc, UWO, MBA; co. pres.; designed, built Miss Supertest series unlimited hydroplanes; developed propellor driven boat that set world record 184.24 mph; with Bob Hayward driving Miss Supertest III won Harmsworth Trophy '59-61; crafts set ntl, BE speed records; ret'd from racing when Hayward was killed in Detroit River Silver Cup race '61; mem. Canada's Sports Hall of Fame; res. London, Ont.

THOMPSON, Jim (shooting): 4 Jan 1941, Horseforth, York, Eng.; given name: James Charlton; m. Marion; c. Claire, Eva; UofT, BA, PhD; UofT chemistry professor; qualified for 4 DCRA Bisley teams, competed 2, coached 2, commandant 1, adjutant 1; capt. 2 of 5 Palma teams; mem. 3 Ont. Bisley teams; represented Canada in New Zealand, West Indies, Australia competitions; won '76 Ont. Lieut.-Gov. match; Ont. govt. special award '85; exec. v-p. DCRA '85-96; outstanding DCRA '98 F-Class competition 5g, 7s, 7b medals; res. Whitevale, Ont.

THOMPSON, Lesley (rowing); b. 20 Sep 1959, Toronto, Ont.; m. Paul Willie; UWO BA, BEd; HS teacher; former gymnast who began rowing at UWO; sweep ntl coxed 4s, 8s title crews '80-83; coxswain ntl teams '80-00; mem. '80, '84, '88, '92, '96, '00 Olympic teams; 1 Olympic gold, 2 silver, 1 bronze; 1 CG gold, 1 World gold, silver, 3 bronze; 4 international regatta titles; coached Ont. team '89 Canada

Games; 2 Dick Ellis team awards; mem. Cdn Olympic, London Sports halls of fame; res. London, Ont.

THOMPSON, Marilyn (figure skating); b. 2 Aug 1942, Ottawa, Ont.; given name Marilyn Joyce Atchison; m. Gordon Thompson; pro skating teacher; made skating debut in solo role Minto Follies age 7; turned to coaching in 20s primarily at Ottawa Minto Club; coached ntl champions Lynn Nightingale, Kim Alletson; frequently without remuneration guided careers of several skaters who achieved ntl, intl success; res. Manotick, Ont.

THOMPSON, Stanley (golf); b. 17 Sep 1893, Toronto, Ont.; d. 4 Jan 1953, Toronto, Ont.; m. 1. Ruth McAinch (d), 2. Helen Duffy; golf course designer; mem. prominent Cdn golfing families; brother Frank twice Cdn Amateur titlist, brother Bill twice Ont., once Cdn amateur titlist, brothers Matt, Nicol long-time golf pros; ranked on par with Robert Trent Jones, Dr. Alister MacKenzie among world's finest course designers; designed more than 200 courses mostly in Canada, but also at such sites as Brazil, Colombia, British West Indies and US; among his designs were Toronto St. George's, Vancouver Capilano, Montebello's Seigniory Club, Nova Scotia's Digby Pines and Jasper, Alta., GC; mem. RCGA Hall of Fame.

THOMPSON, Tiny (hockey); b. 31 May 1905, Sandon, B.C., d. 9 Feb 1981, Calgary, Alta.; given name: Cecil; hockey scout; goalie; Calgary Monarchs jrs., Pacific Grain srs., Bellvue Bulldogs, Duluth, Minneapolis; pro Minneapolis; Boston (NHL) '28-39, Detroit '39-40; lifetime NHL goals-against avg. 2.27 regular season, 2.00 playoffs; 4 times Vezina Trophy; twice both 1st, 2nd all-star teams; vs Toronto '33 worked 104 minutes, 45 seconds of shutout hockey before being beaten 1-0; chief Western scout Chicago; mem. Hockey Hall of Fame.

THOMPSON, Tommy (baseball): b. 16 Jun 1918, Fredericton, N.B.; d. 21 Jul 1987, Fredericton, N.B.; given name: Thomas George; m. Lawanda; men's wear mgr.; involved 48yrs as player, coach, mgr., owner of teams in Fredericton; coached 5 NB, 1 Maritime jr. title teams; coached 2 jr. Vikings ntl title teams; asst. coach '74 ntl jr. titlist Fredericton Condors; coached 6 NB teams in ntl sr. finals, 2 winners; '72 Maritime sr. title; 3 times to sr. ntls; '76 coach-of-yr award; hon. citizen Republic of Madawaska '81; NB recognition certificate '81; baseball field, HS trophy, NB jr. baseball title trophy named in his honor; mem. NB Baseball, Fredericton Sports Wall and NB Sports halls of fame.

THOMPSON, William (skiing); b. 18 May 1905, Westmount, Que.; d. 3 Apr 1994, Ottawa, Ont.; given name: William Brown; m. Margaret Stuart Fraser; McGill, BSc; ret'd chemical consultant; x-country specialist; mem. title winning Westmount HS team '23 Montreal and district HS x-country championships; 3 consecutive Mount Royal x-country race titles; CIAU x-country champion '25, 3rd in ski jumping; Lake Placid college 7-mile titles '26-27; 2nd '27, 3rd '25 Dartmouth Winter Carnival 7-mile race; 2nd (1st Cdn) '27 ntl 10-mile championships; mem. 1st Canadian Olympic ski team '28; x-country; capt. McGill ski team '26-27; secty. Intl Intercollegiate Winter Sports Union '26-27; co-founder, with A.H. Pangman, H.S. Maxwell, McGill Red Birds Ski

Club, pres. '28-31; pres. CASA '33-36; chair. Olympic Ski Team comm. '36; mem. Cdn Skiing Hall of Fame.

THOMSON, Earl (t&f); b. 15 Feb 1895, Birch Hills, Sask., d. 19 May 1971, Oceanside, Calif.; South Carolina, Dartmouth Coll., BSc; as SC freshman set world record 14.8 for 110yd high hurdles; as mem. Royal Flying Corps 5 firsts, 1 2nd, 6 cups, gold medal service track meet Toronto; '19 world 110yd high hurdles mark of 14.4; IC4A high hurdles '19-21, low hurdles title '21; gold high hurdles '20 setting 14.8 Olympic mark; track coach West Virginia 1 year, asst. coach Yale to '27; coach US Naval Academy track teams more than 25 years; mem. Cdn Amateur, Canada's, Sask. Sports halls of fame.

THOMSON, Kay (figure skating); b. 18 Feb 1964, Toronto, Ont.; coached by Louis Stong; '79 ntl jr. title; 2nd '80 jr. worlds; '81 Moscow Skate title; '82-84 ntl sr. titles; silver Skate Canada '83; pro Ice Capades '84; res. Toronto, Ont.

THOMSON, Mabel (golf); b. 28 Sep 1874, Saint John, N.B., d. 13 Aug 1950, Saint John N.B.; given name: Mabel Gordon; Canada's top woman golfer turn of century; ntl Open, amateur titles '02, '05-08; numerous regional, provincial competition honors; mem. RCGA, NB Sports halls of fame.

THORBURN, Cliff (snooker); b. 16 Jan 1948, Victoria, B.C.; given name: Clifford Charles Devlin; m. Barbara Lynn Jalbert; c. James Edouard, Andrew Clifford; pro snooker player; pitched 2 no-hitters leading team to BC Little League baseball title; 9yrs minor soccer, 6yrs minor lacrosse; '70 Toronto snooker title; '71 NA title with 2 perfect 147 games; 3 perfect games in 8 days '73; ntl title '74-76; brought perfect-game total to 9 with 3 '75; world quarterfinalist '75; 1st Cdn ever seeded in world play; world tournament record 13 straight black balls, tied record 2 consecutive century breaks reaching world finals '77; world champion '80, runnerup '83; recorded first 147 (perfect) break in world pro title play '83; world masters titles '83, '85; mem. Order of Canada, BC, Greater Victoria, Canada's Sports halls of fame; res. Markham, Ont.

THORNTON, Bernie (football); b. 18 Jul 1912, Hamilton, Ont.; d. 6 Jun 2001, Wiarton, Ont.; given name: Bernard David; m. June Carr; c. Carr Alison, Bernard Joseph; Queen's; ret'd salesman; mem. Queen's Intercollegiate title team '37; mem. '32 Tiger-Cats Grey Cup champions; end Argos '38-40; all-Cdn '38-39, mem. '38 Grey Cup winner; Big Four all-star outside rcvr '38-40; mem. '41 Winnipeg Grey Cup winner; end all-Argo ('21-41) team.

THORNTON, Dick (football); b. 1 Nov 1939, Chicago, Ill; given name: Richard Quincy; div. Irene Keobke; m. Adelfa; c. Sequeira Jennifer Delle; Northwestern, BSc; coach, writer, business exec.; all-American QB Northwestern; drafted by NFL Cleveland and dealt to St. Louis; also chosen by AFL Dallas; pro Winnipeg '61-66, Toronto '67-72; capt. Memphis Southmen (WFL div. Title '74); versatility saw him perform with great skill as QB, free safety, special teams, cornerback, wide receiver; 4 Grey Cup finals, 2 winners; CFL record: 147 games played, 42 int for 847yds, 8tds; completed 43 of 117 passes for 679yds, 11int, 5tds; recovered 10 fumbles, 1td; blocked 3 kicks; caught 23 passes

for 338yds, 3tds; returned 8 punts for 50yds, 27 kickoffs for 525yds; scored 112pts on 18tds, 4s; 87 carries for 585yds, 6tds; punted 164 times for 6013yds, 3s; cut by Argos he became columnist for Toronto Sun before returning to game as def. capt. Memphis; spent '75 in front office Hawaii WFL club; AD/head coach Memphis Southwestern 3yrs (2 conf. titles); 15yrs Coca-Cola exec; formed own consulting firm coaching business execs; all-time CFL all-star on fan vote '93; 3 CFL records; 3 all-Canadian; nicknamed "Tricky"; mem. Blue Bomber Hall of Fame; res. Makati City, The Philippines.

THORNTON, Joe (hockey); b. 2 Jul 1979, London, Ont.; given name: Joseph Eric; c St. Thomas jr. B '94-95, Sault Ste. Marie (OHL) '95-97; Cdn Major Junior rookie of '96; youngest mem. Team Canada world jr. gold '97; played in '01 worlds, '04 World Cup; 1st overall pick '97 NHL entry draft; NHL Boston '97-03; Bruins capt.; NHL record (through '04) 509 scheduled games, 160g, 261a, 35 playoff games, 6g, 12a; played in Davos Switzerland during '04 labor dispute, won Spengler Cup; res. Boston, Mass.

THURLOW, Jim (shooting); b. 20 May 1948, Bridgewater, N.S.; given name: James Maxwell; m. Deborah Anne Egan; c. Christopher, Karen; Ashbury College, Queen's; garage operator; pistol specialist; NRA ntl title '74; holds several provincial records; specializes in standard pistol, centre-fire competitions; mem. Bentio Juarez Games, Federation of Americas shoot teams '72-73; standard pistol silver, team gold standard pistol, team silver centre-fire world '74; Ottawa RA Gun Club shooting award, NDHQ club championship award, Ottawa Valley League top gun award; res. Edwards, Ont.

TIHANYI, Jeno (coaching/swimming); b. 13 Jul 1936, Nagybaracska, Hungary; m. Catherine Elizabeth Ennis; c. Miklos, Sacha, Andrey; Normal School of PE, Hungary; UBC, BPhE, MPhE; UAlta, PhD; child physiology professor; swim coach 38yrs; prov team coach Alta 1yr, Ont. 6yrs; ntl team coach '78-87, '93; dir./chair. Ont. Swim Coaches Assn. '74-81; v-p. (research) CSA '80; dir/pres. Cdn Swim Coaches Assn. '82-87; coached 54 ntl, 24 CIAU titlists, 13 world record holders, 2 Olympic gold medalists, 11 ntl team members; 4 Swim Ont., Swim Canada coach-of-yr awards; OUAA '90, CIAU '93, CWIAA '94 coach-of-yr awards; 2 fed. govt achievement awards; Air Canada award '94; Ont. special achievement award '94; Sudbury Sportsman of '80; academic, professional, scientific conf. presentations; authored numerous articles, 1 book; life mem. Sudbury Science North Life; mem. Sudbury Kinsmen Sports, Ont. Aquatic, Laurentian Sports halls of fame; res. Sudbury, Ont.

TILDESLEY, Donovan (swimming); b. 24 Jul 1984, Vancouver, B.C.; UBC; broke 2 world short course records '02; 5 gold, 1 silver world championships for swimmers with a disability '02; Paralympic 200m IM bronze '00, silver '04, 400m FS '04, 100m FS bronze '04; res. Vancouver, B.C.

TILLEMAN, Karl (basketball); b. 11 Jan 1960, Ogden, Utah; UCal, BSc, Brigham Young; lawyer; CIAU all-star gd smooth ball handler with deft shooting touch; mem. ntl team '81-88; mem. '83 FISU Games gold medal, '83 PAG '84, '88 Olympic teams; 2 CIAU scoring titles; UCal all-time scoring leader with 2090pts in 79 games; 3 CWUAA all-star, scoring titles; 3 CIAU all-Canadian awards; jersey 30 ret'd by UCal; 2 Mike Moser Memorial CIAU player-of-yr awards; Calgary athlete of '82; tryout Denver (NBA) '84; fed. govt. excellence award '84; mem. UCal Sports Hall of Fame; res. Phoenix, Ariz.

TILLEY, Ray (softball): b. 27 Aug 1953, Toronto, Ont.; given name: Raymond Warren; div. Tracey Hopkins; c. Reagan, David, Evan; m. Deb; correctional officer; with Petrolia Squires won Allan Cup hockey title; smooth fielder and steady hitter; ntl men's fastball team '83-95; 4 PAG gold; 4 ntl sr. titles; ISC World gold, silver, bronze medals; asst. coach Team Canada '03-04; res. Woodstock, Ont.

TILLMAN, Eric (football/administration); b. 24 Jul 1957, Jackson, Miss.; m. Francine; c. 1; Mississippi BA journalism; football exec.; wide receiver, shortstop, avid golfer; began pro administrative career Houston Oilers PR dept. '81; dir. player personnel Montreal Concordes '82; GM B.C. Lions '93-95; GM Toronto Argos '97-99; Ottawa Renegades '01-04; 2 Grey Cup winners; 8yrs ED Mobile Senior Bowl; dir. fb operations World League of American fb '96; TSN analyst '99-01; nickname "CNN"; res. Jackson, Miss.

TIMKO, Brittany (soccer); b. 5 Sep 1985, Vancouver, B.C.; Nebraska; midfielder Coquitlam City -14, Eagle Ridge Westwood Youth -15, -16, Burnaby SC -17, -18 teams; Vancouver Whitecaps W-League; ntl -19 FIFA world silver team; made intl debut vs. Japan '02; competed '02 Women's Gold Cup, '03 Algarve Cup, '03 WC, '04 4-Nations tourney teams; moved to striker, led ntl –19 team as top scorer (7 goals) at '04 Worlds, named all-star; res. Coquitlam, B.C.

TIMMERMAN, Jim (shooting); b. 23 Sep 1950, Amsterdam, Holland; Mount Royal Coll., UCal; accountant, tax consultant; pistol specialist; mem. ntl team '73-74, '77, '79-83; nationally ranked 1st rapid fire '81-82; silver individual rapid fire pistol, bronze team air pistol '82 CG; secty.-treas '78-79, v-p. Alta. Fed. of Shooting Sports; secty. Alta. Handgun Assn. '78-80; pres. Calgary Rifle and Pistol Club '81-85; intl Level IV coaches certificate; ntl Level III officials certificate; res. Calgary, Alta.

TIMMIS, Brian (football); b. 5 Dec 1899, Winnipeg, Man., d. 22 Aug 1971, Hamilton, Ont.; m. Ada Clements; c. Brian Jr.; distillers rep.; hb/fb Ottawa '24, Hamilton '25-35, '37; Grey Cup champions '28, '29, '32; noted for powerful, grinding, battering ram- style rushes; played without helmet and suffered many injuries; coached Hamilton to '43 Grey Cup triumph over Winnipeg; mem. Canadian Football, Ottawa, Canada's Sports halls of fame.

TINDALE, Bill (skiing); b. 10 Jul 1925, Toronto, Ont.; d. 24 Aug 1996, Ottawa, Ont.; m. Barbara; c. Chrystie, Katharine; McGill; ret'd Fisher Scientific; began skiing mid-30s; Ottawa SC Night Rider '42-43; mem. Dawson Coll. CIAU champs '48; mgr. McGill ski team '50; co-chair. McGill Winter Carnival '51; average racer; Osler Bluff SC champion '56; chair. Laurentian Ski Zone competitions '56; conceived 1st race-rating system in Canada; chair. CSA intl competitions comm. '57-59; founded ntl team '57; rewrote constitution/by-laws CASA; pres. CASA '65-67; CASA FIS comm. chair '68;

dir. COA '67-76; helped establish Olympic Trust; established Young Olympians of Canada, jr. Olympics program; played role in bringing Olympics to Montreal '76, Calgary '88; chair. Cdn Ski Museum from '87; Montreal Sportsman's Assn. award of merit '66; Gala des Skiers award '66; Air Canada ntl sports exec of '67; fed. govt. Centennial medal '67; Queen's Jubilee medal '70; hon. life mem. COA; mem. Cdn Skiing Hall of Fame.

TINDALL, Frank (football); b. 16 Oct 1908, Syracuse, N.Y.; d. 5 Oct 1993, Kingston, Ont.; m. Mary; c. Frank Jr., Charles; Syracuse, BA, BPHE; ret'd professor phys-ed, football, basketball coach; '32 all-Eastern gd, hon. mention all-American, Syracuse MVP; '33 all-star lineman Argos, Grey Cup champions; all-time all-star Argos tackle '21-41 era; football coach Queen's Golden Gaels '39-75, basketball '48-75; 8 Intercollegiate football titles, 1 ntl championship '68, OUAA co-champions basketball '56-57; college football coaching record: 112 wins, 84 losses, 2 ties; CAFA-CFL plaque for outstanding services to football in Canada; trophy in his honor awarded annually by CIAU via Carleton Old Crows to CIAU Football coach of year; mem. Canadian Football, Kingston Sports, Queen's Football, Coaches halls of fame.

TINDLE, Janice (tennis); b. 3 Jul 1950, Vancouver, B.C.; given name: Janice Lee; UBC, Arizona BA; avalanche predictor; ex-tennis pro; ntl -16 singles '66, -18 '67, with Michelle Carey -18 doubles '68, Jr. Federation Cup singles '68, ntl women's Closed '72; mem. 3 Federation Cup teams; Pepsi-Cola Sportsmanship Trophy '66; competed briefly as pro; coached Delta Airport Inn and with Tony Bardsley conducted numerous teaching clinics; avid skier, mem. ski patrol; Yukon mining field worker; res. Alta Lake, B.C.

TINLINE, Dorothy (badminton); b. 25 Dec 1921, Scott, Sask.; given name: Dorothy Carol; Brandon College, UofT; ret'd HS phys-ed teacher; 4 ntl open, closed ladies doubles, '62 open mixed, 8 Ont. doubles, '64 Ont. singles, 2 ntl sr. mixed, ladies' doubles, 7 Masters singles, 5 ladies doubles, ntl grand masters singles '81; mem. 3 Uber Cup teams; twice umpire world games, once Uber Cup; Cdn rep. IBF '81; ntl senior ladies's tennis doubles title '65; pres. Toronto Dist. BA '64-65, '73-76; chair. Cdn Badminton Officials Assn. '67-81; 1st Cdn to umpire All-England '73; head badminton staff York seminars '75-81; Ont. coach '73-81; 3 terms pres. OBA; chair. Uber Cup program '69; chair. Devlin Cup championships '68-75; CBA dir. '60-81, pres. '81; Sr. examiner IBA; intl badminton fed. exec. 6yrs; Centennial medal; Canada Winter Games silver team medal; H.I. Evans Memorial award; Ont. awards '71-81; special fitness and amateur sports achievement award; Donald Smythe award; Queen's Jubilee medal; life mem. Badminton Canada; mem. Canadian Amateur Sports Hall of Fame; res. Toronto, Ont.

TINSLEY, Buddy (football); b. 16 Aug 1924, Damon Tex.; given name: Robert Porter Jr.; m. Hazel George Stevens; c. Cynthia Diane, Jack Steven; Baylor, BPhE; ret'd sales mgr.; tackle Los Angeles Dons '49; Winnipeg '50-60, 7 times WFC all-star, 4 all-Cdn 4; capt. Bombers 10 years; mem. 4 East-West Shrine all-star game teams; coached St. James Rams to 2 Western Cdn sr., 1 ntl championship; wife Hazel founded Winnipeg Bomberettes '52; mem.

Canadian, Winnipeg Football, Man. Sports halls of fame; res. Winnipeg, Man.

TIPPETT, Dave (hockey/coaching); b. 25 Aug 1961, Moosimin, Sask.; m. Wendy; c. Nicole, Natalie; N. Dakota; hockey exec.; lw Prince Albert (SJHL) '79-81; UND '81-83; Team Canada '83-84, '92-93; NHL Hartford '84-90, Washington '90-92, Pittsburgh '92-93, Philadelphia '93-94; IHL Houston '94-95; NHL record: 721 scheduled games, 93g, 169a, 62 playoff games, 6g, 16a; '82 NCAA Div. title; Team Canada capt. '84, silver '92 Olympics; began coaching '95; led Houston to '99 Turner Cup; IHL coach of '99 award; Fred Hubner Memorial award; with Hartford Community Service, Unsung Hero, Mr. Hustle, Best Defensive forward awards; asst. coach Los Angeles '99-02; head coach Dallas '02-03; res. Plano, Tex.

TIPPETT, Karen (canoeing); b. 7 Apr 1955, Winnipeg, Man.; given name: Karen Mary; m. Gerry Irving; Carleton; BSc, UWO; chartered accountant; mem. Rideau Canoe Club; ntl team '73-77; ntl sr. K2, K4 titles '73-76; with Sue Holloway NA K2 title '74; mem. '73-75 worlds, '76 Olympic teams; former treas. Gloucester; res. Nepean, Ont.

TKACHUK, Keith (hockey); b. 28 Mar 1972, Melrose, Mass.; m. Chantal; c. Matthew, Braeden; Boston U; all-rookie team '91; Team USA '92, '96, '02 (silver) Olympics, World Cup '96 gold; lw power forward drafted by Winnipeg '90; capt. Jets '93-96, Coyotes '96-00; NHL Winnipeg '91-96, Phoenix '96-01, St. Louis '01-04; NHL record (through '04): 856 scheduled games, 431g, 401a, 81 playoff games, 27g, 26a; twice topped 50g plateau (50 '96, 52 '97); 1st US-born player to lead NHL in goals scored '97; 3 NHL all-star games; nickname "Walt"; Sodertalje Sweden during '04-05 labor dispute; res. Cape Cod, Mass.

TKACZUK, Walt (hockey); b. 29 Sep 1947, Emsdetten, Germany; given name: Walter Robert; m. Valerie Kelford; c. Michael, David, Sarah; co-owner River Valley Golf & Country Club; ctr Kitchener Rangers OHA jrs, 1 MVP award; minor pro Omaha, Buffalo; NYR '68-81; with Bill Fairbairn, Dave Balon formed NYR Bulldog Line; rejected Chicago WHA offer; NHL record: 945 scheduled games, 227g, 451a, 93 playoff games, 19g, 32a; asst. coach Rangers '81-83; res. St. Mary's, Ont.

TOBACCO, Terry (t&f); b. 2 Mar 1936, Cumberland, B.C.; given name: Charles Terrence; m. Norine Irving; c. David, Tom, Judy, Michael; Washington, BA, MSc; teacher; bronze 440, anchor silver 4x400 relay team '54 BEG; semifinalist 400m, anchored 5th-place 4x400 Olympic relay team '56; bronze 440, anchored bronze 4x400 relay team '58 BEG; semifinalist '60 Olympics; 3rd 440 NCAA championships '59; NCAA all-American track team; 3rd-ranked in world for 440 '58-59; ntl 440 champion '54-60; Pacific Coast 440 titlist '56-58; capt. Wash. track team '59; res. Victoria, B.C.

TOBIN, Lee (curling); b. 2 Feb 1922, Huntingdon, Que.; given name: Eileen Herdman; m. Bill Tobin; c. Sharon, Bill Jr., Bob; pitcher Montreal Royals softball team; skipped Ont. tankard runnerup '63, 4 Que. ladies' title rinks '70-75; ntl ladies' title rink '75 beating late Marj Mitchell in playoff;

3rd Que. mixed title rink '76; key role in boosting calibre of jr. curling in Que., NB, NS through clinics; mem. Canadian Curling Hall of Fame; res. Montreal, Que.

TOCCHET, Rick (hockey); b. 9 Apr 1964, Scarborough, Ont.; m. Lynne; c. Trevor; hockey coach; power forward Sault Ste. Marie jrs. '81-84; NHL Philadelphia '84-92 (capt. '91-92), '00-02, Pittsburgh '92-94, Los Angeles '94-96, Boston '96-97, Washington '97, Phoenix '97-00; asst coach Colorado '02-03; head coach Kelowna (WHL) '04; NHL record: 1144 scheduled games, 440g, 512a, 145 playoff games, 52g, 60a; played in 4 NHL all-star games; 1 Stanley Cup winner; mem. Team Canada '87, '91 World, Canada Cup; active softball player; nicknamed "Toe"; res. Kelowna, B.C.

TODD, Dick (hockey, coaching); b. 3 Jun 1945, Toronto, Ont.; given name: Richard Edward; m. Mary Redner; c. Terri-Anne; hockey coach; pitcher Ont. All-stars, '64 Eastern Cdn champs; dreams of pitching ML baseball with Pittsburgh dashed '65 with rotator cup injury; trainer, coach, GM Peterborough Petes 21yrs through '93, resumed coaching Petes '04; asst. NYR '93-98, scout NYR '98-01; asst. '90, head coach '91 Team Canada world jr. gold medal teams; OHL jr. coaching record (to '03) 490-258-54; OHL coach of '88; 4 Leyden div. titles, 2 OHL playoff titles, 3 Memorial Cup finals; 1 Stanley Cup, 1 Memorial Cup, 1 Calder Cup, 2 world title rings; res. Peterborough, Ont.

TODD, Margaret (golf); b. 31 May 1918, Montreal, Que.; given name: Margaret Sutcliffe; m. John Todd; c. John, Rick, David; 13 Victoria, 3 BC Ladies, 2 BC Srs., 2 ntl Srs., 7 Jasper Totem Pole, 3 Empress Hotel, 2 Victoria srs. titles; mem. 9 BC amateur, 8 srs., 5 intl teams; 2yrs club capt., 3 yrs pres. Van. branch BCCLGA, 8yrs. BCCLGA exec.; 3yrs ntl rating dir.; devised rating system for Canada's female golfers '61; ntl teams dir. 3yrs.; CLGA board ntl rules, handicap dir. '83-85; CLGA distinguished service award; life mem. Victoria Golf Club; with husband conducted weekly swim class for blind; mem. RCGA, BC, Greater Victoria Sports halls of fame; res. Victoria, B.C.

TOLCHINSKY, Sol (basketball); b. 2 Jan 1929, Montreal, Que.; m. Margot Blatt; c. Ivy, Neil, Leslie; McGill, BA; exposition service contractor; mem. Eastern Cdn champion, ntl finalist Montreal YMHA juv basketball team '44-45; Eastern Cdn champion, ntl finalist Montreal YMHA jr. team '45-46; Horace Baitle Award jr. team MVP '46; mem. Que. jr. title team '46-47; ntl finalist sr. team '47-48; mem. '48 Olympic, '50, '53 Maccabiah Games teams; Eastern Cdn finalist sr. team '48-49, ntl champions '49-50; mem. Golden Ball champion McGill team '50-51; mem. Montreal YM-YWHA Sports Hall of Fame; res. Westmount, Que.

TOLLESTRUP, Phil (basketball); b. 21 Oct 1949, Raymond, Alta; c. Allen; Brigham Young, Lethbridge BA; teacher; Alta '67-68 Raymond Comets title teams; BYU Conf. title team; CIAU all-Cdn; Lethbridge male athlete of yr; ntl team '71-79; 3 PAG, 1 FISU, 1 Worlds; capt., all-star '76 Olympics; pro Spain '73-74; coached McMaster '78-80; HS coach Milk River, Stirling, Magrath (Alta).; mem. Alta., Raymond, Lethbridge Sports, Cdn Basketball halls of fame; res. Magrath, Alta.

TOMBS, Tina (golf): b. 4 Apr 1962, Montreal, Que.; given name: Tina Tombs; div. Tom Purtzer; c. Sarah, Heidi; m. Joey Rodolfo; Arizona State; 2 titles, twice all-American; won '79 NH jr., '81 NH state title, New England amateur '82, Eastern amateur '84; joined pro tour '87, career low round 64; won LPGA Jamie Farr Toledo Classic '90; res. Minneapolis, Minn.

TOMLINSON, Lesley (cycling): b. 26 Dec 1959, Derbyshire, Eng.; SFU; 6 all-American; full-time athlete; former marketing mgr.; long competitive career in x-country, marathon running before turning energy to mountain-biking and road racing; 11yrs ntl team; 2 ntl silver; TTT gold, road race silver '94; CG team time trial silver '94, '98; competed '96, '00 Olympics, 9 worlds; res. Victoria, B.C.

TOMLINSON, William (administration): b. 31 Jan 1912, Cedar Rapids, Iowa; d. 4 Aug 1991, Thunder Bay, Ont.; given name: William Sherwood; m. Marion Elizabeth McKay (d), m. Hazel Jean Campbell; c. William Sherwood, Laren Campbell, Colin Campbell; St. John's Coll., UMan., Queen's, BSc; construction co. pres.; played football UMan.; avid golfer, duck hunter; owner Port Arthur Arena; pres. Port Arthur Bruins '48 Memorial Cup team; life mem. Port Arthur Golf & Country Club; mem. NWO Sports Hall of Fame.

TOMMY, Andy Jr. (skiing): b. 1 Nov 1932, Ottawa, Ont.; d. 2 Aug 2004, Ottawa, Ont.; given name: Andrew Bailie; m. Marion Dunning; c. Sarah Jane, Randy, Lisa, Michael; ski resort, golf course owner; prominent alpine skier 40s, 50s; mem. ntl team '50 world championship, '56 Olympic teams; ntl alpine champion '50; head coach, mgr. '60 Olympic ski team; mem. Canadian Skiing; Ottawa Sports halls of fame.

TOMMY, Andy Sr. (football): b. 24 Dec 1911, Hartland, N.B., d. 23 Apr 1972, Wakefield, Que.; m. Helen Bailie; c. Andrew B, Arthur, Frederick; agronomist, statistician; backfielder Ottawa Rangers '31-32, Rough Riders '33-45 excluding 2 seasons with Argos WW2; 5 Grey Cup finals, 2 winners; Jeff Russel Memorial Trophy Big Four MVP '40; mem. Ottawa CSRA, NB, Ottawa, Canada's Sports halls of fame.

TOMMY, Art (skiing): b. 15 Dec 1933, Ottawa, Ont.; d. 25 Nov 1994, Ottawa, Ont.; given name: Arthur Roland Bailie; m. Marilyn Thorpe; c. Natalie, Jedson, Lizbeth; merchant, enterpreneur; dominated ntl alpine skiing '52-60; ntl alpine, Arlberg Kandahar, Ottawa Ski Club, Gatineau Zone, NY State, Que. Taschereau, Que., titles, 11th in world as mem. FIS team '54 world championships; mem. ntl team '54-60; broke ankle world's 1st pro ski race; coach Ottawa Ski Club, Gatineau Zone, ntl team; mem. Intl Competitions Comm.; coach Gatineau Zone, Que. teams through '74; mem. Canadian Skiing, Ottawa Sports halls of fame.

TOMMY, Fred (skiing): b. 24 Sep 1941, Ottawa, Ont.; d. 3 Feb 2004, Ottawa, Ont.; m. Heather Gibson; c. Alexandre Frederic; UofOtt, BComm, McGill; chartered acountant, dir., v-p. of finance, realty firm; mem. Canada FIS team '58 world championships, '60 Olympic team.

TOMSETT, Arthur (shooting): b. 19 Feb 1928, Vancouver, B.C.; m. Shirley; c. Terry, Danny, Kevin, Richard, Susan; Vancouver Institute of Engineering; ret'd engineer; mem. gold medal team Canada Games '57; BC indoor, outdoor titles '73, Vancouver Island titles '73-74; mem. ntl handgun team, free-pistol, centre-fire, standard pistol '73-95; mem. Benito Juarez Games, '74 world championships, '75, '79 PAG teams; mem. bronze medal centre-fire team '75 Benito Juarez Games; team gold '79 PAG; '82 SFC golden anniversary award for outstanding contribution to shooting; res. Saanichton, B.C.

TONELLI, John (hockey): b. 23 Mar 1957, Hamilton, Ont.; insurance broker; lw Toronto Marlboros OHA '73-75, Houston WHA '75-78, Team Canada '85 Canada Cup' NHL NYI '78-86, Calgary '86-88, Los Angeles '88-91, Chicago '91-92, Quebec '92; NHL totals: 1028 scheduled games 325g, 511a, 172 playoff games, 40g, 75a; MVP '84 World Cup, NHL all-star; 4 consec. Stanley Cups; Milton sports centre bears his name; res. Milton, Ont.

TONELLO, Jerry (wheelchair basketball): b. 29 Dec 1956, Toronto, Ont.; York, BA, UofT, BEd; financial planner Revenue Canada; 1st able-bodied player to compete in Canadian Wheelchair Basketball ntl championships; mem. Toronto Spitfires WBA team; Team Ont. 6 ntl gold, 3 silver; Canada Games bronze '95; 1 Stoke-Mandeville, 2 Paralympic, 1 Roosevelt Cup gold; 1 WC bronze; coached basketball from '80; ntl team asst. from '91; res. Toronto, Ont.

TONER, Vance (administration): b. 10 Apr 1926, Edmunston, N.B.; m. Pauline; St.Thomas; ret'd prof., dir. Moncton PhE&R dept.; coached intercollegiate hockey, football; founder, 1st dir. '65-76 school of PhE&R and Institut de Leadership, Moncton; NB rep. Ntl Advisory Council on Fitness/Amateur Sport; chair. task force on hockey in NB; mem. NBSHF, Canada's SHF selection comms; mem. Canada's Olympic Hockey comm.; chair NBSHF '70-71; consultant on fed. gvt. Ntl Sports Admin, Centre development, 7yrs dir.; co-author *Master Plan for Sport in NB*; Queen's Jubilee medal; Moncton man of yr; St. Thomas Alumni, CIAU Austin-Matthews, CAHPER Tait McKenzie awards; mem. Order of Canada, Moncton Sports Wall, NB Sports halls of fame; res. Moncton, N.B.

TOOGOOD, Ted (football): b. 27 Aug 1924, Toronto, Ont.; given name: Alex Edgar; m. Joan Davidson; c. Sharon, Sandra, Sylvia, Shirley, Sonya, Glen; UofT, BA, BPHE, West Virginia, MSc; ret'd teacher, Etobicoke HS, RIT AD; pro Toronto (CFL) '50-54, capt. '52, mem. 2 Grey Cup winners; Argos, CFL record for tds scored on punt returns single game with 2 vs Hamilton '50; single-game punt return yardage mark with 155 on dashes of 90 and 65 yds for majors; Eastern all-star '53; mem. UofT Hall of Fame; res. Islington, Ont.

TOOHY, Ralph (football): b. 9 Oct 1926, Montreal, Que.; d. 20 Jul 1998, Oakville, Ont.; given name: Ralph Joseph Edward; m. Teresa Lyon; c. Gary, Gail (d), Sharon, Bruce, Colleen, Ralph Jr., Kevin; Loyola, Colorado Coll.; ret'd salesman; oe/de 5yrs Montreal, 7yrs Hamilton; earned reputation as hard-rock; mem. 3 Grey Cup winners; 3 time CFL all-star; ss/of Snowden Fastball League, MVP, batting titles; Memorial Cup hockey semifinalist; mem. Loyola Sports Hall of Fame.

TORREY, Bill (builder/hockey); b. 23 Jun 1934, Montreal, Que.; given name: William Arthur; div. c. William, Richard, Peter, Arthur; St. Lawrence, BA; ret'd hockey exec.; began NHL career '67 as exec. v-p. expansion California Seals; GM expansion NYI '72-92; built Islanders into dynasty which claimed 4 consec. Stanley Cups; club pres. '80-89, board chair. '89-92; stepped down remaining with club as consultant to '93; pres./GM Florida Panthers '93-02; Panthers reached Stanley Cup finals in their 3rd season, fastest-ever for expansion team; Lester Patrick trophy '83; *SN, HN* exec. of yr. awards; nickname "Bow-Tie Bill"; mem. Long Island, Hockey halls of fame; res. West Palm Beach, Fla.

TOSH, Wayne (football); b. 7 Aug 1947, Kitchener, Ont.; given name: Wayne Kenneth; m. Marlene Grubbs; c. Tim, Amy, Casey; Richmond, BSc, BA; civil servant; Sarnia Northern HS athlete of '67; lettered 4 yrs football Richmond; pro lb Rough Riders '71-77; led EFC in interceptions '75 with 9; EFC all-star '75; mem. Grey Cup winners '73, '76; mem. Athletes in Action; mem. Sarnia/Lambton Sports Hall of Fame; res. Orleans, Ont.

TOTZKE, Bob (bowling); b. 6 Nov 1917, Kitchner, Ont., d. 13 Dec 1980, Kitchener, Ont.; m. Martha; c. Marilyn, John, Steve; bowling proprieter; helped organize K-W 5-pin bowling assn.; hosted ntl 5-pin finals, BPAO convention; 15yrs Zone C pres. BPAO; coach 3 ntl tournament title teams; chairman, treas. 32-team Golden Horseshoe Intercity League 24 years; averaged 255 in '70; mem. 2 Ont. title teams, rolled 21 400-plus singles; Builders of Bowling Industry Award '76; mem. Waterloo sr. baseball exec. '48-54; jr., int., sr. ORFU football; 2 holes-in-one.

TOTZKE, Carl (football/basketball); b. 25 May 1926, Waterloo, Ont.; given name: Carl Andrew; m. Lois Joan Pfeiffer; c. Sarah, Paul, Susan; Waterloo College, BA, McGill; ret'd AD; football, basketball, hockey, t&f Waterloo College '44-49, football at McGill '49-50; K-W Dutchman ORFU titlists '53-55; mem. YMCA ntl int. basketball champions '51-52; coach Waterloo football '54-67; delegate FISU Games '73, '75; CIAU pres. '71-72, '84-85; CAUAD pres. '69-70; CIAU Austin-Matthews award; UW male-athlete-of-yr award bears his name; res. Waterloo, Ont.

TOUSEK, Yvonne (gymnastics): b. 23 Feb 1980, Kitchener, Ont.; given name: Yvonne Natalie; UCLA; 2 all-American; strong on uneven bars, beam, floor exercises; competed 4 Worlds, '96 America Cup; '96, '00 Olympics; team, indiv. floor exercises, uneven bars gold '99 PAG; 2 Gymnastics Canada athlete-of-yr. awards; 2 Cambridge athlete-of-yr. awards; Oktoberfest woman of '99 award; res. Cambridge, Ont.

TOWN, Bob (basketball); b. 4 Oct 1949, Winnipeg, Man.; given name: Robert Frederick; m. Barbara Diane Bock; c. Sean Cameron, Andrew Curtis; UMan, BPhE, BEd, MEd; HS principal; second team all-Cdn UMan '72; mem. ntl team '72-73, '75-76; '76 Olympics; mem. St. Andrews Super Saints ntl sr. men's title team '75-76; 4 times ntl championships all-star; mem. Gillette All-Star touring team '72; plays at Masters level; coach regionally, provincially; mem. Man, Basketball Hall of Fame; res. Winnipeg, Man.

TOWN, Tom (t&f): b. 7 Aug 1893, London, Eng.; d. 29 Mar 1957, White Rock, B.C.; m. Roseta Chapman; c. Jean, Lillian, June, Tom; decorator; began competitive road running career age 10; English all-schoolboy champion, English jr champion at 16; emigrated to Brandon, Man., '10 making presence felt at provincial, local levels before moving into ntl ranks '19; ntl 5-mile champion '19-22; 5000m title '20; 3-mile title '21; 800yd, 1-mile titles '24; competed '20 Olympics; named to '24 Olympic team but lack of funding forced him to decline; offered ChicagoU coaching job; defeated only once in a Cdn championship meet when he lost a shoe in '14 race; awarded permanent possession of Coldwell Cup for winning Manitoba 5-mile Labor Day race so often; mem. Manitoba Sports Hall of Fame.

TOWNS, Tom (football); b. 17 Mar 1953, Edmonton, Alta.; given name: Thomas Leslie; UAlta; mem. varsity wrestling team; impressive rb Golden Bears before switching to lb; twice Western Intercollegiate all-star; CIAU all-Cdn lb '74; on Eskimos protected list '75; mem. Eskimos '75-84; twice WFC all-star; mem. 7 Grey Cup finalists, 6 winners; mem. UAlta Sports Hall of Fame; res. Edmonton, Alta.

TOWNSEND, Billy (boxing): b. 6 May 1909, Durham, Eng.; d. 12 May 1985, Nanaimo, B.C.; came to Canada age 2; began boxing age 14; nicknamed "Blond Tiger"; Cdn lightweight, welterweight titles before turning pro at 16; 300 career bouts, only 22 losses; fought 11 main events (including 4 world champions) at Madison Square Gardens against such big names as Billy Petrolle, Bat Battalino, Tony Canzoneri, Benny Leonard, Joe Glick; ret'd from ring '34 but made comeback '36; had comeback run of 12 straight wins before being beaten on KO in 13th round of 13th bout; regarded by *Ring Magazine* as "greatest lightweight ever produced in Canada"; mem. BC Sports Hall of Fame.

TOWNSEND, Brit (t&f); b. 10 Feb 1957, Copenhagen, Denmark; given name: Brit Lind-Petersen; div. Dale McRoberts; m. Chris Townsend; c. Addy, Dana; SFU BSc; head coach t&f SFU; 800m, 1500m specialist; mem. '79 PAG, capt. '84 Olympic, '86 CG (sidelined by flu), '79, '81 World Cup, '81 Pacific Conf. Games teams; ntl 1500m title '80-81; unbeaten outdoors '80; gold 1500m '81 Pacific Conf. Games; silver, bronze 1500m *Toronto Star, Ottawa Citizen*, gold 800m *Edmonton Journal* indoor Games '81; despite stress fracture in right foot, which sidelined her 7 weeks, claimed Dublin, WC trials gold; 2nd 5th Ave. mile New York with PB 4:28.3 '81, 2nd FA mile '83; broke Paris mile record with 4:23.64 '86; *Toronto Star* 1500m, US ntl mile titles '84; 7 ntl records; PB 800m 2:00.02 (Zurich '83), 1500m 4:03.23 (Kohl, West Germany '83); ntl track athlete of '81 nominee; BC track athlete of '81; BC athlete of '83; Vic Andrew Trophy (Lower Mainland amateur athlete of '81); with husband Chris sold real estate 10yrs; Level 4 coaching certif.; res. Coquitlam, B.C.

TOWNSEND, Cathy (bowling); b. 8 Jun 1937, Campbellton, N.B.; given name: Catherine Champoux; m. Douglas Townsend; bank employee; lefthander; 6th world championships '69; with Joanne Walker of Montreal gold women's doubles FIQ American Zone championships, record 2285 pins, also silver, bronze medals; 3rd Cdn, first woman World Cup title winner '75; all-events title 23-nation

Tournament of Americas '76 with 67,333 for 36 games; with Glen Watson, Diane Langlois, Jean Benard mixed foursome title; bronze women's singles; Montreal's Bowler of Year as chosen by Montreal Sports Writers; mem. Cdn 10-Pin Bowling, Canada's Sports halls of fame; res. St. Thérèse, Que.

TOWNSEND, Stephanie (skiing); b. 21 Mar 1948, Calgary, Alta.; given name: Stephanie Margaret; div. Dexter Williams; m. Gary Bucher; Notre Dame, BA; Alberta juvenile champion '60-61, jr. '62-64; ntl team '65-69; slalom, combined titles Lowell Thomas Classic '68; instructor Aspen, Colo., ski club '69-70; Rotary Sportsman's Award '63, Alta. Sportswoman's Assn. Award '67; res. Houston, Texas.

TRACY, Paul (motorsport); b. 17 Dec 1968, Toronto, Ont.; given name: Paul Anthony; div. Tara; c. Alysha Rachelle, Conrad; m. Liisa Hunter; race car driver; began racing karts age 8; ntl Formula Ford title age 16, youngest FF champion ever; competed in FF2000 '86 becoming youngest ever Can-Am winner at 17; raced in SCCA Escort endurance series, Mosport 24-hour, British Grandstand series '87; entered Indy Lights series '88 winning initial race at Phoenix; won 9 of 14 Indy Lights races '90 setting 4 race records, 6 qualifying records, 7 poles single-season record, Bruce McLaren most-promising-driver award; mem. Dale Coyne, Penske, Newman/Haas, Kool Green racing teams; 10 Indy Lights victories, 8 seconds, 7 thirds, 10 poles in 77 starts; competed on CART circuit from '96; regarded as one of quickest drivers in sport; most improved driver award '93; joined Reynard-Honda team '98-02; with Patrick Carpentier formed all-Cdn Player's-Forsythe team '03; set Michigan 500 track record 234.949mph '00; 1st Cdn to win Vancouver Molson Indy '00, runnerup '02 won again '03, '04; runnerup '02 Indy 500; provided Cdn Team Player's initial CART victory winning '03 season opener Tampa Bay, followed up by winning Monterrey, Long Beach GP; 1st driver in CART history to win 1st 3 races at start of season; won 7 CART races '03, including Toronto Molson Indy; 25 career CART victories; series driving title '03; 4 Long Beach GP titles; res. Scarborough, Ont./Paradise Valley, Ariz.

TRAER, Rick (basketball/administration); b. 14 Oct 1955, Chatham, N.B.; given name: Richard Karl; m. Francine Alexina Lanteigne; c. Zacharie, Catherine; UofO BSc, MPE; administrator; CEO CSTA; 15yrs ntl, prov. sport systems: TD OBA '83-86, Basketball Canada TD '86-88, HPD '88-89, ED '89-97; extensive background in intl. sport includes serving as a mem. COA '93-97, pres. FIBA Americas '00-06), v-p. Assn. of Pan-American Sport Confederations '03-07); led successful bids 3 intl. basketball events, co-chair. bid comm., v-p. '94 men's world basketball championships Toronto; coach minor basketball, soccer; res. Chelsea, Qué.

TRAGER, John (bowling): b. 12 May 1927, Winnipeg, Man.; given name: John Emil Joseph; m. Elsie Hrenchuk; c. Mary Anne, Kathryn, Barbara; ret'd; began 5-pin bowling '44; shifted to 10-pins '48; St. Joseph's league secty from '48; turned talents to administrative end of game '52 as director Winnipeg 10-pin Assn., pres. '61; founding mem. Man. 10-pin BA '94, secty-treas to '95; instrumental in formation Man. 10-pin Fed., pres. 17yrs; founding mem.

Cdn 10-pin Fed, 5yrs sect-treas, 5yrs pres.; exec. mem. FIQ, auditor '87-91; dir. COA; life mem. Cdn, Man 10-Pin Feds; life mem. Winnipeg Bowling Assn.; Man. Sports Federation Outstanding Volunteer award '81; mem. Manitoba Bowling, Sports, Cdn 10-pin halls of fame; res. Winnipeg, Man.

TRAWICK, Herb (football): b. Pittsburgh, Pa.; d. 16 Sep 1986, Hawkesbury, Ont.; ol; one of 1st imports selected by Lew Hayman and Leo Dandurand for new Alouettes team '46; played 12 CFL seasons; noted for quickness he was 1st player 7 times all-Eastern, 5 as tackle, 2 as guard; one of few linemen to score a touchdown in Grey Cup competition; mem. '49 Grey Cup title team; ret'd '57; noted for outstanding charitable work in community; mem. Cdn Football Hall of Fame.

TREGUNNO, Jane (rowing); b. 9 Jul 1962, St. Catharines, Ont.; McMaster BSc, CA; financial analyst Weiler & Co.; Cdn. Henley jr. pairs '78; sweep 8s ntl championships '78, jr. worlds '79; silver coxed 4s '81 Royal Henley; won coxed 4s '83 Head of the Charles; silver coxed 4s '84 Olympics; mem. '80, '84 Olympic teams; res. Guelph, Ont.

TRELLE, Herman (t&f/wrestling); b. 8 Dec 1894, Kendrick, Idaho, d. 4 Sep 1947, Fontana, Calif.; m. Bernice Irene Burdick; c. 1 son, 1 daughter; Blairmore, Alberta College, UAlta; grain grower; 2 ntl field records; Alta. heavyweight wrestling title.

TREMBLAY, Thalie (fencing): b. 6 Jun 1967, Montreal, Que.; m. Denis Lauriault; c. Mathieu, Camille; UofOtt, BA; ex-SRC, self-employed; followed footsteps of grandparents, both world champions for France, by winning 3 ntl jr., sr. women's foil titles; achieved Canada's best-ever performance by placing 7th women's world foils '91; best-ever Cdn Olympic women's foil standing with 14th '92 Olympics; competed '88, '92 Olympic, '90 CG; coached at Uof Ott; res. Hull, Que.

TRIANO, Jay (basketball); b. 21 Sep 1958, Tillsonburg, Ont.; SFU; coach; former Vancouver Grizzlies (NBA) dir. community relations, TV-radio color analyst; ex-SFU basketball coach; son of former Tillsonburg Livingston's star Howie Triano; gd ntl team '78-90; mem. Commonwealth Cup champions '78, FISU gold medal team '83; silver medal pre-Olympic '80, Jones Cup '82; mem. '79, '83 PAG, '80, '84 Olympic, '79, '81, '83 FISU, '82 Brazil tournament teams; BC university athlete of '78; 6th round draft CFL Stampeders, 8th round draft NBA Lakers '81, tryout Jazz '84; coach ntl team '99-04; asst. coach Toronto Raptors '02-05; mem. SFU, Ont., Cdn Basketball, Olympic halls of fame; res. Burnaby, B.C.

TRIFUNOV, Jim (wrestling); b. 18 Jul 1908, Yugoslavia; d. 27 Jun 1993, Winnipeg, Man.; m. Mary; c. Donald; ret'd promotion mgr.; 10 ntl titles (9 bantam, 1 featherweight) '23-32; mem. '24, '28, '32 Olympic teams, bronze '28; gold '30 BEG; coached YMCA jrs., UWpg, Olympic teams '52-60; mgr. ntl teams '54, '70 BE, CG, '66, '70 worlds; pres. MWA 25yrs; v-p. CAWA; sec.-founding dir. Man. Sports Federation; chairman Man. Sports Hall of Fame; pres. Winnipeg Bowling Assn. '51-52; FILA medal '67 PAG organizational work; gold star medal, dip. of honor IAWF for outstanding service to wrestling '76; Man. merit award; Centennial, Jubilee medals; Winnipeg Community Service award; street in Regina named in his honor; life mem. Winnipeg Central YMCA; hon. dir. Man. Sports Fed.; mem. Order of Canada, Cdn Amateur, Sask., Man., Canada's Sports, Cdn Amateur Wrestling halls of fame.

TRIHEY, Harry (hockey); b. 25 Dec 1877, Montreal, Que., d. 9 Dec 1942, Montreal, Que.; given name: Henry Judah; McGill; 1st man to utilize 3-man line leaving rover to roam free and encourage def to carry puck; starred in hockey with McGill, Montreal Shamrocks, rover, capt. Shamrocks Stanley Cup winners '99, '00; ret'd '01 with record of 46 goals in 30 games and 16 in 8 playoff games; secty-treas., later pres. CAHL leading league through disputes with Federal League '04-05; advisor to Wanderers; refereed many league, Stanley Cup playoff games; pre-NHL record of 10 goals in single game during regular season; mem. Hockey Hall of Fame.

TRIPUCKA, Frank (football); b. 8 Dec 1927, Bloomfield, N.J.; given name: Francis Joseph; m. Randy Jewkes; c. Heather, Tracy, Mark, Todd, T.K., Kelly, Chris; Notre Dame, BA; pres. plastics distributing co.; 23yrs beer distributor; pro qb Detroit Lions, Chicago Cardinals, Dallas Texans '49-53; Saskatchewan '53-58, '63, Ottawa '59, Denver Broncos 4yrs, asst coach Denver; 1st pro qb to surpass 3000 passing yds single season; completed 1st td pass in AFL history; all-conf. qb '54; record 216 completions '56 (since topped by Ron Lancaster), 3274yds passing; completed 158 of 257 passes for .615 percentage '55; had 29 intercepted '57; CFL record: 15,506yds on 1090 completions in 1930 attempts, .565 avg., 136 intercepted, 83tds; nickname "The Trip"; active in community affairs; mem. N.J., Colorado Sports, Bloomfield (NJ), Denver Broncos Ring, Ntl Polish Assoc. halls of fame; res. Essex Fells, N.J.

TRITES, Ev (curling/golf): b. 18 Sep 1912, New Glasgow, N.S.; d. 6 May 1984, Saint John, N.B.; given name: Evan Allison; m. Jean; ntl sales dir.; chair. CCA ntl mixed curling comm. '71-76; ntl sr. comm. '77-81; exec. NBCA '73-75, NBMCA '74-76; secty-treas. NBGA '75-83; exec.-dir. CPGA Atlantic Zone '77-83; chair. Saint John Canada Summer Games comm. '77, '85; nicknamed "Mr. Organization"; Moosehead Sports exec. of '78; CCA award of merit '83; mem. Cdn Curling, NB, Saint John Sports halls of fame.

TRITTEN, Karla (wheelchair basketball); b. 17 Apr 1968, Edmonton, Alta.; UofA BPE; phys ed. teacher; began playing '89; ntl team from '02; 4 gold, 5 silver, 2 bronze ntl championships; MVP award ntls '96; 5 ntl championship all-star teams; bronze '04 Paralympics; res. New Sarepta, Alta.

TROTTIER, Bryan (hockey); b. 17 Jul 1956, Redvers, Sask.; given name: Bryan John; div.; c. Bryan Jr., Lindsay Ann, Taylor Noelle; treaty Indian status; hockey coach; jr. Lethbridge Broncos; 2nd choice NYI '74 draft; minor pro Swift Current, Lethbridge (WHL) '72-75; WHL MVP, 1st team all-star ctr '75; Islanders '75-90, Pittsburgh '90-96; Calder Memorial Trophy '76; Ross, Hart trophies '79; Conn Smythe Trophy '80, King Clancy Trophy '89; led Stanley Cup playoff scorers '80 with 29 points; twice NHL 1st team, 2nd team all-star; mem. 6 Stanley Cup winners; competed

8 all-star games; shares NHL record fastest goal from start of game (5sec.), record 27 playoff points consecutive yrs '80-82; holds/shared 6 NHL scoring records; scored 50g '82; asst. coach Pittsburgh '94-97; head coach Portland Pirates (AHL) '97; asst. coach Colorado '98; head coach NYR '02, asst. NYI '04; NHL man of year '88; US citizen '84; mem. Team Canada '81, Team USA '84 Canada Cup series; NHL record: 1279 scheduled games, 524g, 901a, 221 playoff games, 71g, 113a; mem. Cdn Hockey, AHL halls of fame; res. McMurray, Pa.

TRUANT, Ray (football/basketball); b. 10 Oct 1930, Detroit, Mich,; given name: Ray Linard; m. Ann Tuson Birch McCallum; c. Janis Ann, Timothy Ray; Assumption Coll, UWO; ret'd educator, PE dept. head; 1st team all-city basketball honors '48-49 with Windsor Kennedy CI; ORFU jr. finalist with Assumption '49-50; with Bill Pataky, Jack Bruce, Bruno Bitkowski, Bob Simpson mem. Assumption Freshman Five; impressive athletic record UWO as fb quarter, def. back, basketball guard; all-Cdn, OUAA basketball all-star '51-53; 2 CIAU basketball, 1 football title; lone unanimous pick CP all-Cdn as Western won OUAA fb title; Hamilton 1st round draft '53 as def. back; ankle injury forced retirement '57; mem. 2 Grey Cup champions; Schenley top Cdn nominee; coached Brantford CI to sr. city fb crown, also coached basketball, t&f; coached North Park CI to 2 sr, jr, 2 CWOSSA jr. football titles, 1 city midget basketball crown; UWO athlete of yr award; mem. Brantford & Area hall of recognition, UWO, Windsor/Essex Sports halls of fame; res. Brantford, Ont.

TSANG, Tosha (rowing): b. 17 Oct 1970, Saskatoon, Sask.; McGill BA, UAlta. MA; mem. ntl team from '95; gold straight pairs, double sculls '93, quad '94 ntl championships; silver 8s '96 Olympics; McGill University Rowing Club most valuable female player '91-92; Association Quebecois d'Aviron volunteer-of-yr. award '91; res. Victoria, B.C.

TUBMAN, Joe (football); b. 18 Aug 1897, Ottawa, Ont., d. 29 Nov 1975, Ottawa, Ont.; given name: Robert Elmer; m. Madge Whyte (d.); c. Mary; railway employee; hb/k Rough Riders '19-29; capt. '25-26 Grey Cup winners; refereed, umpired interprovincial, ORFU 15 years; ret'd end of '44 season; as canoeist Eastern tandem and ntl war canoe tiltes for New Edinburgh club; played city league lacrosse, cricket, golf, lawn bowling; mem. Canadian Football, Ottawa, Canada's Sports halls of fame.

TUCKER, Murray (golf); b. 2 Nov 1922, Mitchell, Ont.; d. 24 Jun 2002, Markham, Ont.; given name: Murray Carlyle; m. Fleurette Prevost; c. Terry; ret'd golf professional, golf dir. Board of Trade Country Club; asst. pro Mississauga '46-48; head pro Sunningdale '48-53, Rosedale '53-65, Board of Trade '65-89; Ont. Open champion '50, runnerup twice; Ont. PGA champion '58, runnerup twice; mem. Cdn intl teams; mem. Ont. team; CPGA match play champion; 3 OPGA srs. titles; CPGA srs champion '78; tied 1st Que. Open; twice runnerup CPGA; club records Rosedale, Uplands, Box Grove, Cobourg, York Downs, Board of Trade; pres. OPGA, CPGA; Ont., Cdn club pro of year; Canada's 1st Master Golf Professional; instituted CPGA pension plan; authored CPGA employment manuals; mem. Cdn Golf Hall of Fame.

TUCKER, Whit (football); b. 15 Nov 1940, Windsor, Ont.; given name: Whitman; m. Heather McCuaig; c. Ken, Kelly, Diane, Wendy; UWO, BA; resident dir., investment consultant firm; all-city football, basketball Windsor '58-59; Ont. scholastic lj record '58; Royal Arcanum Trophy Windsor's outstanding HS athlete '59; Intercollegiate all-star football '61; pro rcvr Ottawa '62-70; Gruen Award Big Four Cdn rookie of year; all-star twice; 3 Grey Cup finals, 2 winners; CFL record: 272 pass receptions for 6092yds, 52tds; avg. gain 22.5 per-catch, best in CFL; runnerup outstanding Cdn award '68; dir. Ottawa Football Club; trustee Ottawa Sports Hall of Fame; mem. Ottawa Sports, Cdn Football, UWO W-Club, Windsor-Essex halls of fame; res. Ottawa, Ont.

TUDIN, Conny (hockey); b. 21 Sep 1917, Ottawa, Ont.; d. 24 Oct 1988, Ottawa, Ont.; given name: Cornell; m. Lois Darlene Sinnett; c. Terry, Rick; St. Patrick's College; supervisor HS tech. training; mem. Rideau Jrs., 1st team to employ red line, '35-37, Eastern Cdn title '37; Harringay Greyhounds English League champions '38-39, first UK team to have games televised in Eng.; pro Montreal organization '39-40; def/fwd Lachine Rapids, Washington Lyons, New Haven Eagles, Canadiens; mem. RCAF Flyers '42-46, Eastern Cdn Allan Cup finalists; mem. Ottawa Allan Cup finalists '48, champions '49; Smith Falls Rideaus '50-52 Eastern Cdn finalists; '52-53 Brockville St. Lawrence League titlists; organized Ottawa Riverside Park minor hockey league '61 coaching mosquito, peewee, midget teams; coach Glebe midgets Ottawa Cradle League, St. Jean's jr. city league, St. James UC midgets; scoring titles Rideau Jrs, Lachine Rapides, RCAF Flyers; mem. Ottawa Old Timers Hockey comm. '71-88; mem. Hockey Hall of Fame as mem. Flyers and Senators.

TUGNUTT, Ron (hockey); b. 22 Oct 1967, Scarborough, Ont.; given name: Ronald Frederick Bradley; m. Lisa; c. Jacob, Matthew; goalie Toronto Young Nats, Weston Dukes '83-84; OHL Peterborough '84-87, 1 all-star; AHL Fredericton '87-88, Halifax '88-92, Portland '95-96, Utah '04; NHL Quebec '87-92, Edmonton '92-93, Anaheim '93-94, Montreal 94-95, Ottawa '96-00, Columbus '00-02, Dallas '02-04; NHL totals: 537 scheduled games, 29,486 minutes, 186-239-62, 26sho, 25 playoff games, 1482 minutes, 9-13-0, 3sho; OHL Dinty Moore, Dave Pinkney trophies; 1 OHL, NHL all-star; active in Children's Hospital charities; res. Stittsville, Ont.

TULLY, George (fencing); b. 29 Aug 1914, Montreal, Que.; d. (circa 1990), Montreal, Que.; given name: George Victor; m. Rita Lumsden Seale; m. Barbara, Ann, Dianne Olivia, George Cornelius; ret'd salesman; NBYMCA 3-weapon champion '29-35, '37-39; Que. sabre champion '33, '36-39; Que. foil champion '38-39; ntl sabre champion '33, '37-39; ntl foil champion '37-39; ntl épée champion '37-39; Que. duelling sword champion '34; ntl duelling sworld champion '35; Open City (Montreal) 3-weapon champion '39; mem. '36 Olympic team; coached McGill '40-70, BEG team '58; taught fencing 12 years NBYMCA, West Montreal YMCA; OUA men's fencing trophy bears his name.

TUNKS, Jason (t&f); b. 5 Jul 1975, London, Ont.; m. Lieja Koeman; SMU, UWO; discus specialist; began competing in discus, shot put age 15; set ntl jr. record 58.76m '94

Ont. summer games; 7 consec. ntl sr. discus titles; ntl shot title '97; gold '01 Francophone Games, IAAF GP meets Osaka, Rio De Janeiro, Palo Alto, Sacramento, Toronto, pre-Olympic tuneup meet Gold Coast; bronze '98, silver '02 CG, '99 PAG; competed '96, '00, '04 Olympics, '97, '01 worlds; ntl, Commonwealth records; res. Amsterdam, Netherlands/ London, Ont.

TUPPER, Stephen (sailing); b. 6 Feb 1941, Vancouver, B.C.; given name: Stephen McGirr; m. Anne; c. Peter, Paul; UBC, BEd; exec. dir. BC Sailing Assn.; ntl team coach '73-80; 3 national Dragon Class titles; twice 3rd NA Dragon championships; 4th '68 Olympics Dragon Class; mem. Cdn One Ton crew New Zealand '71; mem. Cdn Onion Patch crew Bermuda '74, 2nd place; mem. Cdn Admiral's crew '75; coach 3 Olympic, 2 PAG teams; coach/ortganizer Canada's Cup; ISAF sailing comm.; intl jury Volvo Ocean race; Rolex Sailor of '02; elected CYA Councillor of Honor; res. Vancouver, B.C.

TURCOTTE, Bob (curling): b. 5 Mar 1944, Pembroke, Ont.; m. Kristin Holman; c. Jared, Sean, David, Alison; supervisor Ont. Hydro; competed 12 Ont. Tankards; 3rd for Bob Fedosa '79 Brier; skipped 3 Ont, 3 ntl srs. title rinks; rep. Ont. 2 ntl mixed; wife Kristin 3rd Alison Goring '83 ntl jr., '90 ntl women's title rinks; res. Ajax, Ont.

TURCOTTE, Maryse (weightlifting); b. 23 Feb 1975, Sherbrooke, Qué.; U.Q.A.M., BBA, UMontréal; ntl team from '94; Cdn. record 53kg total, 58kg total, 63kg c&j, total; 11 Cdn. sr. titles including 10 consec. '94-03; silver c&j '98 worlds; '99 PAG gold; competed '00 Olympics; gold 2 FISU, '02 CG; bronze c&j '02, '03 worlds; more than 50 Québec, Cdn. records from '92; competed 8 sr. worlds ranking among the top-7 every time; first American woman to c&j double her bodyweight (110kg '97 worlds); 1st-ever PAG, CG women's 58kg champion (women's weightlifting on program first time '99 PAG, '02 CG); 1st Cdn. woman to compete Olympic weightlifting '00; 14 medals (5 gold, 7 silver, 2 bronze) in 5 FISU championships, most ever by any participant; record 7 successive Sinclair awards for best lifter Cdn. sr. championships; 2 Personality of the Week *LaPresse* awards; res. Brossard, Qué.

TURCOTTE, Mathieu (speed skating); b. 8 Feb 1977, Sherbrooke, Qué.; orthotics/prosthetics technician; pres./founder Apex Racing Skates; relay gold, 1000m bronze '02 Olympics; competed 4 short track worlds; 2 Dick Ellis trophies; Eastern Twps athlete of '02; res. Montréal, Qué.

TURCOTTE, Mel (harness racing): b. 30 Nov 1938, Mattawa, Ont.; m. Barbara; 7th of 10 brothers educated in sport by father Theo; received P license at Batavia '58 but upgraded to A license after winning seven of 1st 10 races; criss-crossed US-Canada border for 12yrs before settling on Northfield Park as base of operations; enjoyed racing success with Essence Bear and Royal Cold; more than 2900 victories with purses exceeding $8M; res. Coconut Creek, Fla.

TURCOTTE, Ron (horse racing); b. 22 Jul 1941, Drummond, N.B.; given name: Ronald Joseph Morel; m. Gaetane; c. 4 daughters; Academie Notre Dame; ntl jockey of '62-63; 1st Cdn jockey to win successive Kentucky Derbys with Riva Ridge, Secretariat; twice winner Kentucky Derby,

Preakness, Belmont; 1 of 3 Cdn jockeys to win thoroughbred racing's Triple Crown with Secretariat '73; Man. Centennial Derby '70; twice winner Cdn International Stakes; other major stakes wins include Wood Memorial, Coaching Club American Oaks; career record: 3032 victories, 2897 seconds, 2559 thirds with purses totalling $28,606,490; career ended with injury sustained in race mishap '78; Cdn horse racing man of yr '78; French-Cdn-athlete-of-'73 award; subject of book *Will to Win;* advocate for disabled; mem. Order of Canada, Canadian Horse Racing, Ntl Museum of Racing (US), Long Island, Canada's, NB Sports halls of fame; res. Grand Falls, N.B.

TURGEON, Mathieu (trampoline); b. 2 Aug 1979, Pointe Claire, Que.; York; kinesiology; gold '96 age group games; 2 gold, 3 silver at ntls; competed '98, '99 worlds, '01 Goodwill Games; '00 (bronze) '04 Olympics; gold '02 Canada Cup; 5 WC synchronized trampoline medals; Gymnastics Can. trampoline/tumbling athlete of '00; res. Unionville, Ont.

TURGEON, Melanie (skiing); b. 21 Oct 1976, Alma, Que.; ntl team from '92; combined bronze '93 world jr. championships; ntl GS title '93; EC Super G silver '93; competed '94, '98 Olympics; WC gold, silver Igls, Austria Super G '00; lone Cdn to record rare WC super-G silver, downhill bronze same day '01; world alpine downhill gold '03; sportswear collection bears her name; res. Quebec City, Que.

TURGEON, Pierre (hockey): b. 29 Aug 1969, Rouyn, Que.; m. Elisabeth; c. Elizabeth, Alexandra, Dominic, Valerie; pitched in Little League World Series; ctr Granby '85-87; Cdn ntl team '86; 1st overall draft pick Buffalo '87-91, NYI '91-95, Montreal '95-96, St. Louis '97-01, Dallas '01-04; QMJHL Michel Bergeron rookie, Mike Bossy top-pro-prospect awards '87; Lady Byng trophy '93; 4 NHL all-star games; scored 58g '93; passed 1000 pts '99; NHL record: (through '04) 1215 scheduled games, 495g, 779a, 104 playoff games, 35g, 60a; res. Rosemere, Que.

TURNBULL, Alex (lacrosse); b. 6 Dec 1883, Paris, Ont., d. 27 Aug 1956, Vancouver, B.C.; top scorer '08 Olympic team; mem. New Westminster Salmonbellies '97-09; 6 championship teams including '00 world title team; mem. Canadian Lacrosse, BC Sports halls of fame.

TURNBULL, Barbara (golf); b. 6 Apr 1933, Saskatoon, Sask; given name: Barbara Lois Stone; m. William Turnbull (d); m. Danahar; 18 Saskatoon Riverside Club titles; from '58 mem. 24 provincial amateur teams; 9 Sask. titles, 6 times runnerup; runnerup ntl women's amateur '69; mem. Sask. team which tied BC for '67 interprovincial title; capt. Women's World Games team '70; mem. '73 international matches team; 13 Saskatoon city titles; low amateur Winnipeg Glendale pro-amateur; Saskatoon sportswoman of '67; mem. Sask., Saskatoon Sports halls of fame; res. Saskatoon, Sask.

TURNBULL, Ian (hockey); b. 22 Dec 1953, Montreal, Que.; given name: Ian Wayne; m. Inge Plug; c. Thea, William; UofOtt; real estate managing partner, hockey coach; Montreal jrs. '69-72 (Memorial Cup); Ottawa 67's '72-73; 3rd Toronto choice, 15th overall '73 amateur draft; minor stints CHL Oklahoma, AHL New Haven, Baltimore;

NHL Maple Leafs '73-81, Los Angeles '81-82, Pittsburgh '82-83; Toronto club record for def with 22 goals '76-77; club, NHL record most goals 1 game by def with 5 vs Detroit 2 Feb '77; NHL record: 628 scheduled games, 123 goals, 317 assists, 55 playoff games, 13 goals, 32 assists; with partners opened Toronto's first wine bar "Grapes" '77; oldtimers hockey with LA alumni; asst. coach Yuma Ramblers '02-03; nickname "Bull"; res. Redondo Beach, Calif.

TURNBULL, Ray (curling); b. 19 Jul 1939, Huntsville, Ont.; given name: Charles William; div Valerie Marcia Kaplan; c. Scott Douglas, Lori Dawn, Leanne Elizabeth; m. Jane; insurance agent, *TSN* curling color commentator from '84; all-star jr. lb; mem. Man, jr. title rink '58; all-star lead '65 Man., Brier title rink, world championships; trained 11 world champions; 1 of 4 ICF umpires; chief umpire 6 world jr., 4 Silver Brooms (worlds); curling clinic conductor; mem. Man., Cdn Curling halls of fame; res. Winnipeg, Man.

TURNER, Dave (soccer); b. 11 Oct 1903, Edinburgh, Scotland; d. 6 Apr 1989, Victoria, B.C.; given name: David Binnie; m. Margaret; c. Sandra Jean, David Robert; UBC, BSA, BA, MA, hon. PhD, Cornwall '46; ret'd deputy minister; standout St. Andrews, Cumberland United; vs ntl champion Nanaimo kicked 5 goals in 2-games series; BC title, Connaught Cup semifinals with Cumberland; 1yr pro in US then joined Toronto Ulster United; rejected '24 offer to join ntl all-stars on Australian tour but accepted '27 invitation for New Zealand tour; 9 seasons New Westminster Royals, 4 ntl titles; mem. BC, Canada's Sports halls of fame.

TURNER, Howie (football); b. 13 Oct 1922, Rocky Mountain, N.C.; d. 5 Nov 2004, Ottawa, Ont.; given name: Howard; m. Phyllis McNamara; c. Wanda, Patricia, Susan, Rosanne, Caroline; N.Carolina; salesman, nursing home owner; from standout career as rb with Tar Heels turned pro Ottawa Rough Riders '47-54; noted for quick, elusive running style he earned nickname "Touchdown"; mem. '51 Grey Cup title team.

TURNER, John (t&f); b. 7 Jun 1929, Richmond, Surrey, Eng; given name: John Napier; m. Geills McCrae Kilgour; c. Elizabeth, Michael, David, Andrew; St. Patrick's College, UBC, BA, Oxford (Rhodes Scholar), BA, BCL., MA, Paris; lawyer (QC), ret'd politician; ntl jr. 100-, 220yd sprint champion '47; mem. English t&f team '50-51; Lib MP '62-76; cabinet minister various portfolios '65-76; Cdn. Prime Minister '84; leader of opposition '84-86; res. Toronto, Ont.

TURNER, Lloyd (builder/hockey); b. 1884 Elmvale, Ont.; d. 7 Apr 1976, Calgary, Alta.; played with Sault Ste. Marie Ont. McNamaras; player/coach/mgr. Ft. William; moving to Calgary had ice installed in old roller rink and organized team and league from which Calgary Tigers emerged to unsuccessfully challenge for '24 Stanley Cup; moved to Minneapolis and Seattle before returning to Calgary and organizing Western Canada League '31; instrumental in resurgence of Allan Cup early '30s; organized Alta. Native tribes into tournament competition; mem. Hockey Hall of Fame.

TURVILLE, Frank (football); b. 23 Sep 1907, Port Arthur, Ont., d. 8 Jan 1984, Toronto, Ont.; given name: Franklin David; m. Reta Lowry; c. Mary Ann, Nancy, William David; UWO, BA, Osgoode Hall, LLD; lawyer, QC; outstanding scholar-athlete Windsor HS '25; rb/rcvr/p Argos '28-31, capt., Jeff Russel award '30; Hamilton Tigers '32-36; mem. '32 Grey Cup winner; mem. 1ˢᵗ *CP* all-star team '32, repeat through '35; powerful punter; 116 CFL career singles, 27 in '32 season; Hamilton alderman '35; mem. W-Club Sports Hall of Fame.

TWADDLE, Tim (harness racing): b. 21 Aug 1962, St. Catharines, Ont.; Niagara College; broke into sport with John Burns stable in '80s; plagued by injuries throughout career, despite heart surgery managed to forge impressive record; through '97 1385 victories with purses exceeding $10M; 27 major stakes race victories; drove Hardie Hanover to '94 Breeders Crown; res. Meadow Lands, Pa.

TYTLER, Donald (sailing); b. 8 Mar 1924, Toronto, Ont.; given name: Donald Milne; m. Elizabeth Osbourne; c. John, Ian, Margaret; UofT, BASc.; ret'd mechanical engineer; crew mem. 6-metre team '52 Olympics, '56 Olympics Dragon team; mem. *Globe and Mail* 6-metre NA title team '54; mem. '46-48 Bartnel Trophy 8-metre title crew for Great Lakes; res. Don Mills, Ont.

UDVARI, Frank (hockey/officiating); b. 2 Jan 1924, Miltec, Yugoslavia; m. Colette Reinhardt; c. Martin, Jane; supervisor NHL officials; officiated OMHA 2yrs, OHA 4yrs; pro '51 refereeing 718 regular season, 70 NHL playoff games, 229 AHL, 7 WHL, 15 EHL, 7 CHL games; AHL referee-in-chief; conducted hockey schools across Canada and US, 2 in Germany for Cdn army; introduced 3-man officiating system to Finland '74; mem. Hockey Hall of Fame selection comm.; mem. Waterloo County, Hockey halls of fame; res. Waterloo, Ont.

ULLMAN, Norm (hockey); b. 26 Dec 1935, Provost, Alta.; given name: Norman Victor Alexander; m. Bibiane Goueffic; c. Gordon, Linda, Lori; business exec.; mem. 2 provincial bantam title teams, leading scorer bantam, peewee, midget, juvenile, junior; mem. provincial midget, juvenile title teams; Memorial Cup finals Edmonton Jr. Oil Kings; jr. league scoring record 55 goals, 46 assists in 36-game schedule; pro ctr Edmonton Flyers (WHL), Detroit (NHL) '55-68, Toronto '68-75, WHA Edmonton Oilers '75-77; p.-pres. NHL Players Assn.; 7th in NHL history to score 400 goals; NHL-WHA record: 537g, 822a, 106 playoff games, 30g, 53a; mem. Toronto Old Stars HC; mem. Hockey, Alta. Sports halls of fame; res. Toronto, Ont.

UMEH, Stella (gymnastics): b. 27 May 1975, Toronto, Ont.; UCLA; called in as last minute replacement '90 CG and led Cdn team to gold medal; subsequently competed in '92 Olympics, worlds, '93 world gymnastics challenge; 2 gold, 1 silver '94 CG; ret'd from intl competition '94; top performer '98 Pac-10 championships; shared floor gold '98 NCAA championships; performed in Sea World's Rhythm on Ice; joined Cirque de Soleil '99; *CBC* color commentator '02 CG; res. Mississauga, Ont.

UNDERHILL, Barbara (figure skating); b. 24 Jun 1963, Pembroke, Ont.; given name: Barbara Ann; m. Rick Gaetz; c. Stephanie (d), Samantha, Matthew; with Paul Martini ntl, world jr. pairs titles '78; International GP; '79 St. Gervais, Oberstdorf; ntl srs. '79-84; St. Ivel, NHK Challenge Cup, Ennia Challenge, Skate America; mem. '79-84 Worlds, '80, '84 Olympic, '79 Moscow Skate teams; bronze '83, gold '84 Worlds; pro '84-98; TV skating analyst; launched Stephanie Gaetz KeepSafe Foundation; mem. Cdn Olympic, Canada's Sports, Cdn Figure Skating halls of fame; res. Mississauga, Ont.

UNDERHILL, Beth (equestrian): b. 5 Sep 1962, Guelph, Ont.; Beth Underhill Stables operator; began riding age 7 at Georgetown Y; despite winning singing awards from Royal Conservatory her riding interests took precedence; following successful junior/amateur career moved into jumper competition at 21 with Sagan, winning Ont. Open jr. titles '84, '86; with Monopoly won 6 World Cup qualifying events; mem. ntl team from '90; mem. 3 Bank of Montreal Nations Cup title teams; team, individual silver '91, team bronze '99 PAG; 3 ntl show jumping titles; Cdn World Cup League champion '93; competed '92 Olympics; was ranked

#1 female rider in world; competed more than 25 Nation's Cup, PAG, Olympic, World Equestrian games; coached by Torchy Millar; res. Schomberg, Ont.

UNDERHILL, Eileen (badminton); b. 1 Apr 1899, Moosomin, Sask; d. 31 Jul 1988, Vancouver, B.C.; given name: Margaret Eileen Stuart George; m. John Edward Underhill (d); c. John Gerald, Charles Stuart; 12 BC singles titles, shared 11 BC ladies' doubles, 5 BC mixed doubles; ntl singles title '27, shared 4 doubles and with husband John 4 mixed doubles; 1st husband-wife team BC Sports Hall of Fame.

UNDERHILL, John (badminton); b. 3 Sep 1902, Vancouver, B.C., d. 3 Sep 1972, Vancouver, B.C.; given name: John Edward; m. Margaret Eileen Stuart George; c. John Gerald, Charles Stuart; 5 BC, 2 ntl singles titles; 5 BC men's doubles, each time with different partner; with wife Eileen 4 ntl mixed doubles titles; first husband-wife team elected to BC Sports Hall of Fame.

UNDERHILL, Pat (speed skating); b. 24 Jul 1928, Edmonton, Alta.; given name: Patricia Gunn; m. John C. Underhill; ntl outdoor titles '55-56, '60-61, indoor '58; NA indoor '56, Alta. outdoor '56, '61, indoor '56-59, '61, Illinois State indoor '56, Montana State indoor '56-58, BC outdoor '59-61, indoor '59, '61, Northwest Intl indoor '60; 4 ntl, 9 Montana records; mem. 2 world championship teams; alternate '60 Olympics; directly responsible for starting, developing clubs in Edmonton, Red Deer, Dawson Creek, Fort St. John, Regina, Calgary; conducted coaching clinics across Canada reactivating clubs in Montreal, Quebec City, Kitchener, Ottawa; mem. ntl exec., pres. CASSA '66; mem. Cdn Speed Skating, Alta Sports halls of fame; res. Toronto, Ont.

UNDERWOOD, Brad (softball): b. 27 May 1959, Owen Sound, Ont.; regarded as one of the outstanding lhps of his era; toiled with variety of top-notch teams including Owen Sound Tiremen, Toronto Gators, Green Bay All-Car; while noted for his brilliant pitching performances he also was a standout hitter; pitched 4 no-hitters in ISC world championship play, including perfect game '91; mem. Gators' '95, Green Bay '94 ISC gold medal teams; mem. 5 ntl title teams; wide array of ISC, ASA MVP awards; mem. ntl team '96, Owen Sound Tiremen '97; won total of 29 ISC tournament games '95; res. Owen Sound, Ont.

UNDERWOOD, Reg (softball); b. 7 May 1951, Sidney, B.C.; given name: Reginald Wayne; m. Julie May Wilson; Camouson College; carpenter; mem. Victoria Russell Cup rugby champions '70-71; Brentwood basketball tournament all-star ctr '67, bantam sportsmanship award '66, Cordova Bay tournament all-star ctr '68, Saanichton tournament all-star ctr '68; Victoria all-star '71, Songhees Totem tour all-star '73; mem. 5- 10-pin title bowling teams '68-75; mem. Victoria Bate fastball team '74-77; Victoria Budget team '78-81; 7 BC, 4 ntl title teams; mem. '76 world, '78 PAG title teams; 2 tournament MVP awards; 11 times tournament all-star; 5 team-of-yr awards; '75 City of Victoria plaque; Brentwood League MVP '71; Stuffy McGinnis Invitational top batter, MVP '73; Senior C batting champion '72; major men's, Campbell River batting titles '73; Victoria all-Native tournament all-star; Tom Longboat top Native athlete award; mem. Greater Victoria Sports Hall of Fame; res. Victoria, B.C.

UNGER, Garry (hockey); b. 7 Dec 1947, Edmonton, Alta.; given name: Garry Douglas; m. Beverly; c. Kim, Jamie, Kristin; hockey coach; wing jr Calgary, London Nationals; pro '66-67 Tulsa (CPHL), Rochester (AHL); Toronto '67-68, Detroit '68-71, St. Louis '71-79, Atlanta '79-80, Los Angeles '80-81, Edmonton '81-83; NHL consec. games played record 914 from 24 Feb '68-21 Dec '79; NHL record: 1105 scheduled games, 413g, 391a, 52 playoff games, 12g, 18a; 7 consec. NHL all-star games; '74 all-star MVP; player/coach Dundee Rockets, Peterborough Pirates (UK) '85-88; coach Phoenix (IHL) '90-92, Tulsa Oilers from '92, '93 CHL champions, CHL coach of '93; coached New Mexico Scorpions (WPHL); res. Tulsa, Okla.

UNGERMAN, Irv (boxing); b. 1 Feb 1923, Toronto, Ont.; given name: Irving; m. Sylvia Rothstein; c. Shelley, Howard, Temmi; ret'd poultry processor, real estate agent, boxing promoter; active soccer, hockey player, boxer at YMCA; fought for Toronto 105lb title '39; during 3 years RCAF service fought at 135lbs, also served as phys-ed officer; managed, promoted careers of numerous fighters including ntl heavyweight champion George Chuvalo, Cdn, Commonwealth welterweight champion Clyde Gray; agent for Trevor Berbick; *All-Canada Sports and City TV* Trophy '73; Jack Allen Trophy for contribution to world boxing '65-66; active fund-raiser Cdn Maccabiah Games Assn.; nicknamed "Chicken King"; mem. WingateU (Israel) Intl, Cdn Boxing halls of fame; res. Toronto, Ont.

UPPER, Wray (baseball); b. 18 May 1931, Port Colborne, Ont.; m. Helen Bartok; c. Cindy, Shawn, Lisa; ret'd supervisor; NY Giants organization '51-52; Sr. IC Galt '53-55, '57-72, Kitchener '56, Brantford '73-74; Sr. IC record: .289 lifetime BA; led league hitters '58 with .413; twice led league in hits, triples, once runs scored; managed Galt '62-67, '70-72, 113-157 record; 1st team all-star 3b 6 times, mgr once, 2nd team 3b 5 times; mem. Ont. team '69 Canada Games; res. Cambridge, Ont.

UPTON, Eric (football); b. 29 Apr 1953, Ottawa, Ont.; given name: Eric Thomas; m. Nancy; Colorado, UofOtt; son of former Rough Rider star Joe Upton; jr. Ottawa Sooners; twice OQIFC all-star og; UofOtt outstanding lineman award '74; pro Edmonton '76-85; WFC all-star guard; mem. 5 Grey Cup winners; mem. Nepean Sports Wall of Fame; res. Kazabazua, Que.

URBAN, Faye (tennis); b. 28 Oct 1945, Windsor, Ont.; m. William Mlacak; Windsor Teachers' College; bank employee; ntl -13 singles '58; with Brenda Nunns -15 doubles '60, -18 doubles, singles '61-62; with Nunns women's doubles, with David Body mixed doubles '65; with Vicki Berner women's doubles '66-69; closed singles '68-69, open singles '69; mem. '66-70 Federation Cup

team, capt. '68; mem. Windsor-Essex County Sports Hall of Fame; res. Toronto, Ont.

URNESS, Ted (football); b. 23 Jun 1937, Regina, Sask; given name: Harold; m. Jacquelyn Joy; c. Mark, Dee Anne, Daniel; Arizona, BSc; pres. auto equipment sales co.; Governor's Trophy UAlta MVP '60;. Roughriders '61-70; all-Cdn ctr '65-70; runnerup Schenley CFL lineman of '68; 3 Grey Cup finals, 1 winner; res. Saskatoon, Sask.

URSEL, Bob (curling); b. 12 Feb 1965, Winnipeg, Man.; given name: Robert James; m. LeeAnne Homme; c. Mitchell, Brady, Spencer, Shea; Manitoba BA; RCMP officer; following footsteps of Brier champ father Jim he skipped 2 Man. jr title rinks; ntl jr. title '84; world jr. title '85, lead '87, skip '01 Cdn Olympic trials; 3rd 2 B.C. men's title rinks; competed 2 Briers; Man. team of yr '85; runnerup Man. athlete of '85; mem. Man. Curling Hall of Fame; res. Kelowna, B.C.

URSEL, Jim (curling); b. 22 Jan 1937, Glenella, Man.; given name: James William; m. Carol; c. Robert, Michael, Jill; ret'd personnel mgr. Air Canada; Man. schoolboy title, ntl final playoff loser '54; all-star third '62 Brier; skipped Que. to 6 Briers, '77 title; finalist '77 Silver Broom (world); '77-78 Kronenbourg Trophy, Switzerland; twice Brier all-star skip; *CBC* championship '75; Ross Harstone Trophy '77 Brier; overall Brier record 48-27; 2 ntl sr. men's titles; coached sons to '84 Pepsi Jr. title rink; coached 3 other ntl jr title, 2 men's world rinks; mem. Man., Cdn Curling, Man. Sports halls of fame; res. Kelowna, B.C.

URSULIAK, Wally (curling); b. 30 Jun 1929, Edmonton, Alta.; m. Kathleen VanKleek; c. Ken, Robin, Kelly; pro curling instructor, freelance broadcaster; Pittsburgh Pirates baseball training camp '51; lead for Hec Gervais '61-62 Briers, Brier, world titles '61; ntl Open, Edmonton Masters, Tournament of Champions titles '65; coached European curlers including world champions Otto Danieli of Switzerland, Kjell Oscarius of Sweden; coached '75 ntl Lassies champion Lee Tobin of Que.; res. Edmonton, Alta.

UTECK, Larry (football/coaching): b. 9 Oct 1952, Thornhill, Ont.; d. 25 Dec 2002, Halifax, N.S.; m. Sue; c. Luke, Cain; Colorado, Wilfrid Laurier; athletic dir., football coach, politician; gd/db in CFL with Toronto '74-76, BC '77, Montreal '78-80; Eastern all-star '75-76; competed in Gator Bowl, Atlantic Bowl; asst. coach Saint Mary's '82, head coach '83-98; AD from '96; 2 Frank Tindall CIAU coach-of-yr awards; ex-Halifax alderman; diagnosed with ALS '98; Halifax named Larry Uteck Blvd. in his honor; CIS renamed Churchill Bowl to Uteck Bowl; mem. Order of Canada.

VACHON, Brian (bobsleigh); b. 10 Aug 1951, Moncton, N.B.; m. Marla Marino; c. Margo; Carleton, BSc; marketing consultant; ot Carleton football team '71-76; mem. natl. team 2- & 4-man crews, generally as brakeman, '72, '77-78 world championships; '76, '80 Olympics; driver '80; TV Olympic sports commentator '88, '92; res. Gloucester, Ont.

VACHON, Mad Dog (wrestling); b. 1929, Montreal, Que.; given name: Maurice; started wrestling age 12; competed at 174lbs '48 Olympics; gold '50 BEG; turned pro with Verne Gagne's American Wrestling Assn.; won world AWA heavyweight title; teamed with brother Paul "The Butcher" for AWA tag team title; later partnered with Fritz Von Goering, Bob Orton, Killer Kowalski, Baron von Raschke, Gagne for added AWA tag team titles; 3 NWA Texas, 1 Southern, Pacific Northwest tag team crowns; 2 AWA world tag team titles; 6 NWA, 5 AWA world, 2 Montreal intl heavyweight crowns; uncle of former WWE/WCW female wrestler Luna Vachon; Iron Mike Mazurki award; lost leg following '87 car accident near Iowa home; mem. Cdn Wrestling Hall of Fame; res. Iowa.

VACHON, Rogie (hockey); b. 8 Sep 1945, Palmarolle, Que.; given name: Rogatien Rosaire; m. Nicole Blanchard; c. Nicholas, Jade, Marie Joie; hockey exec.; jr. Thetford Mines; goalie; pro Quebec (AHL) '65-66, Houston (CPHL) '66-67; Montreal for Stanley Cup playoffs '67; remained until '71, Los Angeles '71-78, Detroit '78-80, Boston '80-82; shared '67-68 Vezina Trophy with Gump Worsley; twice 2nd team all-star; MVP Team Canada '76; Kings' most inspirational player '73; *Hockey News* player of '75; Red Rose award by Hospital Charities Assn., Brian Piccolo award nominee '75; NHL record: 795 scheduled games, 355-291-127, 51so, 2.99 avg., 48 playoff games, 2so, 2.77 avg,; mem. 3 Stanley Cup winners; asst. coach LA '82-84, '95, GM '84-92; asst. to chair Bruce McNall '92-95; LA pres. '95-97; v-p. special projects '97-03; jersey #30 ret'd by Kings; res. Playa del Rey, Calif.

VADNAIS, Carol (hockey); b. 25 Sep 1945, Montreal, Que.; given name: Carol Marcel; hockey scout; jr. Montreal OHA; def Montreal '66-68, Oakland '68-70, California '70-72, Boston '72-75, NYR '75-82, New Jersey '82-83; NHL playing record: 1087 scheduled games, 169g, 418a, 106 playoff games, 10g, 40a; mem. 2 Stanley Cup winners; asst. coach Rangers '83-84; scout/asst coach Canadiens '93-95; res. New York, N.Y.

VAILLANCOURT, Michel (equestrian); b. 26 Jul 1954, St. Felix de Valois, Que.; m. Carolyn; high- performance dir. Jump Canada, course designer; Ottawa Winter Fair puissance title '72; only Cdn to place (3rd) in Lake Placid Grand Prix '75; rode Branch County, a converted race horse, placed high in variety of Rothman's Grand Prix competitions; silver '76 Olympics; mem. bronze jumping team '75 PAG; Royal Winter Fair Nation's Cup '79; Spruce Meadows jumping title '80; team gold Rotterdam Nations

Cup '80; World Cup preliminary title Spruce Meadows '80; ntl, World Cup jumping titles '82; res. Mt. Albert, Ont.

VAIVE, Rick (hockey); b. 14 May 1959, Ottawa, Ont.; given name: Rick Claude; m. Joyce; c. Jeffrey, Justin; hockey coach; fwd jr. Sherbrooke '76-78, Birmingham (WHA) '78-79; 1st Vancouver pick, 5th overall '79 amateur draft; Vancouver '79-80, '92, Toronto '80-87, Chicago '87-89; Buffalo '89-92; scored 54g '82, 51 '83, 52 '84; asst. coach Hamilton Canucks '92; coach/GM South Carolina Stingrays (ECHL) '93-98; head coach Saint John Flames (AHL) '98-99, Mississauga Ice Dogs (OHL) '00-01; NHL record: 877 scheduled games, 441g, 347a, 54 playoff games, 27g, 16a; WHA record: 75 scheduled games, 26g, 33a; played with Dundas Sr. OHA '02; res. Mississauga, Ont.

VALENTAN, Walter (bowling); b. 23 Jun 1929, Graz, Austria; given name: Walter Johann; div. Connie West; c. Monica, Anita; m. Edeltraude Schobel; tool engineer, bowling administrator; pres. Kitchener Bowlers' Assn. '68; dir. Ont. Bowlers' Congress '70, Cdn Bowlers' Congress '70-72; dir. public relations OBC '72-73; ED BPAO '73-04; life mem. OPBA, Conestoga BA; OBC president-of-yr award; Ont. sport achievement award; Builder of Bowling Industry award; listed *Intl Who's Who of Professionals*; mem. Bay of Quinte Bowling, Ont. 5-pin Bowling halls of fame; res. Oshawa, Ont.

VAMPLEW, Des (shooting); b. 20 Aug 1955, Toronto, Ont.; given name: Desmond George Paul; m. Mary Gemorija; c. Timothy, Jonathon; York, BA; sales manager Dansk International Designs; hockey league MVP bantam, midget; '72 Strathcona award Canada's top cadet shooter, ntl prone indoor jr. small-bore titlist '72, '74; ntl jr. high-power champion '73-74; mem. '74 Royal Cdn Army Cadet Bisley team, top cadet honors (Bell Trophy) at Bisley; Lieut.-Gov.'s gold medal '75-76 Que. H-P championships; Que. H-P title '77-78; Ont. H-P '76, '79; Ont. SB '76, '78; Alta. H-P '78; Atlantic H-P '79; mem. ntl full-bore team '77-84; silver '77 ntl H-P, 4th Gov.-Gen.'s match; gold full-bore '78 CG; ntl H-P title '79; bronze '79 Gov.-Gen.'s match; Queen's Prize finalist Bisley '79, '81; mem. world full-bore championships team '80; gold Lord Tedder aggregate Bisley, finalist St. George's Prize Bisley '74, '81; mem. 9 Bisley teams, 3 as coach; mem. ntl small-bore team '82-84; gold English Match '84 Benito Juarez; 7 Ont. achievement awards; 4 Ont. championship certificates; hon. life mem. DCRA, ORA; life gov. ORA; mem. DCRA Hall of Fame; res. Scarborough, Ont.

VAMPLEW, Edith (shooting): b. 15 Jun 1924, Toronto, Ont.; m. Thomas Vamplew (d); c. Patrick, Desmond; UofT; ret'd; full-bore rifle specialist; mem. Ont. team '73 Canada Games; DCRA Tess Spencer award '78; commandant Cdn Bisley team '94; capt. Canada, Commonwealth, -25 match teams; gov. Ont. Army Cadet League; mem. ntl Army Cadet League; life mem. ORA, DCRA; res. Whitby, Ont.

VAMPLEW, Pat (shooting); b. 24 Nov 1952, Toronto, Ont.; given name: Patrick Blakely; m. Donna Maria Marchand; c. Thomas Gil, Katherine Edith; UofT, BPHE, UWO, BEd; teacher; mem. '69 Bisley cadet team; ntl jr. full-bore rifle champion '73; mem. ntl small-bore team from '75; Florida State champion '76; Ont. indoor SB title '76; ntl 3-position title, pre-Olympic gold SB prone '76; team bronze Benito Juarez Games '77, '79-80; ntl open full-bore rifle title, Gov.-Gen.'s gold '77; Ont. air rifle, standard rifle titles, CG full-bore bronze '78, small-bore prone team bronze '82; 3 team silver, 300m prone free-rifle bronze '83, small-bore rifle gold '87 PAG; tied 3rd world full-bore Bisley '80; 4 ntl prone championships; mem. '84, '88 Olympic teams; holder/co-holder 4 ntl records; 23 provincial titles; qualified for 13 Bisley teams; coach '90 cadet Bisley team; 9 provincial achievement awards; 2 Ont. championship certificates; SFC golden anniversary award '82; mem. bantam, midget hockey title teams; MVP awards; x-country runner, winning '71 York League 300m, 3,000m, steeplechase titles, HS most-valuable-runner award '71; mem. Cdn Forces Sports, DCRA halls of fame; res. Whitby, Ont.

VANDERJAGT, Mike (football); b. 24 Mar 1970, Oakville, Ont.; m. Janelyn; c. Jay Michael; Michigan State, Allan Hancock J.C., West Virginia; pro football player; qb/kicker spent 4yrs in CFL with Toronto, Hamilton, Sask. playing on 2 Grey Cup winners; noted for strong leg and great kicking accuracy; 1 season Minnesota (Arena League); NFL Indianapolis Colts from '98; scored in 71 consec. games; only 3rd Colt to win NFL scoring title; club record 125 consec. PAT; only player with 5 consec 100+ point seasons; set NFL record 41 consec. FG to clinch Colts playoff berth '03; NFL record through '03: 94 games, 173FG on 197 attempts, 233PAT on 234 attempts for 752pts; aspiring actor; kicking double for Tony Danza in *The Garbage Pickin' Field Goal Kickin' Philadelphia Phenom*; instructor Colts women's football clinics; AP all-pro'03; Pro Bowl '04; res. Toronto, Ont.

van der KAMP, Anna (rowing): b. 19 Jun 1972, Abbotsford, B.C.; UVic; lifeguard, swimming instructor, recycling education co-ordinator; mem. ntl team from '94; 2 ntl titles; mem. women's 8s silver medal crew '96 Olympics; CARA female crew-of-yr award with UVic '93; res. Port Hardy, B.C.

van der MERWE, Marina (coaching/field hockey); b. 7 Feb 1937, Cape Town, S.A.; Cape Town, Fredensborg, Denmark, Loughborough, Eng., teaching cert., Syracuse, BSc, Iowa, MA, Ohio State, PhD; ret'd asst. prof. York; mem. ntl team '65, '71; coached ntl team '76-95; guided ntl team from 16th ranking '76 to silver medal '83, bronze '86 world championships; coach 3 Olympic team; coach York '77-99; 6 CIS silver, 2 bronze, 7 OUA titles; fed. govt. excellence award '83; Air Canada coach of '83; 2 CIS FH coach-of-yr awards; OUA, York FH awards bear her name; res. Downsview, Ont.

VAN DINE, David (curling); b. 25 Jun 1948, Ottawa, Ont.; Carleton, BA, UofOtt, LLB; personnel mgr.; 3rd for Harry Adams 3 Ont. men's finals, skip for 2 others; competed 6 Ont. mixed finals, 5 as skip, Ont. champion '82, '86; ntl mixed champion '86; all-star skip '82 ntl mixed championships; res. Ottawa, Ont.

VAN HEES, Christie (racquetball); b. 5 Jul 1977, Kelowna, B.C.; Douglas Coll.; 7 ntl jr. titles; doubles gold '95 jr. worlds; 2 gold, 1 silver sr. ntls; bronze '96 sr. worlds; gold US women's open '96. '01; 2 monitoring event gold; US Intercollegiate gold '98; world gold '98; competed '96 Tournament of Americas; '99 PAG silver; res. Kelowna, B.C.

VAN HELLEMOND, Andy (officiating/hockey); b. 16 Feb 1948, Winnipeg, Man.; m. Cheryl MacDonald; c. Susan, Vanessa, Cynthia; ret'd hockey referee, hockey exec.; joined NHL ranks '71 making on-ice debut 22 Nov '72; went on to become one of top senior officials; worked 2 NHL all-star games, Rendez-Vous '87 series; worked 19 Stanley Cup finals; NHL record: 1475 scheduled games, 227 playoff games; as a '96 sendoff gesture on retirement after 25 yrs was fined $250 for incident year previous; v-p. hockey operations East Coast HL; dir. NHL officiating '00-04; officiating consultant; mem. Cdn, Man. Hockey halls of fame; res. Princeton, N.J.

VAN KIEKEBELT, Debbie (t&f); b. 1 Mar 1954, Kitchener, Ont.; m.; c. 3; York, Ryerson PTI; broadcaster; mem. Scarborough Lions Track Club; ntl records midget hj (5'10"), lj (19'5 1/2") '70; 5th hj '70 CG, native, NA women's pentathlon record 5052 points '71; gold '71 PAG penthathlon; mem. '72 Olympic team; shared Bobbie Rosenfeld '71 award with Debbie Brill; res. Toronto, Ont.

van KOEVERDEN, Adam (canoeing); b. 29 Jan. 1982, Toronto, Ont.; given name: Adam Joseph; kinesiology student, McMaster.; sprint kayak; world cup medals '01, silver K-1 1000m '03 worlds; gold, silver '04 world cup Racice, Czech Republic, bronze Duisburg, 2 gold Hazewinkel, '04 Olympics gold K-1 500m, bronze K-1 1000m; Cdn flag bearer '04 Olympics closing ceremonies; Lou Marsh trophy '04; res: Burlington, Ont.

VAN RUYVEN, Andy (rowing); b. 9 Sep 1952, St. Catharines, Ont.; UWO, hons BA; salesman Xerox Canada; mem. Ont. gold medal 4s, 8s, 500m 8s dash '69 Canada Games; mem. ntl team '70-77, '80; mem. '72, '76, '80 Olympic, '71, '75 PAG, 6 world championships teams; gold '72 English Henley, '75 PAG, '76 Lucerne Intl Regatta, Yugoslavian Intl Regatta coxed 4s, '80 Nottingham Intl Regatta coxless 4s; ntl champion '70-77, '80; with '76 crew placed 3rd '03 Head of Charles coxed four masters race; St. Catharines achievement awards '75-76, '80; res. N. Vancouver, B.C.

VAN VLIET, Maury (administration); b. 3 Aug 1913, Bellingham, Wash.; d. 4 Apr 2001, Edmonton, Alta.; m. Virginia Gaddis; c. Vicki, Maury Jr., Katharine Pieter; Oregon, BSc, MSc, UCLA, EdD; hon. LLD UWO, Windsor, UAlta., Dalhousie, Queen's; educator; coached basketball (2 ntl champions, 3 runnersup) t&f, football (6 Western Intercollegiate champions), rugby, gymnastics; responsible for 1st PhD program in PhE in Canada; 1st dean field of PhE in Commonwealth; dir PhE UBC '36-45; UAlta '45-75; pres. CG Foundation '75-78; exec. roles BC, Alta., ntl athletic, academic organizations; hon. pres. CAHPER, Edmonton Paralympic Sports Assn; mem. Cdn Assn. for Sports Sciences, National College PhE Assn. for men; fellow, American College of Sports Medicine; mem. Alta. Sports

Council, chair. Advisory Comm.; Centennial Medal, Alta. Premier's Achievement award, Edmonton builder-of-the-community award, Edmonton meritorious service certificate, Edmonton parks & recreation honor award, Citrus College, Calif. alumnus-of-yr award, ntl, Edmonton CAHPER honor awards, CPSA pre-eminent service recognition; Churchill Bowl MVP award bears his name; mem. Order of Canada, Edmonton Sportsmen's, UBC, Alta., BC, Canada's Sports halls of fame.

VANDERBURG, Helen (synchro swim); b. 12 Jan 1959, Calgary, Alta.; given name: Helen Lena; m. Les Shaw; UCal, BPHE; operator Heaven's Fitness Club; mem. ntl team '71-79; jr. team titles '71-73, sr. team titles '75-77; 11 ntl solo, duet, figures titles; silver team '75, '79 PAG, '76 Pan-Pacific, '79 FINA World Cup; gold duet, solo, figures '78 Worlds; gold solo, duet '79 PAG; gold solo, duet, figures '79 FINA world Cup; gold solo '79 Pan-Pacific; all events sweep '78 worlds, '79 PAG, Pan-Pacific, FINA Cup constituted unprecedented grand slam; Olympic team coach '96; Synchro Canada outstanding-jr. award bears her name; 2 Elaine Tanner, 1 Velma Springstead award; Calgary athlete of '78; 3 times Booster Club of Canada athlete of yr; Aquatic Federation of Canada female athlete of '79; mem. Cdn, World Aquatic, Alta., Cdn Amateur, Canada's Sports halls of fame; res. Calgary, Alta.

VARALEAU, Jack (weightlifting); b. 22 May 1922, Eastview (Vanier), Ont.; given name: James Patrick; rec. dir., ret'd RCAF; mem. '48, '52 Olympic, '50 BEG teams; placed 6th, broke Olympic press record '48; BE championship '48-50; gold '50 BEG; asst. mgr-coach '60 Olympic weightlifting team; Gil O. Julien trophy French Cdn athlete of '50; Ont. Sports Achievement Award; mem. Ottawa, Canadian Forces Sports halls of fame; res. Vancouver, B.C.

VARGO, Ken (football); b. 10 Jul 1934, Martins Ferry, OH; given name: Kenneth William; c. Laura, Bill; Ohio State, BSc; sales Capital Office Interiors; captained Martin's Ferry HS teams in football/basketball/t&f; Wigwam Wisemen ntl HS football all-American; ctr Ohio State '53-55, co-capt, all-Big 10 '55; mem. '54 ntl title team; Hula Bowl, East-West Shrine game participant, Rose Bowl title team '55; ctr Rough Riders (CFL) '56-58, all-star '56; participated East-West game '56; res. Nepean, Ont.

VAUGHAN, Eileen (parachuting); b. 1 Oct 1958, Halifax, N.S.; North Texas State, Dalhousie, BRec; competed in gymnastics, t&f, curling, basketball, volleyball, field hockey, ice hockey, soccer, box lacrosse, parachuting; competed nationally, internationally in box lacrosse; mem. '75 Cdn title team; 1st team accuracy parachuting Ont. Summer Games; 2nd junior style event '80; ranked 8th in world style '82; certified scuba diver; senior parachuting instructor; ntl Level III lacrosse referee; 3 times Canada Fitness award-of-excellence recipient; accomplished musician 5 instruments; made Dean's list North Texas State; technical asst. CSPA '81-82; mem. Cdn Forces Sports Hall of Fame; res. Halifax, N.S.

VAUGHAN, Gerald (football); b. 8 Apr 1970, Abbeville, Miss,; UMiss; db/lb; shone in hs t&f, basketball, baseball, football; UMiss '89-92; CFL Calgary '93-95, Winnipeg '96,

Hamilton '97-01, Ottawa '02-04; standout kick blocker; 3 Grey Cup finals, 1 winner; res. Ottawa, Ont.

VAUGHAN, Kaye (football); b. 30 Jun 1931, Concordia, Kansas; given name: Charles Kaye; m. Lucile Wheeler; c. Myrle, Jake; Tulsa, BA, Kansas, MSc, McGill; school administrator; lineman Tulsa '50-53; pro tackle Ottawa '53-64; team capt.; Schenley lineman of '56-57, runnerup '60; 10 times EFC all-star; mem. '60 Grey Cup winner, recovering fumble for game-winning td; above avg. skier, skilled diver; mem. Ottawa Sports, Canadian Football halls of fame; res. Knowlton, Que.

VAUGHAN, Terry (football); b. 25 Dec 1971, Sumper, S.C.; m. Casandera; c. Tristen, Sydney; Arizona; standout baseball player drafted by NY Yankees but opted for football; sb CFL Calgary '95-98, Edmonton '99-04; ' 3 all-Cdn, 8 West conf., 1 CFLPA all-star; record 8 consec. 1000+yds receiving seasons; CFL record (through '04) 176 scheduled games, 853 receptions, 11,938yds, 64tds; 2 Grey Cup finals, 1 winner; res. Edmonton, Alta.

VAVRA, Greg (football); b. 19 Feb 1961, Red Deer, Alta.; given name: Gregory; m. Jody Jensen; c. Mitchell, Tyler, Jade; UCal, BComm, LLB; self-employed oil/gas consultant, coach; qb HS MVP '79; WIFL leading passer 4yrs, twice player of year; qb'd Calgary Dinosaurs to Vanier Cup '83; Hec Crighton Trophy '83; North American single game passing record 627yds; qb Stampeders '84-85, BC '86-87, Edmonton '88; CFL record: 161 completions in 324 attempts, 1901yds, 10tds, 16 interceptions; jersey #17 ret'd by UCal; Stampeders qb coach '03; Calgary Bantam FB Wall, UCal Sports Hall of Fame; res. Calgary, Alta.

VENTURA, Dawn (curling/softball); b. 23 Apr 1940, Ottawa, Ont.; statistician; catcher sr. softball teams '53-63; mem. 4 Eastern Ont. Sr. title teams, 2 Ottawa Interdepartmental League titles; 3rd 6 OCA divisional mixed title rinks, Ont., ntl titlists '86; '71 OVCA mixed champions, '72 Lady Gilmour Lem Cushing trophy winners, runnerup '73; skipped Ottawa Crystal Pebble grand aggregate title rink '71, 8 Eastern Ont. ladies' championships, 2 Ont. titles; mem. Ottawa RA Curling Club, Rideau CC; 3 times RA curler of year; twice RA female athlete of year; twice Ottawa ACT curling award winner; Ont. achievement award '74; mem. Ottawa, CSRA Sports halls of fame; res. Ottawa, Ont.

VERBEEK, Pat (hockey): b. 24 May 1964, Sarnia, Ont.; m. Dianne; c. Kyle, Stephanie, Kendall, Haley; r/l wing Sudbury (OHL); league MVP '81; chosen by OHL coaches as hardest working player; drafted by New Jersey '82; played NHL with New Jersey '82-89, Hartford '89-95, NYR '95-96, Dallas '96-99, '01-02, Detroit '99-01; 1 Stanley Cup winner; played 2 NHL all-star games; NHL record: 1424 scheduled games, 522g, 541a, 117 playoff games, 26g, 36a; active in Special Olympics, Leukemia Society; res. Avon, CT.

VERBEEK, Tonya (wrestling); b. 14 Aug 1977, Grimsby, Ont.; given name: Tonya Lynn; Brock BR&L, BEd, MEd student; 55 kg; mem. women's ntl team 7yrs; 1st-ever Cdn. Olympic women's wrestling medalist (silver '04); gold '03 Pan-Am Championships., '03 Hans von Zons (Germany), New York Athletic Club tourney, '04 Austrian Ladies

Open, Canada Cup; silver '03 PAG, World Cup; medallist 5 consec. sr ntl championships '99-03; espoir ntl champion '95; #1 woman in weight class in Canada '95, '04; 10yrs on performance, competitive skipping team; 2 Brock athlete of yr, res. Thorold, Ont.

VERCHEVAL, Pierre (football); b. 22 Nov 1964, Quebec City, Que.; c. Samuel; UWO; 2 CIAU all-star; CIAU outstanding lineman '88; Eastern Cdn rep. '88 Shrine Bowl; pro CFL ctr/gd Edmonton '88-92, Toronto '93-96; NFL tryouts New England, Detroit; CFL East, West, Northern all-star; 2 Grey Cup finals, 1 winner; res. Quebec City, Que.

VERGARA, Héctor (soccer/officiating); b. 15 Dec 1966, San Javier, Chile; given name: Héctor Osvaldo; m. Joanne Mucz; c. Natalya, Andres; Manitoba BA, BRS; sales/marketing manager; youth referee level C age 16; FIFA asst. ref. age 26 (ntl ref. '97-03); only official in world to work 6 matches '02 World Cup; 65 intl. matches to Dec '03 including: '97, '99 USA Cup, '98, '02 World Cup qualifying matches, '98 Caribbean Shell Cup, '98 CONCACAF u-20 Worlds qualifier, '95, '99 Canada Cup, '99 CONCACAF Club championships., '00, '02 WC qualifier, '00, '04 Olympic CONCACAF qualifier, '93, '95 u-17 Worlds, '01 u-20 Youth Worlds, '02 Football Confederation Gold Cup, '02 World Cup, '03 CONCACAF Gold Cup Final; MSRA exec.; John Taylor Collegiate volleyball, basketball MVP, athlete of yr; WYSA Recognition Award, '95; CSA Ray Morgan Memorial Award '96; Intl. Achievement Award '02; MSRA Outstanding Contribution Award '97, 10 yr Service, World Cup Recognition, Fox 40 Classic Recognition, Frank Major Award of Merit, FIFA World Cup 3rd/4th place medal '02; Sport Man. Official of '02 award; res. Winnipeg, Man.

VERNON, Mike (hockey); b. 24 Feb 1963, Calgary, Alta.; m. Jane; c. Amelia, Matthew, Dean; goalie (WHL), Oklahoma City, Colorado (CHL), Moncton (AHL), Salt Lake (IHL); drafted by Calgary '81; NHL with Calgary '80-94, '00-02, Detroit '94-97, San Jose '97-99, Florida '00; 2 WHL 1st team all-star, MVP; Hap Emms Memorial Cup top goalie award '83; 5 NHL all-star games; mem. Stanley Cup winners '89, '97; NHL record: 750 scheduled games, 385-273-92, 44,449min, 27sho, 2.98ga avg.138 playoff games, 77-56, 8214min, 6sho; shared William Jennings trophy '96 with Chris Osgoode; Conn Smythe trophy '97; 2 Calgary booster club athlete-of-yr awards; mem. '91 Team Canada World silver medal team; res. Calgary, Alta.

VERNOT, George (swimming); b.27 Feb 1901, Montreal, Que.; d. 22 Nov 1962, Montreal, Que.; McGill BSc; capt. McGill swim team '22-26; high scoring forward McGill water polo team; set school records; 1500m FS silver, 400m FS bronze '20 Olympics; also competed in '24 Olympics; set ntl records in distances from 100yds to 1 mile; ranked among top 3 Cdn male swimmers in half-century poll; mem. McGill Sports Hall of Fame.

VERSFELD, Mark (swimming); 13 Jun 1976, Edmonton, Alta; UBC; mem. Pacific Dolphins; coach Tom Johnson; backstroke specialist; mem. ntl team '94-99; competed '94, '98 CG; 100, 200m gold, 4x100 medley relay bronze '98 CG; set Commonwealth 200m backstroke record 1:59.39; bronze '95, silver, 2 bronze '97 Pan-Pacifics; silver, bronze '98 worlds; gold 100m backstroke '98 summer ntls; relay

bronze '99 PAG; competed '00 Olympics; res. Vancouver, B.C./Fort McMurray, Alta.

VESPAZIANI, Bob (football/administration/coaching); b. 15 Jun 1935, Mt. Vernon, N.Y.; div. June; c. Robert Daniel, Michael, Lori, Joseph, Jennifer; m. Sheila Coul; Springfield (Mass.) BSc, MSc; football consultant/coach; asst. coach Springfield, Bloomfield, N.J. hs 3yrs; East Long Meadow AD/head coach 6yrs; coached Acadia 10yrs; 3 AUAA titles, 2 Atlantic Bowls, 2 Vanier Cup finals; 3 AUAA coach-of-yr awards; varied coaching/admin. roles with CFL Winnipeg '79-84, '92, BC '85, '88-91, Calgary '86-87 (head coach), '94-99, Sask. '94, '00-04 (AGM); 7 Grey Cup finals, 3 winners; mem. Acadia Hall of Fame; res. Calgary, Alta.

VESSELS, Billy (football); b. 22 Mar 1931, Cleveland, Okla; d. 17 Nov 2001, Coral Gables, Fla.; m. Susanne Wilson; c. Jane, Lance, Chase: Oklahoma, BSc; ret'd Mackler Real Estate Dev. Co. exec.; 3 seasons under coach Bud Wilkinson Oklahoma Sooners; all-American rb '50, '52; Heisman Trophy winner '52; college record: 35tds, 2085yds rushing, 21 pass receptions for 391 yds; Sooners record (since broken) 1072yds rushing '52; rushed 100 or more yds single game 7 times, 5 in succession; 1st draft Baltimore Colts '53; opted for Edmonton CFL; initial recipient Schenley outstanding player award '53; joined Colts '56 after sitting out 2 seasons; 1 season with Baltimore, 215yds, 44 carries, 2tds, 11 pass receptions, 16yd avg., 1td; shelved by leg injury; TV football color commentator; avid fisherman; mem. Oklahoma, Sooners Sports halls of fame.

VÉZINA, Georges (hockey); b. 7 Jan 1888, Chicoutimi, Que., d. 26 Mar 1926, Chicoutimi, Que.; nicknamed "Chicoutimi Cucumber"; never missed league or playoff game in 15 NHL seasons; pro Montreal 1910-25; 328 consec. league, 39 playoff games allowing 1267 goals; mem. 5 title teams, 2 Stanley Cup winners; played most of career in era when goalies weren't permitted to drop to knees to muffle shots; trophy in his memory awarded annually to NHL goalie with best goals-against avg.; Chicoutimi arena bears his name; mem. Hockey, Que. Sports halls of fame.

VIDRUK, Kas (builder); b. 6 Oct 1925, Lithuania; d. 21 Oct 1986, Winnipeg, Man.; m. Phyllis; c. Michael, Shirley, Robin, Cheryl; educator; played football in CFL with Winnipeg '42-43, '52-56, Montreal '48-51; officiated CFL '57-74; mem. Man. Amateur Football Officials Assn. '56-76; founding mem. Man. HS Athletic Assn; mem. PAG society facilities board '66-69; chair. Man. Sports Fed '78-81; board mem. SFC '82-85; v.-chair. Man. Sports Hall of Fame '79-85; mem. Man. Sports Hall of Fame.

VIELE, Vincent (jiu jitsu); b. 26 Nov 1938, Niagara Falls, N.Y.; m. Jean Jack; c. Wendy, Cindy, Billy; ironworker; judo brown belt '66-70; 1 year Tae Kwon Do; 4th degree black belt jiu jitsu; 3rd all-Cdn Randori competition '80; chief instructor Niagara College; Ont. distinguished service award '79; res. Niagara Falls, Ont.

VIGARS, Robert (coaching); b. 20 Feb 1944, St. Thomas, Ont.; given name: Robert Joseph; m. Julie Crouch; c. Jessica, Michele; Southern Illinois, BSc, CalState, MA; professor, coach UWO; lettered in HS swimming, gymnastics, basketball, football, t&f; coach UWO men's x-country, t&f team from '68, women's teams from '72; head coach UWO men's, women's gymnastic teams '69-72; head coach London-Western t&f Club from '70; coached 3 CIAU x-country title teams, 3 OUAA x-country title teams, 5 OUAA t&f title teams, 7 ntl individual events t&f champions from '74, 29 OUAA individual events t&f champions from '68; Ont. coach men's decathlon from '74; co-coach ntl team intl decathlon/pentathlon '76; men's, women's Ont. t&f team '76 Olympic trials; Ont. coach women's pentathlon from '77; coach '79, '81 FISU Games; head coach t&f '81 Maccabiah Games; 5 CIAU X-C coach-of-yr awards; outstanding young Londoner award; top level coaching certification; meet dir. 10 gymnastics, 37 x-country, 128 t&f meets '68-80; noted for innovations in t&f programming at Intercollegiate level, particularly indoor meets; res. London, Ont.

VIGER, Andre (t&f); b. 27 Sep 1952, Windsor, Ont.; wheelchair equipment supplier; wheelchair athletics, specialist in long distances; gold 200m, 400m, 800m, 1500m '82 PAG for Disabled; 5 gold ntl championships '83; gold, 2 silver '92 Paralympics; 3 world, 1 PAG records; placed 10th '95 Boston Marathon; Officer Order of Canada '89; mem. Quebec, Terry Fox Sports halls of fame; res. Sherbrooke, Que.

VILAGOS, Penny (synchro swim); b. 17 Apr 1963, Brampton, Ont.; m. Jeff Brown; c. Nicole, Laura; McGill BComm.; marketing mgr.; ntl team '80-85, '90-92; with twin sister Vicky 5 ntl sr., 1 Canada Games, 2 Swiss, 2 Rome, 1 Petro Canada Cup, 1 German, 1 Czechoslovakian, 1 Spanish duet titles; duet silver, team gold '83 PAG; duet silver '92 Olympics; world team gold '82; FINA World Cup team gold '85; world masters gold '89; 1st duet in world to score perfect 10 '80 Swiss Open; fed. govt. world champion award '83, excellence award '84; ret'd '85 then made comeback '90-92; mem. Cdn Aquatic, Olympic Sports halls of fame; res. Beaconsfield, Que.

VILAGOS, Vicky (synchro swim); b. 17 Apr 1963, Brampton, Ont.; m. Alex Staton; c. Allison, Meghan, Claire; McGill BComm.; bilingual motivational speaker; operates own company; mem. Cdn Assn. Professional Speakers; see twin sister Penny for competitive, awards records; mem. Cdn Aquatic, Olympic Sports halls of fame; res. Pte. Claire, Que.

VILLENEUVE, Gilles (motorsport); b. 18 Jan 1952, St. Jean, Que.; d. 8 May 1982, Zolder, Belgium; m. Joanne; c. Melanie, Jacques; racing driver; ntl snowmobile titles '73, '75, world championship '74; Que. Formula Ford title '73; ntl driving title '76-77; US Formula Atlantic title '77; Molson Grand Prix (Trois-Rivieres) beating world class drivers James Hunt, Allan Jones; mem. Marlboro McLaren Formula 1 auto racing team '77; 1st GP victory for Ferrari Montreal '78; other GP victories Kyalami, Long Beach, Watkins Glen '79, Monaco, Spanish '81; in 67 GP starts won 6; runnerup to teammate Jody Scheckter '79 world driving title; fatally injured during qualifying run for Belgian GP when car crashed; shared Que. athlete-of-yr honors with Guy Lafleur '75; Julien Trophy, Lionel Conacher trophy '79; spawned concert, became first patron Cdn Motor Sport Foundation; mem. Cdn Motorsport, Que., Canada's Sports halls of fame.

VILLENEUVE, Jacques (motorsport); b. 9 Apr 1971, St-Jean-sur-Richelieu, Que.; son of late racing great Gilles; Jim Russell racing school Mont-Tremblant Formula Ford 1600 title '86; Spenard-David racing school Shannonville F-2000 title '87; competed Italian Formula 3 circuit '88-91; Japanese Formula 3 circuit '92, 3 victories, 2nd overall; 3rd in first NA event Trois-Rivieres GP; mem. Player's Ltd. IndyCar team '93; won '94 Elkhart Lake 200, '95 Miami IndyCar; won '95 Indianapolis 500, 2nd '94; IndyCar rookie of '94; 1st Cdn winner Indy 500 '95; 3rd Toronto Molson '95; shifted to Formula One circuit with Williams-Renault team '96 placing 2nd initial race then scoring 4 GP race victories in rookie season to place 2nd in top driver race; added Brazilian, Argentinan, Spanish, British, Hungarian, Austrian, Luxembourg GP victories '97 to eclipse father's career GP victory total with 11; 1st Cdn to earn F1 driving championship '97; joined Sauber-Petronas team '04; only driver to win on oval (Indy), permanent road course (Road America), street circuits (Miami, Cleveland); mem. BAR team 4yrs; talented skier; 2 Lou Marsh, 2 Lionel Conacher trophies; mem. Canada's Walk of Fame; res. Monte Carlo, Monaco.

VILLENEUVE, Jacques (motorsport); b. 4 Nov 1955, Chambly, Que.; m. Celine; younger brother of Gilles; Que. snowmobile champion; moved into Formula Ford racing and established strong credentials; rookie of '79 NA Formula Atlantic circuit; NA Formula Atlantic title '81-82; Can-Am series title '83; qualified '84 Indianapolis 500 but accident in practice run kept him from race; world record qualifying for pole position '84 Phoenix IndyCar race; res. St. Cuthbert, Que.

VINCE, Anthony (t&f); b. 30 Jul 1902, Baltimore, Md.; d. circa 1990, Toronto, Ont.; given name: Anthony Joseph; m. Dorothy Margaret Cowan; c. Robert John, Dennis Jordon; UofT, DDS; dentist; sprint specialist; Riverdale HS champion; Broadview YMCA '22 gold medal 100yd dash champion; won '23 ntl YMCA title; gold 100yd dash, silver 200m '23 ntl championships; mem. '24 Olympic team; 3 Ont. 100yd dash gold medals.

VINCENT, Mark (parachuting); b. 12 Aug 1957, Winnipeg, Man.; given name: Mark Kenneth; contractor; m. Carol Whiteman; c. 1 son; 10yrs organized hockey, 3yrs competitive diver, 2yrs baseball; 10yrs competitive water skier, 3yrs snow skier, active gymnast; skydiving from '77; more than 1000 jumps; ntl 8-way, 3rd 4-way '79; ntl 4-way, 8-way '80; 2nd 8-way France '79, 4-way China '80; res. Victoria, B.C.

VINE, Bill (coaching); b. 27 Nov 1910, St. Catharines, Ont., d. 16 Jun 1983, Ottawa, Ont.; m. Winnifred Timmins; c. James, Joseph, William, Douglas; CIMA (Ind. Eng. & Management), IMMS (intl material man. & handling); Atomic Energy Canada; jumping coach Ottawa Uplands Harriers TC from '62; Ont. sr. jumping coach, advisor to Ont. tech. dir. t&f; Ont. official, Grade 5 referee; ntl instructor of officials; referee lj/tj '76 Olympics; officiated 2 Canada Games, provincial, ntl championships, Olympics, AAU meets; mem. jury of appeal Special Olympics '81.

VITARELLI, Dootch (lacrosse/hockey); b. 4 Aug 1921, Peterborough, Ont.; given name: Donato Anthony; m. Betty

McMahon; c. Linda; ret'd salesman; natural athlete starring at rw in hockey, fwd in lacrosse and standout golfer; mem. '49 Legion Ont. Sr. B title hockey team; mem. 3 Ont. Sr. B lacrosse title teams; 3 Mann Cup Sr. A title winners; ret'd as player '53; mem. Peterborough Sports Hall of Fame; res. Peterborough, Ont.

VLOOSWYK, Lisa (golf/trampoline); b. 21 May 1974, Calgary, Alta.; given name: Lisa Ann Lemmens; m. Anton Vlooswyk; UCal BA, BEd; teacher; competed t&f UCal; mem. ntl trampoline team; introduced to golf as teenager and played recreationally early 20's; inspired to play competitively after volunteering for '99 LPGA du Maurier Classic; entered 1st long-drive competition '00; claimed ntl long-drive titles '01-03; capt. Team Canada '02-03 (gold '03) NA championships; competed 3 world championships; 3 Lynx Ridge club titles; longest drive in competition 341yds, 2'5" led to monicker 'Lisa Longball'; writes weekly golf column *Calgary Herald;* internationally-certified tumbling judge; competitive volleyball, softball player; res. Calgary, Alta.

VOGT, Kathy (speed skating); b. 7 Mar 1959, Elkhart, Ind.; m. Gregg; UMan, BPHE, UAlta.; 1 gold, 2 silver, 1 bronze '75 Canada Winter Games; ntl indoor, outdoor jr. champion '75; NA outdoor jr. champion, 3rd NA indoor '75; gold 500m, bronze 1000m, jr. world 500m record '76 world championships; 2nd world indoor championships '76-77; 6th overall, silver 1000m '79 jr. worlds; mem. '76, '80 Olympic, '76-81 world championships teams; Man. jr. athlete of '75; coach '81; res. Edmonton, Alta.

VOLPE, Jon (football); b. 17 Apr 1968, Kincheloe, Mich.; Stanford; business exec.; rb; joined CFL BC '91-93, Las Vegas '94; set CFL rookie record 20 tds '91; CFL record 40 scheduled games, 42tds, 1 2-pt cvt, 511 carries for 2,654yds, 37tds, 100 receptions for 896yds, 6tds; 1 playoff game, 3tds; Jackie Parker, GMC rookie awards; 2 all-Western, 2 all-CFL all-star; 2 CFL rookie records; res. Tucson, Ariz.

VOLPE, Nick (football/administration); b. 23 Feb 1926, Toronto, Ont.; given name: Nicholas Peter; m. Rose Marie Masiello; c. Helen, Donna, Frank, Peter, Steven; UofT, BEd, MEd, BPHE; football administrator; ret'd school superintendent, special education; mem. '48 Yates Cup winner; qb/db/pk Toronto '49-52; led Argos punt returners '49; 53 of 58 convert attempts '50; mem. 2 Grey Cup champions; HS football coach Port Credit 15yrs, 8 TCIAA, 2 all-Toronto titles; coached Lakeshore Bears '55-63, 1 Ont. jr. title; backfield coach Toronto Balmy Beach, '53 ORFU title; backfield coach. scout Argos '53-56; recruited Dick Shatto for Argos; scout Ottawa '56-58; author football text for CAHPER; CFRB radio football broadcasts spotter '65-68; isolation dir. *CTV* football '72-87; Argos player personnel dir. '90-93; Argos dir. college scouting from '94; East York CI athlete of '42, Wm. Burgess gold medal for leadership '44; T award football, basketball; awarded game ball by mates for '50 Grey Cup 13-0 victory in which he kicked 2 field goals and made key tackle of Winnipeg's Lee McPhail on 5yd line to preserve Mud Bowl shutout; res. Mississauga, Ont.

VOSS, Carl (all-around); b. 1 Jan 1907, Chelsea, Mass.; d. 13 Sep 1993, Lake Park, Fla.; given name: Carl Potter;

m. Pearl; Queen's; ret'd hockey official; born of Cdn parents, raised, educated Toronto; mem. '23-24 Queen's Intercollegiate, Grey Cup title team; jr. hockey Kingston, OHA, Eastern Cdn titles, Memorial Cup finalists; 1st player signed to Maple Leafs contract when they purchased St. Pat's club of NHL '27; mem. '32 Buffalo Bisons (IHL) title team; league scoring leader, all-star; Detroit '33, rookie of year, first such NHL award (preceded Calder Trophy); mem. '38 Chicago, Stanley Cup; leading playoff scorer; pres. USHL '49; NHL referee-in-chief '50-65; NHL playing service also took him to NYR, Ottawa, St. Louis, NY Americans, Montreal Maroons; mem. Hockey Hall of Fame.

VOYLES, Carl (football/coaching); b. 11 Aug 1898, McLowd, Okla., d. 11 Jan 1982, Ft. Meyers, Fla.; m. Gertrude M. Hall (d); c. Carl Jr., Robert; m. Dorothy Belknap; Oklahoma State, BSc; coach, realtor; capt. college football team sr. year, basketball team 3yrs; coached HS conf. football, basketball title teams, tied for state wrestling title; coach Southwestern State College 3yrs, guided football team to 22-5-3 record, basketball team to ntl tournament twice; freshman football coach Illinois '25-31, head scout for coach Bob Zuppke; 8yrs asst.-AD, asst. football coach Duke; head coach, AD William and Mary, Southern Conf. title; AD, head coach Auburn '44-47; coach, GM Brooklyn Dodgers (all-American Conf.) '48-49; coach/GM newly-combined Tiger-Cats '50; Grey Cup '53; scout Hamilton '54-80.

WADE, Harry (basketball); b. 12 Mar 1928, Windsor, Ont.; m. Helen Lucas; c. Paul, William; UWO; business exec.; mem. all-Ont. HS basketball champions '47-48; 3 CIAU title teams '49-51; 2yrs football UWO, '49 league champions; mem. ntl sr. basketball champion Tillsonburg Livingstons '51, '52; Olympic team '52; res. Tillsonburg, Ont.

WADSWORTH, Mike (football): b. 4 Jun 1943, Ottawa, Ont.; d. 28 Apr 2004, Rochester, Minn.; m. Bernadette; c. Carolan, Mary, Jane; Notre Dame, BA, Osgoode Hall, LLB, Harvard Business School; ex-AD Notre Dame; son of '36-43 CFL all-star Bunny Wadsworth; attended ND on football scholarship '63-65; dt; CFL Argos '66-70; 1st pres. CFL Players Assn.; practiced law '71-81; *Toronto Star* columnist '72; CFL broadcaster '71-81; v-p. Tyco Laboratories '81-84; v-p. Crownx Inc. '84-89; v-p. Crown Life '87-89; Cdn ambassador to Ireland '89-94; ND Advisory Council for International Activities; lecturer; ND athletic dir. '95-00.

WAGHORNE, Fred (builder/hockey); b. 1866, Tunbridge Wells, Eng.; d. 1956, Toronto, Ont.; over 50yr span officiated more than 2000 hockey, 1500 lacrosse games; earned reputation as innovator; credited with system of dropping puck on faceoffs (previously placed on ice between players sticks), use of whistle to stop play (ringing cow bell previous methiod); noted for unusual no-goal ruling in game in which puck (then two glued together pieces) split on hitting goal post with only half entering net, his argument was a legal size puck did not enter goal; pioneer '11 in what now is Metro Toronto HL; mem. Hockey Hall of Fame.

WAGNER, Barbara (figure skating); b. 5 May 1938, Toronto, Ont.; given name: Barbara Aileen; div. Grogan; c. James David Grogan; m. Michael Hofmann; Ryerson PTI; figure skating coach; with Robert Paul 5 ntl, 4 world, 2 NA, '60 Olympic pairs championships; Lou Marsh Trophy '57; Torch Award Canada's outstanding winter athlete of half-century '76; mem. Cdn, US, World Figure Skating, Cdn Amateur, Canada's Sports halls of fame; res. Valley Home, Calif.

WAGNER, Bill (curling); b. 19 Dec 1919, Wimborne, Alta.; m. Elaine Flynn; c. Darce, Kirk, Wendy, Heather, Douglas; UBC, BSA; civil servant; hockey Nanaimo Clippers '40 Western Canada Int. finalists, '44 Northwest Air Command RCAF champions, Alberta, UBC champions; softball BC sr. titlists '41; skip Ont. seniors champion '75, '77, masters champion '81, '83; ACT trophy Ottawa's outstanding curler '65, ACT curling team trophy '78; res. Ottawa, Ont.

WAGNER, Lauren (squash): b. 6 Jul 1968, Johannesburg, S.A.; accountant/office mgr/coach; South African -19 champion 3yrs; played on provincial A team 7yrs; won provincial -21 title; mem. BC team '96 Cdn championships; mem. '96 Cdn ntl women's team; 1 BC open, 2 closed, 1 Alta open, Pacific Coast open titles; team gold, bronze individual '96 ntl championships; competed '96, '98 worlds; res. Victoria, B.C.

WAGNER, Victor (squash); b. 19 Dec 1958, Ottawa, Ont.; Yale.; men's Que. Criterium title '76; Ont. jr. open champion '76-77; ntl jr. softball title '76-77; mem. first ntl squash racquets men's team; competed Drysdale Cup jr. open tournament London, Eng.,'77; mem. world championships team '77; Man. Open, Ottawa amateur titles '78; NCAA all-American '80; Boodles Open NYC, Yale Invitation titles '80; Intercollegiate all-American, all-Ivy League team '81; mem. Ont. Games jr. gold medal, ntl silver medal field hockey teams '74; mem. Ottawa Ont. Games gold, ntl jr. Olympics bronze teams '75; played field hockey internationally vs Holland '77; twice Little League baseball all-star team mem.; mem. Ont. jr. tennis team; 2 HS tennis trophies; 2 Ottawa ACT squash awards; res. Ottawa, Ont.

WAGNER, Virgil (football); b. 27 Feb 1922, Belleville, Ill.; d. Aug 1997, Belleville, Ill.; given name: Virgil Edwin; m. Mary Jeanette Rothgangel; c. Michael, Martha, Rebecca, Sara; Millikin, BSc US govt. inventory mgr.; all-conf., all-state HS football '38; lettered in football, basketball, baseball at Millikin; all-conf. '40-42, Little all-American '41-42; listed *Who's Who in American Colleges and Universities* '43; football Iowa Seahawks Naval Aircorps service team '43; pro Montreal '46-54; led Big Four scorers '46-49; 4 times all-Big Four, all-Eastern all-star; all-Cdn '46-49; Jeff Russel Memorial Trophy '47; CFL career, Alouettes team record 55tds; mem. Belleville Area, Millikin, Canadian Football halls of fame.

WAINMAN, Tracey (figure skating); b. 27 May 1967, Kirkland Lake, Ont.; div. Jozef Saboucik; coach/dir. York Region Skating Academy; ntl novice title '79, at 14 youngest ntl sr. titlist '81; Skate Canada, St. Ivel titles '81; coached by Doug Leigh; Bobbie Rosenfeld Trophy '81; res. Willowdale, Ont.

WAITE, Gary (squash); b. 9 Sep 1966, Quebec City; pro athlete; British jr. open finalist '84; world jr. hardball champion '85; NA open champion '93; NA open doubles titlist '94; men's, mixed doubles titles '02 worlds; ranked 12 in world, highest ranking ever by Pan-American '93; capt. men's ntl team to highest ever finish world championships '95; 3 gold '95 PAG; Squash Canada delegate for COA from '95; dir. PSA from '95; Viscount Alexander Trophy '86; with Damian Mudge NA open doubles title '03; res. New York, N.Y.

WAITE, Jim (curling/golf); b. 17 Feb 1941, St. Thomas, Ont.; given name: James Frederick; m. Sue Richardson; c. Chris, David; McMaster, UWO, BA, MEd; ret'd PS principal; 1st of 14 Ont. title bids as lead '66; won '68; 3 OCA Challenge Round titles; with Stan Curtis skipping other rink won '70 Gov.-Gen.'s double rink title; with Don Gilbert other skip Ont. Silver Tankard '73, '75; Curl Canada ntl course conductor; gen. chair. '79 Consols; head umpire '81 Air Canada Silver Broom; Worlds head official '89, '91, '92; ntl coach Canada's Worlds teams '93-97; Olympic coach '98; 5 St. Thomas G&CC golf titles; 2 St. Thomas

Early Bird golf titles; '73 father and 3 sons championship; golf coach UWO; res. St. Thomas, Ont.

WALA, George (t&f); b. 5 May 1904, Kuivniemi, Finland; d. 18 Oct 1973, Sudbury, Ont.; given name: Yrjo Vaataja (changed to George Rudolph Wala); m. Fanny Ylitalo; c. Doris; carpenter, miner, lumberjack; shot, discus, javelin specialist; javelin gold, shot bronze '32 ntls; set records in shot, discus, javelin '33 ntl championships, outstanding athlete of meet award; competitor/trainer '34 BEG; silver, bronze '36 ntls; in later years became standout pistol marksman; mem. NWO Sports Hall of Fame.

WALBY, Chris (football): b. 23 Oct 1956, Winnipeg, Man.; given name: Christopher Martin; div.; c. Brandon, Clayton, Christien, Matthew; Dickinson State BSc; pharmaceutical rep. Whitehall-Robins Inc.; *CBC-TV* football analyst; jr. A hockey West Kildonan; tackle 2yrs Winnipeg jr. Rods; drafted by Montreal '81, Winnipeg from '81-96; CFL record: 254 scheduled games, 1 td, 15 tackles, 21 playoff games; 4 Western, 7 Eastern, 9 CFL all-star; 4 Leo Dandurand trophies; 2 CFL outstanding-offensive-lineman awards, 2 runnerup; 3 top-offensive-lineman awards; 5 Grey Cup finals, 3 winners; ret'd '97 to become *CBC-TV* football analyst; produced Walby's Pro Tips for TV; mem. Winnipeg, Cdn Football halls of fame; res. Winnipeg, Man.

WALCHUK, Don (curling): b. 3 Jun 1963, Melville, Sask; stockbroker; m. Shelley; c. Michelle, Chad; began curling age 10; skipped '80 Sask. HS bronze medal rink, '81 Sask. jr men's title rink; competed 6 Briers, 3 winners; all-star lead for Pat Ryan '85 Brier runnerup; all-star 2nd with Ryan '87-89 Briers; 3rd Kevin Martin '96, '97, '00 Briers; all-star 3rd '96; runnerup '87 Olympic Curling trials; competed '02 Olympics; 2 Alta Achievement awards; all-star 2nd '89 world title rink; Dick Ellis team award '89; mem. Cdn Curling Hall of Fame; res. Sherwood Park, Alta.

WALCHUK, Michael (boxing): b. 24 Dec 1978, Kitchener, Ont.; given name: Michael Joseph Vincent; c. Stephania, Athena, Adonis; caregiver; began boxing '96; silver '01, gold '02, '03 ntls; bronze '02 CG; 52-8 as amateur; turned pro '03; 2-0 to Jan. '04; res. Regina, Sask.

WALDEN, Margaret (table tennis): b. 12 Dec 1913, West Nissouri, Ont; d. 12 Feb 2003, Toronto, Ont.; given name: Margaret Isobel Downham; m. Earl Walden; Greg Business Coll.; ret'd Dupont Canada; began playing '37; Ont. Women's singles champ '39-41; served varied roles in Ont. Table Tennis Assn. '47-84; chief liaison with CNE '65-95; CTTA secty/treas. '52-71; ntl tournament chair '52-92; ntl historian from '75; mem. Intl TT standing orders comm. '73-91; 9 times Cdn delegate ITTF Congress; mem. Management comm. Commonwealth TTF '71-91; mgr. Cdn team '71 world championship; led Cdn team on first visit to China in what became known as ping pong diplomacy; hon. life mem. CTTA; Sports Fed. Of Canada Donald King award; 2 Confederation of Can. Medals; ITTF gold merit award for contribution to table tennis; mem. Swaythling Club Intl.; Michigan TTA award; 3 OTTA, 3 CTTA, 2 Air Canada, meit awards.

WALDO, Carolyn (synchro swim): b. 11 Dec 1964, Montreal, Que.; given name: Carolyn Jane; m. Tom Baltzer; c. Brittany, Corey; UCal; TV sports reporter; team gold, figures silver '83 PAG; team gold, figures bronze '83 America Cup; team gold, figures bronze '82 world championships; team gold '81 Pan-Pacific Games; solo silver '84 Olympics; fed. govt. world champion award '83, excellence award '84; flag-bearer, single, duet gold '88 Olympics; Lou Marsh Trophy '88; 2 Bobbie Rosenfeld, 4 Velma Springstead, 2 Dick Ellis team awards; Officer Order of Canada '88; mem. Cdn Amateur, Alta, Que, Intl Swimming, Cdn Aquatic, Canada's Sports halls of fame; res. Kanata, Ont.

WALKER, Bruce (football): b. 16 Apr 1955, Windsor, Ont.; given name: Bruce Michael; div.; c. Cailey; N. Dakota U, Windsor BEd; v-p sales, marketing Ottawa Athletic Club; excelled at football, baseball, basketball, t&f; qb'd Assumption HS to 2 WSSA titles, 2 all-city awards; all-city basketball award; hj, lj, hurdles, sprints standout, competed 3 OFSAA championships, 400m hurdles bronze '74, OUAA lj bronze; 2 MicMac jr. baseball MVP awards, Ont. jr. tourney MVP shortstop, mem. South Windsor Cdn championships team; played in Essex County sr, league; rookie of '76 award, won batting, rbi titles, Cdn championship bronze; declined invitation to ntl team to pursue football career; OUAA Yates Cup finalist; MVP, offensive player '78, '79, best all-around athlete award; all-Cdn wr, OUAA all-star; team capt. Can-Am Bowl '79; CFL Ottawa Rough Riders '79-84, 3000 career yds, 4tds; 1 Grey Cup final; Tom Pate award '83; Ronald McDonald House player of '84 award; active in charity work; hon. chair. Ronald McDonald House Do it for Dad race dir; mem. Windsor-Essex Sports Hall of Fame; res. Orleans, Ont.

WALKER, Elisabeth (swimming): b. 5 Feb 1977, Saskatoon, Sask.; Bruck; as part of physiotherapy began swimming age 1, competing age 13; world 50m butterfly, 100m backstroke record holder; competed '92, '96, '00 Paralympics; 3 gold, 2 WR '00 Paralympics; gold 100 FS '93 Cdn Foresters ntl championships; 5 gold '01 Argentina Cideli competition; mem. '94 CG team; mem. Brock Sports Hall of Fame; res. Toronto, Ont.

WALKER, Gord (administration): b. 17 Jul 1915, Kincardine, Ont.; d. 9 Jul 1988, Toronto, Ont.; given name: Gordon Sinclair; m. Victoria Burgess; c. Gordon Jr., Barry, Terry, Shirley; ret'd; sports writer *Globe* '35-42, *Toronto Star* '42-47, excluding WW2 navy stint, *Globe & Mail* '47-49, '50-73; business mgr. Toronto Maple Leafs baseball club '49; CFL information dir. '73-82; instrumental in organizing Ont. Sportswriters, Sportscasters Assn. '48, initial v-p., later pres., secty-treas.; pres. Intl Baseball League Writers' Assn. '56; prime organizer, 1st pres. Football Reporters of Canada '57; 10yrs FRC secty-treas.; authored 1st Big Four statistical, record manual '55; instrumental in establishing practice of including goal number following scorer's name in NHL summaries; brother Hal sports editor *Toronto Telegram, Calgary Herald*; mem. Canadian Football Reporters Hall of Fame.

WALKER, Jack (hockey): b. 28 Nov 1888, Silver Mountain, Ont., d. 16 Feb 1950, Seattle, Wash.; given name: John Phillip; from '06 mem. 4 consecutive Port Arthur city title teams; mem. Toronto Arenas, Seattle, Victoria Cougars Stanley Cup winners; mem. Moncton, Toronto

Arenas, Seattle, Victoria, Detroit, Edmonton teams '12-30; player-mgr. Hollywood Stars '31-32; ret'd to manage, coach, referee in PCL; originator of hook check; noted for ability to teach young players; 2 PCL, NHL MVP awards; mem. Hockey Hall of Fame.

WALKER, Larry (baseball): b. 1 Dec 1966, Maple Ridge, B.C.; given name: Larry Kenneth Robert; div. Christa Vandenbrink; c. Brittany Marie; m. Angela; of; played goal in minor hockey; mem. ntl jr. baseball team; pro Montreal organization '84; minor league stops Utica, Burlington, West Palm Beach, Jacksonville, Indianapolis, Salem, Colorado Springs; promoted to Expos '87-94, Colorado '95-04, St. Louis '04; ML record (through '04): 1888 scheduled games, 6592ab, 1289r, 2069h, 451db, 61tr, 368hr, 1259rbi, 228sb, .314ba; Expos player of '92; 7 Gold Glove awards; Silver Bat '92; 1st all-star selection '92, '97, '99; *AP, Sporting News* post-season all-star '92; runnerup *CP* male athlete of '92, '97; Lou Marsh, Conacher trophies '98; 9 Tip O'Neill awards; runnerup '97 NL batting race with .366, .720 slugging avg, 49hrs, 130rbi; 1st Cdn named NL MVP '97; became 1st Cdn in modern baseball annals to win NL batting title with .363 '98, repeat '99 with .379, '01 with .350; best Cdn position player in history; combines power with solid defence to rank among game's best rf; youth baseball fields in Maple Ridge, Denver, Ft. Collins named in his honor; mem. Ridge Meadows Hall of Fame; res. Aurora, Colo.

WALKER, Larry (harness racing): b. 5 Apr 1947, Owen Sound, Ont.; regarded by peers as one of the most proficient handlers of trotters; earned that reputation starting with Erin's Jet in '82 Roosevelt International trot; other square gaiters who have enhanced that reputation are Ambro Ermine, Shipps Dream, Armbro Flori, Ashley Jane, Mark's Marathon, Going Smartly and Veras Image; no slouch training pacers either, he guided Witsend Gypsy to Canadian Pacing Derby title '86; through '97 2165 victories with purses seeking $18M; winner of 23 major stakes races; res. Puslinch, Ont.

WALKER, Louise (t&f): b. 21 Mar 1951, Toronto, Ont.; given name: Marilyn Louise Hanna; m. James Douglas Walker; c. Kathryn, Bradley; UofT, BSc, MD, CCFP, dip, Sport Medicine; physician specializing in sports medicine; hj specialist; ntl jr. title '70; ntl sr. titles '73, '75; silver '74 CG, '75 PAG; ntl record 1:87m '75; mem. '72, '76 Olympic teams; finalist '76; switched to rowing '84 won 3 Head of Rideau Masters events; 1st female pres. Cdn Academy of Sport Medicine; v.-chair. Cdn Centre for Ethics in Sport from '03; mem. UofT Sports Hall of Fame; res. Nepean, Ont.

WALKER, Peahead (football/coaching): b. 1899, Birmingham, Ala., d. 16 Jul 1970, Charlotte, N.C.; given name: Douglas Clyde; m. Flonnie; c. Gwen; football exec.; head coach '37-50 Wake Forest compiling 79-47 w-l record; asst. to Herman Hickman Yale 2 seasons; head coach Montreal '52-59, 3 consecutive Grey Cup finals losing each time to Pop Ivy's Eskimos; NY Giants (NFL) scout.

WALKER, Skip (football): b. 11 Sep 1954, Houston, Tex.; given name: Alvin; m. Lisa; Texas A&M; pro rb Montreal '80-81, Ottawa '82-84; twice led CFL ground gainers; Ottawa single-season rushing record 1431yds '83; twice CFL all-star, Carlsberg player of year; Ottawa team MVP '83, *CBC-TV* coaches all-star team '83; brother Cornelius mem. '78 Ottawa club; CFL record '84: 648 carries, 3574yds, 114 receptions, 1625yds, 49 kickoff returns, 1118yds, 41tds; res. Austin, Tex.

WALL, Dave (harness racing): b. 9 Nov 1946, Kincardine, Ont.; in hockey he might be considered a "grinder", a player whose work ethic translates into success; through '03 had drove 6095 winners with purses exceeding $50M; string of 26 consecutive years winning 100+ races and 20 straight years topping $1M purses mark; pacers Okdies Fame, Odds Against and trotters Armbro Luxury and Goodtimes among his best horses; 1 NA Cup, 1 Canadian Pacing Derby, 1 Maple Leaf Trot; 2 Robert Stewart classic, 3 Frank Ryan trot, 3 Simcoe Stakes titles; seriously injured in London track accident '02; nickname "Mr. Ont. Sires Stakes"; mem. Western Fair Raceway Wall of Fame; res. Komoka, Ont.

WALL, Gwen (t&f): b. 16 Jan 1963, Saskatoon, Sask.; m. Brian Ridout; c. Paige, Jay; UofSask, BEd; HS teacher; hurdles specialist; 2 ntl 400m hurdles titles; silver 4x400m relay, bronze 400m hurdles '83 PAG; bronze 400m hurdles '83 FISU Games; mem. '82, '86 CG teams; broke ntl 400m record 13 times '83; 2 ntl jr., sr. records; ret'd '86; mem. UofSask. Wall, Saskatoon Sports Hall of Fame; res. Calgary, Alta.

WALL, Nick (horse racing): b. 18 Dec 1906, Lower Gully, Kelligrews, Conception Bay, Ireland; d. 17 Mar 1983, Bellerose, N.Y.; emigrated to Cape Breton age 9; raised Glace Bay, Montreal; apprentice jockey Montreal; '26-57 rode 11,164 mounts, 1419 1sts, 1305 2nds, 1352 3rds; leading US jockey '38 with purses exceeding $3.5 million; rode in all major US races including Kentucky Derby, Preakness, Belmont Stakes; riding Stagehand '38 Santa Anita Handicap defeated famed Seabiscuit in photo-finish; double winner world's richest stakes race by riding Bay View through sea of mud to defeat Mouland '40; mem. Nfld, Canada's Sports halls of fame.

WALLACE, Ben (harness racing): 29 Jan 1949, Kitchener, Ont.; given name: Benjamin; worked for Bill Wellwood before operating highly successful Ont. stable for several years with little recognition outside of province; status changed '99 when his pacing colt Blissful Hall won Cdn horse-of-yr, Dan Patch pacer-of- yr awards; won harness racing's triple crown (Cane Pace, Little Brown Jug, Messenger Stakes), O'Brien trainer-of-yr award; also trained Camotion; res. Milton, Ont.

WALLACE, Heather (squash): b. 4 Dec 1962, Kitwe, Zambia; Bedford (Eng.) Coll., BSc; squash pro Goodlife Fitness Club; began playing squash age 16; Rhodesian, South African titles; 12 ntl titles, tying Cdn record for consec. ntl title wins in any sport with 12 '97 (knee injury kept her from '98 title play); undefeated by any Cdn woman '87-98; 6 Western Cdn, 5 Pacific Coast Open, 5 Que. Open, 4 Ont. Open, 4 Pacific Rim Open, 1 BC Open titles; '93 Japan, San Francisco Open titles, '95 US Rolex Open, 3 gold '95 PAG; mem. '98 CG team; frequently competed vs. men in tournament play and beat them; mem. ntl team 3 world championships; with Jamie Crombie world doubles bronze '97; ret'd from international stage '98; coach jr. women's ntl team '91-93; level 4 NCCP coach; mem. Ottawa Sports Hall of Fame; res. Ottawa, Ont.

WALLACH, Tim (baseball); b. 14 Sep 1957, Huntington Park, Calif.; given name: Timothy Charles; m; c. 3; Cal State Fullerton; baseball mgr.; 3b; Montreal '80-92, LA Dodgers '93-96, Anaheim '96; asst. coach Cal State Fullerton; ML record: 17yrs, 2212 scheduled games, 8099ab, 908r, 2085h, 432db, 36tr, 260hr, 1125bi, 649bb, 1307k, 51sb, .257ba; 5 all-star, 3 gold gloves; mgr. Rancho Cucamonga (Angels); res. Yorba Linda, Calif.

WALLIN, Terry (softball); b. 19 Feb 1961, Moose Jaw, Sask.; m. Patsy Leah; c. Harrison David Michael; Air Canada station services; mem. Legion 141 Winnipeg ntl jr. baseball champions '81; played fastball Portage Diamonds, Remple Bros, Toronto Gators, Decatur Pride; mem. ntl developmental team '92, ntl team from '94; capt. Rempel Bros '94 ntl title team; PAG gold '95; all-Canadian 2nd baseman '91-92; res. Saskatoon, Sask.

WALLING, Brian (football); b. 16 Sep 1963, Toronto, Ont.; Acadia; rb; CFL Toronto '87, Edmonton '88-95, Saskatchewan '89, Hamilton '96; CFL record: 122 games, 213 carries for 1059yds, 2tds, 32 pass receptions for 219yds, 4tds; 13 playoff games, 3tds, 3 Grey Cup finals, 2 winners; res. Toronto, Ont.

WALLINGFORD, Ron (t&f); b. 13 Sep 1933, Ottawa, Ont.; given name: Ronald Roy; m. Heather Jane Magwood; c. Randy Roy, Anthony Alexander, Roxanne Rae, Cassandra Carmen, Darcy Dale; Michigan, BSc, McMaster, BPhE, Buffalo, MEd, EdD; ret'd dir. PE Laurentian; distance runner, steeplechase specialist; ntl jr. 3-mile record '52, indoor mile, 3000m, steeplechase, 5000m, marathon records; mem. ntl record medley relay; 3rd '64 Boston marathon, 9th '71; mem. '66 CG, '71 PAG teams; 2nd world masters marathon '74; chairman Ont. Coaches Assn. '71-73; marathon race mgr. '76 Olympics; dir. OTFA '71-73; former tech. co-ordinator CTFA; ntl t&f coach '65, '77, '79 FISU Games; res. Sudbury, Ont.

WALLIS, Kevin (harness racing); b. 18 Oct 1956, London, Ont.; enjoyed relative success in Canada before shifting to Hazel Park in Detroit and Pompano Beach in Florida where he is ranked among best catch drivers since '81; leading Hazel Park driver '94-95; career high season '96 posting 651 victories; also conditions solid stable; through '03, 21 consec. 100+ win seasons, earning 7146 victories with purses exceeding $30M; res. Deerfield Beach, Fla./Maidstone, Ont.

WALLS, Earl (boxing); b. 19 Feb 1928, Puce, Ont.; d. 13 Dec 1996, Toronto, Ont; given name: Earl Sylvestre; m. June Palmer; c. Richard, Michael; Cdn heavyweight champion '52-55; Pacific Northwest title; ranked #1 in BE, #5 in World; Ont. Amateur title; posted victories over champions of Scotland, Austria, Belgium; pro record: 32 KOs, 17 in 1st round; ret'd age 27 while still ntl champion; active in humanitarian affairs working on varied charitable projects; initiated project of Walls family working with Toronto police hate crimes division; mem. Essex/Windsor, Etobicoke Sports, Cdn. Boxing, Intl African/American Sports halls of fame.

WALLS, Ken (builder); b. 21 Apr 1907, Elmvale, Ont.; d. 4 Nov 1984, Barrie, Ont.; given name: William Kenneth; Barrie Business Coll., UofT (Victoria Coll.), BA; newspaper publisher; versatile athlete; mem. varied baseball teams, Ont. finalists '35; batted .429 with North Simcoe title team; played intermediate lacrosse '31-33; mem. Barrie Colts hockey team '26-27; played hockey with Victoria Coll., Barrie intermediates; accomplished golfer; with Fred Anderton won '39 Georgian Bay district men's badminton doubles; established *Barrie Examiner* sports desk and played key role in boosting sport profile in region; mem. N. Simcoe baseball league exec. '30-36; publicity chair. Grey-Simcoe baseball league '47; mem. Barrie intermediate hockey club finance comm.; v-p. Barrie Town HL; pres. Barrie Garrison badminton club '47; pres. Georgian Bay District badminton assn.; club capt. Barrie Country Club; mem. Barrie Arena Commission; mem. Barrie Sports Hall of Fame.

WALLS, Mickey (horse racing); b. 1 Jun 1974, Vancouver, B.C.; began race-riding at 16 in Vancouver; after dominating jockey standings at Exhibition (now Hastings) Park moved East '90; although OJC rules prohibit licensing before age 18, his BC license was honored and he went on to win Sovereign apprentice jockey award '90; repeated award victory '91 posting 230 wins and claiming NA Eclipse apprentice jockey award; broken leg cost him much of '92 season; moved to Chicago/Oaklawn Park '94-95 before returning to OJC circuit '96; won two-thirds of Cdn thoroughbred racing's Triple Crown (Prince of Wales, Breeder's Stakes) '96; Sovereign top jockey award '91; outstanding performance Breeders' Cup XIII at Woodbine '96; rode Woodcarver to '99 Queen's Plate; did some racing in Dubai; ret'd as competitive jockey '03; res. Toronto, Ont.

WALSH, Billy Jr. (curling); b. 8 Oct 1948, Winnipeg, Man.; given name: William Joseph; div. Tannys Aspevig; c. Casey, Kiley, Steven; UMan; chartered accountant; skipped Fort Rouge CC Man. bonspiel grand aggregate winner '74; skipped Red Anderson Memorial Trophy winning Ottawa Navy rink '83; finalist '83 Ont. Tankard; skipped Ottawa Rideau rink to third place '93 *TSN* Skins Game; Shorty Jenkins Sportsmanship award '97; ex-wife Tanys 3 time Man. ladies golf champion; baseball scout for LA Dodgers; active on executive Ottawa Nationals minor baseball; Camelot Golf Club championship; res. Ottawa, Ont.

WALSH, Billy Sr. (curling); b. 20 Jan 1917, Haileybury, Ont., d. 7 Oct 1971, Winnipeg, Man.; given name: William James; m. Madeline Mary Metcalfe; c. William Joseph; provincial auditor; skipped Fort Rouge CC to '52 Man. Consols, Brier titles, 10-0 record; unprecedented 17 consecutive Brier playdown victories; won '56 Brier beating Ont. skipped by Alf Phillips Sr. in extra-end playoff; mem. Man., Cdn Curling halls of fame.

WALSH, Brenda (t&f); b. 31 Dec 1952, Edmonton, Alta.; given name: Brenda Constance; UAlta, BPhE; teacher; ntl jr. 400m title '70; ntl indoor jr. 400m record 54.9 '72; world indoor 300m 38.8 '73; ntl open indoor 400m 54.1 '73; mem. '71 PAG, '73 FISU, '74 CG (bronze 4x400m relay) teams; Alta. open record 400m hurdles 59.9 '79; Bakewell Memorial Trophy (UAlta outstanding female athlete), Edmonton athlete of '73; res. Edmonton, Alta.

WALSH, Marty (hockey); b. 1883, Kingston, Ont., d. 1915, Gravenhurst, Ont.; given name: Martin; Queen's, BA; mem.

Queen's OHA team which unsuccessfully challenged Ottawa Silver Seven for '06 Stanley Cup; Ottawa sought his services as replacement for ctr Frank McGee but he elected to go to intl pro league where he broke his leg; with Ottawa '08-12, scored 135 goals 59 games, 26 goals 8 playoff games; mem. 2 Stanley Cup winners; 3 NHA scoring titles; 10 goals 1 game vs Port Arthur '11, 7 vs Montreal '08, 6 vs Galt '10, Renfrew '11, 5 vs Wanderers '08, Shamrocks '10; mem. Hockey Hall of Fame.

WALSH, Tarp (football); b. 21 Sep 1921, Sydney, N.S.; d. 25 Jun 2002, Hamilton, Ont.; given name: Gerald; m. Bernadette Layden; c. Michael, Patricia, Karen, Maureen; St. FX, BSc, McGill, BEng; electrical engineer, ret'd production supervisor Stelco; Jr. hockey Sydney; mem. St. FX Maritime English rugby champions; Maritime heavyweight boxing titlist; end/fb Hamilton Tigers '46-48; St. FX Larkin Trophy; mem. St. FX, NS Sports halls of fame.

WALTER, Ryan (hockey); b. 23 Apr 1958, New Westminster, B.C.; given name: Ryan William; c. 3; broadcaster, motivational speaker; ctr Langley, Kamloops, Seattle, Team Canada; NHL Washington (capt.) '78-82, Montreal '82-91, Vancouver '91-93; NHL totals: 1003 scheduled games, 264g, 382a, 113 playoff games, 16g, 35a; 1 Stanley Cup winner; WCJHL all-star; capt. Team Canada world jrs.; 1 NHL all-star; NHL Bud Man of '92; Vancouver Canucks 25th anniversary ambassador; v-p NHLPA; active Athletes in Action fund-raiser; pres. internet hockey site; mem. BC Hockey Hall of Fame; res. Vancouver, B.C.

WALTERS, Angus (sailing); b. 1882, Lunenburg, N.S., d. 12 Aug 1968, Lunenburg, N.S.; sailor, dairy farmer; from '21-42 managing-owner schooner Bluenose in which he won 5 international races; took Bluenose to Chicago '33 to represent Canada at Century of Progress exhibition; sailed to Eng. '37 to compete in Silver Jubilee of King George V and Queen Mary; mem. NS, Canada's Sports halls of fame.

WALTERS, Dale (boxing); b. 27 Sep 1963, Port Alice, B.C.; m. Kathy Kovacs; c. Trevor; owns/operates Ringside Fitness; established radio/TV boxing commentator; actor; bantamweight; BC Emerald, Silver Gloves titles '73-79; BC jr. Golden Gloves titles '77-79; BC sr. Golden Gloves titles '80-82; ntl bantamweight titles 81-84; mem. '82 Worlds, CG, '83 PAG teams; bantamweight bronze '84 Olympics; Stockholm Open gold '84, outstanding boxer award; brief pro career 7-1 before broken hand suffered as amateur led to retirement; played role of Robert Ritter in 26 episode *CBC-TV* series *Ritter's Cove*; appeared in 6 segments Huckleberry Finn TV series; father Len mem. '50 CG, '52 Olympic Games, Cdn athlete of '51; mem. Cdn Boxing Hall of Fame; res. Vancouver, B.C.

WALTERS, Lisa (golf); b. 9 Jan 1960, Prince Rupert, B.C.; given name: Lisa Evelyn Young; m. Mike Walters; UVic, Florida State, BSc; mem. BC jr. team '76-77; ntl jr. team '77-78; BC jr. title '77; BC Ladies titles '79-81; mem. Cdn Ladies' team British Amateur '81; mem. FSU golf team '78-82; Lady Gator tournament title '80; 1st ranked US college golf '80-81 season; 3rd overall '81 AIWA ntl tournament; led FSU team to '81 AIWA title; all-American, regional SE US team '81; FSU team MVP '80-81; joined pro circuit '83; 2 career holes-in-one; career low 65; LPGA Itoki Hawaiian

Open '92-93; LPGA Oldsmobile Classic '98 with record 23-under par; res. Tampa, Fla.

WALTERS, Rick (football); b. 19 Jul 1971, Mandeville, Jamaica; m. Jana; SFU; teacher; receiver; led SFU rushers 4yrs amassing 3149yds, 27tds; CFL Sask. '94-98, Edmonton '99-03, Calgary '04; CFL record (through '04) 221 receptions, 2629yds, 44 carries, 197yds, 11 career tds; 3 Grey Cup finals, 1 winner; Tom Pate Memorial award '01; volunteer basketball coach McNally HS Edmonton; active in Eskimos Stay in School program; Edmonton Community Service award '01; res. Edmonton, Alta.

WALTON, Brian (cycling); b. 18 Dec 1965, Ottawa, Ont.; Snow Valley coach/dir.; road-racing specialist; 10 ntl championships; rode for 7-11 amateur team before turning pro '89. 2 gold, 1 bronze '95, gold '99 PAG, bronze '94 CG silver '96 Olympic Games; Cdn Individual Pursuit record '94. 2 Canadian Tire overall titles; mem. Team Saturn '93-00; turned in strong performances on European circuit; competed '87, '95, '99 PAG, '88, '96, '00 Olympic, '94 CG; launched Walton's Wheels; mem. Cdn Cycling Hall of Fame; res. North Delta, B.C.

WALTON, Dorothy (badminton); b. 7 Aug 1909, Swift Current, Sask., d. 16 Oct 1981, Toronto, Ont.; given name: Dorothy Louise McKenzie; m. W.R. Walton Jr.; c. 1 son; UofSask, BA, MA; Sask., Western Canada tennis titles; ntl badminton singles titles '36, '38, '40, ladies' doubles '40; world badminton titles '39-47; Bobbie Rosenfeld award '40; 1 of 6 outstanding female athletes of half century '50 CP poll; mem. Order of Canada, Sask., Cdn Amateur, Canada's Sports halls of fame.

WALTON, Mike (hockey); b. 3 Jan 1945, Kirkland Lake, Ont.; given name: Michael Robert; m. Candy Hoult; nicknamed "Shaky"; real estate broker, bar owner; mem. Toronto Marlboro Memorial Cup winners; pro rookie of year Tulsa (CPHL) '65, Rochester (AHL) '66; Maple Leafs '66-71, Bruins '70-73, Minnesota Fighting Saints (WHA) '73-75, Canucks '75-78, St. Louis, Boston, Chicago '78-79; 1 Stanley Cup; WHA scoring title '74; 2nd team ctr WHA all-stars' mem. '74 WHA Team Canada; pro record (NHL, WHA): 799 scheduled games, 337g, 392a, 70 playoff games, 34g, 25a; res. Toronto, Ont.

WAPLES, Keith (harness racing); b. 8 Dec 1923, Victoria Harbour, Ont.; m. Eileen Devitt; c. Barbara, Donna, Karen, Gordon; drove Mighty Dudley to Canada's 1st sub 2:00 mile clocking 1:59.3 on Ωmile Richelieu Park track '59; won '62 Roosevelt International trot with Tie Silk; record 246 wins on Canadian tracks '67; drove Strike Out at Blue Bonnets '72 for 1st $100,000 race win in Canada (standardbred or thoroughbred); with Strike Out won '72 Little Brown Jug, Adios Pace, Prix d'/té, Tattersalls Pace; top Canadian dash winner '67-68; career win record exceeds 3000, purses exceed $5 million; more than 30 sub 2:00 minute miles; active in operation Orangeville (Ont.), Cloverdale (BC) harness tracks; mem. Canada's Sports, Canadian Horse Racing halls of fame; res. Durham, Ont.

WAPLES, Randy (harness racing); b. 31 Jul 1965, Orillia, Ont.; given name: Randall; following footsteps of famed father Ron he began driving '84 but didn't emerge as force until '96 when he posted 151 wins; had season high 550 victories '01; 2 O'Brien driver-of-yr awards; through '03 3609 wins, $46+M in purses; 49 major stakes victories including 1 Cdn Pacing Derby, 1 Breeders Crown; res. Milton, Ont.

WAPLES, Ron (harness racing); b. 21 Jul 1944, Toronto, Ont.; m. Josephine; c. Ronnie, Randy; cousin of Keith; 5 Canadian-horseman-of-yr awards; NA dash champion '79; through '03 6818 victories, purses exceeding $72M; 1st to surpass $1 million in purses racing almost exclusively on Canadian tracks '78; drove Ralph Hanover, pacing triple crown winner, to fastest mile Messenger Stakes history 1:57 Jun '83; 8 Breeders Crown triumphs; drove No Sex Please to 2 world records; among other noteworthy horses Dream Maker, Armbro Dallas, Super Flora, Presidential Ball, Park Avenue Joe, Village Jiffy; 193 major stakes victories, including Hambletonian, 2 Little Brown Jugs, 1 Cane Pace, 1 Messenger, 1 NA Cup, 1 Cdn Pacing Derby, 4 Maple Leaf Trots; mem. Cdn Horse Racing, Harness Racing's Living halls of fame; res. Puslinch, Ont.

WARD, Clint (water skiing); b. 11 Jun 1932, Saskatoon, Sask.; div.; c. Rande, Kim, Clint Jr.; UofSask; ret'd capt. Air Canada; ntl age-group titles '61-74; coach-mgr. ntl team '65-71; organizing chair. 10th world championships '67; pres. CWSA '68-70; pres. Group 1 World Water-Ski Union '71-75; Group 1 secty.-gen. '76-80; exec. v-p. Sports Fed. of Canada '73-74; mem. board of dir. National Sports Administration Centre '74-76; COA administration staff mem. '76 Winter Olympics team; comm. chair World Water Ski championships '77-79; pres. Water Ski Canada '87-91; *CBC* water-ski commentator; with George Athans Jr. authored *Water Skiing*; pres. OWSA '77-79; Air Canada sport merit award '74, finalist '79; Ont. special achievement award '79; mem. '08 Toronto Olympic bid board; chair wakeboard, waterski Hall of Fame; mem. Sask. Sports Hall of Fame; res. Toronto, Ont.

WARD, Pete (baseball); b. 26 Jul 1939, Montreal, Que.; given name: Peter Thomas; Lewis & Clark Coll., Portland, BSc; travel agency operator; infielder; son of Jimmy Ward, former NHL standout with Montreal Maroons; a power-hitter, he played in minors with Vancouver (PCL), Stockton (Class C), Fox Cities (3-I), Little Rock, Ardmore, Rochester (IL), led IL in runs (114), doubles (34) while batting .328 with 22hr; made ML debut with Baltimore '62 as outfielder; dealt to Chicago White Sox '63; *Sporting News* AL rookie of yr '63; injuries suffered in car accident plagued balance of career; dealt to NY Yankees '69-70; ret'd as player '70 but remained with Yankees organization as coach Rochester, mgr. Fort Lauderdale, West Haven, winning pennants '75-76; coach Atlanta '78; ML record: 973 scheduled games over 9 seasons, 3060ab, 345r, 776h, 136d, 17t, 98hr, 427rbi, .254ba; mem. Cdn Baseball Hall of Fame; res. Portland, Ore.

WARD, Peter (swimming): b. 18 Jul 1963, North York, Ont.; given name: Peter Francis; m. Cheryl McArton; c. Rebecca, Rachel; Arkansas, BA; head coach George Mason; butterfly specialist; ntl team '79-88; 3 ntl 200 fly titles; Cdn record 2:00.78 for 200m fly '81; competed '84 Olympic, '87 FISU Games; silver 400m medley relay '87 PAG; silver '81, bronze '83 Pan-Pacific championships; asst. coach

Arkansas '91-95; head swim coach Indiana University of Pa '95-98; Southeast/Southwest Conf. titles; produced 10 all-Americans at NCAA Div II '95; PSAC coach of '98; involved with Special Olympics; mem. American, College Swimming Coaches Assns; assisted DC in 2012 Olympic bid; res. Fairfax, Va.

WARDEN, Donald (archery); b. 27 Dec 1931, Arthur, Ont.; given name: Donald Elgin; m. Jean Marie Brown; c. Donna, David, Dianne, Joan; Guelph Bus. College; real estate; early hockey interests terminated when injured pursuing duties as fireman '74; class III paraplegic; ntl archery records; ntl silver, bronze air rifle, air pistol; 5th Holland archery competition '80; mem. Stayner Rod and Gun Club; proficient in .22 rifle; mem. Base Borden Archery Club; Ont. good citizenship award '81; active in community life, activities for physically handicapped; last known res: Stayner, Ont.

WARNER, Edson (shooting); b. 6 Mar 1930, Sawyerville, Que.; given name: Edson Lyman; m. Edith; c. Patrick, Robert, Terry , Susan; McGill, BComm, Bishop's, BA; ret'd accountant; mem. '52, '60 Olympic, '52, '58, '66 world championships teams; mem. 7 Bisley teams; 13 ntl .22 rifle titles; mem. '74 CG team; 3 Macdonald Stewart silver badge titles, 5 Queen's medals; '56 runnerup Queen's Prize Bisley, Duke of Gloucester award '56; 3 Bisley Argentina medals; p-pres. PQRA; 22yrs service Cdn army militia Sherbrooke Hussars; mem. DCRA Hall Of Fame; res. Lennoxville, Que.

WARREN, Harry (field hockey/t&f/cricket); b. 27 Aug 1904, Anacortes, Wash.; d. 14 Mar 1998, Vancouver, B.C.; given name: Harry Verney; m. Margaret Bessie Tisdall; c. Charlotte Louisa Verney, Victor Henry Verney; UBC, BA, BASc.; hon. DSc, Rhodes Scholar, Oxford, MSc, PhD; joined UBC faculty '32; ret'd geology prof., consulting geological engineer; t&f alternate '28 Olympic team; 100m (on grass) Irish record Tailteann Games, 2 inter-varsity relay records Oxford-Cambridge meet '29; capt. Queen's Coll. AC '28-29; introduced badminton, cricket, rugby, men's field hockey to Cal Tech '29-32; hon. life mem., founder Calif. Wanderers FHC; father of Canadian field hockey; organized UBC club '23; hon. pres. CWFHA; 1st pres., co-founder CFHA '62; instrumental in sending Canada's 1st field hockey entry to Olympics '64; twice UBC Big Block for rugby, track; Oxford track honors; University Hill's Men's Forum award for contribution to amateur sport '65; Warren pitch Thunderbird Park named in his honor '70; BC cricket cap '23; IHF award of merit '77; fellow Royal Society of Canada, Geological Society of America, Geochemical Society; served on UBC senate '39-60, '63-72; mem. Order of Canada, UBC, BC Sports halls of fame.

WARREN, Rod (rodeo); b. 24 Feb 1968, Valleyview, Alta.; m. Jennifer; c. Hayden, Cole; rancher; rose through amateur to pro ranks '88 following path of brother Rick; began with bull riding but soon switched to saddle bronc riding, steer wrestling; Calgary Stampede bronze; Skoal, Bud pro circuit SB titles '94; 7 ntl AA titles; Dodge pro tour SB title '95; ntl SB title '01; 7 Alta. circuit, 2 SK circuit, 3 BC circuit AA titles; Wrangler circuit AA title '96; 2 ntl high-point titles, Stampede bonus title '03; res. Valleyview, Alta.

WARREN, Victor (field hockey); b. 19 Aug 1937, Vancouver, B.C.; given name: Victor Henry Verney; m. Cindy Secord; c. Devon, Davey, Steven;UBC, BA; civil servant; mem. 11 test match ntl teams; '64 Olympic team; mgr. ntl team '74-79; 98 test matches including '74, '79 PAG, '76 Olympics, '78 World Cup; pres. CFHA; res. West Vancouver, B.C.

WARWICK, Bert (football): b. 1902, Fort Chipewyan, NWT; d. 1963, Winnipeg, Man.; as player/coach/exec. at all levels served Cdn football for more than 50yrs; played with St. John's College of Wpg.; coach Western champion Blue Bombers '45; pres. jr. Bombers, chair. CRU/CFL rules comm. 8yrs; life mem. Blue Bombers; CFL commissioner's Western rep at time of death; mem. Cdn Football Hall of Fame.

WARWICK, Billy (hockey); b. 17 Nov 1924, Regina, Sask.; given name: William Harvey; m. Beatrice Powell (d); c. Jane Anne, Linda Caroline; m. Jackie Schoeneich; c. William Christopher, Richard Rudolph (d); publisher *Billy's Guide*; mem. Regina Sask jr. title team; attended Oshawa jr. camp but turned pro NYR organization '42; played in minors with NY Rovers, Hershey, Providence, Philadelphia, Fort Worth, Cleveland, Memphis, Denver, Ottawa, Halifax; NHL with Rangers 14 games, 3g, 3a; ret'd from pro ranks '52; with brothers Dick and Grant formed famed Warwick line which led Penticton Vees to Allan Cup '54 and world title over Russia '55; mem. Intl, BC Hockey, BC, Sask. Sports halls of fame; res. Edmonton, Alta.

WARWICK, Claude (boxing); b. 28 Oct 1922, Regina, Sask.; d. 1 Mar 1945, Montreal, Que.; given name: Claude Carl; Cdn Forces; db Regina Roughriders and Navy football teams; southpaw boxer who reigned as Cdn Navy featherweight champion; won ntl amateur featherweight title '41 with 29th straight victory; died as result of vehicular accident; ring record 51 bouts, 50 wins, 1 draw; mem. Sask. Sports Hall of Fame.

WARWICK, Grant (hockey); b. 11 Oct 1921, Regina, Sask; d. (circa 2002), Edmonton, Alta.; given name: Grant David; div.; c. Grant, William, Gayle; restaurateur; pro Rangers '41-47, Boston '47-49, Montreal '49-50; NHL record: 399 scheduled games, 147g, 142a, 16 playoff games, 2g, 4a; Calder, Jacobson rookie trophy '41; scored 1st goal in inaugural NHL all-star game '47; made history as 1st playing coach to win Allan Cup ('54), World championship ('55) with Penticton Vees; with brothers Billy, Claude, Dick and sister Millie inducted into Sask. Sports Hall of Fame same cermony; mem. International, BC Hockey, BC Sports halls of fame.

WARWICK, Millie (all-around); b. 28 Oct 1922, Regina, Sask.; given name: Mildred Marion; m. Kenneth McAuley (d); c. Ken Jr., Todd; ret'd public servant; versatile athlete who excelled in basketball, t&f, softball, speed skating, 5-pin bowling, curling, baseball; set Sask. HS softball throw record; mem. '51 ntl champion Edmonton Mortons softball team; '38 Sask. speed skating champion; 3b Rockford Peaches in AAGPBL '43-44; with brothers Billy, Claude, Dick, Grant inducted into Sask. Sports Hall of Fame in same ceremony; honored Cooperstown, Cdn Baseball halls of fame; mem. North Battleford Baseball Hall of Fame; res. Edmonton, Alta.

WARWICK, Richard (hockey); b. 28 Apr 1927, Regina, Sask.; given name: Richard McAllister; m. Pam Gates; c. Claude, Sheryl; ret'd Canada Dry sales/restaurateur; fine playmaker/prolific scorer; played jr. Humboldt, Medicine Hat, sr. Nanaimo, Penticton; played key role in formation of Penticton Vees and got brothers Billy and Grant to join him forming famed Warwick line which led Vees to '54 Allan Cup, '55 world championship over Russia; mem. Sask., BC Sports, International, BC Hockey halls of fame; res. Saanichton, B.C.

WASHBURN, LeRoy (t&f): b. 16 Jun 1934, Blackville, N.B.; ret'd AD St. ThomasU; overall NB t&f title '74; t&f official '67 PAG, '76, '96 Olympic, '78, '86 CG; mem. IAAF tech. officials comm '85; CTFA officials comm., NBTFA dir., pres. '84-87; CdM '87 FISU Games; v-p. NB Special Olympics Assn.; active with paralympic athletes; consultant NB Indian Summer Games; Myer Budovitch Memorial trophy Fredericton athlete of '58; Lieut.-Gov. trophy '61; mem. NB Assembly '74; PetroCan coaching excellence award; STU athletic field bears his name; mem. Fredericton Sports Wall, NB Sports Hall of Fame; res. Oromocto, N.B.

WASZCZUK, Henry (fishing/football); b. 26 Aug 1950, Peterborough, Eng.; m. Mary Louise Duncanson; c. Michael, Jessica; Kent, BSc, MA; teacher, TV personality, producer, publisher; emigrated to Canada age 2; ctr Tiger-Cats '75-84; 7 all-Eastern awards; Tom Pate Memorial award recipient; 3 Schenley outstanding lineman nominations; mem. All-time Ticats dream team; co-host *TSN Canadian Sportfishing* series; writer/partner *Canadian Sportfishing* magazine; host *Fins & Skins Classic Adventures; Fishing the Flats* TV shows; authored more than 10 books on fishing; mem. Oshawa Sports Hall of Fame; res. Campbellville, Ont.

WATKINS, Bill (baseball); b. 5 May 1858, Brantford, Ont.; d. 9 Jun 1937, Port Huron, Mich.; given name: William Henry; played briefly as infielder with Indianapolis (AA) '84; same yr became team mgr.; became mgr. Detroit (NL) '85-88, Kansas City (AA) '88-89, St. Louis (NL) '93, Pittsburgh (NL) '98-99; ML managerial record: 914 games, 452-444; mgr. '87 pennant, World Series winner.

WATLING, Wallace (all-around): b. 16 Mar 1888, Chatham, N.B.; d. 19 Sep 1929, Chatham, N.B.; mayor Chatham, N.B.; competed in hockey, t&f, baseball, basketball, rugby, boxing; excelled in 100-, 200yd dashes, 400 relay, bj, shot put; many NB, Maritime titles; capt. Chatham's basketball, football teams; mem. NB Sports Hall of Fame.

WATSON, Bev (parachuting); b. 4 Dec 1953, Montreal, Que.; given name: Beverly Dale; Queen's, BA, York, MBA, CA; chartered accountant; mem. OUAA title ski team '74; provincially-ranked squash player; 1st style Alta. parachuting championships '79; 4th style, accuracy, overall '80 ntl championships; mem. ntl team '80 world championships; silver single '86 Adriatic Cup; women's overall world paraski titlist; European Cup gold '87; combined silver '89 world paraski; res. Calgary, Alta.

WATSON, Harry (hockey); b. 6 May 1923, Saskatoon, Sask.; d. 19 Nov 2002, Toronto, Ont.; given name: Harry Percival; m. Lillian Thomson; c. Barry, Ron, Dale; ret'd sales agency operator; Saskatoon jr. Quakers; pro Brooklyn Americans '41, Detroit '42-43, '45-46, Toronto '46-55, Chicago '55-57; mem. 5 Stanley Cup winners; lw on Leafs' line of Syl Apps Sr., Bill Ezinicki; NHL record: 809 scheduled games, 236g, 207a, 62 playoff games, 16g, 9a; 7 NHL all-star games; 12yrs mgr. Tam O'Shanter hockey school; coach '63 Windsor Bulldogs Allan Cup champions; co-chair. Timmy Tyke hockey tournament; mem. Toronto Oldtimers hockey team 20yrs; mem. Ont. Legends, Sask., Saskatoon Sports, Hockey halls of fame.

WATSON, Ken (curling); b. 12 Aug 1904, Minnedosa, Man.; d. 26 Jul 1986, St. Boniface, Man.; m. Marcella Dowdall; UMan, BA; ret'd insurance exec., teacher; lead 1st Man. bonspiel '23; 1st of 32 major trophies Man. 'spiel '26; 7 MCA grand aggregate titles including unprecedented 6 in succession '42-47; 4 Man. Consols titles; Brier championships '36, '42, '49; promoted, helped organize Scotch Cup '59; founder 1st Man. HS 'spiel '40; authored 4 curling books; hon. life mem. Strathcona CC, MCA, CCA; Elmer Freytag Memorial award; mem. Order of Canada, Man., Canada's Sports, Man., Cdn Curling halls of fame.

WATSON, Mark (soccer): b. 7 Sep 1970, Vancouver, B.C.; given name: Mark Stuart; UBC; made pro debut as defender Ottawa Intrepid CSL '90; mem. Hamilton Steelers '91, Montreal Supra '92, Watford English 1st div.'93-95, Vancouver 86ers A-League, Columbus Crew MSL, New England Revolution '96; also had stints with Sweden Osters, Oxford, DC United, Wolverhampton, Oldham, St. Johnstone, Seattle; scored Canada's lone goal for NA title '00 Gold Cup; international debut age 21; mem. ntl team '91-01; Charleston Battery A-League '02; res. Vancouver, B.C.

WATSON, Moose (hockey); b. 14 Jul 1898, St. John's, Nfld., d. 11 Sep 1957, Toronto, Ont.; given name: Harry; St. Andrew's Coll.; St. Andrew's, Aura Lee jrs; Toronto Dentals '19; Toronto Granites, 2 Allan Cups, '24 Olympic title; totaled IIHF record 36 goals in '24 Olympics; player-coach Toronto National Sea Fleas Allan Cup winner '31; rejected pro offers; mem. IIHF, Hockey halls of fame.

WATSON, Sandy (hockey/builder); b. 28 Mar 1918, Scotland; d. 28 Dec 2003, Ottawa, Ont.; given name: Alexander Gardner; m. Patricia Brown; c. John Alexander; St. Andrews, Harvard, Cambridge, Columbia Presbyterian; eye surgeon; prof. of ophthalmology; Sally Letson Foundation ED 25yrs; Rockcliffe Park councilor; architect/ mgr. RCAF Flyers '48 Eastern Canada League, world, Olympic title teams; mgr. IHF team; mem. COA, former governor Hockey Canada; mem. Order of Canada; with '48 Olympic team mem. Ottawa Sports Hall of Fame, military athletes of 20th Century.

WATSON, Whipper Billy (wrestling); b. 25 Jun 1915, East York, Ont.; d. 4 Feb 1990, Orlando, Fla.; given name: William Potts; m. Eileen; c. John, Georgina, Phillip; pitched, played 2b Legion softball team; def in hockey; football Eastside, Balmy Beach jrs; marathon swimmer CNE, across Hamilton Bay, down Humber River swims; European light-heavyweight champion; twice held world title, beat Bill Longson '47, lost to Lou Thesz '48, reclaimed from Thesz '56, lost in rematch; in 36yrs of wrestling more than 7400

bouts Europe, NA; record 12 NWA British Commonwealth titles; forced into retirement following '70 auto mishap; prominent fund-raiser Ont. Society for Crippled Children, Easter Seals telethon, other charities; B'Nai Brith citizen of '55 award; Ont. good citizenship medal '78; hon. life mem. Easter Seals Society; hon. LLD York; hon. citizen awards from myriad of Cdn cities; mem. TRC Pro Wrestling, Ont. Sports Legends halls of fame.

WATT, David (t&f); b. 24 Feb 1952, Barrie, Ont.; UofT, BA, MA; economist; ntl juv tj title '70-71; ntl jr. title '72; mem. ntl '74-78; ntl sr. tj title '75-77, record 16.05; mem. '75 PAG, FISU, '77 Pacific Conf., '78 CG teams; varsity basketball UofT '71-73, OUAA all-star '73; UofT outstanding athlete '74; treas. OTFA; res. Scarborough, Ont.

WATT, Laird (tennis); b. 21 May 1913, Montreal, Que.; d. 3 May 2001, Montreal, Que.; given name: Malcolm Laird; m. Anne Fraser; c. Nancy, Linda, Sherrill; McGill, BComm; ret'd chartered accountant; playing mem. Davis Cup team '34, '38, '46; number 1 nationally '38-39; with father 3 US father-son titles; 2 Cdn Intercollegiate singles, doubles titles; 2 ntl indoor men's doubles titles; 1 Maryland state men's doubles title; 3 Que. singles titles, 5 men's doubles; 1 Ont. singles, doubles title; pres. CLTA '62-63, QLTA '51-52, ILTC of Canada '65-69; hon. treas. CG Assn. of Canada '53-59, v-p. '59-63; Centennial medal '67; mem. Cdn Amateur Sports, Cdn Tennis halls of fame.

WATT, R.N. (tennis); b. 11 Oct 1885, Tara, Ont., d. 4 Jul 1971, Montreal, Que.; given name: Robert; m. Marguerita Vittie; c. Laird, Robert Jr. (d); business exec.; with son Laird US ntl father-son doubles titles '33, '34, '37; CLTA pres. '37-45; only Cdn pres. Intl Lawn Tennis Federation '57; mem. Cdn Amateur Sports, Cdn Tennis halls of fame.

WATT, Tom (coaching); b. 17 Jun 1935, Toronto, Ont.; m. Mabs MacPherson; c. Kelly, Ruth Anne, Robert; UofT, BPHE, MEd; hockey coach; coached Toronto Jarvis CI '59-64, Monarch Park HS '64-65; asst. football coach UofT '65-73; asst. coach Vancouver '80, head coach '85-87, Winnipeg '81-83, Toronto '90-92; asst coach Calgary '87-89, Anaheim '01-02; NHL coaching record: 490 scheduled games, 176-252-62; 10 playoff games, 1-9; head hockey coach UofT '65-80, '84-85, 11 OUAA, 9 CIAU championships; coach Saint John AHL '94; wrote How to Play Hockey; CIAU coach of '71; TV color commentator '77 world, '84, '94 Olympic hockey tournaments; coach '80 Olympic team; NHL coach of '81-82; scout Toronto '97; mem. UofT Sports Hall of Fame; res. Toronto, Ont.

WATTERS, Lynn (sailing); b. 20 Nov 1916, Montreal, Que.; given name: Lynn Alexander; m. Gretchen; c. Penny, Sally, Alex, Nancy; Lower Canada College, McHill, BEng; chair. Plow & Watters Printing Canada Ltd.; mem. '60, '64, Olympic Dragon, '63 PAG gold Dragon crew; coach '68 Olympic Dragon crew; commodore Royal St. Lawrence Yacht Club; hon. dir. CYA; chair. CYA racing rules comm., NA Yacht Racing Union racing rules comm.; chairman Intl YRU racing rules comm.; dir. for yachting COA; IYRU rep. organizing comm. for yachting Kingston '76; pres. intl jury '67, '75 PAG, F.D. World championships '67, Finn Gold Cup '69, '71; pres. jury Canada Games '69; pres. jury Laser World championships '74; mem. intl jury '71 PAG, '72, '76,

'80 Olympics, Finn Gold Cup '74, Canada Games '77, '81, finalist Air Canada official-of-yr award '78; elected CYA Councillor of Honor; res. Cornwall, Ont.

WATTS, J.C. (football); b. 18 Nov 1957, Eufaula, Okla.; given name: Julius Caesar; m. Frankie; c. 5; Oklahoma BA (journalism); business entrepreneur, ordained minister, former US congressman, chair. house Republican conf.; high-profile US college qb twice led Oklahoma to Orange Bowl victories, twice MVP; joined CFL Ottawa '81, '83-85, Toronto '86; CFL record: 63 scheduled games, completed 785 of 1487 passes for 11,550yds, 59tds, 315 carries for 2106yds, 12tds; 1 Grey Cup final; retiring from football became Baptist youth minister then entered politics becoming 2nd black Republican congressman elected in 60yrs '94; left politics after 4 terms; numerous awards for community service; gifted orator; serves on boards of several organizations; *SN* columnist; mem. Orange Bowl Hall of Honor; Ottawa Sports Hall of Fame; res. Norman, Okla.

WAWRYN, Alexandra (fencing): b. 1 Sep 1978, Warsaw, Poland; following in brother Borys' (former ntl jr. team mem.) footsteps, began as foil fencer then switched to épée. 2 Ont, titles, 2 cadet ntl titles; earned ntl team berth at 15; ntl sr. title '96; set Cdn best-ever performance '95 Cadet worlds in Paris with 2nd; undefeated double medalist '95 Canada Games leading Ont. to team title; Elaine Tanner award '95; res. Ottawa, Ont.

WAY, Kelly Ann (cycling): b. 18 Sep 1964, Windsor, Ont.; Windsor BSc; chiropractic asst/therapist; road-race, pursuit specialist; began racing '75; 1st North American to win Tour de France stage '84, 8th stage; only Cdn woman to have worn leaders yellow jersey '89 Tour de France; competed '88, '92 Olympic, '90 CG, '83 FISU Games, 8 world championships, 6 Tour de L'Aube, 4 Tour de France; gold '87 Tour de L'Aube individual time trial; 5 Ont. Cycling Assn, sportswoman- of-yr awards; mem. UWindsor, Windsor/Essex Sports halls of fame; res. Windsor, Ont.

WEARRING, George (basketball); b. 2 Jun 1928, London, Ont.; given name: George Arthur; m. Marilyn Krueger; c. Matthew, Olin, Andrew, Joel; UWO, BA, SouthernCal, Michigan, MA, UofSask, PhD; ret'd educator; 4yrs basketball, football standout UWO; mem. Ont. all-star basketball, football teams; mem. '52 Olympic team; mem. ntl champion Nortown Tri-Bells '53; res. London, Ont.

WEATHERALL, Jim (football); b. 26 Oct 1929, Texas; d. 2 Aug 1992, Moore, Okla.; m. Ruth Williams; c. Tracy, Clay, Jamie; Oklahoma, BBA; ret'd insurance, securities broker; Sooners all-American lineman '50-51, Outland award '51, East-West Shrine Game '51, Senior Bowl, College all-star games '52; pro Edmonton '54, Grey Cup; Philadelphia (NFL) '55-57, Pro Bowl '55-56, Washington '58-59, Detroit '60-62; mem. Panhandle of Texas, US College Football, Big Eight Football Conf. halls of fame.

WEBB, Don (coaching); b. 7 Apr 1933, Toronto, Ont.; div.; c. Michaele (d), Kelly; diving coach; pro diver at 15 competing in major water shows throughout world; pro high-diving title '63; gymnastics coach '57-59; diving coach from '60; diving coach at 7 Olympic, 7 PAG, 7 CG, 10

FINA World Cup, 7 World championships, 2 FISU Games; personal coach David Bedard; mem. Cdn Amateur Sports halls of fame; res. Pointe Claire, Que.

WEBB, Vanessa (tennis); b. 24 Jan 1976, Toronto, Ont.; Duke; tennis player; joined pro ranks '99 after graduating from Duke as all-American with NCAA sr. player of the year honors; collegiate career included '96-98 first team all-American honors, '96 ITA ntl rookie of the year, '97-98 Atlantic Coast Conference, '98 NCAA singles champ, which earned her wild card into the U.S. Open, Rolex/*Tennis Magazine* collegiate player of '98; career-high #107 on WTA Tour '00; Cdn. Fed Cup team from '00; mem. '00 Olympic team; qualified for the Australian Open 1st time '02, recording 1st Grand Slam match victory over Sanchez; biggest win of career defeating #38 Magui Serna of Spain 1st round Miami '02; 7-1 Fed Cup doubles record; 10 ITF Women's Circuit singles titles; Tennis Canada female doubles player of '02; retd '03; res. Toronto, Ont.

WEBER, Richard (skiing/mountaineering); b. 9 Jun 1959, Edmonton, Alta.; m. Josée Auclair; c. Tessum, Nansen; Vermont, BEng; expedition organizer, lecturer; 3 ntl jr. boys, 4 ntl sr. x-country ski titles; ntl biathlon title '81; mem. Cdn team '77, '79 world jr., '82, '85 world men's championships; with teammate Brent Boddy became 1st Cdns to reach North Pole on foot '86; Cdn team leader '88 Soviet-Canadian transpolar ski 1800km expedition from Northern Siberia to Ellesmere Island ntl park via North Pole; guided '89 environmental group that launched 1st hot air balloon from North Pole; with Russian Misha Malakhov set record 102-day two-way polar journey without benefit of dogs, airplanes, resupplies '92; 1st to reach North Pole four times; with Malakhov lead 1st commercial North Pole expedition '93 when two groups totalling 19 persons from 8 countries skied final 100km to Pole; UNESCO International Fairplay award '89; medal of Friendship of Nations from Soviet govt. '89, '96; Russian medal for personal courage '93; Cdn govt. Confederation Medal '93; meritorious service medal '94; wrote *Polar Attack; Polar Bridge, an Arctic Odyssey*; noted lecturer, photographer, writer; mem. Cdn Skiing Hall of Fame; res. Aylmer, Que.

WEBSTER, Peter (builder/administration/skiing); b. 29 May 1941, Quebec City, Que.; given name: Peter Wynne; m. Nevenka; c. Sheryl, Julia, Brian; Lower Can. Coll, MacDonald Coll (dip. Agriculture), South Dakota State; chair. Petwyn Investments Ltd.; alpine, Nordic ski teams, ski club pres., Lower Canada Coll football team mgr. '57-61; MacDonald Coll. ski, woodsmen teams '61-63; organizing comm. Kaisen Forum Vancouver '95-96; enthusiastic volunteer in skiing serving varied roles from pres., treas., PR officer to mgr Laurentian Zone, ntl team; acting AD Notre Dame (B.C.) '66-67; founding mem/exec Assn. Sports Museums & Halls of Fame from '73; founding mem. CASH '79; volunteerism has spanned myriad of areas involved with regional, prov., ntl, intl sports and Cdn sports heritage; served as exec, trustee, board mem. Alta., Intl Swimming, B.C. Sports (ED '72-83) halls of fame; highly regarded in business and sports communities serving as dir./trustee/exec. of numerous organizations covering wide array of interests; Bill Schroeder (Sports Museums distinguished service) award; Boys & Girls Clubs of Can. awards; B.C. sports lifetime achievement award; alpine ski team alumni of yr.; Queen's Jubilee medal; several other merit/achievement awards; mem. Cdn Skiing Hall of Fame; res. Vancouver, B.C.

WEDGE, Cathy (equestrian); b. 29 Dec 1950, Saskatoon, Sask.; given name: Katherine; UofSask. hons. BA, LLB; lawyer; working hunter title Seattle '69; mem. ntl team '70-78; mem. '71 Pan-Am 3-day event gold team; ntl 3-day title with City Fella '74; mem. '76 Olympic team; injuries prevented participation '72 Olympic, '75 PAG; team gold '78 world championships; US reserve combined title '78; CEF award of merit '78; mem. Saskatoon, Sask. Sports halls of fame; res. Vancouver, B.C.

WEDLEY, Jack (football); b. 19 Sep 1917, England; m. Becky MacDonald; c. Joanne, Jacqueline; ret'd Seagram's sales mgr; mem. 2 Toronto city HS football title teams; pro football, both oe/de Argos, Navy, Regina '37-51; 7 Grey Cup finals, 6 winners; 5 times all-star; mem. 6 Metro Toronto jr., sr. baseball title teams, 2 Maritime titles, 2 Que. titles; scouted by NL teams; 6yrs basketball, 3 Toronto city title teams; mem. ntl champion Navy softball team '42, competed world championships; WW2 Navy phys-ed instructor; helped organize Scarborough Kiwanis Little-4 Fbll Lg; mem. Scarborough P&R Commission; charter mem. Scarborough Rams Fbll exec.; league pres., coach Stouffville Whitchurch baseball title team '73; groom for horses daughter Jacqueline shows on Ont. jumping circuit; res. Gilford, Ont.

WEDMANN, Wilf (t&f); b. 17 Apr 1948, Wagenetz, Germany; SFU, hons BA, Rhodes Scholar, Oxford, MA; AD SFU; ex-pres/CEO Gymnastics Canada; hj specialist; ntl midget HJ champion '63, ntl jr. '67, 4 ntl sr. titles; mem. '68 Olympic, '67, '71 PAG, '69 Pacific Conference Games teams; silver '71 PAG, gold Canada Games '69; ntl jr., sr. record holder; with partner Harry Jerome developed BC premier's sports award program; varied exec. roles '79-88; dir./coach Kajaks TFC '78-85; pres. BC Athletics '81-85; GM/pres./CEO Athletics Canada '85-88; dir. Athletics Canada '83-85; pres./CEO Cdn Sport & Fitness Admin. Centre '88-96; COA dir. '83-93; pres./CEO Gymnastics Canada '97-2000; res. Vancouver, B.C.

WEIDER, Ben (builder); b. 1 Feb 1924, Montreal, Que.; m. Hugette Drouin; c. Eric, Mark, Louis; pres. IFBB, chair. Weider Nutrition Group Canada Ltd.; parlayed grade 7 education into fitness empire; with brother Joe founded IFBB '46; toured world selling body-building as sport; earned recognized IOC status '98; played key role in fight vs. apartheid in S. Africa; IFBB boasts strong anti-drug policy; with Joe organized Mr. Olympia competition won in '75 by Arnold Schwarzenegger; recipient of numerous honorary degrees, including PhD US Sports Academy; advisor to numerous sports, law enforcement, medical research; myriad of distinguished service awards from wide array of countries; recognized world authority on Napoleon Bonaparte, author several books on subject; *Sport Intern* magazine ranked him among top 50 most influential sports personalities in world; Montreal Jewish community centre bears his name; regarded as citizen of world noted for philanthropic works; life mem. Cdn Bodybuilding Fed.; Queen's Silver Jubilee medal; mem. Order of Canada, French Legion of Honour, Knight Ntl

Order of Que., Nobel Peace prize nominee '84, mem. Quebec, Jewish, Maccabiah Sports halls of fame; res. Montreal, Que.

WEIDER, Joe (builder); b. 29 Mar 1920, Montreal, Que.; m. Betty Brosmer; launched what would become major fitness publishing empire with *Your Physique* newsletter at 17; with brother Ben created IFBB '45; created Mr. Olympia competition '65, event won 7 times by Arnold Schwarzenegger; added Ms. Olympia caterory '80, Fitness Olympia category '95; authored several books on body building; developed nutritional products, fitness equipment; publisher of '83 award; Dwight D. Eisenhower fitness award; Calif. Governor's council lifetime achievement award; Boy Scouts of America distinguished citizen award; founded Body Building Hall of Fame '99; res. Woodland Hills, Calif./Las Vegas, Nev.

WEIGHT, Doug (hockey); b. 21 Jan 1971, Warren, Mich.; m. Allison; c. Ryan, Danny; Lake Superior State; began skating age 2; ctr. Bloomfield (NAJHL) '88-89; Lake Superior (CCHA) '89-91; Binghampton (AHL) '91; NHL NYR '91-93, Edmonton '93-01 (capt. '99-01), St. Louis '01-04; Rosenheim Germany '94; Team USA '96 World Cup (gold), '91 World Jr., '93, '94 Worlds; all-American '91; '98, '02 (silver) Olympics; 2 NHL all-star games; Oilers unsung hero award; NHL record (through '04) 912 scheduled games, 224g, 604a, 69 playoff games, 20g, 35a; res. St. Louis, Mo.

WEILAND, Cooney (hockey); b. 5 Nov 1904, Seaforth, Ont.; d. 7 Jul 1985, Boston, Mass.; given name: Ralph; m. Gertrude; Minnesota; ret'd; mem. Owen Sound Memorial Cup winner '24; pro Minneapolis '25-28, NHL Boston '28-32, '35-39, Ottawa '32-33, Detroit '34-35; formed Boston's Dynamite Line with Dit Clapper, Dutch Gainor; Stanley Cup winners '29, '39; NHL record: 509 scheduled games, 173 goals; best season '29-30, 43 goals in 44-game schedule; 2nd team all-star '34-35; coach Bruins, '41 Stanley Cup winners; NHL coaching record: 96 scheduled games, 58-20-18; 17 playoff games, 10-7; coach Harvard to '71 retirement; mem. Hockey Hall of Fame.

WEILER, Willie (gymnastics); b. 1 Mar 1936, Rastatt, Germany; given name: Wilhelm Friedrich; m. Fay Joy Prosser; c. Rick, Kimberley; ret'd soldier, tool and die maker; '56 jr. all-around German gymnastics title; Cdn gymnastics titles '57-58, '60, '62, '66 working without coach; 1st in NA to perform Yamashita vault in competition; '60 US vaulting title; 1st in NA to perform piked back somersault dismount off horizontal bar; 3 gold, 4 silver, 1 bronze '63 PAG; mem. '64, '68 Olympic, '66 worlds teams; mgr '71 PAG gym team; life mem. Cdn Gymnastics Fed.; mem. Order of Canada; mem. Cdn Amateur, Cdn Forces Sports halls of fame; res. London, Ont.

WEINMEISTER, Arnie (football); b. 23 Mar 1923, Rhein, Sask; d. 29 Jun 2000, Seattle, Wash,; Washington; Teamsters Union organizer; dt who began pro career with NY Yankees (AAFC) '48; mem. Brooklyn-NY Yankees (AAFC) '49; became mem. NY Giants in NFL merger '50-53; all-AAFC '49; all-NFL '50-53; BC Lions '54, player-coach '55; mem. 4 Pro Bowl teams; dominant dt of his time; mem. NFL Hall of Fame.

WEIR, Glen (football); b. 23 Jul 1951, London, Ont.; m. Elizabeth; c. Rachel, Jeannette, Jacqueline; pro football player, employee Imperial Tobacco; nicknamed "Fuzzy"; HS wrestling champion; mem. London Lords Sr. ORFU; launched CFL career as def lineman Hamilton '72; dealt to Montreal same season; '72-84 def mainstay with Alouettes/Concordes; runnerup '77 Schenley def award; James McCaffrey EFC def award '77; O'Keefe Cup Alouette player of '77; 5 EFC, 2 CFL all-star awards; res. London, Ont.

WEIR, Mike (golf); b. 12 May 1970, Sarnia, Ont.; m. Bricia; c. Elle Marisa, Lily; Brigham Young; 1st tournament victory Seaforth jr. at 13; Cdn juvenile title '86; Ont. Jr title '88; Ont. Amateur title '90, '92; twice runnerup Cdn amateur; 2nd team all-American, WAC player of '92; turned pro '93; Cdn tour-rookie-of-'93 award; PGA tour mem. from '98; 3 Cdn tour victories through '99; PGA Air Canada '99; qualifying tournament '98; Cdn tour Order of Merit and Stroke Average award '97; won '96 Desert tour event; won American Express Valderrama World Cup title in Spain '00; PGA tour championship tourney '01; Bob Hope Desert Classic, Nissan Open '03-04; 1st Cdn, lefthander to win Masters title beating Len Mattiace in playoff '03; lost 3-hole Cdn Open playoff to Vijay Singh '04; mem. '97 World Cup team, '00 President's Cup team; won '99 Cdn Skins Game title; '03 Lou Marsh trophy; 3 Lionel Conacher awards; 2 Syl Apps (Ont. Athlete of yr) awards; Mike Weir-Dino Ciccarelli Charity Classic tourney held at Huron Oaks club in Bright's Grove; Sarnia park bears his name; nickname "Weirsy"; res. Draper, Utah

WELBOURN, Graham (swimming); b. 11 Jan 1961, Calgary, Alta.; Arizona State, UBC; freestyle sprint specialist; ntl team '77-84; 6 ntl titles, 2 ntl, 2 commonwealth records; 2 silver, 1 bronze '79 PAG, 2 bronze '83 FISU, 1 bronze '82 CG; mem. '80 Olympic, '82 world championships teams; 6 ntl masters records; res. Clareshom, Alta.

WELCH, Barbara (badminton); b. 28 Feb 1948, Toronto, Ont.; given name: Barbara Hood; m. Garry Welch; sports clothing sales; 5 ntl ladies' doubles titles; ntl mixed doubles '73; mem. 3 Uber Cup, '74 CG, '72 People's Republic of China tour teams; '72; ntl jr. ladies' doubles, finalist Danish Open mixed doubles '71; ntl Open ladies', mixed doubles '74; res. Toronto, Ont.

WELCH, Huck (football); b. 12 Dec 1907, Toronto, Ont., d. 15 May 1979, Ancaster, Ont.; given name: Hawley; m. Helen (d); c. Sandra, Patricia, Douglas, Robert; sales mgr. florist shop; twice topped scorers while helping Delta to 3 national interscholastic titles; Hamilton Tigers '28 helping club to interprovincial titles, Grey Cup '28-29; Montreal Winged Wheelers Grey Cup winners '31; Jeff Russel Memorial Trophy '33; frequent Big Four, all-Cdn all-star; rejoined Hamilton '35-37; twice interprovincial scoring champion, twice runnerup; coach Delta CI srs, Eastwood CI jrs; 1st post-war pres. Tigers '46; coach Kelvin CI, Winnipeg '48-50, Regina jrs '53; Hamilton rep. CFL commissioner '59; mem. Collingwood, Canadian Football, Canada's Sports halls of fame.

WELDON, Craig (judo); b. 5 Jul 1960, Scarborough, Ont.; given name: Craig Steven; m. Elizabeth; Concordia, BA; Ministry of Transportation examiner; black belt age 16; 14yrs ntl team; gold ntl jr. championships '77; silver Arizona Desert Open '78, Dutch Open, ntl championships '79; bronze Canada Cup international '79, 3 ntl sr. championships; gold '80 ntl jr. championships; silver '80 Canada Cup international; '86 PAG silver; competed '88 Olympics; Que., British open titles; 5th degree black belt; Michigan governor's award; Ont. sports achievement awards; v-p Judo Canada; Judo Ont. head coach '01; Olympia Sports Camp instructor; res. Whitby, Ont.

WELLS, Jay (hockey); b. 18 May 1959, Paris, Ont.; given name: Gordon Jay; hockey coach; played def Kingston (OHA), Binghamton (AHL) '77-80; OHA 1st team all-star; 1st LA choice '79 draft; NHL with Los Angeles '79-88, Philadelphia '88-90, Buffalo '90-92, NYR '92-95, St. Louis '96, Tampa Bay '96-97; bronze '86 worlds; NHL record: 1098 scheduled games, 47g, 216a, 114 playoff games, 3g, 14a; asst. coach Portland Pirates (AHL) '97-98, Hershey '98-01; active in Oldtimers hockey; res. Portland, Maine.

WELLS, Vernon (baseball); b. 8 Dec 1978, Shreveport, La; of; drafted 1st round Toronto Blue Jays '97; record (through '04) 511 scheduled games, 2008ab, 309r, 581h, 130db, 11tr, 81hr, 298bi, 28sb, 129bb, 281k, .289ba; 1 all-star, 1 gold glove; res. Shreveport, La.

WELLWOOD, William (harness racing); b. 22 Jul 1940, Chatham, Ont.; given name: William Edwin; m. Jean Bailey; c. Paula; began in stable of uncle Harold Wellwood; following 11yr apprenticeship launched own stable; 4 times horseman of year Ont. Jockey Club circuit; 2 CTA horseman-of-yr awards; 2 Cdn O'Brien trainer-of-yr awards; campaigns throughout NA but enjoys greatest success on Greenwood, Mohawk tracks; through '03 (as driver) 2891 victories, $15M in purses, (as trainer) 966 victories, $17M in purses; with Surge Hanover won '73 Batavia Colt & Filly, Hanover Stake, '74 Dexter Cup, Reynolds Memorial Trot; with Village Jiffy won '92. '94 Breeders Crowns; operates training centre Acton, Ont.; mem. Cdn Horse Racing Hall of Fame; res. Cambridge, Ont.

WELSH, Alex (curling); b. 12 Oct 1907, Edinburgh, Scotland, d. 4 Jan 1971, Winnipeg, Man.; m. Edna Howard; c. Judy, Heather, Alexander Jr.; insurance co. mgr.; 3 Man. Consols titles, 3rd for John Douglas '33 Brier, 3rd for brother Jim '47 (title), '54 Brier entries; twice MCA grand aggregate champion.

WELSH, Jim (curling); b. 18 Feb 1910, Leith, Scotland; d/ 23 Oct 1988, Winnipeg, Man.; m. Kathleen Lloyd; c. Kathleen, Patricia; ret'd; 4 Man. Consols titles; 2nd for John Douglas '33 Brier, skipped '37 Brier runnerup, '47 Brier champion (9-0 record), '54 Brier entry; pres. MCA '64-65; 3 MCA bonspiel grand aggregate titles; mem. Man., Cdn Curling halls of fame.

WELTON, John (football); b. 9 Dec 1929, Ottawa, Ont.; m. Joan King; c. John Jr., Dan, Caroline; Wake Forest, BBA, Stanford, MBA; ret'd pres. development co.; Ottawa '52-54, top rookie '52; Toronto '55-58, Eastern all-star '57; Ottawa sr. city basketball '52-54; res. Mississauga, Ont.

WENDEL, Fred (curling); b. 11 May 1909, Neudorf, Sask.; d. 20 Mar 2001, Trail, B.C.; given name: Louis Fred;

m. Betty McLuckie; ret'd smelterman; mem. Trail's BC Consols finalists '39-40, '42; Brier runnerup '47, winner '48; Edmonton carspiel winner '49, runnerup '50; 2nd Cdn Legion title team '70.

WENDLING, Wendy (t&f/football); b. 4 Jun 1901, Brockville, Ont.; d. 26 Nov 1985, Woodstock, Ont.; m. Margaret McKay (d); c. Mary Joan, Peter, Paul; Loyola College, BA, UofT, BPHE; ret'd teacher, business exec.; Que. jr. track champion '16-18; mem. Loyola sr. track champions '19-22; coached Jean Thompson ("The Penetang Pansy") to 880 berth '28 Olympics; coached Woodstock CI to 1st WOSSA championship '29 molding team which scored 408 points while yielding only 6, and no touchdowns all season; repeated title triumphs '30-31; helped organize, coached Oxford Rifles, later called Grads, to ORFU jr. title and defeated Moose Jaw for ntl title '31; coached last provincial title team, the Grads, '36.

WENNINGTON, Bill (basketball); b. 26 Apr 1963, Montreal, Que.; given name: William Percy; St. John's Coll; 7ft ctr ntl team '82-94; mem. '83 FISU Games gold team, '84, '92 Olympic teams; 2nd place Jones Cup team '82; 1st round (16th overall) NBA draft pick Dallas '85; dealt to Sacramento '90; played in Knorr, Bologna, Italy, '91-93; signed as free agent by Chicago '93; with Bulls through '98, 3 NBA title teams; joined Sacramento '99; fed. govt. excellence award '84; mem. Cdn Basketball Hall of Fame; res. Chicage, Ill.

WENZEL, Joan (t&f); b. 24 Dec 1953, Hamilton, Ont.; given name: Joan Evelyn Eddy; div.; Waterloo, BA, UCal, BEd; teacher, coach; ntl jr. 400m record; mem. '71, '75 PAG, '76 Olympic, '74 CG teams; bronze 800m '75 PAG, lost it because she took a cold remedy containing prohibited drug; res. Vancouver, B.C.

WERBENIUK, Bill (snooker); b. 14 Jan 1947, Winnipeg, Man; d. 20 Jan 2003, Vancouver, B.C.; began competing in father's billiard hall age 9; held ntl title '73-76; turned pro '73 and became well-known in Britain, Australia and Canada; noted for his massive girth, 360lbs and consumption of 50 pints of lager daily; the latter was result of medical condition which might have been stabilized with use of beta blocker drug Inderol; that drug was banned by World Professional Billiards and Snooker Assn forcing him to consume lager in vast quantities to enable him to compete.

WERENICH, Ed (curling); b. 23 Jun 1947, Benito, Man.; given name: Edrick; m. Linda Louise Goulsbra; c. Darren, Ryan; Ryerson PTI; fireman; competed in 11 Ont. Consols/Tankard/Nokia Cup championships; 3rd Paul Savage rink 4 Consols, 1 Tankard titles; skipped '83-84, '90, '97 Ont. Tankard (Nokia Cup) winners; 10 Briers, '83, '90 winners; skipped '83, '90 World title winners; twice winner Royal Canadian Classic, Thunder Bay Grand Prix; '82 Molson cashspiel title; skipped 4 *TSN* Skins Game winners; skipped 8 Ont., 4 ntl Firefighters title rinks; ret'd from competitive ranks '01 but made '04 comeback; fed. govt. champions award '83; Ont. team of '83; Dick Ellis team award '83; mem. Cdn Curling Hall of Fame; res. Holland Landing, Ont.

WERTHNER, Penny (t&f); b. 5 Jul 1951, Ottawa, Ont.; given name: Penny Christine; m. John Bales; c. Neill, Elena;

McMaster, BA, Carleton, Waterloo, UofOtt, MSc, PhD; prof UofOtt, sport psychologist; ntl midget 440yds, juvenile, junior 880yds, juv 1500m records; mem. '70, '78 CC, '71, '79 PAG '76 Olympic, '77 FISU Games teams; bronze 800m '71 PAG, 1500m '78 CG, '79 PAG; world 1000m record '72; Bryce Taylor Memorial award '98; mem. Ottawa Sports Hall of Fame; res. Ottawa, Ont.

WESLEY, Glen (hockey); b. 2 Oct 1968, Red Deer, Alta.; m. Barb; c. Amanda, Josh, Matthew; def. Portland WHL '85-85; 2 all-star, best defenceman awards; 1st Boston choice, 3rd overall '87 NHL draft; NHL Boston '87-94, Hartford '94-97, Carolina '97-02, '03-04; Toronto '02-03; all-rookie team '88; NHL record (through '04): 1247 scheduled games, 124g, 382a, 144 playoff games, 15g, 36a; 1 NHL all-star game; res. Red Deer, Alta.

WESLOCK, Nick (golf); b. 13 Dec 1917, Winnipeg, Man.; given name: Nick Wisnock; m. Elsie; c. Sheri-lee; ret'd company owner, pres., sales rep.; US citizen; using borrowed clubs scored 1st tournament victory '39 Southern Ont. amateur; 405 tournament victories including 4 ntl, 8 Ont. amateurs, 7 Ont. opens, 4 ntl, 11 Ont. srs titles; 16 times leading amateur Canadian Open; mem. 25 Ont. Willingdon Cup, 7 America's Cup teams; 40yrs carried RCGA, OGA certified scratch handicap; 4 times invited to US Masters; special players rep., dir., OGA; mem. RCGA, Canada's Sports halls of fame; res. Burlington, Ont.

WEST, Art (football); b. 29 Jul 1918, Newport, Wales; given name: Arthur Philip; m. Veronica Ferriman; c. Arthur Jr.; Michigan State; ret'd distilling industry; cf Maher Shoes Toronto Sr. Baseball League, batting, home-run leader '36-38; gd Broadview Rascals, Simpson Grads Toronto Sr. Basketball League; hb Toronto '36-40, '45-46, 4 Grey Cup champions; '42 Grey Cup champion RCAF Hurricanes; end Montreal '47; captain '40 Argos; league td leader '37-38; CFL single- game interception record with 6 vs Ottawa '36; 1st Argo to return interception for td 6 Oct '36; all-star Lionel Conacher's all-Cdn team '38; hb all-Argo dream team '21-41 era; nicknamed "Whippet"; coach Jr. Argos '48-49, Parkdale Lions Intermediates '50, Balmy Beach ORFU '51, Cobourg Galloping Ghosts Srs. '52; v-p. in charge of coaches, playing personnel Kitchener-Waterloo Dutchmen ORFU '64; res. Thornhill, Ont.

WEST, Dale (football); b. 11 Aug 1941, Cabri, Sask.; given name: Kenneth Dale; div. Gail Anne Young; c. Kelly, Rae; m. Joan Lesley Hambley; c. Ryan, Timothy; U Arizona, U Sask, U Regina, B.Ed, post grad diploma Curriculum and Instruction; ret'd teacher; program coordinator Sask. Sports Hall of Fame & Museum; ntl bantam speed skating title '50; ntl midget t&f champion '56; set ntl long jump record; alternate (as sprinter) '59 PAG team, '60 Olympic speed skating team; lettered in football Arizona '60; western all-star U Sask '61; CFL 7yrs with Sask. Roughriders from '62; western conf. Record 10 interceptions '63; Schenley most valuable Cdn nominee; 3yrs western conf. All-star; mem. Saskatoon, Saskatchewan Sports halls of fame, Sask. Roughriders Plaza of Honor; res. Regina, Sask.

WEST, James (football): b. 19 Dec 1956, Fort Worth, Tex.; Texas Southern; lb; signed/released NFL Oakland '80; Houston Gamblers USFL '85; CFL Calgary '82-84,

Winnipeg '85-92, BC '93; CFL record: 164 scheduled games, 3tds, 21 interceptions, 51.5 qb sacks, 481 tackles, 14 playoff games, 7 qb sacks, 48 tackles; 1 all-Western, 3 all-Eastern, 2 all-CFL all-star; James McCaffrey trophy '87; runnerup Schenley outstanding def player '87; mem. 3 Grey Cup finalists, 2 winners; res. Texas.

WEST, Mike (swimming); b. 31 Aug 1964, Kitchener, Ont.; Waterloo; backstroke specialist; 8 ntl, 1 US titles; 8 ntl sr., 1 CG records; world's best time 200m backstroke 1:57.90 Jan '84; gold 100m backstroke, bronze 200m '82 CG, silver, 2 bronze '83 PAG, gold 100m, silver, bronze '83 FISU Games; silver 4x100 medley relay, bronze 100m backstroke '84 Olympics; fed. govt. excellence awards '83-84; res. Hamilton, Ont.

WESTFALL, Ed (hockey); b. 19 Sep 1940, Belleville, Ont.; broadcaster; d/rw OHA Barrie '57-60, Niagara Falls '60-61, EPHL Kingston '60-63, AHL Providence '64, NHL Boston '61-72, NYI '72-79; NHL totals: 1220 scheduled games, 231g, 394a, 95 playoff games, 22g, 37a; 6 Stanley Cup winners; scored 1st ever NYI goal; 1st ever NYI captain; nicknamed "Shadow"; res. New York.

WEST-MAHONEY, Stacey (golf); b. 8 Sep 1958, Toronto, Ont.; given name: Stacey Louise West; m. Robert Mahoney; Florida, BA; 3 Ont., ntl jr. titles; ntl Ladies amateur '79; twice low amateur Peter Jackson Golf Classic; mem. 2nd-place team world amateur championships '78, Commonwealth championship team '80; mem. 5th ranked UFla. team; res. Thornhill, Ont.

WESTLING, Gunnar (shooting); b. 25 Dec 1907, Trandstrand, Sweden; d. 25 Oct 1997, Vancouver, B.C.; m. Gertrude Norman; c. Kenneth; ret'd welder; from '48 mem. DCRA ntl team specializing in full-bore, small-bore rifles and pistols; qualified 8 times for Cdn Bisley team competing on 7 occasions; Duke of Gloucester prize '60, Clocktower award '72; Bisley aggregate winner '66, with son Ken Bisley Families match '78; silver cross ntl champion '66; rep. Canada 6 times NRA prize meetings; helped team win overseas match '70, '72, Kalapore team match '72; 1 of 7 Canadians to win Bisley Queen's prize; only marksman to win BC title in grand-slam style; 5 BC, 1 Cdn target rifle titles; 4 BC Lieut.-Gov's match titles; won every match, aggregate and team event at least once at BCRA annual prize meet; provincial handgun champion '56, centre-fire titlist twice, small-bore titlist '47; mem. DCRA, BC Sports halls of fame.

WESTLING, Ken (shooting): b. 18 Oct 1942, Vancouver, B.C.; m. Marilyn Orchard; c. Wesley, Warren, Wade; banker; grand aggregate champion DCRA '91 shoot; gold '91, '97, silver '94-95 Cdn target rifle; mem. 3 Cdn Palma teams, 6 Cdn Bisley teams; 2 BC championships; with father Gunnar Bisley Families match '78; mem. DCRA Hall of Fame; res, Vancouver, B.C.

WESTPHAL, Don (curling): 26 Aug 1963, Buckingham, Que.; m. Joanne; c. Mathieu; asst. golf pro; began curling age 13; represented Quebec 4 Briers, 2nd for Pierre Charette '89, '93, skip '96 (semifinalist) '97, 3rd for Guy Hemmings '01 Briers; res. Buckingham, Que.

WESTWICK, Harry (hockey); b. 23 Apr 1876, Ottawa, Ont., d. 3 Apr 1957, Ottawa, Ont.; m. Ruby Duval; c. Bill, Thomas, Barberry, Elaine, Ula, Beatrice; civil servant; at 17 mem. Ottawa's '92-93 title winners; Capitals (Silver Seven) '95-97, '00-08, Waterloo '99; mem. 3 successive Ottawa Stanley Cup winners; best season '04-05, 24 goals 13 games; '06 named to 1st sr. all-star team in Cdn hockey; nicknamed "Rat"; refereed in NHA; mem. '96-04 Ottawa Capitals lacrosse team, 3 world titles; '02 National Lacrosse Union all-star; football Rough Riders; mem. Ottawa, Hockey halls of fame.

WETZEL, Jake (rowing); b. 26 Dec 1976, Saskatoon, Sask.; given name: Jacob.; UCal Berkeley, economics, statistics (double major); grad student/athlete; as dual citizen has rowed at ntl level for both US, Canada; competed pairs '98 worlds; 1st varsity men's coxed eight at 99, '01, '02 IRA Ntl Collegiate championships; joined men's coxed four '03, winning British Henley, Lucerne World Cup, world championships; '04 Olympic men's coxed four silver; as mem. Team USA won gold coxed fours '99 worlds; competed quad sculls '00 Olympics; All Pac-10 conf. team '99, '01; won all but one race in entire collegiate athletic career; undefeated in championship regattas; res. Victoria, B.C.

WHALLEY, Joan (administration); b. 17 Dec 1918, Wolverhampton, Eng.; given name: Joan White; m. Evan Whalley; c. Ellen, Leslie, Geraldine, Doree; pres. Deer Lodge (Winnipeg) CC '59-60, hon. life mem., instrumental in development business girls, jr. girls programs; varied exec, roles MLCA, pres. '66-67; chair. '67 ntl championships; pres. CLCA '75; instrumental in development Curl Canada uniform coaching program; CLCA service award; mem. Man., Cdn Curling, Man. Sports halls of fame; res. Winnipeg, Man.

WHATLEY, Chris (shooting): b. 29 Nov 1970, North York, Ont.; given name: Christopher Russell; Carleton; industrial designer; began competing at 14; mem. Queen's York Rangers Army Cadet Corps; mem. RCAC, Ont., Cdn, under-25 (2) Bisley teams; qualified for 5 ntl Bisley, 1 Palma team; DCRA Patron's, Gatineau match gold, Letson silver; ntl -25 champion '94; competed '93 Bisley Queen's final, '87, '94 St. George's final; twice top 50 Bisley grand aggregate; mem. -25 title team Bisley '87, Canada '89, '91; capt. Ont. team '92 ntls; capt./head coach ntl -25 Bisley team '94; res. Kettleby, Ont.

WHEATLEY-MAGEE, Terry (field hockey); b. 28 Jul 1960, Saskatoon, Sask.; given name: Florence Therese Wheatley; m. Mark Magee; c. Matthew, Chloe, Krista; UofT, BPhE; high performance coordinator Field Hockey Canada; '82 CIS all-star, CIS Champion; Uof T athlete of '83; ntl team '82-85; 4th '84 Olympics; asst. coach Carleton '90-95, head coach '96-01, '04; OUA, CIS coach of '01; mem. Carleton Athletics Hall of Fame; res. Orleans, Ont.

WHEATON, Robert (swimming); b. 28 Dec 1941, Victoria, B.C.; m. Julie Banfield; c. Fraser, Spencer, Ashley; UVic, UBC, SFU; construction co. pres.; backstroke specialist; silver, bronze '58 BEG, relay silver '59 PAG, 4th relay '60 Olympic Games teams; res. Victoria, B.C.

WHEELER, Lucile (skiing); b. 14 Jan 1935, Montreal, Que.; m. Kaye Vaughan; c. Myrle, Jake; ski coach; ntl jr. downhill title age 12; mem. ntl team at 14; 1st Canadian to claim Olympic skiing medal with '56 downhill bronze; downhill, combined Hakenkammen, Kitzbuhel, Austria, titles '57; 1st NA world title winner downhill, GS, silver combined '58; Bobbie Rosenfeld, Lou Marsh trophies '58, Perry medal Ski Club of Great Britain '58; mem. Order of Canada, Que., Cdn Amateur, Canada's Sports, US National, Cdn Skiing halls of fame; res. Knowlton, Que.

WHITAKER, Denis (builder); b. 27 Feb 1915, Calgary, Alta.; d. 30 May 2001, Oakville, Ont.; m. Juanita Bergey (d) c. Gail, Clarke, Michael; m. Shelagh; RMC; ret'd Brig. Gen., O'Keefe Brewery CEO, financial consultant; successful college football career qb for Hamilton Tigers until war intervened; overseas mem. Cdn team which competed vs. US squad in football; turned attention to horses following WW2; key role in developing strong Cdn equestrian program; founded Hamilton Hunt Club; 2 horseman of yr.; chair. Cdn Equestrian team board '60-82; under his guidance Cdn jumping, 3-day event, dressage teams achieved impressive medal collection, Olympic gold, silver, 2 world gold, 1 bronze, 6 PAG gold, 5 silver, 5 bronze; won srs titles in squash, water-skiing; dir. COA; CdM '80 Olympic team; governor Olympic Trust; mem. Royal Winter Fair exec. comm.; author 4 Cdn military history books; John W. Dafoe literary award; actions at Dieppe led to 1st of 2 Distinguished Service Orders; officer French Legion of Honour; mem. Order of Canada, Canada's Sports Hall of Fame.

WHITCROFT, Frederick (hockey); b. 1883, Port Perry, Ont., d. 1931, Vancouver, B.C.; mem. Peterborough Colts '01 OHA jr. champions; rover in 7-man hockey days; capt. Peterborough '06 OHA Int. title team; Kenora Thistles '07 Stanley Cup; capt. Edmonton sr. team which challenged Ottawa for '08 Stanley Cup (losing 2 straight); 49 goals that season; Renfrew Millionaires '09-10 season; mem. Hockey Hall of Fame.

WHITE, Al (t&f); b. 28 Mar 1904, Catlin, Ill.; d. circa 1990, Peterborough, Ont.; given name: Albert; m. Louise (d); c. Don, Scott; Wayne, BA, Michigan Tech, BSc; ret'd engineer; osteomyelitis of right leg at age 8 threatened athletic career almost from outset; turned to racing horses; HS tennis champion '22; Mich. Tech 100, 220, 440 lj awards; qb football squad; mem. world champion rifle team '34; semipro football Detroit '34-40; moved to Canada '56; at son Scott's urging competed in Ont. Masters t&f meet Oshawa '74; gold shot put, discus, javelin, hammer, 4x100 relay; from '74 competed regularly in Masters meets at local, provincial, ntl levels, also New Zealand; among top-10 4 world championships; world pentathlon record for men 76 '80, men 77 '81, surpassing '80 performance by 47 points; Grade V ranking as judge for intl throws, Grade III field referee; officiated Canada, US, Mexico, Sweden, NZ; Gov.-Gen.'s plaque for youth work; founder, exec. mem. Peterborough TC; officiated '76 Olympics; mem. Ont. t&f, Cdn Masters committees.

WHITE, Ben (harness racing); b. 5 Feb 1873, Whitevale, Ont., d. 1958, Orlando, Fla.; given name: Benjamin Franklin; horseman; drove 1st race at 15; groom for Hamlin Village Farm, East Aurora, N.Y.; assisted trainer Edward 'Pops' Geers; head trainer '03-05; drove 4 Hambletonian, 7 Kentucky Futurity winners plus impressive list of other major stakes and futurity winners; noted as developer, trainer of trotting colts; nicknamed "Dean of Colt Trainers"; among his trainees 3-year-old world champion trotter The Abbe; active driver more than 50 years; Ben White Raceway Orlando, Fla., dedicated in his honor; mem. Harness Racing's, Canadian Horse Racing halls of fame.

WHITE, Betty (t&f); b. 14 May 1915, Niagara Falls, Ont.; given name: Elizabeth McCallum; m. Frank Lewington; c. Nancy, Bill; ret'd sales clerk; won 100yd dash Canada vs US meet CNE '32; 2nd 100m, 200m '33 ntl championships, ntl 200m record, outstanding female athlete; mem. gold medal 660yd relay team '34 BEG; res. Hamilton, Ont.

WHITE, Bill (hockey); b. 26 Aug 1939, Toronto, Ont.; given name: William Earl; div. Gail Rice; c. Kimberly, Karrie, Kristen, Kortnee, Kameron; plumbing wholesaler; jr. Toronto Marlboros; def Rochester (AHL) '59-60, '61-62, Sudbury (EPHL) '60-61, Springfield (AHL) '62-63, Los Angeles (NHL) '67-68, Chicago '69-77; 3 times 2nd team all-star; mem. Team Canada '72; coach Chicago '76-77, jr Toronto Marlboros '80-81; NHL playing record: 604 scheduled games, 50g, 215a, 91 playoff games, 7g, 32a; NHL coaching record: 46 scheduled games, 16-24-6; 2 playoff games, 0-2; played 5yrs Labatt's touring team, 7yrs Canadiens touring team; res. Toronto, Ont.

WHITE, Dalt (coaching); b. 6 Jul 1917, Toronto, Ont.; d. 7 Mar 2002, Toronto, Ont.; given name: Alexander Dalton; m. Margaret; c. Peter, Edward, Laurie-Ann, Jeffrey, Brian, Douglas, Janet; UofT, BA, BEd, MEd, OCE; ret'd AD; mem. Orillia ntl jr. lacrosse champions '37; lacrosse Toronto Marlboros, Hamilton Tigers, Brampton Excelsiors, UofT; sr. basketball Toronto West End Y; coached Port Colborne to Central Ont. HS football title '40; Toronto Western Tech city, provincial basketball title teams; asst. dir. P&HE branch Ont. govt. '47-57; asst. football coach UofT '51-55, head coach '56-65; Yates Cup '58, '65; Vanier Cup '65; AD UofT, '70-77; Thomas R. Loudon Award for contribution to OUAA; Dalt White Bursary created in his name; Yates Cup MVP trophy bears his name; mem. UofT Sports Hall of Fame.

WHITE, Dennis (boxing); b. 4 Dec 1898, Waterloo, Que; d. circa 1980, St. Laurent, Que; ret'd railway employee; AAUofC boxing supervisor '28, ntl chair. '37-63; mgr. ntl boxing team '30 BEG; coach '32 Olympic team; mgr. Olympic boxing teams '48, '52, '60; AIBA exec. comm. '71-74; mem. Cdn Amateur Sports, Cdn Boxing halls of fame.

WHITE, Devon (baseball); b. 29 Dec 1962, Kingston, Jamaica; m. Colleen; c. Thaddeus, Davellyn Rae, Anaya Jade; of; drafted by California '81; began pro career Idaho Falls (Pioneer); moved through minors with stops at Danville (A), Peoria (A), Nashua (AA), Redford (A), Midland (AA), Edmonton (AAA); made ML debut with Angels '85, became regular '87 earning berth on Topps all-rookie team; traded to Toronto '91; signed as free agent by Florida '96; traded to Arizona '98, Los Angeles '99-00, Milwaukee '01; ML record: 1941 scheduled games, 7344ab, 1125r, 1934h, 378db, 71tr, 208hr, 846rbi, 346sb,

.263ba; mem. 3 World Series champions; 3 all-star games; 7 Rawlings Gold Glove awards; noted for dramatic catches; res. Mesa, Ariz.

WHITE, Donald (shooting): b. 7 Mar 1908, Grand Falls, N.B.; d. 28 Sep 1988, Victoria, B.C.; given name: Donald Odell; c. Charles; attended 1st DCRA matches at 15; qualified 4 Bisley teams, competed in 3; Gov.-Gen.'s gold medal '32; 5th King's Prize event '33; won MacDonald Challenge Trophy '53; ret'd from competition '55; grand aggregate silver medal '32, '53; mem. NB Sports Hall of Fame.

WHITE, Julie (t&f); b. 1 Jun 1960, Bancroft, Ont.; given name: Julie Margaret; Boston.; hj specialist; 1st BU female athlete to win ntl title; all-American '82; women's t&f MVP '81-82; world age-class record 1.85m '75; ntl jr. record 1.88m '79; US indoor title '76; AIWA pentathlon gold '82; mem. '76 Olympic, '79 PAG, '82 CG teams; ntl jr. pentathlon record 3998 points '78; Mildred Barnes award; mem. BU Sports Hall of Fame; res. Brampton, Ont.

WHITE, Nancy (golf): b. 26 May 1959, Montague, P.E.I.; m. John Brophy; head pro Ivy Hill GC; won '82 Ont. amateur; speed skater turned golfer; just missed qualifying for '80 Olympic speed skating team; joined LPGA tour '84; career low round 66; mem. PEI Sports Hall of Fame; res. Forest, Va.

WHITE, Tommy (baseball); b. 19 Apr 1922, Regina, Sask., d. 27 Feb 1982, St. Thomas, Ont.; given name: Thomas Towersey; m. Sally Anne Jones; c. Thomas Barry, James Joseph; Assumption College; sporting goods store manager, HS phys-ed teacher; pitched Windsor sr. OBA '39, Welland OBA '40; Cleveland farm system Appleton, Wausau, Wis.,. '41-42, London, Ont., army team '43, London Majors Sr.IC '44-53, St. Thomas Elgins Sr. IC player-mgr. '53-60; twice led league won-lost percentage; Sr. IC record: 18 seasons 108 wins, 57 losses; 25-1 record '47; 3 victories 7-game World Sandlot series triumph by London Majors over Fort Wayne '48; frequent IC all-star, MVP '49; mem. Assumption College Eastern Cdn Sr. champion basketball team '45-46.

WHITE, Vance (bobsleigh); b. 26 Oct 1944, Toronto, Ont.; given name: Harvey Vance; m. Margaret Louise Law; Upper Canada College, UofT, BPHE; natural resource exec., pres. Dickenson Mines Ltd.; teenager provincial level diver, swimmer; mem. ntl bobsleigh team '69-73; mgr. ntl team '74-76; res. Toronto, Ont.

WHITEHOUSE, Reg (football); b. 8 Oct 1933, Montreal, Que.; given name: Reginald Alfred; m. Joanne Lee; c. Timber, Lee; self-employed, electrical co.; mem. Notre Dame de Grace '51 Que. champions; Saskatchean (CFL) '52-64, 1st string og/dt/lb/pk 15 seasons; CFL record: 167 converts, 59 field goals; 5 converts '56 all-star game; Tibbits trophy Saskatchewan MVP; WFC record for field goal completion percentage 76.4; organized Saskatchewan players' assn. '64; '66 Grey Cup winner; coached Verdun Invictus to Que. jr. football title '71; res. Cranbrook, B.C.

WHITFIELD, Simon (triathlon); b. 16 May 1975, Kingston, Ont.; full-time athlete; ntl spokesperson for Multiple Sclerosis Society from '01; '95 Cdn jr. title; ntl

team '96-03; 3 ntl titles; bronze '99 PAG, '01 Escape from Alcatraz; won '04 America's Continental Cup; competed '99, '01 worlds; '00 (gold), '04 Olympics, '02 CG; 5 world cup gold, 3 silver; 2 Triathlon Canada athlete of yr. awards; Victoria athlete of '00; Cdn team flag bearer, '00 Olympics closing ceremony; honored by David Foster Foundation for community achievement '02; 3 Cdn World Cup athlete of the year awards; Vancouver Island award of excellence; mem. B.C. Sports Hall of Fame; res. Victoria, B.C.

WHITLEY, Gerry (lawn bowling); b. 22 Apr 1921, Ottawa, Ont.; div.; c. Scott, Steven; Carleton Coll; real estate agent; skipped rinks entry '68 Ont., ntl championships; skipped pairs team to '76 Ont. title, runnerup in ntl championship; res. Ottawa, Ont.

WHITNEY, Ray (hockey); b. 8 May 1972, Fort Saskatchewan, Alta.; m. Brijet; c. Hanna; launched hockey career age 5; lw Spokane (WHL) '88-91, Cologne, Germany '91-92, Team Canada '92, San Diego (IHL) '91-92, Kansas City (IHL) '92-93, Kentucky (AHL) '96-97, Utah (IHL) '96-97; drafted by San Jose '91; NHL San Jose '92-96, Edmonton '97, Florida '97-01, Columbus '01-03, Detroit '03-04; WHL MVP award, Memorial Cup title team '91; NHL record (through '04) 700 scheduled games, 205g, 330a, 41 playoff games, 6g, 11a; res. Edmonton, Alta.

WHITT, Ernie (baseball/coaching); b. 13 Jun 1962, Detroit, Mich.; given name: Leo Ernest; Macomb Comm. Coll.; baseball exec./coach; catcher; Boston '76, Toronto '77-89, Atlanta '90, Baltimore '91; ML record: 15yrs, 1328 scheduled games, 3774ab, 449r, 938h, 176db, 15tr, 134hr, 534bi, 436bb, 491k, .249ba; batting/catching instructor Blue Jays org. from '97; mgr. Team Canada '99 PAG bronze, '00 (dnq), '04 Olympcs; res. Mount Clemons, Mich.

WHITTAKER, Sharon (badminton, tennis); 4 Oct 1939, Victoria, B.C.; m. Alfred Bleuler; sc. John, Jason; UBC, BSc, MPE; U Washington, MS, PhD; sport psychologist; prof emeritus UBC; mem. ntl badminton team '63-70; women's singles silver. Mixed doubles semifinalist '66 Commonwealth Games; ranked 10th in world '66; women's singles finalist US Open '66-67; ntl open singles, doubles titles '68; ntl women's closed singles '65; NE Open title; mem. Uber, Devlin Cup teams; ranked in top 3 singles in Canada '63-70; finalist '65 North of Scotland, all-England; 4 BC women's singles, 6 doubles titles; 4 Ont. women's singles titles; retd from competition '70; won 1st Victoria City women's tennis singles title at 16; ranked #1 BC jr. women's tennis singles, #2 adult women's singles'58; BC open grass court women's doubles title '58; BC public parks (hard court) open doubles title '59; frequent finalist ntl, BC, Western Cdn singles; avid golfer taking up game '85; competed 1 BC, Cdn srs championship; res. Vancouver, B. C.

WHITTALL, Beth (swimming); b. 26 May 1936, Montreal, Que.; div.; c. Lyne, Helen, Marc Couvrette; Purdue, BPharm; pres. Leader Sports Products LSP Inc.; swam for Lafayette SC; silver 400m FS relay, finalist 400m FS '54 BEG; gold 100m butterfly, 400m FS, silver 400m medley relay, 400m FS relay '55 PAG; 7th 100m butterfly '56 Olympics; Lou Marsh Trophy '55; on retirement coached age-group swimmers in Montreal; launched St. Laurent Masters SC

'73; moved to Ont. '76; pres. Ont. Masters comm. '87-88; chair MSO, MSC rules comm.; with Kay Miles Easun helped develop Cdn masters championship; launched Georgian Bay Masters; writer/editor/publisher *Wavelengths* masters quarterly 16yrs; took over *MSC News* '95; holds variety on Ont./ntl records; mem. Cdn Aquatic, Cdn Amateur Sports halls of fame; res. Meaford, Ont.

WHITTIER, Heather (archery); b. 13 Dec 1950, Edmundston, N.B.; given name: Heather Margaret Horricks; m. Carl James Whittier; c. Crystal Louise; UWO hon. BA, UofT, MEd; French immersion teacher; began shooting on husband's team in La Tuque, Que., and, in a span of 4yrs blossomed into a ntl and world champion; a hard-working natural, she has garnered gold at club, regional, provincial, national and world levels and set 3 ntl records; competes in both target and field events and holds records in both; broke all records in FCA FITA field, bowhunter unlimited class championships '98 to qualify for Canada's gold team; 3 ntl CFAA, 1 IFA, 1 NAFA titles; silver '98 US nationals; world field championship '98; Peel Bd of Ed award of excellence '97; res. Caledon East, Ont.

WHITTINGHAM, Dianne (field hockey); b. 27 Apr 1953, Vernon, B.C.; given name: Dianne Louise; UVic, BEd, UBC, MPhE; UAlta; teacher; mem. BC sr. women's field hockey team '70-80, ntl team '72-80; mem. FIH World Cup team '78; mem. BC jr. softball team '73 Canada Games; finalist '74 Victoria female athlete of yr; '79 Vancouver Island women's FHA MVP; '80-81 Vancouver women's FHA MVP; res. Victoria, B.C.

WHITTLE, Doug (gymnastics); b. 25 Mar 1917, Calgary, Alta.; d. 3 Apr 1998, Vancouver, B.C. c. 3; UofT BPHE; Oregon MSc, PhD; ret'd professor UBC; received early gymnastics training Calgary YMCA '35-38; physical dir. Winnipeg Y '38-42; coached gymnastics/swimming/diving/basketball UBC '45-65; organizer/pres. BC Gymnastic Assn '48-62; mgr. ntl team '59 PAG, '62 worlds; ntl gymnastics chair '62; organized 1st international gymnastics clinics in Canada '65; gymnastic men's judge '65-77; aquatic dir. Cranbrook pool '38; rec. dir. Geraldton, Ont., '42; hon. mem. Cdn, BC gymnastic bodies; ntl physical fitness scholarship '49; Cdn Red Cross 25yr service cross; Royal Life Saving Society 25yr cross; Varsity T for gymnastics '43-45.

WHITTON, John (soccer); b. 8 May 1942, Norwich, Eng.; given name: John Michael; m. Noreen Ella Turnham; c. Carie Anne, Amanda Jayne, Michael John; London School of Economics, MSc, Aberystwyth, hons. BA; civil servant; 20yrs competitive soccer in Britain; coached girls soccer taking teams age 11 through sr. to tournament action throughout NA; organized National Capital Invitational girls tournament '83 starting with 2 divisions and 24 teams and growing to 9 divisions and 180 teams and international in scope; ret'd as tournament dir. '02; Cdn. Assn. for Advancement of Women in Sport award '94; Ottawa ACT Gord Trivett Memorial trophy '98; res. Nepean, Ont.

WHYTE, Shauna (biathlon); b. 19 Sep 1967, Hinton, Alta.; given name: Shauna Maria; div. Eric Rauhanen; Lakeside Coll.; full-time athlete, teacher; strong Myriam Bedard challenger until she suffered broken back in horseback accident; 2 additional accidents involving cars threatened

career but she rebounded after each; ntl jr. biathlon title '86; became standout wheelchair racer placing 10th '96 Boston Marathon; resumed biathlon '97; competed in biathlon, XC sit-skiing '98, '02 Paralympics; WC biathlon gold '00, bronze '01; silver '02 WC sit-ski; 5 WC victories; 2 European championship bronze '02; ranked #2 in world; works with Smart Risk's Heroes program; res. Hinton, Alta.

WICKENHEISER, Hayley (hockey); b. 12 Aug 1978, Shaunavon, Sask.; UCal; hockey player; m. Tomas Pacina; c. Noah; competed for Calgary Northwest Bruins boys bantam AA team; bronze with Edmonton Chimos '95 sr. women's nationals; gold Team Alta. '01 Esso ntls, 3 ntl championships MVP awards; ntl team capt. '98-02; MVP in title winning '91 Canada Winter Games match; 7 world, 2 Pacific Rim, 4-Nations Cup gold; mem. '98 Olympic silver, '02 gold medal teams; competed '95 world jr. softball championships; mem. Team Canada '00 Olympic softball squad; referred to as the "Wayne Gretzky of women's hockey"; mem. Olympic Oval high-performance female hockey program; invited to Philadelphia Flyers prospect camp '98-99; played pro Finland 18 months; launched Western Women's HL '04; Stacey Levitt Women & Sport scholarship '97; Bruce Kidd award; res. Shaunavon, Sask.

WICKS, Ron (officiating/hockey); b. 22 Sep 1940, Toronto, Ont.; given name: Ronald Thomas; m. Barb; c. Lisa, Brian; real estate broker; launched officiating career '57 in Sudbury minor hockey; moved to NHL as linesman '60; began refereeing in AHL, IHL '64; made NHL debut as ref '66; NHL career as both ref and linesman spanned '60-86 working 1442 scheduled games, 100 playoff games; officiates NHL old timers games; involved with numerous charity hockey, golf tournaments; res. Brampton, Ont.

WIEBE, Wendy (rowing); b. 6 Jun 1965, St. Catharines, Ont.; m.; began rowing '81; mem. '83 ntl jr team; mem. ntl team from '84; with Colleen Miller 3 consec. worlds double sculls gold; single scull silver '95 PAG; straight 4s bronze '86 CG; single scull gold '93 FISU Games; 1 Cdn, 7 US titles; competed '86 CG, '90 Goodwill, '95 PAG, '96 Olympic Games; res. St. Catharines, Ont.

WIEBUSCH, Harry (boxing); b. 16 Jan 1916, Montreal, Que.; m. Heidi, Karen; UWO; ret'd fuel co. pres.; '33 Que. junior 160lb title; '34-36 Que. 175lb title; boxing coach '36 Olympics; mem. Olympic Club Canada; res. Mount Royal, Que.

WIEDEL, Gerry (fencing); b. 1 May 1933, Germany; m. Pacita Dumenieux; contractor; ntl épée champion '65, foil '65, '69, '70; mem. '67 PAG, '70 CG (bronze team foil), '68, '72 Olympic teams; res. Toronto, Ont.

WIEDEL, Pacita (fencing); b. 31 Mar 1933, Spain; given name; Pacitia Dumenieux; m. Gerry Wiedel; ntl women's foil title '59-64, '66, runnerup '67-68, '71; topped rankings '70-71; 9 Ont. titles; 5th US championships '65, 2nd US team championships '64; mem. '64 Olympic, '63, '67 PAG, bronze individual, team foil '67, '70 CG teams, bronze team '70; res. Toronto, Ont.

WIETZES, Eppie (motorsport); b. 28 May 1938, Groningen, Holland; sep.; c. Michael, Douglas, Marlain;

Ont. Trade School; class A mechanic, owner auto dealership; drove Comstock Mustang, GT40 '65-67; mem. Ford team Winter Rally, Shell 4000; drove Formula 1 Lotus '67 ntl GP rand; ntl Road Racing title with Lola T142 '69; sponsored by Formula Racing, drove McLaren M10B in Canadian, US Formula A competition repeating Cdn triumph; never placed lower than 6th ntl driving title series '70-75; returned to racing with Swiss Chalet team after 6 year retirement '81 and won 1st round CRC Chemical Trans-Am series; mem. Cdn Motorsport Hall of Fame; res. Thornhill, Ont.

WIGSTON, Fran (volleyball); b. 28 May 1935, North Bay, Ont.; given name: Frances Anne; m. John Eberhard; UWO, BA, MA; university prof.; mem. ntl volleyball title teams '66-68, ntl basketball team '67-68; coach-player London Grads basketball team '69-74; basketball silver '67, gold '71 Canada Winter Games; coached UWO 6 Ont., 3 ntl women's volleyball titles, UWO women's t&f team '69-71, team mem. '64-74; coached London Junos volleyball team '71-75, Ont. sr. women's title '73-74, ntl finalists '74; coached sr. men's London Kineldiego volleyball team '73-75; ntl women's volleyball team '73 FISU Games; coached London Lions Olympic t&f Club '64-68; mem. National Advisory Council on Fitness and Amateur Sport; UWO award bears her name; res. Komoka, Ont.

WILHELMSEN, Franz (builder): b. 7 Oct 1918, Trondheim, Norway; d. 30 Apr 1998, Vancouver, B.C.; m. Annette Jean Irvine Seagram; c. Annette Gina, Franz Philip; Norway Business Coll., UBC; businessman, ski resort developer; extensive speed skating/skiing as youngster in Norway; served in Norwegian military; Cdn citizen '47; real estate developer; earned nickname "Whistler's Father" serving as pres. Garibaldi Lifts '60-84, developer of Whistler Mountain; Greater Vancouver man of '66; fed. govt Queen's Medal '77, tourism medallion '84, certificate of merit '88; Canada West Ski Areas Marshall Award; freeman of resort municipality of Whistler; WAC Bennett award; mem. BC Sports, Cdn Skiing halls of fame.

WILKES, Debbi (figure skating); b. 16 Dec 1946, Toronto, Ont.; m. John Darroch; c. Christopher, Jillian; York., hons. BA, Mich. State, MA; journalist; *TSN* skating analyst, columnist; *CTV Sportsnet* broadcaster; with late Guy Revell won Canadian, NA pairs titles '63-64; Olympic silver '64; *CTV* color commentator for international, ntl skating events; Ont. Achievement Award; mem. Cdn Figure Skating hall of fame; res. Scarborough, Ont.

WILKES, Jimmy (baseball); b. 1 Oct 1925, Philadelphia, Pa.; given name: James Eugene; div. Hattie; c. James, Janice, Patricia, Eugene; m. Donna Newton; ret'd municipal employee; mem. Negro American League '45 teaming with Larry Doby, Monte Irvin, Don Newcombe, same league as Jackie Robinson, Josh Gibson, Willie Mays, Satchel Paige, Bob Thurman; Dodgers organization '50, 2 seasons Eastern League at Elmira, N.Y., Trois-Rivieres, Lancaster, Pa., Interstate League; '52 season Hank Aaron teammate Indianapolis Clowns; Brantford (Sr. IC) '53-62; all-star cf; 10yr IC career BA .294; best season '56 batted .344, led league in hits, doubles, times at bat, walks, only player to appear in all league, playoff games; mgr. Brantford '58; mem. 3 pennant winners, 5 playoff champions; umpire Brantford city league '64,

Senior Intercounty '65-86; mem. Brantford & Area Wall of Recognition; res. Brantford, Ont.

WILKINS, Bruce (shooting); b. 29 May 1933, Hamilton, Ont.; d. 26 Oct 2000, Ancaster, Ont.; given name: Bruce Gray; m. Bertha Stewart; c. Sandie, Janet; Mohawk College; ret'd electronics draftsman; ntl open sporting rifle champion '66; ntl indoor standard rifle champion '70; 7 Ont. titles '67-74; mem. ntl champion Inter-Cities teams '63-75; mem. ntl rifle team '69-72; mem. '70 world, '71 PAG teams; Ont. rifle coaching chair. '73-76, ntl chair. '73-97; ntl rifle team mgr.-coach from '76; rifle shooting chair. '76 Olympiad for physically disabled; coach '77 Ont. gold medal Canada Games rifle team; coach 2 CG, 9 world championships, 6 Olympic Games, 8 Benito Juarez, 1 PAG, 5 World Cup, 1 World Air Gun, 1NA championship rifle teams; avid folk music performer.

WILKINSON, Tom (football); b. 4 Jan 1943, Greybull, Wyo.; given name: Thomas Edward; m. Anna Louise Michelena; c. Sherry, Tom Jr., Jodi; Wyoming; carpet salesman; ex-football coach; pro qb Toronto Rifles Continental League '66, Toronto '67-70, BC '71, Edmonton '72-82; led CFL pass completions avg. '72; qb'd Edmonton 9 Grey Cup finals, 6 winners; CFL record: completed 1613 of 2662 pass attempts for 22,579 yds, 154tds, .606 percentage, 126 intercepted; league record holder best single game .905 (19-21) vs. Ottawa '74, single-season .6604 (177-268) '72; Edmonton athlete of '74; Jackie Parker Trophy, Canada Packers Award '72, '74; Schenley outstanding-player award '74, runnerup '78; top qb '79 all-pro voting; head coach UAlta Golden Bears '91-00; mem. Edmonton Eskimo Wall of Honor, UAlta., Cdn Football, Alta. Sports halls of fame; res. Sherwood Park, Alta.

WILLIAMS, Barney (rowing); b. 13 Mar 1977, San Martin de Los Andes, Argentina; given name: Guillermo Barney; m. Buffy Alexander; UVic, BA English & History; Oxford, Diploma of Legal Studies; self-employed; '03 world champion, men's fours; '04 Olympic silver men's fours; gold '03 Lucerne World Cup men's fours; '03 Cdn. Champion men's pairs with Jake Wetzel; most improved player Upper Canada College varsity basketball team '95; most improved rower UVic varsity rowing team '96-97; Cdn. men's pairs crew of '97 with Paul Hawksworth; Centennial medal '03, Rowing Canada; wife Buffy twice Olympian, rowing bronze '00 Olympics; res. Victoria, B.C.

WILLIAMS, David (football): b. 1 Jun 1964, Los Angeles, CA; Illinois; wr; NFL Chicago, Tampa Bay, LA Raiders '86-87, CFL BC '88-89, Ottawa '90, Edmonton '91, Toronto '91-92, Winnipeg '93-95; CFL record: 101 scheduled games, 79tds, 439 receptions for 7197yds, 78tds, 5 playoff games, 2tds; 2 Western, 2 Eastern, 2 CFL all-star; Schenley outstanding-player award '91; Jeff Nicklin Memorial trophy '88; tied 1 CFL record; 3 Grey Cup finals, 1 winner; res. Los Angeles, CA.

WILLIAMS, Dawn (canoeing): b. 13 Nov 1959, Sao Paulo, Brazil; given name: Dawn Elizabeth; m. Mats Zupan; Guelph, BA, MSc, UofT, BEd; teacher, operates Huron Kayak & Canoe; represented Canada 5 world cup marathon canoeing championships; US C2 women's open sprint title '92; amassed 8 gold, 6 silver, 6 bronze in international competition '87-92; with husband Mats formalized Modern Canoeing program specializing in sea kayaking; also x-country ski competitor; res. Paisley, Ont.

WILLIAMS, Desai (t&f); b. 12 Jun 1959, Basseterre, St. Kitts; m. Hazel; York, Clemson; supervisor disaster services American Red Cross; corporate sports medicine marketing dir.; sprint specialist; 2 all-American awards; ntl 200m outdoor title '77, '82, 100m, 200m titles '79-81; mem. '77, '81 Pacific Conf., '78, '82 CG, '79, '83 PAG, '80, '84, '88 Olympic, '83 FISU Games teams; '83 CIAU 300m, 60m titles; silver 4x100m relay '82, gold '86 CG, 100m, 4x100m relay silvers '83 FISU Games; relay silver '85 worlds; bronze 4x100 relay '84 Olympics; ntl sr. record, world best 1:23.97 4x200m relay '83 ntl indoor championships; ntl sr. record 33.53 300m, 6.66 60m '83 CIAU championships; male-athlete-of-meet '82 8-nation invitational; 2 CIAU indoor t&f male-athlete-of-yr awards; 2 CIAU indoor t&f records; res. Baltimore, Md.

WILLIAMS, Dick (baseball); b. 7 May 1929, St. Louis, Mo.; given name: Richard Hirshfeld; m. Norma Marie Mussato; c. Kathi, Ricky, Marc; Pasadena City College; baseball mgr.; minor pro Dodgers organization '47-50; 14 ML seasons of/if Brooklyn, Baltimore, Cleveland, Kansas City, Boston; 1023 games, .260 career BA; '53 World Series; mgr. Toronto Maple Leafs (IL), consecutive Governor's Cup titles '65-66; Red Sox '67-69, coach Expos '70; mgr. Oakland A's '71-73, consecutive AL pennants, World Series victories '72-73; mgr. California Angels '74-76, Expos '76-81, Padres '82-85, Mariners '86-88, 2 AL, 1 NL pennant; ML managerial record: 3023 games, 1571-1451; reached 1000 victory plateau 5 Aug '80 vs Mets in Montreal; ML mgr. of year (*Sporting News*) '67; AL mgr. of year (*AP*) '71; NL mgr. of year (*AP*) '79; res. Tampa, Fla.

WILLIAMS, Freddie (t&f); b. 24 Feb 1962, Cape Town, S.A.; m.; c. Lesley-Ann, Megan; teacher; emigrated to Canada '89; 800m specialist; began competing age 15; ntl sr. 800m record 1:45.13 '93 worlds; 6 NCAA, 11 International Invitational, 4 ntl outdoor, 1 Ont. gold; competed '92 Olympic Games, '93 world indoor, outdoor meets; mem. Toronto Olympic Club; 1st Cdn man to achieve berth in 800m final 8 at either Olympic or outdoor world championships '93 Worlds; TOC athlete of '91; res. Mississauga, Ont.

WILLIAMS, Gizmo (football); b. 31 May 1963, Memphis, Tenn.; given name: Henry; c. Marcus, Henry Jr.; special teams/wr; family plagued by misfortune, mother, uncle, 8 siblings died of MS, father killed in house fire, 1 brother shot, sister drug overdose; 2yrs Northwest Miss jr. coll, 2yrs East Carolina; Memphis Showboats USFL '85; CFL Edmonton '86-88, '90-00, Philadelphia NFL '89; CFL record 1002 punt returns for 11,134yds 24tds, 333 kickoff returns 7291yds 2tds, 58 missed FG returns 1612yds 3tds, 199 receptions 3644yds 21tds; 23,787 all-purpose yds; all-time CFL leader punt return tds; 7 Western, 5 CFL all-star; most punt-return yardage single game (221); most punt-return tds single season (4); set/tied 13 CFL punt-return records, 1 Grey Cup record; 4 Grey Cup finals, 2 winners; 2 Eskimos community service awards; mem. Eskimos Wall of Honor; res. Edmonton, Alta.

WILLIAMS, Jerry (football); b. 1 Nov 1923, Spokane,

Wash.; m. Marian Munroe; c. Jerry Bill, Rebecca Sue, Todd David, Julie Ann, Tyler Laurie; Washington State, BSc, Temple; rancher, ret'd charter flying service owner; football coach; competed East-West Shrine Game, Chicago college all-star game; pro Los Angeles '49-52, world champions '51, Philadelphia '53-54; head coach Montana '55-57; def coach Philadelphia '58-63; asst. coach Calgary (CFL) '64, head coach '65-68, Grey Cup final '68, WFC pennant '65; head coach Philadelphia '69-71, Hamilton '72-75; asst. coach Calgary '81-82; guided '72 Ticats to single season team won-lost record 11-3, Grey Cup victory; CFL coach of '67; Dan Reeves' all-time Rams team; res. Prescott, Ariz.

WILLIAMS, John (motorsport); b. 26 Mar 1939, Toronto; m. Marilyn Lake; c. Greg, Wade, Terry; pro rider, STP team mgr.; 5 world hill-climbing titles; 5 US grand ntl titles; once recognized in *Guinness Book of World Records* as only Cdn world champion in any motor sport in Cdn history; 25 consec. 1-2 finishes '80-81 season; 9 ntl hill-climbing titles; with sons Greg, Wade only Cdn pro hill climbers; mem. Cdn Motorsport Hall of Fame; res. Markham, Ont.

WILLIAMS, Lynn (t&f); b. 11 Jul 1960, Regina, Sask.; given name: Lynn Kanuka; m. Paul Williams; UofSask, San Diego State; TV commentator; 3000m specialist; ntl 3000m title '83; gold 2000m West German Intl meet, 1500m Sweden International meet '83; bronze 3000m '83 FISU, '84 Olympics; 11 Cdn running records; won 5th Ave. mile '85; gold 3000, bronze 1500 '86 CG; bronze '89 World x-country; competed '84, '88 Olympics; 6 BC athlete of yr, BC Premier's awards; Sport BC athlete of '85; Dr. Phil Edwards awards '88-89, Vanier award '90; spokesperson for anti-drug, stay-in-school programs; mem. Cdn Olympic, Sask Sports halls of fame; res. Vancouver, B.C.

WILLIAMS, Paul (t&f); b. 8 Jul 1956, Ottawa, Ont.; given name: Paul Gregory; m. Lynn Kanuka; Guelph, UofT, UBC; mem. OFSAA x-country title team '73; ntl juv x-country title '74; CIAU x-country '77-78, '80; ntl sr. indoor 3000m, outdoor 5000m '79; indoor record 3000m 7:54.1; 3000m steeplechase record 8:35.8 FISU Games '79; mem. '80, '84 Olympic, world x-country teams '80, World Cup team '81; won Toronto Inter-regionals 10,000m '81, Americas' trials 5000m '81, Nice, France 5000m '81, MTRAA Toronto 10 miles '81; 5000m gold '90 Goodwill Games; grandfather Jack Tait mem. '08, '12 Olympic t&f teams; mem. Guelph Sports Hall of Fame; res. Vancouver, B.C.

WILLIAMS, Percy (t&f); b. 19 May 1908, Vancouver, B.C.; d. 29 Nov 1982, Vancouver, B.C.; insurance consultant; gold 100m, 200m '28 Olympics; tied world record 100m (10.6) on grass track '25, tied world mark 100yds (9.6); won 21 of 22 races during 21-day span on US indoor circuit '29; world record 100m (10.3) '30; gold 100yds '30 BEG; mem. '32 Olympic team; ret'd from racing at 22; Canada's t&f athlete of half century; Officer Order of Canada '79; mem. BC, Cdn Amateur, Canada's Sports halls of fame.

WILLIAMS, Roy (basketball); b. 8 Jul 1927, Winnipeg, Man.; given name: Roy Edward; m. Lenore Johannesson;

c. Christopher, Cynthia, Andrea, Alison; UMan, BComm, CLU; ret'd branch mgr. Great West Life; mem. city, provincial HS title teams, team capt. '44-45; mem. Lazy L jr. city league title teams '43-45; UMan Bisons jr. varsity city, provincial title teams '45-46; 4yrs mem. UMan sr. varsity team; Winnipeg sr. league champions '50, Western Cdn titlists, ntl finalist '50; mem. Winnipeg Paulins, twice Winnipeg sr. champs, Western Cdn finalist; mem. league champion Kings Best '55-56, UMan Grads '50-53, 3 consec. league titles, '52 Western Cdn champions, ntl finalists; mem. '52 Olympic team; Winnipeg sr. league MVP '51; all-star team mem. '49-53; Birks Trophy winner '64 Man. bonspiel; Winnipeg Granite Club champion '64; mem. Man. Basketball Hall of Fame; res. W.Vancouver, B.C.

WILLIAMS, Tiger (hockey); b. 3 Feb 1954, Weyburn, Sask.; given name: David James; owner Tigermen Developments; 4yrs jr. Swift Current (WHL); prolific scorer noted for pugilistic efforts as enforcer, hence nickname "Tiger"; NHL Toronto `74-80, Vancouver `80-84, Detroit `84-85, Los Angeles `85-87, Hartford `87-88; NHL record: 962 scheduled games, 241g, 272a, 3966pim, 83 playoff games, 12g, 23a, 455pim; authored *Tiger-A Hockey Story*; dir. 5 public companies; partner snowboard mfgr. One Track; owner Merrick, BC, jr. hockey team; involved with roller hockey as player, team owner; plays regularly in adult sr. league; competed `98 Heroes of Hockey game; coach CHL Top Prospects team '01-02; res. Vancouver, B.C.

WILLIAMSON, Jean (basketball): b. 4 Feb 1919, Edmonton, Alta.; d. 3 Mar 2003, Edmonton, Alta.; m. Thomas Quilley (d); c. Wendy, Ronald; McDougall Commercial; ret'd; competitive swimmer winning numerous medals as youngster; also active in t&f, tennis; member of famed Edmonton Grads basketball team; brother Gordon was "voice" of Grads on radio; standout 5-pin bowler earning several Alta trophies; won Cdn Legion singles title '75; mem. Alta., Cdn Basketball halls of fame.

WILLIAMSON, Peter (speed skating): b. 1 Aug 1946, Winnipeg, Man.; d. 7 Jul 1991, Winnipeg, Man.; m. Lori Toshack; c. Chris, Tyler, Reece, Elizabeth; ski centre mgr.; Calif. jr. x-country running title '62; ntl indoor mass start gold '66-67; mem. Man. team '67 Canada Winter Games; mem. ntl pursuit cycle team '67 PAG; ntl Olympic style speed skating gold '68; mem. Cdn speed skating team '68 Winter Olympics, cycling team Summer Olympics; Man. Olympic style speed skating gold '68; Man. coach/tech. dir. MSSA '83-88; Man. cycling coach '83-87; helped launch Roller Sport Man.; helped found Man. Coaching Assn, 1st pres.; helped launch Snowman Triathlon, Cobblestone Classic; torch bearer '88 Olympic relay; tech. dir CASSA '89-91; CAM coach-of-yr award bears his name; ntl women's short track relay team dedicated '92 Olympic gold to his memory; color commentator *CBC, TSN* world championships; Man. order of sports excellence; mem. Cdn Speed Skating, Man. Sports halls of fame.

WILLS, Stan (shooting); b. 31 Dec 1950, Lethbridge, Alta.; ex-carpenter, family pre-cast concrete co. mgr.; handgun specialist; mem. ntl team from '82; competed 1 world championship, 30 World Cup, 3 Benito Juarez, 2 PAG, 2 CG; with Mark Howkins pairs rapid- fire silver '90, with John

Rochon bronze '94 CG; team air pistol bronze '95 PAG; 3 ntl free-pistol, 1 men's air pistol, 2 rapid fire, 3 standard, 2 centre-fire pistol, 1 Cdn 1800, 2700 centre-fire titles; 3 Crossman air pistol titles, 11 grand aggregate titles; Alta. achievement award; mem. Lethbridge Sports Hall of Fame; res. Lethbridge, Alta.

WILLSEY, Ray (football); b. 30 Sep 1929, Griffin, Sask.; m. Barbara Bigelow; c. Lee Ann, Janet, Louise; California, BSc; ret'd football coach; pro Edmonton '53-55, all-Western db rookie season; mem. coaching staff NFL St. Louis Cardinals, Los Angeles Raiders, WLAF London Monarchs; Seeborg award UC '02; 2 Super Bowl, 2 Grey Cup, 3 NFL Europe/worlds titles; res. Los Angeles, Calif.

WILLSIE, David (rugby); b. 23 Mar 1968, London, Ont.; lumber co. estimator; excelled at semi-pro baseball, XC running, basketball, hockey before hockey accident left him a quadriplegic; hockey referee father encouraged him to compete in wheelchair rugby; mem. ntl team from '97; co-capt. '00 Paralympic team ; competed '99 (bronze), '02 (gold), '03 (silver) worlds; 2 Que. titles; 1 ntl title, 1 silver, 1 bronze; 2 ntl tourney MVP awards; silver '03 US ntls; bronze '03 NZ ntls; competed for Sarasota, Fla. US Atlantic champs '03; res. Belmont, Ont.

WILLSIE, Harry (shooting); b. 20 Dec 1928, Jacksonville, Mo.; d. 3 Jan 2003, Lake Worth, Fla.; div.; c. Billie, Alan, Carol Dean, Debora; Missouri, BA; ret'd real estate agent; p-pres. Cdn Skeet Shooting Assn.; dir. Shooting Federation of Canada; dir. QSSF, COJO Tir Mission '76, QTSA '59-67, Amateur Trap Shooting Assn. of America '59-68; pres. CTSA '63-67; gold, record '74 CG; mem. '64, '68 Olympic, '67, '71, '74 PAG teams; mgr. '78 CG team; 6 ntl trap/skeet titles; only Cdn to score perfect 100x100 in American trap doubles.

WILMSMEYER, Klaus (football); b. 4 Dec 1967, Mississauga, Ont.; m. Deborah Lynn; c. Kasey Nicole; Louisville; banker; punter; lettered in football/soccer at Lorne Park HS; p/pk at Louisville; noted for prodigious punts; AP 1st team all-South Independent '90; career longest punt 84yds '90; tied school record 52yd fg vs. Virginia '89; drafted in NFL by Tampa Bay '92; signed as free agent by San Francisco '92 earning all-rookie status *Football News, Pro Football Weekly, College & Pro Football Newsweekly*; joined New Orleans Saints '95; sat out '97 season then joined Miami '98; best season punting avg 41.4yds '94; best NFL punt 63yds '96; through '97 only 1 of 305 career punts blocked; mem. Super Bowl XXIX title team; res. Louisville, Ky.

WILSON, Al (football); b. 6 Apr 1950, Duncan, B.C.; given name: Alan Douglas; m. Robin Knowles; c. Chelsea, Alana, Colby; Montana State, BA; projects mgr. Vancouver energy co., entrepreneur; all-Big Sky Conf. ctr; mem. BC '72-86; all-WFC, all-Cdn centre '75-81; 3 times Schenley lineman award finalist, winner '77; knee injury suffered '82 season ended remarkable record of never having missed a practice, pre-season or regular- season game in his career, 167 consecutive regular season games with Lions; jersey 52 ret'd by Lions; Duncan park bears his name; mem. BC Place Wall, Cdn Football Hall of Fame; res. N. Vancouver, B.C.

WILSON, Alex (rowing); b. 2 Feb 1931, Toronto, Ont.; m. Sheila Sherman; c. Doug, Bruce, Sandra; Brock; policeman; competed at Cdn, US championship level; coached Olympic rowing team '60; coached HS rowers to Cdn, US schoolboy victories; FISA licensed rowing official; officiated at world, Olympic, PAG level; mem. Cdn Amateur Sports Hall of Fame; res. St. Catharines, Ont.

WILSON, Ben (football); b. 12 Jul 1926, London, Ont.; d. 11 Jan 1995, Toronto, Ont.; given name: Benson Andrus; m. Charlotte Henry Harrington; c. Benson Andrus 2nd, Meredith Jane; UWO, BSc, Oxford, BSc; asst. deputy minister, Ministry of Colleges and Universities; outstanding lineman UWO Mustangs '44-47; '48-50; Oxford basketball team capt. '49-50; University College (Oxford) rugger team, Inter-College Cup semifinalists '49-50; coach football, basketball Ridley College, St. Catharines '50-51.

WILSON, Bruce (soccer); b. 20 Jun 1951, Vancouver, B.C.; sep. Donna Beltley; c. Derek, Colin; soccer coach UVic; minor soccer BC; rejected pro overtures Everton English League; mem. ntl team '74-86; capt. '76-79; pro Vancouver Whitecaps '74-78, Chicago Sting '78-80, NY Cosmos '80, Toronto Blizzard '81-85; mem. NY Soccer Bowl champions '80; capt. Chicago, Toronto, Vancouver teams; NASL "iron man" record playing 161 consec. games '75-80; played every minute of every league and playoff game over 6-yr span; mem. '86 World Cup team; 1st Cdn to receive NASL all-star ranking; 1st team 3, 2nd team 3, hon. mention 1; coach '93 FISU Games team; coach UVic 8yrs; 2 CIAU coach-of-yr awards; named to Pele's '88 world all-star team; lone Cdn named to CONCACAF team of century; mem. Cdn Soccer, NASL, Canada's, BC Sports halls of fame; res. Victoria, B.C.

WILSON, Chris (wrestling): b. 30 Dec 1967, Winnipeg, Man.; SFU; began competing age 13; mem. ntl team '87-94; World Cup 68kg silver '91, bronze '89-90; gold US, Polish Grand Prix '93, Czech GP '92; 5 ntl FS titles; Canada Cup silver '92; competed '90 Goodwill, '92 Olympic, '94 CG; Viscount Alexander award '87; BC male athlete of '87; CAWA wrestler of '90-91; Danny Gallivan Fair Play award '92; BC sr. and overall athlete of '91; Intl Fair Play award '93; Johnny F. Bassett award '93; mem. SFU Sports Hall of Fame; res. Coquitlam, B.C.

WILSON, Doug Jr. (hockey); b. 5 Jul 1957, Ottawa, Ont.; given name: Douglas Frederick; m. Kathy Kovisto; c. Lacey, Douglas III, Chelsea, Charles; hockey exec.; dir. player development San Jose '97-03, GM from '03; former co-ordinator player relations/business development NHLPA; minor hockey Ottawa; jr. Ottawa 67's '74-75; OHA all-star def; Memorial Cup finalist '77; Memorial Cup tournament all-star def '77; pro Chicago '77-91, 1st draft choice, 6th overall, traded to expansion San Jose '91-93, team capt.; mem. Team Canada '84 Canada Cup, '87 Rendez-Vous series; Norris trophy '82; pres. NHLPA '91-93; mem. pension dispute bargaining comm.; 7 all-star games; management consultant 4 Cdn gold medal jr. worlds, '98 Olympic teams; dir. Chicago alumni assn.; NHL record: 1024 scheduled games, 237g, 590a, 95 playoff games, 19g, 61a; Cedarhill Golf Club champion '76; Toronto Thunderbird Invitational '76; co-owner San Jose Rhinos roller hockey team; board mem. CHA, Black Hawks Alumni, San Jose

Children's Shelter; oversees Doug Wilson Scholarship Foundation; Ottawa 67's ret'd his jersey #7; mem. Ottawa, Chicago Sports halls of fame; res. Hinsdale, Ill.

WILSON, Doug Sr. (t&f/hockey); b. 25 Oct 1929, Toronto, Ont.; d. 29 Aug 1983, Ottawa, Ont.; given name: Douglas Frederick; m. Verna Myers; c. Murray, Victoria, Patricia, Douglas Jr.; UWO, BA; staff relations officer Carleton Board of Education; mem. UWO track team; involved with Ottawa 67's hockey organization from inception working with minor league development program; v-p. Man. t&f Assoc.; mem. ntl selection comm.; chief scout Ottawa 67's hockey club '74-78.

WILSON, Harold (speedboat racing); b. 12 Oct 1911, St. Catharines, Ont.; d. 11 Dec 1995, Montserrat, W.I.; given name: Harold Albert; m. Lorna Margaret Reid; c. Ernest, Launi, Marion, Harold, Patricia; Ridley College, UofT, BSc; manufacturer, pres. Ingersoll Machine and Tool Co., pres. Morrow Screw and Nut Co.; world 225-cubic-inch-class title Toronto '33-34 with 1st in series of inboard hydroplanes, Little Miss Canada series boats III, IV, V, VI, before moving up to 12-litre Gold Cup class and competing for this trophy at Lake George and Detroit; won Silver Cup at Detroit, President's Cup Washington with Gold Cup-class hydroplane Miss Canada III; NA speed record for this class, world 12- litre title; challenged for Harmsworth Trophy '47 with unlimited hydroplane Miss Canada IV; world speed record at Picton; also made unofficial 173 mph run; ret'd from competitive races although he drove Miss Canada IV in Gar Wood Memorial race at Detroit and Gravenhurst Antique Boat Show; turned to auto racing; 2 terms pres. Cdn Automobile Sports Clubs; dir., pres. Mosport race track in formative years; avid sail boater; mem. Gulf 100 mph club; life mem. Picton Yacht Club; author *Boats Unlimited*; mem. Gulf Marine, Canada's Sports halls of fame.

WILSON, Jean (speed skating); b. 1910, Glasgow, Scotland, d. 1933, Toronto, Ont.; Toronto indoor, NA champion '31; rep. Canada '32 Olympic demonstration event, 500m in record 58:00, world record for 1500m (2:54.2); died from progressive muscular disease; *Toronto Telegram* donated Jean Wilson Trophy in her memory to fastest indoor woman skater '34; mem. Cdn Speed Skating, Amateur, Canada's Sports halls of fame.

WILSON, Lefty (hockey); b. 15 Oct 1919, Toronto, Ont.; d. 5 Nov 2002, Naples, Fla.; given name: Ross Ingram; m. Lillian Bhowe; c. Ross Martin; ret'd athletic trainer; mem. Toronto Shirley St. School softball title team, Ont. title Brock Grads lacrosse team, KofC juv baseball title team; goal Toronto Lions OHA jr. team; baseball St. Catharines, Niagara district teams '38-43; service softball batting title; minor pro 1b Roanoke Piedmont League, Savannah Sally League; Brantford (Sr.IC); goalie Calder Cup champion Indianapolis (AHL); 3 partial games in NHL as fillin for Boston, Toronto, Detroit; head trainer Red Wings; 3 terms pres. NHL Trainers' Assn.

WILSON, Montgomery (figure skating): b. 20 Aug 1909, Toronto, Ont.; d. 15 Nov 1964, Lincoln, Mass.; m. Mary Ann Winston; c. Marsha, Stewart Kimbrough, Winston; Toronto Skating Club jr. champion '22; 9 sr. men's ntl singles titles; with Constance Wilson Samuel 5 ntl pairs titles; 4 ntl fours titles; 6 NA sr. men's singles titles; 3 NA pairs, 1 NA fours titles; competed 4 world championships earning 1st world medal by Cdn male with singles silver '32; competed '28, '32, '36 Olympics winning 1st Cdn figure skating Olympic medal with bronze '32; turned pro St. Paul, Minn. '39; 18yrs coaching Boston SC; mem. US, Cdn Figure Skating halls of fame.

WILSON, Murray (hockey); b. 7 Nov 1951, Toronto, Ont.; given name: Murray Charles; div. Cathy Lewis; c. Emily, Matthew; Carleton; marketing consultant, Montreal hockey color commentator; jr. A Ottawa 67's; 3rd Montreal choice, 11th overall '71 amateur draft; 1 season Nova Scotia Voyageurs (AHL); lw Montreal '72-78, Los Angeles '78-79; mem. 4 Stanley Cup winners; NHL record: 386 scheduled games, 94g, 95a, 53 playoff games, 5g, 14a; ntl juv discus record; Ottawa HS discus record 51.86m '70; Ottawa Lynx community relations '93-96; mem. Ottawa Sports Hall of Fame; res. Nepean, Ont.

WILSON, Peter (ski jumping); b. 22 Oct 1952, Ottawa, Ont.; m. Lynne Massey; Cariboo Coll., TCOM; electrician; mem. Ottawa Ski Club; ntl ski team '70-77; '72, '76 Olympic teams; world Nordic championships '74, world ski flying championships '72, '73; 2nd NA jumping championships '72; held Cdn distance record of 142m '73-79; mem. Ottawa Rowing Club, ntl jr, sr. cox 4s; avid windsurfer; res. Fernie, B.C.

WILSON, Phat (hockey); b. 29 Dec 1895, Port Arthur, Ont.; d. 26 Jul 1970, Thunder Bay, Ont.; given name: Gordon Allan; amateur throughout career as player, coach; def Port Arthur War Veterans srs '18-20; Iroquois Falls NOHA, league title; Port Arthur Seniors, Allan Cup '25, '26, '29, Western Cdn title '30; coach Bearcats '38, '40; mem. NWO Sports, Hockey halls of fame.

WILSON, Robert (rowing); b. 14 Oct 1935, Kamloops, B.C.; given name: Robert Andrew; m. Barbara Evon Andrews; c. Sharon Marie, Douglas James; UBC, BSc; mem. gold medal 8s '54, '58 BE, CG; silver '56 Olympics; mem. BC Sports Hall of Fame; res. Calgary, Alta.

WILSON, Robin (curling); b. 22 Apr 1951, Vancouver, B.C.; given name: Robin Leigh Knowles; m. Alan Douglas Wilson; c. Chelsea, Alana, Colby; UBC, BComm; marketing consultant; 2nd stone Cdn women's title rinks '76, '79; rink skipped by Lindsay Sparkes placed 3rd in 1st women's world championship; co-ordinated Scott Tournament of Hearts ntl women's championships from '82 when Scott Paper assumed sponsorship; res. N. Vancouver, B.C.

WILSON, Rod (baseball): b. 8 Sep 1938, Fredericton, N.B.; given name: Harold Rodney; m. Judith Marilyn; P.S. v-principal; nicknamed "Silver Fox"; coached St. Stephen HS girls to 8 NB softball titles; St. Stephen Sabres to NB, Atlantic titles (midget) '78, (juv) '79, ntl bronze '79, NB jr. titles '80-81, Marysville Royals to '97 NB sr title; St. Stephen basketball team to NB bantam A crown, Eastern Cdn silver '85; mem. ntl youth baseball coaching staff '87; scout Blue Jays; Intl-Year-of-Child award '79; Moosehead Sports coach of '80; Canada Summer Games merit award '81; Baseball NB coach of '87; NB coach of '89; mem. NB Sports Hall of Fame; res. St. Stephen, N.B.

WILSON, Ron (hockey/coaching); b. 28 May 1955, Windsor, Ont.; m. Maureen; c. Kristen, Lauren; Providence Coll.; fwd/def. led U.S. college scorers '75; 2 all-American; father Larry, uncle Johnny both Stanley Cup winners with Detroit; played Dallas (CHL), N.B. (AHL), Switzerland '80-85; mem. Team USA '75, '81; NHL TML '77-79, Minnesota '85-88; NHL record: 177 scheduled games, 26g, 67a, 20 playoff games, 4g, 13a; coached Team USA to '96 world title, coach Team USA '04; asst. Vancouver 3yrs; head coach Anaheim '93-97, Washington '97-02, San Jose '02-04; res. San Jose, Calif.

WILSON, Ruth (tennis/golf/basketball); b. 27 Apr 1919, Calgary, Alta.; d. 2001, Vancouver, B.C.; given name: Ruth Plant; m. Art Willoughby (d); UBC, BA, Western Washington State College, MEd; teacher, counsellor; gd 4 ntl basketball title teams; coached 3 ntl sr. A titlists (Eilers '50-51, Buzz Bombs '75), bronze '67 PAG; mgr. '59 PAG team; coached basketball 35yrs; catcher 2 women's softball world series, coached a third; mem. 8 BC interprovincial golf teams, 4 ntl titles; mem. 1 international team; runnerup ntl Closed championship '61; BC jr. tennis doubles, mixed doubles; Whistle Award for basketball contributions by BC referees; dir. CABA '52-61, BCABA '76-81; recognized among BC women in sports leaders & legends; UBC Big Block award; mem. BC, UBC Sports halls of fame.

WILSON, Seymour (football/officiating); b. 1911, Hamilton, Ont., d. 23 Sep 1974, India; c. Kerry, Simone; chief clerk treasury dept.; backfielder Victoria Park juv, jr. teams; made ORFU Hamilton Tigers '29 but persuaded by family to forego game because of size; made Tigers as end '30-37; mem. 2 Grey Cup finalists, 1 winner; began officiating '30; IRFU '38-57, CFL '58-70; umpire, head linesman, referee more than 10 Grey Cup finals; mem. Canadian Football Hall of Fame.

WILSON, Stacy (hockey): b. 12 May 1965, Salisbury, N.B.; Acadia BSc; P.E. teacher, coach; fwd Team NB sr. women's ntl championships '87-96, Maritime Sports Blades '94 finals; ntl tournament MVP '95; top scorer '86 ntls, '88 all-star, '90, '96 most sportsmanlike player; MVP, top scorer NB sr. league '90; mem. 7 Team Canada world, 2 Pacific Rim title teams; silver '98 Olympics; ntl '90-98; asst. coach NB '95 Canada Winter Games team; rep. hockey at Cdn Athletes Assn. forum; volunteer with NB women's hockey council; attended Olympic Oval high performance program; asst. coach UMinn.-Duluth; mem. Acadia Sports Hall of Fame; res. Duluth, Minn.

WILSON, Tom (curling); b. 2 Jul 1948, Saskatoon, Sask.; given name: Thomas Robert; UofSaskatoon, BA; sales mgr. Q.S.P. (Reader's Digest/McLean-Hunter); 2nd Rick Folk's ntl mixed title rinks '74, '83, runnerup '81-82; all-star status; mem. Folk's '78-79 ntl men's championship runnerup, '80 Brier, Silver Broom (world) champions; '76 Calgary Grey Cup 'spiel, '77 Edmonton Christmas car 'spiel, '78 Vernon car 'spiel, '80 Lausanne, Switzerland, Classic, Victoria invitational, '81 Scotland international; Dick Ellis team award '80; mem. Saskatchewan Sports Hall of Fame; res. Toronto, Ont.

WILSON, Tracy (figure skating); b. 25 Sep 1961, Lachine, Que.; m. Brad Kinsella; c. 2; TV broadcaster; with Mark

Stokes ntl jr. dance title '80; with Robert McCall 7 straight ntl, 2 Skate Canada dance titles; mem. '84, '88 (bronze) Olympic, '82-84 world (3 bronze) championships teams; pro Stars on Ice; *TSN Women in Sport* show host; BC Women in Sport Leaders & Legends award; BC athlete of '88; Olympic champion award; mem. Order of Canada, Cdn Amateur Sports, Skate Canada halls of fame; res. Port Moody, B.C.

WILTJER, Greg (basketball); b. 26 Nov 1960, Whitehorse, Y.T.; m. Carol; Oregon State, UVic; all-American Idaho Junior College; ctr ntl team '81-86, '91, '94; gold Worlds Fair tournament '82, FISU Games '83; mem. '83 PAG, '84 Olympic teams; 1 CIAU MVP Jack Donohue trophy; 1 CIAU all-Cdn; mem. Canada's '82, '86, '94 World Championships teams; 2nd round draft Chicago NBA '84 but opted to play in Europe with Brescia (Italy), Barcelona (Spain), Madrid (Spain), Thessalonika (Greece); CBA Omaha Racers '89-90; fed. govt. excellence award '84; res. Victoria, B.C.

WILTSHIRE, Kelly (football); b. 28 Jun 1972, Saint-Laurent, Que.; Vanier Coll, Hudson Valley CEGEP, James Madison; linebacker; midget fb Saint-Laurent; also basketball, baseball standout; 2 CEGEP AAA all-star awards; NCAA Div. II, Yankee conf. def. player of '95 awards; attended NFL Jacksonville camp; CFL Toronto '97-99, Montreal '00-01, Ottawa '02-04, Edmonton '05; 2 East div all-star; frequent CFL def-player-of-wk awards; regarded as ironman with 152 consec. games including playoffs; res. Ottawa, Ont.

WINDEYER, Walter (sailing); b. 1900, Toronto, Ont., d. 1964, Toronto, Ont.; mem. Royal Cdn Yacht Club; 4 Townsend Cups for International 14ft dinghies; Canada's 1st International Dragon Class world championship '59; at 19 Douglas Cup; 3 consecutive Wilton Morse Trophies; mem. Cdn entry which won Currie Cup International 14ft class '36; skipper Invader II '32 Canada's Cup challenge; '58 with Corte on Great Lakes; '59 Dragon Gold Cup, O'Keefe Trophy, *Toronto Telegram* Trophy, Olympic trials; Duke of Edinburgh Trophy Lake Ont. '61; permanent possession O'Keefe Trophy with 3rd victory; mem. Canada's Sports Hall of Fame.

WINFIELD, Dave (baseball); b. 3 Oct 1951, St. Paul, Minn; given name: David Mark; m. Tonya Turner; c. Shanel; Minnesota, hon. degree Syracuse; capt. Minn baseball team as p/of; also standout in football, basketball; 1st team all-American, college world series MVP; drafted in baseball by San Diego, football Minnesota, basketball Utah (ABA), Atlanta (NBA); founded David M. Winfield Foundation '77; ML player San Diego '73-80, NY Yankees '81-90, California '90-91, Toronto '92, Minnesota '93-94; passed 3000 hits '93; ML record: 2973 scheduled games, 11,003ab, 1669r, 3110h, 540db, 88tr, 465hr, 1833rbi, 223sb, .283ba; 2 world series, 1 winner; 5 Dick Siebert Upper Midwest player-of-yr awards; 7 Rawlings Gold Glove awards; 2 Silver Slugger awards; outstanding DH award; AL comeback-player-of-yr award '90; 12 consec all-star games; played key role in Toronto '92 World Series victory; v-p San Diego Padres '02; YMCA Brian Piccolo humanitarian award '79; Branch Rickey Community Service award; Arete award '92; Joe Cronin award '93; mem. Baseball Hall of Fame; res. Minnesota.

WINFIELD, Earl (football): b. 6 Aug 1961, Petersburg, Va.; North Carolina; wr; NFL Seattle tryout '86, San Francisco '89; CFL Hamilton '87-96; 3 Eastern, 1 Northern, 1 CFL all-star; Jeff Russell Memorial trophy '88; runnerup Schenley outstanding player award '88; tied CFL record 2td punt returns single game '93; 8 playoff games, 1 Grey Cup final; res. Hamilton, Ont.

WINNING, Craig (parachuting); b. 7 Jan 1950, Windsor, Eng.; given name: Craig Stuart; m. Susan Fry; Waterloo Lutheran, BA; salesman; ntl overall champion '79-80; mem. ntl team world championships '74, '76, '78, '80; silver accuracy '80 Worlds; ntl record 10 consecutive dead-centre landings on electronic accuracy pad '80 world meet; diamond wings (2000+ jumps); coached ntl team '78 world meet; res. Hamilton, Ont.

WINTERS, Shelley (field hockey); b. 24 Jun 1953, Victoria, B.C.; given name: Shelley Ann; m. Rod Andrews; c. Robin, Brendan, Charlotte; UBC, BPhE; teacher; UBC varsity team '71-76; def ntl team '75-86; mem. silver medal World Cup team '83; mem. '84 Olympic team; mem. BC ntl title team '80; mem. 4 World Cup, 2 world championships teams; Oak Bay sportsmanship award '71; UBC female athlete of '76; UBC Joan Livesey sportsmanship award '73; VFHA MVP '72, VIFHA MVP '80, '82; fed. govt. excellence award '83; mem. Greater Victoria Sports Hall of Fame; res. Victoria, B.C.

WIRKOWSKI, Nobby (football); b. 20 Aug 1926, Chicago, Ill.; given name: Norbert; m. Therea Ann Lombardo; c. Linda Mary, Norbie J., Carol Julie, Ricky Patrick; Miami of Ohio, BSc; ret'd AD; mem. '48 Sun Bowl, '51 Salad Bowl champions; pro Toronto '51-54, Hamilton '55-56, Calgary '57-59; qb'd '52 Argos Grey Cup winners; asst. coach Argos '60-61, head coach '62-64, dir. player personnel '66-68; football coach York '68-74; athletic dir. York.; res. Mississauga, Ont.

WISEMAN, Eddie (hockey); b. 28 Dec 1909, Newcastle, N.B., d. 6 May 1977, Red Deer, Alta.; given name: Edward Randall; mem. Regina Pats '30 Memorial Cup winner; pro Chicago Shamrocks (AHL); NHL Detroit '32-35, NY Americans '35-39, Boston '40-42; NHL record: 115 goals, 165 assists; led Bruins playoff goal scorers with 6 en route to '41 Stanley Cup victory; mem. NB Sports Hall of Fame.

WISHART, Carol (fencing); b. 20 Dec 1953, Jonquiere, Que.; given name: Carol Anne; m. Winston Esnard; c. Victoria, Elizabeth; UofOtt, hons BSc; v-p. Tree Canada Foundation from '92; mem. intercollegiate team '72-75; mem. ntl team '78-80; Ont. women's foil champion '79-80; mem. Ont. women's gold medal team '79-80; team gold ntl foil championships '77-78, individual silver; mem. Ont. women's intercollegiate gold foil team '73-74, individual silvers; fencing instructor UofOtt '75-76; secty-treas. Region IV OFA '79-86; holder levels I, II coaching certificates; UofOtt female athlete of '75; nominee RA female athlete of '78; ED freestyle Ski Canada '82-86; ED Cdn Fencing Fed. '86-89; v-p. marketing United Way Canada '89-92; res. Carleton Place, Ont

WISHART, Wyatt (wrestling); b. 10 Jun 1958, Fort William, Ont.; Concordia, BA; weights mfgr.; Pan-Am jr. 100kg FS,

GR titles '76, '78; ntl jr. 100kg FS, GR champion '78; 3 ntl 100kg FS, 1 GR titles; gold 100kg FS '78 CG; bronze '79 PAG 100kg FS; bronze 100kg FS '78-79 Cerro Pelado, silver '80; 4th US Nationals '79; bronze 100kg FS '80 World Cup; gold super- heavyweight '82 CG; outstanding wrestler (Greco Roman) '78 Pan-Am championships; Que. judo titles '80-81; middle guard Concordia football '80; drafted 6th round Edmonton Eskimos '81; competed for Lakehead U Weightlifting Club; mem. NWO Sports Hall of Fame; res. Suzhou, China.

WITTMEIER, Bonnie (gymnastics); b. 15 Sep 1966, Winnipeg, Man.; div. John Withington; 2 ntl all-around, beam, vault, 1 floor, uneven bars titles; 4 Canada Games gold medals; '82 Commonwealth championships floor exercise, team titles; sister Robin ntl diving team mem.; Man. Panthers gym club award bears her name; mem. Man. Sports Hall of Fame; res. N. Vancouver, B.C.

WOHLBERG, Eric (cycling): b. 8 Jan 1965, Sudbury, Ont.; road-racing specialist; mem. ntl team '92-03; won '93 Victoria Grand Prix; established Cdn record while placing 5th in team time trial '94 CG; represented Canada '96, '00 Olympic, '98, '02 CG, 6 World championships; 7 consec. ITT ntl titles, 5 ntl road-race titles; 1 gold, 1 bronze '98 CG; gold '99 PAG; '02 Coconut Grove '00 Tour of Gila, Tour de Hokkaido gold; Cdn Cycling Online male, road cyclist of '98 awards; mem. Saturn team; res. San Jose, Calif.

WOIT, Benny (hockey); b. 1 Jul 1928, Fort William, Ont.; given name: Benedict; m. Julie Franchi; c. Deborah, Denise; St. Michael's Coll.; graintrimmer; d/rw Port Arthur (TBJHL) '44-48, St. Mike's (OHA) '46-47; 2 Memorial Cups; pro AHL Indianapolis '49-51, Rochester '56-58, Providence '59-61, WHL Spokane '58-59; NHL Detroit '51-55, Chicago '55-57; EHL Kingston, Clinton, New Jersey '61-66; OHA Sr. Port Arthur '72-75; NHL record: 334 scheduled games, 7g, 28a, 41 playoff games, 2g, 6a; played '64 all-star game; 4 EHL all-star; coached Westfort (TBJHL) 5yrs, 2 titles; mem. NWO Sports Hall of Fame; res. Thunder Bay, Ont.

WOLF, Walter (motorsport); b. 5 Oct 1939, Graz, Austria; m. Elizabeth; c. Wendy Heather, Alexandra Justin, Walter Maximillian, Fiona Elizabeth; oil equipment supplier; purchased Williams Formula 1 racing team '75; ran '76 F1 world championship under Williams name with varied drivers including Jacky Ickx but scored no points; entered '77 F1 world championships as Walter Wolf Racing with Jody Scheckter as premier driver; won Argentina, Monaco, Mosport races; Scheckter runnerup to Niki Lauda in driver race and Wolf 4th in constructors' championship; entered a Wolf-Dallara in '77 Can-Am Challenge series with Gilles Villeneuve placing 3rd at Road America; Wolf team 5th in '78 constructors' championship; ran '79 F1 earning no points; ran a team in '85-86 Can-Am Motorcycle series; mem. Cdn Motorsport Hall of Fame; res. Austria/Canada.

WOLFF, Doreen (t&f): b. 23 Jul 1931, Kelvington, Sask.; given name: Doreen Mae Dredge; m. Bernard Wolff; c. Diane, Larry, Barbara; teacher's certif.; hj/lj/sprinter; displayed versatility with participation in softball, volleyball, curling, snowmobiling, skiing; set Sask., Cdn hj records; mem. '48 Cdn Olympic team; mem. Sask. Sports Hall of Fame; res. Arizona/Liberty, Sask.

WOLFS, Mike (sailing); b. 2 Sep 1970, Port Credit, Ont.; given name: Michael Anthony; sailmaker; Star class; a string of 2nd places '04 Greek ntls, Star Bacardi Cup and Spa Regatta culminated (with Ross Macdonald) silver '04 Olympics; numerous medals competing in different classes of boats during 11 years on ntl sailing team; Cdn. Rolex sailor of '04; Cdn. sailor male athlete of '04; res. Toronto, Ont.

WONG, Charlene (figure skating); b. 4 Mar 1966, Montreal, Que.; m. Scott Williams; Que. juv champion '75-76; Que. Ladies Novice title '78; Eastern Canada novice '78; 2 Eastern div. titles; runnerup ntl sr. singles '83, '88-90; GP intl title '81; won '88 Skate Electric invitational; guest skater Tour of World Champions Montreal Forum '79, '81; competed at masters level '91-93; conceived concept of American Open pro championships; Que. athlete of '78; res. Pierrefonds, Que.

WONG, Lester (fencing); b. 28 Aug 1944, China; m. Donna; UAlta, BSc; production mgr.; individual silver épée, team bronze '70 CG; ntl épée title '71, foil '75; mem. '71, '75 PAG, '72, '76 Olympic teams; res. Caledon, Ont.

WONG SHUI, Mike (shooting); b. 24 Aug 1952, Montego Bay, Jamaica; given name: Herbert Michael; m. Dianne Ngo; Carleton, BEng; optician; mem. 10 Cdn Bisley teams, 2 others as coach; finalist St. George match, 3rd Queen's Prize '81 Bisley matches; competed ORA 100th matches '81; 3rd Lieut.-Gov.'s final; 4 Palma teams; Ottawa ACT shooting award '82; mem. DCRA Hall of Fame; res. Mississauga, Ont.

WOO, Wes (weightlifting); b. 11 Sep 1939, Vancouver, B.C.; given name: Westley; m. Joyce; UBC, BSP; fitness centre dir.; ntl teenage middleweight lifting title '56; BC jr. champion, record holder '60; UBC record holder; pres. BC Weightlifting Assn. '66-70; mem. ntl Senior Coaches Assn., chair. '74-78; coach ntl teams '68, '76, '80 Olympic, '71, '75 PAG, '74, '77 world championships, '78 CG, '79 IWF world super-heavyweight championships, '81 Commonwealth championships; '71 Canada Winter Games; coach BC teams 13 ntl championships; formed Spartak Weightlifting Club '68; runnerup Air Canada coach of '75; res. Vancouver, B.C.

WOOD, Bryan (curling); b. 10 Mar 1944, Brandon, Man.; given name: Bryan David; m. Thelma Davis; c. Kevin, Robbie; real estate, farming; played for skips Don Duguid, Barry Fry, Rod Hunter as well as 2 seasons skipping own rink; mem. *CBC* televised series winners '70, '71, runnerup '76; Heather carspiel title '70; runnerup with Bob Pickering Toronto Grey Cup 'spiel '74; mem. Duguid's '70, '71 Man. Consols, Brier, Silver Broom (world) champions; mem. '79 Fry Man. Consols, Brier winners; mem. Man Sports, Man., Cdn Curling halls of fame; res. Justice, Man.

WOOD, Howie (curling); b. 8 Jul 1918, Winnipeg, Man.; d. 2 May 2000, Winnipeg, Man.; given name: Howard Francis Jr.; m. Christine Romano; c. Larry, Victor, Betty, Bob, Howie, Bruce, Ken, Dave; ret'd division mgr. Investors' Syndicate; semifinalist Man. 21-and-under championships age 11; with father beat Gordon Hudson for Winnipeg city title age 16; with father 1st carspiel Nipawin '47; 2nd for father '40 Brier winner with 9-0 record; skipped '57 Man. Brier entry comprising Bill Sharpe, Don and Lorne Duguid; skipped '54 Man. Bonspiel winner; Man. seniors title '70; pres. Man. Jr. (21-and-under) CA at 16; mem. Man Curling Hall of Fame.

WOOD, John (canoeing); b. 7 Jun 1950, Toronto, Ont.; given name: John Joseph; UofT, BA; stockbroker; mem. '68, '72, '76 Olympics, silver 500m solo canoe '76; '70, '73, '74, '75, '77 world championships teams, silver C2 (with Gregg Smith) '77; NA CI, C2 100m titles '74; ntl 500m, 1000m CI, C2 titles '72-77; bronze soling class sailing '79 PAG; *CBC-TV* color commentator '84 Olympics; res. Oakville, Ont.

WOOD, Lionel (curling); b. 5 Dec 1924, Winnipeg, Man.; given name: Lionel Lawrence; m. Colleen Margaret Warner; c. Craig Wynn, Paul Daniel, Jayanne; UMan, LLB; ret'd owner-mgr., office equipment; mem. '38 Man. PS softball champions; '39 soccer champions; Man. schoolboy curling title '41; Man. Consols '45; mem. Man.-Lakehead lacrosse champions '47; mem. Man. provincial HS football champions '42; mem. '46-47 Grey Cup finalist Blue Bombers; frequent Man. bonspiel trophy winner including grand aggregate; res. Edmonton, Alta.

WOOD, Nora (curling); b. 19 Jan 1903, Arnprior, Ont.; d. 12 Feb 1988, Arnprior, Ont.; given name: Nora Ward; m. Roy Wood; active curler '20-75; runnerup '52 Tweedsmuir Trophy double rink competition using irons, winner '54 Tweedsmuir using granites; pres. EOLCA '61, '70-72, OLCA '70-71; mem. Canadian Curling Hall of Fame.

WOOD, Pappy (curling); b. 29 Aug 1888, Winnipeg, Man., d. 28 Dec 1978, Winnipeg, Man.; given name: Howard; m. Elizabeth Gillespie; c. Howard Jr., Lionel; business college; pres. contracting firm; mem. Dominion Beavers soccer club '15, 1 of 2 Cdns on all-Scottish team; recognized in *Guinness Book of World Records* for curling longevity by competing in 65 consec. Man. bonspiels '08-72; 8 MCA 'spiel grand aggregate titles; won original Macdonald Brier '25 in conjuction with MCA 'spiel; skipped Brier winners '30, '40, 3rd Jim Congalton's '32 title winner; with son Howie 1st Nipawin carspiel '47; mem. Man., Cdn Curling, Man., Canada's Sports halls of fame.

WOOD, Sharon (mountaineering); b. 10 May 1957, Halifax, N.S.; given name: Sharon Adele; m. Christopher Jon Stethem; c. Robin, Daniel Layne; UCal, hon. LLD; co. pres./mountain guide/motivational speaker; began climbing '68; achieved international recognition as 1st Cdn woman to reach summit Mount Everest '86; in addition to Everest has climbed numerous 20,000+-foot summits around the world; 1st woman to achieve full climbing guide status within Assn. of Cdn Mountain Guides; Tenzing Norgay award as pro mountaineer of yr; Alta. achievement award; Breakthrough Award; *MacLeans* honor roll for outstanding-achievement award; *Outside Magazine* 10-who-made-the-difference award; co-founded Mountain Gate Community School; pres. Canmore Society for Community Education; Bill March Summit of Excellence award; Alta. Sports Hall of Fame special award; res. Canmore, Alta.

WOODCROFT, Greg (wrestling); b. 27 Aug 1970, Hamilton, Ont.; McMaster; teacher; 2 CIAU 52kg titles; mem. ntl team from '89; 9 ntl sr titles; silver '94 Francophone Games; bronze '93 World Cup; competed '93 World Cup, '96 Olympics, '90, '96 Pan-Am championships; res. Hamilton, Ont.

WOODHOUSE, Hedley (horse racing); b. 23 Jan 1920, Vancouver, B.C., d. 29 Dec 1984, New York, N.Y.; given name: Hedley John; m. Elsie Martens; c. Marten, Robert, Deborah; ret'd jockey; apprentice jockey Vancouver at 17; rode initial winner at 20; riding career spanned 31 years and involved every major race track in US, Canada; noted for ability to handle highly- temperamental fillies, mares; 2642 victories including phenomenal 103 stakes races; won all major NY races, except Belmont Stakes, at least once; top year '55 with 148 winners; twice NY riding champion, once runnerup; ret'd age 51; Woodbine Park security guard '72-83; mem. Canadian Horse Racing, BC Sports, BC Thoroughbred Breeders Society halls of fame.

WOODLEY, Erin (synchro swim): b. 6 Jun 1972, Mississauga, Ont.; m. Larry Roland; c. Ella; UofT BA; chef consultant; began competing '81; team silver '91 PAG; competed 2 Petro Canada Cups, 1 Loano, Fina, America Cups; duet gold (Lisa Alexander) '94 CG; 2 silver '95 PAG; team silver '96 Olympics; Unysis quest-for-excellence award '91 Canada Games; res. Etobicoke, Ont.

WOODS, Larry (sailing); b. 2 Aug 1939, Hamilton, Ont.; given name: Larry Earl; m. Elizabeth Helen Pleli; c. Larry David, Todd Michael; McMaster, BA,UofT, MEd; educator; ntl champion Tornado catamaran '74, '78; CORK title '78, in top 3 '76-80; NA champion '73, '80; 7th '76 Olympics; mem. '80 Olympic team; mem. 5 world championships teams; columnist *Sailing World*; res. Winona, Ont.

WOODWARD, Rod (football); b. 22 Sep 1944, Vancouver, B.C.; given name: Rodney William; m. Kay Whitacre; c. Tod William Brian, Carilena Mae; Idaho, BSc; teacher, football coach; all-conf. dh, hon. mention hb Everett Junior College '63-64; pro Montreal '67-69, Ottawa '70-76, Calgary '77, Hamilton '78; CFL record: 39 interceptions; CFL record interceptions 7 consecutive games; twice intercepted 3 passes single game; all-Eastern Conf. 3 times, all-Cdn once; '75 Ottawa Schenley nominee db of year; mem. Athletes in Action; coach Tri-City Bulldogs BC jr. team; res. Burnaby, B.C.

WOOLF, George (horse racing); b. 1910, Cardston, Alta., d. 3 Jan 1946, Santa Anita, Calif; nicknamed "The Iceman"; won '36 Preakness on Bolt Venture, '38 Pimlico Special on Seabiscuit; American Derby, Harve de Grace Handicap, Belmont Futurity, Hollywood Gold Cup 3 consecutive years; '45 Santa Anita Derby on Bymeabond; killed while riding Please Me at Santa Anita '46; in 19yr racing career 721 wins, 589 2nds, 468 3rds; George Woolf Memorial award for most sportsmanlike jockey in his honor; mem. Canada's Sports, American Jockey, Canadian Horse Racing halls of fame.

WOOLLEY, Emily (curling); b. 24 Jan 1899, Sarnia, Ont.; d. 1967, Toronto, Ont.; given name: Emily Clark; m. LeRoy Woolley; c. Jane; lefthanded standout in tennis, golf, badminton, curling; Royal Life Saving Society gold medal swimmer; began curling '32; mem. 14 Ont. Ladies' Tankard winners; with sisters Dadie, Janie, Redd formed famed Clark sisters rink; mem. 13 Toronto Granite Club Robertson Trophies, 7 Seigniory Club 'spiel titles, 5 Ont. title rinks; rep. Ont. '61, '63 ntl Diamond D competitions; SOLCA seniors trophy bears her name; recipient Ont. govt. achievement award; charter mem. Sarnia CC; life mem. Toronto Granite CC; mem. Canadian Curling Hall of Fame.

WOOTTON, Moon (lacrosse): b. 17 Sep 1926, Owen Sound, Ont.; d. 8 Feb 1989, Port Hope, Ont.; given name: William Lloyd; goaltender; played jr. Owen Sound; mem. 5 consec. Mann Cup winners, 1 Owen Sound, 4 Peterborough; ranked top goalie in Canada several seasons; 3 times Mann Cup MVP; played 10 seasons with Peterborough; mem. Cdn Lacrosse, Peterborough Sports halls of fame.

WORRALL, Jim (t&f/administration); b. 23 Jun 1914, Bury, Lancashire, Eng., m. Aileen McGuire (d); c. Anna Jane, Brian, Brenda; div. Lisbet Svensen; c. Ingrid; McGill, BSc, Osgoode Hall, LLB; ret'd lawyer; Rector's Trophy all-around athlete Montreal HS; silver 120yds hurdles '34 BEG; flag-bearer '36 summer Olympics; 2yrs pres. Ont. t&f comm. AAUofC; 8yrs v-p. COA; 1st pres. Cdn Sports Advisory Council; mem. National Advisory Council on Fitness, Amateur Sport '61-66, chair. 2yrs; 1st Cdn IOC exec. board; Officer Order of Canada '76; mem. Cdn Olympic Order, Canadian Amateur, McGill Sports halls of fame; res. Don Mills, Ont.

WORSLEY, Gump (hockey); b. 14 May 1929, Montreal, Que.; given name: Lorne John; m. Doreen; c. Lorne Jr., Dean, Drew, Lianne; ret'd; from NY Sr. Rovers (EHL) to New Haven (AHL), St. Paul (USHL), Saskatoon (PCHL, WHL), Vancouver (WHL); NYR '52-63, Calder Trophy rookie of year, Montreal '63-70, Minnesota '70-74; scout Minnesota; coach Belleville (OHL) '82; NHL record: 860 games, playing 50,201 minutes, 2432g, 43so, 2.91avg., 70 playoff games, 4080 minutes, 192g, 5so, 2.82avg.; 1st, 2nd team all-stars once each; mem. 4 Stanley Cup winners; USHL rookie of year Charles Gardiner Memorial Trophy; WHL MVP; WHL leading goalie; 2 Vezina Trophies ('66 with Charlie Hodge, '68 with Rogie Vachon); mem. AHL, Hockey halls of fame; res. Beloeil, Que.

WORTERS, Roy (hockey); b. 19 Oct 1900, Toronto, Ont., d. 7 Nov 1957, Toronto, Ont.; goalie nicknamed "The Shrimp"; Pittsburgh Yellowjackets (USAHA); Pittsburgh Pirates '26-28, NY Americans '28-29, '30-37, Canadiens '30; averaged 2.36 goals-against in 488 league games, Vezina Trophy '31 with 1.68 avg.; twice 2nd team all-star; 1st goalie to win Hart Trophy (MVP) '28-29 season; 1st goalie to use back of gloves to direct pucks to corners; mem. Hockey Hall of Fame.

WOSTENHOLME, Martin (tennis); b. 11 Oct 1962, Toronto, Ont.; given name: Martin Clark; Yale, BA, NYU (Stern School Business) MBA; pres./CEO ME2 Corp; ; div. 1 Eastern conf. singles '84; ntl -12 doubles '75, -14 singles, doubles '76, -18 doubles (with Glenn Michibata) '78, '80; mem. Galea Cup team '79-81, Davis Cup team '81-93; reached 3rd round '82 Players International; best ATP ranking #84 in '84; Tennis Canada player of '84; pro circuit '84-94; *TSN* color commentator; mem. Cdn Tennis Hall of Fame; res. New York, N.Y.

WOTHERSPOON, Jeremy (speed skating); b. 26 Oct 1976, Humboldt, Sask.; long-track specialist; mem. ntl team from '96; silver 500m '96 world jr; 8 gold, 2 silver world cup; ntl overall gold '96, 500 bronze '97; Cdn, world 500m, 1000m records; 500m silver '98 Olympics; through '01 world 1000m 1:08.28, 500m 34.63 records; won 3 consec. world titles; won 8 consec. 500m WC races, overall WC gold '99; world sprint title '02-05; Cdn long-track male athlete of '99-00, '02; res. Calgary, Alta.

WRIGHT, Doug (wheelchair basketball); b. 4 Feb 1938, Hamilton, Ont.; m. Dannielle; c. Douglas, Michael; CPO1 Cdn navy; played numerous sports for service teams '55-70; football MVP Bluenose conf. '66; Maritime Command athlete of '68; asst. football coach St. Mary's '70-82, 7 AAU titles, Vanier Cup '73; coached SMU Huskies varsity basketball '73-78, 2 ntl titles; head coach NS Flying Wheels, ntl wheelchair basketball silver medal team '81 PAG, bronze medal team '90 Stoke-Mandiville Games; asst coach ntl women's team '76 Olympics; mem. NS, Cdn Forces Sports halls of fame; res. Dartmouth, N.S.

WRIGHT, Harold (t&f/administration); b. 10 Dec 1908, Winnipeg, Man.; d. 11 Dec 1997, Vancouver, B.C.; m. Edna May Robinson; c. Linda Catherine, Lee Madison, James Kirkland; UAlta, Utah, BSc, MSc; UBC, MA, LLD; ret'd engineer; sprinter '32 Olympic team; dir., pres., life mem. Vancouver Olympic Club; pres. CFHA '65-69; pres., dir., COA; governor Olympic Trust '70-97; dir. Montreal Olympics organizing comm.; dir. BC Amateur Sports Council; trustee BC Sports Hall of Fame; gov. Canada's Sports Hall of Fame; dir. Calgary Olympic Development Assn.; mem. Olympic Club Canada; special achievement award BC Sports Fed., Olmpic comm. order of merit, Queen's Jubilee medal, IOC order of merit, silver medal; mem. Order of Canada; mem. BC, Canada's Sports halls of fame.

WRIGHT, Jack (tennis); b. 11 Nov 1901, Nelson, B.C.; d. Sep 1949, Montreal, Que.; given name: John; MD; won Washington, Oregon, Idaho, BC, Northwest, Inland Empire jr. titles; 3 ntl singles titles; with Willard Crocker 3 and Marcel Rainville 1 ntl indoor doubles titles; mem. Cdn Davis Cup team '23-33, Cdn record 40 Cup matches; defeated world #3 ranked Tacheichi Harada of Japan in 3 straight sets; Que. titlist '31; voted Canada's outstanding tennis player of half century by *CP* '50; mem. Cdn Tennis, Canada's, BC Sports halls of fame.

WRIGHT, Joseph Jr. (rowing); b. 28 Mar 1906, Toronto, Ont., d. 7 Jun 1981, Toronto, Ont.; m. Dorothy; c. Dianne; pres. coal co.; ctr/gd Argos '24-36; Grey Cup '33; stroked jr., sr. Argos 8s to Cdn Henley titles; mem. Penn AC crew '25 Middle States regatta title; 3 US ntl sculling titles, record times; 9 ntl titles; diamond sculls Royal Henley, England '28, runnerup '29; flag-bearer, silver, bronze medals '28 Olympics; 2 bronze '32 Olympics; pres. Eastern Football Conf.; mem. Canadian Amateur, Canada's Sports halls of fame.

WRIGHT, Joseph Sr. (all-around); b. 14 Jan 1864, Villanova, Ont., d. 18 Oct 1950, Toronto, Ont; m. Alethea Ainley Spink; c. George, Jessie, Nancy, Margaret, Joseph Jr.; UofT; rowing coach; Canadian amateur heavyweight boxing title at 35; among 1ˢᵗ Canadians to run 100yds in 10:00, ntl shot put, hammer throw records; 18yrs mem. Argos, '11 Grey Cup match with son George; ntl amateur wrestling titlist; ntl billiards champion; stroked 1ˢᵗ Cdn 8s to win US ntl title '01; 1ˢᵗ Cdn to win heat British Henley diamond sculls; Bedford Cup, English amateur singles title '95 (1ˢᵗ-ever by Cdn); US jr. singles 1891, int. singles '92; honored by King of Sweden '12 Olympics; coached sr. 8s '05, '07, '11, int. 8s '05-06, '09-11 Cdn Henley, US ntl titles; coach Penn. '16-26; Cdn oarsman of half century '50 *CP* poll; mem. Cdn Amateur, Canada's Sports halls of fame.

WRIGHT, Ken (builder/all-around); b. 24 Jun 1913, Chaplin, Sask.; d. 8 Apr 1996, New Westminster, B.C.; given name: Kenneth William Thomas; UBC; nicknamed "Hooker" for famed hook shot in basketball; mem. New Westminster Adanacs, UBC Thunderbirds before turning to coaching and administration; founder BC HS boys basketball tournament '45, active comm. mem. 36yrs; co-founder/pres/hon. life mem. BCHSBBA; co-authored written/pictorial history of BCHSBBA tournament; coach BC women's relay team to '52 ntl t&f championship; coached New Westminster t&f club athletes to 5 gold, 3 silver, 2 ntl records '52 Cdn age- class championships; chair. '54 BEG t&f officials; founding mem./governor Cdn Lacrosse Hall of Fame; pres./hon. life mem. New Westminster Tennis Club; mem. BC Sports Hall of Fame.

WRIGHT, Lee (field hockey); b. 28 Aug 1944, Vancouver, B.C.; given name: Lee Madison; m. Thelma Fynn; c. Lindsay, Anthony, Philip, Gillian; UBC, BPhE, SouthernCal, MA; phys-ed co-ordinator/coach; mem. '64, '76 Olympic, '67, '71, '75 PAG teams; more than 60 intl matches; bronze '71, silver '75 PAG; both he and wife Thelma, a 1500m runner, won silver medals '75 PAG; ret'd '76; coached BC team '78-79, '82; coached ntl team Colorado Springs tourney '82; dir. Olympic Club Canada; active fund-raiser UBC artificial turf project; res. Vancouver, B.C.

WRIGHT, Thelma (t&f); b. 9 Oct 1951, Eastbourne, Eng.; given name: Thelma Sonia Fynn; m. Lee Madison Wright; c. Lindsay, Anthony, Philip, Gillian; UBC, BPhE; teacher; ntl team '69-77; 800-3000m specialist; silver '75 FISU (3000m 8:54.9), '75 PAG (1500m 4:22.3), bronze '70 CG (1500m 4:18), '74 CG (1500m 4:12.3), '75 NZ Games (1500m 4:19); 4 ntl 1500m titles; 3 ntl 2 Ω-miles x-country titles; bronze '70 US x-country; '74 Springbank 4 miles, Puerto Rico 6 -mile road race titles; PB: 800m 2:05.1 '74, 1500m 4:10.5 '74, 3000m 8:54.9 '75; ntl open 3000m record '73-75; mem. '72, '76 Olympic, '70, '74, CG, '75 PAG teams; mem.'77 world x-country then ret'd; coach Vancouver Olympic TC, asst. coach UBC track team; mgr. BC t&f team '78-82; mgr. ntl x-country team '80-81; won 3 ntl masters x-country titles; dir. Olympic Club Canada; active fund-raiser UBC artificial turf project; mem. UBC, BC Sports halls of fame; res. Vancouver, B.C.

WRUCK, Larry (football); b. 29 Oct 1962, Saskatoon, Sask.; lb Saskatoon Jr. Hilltops; CFL Edmonton '85-96; CFL record: 213 scheduled games, 673 tackles, 40 qb sacks, 15 fumble recoveries, 13 interceptions, 19 playoff games, 60 tackles; 1 Western all-star; 2 Dr. Beattie Martin trophies; twice CFL most outstanding Canadian runnerup; 4 Grey Cup finals, 2 winners; res. Edmonton, Alta.

WU, Walter (swimming); b. 14 Aug 1972, Vancouver, B.C.; travel agent; B3 blind athlete; strong swimmer in FS, butterfly, backstroke and IM; mem. Pacific Dolphin Swimming Assn.; 5 gold '94 Kinsmen/Kinette Cup; 5 gold IPC World championships '94; 5 gold Superior Propane Cup '95; 5 gold IPC Swim trials '95; 5 gold, 1 bronze '96, 2 gold, 2 silver, 1 bronze '00 Paralympics; 7 gold World Blind championships '98; competed 5 Paralympics; 8 world titles; world records 200, 400m FS, 100m fly; BC Blind Sports Assn. Athlete of '94; mem. Terry Fox Hall of Fame; res. Richmond, B.C.

WURR, Alfred (wrestling); b. 28 Jun 1934, Germany; m. Beverly Bamendine; c. Alfred, Elke; iron worker; competitive at provincial, ntl, international levels '57-72; 11 FS, 8 GR ntl titles; silver '70 CG 163lb GR; mem. '70 world championships, '71 PAG, '72 Olympic Games teams; AAU male athlete of '64; YMCA athlete of '64-65; Man. athlete of '68; mem. Canadian Amateur Wrestling, Man. Sports halls of fame; res. Winnipeg, Man.

WURTELE, Rhoda (skiing); b. 21 Jan 1922, Montreal, Que.; given name: Rhoda Isabella; m. Arnold Eaves; c. David Wurtele, John Ironside, Bruce Arnold; Trafalgar School for Girls, Notre Dame Secretarial School; ski club dir.; mem. '48, '52 Olympic teams; US ntl downhill, combined '47; ntl downhill, slalom, combined '51, Norwegian National Holmenkollen Vos slalom, giant slalom, combined '52, Que. Kandahar, Far West Kandahar, Harriman Cup Sun Valley, Roch Cup Aspen '57, NA combined '57; 3ʳᵈ Arleberg Kandahar downhill Chamonix, France, '48; with twin sister Rhona female athlete of '44, runnerup to Joe Krol Cdn athlete of '45; dir. Ski Jay (1ˢᵗ children's club NA); mem. Que. Srs Golf team '72-78; pro-celebrity ski ballet competition with son John '77; mem. US National Ski, Cdn Amateur Sports, Skiing halls of fame; res. Etobicoke, Ont.

WURTELE, Rhona (skiing/swimming); b. 21 Jan 1922, Montreal, Que.; div. Gene Alan Gillis; c. Christopher Wurtele, Margaret Rose, Nancy Joanne, Jere Alan; Trafalgar School for Girls, Mother House secretarial school, Sir George Williams, Oregon; ski club dir.; Que., ntl 50, 100yd FS swim titles, provincial records in both; Idaho State 1m diving title; with twin sister Rhoda female athlete of '44, runnerup to Joe Krol Cdn athlete of '45, Cdn, US ntl titles slalom, downhill, GS; mem. US FIS team '50; mem. '48 Olympic team; mem. '73 Que. ladies' interprovincial golf team; Summerlea club champion; competed '80 Montreal marathon; mem. US National Ski, Cdn Amateur Sports, Skiing halls of fame; res. Actonvale, Que.

WYATT, Dave (coaching); b. 25 Jan 1940, Sherbrooke, Que.; m. Judith Stone; c. Chris; Queen's, hons BSc; ret'd teacher; Little League baseball coach more than 25yrs; 17 District, 3 provincial, 1 ntl title teams; coach '71 Little League World Series team; Brockville sportsman of '75; mem. Brockville Sports Hall of Fame; res. Brockville, Ont.

WYATT, Jennifer (golf); b. 10 Dec 1965, Vancouver, B.C.; Lamar; graphic artist, teaching golf pro Pacific Golf Academy; competitive hockey player before concentrating on golf; '84 BC jr. title; ranked top jr. in Canada '85-87;

won NZ amateur '87; mem. Cdn Commonwealth team '87; 2 university tournament titles; played on LPGA tour '88-98; career low round 66; won Crestar Farm Fresh Classic '92; 3rd BMO tour Wolf Creek tourney '03; mem. LPGA softball team; res. Vancouver, B.C.

WYDARENY, John (football); b. 15 Feb 1941, Hearst, Ont.; m. Janet Elizabeth Gowans; c. John Christopher, Erin Jean; UWO, BA, UofT, BEd; teacher; Ont. 440yd titles '55-57; OQAA all-star backfielder Western Mustangs; pro Argos '63-65, *Globe and Mail* all-star db each year; Eskimos '66-72; 3 times WFC all-star, twice all-Cdn; Jackie Parker Eskimo's MVP trophy '69; CFL record: 52 interceptions for 747yds; gained 208yds on interceptions '67, 127yds Edmonton at Calgary game '67; 11 interceptions lead WFC, CFL '69-70; mem. UWO W-Club Hall of Fame; res. St. Albert, Alta.

WYKEHAM-MARTIN, Simon (parachuting); b. 23 Dec 1937, Ryde, Isle of Wight, Eng.; d. 1992; given name: Simon Fairfax; div.; c. Cathy Lynn, Douglas Fairfax; ret'd Cdn Forces, safety dir.; mem. Cdn Sports Parachuting Assoc. team '62, '64, '66, '68, '70; world championships '62, '64, '66; 1st Cdn parachute medalist world competition with 2 silver, 1 bronze '66; silver, bronze '70 Worlds; 2 silver, 1 bronze military team European intl meets; former mem., pres., p.-pres. CSPA; ntl overall Sport Parachuting, accuracy champion; qualified CSPA instructor/examiner, rigger; responsible for establishing Cdn Forces Military Freefall Training program and CF parachute team Skyhawks; 5yrs Skyhawks team leader; mem. CF Airborne Trials and Evaluation Section; 2600 free-fall descents; qualified for airborne wings of Belgium, France, U.S.A., Canada; mem. Canadian Forces Sports Hall of Fame.

WYLIE, Bob (golf); b. 25 Sep 1929, Lamont, Alta.; given name: Robert Lenwood Duncan; m. Joan Cuthbert; c. Robert Scott, Michael, Jock; Mt. Royal Coll., Fullerton Jr. Coll.; ret'd steel co. mgr.; 4 Alta. Amateur titles, 3 times runnerup; 2 Alta. Open titles, lost 3rd in playoff, 3 times runnerup; Mexican Amateur title '61, Sask. Open '62; quarterfinalist British Amateur '70; rep. Canada 7 times internationally; mem. 14 Willingdon Cup teams; mem. Alta Sports, RCGA halls of fame; res. Calgary, Alta.

WYLIE, Harvey (football); b. Apr 1933, Lamont, Alta.; m. Pat Muir; c. Barbara, Wesley; Montana State; ret'd engineer; baseball tryout Chicago White Sox; jr. A hockey Calgary; pro football Calgary '56-64; WFC all-star safety 5 successive years; twice all-Cdn; CFL record 5 tds on kickoff returns; 35 career interceptions; 20 fumble recoveries; career record 151 kickoff returns for 4293yds; mem. Montana State, Alta. Sports, Canadian Football halls of fame; res. Rocky Mountain House, Alta.

WYNNE, Ivor (coaching); b. 2 Nov 1918, Wales, d. 1 Nov 1970, Hamilton, Ont.; m. Frances; c. Bob, John; McMaster, BA, Syracuse, MA, OCE; educator; nicknamed "The Driver"; 2 seasons ntl champion Cloverleafs basketball team; athletic dir. McMaster from '48; pres. CIAU, governor OQAA; 16yrs color commentator for pro, intercollegiate football games on radio, TV with sportscaster Norm Marshall; Hamilton Civic Stadium renamed in his honor; McMaster athletic complex bears his name; mem. McMaster Sports Hall of Fame.

YAKUBOWICH, Joyce (t&f); b. 29 May 1953, Toronto, Ont.; given name: Joyce Louise Sadowick; m. Bradley Yakubowich; c. Jennifer, Lee; SFU, UVic; computer support; ntl HS record 54.7 for 400m '70; mem. bronze 4x100m relay team '70 CG; mem. '71, '75 PAG, '72, '76 Olympic, '73 FISU Games, '77 European tour teams; gold 400m, 4x400m relay, bronze 4x100m relay '75 PAG; Pan-Am, ntl records (51.60) in 400m, (23.2) 200m, ntl relay records; ntl 400m titles '71-78, 200m '72, '75; ret'd '78 due to blood disorder; coaches fitness training; mem. SFU Sports Hall of Fame; res. Victoria, B.C.

YALLOP, Frank (soccer); b. 4 Apr 1964, Watford, Eng.; soccer coach; honed talents Port Coquitlam; 14 seasons as def Ipswich Town, Blackpool; moved to MLS with Tampa Bay Mutiny '96-98; MLS coach-of-'01 award; mem. ntl team '90-03; competed '91, '93 Gold Cup, '92-93 World Cup qualifiers; 52 international caps; coach San Jose Earthquakes '01-03, 2 MLS titles; Cdn ntl team '04; mem. Cdn Soccer Hall of Fame; res. Vancouver, B.C.

YASHIN, Alexei (hockey); b. 5 Nov 1973, Sverdlovsk, Russia; ctr; represented Russia '92, '93 world jr, gold '92; competed for Russia 6 world championships, gold '93; competed for Russia '96 World Cup; '98 (silver), '02 (bronze) Olympics; Ottawa 1st choice '92 NHL entry draft; made NHL debut '93; Ottawa '93-01, NYI '01-04; NHL record (through '04): 710 scheduled games, 291g, 374a, 43 playoff games, 11g, 16a; only rookie '93-94 all-star game scoring 2g, including winner; 2 NHL all-star games; donated $1M to National Arts Centre '98, withdrew donation '99 after first $200,000 payment made; Senators team capt. '98-99; *SN* all-star team '99; suspended by Senators for entire '99-00 season for refusal to honor $3.6M contract; court rules he owes Senators another season of play so he returns to fold '00-01; traded to NYI '01-02; res. New York, NY/Kloten, Switzerland.

YEATS, Doug (wrestling); b. 1 Nov 1957, Montreal, Que.; Concordia; engineer; Greco-Roman specialist; 2 ntl 68kg GR, 1 62kg GR titles; 3 US 68kg GR titles; gold 62kg '79 PAG; mem. '79, '83 Pan-Am, '76, '80, '84, '88, '92 Olympic, '77-79, '81-83, '86-87, '91 world championships teams; silver '92 Pan-Am championships; mem. Concordia, Cdn Wrestling halls of fame; res. Montreal, Que.

YETMAN, Wayne (t&f); b. 8 Oct 1946, Toronto, Ont.; given name: Wayne Douglas; UWO, BA, UofT; mgr. creative services; '68 Detroit, '75 Toronto Police Games, '76 National Capital marathon titles; 19th '69, 10th '70 Boston marathons; mem. '76 Olympic team; 2nd '75 Skylon (Buffalo to Niagara Falls) marathon; res. Toronto, Ont.

YOCHUM, Dan (football); b. 19 Aug 1950, Bethlehem, Pa.; Syracuse; hon. mention *AP, UPI* all-American; played college all-star game vs. Dallas Cowboys; drafted by Philadelphia Eagles but opted to join Montreal Alouettes as ot '72; played 9 seasons closing CFL career Edmonton

'80; 7 Eastern all-star, 4 all-Cdn; Schenley outstanding off. lineman award '76; 4 Grey Cup, 3 winners; Pa-NJ all-millennium-athlete-top-100 award; Pennsylvania Sports Legends award; mem. Cdn Football Hall of Fame; res. New Jersey.

YORK, Jason (hockey); b. 20 May 1970, Nepean, Ont.; m. Laurel; c. Jack, Alexandra, Matthew; hockey player; def. OHL Hamilton '87-88, Windsor '88-91, Kitchener '89-90; drafted by Detroit '90; AHL Adirondack '91-95, Cincinnati '03; NHL Detroit '93-95, Anaheim '94-96, '01-02, Ottawa '96-01, Nashville '02-04; NHL record (through '04) 708 scheduled games, 41g, 180a; 34 playoff games, 2g, 7a; res. Kanata, Ont./Nashville, Tenn.

YORK, Patrick (t&f/wrestling); b. 12 Jul 1951, Winnipeg, Man.; blind all-around athlete; brother of ntl team diver Teri; 23 gold BC Games for Disabled '77-81; 5 gold BC indoor games '79; 3 wrestling, 2 t&f, 1 canoeing gold Canada summer games; 3 silver, 1 bronze '78 PAG, relay bronze, 400m gold '80 disabled Olympics; world record 400m; with fellow blind Cdn Joe Lewis refined rules/equipment for Showdown, a form of handball for the blind; res. Vancouver, B.C.

YORK, Teri (diving); b. 11 Nov 1955, Winnipeg, Man.; given name: Theresa Kathleen; SFU, BA; teacher; ntl jr. 3m, 1m diving champion '69-72; mem. '72, '76 Olympic teams; 6th 10m '76 Olympics; bronze '74 Swedish Cup, silver 10m Finnish championships, Czech 3m, US ntl 10m titles '74; ntl 3m, tower titles '73-75; bronze '74 CG; 6th 10m, 7th 3m '75 world championships; Australian 3m title '77; res. White Rock, B.C.

YOST, Ken (coaching); b. 2 Sep 1905, Winnipeg, Man.; d. 12 Jul 1990, Winnipeg, Man.; given name: Elmer Kenneth; m. Leona Pearl Tetrault (d); c. Raymond, Carolyn, Greg; business college; ret'd railroad employee; coach '48 Olympic t&f team; records chair. '52 BEG; p.-pres. Winnipeg AA, Greater Winnipeg Girls' Sr. Softball League, MSA, WCSA, CSA; treas., later secty. AAUofC; convenor Winnipeg Sr. HL; mem. Canadian Amateur Sports Hall of Fame.

YOUNG, Dolores (rowing); b. 2 May 1957, Picton, Ont.; given name: Dolores Robina Mary; m. Robert Bailey; c. Graham, Emma; York, hons. BPhE, Queen's, BEd; ED Manitoba Rowing Assn.; US HS cox 4s, ntl 8s titles '75; mem. '76, '84 Olympic teams; West German cox 4s, 8s titles, bronze 8s '77 world championships; cox 4s title Cdn Henley, 8s Australia International regatta, bronze '78 Worlds; won 8s Amsterdam '79; quad title '80 nationals, '80-82 Cdn Henley, US nationals '83; competed '83 worlds; Ont., ntl jr. single sculls '82; Ont. achievement awards; co-chair rowing '99 PAG; res. Winnipeg, Man.

YOUNG, Don (all-around); b. 15 Feb 1906, Blakney, Ont.; d. 2 Mar 1988, Ottawa, Ont.; m. Frances Boomer (d), Alice Taylor McArton; c. Kenneth (d), Debbie,

Jack McArton, Ron McArton; McGill, MD; general practitioner; starred in basketball, football with McGill; mem. Rideau Aquatic Club sr Cdn basketball titlists '24-25; mem. Rough Riders '25-27. 2 Grey Cup winners; ctr (capt. '30) McGill basketball squad undefeated over 4yrs; Intercollegiate champs '28; captained 3 McGill football squads where he was a backfielder '28-34; 1st Ottawa native named *CP* university football all-star; played outside wing and rated superb tackler; mem. Rideau jr. football club; cousin of basketball inventor James Naismith; also shone in lacrosse, baseball where he caught for Renfrew, Smiths Falls, Ottawa Gunners city champs '31; scored hole-in-one at Ottawa Hunt; served overseas as medic WW2; McGill athlete of yr; OBE; mem. Ottawa, McGill Sports halls of fame.

YOUNG, Frank (rowing/basketball/racquetball); b. 5 Aug 1929, Toronto, Ont.; given name: Frank David; m. Jean Lockhart; c. John, James, Bob, Elizabeth; ret'd insurance agent; mem. heavy 8s '52 Olympics; Sr. A basketball Toronto West End Y '50-54, Sr. B Andy's AC '55-56; mem. Kitchener-Waterloo Ont. Sr. B basketball champions '57-58; Eastern Cdn men's masters racquetball champion '76; Ont. men's masters racquetball titles '77, '80, 3rd '79, '81; co-capt. Central Tech sr. football, basketball teams; res. Hamilton, Ont.

YOUNG, George (swimming); b. 1910, Scotland, d. 6 Aug 1972, Niagara Falls, Ont.; m. 1. Margaret Ravior, 2. Gay Booth, 3. Georgina Stokoe; c. George, Margaret, Thomas; parks commission employee; emigrated to Canada age 2; as amateur won 5 ntl titles; 4 Toronto across-the-bay, 3 Montreal bridge-to-bridge swim titles; Catalina channel in 15:45 '27; nicknamed "Catalina Kid"; staged own Lake Ont. marathon '28 but pulled from water after only 5 miles; failed to finish 3 more CNE swims, won '31; named Canada's outstanding swimmer of half century '50; mem. Canada's Sports, International Marathon Swimmers, Ont. Aquatic halls of fame.

YOUNG, Jim (football); b. 6 Jun 1943, Hamilton, Ont.; given name: James Norman; div.; c.Jamie, Sean, Cory; Queen's, BA; freelance broadcaster, Barter Business Exchange exec.; Omega Trophy OUAA MVP '64; 2yrs Minnesota (NFL); BC Lions '67-79; CFL record: 522 pass receptions for 9248yds, 17.7 avg., 65tds; club records receptions, yds receiving, tds on passes; 5th all-time CFL rcvrs, all-Cdn '72, twice WFC all-star; Schenley outstanding Cdn award '70, '72, runnerup '69; asst. coach BC '89-90; v-p. community relations '90-92; rep. BC in Countdown, Superstars competitions; subject of book *Dirty 30* by Jim Taylor; mem. Cdn, OUAA Football, Canada's, BC Sports halls of fame; res. Coquitlam, B.C.

YOUNG, Joe (t&f); b. 4 May 1920, Hamilton, Ont.; given name: Joseph Riley; m. Mary (Molly) O'Neil; c. Joseph, Jennifer, Martha; McMaster, BA, BPhE, OCE; ret'd supervisor phys ed Hamilton Board of Education; Ont. int. 440yd championship '36, ntl jr. 440yd '38, mem. ntl sr. mile relay champions '38; coached HS teams t&f, basketball, football '46-66 Woodstock, Ottawa, Hamilton; from '60 registered CTFA official; chief starter '76 Olympics, '78 CG, '79 World Cup, '81 Caribbean Games, World Cup Americas II trials; res. Ancaster, Ont.

YOUNG, Preston (football); b. 15 Jul 1954, Regina, Sask.; m. Nadine; c. Daniel; SFU; partner fitness club; mem. undefeated jr. Regina Rams 2yrs; db Sask. '78, Toronto '79-80, '85, Hamilton '81, Montreal '82-84; ranked among premier dbs in CFL; record 134 punt returns 1477yds, 23 interceptions 317yds, 7 fumble returns 100yds, 1td; res. Regina, Sask.

YOUNG, Walter (t&f); b. 14 Mar 1913, Lime Ridge, Que.; m. Muriel Smith; c. Stanley; ret'd fireman; 2 undistinguished Boston Marathon appearances preceded '37 victory; 2nd N.Melford, Mass., 20-mile race '37; Salisbury Beach marathon title '31; mem. '38 BEG team; mem. Montreal Castor AC; welter-, middleweight boxer, 3 pro bouts, won 1, lost 2 by KO; 10 consecutive snowshoe race victories including 10-mile record Hull race; expert marksman; ntl .22 100yd accuracy title '64; res. Longueuil, Que.

YOUNG-BLACK, Stuart (equestrian); b. 21 Jul 1959, Macclesfield, Eng.; short-listed for British jr team; moved to Canada at 17; Ontario jr team '77-80; mem. ntl three-day event team from '87; 1st Canadian to win international advanced 3-day event in foreign country; competed '92, '96 Olympics; team gold '91, silver '87 PAG; res. Millwood, VA.

YOUNGBERG, Jane (badminton); b. 25 Dec 1948, Alysbury, Eng.; given name: Jane Marie Dubord; m. Edward Youngberg; c. Marion, Brett; UBC, BEd; teacher; with Sue Latournier '65 jr. doubles age 15; with Barbara Nash ntl ladies' jr. doubles '67-68; ntl ladies' Open, Closed singles titles, with Barb Welch Open, Closed doubles '74-75, '77; mem. Uber Cup team '72, '75 beating former world champion Etsuko Takenaka of Japan '75; competed '74 Christchurch CG, Devlin Cup Matches vs US; with Sherry Boyce ntl women's doubles '76, quarterfinals all-Eng. singles; '77 Cdn women's singles; World Cup semifinals with Wendy Clarkson; mem. '78 CG silver medal team; res. Surrey, B.C.

YOUNGSON, Les (curling); b. 1900 Neury, County Down, Ireland, d. 28 May 1979, Regina, Sask.; given name: Lesley; m. Muriel Armstrong; c. Dorothy; car salesman; skip '36 Sask. Brier entry; South Sask. champion '43, '48; 43 consec. yrs Regina bonspiel competitor; 3yrs secty. SCA, pres. '43-44; life mem. SCA from '51; pres. Regina CC '49-50; hon. life mem. Regina CC; mem. Sask. Sports Hall of Fame.

YOUNGSON, Muriel (curling); b. 15 Aug 1906, Pearson, Man.; d. 17 Feb 1986, Regina, Sask; given name: Muriel Armstrong; m. Les Youngson (d); c. Dorothy; ret'd nurse; competitive curler '31-62; Regina Ladies' Bonspiel grand aggregate '43, '45; pres. Caledonian Ladies' CC '45-47; active role formation Sask. LCA; mem. exec. council SLCA, pres. '59; exec. mem. WCLCA, pres. '60; key role in formation of CLCA, v-p. '61, pres. '62; with Addie Bright formed Sask. Sr. LCA, pres. '67-71; life mem.Caledonian LCC; with husband Les mem. Sask. Sports Hall of Fame.

YUNG, Darryl (badminton); b. 5 Aug 1972, Victoria, B.C.; CEO Prizm Sports, Multiland Investment Ltd.; mem. ntl team from '94; 2 ntl men's doubles titles; competed '94, '98 CG, '96 Olympic Games, '95 worlds; mixed doubles gold, men's doubles bronze '95 PAG; 2 Thomas Cup teams; mixed/men's doubles titles B.C., Man, Glenmore Intl, Alta. Classic, Can.-Scotland Intl team matches; res. Calgary, Alta.

YZERMAN, Steve (hockey); b. 9 May 1965, Cranbrook, B.C.; m. Lisa Brennan; c. Isabella, Maria, Sophia; came up through Nepean, Ont., minor program to Nepean Raiders (CJHL) then Peterborough Petes (OHL) '81-83; 1st pick Detroit '83 draft; pro Detroit from '83; youngest Red Wing capt. '86-87; NHL rookie team; set several rookie records; L.B. Pearson award '89; mem. Team Canada '83 world jr, '85, '89, '90 worlds, '96 World Cup, '98, '02 (gold) Olympics; scored 50g '88, 65 '89, 62 '90, 51 '91, 58 '93; CJHL div. bears his name; 10 NHL all-star games; NHL record: (through '04) 1453 scheduled games, 678g, 1043a, 192 playoff games, 70g, 111a; capt. '97, '98, '02 Stanley Cup champions; Conn Smythe trophy '98; 8th player to reach 600g also reach 1600 points; Selke award '00; Masterton award '03; Syl Apps Ont. athlete of '02 award; Nepean arena bears his name; mem. Nepean Wall of Fame; res. Bloomington Hills, Mich.

Z

ZACK, Darren (softball); b. 9 Aug 1960, Sault Ste. Marie, Ont.; m. Charlotte Syrette; c. Darren, Molli Ann; natural resources; rhp; mem. NIAA (native) softball champions '84-85, '87, '89, '94; 1st world class exposure in Labatt's Challenge Cup '90; gold '91, '95, '99 PAG; mem. 2 ntl title teams; ISF World title '92; with Toronto Gators ISC world title team '93, '95, with Decatur Pride '01; set world record with '92 Magicians hurling all but 1 inning of team's 9 games winning 7; ISC record 136k in 76 innings, 0.38 ERA; 3rd pitcher in ISC world championship history to win back-to-back outstanding pitcher awards with 15-3 record and 108 strikeouts in 61 innings, hiked record to 150 SO '95; ranked number 1 pitcher in world '92-94; through '03 4 ISC world tourney outstanding pitcher awards; pitched with Tampa Bay Smokers '97-98, Oshawa Gators '99; led Invermere, BC to ntl Indian Athletic Assn. Title '02; featured in movie *Fastpitch* '00; Ntl Aboriginal Achievement award; res. Garden River, Ont.

ZAHAR, Mike (parachuting); b. 30 Oct 1954, Port Alberni, B.C.; m. Marlene Marsin; commercial jet pilot; former master rigger for parachute manufacturer; ntl 10-way title '73, 4-way, 8-way titles '77-80; Australian 4-way '77, French 4-way '79; 2nd French 8-way '79, China 4-way '80; world titles '77, '79; helped develop skydiving stunts for James Bond movies; with Ron Laidlaw developed progressive free-fall system; 2 Leonardo da Vinci diplomas; intl parachuting comm. exec.; dir. CSPA; more than 2500 jumps; res. Paris, France.

ZAIPEC, Chuck (football); b. 1 Jul 1949, Philadelphia, Pa; given name: Charles; m. Mary Roberts; c. Emily, Sydney; Penn State, BA; financial advisor; def. capt., 1st team all-American Penn State '71; 8yrs pro with Dallas, Miami, Kansas City (NFL), Montreal (CFL); radio/TV analyst for NFL/CFL games; res. New Hope, Pa.

ZAMUNER, Rob (hockey); b. 17 Sep 1969, Oakville, Ont.; lw OHL Guelph '86-89, IHL Flint '89-90, AHL Binghamton '90-92, NHL NYR '91, Tampa Bay '92-99, Ottawa '99-00, Boston '01-04; mem. Team Canada '97 (gold), '98 worlds, '98 Olympics; NHL record (through '04): 798 scheduled games, 139g, 172a, 34 playoff games, 4g, 5a; res. Oakville, Ont.

ZEMAN, Joe (builder); b. 6 Feb 1914, Outlook, Sask.; m. Mary Schewan; c. Gary, Dale, Brenda, Blair; UofSask, BEd, BSc; agricultural economist; mgr. ntl baseball team '67 PAG; founding mem. 3 hockey, several baseball organizations; mem. Saskatoon Parks & Rec. board, Sask. P&R Assn. council; board, comm. mem. 18 sports organizations; qualified baseball, hockey coach; dir. Sask. Sport, Sask. Sports Hall of Fame; co-author *Hockey Heritage: 88 Years of Puck Chasing in Saskatchewan;* Kinsmen sportsman of '64 award; mem. UofSask Wall, Sask., Saskatoon Sports, Man. Baseball halls of fame; res. Saskatoon, Sask.

ZENK, Marina (officiating/hockey); b. 6 Nov 1963, Ottawa, Ont.; Seneca Coll., Algonquin Coll.; operations mgr. Hockey Canada, Level VI official; 14yrs officiating women's hockey from minor to international levels; officiated 3 Ont. Winter Games, 2 Ont. Sr. AA, 1 Sr. AAA finals; 4 Sr. women's finals, 2 Nations Cup, 1 Pacific Rim, varied international exhibitions; Canada Winter Games, Esso Women's ntls, European, worlds; officiated 1st- ever women's Olympic hockey '98; CHA, Hockey Canada female officials development co-ordinator from '00; supervisor CHA for Esso ntls, -18 championships; supervisor for Hockey Canada Nations Cup; ref-in-chief, supervisor Cdn University championships '04; active as instructor/supervisor officiating clinics/seminars for ODHA, CHA, Hockey Canada; mem. Hockey Canada officiating policy comm.; supervisor 5yrs OWHA, 9yrs ODWHA, ODHA, 6yrs Hockey Canada ntl program; created/maintained ODWHA web site quiz; recipient Hockey Canada Female Breakthrough Award '01; res. Orleans, Ont.

ZERON, Rick (harness racing); b. 8 Sep 1956, Ottawa, Ont.; honed skills in Ottawa area before switching to Blue Bonnets '82 where he rapidly rose to top billing; from '86-94 leading Blue Bonnets dash winner 7 times; led Blue Bonnets drivers in earnings 7 straight years; won 5 UDR titles; shifted operations to OJC circuit '95; career best season 437 wins '89; also highly regarded trainer; 23 major stakes wins incluided 5 Simcoe, 5 Champlain, 1 Maple Leaf Trot, 1 Robert Stewart; through '03 5247 victories with purses exceeding $44M; res. Oakville, Ont.

ZILBERMAN, Victor (wrestling); b. 28 Mar 1947, Kishinev, USSR; m. Christine Siciliano; c. Victoria, David; educator, coach; USSR jr champion '64-65; gold Israel ntls '74, Finland, Berlin internationals, USSR sr ntls '72, European team championships '73, Cdn sr FS titles '75, '78; silver World Cup Toledo, Spain (Sambo), '78 CG; impressive coaching record with USSR '65-66, Israel '74, Thunder Bay '75-76, Que. provincial '76-80, McGill '77-81, Snowdon YMHA Montreal '80-84, Concordia from '77; 6 ntl titles; CIAU coach of '84. '86, Que. wrestling coach of '85; coached 4 Cdn Olympic teams; pres. Cdn Amateur Wrestling Coaches Assn; Ont., Soviet achievement awards; 5 PetroCan coaching excellence awards; USSR master of sport award; mem. Concordia, YM-YWHA Sports halls of fame; res. Montreal, Que.

ZIMMERMAN, Jeff (baseball); b. 9 Aug 1972, Kelowna, B.C.; given name: Jeffrey Ross; Texas Christian BS, SFU MBA; rhp; pitched in France '94; extensive experience with ntl sr. men's team '95-97; 2 seasons at TCU '92-93; made pro debut Winnipeg '97; Northern League rookie of '97; named to '97 Independent Leagues all-star team by *Baseball America;* pitched for Peoria (Arizona Fall League); joined Texas Rangers organization '98 playing with Charlotte, Tulsa; Nolan Ryan Texas Rangers Minor League pitcher of '98 award; made major league debut '99 quickly establishing himself as premier relief pitcher and earning berth on AL all-star game team as rookie; '99 Tip O'Neill award; 2yrs

Texas, 17-12, 196 scheduled games, 32svs, 228ip, 73bob, 213k, 3.27era; res. Vancouver, B.C.

ZMICH, Rick (football); b. 18 Sep 1958, Ottawa, Ont.; UofOtt, hons Bsc; football coach; qb'd UofOtt Gee-Gees '78-82; noted for strong, accurate passing arm; competed '80 Vanier Cup; all-Cdn '82; Hec Crighton award winner '82; head coach Wilfrid Laurier; CIAU coach of '95; mem. UofOtt Football Hall of Fame; res. Waterloo, Ont.

ZOCK, Bill (football); b. 26 Jan 1918, Toronto, Ont.; d. 29 Apr 1988, Toronto, Ont.; m. Mildred Eason (d); c. William Jr., Gordon, Arlene; steamfitter; hard-nosed guard/tackle who played 18yrs in CFL with Toronto, Edmonton; mem. 7 Grey Cup finals, 6 winners; all-Cdn guard '46-47; coached Balmy Beach, Argos; respected as a tough competitor on the field but true gentleman off field; accomplished singer who was musical dir. Invictones male chorus 20yrs; mem. Cdn Football Hall of Fame.

ZOKOL, Richard (golf); b. 21 Aug 1958, Kitimat, B.C.; Brigham Young; Cdn. amateur champion '81; mem. BYU NCAA title team, 2nd team all-American '81; International amateur champion of Morocco '80; joined PGA tour '81; won '92 Milwaukee Open, Deposit Guaranty Classic; CPGA title '01; nicknamed "Disco Dick"; golf columnist *Vancouver Sun*; spokesman, non-playing capt. Cdn Jr. Golf Assn.; celebrity tournament bears his name; res. White Rock, B.C.

ZUGER, Joe (football); b. 25 Feb 1940, Homestead, Pa.; given name: Joseph Mark; m. Eleanor Townsend; c. Beth, Joe Jr., Amy; Arizona State; ret'd football exec.; led all US colleges in punting, passing; Arizona State MVP '61; pro Hamilton '62 as db until injury to Bernie Faloney provided opportunity to qb team; took team to 2 Grey Cup wins; CFL record '62-71: 1618 passes, 814 completions for 12,676yds, 95 interceptions, 76tds, 1075 punts for 48,930yds, 68 singles, record 45.5 avg.; outstanding player award '67 Grey Cup; mgr. Hamilton Wentworth Curling Club; coached Mount Hamilton peewee hockey teams to 2 league titles; closed playing career Detroit (NFL) '72; asst. coach Hamilton '79, player co-ordinator '80, GM '81-92; 3 div. titles, 4 Grey Cup finals, 1 winner; v.-chair CFL governors '86-92; mem. Ariz. State Sports Hall of Fame; res. Hamilton, Ont.

LIST OF ABBREVIATIONS

a - assist
AA - All Around; Athletic Association
AAFC - All-America Football Conference
AAGPBL - All America Girls Professional Baseball League
AAGPBLPA - All America Girls Professional Baseball League Players Association
AAHA - American Amateur Hockey Association
AASSA - American Amateur Speed Skating Association
AAU - Amateur Athletic Union
AAU of C - Amateur Athletic Union of Canada
ab - at bats
ABA - American Basketball Association
ABC - American Bowling Congress
AC - athletic club
ACHL - Atlantic Coast Hockey League
ACT - Associated Canadian Travellers
AD - athletic director
ADM - Assistant Deputy Minister
AEC - Atomic Energy Commission
AFB - Air Force Base
AFL - American Football League
AFL - Arena Football League
AGM - assistant general manager
AHA - Atlantic Hockey Association
AHL - American Hockey League
AIAW - Association of Intercollegiate Athletics for Women
AIS - Australian Institute of Sport
AIWA - Association of International Women's Athletics
AL - American League
ALCA - Alberta Curling Association
ALCS - American League Championship Series
Alta. - Alberta
AKO - Alpha Kai Omega fraternity
AMA - Automobile Manufacturer's Association
AMBC - American Mountain Bike Cycling
Amer. - American
ANAF - Army, Navy, Air Force
AOSSM - American Orthopaedic Society for Sport Medicine
AP - Associated Press
APAHPER - Atlantic Provinces Association for Health, Physical Education & Recreation
APSL - American Professional Soccer League
APRC - Association of Professional Rodeo Cowboys
ASA - American Softball Association
ASMHF - Association of Sport Museums and Halls of Fame
assn - association
assoc. - associate

asst. - assistant
ATP - Association of Tennis Professionals
AUAA - Atlantic Universities Athletic Association
AUMA - Alberta Urban Municipalities Association
AUT - Austria
avg. - average
AWA - American Wrestling Association

b. - born
b - bronze
BA - batting average
BA - bachelor of arts
BBA - bachelor of business administration
bob - base on balls
BB - bare back (rodeo riding)
BBHOF - Baseball Hall of Fame
BBWAA - Baseball Writers Association of America
B.C. (BC) - British Columbia
BCABA - British Columbia Amateur Basketball Association
BCABA - British Columbia Amateur Boxing Association
BCAHA - British Columbia Amateur Hockey Association
BCASA - British Columbia Amateur Softball Association
BCCLGA - British Columbia Canadian Ladies Golf Association
BCJHL - British Columbia Junior Hockey League
BCLA - British Columbia Lacrosse Assn.
BCPGA - British Columbia Professional Golf Association
BCU - Boston College University
BComm - Bachelor of Commerce
BCrim - Bachelor of Criminology
bd - board
BD - Bachelor of Divinity
BE - British Empire
BE& C - British Empire & Commonwealth
BEc - Bachelor of Economics
BEd - Bachelor of Education
BEG - British Empire Games
BEng - Bachelor of Engineering
bk - balks
BM - Boston Marathon
BMX - Bicycle Motor Cross
BPA - Bowling Proprietor's Association
BPAC - Bowling Proprietor's Association of Canada
BPAO - Bowling Proprietor's Association of Ontario
BPhE - Bachelor of Physical Education
BPharm - Bachelor of Pharmocology
BPHE - Bachelor of Physical, Health Education
BPSc - Bachelor of Political Science

BRS - Bachelor of Recreation Studies
BSc - Bachelor of Science
BSA - Bachelor of Science Agriculture
BScPhE - Bachelor of Science Physical Education
BPsych - Bachelor of Psychology
BR&L - Bachelor of Recreation & Leisure
BScPT - Bachelor of Science Physical Therapy
BYU - Brigham Young University

c. - children
C - centre
C1 - canoe singles
C2 - canoe doubles
C4 - canoe fours
CA - Curling Association
CA - chartered accountant
CAAO - Canadian Association of Amateur Oarsmen
CAAWS - Canadian Association for the Advancement of Women and Sport and Physical Activity
CABA - Canadian Amateur Basketball Association
CABA - Canadian Amateur Boxing Association
CABC - Canadian Association of Basketball Coaches
CABO - Canadian Association of Basketball Officials
CAC - Canadian Association of Coaches
CADA - Canadian Amateur Diving Association
CADORA - Canadian Dressage Owners & Riders Association
CADS - Canadian Association for Disabled Skiing
C.A.E. - Certified Association Executive
CAFA - Canadian Amateur Football Association
CAFC - Canadian Association of Football Coaches
CAHA - Canadian Amateur Hockey Association
CAHL - Canadian Amateur Hockey League
CAHPER - Canadian Association for Health, Physical Education and Recreation
Calif.(CAL) - California
CAM - Club and membership
CANZ - Canada New Zealand
capt. - captain
CARA - Canadian Amateur Rowing Association
CARHA - Canadian Adult Recreational Hockey Association
CART - Championship Auto Racing Teams
CASA - Canadian Amateur Swimming Association; Canadian Amateur Skiing Association

CASH - Canadian Association for Sport Heritage

CASM - Canadian Academy of Sport Medicine

CASSA - Canadian Amateur Speed Skating Association; Canadian Amateur Synchronized Swimming Association

CAUAD - Canadian Association of University Athletic Directors

CAWA - Canadian Amateur Wrestling Association

CBA - Canadian Badminton Association

CBC - Canadian Bowling Congress; Canadian Broadcasting Corporation

CBF - Canadian Boating Federation

CBHL - Cape Breton Hockey League

CBRCCC - Canadian Branch Royal Caledonian Curling Club

CC - curling club

cc - cubic centimetres

CCA - Canadian Canoe Association; Canadian Cricket Association; Canadain Coaching Association; Canadian Curling Association; Canadian Cycling Association

CCAA - Canadian College Athletic Association

CCFP - Certificate College of Family Physicians

CCAM - Canadian Civilian Association of Marksmen

CCF - Co-operative Commonwealth Federation

CCGA - Canadian Commonwealth Games Association

CCHA - Central Conference Hockey Association

CCIFC - Central Canada Intercollegiate Football Conference

CCR - Canadian Curling Reporters

CCSE Canadian Centre for Social Entrepreneurship

CD - Canada decoration

CdM - chef de mission

Cdn - Canadian

CEF - Canadian Equestrian Federation

CEO - Chief executive officer

CF - Canadian Forces

CFA - Canadian Fencing Association; Canadian Football Association

CFAA - Canadian Field Archery Association

CFAB - Canadian Federation of Amateur Baseball

CFB - Canadian Forces Base

CFC Certified Fitness Consultant

CFHA - Canadian Field Hockey Association

CFL - Canadian Football League

CFLPA - Canadian Football League Players Association

CFO - chief financial officer

CFSA - Canadian Figure Skating Association

CFSA- Canadian Federation of Strength Athletes

CFSAC - Canadian Forces Small Arms Competition

CG - Commonwealth Games

cg - complete games

CGA - Certified general accountant

CGF - Canadian Golf Foundation; Canadian Gymnastics Federation; Commonwealth Games Federation

ChFC - Chartered Financial Consultant

CHL - Canadian Hockey League; Central Hockey League

CIAU - Canadian Interuniversity Athletic Union

CI - Collegiate Institute

CIBC - Canadian Imperial Bank of Commerce

CIHU - Canadian Intercollegiate Hockey Union

CIL - Canadian Industries Limited

CIRU - Canadian Intercollegiate Rugby Union

CIS - Canadian Intercollegiate Sport

CISM - Conseil Internationale du Sport Militaire

c&j - clean & jerk

CJA - Canadian Jiu-jitsu Association

CJFL - Canadian Junior Football League

CJHL - Central Junior Hockey League

CKSS - Chatham Kent Secondary School

CLA - Canadian Lacrosse Association

CLBC - Canadian Lawn Bowling Council

CLCA - Canadian Ladies' Curling Association

CLGA - Canadian Ladies' Golf Association

CLGU - Canadian Ladies' Golf Union

CLLBC - Canadian Ladies' Lawn Bowling Council

CLTA - Canadian Lawn Tennis Association

CLU - Chartered Life Underwriter

CMA - Canadian Medical Association; Canadian Motorcycle Association

CMHA - Canadian Minor Hockey Association

CMJHL - Canadian Major Junior Hockey League

CMO - Chief Medical Officer

CMTR Canadian Mental Training Registry

CNE - Canadian National Exhibition

CNR - Canadian National Railways

co. - company

CO - Commanding Officer

COA - Canadian Olympic Association

COC - Canadian Olympic Committee (formerly COA)

CODA - Calgary Olympics Development Association

COF - Canadian Orienteering Federation

CofO - City of Ottawa

COJO - Montreal Olympics organizing committee

coll. - college

Colo. - Colorado

comm. - committee

CONCACAF - Confederation of North, Central American and Caribbean Associations of Football

conf. - conference

consec. - consecutive

COPABA - Confederacion Pan-Americana de Baloncesto

CORK - Canadian Olympic Regatta, Kingston

COS - Canadian Ophthalmological Society

COTHA - Canadian Old-Timers Hockey Association

COWHL - Central Ontario Women's Hockey League

CP - The Canadian Press

CPBF Canadian Professional Boxing Federation

CPCA - Canadian Professional Coaches Association

CPCC - Carleton Place Canoe Club

CPGA - Canadian Professional Golfers Association

CPHL - Central Professional Hockey League

CPRA - Canadian Professional Rodeo Association

CPSA - Canadian Paralympic Sport Association

CRCA - Canadian Race Car Association

CRC - Canadian Rugby Council

CRCS - Canadian Royal College of Surgeons

CRDA - Canadian Race Drivers Association

CRU - Canadian Rugby Union

CSA - Canadian Ski Association; Canadian Soccer Association; Canadian Softball Association; Canadian Standards Association

CSC - Canadian Silver Cross

CSCC - Canadian Snooker Control Council

CSCF - Canadian Ski Coaches Federation

CSCO - Canadian Sports Centre Ontario

CSFA - Canadian Soccer Football Association

CSFAC Canadian Sport and Fitness Administration Centre

CSGA - Canadian Seniors Golf Association

CSIA - Canadian Ski Instructors Alliance

CSL - Canadian Soccer League

CSPA - Canadian Sport Parachuting Association

CSPS - Canadian Ski Patrol System

CSRA - Civil Service Recreation Association

CSSA - Canadian Synchronized Swimming Association

CSSF - Canadian School Sports Federation

CSSIA - Canadian Ski School & Instructors Alliance

CT. - Connecticut

CTA - Canadian Trotting Association

CTF - Canadian Teachers Federation

CTFA - Canadian Track and Field Association

ctr - centre
CTR - Canadian Target Rifle
CTSA - Canadian Trap Shooting Association
CTTA - Canadian Table Tennis Association
CURBAA - Carleton Ravens Basketball Alumni Association
CVA - Canadian Volleyball Association
CVHL - Central Valley Hockey League
cvts. - converts
CWA - Canadian Weightlifting Association
CWBA - Canadian Wheelchair Basketball Association
CWBL - Canadian Wheelchair Basketball League
CWFHA - Canadian Women's Field Hockey Association
CWIAA - Canadian Women's Intercollegiate Athletic Association
CWIAU - Canadian Women's Intercollegiate Athletic Union
CWSA - Canadian Water Skiing Association
CWSA - Canadian Wheelchair Sports Association
Cwlth - Commonwealth
CWUAA - Canadian Women's University Athletic Association
CYA - Canadian Yachting Association

d. - death
(d) - deceased
d or dbs - doubles
D.C. - District of Columbia
DCA - Dominion Curling Association
DCRA - Dominion of Canada Rifle Association
DD - Doctor of Divinity
DDS - Doctor of Dental Surgery
de. - defensive end
DEd - Doctor of Education
def. - defence
dept. - department
d-gs -drop goals (rugby)
dh - downhill
dir. - director
div. - divorced
DL - dart league
DMD - (Gregoire - dentistry degree)
DND - Department of National Defence
DO - orthopedic surgeon
DPhE - Doctor of Physical Education
DPHE - Doctor of Physical and Health Education
DQ or dq - disqualified
D.R. - Dominican Republic
DSA - Doctor Sports Administration
DSc - Doctor of Science
DSO - Distinguished Service Order

EAHL - Eastern Amateur Hockey League
ECAC - Eastern Colleges Athletic Conference
ECAHA - Eastern Canadian Amateur

Hockey Association
ECHL - East Coast Hockey League
ED - Executive Director
EdD - Doctorate of Education
EFC - Eastern Football Conference
EFC - Equestrian Federation of Canada
EHL - Eastern Hockey League
EL - Eastern League
EO - Eastern Ontario
EOLCA - Eastern Ontario Ladies' Curling Association
EOSSA - Eastern Ontario Secondary School Athletics
EOSSA - Eastern Ontario Speed Skating Association
EPBL - Eastern Professional Basketball League
EPHL - Eastern Pro Hockey League
era - earned run average
ERT Emergency Response Team
EWU - East Washington University
exec. - executive
EYTC - East York Track Club

FA - Football Association
F.A.M.E. - Female Athletes Motivating Excellence
FAQ - Federation of Quebec Athletics
FAS - Fitness and Amateur Sport
FAST - Federation for Athletes & Sport Training
fb - fullback
FBF - International Boxing Federation
FBI - Federal Bureau of Investigation
FCA - Federation of Canadian Archers
FCA - Football Coaches Association
FCM - Federation of Canadian Municipalities
FD - Flying Dutchman
fed. - federation or federal
FFKA - Fighting Federation Kickboxing Association
FG (fg) - field goal
FH - field hockey
FHA - Field Hockey Association
FHC - Field Hockey Club
FIA - Federation Internationale de l'Automobile
FIBL - Federation Internationale Bobsleigh & Luge
FIBT - Federation Internationale de Bobsleigh et de Tobaganning
FIE - Federation Internationale de Escrime
FIFA - Federation Internationale de Football Associations
FIH - Federation Internationale de Hockey
FILA - Federation Internationale de Lute Amateur
FINA - Federation Internationale de Natation Amateur
FIQ - Federation Internationale de Quilles
FIS - Federation Internationale de Ski
FISM - Federation Internationale de Medicine Sportive

FISU - World University Games
FITA - International Archery Federation
FIVB - Federation internationale de Volleyball
fl - flanker
Fla. - Florida
fp - fielding percentage
Fr. - Father
FS - Figure Skating; freestyle
FSL - Florida State League
FSR - freestyle record
FSU - Florida State University
Ft (ft) - feet; free throws
Ft. - Fort
ftbll - football

g. - goals; gold
ga - goals against
GB - Great Britain
GBNRA - Great Britain National Rifle Association
GC - golf club
gc. - grandchildren
G&CC - golf and curling club
gd - guard
GF - Gymnastics Federation
GM - general manager
Gov.-Gen. - Governor-General
govt - government
GP - grand prix
GPAC - Great Plains Athletic Conference
GR - Greco-Roman
GS - giant slalom
GT-CN - Grand Trunk-Canadian National

h - hits; hours
hb - halfback
HBA - honors bachelor of arts
H&D - Halifax & District
HJ or hj - high jump
HL - Hockey League
HMCS - Her (His) Majesty's Canadian Ship
HMI - Hockey Ministries International
HN - Hockey News
HNIC - Hockey Night in Canada
hon. - honorary or honorable
hons. - honors
HP - high powered
HPA - Horseshoe Pitching Association
HPD - High Performance Director
HR - home run
HS - high school
HTA - Harness Track Association

IAAA - International Amateur Aquatic Association
IAABO - International Association of Amateur Basketball Officials
IAAF - International Amateur Athletic Federation
IBA - International Boxing Association
IBHOF - International Boxing Hall of Fame

IBSA - International Blind Sport Association

IC - Inter County

ICF - International Curling Federation

IC4A - Intercollegiate Amateur Athletic Association of America

IEF - International Equestrian Federation

IESS - International Equestrian Sport Services

IFA - International Archery Federation

IHF - International Hockey Federation

IHL - International Hockey League

IIHF - International Ice Hockey Federation

IIHFM - International Ice Hockey Hall of Fame & Museum

IIHL - Intercollegiate Ice Hockey League

IL - International League

Ill. - Illinois

ILTC - International Lawn Tennis Championship

ILTF - International Lawn Tennis Federation

IM - individual medley

IMSA - International Motor Sport Association

Inc. - Incorporated

Ind. - Indiana; Industries

INS - International News Service

inst. - institute

int. - interceptions; intermediate

intl. - international

IOC - International Olympic Committee

ip - innings pitched

IP - individual pursuit

IPC - International Paralympic Association

IPRU - Interprovincial Rugby Union

IRFU - Interprovincial Rugby Football Union

IRL - Indy Racing League

ISAKOS - International Society of Arthoscopy, Knee Surgery and Orthopaedic Sports Medicine

ISC - International Softball Congress

ISF - International Softball Federation

ISKA - International Sport Kickboxing Association

ISMTE International Society for Mental Training & Excellence

ISSA - International Swimming Statisticians Association

ISU - International Shooting Union; International Skating Union

ITA - Italy

ITF - International Tennis Federation

ITT - Individual Time Trial

ITTF - International Table Tennis Federation

ITU - International Triathletes Union

IVBF - International Volleyball Federation

IWA - International Wrestling Federation

IWF - International Weightlifting Federation; International Wrestling Federation

IYRU - International Yacht Racing Union

JD - Juris Doctorate

Jpn - Japan

jr. - junior

juve. - juvenile

k - strikeouts

K1 - kayak singles

K2 - kayak doubles

K4 - kayak fours

K of C - Knights of Columbus

kg - kilograms

km - kilometres

KO - knockout or kickoff

KOCR - King's Own Calgary Regiment

KSU - Kentucky State University

K-W - Kitchener-Waterloo

Ky - Kentucky

LA - Los Angeles

lb - linebacker; pound

LBR - Ladies Barrel Racing

LCA - Ladies' Curling Association

LCBO - Liquor Control Board of Ontario

LCC - Ladies Curling Club

lcs - league championship series

lhp - left-handed pitcher

Lib - Liberal

LJ (lj) - long jump

LL - Little League

LLB - Bachelor of Laws

LLD - Doctor of Laws

LLM - Master of Laws

LPGA - Ladies' Professional Golf Association

LSU - Louisiana State University

LT - long track

LTC - Lawn and Tennis Club

Lt.-Gov. - Lieutenant-Governor

lw - leftwing; lightweight

m. - married

m - metres; miles; minutes

MA - Master of Arts

MAAA - Montreal Amateur Athletic Association

MAC - Mid-Atlantic Conference

MAHA - Manitoba Amateur Hockey Association

Man. - Manitoba

ManDak - Manitoba-Dakota

Mass. - Massachusetts

MB - Master Bowler

MBA - Master Bowlers' Association; master of business administration

MBE - Member of the British Empire

MCA - Manitoba Curling Association

MD - Doctor of medicine

mech. - mechanical

MEd - Master of Education

mem. - member

MFA - Manitoba Football Association

mfgr. - manufacturer

MFL - Minor Football League

mgr. - manager

MHA - Minor Hockey Association

MHL - Manitoba Hockey league

Mich. - Michigan

min - minutes

MILL - Major Indoor Lacrosse League

MIT - Massachusetts Institute of Technology

ML - major league

MLA - member legislative assembly

mlb - middle linebacker

MLB - Major League Baseball

MM - Military Medal

MMHL - Maritime Major Hockey League

mos. - months

MP - modern pentathlon

MPhE - Master of Physical Education

MPP - Member Provincial Parliament

MPRA - Manitoba Provincial Rifle Association

MR - medley relay

MRA - Military Rifle Association; Masters of Resource Management

MRE - Master of Religious Education

MRM - Masters of Resource Managment

MSA - Manitoba Softball Association

MSA - Manitoba Soccer Association

MSc - Master of Science

MSL - Metro Soccer League

MSRA - Manitoba Soccer Referees Association

MSSA - Manitoba Speed Skating Association

MSU - Michigan State University

Mt. - Mount

MTB - Mountain Bike

MTHL - Metro Toronto Hockey League

MVD - most valuable defence

MVP - most valuable player

N. - North

NA - North American

NAIA - National Association of Intercollegiate Athletics

NAHL - North American Hockey League

NALA - North American Lacrosse Association

NALCA - Northern Alberta Ladies' Curling Association

NAMLFA - North American Minor League Footabll Alliance

NASCAR - National Association for Stock Car Auto Racing

NASKA - North American Sport Karate Association

NASL - North American Soccer League

NASO - National Association of Sports Officials

N.B.(NB) - New Brunswick

NBA - National Basketball Association

NBABA - New Brunswick Amateur Basketball Association

NBFHA - New Brunswick Field Hockey Association

NBGA - New Brunswick Golf Association

NBLCA - New Brunswick Ladies' Curling

Association
NBOA - New Brunswick Officials Association
NBRA - New Brunswick Rifle Association
NBSA - New Brunswick Softball Association
NBSBL - New Brunswick Senior Baseball League
NBSHF - New Brunswick Sports Hall of Fame
NBTFA - New Brunswick Track & Field Association
N.C.(NC) - North Carolina
NCAA- National Colleagiate Athletic Association
NCAFA - National Capital Amateur Football Association
NCCP - National Coaching Certification Program
NCD - National Capital Division
NCI - National Coaching Institute
NCM - National Capital Marathon
NCRRA - National Capital Region Rifle Association
NCTA - National Capital Tennis Association
ND -Naturopathic Doctor
N.D.(ND) - North Dakota
ND - Notre Dame
NDG - Notre Dame de Grace
NDHQ - National Defence Headquarters
NDHQRA - National Defence Headquarters Rifle Association
NDS - North Dakota State
N.E.(NE) - New England
NEA - News Enterprises of America
NF - Niagara Falls
NFCVI - Niagara Falls Collegiate & Vocational Institute
NFC - Northern Football Conference
NFL - National Football League
Nfld. - Newfoundland
NGU - Never Give Up
NHA - National Hockey Association
NHL - National Hockey League
NHLPA - National Hockey League Players' Association
NHPA - National Horseshoe Pitchers Association
NIT - National Invitation Tournament
N.J.(NJ) - New Jersey
NL - National League
NLL - National Lacrosse League
NO - Northern Ontario
NOCA - Northern Ontario Curling Association
NOHA - Northern Ontario Hockey Association
NOSAA - Northern Ontario School Athletic Association
NORBA   National Off-Road Bicycle Association
NORCECA - North Central America and Caribbean zone

NMMI - New Mexico Military Institute
NPAAO - North Pacific Association of Amateur Oarsmen
NPSL - National Professional Soccer League
NRA - National Rifle Association; National Rodeo Association
NRC - National Research Council
N.S.(NS) - Nova Scotia
NSB - National Speakers Bureau
NSFAS - Nova Scotia Fitness & Amateur Sport
NSR - North Saskatchewan Regiment
NSRC - National Sport & Recreation Centre
NSSA - National Skeet Shooting Association
NSSFL - Nova Scotia Senior Football League
ntl -national
NTS - North Texas State
NWA - National Wrestling Association
NWBA - National Wheelchair Basketball Association
NWBT - National Wheelchair Basketball Tournament
NWOCA - North Western Ontario Curling Association
NWO - North Western Ontario
NWT - Northwest Territories
NWTCA - Northwest Territories Curling Association
NY - New York
NYC - New York City
NYP - New York-Pennsylvania
NYR - New York Rangers
NYU - New York University
N.Z.(NZ) - New Zealand

OAC - Ottawa Athletic Club
OALA - Ontario Amateur Lacrosse Association
OASA - Ontario Amateur Softball Association
OAWF - Ontario Amateur Wrestling Federation
OBA - Ontario Baseball Association
OBC - Ontario Bowling Congress
OBE - Order of the British Empire
OCA - Ontario Curling Association
OCF - Ontario Curling Federation
OCE - Ontario College of Education
OCRAS - Ottawa Carleton Regional Ambulance Service
OCWSA - Ottawa-Carleton Wheelchair Sports Association
O&D - Ottawa and District
ODFA - Ottawa District Football Association
ODHA - Ottawa District Hockey Association
ODGA - Ottawa District Golf Association
OEA - Ontario Educational Association
of - outfielder

OFA - Ontario Fencing Association
OFC - Ontario Football Conference
off - offensive
OFHA - Ontario Field Hockey Association
OFSAA - Ontario Federation of School Athletic Associations
og - offensive guard
OGA - Ontario Golf Association
OGF - Ontario Gymnastics Federation
OHA - Ontario Hockey Association
OHL - Ontario Hockey League
OIAA - Ontario Intercollegiate Athletic Association
OJC - Ontario Jockey Club
OLA - Ontario Lacrose Association
OLBA - Ontario Ladies' Basketball Association
OLCA - Ontario Ladies' Curling Association
OLGA - Ontario Ladies' Golf Association
OLTA - Ontario Lawn Tennis Association
OMJHL - Ontario Major Junior Hockey League
OMSA - Ontario Minor Soccer Association
Ont. - Ontario
OPGA - Ontario Professional Golfers' Association
OPHEA - Ontario Physical & Health Education Association
OPHL - Ontario Professional Hockey League
OPLBA - Ontario Provincial Lawn Bowling Association
ORA - Ontario Rowing Association
OQAA - Ontario-Quebec Athletic Association
OQIFC - Ontario-Quebec Interuniversity Football Conference
ORA - Ontario Rifle Association
Ore. - Oregon
ORFU - Ontario Rugby Football Union
OSC - Ottawa Ski Club
OSL - Ontario Soccer League
OSSA - Ontario Speed Skating Association
OSTFL - Ottawa Senior Touch Football League
ot - offensive tackle; Old Timers
OTA - Ontario Tennis Association
OTFA - Ontario Track & Field Association
OUA - Ontario University Athletics
OUAA - Ontario Universities Athletic Association
OVCA - Ottawa Valley Curling Association
OVGA - Ottawa Valley Golf Association
OWA - Ontario Weightlifting Association
OWFHA - Ontario Women's Field Hockey Association
OWHA - Ontario Women's Hockey Association
OWIAA - Ontario Women's Interuniversity Athletic Association
OWPA - Ontario Water Polo Association
OWSA - Ontario Water Skiing Association
p - pitcher

p. - place
Pa. - Pennsylvania
Pac. - Pacific
Pan-Am - Pan American
PAG - Pan-Am Games
PB - personal best
PC - Progressive Conservative
PCCA - Pacific Coast Curling Association
PCCHL - Peterborough Community Centre Hockey League
PCHA - Pacific Coast Hockey League
PCHL - Pacific Coast Hockey League
PCL - Pacific Coast League
PE - physical education
P.E.I.(PEI) - Prince Edward Island
PEIJHL - Prince Edward Island Junior Hockey League
PEng - Professional Engineer
PESE   Physical Energetics Systems of Equations
PGA - Professional Golfers Association
PhD - Doctor of Philosophy
phys ed - physical education
pim - penalty minutes
PITA - Pacific International Trapshooting Association
PLBA - Provincial Lawn Bowling Association
POM - Piscine Olympique Montreal
POW - Prisoner of War
PPC - Police Pistol Combat
PQ - Province of Quebec
PQFA - Province of Quebec Fencing Association
PQLTA - Province of Quebec Lawn Tennis Association
PR - Puerto Rico
PR - public relations
PRCA - Professional Rodeo Cowboys Association
P&R - parks and recreation
pres. - president
p.-pres - past president
prof. - professor
prov. - province or provincial
PS - public school
PSA - Professional Squash Association
PSAC - Pennsylvania State Athletic Conference
PT - physical training
pts - points
pv - pole vault

QABA - Quebec Amateur Boxing Association
QAHA - Quebec Amateur Hockey Association
QAHL - Quebec Amateur Hockey League
QATFA - Quebec Amateur Track & Field Association
QAWA - Quebec Amateur Wrestling Association
QB, qb - quarterback
QBA - Quebec Badminton Association

QC - Queen's Council
QCA - Quebec Curling Association
QFSAA - Quebec Federation of School Athletic Associations
QGA - Quebec Golf Association
QHL - Quebec Hockey League
QJA - Quebec Judo Association
QJAHL - Quebec Junior Amateur Hockey League
QJHL - Quebec Junior Hockey League
QLTA - Quebec Lawn Tennis Association
QLTF - Quebec Lawn Tennis Federation
QMJHL - Quebec Major Junior Hockey League
QSF - Quebec Sailing Federation
QSHL - Quebec Senior Hockey League
QSM - Quartermaster Sergeant Major
QSSF - Quebec Skeet Shooting Federation
QTF - Quebec Tennis Federation
QTFF - Quebec Track & Field Federation
QTSA - Quebec Trap Shooting Association
Que. - Quebec

r - runs
RA - recreation association
RAF - Royal Air Force
RB - running back
rbi - runs batted in
rbs - rebounds
RC - rowing club; Royal Canadian
RCAF - Royal Canadian Air Force
RCCC - Royal Caledonian Curling Club
RCGA - Royal Canadian Golf Association
RCMP - Royal Canadian Mounted Police
RCN(R) - Royal Canadian Navy (reserve)
RCSSB - Roman Catholic Separate School Board
RDA - Race Drivers Association
recept. - reception
rep. - representative
res. - residence
retd. - retired
RGF - Rhythmic Gymnastic Federation
RHIL - Roller Hockey International League
RHYC - Royal Hamilton Yacht Club
RIT - Ryerson Institute of Technology
RMC - Royal Military College
RPI - Rensselaer Polytechnic Institute
RSA - Republic of South Africa
RVC - Royal Victoria College
rw - rightwing

s - singles; show; silver
SA - Shooting Association
SABR - Society for American Baseball Research
SAIT - Southern Alberta Institute of Technology
SAL - South Atlantic League
Sask (SK) - Saskatchewan
SASSA - Saskatchewan Amateur Speed Skating Association
sb (SB) - saddle bronc, smallbore, slotback; stolen base

SBSA - Saskatchewan Blind Sport Association
SC - swimming club; South Carolina
s-c - step-child(ren)
SCA - Saskatchewan Curling Association
SCCA - Sports Car Club of America
SD - South Dakota
SDSU - San Diego State University
SEC - South East Conference
secty - secretary
sep. - separated
SFC - Shooting Federation of Canada; Sports Federation of Canada
SFU - Simon Fraser University
SFVS - San Fernando Valley State
St.FX - St. Francis Xavier University
SGW - Sir George Williams University
SHL - Southern Hockey League
sho - shutouts
SHSAA - Saskatchewan High School Athletic Association
SJD - Doctor of Juridical Science
SJHL - Saskatchewan Junior Hockey League
SLCA - Saskatchewan Ladies' Curling Association
SLTA - Saskatchewan Lawn Tennis Association
SMU - St. Mary's University
SO - Southern Ontario
so - strikeouts; shutouts
SORC - Southern Ocean Racing Circuit
SOU - Southern League
S.P.O.R.T. - St. Petersburg Olympic Regatta for Training
SPRA - Saskatchewan Provincial Rifle Association
sr. - senior
S&R - sport & recreation
Sr. IC - Senior Intercounty
ss - shortstop
SSA - Speed Skating Association
SSC - Speed Skating Club
SSM - Sault Ste. Marie
ST - short track
St./Ste. - Saint
stl - steals
STOH - Scott Tournament of Hearts
SUNY - State University of New York
sv - saves
SWC - South West Conference
SWE - Sweden

t - tackle; triples
TB - Thunder Bay
TBFPBA - Thunder Bay Five Pin Bowlers Association
TC - track club; tennis club
TCA - Toronto Curling Association
TCIAA - Toronto Collegiate Institute Athletic Association
TCU - Texas Christian University
td (tds) - touchdowns
TDIAA - Toronto District Interscholastic

Athletic Association
TDMSA - Toronto & District Minor Soccer Association
te - tightend
t&f - track and field
TFA - track & field association
TFC - track & field club
tj - triple jump
TKO - Technical Knock Out
TL - Texas League
TML - Toronto Maple Leafs
Tor. - Toronto
TPC - Tour Players' Championship
tr - triples
TRC - The Ring Chronicle
treas. - treasurer
TSN - The Sports Network
TSSAA - Toronto Secondary School Athletic Association
TT - time trials

UAlta - University of Alberta
UBC - University of British Columbia
UBCSC - University of British Columbia Swim Club
UCal - University of Calgary
UCI - Union Cyclist International
UCLA - University of California Los Angeles
UDR - Universal Driver Rating
UDRS - Universal Driver Rating System
UFL - United Football League
UK - United Kingdom
UKOA - British Olympic Association
UMan - University of Manitoba
UMich - University of Michigan
UNB - University of New Brunswick
UNC - University of North Carolina
UND - University of North Dakota
UNLV - University of Nevada Las Vegas
UofOtt - University of Ottawa
UPI - United Press International
UQAM - University of Quebec at Montreal
UQTR - University of Quebec Trois-Rivieres
US - United States
USAC - United States Auto Club
USAHA - United States Amateur Hockey Asociation
UofSask - University of Saskatchewan
USC (SouthernCal) - University of Southern California
USD - University of South Dakota
USFL - United States Football League
USGF - United States Gymnastics Federation
USHHOF - United States Hockey Hall of Fame
USHL - United States Hockey League
USHWA - United States Harness Writers Association
USNRA - United States National Rifle Association

USNRA - United States National Rowing Association
USRRC - United States Road Racing Club
USSR - Union of Soviet Socialist Republics
USTA - United States Trotting Association
USTPA - United States Tour Players Association
UofT - University of Toronto
UTEP - University Texas El Paso
UTS - University of Toronto Schools
UVic - University of Victoria
UVRC - University of Victoria Rowing Club
UWash - University of Washington
UWO - University of Western Ontario

Va. - Virginia
VANOC - Vancouver Organizing Committee
VASC - Vancouver Amateur Swim Club
VB - volleyball
VBA - Volleyball Association
VCRC - Victoria City Rowing Club
v.capt - vice captain
v-p - vice president
V&D - Vancouver & District
VFHA - Vancouver Field Hockey Association
VIFHA - Vancouver Island Field Hockey Association
VRC - Vancouver Rowing Club
vs. - versus
Vt. - Vermont

w - walks; win(s)
WAKO - World Amateur Kickboxing Organization
WBA - World Boxing Association
WBC World Boxing Council
WBL - World Basketball League
WBTF - World Baton Twirling Federation
WC - World Cup; wrestling club
WCBA - World Commission of Boxing Associations
WCC - Winnipeg Canoe Club
WCFPBA - Western Canada Five-Pin Bowling Association
WCG - Western Canada Games
WCIAA - Western Canada Intercollegiate Athletic Association
WCL - Western Canada League
WCLCA - Western Canada Ladies' Curling Association
WCSA - Western Canada Softball Association
WCT - World Curling Tour
WCW - World Championship Wrestling; Western Athletic Conference
WFC - Western Football Conference
WFL - World Football League
WHA - World Hockey Association
WHL - Western Hockey League
WIAU - Western Intercollegiate Athletic Union

WIFU - Western Interprovincial Football Union
WISL - World Indoor Soccer League
WISPA - Women's International Squash Players Association
WKA - World Karate Association
WKA - World Kickboxing Association
WKC - World Karate Commission
WKN - World Kickboxing Network
w-l - wins-losses/won-lost
WLA - Western Lacrosse Association
WLAF - World League of American Football
WLCA - Western Ladies' Curling Association
WLU - Wilfrid Laurier University
W&M - William & Mary
WNBA - Women's National Basketball Association
WO - Western Ontario
WOHA - Western Ontario Hockey Association
WOSSA - Western Ontario Secondary School Athletics
wp - wild pitches
WP - Water Polo
Wpg - Winnipeg
WPKA - World Profi Kickboxing Association
WR - world record
WS - World Series
WSC - Water Ski Canada
WSSA - Windsor Secondary School Athletics
WSU - Washington State University
WTA - World Tennis Association
WW1 - World War 1
WW2 - World War 2
WWE - World Wrestling Entertainment
WWWF - World Wide Wrestling Federation
Wyo. - Wyoming
WYSA - Winnipeg Youth Soccer Association

XC - cross country

YBC - Youth Bowling Council
YC - yacht club
yds - yards
YMCA - Young Men's Christian Association
YMHA - Young Men's Hebrew Association
yr(s) - year(s)
YM-YWCA - Young Men's-Young Women's Christian Association
YTV - Youth Television

CROSS REFERENCE INDEX BY SPORT

deceased

ADMINISTRATION
* Abramowitz, Moe
Ackles, Bob
Adams, Bob
* Adams, Jack
Albrecht, J.I.
* Allan, Maurice
Allen, Keith
* Andersen, Roxy
Anderson, Dave
* Anderson, George
Andru, John
* Antoft, Kell
Armitage, Rolly
Ash, Gord
* Back, Len
Baird, Vaughan
Baker, Bill
Baker, Charles
Bales, John
* Ballard, Harold
Barrow, John
Bastarache, Clarence
* Bastien, Baz
* Bauer, David
* Bayer, Jim
* Beach, Pete
* Bearpark, Bob
* Bedecki, Tom
Beeston, Paul
* Bell, Bobby
Bigras, Sylvie
Binns, Hilda
* Bishop, Jim
Bitz, Ed
Blair, Wren
Bouchard, Butch
Bourne, Bob
* Bowering, Ebbie
* Box, Charlie
* Boyle, Charles
Branch, David
Britton, Bill
Brochu, Claude
* Brock, Henry
* Buddo, Don
* Bulloch, Jim
Burelle, Jacques
Burke, Brian
* Burns, Leo
* Bush, Carmen
Butler, Barry
* Calder, Frank
* Campbell, Clarence
* Campbell, Colin
Capozzi, Herb
* Cavallin, Isabell
* Cavallin, John
Chambers, Mike
Champagne, Chantal
* Chipman, A.U.
Chynoweth, Ed
* Clair, Frank

* Clancy, King
* Clifford, John
* Condon, Eddie
Cook, Murray
Copeland, Jim
Corey, Ron
Costello, Murray
* Crowe, Norton
* Dandurand, Leo
* Davies, Jack
* Dawson, Earl
DeBlonde, Garry
Delvecchio, Alex
Denoncourt, Sonia
* Deschamps, Claude
* Devine, Jack
* Dickeson, Jean
* Dilio, Frank
Dion, Yves
Dojack, Paul
Donaghey, Sam
* Donohue, Jack
Dore, David
Dorsch, Henry
* Dowell, Hanson
Dudley, Rick
* Duncan, Cecil
Dunlap, Jake
* Duthie, George
Eagleson, Alan
Elliott, Allen
* Elliott, Bob
Elliott, Geoff
Embuldeniya, Herb
Enos, Ed
Estabrooks, John
Etcheverry, Sam
Fanning, Jim
* Farmer, Jim
* Farmer, Ken
Farrell, Neil
Fauquier, Harry
Fedoruk, Sylvia
Fennell, Neil
Ferguson, John
Ferguson, Merv
* Firth, Doug
Fitch, Ed
* Fitzpatrick, Allan
Fletcher, Cliff
* Fletcher, Doug
* Fleury, Lionel
Fontana, Don
* Forbes, Bruce
* Foster, Red
* Fournier, Lionel
* Fox, Fred
Francis, Emile
Fraser, Bud
Fripp, John
Frost, Stan
Fryatt, Dave
* Fulton, Greg
Gainey, Bob

Garside, Bert
Gaudaur, Jake Jr.
Gauthier, Pierre
Giardino, Wayne
Gillick, Pat
* Gloag, Norm
Glynn, Hugh
Godbout, Francois
Goplen, Henrietta
Gosset, John
* Goulding, Bev
Gowan, Geoff
Grant, Duncan
Gribbin, Chris
* Griffith, Cal
Grinnell, Rae
Gurowka, Joe
* Halder, Wally
* Halter, G. Sydney
* Hamilton, Jack
* Hammond, Gord
Hansen, Warren
Harris, Susan
Hart, David
* Hart, Nelson
* Hauch, Paul
* Hayman, Lew
Hayter, Ron
Heeney, Walter
Heikkila, Bill
* Helliwell, David
Hendrie, George Jr.
* Hendrie, George Sr.
* Henick, Ed
* Hershfield, Leible
* Hewitson, Bobby
* Hewitt, W.A.
* Hill, Harvey
* Hilton, Geordie
* Histed, Jack
Hoffman, Abby
* Hogarth, Malcolm
Holmes, Derek
Hudson, John
Hume, Ian
* Imlach, Punch
* Irvin, Dick Sr.
Jackson, Roger
Johnson, Don
Johnston, Jerry
Johnston, Marshall
Johnstone, Lori
* Juckes, Gordon
Kierstead, Bob
Kihn, Richard
Kilrea, Brian
Kimball, Norm
King, Peter
* Kingsmith, Ray
Kirkconnell, Herb
Kitts, Charlie
* Kryczka, Joe
* Lamb, Joe
Larose, Bob

* LeBel, Bob
Lee, Tae Eun
* Lefaive, Lou
Lenard, Al
* Letheren, Carol Anne
L'Heureux, Bill
Lindsay, Ted
* Lister, Ralph
* Loaring, John
Logan, Tip
Loiselle, Claude
* Loney, Don
Long, Bill
* Lord, Margaret
Lord, Tom
Love, Drew
* Lumsden, Bill
Lumsden, Neil
Lunsford, Earl
MacAdam, Lane
* MacFarlane, Gus
MacInnes, Kent
Macken, Jim
MacKenzie, Bill
* MacLaggan, James
MacMillan, Billy
Maloney, Phil
Mara, George
Martin, John
Mazurak, Steve
* McBrien, Harry
* McCaffrey, Jimmy
* McCann, Dave
* McCannell, Don
McConachie, John
McConkey, Jim
McCormick, Frank
McCrae, John
McCrae, Judy
McDonald, Dennis
McDonald, Les
* McDonald, Vern
* McEwen, Bill
* McGill, Frank
McHale, John
McKinnon, Frank
McMahon, John
McPherson, Gary
Mellway, Dean
Melvin, Doug
Merklinger, Anne
Miller, Doug Jr.
Miner, Hazel
Mitchell, Doug
Molnar, Bill
* Molson, Hartland
* Montgomery, Ken
* Morris, Fred
Morris, Sid
Morrison, Scotty
Moynihan, Kerry
* Murray, Ken
* Murray, Pere
Nanne, Lou

Neill, Susan
Nesbitt, Keith
Newsham, David
Nicholson, Bob
Nicurity, Bryan
*Nooney, John
Nye, Barry
*Obeck, Vic
*Obodiac, Stan
O'Connor. Zeke
O'Neill, Brian
*O'Quinn, Red
*Osborne, Bob
Ouellette, Bert
Overend, Tom
*Page, Fred
*Page, Percy
Panting, Bill
Parker, Jackie
Parker, Ken
*Patrick, Frank
*Patrick, Lester
*Patrick, Muzz
Pearsall, Shane
*Perry, Norm
*Phillips, Alf Sr.
Pielak, Casmer
Pinder, Gerry
Pinder, Herb
Pipe, Andrew
Poce, Paul
*Poile, Bud
Pollock, Sam
Pomfret, Jack
Popp, Jim
Porter, Ken
Pound, Richard
*Powell, Cliff
*Prentice, Bob
Prentice, Bruce
*Preston, Ken
*Price, Harry
Primrose, John
Proulx, Rita
Pugh, Bob
Pugliese, Dan
Pulford, Bob
*Quigley, Ernest
*Quilty, Silver
Rae, Al
*Ramage, Pat
*Ratcliffe, Frank
Rathwell, Bob
*Rea, Harold
Reed, George
Regan, Larry
Reid, Lefty
Reid, Pat
Renwick, Gordon
Restivo, John
*Richardson, John
Richman, Ruby
Rita, Adam
Roberts, Roy
Robillard, Gene
Robinson, Bill
*Robinson, Bobby
Robinson, Morrie

Rodney, David
Rokosh, Greg
Ruckstuhl, Sandy
Rumbold, Dave
Rutherford, Jim
Ruys, Henk
Ryan, Doreen
*Ryan, Joe
Saunders, Sandy
Savage, Marilyn
Sawula, Lorne
Sazio, Ralph
*Schmalz, Tubby
Schmidt, Milt
Schootman, Teddy
Schreider, Gary
*Schwende, Carl
Scorrar, Doug
Scott, Mike
Seiling, Rod
*Seller, Peggy
Servold, Irvin
*Shatto, Dick
*Shaughnessy, Frank Jr.
*Shaughnessy, Shag
*Shaw, Dan
Shaw, Paul
*Sherwood, Liv
*Shore, Eddie
Short, George
*Simons, Pop
Sinclair, Marjorie
Sinden, Harry
Skinner, Jim
Skinner, Larry Sr.
Slack, Bill
Slavik, Jerry
Smith, Bobby
*Smith, Don
Smith, Gwen
Smith, Neil
*Smith, Stanley
Smyth, Jack
*Smythe, Conn
Soulliere, Bernie
Spack, Mike
*Spencer, Jim
*Spencer, Victor
*Spray, Robert
*Spring, Harry
*Stacey, Nelles
Steadward, Robert
*Stevens, Warren
Stinson, Wally
Stock, Ed
*Stockton, Don
Storey, Bob
Strong, Lawrence
Strumm, Gil
Tapp, Larry
Tatarchuk, Hank
*Taylor, Bryce
*Taylor, Gordon
Tennant, Mark
Thompson, Clif
Thompson, George
*Thompson, William
Tillman, Eric

Tinline, Dorothy
*Tomlinson, William
Toner, Vance
Totzke, Carl
Traer, Rick
*Trifunov, Jim
*Trihey, Harry
Udvari, Frank
Ungerman, Irv
*Van Vliet, Maury
Vespaziani, Bob
Volpe, Nick
*Voss, Carl
*Walden, Margaret
*Walker, Gord
Wallingford, Ron
*Watt, Laird
*Watt, R.N.
Watt, Tom
Watters, Lynn
Webster, Peter
Whalley, Joan
*Willsie, Harry
Wishart, Carol
*Wood, Nora
Worrall, Jim
*Wright, Harold
*Yost, Ed
Zuger, Joe

ALL-AROUND
*Abelson, Jess
*Akervall, Henry
Anderson, Dave
*Bain, Dan
*Bath, Doc
*Bauld, Donald
Beaton, Bob
Beck, Ross
Beckman, Jim
Benson, Lorne
*Box, Charlie
*Brockway, Dot
Bronson, Pat
*Browne, Cec
*Buddo, Don
*Cameron, Jack
Chiarelli, John
Clarkson, Reg
*Conacher, Lionel Sr.
*Connell, Charlie
*Cook, Myrtle
*Cooke, Stan
*Deacon, Tom
Desjardins, Larry
Devenney, Sandra
*Dibben, Hugh
Dunsmore, Fred
Ellefson, Steve
*Elliott, Bob
*Evon, Russ
Fedoruk, Sylvia
*Fletcher, Douglas
Grace, Maureen
Halpenny, Rachelle
Hansen, Rick
Harpell, Winnifred
*Hershfield, Leible

Hill, Jim
Huband, Deb
*Hughes, Billy
Hunt, Ted
*Johnstone, Charlie
Junor, Daisy
*Laing, George
*Leach, Al
*Lister, Ralph
Little, Ken
Lovett, Claire
*MacKinnon, Dan
*Malcolm, Andrew
*McGill, Frank
*McKenzie, Merv
*McKinnon, Archie
McKinnon, Frank
Mellway, Dean
*Milne, Howie
*Mobberley, Herb
*Molson, Percy
*Morris, Jim
*Obodiac, Stan
*Parry, Jack
*Patrick, Lynn
*Patrick, Muzz
Peden, Doug
*Percival, Lloyd
Pomfret, Jack
*Porter, Bob
Provost, Mary Haydon
*Pulford, Harvey
Rathgeb, Chuck
Reimer, Eugene
Richman, Joey
Robertson, Sandy
Ryan, Doreen
*Seller, Peggy
Strumm, Gil
Stulac, George
*Thomas, Fred
*Voss, Carl
Warwick, Millie
*Watling, Wallace
*Wright, Joseph Sr.
*Wright, Ken
*Young, Don

ARCHERY
*Albert, Herb
Allan, Wanda
Anderson, Les
Buscombe, Lisa
Ewert, Elmer
Genge, Ronald
Jackson, Don
Jackson, Rose Ann
Kazienko, Linda
Lemay, Lucille
Lemay, Roger
Lessard, Lucille
Lidstone, Dorothy
Mann, David
Mather, Eddie
McDonald, Joan
Muir, Lela
Pullen, Wayne
Reimer, Eugene

Rusnov, Rob
Sally, Kevin
Warden, Donald
Whittier, Heather

BADMINTON
Backhouse-Sharpe, Claire
*Bauld, Don
Bitten, Mike
Blanshard, Bryan
Butler, Mike
*Cameron, Jack
Carnwath, Jim
Carter, Wendy
Cornish, Ray
Czich, John
Deng, Si-An
Devlin-Hashman, Judy
Fabris, Lucio
Falardeau, Johanne
Fergus, Bert
*Fitzpatrick, Allan
Harris, Lesley
Hermitage, Robbyn
Julien, Denyse
Kanchanaraphi, Raphi
Kaul, Anil
Kirkconnell, Herb
Lovett, Claire
MacDonnell, Wayne
McKee, Jamie
Money, Ken
*Nash, Jack
Paulson, Jamie
Piche, Doris
Priestman, Keith
*Purcell, Jack
*Purdy, Margaret
Ratanaseangsuang,
   Channarong
Roberts, Roy
Rollick, Bruce
Rollick, Judi
Ryan, Doreen
Samis, John
Shedd, Marjory
Skillings-Harney, Sandra
Smythe, Don
Sydie, Iain
Tinline, Dorothy
*Underhill, Eileen
*Underhill, John
*Walton, Dorothy
Welch, Barbara
Whittaker, Sharon
Youngberg, Jane
Yung, Darryl

BALLOONING
Lang, Dale
Rathgeb, Chuck
Ritchie, Dale

BARREL JUMPING
Jolin, Yvon Jr.
*Robson, Fred

BASEBALL
*Abbott, Jack
*Allbon, Ackie
Alomar, Robbie
Alou, Felipe
Ambrose, John
Anderson, Gabby
Ash, Gord
Atkinson, Bill
*Baker, Mary
Barr, Doris
Bawn, Bev
Bay, Jason
*Bedecki, Tom
Beeston, Paul
Bell, George
*Bend, Olive
Benson, Lorne
Bertoia, Reno
*Biasatti, Hank
Boss, Leonard
Boucher, Denis
Bowsfield, Ted
Bronfman, Charles
*Brown, Robert
*Browne, Cec
Burgess, Tim
*Bush, Carmen
*Callaghan, Helen
*Callaghan, Margaret
Carter, Gary
Carter, Joe
Casanova, Bruno
Casanova, Willie
*Cass, Eddie
*Clarke, Nig
Clarkson, Reg
Clemens, Roger
Cleveland, Reggie
*Clifford, Shanty
*Colman, Frank
*Conacher, Lionel Sr.
*Condy, Buddy
*Congalton, William
*Connell, Alex
*Cooke, Jack Kent
*Corkey, Joe
Cormier, Rheal
Cosentino, Frank
Cox, Bobby
Creighton, Dale
Cripps, Ken
Curran, Randy
Dalton, Chuck
Dawson, Andre
Deakin, Bobby
Delgado, Carlos
Dempster, Ryan
Doiron, Phillip
*Ducey, John
*Earley, Ted
Eddie, Arden
*Edwards, Jake
*Elliott, Bob
*Elliott, Chaucer
*Emslie, Bob
*Evon, Russ
Fairs, Jack

Fanning, Jim
*Ferguson, Dorothy
Ferguson, Skit
*Ferguson, Vince
*Fergusson, Layton
Fernandez, Tony
*Finnamore, Arthur
*Ford, Russ
*Fowler, Dick
*Fox, Fred
Frobel, Doug
Gagne, Eric
Gaston, Cito
*Gibson, George
Gillick, Pat
Gillis, Eddie
*Gorbus, Glen
*Gorman, Charles
*Gorman, T.P.
*Graney, Jack
*Greaves, Joe
Green, Shawn
*Griffith, Cal
Grimsley, Ross
Guerrero, Vladimir
*Guzzo, Patrick
Haine, Audrey
Harvey, Scott Jr.
*Harvey, Scott Sr.
Hayter, Ron
*Heath, Jeff
Hentgen, Pat
Hiller, John
Hodgson, Paul
Holman, Sam
Huff, Bruce
Hupp, Howie
*Irwin, Arthur
Jackson, Russ
Jenkins, Ferguson
Johnson, Donnie
*Judd, Oscar
Kane, Frank
*Karpuk, Pete
*Keating, Jack
Kitts, Charlie
Koskie, Corey
Lapthorne, Whitey
*Leader, Al
Leblanc, Eugene
*Lee, Knotty
Leggatt, Art
Leitch, Kerry
*Lister, Ralph
Little, Ken
Mabey, Hap
MacKay, Gerry
MacKenzie, Bill
MacKenzie, Eric
MacLean, Lucella
*Malcolm, Andrew
*Marchildon, Phil
Martinez, Dennis
Martinez, Pedro
*Masters, Wally
*Matoba, Tom
Matthews, John
Mauch, Gene

McCaskill, Kirk
McHale, John
McKay, Dave
*McKay, Roy
McKean, Jim
McKenzie, Tom
McKillop, Bob
McKinnon, Frank
McLeod, Jackie
Melvin, Doug
*Miles, Rollie
*Milne, Howie
Molitor, Paul
Moore, Curt
*Moore, Harry
*Moore, Quip
Moroz, Evelyn
Morris, Greg
*Morris, Jim
Morris, Sid
*Moyer, John
Nicol, Helen
Noga, Arleene
Norton, Wayne
Obey, Arthur
*O'Brien, John
*O'Neill, Tip
*O'Rourke, Frank
Olerud, John
Oliver, Al
Oliver, Murray
Ouellette, Red
Owen, Jon
Palmer, David
Parrish, Larry
*Parry, Jack
Pataky, Bill
Paul, Chuck
*Pearson, Mike
Peden, Doug
*Phillips, Bill
Piche, Ron
Pielak, Casmer
*Plante, Jacques
Pomfret, Jack
*Porter, Bob
Potter, Billy
*Prediger, Pete
*Prentice, Bob
Psutka, Harry
Puhl, Terry
Quantrill, Paul
*Quigley, Ernest
Raines, Tim
Rau, Richard
Raymond, Claude
Richman, Joey
Richman, Ruby
Rizak, Gene
Robertson, Sandy
Robinson, Al
*Robinson, Jackie
Rogers, Steve
*Rosen, Goody
Rousseau, Bobby
Ruiter, Garth
Runge, Paul
Saunders, Billy

500

Schooley, Dennis
Seely, Glen
*Selkirk, George
*Shaughnessy, Shag
Sinclair, Marjorie
Slack, Bill
Slack, Bill
Slack, Stan
*Sleeman, George
*Smith, Pop
*Smith, Robert
Soulliere, Bernie
Speier, Chris
Stairs, Matt
Staub, Rusty
Stead, Ron
*Steele, David
Stieb, Dave
Stoneman, Bill
Strumm, Gil
*Sutherland, Hugh
Takahashi, Masao
Taylor, Ron
*Thomas, Fred
Thomas, Paul
*Thompson, Tommy
Thorburn, Cliff
Upper, Wray
Walker, Bruce
*Walker, Gord
Walker, Larry
Wallach, Tim
Ward, Pete
*Watkins, Bill
Wedley, Jack
Wells, Vernon
West, Art
White, Devon
*White, Tommy
Whitt, Ernie
Wilkes, Jimmy
Williams, Dick
*Wilson, Lefty
Wilson, Rod
Winfield, Dave
Zeaman, Joe
Zimmerman, Jeff

BASKETBALL
*Abramowitz, Moe
Ager, Barry
*Aitchison, Gordon
*Allison, Ian
Andrews, Porky
Armstrong, Paul
*Bailey, Marguerite
*Baker, Norm
*Baldwin, Frank
*Bardsley, Jim
Barnes, Bev
Baryluk, Mitch
*Bauld, Don
Bawden, Betty
Beck, Ross
*Belanger, Babe
*Bennie, Elsie
*Biasatti, Hank
Blackwell, Andrea

Boland, Pat
Boucher, Kelly
*Bowering, Ebbie
*Box, Charlie
Brkovich, Mike
*Brockway, Dot
*Brown, Mae
*Brown, Sophie
*Browne, Ed
Brumpton, Jerry
Bruno, Al
*Bulloch, Jim
Burnham, Faye
Campbell, David
*Campbell, R.D.
Campbell, Woody
Carter, Vince
Casanova, Willie
*Chapman, Art
Chapman, Chuck
Clarkson, Candy
Clarkson, Reg
*Cline, Paddy
Colistro, Peter
*Connell, Charlie
*Cooke, Jack Kent
*Coulson, Evelyn
Coulthard, Bill
Critelli, Chris
Czaja, Mitch
Dales-Schumann, Stacey
Dalton, Chuck
*Daniel, Babe
*Dann, Etta
*Dawson, Eddie
Devlin, Alex
Diffin, Charlie
*Donohue, Jack
Douthwright, Joyce
Dufresne, Coleen
Dukeshire, Kelly
*Dunn, Mary
*Earley, Ted
*Edwards, Ted
*Elliott, Bob
*Elrick, Elizabeth
*Ennis, Peter
Evans, Jodi
*Farmer, Jim
Fedoruk, Sylvia
*Ferraro, John
Fox, Rick
Foxcroft, Ron
Fraser, Bud
*Fry, Gladys
*Gallen, Winnie
*Garrow, Alex
*Gloag, Norm
*Gordon, Frances
Gosset, John
Gurunlian, Varouj
Hallas, Kory
Hansen, Lars
Harris, Merelynn
Heaney, Brian
*Hevenor, George
Horgan, Fred
Horwood, Don

Houbregs, Bob
Howson, Barry
Huband, Deb
Hutchison, Patti
Ingaldson, Fred
*Innis, Jessie
Jerant, Martina
*Johnson, Daisy
*Johnson, Dorothy
Johnston, Cynthia
Karch, Karla
Kazanowski, Gerald
*Kenyon, Jack
*Kinney, Margaret
Kitts. Charlie
Konchalski, Steve
Kootnekoff, John
Kristmanson, Alan
Lands, Ben
Larose, Bob
*Lister, Ralph
Little, Ken
*Livingston, Gerry
Love, Drew
Love, Jon
Lovett, Claire
Lucht, Edward
MacCulloch, Todd
MacDonald, Jackie
MacDonald, Noel
*MacFarlane, Gus
*MacPherson, Kitch
MacRitchie, Kay
*Mayers, Wallace
McBurney, Margaret
*McCormack, Mildred
McCrae, Don
*McDonald, Vern
McFarland, Packy
McKibbon, John
*McNaughton, Duncan
Meretsky, Toots
*Metras, John
*Monnot, Ray
*Milne, Howie
Miner, Hazel
*Mountifield, Eleanor
Mullins, Peter
*Munton, Mabel
*Naismith, James
*Nantais, Red
Nash, Steve
*Neale, Doris
Nicurity, Bryan
Nord, Dennis
Northup, Helen
O'Billovich, Bob
O'Connor, Zeke
Olafsson, Shirley
*Osborne, Bob
*Page, Percy
*Panasis, Rita
Pasquale, Eli
Pataky, Bill
*Patrick, Lynn
*Patrick, Muzz
Peden, Doug
*Perry, Nellie

Pettinger, Glen
Phibbs, Bob
Philp, Jerry
Phinney, Gertrude
Pickard, Leroy
*Pickell, Bob
Pipe, Andrew
Polson, Lynn
Pomfret, Jack
Provost, Mary Haydon
*Pullen, Harry
Pullen, Tom
*Quigley, Ernest
Rae, Al
Raffin, Romel
Rau, Richard
Rautins, Leo
Restivo, John
Reynolds, Warren
Richman, Joey
Richman, Ruby
*Ridd, Carl
Riley, Martin
Ritchie, Bill
Rizak, Gene
Robertson, Sandy
Robinson, Bill
*Rogin, Bill
*Rose, Jimmy
Ross, Betty
Ross, Chucker
Ruiter, Garth
Russell, Jamie
Ryan, Doc
Sankey, Derek
*Scott, Abbie
Shields, Kathy
Shields, Ken
Simpson, Bob
*Singleton, Harvey
Smith, Bev
*Smith, Connie
Smrek, Mike
Sovran, Gino
Spack, Mike
*Spencer, Jim
Sternberg, Gerry
*Stewart, Gordon
Stewart, Susan
Stone, Edith
Stone, Helen
Stoqua, Pat
Strumm, Gil
Stulac, George
Sutton, Warren
Sutton-Brown, Tammy
Suzuki, Arthur
Sweeney, Sylvia
Swords, Shawn
Tatarchuk, Hank
Tatham, Pat
*Thomas, Fred
Thomas, Misty
Thomas, Paul
Tilleman, Karl
*Tindall, Frank
Tolchinsky, Sol
Tollestrup, Phil

Totzke, Carl
Town, Bob
Traer, Rick
Triano, Jay
Truant, Ray
Underwood, Reg
Wade, Harry
Wearring, George
Wedley, Jack
Wennington, Bill
West, Art
*White, Dalt
*White, Tommy
Wigston, Fran
Williams, Roy
*Williamson, Jean
*Wilson, Ruth
Wiltjer, Greg
*Wynne, Ivor
Young, Frank

BATON TWIRLING
Garland, Lynda
Harmen, Wendy
Kopas, Ron

BIATHLON
Bedard, Myriam
Clegg, Robin
McMahon, David
Meloche, Lise
Rauhanen, Eric
Rupertus, Glenn
Whyte, Shauna

**BILLIARDS
/POOL
/SNOOKER**
Budge, Ervin
*Chenier, Georges
*Emerson, Eddie
Mellway, Dean
Miller, Doug Jr.
*Olson, Billy
Thorburn, Cliff
*Werbeniuk, Bill
*Wright, Joe. Sr.

**BOARDSAILING
/WINDSURFING**
Alie, Caroll-Ann
Bolduc, Alain

BOBSLEIGH
Anakin, Doug
Baptiste, Sheridon
Currier, Doug
Emery, John
Emery, Victor
Flynn, Clarke
Frank, Chris
Gilbert, Glenroy
Graham, John
Greenidge, Ricardo
Haydenluck, Greg
Kilburn, Joey
Kirby, Peter
Leblanc, Ken

Lori, Chris
Lueders, Pierre
MacEachern, Dave
MacLachlan, Alan
Pyc, Jack
Rathgeb, Chuck
Storey, Bob
Stovel, Peter
Vachon, Brian
White, Vance

BOCCIA
Gauthier, Paul

BODY BUILDING
Weider, Ben
Weider, Joe

BOWLING
*Bagguley, Howard
Bala, Ray Sr.
Ballantine, Bonny
Bigras, Orv
Blake, Terry
Boehm, Frank
Carey, Jim
Chibi, Tony
Coghill, Sandi
Connerty, Doug
Cripps, Ken
*Cutting, Flo
*Evon, Russ
Fine, Jack
Garside, Bert
*Gaudette, Cecelia
Glasser, Red
Hambly, Fraser
Heeney, Walter
*Hershfield, Leible
*Hohl, Elmer
Hong, Al
Hoult, Billy
Hynduik, Ollie
Lovett, Claire
*Martel, Marty
Martin, John
Matthews, John
McCaw, Doug
Miller, Doug Jr.
Miller, Russ
Mitchell, Ray
Morris, Sid
Most, Joe
*Moyer, John
Noga, Arleene
Pizzey, Blair
*Powell, Bill
Procher, Theda
Reid, Lefty
*Robinson, Blondie
*Ryan, Tommy
Stevenson, Lori
*Totzke, Bob
Townsend, Cathy
Trager, John
Underwood, Reg
Valentan, Walter

BOXING
Alleyne, Jeff
Andersen, Dale
Anderson, Dave
Anderson, Ricky
*Bath, Doc
*Battaglia, Frankie
Beaton, Bob
*Belanger, Frenchy
Benson, Lorne
Bergeron, Jean François
*Boucher, Jerry
*Box, Charlie
*Brosseau, Eugene
*Brouillard, Lou
Brown, Dale
Burke, Jack
*Burns, Leo
*Burns, Tommy
Cadieux, David
*Callura, Jackie
Chuvalo, George
Clyde, Ian
*Conacher, Lionel Sr.
*Connell, Charlie
*Connolly, Edward
*Cotton, Harry
*Coulon, Johnny
Czich, John
Daigle, Nora
Darwin, Howard
*Dècarie, Al
*Delaney, Jack
de Wit, Willie
*Dixon, George
Donison, Lee
Doucet, Paul
Douglas, Jason
Downey, Raymond
*Dugan, Jackie
Durelle, Yvon
*Dwyer, John
Embuldeniya, Herb
Faul, Adam
Fennell, Pat
Ferguson, Merv
Filane, Domenic
Findlay, Dick
Foley, Joe
Gardiner, Tyrone
Gaudet, Benoit
Gauthier, Sebastien
Gibson, Bryan
Glesby, Tom
*Goff, Ken
Gordon, Taylor
Gordon, Wayne
*Graham, Charles
Grant, Otis
Gray, Clyde
*Gwynne, Lefty
Hafey, Art
Hart, Gaétan
Hayter, Ron
*Headley, Ron
*Herlen, Ossie
*Hewitt, Foster
Hilton, Alex

Hilton, Dave Jr.
Hilton, Dave Sr.
Hilton, Matthew
*Howard, Kid
Huard, Camille
Hunt, Ted
Ius, Chris
Johnson, Greg
Keenan, Roy
Kenny, Clayton
*Kerwin, Gale
Kooner, Andrew
Kyvelos, Hercules
*Lablanche, George
Lacelle, Ron
Lalonde, Donny
Lambert, Claude
*Langford, Sam
Leduc, Mark
Leitham, Bobby
Lemieux, Gerald
Lewis, Lennox
*Lifford, Johnny
Lucas, Eric
*Luftspring, Sammy
Martin, Frank
*Matheson, Dan
Matiowski, Buck
*Maughan, George
*McEachern, Archie
McFater, Allan
*McLarnin, Jimmy
McWhirter, Cliff
Mitchell, Pinky
Noel, Leo
Nolan, Frank Jr.
*Nolan, Frank Sr.
Nolan, Steve
O'Sullivan, Shawn
Olson, Scott
Pascal, Jean
*Patrick, Muzz
*Pearce, Bobby
*Pelkey, Arthur
Pelletier, Leo-Charles
*Percival, Lloyd
Pomfret, Jack
*Powell, Bill
*Pulford, Harvey
Raftery, John
*Richardson, Blair
Richman, Joey
Ross, George
Ryan, Vinnie
Sandulo, Joey
Saunders, Jim
*Sauve, Gordon
*Schneider, Bert
Scott, Mike
Senos, Eddie
*Sidders, George
*Silverheels, Jay
*Smylie, Doug
*Stewart, Gordon
Strange, Michael
*Sullivan, Tommy
*Swartman, Mel
*Townsend, Billy

Ungerman, Irv
Walchuk, Michael
*Walls, Earl
*Walsh, Tarp
Walters, Dale
*Warwick, Claude
*White, Dennis
Wiebusch, Harry
*Wright, Joe Sr.
Young, Walter

BROOMBALL
Breton, Skip
MacDuff, Alan
Montgomery, Willie

BUILDER
*Adams, Jacks
*Adamson, Gail
Adkin, Dennis
*Ahearn, Frank
Allen, Keith
*Andersen, Roxy
*Anderson, Nint
Armstrong, Lesley
Aubut, Marcel
*Ballard, Harold
Baird, Vaughan
*Bauer, David
*Bean, Gladys
*Beers, William George
*Bickell, J.P.
*Bonnycastle, Charles
Bronfman, Charles
*Brook, Tom
*Brown, D. Wes
*Brown, Robert
Bryden, Rod
*Bush, Carmen
Butterfield, Jack
*Caithness, Charlie
*Callaghan, Pius
*Campbell, Angus
*Campbell, Clarence
Carnegie, Herb
*Cartwright, Ethel Mary
*Cattarinich, Joseph
*Cavallin, Isabell
*Chick, John
Chynoweth, Ed
Class, Harry
*Clifford, John
*Combe, Harvey
*Condon, Eddie
*Cooper, Ralph
Daniels, Danny
Desjardins, Larry
*Doucet, Evard
*Dudley, George
*Dunn, James
Durrell, Jim
Eagleson, Al
Estabrooks, John
Fabro, Sam
Fennell, Neil
Fink, Hardy
Fireman, Jack
Firestone, Bruce

*Firth, Doug
*Freeman, John
Gage, Bob
*Gibson, Jack
Goodings, Thomas
*Gorman, T.P.
*Griffiths, Frank
*Hanley, Bill
*Hannibal, Frank
*Hart, Stu
*Hatskin, Ben
*Hay, Charles
*Hayman, Lew
Heeney, Walter
*Henick, Ed
*Hill, Harvey
Hind, Terry
*Hogarth, Malcolm
Holman, Sam
Howard, Dick
Huff, Bruce
Hume, Ian
Hurdis, John
Hurley, Bill
*Keffer, Karl
Kelly, Henry
Kielty, Terry
Kinsella, J.J.
*Kinsella, Ray
*Krupp, Charlie
*Kubinec, John
*Leader, Al
*Leah, Vince
Lee, Tae Eun
*Livingston, Gerry
Macdonald, Daniel
MacKay, Gerry
Mackie, Gordie
*Marsh, Lou
*Martitsch, Karl
*Mathers, Frank
Matiowski, Buck
Maxwell, Doug
McConkey, Jim
McDonald, Les
*McEwen, Bill
*McEwen, Cam
McFarlane, Brent
*McKenzie, Ken
*McKenzie, Tait
McNaughton, Don
*McPherson, Don
Mellway, Dean
Miller, Doug Jr.
*Miller, Doug Sr.
*Mitchell, Bill
*Molson, Hartland
Morris, Sid
*Mumford, Peter
*Murchison, Cliff
*Murray, Pere
*Naismith, James
Nesbitt, Keith
*O'Brien, J. Ambrose
O'Dowda, Ernie
*Oberlander, Fred
Oldershaw, Bert
*Orban, Bill

Parker, Ken
Pashby, Tom
*Patrick, Frank
*Patrick, Lester
Paul, Donald
Pelech, Jack
*Percival, Lloyd
*Pickard, Allan
*Pilous, Rudy
Pocklington, Peter
*Poile, Bud
Pollock, Lloyd
*Porter, Muriel
*Potter, John
*Randall, Sam
Ratushny, Ed
Renwick, Gordon
*Reville, Ralph
Richman, Joey
*Ritchie, Alvin
Roberts, Roy
*Robinson, Bobby
*Robinson, Claude
*Roe, Lot
*Rogers, Melville
*Ross, Art
Ross, Dave
*Ross, P.D.
*Rowell, Fred
*Ryan, Joe
*Ryan, Tommy
Sample, Tim
*Sargent, Frank
*Selke, Frank Sr.
*Shaughnessy, Shag
Siciliano, Dave
*Sidwell, Pop
*Simons, Pop
*Simpson, Bill
*Simpson, Jimmy
*Smith, Frank
*Smith-Johannsen, Herman
*Smythe, Conn
*Speers, Jim
*Spencer, Jim
Stauder, Zlatica
Steadward, Robert
*Stevens, Warren
Storey, Bob
*Stronge, Stan
Stukus, Annis
*Sutherland, James
Thierry, Nick
Thompson, Jim
*Thompson, Stanley
Torrey, Bill
*Totzke, Bob
*Trifunov, Jim
*Turner, Lloyd
Underhill, Pat
*Vidruk, Kas
*Waghorne, Fred
*Walker, Gord
*Walls, Ken
*Warren, Harold
*Watson, Sandy
Webster, Peter
Weider, Ben

Weider, Joe
*Wendling, Wendy
*Whitaker, Denis
Wilhelmsen, Franz
*Wright, Ken
*Wykeham-Martin, Simon
Zeman, Joe

CANOEING /KAYAKING
*Amyot, Frank
Bales, John
Barre, Alexandra
Barre, Denis
Barre, Jean
Beedell, John
Behrens, Norman
Bennett, Douglas
Botting, Steve
Boyle, Sheryl
*Brien, Alvin
Brien, Don
*Brigden, William
Brunet, Caroline
Buday, Attila
Buday, Tamas Jr.
Cain, Larry
*Charters, Harvey
*Cleevely, Bill
Crichlow, Renn
Dodge, Ann
Edwards, John
Faloon, Joanna
Findlay, Dave
Fisher, Hugh
Ford, David
Fraser, Martin
Furneaux, Karen
Gibeau, Marie-Josée
Giles, Peter
Giles, Steve
*Groff, Doug
Guay, Lucie
Harris, Susan
Herst, Alison
*Hevenor, George
Hickox, Mac
Holloway, Sue
Homer-Dixon, Marjorie
Howe, Dan
Hunt, Claudia
Kennedy, Corrina
Kerckhoff, Claudia
Kerckhoff, Hermann
Lalonde, Bernie
Lane, Ken
Lee, Scott
*Lewis, Stanley
Lukanovich, Karen
Lukanovich, Louis
MacAskill, Klari
Maxwell, Gavin
McCleery, Alan
*Merrill, Horace
Morris, Alwyn
Morris, Sid
Norman, Larry
Oldershaw, Bert

Oldershaw, Dean
Oldershaw, Scott
Olmsted, Barbara
Olmsted, Nancy
*Pulford, Harvey
Sample, Bonnie
Scott, Mike
Shaw, Colin
*Stroulger, Ken
Tippett, Karen
van Koeverden, Adam
Williams, Dawn
Wood, John

COACHING

Abbott, Marni
Abbruzzi, Pat
*Abel, Sid
*Abramowicz, Moe
Adams, Dick
*Adams, Jack
Adams, Robert
Allan, Robert
Alleyne, Jeff
Alou, Felipe
Anderson, Dave
Anderson, Steve
*Anderson, Verne
Andrews, Porky
*Anthony, Matt
ApSimon, John
Arbour, Al
*Armstrong, Charles
Armstrong, George
Armstrong, Paul
Arseneault, Lise
Arsenault, Paul
Arusoo, Toomas
Backstrom, Ralph
Baert, Jean-Paul
Baillie, Charlie
Bajin, Boris
*Baldwin, Frank
Bales, John
Balon, Dave
Barresi, Jamie
Barry, Cliff
*Bauer, David
Baytor, Terry
Beaton, Bob
Beaton, Ewan
*Bedecki, Tom
*Bell, Bobby
Bennett, Doug
Benning-Reid, Denise
Berenson, Red
Bergey, Kim
Berry, Bob
Blair, Wren
*Blake, Toe
Boadway, Bob
Bodnar, Gus
Boland, Pat
Bonnello, Bonny
Botting, Steve
Bottoms, Lynn
*Boucher, Bob
*Boucher, Frank

Bourne, Bob
*Bowering, Ebbie
Bowman, Scotty
Bowness, Rick
Brabenec, Hana
Brabenec, Josef Sr.
Brain, Karen
Brancato, George
Bratty, Gary
Breck, Ian
*Breen, Joe
Brock, Dieter
*Broda, Turk
Brophy, John
*Brown, Dick
Brown, Hal
*Brown, Wally
*Browne, Cec
*Browne, Ed
Brumpton, Jerry
Bruno, Al
*Buckna, Mike
*Bulloch, Jim
Burchuk, Mike
Burka, Ellen
Burns, Pat
*Bush, Carmen
*Bush, Eddie
Butler, Barry
Cahill, Leo
Campbell, Hugh
*Campbell, R.D.
Casanova, Willie
*Cavallin, Isabell
*Cavallin, John
*Chamberlain, Murph
Chambers, Dave
Cheevers, Gerry
*Clair, Frank
Clark, Jim
Connellan, Peter
Cosentino, Frank
Coulter, Bruce
Cox, Bobby
Crawford, Marc
Crisp, Terrry
Cullen, Ronald
Currie, Gordon
Custis, Bernie
Daigneault, Doug
Daley, Jim
Danyluk, Terry
David, Tracy
Davis, Pat
*Day, Hap
Delahey, Wally
Demers, Jacques
Desclouds, Rick
*Dimitroff, Tom
Dineen, Gord
*Distelmeyer, Wally
Donaghey, Sam
*Donohue, Jack
Drake, Clare
Dudley, Rick
Duff, Alexander
Duguay, Ron
Dussault, Jacques

*Edwards, Ted
Eisler, Laurie
*Elliott, Bob
Elliott, Geoff
*Elmer, Wally
*Ennis, Peter
*Eon, Suzanne
Estay, Ron
Etcheverry, Sam
Eynon, Bob
Faulkner, John
Fedoruk, Sylvia
Filchock, Frank
Findlay, Dave
*Firby, Howard
*Fletcher, Doug
*Foot, Fred
Forder, Anna
Fowlie, Jim
Fracas, Gino
Francis, Bob
Francis, Emile
Fraser, Bud
*Frederickson, Frank
*Freeman, John
Frick, Tim
Fripp, Shaun
Galbraith, Sheldon
*Garvie, Clarence
Gaston, Cito
Gate, George
Geller, Mitch
Gilbert, Don
Gilbert, Greg
Gillis, Eddie
*Glover, Fred
Goermann, Elfriede
Goermann, Monica
*Gold, Otto
Gordon, Jack
Gordon, Taylor
Gordon, Wayne
Gowan, Geoff
Grace, Maureen
*Graham, Barbara
*Graham, Charles
Grant, Bud
Grant, Martha
*Grassick, Greg
Greaves, Sandra
Green, Gary
*Griffing, Dean
*Griffith, Harry
*Griffiths, Joe
Gurney, Helen
Hall, Chris
*Hamilton, Jack
*Hare, Bill
Hargreaves, Doug
*Hart, Stu
Hartley, Bob
Hayes, Bob
*Hayes, John
*Hayman, Lew
Heaney, Brian
*Hedgewick, Mike
Heikkila, Bill
Henley, Garney

Hildebrand, Ike
*Hill, Harvey
Hindmarch, Bob
Hitchcock, Ken
Horwood, Don
Huband, Deb
Hughes, George
Hughes, Karen
Hume, Ian
*Hunt, Lynda Adams
Hyland, Bruce
Hyland, Margaret
*Imlach, Punch
Innes, Cam
*Irvin, Dick Sr.
*Irwin, Arthur
*Ivan, Tommy
*Ivy, Pop
Jackson, Russ
Jacobs, Dave
*Jacobs, Jack
Janzen, Henry
Johnson, Dave
Johnson, Tom
Kadatz, Dennis
Keenan, Mike
Kemp, Nigel
Kemp, Sally
*Kenyon, Jack
*Kerwin, Gale
Keys, Eagle
Kierstead, Bob
Kilrea, Brian
Knight, Tuffy
Konchalski, Steve
Krause, Willi
Kromm, Bobby
Lalonde, Lally
Langlois, Jocelyn
Lee, Tae Eun
L'Heureux, Bill
Leigh, Doug
Leitch, Kerry
Lemaire, Jacques
Lemelin, Reggie
Lenard, Al
Levy, Marv
*Lindquist, Vic
*Loaring, John
*Loney, Don
Long, Bill
Ludwig, Craig
*MacDonald, Irene
MacDonald, Noel
*MacFarlane, Gus
Mach, Gerard
MacKenzie, Bill
MacKenzie, Eric
*MacKenzie, Shanty
MacLean, John
MacMillan, Billy
Main, Lorne
Maloney, Phil
Manning, Peter
*Mantha, Sylvio
Marek, Deb
Marshall, Dru
Martin, Jacques

*Masters, Wally
Matthews, Don
Mauch, Gene
Maurice, Paul
*McCannell, Don
McClintock, Joel
McCrae, Don
McCrae, Judy
McDadi, Hatem
McDonald, Dennis
McFarland, Packy
McFarlane, Brent
McGuire, Pierre
McInnis, Andy
*McKay, Willie
McKee, Walt
McKenzie, Tom
McKillop, Bob
*McKinnon, Archie
McLeod, Jackie
*McNie, Murray
McPhee, Dennis
McWhirter, Cliff
Meeker, Howie
Meiszter, Ernst
Mervyn, Glen
*Metras, John
Michienzi, Pete
Miller, Doug Jr.
*Miller, Leigh
Miller, Shannon
*Milne, Howie
Mitchell, Dale
Mitchell, Doug
Mitchell, Ray
*Mobilio, Dominic
Montgomery, Willie
*Moore, Harry
*Morris, Fred
*Morris, Jim
Morris, Sid
*Morris, Teddy
Morrison, Roland
Morrow, Al
Moss, Joe
Most, Joe
Muckler, John
Muir, Debbie
Mullins, Peter
Murphy, Cal
Murphy, Ron
Murray, Bryan
*Murray, Pere
Murray, Terry
Nadon, Chantal
Nakamura, Hiroshi
*Nantais, Red
*Neilson, Roger
Nelson, Donald
Nettles, Ray
*Newman, Al
*Newman, Bernard
*Nolan, Frank Sr.
*Nooney, John
Nord, Dennis
*Norman, Percy
Norton, Wayne
Nye, Barry

O'Billovich, Bob
*Obeck, Vic
Obey, Arthur
Oldershaw, Dean
O'Malley, Terry
*Osborne, Bob
Ouellette, Bert
Oxenbury, Noel
Oye, Moe
Paddock, John
*Page, Percy
Paopao, Joe
Parker, Jackie
Parker, Ken
*Patrick, Lester
Patterson, Joe
Pearn, Perry
Peden, Sandy
*Percival, Lloyd
Philip, Bob
Philp, Jerry
Phoenix, Skip
Pischke, Garth
*Plante, Jacques
Poce, Paul
*Poile, Bud
Pomfret, Jack
Popp, Jim
*Porter, John
Porter, Ken
*Potter, John
*Primeau, Joe
Pronovost, Jean
Pronovost, Marcel
Pugh, Bob
*Pugh, Lionel
Pyle, Dave
*Quigley, Ernest
*Quilty, Silver
Quenneville, Joel
Quinn, Pat
Raine, Al
Ramsay, Craig
*Rankin, Frank
Ratanaseangsuang,
　　　　　Channarong

Rathgeb, Chuck
*Read, Frank
*Reay, Billy
*Rebholz, Russ
Reid, Pat
Renney, Tom
Resch, Chico
Restivo, John
Richman, Joey
Riley, Martin
Rita, Adam
*Ritchie, Alvin
Ritchie, John
Roberts, Jim
Robinson, Larry
*Rodden, Mike
Rodney, David
Rogers, Doug
*Rogin, Bill
Rokosh, Greg
Rollick, Bruce

*Rose, Jimmy
*Ross, Art
Ross, Dave
Rowan, Sheila
Roy, Aldo
Ruel, Claude
Ruff, Lindy
Ruiter, Garth
Rumbold, Dave
Russell, Ernestine
Ryan, Doc
*Ryder, Gus
Sanderson, Lyle
Sandulo, Joey
Saunders, Billy
*Sauve, Gordon
Savage, Marilyn
Savageau, Daniele
Sawula, Lorne
Sazio, Ralph
*Schleimer, Joe
Schmidt, Milt
Schoenfeld, Jim
Schoenhals, Paul
Schulze, Rudy
Selwood, Brad
Servold, Irvin
*Shaughnessy, Shag
Sheahan, Pat
*Shero, Fred
Shields, Kathy
Shields, Ken
*Shore, Eddie
Sinden, Harry
Skrien, Dave
*Smith, Alf
*Smith, Don
Smith, Gwen
*Smith, Robert
Smith, Sandra
Snelling, Deryk
Sonmor, Glen
*Spencer, Jim
Stanfield, Fred
*Stanley, Barney
Steadward, Robert
*Stevens, Warren
Stewart, Ron
Stratten, Gaye
*Stronge, Stan
Stukus, Annis
*Sullivan, Tommy
Sutton, Warren
*Sztehlo, Zoltan
Takahashi, June
Takahashi, Masao
Takahashi, Ray
Takahashi, Tina
*Templeton, Bert
Tennant, Mark
Tessier, Orv
Thomas, Paul
Thomas, Ted
*Thomson, Earl
Tihanyi, Jeno
*Timmis, Brian
*Tindall, Frank
Tippett, Dave

Todd, Dick
*Tommy, Andy Jr.
*Trifunov, Jim
Truant, Ray
Upper, Wray
Ursuliak, Wally
*Uteck, Larry
van der Merwe, Marina
*Van Vliet, Maury
Vespaziani, Bob
Vigars, Robert
*Vine, Bill
Volpe, Nick
*Voyles, Carl
*Walker, Peahead
*Watson, Moose
Watt, Tom
Webb, Don
*Weiland, Cooney
*Wendling, Wendy
West, Art
*White, Dalt
*White, Dennis
Whitt, Ernie
Wigston, Fran
*Wilkins, Bruce
Williams, Dick
Willsey, Ray
Wilson, Alex
Wilson, Ron
Wirkowski, Nobby
Woit, Benny
Woo, Wes
*Wright, Joe Sr.
Wright, Lee
Wyatt, Dave
*Wynne, Ivor
Yallop, Frank
*Yost, Ken
Young, Joe

CRICKET
Brewster, Ken
*Cameron, Jack
*Fletcher, Doug
*King, Donald
*Laing, John
*Lyon, George
*Martin, Fritz
*Percival, Lloyd
Rathgeb, Chuck
*Saunders, Dyce
*Somerville, Sandy
Stevens, Rick
*Warren, Harry

CURLING
Adams, Diane
*Adams, Harry
Aitken, Don
*Anderson, Nint
Anton, Ron
Armstrong, Jim
Arnott, Jan
*Avery, Frank
Baldwin, Matt
Bartlett, Don
Bartlett, Sue Anne

Base, John
*Bauld, Don
Begin, Terry
Belcourt, Tim
Benson, Lorne
Betker, Jan
Black, Elmer
Bodogh, Marilyn
Bodogh-Jurgenson, Christine
Borst, Cathy
Boyd, Mike
Braunstein, Terry
Bray, Shirley
Brown, Gord
Brown, Ted
Buchan, Ken
Burtnyk, Kerry
*Butterworth, Arnie
*Buxton, Noel
*Calles, Ada
Cameron, Doug
*Campbell, Clarence
*Campbell, Colin
Campbell, Garnet
Carney, Laurie
Carruthers, Bob
Carstairs, Kent
Charette, Agnés
Charette, France
Charette, Pierre
Chernoff, Mike
Chiarelli, John
*Coben, Muriel
Cole, Betty
*Congalton, Jim
Coombe, Eldon
*Corkey, Joe
Corner, Peter
Creber, Bill
Czaja, Mitch
Dacey, Mark
*D'Amour, Frenchy
DeBlonde, Clare
DeBlonde, Garry
Delmage, Al
DeWare, Mabel
Dewitte, Marcel
*Dickeson, Jean
Duguid, Don
*Dunbar, William
*Edwards, Jake
*Elliott, Bob
Fedoruk, Sylvia
Fedosa, Bob
Ferbey, Randy
Ferguson, Reid
Ferguson, Skit
Fletcher, Bill
Folk, Rick
Forgues, Keith
Fraser, Sherry
Fry, Barry
Gallant, Peter
Geiger, Marla
Gellard, Kim
*Gervais, Hec
*Gilbert, Don
Goring, Alison

*Gowanlock, Ab
Gowsell, Paul
*Greaves, Joe
Green, Ron
Gretsinger, Bert
Gudereit, Marcia
*Gunnlaugson, Lloyd
Gurowka, Joe
Hackner, Al
*Hansen, Ina
Hansen, Warren
Harris, Mike
Harrison, Neil
Hemmings, Guy
Herlinveaux, Louise
*Hermann, Tiny
Houck, Norm
Houston, Heather
Houston, Neil
Howard, Glenn
Howard, Russ
Hritzuk, Eugene
Hudson, Bruce
*Hudson, Gordon
Hunter, Rod
Hushagen, Earle
Hushagen, Sandra
Jackson, Virginia
Jenkins, Bill
Jenkins, Peter
Jenkins, Shorty
Jones, Colleen
Jones, Debbie
Karrys, George
Kawaja, John
Keith, Harold
*Kempster, Ray
Kennedy, Bruce
Kennedy, Tracy
*Kingsmith, Ray
Laliberte, Connie
Lang, Lorraine
Lang, Rick
Langlois, Al
LaRocque, Penny
Law, Kelley (Owen)
Lawes, Keith
Lewis, Bill
Little, Ken
Lobel, Art
Lord, Lovel
Lukowich, Ed
*Lumsden, Bill
Mabey, Hap
*Mabey, Harold
*MacDonald, Wen
MacInnes, Bob
MacInnes, Kent
MacKay, Gerry
*Manahan, Cliff
*Mann, Avard
*Mann, Bob
Martin, Flora Greenwood
Martin, Kevin
Maxwell, Doug
Mazinke, Harvey
McCrae, John
McCusker, Joan

*McEwen, Cam
McGrath, Larry
*McKee, Joyce
*McMillan, Roy
*McMurray, Mary
McPhee, Barry
*McTavish, Bill
Meleschuk, Orest
Merklinger, Anne
Merklinger, Bill
Merklinger, Dave
Middaugh, Wayne
Miki, Fuji
Miller, Russ
Miller, Tommy
Millikin, Hugh
Moffatt, Rich
Moore, Linda
Morris, Earle
Morris, John
Morrison, Lee
Munro, Bruce
*Murchison, Cliff
Naimark, Barry
*Nairn, Bill
*Nash, Jack
Nedohin, Dave
Neufeld, Chris
Nicol, Robert
Noga, Arleene
Northcott, Ron
Noseworthy, Mark
O'Neill, Kay
Ogden, Steve
*Oyler, Don
Palmer, Doug
Paterson, Gord
Paul, Chuck
Perroud, Pat
*Perry, Gordon
Peters, Vic
Pettapiece, Jim
Pezer, Vera
Pfeifer, Scott
Phillips, Alf Jr.
*Phillips, Alf Sr.
Phillips, Peter
Piaskoski, Jim
Pickering, Bob
Pidskalny, Diane
Pierce, Glen
*Porter, Muriel
Proulx, Rita
Provost, Barry
Rankin, Heather
Reilly, Keith
Richardson, Arnold
Richardson, Ernie
Richardson, Garnet
Richardson, Wes
Rocque, Marcel
Ross, Chucker
Rowan, Sheila
Ruiter, Garth
Ryan, Pat
*Sargent, Frank
Savage, Paul
*Schmirler, Sandra

Schoenhals, Dorenda
Seltzer, Sheila
Sharples, Jim
*Sinclair, Marjorie
*Smith, David
Sparkes, Bernie
Sparkes, Lindsay
Steeves, Ed
*Stevenson, Forbis
*Stone, Reg
*Stone, Roy
Storey, Fred
Stoughton, Jeff
Tallon, Wayne
Taylor, Russ
*Tetley, Bill
Tetley, Ian
*Thibodeau, Nick
Thomas, Jeff
Thompson, Clif
Tobin, Lee
*Trites, Ev
Turcotte, Bob
Turnbull, Ray
Ursel, Bob
Ursel, Jim
Ursuliak, Wally
Van Dine, David
Ventura, Dawn
Wagner, Bill
Waite, Jim
Walchuk, Don
Walsh, Billy Jr.
*Walsh, Billy Sr.
*Watson, Ken
*Welsh, Alex
*Welsh, Jim
*Wendel, Fred
Werenich, Ed
Westphal, Don
Wilson, Robin
Wilson, Tom
Wood, Bryan
*Wood, Howie
Wood, Lionel
*Wood, Nora
*Wood, Pappy
*Woolley, Emily
*Youngson, Les
*Youngson, Muriel

CYCLING
Atkinson, Lorne
Bauer, Steve
Bessette, Lyne
Blouin, Marc
Boucher, Gaetan
Burka, Sylvia
Carter-Erdman, Kelly Ann
*Davies, Jim
Dietiker, Judy
Dubnicoff, Tanya
Fraser, Gord
Gagne, Maurice
Garneau, Louis
Green, Roland
Harnett, Curt
*Harper, Ted

Harvey, Pierre
Hayman, Ron
Hughes, Clara
Hurley, Bill
Jackson, Linda
Keast, Brian
Larocque, Dominique
Lovell, Jocelyn
Ludtke, Frank
*Mathieu, Wilfrid
*McCulloch, Jack
*McEachern, Archie
McManus, Seamus
McRae, Ed
Muenzer, Lori-Ann
Murphy, Pat
Oland, Erick
Palmer, Sue
Peden, Doug
*Peden, Torchy
Premont, Marie-Helene
Redden, Chrissy
Robinson, Morrie
Samplonius, Anne
Singleton, Gordon
Stieda, Alex
Strong, Karen
Sydor, Alison
Tomlinson, Lesley
Walton, Brian
Way, Kelly Ann
Wohlberg, Eric

DARTS
*Astra, Duke
Cripps, Ken
Miller, Russ
Part, John

DIVING
Armstrong, Ken
Athans, George Sr.
Bedard, David
Bernier, Sylvie
Boys, Bev
Bulmer, Eryn
Carruthers, Liz
Class, Harry
Comtois, Phillipe
Cranham, Scott
*Crighton, Hec
Cuthbert, Linda
Dacyshyn, Anna
Depiero, Mary
Despatie, Alexandre
Dinsley, Tom
Flewwelling, Larry
Friesen, Ron
Fuller, Debbie
Fuller, Wendy
Geller, Mitch
Gordon, Megan
Gordon, Paige
Grout, Glen
Hartley, Blythe
Heymans, Emilie
*Hunt, Lynda Adams
Kiefer, Eniko

Liberty, Jeff
*Little, Laura
*MacDonald, Irene
MacKay, Elizabeth
MacLeod, Tammy
McArton, Jennifer
*McKinnon, Archie
Meissner, Ernie
Montminy, Anne
Morrow, Carol
*Moss, Judy
Napper, Jason
Nash, John
Nutter, Janet
Pelletier, Annie
*Phillips, Alf Sr.
Phoenix, Skip
Robertson, Nancy
Rollo, Kathy
Sageman, Randy
Stott, Arthur
Stulac, George
Webb, Don
York, Teri

DOG-SLEDDING
Martin, Frank
*Montabone, Monty
*St. Godard, Emile

ENTREPRENEUR
*Ballard, Harold
*Bassett, John Jr.
*Berger, Sam
*Cooke, Jack Kent
*Dandurand, Leo
Darwin, Howard
*Gorman, T.P. Tommy
*Nayler, Thomas

EQUESTRIAN
Ashton, Elizabeth
Baker, Charles
Bonnello, Bonny
Boylen, Christilot
Brain, Karen
Cone, Mac
Day, James
Deslauriers, Mario
Dunlap, Moffatt
Dvorak, Tom
Ehrlick, Allan
Elder, Jim
Gayford, Tom
Graham, Hugh
Grant, Martha
Greenough, Gail
Hahn, Robin
Hayes, Jay
Henselwood, Jill
Herbert, Michael
Ishoy, Mark
*Jacobsen, George
Kerr, Barbara
Kozak, Chelan
Lamaze, Eric
Laskin, Mark
Millar, Ian

Millar, Torchy
Neale, Cynthia
Pearce, John
Scott, Barbara Ann
Simpson, John
Smith, Gina
Stubbs, Lorraine
*Sztehlo, Zoltan
Thomas, Shirley
Underhill, Beth
Vaillancourt, Michel
Wedge, Cathy
*Whitaker, Denis
Young-Black, Stuart

FENCING
Andru, John
ApSimon, John
Archibald, Joan
*Archibald, Nancy
Banos, Jean-Marie
Banos, Jean-Paul
*Bakonyi, Peter
Beaudry, Paul
Chatel, Sigrid
Chouinard, Jean-Marc
Conyd, Magdy
*Desjarlais, Robert
Dessureault, Michel
Foxcroft, Bob
Hennyey, Donna
*Hennyey, Imre
*Horn, Alf
Lavoie, Marc
Leblanc, Louise-Marie
MacKay, Sherraine
Meiszter, Ernst
Morrison, Roland
Nagy, Imre
Nowosielski, Dan
Nowosielski, Leszek
Obst, Herbert
Ploudre, Tony
Ransom, James
*Schwende, Carl
Shong, Laurie
Sukunda, Eli
Tremblay, Thalie
*Tully, George
Wawryn, Alexandra
Wiedel, Gerry
Wiedel, Pacita
Wishart, Carol
Wong, Lester

FIELD HOCKEY
Beecroft, Lynne
Benson, Heather
Bissett, David
Blaxland, Jody
Borowy, Janet
Brafield, Leslie
Brewster, Ken
Broderick, Kathleen
Burrows, Pat
Charlton, Nancy
Conn, Michelle
Creelman, Sharon

Crook, Jan
Douthwright, Joyce
Dube, Ajay
Ellis, Phyllis
Faust, Lisa
Forbes, Sarah
Forrest, Robin
Forshaw, Sheila
Gourlay, Jean
Haig, Cathy
Hartley, Errol
Hewlett, Karen
Hobkirk, Alan
Johnson, Jenny
Kanjee, Hashmuk
Kant, Hari
Lambert, Laurie
MacKinnon, Zoe
Mahey, Diane
Marshall, Dru
McCrae, Judy
Motzek, Peter
Mouat, Michael
Neill, Susan
Olafsson, Shirley
Palmer, Alison
Pereira, Ken
Plummer, Reg
Roberts, Rick
Short, Robert
Sparling, Jean
Stoyka, Darlene
van der Merwe, Marina
*Warren, Harry
Warren, Victor
Wheatley-Magee, Terry
Whittingham, Dianne
Winters, Shelley
Wright, Lee

FIGURE SKATING
Albright, Debbie
Alletson, Kim
*Bain, Dan
*Baptie, Norval
*Belyea, Arthur
Benning-Reid, Denise
Berezowski, Barbara
Bezic, Sandra
Bezic, Val
Bourne, Shae-Lynn
*Bowden, Norris
Brasseur, Isabelle
Browning, Kurt
Burka, Ellen
Burka, Petra
Butt, Mark
Carscallen, Susan
Chouinard, Josée
Colman, Ann
Cranston, Toller
Dafoe, Frances
*Distelmeyer, Wally
Dore, David
Dowding, John
Duchesnay, Isabelle
Duchesnay, Paul
Eisler, Lloyd Jr.

Forder, Anna
Galbraith, Sheldon
*Gold, Otto
*Graham, Barbara
Griner, Wendy
Humphry, Jay
Hyland, Bruce
Hyland, Margaret
Irwin, Cathy Lee
Jackson, Donald
Jelinek, Maria
Jelinek, Otto
Jones, Candy
Kemkaren, Heather
Kraatz, Victor
Langdon, Jeff
Leigh, Doug
Leitch, Kerry
Magnussen, Karen
Manley, Elizabeth
Martini, Paul
*McCall, Robert
*McCreath, Ralph
McGillivray, David
*McPherson, Donald
Morrissey, Janet
Morrow, Suzanne
*Mumford, Peter
Nightingale, Lynn
Orser, Brian
Pachl, Carole
Paul, Robert
Pelletier, David
Phillips-Maya, Wendy
*Pockar, Brian
*Reville, Guy
Robinson, Jennifer
*Rogers, Melville
*Rubenstein, Louis
Sale, Jamie
Sandhu, Emanuel
Scott, Barbara Ann
*Scott, Norman
Shaver, Ron
Snelling, Charles
Soper, Barry
Soper, Louise
Stojko, Elvis
Terpenning, Barbara
*Thacker, Mary Rose
Thompson, Marilyn
Thomson, Kay
Underhill, Barbara
Wagner, Barbara
Wainman, Tracey
*Wala, George
Wilkes, Debbi
*Wilson, Montgomery
Wilson, Tracy
Wong, Charlene

FISHING
Deval, Gordon
Labignan, Italo
Rathgeb, Chuck
Waszczuk, Henry

FOOTBALL

Abbruzzi, Pat
Abendschan, Jack
Ackles, Bob
Adams, Dick
*Adelman, Louis
Ah You, Junior
Aird, Stu
Albrecht, J.I.
Aldag, Roger
Aldridge, Dick
Alexander, Ray
Allen, Damon
Anderson, Dave
Andrusyshyn, Zenon
*Anthony, Matt
Arakgi, Nick
Atchison, Ron
Avery, Jeff
*Back, Len
*Bailey, By
Baillie, Charlie
Baker, Bill
Baker, Terry
*Ballard, Harold
Barresi, Jamie
Barrett, Danny
Barrow, John
*Barwell, Gord
Bass, Danny
*Batstone, Harry
Battle, Greg
Bauer, Lyle
*Beach, Ormand
Beck, Ross
Belcher, Val
Belec, Jacques
Belsher, Don
Benefield, David
Bennett, Bruce
Bennett, Paul
Benson, Lorne
*Berger, Sam
Berryman, Tim
*Bevan, Eddie
Bevan, Marv
Beynon, Tom
*Bitkowski, Bruno
Black, Fred
Blair, Don
Blanchard, Leo
Bonk, John
Bottoms, Lynn
*Box, Ab
Brancato, George
Brazley, Carl
Breck, Ian
*Breen, Joe
Brennan, Bernie
*Bright, Johnny
Britton, Bill
Brock, Dieter
Brown, Clayton
*Brown, D. Wes
*Brown, Dick
Brown, Tom
*Browne, Cec
Browne, Less
*Bruce, Lou

Bruno, Al
*Buddo, Don
Buono, Wally
Burden, Willie
Burgess, Tom
Burkholder, Dave
Burns, Chris
Cahill, Leo
Cahoon, Ben
Cain, Jim
Calvillo, Anthony
Cameron, Bob
Campbell, Hugh
Campbell, Jerry
*Campbell, R.D.
Capozzi, Herb
Carpenter, Ken
Casanova, Bruno
Casanova, Willie
*Casey, Tom
Cassata, Rick
Chalupka, Ed
Champion, Tony
*Charlton, Ken
*Chipper, Eric
Chiu, Bryan
Chomyc, Lance
Christie, Steve
*Clair, Frank
Clare, Lou
Claridge, Pat
Clark, Jim
Clark, Ken
Clarke, Bill
Clarkson, Reg
Clements, Tom
Clemons, Mike
Clermont, Jason
Climie, Jock
Coffey, Tommy-Joe
Coleman, Lovell
Collins, Doug
Collins, Merv
Conacher, Lionel Jr.
*Conacher, Lionel Sr.
*Connell, Charlie
Conroy, Jim
*Cooke, Jack Kent
*Cooper, Ralph
Copeland, Jim
Copeland, Royal
Corrigall, Jim
Cosentino, Frank
*Cotton, Harry
Coulter, Bruce
Coulter, Carl
Coulter, Tex
Covington, Grover
*Cox, Ernie
Creighton, Dale
*Crighton, Hec
*Cronin, Carl
Crysdale, Jamiee
*Cummings, Bruce
*Currie, Andy
Curtis, Ulysses
Custis, Bernie
Cutler, Dave

*Cutler, Wes
Cyncar, Marco
Daigneault, Doug
Dalla Riva, Peter
*Dandurand, Leo
Danychuk, Bill
Darch, Art
Dattilio, Gerry
*Davies, Bill
Dawson, Bob
*Deacon, Tom
Deakin, Bobby
Dean, Bob
*Degruchy, John
Dekdebrun, Al
Delahey, Wally
Desjardins, Paul
Dickenson, Dave
*Dimitroff, Tom
DiPietro, Rocky
*Dixon, George
Dojack, Paul
Dorsch, Henry
Dorsey, Dean
Doty, Frederick
*Doucette, Gerry
Drake, Clare
Dublinski, Tom
Dumelie, Larry
*Dumoulin, Seppi
Dunigan, Matt
*Dunlap, Frank
Dunlap, Jake
Dussault, Jacques
*Earley, Ted
Eben, Mike
Ecuyer, Al
*Edwards, Ted
*Elford, Gear
Elgaard, Ray
*Eliowitz, Abe
Ellingson, James
*Elliott, Chaucer
Ellis, Craig
*Elsby, Ted
*Emerson, Eddie
Enos, Ed
Estay, Ron
Etcheverry, Sam
Evanshen, Terry
Exelby, Clare
Fairbanks, Lloyd
Fairs, Jack
*Faloney, Bernie
*Farmer, Jim
*Fear, Cap
Fennell, Dave
*Ferraro, John
Ferrone, Dan
Fieldgate, Norm
Filchock, Frank
*Fisher, Frank
*Flanagan, Flin
Fleming, Joe
Fleming, Sean
Fleming, Willie
Flutie, Darren
Flutie, Doug

Flynn, Chris
Foley, Jim
Ford, Alan
Fort, Neil
*Foster, Red
*Foulds, William C
*Fouts, Dick
Fracas, Gino
Frank, Bill
Fraser, Cam
*Fraser, Frank
*Fraser, George
Fripp, John
*Fritz, Bob
Fry, Jay
Fryer, Brian
*Fulton, Greg
Furlong, Jim
Gabler, Wally
Gabriel, Tony
Gaines, Gene
*Garvie, Clarence
Gaudaur, Jake Jr.
Gerela, Ted
Getty, Don
Giardino, Wayne
Gilbert, Don
*Glasser, Sully
Glenn, Steve
Golab, Tony
Gorrell, Miles
Gotta, Jack
Grace, John
Graham, Milt
Grant, Bud
Grant, Tommy
*Grassick, Greg
Gray, Herb
*Griffing, Dean
*Gurney, Jack
*Halter, G. Sydney
Ham, Tracy
*Hanson, Fritzie
Harper, Glenn
Harrington, Ed
Harris, Wayne
Harrison, Herm
Hatanaka, Bill
Hayes, Bob
*Hayman, Lew
Hedges, Brian
*Hedgewick, Mike
*Hees, George
Hegan, Larry
Hendrickson, Lefty
*Henick, Ed
Henley, Garney
*Hermann, Tiny
*Hershfeld, Leible
*Hevenor, George
Heydenfeldt, Bob
Highbaugh, Larry
Hill, Norman
Hill, Stewart
*Hilzinger, Karl
Hinds, Sterling
Hinton, Tom
Hitchcock, Rob

Hollimon, Joe
Holloway, Condredge
*Howell, Ron
Howes, Bob
Hufnagel, John
Hughes, George
Hunt, Ted
*Hutton, Bouse
Ilesic, Hank
Innes, Cam
Irwin, Al
*Isbister, Robert Jr.
*Isbister, Robert Sr.
Ivory, Clifford
*Ivy, Pop
Jackson, Glen
Jackson, Russ
*Jacobs, Jack
*James, Eddie
James, Gerry
Janzen, Henry
Jauch, Ray
Johnson, William
Jonas, Don
Jones, Tyrone
Joseph, Darren
Jurasin, Bobby
*Kabat, Greg
Kadatz, Dennis
Kapp, Joe
Karcz, Zeno
*Karpuk, Pete
Karrys, Steve
Keeling, Jerry
Kelly, Brian
Kelly, Con
Kelly, Ellison
Kennerd, Trevor
Kepley, Dan
Kerns, John
Kerrigan, Mike
Keys, Eagle
Kielty, Terry
Kimball, Norm
*King, Don
King, Mike
Kiniski, Gene
Kirzinger, Dave
Knight, Lee
Knight, Tuffy
Konihowski, John
Kosmos, Mark
Kraemer, Bob
Krol, Joe
Krouse, Bob
Kruger, Harry
Kulka, Glenn
Kwong, Normie
L'Heureux, Bill
Laird, Stu
Lalonde, Lally
Lancaster, Ron
Landy, Frank
Langford, Harry
Larose, Bob
Lashuk, Mike
*Lawson, Smirle
*Leach, Al

*Leadlay, Pep
*Lear, Les
Learn, Ed
Lehmann, Ken
Lemmerman, Bruce
Lenard, Al
Levantis, Steve
Levy, Marv
Lewis, Leo
Lewis, Loyd
*Lieberman, Moe
Liebrock, Chuck
Lindley, Earl
Liske, Peter
*Lister, Ralph
*Lockhart, Gene
Logan, Tip
*Loney, Don
Lumsden, Jesse
Lumsden, Neil
Lunsford, Earl
Luster, Marv
Luzzi, Don
*MacKenzie, Shanty
Mackie, Baz
Makowsky, Gene
Mandarich, Tony
Mann, Dave
Marshall, Blake
Marshall, Greg
Martin, Peter
Masotti, Paul
*Masters, Wally
Matthews, Don
Maughan, George
Mayes, Rueben
Mazurak, Steve
*McBrien, Harry
*McCaffrey, Jimmy
*McCance, Ches
*McCann, Dave
McConachie, John
*McConnell, Russ
McEachern, Ken
*McEwen, Bill
McFarland, Packy
McFarlane, Bob
McFarlane, Don
McGee, Doug
*McGill, Frank
McGowan, George
*McKay, Willie
McKee, Walt
McKeown, Bob
McLoughlin, Mark
McMann, Chuck
McManus, Danny
McMillan, Leigh
McNamara, Bob
McNeil, Jay
McNichol, Doug
McPhee, Dennis
McQuarters, Ed
McTague, Mike
Mikawos, Stan
Miles, Barron
*Miles, Rollie
Millington, Sean

Mills, James
*Milne, Howie
Mimbs, Robert
Mitchell, Doug
Mitchell, Doug
Moir, Darrell
Montford, Joe
*Montgomery, Ken
Moon, Warren
Moore, Travis
Morris, Chris
Morris, Frank
*Morris, Teddy
*Morrison, Arnie
Morrison, Bernie
Mosca, Angelo
Moses, Paul
Moss, Joe
*Munro, Johnny
Murphy, Cal
Murphy, James
Murphy, Ron
Murray, Eddie
*Murray, Ken
*Nagurski, Bronco
*Nairn, Bill
Narcisse, Donald
*Nelson, Roger
Nettles, Ray
Neumann, Peter
*Newton, Jack
Nielsen, Ken
O'Billovich, Bob
O'Connor, Zeke
*O'Quinn, Red
O'Shea, Micheal
*Obeck, Vic
Okeke, Uzooma
*Oneschuk, Steve
*Orban, Bill
Organ, Gerry
Osbaldiston, Paul
Pajaczkowski, Tony
Paopao, Joe
*Paproski, Steve
Parker, Jackie
Parker, James
Parkin, Lorne
*Parry, Jack
Passaglia, Lui
Pataky, Bill
Paterson, Gord
*Patrick, Lynn
Patrick, Steve
Patterson, Hal
Paul, Chuck
Payton, Elfrid
*Pearson, Mike
Pearson, Paul
Perowne, Ron
*Perrier, Ross
*Perry, Gordon
*Perry, Norm
Pfeifer, Alan
Phibbs, Bob
Philp, Jerry
Piaskoski, Jim
*Pickell, Bob

Pilon, Claude
Pitts, Allen
Pless, Willie
Ploen, Ken
Poirier, Joe
Pomfret, Jack
Poplawski, Joe
Popp, Jim
Pothier, Hector
Potter, Billy
Potter, Dale
*Potter, John
*Prather, Rollie
Prefontaine, Noel
*Preston, Ken
Pringle, Mike
Printers, Casey
Profit, Mel
Pugh, Bob
*Pulford, Harvey
*Pullen, Harry
Pullen, Tom
Pyzer, Doug
*Quigley, Ernest
*Quilty, Silver
Racine, Moe
Raimey, Dave
Ranek, Josh
Reaves, Willard
*Rebholz, Russ
Reed, George
*Reeve, Ted
Ribbins, Peter
Richman, Joey
Ridgway, Dave
Rigney, Frank
Rita, Adam
*Ritchie, Alvin
Ritchie, Dave
Roberts, Jay
Robillard, Gene
Robinson, Bill
Robinson, Larry
*Rodden, Mike
Rodgers, Johnny
*Rogin, Bill
Romano, Rocco
Rokosh, Greg
Rorvig, Ed
*Rote, Tobin
Rountree, Jim
*Rowe, Paul
Rowland, Gordie
Ruby, Martin
Ruckstuhl, Sandy
Ruoff, Bernie
*Russel, Jeff
*Ryan, Joe
Rypien, Mark
Sampson, Darryl
Sandusky, Jim
Sapunjis, Dave
Saunders, Alex
Sazio, Ralph
Schoenhals, Paul
Schreider, Gary
Schriewer, Tex
Schuette, Tom

*Scoccia, Sam
Scott, Tom
*Scott, Vince
Shannon, Carver
*Shatto, Dick
*Shaughnessy, Frank Jr.
*Shaughnessy, Shag
*Shaw, Dan
Shaw, Gerry
Shaw, Wayne
Sheahan, Pat
*Sheridan, Juan
Short, George
*Shouldice, Hap
*Simpson, Ben
Simpson, Bob
*Simpson, Jimmy
*Singleton, Harvey
Skinner, Chris
Skrien, Dave
Smale, Ted
*Smith, Alf
Smith, Darrell K.
Smith, Donn
Smith, Larry
*Smylie, Doug
*Smylie, Rod Jr.
Snipes, Angelo
Soles, Michael
*Sopinka, John
Sowieta, Rick
*Sprague, Dave
St. Germain, Val
*Starr, Harold
Stegall, Milt
Sternberg, Gerry
*Stevens, Warren
*Stevenson, Art
Stevenson, Bill
Stevenson, Douglas Roy
Stevenson, Victor
Stewart, Ron
Stillwagon, Jim
*Stirling, Bummer
*Stone, Rocky
Stoneburgh, Norm
Stoqua, Pat
Storey, Red
Strumm, Gil
Stukus, Annis
Stukus, Bill
Stukus, Frank
Stumon, Gregg
Sugarman, Ken
*Sullivan, Frank
Sunter, Ian
Sutherin, Don
Sutherland, Mike
Sweet, Don
Swift, Bob
Symons, Bill
Taylor, Bobby
*Taylor, Piffles
Theismann, Joe
Thelen, Dave
*Thomas, Fred
Thomas, Jim
Thomas, Willie

*Thornton, Bernie
Thornton, Dick
Tillman, Eric
*Timmis, Brian
*Tindall, Frank
Tinsley, Buddy
*Tommy, Andy Sr.
Toogood, Ted
*Toohy, Ralph
Tosh, Wayne
Totzke, Carl
Towns, Tom
*Trawick, Herb
Tripucka, Frank
Truant, Ray
*Tubman, Joe
Tucker, Whit
*Turner, Howie
*Turville, Frank
Upton, Eric
Urness, Ted
*Uteck, Larry
Vanderjagt, Mike
*Van Vliet, Maury
Vargo, Ken
Vaughn, Gerald
Vaughan, Kaye
Vaughn, Terry
Vavra, Greg
Vercheval, Pierre
Vespaziani, bob
*Vessels, Billy
Volpe, Jon
Volpe, Nick
*Voyles, Carl
*Wadsworth, Mike
*Wagner, Virgil
Walby, Chris
Walker, Bruce
*Walker, Gord
*Walker, Peahead
Walker, Skip
Walling, Brian
*Walsh, Tarp
Walters, Rick
*Warwick, Bert
Waszczuk, Henry
*Watson, Whipper Billy
Watts, J.C.
*Weatherall, Jim
Wedley, Jack
*Weinmeister, Arnie
Weir, Glen
*Welch, Huck
Welton, John
*Wendling, Wendy
West, Art
West, Dale
West, James
*White, Al
Whitehouse, Reg
Wilkinson, Tom
Williams, David
Williams, Gizmo
Williams, Jerry
Willsey, Ray
Wilmsmeyer, Klaus
Wilson, Al

*Wilson, Ben
*Wilson, Seymour
Wiltshire, Kelly
Winfield, Earl
Wirkowski, Nobby
Wood, Lionel
Woodward, Rod
*Wright, Joe Jr.
*Wright, Joe Sr.
Wruck, Larry
Wydareny, John
Wylie, Harvey
Yochum, Dan
Young, Jim
Young, Preston
Zaipec, Chuck
Zambiasi, Ben
Zmich, Rick
*Zock, Bill
Zuger, Joe

GOAL BALL
Alsop, Amy
Hope, Gord
Ljubisic, Lilo

GOLF
Alexander, Keith
Ames, Stephen
Anderson, Jerry
Bagley, June
Balding, Al
Barr, Dave
Bathgate, Andy
Belec, Jacques
Beatty, Lou
Bigras, Adrien
*Black, David
*Black, Ken
*Boes, Allan
Borthwick, Gayle
Bouchard, Rémi
Bourassa, Jocelyne
*Brockway, Dot
*Brydson, Gordie
Bunkowsky, Barbara
Burelle, Jacques
*Butterworth, Arnie
*Cameron, Jack
*Campbell, Dorothy
Carnegie, Herb
*Carrick, Donald
Charette, Agnes
Charette, Pierre
Charlebois, Vera
Coe-Jones, Dawn
Cole, Betty
*Combe, Harvey
Cooke, Graham
Cordukes, Don
Cornish, Geoffrey
*Costello, Ralph
Cowan, Gary
Crowell, Eddie
*Cumming, George
*Darling, Dora
Darling, Judy
*Dickeson, Jean

*Doyle, Jimmy
Driscoll, Mary Ellen
Eathorne, A.J.
*Edey, Marjorie
Ervasti, Ed
Estabrooks, John
Ezinicki, Bill
*Farley, Phil
Fedoruk, Sylvia
*Fletcher, Doug
*Fletcher, Pat
Folk, Rick
*Forbes, Bruce
Fowler, Frank
*Fraser, Alexa Stirling
Fulton, Ken
Gay, Mary
Getliffe, Ray
Girard, Ken
Goulet, Joanne
Graham, Gail
*Grant, Benny
*Gray, Robert Jr.
Guilbault, Michele
Halldorson, Dan
Hamilton, Gar
Harris, Mike
*Harvey, Florence
Harvey, Nancy
*Hedgewick, Mike
Helleur, Kay
*Hevenor, George
Hewson, Joanne
*Hilton, Geordie
*Hilzinger, Karl
Hnatiuk, Glen
Holzscheiter, Herb
Homenuik, Wilf
*Horne, Stan
Howard, Russ
*Huot, Jules
Jensen, Al
Johnston, John
Kane, Lorie
Kay, Jack Jr
*Keffer, Karl
Kern, Ben
*Kerr, Bill
*Knudson, George
*Kolar, Stan
Kuzmich, Heather
*Lamb, Willie
*Leddy, Jack
*Lederhouse, Phil
Leggat, Ian
Leonard, Stan
Lohnes, Rita
Lyle, Dulcie
*Lyon, George
*MacKenzie, Ada
*Martell, Henry
*Martin, Fritz
*Mawhinney, Bill
McElroy, Walter
*McLaughlin, Jack
McLean, Arnold
Meagher, Kathy
Middaugh, Wayne

Mikowetz, Rudy
*Moore, Gail Harvey
Mundinger, Karin
*Murray, Albert
Murray, Bruce
*Murray, Charlie
*Nash, Jack
Nelford, Jim
*Nezan, Andy
*Norman, Moe
*Obodiac, Stan
Olson, Greg
Ouellette, Red
Palmer, Marilyn
Panasik, Bob
*Pattemore, Claude
Paul, Chuck
Post, Sandra
Provost, Mary Haydon
Proulx, Rita
*Reid, Robert
Renaud, Don
*Reville, Ralph
Robinson, Al
*Robson, Lex
Rose, Bob
Ross, Chucker
Rousseau, Bobby
Roxburgh, Doug
Sams, Judy
*Sargent, Frank
*Scott, N orman
Sears, John
Seely, Glen
*Shaughnessy, Frank Jr.
Sherk, Cathy
Silverberg, Doug
*Skinner, Archie
*Somerville, Sandy
*Soper, Alice
Stephenson, Linda
*Stevenson, Forbis
Stewart, Ray
Stimpson, Bob
*Stimpson, Earl
*Stone, Reg
*Stone, Roy
*Streeter, Val
Streit, Marlene Stewart
*Sweeny, Violet
Tallon, Dale
*Taylor, Gordon
*Thompson, Stanley
*Thomson, Mabel
Todd, Margaret
Tombs, Tina
*Trites, Ev
*Tucker, Murray
Turnbull, Barbara
Vlooswyk, Lisa
Waite, Jim
Walters, Lisa
Weir, Mike
Weslock, Nick
West-Mahoney, Stacey
White, Nancy
*Wilson, Ruth
Wyatt, Jennifer

Wylie, Bob
Zokol, Richard

GYMNASTICS
Arsenault, Lise
Bajin, Boris
Burley, Kris
Chartrand, Philippe
Choquette, Jean
Daley, Gail
Delasalle, Philip
Diachun, Jennifer
Dion, Yves
Eagle, Don
Gagnier, Ed
Goermann, Elfriede
Goermann, Monica
Harris, Susan
*Hawco, Sherry
Hibbert, Curtis
Hogarth, Malcolm
Ikeda, Richard
Jeltkov, Alexander
Kelsall, Karen
Kihn, Richard
Kikuchi, David
Lacy, Irene
Larose, Gilbert
Long, Warren
Macdonald, Daniel
MacEachern, Shanyn
Mitruk, Steve
*Newman, Bernard
Nolet, Alan
*Nooney, John
Oryszcyn, Eugene
Purnell, Heather
Richardson, Kate
Rothwell, Nigel
Russell, Ernestine
Savage, Marilyn
Schlegel, Elfi
*Scott, Norman
Shewfelt, Kyle
Stone, Kylie
*Taylor, Bryce
Tousek, Yvonne
Umeh, Stella
Weiler, Willie
*Whittle, Doug
Wittmeier, Bonnie

HANDBALL
de Roussan, Hugues
Deckert, Merv
*Fry, Harry
*Pickell, Bob
St. Martin, Pierre

HARNESS RACING
Armitage, Rolly
Aubin, Marc
*Avery, Earle
*Baldwin, Ralph
Belanger, Bertrand
Brennan, Bernie
Brown, Doug
Burgess, Blair

Campbell, John
*Chapman, John
Christoforou, Chris
Clarke, Keith
Condren, Stephen
Cote, Benoit
Daigneault, Réjean
Doherty, James
*Feagan, Ron
*Filion, Henri
Filion, Hervé
Filion, Sylvain
Filion, Yves
Findley, John
Firlotte, Stewart
*Fleming, Vic
Fontaine, Lucien
Fritz, Bud
Galbraith, Clint
Gale, Bill
Gassien, Reg
Gendron, Gilles
Gilmour, Buddy
*Gorman, T.P.
Grant, Fred
Hamilton, Douglas
Hebert, Jacques
Hennessey, Walter
*Hodgins, Clint
Hudon, Joe Jr.
James, Jeff
Johnson, Danny
Kerr, Randy
Kerr, Terry
Kerwood, Tony
Kopas, Jack
Lachance, Michel
Lamy, Gaetan
Linton, Keith
MacDonell, Paul
*MacKinnon, Dan
Mayotte, Roger
McIntosh, Bob
*McKinley, Harold
*Mehlenbacher, Jack
Miller, James
Morand, Jim
*O'Brien, Joe
O'Donnell, William
Ouellette, Luc
Pinkney, David Sr.
Rankin, Callie
Remmen, Ray
Ritchie, Trevor
Robinson, Bill
*Rowe, Earl
Saftic, Mike
Seiling, Rod
Simard, Richard
Slack, Bill
Turcotte, Mel
Twaddle, Tim
Walker, Larry
Wall, Dave
Wallace, Ben
Wallis, Kevin
Waples, Keith
Waples, Randy

Waples, Ron
Wellwood, William
*White, Ben
Zeron, Rick

HIGHLAND GAMES
Harrington, Dave

HOCKEY
*Abbott, Jack
*Abel, Sid
Acton, Keith
*Adams, Jack
*Ahearn, Frank
Alfredsson, Daniel
Allen, Keith
Anderson, Glenn
Andreychuk, Dave
*Apps, Syl Sr.
Arbour, Al
Armstrong, George
Armstrong, Neil
Arnott, Jason
Ashley, John
*Aurie, Larry
Awrey, Don
Babych, Dave
Babych, Wayne
Backstrom, Ralph
*Bailey, Ace
*Bailey, Garnet "Ace"
*Ballard, Harold
Balon, Dave
Barber, Bill
*Barilko, Leo
Barrie, Rachel
*Barry, Martin
*Bastien, Baz
*Bath, Doc
Bathgate, Andy
*Bauer, Bobby
*Bauer, David
Baun, Bobby
Bawn, Bev
Beaupre, Don
Bedard, Bob
*Bedecki, Tom
Belfour, Ed
Beliveau, Jean
Bellows, Brian
Belsher, Don
*Benedict, Clint
*Bentley, Doug
*Bentley, Max
Berenson, Red
*Bergman, Gary
Berry, Bob
Bertuzzi, Todd
*Beveridge, Bill
*Bickell, J.P.
*Bionda, Jack
*Bishop, Jim
Blair, Wren
Blake, Rob
*Blake, Toe
Bodnar, Gus
Boivin, Leo
Boldirev, Ivan

*Boll, Buzz
Bonk, Radek
Bonney, Wayne
*Boon, Dickie
Boschman, Laurie
Bossy, Mike
Botterill, Cal
Botterill, Jason
Botterill, Jenniferr
Bouchard, Butch
Bouchard, Dan
*Boucher, Bill
*Boucher, Bob
*Boucher, Frank
*Boucher, Frank
*Boucher, George
Bourbonais, Roger
Bourne, Bob
Bourque, Ray
Bower, Johnny
*Bowie, Russell
*Bowman, Scotty
Bowman, Scotty
Bowness, Rick
*Boyle, Charles
Branch, David
Branchaud, Mike
*Brewer, Carl
Brewer, Eric
Brind'Amour, Rod
Brisson, Thérèse
*Broadbent, Punch
*Broda, Turk
Brodeur, Martin
Brophy, John
Brown, Bobby
*Browne, Cec
*Bruneteau, Mud
Bryden, Rod
*Brydson, Gordie
Buchberger, Kelly
*Buckna, Mike
Bucyk, John
Bullard, Mike
*Burch, Billy
Bure, Pavel
Bure, Valeri
Burke, Brian
Burke, Sean
Burns, Pat
*Bush, Eddie
Butterfield, Jack
*Butterworth, Arnie
*Calder, Frank
*Cameron, Harry
*Cameron, Jack
*Campbell, Angus
Campbell, Cassie
*Campbell, Clarence
Carbonneau, Guy
Carlyle, Randy
Carnegie, Herb
Cashman, Wayne
Cassels, Andrew
*Cattarinich, Joseph
*Chabot, Lorne
*Chamberlain, Murph
Champagne, Chantal

Charlebois, Bob
Charron, Guy
Cheevers, Gerry
Chelios, Chris
Cherry, Don
*Chevrefils, Real
Chiarelli, John
Chouinard, Guy
Chynoweth, Ed
Ciccarelli, Dino
*Clancy, King
*Clapper, Dit
Clark, Wendel
Clarke, Bobby
*Cleghorn, Odie
*Cleghorn, Sprague
Coffey, Paul
*Colville, Neil
Conacher, Brian
*Conacher, Charlie
*Conacher, Lionel Sr.
Conacher, Pete
*Conacher, Roy
*Connell, Alex
*Cook, Bill
*Cook, Bun
*Cook, Tommy
Copp, Bobby
Corson, Shayne
*Costello, Les
Costello, Murray
*Coulter, Art
Cournoyer, Yvan
Courtnall, Geoff
Courtnall, Russ
*Cowley, Bill
Craven, Murray
Crawford, Marc
*Crawford, Rusty
Crisp, Terrry
Cristofoli, Ed
*Cronie, Ab
Crosby, Sidney
*Crozier, Roger
Cunneyworth, Randy
*Cunningham, Les
Curry, Floyd
D'Amico, John
Daigle, Alexandre
Damphousse, Vincent
*Dandurand, Leo
Daneyko, Ken
*Darragh, Jack
Darwin, Howard
*Davidson, Bob
*Davidson, Scotty
*Dawson, Earl
*Day, Hap
Daze, Eric
*Deacon, Tom
Deadmarsh, Adam
Delvecchio, Alex
DeMarco, Ab
Demers, Jacques
*Denneny, Corb
*Denneny, Cy
Desjardins, Eric
Desjardins, Gerry

*Devine, Jack
*Dickie, Bill
Diduck, Judy
*Dilio, Frank
Dineen, Bill
Dineen, Gord
Dineen, Kevin
Dionne, Marcel
Doan, Shane
Doiron, Phillip
*Doraty, Ken
*Dowell, Hanson
Drake, Dallas
Draper, Kris
*Drillon, Gord
*Drinkwater, Graham
Drolet, Nancy
Dryden, Dave
Dryden, Ken
Dube, Danielle
Duchesne, Gaétan
*Dudley, George
Dudley, Rick
Duff, Dick
Dugan, Arnie
Duguay, Ron
*Dumart, Woody
*Duncanson, Albert
*Dunderdale, Tommy
*Dunlap, Frank
*Dunn, James
Dupere, Denis
Dupuis, Lori
*Durnan, Bill
*Dutton, Mervyn Red
*Dye, Babe
Eagleson, Alan
*Eddolls, Frank
Ellett, Dave
*Elliott, Chaucer
Ellis, Ron
*Elmer, Wally
*Emms, Hap
Esposito, Phil
Esposito, Tony
*Evon, Russ
Ezinicki, Bill
*Farmer, Ken
Faulkner, Alex
Federko, Bernie
Ferguson, John
Ferguson, Lorne
Ferguson, Skit
*Ferguson, Vince
Ferraro, Ray
Finn, Ron
*Finnigan, Frank
*Fisher, Frank
Fitzgerald, Tom
Flaman, Fern
Fletcher, Cliff
*Fletcher, Doug
*Flett, Bill
*Fleury, Lionel
Fleury, Theoren
Foligno, Mike
Fontinato, Lou
Foote, Adam

Forhan, Bob
*Foster, Red
*Fox, Fred
Fox, Jim
*Foyston, Frank
Francis, Bob
Francis, Emile
Francis, Ron
Fraser, Kerry
*Fredrickson, Frank
Fuhr, Grant
Gadsby, Bill
Gagne, Simon
Gainey, Bob
Galley, Garry
Gamble, Dick
*Gardiner, Charlie
*Gardiner, Herb
*Gardner, Cal
Gare, Danny
Gartner, Mike
Gaudet, Oscar
Gauthier, Gérard
Gauthier, Pierre
Gavillucci, Angelo
Gelinas, Martin
*Gelineau, Jack
Geoffrion, Bernie
*Gerard, Eddie
Getliffe, Ray
Giacomin, Ed
Gibson, Doug
*Gibson, Jack
Gilbert, Greg
Gilbert, Rod
Gill, Todd
Gillies, Clark
*Gilmour, Billy
Gilmour, Doug
Girard, Ken
*Glover, Fred
*Goldham, Bob
*Goldsworthy, Bill
*Goodfellow, Ebbie
Goold, Billy
Gordon, Jackie
Goring, Butch
*Gorman, T. P.
Goulet, Michel
Goyette, Danielle
Goyette, Phil
*Grant, Benny
Grant, Danny
Grant, Mike
*Gravelle, Red
Graves, Adam
Green, Gary
*Green, Shorty
Green, Ted
Gregg, Randy
Grenda, Ed
Greschner, Ron
Gretzky, Wayne
Griffin, Pat
*Griffis, Si
*Griffiths, Frank
Guerin, Bill
*Guzzo, Patrick

Hadfield, Vic
Haight, Jim
*Hainsworth, George
*Halder, Wally
Hall, Glenn
*Hall, Joe
*Halliday, Milton
*Hammond, Alvin
*Hanley, Bill
Harper, Terry
Hartley, Bob
Hartsburg, Craig
Harvey, Buster
*Harvey, Doug
Harvey, Scott Jr.
Hawerchuk, Dale
Hay, Bill
*Hay, Charles
*Hay, George
*Hayes, George
Heaney, Geraldine
Heatley, Dany
Hebenton, Andy
Hedberg, Anders
Hefford, Jayna
Henderson, Paul
*Henry, Camille
*Hern, Riley
*Hewitson, Bobby
*Hewitt, Foster
*Hewitt, W.A.
*Hextall, Bryan Sr.
Hextall, Ron
Hibberd, Ted
Higgins, Tim
Hildebrand, Ike
Hillman, Larry
Hindmarch, Robert
Hitchcock, Ken
Hodge, Ken
*Hollet, Flash
Holmes, Derek
*Holmes, Hap
*Hooper, Tom
Horner, Red
Hood, Bruce
*Horton, Tim
Horvath, Bronco
Hossa, Marian
Houle, Réjean
Housley, Phil
Howe, Gordie
*Howe, Syd
Howell, Harry
*Howell, Ron
Hrudey, Kelly
Huck, Fran
Huddy, Charlie
Huff, Bruce
Hughes, Karen
Hull, Bobby
Hull, Brett
Hull, Dennis
*Hume, Fred
Hunter, Dale
*Hutton, Bouse
*Hyland, Harry
Iginla, Jarome

*Imlach, Punch
Ingarfield, Earl
*Ion, Mickey
*Irvin, Dick Sr.
*Ivan, Tommy
*Jackson, Busher
James, Angela
James, Gerry
Jarvis, Doug
*Johnson, Ching
Johnson, Don
*Johnson, Moose
Johnson, Tom
Johnston, Ed
Johnston, Marshall
*Joliat, Aurel
Joseph, Curtis
Jovanoski, Ed
*Juckes, Gordon
Kane, Frank
Kariya, Paul
Keane, Mike
*Keating, Jack
*Keats, Duke
*Keeling, Butch
Keenan, Mike
Kehoe, Rick
Kellar, Becky
Kelly, Pete
Kelly, Red
Kennedy, Sheldon
Kennedy, Ted
Keon, Dave
Kerr, Tim
Kilrea, Brian
*Kilrea, Hec
*Kilrea, Wally
King, Dave
Klassen, Cindy
Knox, Swede
Koharski, Don
Koivu, Saku
Kromm, Bobby
*Kubinec, John
Kurri, Jari
Kurtenbach, Orland
L'Heureux, Bill
*Labine, Leo
Lach, Elmer
Lafleur, Guy
Lalime, Patrick
Lalonde, Lally
*Lalonde, Newsy
*Lamb, Joe
Lammens, Hank
Laperriére, Andr
Laperriére, Jacques
Lapointe, Guy
Laprade, Edgar
Larmer, Steve
*Larocque, Bunny
Larouche, Pierre
*Laviolette, Jack
Leach, Reg
*Leader, Al
*LeBel, Bob
Leblanc, Eugene
Lecavalier, Vincent

LeClair, John
Lee, Peter
Leeman, Gary
Leetch, Brian
*Lehman, Hughie
Lemaire, Jacques
Lemelin, Reggie
Lemieux, Claude
Lemieux, Mario
Lenardon, Norman
Leschyshyn, Curtis
Lespi, Kusti
*LeSueur, Percy
*Leswick, Tony
Lever, Don
Lewis, Bryan
Lewis, Dave
*Lewis, Herbie
Linden, Trevor
*Lindquist, Vic
Lindros, Eric
Lindsay, Ted
Linseman, Ken
*Liscombe, Carl
Little, Ken
Liut, Mike
Litzenberger, Eddie
*Locking, Norm
Loiselle, Claude
Long, Bill
Lonsberry, Ross
Lord, Herve
Lowe, Kevin
Lowry, Dave
Luce, Don
Ludwig, Craig
*Lumley, Harry
Lund, Pentti
Luongo, Roberto
*MacDonald, Kilby
MacInnis, Al
*MacKay, Mickey
MacKell, Fleming
MacKenzie, Barry
MacLean, John
MacLeish, Rick
MacMillan, Billy
MacNeil, Al
MacTavish, Craig
*Magnuson, Keith
Maher, Peter
Mahovlich, Frank
Mahovlich, Pete
*Malone, Joe
Maloney, Don
Maloney, Phil
Maltby, Kirk
Maniago, Cesare
*Mann, Bob
*Mantha, Sylvio
Mara, George
*Marker, Gus
Marleau, Patrick
Marsh, Brad
Marshall, Don
*Marshall, Jack
Martin, Jacques
Martin, Pit

Martin, Rick
Martin, Seth
Maruk, Dennis
*Masterton, Bill
*Mathers, Frank
Matiowski, Buck
Maurice, Paul
*Maxwell, Steamer
*Mazur, Eddie
*McCaffrey, Jimmy
McComb, Bill
McConachie, John
*McConnell, Russ
McCourt, Dan
McCrimmon, Brad
*McCulloch, Jack
McDonald, Dennis
McDonald, Lanny
*McEwen, Bill
McFarlane, Brian
*McGee, Frank
*McGimsie, Billy
McGuire, Pierre
*McIntyre, Jack
McKechnie, Walt
McKegney, Tony
McKenzie, Johnny
*McKenzie, Ken
McKillop, Bob
McKinnon, Frank
McLean, Kirk
McLelland, Ivan
McLeod, Jackie
McNab, Peter
*McNamara, George
*McNeil, Gerry
*McReavy, Pat
McSorey, Marty
Meeker, Howie
Mellanby, Scott
Mellway, Dean
Meloche, Gilles
Merrick, Wayne
*Merrill, Horace
Messier, Mark
*Metz, Nick
*Mickoski, Nick
Middleton, Rick
Migay, Rudy
Mikita, Stan
*Milford, Jake
Millen, Greg
Miller, Shannon
*Milne, Howie
Mitton, Randy
Mogilny, Alexander
Mohns, Doug
*Molson, Hartland
*Montgomery, Ken
*Monson, Walter
Moog, Andy
*Moog, Don
Moore, Dickie
*Moran, Paddy
*Morenz, Howie
Morris, Greg
Morrow, Brenden
*Mosienko, Bill

Muckler, John
Muller, Kirk
Murphy, Larry
Murphy, Ron
Murray, Bob
Murray, Bryan
Murray, Glen
*Murray Ken
*Murray, Pere
Murray, Terry
Nadin, Robert
Nanne, Lou
Nansen, Derek
Nash, Rick
Naslund, Markus
*Nayler, Thomas
Neale, Harry
Neely, Cam
*Neilson, Roger
Nesterenko, Eric
Nicholls, Bernie
Nicholson, Bob
Niedermayer, Rob
Niedermayer, Scott
Nieuwendyk, Joe
*Nighbor, Frank
Nilsson, Kent
*Noble, Reg
Nolan, Owen
Nolan, Ted
Nystrom, Karen
*O'Brien, J. Ambrose
*O'Connor, Buddy
O'Malley, Terry
O'Neill, Brian
O'Ree, Willie
Oates, Adam
Obey, Arthur
*Obodiac, Stan
Ogrodnick, John
*Oliver, Harry
Oliver, Murray
Olmstead, Bert
*Orban, Bill
Orr, Bobby
Osborne, Mark
Otto, Joel
Ouellette, Caroline
Ouellette, Red
Pachal, Vern
Paddock, John
*Page, Fred
Page, Pierre
Pare, Mark
Parent, Bernie
Park, Brad
*Patrick, Frank
Patrick, James
*Patrick, Lester
*Patrick, Lynn
*Patrick, Muzz
Patrick, Steve Jr.
Paul, Chuck
Pavelich, Matt
Peacosh, Walter
Pearn, Perry
Pearsall, Shane
*Pearson, Mike

Peca, Mike
Pelyk, Mike
Perreault, Gil
Philip, Bob
Phillips, Chris
*Phillips, Tommy
*Pickard, Allan
Pilote, Pierre
*Pilous, Rudy
Pinder, Gerry
Pinder, Herb
*Pitre, Didier
*Plante, Jacques
*Plaxton, Hugh
Pocklington, Peter
*Poile, Bud
Pollock, Sam
Pomfret, Jack
*Porter, Bob
*Porter, John
Potter, Billy
Potvin, Denis
Potvin, Felix
Potvin, Jean
Poulin, Dave
Pounder, Cheryl
Power, Dale
*Pratt, Babe
Prentice, Dean
Price, Noel
*Primeau, Joe
Primeau, Keith
Pronger, Chris
Pronovost, Jean
Pronovost, Marcel
Propp, Brian
Provost, Claude
Prystai, Metro
Psutka, Harry
Pugh, Bob
Pulford, Bob
*Pulford, Harvey
*Quackenbush, Bill
Quenneville, Joel
Quinn, Pat
Quintal, Stephane
Raleigh, Don
Ramage, Rob
Ramsay, Craig
*Rankin, Frank
Ratelle, Jean
*Rayner, Chuck
Reardon, Ken
*Reay, Billy
Recchi, Mark
Redden, Wade
Reddon, Lesley
Redmond, Mickey
Regan, Larry
Regehr, Robyn
*Reid, Bobby
Reid, Lefty
Renaud, Ab
Renwick, Gordon
Resch, Chico
Rheaume, Manon
Ricci, Mike
Richard, Henri

*Richard, Jacques
*Richard, Maurice
Richards, Brad
*Richardson, George
Richardson, Luke
Richer, Stephane
Richman, Ruby
Risebrough, Doug
*Ritchie, Alvin
Roberts, Gary
*Roberts, Gordon
Roberts, Jim
Robinson, Al
*Robinson, Claude
Robinson, Larry
Robitaille, Luc
*Rodden, Mike
Ronning, Cliff
*Ross, Art
Rousseau, Bobby
Roy, Patrick
Rucchin, Steve
Ruel, Claude
Ruff, Lindy
*Russel, Blair
*Russell, Ernest
Rutherford, Jim
*Ruttan, Jack
Sakic, Joe
Salming, Borje
Sanderson, Derek
Sanderson, Geoff
*Sargent, Frank
Saskamoose, Fred
Sather, Glen
Savageau, Daniele
Savard, Denis
Savard, Serge
*Sawchuk, Terry
Scapinello, Ray
Scherer, Sue
*Schmalz, Tubby
Schmidt, Milt
Schock, Ron
Schoenfeld, Jim
*Schriner, Sweeney
*Schroeter, Reg
Schuler, Laura
*Scodellaro, Duke
*Scott, Norman
Secord, Al
*Seibert, Earl
*Seibert, Oliver
Seiling, Rod
Selanne, Teemu
*Selke, Frank Sr.
Selwood, Brad
Shack, Eddie
Shanahan, Brendan
*Shaske, Ed Jr.
*Shaughnessy, Frank Jr.
Sheppard, Gregg
Sheppard, Ray
*Shero, Fred
Shewchuk, Tammy Lee
Shibicky, Alex
*Shields. Al
*Shore, Eddie

Shutt, Steve
Siciliano, Dave
*Siebert, Babe
Simmer, Charlie
*Simpson, Bullet Joe
Simpson, Craig
Sinden, Harry
Sittler, Darryl
Skinner, Jim
Skinner, Larry Jr.
Skinner, Larry Sr.
Sloan, Tod
Small, Sami Jo
*Smeaton, Cooper
*Smith, Alfred E.
Smith, Billy
Smith, Bobby
*Smith, Brian
Smith, Clint
Smith, Dallas
*Smith, Frank
Smith, Gary
*Smith, Hooley
Smith, Murray
Smith, Neil
*Smith, Robert
*Smith, Sid
*Smith, Tommy
Smyl, Stan
*Smylie, Doug
*Smylie, Rod Sr.
Smyth, Ryan
*Smythe, Conn
*Somerville, Sandy
Sonmor, Glen
Sostorics, Colleen
St. Louis, France
St. Louis, Martin
St. Marseilles, Frank
St. Martin, Martin
St. Pierre, Kim
Stanfield, Fred
Stanley, Allen
*Stanley, Barney
Stanowski, Wally
Stapleton, Pat
*Starr, Harold
Stasiuk, Vic
Stastny, Peter
*Steele, David
Steen, Thomas
Stevens, Scott
*Stewart, Black Jack
*Stewart, Nels
Stewart, Ron
Stickle, Leon
Storey, Red
Stothart, Paul
Stoughton, Blaine
*Stuart, Bruce
*Stuart, Hod
Stukus, Annis
*Sullivan, Frank
*Sullivan, Joe
Sullivan, Red
Sundin, Mats
Sunohara, Vicky
Suter, Gary

*Sutherland, Hugh
*Sutherland, James
Sutter, Brent
Sutter, Brian
Sutter, Darryl
Sutter, Duane
Sutter, Ron
Sweeney, Don
Talbot, Jean Guy
Tallon, Dale
Taylor, Bobby
*Taylor, Cyclone
Taylor, Dave
*Templeton, Bert
Tessier, Orv
Theodore, Jose
Thibault, Jocelyn
Thomas, Steve
Thomas, Wayne
*Thompson, Tiny
Thornton, Joe
Tippett, Dave
Tkachuk, Keith
Tkaczuk, Walt
Tocchet, Rick
Todd, Dick
Tonelli, John
Torrey, Bill
*Trihey, Harry
Trottier, Bryan
*Tudin, Conny
Tugnutt, Ron
Turgeon, Pierre
Turnbull, Ian
*Turner, Lloyd
Udvari, Frank
Ullman, Norm
Unger, Garry
Vachon, Rogie
Vadnais, Carol
Vaive, Rick
Van Hellemond, Andy
Verbeek, Pat
Vernon, Mike
*Vezina, Georges
Vitarelli, Dootch
*Voss, Carl
*Waghorne, Fred
*Walker, Jack
*Walsh, Marty
Walter, Ryan
Walton, Mike
Warwick, Billy
*Warwick, Grant
Warwick, Richard
*Watson, Harry
*Watson, Moose
*Watson, Sandy
Weight, Doug
*Weiland, Cooney
Wells, Jay
Wesley, Glen
Westfall, Ed
*Westwick, Harry
*Whitcroft, Frederick
White, Bill
Whitney, Ray
Wickenheiser, Hayley

Wicks, Ron
Williams, Tiger
Wilson, Doug Jr.
*Wilson, Doug Sr.
*Wilson, Lefty
Wilson, Murray
*Wilson, Phat
Wilson, Ron
Wilson, Stacy
*Wiseman, Eddie
Woit, Benny
Worsley, Gump
*Worters, Roy
Yashin, Alexei
York, Jason
Yzerman, Steve
Zamuner, Rob
Zeman, Joe
Zenk, Marina

HORSE RACING
Atkinson, Ted
Attfield, Roger
*Bell, Max
Cheevers, Gerry
*Dandurand, Leo
Elliott, Stewart
Fell, Jeffrey
Ferguson, John
Frostad, Mark
*Gomez, Avelino
*Gorman, T.P.
Hawley, Sandy
Hendrie, George Jr.
*Hendrie, George Sr.
*Hewitt, W.A.
*Huntley, Gordon
Kabel, Todd
Landry, Robert
*Laurin, Lucien
Laurin, Roger
*Levesque, Jean-Louis
*Longden, Johnny
*MacBeth, Donald
*McLaughlin, Sam
Minshall, Barbara
Platts, Robin
*Randall, Sam
Rathgeb, Chuck
*Rogers, Chris
Saunders, William
*Seagram, Joseph
*Smythe, Conn
*Speers, Jim
Stronach, Frank
*Taylor, E.P.
Turcotte, Ron
*Wall, Nick
Walls, Mickey
*Woodhouse, Hedley
*Woolf, George

HORSESHOES
Bigras, Orv
Cantin, Diane
Curtis, Crystal
*Hohl, Elmer
Hohl, Steve

Janssens, Sandy
Kissick, Myrna
LeClerc, Andre
Markle, Jean
Markle, Larry
McLaughlin, Dean
Moisan, Sylvianne
Stevenson, Ross

JIU JITSU
Forrester, Ron
Lariviere, Chelsea
MacLean, Allan
Sylvain, Georges
Viele, Vincent

JUDO
Barry, Michael
Beaton, Ewan
Berger, Mark
Blaney, Fred
Bolger, Pat
Buckingham, Michelle
Cyr, Alain
Doherty, Kevin
Erdman, Wayne
Farnsworth, Terry
Farrow, Brad
Filteau, Nancy
Gill, Nicolas
Greaves, Sandra
Greenway, Tom
Jani, Louis
Kawasaki, Mitch
Lappage, Ron
Lepage, Carolyne
Mascoe, Pat
Morgan, Colin
Morgan, Keith
Morneau, Marie-Josee
Nakamura, Hiroshi
Oye, Moe
Pilon, Claude
Roberge, Patrick
Rogers, Doug
Sheffield, Cathy
Sylvain, Georges
Takahashi, Allyn
Takahashi, June
Takahashi, Masao
Takahashi, Philip
Takahashi, Ray
Takahashi, Tina
Tan, Taro
Weldon, Craig

KARATE
Anderson, Steve
Brown, Selina
Foster, Norma
Laroda, John
Orr, Lindsay
Sabourin, Jamie
Sylvain, Georges

KICK-BOXING
McMahon, John
Nadon, Chantal

Thériault, Jean-Yves
Sabourin, Jamie
Sylvain, Georges

LACROSSE
Aird, Stu
Alexander, Kevin
Allan, Robert
Batley, Jamie
*Beers, William George
Benson, Lorne
*Bionda, Jack
*Bishop, Jim
*Box, Charlie
*Boyle, Charles
*Buddo, Don
Campbell, David
*Cavallin, John
Cavallin, Roy
*Conacher, Lionel Sr.
*Connell, Alex
*Connell, Charlie
*Coombes, Cy
*Crookall, Dot
Dean, Geordie
*Dickinson, William
*Douglas, Jim
Dugan, Arnie
*Ferguson, Arnold
Ferguson, John
Ferguson, Larry
Ferguson, Merv
*Fitzgerald, Billy
*Fletcher, Doug
*Foster, Red
Fulton, Jack
Gait, Gary
Gait, Paul
Gaudaur, Jake Jr.
Gisiger, Michelle
*Goldham, Bob
*Gorman, T.P.
Hall, Chris
Halladay, Del
*Hammond, Gord
Hieltjes, Ben
Hildebrand, Ike
Huff, Bruce
*Hume, Fred
Hunt, Ted
*Hutton, Bouse
*Ion, Mickey
Kells, Morley
Klassen, Cindy
*Lally, Joe
Lalonde, Lally
*Lalonde, Newsy
Large, Bert
*Laviolette, Jack
Marechek, Bill
Marechek, Tom
Miller, Doug Jr.
*Miller, Doug Sr.
Oates, Adam
*Oneschuk, Steve
Parnell, Paul
*Pitre, Didier
Pomfret, Jack

*Porter, Bob
*Powless, Gaylord
*Powless, Ross
*Reeve, Ted
*Sargent, Frank
Sawicki, Ted
*Silverheels, Jay
*Smith, Alf
*Spring, Doughy
*Stewart, Gordon
*Stockton, Don
Tavares, John
*Thompson, George
Thorburn, Cliff
*Turnbull, Alex
Vaughan, Eileen
Vitarelli, Dootch
*White, Dalt
*Wilson, Lefty
*Wootton, Moon

LAWN BOWLING
Au, On-Kow
Boettger, Bill
Clayton, Harold
Creaney, Doreen
Elliff, Jim
Forrest, Robin
*Hart, Nelson
*Kempster, Ray
Martin, Flora Greenwood
Ranger, Melissa
Roney, Jean
Roney, Keith
Stock, Ed
Whitley, Gerry

LUGE
Albrecht, Grant
Bowie, Mary Jane
Crutchfield, Linda
Keyes, Carole
Lauscher, Regan
Poscente, Vincent
Pothier, Eric
Seitz, Tyler

MODERN PENTATHLON
Chornobrywy, Lynn
Keyte, Lawrence
Shong, Laurie

MOTORSPORT
Bentham, Lee
Boyce, Walter
Brack, Bill
Carpentier, Patrick
*Carter, Mo
Duff, Mike
Duhamel, Miguel
Duhamel, Yvon
Empringham, David
*Emerson, Eddie
Fellows, Ron
Goodyear, Scott
Headland, Martin
Heimrath, Ludwig Sr.
Jones, John

Jones, Tom
Kelly, Jim
Kroll, Horst
*Moore, Greg
*Pickell, Bob
Rathgeb, Chuck
Ross, Earl
*Ryan, Peter
Smith, Sheldon
Stewart, Brian
Tagliani, Alex
Tracy, Paul
*Villeneuve, Gilles
Villeneuve, Jacques
Villeneuve, Jacques
Wietzes, Eppie
Williams, John
*Wilson, Harold
Wolf, Walter

MOUNTAINEERING
Amatt, John
Gmoser, Hans
*March, Bill
McDonald, Les
O'Connor, Zeke
Rathgeb, Chuck
Rodney, David
Skreslet, Laurie
Weber, Richard
Wood, Sharon

OFFICIATING
Adams, Robert
Armstrong, Neil
Ashley, John
Beaton, Bob
Bonney, Wayne
*Cameron, Jack
*Campbell, Clarence
Champagne, Chantal
D'Amico, John
Denoncourt, Sonia
Diffin, Charlie
Dojack, Paul
*Earley, Ted
*Elliott, Chaucer
Embuldeniya, Herb
*Emslie, Bob
*Evon, Russ
*Farmer, Jim
*Ferguson, Arnold
Findlay, Dick
Finn, Ron
*Fletcher, Doug
Foxcroft, Ron
Fraser, Kerry
Frost, Barclay
Gauthier, Gérard
*Graham, Barbara
*Gravelle, Red
*Gurney, Jack
*Hammond, Gord
*Hayes, George
*Hedgewick, Mike
*Hewitson, Bobby
*Hill, Harvey
Hood, Bruce

Howard, Gerry
*Ion, Mickey
*Isbister, Bob Sr.
King, Don
Kitts, Charlie
Knox, Swede
Koharski, Don
*Kubinec, John
Lewis, Bryan
*Lindquist, Vic
*Loaring, John
Logan, Tip
Lowery, Ron
*Luftspring, Sammy
Macken, Jim
*Malcolm, Andrew
*Mantha, Sylvio
*Maxwell, Steamer
*McBrien, Harry
McCourt, Dan
*McKay, Willie
McKean, Jim
*Mehlenbacher, Jack
Michienzi, Pete
Miles, Wiff
*Milne, Howie
Mitton, Randy
*Morris, Jim
Morrison, Scotty
Morrow, Suzanne
Nadin, Robert
*Nairn, Bill
Nansen, Derek
Pare, Mark
Paul, Chuck
Pavelich, Matt
*Perrier, Ross
*Porter, Bob
Provost, Mary Haydon
*Quigley, Ernest
*Quilty, Silver
Rae, Al
*Rodden, Mike
*Rogin, Bill
Runge, Paul
*Ruttan, Jack
*Sauve, Gordon
Scapinello, Ray
Shannon, Carver
*Shouldice, Hap
*Simpson, Ben
*Smeaton, Cooper
Smith, Gwen
*Spencer, Jim
*Spray, Robert
*Stack, Frank
Stickle, Leon
Storey, Red
Strumm, Gil
Sylvain, Jules
Tinline, Dorothy
*Trihey, Harry
Turnbull, Ray
Udvari, Frank
Van Hellemond, Andy
Vaughan, Eileen
Vergara, Hector
*Voss, Carl

*Waghorne, Fred
Waite, Jim
*White, Al
Wicks, Ron
Wilkes, Jimmy
Wilson, Alex
*Wilson, Seymour
Young, Joe
Zenk, Marina

ORIENTEERING
Budge, Susan
Demonte, Denise
de St. Croix, Ted
Hunter, Gord
Kaill, Bob
Lowery, Ron
McIntosh, Pam
Robert, Magli

PARACHUTING
Cox, Kathy
Grant, Duncan
Henry, Daryl
Kangas, Katherine
Marchand, Claude
Sutton, Stephen
Taylor, Graham
Vaughan, Eileen
Vincent, Mark
Winning, Craig
*Wykeham-Martin, Simon
Zahar, Mike

POWER LIFTING
Girard, Hugo
Macvicar, Don

RACQUETBALL
Capozzi, Herb
Ceresia, Mike
Grand'Maitre, Josée
Greenfeld, Sherman
Johnstone, Lori
McKay, Heather
McNamara, Bob
Mikowetz, Rudy
*Pickell, Bob
Powell, Lori-Jane
Roy, Simon
Shanks, Vicki
Stupp, Heather
Theismann, Joe
Van Hees, Christie
Young, Frank

RHYTHMIC GYMNASTICS
Bryant, Deborah
Fung, Lori
Fuzesi, Mary
Livingston, Emilie
Martens, Camille
Stauder, Zlatica
Stirton, Erike-Leigh

RINGETTE
Anderson, Tamara
Brisson, Thérèse

Brown, Cara
Brown, Lisa
Coggles, Susan
Diduck, Judy
*Jacks, Sam
Marek, Deb
Reynolds, Shelley

RODEO
Bews, Tom
Bruce, Winston
Butterfield, Joe
Coleman, Mel
Daines, Duane
Dunham, Steve
Eirikson, Tom
*Girletz, Wilf
Gladstone, Jim
Hay, Denny
Hay, Rod
*Kesler, Reg
*Knight, Pete
Lucas, Joe
*McLean, Kenny
Phillips, Jerry
Renger, Debbie
Robinson, Larry
Shapka, Guy
Warren, Rod

ROLLER SKATING
*Bain, Dan
Domik, Bernard
*Lewis, Stanley
*McCulloch, Jack

ROWING
Arnold, Don
Baerg, Cameron
Barber, Darren
Barnes, Kirsten
Battersby, Robert
*Belyea, Arthur
Biesenthal, Laryssa
*Bonnycastle, Charles
Boyes, Dave
Brain, Marilyn
Brown, Clayton
*Brown, George
Cameron, Bev
Cameron, Trice
Catherall, Robin
Clarke, Christine
Clarke, Heather
*Cline, Paddy
Craig-Eaton, Betty
Crosby, Andy
Davidson, Chris
Delahanty, Megan
Doey, Jennifer
Dubois, Theo
Evans, Mark
Evans, Michael
Ford, Bruce
Forgeron, Mike
*Fry, Harry
Gaudaur, Jake Jr.
*Gaudaur, Jake Sr.

Gotfredsen, Leif
Grace, Maureen
Graham, Phil
Green, Peter
*Griffis, Sy
*Guest, Jack
Hallett, Todd
Hamilton, Doug
*Hanlan, Ned
Hassett, Gavin
Hattin, Heather
Heddle, Kathleen
Hegan, Larry
*Helliwell, David
Herschmiller, Tom
Hungerford, George
Jackson, Roger
Jespersen, Julie
*Johnston, Bob
Jonker, Karel
*Kaysmith, Henry
King, Peter
Korn, Alison
Kovits, Herman
Kueber, Philip
Laumann, Silken
Lay, Jeff
Lichty, Kathy
*Logan, Willie
Loomer, Lorne
Mason, Janice
Maunder, Maria
McBean, Marnie
McDermid, Heather
McDonald, Doug
Mervyn, Glen
Miller, Colleen
Mills, Bob
Monckton, Philip
Monroe, Jessica
Morrow, Al
Newman, Pat
*Norris, Edgar
O'Grady, Diane
*O'Neill, John
Parfitt, Adam
Peaker, Brian
*Pearce, Bobby
Porter, Derek
Pratt, Ned
*Pulford, Harvey
*Read, Frank
*Richardson, Bert
*Riley, Con
*Riley, Culver
Robinson, Emma
*Rogers, Shotty
Rokosh, Greg
*Ross, P.D.
*Ryder, Gus
Saunders, Sandy
Schneider, Angela
*Scholes, Louis
*Senkler, Harry
Smith, Glen
Smith, Tricia
*Spencer, Victor
Spowage, Cheryl

*Stacey, Nelles
Stevenson, Greg
Storm, Tim
*Sweeny, Bimbo
Thompson, Lesley
Tregunno, Jane
Tsang, Tosha
van der Kamp, Anna
Van Ruyven, Andy
Wetzel, Jake
Wiebe, Wendy
Williams, Barney
Wilson, Alex
Wilson, Robert
*Wright, Joseph Jr.
*Wright, Joseph Sr.
Young, Dolores
Young, Frank

RUGBY
*Bauld, Donald
*Bedecki, Tom
*Browne, Cec
Burnham, Barrie
Charron, Al
*Conacher, Lionel Sr.
Elliott, Geoff
Evans, Eddie
Gray, Steve
Harper, George
Howe, Bruce
Hunt, Ted
Jackart, Dan
*King, Donald
*Lister, Ralph
Luke, Michael
Moore, Buzz
*Patrick, Lynn
Peden, Doug
Pomfret, Jack
Rees, Gareth
*Spray, Robert
*Sweeny, Bimbo
Taylor, Graham
*Van Vliet, Maury
Willsie, David
*Wilson, Ben

SAILING
Abbott, Bill Jr.
Abbott, Joanne
Bastet, Evert
Bjorn, Tyler
Bruce, Ian
Clarke, Richard
Cochrane, Nigel
Cross, Jay
Davies, Rod
Davis, Penny
Dexter, Glen
*Duggan, Herrick
Eckard, Jeff
Emery, Vic
Fogh, Hans
Green, Donald
Hall, Peter
Henderson, Paul
Innes, Marjorie

Janse, Roy
Jespersen, Eric
Josenhans, Andreas
Kerr, John
Kidd, James
Kirby, Bruce
Konantz, Gordon
Lammens, Hank
Leibel, Allan
Lemieux, Lawrence
MacDonald, Ross
MacMillan, Sandy
Matthews, Tam
*McGill, Frank
McLaughlin, Frank
*McLaughlin, Sam
McLaughlin, Terry
Miller, Dave
Moberg-Parker, Tine
Moss-Lovshin, Shona
Neilson, Terry
Roy, Andy
*Sherwood, Liv
Stock, Ed
Tupper, Stephen
Tytler, Donald
*Walters, Angus
Watters, Lynn
*Windeyer, Walter
Wolfs, Mike
Woods, Larry

SHOOTING
Adlhoch, Hans
Alexander, Jeremy
Altmann, Fred
Arnold, Sherman
Ashcroft, Christina
Ashcroft, Michael
*Bain, Dan
Baldwin, Bill
Barwise, Bob
*Beckett, Norman
Best, Bob
Bissonnette, Serge
*Boa, Andrew
*Boa, Gil
*Boa, James Sr.
Boa, Sandy
*Boa, Stuart
Boa, Vicki
Boll, Rod
Bowes, Sharon
Bowman, Gary
Brown, Colin
Bullock, Bruce
Bullock, Jim
*Burke, Des
Caldwell, Earl
Carty, Hank
Carver, Julie
Chase, George
*Clifford, William
*Colville, Nelson
Cozzarin, Sharon
Cunningham, Keith
D'Amour, Léo
Dahlstrom, Clint

Dahlstrom, Patricia
Decsi, Laszlo
Dion, Michel
Dombroski, Ben
Eagles, Kim
*Ewing, Walter
Ferguson, Bruce
Ferguson, Ken
Fitch, Ed
Frazer, Gerry
Frost, Stan
Gabriel, Brian
*Genereux, George
*George, Ed
George, Ron
Graham, Sally
Grundy, Art
Guinn, Tom
*Gunter, Andy
Gutnick, Paul
*Hampton, Richard
Hare, Dorothy
*Hare, William
Harper, George
Hartl, Gus
Hartman, Barney
*Hayhurst, Tom
Henderson, Gil
*Houlden, Jim
Howkins, Mark
Huot, Jean-Pierre
Igorov, Metodi
Jans, Edward
Jasiak, Andrew
Jmaeff, Peter
Johnson, Cari Lynne
Kelly, Steven
Kierstead, Bob
Kwasnycia, Don
Langlois, Jocelyn
Laporte, Paul
*Lea, Mary
Leary, George
Lorion, Guy
*Mann, Avard
*Mann, Bob
Marin, Violaine
Marion, Alain
Mayer, Alfons
McCormick, Frank
McMahon, Gary
Meyer, Cynthia
Miller, Clayton
Miller, Linda
Mitchell, Kurt
Molnar, Bill
Murray, Scott
Nadeau, Daniel
Nattrass, Sue
Opsal, Frank
*Ouellette, Gerry
Papasideris, Peter
Parks, Arnold
Paton, Jim
Peden, Sandy
Pitcairn, Bob
Primrose, John
Rochon, John

Rumbold, Dave
Sanderlin, Don
Sanderson, Gus
Schulze, Rudy
Senecal, Jean-Francois
Sewell, Don
Sewell, Doran
*Shaske, Ed Jr.
Shaw, Paul
*Shea, Stu
Smith, Helen
Sobrian, Jules
Sorensen, Arne
Sorensen, Wayne
Spratley, Jim
Strachan, Bill
Surette, Ron
Terry, Jackie
*Thibodeau, Nick
Thom, Linda
Thompson, Jim
Thurlow, Jim
Timmerman, Jim
Tomsett, Arthur
Vamplew, Des
Vamplew, Edith
Vamplew, Pat
Warner, Edson
*Westling, Gunnar
Westling, Ken
Whatley, Chris
*White, Al
*White, Donald
*Wilkins, Bruce
Wills, Stan
*Willsie, Harry
Wong Shui, Mike
Young, Walter

SHUFFLEBOARD
Mattson, Dale

SKATEBOARD
Regnier, Claude

SKIING
*Anderson, Verne
*Antoft, Kell
Asselin, Marie-Claude
Athans, Gary
Athans, George Jr.
Athans, Greg
*Bagguley, Howard
*Bott, Punch
Boyd, Rob
Brassard, Jean-Luc
Brenner, Veronica
Brooker, Todd
Champagne, Ed
Chapman, Currie
*Clark, Bud
Clifford, Betsy
*Clifford, Harvey
*Clifford, John
Cochand, Louis
*Condon, Eddie
Cousineau, Alain
Crawford, Judy

Crutchfield, Linda
Culver, Diane
Dionne, Deidra
Downs, Darcy
Dubois, Luc
Eaves, John
*Firth, Doug
Firth, Sharon
Firth, Shirley
Fontaine, Nicolas
Fraser, Anna
Fripp, John
Fripp, Kim
Fripp, Shaun
Gilmour, Bob
Gmoser, Hans
Goodman, Russell
Graham, Laurie
Grandi, Thomas
Greene, Nancy
Grinnell, Rae
*Groff, Doug
Gudwer, Doug
Haight, Didi
Harvey, Pierre
Heggtveit, Anne
*Heggtveit, Halvor
Heil, Jennifer
Henderson, Scott
Herschmiller, Tom
Hewson, Joanne
*Hilzinger, Karl
Holloway, Sue
Hunter, Jim
Hunter, Malcolm
Irwin, Bert
Irwin, Dave
Jacobs, Dave
*Jacobsen, George
Johnson, Don
Johnston, Jerry
Keenan, Bill
Kent, Chris
Kerckhoff, Claudia
Kirby, Peter
Konantz, Gordon
Kreiner, Kathy
Kreiner, Laurie
Lalonde, Bernie
Langlois, Lloyd
Laroche, Alain
Laroche, Philippe
Laroche, Yves
Lee-Gartner, Kerrin
Lyon, Don
McCleery, Alan
McConkey, Jim
McDonald, Les
McMahon, David
Meloche, Lise
Midgley, Arnold
Miller, Esther
Monod, Peter
Mullen, Gary
*Murray, Dave
Nemesvary, Mike
Nesbitt, Keith
Olivier, Caroline

Pace, Kate
*Pangman, Arthur
Pelchat, Ann-Marie
Percy, Karen
Pilcher, Al
Podborski, Steve
Podivinsky, Edi
Poscente, Vincent
Raine, Al
*Ramage, Pat
*Read, Dee
Read, Ken
Rees, David
Ritchie, John
Rochon, Stephane
*Ryan, Peter
Savijarvi, Liisa
Schmidt-Foster, Angela
Scott, Beckie
Servold, Clarence
Servold, Irvin
Simboli, Chris
*Smith-Johannsen, Herman
Sorensen, Gerry
Stemmle, Brian
Stemmle, Karen
*Taylor, John
*Thompson, William
*Tindale, Bill
*Tommy, Andy Jr.
*Tommy, Art
*Tommy, Fred
Townsend, Stephanie
Turgeon, Melanie
Weber, Richard
Webster, Peter
Wheeler, Lucile
Whyte, Shauna
Wurtele, Rhoda
Wurtele, Rhona

SKI JUMPING
*Bagguley, Howard
Bulau, Horst
Charland, Jacques
Collins, Steve
Gravelle, Gérard
Graves, Richard
Hunt, Ted
*Morris, Fred
Servold, Irvin
Wilson, Peter

SNOWBOARDING
Anderson, Jasey Jay
Andrew, Trevor
Fawcett, Mark
Glazier, Lori
Rebagliati, Ross
Ricker, Maelle

SNOWMOBILING
Duhamel, Yvon
*Villeneuve, Gilles
Villeneuve, Jacques

SNOWSHOES
*Ball, Jim
*Buddo, Don

Grenda, Ed
*Mathieu, Wilfrid
*Montabone, Monty
Young, Walter

SOARING
*Audette, Julien

SOCCER
Albrecht, J.I.
Anderson, Dave
*Anderson, George
*Bearpark, Bob
Belanger, Josee
Brewster, Ken
Bunbury, Alex
*Caithness, Charlie
Capozzi, Herb
Chursky, Tony
Corazzin, Carlo
*Cowan, Jack
Crossan, Errol
Dasovic, Nick
David, Tracy
*Deacon, Tom
Denoncourt, Sonia
deVos, Jason
Dolan, Paul
Donaghey, Sam
*Draffin, Ernie
Etchegary, Gus
*Fitzpatrick, Allan
Forrest, Craig
*Forsyth, David
Fraser, Iain
Fryatt, Dave
Gray, Gerry
Grenda, Ed
*Hayes, John
*Hershfield, Leible
Hooper, Charmaine
Hooper, Lyndon
Howard, Dick
*Hume, Fred
Jamani, Aysha
*Kennaway, Joe
Kiss, Kristina
Kouzmanis, Tom
*Kulai, Dan
Lang, Kara
Lenarduzzi, Bob
Lenarduzzi, Sam
Letteri, Tony
Limniatis, John
Maranda, Veronique
*Mayers, Wallace
McKee, Walt
McMahon, John
Miller, Colin
Mitchell, Dale
*Mobilio, Domenic
*Morris, Jim
Neil, Andrea
Newsham, David
Nicholl, Jimmy
Peschisolido, Paul
Pomfret, Jack
*Reid, Bobby

Robertson, Sandy
Ruys, Henk
Samuel, Randy
*Sanford, Aubrey
Sangster-Daley, Rose Mary
*Simpson, Bill
Sinclair, Christine
Skinner, Larry Sr.
*Spencer, Jim
*Spring, Harry
*Steele, David
*Stewart, Gordon
*Stronge, Stan
Thorburn, Cliff
Timko, Brittany
*Turner, Dave
Watson, Mark
Whitton, John
Wilson, Bruce
Yallop, Frank

SOFTBALL
*Baker, Mary
*Bath, Doc
Bay, Lauren
Baytor, Terry
*Bend, Olive
Bitz, Ed
Bodashefsky, Larry
Bottoms, Lynn
Branchaud, Mike
Burrows, Bob
Casselman, Bruce
Challis, Terry
Chiarelli, John
Clayton, Juanita
*Coben, Muriel
Coggles, Susan
*Cooke, Myrtle
Cooperband, Mary
*Corbett, Ed
Cowdrey, Jim
Dealy, Wendy
Desabrais, Paul
*Deschamps, Claude
Domik, Bob
*Durnan, Bill
Fedoruk, Sylvia
Fennell, Neil
*Fletcher, Doug
*Foster, Red
*Fox, Fred
French, Joan
Fuller, Rose
*Gibbons, Pops
Gibson, Doug
Gillett, George
Gosset, John
*Guzzo, Patrick
Hames, Dick
Hearn, Eugene
*Hershfield, Leible
Holness, Bob
Howard, Gerry
Huband, Deb
Huff, Bruce
Jones, Chris
Jones, Jim

Kalailieff, Bette Jean
Kelland, Kelly
Kellar, Becky
Kelly, Henry
Kern, Stan
Kernaghan, Marty
Lance, Jackie
Landers, Pete
Lands, Ben
*Leach, Al
Leblanc, Vicky
Mabey, Hap
Martin, Flora Greenwood
*Matoba, Tom
Maurice, Pauline
*McKee, Joyce
McKinnon, Frank
Morrison, Lee
Neill, Cliff
Noga, Arleene
*Obodiac, Stan
*Panasis, Rita
Parris-Washington, Christine
Paton, Brian
Patterson, Joe
Pearce, Dave
Pezer, Vera
Pickard, Leroy
Pomfret, Jack
*Porter, Bob
Price, Steve
*Pullen, Harry
Pyzer, Doug
Rau, Richard
Reid, Lefty
Richman, Ruby
Rowan, Sheila
Ruiter, Garth
Ryan, Doreen
Scherer, Sue
*Simons, Pop
Sippel, Lori
Skinner, Grant
Skinner, Larry Jr.
Skinner, Larry Sr.
Smith, Adam
*Smith, Ethel
Smith, Mark
Snelgrove, Karen
Sonnenberg, Debbie
*Strike, Hilda
Strumm, Gil
*Thomas, Fred
Tilley, Ray
Tobin, Lee
*Toohy, Ralph
Underwood, Brad
Underwood, Reg
Ventura, Dawn
Vergara, Hector
Wallin, Terry
*Watson, Whipper Billy
*Wilson, Lefty
Zack, Darren

SPEED SKATING
Appleby, Elizabeth
Auch, Susan

Audley, Gordon
*Baptie, Norval
*Barber, Jack
Baril, Benoit
Barron, Andy
Bédard, Eric
*Belyea, Arthur
Blackburn, Frédéric
Boshuck, Wally
Bouchard, Sylvain
Boucher, Gaétan
*Brooks, Lela
Burka, Sylvia
Campbell, Derrick
Cassan, Gerry
Cassidy, John
Charest, Isabelle
*Cody, Harry
Cutrone, Angela
Daigle, Sylvie
Daignault, Michel
Dietiker, Judy
Donatelli, Eden
Drolet, François
Fitzgerald, Marie
*Flack, Herb
Gagné, Maurice
Gagnon, Marc
Gagnon, Sylvain
Goplen, Henrietta
*Gorman, Charles
Grenier, Louis
Groves, Kristina
Hearn, Eugene
Hennigar, Carl
Hodges, Bob
Hughes, Clara
*Hurd, Alex
Hurdis, John
Ireland, Mike
Ireland, Sean
*Johnston, Percy
Kelly, Con
Kelly, Patrick
Klassen, Cindy
Lambert, Nathalie
Larocque, Dominique
Le May-Doan, Catriona
Liepa, Ingrid
*Logan, Freddie
*Logan, Willie
Ludtke, Frank
MacKay, Craig
Marshall, Neal
*Mathieu, Wilfrid
*McCannell, Don
McCannell, Donna
McCannell, Doreen
*McCulloch, Jack
Olin, Ralf
Olson, Betty
Overend, Alan
Overend, Bill
Overend, Clara
Overend, Howard
Overend, Tom
Overland, Kevin
Panting, Bill

Perreault, Annie
Priestner, Cathy
Richards, Eileen
*Robson, Fred
*Roe, Lot
*Roughton, William
Ryan, Doreen
Sands, Johnny
Sevigny, Chantal
*Smyth, Harry
*Stack, Frank
Thibault, Jacques
Turcotte, Mathieu
Underhill, Pat
Vogt, Kathy
*Williamson, Peter
*Wilson, Jean
Wotherspoon, Jeremy

SPEED BOAT RACING
*Ballard, Harold
*Foster, Red
*Hayward, Bob
*Hutchison, Jim
*Lombardo, Guy
Rathgeb, Chuck
Thompson, Jim
*Wilson, Harold

SPORTS MEDICINE
Botterill, Cal
Faloon, Joanna
*Firth, Doug
Fowler, Peter
Grace, Maureen
Johnson, Don
Lalonde. Bernie
*Orban, Bill
Pashby, Tom
Pipe, Andrew
Walker, Louise

SQUASH
Adair, Colin
Cooper, Barbara Ann
Crombie, Jamie
Glover, Penny
Henderson, Paul
Ives, Charles
Jans, Melanie
Khan, Sharif
Macken, Brendan
McKay, Heather
Power, Jonathon
*Pulford, Harvey
Robertson, Sandy
Rosen, David
Ryding, Graham
Souchereau, Kelsey
Styner, Dale
Styner, Lori
Wagner, Lauren
Wagner, Victor
Waite, Gary
Wallace, Heather

SWIMMING
Abbott, Marni

Abdo, Reema
Amey, Jessica
Amundrud, Gail
Anderson, Gary
Arusoo, Toomas
*Aubin, Jack
Baker, Joann
Bald, Kathy
Barber, Sara
Barr, Irene
Bastarache, Clarence
Baumann, Alex
Bell, Marilyn
*Bieber, Ethel
Boadway, Bob
Borsholt, Lisa
*Bourne, Munroe
Brafield, Leslie
Braknis, Robert
Buckboro, Dean
Campbell, Jennifer
Campbell, Shirley
Campo, Danielle
Chenard, Line
Clarke, Stephen
Cleveland, Jon
Cliff, Leslie
Cloutier, Guylaine
Cole, Andrea
Corsiglia, Robin
Cote, Kirby
Coughlan, Angela
Daigneault, Julie
*Davis, Victor
Deglau, Jessica
*Dewar, Phyllis
Dixon, Stephanie
Dockerill, Sylvia
Draxinger, Kevin
Dryden, Nikki
Duggan, Keltie
*Duthie, George
Edwards, Betty
Emery, John
Evans, Clay
*Evon, Russ
Eynon, Bob
Faulkner, John
*Firby, Howard
Flemons, Wade
Flood, Lisa
Ford, Albert
Fowler, Peter
Fowlie, Jim
Garapick, Nancy
Gate, George
Gery, Marcel
Gibson, Cheryl
Giguere, Nathalie
Goss, Sandy
Gotell, Chelsey
Grace, Maureen
Grant, Martha
*Griffin, Audrey
*Griffiths, Joe
Grout, Cameron
Gurr, Donna-Marie
Hainey, Tom

Haley, Andrew
Hartzell, Irene
*Haslam, Phyllis
*Hauch, Paul
Henning, Cam
Herschmiller, Tom
Higson, Allison
*Hodgson, George
Hogg, Wendy
Huband, Deb
Hunt, Helen
Huot, Benoit
Hutton, Ralph
Jardin, Anne
Johnson, Dave
Johnson, Marian
Johnson, Tom
Kasting, Robert
Keith, Vicki
Kemp, Nigel
Kennedy, Bill
Kennedy, Louise
Ker, Michael
Kerr, Cay
Kerr, Jane
King, Vivian
Klimpel, Carol
Lay, Marion
*Leach, Al
*Leuszler, Winnie Roach
Limpert, Marianne
*Loaring, John
*Lockhart, Gene
*Lumsdon, Cliff
Lumsdon, Kim
MacDonald, Byron
MacDonald, Gary
MacPherson, Michelle
Mahony, Bill
Malar, Joanne
Martin, Doug
Mason, Susan
*Mayers, Wallace
McArton, Cheryl
McIsaac, Tim
*McKinnon, Archie
McNamee, Kathleen
Meraw, Ann
Merklinger, Anne
Michel, Yvette
Miles, Kay
Mindorff, Philip
Mintenko, Mike
Myden, Curtis
Nicholas, Cindy
*Norman, Percy
Nugent, Andrea
Ottenbrite, Anne
Oxenbury, Noel
Parenti, Eddie
Pickell, Stephen
Polinario, Anne
Pomfret, Jack
Ponting, Tom
Pound, Richard
Priestley, Gladys
*Puddy, Bill
Quirk, Wendy

Reimer, Eugene
Renaud, Chris
Richardson, Kathy
Richardson, Stephanie
Ritchie, Andy
Robertson, Bruce
Rogers, Bruce
Rogers, Danny
Ross, Marie Claire
*Ryder, Gus
Sawchuk, Bill
Say, Rick
Schootman, Teddy
Shakespeare, Shannon
Shockey-Milanese, Barbara
*Sidwell, Pop
Slater, Bill
Sloan, Susan
Smith, Becky
Smith, George
Smith, Graham
Smith, Gwen
Smith, Sandra
Smith, Shannon
Smith, Sue
Snelling, Deryk
Stewart, Mary
Stratten, Gaye
Stulac, George
Sweetnam, Nancy
Szmidt, Peter
Tanner, Elaine
Tapp, Jay
Tapp, Larry
Tewksbury, Mark
Thierry, Nick
Thomas, Ted
Thompson, Dan
Tihanyi, Jeno
Tildesley, Donovan
*Vernot, George
Versfeld, Mark
Walker, Elisabeth
Ward, Peter
*Watson, Whipper Billy
Welbourn, Graham
West, Mike
Wheaton, Robert
Whittall, Beth
Wu, Walter
Wurtele, Rhona
Young, George

**SYNCHRONIZED
SWIMMING**
*Adamson, Gail
Alexander, Lisa
Barber, Wendy
Bedard, Nancy
Bremner, Janice
Calkins, Michelle
Cameron, Michelle
Carrier, Lyna
Carrier, Lyne
Carver-Dias, Claire
Clark, Karen
*Cody, Della
*Eon, Suzanne

Fonteyne, Karen
*Forbes, Pansy
Fortier, Sylvie
Frechette, Sylvie
Glen, Kathy
Hambrook, Sharon
Harris, Susan
Hartzell, Irene
Hermanson, Myrna
Hould-Marchand, Valerie
Kryczka, Kelly
Kuleza, Kasia
Larsen, Christine
Letourneau, Fanny
Muir, Debbie
Oxenbury, Noel
Read, Cari
*Seller, Peggy
Simard, Martine
Thivierge, Jojo
Vanderburg, Helen
Vilagos, Penny
Vilagos, Vicky
Waldo, Carolyn
Woodley, Erin

TABLE TENNIS
Barton, Julie
*Bauld, Donald
Bédard, Hélène
Cada, Petra
Caetano, Errol
Chiu, Barbara
Domonkos, Mariann
Geng, Lijuan
Heap, Alan
Hsu, Gloria
Huang, Johnny
Johnson, Julia
Kosanovic, Zoran
*Marinko, Max
Nesukaitis, Violetta
Ng, Gideon Joe
Normandin, Pierre
Pintea, Horatio

TAEKWONDO
Bosshart, Dominique
Lee, Tae Eun
Norman, Clint

TENNIS
*Babbitt, Ethel
*Babbitt, John
Barclay, Ann
*Bardsley, Jim
Barlow, Wendy
Bassett, Carling
*Bauld, Donald
Bedard, Bob
Belkin, Mike
Blackwood, Marjorie
Blais, Thérèse
Bonneau, Bonny
Bonneau, Stéphane
Boyce, Jim
Brabenec, Hana
Brabenec, Josef Jr.

Brabenec, Josef Sr.
*Brockway, Dot
*Brown, Louise
Butler, Barry
Butt, Susan
Carpenter, Keith
Chang, Albert
*Condon, Eddie
Connell, Grant
*Crocker, Willard
Dancevic, Frank
Dewis, Karen
Drake, Maureen
Ebbels, Bill
Fairs, Jack
Fauquier, Harry
Fontana, Don
Genois, Réjean
Godbout, François
*Halder, Wally
Harris, Lesley
Hetherington, Jill
Howson, Barry
Hy, Patricia
Januskova, Eva
Jeyaseelan, Sonja
Kelesi, Helen
Kolbovic, Renata
Lareau, Sebastien
Larose, Simon
*Leeming, Marjorie
Lovett, Claire
Macken, Brendan
Macken, Jim
Macken, Patricia
Main, Lorne
*Martell, Henry
Matthews, John
*Mayers, Wallace
McDadi, Hatem
*McDiarmid, Don
Mellway, Dean
Michibata, Glenn
Mikowetz, Rudy
Nejedly, Jana
Nestor, Daniel
Niemeyer, Frederic
Nunns, Brenda
*Nunns, Gilbert
O'Hara, Jane
Ouellette, Bert
*Percival, Lloyd
Phinney, Gertrude
Power, Dale
Pridham, Chris
*Purdy, Margaret
Rainville, Marcel
Richman, Joey
Robillard, Gene
Rochon, Henri
*Rosenfeld, Bobbie
Rubes, Jan
Rusedski, Greg
*Schwengers, Bernie
Simpson, Rene
Sinclair, Ken
Strong, Lawrence
Sznajder, Andrew

Tindle, Janice
Urban, Faye
*Walton, Dorothy
*Watt, Laird
*Watt, R.N.
Webb, Vanessa
*White, Al
Whittaker, Sharon
*Wilson, Ruth
Wostenholme, Martin
*Wright, Jack

TOUCH FOOTBALL
Belsher, Don
Huband, Deb
Robinson, Bill

TRACK & FIELD
*Acoose, Paul
Adams, Jeff
Adams, Robert
*Andersen, Roxy
Anderson, Kate
Andrusyshyn, Zenon
*Apps, Syl Sr.
Armstrong, Brian
Babits, Laslo
Baert, Jean-Paul
Bailey, Angela
Bailey, Dave
Bailey, Donovan
Bailey, Marjorie
Baker, Alison
*Ball, James
Bannon, Paul
*Barnes, Rolph
Bastarache, Clarence
*Bath, Doc
Bauck, Dean
Beaton, Bob
Beaudoin, Andre
Beers, John
*Bell, Jane
*Benevoy, Charles
Bergeron, Dean
Berrett, Tim
Binns, Hilda
Blackman, Craig
Boateng, Kwabu
Bogue, Glenn
Boileau, Art
Boldt, Arnold
Bond-Mills, Catherine
Boswell, Mark
Boucher, Alain
Bourdeau, Yvan
Bourgeois, Joel
Bowen, Stacy
Boychuk, Andy
Boyd, Barry
*Boyle, Charles
Bradley-Kameli, Sue
Branch, Cecilia
*Bricker, Cal
Brill, Debbie
Brothers, Tanya
Brown, Hal
Brown, Larry

*Brown, Wally
*Buddo, Don
*Burns, Leo
 Butler, Kathy
*Caffery, Jack
*Cameron, Fred
 Campbell, Debbie
 Campbell, Rachelle
*Campbell, R.D.
 Casanova, Willie
*Catherwood, Ethel
 Chalmers, Angela
 Chambers, Carlton
 Chambul, Borys
 Charette, Richard
 Cheater, Millie
*Christie, Alan
 Clark, Paul
 Clark, Ranza
 Clarke, Karen
 Clement, Diane
 Clement, Doug
*Coaffee, Cyril
*Cohen, Laurie
 Colistro, Peter
 Connor, Earle
*Cook, Myrtle
 Cooperband, Mary
 Corazza, John
*Coté , Gérard
*Courtwright, Jim
*Coy, Eric
 Craig, John
 Craig, Paul
 Crooks, Charmaine
 Crothers, Bill
 Crowley, Maureen
*Crummer, Keith
 Daniels, Danny
*Davies, Jack
 Deacon, Bruce
*Desmarteau, Etienne
 Devonish, Nicole
 Dickson, Gordon
*Docherty, Alexander
 Dolegiewicz, Bishop
 Donahue, Jake
 Dowds, Maureen
 Drayton, Jerome
*Duffy, James
*Duhaime, Greg
 Dunkerly, Jason
 Duprey, Donalda
 Eckel, Shirley
 Edeh, Rosey
*Edwards, Phil
 Egerton, Stan
 Elliott, Geoff
 Elmer, Ken
 Enright, Jim
 Esmie, Robert
 Estwick, Leslie
*Eville, Vern
*Fabre, Edouard
 Farrell, Neil
 Fedoruk, Sylvia
 Fee, Earl
 Felicien, Perdita

 Fell, Graeme
*Ferguson, Rich
 Ferguson, Tracey
 Finlay, Robert
 Fitzgerald, Mel
 Floreal, Edrick
 Fonseca, Peter
*Foot, Fred
 Forrester, Nicole
*Fournier, Lionel
*Fox, Fred
*Fox, Terry
 Franks, Lisa
 Fraser, Bud
 Fraser, Hugh
*Freeman, John
*Fritz, Bill
 Frost, Barclay
 Gagne, France
 Gairdner, Bill
 Gallant, Georgie
 Gareau, Jacqueline
*Garvie, Clarence
 Gavillucci, Angelo
 Gendron, Francine
 Gerein, Clayton
 Gilbert, Glenroy
*Gillis, Duncan
 Good, Norah
*Goulding, George
 Gowan, Geoff
 Grace, Maureen
 Graham, John
*Gray, George
 Gray, Rob
 Greenidge, Ricardo
*Griffiths, Joe
 Haist, Jane
 Halvorsen, John
*Hammond, Alvin
 Harding, Dick
 Harper, George
 Harrison-Tucker, Ardin
 Haslam, Eleanor
 Hawkins, John
 Haydenluck, Greg
 Heikkila, Bill
 Hendry, Joan
 Herman. Wally
*Hershfield, Leible
*Higgins, Robina
 Highbaugh, Larry
 Hinds, Sterling
*Histed, Jack
 Hoffman, Abby
 Hood, Graham
 Hoogewerf, Simon
 Howard, Tom
 Howie, Al
 Hudson, John
*Humber, Bruce
 Hume, Ian
 Hutchins, Jack
 Issajenko, Angella Taylor
 Jackes, Arthur
*Jerome, Harry
 Jerome, Valerie
 Jobin, Marcel

 Johnson, Ben
 Johnson, Don
 Joy, Greg
 Keating, Murray
*Keeper, Joe
 Kern, Laurie
*Kerr, Bobby
 Kidd, Bruce
 Killingbeck, Molly
*King, Donald
 Knight, Courtney
*Knox, Walter
*Komonen, Dave
 Konihowski, Diane
 Konihowski, John
 Krause, Willi
 Kroeker, Tim
 Kyle, Doug
 Lachance, Jason
 Landry, Denis
 Lane, Sharon
 Lariviere, Chelsea
 Latulippe, Phil
 LeBlanc, Guillaume
 Lee, Scott
 Lefrancois, Charles
 Lenover, Max
 Lewington, Nancy
*Lewis, Ray
*Loaring, John
 Lockett, Donna
*Longboat, Tom
 Lord, Herv
 Lord, Tom
 Loverock, Patty
 MacDonald, Jackie
 MacGowan, Margaret
 Mach, Gerard
 Mackie-Morelli, Anne
 Maddin, Janet
*Mah, Sy
 Maher, Peter
 Mahorn, Atlee
 Makolosky, Randy
*Malcolm, Andrew
 Manning, Peter
 Marquette, Ulla
 Martin, Carol
 Martin, Robert
 Mather, Eddie
 Matthias, Brendan
*Maughan, George
*Maxwell, Brian
*Maynes, Billy
 McBlain, Liz
 McCaffrey, Janice
 McCloy, Paul
 McCredie, Nancy
 McCubbins, Chris
 McEwen, Don
 McFarlane, Bob
 McFarlane, Brent
 McFarlane, Don
 McGee, Doug
*McGill, Frank
 McGillivray, David
 McInnis, Andy
*McKay, Willie

*McKinnon, Archie
 McKinnon, Frank
 McKoy, Mark
 McLaren, Grant
 McLaren, Robert
 McLeod, Barbara
*McNaughton, Duncan
*McNie, Murray
*Meagher, Aileen
 Meagher, Robyn
 Meldrum, Jenny
 Michel, Yvette
*Miles, Johnny
*Miller, Leigh
*Miller, Zan
 Minor, Ron
 Money, Ken
*Montabone, Monty
 Moore, Bob
 Moreau, Lucette
 Morris, Sid
 Mullins, Joe
 Neilson, Scott
 Newhouse, Ian
 Nicks, Frank
 Oakley, Alex
*O'Connor, Larry
 Ogden, Steve
 Ogilvie, Peter
 Olafsson, Shirley
 Olesen, Marc
*Oliver, Roy
 Olsen, Phil
 Olson, Betty
*Orton, George
 Ottey, Milt
 Page, Andrea
 Palmason, Diane
 Palmer, Lillian
 Parker, Ken
 Parnell, Bill
*Parry, Jack
*Patrick, Muzz
 Pauletto, Bruno
 Payne, Marita
 Peden, Doug
 Peel, Ann
 Pells, Leah
*Percival, Lloyd
 Petitclerc, Chantal
 Phibbs, Bob
 Phillips-Maya, Wendy
 Phinney, Gertrude
*Pickard, Vic
 Pidskalny, Diane
 Pilon, Jacques
 Piotrowski, Irene
 Pirnie, Bruce
 Poce, Paul
 Poitras, Tina
 Porter, Ken
 Provost, Mary Haydon
*Pugh, Lionel
 Pullen, Tom
 Puntous, Patricia
 Puntous, Sylviane
 Purnell, Ashley
 Pyzer, Doug

Quessy, Marc
Radmore, Joey
Raike, Stan
*Rankine, Scotty
Rau, Richard
Reed, Georgette
Reid, Patrick
Reimer, Eugene
Reiser, Glenda
Richardson, Jillian
Richman, Joey
*Robinson, Bobby
Rock, Richard
*Roe, Lot
*Rogin, Bill
Roost, Ain
*Rosenfeld, Bobbie
Ross-Giffen, Jill
Roy, Diane
Ruegger, Silvia
Ryan, Doreen
Sanderson, Lyle
Saunders, Bryan
Sax, Joe
Schnurr, Paula
Scorrar, Doug
Scott, Debbie
*Seller, Peggy
Seltzer, Sheila
Shannon, Carver
Sharpe, Tony
Shepherd, George
*Sherring, William
Short, George
*Shrubb, Alf
*Sigfusson, Svein
Simpson, Bruce
*Singleton, Harvey
Slavik, Jerry
*Smith, Ethel
Smith, Kelly
Smith, Michael
*Smylie, Rod Sr.
Smyth, Jack
Snyder, Brad
Sovran, Gino
Sparling, Jean
Spir, Peter
Spowage, Cheryl
*Sprague, Dave
*Springstead, Velma
St. Pierre, Martin
Steen, Dave
Steen, Dave
*Stevenson, Art
Stewart, Gordon
*Storey, Irene
Stovel, Peter
Stride, Bryan
*Strike, Hilda
Sullivan, Kevin
Surin, Bruny
Tashlin, Lesley
*Taylor, Betty
*Thomson, Earl
Tobacco, Terry
*Town, Tom
Townsend, (McRoberts), Brit

*Trelle, Herman
*Tunks, Jason
Turner, John
*Van Vliet, Maury
Vigars, Bob
Viger, Andre
*Vince, Anthony
*Vine, Bill
Vlooswyk, Lisa
*Wala, George
Walker, Bruce
Walker, Louise
Wall, Gwen
Wallingford, Ron
Walsh, Brenda
*Warren, Harry
Washburn, Leroy
Watt, David
Wedmann, Wilf
*Wendling, Wendy
Wenzel, Joan
Werthner, Penny
*White, Al
White, Betty
White, Julie
Whyte, Shauna
Williams, Desai
Williams, Freddie
Williams, Lynn
Williams, Paul
*Williams, Percy
*Wilson, Doug Sr.
Wilson, Murray
Wolff, Doreen
Worrall, Jim
*Wright, Harold
*Wright, Joe Sr.
Wright, Thelma
Yakubowich, Joyce
Yetman, Wayne
York, Patrick
Young, Joe
Young, Walter

TRAMPOLINE
Cockburn, Karen
McManus, Heather
Nemesvary, Mike
Ross, Dave
Turgeon, Mathieu
Vlooswyk, Lisa

TRIATHLON
Bates, Mark
Bermel, Lynne
Bowden, Lori
Donnelly, Sharon
Fuhr, Heather
Hellard, Rick
MacMartin, Andrew
McDonald, Les
McNicoll, Bruce
Montgomery, Carol
Reid, Peter
Ritchie, Jo-Anne
Whitfield, Simon

VOLLEYBALL

Anderson, Randy
Baydock, Donna
Bigras, Sylvie
Bishop, Carole
Bridle, Wezer
Buchberger, Kerri Ann
Burchuk, Mike
Child, John
Danyluk, Terry
Davis, Pat
Drakich, Ed
Dunn, Marc
Eisler, Laurie
Gratton, Paul
Heese, Mark
Hitchcock, Dean
Hitchcock, Monica
Hunt, Helen
Kelly, Janis
Leinemann, Conrad
Mellway, Dean
Nord, Dennis
Pischke, Garth
Reimer, Eugene
Russo, Erminia
Sawula, Lorne
Tennant, Mark
Wigston, Fran

WATER POLO
Gifford, Heather
*Gilbey, Janice
Gross, George Jr.
Gunell, Roy
Hart, David
Horn-Miller, Waneek
McCleery, Alan
*McGill, Frank
Meyer, Bill
Pugliese, Rick
*Richardson, John
*Seller, Peggy

WATER SKIING
Athans, Gary
Athans, George Jr.
Athans, Greg
*Clifford, John
Crutchfield, Linda
*Duthie, Carol Ann
Gregoire, Hélène
Hazzard, Elmer
Ito, Don
Llewellyn, Jaret
McClintock, Joel
McClintock, Judy
Messner, Joe
Messner, Pat
Nehohin, Dave
Reid, Bruce
Reid, Ian
Ward, Clint

WEIGHTLIFTING
*Allan, Maurice
Bilodeau, Alain
Bratty, Gary
Burke, Larry

Cardinal, Marc
*Cyr, Louis
*Delamarre, Victor
Demers, Jacques
Flynn, Clarke
Gilchrist, Jack
Girard, Hugo
Hadlow, Terry
*Hepburn, Doug
*Hill, Harvey
Legace, Francois
Lipari, Michel
Macvicar, Don
McCarthy, Scott
Mercier, Michel
Morris, Price
Nesbitt, Keith
Parente, Mario
Pietracupa, Michel
Prior, Russ
Reimer, Eugene
Robertson, Doug
Robitaille, Daniel
Roy, Aldo
Roy, Kevin
Salter, Allen
Sandor, Akos
Smith, Rosaire
Smith, Wayne
Squires, Bert
Sylvain, Jules
Turcotte, Maryse
Varaleau, Jack
Woo, Wes

**WHEELCHAIR BASKET-
BALL**
Abbott, Marni
Anderson, Patrick
Bastarache, Clarence
Benoit, Chantal
Borisoff, Jaimie
Bowden, Bradley
Butler, Barry
Durepos, Dave
Enright, Jim
Ferguson, Tracey
Frick, Tim
Gaertner, Travis
Gavillucci, Angelo
Golden, Shira
Griffin, Pat
Hansen, Rick
Henderson, Roy
Johnson, Joey
Kelly, Joanne
Krempien, Jennifer
Kutrowski, Linda
Lancia, Adam
Lapalme, Denis
Lord, Herv
McClellan, Reg
McNeney, Arley
McPherson, Gary
Mellway, Dean
Minor, Ron
Norton, Ross
Ohama, Kendra

Peers, Danielle
Peter, Richard
Pettinicchi, Sabrina
Pidskalny, Diane
Radke, Lori
Reimer, Eugene
Stoutenburg, Chris
Tonello, Jerry
Tritten, Karla
Wright, Doug

WRESTLING
Abdou, Justin
Anderson, Dave
Barry, Michael
Beiler, Egon
Bergey, Kim
Bertie, Gordon
Bianco, Scott
Boese, Kurt
Bohay, Gary
Bolger, Pat
Borodow, Andy
Calder, Marty
*Conacher, Lionel Sr.
Cox, Doug
*Cummings, Dave
Daniar, Stephen
Davis, Clark
DeBenedetti, Tania
Deschatelets, Richard
Donison, Butch
Donison, Danny
Donison, Lee
*Flanagan, Pat
*Garvie, Clarence
*Garvie, Gord
Geris, Harry
Hart, Bret
*Hart, Stu
Hohl, David
Hope, Gord
Huff, Bruce
Iacovelli, Orlando
Igali, Daniel
Johl, Yogi
Kallos, Garry
Kawasaki, Mitch
Kiniski, Gene
Kowalski, Killer
Ladik, Oleg
Lappage, Ron
*Layton, Lord Athol
Leyshon, Glynn
*Matheson, Dan
*McCready, Earl
Michienzi, Peter
Mitchell, Doug
Molle, Bob
Mosca, Angelo
Nordhagen, Christine
Nye, Barry
*Oberlander, Fred
Oberlander, Phil
*Pettigrew, Vern
Pilon, Claude
Pyle, Dave
Renken, Brian

Renken, Lloyd
Rinke, Chris
*Robert, Yvon Sr.
Robinson, Bob
Rokosh, Greg
*Schleimer, Joseph
Sissaouri, Guivi
Sorensen, Ole
Steckle, Bob
*Stockton, Donald
Stupp, Howard
Takahashi, Ray
Tam, Selwyn
*Thomas, Howard
*Trelle, Herman
*Trifunov, Jim
Vachon, Mad Dog
Verbeek, Tonya
*Watson, Whipper Billy
Wilson, Chris
Wishart, Wyatt
Woodcroft, Greg
*Wright, Joe Sr.
Wurr, Alfred
Yeats, Doug
York, Patrick
Zilberman, Victor

List of Canadian Champions, Award Winners, and Medallists

List of Canadian Champions, Award Winners, and Medallists

HOCKEY

Stanley Cup 527

Memorial Cup 528

FOOTBALL

Grey Cup 528

Vanier Cup 529

CURLING

The Brier (Men's) 530

Scott Tournament of Hearts (Women's) 531

NATIONAL AWARDS

Lou Marsh 532

Lionel Conacher 533

Bobbie Rosenfeld 533

AMATEUR SPORTS AWARDS

Velma Springstead 534

Norton Crowe 534

OLYMPIC MEDALLISTS

Summer Games 535

Winter Games 538

Pan American Games Medallists 539

British Empire / Commonwealth Games Medallists 555

PARALYMPICS MEDALLISTS

Summer Games 569

Winter Games 578

HOCKEY
Stanley Cup

Year	Winner	Finalist	Series Margin	Year	Winner	Finalist	Series Margin
1893	Montreal AAA			1947	Toronto Maple Leafs	Montreal	4-2
1894	Montreal AAA			1948	Toronto Maple Leafs	Detroit	4-0
1895	Montreal Victorias			1949	Toronto Maple Leafs	Detroit	4-0
1896	Winnipeg Victorias (Feb)			1950	Detroit Red Wings	New York Rangers	4-3
1896	Montreal Victorias (Dec)			1951	Toronto Maple Leafs	Montreal	4-1
1897	Montreal Victorias			1952	Detroit Red Wings	Montreal	4-0
1898	Montreal Victorias			1953	Montreal Canadiens	Boston	4-1
1899	Montreal Shamrocks			1954	Detroit Red Wings	Montreal	4-3
1900	Montreal Shamrocks			1955	Detroit Red Wings	Montreal	4-3
1901	Winnipeg Victorias			1956	Montreal Canadiens	Detroit	4-1
1902	Montreal AAA			1957	Montreal Canadiens	Boston	4-1
1903	Ottawa Silver Seven			1958	Montreal Canadiens	Boston	4-2
1904	Ottawa Silver Seven			1959	Montreal Canadiens	Toronto	4-1
1905	Ottawa Silver Seven			1960	Montreal Canadiens	Toronto	4-0
1906	Montreal Wanderers			1961	Chicago Black Hawks	Detroit	4-2
1907	Kenora Thistles (Jan)			1962	Toronto Maple Leafs	Chicago	4-2
1907	Montreal Wanderers (Mar)			1963	Toronto Maple Leafs	Detroit	4-1
1908	Montreal Wanderers			1964	Toronto Maple Leafs	Detroit	4-3
1909	Ottawa Senators			1965	Montreal Canadiens	Chicago	4-3
1910	Montreal Wanderers			1966	Montreal Canadiens	Detroit	4-2
1911	Ottawa Senators			1967	Toronto Maple Leafs	Montreal	4-2
1912	Ottawa Senators			1968	Montreal Canadiens	St. Louis	4-0
1913	Quebec Bulldogs			1969	Montreal Canadiens	St. Louis	4-0
1914	Toronto Blueshirts			1970	Boston Bruins	St. Louis	4-0
1915	Vancouver Millionaires			1971	Montreal Canadiens	Chicago	4-3
1916	Montreal Canadiens			1972	Boston Bruins	New York Rangers	4-2
1917	Seattle Metropolitans			1973	Montreal Canadiens	Chicago	4-2
1918	Toronto Arenas	Vancouver Millionaires	3-2	1974	Philadelphia Flyers	Boston	4-2
1919	*no decision**			1975	Philadelphia Flyers	B uffalo	4-2
1920	Ottawa Senators	Seattle	3-2	1976	Montreal Canadiens	Philadelphia	4-0
1921	Ottawa Senators	Vancouver Millionaires	3-2	1977	Montreal Canadiens	Boston	4-0
1922	Toronto St. Pat's	Vancouver Millionaires	3-2	1978	Montreal Canadiens	Boston	4-2
1923	Ottawa Senators	Edm. Eskimos/Vancouver 2-0/3-1		1979	Montreal Canadiens	New York Rangers	4-1
1924	Montreal Canadiens	Calgary/Van. Maroons 2-0/2-0		1980	New York Islanders	Philadelphia	4-2
1925	Victoria Cougars	Montreal	3-1	1981	New York Islanders	Minnesota	4-1
1926	Montreal Maroons	Victoria	3-1	1982	New York Islanders	Vancouver	4-0
NHL assumed control of Stanley Cup competitions after '26				1983	New York Islanders	Edmonton	4-0
1927	Ottawa Senators	Boston	2-0-2	1984	Edmonton Oilers	New York Islanders	4-1
1928	New York Rangers	Montreal Maroons	3-2	1985	Edmonton Oilers	Philadelphia	4-1
1929	Boston Bruins	New York Rangers	2-0	1986	Montreal Canadiens	Calgary	4-1
1930	Montreal Canadiens	Boston	2-0	1987	Edmonton Oilers	Philadelphia	4-3
1931	Montreal Canadiens	Chicago	3-2	1988	Edmonton Oilers	Boston	4-0
1932	Toronto Maple Leafs	New York Rangers	3-0	1989	Calgary Flames	Montreal	4-2
1933	New York Rangers	Toronto	3-1	1990	Edmonton Oilers	Boston	4-1
1934	Chicago Black Hawks	Detroit	3-1	1991	Pittsburgh Penguins	Minnesota	4-2
1935	Montreal Maroons	Toronto	3-0	1992	Pittsburgh Penguins	Chicago	4-0
1936	Detroit Red Wings	Toronto	3-1	1993	Montreal Canadiens	Los Angeles	4-1
1937	Detroit Red Wings	New York Rangers	3-2	1994	New York Rangers	Vancouver	4-3
1938	Chicago Black Hawks	Toronto	3-1	1995	New Jersey Devils	Detroit	4-0
1939	Boston Bruins	Toronto	4-1	1996	Colorado Avalanche	Florida	4-0
1940	New York Rangers	Toronto	4-2	1997	Detroit Red Wings	Philadelphia	4-0
1941	Boston Bruins	Detroit	4-0	1998	Detroit Red Wings	Washington	4-0
1942	Toronto Maple Leafs	Detroit	4-3	1999	Dallas Stars	Buffalo	4-2
1943	Detroit Red Wings	Boston	4-0	2000	New Jersey Devils	Dallas	4-2
1944	Montreal Canadiens	Chicago	4-0	2001	Colorado Avalanche	New Jersey	4-3
1945	Toronto Maple Leafs	Detroit	4-3	2002	Detroit Red Wings	Carolina Hurricanes	4-1
1946	Montreal Canadiens	Boston	4-1	2003	New Jersey Devils	Anaheim Mighty Ducks	4-3
				2004	Tampa Bay	Calgary Flames	4-3
				2005	*No winner, season cancelled by labor dispute*		

* (Information supplied by National Hockey League)

Memorial Cup

Year	Winner	Year	Winner	Year	Winner
1919	University of Toronto Schools	1948	Port Arthur West End	1977	New Westminster Bruins
1920	Toronto Canoe Club	1949	Montreal Royals	1978	New Westminster Bruins
1921	Winnipeg Falcons	1950	Montreal (Jr.) Canadiens	1979	Peterborough Petes
1922	Fort William War Veterans	1951	Barrie Flyers	1980	Cornwall Royals
1923	University of Manitoba	1952	Guelph Biltmores	1981	Cornwall Royals
1924	Owen Sound Greys	1953	Barrie Flyers	1982	Kitchener Rangers
1925	Regina Pats	1954	St. Catharines Tee Pees	1983	Portland Winter Hawks
1926	Calgary Canadians	1955	Toronto Marlboros	1984	Ottawa 67's
1927	Owen Sound	1956	Toronto Marlboros	1985	Prince Albert Raiders
1928	Regina Monarchs	1957	Flin Flon Bombers	1986	Guelph Platers
1929	Toronto Marlboros	1958	Ottawa-Hull Canadiens	1987	Medicine Hat Tigers
1930	Regina Pats	1959	Winnipeg Braves	1988	Medicine Hat Tigers
1931	Winnipeg Elmwoods	1960	St. Catharines Tee Pees	1989	Swift Current Broncos
1932	Sudbury Bruins	1961	St. Michael's Majors	1990	Oshawa Generals
1933	Newmarket	1962	Hamilton Red Wings	1991	Spokane Chiefs
1934	Toronto St. Michael's	1963	Edmonton Oil Kings	1992	Kamloops Blazers
1935	Winnipeg Monarchs	1964	Toronto Marlboros	1993	Sault Ste. Marie Greyhounds
1936	West Toronto Redmen	1965	Niagara Falls Flyers	1994	Kamloops Blazers
1937	Winnipeg Monarchs	1966	Edmonton Oil Kings	1995	Kamloops Blazers
1938	St. Boniface Seals	1967	Toronto Marlboros	1996	Granby Predateurs
1939	Oshawa Generals	1968	Niagara Falls Flyers	1997	Hull Olympiques
1940	Oshawa Generals	1969	Montreal Jr. Canadiens	1998	Portland Winter Hawks
1941	Winnipeg Rangers	1970	Montreal Jr. Canadiens	1999	Ottawa 67's
1942	Portage La Prairie	1971	Quebec Remparts	2000	Rimouski Oceanic
1943	Winnipeg Rangers	1972	Cornwall Royals	2001	Red Deer Rebels
1944	Oshawa Generals	1973	Toronto Marlboros	2002	Kootenay Ice
1945	Toronto St. Michael's	1974	Regina Pats	2003	Kitchener Rangers
1946	Winnipeg Monarchs	1975	Toronto Marlboros	2004	Kelowna
1947	Toronto St. Michael's	1976	Hamilton Fincups		

FOOTBALL
Grey Cup

Year		Result			Year		Result		
1909	U of Toronto	26	Parkdale	4	1936	Sarnia	26	Ottawa	20
1910	U of Toronto	16	Hamilton	7	1937	Toronto	4	Winnipeg	3
1911	U of Toronto	14	Toronto Argos	7	1938	Toronto	30	Winnipeg	7
1912	Hamilton	11	Toronto	4	1939	Winnipeg	8	Ottawa	7
1913	Hamilton	44	Parkdale	2	1940	Ottawa	8	Balmy Beach	2
1914	Toronto	14	U of Toronto	2		Ottawa	12	Balmy Beach	5
1915	Hamilton	13	Toronto	7	1941	Winnipeg	18	Ottawa	16
1916-19 - No games, World War 1					1942	Toronto	8	Winnipeg	5
1920	U of Toronto	16	Toronto	3	1943	Hamilton	23	Winnipeg	14
1921	Toronto	23	Edmonton	0	1944	Montreal	7	Hamilton	6
1922	Queen's U	13	Edmonton	1	1945	Toronto	35	Winnipeg	0
1923	Queen's U	54	Regina	0	1946	Toronto	28	Winnipeg	6
1924	Queen's U	11	Balmy Beach	3	1947	Toronto	10	Winnipeg	9
1925	Ottawa	24	Winnipeg	1	1948	Calgary	12	Ottawa	7
1926	Ottawa	10	U of Toronto	7	1949	Montreal	28	Calgary	15
1927	Balmy Beach	9	Hamilton	6	1950	Toronto	13	Winnipeg	0
1928	Hamilton	30	Regina	0	1951	Ottawa	21	Saskatchewan	14
1929	Hamilton	14	Regina	3	1952	Toronto	21	Edmonton	11
1930	Balmy Beach	11	Regina	6	1953	Hamilton	12	Winnipeg	6
1931	Montreal	22	Regina	0	1954	Edmonton	26	Montreal	25
1932	Hamilton	25	Regina	6	1955	Edmonton	34	Montreal	19
1933	Toronto	4	Sarnia	3	1956	Edmonton	50	Montreal	27
1934	Sarnia	20	Regina	12	1957	Hamilton	32	Winnipeg	7
1935	Winnipeg	18	Hamilton	12	1958	Winnipeg	35	Hamilton	28

Year	Result				Year	Result			
1959	Winnipeg	21	Hamilton	7	1982	Edmonton	32	Toronto	16
1960	Ottawa	16	Edmonton	6	1983	Toronto	18	B.C.	17
1961	Winnipeg	21	Hamilton	14	1984	Winnipeg	47	Hamilton	17
1962	Winnipeg	28	Hamilton	27	1985	B.C.	37	Hamilton	24
1963	Hamilton	21	B.C.	10	1986	Hamilton	39	Edmonton	15
1964	B.C.	34	Hamilton	24	1987	Edmonton	38	Toronto	36
1965	Hamilton	22	Winnipeg	16	1988	Winnipeg	22	B.C.	21
1966	Saskatchewan	29	Ottawa	14	1989	Saskatchewan	43	Hamilton	40
1967	Hamilton	24	Saskatchewan	1	1990	Winnipeg	50	Edmonton	11
1968	Ottawa	24	Calgary	21	1991	Toronto	36	Calgary	21
1969	Ottawa	29	Saskatchewan	11	1992	Calgary	24	Winnipeg	10
1970	Montreal	23	Calgary	10	1993	Edmonton	33	Winnipeg	23
1971	Calgary	14	Toronto	11	1994	B.C.	26	Baltimore	23
1972	Hamilton	13	Saskatchewan	10	1995	Baltimore	37	Calgary	20
1973	Ottawa	22	Edmonton	18	1996	Toronto	43	Edmonton	37
1974	Montreal	20	Edmonton	7	1997	Toronto	47	Saskatchewan	23
1975	Edmonton	9	Montreal	8	1998	Calgary	26	Hamilton	24
1976	Ottawa	23	Saskatchewan	20	1999	Hamilton	32	Calgary	21
1977	Montreal	41	Edmonton	6	2000	B.C.	28	Montreal	26
1978	Edmonton	20	Montreal	13	2001	Calgary	27	Winnipeg	19
1979	Edmonton	17	Montreal	9	2002	Montreal	25	Edmonton	16
1980	Edmonton	48	Hamilton	10	2003	Edmonton	34	Montreal	22
1981	Edmonton	26	Ottawa	23	2004	Toronto	27	B.C.	19

University — Vanier Cup

1967	Alberta	10	McMaster	9	1986	UBC	25	Western	23
1968	Queen's	42	Waterloo Lut.	14	1987	McGill	47	UBC	11
1969	Manitoba	24	McGill	15	1988	Calgary	52	St. Mary's	23
1970	Manitoba	38	Ottawa	11	1989	Western	35	Saskatchewan	10
1971	Western	15	Alberta	14	1990	Saskatchewan	24	St. Mary's	21
1972	Alberta	20	Waterloo Lut.	7	1991	Wilfrid Laurier	25	Mt. Allison	18
1973	Saint Mary's	14	McGill	6	1992	Queen's	31	Saint Mary's	0
1974	Western	19	Toronto	15	1993	Toronto	37	Calgary	34
1975	Ottawa	14	Calgary	9	1994	Western	50	Saskatchewan	40
1976	Western	29	Acadia	13	1995	Calgary	54	Western	24
1977	Western	48	Acadia	15	1996	Saskatchewan	31	St. FX	17
1978	Queen's	16	UBC	3	1997	UBC	39	Ottawa	23
1979	Acadia	34	Western	12	1998	Saskatchewan	24	Concordia	17
1980	Alberta	40	Ottawa	21	1999	Laval	14	Saint Mary's	10
1981	Acadia	18	Alberta	12	2000	Ottawa	42	Regina	39
1982	UBC	39	Western	14	2001	Saint Mary's	42	Manitoba	16
1983	Calgary	31	Queen's	21	2002	Saint Mary's	33	Saskatchewan	21
1984	Guelph	22	Mt. Allison	13	2003	Laval	14	Saint Mary's	7
1985	Calgary	25	Western	6	2004	Laval	7	Saskatchewan	1

CURLING
The Brier
Canadian men's championships
1927-2005
Sponsors: 1927-79 Macdonald Tobacco, 1980-00 Labatt Breweries, 2001-04 Nokia, 2005- Tim Hortons

1927	Nova Scotia	Murray Macneill, Al MacInnes, Cliff Torey, Jim Donahoe
1928	Manitoba	Gordon Hudson, Sam Penwarden, Ron Singbusch, Bill Grant
1929	Manitoba	Gordon Hudson, Don Rollo, Ron Singbusch, Bill Grant
1930	Manitoba	Howard Wood, Jimmy Congalton, Victor Wood, Lionel Wood
1931	Manitoba	Bob Gourlay, Ernie Pollard, Arnold Lockerbie, Ray Stewart
1932	Manitoba	Jimmy Congalton, Howard Wood, Bill Noble, Harry Mawhinney
1933	Alberta	Cliff Manahan, Harold Deeton, Harold Wolfe, Bert Ross
1934	Manitoba	Leo Johnson, Lorne Stewart, Linc Johnson, Marno Frederickson
1935	Ontario	Gordon Campbell, Don Campbell, Gord Coates, Duncan Campbell
1936	Manitoba	Ken Watson, Grant Watson, Marvin McIntyre, Charles Kerr
1937	Alberta	Cliff Manahan, Wes Robinson, Ross Manahan, Lloyd McIntyre
1938	Manitoba	Ab Gowanlock, Bung Cartwell, Bill McKnight, Tom Knight
1939	Ontario	Bert Hall, Perry Hall, Ernie Parkes, Cam Seagram
1940	Manitoba	Howard Wood, Ernie Pollard, Howard Wood Jr., Roy Enman
1941	Alberta	Howard Palmer, Jack Lebeau, Art Gooder, Claire Webb
1942	Manitoba	Ken Watson, Grant Watson, Charlie Scrymgeour, Jim Grant
1943 - 1945		*No competition war years*
1946	Alberta	Bill Rose, Bart Swelin, Austin Smith, George Crooks
1947	Manitoba	Jimmy Welsh, Alex Welsh, Jack Reid, Harry Monk
1948	B.C.	Frenchy D'Amour, Bob McGhie, Fred Wendell, Jim Mark
1949	Manitoba	Ken Watson, Grant Watson, Lyle Dyker, Charles Read
1950	N. Ontario	Tim Ramsay, Len Williamson, Bill Weston, Bill Kenny
1951	Nova Scotia	Don Oyler, George Hanson, Fred Dyke, Wally Knock
1952	Manitoba	Billy Walsh, Al Langlois, Andy McWilliams, John Watson
1953	Manitoba	Ab Gowanlock, Jim Williams, Art Pollon, Russ Jackman
1954	Alberta	Matt Baldwin, Glenn Gray, Pete Ferry, Jim Collins
1955	Saskatchewan	Garnet Campbell, Don Campbell, Glenn Campbell, Lloyd Campbell
1956	Manitoba	Billy Walsh, Al Langlois, Cy White, Andy McWilliams
1957	Alberta	Matt Baldwin, Gordon Haynes, Art Kleinmeyer, Bill Price
1958	Alberta	Matt Baldwin, Jack Geddes, Gordon Haynes, Bill Price
1959	Saskatchewan	Ernie Richardson, Arnold Richardson, Garnet Richardson, Wes Richardson
1960	Saskatchewan	Ernie Richardson, Arnold Richardson, Garnet Richardson, Wes Richardson
1961	Alberta	Hec Gervais, Ron Anton, Ray Werner, Wally Ursuliak
1962	Saskatchewan	Ernie Richardson, Arnold Richardson, Garnet Richardson, Wes Richardson
1963	Saskatchewan	Ernie Richardson, Arnold Richardson, Garnet Richardson, Mel Perry
1964	B.C.	Lyall Dagg, Leo Hebert, Fred Britton, Barry Naimark
1965	Manitoba	Terry Braunstein, Don Duguid, Ron Braunstein, Ray Turnbull
1966	Alberta	Ron Northcott, George Fink, Bernie Sparkes, Fred Storey
1967	Ontario	Alf Phillips Jr., John Ross, Ron Manning, Keith Reilly
1968	Alberta	Ron Northcott, Jim Shields, Bernie Sparkes, Fred Storey
1969	Alberta	Ron Northcott, Dave Gerlach, Bernie Sparkes, Fred Storey
1970	Manitoba	Don Duguid, Rod Hunter, Jim Pettapiece, Bryan Wood
1971	Manitoba	Don Duguid, Rod Hunter, Jim Pettapiece, Bryan Wood
1972	Manitoba	Orest Meleschuk, Dave Romano, John Hanesiak, Pat Hailley
1973	Saskatchewan	Harvey Mazinke, Billy Martin, George Achtymichuk, Dan Klippenstein
1974	Alberta	Hec Gervais, Ron Anton, Warren Hansen, Darrel Sutton
1975	N. Ontario	Bill Tetley, Rick Lang, Bill Hodgson, Peter Hnatiw
1976	Newfoundland	Jack MacDuff, Toby McDonald, Doug Hudson, Ken Templeton
1977	Quebec	Jim Ursel, Art Lobel, Don Aitken, Brian Ross
1978	Alberta	Ed Lukowich, Mike Chernoff, Dale Johnston, Ron Schindle
1979	Manitoba	Barry Fry, Bill Carey, Gord Sparkes, Bryan Wood
1980	Saskatchewan	Rick Folk, Ron Mills, Tom Wilson, Jim Wilson
1981	Manitoba	Kerry Burtnyk, Mark Olson, Jim Spencer, Ron Kammerlock
1982	N. Ontario	Al Hackner, Rick Lang, Bob Nicol, Bruce Kennedy
1983	Ontario	Ed Werenich, Paul Savage, John Kawaja, Neil Harrison
1984	Manitoba	Mike Riley, Brian Toews,

1985	N. Ontario	John Helston, Russ Wookey Al Hackner, Rick Lang, Ian Tetley, Pat Perroud
1986	Alberta	Ed Lukowich, John Ferguson, Neil Houston, Brent Syme
1987	Ontario	Russ Howard, Glenn Howard, Tim Belcourt, Kent Carstairs
1988	Alberta	Pat Ryan, Randy Ferby, Don Walchuk, Don McKenzie
1989	Alberta	Pat Ryan, Randy Ferby, Don Walchuk, Don McKenzie
1990	Ontario	Ed Werenich, John Kawaja, Ian Tetley, Pat Perroud
1991	Alberta	Kevin Martin, Kevin Park, Dan Petryk, Don Bartlett
1992	Manitoba	Vic Peters, Dan Carey, Chris Neufeld, Don Rudd
1993	Ontario	Russ Howard, Glenn Howard, Wayne Middaugh, Peter Corner
1994	B.C.	Rick Folk, Pat Ryan, Bert Gretzinger, Gerry Richard

1995	Manitoba	Kerry Burtnyk, Jeff Ryan, Rob Meakin, Keith Fenton
1996	Manitoba	Jeff Stoughton, Ken Tresoor, Garry Vandenberghe, Steve Gould
1997	Alberta	Kevin Martin, Don Walchuk, Rudy Ramcheran, DonBartlett
1998	Ontario	Wayne Middaugh, Graeme McCarrel, Ian Tetley, Scott Bailey
1999	Manitoba	Jeff Stoughton, Jon Mead, Garry Vandenberghe, Doug Armstrong
2000	B.C	Greg McAuley, Brent Pierce, Bryon Miki, Jody Sveistrup
2001	Alberta	Randy Ferbey, Dave Nedohin, Scott Pfeifer, Marcel Rocque
2002	Alberta	Randy Ferbey, Dave Nedohin, Scott Pfeifer, Marcel Rocque
2003	Alberta	Randy Ferbey, Dave Nedohin, Scott Pfeifer, Marcel Rocque
2004	Nova Scotia	Mark Dacey, Bruce Lohnes Rob Harris, Andrew Gibson
2005	Alberta	Randy Ferbey, Dave Nedohin Scott Pfeifer, Marcel Rocque

Scott Tournament of Hearts
Canadian women's championships
1961-2005
From 1961-67 known as Diamond D championships.
From 1968-71, 1980-81 the CLCA championships.
From 1972-79 the MacDonald Lassie and
from 1982 Scott Paper Ltd. has sponsored the Scott Tournament of Hearts.

1961	Saskatchewan	Joyce McKee, Sylvia Fedoruk, Barbara MacNevin, Rosa McFee
1962	B.C.	Ina Hansen, Ada Callas, Isabel Leith, May Shaw
1963	New Brunswick	Mabel DeWare, Harriet Stratton, Forbis Stevenson, Marjorie Fraser
1964	B.C.	Ina Hansen, Ada Callas, Isabel Leith, May Shaw
1965	Manitoba	Peggy Casselman, Val Taylor, Pat MacDonald, Pat Scott
1966	Alberta	Gail Lee, Hazel Jamieson, Sharon Harrington, June Coyle
1967	Manitoba	Betty Duguid, Joan Ingram, Laurie Bradawaski, Dot Rose
1968	Alberta	Hazel Jamieson, Gail Lee, Jackie Spencer, June Coyle
1969	Saskatchewan	Joyce McKee, Vera Pezer, Lenore Morrison, Jennifer Falk
1970	Saskatchewan	Dorenda Schoenhals, Cheryl Stirton, Linda Burnham, Joan Anderson
1971	Saskatchewan	Vera Pezer, Sheila Rowan, Joyce McKee, Lenore Morrison
1972	Saskatchewan	Vera Pezer, Sheila Rowan, Joyce McKee, Lenore Morrison
1973	Saskatchewan	Vera Pezer, Sheila Rowan, Joyce McKee, Lenore Morrison
1974	Saskatchewan	Emily Farnham, Linda Saunders, Pat McBeath, Donna Collins
1975	Quebec	Lee Tobin, Marilyn McNeil, Michelle Garneau, Laurie Ross
1976	B.C.	Lindsay Davie, Dawn Knowles, Robin Klassen, Lorraine Bowles

1977	Alberta	Myrna McQuarrie, Rita Tarnava, Barb Davis, Jane Rempel
1978	Manitoba	Cathy Pidzarko, Chris Pidzarko, Iris Armstrong, Patty Vanderkerckhove
1979	B.C.	Lindsay Sparkes, Dawn Knowles, Robin Wilson, Lorraine Bowles
1980	Saskatchewan	Marj Mitchell, Nancy Kerr, Shirley McKendry, Wendy Leach
1981	Alberta	Susan Seitz, Judy Erickson, Myrna McKay, Betty McCracken
1982	Nova Scotia	Colleen Jones, Kay Smith, Monica Jones, Barbara Jones-Gordon
1983	Nova Scotia	Penny LaRocque, Sharon Horne, Cathy Caudle, Pam Sanford
1984	Manitoba	Connie Laliberte, Chris More, Corinne Peters, Janet Arnott
1985	B.C.	Linda Moore, Lindsay Sparkes, Debbie Jones, Laurie Carney
1986	Ontario	Marilyn Darte, Kathy McEdwards, Chris Jurgenson, Jan Augustyn
1987	B.C.	Pat Sanders, Georgina Hawkes, Louise Herlinveaux, Deb Massullo
1988	Ontario	Heather Houston, Lorraine Lang, Diane Adams, Tracy Kennedy
1989	Team Canada	Heather Houston, Lorraine Lang, Diane Adams, Tracy Kennedy
1990	Ontario	Alison Goring, Kristin Turcotte, Andrea Lawes, Cheryl McPherson
1991	B.C.	Julie Sutton, Jodie Sutton, Melissa Soligo, Karri Willms
1992	Manitoba	Connie Laliberte, Laurie Allen, Cathy Gauthier, Janet Arnott

1993	Saskatchewan	Sandra Peterson, Jan Betker, Joan McCusker, Marcia Gudereit
1994	Team Canada	Sandra Peterson, Jan Betker, Joan McCusker, Marcia Gudereit
1995	Manitoba	Connie Laliberte, Cathy Clapham, Cathy Gauthier, Janet Arnot
1996	Ontario	Marilyn Bodogh, Kim Gellard, Corie Beveridge, Jane Hooper Perroud
1997	Saskatchewan	Sandra Schmirler, Jan Betker, Joan McCusker, Marcia Gudereit
1998	Alberta	Cathy Borst, Heather Godberson, Brenda Behmer, Kate Horne
1999	Nova Scotia	Colleen Jones, Kim Kelly, Mary-Jane Waye, Nancy Delahunt

2000	B.C.	Kelley Law, Julie Skinner, Georgina Wheatcroft, Diane Nelson
2001	Nova Scotia	Colleen Jones, Kim Kelly, Mary-Jane Waye, Nancy Delahunt
2002	Team Canada	Colleen Jones, Kim Kelly, Mary-Jane Waye, Nancy Delahunt
2003	Team Canada	Colleen Jones, Kim Kelly, Mary-Jane Waye, Nancy Delahunt
2004	Team Canada	Colleen Jones, Kim Kelly, Mary-Jane Waye, Nancy Delahunt
2005	Manitoba	Jennifer Jones, Cathy Overton-Clapham, Jill Officer, Cathy Gauthier

NATIONAL AWARDS
(Information supplied by Toronto Star, Canadian Press, Canadian Centre for Ethics in Sport)

Lou Marsh Trophy
Canadian athlete of year

Year	Athlete	Sport
1936	Phil Edwards	t&f
1937	Marshall Cleland	equestrian
1938	Bob Pearce	rowing
1939	Bob Pirie	swimming
1940	Gérard Côté	t&f
1941	Theo Dubois	rowing
1942-44	*No awards WWII*	
1945	Barbara Ann Scott	figure skating
1946	Joe Krol	football
1947	Barbara Ann Scott	figure skating
1948	Barbara Ann Scott	figure skating
1949	Cliff Lumsdon	swimming
1950	Bob McFarlane	t&f/football
1951	Marlene Stewart	golf
1952	George Genereux	shooting
1953	Doug Hepburn	weightlifting
1954	Marilyn Bell	swimming
1955	Beth Whittall	swimming
1956	Marlene Stewart Streit	golf
1957	Maurice Richard	hockey
1958	Lucile Wheeler	skiing
1959	Barbara Wagner/Robert Paul	figure skating
1960	Anne Heggtveit	skiing
1961	Bruce Kidd	t&f
1962	Donald Jackson	figure skating
1963	Bill Crothers	t&f
1964	George Hungerford/Roger Jackson	rowing
1965	Petra Burka	figure skating
1966	Elaine Tanner	swimming
1967	Nancy Greene	skiing
1968	Nancy Greene	skiing
1969	Russ Jackson	football
1970	Bobby Orr	hockey
1971	Hervé Filion	harness racing
1972	Phil Esposito	hockey

Year	Athlete	Sport
1973	Sandy Hawley	horse racing
1974	Ferguson Jenkins	baseball
1975	Bobby Clarke	hockey
1976	Sandy Hawley	horse racing
1977	Guy Lafleur	hockey
1978	Graham Smith	swimming
	Ken Read	skiing
1979	Sandra Post	golf
1980	Terry Fox	Marathon of Hope
1981	Susan Nattrass	shooting
1982	Wayne Gretzky	hockey
1983	Wayne Gretzky	hockey
1984	Gaetan Boucher	speed skating
1985	Wayne Gretzky	hockey
1986	Ben Johnson	t&f
1987	Ben Johnson	t&f
1988	Carolyn Waldo	synchro swim
1989	Wayne Gretzky	hockey
1990	Kurt Browning	figure skating
1991	Silken Laumann	rowing
1992	Mark Tewksbury	swimming
1993	Mario Lemieux	hockey
1994	Myriam Bedard	biathlon
1995	Jacques Villeneuve	auto racing
1996	Donovan Bailey	t&f
1997	Jacques Villeneuve	auto racing
1998	Larry Walker	baseball
1999	Carolyn Brunet	kayak
2000	Daniel Igali	wrestling
2001	Jamie Sale/David Pelletier	figure skating
2002	Catriona LeMay Doan	speed skating
2003	Mike Weir	golf
2004	Adam van Koeverden	canoeing

Lionel Conacher Trophy
CP Male Athlete of the Year

Year	Athlete	Sport
1932	Sandy Somerville	golf
1933	Dave Komonen	t&f
1934	Harold Webster	t&f
1935	Scotty Rankine	t&f
1936	Phil Edwards	t&f
1937	Syl Apps	hockey
1938	Bummer Stirling	football
1939	Fritzie Hanson	football
1940	Gerard Cote	t&f
1941	Tony Golab	football
1942-45	*No awards WWII*	
1946	Joe Krol	football
1947	Joe Krol	football
1948	Buddy O'Connor	hockey
1949	Frank Filchock	football
1950	Lionel Conacher - athlete of half century	
		football/hockey
1951	*No award*	
1952	Maurice Richard	hockey
1953	Doug Hepburn	weightlifting
1954	Rich Ferguson	t&f
1955	Normie Kwong	football
1956	Jean Beliveau	hockey
1957	Maurice Richard	hockey
1958	Maurice Richard	hockey
1959	Russ Jackson	football
1960	Ron Stewart	football
1961	Bruce Kidd	t&f
1962	Bruce Kidd	t&f
1963	Gordie Howe	hockey
1964	Bill Crothers	t&f
1965	Bobby Hull	hockey
1966	Bobby Hull	hockey
1967	Ferguson Jenkins	baseball
1968	Ferguson Jenkins	baseball
1969	Russ Jackson	football

Year	Athlete	Sport
1970	Bobby Orr	hockey
1971	Ferguson Jenkins	baseball
1972	Phil Esposito	hockey
1973	Phil Esposito	hockey
1974	Ferguson Jenkins	baseball
1975	Bobby Clarke	hockey
1976	Greg Joy	t&f
1977	Guy Lafleur	hockey
1978	Graham Smith	swimming
1979	Gilles Villeneuve	auto racing
1980	Wayne Gretzky	hockey
1981	Wayne Gretzky	hockey
1982	Wayne Gretzky	hockey
1983	Wayne Gretzky	hockey
1984	Alex Baumann	swimming
1985	Wayne Gretzky	hockey
1986	Ben Johnson	t&f
1987	Ben Johnson	t&f
1988	Mario Lemieux	hockey
1989	Wayne Gretzky	hockey
1990	Kurt Browning	figure skating
1991	Kurt Browning	figure skating
1992	Mark Tewksbury	swimming
1993	Mario Lemieux	hockey
1994	Elvis Stojko	figure skating
1995	Jacques Villeneuve	auto racing
1996	Donovan Bailey	t&f
1997	Jacques Villeneuve	auto racing
1998	Larry Walker	baseball
1999	Wayne Gretzky - athlete of century	hockey
2000	Mike Weir	golf
2001	Mike Weir	golf
2002	Steve Nash	basketball
2003	Mike Weir	golf
2004	Kyle Shewfelt	gymnastics

Bobbie Rosenfeld Trophy
CP Female Athlete of the Year

Year	Athlete	Sport
1933	Ada Mackenzie	golf
1934	Phyllis Dewar	swimming
1935	Aileen Meagher	t&f
1936	Betty Taylor	t&f
1937	Robina Higgins	t&f
1938	Noel Macdonald	basketball
1939	Mary Rose Thacker	figure skating
1940	Dorothy Walton	badminton
1941	Mary Rose Thacker	figure skating
1942-45	*No awards WWII*	
1946	Barbara Ann Scott	figure skating
1947	Barbara Ann Scott	figure skating
1948	Barbara Ann Scott	figure skating
1949	Irene Strong	swimming
1950	Bobbie Rosenfeld - athlete of half century	
		t&f
1951	*No award*	

Year	Athlete	Sport
1952	Marlene Stewart	golf
1953	Marlene Stewart	golf
1954	Marilyn Bell	swimming
1955	Marilyn Bell	swimming
1956	Marlene Stewart	golf
1957	Marlene Stewart	golf
1958	Lucile Wheeler	skiing
1959	Anne Heggtveit	skiing
1960	Anne Heggtveit	skiing
1961	Mary Stewart	swimming
1962	Mary Stewart	swimming
1963	Marlene Stewart Streit	golf
1964	Petra Burka	figure skating
1965	Petra Burka	figure skating
1966	Elaine Tanner	swimming
1967	Nancy Greene	skiing
1968	Nancy Greene	skiing

Year	Athlete	Sport
1969	Bev Boys	diving
1970	Bev Boys	diving
1971	Debbie Van Kiekebelt	t&f
	Debbie Brill	t&f
1972	Jocelyn Bourassa	golf
1973	Karen Magnussen	figure skating
1974	Wendy Cook	swimming
1975	Nancy Garapick	swimming
1976	Kathy Kreiner	skiing
1977	Cindy Nicholas	swimming
1978	Diane Jones Konihowski	t&f
1979	Sandra Post	golf
1980	Sandra Post	golf
1981	Tracey Wainman	figure skating
1982	Gerry Sorensen	skiing
1983	Carling Bassett	tennis
1984	Sylvie Bernier	diving
1985	Carling Bassett	tennis
1986	Laurie Graham	skiing

Year	Athlete	Sport
1987	Carolyn Waldo	synchro swim
1988	Carolyn Waldo	synchro swim
1989	Helen Kelesi	tennis
1990	Helen Kelesi	tennis
1991	Silken Laumann	rowing
1992	Silken Laumann	rowing
1993	Kate Pace	skiing
1994	Myriam Bedard	biathlon
1995	Susan Auch	speed skating
1996	Alison Sydor	cycling
1997	Lorie Kane	golf
1998	Catriona LeMay Doan	speed skating
1999	Nancy Greene - athlete of century	skiing
2000	Lorie Kane	golf
2001	Catriona LeMay Doan	speed skating
2002	Catriona LeMay Doan	speed skating
2003	Perdita Felicien	t&f
2004	Lori Anne Muenzer	cycling

AMATEUR SPORTS AWARDS

Velma Springstead Award
Outstanding female athlete

Year	Athlete	Sport
1972	Karen Magnussen	figure skating
1973	Karen Magnussen	figure skating
1974	Wendy Cook	swimming
1975	Nancy Garapick	swimming
	Diane Jones	t&f
1976	Cheryl Gibson	swimming
1977	Sylvia Burka	cycling
	Susan Nattrass	shooting
1978	Diane Jones Konihowski	t&f
	Cathy Sherk	golf
1979	Helen Vanderburg	synchro swim
1980	Angella Taylor	t&f
1981	Susan Nattrass	shooting
1982	Angella Taylor	t&f
1983	Lynn Chornobrywy	modern pentathlon
1984	Linda Thom	shooting
1985	Carolyn Waldo	synchro swim
1986	Carolyn Waldo	synchro swim
1987	Carolyn Waldo	synchro swim
1988	Carolyn Waldo	synchro swim
1989	Heather Houston	curling
1990	Sylvie Daigle	speed skating
1991	Silken Laumann	rowing
1992	Kerrin Lee-Gartner	skiing
1993	Kate Pace	skiing
1994	Myriam Bedard	biathlon
1995	Alison Sydor	cycling
1996	Alison Sydor	cycling
1997	Caroline Brunet	kayak
1998	Catriona LeMay Doan	speed skating
1999	Catriona LeMay Doan	speed skating
2000	Caroline Brunet	kayak
2001	Catriona LeMay Doan	speed skating
2002	Catriona LeMay Doan	speed skating
2003	Perdita Felicien	t&f
2004	Chantal Petticlerc	t&f

Norton Crowe Award
Outstanding male athlete

Year	Athlete	Sport
1972	Eugene Reimer	all-around
1973	George Athans Jr	water skiing
	Bruce Robertson	swimming
1974	Toller Cranston	figure skating
1975	Jocelyn Lovell	cycling
1976	Greg Joy	t&f
1977	Jerome Drayton	t&f
1978	Graham Smith	swimming
1979	Ken Read	skiing
1980	Mel Fitzgerald	wheelchair t&f
1981	Steve Podborski	skiing
1982	Steve Podborski	skiing
1983	Louis Grenier	speed skating
1984	Gaetan Boucher	speed skating
1985	Ben Johnson	t&f
1986	Ben Johnson	t&f
1987	Ben Johnson	t&f
1988	Lennox Lewis	boxing
1989	Kurt Browning	figure skating
1990	Kurt Browning	figure skating
1991	Kurt Browning	figure skating
1992	Mark Tewksbury	swimming
1993	Kurt Browning	figure skating
1994	Elvis Stojko	figure skating
1995	Donovan Bailey	t&f
1996	Donovan Bailey	t&f
1997	Elvis Stojko	figure skating
1998	Peter Reid	triathlon
1999	Daniel Igali	wrestling
2000	Daniel Igali	wrestling
2001	Roland Green	cycling
2002	Roland Green	cycling
2003	David Ford	canoe
2004	Kyle Shewfelt	gymnastics

CANADA'S OLYMPIC MEDALLISTS
Summer Games

Gold

Year	Name	Event/Sport
1900	George Orton*	3000m steeplechase
	Orton, a Canadian, competed for the U S as Canada had no team	
1904	Etienne Desmarteau	56-pound weight toss
	Galt Football Club (Soccer)	
	George S. Lyon	golf
	Winnipeg Shamrock	lacrosse
1906*	William Sherring	marathon
	not an official Olympiad	
1908	Bobby Kerr	200m run
	Walter Ewing	trap shooting
	Lacrosse - All Canada's team	
1912	George Goulding	10,000m walk
	George Hodgson	400m swim
	George Hodgson	1500m swim
1920	Earl Thomson	100m hurdles
	Bert Schneider	welterweight boxing
1928	Percy Williams	100m run
	Percy Williams	200m run
	Ethel Catherwood	women's high jump
	Bobbie Rosenfeld,	women's 4x100m relay run
	Ethel Smith, Florence Bell,	
	Myrtle Cook	
1932	Duncan McNaughton	men's high jump
	Lefty Gwynne	bantamweight boxing
1936	Frank Amyot	canoeing 1000m single
1952	George Genereux	trap shooting
1956	Don Arnold,	rowing - UBC coxless fours
	Lorne Loomer,	
	Walter d'Hondt,	
	Archie McKinnon	
	Gerry Ouellette	small-bore prone rifle
1964	Roger Jackson,	rowing - UBC coxless pair
	George Hungerford	
1968	Jim Day, Jim Elder,	equestrian Prix des Nations
	Tom Gayford	
1984	Linda Thom	women's sport pistol
	Alex Baumann	400m IM swim
	Alex Baumann	200m IM swim
	Anne Ottenbrite	200m breaststroke swim
	Victor Davis	200m breaststroke swim
	Blair Horn,	coxed heavy eights
	Dean Crawford, Mike Evans,	
	Paul Steele, Grant Main,	
	Mark Evans, Kevin Neufeld,	
	Pat Turner, Brian McMahon	
	Sylvie Bernier	3m springboard diving
	Larry Cain	500m C1
	Hugh Fisher, Alwyn Morris	men's 1000m K2
	Lori Fung	rhythmic gymnastics
1988	Lennox Lewis	boxing +91kg
	Carolyn Waldo	synchro swim solo
	Carolyn Waldo,	synchro swim duet
	Michelle Cameron	
	Ben Johnson	100m sprint*
	stripped of medal due to doping infraction	

Year	Name	Event/Sport
1992	Mark McKoy	110m hurdle
	Mark Tewksbury	100m backstroke
1988	Marnie McBean,	women's pair rowing
	Kathleen Heddle,	
	Kirsten Barnes,	women's rowing fours
	Brenda Taylor,	
	Jessica Monroe, Kay Worthington	
	Kirsten Barnes,	women's rowing eights
	Brenda Taylor, Megan Delahanty,	
	Shannon Crawford, Marnie McBean,	
	Kay Worthington, Jessica Monroe,	
	Kathleen Heddle, Lesley Thompson	
	John Wallace,	men's rowing eights
	Bruce Robertson,	
	Michael Forgeron, Darren Barber,	
	Robert Marland, Michael Rascher,	
	Andy Crosby, Derek Porter, Terry Paul	
1996	Sylvie Frechette	synchro swim solo
	Donovan Bailey	100m sprint*
	world record 9.84 sec	
	Kathleen Heddle,	double sculls
	Marnie McBean	
	Robert Esmie,	4x100 relay
	Glenroy Gilbert,	
	Bruny Surin, Donovan Bailey	
2000	Daniel Nestor,	tennis men's doubles
	Sebastien Lareau	
	Simon Whitfield	men's triathlon
	Daniel Igali	wrestling 69kg freestyle
2004	Kyle Shewfelt	gymnastics floor exercise
	Lori-Ann Muenzer	women's cycling sprint
	Andrew van Koeverden	men's K1 500m
	Chantal Petticlerc	800m wheelchair race (demonstration)

Silver

Year	Name	Event/Sport
1904	Toronto Argonauts	rowing heavy eights
1906*	Donald Linden	1500m walk
	not an official Olympiad	
1908	Garfield McDonald	hop, step and jump (triple jump)
	Con Walsh	hammer throw
	George Beattie	trap shooting
	Team trap shooting	
1912	Cal Bricker	running long jump
	Duncan Gillis	hammer throw
1920	Charles Graham	bantamweight boxing
	Georges Prud'Homme	middleweight boxing
	George Vernot	1500m swim
1924	William Wood,	coxless fours
	Colin Finlayson,	
	George McKay, Archie Black	
	(Vancouver Rowing Club)	
	University of Toronto	rowing heavy eights
	Team trap shooting	
1928	Jack Guest, Joe Wright Jr.	double sculls

Year	Name	Event/Sport
	Jim Ball	400m run
	Bobbie Rosenfeld	100m run
	Don Stockton	wrestling
1932	Alex Wilson	800m run
	Hilda Strike	100m run
	Mildred Frizzell,	4x100m relay
	Mary Frizzell, Lillian Palmer,	
	Hilda Strike	
	Dan MacDonald	welterweight wrestling
	8-metre International yachting	
1936	John Loaring	400m hurdles
	Frank Saker,	
	Harvey Charters	10,000m canoeing doubles
	Men's basketball	
1948	Doug Bennett	1000m canoeing singles
1952	Gerald Gratton	75kg weightlifting
	Ken Lane, Don Hawgood	10,000m canoeing doubles
1956	UBC Eights	rowing heavy eights
1960	UBC Eights	rowing heavy eights
1964	Bill Crothers	800m run
	Doug Rogers	judo
1968	Elaine Tanner	100m backstroke
	Elaine Tanner	200m backstroke
	Ralph Hutton	400m freestyle
1972	Bruce Robertson	100m butterfly
	Leslie Cliff	400m IM
1976	Greg Joy	men's high jump
	John Wood	500m C1
	Michel Vaillancourt	equestrian jumping
	Cheryl Gibson	400m IM
	Clay Evans,	men's 4x100 medley relay
	Gary MacDonald,	
	Stephen Pickell, Graham Smith	
1984	Victor Davis	100m breaststroke
	Steve Bauer	190km cycling road race
	Curt Harnett	1000m cycling time trial
	Anne Ottenbrite	100m breaststroke
	Jacques Demers	75kg weightlifting
	Tricia Smith, Betty Craig	women's coxless pairs
	Marilyn Brain,	women's coxed fours
	Angela Schneider,	
	Barbara Armbrust, Jane Tregunno,	
	Lesley Thompson (cox)	
	Mike West, Victor Davis,	men's 4x100m medley relay
	Tom Ponting, Sandy Goss	
	Terry McLaughlin,	Flying Dutchman yachting
	Evert Bastet	
	Larry Cain	men's 1000m C1
	Alexandra Barre,	women's 500m K2
	Sue Holloway	
	Bob Molle	100+kg wrestling
	Willie deWit	91kg boxing
	Shawn O'Sullivan	71kg boxing
	Sharon Hambrook,	synchro swim duet
	Kelly Kryczka	
	Carolyn Waldo	synchro swim solo
	Angela Bailey,	women's 4x100m relay
	Marita Payne,	
	Angella Taylor, France Gareau	
	Molly Killingbeck,	women's 4x400m relay
	Jillian Richardson,	
	Charmaine Crooks, Marita Payne	
1988	Egerton Marcus	boxing 75kg

Year	Name	Event/Sport
	Mark Tewksbury,	4x100 medley relay
	Victor Davis,	
	Tom Ponting, Sandy Goss	
1992	Marc Leduc	light weltertweight
		63.5kg boxing
	Penny and Vicky Vilagos	synchro swim duet
	Marcia King	taekwondo (demonstration)
	Guillaume Leblanc	20m racewalk
	Jeff Thue	130kg FS wrestling
1996	Marianne Limpert	200IM swim
	Derek Porter	men's single sculls
	Silken Laumann	women's single sculls
	Brian Walton	men's cycling point race
	David Boyes,	men's lightweight fours
	Gavin Hassett, Jeff Lay,	
	Brian Peaker	
	Women's rowing eights	
	Caroline Brunet	women's 500m K1
	Alison Sydor	women's mountain biking
	Giuvi Sissaouri	57kg freestyle wrestling
	David Defiagbon	91kg boxing
	Women's synchro swim team	
2000	Caroline Brunet	women's 500m K1
	Emelie Heymans,	synchronized diving team
	Anne Montminy	women's 10m
	Nicolas Gill	judo 100kg
2004	Karen Cockburn	women's trampoline
	Cameron Baerg,	men's coxless fours rowing
	Thomas Herschmiller	
	Jake Wetzel, Barney Williams	
	Tonya Verbeek	women's 55kg FS wrestling
	Alexandre Despatie	men's 3m springboard
	Marrie-Helene Premont	women's mountain bike
	Ross Macdonald,	men's Star sailing
	Mike Wolfs	

Bronze

Year	Name	Event/Sport
1900	George Orton	400m hurdles
1904	Mohawk Indians	lacrosse
1908	Bobby Kerr	100m run
	Cal Bricker	running long jump
	Ed Archibald	pole vault
	Aubert Cote	wrestling
	N.B.Jacks, F.P.Toms	coxless pairs
	Team shooting	
	Team cycling pursuit	
	Con Walsh	hammer
	Men's rowing eights	
1912	Bill Happeny (tie)	pole vault
	Frank Lukeman	pentathlon
	Everard Butler	single sculls rowing
1920	Chris Newton	lightweight boxing
	Moe Herscovitch	middleweight boxing
	George Vernot	400m freestyle swim
1924	Douglas Lewis	welterweight boxing
1928	Alex Wilson, Phil Edwards,	4x400 relay
	Stan Glover, Jim Ball	
	Ethel Smith	100m sprint
	Jim Trifunov	56kg wrestling
	Maurice Letchford	72kg wrestling
	Ray Smillie	welterweight boxing

Year	Name	Event/Sport
	Munroe Bourne, Jim Thompson, Garnet Ault, Walter Spence	4x200 FS swim relay
	Argonaut Rowing Club	heavy eights
1932	Alex Wilson	400m run
	Phil Edwards	800m run
	Phil Edwards	1500m run
	Ray Lewis, Phil Edwards, Jim Ball, Alex Wilson	4x400 relay
	Eva Dawes	women's high jump
	Noel de Mille, Charles "Ned" Pratt	double sculls
	Hamilton Leanders	rowing heavy eights
	6-metre R Class yachting	
1936	Phil Edwards	800m run
	Betty Taylor	80m hurdles
	Dorothy Brookshaw, Jeanette Dolson, Hilda Cameron, Aileen Meagher	4x100m relay
	Joe Schleimer	welterweight wrestling
	Frank Saker, Harvey Charters	1000m C2
1948	Viola Myers, Nancy McKay, Dianne Foster, Patricia Jones	women's 4x100m relay
	Norm Lane	10,000m canoeing singles
1956	Gil Boa	small-bore prone rifle
	Irene MacDonald	3m springboard diving
	John Rumble, Brian Herbinson, Jim Elder	equestrian 3-day event
1964	Harry Jerome	100m sprint
1968	Marilyn Corson, Angela Coughlan, Elaine Tanner, Marion Lay	women's 4x100 FS relay
1968	Erik Fish, Bob Kasting, Bill Mahony, Bruce Robertson	men's 4x100 medley relay
1972	Donna-Marie Gurr	200m backstroke
	Paul Cote, John Ekels, David Miller	Soling yachting
1976	Nancy Garapick	100m backstroke
	Nancy Garapick	200m backstroke
	Shannon Smith	400m freestyle
	Becky Smith	400m IM
	Gail Amundrud, Barbara Clark, Anne Jardin, Becky Smith	women's 4x100 FS relay
	Robin Corsiglia, Wendy Hogg, Anne Jardin, Susan Sloan	women's 4x100 med.relay
1984	Reema Abdo, Anne Ottenbrite, Michelle MacPherson, Pam Rai	women's 4x100 med. relay
	Cam Henning	200m backstroke
	Mike West	100m backstroke
	Daniele Laumann, Silken Laumann	double sculls
	Ben Johnson	men's 100m sprint
	Ben Johnson, Tony Sharpe, Desai Williams, Sterling Hinds	men's 4x100m relay
	Bob Mills	men's single sculls
	Bruce Ford, Phil Monckton, Mike Hughes, Doug Hamilton	men's coxless quad sculls

Year	Name	Event/Sport
	Hugh Fisher, Alwyn Morris	men's 500m K2
	Mark Berger	judo +95kg
	Lynn Williams	women's 3000m run
	Dale Walters	54kg boxing
1984	Alexandra Barre, Sue Holloway, Lucie Guay, Barb Olmstead	women's 500m K4
	Chris Rinke	82kg wrestling
	Terry Neilson	Finn yachting
	Hans Fogh, Steve Calder, John Kerr	Soling yachting
1988	Dave Steen	decathlon
	Raymond Downey	boxing 71kg
	Cynthia Ishoy, Eva-Marie Pracht, Gina Smith, Ashley Nicoll	equestrian team dressage
1988	Lori Melien, Allison Higson, Jane Kerr, Andrea Nugent	women's 4x100 med. relay
	Frank McLaughlin, John Millen	Flying Dutchman yachting
1992	Chris Johnson	middleweight boxing
	Curt Harnett	individual sprint cycling
	Nicolas Gill	middleweight judo
	Silken Laumann	women's single scull rowing
	Mark Tewksbury, Jon Cleveland, Marcel Gery, Stephen Clarke	men's 4x100m medley relay
	Angela Chalmers	3000m run
	Ross MacDonald, Eric Jesperson,	Star yachting
1996	Clara Hughes	women's cycling road race
	Clara Hughes	women's indiv. time trial
	Curtis Myden	400 IM swimming
	Curtis Myden	200 IM swimming
	John Child, Mark Heese	men's beach volleyball
	Curt Harnett	men's cycling sprint
	Marnie McBean, Kathleen Heddle, Laryssa Biesenthal, Diane O'Grady	women's quad sculls
	Annie Pelletier	women's 3m springboard
2000	Anne Montminy	women's 10m platform
	Curtis Myden	400 IM swimming
	Lyne Beaumont, Claire Carver-Dias, Erin Chan, Jessica Chase, Catherine Garceau, Fanny Letourneau, Kirstin Normand, Jacinthe Taillon, Reidun Tatham	synchro swim team
	Mathieu Turgeon	men's trampoline
	Karen Cockburn	women's trampoline
	Steve Giles	1000m C1 sprint
	Buffy Alexander, Laryssa Biesenthal, Heather Davis, Alison Korn, Theresa Luke, Heather McDermid, Emma Robinson, Leskey Thompson, Dorota Urbaniak	women's coxed eight
	Dominique Bosshart	taekwondo 67+kg
2004	Blythe Hartley, Emilie Heymans	women's 10m synchronized diving
	Caroline Brunet	women's K1 5oom
	Adam van Koeverden	men's K1 1000m

Winter Games

Gold

Year	Name	Event/Sport
1920*	Hockey - Winnipeg Falcons	
	Although Winter Games did not begin until 1924, hockey was an official event at the 1920 Summer Games.	
1924	Hockey - Toronto Granites	
1928	Hockey - U of T Grads	
1932	Hockey - Winnipeg	
1948	Hockey - RCAF Flyers	
	Barbara Ann Scott	women's figure skating
1952	Hockey - Edmonton Mercurys	
1960	Anne Heggtveit	women's slalom skiing
	Barbara Paul, Bob Wagner	figure skating pairs
	Vic Emery, John Emery,	4-man bobsled
	Doug Anakin, Peter Kirby	
1968	Nancy Greene	women's giant slalom skiing
1976	Kathy Kreiner	women's giant slalom skiing
1984	Gaetan Boucher	men's speedskating 1000m
	Gaetan Boucher	men's speedskating 1500m
1992	Kerrin Lee-Gartner	women's downhill skiing
	Angela Cutrone,	women's speed skating (ST)
	Sylvie Daigle,	3000m relay
	Nathalie Lambert, Annie Perreault	
1994	Myriam Bedard	biathlon 7.5km
	Myriam Bedard	biathlon 15km
	Jean-Luc Brassard	freestyle skiing moguls
1998	Ross Rebagliati	snowboarding giant slalom
	Catriona Le May Doan	speedskating (LT) 500m (OR)
	Sandra Schmirler,	women's curling
	Jan Betker, Joan McCusker,	
	Marcia Gudereit, Atina Ford	
	Pierre Lueders,	two-man bobsleigh
	Dave MacEachern	
	Annie Pereault	speedskating (ST) 500m
1998	Marc Gagnon,	men's speedskating (ST)
	Derrick Campbell,	5000m relay
	Francois Drolet, Eric Bedard	
2002	Jamie Sale, David Pelletier	figure skating pairs
	Catriona Le May Doan	speedskating (LT) 500m
	Marc Gagnon	speedskating (ST) 500m
	Marc Gagnon,	men's speedskating (ST)
	Eric Bedard,	5000m relay
	Francois-Louis Tremblay,	
	Jonathan Guilmette	
	Men's hockey	
	Women's hockey	
	Beckie Scott*	women's cross-country skiing pursuit
		*(upgraded from bronze)

Silver

Year	Name	Event/Sport
1932	Alex Hurd	men's speedskating 1500m
1936	Hockey - Port Arthur Bearcats	
1956	Frances Dafoe,	figure skating pairs
	Norris Bowden	
1960	Hockey - Kitchener-Waterloo Flying Dutchmen	

Year	Name	Event/Sport
1968	Nancy Greene	women's slalom skiing
1972	Karen Magnussen	women's figure skating
	Cathy Priestner	women's speedskating 500m
1980	Gaetan Boucher	men's speedskating 1000m
1984	Brian Orser	men's figure skating
1988	Brian Orser	men's figure skating
	Elizabeth Manley	women's figure skating
1992	Hockey - National Team	
	Frederic Blackburn	men's speed skating (ST) 1000m
	Frederic Blackburn,	men's speedskating (ST)
	Michel Daignault,	5000m relay
	Mark Lackie, Sylvain Gagnon	
1994	Elvis Stojko	figure skating men's
	Philippe Laroche	freestyle skiing aerials
	Nathalie Lambert	speed skating (ST) 1000m
	Christine Boudrias,	women's speedskating (ST)
	Isabelle Charest,	3000m relay
	Sylvie Daigle, Nathalie Lambert	
	Susan Auch	speedskating (LT) 500m
	Hockey - National team	
1998	Jeremy Wotherspoon	speedskating (LT) 500m
	Susan Auch	speedskating (LT) 500m
	Elvis Stojko	men's figure skating singles
	Mike Harris,	men's curling
	Richard Hart, Collin Mitchell,	
	George Karrys, Paul Savage	
	Women's hockey - National team	
2002	Kevin Martin,	men's curling
	Don Walchuk,	
	Carter Rycroft, Don Bartlett	
	Jonathan Guillmette	speedskating (LT) 500m
	Veronica Brenner	women's freestyle aerials

Bronze

Year	Name	Event/Sport
1932	Montgomery Wilson	men's singles figure skating
	Alex Hurd	men's 500m speedskating
	William Logan	men's 1500m speedskating
	William Logan	men's 5000m speedskating
	Frank Stack	men's 10,000m speedskating
1948	Suzanne Morrow,	figure skating - pairs
	Wally Diestelmeyer	
1952	Gordon Audley	men's 500m speedskating
1956	Lucile Wheeler	women's downhill skiing
	Hockey - Kitchener-Waterloo Flying Dutchmen	
1960	Donald Jackson	men's figure skating
1964	Debbi Wilkes, Guy Revell	figure skating - pairs
	Petra Burka	women's figure skating
1968	Hockey - National Team	
1976	Toller Cranston	men's figure skating
1980	Steve Podborski	men's downhill skiing
1984	Gaetan Boucher	men's 500m speedskating
1988	Karen Percy	women's downhill skiing
	Karen Percy	women's Super-G skiing
	Tracy Wilson, Rob McCall	figure skating - ice dance
1992	Myriam Bedard	15km biathlon
	Isabelle Brasseur,	figure skating - pairs
	Lloyd Eisler	

Year	Name	Event/Sport
1994	Edi Podivinsky	skiing downhill
	Isabelle Brasseur,	figure skating - pairs
	Lloyd Eisler	
	Lloyd Langlois	freestyle skiing aerials
	Marc Gagnon	speedskating (ST) 1000m
1998	Kevin Overland	speedskating (LT) 500m
	Eric Bedard	speedskating (ST) 1000m
	Christine Boudrias,	speedskating (ST)
	Isabelle Charest,	3000m relay
	Annie Perreault, Tania Vicent	
	Catriona Le May Doan	speedskating (LT) 1000m

Year	Name	Event/Sport
2002	Marc Gagnon	speedskating (LT) 1500m
	Kelly Law, Julie Skinner,	women's curling
	Georgina Wheatcraft,	
	Diane Nelson	
	Deidra Dionne	free style skiing aerials
	Cindy Klassen	speedskasting (LT) 3000m
	Clara Hughes	speedskating (LT) 5000m
	Mathieu Turcotte	speedskating (ST) 1000m
	Alana Kraus,	speedskating (ST)
	Marie-Eve Drolet,	3000m relay
	Amelie Goulet-Nadon, Isabelle Charest	

PAN AMERICAN GAMES MEDALLISTS

Gold

Year	Name	Event/Sport
1955	Helen Stewart	100m FS
	Beth Whittall	400m FS, 100m butterfly
	Leonore Fisher	100m backstroke
1959	Equestrian team 3-day event	
	Ernestine Russell	women's gymnastics all-around, vault, uneven bars, balance beam
1963	Don Bertoia	800m run
	Alex Oakley	20km walk
	Abby Hoffman	800m run
	Nancy McCredie	shot put, discus
	Tom Dinsley	men's springboard diving
	Willie Weiler	men's gymnastics all-around, floor, vault
	Men's coxed eights	
1967	Harry Jerome	100m sprint
	Andy Boychuk	marathon
	Nancy McCredie	shot put
	Marcel Roy	cycling road race
	Jim Day	equestrian individ. jumping
	Susan McDonnell	gymnastics uneven bars
	Michael Johnson	95kg judo
	Doug Rogers	open judo
	Alf Mayer	small-bore prone rifle
	Ralph Hutton	200m backstroke
	Elaine Tanner	100m, 200m backstroke
1971	Stephanie Berto	200m sprint
	Abby Hoffman	800m run
	Debbie Brill	high jump
	Brenda Eisler	long jump
	Debbie Van Kiekebelt	pentathlon
	Jocelyn Lovell	1,000m time trial
	Liz Carruthers	women's springboard
	Nancy Robertson	women's platform
	Christilot Hanson	individual dressage
	Equestrian team dressage	
	Equestrian team jumping	
	Equestrian team 3-day event	
	Donna-Marie Gurr	100m, 200m backstroke
	Sylvia Dockerill	100m breaststroke
	Leslie Cliff	200m, 400m IM
	Women's 4x100 medley relay	
1975	Bruce Pirnie	shot put

Year	Name	Event/Sport
	Joyce Yakubowich	400m run
	Marg MacGowan,	4x400m relay
	Joanne McTaggert,	
	Rachelle Campbell,	
	Joyce Yakubowich	
	Diane Jones	pentathlon
	Chris Clarke	lightweight boxing
	Jocelyn Lovell	cycling 1,000m time trial
	Janet Nutter	women's platform diving
	Christilot Boylen	equestrian individ. dressage
	Brad Farrow	65kg judo
	Wayne Erdman	71kg judo
	Rainer Fisher	86kg judo
	Four-oared shell with coxswain	
	Line Chenard	100m backstroke
	Russ Prior	weightlifting overall total, snatch, clean & jerk
	Egon Beiler	62kg FS wrestling
	Howard Stupp	62kg Greco-Roman wrestling
1979	Scott Nielson	hammer throw
	Diane Konihowski	pentathlon
	Bruce Simpson,	pole vault
	Gord Singleton,	1km time trial
	Gord Singleton	sprint
	Claude Langlois	4,000m industrial pursuit
	Monica Goermann,	women's team gymnastics
	Elfi Schlegel, Sherry Hawco,	
	Diana Carnegie, Ellen Stewart,	
	Carmen Alie	
	Monica Goermann	uneven bars, individual all-around
	Sherry Hawco	balance beam
	Brad Farrow	65kg judo
	Louis Jani	86kg judo
	Bruce Ford, Pat Walter	double sculls
	Brian Dick, Tim Storm	coxless pairs
	Guy Lorion	individual air rifle
	Tom Guinn, Ed Jans,	free pistol team
	Art Tomsett, Manley Wolochow	
	Men's softball team	
	Anne Gagnon	200m breaststroke
	Helen Vanderburg,	solo synchro swim

Year	Name	Event/Sport
	Helen Vanderburg, Kelly Kryczka	duet synchro swim
	Howard Stupp	68kg freestyle wrestling
	Doug Yeats	62kg Greco-Roman wrestling
	Terry Neilson	Laser yachting
1983	Dave Steen	decathlon
	Lazlo Babits	javelin
	Charmaine Crooks	400m
	Ranza Clark	1,500m
	Men's field hockey	
	Louis Jani	86kg judo
	Mark Berger	+95kg judo
	Phil Haggerty	double sculls
	Bob Mills	
	Phil Haggerty, Mel LaForme, Bob Mills, Greg Murphy	quadruple sculls
	Men's Softball team	
	Women's softball team	
	Anne Ottenbrite	100m breaststroke
	Kathy Bald	200m breaststroke
	Synchro Swim team	
	Guy Greavette	82.5kg weightlifting
	Ray Takahashi	52kg freestyle wrestling
	Jeff Stuebing	74kg Greco-Roman wrestling
	Gary Kallos	90kg Greco-Roman wrestling
1987	Jack Chubaty, Max Tracy	C2 1000m
	Curt Harnett	1km individual time trial
	Ian Millar	individual jumping
	Ian Millar, Lisa Carlsen, Laura Balisky, Hugh Graham	team jumping
	Christilot Boylen	individual dressage
	Diana Billes, Christilot Boylen, Eva-Marie Pracht, Martina Pracht	team dressage
	Jean-Paul Banos	individual sabre
	Men's field hockey team	
	Sandra Greaves	66kg judo
	Silken Laumann	single sculls
	Kirsten Barnes, Kathleen Heddle	coxless pairs
	Michele Murphy	lightweight single sculls
	John Murphy, Brian Thorne	lightweight double sculls
	Sharon Bowes	women's air rifle
	Pat Vamplew	prone free rifle
	Michael Ashcroft, J.F. Senecal, Pat Vamplew	free rifle team
	Guy Lorion	air rifle
	Mart Klepp, Guy Lorion, J.F. Senecal	air rifle team
	Men's softball team	
	Keltie Duggan	100m breaststroke
	Gideon Joe Ng	table tennis men's singles
	Horatio Pintea, Gideon Joe Ng	men's doubles
	Denis Garon	100kg total, snatch, c&j weightlifting

Year	Name	Event/Sport
	David Bolduc	110kg total, snatch, c&j weightlifting
	Doug Cox	90kg wrestling
	Bruce MacDonald, Ross MacDonald	Star yachting
1991	Corinna Kennedy	K1 500m
	Tessa Desouza, Corrina Kennedy	K2 500m
	Richard Young	cycling sprint
	Tanya Dubnicoff,	cycling sprint
	Lorraine Stubbs	dressage
	Ashley Munro, Lorraine Stubbs, Gina Smith, Leslie Reid	team dressage
	Danny Foster	individual jumping
	Mary Fuzesi	rhythmic gymnastics hoop
	Rhythmic gymnastics team	
	Ian Swan, Andrew Lamont, Dave Brown, Dave Miege, Bruce Boulter	men's coxed fours
	Nori Doobenen, Laurie Featherstone	lightweight double sculls
	Rod Colwell, John Rochon, Jean-Pierre Huot	free pistol team
	Sharon Cozzarin	women's air pistol
	George Leary, Curtis Wennberg, Ron Bonotto	trap team
	Guy Lorion, Mart Klepp, Michel Dion	team air rifle
	Men's softball team	
	Kristen Topham	50m FS, 100m butterfly
	Jae Hoon Lee	76kg taekwondo
	Jeff Eckard, Nigel Cochrane	470 yachting
	Lawrence Lemieux	Finn yachting
	Shona Moss	Laser yachting
1995	Rob Rusnov	men's 70m, 90m archery
	Glenroy Gilbert	100m sprint
	Jamie Dawson	badminton men's singles
	Anil Kaul, Iain Sydie	badminton men's doubles
	Sian Deng, Denyse Julien	badminton women's doubles
	Denyse Julien	badminton women's singles
	Denyse Julien, Darryl Yung	badminton mixed doubles
	Catharine Willis	women's bowling singles
	Sandra Lowe, Anne Saasto, Debbie Ship, Catharine Willis	women's bowling team
	Bill Rowe	men's bowling singles
	Cathy Breckenridge, Jessica Ferguson, Marie-Josee Gibeau, Danica Rice	K4 500m
	Danny Howe, Mike Oryschak	C2 500m
	Alison Sydor	women's mountain bike
	Tanya Dubnicoff	women's sprint
	Brian Walton	men's points race, road race
	Ewan Beaton	60kg judo
	Nicolas Gill	86kg judo

Year	Name	Event/Sport
	Keith Morgan	95kg judo
	Nicole Poirier	52kg kumite
	Silken Laumann	single sculls
	Marnie McBean,	double sculls
	Diane O'Grady	
	*Silken Laumann,	women's coxless fours
	Marnie McBean,	
	Diane O'Grady, Wendy Weibe	
	*stripped of medal due to inadvertent doping infraction	
	Alex Gyori	individual double trap
	Rod Boll, Alex Gyori,	double trap team
	Kirk Reynolds	
	Men's softball team	
	Heather Wallace	women's squash singles
	Heather Wallace,	squash women's team
	Anita Soni,	
	Kelsy Souchereau,	
	Melanie Jans	
	Gary Waite	squash men's singles
	Gary Waite,	squash men's team
	Jaimie Crombie, Sabir Butt,	
	Jonathon Power	
	Heather Wallace,	squash mixed
	Anita Soni,	grand champion
	Kelsy Souchereau, Melanie Jans,	
	Gary White, Jaimie Crombie,	
	Sabir Butt, Jonathon Power,	
	Annie Pelletier,	3m springboard
	Anne Montminy	10m platform
	Lisa Flood	100m breaststroke
	Joanne Malar	200m, 400m IM
	Curtis Myden	200m, 400m IM
	Lijuan Geng	table tennis women's singles
	Barbara Chiu, Lijuan Geng	table tennis women's doubles
	Lijuan Geng,	table tennis women's team
	Chris Ngo Xu,	
	Barbara Chiu, Petra Cada	
	Horatio Pintea,	table tennis mixed doubles
	Lijuan Geng	
	Kristie Otto, Fiona Cribb	triathlon women's team
	Jaret Llewellyn	water skiing men's tricks, jumps
	Jaret Llewellyn,	water skiing mixed team
	Kreg Llewellyn, Jim Clunie,	
	Drew Ross, Susi Graham,	
	Kim De Macedo	
	Caroll-Ann Alie	Mistral yachting
	Penny Davis,	women's 470 yachting
	Leigh Pearson	
1999	Jody Holden,	men's beach volleyball
	Conrad Leinemann	
	Alexander Jeltkov	horizontal bars
	Lise Leveille	balance beam
	Yvonne Tousek	floor exercises
	Yvonne Tousek	uneven bars
	Yvonne Tousek,	women's team
	Julie Beaulieu,	
	Michelle Conway,	
	Emilie Fournier,	
	Lise Leveille,	
	Kate Richardson	

Year	Name	Event/Sport
	Graham Hood	1500m
	Joel Bourgeois	3000m steeplechase
	Mark Boswell,	men's high jump
	Kwaku Boateng (tie)	
	Emilie Livingston	rhythmic gymnastics individual all-around
	Brent Olynyk, Iain Sydie	badminton men's doubles
	Robbyn Hermitage,	badminton women's doubles
	Milaine Cloutier	
	Iain Sydie, Denyse Julien	badminton women's doubles
	Stephen Giles	men's C1 1000m
	Karen Furneaux	women's K1 500m
	Carerie Lightbound,	women's K2 500m
	Marie-Josee Gibeau-Ouimet,	
	Karen Furneaux,	women's K4 500m
	Liza Racine,	
	Carrie Lightbound,	
	M-J Gibeau-Ouimet	
	Eric Wohlberg	men's ITT
	Brian Walton	men's road race
	Tanya Dubnicoff	women's sprint
	Tanya Dubnicoff	women's 500m time trial
	Emilie Heymans	women's 10m platform
	Eryn Bulmer	women's 3m springboard
	Ian Millar	individual station jump
	Michel Boulos,	men's sabre team
	Marc-Olivier Hassoun,	
	Evens Gravel	
	Richard Clarke	men's Finn class sailing
	Kelly Hand	women's Laser Radial sailing
	Oskar Johansson	singlehanded Sunfish sailing
	Derek Porter	men's single sculls
	Marnie McBean	women's single sculls
	Theresa Luke,	women's coxless pairs
	Emma Robinson	
	Larissa Biesenthal,	women's double sculls
	Jenna Browett	
	Guivi Sissaouri	58kg freestyle wrestling
	Maryse Turcotte	women's 58kg weightlifting
	Miel McGerrigle	women's 63kg weightlifting
	Andrew Ross	men's waterski slalom
	Jaret Llewellyn	men's waterski tricks
	Josee Marsolais,	women's water polo
	Johanne Begin,	
	Waneek Horn-Miller,	
	Kaliya Young, Ann Dow,	
	Melissa Collins,	
	Cora Campbell,	
	Marc-Luc Arpin,	
	Sandra Lize,	
	Lila Fraser,	
	Marie-Claude Deslieres	
	Sharon Donnelly	women's triathlon
	Roxanne Forget	women's 49kg taekwondo
	Shamek Pietucha	men's 200m butterfly
	Morgan Knabe	men's 200m breaststroke
	Curtis Myden	men's 200m IM
	Curtis Myden	men's 400m IM
	Jessica Deglau	women's 200m butterfly
	Laura Nicholls	women's 100m FS
	Jessica Deglau	200m FS

Year	Name	Event/Sport
	Lauren Van Oosten	200m breaststroke
	Joanne Malar	200m IM
	Joanne Malar	400m IM
	Kelly Stefanyshyn	women's 100m backstroke
	Sarah Evanetz,	women's 4x100 FS relay
	Jessica Deglau,	
	Laura Nicholls,	
	Marianne Limpert	
	Jessica Deglau,	women's 4x200 FS relay
	Joanne Malar,	
	Marianne Limpert,	
	Laura Nicholls	
	Jamie Crombie,	men's squash team
	Kelly Patrick,	
	Jonathon Power,	
	Graham Ryding	
	Graham Ryding	men's squash singles
	Marnie Baizley,	women's squash team
	Melanie Jans,	
	Kelly Souchereau,	
	Carolyn Russell	
	Melanie Jans	women's squash singles
	Colin Abbott,	men's softball
	Kevin Bobroskie, Craig Crawford,	
	Randy Peck, Todd Martin,	
	Paul Rosebush, Adam Smith,	
	Doug Chase, Jody Hennigar,	
	Chris Jones, Todd King,	
	Michael Piechnik, Steve Price,	
	Brian Paton, Darren Zack	
	Kim Eagles	women's air pistol
	Robert Bird, Chris Gifford,	men's field hockey
	Hari Kant, Bindi Kullar,	
	Ken Pereira, Richard Roberts,	
	Paul Wettlaufer, Sean Campbell,	
	Andrew Griffiths, Singh Jagday,	
	Scott Mosher, Robert Short,	
	Alan Brahmst, Robin D'Abreo,	
	Mike Mahood, Peter Milkovich	
	Nicholas Gill	men's 100kg judo
	Claire Carver-Dias,	synchro swim duet
	Fanny Letourneau	
	Lyne Beaumont,	synchro swim team
	Jessica Chase, Valerie Hould-Marchand,	
	Kirstin Normand, Jacinthe Taillon,	
	Reidun Tatham, Lesley Wright	
	*Men's in-line roller hockey team.	
	stripped of medal when goaler Steve Vezina fails drug test.	
2003	Philippe Comtois	3m, 10m synchronized diving
	Alexandre Despatie	3m springboard, 3m, 10m synchronized diving
	Blythe Hartley	3m springboard, 3m synchronized diving
	Emilie Heymans	10m plat6form, 3m, 10m synchronized diving
	Marie-Eve Marleau	10m synchronized diving
	Audrey Lacroix,	200m butterfly
	Joanne Malar-Morreale	200m IM
	Brandon O'Neill	artistic gymnastics floor
	Alice Falaiye	women's long jump
	Eric Forshaw	men's discus

Year	Name	Event/Sport
	Achraf Tadili	men's 800m
	Mike Beres	badminton men's singles
	Philippe Bourret, Denyse Julien	badminton mixed doubles
	Helen Nichol, Charmaine Reid	badminton women's doubles
	Jen Adamson, Jill D'Alessio, Emilie Fournel, Victoria Tuttle	women's K4 500m
	Clara Hughes	women's cycling points race
	Leslie Reid	individual dressage
	Gen Meredith, Fiona Milne	women's lightweight double sculls
	Stacey Norwood, Marilyn Taylor	women's double sculls
	Terry Challis, Bob Court, Craig Crawford, Mike Crawford, Trevor Ethier, Rob Giesbrecht, Gary Hermsen, Darryl Joy, Daniel Loney, Keith Mackintosh, Tim Macumber, Evan Potskin, Jeff Seed, Rick Smith, Harvey Stevenson Jr., Nick Underhill, Ron White, Sean Whitten	men's softball team
	Viktor Berg, Graham Ryding, Shahier Razik	men's squash team
	Shahier Razik	men's squash singles
	Jill Savege	women's triathlon
	Jaret Llewellyn	men's water ski tricks
	Drew Ross	men's water ski slalom
	Karissa Wedd	women's water ski jump

Silver

Year	Name	Event/Sport
1955	George Park	100m FS swim
	4x200m FS men's relay	
	4x100m FS women's relay	
	4x100m women's medley relay	
	Synchro swim team	
1959	Doug Kyle	10,000m run
	Alice Whitty	women's high jump
	Men's gymnastic team	
	Richard Montpetit	gymnastics pommel horse, vault
	Nino Marion, Women's gymnastics team	gymnastics rope climbing
	Ernestine Russell	gymnastics floor exercises
	Tony Biernacki, Rowing men's coxed eights	rowing skiff
	Gerry Ouelette Men's 4x100m medley relay	small-bore rifle 3-positions
	Sara Barber Women's 4x100 FS, medley relays	100m backstroke
	Bob Bedard	men's tennis singles
	Bruno Ochman	73kg FS wrestling
	Rod Carrow	87kg FS wrestling
	Keith Maltman	+87kg FS wrestling
	Melville Gould	5.5 Metre yachting
	Angus MacDonald	Flying Dutchman yachting
1963	Sigmar Ohlemann	800m run
	Nicola Marrone	20km walk
	Bill Gairdner	decathlon

Year	Name	Event/Sport
	Jenny Wingerson	80m hurdles
	Dianne Gerace	high jump
	Judy Stewart	women's springboard
	Gymnastics	men's & women's teams
	Willie Weiler	pommel horse, parallel bars, high bar
	Dorothy Haworth	balance beam
	Susan McDonnell	floor exercises
	Men's smallbor	rifle 3-position, centre-fire pistol, free pistol teams
	Garfield McMahon	free pistol individual
	John Gilchrist	1500m FS
	Men's 4x200m FS relay team	
	Mary Stewart	100m FS, butterfly
	Women's 4x100m FS, medley relays	
	Bob Steckle	87kg FS wrestling
	Sam MacDonald	Dragon yachting
1967	Bill Crothers	800m
	Felix Capella	50km walk
	Ross MacKenzie,	4x400m relay
	Brian MacLaren,	
	Bob MacLaren, Bill Crothers	
	Bob Raftis	pole vault
	Janet Maddin,	4x100m relay
	Judy Dallimore,	
	Jenny Meldrum,	
	Irene Piotrowski	
	Sue Nigh	high jump
	Carol Martin	discus
	Jenny Meldrum	pentathlon
	Bev Boys	platform diving
	Equestrian	team jumping
	Norm Elder	individual equestrian 3-day event
	Women's gymnastics team	
	Pat Bolger	65kg judo
	Doug Rogers	95+kg judo
	Double sculls rowing	
	Men's coxless pairs rowing	
	Men's coxless fours rowing	
	Men's coxed 8's rowing	
	Men's small-bore rifle prone, 3-position, centre-fire pistol teams	
	Gerry Ouellette	small-bore 3-position rifle individual
	Ralph Hutton	200, 400, 1500m FS
	Toomas Arusoo	200m butterfly
	Men's 4x100,4x200m FS, 4x100m medley relays	
	Marion Lay	100m, 200m FS
	Elaine Tanner	100m butterfly
	Women's 4x100FS, medley relays	
	Paul Bjarnson	middle heavyweight weightlifting
	Ray Loughead	70kg FS wrestling
	Bob Chambreault	97+kg FS wrestling
1971	Bill Smart	3000m run
	Wilf Wedmann	high jump
	Stephanie Berto,	100m sprint
	Penny May	pentathlon
	Bev Boys	platform diving
	Clint Bambury	individual equestrian 3-day event

Year	Name	Event/Sport
	Gil Boa	small-bore rifle prone position
	Men's centre-fire pistol team	
	Men's 4x100, 200 FS, 4x100 medley relays	
	Angela Coughlan	100m, 200m FS
	Jan Wright	200m backstroke
	Leslie Cliff	100m butterfly
	Women's 4x100m FS relay	
	Jojo Carrier	synchro swim solo
	Jojo Carrier, Mado Ramsey	synchro swim duet
	Synchro swim team	
1975	John Beers	high jump
	Bruce Simpson	pole vault
	Bishop Dolegiewcz	shot put
	Patti Loverock	100m sprint
	Abby Hoffman	800m run
	Thelma Wright	1500m run
	Louise Walker	high jump
	Michael Prevost	light middleweight boxing
	Liz Carruthers	springboard diving
	Equestrian dressage team	
	Equestrian 3-day event team	
	Donna Hennyey,	women's foil team
	Fleurette Leblanc,	
	Susan Stewart, Chantal Gilbert	
	Men's field hockey team	
	Men's coxed pairs rowing	
	Men's free pistol team	
	Jules Sobrian	rapid-fire pistol
	Men's trap team	
	Mike Scarth	200m backstroke
	Dave Heinbuch	200m breaststroke
	Men's 4x100	4x200 FS, 4x100 medley relays
	Gail Amundrud	200m FS
	Line Chenard	200m backstroke
	Joann Baker	200m breaststroke
	Cheryl Gibson	200m butterfly, 400m IM
	Women's 4x100m FS, medley relays	
	Sylvie Fortier	synchro swim solo
	Carol Stuart, Laura Wilkin	synchro swim duet
	Synchro swim team	
	Clive Llewellyn	68kg FS wrestling
	Richard Deschatelets	82kg FS wrestling
	Jamie Kidd	Flying Dutchman yachting
1979	Stan Siatkowski,	men's archery team
	Daniel Desnoyers,	
	Chris Smith	
	Joan McDonald,	women's archery team
	Linda Kazienko,	
	Marie-Claude Pitre	
	Bishop Dolegiewicz	shot put
	Angella Taylor	300m
	Sharon Lane	100m hurdles
	Ian Millar, Terry Leibel,	team grand prix jumping
	John Simpson,	
	MichelVaillancourt	
	Jacynthe Poirier,	women's foil team
	Louise LeBlanc,	
	Patricia Balz, Chantal Payer	
	Men's field hockey team	

Year	Name	Event/Sport	Year	Name	Event/Sport
	Warren Long,	men's gymnastics team		Andrea Page, Gwen Wall,	4x400m relay
	Jean Choquette,			Christine Slythe,	
	Marc Epprecht,			Jillian Richardson	
	Nigel Rothwell,			Jim Elder	individual jumping
	Pierre Clavel,			Ian Millar, Hugh Graham,	jumping team
	Andre Vallerand			Jim Elder, Torchy Millar	
	Warren Long	floor exercises, vault		J.M. Chouinard	individual épée
	Elfi Schlegel	vault		J.M. Chouinard,	team épée
	Kevin Doherty	71kg judo		Daniel Perreault,	
	Phil Monckton	rowing single sculls		Jacques Cardyn,	
	Robert Cherwinski,	coxed fours		Alain Cote,	
	Mel LaForme, Doug Turton,			Michel Dessureault	
	Carl Zintel, Miles Cohen			Fred Blaney	open judo
	Rowing coxed eights			Mandy Clayton	52kg judo
	Hans Adlhoch,	3-positions rifle team		Lorraine Methot	66kg judo
	Guy Lorion,			Nancy Jewitt	72kg judo
	Alfons Mayer,			Mel LaForme	single sculls
	Arne Sorensen			Marie-Claude Gaudet,	double sculls
	Ed Jans, Steve Kelly,	centre-fire team		Heather Hattin	
	Jules Sobrian,			Joelle Fefer, Jackie Terry,	air rifle team
	Robert Zimmer			Christina Schulze	
	Joanne Bedard	200m breaststroke		Guy Lorion, Alfons Mayer,	air rifle team
	Nancy Garapick	200m IM		J.F. Senecal	
	Gail Amundrud,	400m medley relay		Michel Dion, Glen Hewitt,	English match 50m team
	Anne Gagnon,			Pat Vamplew	
	Nancy Garapick,			J.F. Senecal, Glen Hewitt,	English match 300m team
	Cheryl Gibson			Pat Vamplew	
	Gail Amundrud,	400m FS relay		Michel Dion, J.F. Senecal,	free rifle 300m team
	Anne Gagnon,			Pat Vamplew	
	Carol Klimpel,			Joelle Fefer, Jackie Terry	standard rifle team
	Wendy Quirk			Christina Schulze	
	Cheryl Gibson	100m, 200m backstroke		Linda Thom	match pistol
	Dan Thompson	100m butterfly		Mike West,	4x100 medley relay
	George Nagy	200m butterfly		Marco Veilleux,	
	Graham Smith	200m IM		Tom Ponting,	
	Bill Sawchuk	400m IM		Dave Churchill	
	Stephen Pickell,	4x100m medley relay		Jane Kerr	100m FS
	Graham Smith,			Kathy Bald	100m breaststroke
	Peter Szmidt,			Michelle Macpherson	100m butterfly, 200m IM
	Dan Thompson			Carol Klimpel, Kathy Bald,	4x199m FS relay
	Bill Sawchuk,	4x100m FS relay		Pam Rai, Jane Kerr	
	Peter Szmidt,			Barbara McBain,	4x100m medley relay
	Dan Thompson,			Anne Ottenbrite,	
	Graham Welbourn			Michelle Macpherson,	
	Synchro Swim team			Jane Kerr	
	Nicole Marois,	tennis women's doubles		Penny Vilagos,	synchro swim duet
	Helene Pelletier			Vicky Vilagos	
	Eric Rogers	75kg weightlifting		Sharon Hambrook	synchro swim solo
	Terry Hadlow	90kg weightlifting		Alain Bourbonnais,	table tennis men's team
	Marc Cardinal	super heavyweight weightlifting		Gideon-Joe Ng,	
				Horatio Pintea	
	Clark Davis	82kg wrestling		Mariann Domonkos,	table tennis mixed doubles
	Gordon Crothers,	Lightning yachting		Horatio Pintea	
	Peter Jones, Gil Mercier			Jacques Demers	76kg weightlifting
1983	Daniel Desnoyers,	men's archery team		Mario Parente	90kg weightlifting
	Roger Lemay, Eric Amos			Kevin Roy	110kg weightlifting
	Linda Kazienko,	women's archery team		Richard Deschatelets	100kg FS wrestling
	Lucille Lemay,			Louis Santerre	82kg Greco-Roman wrestling
	Roberta Barker				
	Harold Willers	hammer		Andy Roy	Laser yachting
	Ranza Clark	800m		Gord Anderson,	Soling yachting

Year	Name	Event/Sport
	Bill Abbott Jr.,	J-24 yachting
	Larry Abbott, Gord Crothers,	
	Peter Candish, Harry Jemmett,	
	Peter Jones, David Roy	
1987	Denis Canuel	archery individual men
	Ann Peel,	10,000m walk
	Connie Polman-Tuin	heptathlon
	Charmaine Crooks,	4x400m relay
	Molly Killingbeck,	
	Marita Payne,	
	Jillian Richardson	
	Nancy Tinari	10,000m
	Angela Chalmers	3,000m
	Debbie Bowker	1,500m
	Jillian Richardson	400m
	Otis Grant	75kg boxing
	Lennox Lewis	+91kg boxing
	Stephen Wasteneys	C1 500m
	Jack Chubaty, Max Tracy	C2 500m
	Erika Revesz	K1 500m
	Louise Hine,	K2 500m
	Cindy Leonard	
	Erica Revesz,	K4 500m
	Cindy Leonard,	
	Louise Hine,	
	Alexandra Rubinger	
	Kelly Carter	women's individual pursuit
	Wendy Fuller	women's 10m platform
	Martina Pracht	individual dressage
	Phil Desourdy,	3-day event
	Stuart Black, Moira Tone,	
	James Smart	
	Madeleine Philion	individual foil
	Stephen Angers,	team foil
	Benoit Giasson,	
	Luc Rocheleau,	
	Dan Nowosielski	
	Women's handball team	
	Joe Meli	95kg judo
	Alison Webb	72kg judo
	Barry Kennedy	modern pentathlon
	Mary Fuzesi	rhythmic gymnastics, clubs
	Siobhan Herron,	double scull
	Marlene Van Der Horst	
	Diane Sinnige,	lightweight coxless pairs
	Karen Smyte	
	Darcel Berkhout,	coxless pairs
	Jamie Schaffer	
	Chris Flood,	lightweight coxless pairs
	Wayne MacFarlane	
	Jean-Francois Senecal	free rifle prone
	Mart Klepp	free rifle 3-position individual
	Mart Klepp, Guy Lorion,	free rifle 3-position team
	J.F. Senecal	
	John Primrose, Paul Shaw,	trap team
	Fred White	
	Denise Gereghty,	4x100m FS relay
	Cheryl McArton,	
	Robin Ruggiero,	
	Manon Simard	
	Keltie Duggan,	4x100m medley relay
	Cheryl McArton,	
	Robin Ruggiero,	
	Manon Simard	
	Brad Creelman,	4x100m FSS relay
	Claude Lamy,	
	Gary Vandermeulen,	
	Darren Ward	
	Chris Chalmers,	4x200m FS relay
	Mike Meldrum,	
	Gary Vandermeulen,	
	Darren Ward	
	Ray Brown, Claude Lamy,	4x100m medley relay
	Darcy Wallingford,	
	Darren Ward	
	Sylvie Frechette	synchro swim solo
	Karen Fonteyne,	synchro swim duet
	Karen Sribney	
	Synchro swim team	
	Mariann Domonkos	table tennis women's singles
	Mariann Domonkos,	table tennis women's doubles
	Thanh Mach	
	Ray Mourad	taekwondo 54-58kg
	Ferrere Clerveaux	taekwondo 76-83kg
	Paramjit Gill	90kg total, snatch, c&j weightlifting
	Langis Cote	52kg snatch weightlifting
	Robert Dawson	57kg wrestling
	Joe Domarchuck	62kg wrestling
	Lou Kok	82kg wrestling
	Steve Calder, Hans Fogh,	Soling yachting
	Mark Lammens	
	Alain Boucher, Peter Hall,	Lightning yachting
	Scott Morgan	
	Caroll-Ann Alie	women's sailboard
1991	Everton Anderson,	4x100m relay
	Mike Dwyer,	
	Oral O'Gilvie,	
	Donovan Bailey	
	Doug Wood	pole vault
	Lisa Harvey	10,000m
	Greg Johnson	67kg boxing
	Chris Johnson	75kg boxing
	Paul Pageau	C1 500m, 1000m
	Scott Kerrigan,	K4 500m
	Jason Moffat,	
	Jeff Allbon,	
	Ashley McColgan	
	Tessa Desouza,	K4 500m
	Corrina Kennedy,	
	Lucy Slade,	
	Leslie-Ann Young	
	Clara Hughes	3,000m pursuit
	Paige Gordon	3m springboard diving
	Ashley Munro	individual dressage
	Beth Underhill	individual jumping
	Beth Underhill,	team jumping
	Sandra Anderson,	
	Danny Foster, Ian Millar	
	Men's field hockey team	
	Women's field hockey team	
	Mylene Fleury	gymnastics uneven bars
	Ewan Beaton	60kg judo

Year	Name	Event/Sport
	Jean Cantin	65kg judo
	Mary Fuzesi	rhythmic gymnastics all-around, rope, balls
	Stephen Frisch, Mike Forgeron	lightweight double sculls
	Dave Dickison, Don Dickison	double sculls
	Shannon Crawford, Julie Jesperson	double sculls
	Sharon Cozzarin, Claudine Tanguay, Helen Smith	team air pistol
	Christina Ashcroft	standard rifle
	Sharon Bowes, Christina Ashcroft, Therese Lander	team air rifle
	George Leary	open trap
	Women's softball team	
	Reggie Lacoursiere, Ron Page, Stephen Clarke, Steven Vander Meulen	4x100m FS relay
	Chantal Dubois	200m breaststroke
	Nikki Dryden	100m, 200m backstroke
	Joanne Malar	200m, 400m IM
	Sharon Turner, Kristin Topham, Joanne Malar, Kim Paton	4x100m FS relay
	Kim Paton, Joanne Malar, Nikki Dryden, Tara Seymour	4x200m FS relay
	Synchro Swim team	
	Gideon Joe Ng, Horatio Pintea	table tennis men's doubles
	Stephen Goodwin	64kg taekwondo
	John Matile	100kg wrestling
	Andy Borodow	130kg wrestling
	Edithe Trepanier	women's sailboard
	Alison Keagan,	artistic roller skating women's singles
	Heather Paterson, Jaime Crouch	artistic roller skating dance
1995	Jeannot Robitaille	men's 90m archery
	Sarah Howell	1500m run
	Carol Montgomery	10,000m run
	Donalda Duprey	100m hurdles
	Sian Deng	badminton women's singles
	Milaine Cloutier, Robbyn Hermitage	badminton women's doubles
	Iain Sydie	badminton men's singles
	Anil Kaul, Sian Deng	badminton mixed doubles
	Jean-Francois Bergeron	91+kg boxing
	Marie-Josee Gibeau, Kelly O'Leary	K2 500m
	Attila Buday	C1 500m
	Tamas Buday, Attila Buday	C2 1000m
	Emmanuel Auger	K1 500m
	Clara Hughes	cycling road race
	Annie Pelletier	1m springboard
	Men's field hockey team	
	Women's handball team	
	Carolyne Lepage	48kg judo

Year	Name	Event/Sport
	Michelle Buckingham	61kg judo
	Vicki Shanks, Debbie Ward	racquetball women's doubles
	Women's, men's racquetball teams	
	Jacques Demers, Chris Brumwell	racquetball men's doubles
	Sally Green, Keith Hickman	roller skating mixed dance
	Wendy Wiebe	women's lightweight single sculls
	Jeff Lay, Rob Fontaine	men's lightweight double sculls
	Greg Stevenson, Ken Kozel, Adam Parfitt, Phil Graham	men's coxless fours
	Jay Bertagnolli, Scott Brodie, Pat Bryden, Henry Hering, Mark Platt	men's coxed fours
	Chris Davidson, Rob Fontaine, Geoff Johns, Jeff Lay	lightweight coxless fours
	Men's coxed eights	
	Sharon Bowes	50m standard rifle
	Jean-Francois Senecal	10m air rifle
	Michel Dion, J.F. Senecal, Wayne Sorensen	10m air rifle team
	Kirk Reynolds	men's double trap
	Sue Nattrass	women's double trap
	George Leary, John Primrose, Paul Shaw	men's trap team
	Jason Caswell, Don Kwanycia, Derrick Nixon	skeet team
	Jonathan Power	squash men's individual
	Shannon Shakespeare	50m FS
	Marianne Limpert	200m FS, IM
	Guylaine Cloutier	100m, 200m breaststroke
	Shannon Shakespeare, Katie Brambley, Joanne Malar, Marianne Limpert	4x100, 4x200 FS relays
	Joanne Malar, Shannon Shakespeare, Lisa Flood, Marianne Limpert	4x100 medley relay
	Jon Cleveland	100m breaststroke
	Karen Clark	synchro swim solo
	Lisa Alexander, Erin Woodley	synchro swim duet
	Synchro swim team	
	Roxanne Forget	51kg taekwondo
	Kristie Otto	individual women's triathlon
	Mark Bates	individual men's triathlon
	Susi Graham	women's waterski slalom
	Kim De Macedo	women's waterski tricks, jumps
	Kreg Llewellyn	men's waterski slalom
	Paul Ragusa	48kg FS wrestling
	Rob Dawson	57kg FS wrestling

Year	Name	Event/Sport
	Craig Roberts	68kg FS wrestling
	David Hohl	74kg FS wrestling
1999	Donovan Bailey,	4x100m relay
	Trevino Betty,	
	Brad McCuaig,	
	Glenroy Gilbert	
	Leah Pells	1500m
	Alexander Jeltkov	men's individual all-around
	Michelle Comway	women's floor exercises
	Michelle Conway	women's individual all-around
	Julie Beaulieu	women's uneven bars
	Arthur Stuart	men's badminton singles
	Charmaine Reid,	women's badminton doubles
	Denyse Julien	
	Charmaine Reid	women's singles
	Brent Olynyk,	mixed badminton doubles
	Robbyn Herimitage	
	Michelle Hendry,	women's basketball
	Tammy Sutton-Brown,	
	Joby McKenzie, Kelly Boucher,	
	Dianne Norman, Cynthia Johnston,	
	Teresa Kleindienst, Elizabeth Hart,	
	Nikki Johnson, Stacey Dales,	
	Cal Bouchard	
	Stephen Giles	C1 500m
	Tamas Buday Jr.,	C2 1000m
	Attila Buday	
	Maxime Boilard,	C2 500m
	Howard Pellerin	
	Dominique Boivin,	women's team handball
	Julie Hebert, Debra Dyckow,	
	Nadia Lefebre, Julie Brisebois,	
	Fabienne Raphael, Nancy Karpinsky,	
	Mirjana Jurcic, Marie-Claude Gibeau,	
	Martine Gagnon, Carole Cote,	
	Amelie Champagne, Nathalie Brochu	
	Nichole Jenkins	78kg women's judo
	Wayne Sorensen	men's prone free rifle
	Sharon Bowes	women's air rifle
	Denise Carriere,	women's softball
	Stacey Fertile, Nathalie Fradette,	
	Cherene Hiesl, Katherine Iggulden,	
	Sandra Newsham, Jackilee Nichol,	
	Colleen Smith, Carmelina Vairo,	
	Sommer West, Meaggan Wilton,	
	Erin Woods, Jackie Lance,	
	Vicky Bastarache, Christine Parris-Washington	
	Shamek Pietucha	men's 100m butterfly
	Morgan Knabe	men's 100m breaststroke
	Jessica Deglau	women's 100m butterfly
	Jennifer Button	women's 200m butterfly
	Lauren Van Oosten,	women's 4x100 medley relay
	Jessica Deglau,	
	Kelly Stefanyshyn,	
	Laura Nicholls	
	Barbara Pak,	67kg taekwondo
	Jaret Llewellyn	water ski men's tricks
	Kreg Lewellyn	water ski men's slalom
	Susan Graham	water ski women's slalom
	Nancy Niro	58kg women's weightlifting
	Paul Ragusa	54kg FS wrestling

Year	Name	Event/Sport
	Gary Holmes	85kg FS wrestling
	Kyle Warrington,	men's rowing lightweight doubles
	Andrew Borden	
	Tracy Duncan	women's rowing lightweight single sculls
	Caroll-Ann Alie	women's Mistral sailing
	Heather Landymore,	women's team épée
	Sherraine Schalm,	
	Monique Kavelaars	
	Shannon Oldham-Dueck	individual dressage
	Blythe Hartley	women's 10m diving
	Gord Fraser	men's road race
	Alison Sydor	women's mountain bike
	Lyne Bessette	women's ITT
	Chris Xu, Petra Cada,	women's table tennis team
	Lijuan Geng	
	Lijuan Geng	women's singles
	Mathieu Chouinard,	men's 10-pin bowling team
	Jean-Sebastien Lessard,	
	Alan Tone, Marc Doi	
	Roger Harripersad,	men's racquetball doubles
	Kelly Kerr	
	Lori-Jane Powell,	women's racquetball doubles
	Deborah Ward	
	Christie Van Hees	women's racquetball singles
	Zayas Younan	57kg boxing
	Dana Laframboise	60kg boxing
	Jeremy Molitor	67kg boxing
	Scott MacIntosh	71kg boxing
	Mark Simmons	91kg boxing
	Shawn Riggs,	men's team archery
	Robert Rusnov,	
	David Dalziel	
2003	Emelie Heymans	3m springboard
	Lisa Blackburn	200m breaststroke
	Elizabeth Collins	4x100 medley relay, 4x100 FS relay
	Kelly Doody	4x100 FS relay
	Audrey Lacroix	100m butterfly, 4x100 medley relay, 4x100 FS relay
	Joanne Malar-Morreale	4x100 medley relay, 4x100 FS relay
	Kathleen Stoody	4x100 medley relay
	Lindsay Cargill,	synchro swim team
	Amy Caskey,	
	Erin Chan, Jessica Chase,	
	Marie-Pierre Gagne, Lynn Johnson,	
	Fanny Letourneau, Shayna Nackoney,	
	Courtenay Stewart	
	Fanny Letourneau,	synchro swim duet
	Courtenay Stewart	
	Marie-Luc Arpin,	women's water polo team
	Christi Bardecki, Johanne Begin,	
	Cora Campbell, Melissa Collins,	
	Andrea Dewar, Valerie Dionne,	
	Ann Dow, Sue Gardiner,	
	Marianne Illing, Whynter Lamarre,	
	Rachel Riddell, Jana Salat	

Year	Name	Event/Sport
	Mel Banville, Gael Mackie, Heather Purnell, Richelle Simpson, Kylie Stone, Lydia Williams	women's artistic gymnastics team
	Joel Bourgeois	3,000m steeplechase
	Bruce Deacon	men's marathon
	Perdita Felicien	women's 100m hurdles
	Nicole Haynes	women's heptathlon
	Mike Beres, Jody Patrick	badminton mixed doubles
	Andrew Dabeka	badminton men's singles
	Denyse Julien, Anna Rice	badminton women's doubles
	Anna Rice	badminton women's singles
	Danyck Briere, George Lambert IV	men's bowling doubles
	Jill D'Alessio, Emilie Fournel	women's K2 500m
	Scott Dickey	men's C1 500m
	Clara Hughes	women's individual road time trial
	Jacqueline Brooks, Ashley Holzer, Leslie Reid, Evi Strasser	team dressage
	Sherraine Mackay	women's individual épée
	Robin D'Abreo, Steve Davis,Ranjeev Deol, Wayne Fernandes, Ronnie Jagday, Dave Jameson, Ravi Kahlon, Michael Lee, Jon Mackinnon, Mike Mahood, Mike Oliver, Ken Pereira, Scott Sandison, Peter Short, Rob Short, Paul Wettlaufer	men's field hockey
	Josee Belanger, Lisa Collison, Linda Consolante, Tanya Dennia, Robyn Gayle, Kelly Haxton, Selenia Iachelli, Kathleen Johnston, Kristina Kiss, Steph Labbe, Justine Labrecque, Holly Lincoln, Veronique Maranda, Katie Radchuck, Leah Robinson, Taryn Swiatek, Katie Thorlakson, Rhian Wilkinson	women's soccer team
	Nicolas Gill	men's judo 100kg
	Carolyne Lepage	women's judo 48kg
	Keith Morgan	men's judo 90kg
	Saeed Baghbani	men's karate kumite 68kg
	Btissama Essadiqi	men's karate kumite 58kg
	Mike Green	men's racquetball singles
	Roxy Cervantes, Ira Funtikova, Pam Jewell Emilie Livingstone, Sarah Stock, Alex Orlando	women's rhythmic gymnastics group all-around
	Alex Orlando	rhythmic gymnastics club, hoop, ribbon
	Jay Allan, Hugo Belanger, Bill Boyes, Jamie Cooke, Ben Frank, Victor Gervais, Scott Humphrey, Brett Leggat, Brent Thurston, Mark Woolf, Neil Armour,	men's in-line hockey team
	Iain Brambell, Kevin Burt, Chris Davidson, Geoff Hodgson, David Kay, Mike Lewis, Michael Simonson, Dallas Smith	men's eights with cox
	Gen Meredith	women's lightweight single sculls

Year	Name	Event/Sport
	Fiona Milne	women's single sculls
	Bernard Luttmer	men's laser sailing
	Keamia Rasa	women's laser radial
	Dominique Vallee	women's sailboard mistral
	Cynthia Meyer	women's trap, double trap shooting
	Alison Bradley, Erin Cumpstone, Cindy Eadie, Melissa Finley, Kaila Holtz, Tamara Howren, Sheena Lawrick, Angela Lichty, Kristy Odamura, Sasha Olson, Tiffany Patteson, Shannon Rossiter, Kim Sarrazin, Rachel Schill, Auburn Sigurdson, Erin White, Meaggan Wilton, Kelly Zeilstra,	women's softball team
	Marnie Baizley, Melanie Jans, Carolyn Russell,	squash women's team
	Melanie Jans	squash women's singles
	Graham Ryding	squash men's singles
	Jaret Llewellyn	water ski men's jump
	Ohenewa Akuffo	women's FS wrestling 72kg
	Lindsay Belisle,	women's FS wrestling 48kg
	Tonya Verbeek	women's FS wrestling 55kg
	Viola Yanik	women's FS wrestling 63kg
	Carl Rainville	men's FS wrestling 84kg
	Gia Sissaouri	men's FS wrestling 60kg

Bronze

Year	Name	Event/Sport
1955	Virginia Grant	100m FS
	Diane Baker, Bev McKnight	synchro swim duet
1959	Doug Kyle	5000m run
	Gord Dickson	marathon
	George Stulac	decathlon
	Sally McCallum	200m sprint
	Marian Munroe	80m hurdles
	Heather Campbell, Maureen Rever, Sally McCallum, Valerie Jerome	4x100 relay
	Ignaz Lindmoser	light heavyweight boxing
	Norm Elder	equestrian individual 3-day event
	John Andru, Jack Dalton, Bob Foxcroft, Carl Schwende	men's team foil
	John Andru, Joseph Vidz, Paul Szabolcsy, Carl Schwende	men's team sabre
	Nino Marion	men's gymnastics rings
	Richard Montpetit	men's gymnastics rope climbing
	Marie-Claire Larsen	women's all-around gymnastics, uneven bars
	Louise Parker	gymnastics vault
	Men's small-bore rifle	prone position, 3-position, free pistol teams
	Garfield McMahon	centre-fire pistol
	Barney Hartman	skeet

Year	Name	Event/Sport
	Men's 4x200m FS relay	
	Ralph Caspenson	62kg FS wrestling
	Arnold Massey	Dragon yachting
1963	Don Bertoia,	1500m run
	Noreen Deulina	800m run
	Richard Montpetit	gymnastics pommel horse
	Willie Weiler	gymnastics rings
	Gail Daley	gymnastics balance beam
	Clint Dahlstrom	free rifle
	Garfield McMahon	centre-fire pistol
	Barney Hartman	individual skeet
	Men's skeet shooting team	
	Dan Sherry	100m FS
	John Gilchrist	400m FS
	Ralph Hutton	1500m FS
	John Kelso	200m breaststroke
	Men's 4x100 medley relay	
	Lynne Pomfret	200m, 400m FS
	Eileen Weir	100m backstroke
	Marjon Wilmink	200m breaststroke
	Sandra Marks	synchro swim solo
	Marilyn Malenfant,	synchro swim duet
	Sandra Marks	
	Pierre Saint-Jean	middleweight weightlifting
	Michel Lipari	light heavyweight weightlifting
	John Lewis	middle heavyweight weightlifting
	Ernest Chomomydz	57kg FS wrestling
	Kurt Boese	70kg FS wrestling
	Anton Zegers	Flying Dutchman yachting
1967	Don Domansky	400m run
	Brian MacLaren	800m run
	Dave Bailey	1500m run
	Dave Ellis	10,000m run
	Bob MacLaren	400m hurdles
	Felix Capella	20km walk
	Robert Yard	pole vault
	Dave Steen	shot put
	George Puce	discus
	Irene Piotrowski	100m run
	Abby Hoffman	800m run
	Maureen Dowds	shot put
	Jane Dahlgren	javelin
	Women's basketball team	
	Walter Henry	flyweight boxing
	Donato Paduano	light middleweight boxing
	Morigan Kholar,	light heavyweight boxing
	Kathy McDonald	springboard divingg
	Equestrian dressage team	
	Les Samek	individual men's sabre
	Men's sabre team	
	Pacita Wiedel	individual women's foil
	Women's foil team	
	Roger Dion	gymnastics men's vault
	Gordon Battle	86kg judo
	Jules Sobrian	centre-fire pistol
	Sandy Gilchrist	100m FS, 200m, 400m IM
	Jim Shaw	100m backstroke
	Angela Coughlan	200m, 400m, 800m FS
	Shirley Cazalet	100m backstroke
	Marilyn Corson	100m, 200m butterfly, 400m IM

Year	Name	Event/Sport
	Sandra Dowler	200m IM
	Vicki Berner, Faye Urban	tennis women's doubles
	Pierre Saint-Jean	light heavyweight weightlifting
	Nick Schori	78kg FS wrestling
	Alan Clarke	Finn yachting
	Peter Byrne	Flying Dutchman yachting
1971	Mike Mason	long jump
	Bruce Simpson	pole vault
	Michael Mercer	shot put
	Ain Roost	discus
	Penny Werthner	800m run
	Penny May	100m hurdles
	Carol Martin	discus
	Bernard Guindon	light middleweight boxing
	Bill Titley	light heavyweight boxing
	Bev Boys	springboard diving
	Torchy Millar	individual equestrian jumping
	Men's gymnastics team	
	Andre Simard	gymnastics rings
	Women's gymnastic team	
	Lise Arsenault	gymnastics floor exercises
	Jennifer Diachun	gymnastics floor exercises
	Men's field hockey team	
	Men's coxed 8s rowing	
	Alf Mayer	small-bore prone rifle
	Men's small-bore prone rifle team	
	Jules Sobrian	centre-fire pistol
	Bob Kasting	100m FS
	Ralph Hutton	200m, 400m FS
	Bill Kennedy	100m backstroke
	John Hawkes	200m backstroke
	Byron MacDonald	100m butterfly
	Karen James	100m FS
	Angela Coughlan	400m FS
	Susan Smith	200m butterfly
	Chun Hon Chan	flyweight weightlifting
	Wayne Wilson	middle heavyweight weightlifting
	Ernest Morris	super heavyweight weightlifting
	Pat Bolger	62kg FS wrestling
	Taras Hyrb	82kg FS wrestling
	Don Allen	Lightning yachting
1975	Tom Howard, marathon	
	Hugh Fraser,	4x100m relay
	Marvin Nash,	
	Bob Dukowski,	
	Bob Martin	
	Glenn Bogue,	4x400m relay
	Ron Jackson,	
	Bryan Saunders,	
	Bob Dukowski	
	Rick Cuttell	high jump
	Scott Neilson	hammer
	Marjorie Bailey	100m sprint
	Abby Hoffman,	500m run
	Marjorie Bailey,	4x100m relay
	Patti Loverock,	
	Joanne McTaggart,	
	Joyce Yakubowich	

Year	Name	Event/Sport
	Lucette Moreau	shot put
	Jane Haist	discus
	Linda Cuthbert	platform diving
	Equestrian jumping team	
	Men's coxless fours rowing	
	Men's small-bore rifle 3-positions team	
	Jules Sobrian	rapid-fire pistol
	Bruce Robertson	100m FS, 100m butterfly
	Bill Sawchuk	200m IM
	Jill Quirk	100m FS
	Anne Jardin	200m FS
	Michele Oliver	400m FS
	Janice Stenhouse	800m FS
	Cheryl Gibson	200m backstroke
	Marian Stuart	100m breaststroke
	Wendy Quirk	100m butterfly
	Cheryl Gibson	200m IM
	Dan Robitaille	middleweight weightlifting total, snatch, C&J
	Jim Miller	74kg FS wrestling
	Terry Paice	90kg FS wrestling
	Claude Pilon	100kg FS wrestling
	John McPherson	68kg GR wrestling
	Harry Geris	+100kg GR wrestling
1979	Stan Siatkowski	archery individual men
	Joan McDonald	archery individual women
	Bruno Pauletto	shot put
	Dick Hughson	marathon
	Micheline Racette, Marita Payne, Janette Wood, Anne Mackie-Morelli	4x400m relay
	Debbie Brill	high jump
	Carmen Ionesco	discus, shot put
	Jill Ross	pentathlon
	Angella Taylor	100m
	Penny Werthner	1,500m
	Geraldine Fitch	3,000m
	Milt Ottey	high jump
	Zenon Smiechowski	decathlon
	Women's basketball team	
	Ian Clyde	51kg boxing
	Pat Fennell	81kg boxing
	Eon D'Ornellas, Pierre Harvey, Bernard Willock, Normand St. Aubin	100km team time trial
	Janet Nutter	3m springboard
	Linda Cuthbert	10m platform
	Ian Millar	individual grand prix jumping
	Warren Long	horizontal bars, individual all-around
	Jean Choquette	pommel horse
	Elfi Schlegel	uneven bars, individual all-around
	Phil Takahashi	60kg judo
	Joe Meli	open judo
	Sylvie Gingras	roller skating artistic singles
	Guy Aubin	roller skating artistic singles
	Guy Aubin, Sylvie Gingras	freestyle pairs
	Lori Beal, Robert Dalgleish	freestyle dance
	Tom Guinn	individual free pistol

Year	Name	Event/Sport
	George Leary	individual trap
	John Cowan, Jim Kagan, George Leary, John Primrose	team trap
	Guy Lorion	individual 3-positions rifle
	Kurt Mitchell	individual air rifle
	Anne Gagnon	100m breaststroke
	Nancy Garapick	100m, 200m butterfly, 400m IM
	Gail Amundrud	100m, 200m FS
	Wendy Quirk	400m FS
	Barbara Shockey	800m FS
	Peter Szmidt	400m FS
	Stephen Pickell	100m backstroke
	Graham Smith	100m breaststroke
	Clay Evans	100m butterfly
	Bill Sawchuk	200m butterfly
	Alex Baumann	400m IM
	Dennis Corcoran, Bill Sawchuk, Peter Szmidt, Graham Welbourn	4x200 FS relay
	Men's volleyball team	
	Men's water polo team	
	John Park	62kg wrestling
	Egon Beiler	68kg wrestling
	Marc Mongeon	74kg wrestling
	Richard Deschatelets	90kg wrestling
	Michael Kappel	100kg wrestling
	Wyatt Wishart	super heavyweight wrestling
	Brian Renken	74kg Greco-Roman wrestling
	Louis Santerre	82kg Greco-Roman wrestling
	Stephen Daniar	90kg Greco-Roman wrestling
	Charles Robitaille, Jerry Rouffs	470 yachting
	James Beatty, John Dakin, John Wood	Soling yachting
1983	Linda Kazienko	individual women's archery
	Greg Duhaime	3,000m steeplechase
	Gwen Wall	400m hurdles
	Molly Killingbeck, Karen Nelson, Charmaine Crooks, Tanya Brothers	4x100m relay
	Sylvie Bernier	springboard diving
	J.P. Banos	individual sabre
	J.M. Banos, J.P. Banos, Claude Marcil, Eli Sukunda, Marc Lavoie	sabre team
	Yves Dion, Curtis Hibbert, Guy Lemelin, Marshall Garfield, Dave Arnold, Jim Rozon	men's gymnastic team
	Phil Takahashi	60kg judo
	Tina Takahashi	48kg judo
	Diane Amyot	61kg judo
	Sara Rives	open judo
	Ron Burak, Blair Horn, Paul Steele, Nick Toulmin, Paul Tessier	coxed fours

Year	Name	Event/Sport
	Gary May, Fred Loucks, Mark Thomas, Joe Wilhelm Men's coxed eights	coxless fours
	Maureen Grace	single sculls
	Guy Lorion, Alfons Mayer, J.F. Senecal	free rifle team
	Guy Lorion	air rifle
	Pat Vamplew	English match 300m rifle
	Joelle Fefer, Sheila McQuarrie, Christina Schulze	English match team
	Christina Schulze	standard rifle
	Linda Thom	air pistol
	Mike West	100m, 200m backstroke
	Peter Dobson	400m IM
	Julie Daigneault	200m, 400m, 800m FS
	Kathy Bald	100m FS
	Barbara McBain	100m, 200m backstrokee
	Marie Moore	200m butterfly
	Michelle Macpherson	400m IM
	Mariann Domonkos, Thanh Mach	table tennis women's doubles
	Mariann Domonkos, Gloria Hsu, Thanh Mach Men's Water polo team	table tennis women's team
	Michel Viau	67.5kg weightlifting
	Bob Robinson	62kg wrestling
	Pat Sullivan	68kg wrestling
	Ken Bradford	74kg wrestling
	Chris Rinke	82kg wrestling
	Bob Molle	+100kg wrestling
	Raines Koby	windglider
	Steve Fleckenstein, Mike Grant	Star yachting
	Frank McLaughlin, Martin Tenhove	470 yachting
1987	Denis Canuel, John McDonald, David Viney	men's archery team
	Brit McRoberts	1,500m
	Paul McCloy	10,000m
	Gord Orlikow	decathlon
	Women's basketball team	
	Jeff Houser	K1 500m
	Tom Ladanyi	K2 500m
	Stephen Wasteneys	C1 1000m
	Jeff Houser, Liam Jewell	K2 1000m
	Curt Harnett	cycling sprint
	Pat Beauchemin	individual pursuit
	Sara Neil	individual road race
	Debbie Fuller	women's springboard
	David Bedard	men's 10m platform
	Jean-Marie Banos	individual sabre
	J.M. Banos, J.P. Banos, Wulfe Balk, Luc Rocheleau	team sabre
	Jean Marc Chouinard	individual épée
	Andrea Conway, Yanic Giguere, Iidiko Hattayer, Theresa MacKenzie, Amelie Major, Daphne Vallieres	women's team gymnastics
	Women's field hockey team	
	Fred Blaney	+95kg judo

Year	Name	Event/Sport
	Lyne Poirier	48kg judo
	Kathryn Hubble	52kg judo
	Nathalie Gosselin	56kg judo
	Mary Fuzesi	rhythmic gymnastics women's all-around, hoop, ribbon
	Jim Crouch, Heather Paterson	roller skating artistic dance
	Karen Ashford, Connie Delisle	double sculls
	Ray Collier, Scott Drossos, Mike Rascher, Bruce Robertson	coxless fours
	Scott Anderson, Chris Flood, Tom Kent, Wayne MacFarlane Men's coxed eights	lightweight coxless fours
	Joelle Fefer	standard rifle prone
	Mark Bedlington	running game rifle
	Paul Shaw	open trap
	Brian Gabriel	skeet
	Fred Altmann, Brian Gabriel, Don Kwasnycia	skeet team
	Women's softball team	
	Megan Holliday	400m, 800m FS
	Robin Ruggiero	100m butterfly
	Shay McNicol	200m butterfly
	Karen Helmstaedt	200m, 400m IM
	Anne-Marie Andersen, Denise Gereghty, Sally Gilbert, Cheryl McArton	4x200m FS relay
	Chris Chalmers	1,500m FS
	Ray Brown	200m backstroke
	Darcy Wallingford	100m, 200m breaststroke
	Mike Meldrum	400m IM
	Mariann Domonkos, Thanh Mach, Helene Bedard	table tennis women's team
	Gideon Joe Ng, Horatio Pintea, Chris Chu	table tennis men's team
	Gideon Joe Ng, Mariann Domonkos	table tennis mixed doubles
	Gilles Desmarais	60kg total, snatch, c&j weightlifting
	Langis Cote	67.5kg total weightlifting
	Guy Greavette	82.5kg total, snatch weightlifting
	Glen Dodds	82.5kg clean & jerk weightlifting
	Chris Woodcroft	52kg FS wrestling
	Pat Sullivan	68kg FS wrestling
	Gary Holmes	74kg FS wrestling
	Gavin Carrow	100kg FS wrestling
	Daniel Payne	130kg FS wrestling
	Doug Cox	90kg Greco-Roman wrestling
	Steve Marshall	100kg Greco-Roman wrestling
	Daniel Payne	130kg Greco-Roman wrestling
	Richard Myerscough	men's sailboard

Year	Name	Event/Sport
1991	Dan Bertoia	1,500m
	Sarah Howell	1,500m
	Tom Glesby	91kg boxing
	Terry Campbell	+91kg boxing
	Gavin Maxwell, Craig O'Leary	C2 500m, 1000m
	Scott Kerrigan	K1 500m
	Peter Giles	K1 1000m
	Peter Giles, Alan Gibb	K2 1000m
	Scott Kerrigan, Alan Gibb, Ashley McColgan, Peter Giles	K4 1000m
	Edie Fisher, Clara Hughes, Denise Kelly, Sharon Keogh	women's team time trial
	Men's team foil	
	Dan Nowosielski	individual épée
	Jean-Marie Banos	individual sabre
	Men's team sabre	
	Jennifer Wood	gymnastics vault
	Women's gymnastics team	
	Brigitte Lastrade	48kg judo
	Susie Cushman	rhythmic gymnastics all-around, hoop
	Rhythmic gymnastics group	
	Mike Koski, Jon Siebert, Greg Stevenson, Chris Spooner	coxless fours
	Todd Hallett	single sculls
	Men's coxed eights	
	Men's coxed fours	
	Rod Colwell	free pistol
	Guy Lorion	men's air rifle
	Sharon Bowes	women's air rifle
	Jasen Pratt	400m IM
	Kristen Topham	100m FS
	Kim Paton	200m FS
	Tara-Lynn Seymour	400m, 800m FS
	Lisa Flood	100m, 200m breaststroke
	Joanne Malar	200m backstroke
	Beth Hazel	200m butterfly
	Julie Bibby, Corinne Keddie	synchro swim duet
	Horatio Pintea	table tennis men's singles
	Men's table tennis team	
	Julie Barton, Caroline Sylvestre	table tennis women's doubles
	Gideon Joe Ng, Julie Barton	table tennis mixed doubles
	Michael Popowich	70kg taekwondo
	Robert Dawson	57kg FS wrestling
	David Hohl	82kg FS wrestling
	Greg Edgelow	90kg FS, Greco-Roman wrestling
	John Matile	100kg Greco-Roman wrestling
	Andy Borodow	130kg Greco-Roman wrestling
	Murray McCaig	men's sailboard
	Shayne Bayford	artistic rollerskating men's singles

Year	Name	Event/Sport
1995	Rob Rusnov,	archery men's 30m, 50m, individual Olympic round
	Jeannot Robitaille,	archery Olympic round men's team
	Rob Rusnov, Kevin Sally	
	Veronique Dufour, Sylvie Plante, Caroline Labrecque	archery Olympic round women's team
	Carol Montgomery	5000m run
	Valerie Tulloch	javelin
	Darryl Yung, Jamie Dawson	badminton men's doubles
	Marc Doi, Bill Rowe	bowling men's doubles
	Marc Doi, Bill Rowe, Paul Gyarmati, Doug Shatz	bowling men's team
	Claude Lambert	54kg boxing
	Mike Strange	60kg boxing
	Hercules Kyvelos	67kg boxing
	Jason Smith	71kg boxing
	Dan Howe	C1 1000m
	Clara Hughes	individual road time trial
	Brian Walton	individual pursuit
	Bobbi-Ann MacPherson	3m springboard
	David Bedard	3m springboard
	Victoria Winter, Stefan Von Schalburg, Nancy MacLachlan, Louise Miechowsky	equestrian dressage team
	Victoria Winter	individual dressage
	Maureen Griffin, Sherraine Schalm, Heather Landymore, Marie-Francoise Hervieu	fencing épée team
	Jean-Marc Banos, Leszek Nowosielski, Tony Ploudre, Maxime Soucy	fencing sabre team
	Women's field hockey team	
	Richard Ikeda	gymnastics pommel horse
	Kris Burley	gymnastics floor exercixes, vault
	Men's gymnastic team	
	Nathalie Gosselin	52kg judo
	Renee Hock	56kg judo
	Nancy Filteault	+72kg judo
	Taro Tan	65kg judo
	Jean-Pierre Cantin	71kg judo
	Colin Morgan	78kg judo
	Carol McFetridge	individual women's racquetball
	Sherman Greenfeld	individual men's racquetball
	Jason Moreton	roller skating artistic figures
	Henry Hering, Todd Hallett	men's double sculls
	James Brambell	lightweight single sculls
	Brian Thompson, James Brambell	lightweight double sculls
	George Leary	individual trap shooting
	Jean-Pierre Huot, John Rochon, Stan Wills	10m air pistol team
	Michel Dion	50m free pistol
	Derrick Nixon	individual skeet

Year	Name	Event/Sport
	Andrea Moody	50m FS
	Marianne Limpert	100m FS
	Katie Brambley	400m FS
	Joanne Malar	200m backstroke
	Curtis Myden	200m breaststroke
	Chris Renaud,	4x100m medley relay
	Jon Cleveland,	
	Eddie Parenti,	
	Curtis Myden	
	Barbara Chiu	table tennis women's singles
	Horatio Pintea	table tennis men's singles
	Joe Ng, Horatio Pintea	table tennis men's doubles
	Joe Ng, Horatio Pintea,	table tennis men's team
	Dennis Su, Francis Trudel	
	Joe Ng, Barbara Chiu	table tennis mixed doubles
	Miranda Hall	47kg taekwondo
	Marcia King	70kg taekwondo
	Dominique Bosshart	+70kg taekwondo
	Tino Dossantos	64kg taekwondo
	Stephen Goodwin	75kg taekwondo
	Fiona Cribb	individual triathlon
	Women's volleyball team	
	Kim De Macedo	water skiing women's slalom
	Selwyn Tam	52kg FS wrestling
	Gavin Carrow	100kg FS wrestling
	Andy Borodow	130kg FS, GR wrestling
	Murray McCaig	Mistral yachting
	Jason Rhodes	Laser yachting
1999	Kara Grant	women's modern pentathlon
	Ron Woods, Sherri Bint	roller sports dance
	Renata Kolbovic,	women's tennis doubles
	Aneta Soukup	
	Zach Whitmarsh	800m
	Jeff Schiebler	5000m
	Jean-Nicolas Duval	3000m steeplechase
	Jason Pearce	men's pole vault
	Bradley Snyder	men's shot put
	Jason Tunks	men's discus
	Tina Connelly	women's 10,000m
	Nicole Forrester	women's high jump
	Caroline Wittrin	women's hammer
	Kris Burley	men's vault
	Roshan Amendra,	men's team gymnastics
	Alexander Jeltkov,	
	Richard Ikeda,	
	Darin Good,	
	Grant Golding,	
	Kris Burley	
	Mike Beres,	men's badminton doubles
	Bryan Moody	
	Kara Solmundson,	women's badminton singles
	Denyse Julien	(tie)
	Adrian Richardson	men's K1 1000m
	Maxime Roberge	81kg men's judo
	Keith Morgan	90kg men's judo
	Luce Baillargeon	52kg women's judo
	Brigitte Lastrade	57kg women's judo
	Susan Armstrong,	women's field hockey
	Michelle Bowyer, Lisa Faust,	
	Sarah Forbes, Aoibhinn Grimes,	
	Ann Harada, Christine Hunter,	
	Karen MacNeill, Carla Somerville,	

Year	Name	Event/Sport
	Kristen Taunton, Suzanne Tingley,	
	Jenny Zinkan-McGrade, Amy MacFarlane,	
	Bobbi Steadward, Julia Wong,	
	Laurelee Kopeck	
	Wayne Sorensen	men's air rifle
	Henry Gerow	men's free rifle prone
	Clayton Miller	men's skeet
	George Leary	men's trap
	Christina Ashcroft	women's 3-position sport rifle
	Marnie Baizley	women's squash singles
	Mark Johnston	men's 200m FS
	Richard Say	men's 400m FS
	Owen Von Richter	men's 200m IM
	Owen Von Richter	men's 400m IM
	Karine Chevrier	women's 100m butterfly
	Laura Nicholls	women's 50m FS
	Marianne Limpert	women's 100m FS
	Joanne Malar	women's 400 FS
	Lindsay Beavers	women's 800m FS
	Lauren Van Oosten	100m breaststroke
	Marianne Limpert	women's 200m IM
	Kelly Stefanyshyn	women's 200m backstroke
	Mark Johnston,	men's 200m FS relay
	Brian Johns,	
	Yannick Lupien,	
	Richard Say	
	Mark Versfeld,	men's 100m medley relay
	Morgan Knabe,	
	Shamek Pietucha,	
	Yannick Lupien	
	Raymond Mourad	58kg men's taekwondo
	Darrell Henegan	80kg men's taekwondo
	Gael Texier	women's 57kg taekwondo
	Dominique Bosshart	women's 67kg taekwondo
	Simon Whitfield	men's traithlon
	Carol Montgomery	women's triathlon
	Garrett Head, Mikael Sabo,	men's water polo
	Alex Thibeault, Darryl Bourne,	
	Yannick Lize, Christopher Lovett,	
	Adam Sidky, Ted Bader,	
	Adam Deffett, Kent Hardisty,	
	Mark Block, Nathaniel Miller,	
	Zoltan Csepregi	
	Kim deMacedo	women's water ski jump
	Jean Lassen	women's 75kg weightlifting
	Marty Calder	63kg FS wrestling
	Daniel Igali	69kg FS wrestling
	Dean Schmeichel	97kg FS wrestling
	Wayne Weathers	130kg FS wrestling
	Colbie Bell	97kg GR wrestling
	Phil Graham,	men's coxless pairs
	Kevin White,	
	Phil Graham,	men's coxless fours
	Andrew Hoskins,	
	Ken Kozel,	
	Kevin White	
	Katrina Scott,	women's lightweight double sculls
	Nathalie Benzing	
	Renata Troc,	women's lightweight quadruple sculls
	Nathalie Benzing,	
	Katrina Scott,	
	Tracy Duncan	

Year	Name	Event/Sport
	Larry MacDonald, Julie-Marie Innes-MacDonald, Trevor Born	three hand Lightning sailing
	David Sweeney, Kevin Smith	catam hobie 16 open sailing
	Laurie Shong	men's épée
	Michel Boulos	men's sabre
	Julie Mahoney	women's foil
	Eric Lamaze, Jill Henselwood, Beth Underhill, Ian Millar	stadium team jump
	Blythe Hartley	women's 3m diving
	Chris Sheppard	men's mountain bike
	Doug Baron	men's 1km cycle TT
	Btissima Es-Sadiqi	women's 53kg karate
	Lisa Ling	women's 60kg karate
	Matt Stockman, Colon Dixon, Troy Fortin, Dave Ross, Greg Morrison, Mike Myers, Clint Lawrence, Chad Ricketts, Jason Gooding, Andy Stewart, Jason Green, Steve Green, Todd Betts, Chris Mears, Ryan Radmanovich, Jeremt Ware, Julien Lepine, Mark Randall, Yan Lachapelle, Matt Logan, Stubby Clapp, Aaron Guiel, Lee Delfino	men's baseball
	Pradeeban Peter-Paul, Horatio Pintea, Xavier Therien	men's table tennis team
	Petra Cada	women's table tennis singles
	Marc Doi	men's 10-pin masters
	Jennifer Willis	women's 10-pin masters
	Jason Trepanier, Steve Brinkman, Doug Bruce, Paul Duerden, Bruce Edwards, Murray Grapentine, David Kantor, Scott Koskie, Jules Martens, Keith Sanheim, Andrew Zurawsky, Dustin Reid	men's volleyball
	Troy Amos Ross	81kg boxing
	Julie Hayward, Katie Iafolla, Joanna Krecsy, Jenny Pudavick, Andrea Sellen	rhythmic gymnastics group
2003	Alexandre Despatie	men's 10m platform
	Blythe Hartley	women's 10m platform
	Maya Beaudry, Elizabeth Collins, Kelly Doody, Joanne Malar-Morreale	women's 4x200 FS relay
	Scott Dickens, Brian Edey, Chad Murray, Tobias Oriwol, Matt Rose, Sean Sepulis	men's 4x100m medley relay
	Scott Dickens, Brian Edey, Tobias Oriwol, Colin Russell, Chad Murray,	men's 4x200m FS relay
	Tobias Oriwol, Matt Rose, Colin Russell	men's 4x100m FS relay
	Kathleen Stoody	100m, 200m breaststroke

Year	Name	Event/Sport
	Vladimir Cosic, Adam Deffett, Mike Gordon, Kent Hardisty, Garrett Head, Iain Lark, Dusan Lazarevic, Thomas Marks, Nathaniel Miller, Noah Miller, Kevin Mitchell, Mikael Sabo, Nic Youngblud	men's water polo team
	Anson Henry	men's 100m sprint
	Stephanie McCann	women's pole vault
	Brad Snyder	men's shot put
	Mike Beres, Kyle Hunter	badminton men's doubles
	Kyle Hunter	badminton men's singles
	Jason Douglas	91kg boxing
	Andrew Kooner,	54kg boxing
	Jean Pascal	75kg boxing
	Jill D'Alessio	women's K1 500m
	Mark De Jonge	men's K1 500m
	Tom Hall, Ian Mortimer	men's C2 500m
	Clara Hughes	women;s individual pursuit
	Michel Boulos	men's saber
	Catherine Dunnette, raine Mackay, Marie-Eve Pelletier	women's team épée Sher-
	Olia Berger	women's judo +78kg
	Amy Cotton	women's judo 78kg
	Jean-Francois Marceau	men's judo 73kg
	Isabelle Pearson	women's judo 63kg
	Nassim Varasteh	karate kumite 58kg
	Josee Grand'maitre, Julie Neubauer	women's racquetball doubles
	Corey Osborne, Francois Viens	men's racquetball doubles
	Lori-Jane Powell	women's racquetball singles
	Roxy Cervantes, Ira Funtikova, Pam Jewell, Emilie Livingstone, Sarah Stock,	rhythmic gymnastics group, 3 hoops, 2 balls
	Roxy Cervantes,	rhythmic gymnastics, group 5 ribbons
	Ira Funtikova, Pam Jewell, Emilie Livingstone, Alex Orlando	
	Neil Armour, Kevin Burt, Geoff Hodgson, David Kay	men's coxless fours
	Kevin Stittle	men's sailboard mistral
	Linda Conley	women's skeet
	Lynda Hare	women's 10m air pistol
	Susan Nattrass	women's double trap
	Marnie Baizley	women's squash singles
	Ryan Dodd	men's water ski jump
	Zoltan Hunyady	men's FS wrestling 74kg
	Mischa Japaridze	men's FS wrestling 55kg

BRITISH EMPIRE/COMMONWEALTH GAMES MEDALLISTS

Gold

Year	Name	Event/Sport
1930	Percy Williams	100yd sprint
	Alex Wilson	440yd run
	John Brown, Leigh Miller, Ralph Adams, John Fitzpatrick	4x100yd relay
	Len Hutton	long jump
	Gordon Smallacome	triple jump
	Vic Pickard	pole vault
	Alf Phillips	3 & 10m diving
	Pearl Stoneham	10m diving
	Elswood Boles, Bob Richards	double sculls rowing
	Munro Bourne	100yd freestyle swim
	Jack Aubin	200yd breaststroke
	Munroe Bourne, Al Gibson, George Burleigh, James Thompson	4x200yd FS relay
	Jim Trifunov	57kg wrestling
	Cliff Chilcott	62kg wrestling
	Howard Thomas	68kg wrestling
	Reg Priestley	74kg wrestling
	Mike Chepwick	82kg wrestling
	L. McIntyre	90kg wrestling
	Earl McCready	100kg wrestling
1934	Harold Webster	marathon
	Sam Richardson	long jump
	Syl Apps	pole vault
	Lillian Palmer, Aileen Meagher, Betty White, Audrey Dearnley	660yd relay
	Robert Dixon	javelin
	Robert McLeod	cycling 10-mile road race
	Judy Moss	3m diving
	George Burleigh	100yd FS swim
	Phyllis Dewar	100 & 440yd FS swim
	George Larson, Robert Hooper, Robert Pirie, George Burleigh	4x200yd FS relay
	Ben Gazell, George Burleigh, Bill Puddy	3x100yd medley relay
	Margaret Hutton, Phyllis Haslam, Phyllis Dewar	3x100yd medley relay
	Phyllis Dewar, Florence Humble, Irene Pirie, Margaret Hutton	4x100yd FS relay
	Robert McNab	62kg wrestling
	Joe Schleimer	74kg wrestling
	Terry Evans	82kg wrestling
1938	John Brown, Pat Haley, John Loaring, Larry O'Connor	4x100yd relay

Year	Name	Event/Sport
	William Dale, John Frazer, John Loaring, John Lee Orr	4x440yd relay
	John Loaring	440yd hurdles
	Eric Coy	discus
	Harold Brown	long jump
	Jim Courtwright	javelin
	Robina Higgins	women's javelin
	George Sutherland	hammer
	Thomas Osborne	+81kg boxing
	Robert Pirie	100 & 440yd FS swim
	Florence Humble, Dorothy Lyon, Noel Oxenbury, Phyllis Dewar	4x110yd FS relay
	Terry Evans	82kg wrestling
1950	Bill Parnell	1 mile run
	Leo Roininen	javelin
	George Athans Sr.	3m diving
	Peter Salmon	110yd FS swim
	Gerard Gratton	75kg weightlifting
	Jack Varaleau	82.5kg weightlifting
	Henry Hudson	74kg wrestling
	Maurice Vachon	82kg wrestling
1954	Don Stonehouse, Bruce Springbett, Harry Nelson, Don McFarlane	4x110yd relay
	Mickey Bergin	63,5kg boxing
	Wilf Greaves	71kg boxing
	Bill Patrick	10m diving
	Roland Asselin, Leslie Krasa, Carl Schwende	team sabre
	Glen Smith, Tom Harris, Tom Toynbee, Doug McDonald, Lawrence West, Herman Zioklikovits, Ken Drummond, Bob Wilson, Ray Sieroina	rowing coxed eights
	Gerard Gratton	82.5kg weightlifting
	Keevil Daly	90kg weightlifting
	Doug Hepburn,	110kg weightlifting
1958	Don Arnold, Wayne Pretty, Glen Mervyn, Walter d'Hondt, Bill McKerlick, Archie MacKinnon, Lorne Loomer, Bob Wilson, Sohen Biln	rowing coxed eights
1962	Bruce Kidd	6-mile run
	Harold Mann	71kg boxing
	Richard Pound	110yd FS swim
	Mary Stewart	110yd butterfly
1966	Harry Jerome	100yd sprint
	Dave Steen	shot put
	Abby Hoffman	880yd run
	Gil Boa	small-bore rifle
	Jim Lee	centre-fire pistol
	Ron Jacks	110yd butterfly
	Ralph Hutton, Len Chase, Ron Jacks, John Gilchrist	4x110yd medley relay

Year	Name	Event/Sport
	Marion Lay,	110yd freestyle swim
	Elaine Tanner,	4x110yd FS relay
	Jane Hughes,	
	Louise Kennedy,	
	Marion Lay	
	Elaine Tanner	110 & 220yd butterfly
		440yd IM
	Pierre St. Jean	75kg weightlifting
	Robert Chamberot,	90kg wrestling
1970	Dave Steen	shot put
	George Puce	discus
	Debbie Brill	high jump
	Jamie Paulson	men's badminton singles
	Jocelyn Lovell	10-mile cycling road race
	Bev Boys	3 & 10m diving
	Bill Kennedy	100m backstroke
	Bill Mahony	100 & 200m breaststroke
	Byron MacDonald	100m butterfly
	Toomas Arusoo	200m butterfly
	George Smith	200 & 400m IM
	Bill Kennedy, Bill Mahony,	4x100m medley relay
	Byron MacDonald,	
	Bob Kasting	
	Angela Coughlan	100m freestyle
	Russ Prior	110kg weightlifting
	Ed Millard	100kg wrestling
1974	Yvonne Saunders	400m run
	Glenda Reiser	1500m run
	Jane Haist	shot put
	Cindy Shatto	3m diving
	Bev Boys	10m diving
	John Primrose	clay pigeon
	Harry Willsie	skeet shooting
	Jules Sobrian	free pistol
	Bill Hare	rapid-fire pistol
	Bruce Robertson,	4x100 FS relay
	Ian MacKenzie,	
	Gary MacDonald,	
	Brian Phillips	
	Gail Amundrud,	4x100 FS relay
	Becky Smith,	
	Anne Jardin, Judith Wright	
	Steve Pickell, Bill Mahony,	4x100m medley relay
	Bruce Robertson,	
	Brian Phillips	
	Wendy Cook,	4x100m medley relay
	Marion Stuart,	
	Patti Stenhouse,	
	Gail Amundrud	
	Wendy Cook	100 & 200m backstroke
	Patti Stenhouse	100m butterfly
	Leslie Cliff	200 & 400m IM
	Russ Prior	110kg weightlifting
	Mitch Kawasaki	48kg wrestling
	Egon Beiler	62kg wrestling
	Terry Paice	90kg wrestling
	Claude Pilon	100kg wrestling
	Bill Benko	+100kg wrestling
1978	Borys Chambul	discus
	Carmen Ionescu	women's discus
	Phil Olson	javelin
	Claude Ferrange	high jump
	Bruce Simpson	pole vault

Year	Name	Event/Sport
	Diane Jones Konihowski	pentathlon
	Kelly Perlette	71kg boxing
	Roger Fortin	81kg boxing
	Jocelyn Lovell	1000m time trial
		& 10-mile road race
	Jocelyn Lovell,	tandem sprint
	Gord Singleton	
	Janet Nutter	3m diving
	Linda Cuthbert	10m diving
	Karen Kelsall,	women's gymnastics team
	Elfi Schlegel,	
	Monica Goermann,	
	Sherry Hawco	
	Nigel Rothwell,	men's gymnastics team
	Owen Walstrom,	
	Jean Choquette,	
	Philip Delesalle	
	Elfi Schlegel	individual women's
		gymnastics
	Philip Delesalle	individual men's gymnastics
	John Primrose	trap shooting
	Yvon Trempe	free pistol
	Jules Sobrian	rapid-fire pistol
	Des Vamplew	full-bore rifle
	Graham Smith	100/200m breaststroke,
		200/400m IM
	Robin Corsiglia	100m breaststroke
	Lisa Borsholt	200m breaststroke
	Dan Thompson	100m butterfly
	Wendy Quirk	100m butterfly
	George Nagy	200m butterfly
	Carol Klimpel	100m freestyle
	Cheryl Gibson	200m backstroke
	Bill Sawchuck,	4x100m FS relay
	Graham Smith,	
	Gary MacDonald,	
	Peter Szmidt	
	Gail Amundrud,	4x100m FS relay
	Carol Klimpel,	
	Susan Sloan,	
	Wendy Quirk	
	Jay Tapp, Graham Smith,	4x100 medley relay
	Dan Thompson,	
	Bill Sawchuck,	
	Helene Boivin,	4x100m medley relay
	Marion Stuart,	
	Wendy Quirk,	
	Carol Klimpel	
	Michel Mercier	60kg weightlifting
	Russ Prior	110kg weightlifting
	Marc Cardinal	+110kg weightlifting
	Ray Takahashi	52kg wrestling
	Egon Beiler	62kg wrestling
	Richard Deschatelets	82kg wrestling
	Stephen Daniar	90kg wrestling
	Wyatt Wishart	100kg wrestling
	Robert Gibbons	+100kg wrestling
1982	Angella Taylor	100m sprint
	Charmaine Crooks,	4x400 relay
	Jillian Richardson,	
	Molly Killingbeck,	
	Angella Taylor	
	Debbie Brill	high jump

Year	Name	Event/Sport
	Milt Ottey	high jump
	Mark McKoy	110m hurdles
	Bruno Pauletto	shot put
	Claire Backhouse,	badminton women's doubles
	Johanne Falardeau,	
	Shawn O'Sullivan	71kg boxing
	Willie de Wit	+81kg boxing
	Tom Guinn	free pistol
	Jean-Francois Senecal	men's air rifle
	Brian Gabriel,	skeet team
	Fred Altmann	
	Kathy Bald	100m breaststroke
	Anne Ottenbrite	200m breaststroke
	Victor Davis,	200m breaststroke
	Cheryl Gibson,	4x100 medley relay
	Anne Ottenbrite,	
	Michelle MacPherson,	
	Maureen New	
	Mike West	100m backstroke
	Dan Thompson	100m butterfly
	Cameron Henning	200m backstroke
	Alex Baumann	200m, 400m IM
	Bob Robinson	62kg wrestling
	Chris Rinke	82kg wrestling
	Clark Davis	90kg wrestling
	Richard Deschatelets	100kg wrestling
	Wyatt Wishart	+100kg wrestling
1986	Ben Johnson	100m sprint
	Angella Issajenko	200m sprint
	Lynn Williams	3000m run
	Graeme Fell	300m steeplechase
	Mark McKoy	110m hurdles
	Ben Johnson,	4x100m relay
	Mark McKoy,	
	Atlee Mahorn,	
	Desai Williams	
	Charmaine Crooks,	4x400m relay
	Molly Killingbeck,	
	Marita Oayne,	
	Jillian Richardson	
	Ray Lazdins	discus
	Milt Ottey,	high jump
	Scott Olson	48kg boxing
	Billy Downey	57kg boxing
	Asif Dar	60kg boxing
	Howard Grant	63.5kg boxing
	Dan Sherry	71kg boxing
	Lennox Lewis	+91kg boxing
	Debbie Fuller	3m, 10m diving
	Kathryn Barr,	coxless pair
	Andrea Schreiner	
	Bruce Ford, Pat Walter	double sculls
	Tina Clarke,	coxed four
	Tricia Smith,	
	Lesley Thompson,	
	Jane Tregunno,	
	Jenny Wallinga	
	Grant Main,	coxless four
	Kevin Neufeld,	
	Paul Steele, Pat Turner	
	Guy Lorion	air rifle
	Sharon Bowes,	air rifle team
	Guy Lorion	

Year	Name	Event/Sport
	Bill Baldwin,	full-bore rifle team
	Alain Marion	
	Claude Beaulieu,	free pistol team
	Tom Guinn	
	Michael Ashcroft,	prone rifle team
	Gale Stewart	
	Mark Tewksbury	100m backstroke
	Sandy Goss	200m backstroke
	Victor Davis	100m breaststroke
	Allison Higson	100, 200m breaststroke
	Donna McGinnis	200m butterfly
	Jane Kerr	100m freestyle
	Alex Baumann	200, 400m IM
	Jane Kerr, Trish Noall,	4x100 freestyle relay
	Andrea Nugent, Pam Rai	
	Alex Baumann,	4x100 medley relay
	Victor Davis,	
	Tom Ponting,	
	Mark Tewksbury	
	Michelle Cameron,	synchro swim duet
	Carolyn Waldo	
	Sylvie Frechette	synchro swim solo
	Denis Garon	100kg weightlifting
	Kevin Roy	110kg weightlifting
	Ron Moncur	48kg wrestling
	Chris Woodcroft	52kg wrestling
	Mitch Ostberg	57kg wrestling
	Paul Hughes	62kg wrestling
	Dave McKay	68kg wrestling
	Gary Holmes	74kg wrestling
	Chris Rinke	82kg wrestling
	Clark Davis	100kg wrestling
	Wayne Brightwell	+100kg wrestling
1990	Guillaume LeBlanc	30km road walk
	Michael Smith	decathlon
	Angela Chalmers	1500, 3000m runs
	Chris Johnson	75kg boxing
	Mary Depiero	1m springboard diving
	Anna Dacyshyn	10m diving
	Curtis Hibbert, Alan Nolet,	men's gymnastics team
	Claude Latendresse,	
	Lorne Bobkin	
	Curtis Hibbert	individual all-around, horizontal bar (tie), parallel bar, rings
	Alan Nolet	horizontal bar (tie)
	Larissa Lowing,	women's gymnastic team
	Janet Morin,	
	Lori Strong, Stella Umeh	
	Lori Strong	individual all-around, balance beam, floor
	Mary Fuzesi	rhythmic gymnastics all-around, hoop, ribbon
	Madonna Gimotea	rhythmic gymnastics ball
	Guy Lorion	10m air rifle
	Guy Lorion, Mart Klepp	10m air rifle team
	Mart Klepp	50m free rifle 3-position
	Mart Klepp,	50m free rifle 3-position team
	Jean-Francois Senecal	
	Mark Tewksbury	100m backstroke
	Gary Anderson	200m backstroke, 200m IM
	Jon Cleveland	200m breaststroke
	Jon Cleveland,	4x100 medley relay

Year	Name	Event/Sport
	Marcel Gery,	
	Tom Ponting,	
	Mark Tewksbury	
	Keltie Duggan	100m breaststroke
	Nathalie Giguere	200m breaststroke
	Nancy Sweetnam	200m IM
	Sylvie Frechette	synchro swim figures, solo
	Kathy Glen,	synchro swim duet
	Christine Larsen	
1994	Jeff Adams	wheelchair 800m, 1500m
	Donovan Bailey,	4x100m relay
	Glenroy Gilbert,	
	Carleton Chambers,	
	Bruny Surin	
	Michael Smith	decathlon
	Angela Chalmers	3000m
	Carole Rouillard	marathon
	Casey Patton	57kg boxing
	Mike Strange	60kg boxing
	Rowan Donaldson	75kg boxing
	Dale Brown	81kg boxing
	Tanya Dubnicoff	1000m sprint cycling
	Annie Pelletier	1m, 3m springboard
	Anne Montminy	10m platform
	Travis Romagnoli,	men's gymnastics team
	Kris Burley, Richard Ikeda,	
	Alan Nolet	
	Alan Nolet	horizontal bar gymnastics
	Stacey Galloway,	women's gymnastic team
	Jaime Hill,	
	Lisa Simes, Stella Umeh	
	Stella Umeh	women's individual all-around, vault gymnastics
	Lindsay Richards,	rhythmic gymnastics team
	Camille Martens,	
	Gretchen McLennan	
	Mark Bedlington,	pairs running target shooting
	Matthew Bedlington	
	Jean Pierre Huot	men's air pistol
	Michel Dion	men's small-bore 3-position rifle
	Wayne Sorensen,	men's pairs small-bore
	Michel Dion	3-position rifle
	Jean-Francois Senecal,	men's pairs air rifle
	Wayne Sorensen	
	Helen Smith	women's air pistol
	Sharon Bowes	women's small-bore rifle
	Sharon Bowes,	women's pairs small-bore
	Christina Ashcroft	3-position rifle
	Stephen Clarke	100m freestyle swimming
	Andrew Haley	100m freestyle disabled swimming
	Lisa Alexander	synchro swim solo
	Lisa Alexander	synchro swim duet
	Erin Woodley	
	Selwyn Tam	52kg wrestling
	Robert Dawson	57kg wrestling
	Marty Calder	62kg wrestling
	Chris Wilson	68kg wrestling
	David Hohl	74kg wrestling
	Justin Abdou	82kg wrestling
	Scott Bianco	90kg wrestling

Year	Name	Event/Sport
	Greg Edgelow	100kg wrestling
	Andrew Borodow	130kg wrestling
1998	Michael Strange	63.5kg boxing
	Jeremy Molitor	67kg boxing
	Mark Simmons	91kg boxing
	Eric Wohlberg	cycling, 42km road race
	Lyne Bessette	cycling, 94km road race
	Tanya Dubnicoff	women's sprint cycling
	Alexandre Despatie	high dive
	Eryn Bulmer	springboard diving
	Alexander Jeltkov	men's horizontal bar
	Erika Leigh Stirton	rhythmic gymnastics all round
	Erika Leigh Stirton	rhythmic gymnastics clubs
	Erika Leigh Stirton	rhythmic gymnastics hoop
	Erika Leigh Stirton	rhythmic gymnastics ribbon
	Erika Leigh Stirton	rhythmic gymnastics rope
	Christina Ashcroft,	air rifle team
	Sharon Bowes	
	James Paton	full-bore rifle
	Metodi Igorov	rapid-fire pistol
	Michel Dion,	small-bore rifle team
	Wayne Sorensen	
	Christina Ashcroft,	small-bore sport rifle team
	Sharon Bowes	
	Mark Versfeld	100m backstroke
	Mark Versfeld	200m backstroke
	Marianne Limpert	200m individual medley
	Joanne Malar	400m individual medley
	Jacinthe Taillon,	synchro swim duet figures
	Kasia Kulesza	
	Valerie Hould Marchand	synchro swim solo figures
	Sebastien Groulx	69kg weightlifting, combined
	Sebastien Groulx	69kg weightlifting, snatch
	Akos Sandor	105kg weightlifting, clean and jerk
	Akos Sandor	105kg weightlifting, combined
	Akos Sandor	105kg weightlifting, snatch
2002	Chantal Petitclerc	wheelchair 800m
	Mark Boswell	high jump
	Jason Douglas	91kg boxing
	Jean Thenistor Pascal	71kg boxing
	Roland Green	cycling, cross country
	Chrissy Redden	cycling, cross country
	Clara Hughes	cycling, road race time trial
	Alexandre Despatie	1m springboard diving
	Alexandre Despatie	springboard diving
	Kate Richardson	gymnastics balance beam
	Kyle Shewfelt	men's gymnastic floor exercise
	Kate Richardson	gymnastics women's individual
	Kyle Shewfelt	gymnastics men's vault
	Nicolas Gill	100kg judo
	Carolyne Lepage	48kg judo
	Kim Eagles,	air pistol team
	Dorothy Hare	
	Cynthia Meyer	clay pigeon trap
	Metodi Igorov	rapid-fire pistol
	Clayton Miller	skeet
	Jonathon Power	men's singles squash
	Claire Carver-Dias,	synchro swim duet figures

Year	Name	Event/Sport
	Fanny Letourneau	
	Claire Carver-Dias	synchro swim solo figures
	Simon Whitfield	triathlon
	Carol Montgomery	triathlon
	Maryse Turcotte	58kg women's weightlifting, clean and jerk
	Maryse Turcotte	58kg women's weightlifting, combined
	Pascale Dorcelus	63kg women's weightlifting, snatch
	Guivi Sissaouri	60kg wrestling
	Daniel Igali	74kg wrestling
	Nicholas Ugoalah	84kg wrestling
	Dean Schmeichel	96kg wrestling

Silver

Year	Name	Event/Sport
1930	John Fitzpatrick	220yd run
	Doral Pilling	javelin
	M.C. Herman, discus	
	Alexander Wilson,	4x400yd relay
	Arthur Scott,	
	Stanley Glover,	
	James Ball	
	Cosmos Canzano	60kg boxing
	Howard Williams	67kg boxing
	William Skimming	+81kg boxing
	Helen McCormack	10m diving
	Samuel Walker,	10m diving
	Doris Ogilvie	3m diving
	Jimmy Campbell,	lawn bowling fours
	Mitch Thomas, W. Rae,	
	Harry Allen	
	J. Callaghan, J, Fleming,	coxless four
	O. Belyer, H. Pelam,	
	B.L. Gates, R.S. Evans,	coxed four
	J.A. Butler, H.R.McCuaig,	
	A. Miles	
	Irene Pirie, Betty Edwards,	4x100yd freestyle relay
	Marjorie Linton,	
	Peggy Bailey	
1934	Robert Rankine	6 mile run
	Birchall Pearson,	4x110yd relay
	Allan Poole,	
	Frank Nicks,	
	William Christie	
	Bill Fritz, Arthur Scott,	4x440yd relay
	Joseph Addison, Ray Lewis	
	Jim Worrall	120yd hurdles
	Joe Haley	high jump
	Eva Dawes	high jump
	A. Gilbert	pole vault
	George Sutherland	hammer
	Aileen Meagher	220yd dash
	Betty Taylor	80m hurdles
	Audrey Dearnley,	440yd relay
	Aileen Meagher,	
	Hilda Strike	
	Hilda Strike	100yd dash
	Sam Richardson	triple jump
	Evelyn Goshawk	long jump

Year	Name	Event/Sport
	Maxie Berger	51kg boxing
	Leonard Wadsworth	75kg boxing
	Robert McLeod	1000m time trial cycling
	W.S. Macdonald	lawn bowling singles
	W.G. Hutchinson,	lawn bowling pairs
	A.A. Langford	
	George Larsen	100yd freestyle swim
	Robert Pirie	1500yd freestyle
	Irene Pirie	100yd freestyle
	Phyllis Haslam	200yd breaststroke
	Ted McKinley	57kg wrestling
	Pat Meehan	100kg wrestling
1938	Bill Fritz	440yd dash
	Robert Rankine	6 mile run
	Larry O'Connor	120yd hurdles
	Jim Panton	long jump
	Eric Coy	shot put
	Aileen Meagher,	440yd relay
	Jeannette Dolson,	
	Barbara Howard	
	Joseph Gagnon	51kg boxing
	Henry Hurst	60kg boxing
	Lynda Adams	3m, 10m diving
	Robert Pirie	1650yd freestyle swim
	George Burleigh,	4x220yd freestyle relay
	Robert Hooper,	
	Gord Devlin,	
	Robert Pirie	
	Gordon Kerr	110yd backstroke
	Gordon Kerr,	3x110yd medley relay
	Jimmy Prentice,	
	Robert Pirie	
	Vernon Blake	57kg wrestling
	Larry Clarke	62kg wrestling
1950	Jack Hutchins	880yd run
	Stan Egerton	pole vault
	George Athans Sr.	10m diving
	Robert Desjarlais,	sabre team
	George Pouliot,	
	Edward Brooke	
	James Portelance	1650yd freestyle
	Lucien Beaumont,	3x110yd medley relay
	Peter Salmon,	
	Allan Gilchrist	
	Rosaire Smith	56kg weightlifting
	Roland Milord	62kg wrestling
	Morgan Pumb	68kg wrestling
1954	Don McFarlane	100yd dash
	Laird Sloan,	4x440yd relay
	Doug Clement,	
	Joe Foreman,	
	Terry Tobacco	
	Ronald Miller	pole vault
	John Pavelich	shot put
	Jackie MacDonald	women's shot put
	Roy Pella	discus
	Gwen Hobbins	80m hurdles
	Gerald Buchanan	+81kg boxing
	Roland Asselin,	épée team
	Ed Brooke,	
	Carl Schwende	
	Sam Gardiner,	lawn bowling pairs
	Richard Williams	

Year	Name	Event/Sport
	Gerry McNamee,	4x220yd freestyle relay
	Ed Simpson,	
	Allan Gilchrist,	
	George Park	
	Virginia Grant	110yd freestyle
	Gladys Priestley	440yd freestyle
	Virginia Grant,	4x110yd freestyle relay
	Gladys Priestley,	
	Helen Stewart,	
	Beth Whittall	
	Jules Sylvain	60kg weightlifting
	Dave Baillie	110kg weightlifting
	Ruby Leibovitch	68kg wrestling
	James Christie	82kg wrestling
	Robert Steckle	90kg wrestling
	Keith Maltman	100kg wrestling
1958	John Smyth	triple jump
	Robert Reid	pole vault
	Bill Patrick	3m diving
	Irene MacDonald	3m diving
	Carl Schwende,	épée team
	John Andru	
	Roland Asselin	
	Glen Smith,	coxless four
	Malcolm Turnbull,	
	Richard McClure,	
	John Madden	
	Don Arnold,	coxed four
	Walter d'Hondt,	
	Dave Helliwell,	
	Larry Stapleton,	
	Sohen Biln	
	Robert Wheaton,	4x110yd medley relay
	Peter Bell,	
	George Park,	
	Cameron Grout	
	Sara Barber,	4x110yd freestyle relay
	Margaret Iwasaki,	
	Gladys Priestley,	
	Susan Sangster	
	Dave Baillie	110kg weightlifting
1962	Tom Dinsley	3m diving
	Benedek Simo	individual sabre
	John Andru,	sabre team
	Benedek Simo,	
	Carl Schwende,	
	Bob Foxcroft	
	Aldwin Meinhardt,	4x110yd freestyle relay
	John Kelso,	
	John Gilchrist,	
	Dick Pound	
	Pat Thomson,	4x110yd freestyle relay
	Sara Barber,	
	Madeleine Sevigny,	
	Mary Stewart	
	John Kelso,	4x220yd freestyle relay
	Aldwin Meinhardt,	
	Dick Pound,	
	John Gilchrist	
	Allan Salter	56kg weightlifting
	Pierre St. Jean	75kg weightlifting
	Cosford White	90kg weightlifting
	Peter Michienzi,	52kg wrestling

Year	Name	Event/Sport
	Matti Jutila	62kg wrestling
	Phil Oberlander	74kg wrestling
1966	Ross McKenzie,	4x440yd relay
	Brian McLaren,	
	Don Domansky,	
	Bill Crothers	
	George Puce	discus
	Irene Piotrowski,	100yd dash
	Sharon Whittaker	badminton women's singles
	Bev Boys	3m diving
	John Andru,	épée team
	Konrad Widmaier,	
	Peter Bakonyi	
	Jules Sobrian	free pistol
	John Gilchrist	1650yd freestyle swim
	Robert Kasting,	4x110, 4x220yd freestyle
	Ralph Hutton,	relays
	Ron Jacks,	
	John Gilchrist	
	Ralph Hutton	110, 220yd backstroke,
		440yd IM
	Elaine Tanner	110, 220yd backstroke
	Marilyn Corson	220yd butterfly
	Louise Kennedy,	4x1100yd medley relay
	Donna Ross,	
	Elaine Tanner,	
	Marion Lay	
	Ray Lougheed	68kg wrestling
	Richard Bryant	74kg wrestling
	Sebastien Donison	82kg wrestling
1970	John Hawkins	high jump
	Allan Kane	pole vault
	Jocelyn Lovell,	cycling tandem sprint
	Barry Harvey	
	Ken Sully	3m diving
	Liz Carruthers	3m diving
	Nancy Robertson	10m diving
	Lester Wong	épée
	Ralph Hutton	200, 400m freestyle
	Angela Coughlan	200m freestyle
	Ralph Hutton,	4x100, 4x200m freestyle
	George Smith,	relays
	Ron Jacks,	
	Robert Kasting	
	Peter Cross	100m breaststroke
	Susan Smith,	4x100 freestyle relay
	Linda Hall,	
	Karen James,	
	Angela Coughlan	
	Ken Campbell	200m IM
	Donna-Marie Gurr	200m backstroke
	Robert Santavy	90kg weightlifting
	Ken Shand	48kg wrestling
	Herbert Singerman	57kg wrestling
	Pat Bolger	62kg wrestling
	Alfred Wurr	74kg wrestling
	Nicholas Schori	82kg wrestling
1974	Louise Hanna	high jump
	Brenda Eisler,	long jump
	Jamie Paulson	badminton singles
	Scott Cranham	3m diving
	Bev Boys	3m diving
	Jules Sobrian	rapid-fire pistol

Year	Name	Event/Sport		Year	Name	Event/Sport
	Bruce Robertson	100, 200m freestyle			Desai Williams,	
	Gail Amundrud	100m freestyle			Mark McKoy	
	Steve Pickell	100m backstroke			Ben Johnson	100m sprint
	Donna-Marie Gurr	100m backstroke			Rob Gray	discus
	Byron MacDonald	100m butterfly			Laslo Babits	javelin
	Wendy Quirk	400m freestyle			Dave Steen	decathlon
	Marion Stuart	100m breaststroke			Marcel Jobin	30km walk
	Patti Stenhouse	200m butterfly			Claire Backhouse,	badminton team
	Becky Smith	200, 400m IM			Johanne Falardeau, Mark Freitag,	
	Yves Carignan	56kg weightlifting			Paul Johnson, Denyse Julien,	
	Gordon Bertie	52kg wrestling			Robert MacDougall, Keith Priestman,	
1978	Jerome Drayton	marathon			Sandra Skillings, Patrick Tyron,	
	Bruno Pauletto	shot put			Jane Youngberg,	
	Carmen Ionesco	shot put			Steve Bauer	cycling road race
	Scott Neilson	hammer			Sylvie Bernier	3m diving
	Greg Joy	high jump			Jennifer McArton	10m diving
	Debbie Brill	high jump			Jim Timmerman	rapid-fire pistol
	Alison Hayward	javelin			Guy Lorion,	3-position rifle team
	Angela Bailey,	4x100m relay			Jean-Francois Senecal	
	Patty Loverock,				Anne Ottenbrite	100m breaststroke
	Margaret Howe,				Victor Davis	100m breaststroke
	Marjorie Bailey				Kathy Bald	200m breaststroke
	Jamie McKee,	badminton team			Cheryl Gibson	200m IM
	John Czich,				Cam Henning	100m backstroke
	Ken Priestman,				Peter Szmidt	200, 400m freestyle
	Greg Carter,				Guy Greavette	82.5kg weightlifting
	Wendy Clarkson,				Ray Takahashi	52kg wrestling
	Jane Youngberg,			1986	Jillian Richardson	400m run
	Johanne Falardeau,				Debbie Scott-Bowker	1500, 3000m runs
	Sharon Crawford,				Donalda Duprey	400m hurdles
	Claire Backhouse,				Guillaume Leblanc	30km walk
	Lucio Fabris				Angela Bailey,	4x100 relay
	Jane Youngberg,	badminton women's doubles			Angella Issajenko,	
	Claire Backhouse				Esmie Lawrence,	
	Ian Clyde	51kg boxing			Angela Phipps	
	Pierre Harvey	cycling road race			Dave Steen	decathlon
	Bev Boys	3m diving			Dave Edge	marathon
	Scott Cranham	3m diving			Bob Ferguson	pole vault
	Ken Armstrong	10m diving			Johanne Falardeau,	badminton women's doubles
	Sherry Hawco	individual gymnastics			Denyse Julien	
	Monica Goermann	individual gymnastics			Claire Backhouse-Sharpe,	badminton team
	George Leary	trapshooting			Mike Butler, Linda Cloutier,	
	Ed Jans	free pistol			Michael de Belle, Johanne Falardeau,	
	Bill Sawchuck	100m freestyle, 200m IM			John Goss, Denyse Julien, Ken Poole,	
	Claus Bredschneider	200m butterfly			Sandra Skillings	
	Wendy Quirk	200m butterfly			Alex Ongaro	cycling sprint
	Helene Boivin	100m backstroke			John Nash	3m diving
	Becky Smith	400m IM			David Bedard	10m diving
	Bill Sawchuck,	4x100m freestyle relay			Bill Boettger, Ron Jones	lawn bowling pairs
	Dennis Corcoran,				Dave Brown,	lawn bowling fours
	Robert Baylis,				Dave Duncalf,	
	Peter Szmidt				Dave Houtby,	
	Terry Hadlow	90kg weightlifting			Dan Milligan	
	Wayne Smith	110kg weightlifting			Lisa Wright	single scull rowing
	George Gunovski	48kg wrestling			Peter Tatersall	lightweight single scull
	Michael Barry	57kg wrestling			Heather Clarke,	double sculls
	Victor Zilberman	74kg wrestling			Lisa Robertson	
1982	Roger Lemay	individual archery			Tom Guinn	air pistol
	Angela Bailey,	4x100m relay			Sharon Bowes	air rifle
	Marita Payne,				Alain Marion	full-bore rifle
	Angella Taylor,				Brian Gabriel,	skeet team
	Molly Killingbeck,				Don Kwasnycia	
	Ben Johnson, Tony Sharpe,	4x100m relay			Michel Dion,	3-position rifle

Year	Name	Event/Sport
	Jean-Francois Senecal	
	Victor Davis	200m breaststroke
	Cindy Ounpuu	200m breaststroke
	Tom Ponting	200m butterfly
	Jane Kerr	200m freestyle
	Alex Baumann,	4x100m freestyle relay
	Vlastimil Cerny,	
	Sandy Goss,	
	Blair Hicken	
	Scott Flowers, Sandy Goss,	4x200m freestyle relay
	Tom Ponting, Paul Szekula	
	Allison Higson, Jane Kerr,	4x100 medley relay
	Barb McBain,	
	Donna McGinnis	
	Louis Payer,	75kg weightlifting
	David Bolduc	+110kg weightlifting
	Doug Cox	90kg wrestling
1990	Denyse Julien	badminton singles
	Mike Bitten,	badminton team
	Bryan Blanshard, Mike Butler;	
	Anil Kaul, Dave Humble,	
	Johanne Falardeau, Denyse	
	Julien, Claire Backhouse-Sharpe,	
	Doris Piche, Linda Cloutier	
	Geronimo Bie	54kg boxing
	Greg Johnson	67kg boxing
	Ray Downey	71kg boxing
	Dale Brown	81kg boxing
	Pat Jordan	91kg boxing
	Chris Koberstein,	100km cycling team time trial
	David Spears,	
	Peter Verhessen, Sean Way	
	Curt Harnett	1000m cycling sprint
	David Bedard	1m, 10m diving
	Mark Rourke	3m diving
	Barb Bush	3m diving
	Alan Nolet,	gymnastics individual all-around, floor exercise
	Curtis Hibbert	gymnastics vault
	Larissa Lowing	balance beam, floor exercise
	Lori Strong	uneven bars, vault
	Kevin West	-60kg judo
	Tom Greenway	+95kg judo
	Mario Laroche	open judo
	Karen Hayde	-66kg judo
	Alison Webb	-72kg judo
	Jane Patterson	open judo
	Alf Wallace,	lawn bowl pairs
	George Boxwell	
	Madonna Gimotea,	rhythmic gymnastics all-around, hoop, ribbon, rope
	Mary Fuzesi	rhythmic gymnastics ball
	Mark Howkins, Stan Wills	25m rapid-fire pistol
	Mark Bedlington,	10m running target
	David Lee	
	Michael Ashcroft,	50m free rifle prone team
	Barry Sutherland	
	Gary Anderson	100m backstroke
	Marcel Gery	100m butterfly
	Jon Kelly,	4x200 freestyle relay
	Turlough O'Hare,	

Year	Name	Event/Sport
	Eddie Parenti,	
	Gary Vander Meulen,	
	Guylaine Cloutier	100, 200m breaststroke
	Allison Higson,	4x100m freestyle relay
	Erin Murphy	
	Patricia Noall, Kim Patton	
	Kathy Glen	synchro swim figures
1994	Kevin Sullivan	1500m run
	Tim Berrett	30km road walk
	Curtis Heywood	pole vault
	Charmaine Crooks	800m run
	Paula Schnurr	1500m run
	Robyn Meagher	3000m run
	Lizanne Bussieres	marathon
	Si-An Deng	badminton women's singles
	Stephen Gallinger	91kg boxing
	Curt Harnett	1000m cycling sprint
	Clara Hughes,	cycling team time trial
	Anne Samplonius,	
	Alison Sydor,	
	Lesley Tomlinson	
	Linda Jackson	cycling road race
	Paige Gordon	3m, 10m diving
	Kris Burley	gymnastics floor exercise, parallel bars, vault
	Richard Ikeda	gymnastics horizontal bar
	Stacey Galloway,	gymnastics women's team
	Jaime Hill,	
	Liza Simes, Stella Umeh	
	Stella Umeh	gymnastics uneven bars
	Camille Martens	rhythmic gymnastics individual all-around, ball, ribbon
	Lindsay Richards	rhythmic gymnastics hoop
	Mark Bedlington	individual running target
	Jean-Pierre Huot,	air pistol pairs
	John Rochon	
	Wayne Sorensen	individual small-bore rifle 3-position
	Jean-Francois Senecal	individual air rifle
	Sharon Cozzarin,	sport pistol pairs
	Helen Smith	
	George Leary	individual open trap
	Ron Bonotto,	open trap pairs
	George Leary	
	Kevin Draxinger	200m backstroke
	Stephen Clarke	100m butterfly
	Curtis Myden	200m, 400m IM
	Chris Renaud,	4x100 medley relay
	Jon Cleveland,	
	Stephen Clarke,	
	Robert Braknis	
	Andrea Nugent	50m freestyle
	Marianne Limpert	200m IM
	Nancy Sweetnam	400m IM
	Serge Tremblay	76kg weightlifting snatch
	Paul Ragusa,	48kg wrestling
1998	Philomena Mensah	100m run
	Nicholas "Nick" A'Hearn	20km walk
	Brad McCuaig,	4x100m relay
	Glenroy Gilbert,	
	O'Brian Gibbons,	

Year	Name	Event/Sport
	Trevino Betty	
	Marty O'Donnel	57kg boxing
	Scott MacIntosh	71kg boxing
	Troy Amos	81kg boxing
	Linda Jackson	28 km cycling, road race
	Blythe Hartley	1m springboard diving
	Myriam Boileau	high dive
	Kris Burley	gymnastics horizontal bars
	Richard Ikede	gymnastics parallel
	Richard Ikede	gymnastics pommel horse
	Katie Iafolla,	rhythmic gymnastics team
	Emilie Livingston,	
	Erika Leigh Stirton	
	Veronique Leeleve	gymnastics uneven bars
	Sharon Bowes	air rifle
	John Rochon,	centre fire-pistol team
	Metodi Igorov	
	James Paton,	full-bore rifle pairs
	Alain Marion	
	Joe Trinci	skeet
	Wayne Sorensen	small-bore rifle
	Sharon Bowes	small-bore sport rifle
	Christina Ashcroft,	small-bore sport rifle prone team
	Maureen Spinney	
	Jonathon Power	singles squash
	Kelly Stefanshyn	100m backstroke
	Courtenay Chuy	200m breaststroke
	Joanne Maler	200m individual medley
	Elizabeth Warden	400m individual medley
	Stephen Clarke,	4x100m freestyle relay
	Craig Hutchison,	
	Garret Pulle,	
	Robbie Taylor	
	Jessica Deglau,	4x100m medley relay
	Laura Nicholls,	
	Kelly Stefanyshyn,	
	Lauren Van Oosten,	
	Joanne Malar	800m freestyle
	William Rowe	tenpin bowling
	Sebastien Groulx	69kg weightlifting clean and jerk
2002	Shane Niemi	400m run
	Diane Cummins	800m run
	Jason Tunks	discus
	Kwaku Boateng	high jump
	Scott Russell	javelin
	Andrew Kooner	54kg boxing
	David Cadieux	+91kg boxing
	Seamus McGrath	cycling, cross country
	Lori-Ann Muenzer	cycling, sprint
	Susan Palmer-Komar	93.6km cycling road race
	Blythe Hartley	1m springboard diving
	Emilie Heymans	high dive
	Emilie Heymans	springboard diving
	David Kikuchi	gymnastics parallel
	team event	gymnastics men's team event
	Catherine Roberge	70kg judo
	Keith Morgan	90kg judo
	Shirley Fitzpatrick-Wong,	women's rinks/fours lawn bowling
	Anita Nivala,	
	Melissa Ranger,	
	Andrea Weigand	

Year	Name	Event/Sport
	Dorothy Hare	air pistol
	Kim Eagles,	air pistol team
	Dorothy Hare	
	Cynthia Meyer,	double trap pairs
	Susan Nattrass	
	Morgan Knabe	100m breaststroke
	Mike Mintenko	100m butterfly
	Stephanie Dixon	100m multi disability freestyle
	Brian Johns	400m individual medley team, 4x200m freestyle relay
	Jennifer Carroll	50m backstroke
	Philippe Gagnon	50m multi disability freestyle
	Stephanie Dixon	50m multi disability freestyle
	Johnny Huang	table tennis single
	Karine Turcotte	48kg weightlifting clean and jerk
	Karine Turcotte	48kg weightlifting combined
	Karine Turcotte	48kg weightlifting snatch
	Maryse Turcotte	58kg weightlifting snatch
	Julien Galipeau	94kg weightlifting clean and jerk
	Akos Sandor	105kg weightlifting clean and jerk
	Akos Sandor	105kg weightlifting combined
	Akos Sandor	105kg weightlifting snatch
	Mikheil Japaridze	55kg wrestling
	Graham Neal Ewers	66kg wrestling
	Eric Ronald Kirschner	120kg wrestling

Bronze

Year	Name	Event/Sport
1930	John Fitzpatrick	100yd dash
	M.C. Herman	shot put
	Robert Stoddart	pole vault
	Alex Wilson	880yd run
	Leonard Hutton,	triple jump
	Jack Cameron	hammer
	William Stargratt	high jump
	John Miles	marathon
	Ross Galloway	51kg boxing
	John Keller	54kg boxing
	Al Pitcher	81kg boxing
	Arthur Stott	3m diving
	Mollie Bailey	3m diving
	A.S. Reid, W.W. Moore	lawn bowling men's pairs
	Leslie McDonald,	coxed eight
	Earl Eastwood, Albert Taylor,	
	Dan Doal, William Thoburn,	
	Joseph Zabinsky, Harry Fry,	
	Joseph Bowkes, William Moore	
	Albert Gibson	100yd freestyle swim
	George Burleigh	400, 1500yd freestyle swim
1934	Margaret Bell	high jump
	Harry Class	3m diving
	Doris Ogilvie	3m diving
	Robert Pirie	440yd freestyle swim
	Irene Pirie	440yd freestyle swim
	Ben Gazell	100yd backstroke
	Bill Puddy	200yd breaststroke
	Howard Thomas	68kg wrestling

Year	Name	Event/Sport
	Alex Watt	90kg wrestling
1938	William Dale	880yd run
	Scotty Rankine	3 mile run
	Stuart Frid	pole vault
	George Sutherland	discus
	Jeannette Dolson	100yd dash
	Violet Montgomery,	660yd relay
	Barbara Howard,	
	Aileen Meagher,	
	Jeannette Dolson	
	Rex Carey	75kg boxing
	George Athans Sr	3m, 10m diving
	Marie Sharkey	3m diving
	James Temple,	coxed four
	Max Winkler,	
	Don Davis,	
	John McDonald,	
	Ken Jaggard	
	Dorothy Lyon	110yd freestyle swim
	James Prentice	220yd breaststroke
	Joan Langdon	220yd breaststroke
	John Whelan	100kg wrestling
1950	Donald Pettie	100yd dash
	Bill Parnell	880yd run
	Leo Roininen	shot put
	Svein Sigfusson	discus
	Doug Robinson	javelin
	Eleanor McKenzie,	660yd relay
	Gerry Bernister,	
	Pat Jones,	
	Elaine Silburn	
	Len Walters	54kg boxing
	Ed Haddad	60kg boxing
	Bill Pinkus,	75kg boxing
	Lynda Hunt	3m diving
	George Pouliot	individual foil
	Robert Desjarlais,	foil, épée teams
	George Pouliot,	
	Ed Brooke	
	George Pouliot	individual sabre
1954	Terry Tobacco	440yd run
	Rich Ferguson	1 mile run
	Norm Williams,	120yd hurdles
	Margery Squires,	4x110yd relay
	Dorothy Kozak,	
	Annabelle Murray,	
	Geraldine Bernister	
	Alice Whitty	high jump
	Marie Dupree	discus
	Shirley Couzens	javelin
	Marcel Piau	75kg boxing
	Bill Misselbrooke	81kg boxing
	Irene MacDonald	3m diving
	John Alan Howard,	foil team
	Carl Schwende,	
	Roland Asselin,	
	Ed Brooke	
	Carl Schwende	individual épée
	Robert Williams	single sculls
	Don Guest,	double sculls
	Lawrence David Stephan	
1958	Mike Agostini	100yd dash
	Terry Tobacco	440yd run

Year	Name	Event/Sport
	Hans Moks	javelin
	Diane Matheson,	4x110yd relay
	Eleanor Haslam,	
	Maureen Rever,	
	Freyda Berman	
	Jackie Gelling	shot put
	Ray Galante	63.5kg boxing
	James Walters	71kg boxing
	Robert Piau	75kg boxing
	Ken Williams, Peter Bell,	4x220yd freestyle relay
	Cameron Grout, Bill Slater	
	Robert Wheaton	110yd backstroke
	Margaret Iwasaki	110yd butterfly
	Sara Barber, Irene Service,	4x110yd medley relay
	Margaret Iwasaki,	
	Gladys Priestley	
	Marcel Gosselin	56kg weightlifting
	Adrien Gilbert	75kg weightlifting
	Frederick Flannery	52kg wrestling
	Robert Steckle	90kg wrestling
1962	Bruce Kidd	3 mile run
	Dave Steen	shot put
	Harvey Reti	63.5kg boxing
	Ernie Meissner	3m diving
	Carl Schwende,	team foil
	Benedek Simo,	
	John Andru	
	Carl Schwende,	team épée
	Peter Bakonyi,	
	Bob Foxcroft	
	John Andru	individual sabre
	Eldon Worobieff,	coxless four
	Tom Gray,	
	Tom Stokes,	
	Ray McIntosh	
	Stephen Rabinovitch	110yd breaststroke
	Aldwin Meinhardt,	110yd butterfly
	John Kelso	440yd IM
	Mary Stewart	110yd freestyle
	John Kelso,	4x110yd medley relay
	Stephen Rabinovitch,	
	Aldwin Meinhardt,	
	Dick Pound	
	Sara Barber,	4x110yd medley relay
	Alison Glendenning,	
	Mary Stewart,	
	Patricia Thompson	
	Kurt Boese	68kg wrestling
1966	Don Domansky	440yd run
	Gerry Moro	pole vault, decathlon
	George Puce	shot put
	Nancy McCredie	shot put
	Irene Piotrowski	220yd run
	Jenny Wingerson	80m hurdles
	Carol Martin	discus
	Judy Dahlgren	javelin
	Frank Scott	51kg boxing
	Bev Boys	10m diving
	Les Samek, John Andru,	team sabre
	Bob Foxcroft,	
	Garfield McMahon	free pistol
	Jules Sobrian	rapid-fire pistol
	Ralph Hutton	440, 1650yd freestyle

Year	Name	Event/Sport
	Bill Mahony	220yd breaststroke
	Toomas Arusso	200m butterfly
	Jane Hughes	440yd IM
	John Gilchrist	440yd IM
	Chun Hon Chan	56kg weightlifting
	Allen Salter	60kg weightlifting
	Pete Michenzi	52kg wrestling
1970	Bill Stewart	800m run
	Bob Raftis	pole vault
	Thelma Fynn	1500m run
	Joan Hendry,	4x100m relay
	Joyce Sadowick,	
	Patty Loverock,	
	Stephanie Berto	
	Joan Hendry	long jump
	Carol Martin	discus
	Judy Dahlgren	javelin
	Jenny Meldrum	pentathlon
	Jamie Paulson, Yves Pare	badminton men's doubles
	Jack Meda	81kg boxing
	Jocelyn Lovell	1000m time trial
	Ron Friesen	3m diving
	Gerry Wiedel,	foil team
	Magdy Conyd,	
	Konrad Widmaier	
	Fleurette Comeau,	foil team
	Pacita Wiedel,	
	Kyoko Aoyama	
	Peter Bakonyi,	épée team
	Lester Wong,	
	Konrad Widmaier	
	Eric Fish	100m backstroke
	Ron Jacks	100m butterfly
	Donna-Marie Gurr	100m backstroke
	Donna-Marie Gurr,	4x100 medley relay
	Sylvie Dockerill,	
	Susan Smith,	
	Angela Coughlan	
	Pierre St. Jean	75kg weightlifting
	Price Morris	110kg weightlifting
	David Stitt	52kg wrestling
	Ole Sorensen	68kg wrestling
	Claude Pilon	90kg wrestling
1974	Claude Ferragne	high jump
	Bruce Pirnie	shot put
	Thelma Wright	1500m run
	Yvonne Saunders,	4x400m relay
	Brenda Walsh,	
	Margaret MacGowan,	
	Maureen Crowley	
	Brigitte Bittner	high jump
	Carol Martin	discus
	Dale Anderson	57kg boxing
	Teri York	3m diving
	Scott Cranham	10m diving
	Brian Phillips	100m freestyle
	Judy Wright	100m freestyle
	Ian MacKenzie,	4x200 freestyle relay
	Gary MacDonald,	
	Jim Fowlie,	
	Bruce Robertson	
	Bruce Robertson	100m butterfly
	Gary MacDonald	200m IM

Year	Name	Event/Sport
	Gail Amundrud	200m IM
	Donna-Marie Gurr	200m backstroke
	Stephen Martin	68kg wrestling
	Tarah Hryb	82kg wrestling
1978	Glenn Bogue	400m run
	Paul Bannon	marathon
	Bishop Dolegiewicz	shot put
	Robert Gray	discus
	Lucette Moreau	discus
	Dean Bauck	high jump
	Julie White	high jump
	Penny Werthner	1500m run
	Laurie Kern	javelin
	Margaret Stride,	4x400m relay
	Debbie Campbell,	
	Anne Mackie-Morelli,	
	Rachelle Campbell	
	Wendy Clarkson	badminton singles
	Bill Rannelli	54kg boxing
	Guy Boutin	57kg boxing
	John Raftery	63kg boxingg
	Derrick Hoyt	67kg boxing
	Roddy McDonald	75kg boxing
	Gord Singleton	100m time trial
	Eniko Kiefer	3m diving
	Scott Cranham	10m diving
	Janet Nutter	10m diving
	Jean Choquette	individual gymnastics
	Pat Vamplew	full-bore rifle
	Gary MacDonald	100m freestyle swim
	Wendy Quirk	100m freestyle
	Jay Tapp	100m backstroke
	Bill Sawchuk	400M IM, 100m butterfly
	Cheryl Gibson	100m backstroke, 400m IM
	Marian Stuart	100m breaststroke
	Becky Smith	200m IM
	Darrell Schultz	60kg weightlifting
	Bob Santavy	100kg weightlifting
1982	Lucille Lemay	individual archery
	Angella Taylor	200m dash
	Susan Kamelli	100m hurdles
	Rosemarie Hauch	shot put
	Luby Chambul	shot put
	Jill Ross	heptathlon
	Greg Duhaime	3000m steeplechase
	Bishop Dolegiewicz	discus
	Guillaume Leblanc	30km walk
	Patrick Tryon,	badminton men's doubles
	Paul Johnson	
	Kevin McDermott	75kg boxing
	Alex Stieda	individual cycling pursuit
	Kathy Kelemen	10m diving
	John Nash	10m diving
	Guy Lorion	3-position rifle
	Tom Guinn	air pistol
	Pat Vamplew,	prone rifle team
	Ernest Sopsich,	air pistol team
	Jim Timmerman,	
	Tom Guinn	
	Michelle MacPherson	100m butterfly, 400m IM
	Tom Ponting	100m butterfly
	Cheryl Gibson	200m backstroke
	Mike West	200m backstroke

Year	Name	Event/Sport	Year	Name	Event/Sport
	Kathy Richardson	200m breaststroke		Mike Bitten	
	Wade Flemons	100m backstroke		Johanne Falardeau,	badminton women's doubles
	Jeff Sheehan	200m IM		Denyse Julien	
	Alex Baumann,	4x100m freestyle relay		Domenic (Filane)	
	Blair Hicken,			Figliomeni	48kg boxing
	Graham Welbourn,			Vern Linklater	+91kg boxing
	Peter Szmidt			Scott Goguen	men's cycling road race
	Jacques Demers	75kg weightlifting		Kelly-Ann Way	3000m individual pursuit
	Kevin Roy	100kg weightlifting		Larry Flewwelling	3m diving
	Mario Leblanc	110kg weightlifting		Bruno Fournier	10m diving
	Maldwyn Cooper	48kg wrestling		Paige Gordon,	10m diving
	Lloyd Renken	68kg wrestling		Curtis Hibbert,	gymnastics floor exercise,
	Brian Renken	74kg wrestling		Jean-Pierre Cantin,	-65kg judo
1986	Angella Issajenko	100m sprint		Roger Cote	-75kg judo
	Ben Johnson	200m sprint		James Kendrick	-95kg judo
	Dave Campbell	1500m run		Mandy Clayton	-61kg judo
	Lynn Williams	1500m run		Mary Fuzesi	rhythmic gymnastics rope
	John Graham,	400m hurdles		Mart Klepp	10m air rifle
	John Graham,	4x400m relay		Chris Bowie	400m freestyle
	Atlee Mahorn,			Jon Kelly	200m butterfly, 400m IM
	Anton Skerritt,			Marcel Gery,	4x100 freestyle relay
	Andre Smith			Stephane Hebert,	
	Alain Metellus	high jump		Steven Vander Meulen,	
	Kyle McDuffie	long jump		Darren Ward	
	Odette Lapierre	marathon		Andrea Nugent	50m freestyle
	Steve Beaupre	51kg boxing		Patricia Noall	100, 200m freestyle
	John Shaw	67kg boxing		Keltie Duggan,	4x100m medley relay
	Brent Kosolofski	81kg boxing		Lori Melien,	
	Domenic D'Amico,	91kg boxing		Patricia Noall,	
	Kathy Kelemen	3m diving		Nancy Sweetnam	
	Anne Drost,	lightweight coxless fours		Christine Larsen	synchro swim figures
	Marni Hamilton,			Denis Aumais	weightlifting 56kg snatch
	Marlene van der Horst,			Benoit Gagne	75kg weightlifting
	Wendy Wiebe			Sylvain Leblanc	weightlifting 82.5kg snatch
	Dave Henry, Brian Peaker,	lightweight coxless fours		Guy Greavette	100kg weightlifting, snatch,
	Bob Thomas, Ryan Tierney				c&j
	Heather Hattin	lightweight single scull	1994	Graeme Fell	3000m steeplechase
	Jean-Francois Senecal	3-position rifle		Ian James	long jump
	Mark Howkins	rapid-fire pistol		Anne Yakiwchuk,	4x400m relay
	Andre Chevrefils,	rapid-fire pistol team		Stacey Bowen,	
	Mark Howkins			Donalda Duprey,	
	Brian Gabriel	skeet		Charmaine Crooks	
	Mike West	100m backstroke		Janice McCaffrey	10km road walk
	Sean Murphy,	200m backstroke		Catherine Bond-Mills	heptathlon
	Tom Ponting	100m butterfly		Denyse Julien,	badminton women's doubles
	Jill Horstead	200m butterfly		Si-An Deng	
	Chris Chalmers	1500m freestyle		Domenic Filane	48kg boxing
	Jane Kerr	200m IM		Wald Fleming	67kg boxing
	Sophie Dufour,	4x200m freestyle relay		Brian Walton	10-mile cycling scratch race
	Jane Kerr,			Alison Sydor	women's cycling road race
	Donna McGinnis,			Jason Napper	3m diving
	Trish Noall			Claude Villeneuve	10m diving
	Langis Cote	67.5kg weightlifting		Mary Depiero	1m diving
	Guy Greavette	90kg weightlifting		Myriam Boileau	10m diving
1990	Bruny Surin	100m sprint		Alan Nolet	gymnastics floor exercise
	Paul Williams	10,000m run		Richard Ikeda	gymnastics pommel horse,
	John Graham	400m hurdles			rings
	Milt Ottey	high jump		Lisa Simes	gymnastics floor exercises,
	Edrick Floreal	triple jump			vault
	Rosey Edeh,	4x400m relay		Gretchen McLennan	rhythmic gymnastics ball,
	France Gareau,				ribbon
	Cheryl Allen, Gail Harris			Michel Dion	individual small-bore
	Bryan Blanshard,	badminton men's doubles			prone rifle

Year	Name	Event/Sport	Year	Name	Event/Sport
	Stanley Wills, John Rochon	men's centre-fire pairs pistol		Katie Rowland John Rochon, Jean-Pierre Huot	men's air-pistol team
	Sharon Cozzarin	individual air pistol		John Rochon	centre fire pistol
	Sharon Bowes	individual air rifle		John Rochon, Jean-Pierre Huot	men's free pistol team
	Christina Ashcroft, Sharon Bowes	women's air rifle pairs			
	Christina Ashcroft, Linda Szulga	small-bore rifle prone pairs		Douglas McCutcheon, Joe Trinici	men's skeet team
	Christina Ashcroft	individual small-bore rifle		Kimberley Eagles	sport pistol
	Jon Cleveland	100, 200m breaststroke		Chris Renaud	100m backstroke
	Shannon Shakespeare	50m freestyle		Lauren Van Oosten	100m breaststroke
	Marianne Limpert	100m freestyle		Greg Hamm	200m backstroke
	Nikki Dryden	800m freestyle		Lauren Van Oosten	200m breaststroke
	Lisa Flood	200m breaststroke		Jessica Deglau	200m butterfly
	Nancy Sweetnam	200m IM		Jessica Deglau	200m freestyle
	Marianne Limpert, Shannon Shakespeare, Jessica Amey, Glencora Maughan	4x100m freestyle relay		Joanne Malar	400m freestyle
	Stephanie Richardson, Donna Wu, Joanne Malar, Marianne Limpert	4x200 freestyle relay		Laura Nicholls, Marianne Limpert, Jessica Deglau, Nicole Davey	4x100m medley relay
	Beth Hazel, Lisa Flood, Jessica Amey, Marianne Limpert	4x100 medley relay		Jessica Deglau, Joanne Malar, Laura Nicholls, Andrea Schwartz	4x200m freestyle relay
	Francois Lagace,	54kg snatch, overall weightlifting		Bill Rowe, Jane Amlinger	tenpin bowling mixed doubles
	Denis Aumais,	59kg snatch, overall weightlifting		Waren Rennox	tenpin bowling
				Alain Bilodeau	77kg weightlifting clean and jerk
	Serge Tremblay	76kg clean & jerk, overall weightlifting		Alain Bilodeau	77kg weightlifting combined
	Yvan Darsigny	83kg snatch, overall weightlifting	2002	Pierre Browne	100m run
				Karlene Haughton	400m hurdles
1998	Keturah "Katie" Anderson	100m hurdles		Timothy "Tim" Berrett	50km walk
	Karlene Haughton	400m hurdles		Nicole Forrester	high jump
	Karlene Haughton, Diane Cummins, Ladonna Antoine, Foy Williams	4x400m relay		Stephanie McCann	pole vault
				Sebastien Gauthier	51kg boxing
	Michael Cameron Smith	decathlon		Benoit Gaudet	57kg boxing
	Jason Tunks	discus		Michael Walchuk	75kg boxing
	Caroline Wittrin	hammer throw		Clara Hughes	25km cycling points race
	Trista Bernier	pole vault		Lori-Ann Muenzer	500m time trial
	Andrew Kooner	54kg boxing		Lyne Bessette	23.4km road time trial
	Trevor Stewardson	75kg boxing		Alexander Despatie	high dive
	Eric Wohlberg	184km cycling road race		Blythe Hartley	high dive
	Annie Gariepy	24km cycling point race		Kylie Stone	gymnastics floor
	Lori Muenzer	cycling sprint		Alexander Jeltkov	gymnastics horizontal bar
	Eryn Bulmer	1m springboard		Alexander Jeltkov	gymnastics individual
	Myriam Boileau	springboard		team event	gymnastics women's team event
	Anne Montminy	high dive			
	Liza Leveille	gymnastics balance beam		Vanessa Meloche	gymnastics uneven bars
	Emilie Livingston	rhythmic gymnastics clubs		Vanessa Meloche	gymnastics vault
	Kristan Burley, Alexandre Jeltkov, Grant Golding, Richard Ikeda, Peter Schmid	gymnastics men's team event		Luce Baillargeon	57kg judo
				Daniel Simard	60kg judo
				Jean-Francois Marceau	73kg judo
				Jacynthe Maloney	78kg judo
				Vivian Berkeley	lawn bowling singles blind
	Emilie Fournier, Crystal Gilmore, Veronique Lecler, Lisa Leveille,	gymnastics women's team event		Susan Nattrass	clay pigeon trap
				Cynthia Meyer	double trap
				Sharon Bowes, Jaclyn Mecredy	small-bore rifle team
				Cynthia Meyer, Susan Nattrass	trap team
				Jennifer Button	100m butterfly
				Kirby Cote	100m multi disability free style

Year	Name	Event/Sport
	Michael Brown	200m breaststroke
	Rick Say	200m freestyle
	Marianne Limpert	200m individual medley
	team event	team 4x100m freestyle
	team event	relay team
	team event	4x100m freestyle relay
	team event	team 4x100m medley relay
	Benoit Huot	50m multi disability freestyle
	Danielle Campo	50m multi disability freestyle
		team event table tennis
	Christine Girard	65kg weightlifting clean and jerk
	Pascale Dorcelus	65kg weightlifting combined
	Scott McCarthy	77kg weightlifting clean and jerk
	Scott McCarthy	77kg weightlifting combined
	Julien Galipeau	94kg weightlifting combined

PARALYMPICS - MEDALLISTS
Summer Games

Gold

Year	Name	Event/Sport
1968	Hilda Binns	wheelchair novice 60m, 25m FS swim *
	Gordon Patterson	wheelchair novice 60m
	Doug Wilson	wheelchair novice 60m
	Eugene Reimer	men's club*, discus *
1972	Doug Bovee	men's wheelchair slalom
	Bob Simpson	men's wheelchair 100m
	Canada	men's wheelchair 4x60m relay
	Eugene Reimer	men's pentathlon
	Eugene Reimer	men's discus*
	Richard Wasnok	men's 3x25m IM swim
1976	Tom Parker	archery advanced metric tetraplegic
	Bev Stanger	women's blind A high jump
	Gerry Bloomfield	women's blind B high jump
	J. Pacquette	women's blind A pentathlon, discus, javelin
	Lucille Baillargeon	women's blind B pentathlon, javelin
	Diane Pidskalny	women's amputee D javelin
	Joe Harrison	men's amputee D 100m
	Peter Colisto	men's wheelchair 800m
	Arnold Boldt	men's amputee high jump, long jump
	Doug Lyons	men's shot put*
	F. Widgory	men's amputee lawn bowls singles
	P. Lynn	men's blind B lawn bowl singles
	P. Lynn/Victor Goetz	men's blind B lawn bowls team
	J. Byrns	open rifle
	Ralph Thibodeau	quadriplegic rifle
	Dean Mellway	open snooker
	Doris Choptain	women's blind B 100M backstroke, breaststroke, 4x100IM
	Canada	women's 4x100 medley relay
	Timothy McIsaac	men's blind A 4x100IM
	George Crhak	men's amputee D table tennis singles
1980	Tom Parker	men's archery double Fita
	Anne Farrell	women's amputee C 100m*, long jump*, shot put*, javelin*, discus*
	Giselle Cole	women's amputee F1 100m *, 400m*, long jump*
	Joanne McDonald	women's wheelchair slalom*
	Cheryl Hurd	women's blind A 3km walk*
	Sue Grimstead	women's amputee D high jump. long jump*

Year	Name	Event/Sport
	Stephania Balta	women's amputee D pentathlon, discus*, javelin, shot put*
	Sarah Baker	women's amputee C1 discus*, javelin*
	Magella Belanger	men's amputee C 100m
	Denis Lapalme	men's amputee C1 100m, javelin*, 100m backstroke*
	Joe Harrison	men's amputee D 400m
	Parick York	men's blind A 400m*
	Jacques Pilon	men's blind A 1500m*
	Paul English	men's blind B 1500m*
	Rick Hansen	men's wheelchair 800m*
	Mel Fitzgerald	men's wheelchair 800m*, 1500m*
	Arnold Boldt	men's amputee D high jump *, long jump
	Ernie Lambier	men's blind A high jump
	Al Heaver	men's amputee C pentathlon
	Chris Facey	men's amputee E pentathlon
	Dan Leonard	men's amputee F pentathlon, javelin*
	Eugene Reimer	men's discus
	Doug Lyons	men's shotput*
	Marjorie Seargeant	women's amputee F 50m FS swim*, 50m breaststroke*
	Josee Lake	women's amputee J 50m FS * 50m backstroke*, 50m breaststroke*
	Yvette Michel	women's blind A 100m FS*, 100m backstroke*, 100m breaststroke *, 4x50IM
	Jackie Mitchell	women's amputee C-D 400m FS*
	Cheryl Kristiansen	women's amputee C 100m breaststroke*, 100m fly*, 4x50IM*
	Andrea Rossi	women's blind A 100 fly*
	Canada	women's amputee C-D 4x100 FS relay
	Kim Kilpatrick	women's blind A 4x100IM
	Mark Burger	men's 25m FS swim, 25m breaststroke
	Gary Collins-Simpson	men's amputee C-D 100m backstroke*, 4x50IM*
	Tim McIsaac	men's blind A 100m breaststroke, 100m fly*, 4x50IM, 4x100IM*
	S. Breddlove	men's up to 57kg wrestling
1984	David Barefoot	men's C1-C2 double Fita archery
	Laura Misciagna	women's C2 60m dash*, 200m, slalom (leg)*
	Christine Nicholas	women's B2 1500m, 3000m*
	Cheryl Hurd	women's B1 3000m*

Year	Name	Event/Sport
	Norah Good	women's B3 3000m*
	T. Simpson	women's 1C slalom*, 100m*, 200m*, 400m*, 800m
	N. Gustafson	women's wheelchair 1A 100m*, 200m*, 400m*, 800m*, discus
	Debbi Kostelyk	women's wheelchair 3 100m*, 400m
	A. Lerretti	women's wheelchair 5 800m, 1500m*, 5000m*
	Canada	women's wheelchair 2 4x100m relay*
	Stephania Balta	women's A2 discus, shotput
	Anne Farrell	women's C5 javelin*
	Joanne Bouw	women's C7 javelin*, shotput*
	Judy Goodrich	women's C8 javelin*
	Brian Kelly	men's C2 (arm) 20m*
	Robert Easton	men's C4 100m, 400m*, 800m
	Robert Mearns	men's C8 800m*, cross-country 1500m
	Canada	men's C4 4x100m relay
	Ron Minor	men's wheelchair 4 200m*, 400m*, 800m*
	Paul Clark	men's wheelchair 2 800m
	Rick Hansen	men's wheelchair 4 1500m, marathon
	Canada	men's wheelchair 1A 4x200m relay*
	Andre Viger	men's wheelchair 2 marathon
	Mel Fitzgerald	men's wheelchair 5 marathon
	Arnold Boldt	men's A2 high jump
	Yvan Bourdeau	men's B1 long jump*
	Dan Leonard	men's A6-8 discus*
	Jacques Martin	men's 4 shotput*
	Leslie Lord	women's 1500m tricycle
	M. Gustafson	women's 1B 25m FS swim*
	Susie Chick	women's C6 25m FS swim*, 50m FS*
	Debbie Willows	women's C1 25m FS
	J. Fauche	women's 2 50m FS, 200m FS, 25m fly, 4x25m IM
	Judy Goodrich	women's C8 50m FS, 100m FS*, 50m backstroke*
	Josee Lake	women's A9 100m FS*, 50m backstroke*, 50m breaststroke*, 150m IM*
	Yvette Michel	women's B1 100m FS*, 100m backstroke, 200m IM*
	Andrea Rossi	women's B1 400m IM
	Canada	women's C1-C8 4x50m FS relay
	Tom Hainey	men's 6 100m FS, 400m FS, 100m breaststroke*, 4x50 IM*
	Bill Parry	men's C8 50m backstroke*,

Year	Name	Event/Sport
	Gary Simpson	men's A4 100m backstroke*
	Mark Hoyle	men's B3 100 breaststroke*, 400m breaststroke*
	Timothy McIsaac	men's B1 400m breaststroke*, 400m IM*
	Michael Edgson	men's B3 100m fly*, 200m IM*, 400m IM*
	Canada	men's B1 4x100 FS relay*, 4x100 medley relay (WR)
	Wayne Bell	men's up to 48kg wrestling
	Eddie Morten	men's up to 68kg wrestling
1988	Claude Poumerol	women's A4, 49 100m*
	Sylvie Bergeron	women's C8 200m*
	Joanne Bouw	women's C7 discus, javelin*, shotput*
	Jeffrey Tiessen	men's A5, A7 400m*
	Daniel Westley	men's A1, A2, A3, A9, L2 wheelchair 100m*, 800m*
	Jamie Bone	men's C3 wheelchair 100m*, 200m*, 400m*
	Robert Easton	men's C4, C5 wheelchair 100m, 200m, 400m
	Serge Raymond	men's 1B wheelchair 200m*, 1500m, marathon
	Andre Beaudoin	men's 1C wheelchair 200m
	Clayton Gerein	men's 1B wheelchair 400m*, 800m*, 5000m
	Paul Clark	men's 2 wheelchair 800m*
	Marc Quessy	men's 2 marathon
	Andre Viger	men's 3 marathon
	Arnold Boldt	men's A2, A9 high jump
	Rick Reelie	men's 1B discus, javelin*, shotput*
	Jacques Martin	men's 4 shotput*
	Dwyer, Dean	men's LC3 cycling 60km
	Halldor Bjamason	men's C5/C6 cycling 1500m tricycle*
	Tammy Barker	women's C4 100m FS*, 200m FS
	Joanne Mucz	women's A4 400m FS*
	Yvette Weicker	women's B1 100m backstroke
	Michael Edgson	men's B3 50m FS, 100m FS, 400m FS, 100m backstroke*, 100 fly*, 200m IM*,400m IM*, blind open 4x100 FS relay*, 4x100 medley relay
	Stephane Lecours	men's A2 400m FS, 100m backstroke*, 100m breaststroke, 100m fly*, 200m IM*
	Tim McIsaac	men's B1 400m FS, 100m backstroke, 100m fly, 200m IM, blind open 4x100 FS relay*, 4x100m medley relay
	Lee Grenon	men's B2 400m FS, 100m fly, blind open 4x100 FS relay*, 4x100 medley relay
	Adrian Peirson	men's blind open 4x100 FS relay*, 4x100 medley relay

Year	Name	Event/Sport
1992	Kristine Harder	women's TW2, wheelchair 200m*, 400m*
	Ljiljana Ljubisic	women's B1 discus*
	Joanne Bouw	women's C5-C8 discus*, javelin*, shotput*
	Frank Bruno	men's C8 100m, 200m, 400m*
	Rick Reelie	men's TW2 wheelchair 400m*, 800m*
	Clayton Gerein	men's TW2 wheelchair 5000m*, marathon
	Andre Viger	men's TW3 wheelchair 10,000m
	Arnold Boldt	men's high jump
	Jacques Martin	men's THW5 discus*
	Marni Abott, Chantal Benoit, Tracey Ferguson, Judy Goodrich, Patti Jones, Jennifer Krempien, Linda Kutrowski, Jodie Millard, Kendra Ohama, Diane Rakiecki, Helene Simard, Irene Wowtuk	Women's basketball
	Patrice Bonneau	men's LC2 cycling road race
	Laszlo Desci	mixed SH1-SH3 free pistol
	Joanne Mucz	women's S9 100m FS*, 400m FS*, 100m breaststroke*, 100m fly*, 200IM*
	Michael Edgson	men's B3 100m backstroke, 100m fly, 200m IM*, 400m IM
1996	Chantal Petitclerc	women's T53 wheelchair 100m*, 200m
	Dean Bergeron	men's T51 wheelchair 200m
	Jeff Adams	men's T53 wheelchair 800m
	Clayton Gerein	men's T51 wheelchair 1500m
	Brent McMahon	men's T51 marathon
	James Shaw	men's F34-37 discus*
	Jacques Martin	men's F54 discus
	Jason Delesalle	men's F12 pentathlon
	Marni Abott, Chantal Benoit, Renee Delcolle, Tracey Ferguson, Jennifer Krempien, Kelly Krywa, Linda Kutrowski, Kendra Ohama, Sabrina Pettinicchi, Lori Radke, Marnie Smithies, Lisa Stevens.	Women's basketball
	Gary Longhi	men's Div. 3 bicycle 5000m
	Larouche/Cournoyer	women's tendem 50/60 road
	Cloutier/Cournoyer	mixed tandem 60/70 road
	Lance MacDonald	men's lawn bowls singles
	Rebeccah Bornemann	women's S7 400m FS
	Marie-Claire Ross	women's B3 100m breaststroke*, 200m IM*
	Tony Alexandre	men's S7 50m FS
	Walter Wu	men's B3 100m FS, 400m FS*, 100m backstroke*, 100m fly, 200IM
2000	Jeff Adams	men's T54 800m, 1500m
	Earle Connor	men's T42 100m*
	Clayton Gerein	men's T52 marathon
	Jason Lachance	men's T34 200m
	James Shaw	men's F38 discus
	Lisa Franks	women's T52 200m, 400m, 800m, 1500m
	Chantal Petitclerc	women's T54 200m, 800m
	Danielle Campo	women's S7/SB7/SM7 100FS*, 4x100m FS relay*, 50m FS
	Stephanie Dixon	women's S9/SB8/SM9 400m FS*, 100m FS*, 100m backstroke*, 4x100 medley relay*
	Jessica Sloan	women's S10/SB9/SM10 50m FS*, 100m FS*, 100m breaststroke*, 200IM*
	Elizabeth Walker	women's S7/SB7/SM7 50m fly, 200m IM*
	Dara Geigre, Stephanie Dixon, Jessica Sloan, Elizabeth Walker	women's 4x100 medley relay
	Danielle Campo, Andrea Cole, Stephanie Dixon, Jessica Sloan	women's 4x100 FS relay
	Kirby Cote	men's S13/SE13/SM13 200IM*, 100m breaststroke*
	Philippe Gagnon	men's S10/SB9/SM10 100m FS*, 400m FS
	Benoit Huot	men's S13/SB13/SM10 50m FS*, 200m IM
	Adam Purdy	men's S5/SB6/SM6 100m backstroke, 4x100 medley relay*
	Walter Wu	men's S13/SB13/SM13 100m fly*, 100m backstroke
	Andrew Haley, Benoit Huot, Adam Purdy, Philippe Gagnon	men's 4x100 medley relay
	Marni Abott, Chantal Benoit, Renee Delcolle, Tracey Ferguson, Joanne Kelly, Jennifer Krempien, Linda Kutrowski, Kendra Ohama, Marnie Peters, Sabrina Pettinicchi, Lori Radke, Michelle Stilwell	women's basketball
	Patrick Anderson, Jaimie Bonsoff, Jeffrey Dennis, David Durepos, Travis Gaertner, Ken Hall, Roy Henderson, Joey Johnson, Ross Norton, Richard Peter, Chris Stoutenburg, James Treuer	men's basketball
	Amy Alsop, Carrie Anton, Nathalie Chartrand, Viviane Forest, Nancy Morin, Contessa Scott	women's goalball
2004	Benoit Huot	100m butterfly (WR), 100m FS (WR), 50m FS (WR), 200m IM, 400m FS
	Kirby Cote	400m FS, 100m butterfly, 100m FS, 200m IM, 50m FS
	Chantal Petticlerc	100m (WR), 800m (WR), 1500m, 400m (WR), 200m

Year	Name	Event/Sport
	Walter Wu	400m FS
	Chelsea Clark	100m, 200m sprint
	Anne Polinario	100m, 50m FS
	Lisa Franks	200m, 400m sprint
	Stephanie Dixon	100m backstroke (WR)
	Chelsey Gotell	100m backstroke
	Paul Gauthier	boccia singles
	Andre Beaudoin	200m sprint
	Amy Alsop,	women's goalball
	Viviane Forest, Kelley Hannett,	
	Annette Lisabeth, Nancy Morin,	
	Contessa Scott	
	Patrick Anderson,	men's basketball
	Jaimie Borisoff,	
	Bradley Bowden, Davis Durepos,	
	David Eng, Travis Gaertner,	
	Roy Henderson, Joey Johnson,	
	Adam Lancia, Ross Norton,	
	Richard Peter, Chris Stoutenberg	

* denotes World Record

Silver

Year	Name	Event/Sport
1968	Hilda Binns	women's B slalom
	Walter Dann	men's C novices 60m
	Gary Neault	men's D club
	Eugene Reimer	men's B javelin
	Karen McPherson	women's 3 50m backstroke
	Irene Miller	women's 4 50m backstroke
1972	Hilda Binns	women's 3 slalom
	Hilda Binns	women's 3 60m
	Joyce Murland	women's 1A javelin
	Doug Bovee	men's 1A 60m
	Reg Muise	men's 1B shotput
1976	J. Pacquette	women's A 60m
	Joanne McDonald	women's 5 slalom
	Lucille Baillargeon	women's blind B long jump
	Bev Stanger	women's blind A pentathlon, javelin
	Simmons	women's blind B pentathlon
	L. Lahey	women's blind B discus
	Lucie Raiche	women's 4 discus
	Magella Belanger	men's amputee C 100m
	Stan Holcomb	men's amputee D 100m
	Steve Little	men's amputee D1 100m prosthesis
	Peter Colisto	men's 5 1500m
	Dennis Cherenko	men's 1B pentathlon
	Victor Goetz	men's blind B 1500m walk
	Eugene Reimer	men's 4 pentathlon, discus
	Reg Muise	men's 1B club
	Chris Facey	men's amputee E precision javelin
	Magella Belanger	men's amputee C lawn bowls teams
	F. Widgory	men's amputee C lawn bowls teams
	Joyce Murland	women's 1A-1C rifle quadriplegic

Year	Name	Event/Sport
	Simmons	womens blind B 100m FS, 4x100IM
	Doris Choptain	women's blind B 100m fly
	Tom Parker	men's 1C 25m backstroke
	Barney Fegyverneki	men's 4 50m backstroke
	Denis Lapalme	men's amputee C1 100m FS
	Tim McIsaac	men's blind A 100m fly
	Canada	men's blind A 4x100 medley relay
	B. Arthur	men's blind B 4x100IM
	Diane Pidskalny	women's amputee D table tennis singles
	Lesile Lam	men's 2 table tennis singles
1980	Karen Gillis	women's amputee C 100m
	Lucille Baillargeon	women's blind B pentathlon
	Tony Wills	men's amputee C 100m, high jump
	Joe Harrison	men's amputee D 400m
	Charles Peart	men's amputee F1 400m, long jump
	Chris Facey	men's amputee E 1500m
	Gary Birch	men's 1A wheelchair 60m
	Mel Fitzgerald	men's 5 wheelchair 100m
	Rick Hansen	men's 4 wheelchair 1500m
	Al Heaver	men's amputee C discus, javelin
	Dan Leonard	men's amputee F discus, shotput
	Gilles Marois	men's blind B javelin
	Yvon Page	mixed 1A, 1B, 1C air rifle standing, prone
	Laszlo Desci	men's amputee open air pistol
	Jackie Mitchell	women's amputee C-D 100m FS, 100m breaststroke
	Marjorie Seargeant	men's amputee F 50m backstroke
	L. Bentz	men's blind B 100m breaststroke
	Marjorie Nicholson	women's amputee D 100m fly, 4x50IM
	Andrea Rossi	women's blind A 4x50IM
	Canada	women's blind A 4x100 medley relay
	Tim McIsaac	men's blind A 100m FS
	Denis Lapalme	men's amputee C1-D1 100m breaststroke
	Larry Gardner	men's amputee D 100m breaststroke
	Jeff Standfield	men's 4 100m breaststroke
	Gary Collins-Simpson	men's amputee C 100m fly
	Canada	men's 1A, 1B, 1C 3x25m FS relay
	Canada	men's blind A-B 4x100 medley relay
1984	Irene Larochelle	women's C5 100m
	Cheryl Hurd	women's B1 1500m
	Norah Good	women's B3 1500m
	Debbi Kostelyk	women's 3 wheelchair 200m
	Angela Ieriti	women's 5 wheelchair 200m, 400m
	Diane Rakiecki	women's 4 wheelchair 800m

Year	Name	Event/Sport
	Stephania Balta	women's A2 javelin
	Debbie Willows	women's C1 precision throw
	Judy Zelman	women's 1C shotput
	Canada	mixed C2-C3 3x60m relay
	Yvan Bourdeau	men's B1 100m
	Robert Mearns	men's C7 400m
	Chris Stoddard	men's 3 slalom
	Robert Easton	men's C4 slalom
	Paul Clark	men's 2 wheelchair 200m, 400m, 1500m, 5000m, marathon
	Mel Fitzgerald	men's 5 wheelchair 1500, 5000m, marathon
	Canada	men's 2-5 wheelchair 4x200m relay
	Canada	men's 2 wheelchair 4x400 relay
	Jeffrey Tiessen	men's A5 high jump
	Walter Butt	men's C6 discus
	Dan Leonard	men's A6-A8 distance throw, shotput
	John Donahue	men's 1B shotput
	John Belanger	men's A1 shotput
	Denis Sevigny	men's C8 shotput
	Russell Cecchini	men's C1 boccia singles
	Gord Hamilton	men's C2 boccia singles
	Dean Dwyer	men's bicycle 1500m, 5000m
	Arlene Aiken	C1-C2 equestrian elementary walk
	Tim Hamilton	C1-C3 equestrian obstacle course
	Canada	women's goalball
	Al Slater	up to 82.5kg powerlifting
	Gino Vendetti	up to 90kg powerlifting
	Canada	wheelchair soccer
	Tamara Boccacciio	women's B1 50m FS
	Patricia Hennin	women's C4 50m FS, 200m FS
	Helene Binet	women's C6 50m FS
	Sigrid Voth	women's 5 400m FS, 100m breaststroke
	Yvette Michel	women's B1 400m FS, 100m breaststroke
	Martha Gustafson	women's 1B 25m backstroke
	Jose Fauche	women's 2 50m backstroke
	Judy Goodrich	women's C8 100m backstroke
	Susan Smith	women's C8 50m breaststroke
	Andrea Rossi	women's B1 200IM
	Mickey Macri	men's L2 25m FS, 25m backstroke
	Brian Kelly	men's C1 25m FS
	Ken Booth	men's B1 50m FS
	Joe Higgins	men's C4 50m FS, 100m FS, 200m FS
	Dennis Quenneville	men's A2 400m FS
	Timothy McIsaac	men's B1 400m FS, 100m breaststroke, 200IM
	Lee Grenon	men's B2 400m FS, 100m fly
	Phillip Mindorff	men's A8 100m backstroke

Year	Name	Event/Sport
	Greg Thompson	men's B1 100m backstroke
	Michael Edgson	men's B3 100m backstroke
	Bill Parry	men's C8 50m breaststroke, 50m fly
	Bruce Vandermolen	men's B2 100m breaststroke
	Tom Hainey	men's 6 100m fly
	Scott Herron	men's B1 400IM
	Canada	men's B1-B3 4x100m FS relay
	Canada	men's A1 4x100m medley relay
	Chris Gabriel	men's up to 52kg wrestling
	Gord Hope	men's up to 57kg wrestling
	Pier Morten	men's up to 62kg wrestling
	Frank Dipierdomenico	-74kg wrestling
	Wayne Prymych	-82kg wrestling
	Dave Duncan	-90kg wrestling
1988	Claude Poumerol	women's A4, 49 200m
	Sylvie Bergeron	women's C8 400m
	Norma Lorincz	women's C7 800m
	Debbi Kostelyk	women's 3 wheelchair 100m
	Linda Hamilton	women's A1, A2, A3, A9, L2 wheelchair 400m, 800m
	William Wiebe	men's A6, A8, A9, L4 100m
	Andre Beaudoin	men's 1C wheelchair 100m, 400m
	Marc Quessy	men's 2 wheelchair 100m
	Michael Johner	men's C4-5 wheelchair 100m
	Daniel Westley	men's A1, A2, A3, A9, L2 wheelchair 200m, 400m, 1500m, 5000m
	Gino Vendetti	men's C4-C5 wheelchair 200m, 400m
	Daniel Stubel	men's 1B wheelchair 400m
	Clayton Gerein	men's 1B wheelchair 1500m
	Paul Clark	men's 2 wheelchair 1500m, marathon
	Andre Viger	men's 3 wheelchair 10,000m
	Arnold Boldt	men's A2, A9 long jump
	Gary Schaff	men's 2 discus
	Stuart McKeown	men's 3 discus
	John Belanger	men's A1, A2, A3, A9, L2 discus, javelin
	Jim Enright	men's A4, A9 javelin
	Halldor Bjamason	men's C5/C6 3000 tricycle
	Michael Johnson	-82.5kg powerlifting
	Heather Kuttai	women's 2-6 air pistol, open air pistol team
	Bernard Gehring	open air pistol team
	Richard Schell	open air pistol team
	Joanne Mucz	women's A4 100m FS, 100m backstroke
	Yvette Weicker	women's B1 100m FS
	Tammy Barker	women's C4 100m backstroke
	Judy Goodrich	women's C8 100m backstroke
	Tom Hainey	men's 6 100m FS, 400m FS, 100m fly, 200IM
	Jeff Worobetz	men's C6 50m breaststroke

Year	Name	Event/Sport
1992	Kristine Harder	women's TW2 wheelchair 200m
	Ljlijana Ljubisic	women's B1 shotput
	David Howe	men's C5-C8 5000m
	Andre Beaudoin	men's TW2 wheelchair 100m
	Rick Reelie	men's TW2 wheelchair 200m, 1500m
	Marc Quessy	men's TW3 wheelchair 200m, 400m
	Jeff Adams	men's TW4 wheelchair 800m
	Canada	men's TW3, TW4
	James Baker,	wheelchair 4x100m relay
	Marc Quessy,	
	Andre Viger, Daniel Westley	
	Canada	men's TW3, TW4
	Jeff Adams,	wheelchair 4x400 relay
	Luke Gingras,	
	Marc Quessy, Andre Viger	
	France Gagne	men's B3 discus
	Jason Delasalle	men's B3 javelin
	Jacques Martin	men's THW5 javelin
	Rick Gronhan	men's C7 shotput
	Monique Glasgom	women's 5000m cycling
	Gary Longhi	men's Div 3 5000m cycling
	Yvette Weicker	women's B1 50m FS
	Marie Claire Ross	women's B32 100m breaststroke
	Irene Irvine,	women's B1-B3 4x100
	Carla Qualtrough,	medley relay
	Marie Claire Ross,	
	Yvette Weicker	
	Jeremy Gervan	men's S6 200m FS
	Michael Edgson	men's B3 200m backstroke
1996	Tracey Melesko	women's 200m, long jump
	Chantal Petitclerc	women's T53 wheelchair 400m, 800m 1500m
	Courtney Knight	women's F12 discus
	Joey Radmore	men's T32 wheelchair 100m
	Andre Beaudoin	men's T51 wheelchair 100m, 400m
	Jeff Adams	men's T53 wheelchair 400m
	Dean Bergeron	men's T51 wheelchaire 800m, 1500m, 400m
	Stuart McGregor	men's T12 1500m
	Marc Quessy	men's T52 wheelchair 800m
	Clayton Gerein	men's T51 wheelchair marathon
	France Gagne	men's F12 javelin
	Jacques Martin	men's F54 javelin
	Larouche/Cournoyer	women's tandem individual pursuit
	Mario Caron	men's goalball
	Jeff Christy,	
	Jean-Francois Crepault,	
	Rob Gaunt, Eric Houle,	
	Dean Kozak	
	Vivian Berkeley	women's lawn bowls singles
	Marie Claire Ross	women's B3 100m backstroke
	Tony Alexandre	men's S7 100m FS
	Dany Belanger	men's wheelchair rugby
	Garrett Hickling,	
	Kirby Kranabetter,	
	Raymond Lizotta,	
	Brian McPhate,	
	Alan Semeniuk,	
	David Stubel,	
	David Tweed	
	David Cook	sailing crew boat
	Ken Kelly,	
	John McRoberts,	
	Kirk Westergaard	
2000	Jeff Adams	men's T52 400m, 4x100m relay
	Andre Beaudoin	men's T52 200m
	Earle Connor	men's T42 200m
	Jason Dunkerley	men's T11 1500m*
	Rick Reeve	T52 800m
	France Gagne	men's F13 javelin
	Jason Lachance	men's T34 100m, 200m, 400m
	Jacques Martin	men's F55 discus
	Kyle Pettey	men's F35 discus, shotput
	Jeff Adams	men's T54 4x100 relay
	Barry Patriguin,	
	Mathieu Parent,	
	Mathieu Blanchette	
	Courtney Knight	women's F12 pentathlon
	Chantal Petitclerc	women's T54 100m, 400m
	Lisa Franks	women's T52 110m
	Julie Cournoyer	open mixed tandem 60/70km road race
	Jean Quevillon	men's D3 5km bicycle time trial
	Danielle Campo	women's S7/SB6/SM7 400m FS
	Andrea Cole	women's S8/SB9/SM8 100m fly
	Stephanie Dixon	women's S9/SB8/SM9 50m FS, 200IM
	Chelsay Gottell	women's S132/SB13/SM13 100m breaststroke
	Jessica Tuomela	men's S11/Sb11/Sm11 50m FS
	Kirby Cote	men's S13/SB13/SM13 50m FS, 100m FS
	Philippe Gagnon	men's S10/SB9/SM10 100m fly
	Brian Hill	men's S13/SB13/SM13 100m fly
	Benoit Huot	men's S10/SB9/SM10 100m FS, 400m FS, 100 backstroke
	Walter Wu	men's S13/SB13/SM13 400m FS, 200IM
	Mikael Bartholdy	men's volleyball
	Wayne Epp, Lawrence Flynn,	
	Geoff Hammond, Neil Johnaon,	
	Larry Matthews, Jason Migchels,	
	John Przybyszewski, Tony Quarin,	
	Jose Rebela, Joey Stabner	

Year	Name	Event/Sport
2004	Stephanie Dixon	100m FS, 100m butterfly, 200m IM, 400m FS, 4x100m FS, 4x100m medley
	Donovan Tildesley	400m FS, 200m IM
	Chelsea Larivere	100m sprint
	Jason Dunkerley	1500m
	Andre Beaudoin	400m sprint
	Walter Wu	200m IM, 100m basckstroke
	Bernie Huot	100m backstroke
	Anne Polinario	100m backstroke, 4x100m FS, 4x100m medley
	Kirby Cote	100m breast, 100m back
	Andrea Cole	4x100m FS
	Danielle Campo	4x100m FS
	Elizabeth Walker	4x100m medley
	Darda Geiger	4x100m medley
	Kelly Smith	men's marathon
	Mike Bacon, Ian Chan, Allan Chartrand, Jared Funk, Garett Hickling, Fabien Lavoie, Raymond Lizotte, Daniel Paradis, Allan Semeniuk, Patrice Simard, Michael Whitehead, David Willsie	men's wheelchair rugby

Bronze

Year	Name	Event/Sport
1968	Glendine "Snooky" Seeley	women's C club, javelin
	Orene Bourne	men's B novices 60m
	Walter Schmid	lawn bowls open singles
	Karen McPherson	women's 3 50m breaststroke, 100m breaststroke
	Gunther Schuster	men's 3 50m FS
1972	Sharon Long	women's 1B slalom
	Hilda Binns	women's 3 pentathlon
	Joyce Murland	women's 1A shotput
	Doug Bovee	men's 1A shotput
	Veronica Demarakas	women's 1A 25m backstroke, table tennis singles, women's doubles
	Angel	women's 1A table tennis singles
	Sharon Long	women's 1A-1B table tennis women's doubles
	Canada	women's 3 table tennis teams
1976	Ralph Thibodeau	men's 1A-1C archery tetraplegic round
	T. Stevenson	women's blind A 60m, long jump, pentathlon
	Gerry Bloomfield	women's blind B pentathlon, javelin
	Diane Crow	women's 3 pentathlon
	Elaine Ell	women's 4 pentathlon, javelin
	Joyce Murland	women's 1A club, discus
	Diane Pidskalny	women's amputee D discus, precision javelin, shotput
	Lucille Baillargeon	women's blind B shotput
	Ed Batt	men's 1A slalom
	Chris Stoddard	men's 4 slalom, 800m
	Chris Facey	men's amputee E pentathlon

Year	Name	Event/Sport
	Clarence Bastarache	men's 2 pentathlon
	Reg Muise	men's 1B discus
	Doug Lyons	men's 2 discus
	Eugene Reimer	men's 4 javelin
	L. Lahey	women's blind B lawn bowls team
	Doris Choptain	women's blind B lawn bowls team
	Jacques Pilon	men's blind A lawn bowls singles
	Jackie Mitchell	women's amputee D 100m backstroke
	Tim McIsaac	men's blind A 100m FS
	Barnard	women's 3 table tennis teams
	Stewart	women's 3 table tennis teams
	John Donahue	men's 1B table tennis teams
	Jerry Terwin	men's 1B table tennis teams
	Noor Jamal	men's 3 table tennis teams
	Leslie Lam	men's 3 table tennis teams
1980	Lucy Wong	women's blind B 800m, javelin
	Pam Frazee	women's 3 wheelchair 400m
	Cheryl Hurd	women's blind A high jump
	Anna Ostapa	women's blind B high jump
	Karen Gillis	women's amputee C long jump
	Charles Peart	men's amputee F1 400m
	Ed Batt	men's 1A slalom
	Ron Minor	men's 4 slalom
	Canada	men's 2-5 4x100m wheelchair relay
	Eddie Morten	men's blind B 5km walk
	Yvan Bourdeau	men's blind A long jump
	Rodney Hersey	men's blind A pentathlon
	Dennis Cherenko	men's 1B club
	Dale Vincent	men's amputee J discus, shotput
	John Donahue	men's 1B shotput
	Yvon Page	mixed 1A, 1B, 1C air rifle 3 positions
	Sarah Baker	women's amputee C1-D1 100m FS
	Margaret Nicholson	women's amputee C-D 400m FS
	Andrea Rossi	women's blind A 100m backstroke
	Irene Wownuk	women's 4 25m fly
	Denis Lapalme	men's amputee C1-D1 100m FS
	Gary Birch	men's 1A 25m backstroke
	Mark Burger	men's 1B 25m backstroke
	Jeff Standfield	men's 4 100m breaststroke
	Larry Gardner	men's amputee D 100m fly
	Canada	men's blind A-B 4x100m FS relay
	Lee Grenon	men's blind B 4x100IM
	George Chrak	men's amputee D table tennis singles
1984	Anne Farrell	women's A4 100m, 400m
	Sandy Morgan	women's C5 100m

Year	Name	Event/Sport	Year	Name	Event/Sport
	Elaine Hewirr	women's C3 200m		Canada	men's B1 4x100 medley relay
	Kim Umbach	women's B3 3000m			
	Judy Zelman	women's 1C wheelchair 200m, 400m, javelin		Martha Johnson	women's C3 table tennis singles
	Cheril Barren	women's A2 long jump	1988	Lynette Wildeman	women's A6, A8, A9, L4 100m, 200m
	Joanne Bouw	women's C7 long kump, discus		Sylvie Sauve	women's C6 100m
	Susan Smith	women's C5 discus, javelin		Sonia Atkins	women's C7 400m
	Debbie Willows	women's C1 distance throw, boccia singles		Racquel Head	women's C7 800m
	Harriet Lahman	women's C2 distance throw, medicine ball thrust		Linda Hamilton	women's A1, A2, A3, A9, L2 wheelchair 100m, 200m, 1500m
	Martha Johnson	women's C5 shotput		Jacquie Towes	women's B discus
	Ken Thomas	men's C2 slalom (leg)		Trish Lovegrove	women's B1 shotput
	Brian Kelly	men's C2 slalom		Ljlijana Ljubisic	women's B2 shotput
	Terry Gehlert	men's 1B wheelchair 100m		Marjorie Lynch	women's C4 shotput
	Ron Minor	men's 4 wheelchair 100m		Keith Myette	men's B1 800m
	Mel Fitzgerald	men's 5 wheelchair 800m		Robert Mearns	men's C7 800m. 1500m
	Andre Viger	men's 3 wheelchair 1500m, marathon		David Howe	men's C5-C8 5000 cross-country
	Ross Sampson	men's 3 wheelchair marathon		Terry Robinson	men's C1 slalom
	Denis Sevigny	men's C8 discus		David Severin	men's C3 wheelchair 100m, 400m
	Bob Schmid	men's 1B shotput		Michael Johner	men's C4-C5 wheelchair 200m
	John Palubicki	men's A3 shotput			
	Glenn Whitford	men's C4 shotpuit		Ted Vince	men's A1, A2, A3, A9, L2 wheelchair 400m
	Tim Hamilton	C1-C2 equestrian elementary walk		Andre Beaudoin	men's 1C wheelchair 800m
	Eileen Larochelle	C4-C5 equestrian elementary walk/trot, advanced walk/trot		Andre Viger	men's 3 wheelchair 800m, 5000m
	Arlene Aiken	C1-C3 equestrian obstacle course		Jeff Adams	men's 5-6 wheelchair 800m, 1500m
	Martha Johnson	women's C5 50m FS		Ken Thomas	men's C2 800m
	Sigrid Voth	women's 5 100m FS, 100m backstroke, 4x50IM		Canada	mixed C2-3 4x100m wheelchair relay
	Patricia Hennin	women's C4 100m FS		Jamie Bone, David Severin, Andre Lavallee, Laura Misciagna	
	Andrea Rossi	women's B1 400m FS, 400m breaststroke, 100m fly		Clayton Gerein	men's 1B marathon
	Susie Chick	women's C6 25m backstroke		Ted Vince	men's A1, A2, A3, A9, L2 marathon
	Jennifer Veenboer	women's A9 50m backstroke, 50m breaststroke, 150IM		Jim Enright	men's A4, A9 high jump
				Jacques Martin	men's 4 discus
	Rob Scrace	men's C6 25m FS, 50m FS		Stuart McKeown	men's 3 shot put
	Russell Cecchini	men's C1 25m FS		John Belanger	men's A1, A2, A3, A9, L2 shotput
	Ken Thomas	men's C2 25m FS		Patsy Campion	women's goalball
	Bill Parry	men's C8 50mFS		Lucy Greco, Danielle Lessard, Diane Robitaille, Helena Rooyakers, Lisa Wade	
	Mark Ludbrook	men's A4 100m FS			
	Mark Hoyle	men's B3 400m FS			
	Joe Higgins	men's C4 50m backstroke		Pier Morten	men's up to 65kg judo
	Jeff Standfield	men's 4 100m backstroke, 100m breaststroke		Eddie Morten	men's up to 71kg judo
	Rick Gronman	men's C8 50m breaststroke		Adam Salamandyj	men's 1A, 1B, 1C air rifle, air rifle kneeling
	Jim Visser	men's B2 50m breaststroke, 400m breaststroke		Yvette Weicker	women's B1 50m FS, 50m breaststroke, 100m breaststroke, 200IM, 4x100 medley relay
	Dennis Quenneville	men's A2 100m breaststroke			
	Ken Booth	men's B1 100m fly			
	Gary Simpson	men's A4 200IM		Susie Chick	women's C6 100m FS
	Lee Grenon	men's B2 400IM		Judy Goodrich	women's C8 100mFS
	Canada	men's A1 4x100 medley relay			

Year	Name	Event/Sport	Year	Name	Event/Sport
	Michelle Arnold	women's B3 400m FS, 100m backstroke, 200IM, 400IM, 4x100m medley relay		Larouche/Cournoyer	women's tandem cycling 1km sprint
				Gary Longhi	men's Div 3 20km road race
	Tamara Boccaccio	women's B1 200m breaststroke, 4x100m medley relay		Patrice Bonneau	men's LC2 55/65 bicycle road race
				Marie Claire Ross	women's B3 50m FS, 100m FS, 100m fly
	Chris Qualtrough	women's blind open 4x100m medley relay		Elizabeth Walker	women's S7 100m backstroke
	Timothy McIsaac	men's B1 50m FS, 100m FS, 200m breaststroke		Walter Wu	men's B3 50m FS
				Andrew Haley	men's S9 400m FS, 100m fly
	Phillip Mindorff	men's A8 100m backstroke			
	Lee Grenon	men's B1 400IM		Garth Harris	men's SB3 50m breaststroke
1992	Colette Bourgonje	women's TW3 wheelchair 100m, 800m	2000	Jeff Adams	men's T54 5000m
				Andre Beaudoin	men's T52 100m
	Chantal Petitclerc	women's TW4 wheelchair 200m, 800m		Dean Bergeron	men's T52 200m, 400m
				France Gagne	men's F13 discus
	Joe Zuppanic	men's C3, C4 100m		Stuart McGregor	men's T13 800m
	Jeffrey Tiessen	men's T53 400m		Rick Reelie	men's T52 5000m
	Andre Beaudoin	men's TW2 wheelchair 200m		Tracey Melesko	women's T20/F20 200m
				Caitlin Renneson	women's T34 400m
	Luc Gingras	men's TW3 wheelchair 200m, 800m		Paul Gauthier	mixed BC3 boccia individual, pairs
	Clayton Gerein	men's TW2 wheelchair 800m, 1500m		Julie Cournoyer	women's B2 mixed tandem individual pursuit
	Steve Brooks	men's B1 marathon		Pier Morten	men's B1 73kg judo
	Hal Merrill	men's THW2 shotput		Chelsey Gottell	women's S13/SB13/SM13 50m FS, 200IM
	Jacques Martin	men's THW5 shotput			
	Agnes Meszaros	women's cycling 5000m		Moorea Longstaff	women's S7/SB6/SM7 400m FS
	Patricia Campion	women's goalball			
	Natalie Chartrand, Eva Gill-Sager, Anne Jarry, Teresa Lloy, Helena Rooyakers			Anne Polinario	women's S10/SB9/SM10 100m FS, 100m backstroke, 50m FS
	Pier Morten	men's up to 71kg judo		Tyler Emmatt	men's S13/ SB13/SM13 200IM
	Heather Kuttai	mixed SH 1-SH3 air pistol		Andrew Haley	men's S9/SB9/SM9 100m fly
	Marie Claire Ross	women's B3 50m FS			
	Rebeccah Bornemann	women's S8 100m FS, 400 FS		Donovan Tildesley	men's S11/SB11/SM11 200IM
	Nora Sednarski	S7 50m fly		Walter Wu	men's S13/SE13/SM13 100m FS
	Irene Irvine, Carla Qualtrough, Marie Claire Ross, Yvette Weicker	women's B1-B3 4x100m FS relay		Brian MacDonald, Paul Tingley, David Williams	mixed 7 three person keelboat sailing
	Andrew Haley	men's S9 400m FS		Paul Gauthier	mixed boccia
1996	Colette Bourgonje	women's T52 wheelchair 100m, 200m		Alison Kabush	
			2004	Brian Hill	400m FS, 100m back
	Ljiljana Ljubisic	women's F10-11 shotput, discus		Andrea Cole	100m fly (CR)
				Karen Brain	equestrian dressage, individual FS test
	Kris Hodgins	women's F34-35 discus		Jessica Matassa	800m
	Dean Bergeron	men's T51 wheelchair 100m		Chelsey Gotell	100m FS, 50m FS, 200m IM
	Andre Beaudoin	men's T51 wheelchair 400m		Jeff Adams	400m sprint
	Clayton Gerein	men's T51 wheelchair 1500m		Danielle Campo	400m FS, 50m FS
	Jeff Adams, Carl Marquis, Colin Matheson, Marc Quessy	men's T52, T53 wheelchair 4x400m relay		Courtney Knight	women's discus
				France Gagne	men's javelin
				Donovan Tildesley	100m FS
				Andre Beaudoin	100m sprint
	Hal Merrill	men's F51 shotput		Diane Roy	1500m, 400m
	Jason Delasalle	men's F12 discus		Elizabeth Walker	50m fly
	James Shaw	men's F34-37 javelin		Dean Bergeron	800m
				Clayton Gerein	men's marathon

Stephanie Dixon	50m FS	
Stuart McGregor	800m	
Paul Gauthier,	boccia pairs	
Alison Kabush		
Marni Abbott,	women's basketball	
Chantal Benoit, Tracey Ferguson,		
Shira Golden, Jennifer Krempien,		
Linda Kutrowski, Arley McNeney,		
Kendra Ohama, Danielle Peers,		
Sabrina Pettinicchi, Lori Radke,		
Karla Tritten		

Winter Games
Gold

Year	Name	Event/Sport
1976	John Gow	men's alpine skiing
	Lorna Manzer	women's cross-country skiing
1980	Lana Spreeman	women's alpine skiing
	Lorna Manzer	women's alpine skiing
1984	Mark Bentz	men's alpine skiing
1988	Lynda Chyzyk	women's alpine skiing
	Francine Lemire	women's cross-country skiing
	Sandra Lecour	women's cross-country skiing
1992	Jeff Dickson	men's alpine skiing
1994	Stacy Kohut	women's alpine skiing
1998	Daniel Wesley	men's alpine skiing
2002	Bill Harriott	men's alpine skiing
	Chris Williamson	men's alpine skiing
	Daniel Wesley	men's alpine skiing
	Lauren Woolstencroft	women's alpine skiing
	Brian McKeever	men's cross-country skiing
	Robin McKeever	women's cross-country skiing

Silver

Year	Name	Event/Sport
1980	Greg Oswald	men's alpine skiing
	Jim Cullen	men's alpine skiing
	Lorna Manzer	women's alpine skiing
1984	Lana Spreeman	women's alpine skiing
	Lynda Chyzyk	women's alpine skiing
	Rodney Hersey	men's alpine skiing
	Uli Rompel	men's alpine skiing
	Wayne Burton	men's alpine skiing
1988	Lana Spreeman	women's alpine skiing
	Uli Rompel	men's alpine skiing
1992	Lana Spreeman	women's alpine skiing
	Sandra Lynes	women's alpine skiing
1994	Lana Spreeman	women's alpine skiing
	Ramona Hoh	women's alpine skiing
1998	Dale Winder	men's alpine skiing
	Karolina Wisniewska	women's alpine skiing
	Marni Winder	women's alpine skiing
	Stacy Kohut	women's alpine skiing
	David Eamer, Dean Delaurier,	
	Dean Mellway, Herve Lord,	
	Jamie Eddy, Jean Labonte,	
	Pierre Pichette, Rob Lagace,	

Year	Name	Event/Sport
	Shawn Matheson, Todd Nicholson,	
	Warren Martin, Yves Carrier	
2002	Daniel Wesley	men's alpine skiing
	Karolina Wisniewska	women's alpine skiing
	Brian McKeever	men's cross country skiing
	Robin McKeever	women's cross-country skiing

Bronze

Year	Name	Event/Sport
1976	Lorna Manzer	women's alpine skiing
1980	Dawn Coyle	women's cross-country skiing
	Janet Schuster	womew's cross-country skiing
	Judy Shaw	women's cross-country skiing
	Mary Bruner	women's cross-country skiing
1984	Lynda Chyzyk	women's alpine skiing
	Murray Bedel	men's alpine skiing
	Wayne Burton	men's alpine skiing
1988	John Houston	men's alpine skiing
	Lana Spreeman	women's alpine skiing
	Michel Duranceau	men's alpine skiing
	Steve Ellefson	men's alpine skiing
1992	Caroline Viau	women's alpine skiing
	Jeff Dickson	men's alpine skiing
	Lana Spreeman	women's alpine skiing
1994	Lana Spreeman	women's alpine skiing
	Ramona Hoh	women's alpine skiing
	Angelo Gavillucci,	men's sledge hockey team
	Dan Jansen, Claude,	
	Herve Lord, Jamie Eddy,	
	Jean Chan-Chiang, John Belanger,	
	Ken Schneider, Lou Mulvihill,	
	Pat Griffin, Pierre Pichette,	
	Rob Lagace, Shawn Matheson,	
	Todd Nicholson, Yves Carrier	
1998	Dale Winder	men's alpine skiing
	Daniel Wesley	men's alpine skiing
	Mark Ludbrook	men's alpine skiing
	Marni Winder	women's alpine skiing
	Ramona Hoh	women's alpine skiing
2002	Daniel Wesley	men's alpine skiing
	Karolina Wisniewska	women's alpine skiing
	Lauren Woolstencroft	women's alpine skiing
	Scott Patterson	men's alpine skiing

WHO'S WHO IN CANADIAN SPORT

5 Catterick Cresc., Kanata, ON K2K 3M5 Phone/Fax (613) 271-8690
e-mail: fergwho@rogers.com **web: www.sportingfacts.com**

Please complete information form fully and return to Bob Ferguson at above address:

SPORT _____

NAME (in full) _____

BIRTH (day/month/year/place) _____

DEATH (where applicable d/m/y/p) _____

SPOUSE (full/maiden name) _____

CHILDREN (names) _____

EDUCATION (schools/degrees/etc/) _____

OCCUPATION _____

_____

HOME ADDRESS _____

_____

TELEPHONE _____ **FAX** _____

EMAIL _____

ATHLETIC/PERSONAL HISTORY (include all sports/special awards)

_____

_____

_____

_____

_____

_____

_____

_____

_____